Contents

The MILEPOST®
All-The-North Travel Guide®

2014 Digital MILEPOST

Congratulations on your purchase of the 66th edition of The MILEPOST®

You have joined millions of travelers who've used The MILEPOST® as their exclusive guide to exploring the highways and byways of Alaska and western Canada.

We invite you to register to join The MILEPOST® VIP Travelers Club for your

FREE ACCESS

to The MILEPOST® Digital Edition.

The MILEPOST® Digital Edition is a comprehensive eBook trip planning resource for Alaska and western Canada.

> *These are the same pages found in the print edition with the added benefit to explore thousands of websites for the most informed travel planning*

Go to www.themilepost.com to begin your adventure!

Step 1:

Simply go to **www.themilepost.com/vip_login** to register as a VIP member. You will receive your password via email
(check your spam folder if delayed).

Step 2:

Log on and finish registering using your exclusive, priority access code located below.

Trip planning on a whole new level!

> Includes all the content from the print edition. Easy search and navigation allow you to explore all the pages of The MILEPOST® right from your computer.

> Hyperlinked content offers quick access to advertisers, destinations, ferry schedules, and much more.

> Downloadable PDF and **FREE access to iPad and Android apps.** Once you have registered as a VIP member, download the FREE MILEPOST app from the iTunes™, Google Play™ or Amazon™ app stores and login using your VIP account login information.

2014 The MILEPOST® VIP Travelers Club

Start your Free Registration Now!

1. Go to *www.themilepost.com/vip_login*

2. Create an account. Then using this **Priority Access Code:** register to access The MILEPOST® Digital Edition. **66MP4316**

Publisher, William S. Morris III

Editor, Kris Valencia
Art Director/Production Mgr., David L. Ranta
Assistant Editor, Claire Torgerson
Senior Field Editor, Sharon Paul Nault
Editorial Contributors: John Erskine, Helen Edwards, Meghan Mackey, Michael Robb, J.V. Teague
Advertising Traffic Coordinator, Brian Keith
Advertising Representatives, Judy Nadon, Lynn Owen, Sean Simmons,
Advertising Sales Director, Steve Sauder
Director of Anchorage Business Operations, Tracy Allison
Alaska Regional Vice President, Lee Leschper

To order a copy of *The MILEPOST®* and related products, phone 1-800-726-4707; email books@themilepost.com; or visit our book catalog at www.themilepost.com. Distributed by Globe Pequot Press.

A PUBLICATION OF THE MAGAZINE DIVISION OF MORRIS COMMUNICATIONS COMPANY LLC,

ALSO PUBLISHER OF:

Alaska where Alaska
The Magazine of Life on the Last Frontier

EDITORIAL AND ADVERTISING SALES OFFICES:
301 Arctic Slope Ave., Suite 300
Anchorage, AK 99518
Phone (907) 272-6070 • Fax (907) 275-2117
HEAD OFFICE:
735 Broad Street, Augusta, GA 30901

ISBN: 978-1-892154-31-6   ISSN: 0361-1361
Key title: The Milepost   Printed in U.S.A.

Cover Photo: Seward Highway along Turnagain Arm. (©Lucas Payne/AlaskaStock.com)

Questions, comments, complaints: Contact the Editor at our office in Anchorage (address above); direct phone line (907) 275-2111; email mpedit@ themilepost.com.

Photo submissions: Photo submission guidelines must be requested before submitting photos; contact the Editor. *The MILEPOST®* assumes no responsibility for unsolicited materials.

Advertising and Editorial Policy: *The MILEPOST®* does not endorse or guarantee any advertised service or facility. A sincere effort is made to give complete, accurate and annually up-to-date travel information for this immense segment of North America. However, between the time of our field surveys and the time of the readers' trip, many things may change. In all such cases, the publisher will not be held responsible.

How to Use The MILEPOST®

The *MILEPOST®* provides mile-by-mile descriptions of all major highways and roads in Alaska and northwestern Canada; detailed information on all major destinations (cities, communities, national parks, attractions) and how-to help for various modes of transportation (air, ferry, railroads, etc.). Refer to the Contents page and Index for subjects and destinations.

The *MILEPOST®* will work for you regardless of how you plan to travel—whether by car, by plane, on a tour bus, ferry, or by bicycle. It will help you plan your trip, as well as acting as a valuable guide during your trip.

The backbone of *The MILEPOST®* are the highway logs. In these mile-by-mile descriptions of the highways and byways of the North, you will find campgrounds; food, lodging, gas and other services; attractions; fishing spots; road conditions; geography and history; and much more.

The Key to Highways maps on pages 9-11 show you driving distances and which highways are covered in *The MILEPOST®*. The Basic Itineraries on pages 747-750 give you an idea of how to put together your trip.

To the right is an abbreviated version of part of the Parks Highway log, keyed to help you understand how to read all highway logs in *The MILEPOST®*.

1. A boldface paragraph appears at the beginning of each highway log in *The MILEPOST®* that explains which beginning and ending destinations are used, and which boldface letters represent those destinations. In this log A represents **Anchorage**, C is **Cantwell** and F is **Fairbanks**.

2. The boldface numbers following the letters represent the distance in miles from the beginning and ending destinations. (In Canada, the metric equivalent in kilometres follows the boldface mileage.) In this example, the Denali National Park entrance is located at **A 237.4 C 27.4 F 124.6** or 237.4 miles from Anchorage, 27.4 miles from Cantwell and 124.6 miles from Fairbanks.

3. **Junctions** with other logged roads are indented with a color bar. The cross-referenced section is always uppercased. In this example, the DENALI NATIONAL PARK section is referenced. (If a page number is not given, refer to the Contents page.)

4. Display advertisements are keyed in the log by a boldface entry at their highway locations, followed by the words "See display ad." Their advertisement will appear near this entry or a page or section will be referenced.

5. "Log" advertisements are classified-type advertisements that appear in the text. These are identified by the boldface name of the business at the beginning of the entry and "[ADVERTISEMENT]" at the end. These log advertisements are written by the advertisers.

It may also help you to know how our field editors log the highways. *The MILEPOST®* field editors drive each highway, taking notes on facilities, features and attractions along the way and noting the mile at which they appear. Mileages are measured from the beginning of the highway, which is generally at a junction or the city limits, to the end of the highway, also usually a junction or city limits. Most highways in *The MILEPOST®* are logged either south to north or east to west. If you are traveling the opposite direction of the log, you will read the log back to front. To determine driving distance between 2 points,

simply subtract the first mileage figures.

The introduction to each highway logged in *The MILEPOST®* includes a chart of mileages between major points (see example).

Maps also accompany highways logged in *The MILEPOST®*, each with a key explaining the abbreviations (see example at bottom). Key to mileage boxes reflect rounded off mileages.

The following symbols appear in *The MILEPOST®* logs:

- 🅐 Campground
- 🖾 Fishing
- ➕ Medical aid
- 🅖 Gas station
- 🅓 Gas station with diesel
- 🙢 Wildlife viewing

Parks Highway Log

Distance from Anchorage (A) is followed by distance from Cantwell (C) and distance from Fairbanks (F). ❶

❷ **A 237.4 C 27.4 F 124.6 Denali National Park and Preserve** entrance. Turnoff to west on Park Road for access to Denali National Park and Preserve. There is a double-ended parking area by the Denali Park sign, located just west of the turnoff here, that is a popular stop for photos.

❸ **Junction** 92-mile-long Park Road, which provides access to visitor services and attractions in Denali National Park. See DENALI NATIONAL PARK section on page 469 for Park Road log and details on park entrance fee, campgrounds, transportation and activities in the park.

Begin paved pedestrian path on west side of Parks Highway, which leads north along the highway to Denali Park commercial area.

A 237.7 C 27.7 F 124.4 Turnout by Denali National Park sign southbound.

A 238 C 28 F 124 Access to west for double-ended Mile 238 Rest Area (description follows). Access to east for **Era Helicopters Denali Flightseeing**.

Cabins at Denali. See display ad page 473 in the DENALI NATIONAL PARK section.

❹ **Nenana Raft Adventures.** See display ad page 477 in the DENALI NATIONAL PARK section.

Era Helicopters Denali Flightseeing. See display ad this page.

A 238.1 C 28.1 F 123.9 Kingfisher Creek. Grande Drive to east to Grande Denali Lodge.

❺ **Grande Denali Lodge.** Authentically Alaskan. Extraordinary views of the Denali Park wilderness. Located just north of the Denali National Park entrance, perched high atop Sugarloaf Mountain. Featuring timbered greatroom with stone fireplace, Alpenglow Restaurant, Peak Spirits Lounge, espresso bar, tour desk, shuttle, laundry and gift shop. Phone toll-free 1-866-683-8500 or www.denali alaska.com. [ADVERTISEMENT]

Distance in miles	Anchorage	Denali Park	Fairbanks	Talkeetna	Wasilla
Anchorage		237	362	113	42
Denali Park	237		125	153	195
Fairbanks	362	125		278	320
Talkeetna	113	153	278		71
Wasilla	42	195	320	71	

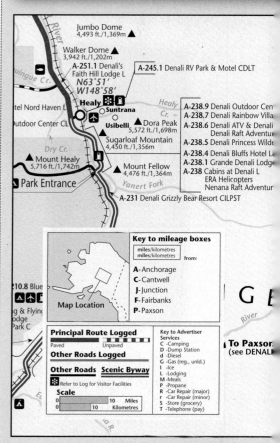

Key to mileage boxes

miles/kilometres
miles/kilometres from:

- **A** -Anchorage
- **C** -Cantwell
- **J** -Junction
- **F** -Fairbanks
- **P** -Paxson

Principal Route Logged
Paved   Unpaved

Other Roads Logged

Other Roads   **Scenic Byway**
🙢 Refer to Log for Visitor Facilities

Key to Advertiser Services
- **C** -Camping
- **D** -Dump Station
- **d** -Diesel
- **G** -Gas (reg., unld.)
- **I** -Ice
- **L** -Lodging
- **M** -Meals
- **P** -Propane
- **R** -Car Repair (major)
- **r** -Car Repair (minor)
- **S** -Store (grocery)
- **T** -Telephone (pay)

Scale
0   10   Miles
0   10   Kilometres

Welcome to the North Country

Dall sheep photographed in Savage River Valley, Denali National Park.
(©Michael F. Jones)

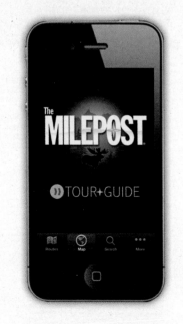

The MILEPOST®

))TOUR+GUIDE

Routes   Map   Search   More

Find our *NEW* iPhone™App on the App Store in iTunes!

The North Country is the land north of 51° 16' latitude. Geographically, it encompasses Alaska, Yukon, Northwest Territories, northern British Columbia and Alberta. Following are some facts and figures about each of these areas.

Alaska

Population: 735,132
Capital: Juneau
Largest City: Anchorage
Area: 571,951 square miles
Coastline: 33,904 miles
Highest Point: Mount McKinley, 20,320 feet
Lowest Point: Pacific Ocean, sea level
State Flower: Forget-me-not
State Tree: Sitka spruce
State Bird: Willow ptarmigan
State Motto: "North to the Future"
Major Industries: Tourism, petroleum, fishing
Drinking age: 21. *(NOTE: The sale and/or importation of alcoholic beverages is prohibited in more than 100 bush communities.)*
Visitor Information: Alaska Travel Industry Association, 2600 Cordova St., Suite 201 Anchorage, AK 99503; phone (907) 929-2842; www.travelalaska.com; or http://alaska.gov/visitorHome.html

Alaska is the largest state in the union in area (twice the size of Texas), but ranks

47th in population, based on the 2010 U.S. census estimate. Approximately 16 percent of the population is Alaska Native: Inupiaq, Yupik, Cupik, Aleut, Alutiiq, Athabascan, Tlingit, Haida, Tsimshian.

Alaska has 17 of the 20 highest mountains in the United States, including the highest peak in North America—Mount McKinley/Denali, the crown jewel of Denali National Park, elev. 20,237 feet. (This elevation is the result of a September 2013 survey which changed the 20,320 feet recorded in 1952 by 83 feet; 20,320 is still used throughout our text and will be corrected in the 2015 edition.) Named by a prospector in 1896, for presidential nominee William McKinley of Ohio, the mountain returned to its original name—Denali—with passage of the Alaska National Interest Lands Conservation Act of 1980. However, it is still McKinley according to the U.S. Board of Geographic Names.

The state falls into 6 natural geographical regions: Southeastern, Southcentral, the Interior, Southwestern, Western and the Brooks Range/Arctic.

Southeastern Alaska is a moist, luxuriantly forested panhandle extending some 500 miles from Dixon Entrance south of Ketchikan to Icy Bay on the Gulf of Alaska coast. This narrow strip of coast, separated from the mainland and Canada by the Coast Mountains, and the hundreds of islands of the Alexander Archipelago, form the Inside Passage water route used by ships and ferries. Cruise ships bring nearly 1 million passengers through the Inside Passage each summer. Alaska's capital city, Juneau, is the largest city in Southeast. Prince of Wales Island is the 3rd largest island in the nation (behind Hawaii and Kodiak).

The Southcentral region of Alaska curves 650 miles north and west from the Gulf of Alaska coast to the Alaska Range. This region's geographic variety includes the Matanuska–Susitna river valleys, the Chugach and Wrangell–St. Elias mountain ranges, the Kenai Peninsula and the Prince William Sound glaciers. Anchorage, the state's largest city, is the hub of Southcentral.

Interior Alaska lies cradled between the Brooks Range to the north and the Alaska Range to the south, a vast area that drains to the Yukon River, the Kuskokwim River and its tributaries. It is a climate of extremes, holding both the record high (100°F at Fort Yukon) and the record low (-80°F at Prospect Creek). Fairbanks is the hub of the Interior and a jump-off point for bush communities in both the Interior and Arctic.

Southwestern Alaska takes in Kodiak Island, the Alaska Peninsula and Aleutian Islands. Kodiak, less than an hour's flight from Anchorage and 9.5 hours by ferry from Homer, is the largest island in Alaska and second largest in the United States (the largest being Hawaii). Kodiak was Russian

Alaska's first capital city and is home to the largest bears in the world. Brown bear viewing is an attraction on Kodiak and at Katmai National Park and Preserve near King Salmon. The Alaska Marine Highway Southwest/Aleutian route, provides ferry service from Kodiak to Unalaska/Dutch Harbor.

Western Alaska stretches from the head of Bristol Bay north along the Bering Sea coast to the Seward Peninsula near the Arctic Circle. This region extends inland from the coast to encompass the Yukon–Kuskokwim Delta. Nome is one of the best known destinations in Western Alaska.

Arctic Alaska lies above the Arctic Circle (latitude 66°33'), between the Brooks Range to the south and the Arctic sea coast to the north, and from the Canadian border to the east westward to Kotzebue. Day and overnight trips to Nome, Barrow and Prudhoe Bay are popular packages offered out of Anchorage and Fairbanks.

If you include the Alaska Marine Highway System, all regions of Alaska are connected by highway with the exception of Western Alaska. And that region's hub cities—Bethel and Nome—are less than 2 hours from Anchorage by air.

Icefields Parkway straddles the British Columbia–Alberta border. (©Michael K. Robb)

Yukon

Population: 36,304
Capital: Whitehorse
Largest City: Whitehorse
Area: 186,661 square miles/483,450 square km
Highest Point: Mount Logan, 19,550 feet/5,959m
Lowest Point: Beaufort Sea/Arctic Ocean, sea level
Territorial Flower: Fireweed
Territorial Bird: Raven
Territorial Tree: Subalpine Fir
Major Industries: Tourism, mining
Drinking age: 19. Packaged liquor, beer and wine are sold in government liquor stores and licensed off-sales outlets.
Visitor Information: Tourism Yukon, Box 2703, Whitehorse, YT Y1A 2C6; phone 1-800-661-0494; email vacation@gov.yk.ca; www.travelyukon.com

Shaped somewhat like a right triangle, Yukon is bordered on the west by Alaska at 141° longitude; on the north by the Beaufort Sea/Arctic Ocean; on the south by British Columbia at latitude 60°; and on the east by the Northwest Territories.

Indigenous peoples of Yukon are referred to as First Nations. These aboriginal groups are Gwich'in, Han, Northern Tutchone, Southern Tutchone, Kaska, Tagish, Inland Tlingit and Upper Tanana. Their languages derive from the Athapaskan and Tlingit linguistic families. First Nations are organized around a community or region, such as Carcross/Tagish First Nations, Selkirk First Nation (Pelly Crossing), and Champagne/Aishihik First Nations. Indigenous peoples presence in Yukon is thought to date back 30,000–50,000 years, according to Yukon Tourism.

Yukon was made a district of the Northwest Territories in 1895, and became a separate territory in June of 1898, propelled by the influx of people and commerce that arrived with the great Klondike Gold Rush.

News of the gold strike on Rabbit Creek (later renamed Bonanza Creek) in 1896 had filtered to the outside world, provoking a frenzied stampede. In 1897–98, thousands of gold seekers landed at Haines or Skagway, AK, climbed Chilkoot Pass or White Pass, and headed for the Klondike gold fields.

A contingent of North West Mounted Police, forerunner of today's Royal Canadian Mounted Police (RCMP) had been sent to Yukon in 1894, to help establish law and order among miners. With the advent of the Klondike Gold Rush, permanent detachments were stationed at the summits of Chilkoot and White passes, both to maintain law and order and to assert Canadian sovereignty at these 2 borders.

Dawson City, in the heart of the Klondike, became the new territory's first capital. Dawson City's downtown Dawson Historical Complex, sternwheeler *SS Keno* and Dredge No. 4 and Discovery Claim make up the 4 National Historic Sites of Canada in the Klondike.

At the height of the gold rush, an estimated 30,000 people lived in Dawson City. By 1903, as other gold stampedes drew off much of Dawson's population, the city's boom days were over, although mining continued to support the community for many years. Whitehorse, however, was thriving, both as terminus of the White Pass & Yukon Route railway from Skagway and as a major service stop on the Alaska Highway, which had opened to public travel in 1948. Whitehorse also had a large airport—today's Erik Nielsen Whitehorse International Airport—and on March 31, 1953, Whitehorse replaced Dawson City as capital of Yukon.

Yukon has 3 national parks. Kluane National Park, a UNESCO World Heritage Site, accessible from the Haines and Alaska highways, contains Canada's highest peak, Mount Logan (elev. 19,545 feet/5,959m). Vuntut National Park of Canada is located in the northwestern corner of Yukon. Ivvavik National Park of Canada was the first national park in Canada to be created as a result of a Yukon First Nation land claim agreement (1995). It protects a portion of the calving ground for the Porcupine Caribou Herd.

British Columbia

Population: 4,573,300
Capital: Victoria
Largest City: Vancouver
Area: 364,764 square miles/944,735 square km
Highest Point: Fairweather Mountain 15,299 feet/4,663m
Lowest Point: Pacific Ocean, sea level
Provincial Flower: Pacific dogwood
Provincial Tree: Western redcedar
Provincial Bird: Steller's jay
Provincial Mammal: Spirit Bear (also known as the Kermode Bear)
Provincial Motto: Splendour Without Diminishment
Major Industries: Construction, manufacturing, forestry, mining and energy, tourism, film and television productions, food processing, agriculture, seafood products
Drinking age: 19. Packaged liquor, beer and wine are sold in government liquor stores and various private retail outlets.
Visitor Information: Tourism British Columbia. Phone 1-800-435-5622; Website: www.hellobc.com.

Canada's most westerly and third largest province, British Columbia stretches 808 miles/1,300 km from its southern border with the United States to the northern boundaries with Yukon and Northwest Territory. It is bounded on the east by Alberta and on the west by the Pacific Ocean. The province encompasses Vancouver Island, site of the capital city of Victoria. Slightly more than half the province's population resides in the Victoria–Vancouver area.

The region was important in early fur trade, and expansion of the province came with the 1860s Cariboo gold rush, followed by the completion of Canada's first trans-

Eroded mountains form fantastical rock formations along the Dempster Highway between Yukon and Northwest Territories. *(©Tim Grams)*

continental railway—the Canadian Pacific. British Columbia entered the Dominion of Canada on July 20, 1871, as the 6th province.

Popular tourist destinations include Vancouver and Whistler; Victoria and Vancouver Island; the Gulf Islands; the Sunshine Coast; the Okanagan Valley: the Cariboo; the Kootenay Rockies; Northern BC and Haida Gwaii. BC has 7 national parks, one marine conservation area, 13 National Historic Sites and 1,030 parks, reserves, protected areas, conservancies and recreation sites. The province's national parks—Glacier, Gulf Islands, Gwaii Haanas, Mount Revelstoke, Kootenay, Pacific Rim and Yoho—are among the most spectacular in North America.

Mile Zero of the Alaska Highway is located in Dawson Creek, BC (not to be confused with Dawson City, YT), in the northeastern part of the province.

Alberta

Population: 3,632,483
Capital: Edmonton
Largest City: Calgary
Area: 255,303 square miles/661,185 square km
Highest Point: Mount Columbia, 12,294 feet/3,747m
Lowest Point: Salt River at the border with Northwest Territories, 600 feet/183m
Provincial Flower: Wild rose
Provincial Tree: Lodgepole pine
Provincial Bird: Great horned owl
Provincial Motto: Strong and free
Major Industries: Petrochemicals, forest products, food processing, tourism, machinery, electronics and telecommunications, business services.
Drinking age: 18. Liquor, beer and wine are sold in private liquor stores.

Visitor Information: Travel Alberta, Edmonton; Phone 1-800-ALBERTA; travelinfo@travelalberta.com; www.travelalberta.com.

The Province of Alberta is bordered to the west by British Columbia, to the south by Montana, to the east by Saskatchewan and to the north by the Northwest Territories. Among the dramatic features of this geographically fascinating area are the vast Canadian Rocky Mountains, the Columbia Icefields, and the bizarre rock formations of the badlands and Drumheller, home to some of the largest dinosaur findings.

Native inhabitants included Assiniboine, Blackfoot, Cree and Sarcee Indians. The first European settlers—fur traders—arrived in the 18th century. In 1905, Alberta became a province of Canada. Discoveries of oil and natural gas deposits in the 1930s caused economic growth, and in the 1970s and 1980s, these same deposits brought new industries and a resulting rise in population to the area.

Edmonton in central Alberta and Calgary to the south are the most populous cities and major destinations. Banff and Jasper are 2 of Alberta's 5 national parks and are located in the Canadian Rockies. These parks host several million visitors a year. Alberta offers 14 National Historic Sites

Northwest Territories

Population: 43,439
Capital: Yellowknife
Largest City: Yellowknife
Area: 452,480 square miles/1,171,918 square km
Highest Point: Cirque of the Unclimbables Mountain, 9,062 feet/2,762m
Lowest Point: Beaufort Sea, sea level
Territorial Flower: Mountain aven
Territorial Tree: Tamarack
Territorial Bird: Gyrfalcon
Major Industries: Mining, manufacturing, fishing, tourism
Drinking age: 19. Packaged liquor, beer and wine are sold in government liquor stores. Sale and possession of alcohol is prohibited in several communities.
Visitor Information: Northwest Territories Tourism, Yellowknife; Phone (867) 873-7200 or toll-free within the U.S. and Canada at 1-800-661-0788; email info@spectacularnwt.com; www.spectacularnwt.com.

On April 1, 1999, Northwest Territories was divided into 2 territories. This division created Nunavut and its capital, Iqaluit on Baffin Island, in what was the eastern half of the old Northwest Territories. The new Northwest Territories—the western half of the former Northwest Territories—comprises a sixth of Canada and is about the size of Alaska. Roughly half of the population of Northwest Territories is Aboriginal, including Dene, Dogrib, Dehcho, Inuvialuit, Inuit, Gwich'in and Metis.

Northwest Territories' Wood Buffalo National Park, established in 1922, is one of the largest national parks in the world. The Territories include 4 other National Parks and 1 National Historic Site.

Access to Northwest Territories is from Alberta via the Mackenzie Highway, from British Columbia via the Liard Highway, and from Yukon via the Dempster Highway. A major road-building project in the 1960s constructed most of the highway system in western Northwest Territories. Many roads are paved or scheduled to be paved in the coming years. The Deh Cho Bridge across the Mackenzie River officially opened Nov. 30, 2012, allowing year-round, all-road access to Yellowknife.

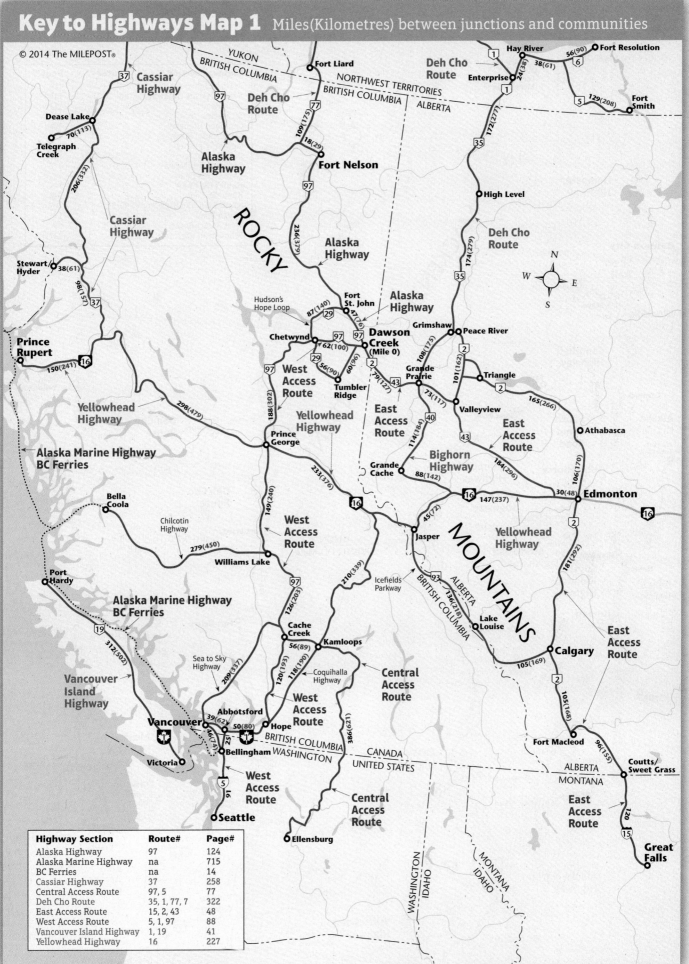

© 2014 The MILEPOST®

YUKON
BRITISH COLUMBIA
NORTHWEST TERRITORIES
BRITISH COLUMBIA
ALBERTA

37 Cassiar Highway

Fort Liard

Deh Cho Route

Hay River
56(90) Fort Resolution
1
24(38)
Enterprise
38(61)
6
172(277)
5
129(208) Fort Smith

Dease Lake
70(113)
Telegraph Creek
206(332)

97
97
Deh Cho Route
77
109(175)
18(29)
Alaska Highway
Fort Nelson
97

35

High Level

Cassiar Highway
ROCKY

Deh Cho Route
174(279)

236(379)

Stewart/Hyder
38(61)
98(157)
37

Alaska Highway

35

N
W E
S

Prince Rupert
16
150(241)

Hudson's Hope Loop
87(140)
Fort St. John
47(76)
Alaska Highway

29
Chetwynd
97
97
Dawson Creek (Mile 0)

Grimshaw
Peace River
108(175)
2
101(162)
Triangle
2
165(266)

Yellowhead Highway
298(479)

62(100)
60(96)
29
56(90)
Tumbler Ridge
2
79(127)
43
Grande Prairie
73(117)
Valleyview
40
43
East Access Route

97
West Access Route
188(302)

Yellowhead Highway

East Access Route
114(184)

Athabasca

Alaska Marine Highway
BC Ferries

Prince George
233(376)

Grande Cache
88(142)
Bighorn Highway
184(296)
106(170)

16
147(237)
30(48)
Edmonton
16

Bella Coola
149(240)

West Access Route

Chilcotin Highway
279(450)

Williams Lake

45(72)
Jasper
210(339)
Icefields Parkway
93
136(218)
Lake Louise
MOUNTAINS
Yellowhead Highway
184(296)
181(292)

East Access Route

Port Hardy
312(502)
19

Alaska Marine Highway
BC Ferries

97
126(203)
Cache Creek
56(89)
Kamloops
Coquihalla Highway
120(193)
118(190)
Central Access Route
105(169)
Calgary
2

Vancouver Island Highway

Sea to Sky Highway
209(337)
West Access Route

Abbotsford
39(62)
50(80)
Hope
46(74)
25
Bellingham

Vancouver
Victoria

BRITISH COLUMBIA
WASHINGTON
CANADA
UNITED STATES

5
91
West Access Route

386(621)

Central Access Route

Fort Macleod
96(155)
Coutts/Sweet Grass
ALBERTA
MONTANA

East Access Route
4
15

Seattle
Ellensburg

WASHINGTON IDAHO
MONTANA
IDAHO

Great Falls

East Access Route

Highway Section	Route#	Page#
Alaska Highway	97	124
Alaska Marine Highway	na	715
BC Ferries	na	14
Cassiar Highway	37	258
Central Access Route	97, 5	77
Deh Cho Route	35, 1, 77, 7	322
East Access Route	15, 2, 43	48
West Access Route	5, 1, 97	88
Vancouver Island Highway	1, 19	41
Yellowhead Highway	16	227

Key to Highways Map 2 Miles(Kilometres) between junctions and communities

© 2014 The MILEPOST®

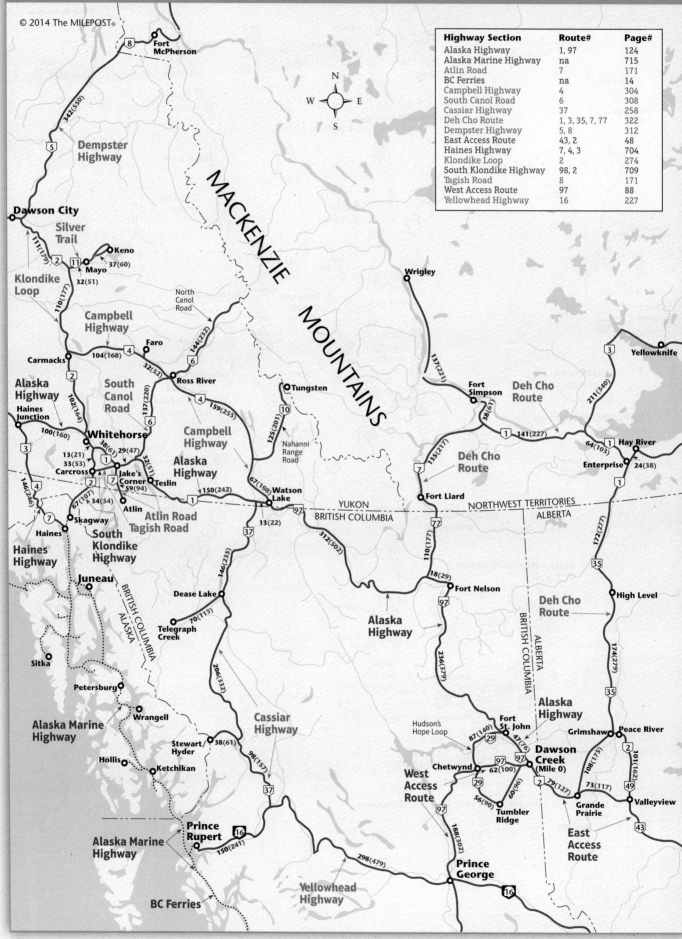

Highway Section	Route#	Page#
Alaska Highway	1, 97	124
Alaska Marine Highway	na	715
Atlin Road	7	171
BC Ferries	na	14
Campbell Highway	4	304
South Canol Road	6	308
Cassiar Highway	37	258
Deh Cho Route	1, 3, 35, 7, 77	322
Dempster Highway	5, 8	312
East Access Route	43, 2	48
Haines Highway	7, 4, 3	704
Klondike Loop	2	274
South Klondike Highway	98, 2	709
Tagish Road	8	171
West Access Route	97	88
Yellowhead Highway	16	227

Fort McPherson

MACKENZIE MOUNTAINS

342(550)

Dempster Highway

Dawson City

111(179)

Silver Trail

Keno
37(60)
Mayo
32(51)

Klondike Loop

110(177)

Campbell Highway

Carmacks

104(168)

Faro

32(52)

Alaska Highway

102(164)

Haines Junction

100(160)

South Canol Road

137(220)

Ross River

144(232)

North Canol Road

Wrigley

137(221)

Fort Simpson

38(61)

Deh Cho Route

Yellowknife

3

211(340)

Tungsten

Campbell Highway

125(201)

Nahanni Range Road

141(227)

64(103)

Hay River

24(38)

1

Enterprise

Whitehorse

38(61)
29(47)

13(21)
33(53)

Carcross

Jake's Corner
59(94)
Teslin

32(51)

Alaska Highway

67(108)

150(242)

Watson Lake

97

135(217)

Deh Cho Route

Fort Liard

YUKON
BRITISH COLUMBIA

NORTHWEST TERRITORIES
ALBERTA

7

1

3

146(246)

34(54)

Atlin

Atlin Road
Tagish Road

13(22)

Skagway

South Klondike Highway

37

312(502)

77

110(177)

172(277)

35

Haines

Haines Highway

146(235)

Juneau

Dease Lake

18(29)

Fort Nelson

97

High Level

BRITISH COLUMBIA
ALASKA

70(113)

Telegraph Creek

Alaska Highway

Deh Cho Route

Sitka

206(332)

236(379)

174(279)

Petersburg

Cassiar Highway

BRITISH COLUMBIA
ALBERTA

35

Wrangell

Alaska Marine Highway

Hudson's Hope Loop

Alaska Highway

Grimshaw

Peace River

Hollis

Stewart/Hyder

38(61)

87(140)

29

Fort St. John

47(76)

2

Ketchikan

98(157)

West Access Route

Chetwynd

97

62(100)

Dawson Creek (Mile 0)

108(175)

73(117)

49

101(162)

37

29

60(96)

79(127)

Valleyview

56(90)

Tumbler Ridge

Grande Prairie

43

Prince Rupert

16

97

East Access Route

Alaska Marine Highway

150(241)

188(302)

298(479)

Prince George

16

Yellowhead Highway

BC Ferries

N
W E
S

Key to Highways Map 3 Miles(Kilometres) between junctions and communities

Highway Section	Route#	Page#
Alaska Highway	1, 2	124
Alaska Marine Highway	na	715
Atlin Road	7	171
Campbell Highway	4	304
Dalton Highway	11	532
Dempster Highway	5, 8	312
Denali Highway	8	509
Edgerton Highway/ McCarthy Road	10	500
Elliott Highway	2	525
Glenn Highway	1, 4	342
Haines Highway	7, 4, 3	704
Klondike Loop	2, 9, 5	274
Parks Highway	3	407
Richardson Highway	4, 2	481
Seward Highway	1, 9	551
South Klondike Highway	98, 2	709
Steese Highway	6	517
Sterling Highway	1	581
Tagish Road	8	171
Taylor Highway	5	274
Tok Cutoff	3	342
Top of the World Highway	9	274

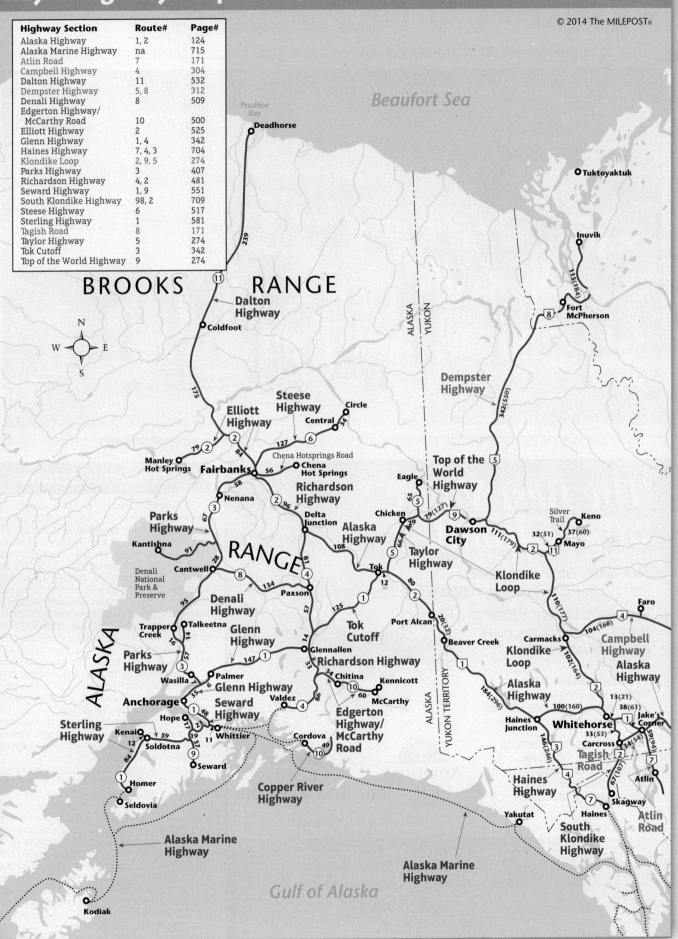

Travel Planning

The Fortymile caribou herd on the Taylor Highway. (©Tim Grams)

Accommodations

Accommodations in the North—as anywhere else—can range from luxurious to utilitarian to downright funky. You will find lodging in fine lodges and major-chain hotels/motels (Princess Lodges, Westmark Hotels, Best Value Inns, Super 8's and others); in bed and breakfasts; in hostels; in rustic log cabins; and in mobile homes. When visitors consider the remoteness of many communities and the seasonal nature of Northern travel, they are often surprised at the wide variety of lodging available.

The larger cities, such as Anchorage, Fairbanks and Whitehorse, for example, have more to choose from than the smaller, more remote communities. But in midsummer, even those locations with greater numbers of rooms available can fill up quickly. You should consider making reservations ahead of time during the busy summer season, whether your destination is a major city or a small highway community.

Some facilities along highways of the North may be a bit on the rustic side compared to what you are used to. This is, after all, the Last Frontier. You will also find some first-class establishments in surprisingly remote locations along our highways, accommodations deemed interesting enough and charming enough to be included in the "best of" lists of various travel publications. The frills of city travel may sometimes be missing, but the hospitality of the North more than makes up for it.

We do not rate accommodations. In our experience, you can have a 5-star experience in a 1-star hotel (or vice versa), and

sometimes the remote location and lack of choices in lodging make ratings moot anyway. Paid advertisements for accommodations appearing in *The MILEPOST®*—whether display ads or "log ads" placed in the highway log—are written by the advertisers themselves. We do not endorse or guarantee any of these facilities or services, although we trust the advertisers will live up to their promises. If they do not, please write, phone or email us. We do not mediate disputes, but if we get enough complaints about a business not living up to its advertisement, we will ask the advertiser to do a reality check. Keep in mind that businesses may close and ownership, season and rates may change.

Air Travel

Slightly more than half of all visitors to Alaska arrive by air. Air travel is also one of the most common forms of transportation within the North. You can fly just about anywhere by wheel or floatplane (some floatplanes will have wheels embedded in their floats and those are called "amphibs," short for amphibian). If there is no scheduled service to where you want to go and for what you want to do, you can almost always charter a plane.

You will find charter planes at the local airstrip. Most communities have a state-maintained airstrip or private airstrip. But keep in mind that not all airstrips have airports. You will find links to Alaska airport information at http://dot.alaska.gov/airport-portal.shtml.

Major communities such as Anchorage, Fairbanks and Juneau have a selection of companies offering air tours to glaciers and mountaintops in fixed-wing aircraft or helicopters. Other tour options include wildlife viewing (see more in the Wildlife Viewing section further on in this section). For example, Rust's Flying Service out of Anchorage offers bear viewing tours that fly across Cook Inlet to Katmai National Park on a guided day tour.

An air carrier must be licensed by the Federal Aviation Administration to fly passengers commercially. Many offer flights in small planes under Visual Flight Rules (VFR), which means the flight can take place only when weather and visual conditions permit the pilot to see 2 miles ahead, and the ceiling is at least 1000 feet. Passengers should be prepared to have a flight postponed or canceled if conditions are not favorable. For information on the FAA's Circle of Safety aviation education program, visit avcams.faa.gov/index.php or phone 1-866-357-4704.

Airlines flying within Alaska include Alaska Airlines, Corvus Airlines (formerly Era Aviation), Ravn Connect (formerly Hageland Aviation and Frontier Flying Service), Grant Aviation and PenAir. Airlines serving Alaska include Air Canada, Alaska Airlines, American Airlines, Condor, BP/ConocoPhillips, Continental, Delta Airlines, Japan Airlines, JetBlue, Korean Air, Northwest, PenAir, Sun Country, TransNorthern, United Airlines, US Airways, Yakutia Airlines.

Air Canada, Air North, Edelweiss Air and Condor, Air North and West Jet serve Whitehorse, YT, while several major carriers serve larger cities such as Edmonton and Calgary, AB. International carriers from Asia and Russia also offer regularly scheduled or charter flights.

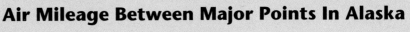

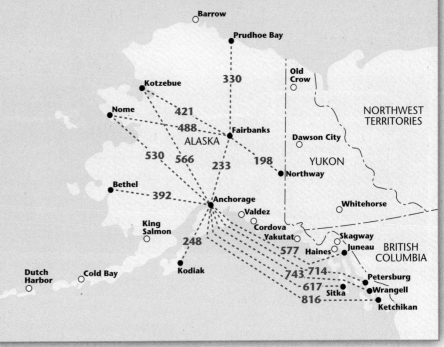

There are more than 250 certified charter/air taxi operators in Alaska. Check the advertisements for scheduled and charter air service in the communities covered in *The MILEPOST®*. There are many to choose from.

Air taxi rates may vary from carrier to carrier. Most operators charge an hourly rate either per plane load or per passenger; others may charge on a per-mile basis.

Aside from offering transportation from

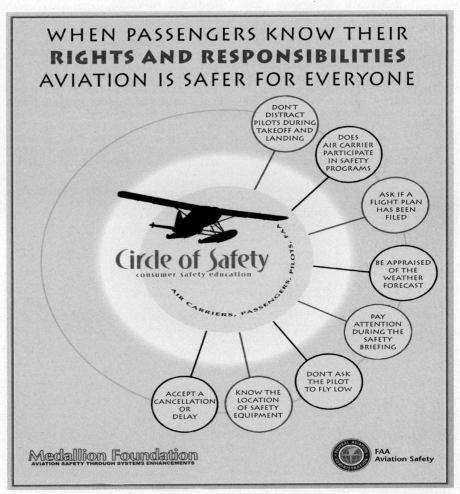

Visitors fly into and out of Coldfoot Airport on the Dalton Highway. (©Sharon Nault)

one place to another, many flying services also offer—or specialize in—flightseeing. For a fixed fee, you can fly around mountains, look for wildlife, or land on a glacier and go dogsledding or hiking. Flightseeing trips to area attractions are often available at a fixed price per passenger.

Charter fares vary greatly between companies, planes and destinations. Planes may be on wheels, floats or skis (luggage space is often limited and dependent on number of passengers). Don't be offended when the pilot or ticketing agent asks your weight; they need that to ensure an accurate balance within the plane. Contact local companies and see ads in *The MILEPOST®* for more information on charters.

The MILEPOST® highway logs include the location of most airstrips along the highways and in communities. *NOTE: The brief description of airstrips given in* The MILEPOST® *is in no way intended as a guide for pilots.* Pilots should have a current copy of the *Alaska Supplement* and charts.

BC Ferries

BC Ferries provides year-round service on 25 routes throughout coastal British Columbia, with a fleet of 36 passenger- and vehicle-carrying ferries. The ferry route of special interest to Alaska-bound travelers is the "Inside Passage" service between Port Hardy and Prince Rupert, and service to Vancouver Island from mainland ports at Tsawwassen and Horseshoe Bay. In addition, Alaska-bound travelers may use "Discovery Coast" service between Port Hardy and Bella Coola.

Inside Passage service between Port Hardy, on Vancouver Island, and Prince Rupert offers a convenient connection with the Alaska Marine Highway at Prince Rupert. Prince Rupert is located 450 miles/724 km west of Prince George via the Yellowhead Highway (see YELLOWHEAD HIGHWAY 16 section). Port Hardy is 312 miles/502 km

north of Victoria via Trans-Canada Highway 1 and BC Highway 19 *(see "Vancouver Island Highway" log on pages 41-47).* NOTE: The ferry leaves from Bear Cove terminal, 6 miles from Port Hardy.

Inside Passage summer service between Port Hardy and Prince Rupert is aboard the *Northern Expedition,* carrying 600 passengers and 130 vehicles. This ferry has an expanded range of cruise-ship-like food service options to include a fine dining buffet, a relaxed atmosphere grill/cafeteria, as well as solarium seating, a gift shop, lounge, children's playroom, 55 modern staterooms, travel information, telephone, and many other amenities. Summer service on this route is during daylight hours, so cabins are not necessary for the 15-hour trip, although cabins are available for day-use or round-trip passengers. The ferry goes up one day and comes back the next. (Winter sailings include an overnight aboard the *Northern Adventure* with fewer scheduled sailings than in summer.) Check-in time is 2 hours before departure.

Inside Passage travelers can extend their visit from Prince Rupert out to Haida Gwaii (the Queen Charlotte Islands) via the *Northern Adventure.* BC Ferries provides 6-day-a-week service to Skidegate on Graham Island in Haida Gwaii. Crossing time is about 7 hours, with one sailing a week an overnight (cabins are available).

Another travel option for Alaska-bound motorists is Discovery Coast service aboard the *Queen of Chilliwack* between Port Hardy and Bella Coola. The *Queen of Chilliwack* features a cafeteria, gift shop, lounge, reclining seats and showers. This summer-only service connects Port Hardy on Vancouver Island with Bella Coola on the Chilcotin Highway, with stops at Bella Bella, Shearwater, Ocean Falls and Klemtu. The Chilcotin Highway connects Bella Coola with the WEST ACCESS ROUTE to the Alaska Highway *(see pages 104-105 for log of the Chilcotin Highway).*

To reach Vancouver Island, travelers may use the passenger and vehicle ferry service to Victoria out of Port Angeles, WA, available from Black Ball, or take BC Ferries passenger and vehicle service from Tsawwassen, south of Vancouver, to Swartz Bay.

Travelers may also take BC Ferries service from Tsawwassen to Duke Point/Nanaimo (2 hours) or from Horseshoe Bay, west of Vancouver, to Departure Bay/Nanaimo. From Nanaimo it is 251 miles/405 km—or about 5 hours' driving time—to Port Hardy, departure point for Inside Passage and Discovery Coast ferries. If you are driving from Victoria to Port Hardy, allow at least 7 hours. (Vancouver Island is a popular destination for vacationing mainland residents.) Ferry routes connecting Vancouver and Vancouver Island are serviced by a modern fleet of ferries including 3 Super C class vessels providing the ultimate in comfort for your passage.

Schedules: BC Ferries Summer 2014 Inside Passage (Port Hardy–Prince Rupert) and Discovery Coast (Port Hardy–Bella Coola) schedules appear on these pages. Sailing schedules for other months are available online at www.bcferries.com. The Discovery Coast Passage is under-review for the 2014 season. Travelers are advised to check the online schedule prior to traveling.

Tsawwassen–Swartz Bay, Horseshoe Bay–Departure Bay, and Tsawwassen–Duke Point ferries sail daily year-round, with hourly sailings from early morning to late evening

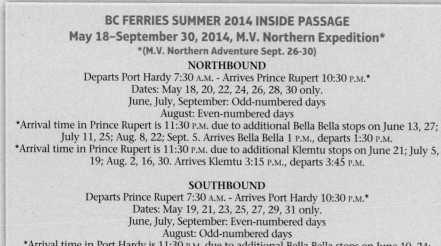

BC FERRIES SUMMER 2014 INSIDE PASSAGE
May 18–September 30, 2014, M.V. Northern Expedition*
*(M.V. Northern Adventure Sept. 26-30)
NORTHBOUND
Departs Port Hardy 7:30 A.M. - Arrives Prince Rupert 10:30 P.M.*
Dates: May 18, 20, 22, 24, 26, 28, 30 only.
June, July, September: Odd-numbered days
August: Even-numbered days
*Arrival time in Prince Rupert is 11:30 P.M. due to additional Bella Bella stops on June 13, 27;
July 11, 25; Aug. 8, 22; Sept. 5. Arrives Bella Bella 1 P.M., departs 1:30 P.M.
*Arrival time in Prince Rupert is 11:30 P.M. due to additional Klemtu stops on June 21; July 5,
19; Aug. 2, 16, 30. Arrives Klemtu 3:15 P.M., departs 3:45 P.M.

SOUTHBOUND
Departs Prince Rupert 7:30 A.M. - Arrives Port Hardy 10:30 P.M.*
Dates: May 19, 21, 23, 25, 27, 29, 31 only.
June, July, September: Even-numbered days
August: Odd-numbered days
*Arrival time in Port Hardy is 11:30 P.M. due to additional Bella Bella stops on June 10, 24;
July 8, 22; Aug. 5, 19; Sept. 2. Arrives Bella Bella 5:30 P.M., departs 6 P.M.
*Arrival time in Port Hardy is 11:30 P.M. due to additional Klemtu stops on June 21; July 5, 19;
Aug. 2, 16, 30. Arrives Klemtu 3:15 P.M., departs 3:45 P.M.

during summer with naturalists onboard in summer. Printed schedules are *not* available: Visit www.bcferries.com for current schedules on all routes.

Fares: Inside Passage and Discovery Coast peak (regular) season passenger fares are from May 1 to September 30. Shoulder and off-peak season rates are reduced. These lower fares are available during the fall, winter and spring when service is less frequent.

All fares shown are in Canadian funds. Terminals accept Visa, Mastercard and American Express, but most terminals cannot accept debit cards (the exceptions are Port Hardy/Bear Cove and McLoughlin Bay, which can accept debit cards for payment).

At presstime, Inside Passage peak/regular passenger fares one-way to/from Port Hardy and Prince Rupert were: $194.75 adult passenger; $97.50 child, 5 to 11 years; under 5 years of age, free. (Special fares apply for BC residents on school events and for disabled and senior BC residents.) Vehicle fares one-way for vehicles up to 7 feet high, up to 20 feet in length: $444.50, plus $22.25 each extra foot over 20 feet. One-way fares for overheight vehicles (over 7 feet high—which includes most RVs—and up to 20 feet in length): $760, plus $38 each extra foot more than 20 feet. Other one-way fares: Motorcycle, $222.25 (with sidecar or trailer, $338.25); bicycle, $5; stowage (canoe, kayak, etc.), $10.

Discovery Coast peak/regular season passenger fares, one-way to/from Port Hardy and Bella Coola are: $192.50 adult passenger; $96.25 child, 5 to 11 years; under 5 years of age, free. (Special fares apply for BC residents on school events and for disabled and senior BC residents.) One-way vehicle fares are as follows: up to 7 feet high, up to 20 feet in length, $385.25, plus $19.25 each extra foot; overheight vehicles (over 7 feet high, up to 20 feet in length), $515.25 plus $25.75 each extra foot more than 20 feet. Other one-way fares: Motorcycle, $192.75 (with sidecar or trailer, $286.25); bicycle, $5; stowage (canoe, kayak, etc.), $10.

Summer cabin rates for the *Northern Expedition* day-cruise between Port Hardy and Prince Rupert are: Inboard cabins, $90; outboard cabins and wheelchair cabins, $120.

Reservations: Passenger and vehicle (private passenger or recreational vehicle with or without a trailer) reservations are strongly advised for the Inside Passage, Discovery Coast Passage and the Haida Gwaii (Queen Charlotte Islands). For reservations, phone toll-free in North America 1-888-223-3779; from outside North America, phone 250-386-3431. Reservations can be made online at www.bcferries.com. Cancellations made fewer than 30 days prior to departure are subject to a cancellation fee.

Information: BC Ferries phone toll-free in North America 1-888-223-3779; from outside North America, phone 250-386-3431; email customerservice@bcferries.com; online at www.bcferries.com. For fully packaged vacation options please visit www.bcferries vacations.com

Bus Lines

Transportation in this category ranges from no frills shuttle van service to narrated motorcoach tours. Most scheduled bus service between or to cities in the North is

seasonal (summer-only).

Alaska Bus Guy, phone (907) 720-6541; www.alaskabusguy.com. Departs from Egan Center at 5th Ave. and F St. in Anchorage at 7 A.M. for Wasilla, Talkeetna and arriving Denali National Park at 1 P.M., arriving back in Anchorage at 6:30 P.M. from Denali. One-way and round-trip fares. Scenic and wildlife

photo stops. Reservations recommended.

Alaska Park Connection/Alaska Tour & Travel, P.O. Box 22-1011, Anchorage, AK 99522. 1-800-266-8625; www.alaskacoach.com. Twice daily deluxe motorcoach service between Anchorage, Whittier, Seward, Talkeetna and Denali National Park. Custom tour packages also available.

A beautiful day along the Inside Passage route in British Columbia. (©Claire Torgerson, staff)

BC FERRIES SUMMER 2014 DISCOVERY COAST
June 10–September 8, 2014

NORTHBOUND
Tuesdays (June 1–September 2)
Departs Port Hardy 10:15 A.M. — Arrives Bella Bella 8:30 P.M.
Departs Bella Bella 9:45 P.M. — Arrives Shearwater 10:30 P.M.
Departs Shearwater 11 P.M.— Arrives Bella Coola Wed. 6:30 A.M.

Thursdays (June 12–September 4)
Departs Port Hardy 10:15 A.M. — Arrives Bella Coola 11 P.M.

Saturdays (June 14–September 6)
Departs Port Hardy 9:30 P.M. — Arrives Bella Bella Sun. 8:30 A.M.
Departs Bella Bella Sun. 9:30 A.M. — Arrives Shearwater Sun. 10:15 A.M.
Departs Shearwater Sun. 10:45 A.M.— Arrives Klemtu Sun. 3 P.M.
Departs Klemtu Sun. 6 P.M.* — Arrives Ocean Falls Mon. 12:45 A.M.
Departs Ocean Falls Mon. 1:15 A.M.— Arrives Bella Coola Mon. 6:30 A.M.

*6 P.M. departure from Klemtu: Available transfer to 8 A.M. southbound sailing Monday from Bella Coola to Port Hardy.

SOUTHBOUND
Wednesdays (June 11–September 3)
Departs Bella Coola 8 A.M. — Arrives Shearwater 3 P.M.
Departs Shearwater 5 P.M. — Arrives Bella Bella 5:45 P.M.
Departs Bella Bella 7:45 P.M.— Arrives Port Hardy Thurs. 7:45 A.M.

Fridays (June 13–September 5)
Departs Bella Coola 8 A.M. — Arrives Ocean Falls 2 P.M.
Departs Ocean Falls 4 P.M. — Arrives Shearwater 7:30 P.M.
Departs Shearwater 8:15 P.M. — Arrives Bella Bella 9 P.M.
Departs Bella Bella 11 P.M.— Arrives Port Hardy Sat. 9 A.M.

Mondays (June 16–September 8)
Departs Bella Coola 8 A.M. — Arrives Port Hardy 9 P.M.

Schedules are subject to change without notice. Please check before going to the terminal.

Alaska/Yukon Trails, P.O. Box 84608, Fairbanks, AK 99708. Toll-free 1-800-770-7275; AlaskaShuttle@yahoo.com; www.alaskashuttle.com/. Service between Whitehorse, Dawson City and Fairbanks; daily shuttle Anchorage–Talkeetna–Denali–Fairbanks. Group charters available.

Dalton Highway Express, P.O. Box 71665, Fairbanks, AK 99707. (907) 474-3555; adventure@northernalaska.com; www.daltonhighwayexpress.com. One-day van service in summer between Fairbanks and Deadhorse/Prudhoe Bay with stops at Yukon River, Arctic Circle, Coldfoot, Wiseman and Galbraith Lake. Drop-offs and pickups for bicyclists arranged. Departs Fairbanks at 6 A.M., arrives Deadhorse 10 P.M. Advance reservations strongly recommended to ensure service.

Denali Overland Transportation Co., P.O. Box 330, Talkeetna, AK 99676. Phone (907)733-2384; fax (907)733-2385; info@denalioverland.com; www.denalioverland.com. Charter van service based in Talkeetna offers 24-hour daily service April 1 to October 1 between Anchorage, Talkeetna and Denali National Park.

Gray Line of Alaska, 800 5th Ave. Suite 2600, Seattle, WA 98104; 1-888-425-1737; or in Anchorage (907) 277-5581 or 550-7711 (mid-May to mid-Sept.); www.graylineofalaska.com. Sightseeing and package motorcoach tours throughout Alaska and Yukon.

Greyhound Canada Transportation Corp., 2191 2nd Ave., Whitehorse, YT Y1A 3T8. (867) 667-2223; www.greyhound.ca. Scheduled service to Whitehorse from all U.S.-Canada border crossings with stops at Alaska Highway communities including Dawson Creek, Fort Nelson and Watson Lake. Whitehorse depot has carriers to Dawson City and Alaska destinations.

Kennicott Shuttle, HC 60 Box 148T, Copper Center, AK 99573. Phone (907) 822-5292; kennicottshuttle@gmail.com; www.kennicottshuttle.com. Shuttle service connecting Glennallen, Copper Center, Kenny Lake, Chitina Airport, and Chitina Wayside to Kennicott River Footbridge. (Transportation from footbridge to Kennicott and McCarthy provided by local van services like Wrangell Mountain Air.)

Seward Alaska Bus Company, phone (907) 350-6010, toll-free 1-888-257-8527; info@alaskacruisetransfer.com; www.sewardalaskabus.com. Provides narrated day tours and direct transfers between Seward and Anchorage. Narrated direct transfer picks up at Seward port at 8 A.M., drop off in Anchorage at 10:30 A.M. Narrated Wildlife Tour picks up at Seward 8 A.M., drop off in Anchorage at 11:45 A.M.; Anchorage pick up at noon, drop off in Seward 4:30 P.M. Also all day 8-hour tour between Seward and Anchorage.

Seward Bus Line, depot locations at 539 3rd Ave., Seward and 3333 Fairbanks St., Anchorage; toll-free phone 1-888-420-7788; phone in Seward, (907) 224-3608; phone in Anchorage, (907) 563-0800; sewardbuslines@

acsalaksa.net; www.sewardbuslines.net. Daily summer (May 1–Sept. 15) schedule has twice daily departures from Anchorage (9:30 A.M. and 2 P.M.) and Seward (9:30 A.M. and 2 P.M.). Also transportation between Anchorage and Whittier ferry terminal and Seward and Whittier ferry terminal.

The Stage Line, 1213 Ocean Dr. Homer, AK, 99603; and 412 W 53rd, Anchorage, AK 99528; phone in Homer (907) 235-2252; phone in Anchorage (907) 868-3914; http://stagelineinhomer.com. Passenger transportation, freight, parcel, and courier service, between Anchorage and the Kenai Peninsula and between Kenai Peninsula communities.

Calendar of Events

Following are dates for some of the special events and all observed holidays in 2014 beginning in March. (For events and holidays that take place in January and February, check individual websites for 2015 dates.) Be sure to check for other special events under Attractions in each of the community descriptions in *The MILEPOST®*.

January
Haines—Alcan 200 Snowmobile Rally, http://www.alcan200.org/. **Seward**—Annual Polar Bear Jump, http://community.acsevents.org/.
Holidays: New Year's Day; Martin Luther King, Jr. Day (USA)

February
Anchorage—Fur Rendezvous, a 10-day-long festival held the end of February through the first weekend in March that includes Running with the Reindeer, Frostbite Footrace, snow sculpture contest, sled dog races and more; www.furrondy.net. **Fairbanks**—Iron Dog, world's longest snowmobile race; www.irondograce.org. Yukon Quest Sled Dog Race started here in 2014, and ended in Whitehorse, YT (www.yukonquest.com for dates). **Nenana**—Tripod Raising Festival takes place the last weekend in February. **Whitehorse, YT**—Sourdough Rendezvous, www.yukonrendezvous.com. Yukon Quest Sled Dog Race starts here in 2015, finishes in Fairbanks, AK (www.yukonquest.com for dates).
Holidays: Presidents Day (USA) February 16.

March
Anchorage/Willow—Iditarod Trail Sled Dog Race® to Nome, ceremonial start in Anchorage on the first Saturday in March, followed by the re-start the next day in Willow, 70 miles north of Anchorage; www.iditarod.com. **Fairbanks**—BP World Ice Art Championships, late February to late March; www.icealaska.com. **Skagway**—Buckwheat Cross-Country Ski Classic, March 29; http://buckwheatskiclassic.com/.
Holidays: March 30 Seward's Day (Alaska),

April
Girdwood—Alyeska Spring Carnival & Slush Cup, April 11-13 (Slush Cup is on Saturday April 12). **Kodiak**—ComFish Alaska, April 17-19; Whalefest, for dates go to www.whalefestkodiak.org. **Summit Lake**—Tesoro Arctic Man Classic, April 8-14 (www.arcticman.com). **Whitehorse**—A Celebration of Swans, April 13-21, at Marsh Lake. **Wrangell**—Stikine River Birding Festival.
Holidays: April 18 Good Friday, Easter Sunday April 20, April 21, Easter Monday (Canada).

May
Anchorage—Gold Nugget Triathlon May 18 (www.goldnuggettriathlon.com).

Cordova—Copper River Delta Shorebird Festival. **Dawson City, YT**—Dawson City Gold Show, May 16-17. **Faro, YT**—Crane & Sheep Festival (www.faroyukon.ca). **Haines**—Great Alaska Craft Beer & Homebrew Festival, May 23-24. **Homer**—Kachemak Bay Shorebird Festival, May 9-11; Homer Halibut Derby, May 15 through Aug.15 (www.homerhalibutderby.com). **Ketchikan**—King Salmon Derby, May and June (http://ketchikansalmonderby.com). **Kodiak**—King Crab Festival, May 22-26. **Petersburg**—Little Norway Festival, May 15-18; King Salmon Derby, Memorial Day weekend. **Valdez**—Halibut Derby, May 18 to Sept. 1 (www.valdezfishderbies.com). **Soldotna**—Kenai Birding Festival, May 15-18. **Whittier**—Fish Derby, May 1-Sept. 15; www.whittieralaskafishderby.org.
Holidays: May 19 Victoria Day (Canada); May 26 Memorial Day (USA)

June
Anchorage—Alaska Run For Women June 7 (www.akrfw.org); Mayor's Midnight Sun Marathon, June 21. **Fairbanks**—Midnight Sun Baseball Game, June 21. **Haines Junction, YT/Haines, AK**—Kluane to Chilkat International Bike Relay, June 15. **Ketchikan**—King Salmon Derby, May and June (http://ketchikansalmonderby.com). **Palmer**—Colony Days, June 13-15 (http://palmerchamber.net/events/colony-days.html). **Prince Rupert, BC**—Seafest, second weekend in June. **Sitka**—Summer Music Festival, June 6–July 5 (www.sitkamusicfestival.org). **Soldotna**—Kenai River Festival, June 6-8 (www.kenaiwatershed.org/kenairiverfestival.html). **Whitehorse, YT**—Kluane Mountain Bluegrass Festival, June 7-9 (www.yukonbluegrass.com); 24 Hours of Light Mountain Bike Festival, June 21-23 (www.24hoursoflight.ca); Yukon River Quest Canoe & Kayak Race to Dawson City, June 25-29 (www.yukonriverquest.com).

July
Calgary—Calgary Stampede, July 4-13; www.calgarystampede.com. **Dawson City, YT**—Yukon Gold Panning Championship July 1st; Dawson City Music Festival, July 18-20 (www.dcmf.com); International Dome Race July 19. **Eagle River**—Bear Paw Festival, July 9-13 (www.bearpawfestival.org). **Fairbanks**—Golden Days, July 16-20; Fairbanks Summer Arts Festival, July 13-27 (www.fsaf.org); World Eskimo-Indian Olympics, July (www.weio.org). **Girdwood**—Forest Fair, for dates www.girdwoodforestfair.com/. **Haines**—Southeast Alaska State Fair, July 31-Aug. 3 (www.seakfair.org). **Homer**—Concert on the Lawn, July 28-29 (www.kbbi.org). **Inuvik, NWT**—Great Northern Arts Festival, July 11-20 (www.gnaf.org). **Palmer**—Palmer Pride Picnic, July 23. **Seward**—Mount Marathon Race®, July 4. **Sitka**—Summer Music Festival, (www.sitkamusicfestival.org). **Soldotna**—Progress Days, July 26-27. **Valdez**—Silver Salmon Derby, July 19-Aug. 31 (www.valdezfishderbies.com). **Whitehorse, YT**—Yukon 1000 Canoe and Kayak Races, July 21 (www.yukon1000.com).
Holidays: July 1 Canada Day (Canada); July 4 Independence Day (USA).

August
Dawson City, YT—Discovery Days, August 15-17; Labour Day Mixed Slowpitch Classic, Aug. 31 (www.dawsoncity.ca). **Edmonton**—International Fringe Theatre Festival, August 14-24 (http://fringetheatreadventures.ca/festival.php). **Fairbanks**—Tanana

Valley State Fair, Aug. 2-11 (www.tanana valleystatefair.org). **Juneau**—Golden North Salmon Derby, Aug. 9-11 (www.goldennorth salmonderby.org). **Ketchikan**—Blueberry Arts Festival first weekend in August (http://ketchikanarts.org); Gigglefeet Dance Festival, Aug. 2-4. **Kodiak**—St. Herman's Pilgrimage (www.dioceseofalaska.org). **Ninilchik**—Kenai Peninsula Fair, Aug. 16-18; www.kenaipeninsulafair.com. **Palmer**—The Alaska State Fair, Alaska's largest annual event, features headline entertainers, midway rides, carnival games, hundreds of food and vendor booths, 4H livestock, pig racing, exhibits ranging from quilts to goats, giant veggies, and more; Aug.21-Sept. 1; www.alaskastatefair.org. **Seward**—Silver Salmon Derby®. Aug. 9-17.
Holidays: August 4 Civic Holiday (Canada); August 18 Discovery Day (Yukon)

September

Dawson City, YT—Great Klondike Outhouse Race (www.dawsoncity.ca); White Ram Poker Tournament, Sept. 5-8. **Skagway, AK/Whitehorse, YT**—Klondike Trail of '98 International Road Relay, Sept. 5-6 (www.klondikeroadrelay.com).
Holidays: Sept. 1 Labor Day (USA)/Labour Day (Canada)

October

Sitka—Alaska Day Celebration, (www.alaskadayfestival.org); Whalefest, Oct. 30–Nov. 2; www.sitkascience.org.
Holidays: October 13 Columbus Day (USA)/ Thanksgiving (Canada); Oct. 18 Alaska Day (Alaska)

November

Anchorage—Carrs/Safeway Great Alaska Shootout, Nov. 25-26. **Haines**—Alaska Bald Eagle Festival, Nov. 10-16 (http://baldeagles.org/festival).
Holidays: Nov. 10 Veterans Day (USA), Nov. 11 Remembrance Day (Canada); Nov. 27 Thanksgiving Day (USA)

December

Check locally for events such as holiday bazaars and fireworks displays.
Holidays: Dec. 25 Christmas Day (USA/ Canada); Dec. 26 Boxing Day (Canada)

Camping

Alaska and Canada have both government and private campgrounds. With few exceptions, these campgrounds are located along the road system, and most roadside campgrounds accommodate both tents and RVs. Wilderness camping is also available in most state, federal and provincial parklands.

The MILEPOST® logs all public roadside campgrounds, and includes facilities (water, firewood, tables, firepits, etc.), camping fees, length of stay limits and other information. *The MILEPOST®* highway logs also include private campgrounds. Keep in mind that government campgrounds generally do not offer hookups or other amenities, and may not be able to accommodate large RVs and 5th-wheelers. Additionally, each location may have hours when their electricity and/or water services are curtailed. Be sure to read posted notices or inquire with campground host, if you are concerned.

Season dates for most campgrounds in the North depend on weather, i.e. freezing temperatures can freeze water-lines. Campgrounds are open from mid- to late-May until early September. The farther north the campground, the shorter the season.

NOTE: Campers are urged to use established

Campground hosts greet visitors to many Alaska state and federal campgrounds.
(©Sharon Nault)

campgrounds. Overnighting in rest areas and turnouts may be unsafe and is illegal unless otherwise posted. Something else to consider before adventuring out is the midnight sun these areas experience. If you have difficulty sleeping in light, you may want to bring blackout shades for your RV or a sleeping mask for camping.

The MILEPOST® indicates both private and public campgrounds with tent symbols in the highway logs.

Alaska

Government agencies offering recreational campsites in Alaska are the Alaska Dept. of Natural Resources' (DNR) Alaska State Parks, the Bureau of Land Management (BLM), the National Park Service (NPS), the U.S. Forest Service (USFS) and the U.S. Fish & Wildlife Service (USF&WS).

Alaska State Parks. The largest state park system in the United States, DNR maintains more than 3,000 campsites within the 119-unit state park system. Camping is available at 40 state recreation sites, 5 state parks (Chugach, Denali, Chilkat, Kachemak Bay, Wood-Tikchik), 14 state recreation areas and a state historic park. State campgrounds, as a rule, do not accept reservations, although state campgrounds operated by private contractors may have a reservation system in place.

Camping fees (subject to change) range from $10 to $28 per night. Day-use parking fees are $5 to $10 per vehicle. Boat launch fees are $5 to $10 per day. There are also fees for dump stations and firewood.

State campgrounds and recreation areas are all operated by private contractors and there are no longer annual camping passes to purchase for entrance. To obtain annual day-use and boat launch passes, go to www.alaskastate parks.org and click on Parks Pass under Fees for details, then click either online parks pass order form or paper park pass order form. Annual park passes may also be purchased in person (see list of locations online). Paper forms are mailed with check or money order payable to the State of Alaska, to DNR Public Information Center, Alaska Park Pass, 550 W. 7th Ave., Ste. 1260, Anchorage, AK 99501. Online passes may

be purchased with a credit card. Decals are mailed within 2 business days of receipt of online request. Requests for passes can also be faxed to (907) 269-8901. Phone the Anchorage Public Information Center at (907) 269-8400 with any questions.

BLM maintains 15 campgrounds; fees are charged at some. Unless otherwise posted, all undeveloped BLM public lands are open to free camping, usually for a maximum of 14 days per stay. The Bureau of Land Management, Alaska State Office is located at 222 W. 7th Ave., Suite 13, Anchorage, AK 99513-7599; phone (907) 271-5960 and has a public information center, open 8 A.M. to 4 P.M. weekdays (closed holidays) at 605 W. 4th St.; (907) 644-3661. In Fairbanks, stop by the BLM office at 1150 University Ave., phone (907) 474-2200. In Glennallen, stop by the BLM office at Mile 186.5 Glenn Highway. Open 8 A.M. to 4:30 P.M. weekdays, phone (907) 822-3217; www.blm.gov/ak.

The **National Park Service** maintains 6 campgrounds in Denali National Park and Preserve (see DENALI NATIONAL PARK

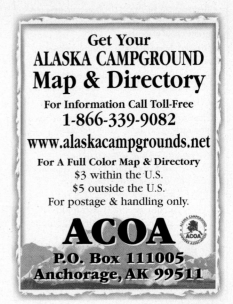

Firewood

Firewood can harbor many different kinds of invasive pests and diseases that are harmful to Alaska's trees—both in forest and urban settings. Inadvertent transportation of insect larvae and tree diseases in infested materials by people has greatly increased the distribution of pests and diseases such as gypsy moth, oak wilt, and the emerald ash borer that hitch-hike on firewood, making their way into previously unaffected, healthy areas. This poses a serious threat to trees such that several states have firewood and quarantine regulations in place to try to slow the spread of wood pests. In fact, on October 22, 2008, APHIS issued a Federal Order requiring heat treatment for shipments of all firewood made of hardwood species entering the United States from Canada.

The emerald ash borer (*Agrilus planipennis*), an invasive, wood-boring beetle that attacks ash trees (*Fraxinus spp.*), including white, green, black, and blue ash. Mountain ash (*Sorbus spp.*), not a true ash, is unaffected. While ash trees are not part of Alaska's natural hardwood forest component, hundreds of ash trees are planted throughout the urban landscape. Early detection and isolation of infestations are the best defenses against the ecological and economic damage caused by wood pests and diseases. Stay alert to large or colorful insects such as the Asian longhorn beetle and emerald ash borer.

Campers and visitors are encouraged to take a role in helping ensure the healthy future of the state's parks, forests, and trees.

Please report unusual or suspect materials or insects immediately by calling UAF Cooperative Extension Service at (contact info for Anchorage (907) 786-6300; Juneau (907) 796-6221, and Fairbanks (907) 474-5211.

To protect our forests and cities from these firewood hitch hikers, do not transport firewood across state lines. Burn what you buy or collect, where you acquire it. Scrap lumber is a good alternative for campfires as it is fully dried and debarked and cannot harbor pests and diseases of living trees like raw wood or logs can. Minimally processed wood, such as full or partial pallets, skids,

©Kris Valencia, staff

or slabs, are cut wood, but they can be fresh enough or have enough attached bark that they can harbor pests or diseases.

NOTE: *Painted, treated, or composites of wood and glue such as chipboard and plywood should not be burned as doing so can create a serious health hazard.*

Emerald Ash Borer

Firewood Can Transport Harmful Pests!

Don't Destroy Alaska's Beautiful Trees

• To protect our forests and city trees from these firewood hitchhikers, do not bring firewood along with you into or out of the state.

• Firewood should be purchased or collected at or near your destination.

• Any unused firewood should be left behind, to be used/burned; do not transport it to a new location.

• Untreated scrap lumber is a good alternative.

• Please report unusual or suspect materials or insects immediately by calling University of Alaska Cooperative Extension Service.

Visit *http://na.fs.fed.us/firewood* or Contact University of Alaska Cooperative Extension Service for more information.

Fairbanks (907) 474-5211
Anchorage (907) 786-6300
Juneau (907) 796-6221

section); fees are charged. Golden Eagle, Golden Age, and Golden Access passes, while still honored at most campgrounds, have been discontinued and replaced with America the Beautiful, annual, military, senior and access passes. Other national parks included in *The MILEPOST®* are: Glacier Bay and Kenai Fjords (accessible by tour boat); Klondike Gold Rush National Park in Skagway; and Wrangell-St. Elias National Park & Preserve (see page 508). For more information, go to www.nps.gov.

U.S. Forest Service campgrounds are available in Alaska's 2 national forests: Tongass and Chugach. USFS campgrounds charge a fee of $6 to $24 per night depending on facilities. There is a 14-day limit at most campgrounds. Some campsites may be reserved. For more information and reservations, visit the National Recreation Reservation Service (NRRS) at www.recreation.gov, phone toll-free 1-877-444-6777. For information on all recreation in Alaska's national forests, visit www.fs.usda.gov/chugach/ and www.fs.usda.gov/tongass/.

U.S. Fish & Wildlife Service manages camping areas along Skilak Lake Road and Swanson River/Swan Lake Roads within Kenai National Wildlife Refuge. Contact the Refuge Manager, Kenai National Wildlife Refuge, Box 2139, MS 519, Soldotna, AK 99669, phone (907) 262-7021; or visit http://alaska.fws.gov.

Alaska camping information can also be obtained through the Alaska Public Lands Information Centers at www.nps.gov/aplic or call toll-free 1-866-869-6887, (907) 644-3661. Forest service campground and cabin reservations may be made at www.recreation.gov.

Canada

Provincial and territorial government campgrounds and recreation sites as well as private campgrounds are readily available along the Alaska Highway and connecting routes in British Columbia, Alberta, Yukon and Northwest Territory.

Yukon has more than 50 government campgrounds and recreation sites located along its road system. These well-maintained campgrounds have picnic tables, firepits, firewood, outhouses, well water, a picnic shelter and often, boat launches. There is a 14-day limit in any 30-day period, per Yukon Government Campground. A camping permit ($12/night) and nightly self-registration is required. Visitors may purchase daily campground permits in advance at many highway lodges, gas stations, retail stores, in liquor stores (outside Whitehorse) and at all Environment Yukon offices. Or visitors may pay the camping fee when they self-register at Yukon government campgrounds. (Instructions are posted.) There are no dump stations in Yukon Government campgrounds. The Yukon Parks web page lists all government campgrounds, recreation sites and dump site locations.

For more information, contact Yukon Parks at Environment Yukon, phone (867) 667-5648; toll-free in Yukon 1-800-661-0408 ext. 5648; email yukon.parks@gov.yk.ca; or visit www.yukonparks.ca.

British Columbia has an extensive provincial park system, with camping available at more than 340 vehicle accessible campgrounds. Park gates are generally open from 7 A.M. to 11 P.M. Camping fees range from $10 to $30 per camping party per night, depending on facilities. There is a 14-day limit for most parks. Some campsites may be reserved; visit www.discovercamping.ca for a list of provincial parks accepting campsite reservations (campsite and yurt reservations begin March 15, 2014).

In all provincial parks, conservancies, protected areas and recreational areas, generators are restricted to use between 9 A.M.–11 A.M. and from 6 P.M.–8 P.M. Generators must be placed on designated campsite pads and not in surrounding vegetation. Generators will not be allowed in walk-in campsites.

For more information on BC Parks, visit www.bcparks.ca. Reservations can be made 24 hours/day online at www.discovercamping.ca. Or phone toll-free in Canada 1-800-689-9025, or outside Canada

(519) 826-6850, weekdays 7 A.M. to 7 P.M. (PDT) and Saturday, Sunday and holidays 9 A.M. to 5 P.M. For information regarding RVing in BC, go to www.camping RVbc.com. For information on BC's recreations sites and trails, go to www.sitesand trailsbc.ca.

Alberta also has a provincial park system with 108 provincial parks and recreation area campgrounds and 79 forest provincial recreation areas. Online booking for provincial parks is available at www.albertaparks. ca. To receive a campground guide, call Travel Alberta toll–free at 1-800-252-3782.

Northwest Territories operates more than 20 public campgrounds, many with walking trails and natural features, such as waterfalls. Fees range from $15 to $32 per night and payment is in Canadian currency or by Canadian check only. Fred Henne, Prelude and Hay River Territorial parks have a 14–day limit during peak season. Firewood is available for a fee. Visit www.spectacularnwt.com (go to Where to Stay), www.iti.gov.nt.ca/tourismparks/ generalparkservices.shtml or www.camping nwt.ca for reservations.

Multiple day-use areas are available for highway travelers to enjoy an open-air picnic or stretch their legs.

There are also 4 national parks in NWT operated by the federal government: Tutkut Nogait, Aulavik, Nahanni and Wood Buffalo. The only national park with highway access, however, is Wood Buffalo. Go to www.parks canada.ca for more information.

Across Canada, a park sticker, available at entrance stations, is required for motorists staying overnight in the national parks. National Park campgrounds may have electrical service (standard 60 cycle). Firewood is supplied for free, but bring your own ax to split kindling. "Serviced" campgrounds have caretakers/hosts. For more information, visit www.parkscanada.ca.

CB Radios/FSR Radios

There is no license required to use unmodified CB or a hand–held FSR Radio (Family Service Radio) in Canada or Alaska. Many travelers have recently noted the convenience of an FSR Radio for caravan travel (these are more common than a CB Radio, which are typically used by truckers). The FSR radio may be purchased in many big-box stores or electronics stores. They cost upwards of $30 and have a distance range of 3 miles or more. One of *The MILEPOST*® editors used a Uniden set of radios to travel highways and notes: "The convenience of communication between vehicles was invaluable as stops were approached or needed, or just to share the beauty of the road." The only difficulty is that the batteries can run out much faster than the conversation, and she recommends an inverter that can charge the radio through the power socket while traveling or a radio that can plug directly into the socket.

Cell Phones/Internet

Cell phone coverage and reception is unpredictable and sporadic outside the cities. We've received and placed calls on our cell phones in the middle of the Alaska Range and up at Deadhorse, but have been unable to raise a signal just a few miles outside Fair-

Highway signage in Canada is in metric, like this kilometrepost near Cache Creek, BC.
(©Kris Valencia, staff)

banks or south of Anchorage along Turn-again Arm. Adding to the unpredictability is your cell phone provider's roaming agreements, which may black out certain areas.

Most hotels, motels, lodges, bed-and-breakfasts, hostels and RV parks offer some form of Internet access for their guests. Internet cafes dot many northern communities—large and small. WiFi is increasingly available at hotels, local libraries, visitor centers and even campgrounds. Schools and community centers may also offer Internet access for travelers.

In remote spots in the North, of which there are many, Internet use is provided by satellite and usage is often limited to 10MB. You may be asked by the provider to refrain from using certain websites, sending videos or photos, playing games and other high usage activites.

For more information on Internet access along the highways, see highway businesses advertising in *The MILEPOST*®.

Use 10-digit phone numbers for all calls in Alberta and British Columbia.

British Columbia, Yukon, Alberta and Northwest Territories have laws against the use of handheld cell phones or other electronic devices while driving.

Crossing the Border

Travel between the United States and Canada is usually fairly straightforward, although there are various documentation requirements and a daunting number of regulations pertaining to importation of agricultural and/or wildlife products, commercial goods, alcohol, tobacco and firearms. All travelers and their vehicles may be searched at the discretion of the customs officials whether or not the traveler feels that he or she has complied with customs requirements. When in doubt, declare it.

Following is a brief description of border crossing requirements for the U.S. and Canada. Regulations and procedures change frequently. Due to increased security, travelers are urged to check with customs offices or online sources for the most current

restrictions and regulations prior to traveling. For Canada customs information, go to the Canada Border Services Agency website at http://www.cbsa.gc.ca and click on non-Canadians (the direct link is www.cbsa. gc.ca/travel-voyage/ivc-rnc-eng.html) or click on Contact Us. You may also contact Canada Border Services Agency, through the 24-hour BIS line at 1-800-461-9999 within Canada; (204) 983-3500 outside Canada.

For detailed U.S. customs information go to the Travel section of the U.S. Customs & Border Protection website at www.cbp. gov. You may also contact your nearest U.S. customs office; toll-free 1-877-CBP-5511 or write U.S. Customs and Border Protection, 1300 Pennsylvania Ave., N.W., Washington, D.C. 20229.

Entry into Canada from the U.S.

Identification: If you are a U.S. citizen, you do not need a passport to enter Canada; however, to cross the border back into the U.S., a passport (or other approved WHTI-compliant document) WILL BE REQUIRED, so crossing into Canada without one of these is ill-advised. Entering Canada requires that you carry proof of your citizenship, such as a birth certificate, a certificate of citizenship or naturalization or a Certificate of Indian Status, as well as a photo ID. If you are a permanent resident of the United States (i.e., a foreigner), you must have your permanent resident card (i.e. green card).

All travellers should visit http://www. cbp.gov/xp/cgov/travel/ (click on "Know Before You Go") and http://getyouhome.gov for information on the U.S. Western Hemisphere Travel Initiative (WHTI) and requirements to *enter or return to the United States*.

Travelling with children: Children under the age of 18 are classified as minors and are subject to the entry requirements set out under the Immigration and Refugee Protection Act.

Minors travelling alone must have proof of citizenship. We strongly recommend that they have a letter from both parents (where applicable or whomever has guardianship of the child) detailing the length of stay, providing the parents' telephone number and

Canada Customs on Highway 37A between Stewart, BC, and Hyder, AK. (©Kris Valencia, staff)

authorizing the person waiting for them to take care of them while they are in Canada.

If you are travelling with minors, you must carry proper identification for each child such as a birth certificate, passport, citizenship card, permanent resident card or Certificate of Indian Status. If you are not the parent or guardian of the children, you should also have written permission from the parent/guardian authorizing the trip. The letter should include addresses and telephone numbers of where the parents or guardian can be reached. Divorced or separated parents should carry copies of the legal custody agreements for the children. If you are travelling with a group of vehicles, make sure you arrive at the border in the same vehicle as your children to avoid any confusion.

Admissibility: Admissibility of all travelers seeking to enter Canada is considered on a case-by-case basis and based on the specific facts presented by the applicant at the time of entry. Under the Immigration and Refugee Protection Act (IRPOA), a person may be deemed inadmissible for a number of reasons. A criminal conviction—including a conviction of Driving Under the Influence (DUI)—could make a person inadmissible to Canada. For that reason, be prepared to discuss your criminal history with a border services officer when arriving in Canada. If planning a trip to Canada, visitors are encouraged to visit the CBSA or Citizenship and Immigration Canada (CIC) websites in order to ensure that they are admissible to Canada. People with criminal convictions can apply to be deemed rehabilitated or they may be eligible for a temporary resident permit. For more information on overcoming criminal inadmissibility please visit the CIC website at http://www.cic.gc.ca/english/information/inadmissibility/conviction.asp.

All provinces in Canada require visiting motorists to produce evidence of financial responsibility should they be involved in an accident. Financial responsibility limits vary by province. U.S. motorists are advised to obtain a Canadian Nonresident Interprovincial Motor Vehicle Liability Insurance Card. This card is available only in the U.S. through insurance companies or their agents. Check with your insurance company prior to entering Canada to find out what your current coverage includes.

What you can bring: Visitors may bring "personal baggage" into Canada free of duty. This includes clothing, camping and sports equipment, cameras, CD players and iPods, computers, vehicles, boats, etc. Gifts up to $60 (CN) per gift, excluding alcohol and tobacco, permitted, duty free. Alcohol and tobacco are admitted if the visitor meets the age requirements of the province or territory where they are entering Canada. Visitors are permitted the following amounts without paying duty, on all of the following: 200 cigarettes, 50 cigars or cigarillos, 200 tobacco sticks and 200 grams (7 oz.) of manufactured tobacco. Visitors are permitted the following amounts without paying duty on only 1 of the following: 1.5 litres of wine or 1.14 litres (40 oz.) of liquor, or 24 355-ml (12 oz.) cans or bottles (8.5 litres) of beer or ale provided that it is for personal use. You may bring additional quantities but you will have to pay full duty and taxes on the excess.

Canada has restrictions and limitations that apply to importing meat, eggs, dairy products, fresh fruit, vegetables, dog food (see "Pets" on page 34) and other food and non-food items. Details at www.beaware.gc.ca/english/toce.shtml; follow links specifically pertaining to the commodity for which you are importing.

Canada also follows CITES guidelines regarding the import/export of endangered species of wild fauna and flora including parts or products. For details on CITES restrictions and permits, visit http://www.cites.ca/.

Pets: Dogs and cats from the U.S. that are at least 3 months old need signed and dated certificates from a veterinarian verifying that they have a current vaccination against rabies and also a health certificate, issued not more than 30 days prior to crossing the border, and stating that your pet is healthy. Both certificates must clearly identify the animal in your possession. While these certificates are not always reviewed, the lack of them may result in longer wait times at the border and inadmissibility of your pet.

Firearms: Canada vigorously enforces its firearms importation laws. Border officials may, at their discretion, search any vehicle for undeclared firearms and seize any vehicle and firearm where such firearms are found.

Complete a Non-Resident Firearm Declaration form before you reach the border. To obtain this form, email cfp-pcaf@rcmp-grc.gc.ca or phone 1-800-731-4000.

Firearms in Canada are classified as restricted, non–restricted and prohibited. ALL handguns are either restricted or prohibited. Visitors CANNOT import a prohibited firearm into Canada. They must be at least 18 to import other firearms. Restricted firearms are only allowed for approved purposes such as participation in target–shooting competitions where the importation is allowed for special purposes, with a temporary registration (nonresident fee of $25).

Pepper spray is allowed if it is clearly labeled as an animal repellent, e.g. bear spray. "Mace" and similar products intended to incapacitate a person are prohibited.

Visit the Canada Firearms Centre online at www.rcmp-grc.gc.ca/cfp-pcaf/ or phone 1-800-731-4000 for details and documents required to lawfully import and possess firearms in Canada, as well as the rules for storing and transporting firearms. Visit the Canada Border Services Agency online at www.cbsa.gc.ca for information on border controls or call the BIS line.

Fireworks: An import permit issued by Natural Resources Canada is required.

Returning Canadian Residents: Personal exemptions from duty on imported goods is based on how long you have been absent: $50 worth of goods for 24 hours (does not apply to tobacco products and alcoholic beverages); $400 of goods for 48 hours; and $750 for 7 days or more.

Entry into the U.S. from Canada

Identification: All U.S. residents and Canadian citizens, aged 16 and older, must present a valid, acceptable travel document that denotes both identity and citizenship when entering the United States by land or sea. U.S. and Canadian citizens under 16 must have a birth certificate issued by federal, state, provincial, county or municipal authority or alternative proof of citizenship when entering by land or sea. WHTI-compliant documents include U.S. or Canadian passports, Trusted Traveler Card (NEXUS, SENTRI, or FAST/EXPRES), U.S. Passport Card, state or province-issued enhanced driver's license when and where available. For more information please visit http://getyouhome.gov.

A valid, unexpired passport and visa are required for all other foreign nationals. Nationals of countries participating in the Visa Waiver Program may present unexpired machine-readable passports. The Electronic System for Travel Authorization (ESTA) is accessible via Internet for citizens and eligible nationals of Visa Waiver Program (VWP) countries to apply for advance authorization to travel to U.S. under VWP. Certain persons may require specific supporting documentation such as an employment petition, student authorization, or approval notice. For more details, go to www.travel.state.gov.

Foreign visitors entering the U.S. for the first time are required to pay a paper processing fee of $6 U.S. per person. (This fee does not apply to citizens of Canada.) This fee is payable in U.S. currency or U.S. travelers

checks only. Have U.S. funds prior to arriving at the U.S. border.

What you can bring: Visitors to the U.S. may bring in duty-free all personal effects (wearing apparel, jewelry, hunting and fishing equipment, cameras, portable radios, etc.), household effects (furnishings, dishes, linens, books, etc.), and vehicles for personal use and not for resale.

Non-residents who are at least 21 years old may bring in, free of duty, up to 1 litre of alcoholic beverage (beer, wine, liquor) for personal use. Quantities above 1 litre are subject to duty and internal revenue tax. Tobacco products included in your personal exemption are 200 cigarettes (one carton) or 50 cigars or 2 kg. (4.4 lbs.) of smoking tobacco, or proportional amounts of each.

If you require medicine containing habit-forming drugs, carry only the quantity normally needed and properly identified, and have a prescription or written statement from your personal physician that the medicine is necessary for your physical well-being.

The U.S. Dept. of Agriculture's Animal and Plant Health Inspection Service (APHIS) requires that travelers entering the United States from a foreign country declare all fruit, vegetables, plants and plant products, meat and meat products, animals, birds and eggs. This includes agricultural products of U.S. origin. Fruits, vegetables, meats, and birds taken out of the United States cannot always be reentered into the country. APHIS offers traveler tips for facilitating inspection at the international border at www.aphis.usda.gov/ppq/permits.

Travelers purchasing Alaska Native arts made with wildlife parts while in Alaska who drive back through Canada to the Lower 48 with these items, should check regulations beforehand. (Mammoth and mastodon ivory require no paperwork, but walrus ivory does). The U.S. Fish & Wildlife Service and Alaska State Council on the Arts have issued a *Customs Guide to Alaska Native Arts*. View or download the guide at www.eed.state.ak.us/aksca/pdf/customs_guide_to_ak_native_arts.pdf. You may also request a copy by phoning 1-800-858-7621. The U.S. Fish and Wildlife Service Import Export Office is located in Anchorage; phone (907) 271-6198.

Other restricted or prohibited items may include: Cuban cigars, liquor-filled candy; firearms and ammunition; hazardous articles (fireworks, dangerous toys, toxic or poisonous substances); lottery tickets; exotic pets; pet birds; obscene articles and publications; switchblade knives; trademarked items; wildlife and endangered species, including any part or product.

Personal exemptions for U.S. residents depend on how long you have been out of the country; if you have been out of the country more than once in a 30-day period; and the total value of the merchandise you are bringing back with you, as well as its country of origin. Personal exemptions are $200, $800, or $1,600. There are limits on the amount of alcoholic beverages, cigarettes, cigars, and other tobacco products that may be included in a resident's personal exemption. Differences are explained in "Know Before You Go" at http://www.cbp.gov/xp/cgov/travel/id_visa/kbyg//.

Pets: A valid rabies vaccination certificate must accompany dogs and both dogs and cats must be in apparent good health. It is quite possible that you will be asked for a Veterinary's health certificate, proving

a health inspection within the past 30 days (prior to your arrival at the border crossing). These are no longer mandatory but if there is any question regarding your pets health you may be denied entry if you do not have the certificate.

Invasive Species: Be aware that when crossing the border by ferry or automobile, you may unintentionally transport invasive weeds and other pests that can damage Alaska's ecosystems. Learn about the risks that invasive species pose and simple steps you can take to avoid facilitating their spread. Alaska has a unique opportunity to prevent the introduction of species that have harmed natural resources elsewhere.

Resource managers in Alaska have identified spotted knapweed as a high priority species for prevention and eradication, due to its potential to severely harm moose, deer, caribou, elk and salmon. Introduced to North America a couple hundred years ago, spotted knapweed has severely infested the northwestern United States and Southern British Columbia. Knapweeds replace native grass species, which can decrease forage for livestock and wildlife. It also increases soil erosion, which degrades fish habitat. Once established, controlling spotted knapweed is difficult and costly.

Small populations of spotted knapweed have been found in Alaska. We encourage you to employ the following practices to prevent the spread of spotted knapweed and other unwanted invasives. Wash vehicles thoroughly and often, especially before entering Alaska; pay special attention to areas where soil is likely to be trapped, such as on the insides of wheels and anywhere beneath the vehicle; clean ATVs, trailers, bicycles, boats, and footwear thoroughly after use and before resuming travel.

Report spotted knapweed and other high priority invasive weeds. Visit www.alaskainvasives.org for a free pocket weed guide.

Cruising to Alaska

Alaska's massive coastline features extraordinary beauty and quaint, small-

town ports to explore. A destination sought after by many, cruises to Alaska combine the comfort of a largely prepaid and often luxurious accommodation with the wild beauty of Alaska. And the choices of port-side experiences vary to suit any cruiser. Whether your passion is to shop for Alaska jewelry or Alaska Native artwork, flightsee over natural wonders, take a thrilling zipline tour, kayak in glacial waters, take a dogsled ride or glacier hike, the options are seemingly endless.

The most common choice for cruisers is the week-long Inside Passage itinerary which departs from Seattle or Vancouver, with stops at several Southeast Alaska ports and a return to the departure city. The second most common would be a one-way, either traveling north or southbound through the Inside Passage and crossing the Gulf, with one direction traveled by cruiseship and the other by airplane. And lastly, there are a wide array of shorter and longer trips that range from sailing to cruising, often in a more boutique-styled vessel. These may stay solely in the Inside Passage, Cross Sound or the Prince William Sound area. A few longer voyages include those that cross trans-Pacific to Russia or Japan while including the Alaska Gulf, Aleutian Islands and Southwest Alaska ports.

Among the choices to make in this vacation decision are what size of vessel and quantity of fellow travelers appeal to you? Ships to Alaska vary from nearly 3000 passengers on mega cruiseships down to just a handful of fellow travelers on the smallest boats. Next, when do you want to cruise? Cruising season is largely mid-May to mid-September for the most options but both pre-season and post-season choices can offer unusual port stops and extraordinary experiences. The warmest weather is likely in July or August but salmon runs and whale watching may be better in June or September. And lastly, which type of experience are you after and which ports do you hope to visit? With those decisions made, you can begin to examine the options of cruiseline and sailing date that works best for you.

See general details and contact information in the following overview of

Silversea's Silver Shadow stops in Homer on its May sailing between Tokyo and Seward.
(©Sharon Nault)

A cruise ship sails down Gastineau Channel from Juneau. (©Sharon Nault)

cruise companies serving Alaska in 2014. Additional choices, information and booking opportunities are available by calling or going to the websites that are included.

Large to "Mega" Cruiseships

Carnival Cruiselines: The Carnival *Miracle* (2,124 passengers/963 ft. in length) offers summer-long Tuesday departures from Seattle (beginning late May) and docks at Ketchikan, Juneau and Skagway with a trip through Glacier Bay and a return to Victoria, BC. Information at 1-800-CARNIVAL; www. Carnival.com.

Celebrity Cruiselines: The *Century*, *Millennium* and *Solstice* all tour Alaska waters (approx. 1,814 passengers/843 ft. in length) with so many options, they're impossible to list. Cruises range from 7-16 days in length with multiple focuses to choose between. Information from 1-800-647-2251; www.celebritycruises.com.

Disney Cruiselines: the Disney's *Wonder* departs Vancouver, BC, in summer season on Mondays (2,400 passenger/964 ft. in length). The 7-day roundtrip cruise goes through Tracy Arm to Juneau, Skagway and Ketchikan. Additional information at 1-800-951-3532, www.disneycruise.com.

Holland America: is like a small-sized Large/Mega cruiseline with approx. 1,400 passengers/800 ft. in length. Typical stops for these 7-14 day cruises include Ketchikan, Juneau and Skagway with variations that include cross gulf travel to Whittier or Seward. Land and Sea packages make this stand out for guests looking for longer vacations (10-20 day) and the addition of interior experiences. Information from 1-877-932-4259; www.hollandamerica.com.

Norwegian Cruiselines: The *Norwegian Sun* and *Norwegian Jewel* (approx. 2,394 passengers/695 ft. in length) Offering cruises from 5-14 days in length, departure ports include Seattle, WA, Vancouver, BC and Whittier, AK. Both one-way north or southbound, and roundtrip options are available. The longer cruises include more time at glacial viewing locations with options to see wildlife and spend more time ashore. Information from 1-866-234-7350; www.ncl.com.

Princess Cruiselines: This cruiseline schedules 6 ships for Alaska itineraries (approx. 2,590 passengers/935 ft. in length) and offers roundtrips from Seattle, WA, and San Francisco, CA, and north or southbound sailings from Vancouver, BC, or Whittier, AK. Trips vary from 7 to 11 days in length with the 11 day itineraries roundtrip from San Francisco. Information from 1-800-774-6237; www.princess.com.

Royal Caribbean Cruiseline: *Radiance of the Seas* and *Rhapsody of the Seas* (approx. 2,139 passengers/962. ft in length). These two ships depart from Vancouver, BC, Seattle WA, and Seward, AK for 7 night voyages that include Skagway, Tracy Arm Fjord, Victoria and the Hubbard Glacier. Information from 1-866-562-7625; www.royalcaribbean.com.

Mid-Size Cruise Vessels

Oceania Cruiseline: Offering a limited number of 10-night cruises, the *Regatta* departs Seattle, WA and returns to Victoria, BC or departs Vancouver, BC and returns to Seattle, WA. En route it cruises the Inside and Outside Passage, stops in some of the lesser visited ports and offers a luxurious onboard experience. For more information call/go to: 1-800-386-9283; www.cruiseoceania.com.

Regent Seven Seas Cruises: The *Navigator* travels Alaska waters in 2014. These trips are 7-days in length, one-ways from Seward, AK, crossing the Gulf of Alaska and through the Inside Passage to Vancouver, BC or in reverse. This cruise company offers all-inclusive packages with free unlimited shore excursions. Additional information from 1-844-473-4368; www.RSSC.com.

Silversea Cruises: From Vancouver, BC to Seward, AK (or in reverse), the *Silver Shadow* offers 7-day voyages throughout the summer. The routes include Ketchikan, Juneau, Skagway, Sitka, Tracy Arm, Prince Rupert and Victoria, BC. For more information call/go to: 1-877-215-9986; www.silversea.com.

Small Cruise Vessels

Alaska Coastal Quest: This single-ship cruiseline offers some of the most diverse cruising in Southeast Alaska. The expedition-class *Misty Fjord* offers accommodations for 12 guests in 5 staterooms. Varied full-ship charters are offered to groups and individuals; unbooked cabins are then opened to the general public. At press time, the ship was open in April–early June and mid-July–late July as well as late August. Trips range from Ketchikan to Sitka, Sitka to Petersburg, and roundtrip Petersburg. For more information call/go to: Phone (907) 225-3498; www.akquest.com.

Alaska Dream Cruises: The *Alaskan Dream*, *Admiralty Dream* and *Baranof Dream* offer 5 cruise options (approx. 40-60 passengers/100-144 ft. in length). They are the: 13-day Alaska Glacier Bay & Inside Passage Voyage; the 11-day Admiralty, Baranof and Chichagof Explorer; the 11-day Alaska's Southeast Explorer; the 9-day Alaska's Inside Passage Sojourn; the 8-day Alaska's Glacier Bay & Island Adventure; and the 6-day Tracy Arm Fjord Trek. For more information call/go to: 1-855-747-8100; www.AlaskanDreamCruises.com.

AllAboard Yacht Charters: The historic 87-foot, 6 cabin, 1931-vintage yacht *Discovery* features 7-night/8-day Inside Passage cruises north or south between Ketchikan and Juneau, and Juneau and Sitka, and round-trip voyages from Juneau. These cruises provide fishing opportunities, wildlife viewing, rowing skiffs and kayaks for guest adventures. NOTE: All but the final, repositioning trip in Sept. 2014 was fully booked at press time. Book early to travel in 2015 with this provider. For more information call/go to: 1-800-767-1024; www.AlaskaCharters.com.

American Cruise Lines: Embarking Saturdays for 2 itineraries aboard the 100-passenger *American Spirit*. First and last sailings of season are 11-night/12-day 1,000-mile cruises departing from Seattle to Alaska and in reverse, at the beginning and end of season. The line has scheduled 11 7-night/8-day core season Southeast Alaska cruises which include Glacier Bay, Haines, Skagway, Petersburg, and Tracy Arm/South Sawyer Glacier with return to Juneau. For more information call/go to: 1-800-460-4518; www.americancruiselines.com.

The Boat Company: This cruiseline emphasizes environmental awareness. Two vessels—the 20-guest *Liseron*, a now-upscale converted 1940s minesweeper, and the 24-guest *Mist Cove*, a decidedly upscale replica—sail 7-night/8-day voyages between Sitka and Juneau. The itinerary is flexible and spontaneous. Passengers can spend as much time off the boat as they like, hiking, fishing, canoeing, kayaking or beachcombing. For more information call/go to: 1-877-647-8268; www.theboatcompany.org.

Discovery Voyages: This pioneering small ship cruise company operates the comfortably refurbished former missionary vessel *Discovery* in Prince William Sound. Cruise and cruise-tour itineraries range from 3 to 13 days. Its varied-length sightseeing vessel trips include a hike and kayak voyage, Sierra Club Classic Discovery, Grand Alaska Journey (includes Denali National Park), Photo Voyages and more. For more information call/go to: 1-800-324-7602; www.discoveryvoyages.com.

Fantasy Cruises: A full summer season of mostly 8-night/9-day voyages aboard the *Island Spirit*. Sailings are a series of alternating southbound or northbound trips between Sitka and Petersburg. All trips include glacier viewing, beach hikes, explor-

ing small coves, forest trail walks, and other outdoor activities. Initial and final voyages for the year will be a Juneau to Seattle voyage For more information call/go to: 1-800-234-3861; www.smallalaskaship.com.

Lindblad Expeditions/National Geographic: The *Sea Bird* and *Sea Lion* both provide 62 passenger accommodations in 31 outside suites. The 8- or 15- day journeys feature Tracy Arm fjord and Sawyer glaciers, Ford's Terror wilderness, Petersburg, whale watching in Frederick Sound, Chatham Strait, Point Adolphus, and Inian Pass plus cruising a full day in Glacier Bay. For more information call/go to: 1-800-397-3348; www.expeditions.com.

Maple Leaf Adventures: A 92-foot "tall ship" sailing schooner, the *Maple Leaf*, accommodates 8-9 guests. This historic vessel has sailed the waters of Alaska and British Columbia since 1904. 2014 trips are already sold out on some dates so trips must be booked in advance. Ports of call include Ketchikan, Petersburg and Baranof in Warm Springs Bay. For more information call/go to: 1-888-599-5323; www.MapleLeafAdventures.com.

Sea Wolf Adventures: The 12 passenger/97 ft *Sea Wolf* accommodates and specializes in cruises that are 6- and 10-day Glacier Bay trips, 10-day Inside Passage, and 11-day Great Bear Exploring BC's Inside Passage. This small-group offers customized options like beach strolls and mountain climbs as well as sea life viewing and kayaking. For more information call/go to: (907) 957-1438; www.seawolfadventures.net.

Sound Sailing: The vessel is a modern, fast Catalina/Morgan 50-foot sailboat, with 3 guest cabins (large double berth with private head and shower). They offer itineraries for 6- or 9-day trips, customizing each trip to match passenger interests. For more information call/go to: (907) 887-9446 or www.soundsailing.com.

Un-Cruise Adventures: From April to September, these boats (22-86 passengers) will sail 11 different itineraries that range from 7 to 21 nights. Some of these cruises focus on gold rush history and Inside Passage culture. Other cruises feature expedition-style explorations, including kayaking and paddle-boarding. The luxury cruise options have extra amenities, soft-adventure, and exclusive excursions. For more information call/go to: 1-888-862-8881 or www.un-cruise.com.

Driving North

Driving to the North is no longer the ordeal it was in the early days. Those old images of the Alaska Highway with vehicles stuck in mud up to their hubcaps are far removed from the asphalt-surfaced Alaska Highway of today.

Motorists can still expect road construction and some rough road. But have patience! Ongoing projects are helping to improve severely deteriorated sections of road.

Roads in the North range from multi-lane freeways to 1-lane dirt and gravel roads. The more remote roads are gravel. Motorists are much farther from assistance, and more preparation is required for these roads.

Major highways in Alaska are paved with the exception of the following highways that are at least partially gravel: Steese Highway (Alaska Route 6), Taylor Highway

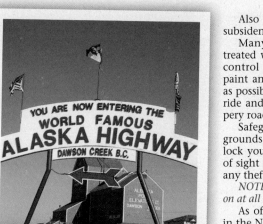

Alaska Highway Mile 0 cairn in Dawson Creek, BC. (©Kris Valencia, staff)

(Alaska Route 5), Elliott Highway (Alaska Route 2), Dalton Highway (Alaska Route 11) and Denali Highway (Alaska Route 8).

In Yukon, the Alaska Highway, the Haines Highway and the Klondike Highway from Skagway to Dawson City are asphalt-surfaced.

Major routes through Alberta and British Columbia are paved. The Cassiar Highway (BC Highway 37) is paved with occasional gravel breaks. The Liard Highway connecting British Columbia and Northwest Territories is both gravel and pavement. Paving has been completed on NWT Highway 3 to Yellowknife, and NWT Highway 1 is paved from its junction with Highway 3 to the Alberta border.

RV owners should be aware of the height of their vehicles in metric measurements, as bridge heights in Canada are noted in meters.

Know your vehicle and its limitations. Some Northern roads may not be suitable for a large motorhome or trailer, but most roads will present no problem to a motorist who allots adequate time and uses common sense. It is always a good idea to empty your gray water tanks before you embark, to decrease weight on tougher roads.

Keep in mind the variable nature of road conditions. Some sections of road may be in poor condition because of current construction or recent bad weather. Other highways—particularly gravel roads closed in winter—may be very rough or very smooth, depending on when maintenance crews last worked on the road.

Asphalt surfacing for most Northern roads is Bituminous Surface Treatment (BST), an alternative to hot-mix pavement which involves application of aggregates and emulsified asphalt. Also known as "chip seal," recently applied or repaired BST is as smooth as any Lower 48 superhighway. However, weather and other factors can lead to failures in the surfacing including potholes and loss of aggregate.

Also watch for "frost heaves" caused by subsidence of the ground under the road.

Many gravel roads in the North are treated with magnesium chloride as a dust-control measure. This substance corrodes paint and metal; wash your vehicle as soon as possible. In heavy rains, magnesium chloride and mud combine to make a very slippery road surface; drive carefully!

Safeguard against theft while at campgrounds, rest stops or in the cities. Always lock your vehicle, be sure valuables are out of sight in an unattended vehicle and report any thefts to the authorities.

NOTE: Drive with headlights and seat belts on at all times.

As often as we give advice about driving in the North Country, we also hear from our readers who have additional comments that may be helpful to others. Gerry Kreimeyer had this to say about protecting RVs.

"Dirty windows, damaged paint or finishes, and constant cleaning can all take away from the enjoyment of seeing Canada and Alaska on your trip north. There are some preparations and precautions you can take before you leave home that will lessen the workload. Whether you own or rent an RV, keeping the RV clean and damage-free is easier when you plan ahead.

"First: Make sure the RV is water tight. Check and reseal any caulk that is cracked, damaged or missing. A good self-leveling lap sealant is best.

"Second: Wash, degrease, clean and wax. There are products made for fiberglass boats in salt-water (go to www.collinitemarine.com for wax and cleaner/degreaser) that work great for RVs.

"Third: Apply a barrier to help prevent or minimize damage from rocks, dirt and bugs. Inexpensive surface protectors like www.surfacearmor.com work well on RVs."

Gasoline/Diesel

Gasoline and diesel are readily available in Alaska and Canada. Good advice for travelers: Gas up/fuel up whenever possible.

In the North, as elsewhere, gas prices vary. Generally, gas prices are slightly higher in Canada and Alaska than the Lower 48, but this is not a hard and fast rule. You may find gas in Anchorage or other Alaska cities the same price—or even lower—than in Lower 48 communities. A general rule of thumb: The more remote the gas station, the higher the price. Gas prices may vary considerably at service stations within the same community. And don't forget to factor in prevailing exchange rates (see accompanying chart) and credit card company

It is a good idea to carry cash, since a few gas stations in Alaska and along some Canadian highways are independents and may not accept credit cards, although most if not all gas stations—including Chevron, Shell/Texaco, Petro-Canada, North 60 Express Petro, Esso and Tesoro stations—will accept VISA and MasterCard. Watch for posted gas prices that are for cash, but not noted as such. Some northern Canadian gas stations have begun "pay inside only" due to drivers leaving without paying. Some stations are automated and there is no attendant on duty. Gas stations may have dollar limits on number of gallons pumped using a credit card or they may put a "hold" for a fixed amount on your credit card but charge the correct or pump total when collecting charges.

IMPORTANT: Make sure you are at the

Gas Cost in U.S. Funds per Gallon

Canadian price per litre at the pump	Exchange Rate: If $1.00 U.S. equals this Canadian fund amount, your price per gallon based on price per litre will be:				
	$.95	$1.00	$1.05	$1.10	$1.15
$0.85	$3.39	$3.22	$3.06	$2.92	$2.80
$0.89	$3.55	$3.37	$3.21	$3.06	$2.93
$0.93	$3.71	$3.52	$3.35	$3.20	$3.06
$0.97	$3.86	$3.67	$3.50	$3.34	$3.19
$1.01	$4.02	$3.82	$3.64	$3.48	$3.32
$1.05	$4.18	$3.97	$3.79	$3.61	$3.46
$1.09	$4.34	$4.13	$3.93	$3.75	$3.59
$1.13	$4.50	$4.28	$4.07	$3.89	$3.72
$1.17	$4.66	$4.43	$4.22	$4.03	$3.85
$1.21	$4.82	$4.58	$4.36	$4.16	$3.98
$1.25	$4.98	$4.73	$4.51	$4.30	$4.11
$1.29	$5.14	$4.88	$4.65	$4.44	$4.25
$1.34	$5.34	$5.07	$4.83	$4.61	$4.41
$1.39	$5.54	$5.26	$5.01	$4.78	$4.57
$1.44	$5.74	$5.45	$5.19	$4.95	$4.74
$1.49	$5.94	$5.64	$5.37	$5.13	$4.90
$1.54	$6.14	$5.83	$5.55	$5.30	$5.07
$1.58	$6.30	$5.98	$5.70	$5.44	$5.20
$1.62	$6.45	$6.13	$5.84	$5.57	$5.33
$1.66	$6.61	$6.28	$5.98	$5.71	$5.46
$1.70	$6.77	$6.43	$6.13	$5.85	$5.60
$1.74	$6.93	$6.59	$6.27	$5.99	$5.73
$1.78	$7.09	$6.74	$6.42	$6.12	$5.86
$1.82	$7.25	$6.89	$6.56	$6.26	$5.99
$1.86	$7.41	$7.04	$6.70	$6.40	$6.12
$1.90	$7.57	$7.19	$6.85	$6.54	$6.25
$1.94	$7.73	$7.34	$6.99	$6.68	$6.39
$1.98	$7.89	$7.49	$7.14	$6.81	$6.52

right pump for the fuel you need and double-check with attendant if diesel and gas are not clearly identified. Do not assume type of gas by pump handle color. Diesel is usually identified by a green pump handle in the U.S., while in Canada a green handle is gas and a yellow or red pump handle is diesel. But even color coding cannot be relied upon, since pumps may be repurposed by the gas station so that the diesel pump pumps gas, for example, and a note to this effect is probably taped to the front of the pump.

Canadian gas stations use the metric system; quantity/price are based on litres. There are 3.785 litres per U.S. gallon or .2642 gallons per litre. The chart above shows cost per litre in U.S. funds depending on exchange rate. Canadian gas stations, like U.S. stations, grade gasoline according to the octane rating, but they use the designations Bronze (87), Silver (89) and Gold (91) instead of regular, plus, and super/supreme/premium. Some northern gas stations may *only* have regular gas available. Consider bringing a booster additive with you if your vehicle requires a super/supreme level gas. ULSD (Ultra Low Sulfur Diesel) is available by law across Canada and Alaska.

Emergency Services Along the Way

Major cities and many mid-size towns in the North have hospitals, ambulance service and police on the 911 system. Out on the highway it is often a different story, with stretches of road that may not be included in a 911 service area or even have cell phone reception. **Emergency Services** are noted in all highway communities in *The MILEPOST®*, with phone numbers for Alaska State Troopers and RCMP, city police, ambulances, hospitals and health clinics. In the event of an injury accident, first try 911, then the number of the nearest law enforcement.

Because of the long distances between services on most Northern highways and byways, there is a tradition in the North of stopping to help motorists in trouble. Local residents will usually jump into action and lend a helping hand.

Highway Safety Tips

Carry an emergency road kit with flares and/or reflectors. In the event of an accident or vehicle breakdown, create a safety zone around the vehicle using at least 3 flares. Place flares/reflectors starting 300 feet behind your vehicle on the edge of the roadway to adequately warn oncoming traffic. Tie a white cloth to the radio antenna or a door handle. Make sure it is clearly visible.

If you do not have flares/reflectors, turn on your vehicle's emergency flashers or leave your headlights on low beam and turn on your turn signal. Put up the hood

of the car. The highway flares, white cloth and flashers are all distress signals that will let law enforcement officers know that you need help.

If possible pull your vehicle off the main highway onto the shoulder or use a turnout (turnouts are logged in *The MILEPOST®*). Injury and fatality accidents often occur after someone has stopped along the road either because they are in trouble or have stopped to help someone else in trouble.

Stay with your vehicle until help comes. If you must leave your vehicle, carry a flashlight or lightstick. Walk on road shoulder, facing traffic.

Insurance

Auto insurance is mandatory in Alaska and all Canadian provinces and territories. The minimum liability insurance requirement in Canada is $200,000 Canadian. Drivers should carry adequate car insurance before entering the country. Visiting motorists are required to produce evidence of financial responsibility should they be involved in an accident. There is an automatic fine if visitors involved in an accident are found to be uninsured. Your car could be impounded.

Ask your insurance company about providing you with some tangible proof of insurance coverage that would be evidence of financial responsibility.

Motorcycles

Almost every make of motorcycle, in every shape and size, has made the trip to Alaska. The most common concern expressed by motorcyclists we've talked to along the way was the distance between gas stops. Many were using *The MILEPOST®* to figure their gas stops in advance of each day's travel. Some also carried auxiliary gas tanks.

Many motorcyclists were pulling trailers and there were no significant challenges to report despite driving many miles of road that included stretches of gravel, potholes and frost heaves. We did meet up with a motorcyclist on the Alaska Highway one year who was on the return portion of his trip back to the Lower 48. He had found out the hard way that he was pulling too heavy a trailer for Northern roads. He had had a miserable time negotiating the frost heaves and potholes that plague some roads.

Lighter bikes are more suitable for gravel roads while larger bikes are definitely more comfortable for long highway trips. If you prefer, you can fly or cruise to Alaska then rent a motorcycle from Alaska Rider Motorcycle Tours out of Anchorage and skip the extra miles and wear on your own bike. Power cruisers and touring bikes are popular choices, especially with those pulling trailers.

Regardless of what you ride, perform major maintenance on your bike before heading North. If you break down on the road, towing distances to the next repair shop can be several hundred miles.

There are motorcycle repair shops in Alaska and Canada, but you will usually find well-stocked motorcycle shops only in the cities. Many riders prefer the comfort designed models made for touring and these are serviced in major cities, just as they would in the lower 48. For service for Harley-Riders, or just for the location of that next great Harley collectible T-shirt, there is Harley-Davidson Motorcycles in Fairbanks;

Denali Harley-Davidson Shop at Mile 37.5 Parks Highway in Wasilla; House of Harley-Davidson and Buell in Anchorage and adjacent it, Alaska Rider and MotoQuest Tours; Kenai Peninsula Harley-Davidson, Soldotna; Yukon Harley-Davidson, Whitehorse, YT; and Trails End Harley-Davidson in Yellowknife, NWT.

Windshields are essential to protect riders from gravel and dust. Some bikers also use plexiglas headlight shields and hand guards. A fairing, while not completely protecting you from rocks, will offer good protection against insects, rain, wind and cold. Case guards are good insurance against damage to the bike should you go down. Consider taking a good competition air filter to improve engine performance and gas mileage. Heated handgrips are also recommended for colder temperatures. A skid plate will help protect the engine from rocks kicked up by the front wheel, and a center stand can be a great help when parking on gravel, fixing a flat or lubing a chain. For additional security, carry a light nylon cover for your bike. Keep your radiator safe from flying rocks with a perforated guard in front of it, as suggested by riders we met on the road.

As far as gas tanks go, the bigger, the better. While gas is readily available on major routes, fuel stops are few and far between in more remote areas. An auxiliary tank or additional gas cans may be necessary.

Gravel roads are rough on tires, and flats are common, so start out with new tires. A complete tire repair kit is essential. Also, bring a valve stem tool, a mini bicycle pump and dish soap to aid in tire changes.

Some northern bridges present challenges to motorcyclists. There are numerous narrow 2-lane bridges, many with metal-grated decks that can be *very slippery* when wet and have longitudinal grooves that tend to cause motorcycles to sway. Go with the sway rather than fighting it. There are also wood-deck bridges that are very slippery when wet. Slow down when crossing these bridges.

Be wary when driving on roads with rumble strips. Some roads will have rumble strips down the center lines so that people who wander into the center of the highway will be alerted to their location. These rumble strips can startle a biker while pulling out to pass a vehicle ahead and cause them to overcorrect. These grooves have been studied and determined to not be a danger in and of themselves for motorcyclists, but when taken by surprise by them, can impact a rider.

We have met many groups of riders out on the road who were having fantastic trips with nary a problem. But there have also been fatal motorcycle accidents caused by moose, other cars and rough roads.

In 2012, a rider named Richard Seay, who we had first met, along with his buddy John Conniff, at a rest stop on the Tok Cutoff, emailed us about a serious accident he had on the Dalton Highway (more on that below).

We don't need to warn experienced motorcyclists about the dangers of the road, but we do need to remind motorcyclists about the unique challenges of riding in the North. As Richard noted in his email to us about his accident, "I have a new respect for the Canadian and Alaskan roads."

Richard's story: "We were on a 200-mile ride north out of Fairbanks to the Arctic

Gas stations come in all shapes and sizes in the North, like this one at Deadhorse.
(©Sharon Nault)

Circle for a photo-op at the Arctic Circle sign. We had rented 3 BMW dual-sport motorcycles for the ride up the Dalton Highway. It was a beautiful day, great riding and the road was in good condition.

"I was leading the group, about 30 miles south of the Arctic Circle, when I came up on 4 huge potholes (actually looked like bomb craters). I could not stop in time and there was a motorhome in the southbound lane that eliminated my plan to swerve around the potholes. I hit the potholes and went over the handlebars at 50mph." Richard's bike was totaled and he suffered life-threatening injuries.

"An Alyeska pipeline environmental engineer stopped in a pickup truck and offered to drive me South to Pump Station #6 (on the Yukon River) where they had EMTs. He did and they were waiting for us to arrive. The EMT checked me out and said I had obvious broken bones but he also suspected internal injuries and bleeding and said I needed to get to a hospital quickly. He suggested either they take me in the Alyeska ambulance south down the Dalton Highway or they take me north to Pump Station #5 where they had an airport and Alyeska medi-vac airplane to take me to Fairbanks. He recommended the airplane and that is what we did. I did get to cross the Arctic Circle, but in the ambulance!

"At Fairbanks they did X-rays and scans when I arrived. Monday morning they decided to Medivac me to Anchorage Providence Hospital.

"I am very grateful to the Alyeska EMT who saved my life with his assessment of my injuries and recommendation to get to a hospital promptly. I am really grateful to Alyeska for their EMT treatment and the flight from Pump Station #5 to Fairbanks. Fortunately, I had good medical and vehicle insurance."

Richard spent another week in the hospital in Anchorage undergoing treatment, then flew home to Texas. His buddy John took care of shipping their bikes.

Final word to both motorcyclists and

vehicle drivers: Be safe out there! Watch out for wildlife. There are quite a few moose-vehicle collisions each year and some stretches of highway are designated Moose Danger Zones. We met a young woman who totaled her car after hitting a grizzly along Kluane Lake (the bear ran off). Be alert for potholes, loose gravel on pavement and other road damage such as frost heaves and deeply rutted pavement that can fatally hinder your ability to maneuver at normal driving speeds.

Planning your trip

Depending on where you want to stop and how much time you have to spend, you can count on driving anywhere from 150 to 500 miles a day. On most roads in the North, you can figure on comfortably driving 250 to 300 miles a day.

In the individual highway sections, log mileages are keyed on the highway strip maps which accompany each highway section in *The MILEPOST*. You may also use the mileage boxes on these maps to calculate mileages between points, or refer to the mileage box at the beginning of the highway as well. There is a Mileage Chart on the back of the Plan-A-Trip Map, and mileages between junctions and communities are also given on the Key to Highways maps *appearing on pages 9-11.*

Four suggested itineraries are located in the back of the book, *pages 747-750,* to serve as trip ideas for those looking for a bit more instruction. These basic routes include varied inbound and outbound routes to maximize your Alaska/Canada experience by not having to retrace your steps. The major attractions are listed with each itinerary to assist you with your decision.

Gas prices can fluctuate drastically throughout the year and in various locations along the highways. For current gas prices visit www.gasbuddy.com or got to www.themilepost.com and click on Alaska, British Columbia and Alberta gas price links at the bottom of the home page. Also use our gas chart this sec-

Expect traffic delays at road construction projects along Northern roads. (©Kris Valencia, staff)

tion to help you determine price per litre when in Canada.

Normally, May through October is the best time to drive to Alaska. A severe winter or wet spring may affect road conditions, and there may be some rough road until road maintenance crews get out to upgrade and repair. Motels, hotels, gas stations and restaurants are open year-round in the cities and on many highways. On more remote routes, such as the Cassiar Highway, not all businesses are open year-round. Check road conditions and weather outlook before traveling. Also call ahead for accommodations and gas if traveling these roads in winter.

VISA and MasterCard are readily accepted all along the highways of Alaska and Canada. Still, it is wise to carry enough cash for souvenirs, gas or lodging at that random place that may not accept plastic.

Police

The 2 police forces travelers will see along the highways of the North are the Alaska State Troopers in Alaska and the Royal Canadian Mounted Police (RCMP) in Canada. In addition, many Northern communities have city or municipal police.

The RCMP was established in Yukon during the Klondike Gold Rush, when it was called the Northwest Mounted Police. Later the RCMP began patrolling the newly constructed Alaska Highway in the 1940s, with detachments at Whitehorse, Haines Junction, Teslin and Watson Lake. Today, the RCMP is responsible for providing policing services at the federal, provincial and municipal level throughout Canada, and has more than a dozen detachments in Yukon.

The Alaska State Troopers is a statewide law enforcement agency with Trooper Posts throughout the state and Detachments in Ketchikan, Palmer, Anchorage, Fairbanks and Soldotna.

Like their Canadian counterparts, Alaska's law enforcement evolved largely in response to the influx of gold seekers, followed by the need to patrol the state's growing number of roads in the 1940s. The Territory of Alaska Highway Patrol was established in 1941, and given policing powers in 1948. The Alaska State Trooper Museum in Anchorage traces the history of this public safety division.

Phone numbers for city police, RCMP detachments and Alaska State Troopers posts are noted in community descriptions.

Road Condition Reports

General road conditions are noted in the introduction to each highway in *The MILE-POST*®. Specific areas of concern are also called out in the logs. Current seasonal road conditions provided by government agencies may be obtained at www.themilepost.com. Or contact the following:

Alaska road conditions. The Alaska DOT has a telephone- and web-based travel information system: 511 Travel in the Know. The 511 system provides current driving conditions, current and future road construction, closures, incidents and urgent reports, weather cameras, winter driving tips, route summary reports and mountain pass locations. Phone 511, or visit their website at http://511.alaska.gov. (The National Weather Service also provides weather information at www.arh.noaa.gov/.)

Statewide updates for Very Difficult and/or Hazardous driving condition will be tweeted to the Twitter handle @alaska511. Travelers can follow either the statewide handle @alaska511 or the folllowing area Twitter accounts preceded by ak511_ (for example ak511_Anchorage): Anchorage, Fairbanks, Southeast, Peninsula, Mat-Su, Tok, Tazlina, Valdez, Dalton, Denali.

Current road conditions available at http://dot.alaska.gov.traveler.shtml; click 511 Traveler Information then click on icons for details. Or choose an area or corridor map at http://www.dot.state.ak.us/iways/roadweather/forms/AreaSelectForm.html then click on blue icons: It will give you the temperature of the road.

Yukon road conditions: For year-round daily recorded updates, phone (867) 456-7623 toll-free in YT only. Yukon Highways & Public Works Dept.'s Road Report online at www.511yukon.ca/. Reports are up-to-the-minute and include road construction. Also visit the Visitor Centres for reports and conditions.

British Columbia road conditions: General automated road information is available 24 hours-a-day toll-free 1-800-550-4997 (cell *4997); or dial 511 in BC for road reports. Or go to www.drivebc.ca.

Northwest Territories road conditions: Phone toll-free 1-800-661-0750 or go to www.dot.gov.nt.ca and click on "Highway/Ferry Conditions" under the Drivers/Vehicles subhead (http://www.dot.gov.nt.ca/_live/pages/wpPages/roadConditions.aspx).

Alberta road conditions: The Alberta Motor Association's website at www.ama.ab.ca has road reports under the Auto & Driving subhead for specific routes. Or go to or go to http://511.alberta.ca/ab/en.html.

Roundabouts

Since 2000, the Alaska Dept. of Transportation has built more than a dozen roundabouts—in Anchorage, Fairbanks, Juneau and Sitka—and more are planned, so both residents and visiting motorists need to know how to negotiate these unique traffic patterns. Essentially, roundabouts are 1- to 2-lane continuous traffic intersections. Traffic moves in a counter-clockwise direction and there are no traffic signals. The most important rule to remember is: Motorists already in the roundabout have the right-of-way. Vehicles entering the roundabout must yield to vehicles already in the roundabout.

While traffic in the roundabout has the right-of-way and should not stop, in practice roundabout drivers will slow to allow drivers waiting at the yield lines to enter the roundabout during periods of heavy traffic, such as rush hour.

Finally, follow posted speed limits; stop for pedestrians; watch for bicyclists; and drive defensively. For more information, go to www.alaskaroundabouts.com.

Speed Limits/Driving Laws

Travelers may plan to average 55 mph on paved highways. For more remote gravel roads, such as the Taylor Highway and Denali Highway, a safe average might be 40 to 45 mph.

Actual driving time may vary due to weather, road construction, road conditions, traffic, time of day, season, driver ability and rest stops, but 55 mph is a reliable average for the main routes.

The MILEPOST® references speed limits on some sections of highways to give an idea of travel time. But on the whole, we do not include posted speed limits, which on paved highways in Alaska range from 55 to 65 mph on major highways to 35 mph through communities.

In British Columbia, if you are caught speeding more than 40 kmph/25 mph above the speed limit, your vehicle will be impounded for 7 days. The cost of towing and the impound storage fee is at least $210, in addition to your fine.

Of particular note because of its severity compared to other provinces, territories and states, is British Columbia's drinking limits allowable for drivers. A 0.05 blood alcohol concentration has a first offense of 3-days driving ban, $200 fine, possible vehicle impound for 3 days (with $150 fee associated) and a $250 reinstatement fee for your driver's license (this totals at least $600 for the first offense).

Distracted Driving laws are in place in Yukon, British Columbia, Alberta and Northwest Territories banning the use of

handheld cell phones and other electronic devices including iPods, laptops and GPS units. Fines range from $100 to $250 and 0 to 3 demerits, depending on the province, against your record. One-touch or voice activated phones are allowed. See http://distracteddriving.caa.ca/education/distracted-driving-laws-in-canada.php for specifics.

Tires

On gravel, the faster you drive, the faster your tires will wear out. So take it easy, and you should have no tire problems, provided you have the right size for your vehicle, with the right pressure, not overloaded, and not already overly worn. Belted bias or radial ply tires are recommended for gravel roads. Studded tires are legal in Alaska from Sept. 15 to May 1 and from Oct. 1–April 30 in BC. Yukon is in conjunction with Alaska and BC.

Carry 1 good spare. Consider 2 spares if you are traveling remote gravel roads such as the Dempster, Taylor and Dalton highways. The space-saver (doughnut) spare tires found in some passenger cars are not adequate for travel on gravel roads.

Our RVing friend Gerald Kreimeyer says: "Check your tires' manufacture date. If the tires are 4 or 5 years old or show signs of cracking, you need new ones, especially driving Northern Roads. It is not just the inconvenience of a flat tire: Tire blowouts can inflict tremendous damage to the under carriage of your rig and, if a rear dually is affected, can wipe out electric, plumbing or even worse."

Vehicle Preparation

Make sure your vehicle and tires are in good condition. Paved highways have cut down on the problems with dust and mud in the North, though you may run into both on gravel roads or in construction areas. When driving gravel in dry weather, keep the windows on your vehicle closed and check your air filter periodically.

A high clearance vehicle is best for some of the rougher gravel roads. Good windshield wipers and a full windshield washer (or a bottle of wash and a squeegee) will make travel safer.

On gravel roads, drive at slow, safe speeds to keep down the dust for drivers behind you, and avoid spraying other vehicles with gravel. Gravel breaks are noted by "Loose Gravel" signs. *Slow down for gravel breaks!*

Although auto shops in Northern communities are generally well-stocked with parts, carry tools and a first-aid kit. If you are driving a vehicle which may require parts not readily available up North, carry whatever you think necessary. You may wish to carry a few extra gallons of gas, water, and fluid for brakes, power steering and automatic transmissions.

RV preparation tips: Diesel pushers can suffer from a "street sweeping" type of injury when traveling through gravel. The mud/rock guards that are installed on most of these RVs can actually end up bouncing rocks and gravel back into the fan, which then propels those items into the radiator at penetrable speeds. To prevent this, Alaska Performance RV's owner, Tim Anderson says, to "consider installing rock guards behind the rear wheels, install tow car shields, and if possible, install protection around the radiator and fan blades." Simple aluminum screening on both sides of the RV, held in place by plastic wire wraps is one reader's fix for this problem. Towing costs and repair costs can be exorbitant in out-of-the-way places, so plan ahead.

In Ronald Jones' *RVing to Alaka*, Mr. Jones includes tips from his travels to Alaska, in a 42-foot rig with tow vehicle. Now in it's second edition, he referred to his experience towing a vehicle on his first trip to Alaska: "I had lots of chipped paint along the front and leading edge of my hood, my windshield had six big 'stars' where rocks hit. I had the equivalent of a small bucket of rocks scatterered around and laying on every nook and cranny of the engine area." For his second trip to Alaska, he used a car cover over his tow vehicle and kept the paint and windshield protected from rocks his RV kicked up. He also adds in his book that he recommends "extra filters and belts for the engine, generator, and AquaHot as these can often be changed by roadside assiantce. Those with diesel pushers often carry a spare set of filters and belts for their engines and generator. Even in the Lower 48, a service facility may not have the exact part you need in stock. Carrying a spare set solves this problem." He also carries a total of 60 feet of air hose to reach all tires on his tow car without unhooking it.

If your vehicle should break down on the highway, and tow truck service is needed, you will normally be able to flag down a passing motorist. Travelers in the North are generally helpful in such situations. If you are the only person traveling in the disabled vehicle, leave a note on your windshield indicating when you left the vehicle and in which direction you planned to travel.

Winter Driving

In addition to the usual precautions taken when driving in winter, such as keeping the windshield clear of ice, checking antifreeze and reducing driving speeds on icy pavement, equip your vehicle with the following survival gear: traction material (ashes, kitty litter, wood chips); chains (even with snow tires); shovel, ice scraper, flashlight, flares; fire extinguisher; extra warm clothing (including gloves, boots, hat and extra socks); blankets or sleeping bags; food; tools; first-aid kit; and an extension cord to plug the car into a block heater. Other items which may be added to your survival gear are a tow rope or cable, ax, jumper cables and extra gas.

Extremely low temperatures occur in the North. A motorist may start out in -35° to -40°F weather and hit cold pockets along the road where temperatures drop to -60°F or more. If you do become stranded in weather like this, do not leave your vehicle; wait for aid. DO NOT attempt to drive unmaintained secondary roads or highways in winter (e.g.

10 Highest Highway Passes in Alaska

Cleary Summit
Steese Highway
(2,233 ft./681m)

Thompson Pass
Richardson Highway
(2,678 ft./816m)

Twelvemile Summit
Steese Highway
(2,982 ft./909m)

Isabel Pass
Richardson Highway
(3,000 ft./914m)

Tahneta Pass
Glenn Highway
(3,000 ft./914m)

White Pass
Klondike Highway 2
(3,290 ft./1,003m)

Eureka Summit
Glenn Highway
(3,322 ft./1,012m)

Eagle Summit
Steese Highway
(3,624 ft./1,105m)

Maclaren Summit
Denali Highway
(4,086 ft./1,245m)

Atigun Pass
Dalton Highway
(4,800 ft./1,463m)

The solarium deck is a popular gathering place on Alaska State Ferries. *(©Sharon Nault)*.

Denali Highway, Top of the World Highway), even if the roads look clear of snow.

An experienced traveler offered the following practical suggestions for others planning to drive northern roads during winter months:

1) Always carry extra car keys in case you start your car to warm it up and want to lock it before departure. 2) A lock de-icer is inexpensive and can be a life saver. 3) Have a bottle of gasline antifreeze to add to your

tank when it is cold—very helpful at below-zero temperatures. 4) A dipstick oilpan heater is useful as a supplement to a block heater and/or a battery blanket; the oilpan heater will expedite the time required for oil pressure to come up. Proper oil weight is also an important factor. 5) Be aware that unprotected wiring beneath your vehicle may be torn up by snow, ice, gravel, road salt and cold temperatures. Check regularly for possible damage. 6) Do not assume you

will make it to the next gas stop based on your typical tank mileage. In extremely cold weather, you are usually driving in a lower gear and getting lower gas mileage. Also, starting your car to warm it up burns a significant amount of fuel; allow for the difference and do not get caught short.

For additional winter driving tips, go to http://511.gov.

Ferry Travel

Ferry travel to and within Alaska is provided by the state ferry system—the Alaska Marine Highway System (AMHS)—which serves Bellingham, WA, Prince Rupert, BC, and 30 coastal Alaska communities from Ketchikan to Unalaska. (The state's Alaska Marine Highway System celebrated 50 years of service last year; see "History of the AMHS" *on page 721*.) The Inside Passage water route the ferries follow from Bellingham, WA, to Skagway, AK, is also referred to as the Alaska Marine Highway. The South-central/Southwest systems serve Prince William Sound, Homer, Kodiak and the Aleutian Islands. *(See maps on pages 716-718.)*

The Inside Passage route for the Alaska Marine Highway, follows the coast of British Columbia and uses the protected waterways between the islands and the mainland of southeastern Alaska. (The Inside Passage is also commonly used to refer to Southeast Alaska and its communities.) The Tongass National Forest places naturalists aboard selected Alaska State Ferries sailing from Bellingham, WA and within Southeast Alaska from Memorial Day to Labor Day, who offer wildlife, marine mammal geology, history, community presentations and will answer questions. Check the Tongass National Forest website for current information (www.fs.usda.gov/tongass).

BC Ferries also serve the Inside Passage, providing passenger/vehicle ferry service between Port Hardy and Prince Rupert, BC. Port Hardy is located at the north end of Vancouver Island, 312 miles/502 km north of Victoria via Trans-Canada Highway 1 and BC Highway 19; the ferry terminal is at Bear Cove *(see "Vancouver Island Highway" log on pages 41-47)*. Prince Rupert is also the farthest north of the 47 ports served by BC Ferries, and the southern port for many Alaska state ferries serving Southeast Alaska.

BC Ferries schedules, information and reservations for Inside Passage and Discovery Coast service, along with details on tariffs and vessels, appear under "BC Ferries" *beginning on page 14 this section*. Visit BC Ferries online at www.bc ferries.com or phone 1-888-223-3779.

Motorists often use the Inside Passage northbound or southbound as an alternative to driving all of the Alaska Highway and its access routes. By using the Alaska Marine Highway System and BC Ferries, travelers can eliminate between 700 and 1,700 miles of highway driving, depending on their itinerary. The water route also allows travelers the opportunity to take in the magnificent scenery and picturesque communities of the Inside Passage. Cross-Gulf trips between Juneau and Whittier save additional highway mileage.

Alaska-bound motorists should keep in mind that only 2 Inside Passage ports connect to the Alaska Highway: Haines, via the Haines Highway; and Skagway, via the South Klondike Highway.

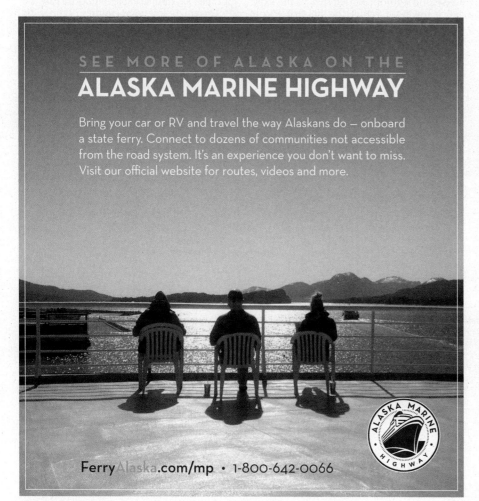

Also providing passenger/vehicle ferry service within Alaska's southeastern region is the Inter-Island Ferry Authority. Details and summer schedule appear on this page.

Alaska State Ferries

The Alaska Marine Highway System's fleet of state ferries provides passenger/vehicle ferry service in 3 regions: Southeast, Southcentral/Prince William Sound and Southcentral/Southwest. There is also Cross-Gulf service in summer connecting Juneau in Southeast and Whittier in Southcentral.

The Alaska state ferry system has 2 seasons: May 1 to Sept. 30 (summer), when sailings are most frequent; and Oct. 1 to April 30 (fall/winter/spring), when service is less frequent. Summer 2014 schedules and tariffs available at our presstime appear in the ALASKA MARINE HIGHWAY section beginning on page 715.

For updates in the summer schedules, schedules for routes and tariffs not shown, fare specials, to make online reservations or for answers to frequently-asked questions, go to the DOT website at www.ferryalaska.com. Email questions to the Alaska Marine Highway System at dot.ask.amhs@alaska.gov or phone the central reservations office in Juneau at 1-800-642-0066.

Reservations: The Alaska state ferries are very popular in summer. Walk-on traffic is usually accommodated, but reservations are advised, especially for those traveling with a vehicle or wanting a cabin. The reservation offices of the Alaska Marine Highway System are at 6858 Glacier Highway in Juneau. Write to P.O. Box 112505, Juneau, AK 99811-2505; local phone (907) 465-3941; phone toll-free 1-800-642-0066; fax (907) 465-8824; TDD 1-800-764-3779. Or make reservations online at www.ferryalaska.com.

If you do not have cabin space on overnight ferry sailings, you will have to go deck passage. For more details on deck passage, reservations, fare payment, cabins and other topics, read the ALASKA MARINE HIGHWAY section beginning on page 715.

Vehicles: Reservations are strongly recommended. Any vehicle that may be driven legally on the high-

Inter-Island Ferry Authority (IFA)

Formed in 1997 to improve transportation to island communities in southern Southeast Alaska, the IFA is a public corporation organized under Alaska's Municipal Port Authority Act.

The IFA's MV *Stikine* or MV *Prince of Wales* offer daily passenger and vehicle service between Ketchikan and Hollis/Clark Bay on Prince of Wales Island. Crossing time is about 3 hours. The IFA ferry departs Ketchikan from a dock adjacent the Alaska Marine Highway terminal. An IFA reservation desk is located inside the Alaska Marine Highway Ketchikan terminal building. IFA maintains its own terminal at Hollis/Clark Bay.

A paved highway begins at the Clark Bay ferry terminal near Hollis on Prince of Wales Island and leads 23 miles to the coast at Klawock with connections to Craig, Hydaburg, Thorne Bay, Coffman Cove, Naukati and Whale Pass; this route takes motorists through the temperate rainforest environment typical of Southeast Alaska. Roads are 2-lane black top, except to Naukati and

Whale Pass, which is gravel and under reconstruction this summer (anticipate delays); see Prince of Wales Island description and road logs on pages 660-668. NOTE: The IFA will be using the Coffman Cove ferry dock on Prince of Wales Island as an alternate to the Hollis dock for approximately 2 weeks in September 2014, while that facility is out of service for upgrading. Daily ferry service between Ketchikan and Prince of Wales Island will operate with the same departure times during this period. Cruising time will be about 5 hours in each direction. Call for more updated information.

Shuttle service once in port may be reached at (907) 401-1414.

For information and reservations on IFA vessels, phone toll-free 1-866-308-4848 or visit www.interislandferry.com.

IFA Terminal Phone #s
Clark Bay/Hollis Terminal:
  Phone (907) 530-4848
Ketchikan Terminal:
  Phone (907) 225-4848

KETCHIKAN TO HOLLIS
MV *Stikine* or MV *Prince of Wales*

Daily year-round service
(except for Thanksgiving Day & Christmas Day)

Depart Hollis 8:00 A.M. - Arrive Ketchikan 11:00 A.M.
Depart Ketchikan 3:30 P.M. - Arrive Hollis 6:30 P.M.

---

way is acceptable for transport. Most vessels on the Southeast system can load vehicles up to 70 feet long with special arrangements. Maximum length on the *Tustumena* is 40 feet. Vehicle fares are determined by the overall length and width of the vehicle. For more details on vehicles, read the ALASKA MARINE HIGHWAY sec-

tion beginning on page 715. The *Tustumena* also has very limited cabin space so if you intend to take the Aleutian Island route, be sure to book well in advance to reserve a cabin.

Schedules: For Summer 2014 sailing schedules and passenger/vehicle/cabin rates for Inside Passage, Southeast, Cross-Gulf,

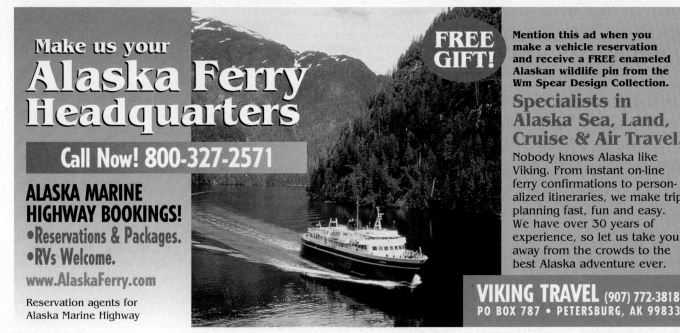

Gold Mining in Alaska

Learning to gold pan from an expert at Gold Dredge 8 near Fairbanks. (©Kris Valencia, staff)

Alaska, known for its historic gold rushes and current mining opportunities, offers the chance to pan for gold and to learn about recreational gold mining. Locals and visitors alike can get caught up in the hunt for this elusive yet valuable (more than $1,200 per ounce at press time!) metal.

It is important to familiarize yourself with the current regulations before you begin. Panning, sluicing and suction dredging on private property, established mining claims or on Alaska Native owned lands is considered trespassing unless you have the consent of the owner. Recreational gold panning, mineral prospecting or mining using light portable field equipment (e.g. hand-operated pick, shovel, pan, earth auger or backpack power drill or auger) is allowed without mining claims in designated recreational mining areas managed by the Dept. of Natural Resources. Motorized gold

panning on public lands set aside for recreational mining and panning is not allowed. This means, if you wish to do some gold panning of your own, you'll need to do it with gold pans, or sluice and rocker boxes. Sluice boxes are available are available at many Alaska sporting goods stores or online from Micro-Sluice Gold Products (www.micro-sluice.com). For further information on working streams on public lands, check out the Bureau of Land Management's website at http://www.blm.gov/ak/st/en/prog/recreation/activities/gold_panning.html.

Panning can be a great outdoor activity, but to ensure that you have a good experience you'll need the proper equipment. Plan on dressing in layers to prepare for changing temperatures; carry effective rain gear and waterproof boots; have insulated gloves for working in Alaska's ice cold streams; and have plenty of bug spray on hand.

There are public lands in Southcentral set aside for recreational gold panning, such as on the Kenai Peninsula, where 4 different gold producing creeks are known to provide "colors" or gold: Bertha Creek at **Milepost S 65.4** Seward Highway; Sixmile Creek on the Hope Highway; Resurrection Creek, off the Hope Highway; and Crescent Creek (Quartz Creek Road off the Sterling Highway). There is an informative document on this area and opportunities for mining at www.fs.usda.gov/Internet/FSE_DOCUMENTS/stelprdb5195151.pdf.

Petersville Recreational Mining Area on Petersville Road (turnoff at **Milepost A 114.9** Parks Highway) and Caribou Creek Recreational Mining Area (access from **Milepost A 106** Glenn Highway) have areas that allow for independent recreational mining. For fact sheets on these areas, go to www.dnr.state.ak.us/mlw/factsht/index.htm.

In the Interior, recreational mining is allowed in the Nome Creek Valley of White Mountains National Recreation Area. This area is accessed via 11 miles of gravel road from **Milepost F 57** Steese Highway and is

managed by the Bureau of Land Management. Recreational gold panning is also allowed (no mechanical devices) on the west side of Pedro Creek, directly across from the Felix Pedro Monument, at **Milepost F 16.6** Steese Highway. Check with the Alaska Public Lands Center in Fairbanks or go to www.blm.gov/ak/st/en/prog/nlcs/white_mtns/summer_recreation/gold_panning.html.

One of the easier ways to learn about gold panning and mining history in Alaska is to visit a commercial operation. They guarantee that you will find gold!

In Southcentral, the Indian Valley Gold Mine at **Milepost S 104** Seward Highway lets you pan and sluice for gold in their troughs or from a proven, gold-producing stream. Just a few miles away, the Crow Creek Mine off the Alyeska Highway also let's you try your hand at some gold panning along with demonstrating gold panning techniques in the same waters that they work for gold extraction. South of here, at **Milepost S 56.3**, turn off on the Hope Highway to go to Hope Historical Museum, where it is possible to do some panning for gold with an old-time prospector. Hope was the location for the first gold rush in Alaska.

North of Anchorage, the 271-acre Independence Mine and State Historical Park (215 miles roundtrip from Anchorage) includes several restored mine buildings and old mining machinery. Alaska Pacific Consolidated Mine Co., one of the largest gold producers in the Willow Creek mining district, operated here from 1938 through 1941. Although there is no gold panning here, it is well worth a visit for the history of this area and of gold mining.

In Interior Alaska's capital, Fairbanks, gold panning is offered at Pioneer Park, which also has displays of gold mining equipment. Northeast of Fairbanks via the Steese Highway there is Gold Dredge 8, a National Historic Site. Their tour includes a narrated train ride past Gold Dredge No. 8, plenty of Interior mining history, gold panning lessons and gold pans for sale. The turnoff for Gold Dredge 8 is at **Milepost F 9.5** on the Steese Highway.

The Taylor Highway provides access to the historic Fortymile gold mining district, where active gold mining is still underway. Take the Taylor Highway to Chicken, AK, and visit the Gold Panner for free goldpanning on Chicken Creek, and Chicken Gold Camp for tours of the Pedro gold dredge, gold panning lessons and recreational mining opportunities.

Continue up the Taylor Highway and across Top of the World Highway to Dawson City, YT. Rocker box demonstrations are offered twice daily at the Dawson City Museum. Free gold panning (bring your own pan) is available at Claim No. 6 on Bonanza Creek just outside of Dawson City, sponsored by the Klondike Visitors Association.

Prince William Sound and Southwest/Aleutian Chain, turn to the ALASKA MARINE HIGHWAY section beginning on page 715.

Hunting & Fishing

Hunting and fishing are popular sports in the North and a way of life for many residents. Both resident and nonresident sportfishermen and hunters must be aware of rules and regulations before going out in the field. Failure to comply with Fish & Game regulations can result in monetary fines and loss of trophies or property.

Regulation booklets are available from the government sources listed below and may also be found at a variety of different outlets, from supermarkets to foodmarts.

Alaska Dept. of Fish & Game: Located at 1255 W. 8th Street, in Juneau; mailing address is P.O. Box 115526, Juneau, AK 99811-5526; license information, phone (907) 465-2376; licensing fax (907) 465-2440; email adfg.license@alaska.gov; www.adfg.state.ak.us. Hunting and fishing licenses are available through one of 1,100 license vendors throughout Alaska. Licenses may also be obtained by mail or online at https://www.adfg.alaska.gov/store/.

Alberta Fish & Game: Sustainable Resource Development, Information Centre, phone toll-free 1-800-310-3773 or (780) 944-0313 outside of North America; www.srd.gov.ab.ca for hunting and fishing regulations.

British Columbia Fish & Game: Fish & Wildlife Branch, Ministry of Environment, P.O. Box 9391, Stn. Prov. Govt., Victoria, BC V8W 9M8; phone (250) 387-9771, www.env.gov.bc.ca/fw/ for hunting and fishing regulations.

NWT Fish & Game: Wildlife & Fisheries, Dept. of Environment & Natural Resources, 600, 5102–50th Ave., Yellowknife, NT X1A 3S8; phone (867) 920-8064; www.enr.gov.nt.ca/_live/pages/wpPages/regulations.aspx for hunting and fishing regulations.

Yukon Fish & Game: Hunting, Fishing and Wildlife Viewing: Dept. of Environment, Fish & Wildlife Branch, Box 2703 (V-3A), Whitehorse, Yukon, Y1A 2C6, phone (867) 667-5652; www.environmentyukon.gov.yk.ca. Yukon government issues an abbreviated guide to current regulations and information, available wherever fishing licenses are sold, as well as at the main office at 10 Burns Road, Whitehorse, YT Y1A 2C6; phone toll-free in Yukon 1-800-661-0408, ext. 5652, or (867) 667-5652. Email: environment.yukon@gov.yk.ca.

Fishing (Alaska)

The biggest challenge for visiting fishermen is the sheer number and variety of fishing opportunities available. The Alaska Dept. of Fish and Game has hundreds of pamphlets on fishing regional waters, as well as online regional sport fishing updates. A nonresident fishing license (annual) is $145; resident is $24. To fish for king salmon you also purchase a "king stamp" for $10 (residents) or $10 to $100 depending on days needed/chosen for fishing (nonresident).

Salmon are the most popular sport fish in Alaska, with all 5 species of Pacific salmon found here: king (chinook), silver (coho), pink (humpy), chum (dog) and red (sockeye). Other sport fish include halibut, rainbow and steelhead, Dolly Varden and arctic char, cutthroat and brook trout, northern

Fly-in fishermen deplane on an Admiralty Island trip in Southeast. (©Terry Sheely)

pike, and lake trout.

Knowing the kind of fish and fishing you want may help plan your trip. For example, king salmon fishing in Southeast is restricted to salt water, but cutthroat are common on the mainland and every major island in Southeast. Alaska's Interior has the largest arctic grayling fishery in North America. Northern pike is the most sought-after indigenous sport fish in Interior Alaska after the arctic grayling. These fish are the main sport fish species in the Tanana River drainage.

Excellent fishing is available within a day's drive of Anchorage. The Kenai Peninsula offers streams where king, red, silver, pink and chum salmon may be caught during the summer. Dolly Varden, steelhead and rainbow also run in Peninsula streams. Several lakes contain trout and landlocked salmon. In-season saltwater fishing for halibut, rockfish and several salmon species is excellent at many spots along the Peninsula and out of Whittier, Homer, Seward and Valdez. For specific fishing spots both north and south of Anchorage, see the PRINCE WILLIAM SOUND, SEWARD, STERLING, GLENN and PARKS HIGHWAY sections. Because of the importance of fishing to Alaska, both commercially and for sport, regulations are updated yearly by the state and are strictly enforced, so it is wise to obtain a current regulations book. Check the ADF&G home page, www.adfg.alaska.gov, under Fishing subhead, Licenses & Permits.

Most fishing enthusiasts focus their trips between April and October, when the weather is milder, but anglers have great success during the colder months as well. The Alaska Dept. of Fish and Game Sport Fish Division gives a run timing for all fisheries by region. Also check local newspapers for ADF&G regional fishing updates.

Where to fish is probably the most difficult choice, with the huge number of fishing destinations available. Throughout *The MILEPOST®* you will see the friendly little fish symbol at the end of some paragraphs. Wherever you see one, you will find a description of the fishing at that point. Fishing spots are also listed under Area Fishing in the Attractions section of each community.

You can fish any body of water with fish in it as long as it is legal, but local knowledge greatly increases chances for success. Many fishing guides and charter operators advertise in *The MILEPOST®*.

There is a long tradition of harvesting shellfish in Alaska. However, *shellfish harvested in Alaska waters can contain the toxin causing PSP (paralytic shellfish poisoning).* This includes clams, mussels, oysters, cockles, geoducks and scallops. Crabmeat is not known to contain the toxin causing PSP, but crab viscera can contain unsafe levels of toxin and should be discarded. According to the Alaska Dept. of Health and Social Services, the toxin that causes PSP cannot be cooked, cleaned or frozen out of shellfish. Early signs of PSP include tingling of the lips and tongues, which may progress to tingling of fingers and toes, logss of control of arms and legs, followed by difficulty breathing. PSP can be fatal in as little as 2 hours.

Hunting (Alaska)

Nonresident hunters in Alaska must be accompanied by a registered guide or a close relative over 19 who is an Alaska resident, when hunting brown bear, Dall sheep or mountain goats. A non-resident hunting license is $85; resident is $25.

There are 26 game management units in Alaska and a wide variation in both seasons and bag limits for various species. Check for special regulations in each unit.

Big game includes black and brown/grizzly bears, deer, elk, mountain goats, moose, wolves and wolverines, caribou, Dall sheep, musk-oxen and bison. Big game tags are required for residents hunting musk-ox and brown/grizzly bear and for nonresidents hunting any big game animal. These nonrefundable, nontransferable metal locking tags (valid for the calendar year) must be purchased prior to the taking of the animal. A tag may be used for any species for which the tag fee is of equal or lesser value. Examples of non-resident tag prices: brown/grizzly bear/$500, Dall sheep/$425, and mountain goat/$300.

Small game animals include grouse, ptarmigan and hares. Fur animals that may be

Canadian and U.S. currencies are similar but there are differences. (©Kris Valencia, staff)

METRIC CONVERSIONS
Temperatures, distance and speed limits

Fahrenheit	Celsius
122°	50°
120°	49°
110°	43°
104°	40°
100°	38°
90°	32°
86°	30°
80°	27°
70°	21°
68°	20°
60°	16°
50°	10°
40°	4°
32°	0°
30°	-1°
20°	-7°
14°	-10°
10°	-12°
0°	-18°
-4°	-20°
-10°	-23°
-20°	-29°
-22°	-30°
-30°	-34°
-40°	-40°

Miles	Kilometers
1	1.6
2	3.2
3	4.8
4	6.4
5	8.0
6	9.7
7	11.3
8	12.9
9	14.5
10	16.1
20	32.2
30	48.3
40	64.4
50	80.5
60	96.5
70	112.6
80	128.7
90	144.8
100	160.9

Kilometers	Miles
1	0.6
2	1.2
3	1.9
4	2.5
5	3.1
6	3.7
7	4.3
8	5.0
9	5.6
10	6.2
20	12.4
30	18.6
40	24.8
50	31.0
60	37.2
70	43.4
80	49.6
90	55.8
100	62.0

KPH	MPH
30	20
50	30
70	40
90	55
100	60

hunted are the coyote, fox and lynx. Waterfowl are also abundant. There is no recreational hunting of polar bear, walrus or other marine animals.

The Alaska Department of Fish and Game's Division of Wildlife Conservation has an entire web section devoted to providing information for hunters/trappers. Go to www.adfg.alaska.gov and find Trapping in the Hunting subhead menu.

Medical Services

From clinics to hospitals, chiropractors to acupuncturists, large cities in Alaska and Canada have all of the typical health care choices. Smaller cities may also have hospital facilities and urgent care clinics. Highway communities usually have ambulance service and a local health clinic. Available medical services are included in community descriptions in *The MILEPOST®* and noted in the highway logs with a red cross symbol: ✚

If you are having a medical emergency dial 911. Most communities and many highways in Alaska and Canada have 911 service, although keep in mind that cell phone service on the highways is sporadic.

Local phone numbers for emergency services and 911 service are noted in the introduction to each highway in *The MILEPOST®* in the **Emergency Medical Services** paragraph. Emergency call boxes are located and marked along Alaskan highways. These emergency phones are noted in our logs. If an emergency arises when you are outside cell phone signal range, locate the nearest emergency callbox or flag down help.

Add prescriptions and insurance card to your *To Pack* list. If you suffer from a serious chronic illness, pack your medical records as well. An insurance card is vital as you cross into Canada, especially as non-Canadian citizens cannot receive health care without some form of insurance to cover medical expenses.

Bring enough of your prescription medications to last the length of your trip. If you do run out, you can usually get your prescription filled at an Alaska pharmacy if it is from out of state. You cannot transfer your prescription to Alaska from another country. (The same applies for U.S. citizens wanting to refill a prescription in Canada.)

Chain pharmacy services in Alaska include Costco (Anchorage, 2; Fairbanks 1) and Walmart (multiple in Anchorage, Fairbanks and 1 in Wasilla); Fred Meyer's, with locations in Anchorage (4 stores), Wasilla, Palmer, Soldotna and Fairbanks (2 stores); Walgreens (5 in Anchorage, 1 in Eagle River, 1 in Wasilla); and Carrs/Safeway, with pharmacies at their 9 Anchorage stores, 2 Fairbanks stores and 1 each in Eagle River, Palmer and Wasilla.

Remember to store prescription medications in original containers with your name and drug identification attached. If you use syringes it is especially important to have proof of prescription when crossing the border.

Metric System

Metric conversions of special interest to cross-Canada travelers are as follows: 1 mile=1.609 kilometers; 1 kilometer=0.621 miles; 1 meter=3.3 feet; 1 yard=0.9 meters; 1 gallon=3.785 liters; 1 liter=.2642 gallons. See chart to right for additional conversions.

Money/Credit Cards

The money system in Canada is based on dollars and cents, but there are differences. Canada has nickels, dimes, quarters, 1-dollar coins ("loonies") and 2-dollar coins ("toonies"), but no longer uses pennies, so cashiers round-off up or down as needed. Paper currency comes in $5, $10, $20, $50, $100, etc. bills.

U.S. currency is accepted as payment in many places in Canada, but merchants will give you change in Canadian currency and they may or may not give you the prevailing exchange rate. Businesses in Alaska do not accept Canadian currency.

The Canadian dollar and American dollar are 2 separate currencies and the rate of exchange varies. It has been close to par in recent years, although sometimes falling slightly in favor of one currency over the

other. Not all banks in the U.S. have foreign currency on hand, so exchange your U.S. currency for Canadian curency at a bank in Canada. You will probably get a better rate of exchange at a bank, although there is still a fee.

Major American bank and credit cards are accepted in Canada. Credit card purchases are billed at the U.S. dollar equivalent of the Canadian price at the full exchange rate for the day of billing, and often a "Foreign Transaction Fee" is included.

Many cities in Alaska and Canada have automated teller machines (ATMs)—MasterCard/Cirrus ATM Network, Nexxus and others—and they usually accept bank debit cards regardless of country of origin. It is important to carry cash since some merchants may not accept plastic.

Mosquitoes

An often asked question about travel to the North is "What's the best time to avoid mosquitoes?" The answer is probably mid-winter. Summer is bug season and you will run into mosquitoes, black flies (also called white-sox, simulids and buffalo gnats) and no-see-ums (also known as punkies).

Mosquitoes emerge from hibernation before the snow has entirely disappeared. They peak in about June but continue to harass humans and wildlife through the fall. Mosquitoes are especially active in the early morning and at dusk. They hatch their eggs in water, so the North—with its marshy tundra and many lakes—is a good breeding ground.

You cannot plan your summer vacation around the mosquito. You can take steps to avoid them. The USDA recommends a light weight hooded parka, tight fitting at the wrists with a drawstring hood so it fits snugly around the face and trousers tucked into socks to reduce bites. Mosquitoes can bite through thin material so wear some heavier protection when and where mosquitoes are active. Locating campsites away from water and where there is a breeze is helpful. The USDA states that repellents containing diethyl-meta-toluamide (DEET) are most effective. Make sure you apply this to all exposed skin. The repellent is less effective for black flies and no-see-ums however they are deterred by wind and relative low humidity.

Museums & Cultural Centers

The history of the North is still very much in evidence in Alaska and northwestern Canada. Artifacts from the gold rush litter the landscape. Monuments and markers commemorate important events, from the Russian fur trade to WWII and construction of the Alaska Highway. But it is the museums along the highways and in the communities that provide travelers with a deeper understanding of the people and places they are visiting. And there is a museum for every interest. Listed below are a top 10 of what is available (not in order).

Take your penchant for small planes to the Alaska Aviation Museum in Anchorage and learn how aviation affected Alaska pre-statehood, through WWII and more. There are 2 theaters and a restoration hangar to

Woolly mammoth statue stands outside Beringia and Yukon Transportation museums in Whitehorse. (©Kris Valencia, staff)

round out your experience.

The major museum in Anchorage is the Anchorage Museum, home to the Smithsonian Arctic Studies Center, an extensive collection of Northern artifacts with state-of-the-art interactive interpretation.

The Alaska Native Heritage Center in Anchorage introduces Alaska's Native peoples. Visitors experience Alaska Native culture first-hand through storytelling, authentic Native song and dance, and artist demonstrations. A theater offers a film introduction to Native history and culture. Outdoors, and surrounding a small scenic lake, is a path that leads through life-sized traditional style dwellings from 6 different Native groups in Alaska.

In Fairbanks, the Museum of the North at the University of Alaska has 2,000 years of Alaskan art and more than a million artifacts from Alaska's past housed in an architecturally striking building. A note-worthy stop. The "Dynamic Aurora" film in the museum theatre is a favorite with visitors.

Fairbanks' newest museum is the **Fountainhead Antique Auto Museum**, a collection of some 70 historically significant automobiles. Vintage fashion displays accompany and complement many of the cars on display, as do historic photographs. The first car to come to Alaska is currently on display. For more information, go to www.FountainheadMuseum.com. See description in FAIRBANKS Attractions.

Homer, at the end of the Sterling Highway, has two important natural history museums: the Pratt Museum and the Alaska Islands & Ocean Visitor Center. The Pratt Museum focuses on the history, culture, art and science of Homer and Kachemak Bay. Their live web cams are a favorite for watching far-off wildlife like brown bears at McNeil River. Alaska Islands and Oceans Visitor Center is an interpretive and educational facility for the Alaska Maritime National Wildlife Refuge and the Kachemak Bay Research Reserve. Visitors virtually visit the remote Alaska coastline through interactive exhibits.

The George Johnston Museum is a favorite with Alaska Highway travelers.

The 3,000-square-foot facility in Teslin, YT, is named for a Tlingit Indian who captured the life of Tlingit people in this area between 1910 and 1940. Johnston also brought the first car to Teslin, a 1928 Chevrolet, that is display at the museum. Also in Teslin is the Teslin Tlingit Heritage Centre, where travelers can experience the exciting traditions of the Tlingit people.

A wealth of museums greet you in Whitehorse, YT: the Yukon Transportation Museum, the Old Log Church Museum, the Yukon Beringia Interpretive Centre and MacBride Museum of Yukon History. Each focuses on an aspect of northwestern Canada's rich cultural and physical history.

Dawson City, Yukon's first capital, was declared a National Historic Site in the early 1960s, with many of its original structures restored or reconstructed. The Old Territorial Administration Building houses the Dawson City Museum, which features First Nations and gold mining history.

The MILEPOST® includes detailed descriptions of all these museums and many more in the communities and along the highways of the North, like the Hammer Museum in Haines, AK; the Prince William Sound Museum in Whittier, AK; and many others. Many visitor centers in the North, such as the Da Ku Cultural Centre in Haines Junction, have museum-like cultural displays.

Travelers with their leashed dogs at Beautiful Downtown Chicken. (©Kris Valencia, staff)

Pets

For those traveling with pets, here's some helpful advice from other pet-loving Alaska travelers.

Keep your pets on leashes whenever they are outside your vehicle. Make sure your pet is microchipped and has current ID tags on its collar, so that if you lose a pet and it is found, the rescuer knows where to find/reach you. One tip provided by Ronald Jones in *Rving to Alaska*, is to "put emergency contact information and a picture of your animal somewhere in the coach—a sort of mini-passport... If the animal has an identification chip, include that information... If you use a special pet food, bring enough to feed the animal for the entire trip because you might not be able to get it in Canada or Alaska." (Editor's NOTE: Be sure to leave the food in its original bag with ingredients listed. If you don't, it may be confiscated at the border for unknown content. Additionally, Canada's rule limits import to 20 kg/44 lbs of pet food).

If you do lose your dog, check with the vet's office or animal shelter in the next town. Animal shelters are generally found only in the larger communities and not all communities have vets, so if the town has neither one, ask around. Also ask about broadcasting a lost dog message on the local radio station.

It is important to have proper proof of rabies vaccination documentation for your pet when crossing the U.S.–Canada border. Not all customs officers will ask for documentation, but it is best to be prepared, as they can deny your pet entry without proper documentation. Get your pet checked by a vet and obtain a health certificate no more than 30 days prior to travel as this also may be required at the border and may also be required for Alaska State ferry travel out of Bellingham, WA. You are encouraged to use a top spot treatment or flea and tick shampoo before traveling north as Alaska has no fleas or ticks. Please do not bring them with you.

Please respect the highway businesses who are tired of picking up after canine visitors and have posted notices requesting that pets stay in their vehicles.

Most communities allow leashed dogs in outdoor public areas, unless otherwise posted. In Anchorage, selected city parks allow dogs off-leash if they are under voice control. Municipal laws require that you pick up after your pet.

Pet policies at hotels, motels, and bed and breakfasts in the North range from "no pets" to "pets okay" to "it depends on the size and good manners of your dog." Check lodging advertisements in *The MILEPOST®* for pet policies, and check business websites for pet policies. As a rule, private RV parks generally accept pets. If in doubt, email or phone ahead of time to confirm pet policies.

Finding kennels and even "doggie day-cares" is simple in large communities but vets can help you locate them or kennel your pet, in smaller cities. Some RV parks and lodges may offer dog shelters or pens for limited use, especially those near major attractions like Denali National Park. Leaving your dog in the car or RV may be your only option, but keep in mind that nights can be quite cold in the North during spring and fall, and summer days can be suffocatingly hot. Cracking the windows in your car on a hot day may not provide adequate ventilation to keep temperatures down.

When hiking with your pet, always carry fresh water and take frequent rests. Northern summer days can be very hot, particularly in the interior. There have been numerous cases of dogs dying from heat exhaustion and stroke on what their owners thought were short, easy hikes on local trails. Keep in mind what your friend is used to and if it is a life on the couch, realize the difference in activity level and plan accordingly. Another thing to consider when hiking with your dog is bringing an insect repellent for them like "Bite Blocker," which is made for pets and repels mosquitoes and other pests.

If you are traveling on the Alaska Marine Highway (ferry) System, your pet(s) must be transported in your vehicle on the vehicle deck. Pets are not allowed above deck. On the longer voyages, you may visit your pet only during 15-minute "car-deck calls"—which are given 2 or 3 times daily—during which time dog owners may feed and water their pets, and walk them around the car deck. (Paper towels are on hand so that you can clean up after your pet.) The dogs seem to do fine on the ferry, although some refuse to relieve themselves on the unfamiliar decking. Keep in mind that it is *very* close quarters on the car deck. If your dog doesn't like other dogs, a muzzle is a good idea. The 37-hour Bellingham to Ketchikan run is the longest ferry trip without a port call. The Cross-Gulf trip has 2 long stretches—of about 20 hours each—between Whittier, Yakutat and Juneau.

Animal injuries occur in the North as they do anywhere else, but there are a few special considerations to keep in mind. Smaller communities may not have a resident vet. If your dog is injured, help may be several hours away. Bring a pet first aid kit that includes self-sticking bandage tape, gauze, antiseptic, triple antibiotic cream, Benedryl, liquid skin and a non-steroidal anti-inflammatory like Rimadyl (doggie Advil). You may want to download in advance, the American Red Cross app to help with pet first aid (http://www.redcross.org/mobile-apps/pet-first-aid-app).

Small dogs are vulnerable to predation by eagles and foxes. Bears and moose will go after any size dog if provoked. Also keep an eye out for porcupines. Dog fights with loose and unfriendly local dogs are also a common cause of dog injuries.

If you take your pet fishing, boat and water safety should apply to both pet and owner. Fast-moving, powerful rivers, such as the Kenai, are difficult for even strong swimmers (canine or human) to negotiate. Consider a life preserver for your dog.

Railroads

Although no railroads connect Alaska or the Yukon with the Lower 48, there are 2 railroads in the North—the Alaska Railroad and the White Pass & Yukon Route. Trans-Canada service is provided by VIA Rail.

Construction of the Alaska Railroad began in 1915 under Pres. Woodrow Wilson. On July 15, 1923, Pres. Warren G. Harding drove the golden spike at Nenana, signifying completion of the Railroad. The main line extends 470 miles from Seward to Fairbanks, with spurs to Whittier and Palmer.

The Alaska Railroad is an iconic part of Alaska history, connecting some of Alaska's best-loved destinations for over 90 years! The Alaska Railroad operates daily summer service between Anchorage, Denali Park, Fairbanks, Seward, Girdwood, Whittier, Portage, Grandview and Spencer Glacier, and year-round service between Anchorage and Fairbanks.

The White Pass & Yukon Route (WP&YR) is a narrow-gauge (36-inch) privately owned railroad built during the Klondike Gold Rush. Construction of the WP&YR began in May 1898 and reached White Pass in February 1899 and Whitehorse in July 1900. It was the first railroad in Alaska and at the time the most northern of any railroad in North America.

The WP&YR has one of the steepest railroad grades in North America. Starting at sea level in Skagway the railroad climbs to 2,865 feet/873m at the Summit of the White Pass in only 20 miles/32 km of track. In 1994, it was declared an International Historic Civil Engineering Landmark, one of only 42 in the world today. From 1900 until 1982, the WP&YR provided passenger and freight service between Skagway, AK,

and Whitehorse, YT.

The WP&YR offers daily train service and sightseeing excursions from May through September (see details on next page under White Pass and Yukon Route heading).

VIA Rail operates Canada's only national passenger rail service. VIA Rail serves all regions of Canada, from the Atlantic to the Pacific. VIA Rail's Jasper/Prince Rupert service may be included in itineraries for Alaska-bound travelers departing from Prince Rupert, BC, on the Alaska Marine Highway System. VIA Rail's Canadian transcontinental service, "the ultimate Canada train trip," connects Toronto, ON, with Vancouver, BC, departure point for some Alaska-bound cruise ships.

The Alaska Railroad

Following are schedules and adult fares (peak season) on Alaska Railroad routes in summer 2014. (Peak Season is May 31 to August 31, 2014; Value Season is May 14-30 and Sept. 1-14, 2014.) Children ages 2 through 11 ride for 50 percent of adult fare; under 2 ride free. Alaska residents and U.S. Military receive 20 percent discount off retail rail fares with proper ID required at boarding.

The following schedules and fares are subject to change without notice. Check train schedules at www.AlaskaRailroad.com for updates.

Reservations and information: Reservations are recommended on all routes. Tickets may be purchased in advance by mail. Checks, VISA, MasterCard, AMEX and Discover are accepted. Phone (907) 265-2494; toll-free 1-800-544-0552; www.AlaskaRailroad.com.

A photo ID is required at depot check-in. Passengers may have 2 pieces of checked baggage and 1 carry-on for no charge; 2 extra pieces of baggage (for a total of 4) for an additional fee. No single piece may weigh more than 50 lbs. A special handling fee of $20 per item applies to oversized bags, bicycles and other recreational equipment. Special firearms restrictions apply. Camping fuel, motor fuel and other hazardous items are not permitted. Animals must be transported in kennels in the baggage car. The Alaska Railroad accommodates visitors with disabilities

Anchorage–Wasilla–Talkeetna–Denali–Fairbanks (Denali Star Train): Daily passenger service on the Denali Star from May 14 to Sept. 14, 2014. Dining, baggage service, no-smoking cars, wheelchair access.

Northbound train departs Anchorage at 8:15 A.M., arrives Wasilla 9:30 A.M., departs Wasilla at 9:35 A.M., arrives Talkeetna 11:05 A.M., departs Talkeetna at 11:20 A.M., arrives Denali Park 3:40 P.M., departs Denali Park at 4 P.M. and arrives Fairbanks 8 P.M.

Southbound train departs Fairbanks at 8:15 A.M., arrives Denali Park at 12:10 P.M., departs Denali Park at 12:30 P.M., arrives Talkeetna at 4:40 P.M., departs Talkeetna at 4:55 P.M., arrives Wasilla 6:10 P.M., departs Wasilla at 6:15 P.M., and arrives Anchorage 8 P.M.

One-way peak season (June 1–Aug. 31) fares are: Anchorage–Fairbanks, $224; Anchorage–Talkeetna, $95; Anchorage–Denali Park, $156; Fairbanks–Denali Park, $68.

Luxury railcars are also available on this route through Gray Line of Alaska (Holland America Lines/Westours) and Princess Tours.

Talkeetna–Hurricane (Hurricane Turn Train): Round-trip summer service between Talkeetna and Hurricane Gulch operates May 15 to Sept. 14, 2014, Thursdays through Sundays and Memorial Day, Fourth of July and Labor Day. One of America's last flag stop trains, the Hurricane Turn takes you into rural Alaska and provides an opportunity to meet local residents who have used the train for transportation to their homes or recreational property since 1923. A great day trip for visitors.

Departs Talkeetna 12:45 P.M., arrives Hurricane 3 P.M., leaves Hurricane at 4 P.M. arrives back in Talkeetna at 7 P.M. (all times are approximate). Roundtrip fares from Hurricane to Talkeetna are $96. The Hurricane Turn will stop wherever people want to get on or off. There is no dining on the Hurricane Turn Train.

Anchorage–Girdwood–Seward (Coastal Classic Train): Operates daily in summer from May 10 to Sept. 14, 2014. Dining, baggage service, no-smoking cars, wheelchair access.

Southbound train departs Anchorage at 6:45 A.M., arrives Girdwood 7:55 A.M., arrives Seward 11:05 A.M. Northbound train departs Seward at 6 P.M., arrives Girdwood 8:50 P.M., arrives Anchorage 10:15 P.M.

Round-trip adult fare from Anchorage or Girdwood to Seward is $135 Adventure Class, $235 GoldStar Service. One-way fare from Anchorage to Girdwood is $65. One-way adult fare Anchorage to Seward is $85 Adventure Class, $140 Goldstar Service .

Anchorage–Whittier–Portage (Glacier Discovery Train): Round-trip service daily in summer, from June 1 to Sept. 14, 2014, between Anchorage, Girdwood, Portage and Whittier, with 1-way service (motorcoach return from Portage to Anchorage or Girdwood) to Spencer Glacier/Whistle Stop service and Grandview. (The Glacier Discovery will operate round trip from Anchorage to Whittier only on the following dates: May 17, May 24, May 31, 2014.) Dining, baggage service, no-smoking cars, wheelchair access.

The Glacier Discovery follows Turnagain Arm to Portage, then goes through the Anton Anderson Memorial Tunnel to Whittier. The train backtracks to Portage to board passengers before continuing on to Spencer Glacier Whistle Stop, where there is a boarding platform, shelter, restrooms, interpretive signs and trail. Guided hike is led by a U.S. Forest Service ranger. At the glacier the railroad also offers an optional Rafting Tour; advance reservations required. The train then climbs some of the railroad's steepest grade to Grandview (stunning alpine views).

Departs Anchorage at 9:45 A.M., arrives Girdwood 10:55 A.M., departs Girdwood 11:00 A.M., arrives Portage 11:30 A.M., departs Portage 11:35 A.M., arrives Whittier 12:05 P.M., departs Whittier 12:45 P.M., arrives Portage at 1:15 P.M., departs Portage at 1:25 P.M., arrives Spencer Glacier 1:45 P.M., departs Spencer Glacier 1:55 P.M., arrives Grandview 3:20 P.M.

Return train departs Grandview at 3:30 P.M., arrives at Spencer Glacier at 4:30 P.M., departs Spencer Glacier 4:40 P.M., arrives Portage at 5:15 P.M., departs Portage at 5:30 P.M., arrives Whittier at 6:05 P.M., departs Whittier at 6:45 P.M., arrives Portage at 7:05 P.M., departs Portage at 7:20 P.M., arrives Girdwood at 7:35 P.M., departs Girdwood at 7:40 P.M. and arrives Anchorage 9:15 P.M. (Rafting participants as well as Grandview sightseeing guests disembark in Portage for motorcoach transfer to Anchorage, arriving 6:45 P.M.)

Round-trip adult fares from Anchorage to Girdwood, $93. Anchorage to Spencer Glacier Whistle Stop, $110, or to Grandview $120 (both include motorcoach transfer from Portage to either Anchorage or Girdwood).

Reservations and information: Reservations are recommended on all routes. Tickets may be purchased in advance by mail. Checks, VISA, MasterCard, AMEX and Discover are accepted. Trains are cashless so all purchases onboard must be made with credit card. Phone (907) 265-2494; toll-free 1-800-544-0552; www.AlaskaRailroad.com.

A photo ID is required at depot check-in. Passengers may have 2 pieces of checked baggage and 1 carry-on for no charge, 2 extra pieces of baggage (for a total of 4) for an additional fee. No single piece may weigh more than 50 lbs. A special handling fee of $20 per item applies to oversized bags, bicycles and other recreational equipment.

Special firearms restrictions apply. Camping fuel, motor fuel and other hazardous items are not permitted. Animals must be transported in kennels in the baggage car. The Alaska Railroad accommodates visitors with disabilities.

White Pass & Yukon Route

Following are schedules and fares for White Pass & Yukon Route in 2014. All times indicated in schedules are Alaska time. Skagway is on Alaska Time, which is 1 hour earlier than Whitehorse, which is on Pacific Time. Reservations a must!

Fares in U.S. dollars and include taxes; half price for children 12 and under. Cancellation fees apply. Schedules and fares are subject to change without notice.

Contact the White Pass & Yukon Route at PO Box 435, Skagway, AK 99840. Phone (907) 983-2217 or toll free 1-800-343-7373; email at info@wpyr.com; www.wpyr.com.

Do not miss taking a ride on the White Pass & Yukon Route out of Skagway. (©Sharon Nault)

White Pass Summit Excursion: Available May 2 to Sept. 25, 2014. This 3-hour, 40-mile fully narrated round-trip features 2 tunnels, trestles, waterfalls and more. Departs Skagway 8:15 A.M. and 12:45 P.M. daily. (There is a 4:30 P.M. departure Tuesday and Wednesday from May 27 to Sept. 3, 2014. Adults $119, children $59.50. Passport not required. Train is wheelchair accessible. Visit www.wpyr.com/summitexcursion.html for additional information on availability and exceptions to schedule.

Fraser Meadows: Passport required. This 4-hour trip by steam locomotive travels 6 miles beyond White Pass to Fraser Meadows, for a total of 54 miles round-trip. Departs at noon on Thursdays & Fridays and at either 8 A.M. or noon on Mondays between May 16 and Sept. 8, 2014. Adults $159, children $79.50. For additional days of service and departure times and exceptions to schedule

for steam service visit www.wpyr.com/fraser meadows.html.

Bennett Scenic Journey: Passport required. Follow the trail of the Klondike stampeders between Skagway, AK, and Carcross, YT. A 1 hour 15 minute layout at Bennett for lunch at restored 1903 Bennett Station House and self-guided walking tour of historic gold rush townsite. Motorcoach transfer to/from Skagway via the Klondike Highway with a stop at Emerald Lake available. Available May 28 to Sept. 5, 2014. Departs 7:30 A.M. Wednesdays, Thursdays and Saturdays, and 8:30 A.M. Tuesdays and Fridays. Adults $229, children $114.50. Visit www.wpyr.com/bennettscenicjourney.html.

Train and Motorcoach Connections via Carcross: Passport required. There are several options, including Skagway to Whitehorse via Carcross Train/Bus one-way; Whitehorse to Skagway via

Carcross Bus/Train one-way; Skagway to Whitehorse via Carcross with bus return (overnight); the Canadian Loop; the Carcross Loop; and the Carcross to Skagway Train with bus return (an overnight). A hot lunch at Lake Bennett is included in all tours. For details visit www.wpyr.com/trainandmotorcoachconnectionsvia carcross.html.

Laughton Glacier Hiker Service: Passport required. This 14-mile train ride leads to a 5- to 8-mile self-guided hike through old growth forest to Laughton Glacier. Departs Skagway daily at 8 A.M. and 12:30 P.M. between May 2 and Sept. 25, 2014. Adults $68, children $34. Visit www.wpyr.com/skagwaytolaughton.html for exceptions to schedule and more information.

Denver Glacier Service: Passport required. Board in Skagway for a round-trip train to the Denver trailhead. Self-guided walking tour to view Denver Glacier, recommended for those in fair physical conditions. Departs Skagway daily at 8 A.M. and 12:30 P.M. between May 2 and Sept. 25, 2014. Adults $34, children $17. Visit www.wpyr.com/hikers.html for exceptions to schedule and more information.

Chilkoot Trail Hiker Service: Passport required. Operates May 28 to September 5, 2014. Northbound train departs Bennett on Wednesdays, Thursdays and Saturdays at 11:30 A.M. for Carcross. Southbound train departs Bennett on Tuesdays and Fridays at 2:10 P.M. for Fraser and Skagway. For details visit www.wpyr.com/chilkoottrail.html. Hot lunch is available for advance purchase.

VIA Rail

VIA Rail's famous *Canadian* departs Toronto for Vancouver on Tuesdays, Thursdays and Saturdays during peak season (April 27 to Oct. 31, 2014) with stops in Winnipeg, Saskatoon, Edmonton and Jasper over the train's 3-day, 4-night journey. The *Canadian*'s schedule provides for same-day connections in Toronto and other eastern destinations and daylight viewing of the Canadian Rockies. Travelers can choose between Economy class or Sleeper Plus class, VIA's premier service with sleeping car accommodations, delicious meals prepared by onboard chefs, showers, and dome cars.

The other Rockies and Pacific VIA service in Western Canada is between Jasper, AB, and Prince Rupert, BC, with an overnight layover in Prince George (passengers must book their own hotel room). The 2-day trips departs 3 times per week on Wednesdays, Fridays, and Sundays. Economy or Touring class to choose from. Touring class is available mid-June to late September and includes at-your-seat service as well as access to a domed observation car.

Reservations and information: For more information, schedules and fares, phone 1-888-VIA-RAIL (1-888-842-7245), or go online to www.viarail.ca.

Renting an RV

"It's really just as easy to drive a 30-foot rig as it is a 22-foot RV," I was assured by the rental agent in Anchorage, while making arrangements for a June camping trip in Alaska a few years ago. It was my first time driving an RV, part of my research to assure any *MILEPOST®* readers planning to do the same thing that if I could do it, they could do it. The only RV available the weekend of

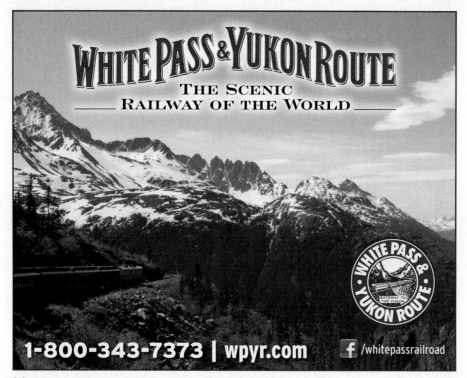

my trip was 30 feet long.

For first-timers, be assured that it really isn't that hard to drive the "big rigs." The pros at rental agencies in Anchorage say you get the hang of it either 15 minutes out of town or by the time you get to Talkeetna. I didn't really relax until I'd made it to Denali Park. But it was much easier than I expected to drive a vehicle more than twice as long as my own. And staying in an RV is far more luxurious than car camping or sleeping in a tent.

If you have a large group, or do not want to be restricted by hotel reservation dates, renting an RV can be a relatively economical way to explore the state at your own pace, enjoying the solitude that camping offers from the soft bed of a motorhome.

The rental agency should demonstrate the basic operation of the motorhome for you before you take off. The 30-minute video you are required to watch at Great Alaskan Holidays is a great help in preparing for "off tracking," "swing out" (or "tail swing") and the other effects of driving a 10-foot-wide vehicle with 12 or more feet of overhang behind the rear wheels.

Some of the key points to remember in driving an RV: Do not start turning until your back wheels are past the obstacle; drive slowly and at an angle over dips in the road, such as gutters, so that the overhang doesn't "bottom out"; accelerate slowly; and allow 4 to 5 times the stopping and following distance you do in a car. It is also recommended you use an outside spotter when backing up, in addition to the rearview mirrors, and that you make sure to check for obstructions at campsites. Trees and tree branches are the number one cause of damage to rental RVs.

Upon making your reservation, a deposit is usually required and you may be given a check-in time frame to pick up your rental vehicle, as well as a return time. Do not plan to put in a lot of miles the first day of your trip. You will spend some time doing paperwork, familiarizing yourself with the RV, packing up the RV, buying food and other supplies, then driving through town traffic before you reach the open road.

The RV should come supplied with linens, towels, pots and pans, cutlery and dishes. Toasters and coffee makers may be made available free on request or for an extra charge. Other items often available for rent include ice chests, extra lawn chairs, bike racks and fishing rods.

There are a number of reputable rental agencies to choose from in Anchorage, where most visitors land, including Great Alaskan Holidays (www.greatalaskanholidays.com); Alaska Motorhome Rentals (www.BestofAlaskaTravel.com); ABC Motorhome & Car Rentals (www.abcmotorhome.com); and Clippership Motorhome Rentals (www.clippershiprv.com).

You will find most RV rental rates are quite comparable. Generally, rates vary depending on the size of the RV, with the daily rate higher in mid-summer and lower at the beginning of the season (April–May) and at the end of the season (September–October). Daily rates are usually based on a 7 days or more rental period; expect to pay an extra charge for 4- to 6-day rentals.

Mileage options may be offered as well, with a daily rate plus per mile charge or a higher daily rate with unlimited mileage. Additional costs may be incurred if you do not return the RV with full gas and propane tanks.

Ask what kind of extra services and items they supply. Do they have courtesy van service to and from the airport? What is included in the basic rental fee? What are the extra costs, such as cleaning fees?

Also ask about insurance coverage. Most dealers include comprehensive coverage, but with a high deductible. Talk to your own insurance agent about whether you should purchase the dealer's Collision Damage Waiver or if your policy will cover the deductible.

When choosing a vendor, you will need to look at what they have available in terms of makes and models of RVs. Check web sites and brochures for particulars on their rental RVs. How many does the unit sleep? Do they have slideouts? Also key to making a decision is what units are available for your vacation dates.

A good dealer will provide you with plenty of information upon receiving your inquiry and even more information after taking your reservation. I received a confirmation packet from Great Alaskan Holidays that detailed my motorhome pickup time and all fees to be charged. This 10-page booklet included general arrival information, what to do if arriving after hours, pickup particulars, credit card requirements, return times, driver's license requirements, and answers to some commonly asked questions.

If you have only a week or two, have some kind of itinerary in mind before you arrive. Alaska's road system is relatively limited, and distances are not great, but there's a lot to see. And you may want to make advance reservations for the Alaska State ferry across Prince William Sound between Whittier and Valdez, or for campsites in popular areas like Denali Park and the Kenai Peninsula.

If you arrive in Anchorage, you can take off in 3 directions: South down the Seward Highway; east on the Glenn Highway; and north up the Parks Highway (see Key to Highways Map 3 on page 11). Read through the highway logs in The MILEPOST®, noting campground locations, attractions, fishing opportunities, and mileages between points, to come up with a trip that will fit your interests and your timetable.

One-way RV rentals to Alaska are hard to find but inquire with ABC Motorhomes about RVs departing from Elkhart, IN, that can be driven to Anchorage. Phone 1-800-421-7456.

Shipping

Whether you are moving to Alaska, or planning to ship your vehicle one way and drive the other, there is a shipper to accommodate your needs.

Vehicles: Carriers that will ship cars, campers, trailers and motorhomes between Anchorage and Seattle/Tacoma include the following:

Alaska Vehicle Transport (a division of United Road Services Inc.), in Anchorage phone (907) 561-2899 or 1-800-354-6007; in Tacoma phone (253) 874-9919 or toll-free 1-800-422-7925; www.alaskavehicletransport.com.

Horizon Lines of Alaska, 1717 Tidewater Rd., Anchorage, AK 99501, phone (907) 263-5073, or 1675 Lincoln Ave., Building 300, Tacoma, WA 98421; phone (253) 882-1600.

Toll-free 1-877-678-7447; www.horizonlines.com.

Totem Ocean Trailer Express Inc. (TOTE), 2511 Tidewater, Anchorage, AK 99501, or 500 Alexander Ave., Tacoma, WA 98421. Toll-free 1-800-426-0074; www.totemocean.com.

Between southeastern Alaska and Seattle, vehicle transport and shipping services are provided by Lynden's Alaska Marine Lines/Northland Services at 5615 W. Marginal Way SW, Seattle, WA 98106, phone (206) 764-8346 or toll-free 1-800-950-4265 or 1-800-326-8346; www.lynden.com/aml/. Direct service twice weekly to Ketchikan, Petersburg, Sitka, Juneau. Also weekly service between Seattle and Haines, Skagway, Whitehorse & Yukon, Wrangell, Prince of Wales, Kensington, Kake, Hawk Inlet. Also weekly service to Anchorage, Cordova, Fairbanks, Kenai, Palmer, Seward, Valdez and Wasilla. Seasonal service offered to Angoon, Excursion Inlet, Hoonah, Tenakee and Yakutat.

Persons shipping vehicles between Seattle/Tacoma and Anchorage are advised to shop around for the carrier that offers the services and rates most suited to the shipper's needs. Freight charges vary depending upon the carrier and the size of the vehicle.

Not all carriers accept rented moving trucks and trailers, and a few of those that do require authorization from the rental company to carry its equipment to Alaska. Check with the carrier and your rental company before booking service.

Book your reservation in advance and prepare to have the vehicle at the carrier's loading facility 2 days prior to sailing. Carriers differ on what non-vehicle items they allow to travel inside, from nothing at all to goods packaged and addressed separately. Regulations forbid the transport of vehicles holding more than ¼ tank of gas; so make sure your gas tank is under that requirement when you arrive. (It can take a surprisingly long time to drive off that extra gas, and the carriers do not make exceptions.) None of the carriers listed above allows owners to accompany their vehicles in transit. Remember to have fresh antifreeze installed in your car or truck prior to sailing!

Household Goods and Personal Effects: Most moving van lines have service to and from Alaska through their agency connections in most Alaska and Lower 48 cities. To initiate service, contact the van line agents nearest your origin point.

Northbound goods are shipped to Seattle and transferred through a port agent to a water vessel for carriage to Alaska. Few shipments go over the road to Alaska. Southbound shipments are processed in a like manner through Alaska ports to Seattle, then on to the destination.

U-Haul (www.uhaul.com) provides service into the North Country for those who prefer to move their goods themselves. There are many U-Haul dealerships in Alaska and several in northwestern Canada for over-the-road service.

Time Zones

Most of Alaska is on Alaska Standard Time, which is 1 hour earlier than Pacific Standard Time, 2 hours earlier than Mountain Standard Time, 3 hours earlier than Central Standard Time and 4 hours earlier than Eastern Standard Time. St. Lawrence

DAYLIGHT HOURS

Summer Maximum

	Sunrise	Sunset	Daylight
Barrow	May 10	Aug. 2	continuous
Fairbanks	2:58 A.M.	12:47 A.M.	21:45 hours
Anchorage	4:21 A.M.	11:39 P.M.	19:17 hours
Juneau	3:51 A.M.	10:08 P.M.	18:17 hours
Ketchikan	4:04 A.M.	9:32 P.M.	17:26 hours
Adak	6:27 A.M.	11:10 P.M.	16:43 hours

Winter Minimum

	Sunrise	Sunset	Daylight
Barrow	Jan. 22	Nov. 18	none
Fairbanks	10:58 A.M.	2:39 P.M.	3:37 hours
Anchorage	10:14 A.M.	3:42 P.M.	5:28 hours
Juneau	8:44 A.M.	3:07 P.M.	6:21 hours
Ketchikan	8:11 A.M.	3:18 P.M.	7:07 hours
Adak	9:52 A.M.	5:38 P.M.	7:46 hours

Island and part of the Aleutian Islands are on Hawaii–Aleutian Standard Time.

Canada uses 6 primary time zones. From east to west they are: Newfoundland Time Zone, Atlantic Time Zone, Eastern Time, Central Time Zone, Mountain Time Zone, and Pacific Time Zone.

Yukon and most of British Columbia are on Pacific Standard Time. (Exceptions in British Columbia include Rocky Mountain communities and the Dawson Creek area, which observe Mountain Standard Time.)

Northwest Territories and Alberta are on Mountain Standard Time (MST).

Daylight Saving Time in the U.S. and Canada begins on the second Sunday in March and ends on the first Sunday in November. Daylight Saving Time is observed in Alaska except in the Aleutian Islands and St. Lawrence Island.

Time zone changes are posted along the highways. Time zone changes are noted in *The MILEPOST® highway logs.

Tours

Packaged tours are multi-day itineraries which may use several different vendors to provide transportation, accommodations and sightseeing/activities. Tour costs vary and may or may not include all transportation, lodging and activities, meals, tips, taxes, etc. These types of tours are usually not cheap, although for many travelers the expense of a packaged tour is offset by the convenience of reserved lodging and pre-arranged transportation and activities.

Package tours often offer a number of options as to method of transportation (cruise; fly/cruise; cruise plus land tour by motorcoach, rail, etc.) and arrangement of the itinerary, and may be customized with optional add-ons, such as destinations and activities that are not part of the basic package.

Tour packages may be put together by a tour company, a travel agent, a travel wholesaler or you, the independent traveler. There is an incredible list of travel options to choose from in Alaska, as well as a huge geographical area. Your time, budget and interests will help narrow down the choices.

The larger tour companies in Alaska offer package tours using their own motorcoaches, cruiseships, railcars and motels. Other major Alaska tour companies use their own facilities (ships, motorcoaches, etc.) as well as other vendors to provide transportation, lodging, sightseeing and activities on their packaged tours.

A travel agent can also acquaint you with what package tours are available and their cost. If you are considering a package tour to Alaska by cruise ship, see "Cruising to Alaska" page 21. Travelers who do not wish to join a large tour may customize their own package tour, either with the help of a travel agent or *The MILEPOST®.

Read through the descriptions of major destinations in Alaska, such as Southeast/Inside Passage, Prince William Sound, Denali National Park, Kenai Peninsula, Anchorage, Fairbanks, etc. Everything from half-day motorcoach trips, sightseeing cruises or fly-in bear viewing to overnights on islands or on the North Slope, are covered in both the editorial and in the advertising.

Independent travelers can book any tour that might interest them, but they may also have to make arrangements for additional lodging and transportation. For example, a visitor might make independent arrangements for a flight to Anchorage and lodging for a night, then book a tour to Denali Park or Barrow or some other destination that would include transportation and lodging. The options are almost limitless. You can even purchase portions of the packaged tours (if space is available), such as the land tour portion of a cruise/tour.

Weather/When to go

One of the most often asked questions is, "When is the best time to travel?" Many Alaskans recommend May and June as the most favorable months for travel to the North, as well as probably the most promising period for views of Mount McKinley. The high season for travel in the North is June through August, usually the warmest months. But summer can also be the wettest months. The weather is as variable and unpredictable in the North as anywhere else.

The National Weather Service website for Alaska is www.arh.noaa.gov. Or phone the Alaska Weather Information Line: in Anchorage or from Outside, phone (907) 266-5105 and press option 1 for recorded forecast. To view weather conditions at various airports in Alaska, go to the FAA web site at http://akweathercams.faa.gov. For seasonal weather data, go to the Alaska Climate Research Center at http://climate.gi.alaska.edu. For Road Weather Information System (RWIS) reports, choose an area or corridor map at http://www.dot.state.ak.us/iways/roadweather/forms/AreaSelectForm.html then click on blue icons: It will give you the temperature of the road.

Current weather and 5-day forecasts for Alberta, British Columbia and Yukon communities are available from Environment Canada at www.weatheroffice.ec.gc.ca/canada_e.html. 24-hour recorded weather reports and forecasts are available by phone for: Whitehorse, YT, (867) 456-7623 (includes road report); Fort Nelson, BC, (250) 774-6461; and for Dawson Creek, Chetwynd, Fort St. John and Fort Nelson, BC, Peace River and Grande Prairie, AB, by phoning (250) 785-7669.

One advantage of summer travel to the North is the long hours of daylight: 19 hours and 21 minutes in Anchorage at summer solstice (June 21) and nearly 22 hours of daylight in Fairbanks. If you are traveling in winter, the reverse is true: 3 hours and 39 minutes of daylight in Fairbanks at winter solstice (December 21) and about 5½ hours in Anchorage. The farther north you go, the longer (or shorter) the days get. *See chart on this page.*

You can obtain a table of the times of sunrise/sunset, moonrise/moonset, or the beginning and end of twilight, for any year between 1700 and 2100 at http://aa.usno.navy.mil/data/docs/RS_OneYear.php.

Because most people travel in the summer and fill up hotels, motels, campgrounds and ferries, you might consider an early spring (April or May) or fall (late August into October) trip, when there's usually more room at lodges, campgrounds and on the ferries. Keep in mind, however, that some tours, attractions, lodges, campgrounds and other businesses may not be open in shoulder seasons. Check the advertisements in *The MILEPOST®* for details on seasonal opening and closing dates. Also, snowstorms are not uncommon in spring and fall in the North.

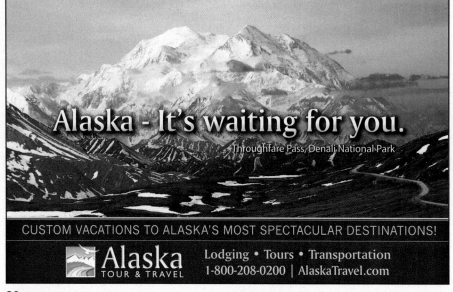

Alaska - It's waiting for you.

Throughfare Pass, Denali National Park

CUSTOM VACATIONS TO ALASKA'S MOST SPECTACULAR DESTINATIONS!

Alaska TOUR & TRAVEL

Lodging • Tours • Transportation

1-800-208-0200 | AlaskaTravel.com

Wildlife Viewing

The opportunity to see wildlife is a major attraction for many visitors to the North Country. *The MILEPOST®* highway logs point out spots along the highways where travelers may see Dall sheep, moose, caribou, and other mammals. Wildlife viewing areas of particular interest are highlighted by this symbol:

Booking agents packaging custom Alaska vacations can include wildlife touring on your trip. Alaska Heritage Tours and Phillips Cruises and Tours in Anchorage can help you package a trip. Also check with tour desks at motels/hotels or ask your bed-and-breakfast or campground host about wildlife viewing tour operators available locally.

A good resource for wildlife viewing information is the Alaska Dept. of Fish and Game (ADF&G). Check out their list of Alaska wildlife viewing sites at www.adfg.alaska.gov/ at "Where to Go" under the Viewing subhead.

The ADF&G has teamed up with the U.S. Forest Service, the Alaska Marine Highway System and other partners to produce a series of regional guidebooks and community-based brochures that highlight wildlife viewing sites in and near communities. Those included are: Anchorage, Fairbanks, the Kenai Peninsula and coastal communities from Ketchikan in Southeast Alaska to Dutch Harbor/Unalaska on the Aleutian Islands.

Birding

Alaska has 493 species of birds, so visitors have a good chance of seeing many varieties without even trying. Birding newsletters and statewide bird checklists are available at the Alaska Dept. of Fish and Game's Wings Over Alaska web site at www.birding.alaska.gov. Audubon Alaska offers information on how to obtain birding trail maps from local chapters in Kodiak, Fairbanks and Anchorage, on their website at http://ak.audubon.org. Or see "Checklist of Alaska Birds" at www.universityofalaskamuseumbirds.org.

St. Paul Island, boasts 248 species of birds, and is an incredible location for bird watching. In Alaska's Pribilof Islands, St. Paul is the largest of the Pribilof Islands and lies 300 miles off the coast of Alaska in the heart of the Bering Sea. Check out www.stpaultour.com for tour packages (see display ad this page).

There's good bird watching in summer in Fairbanks at Creamer's Field Migratory Waterfowl Refuge (www.creamersfield.org).

Another popular bird watching spot is Potter Point State Game Refuge just south of Anchorage off the Seward Highway. Also called "Potter Marsh," the refuge supports many species of ducks and other water birds.

The Copper River Delta Shorebird Festival in Cordova and the Kachemak Bay Shorebird Festival in Homer both take place in May and offer an opportunity to see great numbers of migrating shorebirds. The Alaska Bald Eagle Festival takes place in Haines in November and celebrates the winter gathering of more than 3,500 bald eagles on the Alaska Chilkat Bald Eagle Preserve.

Bear Viewing

There are 3 types of bears in Alaska: polar bears, black bears and brown bears. Polar bears *(Ursus maritimus),* classified as a marine mammal, are found along the northern coastline of Alaska and Canada, nearly always in association with sea ice. Brown bears *(Ursus arctos),* which are closely related to polar bears, are found throughout Alaska, with the exception of some islands in Southeast Alaska, the Aleutians and the Bering Sea. Black bears *(Ursus americanus),* are the most abundant and widely distributed of the 3 species of North American bears, as well as the smallest, according to the Alaska Dept. of Fish and Game (ADF&G).

Viewing *Ursus arctos,* the brown bear or grizzly, ranks high on visitors' wish lists of activities during a trip to Alaska. Both government agencies and private businesses in Alaska offer brown bear viewing opportunities for the public.

Most private bear viewing businesses offer day trips to see brown bears, although overnight and multi-day trips with lodging or camping are available. The hot spots for bear viewing tours in Southcentral and Southwestern Alaska are West Cook Inlet, Kodiak Island and the Alaska Peninsula, where coastal brown bears congregate in large numbers to fish at stream mouths or graze sedge fields.

Access is mainly by small plane, on floats or wheels, out of Homer, Kodiak, Kenai–Soldotna, King Salmon, Anchorage and Seward. Air services offer aerial bear viewing, guided land-based bear viewing tours and round-trip transportation to bear viewing camps and lodges. Tour operators often offer sport fishing, bird watching and other activities along with bear viewing. A few tour operators offer coastal brown bear viewing by boat.

A number of camps and lodges emphasize bear viewing as one of their major attractions. Silver Salmon Creek Lodge, a private lodge in Lake Clark National Park, offers 1-day tours or multi-night stays in their lodge on the west side of Cook Inlet. Afognak Wilderness Lodge offers bear viewing on Afognak Island north of Kodiak Island.

Air service to these and other bear view-

See you on the road!

©Kris Valencia, staff

We met many travelers (like the father and son pictured above with our MILEPOST truck) on the highway in summer 2013, when we were logging the roads, updating information for this edition. Thanks to all of you who shared your trip highlights with us, posed for a photo with our camper, expressed your enthusiasm for Northern travel and voiced your appreciation for this publication. It is always humbling and uplifting to hear from our readers. We very much appreciate your comments and suggestions.

It is a pleasure sharing these beautiful roads with equally passionate travelers from around the world. We hope to meet many more of you this summer in 2014. See you on the road or around the campfire!

ing destinations is offered by Andrew Airways, and Sea Hawk Air out of Kodiak; Alaska Bear Adventures with Kachemak Bay Air and Bald Mountain Air Service out of Homer; Natron Air in Soldotna; several charters out of Seward; and **Rust's Flying Service** out of Anchorage (see display ad on page 39).

Alaska's public parklands also have bear viewing. In southcentral Alaska, the 2,812-square-mile Kodiak National Wildlife Refuge, accessible by air charter or boat, is home to about 3,000 bears. The refuge now offers a bear viewing platform at the O'Malley River where visitors can observe bears in the wild. Contact the refuge for details at http://kodiak.fws.gov. On the Alaska Peninsula, numerous bears congregate at Brooks Falls, near Brooks Camp in Katmai National Park (www.nps.gov/katm/index.htm), for the red salmon run. Accommodations are available at Brooks Lodge through the park concessionaire.

The McNeil River State Game Sanctuary, about 100 miles southwest of Anchorage, is a favorite site of photographers and videographers intent on documenting brown bears. Visits to McNeil are by permit only, selected in an annual lottery. Information on permits is available online from Alaska Dept. of Fish and Game at www.adfg.alaska.gov/index.cfm?adfg=mcneilriver.main (open permits tab). The ADF&G also oversees Wolverine Creek on the west side of Cook Inlet, a popular destination for bear viewing and fishing by chartered skiff.

Off of the Parks Highway, in Talkeetna, several flightseeing services offer bear and wildlife viewing options.

In Southeast Alaska, the U.S. Forest Service manages 3 bear viewing sites: Anan Wildlife Observatory, located southeast of Wrangell; Stan Price State Wildlife Sanctuary at Pack Creek, located on Admiralty Island (co-managed by the ADF & G and USFS); and Fish Creek Wildlife Observatory near Hyder. For general information on these bear viewing destinations and links to related sites, visit www.fs.usda.gov/tongass (click on Recreation, then Nature Viewing, then Wildlife Viewing.

Anan Observatory is accessible by boat from Wrangell. Summer visitors can watch bears catch salmon headed for upstream spawning grounds. Breakaway Adventures (www.breakawayadventures.com) offers trips to Anan from Wrangell.

Both the Forest Service and ADF&G provide information about Pack Creek, where brown bears feed on salmon from June to early September. Pack Creek is a 30-minute flight by floatplane from Juneau and visits are by permit only. For more information visit www.fs.usda.gov/activity/tongass/recreation/natureviewing.

Also in Southeast Alaska, accessed via Cassiar Highway 37, is the Fish Creek Wildlife Observatory, located near Hyder. A U.S. Forest Service day-use recreation area is located at Fish Creek. Both brown and black bears may be photographed here as they fish for salmon from mid-July to early September. For more information visit www.fs.usda.gov/activity/tongass/recreation/nature viewing.

For those wanting to see bears but not wanting to go on a tour to do it, wherever the salmon are, you can typically also find bears. Bears are frequently in residence, for example, at the Russian River on the Kenai peninsula, during the salmon runs. If you drive down the peninsula and see bunches of fishermen, it means the fishing is good, so bear viewing will likely be also.

If you are fishing (or just viewing) where bears are present, be sure to read and follow posted instructions regarding bear etiquette. The best defense against bears: Do not surprise them, do not approach them, and do not underestimate their speed or destructive potential. Be "Bear Aware" at all times—the streams that cross Anchorage, for example, are salmon spawning routes in summer, and bears follow those streams to find their food source. *Remember: feeding wildlife is illegal.*

Wildlife Cruises

Both charter cruises and scheduled day cruises are available to view wildlife along Alaska's magnificent coastline. Passengers on day cruises have the opportunity to see some of Alaska's most famous glaciers and also its wildlife. Commonly seen on these cruises are sea otters, Steller sea lions, dolphins, harbor seals, Dall porpoises, whales (minke, gray, fin, humpback), puffins, eagles, black-legged kittiwakes, common murres, cormorants, and parakeet and rhinoceros auklets.

In Southeast Alaska, day cruises concentrate on whale watching and sightseeing in such gems as Misty Fjords National Monument (out of Ketchikan), Tracy Arm (out of Juneau) and Glacier Bay (also out of Juneau). Juneau's *Adventure Bound* Alaska Cruises offer daily trips to Tracy Arm, a long, narrow fjord that extends into the heavily glaciated Coast Mountain Range, 50 miles southeast

of Juneau, to see wildlife, waterfalls and glaciers. Adventures with Whales, Orca Enterprises offers wildlife and whale watching cruises around Juneau.

Whale watching, glacier tours and custom sightseeing are offered by Whale Song Cruises out of Petersburg. Viking Travel in Petersburg also arranges whale-watching and custom sightseeing trips.

Glacier Bay National Park offers wildlife and spectacular glacier scenery. Glacier Bay is on the itinerary of most Inside Passage cruise ships and now on the Alaska Marine Highway ferry route, and it is also a popular destination for day cruises out of Juneau. Charter boat tours of Glacier Bay, Icy Strait and Point Adolphus are available in Gustavus, the small community just outside the park boundary. Wildlife cruises may be arranged through local accommodations, such as Annie Mae Lodge.

In southcentral Alaska, charter and scheduled wildlife cruises depart from Whittier, Seward, Ninilchik, Homer and Seldovia for sightseeing Prince William Sound, Resurrection Bay, Cook Inlet and Kachemak Bay. Full-day, half-day and dinner cruises of Kenai Fjords National Park depart daily from Seward, located 127 miles south from Anchorage. These scheduled cruises explore the park's glaciated coastline and the substantial populations of marine mammals and birds that make their home there. Full-day cruises also visit Chiswell Islands National Wildlife Refuge. Charter boats are also available out of Seward for wildlife viewing. Scheduled cruise tours and charter service out of Seward for wildlife viewing include: Kenai Fjords Tours; Major Marine Tours; Kayak Adventures Worldwide; and Sunny Cove Sea Kayaking Co. And while you are in Seward, visit the Alaska SeaLife Center and learn about the the birds and mammals of coastal Alaska.

Daily scheduled cruise tours and custom sightseeing cruises of Prince William Sound's glaciers and wildlife depart from Whittier and Valdez. Prince William Sound tour operators include: Phillips' Cruises & Tours; Stan Stephens Glacier & Wildlife Cruises; Major Marine Tours; Prince William Sound Cruises & Tours; and *Lu-Lu Belle* Glacier Wildlife Cruises.

Marine wildlife cruises out of Homer travel to destinations around Kachemak Bay. Both the Seldovia Bay Ferry and the *Danny J* to Halibut Cove cruise Gull Island.

Wildlife Parks & Tours

The Alaska Wildlife Conservation Center at **Milepost S 79** Seward Highway, 48 miles south of Anchorage is a drive-through animal park, the center is dedicated to the rehabilitation of wild orphaned and injured animals. Rescued bears, lynx, caribou, moose, musk-oxen, bison, elk, Sitka black-tailed deer, eagles and owls are among the residents at the park.

Two destinations specializing in musk-ox viewing are the Musk-Ox Farm in Palmer (which also houses a gift shop of Musk-Ox qiviut items) and the UAF Large Animal Research Station in Fairbanks. Both locations offer guided tours of these ancient animals.

The Yukon Wildlife Preserve, located about a half-hour's drive from Whitehorse, is a 700-acre animal park. A 1½-hour passenger van tour reveals mountain goats, caribou, moose, elk, wood bison, musk-oxen, mule deer and mountain sheep in their natural habitat. For more information, go to its website: www.yukonwildlife.ca.

Vancouver Island Highway

CONNECTS: Victoria to Port Hardy, BC

Length: 312 miles   Road Surface: Paved   Season: Open all year

(See map, page 42)

19

Good view from Malahat Summit Lookout of Saanich Peninsula.
(©Kris Valencia, staff)

Major Attractions:

©Kris Valencia, staff

*Victoria,
Butchart Gardens,
Pacific Rim National Park*

Highest Summit:
*Malahat Summit
1,156 ft./352m*

Alaska-bound travellers taking BC Ferries Inside Passage service from Port Hardy to Prince Rupert, or the Discovery Coast service from Port Hardy to Bella Coola, must drive to the northeast coast of Vancouver Island. Prince Rupert, at the west end of the Yellowhead Highway, is the departure point for Alaska State Ferries sailing the Inside Passage north. *(See description of Prince Rupert beginning on page 255.)* Bella Coola, at the end of the Chilcotin Highway, may be added to your itinerary as either a stopover or as a debarkation point. *(Descriptions of the Chilcotin Highway and Bella Coola on pages 104-105.)* This itinerary may also be driven in reverse for return travelers, and makes an especially logical choice for motorists coming down the Cassiar Highway.

Most motorists begin their drive to Port Hardy—located on the "north island"—from Victoria, located at the south end of the island, a 312-mile/502-km drive, or from Nanaimo, a 246-mile/396-km drive.

Allow plenty of time for the drive. A world-renowned travel destination, Vancouver Island offers Alaska travellers many distractions, enough to keep them on the island for several days, so plan accordingly.

Ferries from the mainland to south Vancouver Island (see map) land at Victoria (from Port Angeles, WA), Swartz Bay (from Tsawwassen), Sidney (from Anacortes, WA), Nanaimo/Duke Point (from Tsawwassen) and Nanaimo/Departure Bay (from Horseshoe Bay). Trans-Canada Highway 1 connects Victoria and Nanaimo, and Highway 19 connects Nanaimo with Port Hardy. See BC Ferries schedule page 14 for service to/

Distance in miles	Campbell River	Duncan	Nanaimo	Port Hardy	Port McNeill	Victoria
Campbell River		128	96	146	121	166
Duncan	128		32	274	249	38
Nanaimo	96	32		242	217	70
Port Hardy	146	274	242		25	312
Port McNeill	121	249	217	25		287
Victoria	166	38	70	312	287	

Vancouver Island Highway Victoria, BC, to Port Hardy, BC

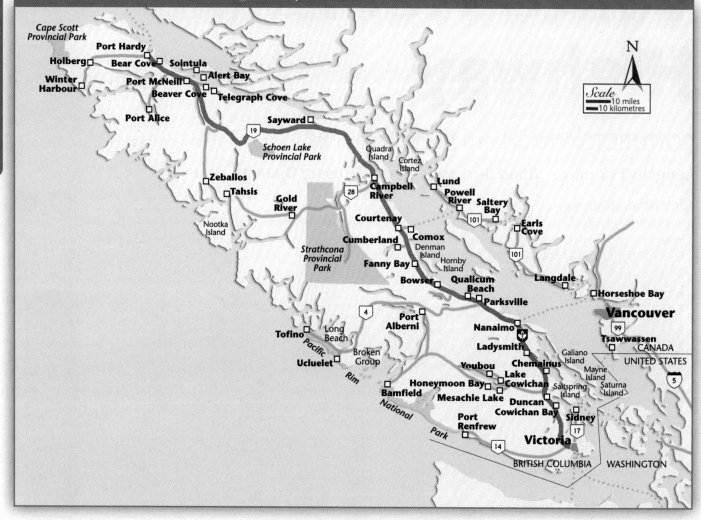

from Port Hardy/Bear Cove ferry terminal.

Distance in miles from Victoria (V) is followed by distance in miles from Port Hardy (PH). *Kilometreage for distance from Victoria reflects existing physical kilometreposts as noted in the log.*

Victoria

V 0 PH 312.3 (502.6 km) Douglas Street at Belleville in downtown Victoria. **Population:** 78,057. Seat of British Columbia's provincial government, Victoria is a major tourist destination for international travellers. As such, the city offers an extensive array of accommodations, dining experiences, shopping and sightseeing opportunities. It is a busy city, but parking is available: View parking map at www.downtownvictoria.ca/park. RV parking is a little more challenging, although there are some parking areas that accommodate RVs.

Visitor Information: www.tourism victoria.com, www.vancouverisland.com; or stop by the visitor centre at 812 Wharf Street, overlooking the Inner Harbor; phone (250) 953-2033.

Attractions include the Legislative Buildings and the Royal British Columbia

©Kris Valencia, staff

Museum. Have tea at the Empress, overlooking Victoria's Inner Harbor. Rent bikes and ride the Galloping Goose trail. Buy a Tilley hat, visit Murchie's Tea & Coffee, shop the Bay Centre. Take a land and water tour of Victoria. Take a Grayline tour or drive yourself to Brentwood Bay to visit famous Butchart Gardens (not to be missed) and the nearby Butterfly World (especially fun for kids). Get driving directions to Butchart from the visitor centre before departing Victoria. Plenty of RV parking at Butchart Gardens.

NOTE: Mile 0 of Trans-Canada Highway 1 is at the junction of Douglas Street and Dallas in Victoria. Head north via Douglas Street for Trans-Canada Highway 1 to Nanaimo. (Head north via Blanchard Street for Highway 17 to Swartz Bay; this is also the access to Butchart Gardens.)

TRANS-CANADA HIGHWAY 1

V 2.1 PH 310.2 (499.2 km) Traffic light at Cloverdale; signs direct northbound traffic to turn for BC Highway 17 to Sidney/Swartz Bay ferry terminals. Trans-Canada 1 becomes Douglas Street in Victoria. Blanchard becomes Highway 17 in Victoria.

V 2.3 PH 310 (499.2 km) Traffic light at Saanich; access to Highway 17 (follow signs).

V 2.7 PH 309.6 (498.2 km) Distance marker northbound shows Duncan 58 km/36 miles, Nanaimo 109 km/68 miles.

V 4.8 PH 307.5 (494.8 km) Exit 8 for Helmcken Road, View Royal; hospital.

NOTE: Trans-Canada 1 between Victoria and Nanaimo has 2- and 4-lane divided and undivided highway as well as 3-lane road with intermittent north- and southbound passing lanes. Sections of highway divided by concrete barriers restrict left-hand turns. Watch for U-turn routes: these are narrow with short turning radius and may be difficult if not impossible for large RVs and trailers to negotiate. Posted speed limits from 50 to 100 kmph/31 to 62 mph, with speed zones and curves as posted. Narrow road shoulders. CAUTION: Watch for bicyclists along the highway, day and night!

Freeway portions of highway have both exit ramps and traffic lights controlling 3-way and 4-way stops at junctions.

V 5.6 (10 km) PH 306.7 (493.5 km) Exit 10 to View Royal, Collwood, Fort Rodd Hill,

Thetis Lake.

V 8 (14 km) **PH 304.3** (489.7 km) Exit 14 to Langford, Port Renfrew, Sooke.

V 9 (15 km) **PH 303.3** (488.1 km) Exit 15 to McCallum; Shell gas station to east.

End 4-lane divided highway, begin 2-lane highway, northbound.

V 9.3 (16 km) **PH 303** (487.6 km) Exit 16 to Leigh Road.

V 10.6 (17 km) **PH 301.7** (485.5 km) Traffic light at West Shore Parkway; Shell gas station, Tim Hortons. Goldstream Provincial Park to west. Distance marker shows Duncan 45 km/28 miles, Nanaimo 95 km/59 miles. *NOTE: A few physical kilometreposts northbound measure from this junction and are added to this log as landmarks.*

V 11.2 (19 km) **PH 301.1** (484.5 km) Physical Kilometrepost 1 (measured from West Shore Parkway). *Slow for 60-kmph/ 37-mph curves northbound. Begin narrow, winding road with high traffic volume, highway climbs to Malahat Summit. Hitch-hiking and picking up hitch-hikers is illegal.*

V 12.4 (21 km) **PH 299.9** (482.6 km) Goldstream day-use area to east at end of northbound curve.

V 12.5 (21.2 km) **PH 299.8** (482.4 km) Physical Kilometrepost 3. Gravel turnout to east for northbound traffic

V 16.9 (28.5 km) **PH 295.4** (475.4 km) Physical Kilometrepost 10.

V 17.2 (28.7 km) **PH 295.1** (474.9 km) Victoria West KOA up hill to west, gas station to east. Malahat Mountain Inn to north of gas station is closed.

V 19.2 (32 km) **PH 293.1** (471.7 km) South Shawnigan Lake Road leads northwest to West Shawnigan Lake Provincial Park.

V 19.7 (32.8 km) **PH 292.6** (470.9 km) Northbound traffic-only viewpoint to east at **Malahat Summit** (elev. 1,156 feet/352 m).

V 21.2 (35.2 km) **PH 291.1** (468.5 km) Northbound-only rest area with toilets to east.

V 21.6 (35.8 km) **PH 290.7** (467.8 km) Malahat Lookout viewpoint to east for northbound traffic only.

Begin 8 percent downgrade northbound.

V 22.8 (37.7 km) **PH 289.5** (465.9 km) *End 2-lane highway, begin 4-lane divided highway, northbound.*

V 23.6 (39 km) **PH 288.7** (464.6 km) Exit for Bamberton, Mill Bay Road, Brentwood Ferry. Bamberton Provincial Park has camping, sandy beach, swimming, fishing.

V 26.7 (44 km) **PH 284.1** (457.2 km) Traffic light at Deloume Road; Shell gas station at southwest corner, Co-op Gas at northeast corner; fast food, South Cowichan

Visitor Booth, Mill Bay Shopping Centre. Mill Bay Road to Brentwood Ferry.

V 26.9 (44.3 km) **PH 285.4** (459.3 km) Traffic light at Shawnigan Lake-Mill Bay Road junction; Pioneer Square Mall. Access to the **Kinsol Trestle**, one of 8 trestles on the Cowichan Valley Trail and one of the tallest free-standing timber rail trestle structures in the world. To reach the Trestle: Head west through Shawnigan Village and turn right on Shawnigan Lake Road which becomes Renfrew Road; turn right on Glen Eagles Road to reach parking lot trailhead at corner of Shelby Road.

V 27.5 (45.5 km) **PH 284.8** (458.3 km) Traffic light at Cobble Hill Road; Petro-Canada gas station to west. Access to Kinsol Trestle (see **Milepost V 26.9**).

V 30.2 (49.4 km) **PH 282.1** (454 km) Traffic light; gas station.

V 31.3 (51.1 km) **PH 281** (452.2 km) Rest area to east for northbound traffic only.

V 34.5 (56 km) **PH 277.8** (447.1 km) Whippletree Junction to east on frontage road; family-owned Double Barrel Coffee Company is open 7 days a week.

V 35.1 (57.2 km) **PH 277.2** (446.1 km) Traffic light at Bend Road; Save On gas station to east.

V 37.4 (60.9 km) **PH 274.9** (442.4 km) Traffic light at Allenby/Chaster Roads; Super 8 to east.

V 37.7 (61.6 km) **PH 274.6** (441.9 km) Traffic light at Boyes Road. Access to Duncan RV Park. Sun Valley Mall to west.

Duncan

V 38.2 (62.4 km) **PH 272.7** (438.8 km) Traffic light at Trunk Road/Government Street; Coop, Petro Canada, Shell and Mohawk gas stations; convenience stores, fast food, Safeway. Access west to downtown Duncan.

Population: 4,986.
Visitor information: at Coronation Street (next traffic light northbound); www.tourismcowichan.com, phone 1-888-303-3337.

Gateway to the Cowichan Valley region, Duncan has all visitor services, a post office, medical clinics, RCMP, police and churches. Shopping and services are found along Trans-Canada 1. Unique shops and artisanal shopping is in the downtown area (access west via Trunk Road/Government Street or Coronation Avenue.) Cowichan Valley Museum is located in the Duncan Train Station at 130 Canada Avenue; phone 250-746-

City Square in Duncan is the site of a popular Farmers' Market. (©Tourism Cowichan)

6612, or visit www.cowichanvalleymuseum.bc.ca. Guided totem tours are offered on the hour from June to September from the train station on Canada Avenue.

The Farmers' Market in City Square, Saturdays from 9 A.M. to 2 P.M., is the largest on the island; arts, entertainment, produce. Major attractions in the area include wineries (visit http://wines.cowichan.net), and there are also several intriguing agricultural and culinary attractions, such as True Grain Bread in Cowichan Bay Village (www.truegrain.ca) and the Lavender Labyrinth.

Outdoor recreation includes 3 championship golf courses. Bicyclists will enjoy the Cowichan Valley Trail/Trans Canada Trail that starts at the south end of Shawnigan Lake and goes west to Cowichan Lake then east to North Cowichan and Ladysmith. Or just walk the Kinsol Trestle (see **Milepost V 26.9**) on the trail. Lake Cowichan on Highway 18 is a popular summer recreation spot.

TRANS-CANADA HIGHWAY 1
(continued)

V 38.3 (62.5 km) **PH 274** (440.9 km) Traffic light at Coronation; Shell gas on southeast corner. Visitor information and downtown Duncan to west.

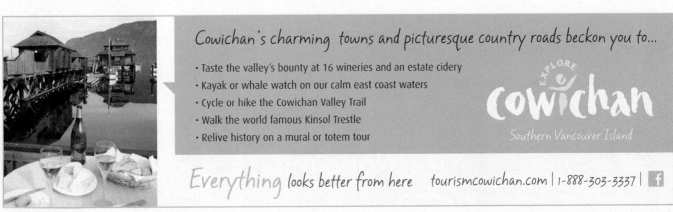

Nanaimo's Harbourfront Walkway is one of the city's most appealing attractions.
(©Kris Valencia, staff)

V 38.6 (63 km) **PH 273.7** (440.5 km) Traffic light at James Street; Boston Pizza, Pizza Hut, McDonalds, Tim Hortons. Downtown Duncan to west.

V 39 (63.6 km) **PH 273.3** (439.8 km) Traffic light at Beverly Street; Sears to east, shopping mall and Starbucks to west. Vancouver Island also boasts its own chain of coffee shops, Serious Coffee.

V 39.8 (64.9 km) **PH 272.5** (438.5 km) Rest area with litter barrels to east.

V 40.3 (65.7 km) **PH 272** (437.7 km) Traffic light at Drinkwater Road; Cowichan Commons, Walmart, Canadian Tire.

BC Forest Discovery Center to east (www. discoveryforest.com), open daily 10 A.M. to 4:30 P.M. from May 30 to Labour Day. Steam train rides daily in July and August.

V 41.2 (67.1 km) **PH 271.1** (436.3 km) Traffic light at **junction** with Highway 18/ Cowichan Valley Highway/Herd Road. Drive west to Lake Cowichan Recreation Area. Also access to Mount Prevost Memorial Park and Averill Creeks and Deol Estate wineries. A 55-km/34-mile road connects Lake Cowichan and Port Renfrew on Pacific Rim National Park coast.

V 42.6 (69.3 km) **PH 269.7** (434 km) Traffic light at Mays Road; Chevron and Co-op Commercial Cardlock gas stations.

V 45.5 (74 km) **PH 266.8** (429.4 km) Traffic light at Mount Sicker Road; FasGas with convenience store to west. Turnoff for Crofton and Salt Spring Island Ferry.

V 48.2 (78.4 km) **PH 264.1** (425 km) Traffic light at Henry Road; Co-op gas with convenience store at northwest corner. Exit east for **CHEMAINUS** (pop. 3,900), famous for its 39 outdoor murals and for the Boeing 737 which was sunk off the coast there as an artificial reef for scuba divers. All services available.

V 54.4 (88.3 km) **PH 257.9** (415 km) Traffic light at Davis Road; Safeway and other services to west.

V 55.7 (90.4 km) **PH 256.6** (412.9 km) Traffic light at Roberts Street. Drive west on Roberts Street to First Avenue and downtown **LADYSMITH** (pop. 8,328); all services. Ladysmith is known as the "prettiest town in British Columbia." Old Towne Bakery here is the most popular bakery on Vancouver Island. www.ladysmith.ca.

V 55.9 (90.7 km) **PH 256.4** (412.6 km) Shell gas station to west for southbound traffic only.

V 58 (94 km) **PH 254.3** (409.2 km) Ivy Green Husky/A&W gas station to east for northbound traffic only just south of traffic light at Oyster Sto Lo Road.

V 61.2 (99.3 km) **PH 251.1** (404.1 km) Spitfire Way; Nanaimo airport to east.

V 62.1 (100 km) **PH 250.2** (402.6 km) Northbound-only rest area to east; toilets, litter bins, large parking area.

V 62.4 (100.5 km) **PH 249.9** (402.2 km) Nanaimo River bridge.

V 64 (103.5 km) **PH 248.3** (399.5 km)

Traffic light at Morden Road; Gas & Go station to west.

V 65.3 (106 km) **PH 247** (397.5 km) **Duke Point Interchange.** Exit to BC Ferries/Duke Point terminal (5 miles/8 km) via Highway 19 East for ferry service to/from Tsawwassen.

V 66.2 (107.3 km) **PH 246.1** (396 km) Highway splits northbound: Keep to left for Highway 19 North to Parksville, Campbell River and Port Hardy; keep to right for Trans-Canada Highway 1/Highway 19A (log follows) for Nanaimo city centre (description follows) and BC Ferries Departure Bay terminal for ferry service to/from Horseshoe Bay. *Port Hardy-bound travelers exit from Trans-Canada Highway 1 to continue north on Highway 19/ Nanaimo Parkway. Kmposts northbound show distance from Duke Point.*

Trans-Canada Highway 1/Highway 19A log to Nanaimo as follows. Food, gas, lodging and other services available along the highway.

Mile 0.4 Traffic light at Cedar Road.

Mile 0.7 Traffic light at Cranberry.

Mile 0.9 Traffic light at Maki Road/10th Street; South Parkway Mall to west. Chevron commercial cardlock to east. Living Forest RV Park is 0.3 mile/0.5 km east.

Mile 1.7 Petroglyph Park hiking trail.

Mile 2.6 Traffic light at Needham; car wash to east.

Mile 2.9 Dairy Queen, gas station to west.

Mile 3 Shell gas station to east.

Mile 3.4 Esplanade/Gordon Street; Casino Nanimo, Port Place Mall (Thrifty Foods, London Drugs, BC Liquor Store).

Mile 3.7 Traffic light at Commercial. City centre.

Mile 3.8 Traffic light at Comox Road; Mr. Lube. Turn east for Maffeo Sutton Park (passenger ferry to Newcastle Island). Highway 19A/Island Highway continues as Terminal Avenue to rejoin Highway 19 just north of Exit 28/Aulds Road.

Nanaimo

Located on the east coast of Vancouver Island, Nanaimo is the third oldest city in British Columbia. **Population:** 78,692. Nanaimo is an important port city, connecting passengers and vehicles to/from the mainland via BC Ferries Tsawwassen–Duke Point service, and Horseshoe Bay–Departure Bay service.

Visitor Information: Visitor Centre on

Commercial near waterfront. Downtown visitor kiosk with maps, brochures, guides and event information (seasonal location). www.tourismnanaimo.com.

This is a good-sized city with complete tourist facilities including major-chain hotels/motels, restaurants and retail stores. The downtown area fronts Nanaimo Harbour and features one of the city's most appealing attractions: the 5-km-/3-mile-long Nanaimo Harbourfront Walkway. Passenger ferries also connect the downtown waterfront with Protection Island (famous for its floating pub) and Newcastle Island.

The Nanaimo Bar Trail is a different kind of walk, offering places to stop for Nanimo Bars (including a deep-fried version). Nanaimo is the home of the Nanaimo Bar, and the Nanaimo Museum at 100 Museum Way (adjacent Serious Coffee) The Tourism Nanaimo website has a Nanimo Bar recipe.

Nanaimo boasts a honey farm, herb farm and 4 farmers' markets. The Pioneer Plaza Farmers' Market downtown takes place from May to October, Fridays 10 A.M. to 2 P.M. (to 3 P.M. when cruise ships are in port); www.nanaimofarmersmarket.com.

Nanimo has some 200 parks, 130 kms/81 miles of trails, and 9 off-leash dog parks. Nanaimo Aquatic Center (Exit 18 on Highway 19) is the largest west of Edmonton; wave pool, lots of parking.

HIGHWAY 19

V 66.2 (107.3 km) **PH 246.1** (396 km) **Junction** of Highway 19 and Highway 19A/Trans-Canada Highway 1. Continue north on Highway 19 for Campbell River, Port McNeill and Port Hardy. *Physical kilometreposts northbound show distance from Duke Point and are added to this log.*

V 70 (16 km) **PH 242.3** (389.9 km) Traffic light at Exit 16 Fifth Street/College Drive.

V 71.2 (18 km) **PH 241.1** (388 km) Traffic light at Exit 18 Jingle Pot Road east to Aquatic Centre and Nanaimo City Centre.

Northbound, the Parkway Trail (multiuse) parallels Highway 19 to Exit 28.

V 73 (21 km) **PH 239.3** (385.1 km) Traffic light at Exit 21 Northfield Road east.

V 75 (24 km) **PH 237.3** (381.9 km) Traffic light at Exit 24 Mostar Road east to Highway 19A/Island Highway and Jingle Pot Road west to camping.

V 77.3 (28 km) **PH 235** (378.2 km) Traffic light at Exit 28 Aulds Road. Walmart/Woodgrove Centre, the island's largest shopping mall, to east.

V 77.5 (28.3 km) **PH 234.8** (378 km) Northbound access east to Walmart via Mary Ellen Drive.

V 78 (29 km) **PH 234.3** (377 km) Traffic light at **junction** with Highway 19A/Island Highway southbound for downtown Nanaimo and Departure Bay ferry terminal. Victoria-bound travelers continue on Highway 19/Nanaimo Parkway southbound.

V 78.8 (30.3 km) **PH 233.5** (375.7 km) Traffic light at Ware Road to Lantzville.

V 80 (32.2 km) **PH 232.3** (373.8 km) Traffic light at Superior Road to village of Lantzville to east.

V 83.2 (37.3 km) **PH 229.1** (368.7 km) Southbound-only rest area to west with picnic tables, litter barrels, grassy area.

V 84.7 (39.7 km) **PH 227.6** (366.3 km) Traffic light at Northwest Bay Road; Petro-Canada gas station at northeast corner. [i]

V 86.7 (42.9 km) **PH 225.6** (363 km)

Southbound-only access to Chevron gas station to west. [gas]

V 88.3 (45.5 km) **PH 224** (360.5 km) Exit 46 to **PARKSVILLE** and **junction** with Highway 19A North/Oceanside Route, a 2-lane highway that gives access to a string of resorts, beaches and tourist facilities between Parksville and Qualicum Beach. Attractions along here include Rathtrevor Beach at low tide; Second Avenue in Qualicum Beach, with local shops and no chain stores allowed; **Paradise Adventure Mini-Golf &**

©Kris Valencia, staff

RV Park has a well-maintained and colorful miniature golf course; they are celebrating their 27th anniversary in 2014.

V 91.2 (50.3 km) **PH 221.1** (355.8) Exit 51 to Parksville/Coombs and Highway 4A/Port Alberni. Recommended side trip (description follows) to Englishman River Falls and Goat on the Roof Market.

Exit west and follow Highway 4A north 1.5 miles and turn left (west) on Errington Road. It is approximately 5 miles/9 km to **Englishman River Falls Provincial Park**. Beautiful area of tall trees; large parking area and short walk to falls. Includes a 105 campsites in addition to the day-use area.

Returning to Highway 4A, continue north 2.5 miles to Coombs to visit the very

©Kris Valencia, staff

popular **Goat on the Roof Market**. This small complex, just south of Coombs River Bridge, has fresh fruit and vegetables and a variety of small shops that attract a big crowd, even on weekdays. Parking for cars is extensive up a narrow side street at the market; or park along Highway 4A; or follow RV/bus parking signs.

From Coombs, continue north on Highway 4A 1.5 miles to junction with Highway 4; turn east and continue 1.5 miles to return to Highway 19 at Exit 60, or turn west on Highway 4 for Little Qualicum Falls/Cameron Lake, Cathedral Grove and Pacific Rim National Park.

V 96.7 (52 km) **PH 215.6** (347 km) Exit 60 to Highway 4 to Port Alberni, Tofino, and Pacific Rim National Park. Other major attractions west off this exit include Little Qualicum Falls (camping; day-use areas on Cameron Lake), and MacMillan Park, which contains the famous Cathedral Grove stand of douglas fir. Exit east for Qualicum Beach and Highway 19A.

V 101.7 (67 km) **PH 210.6** (338.9 km)

Englishman River Falls. (©Kris Valencia, staff)

Little Qualicum River.

NOTE: Signed river crossings northbound are included in this log. Creek crossings (of which there are many) are not included.

V 106.3 (74.5 km) **PH 206** (331.5 km) Exit 75 Horne Lake Road west to Spider Lake Provincial Park (5.5 miles/9 km) and Horne Lake Caves Provincial Park (9.5 miles/15 km). Exit east for Highway 19A/Qualicum Beach.

V 107.6 (76.6 km) **PH 204.7** (329.4 km) Big Qualicum River.

V 108.5 (78 km) **PH 203.8** (328 km) Northbound-only turnout to east.

V 113.8 (86.5 km) **PH 198.5** (319.4 km) Exit 87 Cooke Creek Road to Highway 19A, Deep Bay, Fanny Bay. Rosewall Creek Provincial Park day-use area.

V 122.1 (100 km) **PH 190.2** (306.1 km) Exit 101 east to Buckley Bay, Union, Royston. Buckley Bay ferry and junction with Highway 19A/Oceanside Route. Rest area with bike path.

V 130.2 (113 km) **PH 182.1** (293 km) Trent River.

V 132.6 (116.8 km) **PH 179.7** (289.2 km) Exit 117 to Cumberland, Courtenay and Comox. Hospital, police, ferry, visitor centre, airport.

V 137.2 (124 km) **PH 175.1** (281.8 km) Puntledge River.

V 138.4 (126 km) **PH 173.9** (279.9 km) Browns River.

V 138.8 (126.6 km) **PH 173.5** (279.2 km) Traffic light at Exit 127 Piercy Road, Courtenay, Comox.

V 141.1 (130.3 km) **PH 171.2** (275.5 km) Exit 130 to Mount Washington Alpine Resort, Strathcona Parkway.

V 145.7 (137.4 km) **PH 166.6** (268.1 km) Tsolum River.

V 149.4 (143.5 km) **PH 162.9** (262.2 km) Traffic light at Exit 144 Hamn Road; Saratoga Beach, Oyster Bay and Miracle Beach Provincial Park (8 km/5 miles), one of Vancouver Island's most popular parks. Camping and day-use. [camp]

V 154.8 (152 km) PH 157.5 (253.5 km) Oyster River.

V 155.5 (153.3 km) PH 156.8 (252.3 km) Traffic light at Cranberry Road.

V 156.3 (154.5 km) PH 156 (251 km) Little Oyster River.

V 160.2 (161.6 km) PH 152.1 (244.8 km) Exit 161 to Jubilee Parkway, Highway 19A/Oceanside Route.

V 164.2 (167 km) PH 148.1 (238.3 km) Traffic light at Exit 167 Willis Road; Shell gas station to west.

Highway splits northbound: Begin 1-way Tamarac Street northbound. End 1-way Willow Street southbound.

V 165.6 (169.3 km) PH 146.7 (236.1 km) Traffic light at 14th Avenue. Access east to Campbell River city centre.

V 165.7 (169.5 km) PH 146.6 (235.9 km) Traffic light at 16th Avenue; Esso and Chevron gas stations, McDonalds. Access east to Campbell River city centre.

V 165.8 (169.7 km) PH 146.5 (235.7 km) Traffic light at **junction** of Highway 19 with Highway 19A/Island Highway east to Campbell River (description follows), and Highway 28 west. Walmart is 0.8 miles/1.3 km east on Highway 19A, which continues to Visitor Centre and Campbell River waterfront.

Campbell River

Located on the east coast of North Vancouver Island, 3-hour drive from Victoria and less than 2 hours north of Nanaimo. **Population:** 36,096. **Emergency Services:** Police, Fire Dept. and Ambulance, phone 911. **Hospital:** Campbell River Hospital, phone 250-850-2141.

©Kris Valencia, staff

Visitor Information: Tourism Campbell River Visitor Center is housed in the same building as the Art Gallery, at 1235 Shoppers Row; phone 1-877-286-5707; website http://campbellrivertourism.com. Free 2-hour vehi-

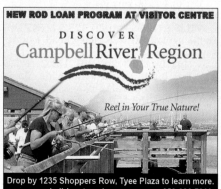

cle and RV parking is available behind the visitor centre at Tyee Place Shopping Centre; Shoppers Drugmart.

Climate: Moderate, with an average temperature of 8°C/46.4°F, and an average annual precipitation of 140 cm/55 inches.

Full visitor services are available, including accommodations (from budget hotels to the world-famous Painter's Lodge), fine dining, fast-food, major chain stores and interesting locally-owned shops. Oceanside camping at Thunderbird RV Park, phone 250-286-3344.

Campbell River is located at the entrance to Discovery Passage, the primary route for marine traffic between the Pacific Ocean to the north and the Strait of Georgia to the south. Cruise ships, deep sea freighters and barges in transit to Alaska, along with sailboats, yachts and other pleasure boats, pass through Discovery Passage. Not surprisingly, the city has a busy waterfront scene, with marinas, the landmark Discovery Pier, multi-use trails and parking. There is also ferry service to Quadra Island and Cortes Island; whale watching and kayak tours.

HIGHWAY 19
(continued)

V 165.8 (169.7 km) PH 146.5 (235.7 km) Traffic light at **junction** of Highway 19 with Highway 19A and Highway 28 (Gold River Highway). Access to Parkside Campground & R.V. Park, 5 mi/3 miles west.

V 165.9 (169.9 km) PH 146.4 (235.5 km) Campbell River Bridge.

V 166.7 (171.2 km) PH 145.6 (234.3 km) *End 4-lane highway, begin 2-lane highway, northbound. Highway 19 becomes North Island Highway: Road narrows; limited services between communities; watch for deer!*

Highway splits southbound: Begin 1-way Willow Street southbound. End 1-way Tamarac Street northbound.

V 167.7 (173 km) PH 144.6 (232.7 km) Gas station with diesel.

V 172.6 (180.8 km) PH 139.7 (224.8 km) Turnout to east with point-of-interest sign.

V 174.9 (184.5 km) PH 137.4 (221.1 km) Turnoff for Morton Lake Provincial Park, 16 km/10 miles west; 24 lakeside campsites, rustic.

V 176.3 (186.8 km) PH 136 (218.9 km) Ripple Rock Recreation Hiking Trailhead to east; parking.

V 177.5 (188.7 km) PH 134.8 (216.9 km) Turnoff for Ripple Rock RV Park, Browns Bay Resort.

V 181.5 (195 km) PH 130.8 (210.5 km) Distance marker northbound shows Port Hardy 208 km/129 miles.

V 185.6 (201.6 km) PH 126.7 (203.9 km) Turnoff east to Roberts Lake Rest Area with litter bins and toilets.

V 204.9 (233 km) PH 107.4 (172.8 km) Salmon River.

V 205.7 (233.7 km) PH 106.6 (171.6 km) **Sayward Junction**; convenience store and gas/diesel. Turnoff for village of Sayward (5 miles/8 km).

V 206.3 (234.7 km) PH 106 (170.6 km) Sayward Hill winter chain-up area to east for northbound traffic.

V 206.5 (235 km) PH 105.8 (170.3 km) Highway climbs Sayward Hill northbound.

NOTE: Grades to 7 percent northbound.

Speed limit 100 kmph/62 mph or as posted. 2-lane road with some passing lanes on hills. Drive with headlights on at all times. Watch for logging trucks and for deer. Some patched and bumpy pavement. Sporadic cell phone service.

V 208.9 (238.9 km) PH 103.4 (166.4 km) Brake check area to west for southbound traffic descending Sayward Hill.

V 211.4 (242.8 km) PH 100.9 (162.4 km) Keta Lake Rest Area with litter bins, picnic table and outhouses.

V 217.7 (252.7 km) PH 94.6 (152.2 km) Adam River.

V 223.5 (262 km) PH 88.8 (142.9 km) Turnoff for rest area to east.

V 240.1 (288.5 km) PH 72.2 (116.2 km) Turnoff west on gravel road for Schoen Lake Provincial Park, one of the most scenic lakes on Vancouver Island; 9 vehicle accessible campsites. Mount Caine Ski Area access.

V 242.8 (292.7 km) PH 69.5 (111.8 km) Hoomak Lake rest area to west with toilets, litter bin.

V 244.3 (295 km) PH 68 (109.4 km) Distance marker northbound shows Port McNeill 69 km/40 miles, Port Hardy 108 km/67 miles.

V 246.8 (299.2 km) PH 65.5 (105.4 km) Woss Cutoff: road leads 1 mile/1.6 km south to community of Woss with gas station and general store.

V 250.5 (305.2 km) PH 61.8 (99.5 km) Eagles Nest roadside rest area to west with toilet and litter barrel.

V 251.6 (306.9 km) PH 60.7 (97.7 km) Double-ended turnout to west.

Highway climbs northbound; passing lane.

V 258 (317.1 km) PH 54.3 (87.4 km) Double-ended viewpoint to west.

Highway descends northbound. End uphill passing lane southbound.

V 260.3 (320.6 km) PH 52 (83.7 km) **Zeballos junction.** Zeballos is a logging town located 42 km/26 miles southwest via a gravel road.

V 272.3 (339.8 km) PH 40 (64.4 km) Gravel turnout to west.

V 282.1 (355.3 km) PH 30.2 (48.6 km) Paved road east leads 15 km/9 miles to **TELEGRAPH COVE** (pop. 20). This his-

©Claire Torgerson, staff

toric boardwalk village is probably the most picturesque community on Vancouver Island and a popular tourist destination in summer. Whale watching tours available from May to October.

V 283.2 (357.1 km) PH 29.1 (46.8 km) Nimpkish River bridge; turnout with litter bins to east at north end.

V 284.1 (358.7 km) PH 28.2 (45.4 km) Hyde Creek. Petro Canada station to east.

V 286.5 (362.5 km) PH 25.8 (41.5 km) Turnout with litter bin to east and information sign for Alert Bay.

V 286.6 (362.7 km) PH 25.7 (41.3 km) Turnoff for Port McNeill via Campbell Way (1.6 miles/2.6 km); description follows.

Port McNeill

Located on on the northeast coast of Vancouver Island on Broughton Strait. Port McNeill is 6 hours from Victoria, 4 hours from Nanimo and 30 minutes from Port Hardy by highway. **Population:** 2,600. **Emergency Services:** RCMP, Fire Dept., ambulance, hospital, pharmacy, medical and dental clinics.

Visitor Information: Port McNeill Visitor Centre, 1594 Beach Drive (on the waterfront); phone 250-956-3131 or 1-888-956-3131. Website www.portmcneill.net.

Climate: Typical west coast marine climate, with temperatures averaging 17.4°C/63°F in July and August.

Port McNeill has complete tourist services. Groceries, clothing, hardware, fishing and sporting goods, and gifts are available in local stores, many within walking distance of the Visitor Center. Pick up a town map at the Visitor Centre along with a list of popular local hiking and walking trails.

With its full service harbour facility, Port McNeill plays host to Inside Passage marine traffic and is also a gateway to a variety of activities, from salmon fishing to whale watching and kayaking. Campers and outdoor enthusiasts will find everything they require in this full facility community.

Special events include **Orca Fest**, scheduled for August 16 in 2014.

Port McNeill is home to 2 of the world's largest burls. The largest is just north of the Visitor Centre in the Community Hall parking lot. Continue past the Community Hall and turn left up hill for Broughton RV Park.

Ferry service from Port McNeill to Alert Bay (www.alertbay.ca) and Sointula (www.sointulainfo.ca).

HIGHWAY 19
(continued)

V 287.2 (363.6 km) **PH 25.1** (40.4 km) Turnout to west with information sign on Port McNeill.

V 292.3 (371.8 km) **PH 20** (32.1 km) Turnoff to east for Cluxewe Resort, 0.7 mile/1.1 km via gravel road; popular seaside RV park, cabins, cafe.

V 294.4 (375.2 km) **PH 17.9** (28.8 km) Viewpoint to east; North Vancouver Island map, litter bins.

V 297.2 (379.8 km) **PH 15.1** (24.3 km) Rest area to east.

V 298.7 (382.3 km) **PH 13.6** (21.9 km) Keogh River.

V 298.9 (382.6 km) **PH 13.4** (21.6 km) **Junction** with Highway 30 which leads west 18 miles/30 km to **Port Alice**, a full-service community known as the "gateway to the Wild West Coast"; www.portalice.ca. Camping at Marble River Provincial Park, Link

Port McNeill's visitor information centre is located on the waterfront. (©Claire Torgerson, staff)

River Regional Park and Port Alice RV & Campground.

V 309.2 (399 km) **PH 3.1** (5 km) Welcome to Port Hardy turnout at **junction** with Bear Cove Highway, which leads east 3 miles/5 km to **BC Ferries terminal** at Bear Cove. Also access this turnoff to Wildwoods Campground (Mile 1.1), Bear Cove Cottages (Mile 2.3), Bear Cove Park day-use area (Mile 2.7). Distance marker leaving ferry terminal shows Port Hardy 10 km/6 miles, Nanaimo 387 km/240 miles, Victoria 495 km/308 miles.

NOTE: End physical kilometreposts on Highway 19. Kilometres from Victoria now reflect metric conversion of mileage. Kilometreposts continue on Bear Cove Highway and reflect distance from Duke Point ferry terminal in Nanaimo, with Kilometrepost 405 just before the ferry terminal entrance.

V 309.8 (400 km) **PH 2.5** (4 km) Port Hardy RV Resort. *NOTE: Because the ferry from Prince Rupert arrives late in the evening, area campground owners generally are at the front gate with a flashlight to greet campers.*

V 309.9 (498.7 km) **PH 2.4** (3.9 km) Quatse River bridge then **junction** with Hardy Bay Road to northeast and Coal Harbour Road to southwest. Lodging on Hardy Bay Road: Glen Lion Inn and Quarterdeck Inn. Quatse Salmon Centre and Quatse River Campground are 0.5 mile/0.8 km southwest on Byng Road. Salmon Centre open mid-May through September, from 10 A.M. to 5 P.M., Wed.–Sun.; admission fee.

V 310.5 (499.7 km) **PH 1.8** (2.9 km) Holberg Road to Cape Scott Provincial Park (39 miles/63 km).

V 311.8 (501.8 km) **PH 0.5** (0.8 km) 4-way stoplight: Turn east on Granville for Chevron and Esso gas stations, Thunderbird Mall (Overwatea Foods, Peoples Drugmart, Subway, A&W), Providence Inn and Port Hardy Inn. Granville junctions with Market Street in downtown Port Hardy.

V 312.3 (502.6 km) **PH 0** Highway 19 ends/begins at junction with Market Street in Port Hardy; description follows.

Port Hardy

Located on Hardy Bay on the northeast coast of Vancouver Island. **Population:** 4,008. **Emergency Services:** Phone 911 for RCMP, Ambulance and Fire Dept. **Visitor Information:** Port Hardy & District Chamber of Commerce/Visitor Information Centre, 7250 Market (at the bottom of Main Street); phone 250-949-7622, website www.ph-chamber.bc.ca.

Port Hardy has all visitors services including hotels, motels, cabins, bed-and-breakfasts and campgrounds; restaurants and fast-food outlets; gas stations; marine supplies; and retail services. 24-hour ATMs inside lobbies of bank and credit union. WiFi at Guido's coffee shop and elsewhere (ask at visitor centre).

This is a base for outdoor adventures such as hiking, kayaking and fishing. The North Coast Trail here is an extension of the Cape Scott Trail and one of the longest backpacking wilderness trails on Vancouver Island. Port Hardy is also home to the award-winning Quatse Salmon Stewardship Centre, a community museum, local craft shop and galleries.

Alaska Highway via
East Access Route

CONNECTS: Great Falls, MT, to Dawson Creek, BC

Length: 872 miles **Road Surface:** Paved **Season:** Open all year

(See map, pages 49-50)

15 **2** **3** **4** **43**

Alberta's agriculture is on display along its highways. This hay field is in the Peace River region. (©Michael K. Robb)

Distance in miles	Calgary	Dawson Creek	Edmonton	Grande Prairie	Great Falls	Lethbridge	Valleyview
Calgary		553	174	471	320	137	398
Dawson Creek	553		379	82	872	690	155
Edmonton	174	379		297	494	311	224
Grande Prairie	471	82	297		791	608	73
Great Falls	320	872	494	791		183	718
Lethbridge	137	690	311	608	183		535
Valleyview	398	155	224	73	718	535	

The East Access Route is one of 3 major access routes to the Alaska Highway logged in *The MILEPOST®* (the others are the West Access Route and Central Access Route). This was the first and only access route to Dawson Creek, BC—and the start of the Alaska Highway—when the Alaska Highway opened to civilian traffic in 1948. The original route differed somewhat from today's because Highway 43 was not completed until 1955. Instead, motorists had to drive north from Edmonton via Highway 2 to Athabasca, then west to High Prairie, then south to Grande Prairie, AB. Today's route goes directly from Edmonton to Grande Prairie and Dawson Creek via Highway 43 through Whitecourt and Valleyview. Total driving distance via East Access Route is 872 miles/1,403 km.

Side trips and alternate routes in Alberta featured in the East Access Route section are: the Icefields Parkway (see "Canadian Rockies Alternate Route" from Calgary); Highways 72 and 9 to Drumheller in the Canadian Badlands; the Devonian Way Bypass at Edmonton; and Heritage Highway South to Tumbler Ridge, BC, and Monkman Provincial Park.

The following driving log of the East Access Route is divided into 3 sections: Great Falls, MT, to the U.S.-Canada shared border crossing station at Sweetgrass, MT/Coutts, AB; from the border to Edmonton; and from

Major Attractions:

©Earl L. Brown

Calgary Heritage Park, Royal Tyrrell Museum, Icefields Parkway, West Edmonton Mall

East Access Route Great Falls, MT, to Edmonton, AB (includes Icefields Parkway)

© 2014 The MILEPOST®

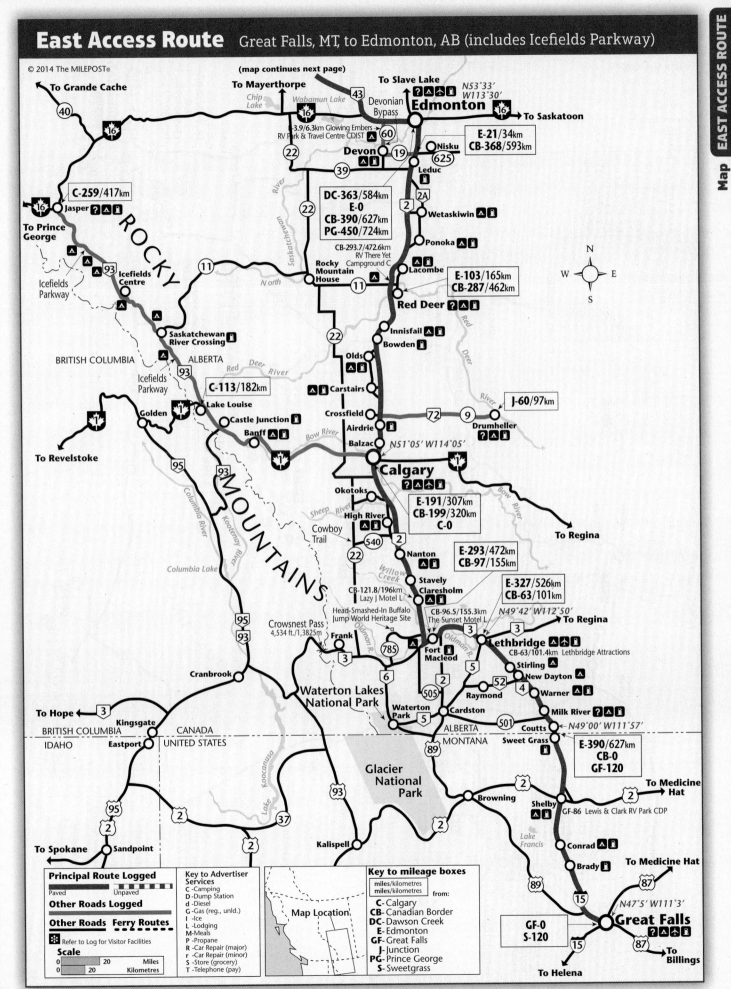

(map continues next page)

To Grande Cache

To Mayerthorpe

To Slave Lake

Devonian Bypass

N53°33'
W113°30'

Edmonton

To Saskatoon

43

16

Chip Lake

Wabamun Lake

E-3.9/6.3km Glowing Embers
RV Park & Travel Centre CDIST

60

Devon

19

Nisku

E-21/34km
CB-368/593km

625

22

39

Leduc

2A

16

C-259/417km

16

2

Jasper

To Prince George

DC-363/584km
E-0
CB-390/627km
PG-450/724km

Wetaskiwin

ROCKY

Saskatchewan River

Ponoka

93

11

CB-293.7/472.6km
RV There Yet
Campground C

Lacombe

Icefields Centre

Icefields Parkway

North

Rocky Mountain House

11

E-103/165km
CB-287/462km

Red Deer

W   E

N

S

Saskatchewan River Crossing

Innisfail

Bowden

Red

Deer

River

BRITISH COLUMBIA

ALBERTA

22

Olds

93

Icefields Parkway

Red   Deer   River

Carstairs

C-113/182km

J-60/97km

Golden

1

Lake Louise

Crossfield

72

9

Drumheller

Castle Junction

Airdrie

95

93

Banff

Balzac

N51°05' W114°05'

1

Calgary

To Revelstoke

Columbia River

MOUNTAINS

Bow River

Okotoks

E-191/307km
CB-199/320km
C-0

Bow River

To Regina

Columbia Lake

Columbia Lake

High River

Sheep   River

540

2

95

93

Kootenay River

Cowboy Trail

22

Nanton

E-293/472km
CB-97/155km

Willow Creek

Stavely

CB-121.8/196km
Lazy J Motel L

Claresholm

E-327/526km
CB-63/101km

Head-Smashed-In Buffalo
Jump World Heritage Site

CB-96.5/155.3km
The Sunset Motel L

N49°42'W112°50'

To Regina

Crowsnest Pass
4,534 ft./1,825m

Frank

3

785

Oldman R.

Fort Macleod

Oldman R.

3

Lethbridge

CB-63/101.4km Lethbridge Attractions

Cranbrook

6

2

5

Stirling

52

New Dayton

To Hope

3

Kingsgate

505

4

Warner

Raymond

BRITISH COLUMBIA

CANADA

Waterton Lakes
National Park

Cardston

Milk River

IDAHO

Eastport

UNITED STATES

Waterton Park

5

501

Coutts

N49°00' W111°57'

Lake   Koocanusa

89

ALBERTA
MONTANA

Sweet Grass

E-390/627km
CB-0
GF-120

To Medicine Hat

Glacier National Park

Browning

2

To Spokane

95

2

37

93

2

Shelby

GF-86 Lewis & Clark RV Park CDP

89

Sandpoint

2

Kalispell

Conrad

To Medicine Hat

87

Brady

15

GF-0
S-120

N47°5'W111°3'

Great Falls

To Helena

15

87

To Billings

Principal Route Logged
Paved ——— Unpaved ▬▬▬

Other Roads Logged

Other Roads ——— Ferry Routes ━ ━ ━

✦ Refer to Log for Visitor Facilities

Scale
0   20   Miles
0   20   Kilometres

Key to Advertiser Services
C - Camping
D - Dump Station
d - Diesel
G - Gas (reg., unld.)
I - Ice
L - Lodging
M - Meals
P - Propane
R - Car Repair (major)
r - Car Repair (minor)
S - Store (grocery)
T - Telephone (pay)

Map Location

Key to mileage boxes
miles/kilometres
miles/kilometres
from:
C - Calgary
CB - Canadian Border
DC - Dawson Creek
E - Edmonton
GF - Great Falls
J - Junction
PG - Prince George
S - Sweetgrass

East Access Route Edmonton, AB, to Dawson Creek, BC

© 2014 The MILEPOST®

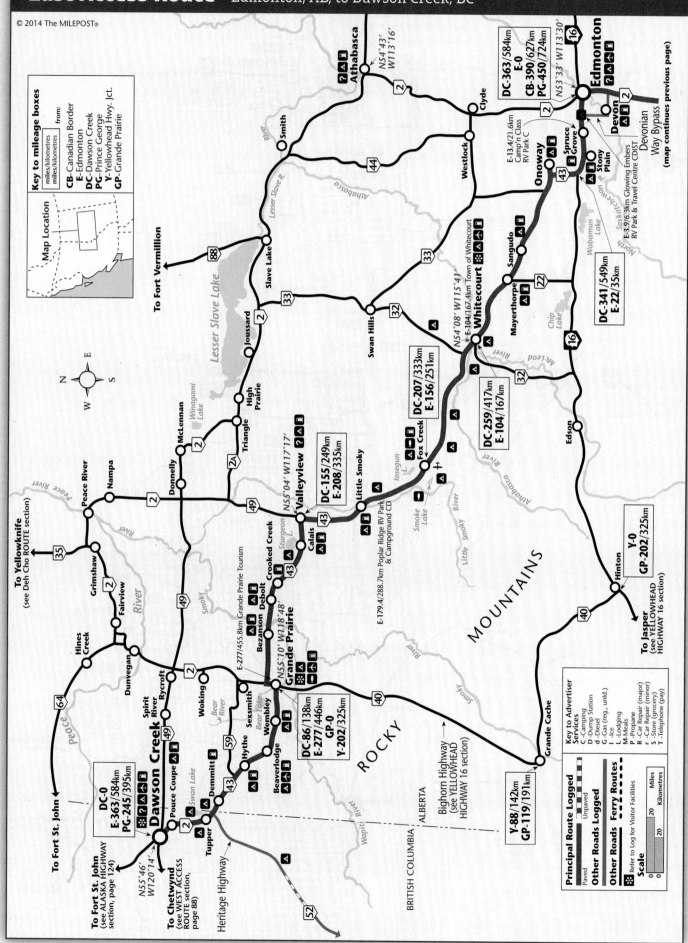

Key to mileage boxes   from:
miles/kilometres
miles/kilometres
CB-Canadian Border
E-Edmonton
DC-Dawson Creek
PG-Prince George
Y-Yellowhead Hwy. Jct.
GP-Grande Prairie

Map Location

DC-363/584km
E-0
CB-390/627km
PG-450/724km

N53°33' W113°30'

(map continues previous page)

N54°43'
W113°16'

Athabasca

Smith

Clyde

Westlock

E-13.4/21.6km
Camp'n Class
RV Park C

Onoway

Spruce
Grove

Stony
Plain

Devon

Devonian
Way Bypass

E-3.9/6.3km Glowing Embers
RV Park & Travel Centre CDIST

To Fort Vermillion

Lesser Slave Lake

Slave Lake

Joussard

High Prairie

Winagami
Lake

McLennan

Triangle

Donnelly

Nampa

Peace River

Grimshaw

Fairview

Hines
Creek

Dunvegan

Spirit
River

Rycroft

Woking

Sexsmith

Wembley

Hythe

Beaverlodge

Demmitt

Tupper

To Fort St. John
(see ALASKA HIGHWAY
section, page 124)

To Chetwynd
(see WEST ACCESS
ROUTE section, page 88)

Heritage Highway

N55°46'
W120°14'

DC-0
E-363/584km
PG-245/395km

Dawson Creek

Pouce Coupe

Swan Lake

To Yellowknife
(see Deh Cho ROUTE section)

To Yellowknife

Peace River

Smoky
River

Bear
River

Bear Lake

Sturgeon
L.

N55°10' W118°48'

Grande Prairie

E-277/455.8km Grande Prairie Tourism

Bezanson

Debolt

Crooked Creek

Calais

Valleyview

N55°04' W117°17'

DC-155/249km
E-208/335km

Little Smoky

Smoke
L.

losegun
L.

Fox Creek

DC-207/333km
E-156/251km

DC-259/417km
E-104/167km

Swan Hills

Sangudo

Mayerthorpe

Chip
Lake

Whitecourt

N54°08' W115°41'
E-104/167.4km Town of Whitecourt
E-104/167.4km Town of Whitecourt

DC-341/549km
E-22/35km

Wabamun
Lake

North
Saskatchewan R.

McLeod

River

Athabasca
River

Edson

Hinton

Y-0
GP-202/325km

To Jasper
(see YELLOWHEAD
HIGHWAY 16 section)

MOUNTAINS

ROCKY

Little Smoky
River

Smoky

Wapiti River

River

Kakwa
River

Grande Cache

Bighorn Highway
(see YELLOWHEAD
HIGHWAY 16 section)

ALBERTA

BRITISH COLUMBIA

Y-88/142km
GP-119/191km

DC-86/138km
E-277/446km
GP-202/325km

E-179.4/288.7km Poplar Ridge RV Park
& Campground CD

Key to Advertiser
Services
C -Camping
D -Dump Station
d -Diesel
G -Gas (reg., unld.)
I -Ice
L -Lodging
M -Meals
P -Propane
R -Car Repair (major)
r -Car Repair (minor)
S -Store (grocery)
T -Telephone (pay)

Principal Route Logged
Paved
Unpaved
Other Roads Logged
Ferry Routes
Refer to Log for Visitor Facilities

Scale
0   20 Miles
0   20 Kilometres

Edmonton to Dawson Creek, BC, via Valleyview and Grande Prairie.

All highways logged in this section are paved primary routes, with visitor services readily available along the way.

East Access Route Log

Distance from Great Falls (GF) followed by distance from international border crossing at Sweetgrass (S).
Exit numbers and mileposts on Interstate 15 reflect distance from Idaho–Montana border. Most of the East Access Route is multi-lane divided highway.

INTERSTATE HIGHWAY 15

GF 0 S 119.5 Exit 278 to **GREAT FALLS** (pop. 58,950 elev. 3,300 feet) via 10th Avenue South. Exit here for food, gas/diesel, lodging, private RV park, Market Place shopping mall and hospital.

Visitor Information: Great Falls Visitor Center, located about 2 miles east of this exit via 10th Avenue South to Overlook Drive/River Road (turn right after crossing the Missouri River). Open daily in summer 10 A.M.–6 P.M. weekdays and 10 A.M.–4 P.M. weekends; picnic tables and Broadwater Overlook. Trolley tours depart from this location throughout the day.

Great Falls, located at the confluence of the Sun and Missouri rivers, is Montana's third largest city (after Billings and Missoula). MSU's College of Technology and Malmstrom AFB are located here. Local attractions include Electric City Water Park and Riverside Railyard Skateboard Park. Major attractions are the Lewis and Clark National Historic Trail Interpretive Center, the Charles M. Russell Museum and Giant Springs Heritage State Park.

GF 2 S 117.5 Exit 280 to Great Falls City Center via Central Avenue West/U.S. 87 North. Access this exit to Gibson Park and Elk's Riverside Park; Giant Springs State Park (day-use only); the C.M. Russell Interpretive Center; Children's Museum of Montana; downtown shopping, dining and lodging; and the Paris Gibson Square Museum of Art (between 14th and 15th streets).

Continue north on Interstate 15 for the Canadian border. The posted speed limit is 75 mph (65 mph for trucks).

GF 5 S 114.5 Distance marker northbound shows Vaughn 7 miles, Shelby 80 miles, Lethbridge 179 miles.

GF 6 S 113.5 Paved turnout to east.

GF 8 S 111.5 Exit 286 to Manchester.

GF 12 S 107.5 Vaughn. Exit 290 to U.S. Highway 89 North/MT Highway 200 West; to Choteau and Missoula. Gas/diesel, lodging, camping, restaurants, Lewis and Clark Trail.

GF 13 S 106.5 Distance marker northbound shows Dutton 22 miles, Shelby 72 miles, Lethbridge 171 miles.

GF 19 S 100.5 Exit 297 to Gordon; no services.

GF 20.2 S 99.3 Distance marker northbound shows Power 5 miles, Conrad 40 miles, Lethbridge 164 miles.

GF 24 S 95.5 Exit 302 to Power and Highway 431. Teton County.

GF 25 S 94.5 Distance marker northbound shows Dutton 10 miles, Shelby 60 miles, Lethbridge 159 miles.

GF 35 S 84.5 Exit 313 to Highway 379 East and Highway 221 West to Dutton (gas, phone, picnic tables and food).

GF 36.2 S 83.3 Distance marker northbound shows Brady 14 miles, Conrad 25 miles, Lethbridge 148 miles.

GF 40.7 S 78.8 Rest areas both sides of freeway at Teton River bridge. Next rest area 80 miles.

GF 42.8 S 76.7 Exit 321 to Collins; no services.

GF 44 S 75.5 Distance marker northbound shows Brady 6 miles, Shelby 41 miles, Lethbridge 140 miles.

GF 49.5 S 70 Exit 328 west to Brady (gas) and east to Highway 365.

GF 50.5 S 69 Distance marker northbound shows Conrad 10 miles, Shelby 34 miles, Lethbridge 133 miles.

GF 57 S 62.5 Exit 335 to Midway Road, Conrad (4 miles) via Business Loop 15.

GF 61 S 58.5 Exit 339 to **CONRAD** (pop. 2,488); food, gas, diesel, lodging (Super 8) and RV park. Hospital.

GF 62.2 S 57.3 Distance marker northbound shows Ledger Road 5 miles, Shelby 23 miles, Lethbridge 122 miles.

GF 67 S 52.5 Exit 345 to Highway 366 east, Ledger Road and Tiber Dam; no services.

GF 70 S 49.5 Exit 348 to junction with MT Highway 44 west to Valier Road and Lake Frances Recreation Area.

GF 71 S 48.5 Distance marker northbound shows Shelby 14 miles, Kevin-Oilmont 30 miles, Lethbridge 113 miles.

GF 74 S 45.5 Exit 352 to Bullhead Road; no services.

GF 77.5 S 42 *Highway descends 7 percent grade northbound. Watch for deer next 3 miles.*

GF 79 S 40.5 Marias River.

GF 80.5 S 39 Exit 358 to Marias Valley Road to east, camping; Golf Course Road to west.

GF 81 S 38.5 Distance marker northbound shows Shelby 4 miles, Kevin-Oilmont 20 miles, Lethbridge 103 miles.

GF 83 S 36.5 Double-ended roadside parking area northbound with litter barrel.

GF 85 S 34.5 Exit 363 to Business Loop 15 to **SHELBY** (pop. 3,376); food, gas, diesel, lodging; access to Marias Medical Center. Visitor information at the Chamber of Commerce. Camping at Lewis & Clark RV Park (see Exit 364). Marias Museum of History and Art located across from city park.

Junction with U.S. Highway 2 to Cut Bank and Glacier National Park at this exit.

GF 86 S 33.5 Exit 364 to Shelby via Business Route 15; access to airport and to **Lewis & Clark RV Park**; pull-throughs, laundry, propane, satellite TV.

Lewis & Clark RV Park. See display ad this page.

GF 87.2 S 32.3 Distance marker northbound shows Sunburst 24 miles, Sweetgrass 32 miles, Lethbridge 98 miles.

GF 90.6 S 28.9 Exit 369 to Bronken Road; no services.

GF 92 S 27.5 Distance marker northbound shows Kevin-Oilmont 9 miles, Sweetgrass 27 miles, Lethbridge 93 miles.

GF 95 S 24.5 Exit 373 to Potter Road; no services.

GF 96 S 23.5 Distance marker northbound shows Kevin-Oilmont 5 miles, Sweetgrass 23 miles, Lethbridge 89 miles.

Rest area off Exit 397 at Sweetgrass, just south of international border. (©Michael K. Robb)

Relax with us

Canada's Mormon Trail

Wild Past. Peaceful Present.

From the Montana border, drive the peaceful highways of Canada's Mormon Trail. Enjoy serene RV sites and great bird watching in one of the sunniest parts of Canada!

Then visit Lethbridge, experience fur trading history at Fort Whoop Up, modern history at the Galt, and ancient serenity at the Japanese gardens.

Lethbridge Attractions

Lethbridge Attractions:
FortWhoopUp.com | NikkaYuko.com | GaltMuseum.com

Canada's Mormon Trail:
TheMormonTrail.ca

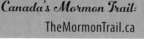

In partnership with

FORT WHOOP-UP NATIONAL HISTORIC SITE · INDIAN BATTLE PARK, LETHBRIDGE, ALBERTA, CANADA

Nikka Yuko Japanese Garden

Galt MUSEUM & ARCHIVES

Travel Alberta Canada

GF 101 S 18.5 Exit 379 to Kevin/Highway 215 and Oilmont/Highway 343; restaurants and other services.

GF 102 S 17.5 Distance marker northbound shows Sunburst 9 miles, Sweetgrass 17 miles, Lethbridge 83 miles.

GF 106.8 S 12.7 Exit 385 to Swayze Road; no services.

GF 111.5 S 8 Exit 389 to city of Sunburst/Highway 552, all services.

GF 112.5 S 7 Distance marker northbound shows Sweetgrass 7 miles, Lethbridge 73 miles.

GF 116.5 S 3 Exit 394 Ranch access; no services. *CAUTION: Watch for deer.*

GF 119 S 0.5 Exit 397 to Sweetgrass; food, gas, diesel, lodging, rest area. Last turn back northbound before border. Southbound, the rest area is to the right, immediately after going through customs.

GF 119.5 S 0 Shared 24-hour U.S.–Canada Port-of-Entry at international border (Sweetgrass, MT/Coutts, AB). Make sure you have your passport. *See Crossing the Border in the TRAVEL PLANNING section for more details on customs requirements.*

ALBERTA HIGHWAY 4

Distance from U.S.–Canada border (CB) is followed by distance from junction with Highway 16A at Edmonton (E).

CB 0 E 389.7 (627 km) Shared 24-hour U.S.–Canada Port-of-Entry at international border. Duty-free shop southbound. Community of **COUTTS** (pop. 305); Coutts Traveller Operations, phone 403-344-3766, www.villagecoutts.ab.ca. Nearest hospital is in Milk River, phone 403-647-3500.

NOTE: Seat belts are required in Alberta. Speed limits in Alberta are in metric. Posted highway speed limit is 110 kmph/68 mph on 4-lane highway northbound.

CB 0.6 (1 km) **E 389.1** (626.2 km) Vehicle inspection to west (RVs and autos exempt); County of Warner roadside turnout and Welcome to Alberta sign to east.

CB 0.8 (1.3 km) **E 388.9** (625.8 km) Exit for Highway 500 East to Aden and Highway 880 (30 miles/49 km).

CB 1.5 (2.4 km) **E 388.2** (624.6 km) Distance marker northbound shows Milk River 18 km/11 miles, Lethbridge 103 km/64 miles.

CB 7.5 (12.1 km) **E 382.2** (615 km) Turnoff for private campground 4 km/2.5 miles east.

CB 10 (16.1 km) **E 379.7** (610.9 km) **Junction** with Highway 501 to Del Bonita which leads 67 miles/108 km west to junction with Highways 2 and 5 at Cardston, home of the **Remington–Alberta Carriage Centre**, one of the world's foremost collections of horse-drawn vehicles. From Cardston, Highway 5 leads 25 miles/40 km west to Waterton Park, tourist centre for Waterton Lakes National Park.

CB 12 (19.3 km) **E 377.7** (607.7 km) **Milk River Travel Information Centre** to east is open mid-May to mid-Oct.; parking, pay phone, restrooms, picnic tables, sani-dump; 403-647-3938. The large dinosaur model on display here makes a good photo subject.

CB 12.3 (19.8 km) **E 377.4** (607.2 km) Under 8 Flags Campground to east; picnic tables, dump station, campsites and hookups. The 8 flags flying over the campground

represent 7 countries and the Hudson's Bay Co., all of which once laid claim to the Milk River area.

CB 12.5 (20.1 km) **E 377.2** (606.9 km) Grain elevators.

CB 12.6 (20.3 km) **E 377.1** (606.8 km) **Junction** with Highway 501 east to **Writing-on-Stone Provincial Park**, 26 miles/42 km; camping, Indian petroglyphs.

CB 13.1 (21.1 km) **E 376.6** (605.9 km) **MILK RIVER** (pop. 846); restaurant, motel and truck stop east side of highway. All services.

CB 23.6 (38 km) **E 366.1** (589.1 km) **Junction** with Highway 36 north to Taber and Brooks. Access west to **WARNER** (pop. 383); food, gas, restaurant and RV park. Dinosaur eggs and fossilized fish and reptiles were discovered in this area in 1987. Warner is considered the gateway to the Devil's Coulee dinosaur egg site. The Devil's Coulee Dinosaur Heritage Museum is open from late-May to early-September.

CB 23.8 (38.3 km) **E 365.9** (588.9 km) Distance marker northbound shows New Dayton 20 km/12 miles, Lethbridge 69 km/43 miles.

CB 28.6 (46 km) **E 361.1** (581.1 km) Exit for Secondary Road 505 West to Milk River Ridge Reservoir (15 miles/24 km).

CB 28.8 (46.3 km) **E 360.9** (580.8 km) Distance marker northbound Stirling 25 km/16 miles, Lethbridge 52 km/32 miles.

CB 29.6 (47.6 km) **E 360.1** (579.4 km) Large double-ended turnouts with litter barrels, toilets both sides of highway.

CB 31.8 (51.2 km) **E 357.9** (576 km) Access west to Tyrrell Lake east.

CB 33 (53.1 km) **E 356.7** (574 km) Tyrrell Lake with fishing and boat access.

CB 36.8 (59.2 km) **E 352.9** (567.9 km) New Dayton; camping and groceries.

CB 36.9 (59.4 km) **E 352.8** (567.8 km) Distance marker northbound shows Stirling 13 km/8 miles, Lethbridge 45 km/28 miles.

CB 41 (66 km) **E 348.7** (561.2 km) **Junction** with Highway 52 west to Raymond (10 miles/16 km); Magrath (20 miles/32 km); Cardston (46 miles/74 km); and Waterton Lakes National Park (74 miles/119 km).

CB 41.1 (66.1 km) **E 348.6** (561 km) Distance marker northbound shows Stirling 6 km/4 miles, Lethbridge 39 km/24 miles.

CB 41.2 (66.3 km) **E 348.5** (560.9 km) Craddock elevators.

CB 44.3 (71.3 km) **E 345.4** (555.9 km) Distance marker northbound shows Stirling 15 km/9 miles. Distance marker southbound shows Milk River 67 km/42 miles, U.S. border 87 km/54 miles.

CB 44.4 (71.4 km) **E 345.3** (555.6 km) **STIRLING** (pop. 1,157), 1 km/0.6 mile west, is the oldest, best-preserved Mormon settlement in Canada. Many Mormons came to Southern Alberta at the insistence of their church. Their mission was to build settlements on the dry, windy prairie. They began the irrigation canal system that helped create the rich farmland seen today. Mormons also built the towns of Cardston, Magrath, Raymond and Stirling.

The "**Mormon Trail**" is a self-guided drive that features a mix of national and provincial historic sites, walkable communities, and a unique cultural heritage. Stops include the Mormon Temple in Cardston. For details see www.themormontrail.ca.

Stirling has the Galt Historic Railway Park and a municipal campground.

CB 45.3 (72.9 km) **E 344.4** (554.2 km) Stirling elevators to east.

CB 46.2 (74.3 km) **E 343.5** (552.8 km) **Junction** with Highway 61 east to Cypress Hills. Distance marker northbound shows Lethbridge 29 km/18 miles.

CB 53.8 (86.6 km) **E 335.9** (540.5 km) **Junction** with Highway 845 North to Coaldale and Raymond; Alberta Birds of Prey Centre 17 km/11 miles via this exit.

CB 55.3 (89 km) **E 334.4** (538 km) **Junction** with Highway 508 West by elevators.

CB 56.5 (90.9 km) **E 333.2** (536.2 km) Harvest Market U-Pick 4 km/2.5 miles east of highway.

CB 57.1 (91.9 km) **E 332.6** (535.2 km) Southbound-only roadside turnout with litter bins to west with information sign about irrigation.

CB 57.8 (93 km) **E 331.9** (534.1 km) Lethbridge airport to west.

CB 60.3 (97 km) **E 329.4** (530 km) *Begin 80 kmph/50 mph speed zone northbound.*

CB 62 (99.8 km) **E 327.7** (527.3 km) Turnoff to 43 Street in Lethbridge, the truck route north to Highway 3. Bypass route to Fort Macleod and Calgary.

CB 62.3 (100.3 km) **E 327.4** (526.9 km) *Begin 60 kmph/37 mph speed zone northbound.*

CB 62.7 (100.9 km) **E 327** (526.3 km) Stoplight at **junction** of Highways 4 with 5 and Mayor Magrath Drive in Lethbridge. Highway 5 leads south to Cardston (48 miles/77 km) and Waterton Park (81 miles/131 km).

Tourist Information Centre located at the northwest corner of this intersection on Scenic Drive; open year-round, RV parking, restrooms, picnic shelter, playground, dump station and dumpster available.

Northbound travelers turn right at this intersection for Lethbridge services (food, gas, lodging, hospital) and continuation of East Access Route via Mayor Magrath Drive to Crowsnest Trail (Highway 3). It is 2.3 miles from this

intersection to Highway 3 via Mayor Magrath Drive. Description of Lethbridge follows.

Northbound motorists may also continue straight through this intersection and follow the Scenic Drive route to Crowsnest Trail; see Lethbridge map. It is 4.3 miles from this intersection to Highway 3 via Scenic Drive.

Log continues on page 54 for northbound travelers.

Lethbridge

CB 63 (101.4 km) **E 326.7** (525.7 km) Located at the **junction** of Highways 3, 4 and 5. **Population:** 87,882. **Elevation:** 3,048 feet/ 929m. **Emergency Services:** Phone 911 for police, ambulance and fire department. **Police:** 135 1st Ave. South, phone 403-327-2210; **RCMP,** 427 Stafford Drive South, phone 403-329-5010. **Hospital:** Chinook Regional, 960–19th St. South. Phone 403-388-6111.

Visitor Information: Chinook Country Tourist Assoc. at 2805 Scenic Drive/Highway 4; open year-round. RV parking, restrooms, picnic shelter, playground and interpretive panels, dump station and dumpster available. Phone 403-320-1222 or 1-800-661-1222. Email info@chinookcountry.com. Websites: www.lethbridge.ca, www.visitlethbridge.com, www.exploresouthwestalberta.ca. **Newspaper:** *Lethbridge Herald* (daily).

Private Aircraft: Airport 4 miles/6.4 km southeast; elev. 3,047 feet/929m; length 6,500 feet/1,981m; paved, fuel 100, jet. FSS.

The Lethbridge region was home to 3 Indian nations: the Sik-sika (Blackfoot), Kainai (Many Leaders, now called Bloods), and Pikani (including the Ammsskaapi-piikain in Montana and Apatohsipiikani in Souther Alberta, also called Peigan). Collectively, they formed the Sow-ki'tapi (Prairie People). Because European fur traders along the North Saskatchewan River first came into contact with the Blackfoot, that tribal name came to be applied to the entire confederacy.

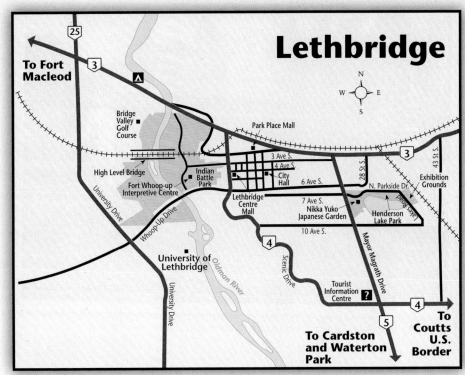

Lethbridge

To Fort Macleod

Bridge Valley Golf Course

Park Place Mall

High Level Bridge

Fort Whoop-up Interpretive Centre

Indian Battle Park

City Hall

3 Ave S.
4 Ave S.
6 Ave S.

43 St. S.

N. Parkside Dr.

Exhibition Grounds

University Drive

Lethbridge Centre Mall

Nikka Yuko Japanese Garden

7 Ave S.

Henderson Lake Park

10 Ave S.

Whoop-Up Drive

University of Lethbridge

Oldman River

University Drive

Scenic Drive

Mayor Magrath Drive

Tourist Information Centre

To Cardston and Waterton Park

To Coutts U.S. Border

Nikka Yuko Japanese Garden in Lethbridge. (©Claire Torgerson, staff)

In 1869, the American Army decided to stop trade in alcohol with Indians on reservations across Montana. In December 1869, 2 American traders, John J. Healy and Alfred B. Hamilton, built a trading post at the junction of the St. Mary and Belly (now Oldman) rivers, near the future site of Lethbridge. The post, named Fort Hamilton, became known as Fort Whoop-Up. It was the most notorious of some 44 trading posts built in southern Alberta from 1869 to 1874. An important trade commodity "whiskey," was a concoction of 9 parts river water to 1 part pure alcohol, to which was added a plug of chewing tobacco for colour and a can of lye for more taste.

Alarmed by the activities of the whiskey traders, Prime Minister Sir John A. Macdonald formed the North West Mounted Police (NWMP), now the Royal Canadian Mounted Police, to bring law and order to the West. The NWMP reached Fort Whoop-Up on Oct. 9, 1874, and immediately put a stop to the whiskey trade.

Early development of Lethbridge commenced in 1874 with the arrival of Nicholas Sheran in search of gold. The gold turned out to be black gold—coal—and by the late 1870s a steady coal market and permanent settlement had developed.

The climax of the early development of Lethbridge came with the CPR construction in 1909 of the High Level Bridge that today carries freight shipments by rail west to Vancouver. The "Bridge"—with a mile-long span and 300-foot elevation—is still the longest and highest bridge of its kind in the world.

Today, Lethbridge is Alberta's fourth largest city. It has a strong agricultural economy and is home to the University of Lethbridge and Lethbridge College. The city's ENMAX Centre, a sports and special events venue, is home to the Lethbridge Hurricanes hockey team and the Spitz Stadium is home to the Lethbridge Bulls baseball team.

Lodging & Services

As southwest Alberta's service and shopping centre, Lethbridge has several malls and a variety of retail businesses and visitor facilities. Major-chain motels/hotels (Days Inn, Holiday Inn, Sandman, etc.), restaurants, fast-food outlets and gas/diesel stations are primarily located on Mayor Magrath Drive.

Camping

Camping at Bridgeview RV Resort, located on the banks of the Oldman River, with access from Highway 3; phone 403-381-2357.

Attractions

Fort Whoop-Up Interpretive Centre (www.fortwhoopup.com) is located 0.8 miles/1 km west of Scenic Drive (turn at 3rd Avenue) in Indian Battle Park. Fort Whoop-Up is a re-creation of the original trading post for trappers and Indians and NWMP fort that served this area in the late 1800s. It gained its name from brisk whiskey sales. Historical reenactments are held in summer. Admission charged. Phone 403-329-0444.

Galt Museum (www.galtmuseum.com), features regional history and art and offers a fantastic view of the High Level Bridge. Located at 502 1st St South, at the west end of 5th Avenue South off Scenic Drive. (For parking, use the 4th Avenue turnoff from Scenic Drive.) Phone 403-320-4248. Admission is $6/adults. Open daily, 10 A.M.–5 P.M. Monday through Saturday (to 9 P.M. Thursdays) and Sundays and holidays 1 P.M.–5 P.M.

Scenic Drive Dog Run, located 2.2 miles from the visitor centre at the Highway 4/5 junction on Scenic Drive, is one of 3 designated off-leash dog parks in Lethbridge. It is part of the 200-acre Botterill Bottom Park, which includes the Coal Banks Trail. There are fine views of the University of Lethbridge from Scenic Drive.

Henderson Lake Park on Mayor Magrath Drive includes a golf course, swimming pool, picnic area and rose gardens. Open daily May–September.

Adjacent to the park, and best accessed via Mayor Magrath Drive and 9th Avenue South is the site of the **Nikka Yuko Japanese Garden** (www.nikkayuko.com). The 4-acre garden, which opened in 1967 as part of Canada's Centennial celebration, contains traditional features of Japanese garden design. Hours are 9 A.M.–5 P.M. daily, May (beginning Mother's Day) to mid-Oct. Admission charged.

The **Helen Schuler Nature Centre** (www.lethbridge.ca/hsnc) has self-guided trails which explore the beautiful Oldman River valley. It has interactive, hands-on exhibits for learning about local wildlife. Off of 3rd Avenue South. Phone 403-320-3064. Open daily 10 A.M.–6 P.M. June–Aug.; 1 P.M.–4 P.M. Sept.–May (closed Mondays).

Southern Alberta Art Gallery, located downtown Lethbridge, offers a dynamic variety of changing exhibitions of contemporary art. It is one of Canada's top ten contemporary galleries, (and has been recognized at an international level) located in downtown Lethbridge. Open year round, Tuesday-Saturday: 10 A.M.–5 P.M. Sunday; 1 P.M.–5 P.M. Admission charged, free on Sundays. Web address: www.saag.ca.

New West Theatre is Lethbridge's professional theatre company and offers more than 100 performances of original music-comedy revue shows every summer at Yates Theatre. The winter season includes a litany of performances designed to combat winter blues. Web address: www.newwesttheatre. com; 403-329-SEAT (7328) for tickets.

Alberta Birds of Prey Centre, a 10-minute drive east of Lethbridge in Coaldale, is a rescue and rehabilitation centre featuring hawks, falcons, eagles and owls, the majority of which have been rescued from traumatic events and rehabilitated for hopeful release to the wild. Daily flight shows (weather permitting) and tours of the facilities. Open daily May to September. Admission $8.50 adults, reduced price for seniors and kids. Phone 403-345-4262; www. burrowingowl.ca.

Remington Carriage Museum, North America's largest collection of horse drawn vehicle carriage museum, is located in Cardston, a 45-minute drive south from Lethbridge via Highway 5. The museum is on the "Mormon Trail" and features Mormon Pioneer wagon rides through town at 1 P.M. Friday through Sunday during summer. The museum is open daily; admission charged. Phone 403-653-5139 for more information.

Lethbridge Attractions. See display ad on page 52.

East Access Route Log
(continued)

CB 65 (104.6 km) **E 324.7** (522.5 km) Mayor Magrath Drive/Lethbridge exit/on-ramp to Crowsnest Trail (Highway 3 West). Southbound travelers exit here for Lethbridge services. Northbound travelers merge onto Highway 3 West here.

Resume divided 4-lane highway northbound.

CROWSNEST HIGHWAY 3 WEST

CB 66 (106.2 km) **E 323.7** (520.9 km) Stafford Drive/Lethbridge exit.

CB 67 (107.8 km) **E 322.7** (519.3 km) 1st Avenue South exit to Lethbridge City Centre and Highways 4/5. (This exit southbound junctions with Scenic Drive in 1 mile).

CB 67.6 (108.8 km) **E 322.1** (518.3 km) Oldman River Bridge.

CB 67.8 (109.1 km) **E 321.9** (517.5 km) Bridge Drive/Highway 3A exit to West Lethbridge and access to Bridgeview RV Resort.

CB 69 (111 km) **E 320.7** (516 km) Exit to Highway 25 North to Picture Butte (22 km/14 miles) and University Drive south to

West Lethbridge.

CB 71.3 (114.7 km) **E 318.4** (512.3 km) Northbound-only roadside turnout to east with litter and recycle bins and historical information sign about Coalhurst.

CB 72 (115.8 km) **E 317.7** (511.2 km) Community of **COALHURST** (pop. 1,523) just north of highway; Shell gas station, dump station and campground at the Miners Memorial Park (showers, kitchen shelter, picnic tables) $10 per night. Call ahead, some reservations for groups are accepted and can include the entire campground.

CB 73.3 (118 km) **E 316.4** (509 km) Exit for Highway 509 South to Stand Off and Highway 2 (30 miles/49 km).

CB 73.4 (118.1 km) **E 316.3** (508.9 km) Distance marker shows Monarch 12 km/8 miles, Fort Macleod 38 km/24 miles, Calgary 216 km/134 miles.

CB 75.3 (121.2 km) **E 315.4** (507.6 km) Large, long turnout southbound with interpretive signs, litter and recycling bins. Nice view of the valley below.

CB 76.9 (123.7 km) **E 312.8** (503.3 km) Large turnout northbound with Southern Alberta historic sites tour route map and litter and recycling bins.

CB 78 (125.5 km) **E 311.7** (501.6 km) Exit to Highway 23 north to Vulcan and Highway 3A west to Monarch.

CB 81 (130.3 km) **E 308.7** (496.7 km) Oldman River bridge.

CB 82.4 (132.6 km) **E 307.3** (494.5 km) Turnoff for Highway 3A East to Monarch and Highway 23 north.

CB 82.5 (132.8 km) **E 307.2** (494.4 km) Distance marker shows Fort Macleod 22 km/14 miles, Crowsnest Pass 99 km/62 miles and Calgary 189 km/117 miles.

CB 95.2 (153.2 km) **E 294.5** (473.9 km) **Junction** with Highway 2 South for Cardston and Waterton Lakes. Northbound travelers continue on Highway 3 for Fort Macleod businesses and historic district and Highway 2 North to Calgary. Southbound travelers take Highway 3 East to Lethbridge.

Through the town of Fort Macleod, Highway 3 West becomes 25th Street also known as Jerry Potts Blvd. (1–way) and Highway 3 East becomes 23rd Street also known as Chief Red Crow Blvd. (1–way).

CB 95.5 (153.7 km) **E 294.2** (473.5 km) *NOTE: Begin 50 kmph/30 mph speed zone northbound as Highway 3 winds through Fort Macleod.*

CB 96.5 (155.3 km) **E 293.2** (471.8 km) Fort Macleod Museum parking and access to historic Main Street. Description of Fort Macleod follows.

Fort Macleod

CB 96.5 (155.3 km) **E 293.2** (471.8 km) Located at the **junction** of Highways 3 and 2. **Population:** 3,072. **Elevation:** 3,300 feet/1,006m. **Emergency Services:** Phone 911 for police, fire and ambulance. **Hospital:** Fort Macleod Health Centre. Phone 403-553-5311.

Visitor Information: Visitor Information Services provided at the Fort–Museum. Hours are 9 A.M. to 5 P.M. daily from early May through June; 9 A.M. to 6 P.M. daily, July to Labour Day; and 10 A.M. to 4 P.M. Wednes-

day–Sunday, early May and September–October. The museum is closed November to April.

Fort Macleod has lodging, campgrounds, restaurants, fast-food, shopping facilities, laundromats, car wash and gas/diesel stations. Fort Macleod Golf & Country Club is western Canada's oldest golf course (established 1890).

The town's Main Street is Alberta's only provincially designated historic area. The historic Empress Theatre on Main Street is the oldest continuously operating theatre west of Winnipeg.

The Fort–Museum of the North West Mounted Police, a replica of the original Fort Macleod, features the history of the North West Mounted Police, local Native cultures and early pioneers. The original fort, named for Colonel J.F. Macleod, was built in 1874 and was the first outpost of the North West Mounted Police (later the Royal Canadian Mounted Police) in western Canada. The 30-acre North West Mounted Police 1884 Barracks Provincial Historic Site preserves 3 reconstructed buildings housing period displays and artifacts.

During July and August, the museum features a local re-creation of the official RCMP Musical Ride: Youth in NWMP uniforms execute drills on horseback in a colorful display (at 10 A.M., 11:30 A.M., 2 P.M. and 3:30 P.M., weather permitting–July through August). An award-winning play, "March of the Red Coats," is presented twice daily in summer at 10:45 A.M. and 2:45 P.M..

The museum and visitor information are open 9 A.M. to 5 P.M. daily from May through June; 9 A.M. to 6 P.M. daily, July to Labour Day; and 10 A.M. to 4 P.M. Wednesday–Sunday, September to mid-October. The museum is closed November to April. Admission charged. Web address: info@nwmpmuseum.com for more information.

The Sunset Motel in Fort Macleod offers clean, comfortable, reasonably priced AAA/CAA approved 1- and 2-room units with air conditioning, 40" flat screens, fridges, microwaves, coffee makers and WiFi. Park at your door. Easy highway access. Closest motel to Head-Smashed-In Buffalo Jump. Show *The MILEPOST®* to save 10 percent. Phone 403-553-4448. Email: rooms@sunset

motel.ca. [ADVERTISEMENT]

East Access Route Log
(continued)

CB 96.8 (155.8 km) **E 292.9** (471.3 km) Gas west, campground to east.

CB 98.1 (157.8 km) **E 291.6** (469.2 km) **Junction** with Highway 2 North. Northbound travelers on Highway 3 West exit here for Highway 2 North to Calgary and Edmonton. View of wind turbine. There are 24 operational wind farms in Alberta and more are planned.

Southbound travelers exit to Highway 3 (Crowsnest Trail) East for Lethbridge.

Highway 3 West continues 600 miles/966 km to Hope, BC. The highway takes its name from Crowsnest Pass (elev. 4,534 feet/1,382m) located 66 miles/106 km west of here.

ALBERTA HIGHWAY 2
CB 98.3 (158.2 km) **E 291.4** (469 km) Distance marker northbound shows Claresholm 37 km/23 miles, High River 110 km/68 miles and Calgary 165 km/102 miles.

CB 98.7 (158.8 km) **E 291** (468.2 km) Access to private campgrounds.

CB 99 (159.3 km) **E 290.7** (467.7 km) Oldman River bridge.

CB 99.7 (160.4 km) **E 290** (466.6 km) Turnoff to west on Highway 785 for 10 miles/16 km west to reach the UNESCO World Heritage Site, **Head-Smashed-In Buffalo Jump.** The 1,000-foot/305-m-long cliff is one of the oldest, largest and best-preserved buffalo jumps in the world and is descriptively named. Here, Plains peoples stampeded buffalo to their deaths for nearly 6,000 years.

An interpretive centre houses artifacts and displays describing the buffalo hunting culture. First Nations interpretive guides available on site. Guided walks available twice daily during July and August. Gift shop, cafe and theatre. Open daily year-round; 9 A.M. to 6 P.M., May 15 to Labour Day; 10 A.M. to 5 P.M., Labour Day to May 14; closed major holidays. Admission fee of $10 adults, discounted for kids and seniors.

CB 101.2 (162.8 km) **E 288.5** (464.2 km) Northbound roadside turnout with litter

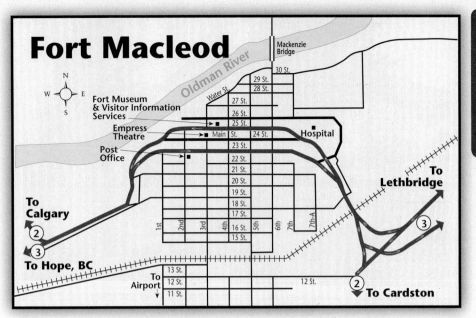

The historic railroad station houses Claresholm Museum and visitor information centre.

(©Michael K. Robb)

barrels.

CB 105.2 (169.3 km) **E 284.5** (457.9 km) Willow Creek.

CB 110.7 (178.1 km) **E 279** (448.9 km) **Junction** with Highway 519 East to **GRANUM** (pop. 445); camping, diesel, gas, propane, dump station and groceries.

CB 110.9 (178.5 km) **E 278.8** (448.7 km) Distance marker northbound shows Claresholm 18 km/11 miles, Nanton 58 km/36 miles, Calgary 142 km/88 miles.

CB 120.5 (193.9 km) **E 269.2** (433.1 km) *Begin 70 kmph/43 mph speed zone northbound.*

CB 120.8 (194.4 km) **E 268.9** (432.7 km) *Begin 50 kmph/31 mph speed zone northbound.*

CB 121.2 (195 km) **E 268.5** (432 km) **Junction** with Highway 520.

CB 121.8 (196 km) **E 267.9** (431.1 km) **CLARESHOLM** (pop. 3,758) whose major employer is the health care sector, has all visitor facilities including motels (**Lazy J Motel** located on highway), restaurants, fast-food, gas stations with diesel, 2 supermarkets and 2 laundromats. **Emergency Services:** Phone 911.

Lazy J Motel. See display ad this page.

Visitor Information: This historic railway station served as half of the Calgary railway station from 1893-1910, when it was outgrown. The half you see today was moved to Claresholm and its other half moved to High River to serve as these smaller communities' railway stations. It now houses the visitor centre and Claresholm Museum. The city also has an 18-hole golf course and murals painted on buildings lining First Street. Claresholm also has the Appaloosa Horse Museum.

Camping at Centennial Park; 28 sites, dump station, playground, showers, spray park.

CB 122.1 (196.5 km) **E 267.6** (430.6 km) Vehicle inspection station northbound, Alberta History interpretive signs, also roadside turnout with litter bins.

CB 125.3 (201.6 km) **E 264.4** (425.4 km) Roadside turnout northbound with litter cans and historic sign about Willow Creek.

CB 130.8 (210.5 km) **E 258.9** (416.6 km) Community of Stavely to the east. All services.

CB 131 (210.8 km) **E 258.7** (416.3 km) Roadside turnout southbound with litter barrels.

CB 131.3 (211.3 km) **E 258.4** (415.8 km) Roadside turnout northbound with litter barrels and historic sign about Stavely.

CB 131.7 (211.9 km) **E 258** (415.1 km) **Junction** with Highway 527 West to Willow Creek Provincial Park (10 miles/16 km).

CB 132.2 (212.8 km) **E 257.5** (414.4 km) Southbound turnout with litter barrels.

CB 135.8 (218.5 km) **E 253.9** (408.5 km) **Junction** with Highway 529 East to Little Bow Provincial Park (35 miles/57 km).

CB 137.7 (221.6 km) **E 252** (405.5 km) Exit to Parkland (no services).

CB 139.2 (224 km) **E 250.5** (403.1 km) Roadside turnout southbound with litter and recycling bins.

CB 145.8 (234.6km) **E 243.9** (392.4 km) **Junction** with Highway 533 West to **Chain Lakes Provincial Park**.

Begin 70 to 50 kmph/43 to 31 mph speed zones northbound entering Nanton.

CB 146.6 (235.93 km) **E 243.1** (391.1 km) **NANTON** (pop. 2,124). All visitor facilities available, including gas and diesel stations with propane, supermarket and fast-food outlets. Nanton campground (75 sites) is located at the junction with Highway 533 East. Nanton Golf Club 18-hole golf course is nearby. **Visitor Information:** Visitor Centre open May to Septem-

ber; websites www.nantonchamber.com or www.nanton.ca.

Nanton's well preserved history is on display at the Antique & Art Walk of Alberta (open daily), and along Main Street, with its restored turn-of-the-century buildings. Nanton is also home to the Big Sky Garden Railway, the largest garden railway in Canada, and Bomber Command Museum of Canada, located on Highway 2. The Bomber Command Museum houses an impressive display of WWII aircraft and artifacts. The centerpiece of the 26,000-square-foot museum is a 1945 Lancaster Bomber, one of the few in the world that is still intact. The museum is open daily from April 16 to October 15. Weekends only the remainder of the year. See main website at www.bombercommandmuseum.ca.

Museum of Miniatures is located behind the Big Sky Garden Railway (corner of Highway 2 South and 19th Street). History at $1/12$ scale. Open daily May 1 to October 31, 10 A.M. to 6 P.M.

The Canadian Grain Elevator Discovery Centre offers a popular tour; www.nantonelevators.com and the Nanton Agricultural Society hosts rodeo events throughout the summer www.nantonagsociety.com.

CB 147.3 (237 km) **E 242.4** (390 km) Exit to Highway 533 East to Vulcan and Highway 23 (25 miles/41 km).

CB 147.5 (237.3 km) **E 242.2** (389.8 km) Distance marker northbound shows High River 31 km/19 miles, Calgary 85 km/53 miles.

CB 148.5 (239 km) **E 241.2** (388.2 km) Mosquito Creek.

CB 151 (243 km) **E 238.7** (384.2 km) Distance marker southbound shows Nanton 8 km/5 miles, Claresholm 46 km/29 miles, Fort Macleod 89 km/55 miles.

CB 152.9 (246.1 km) **E 236.8** (381.2 km) Exit west to Cayley (1.9 miles/3 km).

CB 156.9 (252.5 km) **E 232.8** (374.6 km) Exit to Highway 540 West to Alberta Highway 22 ("Cowboy Trail") and access to Bar U Ranch National Historic Site (21 miles/34 km), a living history ranch preserving Canada's "old west." Open late May to early October; restaurant, gift shop, 35 historic structures.

CB 162.7 (261.8 km) **E 227** (365.2 km) Exit 194A to Highway 23/Vulcan.

CB 164 (263.9 km) **E 225.7** (363.2 km) Exit 194B west to **HIGH RIVER** (pop. 12,920); all visitor facilities. **Visitor Information:** Town of High River, phone 403-603-3101, 1-877-603-3101 or visit http://highriver.ca or www.highrivertourism.ca.

Once the centre of a harness-making industry, High River has historical murals, the Museum of the Highwood, Sheppard Family Park and an extensive trail system with the visitor centre located in the Munroe Barn. The downtown area has art galleries, boutiques, specialty stores, restaurants and coffeehouses. George Lane Park on the Highwood River offers a 55-site campground, dump stations, showers, playground and horseshoe pits.

Begin 5-lane divided highway northbound.

CB 164.1 (264 km) **E 225.6** (363 km) Northbound roadside turnout with litter barrels and sign about Alberta's history.

CB 170.2 (273.9 km) **E 219.5** (353.2 km) Highwood River.

CB 172 (276.8 km) **E 217.7** (350.3 km) Exit 209 to Highways 7/547 to Okotoks. The

Okotoks Erratic, located west of town, is the largest known glacial erratic in the world.

CB 173.6 (279.3 km) **E 216.1** (347.7 km) Sheep River.

CB 173.9 (279.8 km) **E 215.8** (347.2 km) Turnoff for private campground.

CB 175.2 (281.9 km) **E 214.5** (345.2 km) *Begin 6-lane divided highway northbound.*

CB 176.3 (283.7 km) **E 213.4** (343.4 km) U-pick, Saskatoon farm and another U-pick farm 5 miles/8 km north.

CB 180.5 (290.4 km) **E 209.2** (336.6 km) Exit 222 for Highway 2A South to Okotoks; all visitor services.

CB 182 (292.8 km) **E 207.7** (334.2 km) *NOTE: Highway 2 North divides into Macleod Trail (2A) and Deerfoot Trail (2). Macleod Trail provides access to suburban malls and services, downtown Calgary and junctions with Trans-Canada Highway 1.*

Northbound travelers following this log take Deerfoot Trail for continuation of Highway 2 North to Red Deer and Edmonton, and for access to Trans-Canada Highway 1 to Banff/Lake Louise and the Icefields Parkway to Jasper (see "Canadian Rockies Alternate Route" on page 59).

CB 183.3 (294.9 km) **E 206.4** (332.1 km) Exit 227, golf courses, Dunbow Road, De Winton.

CB 184.9 (297.5 km) **E 204.8** (329.5 km) Bow River.

CB 186.4 (300 km) **E 203.3** (327.2 km) Exit 232 for Cranston Avenue and Seton Blvd.

CB 187.6 (301.8 km) **E 202.1** (325.2 km) Exit 234 Marquis of Lorne Trail 22X/Stoney Trail. *Access to East Calgary Bypass (Highway 201); planned opening 2014.*

CB 189 (304.1 km) **E 200.7** (322.9 km) Exit 236 McKenzie Lake Blvd. and McKenzie Town Blvd.

CB 190.1 (305.9 km) **E 199.6** (321 km) Exit 238 130 Avenue SE. South Trail Crossing shopping mall east off exit.

CB 191.4 (308 km) **E 198.3** (319.1 km) Exit 240 Barlow Trail North.

CB 192.4 (309.6 km) **E 197.3** (317.5 km) Exit 241 Douglasdale Blvd./24 Street E.

CB 192.6 (310 km) **E 197.1** (317.2 km) Ivor Strong Bridge.

CB 193.3 (311.1 km) **E 196.4** (316.1 km) Exit 243 Anderson Road/Bow Bottom Trail.

CB 194.3 (312.7 km) **E 195.4** (314.5 km) Exit 245 Southland Drive.

CB 195.4 (314.5 km) **E 194.3** (312.7 km) Exit 247 Glenmore Trail. Shopping centre to west. Heritage Park Historical Village west off this exit.

CB 196.2 (315.8 km) **E 193.5** (311.4 km) Exit 248 East Glenmore Trail.

CB 198.6 (319.6 km) **E 191.1** (307.6 km) Exit 251 Peigan Trail East/Barlow Trail South.

CB 199.5 (321.1 km) **E 190.2** (306.1 km) Exit 254 Blackfoot Trail/Calgary City Centre/17th Avenue.

Description of Calgary follows. Log of East Access Route to Edmonton continues on page 58.

Calgary

CB 199.5 (321.1 km) **E 190.2** (306.1 km) Located at the confluence of the Bow and Elbow rivers, where the foothills of the Canadian Rockies meet the prairie. **Population:** 1,065,455. **Emergency Services:** Phone 911. Hos-

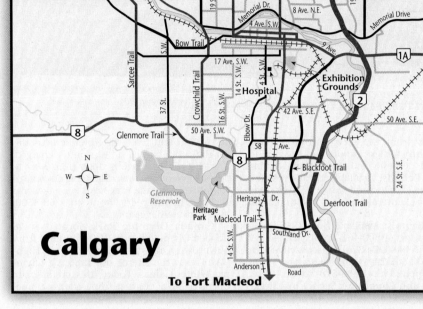

pitals: Alberta Children's Hospital, 2888 Shaganappi Trail NW; Rockyview General Hospital, 7007–14 St. SW; Peter Lougheed Center, 3500–26 Ave. NE; Foothills Medical Center, 1403–29 St. NW.

Visitor Information: At the arrivals level across from baggage carousel #4 in Calgary International Airport (open 6 A.M. to 11 P.M. year-round). Also at the base of Calgary Tower at 101–9 Ave. S.W., open 9 A.M. to 7 P.M. in summer, 9 A.M. to 5 P.M. in winter; phone 403-750-2362. Call Tourism Calgary at 403-263-8510 (local) or toll-free in North America 1-800-661-1678; www.visitcalgary.com.

Elevation: 3,736 feet/1,139m. **Climate:** Moderate 4-season climate with the most sunny days of any major Canadian city. Summer days average 72°F/22°C; fall days, 52°F/11°C; winter days, 9°F/-15°C; spring days, 42°F/9°C. **Newspapers:** *Calgary Herald* and *Calgary Sun*.

Private Aircraft: Calgary International Airport, 10.6 miles/17 km northeast of downtown Calgary; elev. 3,736 feet/1,139m; 3 runways. See Canadian Flight Supplement.

Originally established in 1875 as a fort by a contingent of the NWMP, Calgary has grown from a frontier settlement to a world-class destination. One of Alberta's 2 major population centers (the other being the provincial capital of Edmonton), Calgary uniquely mixes cosmopolitan flair and big city energy with rich western heritage and famous cultural traditions. The city boasts its own Philharmonic Orchestra and ballet, while its rich western heritage is preserved in its attractions, such as Fort Calgary, Heritage Park Historical Village and the annual Calgary Stampede.

Calgary is the gateway to the Canadian Rockies. Summer activities in the Kananaskis, Canmore, Banff and Lake Louise area include hiking, biking, kayaking, whitewater rafting, camping, horseback riding, mountain climbing, golfing, hang gliding and more. Winter activities include downhill skiing, snowboarding, cross-country skiing, dog sledding, snowshoeing and ice climbing.

Lodging & Services

Accommodations are located downtown; near the airport in northeast Calgary; on Highway 2 south (Macleod Trail); on Trans-Canada Highway 1 north (16th Avenue); and on Alternate 1A (Motel Village).

Calgary's restaurants include everything from major-chain fast-food outlets to upscale restaurants serving world-famous Alberta beef and various other award-winning cuisine.

Camping

There are several campgrounds in and around the city; phone for details on facilities and season. Calaway R.V. Park & Campground, 6.2 miles/10 kms west on Trans-Canada Highway 1, phone 403-240-3822, www.calawaypark.com; Calgary West Campground, west of Canada Olympic Park on Trans-Canada Highway 1, phone 1-888-562-0842, http://calgarycampground.com; and Mountain View Camping Ltd., phone 403-293-6640, www.calgarycamping.com. For additional camping options see www.visitcalgary.com under accommodations tab.

Transportation

Air: Calgary International Airport, 20

Heritage Park Historical Village celebrates its 50th anniversary in 2014. (©Michael K. Robb)

minutes from the city centre, is Canada's fourth busiest airport and the hub for regional, domestic and international airlines.

Car Rentals: Available through Alamo, Avis, Budget, Discount Car and Truck, Driving Force, Enterprise, Hertz, National and Thrifty.

RV Rentals: Available from CanaDream Campers Inc. (1-800-461-7368), Candan R.V. Center (1-800-922-6326), Fraserway RV Rentals (1-800-661-2441) and Westcoast Mountain Campers Ltd. (1-888-878-3200).

Taxi and Limousine: Service by Checker Group/Ambassador, phone 1-800-867-4497; Lawson's Carey Limousine, 1-800-779-2279; Blue Sky Limos, 1-866-261-3872; Allied Sedan & Limousine Service & Associated Cabs, 1-877-299-9555; and M.C. Limousine & Sedan Ltd., 1-866-652-5004.

Bus: Greyhound Canada is the largest inter-city bus company and has scheduled service to most points in Canada and the U.S.; phone 1-800-661-8747; www.greyhound.ca. Red Arrow to Edmonton, Red Deer and Fort McMurray, phone 1-800-232-1958; www.redarrow.ca. Independent package tours offered by more than 20 companies; for details, visit Tourism Calgary at www.visitcalgary.com.

Attractions

Heritage Park Historical Village, located on Heritage Drive SW, is Canada's largest living history museum, with more than 150 historical exhibits and 127 acres of parkland. This award-winning park celebrates its 50th anniversary in 2014.

©Michael K. Robb

Experience the sights and sounds of life in turn-of-the-century Western Canada: An authentic steam locomotive; an antique midway; the S.S. *Moyie* sternwheeler; Gasoline Alley Museum, various shops, cafe and

restaurant; and lively interpretive activities for the entire family. Admission fee charged. The Historical Village is open from May to October. Heritage Town Square is open year-round and Heritage Park hosts special events throughout the year. Phone 403-268-8500; visit www.heritagepark.ca.

Canada Olympic Park, located at 88 Canada Olympic Road SW, 15 minutes from downtown Calgary on Trans-Canada Highway 1, was the site of the 1988 XV Olympic Winter Games. Today, this premier site operates as a competition, training, recreation and hospitality area designed for year-round use by athletes and the general public. Summer attractions for the general public include mini golf, a childrens activity area with climbing wall, and the **Ski Jump Tower Tour**. Ride a glass elevator to the highest vantage point in Calgary, stepping outside onto the deck of the 1988 Winter Olympic's biggest ski jump. The observation level also features Olympic ski jumping memorabilia. Tickets are available for purchase at Guest Services or directly at the Ski Jump Tower

Winter facilities include world-class sliding track, a freestyle venue and super half-pipe. Open daily except Dec. 25. Free admission; pay per activity. For information, phone 403-247-5452 or visit www.winsportcanada.ca.

Calgary Zoo, Botanical Garden and Prehistoric Park, located at 1300 Zoo Road N.E. has more than 1,100 live animals and a prehistoric park with life-size replicas of dinosaurs. Journey through Destination Africa and see western lowland gorillas up close. Open year-round, 9 A.M. to 5 P.M. daily. For more information, phone 1-800-588-9993; or visit www.calgaryzoo.org.

Glenbow Museum. Western Canada's largest museum traces the history of Canada's West, from its First People to the arrival of European settlers. International collections; Blackfoot Gallery, "Nitsitapiisinni: Our Way of Life," and "Mavericks: an Incorrigible History of Alberta" (interactive exhibit). Open year-round. Admission charged. Located at 130–9 Ave. SE. For more information, phone 403-268-4100, or visit www.glenbow.org.

Fort Calgary, located at 750–9th Ave. SE. Stroll through Calgary from 1875 to 1940. Authentic reconstruction of the 1875 Fort

and 1888 Barracks, with interpretive centre and activities. Live a day in the life of a North West Mounted Police. Deane House Historic Site/Restaurant. Open year-round except for primary holidays. Admission charged. For more information, phone 403-290-1875 or visit www.fortcalgary.com.

Calgary Tower. Two 18-passenger high-speed elevators take visitors to the top of Calgary Tower (525 feet/160m) in 62 seconds. Sweeping views of city and mountains; look through glass floor at the street far below. Revolving Sky360 Restaurant. Located in the heart of downtown at 101–9 Ave. SW. Open year-round except Christmas Day. Admission charged. For information, phone 403-266-7171 or visit www.calgary tower.com.

Calgary Stampede. The city's best-known and oldest event is the annual Calgary Stampede, "the Greatest Outdoor Show on Earth," which takes place July 4–13, 2014, at the Exhibition Grounds. The 10-day citywide celebration of Calgary's western heritage includes a parade, daily rodeo (the world's richest outdoor rodeo), Chuckwagon races, musical performances and evening Grandstand Show extravaganza. For information and tickets, phone 1-800-661-1767, 403-269-9822 or visit www.calgarystampede.com.

Aero Space Museum, founded in 1975 by former WWII pilots and aviation enthusiasts, preserves the history of aviation and space industry in Western Canada. Try your hand on the flight simulators, learn about the Canadian Space programs and examine the aircraft up close. The museum's aircraft collection includes a Sopwith Triplane from WWI, 5 aircraft from WWII, civil and recreational aviation aircraft, helicopters and a collection of 58 aeronautical engines. Gift shop, classic movie night, The Aero Space Museum is located near the Calgary International Airport, off McKnight Boulevard NE. Phone 403-250-3752; www.asmac.ab.ca.

East Access Route Log
(continued)

ALBERTA HIGHWAY 2
Queen Elizabeth II Highway
Distance from U.S.–Canada border (CB) is followed by distance from junction with Highway 16A at Edmonton (E).
Exit numbers reflect distance in kilometres from U.S. border (Carway/Port of Peigan crossing) via Highway 2.

CB 199.5 (321.1 km) E 190.2 (306.1 km) Exit 254 Blackfoot Trail/Calgary City Centre/17th Avenue. *Description of Calgary begins on page 57.*

CB 200 (321.8 km) E 189.7 (305.3 km) Exit 256 Memorial Drive to Calgary Zoo, Calgary Herald and City Centre.

CB 201.5 (324.3 km) E 188.2 (302.9 km) Exit 258 to Trans-Canada Highway 1 and 16 Avenue North going east and west. Continue north on Highway 2 for Red Deer and Edmonton (log follows).

Junction with Trans-Canada Highway 1 West for Lake Louise and the Icefields Parkway to Jasper. See log of this route in "Canadian Rockies Alternate Route" beginning on facing page.

CB 202.4 (325.7 km) E 187.3 (301.4 km) Exit 260 to 32nd Avenue North.

(Continues on page 62)

Canadian Rockies Alternate Route: Icefields Parkway

An alternate route for East Access Route motorists is to take Trans-Canada Highway 1 west 114 miles/184 km from Calgary to Highway 93 North, then drive 146 miles/235 km to Jasper. From Jasper, drive 45 miles/72 km east via Yellowhead Highway 16 to the Highway 40 junction and take the Bighorn Route 202 miles/325 km to Grande Prairie, where you will rejoin the East Access Route to Dawson Creek, BC, and the start of the Alaska Highway. Total driving distance from Calgary to Grande Prairie via this route is 462 miles/744 km, versus 471 miles/758 km via Edmonton.

The stretch of Highway 93 between Lake Louise and Jasper is called the Icefields Parkway, and it is one of the most scenic drives in North America, traversing Alberta's Banff and Jasper national parks in the central Canadian Rockies. Icefields Parkway accesses campgrounds and major attractions in Jasper and Banff national parks, so the roadway may be busy with tourist traffic in summer.

Snow may still be on the ground well into May. Most park campgrounds are open from May through September and early reservations are recommended. Go to the Parks Canada website at www.pccamping.ca to reserve a campsite.

This route is recommended for summer travel only; there are no services along the Icefields Parkway between Banff and Jasper from November to March. Fill your gas tank in Banff before heading north on the Icefields Parkway, or in Jasper before heading south. The only other gas stop on the Icefields Parkway is at Saskatchewan Crossing (summer only). For current road reports, visit http://511.alberta.ca.

Emergency services: Phone 911; RCMP in Banff, phone 403-762-2226; RCMP in Jasper, phone 780-852-4848 (for 24-hour dispatch).

TRANS-CANADA HIGHWAY 1

Distance from Calgary(C) is followed by distance from Jasper (J).

C 0 J 259 (416.8 km) **Junction** of Highway 2 (Deerfoot Trail) and Trans-Canada 1 West at **Milepost CB 201.5.** Follow Trans-Canada 1 West; services and shopping first 4 miles/6.4 km. Good 2-lane highway, posted 90 kmph/55 mph.

C 8.8 (14.1 km) **J 250.2** (402.6 km) Olympic Park to south.

C 9.5 (15.3 km) **J 249.5** (401.5 km) KOA Campground to south.

C 11 (17.7) **J 248** (399.1 km) Calgary city limit (sign).

C 12.1 (19.5 km) **J 246.9** (397.3 km) Exit 172.

C 14.5 (23.3 km) **J 244.5** (393.5 km) Exit 169 to Calaway Park, Western Canada's largest outdoor family amusement park, with 30 rides, live musical stage show, miniature golf and other attractions. All inclusive admission. Campground. Open daily July–August; weekends May–June and September. www.calawaypark.com.

C 19.5 (31.4) **J 239.5** (385.4 km) Exits for Cochrane/Highway 22 North and Bragg Creek/Highway 22 South.

C 20.2 (32.5 km) **J 238.8** (384.3 km) Roadside turnout westbound.

C 23 (37 km) **J 236** (379.8 km) Jumpingpound Creek.

C 27.7 (44.6 km) **J 231.3** (372.2 km) Weigh station, eastbound.

C 30.2 (48.6 km) **J 228.8** (368.2 km) Exit 143 Sibbald Creek Trail/Highway 68 South.

C 32 (51.5 km) **J 227** (365.3 km) Roadside turnout westbound.

C 32.4 (52.1 km) **J 226.6** (364.7 km) Stoney Indian Reserve boundary.

C 34.5 (55.5 km) **J 224.5** (361.3 km) Bear Hill Road exit.

C 37.5 (60.3 km) **J 221.5** (356.5 km) Chiniki Village/Morley Road exit; food and gas at exit.

C 38.4 (61.8 km) **J 220.6** (355 km) Distance marker westbound shows Canmore 45 km/30 miles, Banff 66 km/41 miles.

C 43.8 (70.5 km) **J 215.2** (346.3 km) Roadside turnout westbound.

C 46 (74 km) **J 213** (342.8 km) Exit to Highway 40 South for access to Barrier Lake Travel Information Center (4.3 miles/7 km), Barrier Dam picnic area and boating (5.5 miles/8.8 km), Barrier Lake picnic area and boating (7 miles/11.3 km), Kananaskis Village (14.3 miles/23 km), Boundary Ranch (15.7 miles/25.3 km) and Kananaskis Country Golf Course (16.4 miles/26.4 km).

The 36-hole Kananaskis Country Golf Course is one of the most spectacular courses in North America. Open to the public; club rentals, lessons, pro shop available. Phone 403-591-7272 or toll-free 1-877-591-2525.

C 48 (77.2 km) **J 211** (339.6 km) Kananaskis River.

C 48.5 (78 km) **J 210.5** (338.8 km) Exit to Seebee and Exshaw via Highway 1A; access to Bow Valley Provincial Campground.

C 49 (79 km) **J 210** (338 km) Distance marker westbound shows Canmore 27 km/17 miles, Banff 48 km/30 miles.

C 53.7 (86.4 km) **J 205.3** (330.4 km) Exit 105 to Lac Des Arcs Campground. Pay phone.

C 55.2 (88.8 km) **J 203.8** (328 km) Roadside turnouts both sides of highway next mile westbound.

C 56 (90.1 km) **J 203** (326.7 km) *CAUTION: Wildlife on highway.*

C 58.6 (94.3 km) **J 200.4** (322.5 km) Exit 98 Dead Man's Flats, Three Sisters Campground; gas, lodging, sani-dump.

C 61 (98.2 km) **J 198** (318.6 km) Three Sisters Mountain Village, Bow River Campground.

C 62 (99.8 km) **J 197** (317 km) Bow River.

C 63 (101.4 km) **J 196** (315.4 km) Exit 91 for Highway 1 A, Canmore.

C 63.2 (101.7 km) **J 195.8** (315.1 km) *CAUTION: Elk crossing next 2 km/1.2 miles westbound.*

C 64.2 (103.3 km) **J 194.8** (313.5 km) Exit 89 for Canmore town centre/Silvertip Resort exit. **CANMORE** (pop. 12,226, plus approximately 5,000 seasonal residents) is a year-round resort community with full tourist facilities.

C 65.6 (105.5 km) **J 193.4** (311.2 km) Exit 86 for Canmore/Trans-Canada Highway 1A (Bow Valley Trail). Access to visitor info centre, food, gas/diesel and lodging.

C 68 (107.8 km) **J 191** (307.4 km) **East entrance gate** for the national parks. Motorists staying in Jasper or Banff national parks or driving the Icefields Parkway must

The scenic Bow River in Canmore. This attractive community offers full tourist facilities.
(©Michael K. Robb)

Canoeing the turquoise-colored waters of Lake Louise is a popular summer activity.
(©Michael K. Robb)

purchase a park pass ($19.60 in 2011 for car regardless of number of passengers or $9.80 for 1 adult only). Banff Park radio station is 101.1 FM.

C 69.1 (111.2 km) J 189.9 (305.6 km) Tunnel Mountain/Minnewanka Loop exit. Access to Minnewanka Lake (boat tours) and Two Jack Lake campground via Minnewanka Loop Road.

Access to Tunnel Mountain Campground via Tunnel Mountain Road.

C 76.2 (122.6 km) J 182.8 (294.2 km) Banff, Tunnel Mountain/Minnewanka Loop exit. Access to Minnewanka Lake (boat tours) and Two Jack Lake campground via Minnewanka Loop Road. Access to Tunnel Mountain Campground via Tunnel Mountain Road.

C 78.8 (126.8 km) J 180.2 (290 km) Exit to **BANFF** (pop. 8,721) townsite and headquarters for Banff National Park. **Visitor Information:** Banff Visitor Centre, 224 Banff Ave., phone 403-762-1550. **Elevation:** 4,540 feet/1,384m. RCMP, phone 403-762-2228.

This scenic resort town attracts 2.5 million visitors every year, in summer for the scenery, and in winter for the skiing at nearby Mount Norquay (also accessible via this exit), Sunshine Village and Lake Louise. Banff offers food, gas, diesel and lodging year-round. Local attractions include the Banff Park Museum and National Historic Site and the hot springs at Cave & Basin National Historic Site.

C 82.4 (132.6 km) J 176.6 (284.2 km) Bow Valley Parkway/Highway 1A exit; access to Johnston Canyon, Castle Mountain and Protection Mountain campgrounds (waterfalls along this route).

C 82.9 (133.4 km) J 176.1 (283.4 km) Distance marker westbound shows Lake Louise 48 km/30 miles, Radium Hot Springs 126 km/78 miles.

C 83 (133.6 km) J 176 (283.2 km) Roadside turnout westbound.

C 83.7 (134.7 km) J 175.3 (282.1 km) Sunshine Village ski area exit; food, lodging, hiking trails and gondola rides in summer.

C 85.3 (137.3 km) J 173.7 (279.5 km) Large animal overpass. Much of this stretch of highway is fenced for the safety of both the wildlife and motorists. This overpass (and 23 others), covered in sod and made to look like natural rock, was built to allow large animals to cross the busy highway without getting hit by vehicles. Currently it is used by 11 species of large mammals.

C 85.5 (137.6 km) J 173.5 (279.2 km) Distance marker shows Banff 20 km/12 miles, Lake Louise 45 km/28 miles.

C 86.1 (138.6 km) J 172.9 (278.2 km) Bourgeau Lake; summer hiking trail.

C 90.1 (145 km) J 168.9 (271.8 km) Large animal overpass.

C 90.2 (145.2 km) J 168.8 (271.6 km) Redearth Creek; picnicking and hiking in summer.

C 91.9 (147.9 km) J 167.1 (268.9 km) Rest area westbound with toilets, litter barrels and scenic view of Castle Mountain.

C 97.3 (156.6 km) J 161.7 (260.2 km) **Castle Junction:** Trans-Canada Highway 1 junctions with Highway 93 South to Radium Hot Springs. Highways 1 and 93 share a common alignment between Castle Junction and Lake Louise.

C 98.1 (157.9 km) J 160.9 (258.9 km) *End 4-lane divided highway westbound, begin 2-lane undivided highway with passing lanes.*

C 98.5 (158.5 km) J 160.5 (258.3 km) Distance marker westbound shows Lake Louise 25 km/15 miles, Jasper 257 km/160 miles.

C 102.5 (165 km) J 156.5 (251.9 km) Rest area westbound overlooking Bow River; picnic tables.

C 109.1 (175.6 km) J 149.9 (241.2 km) *Begin 4-lane divided and fenced highway.*

C 110.8 (178.3 km) J 148.2 (238.5 km) Overflow camping area to south.

C 113 (181.9 km) J 146 (235 km) Exit to Lake Louise village (description follows) via Lake Louise Drive. Access to **Moraine Lake** and Valley of Ten Peaks from Lake Louise Drive. This is also the exit for Highway 1A/ Bow River Parkway, an alternate route to Castle Junction and Banff. **LAKE LOUISE** (pop. 1,500) is a popular destination resort serving summer tourists and winter skiers; food, gas, diesel, lodging and shopping. **Visi-**

tor Information: Lake Louise Visitor Centre by Samson Mall, phone 403-522-3833; www.banfflakelouise.com. The baronial Chateau Lake Louise and the much-photographed alpine lake of the same name, are located 2.5 miles/4 km from Lake Louise village via Lake Louise Drive.

C 114.1 (183.6 km) J 144.9 (233.2 km) **Junction** with Highway 93 North to Jasper (207 km/128 miles) via Icefields Parkway; gas, diesel. *Next gas northbound (summer only) is 77 km/48 miles from here.*

HIGHWAY 93 NORTH (ICEFIELDS PARKWAY)

C 115.3 (185.6 km) J 143.7 (231.3 km) Distance marker northound shows Icefields Centre 125 km/78 miles.

C 115.4 (185.7 km) J 143.6 (231.1 km) Park Gate. Stop and purchase park pass. Good 2-lane highway, posted 90 kmph/55 mph; driving conditions posted here.

C 116.8 (188 km) J 142.2 (228.8 km) Herbert Lake picnic area. The lake is known as a "sink" because it has no visible outlet; popular for swimming.

C 126.4 (203.4 km) J 132.6 (213.4 km) Hector Lake viewpoint. Pulpit Peak (elev. 8,940 feet/2,725m) rises above the lake's north end.

C 129.6 (208.6 km) J 129.4 (208.2 km) Mosquito Creek campground (32 sites) and hostel. Molar Pass trailhead.

C 135.2 (217.6 km) J 123.8 (199.2 km) Crowfoot Glacier viewpoint and trailhead for Helen Lake (3.7 mile-/6-km hike) and Dolomite Pass.

C 136.1 (219 km) J 122.9 (197.8 km) **Bow Lake** viewpoint and picnic area. Ice-covered until June, the turquoise-colored Bow Lake is headwater for the Bow River.

C 136.7 (220 km) J 122.3 (196.8 km) Turnoff for Num-ti-jah Lodge; food, lodging and phone. Num-ti-jah Lodge was built in the 1920s by pioneer guide Jimmy Simpson. The mountain above the lake was named after him. Access to Bow Glacier Falls trail.

C 139.9 (225.1 km) J 119.1 (191.7 km) **Bow Summit** (elev. 6,849 feet/2,088m— highest point on the Icefield's Parkway). Short side road west to **Peyto Lake** viewpoint. The glacial meltwater lake, a brilliant turquoise from suspended glacial sediments, lies several hundred feet below the viewpoint. Short, steep trail from viewpoint to lakeshore.

C 141.5 (227.7 km) J 117.5 (189.1 km) Small gravel turnouts both sides of road next several miles northbound.

C 146.7 (236 km) J 112.3 (180.7 km) Overflow camping.

C 146.9 (236.4 km) J 112.1 (180.4 km) Double-ended turnoff to east.

C 149.3 (240.3 km) J 109.7 (176.5 km) The highway runs beside Lower Waterfowl Lake, and there are several good turnouts for photography and wildlife observation.

C 150.1 (241.6 km) J 108.9 (175.3 km) **Waterfowl Lake campground** (116 sites, $21.50 per night); kitchen shelters, hiking trails to Cirque and Chephren lakes.

C 151.6 (244 km) J 107.4 (172.8 km) Turnoff with litter barrels to east next to Waterfowl Lake.

C 154.2 (248.2 km) J 104.8 (168.7 km) Nice gravel turnoff to east, paved turnoff to west.

C 157.4 (253.3 km) **J 101.6** (163.5 km)
Paved turnoff with litter barrels.

C 158.8 (255.6 km) **J 100.2** (161.3 km)
Turnout and trail to **Mistaya Canyon**, a
10-minute walk. Here the river has worn a
deep, twisting gorge into the limestone bedrock, and tumbling boulders have created
potholes and a natural arch in the canyon
sides.

C 160.7 (258.6 km) **J 98.3** (158.2 km)
Saskatchewan Crossing warden station;
emergency aid. ✚

C 161.5 (259.9 km) **J 97.5** (156.9 km)
Avalanche gates.

C 162.1 (260.9 km) **J 96.9** (155.9 km)
Treed rest stop with litter barrels, restrooms,
picnic tables.

C 162.4 (261.4 km) **J 96.6** (155.5 km)
SASKATCHEWAN CROSSING; food, full-
service gas, diesel, lodging, pub, dining,
phone, sani-dump, spa facilities and laundry. Open mid-March–mid-Nov. The
Mistaya, Howse and North Saskatchewan
rivers converge here. *Next gas northbound is
158 km/98 miles from here.* ⛽

Junction with Highway 11 (David
Thompson Highway), which goes east to
the old mining town of Nordegg, now a
Provincial Historic Site; Rocky Mountain
House, 112 miles/180 km; and Red Deer, 160
miles/257 km.

C 162.9 (262.2 km) **J 96.1** (154.7 km) Trail
to Glacier Lake (5.5 miles/9 km).

C 165.2 (265.9 km) **J 93.8** (151 km)
Gravel turnoff to east.

C 169.7 (273 km) **J 89.3** (143.7 km)
Rampart Creek campground (50 sites) and
hostel to the east. ⛺

Highway follows the North Saskatchewan
River north. Watch for moose.

C 170.3 (274.1 km) **J 88.7** (142.7 km)
Turnoff with litter barrels and view to west.

C 170.8 (274.9 km) **J 88.2** (141.9 km)
Mountain viewpoints of Mount Amery (elev.
10,941 feet/3,335m), Mount Saskatchewan
(elev. 10,964 feet/ 3,342m) and Cleopatra's
Needle, a dolomite pinnacle also known as
the Lighthouse Tower.

C 171.1 (275.4 km) **J 87.9** (141.5 km)
Mount Coleman viewpoint.

C 172.5 (277.6 km) **J 86.5** (139.2 km)
Trailhead to Sunset Pass and Sunset Lookout.

C 176.5 (284 km) **J 82.5** (132.8 km)
Coleman Creek picnic area.

C 177.2 (285.2 km) **J 81.8** (131.6 km)
Turnout with views of mountains.

C 178.9 (287.9 km) **J 80.1** (128.9 km)
Viewpoint. Cirrus Mountain and North Saskatchewan River. Litter barrels.

C 179.9 (289.5 km) **J 79.1** (127.3 km)
Weeping Wall viewpoint. Water from melting snowfields high above the Cirrus Mountain cliffs finds its way through cracks in
the wall and emerges as a series of graceful
waterfalls.

C 185.3 (298.2 km) **J 73.7** (118.6 km)
Northbound turnout. Highway climbs "Big
Bend," a steep switchbacked stretch of road
next 0.8 mile/1.2 km northbound.

C 186.1 (299.5 km) **J 72.9** (117.3 km)
Turnout overlooking North Saskatchewan
River valley. Switchbacked descent of "Big
Bend" for southbound motorists.

C 186.4 (300 km) **J 72.6** (116.8 km)
Bridal Veil Falls viewpoint.

C 188.3 (303 km) **J 70.7** (113.8 km) Turnout at trailhead for Nigel Pass (4.5 miles/7.2
km 1-way).

Athabasca Falls may be viewed by driving a short access road off the Icefields Parkway, just 18 miles south of Jasper. (©Michael K. Robb)

C 189.5 (305 km) **J 69.5** (111.8 km)
Parker Ridge trail (3.4 miles/5.4 km round-
trip); a short steep hiking with great view of
Saskatchewan Glacier. Restrooms, information board.

C 190 (305.8 km) **J 69** (111 km) Hilda
Creek hostel. Key access only. Call 1-866-
762-4122.

C 193.3 (311.1 km) **J 65.7** (105.7 km)
Turnout at **Sunwapta Pass** (elev. 6,676
feet/2,035m), the boundary between Banff
and Jasper national parks and the second
highest point on the Icefields Parkway.

C 193.6 (311.5 km) **J 65.4** (105.2 km)
Avalanche area northbound. Avoid stopping
along this stretch of road.

C 194.3 (312.7 km) **J 64.7** (104.1 km)
Wilcox Creek campground suitable for units
up to 25 feet (46 sites/$18 per night, unser-
viced sites) and trailhead. Toilets. ⛺

C 194.9 (313.6 km) **J 64.1** (103.2 km)
Columbia Icefield campground tents only
(33 tent sites/$18 per night, unserviced
sites); hiking trail. ⛺

C 195.6 (314.8 km) **J 63.4** (102 km)
Icefield Centre on east side of highway
features Parks Canada interpretive displays
about the Columbia Icefield as well as information services, food, lodging, restrooms
and public phone. The centre is open mid-
April–mid-Oct.; phone 1-877-423-7433/403-
762-6700 or the Parks Canada desk:
780-852-6288. Snocoach tours of glaciers
available. Parking and glacier views west
side of highway. The glaciers visible from
the road are fingers of the giant Columbia
Icefield, which covers 241 square miles/388
square km. RV camping. Can accomodate all
sizes. $18 for unserviced parking. ⛺

C 196 (315.4 km) **J 63** (101.4 km) Parking and viewpoint to west.

C 197.2 (317.4 km) **J 61.8** (99.5 km)
Distance marker northbound shows Jasper
102 km/63 miles.

C 198.5 (319.5 km) **J 60.5** (97.4 km)
Highway climbs northbound.

C 199.6 (321.3 km) **J 59.4** (95.6 km)

Mount Kitchener/Sunwapta Canyon Lookout to west; pull-out. New (opening May
2014) Glacier Skywalk includes cliff-edge
walkway that leads to a glass-floored observation platform 918 feet/280m above the
Sunwapta Valley. Visitors can take in the
view from the north end of the pull-out, or
buy a ticket to go on a guided interpretive
tour of the walkway and out onto the platform (more at http://glacierskywalk.ca/).
*CAUTION: Highway descends steeply north-
bound with 30-mph/50-kmph curves. Loose
gravel and rocks on roadway.*

C 200.4 (322.5 km) **J 58.6** (94.3 km) Two
pullouts with restrooms and litter barrels.

C 200.9 (323.3 km) **J 58.1** (93.5 km)
Tangle Creek Maintenance Campground.

C 201.6 (324.4 km) **J 57.4** (92.3 km)
Double-ended viewpoint; Mt. Kitchener
(elev. 11,397 feet/3,474m).

C 205.8 (331.2 km) **J 53.2** (85.6 km)
Turnout at trailhead for Beauty Creek/Stan-
ley Falls.

C 207.1 (333.3 km) **J 51.9** (83.5 km)
Beauty Creek hostel and campground to
east. ⛺

C 208.1 (334.9 km) **J 50.9** (81.9 km)
Roadside turnout and interpretive sign for
Mushroom and Diadem Peaks.

C 212.7 (342.7 km) **J 46.3** (74.5 km)
Jonas Creek campground with group shelter
(25 sites suitable for units up to 25 feet), $18
for unserviced site. ⛺

C 215.8 (347.3 km) **J 43.2** (69.5 km)
Sunwapta station; emergency aid. Trailhead–
Pobokton.

C 220.4 (354.7 km) **J 38.6** (62.1 km)
Rafting turnoff.

C 222.7 (358.4 km) **J 36.3** (58.4 km)
Bubbling Springs picnic site, toilets, phone.

C 226.4 (364.4 km) **J 32.6** (52.5 km)
Sunwapta Falls Lodge; food and lodging in
summer. Turnoff on side road adjacent lodge
for **Sunwapta Falls** viewpoint and picnic
area (0.6 mile/1 km); parking, toilets, short
walk to falls.

C 226.6 (364.7 km) **J 32.4** (52.1 km)
Distance marker northbound shows Jasper

Watch for wildlife. (©Sharon Nault)

53 km/33 miles.

C **227.9** (366.8 km) J **31.1** (50 km) Trailhead for Buck and Osprey lakes.

C **228.6** (367.9 km) J **30.4** (48.9 km) Honeymoon Lake campground (35 sites suitable for units up to 25 feet). $18 for unserviced sites. ▲

C **229** (368.5 km) J **30** (48.3 km) Paved turnoff with litter barrels to east.

C **231.7** (372.9 km) J **27.3** (43.9 km) View of Mount Christie (elev. 10,180 feet/ 3,103m).

C **234.7** (377.7 km) J **24.3** (39.1 km) Picnic area beside Athabasca River to south.

C **236.6** (380.8 km) J **22.4** (36 km) Goat Lookout, a popular animal lick. *Slow to 50 kmph/31 mph here due to travelers stopping to look at mountain goats.* View of Mt. Fryatt.

C **237** (381.4 km) J **22** (35.4 km) Viewpoint for Mount Kerkeslin (elev. 9,698 feet/ 2,956m).

C **238.5** (383.8 km) J **20.5** (33 km) Mount Kerkeslin campground (42 sites suitable for units up to 25 feet). $18 camping fee. ▲

C **240.1** (386.4 km) J **18.9** (30.4 km) Athabasca station (emergency aid) to the west.

C **240.3** (386.7 km) J **18.7** (30.1 km) Athabasca hostel.

C **240.9** (387.7 km) J **18.1** (29.1 km) **Junction** with south end of Highway 93A; a 15-mile/24-km alternate route which rejoins the main highway at **Milepost C 258.6.** Turnoff on Highway 93A for access to **Athabasca Falls**: It is 0.4 mile/0.6 km from main highway to parking area (follow signs). Athabasca Falls drops just 40 feet/12m, but it is through a short, narrow canyon and the sight is worth the stop; parking, picnic site and toilets at falls.

C **241.2** (388.2 km) J **17.8** (28.6 km) Distance marker northbound shows Jasper 30 km/19 miles.

C **243** (391.1 km) J **16** (25.7 km) Steep turnout and parking (toilets) for Horseshoe Lake under the cliffs of Mount Hardisty.

C **244.2** (393 km) J **14.8** (23.8 km) Viewpoints of Mounts Edith Cavell and Hardisty.

C **244.4** (393.3 km) J **14.6** (23.5 km) Viewpoint of Mount Kerkeslin.

C **250.9** (403.8 km) J **8.1** (13 km)

Trailhead for Wabasso Lake, Shovel Pass and the Maligne Valley.

C **254.2** (409 km) J **4.8** (7.7 km) Trailhead parking to east for Valley of the Five Lakes trail.

C **255** (410.4 km) J **4** (6.4 km) Athabasca River.

C **255.7** (411.5 km) J **3.3** (5.3 km) **Junction** with Highway 93A, a 15-mile/24-km alternate route which also intersects Highway 93 at **Milepost C 240.9** and at **Milepost C 258.6.** Highway 93A provides access to Marmot Basin ski area and Wabasso campground (231 sites/suitable for units up to 45 feet); 51 with electrical hook up for $28, $22 for unserviced sites. ▲

C **255.8** (411.7 km) J **3.2** (5.1 km) Southbound tollgate for Icefields Parkway.

C **256.1** (412.1 km) J **2.9** (4.7 km) Turnout to east with area maps, information boards from the Lions Club.

C **256.6** (413 km) J **2.4** (3.9 km) Becker's Chalets (lodging).

C **257.5** (414.4 km) J **1.5** (2.4 km) Turnoff for Wapiti campground (362 sites suitable for units up to 45 feet, 86 with electrical hookup; $27-$32 per night), sani-station, hot showers, interpretive programs. Elk (wapiti) frequent this valley in fall and winter. ▲

C **258** (415.2 km) J **1** (1.6 km) Jasper House Bungalows (lodging).

C **258.4** (415.9 km) J **0.6** (1 km) **Junction** with road west to Whistlers campground (781 sites, 120 full hook-up, 126 elec. only: no services $28, power only $33, all hook-ups $39) and Jasper Tramway up Whistler Mountain to the 7,496-foot/2,285-m level. The tramway is open March through October. At the top of the lift are a restaurant, an interpretive area and trail to summit. ▲

C **258.6** (416.2 km) J **0.4** (0.6 km) North **junction** of Highway 93A. South junction is at **Milepost C 240.9.**

C **258.8** (416.5 km) J **0.2** (0.3 km) Miette River.

C **259** (416.8 km) J **0** **Junction** of Highway 93 and Highway 16. Continue north across Highway 16 for Jasper (description follows). Turn west for Prince George, east for Edmonton, on Highway 16.

Junction with Yellowhead Highway 16. Turn to **Milepost E 219.9** on page 237 in the YELLOWHEAD HIGHWAY section for log.

JASPER (pop. 4,745) townsite and park headquarters for Jasper National Park. **Visitor information:** Brochures, maps and permits at Jasper National Park Information Centre, housed in historic 1914 building. Open year-round; phone 780-852-6176. RCMP, phone 780-852-4848.

Restaurants, shopping, gas/diesel and lodging available year-round, with accommodations ranging from bungalows to luxury lodges like Jasper Park Lodge. *Next gas southbound is 158 km/98 miles from here.* 🅱

A popular ski area in winter, Jasper also offers a variety of summer attractions, including fishing, horseback riding, rafting, boating and cruises on Maligne Lake, shopping and tram rides to alpine hiking trails.

**Turn to Milepost E 219.9
Yellowhead Highway**

(Continued from page 58)

CB **203.6** (327.6 km) E **186.1** (299.5 km) Exit 261A McKnight Blvd. East; access to Aero Space Museum.

CB **203.7** (327.8 km) E **186** (299.3 km) Exit 261B McKnight Blvd. West.

CB **204.5** (329.1 km) E **185.2** (298 km) Exit 263 for 64th Avenue North.

CB **205.5** (330.7 km) E **184.2** (296.4 km) Exit 265 Beddington Trail West. CB **206.9** (332.9 km) E **182.8** (294.2 km) Exit 266 Airport Trail, Calgary International Airport to east.

CB **207.9** (334.6 km) E **181.8** (292.6 km) Exit 268 Country Hills Blvd.; access east to Calgary International Airport.

CB **208.1** (334.9 km) E **181.6** (292.3 km) Exit 271 Highway 201/Stoney Trail. This route links 16 Avenue (Trans-Canada Highway 1) and Deerfoot Trail (Highway 2).

CB **210.2** (338.3 km) E **179.5** (288.9 km) Calgary northern city limits (sign).

CB **212.2** (341.5 km) E **177.5** (285.6 km) Exit 275 to Balzac.

CB **213.5** (343.6 km) E **176.2** (283.6 km) Northbound vehicle inspection station; pay phone.

CB **215.1** (346.2 km) E **174.6** (281 km) Exit 282 to **AIRDRIE** (pop. 39,882); gas, diesel, lodging and restaurants to east. 🅱

CB **216.2** (347.9 km) E **173.5** (279.2 km) Exit 284 to East Airdrie Industrial; gas, diesel and restaurants east off exit. 🅱

CB **218.4** (351.5 km) E **171.3** (275.7 km) Exit 285 to Highway 567 west to city centre for lodging, gas, diesel, restaurants and shopping or east to industrial centre. 🅱

CB **223.6** (359.8 km) E **166.1** (267.3 km) Dickson–Stephansson Stopping House on Old Calgary Trail (southbound-only) rest area and tourist information to west side, well away from the highway. Pay phones.

CB **224.3** (361 km) E **165.4** (266.2 km) Exit 295 to West 2A Crossfield and Highway 72 to Drumheller.

Junction with Highway 72 east to Drumheller, 60 miles/97 km. See "Side Trip to the Canadian Badlands" facing page for log of this route.

CB **226.2** (364 km) E **163.5** (263.1 km) Esso gas, diesel and restaurant east side of highway. 🅱

CB **230.7** (371.3 km) E **159** (255.9 km) Exit 305 to **CROSSFIELD** (pop. 2,648); visitor services; 18–hole golf course, Farmer's Market.

CB **236.6** (380.7 km) E **153.1** (246.4 km) Exit 315 west to Highway 581 and **CARSTAIRS** (pop. 2,656); visitor services, 2 golf courses, museum with visitor information centre. Municipal Campground with showers and potable water, $25 per night per RV; $20 for tent; $1 for sewage dump and potable water. 🅱 ▲

CB **243.8** (392.4 km) E **145.9** (234.8 km) Exit 326 to **DIDSBURY** (pop. 4,599) on Highway 582; visitor services available. Gas and diesel at Fas Gas. Camping at the municipal Rosebud Valley Campground, $20 tenting, $25 power hookup, showers. The Didsbury Museum housed in a 2-storey red brick and sandstone building, with bell tower, built in 1907 as a school. 🅱 ▲

CB 245.8 (395.6 km) **E 143.9** (231.6 km) Roadside turnout southbound with litter and recycling bins.

CB 252.9 (407 km) **E 136.8** (220.2 km) Exit 340A to Highway 27 East.

CB 253.1 (407.3 km) **E 136.6** (219.8 km) Exit 340B to Highway 27 West for Olds and Sundry. **OLDS** (pop. 7,248); visitor services. O.R. Hedges Lions Campground (45 sites) across from Centennial Park. 🏕🏕

CB 257 (413.6 km) **E 132.7** (213.6 km) Gas and food 3.7 miles/6 km to the west, southbound. ⛽

CB 257.8 (414.9 km) **E 131.9** (212.2 km) Turnout northbound with litter bins.

CB 262.9 (423.1 km) **E 126.8** (204.1 km) Exit 357 to Highway 587 West to **BOWDEN** (pop. 1,236) food, gas and lodging. **Red Lodge Provincial Park** west on Highway 587 (9.3 miles/15 km).

CB 263 (423.3 km) **E 126.7** (203.9 km) Heritage rest area southbound, Pioneer Museum and golf course. Across from Fas Gas station with gas and diesel. ⛽

CB 268.4 (431.9 km) **E 121.3** (195.2 km) Exit 365. Exit east and follow signs for RCMP Police Dog Service Training Centre. The only dog training centre in Canada, free 45-minute tours are offered to the public on Wednesdays at 2 P.M. between Victoria Day and Labour Day. Confirm hours before arrival by phoning 403-227-3346.

CB 270.9 (436 km) **E 118.8** (191.2 km) Exit 368A Highway 590 East/Big Valley; Exit 368B Highway 54 West to **INNISFAIL** (pop. 7,883); all visitor facilities. Attractions include the Danish Gardens, multiple museums, a Historical Village and the Discovery Wildlife Park, home to some famous bears. **Visitor Information:** Tourist booth at junction of Highway 54 and 50th Street (5204 50th St.), phone 403-227-1177 (town office: phone 403-227-3376).

Camping at the Anthony Henday Municipal Campground (45 sites), power sites $20, tent $10 (showers). End of May–early Oct. Phone 403-227-3376. 🏕🏕

CB 273.3 (440 km) **E 116.4** (187.3 km) Turnouts both sides with litter bins. Southbound also has interpretive signs regarding Alberta history.

CB 275.5 (443.4 km) **E 114.2** (183.7 km) U-Pick farm 1.9 km/3 km west.

CB 280.7 (451.6 km) **E 109** (175.4 km) Exit 384 to Highway 42 West; Penhold, Pine Lake, Stephansson House Historic Site at Markerville, also Red Deer Regional Airport.

CB 282.3 (454.3 km) **E 107.4** (172.8 km) Northbound-only roadside turnout and Welcome to Red Deer.

CB 283.8 (456.7 km) **E 105.9** (170.4 km) Exit 391 to "Gasoline Alley" (first exit northbound), a tourist service area with gas stations, restaurants, fast food, lodging and retail outlets. 🏕

CB 285 (458.6 km) **E 104.7** (168.5 km) Second exit northbound to Gasoline Alley.

CB 286.2 (460.6 km) **E 103.5** (166.7 km) Exit 394 to Highway 2A/Gaetz Avenue to Red Deer (description follows); shopping and all services this exit. *NOTE: Northbound traffic use exit at Milepost CB 288.5 for Visitor Centre; southbound traffic use Exit 397.*

Side Trip to the Canadian Badlands

Alberta Highways 72 and 9 lead 60 miles/97 km east to Drumheller in the Canadian Badlands—a region characterized by scanty vegetation and intricate erosional features. Besides its fantastic scenery, the Badlands are also famous for dinosaurs, on display at the Royal Tyrrell Museum and in Drumheller.

Distance from Highway 2 junction (J) is shown.

ALBERTA HIGHWAY 72 EAST

J 0 Junction with Alberta Highway 2 at **Milepost CB 224.3** (approximately 25 miles/40.5 km north of Calgary).

J 0.3 (0.5 km) Distance marker shows Beiseker 33 km/21 miles, Drumheller 93 km/58 miles.

J 7.5 (12.1 km) **Junction** with Highway 791, which leads to the Fairview Colony.

J 13.8 (22.2 km) Rosebud River.

J 14 (22.6 km) Beiseker Colony.

J 20.7 (33.4 km) **BEISEKER** (pop. 837); all services available. See www.beiseker. com for more information. Beiseker Railway Museum is in a renovated 1911 CPR Station building. Highway 72 becomes Highway 9 eastbound. ⛽

J 21.4 (34.4 km) Beiseker municipal RV park; 50 sites (30 powered, 20 without power) and day-use area. 🏕

J 33.1 (53.3 km) Distance marker shows Drumheller 45 km/28 miles, Hanna 121 km/75 miles.

ALBERTA HIGHWAY 9 EAST

J 33.2 (53.5 km) **Junction** with Highway 21 to Three Hills and Trans-Canada Highway 1.

J 37.3 (60.1 km) **Junction** with Highway 836; food and gas available. Carbon Recreation Area and Campground 13 km/8 miles north, Rockyford 18 km/11 miles south. ⛽

J 45.1 (72.6 km) **Junction** with Highway 840 to Rosebud and Standard.

J 50.6 (81.5 km) **Horseshoe Canyon Viewpoint**; restrooms, picnic tables, litter barrels, area map, hiking trails. Very scenic area, good photo-ops. In wet weather be careful of slick surfaces.

J 52.7 (84.8 km) Nacmine 8 km/5 miles north.

J 54.8 (88.2 km) **Junction** with 841 South to Dalum.

J 54.9 (88.4 km) Distance marker shows Drumheller 9 km/6 miles, Hanna 86 km/53 miles, Stettler 106 km/66 miles.

J 57.2 (92.1 km) Roadside turnout at Drumheller city limits; litter barrels and information board.

J 57.8 (93 km) *CAUTION: 8 percent downgrade eastbound, trucks use lower gears.*

J 60.1 (96.8 km) **DRUMHELLER** (pop. 8,029). **Visitor Information:** A Visitor Information Centre is located at 60 1st Avenue West. Mailing address is: Box 999, Drumheller, Alberta T0J 0Y0; phone toll-free 1-866-823-8100; website www.traveldrumheller.com; email tourisminfo@drumheller chamber.com.

Drumheller, in the heart of the Canadian Badlands, has all visitor facilities available, including restaurants, gas stations, accommodations and campgrounds. 🏕🏕

The town is strewn with dinosaur replicas—and photo opportunities abound. Climb into the mouth of the world's largest dinosaur for a panoramic view of the Drumheller Valley. While in Drumheller, visit the Badlands Historical Centre, Reptile World and the Valley Doll Museum.

The first dinosaur fossil found in the Badlands was an Albertosaurus (a slightly smaller version of the Tyrannosaurus), unearthed in 1884 by Joseph Burr Tyrrell (pronounced TEER-ell), just east of what is Drumheller today. The "Great Canadian Dinosaur Rush" followed, as famous fossil hunters Barnum Brown, Joseph Sternberg and others vied for trophies.

Today, the major attraction in Drumheller is the **Royal Tyrrell Museum**, located in Midland Provincial Park just outside the town limits on Highway 838. The museum boasts an outstanding fossil collection presented in stunning displays. More than 40 complete dinosaur skeletons, as well as flying reptiles, prehistoric mammals and marine invertebrates are displayed. The Cretaceous Garden, a tropical plant conservatory, has more than 600 species of plants simulating the botanical world of the dinosaurs. A viewing window in the main laboratory allows visitors to watch scientists at work. The museum has a cafeteria and gift shop. Spring/summer hours are 9 A.M. to 9 P.M. daily from May 15 to August 31. Fall/winter hours are Tue.–Sun., 10 A.M. to 5 P.M. Sept. 1 to May 14. Admission adult $11, senior $8, youth $6, family $30. For more information phone 403-823-7707 or to to www.tyrrellmuseum.com.

Other attractions and activities include the Homestead Museum, Bumper Boat Amusements, Fossil World Discovery Centre, the Little Church, Dinosaur Trail Golf and Country Club, Badlands Go-Kart Park, Horsethief Canyon and the Bleriot Ferry (connects South and North Dinosaur Trails).

The Canadian Badlands Passion Play, presented in a 2,700-seat natural amphitheatre, takes places in July. Performance scheduled for July 11-13 and 18-20 in 2014; details at www.canadianpassionplay.com.

Much of the famous, yet eerie landscape of the Canadian Badlands can be seen along the Hoodoo Trail (Highway 10 East), another of the Drumheller Valley's scenic driving tours. On the trail, see the strange sandstone formations called hoodoos, as well as the Rosedale Suspension Bridge, the Last Chance Saloon in Wayne, the Atlas Coal Mine National Historic Site, (15 minutes from downtown Drumheller, phone 403-822-2220) and the East Coulee School Museum. Ask at the Visitors Information Centre for additional locations.

**Return to Milepost CB 224.3
East Access Route**

Hockey display inside Red Deer's Sports Hall of Fame. (©Brian Stein)

Red Deer

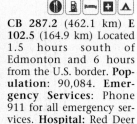

CB 287.2 (462.1 km) **E 102.5** (164.9 km) Located 1.5 hours south of Edmonton and 6 hours from the U.S. border. **Population**: 90,084. **Emergency Services**: Phone 911 for all emergency services. **Hospital**: Red Deer Regional Hospital, phone 403-343-4422.

Visitor Information: Tourism Red Deer Visitor Centre, located at 101 4200 Highway 2. Open daily year-round; phone 403-346-0180; website www.tourismreddeer.com.

Red Deer has all services, including major chain motels and restaurants, retail outlets and a hospital. Collicutt Leisure Centre features a wave pool, waterslide and indoor tennis. Camping at private RV parks and at Lions Municipal Campground.

Attractions in Red Deer include Fort Normandeau; Kerry Wood Nature Centre; Bower Ponds (picnicking, paddle boats); Discovery Canyon; Heritage Square, a collection of historic buildings in a park setting; and Red Deer & District Museum. The architecture of Douglas Cardinal's St. Mary's Church may be seen at 38th Street and Mitchell Avenue. Visit the Historical Ghosts in the downtown core and throughout the parks system. Events throughout summer.

East Access Route Log

(continued)

CB 288.3 (464 km) **E 101.4** (163.2 km) Southbound Exit 397 32nd Street/Fort Normandeau; access to rest area, Visitor Centre, Alberta Sports Hall of Fame & Museum and Heritage Ranch (equestrian centre).

CB 288.5 (464.3 km) **E 101.2** (162.9 km) Northbound-only exit to Tourism Red Deer Visitor Centre and Sports Hall of Fame. Open year-round; restrooms, snack shop, gift shop and sports museum. It is a family friendly interactive experience. Adjacent park has ample parking, a playground and picnic sites. Loop road through park accesses the Heritage Ranch equestrian centre; www.heritageranch.ca, pre-booking necessary for

trail rides, carriage or sleigh rides. Cafe/restaurant on site, open daily. Parking for the Waskasoo Park trail system. Also access to roadside turnouts, both sides of highway, with litter barrels and recycling.

CB 289.2 (465.4 km) **E 100.5** (161.7 km) Red Deer River.

CB 292.5 (470.7 km) **E 97.2** (157 km) Exit 401 Highway 11 West to Sylvan Lake (10 miles/16 km). Highway 11 continues 48 miles/78 km west to the town of Rocky Mountain House and to Rocky Mountain House National Historic Park. The park preserves the sites of 4 fur trading posts that operated between 1799 and 1875. Interpretive trails and demonstrations, visitor centre with exhibits. Open daily, 10 A.M. to 5 P.M., mid–May to early September; 10 A.M. to 5 P.M., Monday–Friday September to early October. Rocky Mountain House Visitor Centre phone 403-845-2412.

CB 293.5 (472.3 km) **E 96.2** (154.8 km) Exit 405A Highway 11A, East to Red Deer.

CB 293.7 (472.6 km) **E 96** (154.5 km) Exit 405B Highway 11A West, Sylvan Lake. Many visitor attractions including camping at **RV There Yet Campground**.

CB 294.7 (474.3 km) **E 95** (152.9 km) Southbound roadside turnout with information boards and litter barrels.

CB 295.8 (476 km) **E 93.9** (151.1 km) Blindman River.

CB 296.9 (477.8 km) **E 92.8** (149.3 km) Distance marker southbound shows Red Deer 16 km/10 miles, Calgary 157 km/98 miles.

CB 297.1 (478.1 km) **E 92.6** (149 km) Exit 412 Blackfalds/Highway 597 East, Joffre. Teepee camping, water spray park.

CB 304.4 (489.9 km) **E 85.3** (137.3 km) Exit 422A Highway 12 East to **LACOMBE** (pop. 11,562); all visitor facilities, corn maze, municipal Michener Park (57 sites), power hookup $20, tenting $15.

CB 304.6 (490.2 km) **E 85.1** (137 km) Exit 422B Highway 12 West to Aspen Beach Provincial Park at Gull Lake (6 miles/10 km) and Bentley.

CB 308.1 (495.8 km) **E 81.6** (131.3 km) Large, double-ended, gravel turnout southbound.

CB 309.6 (498.3 km) **E 80.1** (129 km) Exit 431 Highway 2A South, 4.3 miles/7 km east to Lacombe (all visitor facilities) and Stettler.

CB 313.3 (504.2 km) **E 76.4** (123 km) Exit 437 to Highway 2A North/East to Ponoka and Wetaskiwin.

CB 314.5 (506.1 km) **E 75.2** (121 km) Distance marker southbound shows Red Deer 43 km/27 miles, Calgary 184 km/114 miles.

CB 314.7 (506.5 km) **E 75** (120.7 km) Exit 439 Wolf Creek Golf Resort 0.6 mile/1 km to east, Highway 604.

CB 316.7 (509.7 km) **E 73** (117.5 km) Roadside turnout southbound with litter bins and pay phone.

CB 317.6 (511.1 km) **E 72.1** (116 km) *CAUTION: Deer crossing southbound.*

CB 319.2 (513.7 km) **E 70.5** (113.4 km) Distance marker southbound shows Red Deer 50 km/31 miles, Calgary 191 km/119 miles.

CB 320.3 (515.5 km) **E 69.4** (111.7 km) Battle River.

CB 321.4 (517.2 km) **E 68.3** (110 km) Exit 450A Highway 53 East to **PONOKA** (pop. 6,576); all visitor facilities. Ponoka Stampede Campground.

CB 321.8 (517.9 km) **E 67.9** (109.3 km) Exit 450B West Rimbey. Truck museum.

CB 324.9 (522.9 km) **E 64.8** (104.3 km) Turnout northbound with litter bins.

CB 325.9 (524.5 km) **E 63.8** (102.7 km) Turnout southbound with litter bins.

CB 328.8 (529.1 km) **E 60.9** (98 km) Exit 462 Meniak Road.

CB 329 (529.5 km) **E 60.7** (97.7 km) Distance marker southbound shows Ponoka 16 km/10 miles, Red Deer 66 km/41 miles, Calgary 207 km/129 miles.

CB 329.5 (530.3 km) **E 60.2** (96.9 km) Distance marker northbound shows Leduc 55 km/34 miles, Edmonton 89 km/55 miles.

CB 330.3 (531.6 km) **E 59.4** (95.6 km) Southbound turnout with litter bins.

CB 332.8 (535.6 km) **E 56.9** (91.6 km) Exit 469 to Highway 611 east to Hobbema.

CB 336.8 (542 km) **E 52.9** (85.1 km) Northbound-only access to Mayfield rest area; diner, picnic tables, restrooms.

CB 341.2 (549.1 km) **E 48.5** (78.1 km) Exit 482A Highway 13 East to community of **WETASKIWIN** (pop. 12,285). Wetaskiwin provides all services, major hotels, 2 RV Campgrounds, numerous restaurants, 4 museums (including the world class Provincial Reynolds-Alberta Museum, biannual air show, several annual events and a fascinating historic downtown with 13 turn-of-the-century buildings including the 1907 historic courthouse which serves as City Hall. Visitor Information Centre is in the Chamber of Commerce Office on 55A Street across from the water tower. For more information www.wetaskiwin.ca.

CB 342 (550.3 km) **E 47.7** (76.7 km) Exit 482B Highway 13 West.

CB 345 (555.2 km) **E 43.7** (70.3 km) Distance marker southbound shows Red Deer 93 km/58 miles, Calgary 234 km/145 miles.

CB 345.2 (555.5 km) **E 43.5** (70 km) Exit 488 Correction Line Road.

CB 347.6 (559.4 km) **E 41.1** (66.1 km) Roadside turnout southbound with litter bins and recycling barrels.

CB 350.6 (564.2 km) **E 38.1** (61.3 km) Exit to Highway 616 to Millet.

CB 353.3 (568.4 km) **E 36.4** (58.6 km) Northbound-only turnout to east with litter bins and recycle bins.

E 357.5 (575.3 km) **E 32.2** (51.8 km) Distance marker southbound shows Red Deer 113 km/70 miles, Calgary 215 km/134 miles.

CB 357.9 (576 km) **E 31.8** (51.2 km) Exit 508 for Glen Park and Cavanaugh; Green Valley Farms, U-pick.

CB 361.1 (581.1 km) **E 28.6** (46 km) Southbound-only truck weigh station.

CB 362.4 (583.2 km) **E 27.3** (43.9 km) Exit 516 Highway 2A South/Leduc. First of 3 exits northbound for Leduc.

CB 363.1 (584.4 km) **E 26.6** (42.8 km) Exit 517 to Leduc City Centre via Highway 2A and to Highway 39 West Drayton Valley. Leduc was founded and named for the Leduc oil field. The 200-million barrel oil field was the first of a series of oil and natural gas finds that changed the economy of Alberta.

CB 364.8 (587.1 km) **E 24.9** (40.1 km) Exit 519 to **LEDUC** (pop. 23,293); access to visitor information centre, motels, restaurants, fast-food, gas stations with diesel and shopping on 50th Street (Highway 2A). Leduc Lions Campground (69 sites); go south on 50th Street, then 1.2 miles/2 km east on Rolly View Road.

CB 365.8 (588.7 km) **E 23.9** (38.5 km) Leduc North sector exit; 24-hour truck and tourist services with gas and diesel.

CB 366.1 (589.2 km) **E 23.6** (38 km) Exit 522 to International Airport; access to services on Highway 2A.

CB 368.3 (592.6 km) **E 21.4** (34.4 km) Exit 525 Devon Bypass/Highway 19; gas stations with diesel and fast-food east off exit. Access west to Leduc No. 1 Well Historic Site.

Junction with Highway 19 west and Edmonton Bypass route. See "Devonian Way Bypass" on this page.

*NOTE: Northbound motorists wishing to avoid heavy traffic through Edmonton may exit west on Highway 19 (Devonian Way) for Devon Bypass route. Drive 8.2 miles/13.2 km west on Highway 19, then 14.5 miles/23.3 km north through Devon via Highway 60 to junction with Yellowhead Highway 16 approximately 10 miles/16 km west of Edmonton (see **Milepost E 3.9** on page 68 this section for continuation of East Access Route northbound log).*

CB 373.2 (600.6 km) **E 16.5** (26.6 km) Welcome to Edmonton northbound sign.

CB 373.5 (601.1 km) **E 16.2** (26.1 km) Left lane exit to **Edmonton Tourism's Gateway Park Visitor Centre**, open year-round, daily; pay phones, restrooms, dump station. The downtown location is *not* open weekends except during July and August.

Devonian Way Bypass

This 21 mile/33 km bypass route circles the southwest edge of Edmonton, connecting Highway 2 and Highway 16 via Highway 19 and Highway 60, known as the Devonian Way. There are several stops of interest along the way.
Distance from Highway 2 and Devonian Way junction (J) is shown.

J 0 Junction with Highway 19, Devonian Way, at **Milepost CB 368.3**. Follow Devonian Way west.

J 0.4 (0.7 km) Rest area to south.

J 1.4 (2.3 km) Castrol Raceway to south, Amberlea Meadows equestrian facility to north.

J 4.5 (7.2 km) Rabbit Hill Ski Resort 7 km/4.3 miles west and Shalom Waterskiing Park 7 km/4.3 miles to the north.

J 7.4 (11.9 km) **Junction** with Highway 60 (Edmonton truck bypass). Turn north on Highway 60 for Devon and Yellowhead Highway; turn south at intersection and drive 3.7 mile/6 km for Leduc #1 Energy Discovery Centre (descriptions follow).

The **Leduc Well** was brought in on Feb. 13, 1947. It was the 134th try for Imperial Oil after drilling 133 dry wells, and it was wildly successful, making Edmonton the "Oil Capital of Canada." A 174-foot/53-m derrick marks the site. Visitors may climb to the drilling floor to view drilling equipment.
Leduc #1 Energy Discovery Centre has museum displays, models and fossils. Knowledgeable guides make it a memorable learning experience. Open 9 A.M.–5 P.M. daily year-round. Admission charged. Campground with hookups and showers. Phone 1-866-987-4323; www.leducnumber1.com.

J 7.8 (12.5 km) Dump station off of Derrick Drive.

J 8.6 (13.8 km) Turn east on Athabasca Avenue for downtown **DEVON** (pop. 6,534). This small, relaxed community, newly branded as Bike Town Alberta, boasts several circuits for the cycling enthusiast. It has all visitor services, including hotel and B & B accommodations, restaurants, fast-food outlets, gas stations, grocery stores, mountain bike skills park and skateboard park, outdoor pool, trail systems, RV parking, river tours, fishing, canoeing, campground (237 sites), boat launch, day-use area (Voyageur Park), gold panning, Farmer's Market (Thursday

NOTE: From here north to 23rd Avenue, traffic will be controlled by signals with 2 through lanes, one left-turn lane and one through OR left turn lane.

CB 374.8 (603.1 km) **E 14.9** (24 km) Ellerslie Road exit.

CB 375.3 (604 km) **E 14.4** (23.2 km) Left lanes provide exit for Anthony Henday/Highway 216, another bypass that avoids downtown traffic but provides easy access to businesses, including West Edmonton Mall, en route to Highway 16 westbound. Other lanes continue northbound as Gateway Boulevard.

CB 376.8 (606.3 km) **E 12.9** (20.8 km) Stoplight at 19th Avenue; big box stores to east.

afternoons in summer and fall), splash park, an 18-hole golf course and a conference centre.

J 9 (14.5 km) Bridge over North Saskatchewan River.

J 11.8 (19 km) **Devonian Botanic Garden**; Japanese garden, alpine garden, herb garden, rose garden and other special collections gardens set in natural landscape (total of 190 acres). Tours available. Indoor display house include a butterfly house. Concession and gift shop. Open daily from 10 A.M. May to mid-Oct. Call 780-987-3054 for hours. Fee charged.

J 12.6 (20.3 km) Clifford E. Lee Nature Sanctuary 2 km/1.2 miles to west.

J 14.1 (22.7 km) Distance marker southbound shows Devon 11 km/7 miles, Leduc 34 km/21 miles .

J 14.9 (24 km) **Junction** with Secondary Highway 627; turn east for Edmonton.

J 20.2 (32.5 km) Distance marker shows Devon 21 km/13 miles.

J 20.7 (33.3 km) **Junction** with Yellowhead Highway 16A.

**Turn to Milepost E 3.9
East Access Route**

CB 377.4 (607.2 km) **E 12.3** (19.8 km) Exit 539 23rd Avenue; shopping mall access.

CB 378.3 (608.7 km) **E 11.4** (18.3 km) Stoplight at 34th Avenue.

CB 379.2 (610.1 km) **E 10.5** (16.9 km) **Junction** with Whitemud Drive West/Highway 2. Continue straight ahead for downtown Edmonton (description follows). *To continue with East Access Route log, northbound travelers turn left here and follow Whitemud Drive/Highway 2 west; see map on page 66.*

CB 384 (617.9 km) **E 5.7** (9.2 km) Saskatchewan River.

CB 386 (621.1 km) **E 3.7** (6 km) Exit for **West Edmonton Mall**/N 170th Street (Highway 2). See description of West Edmonton Mall in Edmonton Attractions.

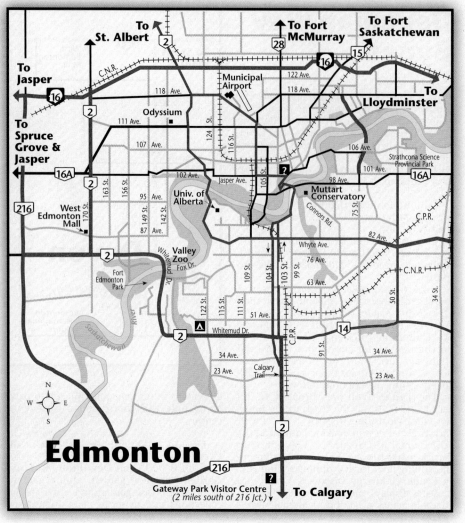

To St. Albert
To Fort McMurray
To Fort Saskatchewan
To Jasper
C.N.R.
Municipal Airport
122 Ave.
118 Ave.
118 Ave.
To Lloydminster
Odyssium
111 Ave.
124 St.
116 St.
107 Ave.
106 Ave.
To Spruce Grove & Jasper
Strathcona Science Provincial Park
102 Ave.
Jasper Ave.
101 Ave.
163 St.
156 St.
Univ. of Alberta
Muttart Conservatory
98 Ave.
95 Ave.
West Edmonton Mall
170 St.
149 St.
142 St.
Connors Rd.
75 St.
82 Ave.
C.P.R.
87 Ave.
Valley Zoo
Fox Dr.
Whitemud Dr.
Whyte Ave.
76 Ave.
63 Ave.
C.N.R.
River
Saskatchewan
Fort Edmonton Park
122 St.
115 St.
111 St.
109 St.
104 St.
103 St.
99 St.
50 St.
34 St.
51 Ave.
C.P.R.
Whitemud Dr.
91 St.
34 Ave.
34 Ave.
23 Ave.
Calgary Trail
23 Ave.
N W E S
Edmonton
Gateway Park Visitor Centre
(2 miles south of 216 Jct.)
To Calgary

CB 387.5 (623.5 km) **E 2.2** (3.5 km) Northbound travelers exit to Anthony Henday Drive North/Highway 216.

CB 389.7 (627 km) **E 0 Junction** with Highway 16A West (Stony Plain Road). Dawson Creek-bound travelers follow Highway 16A West. *Log continues on page 68.*

Edmonton

Capital of Alberta, 180 miles/290 km from Calgary; 363 miles/584 km from Dawson Creek, BC; 1,853 miles/2,982 km from Fairbanks, AK. **Population:** 782,439; area 1,034,945. **Emergency Services:** Phone 911 for all emergency services. **Hospitals:** Grey Nuns Community Hospital, 1100 Youville Dr., phone 780-735-7000; Misericordia Community Hospital, 16940–87th Ave., phone 780-735-2611; Royal Alexandra Hospital, 10240 Kingsway Ave., phone 780-735-4111; University of Alberta Hospital, 8440–112 St., phone 780-407-8822.

Visitor Information: Contact Edmonton Tourism, phone 780-496-8400 or toll-free 1-800-463-4667, or visit their web site at www.edmonton.com or www.TravelAlbertaEdmonton.com; email gateway@edmonton.com;. Edmonton Tourism operates visitor information centres downtown at the World Trade Centre and on Highway 2 at Gateway Park. Be sure to pick up an Edmonton Attractions Brochure, available at Edmonton's visitor centres; the brochure includes a map, coupons and current listings for festivals and events.

Elevation: 2,182 feet/668m. **Climate:** Average temperatures in July range between 60–72°F/16–22°C. Average high is 73°F/23°C. In January from 0 to 16°F/-18 to -9°C with an average high of 16°F/-8°C. Average annual precipitation includes 13 inches of rain and 55 inches of snow. Edmonton is located on the 53rd latitude and enjoys 17 hours of daylight in mid-summer. **Newspaper:** *Edmonton Sun* (daily), *Edmonton Journal* (daily), *Edmonton Examiner* (weekly).

Private Aircraft: Edmonton International Airport 11 miles/17 km south of the Edmonton City limits. See Canadian Flight Supplement and www.flyeia.com.

Edmonton traces its roots back to 1795 beginning as a fur-trading outpost. Just over 100 years later, and during the 1897 Klondike Gold Rush, prospectors boosted Edmonton's fortune as they stopped in Edmonton for supplies en route to the Yukon. Many would also make Edmonton their permanent home increasing the population to 6 times its previous size.

The discovery of oil in 1947 just outside of Edmonton in Leduc county made Edmonton the "Oil Capital of Canada." Today the city, which sits in the geographic centre of the province, is the hub for energy development and petrochemicals for Alberta. It has become a centre of excellence in research through the University of Alberta and the high technology industries located in the region such as the National Institute of Nan-

otechnology.

Historic Edmonton is seen in its magnificent Alberta Legislative building and grounds, throughout downtown, in Fort Edmonton Park, and in walking tours of Old Strathcona. Modern-day Edmonton is reflected in the scale of West Edmonton Mall and the dramatic architecture of many buildings throughout the city.

The North Saskatchewan River winds through the centre of Edmonton. Flanked on both banks by swaths of green, it is the focal point of a series of parks and bikeways and the largest stretch of urban parkland in North America, 22 times the size of New York's Central Park. Located along the river's parkland is Victoria Golf Course, the oldest municipal golf course in Canada, est. 1907. William Hawrelak Park in the river valley has a lake and is home to the Heritage Amphitheatre, which hosts a number of special events.

A sports-minded city, Edmonton is home to the Edmonton Oilers of the National Hockey League (NHL) and Edmonton Eskimos of the Canadian Football League (CFL).

Lodging & Services

There are more than 13,000 hotel/ motel/ bed & breakfast rooms in Edmonton and approximately 3,500 restaurants in the region.

Camping

Camping is available at **Glowing Embers Travel Centre**; see ad on facing page.

Transportation

Air: Edmonton International Airport, located approximately 11 miles/17 km south of the city centre, is the fifth busiest airport in Canada. Major airlines serving Edmonton include Air Canada, Delta/Northwest Airlines, Horizon/Alaska Airlines, WestJet and United Airlines. Air North offers nonstop service to Whitehorse, YT. Phone 1-800-268-7134; www.flyeia.com.

Bus: Greyhound Canada scheduled service to destinations throughout Canada and the U.S.; phone 780-420-2400, toll free 1-800-661-8747; www.greyhound.ca. Red Arrow provides service to Calgary, Red Deer Lethbridge, Banff, Lake Louise and Fort McMurray; phone 1-800-232-1958; www.redarrow.ca.

Railroad: Edmonton is on VIA Rail's Canadian route with service to Saskatoon, Winnipeg, Toronto, Jasper and Vancouver. The Edmonton terminal is located at 12360–121 St. off the Yellowhead Highway. Phone 1-888-842-7245; www.viarail.ca.

Attractions

West Edmonton Mall. Topping the list of major attractions for visitors to Edmonton is the North America's largest shopping and entertainment centre and Alberta's #1 tourist attraction. West Edmonton Mall features over 800 stores and services, 100 eating establishments, 2 hotels and 10 theme park attractions. There is an enormous indoor water park; a full-scale amusement park; an ice skating rink; 2 18-hole miniature golf courses (one is the neon Putt'n'Glow); bowling, billiards and bingo; bumper boats; and a sea lion show and underground aquarium at Sea Life Caverns. Also located in the mall are Palace Casino, Jubilations Dinner Theatre and the IMAX 3D Theatre. Located on 87–90 Avenue at 170–178 Street, the shopping mall is open 7 days a week; www.westedmonton

mall.com.

Sir Winston Churchill Square is an entertainment destination, providing events and festivals throughout the year. Churchill Square is located in the heart of Edmonton's vibrant downtown. The Square is bound by 99 and 100 streets and 102A and 102 avenues.

Surrounding the square are: City Hall; the Stanley A. Milner Library; the Francis Winspear Centre for Music, home to the Edmonton Symphony Orchestra and the Davis Concert Organ (www.winspearcentre.com); the Citadel Theatre, presenting mainstage and special live theatre series (www.citadel theatre.com); and the Art Gallery of Alberta (see description following).

Art Gallery of Alberta, known for its exhibits of contemporary and historical Canadian art, the AGA maintains a collection of over 6,000 objects. It is the oldest cultural institution in Alberta and the only museum in the province solely dedicated to the exhibition and preservation of art and visual culture.

The gallery underwent a major reconstruction designed by Los Angeles architect Randall Stout. The ultra-modern structure of steel and glass is 85,000 square feet and includes gift shops and a restaurant. For current hours and exhibits. Phone 780-422-6223; www.youraga.com

Alberta Legislature: Alberta's parliamentary tradition is on display at this imposing public building. Discover the Alberta Legislature Building on a free guided tour. Tours are available 362 days of the year and start at the interpretive centre and gift shop north of the fountains. Visitors may also enjoy self-guided grounds tours, taking a dip in the wading pools during the summer, skating on the rink in winter, or taking in one of the many special events year-round. The Alberta Legislature Building is located at 10820–98 Ave. For more information, phone 780-427-7362; www.assembly.ab.ca.

Fort Edmonton Park is Canada's largest living history park. Costumed staff re-create life as it was in an 1846 Hudson's Bay trading post and Cree encampment, and as it was on the streets of 1885, 1905 and 1920. Period restaurants and retail shops are located in the park. The steam train and streetcar rides are included in the admission price. Accommodations available in the park at Hotel Selkirk.

The park opens at 10 A.M. daily, May to September. Located at Fox Drive and Whitemud Drive. For more information, phone 780-496-5311; www.fortedmontonpark.ca.

Special Events. Known as "Canada's Festival City," Edmonton hosts more than 30 annual music, arts and cultural festivals throughout the year, in addition to regular theatre and symphony seasons. Among the popular events scheduled for 2014 are the International Jazz Festival (June 20-29); International Street Performers Festival (July 4-13); A Taste of Edmonton (July 17-26); Folk Music Festival (August 7-10); and the International Fringe Theatre Festival (August 14-24). Confirm dates online at www.edmonton.ca/attractions_recreation/festivals-events.aspx.

Edmonton Valley Zoo is a great destination for travelers with children, with its birds of prey demonstrations and "Let's Talk Animals" programs, pony rides and paddle boats. The zoo has more than 100 exotic, endangered and native animals. Board the mini-train for a tour through the zoo; open

"City of Champions" is an official slogan based on Edmonton's response to destruction from a 1987 tornado. (©Michael K. Robb)

daily and located at 13315 Buena Vista Road (87 Avenue); phone 780-442-5311; www.valleyzoo.ca.

Muttart Conservatory. The 4 spectacular glass pyramids of Muttart Conservatory showcase plants from the temperate, tropical and arid climates of the world. Open daily. The newly renovated conservatory has a cafe, gift shop and outdoor courtyard for programs. Perfect for family picnics, walking or biking in this beautiful river valley. Located at 9626–96A Street, phone 780-442-5311; www.muttartconservatory.ca.

The Royal Alberta Museum, at 12845–102 Ave., features the Syncrude Gallery of Aboriginal Culture, the Natural History Gallery, the Bug Room and Wild Alberta. Internationally touring exhibitions and special

Rochfort Bridge trestle is the second longest wooden railway trestle in the world.
(©Michael K. Robb)

features on Alberta artists are also in constant rotation. Gift shop, cafe and a 400-seat theatre. Open daily 9 A.M.–5 P.M., closed only Dec. 24–25; phone 780-453-9100; www.royalalbertamuseum.ca.

The **TELUS World of Science–Edmonton** is the city's space and science centre, boasting the largest planetarium dome in North America, an IMAX theatre, and 5 interactive exhibit galleries. It is located at 11211–142 St. NW; phone 780-451-3344; www.edmontonscience.com.

East Access Route Log

(continued)
Distance from Edmonton (E) is followed by distance from Dawson Creek (DC).

YELLOWHEAD HIGHWAY 16A WEST

E 0 DC 363 (584.2 km) **Junction** of Anthony Henday Drive North/Highway 216 with Highway 16A West/Stony Plain Road. *NOTE: Southbound travelers may bypass Edmonton city centre by taking Highway 216 south, skirting downtown but accessing businesses like West Edmonton Mall. You will rejoin the East Access Route at Milepost CB 375.3; see page 65.*

E 3.9 (6.3 km) **DC 359.1** (577.8 km) Exit to Devon Bypass/Highway 60. Access to **Glowing Embers RV Park** this exit.

Glowing Embers RV Park & Travel Centre. See display ad on page 67. [A]

NOTE: Southbound travelers may bypass Edmonton by taking Highway 60 south, then Highway 19 east to Highway 2 (Devonian Way Bypass).

Junction with Highway 60 south to Highway 19 east and Edmonton Bypass route. See "Devonian Way Bypass" on page 65 and read log back to front.

E 6.4 (10.3 km) **DC 356.6** (573.9 km) Several U-pick farm locations near here.

E 9.2 (14.8 km) **DC 353.8** (569.4 km) Tour the **Spruce Grove Grain Elevator, Water Tower and Archives.** The Spruce Grove Grain Elevator Museum, one of Alberta's last remaining wooden grain elevators and still in working condition, was built in 1958. See the historical water tower, originally set up on Spruce Grove in 1957, dismantled in 1978 and restored in 2011. To get there, go south on Golden Spike Road, then east on Railway Ave. Elevator and water tower are visible from Highway 16A/Parkland Highway. Open Tuesday–Saturday 9 A.M.–3 P.M.; phone 780-960-4600; visit sprucegroveagsociety.com for more information.

E 10.2 (16.4 km) **DC 352.8** (567.8 km) Stoplight at Campsite Road in **SPRUCE GROVE** (pop. 24,646). All visitor facilities including hotels, motels, restaurants, fast-food, gas stations with diesel, shopping malls and all emergency services. Chamber of Commerce tourist information building at northwest edge of Rotary Park on Highway 16A/Parkland Highway, open year-round, weekends only; phone 780-962-2561. The tourist information booth has a nice picnic area and is located just to the west of Walmart, Subway, and other businesses. [B]

E 11.1 (17.9 km) **DC 351.9** (566.3 km) Distance marker westbound shows Stony Plain 6 km/4 miles, Edson 178 km/111 miles, Jasper 338 km/210 miles.

E 11.5 (18.5 km) **DC 351.5** (565.7 km) Rotary Park to south.

E 11.6 (18.7 km) **DC 351.4** (565.5 km) Turnout and Welcome to Spruce Grove sign for eastbound motorists. Spruce Grove visitor centre.

E 12.7 (20.4 km) **DC 350.3** (563.7 km) Entering Stony Plain westbound.

E 13.4 (21.6 km) **DC 349.6** (562.5 km) Turnoff for business park in **STONY PLAIN** (pop. 14,117). **Emergency Services**: RCMP, Fire Station and hospital dial 911. All visitor facilities including hotels, motels, restaurants, supermarkets, shopping mall and gas stations with diesel and major repair service. Camping at **Camp 'n Class RV Park** (see ad in YELLOWHEAD section), phone 855-455-2299; and Lions RV Park and Campground phone 780-963-4505. [B][A]

Attractions in Stony Plain include 31 historic outdoor murals; Oppertshauser Art Gallery; and the Pioneer Museum. The Multicultural Heritage Centre here has historical archives, a craft shop and home-cooked meals.

E 14.3 (23 km) **DC 348.7** (561.1 km) Exit on Highway 779 for Stony Plain visitor centre (2 km/1.2 miles), housed in the Dog Rump Creek railway station at the Rotary Park rest area 4815–44th Ave. Open July and August 8:30 A.M. to 5:30 P.M. weekdays, 9:30 A.M. to 5:30 P.M. weekends; September and June weekdays only. Phone 780-963-4545.

E 17.3 (27.8 km) **DC 345.7** (556.2 km) Allan Beach Resort turnoff to north.

E 18 (29 km) **DC 345** (555.1 km) Turnoff for Hasse Lake Parkland County day-use area (10 km/6 miles south).

E 18.5 (29.8 km) **DC 344.5** (554.3 km) Turnoff for Hubbles Lake, 2 km/1.2 miles north; camping. Spring Lake to the south (shopping, gas). [B][A]

E 20.1 (30.3 km) **DC 342.9** (551.8 km) Beach Corner, gas, diesel, auto repair, propane, cafe, store and liquor to north. [B]

E 21.9 (35.2 km) **DC 341.1** (548.9 km)

Junction of Yellowhead Highway 16A with Highway 43 North. If you are continuing west for Prince George or Prince Rupert, BC, turn to **Milepost E 21.9** on page 231 the YELLOWHEAD HIGHWAY section for log of that route.

Northbound travelers turn onto Highway 43 and continue with this log for Dawson Creek, BC.
Southbound travelers take Exit 344, Highway 16A East for Edmonton and read log back to front.

ALBERTA HIGHWAY 43

E 27.5 (44.2 km) **DC 335.5** (539.9 km) Turnout northbound with litter barrel and historical information sign about construction of the Alaska Highway and Alberta Beach.

E 29.1 (46.8 km) **DC 333.9** (537.3 km) Race Trac gas station to east. [B]

E 33.2 (53.4 km) **DC 329.8** (530.8 km) Highway 633 west 6 miles/10 km to Alberta Beach Recreation Area on Lac Ste. Anne. Facilities include a municipal campground (94 sites), open May to September. [A]

E 35.9 (57.8 km) **DC 327.1** (526.4 km) Access to **ONOWAY** (pop. 1,021) has a medical clinic, ambulance, dentist and veterinary clinics. Other visitor services include gas, diesel, propane, 2 gas stations, banks and ATM machines, post office, library, grocery stores, liquor store, laundromat, pharmacy, restaurants, motel, hotel churches and car wash. The Onoway Museum has recently opened in the "Red Brick School" and houses the tourist information booth. Part of this expansion includes signs posted throughout the area that recognize former one-room schoolhouses.

There are 15 golf courses within a 10-minute radius of Onoway. Many local lakes provide fishing, boating, canoeing, swimming and sailing. Onoway is served by Highways 43 and 37. Highway 16 to Jasper National Park is 10 minutes away.

Camping at Imrie Park 4.3 miles/7 km east of Onoway. Fishing at Salter Lake 1.2 miles/2 km south of Onoway. [B][A]

E 36 (57.9 km) **DC 327** (526.2 km) Distance marker southbound shows Stony Plain 33 km/21 miles, Spruce Grove 38 km/24 miles, Edmonton 66 km/41 miles.

E 36.1 (58.1 km) **DC 326.9** (526.1 km) Turnouts for north- and southbound traffic with information panels regarding this area.

E 38 (61.2 km) **DC 325** (523 km) Junction with Highway 37 East to Fort Saskatchewan (43 miles/70 km).

E 38.2 (61.5 km) **DC 324.8** (522.7 km) Distance marker northbound shows Gunn 7 km/4 miles, Whitecourt 105 km/65 miles.

E 39.5 (63.6 km) **DC 323.5** (520.6 km) Sturgeon River.

E 41.6 (66.9 km) **DC 321.4** (517.2 km) Distance marker southbound shows Onoway 11 km/7 miles, Edmonton 73 km/45 miles.

E 41.9 (67.4 km) **DC 321.1** (516.7 km) Distance marker northbound shows Mayerthorpe 61 km/38 miles.

E 42 (67.6 km) **DC 321** (516.6 km) **Junction** with Highway 33 (Grizzly Trail). Continue on Highway 43 northbound for Dawson Creek.

E 42.5 (68.4 km) **DC 320.5** (515.8 km) Restaurant and gas station. Lac Ste. Anne to south; fishing. Also access to Gunn 1 km/0.6 mile, Alberta Beach 6 km/3.7 miles to the south.

E 45.1 (72.6 km) **DC 317.9** (511.6 km) Lessard Lake Campground (50 sites), County of Lac Ste. Anne, 1.9 miles/3 km south; water, showers, playground, boat launch, fishing for pike and perch.

E 54 (86.9 km) **DC 309** (497.3 km) Exit to Highway 765 South to Darwell (16 miles/26 km) and Highway 16.

E 58 (93.3 km) **DC 305** (490 km) Access to Cherhill, 1 km/0.6 mile to south at junction with Highway 764; food, gas, lodging, dining.

E 64.6 (104 km) **DC 298.4** (480.2 km) Northbound large, double ended rest area with toilets and litter barrels.

E 68.2 (109.8 km) **DC 294.8** (474.8 km) Distance marker southbound shows Cherhill 17 km/11 miles, Gunn 43 km/27 miles, Edmonton 117 km/73 miles.

E 68.6 (110.4 km) **DC 294.4** (473.8 km) Exit to Highway 757 and access to **SANGUDO** (pop. 398), located south of Highway 43 on the Pembina River. Sangudo has restaurants, motel and hotel accommodations, a B & B south of town, gas/diesel station, grocery and liquor stores, banks, post office, pharmacy, laundromat and car wash. Stop at Sangudo Visitor's Bureau for more information; open late May to early September. Camping with playground, ball diamonds, skateboard park, beach volleyball, horseshoe pits, river access and dump station at the Sports Grounds on the shores of the Pembina River.

E 68.7 (110.7 km) **DC 294.3** (473.6 km) Pembina River bridge.

E 72.9 (117.3 km) **DC 290.1** (466.9 km) Distance marker northbound shows Valleyview 226 km/140 miles, Grande Prairie 338 km/210 miles.

E 73.4 (118.1 km) **DC 289.6** (466.1 km) Northbound rest area with toilets and litter barrels.

E 73.7 (118.6 km) **DC 289.3** (465.6 km) Second longest wooden railway trestle in the world crosses highway and Paddle River. The **C.N.R. Rochfort Bridge trestle** is 2,414 feet/736m long and was originally built in 1914.

E 74.6 (120 km) **DC 288.4** (464 km) **ROCHFORT BRIDGE.** Highway rest area at Rochfort Bridge Trading Post; gift shop, restaurant, phone, camping, museum.

E 77.8 (125.2 km) **DC 285.2** (459 km)

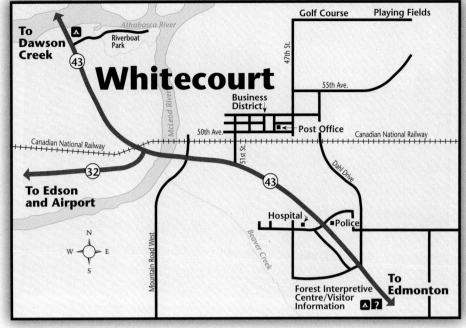

Paved turnout southbound with handicap accessible toilets and litter barrels.

E 79 (127.1 km) **DC 284** (457 km) Exit south to Highway 22 and access north to **MAYERTHORPE** (pop. 1,474). **Emergency Services:** Phone 911. **Visitor Information:** Tourist Information Booth located at the **Fallen Four Memorial Park.** Virtual tours of the town at www.mayerthorpe.ca. There are 2 hotels/motels, 6 restaurants, grocery stores, 3 gas stations, vehicle repair, laundromat, car wash, 2 liquor stores and 2 banks. Services are located on 50th Street, the main entrance to town off of Highway 43. Camping is available south of town at the golf course.

Mayerthorpe is primarily a service center for the surrounding agricultural district. Area farms raise everything from wild game (elk, buffalo, emu, wild boar) to cattle, pigs and sheep. Major lumber mills are located west of town. Oil and gas exploration is on the increase here.

Summer recreation includes swimming at the outdoor pool, canoeing on the Pembina and McLeod rivers, golfing at the 9-hole golf course, fishing and camping. Big game hunting is popular in the fall.

Curling, hockey, snowmobiling, downhill skiing, cross-country skiing and ice fishing are the major winter sports here.

E 85 (136.8 km) **DC 278** (447.4 km) Exit east to Greencourt and Highway 18 east to Barrhead (37 miles/59 km).

E 91.6 (147.4 km) **DC 271.4** (436.8 km) **Junction** with Highway 658; dining, Esso gas, diesel, convenience store.

E 93.2 (150 km) **DC 269.8** (434.2 km) Exit Highway 751 south to Nojack on Highway 16 (38 miles/61 km).

E 101 (162.5 km) **DC 262** (421.6 km) Turnout (northbound-only) with litter barrels and information boards.

E 103 (165.7 km) **DC 260** (418.3 km) **Whitecourt & District Forest Interpretive Centre & Visitor Centre.** Access to **Lions Club Campground**; 60 sites, camping fee, flush toilets, showers, water, tables, dump station, firewood and firepits.

Whitecourt

E 104 (167.4 km) **DC 259** (416.8 km). Located two hours from Edmonton. **Population:** 9,202. **Emergency Services:** For emergencies, phone 911. **Police**, phone 780-778-5454. **Fire Department,** phone 780-778-2342. **Hospital:** Whitecourt Healthcare Centre at Sunset Blvd., phone 780-778-2285. **Ambulance service** 780-778-4257.

Visitor Information: Tourist information in the **Forest Interpretive Centre** at the east end of town just off Highway 43, across from Lion's Campground. Open daily in summer, weekdays in winter; ample parking for large RVs and bus tours. Phone 780-778-3433; toll-free 1-800-313-7383; www.whitecourt.ca, www.woodlands.ab.ca.

Elevation: 2,567 feet/782m. **Radio:** 96.7 CFXW-FM, 105.3 CIXM-FM. **Television:** 57 channels. **Newspaper:** *Whitecourt Star.*

Private Aircraft: Airport 3.1 miles/5 km west of Whitecourt; elev. 2,567 feet/782m; length 5,800 feet/1,768m; paved; fuel 80, 100, jet (24-hour, self-serve). Aircraft maintenance, 24-hour flight service station, all-weather facility.

Transportation: Air—Local charter air service available; helicopter and fixed-wing aircraft. **Bus**—Greyhound provides intercommunity service.

Located at the junction of Highways 43 and 32, Whitecourt dubs itself the "Gateway to the Alaska Highway and the fabulous North." It is also known as the Snowmobile Capital of Alberta, with the Whitecourt Trailblazers Snowmobile Club grooming hundreds of miles of trails each winter. Established as a small trading, trapping and forestry centre, Whitecourt became

WHITECOURT ADVERTISERS

Stop by Whitecourt's Forest Interpretive Centre. (©Michael K. Robb)

an important stop for Alaska Highway travelers when a 106-mile section of Highway 43 connecting Whitecourt and Valleyview was completed in October 1955. This new route was 72 miles shorter than the old Edmonton to Dawson Creek route via Slave Lake.

The Whitecourt & District Forest Interpretive Centre and Heritage Park at the east end of town celebrates Alberta's forest industry with artifacts and audio-visual exhibits.

There are 16 hotels/motels, 39 restaurants and fast-food outlets (Taco Time, Boston Pizza, McDonalds, etc.), 14 gas stations, 3 laundromats, 5 malls, 6 liquor stores and 5 banks. Most services are located on the highway or 2 blocks north in the downtown business district. 5 gas stations are open 24 hours. Camping available in 3 locations including a downtown RV park and Lion's Club Campground at the southeast end of town. Carson Pegasus Provincial Park is at **Milepost E 111.1.** There are dump stations at the Husky, behind the car wash; across from the Dairy Queen at Canadian Tire and at the Forest Interpretive Centre outside of town. Private campgrounds are also available.

This full-service community also supports a library and 11 churches. Service clubs and community organizations (Masons, Knights of Columbus, Rotary) welcome visitors.

Whitecourt & District Forest Interpretive Centre & Visitor Information Centre

just off Highway 43 (across from the Lion's Campground), explores the role of the forest in the growth and development of Whitecourt. Stop by and visit the 7,300 sq. ft. facility with museum, the outdoor displays of equipment, the Interpretive Trail or pick up some helpful brochures on the area. Open daily in summer.

The **Allan & Jean Millar Centre** is an aquatic centre and fitness centre with indoor fieldhouse and track. Enjoy a respite from the summer heat with a stop at **Rotary Park,** which features a covered pavilion with picnic tables, and a popular man-made creek with a series of pools and drops that makes for excellent tubing. Stocked fishing pond here is cleared for skating in winter.

Other attractions include Eagle River Casino and an 18-hole public golf course.

Recreation includes fishing in area creeks, rivers and lakes (boat rentals at Carson–Pegasus Provincial Park). Swimming, tubing down McLeod River, in-line skating, tennis, walking trails, and river boating are also enjoyed in summer. In the fall, big game hunting is very popular.

During the winter there is ice fishing, snowmobiling and cross-country skiing on area trails, skating and curling, bowling and swimming at the indoor pool.

East Access Route Log
(continued)

E 104.1 (167.5 km) DC 258.9 (416.6 km) Private RV park.

E 104.3 (167.9 km) DC 258.7 (416.3 km) McLeod River.

E 104.4 (168 km) DC 258.6 (416.2 km) **Junction** with Highway 32 South (paved). Highway 32 leads 42 miles/68 km to junction with Yellowhead Highway 16 at **Milepost E 97.5** (see the YELLOWHEAD HIGHWAY section).

E 106.9 (172 km) DC 256.1 (412.1 km) Gas stations with diesel, both sides of highway. Tim Horton's, KFC and other dining locations near here.

E 107.2 (172.5 km) DC 255.8 (411.6 km) Turnoff to north for Sagitawah RV Park (camping) and Riverboat Park (picnicking, boat launch), both at the confluence of the McLeod and Athabasca rivers.

E 107.6 (173.1 km) DC 255.4 (410.9 km) Athabasca River bridge.

E 109.6 (176.3 km) DC 253.4 (407.7 km) Vehicle inspection station exit to left for both south and northbound traffic.

E 111.1 (178.8 km) DC 251.9 (405.3 km) **Junction** with Highway 32 North (paved) to Eric S. Huestis Demonstration Forest, provincial parks and fishing lakes (descriptions follow). The demonstration forest has 4.3 miles/7 km of self-guided trails with information signs describing forest management and forest life-cycle.

Carson–Pegasus Provincial Park, 9.3 miles/15 km north, has 182 campsites, electrical hookups, tables, flush toilets, showers, water, dump station, firewood and playground. Boat launch, boat rentals and rainbow trout fishing are available. There are 2 lakes at the park: **McLeod (Carson) Lake,** stocked with rainbow, which has a speed limit of 12 kmph for boaters; and **Little McLeod (Pegasus) Lake,** with northern pike and whitefish, electric motors and canoes only.

E 111.6 (179.6 km) DC 251.4 (404.5 km) Alberta Newsprint Co. to south.

E 116 (186.6 km) DC 247 (397.4 km) Turnout southbound with litter bins, toilets. Turnout northbound with litter barrels.

E 116.7 (187.8 km) DC 246.3 (396.4 km) Chickadee Creek.

E 129.1 (207.7 km) DC 233.9 (376.4 km) Rest area northbound, toilets, litter bins.

E 132.4 (213.1 km) DC 230.6 (371.1 km) Rainbow Creek.

E 132.9 (213.8 km) DC 230.1 (370.3 km) Two Creeks.

E 136.5 (219.6 km) DC 226.5 (364.4 km) Turnout northbound with litter bins and recycling bins.

E 137 (220.4 km) DC 226 (363.6 km) Two Creeks rest area southbound with toilets, litter bin and recycling bin.

E 144.4 (232.4 km) DC 218.6 (351.8 km) Iosegun River bridge.

E 145.5 (234.2 km) DC 217.5 (350 km) Distance marker southbound Whitecourt 65 km/40 miles.

E 145.6 (234.4 km) DC 217.4 (349.8 km) Exit to Highway 947 South to Athabasca River (12 miles/19 km) and Forestry Road to Highway 16.

E 148.2 (238.5 km) DC 214.8 (345.7 km) Turnout northbound with litter bins.

E 153 (246.2 km) DC 210 (337.9 km) Fox Creek airport.

E 153.6 (247.2 km) DC 209.4 (337 km)

Welcome to Fox Creek, northbound.

Fox Creek

E 156 (251 km) DC 207 (333.1 km) **Population**: 2,278. **Elevation**: 2,278 feet/853m. **Emergency Services**: Phone 911 for all emergency services. RCMP, phone 780-622-3740. Fire Department, 780-622-3757. Ambulance, phone 780-622-5212. **Hospital**, phone 780-622-3545.

Visitor Information: The Visitor Information Centre is at the north end of town and behind Winks gas station, open late May to Labour Day weekend; phone 780-622-2000. The centre is conveniently located on Don Nicolson Walking Trail for stretching legs and walking your dog and has a playground and covered picnic area. Fox Creek Museum, across from the visitor centre, features displays on area wildlife, industry and pioneer history. The museum is open in the summer and by appointment (780-622-3438).

Private Aircraft: Fox Creek airport, 3 miles/4.8 km south on Highway 43; elev. 2,840 feet/866m; length, 2,950 feet/899m; paved; no fuel. Unattended.

Fox Creek, a centre of oil and gas exploration and production, has all visitor facilities, including more than 330 rooms in hotels/motels, bed and breakfasts. Multiple gas stations with repair service. Grocery store, convenience stores, pharmacy, laundromats, liquor stores, restaurants and banks. Fox Creek has an outdoor pool, library and 9-hole golf course (Silver Birch Golf Club).

Camping west of town at Poplar Ridge RV Park & Campground from May to September. Camping in town at the municipal campground near the visitor centre; 26 sites, 7 with full hookups; showers, dump station; open year-round.

Fox Creek is also a popular outdoor recreation area. Two local lakes popular with residents and visitors are **Iosegun** and **Smoke lakes**, which are located within 10 miles/16 km on either side of the townsite on good gravel road, both have campgrounds with unserviced sites.

East Access Route Log

(continued)

E 159.9 (257.3 km) DC 203.1 (326.8 km) Turnout northbound with litter barrels.

E 171.8 (276.5 km) DC 191.2 (307.7 km) Rest area northbound. Toilets, litter barrels.

E 172.8 (278.1 km) DC 190.2 (306.1 km) Rest area southbound. Toilets, litter barrels.

E 179.4 (288.7 km) DC 183.6 (295.5 km) **Poplar Ridge RV Park & Campground.** See display ad this page.

E 184.5 (297 km) DC 178.5 (287.3 km) Distance marker southbound shows Fox Creek 47 km/29 miles, Whitecourt 129 km/80 miles, Edmonton 308 km/191 miles.

E 186 (299.3 km) DC 177 (284.8 km) LITTLE SMOKY (pop. 34) village. Motel, RV park, gift shop, pay phone, propane, grocery store, ice cream shop, service station and post office. Country Music Jamboree every 3rd Friday. Turnoff to north on Range Road 215Λ (0.5 km north of Little Smoky) for **Waskahigan River Provincial Recreation Area**; campground (20 sites, self-register), toilets, water pump, fishing, tables, firepits, firewood and day-use shelter.

E 186.2 (299.6 km) DC 176.8 (284.5 km) Little Smoky River bridge.

E 187.5 (301.7 km) DC 175.5 (282.4 km) Waskahigan (House) River bridge at confluence with Smoky River.

E 195.6 (314.8 km) DC 167.4 (269.4 km) Asplund Creek.

E 196.4 (316.1 km) DC 166.6 (268.1 km) Grave Creek.

E 200.7 (322.9 km) DC 162.3 (261.1 km) Turnout northbound with litter barrel.

E 202.5 (325.8 km) DC 160.5 (258.2 km) Peace pipeline storage tanks.

E 204.6 (329.2 km) DC 158.4 (254.8 km) Exit to Highway 665 East to Highway 747 (15 miles/24 km).

E 204.8 (329.5 km) DC 158.2 (254.5 km) Valleyview Riverside golf course.

E 207.2 (333.4 km) DC 155.8 (250.7 km) Valleyview & District Chamber of Commerce Visitor Information Centre has local, regional, provincial and Canada-wide travel information; pay phone, postal stamps available; souvenir gift shop with a good selection of books, including regional, Northern and local authors; picnic tables, water, handicap accessible flush toilets, dump station. Open daily 8 A.M. to 7 P.M. from May 1 to September's long weekend, and then 10 A.M. to 6 P.M. to October's long weekend

E 207.4 (333.7 km) DC 155.6 (250.4 km) Valleyview airport to west.

Private Aircraft: Valleyview airport; elev. 2,434 feet/742m; length, 3,300 feet/1,006m; paved; fuel. Unattended.

Valleyview

E 208.1 (334.8 km) DC 154.9 (249.2 km) Approximately 3 ½ hour drive time from Edmonton. **Population**: 1,884. **Emergency Services**: Phone 911 for all emergency services. RCMP, phone 780-524-3345. **Hospital**, Valleyview General, phone 780-524-3356.

Visitor Information: Major tourist information centre and rest stop located 0.9 mile/1.5 km south of Valleyview on Highway 43. Open daily, 8 A.M. to 7 P.M. from May through Labour Day weekend; phone 780-524-2410; Visitor Centre: vdcc @telus.net or Town Office at http://valleyview.govoffice.com; in winter months contact the town office at 780-524-5150 for information. The visitor centre sells postage stamps, souvenirs and refreshments, along with serving complimentary coffee. Information on regional and provincial travel and community events and services.

Elevation: 2247 feet/685m. **Newspaper**: *Valley Views* (weekly). **Transportation: Air**—Airport 0.7 mile/1.1 km south. **Bus**—Greyhound.

Valleyview, known as the "Portal to the Peace Country" of northwestern Alberta, is located at the junction of Highways 43 and 49. From Valleyview, Highway 43 continues west to Grande Prairie and Dawson Creek. Highway 49 leads north to connect with Highway 2 east to Athabasca and north to Peace River. From Peace River, travelers may follow the Mackenzie Highway 35 to Northwest Territories (see the DEH CHO ROUTE section for details).

Originally called Red Willow when it was homesteaded in 1916, Valleyview boomed with the discovery of oil and gas in the 1950s, and services grew along with the population. Today, Valleyview's economy has diversified to include the oil and gas industry, forestry, tourism, agriculture and government services. Farming consists mainly of grain, oilseed, beef cattle and forage production.

The community has a full range of ser-

Silos along Highway 43 reflect region's agriculture industry. *(©Sharon Nault)*

Grande Prairie Museum features pioneer structures like this barn. (©Michael K. Robb)

vices including banks, automatic teller machines, post office, several churches and a Public Library with Internet access (open Tuesday–Saturday). The library's Art Gallery has a terrific display of more than 900 historical photos (visitors welcome).

All visitor facilities available, including motels, hotels, several restaurants, gas stations (many with major repair service, propane, diesel and 24-hour service), laundromat, grocery, liquor stores, clothing and hardware stores, gift shops and a golf course. Valleyview municipal campground at north end of town (end of 50th Street).

The area boasts many lakes and streams, abundant wildlife, and lush vegetation, including berries. Summer travelers can take advantage of the long summer days here by attending local rodeos, fairs and festivals; playing a round of golf on one of the local golf courses; visiting one of the provincial parks along Sturgeon Lake; cooling off in the outdoor swimming pool or splash park in town; or exploring the wilderness by all-terrain vehicle, horse, canoe or hiking trail.

East Access Route Log
(continued)

E 210 (337.9 km) **DC 153** (246.2 km) **Junction.** Highways 49/2 leads north 88 miles/142 km to the scenic community of **Peace River** and to the Mackenzie Highway 35 (13 miles/21 km west of Peace River) to Northwest Territories.

> **Junction** with Highways 49/2 north to Peace River and the Mackenzie Highway 35 to Northwest Territories. Turn to the DEH CHO ROUTE for log.

A side trip loop north to Peace River then south from Grimshaw to Grande Prairie via Highways 49 and 2, gives travelers a chance to take in historic Peace River and stop at **Historic Dunvegan**. This side trip is 212 miles/341 km in length. Follow the logs in the DEH CHO ROUTE section. Continue west on Highway 43 for Dawson Creek.

E 214.5 (345.2 km) **DC 148.5** (238.8 km) Woodpecker Creek.

E 218.4 (351.5 km) **DC 144.6** (232.7 km) Access road to Sturgeon Lake (fishing and

camping) and **CALAIS** (pop. about 550); post office, fireworks, gas and diesel and grocery store.

E 218.5 (351.6 km) **DC 144.5** (232.5 km) Turnout southbound with litter barrel.

E 220.5 (354.9 km) **DC 142.5** (229.3 km) North access to **Sturgeon Lake** (fishing) and to golf course. Also, **Williamson Provincial Park** (1.2 miles/2 km); 67 campsites (some with electrical hookups), boat launch, dump station, day-use area for picnics. Fishing for perch, pickerel, northern pike, whitefish.

E 223.7 (360 km) **DC 139.3** (224.2 km) Greenview Golf Resort; golfing, dining. Camping at Cozy Cove Campground, sani-dump.

E 224.4 (361.1 km) **DC 138.6** (223 km) *New 4-lane divided highway westbound. Work continues on the twinning (creating a divided 4-lane highway) of Highway 43 to the Alberta/BC border. Watch for continued construction westbound in 2014.*

E 226 (363.6 km) **DC 137** (220.4 km) Sturgeon Heights. Turnoff for **Youngs Point Provincial Park**, 6 miles/10 km northeast; 92 campsites, day-use area boat launch, fishing in **Sturgeon Lake**.

E 228.3 (367.4 km) **DC 134.7** (216.8 km) Turnout north side of highway at top of Clarkson Hill; historic point of interest. Access to **Swan Lake**, 4 miles west, 2.5 miles south. Day-use area, campground with 6 sites, toilets and boat launch (Canfor; phone 780-538-7736). Fishing for rainbow.

E 232.2 (373.7 km) **DC 130.8** (210.5 km) Large double-ended turnout for southbound traffic; restrooms.

E 235.9 (379.6 km) **DC 127.1** (204.5 km) **CROOKED CREEK** store to south with gas, diesel, groceries and local crafts and products from the Sturgeon Lake Native Reserve. Post office.

E 241.6 (388.7 km) **DC 121.4** (195.4 km) Access to DeBolt (1 km) and junction with Highway 736. **DEBOLT** (pop. 150) is a small farming community north of highway with

a general store, gas station, pub, ice cream store in summer, post office, campground, library, golf course (par 3) and district museum.

E 242.5 (390.3 km) **DC 120.5** (193.9 km) Distance marker northbound shows Bezanson 25 km/16 miles, Grande Prairie 59 km/37 miles, Dawson Creek 188 km/117 miles.

E 248.3 (399.6 km) **DC 114.7** (184.6 km) Private RV park to north. Forestry Road leads south 96 miles/155 km to Highway 40.

E 248.6 (400.1 km) **DC 114.4** (184.1 km) Distance marker northbound shows Grande Prairie 46 km/29 miles, Dawson Creek 176 km/109 miles.

E 249.7 (401.8 km) **DC 113.3** (182.3 km) Chain on area with litter bins, both sides of highway and recycling bins.

E 252.4 (406.2 km) **DC 110.6** (178 km) Smoky River bridge.

E 255.2 (410.7 km) **DC 107.8** (173.5 km) Turnouts both sides of highway; litter barrels, chain-up areas in winter.

E 256.6 (412.9 km) **DC 106.4** (171.2 km) Exit south to **BEZANSON** (pop. 85, community of 1,200). Easy access to town. Post office, gas station with diesel, cafe, liquor store, grocery, general store, propane, municipal campground (20 sites).

E 257.7 (414.7 km) **DC 105.3** (169.5 km) Exit to Highway 670 South and Highway 733 North to Teepee Creek (7 miles/11 km) and Wanham on Highway 49 (38 miles/61 km).

E 263 (423.2 km) **DC 100** (160.9 km) Kleskun Hills Park to north 3 miles/5 km (gravel). The park features an ancient sea bottom with fossils of dinosaurs and marine life, a native burial ground, walking trails, and 9 unserviced campsites here (tap water, washrooms). Also, the preserved buildings of the Heritage Village Historic Site.

E 263.3 (423.7 km) **DC 99.7** (160.5 km) Turnout to north with litter bins, recycling and historical sign about Alberta's Kleskun Hills.

E 267.9 (431.1 km) **DC 95.1** (153 km) Turnout northbound only with litter bins, recycling bins and history sign about Grande Prairie.

E 273.9 (440.8) **DC 89.1** (143.4 km) Exit Highway 2 North to Peace River and Dunvegan (57 miles/91 km), a historic Hudson's Bay Co. post, and Grimshaw (108 miles/174 km), Mile Zero of the Mackenzie Highway, part of the Deh Cho Route to the Alaska Highway via Northwest Territories.

E 274.2 (441.3 km) **DC 88.8** (142.9 km) *IMPORTANT: Westbound traffic can take city centre exit or continue straight for bypass. The bypass continues about 2 miles west from this intersection, then signage will demonstrate necessary detour south into city. For access to* **Country Roads RV Park** *for westbound travelers, reduce speed and continue straight ahead.*

> **Junction** with Highway 2 to Grimshaw and the Mackenzie Highway to Northwest Territories. See the DEH CHO ROUTE for log.

Travelers bound for the Deh Cho Route via Grimshaw should exit north onto Highway 2 from here. A side trip loop north to Grimshaw then south from Peace River

to Valleyview via Highways 2 and 49, gives travelers a chance to take in historic Dunvegan and Peace River. This side trip is 212 miles/341 km in length. Follow the logs in the DEH CHO ROUTE section.

Grande Prairie

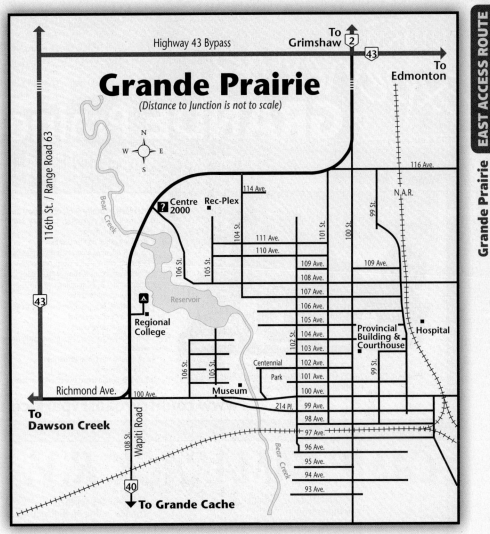

Grande Prairie
(Distance to Junction is not to scale)

E 277 (445.8 km) DC 86 (138.4 km). Located at the junction of Highways 43 and 2 on east and 40 and 43 on the west. **Population**: 55,000. **Emergency Services**: RCMP, phone 780-830-5700. **Fire Department**, phone 911. Ambulance, phone 780-532-4441. **Hospital**, Queen Elizabeth II, 10409 98th St., phone 780-538-7100.

Visitor Information: In the Centre 2000 building, just off of the Highway 43 bypass at 106th Street. The Centre is an excellent information stop with staffed counter and reference materials. **Heritage Discovery Centre** on the lower level of Centre 2000 has interactive displays and movies depicting the area's history from prehistoric to modern day. Piper, the animatronics dinosaur, galleries, movies and hands-on exhibits round out this part of the Centre. There is plenty of parking and sani-dump on the south side of the centre at the Bear Creek Reservoir. The Centre is open 8:30 A.M. to 7 P.M., May to September; 8:30 A.M. to 4:30 P.M. the rest of the year. Phone 780-539-7688 or toll-free 1-866-202-2202. www.gptourism.ca.

Grande Prairie Regional Tourism Association hosts a free Meat & Greet BBQ in summer on Wednesdays from 4–6 P.M. Also check with the visitor centre about free Rotary Club bus tours of the city and industrial area on Mondays, Tuesdays and Thursdays at 7 P.M. from June through August.

Private Aircraft: Airport 3 miles/4.8 km west; elev. 2,195 feet/669m; length 6,500 feet/1,981m; paved; fuel 80, 100, jet. 24-hour flight service station.

Elevation: 2,198 feet/670m. **Transportation**: Air—Scheduled air service to Vancouver, BC, Edmonton, Calgary, and points north. **Bus**—Greyhound. **Newspaper**—Daily Herald Tribune. **Radio**—93.1 Big Country-FM, Rock 97.0, 97.7 SUN-FM, 98.9 Q 99, 103.4 Free FM, 96.3 Shine FM.

Grande Prairie was first incorporated as a village in 1911, as a town in 1919, and as a city in 1958.

The city is booming today, with a strong and diverse economy based on agriculture (canola, cereal grains, fescue, honey, livestock), forestry (a bleached kraft pulp mill, sawmill and oriented strand board plant), and oil and gas. Grande Prairie is a regional centre for much of northwestern Alberta and northeastern British Columbia. The trumpeter swan is the symbol of Grande Prairie and is featured throughout the city.

Lodging & Services

Grande Prairie has all visitor facilities including major chain motels/hotels (Sandman, Service Plus Inns & Suites, Quality Hotel), B&B's, restaurants and fast food outlets, Starbucks, and "big box" stores like Walmart and Costco. The Prairie Mall has over 90 stores and a 650-seat food court. There are more than 400 shops and businesses in the downtown core.

Recreation facilities include the Eastlink Centre, one of the largest aquatic, fit-

ness and adventure facilities in Canada; 18-hole, 9-hole and par 3 golf courses; disc golf course; indoor/outdoor soccer; twin ice arenas; gymnastic facility; curling rink; amusement parks; tennis courts; a public library; and both public and private art galleries. The Nitehawk Ski Hill is a multipurpose recreational area and year round RV Park.

Churches representing almost every denomination are located in Grande Prairie. There are several public schools and a regional college.

Camping

Camping at Rotary Park (59 sites), located on Highway 43; turn into the Regional College (this distinctive structure was designed by Douglas Cardinal) then make an immediate left turn.

Private campgrounds include: **Country Roads R.V. Park** (115 sites), which has an 8-acre cornfield maze and is located near the junction of Highways 43 and 2; **Camp Tamarack RV Park** (89 sites), located 5 miles/8.5 km south of Grande Prairie on Highway 40; and **Nitehawk Wilderness RV Park**, also south of Grande Prairie on Highway 40, overlooking the Wapiti River.

Attractions

Area attractions include **Muskoseepi Park**, which follows the Bear Creek corridor. The park has 17.4 miles/28 km of trails for walking and biking; a bird sanctuary at

Crystal Lake; picnic areas; swimming pool; lawn bowling; mini-golf; and a stocked fishing pond and playground for children. The Grande Prairie Museum is in Muskoseepi Park, across Bear Creek from Centennial Park, and features a Heritage Village.

The paved trail—popular with walkers, joggers, skaters and bicyclists—circles the reservoir and follows Bear Creek. You can access the trail from the Rotary Park campground.

Annual events include the Stompede, a major rodeo held the first weekend in June; Canada Day celebrations on July 1; street performers festival and jet boat racing in July. There are also smaller rodeos, Highland Games, pari-mutuel racing, a Street Performers Festival and many other events. For a complete list of events visit Grande Prairie Regional Tourism's website at www.gptourism.ca or email info@gptourism.ca.

GRANDE PRAIRIE ADVERTISERS

Camp Tamarack RV Park .... Ph. 780-532-9998
Country Roads RV Park .... Ph. 780-532-6323
GP Museum .... Ph. 780-532-5482
Grande Prairie Regional
  Tourism Assoc. .... Ph. 1-866-202-2202
Heritage Discovery Centre .... Ph. 780-532-5790
Nitehawk Wilderness
  RV Park .... Ph. 780-532-6637

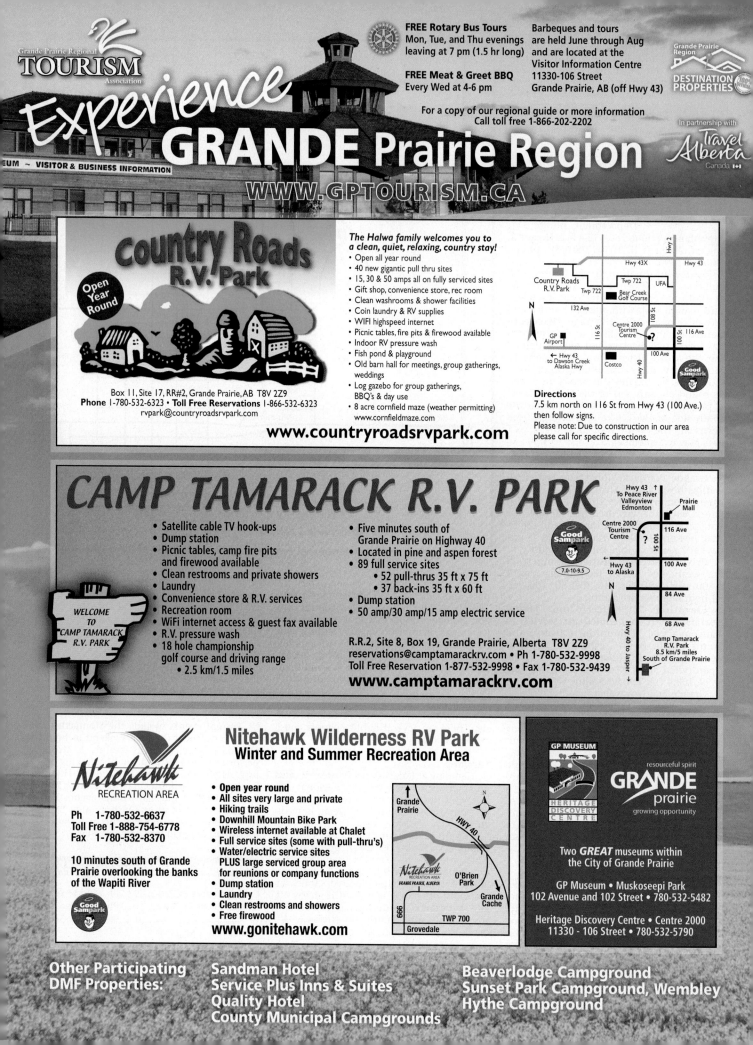

East Access Route Log

(continued)

E 281 (452.1 km) **DC 82** (131.9 km) **Junction** of Highway 43 Bypass (116th Ave./43W). Gateway Shopping Center, Westend Plaza; all services. Bighorn Highway 40 connects Grande Prairie with Grande Cache (114 miles/184 km) and Yellowhead Highway 16 (202 miles/325 km). Access south to **Camp Tamarack RV Park**. If you are headed south on the Bighorn Route, fuel up in Grande Prairie, because there is no gas until Grande Cache. **Nitehawk Wilderness RV Park** is along this route.

> **Junction** with Highway 40 South. Turn to end of "Bighorn Route" log on page 237 in the YELLOWHEAD HIGHWAY section and read log back to front.

E 282.7 (454.9 km) **DC 80.3** (129.2 km) Distance marker northbound shows Wembley 19 km/12 miles, Beaverlodge 39 km/24 miles, Hythe 54 km/34 miles, Dawson Creek 127 km/79 miles.

E 284 (457 km) **DC 79** (127.1 km) Grande Prairie city limit.

E 288.6 (464.5 km) **DC 76.4** (122.9 km) Legion Park campground to north.

E 292 (469.8 km) **DC 71** (114.2 km) **Saskatoon Island Provincial Park** is 2.5 miles/4 km north on park road; 103 campsites, dump station, boat launch, swimming, playground. Saskatoon berry picking in July. This park is a game preserve for trumpeter swans. A Swan Festival is held here the last weekend in April; phone 780-766-2636 for more information.

E 292.7 (471.1 km) **DC 70.3** (113.1 km) South access to town of Wembley and private golf course and campground.

E 293.5 (472.3 km) **DC 69.5** (111.8 km) Exit north to Highway 724 to La Glace on Highway 59 (17 miles/28 km) and exit south for **WEMBLEY** (pop. 1,443) with 1 hotel, 2 liquor stores (1 at hotel), bank, post office, grocery store, gas stop (with diesel), car wash and restaurants. There are 3 area churches and 2 schools. A recreation complex has a fitness centre with a hockey rink. There are tennis courts and a skateboard park. The library (in the Helen E. Taylor School) has 2 public-use computers with internet available. For more information, visit www.wembley.ca.

Sunset Park Campground in town has a dump station and picnicking. Camping May 1 to Oct. 15 at Pipestone Creek County Park, 9 miles/14.5 km south; 99 sites, showers, flush toilets, dump station, boat launch, firewood, fishing, playground with children's water park, fossil display and an 18-hole golf course with grass greens nearby. Bird watching is good here for red-winged blackbirds and yellow-headed blackbirds.

E 294 (473 km) **DC 69** (111 km) Distance marker northbound shows Hythe 34 km/21 miles, Dawson Creek 108 km/67 miles.

E 298.6 (480.5 km) **DC 64.4** (103.6 km) Access south to Huallen.

E 300.4 (483.4 km) **DC 62.6** (100.7 km) Saskatoon Mountain Recreation Area to the north.

E 302.1 (486.2 km) **DC 60.9** (98 km) *End divided 4-lane highway, begin 2-lane undivided highway, westbound.*
   CAUTION: Watch for deer.

E 303.1 (487.8 km) **DC 59.9** (96.4 km) Exit to Highway 723 North to Valhalla Centre and Highway 59 (16 miles/25 km).

Beaverlodge

E 305.5 (491.5 km) **DC 57.5** (92.5 km) Welcome to Beaverlodge (northbound sign). **Population:** 2,264. **Elevation:** 2,264feet/737m. **Emergency Services:** RCMP, phone 911. **Ambulance,** phone 911. **Hospital,** Beaverlodge Municipal Hospital, phone 780-354-2136. Medical and dental clinic.

Visitor Information: Located in the Beaverlodge and Area Cultural Centre on the east side of Highway 43 at the east end of town next to the giant beaver statue. For more information, visit www.beaverlodge.ca.

Private Aircraft: DeWit Airpark 2 miles/3.2 km south; elev. 2,289 feet/1,698m; length 3,000 feet/914m; paved; no fuel. The Beaverlodge airport is a popular stopover on the flying route to Alaska.

Home to Canada's most northerly Agricultural Research Station (open to the public), Beaverlodge serves as regional centre for grain transportation, seed cleaning and seed production. Cereal grains, such as wheat, barley and oats, are the main crops in the area. The PRT Alberta Inc., visible from the highway as you enter town, is a reforestation nursery, growing about 11 million seedlings a year.

Visitor services include 3 motels, 7 restaurants and 3 gas stations. There are 2 supermarkets, 2 banks, a drugstore, post office, veterinary clinic, pharmacy, car wash and sporting goods store. Camping is available at the Pioneer Campground (see **Milepost E 306.6**) at the west end of town (19 sites).

Beaverlodge Area Cultural Centre, featuring local arts and crafts and a tea room, is located on Highway 43 in town. It is hard to miss the cultural centre, thanks to a 15–foot/4.6–metre–high beaver perched on a 19–foot/6m log out in front.

East Access Route Log

(continued)

E 306.6 (493.3 km) **DC 56.4** (90.7 km) Pioneer Municipal Campground on the northeast side of Highway 43 has 19 sites (10 full-service), showers, dump station and electrical hookups. Phone 780-354-2201. Nice grassy, treed area; pioneer buildings.

E 307 (494 km) **DC 56** (90.1 km) Distance marker northbound shows Hythe 13 km/8 miles, Dawson Creek 89 km/55 miles.

E 307.7 (495.2 km) **DC 55.3** (89 km) Welcome to Beaverlodge, southbound.

E 308 (495.6 km) **DC 55** (88.5 km) **South Peace Centennial Museum** to east, 40-acre pioneer village, open daily in summer; phone 780-354-8869. Well worth a stop, the South Peace Centennial Museum features vintage vehicles and working steam-powered farm equipment from the early 1900s. Open daily 10 A.M. to 6 P.M., mid–May to early September. Admission charged. The annual Pioneer Day celebration, held here the third Sunday in July, attracts several thousand visitors. Website: www.spcm.ca. Camping for $10 per night (self-contained only).

E 310.4 (499.4 km) **DC 52.6** (84.6 km)

Farmers Market to the north, held Thursdays in summer from noon to 3 P.M. Also River Bend Golf & Country Club; the clubhouse is a retired NAR station.

E 311 (500.4 km) **DC 52** (83.6 km) Exit to Highway 671 West to Goodfare (8 miles/13 km).

Distance marker westbound shows BC Border 17 miles/28 km.

E 312 (502.1 km) **DC 51** (82.1 km) Hommy county park to west; camping with RV power, pump water, pit toilets ($20) and picnicking.

E 315.2 (507.3 km) **DC 47.8** (76.9 km) Exit to Highway 672 west to Lymburn (10 miles/16 km) and east to Highway 2 to Sexsmith.

E 316 (508.4 km) **DC 47** (75.6 km) **HYTHE** (pop. 820). **Visitor Information:** Hythe Historical Information Centre, located in an old 1910 tack shop, staffed by volunteers and 1 full-time staffer in summer; visit their website at www.hythe.ca. Hythe is an agricultural service community and processing center for fruit and berry crops, especially Saskatoon berries. Canola is also a major crop.

The town has a motel, 2 restaurants, laundromat, Esso and Husky stations, tire repair, car wash and shopping. Hythe Campground on west side of town.

E 316.5 (509.2 km) **DC 46.5** (74.8 km) Hythe Municipal Campground; 24 sites, (20 have power) showers, drinking water, dump station and playground. 2 group shelters. It has a former NAR (Northern Alberta Railroad) car on display. Camping fee is $20 per night, includes firewood.

E 316.6 (509.4 km) **DC 46.4** (74.7 km) Turnoff for Spring Lake Recreation Area. Camping.

E 317 (510.1 km) **DC 46** (74 km) Welcome to Hythe (southbound sign).

E 324 (521.3 km) **DC 39** (62.8 km) Exit to Highway 59 east to Sexsmith on Highway 2 (39 miles/63 km).

Distance marker northbound shows Demmitt 13 km/8 miles, Pouce Coupe 52 km/32 miles, Dawson Creek 62 km/38 miles.

E 332 (534.2 km) **DC 31** (49.9 km) Turnoff to west for **Demmitt**, an older settlement with post office, cafe and gas. Camping at Demmitt County Park just north of the city on Highway 43.

E 334.2 (537.8 km) **DC 28.8** (46.3 km) Camping at Demmitt Provincial Recreation Area on Highway 43. Picnic tables, group shelter, toilets. $10 per vehicle/night.

E 334.4 (538.6 km) **DC 28.6** (46 km) Weigh station to west.

E 335 (539.1 km) **DC 28** (45.1 km) Fas–Gas gas, diesel, convenience store.

E 336.2 (541.1 km) **DC 26.8** (43.1 km) **Alberta–British Columbia border.** Long northbound turnout with litter barrels.

TIME ZONE CHANGE: Alberta is on Mountain time. Most of British Columbia is on Pacific time. Both observe daylight savings time from March to November. Exceptions in BC are the Alaska Highway communities of Dawson Creek, Charlie Lake, Taylor and Fort St. John, which are on Mountain time in winter and Pacific time in summer.

Heritage Highway 52 South

Heritage Highway 52 South (paved with approximately 23 miles of gravel) leads 91 miles/146 km to Tumbler Ridge townsite and provides access to Monkman Provincial Park, site of spectacular Kinuseo Falls. There are no services available along the road until Tumbler Ridge.

The speed limit is 80 kmph/50 mph. Many gravel roads intersect this road, most of which are oil production pumping stations for companies such as ConocoPhillips.

The Heritage Highway loops north to connect with Highway 97.

Distance from Highway 43 junction at Milepost E 338 (J) is shown.

HIGHWAY 52 SOUTH

J 0.1 (0.2 k) Distance marker shows Tumbler Ridge 145 km/90 miles. Posted speed limit is 80 kmph/50 mph.

J 6 (9.7 km) *CAUTION: Narrow bridge and dangerous curves.*

J 6.2 (10 km) **One Island Lake Provincial Park**; 30 campsites, camping fee, picnicking, open May–September, trout fishing, boating.

J 7.4 (12 km) *CAUTION: Winding road and 7 percent downgrade southbound.*

J 7.9 (12.7 km) Narrow bridge.

J 8.5 (13.7 km) Watch for domestic buffalo grazing in adjacent pasture lands.

J 15.1 (24.3 km) Gravel turnout to west.

J 18.1 (29.1 km) Distance marker southbound shows Tumbler Ridge 116 km/72 miles.

J 20.3 (32.7 km) Kelly Lake Road.

J 23.4 (37.6 km) Foot Lake Provincial Park, 19 km/11.8 miles to the west; camping for RV and tent; fishing.

J 27.5 (44.2 km) Bridge over unnamed creek.

J 30.7 (49.4 km) *CAUTION: Gravel road with unexpected breaks from here to Mile 60.*

J 39.5 (63.6 km) *CAUTION: 6 percent downgrade southbound (short but steep).*

J 40.8 (65.6 km) Thunder Creek Campground to west 0.8 mile/1.3 km; fishing, tent and RV campsites.

J 42.3 (68.1 km) Bridge over unnamed creek.

J 42.8 (68.9 km) Redwillow River recreation area to east; picnic tables, camping and fishing.

J 44.3 (71.3 km) Red Willow Industrial Lodge for oil workers.

J 53.4 (85.9 km) Rat Lake road to east.

J 58 (93.3 km) Stony Lake to east 1 mile/1.6 km. Distance marker southbound shows Tumbler Ridge 55 km/34 miles.

J 64 (103 km) Rough road with breaks and frost heaves next 2 miles.

J 66 (106.2 km) Beaver dam in pond.

J 67 (107.8 km) Gas processing plant.

J 67.6 (108.8 km) Very large paved turnout.

J 68.9 (110.8 km) Turnout to west.

J 69.2 (111.4 km) *CAUTION: Slow for winding road and 6 to 8 percent downgrades next 2.5 miles/4 km southbound.*

J 70.3 (113.1 km) Flatbed Creek Recreation Site; camping, picnic tables.

J 70.4 (113.3 km) Flatbed Creek.

J 75.8 (122 km) Small gravel turnout to west.

J 77.8 (125.2 km) Entering Tumbler Ridge District.

J 77.9 (125.4 km) Gravel turnouts to east with river views.

J 81.3 (130.8 km) Gravel turnout to west.

J 82.2 (132.3 km) Airport to west.

J 82.7 (133.1 km) Signed turnoff for Quinette Company and for **Monkman Provincial Park** (to east); hiking, camping, $16 fee, free firewood. Spectacular **Kinuseo Falls** in Monkman Provincial Park is located 35 miles/56 km southwest; the first 3 miles/4.8 km are paved, the remainder is gravel.

J 83.7 (134.7 km) Peace River coal haulout to east.

J 85.6 (137.8 km) *CAUTION: 8 percent downgrade next 1.2 miles/2 km southbound, trucks use lower gears.*

J 89.8 (144.5 km) **Junction** with Highway 52 North, which leads north 60 miles/96 km to junction with Highway 97 12 miles/19 km west of Dawson Creek.

Junction with Highway 52 North. Turn to page 123 in the West Access for continuation of Heritage Highway 52 loop north to Highway 97.

J 90.3 (145.3 km) Turnout with litter barrel at Flathead Falls Regional Park.

J 90.4 (145.5 km) Welcome to Tumbler Ridge sign; information boards.

J 91.3 (146.9 km) **Tumbler Ridge** town centre. See description of Tumbler Ridge on page 123 in the WEST ACCESS ROUTE.

BC HIGHWAY 2 NORTH

E 336.8 (542 km) **DC 26.2** (42.2 km) *Road widening underway next 3.6 miles/6 km westbound in 2013. Expect continued construction or improved highway in summer 2014.*

E 337.5 (543.2 km) **DC 25.5** (40 km) **Junction** with Heritage Highway 52, which leads 91 miles/146 km southwest from Highway 2 to Tumbler Ridge townsite and access to Monkman Provincial Park, site of spectacular Kinuseo Falls. Heritage Highway 52 loops north 59.6 miles/96 km from Tumbler Ridge to join Highway 97 just west of Dawson Creek. (For description of Tumbler Ridge and log of Highway 52 loop north, see pages 122-123 in the WEST ACCESS ROUTE section.)

Junction with Heritage Highway 52 South to Tumbler Ridge. See log above this page.

Distance marker northbound shows Dawson Creek 37 km/23 miles, Fort St. John 112 km/70 miles, Chetwynd 137 km/85 miles.

E 338.7 (545 km) **DC 24.3** (39.1 km) Tupper Creek bridge.

E 340 (547.1 km) **DC 23** (37 km) Tupper Creek (unincorporated).

E 341.7 (549.8 km) **DC 21.3** (34.3 km) Tomslake (unincorporated).

E 342.3 (550.8 km) **DC 20.7** (33.3 km) **Swan Lake Provincial Park**, 2.5 miles/4 km northeast, open May–October; 42 campsites, pit toilets, picnic area, baseball diamonds, playground and boat launch. **Sudeten Heritage Park**, turnoff to southwest; 14 campsites, picnic tables, open May–October. Plaque tells of immigration to this valley of displaced residents of Sudetenland in 1938–39.

E 343.3 (552.4 km) **DC 19.7** (31.7 km) Tate Creek bridge.

E 347.8 (559.7 km) **DC 15.2** (24.5 km) Double ended turnout to east at Swan Lake.

E 350.6 (564.1 km) **DC 12.4** (20 km) Turnout to east with litter barrel and information boards on Pouce Coupe.

E 354 (569.6 km) **DC 9** (14.5 km) Weigh scales to east.

E 354.5 (570.4 km) **DC 8.5** (13.7 km) Bissette Creek bridge. **Pouce Coupe Regional Park** east at south end of bridge. Very nice, very large, grassy picnic area with tables. Campsites on loop road. Camping fee is $13, $18 with power. Pets on leash. Gates locked 11 P.M. to 7 A.M.

Slow for 30 kmph/18 mph speed zone northbound as highway winds through Pouce Coupe.

E 355 (571.2 km) **DC 8** (12.9 km) **POUCE COUPE** (pop. 741; elev. 2,118 feet/646m). **Visitor Information:** Tourist Bureau Office located in Pouce Coupe Museum, 5006 49th Ave. (1 block south of Highway 2). Open 8 A.M. to 5 P.M., May to August. Phone 250-786-5555. Historical artifacts are displayed at the **Pouce Coupe Museum**, located in the old NAR railroad station.

The Pouce Coupe area was first settled in 1898 by a French Canadian, Hector Tremblay, who set up a trading post in 1908. The Edson Trail, completed in 1911, brought in the main influx of settlers from Edmonton in 1912.

The village has a motel, hotel, restaurant, post office, gas station, car wash, municipal office, library, schools and food store. Camping and picnicking at Pouce Coupe Regional Park south of town.

E 356 (572.8 km) **DC 7** (11.3 km) Distance marker northbound shows Dawson Creek 10 km/6 miles, Fort St. John 85 km/53 miles, Prince George 422 km/262 miles.

E 358.5 (576.8 km) **DC 4.5** (7.2 km) Dawson Creek airport.

E 359.6 (578.6 km) **DC 3.4** (5.5 km) Distance marker southbound shows Pouce Coupe 8 km/5 miles, Grande Prairie 130 km/81 miles, Edmonton 608 km/378 miles.

E 361 (580.8 km) **DC 2** (3.2 km) Dawson Mall.

E 361.5 (581.7 km) **DC 1.5** (2.4 km) **Junction** of Highways 2, 97 and 49. This is a busy roundabout: *Drive carefully.*

E 361.6 (581.8 km) **DC 1.4** (2.3 km) Mile "0" monument at 10th Street in downtown Dawson Creek.

E 363 (584.1 km) **DC 0 Junction** with Highway 97 South (Hart Highway).

Turn to page 132 in the ALASKA HIGHWAY section for description of Dawson Creek and log of the Alaska Highway (Highway 97 North). Turn to page 119 at the end of the WEST ACCESS ROUTE and read log back to front for log of Highway 97 South to Prince George.

Central Access Route

CONNECTS: I-90 Junction, WA, to Yellowhead Hwy. 16 Jct., BC

Length: 596 miles   **Road Surface: Paved**   **Season: Open all year**

(See map, page 78)

97 5

Helmcken Falls in Wells Gray Provincial Park. (©Michael K. Robb)

Major Attractions:

©Kris Valencia, staff

Historic O'Keefe Ranch, Wells Gray Provincial Park, The Okanagan

The Central Access Route extends from Ellensburg, WA, on Interstate 90 (106 miles east of Seattle) through northcentral Washington and southcentral British Columbia to junction with Yellowhead Highway 16, a distance of 596.4 miles/959.8 km. This is a mostly 2-lane road through towns, vineyards, orchards, and pine-scented hills, past beautiful lakes offering swimming, beaches and picturesque venues for other water sports. *Watch for deer along this route.*

From Tete Jaune Cache, travelers have 2 choices to reach Dawson Creek and the start of the Alaska Highway. One way is west on Yellowhead Highway 16 to Prince George, then north on Highway 97 to Dawson Creek, a distance of 416 miles/669 km. The other choice is to drive east on Yellowhead Highway 16 through the northern edge of Jasper National Park to Hinton, then take the Bighorn Route north to Grande Prairie (this turnoff is about 5 miles west of Hinton), then Highways 43/2 to Dawson Creek, for a total driving distance of 390 miles/628 km.

The multi-lane Coquihalla Highway between Hope and Kamloops is logged as a side road in this section. Central Access Route travelers can catch the Coquihalla at Kamloops or west from Highway 97 south of Kelowna via Highway 97C (the Okana-

Distance in miles	Clearwater	Ellensburg	Kamloops	Kelowna	Osoyoos	Vernon	Yellowhead 16
Clearwater		462	76	181	258	148	135
Ellensburg	462		386	281	204	314	596
Kamloops	76	386		105	182	72	210
Kelowna	181	281	105		77	33	315
Osoyoos	258	204	182	77		110	392
Vernon	148	314	72	33	110		282
Yellowhead 16	135	596	210	315	392	282	

gan Connector). Beginning near sea level at the confluence of the Coquihalla and Fraser rivers at Hope, it rises 70 miles/112 km up the Coquihalla River and Boston Bar Creek valleys, then drops down the Coldwater River drainage to the town of Merritt. From Merritt, it climbs to the Nicola Plateau

Central Access Route

Ellensburg, WA, to Yellowhead Hwy 16 Junction, BC (includes Coquihalla Highway)

© 2014 The MILEPOST®

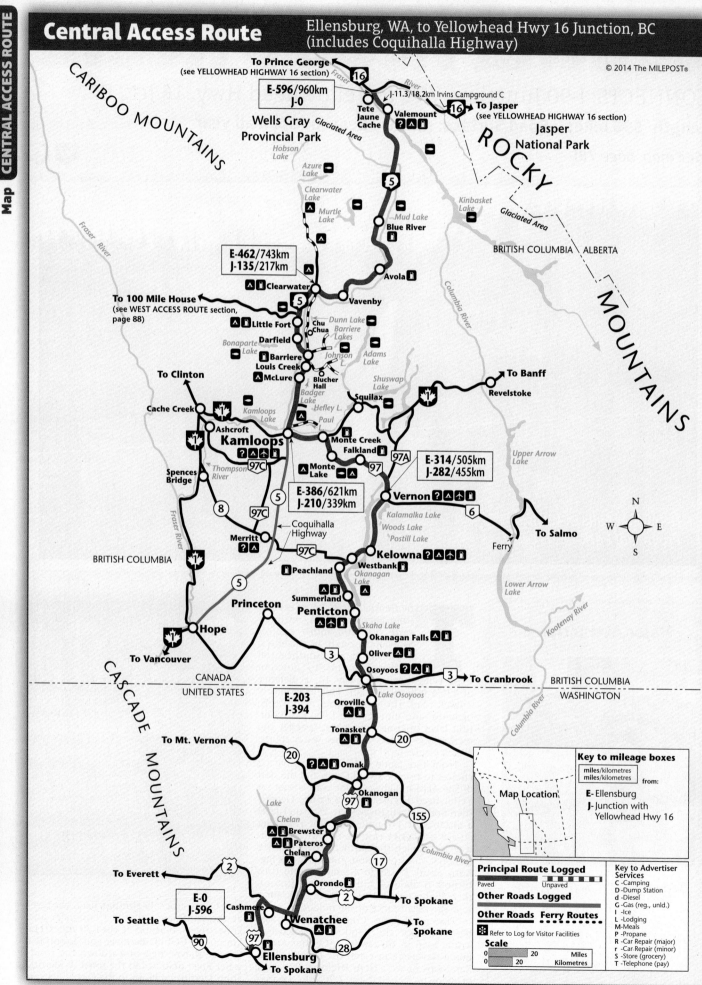

To Prince George
(see YELLOWHEAD HIGHWAY 16 section)

E-596/960km
J-0

J-11.3/18.2km Irvins Campground C

To Jasper
(see YELLOWHEAD HIGHWAY 16 section)

CARIBOO MOUNTAINS

Wells Gray Provincial Park

Tete Jaune Cache
Valemount
Glaciated Area
Hobson Lake

ROCKY

Jasper National Park

MOUNTAINS

Azure Lake
Clearwater Lake
Murtle Lake
Blue River
Mud Lake

Kinbasket Lake
Glaciated Area

BRITISH COLUMBIA | ALBERTA

E-462/743km
J-135/217km

Avola

Columbia River

To 100 Mile House
(see WEST ACCESS ROUTE section, page 88)

Clearwater
Vavenby
Little Fort
Chu Chua
Dunn Lake
Barriere Lakes
Darfield
Bonaparte Lake
Barriere
Louis Creek
Johnson L.
Adams Lake
McLure
Blucher Hall
Badger Lake
Shuswap Lake
Hefley L.
Squilax

To Banff
Revelstoke

To Clinton

Cache Creek
Ashcroft
Kamloops
97C
Kamloops Lake
Paul
Monte Creek
Falkland
97
97A

Upper Arrow Lake

E-314/505km
J-282/455km

Spences Bridge
Thompson River
Monte Lake
8
97C
5
E-386/621km
J-210/339km
Vernon
6
Kalamalka Lake
Woods Lake
Postill Lake

To Salmo

Ferry

Coquihalla Highway

Merritt
97C

BRITISH COLUMBIA

5

Kelowna
Westbank
Okanagan Lake

Lower Arrow Lake

Kootenay River

Peachland
Summerland
Penticton
Skaha Lake

Princeton

Hope

3

Okanagan Falls
Oliver
Osoyoos
3
To Cranbrook
BRITISH COLUMBIA | WASHINGTON

To Vancouver

CANADA
UNITED STATES

CASCADE

Lake Osoyoos

Columbia River

E-203
J-394

Oroville

To Mt. Vernon

Tonasket

20

20
Omak

MOUNTAINS

97
Okanogan

155

Lake Chelan

17

Brewster
Pateros
Chelan

Columbia River

To Everett

2

Orondo

To Spokane

E-0
J-596

Cashmere

2

To Seattle

90
97
Wenatchee

28

To Spokane

Ellensburg
To Spokane

Key to mileage boxes

miles/kilometres
miles/kilometres

Map Location

from:

E- Ellensburg
J- Junction with Yellowhead Hwy 16

Principal Route Logged

Paved | Unpaved

Other Roads Logged

Other Roads | Ferry Routes

⊠ Refer to Log for Visitor Facilities

Key to Advertiser Services

C -Camping
D -Dump Station
d -Diesel
G -Gas (reg., unld.)
I -Ice
L -Lodging
M -Meals
P -Propane
R -Car Repair (major)
r -Car Repair (minor)
S -Store (grocery)
T -Telephone (pay)

Scale

0   20   Miles
0   20   Kilometres

N
W — E
S

www.themilepost.com

before dropping into the Thompson River Valley at Kamloops.

Central Access Route Log

Distance from I-90 junction at Ellensburg (E) is followed by milepost (MP) and distance from Yellowhead Highway 16 junction (J). *Physical mileposts on most of U.S. Highway 97 in Washington reflect distance from Washington–Oregon border.*

U.S. HIGHWAY 97 NORTH

E 0 MP 134 J 596.4 **Junction** of Interstate 90 and Highway 97 North at Exit 106 on I-90. Food, gas/diesel and lodging north off exit (see next entry). Access via 4-mile Business Loop—or use Exit 109 off I-90 for more direct access—to **ELLENSBURG** (pop. 18,174); all services. Ellensburg is home to Central Washington University. The historic downtown is well worth a stop. The annual Ellensburg Rodeo and Kittitas County Fair is held Labor Day weekend.

Frequent turnouts along this initial stretch—not all are mentioned for space.

E 0.1 MP 134.1 J 596.3 Stop sign. Food (Subway, ihop, Perkins), gas (Chevron, Conoco), lodging (Hampton Inn) and truck/RV wash are found here.

Turn left (north) for Highway 97 North. *NOTE: Highway 97 makes a few of these sharp turns the next 15 miles northbound, so watch for 97N signs.*

E 1.3 MP 135.3 J 595.1 Four-way stop. Turn left northbound for Highway 97 North (or right, southbound).

E 2.6 MP 136.6 J 593.8 Turn right northbound for Highway 97 North (or left southbound).

E 2.8 MP 136.8 J 593.6 Distance marker northbound shows Wenatchee 66 miles.

Good 2-lane road northbound with easy curves and grades.

E 8 MP 142 J 588.4 Wind turbines visible on slopes to east belong to Puget Sound Energy's Wild Horse Wind and Solar Facility (Kittitas County), one of the utility's 3 wind farms in the state. This facility's 149 turbines, spanning 10,000 acres, can generate up to 273 megawatts of electricity, enough to serve more than 80,000 homes. Wild Horse came on line in December 2006, and was expanded in 2009.

E 12.2 MP 146.2 J 584.2 Turn right northbound for continuation of Highway 97 North (continue straight ahead for Cle Elum).

E 13 MP 147 J 583.4 Highway 97 northbound leaves the sagebrush flatlands and heads into the pine-scented foothills of the Cascade mountains.

E 15.8 MP 149.8 J 580.6 Stop sign: Turn right for continuation of Highway 97N.

Watch for deer next 30 miles northbound.

E 16.2 MP 150.2 J 580.2 First Creek

E 16.3 MP 150.3 J 580.1 Distance marker northbound shows Wenatchee 53 miles.

E 17.3 MP 151.3 J 579.1 Liberty Cafe.

E 18.8 MP 152.8 J 577.6 **Junction** with Liberty Road which leads east 2 miles to Historic Townsite of Liberty.

Entering Wenatchee National Forest northbound.

E 19.3 MP 153.3 E 577.1 Turnout to west.

E 20.4 MP 154.4 E 576 Begin 0.4 mile passing lane northbound.

E 22.3 MP 156.3 J 574.1 Mineral Springs restaurant to east. Turnoff for Government Mineral Springs Recreation Area U.S. Forest Service campground with 5 sites to west, camping fee $5 per night. Pay phone.

Mule deer and elk are frequently spotted from Highway 97 and there is a wildlife viewing area.

E 22.6 MP 156.6 J 573.8 Turnout.

E 23.6 MP 157.6 J 572.8 Parking east side of road

E 24.8 MP 158.8 J 571.6 Turnout to west.

E 25.3 MP 159.3 J 571.1 Old Blewett Road. Not recommended for vehicles.

E 25.8 MP 159.8 J 570.6 Turnoff to east for Swauk USFS Campground; 22 campsites.

E 26.6 MP 160.6 J 569.8 Large turnout to east for slow vehicles.

E 27.7 MP 161.7 J 568.7 *Highway climbs northbound; grades to 6 percent. Passing lanes provided.*

E 28.3 MP 162.3 J 568.1 Pine Creek Sno-Park.

E 28.7 MP 162.7 J 567.7 Large turnout to east.

E 29.3 MP 163.3 J 567.1 Turnout to east.

E 29.9 MP 163.9 J 566.5 Turnout to east at summit of Blewett Pass (elev. 4,102 feet). Sno-Park area in winter. Trailhead for Forest Discovery Trail. Forest Service Roads 7324 to west and 9716 to east.

Highway descends northbound.

E 34 MP 168 J 562.4 Turnout.

E 34.2 MP 168.2 J 562.2 Large turnout to east.

E 36.7 MP 170.7 J 559.7 Slow vehicle turnout to east for northbound traffic.

E 38 MP 172 J 558.4 Large turnout to west.

E 39 MP 173 J 557.4 Slow for curves northbound.

E 40 MP 174 J 556.4 Turnout to west with Blewett Historical marker.

Slow for curves northbound and southbound.

E 41.1 MP 175.1 J 555.3 Slow-vehicle turnout to west for southbound traffic.

E 42 MP 176 J 554.4 Slow-vehicle turnout. Slow for 45-mph curves northbound.

E 43.1 MP 177.1 J 553.3 Leaving Wenatchee National Forest northbound.

E 43.3 MP 177.3 J 553.1 Long turnout east side of highway for slow vehicle traffic northbound.

E 43.5 MP 177.5 J 552.9 Long turnout west side of highway for slow vehicle traffic southbound.

E 44 MP 178 J 552.4 Ingalls Creek. Lodge (closed).

E 44.1 MP 178.1 J 552.3 Shasta RV Park to west.

E 44.5 MP 178.5 J 551.9 Old Blewett Road.

E 49.1 MP 183.1 J 547.3 Fruit stands in season.

E 51.1 MP 185.1 J 545.3 **Junction** U.S. Highways 97 and 2. Turn right northbound for continuation of Highway 97, which shares a common alignment with Highway 2 eastbound through the Wenatchee River valley to Wenatchee.

NOTE: Physical mileposts eastbound now reflect distance from Interstate 5 via Highway 2 and are included in this log.

E 51.5 MP 105.2 J 544.9 Shell gas station. Begin 4-lane divided highway eastbound.

E 52.3 MP 105.9 J 544.1 Crossing the Wenatchee River.

E 52.9 MP 106.5 J 543.5 Stoplight in **Dryden**, a small fruit-growing town. Turnoff for services; gas, diesel, food and groceries available.

E 55.2 MP 108.8 J 541.2 Turnoff for Peshastin Pinnacle State Park, a popular spot with rock climbers. Day-use only, with pit toilets, picnic area with pay phone, no water available. 1.5 miles of hiking trails.

E 56.5 MP 110 J 539.9 Eastbound-only exit to Cashmere Business Loop/Aplets Way via Goodwin Road.

E 56.6 MP 110.1 J 539.8 Stoplight at Hay Canyon Road.

E 57.6 MP 111.1 J 538.8 Stoplight at Aplets Way and access south to downtown **CASHMERE** (pop. 3,063) via Aplets Way/North Division Street. Cashmere is probably best known as the home of Aplets & Cotlets, a confection made with apples, apricots and walnuts by Liberty Orchards.

©Kris Valencia, staff

Tour the famous **Aplets & Cotlets Candy Kitchen and Country Store**, located south on Aplets Way/North Division at Mission. The store is open daily, April through December, and, weekdays January through March; phone (509) 782-4088; www.liberty-orchards.com. Tours of the candy kitchens are offered every 20 minutes and lots of free samples are available in the store.

E 58.4 MP 112 J 538 Stoplight at Cotlets Way; Shell and Chevron gas/diesel stations, supermarket. Access to Cashmere Historic District, Chelan County Museum via Cottage Avenue.

E 61.6 MP 115 J 534.8 Stoplight at Main Street of **Monitor**.

E 62 MP 115.5 J 534.4 Turnoff for Wenatchee River County Park. The park is in a beautiful setting between river and highway with full hookup sites, picnic shelter, play areas, day-use and restrooms. The river is fished in summer for trout and in fall and early winter for steelhead and salmon.

E 65.4 MP 118.7 J 531 *NOTE: Northbound traffic exits.* Follow signs for Highway 97 North/Okanogan.

Continue straight ahead on North Wenatchee Avenue/SR 285 for access to city of **WENATCHEE** (pop. 31,925), all visitor facilities available.

E 65.7 MP 119 J 530.7 Exit right northbound for Wenatchee Confluence State Park and Visitor Center to south.

E 65.8 MP 119.1 J 530.6 Stoplight at Easy Street. Continue straight ahead for continuation of Highway 97 North.

E 66.4 MP 119.7 J 530 Exit for Ohme Gardens, Rocky Reach Dam, Entiat and Chelan via Highway 97A, an alternate route up the west side of the Columbia River. Log of U.S. Highway 97/2 north via the east side

Irrigated pockets of apple orchards dot Highway 97 as it winds along the Columbia River.
(©Kris Valencia, staff)

of the Columbia River/Lake Entiat continues.

E 66.7 MP 119.9 J 529.7 Crossing the Columbia River, which forms the boundary between Chelan and Douglas counties.

E 67.6 MP 127.8 J 528.8 Stoplight at **junction** with Washington Highway 28/ Sunset Highway, which leads south 4 miles to East Wenatchee. *IMPORTANT: Northbound traffic get in left lane for left turn* and continuation of Highway 97 North/Highway 2 East.

NOTE: Physical mileposts northbound reflect an 8 mile discrepancy for Highway 2 mileages between Chelan and Douglas counties.

E 67.8 MP 128 J 528.6 Distance marker northbound shows Okanogan 87 miles.

Northbound the highway passes some of the apple orchards for which the Wenatchee area is known. Small turnouts each side of road.

E 72 MP 132.3 J 524.4 Shell gas/diesel station with propane.

E 72.2 MP 132.5 J 524.2 Lincoln Rock State Park and Rocky Reach Dam. The park offers 67 RV and 27 tent sites (camping fees $14-28 per night), picnic areas, boat launch, sani-dump and handicap-accessible facilities. Generator use limited to 8 A.M.–9 P.M. Steelhead and trout fishing.

E 79.5 MP 213 J 516.9 Junction with U.S. Highway 2 East to Spokane and Waterville and continuation of Highway 97 North to Chelan and Okanogan. **Orondo**, an orchard town with roadside fruit and vegetable stands in season.

NOTE: Mileposts northbound now reflect distance from Oregon border via Highway 97 and are included in this log.

Mileposts southbound reflect distance from Interstate 5 via U.S. Highway 2., which shares a common alignment with U.S. Highway 97 to Milepost E 51.1.

E 82 MP 215.5 J 514.4 Orondo River Park; pleasant grassy campsites, 13 RV with electric/water, 14 tent sites on narrow stretch of land between highway and lake; showers, picnic areas, volleyball, toilets and boat launch on Lake Entiat.

E 85.4 MP 219.5 J 511 Daroga State Park.

A beautiful waterside park with 28 RV and 17 tent sites (camping fee $14-28 per night), large playfields, swimming, picnic tables, boat launch and handicap-accessible facilities. Sani-dump. Huge group camping site is located 0.6 mile south of here.

E 89 MP 223 J 507.4 Begin 0.8-mile passing lane northbound.

E 101 MP 234.6 J 495.4 Beebe Bridge Park. Camping in 46 tent/RV sites with water and electric (camping fee $20/night in off-season, $25 high season), sani-dump, showers, playground, day-use, picnic and swimming areas, boat launch and handicap-accessible facilities.

E 101.2 MP 234.8 J 495.2 Columbia River bridge.

E 101.5 MP 235 J 494.9 Junction with Washington Highway 150 which leads 5 miles (winding uphill start from Highway 97) to downtown **CHELAN** (pop. 3,890), a popular vacation destination, located on one of the state's most beautiful and most heavily used lakes. Lake Chelan is the largest natural lake in Washington. The city offers motels, resorts, restaurants, gas stations, grocery and variety stores. Chamber of Commerce Visitor Information Center located at Woodin Avenue/U.S. 97A and Sanders Street.

Don Morse City Park in Chelan has **Lakeshore RV Park**; beautiful shaded campground; don't expect to drive in late on a busy summer weekend and find a site, call ahead at (509) 682-8023 or visit www.chelancityparks.com. There is also camping at Chelan State Park, one of the most popular campgrounds in Washington. Southbound from Chelan take Highway 97A south 3 miles, then turn right on South Lakeshore Road and continue 6 miles to park; 109 tent spaces, 18 water and electric sites, 17 full hook-up sites, and a dump station (utility sites are not designed for the modern RV, and RVs longer than 30 feet will not be able to enter or use the facilities at the state park; use Lakeshore RV Park instead).

E 106.6 MP 240.1 J 489.8 North **junction** with Highway 97A.

E 112.6 MP 246.1 J 483.8 Turnoff to east for Wells Dam Public Utility District. Day-use area with picnic tables, toilets, information center.

E 115.2 MP 248.7 J 481.2 Sharp turn to east across railroad tracks for Starr Boat Launch, a large gravel parking area that includes the boat ramp, toilet and dumpster.

E 119.4 MP 253 J 477 Sign about "The China Ditch." *Begin 45 mph speed zone northbound into Pateros.*

E 119.8 MP 253.4 J 476.6 Junction with Washington Highway 153/20 to Twisp (31 miles) via the Methow River valley. Access to Alta Lake State Park, located 3 miles north from here on Highway 153; camping and boating.

E 120 MP 253.6 J 476.4 Methow River bridge.

E 120.1 MP 253.7 J 476.3 Entering **PATEROS** (pop. 667) northbound; food, gas/ diesel (Chevron), lodging and camping. First right as you drive northbound will take you to Riverside Park; overnight on-street parking (fee charged) adjacent the park. which has a playground and restrooms. Visitor information center; www.pateros.com.

E 126.4 MP 260 J 470 *Slow for 40-mph speed zone through* **BREWSTER** (pop. 2,370); motel, RV park, gas/diesel stations (Chevron, 76), fast-food (Subway, McDonalds), drugstore, hardware store, hospital and other services. This is a large apple processing location. Access to Columbia River.

E 127.1 MP 260.4 J 469.3 Junction with Washington Highway 173 to Bridgeport and Chief Joseph Dam on the Columbia River.

E 130.4 MP 264.1 J 466 Okanogan River bridge.

E 131.5 MP 265.2 J 464.9 Junction with Washington Highway 17 South; weigh station. Fort Okanogan Interpretive Center, just southeast of this junction, is open in summer. Continue south 8 miles via Highway 17 for Chief Joseph Dam, Bridgeport and Bridgeport State Park.

E 144.9 MP 278.6 J 451.5 Turnoff for **Malott** (unincorporated), a small community on the west side of the river with limited services. Well-known Johnny Appleseed and other early settlers planted apple trees here in the initial settlement of this area.

E 148.9 MP 282.6 J 447.5 Cariboo Trail Historical Marker at turnout to west; picnic table.

E 150.7 MP 284.3 J 445.7 Large turnout to west.

E 152.6 MP 286.2 J 443.8 Turnoff for Highway 97 Business Loop west to downtown Okanogan via 2nd Avenue South/ Washington Highway 20. Washington Highway 20, also called North Cascades Highway, leads to Twisp. Okanogan Bingo Casino to west on Apple Way Road.

E 153.2 MP 286.6 J 443.2 Distance marker northbound shows Omak 5 miles, Canadian border 50 miles, Penticton 89 miles.

E 153.5 MP 286.9 J 442.9 Exit to frontage road for downtown Okanogan via Oak Street. **OKANOGAN** (pop. 2,552) is the county seat of Okanogan County and offers all traveler services. The historic district transports visitors back to views of the early 1900s.

E 154.4 MP 287.8 J 442 Okanogan Fairgrounds and RV park to west on Rodeo Trail Road.

E 154.4 MP 289.7 J 440 Second turnoff northbound for Okanogan Fairgrounds and RV park to west on Rodeo Trail Road.

E 155.5 MP 290.8 J 438.9 Travel plaza gas station to east.

E 155.9 MP 291.2 J 438.5 Stoplight. Dining, shopping, visitor information to west. Access to Omak Stampede arena. Carl Precht Memorial RV Park (open year-round) and downtown Omak to west. **OMAK** (pop. 4,845) offers food, gas/diesel and lodging. The annual Omak Stampede and World Famous Suicide Race is held the second week in August. East Side Park is open to self-contained campers during Stampede Weekend (fee charged). The Visitor Information Center is inside this park and has a popular photo-op of the "Naming of the Animals" monument; www.omakchamber.com; phone 1-800-225-6625.

Junction with Washington Highway 155 South to Grand Coulee Dam.

E 156.4 MP 291.7 J 438 Crossing highway bridge; view of Stampede Grounds.

E 156.6 MP 291.9 J 437.8 Okanogan River bridge.

E 157.1 MP 292.4 J 437.3 Stoplight: Omak Riverside/Engh Road intersection. McDonalds, Walmart and Home Depot to east, Shopping Mall to west. Also available to west: Arby's, Dairy Queen, Pizza Hut, Taco Bell/Kentucky Fried Chicken, Exxon and Texaco gas stations, Safeway.

E 157.4 MP 292.7 J 437 Turnoff to west for Best Western motel, Subway, Omak Inn, Steakhouse and Omak Clinic.

Distance marker northbound shows Tonasket 22 miles, Penticton 84 miles.

E 157.9 MP 293.3 J 436.5 Turnoff to west for Big R Store and Omak Airport.

E 165.1 MP 298.7 J 431.3 RIVERSIDE (pop. 280) is a small agricultural community. Detros Western Store on Main Street.

E 165.4 MP 299.1 J 431 Turnoff to Conconully State Park (15 miles west); camping, swimming, boating.

E 165.6 MP 299.3 J 430.8 *CAUTION: High kill area for deer. Watch for deer next 13 miles northbound.*

E 167 MP 300.7 J 429.4 Turnout to west. Distance marker northbound shows Tonasket 15 miles, Oroville 32 miles, Penticton 78 miles.

E 171.1 MP 304.8 J 425.3 South Pine Creek. Turnoff to Fish Lake to west.

E 177 MP 310.6 J 419.4 Okanogan River bridge.

E 181.1 MP 314.3 J 415.3 *Slow for 35- and 25-mph speed zones northbound* entering Tonasket.

E 181.2 MP 314.8 J 415.2 Junction with Highway 20 East/6th Avenue. Fast-food outlets, shopping, gas stations with diesel (Exxon, Mobil).

E 181.8 MP 315.1 J 414.6 TONASKET (pop. 1,032); visitor information center (www.tonasketwa.org). Tonasket has fast-food outlets, gas/diesel, supermarket, hardware store, RV park, banks and hospital available.

E 187.4 MP 321 J 409 Old Okanogan Mission Historical Marker and Indian cemetery are located behind Ellisforde's church.

E 187.8 MP 321.4 J 408.6 Ellisforde junction; small grocery. Turnoff for Spectacle Lake.

E 196.4 MP 330.5 J 400 Okanogan River bridge.

E 197.1 MP 331.2 J 399.3 *Slow for 35-mph speed zone northbound* entering Oroville.

E 197.7 MP 331.8 J 398.7 OROVILLE (pop. 1,686); Depot Museum, visitor information (www.orovillewashington.org). Oroville's Main Street has restaurants, shopping, a pharmacy, 24-hour gas station, lodging, veterinary clinic. There are murals in multiple locations in town. An orchard and vineyard industries town, Oroville is the last U.S. town before crossing the border into Canada. It is located at the south end of Osoyoos Lake, which straddles the international border.

E 199 MP 332.6 T J 397.4 Prince's Center shopping mall, gas station, at north end of Oroville. Osoyoos Veteran's Memorial Park at the south end of the lake has 86 campsites, showers and toilets, swimming beach and a boat launch. Excellent smallmouth bass fishing.

E 202.5 MP 336.1 J 393.9 Gas stations with diesel.

E 202.8 MP 336.4 J 393.6 Duty-free store to west.

E 202.9 MP 336.5 J 393.5 U.S.–Canada international border, open 24 hours daily. *Make sure you have your passport and rabies certificate for dogs. For more details on customs requirements, see Crossing the Border in the TRAVEL PLANNING section.*

CANADA HIGHWAY 97 NORTH

E 203.8 (328 km) J 392.6 (631.8 km) Turnoff for **Haynes Point Provincial Park** on Osoyoos Lake. Drive east 0.5 mile (follow signs) through residential area to park entrance. Day-use area for picnicking, swimming, waterskiing and fishing (bass and rainbow); 41 campsites, pit and flush toilets, tap water, boat launch, hiking trail. Camping fee $30. Gates closed 11 P.M. to 7 A.M. Campground season is April to October. Campsite reservations accepted for mid-May to first week in September; go to www.discovercamping.ca. This is a very popular campground in summer.

E 204.3 (328.8 km) J 392.1 (631 km) Access road leads 1 mile/1.6 km east to **OSOYOOS** (pop. 5,044) town centre; all traveler services.

Watch for fruit stands (open when produce is in season) northbound.

E 205.6 (330.9 km) J 390.8 (628.9 km) Stoplight at **junction** of Highway 97 and Crowsnest Highway 3 (Princeton and Hope)/Main Street. Easy access to gas with diesel stations (Shell, Husky), fast-food outlets, truck stop cafe and shopping mall.

BC Visitor Centre/Osoyoos at northeast of corner of intersection is a major stop for tourists entering British Columbia's Okanagan region.

E 207.3 (333.5 km) J 389.1 (626.1 km) Winery section has 4 lanes for passing. Common wine tasting hours at these places are 10 A.M.–6 P.M.

E 209.4 (337 km) J 387 (622.8 km) Leaving Osoyoos northbound, Highway 97 enters the Okanagan's agricultural area, with plenty of vineyards and orchards. Watch for fruit stands along the highway in season.

E 217.7 (350.3 km) J 378.7 (609.4 km) Stoplight at **OLIVER** (pop. 4,564); Oliver Place Mall, fast-food outlets, gas, diesel, lodging and other services.

The town was named for Premier John Oliver, who encouraged a soldier settlement and irrigation scheme here in 1919 that turned the dry sagebrush slopes into rich orchards. Local attractions include Tuc-El-Nuit Lake (swimming, camping), Okanagan River bike trail, and old Fairview gold-mining town. The town's motto is "Wine Capital of Canada." There are *many* wineries along Highway 97, most offering tasting rooms and tours.

E 218 (350.8 km) J 378.4 (609 km) Stoplight; fast-food outlets, shopping, visitor information. Turnoff for Mount Baldy ski area.

E 218.6 (351.8 km) J 377.8 (608 km) Oliver Lions Park (day-use).

E 221.6 (356.6 km) J 374.8 (603.2 km) Turnoff to **Inkaneep Provincial Park** to north; 7 campsites, swimming, fishing. Open late June to early September.

E 222.1 (357.4 km) J 374.3 (602.4 km) Turnoff to Tuc-El-Nuit Lake. Private camping resorts along the lake.

Road widening underway in 2013. Expect improved highway northbound in summer 2014.

E 225.5 (362.9 km) J 370.9 (596.9 km) South end of Vaseux Lake, a federal wildlife sanctuary; resort and beach. British Columbia's largest herd of California bighorn sheep makes its home in the rocky hills. Watch for them by the lake for water in the evenings and early mornings.

Slow for 25-mph/40-kmph curves northbound.

E 227.3 (365.8 km) J 369.1 (594 km) **Vaseux Lake Provincial Park**; 12 campsites, swimming and fishing (largemouth bass, rainbow, perch and whitefish). No motors allowed on the lake. Camping fee April–Oct. Water must be boiled here for drinking. Camping fee $16 per night.

E 227.7 (366.4 km) J 368.7 (593.3 km) Dirt parking area at Vaseux Wildlife Center; interpretive panels, trails and bird blind to west.

E 231 (371.7 km) J 365.4 (588 km) Tickleberry's (www.tickleberrys.com), a popular sweet shop featuring ice cream and other goodies, is on your right entering **OKANAGAN FALLS** (pop. 1,700). *Slow for 50-kmph/31-mph speed zone through town.*

Okanagan Falls is a small resort community at the south end of Skaha Lake. It is known for its antique shops and flea markets. Food, gas/diesel (Esso) and lodging available. Turn off for Okanagan Provincial Park.

E 231.1 (371.9 km) **J 365.3** (587.9 km) Flashing traffic light: Northbound travelers turn to continue on Highway 97 North.

E 231.2 (372.1 km) **J 365.2** (587.7 km) IGA supermarket and Visitor Information.

E 231.3 (372.2 km) **J 365.1** (587.5 km) Okanagan River bridge.

E 235 (378.2 km) **J 361.4** (581.6 km) **Junction** with Highway 3A to Keremeos and Crowsnest Highway 3 to west. Access to Dominion Observatory.

E 235.6 (379.1 km) **J 360.8** (580.5 km) Petro-Canada with gas/diesel, propane and convenience store.

E 237.3 (381.8 km) **J 359.1** (577.8 km) Double-ended turnout to east.

E 237.9 (382.9 km) **J 358.5** (576.9 km) Viewpoint over lake with picnic tables, litter bins, toilets and sign about the founding of Penticton by rancher Tom Ellis (northbound access only to the east).

E 239.8 (385.9 km) **J 356.6** (573.9 km) Wrights Beach Camp.

E 240 (386.2 km) **J 356.4** (573.6 km) Traffic light. Public beach on south side of road at north end of Skaha Lake. Penticton airport to north.

E 240.3 (386.7 km) **J 356.1** (573.1 km) Traffic light as Highway 97/Skaha Lake Road turns north, becoming Highway 97/Channel Parkway and bypassing Penticton city centre. Highway 97/Channel Parkway runs beside the channel that connects Okanagan and Skaha lakes.

©Kris Valencia, staff

A favorite summer pastime is to float down the river on inner tubes or air mattresses from the Riverside Drive at the north end of town down to Skaha Lake. A bike and walking path parallels the channel.

From this junction, continue straight on Skaha Lake Road to reach the Main Street of **PENTICTON** (pop. 32,993), a major tourist destination and the heart of the Okanagan's wine country with more than 50 wineries within 20 minutes of the city's centre. It is a retirement haven as well as a centre for fruit packing and canning. Penticton has excellent sandy beaches on 2 lakes; fine scenery, dependable hot summer weather; and complete visitor facilities. It is also famous as the venue of the Ironman Canada Triathlon, held annually in late August.

E 242.2 (389.8 km) **J 354.2** (570 km) Traffic light; gas (Shell), Tim Horton's, and other businesses.

E 243.3 (391.5 km) **J 353.1** (568.2 km) Traffic light; Penticton & Wine Country Visitor Centre, gas (Chevron). Northbound travelers turn left here to continue on Highway 97 North/Eckhardt Avenue West.

E 243.5 (391.9 km) **J 352.9** (568 km) South Okanagan Events Centre.

E 243.6 (392 km) **J 352.7** (567.8 km) Petro Canada gas station on right south-bound.

E 243.7 (392.2 km) **J 352.5** (567.6 km) Ramada Inn on right southbound.

E 243.8 (392.3 km) **J 352.6** (567.4 km) Traffic light; Petro Canada gas station on right northbound.

E 243.9 (392.5 km) **J 352.5** (567.2 km) Starbucks on right northbound in Riverside mall; shopping, fast-food outlets. Access via Riverside Drive.

Watch for more rafters as you cross the channel northbound.

E 247.1 (397.7 km) **J 349.3** (562.1 km) Kickininee picnic area, Kickininee Provincial Park, to east on Okanagan Lake.

E 247.4 (398.1 km) **J 349** (561.6 km) Soorimpt picnic area, Kickininee Provincial Park, to east on Okanagan Lake; boat launch.

E 248 (399.1 km) **J 348.4** (560.7 km) Pyramid picnic area, Kickininee Provincial Park, to east on Okanagan Lake.

E 249.2 (401 km) **J 347.2** (558.7 km) Sun-Oka Beach Provincial Park picnic area to east has one of the best swimming beaches in the Okanagan. Welcome to Summerland.

E 249.6 (401.7 km) **J 346.8** (558.1 km) Traffic light. Johnson Street. Esso gas/diesel station with propane and market.

E 249.8 (401.9 km) **J 346.6** (557.7 km) Double-ended turnout northbound.

E 252.5 (406.3 km) **J 343.9** (553.4 km) Traffic light. Access to medical clinic and shopping.

E 253.1 (407.3 km) **J 343.3** (552.5 km) Traffic light; gas, shopping. Downtown **SUMMERLAND** (pop. 11,110); all services available. **Visitor information:** Summerland Chamber & Visitor Center on Highway 97; www.summerlandchamber.bc.ca.

The first commercial orchard in the Okanagan was planted here in 1890, and Summerland, a small but busy village with a mock-Tudor look, is still dominated by the fruit and wine industry. There are several wineries and vineyards in the area. Summerland Sweets (www.summerlandsweets.com), on Canyonview Road, manufactures fruit candy, jams and syrups; open year-round.

E 253.2 (407.4 km) **J 343.2** (552.2 km) 50 Classic Cars, Car Museum.

E 259.1 (417 km) **J 337.3** (542.8 km) Turnoff to South Campground in **Okanagan Lake Provincial Park**; picnic tables, sani-station, fishing, swimming and boat launch. A shady oasis with a great beach. Campsite reservations accepted for mid-May to first week in September; go to www.discovercamping.ca. This is a very popular campground in summer.

E 259.8 (418 km) **J 336.6** (541.7 km) Turnoff to North Campground in **Okanagan Lake Provincial Park**; picnic tables, sani-station, fishing, swimming and boat launch. Campsite reservations accepted for mid-May to first week in September; go to www.discovercamping.ca. This is a very popular campground in summer.

E 262.8 (422.9 km) **J 333.6** (536.9 km) Turnout to east with litter bin.

E 263.7 (424.4 km) **J 332.7** (535.4 km) Antler Beach Regional park; picnicking and swimming beach. Northbound sign "Welcome to Peachland."

E 266 (428 km) **J 330.4** (531.7 km) Turn-out and picnic area with small swimming beach. Traffic light: **Junction** with access road to **PEACHLAND** (pop. 5,233), a small fruit-growing settlement with all services available.

E 267.6 (430.6 km) **J 328.8** (529.1 km) Gas, fast-food and market.

E 270.7 (435.6 km) **J 325.7** (524.1 km) **Junction** with Highway 97C (Coquihalla Connector), which leads west 67 miles/108 km to Merritt at **Milepost H 71.5** on Highway 5. *See "Coquihalla Highway" log this section.*

E 272.8 (439 km) **J 323.6** (520.8 km) Welcome to Westbank (northbound sign); gas/diesel, all services, fast-food. **Westbank** is a booming suburb of Kelowna.

E 273 (439.3 km) **J 323.4** (520.4 km) Traffic light. Shopping center to south includes Shoppers Drug Mart, liquor store, bank and Starbucks.

E 273.1 (439.5 km) **J 323.3** (520.2 km) Traffic light; Brown Road. Visitor Centre and Chamber of Commerce building is to the west.

E 273.5 (440.1 km) **J 322.9** (519.6 km) Traffic light. McDonalds, Westbank Shopping Centre.

E 274.3 (441.4 km) **J 322.1** (518.4 km) Westbank Hub Centre; Home Depot, Tim Hortons and other businesses.

E 275.6 (443.5 km) **J 320.8** (516.3 km) Westbank Industrial turnoff.

E 276.2 (444.4 km) **J 320.2** (515.2 km) Ross Road to west. Husky gas with diesel and propane.

E 278.4 (448 km) **J 318** (511.8 km) Traffic light. Esso gas station.

E 279.1 (449.2 km) **J 317.3** (510.6 km) Traffic light at **junction** with Westside Road, which goes up the west side of Okanagan Lake. Access to **Bear Creek Provincial Park**, 4 miles/7 km from junction, with 122 campsites, sani-station, swimming, fishing and hiking. Also access to **Fintry Provincial Park**, 21 miles/34 km north, with 100 campsites. Campsite reservations accepted at both parks for mid-May to first week in September; go to www.discovercamping.ca.

E 280.4 (451.2 km) **J 316** (508.5 km) William Bennett bridge crosses Okanagan Lake.

E 281.2 (452.5 km) **J 315.2** (507.3 km) Traffic light at city centre turnoff for Kelowna (description follows). Highway 97 North continues through Kelowna as 6-lane divided highway lined with motels, restaurants and shopping.

Kelowna

E 281.2 (452.5 km) **J 315.2** (507.3 km) Located on the shore of Okanagan Lake, midway between Penticton and Vernon. **Population:** 115,000. **Elevation:** 1,130 feet/344m. **Emergency Services:** Phone 911 for all emergency services. **Hospital,** phone (250) 862-4000. Veterinary, Kelowna Veterinary Hospital (250) 860-2408.

Visitor Information: Tourist information centre just off Highway 97 at 544 Harvey Ave., (250) 861-1515. www.tourism kelowna.com

The largest community in the Okanagan,

Kelowna offers excellent accommodations—from luxury resorts to campgrounds—as well as many great restaurants and good shopping.

Settlement started here in 1859 when Oblate missionaries Father Charles Pandosy, Father Richard and Brother Sorel founded a mission on a creek at L'Anse au Sable (Sandy Bay), built a tiny church and a school and planted apple trees and vines.

Today, Kelowna's burgeoning economy is based on fruit growing (a third of Canada's fruit exports come from this area), healthcare, tourism, manufacturing (plywood plant), construction and forestry/fishing/mining/oil and gas. Kelowna has 17 golf courses and more than 60 parks.

Attractions include a booming wine industry; golfing; the largest farmer's market in BC; a cultural district with museums, art galleries, boutiques and studios; an indoor water park; and the valley's oldest winery (Calona Winery).

Central Access Route Log
(continued)

E 284.6 (458 km) **J 311.8** (501.8 km) Traffic light at Leckie Road. Safeway supermarket.

E 284.9 (458.5 km) **J 311.5** (501.3 km) Traffic light. Walmart, Holiday Inn.

E 285.2 (459 km) **J 311.2** (500.8 km) Traffic light at **junction** with BC Highway 33 south to Big White Ski Area and on to Crowsnest Highway 3. Costco and Chevron gas/diesel station at this intersection.

E 286.1 (460.4 km) **J 310.3** (499.4 km) Traffic light at McCurdy's Road. Kane's Harley Davidson store.

E 287.7 (463 km) **J 308.7** (496.8 km) Traffic light at Sexsmith Road. Access to Kelowna Springs golf course.

E 288.8 (464.8 km) **J 307.6** (495 km) Exit to University of British Columbia/Okanagan campus.

E 290.1 (466.8 km) **J 306.3** (492.9 km) Traffic light. Turnoff for Kelowna airport.

Begin 4-lane undivided highway northbound.

E 292.4 (470.5 km) **J 304** (489.2 km) Large turnout to east overlooking Duck Lake.

E 293.2 (471.8 km) **J 303.2** (487.9 km) Large turnout to east overlooking Duck Lake.

E 295.1 (474.9 km) **J 301.3** (484.9 km) Traffic light at Beaver Lake Road; turnoff for visitor centre, Shell gas and lodging at **Lake Country/Winfield.**

E 295.5 (475.5 km) **J 300.9** (484.2 km) Traffic light. Petro-Canada gas station.

E 296.1 (476.5 km) **J 300.3** (483.3 km) Husky gas station on right southbound.

E 297.5 (478.8 km) **J 298.9** (481 km) Traffic light. Lakewood Mall, SuperSave gas station.

E 297.7 (479 km) **J 298.7** (480.7 km) Esso gas station on right northbound.

Improved 4-lane highway northbound. This stretch of highway between Oyama and Winfield opened in summer 2013. The narrow, 2-lane stretch of old highway along Wood Lake is under development as the multi-use "Pelmewash Parkway."

E 309 (497.3 km) **J 287.4** (462.5 km) Turnoff for **Kekuli Bay Provincial Park** on Kalamalka Lake; 70 campsites, swimming,

boat launch. Campsite reservations accepted for mid-May to first week in September; go to www.discovercamping.ca.

E 312.3 (502.6 km) **J 284.1** (457.2 km) Traffic light at College Way. Turnoff for Kalamalka Lake Provincial Park; picnicking, swimming, views, boat launch and fishing.

E 313 (503.7 km) **J 283.4** (456.1 km) Vernon Visitor Information Centre offers reservation services.

E 313.6 (504.7 km) **J 282.8** (455.1 km) Turnoff for Vernon Jubilee Hospital to east.

E 314 (505.3 km) **J 282.4** (454.5 km) Traffic light at 25th Avenue/BC Highway 6 to Nelson in downtown Vernon. Polson Park is on your right northbound (southeast corner of intersection). Strip mall at northeast corner of intersection has a Starbucks, A&W, drugstore, Subway, Little Caesar's Pizza and walk-in medical clinic.

E 314.1 (505.5 km) **J 282.3** (454.3 km) Traffic light at 30th Avenue in downtown Vernon; shopping, dining to west.

E 314.2 (505.7 km) **J 282.2** (454.1 km) Traffic light at 32nd Avenue in downtown Vernon; gas stations with diesel (Chevron, Esso, Husky, Shell, Petro-Canada, SuperSave), Best Western, Sandman, and Tim Horton's along Okanagan Highway 97/32nd Street.

Vernon

E 314.2 (505.7 km) **J 282.2** (454.1 km) Vernon is located 33 miles/53 km north of Kelowna in the Okanagan. **Population:** 38,444. **Elevation:** 1,824 feet/556m. **Emergency Services:** Phone 911 for all emergency services. **Hospital,** Vernon Jubilee Hospital south edge of town on highway, phone 250-545-2211.

Visitor Information: Visitor Information at 701 Highway 97 South; phone 250-542-1415, toll-free 1-800-665-0795; www.vernon tourism.com

Situated between Kalamalka and Okana-

gan lakes, Vernon is a popular tourist destination with a wide range of tourist services and activities. Summer temperatures average 68°F/20°C, with a record high in July of 101.3°F/38.5°C.

Vernon is the Okanagan's oldest city, settled in 1867 by Luc Girouard. As head of the Okanagan Lake paddle-wheeler service, Vernon grew in importance with the construction of a branch line of the Canadian Pacific Railway. Later, irrigation made commercial agriculture possible and the area exploded.

Visit Polson Park, a green oasis lined with weeping willows and with a unique floral clock. See the historic turn-of-the-century courthouse surrounded by a flowery courtyard and waterfalls. Stop at Davison Orchards Country Village, family-owned and operated since 1933, for fresh produce, orchard tours, shopping at their gift shop or enjoying special seasonal events. Open daily from 8 A.M. to 6 P.M., May 1 to October 31; www.davisonorchards.ca. You can reach Davison Orchards from Highway 97 by turning west on 30th Avenue to Bella Vista Road, then right on Davison Road.

Central Access Route Log
(continued)

E 315 (506.9 km) **J 281.4** (452.9 km) Traffic light at 43rd Ave. in Vernon; Super 8, Safeway.

E 315.5 (507.7 km) **J 280.9** (452 km) **Junction** with road east to Silver Star Resort. Access to Walmart, Home Depot, Holiday Inn Express and Marriott from this intersection.

Begin 4-lane highway northbound.

E 317 (510.1 km) **J 279.4** (449.6 km) Silver Star RV Park to west.

E 320 (515 km) **J 276.4** (444.8 km) **Junction** with BC Highway 97A to Sicamous on Trans-Canada Highway 1. Northbound travelers exit here for BC Highway 97 to Trans-Canada Highway 1 and Kamloops (continue with this log). Distance marker northbound shows Kamloops 105 kms/65 miles.

Begin 2-lane highway northbound. Sec-

Shaded picnic spots and access to beaches are found at British Columbia's Okanagan parks.
(©Kris Valencia, staff)

tions of winding road, passing lanes and uphill grades.

E 323.1 (520 km) **J 273.3** (439.8 km) **Historic O'Keefe Ranch** heritage site, a recommended stop of interest. *CAUTION: Turnoff to ranch is on a tight turn.*

©Kris Valencia, staff

One of the earliest cattle empires in British Columbia, this spread was staked in 1867. Tours of the O'Keefe Mansion. Several of the ranch buildings, including St. Anne's Church, which dates from 1886, the original log cabin and a fascinating general store, have been restored and are open to the public. Great display of old farming/ranching equipment.

O'Keefe Ranch is open daily between Mother's Day (first Sunday in May) to Thanksgiving Day (the last Sunday in October). Hours are 10 A.M. to 6 P.M. in July and August, and 10 A.M. to 5 P.M. the rest of the time; admission fee charged. Restaurant, gift shop, horseback and pony rides and picnic facilities on site. www.okeeferanch.ca.

E 324.8 (522.7 km) **J 271.6** (437.1 km) Sun Valley Speedway, sprint track.

E 333.8 (537.2 km) **J 262.6** (422.6 km) Whispering Pines Cafe.

E 335.5 (539.6 km) **J 260.9** (419.9 km) Una rest area (eastbound-only traffic). Toilets, litter bins, picnic tables, signs about invasive weeds.

E 341.2 (549.1 km) **J 255.2** (410.7 km) Turnoff to east for Bolean, Spa and Arthur lakes; rainbow.

E 341.7 (549.9 km) **J 254.7** (409.9 km) *Reduce speed to 30 mph/50 kmph speed zone entering* **Falkland**, a small ranching community. Heritage Park and Museum. Services include a pub, coffee shop/restaurant, motel and Petro-Canada gas station with diesel.

E 342.2 (550.7 km) **J 254.2** (409.1 km) Falkland Stampede Grounds. An annual 2-day stampede is held Victoria Day weekend.

E 342.9 (551.8 km) **J 253.5** (408 km) Entering Falkland (southbound sign).

E 344.1 (553.7 km) **J 252.3** (406 km) Railroad tracks. Gravel turnout to east after crossing tracks.

E 350.2 (563.6 km) **J 246.2** (396.2 km) Road west to Pinaus, Ladyking and Square lakes, 6.6 miles/11 km; rainbow fishing.

E 350.6 (564.2 km) **J 245.8** (395.6 km) Slow for S-curves and 44-mph/70-kmph speed zone entering Westwold (northbound sign).

E 352.3 (567 km) **J 244.1** (392.8 km) **Westwold** (unincorporated) Community Hall. This small farm and logging community is situated in a beautiful valley.

E 352.8 (567.8 km) **J 243.6** (392 km) Route 97 Diner.

E 353 (568.1 km) **J 243.4** (391.7 km) General store, cafe. Salmon Lake Resort turnoff.

E 353.6 (569 km) **J 242.8** (390.7 km) Watch for deer, slow for curves, leaving Westwold northbound.

E 355.6 (572.3 km) **J 240.8** (387.5 km) *Highway crosses railroad tracks, slow for curve.*

E 356.2 (573.2 km) **J 240.2** (386.5 km) South end of Monte Lake. Highway winds along east shore of lake northbound; informal gravel turnouts overlooking lake.

E 356.9 (574.4 km) **J 239.5** (385.4 km) **Monte Lake** (unincorporated). RV park to east.

E 357.2 (575 km) **J 239.2** (384.8 km) RV park to east.

E 358.7 (577.3 km) **J 237.7** (382.5 km) Hillside store, SuperSave gas station, post office

Winding 2-lane highway with 37-mph/60-kmph curves northbound. Good shoulders but no turnouts.

E 368.1 (592.4 km) **J 228.3** (367.4 km) Brake check area to east for northbound traffic with travel information board. 8 percent downgrade northbound.

Rest area to west for southbound traffic; toilets, litter bins.

E 369.5 (594.6 km) **J 226.9** (365.2 km) Northbound travelers exit here for Trans-Canada Highway 1 West. Southbound travelers use exit 399 to get onto Highway 97 to Vernon. BC Highway 97 shares a common alignment with Trans-Canada Highway 1 west to Cache Creek.

Begin 4-lane divided highway westbound on Trans-Canada 1.

TRANS-CANADA HIGHWAY 1

E 371.3 (597.5 km) **J 225.1** (362.3 km) Exit 397 Hook Road; no services. Trans-Canada Highway 1 parallels the Thompson River (seen to the north) westbound to Kamloops. Notice the eroded clay hoodoos along the river.

E 375 (603.5 km) **J 221.4** (356.3 km) Exit 391 is westbound access to RV Park and **BC Wildlife Park** to south (eastbound motorists iuse Exit 390). See grizzly bears, cougars, gray wolves, moose and other wildlife of British Columbia. Birds of Prey show in outdoor amphitheatre during summer. Splash Water Park and train rides. Open daily, 9:30 A.M. to 5 P.M., May 1 to Sept. 2; and 9:30 A.M. to 4 P.M. March–April and September 3 through October; weekends and holidays during winter. Admission charged.

E 377.6 (607.7 km) **J 218.8** (352.1 km) Exit 388 Flying J Travel Plaza, Denny's, to north; food, gas/diesel.

E 382.9 (616.2 km) **J 213.5** (343.6 km) Stoplight at Tanager Drive. *Reduce speed to 80 kmph/50 mph westbound.*

E 383.6 (617.3 km) **J 212.8** (342.5 km) Stoplight at River Road.

E 384.1 (618.1 km) **J 212.3** (341.6 km) Stoplight at Highland Road. Access to Valleyview Square shopping mall to south.

E 384.5 (618.8 km) **J 211.9** (341 km) Stoplight at Oriole Road; access south to frontage road services (food, gas, lodging).

E 385.1 (619.7 km) **J 211.3** (340 km) Stoplight at Vicars Road; access south to frontage road services (food, gas, lodging).

E 385.6 (620.6 km) **J 210.8** (339.2 km) Exit 375 Kamloops City Centre exit for westbound motorists.

E 386 (621.2 km) **J 210.4** (338.6 km) Exit 374 to Kamloops and to Yellowhead Highway 5 North to Tete Jaune Cache on Yellowhead Highway 16. *Continue north on Yellowhead Highway 5 to follow this log.*

Highways 1, 97 and 5 share a common alignment westbound on a controlled-access freeway which bypasses the city of Kamloops. Highway 5 South (Coquihalla Highway) exits Trans-Canada Highway south at Exit 362 (see "Coquihalla Highway" log on facing page).

Trans-Canada Highway 1/97 continues west 53 miles/84 km to Cache Creek at the start of Highway 97North/Cariboo Highway (turn to page 100 in the WEST ACCESS ROUTE section). *Trans-Canada Highway 1 west of Highway 5 South junction is a winding 2-lane highway with passing lanes. Gas in Kamloops, Savona and Cache Creek.*

Kamloops

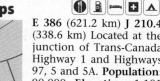

E 386 (621.2 km) **J 210.4** (338.6 km) Located at the junction of Trans-Canada Highway 1 and Highways 97, 5 and 5A. **Population:** 90,000. **Elevation:** 1,181 feet/360m. **Emergency Services:** Phone 911 for all emergency services. **Hospital**, phone (250) 374-5111.

Visitor Information: Kamloops Visitor Centre at 1290 W. Trans Canada Highway (Exit 386, from Highway 1) and is open daily June to Sept., weekdays Sept. through May; phone (250) 374-3377. Email: tourism@kamloopschamber.ca; www.tourismkamloops.com.

Established by fur traders as Fort Kamloops in 1811, Kamloops is located at the confluence of the North and South Thompson rivers. Kamloops boomed with the arrival of the Canadian Pacific Railway in 1885. Today it is British Columbia's 4th largest settlement, a bustling city with excellent shopping and tourist facilities at the crossroads of 2 major tourist routes: Trans-Canada Highway 1 and Highway 5.

Attractions include BC Wildlife Park, Kamloops Heritage Railway, Secwepemc Native Museum and Ethnobotanic Park, Kamloops Museum, Old Courthouse Cultural Centre, Kamloops Art Gallery, BIG Little Science Centre and Riverside Park. Shakespeare in the Park, Nature Photography Tours, Segway Tours, Fishing Packages, Motorcycle Circle Tour Route and much more is available. Music in the Park, 13 golf courses and fishing at over 100 lakes within an hour's drive of the city all draw visitors.

Central Access Route Log
(continued)

YELLOWHEAD HIGHWAY 5

E 386.3 (621.6 km) **J 210.1** (338.1 km) Crossing the Thompson River.

E 386.6 (622.2 km) **J 209.8** (337.6 km) Turnoff to east for gas station, RCMP and access to Secwepemc Native Heritage Park & Museum (follow signs for "Museum" 0.9 mile/1.4 km).

E 389 (626 km) **J 207.4** (333.8 km) Husky and Esso gas/diesel stations at Lake Paul Road **junction** with road east to Harper Mountain Ski Area and **Paul Lake Provincial Park** (11 miles/18 km).

Coquihalla Highway

The Coquihalla Highway connects Hope, at the junction of Highways 1 and 3, with Kamloops on Trans-Canada Highway 1. Created as a more direct route to the Interior of the province, the multi-lane Coquihalla may be used as an alternate route (either northbound or southbound) for both Central Access Route and West Access Route motorists.

Note that food, gas, lodging and camping along the highway are found only by exiting the freeway to Hope, Merritt or Kamloops. There are designated rest areas, chain-up and brake check areas.

This is a 4-lane, divided, limited access freeway; no U-turns except where indicated. Posted speed limit is 110 kmph/68 mph. There are some long grades with truck passing lanes.

The highway may be closed in winter due to slides; check road status prior to travel at www.drivebc.ca.

Distance from Hope (H) is followed by distance from Kamloops (K).

BC HIGHWAY 5

H 0 (0 km) **K 118** (189.9 km) **Junction** of Highway 3/Crowsnest and Trans-Canada Highway 1. Exit 170 to Trans-Canada Highway 1 East to Hope (see page 97 in the WEST ACCESS ROUTE section). Follow Highway 3 east for Coquihalla Highway access.

H 1.5 (2.4 km) **K 116.5** (187.5 km) Exit 173 to Hope.

H 4 (6.4 km) **K 114** (183.4 km) Exit 177 for Highway 3 East (Crowsnest) to Penticton. Westbound travelers continue straight for BC Highway 5/Coquihalla to Merritt and Kamloops.

H 4.3 (6.9 km) **K 113.7** (183 km) Nicolum River bridge.

Kilometreposts northbound reflect distance from this turnoff, not from the junction where this road log begins (4.3 miles south).

H 7.5 (12.1 km) **K 110.5** (178 km) Exit 183, Othello Road Kawkawa Lake and Coquihalla Canyon Provincial Recreation Area; picnic area, restrooms. The former Kettle Valley Railway here has been restored as a walking trail through 3 of 5 original railroad tunnels. Restrooms at parking lot. Kawkawa Lake is a popular destination for picnics, swimming and boating.

H 11.5 (18.5 km) **K 106.5** (171.4 km) Deneau Creek bridge.

H 13 (20.9 km) **K 105** (168.5 km) Large turnout by Coquihalla River, east side of highway, used by fishermen. Dolly Varden in spring and fall; silvers in fall; and steelhead in the upper reaches in summer, lower reaches in winter. Fly-fishing only; river closures, catch and bait restrictions apply.

H 13.5 (21.7 km) **K 104.5** (168.1 km) Exit 192 for Sowaqua Creek near the former Kettle Valley railway station of Jessica.

H 14 (22.5 km) **K 104** (167.3 km) Chain-up area.

H 15.3 (24.6 km) **K 102.7** (165.2 km) Dewdney Creek.

H 16 (25.7 km) **K 102** (164.1 km) Exit 195 for Carolin Mine Road (an operating gold mine). Northbound travelers make U-turn to Coquihalla River Provincial Recreation Area located southwest of the highway; picnic tables, fishing and hiking.

Entering avalanche area northbound.

H 17 (27.4 km) **K 101** (162.5 km) Ladner Creek bridge.

H 19 (30.6 km) **K 99** (159.3 km) Exit 202 for Shylock Road overpass (to gravel pit) and U-turn route for southbound traffic. Nearby is a stop of interest marker about the Kettle Valley Railway. This marks the approximate location of the station of Portia.

H 20 (32.2 km) **K 98** (157.7 km) Portia chain-up area for northbound vehicles; snow on slopes into June.

H 24 (38.6 km) **K 94** (151.3 km) From here to the summit is the most avalanche prone; 11 major avalanche tracks cross the highway alignment. Box Canyon, to west, holds the record for the deepest snowfall of the route: 15 feet in March of 1976.

H 24.5 (39.4 km) **K 93.5** (150.4 km) Box Canyon chain-up area with litter bins and toilets.

H 25.5 (41 km) **K 92.5** (148.8 km) South portal of Great Bear snowshed, among the world's longest at nearly 1,000 feet/300m. Concrete lintels are decorated with incised figures of bears.

H 28 (45 km) **K 90** (144.8 km) Exit 217 to west to rest area under the towering rock slab of Zopkios Ridge; picnic site, washrooms, brake check.

H 29 (46.6 km) **K 89** (143.2 km) Parking area (no services), Boston Bar Creek summit above Romeo railway stop.

H 30 (48.2 km) **K 88** (141.6 km) Coquihalla Highway Summit (elev. 4,081 feet/1,244m).

H 31.5 (50.7 km) **K 86.5** (139.2 km) Exit 221 northbound for Falls Lake picnic area.

H 32 (51.5 km) **K 86** (138.4 km) Dry Gulch bridge.

H 33.5 (53.9 km) **K 84.5** (136 km) Rest areas both sides of the road. Former toll collection site (discontinued in 2008).

H 35 (56.3 km) **K 83** (133.5 km) Exit 228 for Britton Creek rest area; washrooms, picnic tables in trees north of Coquihalla Lakes.

H 35.5 (57.1 km) **K 82.5** (132.7 km) Coldwater River bridge.

H 36 (58 km) **K 82** (132 km) Distance marker northbound shows Merritt 62 km/39 miles, Kamloops 144 km/89 miles, Kelowna 183 km/114 miles.

H 38.4 (61.8 km) **K 79.6** (128.1 km) Exit southbound for Hills Creek Road.

H 41.5 (66.8 km) **K 76.5** (123 km) Bridge over Juliet Creek; exit 238 north of bridge for Coldwater River Provincial Recreation Area; picnicking, fishing (rainbow and Dolly Varden) July to November.

H 49 (78.8 km) **K 69** (111 km) Exit 250 Larson Hill, forestry access.

H 50.5 (81.3 km) **K 67.5** (108.6 km) Begin 6 percent downhill grade northbound.

H 53.3 (85.8 km) **K 64.7** (104.1 km) Kingsvale Bridge. Exit 256 Coldwater Road. U-turn route.

H 54 (86.9 km) **K 64** (103 km) Exit to Gillis Lake and Kane Valley Road to Highway 5A south of Merritt.

H 65.5 (105.4 km) **K 51.5** (82.9 km) Exit 276 Comstock Road.

H 66.1 (106.4 km) **K 50.9** (81.9 km) Distance marker northbound shows Merritt

13 km/8 miles, Kamloops 93 km/58 miles, Kelowna 132 km/82 miles.

Northbound, the highway descends into the dry Interior Plateau.

H 71.5 (115 km) **K 46.5** (74.8 km) Exit 286 to Highway 5A South to Princeton, Highway 8 to Spences Bridge, and 97C (Okanagan Connector) east 67 miles/108 km to Peachland and northwest to Logan Lake (45 miles/72 km) and Ashcroft (81 miles/130 km). Access **MERRITT** (pop. 7,000), elev. 1,952 feet/595m, "Country Music Capital of Canada." Merritt has all visitor services. Visitor information at Merritt Visitor Centre and at www.tourismmerritt.com. Merritt is at the center of 3 historic cattle ranches: Nicola Ranch, Quilchena Cattle Co. and Douglas Lake Cattle Co., Canada's largest.

H 72.5 (116.6 km) **K 45.5** (73.2 km) Nicola River bridge.

H 73 (117.5 km) **K 45** (72.4 km) North exit for Merritt; also exit for Highway 5A North to Nicola, Qulichena, Monck Provincial Park, and Kamloops.

H 76 (122.3 km) **K 42** (67.6 km) Chain-up area with litter bins and toilets; highway north starts a long, steady climb up Clapperton Creek into the high forests of the Nicola Plateau.

H 85.5 (137.6 km) **K 32.5** (52.3 km) Southbound chain-up and brake check area with litter bins and toilets. Summit (elev. 4,741 feet/1,445m).

H 89.6 (144.2 km) **K 28.4** (45.7 km) Helmer Road exit 315 to Helmer Lake.

H 93.6 (150.6 km) **K 24.4** (39.3 km) Surrey Lake Summit 4,738 feet/1,444m.

H 96.5 (155.3 km) **K 21.5** (34.6 km) Begin 6 percent downhill grade for next 3 miles/4.5 km northbound.

H 102 (164.2 km) **K 16** (25.7 km) Exit 336 to Highway 97C west to Logan and Ashcroft.

H 108 (173.8 km) **K 10** (16.1 km) Highway begins 6 percent downgrade northbound as it descends from the plateau into the Thompson Valley.

H 108.6 (174.7 km) **K 9.4** (15.1 km) Brake check area with litter bins and toilet.

H 113.5 (182.6 km) **K 4.5** (7.2 km) Exit 355 for Inks Lake; U-turn route.

H 118 (189.9 km) **K 0**: Exit 362 for junction with Trans-Canada Highway 1 at Kamloops. Central Access Route log continues northbound from Kamloops via Yellowhead 5; see log this section.

© Kris Valencia, staff

Travelers may choose to join the West Access Route at Cache Creek, 53 miles/85 km west of Kamloops via Trans-Canada Highway 1, which becomes a 2-lane road that winds through some spectacular high-desert country (pictured above). Gas in Kamloops, Savona and Cache Creek.

E 395.3 (636.2 km) **J 201.1** (323.6 km) Petro-Canada gas/diesel station.

E 411.4 (662.1 km) **J 185** (297.7 km) Private campground.

E 412.9 (664.5 km) **J 183.5** (295.3 km) Fruit stand at access road west to McLure Ferry across the North Thompson River to Westsyde Road, which goes south to Kamloops and north to Barriere.

E 414.6 (667.2 km) **J 181.8** (292.6 km) Small community of **McLure**; restaurant.

E 416.1 (669.6 km) **J 180.3** (290.2 km) Fish Trap rest area.

E 419.5 (675.1 km) **J 176.9** (284.7 km) Thompson River overlook. The North Thompson River rises in the Cariboo Mountains and flows southward to meet the South Thompson at Kamloops. The route was made famous by a small group of Overlanders, led by Thomas McMicking, who turned south at Tete Jaune Cache and headed for Fort Kamloops on their way to the Cariboo goldfields in 1862. It took the party of 32 men and 1 pregnant woman with 3 children almost a month to reach the fort. The day after their arrival, Mrs. Catherine Schubert delivered her fourth child, Rose. The story of their trip is one of incredible privation and courage.

E 422.3 (679.6 km) **J 174.1** (280.2 km) Louis Creek (unincorporated) antique store. Information boards adjacent store.

E 424 (682.3 km) **J 172.4** (277.4 km) Entering community of Barriere northbound; Esso to west and Fas Gas stations with gas/diesel, propane and open 24-hours. RV park.

E 424.9 (683.8 km) **J 171.5** (276 km) BARRIERE (area pop. 5,000); Petro-Canada gas station with diesel, A&W, restaurants, motels, liquor store and other services. Visitor information centre.

E 425.7 (685.1 km) **J 170.7** (274.7 km) Private RV park.

E 426.2 (685.9 km) **J 170.2** (273.9 km) Turnout with litter bin and information sign.

E 431.3 (694.1 km) **J 165.1** (265.7 km) Large turnout with litter bin and view of Thompson River.

E 432.4 (695.9 km) **J 164** (263.9 km) Unincorporated community of Darfield.

E 440.3 (708.6 km) **J 156.1** (251.2 km) Private RV park.

E 443.5 (713.7 km) **J 152.9** (246.1 km) LITTLE FORT (pop. 200); general store/ Husky gas station with diesel, Subway sandwich shop and lodging in small motels and RV Parks.

E 443.6 (713.9 km) **J 152.8** (245.9 km) **Junction** with Highway 24, which leads west 60 miles/97 km to Highway 97 near 100 Mile House on the West Access Route. This road gives access to great rainbow fishing in many lakes, including Bridge and Sheridan lakes.

E 443.8 (714.2 km) **J 152.6** (245.6 km) Turnoff for creekside rest area.

E 446.2 (718.1 km) **J 150.2** (241.7 km) Rivermont Motel, cafe, camping.

E 446.6 (718.7 km) **J 149.8** (241.1 km) Highway parallels North Thompson River.

Roadside turnout beside river with litter bins.

E 447.2 (719.7 km) **J 149.2** (240.1 km) Roadside turnout with litter bin beside river.

E 453.2 (729.2 km) **J 143.2** (230.4 km) Roadside turnout with litter bin beside river.

E 457.4 (736.1 km) **J 139** (223.7 km) **Junction** with North Thompson Highway.

E 459.4 (739.3 km) **J 137** (220.5 km) **North Thompson River Provincial Park**, 61 campsites, sani-station $5, picnic area and fishing at the mouth of the Clearwater River. Camping fee $21 per night. River trail is 1.2 km.

E 460.4 (740.9 km) **J 136** (218.9 km) Clearwater River bridge. The Overlanders named this river after its crystal-clear waters that contrasted strongly with the muddy Thompson.

E 461.8 (743.2 km) **J 134.6** (216.6 km) **Junction** with Village Road at **CLEARWATER** (pop. 7,000); lodging, restaurant, camping options and liquor store at this intersection. The village road (Old North Thompson Highway) leads west approximately 1 mile to a small business area with gas stations, grocery, liquor store, restaurant, and banks. Also access to RCMP and lodging to west. Access to post office and village office to east. **Emergency Services**: Phone 911 for all emergencies. **Police**, phone 250-674-2237.

Visitor information: Clearwater & District Chamber of Commerce, phone 250-674-2646, www.clearwaterbcchamber.com or www.wellsgray.ca. Stop by the Visitor Infocentre at **Milepost E 462.4**. As the gateway to Wells Gray Provincial Park, Clearwater offers many traveler services and a variety of recreational opportunities year-round. Clearwater is a popular stopover for Jasper-bound travelers.

E 462.4 (744.1 km) **J 134** (215.6 km) Roundabout at **junction** with **Clearwater Valley Road** to Wells Gray Provincial Park. Park road is narrow and paved to turnoff for Helmcken Falls at Mile 26.4/42.5 km, then continues as a gravel road 16.3 miles/26.3 km more to end at Clearwater Lake. Motels, pub, restaurants, grocery and gas stations at this intersection. A KOA campground is located 0.1 mile west on this road; a bakery/cafe is 0.2 mile west.

Wells Gray Provincial Park is a magnificent wilderness in the Cariboo Mountains. The park information centre is located at the northwest corner of this intersection. Stop in for a map and detailed information on camping, hiking and lodging in the park. The park has campgrounds (Pyramid 50 units; Clearwater Lake 39 units; Falls Creek 41 units; Mayhood Lake, 32 units and 5 double units), several picnic areas and more than a dozen hiking trails, but is perhaps best known for its spectacular waterfalls, easily accessible from this side road. These are: Spahats Falls, at Mile 6.4/10.3 km (10 minute walk to viewpoint); Dawson Falls, at Mile 25.4/40.9 km (10 minute walk on broad trail to view); and Helmcken Falls, 26.4 miles/42.5 km to turnoff and 2.5 miles/4 km to parking area. Helmcken Falls Lodge, built in 1948, offers accommodations and dinner at Mile 21.5/34.6 km on the park access road.

NOTE: Make sure you fill your gas tank in Clearwater; there is no gas on the road into the

park.

E 462.7 (744.6 km) **J 133.7** (215.2 km) Business frontage road access to motel, gas station and Dairy Queen.

E 465.5 (749 km) **J 130.9** (210.6 km) Stop of interest, Raft River, riparian zone.

E 468.8 (754.4 km) **J 127.6** (205.3 km) Turn downhill to east for Birch Island rest area with litter bins and viewpoint over the Thompson River valley.

E 469.5 (755.6 km) **J 126.9** (204.2 km) Private campground.

E 474.5 (763.6 km) **J 121.9** (196.2 km) Turnout with litter bin to east.

E 477.7 (768.8 km) **J 118.7** (191 km) Road east to community of **Vavenby**, centre of valley sheep farming.

E 486.8 (783.4 km) **J 109.6** (176.4 km) Mad River bridge. The river gives its name to the rapids in the river below, where the weary Overlanders had to portage their rafts.

E 492.8 (793.1 km) **J 103.6** (166.7 km) Turnout with litter bins to east beside Thompson River.

E 493.5 (794.2 km) **J 102.9** (165.6 km) Roadside turnout to west.

E 495.4 (797.2 km) **J 101** (162.5 km) Turnoff to east for large rest area with litter bins and picnic tables beside Thompson River. Children's playground.

E 495.6 (797.6 km) **J 100.8** (162.2 km) Roadside turnout to east.

E 503.4 (810.1 km) **J 93** (149.7 km) Roadside turnout with litter bin to east.

E 504 (811.1 km) **J 92.4** (148.7 km) Community of **AVOLA**; gas station and food store, restaurant and lodging.

E 504.2 (811.4 km) **J 92.2** (148.4 km) North Thompson River Bridge.

E 504.6 (812.1 km) **J 91.8** (147.7 km) Roadside turnout with litter bin to west.

E 505.5 (813.5 km) **J 90.9** (146.3 km) Roadside turnout with litter bin to west.

E 513.7 (826.7 km) **J 82.7** (133.1 km) Paved chain-up/parking area both sides of highway.

E 514.6 (828.1 km) **J 81.8** (131.6 km) Access road leads 2 miles/3 km to Little Hell's Gate Regional Park and view of Porte d'Enfer, or Hell's Gate canyon, below the highway. The Thompson River turns abruptly through a narrow canyon and emerges south into tempestuous whirlpools. Here the Overlanders had to abandon their rafts (after a member of the party and all the horses were drowned) and go around the rapids on foot. It took them 3 days to make the 8.5-mile/14-km walk.

E 515.4 (839.4 km) **J 81** (130.4 km) Turnout to west with litter bin and toilet. Highway descends next 2.5 miles/4 km northbound from Mesiter Summit (elev. 2,411 feet/735m). View south of North Thompson River valley with the Monashee Mountains to the east, the Cariboo Mountains to the west.

E 521.8 (839.8 km) **J 74.6** (120.1 km) North Thompson River Bridge.

E 527.7 (849.2 km) **J 68.7** (110.6 km) Roadside turnouts with litter bins both sides of highway.

Slow for 70-kmph/43-mph speed zone northbound.

E 528.1 (849.9 km) **J 68.3** (109.9 km) Entering Blue River northbound; Husky gas station and restaurant, Sandman Inn and Tony's Grill restaurant.

E 528.5 (850.5 km) **J 67.9** (109.3 km) Petro-Canada gas station and Rocky Mountain Deli and Glacier Mountain Lodge. **BLUE RIVER** (area pop. 300) began as a divisional point on the Canadian National Railway and is today a jumping-off point for heli-skiing, snowmobiling, backcountry skiing, hiking and fishing in the Monashee and Cariboo mountains.

E 528.9 (851.2 km) **J 67.5** (108.6 km) **Junction** with Murtle Lake Road (gravel) which leads west 15 miles/24 km to Wells Gray Provincial Park's Murtle Lake (accessible by hiking trail), considered to be one of the most beautiful, canoe only, wilderness lakes in British Columbia. Also access this side road to Saddle Mountain, motel and Blue River campground.

E 529.1 (851.5 km) **J 67.3** (108.3 km) Blue River bridge.

E 529.8 (852.6 km) **J 66.6** (107.2 km) Roadside turnout to west with litter bin and Blue River information sign.

E 534.5 (860.2 km) **J 61.9** (99.6 km) Whitewater River.

E 536.3 (862.9 km) **J 60.1** (96.7 km) Gravel turnout to east.

E 537.5 (865 km) **J 58.9** (94.8 km) Thunder River, a tributary of the Thompson River.

E 537.7 (865.3 km) **J 58.7** (94.5 km) Turnoff to west for rest area by Thunder River.

E 540.6 (870 km) **J 55.8** (89.8 km) Roadside turnout with litter bin to east.

E 542.3 (873.4 km) **J 53.6** (86.2 km) Mileage Creek.

E 549.8 (884.8 km) **J 46.6** (75 km) Roadside turnout with litter bin to east.

E 553 (889.8 km) **J 43.4** (69.8 km) North Thompson River Crossing.

E 554 (892.5 km) **J 41.7** (67.1 km) North Thompson River Crossing (again).

E 556.3 (895.1 km) **J 40.1** (64.5 km) North Thompson River, steel girder bridge.

E 556.8 (896.1 km) **J 39.6** (63.7 km) Albreda River bridge.

E 557.8 (897.5 km) **J 38.6** (62.1 km) Dominion Creek.

E 559.9 (901 km) **J 36.5** (58.7 km) Roadside turnout with litter bin to east.

E 564.2 (908 km) **J 32.2** (51.8 km) Large turnout to west.

E 566.7 (912 km) **J 29.7** (47.8 km) Large turnout to west with litter bin. Good view southbound of Albreda Glacier. Northbound, the highway enters the Rocky Mountain Trench.

E 570.8 (918.6 km) **J 25.6** (41.2 km) Summit River Lodge.

E 576.7 (927.9 km) **J 19.7** (31.7 km) Gravel pull through to west.

E 577.8 (929.9 km) **J 18.6** (29.9 km) Paved parking both sides of highway.

E 579.5 (932.6 km) **J 16.9** (27.2 km) Canoe River bridge.

E 580.1 (933.6 km) **J 16.3** (26.2 km) Canoe River campground.

E 581.5 (935.8 km) **J 14.9** (24 km) Cedarside Regional Park. Parking area, swimming beach, picnic tables and fire pits. It has easy access.

E 581.9 (936.5 km) **J 14.5** (23.3 km) Kinbasket Lake turnoff. Follow the East Canoe Forest Service Road until you reach Km 21/13 miles and the Valemount Marina with boat launch. Campsites nearby.

E 583 (938 km) **J 13.4** (21.6 km) *Slow for 70-kmph/43-mph speed zone northbound entering Valemount.*

E 583.1 (938.4 km) **J 13.3** (21.4 km) Best Western Valemount Inn & Suites. Robert W. Starratt Wildlife Sanctuary a Ducks Unlimited project with trails and walkways. Two viewing sites with observation towers. Use trail across dike.

E 584 (939.8 km) **J 12.4** (20 km) Frontage road exit northbound to Co-op Cardlock gas station, auto parts and supplies, post office, coffee shop and hotels and motels. West to Shell gas/diesel station.

Valemount

E 584.3 (940.3 km) **J 12.1** (19.5 km) Located on Highway 5, midway between Kamloops and Prince George. **Population:** 1,100. **Elevation:** 2,667 ft/800m. **Emergency Services:** Phone 911 for all emergency services. Hospital, phone 250-566-9138.

Visitor Information: Valemount Visitor Information Centre just off of Highway 5 at 785 Cranberry Lake Road, 250-566-9893; open May–Sept. www.visitvalemount.ca. The Centre has interpretive displays on the natural history of the area, a gallery, and a store with local arts and crafts and Valemount and B.C. souvenirs. Get trip planning help and book local activities here. Discounted tickets for provincial attractions and accommodation reservations available.

Like a number of communities in northern British Columbia, Valemount relied on forestry for the past 100 years. Due to its strategic location, however, Valemount has diversified its economy to include tourism, with hotels, bed and breakfasts and several restaurants providing hospitality services. There is white-water rafting, guided fishing, horseback riding, ATV tours and helicopter tours.

Area attractions include Mount Robson Provincial Park (tallest peak in the Canadian Rockies and World Heritage Site) and Robert W. Starratt Wildlife Sanctuary, which has more than 90 species of birds and animals. Valemount Museum is located in a restored 1914 Railway Station and features a trapper's cabin, a model railroad and

local history.

Central Access Route Log

(continued)

E 584.7 (941 km) **J 11.7** (18.8 km) Private campgrounds both sides of highway and a bed and breakfast.

E 585 (941.4 km) **J 11.4** (18.3 km) Turnouts with litter bins both sides of highway.

E 585.1 (941.6 km) **J 11.3** (18.2 km) Turnoff to east for **Irvin's RV Park**. Full range of facilities for all sizes of RV rigs. Web address: www.irvinsrvpark.com.

Irvin's RV Park. See display ad on page 239 in YELLOWHEAD section.

E 587 (944.5 km) **J 9.4** (15.1 km) Helitours offered to the east.

E 588.3 (946.7 km) **J 8.1** (13 km) **Mount Terry Fox Viewpoint** and rest area, toilets, recycling and litter bins to west. The mountain was named in 1981 for Terry Fox, a young Canadian who started an epic run across Canada on 1 leg to raise funds for cancer research. Before a recurrence of cancer took his life midway through the run, Fox raised some $25 million.

E 592.4 (953.3 km) **J 4** (6.4 km) Turnoff for Jackman Flats Provincial Park picnic area. Unique ecosystem, several short hiking trails (some with bird watching and plant identification signs).

E 595.9 (959 km) **J 0.5** (0.8 km) **Tete Jaune Cache** (pronounced Tee John Cash) Access Road leads west; limited services, 2 mountain lodges. *Tete Jaune* is French for "yellow head." Reputedly, a fair-haired trapper regularly cached his furs here in the 18th century.

E 596.2 (959.5 km) **J 0.2** (0.3 km) Fraser River bridge.

E 596.4 (959.8 km) **J 0** Yellowhead 5 ends northbound at a cloverleaf **junction** with Yellowhead Highway 16. Prince George, BC, is 171 miles/275 km west from this junction; Jasper, AB, is 63 miles/101 km east from here.

Junction with Yellowhead Highway 16. Turn to **Milepost E 282.9** on page 239 in the YELLOWHEAD HIGHWAY section for log of highway to Prince George.

Valemount has food, gas, lodging and camping for Yellowhead Highway 5 travelers.
(©Kris Valencia, staff)

Alaska Highway via
West Access Route

CONNECTS: Seattle, WA, to Dawson Creek, BC

Length: 807 miles   **Road Surface:** Paved   **Season:** Open all year

(See maps, pages 89-90)

(See maps, pages 89-90)

5   🍁   97

British Columbia's Cariboo Country along Highway 97. (©Kris Valencia, staff)

Distance in miles	Cache Creek	Dawson Creek	Prince George	Seattle
Cache Creek		519	274	288
Dawson Creek	519		245	807
Prince George	274	245		562
Seattle	288	807	562	

Canadian border crossing at Sumas via I-5 and Washington Highways 539 and 546; Trans-Canada Highway 1 from Abbotsford to Cache Creek; Highway 97, the "Cariboo Highway," from Cache Creek to Prince George; and the John Hart Highway (also Highway 97) from Prince George to Dawson Creek.

Distances via this 807-mile route between Seattle, WA, and Dawson Creek, BC, are: Seattle to Abbotsford, 118 miles; Abbotsford to Cache Creek, 170 miles; Cache Creek to Prince George, 274 miles; and Prince George to Dawson Creek, 245 miles.

The West Access Route junctions with Yellowhead Highway 16 at Prince George. This east–west highway connects Prince George with Prince Rupert, departure point for the Alaska Marine Highway System and BC Ferries. Yellowhead Highway 16 also connects Prince George, BC, with Edmonton, AB, on the East Access Route to the Alaska Highway. Turn to the YELLOWHEAD HIGHWAY 16 section for a complete log of that route.

The West Access Route offers several interesting side trips and alternate routes for northbound travelers. Also logged in this section for your consideration are: the continuation of the Interstate 5 log for those traveling from Bellingham to Van-

For West Coast motorists, the West Access Route has been the most direct route to Dawson Creek, BC, and the start of the Alaska Highway since 1952, when the John Hart Highway connecting Prince George and Dawson Creek was completed. Prior to that, all Alaska Highway-bound traffic had to go through Edmonton, AB.

The West Access Route links Interstate 5, Trans-Canada Highway 1 and BC Highway 97. *The MILEPOST®* log of this route is divided into 4 sections: Seattle to the

Major Attractions:

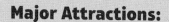

©Kris Valencia, staff

Fraser River Canyon/Hell's Gate, Barkerville Provincial Historic Town

Highest Summit:

Begbie Summit 4,042 ft.

West Access Route — Seattle, WA, to Lac La Hache, BC (includes Sea to Sky Highway)

© 2014 The MILEPOST®

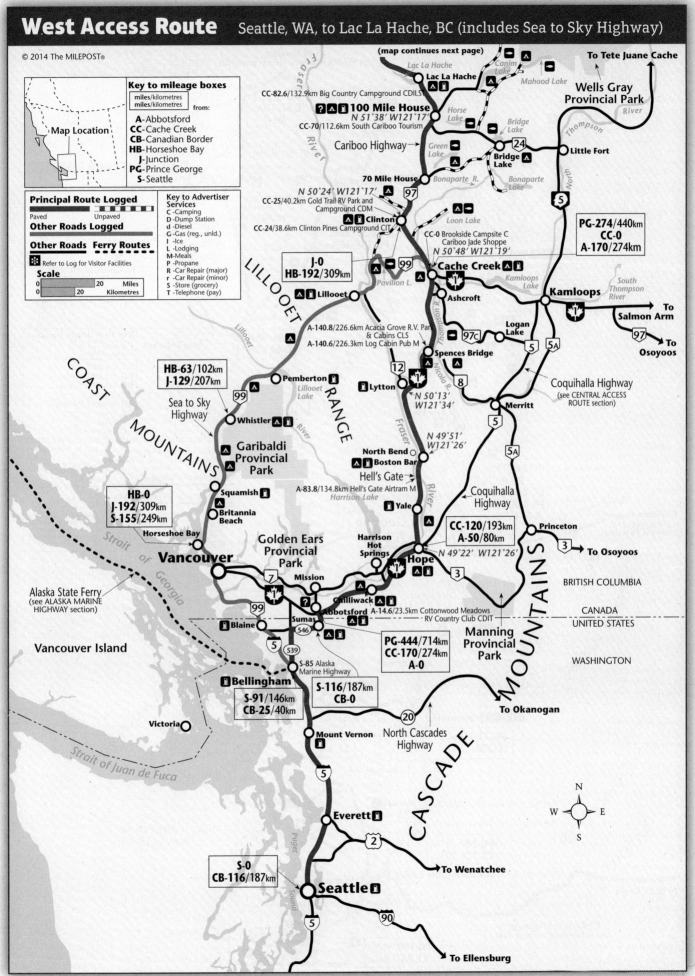

Key to mileage boxes

miles/kilometres
miles/kilometres   from:

A - Abbotsford
CC - Cache Creek
CB - Canadian Border
HB - Horseshoe Bay
J - Junction
PG - Prince George
S - Seattle

Map Location

Principal Route Logged
Paved ▬▬▬   Unpaved ▬ ▬ ▬

Other Roads Logged ▬▬▬

Other Roads ▬▬▬   **Ferry Routes** ▬ ▬ ▬

✴ Refer to Log for Visitor Facilities

Scale
0 ———— 20 Miles
0 ———— 20 Kilometres

Key to Advertiser Services
C - Camping
D - Dump Station
d - Diesel
G - Gas (reg., unld.)
I - Ice
L - Lodging
M - Meals
P - Propane
R - Car Repair (major)
r - Car Repair (minor)
S - Store (grocery)
T - Telephone (pay)

(map continues next page)

To Tete Juane Cache

Wells Gray Provincial Park

Lac La Hache
CC-82.6/132.9km Big Country Campground CDILST

100 Mile House
N 51°38' W121°17'
CC-70/112.6km South Cariboo Tourism

Cariboo Highway

Little Fort

70 Mile House
N 50°24' W121°17'
CC-25/40.2km Gold Trail RV Park and Campground CDM

Clinton
CC-24/38.6km Clinton Pines Campground CIT

J-0
HB-192/309km

Lillooet

CC-0 Brookside Campsite C
Cariboo Jade Shoppe
N 50°48' W121°19'

PG-274/440km
CC-0
A-170/274km

Cache Creek

Ashcroft

Kamloops

To Salmon Arm

HB-63/102km
J-129/207km

Sea to Sky Highway

Pemberton

A-140.8/226.6km Acacia Grove R.V. Park & Cabins CLS
A-140.6/226.3km Log Cabin Pub M

Spences Bridge

Logan Lake

To Osoyoos

Whistler

Lytton
N 50°13' W121°34'

Merritt

Coquihalla Highway
(see CENTRAL ACCESS ROUTE section)

Garibaldi Provincial Park

N 49°51' W121°26'

North Bend
Boston Bar

Hell's Gate

HB-0
J-192/309km
S-155/249km

Squamish

Britannia Beach

Horseshoe Bay

A-83.8/134.8km Hell's Gate Airtram M

Yale

Coquihalla Highway

Princeton

CC-120/193km
A-50/80km
N 49°22' W121°26'

To Osoyoos

Golden Ears Provincial Park

Harrison Hot Springs

Hope

BRITISH COLUMBIA

Vancouver

Alaska State Ferry
(see ALASKA MARINE HIGHWAY section)

Mission

Chilliwack

CANADA
UNITED STATES

Blaine

Sumas

Abbotsford
A-14.6/23.5km Cottonwood Meadows
RV Country Club CDIT

Manning Provincial Park

PG-444/714km
CC-170/274km
A-0

WASHINGTON

Vancouver Island

S-85 Alaska Marine Highway

Bellingham

S-116/187km
CB-0

S-91/146km
CB-25/40km

To Okanogan

Victoria

Mount Vernon

North Cascades Highway

Everett

To Wenatchee

S-0
CB-116/187km

Seattle

To Ellensburg

COAST MOUNTAINS

LILLOOET RANGE

CASCADE MOUNTAINS

Strait of Georgia

Strait of Juan de Fuca

Puget Sound

Fraser River

Lillooet River

Lillooet Lake

Thompson River

Nicola R.

Fraser River

Harrison Lake

Lac La Hache
Canim Lake
Mahood Lake
Horse Lake
Bridge Lake
Green Lake
Bonaparte R.
Bridge Lake
Bonaparte Lake
Loon Lake
Pavilion L.
Kamloops Lake
South Thompson River
Thompson River
North Thompson River

N
W   E
S

West Access Route

Lac La Hache, BC, to Dawson Creek, BC (includes Chilcotin Hwy., Hwy. 26 to Barkerville, Hudson's Hope Loop, Tumbler Ridge Loop)

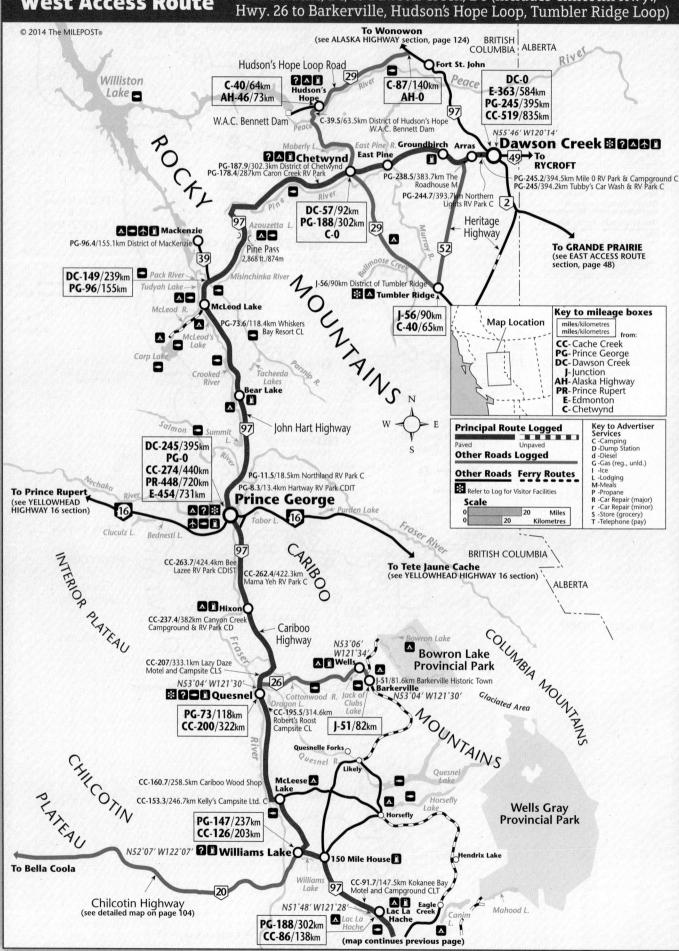

© 2014 The MILEPOST®

To Wonowon
(see ALASKA HIGHWAY section, page 124)

BRITISH COLUMBIA | ALBERTA

River

Williston Lake

Hudson's Hope Loop Road

Fort St. John

29

C-40/64km
AH-46/73km

Hudson's Hope

C-87/140km
AH-0

97

DC-0
E-363/584km
PG-245/395km
CC-519/835km

Peace River

W.A.C. Bennett Dam

C-39.5/63.5km District of Hudson's Hope
W.A.C. Bennett Dam

N55°46' W120°14'

Moberly L.

East Pine R.

Groundbirch

Arras

Dawson Creek

ROCKY

Chetwynd
PG-187.9/302.3km District of Chetwynd
PG-178.4/287km Caron Creek RV Park

East Pine

PG-238.5/383.7km The Roadhouse M

49

To RYCROFT

PG-245.2/394.5km Mile 0 RV Park & Campground C
PG-245/394.2km Tubby's Car Wash & RV Park C

Pine River

DC-57/92km
PG-188/302km
C-0

29

PG-244.7/393.7km Northern Lights RV Park C

2

97

Mackenzie
PG-96.4/155.1km District of MacKenzie

Azouzetta L.

Murray R.

Heritage Highway

52

To GRANDE PRAIRIE
(see EAST ACCESS ROUTE section, page 48)

39

Pine Pass
2,868 ft./874m

Bullmoose Creek

DC-149/239km
PG-96/155km

Pack River

Misinchinka River

J-56/90km District of Tumbler Ridge

Tumbler Ridge

Tudyah Lake

MOUNTAINS

J-56/90km
C-40/65km

McLeod R.

McLeod Lake

PG-73.6/118.4km Whiskers Bay Resort CL

Key to mileage boxes
miles/kilometres
miles/kilometres from:
CC- Cache Creek
PG- Prince George
DC- Dawson Creek
J- Junction
AH- Alaska Highway
PR- Prince Rupert
E- Edmonton
C- Chetwynd

McLeod's Lake

Carp Lake

Parsnip R.

Map Location

Crooked River

Tacheeda Lakes

Bear Lake

John Hart Highway

N
W   E
S

Salmon River

Summit L.

97

DC-245/395km
PG-0
CC-274/440km
PR-448/720km
E-454/731km

Nechako River

PG-11.5/18.5km Northland RV Park C
PG-8.3/13.4km Hartway RV Park CDIT

Prince George

Key to Advertiser Services
C- Camping
D- Dump Station
d- Diesel
G- Gas (reg., unld.)
I- Ice
L- Lodging
M- Meals
P- Propane
R- Car Repair (major)
r- Car Repair (minor)
S- Store (grocery)
T- Telephone (pay)

Principal Route Logged
Paved   Unpaved
Other Roads Logged
Other Roads   Ferry Routes
Refer to Log for Visitor Facilities
Scale
0   20   Miles
0   20   Kilometres

To Prince Rupert
(see YELLOWHEAD HIGHWAY 16 section)

16

Cluculz L.

Bednesti L.

Tabor L.

16

Purden Lake

Fraser River

To Tete Jaune Cache
(see YELLOWHEAD HIGHWAY 16 section)

BRITISH COLUMBIA

ALBERTA

CARIBOO

97

CC-263.7/424.4km Bee Lazee RV Park CDIST
CC-262.4/422.3km Mama Yeh RV Park C

Hixon

CC-237.4/382km Canyon Creek Campground & RV Park CD

Cariboo Highway

Bowron Lake

Bowron Lake Provincial Park

COLUMBIA MOUNTAINS

N53°06' W121°34'

Wells

J-51/81.6km Barkerville Historic Town

CC-207/333.1km Lazy Daze Motel and Campsite CLS

26

Cottonwood R.

Barkerville
N53°04' W121°30'

Glaciated Area

N53°04' W121°30'

Quesnel

Jack of Clubs Lake

Dragon L.

PG-73/118km
CC-200/322km

CC-195.5/314.6km Robert's Roost Campsite CL

J-51/82km

Fraser River

Quesnel R.

Quesnelle Forks

Likely

Quesnel Lake

Wells Gray Provincial Park

CC-160.7/258.5km Cariboo Wood Shop

McLeese Lake

MOUNTAINS

CHILCOTIN

CC-153.3/246.7km Kelly's Campsite Ltd. C

Horsefly Lake

PLATEAU

INTERIOR PLATEAU

Horsefly

PG-147/237km
CC-126/203km

N52°07' W122°07'

Williams Lake

150 Mile House

Hendrix Lake

To Bella Coola

20

Chilcotin Highway
(see detailed map on page 104)

Williams Lake

97

CC-91.7/147.5km Kokanee Bay Motel and Campground CLT

Eagle Creek

Canim L.

Mahood L.

N51°48' W121°28'

Lac La Hache

PG-188/302km
CC-86/138km

Lac La Hache

(map continues previous page)

I-5: Bellingham to Vancouver

West Access Route travelers may choose to continue north on Interstate 5 and cross the international border at Blaine—rather than cross at Sumas (as logged on the main West Access Route)—following Highway 99 to Vancouver, British Columbia's largest city. Vancouver has many major attractions, a beautiful setting and international flavor.

From Vancouver, Alaska-bound travelers may connect with the Sea to Sky Highway (refer to the "Sea to Sky Highway" log beginning on page 94). Allow about an hour-and-a-half driving time from the international border at Blaine to the start of the Sea to Sky Highway.

Another option: Take BC Ferries from either Tswawwassen or Horseshoe Bay to Vancouver Island, and drive north to Port Hardy for B.C. Ferries service to Prince Rupert (see Index for Vancouver Island Highway log).

Distance in miles from Seattle (S) is shown.

INTERSTATE 5

S 91 Exit 256A to **junction** with SR 539N/Guide-Meridian Road to Lynden and Canadian border crossing at Sumas (*see page 92 for log*). Exit 256B to Bellis Fair Mall Parkway. Food, gas and lodging at this exit.

S 92 Exit 257 to Northwest Avenue.

S 93 Exit 258 to Bakerview Road and Bellingham International Airport; food, lodging, gas and diesel at exit. Southbound access to Bellis Fair Mall.

S 95 Exit 260 to Slater Road, Lummi Island. Access to mini-mart with gas/diesel.

S 97 Exit 262 to Main Street/Ferndale city center. Gas and diesel.

S 98 Exit 263 to Portal Way and Ferndale; 24-hour gas and diesel to east.

S 101 Exit 266 to Custer, Grandview Road, SR 548 North.

S 102.5 Rest area.

S 105 Exit 270 to Lynden and Birch Bay; 24-hour gas and diesel at exit. Shopping mall to west. Birch Bay-Lynden Road leads 8 miles east to **junction** with SR 539 (Guide-Meridian Road).

S 109 Exit 274 to Blaine via Loomis Trail Road, Blaine Road and Peace Portal Drive; access to Semiahmoo Resort.

S 110 Exit 275 to Truck Customs (all buses and commercial vehicles) via SR 543 North 2 miles to 24-hour Customs. Access to Blaine via H Street.

S 111 Exit 276 to **BLAINE** (pop. 5,062, area 12,533) city center. This is the last exit northbound before the international border; food, gas, diesel, lodging. Visitor information available.

Freeway ends northbound.

S 111.5 U.S. Customs. **Peace Arch State Park**, dedicated in 1921, lies on the boundary between the U.S. and Canada. One half of the 67-foot-high Peace Arch rests in each country. Picnic areas and Japanese garden, open daily 8 A.M. until dusk. Views of Semiahmoo Bay, Blaine, WA and White Rock, BC.

S 112 Canadian customs. Peak hours for crossing have wait times more than an hour.

Begin 4-lane divided freeway northbound.

BC HIGHWAY 99

S 112.5 Exit 2 to 8th Ave. and **junction** with Trans-Canada Highway 1 to Hope.

S 117.4 Exit 10 King George Highway, Surrey City centre.

S 121.1 Exit 16 North Delta, New Westminster. Alternate Route 91 North to Vancouver.

S 123.5 Exit 20 Ladner, Point Roberts, Boundary Bay Airport; gas.

S 128.3 Exit 28 River Road to Tswawwassen and B.C. Ferries to Vancouver Island; gas, lodging. See "Vancouver Island Highway to

Port Hardy" for description of the route to Port Hardy and ferry service to Prince Rupert.

S 129.6 Tunnel next 0.5 miles/0.8 km northbound.

S 130.4 Richmond Visitor Centre.

S 130.8 Exit 32 Steveston Highway.

S 133 Exit 36 Westminster Highway.

S 133.4 Exit 37 to Highway 91.

S 134.9 Exit 39 Bridgeport Road, Vancouver International Airport.

Entering City of Vancouver. *Freeway ends northbound. Follow signs for Whistler/BC Ferries (Horseshoe Bay) for continuation of Highway 99/Sea to Sky Highway.*

S 138.1 Turn left northbound on West 41st Street.

S 138.6 Turn right northbound on Granville Street.

S 141 Crossing Granville Bridge.

S 141.4 Exit to Seymour Street/99N at end of bridge.

S 142.2 Turn left northbound on to Georgia Street/99N.

S 143.4 Road forks northbound to Stanley Park. North to Lions Gate Bridge.

S 144.8 South end of Lions Gate Bridge.

S 145.7 North end of Lions Gate Bridge. Exit for West Vancouver/99N, BC Ferries, Horseshoe Bay.

S 146.4 Turn right northbound on Taylor Way/99/1A. (*If you miss this turn, Park Royal Shopping Centre will be on either side of Marine Drive: backtrack to Taylor Way.*)

S 147 **Junction** with BC Highway 99/Trans-Canada Highway 1 West (Upper Levels Highway).

S 154.5 Exit 3 (only for traffic coming from Vancouver) on Trans-Canada Highway 1 to Horseshoe Bay/BC Ferries service to Nanaimo on Vancouver Island. Trans-Canada Highway 1 ends here, becoming the toll lanes for B.C. Ferries, then continues on Vancouver Island from Nanaimo south to Victoria.

Sea to Sky Highway/BC Highway 99 rather seamlessly begins and ends here. Distance to Squamish (27 miles/43 km), Whistler (63 miles/102 km), Pemberton 83 miles/134 km, and junction with Highway 97 near Cache Creek (192 miles/309 km).

See "Sea to Sky Highway" log on page 94.

---

couver; Highway 99, the "Sea to Sky Highway," a scenic, mountainous route between Vancouver and the Cariboo; Highway 26 to Barkerville, a provincial historic town dating back to the 1860s; scenic Chilcotin Highway 20 to Bella Coola; Highway 29 south to Tumbler Ridge and access to Kinuseo Falls, logged as "Tumbler Ridge Loop"; and Highway 29 north from Chetwynd to the Alaska Highway via Hudson's Hope, with access to W.A.C. Bennett Dam, which is logged as the "Hudson's Hope Loop."

West Access Route Log

This section of the log shows distance from Seattle (S) followed by distance from the Canadian border (CB) at Sumas.

INTERSTATE HIGHWAY 5 NORTH

Physical mileposts (and exit numbers) on

Interstate Highway 5 reflect distance from the Washington–Oregon border.

S 0 CB 116 Exit 165 northbound (165B southbound) to downtown **SEATTLE** (pop. 620,778). Seattle exits next 10 miles northbound on Interstate 5.

S 11 CB 105 Exit 176 to NE 175 St. and Highway 99, Shoreline; all services.

S 12 CB 104 Exit 177 to 244th/Lake Forest Park to east and west 4.5 miles to Edmonds and Kingston Ferry. Food, gas, diesel east off exit.

S 14 CB 102 Exit 179 220th Street; gas and diesel west off exit. Hospital 2 miles west.

S 15.5 CB 100.5 Exit 181A to Lynnwood/44th Avenue, Brier, Edmonds Community College.

S 16 CB 100 Exit 181B to Alderwood Mall Parkway; shopping.

S 17 CB 99 Exit 182 to **junction** with Interstate 405 South to Bellevue/Renton and

to Highway 525/99 northwest to Mukilteo with access to Alderwood Mall Parkway.

S 18 CB 98 Exit 183 to 164th St. SW; Walmart, major-chain motel and fast-food outlets.

S 21 CB 95 Exit 186 to 128th St. SW/96E; 24-hour gas, diesel, food and lodging.

S 23 CB 93 Exit 188 Weigh station both sides, 24-hour truck stop, Silver Lake rest area southbound.

S 24 CB 92 Exit 189 to Everett Mall Way, Highways 527/99/526; lodging east off exit. Also access to food, gas, and diesel. Everett Mall is a major shopping destination.

S 27 CB 89 Exit 192 to Broadway/41st St., Everett city center; food, gas, diesel, lodging.

S 28 CB 88 Exit 193 Pacific Avenue/SR 529/US Hwy. 2E. Access to **EVERETT** (pop. 104,295) city center and Everett Events Center; all services.

S 29 CB 87 Exit 194 to U.S. Highway 2

Built for the 1964 World's Fair, Seattle's Space Needle offers bird's-eye views of the city.
(©John Erskine)

East to Snohomish.

S 29.5 CB 86.5 Exit 195 northbound to Port of Everett, Marine View Drive.

S 30 CB 85 Snohomish River.

S 32 CB 83 Union Slough.

S 34 CB 82 Exit 199 to SR 528 and **MARYSVILLE** (pop. 60,785); easy on-off for food, gas, diesel, lodging both sides of freeway.

S 35 CB 81 Exit 200 to 88th St. NE/ Quil Ceda Way; gas/diesel and 24-hour grocery and pharmacy east off exit. Quil Ceda Village (Walmart, Home Depot) and Tulalip Casino west off exit, with access to Seattle Premium Outlets mall.

S 37 CB 79 Exit 202 116th Street NE; State Patrol; gas stations, food and access west to Seattle Premium Outlets mall.

S 41 CB 75 Exit 206 to Lakewood, Smokey Point and Arlington Airport; 24-hour gas, diesel, food, shopping east off exit. Costco, Target to west. Visitor information.

S 42 CB 74 Milepost 207. Rest areas both sides of interstate. The northbound rest area has a giant arborvitae.

S 43 CB 73 Exit 208 to Silvana, Arlington, Darrington and SR 530; easy on-off to food, gas/diesel, lodging.

S 44.5 CB 71.5 Stillaguamish River. A popular fishing river it offers cutthroat trout, king and silver salmon, and steelhead. Summer fly-fishing only. Check state regulations before fishing.

S 45 CB 71 Exit 210 to 236th St. NE; Angel of the Winds Casino.

S 47 CB 69 Exit 212 to Stanwood, Camano Island, SRS 232W; easy access to gas/diesel and 24-hour supermarket west off exit.

S 49 CB 67 Milepost 214. Weigh station northbound.

S 50 CB 66 Exit 215 to 300th St. NW.

S 52.5 CB 63.5 Entering Skagit County northbound.

S 53 CB 63 Exit 218 to Starbird Road; no services.

S 56 CB 60 Exit 221 to Conway, La Conner (11 miles), SR 534, Lake McMurray; easy access to gas/diesel stations east and west off exit.

S 59 CB 57 Exit 224 to Old Highway 99S. Food, gas, diesel, services.

S 60 CB 56 Exit 225 to Anderson Road; easy access to gas/diesel stations east and west off exit.

S 61 CB 55 Exit 226 to SR 536W, Kincaid Street, **MOUNT VERNON** (pop. 32,070) city center; all services.

S 62 CB 54 Exit 227 to College Way, SR 538E; easy access to food, gas/diesel, lodging and shopping just off exit.

S 63.5 CB 52.5 Skagit River.

S 64 CB 52 Exit 229 George Hopper Road; access to shopping malls.

S 65 CB 51 Exit 230 east to Burlington, North Cascades Hwy.; west to Anacortes. Shopping, food, gas/diesel, lodging, 24-hour supermarket at exit.

S 66 CB 50 Exit 231 to Bow-Edison, Chuckanut Drive/SR 11N scenic route.

S 67 CB 49 Exit 232 to Cook Road, Sedro Woolley; easy access to 24-hour gas and diesel (Shell, 76), food (DQ, Subway), lodging and camping (Burlington KOA). For campground, exit east to light, then turn north and follow signs 3.5 miles on North Green Road.

S 69 CB 47 Samish River.

S 71 CB 45 Exit 236 to Bow-Edison and Bow Hill Road. Exit east for The Skagit (casino with lodging, dining and entertainment). Also access this exit to Burlington KOA (follow signs east then south on North Green Road).

S 73 CB 43 Milepost 238. Bow Hill rest area to east for northbound traffic.

S 73.5 CB 42.5 Bow Hill rest area to west for southbound traffic.

S 75 CB 41 Exit 240 to Alger; easy gas and diesel east off exit.

S 76 CB 40 Entering Skagit County

southbound.

S 77 CB 39 Exit 242 Nalle Road, South Lake Samish. Entering Whatcom County northbound.

Winding road northbound.

S 81 CB 35 Exit 246 to North Lake Samish and Lake Padden Recreation Area; diesel, gas and groceries west off exit.

S 85 CB 31 Exit 250 South Chuckanut Drive (Fairhaven Parkway); food, pharmacy and gas west off exit. Access to Bellingham's Fairhaven shopping district and to **Bellingham Cruise Terminal**, departure point for Alaska State Ferries. Follow Fairhaven Parkway west 1.3 miles to stoplight at 12th Street; go straight 0.6 mile for ferry terminal (follow signs) or turn on 12th Street for Fairhaven shopping district.

Alaska State Ferries depart Bellingham's Cruise Terminal for Southeast Alaska year-round, with twice-weekly sailings in summer. See "Ferry Travel" in the TRAVEL PLANNING section.

S 87 CB 29 Exit 252 Samish Way, Western Washington University; access to food, gas and diesel and services west off exit.

S 88 CB 28 Exit 253 to Lakeway Drive in **BELLINGHAM** (pop. 81,862); all services. Access east off exit to Bellingham/Whatcom County Visitor Info Center; www.bellingham.org.

S 89 CB 27 Exit 254 to State Street/Iowa Street in Bellingham. Gas and fast-food at exit.

S 90 CB 26 Exit 255 to Sunset Drive, SR 542E (Mount Baker Hwy.). Hospital west off exit. Shopping center, fast food, 24-hour gas station with diesel east off exit.

S 91 CB 25 Exit 256A to **junction** with SR 539N (Meridian St.) to Lynden and Canadian border crossing at Sumas. Exit 256B to Bellis Fair Mall Parkway. Food, gas and lodging at this exit.

The MILEPOST® West Access Route main log exits here to follow Highway 539/Guide-Meridian (12.6 miles), Highway 546 (8 miles) and Highway 9 (4.5 miles) to the international border crossing at Sumas, WA/Abbotsford-Huntingdon, BC, and the junction with Trans-Canada Highway 1 east. Highways 539/546 and 9 are fairly busy 2-lane roads through a semi-rural area with services available in towns along the way.

Northbound travelers who wish to continue on Interstate 5 north to the border crossing at Blaine, WA, and junction with Highway 99 north to Vancouver, BC, see "I-5: Bellingham to Vancouver" page 91. From Vancouver, Highway 99 continues north and east as the "Sea to Sky Highway" to junction with the main West Access Route north of Cache Creek. See "Sea to Sky Highway" log beginning on page 94.

This section of the log shows distance from Interstate 5 junction (J) at Exit 256A followed by distance from the Canadian border (CB) at Sumas.

Highways 539, 546 and 9 are each 2-lane highways through well-populated rural areas with fairly heavy local traffic.

WASHINGTON HIGHWAYS 539, 546 & 9

J 0 CB 23 Exit 256 from Interstate 5 east to Guide-Meridian/Highway 539 North in

Bellingham and access to Bellis Fair Mall.

J 0.1 CB 22.9 Traffic light at Telegraph Road; Denny's restaurant to south, Bellis Fair Mall to north.

J 0.2 CB 22.8 Traffic light; access north to Bellis Fair Mall via Bellis Fair Parkway; access south to shopping and services (Walgreens, Petco, etc.).

J 0.4 CB 22.6 Traffic light; access to lodging, shopping and other services.

J 0.6 CB 22.4 Traffic light; access to lodging, shopping and other services.

J 0.8 CB 22.2 Traffic light; access to lodging, shopping and other services.

J 1 CB 22 Costco to north.

J 1.2 CB 21.8 Traffic light at East Stuart Road; shopping malls both sides of highway.

J 1.3 CB 21.7 Walmart to south.

J 2.3 CB 20.7 Entering Bellingham westbound on SR 539S.

J 3.5 CB 19.5 Traffic light at Smith Road; Chevron gas station.

J 4.5 CB 18.5 Traffic light at Axton Road.

J 5.1 CB 17.9 Traffic light at Laurel Road; 76 gas station.

J 5.8 CB 17.2 Ten Mile Creek.

J 5.9 CB 17.1 Four Mile Creek.

J 6 CB 17 Ten Mile Road roundabout; continue straight through roundabout.

J 7.6 CB 15.4 East Pole Road roundabout. Shell gas station and independent gas station. Continue straight through roundabout on SR 539N/S.

J 8.5 CB 14.5 Wiser Lake Roud roundabout, continue straight through roundabout.

J 9.4 CB 13.6 Nooksack River bridge.

J 9.8 CB 13.2 River Road roundabout, continue straight through roundabout.

J 10.4 CB 12.6 Fish Trap Creek.

J 10.7 CB 12.3 Traffic light at Birch Bay-Lynden Road/Kok Road. Shopping malls and fast-food both sides of highway: Safeway supermarket, DQ, McDonalds, Burger King), Starbucks, drugstore. Continue straight ahead on SR 539N/S.

J 11 CB 12 Traffic light at Front Street access to downtown Lynden. Turnoff to east for city centre. Continue straight ahead on SR 539N/S.

LYNDEN (pop. 12,104) has all services. Lynden's Dutch heritage is evident in its shops and festivals and 72-foot-high windmill in downtown (www.lynden.org).

J 11.5 CB 11.5 Traffic light at Main Street access to downtown Lynden. Turnoff to east for city centre. Continue straight ahead on SR 539N/S.

J 12.6 CB 10.4 Traffic light at **junction** of Highway 539 to/from Bellingham and Highway 546. Travelers bound for the border crossing at Sumas turn right on SR 546. Travelers bound for Interstate 5 turn left on SR 539 (Guide-Meridian) for Bellingham. Posted speed limit is 55mph.

Distance marker eastbound shows Sumas 12 miles, Abbotsford 16 miles.

J 13.1 CB 9.9 Double Ditch Road.

J 13.7 CB 9.3 Benson Road. Physical Milepost 1 on SR 546 indicates distance from junction with SR 539.

J 14.1 CB 8.9 Depot Road roundabout: Continue straight through roundabout. Depot Road leads 1.7 miles south to Front Street in Lynden.

J 14.4 CB 8.6 Bender Road roundabout: Continue straight through roundabout.

J 14.7 CB 8.3 Milepost 2. Shell gas station.

J 15.7 CB 7.3 Milepost 3. Sign for Lynden/Bellingham KOA.

J 20.6 CB 4.4 Traffic light at junction of Highway 546 and Highway 9; Nooksack Valley School. (Do NOT go south on SR 9 if you are following this log!) Northbound travelers continue straight ahead on SR 9 for Sumas and Canadian border. (Mileposts on SR 9 reflect distance from its junction with Highway 522 near Bothell.)

Westbound travelers continue straight ahead on SR 546 West for SR 539 to Bellingham and Interstate 5.

J 22 CB 1 25 mph speed zone northbound through Sumas.

J 23 CB 0 SUMAS (pop. 1,232) has food, gas, lodging, shopping and services. Camping at Sumas RV Park south side of town.

U.S.–Canada international border. The Sumas, WA–Abbotsford-Huntingdon, BC, border crossing is open 24 hours.

Continue north on BC Highway 11 for continuation of West Access Route northbound via Trans-Canada Highway 1 East. Food, shopping and other services are located along BC Highway 11 between the border crossing at Sumas and Trans-Canada Highway 1.

J 25 CB 2 BC Highway 11 junctions with Trans-Canada Highway 1 east. Merge on to Trans-Canada Highway 1 East for Hope and continuation of West Access Route log. (BC Highway 11 continues north to downtown Abbotsford. Trans-Canada Highway 1 West continues to Vancouver.)

This section of the log shows distance from Abbotsford (A) followed by distance from Cache Creek (CC).

TRANS-CANADA HIGHWAY 1 EAST

A 0 CC 170 (273.6 km) Exit 92 to Abbotsford, Mission and Highway 11 south 3 miles/4.8 km to Sumas and the international border. Highway 11 north to **ABBOTSFORD** (pop. 123,864), all visitor services. Abbotsford is the "Raspberry Capital of Canada" and is the home of the Abbotsford International Airshow in August. **Visitor Information:** Use Exit 92 Sumas Way for Abbotsford Visitor Centre at 34561 Delair Rd.; phone 1-888-332-2229; website www.tourismabbotsford.ca; email: info@ tourismabbotsford.ca. A Circle Farm Tour brochure found at the Centre is a great self-guiding tool to use to see this area's agriculture.

Highway 11 north crosses the bridge over the Fraser River to Mission (7.2 miles/11.9 km north), and connects with Highway 7 to Harrison Hot Springs (41 miles/66 km). This 2-lane highway traverses the rural farmland on the north side of the Fraser River, rejoining Trans-Canada Highway 1 at Hope (56 miles/90 km).

A 2 (3.2 km) **CC 168** (270.3 km) Exit 95 to Whatcom Road and westbound access to rest area to south; gas/diesel, food, tourist attractions and lodging north of exit.

A 4 (6.4 km) **CC 166** (267.1 km) Exit 99 (eastbound only) to rest area with phone, picnic tablees, sani-dump.

A 7.5 (12.1 km) **CC 162.5** (261.5 km) Exit 104 to small farming community of Yarrow and No. 3 Road; access to Cultus Lake Rec. Area.

A 10.2 (16.4 km) **CC 159.8** (257.1 km) Vedder Canal.

A 11 (17.7 km) **CC 159** (255.9 km) Exit 109 Yale Road West. Exit for Great Blue Heron Nature Reserve along the Vedder River. Take Yale Road West to Sumas Prairie Road and drive south to road end.

A 14.6 (23.5 km) **CC 155.4** (250 km) Exit 116 to Lickman Road and **CHILLIWACK** (pop. 81,000). **Visitor Information:** Exit south for Chilliwack Visitor Centre, open 9 A.M. to 5 P.M. weekdays year-round, and weekends mid-May to Labour Day; phone 1-800-567-9535; www.tourismchilliwack.com. Visitor Centre has picnic grounds and sani-dump stations open April–Oct. Chilliwack Heritage Park and Chilliwack Antique Powerland located behind the Visitor Centre. Chilliwack has

(Continues on page 97)

Downtown Lynden windmill reflects the community's Dutch heritage. (©Kris Valencia, staff)

Sea to Sky Highway

Highway 99 from Vancouver winds up and over the Coast Mountains. (©Kris Valencia, staff)

The Sea to Sky Highway, an extension of BC Highway 99, is a former logging road that now connects Vancouver, Squamish and Whistler with Lillooet. Completely paved, this scenic 192-mile/309-km highway offers motorists an alternate route from the Fraser River Valley to the BC Interior, connecting with Highway 97 (the Cariboo Highway) just north of Cache Creek. Driving time from Horseshoe Bay to the Highway 97 junction is about 5 hours.

Sea to Sky Highway begins as a winding, 4-lane road along the east shore of stunning Howe Sound, squeezed between the sea and the mountains in a high rainfall area. The highway then climbs up into the coastal mountains with intermittent passing lanes and stretches of 4-lane highway (both divided and undivided), past popular hiking and mountain biking trails, provincial park campgrounds, fishing spots, swimming lakes and rafting rivers. Located on Sea to Sky about an hour's drive from Vancouver is Whistler, a major ski resort in winter as well as a summer destination for thousands of visitors.

Beyond Pemberton, the highway follows the former logging road up and over the Coast Mountains to enter the dramatically different landscape of British Columbia's Interior Plateau. *Between Pemberton and Lillooet, there are long steep grades (9 to 11 percent) with narrow winding road and some hairpin turns.* This highway offers spectacular scenery, and has been significantly improved, but it is not always a relaxing drive. It is busy with fast-moving traffic between Vancouver and Pemberton, and requires alert driving on the narrow, winding sections between Pemberton and the Highway 97 junction. For road reports, go to www.drivebc.ca, which also alerts motorists to special events that may affect traffic .

It is approximately 43 miles/69 km via Highway 99 from the U.S. border to the start of the Sea to Sky Highway at Horseshoe Bay.

Sea to Sky Log

Distance in miles from Horseshoe Bay (HB) is followed by distance in miles from junction with Highway 97 (J).

BC HIGHWAY 99

HB 0 J 192 (308.7 km) Exit 3 (only for traffic coming from Vancouver) on Trans-Canada Highway 1/BC Highway 99 to Horseshoe Bay/BC Ferries service to Nanaimo on Vancouver Island. Trans-Canada Highway 1 ends here, becoming the toll lanes for B.C. Ferries, then continues on Vancouver Island from Nanaimo south to Victoria. Sea to Sky Highway rather seamlessly begins and ends here. Motorists bound for Whistler, Pemberton, Lillooet and Highway 97 junction do NOT exit here, but continue on Highway 99/Sea to Sky Highway. Intermittent passing lanes and 4-lane stretches of highway from here northeast to Pemberton on Highway 99.

IMPORTANT: Traffic on Sea to Sky Highway coming from the direction of Whistler and wishing to exit to Horseshoe Bay for BC Ferries service must proceed to Exit 4 on Trans-Canada Highway 1/BC Highway 99, then follow signs for Horseshoe Bay ferries. You end up returning to Trans-Canada Highway 1 and back-tracking to Exit 3.

HB 9.2 (14.8 km) J 182.8 (294.2 km) Viewpoint to north for southwest-bound traffic only. Good view of Howe Sound, parking, litter bin and point-of-interest signs. A plaque here commemorates completion of the 2009 Sea to Sky Improvement Project.

HB 15.2 (24.4 km) J 176.8 (284.5 km) **Porteau Cove Provincial Park**; 44 vehicle campsites and 16 walk-in sites, hot showers, reservations recommended in summer (Discover Camping), picnicking, swimming, boat launch. Popular scuba diving spot; an old ship has been sunk here to attract marine life. ▲

HB 16.6 (26.7 km) J 175.4 (282.3 km) Furry Creek Drive northbound-only exit. Southbound-only viewpoint of Furry Cove.

HB 17.7 (28.5 km) J 174.3 (280.5 km) Furry Creek Drive southbound-only exit, U-turn route.

HB 20.3 (32.7 km) J 171.7 (276.3 km) Traffic light at access to **BRITANNIA BEACH** (pop. about 300); restaurants and shopping. From 1930 to 1935, Britannia Beach was the British Empire's largest producer of copper. Visit the **BC Museum of Mining**, open daily in summer. Admission charged. *Highway climbs northbound.*

HB 21 (33.8 km) J 171 (275.2 km) Viewpoint with litter bin for southbound traffic.

HB 22.1 (35.6 km) J 169.9 (273.4 km) Turnoff for **Murrin Provincial Park**, a pretty day-use area with swimming, fishing, picnicking, walking trails, steep cliffs suitable for rock climbing, picturesque jewel of Browning Lake within the park and walking trail to nearby Petgill Lake outside the park.

HB 23 (37 km) J 169 (272 km) Viewpoint to west for southbound traffic.

HB 24 (38.6 km) J 168 (270.4 km) Pullout with litter bin for northbound traffic only.

HB 24.1 (38.8 km) J 167.9 (270.2 km) Pullout with litter bin to west for southbound traffic only.

HB 24.8 (39.9 km) J 167.2 (269 km) Traffic light; access to **Shannon Falls Provincial Park.** Very popular day-use park for hiking and picnicking. Falls plunge 1,105 feet/335m, third largest falls in BC. Good walking trails and photo opportunities.

HB 25.4 (40.9 km) J 166.6 (268.1 km) Main parking area for **Stawamus Chief Provincial Park**; day-use area, campground and hiking trails. The park has 15 vehicle campsites (not suitable for RVs) and 45 walk-in campsites. Stawamus Chief is the world's second largest granite monolith (elev. 2,139 feet/652m) known internationally for its challenging rock climbing and a hiking trail for non-climbers, up the backside. ▲

HB 25.7 (41.4 km) J 166.3 (267.6 km) Parking areas both sides of highway; pedestrian bridge.

HB 26.4 (42.5 km) J 165.6 (266.5 km) Traffic light at Valley Drive; gas station with diesel, Chances gaming casino. 🗟

HB 26.7 (43 km) J 165.3 (266 km) Traffic light at Clarke Drive. Parking area.

HB 26.9 (43.3 km) J 165.1 (265.7 km) Shell gas station, fast food. Distance marker westbound shows Horseshoe Bay 43 km/27 miles, Vancouver 64 km/40 miles. 🗟

HB 27.2 (43.7 km) J 164.8 (265.2 km) Mamquam Blind Channel bridge.

HB 27.3 (43.9 km) J 164.7 (265.1 km) Traffic light at Cleveland Avenue in **SQUAMISH** (pop. 14,949); Shopping mall with supermarket, Starbucks and other services; fast-food includes McDonalds and A&W. Follow Cleveland Avenue to downtown Squamish.

Squamish, located at the head of Howe

Sound and overlooked by Mount Garibaldi and Stawamus Chief, has all visitor services. **Visitor information**: www.tourismsquamish.com.

Dubbed the Outdoor Recreation Capital of Canada, Squamish is known for its wind surfing and kite boarding at Squamish Spit, rock climbing in nearby Stawamus Chief Provincial Park and mountain biking opportunities. There is excellent birding (bald eagles) from dikes in Squamish estuary and peregrine falcons nest on Stawamus Chief. The West Coast Heritage Railway Park here has Western Canada's largest collection of heritage railway equipment, including the Royal Hudson steam train in which you may ride the rail for a 3 km route.

HB 28.3 (45.5 km) **J 163.7** (263.4 km) Traffic light at Industrial Way; food, gas and lodging (Wendys, Tim Hortons, Best Western, Chevron).

HB 28.6 (46 km) **J 163.4** (263 km) Traffic light at Commercial Way; Walmart access.

HB 29 (46.7 km) **J 163** (262.3 km) Turnoff for Eagle Vista RV Resort & Campground.

HB 29.2 (47 km) **J 162.8** (262 km) Manaquan River bridge.

HB 29.7 (47.8 km) **J 162.3** (261.2 km) Traffic light at Mamquam Road; Garibaldi Village shopping (food, cinema, shops), Canadian Tire. Mamquam Road leads east 10 miles/16 km to Diamond Head in Garibaldi Provincial Park, 1 of 5 park access points from the highway for this park's backcountry hiking and camping.

HB 30.1 (48.2 km) **J 161.9** (260.5 km) Traffic light at Garibaldi Way; gas, lodging, BC liquor store, London Drugs, Boston Pizza.

HB 31.9 (51.1 km) **J 160.1** (257.6 km) Traffic light at Depot Road, access to **BRACKENDALE** (pop. about 1,000). Brackendale is home to Brackendale Eagles Provincial Park (no visitor facilities), which has one of the largest gatherings of wintering bald eagles in the world.

HB 33.4 (53.5 km) **J 158.6** (255.2 km) Traffic light at Squamish Valley Road (access north to Tenderfoot Hatchery on Midnight Road) and Alice Lake Road south to **Alice Lake Provincial Park**; 108 campsites amid trees with grassy areas, picnicking, swimming, canoeing, birding. Reservations highly recommended in summer for campsites at Alice Lake.

HB 33.6 (53.8 km) **J 158.4** (254.9 km) Turnout with litter bin to south for northeast-bound traffic only, chain-up area in winter. Cheekeye Creek.

HB 36.3 (58.2 km) **J 155.7** (250.5 km) **Brohm Lake** interpretive forest with picnicking and fishing to north.

HB 38.3 (61.4 km) **J 153.7** (247.3 km) Tantalus Lookout (elev. 320m/1,050 feet) for southwest-bound traffic only; parking, litter bins, viewpoint.

HB 43,6 (69.9 km) **J 148.4** (238.8 km) Gravel turnout to north for southwest-bound traffic, viewpoint.

HB 44.2 (70.8 km) **J 147.8** (237.9 km) Viewpoint to north for southwest-bound traffic.

HB 44 (72.1 km) **J 147** (236.6 km) Pull-out to north for southwest-bound traffic.

HB 45.3 (72.6 km) **J 146.7** (236.1 km) Turnout with litter bin to north for south-

west-bound traffic.

HB 46 (73.7 km) **J 146** (235 km) Turnout to south with litter bin for northeast-bound traffic. Chain-up area in winter.

HB 47.9 (76.8 km) **J 144.1** (231.9 km) Turnoff for Garibaldi Lake/Black Tusk in **Garibaldi Provincial Park** via paved road, 1.5 miles/2.5 km to trailhead parking. It is 6 miles/11 km from parking lot to Garibaldi Lake via a well-graded trail. It is 4.6 miles/7.5 km from the parking lot to Taylor Meadows. Both areas have tent spaces and pit toilets. No pets or motorized vehicles allowed in Garibaldi park.

HB 51.5 (82.6 km) **J 140.5** (226.1 km) Pull-out with litter bin and point-of-interest signs to north for southwestbound traffic only.

HB 52.8 (84.7 km) **J 139.2** (224 km) **Brandywine Falls Provincial Park to south**; picnicking, fishing, hiking and biking trails. Falls are 230 feet/66m high, and well worth the 10-minute walk from the road. Good view of Daisy Lake and surrounding mountains. Access to Sea to Sky mountain bike trail.

HB 53.4 (85.7 km) **J 138.6** (223 km) Whistler RV Park campground to north.

HB 56.3 (90.3 km) **J 135.7** (218.4 km) Turnout to south for northeastbound traffic only. Distance marker southwestbound shows Squamish 47 km/29 miles, Vancouver 111 km/69 miles.

HB 58.7 (94.3 km) **J 133.3** (214.5 km) Function Junction. Traffic light at **junction** with Alpha Lake Road and Cheakamus Lake Road. Cheakamus Lake Road leads 5 miles/8.5 km to trailhead parking for easy 1.8-mile/3-km hike to spectacular glacier-fed Cheakamus Lake in Garibaldi Provincial Park.

HB 60.5 (97.1 km) **J 131.5** (211.6 km) Traffic light at Bayshore Drive.

HB 60.9 (97.7 km) **J 131.1** (211 km) Traffic light at Lake Placid Road. Husky gas station with diesel to north, Boston Pizza to south. Whistler Creek.

Northbound, Highway 99 passes a number of residential neighbourhoods—Whistler Creek, Nordic Estates, Highlands, Alta Vista, Blueberry Hill, etc.—that comprise Whistler Resort. A paved walking and cycling trail parallels the highway.

HB 62.6 (100.5 km) **J 129.4** (208.2 km) Traffic light at Blueberry Road.

HB 63.4 (101.7 km) **J 128.6** (207 km) Traffic light at Village Gate Blvd., main entrance to **WHISTLER VILLAGE** (pop. 9,248). *Follow boulevard to public parking areas: There are several very large parking lots, although parking for RVs is somewhat limited.* Whistler is a European-style village, with cobbled streets and pedestrian-only plazas: You will have to park and get out and walk to enjoy the outdoor cafes, exclusive shops and fine restaurants. Whistler offers a variety of upscale accommodations, the most famous of which is Fairmont Chateau Whistler, a 12-storey "castle in the mountains" reminiscent of the turn-of-the-century hotels built by the Canadian Pacific Railway. **Visitor Information:** Visitor Centre at 4230 Gateway Dr., 8 A.M.–10 P.M. daily. www.whistler.com; phone 604-935-3357; 1-800-944-7583.

Whistler Village and adjacent Village North and Upper Village lie between 2 famous side-by-side ski hills, Whistler and Blackcomb (www.whistlerblackcomb.com). Whistler Resort is consistently rated the top ski resort in North America and is the only one to offer summer skiing and snow-boarding (by helicoptering to Horstman Glacier). Whistler hosted the 2010 Winter Olympics and Paralympic Winter Games.

In summer, Whistler boasts some of the world's best golf courses and mountain bike trails. Ride the chairlifts and gondolas for nature walking, alpine hiking and paragliding. Access to Singing Pass hiking trail to Garibaldi Provincial Park from Whistler Village day parking area.

HB 63.8 (102.4 km) **J 128.2** (206.3 km) Traffic light at Lorimer Blvd., turnoff for Upper Whistler Village, medical clinic.

HB 64.1 (102.9 km) **J 127.9** (205.8 km) Traffic light at Nancy Greene Drive/Nesters Road.

Shops and flowers brighten main street of downtown Squamish. (© Kris Valencia, staff).

Sea to Sky Highway

(Continued)

HB 64.6 (103.7 km) **J 127.4** (205 km) Traffic light at Nesters Road West/Spring Grove Way East; exit east for Riverside RV Resort. ▲

HB 65 (104.3 km) **J 127** (204.4 km) Mons Railroad bridge overpass.

HB 65.3 (104.8 km) **J 126.7** (203.9 km) Traffic light at Nicklaus Blvd.

HB 65.8 (105.6 km) **J 126.2** (203.1 km) Traffic light at Alpine Way.

HB 65.9 (105.8 km) **J 126.1** (202.9 km) 19 Mile Creek.

HB 66.6 (106.9) **J 125.4** (201.8 km) Traffic light at turnoff to north for Crazy Canuck residential area.

HB 67 (107.6 km) **J 125** (201.1 km) Interpretive turnoff to south with litter bins, information signs on Green Lake. Good waterfowl watching and boating.

HB 70.6 (113.3 km) **J 121.4** (195.4 km) Access road to parking for Wedgemount Lake trail in Garibaldi Provincial Park.

HB 73.4 (117.8 km) **J 118.6** (190.9 km) Shadow Lake Interpretive Forest to north.

HB 77.3 (124.1 km) **J 114.7** (184.6 km) Soo River Bridge.

Intermittent passing lanes and stretches of 4-lane highway begin westbound and continue to junction with Trans-Canada Highway 1.

HB 78.3 (125.7 km) **J 113.7** (183 km) Rutherford Creek bridge.

HB 81.4 (130.7 km) **J 110.6** (178 km) **Nairn Falls Provincial Park**; 94 campsites. An elevated 0.9 mile/1.5 km riverside trail leads to the falls which plummet 197 feet/60m into jade-coloured Green River. ▲

HB 83.2 (133.7 km) **J 108.8** (175 km) Traffic light at **PEMBERTON** (pop. 2,192); lodging, Husky and Petro-Canada gas stations. The Visitor Centre is on Highway 99, just across from the Petro-Canada station (gas/diesel); open early May–late Sept. 9 A.M.–5 P.M.; phone 604-894-6175. This farming village has become a bedroom community for Whistler. It is an outdoor recreation destination of its own for hiking, biking, boating, fishing and mountain adventures. Pemberton Museum features the gold rush and native culture. ⛽

HB 84.6 (135.9 km) **J 107.4** (172.8 km) Lillooet River Bridge. Lillooet River flows east to Lillooet Lake. Eastbound, Highway 99 winds through rural residential area, headquarters of the Lil'wat group of the Stl'atl'imx Nation. Watch your speed!

HB 87.2 (140.1 km) **J 104.8** (168.6 km) "T" junction. For eastbound travelers, Highway 99 turns sharply right and then begins its climb into the Cayoosh Range of the Coast Mountains. For westbound travelers, turn left for Whistler.

HB 93.2 (149.7 km) **J 98.8** (159 km) Birkenhead River. Westbound, Highway 99 winds through flatlands of the Stl'atl'imx Nation. *Speed limit is 60 kmph/37 mph, narrow road, no passing, watch for horses.*

HB 93.9 (150.8 km) **J 98.1** (157.9 km) Avalanche gates.

CAUTION: Steep uphill grades, narrow winding road with 20-kmph/12-mph curves, eastbound.

HB 94.1 (151.1 km) **J 97.9** (157.6 km) Lower Joffre Creek.

HB 96 (154.2 km) **J 96** (154.5 km) A second westbound brake-check area.

HB 98.6 (158.4 km) **J 93.4** (150.3 km) Large gravel turnout to north.

HB 101.6 (163.2 km) **J 90.4** (145.5 km) Westbound brake-check area. *CAUTION: Steep downgrades, narrow winding road with 20-kmph/12-mph curves, westbound. Runaway truck lanes.*

Distance marker westbound shows Pemberton 30 km/19 miles, Whistler 64 km/40 miles, Vancouver 185 km/115 miles.

HB 102 (163.9 km) **J 90** (144.8 km) **Joffre Lakes Provincial Park**; 24 walk-in campsites. The 3 alpine lakes in the chain can be reached by a 3-mile/5-km trail, with an elevation gain of more than 1,300 feet/400m (4 to 6 hours round-trip.) Best view of glacier for photos is from your vehicle on the highway looking over the parking lot. ▲

HB 102.3 (164.3 km) **J 89.7** (144.4 km) *11 percent grades westbound as Highway 99 descends.*

HB 104 (167.1 km) **J 88** (141.6 km) Bridge over Cayoosh Creek. *Slow for curve.* Views of Joffre Peaks.

HB 104.5 (167.9 km) **J 87.5** (140.8 km) Avalanche gates.

HB 106.7 (171.4 km) **J 85.3** (137.3 km) Large shoulder parking area.

HB 109 (175.1 km) **J 83** (133.6 km) Cayoosh Creek #3 bridge (narrow). Turnout to south at west end of bridge. *Highway descends eastbound, highway climbs westbound.*

HB 109.7 (176.3 km) **J 82.3** (132.4 km) Van Horlick Creek. Note transition between wet coastal forest and dry interior highland plateau.

HB 111.7 (179.5 km) **J 80.3** (129.2 km) Turnout overlooking lake.

HB 112.1 (180.1 km) **J 79.9** (128.6 km) Steep Creek on highway curve.

HB 112.4 (180.6 km) **J 79.6** (128.1 km) Priester Creek.

HB 112.6 (181 km) **J 79.4** (127.8 km) Turnout to north.

HB 113.1 (181.7 km) **J 78.9** (127 km) Large gravel turnout to north overlooking Duffey Lake.

HB 113.6 (182.5 km) **J 78.4** (126.2 km) Large gravel turnout to north overlooking Duffey Lake.

HB 113.8 (182.9 km) **J 78.2** (125.8 km) East end of Duffey Lake is marked by a massive log jam. Gravel turnout, boat launch.

HB 115.4 (185.4 km) **J 76.6** (123.3 km) Blowdown Creek. Gravel turnout to north. *Slow for 30-kmph/19-mph curves westbound.*

HB 115.8 (185.9 km) **J 76.2** (122.8 km) Kane Creek.

HB 116.3 (186.9 km) **J 75.7** (121.8 km) Distance markers eastbound and westbound. Avalanche gate. Blowdown Creek Forest Service Road.

HB 117.1 (188.2 km) **J 74.9** (120.5 km) Creek bridge.

HB 119.4 (191.9 km) **J 72.6** (116.8 km) Channel Creek bridge.

HB 121.8 (195.7 km) **J 70.2** (113 km) Cayoosh Creek bridge. Highway 99 follows Cayoosh Creek to Lillooet, crossing the creek several times via mostly narrow 1-lane bridges.

HB 124.2 (199.6 km) **J 67.8** (109.1 km) Sharp curve and one of 2 turnoffs to south to Rogers Creek B.C. Recreation Site camping area; see description next Milepost.

Improved road surface westbound.

HB 124.6 (200.2 km) **J 67.4** (108.5 km) One of 2 turnoffs to south to Rogers Creek B.C. Recreation Site; 14 campsites in 2 camping areas, tables, toilets, no fee. Popular picnic stop. ▲

HB 124.8 (200.6 km) **J 67.2** (108.1 km) Cayoosh Creek 1-lane bridge.

HB 125.5 (201.7 km) **J 66.5** (107 km) Gott Creek B.C. Recreation Site; small 4-vehicle campground with tables, toilets, no fee. ▲

HB 125.6 (201.9 km) **J 66.4** (106.8 km) Gott Creek bridge.

HB 127 (204.1 km) **J 65** (104.6 km) Large gravel turnout to north.

HB 127.1 (204.3 km) **J 64.9** (104.4 km) Boulder Creek 1-lane bridge.

HB 130.1 (209.1 km) **J 61.9** (99.6 km) Cottonwood Creek B.C. Recreation Site; 14 campsites, tables, toilets, no fee. ▲

HB 132.3 (212.68 km) **J 59.7** (96.1 km) Cinnamon B.C. Recreation Site; 11 campsites, tables, toilets, no fee. ▲

HB 135.1 (217.1 km) **J 56.9** (91.6 km) Gravel turnout to north at top of 13 percent grade.

HB 136.4 (219.2 km) **J 55.6** (89.5 km) Cayoosh Creek 1-lane bridge.

HB 137.4 (220.8 km) **J 54.6** (87.9 km) Large turnout to south.

HB 137.8 (221.5 km) **J 54.2** (87.2 km) Large turnout to south.

HB 139.2 (223.7 km) **J 52.8** (85 km) *CAUTION: 20-kmph/13-mph curve as highway climbs 13 percent uphill grade westbound. Narrow winding road with steep grades, no shoulder and few turnouts westbound to Pemberton.*

HB 140.4 (225.7 km) **J 51.6** (83 km) Avalanche gates.

HB 140.6 (226 km) **J 51.4** (82.7) Large gravel turnout to north with scenic view of Seton Lake.

©Kris Valencia, staff

HB 141.4 (227.3 km) **J 50.6** (81.4 km) B.C. Hydro **Seton Lake Recreation Area**; scenic viewpoint overlooking jade-green Seton Lake; parking area (not much room for large RVs), picnic site and access to beach. Boat rentals.

HB 141.8 (227.9 km) **J 50.2** (80.8 km) B.C. Hydro Seton Lake campground. ▲

HB 142.1 (228.4 km) **J 49.9** (80.3 km) Power Canal 1-lane bridge.

HB 142.3 (228.7 km) **J 49.7** (80 km) B.C. Hydro **Naxwit picnic site**; paved day-use area along river, information signs, picnic tables, RV turnaround. Very nice spot.

HB 142.5 (232 km) **J 49.5** (76.7 km)

Cayoosh Creek 1-lane bridge. Slow for 30-kmph/19-mph curve.

HB 143.3 (230.3 km) **J 48.7** (78.4 km) Gravel turnout to north with sign about Seton Creek Salmon Project.

Improved pavement eastbound. Fair pavement with rough patches westbound.

HB 143.8 (231.2 km) **J 48.2** (77.5 km) Lightfoot Gas & Convenience Store; modern facility with free coffee, picnic tables, gas and diesel. Last gas westbound for 60 miles/100 km (Pemberton).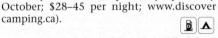

HB 144.1 (231.6 km) **J 47.9** (77.1 km) Turnoff for golf course.

HB 144.3 (231.9 km) **J 47.7** (76.8 km) Seton River 1-lane bridge.

HB 144.4 (232.1 km) **J 47.6** (76.6 km) **Junction** with road which leads 0.5-mile up an 8 percent grade to the Main Street of Lillooet (description of town follows) and continues on to Gold Bridge (106 km). *Northbound travelers turn right for continuation of Highway 99 across the Fraser River (southbound travelers turn left). Drive up hill for downtown Lillooet and visitor services.*

Cayoosh Creek Campground is located on Highway 99 as you turn northbound to cross the Fraser River.

LILLOOET (pop. 2,324), (elev. 784 feet/239m) is perched high above the Fraser River at its confluence with Cayoosh Creek. **Visitor Information:** www.lillooetbc.ca. Lillooet shares the highest temperature ever recorded in Canada: 111.9˚ F/44.4˚ C, in July 1941. The town dates back to the Cariboo gold rush.

Stop by the excellent Lillooet Museum and take in the town's historic points of interest on a walking tour which includes a "jade walk" through town accented by examples of locally found jade. Lillooet offers travelers overnight accommodations, restaurants, a gas station with diesel and other visitor services. First Nations cultural tours, local vineyards, golf and sturgeon fishing is available. Views of the city are from multiple turnouts to the north, above the Fraser River.

The Mount McLean wildfire caused a city-wide evacuation in Aug. 2009. Little evidence of this may be seen from the road as it occurred on ridges just out of sight. The fire came within feet of city limits and homes were spared largely due to firefighters utilizing backfires near the city to reduce the fuel for the wildfire.

HB 144.6 (232.5 km) **J 47.4** (76.2 km) Turnout to north with point-of-interest signs and a Pelton Wheel.

HB 144.8 (232.7 km) **J 47.2** (76 km) Midspan of the Fraser River Bridge.

HB 145.3 (233.6 km) **J 46.7** (75.1 km) **Junction** of Highway 99 with Highway 12, which leads south along the Fraser River 40 miles/65 km to Lytton and Trans-Canada 1.

HB 145.6 (234.4 km) **J 46.4** (74.7 km) Fort Berens Estate Winery to north; tasting room.

HB 146.5 (235.5 km) **J 45.5** (73.2 km) Turnoff for Fraser Cove Campground.

HB 147.4 (236 km) **J 44.6** (71.8 km) Larged paved turnout to north with litter bin; good view of Lilloett and Fraser River.

Slow for 50 kmph/30-mph curves westbound.

HB 147.8 (237.6 km) **J 44.2** (71.1 km) Entering Lillooet, 911 area, westbound (sign).

HB 150.3 (241.6 km) **J 41.7** (67.1 km)

Large gravel turnout to north.

HB 153.7 (247.1 km) **J 38.3** (61.6 km) Fountain Flat Trading Post & Gas Bar; Race Trac gas station and convenience store to north.

HB 154.6 (248.5 km) **J 37.4** (60.2 km) *Slow for 20 kmph curve and 1-lane tunnel* under railway.

Westbound, watch for livestock; 9 percent downgrade.

©Kris Valencia, staff

HB 156.2 (251.1 km) **J 35.8** (57.6 km) *Slow for 30 kmph curve and 1-lane tunnel* under railway. Northbound, Highway 99 leapfrogs B.C. Railway a few more times using underpasses and overpasses. You are now driving through the semi-desert benchlands of the upper Fraser River canyon.

HB 158.8 (255.3 km) **J 33.2** (53.4 km) Sallus Creek.

HB 172.1 (276.7 km) **J 19.9** (32 km) Turnout with information board on Pavilion Lake. Highway 99 follows the shoreline of Pavilion Lake for approximately 4 miles/ 6 km.

HB 173.8 (279.4 km) **J 18.2** (29.3 km) Distance marker westbound shows Lillooet 45 km/28 miles, Pemberton 145 km/90 miles, Whistler 179 km/111 miles, Vancouver 300 km/186 miles.

HB 174.3 (280 km) **J 17.7** (28.5 km) Crown Lake.

HB 174.6 (281 km) **J 17.4** (28 km) Turnoff to south for **Marble Canyon Provincial Park** at Crown and Turquoise Lakes: 30 delightful campsites, towering yellow and red limestone cliffs, picturesque lakes. Picnicking, walking trails, swimming, fishing.

HB 177.8 (286 km) **J 14.2** (22.8 km) Graymont Pavilion Plant produces a range of lime and limestone products including high calcium quicklime and screened limestone.

HB 191.6 (308.2 km) **J 0.4** (0.6 km) Historic **Hat Creek Ranch** built in 1861 as a roadhouse stop on the original Cariboo Wagon Road. Hat Creek Ranch has a restaurant, gift shop, cabin rentals, shower facilities, campground with hookups, trail rides, stagecoach rides, guided tours, open-air museum, and First Nations culture. www.hatcreekranch.com.

HB 191.8 (308.4 km) **J 0.2** (0.3 km) Distance marker westbound shows Lillooet 73 km/45 miles, Pemberton 173 km/ 108 miles, Whistler 207 km/129 miles, Squamish 261 km/162 miles, Vancouver 328 km/204 miles.

HB 192 (308.7 km) **J 0 Junction** with Highway 97, 7 miles/11 km north of Cache Creek.

Turn to **Milepost CC 7** *on page 101 this section for continuation of main WEST ACCESS ROUTE log.*

Return to Milepost CC 7
West Access Route Log

(Continued from page 93)
hotels, motels, bed and breakfasts, restaurants, shopping malls, movie theatres, banks, gas stations with diesel and other services. Minter Gardens, which closed in October 2013 after 33 years, continues to operate their Country Garden store on Young Road in Chilliwack.

Camping at **Cottonwood Meadows RV Country Club** (description follows); exit south at Exit 116 and turn left at first traffic light (Luckak uck Way), then drive past Heritage Museum for entrance Cottonwood Meadows RV park.

©Kris Valencia, staff

Cottonwood Meadows RV Country Club. Exit 116. Highly rated, recommended by Good Sam, Woodalls, Tourism B.C. New, secure, clean, well-maintained, full service park. Easy access, electronic gates, well lit, well managed. Lazy stream, full hookups (15/30/50 amp), cable TV, free WiFi all through park, wide level sites, paved roadways. Nicest washrooms, laundromat, clubhouse, Jacuzzi, pull-throughs, near all amenities, golf, fishing, shopping, watersports. Bird watching on site. Next to Chilliwack Heritage Park and Cheam Golf Course. Open year-round. Near U.S. border crossing. Visa, MasterCard. 44280 Luckakuck Way, Chilliwack, BC V2R 4A7. Phone 604-824-PARK (7275). Email: camping@cottonwoodRVpark.com. www.cottonwoodRVpark.com. [ADVERTISEMENT]

A 15.7 (25.3 km) **CC 154.3** (248.3 km) Exit 118 to Evans Road (head north for Walmart).

A 16.7 (26.9 km) **CC 153.3** (246.7 km) Exit 119 to Vedder Road, Yale Road and Chilliwack city centre; food, gas/diesel, lodging and shopping (head south for Cottonwood Mall and Safeway). Also access to Chilliwack Lake Provincial Park, Cultus Lake Provincial Park and Cultus Lake resort area including several campgrounds (some campsites may be reserved, open early April–early October; $28–45 per night; www.discovercamping.ca).

A 17.6 (28.3 km) **CC 152.4** (245.3 km) Exit 120 westbound only to Young Road, Chilliwack.

A 18.8 (30.3 km) **CC 151.2** (243.3 km) Exit 123 Prest Road north to Rosedale, south to Ryder Lake; no services.

A 22.8 (36.7 km) **CC 147.2** (236.9 km) Exit 129 for Annis Road/Rosedale.

A 26.5 (42.5 km) **CC 143.5** (230.9 km) Exit 135 to **junction** with Highway 9 to Agassiz and Harrison Hot Springs (14 km/8.5 miles). Eastbound access to **Bridal Veil Falls Provincial Park** ½ mile south of highway (follow blue signs); picnicking, trail to base of falls (15 minutes round-trip). Also access to waterpark, food, gas/diesel, lodging and camping.

A 28.5 (45.9 km) **CC 141.5** (227.7 km) Exit 138 to Popkum Road. Access to Bridal Veil Falls (follow signs).

A 33.6 (54.1 km) **CC 136.4** (219.5 km) Exit 146 Herrling Island; no services.

A 36.5 (58.7 km) **CC 133.5** (214.8 km) Exit 151 to Peters Road.

A 38 (61.2 km) **CC 132** (212.4 km) Exit 153 to Laidlaw Road and to Jones Lake (4-wheel drive required).

A 41.5 (66.8 km) **CC 128.5** (206.8 km) Westbound truck weigh scales.

A 42 (67.6 km) **CC 128** (206 km) Exit 160 to Hunter Creek rest area; tables, toilet, pay phone, information kiosk.

A 44.5 (71.6 km) **CC 125.5** (202 km) Exit 165 Access to Flood–Hope Road. This is the business route with access to camping, food and gas/diesel.

A 47 (75.6 km) **CC 123** (197.9 km) Exit 168 westbound access to Flood–Hope Road/ Silver Hope Creek; gas stations. Food, gas/ diesel, lodging and camping. Access to **Skagit Valley Provincial Park** with 3 campgrounds (total 142 sites) and **Silver Lake Provincial Park** (25 sites). Camping fee $16 per night, May 1–mid-Oct. It is illegal to gather firewood around your campsites here, you may purchase firewood or bring your own. Amenities include pit toilets, hand pump drinking water, swimming, fishing for steelhead, Dolly Varden and rainbow.

A 48.5 (78 km) **CC 121.5** (195.4 km) Exit 170 to Hope. *West Access Route travelers take this exit for Hope (description follows) and Trans-Canada Highway 1 East to Cache Creek. (Although you are driving north toward Cache Creek, highway directional signs indicate "East.")*

NOTE: Northbound travelers on the West Access Route may also choose to continue east on Highway 3 and take the Coquihalla Highway north to Kamloops, then rejoin the main West Access Route by driving 52 miles/84 km west on Trans-Canada Highway 1 to Cache Creek. (Continue east 4 miles for start of the Coquihalla Highway.) This is an alternate route which avoids the Fraser River Canyon. See "Coquihalla Highway" log on page 85 in the CENTRAL ACCESS ROUTE section.

TRANS-CANADA HIGHWAY 1 EAST

A 50 (80.5 km) **CC 120** (193.1 km) **HOPE** (pop. 6,667) is located on the Fraser River at the **junction** of Trans-Canada Highway 1, Highway 3 (Crowsnest Highway) and Highway 5 (Yellowhead/Coquihalla Highway). **Visitor Information**: Visitor Centre and museum building, corner of Hudson Bay Street and Water Avenue, on right northbound as you enter town on Trans-Canada Highway 1 East. Tenting campground just beyond between river and highway.

Hope is a convenient stop with all visitor services, including food, gas/diesel and lodging. Views of the Fraser River available along Trans-Canada Highway 1. Shopping, restaurants, town offices, public park and a number of chainsaw carvings are found on Hope's Main Street.

A 51 (82 km) **CC 119** (191.5 km) Bridge over Fraser River.

A 51.3 (82.5 km) **CC 118.7** (191 km) Double-ended turnout to east with litter bin.

A 51.8 (83.4 km) **CC 118.2** (190.2 km) **Junction** with Highway 7 west to Harrison

Hot Springs, an interesting side trip.

A 53.4 (85.9 km) **CC 116.6** (187.6 km) Rest area with picnic tables, toilets, info boards, at Lake of the Woods. This rest area now has eastbound access to enter but no eastbound access to exit.

A 59.1 (95.1 km) **CC 110.9** (178.5 km) Gas/diesel station, cafe.

A 61.2 (98.5 km) **CC 108.8** (175.1 km) Esso gas station with diesel and Hope River General Store & RV Park to west. Turnoff to east for **Yale Campground** and Emory Creek Campground; 34 level gravel sites in trees, water taps, fire rings, picnic tables, firewood ($5 per bundle), flush toilets, litter bins. Camping fee $21 per night. Open mid-May to mid-October. Hiking and walking trails. Gold panning and fishing in **Fraser River**.

A 64.8 (104.3 km) **CC 105.2** (169.3 km) Turnout with historic sign to east.

NOTE: Slow for 50 kmp/31 mph speed zone northbound through Yale.

A 65 (104.6 km) **CC 105** (169 km) Traffic light in historic **YALE** (pop. 200); convenience store and Race Trac gas/diesel station. **Emergency Services**: Phone 911. **Visitor Information**: At museum. Yale is a popular starting point for river rafters on the Fraser River. Historically, Yale was the head of navigation for the Lower Fraser River and the beginning of the overland gold rush trail to British Columbia's goldfields.

The Anglican Church of Saint John the Divine here was built for the miners in 1863 and is the second oldest church still on its original foundation in mainland British Columbia. Next to the church is Yale Museum and a bronze plaque honouring Chinese construction workers who helped build the Canadian Pacific Railway. Walking around town, look for the several plaques relating Yale's history.

A 65.3 (105.1 km) **CC 104.7** (168.5 km) Yale Creek.

A 65.7 (105.7 km) **CC 104.3** (167.8 km) **Yale Tunnel**, first of 7 tunnels northbound through the Fraser Canyon. Turnout to east at south end of tunnel.

Northbound, the highway winds through the dramatic scenery of the **Fraser River Canyon**. The Fraser River and canyon were named for Simon Fraser (1776–1862), the first white man to descend the river in 1808. This is the dry forest region of British Columbia, and it can be a hot drive in summer. The scenic Fraser Canyon travelers drive through today was a formidable obstacle for railroad engineers in 1881.

A 66.6 (107.2 km) **CC 103.4** (166.4 km) Signed turnoff to east with litter bins.

A 66.7 (107.3 km) **CC 103.3** (166.3 km) *CAUTION: Dangerous curve.*

A 67.3 (108.3 km) **CC 102.7** (165.2 km) Signed turnoff to east with litter bins.

A 68.4 (110.1 km) **CC 101.6** (163.5 km) **Saddle Rock Tunnel**. This 480-foot/146-m tunnel was constructed from 1957–58.

A 71.1 (114.4 km) **CC 98.9** (159.1 km) Gravel turnout to east.

A 72 (115.9 km) **CC 98** (157.7 km) **Sailor Bar Tunnel**, nearly 984 feet/300m long. There were dozens of bar claims along the Fraser River in the 1850s bearing colourful names such as Sailor Bar.

A 73 (117.5 km) **CC 97** (156 km) Turnoff to east; avalanche gates southbound.

A 76.9 (123.7 km) **CC 93.1** (149.8 km)

Signed turnoff with litter bin. Point-of-interest sign and cairn at south end of Alexandra Bridge across Fraser River. Built in 1962, Alexandra Bridge is the second largest fixed arch span in the world at more than 1,640 feet/500m in length.

A 77.5 (124.7 km) **CC 92.5** (148.9 km) **Alexandra Bridge Provincial Park**, picnic area and rest stop on west side of highway. Hiking trail down to the old Alexandra Bridge, still intact. This suspension bridge was built in 1926, replacing the original built in 1863.

A 78.3 (126.1 km) **CC 91.7** (147.6 km) Turnoff to west.

A 78.4 (126.2 km) **CC 91.6** (147.4 km) Historic Alexandra Lodge (now a private residence), one of the last surviving original roadhouse buildings on the Cariboo Waggon Road.

The Cariboo Waggon Road connected Yale with the Cariboo goldfields near Barkerville. Built between 1861 and 1863 by the Royal Engineers, it replaced an earlier route to the goldfields—also called the Cariboo Waggon Road—which started from Lillooet.

A 79.4 (127.8 km) **CC 90.6** (145.8 km) Alexandra Tunnel.

Good views northbound of the tracks of the Canadian National and Canadian Pacific railways as they wind through the Fraser River Canyon. Construction of the CPR—Canada's first transcontinental railway—played a significant role in the history of the Fraser and Thompson river valleys. Begun in 1880, the CPR line between Kamloops and Port Moody was contracted to Andrew Onderdonk.

CAUTION: Winding road northbound to Spences Bridge.

A 81.6 (131.3 km) **CC 88.4** (142.3 km) Turnoff with litter bins to east.

A 82.4 (132.6 km) **CC 87.6** (141 km) Hell's Gate Tunnel (328 feet/100m long).

A 82.6 (132.9 km) **CC 87.4** (140.6 km) Ferrabee Tunnel (328 feet/100m long).

A 83.4 (134.2 km) **CC 86.6** (139.4 km) Turnoff with litter bins to west.

A 83.6 (134.5 km) **CC 86.4** (139 km) Northbound parking on east side of road for Hell's Gate Airtram; see description next milepost.

A 83.8 (134.8 km) **CC 86.2** (138.7 km) Southbound parking on west side of road for Hell's Gate Airtram. Here, two 25-passenger airtrams take visitors 500 feet down across the river to a cafe and shop complex overlooking Hell's Gate, the narrowest point on the Fraser River. There is also a steep trail down to the suspension bridge; strenuous hike. Footbridge across river to view fishways through which millions of salmon pass each year. An education center details the life cycle of the salmon, the construction of the International Fishways and the history of Hell's Gate. From the footbridge, visitors may also see rafters running Hell's Gate. The trams operate daily, April to October; phone 604-867-9277 or visit www.hellsgateairtram.com for 2014 dates. The complex is open 10 A.M. to 5 P.M. daily, June–August and 10 A.M. to 4 P.M. daily during shoulder season.

Hell's Gate was by far the most difficult terrain for construction of both the highway and the railway. To haul supplies for the railway upstream of Hell's Gate, Andrew Onderdonk built the stern-wheel steamer *Skuzzy*. The SS *Skuzzy* made its way upstream through Hell's Gate in 1882, hauled by ropes attached to the canyon walls by bolts.

Hell's Gate Airtram. See display ad

this page.

A 84.7 (136.3 km) **CC 85.3** (137.3 km) Turnout to east with litter bin. It is also a turnaround for travelers who miss the Hell's Gate parking lot or want handicap accessible parking. You have to be traveling southbound to get into the parking area in front of the Hell's Gate building.

A 85.4 (137.4 km) **CC 84.6** (136.1 km) China Bar Tunnel, built in 1960. It is almost 2,300 feet/700m long, one of the longest tunnels in North America.

A 88.4 (142.3 km) **CC 81.6** (131.3 km) Anderson Creek Campground. 🏕️

A 88.6 (142.6 km) **CC 81.4** (131 km) Anderson River.

A 89.4 (143.9 km) **CC 80.6** (129.7 km) Turnout with litter barrel to west. Avalanche gate just south.

A 90.8 (146.1 km) **CC 79.2** (127.5 km) **BOSTON BAR** (pop. 885). **Emergency Services: Police** and **ambulance**, phone 911. Services include 3 gas stations, grocery, restaurant, pub, motels and RV park. Boston Bar was the southern landing for the steamer *Skuzzy*, which plied the Fraser River between here and Lytton during construction of the CPR. Celebrations include May Day the 3rd weekend of May each year. ⛽🏕️

A 92 (148 km) **CC 78** (125.5 km) Turnout with litter bin to west.

A 93.1 (149.8 km) **CC 76.9** (123.7 km) Turnout with litter bin to east.

A 94 (151.3 km) **CC 76** (122.3 km) Canyon Alpine Motel and restaurant (food served 6 A.M. to 10 P.M. year-round). Also Canyon Alpine RV Park & Campground here, open April-Oct. 🏕️

A 95.9 (154.3 km) **CC 74.1** (119.2 km) Turnout with litter bins and canyon/river views to west.

A 103.7 (167 km) **CC 66.3** (106.7 km) Large gravel turnouts both sides of highway. There are *several* pullouts northbound on both sides of the highway as it winds through the Fraser Canyon. Litter bins to east.

CAUTION: Winding roads, grades, truck traffic and falling rock northbound. Watch for deer.

A 106.5 (171.4 km) **CC 63.5** (102.2 km) Jackass Mountain summit; small turnout to west with litter bins.

A 110.8 (178.3 km) **CC 59.2** (95.3 km) Turnoff to west for Siska.

A 112 (180.2 km) **CC 58** (93.3 km) Turnoff to west. View to west of Canadian National and Canadian Pacific railway crossing of the Fraser River at Siska.

A 114.6 (184.4 km) **CC 55.4** (89.2 km) Skuppah rest area (northbound only); information signs, toilets, tables, litter bins.

A 116.2 (187 km) **CC 53.8** (85.6 km) Large turnout to east.

A 117.2 (188.6 km) **CC 52.8** (85 km) **Junction** with Highway 12; Esso gas/diesel station. Access to **Lytton** (description follows) and **Lillooet**, a historic community with plenty of adventure opportunities (see description of Lillooet on page 97 in the "Sea to Sky Highway" log). ⛽

LYTTON (pop. 235; elev. 656 feet/200m) is located at the confluence of the Thompson and Fraser rivers. **Emergency Services:** Phone 911. **Visitor Information:** Visitor Centre, 400 Fraser St., phone 250-455-2523. Food, gas, lodging and other services avail-

able. Lytton acts as headquarters for river raft trips on the Thompson and Fraser rivers. The community also boasts a museum, art gallery and one of the last reaction ferries in the province. Historically, sand bars at Lytton yielded much gold, and river frontage has been set aside for recreational gold panning. Lytton shares the record high temperature for British Columbia: 111.9°F/44.4°C in July 1941.

A 118.3 (190 .3 km) **CC 51.7** (83.2 km) Gravel turnout to west.

A 122 (196.3 km) **CC 48** (77.2 km) **Skihist Provincial Park** to east; 58 campsites on east side of highway with water, flush and pit toilets, telephone and dump station ($5 fee). Picnic area on west side of highway (good place to watch the trains go by); wheelchair-accessible restrooms. 🏕️

A 124.3 (200 km) **CC 45.7** (73.5 km) Turnout with litter bins to west. There are several pullouts to the west the next 6.4 miles/10.3 km northbound.

A 126 (202.8 km) **CC 44** (70.8 km) *CAUTION: Extremely narrow, winding section of highway next 2 miles northbound.*

A 128 (206 km) **CC 42** (67.5 km) Nicomen River.

A 130 (209.2 km) **CC 40** (64.4 km) Large gravel turnout to west with view.

A 131 (210.8 km) **CC 39** (62.8 km) Large gravel turnout to west with view, litter bin.

A 134 (216.6 km) **CC 36** (57.9 km) Turnout at entrance to **Goldpan Provincial Park** to west offers good view of railroad tunnels. The provincial park is located alongside the Thompson River; open May 1–Sept., 14 campsites, $16 per night, picnic area, hand pump water, fishing. 🎣🏕️

Turnout on highway near park entrance with good view of railroad tunnels in Thompson River canyon.

A 136.1 (219 km) **CC 33.9** (54.5 km) Big Horn Trading post to east.

Northbound watch for fruit and vegetable stands in season.

A 139.3 (224.2 km) **CC 30.7** (49.4 km) **Junction** with Highway 8 to Merritt (43 miles/69 km east).

First northbound access (south access road) to **Spences Bridge**; description fol-

lows. See also Spences Bridge description at **Milepost A 140.4.**

Plaque at junction about the great landslide of 1905 reads: "Suddenly on the afternoon of August 13, 1905, the lower side of the mountain slid away. Rumbling across the valley in seconds, the slide buried alive 5 Indians and dammed the Thompson River for over 4 hours. The trapped waters swept over the nearby Indian village drowning 13 persons."

A 139.5 (224.5 km) **CC 30.5** (49.1 km) Turnout to west with litter bin.

A 139.6 (224.6 km) **CC 30.4** (48.9 km) Thompson River bridge.

A 140.4 (226 km) **CC 29.6** (47.6 km) Turnoff for residential **SPENCES BRIDGE** (pop. 25). Spences Bridge (elev. 850 feet/259m) is located at the confluence of the Thompson and Nicola rivers is an easy half-day drive from the Washington border or the Vancouver airport. Highway services include the **Log Cabin Pub**, the Historic Packing House, and a grocery with tackle, supplies and fishing licenses. Camping and cabins at **Acacia Grove RV Park & Cabins**, 1 block off the highway. It is the home of the largest continually operating hotel in British Columbia. Well-known for steelhead fishing, a record 30-lb., 5-oz. steelhead was caught in the Thompson River in 1984. Bighorn sheep frequent the city limits in spring and fall and seasonal produce stands provide a taste of this fertile area. 🎣🏕️

A 140.6 (226.3 km) **CC 29.4** (47.3 km) **Log Cabin Pub.** You will appreciate this

Experience Fraser River Canyon up-close on Hell's Gate Airtram. (©Claire Torgerson, staff)

Watch for wildlife along Highway 97. These wild sheep are just south of Cache Creek.
(©Kris Valencia, staff)

unique log structure. The logs were specially selected and prepared locally, some spanning 50 feet. This pub combines the rustic charm of a turn-of-the-century roadhouse with all the amenities of a neighborhood pub. Excellent food and hospitality by your hosts John and Laurie Kingston. Visit us on the web at www.logcabinpub.com. [ADVERTISEMENT]

A 140.8 (226.6 km) **CC 29.2** (47 km) **Acacia Grove R.V. Park & Cabins.** One block off Highway 1. RV park, cabins with kitchens, tenting. Lush setting overlooking the scenic Thompson River, famous for steelhead fishing and whitewater rafting. Visited by mountain sheep, August to May. Full hookups, pull-throughs, laundromat, free hot showers, flush toilets, small convenience/grocery store, pay phone, game room, horseshoes, lawn bowling, volleyball and much more. Pets welcome (leashed). Your hosts Sarah and Roy, VISA/MC/ Interac. Toll-free phone/fax 1-800-833-7508. Email: acaciagrove@telus.net. Website: www. acacia–rvpark–cabins.com. 3814 Riverview Avenue E., Box 69, Spences Bridge, BC V0K 2L0. Latitude N50°42'488," Longitude W121°33'491." [ADVERTISEMENT]

A 147 (2336.5 km) **CC 23** (37 km) *CAUTION: Slow for narrow and winding section of highway. Road descends northbound with 40 mph/60 kmph curves.*

A 147.8 (237.8 km) **CC 22.2** (35.7 km) Pullouts both sides of highway.

CAUTION: Winding upgrade southbound

with *40 mph/60 kmph curves.*

A 149.4 (240.4 km) **CC 20.6** (33.1 km) Turnoff to east. Distance marker northbound shows Ashcroft 29 kms/18 miles, Cache Creek 32 kms/20 miles.

Winding uphill northbound with 7 percent grade.

A 152.3 (245.1 km) **CC 17.7** (28.5 km) Viewpoint to east with litter barrel overlooking Thompson River with plaque about the Canadian Northern Pacific's Last Spike reads:

"Canada's third trans-continental rail link was completed near Basque on January 23, 1915. In a simple ceremony the last spike was driven, witnessed by a small group of engineers and workmen. The line later became part of the Federal Government's consolidated Canadian Nation Railways system."

A 157.4 (253.3 km) **CC 12.6** (20.3 km) Red Hill rest area to east; information about Ashcroft, tables, toilets, litter bins, nice picnic area.

A 163.4 (263 km) **CC 6.6** (10.6 km) Stop of interest sign to east describes **Ashcroft Manor Historic Site**, British Columbia's oldest roadhouse, established in 1862 by C.F. and H.P. Cornwall. The ranch with its grist and saw mills supplied Cariboo miners. The manor house was destroyed by fire in 1943 but the roadhouse survived. Clement Cornwall became one of BC's first senators after confederation with Canada in 1871 and Lieutenant Governor of BC in 1881.

Summer temperatures in this dry and desert-like region typically reach the high 80s and 90s (26°C to 32°C).

A 163.6 (263.3 km) **CC 6.4** (10.3 km) **Junction** with Highway 97C to Ashcroft (description follows) and Logan Lake (39 miles//63 km east). Great viewpoint of Highland Valley Coppermine 29 miles/47 km east of here on Highway 97C (winding road with 8 to 11 percent grades).

ASHCROFT (pop. 1,700), a village on the Thompson River about 4 miles east of Highway 1, supplanted Yale as gateway to the Cariboo with the arrival of the Canadian Pacific Railway in 1885. There are a number of original buildings. Ashcroft Museum houses a collection of artifacts tracing the

history of the region. Camping (May–Oct.) at Legacy Park on the Thompson River. **Visitor Information:** www.ashcroftbc.ca.

A 167.4 (269.4 km) **CC 2.6** (4.2 km) Second turnoff northbound for Ashcroft and **junction** with Highway 97C to Logan Lake.

NOTE: Slow for speed zone northbound through Cache Creek.

Cache Creek

A 170 (273.6 km) **PG 273.6** (440.4 km) Located at the **junction** of Trans-Canada Highway 1 and Highway 97; a 6-hour drive from U.S. border. **Population:** 1,050. **Emergency Services:** Phone 911 for **RCMP** and **ambulance. Hospital,** phone 250-453-5306.

Visitor Information: Open in summer, phone 250-457-7661 or toll-free 1-888-457-7661. Write P.O. Box 460, Cache Creek, BC V0K 1H0; fax 250-457-9668. Or visit www. cachecreekvillage.com.

Elevation: 1,299 feet/396m. **Climate:** Called the Arizona of Canada, Cache Creek's climate is characterized as semi-arid, with hot, dry summers and cold, dry winters. Mean temperature in July is 85°F/30°C, with highs in the 90s°F/ 32s°C. Mean temperature in January is 21°F/-6°C.

An oasis of traveler services in the middle of desert-like country, Cache Creek boasts major chain fast-food outlets (Subway, A&W), motels, gas stations with diesel (Petro-Canada, Chevron), a grocery store and shopping. Camping at **Brookside Campsite,** located east of Cache Creek on Trans-Canada Highway 1 (across from the golf course); see description following.

Check out the 2,850 lb/1,293 kg jade boulder at the **Cariboo Jade Shoppe.**

Brookside Campsite. 1 km east of Cache Creek on Highway 1, full (30 amp) and partial hookups, shady pull-throughs, tent sites, free WiFi, super-clean washrooms, laundry, free showers, sani-station, store, playground, heated pool, golf course adjacent, pets on leash, pay phone. *No trains!* VISA, MasterCard. Phone/fax: 250-457-6633. Email: info@brooksidecamp site.com; website: brooksidecampsite.com. [ADVERTISEMENT]

The settlement grew up around the confluence of Cache Creek and the Bonaparte River. Cache Creek became a major supply point on the Cariboo Waggon Road. Today, agriculture, logging and tourism support the community. Area soils are dry but fertile. Residents claim that with irrigation nearly anything can be grown here.

West Access Route Log
(continued)
This section of the log shows distance from Cache Creek (CC) followed by distance from Prince George (PG).

BC HIGHWAY 97 NORTH

CC 0 PG 273.6 (440.2 km) **Junction** of Trans-Canada Highway 1 and Highway 97 at Cache Creek. Southbound travelers follow

Trans-Canada Highway 1 West. Northbound travelers follow Highway 97 North, the "Gold Rush Trail."

NOTE: Southbound travelers on the West Access Route may choose to drive east 52 miles/84 km on Highway 1 to Kamloops then take the Coquihalla Highway south to Highway 3, rejoining the main West Access Route at Hope. Interesting drive to Kamloops through high desert country of central British Columbia; some dramatic scenery, 2- and 4-lane highway. This is an alternate route which avoids the Fraser River Canyon. See "Coquihalla Highway" description on page 85 in the CENTRAL ACCESS ROUTE section and read log from back to front.

NOTE: Cariboo Connector 4-Lane Upgrade between Cache Creek and Prince George has created many long 4-lane stretches of highway in addition to numerous northbound-only and southbound-only passing lanes.

Watch for deer.

CC 0.4 (0.6 km) **PG 273.2** (439.6 km) Bonaparte River.

CC 0.7 (1.1 km) **PG 272.9** (439.2 km) Gas/diesel station with propane and restaurant to east.

CC 1.2 (1.9 km) **PG 272.4** (438.3 km) Turnout with litter bin and area map to west.

CC 3.7 (6 km) **PG 269.9** (434.4 km) Bonaparte River.

CC 7 (11.3 km) **PG 266.6** (429 km) Junction with Highway 99 to historic **Hat Creek Ranch**, 0.4 mile/0.7 km west (description follows); **Marble Canyon Provincial Park**; Pavilion Lake; **Lillooet** (47 miles/76 km west); and Whistler.

Junction with Highway 99, the "Sea to Sky Highway," to Vancouver via Whistler. Southbound travelers interested in this route turn to page 94 and read description, then follow log back to front from page 97.

Hat Creek Ranch heritage site offers interpretive tours, stagecoach rides and demonstrations. Admission fee charged. Trail rides, licensed restaurant, camping and cabins also available. Open daily from 9 A.M. to 5 P.M., May to September (6 P.M. in July and August).

CC 9.5 (15.3 km) **PG 264.1** (424.9 km) Turnout to west has views of Painted Hills with litter bins and plaque about "B.X.":

"Connecting Barkerville with the outside world, the B.X. stage coaches served [the] Cariboo for over 50 years. The terminus was moved from Yale to Ashcroft after C.P.R. construction destroyed the wagon road through the Fraser Canyon. The red and yellow coaches left Ashcroft at 4 A.M., and 4 days and 280 miles later reached the end of the road at Barkerville."

CC 13.2 (21.2 km) **PG 260.4** (419 km) Turnoff for **Loon Lake**, located 16 miles/26 km east; camping, fishing, resorts.

CC 19.1 (30.9 km) **PG 254.5** (409.4 km) Large turnout with picnic table, litter bins and point-of-interest sign beside 6 Mile Lake. Nice spot.

CC 19.8 (32 km) **PG 253.8** (408.4 km) Willow Springs Campsite.

CC 24 (38.6 km) **PG 249.6** (401.6 km) **Clinton Pines Campground.** Easy access. Quiet and very relaxing. Large shady sites, pull-throughs. Full and partial hookups. Laundry. Free showers, washrooms. WiFi and firewood. Walking distance to town. Open April–November. Hiking trails, horse-

shoes. Beautiful scenery. Pets welcome. Credit cards/Interac accepted. Owner operated. Located south end of Clinton on east side of Highway 97. Phone 250-459-0030; email clintonpines@xplornet.com.

CC 24.7 (39.7 km) **PG 248.9** (400.5 km) Petro-Canada with gas/diesel and propane. Turnoff to west for Pavilion–Clinton Road to **Downing Provincial Park** (11 miles/17 km) on popular Kelly Lake; 18 campsites, picnic area, swimming beach and fishing for rainbows. Open June–September.

Slow for speed zone northbound through Clinton.

Southbound watch for wild sheep alongside highway.

CC 25 (40.2 km) **PG 248.6** (400 km) **CLINTON** (pop. 740, area 4,000; elev. 2,911 feet/887m). **Visitor Information**: Village of Clinton, phone 250-459-2261; www.village .clinton.bc.ca. Visitor information also available in the museum.

This charming community was originally a stopping place at the junction of 2 roads leading to the Cariboo goldfields, the Cariboo Trail from Lillooet and the Cariboo Road from Ashcroft. **Clinton Museum**, housed in a red brick building that once served as a courthouse, has fine displays of pioneer tools and items from the gold rush days.

Clinton offers a historic walking tour of the Village with pictures of original buildings, plus a full handbook guide.

Clinton has all visitor facilities, including motels, a credit union, gas/diesel stations (Shell, Petro-Canada), liquor stores, grocery stores and restaurants. Public washrooms are available in downtown and at the Reg Conn Park. Camping in town at **Gold Trail RV Park and Campground** and south of town at **Clinton Pines Campground.**

Gold Trail RV Park and Campground. 2014 special: From $15 for full hookups, for everyone. Extra large pull-throughs, grassy sites, laundromat, easy in/out, in the village on Highway 97. BBQ buffet every night from $9.99. Cleanest and greenest park in Clinton. Hot showers, WiFi, sani-dump. Community firepit. Host Micheal Dier. goldpark@telus.net. Phone 250-459-2638. www.goldtrailrvpark.ca.

Clinton is the original site of the 47 Mile Roadhouse, a gold-rush settlement on the Cariboo Waggon Road from Lillooet. Clinton boasts the oldest continuously held event of its kind in the province, the Clinton Ball (in May the Saturday preceding Victoria Day). The ball, an annual event since 1868, is the first event of Western Heritage Week, which concludes with a 2–day rodeo.

Slow for speed zone southbound through Clinton.

CC 25.8 (41.5 km) **PG 247.8** (398.8 km) Turnout with litter bins and information boards to west.

NOTE: 2- and 4-lane highway northbound with 6 to 7 percent grades and easy S-curves. Watch for deer.

CC 30.7 (49.4 km) **PG 242.9** (390.1 km) Turnoff to west for **Big Bar Lake Provincial Park** (21 miles/34 km), a popular destination with area residents, offering 2 campgrounds, picnicking, swimming, playground, boat launch and rainbow fishing. Open mid-

May through September.

CC 30.8 (49.6 km) **PG 242.8** (390.7 km) Rest area to east just north of Big Bar Lake turnoff has large double-ended parking area, toilets, tables, litter barrels. NOTE: No access southbound.

CC 33.9 (54.5 km) **PG 239.7** (385.7 km) Turnoff for south end of loop road that leads east 2.5 miles/4 km to **Chasm Provincial Park**. There is a viewpoint and parking at the park, pit toilets, picnic area. Successive lava flows in Chasm Creek Valley formed layers in varying tones of red, brown, yellow and purple, which have been revealed in the steep canyon walls cut by erosion over the past 10 million years. Look for bighorn sheep, moose, mule deer and other animals in this area.

CC 34.7 (55.8 km) **PG 238.9** (384.4 km) Turnoff to west for Beaver Dam Lake, Meadow Lakes and other area fishing lakes or further to Canoe and Dog Creek.

CC 38.2 (61.5 km) **PG 235.4** (378.8 km) North end of Chasm Loop Road (see description at **Milepost CC 34.3**).

CC 44.4 (71.4 km) **PG 229.2** (368.8 km) Turnoff to east for Green Lake at **70 MILE HOUSE** (pop. 450, elev. 3,609 feet/100m); General Store, gas station. Originally a stage stop on the Cariboo Wagon Road, 70 Mile House was named for its distance from Lillooet.

Green Lake Provincial Park to east has 3 campgrounds with 121 total sites and 66 sites that may be reserved. (www.discover camping.ca) Picnic areas, swimming, fishing, boat launch. Open May 15–Sept. 30, camping fee $16 per night, $5 for sani-station. Green Lake is a popular waterskiing lake. The area offers lodging, dining and camping.

NOTE: 70 Mile North 4-Lane Project underway in 2013. Expect continued construction and/or improved highway summer 2014.

CC 56.5 (90.9 km) **PG 217.1** (349.3 km) *8 percent grades approaching* Mount Begbie Summit (4,042 feet/1,232m). Turn on Lookout Road for parking and picnic tables at trailhead for **Mount Begbie Lookout**. Built in 1923 as part of a system to detect forest fires, the tower atop Mount Begbie (elev. 4,187 feet/1,276m) is open to visitors daily in summer, 8 A.M. to 5 P.M. Panoramic views of the South Cariboo. Take the short, steep, interpretive trail up to the tower from the rest area (10 to 15 minute walk).

CC 63.9 (102.8 km) **PG 209.7** (337.5) 93 Mile House; no services.

CC 64.3 (103.5 km) **PG 209.3** (336.8 km) **Junction** with **Highway 24** east to Little Fort on Yellowhead Highway 5 (65 miles/105 km). Travelers may use Highway 24 as a scenic paved route connecting Yellowhead Highway 5 and Highway 97. Known as "the Fishing Highway," Highway 24 provides access to resorts and fishing at 4 main lakes—Fawn, Sheridan, Bridge and Lac des Roches—as well as dozens of other area lakes. Cabins, full-service RV parks, restaurants, boat rentals and other facilities are available along Highway 24. **Bridge Lake Provincial Park** (31 miles/50 km east) has 16 campsites, a boat launch and fishing for rainbow, lake trout and burbot. Moondance Bay (also on Bridge Lake) offers a beautiful RV park and fishing for kokanee.

CC 67 (107.8 km) **PG 206.6** (332.5 km)

Begin 6 percent downgrade northbound.

CC 67.1 (108 km) **PG 206.5** (332.3 km) Entering 100 Mile House (sign) northbound.

CC 68.1 (109.6 km) **PG 205.5** (330.7 km) Highway crosses over CN Railway tracks.

CC 68.6 (110.4 km) **PG 205** (329.9 km) *NOTE: Begin 70 kmph/45 mph speed zone northbound, closely followed by a 50 kmph/30 mph speed zone.*

CC 68.9 (110.9 km) **PG 204.7** (329.4 km) Access to Super 8 Motel and Ramada Inn via frontage road.

Highway climbs 6 percent grade southbound with passing lane.

CC 69.5 (111.8 km) **PG 204.1** (328.5 km) Traffic light at Horse Lake Road, which leads east to **Horse Lake** (rainbow) and connects with Highway 24, the "fishing highway."

CC 69.8 (112.3 km) **PG 203.8** (328 km) Traffic light at 4th Avenue, downtown 100 Mile House; food, gas/diesel, lodging. Visitor Centre to west with giant skis.

100 Mile House

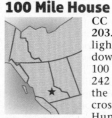

CC 70 (112.6 km) **PG 203.6** (327.6 km) Traffic light at First Avenue downtown; all services. 100 Mile House is located 242 miles/389 km from the international border crossing at Abbotsford-Huntingdon, BC, and Sumas, WA, or about a 5 hour drive. It is a 3 1/2-hour drive to Prince George from 100 Mile House. **Population:** 1,200. **Elevation:** 3,050 feet/ 930m. **Emergency Services:** Phone 911 for all Police, Fire and Ambulance. **Hospital**, phone 250-395-7600.

Visitor Information: At South Cariboo Visitor Centre, located in the log building by 100 Mile House Marsh (a bird sanctuary at the centre of town). Look for the 39-foot-/12-m-long cross-country skis! Write Box 340, 100 Mile House, BC, V0K 2E0; phone 250-395-5353 or toll free 1-877-511-5353; visit www.SouthCaribooTourism.ca.

Visitor services in this bustling community include supermarket (Save On Foods), fast-food outlets (A&W, Subway), restaurants (Tim Horton's), motels, gas/diesel stations (Chevon, Petro-Canada, Husky), repair services, stores, a post office, 2 golf courses, a theatre, a government liquor store, 3 supermarkets, banks and ATMs. Dry site camping at the Municipal Campground for small to mid-size RVs seasonally.

Centennial Park has picnic sites, playground and a scenic walking trail to Bridge Creek Falls, a 10-minute hike. Parking area will accommodate large RVs.

100 Mile House is the service centre for the South Cariboo, an area stretching north from Clinton to 140 Mile House, west to the Fraser River and east to Lac des Roches, with a population of approximately 24,000.

100 Mile House was established as a post house on the Cariboo Waggon Road to the goldfields. In 1930, the Marquess of Exeter established the 15,000-acre Bridge Creek Ranch here. Today, the 100 Mile House area has 2 lumber mills and an Oriented Strand Board (OSB) plant. It is also the "hand-crafted log home capital of North America," with an extensive log home industry. (Inquire at the Visitor Centre about log home sites.)

An infestation of mountain pine beetle in British Columbia's Interior has impacted forests and the timber industry in the prov-

ince. Mountain pine beetles prefer mature (80 years old or more) lodgepole pine trees. Lodgepole pine forest accounts for 25 percent of the province's forestland (forestland covers two-thirds of the province). The mountain pine beetle epidemic is attributed to a number of factors, including more mature lodgepole pine, successful fire fighting, recent mild winters that have lowered normal mortality rates for beetle larvae, and trees weakened by recent drought stress. Current management emphasizes quickly removing dead trees and harvesting still salvageable timber.

South Cariboo Tourism. See display ad this page.

West Access Route Log
(continued)

BC HIGHWAY 97 NORTH
CC 70.3 (113.1 km) **PG 203.3** (327.1 km) Traffic light at Exeter Station Road.

Highway climbs next 1.2 miles/1.9 km northbound. CAUTION: Watch for deer.

Intermittent passing lane northbound. Passing lanes are indicated 2 km before they begin.

CC 71.5 (115.1 km) **PG 202.1** (325.2 km) Traffic light at Canim Hendrix Lake Road. *Highway descends next 1.2 miles/1.9 km southbound.*

Junction with road east to **Ruth**, **Canim**, **Mahood** and other lakes; numerous fishing and camping resorts. Mahood Lake, 55 miles/88 km via paved and gravel roads, is located in the southwestern corner of immense Wells Grey Provincial Park. **Mahood Lake Provincial Park** campground offers camping, fishing and swimming; drinking water, playground, short, easy trails to waterfalls at Canim, Mahood and Deception Falls. Well worth the drive. See www.bcparks.com for more information.

Ducks Unlimited nesting area at northwest corner of this junction; parking and trails.

CC 76.5 (123.1 km) **PG 197.1** (317.1 km) Turnoff to west for 108 Resort; gas station with diesel and propane, phone, convenience store and some shopping. Once a cattle ranch, 108 Mile Ranch became a recreational community in the 1970s.

CC 76.7 (123.4 km) **PG 196.9** (316.8 km) Paved turnout with litter bins to west.

CC 76.9 (123.8 km) **PG 196.7** (316.6 km) Paved turnout with litter bins to west.

CC 78.5 (126.3 km) **PG 195.1** (313.9 km) **108 Mile Ranch Heritage Site** and rest area to west; open Memorial Day to Labour Day. This is one of the nicest rest areas along this route, with parking and restrooms adjacent the heritage site overlooking 108 Mile Lake. Walking/biking trail around lake.

©Kris Valencia, staff

There are 13 historical buildings here, including structures from the old 108 Mile Ranch and the 105 Mile Roadhouse.

Interpretive sign here explains that this site began as a post house on the Cariboo Trail in 1867. During the 1900s, it was both a horse and cattle ranch and later the land was logged during the lumber boom of the 1950s.

CC 81.3 (130.8 km) **PG 192.3** (309.5 km) Spring Lake Guest Ranch; trail rides (phone 250-791-5776).

CC 82.6 (132.9 km) **PG 191** (307.3 km) **Big Country Campground & RV Park.** 3 miles south of Lac La Hache on Highway 97. Heated pool (seasonal), free showers, store, laundromat, rec room. Extra-long pull-throughs; 15-, 30- and 50-amp service; tent sites; cabins; limited cable TV; WiFi; phone. VISA, MasterCard. www.100mile house.ca. 250-396-4181. Box 68, Lac La Hache, BC V0K 1T0. [ADVERTISEMENT]

CC 84.8 (136.4 km) **PG 188.8** (303.8 km) Long paved shoulder parking to east with litter bins.

CC 85.7 (137.9 km) **PG 187.9** (302.3 km) **LAC LA HACHE** (pop. 400; elev. 2,749 feet/838m). Also known as the "longest town in the Cariboo," the community of Lac La Hache stretches along some 11 miles of Highway 97. Lac La Hache, the body of water, is one of the most popular recreation lakes along Highway 97. A beautiful spot. Visitor services here include lodging, Husky gas/diesel station, general store (with liquor store), cafes and lakeside resorts. Fruit stands (in season) along Highway 97.

There are many stories of how the lake got its name, but a local historian says it was named by a French–Canadian *coureur de bois* (voyageur) "because of a small ax he found on its shores." Lac La Hache is French for "Lake of the Ax." **Lac La Hache** has lake char, rainbow and kokanee; good fishing in summer, great ice fishing in winter. Community fishing derby in June. Access to **Timothy Lake** (12 miles/20 km east) via Timothy Lake Road; resorts, swimming, fishing for rainbows. Access to Spout Lake.

©Kris Valencia, staff

CC 91.7 (147.5 km) **PG 181.9** (292.7 km) **Kokanee Bay Motel and Campground.** Relaxation at its finest right on the lakeshore. Fish for kokanee and char or take a refreshing dip. We have a modern, comfortable motel, cabins. Full trailer hookups, grassy tenting area, hot showers, laundromat. Aquabike, boat and canoe rentals. Fishing tackle and ice. Phone 250-396-7345. Fax 250-396-4990. www.kokaneebay cariboo.com. [ADVERTISEMENT]

Also, Esso with diesel across from Kokanee Bay Motel and Campground.

CC 94.5 (152.1 km) **PG 179.1** (288.2 km) **Lac La Hache Provincial Park:** Turnoff to east for campground, turnoff to west for picnic area. Provincial Park campground

Go for a horseback ride at one of the ranches in the Cariboo. (©Kris Valencia, staff)

has 83 sites, tap water, flush and pit toilets, dump station and hiking trails. Open May 15 to Sept. 30. Sites are $15 per night, there are no hook-ups. Provincial park picnic area has boat launch, swimming, playground and excellent fishing on west side of highway. Self-guiding nature trail. Open May 15–Sept. Accepts reservations at www.discovercamp ing.ca.

CC 97.7 (157.2 km) **PG 175.9** (283 km) Turnout to west with litter barrel.

Ribbon-like San Jose River winds through valley to the west of the highway. Canadian artist A.Y. Jackson painted in this valley.

CC 99.8 (160.6 km) **PG 173.8** (279.6 km) 130 Mile Wetlands Conservation Project (sign). This is an important waterfowl breeding area in Canada. Watch for ducks in roadside ponds. Also good bird watching for bald eagles, osprey, great horned owls, American kestrels and pileated woodpeckers.

CAUTION: Watch for deer on highway, especially at dusk.

CC 100.6 (161.9 km) **PG 173** (278.4 km) Large turnout with litter bins to east.

CC 102.5 (164.9 km) **PG 171.1** (275.3 km) Turnout to west with litter bin and point-of-interest sign commemorating the miners, traders and adventurers who came this way to the Cariboo goldfields in the 1860s.

CC 116.4 (187.3 km) **PG 157.2** (252.9 km) Husky gas station with diesel at **150 MILE HOUSE** (pop. 1,275), which also has groceries, a pub, cafe and restaurant in the historic roadhouse. The town was named because it was 150 miles from Lillooet on the Cariboo Waggon Road. Post office was established in 1871.

CC 117.3 (188.7 km) **PG 156.3** (251.5 km) **Junction** with Likely Road to Quesnel and Horsefly lakes and to communities of Horsefly (35 miles/56 km) and Likely (50 miles/80 km). Quesnelle Forks, a gold rush heritage site, is located near Likely. Cedar Point Provincial Park on Quesnel Lake is 3.7 miles/6 km from Likely; 40 campsites, picnicking, boat launch, waterskiing, swim-

ming, fishing and outdoor mining museum. Horsefly Lake Provincial Park (40 miles/65 km) has a popular 23-site campground plus 7 walk-in campsites (this campground requires reservations done through visitor centre or online at http://secure.camis.com/Discovercamping/) and a picnic area. Fishing for rainbow. Open May 15 to Sept. 15.

CC 120.6 (194 km) **PG 153** (246.2 km) The Chief Will-Yum, gas bar with diesel, RV park to east.

CC 121.3 (195.2 km) **PG 152.3** (245.1 km) Golf course to east.

CC 122.5 (197.1 km) **PG 151.1** (243.1 km) Welcome to Williams Lake (northbound sign); double-ended turnout to east with litter bins, recycle bins, toilets, info boards.

CC 123 (197.9 km) **PG 150.6** (242.3 km) Large turnout with litter bins to west.

CC 124.6 (200.5 km) **PG 149** (239.8 km) Turnoff on frontage road for access to Super 8, Best Western and Super Save gas station with diesel.

©Kris Valencia, staff

CC 124.7 (200.7 km) **PG 148.9** (239.6 km) The **Tourism Discovery Centre**, on east side of highway; motorists turn left at entrance to Centre and drive around the back of the building for parking (will accommodate large RVs). Very nice facility with helpful staff offering visitor information on Williams Lake and Cariboo Chilcotin Coast, a coffee bar, gift shop, restrooms and numerous interactive features. Picnic area, litter bins; pets welcome. Open year-(Continues on page 106)

Chilcotin Highway (BC Highway 20)

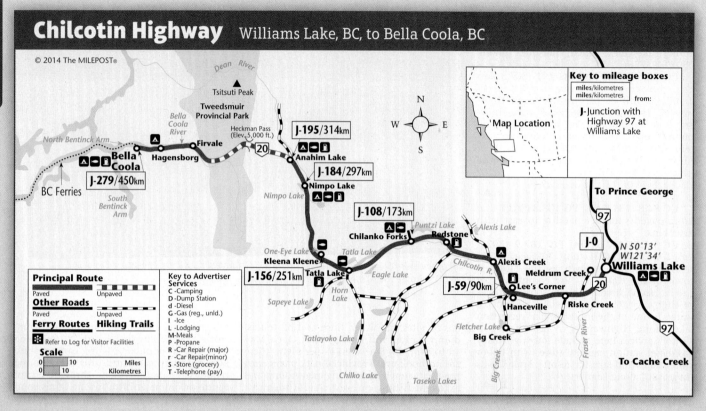

Chilcotin Highway Williams Lake, BC, to Bella Coola, BC

© 2014 The MILEPOST®

Key to mileage boxes
miles/kilometres
miles/kilometres from:
J-Junction with Highway 97 at Williams Lake

Map Location

Principal Route
Paved — Unpaved
Other Roads
Paved — Unpaved
Ferry Routes **Hiking Trails**
Refer to Log for Visitor Facilities
Scale
0   10   Miles
0   10   Kilometres

Key to Advertiser Services
C -Camping
D -Dump Station
d -Diesel
G -Gas (reg., unld.)
I -Ice
L -Lodging
M -Meals
P -Propane
R -Car Repair (major)
r -Car Repair(minor)
S -Store (grocery)
T -Telephone (pay)

J-195/314km
J-184/297km
J-108/173km
J-279/450km
J-156/251km
J-59/90km
J-0

N 50°13'
W121°34'

To Prince George
To Cache Creek

The scenic Chilcotin Highway (BC Highway 20) leads 279.3 miles/449.5 km west from Williams Lake to Bella Coola. Called "Freedom Road" by residents, the highway was bulldozed across the mountains in the 1950s by local volunteers tired of waiting for the government to build a road.

Once a test of endurance, much of today's road is paved and in good condition. There is still "The Hill," a narrow, 11.2-mile/18-km, gravel switchback descent from the top of Heckman Pass (elev. 5,000 feet/ 1,524m) into the Bella Coola Valley with 12 to 18 percent grades. Vehicles towing fifth wheelers or travel trailers test your brakes before attempting The Hill.
Distance from junction (J) with Highway 97 at Williams Lake is shown.

J 0 Junction with Highway 97 at Williams Lake (see description page 106).

©Kris Valencia, staff

Access to Stampede Grounds (watch for turn); camping.

J 1.5 (2.5 km) Road south to Alkali Lake and Dog Creek. Road closure sign warns if Heckman Pass is closed. Westbound, Highway 20 climbs to plateau, then drops down a 5 percent grade to the Fraser River.
J 15 (24 km) Viewpoint at east end of

Sheep Creek bridge over Fraser River.
Begin 6 percent grade westbound.
J 17.4 (28 km) Small turnout with map of Chilcotin wildlife viewing areas and information on the Chilcotin grasslands.
J 20.3 (32.7 km) Turnout with toilets and litter barrels. Begin steep downgrade eastbound; watch for logging trucks.

To the west is the great Fraser Plateau, with the snowcapped peaks of the Coast Range visible on the horizon. The country west of the Fraser is known as the Chilcotin, taking its name from the river that cuts through the plateau. The country is chiefly range land for cattle, though forestry is also important.
J 27.5 (44.4 km) Gravel road loops south and rejoins Highway 20 at Lee's Corner (50-mile/80-km drive). Follow this winding side road south 10 miles/16 km to Farwell Canyon bridge on the Chilcotin River.
J 28.7 (46.3 km) Riske Creek.
J 29.4 (47.3 km) Stack Valley Road to Historic Chilcotin Lodge, now a bed and breakfast. Camping.

J 30.4 (48.9 km) Forest Service recreation area; at Becher Dam; fishing for small rainbow, picnic tables.

J 35.6 (57.4 km) Riske Creek rodeo grounds. Stampede held in mid-June.
J 42.2 (68 km) Gravel road north to Forest Service recreation area on Raven and Palmer lakes; fishing; boat launch.

J 50.9 (81.9 km) Hanceville Recreation Area to south; rest area with toilet, litter barrel and historic marker about Norman Lee and ill-fated Yukon cattle drive of 1898.
Begin 9 percent downgrade westbound.
J 56 (90.1 km) **Lee's Corner**, on site of Norman Lee's ranch house. Hanceville post

office, gas, diesel, propane, groceries and food in old-fashioned general store.

Turnoff south for old settlement of Hanceville, named for Tom Hance, the original settler and author of *Klondike Cattle Drive*. Gravel road continues south across Chilcotin River (a favorite with river rafters) to Fletcher Lake Forest Service Recreation Area; canoeing and fishing. Road loops back to the highway at Milepost J 27.5.
J 62.5 (100.6 km) Store, gas and diesel at **Anaham Village** (TL'etinqox), the largest of 6 Indian reserves in the Chilcotin. *Speed limit 45 mph/70 kmph through reserve.*

J 69.5 (112 km) Turnout to north with information sign.
J 69.8 (112.3 km) **ALEXIS CREEK** (pop. 140); vehicle repair, groceries, ATM, post office, cafe, RV sites, hotel, stores, RCMP outpost, medical centre.

J 72.8 (117.3 km) *Steep downgrade westbound.* View of Chilcotin River and volcanic cliffs of Battle Mountain.
J 74.8 (120.5 km) Bull Canyon Provincial Recreation Area; picnic tables, outhouses, 20 campsites in aspen forest beside Chilcotin River. Beautiful spot. Kayaking, rafting and fishing are popular. Camping fee charged. Open June 16–Sept. 14.

J 90.2 (145.2 km) Chilcotin River bridge; Westbound, the Chilanko River is to the south of the highway.
J 103.3 (166.3 km) Native community of **Redstone**; general store, gas and diesel.

J 105 (169 km) Stunning views westbound of snowcapped Coast Mountains.
J 107.6 (173.3 km) **Chilanko Forks**. Road north to **Puntzi Lake** (4.5 miles/7 km);

resorts, campgrounds, fishing. Birds at Puntzi Lake include pelicans and loons.

J 109 (175.5 km) Puntzi airport road leads to Chilanko Marsh Wildlife Area.

J 113.4 (182.5 km) Gravel road south to **Pyper Lake Recreation Area**; picnic tables and fishing.

J 115.7 (186.3 km) Gravel turnout with view of the long, deep valley of Tatla Lake.

J 129.2 (208 km) Viewpoint.

J 130.5 (210 km) Rest area with picnic tables and outhouse at **Pollywog Marsh**, a wetlands conservation area (Ducks Unlimited).

J 131.6 (211.9 km) Road north to **Tatla Lake** Recreation Area; fishing and boat launch.

J 131.8 (212.2 km) Side road south to Eagle Lake.

J 133.1 (214.3 km) Road south to **Pinto Lake Recreation Area**; picnic tables, boating.

J 137 (220.6 km) Side road south to **Tatlayoko Lake** (21.5 miles/35 km), jumping-off point for expeditions to **Mount Waddington** (elev. 13,100 feet/3,994m), highest peak in the province, also known as Mystery Mountain.

J 137.9 (222 km) **Tatla Lake**; food, gas, lodging, store, post office and clinic. Historic Graham Inn.

J 146.1 (235.2 km) Bridge across Klinaklini River.

J 152.5 (245.5 km) Road north to **One Eye Lake** Recreation Area; fishing and boating.

J 155.7 (250.7 km) Small community of **Kleena Kleene**; phone.

J 156 (251.1 km) Kleena Kleene bridge. Turnout at west end.

J 159 (256 km) Clearwater Lake Resort and provincial recreation site.

J 162.5 (261.5 km) Bridge over McClinchy Creek, a tributary of the Dean River. *CAUTION: Cattle at large.*

J 177.7 (286.1 km) Road south to Charlotte Lake (12 miles/20 km); rainbow fishing and lodging.

J 180.8 (291.1 km) Turnout to north with information sign about Nimpo Lake.

J 184.3 (296.6 km) **NIMPO LAKE**; called the "Freshwater floatplane capital of B.C.". Visitor services include a general store, gas, propane, phone, RV park, restaurant and fishing resorts. The 7.5-mile/12-km-long lake contains rainbows.

J 187.4 (301.6 km) **Dean River** bridge. Forest Service recreation site turnout; canoeing and fishing.

J 190.2 (306.1 km) Anahim Lake Resort.

J 195.2 (314.2 km) **ANAHIM LAKE**, (pop. 1,500) largest community in the Chilcotin; daily 1-hour flights to/from Vancouver. Anahim Lake is a centre for guided wilderness hiking and fishing trips. Groceries at Christensen's general store. Food, gas and lodging available. Annual stampede held in mid-July. Early ranching in this area is described in the classic, *Grass Beyond the Mountains*, by Richmond Hobson.

The Anahim area is a major stop on the Pacific Interior Flyway. Good bird watching on **Eagle's Nest Marsh Trail**, southwest side of Anahim Lake, for American white pelicans, eagles and osprey, great horned and great grey owls, goshawks, trumpeter swans and sandhill cranes.

J 196 (315.5 km) *Pavement ends, hardpacked dirt and gravel begins, westbound.*

J 201.6 (324.5 km) Eagles Nest Resort.

J 212.5 (342.1 km) Louie Creek; turnout at west end.

J 215.1 (346.2 km) Turnout with information sign on the West Chilcotin.

J 217.1 (349.5 km) East entrance to **Tweedsmuir Provincial Park**, the largest park in British Columbia. Highway 20 borders the park for the next 34 miles/54 km westbound. Best known features in Tweedsmuir are Hunlen Falls (Canada's second highest waterfall) and the Monarch Ice Fields (accessible by flightseeing).

View to north of Rainbow Mountains.

J 221 (355.7 km) Trailhead and picnic site with outhouse and information sign.

J 221.5 (356.4 km) Summit of **Heckman Pass** (elev. 5,000 feet/1,524m). The pass is kept open year-round.

J 221.9 (357.1 km) Brake check area and road closure gate. *CAUTION: Highway begins steep 2-part descent westbound; 18 percent grade, narrow road, rock slides, hairpin bends. Use low gear. Use turnouts.*

J 225.2 (362.4 km) Bridge over Young Creek; turnout at east end.

J 232.7 (374.5 km) *Begin steep climb.*

J 233.3 (375.5 km) Hunlen Falls/Turner Lakes trailhead.

J 233.6 (376 km) Turnout with litter barrels and information signs.

J 234.1 (376.8 km) **Atnarko River Campground**; 28 campsites, sani-station, camping fee, fishing. Old growth Douglas fir.

J 234.5 (377.4 km) Tweedsmuir Provincial Park headquarters. Dump station.

J 236.5 (380.6 km) Tweedsmuir Trailhead on Mosher Creek.

J 241.1 (388.1 km) Big Rock Picnic Area and Kettle Pond trailhead (1-hour loop).

J 243.3 (391.6 km) Tweedsmuir Lodge.

J 243.8 (392.4 km) **Fisheries Pool Campground**; 14 campsites, fee, boat launch and picnic area beside Atnarko River. Salmon spawning channels and viewing pool.

J 246.8 (397.2 km) Boat launch.

J 247 (397.6 km) Horsetail Falls Creek.

J 249.7 (402 km) Heritage Mackenzie/Grease trailhead and picnic area; water, litter barrels. Valley View loop trail (1 to 1-1/2 hours) along a portion of the Grease Trail leads to a good viewpoint of the river and Stupendous Mountain (elev. 8,800 feet/2,700m).

J 249.9 (402.2 km) Burnt Bridge. West boundary of Tweedsmuir Provincial Park.

J 254.4 (409.4 km) Settlement of **Firvale**.

J 259.1 (417 km) Bella Coola bridge.

J 268.4 (432 km) **HAGENSBORG** (pop. 279), food, gas, RV parks, groceries and lodging. Settled in 1894 by Norwegians from Minnesota, who found the country similar to the fjords of their homeland. Notable here are the **Augsburg Church** (built in 1904 and still in use) and the Hagensborg Norwegian Heritage House, built by Andrew Svisdahl in the early 1900s. Furnished as a typical Norwegian home of that time period, it is well worth a visit.

J 269.6 (434 km) Private RV Park & Campground.

J 271.2 (436.5 km) Turnoff to Bella Coola airport.

J 272.4 (438 km) Snootli Creek Fish Hatchery.

J 274.2 (441.3 km) Eagle Lodge and Campground.

J 276.2 (444.5 km) Road south up Thorsen Creek leads to one of the most extensive collections of ancient rock carvings in the world. This site has more than 100 glyphs. Inquire locally for directions.

J 277 (446 km) Acwsalcta, School of the Nuxalk Nation, constructed of cedar with Indian graphic designs and carvings; well worth a stop.

Bella Coola

J 279.3 (449.5 km) Entering Bella Coola via Highway 20. Paved road continues around the tidewater flats at the head of the inlet for 1.2 miles/2 km to the fishing harbor and B.C. Ferries dock. **Population**: 2,200 (Bella Coola Valley).

Visitor Information: Visitor information centre is in the Co-op store on Mackenzie Street. Local businesses, such as the Kopas Store, are helpful. Visit www.bella coola.ca

Transportation: Air—One-hour flights to Vancouver, daily year-round, twice daily in summer; local charter service; helicopter base. **Ferry**—B.C. Ferries vessels link Bella Coola and other coastal communities with Port Hardy on the north tip of Vancouver Island. Go to www.bcferries.com for current schedule.

Bella Coola has all visitor services, including lodging, camping and dining at local inns and motels/hotels. Bed-and-breakfast accommodations also available.

Alexander Mackenzie was the second white man to visit this settlement at the head of North Bentinck Arm in 1793 (Captain George Vancouver and crew beat him by 2 weeks). The Hudson's Bay Co. established a trading post here in 1869.

Attractions in the Bella Coola Valley include the spectacular scenery (Hunlen Falls is Canada's third highest single-drop waterfall in Canada); the Kopas Store, established in 1937 (Cliff Kopas is author of *Bella Coola History*); totem pole at the old band office in town and murals at the First Nations' Acwsalcta School; and the Bella Coola Museum, which displays Hudson's Bay Co. relics and items brought by Norwegian settlers, and has a good photo display of the building of "The Freedom Road." Town is home to Bella Coola Band/Nuxalk Nation.

The area offers hiking, mountain biking, rock climbing and heli-skiing. Boat trips to Alexander Mackenzie Historic Park in Dean Channel, where the explorer left a record of his momentous journey: "From Canada by Land, 22nd July, 1793," inscribed on a rock.

Special events include the annual Bella Coola rodeo, one of the largest amateur rodeos in Western Canada, held the July 1st weekend; the Discovery Coast Music Festival, which takes place in mid-July; and the annual Bella Coola Fall Fair Day and Logger's Sports event, held Labour Day weekend.

Return to Milepost CC 126.2 West Access Route

(Continued from page 103)
round.

Signal Point Gaming is adjacent the Discovery Centre; slot machines, bingo, restaurant.

CC 126.2 (203.1 km) **PG 147.4** (237.2 km) Traffic light at Oliver Street; Chevron gas station, Denny's, A&W, Tim Hortons. Northbound travelers turn right uphill for continuation of Highway 97 north to Quesnel and Prince George. Go straight ahead on Oliver Street for Williams Lake city centre; supermarkets (Save-on Foods/Pharmacy, Safeway), liquor store, motels, museum, RCMP, etc.

Junction with BC Highway 20/Chilcotin Highway. Access to Williams Lake Stampede Campground is via Highway 20 to right turn on Mackenzie Avenue South then follow signs.

Junction with BC Highway 20, which leads 279 miles/450 km west to Bella Coola. See "Chilcotin Highway" beginning on page 104 for log of that route.

Williams Lake

CC 126.2 (203.1 km) **PG 147.4** (237.2 km) Located on the shore of Williams Lake, at the junction of Highways 97 and 20. Williams Lake is 74 miles/119 km south of Quesnel; 246 miles/396 km north of Hope; and 298 miles/480 km from the international border at Abbotsford-Huntingdon, BC, and Sumas, WA. **Population:** 12,000. **Elevation:** 1,922 feet/586m. **Emergency Services:** dial 911. **Police,** phone 250-392-6211. **Hospital,** phone 250-392-4411. **Ambulance,** phone 250-392-5402.

Visitor Information: Stop by the Tourism Discovery Centre 9 A.M.–6 P.M. daily in summer (description follows). Or contact Williams Lake Chamber of Commerce, Box 4878, Williams Lake, BC V2G 2V8; email visitors@telus.net; physical address 1660 S. Broadway, Williams Lake, BC V2G 2W4; 1-877-967-5253; www.williamslakechamber.com.

The 13,000-square-foot Tourism Discovery Centre, built by 2 local world-renowned log home companies, is home to a Visitor Centre and a coffee bar/gift store that features unique local products. The Centre is located at the south entrance to Williams Lake on Highway 97 and offers pull-through parking for RVs. Maps, tourist guides, interactive display featuring area history and culture, and knowledgeable staff on hand to answer questions. There is a postal drop on the Centre's exterior and a pay phone.

Williams Lake was named for Shuswap Indian Chief Willyum. The town grew with the advent of the Pacific Great Eastern Railway (later British Columbia Railway) in 1919, rapidly becoming the major cattle marketing and shipping centre for the Cariboo–Chilcotin.

Williams Lake has complete visitor services, including hotels/motels, gas stations, fast-food outlets and restaurants. Boitanio Mall on Oliver Street offers shopping. The public library has free Internet access on their computers. There is a bowling alley on First Avenue and a 4-screen movie theatre on Third Avenue. Slot machines and bingo at Signal Point Gaming adjacent the Discovery Centre just south of Williams Lake on Highway 97. Recreation includes an 18-hole golf course, a 9-hole golf course and a par-3 golf course, and a twin sheet arena and pool complex.

Camping at Williams Lake Stampede Campground (dry camping and hookups); phone 250-398-6718. Follow Highway 20 a short distance west and take first right turn then follow signs. (You can see the Stampede grounds from Oliver Street overlook.)

The famous **Williams Lake Stampede**, British Columbia's premier rodeo, is held here annually near the July 1 holiday (call the Visitor Centre for exact dates). The 4-day event draws contestants from all over Canada and the United States. The rodeo grounds are located in the city and accessed from Highway 20.

©Kris Valencia, staff

The **Museum of the Cariboo Chilcotin** is the only museum in British Columbia to focus on ranching and rodeo. The museum is home to the **BC Cowboy Hall of Fame** which features photos, biographies and memorabilia of the province's outstanding cowboys. Great collection of saddles here. Located at 113 North 4th Avenue; phone 250-392-7404; www.cowboymuseum.com. Open 10 A.M. to 4 P.M. Monday through Saturday from June through August; 11 A.M. to 4 P.M. Tuesday through Saturday from September through May; Admission fee $2 adults.

Walk the **River Valley Trail** from Williams Lake to the Fraser River. This 6.8-mile/11-km multi-use path meanders through forest and grassland, offering both river and mountain views. Stop by the Info centre for more details.

At the west end of Williams Lake is Scout Island Nature Centre. The island is reached by a causeway, with boardwalks providing access to the marshes. A nature house is open May to August.

West Access Route Log
(continued)

BC HIGHWAY 97 NORTH

CC 125.8 (202.4 km) **PG 147.8** (237.8 km) Traffic light at Oliver Street; Chevron gas station, Denny's, A&W, Tim Hortons. Southbound travelers turn left for continuation of Highway 97 South to Cache Creek. Turn right on Oliver Street for Williams Lake city centre; supermarkets (Save-on Foods/Pharmacy, Safeway), liquor store, motels, museum, RCMP, etc.

Junction with BC Highway 20/Chilcotin Highway. Access to Williams Lake Stampede Grounds is via Highway 20 to right turn on Mackenzie Avenue South then follow signs.

Begin long uphill grade next 3 miles/4.8 km northbound.

CC 128.6 (206.9 km) **PG 145** (233.3 km) Traffic light at Mackenzie Ave. Welcome to Williams Lake (southbound sign). *Begin 3-mile/4.8-km descent to Williams Lake southbound.*

CC 128.7 (207.1 km) **PG 144.9** (233.1 km) Truck brake check area turnout to west, toilets, litter bins, recycling bins.

CC 130.6 (210.1 km) **PG 143** (230 km) Double-ended turnout to east with litter bin; careful on approach northbound.

CC 132.4 (213 km) **PG 141.2** (227.2 km) Turnoff to Williams Lake airport to east.

CC 134.1 (215.8 km) **PG 139.5** (224.5 km) Race Trac gas and diesel to east, mobile home park with RV sites.

CC 136 (218.8 km) **PG 137.6** (221.4 km) Turnout with litter bin to west.

CC 140 (225.3 km) **PG 133.6** (215 km) Sun Valley gas, diesel, groceries.

CC 142.7 (229.6 km) **PG 130.9** (210.6 km) Large turnout to west with litter bins. *CAUTION: Watch for deer.*

CC 150.3 (241.8 km) **PG 123.3** (198.4 km) McLeese Lake recreation centre.

CC 153.3 (246.7 km) **PG 120.3** (193.6 km) *Slow for 60 kmph/35 mph speed zone through* **McLEESE LAKE** (pop. 300), a small community with general store, post office, liquor store, **Kelly's Campsite** (description follows) and motels on McLeese Lake. Cafe, pub and restaurants.

Kelly's Campsite Ltd., located just off Highway 97 on McLeese Lake. Turn at Sunny Road, proceed 100m, entrance under the log arch. Lakeside, 40 sites, easy RV access, full hookups, pull-throughs, tent sites, WiFi, playground, horseshoes, beach, swimming, boat launch/dock, showers, firepits, firewood available. Open May–Sept. 250-297-6599 or kellyscampsite@xplornet.com. [ADVERTISEMENT]

McLeese Lake was named for a Fraser River steamboat skipper. **McLeese Lake**, rainbow to 2 lbs., troll using a flasher, worms or flatfish lure.

CC 153.8 (247.5 km) **PG 119.8** (192.8 km) **Junction** with road to **Beaver Lake**.

CC 154 (247.8 km) **PG 119.6** (192.4 km) McLeese Lake Rest Area to west is a small double-ended parking area with picnic tables, litter bins and restrooms overlooking McLeese Lake. Interpretive sign about pine beetle infestation in British Columbia.

CC 157.8 (253.9 km) **PG 115.8** (186.3 km) Large double-ended turnout with litter bin to west with plaque about paddle-wheelers overlooks Fraser River.

CC 160.7 (258.5 km) **PG 112.9** (181.7 km) **Cariboo Wood Shop.** A gift shop you must stop at. We specialize in Canadian-made gifts and our woodshop produces quality furniture and accessories. There are gifts for everyone—plush animals, local pottery, B.C. honey, local area books, wood art, jewelry door knockers, candles and much more. Best of all, our famous fresh fudge. 20 flavours to choose from, including Maple Nut, Cariboo Gold, Heavenly Goo and many more! Ask for a free taste. Sugar-free candy, fresh cappuccinos, lattes, and coffees too. Come in for a visit and treat yourself to a relaxing atmosphere and friendly staff. Easy access drive-through loop for every size of RV. Open 7 days a week, 9 A.M. to 5 P.M. Groups welcome. Phone (250) 747-8397.

www.cariboowoodshop.com.

CC 163.4 (263 km) **PG 110.2** (177.3 km) Castle Cariboo.

CC 164 (263.9 km) **PG 109.6** (176.3 km) Turnout with litter bins to east.

CC 166.3 (267.6 km) **PG 107.3** (172.6 km) Basalt columns to east of highway create a formation known as the Devil's Palisades. Cliff swallows nest in the columns. Viewable northbound (south facing columns).

CC 167.7 (269 km) **PG 105.9** (170.4 km) Stone cairn at double-ended turnout with litter bins to west commemorates **Fort Alexandria**. Built in 1821, it was the last North West Co. fur-trading post established west of the Rockies. The actual site of the fort is across the river. Cairn also marks the approximate farthest point reached by Alexander Mackenzie in his descent of the Fraser in 1793. Alexandria Cafe adjacent.

CC 171.8 (276.5 km) **PG 101.8** (163.8 km) Jade Town.

CC 177.5 (285.6 km) **PG 96.1** (154.6 km) Very nice rest area to west with toilets, picnic tables, litter bins and interpretive signs.

CC 186.2 (299.6 km) **PG 87.4** (140.6 km) Kersley (unincorporated); restaurant, store, motel, gas/diesel, fire department.

CC 188.6 (303.5 km) **PG 85** (136.7 km) Double-ended turnout with litter bin to east.

CC 192.4 (309.6 km) **PG 81.2** (130.6 km) Antique farm machinery park to east.

CC 195.5 (314.6 km) **PG 78.1** (125.7 km) **Robert's Roost Campsite**, located 6 km south of Quesnel and 2 km east of Highway 97 in a park-like setting on Dragon Lake. Partial and fully serviced. 15- and 30-amp sites. Sani-dump, fishing, boat rental, horseshoes, playground, showers and laundromat. Cablevision. Limited accommodations. Close to golfing and shopping. 3121 Gook Road, Quesnel, BC V2J 4K7. Phone 1-888-227-8877; www.robertsroostrvpark.ca.

CC 196 (315.4 km) **PG 77.6** (124.9 km) Traffic light. Sandman Hotel, Denny's restaurant and access to Walmart and gas stations (Petro-Canada, Mohawk). Food (A&W, Boston Pizza, Tim Hortons), gas, diesel, lodging and other services along highway next 1.5 miles/2.4 km northbound.

CC 196.4 (316 km) **PG 77.2** (124.2 km) Stoplight. Canadian Tire and Staples to east.

CC 196.7 (316.5 km) **PG 76.9** (123.7 km) Shell gas/diesel station, motel via frontage road.

CC 197.3 (317.5 km) **PG 76.3** (122.8 km) Super 8 Motel and restaurant to east on Valhalla Road.

Highway descends northbound to Quesnel River. Watch for deer.

CC 198.2 (318.9 km) **PG 75.4** (121.3 km) North Star Road cloverleaf.

CC 198.8 (319.9 km) **PG 74.8** (120.4 km) Quesnel River bridge.

CC 199.4 (320.8 km) **PG 74.2** (119.4 km) **Quesnel Visitor Information Centre** and **Quesnel Museum** on west side of highway in Le Bourdais Park. Both the museum and the information centre are open year-round. Quesnel Museum has an excellent collection of area artifacts and is considered one of the top museums in the province.

Northbound travelers may continue straightahead for Quesnel city centre via

World's longest wooden truss walking bridge crosses Fraser River at Quesnel.
(©Kris Valencia, staff)

Carson Avenue (see map). Highway 97 North becomes Front Street at Heritage Corner. Access to shopping and services from Highway 97.

Quesnel

CC 199.6 (321.2 km) **PG 74** (119 km) Highway 97/ Caribou Highway winds through Quesnel as Carson Avenue and Front Street. **Population**: 10,561. **Elevation**: 1,555 feet/474m. **Emergency Services**: Emergency only, phone 911. **RCMP**, phone 250-992-9211. **Ambulance**, phone 250-992-3211. **Hospital**, phone 250-985-5600.

Visitor Information: At Quesnel Museum and Visitor Centre on the west side of Highway 97 in LeBourdais Park. Or write Quesnel Visitor Centre, 705 Carson Ave., Quesnel, BC V2J 2B6; phone 250-992-8716, toll free 1-800-992-4922. For information on BC's Central Region, contact the Cariboo Chilcotin Coast, 204-350 Barnard St., Williams Lake, BC V2G 4T9; phone toll free 1-800-663-5885.

Visitor services include hotels/motels, several B&Bs, campgrounds and numerous restaurants offering everything from fast food to fine dining. There are gas stations (with diesel and propane), 2 shopping malls, 5 banks, a credit union, laundromats and car washes. Golf and a recreation centre with pool are available.

Quesnel (kwe NEL) is located at the confluence of the Fraser and Quesnel rivers. It began as a supply town for miners during the Cariboo gold rush in the 1860s. The city was named after the Quesnel River, which was named by the explorer, Simon Fraser, after his clerk Jules Maurice Quesnel, a member of Simon Fraser's 1808 expedition down the Fraser River. Explorer Alexander Mackenzie also left his mark here. Mackenzie, the first white man to cross the North American continent, left Lake Athabaska in 1793 to find a trade route to the Pacific. His journey took 72 days through 1,200 miles/2,000 km of unmapped territory. The

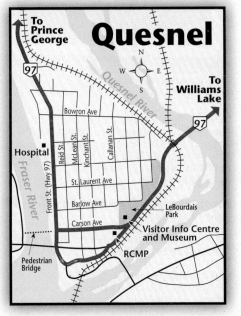

260-mile/420-km trail blazed by explorer Alexander Mackenzie from Quesnel has been retraced and restored in a joint federal, provincial and regional project as the Nuxalk–Carrier Route. The land trail terminates near Burnt Creek bridge on the Chilcotin Highway.

Today, forestry is the dominant economic force in Quesnel, with 2 pulp mills, a plywood plant, and 5 sawmills, planer mills and an MDF plant. Stop by the Forestry Industry Observatory on Highway 97 at the north end of town.

Stop and take a walk along Quesnel's scenic **Riverfront Park** trail system, visible from Highway 97 (Front Street) in

QUESNEL ADVERTISERS

Highway 26 to Barkerville

Gold Rush-era church is preserved at Barkerville. (©Claire Torgerson, staff)

This 51-mile/82-km paved road leads to Barkerville Historic Town in the Cariboo gold fields. Highway 26 follows the route of the original Cariboo Waggon Road. It is winding and hilly. Watch for deer. Gas is available in Wells.

Distance from Highway 97 junction (J) is shown.

J 0 Junction with Highway 97 at Milepost CC 202.9, just north of Quesnel.

J 13 (21 km) Gravel turnout and interpretive trails to south.

J 16.2 (26.1 km) **Historic Cottonwood House** is a roadhouse complex built in 1864 to accommodate miners and stagecoach passengers on the Cariboo Waggon Road. Museum, camping, gift shop and restaurant. May to August daily 10 A.M. to 5 P.M.

J 20.1 (32.4 km) Swift River Forest Road leads 0.2 mile/0.3 km to Lightning Creek Forest Service recreation site (first turn on left); free camping, 14-day limit. *Active logging road, drive with headlights on.* ▲

J 21.4 (34.5 km) Lover's Leap viewpoint to the south with litter bins and info boards. Mexican Hill Summit, one of the steepest grades on the original Cariboo Waggon Road, to the south.

J 24.8 (39.9 km) Ramos Creek and turnout to south.

J 26.4 (42.5 km) Robbers Roost, turnout to north with litter bins.

J 27.1 (43.6 km) Historical stop of interest marker (with litter bins) for **Blessing's Grave**. Charles Morgan Blessing was murdered in 1866 while on his way to Barkerville. His killer, James Barry, was caught when he gave Blessing's keepsake gold nugget stickpin, in the shape of a skull, to a

Barkerville dance-hall girl. James Barry was the only white man hanged on Williams Creek during the gold rush.

J 37.3 (60.1 km) **Junction** with Stanley Road (1.9-mile/3-km loop) to gold-rush ghost towns of Stanley and Van Winkle.

J 40.2 (64.7 km) Devil's Canyon paved turnout to south. Begin 8 percent downgrade and avalanche zone, with no stopping for 2 km.

J 44.9 (72.2 km) Paved turnout to litter barrel to south. **Jack of Clubs Lake**; fishing for rainbows, lake trout and Dolly Varden. ➡

J 45.2 (72.7 km) Jack of Clubs rest area on peninsula to south; picnic tables, information signs, pit toilets and boat launch.

J 45.7 (73.6 km) Paved turnout with litter barrels to south.

J 46.1 (74.2 km) Double-ended lakeshore turnout with information sign.

J 46.7 (75.2 km) **WELLS** (pop. 235) was built in the 1930s when the Cariboo Gold Quartz Mine, promoted and developed by Fred Wells, brought hundreds of workers to this valley. The mine closed in 1967, but the town has continued as a service centre and attraction for tourists, with its picturesque old homes and structures. Food, gas, lodging and camping and available. **Visitor Information:** Phone 1-877-451-9355, www.wellsbc.com. ⛽▲

J 48.6 (78.2 km) Turnout north with litter barrels, interpretive signs and map. Lowhee (Barkerville) Campground to south; 87 sites, playground and flush toilets. ▲

J 49.8 (80.1 km) Dump station, information boards.

J 50 (80.5 km) Bowron Lake Road (gravel) leads north 1 km to Forest Rose Campground and 17 miles/28 km to Bowron Lake Provincial Park, noted for its 72-mile/116-km canoe circuit. Forest Rose (Barkerville) Campground has 54 campsites (some pullthrough), showers and flush toilets. Bowron Lake Provincial Park has 25 sites, water, pit toilets, firewood and a boat launch. Also swimming, fishing, and hiking. ➡🏊▲

J 51 (82.1 km) **BARKERVILLE**. A National Historic Site, an admission fee is charged during summer season. You can visit Barkerville year-round, although it is best to visit between mid-May and September, when all exhibits are open and shows are held multiple times daily. **Visitor Information**: At the Reception Centre; phone toll-free 1-888-994-3332; www.barkerville.ca.

Barkerville was named for miner Billy Barker, who struck gold on Williams Creek. The resulting gold rush in 1862 created Barkerville. More than 130 buildings have been restored or recreated so that visitors may relive the excitement of a 19th-century gold rush town in an authentic setting. Dining, entertainment, lodging. Live musical theatre and historic drama is presented daily in summer by the Theatre Royal. Costumed interpreters conduct walking tours. *NOTE: No pets allowed in Barkerville with the exception of service dogs.*

Return to Milepost CC 202.9
West Access Route

downtown Quesnel. **Heritage Corner**, at Carson and Front streets near the Quesnel footbridge, contains historic artifacts from Quesnel's past.

Quesnel & District Museum and Archives. Explore yesterday, today. Learn the secrets of "Mandy, the Haunted Doll." Hear the stories of Chinese and First Nations Elders at video installations. Meet the residents of early Quesnel through the remarkable photographs of C.D. Hoy. Located with the Visitor Centre on Highway 97, the Museum offers innovative exhibits, children's activities and an excellent gift shop. Rated one of the top 10 museums in BC! 1-250-992-9580; www.quesnelmuseum.ca. [ADVERTISEMENT]

Quesnel Farmers Markets. Runs Saturdays, May to October, on the corner of Kinchant and Carson. 40+ vendors selling the freshest veggies, fruits, flowers, bedding plants, woodwork, herbs and much more. Homemade: everything made, baked or grown in the Cariboo. Stop by between 8:30 A.M. and 1 P.M. every Saturday. [ADVERTISEMENT]

There are some interesting hoodoo formations and scenic canyon views at nearby **Pinnacles Provincial Park**, 4.4 miles/7 km west of Quesnel. It is an easy 0.46-mile/.75 km walk on a well-maintained trail from the parking lot out to the viewpoint.

Billy Barker Days, a 4-day event held the third full weekend in July, commemorates the discovery of gold at Barkerville in 1862. Held in conjunction with the Quesnel Rodeo, Billy Barker Days is the third largest outdoor family festival in the province. For more information, write Box 4441, Quesnel, BC V2J 3J4.

A worthwhile side trip is **Highway 26**, which intersects Highway 97 just north of town and provides access to **Barkerville Historic Town** (allow one hour for drive). A reconstructed and restored Cariboo gold rush town, Barkerville offers guided tours, stage coach rides, live theatre and the opportunity to experience an 1800s gold rush town. On the way to Barkerville, stop at Cottonwood House Historic Site. See "Highway 26 to Barkerville" feature on this page for detailed log of this side trip.

West Access Route Log
(continued)

BC HIGHWAY 97

CC 199.8 (321.5 km) **PG 73.8** (118.8 km) Stoplight at Carson Avenue and Highway 97/Front Street; Heritage Corner.

Southbound travelers can continue straight ahead for Highway 97 South Bypass via Front Street (follow signs) or turn on Carson Avenue.

CC 202 (325 km) **PG 71.6** (115.2 km) Signed turnoff for Quesnel's Forestry Industry Observatory.

CC 202.8 (326.3 km) **PG 70.8** (113.9 km) Large paved turnout to east. World's Largest Gold Pan on display here.

CC 202.9 (326.5 km) **PG 70.7** (113.8 km) Quesnel airport access and turnoff for Highway 26 to Cottonwood House Historic Site, Wells and **Barkerville Historic Town**, a major attraction.

Junction with Highway 26 to Barkerville. See "Highway 26 to Barkerville" log on this page.

NOTE: Begin series of 6 and 7 percent grades

northbound on Highway 97; moderate curves. Intermittent but fairly frequent passing lanes with stretches of improved 4-lane highway to Prince George. Watch for deer.

CC 207 (333.1 km) **PG 66.6** (107.2 km) Turnoff to west for paved side road which leads to **Lazy Daze Resort** (description follows) and to **10 Mile Lake Provincial Park** (0.6 mile/1 km); picnicking, camping, swimming, fishing.

CC 211 (339.5 km) **PG 62.6** (100.7 km) Cottonwood River bridge.

CC 211.2 (339.9 km) **PG 62.4** (100.4 km) Turnout with litter bin to east.

CC 212.5 (342 km) **PG 61.1** (98.3 km) Bello's railroad overpass (clearance 16.3 feet/4.96m).

CC 215.4 (346.6 km) **PG 58.2** (93.6 km) Short access road leads west to rest area by small lake; toilets, tables, litter bins.

CC 217.6 (350.2 km) **PG 56** (90.1 km) Triple J Ranch; 2-hour and full-day horseback rides (250-998-4746).

CC 222.2 (357.5 km) **PG 51.4** (82.7 km) General store, groceries, fireworks, gifts and souvenirs.

CC 232.3 (373.8 km) **PG 41.3** (66.5 km) Shaded turnout with litter bin to east.

CC 237 (381.3 km) **PG 36.6** (58.9 km) *Slow for 60 kmph/35 mph speed zone through* **HIXON** (pop. about 500), a pleasant community on Hixon Creek with grocery store, take-out food, gas/diesel, lodging and camping; liquor outlet; community hall and post office. **Canyon Creek Campground & RV Park** just north of here on Highway 97. Hixon is the Cariboo's most northerly community. Extensive placer mining began here in the early 1900s.

CC 237.1 (381.5 km) **PG 36.5** (58.7 km) Canyon Creek bridge.

CC 237.4 (382 km) **PG 36.2** (58.2 km) **Canyon Creek Campground & RV Park.** See display ad on this page.

CC 237.6 (382.4 km) **PG 36** (57.9 km) Hixon Creek bridge.

CC 242.9 (390.8 km) **PG 30.7** (49.4 km) Woodpecker rest area downhill to west with toilets, tables, litter bins.

CC 249.8 (402 km) **PG 23.8** (38.3 km) Stoner railroad overpass.

CC 254.7 (409.9 km) **PG 18.9** (30.4 km) *Slow for curve under railroad overpass.*

CC 256.5 (412.8 km) **PG 17.1** (27.5 km) Red Rock Median truck scale.

CC 262.6 (422.6 km) **PG 11.4** (18.3 km) **Mama Yeh RV Park.** See display ad page 112.

CC 263.7 (424.4 km) **PG 9.9** (16 km) **Bee Lazee RV Park, Campground.** See display ad on this page.

CC 266.4 (428.6 km) **PG 7.2** (11.6 km) **"Y" junction** with bypass route to Yellowhead 16 East to Jasper and Edmonton (see **Milepost E 448.1** on page 240 in the

Frontage roads along Highway 97 in Prince George offer food, gas, lodging, shopping and services. (©Kris Valencia, staff)

YELLOWHEAD HIGHWAY section). Stay on Highway 97 North for Prince George and for Yellowhead Highway west to Prince Rupert.

CC 268.6 (432.2 km) **PG 5** (8 km) Southpark RV Park.

CC 269.3 (433.3 km) **PG 4.3** (6.9 km) Stoplight. Gas station to west. Turnoff to east for Prince George airport (3 miles/4.8 km).

CC 269.6 (433.8 km) **PG 4** (6.4 km) Sintich RV Park.

CC 271.4 (436.7 km) **PG 2.2** (3.5 km) Pacific Avenue. Husky gas station to east.

CC 271.6 (437 km) **PG 2** (3.2 km) Stoplight at Terminal Blvd; Shell and Super Save Gas gas stations with diesel and dump station to east.

CC 272.2 (438 km) **PG 1.1** (1.8 km) Stoplight at Railway Avenue; gas station to west.

CC 272.7 (438.8 km) **PG 0.9** (1.4 km) Mid-span of Fraser River Bridge.

CC 273 (439.3 km) **PG 0.6** (1 km) Turn offs at north end of bridge for Prince George city centre via Queensway (southbound U-turn exit for Highway 97).

Northbound travelers continue straight ahead on Highway 97 North for Highway 16 West entrance to city.

CC 273.2 (439.6 km) **PG 0.4** (0.6 km) Northbound-only access to motel, restaurants and Esso station.

CC 273.4 (439.9 km) **PG 0.2** (0.3 km) Treasure Cove Casino and Hotel occupies the southwest corner of the Highways 16 and 97 junction, with access from both highways. RV parking available. Casino is open Sun.–Thurs. 9 A.M.–2 A.M., Fri.–Sat. to 4 A.M.

NOTE: Cariboo Connector 4-Lane Upgrade between Prince George and Cache Creek has created many long 4-lane stretches of highway in addition to intermittent northbound-only and southbound-only passing lanes on 2-lane sections of highway.

CC 273.6 (440.2 km) **PG 0 Junction**

of Highway 97 with Yellowhead 16 West to Prince Rupert and Yellowhead Highway 16 East/20th Avenue through downtown Prince George and continuation to Edmonton, Alberta.

Prince George services—food, gas, lodging, shopping, etc.—are located along 20th

Avenue in downtown Prince George; along Trans-Canada Highway 16 West; and on frontage roads along Highway 97 the next 2 miles northbound. *See continuation of Highway 97 North log beginning on page 114. See map of Prince George to right on this page.*

Look for "Mr. P.G." at this intersection. The 26-foot/8-metre-high statue has been a symbol of the importance of the forest industry to Prince George since it was constructed in 1960.

If you are headed west on Yellowhead Highway 16 for Prince Rupert (port-of-call for Alaska state ferries) or east for Edmonton, Alberta, turn to **Milepost PG 0** on page 240 in the YELLOWHEAD HIGHWAY 16 section for log.

Prince George

CC 273.6 (440.2 km) PG 0 DC 245.2 (394.5 km) Located at the confluence of the Nechako and Fraser rivers, near the geographical centre of the province. **Population:** 85,035, trading area 313,556. **Emergency Services:** Phone 911 for all emergency services. **RCMP**, phone 250-561-3300. **Fire Dept.**, phone 250-561-7664. **Ambulance**, phone 250-562-7241. **Poison Control Centre**, phone 1-800-567-8911. **Hospital**, University Hospital of Northern B.C., phone 250-565-2000.

©Kris Valencia, staff

Visitor Information: At the downtown Tourism Prince George Visitor Information Centre, 1300 First Avenue. The centre offers visitor information and showcases local artisans work. A variety of services available

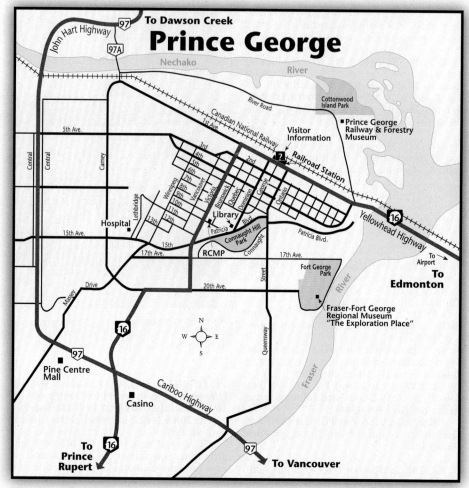

including reservations for accommodations and BC Ferries, free fishing rod use and bike rentals. Phone 250-562-3700 or toll-free 1-800-668-7646; fax 250-564-9807; or visit their website at www.tourismpg.com.

Elevation: 1,886 feet/575m. **Climate:** The inland location is tempered by the protection of mountains. The average annual frost-free period is 85 days, with 1,793 hours of bright sunshine. Dry in summer; chinooks off and on during winter which, accompanied by a western flow of air, break up the cold weather. Average summer highs 68°F/20°C, lows to 44°F/7°C. Average winter highs 38°F/3°C, lows –12°F/11°C. **Radio:** 91.5-FM CBC, 93.1-FM CFIS, 94.3X-FM, 97.3-FM The Wolf, 99.3-FM The Drive, 101.3-FM The River, CFIS-FM 93.1. **Television:** 36 channels via cable. **Newspaper:** *The Citizen* (daily except Sunday); *Free Press* (Wednesday and Friday).

Prince George is British Columbia's 4th largest city and a hub for trade and travel routes in the region. Prince George is located at the junction of Yellowhead Highway 16—linking Prince Rupert on the west coast with the Interior of Canada—and Highway 97, which runs south to Vancouver and north to Dawson Creek.

In the early 1800s, Simon Fraser of the North West Trading Co. erected a post here which he named Fort George in honour of the reigning English monarch. In 1906, survey parties for the transcontinental Grand Trunk Pacific Railway (later Canadian National Railways) passed through the area, and, with the building of the railroad, a great land boom took place. The city was incorporated in 1915 under the name Prince

George. Old Fort George is now a park and picnic spot and the site of The Exploration Place, a history and science museum.

Prince George has emerged as the centre of business, education, health and culture for Northern B.C. The Prince George Forest Region is the largest in the province, and the lumber industry, oil refining, mining and heavy construction are other major area industries.

Prince George offers a diverse blend of urban services that include the University of Northern British Columbia, located at the top of Cranbrook Hill. UNBC opened here in the fall of 1994. It was at that time the first new university to be built in Canada in more than 25 years.

The Nechako and Fraser rivers converge here, providing a landscape that offers an array of recreation and outdoor experiences mentioned under "attractions."

Agriculture in central British Columbia is primarily a forage-livestock business, for which the climate and soils are well suited. Dairying and beef are the major livestock enterprises, with minor production in sheep and poultry.

Lodging & Services

Prince George has all visitor services including more than 30 hotels/motels, 20 bed and breakfasts, 140 restaurants including major chain fast-food outlets, gas stations and "big box" stores.

Camping

Campgrounds located south of the city on Highway 97 include: **Bee Lazee RV park** (10 miles), **MamaYeh RV Park** (11 miles)

and **Hixon's Canyon Creek Campground** (36 miles south). North of the city on Highway 97/Hart Highway are **Hartway RV Park** (8 miles north of Prince George) and **Northland RV Park** (11.5 miles north of Prince George). West of the city is **Blue Cedars Campground** (3 miles) on Kimball Road.

Transportation

Air: Prince George airport is 6.8 miles/11 km southeast of the city centre, serviced by Air Canada Regional, Central Mountain Air, and West Jet. Airport shuttle, phone 250-563-2220. Flightlink service daily from Greyhound; phone 250-564-5454.

Taxi: Emerald Taxi (250-563-3333) and Prince George Taxi (250-564-4444).

Railroad: VIA Rail's "Skeena" service connects Prince George with Prince Rupert and Jasper, AB. For schedules see web site at www.viarail.ca. Train station is located at 1300 1st Avenue.

Bus: Greyhound Canada service to Dawson Creek, Edmonton, Prince Rupert and points south. For more information phone 1-800-661-8747, or visit www.greyhound.ca. City bus service by BC Transit, phone 250-563-0011, www.busonline.ca.

Attractions

The Exploration Place at 333 Becott Place, just off 20th Avenue in Fort George Park. Open 10 A.M. to 5 P.M. daily year round. Galleries include Hands On Science, Demonstrations, Paleontology, Local History and Traveling Exhibitions. A good place to learn about the Northern Interior of British Columbia. Friendly staff, atrium with food service and gift shop. Phone 1-866-562-1612; www.theexplorationplace.com. Admission is charged.

Central British Columbia Railway and Forestry Museum features a dozen original railway buildings, including 2 stations. Among the 50 pieces of rolling stock are 5 locomotives, a 1903 snow plow, a 1913 100-ton steam wrecking crane and a 90-foot 100-ton turntable. Items from 8 past and present railway companies are displayed. There is also a small collection of forestry, mining and agricultural machinery. Located at 850 River Road next to Cottonwood Island Nature Park on the Nechako River. Admission fee charged, open daily May to September from 10 A.M. to 5 P.M. Phone 250-563-7351.

Fort George Park has miles of paved walking trails along the Fraser and Nechako rivers; picnic tables, barbecue facilities; playgrounds and a spray park. Open daily year-round. Free parking for cars and RVs. Wheelchair accessible. No admission fee charged. There are public tennis courts near the park entrance on 20th Avenue. For more information phone 250-562-1612.

City Landmarks: Centennial Fountain, corner of 7th Avenue and Dominion Street, depicts the early history of Prince George in mosaic tile and a statue memorializes Terry Fox. A cairn at Fort George Park commemorates Sir Alexander Mackenzie.

Connaught Hill Park offers colorful flower gardens and views (somewhat obscured by trees) of the city and Fraser River Bridge. Follow Connaught Drive to the park. No parking for big rigs at this park.

City Parks. There are 120 parks and 65 playgrounds, 7 nature parks, 7 athletic parks, 97 sports fields, 73 tennis courts and 66 miles/106 km of trails. Forests for the World

Connaught Hill Park offers shady picnic spots. (©Kris Valencia, staff)

park, minutes from downtown, has more than 9 miles/15 km of trails through various habitats; self-guided nature walks, hiking, biking and picnics. The upper lookout at Shane Lake has a great view of the city. For park information and trail maps, phone 250-562-3700.

Two Rivers Gallery, modeled after Prince George's natural landscape, is a public gallery featuring exhibitions by local, regional and national artists. Shop at the Gallery featuring unique, handmade artwork. Two Rivers Gallery is located downtown in the Civic Centre Plaza. Hours are 10 A.M. to 5 P.M. every day but Thursday; 10 A.M. to 9 P.M. Thursday. Admission charged (free admission Thursdays). Phone 250-614-7800.

Swimming. Four Seasons Swimming Pool at the corner of 7th Avenue and Dominion Street has a pool, waterslide, diving tank and fitness centre. Open to the public from 9 A.M.–8 P.M. Mon.–Fri., and 1 P.M.–5 P.M. weekends. Or check out the Aquatic Centre at 1770 George Paul Lane. It's equipped with a leisure-style wave pool, river channel and a 10-metre diving tower. Open Mon.–Fri. 6:15 A.M.–10 P.M. and weekends 10 A.M.–9 P.M.

Golf Courses. Aberdeen Glen Golf Club is located just north of Prince George, 0.6 mile/1 km off Highway 97 North. Aspen Grove Golf Club is on Highway 97 South. The Prince George Golf & Country Club is located in the heart of the city. Links of Maggie May Golf Course is located 4 miles/6.5 km from the junction of Shelley Road and Yellowhead Highway 16 East. Alder Hills Golf Club located on the east side of Prince George, 4.1 km/2.54 miles on Highway 16 East. Pine Valley Golf Club, Yellowhead Grove Golf Course, Prince George Golf and Curling Club are on Yellowhead Highway 16 West.

Special Events: Elks May Day celebration; Resource Expo in May (even years); Canada Day (July 1); Summerfest in August; BC Rivers Day in September; Studio Fair and Festival of Trees and Winter Lights Festival in November; Cercle des Canadiens Francais Winter Festival in February. Details on these and other events are available from Tourism

Prince George, phone 250-562-3700.

Huble Homestead, next to the scenic Fraser River and the Giscome Portage Regional Park, dates from 1912. These original and reconstructed buildings are surrounded by grazing land and forest. Picnic tables, concession and gift shop. Open every day 10 A.M.–5 P.M. May–Sept. with guided interpretive tours May–October; admission by donation. Located north of Prince George on Highway 97; turn east off the highway at **Milepost PG 25.4** and drive 3.7 miles/6 km on Mitchell Road. www.hublehomestead.ca.

AREA FISHING: Highways 16 and 97 are the ideal routes for the sportsman, with year-round fishing and easy access to lakes and rivers. Hunters and fishermen stop over in Prince George as the jumping-off place for some of North America's finest big game hunting and fishing.

The local fishery releases rainbows into Ferguson Lake and Shane Lake in "Forests For the World." Both lakes lie within the city limits and are stocked to encourage the development of local fishing. Both are small lakes and no motors are permitted. For more information contact Fish & Wildlife at 250-565-6145, or Tourism Prince George, phone 250-562-3700; 1-800-668-7646; www.tourismpg.com.

PRINCE GEORGE

British Columbia – Canada

Need to stretch your legs?

Take a break from your travels and stay a while in Prince George: restock the camper, play a round of golf, stroll around the park or reel in a fish. Don't forget to stop at the Visitor Information Centre where our helpful staff can direct you to local attractions or events and even lend you a bike, fishing rod, or life jacket!

If you are looking for more activities visit **www.takeonPG.com** where we have a list of 365 things to do right here in Prince George!

Don't have time to stop? Make sure you visit us online at **www.tourismpg.com** or find us on **Facebook** or **Twitter @tourismpg**

Northern British Columbia
REGION

SUPER, NATURAL
BRITISH COLUMBIA®
CANADA

West Access Route Log
(continued)

BC HIGHWAY 97/HART HIGHWAY

The John Hart Highway, completed in 1952, was named for the former B.C. premier who sponsored its construction. This paved highway, mostly 2-lanes, with both straight and winding stretches and some steep grades, crests the Rocky Mountains at Pine Pass.

This section of the log shows distance from Prince George (PG) followed by distance from Dawson Creek (DC).

PG 0 DC 245.2 (394.5 km) Junction of Highway 97 and Yellowhead Highway 16 (20th Avenue) in Prince George.

PG 0.3 (0.5 km) DC 244.9 (394 km) Pine Centre shopping mall to west (southbound access).

PG 0.7 (1.1 km) DC 244.5 (393.4 km) Stoplight. Turnoff for College of New Caledonia and Pine Centre shopping mall (northbound access).

PG 1.2 (1.9 km) DC 244 (392.6 km) Stoplight at 15th Avenue; access west to fast food, gas and shopping; access east to City Centre. Also access west to University of Northern British Columbia (follow signs).

PG 1.5 (2.4 km) DC 243.7 (392.1 km) Stoplight at 10th Avenue. Access to food, gas/diesel and lodging.

PG 1.9 (3.1 km) DC 243.3 (391.5 km) Stoplight at 5th Avenue. City Centre to east. Gas/diesel to west. Also access to Spruceland shopping centre

PG 2.3 (3.7 km) DC 242.9 (390.8 km) John Hart Bridge over the Nechako River.

PG 4 (6.4 km) DC 241.2 (388.2 km) Truck weigh scales to west. Mohawk gas station with diesel to east.

PG 4.2 (6.7 km) DC 241 (387.8 km) Stoplight; Chevron gas station with diesel. Access to Aberdeen Glen Golf Club.

PG 6.2 (10 km) DC 239 (384.6 km) Race Trac gas station to east.

PG 6.8 (10.9 km) DC 238.4 (383.6 km) Stoplight. Restaurant to east.

PG 7.7 (12.4 km) DC 237.5 (382.2 km) Stoplight. Petro-Canada (gas/diesel), Tim Hortons, supermarket (to west).

PG 8.3 (13.4 km) DC 236.9 (381.2 km) Stoplight; Esso gas station. Turn west for **Hartway RV Park** and The Treasure Cheset Country Store (antiques); description follow).

PG 8.8 (14.2 km) DC 236.4 (380.4 km) Junction with Chief Lake Road. Husky gas/diesel station. Eskers Provincial Park.

PG 9.1 (14.6 km) DC 236.1 (380 km) *End*

4-lane highway, begin 2-lane highway northbound.,

Distance marker northbound shows Chetwynd 292 km/181 miles, Dawson Creek 394 km/244 miles.

PG 11.5 (18.5 km) DC 233.7 (376 km) Northland RV Park; camping.

PG 16.8 (27 km) DC 228.4 (367.5 km) Wright Creek.

PG 17.2 (27.7 km) DC 228 (366.9 km) Salmon River bridge. *Highway climbs 6 percent northbound, passing lane.*

PG 18.8 (30.3 km) DC 226.4 (364.3 km) Highway bridge crosses railroad.

PG 21.7 (34.9 km) DC 223.5 (359.6 km) Turnoff to west for Goodsir Nature Park; 1.5 miles/2.4 km from highway via Old Summit Lake Road (gravel). This 160-acre park features 6 miles/10 km of nature trails, picnic tables. Open May to October, 8 A.M. to dusk; admission by donation. Adjacent owner's home; be respectful. Limited parking, bug repellent is essential.

PG 24.6 (39.6 km) DC 220.6 (354.9 km) Gravel turnouts both sides of highway. The east side has litter bins.

PG 25.4 (40.9 km) DC 219.8 (353.7 km) Paved turnout to east with litter bins and point-of-interest sign about Crooked River Forest Recreation Area on access road to **Huble Homestead Historic Site** in Giscome Portage Regional Park, 3.7 miles/6 km east via Mitchell Road. The pioneer Huble Homestead and trading post preserves the oldest home in the region. Guided interpretive tours of the original log buildings available May–October. Picnic areas, concession, gift shop and farm animals. Admission by donation. Phone (250) 564-7033; website www.hublehomestead.ca.

PG 28.1 (45.2 km) DC 217.1 (349.4 km) Highway passes under powerlines.

PG 28.9 (46.5 km) DC 216.3 (348 km) Paved double-ended turnout to east with litter bins.

PG 30.6 (49.2 km) DC 214.6 (345.4 km) First of 2 turnoffs northbound to west for **Summit Lake**, a resort area popular with Prince George residents; no services. Lake char and rainbow fishing spring and fall.

PG 31.5 (50.7 km) DC 213.7 (343.9 km) Spectra Energy Compressor Site.

PG 33 (53.1 km) DC 212.2 (341.4 km) Summit Lake turnoff to west.

PG 44.4 (71.4 km) DC 200.8 (323.1 km) *CAUTION: Slow for railroad crossing on curve.*

PG 46.3 (74.5 km) DC 198.9 (320 km) Turnoff to west for **Crooked River (Bear Lake) Provincial Park.** Open May 15–Sept. 8. The centre of activity at this park is Bear Lake. According to BC Parks, Bear Lake's sandy beaches are some of the best in the region. 65 sites, a picnic area and shelter, flush toilets, showers, tables, firepits, dump station, playground and telephone. *No pets or alcohol allowed in day-use area.* Camping fee $16/sani-dump $5. Some sites may be reserved at www.discovercamping.ca. Powerboats are prohibited. Good fishing for rainbows, Dolly Varden, Rocky Mountain whitefish.

Highway 97 follows the Crooked River north to McLeod Lake.

PG 47.4 (76.3 km) DC 197.8 (318.3 km) BEAR LAKE (pop. 300). Gas station with convenience store, restaurant, motel and

liquor store. Greyhound bus stop.

PG 56.7 (91.2 km) DC 188.5 (303.3 km) Red Rock Creek.

PG 57.6 (92.7 km) DC 187.6 (301.8 km) Red Rocky Lake to west.

PG 67 (107.8 km) DC 178.2 (286.7 km) Altezega Creek.

PG 70 (112.6 km) DC 175.2 (281.9 km) Large, double-ended, paved rest area to west beside Crooked River; litter bins, picnic tables and pit toilets.

PG 71 (114.2 km) DC 174.2 (280.3 km) 42-Mile Creek.

PG 73.6 (118.4 km) DC 171.6 (276.1 km) Whiskers Bay Resort has beautiful lakeside camping spots on a quiet bay, some with electricity and water. Hot showers. Cabins with showers, fridges and cooking facilities. Fishing is right off our dock or in many surrounding lakes. Sunsets are sensational, and hummingbirds are bountiful. For real northern hospitality. Come visit us! [ADVERTISEMENT]

PG 78 (125.5 km) DC 167.2 (269 km) View northbound of sandy beach at Whisker's Point on McLeod Lake

PG 78.7 (126.6 km) DC 166.5 (267.9 km) Whiskers Point Provincial Park to west on McLeod Lake; paved loop road, 69 level gravel sites, tap water, flush toilets, boat ramp, fire rings and picnic tables. Also horseshoe pits, volleyball, playground and picnic shelter. Camping fee $16. Late-May to Sept. 8. Open, but no services provided after those dates. Self-guided nature trail loop takes 20 minutes. Boat launch, swimming and sandy beach. **McLeod Lake** has fair fishing for rainbows and Dolly Varden.

PG 85.5 (137.5 km) DC 159.7 (256.9 km) McLEOD LAKE (pop. 70), general store and post office to west. A cairn in front of the store commemorates the first European settlement west of the Rockies and the longest continuously occupied European settlement in British Columbia. The first fur trading post west of the Rockies was established here in 1805 by Simon Fraser for the North West Trading Co., and named by Fraser for Archie McLeod.

PG 86.2 (138.6 km) DC 159 (255.8 km) Turnoff for **Carp Lake Provincial Park**, 20 miles/32 km west via gravel road; 90 tent/RV sites on Carp Lake, 12 sites at War Lake (not suitable for long units) 3 island campsites for those with water transport. Camping fee $16, sani-dump fee is $5. Boating and *excellent* trout fishing.

PG 86.9 (139.8 km) DC 158.3 (254.7 km) Gravel turnout with litter bin to west, welcome to McLeod Lake southbound.

PG 89 (143.2 km) DC 156.2 (251.3 km) Spectra Energy compressor station.

PG 89.7 (144.3 km) DC 155.5 (250.2 km) Entering Mackenzie Forest District northbound.

PG 91 (146.4 km) DC 154.2 (248.1 km) Turnoff to west for **Tudyah Lake Provincial Park**; 36 campsites with picnic tables, fire rings, pit toilets and drinking water. Day-use area with horseshoes, camping in trees for groups, boat launch, swimming and waterskiing. Open mid-May to Sept. 8 for full services, no services but open till Oct. 30. Camping fee $11. Tudyah Lake and nearby **Parsnip River** offer good fishing for rainbow, Dolly Varden and some grayling in summer.

PG 91.7 (146.7 km) **DC 153.5** (247 km) Bear Creek.

PG 91.9 (147.9 km) **DC 153.3** (246.7 km) *Begin 1-mile-long passing lane northbound.*

PG 95.2 (153.2 km) **DC 150** (241.4 km) Windy Point Inn; gas, diesel, restaurant, lodging, store.

Highway makes winding descent northbound to Parsnip River.

PG 96 (154.5 km) **DC 149.2** (240.1 km) Parsnip River bridge (clearance 16.6 feet/5.06m).

Highway climbs southbound, passing lane.

This is the Rocky Mountain Trench, marking the western boundary of the Rocky Mountains. Northbound motorists begin gradual climb through the Misinchinka then Hart ranges of the Rocky Mountains. *Passing lane northbound.*

PG 96.4 (155.1 km) **DC 148.8** (239.4 km) **Junction** with Highway 39; Mackenzie Junction; cafe, gas and diesel.

MACKENZIE (pop. 3,300) is located 18 miles/29 km north on Highway 39. **Visitor Information:** Visitor Centre located in a former train car at this junction; picnic tables, toilets. Phone toll-free 1-877-997-9940, www.district.mackenzie.bc.ca.

The District of Mackenzie lies at the southern end of Williston Lake, the largest man-made reservoir in North America, formed by the WAC Bennett Dam on the Peace River. The town was named for the famous explorer Alexander Mackenzie, who camped near the town site on his epic journey to the Pacific in 1793. The town is home to natural, unspoiled wilderness which provides hiking, mountain biking, camping, wildlife and photography. It is a fisherman's paradise.

Mackenzie attractions include the World's Largest Tree Crusher, Mackenzie Nature Observatory, a 9-hole scenic golf course, recreation centre and the "blue jewel" Morfee Lake (2 km/1.2 miles from town). The downtown commercial core offers all visitor services including the Williston Lake Lodge in downtown. Mackenzie & District Museum (www.mackenziemuseum.ca) is located on Centennial Drive; phone 250-997-3021.

District of Mackenzie. See display ad this page.

PG 96.8 (155.8 km) **DC 148.4** (238.8 km) Highway crosses railroad tracks.

PG 97.1 (156.2 km) **DC 148.1** (238.3 km) *CAUTION: High mountain road with sudden weather changes (northbound sign).*

PG 100 (160.9 km) **DC 145.2** (233.6 km) Large double-ended gravel turnout to east.

PG 107.1 (172.3 km) **DC 138.1** (222.2 km) Large gravel turnout to east.

PG 109.4 (176 km) **DC 135.8** (218.5 km) Highway maintenance yard.

PG 109.6 (176.3 km) **DC 135.6** (218.2 km) Honeymoon Creek.

PG 110.7 (178.1 km) **DC 134.5** (216.4 km) Powerlines crossing highway carry electricity south from hydro dams in the Hudson's Hope area.

PG 111.6 (179.6 km) **DC 133.6** (215 km) *CAUTION: SLOW DOWN for sharp curve across railroad tracks.*

PG 112.4 (180.9 km) **DC 132.8** (213.7 km) **Misinchinka River**, southeast of highway; fishing for grayling, whitefish and Dolly Varden.

PG 113.4 (182.5 km) **DC 131.8** (212.1 km) Rolston Creek bridge.

Bijoux Falls Provincial Park is a popular shady rest stop for travelers. (©Kris Valencia, staff)

PG 116.3 (187.1 km) **DC 128.9** (207.4 km) Gravel turnout to east. Turnoff to west for **Bijoux Falls Provincial Park**; fair-sized parking area with plenty of turn-around space if it is not packed by visitors, picnic tables, toilets (wheelchair accessible). A pleasant stop to view the falls and spot Steller's jays. Good photo opportunities. Day-use only.

PG 117 (188.3 km) **DC 128.2** (206.3 km) Highway climbs 6 to 10 percent grade next 3.5 miles/5.6 km northbound to Pine Pass. *Passing lane northbound.*

PG 117.2 (188.6 km) **DC 128** (206 km) Highway crosses under railroad. Height is 5.68m/18.6 ft.

PG 120.2 (193.4 km) **DC 125** (201.1 km) Northbound sign for **Pine Pass** (elev. 3,061 feet/933m), the highest point on the John Hart Highway. Beautiful view of the Rockies

Stunning Azouzetta Lake from turnout at Milepost PG 122.4. (©Michael K. Robb)

to the northeast. Good highway over pass.

Highway descends 6 to 10 percent down-grade next 3.5 miles/5.6 km southbound.

PG 120.5 (193.9 km) **DC 124.7** (200.6 km) Turnoff to Powder King ski area. Skiing early December to April; chairlift and T-bars (operate Thursday to Sunday, daylight hours), novice to advanced skiing, snow-boarding; ski school, day lodge; restaurants, pub; rentals and repair. Powder King Mountain Resort, phone toll-free 1-866-769-5464. This area receives an average annual snow-fall of 41 feet/1250 cm.

PG 122.4 (194 km) **DC 123.5** (198.7 km) Paved turnout to east with view of picturesque **Azouzetta Lake**.

PG 122.9 (196.9 km) **DC 122.8** (197.6 km) Azouzetta Lake Lodge.

PG 125.9 (202.6 km) **DC 119.3** (192 km) Spectra Energy compressor station.

Highway climbs southbound, passing lane.

PG 129 (207.6 km) **DC 116.2** (187 km) Highway crosses under power lines.

Highway climbs northbound; passing lane, winding road.

PG 131.4 (211 km) **DC 113.8** (183.1 km) Dirt turnout to west.

Highway narrows and makes winding descent northbound.

PG 137.6 (221.4 km) **DC 107.6** (173.1 km) *CAUTION: Watch for moose next 40 km/25 miles northbound.*

Highway makes narrow winding ascent southbound.

PG 139.8 (224.9 km) **DC 105.4** (169.6 km) Link Creek.

PG 142 (228.5 km) **DC 103.2** (166 km) Pine River bridge.

PG 142.3 (229 km) **DC 102.9** (165.6 km) Pine River bridge.

PG 142.9 (229.9 km) **DC 102.3** (164.6 km) West Pine Rest Area to west has a large, double-ended paved park area with picnic tables, litter bins and pit toilets.

PG 143.4 (230.7 km) **DC 101.8** (163.8 km) **Heart Lake** Forestry campground to east; toilets, tables, firepits and litter bins. Fishing for stocked trout.

PG 143.7 (231.2 km) **DC 101.5** (163.3 km) Bridge over West Pine River.

PG 143.8 (231.4 km) **DC 101.4** (163.2 km) B.C. Railway overpass. Height 4.92m/16.1 ft.

PG 143.9 (231.5 km) **DC 101.3** (163 km) Private RV park.

PG 146.4 (235.6 km) **DC 98.8** (159 km) Cairns Creek dumps into Pine River. Massive trees have been brought down this river at high water and left strewn behind, a testament to the power of current.

CAUTION: Slow for curves northbound. Watch for moose and deer in area, especially at dusk and night. Pipeline crosses road.

PG 148.5 (238.9 km) **DC 96.7** (155.6 km) Mount LeMoray (unincorporated); no services. Highway maintenance camp.

PG 149.1 (239.9 km) **DC 96.1** (154.6 km) Lilico Creek.

PG 150 (241.4 km) **DC 95.2** (153.2 km) Martin Creek.

PG 150.7 (242.5 km) **DC 94.5** (152.1 km) Big Boulder Creek.

PG 156.5 (251.8 km) **DC 88.7** (142.7 km) Fisher Creek.

PG 157.2 (252.2 km) **DC 88** (141.6 km) Large gravel turnout with litter bin to south beside Pine River.

PG 160.1 (257.6 km) **DC 85.1** (136.9 km) Willow Creek Mine. Crassier Creek.

PG 161.9 (260.5 km) **DC 83.3** (134 km) Spectra Energy compressor station.

PG 169.7 (273 km) **DC 75.5** (121.5 km) Turnout with picnic tables and litter barrel to south at Jack Pine Point overlooking the beautiful Pine River valley. "Peace Foothills" information board.

Highway climbs northbound. View of the Canadian Rocky Mountain foothills to the south and west.

PG 172.6 (277.7 km) **DC 72.6** (116.8 km) Spectra Pine River gas plant, road to east.

PG 177.6 (285.8 km) **DC 67.6** (108.8 km) Double ended and paved turnout with litter bin to east.

PG 178.4 (287 km) **DC 66.8** (107.5 km) **Caron Creek RV Park**. 7537 Highway 97S; 16 km (10 miles) west of Chetwynd. 30-amp and 15-amp fully-serviced pull-through sites, free WiFi, free hot showers. Laundromat. Discounts for seniors and all club members. Open all year-round. Email: josef-karcher@hotmail.com; website www. caron-creek.com. Phone: 250-788-2522.

[ADVERTISEMENT]

PG 181.6 (292.2 km) **DC 63.6** (102.3 km)

CAUTION: Slow for curve.

PG 182 (292.2 km) **DC 63.2** (101.7 km) Bissette Creek.

PG 183.6 (295.4 km) **DC 61.6** (99.1 km) Wildmare Creek.

PG 186.5 (300.1 km) **DC 58.7** (94.4 km) Paved turnout to south at Welcome to Chetwynd (northbound) sign.

PG 187.1 (301 km) **DC 58.1** (93.5 km) Turnoff for Little Prairie Heritage Museum located in a 1949 post office building. The museum is open Tue.–Sat. in July–August; phone 250-788-3358. Sani dump is located at the museum.

Begin 50 kmph/30 mph speed zone east-bound.

PG 187.8 (302.2 km) **DC 57.4** (92.4 km) Turnoff to north for Chetwynd services and visitor information.

PG 187.9 (302.3 km) **DC 57.3** (92.2 km) Chetwynd town centre turnoff.

Chetwynd

PG 187.9 (302.3 km) **DC 57.3** (92.2 km) Located on Highway 97 at the junction with Highway 29 north to the Alaska Highway via Hudson's Hope, and south to Tumbler Ridge. **Population**: 3,119; area 9,000. **Emergency Services**: Phone 911.

Visitor Information: Chetwynd Visitor Centre open year-round. Free Internet access and information regarding free sani-dump is available for travelers at the Visitor Centre. Contact the Chetwynd Visitor Centre at P.O. Box 594, Chetwynd V0C 1J0; phone 250-788-1943; fax 250-788-1846. Email: tourist@gochetwynd.com. Website: www. gochetwynd.com

Elevation: 2,017 feet/615m. **Radio**: Peace FM 94.5/104.1, CISN-FM 103.9, CJDC 890, CKNL 560, CBC-FM 93.5. **Television**: 7 channels (includes CBC, BCTV, ABC, CBS, CHETTV and NBC) plus pay cable.

The town, formerly known as Little Prairie, is a division point on the British Columbia Railway. The name was changed to honour the late British Columbia Minister of Railways, Ralph Chetwynd, who was instrumental in the northward extension of the province-owned railway.

Chetwynd is the "most livable small community" in British Columbia, according to one poll. Forestry, mining, natural gas processing, ranching, farming and wind energy are the main industries in Chetwynd. Chetwynd lies at the northern end of the North East Coal resource, one of the largest known coal deposits on earth. Quintette Mine, south of Chetwynd near Tumbler Ridge, the world's largest computerized open pit coal mine, shut down in 2000; plans were underway in 2012 to reopen the mine in 2013.

Local radio station Peace-FM 94.5/104.1 was the first community radio station in Canada to be licensed under the 1997 legislation allowing low power community stations. Peace-FM transmits to Chetwynd and Dawson Creek.

A good traveler's stop with easy access to all services, Chetwynd has several motels, fast-food outlets, restaurants, banks and bank machines, post office, laundromats, gas stations, supermarkets and two 9-hole golf courses. The public library has free internet access. (Heavy commercial and industrial traffic often fill up local motels and camp-

Chetwynd

A four season outdoor adventure destination.

Located in the eastern foothills of the Northern Rocky Mountains, Chetwynd offers a unique balance of prairies, mountains, wilderness and a full service community.

The area is well known for its breathtaking scenery and countryside. The surrounding area contains mountains for hiking and skiing, lakes and rivers for swimming, canoeing and fishing, and a countryside and park system that produces some of the best camping, snowmobiling, hunting, and wildlife spotting in Canada.

**CHAINSAW CARVING TOUR | GREENSPACE TRAIL SYSTEM | GOLF | SWIMMING | CAMPING | FISHING | HUNTING
CROSS-COUNTRY SKIING | SNOWMOBILING | MOUNTAIN BIKING**

10th annual INTERNATIONAL CHAINSAW CARVING CHAMPIONSHIP
JUNE 12 - 14, 2014

Watch the artists in action

2013 1st Place

2013 2nd Place

2013 Carvers

The Annual Chetwynd International Chainsaw Carving Championship has visually shaped Chetwynd into a one-of-a-kind locale. Artists from all over the world compete in this unique competition. The District of Chetwynd keeps each intricately carved piece from the championship and places them throughout town.

- Spectators can watch the artists create their works of art over the three days from start to finish
- Today, competitors come from as far as Wales, North Wales and Japan to compete
- Don't miss the quick carve competition held on Sunday and your chance to bid on a piece at the auction!
- Take a self-guided walking tour ■ 120 carvings and more added each year - a must-see!

Pick up a brochure at the Visitor Centre and take a self-guided tour of the carvings.

Chetwynd Visitor Centre

Tel: 250.788.1943
Fax: 250.788.1846
tourist@gochetwynd.com

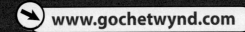
www.gochetwynd.com

Northern
British Columbia
REGION

SUPER, NATURAL
BRITISH COLUMBIA®
CANADA

Each year, new and fantastical wood carvings are added to Chetwynd's collection.
(©Kris Valencia, staff)

grounds; reserve ahead.) There are private RV parks in town and on Highway 97.

Chain saw sculptures. Chetwynd's collection of carvings always stops traffic: Do not miss the display in front of the Visitor Centre on Highway 97. Approximately 12 new sculptures are on display each year before joining the other carvings placed throughout Chetwynd. (In 2013, there were 134 carvings.) Chetwynd's slogan is "Community Carved by Success." The International Chainsaw Carving Championship takes place here June 12-14, 2014.

Moberly Lake Provincial Park is 12 miles/19.3 km north of Chetwynd via Highway 29 north. The park has 109 campsites, beach, picnic area, playground, nature trail, boat launch and a private marina next door with RV sites, boat rental and concession. Good swimming at Moberly Lake on a warm summer day. Worth the drive. (See "Hudson's Hope Loop" log on pages 119-121.)

Tumbler Ridge side trip. Highway 97 travelers can make a loop trip south by driving 57 miles/91 km south on Highway 29 to the town of Tumbler Ridge, the site of some important recent dinosaur fossil finds. A major attraction in the area is spectacular Kinuseo Falls. (See "Tumbler Ridge Loop" on pages 122-123.)

Chetwynd Recreation Centre has a pool with wave machine, whirlpool, gym, hockey arena, curling rink, walking track, climbing wall, squash/racquetball court and weight room. Open daily, visitors welcome.

There is a **Farmer's Market** every Thursday in summer at the Recreation Centre.

District of Chetwynd. See display ad on page 117.

West Access Route Log

(continued)

PG 188 (302.5 km) **DC 57.2** (92 km) Traffic light at **junction** with Highway 29 North to Moberly Lake, Peace River Provincial Recreation Area, Peace Canyon Dam, Hudson's Hope and **W.A.C. Bennett Dam.** Highway 29 connects with the Alaska Highway 53.7 miles/86.4 km north of Dawson Creek.

Junction with Highway 29 north to Hudson's Hope. See "Hudson's Hope Loop" log beginning on page 119.

Highway 97 climbs next 12 miles/19 km for Dawson Creek-bound motorists.

PG 188.1 (302.7 km) **DC 57.1** (91.9 km) Highway crosses railroad tracks.

PG 188.2 (302.8 km) **DC 57** (91.7 km) Traffic light. Industrial Park and airport turnoff to north.

PG 188.3 (303 km) **DC 56.9** (91.6 km) Chetwynd Recreation Centre to north.

PG 188.6 (303.5 km) **DC 56.6** (91.1 km) Centurion Creek.

PG 189 (304.1 km) **DC 56.2** (90.4 km) Private RV Park. ▲

Highway climbs northbound, passing lane.

PG 189.3 (304.6 km) **DC 55.9** (89.9 km) Welcome to Chetwynd (southbound sign).

PG 189.6 (305.1 km) **DC 55.6** (89.5 km) Turnoff to south for Highway 29 South to Gwillim Lake and Tumbler Ridge. Tumbler Ridge is the site of some important recent dinosaur fossil finds and is the gateway to Kinuseo Falls in Monkman Provincial Park.

Junction with Highway 29 South. See beginning of "Tumbler Ridge Loop" log beginning on page 122.

PG 192.1 (309.1 km) **DC 53.1** (85.5 km) Large paved turnout to north (westbound traffic only) with information sign. Brake-check area: Steep downgrade westbound into Chetwynd.

PG 199.2 (320.5 km) **DC 46** (74 km) Double-ended, narrow gravel turnouts both sides of highway.

PG 201 (323.4 km) **DC 44.2** (71.1 km) *CAUTION: Slow down for curve across railroad tracks.*

PG 204.3 (328.7 km) **DC 40.9** (65.8 km) Tembec Pulp Mill to north.

PG 205.7 (331 km) **DC 39.5** (63.6 km) East Pine turnout with litter bin to south.

Begin 6 percent downgrade with curves eastbound; passing lane. CAUTION: Watch for deer.

PG 207.5 (333.9 km) **DC 37.7** (60.7 km) Views of East Pine River Valley and Table Mountain. *CAUTION: Slow for sharp curves next 1.7 miles/2.7 km as highway descends eastbound.*

PG 207.9 (334.5 km) **DC 37.3** (60 km) *Slow for 30 kmph/20 mph curve approaching East Pine River bridge eastbound.*

East Pine River Rest Area to south at west end of East Pine River bridge. Rest area is a large gravel parking area with litter bins located at the entrance to **East Pine Provincial Park** (0.5 mile south on gravel road). The provincial park has a boat launch which provides access to the East Pine and Murray rivers.

PG 208.1 (334.8 km) **DC 37.1** (59.7 km) East Pine River bridge.

Highway climbs 6 percent winding grade next 2.5 miles/4 km westbound. Slow for sharp curves. Passing lane.

Highway climbs eastbound with passing lane.

PG 209.7 (337.4 km) **DC 45.5** (57.1 km) East Pine (unincorporated); no services.

PG 211.6 (340.5 km) **DC 33.6** (54.1 km) Rest area with toilets and litter barrel to north. Westbound use as brake-check area.

Highway descends westbound. Passing lane ends eastbound.

PG 221.4 (356.2 km) **DC 23.8** (38.3 km) Turnouts both sides of highway.

PG 222.5 (358 km) **DC 22.7** (36.5 km) **GROUNDBIRCH** (unincorporated); store, liquor outlet, gas, propane, diesel and post office. Greyhound bus stop.

PG 225.5 (362.8 km) **DC 19.7** (31.7 km) Turn north to McLeod.

PG 230.8 (371.4 km) **DC 14.4** (23.2 km) Progress (unincorporated); no services.

PG 237.5 (382.1 km) **DC 7.7** (12.4 km) **Junction** with Heritage Highway 52, which leads 59.6 miles/96 km south to the community of Tumbler Ridge.

From Tumbler Ridge, Heritage Highway 52 continues 92 miles/148 km east and north to connect with Highway 2 southeast of Dawson Creek.

Junction with Highway 52 South. See end of "Tumbler Ridge Loop" log on page 123.

PG 237.8 (382.6 km) **DC 7.4** (11.9 km) Kiskatinaw River bridge.

PG 238.5 (383.7 km) **DC 6.7** (10.8 km) **ARRAS** (unincorporated). The Roadhouse truck stop restaurant, open late year-round. Junction with Mason Road.

The Roadhouse. See display ad on page 118.

PG 243.2 (391.3 km) **DC 2** (3.2 km) Small turnout to south with litter barrel and point of interest sign about Dawson Creek.

PG 244.7 (393.7 km) **DC 1.5** (2.4 km) **Northern Lights RV Park.** "Where adventure begins." Mike and Annette Jalbert welcome you to their 92-fully serviced sites with large pull-thrus, "state of the art" washrooms/showers/laundromat, WiFi, great views and beautiful sunsets. Located on 97S just 1.5 miles from junction with 97N in Dawson Creek. 250-782-9433; nlrv2010@gmail.com; www.nlrv.com. See display ad on page 136 in the ALASKA HIGHWAY section. [ADVERTISEMENT]

PG 244.9 (394.1 km) **DC 0.3** (0.5 km) Left turn for Dangerous Goods route to bypass Dawson Creek going west on 97.

PG 245 (394.2 km) **DC 0.2** (0.3 km) Entering Dawson Creek. **Rotary Lake Park** on north side of highway, Tubby's Car Wash & RV Park to south.

Tubby's Car Wash & RV Park. See display ad on page 136 in the ALASKA HIGHWAY section.

PG 245.2 (394.5 km) **DC 0 Junction** of the John Hart Highway 97 and Alaska Highway 97. Turn right for downtown Dawson Creek.

Turn to ALASKA HIGHWAY section beginning on page 124 for description of Dawson Creek and log of the Alaska Highway.

Turn left for entrance to **Mile "0" RV Park & Campground;** treed sites, full hookups, hot showers, free WiFi, sanidump, pay phone.

Mile "0" RV Park & Campground. See display ad on page 136 in the ALASKA HIGHWAY section.

Hudson's Hope Loop

BC Hydro offers tours of its W.A.C. Bennett Dam. (©Michael K. Robb)

The Hudson's Hope Loop (BC Highway 29) links the John Hart Highway (Highway 97) with the Alaska Highway (also Highway 97), bypassing Dawson Creek. The south end of Hudson's Hope Loop is at Chetwynd, the north end intersects the Alaska Highway at **Milepost DC 53.6** just north of Fort St. John across from Charlie Lake Provincial Park.

This 85-mile/136.8-km paved loop road provides year-round access to the town of Hudson's Hope, W.A.C. Bennett Dam, Peace Canyon Dam and Moberly Lake.

Highway 29 is a good, scenic 2-lane road with a few steep and winding sections adjacent the scenic Peace River.

HIGHWAY 29 NORTH

Distance from Chetwynd (C) is followed by distance from Alaska Highway junction (AH).

C 0 AH 85 (136.8 km) Traffic light at **junction** of Highways 29 and 97 at Chetwynd, **Milepost PG 188** on Highway 97 (Hart Highway). *See description of Chetwynd beginning on page 116.*

C 1.2 (1.9 km) **AH 83.8** (134.9 km) Truck weigh scales to west.

C 1.5 (2.4 km) **AH 83.5** (134.4 km) *Highway climbs 6 percent grade with passing lanes next 3.3 miles/5.3 km northbound.*

C 2.1 (3.4 km) **AH 82.9** (133.4 km) Jackfish Road to east.

C 4.8 (7.7 km) **AH 80.2** (129.1 km) *Highway descends 6 percent downgrade southbound.*

C 7.7 (12.4 km) **AH 77.3** (124.4 km) Large paved turnout to west.

Passing lanes southbound next 2 miles. Watch for moose.

C 11.7 (18.8 km) **AH 73.3** (118 km) Paved access road leads 2.2 miles/3.5 km west to **Moberly Lake Provincial Park** on south shore; 109 campsites, swimming,

waterskiing, picnicking, drinking water, dump station, boat launch, $16 camping fee ($5 sani-station). This beautiful 9-mile-/15-km-long lake drains into Moberly River. Fishing for lake trout, Dolly Varden and whitefish.

C 11.9 (19.2 km) **AH 73.1** (117.6 km) Moberly River bridge; parking area with litter barrel at south end.

C 12.5 (20.1 km) **AH 72.5** (116.7 km) Crow Feathers store and gas station.

C 15.4 (24.8 km) **AH 69.6** (112 km) **MOBERLY LAKE.** General store and Evergreen Fuel with gas and diesel.

C 15.6 (25.1 km) **AH 69.4** (111.7 km) Historic site for Moberly lake with picnic tables, historic cairn, info panel.

C 17.8 (28.6 km) **AH 67.2** (108.1 km) Moberly Lake and District Golf Club, 0.7 mile/1.1 km east; 9 holes, grass greens, rentals, clubhouse, licensed lounge. Open May to September.

C 24.8 (39.9 km) **AH 60.2** (96.9 km) **Cameron Lake Campground** with 19 campsites; tables, toilets, playground, boat launch (no motorboats or power driven water sports) and swimming. No powerboats. Camping fee $15/night (includes firewood). Open May to September.

C 30 (48.3 km) **AH 55** (88.5 km) Paved turnout with litter bin to east. *Begin 5-mile downgrade northbound to Peace River.*

C 35.2 (56.6 km) **AH 49.8** (80.1 km) Suspension bridge over Peace River; paved turnouts with litter bins at both ends of bridge have concrete totem pole sculptures. View of Peace Canyon Dam.

Begin 5-mile upgrade with passing lanes southbound.

C 35.7 (57.4 km) **AH 49.3** (79.3 km) Turnoff to west for Dinosaur Lake Camp-

Hudson's Hope Loop

(Continued)

ground and **B.C. Hydro Peace Canyon Dam Visitor Centre** (0.6 mile/1 km) adjacent the Powerhouse. The dam's visitor centre is open from 8 A.M. to 4 P.M. daily from late May through Labour Day; weekdays the rest of the year (closed holidays). Self-guided tour includes a full-scale model of duck-billed dinosaurs and a tableau portraying Alexander Mackenzie's discovery of

the Peace River canyon. A pictorial display traces the construction of the Peace Canyon Dam. No admission charged. Tour guides on duty from May to September. For more information, phone 1-888-333-6667; or www.bchydro.com/recreation.

Dinosaur Lake Campground, on Dinosaur Lake, has 16 campsites, firepits, toilets and tables. Boat launch and swimming area. Camping fee of $15/night (includes firewood). Open May to September.

C 37.5 (60.3 km) **AH 47.5** (76.4 km) Alwin Holland Memorial Park (0.5 mile/0.8 km east of highway) is named for the first teacher in Hudson's Hope, who willed his property, known locally as The Glen, to be used as a public park. There are 9 campsites, picnic grounds and barbecues. Camping fee

of $15/night (firewood included).

C 38.5 (62 km) **AH 46.5** (74.8 km) Turnout to east with litter bin and map of Hudson's Hope.

C 38.7 (62.3 km) **AH 46.3** (74.5 km) King Gething Park; small campground with 10 grassy sites, picnic tables, cookhouse, potable water, flush toilets, showers and dump station east side of highway. Camping fee of $15/night (includes firewood).

C 39.3 (63.2 km) **AH 45.7** (73.7 km) Gas station with diesel.

Hudson's Hope

C 39.5 (63.5 km) **AH 45.5** (73.2 km) Beattie Park Visitor Centre, on left northbound, across from Hudson's Hope Museum and St. Peter's Church. **Population:** 1,012. **Emergency Services:** Hospital, Phone 911. **Visitor Information:** Visitor Centre in log building at Beattie Park; open May 1 to Sept. 30. Hours are 8:30 A.M. to 5 P.M. daily May through September; Visitor Centre 250-783-9154 (summer) or District of Hudson's Hope Office info hotline 250-783-9901 (winter); website www.hudsonshope.ca.

Elevation: 1,707 feet/520m. **Climate:** Summer temperatures range from 60°F/ 16°C to 90°F/32°C, with an average of 135 frost-free days annually. **Radio:** CBC 940,CBC-FM 88.3, Energy 98-FM 98.5, The Bear 101.5. **Television:** Channels: satellite or cable.

Private Aircraft: Hudson's Hope airstrip, 3.7 miles/6 km west; elev. 2,200 feet/671m; length 5,200 feet/1,585m; asphalt.

Visitor services in Hudson's Hope include 2 hotels, 4 restaurants, 2 service stations, laundromat, a bank, post office, supermarket, convenience and hardware stores, hairdresser, gift store and a medical clinic. One resort at nearby Williston Lake: Williston Lake Resort.

The Hudson's Hope area was first visited in 1793 by Alexander Mackenzie. In 1805, a Northwest Company trading post was established here by Simon Fraser. In 1821, it, and the Hudson Bay Company combined, creating the currently named Hudson Bay Company (previously named Rocky Mountain Portage House). In 1916, after the fur-trading days were over, a major influx of settlers arrived in the area. It was the head of navigation for steamboats on the lower Peace River until 1936, the year of the last scheduled steamboat run. Area coal mines supplied Alaska Highway maintenance camps during the 1940s.

The historic log St. Peter's Anglican United Church is located next door to the Hudson's Hope Museum. The town's museum, housed in the former Hudson's Bay Post store, has several exhibits including an extensive fossil and prehistoric collection; pioneer displays in on-site buildings; and an arrowhead/projectile point collection. The Museum shop offers a large selection of books, souvenirs and gift items.

HUDSON'S HOPE ADVERTISERS

BC Hydro/W.A.C. Bennett Dam Ph. 1-888-333-6667
District of Hudson's Hope .... Ph. 250-783-9154

©Michael R. Robb

Admission by donation; phone 250-783-5735.

Modern development of Hudson's Hope was spurred by construction of the Peace Power project in the 1960s. Today the area's principal claim to fame is BC Hydro's 600-foot/183-m-high **W.A.C. Bennett Dam** at the upper end of the Peace River canyon, 15 miles/24 km west of Hudson's Hope. The 100-million-ton dam is one of the largest earth-fill structures in the world, and Williston Lake, behind it, is the largest body of fresh water in British Columbia. The dam provides 25 percent of British Columbia's hydroelectricity. Guided, one-hour bus tours of the powerhouse (fee charged). The W.A.C. Bennett Dam Visitor Centre is open daily from 10 A.M. to 5 P.M., Victoria Day weekend (mid-May) through Labour Day (early Sept.). Bus tours depart daily (in season) on the half-hour between 10:30 A.M. and 4:30 P.M. Phone 1-888-333-6667 or visit bchydro.com/recreation to confirm tour times.

Hudson's Hope Loop Log

(continued)

C **39.6** (63.7 km) AH **45.4** (73 km) **Junction** of Highway 29 and W.A.C. Bennett access (Canyon Drive) in Hudson's Hope; Chetwynd-bound travelers turn south here. Gas station and Hudson's Hope post office.

C **40.3** (64.8 km) AH **44.7** (71.9 km) Turnout to north with litter bin and Hudson's Hope visitor map.
CAUTION: Watch for deer between here and the Alaska Highway, especially at dusk and at night.

C **43.6** (70.2 km) AH **41.4** (66.6 km) Lynx Creek crossing followed by Lynx Creek RV campground.

C **47.3** (76.1 km) AH **37.7** (60.7 km) Turnout to south with litter bin and view of the Peace River.

C **49.9** (80.3 km) AH **35.1** (56.5 km) Farrell Creek bridge.
Highway climbs 10 percent grade eastbound.

C **50.2** (80.8 km) AH **34.8** (56 km) *Highway descends 10 percent grade westbound, slow for 50 kmph curve.*

C **55.4** (89.2 km) AH **29.6** (47.6 km) Double-ended turnout to south long, narrow, with litter bin. View of Peace River valley.

C **56** (90.1 km) AH **29** (46.6 km) Turnout to south with litter barrels and view of Peace River valley.

C **58.1** (93.5 km) AH **26.9** (43.3 km) Turnoff to south to spot with litter bin.

C **61.4** (98.8 km) AH **23.6** (38 km) Distance marker westbound shows Hudson's Hope 40 km/25 miles, W.A.C. Bennett Dam 65 km/40 miles, Chetwynd 106 km/66 miles.

C **63.4** (102 km) AH **21.6** (34.7 km) Half-way River.

C **64.8** (104.3 km) AH **20.2** (32.5 km) *Begin 10 percent upgrade eastbound.*

C **65.9** (106.1 km) AH **19.1** (30.7 km) Rest area to south with litter bin, outhouse and picnic tables. Limited access but great view with viewing platform.

C **66** (106.2 km) AH **19** (30.5 km) *Begin 10 percent downgrade westbound.*

C **73** (117.5 km) AH **12** (19.3 km) Bridge over Cache Creek.

C **74** (119.1 km) AH **11** (17.7 km) Highway begins long, winding climb eastbound. *CAUTION: Watch for deer next 5 miles/8 km westbound.*

C **77** (123.9 km) AH **8** (12.9 km) Turnout with litter bin at highest point on Highway 29 (2,750 feet/838m).

Westbound, the highway descends a 10 percent grade: *Slow for 25- to 37-mph/40- to 60-kmph curves.* Views of Peace River Plateau.

C **85** (136.8 km) AH **0** Junction with the Alaska Highway, 6.7 miles/10.8 km north of Fort St. John at **Milepost DC 53.6** Truck stop at junction; food, gas, diesel, propane, store. Camping at Charlie Lake Provincial Park (across highway) and Rotary RV Park (2.7 miles/4 km south).

Distance marker westbound shows Hudson's Hope 50 miles/80 km, W.A.C. Bennett Dam 65 miles/105 km, Chetwynd 91 miles/146 km.

Return to Milepost PG 188 West Access Route or Milepost DC 53.6 Alaska Highway

Tumbler Ridge Loop

Gravel road south from Tumbler Ridge leads to Kinuseo Falls and this view of Murray River basin in Monkman Provincial Park. (©Michael K. Robb)

Highway 97 travelers can make a loop trip by taking Highway 29 South from **Milepost PG 189.6** just east of Chetwynd, to the town of Tumbler Ridge, and returning to Highway 97 via Highway 52 (the Heritage Highway). Tumbler Ridge is the site of some important recent dinosaur fossil finds. The major attraction in the area is spectacular Kinuseo Falls (213 feet/65m), located off of Heritage Highway 52 South (*see log on page 76 in EAST ACCESS section*) via a 35 mile/56 km mostly bumpy gravel road. Inquire locally for directions to the falls; the turnoff is about 7 miles east of Tumbler Ridge.

Highway 29 South is a paved road that leads 55.9 miles/90 km from **Milepost PG 189.6** to the community of Tumbler Ridge. Highway 52, the Heritage Highway, is also a paved road leading 59.6 miles/96 km from Tumbler Ridge to junction with Highway 97 at **Milepost PG 237.5**, just west of Dawson Creek. Highway 52 has many rolling hills, some 8 percent grades and several S curves.

HIGHWAY 29 SOUTH
Distance from Highway 97 junction at Milepost PG 189.6 (J) is shown.

J 0 Junction with Highway 97 at **Milepost PG 189.6**.

J 0.1 (0.2 km) Turnout with litter barrels to east. Highway 29 climbs next 2.3 miles/3.7 km southbound.

J 1.9 (3.1 km) Distance marker indicates Tumbler Ridge 55 miles/88 km; Dawson Creek 129 miles/208 km.

J 2.8 (4.5 km) Sign: Trucks check brakes, steep hill ahead.

J 3 (4.8 km) Large gravel turnouts with litter barrels both sides of highway.

J 5.5 (8.8 km) Twidwell Bend bridge over Pine River.

J 5.6 (9 km) Access road east to Long Prairie (8 miles/12.9 km).

J 6.6 (10.6 km) Highway parallels Sukunka River to west.

J 8.2 (13.2 km) Zonnebeke Creek.

J 8.5 (13.7 km) Natural Springs Resort; 9-hole golf course.

J 10.6 (17 km) Bridge over Dickebush Creek.

J 11 (17.7 km) Sanctuary Ranch.

J 13.7 (22 km) **Junction** with Sukunka Forest Road, which leads west 11 miles/17.7 km to Sukunka Falls. *NOTE: Radio-controlled road, travelers must monitor channel 151.325 MHz.*

J 13.8 (22.2 km) Highway climbs next 3 miles/4.8 km southbound.

J 16.7 (26.9 km) Turnouts both sides of highway.

J 21.6 (34.8 km) Turnout to east.

J 26.9 (43.3 km) Turnouts both sides with litter bin to east.

J 28.8 (46.3 km) Paved road leads east 1.2 miles/1.9 km to **Gwillim Lake Provincial Park**, open May 20–to Sept. 15; 49 campsites, picnic tables, hand pump water and firepits. Day-use area with playground and boat launch. Fishing for lake trout, whitefish, burbot, grayling and pike. Camping fee $16 per night, charged.

J 40.1 (64.5 km) Moose Lake, camping fishing off of Forest Road.

J 41.5 (66.7 km) Access road leads west 9 miles/14.5 km to the Bullmoose Mountain and old Bullmoose mine site (closed).

J 41.8 (67.3 km) Turnout to east. Bullmoose Marshes Wetland Interpretive Area.

J 42.1 (67.8 km) Bridge over Bullmoose Flats River.

J 46.7 (75.1 km) Turnout to east. Phillips Way Summit, elev. 3,695 feet/1,126m.

J 51.9 (83.5 km) Bullmoose Creek bridge.

J 53.3 (85.8 km) Wolverine River bridge. Park on the north side of the bridge between railway and highway to access trail to Wolverine Dinosaur Trackway.

J 54.9 (88.3 km) Murray River bridge.

J 55.6 (89.5 km) Flatbed Creek bridge.

J 55.7 (889.6 km) Lion's Club Flatbed Creek Campground; 40 sites, water, flush toilets, coin showers, dump station, picnic tables and playground. Flatbed Falls trail. Camping fee $15.

J 56.7 (91.2 km) Turnoff for community of Tumbler Ridge (description follows).

Tumbler Ridge

Located 73 miles/117 km southwest of Dawson Creek via Highways 97 and 52; 55 miles/89 km southeast of Chetwynd via Highway 29; and 91 miles/147 km southwest of BC Highway 2 via the Heritage Highway. **Population**: 3,500. **Elevation**: 2,700 feet/830m. **Emergency Services**: Phone 911 Police, Fire and Ambulance. **Medical Centre**, phone (250) 242-4251.

Visitor Information: For the Visitor Centre at 270 Southgate, phone 250-242-3123 or toll-free 1-877-SAW-DINO. For the Community Centre, phone 250-242-4246. For the Town Office, phone 250-242-4242 or write District of Tumbler Ridge, Visitor Centre, P.O. Box 100, Tumbler Ridge, BC V0C 2W0; www.VisitTumblerRidge.ca.

Tumbler Ridge was incorporated April 9, 1981, making it British Columbia's newest community. The town was built in conjunction with development of the Northeast Coal resource. It was created in typical mining town style and layered in 3 tiers (or benches). The primary services area is on the second or middle tier.

The Quintette Mine south of town was the world's largest computerized open coal pit mine until it was shut down in the fall of 2000. Quintette is on track to re-open in the future if and when the steelmaking coal market recovers.

The discovery of dinosaur tracks and later bones in the Tumbler Ridge area led to British Columbia's first dinosaur dig in 2003. Exploration of Tumbler Ridge's canyons and rock exposures has turned up many remarkable discoveries, including dinosaur footprints with skin impressions. The Tumbler Ridge Museum Foundation has established a Dinosaur Discovery Gallery where the expanding collection of dinosaur bones and other fossils is displayed.

Visitors should check with the Visitor Centre about current events and tours associated with the dig. The Gallery is on the upper tier of the town in a former elementary school building. Open May–August, daily 8 A.M.-5 P.M.; during the rest of the year it is closed Tuesdays and Wednesdays.

Visitor facilities include 3 hotels, a bed-and-breakfast, 7 restaurants, a convenience store, retail and grocery outlets, a drugstore, hardware store, service stations, major automotive repairs, propane, and 2 car washes.

Dinosaur footprints fascinate a group of visitors outside the Dinosaur Discovery Gallery.
(©Earl L. Brown)

Recreational facilities include a Community Centre with ice arena, climbing wall, curling rink, weight room, indoor pool, racquet and squash courts, and a library (Internet access available). Outdoor facilities include tennis courts, skateboard park, ball diamonds and a 9-hole golf course.

Camping at the Lions Flatbed Creek Campground at the edge of town; 40 sites, $15/night camping fee (no hook-ups). Monkman RV Park in town has 56 full-service sites for $27 per night. There are 10 user maintained (free) Recreation Site campsites in the area.

There is a 42-site provincial park campground. Not all sites may be open due to beetle killed trees posing a danger to campers. Campground is not charging a fee at this time. It is located 37 miles/60 km south from town via a gravel road and is near the area's major attraction, spectacular 213-foot/65-m **Kinuseo Falls**, located in the northern section of Monkman Provincial Park. Kinuseo Falls is formed by the Murray River, which plunges 60m/197 feet over a geological fault to the river bed below. This thunderous cascade of water provides many visitors with the highlight of their trip, and the Murray River Basin is equally as scenic.

The campground is 1.8 miles from the viewing platform of the falls and the trail from parking lot to viewing platform extends from the lot beyond the pit toilets. If you want to climb down to the base of the falls, that trail also leads from the parking lot, NOT off of and to the right of the viewing platform trail. Both park service trails are marked and depart from the parking lot.

Hiking is a popular activity in Tumbler Ridge, which has nearly 50 named and maintained trails, many offering easy day hikes to scenic waterfalls. The 39-mile/63-km Monkman Pass Memorial Trail offers a 6-day trek from Kinuseo Falls to near Prince George.

Stop by or phone the Tumbler Ridge Visitor Centre at 250-242-3123 for more information on area services and attractions.

District of Tumbler Ridge. See display ad on facing page.

HIGHWAY 52 NORTH

Highway 52 North (log follows) takes you back to Highway 97, about 12 miles/19 km from Dawson Creek. Highway 52 South (logged on page 76) loops you over to Highway 2 near the BC–Alberta border.

Distance from Tumbler Ridge (T) is shown.

T 0 Town of Tumbler Ridge.

T 2.9 (4.7 km) Small turnout to west with litter barrels. Trailhead for Quality Canyon and Quality Mouth hiking trails.

T 3.7 (6 km) Turnout to west at **Quality Falls** trailhead. This is an easy 1.5-mile/2.5-km hike through spruce forest to a picnic area and viewpoint overlooking the falls.

T 9.9 (16 km) Large turnout to west with view of Murray River Valley and Rocky Mountains.

T 10.3 (16.5 km) **Heritage Highway Summit**, elev. 4,150 foot/1,265m.

T 14.9 (24 km) **Murray Canyon Overlook** trailhead. This is an easy 3.7-mile/6-km hike over relatively flat terrain to the overlook. Interpretive trail guides available at trailhead and at the visitor's centre in Tumbler Ridge.

T 21.7 (35 km) Turnout to west at **Tepee Falls** trailhead. This is an easy 3.7-mile/6-km hike to a beautiful waterfall; great views of Murray River Valley.

T 29.3 (47.2 km) *Pavement breaks and dips in road; reduce speed. Slide area.*

T 33.3 (53.7 km) Large turnout to west with litter barrels.

T 35.6 (57.5 km) Salt Creek Valley.

T 41.1 (66.1 km) Large turnout to west with litter barrels.

T 43.1 (69.5 km) Brassey Creek. **T 43.3** (69.7 km) Large turnout to east with litter barrels.

T 46.1 (74.2 km) Turnout to west.

T 46.9 (75.5 km) *CAUTION: Watch for livestock.*

T 52.3 (84.3 km) *CAUTION: Watch for trucks turning at logging road.*

T 56.5 (90.9 km) Turnout to east.

T 59.6 (96 km) **Junction** with Highway 97 at **Milepost PG 237.5**.

Return to Milepost PG 237.5 or 189.6 West Access Route

Alaska Highway

CONNECTS: Dawson Creek, BC, to Delta Junction, AK
(includes Richardson Highway to Fairbanks)

Length: 1,390 miles   **Road Surface:** Paved   **Season:** Open all year

(See maps, pages 125-129)

97 1 2

The Alaska Highway winds along the shore of Yukon's Kluane Lake. (©Kris Valencia, staff)

Distances in miles	Dawson Cr.	Delta Jct.	Fairbanks	Ft. Nelson	Haines Jct.	Tok	Watson Lk.	Whitehorse
Dawson Cr.		1390	1488	283	985	1282	613	895
Delta Jct.	1390		98	1107	405	108	777	495
Fairbanks	1488	98		1205	503	206	875	603
Ft. Nelson	283	1107	1205		702	999	330	612
Haines Jct.	985	405	503	702		297	372	100
Tok	1282	108	206	999	297		669	387
Watson Lk.	613	777	875	330	372	669		282
Whitehorse	895	495	603	612	100	387	282	

crosses can't fail to impress you. It is truly a marvelous journey across a great expanse of North America. And if you take time to stop and meet the people and see the sights along the way, it can be the trip of a lifetime.

Following are some facts about the Alaska Highway and answers to common questions about driving the highway. For a look at the history of the Alaska Highway, see "The History of the Alaska Highway" on page 220.

Alaska Highway facts

The Alaska Highway begins at Mile 0 in Dawson Creek, BC. The first 613 miles/987 km of the Alaska Highway are in British Columbia, where it is designated BC Highway 97 North, and travel in a northwesterly direction to the Yukon Territory border near Watson Lake, YT (**Historical Mile 635**). From there the Alaska Highway continues as Yukon Highway 1, crossing 577 miles/929 km of Yukon Territory to Port Alcan on the Alaska border. The Alaska Highway crosses into Alaska at **Historical Mile 1221.8**, where it becomes Alaska Route 2. From this international border, it is 200 miles to Delta Junction, AK (**Historical Mile 1422**), the official end of the Alaska Highway, and *(Continues on page 130)*

or many people, the Alaska Highway is a great adventure. For others, it is a long drive. But whether you fall into the first group or the second, the vastness of wilderness this pioneer road

Major Attractions:

©Kris Valencia, staff

*Muncho Lake,
Liard Hotsprings,
Watson Lake
Signpost Forest,
SS Klondike, Kluane Lake*

Highest Summit:
*Summit Lake
4,250 ft.*

Alaska Highway Dawson Creek, BC, to Milepost DC 409

© 2014 The MILEPOST®

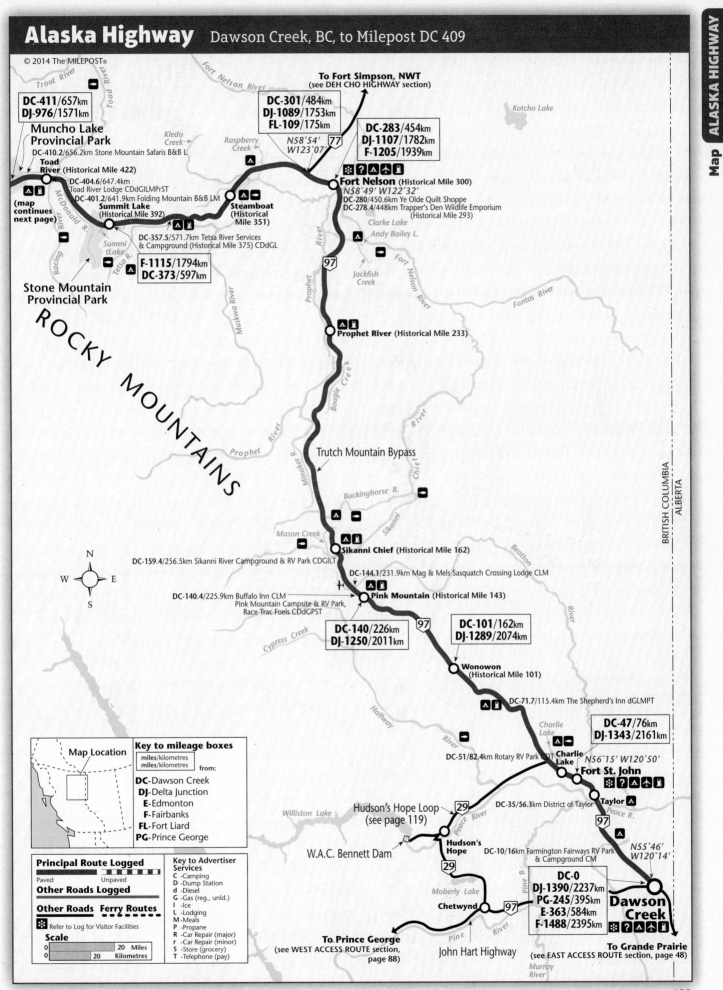

DC-411/657km
DJ-976/1571km
Muncho Lake Provincial Park
DC-410.2/656.2km Stone Mountain Safaris B&B L

Toad River (Historical Mile 422)
DC-404.6/647.4km Toad River Lodge CDdGILMPrST
DC-401.2/641.9km Folding Mountain B&B LM

(map continues next page)

Summit Lake (Historical Mile 392)
DC-357.5/571.7km Tetsa River Services & Campground (Historical Mile 375) CDdGL

F-1115/1794km
DC-373/597km

Stone Mountain Provincial Park

ROCKY MOUNTAINS

DC-301/484km
DJ-1089/1753km
FL-109/175km

77

N58°54' W123°07'

Steamboat (Historical Mile 351)

DC-283/454km
DJ-1107/1782km
F-1205/1939km

Fort Nelson (Historical Mile 300)
N58°49' W122°32'
DC-280/450.6km Ye Olde Quilt Shoppe
DC-278.4/448km Trapper's Den Wildlife Emporium (Historical Mile 293)

To Fort Simpson, NWT (see DEH CHO HIGHWAY section)

97

Prophet River (Historical Mile 233)

Trutch Mountain Bypass

Sikanni Chief (Historical Mile 162)
DC-159.4/256.5km Sikanni River Campground & RV Park CDGILT
DC-144.1/231.9km Mag & Mels Sasquatch Crossing Lodge CLM

DC-140.4/225.9km Buffalo Inn CLM
Pink Mountain Campsite & RV Park, Race Trac Fuels CDdGPST
Pink Mountain (Historical Mile 143)

DC-140/226km
DJ-1250/2011km

97

DC-101/162km
DJ-1289/2074km

Wonowon (Historical Mile 101)

DC-71.7/115.4km The Shepherd's Inn dGLMPT

DC-51/82.4km Rotary RV Park CDT
Charlie Lake

DC-47/76km
DJ-1343/2161km
N56°15' W120°50'
Fort St. John

Hudson's Hope Loop (see page 119)

29

DC-35/56.3km District of Taylor
Taylor

97

W.A.C. Bennett Dam

Hudson's Hope

29

DC-10/16km Farmington Fairways RV Park & Campground CM

N55°46' W120°14'

Chetwynd

97

DC-0
DJ-1390/2237km
PG-245/395km
E-363/584km
F-1488/2395km

Dawson Creek

To Prince George (see WEST ACCESS ROUTE section, page 88)

John Hart Highway

To Grande Prairie (see EAST ACCESS ROUTE section, page 48)

BRITISH COLUMBIA
ALBERTA

Map Location

Key to mileage boxes
miles/kilometres
miles/kilometres   from:

DC-Dawson Creek
DJ-Delta Junction
E-Edmonton
F-Fairbanks
FL-Fort Liard
PG-Prince George

Principal Route Logged
Paved   Unpaved
Other Roads Logged
Other Roads   Ferry Routes
Refer to Log for Visitor Facilities

Scale
0   20 Miles
0   20 Kilometres

Key to Advertiser Services
C - Camping
D - Dump Station
d - Diesel
G - Gas (reg., unld.)
I - Ice
L - Lodging
M - Meals
P - Propane
R - Car Repair (major)
r - Car Repair (minor)
S - Store (grocery)
T - Telephone (pay)

Alaska Highway · Milepost DC 409 to Teslin, YT

© 2014 The MILEPOST®

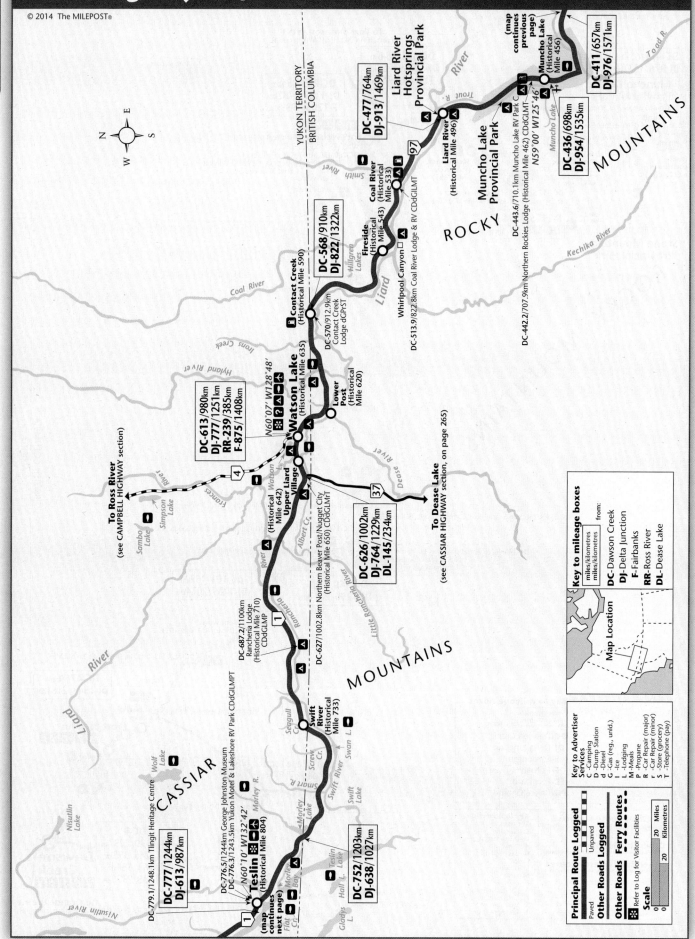

N

W · E

S

(map continues previous page)

Muncho Lake (Historical Mile 456)

DC-411/657km
DJ-976/1571km

ROCKY

MOUNTAINS

Toad R.

River

Trout R.

Liard River Hotsprings Provincial Park

DC-477/764km
DJ-913/1469km

Liard River (Historical Mile 496)

Muncho Lake Provincial Park

DC-436/698km
DJ-954/1535km

N59°00' W125°46'

Muncho Lake

DC-443.6/710.1km Muncho Lake RV Park C
DC-442.2/707.9km Northern Rockies Lodge (Historical Mile 462) CDdGLMT
DC-513.9/822.8km Coal River Lodge & RV CDdGILMT

Kechika River

97

Smith River

Coal River (Historical Mile 533)

Fireside (Historical Mile 543)

Whirlpool Canyon

Liard

YUKON TERRITORY
BRITISH COLUMBIA

DC-568/910km
DJ-822/1322km

Contact Creek (Historical Mile 590)

DC-570/912.9km
Contact Creek Lodge dGPrST

Hilgren Lakes

Coal River

Irons Creek

Hyland River

DC-613/980km
DJ-777/1251km
RR-239/385km
F-875/1408km

N60°07' W128°48'

Watson Lake (Historical Mile 635)

Lower Post (Historical Mile 620)

Dease River

To Ross River
(see CAMPBELL HIGHWAY section)

4

Upper Liard Village

(Historical Watson Mile 642)

To Dease Lake
(see CASSIAR HIGHWAY section, on page 265)

37

DC-626/1002km
DJ-764/1229km
DL-145/234km

DC-627/1002.8km Northern Beaver Post/Nugget City
(Historical Mile 650) CDdGLMrT

Simpson Lake

Sambo Lake

Frances River

Albert Cr.

Little Rancheria River

DC-687.2/1100km
Rancheria Lodge
(Historical Mile 710)
CDdGLMP

1

Rancheria River

MOUNTAINS

Liard River

CASSIAR

Seagull Cr.

Swift River (Historical Mile 733)

Morley R.

Wolf Lake

Smart R.

Screw Cr.

Swift River

Swift Lake

Swan L.

DC-777/1244km George Johnston Museum
DC-776.5/1244km
DC-776.3/1243.5km Yukon Motel & Lakeshore RV Park CDdGILMPT

DC-779.1/1248.1km Tlingit Heritage Centre

Teslin (Historical Mile 804)

N60°10' W132°42'

Nisutlin Lake

DC-777/1244km
DJ-613/987km

Morley Bay

Morley Lake

Teslin Lake

Nisutlin River

Flat Creek

Gladys Hall L.

DC-752/1203km
DJ-638/1027km

1

(map continues next page)

To Ross River (see CAMPBELL HIGHWAY section)
To Dease Lake (see CASSIAR HIGHWAY section, on page 265)
(map continues previous page)
(map continues next page)

Key to mileage boxes

miles/kilometres	from:
miles/kilometres	

DC-Dawson Creek
DJ-Delta Junction
F-Fairbanks
RR-Ross River
DL-Dease Lake

Map Location

Key to Advertiser Services
C -Camping
D -Dump Station
d -Diesel
G -Gas (reg., unld.)
I -Ice
L -Lodging
M -Meals
P -Propane
R -Car Repair (major)
r -Car Repair (minor)
S -Store (grocery)
T -Telephone (pay)

Principal Route Logged
Paved
Unpaved

Other Roads Logged
Other Roads   Ferry Routes

Refer to Log for Visitor Facilities

Scale
0   20   Miles
0   20   Kilometres

Alaska Highway   Teslin, YT, to Milepost DC 1136

© 2014 The MILEPOST®

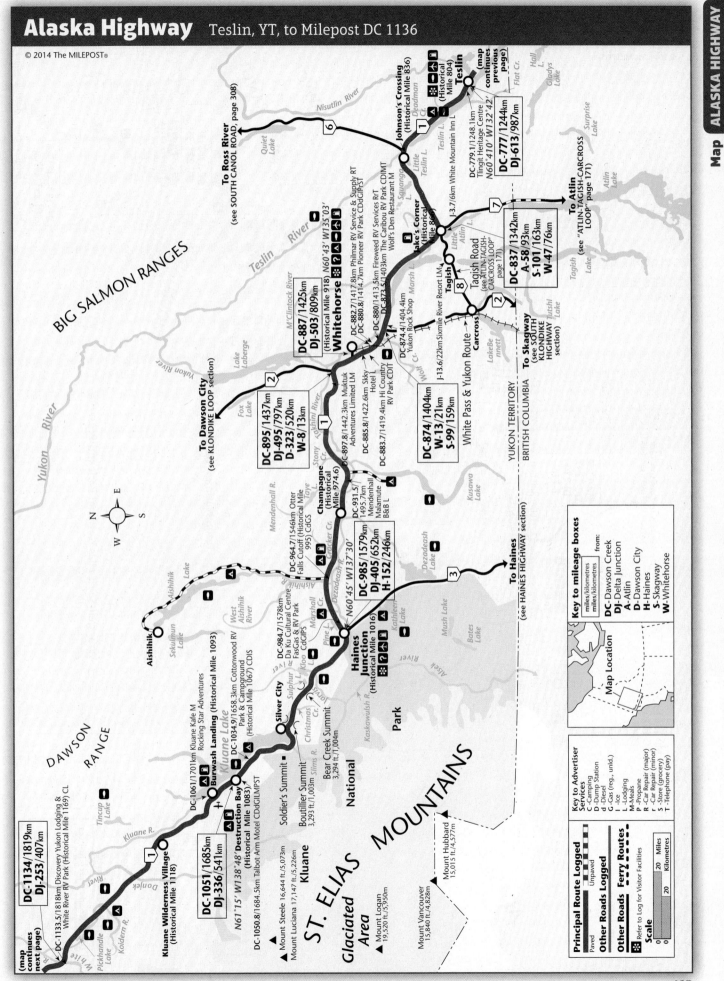

To Ross River
(see SOUTH CANOL ROAD section)

Johnson's Crossing (Historical Mile 836)

(map continues previous page)

Teslin (Historical Mile 804)

DC-779.1/1248.1km
Tlingit Heritage Centre
N60°410' W132°42'

DC-777/1244km
DJ-613/987km

To Atlin
(see "ATLIN-TAGISH-CARCROSS LOOP" page 171)

DC-837/1342km
A-58/93km
S-101/163km
W-47/76km

DC-882.7/1417.8km Philmar RV Service & Supply RT
DC-880.8/1414.7km Pioneer RV Park CDdGIPST
DC-873.5/1403km The Caribou RV Park CDlMT
Wolf's Den Restaurant M

Jake's Corner (Historical Mile 866)

Tagish Road
(see "ATLIN-TAGISH-CARCROSS LOOP" page 171)

Sixmile River Resort LM

Tagish

Carcross

Yukon Rock Shop

J-13.6/22km Sixmile River Resort LM

White Pass & Yukon Route

To Skagway
(see SOUTH KLONDIKE HIGHWAY section)

YUKON TERRITORY
BRITISH COLUMBIA

BIG SALMON RANGES

Teslin River

M'Clintock River

(Historical Mile 918)
Whitehorse

DC-887/1425km
DJ-503/809km

To Dawson City
(see KLONDIKE LOOP section)

DC-895/1437km
DJ-495/797km
D-323/520km
W-8/13km

DC-897.8/1442.3km Muktuk Adventures Limited LM
DC-885.8/1422.6km Skky Hotel L
DC-883.7/1419.4km Hi Country RV Park CDIT

DC-874/1404km
W-13/21km
S-99/159km

Champagne (Historical Mile 974.6)

DC-964.7/1546km Otter Falls Cutoff (Historical Mile 995) CDgGS

DC-931.5/1495.7km Mendenhall Malamute B&B L

DC-985/1579km
DJ-405/652km
H-152/246km

N60°45' W137°30'

To Haines
(see HAINES HIGHWAY section)

Kluane National Park

DAWSON RANGE

Aishihik

DC-1061/1701km Kluane Kafe M
Rocking Star Adventures

Burwash Landing (Historical Mile 1093)

DC-1049/1658.3km Cottonwood RV Park & Campground (Historical Mile 1067) CDIS

DC-984.7/1578km
Kluane Park & Da Ku Cultural Centre
FasGas & RV Park
Kloo CdGIPS

Silver City

Haines Junction (Historical Mile 1016)

DC-1051/1685km
DJ-336/541km

DC-1050.8/1684.5km Talbot Arm Motel CDdGILMPST

N61°15' W138°48' Destruction Bay (Historical Mile 1083)

Soldier's Summit

Boutillier Summit
3,293 ft./1,003m

Bear Creek Summit
3,294 ft./1,004m

▲ Mount Steele 16,644 ft./5,073m
▲ Mount Luciana 17,147 ft./5,226m

ST. ELIAS MOUNTAINS
Glaciated Area

▲ Mount Logan 19,520 ft./5,950m

▲ Mount Vancouver 15,840 ft./4,828m

Mount Hubbard 15,015 ft./4,577m

DC-1134/1819km
DJ-253/407km

DC-1133.5/1818km Discovery Yukon Lodging &
White River RV Park (Historical Mile 1169) CL

Kluane Wilderness Village (Historical Mile 1118)

DC-1050.8/1684.5km Talbot Arm Motel CDdGILMPST

(map continues next page)

Alaska Highway Milepost 1136 to Milepost 1378

© 2014 The MILEPOST®

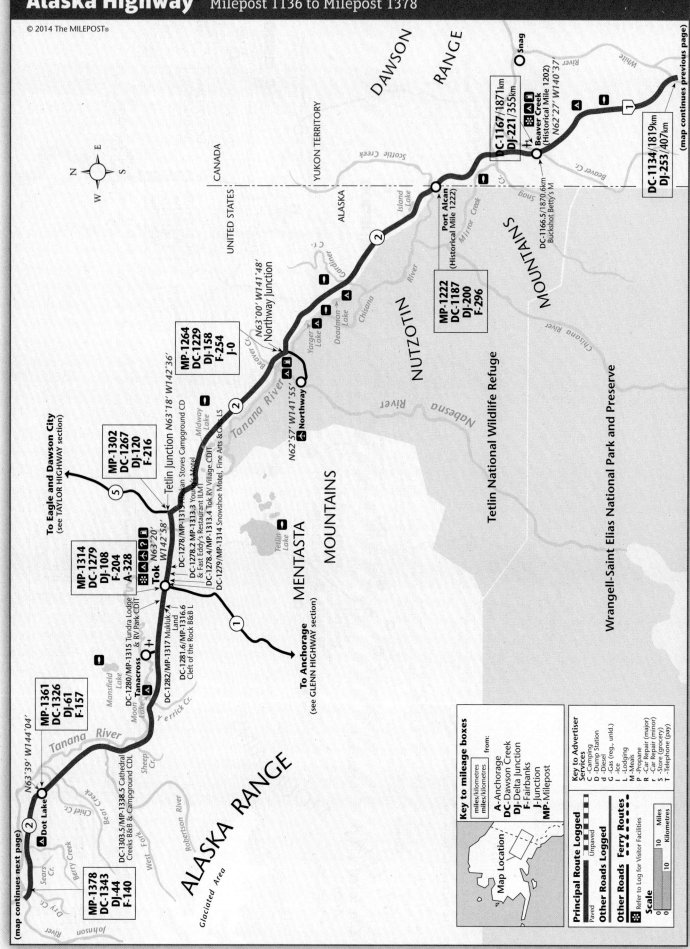

(map continues previous page)

DAWSON RANGE

○ Snag

DC-1167/1871km
DJ-221/355km
Beaver Creek
(Historical Mile 1202)
N62°27' W140°37'

DC-1134/1819km
DJ-253/407km

White River

1

YUKON TERRITORY

Scottie Creek

CANADA
UNITED STATES

ALASKA

DC-1166.5/1870.6km
Buckshot Betty's M

Snag
Mirror Creek

Island Lake

Port Alcan
(Historical Mile 1222)

MOUNTAINS

2

Beaver Cr.

Gardiner Cr.

MP-1222
DC-1187
DJ-200
F-296

Chisana River

NUTZOTIN MOUNTAINS

N63°00' W141°48'
Northway Junction

Deadman Lake

Yarger Lake

Chisana River

Wrangell-Saint Elias National Park and Preserve

N

E
W
S

MP-1264
DC-1229
DJ-158
F-254
J-0

Beaver Cr.

Tetlin National Wildlife Refuge

2

Midway Lake

Tanana River

N63°18' W142°36'
Tetlin Junction

Nabesna River

MP-1302
DC-1267
DJ-120
F-216

To Eagle and Dawson City
(see TAYLOR HIGHWAY section)

5

Dan Stoves Campground CD
DC-1278/MP-1313 Young's Motel
DC-1278.2 MP-1313.3 Young's Motel
& Fast Eddy's Restaurant ILMl
DC-1278.4/MP-1313.4 Tok RV Village CDIT
DC-1279/MP-1314 Snowshoe Motel, Fine Arts & Crafts LS

N63°20'
W142°58'

Tok

N62°57' W141°55'
☓ Northway

N63°00' W141°48'

Tetlin Lake

MENTASTA MOUNTAINS

MP-1314
DC-1279
DJ-108
F-204
A-328

DC-1280/MP-1315 Tundra Lodge
& RV Park CDIT

Tanacross ○╪

DC-1282/MP-1317 Mukluk
Land
DC-1281.6/MP-1316.6
Cleft of the Rock B&B L

1

To Anchorage
(see GLENN HIGHWAY section)

Mansfield Lake

Moon Lake

Yerrick Cr.

MP-1361
DC-1326
DJ-61
F-157

ALASKA RANGE

Tanana River

Sheep Cr.

West Fork

Robertson River

DC-1303.5/MP-1338.5 Cathedral
Creeks B&B & Campground CDL

N63°39' W144°04'

Dot Lake

2

Chief Cr.

Bear Creek

Berry Creek

Sears Cr.

Dry Cr.

Johnson River

(map continues next page)

Glaciated Area

MP-1378
DC-1343
DJ-44
F-140

Key to mileage boxes

miles/kilometres
miles/kilometres from:

A-Anchorage
DC-Dawson Creek
DJ-Delta Junction
F-Fairbanks
J-Junction
MP-Milepost

Key to Advertiser Services

C -Camping
D -Dump Station
G -Gas (reg., unld.)
I -Ice
L -Lodging
M -Meals
P -Propane
R -Car Repair (major)
r -Car Repair (minor)
S -Store (grocery)
T -Telephone (pay)

Map Location

Principal Route Logged
Paved
Unpaved
Other Roads Logged
Other Roads   Ferry Routes
▣ Refer to Log for Visitor Facilities

Scale
Miles
0   10
Kilometres
0   10

Alaska Highway   Milepost 1378 to Fairbanks, AK

© 2014 The MILEPOST®

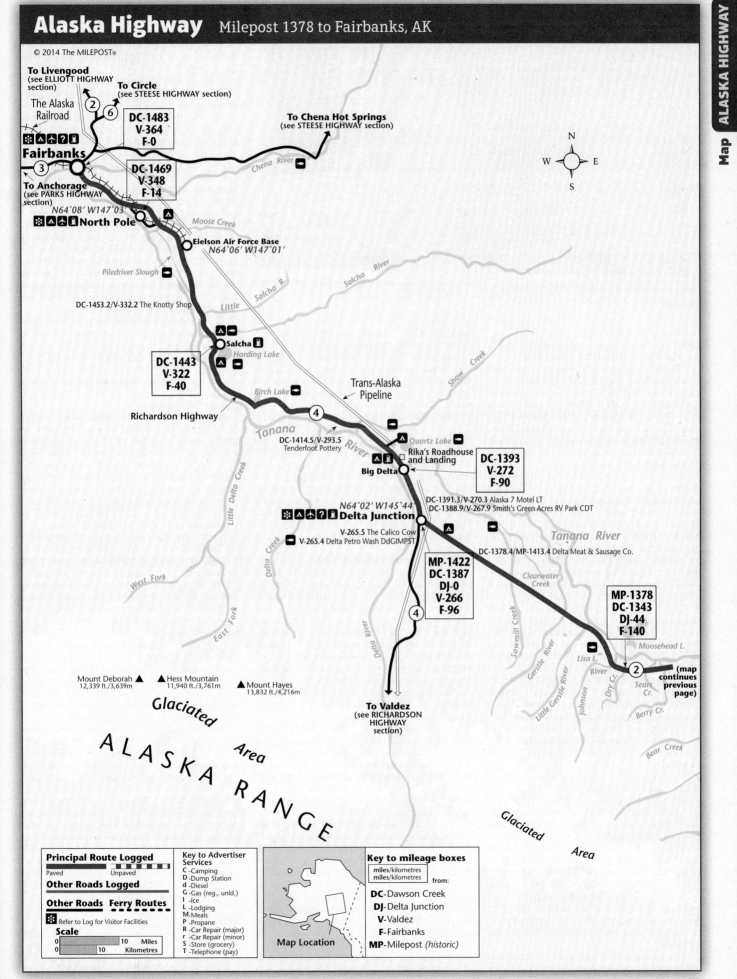

To Livengood
(see ELLIOTT HIGHWAY section)

To Circle
(see STEESE HIGHWAY section)

The Alaska Railroad

2

6

DC-1483
V-364
F-0

To Chena Hot Springs
(see STEESE HIGHWAY section)

Fairbanks

Chena River

DC-1469
V-348
F-14

3

To Anchorage
(see PARKS HIGHWAY section)

N64°08' W147°03'

North Pole

Moose Creek

Eielson Air Force Base
N64°06' W147°01'

Piledriver Slough

Salcha R.

Salcha River

DC-1453.2/V-332.2 The Knotty Shop

Little

Salcha

DC-1443
V-322
F-40

Harding Lake

Shaw Creek

Birch Lake

Trans-Alaska
Pipeline

Richardson Highway

4

Tanana

River

DC-1414.5/V-293.5
Tenderfoot Pottery

Quartz Lake

Rika's Roadhouse
and Landing

Big Delta

DC-1393
V-272
F-90

DC-1391.3/V-270.3 Alaska 7 Motel LT
DC-1388.9/V-267.9 Smith's Green Acres RV Park CDT

N64°02' W145°44'   Delta Junction

V-265.5 The Calico Cow
V-265.4 Delta Petro Wash DdGIMPST

Little Delta Creek

Delta Creek

Tanana River

Clearwater
Creek

DC-1378.4/MP-1413.4 Delta Meat & Sausage Co.

MP-1422
DC-1387
DJ-0
V-266
F-96

West Fork

4

East Fork

To Valdez
(see RICHARDSON HIGHWAY section)

Sawmill Creek

Gerstle River

Little Gerstle River

Johnson River

Dry Cr.

Lisa L.

MP-1378
DC-1343
DJ-44
F-140

Moosehead L.

2

Sears Cr.

Berry Cr.

(map continues previous page)

Bear Creek

Mount Deborah ▲
12,339 ft./3,639m

▲ Hess Mountain
11,940 ft./3,761m

▲ Mount Hayes
13,832 ft./4,216m

Glaciated   Area

ALASKA RANGE

Glaciated   Area

Principal Route Logged

Paved   Unpaved

Other Roads Logged

Other Roads   Ferry Routes

Refer to Log for Visitor Facilities

Scale

0 ———— 10 Miles
0 ———— 10 Kilometres

Key to Advertiser Services
C -Camping
D -Dump Station
d -Diesel
G -Gas (reg., unld.)
I -Ice
L -Lodging
M -Meals
P -Propane
R -Car Repair (major)
r -Car Repair (minor)
S -Store (grocery)
T -Telephone (pay)

Key to mileage boxes
miles/kilometres
miles/kilometres   from:

DC-Dawson Creek
DJ-Delta Junction
V-Valdez
F-Fairbanks
MP-Milepost (historic)

Map Location

Expect construction along the Alaska Highway in summer. (©Sharon Nault)

(Continued from page 124)
296 miles to Fairbanks, the unofficial end of the highway at **Historical Mile 1523**.

The 96-mile stretch of highway between Delta Junction and Fairbanks is part of the Richardson Highway from Valdez, although it is designated Alaska Route 2 and treated as a natural extension of the Alaska Highway. The Richardson Highway (Alaska Route 4) was originally known as the Richardson Trail and predates construction of the Alaska Highway by some 50 years.

Some people still refer to the Alaska Highway as the "Alcan" Highway. ALCAN was the military's name for the pioneer road at its completion in 1942, an acronym for Alaska-Canada military highway. But it was not a popular name with many Alaskans, who were unhappy with restrictions placed on civilian traffic on the highway during the war years. The pioneer road was officially renamed the Alaska Highway in March 1943. It opened to the public in 1948.

Towns and businesses along the Alaska Highway still use their Historical Mile to identify their location, although these figures reflect historical driving distances—not actual driving distances—along the Alaska Highway.

The Alaska Highway is about 35 miles shorter today than it was in the 1940s, thanks to reconstruction and rerouting. And it continues to get shorter, as reconstruction on various sections of the road shaves off more miles. (Refer to "Mileposts and Kilometreposts" this section for more on the subject.)

Is the Alaska Highway paved?

All of the Alaska Highway is paved, although highway improvement projects often mean motorists have to drive a few miles of gravel road.

The most extensive reconstruction of the Alaska Highway in the last couple of years has been along Kluane Lake near Sheep Mountain, where the narrow winding road alongside the lake has been widened and straightened. Rest areas were added or enlarged; a multi-use path constructed next to the road and the Slims River bridge was replaced.

The most challenging reconstruction continues to be between Destruction Bay and the AK–YT border, where several sections of road that had previously been brought up to BST (Bituminous Surface Treatment) standard as part of the Shakwak Highway Project had developed severe frost heaves, making for a very slow and bumpy drive. Each summer road crews are out repairing damage along this length of road.

Despite the ongoing challenges of maintaining a major highway that crosses dramatically varied terrain, and that is subject to extreme temperature fluctuations, the Alaska Highway continued to improve over the years. During the 1980s, many rerouting and paving projects were completed, and by 1992—the 50th anniversary of the Alaska Highway—the last section of original gravel road was rerouted and paved.

What are road conditions like?

Road conditions on the Alaska Highway are not unlike road conditions on many secondary roads in the Lower 48 and Canada. It is the tremendous length of the highway, combined with its remoteness and the extremes of the Northern climate, that often result in surprises along this road. Historically speaking, however, the Alaska Highway has rarely been closed by any weather-related event, and even then usually not longer than a day. (For winter road conditions, see "Driving the highway in winter" this section.)

The MILEPOST® log of the Alaska Highway reflects driving conditions as they existed when our field editors logged the road, which was summer and fall of last year. Keep in mind that any stretch of road can change dramatically—for better or for worse—in a very short time due to weather or construction.

The asphalt surfacing of the Alaska Highway ranges from poor to excellent. Much of the highway is in fair condition, with older patched pavement and a minimum of gravel breaks and chuckholes. Recently upgraded sections of road offer excellent surfacing. Relatively few stretches of road fall into the "poor" category, i.e. chuckholes, gravel breaks, deteriorated shoulders, bumps and frost heaves.

It is difficult to predict road conditions on the Alaska Highway. A hard winter or heavy rains can quickly undermine what was good roadbed, while road crews can just as quickly improve a previously substandard stretch of road.

It is also difficult to offer a summary description of 1,500-plus miles of road, but we will try.

There's a lot of straight road the first 300 miles of highway, between Dawson Creek and Fort Nelson.

North of Fort Nelson, the Alaska Highway crosses the Rocky Mountains: Expect about 150 miles of narrow road with curves and hills and few passing lanes. This stretch of road also has some spectacular scenery, as the highway crosses Summit Pass (**Historic Milepost 392**), highest summit on the Alaska Highway at 4,250 feet elevation, where you can expect the odd snowstorm even in July.

After Summit, the highway winds through a rocky limestone gorge high above the MacDonald River valley. Beautiful scenery, but keep your eyes on the road: there are few guardrails on this section and caribou and stone sheep may be in the middle of the road. The highway straightens out again for the next 140 miles into Watson Lake, YT.

The stretch of road between Watson Lake and Whitehorse, roughly another 300 miles, is in good shape and follows easy curves through wide river valleys and along lakes.

From Whitehorse to Haines Junction, a distance of approximately 100 miles, it is straight road with fair surfacing over some rolling frost heaves.

The next 200 driving miles, from Haines Junction to the Alaska border, consists of long straight stretches of improved highway with wide lanes and generous shoulders; a recently improved stretch following the shore of Kluane Lake; and a long, typically bumpy (depending on the severity of developing frost heaves) stretch of road with easy curves through the Shakwak Valley between Destruction Bay and the Alaska border.

From the Alaska–Yukon Territory border to Delta Junction, the Alaska Highway is in fair to good condition, with some frost heaves and gravel breaks where road crews are repairing damaged road. The Richardson-Alaska Highway between Delta Junction and Fairbanks is also in fair condition. Both these stretches of road have straight stretches interrupted by easy curves.

Highway businesses and other travelers are often helpful sources of information for current road conditions. Always inquire locally about what road conditions may be like up ahead of you and—in the off-season—what facilities are available, since many businesses operate seasonally.

For daily recorded road conditions along the Alaska Highway in Alaska, phone (907) 456-7623 or go to http://511.alaska.gov/. For conditions along the Yukon portion of the Alaska Highway, phone 511 or from outside the Yukon call toll-free 1-877-456-7623, or go to www.511Yukon.ca. For conditions on the BC portion of the Alaska Highway, go to www.drivebc.ca then click on the Alaska Highway. You may view conditions on the Alaska Highway at Fort St. John by clicking on the highway cams. (Links to these agencies are also provided at www.themilepost.com; click on "Road Conditions" in the Features pull-down menu.)

Driving advice

Today's Alaska Highway is a 2-lane highway that winds and rolls across the Northern wilderness. The best advice is to take your time; drive with your headlights on at

all times (it is the law in Canada); keep to the right on hills and corners; use turnouts; watch for wildlife on the road; and—as you would on any highway anywhere else—drive defensively.

There are few steep grades on the Alaska Highway. Most of the 6 to 10 percent grades occur between Fort Nelson, BC, and Watson Lake, YT, where the Alaska Highway crosses the Rocky Mountains.

There are relatively few high summits on the Alaska Highway. The highest summit on the highway is at Summit Lake, elev. 4,250 feet/1,295m, located at **Historic Milepost 392** in the Rocky Mountains. Weather may affect driving conditions at Summit Lake, where it is not unusual to run into fog or sleet and snow conditions in summer.

Drivers may also run into short stretches of loose gravel in areas where chip-seal repairs are under way. *IMPORTANT: Slow down approaching stretches of loose gravel. Sudden braking or excessive speed on gravel can lead to loss of control of your vehicle and roll-overs.*

Always be alert for bumps, dips and pot-holes in the road and for abrupt changes in highway surfacing. Many—but not all—of these surface irregularities are signed, or flagged with small, orange pennants. *Slow down if you see "Rough Road" and "Loose Gravel" signs or roadside flags.*

There are stretches of narrow, winding road without shoulders, particularly in the stretch of highway through the Rocky Mountains. Watch out for soft shoulders when pulling over to the side of the road. It is better to use formal turnouts instead of road shoulders, if possible.

Always watch for construction crews along the Alaska Highway. Extensive road construction may require a detour, or travelers may be delayed briefly while waiting for a pilot car to guide them through the construction. Motorists may encounter rough driving at construction areas, and muddy roadways if there are heavy rains while the roadbed is torn up.

Avoid tickets by paying attention to speed limits, particularly through the small communities along the highway. Alaska State Troopers and the Royal Canadian Mounted Police (RCMP) have a "zero tolerance" policy regarding drinking and driving, aggressive driving and passengers not wearing seatbelts, which are mandatory.

How far apart are services?

Gas, diesel, food and lodging are found in towns and cities along the Alaska Highway, as well as at smaller unincorporated communities, roadhouses and lodges located between the larger population centers. With the closure of several long-time roadhouses in recent years, and the seasonal nature of others, motorists can be looking at 100 to 150 miles between services on a couple stretches of highway. Pay attention to your gas tank and fill up when near a pump.

Motorists should also keep in mind that not all highway businesses are open year-round, nor are most services available 24 hours a day.

There are dozens of government and private campgrounds along the Alaska Highway; these are described at their mile location in the highway log. Most campgrounds are open from mid-May or early June to September. See also "Camping" in the TRAVEL PLANNING section.

Remember that you will be driving in

Caribou trot down the Alaska Highway near Muncho Lake. Stone sheep, caribou, moose and bears cross the Alaska Highway. Watch for wildlife! (©Judy Nadon, staff)

2 different countries that use 2 different currencies. Many if not most Canadian businesses will take U.S. dollars, but they will give you change in Canadian dollars. ATMs are prevalent in many cities and you can get Canadian dollars with a U.S. bank card. U.S. businesses do not take Canadian dollars. Most businesses (but not all) will take major credit cards. Be aware that credit card companies tack on a fee for foreign currency transactions. See also "Money" in the TRAVEL PLANNING section.

NOTE: There are long stretches of highway without cell phone service. Service may also depend on your U.S. provider's coverage in Canada or your Canadian provider's coverage in the U.S.

Mileposts and Kilometreposts

Mileposts were first put up at communities and lodges along the Alaska Highway in the 1940s to help motorists know where they were in this vast wilderness. Today, those original mileposts remain a tradition with communities and businesses on the highway and are still used as mailing addresses and reference points, although the figures no longer accurately reflect driving distance.

When Canada switched to the metric system in the mid-1970s, the mileposts in British Columbia and Yukon Territory were replaced by kilometreposts. Historian and writer Kenneth Coates recalls that as an employee of the Department of Highways, Yukon Territorial Government, he was assigned to lead a 2-person crew to remove mileposts and put up new kilometreposts in 1975.

"The job was simple enough," Coates recalls. "A driver working a day or two ahead of us marked off every two kilometers along the highway. Since he started at the BC–Yukon border and not at Dawson Creek, the distances did not quite jive. Our pickup was stacked high with the new posts, creosoted and painted. All we had to do was dig a hole, drop in the post, prop it up and pack it down."

But "the job description did not match the work precisely," Coates continues. "As the first highway workers discovered, the

Alaska Highway traverses some challenging terrain in North America: rocks, mud, muskeg, and mosquito-infested swamps. We earned our pay over the couple of weeks we spent enroute, enjoying the scenery and remarkable countryside, but exhausting ourselves with back-breaking labour. The hardest part was the abuse. People stopped to curse at us for removing the mileposts."

Kilometreposts on the British Columbia portion of the Alaska Highway were recalibrated in 1990 to reflect current driving distances rather than historical mileposts. These kilometreposts appear about every 5 kilometres on the BC portion of the highway.

Kilometreposts along the Yukon Territory portion of the Alaska Highway have been recalibrated to the Alaska border to reflect actual driving distance. These kilometreposts are placed every 2 kilometres.

In addition to the kilometreposts in Canada, the governments of British Columbia and Yukon installed commemorative mileposts as part of the 50th anniversary celebration of the Alaska Highway in 1992. Many of these historical mile markers are accompanied by Northwest Highway System signs and interpretive panels.

Physical mileposts on the Alaska portion of the highway—between Port Alcan and Delta Junction—reflect historical mileposts. Thus, a discrepancy of 35 miles exists at the AK–YT border between actual driving distance and the physical milepost. (Physical mileposts on the Richardson Highway between Delta Junction and Fairbanks reflect distance from Valdez.)

Kilometreposts and mileposts may be missing on some sections of the Alaska Highway due to road construction, vandalism or because they have succumbed to the elements.

Reading the Alaska Highway log

The MILEPOST® log of the Alaska Highway takes into account physical mileposts and kilometreposts, historical mileposts and actual driving distance.

On the Canadian portion of the highway, *The MILEPOST*® log gives distance to the AK–YT border from Dawson Creek (DC)

An early snowfall along the Alaska Highway in mid-September. (©Kris Valencia, staff)

as actual driving distance in miles followed by kilometre distance based on the kilometreposts *(which is not necessarily a metric conversion of the first figure)*. Use our mileage figure from Dawson Creek to figure correct distance between points on the Alaska Highway within Canada. Use our kilometre figure from Dawson Creek to pinpoint location in reference to physical kilometreposts on the Alaska Highway in Canada.

Traditional milepost figures in Canada are indicated in the text as **Historic Mile**. If there is a commemorative milepost the text will read **Historical Mile.**

On the Alaska portion of the highway between Port Alcan and Delta Junction, *The MILEPOST* log gives driving distance from Dawson Creek followed by distance based on the physical mileposts. The mileposts on this section of the highway reflect traditional mileages—not actual driving distance—from Dawson Creek. Thus when you reach the AK–YT border at **Historical Mile 1221.8**, it is **Milepost DC 1189.8** (the actual driving distance from Dawson Creek) and **MP 1221.8** reflecting the physical milepost in Alaska.

On the Richardson Highway between Delta Junction and Fairbanks, driving distance from Dawson Creek is followed by distance based on the physical mileposts, which reflect distance from Valdez.

When driving the highway and reading the log, it helps to pay attention to all landmarks, not just the mileposts and kilometreposts. If the highway log indicates a campground is 2 miles north of a certain river crossing, then it will be 2 miles north of that river, regardless of the presence or absence of a milepost or kilometrepost.

Weather information

Since the weather frequently influences road conditions along the Alaska Highway, weather reports may be crucial to highway travelers. Current weather and regional forecasts are broadcast on local TV and radio stations; supplied to local visitor information centers, hotels, motels and lodges along the highway; posted on the Internet; and available by phone.

Weather information for the Canadian portion of the Alaska Highway is available from Environment Canada. Current weather conditions and 5-day forecasts for communities throughout British Columbia, Yukon and Alberta are posted at www.weatheroffice.ec.gc.ca. A link to weather forecasts is also available at www.511yukon.ca.

Web cams along the BC Highway 97 portion of the Alaska Highway can be viewed at http://images.drivebc.ca/bchighwaycam/pub/html/www/10.html.

Travelers may get 24-hour recorded weather reports and forecasts by phone from Environment Canada. For the north Peace River region (Dawson Creek, Fort St. John, Fort Nelson, Grande Prairie and Chetwynd), phone 250-785-7669. For Whitehorse, western Yukon and northwestern British Columbia, phone 867-668-6061.

Driving the highway in winter

The Alaska Highway is open year-round, and winter drivers can expect a fair number of big rigs, along with local traffic, to be on the road.

Long-time *MILEPOST* field editor Earl Brown, a year-round resident of Toad River, BC, and a lifelong Alaska Highway resident, says road conditions in winter can be "excellent," with the highway surface smoothed of potholes with graded snow. "Highway crews are generally quick to be out on the road plowing after snowfalls along the Alaska Highway," says Earl.

Here are a few more suggestions from Earl for motorists driving the Alaska Highway in winter.

"Be on the watch for wildlife, like moose, caribou, buffalo and sheep. And when the road signs say to slow down for dangerous curves, *Slow down!*

"Be sure to travel on the top half of your tank. Lots of places along the highway are only seasonal operations. There are about 120 to 150 miles between open-year-round service outlets.

"If you do hit –50° temperatures, you'll want to be sure you can handle keeping warm enough should you hit the ditch. I always carry an extra long set of booster cables, tow rope, snow shovel and lots of warm clothing. It's a good idea to check

with the gas station attendant when you are filling up for what the word is about road conditions ahead.

"Phone ahead to confirm accommodations. *The MILEPOST* log indicates those businesses that plan to be open year-round, but you don't want to be counting on staying overnight some place only to find they've decided to close for the season after all. And keep in mind there are not many businesses along the Alaska Highway that are open 24 hours a day.

"Make sure that your vehicle has a block heater installed so it can be plugged in for cold weather starts. It's a lot easier on your vehicle, and may mean the difference between starting your engine or not the morning after an overnight stop.

"Remember that there are long stretches of highway where there is no cell phone service."

And Earl's last piece of advice: "Plan to take a winter dip at Liard Hotsprings.... It will probably be a highlight of your trip!"

Dawson Creek

©Kris Valencia, staff

Milepost 0 of the Alaska Highway; 367 miles/591 km northwest of Edmonton, AB; 250 miles/402 km northeast of Prince George, BC; 283 miles/455 km south of Fort Nelson; and 46 miles/74 km south of Fort St. John. **Population**: 11,800, area 27,000. **Emergency Services**: Phone 911 for all emergency services.

Visitor Information: At NAR (Northern Alberta Railways) Park, on Alaska Avenue at 10th Street (one block west of the traffic circle), in the red railroad station. Open year-round, 8 A.M. to 5:30 P.M. daily in summer, 10 A.M. to 5 P.M. Tuesday through Saturday in winter. Phone 250-782-9595 or toll-free 1-866-645-3022, or email info@tourismdawsoncreek.com. Trained visitor information counselors can answer questions about weather and road conditions, local events and attractions. Plenty of large vehicle parking in front of the refurbished grain elevator that houses the Dawson Creek Art Gallery.

Elevation: 2,186 feet/666m. **Climate:** Average temperature in January is 0°F/-18°C; in July it is 60°F/15°C. The average annual snowfall is 72 inches with the average depth of snow in midwinter at 19.7 inches. Frost-free days total about 100, with the first frost of the year occurring about the first week of September. **Radio:** CJDC 890, Peace FM 104.1. **Television:** 49 cable channels. **Newspaper:** Dawson Creek Daily News.

NOTE: Dawson Creek is on Mountain Standard Time (same time as Alberta) in the winter. In summer, Dawson Creek does not observe Daylight Savings Time and is therefore on Pacific Standard Time (same time as Prince

George and Vancouver).

Private Aircraft: Dawson Creek airport, 2 SE; elev. 2,148 feet/655m; length 5,000 feet/1,524m and 2,300 feet/701m; asphalt; fuel 100, jet.

Dawson Creek (like Dawson City in the Yukon Territory) was named for George Mercer Dawson of the Geological Survey of Canada, whose geodetic surveys of this region in 1879 helped lead to its development as an agricultural settlement. The open, level townsite is surrounded by rolling farmland, part of the government-designated Peace River Block.

The Peace River Block consists of 3.5 million acres of arable land in northeastern British Columbia, which the province gave to the Dominion Government in 1883 in return for financial aid toward construction of the Canadian Pacific Railway. (While a route through the Peace River country was surveyed by CPR in 1878, the railroad was eventually routed west from Calgary through Kicking Horse Pass.) The Peace River Block was held in reserve by the Dominion Government until 1920, when some of the land was opened for homesteading. The federal government restored the Peace River Block to the province of British Columbia in 1930.

Visitors may notice the fields of bright yellow flowers (in season) in the agricultural area surrounding Dawson Creek. These fields are planted with canola, a hybrid of rapeseed that was developed as a low-cholesterol oil seed. Raw seed is processed in Alberta and Japan. The Peace River region also produces most of the province's cereal grain, along with forage, beef cattle and dairy cattle. Other agricultural industries include the production of honey, hogs, eggs and poultry. Some potato and vegetable farming is also done here.

On the British Columbia Railway line, Dawson Creek is also the hub of 4 major highways: the John Hart Highway (Highway 97 South) to Prince George; the Alaska Highway (Highway 97 North); Highway 2, which leads east to Grande Prairie, AB; and Highway 49, which leads east to Spirit River and Donnelly.

The Northern Alberta Railway reached Dawson Creek in 1931. As a railhead, Dawson Creek was an important funnel for supplies and equipment during construction of the Alaska Highway in 1942. Some 600 carloads arrived by rail within a period of five weeks in preparation for the construction program, according to a report by the Public Roads Administration in 1942. A "rutted provincial road" linked Dawson Creek with Fort St. John, affording the only approach to the southern base of operations. Field headquarters were established at Fort St. John and Whitehorse. Meanwhile, men and machines continued to arrive at Dawson Creek. By May of 1942, 4,720 carloads of equipment had arrived by rail at Dawson Creek for dispersal to troops and civilian engineers to the north.

With the completion of the Alaska Highway in 1942 (and opening to the public in 1948) and the John Hart Highway in 1952, Dawson Creek expanded both as a distribu-

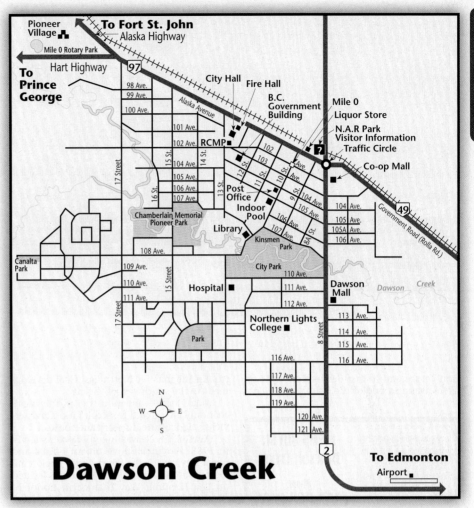

Dawson Creek

DAWSON CREEK ADVERTISERS

Chances Gaming Entertainment Centre	Ph. 250-782-7752
Dawson Creek Art Gallery	Ph. 250-782-2601
Foster's RV & Trailer Sales	Ph. 1-800-661-6623
George Dawson Inn, The	Ph. 250-782-9151
Inn on the Creek	Ph. 250-782-8259
Mile "0" Park & Campground	Ph. 250-782-2590
Northern Lights RV Park	Ph. 250-782-9433
Super 8 Motel	Ph. 250-782-8899
Tourism Dawson Creek	Ph. 1-866-645-3022
Tubby's Car Wash & RV Park	Ph. 250-782-2584
United Spring & Brake Ltd.	Ph. 1-800-283-5040

Favorite photo-op, the Mile Zero post dates back to the 1940s. (©Kris Valencia, staff)

arenas, a curling rink, 18-hole golf course, tennis courts and an outdoor gym and pool at Rotary Lake Park. Downhill skiing, and snowmobile and cross-country ski trails are available in winter.

There are numerous churches in Dawson Creek; check at the Visitor Centre for location and hours of worship.

Lodging & Services

There are more than a dozen hotels/motels, several bed and breakfasts, and dozens of restaurants; department stores, banks, grocery, drug and hardware stores, antique shops and other specialty shops. Shopping is downtown and in the 2 shopping centres, Co-op Mall and Dawson Mall. Visitors will also find laundromats, car and RV washes, gas stations and automotive repair shops. The liquor store is adjacent the Visitor Centre on Alaska Avenue. Contact the Visitor Centre for a complete listing of all services in the Dawson Creek area.

Enjoy free wireless Internet access for your laptop or PDA in Dawson Creek. Wireless hotspots include the Visitor Centre and Alaska Highway House.

Camping

Camping in Dawson Creek at **Mile "0" RV Park** at the junction of the Hart Highway and the Alaska Highway, and at **Tubby's RV Park** on the Hart Highway. **Northern Lights RV Park** is also located on the Hart Highway, 1.4 miles/2.3 km west of the Alaska Highway junction. There are private and provincial campgrounds north of Dawson Creek on the Alaska Highway.

Transportation

Air: Scheduled service from Dawson Creek airport to Vancouver via Central Mountain Air. The airport is located 2 miles/3.2 km south of the Alaska Avenue traffic circle via 8th Street/Highway 2; there is a small terminal at the airport.

Railroad: C.N. Rail provides freight service only.

Bus: Greyhound service to Prince George and Vancouver, BC; Edmonton, AB; and Whitehorse, YT. Dawson Creek also has a city bus transit system.

Taxi: Available.

Car Rental: Available.

tion centre and tourist destination. Dawson Creek was also one of the major supply centres for the massive North East Coal development to the southwest of the city.

Today, significant industries in this area's economy are oil and gas exploration and servicing, agriculture, forestry and tourism.

Dawson Creek was incorporated as a city in 1958. Provincial government offices and social services for the South Peace Region are located in Dawson Creek. City Hall is located on Ben Heppner Way (named in honor of the famous opera tenor, who comes from this area).

The city has a modern hospital, a public library, art gallery, a museum and a college (Northern Lights, associated with the University of Northern BC in Prince George).

Recreational facilities in Dawson Creek include 3 fitness centres, racquetball courts, a bowling alley, indoor swimming pool, 2 ice

Construction of the Alaska Highway began on March 9, 1942, and ended on Oct. 25th the same year.

Attractions

Milepost 0 Alaska Highway monument. Located in downtown Dawson Creek, at 10th Street and 102nd Avenue, across from the Alaska Highway House and one block from NAR Park. This colorful monument has been a favorite photo subject for Alaska Highway travelers since the original was first erected in the 1940s.

Historical Milepost 0 of the Alaska Highway is marked by a cairn and arch located at the east end of the large parking lot in NAR Park (see description following). Interpretive plaques surround the cairn. Excellent photo-op for Alaska Highway travelers.

Northern Alberta Railways (NAR) Park, on Alaska Avenue at 10th Street (near the traffic circle), is the site of the **Visitor Centre,** a popular meeting place for travelers from all over the world; phone 250-782-9595. Housed in a restored railway station, the Visitor Centre has a gift shop, public restrooms, free email check kiosk and the answers to all your travel questions. Pick up a free copy of the Self-Guided Historic Walking Tour brochure. Using this as your guide, stroll the downtown core and view historic photos while reading about Dawson Creek's colorful past.

Also at the railway station is the **Dawson Creek Station Museum,** operated by the South Peace Historical Society. The museum contains pioneer artifacts and wildlife displays, including a collection of more than 50 birds' eggs from this area. Museum admission by donation.

Dawson Creek Art Gallery is housed in a huge wooden grain elevator, the last of Dawson Creek's heritage elevators, moved to its present location through the efforts of community organizations. Art exhibitions featuring local and regional artists are on display and there is an impressive display of historical Alaska Highway construction photos, as well as a large gift shop featuring the work of local artisans. Open year-round, admission is by donation; www.dcartgallery.ca.

There is an outdoor **Farmer's Market** at 1444 102 Avenue on Saturdays, throughout May to October, 8:30 A.M.–12:30 P.M., in summer. Flowers, produce, baked goods and crafts are for sale.

Walter Wright Pioneer Village and Mile 0 Rotary Park. The pioneer village

contains an impressive collection of local pioneer buildings as well as recently built replicas like the fire hall and telegraph office. The entrance to the village is highlighted by Gardens North, consisting of 11 separate themed gardens, including a memorial rose garden. Bring a camera to capture the amazing variety of perennials and annuals that grow in the North. Admission to the village is by donation.

Pick up a free walking tour brochure that will take you back in time through original photos and narrative text. This seasonal attraction is open from May to September. For details, check with the Visitor Centre, phone 250-782-9595.

The Alaska Highway House. Exhibits here showcase the Alaska Highway, from its inception after the bombing of Pearl Harbour and the Japanese invasion of Attu and Kiska islands in Alaska's Aleutians, through its construction in 1942–43, to its role today as a vital transportation route to the North and the driving adventure of a lifetime. Showings of the PBS documentary "American Experience: Building the Alaska Highway."

The Alaska Highway House is located on the corner of 10th Street and 102nd Avenue in downtown Dawson Creek. Hours are 9 A.M. to 5 P.M. daily in summer. Admission by donation. Phone 250-782-4714; www.alaska highwayhouse.com.

Dawson Creek Walking Path, a community project to restore the creek, provides a peaceful path for travelers to stretch their legs and take in some local scenery. The path connects Rotary Park at the junction of the Alaska and Hart highways, with Kinsmen Park on 8th Street. Ask at the Visitor Centre for directions.

Tour Dawson Creek's murals. The Historic Walking Tour brochure, available at the Visitor Centre, includes details on the city's murals. Sponsored annually by the Art Gallery, South Peace Art Society and the City of Dawson Creek, the murals portray the city's history, from pioneer days through WWII and construction of the Alaska Highway.

Rotary Lake, an outdoor man-made swimming facility with restrooms and picnic areas, is popular with visitors and residents alike on hot summer days. (No lifeguard on duty.) Mile 0 Rotary Park is at the junction of the Hart and Alaska highways.

Side trips from Dawson Creek include Tumbler Ridge (dinosaur fossils, Kinuseo waterfall), Chetwynd (chainsaw carvings), Hudson's Hope Loop (BC Hydro dam tours) and other destinations. An area map and information are available at the Visitor Centre at NAR Park on Alaska Avenue.

Tumbler Ridge, originally built in conjunction with development of the Quintette Coal Mine, is in the middle of British Columbia's first dinosaur dig, with thousands of dinosaur bones recently uncovered. The town is also known as the gateway to spectacular Kinuseo Falls in Monkman Provincial Park. Tumbler Ridge is 72 miles/115 km from Dawson Creek by the most direct route: 11.9 miles/19.2 km west via Highway 97, then 59.6 miles/96 km south via Highway 52. Or drive to Chetwynd, home of the International Chainsaw Carving Championship in June, and drive Highway 29 South to Tumbler Ridge. See pages 122-123 in the WEST ACCESS ROUTE for log.

BC Hydro offers tours of one of the

Stop by the Dawson Creek Visitor Centre for trip planning help. (©Kris Valencia, staff)

Historic Kiskatinaw River Bridge is the only original timber bridge built along the Alaska Highway that is still in use today. (©Claire Torgerson staff)

world's largest earthen dams at W.A.C. Bennett Dam, and a life-size Hadrosaur at Peace Canyon Dam. Both dams are accessible via the Hudson's Hope Loop; see pages 119-121 in the WEST ACCESS ROUTE for log.

Alaska Highway Log

Distance from Dawson Creek (DC) is followed by distance from Delta Junction (DJ), official end of the Alaska Highway. Distance from Fairbanks (F) is given at towns and junctions. Historical mileposts are indicated in the text as Historical Mile.

In the Canada portion of *The MILE-POST®* Alaska Highway log, mileages from Dawson Creek are based on actual driving distance and kilometres are based on physical kilometreposts.

BC HIGHWAY 97 NORTH

DC 0 DJ 1387 (2232 km) F 1483 (2386.5 km) **Junction** of Highway 97 (Alaska Avenue), Highway 2 (8th Avenue) and Highway 49 (roundabout).

Northbound: Good pavement approximately next 284 miles/457 km (through Fort Nelson). *CAUTION: Heavy traffic, 2-lane stretches of highway, few passing lanes, to Fort St. John. Drive defensively.*

DC 1.2 (1.9 km) DJ 1385.8 (2230 km) F 1481.8 (2384.7 km) Alaska and Hart highways **junction**.

Tubby's RV Park is just west of here on the Hart Highway/97S; **Northern Lights RV Park** is 1.5 miles west from this junction on Highway 97 South.

Junction of the Alaska Highway and Highway 97 South/Hart Highway to Prince George. Westbound travelers turn to page 119 for the end of the log of the WEST ACCESS ROUTE and read log back to front. Alaska-bound travelers continue with this log.

DC 1.5 (2.4 km) DJ 1385.5 (2229.7 km)

Mile 0 Rotary Park (picnicking and swimming), Walter Wright Pioneer Village and **Mile 0 RV Park & Campground** to west.

Mile 0 RV Park & Campground. See display ad on page 136.

DC 1.7 (2.7 km) DJ 1385.3 (2229.4 km) **Historic Milepost 2.** Turnout to west, interpretive sign about Cantel Repeater Station. The U.S. Army constructed the Alaska Highway telephone system—officially known as Cantel—in 1942-43. The 2,850-mile line stretched from Dunvegan, northwest of Edmonton, Alberta, to Fairbanks, AK, and included a 600-mile circuit to Norman Wells. According to John Schmidt's *This Was No #@&! Picnic*, each repeater station was a small community in itself, with a crew to man the circuits 24 hours a day and tons of equipment to keep messages moving to some 1,600 army phones and teletypes. One of the world's longest open-wire toll circuits at the time, the Cantel system was the forerunner of today's communications system.

DC 2 (3.2 km) DJ 1385 (2228.9 km) Recreation centre and golf course to west. Louisiana Pacific waferboard plant to east.

DC 2.9 (4.7 km) DJ 1384.1 (2227.5 km) Northern Alberta Railway (NAR) tracks.

DC 3.3 (5.3 km) DC 1383.7 (2226.8 km) Turnout to east at **Historic Milepost 3.** Sign marks Curan & Briggs Ltd. Construction Camp, U.S. Army Traffic Control Centre.

DC 10 (16 km) DJ 1377 (2216 km) **Farmington Fairways RV Park and Campground.** Stay and play at our scenic 9-hole golf course just 10 miles north of Dawson Creek and save 20 percent off golf fees. 8 full-service, 23 power/water, 28 campsites, fully-licensed restaurant, free WiFi, 30 amp, coin laundry, showerhouse, large group shelter. Phone 250-843-7774. Farmingtonfairways@hotmail.com; www.farmingtonfairways.com. [ADVERTISEMENT]

DC 10.5 (16.9 km) DJ 1376.5 (2215.2 km) *CAUTION: Watch for moose, next 4 km.*

DC 11.2 (18 km) DJ 1375.8 (2214.1 km) Turnout to west.

DC 11.5 (18.5 km) DJ 1375.5 (2213.6 km) Turnout to east.

DC 14.8 (24 km) DJ 1372.2 (2208.3 km) Farmington (unincorporated).

DC 15.8 (25.4 km) DJ 1371.2 (2206.7 km) Farmington store to west; gas, diesel, groceries.

DC 17.3 (27.8 km) DJ 1369.7 (2204.3 km) Exit east for loop road to **Kiskatinaw Provincial Park**. Follow 2-lane paved road (old Alaska Highway) 3 miles/5 km for provincial park; 28 campsites, drinking water, firewood, picnic tables, fire rings, toilets, garbage containers. Camping fee $16.

This interesting side road gives travelers the opportunity to drive the original old Alaska Highway and to cross the curved, wooden, **Historic Kiskatinaw River Bridge.** A sign at the bridge notes that this 531-foot/162-m-long structure is the only original timber bridge built along the Alaska Highway that is still in use today.

DC 17.5 (28.2 km) DJ 1369.5 (2204 km) Distance marker indicates Fort St. John 29 miles/47 km.

CAUTION: Watch for deer.

DC 19.4 (31.2 km) DJ 1367.6 (2200.9 km) Paved turnout to east.

DC 19.8 (31.9 km) DJ 1367.2 (2200.2 km) Highway descends northbound to Kiskatinaw River.

DC 20.9 (33.6 km) DJ 1366.1 (2198.5 km) Kiskatinaw River bridge.

CAUTION: Strong crosswinds on bridge.

Turnout with picnic tables and pit toilets to east at north end of bridge. View of unique bridge support.

DC 22.5 (36.2 km) DJ 1364.5 (2195.9 km) Loop road to Kiskatinaw Provincial Park and Kiskatinaw River bridge (see **Milepost DC 17.3**).

DC 25.4 (41 km) DJ 1361.6 (2191.2 km) NorthwesTel microwave tower to east. Alaska Highway travelers will be seeing many of these towers as they drive north. The original Cantel land line (see **Milepost DC 1.7**) between Grande Prairie, AB, and the YT–AK border was replaced by 42 microwave relay stations by Canadian National Telecommunications (now NorthwesTel) in 1963.

DC 30.5 (49.1 km) DJ 1356.5 (2183 km) Turnout to east with litter barrels, pit toilet and historical marker about explorer Alexander Mackenzie. Turnout to west.

As the highway descends Peace River Hill to the Peace River bridge, there are good views of the Peace River valley and the industrial community of Taylor to the northeast.

CAUTION: South Taylor Hill. Steep winding descent next 4 miles/6.4 km northbound with 6 to 10 percent grade. Slow for 70 kmph/43 mph curve. Truck traffic (trucks check your brakes); a challenging stretch at night with traffic.

DC 32.1 (51.6 km) DJ 1354.9 (2180.4 km) Paved turnout with litter barrels and view of Peace River, bridge and Taylor.

DC 33.8 (54.4 km) DJ 1353.2 (2177.7 km) Pingle Creek.

DC 34 (54.7 km) DJ 1353 (2177.4 km) Access to **Peace Island Park**, 0.5 mile/0.8 km west of the highway, situated on an island in the Peace River connected to the south shore by a causeway. Peace Island Park has 35 shaded campsites with gravel pads, firewood, fire rings, picnic tables, picnic shelter, toilets, potable water, playground, horseshoe pits and a boat launch. There are also 4 large picnic areas and a tenting area. Camping fee. Open mid-April to mid-September, weather

permitting. Nature trail, bird watching and fishing. *Boaters should use caution on the Peace River since both parks are downstream from the W.A.C. Bennett and Peace Canyon dams and water levels may fluctuate rapidly.*

DC 34.4 (55.4 km) **DJ 1352.6** (2176.7 km) **Peace River Bridge**, the longest water span on the Alaska Highway. *Metal grating bridge deck.* Bridging the Peace was one of the first goals of Alaska Highway engineers in 1942. Traffic moving north from Dawson Creek was limited by the Peace River crossing, where 2 ferries with a capacity of 10 trucks per hour were operating in May. Three different pile trestles were constructed across the Peace River, only to be washed out by high water. Work on the permanent 2,130-foot suspension bridge began in December 1942 and was completed in July 1943. One of 2 suspension bridges on the Alaska Highway, the Peace River bridge collapsed in 1957 after erosion undermined the north anchor block of the bridge. The cantilever and truss-type bridge that crosses the Peace River today was completed in 1960. Gas pipeline bridge is visible to east.

DC 35 (56.3 km) **DJ 1352** (2175.8 km) **Historic Milepost 35** at community of **Taylor** (description follows). This location was the 1st Main Army Camp, 341st Engineers, during construction of the Alaska Highway. Before the Peace River was bridged in 1943, the ferry from Taylor served as the major link across the river.

TAYLOR (pop. 1,300; elev. 1,804 feet/550m), is located on the north bank of the Peace River. **Visitor Information:** Infocentre on left northbound on the Alaska Highway, has helpful staff waiting to assist travelers. Stop and photograph the Gold Panner statue. The infocentre is open May to September; phone 250-789-9015. Also inquire here about industrial tours.

A hotel, motels, cafes, grocery store with liquor store, private RV park, gas/diesel station and post office are located here. Free municipal dump station and potable water located behind the North Taylor Inn.

Taylor is a unique community, offering both a pleasant rural lifestyle and tremendous recreational facilities as well as a strong industrial tax base. There is a Spectra gas transmission and processing plant, the Alta Gas Extraction plant and the Canfor (Taylor) pulp mill. The Spectra Energy natural gas pipeline reaches from here to Vancouver, BC, with a branch to western Washington.

Recreation facilities include the 18-hole, par 72 **Lone Wolf golf course** (home of the world's largest golf ball); RV and tent camping at Peace Island Park Campground (see **Milepost DC 34**); tennis courts; a motocross track; and a recreation complex with swimming pool, curling rink and district ice centre for skating (open year-round). The **World's Invitational Gold Panning Championships** are held at Peace Island Park on the weekend preceding British Columbia Day (first Monday of August). The fertile Taylor Flats area has market gardens and roadside stands in summer.

District of Taylor. See display ad this page.

DC 36.3 (58.4 km) **DJ 1350.7** (2173.7 km) Railroad tracks. Taylor Pool and Curling Ice Centre to west.

DC 37.9 (61 km) **DJ 1349.1** (2171.1 km) Turnout with litter bin to west.

DC 40 (64.5 km) **DJ 1347** (2167.7 km) **Historical Mile 41**. Post office.

DC 40.3 (64.9 km) **DJ 1346.7** (2167.2 km) Exit east for Fort St. John airport.

DC 40.4 (65 km) **DJ 1346.6** (2167.1 km) C.N. Railway overhead tracks (5.5m height).

DC 40.9 (65.8 km) **DJ 1346.1** (2166.3 km) **Historic Milepost 42** Access road to Fort St. John Airport.

DC 44.6 (71.7 km) **DJ 132.4** (2160.3 km) 86th Street, access to municipal sani-dump.

Entering Fort St. John business district northbound. A number of visitor services, such as motels, gas/diesel stations, steakhouse and fast-food outlets, are located on the frontage roads Alaska Road North and Alaska Road South. *Divided 4-lane highway, 43 mph/70 kmph speed zone, northbound.*

DC 45.7 (73.5 km) **DJ 1341.3** (2158.5 km) 96th Street; access northeast to Super 8, Shell gas station, a Walmart pharmacy, the Totem Mall and spacious Pomeroy SportCentre.

DC 45.8 (73.7 km) **DJ 1341.2** (2158.4 km) Traffic light at 100 Street. Access north to Museum and downtown Fort St. John via 100 Street; frontage road access north to Safeway (with Starbucks) and gas station. Follow 100 Street south 2 miles/3.2 km for Peace River viewpoint.

DC 46.4 (74.6 km) **DJ 1340.6** (2157.4 km) Traffic light at 108 Street/109 Street. Access to gas stations and fast-food.

Fort St. John visitor services are found on frontage roads along the Alaska Highway and off the highway in commercial areas. (©Kris Valencia, staff)

DC 47 (75.6 km) **DJ 1340** (2156.5 km) **Historical Mile 48**. Traffic light at 100 Ave. Access northeast to Fort St. John City Centre and airport via 100th Avenue. Chances Gaming and Pomeroy Hotel with Tony Romas.

Fort St. John

DC 47 (75.6 km) **DJ 1340** (2156.5 km) **F 1436** (2311 km) **Historic Milepost 47**. Dubbed the "Energetic City," Fort St. John is located approximately 236 miles/380 km south of Fort Nelson. **Population:** 18,000; area 55,000. **Emergency Services:** For all emergency service phone 911. **RCMP**, phone 250-787-8100. **Hospital**, on 100th Avenue and 98th Street, phone 250-785-6611.

Visitor Information: The Visitor Centre, located at the corner of 100 St. and 96 Avenue, offers a wide selection of brochures, computer access and WiFi for travelers, a gift shop, picnic area and restrooms. Write them at 9523–100 Street, Fort St. John, BC V1J 4N4; phone 250-785-3033 or toll-free 1-877-785-6037; visitorinfo@fortstjohn.ca; www.fortstjohn.ca. Open daily June–August, weekdays rest of year.

RV Round-up! held on Saturdays, June through August, RVers are welcome to meet at the North Peace Leisure Pool parking lot,

a large lot with easy RV access and just steps from the Visitor Centre. Wander over to the Visitor Centre for free coffee and learn about special events, free attraction passes just for RVers, and what attractions are within walking distance.

For information on wilderness hiking and camping opportunities, contact BC Parks (Ministry of Environment), Peace Region, #400, 10003–110th Ave., Fort St. John, BC V1J 6M7, phone 250-787-3411; www.gov.bc.ca/env/.

Direct hunting and fishing queries to the Ministry of Environment, #400, 10003–110th Ave., Fort St. John, BC V1J 6M7; phone 250-787-3411.

Elevation: 2,275 feet/693m. **Climate**: Average high temperature in July, 73°F/23°C, average low 50°F/10°C. In January, average high is 12°F/-11°C; low is -2°F/-19°C. **Radio**: CBC 88.3 FM, Sunrise Radio 92.5 FM, Energy 98.5 FM, The Moose 100.1 FM, The Bear 101.5 FM. **Television**: Cable. **Newspaper**: *Alaska Highway News* (daily), *The Northerner* (weekly), *Northeast News* (weekly)

Private Aircraft: Fort St. John airport, 3.8 E; elev. 2,280 feet/695m; length 6,900 feet/2,103m and 6,700 feet/2,042m; asphalt; fuel 100, Jet. Charlie Lake airstrip, 6.7 NW; elev. 2,680 feet/817m; length 1,800 feet/549m; gravel; fuel 100.

Fort St. John is set in the low, rolling hills of the Peace River Valley. The original Fort St. John was established as Rocky

Mountain Fort in 1794, making Fort St. John the oldest white settlement in mainland British Columbia.

The Peace region was homesteaded in the early 1900s. The town's early commercial development centered around a store established by settler C.M. Finch. His stepson, Clement Brooks, carried on Finch's entrepreneurship, starting several businesses in Fort St. John after WWII.

In 1942, Fort St. John became field headquarters for U.S. Army troops and civilian engineers working on construction of the Alaska Highway in the eastern sector. "Camp Alcan" at Fort St. John (along with Whitehorse, headquarters for the western sector) was the largest of the dozen or so construction camps along the highway. What had been home to 200 became a temporary base for more than 6,000. Much of the field housing, road building equipment and even office supplies were scrounged from old Civilian Conservation Corps camps and the Work Projects Administration.

The Alaska Highway was opened to the traveling public in 1948, attracting vacationers and homesteaders. An immense natural oil and gas field discovered in 1951 made Fort St. John the oil capital of British Columbia. "Energetic City," referring to the natural energy resources and the city's potential for positive growth, became the slogan for the city.

An extension of the Pacific Great Eastern Railway, now called C.N. Rail, from Prince George in 1958 (continued to Fort Nelson in 1971), gave Fort St. John a link with the rail yards and docks at North Vancouver.

Today, Fort St. John's booming economy is based primarily on oil and gas, as well as agriculture, forestry, tourism, hydro-electric power generation, and consumer and public services. Fort St. John is northeastern BC's shopping and service centre, with everything from boutique shops to large chain stores.

Transportation

Air: Fort St. John Airport (www.fsjairport.com) is served by Air Canada, Central Mountain Air and Swanberg Air. Connecting flights to Fort Nelson, Vancouver, Edmonton and Prince George. **Bus**: Coachways service to Prince George, Vancouver, Edmonton and Whitehorse; depot at 10355 101st Ave., phone 250-785-6695.

Lodging & Services

Visitor services are located just off the Alaska Highway and in the city centre, several blocks north of the highway. There are 15 motels/hotels in the Fort St. John area, including the **Blue Belle Motel and Super 8**. *(NOTE: Lodging fills up fast, phone ahead for reservations.)* Restaurants, fast-food outlets and full-service gas stations are located on the Alaska Highway and in town. Shopping malls include Totem Mall, MacKenzie Mall,

Co-op Mall, Northgate Mall, the Sobey's complex and Price Smart complex.

Fort St. John has 4 supermarkets; 2 laundromats; all major Canadian banks (automatic teller machines at Totem Mall and downtown at Charter Banks) and a Credit Union; car washes; a bowling alley; a 5-plex movie theatre; and a gaming entertainment centre (bingo, slot machines).

Recreation facilities include the Pomeroy SportCentre and the North Peace Recreation Centre (see descriptions under Attractions).

Camping

There is one private campground in Fort St. John on Alaska Road. **Rotary R.V. Park** is located just north of town on Charlie Lake at **Milepost DC 51** Alaska Highway.

There is also camping at Beatton Provincial Park, 5 miles east of **Milepost DC 49.5**, and at Charlie Lake Provincial Park, **Milepost DC 53.7** Alaska Highway.

Fresh water fill-up and dump station located at the northeast corner of 86th Street and the Alaska Highway.

Attractions

Centennial Park, located on 100th Street, is home to several recreation facilities, including **Rotary Spray Park**, open 10 A.M. to 9 P.M. during summer; a Skateboard Park; the 8-sheet Fort St. John Curling Club in winter; a volleyball court; and swimming pool. The North Peace Leisure Pool, at 9505 100th Street, has a lap pool, diving boards, waterslide, wave pool and fitness room; phone 250-787-8178 or 250-785-POOL.

A granite monument in Centennial Park commemorates Sir Alexander Mackenzie's

stop here on his journey west to the Pacific Ocean in 1793.

The **Fort St. John North Peace Museum**, at 9323 100th Street, features more than 10,000 artifacts from the region, including archeological artifacts from the fur trade, an early-day schoolroom, a dentist office and a blacksmith shop. Historic buildings include a missionary chapel, a trapper's cabin, and

the British Columbia Police Barracks. The museum gift shop offers a good selection of local and Northwest books, DVDs, clothing, and many souvenir items. The museum is open 9 A.M. to 5 P.M. daily except Sunday year-round; phone 250-787-0430.

Pioneer Pathway Walking Tour. The Energetic City revisits its past through heritage panels located in the downtown area.

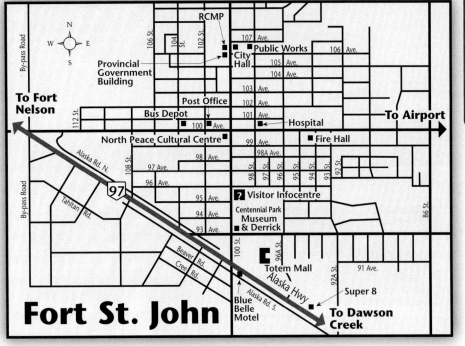

Fort St. John's North Peace Recreation Center complex includes a pool. *(©Judy Nadon, staff)*

The panels feature historic photos and stories of Fort St. John beginning in the 1920s. Start the walking tour at the Visitor Centre, where you can pick up a map.

North Peace Cultural Centre, at 10015 100th Ave., houses Fort St. John Public Library (phone 250-785-3731); a 413-seat theatre which showcases musical, theatrical and other live performances throughout the year; an art gallery; and a cafe. Phone 250-785-1992; www.npcc.bc.ca.

North Peace Recreation Centre, located on 96 Avenue in Centennial Park, has winter ice skating rink. A Farmer's Market is held in the lobby on Saturdays, 9 A.M. to 4 P.M., May–December. The North Peace Leisure Pool, on the other side of the recreation centre, has a waterslide, wave pool, lap pool, diving boards, a sauna and steam room; phone 250-787-8178. The outdoor Rotary Spray Park is located beside the pool.

Pomeroy Sport Centre, at 9324 96 Street, features 2 NHL-sized ice rinks, an indoor Olympic-sized speed skating oval and a 3-lane, 380-metre-/1,247-foot-long rubberized track for community use year-round. This enormous facility has extensive parking and a rainwater harvesting system that will channel rainwater from the roof to holding tanks for use in the facility's landscaping and irrigation needs.

Walking trails. Fish Creek Community Forest, adjacent to Northern Lights College, has 3 interpretive trails to learn more about the forest and forestry management. To reach the college from the Alaska Highway, follow 100th Street north 1.2 miles/2 km and turn right on the Bypass Road just before the railway tracks. Take the first left and park behind Northern Lights College. Or stop by the Visitor Centre for driving directions and trail maps.

Trail System. More than 6 miles/10 km of paved trail loop around the perimeter of the city. Great for joggers, bicyclists and walkers. Trailheads for access to this trail are located at 100 Street and Bypass Road and at Surerus Park, 86 Street and 102 Avenue. There is also trail access from Northern Lights College.

Special Events. Hundreds of events happen in the Energetic City each year, from arts to musical performances, baseball games, ice sculpting and more. Check with the Visitor Centre or visit www.fortstjohn.ca.

Play golf. Fort St. John's only in-town golf course is Links Golf Course, just off the Bypass Road at 86 Street; 9 holes, pro shop and lounge; phone 250-785-9995.

The Lakepoint Golf Course, on Golf Course Road at Charlie Lake, has 18 holes, pro shop, lounge and restaurant; phone 250-785-5566.

W.A.C. Bennett Dam is a major attraction in the area. For an interesting side-trip, drive north from Fort St. John on the Alaska Highway to Milepost DC 53.7 and take Highway 29 west 45.4 miles/73 km to junction with the W.A.C. Bennett access road in Hudson's Hope.

Highway 29 follows the original Canadian government telegraph trail of 1918. Hudson's Hope, formerly a pioneer community established in 1805 by explorer Simon Fraser, grew with construction of the W.A.C. Bennett Dam, which is located 15 miles/24 km west of town. B.C. Hydro's Peace Canyon dam is located approximately 4 miles/6.4 km south of Hudson's Hope. See log on pages 119-121.

Alaska Highway Log
(continued)

BC HIGHWAY 97 NORTH

Distance from Dawson Creek (DC) is followed by distance from Delta Junction (DJ). Distance from Fairbanks (F) is given at towns and junctions. Historical mileposts are indicated in the text as Historical Mile.

In the Canada portion of *The MILEPOST®* Alaska Highway log, mileages from Dawson Creek are based on actual driving distance and kilometres are based on physical kilometreposts.

DC 45.8 (73.7 km) **DJ 1341.2** (2158.4 km) Traffic light at 100 Street. Access north to Museum and downtown Fort St. John via 100 Street; frontage road access north to Safeway/Starbucks, gas station and **Integra Tire** service (car/RV brakes, shocks, alignments). Follow 100 Street south 2 miles/3.2 km for Peace River viewpoint. 🛢

DC 46.4 (74.6 km) **DJ 1340.6** (2157.4 km) Traffic light at 108 Street/109 Street. Access to gas stations and fast-food. 🛢

DC 47 (75.6 km) **DJ 1340** (2156.5 km) **Historical Mile 48.** Traffic light at 100 Ave. Access northeast to Fort St. John City Centre.

DC 47.3 (76.1 km) **DJ 1339.7** (2156 km) Petro Canada gas station. 🛢

DC 48.2 (77.6 km) **DJ 1338.8** (2154.5 km) Traffic light. Road 269/Business Frontage.

DC 48.6 (78.2 km) **DJ 1338.4** (2153.9 km) **Historic Milepost 49** historic sign:

Camp Alcan and the Public Roads Administration Headquarters/Okes Management Contracting Headquarters—Standard Salt & Cement Co., Coghlan Construction Co., M.G. Astleford Co., Southern Minnesota Construction Co., Art Colier, Sorenson & Volden, R.M. Smith Headquarters. "As the southern sector headquarters for the United States Military and Public Roads Administration, Fort St. John was the site of two large construction camps—pyramid tents and Quonset huts—erected in open fields just outside of town."

DC 49.5 (79.6 km) **DJ 1337.5** (2152.4 km) Traffic light, Road 271. **Beatton Provincial Park** (5 miles/8 km) east via paved road; 37 campsites, picnic shelter, horseshoe pits, playground, sports field, sandy beach, swimming and boat launch. Camping fee $16. Fishing for northern pike, walleye (July best) and yellow perch in **Charlie Lake**. 🚤 ⛺

DC 50.1 (81.4 km) **DJ 1336.9** (2151.5

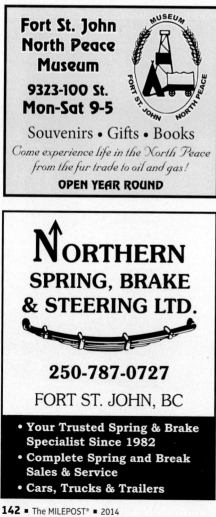

km) City limit for **Charlie Lake** (unincorporated).

DC 51 (82.4 km) **DJ 1336** (2150 km) Turnoff to east and follow signs for **Rotary R.V. Park** campground (full service and pull-through sites), Rotary Park day-use area and **Alaska Highway monument** (description follows). The day-use area on **Charlie Lake** has parking, restrooms, a playground, lake trail, boat launch and fishing.

Rotary R.V. Park. See display ad this page.

The Alaska Highway monument on Charlie Lake memorializes 12 American soldiers who drowned May 14, 1942, when their pontoon boat sank while crossing the lake. The soldiers, part of the 341st Engineers and the 74th Light Pontoon, were working on construction of the highway.

DC 51.3 (82.9 km) **DJ 1335.7** (2149.5 km) **Historic Milepost 52.** NWHS sign commemorates Charlie Lake, Mile 0 Army Tote Road. Site of a major distribution camp for workers and supplies heading north.

DC 51.5 (83 km) **DJ 1335.6** (2149 km) Turnoff for Charlie Lake and Leisure RV Park.

DC 51.8 (83.4 km) **DJ 1335.2** (2148.7 km) *End 4-lane highway, begin passing lane northbound.*

Begin 4-lane highway southbound through Charlie Lake and Fort St. John.

DC 52.6 (86 km) **DJ 1334.4** (2147.4 km) Spectra Energy Charlie Lake.

DC 53.6 (86.3 km) **DJ 1333.4** (2145.8 km) Highway 29 **junction** to west; truck stop with gas/diesel and propane.

Junction with Highway 29, which leads west 47 miles/76 km to Hudson's Hope and the W.A.C. Bennett Dam, then south to connect with the Hart Highway at Chetwynd. Turn to page 121 and read "Hudson's Hope Loop" log from back to front.

Turn east for **Charlie Lake Provincial Park**, just off highway; paved loop road (with speed bumps) leads through campground. There are 58 shaded sites, picnic tables, kitchen shelter with wood stove, firepits, firewood ($8), outhouses, dump station ($5), water and garbage containers. *See posted restrictions on generator use.* Level gravel sites, some will accommodate 2 large RVs. Camping fee $16, reservations accepted (go to http://www.env.gov.bc.ca/bcparks/ or https://secure.camis.com/Discovercamping/).

The provincial park has a playfield, playground, horseshoe pits, volleyball net and a 1.2-mile/2-km hiking trail down to lake. Watch for wildflowers. Because of the wide variety of plants here, including some that may not be seen elsewhere along the Alaska Highway, Verna E. Pratt's *Wildflowers Along the Alaska Highway* includes a special list of species for this park. Fishing in Charlie Lake for walleye, northern pike and yellow perch. Access to the lake for vehicles and boats is from the Alaska Highway just east of the park entrance. Boat launch and picnic area at lake.

DC 53.7 (86.4 km) **DJ 1333.3** (2145.7 km) **F 1429.3** (2300 km) Truck weigh scales east side of highway.

DC 54.3 (87 km) **DJ 1332.7** (2145 km) *End passing lane, begin 2-lane highway, northbound.*

DC 59.9 (96 km) **DJ 1327.1** (2135.7 km)

Turnouts both sides of highway. Litter bins on the east side.

DC 62.4 (100.4 km) **DJ 1324.6** (2131.7 km) A 30-foot/9-m statue of a lumberjack marks Clarke Sawmill to west. (The statue wears a Santa suit at Christmas.)

DC 64.8 (104 km) **DJ 1322.2** (2127.8 km) Spectra compressor station.

DC 65.4 (105 km) **DJ 1321.6** (2126.8 km) Double-ended paved turnout to west.

DC 71.7 (115.4 km) **DJ 1315.3** (2116.7 km) **Historical Mile 72. The Shepherd's Inn** (description follows); a very popular food stop with gas and lodging. Husky gas/diesel station.

©Sharon Nault

The Shepherd's Inn. A great place to stop! We specialize in making folks at home, offering regular and breakfast specials,

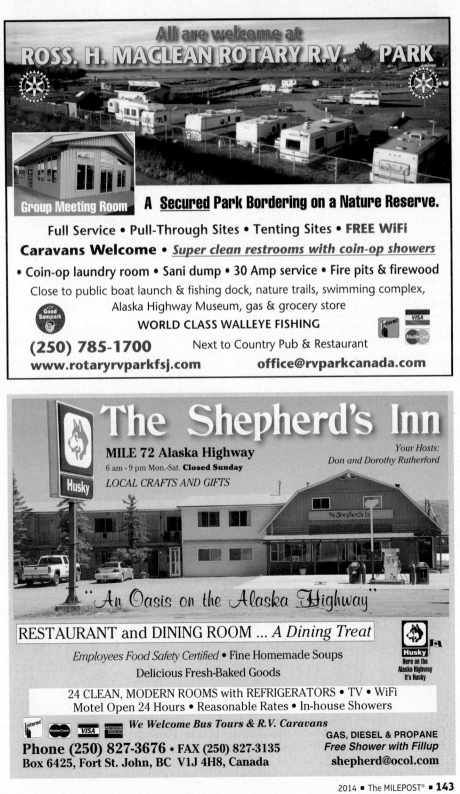

Easy grades and curves characterize the Alaska Highway between Fort St. John and Fort Nelson. (©Kris Valencia, staff)

complete lunch and dinner menu. Low-fat buffalo burgers. A real treat: Russian borscht. Our specialties: homemade soups (no msg), home-baked sweet rolls, cinnamon rolls, blueberry and bran muffins, bread, biscuits and trappers bannock. Delicious desserts, rhubarb-strawberry, Dutch apple, chocolate dream and pumpkin pies, cherry cheesecake. Hard ice cream. Refreshing fruit drinks from local fruits: blueberry and raspberry coolers. Attention caravaners and bus tours ... a convenient and delightful stop on your Alaska Highway adventure! You may reserve your stop–break with us. Motel service 24 hours. NOTE: Highway 29 traffic from Hudson's Hope northbound entering Alaska Highway ... your first motel stop. Southbound ... your last motel selection. Quality Husky products. Phone 250-827-3676. Email shepherd@ocol.com. An oasis on the Alcan at Mile 72. See display ad on page 143.

[ADVERTISEMENT]

DC 72.8 (117.1 km) **DJ 1314.2** (2114.9 km) **Historic Milepost 73** commemorates Beatton River Flight Strip, 1 of 4 gravel airstrips built for American military aircraft during WWII. Road to Prespetu and Buick, access to oil and gas well sites.

DC 79.1 (127.3 km) **DJ 1307.9** (2104.8 km) **Historical Mile 80** paved, shaded, rest area to west with heated restrooms, litter and recycle bins, picnic tables, playground and flush toilets.

DC 81.4 (131 km) **DJ 1305.6** (2101 km) Distance marker northbound shows Wonowon 31 km/19 miles, Fort Nelson 319 km/198 miles, Whitehorse 1297 km/806 miles.

DC 90.1 (145 km) **DJ 1296.9** (2087.1 km) Inga Lake to the west, recreation site, picnicking and camping.

DC 91.4 (147.1 km) **DJ 1295.6** (2085 km) **Historical Mile 92**. Spectra Energy compres-

sor station to west.

Travelers may notice natural gas exploration wells between Dawson Creek and Fort Nelson. Gas exploration along the Alaska Highway corridor in British Columbia and into Yukon and the Northwest Territories has been booming in recent years.

DC 94.6 (152.2 km) **DJ 1292.4** (2079.8 km) Turnoff for Upper Halfway Road. This 34.5-mile/55.5-km side road (paved) leads in a southwesterly direction to area ranches.

DC 98.7 (159 km) **DJ 1288.3** (2073.3 km) Microwave tower to east.

Slow for 70 kmph/43 mph speed zone northbound.

DC 101 (161.7 km) **DJ 1286** (2069.5 km) **WONOWON** (pop. 150), unincorporated, has an Esso gas station with diesel, general store and post office, and Chester's Chicken to west. Wonowon Lodge to east is an open camp facility offering a 24-hour dining room and 208 rooms in modular units.

Historic Milepost 101. The historic sign and interpretive panel here commemorate Blueberry Control Station, "site of the Blueberry Control Gate, a 24-hour military checkpoint operated by U.S. Army personnel through the war years."

The Alaska Highway follows the Blueberry and Prophet river drainages north to Fort Nelson. The Blueberry River, not visible from the highway, lies a few miles east of Wonowon. There is considerable oil and gas exploration along the Alaska Highway north of Fort St. John, and motorists will notice signs marking oil and gas patch access at side roads.

DC 103.5 (166.5 km) **DJ 1283.5** (2065.5 km) **Historic Milepost 104** marks start of Adolphson, Huseth, Layer & Welch contract during Alaska Highway construction.

DC 114 (183.2 km) **DJ 1273** (2048.6 km) Paved turnout with litter bin to east side of road. Beetle kill is obvious in this area.

DC 124.3 (200.5 km) **DJ 1262.7** (2032.1 km) The Cut (highway goes through a small rock cut). Relatively few rock cuts were necessary during construction of the Alaska Highway in 1942–43. However, rock excavation was often made outside of the roadway to obtain gravel fill for the new roadbed.

Highway descends long grades to 6 percent north- and southbound. Slow for dangerous curves. Beetle killed pines are obvious as you descend northbound.

DC 140.4 (226 km) **DJ 1246.6** (2006.2 km) **Historical Mile 143. PINK MOUNTAIN** (pop. 99, area 300; elev. 3,600 feet/ 1,097m). Restaurant, pub, lodging and RV camping to east at **Buffalo Inn**. Post office, Race Trac gas station (diesel, propane), liquor store, groceries, and RV camping to west at **Pink Mountain Campsite & R.V. Park** (description follows).

Pink Mountain Campsite & R.V. Park, Race Trac Fuels. Relax folks, you've arrived at one of the nicest campgrounds on the Alaska Highway. Located

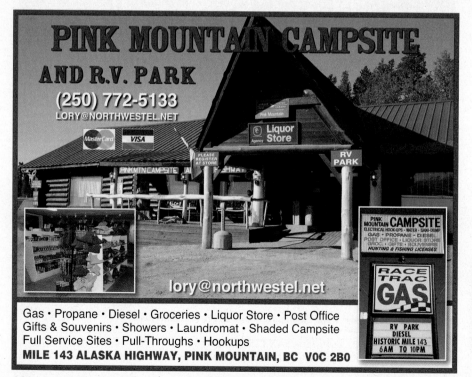

at mile marker 143, we have something to

offer everyone. Propane, gas, diesel, along with Canada Post and BC Government Liquor Store. With shaded sites and firepits, a new laundromat and clean hot showers. All tenters and RVers are welcome. Open year-round. Call Korey or Lory; phone 250-772-5133. Email: lory@northwestel.net. Major credit cards accepted. Thank you! See display ad on page 144. [ADVERTISEMENT]

Buffalo Inn. See display ad this page.

Pink Mountain is home to Darryl Mills, Canadian champion bullrider. According to local resident Ron Tyerman, Pink Mountain gets its name from the local fall foliage, when red-barked willows give the mountain a pink colour in the morning sun. Another source attributes the pink colour of the mountain—and thus the name—to concentrations of feldspar.

DC 142.3 (229 km) **DJ 1244.7** (2003.1 km) Large, gravel turnout to east.

DC 144.1 (231.9 km) **DJ 1242.9** (2002.2 km) **Historical Mile 147. Sasquatch Crossing Lodge**; lodging and camping, restaurant, gift shop.

Sasquatch Crossing Lodge. See display ad this page.

DC 144.5 (232.5 km) **DJ 1242.5** (1999.6 km) Mae's Kitchen.

DC 144.7 (232.7 km) **DJ 1242.3** (1999.2 km) Beatton River bridge. The Beatton River was named for Frank Beatton, a Hudson's Bay Co. employee. The Beatton River flows into the Peace River system.

DC 145.1 (233.4 km) **DJ 1241.9** (1998.6 km) **Historic Milepost 148** double-ended turnout to east with litter bins and sign commemorating Suicide Hill, one of the most treacherous hills on the original highway, noted for its ominous greeting: "Prepare to meet thy maker."

DC 145.5 (234 km) **DJ 1241.5** (1997.9 km) **Private Aircraft**: Sikanni Chief flight strip to east; elev. 3,258 feet/993m; length, 6,000 feet/1,829m; gravel, current status unknown. Well-known local pilot Jimmy "Midnight" Anderson used the Sikanni Chief airstrip, which was the southernmost airfield in the Northwest Staging Route used during WWII.

DC 147.9 (238 km) **DJ 1239.1** (1994.1 km) Distance marker southbound shows Wonowon 74 km/46 miles, Fort St. John 162 km/101 miles.

Distance marker northbound shows Buckinghorse 40 km/25 miles, Fort Nelson 222 km/138 miles.

CAUTION: Watch for moose and deer, especially at dusk and at night.

DC 154.5 (248.6 km) **DJ 1232.5** (1983.5 km) Turnoff for **Duhu Lake Provincial Park** 5.8 km/3.6 miles west. Camping and picnicking.

DC 156 (251 km) **DJ 1231** (1981 km) Large double-ended, gravel turnout/brake check area with litter bins to east at top of Sikanni Hill. Winter chain-up/chain removal area. *CAUTION: Slow for 6 to 9 percent winding downgrade northbound to Sikanni Chief River bridge.*

Section of the old Alaska Highway is visible to east; no access.

DC 159.2 (256.2 km) **DJ 1227.8** (1975.9 km) **Sikanni Chief River Bridge** (elev. 2,662 feet/811m). Steel stanchions to west are all that remain of the historic wooden Sikanni bridge, which was destroyed by arson July 10, 1992. The original timber truss bridge across the Sikanni Chief River was completed on

October 28, 1942, by African American army engineers. It was the first permanent structure completed on the Alaska Highway. Highway construction crews rerouted much of the pioneer road built in 1942 and replaced temporary bridges with 133 steel permanent structures in 1943.

The Sikanni Chief River flows east and then north into the Fort Nelson River, which flows into the Liard River and on to the Mackenzie River, which empties into the Arctic Ocean. Check at the lodge for information on Sikanni Chief Falls (see **Milepost DC 168.5**).

Sikanni Chief River, fair fishing at mouth of tributaries in summer for grayling to 2½ lbs.; whitefish to 2 lbs.

Winding 6 to 9 percent uphill grade southbound.

DC 159.4 (256.5 km) **DJ 1227.6** (1975.6 km) **Historical Mile 162. SIKANNI CHIEF. Sikanni River Campground & RV Park** (description follows); seasonal gas, lodging and camping. Historic highway lodge location: Sikanni Chief Lodge first appeared in the 1949 edition of *The MILEPOST®*.

Watch for moose and other wildlife along the Alaska Highway. *(©Judy Nadon, staff)*

Sikanni River Campground & RV Park is surrounded by natural beauty and offers easy access to riverside camping. Sites are long and level; serviced or non-serviced; pull-through or back-in. WiFi, coin laundry, free showers, clean washrooms, sani-dump, playground and more! Kitchenette cabins, too! The resident owners/operators are happy to welcome many returning guests. Truly a camper's paradise! Phone 250-772-5400; www.sikanni rivercampground.ca. [ADVERTISEMENT]

Highway climbs northbound.

DC 160 (257.5 km) **DJ 1227** (1974.6 km) Turnout with litter bin to west. "Drunken Forest" on hillside to west is shallow-rooted black spruce trees growing in unstable clay-based soil that is subject to slide activity in wet weather. Brake check area.

DC 168.5 (270.3 km) **DJ 1218.5** (1960.9 km) Gravel road west to Sikanni Chief Falls Protected Area. Drive in 10.5 miles/16.9 km to small parking area at trailhead for 0.9-mile/1.5-km hike on well-marked trail to view the 98-foot/30-m falls. Access road has steep hills and 1-lane bridge: *Do not travel this side road in wet weather. Side road is not recommended for large RVs or vehicles with trailers.*

CAUTION: Watch for moose on highway northbound to Milepost DC 200, especially at dusk. Drive carefully!

DC 172.5 (277.6 km) **DJ 1214.5** (1954.5 km) Polka Dot Creek.

DC 172.7 (277.9 km) **DJ 1214.3** (1954.2 km) **Historic Milepost 175**.

DC 173.2 (278.2 km) **DJ 1213.8** (1953.4 km) Buckinghorse River bridge; access to river at north end of bridge.

DC 173.3 (278.4 km) **DJ 1213.7** (1953.2 km) Turnoff to east for **Buckinghorse River Wayside Provincial Park**. Follow the narrow gravel road 0.7 mile/1.1 km along river to camping and picnic area. The park has 33 campsites, picnic tables, side-by-side camper parking, fire rings (firewood may be purchased from park attendant), water pump, outhouses and litter bins; open May to Sept. 30, camping fee $16. Fishing for grayling in Buckinghorse River. Swimming in downstream pools.

DC 173.4 (279 km) **DJ 1213.6** (1953 km) **Historical Mile 175**. Buckinghorse River Lodge west side of highway; food, lodging. The camp complex east from Buckinghorse River Lodge (on right northbound) has gas and lodging and services for gas-patch crews. Seasonal camping at nearby Buckinghorse River Wayside Provincial Park (see **Milepost DC 173.3**).

DC 176 (282.3 km) **DJ 1211** (1948.9 km) Double ended gravel turnout to the east with litter bins and outhouses on south end of 27-mile/43-km Trutch Mountain Bypass, completed in 1987, which rerouted the Alaska Highway around Trutch Mountain, eliminating the steep, winding climb over the mountain. (The "old road" over Trutch is narrow gravel, used by gas and oil patch crews.) The "new" roadbed of the Alaska Highway cuts a wide swath through the flat Minnaker River valley. The river, not visible to motorists, is west of the highway; and was named for local trapper George Minnaker.

Historic Milepost 191. Trutch Mountain, to the east of the highway, was the second highest summit on the Alaska Highway before the highway was rerouted, with an elevation of 4,134 feet/1,260m. It was named for Joseph W. Trutch, civil engineer and first governor of British Columbia.

DC 177.2 (285.2 km) **DJ 1209.8** (1946.9 km) Turnoff to west for an arduous 42-mile/68-km-long all-terrain-vehicle-only trail to Redfern-Keily Provincial Park; hiking, 26 primitive campsites.

DC 182.8 (293.2 km) **DJ 1204.2** (1937.9 km) Large gravel turnout to west with litter bin.

DC 184.5 (297 km) **DJ 1202.5** (1935 km) Distance marker northbound shows Prophet River 68 km/42 miles, Fort Nelson 156 km/97 miles.

DC 199.1 (319.8 km) **DJ 1187.9** (1911.7 km) **Historic Milepost 202**. Large gravel turnout with litter bins to west.

CAUTION: Watch for moose on highway, especially at dusk. Drive carefully!

DC 199.2 (320 km) **DJ 1187.8** (1911.9 km) Welcome to Fort Nelson Forest District (northbound sign).

DC 204.2 (328 km) **DJ 1182.8** (1903.5

km) *Highway descends to* **Beaver Creek**; fishing for grayling to 2½ lbs.

DC 216.6 (348.2 km) **DJ 1170.4** (1883.5 km) Distance marker southbound shows Buckinghorse River 70 km/43 miles, Fort St. John 272 km/169 miles.

DC 217.2 (349.3 km) **DJ 1169.8** (1882.5 km) Gravel side road leads west 0.4 mile/0.6 km through trembling aspen stands and mature white spruce to former Prophet River Wayside Provincial Park (no facilities or services). The park access road crosses an airstrip, originally an emergency airstrip on the Northwest Air Staging Route. This was once part of the old Alaska Highway (known as the Alcan).

The Alaska Highway roughly parallels the Prophet River from here north to the Muskwa River south of Fort Nelson.

Private Aircraft: Prophet River emergency airstrip; elev. 1,954 feet/596m; length 6,000 feet/1,829m; gravel; no services.

DC 219.2 (352.4 km) **DJ 1167.8** (1879.3 km) **Historic Milepost 224**.

DC 222.3 (357.2 km) **DJ 1164.7** (1874.3 km) *Highway descends northbound* to Bougie Creek bridge. Steep dirt access road at south end of bridge leads to informal turnout beside creek.

DC 223.2 (358.6 km) **DJ 1163.8** (1872.9 km) Double ended, gravel turnout to west.

DC 226.2 (363.4 km) **DJ 1160.8** (1868.1 km) Prophet River Indian Reserve to east.

DC 226.5 (363.9 km) **DJ 1160.5** (1867.6 km) **Historical Mile 232**. St. Paul's Roman Catholic Church to east.

DC 227 (364.7 km) **DJ 1160** (1866.8 km) **Historical Mile 233. PROPHET RIVER.**

Northbound: Good pavement, long straight sections of highway, to Fort Nelson.

Southbound: Good pavement, easy curves, some long 6 percent grades.

DC 227.6 (365.6 km) **DJ 1159.4** (1865.8 km) Double-ended turnout with litter bin to east at **Historic Milepost 234**, Adsett Creek Highway Realignment. This major rerouting, completed in 1992, eliminated 132 curves on the stretch of highway that originally ran between Mile 234 and Mile 275.

DC 227.7 (365.8 km) **DJ 1159.3** (1865.6 km) Adsett Creek.

Highway climbs northbound.

DC 230.7 (371.3 km) **DJ 1156.3** (1860.8 km) Natural gas pipeline crosses beneath highway.

DC 230.9 (373.2 km) **DJ 1156.1** (1860.5 km) Distance marker southbound shows Prophet River 8 km/5 miles, Fort St. John 300 km/186 miles.

DC 232.9 (374.8 km) **DJ 1154.1** (1857.3 km) Turnout to west with dumpster and litter bins. Good views northbound of mesa-like topography of Mount Yakatchie.

DC 234.1 (376.5 km) **DJ 1152.9** (1855.4 km) Distance marker northbound shows Fort Nelson 80 km/50 miles, Watson Lake 600 km/373 miles.

DC 241.5 (388 km) **DJ 1145.5** (1843.4 km) Parker Creek.

DC 242.7 (390 km) **DJ 1144.3** (1841.5 km) **Historic Milepost 249**. Little Beaver Creek.

DC 246.5 (396.3 km) **DJ 1140.5** (1835.4 km) *CAUTION: Watch for deer.*

Long straight stretch of highway northbound to Fort Nelson.

DC 248.5 (400 km) **DJ 1138.5** (1832.2 km) Big Beaver Creek.

DC 261.1 (420.2 km) **DJ 1125.9** (1811.9 km) Long double-ended dirt turnout to east

with litter bins.

DC 264.6 (425.2 km) **DJ 1122.4** (1806.3 km) Highway descends to Jackfish Creek bridge then climbs northbound. Note the variety of trembling aspen stands and the white spruce seedlings under them.

DC 265.5 (426.5 km) **DJ 1121.5** (1804.8 km) Turnoff to east for **Andy Bailey Regional Park** via 6.9-mile/12-km dirt and gravel access road (keep to right at "T" at Mile 1.7 on access road). *Large RVs and trailers note: Only turnaround space on access road is approximately halfway in.* The park is located on Andy Bailey Lake; 5 campsites (not suitable for large RVs or trailers), picnic sites, picnic tables, fire rings, firewood, water, outhouses, litter bins, boat launch (no powerboats), swimming and fair fishing for northern pike. Camping fee $17. *Bring insect repellent!*

DC 270.8 (435.1 km) **DJ 1116.2** (1796.3 km) Sulfur gas pipeline crosses highway overhead (7.5m height).

DC 271 (435.4 km) **DJ 1116** (1796 km) Spectra Energy gas processing plant to east. Sulfur pelletizing to west.

DC 276.2 (443.8 km) **DJ 1110.8** (1787.6 km) Rodeo grounds to west. The rodeo is held in August.

DC 276.7 (444.6 km) **DJ 1110.3** (1786.8 km) Railroad tracks.

DC 277.5 (446.2 km) **DJ 1109.5** (1785.5 km) **Muskwa Heights** (unincorporated), an industrial area with rail yard and bulk fuel outlets. Playground and baseball field.

DC 278.1 (447.5 km) **DJ 1108.9** (1784.5 km) Truck scales to west.

DC 278.4 (448 km) **DJ 1108.6** (1784.1 km) **Trapper's Den Wildlife Emporium**, Historical Mile 293 Alaska Highway. Owned and operated by a local trapping family. Native crafts, moccasins, mukluks, smoke-tanned moosehide, birchbark bas-

kets, caribou-hair tuftings, fur hats, mitts, headbands, earmuffs, gauntlets. Wild furs. Diamond Willow. Northern books and art. Antler carvings. Quality backpacking, fly-fishing gear, axes. Photographers welcome. Alaskans shop here! Located across highway from weigh scales, 6 miles south of Fort Nelson. Open 10 A.M.–5 P.M. Monday–Friday, 10 A.M.–4 P.M. Saturday. Phone 250-774-3400. Authentic and unique. www.trappersden.ca. Recommended. [ADVERTISEMENT]

DC 278.8 (448.6 km) **DJ 1108.2** (1783.4 km) **Historic Milepost 295**, Northwest Highway System sign.

DC 279 (448.9 km) **DJ 1108** (1783.1 km) Site of oriented strand board plant processing aspen and balsam poplar.

DC 280 (450.6 km) **DJ 1107** (1781.5 km) Turnoff on Sikanni Road for **Ye Olde Quilt Shoppe** (follow signs). Quilters from all over the world stop here and sign the guestbook; phone 250-774-2773.

Ye Olde Quilt Shoppe. See display ad this page.

DC 281 (451.4 km) **DJ 1106** (1779.9 km) Highway descends northbound to **Muskwa River** bridge, lowest point on the Alaska Highway (elev. 1,000 feet/305m); acesss to

Stop by the Fort Nelson Visitor Center at the Northern Rockies Regional Recreation Centre.
(©Earl L. Brown)

river, boat launch. The Muskwa River flows to the Fort Nelson River. Fair fishing at the mouth of tributaries for northern pike; some goldeye. The Fort Nelson River is too muddy for fishing. The Muskwa River valley exhibits typical river bottom balsam poplar and white spruce stands.

The Alaska Highway swings west at Fort Nelson above the Muskwa River, winding through the Canadian Rockies.

DC 281.8 (452.4 km) **DJ 1105.2** (1778.6 km) Traffic light at turnoff for Fort Nelson Airport. *NOTE: Begin 50 kmph/30 mph speed zone northbound.*

DC 283 (454.3 km) **DJ 1104** (1776.7 km) Entering Fort Nelson northbound. Fort Nelson's central business district extends along both sides of the Alaska Highway (see map on page 149).

Fort Nelson

DC 283 (454.3 km) **DJ 1104** (1776.7 km) **F 1200** (1931 km) Located at **Historical Mile 300** of the Alaska Highway, 237 miles/381 km north of Fort St. John; 330 miles/531 km south of Watson Lake, YT. **Population:** 6,147. **Emergency Services:** RCMP, phone 250-774-2777; **Fire Department,** phone 250-774-2222; **Hospital,** phone 250-774-8100; **Ambulance,** phone 250-774-2344. *NOTE: There is no 911 service in Fort Nelson or in the Northern Rockies Regional Municipality.* **Medical**, **dental**, **optometric clinics** available.

Visitor Information: The Visitor Centre is located at the west end of town in the Northern Rockies Regional Recreation Centre, at the corner of the Alaska Highway and Simpson Trail, 5500 Alaska Highway. Look for the Mile 300 marker. It is open daily, 7:30 A.M. to 7:30 P.M., in summer, and weekdays, 8:30 A.M. to 4:30 P.M., the rest of the year. Inquire here about local attractions, a guide to local hiking trails, information about the Liard Highway and current events. Contact Tourism Northern Rockies by writing Bag Service 399, Fort Nelson, BC V0C 1R0; phone 250-774-6400; tourism@northern rockies.ca; www.tourismnorthernrockies.ca.

Another good source for local information is the Fort Nelson Heritage Museum, located across the Alaska Highway from the Visitor Centre. Visit the museum for authentic displays of pioneer artifacts and to see an amazing collection of historic vehicles.

Elevation: 1,383 feet/422m. **Climate**: Winters are cold with short days. Summers are hot and the days are long. In mid-June (summer solstice), twilight continues throughout the night. The average number

The history of the Alaska Highway is featured at Fort Nelson Heritage Museum. (©Earl L. Brown)

of frost-free days annually is 116. Last frost occurs about May 11, and the first frost Sept. 21. Average annual precipitation of 17.7 inches. **Radio**: CBC 88.3-FM, The Bear 102.3-FM. **Television**: Channel 8 and cable. **Newspaper**: *Fort Nelson News* (weekly).

Transportation: Air—Scheduled service to Edmonton, Calgary, Grande Prairie, Prince George and Vancouver via Central Mountain Air. Charter service available. **Bus**—Greyhound service. **Railroad**—Canadian National Railway (freight service only).

Private Aircraft: Fort Nelson airport, 3.8 ENE; elev. 1,253 feet/382m; length 6,400 feet/1,950m; asphalt; fuel 100, Jet.

Fort Nelson is located in the lee of the Rocky Mountains, surrounded by the Muskwa, Fort Nelson and Prophet rivers. The area is heavily forested with white spruce, poplar and aspen. Geographically, the town is located about 59° north latitude and 122° west longitude.

Flowing east and north, the Muskwa, Prophet and Sikanni Chief rivers converge to form the Fort Nelson River, which flows into the Liard River, then on to the Mackenzie River, which empties into the Arctic Ocean. Rivers provided the only means of transportation in both summer and winter in this isolated region until 1922, when the Godsell Trail opened, connecting Fort Nelson with Fort St. John. The Alaska Highway linked Fort Nelson with the Outside in 1942.

In the spring, the Muskwa River frequently floods the low country around Fort Nelson and can rise more than 20 feet/6m. At an elevation of 1,000 feet/305m, the Muskwa (which means "bear") is the lowest point on the Alaska Highway. There was a danger of the Muskwa River bridge washing out every June during spring runoff until 1970, when a higher bridge—with piers arranged to prevent log jams—was built.

Fort Nelson's existence was originally based on the fur trade. In the 1920s, trapping was the main business in this isolated pioneer community populated with fewer than 200 aboriginals and a few white men. Trappers still harvest beaver, wolverine, weasel, wolf, fox, lynx, mink, muskrat and marten. Other area wildlife includes black bear, which are plentiful, some deer, caribou and a few grizzly bears. Moose remains an important food source for First Nations residents.

Fort Nelson aboriginal people are mostly Dene, who arrived here about 1775 from the Great Slave Lake area. The Dene speak an Athabascan dialect.

Fort Nelson was first established in 1805 by the North West Fur Trading Co. The post, believed to have been located about 80 miles/129 km south of Nelson Forks, was named for Lord Horatio Nelson, the English admiral who won the Battle of Trafalgar.

A second Fort Nelson was later located south of the first fort, but was destroyed by fire in 1813 after aboriginals massacred its 8 settlers. A third Fort Nelson was established

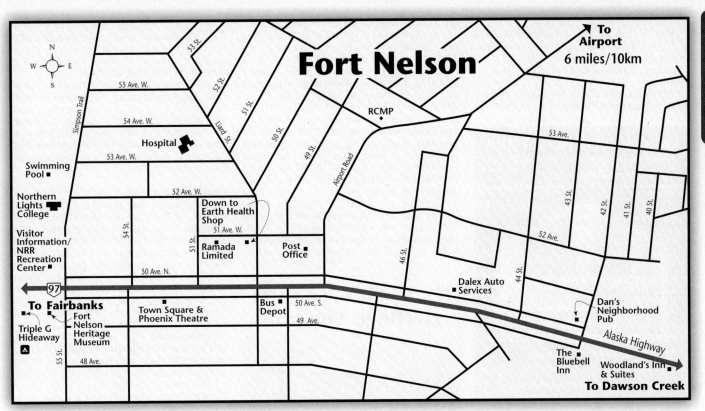

Fort Nelson

To Airport
6 miles/10km

RCMP

To Fairbanks

97

To Dawson Creek

Alaska Highway

(Map labels: 55 Ave. W., 54 Ave. W., 53 Ave. W., 52 Ave. W., 50 Ave. N., Simpson Trail, 55 St., 54 St., 53 St., 52 St., 51 St., 50 St., 49 St., Liard St., Airport Road, 46 St., 44 St., 43 St., 42 St., 41 St., 40 St., 53 Ave., 52 Ave., Hospital, Swimming Pool, Northern Lights College, Visitor Information/NRR Recreation Center, Down to Earth Health Shop, 51 Ave. W., Ramada Limited, Post Office, Town Square & Phoenix Theatre, Bus Depot, 50 Ave. S., 49 Ave., Dalex Auto Services, Dan's Neighborhood Pub, The Bluebell Inn, Woodland's Inn & Suites, Triple G Hideaway, Fort Nelson Heritage Museum, 48 Ave.)

in 1865 on the Fort Nelson River's west bank (1 mile from the present Fort Nelson airport) by W. Cornwallis King, a Hudson's Bay Co. clerk. This trading post was built to keep out the free traders who were filtering in from the Mackenzie River and Fort St. John areas. The free traders' higher fur prices were a threat to the Hudson's Bay Co., which in 1821 had absorbed the rival North West Fur Trading Co. and gained a monopoly on the fur trade in Canada.

This Hudson's Bay Co. trading post was destroyed by a flood in 1890 and a fourth Fort Nelson was established on higher ground upstream and across the river, which is now known as Old Fort Nelson. The present town of Fort Nelson is the fifth site.

Fort Nelson saw its first mail service in 1936. Scheduled air service to Fort Nelson—by ski- and floatplane—also was begun in the 1930s by Yukon Southern Air (which was later absorbed by CPAir, now Air Canada). The Canadian government began construction of an airport in 1941 as part of the Northwest Air Staging Route, and this was followed by perhaps the biggest boom to Fort Nelson—the construction of the Alaska Highway in 1942. About 2,000 soldiers were

bivouacked in Fort Nelson, which they referred to as Zero, as it was the beginning of a road to Whitehorse and another road to Fort Simpson. Later Dawson Creek became Mile 0 and Fort Nelson Mile 300.

Fort Nelson expanded in the 1940s and 1950s as people came here to work for the government or to start their own small businesses: trucking, barging, aviation, construction, garages, stores, cafes, motels and sawmills. It is surprising to consider that as recently as the 1950s Fort Nelson was still a pioneer community without power, phones, running water, refrigerators or doctors.

Fort Nelson was an unorganized territory until 1957 when it was declared an Improvement District. Fort Nelson took on village status in 1971 and town status in 1987. In 2009, the town of Fort Nelson was amalgamated with the Northern Rockies Regional District to become the Northern Rockies Regional Municipality, the first such local

FORT NELSON ADVERTISERS

Bluebell Inn, The .... Ph. 1-800-663-5267
Dalex Auto Services .... Ph. 250-774-6804
Dan's Neighborhood Pub .... Ph. 250-774-3929
Down to Earth Health Shop .... Ph. 250-774-7203
Fort Nelson Heritage
    Museum.. Ph. 250-774-3536
Northern Rockies Tourism .... Ph. 250-774-6400
Ramada Limited........................... Ph. 1-866-774-2844
Trapper's Den Wildlife
    Emporium..................................... Ph. 250-774-3400
Triple "G" Hideaway .... Ph. 250-774-2340
Woodlands Inn & Suites .... Ph. 1-866-966-3466
Ye Olde Quilt Shoppe .... Ph. 250-774-2773

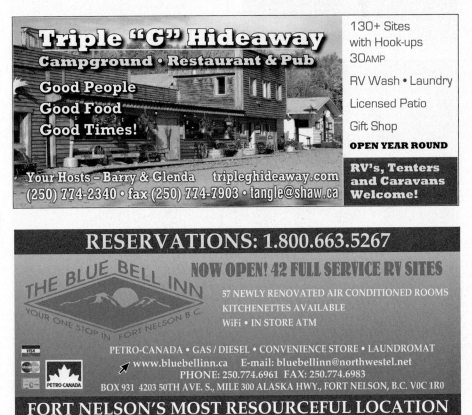

government in British Columbia.

Fort Nelson became a railhead in 1971 with the completion of a 250-mile extension of the Pacific Great Eastern Railway (now Canadian National Railway) from Fort St. John.

Agriculture is under development here with the establishment of the 55,000-acre McConachie Creek agricultural subdivision.

Northeastern British Columbia is the only sedimentary area in the province currently producing oil and gas. Oil seeps in the Fort Nelson area were noted by early residents. Major gas discoveries were made in the 1960s—when the Clarke Lake, Yoyo/Kotcho, Beaver River and Pointed Mountain gas reserves were developed—and in the 1990s. A massive discovery of unconventional shale gas 60 miles north of Fort Nelson in the Horn River Basin has further spurred economic interest in the area, with several multi-billion dollar infrastructure investments underway.

The Spectra Energy natural gas processing plant at Fort Nelson, the largest in North America, was constructed in 1964. This plant purifies the gas before sending it south through the 800-mile-long pipeline that connects the Fort Nelson area with the British Columbia lower mainland. Sulfur, a byproduct of natural gas processing, is processed in a recovery plant and shipped to outside markets in pellet form.

In 1998, the BC government created the Muskwa-Kechika Management Area west of Fort Nelson. This 6.4 million hectares of Northern Rockies wilderness is called the "Serengeti of the North." The information office is in Fort St. John; phone 250-262-0065, or visit www.muskwa-kechika.com.

Lodging & Services

Fort Nelson has about a dozen hotels/motels, including the **Woodlands Inn**, **Ramada Limited** and **The Bluebell Inn**. Most stores and other services are located on frontage roads just off the Alaska Highway. There are gas stations, grocery, general merchandise and health-food at the **Down to Earth Health Shop** (in its award-winning green building), laundromats, auto supply stores and auto repair (**Dalex**). Dining at several local restaurants, including **Dan's Neighborhood Pub** and the **Woodlands Inn's One Restaurant**. **Triple "G" Hideaway**, an RV park, also has a licensed restaurant. See ads and descriptions this section.

The post office and liquor store are on Airport Drive. There is also a liquor store attached to the Woodlands Inn, one at Dan's Neighborhood Pub and one at the Backroads Sports. There are 3 banks, all with ATMs, and a credit union on the business frontage road along the north side of the highway. Internet access is available at the library, located at Town Square, and at the Visitor Centre.

Camping

Camping at **Triple "G" Hideaway**, located at the northwest end of town adjacent the museum. Gravel RV sites available at the Bluebell Inn. Fresh water fill-up and free municipal dump station adjacent the Fort Nelson Recreation Centre at the west end of town.

Triple "G" Hideaway RV Park welcomes RVers, tenters and caravans. Located next to the museum. 130-plus sites, most with full hookups. WiFi Hotspot, some sites with cable, some pull-throughs, coin-op showers, new laundromat, RV pressure wash, licensed restaurant, licensed patio. Phone 250-774-2340; fax 250-774-7903; tangle@shaw.ca. See display ad previous page. [ADVERTISEMENT]

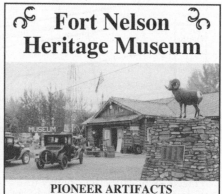

Attractions

Welcome Visitor Program: Learn more about Fort Nelson and the Northern Rockies at the Visitor Centre, located at the Northern Rockies Recreation Centre across from the Fort Nelson Heritage Museum (both are at the northwest end of town alongside the Alaska Highway). These interesting and entertaining presentations have been welcoming visitors to Fort Nelson since 1985. Programs for large groups may be organized by contacting the Visitor Center in advance; phone 250-774-6400. Open year-round

Fort Nelson Heritage Museum, on the south side of the highway at the west end of town, has excellent displays of pioneer artifacts as well as what the *Yukon News* calls "one of the most impressive collections of antique cars in British Columbia." Marl Brown, founder and curator of the museum, keeps many of the vehicles in working condition, including a 1908 Buick, which he drove to Whitehorse in June 2008.

The museum also features displays of wildlife (including an albino moose) and Alaska Highway history. Outside the museum is the Chadwick Ram, a bronze sculpture by Rick Taylor. The statue commemorates the world-record Stone sheep taken in the Muskwa Valley area in 1936.

If you have a connection with the history of the Alaska Highway, this is a must stop! Have your photo taken in front of the Alaska Highway Veterans and Builders Monument, which commemorates the workers who helped build the Alaska Highway in 1942.

This nonprofit museum charges a modest admission fee. Souvenirs and books are sold here.

Northern Rockies Regional Recreation Centre houses Fort Nelson's visitor information, a community hall, 2 ice arenas, a curling rink and fitness and meeting rooms. It is located at 5500 Alaska Highway. Fort Nelson's Skateboard Park is conveniently located next to the Recreation Centre on Simpson Trail. The Fort Nelson Aquatic Centre on Simpson Trail has a 25m swimming pool, 2 slides, whirlpool and sauna. (A new aquatic centre currently under construction is expected to open in 2015.) Phone information on any recreation centre facilities, phone 250-774-2541.

Art Fraser Memorial Park is popular with residents and visitors alike. The park boasts 2 baseball diamonds, picnic tables and firepits, volleyball and tennis courts, playground equipment, restrooms and the Rotary Spray Park (a good place to cool off on a hot day).

A paved 3-mile/5-km community walking trail begins on the Simpson Trail and connects with the Alaska Highway at the east end of town.

For golfers, the Poplar Hills Golf and Country Club, just north of town on the Old Alaska Highway, is a beautiful 9-hole course with grass greens; open daily.

Special Events. Fort Nelson hosts a number of annual benefits, dances, tournaments and exhibits. Check locally for details and dates on all events. **Canada Day** celebration July 1st, with a big parade.

Winter events include the Trappers Rendezvous in February. The Canadian Open Sled Dog Races take place in late December.

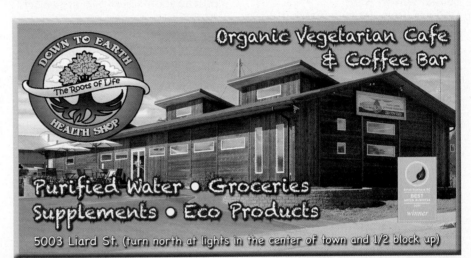

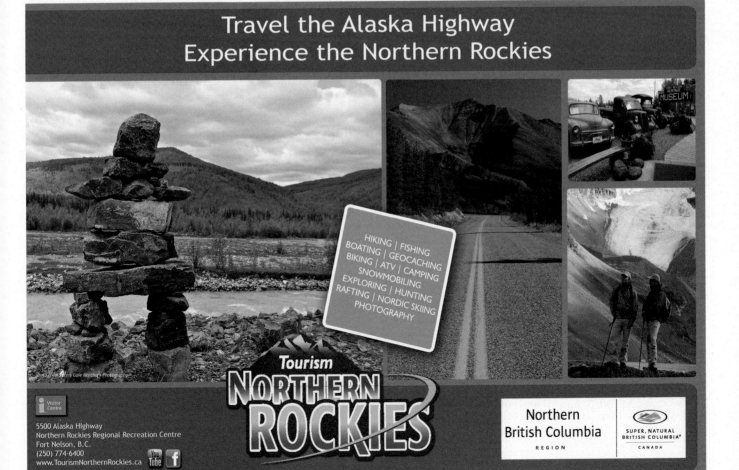

Fort Nelson's Streeper Kennels is well known on the sled dog racing circuit: Terry Streeper won more than 30 major races in 6 countries during the 1990s, and his son Blayne Streeper now carries the torch, competing in international events.

Demonstration Forest: The "Demo Forest" has a well-signed network of trails augmented with interpretive signage and a small pond. Check at the Visitor Centre for more information.

Native crafts are displayed at the **Fort Nelson Aboriginal Friendship Centre**, located on 49th Avenue.

Alaska Highway Log
(continued)

BC HIGHWAY 97 WEST
Distance from Dawson Creek (DC) is followed by distance from Delta Junction (DJ). Original mileposts are indicated in the text as Historical Mile.

In the Canada portion of *The MILEPOST®* Alaska Highway log, mileages from Dawson Creek are based on actual driving distance and kilometres are based on physical kilometreposts.

DC 284 (456.4 km) **DJ 1103** (1775.1 km) **Historic Milepost 300**, historic sign and interpretive panel at west end of Fort Nelson. Visitor information on right northbound in the Northern Rockies Regional Recreation Centre. **Fort Nelson Museum** is across the street on the south side of highway. **Triple "G" Hideaway RV Park** and public freshwater fill-up are adjacent museum. ▲

Northbound: Expect occasional rough pavement and long stretches of improved highway between Fort Nelson and Watson Lake, YT (next 327 miles/526 km). Narrow, winding road with steep grades as the Alaska Highway winds through the Rocky Mountains. Not unusual to run into foggy conditions at higher elevations. Slow for icy conditions in winter.

Leaving Fort Nelson, the highway veers to the west and winds through the northern Canadian Rockies for the next 200 miles. In this densely forested region, there are many scenic vistas, where rivers meander through the wilderness to disappear in the haze of horizons 100 miles distant. Opportunities for many fine photos are offered by the beautiful scenery along this part of the highway, and fortunate travelers occasionally see moose, bear, caribou and Stone sheep.

Southbound: Good pavement, wide road, next 284 miles/457 km (to Dawson Creek). Slow for 50 kmph/31 mph speed limit through Fort Nelson.

DC 284.7 (457.4 km) **DJ 1102.3** (1773.9 km) **Junction** with south end of Old Alaska Highway (Mile 301–308), which was bypassed in 1992 when the Muskwa Valley bypass route opened. Access to Poplar Hills Golf and Country Club on Radar Road via Old Alaska Highway; 9-hole golf course, driving range, grass greens, clubhouse (licensed), golf club rentals. Open 8 A.M. to dusk, May to October.

DC 284.8 (457.7 km) **DJ 1102.1** (1773.6 km) Welcome to Fort Nelson (southbound sign). Watch for bison ranches along highway northbound.

CAUTION: Watch for deer northbound. Slow for 70 kmph/43 mph speed limit southbound.

DC 291 (467.6 km) **DJ 1096** (1763.8 km) **Junction** with north end of Old Alaska

Highway (Mile 308–301), Parker Lake Road.

DC 301 (483.5 km) **DJ 1086** (1747.7 km) **Junction** with Liard Highway, also known as the Liard Trail (BC Highway 77/NWT Highway 7), which leads north to Fort Liard (113 miles/181 km); the Mackenzie Highway/NWT 1 to Fort Simpson (282 miles/454 km); and NWT Highways 1 and 3 to Yellowknife (596 miles/959 km). Gas is available at Fort Liard, Fort Simpson and at Fort Providence on NWT 3. Inquire in Fort Nelson about current road conditions.

> **Junction** with Liard Highway (BC Highway 77) north to Fort Liard and Mackenzie Highway to Fort Simpson and other Northwest Territories destinations. See DEH CHO ROUTE section; turn to page 341 and read log back to front.

DC 304.1 (489.4 km) **DJ 1082.9** (1742.7 km) **Historic Milepost 320**. Start of Reese & Olson contract during construction of the Alaska Highway.

DC 308.2 (495.5 km) **DJ 1078.8** (1736.1 km) Raspberry Creek.

DC 318.4 (509.1 km) **DJ 1068.6** (1719.7 km) Kledo Creek bridge. The Kledo River is a tributary of the Muskwa River. This is a popular hunting area in the fall.

DC 318.7 (509.5 km) **DJ 1068.3** (1719.2 km) Kledo Creek wayside rest area to north with litter bin.

DC 319.5 (514 km) **DJ 1067.5** (1719 km) Sign states Muskwa Recreation Area to west with boat launch and picnicking. Not recommended due to narrow, unmaintained dirt road.

DC 322.7 (516 km) **DJ 1064.3** (1712.8 km) Steamboat Creek bridge.

DC 329 (526.1 km) **DJ 1058** (1702.6 km) Double-ended turnout with litter bin to south.

Highway climbs next 6.7 miles/10.8 km northbound; winding road, 8 percent grades.

DC 332.7 (531.6 km) **DJ 1054.3** (1696.7 km) **Historical Milepost 351. STEAMBOAT** (unincorporated). Steamboat Mountain Lodge (closed). A sign here marks start of Curran & Briggs Ltd. contract during construction of the Alaska Highway.

DC 333.7 (533.2 km) **DJ 1053.3** (1695.1 km) Large turnout to south, view of Muskwa River Valley.

DC 335 (535.3 km) **DJ 1052** (1693 km) Large turnout to south; viewpoint for Muskwa River Valley.

DC 335.5 (536.1 km) **DJ 1051.5** (1692.2 km) Distance marker southbound shows Fort Nelson 80 km/50 miles, Fort St. John 488 km/303 miles.

Highway descends 8 percent winding downgrade next 6.7 miles/10.8 km southbound.

DC 335.7 (536.8 km) **DJ 1051.3** (1691.8 km) Large turnouts both sides of highway near Steamboat Mountain summit (elev. 3,500 feet/1,067m); brake check area with litter bins, toilet, information signs.

Rest area to south has a viewing platform with information panels on the Muskwa-Kechika Management Area. Views of Muskwa River Valley and Rocky Mountains to the southwest. Steamboat Mountain was named because of its resemblance to a steamship. *CAUTION: Watch for bears. Do not feed bears! A fed bear is a dead bear.*

View of Indian Head Mountain as highway descends northbound.

DC 341 (545.4 km) **DJ 1046** (1683.3 km) Double-ended dirt turnout to south. View of

Indian Head Mountain, a high crag resembling the classic Indian profile.

DC 341.5 (546.2 km) **DJ 1045.5** (1682.5 km) Gardner Creek (culvert), named after trapper and guide, Archie Gairdner. In Earl Brown's *Alcan Trailblazers*, about the construction of the Alaska Highway, Harry Spiegel recalls a recon trip in 1942 with Archie Gairdner:

"An old trapper by the name of Archie Gairdner, who has lived up here all his life, is the wrangler and is in charge of the string. He wears homemade moose-hide beaded moccasins, 'Kentucky-jean' pants, [and] a big beaten slouch hat. A hank of gray hair always protrudes from under his old hat and half covers his eyes. He sports a half growth of stubbly gray whiskers and smokes a crooked, big-bowled, sweet smelling pipe… Archie is 62 years old, and even though quite thin and weatherbeaten, he is as straight as a spruce tree and as nimble as a boy in his teens… Archie knows this country like a book and I'm sure his knowledge of this terrain is going to be very helpful for our work."

DC 343.2 (548.9 km) **DJ 1043.8** (1679.8 km) **Teetering Rock** viewpoint (watch for hiking sign) to north; litter bin and outhouses. Teetering Rock is accessible via the 7.6-mile/12.3-km **Teetering Rock Trail**; Steep climb, rated difficult, stay on marked trail and keep pets on leash.

DC 344.7 (551.4 km) **DJ 1042.3** (1677.4 km) Turnoff to south for **Tetsa River Campground Regional Park**, 1.2 miles/1.9 km via gravel road. Grass tenting area, 25 level gravel sites in trees, picnic tables, fire rings, firewood ($5/bundle), outhouses, water and bear-proof garbage containers. Camping fee $17. The Tetsa River offers good fishing for grayling to 4 lbs., average 1½ lbs., flies or spin cast with lures; Dolly Varden to 7 lbs., average 3 lbs., spin cast or flies; whitefish, small but plentiful, use flies or eggs, summer.

◀ ▲

NOTE: Actual driving distance between kilometrepost 555 and 560 is 2.9 kilometres.

DC 357.5 (571.7 km) **DJ 1029.5** (1656.8 km) **Historical Mile 375. Tetsa River Services and Campground** (description follows); gas, diesel, cabins, campground. Popular cinnamon bun stop (Ben Andrew rolls out the cinnamon roll dough in this photo).

🅱 ▲

©Judy Nadon, staff

Tetsa River Services and Campground. A must stop on your Alaska Highway vacation. We're third generation, family-run hosts, the Andrews, and we'll be happy to serve you our world-famous cinnamon buns (said by thousands to be the best they ever had) or homemade breads and pastries. Check in to our campground—country atmosphere (a creek runs through the property), with plenty of pull-through treed sites, power, WiFi, fresh well-water, showers and sani-dump all included in fee. Laundromat on location. Great for tenting or stay in one of our rustic cabins. This historic location originated with the building of the Alaska

Highway, and there are pieces of original equipment still here, left behind by the U.S. troops. All animals are welcome, and we board horses overnight. Be sure to check out our gift shop with many local crafts, a must-see art gallery with exclusive local artists' watercolour paintings. Reservations: tetsariverlodge@gmail.com, phone 250-774-1005. See display ad this page. [ADVERTISEMENT]

DC 358.9 (573.9 km) **DJ 1028.1** (1654.5 km) Gravel turnout alongside the Tetsa River, one of several as the highway follows the Tetsa River westbound. The Tetsa heads near Summit Lake in the Canadian Rockies.

DC 360.3 (576.1 km) **DJ 1026.7** (1652.3 km) Turnout with dumpster to west. Note the aspen-dominated slopes on the north side of the Tetsa River and the white spruce on the south side. Signed "riparian zones" northbound.

Slow for 40 kmph/25 mph curves.

DC 365.6 (584.6 km) **DJ 1021.4** (1643.7 km) Tetsa River bridge No. 1, clearance 17 feet/5.2m. *CAUTION: Metal grating on bridge deck.* Tetsa #1 trailhead. Parking to south at east end of bridge. The 1.2-mile/2- km trail begins across the highway and is rated as moderately easy.

DC 365.9 (585.4 km) **DJ 1021.1** (16433.2 km) Large turnout with litter bin to north.

DC 366.3 (585.6 km) **DJ 1020.7** (1642.6 km) Beaver lodges to north.

DC 367.4 (587.3 km) **DJ 1019.6** (1640.8 km) Tetsa River bridge No. 2. Turnout at south end of bridge.

The high bare peaks of the central Canadian Rockies are visible ahead westbound.

Northbound winter drivers: Carry chains or use good winter-tread tires beyond this point.

DC 371.5 (594.2 km) **DJ 1015.5** (1634.2 km) East boundary of **Stone Mountain Provincial Park.** Stone Mountain Park encompasses the Summit Pass area and extends south to include Wokkpash Protected Area. Access is via MacDonald Creek hiking trail and by 4-wheel drive from 113 Creek (**see Milepost DC 382.2**) to Wokkpash Creek trail. Contact BC Parks District Office in Fort St. John; phone 250-787-3407.

Stone sheep are frequently sighted in this area; *please reduce your speed.* Stone sheep are indigenous to the mountains of northern British Columbia and southern Yukon Territory. Darker and somewhat slighter than the bighorn sheep found in the Rocky Mountains, they are often mistaken for mountain goats, which are not found in this area. Dall or white sheep are found in the mountains of Yukon, Alaska and Northwest Territories.

DC 372.2 (595.2 km) **DJ 1014.8** (1633.1 km) **Historical Mile 390.** North Tetsa River flows under road through large culverts.

DC 372.7 (596 km) **DJ 1014.3** (1632.3 km) Pull-through turnout with litter bin to north; brake check area. Steep access to Tetsa River canyon.

DC 373.3 (597 km) **DJ 1013.7** (1631.3 km) **Historical Mile 392. SUMMIT LAKE** (unincorporated). Summit Lake Lodge has been closed for many years. *NOTE: The Summit area is known for dramatic and sudden weather changes.* The peak behind Summit Lake is Mount St. George (elev. 7,419 feet/2,261m) in the Stone Mountain range.

CAUTION: Watch for caribou and Stone sheep along the highway. DO NOT FEED WILDLIFE. Do not stop vehicles on the highway to take photos; use shoulders or turnouts. You are now in bear country ... a fed bear is a dead bear—don't feed bears!

Watch for Stone sheep and other wildlife along the highway north of Fort Nelson.
(©Sharon Nault)

DC 373.5 (597.4 km) **DJ 1013.5** (1631 km) Rough gravel side road leads 1.5 miles/2.5 km to **Flower Springs Lake trailhead;** 3.5-mile/5.7-km roundtrip hike to alpine lakes, flowers and waterfalls. *NOTE: Snow may remain on this side road well into summer.*

DC 373.6 (597.6 km) **DJ 1013.4** (1630.9 km) **Historic Milepost 392 Summit Pass** (elev. 4,250 feet/1,295m); double-ended gravel turnout to north (across from campground entrance) with toilets, litter bin, point-of-interest sign and historical milepost. This is the highest summit on the Alaska Highway; there may be ice on the lake into June. A very beautiful area of bare rocky peaks (which can be snow-covered any time of the year).

Summit Lake (Stone Mountain) Provincial Campground to south at east end of lake; campground host; 28 level gravel sites; camping fee $16; picnic tables; water and garbage containers; information shelter; boat launch. Fair fishing for lake trout, whitefish and rainbows. Area hiking trails include: Summit Peak, 4 miles/6.7 km roundtrip to upper viewpoint, rated moderately difficult; Flower Springs Trail, 8.4 miles/13.6 km roundtrip to lake edge, rated moderately easy (also see **Milepost DC 373.5**); and Summit Tower Road, 7.4 miles/12 km roundtrip, rated moderately easy.

DC 375.6 (600.8 km) **DJ 1011.4** (1627.6 km) Turnout to north.

DC 375.9 (601.3 km) **DJ 1011.1** (1627.2 km) Picnic site to south with tables and dumpster on Rocky Crest Lake. Nice spot for photos; good reflections in lake when calm.

DC 376 (601.5 km) **DJ 1011** (1627 km) Large turnout to south, Erosion Pillar Trail to north is an easy 0.6-mile/1-km hike to see erosion pillars (hoodoos).

Northbound, the highway winds through a rocky limestone gorge before descending into the wide and picturesque MacDonald River valley. *CAUTION: 8 percent grade, intermittant guardrails, winding road, wildlife on road.* Watch for safe turnouts next 2.5 miles/4 km northbound with views of the valley. Stone sheep are frequently sighted

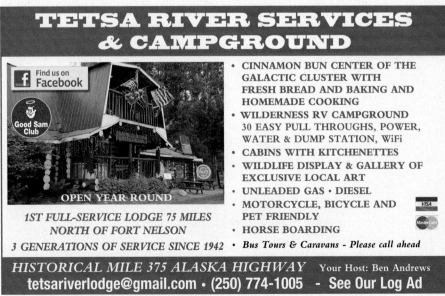

The scenery is spectacular as the Alaska Highway crosses the Canadian Rockies. (©Sharon Nault)

along this stretch of road. Also watch for caribou. Utilize your hazard lights to warn other travelers of wildlife on the road.

DC 378.2 (605.1 km) DJ 1008.8 (1623.5 km) Baba Canyon trailhead parking to north. Popular hiking trail; 3.4 miles/5.5 km round trip to first viewpoint, 6.8 miles/11 km to second viewpoint, rated moderate.

CAUTION: Stone sheep on highway.

DC 378.6 (605.7 km) DJ 1008.4 (1622.8 km) **Historical Mile 397.** Rocky Mountain Lodge. If open, gas is available here.

DC 379.7 (607.4 km) DJ 1007.3 (1621 km) Large gravel turnout to south.

DC 380.7 (609 km) DJ 1006.3 (1619.4 km) West boundary of **Stone Mountain Provincial Park** (see description at the east boundary of the park at **Milepost DC 371.5**). *CAUTION: Southbound, watch for wildlife alongside and on the road. DO NOT FEED WILDLIFE.*

DC 381.2 (611.2 km) DJ 1005.8 (1618.6 km) Highway winds along above the wide rocky valley of MacDonald Creek. MacDonald Creek and river were named for Charlie MacDonald, a Cree Indian credited with helping Alaska Highway survey crews locate the best route for the pioneer road.

DC 382.6 (613.4 km) DJ 1004.4 (1616.4 km) Distance marker northbound shows Toad River 35 km/22 miles, Watson Lake 365 km/227 miles.

Distance marker southbound shows Summit Lake 14 km/8 miles, Fort Nelson 162 km/101 miles.

DC 383.2 (614.4 km) DJ 1003.8 (1615.4 km) Trail access via abandoned Churchill Copper Mine Road (4-wheel drive only beyond river) to **Wokkpash Protected Area**, located 12 miles/20 km south of the highway. This remote area features extensive hoodoos (erosion pillars) in Wokkpash Gorge, and the scenic Forlorn Gorge and Stepped Lakes. Excellent hiking opportunities. Wokkpash Creek hiking trail follows Wokkpash Creek to Wokkpash Lake: 9 miles/15 km.

The Wokkpash is part of Northern Rocky Mountains Provincial Park. Pick up a copy of the *Hiking & Motorized Trail Guide* from the Northern Rockies Regional District or download trail maps at www.tourismnorthernrockies.ca/things_hikebikeride.php. Also visit www.env.gov.bc.ca/bcparks/explore/parkpgs/n_rocky/.

DC 383.3 (614.6 km) DJ 1003.7 (1615.3 km) 113 Creek. The creek was named during construction of the Alaska Highway for its distance from Mile 0 at Fort Nelson. While Dawson Creek was to become Mile 0 on

the completed pioneer road, clearing crews began their work at Fort Nelson, since a rough winter road already existed between Dawson Creek and Fort Nelson. Stone Range to the northeast and Muskwa Ranges of the Rocky Mountains to the west.

DC 384.2 (615.4 km) DJ 1002.8 (1613.8 km) Side road to 115 Creek and **MacDonald Creek**; informal camping. Beaver dams nearby. Fishing for grayling and Dolly Varden.

DC 385.4 (616.6 km) DJ 1001.6 (1611.9 km) 115 Creek bridge. Double-ended turnout with dumpster to south at east end of bridge. Like 113 Creek, 115 Creek was named during construction of the Alaska Highway for its distance from Fort Nelson, Mile 0 for clearing crews.

DC 386.6 (618.5 km) DJ 1000.4 (1609.9 km) Turnout above MacDonald River.

DC 390.5 (624.8 km) DJ 996.5 (1603.7 km) **Historical Mile 408**; Northwest Highway System commemorative sign for "Camp 120." MacDonald River Services (closed for many years).

DC 392.5 (627.8 km) DJ 994.5 (1600.4 km) MacDonald River bridge, clearance 17 feet/5.2m. *CAUTION: Metal grating bridge deck.* Large, informal, gravel turnout to north at east end of bridge; access to MacDonald River. Fair fishing from May to July for Dolly Varden and grayling.

Narrow road, loose gravel patches, eroded road shoulders. Highway winds through narrow valley northbound. Magnificent mountain views and photo ops for travelers.

DC 399.1 (638.6 km) DJ 987.9 (1589.8 km) Stringer Creek bridge.

DC 400.7 (641.1 km) DJ 986.3 (1587.2 km) **Racing River** bridge, clearance 17 feet/5.2m, posted speed limit 50 Kmph on bridge. *CAUTION: Bridge deck is metal grate. slow for curve at east end of bridge.* Turnout with dumpster to north at east end of bridge. The Racing River forms the boundary between the Sentinel Range and the Stone Range, both of which are composed of folded and sedimentary rock.

Note the open south-facing slopes on the north side of the river that are used as winter range by Stone sheep, elk and deer. Periodic controlled burns encourage the growth of forage grasses and shrubs, and also allow chinook winds to clear snow from grazing grounds in winter. *CAUTION: Watch for horses and wildlife on highway.* Racing River, grayling to 16 inches; Dolly Varden to 2 lbs., use flies, July through September.

DC 401.2 (641.9 km) DJ 985.8 (1586.4 km) **Historical Mile 419**. **Folding Mountain Bed and Breakfast** welcomes you year-round. From our guestbook: "Blair and Rebecca extended a warm welcome the minute we arrived and made sure our every need was met until we left. The beautifully built log lodge was clean and comfortable, the scenery breathtaking—wildife in the back fields. We felt truly out in the wilderness yet had all the comfort and safety of home." Experience it yourself! Phone 250-232-5451. www.foldingmtnbnb.com. See display ad this page.

DC 404.1 (646.6 km) DJ 982.9 (1581.8 km) Welcome to Toad River (northbound sign). *Slow for 70- to 50-kmph/43- to 31-mph speed zones northbound.*

DC 404.6 (647.4 km) DJ 982.4 (1581

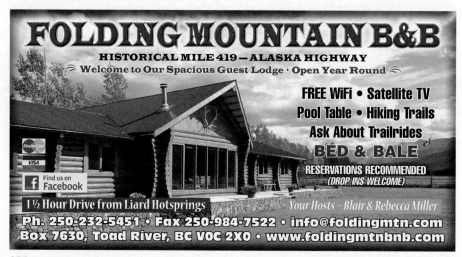

km) **Historical Mile 422. TOAD RIVER** (unincorporated). Situated in a picturesque valley, Toad River has a highway maintenance camp, school and **Toad River Lodge**, which has been a fixture on the highway since the 1940s. The historic lodge, on the southwest side of highway, has a restaurant,

©Judy Nadon, staff

modern motel and cabins (see photo above), gas, diesel, propane, tire repair, and RV and tent campsites nestled on Reflection Lake. Toad River Lodge is known for its collection of hats, which numbered 8,900 in 2013. Post office and phone in lodge, which is also a Greyhound bus stop. Inquire at the lodge about wildlife viewing, fishing and hunting guide outfitters in the area.

Toad River Lodge & RV Park. See display ad this page. 🅿 🅰

Private Aircraft: Toad River airstrip; elev. 2,400 feet/732m; length 3,000 feet/914m. Unattended; no fuel; prior permission to land required.

DC 405.5 (648.8 km) **DJ 981.5** (1579.5 km) Turnout to south with **Historic Milepost 422**. Sign and interpretive panel commemorate Toad River/Camp 138 Jupp Construction.

DC 406.3 (650.1 km) **DJ 980.7** (1578.2 km) Turnout with dumpster.

DC 406.4 (650.3 km) **DJ 980.6** (1578.1 km) Wood Creek culvert.

DC 406.9 (651.1 km) **DJ 980.1** (1577.3 km) 141 Creek culvert.

DC 407.5 (652 km) **DJ 979.5** (1576.3 km) **Historical Mile 426**. Camping, cabins. 🅰

DC 409.2 (654.6 km) **DJ 977.8** (1573.6 km) South boundary of **Muncho Lake Provincial Park**. (The north boundary is at **Milepost DC 460.7**.) The park straddles the Alaska Highway, encompassing the alpine peaks and valleys around Muncho Lake.

DC 410.2 (656.2 km) **DJ 976.8** (1572 km) **Stone Mountain Safaris Bed and Breakfast.** Enjoy a relaxing stay in a beautiful mountain setting at our cedar lodge just 5 km in off the Alaska Highway. Each of our 4 guest rooms is furnished with a queen and at least one twin bed, and all 4 rooms share 2 bathrooms. We also board horses. Book hiking treks, custom-tailored excursions and adventures, weddings, corporate and personal retreats. Open year-round. Your hosts, Leif and Kellie Olsen. bnb@stonemountain-safaris.com; phone 250-232-5469. www.stonemountainsafaris.com. [ADVERTISEMENT]

DC 410.6 (656.8 km) **DJ 976.4** (1571.3 km) Large gravel turnout with information panel on Folded Mountain:

"Originally, all of the rock of the Canadian Rockies lay flat on the shallow sea bed of the western continental shelf, where it had accumulated grain by grain for over a billion years. About 175 million years ago, the continent of North America began to move westward, overriding the Pacific floor and colliding with offshore chains of islands.

"The continental shelf was caught in the squeeze.

The flat-lying layers slowly buckled into folds like those you see here. As time passed, folded mountain ranges sprang up across British Columbia. By 120 million years ago, the Rockies were showing above the sea. They grew for another 75 million years, rising faster than erosion could tear them down—likely reaching Himalayan heights. Active mountain building ended in the Canadian Rockies some 45 million years ago. The peaks have since been eroded to a small fraction of their original size."

DC 411 (657.4 km) **DJ 976** (1570.7 km) *Watch for caribou.* The highway follows beautiful turquoise-coloured **Toad River** westbound. Fishing for grayling to 16 inches; Dolly Varden to 10 lbs., use flies, July through September. 🐟

DC 413.4 (661.3 km) **DJ 973.6** (1566.8 km) **Historic Milepost 431**.

DC 415.5 (664.7 km) **DJ 971.5** (1563.4 km) 150 Creek culvert.

DC 416.9 (667.1 km) **DJ 970.1** (1561.2 km) 151 Creek culvert.

DC 417.6 (668.2 km) **DJ 969.4** (1560 km) Gravel turnout to north with sign about flash floods (excerpt follows).

"The northern Canadian Rockies are famous for their summer downpours. When heavy rains fall on mountains largely bare of trees and other soil-holding vegetation, the water carries sand, gravel and even boulders into the gullies between the peaks. Everything washes out onto the flat valley floors.

"This is one such deposit. It is called an alluvial fan because its outline resembles an open fan. Material carried by streams is called alluvium. This becomes distributed evenly over the fan as the stream [word obscured] sweeps back and forth, changing its position constantly."

Centennial Falls to south. (Waterfall dries

The blue-green waters of Muncho Lake are a photographer's delight. (©Earl L. Brown)

up in summer, unless it is raining.)

DC 419.8 (671.7 km) **DJ 967.2** (1556.5 km) **Toad River** bridge. Turnout to south at west end of bridge; fishing.

CAUTION: Watch for Stone sheep and caribou along the highway (or standing in the middle of the highway). DO NOT FEED WILD-LIFE. Do not stop vehicles on the highway to take photos; use shoulders or turnouts.

DC 421.9 (675 km) **DJ 965.1** (1553.1 km) Watch for moose in boggy areas alongside road; morning or evening best.

Narrow winding road with 60-kmph/37-mph curves southbound.

DC 422.9 (677 km) **DJ 964.1** (1551.5 km) Double-ended gravel turnout to east. Winter travelers put on chains here (a sign to this effect in French is here). Distance marker northbound shows Muncho Lake 21 km/13 miles, Watson Lake 300 km/186 miles.

Highway climbs long winding grades to 7 percent next 6.5 miles/11 km northbound.

The highway swings north for Alaska-bound travelers. For Dawson Creek-bound travelers, the highway follows an easterly direction.

DC 424 (678.6 km) **DJ 963** (1549.8 km) **Historic Milepost 443** at Peterson Creek No. 1 bridge. The creek was named for local trapper Pete Peterson, who helped Alaska Highway construction crews select a route through this area. Historic sign marks start of Campbell Construction Co. Ltd. contract during construction of the Alaska Highway.

DC 424.3 (679 km) **DC 962.7** (1549.3 km) The Village, Historical Mile 442, has been closed for many years.

DC 429.5 (687.4 km) **DJ 957.5** (1540.9 km) Double-ended gravel turnout to northeast with view of Sawtooth Mountains, information shelter and dumpster.

Chain removal area in winter for southbound traffic.

DC 432.5 (692.7 km) **DJ 954.5** (1536.1 km) Large gravel turnout to northeast.

DC 433.7 (694.6 km) **DJ 953.3** (1534.1 km) Distance marker southbound shows Toad River 45 km/28 miles, Fort Nelson 241 km/150 miles.

DC 434.1 (695 km) **DJ 952.9** (1533.5 km)

Muncho Creek.

DC 436 (698 km) **DJ 951** (1530.4 km) **Historic Milepost 456**. A historic sign and interpretive panel mark Muncho Lake/Refueling Stop, Checkpoint during Alaska Highway construction.

The highway along Muncho Lake required considerable rock excavation by the Army in 1942. Horses were used to haul away the rocks. The original route went along the top of the cliffs, which proved particularly hazardous. (Portions of this hair-raising road can be seen high above the lake; local residents use it for mountain biking.) The Army relocated the road by benching into the cliffs a few feet above lake level.

CAUTION: Watch for Stone sheep and caribou on the highway north of here. Please DO NOT FEED WILDLIFE. Do not stop on the highway to take photos; use turnouts.

DC 436.5 (698.7 km) **DJ 950.5** (1529.6 km) Entering **MUNCHO LAKE** (pop. 29) northbound. Double G Services to northeast; lodging, restaurant and gas.

DC 436.9 (699.2 km) **DJ 950.1** (1529 km) Gravel airstrip to west; length 1,200 feet/366m.

NOTE: Highway narrows northbound as road winds along Muncho Lake. Slow for 30 kmph/18 mph curves. No guard rails. Use roadside turnouts to take photos. Watch for falling rock.

DC 437.3 (700 km) **DJ 949.7** (1528.4 km) South end of **Muncho Lake**, known for its beautiful deep green and blue waters, is 7.5 miles/12 km in length, and 1 mile/1.6 km in width; elevation is 2,680 feet/817m. "Muncho" means "big lake" in the Kaska language, and it certainly is one of the largest natural lakes in the Canadian Rockies. The colours are attributed to copper oxide leaching into the lake. Deepest point has been reported to be 730 feet/223m, although government tests have not located any point deeper than 400 feet/122m. The lake drains the Sentinel Range to the east and the Terminal Range to the west, feeding the raging Trout River in its 1,000-foot/305-m drop to the mighty Liard River. The mountains surrounding the lake are approx-

imately 7,000 feet/2,134m high.

For fishermen, Muncho Lake offers Dolly Varden; some grayling; rainbow trout; whitefish to 12 inches; and lake trout. Record lake trout is 50 lbs. Make sure you have a current British Columbia fishing license and a copy of the current regulations.

DC 437.6 (700.5 km) **DJ 949.4** (1527.9 km) Strawberry Flats Campground, Muncho Lake Provincial Park; 15 sites on rocky lakeshore, picnic tables, outhouses, garbage containers. Camping fee $16. Old Alaska Highway Trail (1.2 miles/2 km). *CAUTION: Bears in area.*

DC 440 (704.4 km) **DJ 947** (1524 km) Double-ended gravel turnout with information panels on Stone Sheep (excerpts follow), including a map showing the geographic divide between Stone and Bighorn sheep:

"An easy way to identify male and female Stone sheep is to look at the horns. Rams (males) have large, strongly curved horns; ewes (females) have smaller, straighter horns. Sheep horns continue to grow throughout their lives and do not fall off like antlers of the deer family. The larger its horns, the more status a ram has in a herd. Stone sheep rams use their horns for battering each other during the fall mating season. Larger rams usually have the first opportunity for mating.

"Named after the American hunter-explorer, Andrew J. Stone, Stone sheep are a subspecies of the pure white Dall sheep found in the Yukon (Ovis dalli dalli). These sheep are sometimes called "thinhorn," because their horns are smaller than those of bighorn sheep found further south. Stone sheep eat grass, wildflowers and leaves of shrubs. The sheep are often seen along the roadsides licking natural and artificial accumulations of salt."

Watch for caribou and sheep on highway. Trailhead for Stone Sheep hiking trail at outwash plain at this turnout.

CAUTION: Watch for falling rock.

DC 442.2 (707.9 km) **DJ 944.8** (1520.8 km) **Historical Mile 462**; historic highway lodge location. **Northern Rockies Lodge Ltd.** (description follows) is open year-round. The lodge offers accommodations, a full-service restaurant (try their spaetzle!), gas and diesel, seasonal camping (with and without hookups) and a flying service. Inside the main lodge, the restaurant features a hand-carved map of the region, with lights reflecting the flight path of the lodge's charter service planes. Flights with Liard Air range from an afternoon of flightseeing the Northern Rockies to all day fishing trips and visits to Virginia Falls in Nahanni National Park.

©Kris Valencia, staff

The Northern Rockies Lodge is considered by travellers to be the best place to stay on the Alaska Highway. Clean, comfortable hotel rooms are open year-round and feature full ensuite washrooms and TV. With full service hotel, RV campsites, dining room, lounge and beautiful lakeshore chalets, the Northern Rockies Lodge is the most popular

stop for motorcyclists, campers, families and couples alike. The one-of-a-kind log building stands four stories tall in a park-like setting between the Alcan and the shores of Muncho Lake. Unique wooden carvings in the dining room include an impressive 20-foot, hand-carved map of the region. The Northern Rockies Lodge also operates tours in the area including flightseeing, fly-in fishing and day trips to Virginia Falls in Nahanni Naitonal Park. Please visit www.northernrockieslodge.com or call 1-800-663-5269. See display ad this page. [ADVERTISEMENT]

DC 442.9 (709 km) DJ 944.1 (1519.3 km) Turnoff to west for MacDonald campground, Muncho Lake Provincial Park; 15 level gravel sites, firewood, picnic tables, outhouses, boat launch, information shelter, pump water, litter bins. Camping fee $16. *CAUTION: Watch for bears in area.*

DC 443.6 (710.1 km) DJ 943.4 (1518.4 km) **Historical Mile 463**. Muncho Lake Lodge, a historic highway lodge closed for many years, is now **Muncho Lake RV Park**; full-service sites, tenting, showers.

Muncho Lake RV Park. See display ad this page.

DC 444.9 (712.2 km) DJ 942.1 (1516.1 km) **Muncho Lake viewpoint** to southwest with **Historic Milepost 463**; large parking area, litter bins. Information panels include facts about Muncho Lake and construction of the Alaska Highway along the lake. Sign points out the location of Peterson Mountain (at the south end of lake), the Terminal Range (to the west of the lake) and the Sentinal Range (to the east). The island you see is Honeymoon Island. Memorial to Ernie Birkbeck (1939–2000), who worked as a Contractor Inspector on the Alaska Highway for 26 years. *CAUTION: Watch for Stone sheep on highway next 10 miles/16 km northbound.*

DC 447.9 (717 km) DJ 939.1 (1511.3 km) Long double-ended gravel turnout to east at outwash plain. Boulder Canyon hiking trailhead at south end of turnout.

DC 453.3 (725.6 km) DJ 933.7 (1502.6 km) Turnout to east.

DC 454 (726.7 km) DJ 933 (1501.5 km) Mineral lick; watch for Stone sheep. Hiking trail to west is a 5- to 10-minute loop hike to viewpoints overlooking the Trout River. Trail is slippery when wet and has steep banks; use caution when hiking and bring insect repellent. Sheep, goats, caribou and elk frequent the steep mineral-laden banks. Good photo opportunities, early morning best.

DC 455.5 (729.2 km) DJ 931.5 (1499.1 km) Large turnout with litter bin and park information sign to west. Brake check area for northbound trucks; chain removal area

A favorite stop with Alaska Highway travelers: Liard River Hotsprings. *(©Kris Valencia, staff)*

in winter for southbound vehicles.

Beautiful views northbound of Trout River valley as highway descends. Watch for black bears feeding on grassy highway verge in summer. *CAUTION: Watch for Stone sheep on highway next 10 miles/16 km southbound!*

Highway descends 9 percent grade next 2.2 miles/3.5 km northbound.

DC 457.7 (732.7 km) **DJ 929.3** (1495.5 km) **Trout River bridge.** The Trout River flows into the Liard River. The Trout River offers rafting: Grade II from Muncho Lake to the bridge here; Grade III to Liard River. Inquire locally for river conditions. Trout River, grayling and whitefish; May, June and August best.

The Alaska Highway follows the Trout River for several miles northbound. *Highway climbs 9 percent grade next 2.2 miles/3.5 km southbound. Chains recommended in winter.*

DC 459.8 (734.8 km) **DJ 927.2** (1492.1 km) **Historic Milepost 477.** Gravel turnout to east by Trout River. Leaving Muncho Lake Provincial Park southbound.

DC 461.6 (737.6 km) **DJ 925.4** (1489.2 km) Prochniak Creek bridge. The creek was named for a member of Company A, 648th Engineers Topographic Battalion, during construction of the Alaska Highway. North boundary of Muncho Lake Provincial Park.

DC 463.4 (740.5 km) **DJ 923.6** (1486.3 km) Large gravel turnout to southwest.

NOTE: Slow for 40 kmph/25 mph S-curves and watch for falling rock next 6 miles/10 km northbound.

DC 469.5 (749.5 km) **DJ 917.5** (1476.5 km) Double-ended turnout with litter bin to northeast.

A fire in 1959 swept across the valley bottom here. Lodgepole pine, trembling aspen and paper birch are the dominant species that re-established this area.

DC 471.4 (754 km) **DJ 915.6** (1473.5 km) Gravel turnout to west.

DC 472.5 (756 km) **DJ 914.5** (1471.7 km) Washout Creek (signed).

Sweeping view of Liard River alley as highway descends northbound. The mighty Liard River was named by French-Canadian voyageurs for the poplar ("liard") that line the banks of the lower river. The Alaska Highway parallels the Liard River from here

north to Watson Lake. The river offered engineers a natural line to follow during routing and construction of the Alaska Highway in 1942.

DC 473 (756.6 km) **DJ 914** (1470.9 km) Gravel turnout to west.

Begin 2.1-mile/3.4 km southbound passing lane on uphill grade. Slow vehicles keep to right.

DC 475.3 (760.8 km) **DJ 911.7** (1467.2 km) **Historic Milepost 493.**

DC 476.7 (763 km) **DJ 910.3** (1464.9 km) Lower Liard River bridge (elev. 1,400 feet/427m). This is the only remaining suspension bridge on the Alaska Highway. The 1,143-foot suspension bridge was built by the American Bridge Co. and McNamara Construction Co. of Toronto in 1943.

The **Liard River** flows eastward toward the Fort Nelson River and parallels the Alaska Highway from the Lower Liard River bridge to the BC–YT border. The scenic Grand Canyon of the Liard is to the east and not visible from the highway. Many early fur traders lost their lives negotiating the wild waters of the Liard. The river offers good fishing for Dolly Varden, grayling, northern pike and whitefish.

DC 477.1 (763.8 km) **DJ 909.9** (1464.3 km) **Historical Mile 496.** Entering **LIARD RIVER** (unincorporated) northbound.

DC 477.7 (764.7 km) **DJ 909.3** (1463.3 km) Large double-ended parking area to southwest with pay phone, NWHS sign and **Historic Milepost 496**, across the highway from entrance to **Liard River Hotsprings Provincial Park** to the northeast (description follows).

Liard River Hotsprings has long been a favorite stop for Alaska Highway travelers. Open year-round, Liard River Hotsprings Provincial Park has 53 large, shaded, level gravel sites (some will accommodate 2 RVs), picnic tables, picnic shelter, water pump, garbage containers, firewood, fire rings, playground and restrooms at the hot springs with wheelchair-accessible toilet. Fees charged (cash only) are as follows: Camping fee (which includes use of hot springs pools), $21 from May 1 to October; day-use fee $5/person or $10/vehicle; annual family hot springs pool pass $20, single adult $10. Off-

season rates as posted. Emergency phone at park headquarters. Park gate closes at 10 P.M. and opens at 6 A.M. *CAUTION: Beware of bears!*

A short walk leads to the pools, about a 0.4-mile/0.6-km walk. Plenty of parking at trailhead. The boardwalk trail crosses a wetlands environment that supports more than 250 boreal forest plants, including 14 orchid species and 14 plants that survive at this latitude because of the hot springs. Watch for moose feeding in the wetlands. There are 2 hot springs pools (Alpha and Beta pools) with water temperatures ranging from 108° to 126°F/42° to 52°C. *NOTE: No pets on boardwalk trail or at pools and you may want to leave silver jewelry off. One reader noted that the sulphur water oxidizes it and turns it black in a few minutes.*

DC 477.8 (764.9 km) **DJ 909.2** (1463.2 km) **Historical Mile 497.** Liard Hotsprings Lodge.

NORTHBOUND: Watch for buffalo on road next 56 miles/90 km! Use EXTREME CAUTION at night and in fog or other poor driving conditions.

SOUTHBOUND: Slow for 70- to 50-kmph/43- to 31-mph speed zones.

DC 480 (768.3 km) **DJ 907** (1459.6 km) Mould Creek. Named for trapper Tom Mould who assisted troops during construction of the Alaska Highway.

DC 482.8 (772.9 km) **DJ 904.2** (1455.1 km) Teeter Creek; named for one of the surveyors with Company A, 648 Topographical Battalion, during construction of the Alaska Highway. A footpath leads upstream; 10-minute walk to falls. Grayling fishing.

DC 489 (783.6 km) **DJ 898** (1445.2 km) **Private Aircraft**: Liard River airstrip; elev. 1,400 feet/427m; length 4,000 feet/1,219m; gravel; no fuel.

DC 495 (792.3 km) **DJ 892** (1435.5 km) **Historic Milepost 514.** Smith River bridge, clearance 17 feet/5.2m.

DC 495.2 (792.6 km) **DJ 891.8** (1435.2 km) Access to **Smith River Falls** via 1.6-mile/2.6-km gravel road; not recommended for large RVs or trailers or in wet weather. Hiking trail (current status unknown) down to 2-tiered Smith River Falls from the parking area. Grayling fishing.

DC 497.1 (795.7 km) **DJ 889.9** (1432.1 km) Historic sign here commemorates

Smith River Airport, part of the Northwest Staging Route, located about 25 miles/40 km from the highway (accessible by 4-wheel drive only). In the early days of the Northwest Staging Route—the system of airfields used to ferry supplies and aircraft to Alaska and on to Russia during WWII—there were no aeronautical maps to guide pilots flying between Edmonton and Whitehorse. The young and relatively inexperienced pilots were given hand-drawn maps showing rivers and lakes and sent on their way with a cheery "you can't miss it!", according to the book, *Wings Over the Alaska Highway: A Photographic History of Aviation on the Alaska Highway*. This kind of navigation led to some misadventures. In January 1942, three B-26 Martin Marauder bombers, lost and out of fuel in a storm, crash-landed in the Million Dollar Valley west of here. All crew members survived and the incident became one of the more popular stories from that time. The bombers were salvaged in the early 1970s.

DC 507.7 (812.9 km) DJ 879.3 (1415.2 km) Double-ended turnout to west alongside Liard River.

DC 509.4 (815.6 km) DJ 877.6 (1412.3 km) Large double-ended turnout with dumpster to west.

DC 513.5 (822 km) DJ 873.5 (1405.7 km) Distance marker southbound shows Liard River 58 km/36 miles, Fort Nelson 365 km/227 miles.

Watch for bison on the highway between Liard Hotsprings and Contact Creek.
(©Kris Valencia, staff)

©Kris Valencia, staff

DC 513.9 (822.8 km) DJ 873.1 (1405 km) **Historical Mile 533. COAL RIVER. Coal River Lodge**; food (good buffalo burgers), gas, diesel, lodging and camping May-Sept. Historic highway lodge location: Coal River Lodge dates back to 1949.

🅱 🅰

Coal River Lodge & RV. See display ad this page.

DC 514.2 (823.2 km) DJ 872.8 (1404.6 km) **Historical Mile 533.2.** Coal River bridge. The Coal River flows into the Liard River south of the bridge.

DC 519.5 (831.7 km) DJ 867.5 (1396.1 km) Turnoff to southwest for **Whirlpool Canyon.** Short, unpaved side road leads to small gravel parking area with litter bin, and view of Liard River rapids (not visible from the highway). Primitive campsites in trees. *NOTE: Limited turnaround space, not recommended for large vehicles or vehicles towing trailers.*

Although identified by one astute reader as Mountain Portage Rapids, Whirlpool Canyon (actually located farther downstream) is a more apt description of this location. Here, the Liard River—and any debris in the water—swirls violently around a backwater created by the riverbank, while white-water rapids characterize the main channel.

🅰

DC 524.2 (839.2 km) DJ 862.8 (1388.5 km) **Historical Mile 543. FIRESIDE**; no services. This community was partially

destroyed by fire in the summer of 1982. Evidence of the fire can still be seen from south of Fireside north to Lower Post. The 1982 burn, known as the Eg fire, was the second largest fire in British Columbia history, destroying more than 400,000 acres.

Evidence of a more recent fire may be seen between Fireside and Liard Hot Springs. The summer 2009 burn jumped the highway and briefly halted traffic.

DC 524.7 (840.3 km) DJ 862.3 (1387.7 km) Turnout above Liard River's Cranberry Rapids to west. There are additional gravel turnouts northbound not included in log.

DC 533.1 (853 km) DJ 853.9 (1374.2 km) Turnouts with litter bins to southwest and northeast (about 0.1 mile apart) at summit overlooking the Liard River. Brake check and chain removal area for traffic. *Begin 9 percent downgrade southbound.*

DC 536 (857.8) DJ 851 (1369.5 km) Distance marker southbound shows Fireside 14 km/8 miles, Fort Nelson 398 km/247 miles, Coal River 30 km/18 miles.

DC 550.9 (880 km) DJ 836.1 (1345.5 km) **Historical Mile 570, Allen's Lookout.** Very large gravel parking area to west with picnic tables, firepit, outhouse and litter bin. Goat Mountain is to west.

Legend has it that a band of outlaws took advantage of this sweeping view of the Liard River to attack and rob riverboats. A cairn near the picnic area is dedicated to the surveyors of the Alaska Highway. It shows the elevation and latitude and longitude of Allen's Lookout (N59°52'34", W127°24'21").

EXTREME CAUTION: Watch for bison next 73 miles/117 km southbound to Liard Hotsprings.

DC 558 (893.4 km) DJ 829 (1334.1 km) Highway swings west for Alaska-bound travelers. The Alaska Highway crosses the BC–YT border 6 times before reaching the official border at Historic Milepost 627.

Watch for grizzly bears feeding on grassy highway verge.

DC 560.4 (902.2 km) DJ 826.6 (1330.2 km) Scoby Creek.

DC 561 (903 km) DJ 826 (1329.3 km) Welcome to Fort Nelson Forest District (southbound sign).

DC 562.3 (905 km) DJ 824.7 (1327.2 km) **Historic Milepost 585** cairn. Large gravel turnout.

DC 567.9 (909.4 km) DJ 819.1 (1318.2 km) **Historic Milepost 588, Contact Creek.** Gravel turnout to west; interpretive panel. Access to creek to east at north end of creek crossing.

Contact Creek was named by soldiers of the 35th Regiment from the south and the 340th Regiment from the north who met

here in September 1942, completing the southern sector of the Alaska Highway. A personal reminiscence about the work of A Company 35th Combat Engineers is found in Chester Russell's *Tales of a Catskinner*.

CAUTION: Watch for bison on road.

DC 570 (912.9 km) **DJ 817** (1314.8 km) **Historical Mile 590. CONTACT CREEK.** Contact Creek Lodge (pictured above) is open year-round; snacks, gas, diesel, propane, minor vehicle repairs, 24-hour towing and pay phone. Historic highway lodge location.

Contact Creek Lodge. See display ad this page.

NOTE: Slow for 70 kmph/43 mph speed zone through Contact Creek.

DC 571.9 (915.7 km) **DJ 815.1** (1311.7 km) Cosh Creek.

DC 573.9 (918.9 km) **DJ 813.1** (1308.5 km) Highway crosses Irons Creek. A temporary single-lane bridge replaced the Iron Creek culvert here after it collapsed in June 2001. The culvert, which had been installed in 1998, was one of the largest culverts in the world at 25 feet high, 135 feet long and 62 feet wide. The culvert failure closed the Alaska Highway for 2 days.

According to local sources, Iron Creek was named during construction of the Alaska Highway for the trucks that stopped here to put on tire irons (chains) in order to make it up the hill.

DC 575.9 (922 km) **DJ 811.1** (1305.3 km) **Historical Mile 596.** Iron Creek Lodge (closed).

DC 585 (937.2 km) **DJ 802** (1290.6 km) **Historical Mile 605.9.** Hyland River bridge. The **Hyland River**, a tributary of the Liard River, was named for Frank Hyland, an early-day trader at Telegraph Creek on the Stikine River. Hyland operated trading posts throughout northern British Columbia, competing successfully with the Hudson's Bay Co.

Good fishing for rainbow, Dolly Varden and grayling.

DC 598.5 (956.6 km) **DJ 788.5** (1268.9 km) Mayfield Creek.

DC 602.8 (963.5 km) **DJ 784.2** (1262 km) Turnout with litter bin to southwest.

DC 603.1 (964 km) **DJ 783.9** (1261.5 km) *CAUTION: Watch for bison on highway southbound between Kilometreposts 750 and 680* (readerboard here in summer 2013).

YUKON HIGHWAY 1

The Alaska Highway (Yukon Highway 1) dips back into British Columbia several times before making its final crossing into the Yukon Territory near Morley Lake.

DC 603.3 (964.5 km) **DJ 783.7** (1261.2 km) Welcome to British Columbia (southbound sign) at turnout to southwest; point-of-interest signs.

DC 604.3 (966.1 km) **DJ 782.7** (1259.6 km) Southbound signs: Use winter tires or carry chains beyond this point Oct. 1–April 30. Commercial vehicles must carry chains.

DC 605.4 (968 km) **DJ 781.6** (1257.8 km) Distance marker northbound shows Watson Lake 12 km/7 miles, Whitehorse 457 km/284 miles.

DC 605.6 (968.4 km) **DJ 781.4** (1257.5 km) Double-ended rest area to southwest; toilets.

DC 605.9 (968.9 km) **DJ 781.1** (1257 km) Distance marker southbound shows Fort Nelson 512 km/318 miles, Dawson Creek

968 km/602 miles.

DC 607 (970.6 km) **DJ 780** (1255.3 km) Long double-ended turnout to northeast with Welcome to Yukon sign. Across the highway to the southwest is the parking lot for **Lucky Lake** and **Liard Canyon Recreation Site** (description follows).

Relatively shallow, Lucky Lake warms up quickly in summer, making it a popular local swimming hole. This is a very nice spot with a picnic area, waterslide and adjacent ball diamond. Lucky Lake is stocked with rainbow trout; excellent fishing. A 1.4-mile/2.2-km hiking trail through mature pine and spruce forest down to observation platform overlooking the Liard River. Information panels on natural features of the area. Allow at least an hour for hike. Watch for gray jays, Northern flickers and black-capped and boreal chickadees.

DC 609.5 (974.3 km) **DJ 777.5** (1251.2 km) Watson Lake 2 km/1.2 miles (northbound sign). Easy-to-miss turnoff to southwest for **Watson Lake Riding Association Equestrian Centre.** (Look for pink metal horse southbound; look for distance sign northbound.)

The facility offers reasonably priced overnight boarding (indoor and outdoor 12x12 pens) for horses, and horse owners may camp on the grounds; phone Cheryl O'Brien at (250) 536-2099 for details. The Centre hosts summer classes (in gymkhana, vaulting and canoeing), boards local horses, and has a horse show in July.

DC 610.4 (976 km) **DJ 776.6** (1249.8 km) Welcome to Watson Lake (northbound sign). Entrance to weigh station.

Slow for 70 kmph/43mph then 30 kmph/ 18 mph speed zones northbound through Watson Lake.

Resume 100 kmph/62 mph speed limit southbound.

DC 610.5 (976.3 km) **DJ 776.5** (1249.6 km) **Historical Mile 632.5.** Campground Services. Store and RV park were closed summer 2013; gas station was open.

DC 610.9 (977 km) **DJ 776.1** (1249 km) **Air Force Lodge**, on right northbound; use frontage road access.

DC 611.2 (977.5 km) **DJ 775.8** (1248.5 km) RCMP on right northbound; outside public pay phone.

Watson Lake

DC 612.9 (980 km) DJ 774.1 (1245.7 km) F 870.1 (1400.3 km) Historic Milepost 635, "Gateway to the Yukon," located 330 miles/531 km northwest of Fort Nelson and 275 miles/443 km southeast of Whitehorse. At the **junction** of the Alaska Highway (Yukon Highway 1) and the Campbell Highway (Yukon Highway 4). **Population:** 1,563. **Emergency Services: RCMP**, phone (867) 536-5555 (if no answer call 867/667-5555). **Fire Department**, phone (867) 536-2222. **Ambulance**, phone (867) 536-4444. **Hospital**, phone (867) 536-4444.

Visitor Information: Located in the Alaska Highway Interpretive Centre behind the Signpost Forest, north of the Alaska Highway; access to the centre is from the Campbell Highway. Open daily from beginning of May until third week in September, with hours of operation from 10 A.M. to 6 P.M. and 8 A.M. to 8 P.M. daily, mid-May to mid-September. Phone (867) 536-7469; fax (867) 536-2003. Pay phone with data port. Pick up a copy of the *Watson Lake Walking Tour* brochure here.

Yukon Government campground permits are available locally. These permits are sold at stores and other vendors and are transferable. Or campers may self register at Yukon Government campgrounds and pay the nightly fee.

Elevation: 2,254 feet/687m. **Climate:** Average daily temperature in January is -11°F/-24°C, in July 59°F/15°C. Record high temperature 93°F/34°C in May 1983, record low -74°F/-59°C in January 1947. Annual snowfall is 90.6 inches. Driest month is April, wettest month is September. Average date of last spring frost is June 2; average date of first fall frost is Sept. 14. **Radio:** CBC 990. **Television:** CBC and satellite.

Private Aircraft: Watson Lake airport, 8 miles/12.9 km north on Campbell Highway; elev. 2,262 feet/689m; length 5,500 feet/ 1,676m and 3,530 feet/1,076m; asphalt; fuel 100, jet. Heliport and floatplane bases also located here. Watson Lake is a major port of entry for aircraft.

Watson Lake is an important service stop on the Alaska and Campbell highways (Campbell Highway travelers, fill your gas tanks here!). The community is also a communication and distribution centre for the southern Yukon; a base for trappers, hunters and fishermen; and a supply point for area mining and mineral exploration.

Watson Lake businesses are located along either side of the Alaska Highway. Watson Lake—the body of water—is not visible from the Alaska Highway, although motorists can see Wye Lake. Access to the lake, airport, hospital and Ski Hill is via the Campbell Highway (locally referred to as Airport Road). The ski area is about 4 miles/6.4 km out the Campbell Highway from town.

Originally known as Fish Lake, Watson Lake was renamed for Frank Watson, who settled here in 1898 with his wife, Adela Stone, of Kaska First Nations heritage. Watson, who was born in Tahoe City, California, had come north looking for gold.

Watson Lake was an important point during construction of the Alaska Highway in 1942. The airport, built in 1941, was one of the major refueling stops along the Northwest Staging Route, the system of airfields through Canada to ferry supplies to Alaska and later lend-lease aircraft to Russia. Of the nearly 8,000 aircraft ferried through Canada, 2,618 were Bell P–39 Airacobras.

The Alaska Highway helped bring both people and commerce to this once isolated settlement. A post office opened here in July 1942. Today, the economy of Watson Lake is based on services to mining exploration and on tourism.

The community of Watson Lake takes full advantage of its short summer growing season by participating in Canada's Communities in Bloom program.

Lodging & Services

There are several fine lodging choices in Watson Lake: **Air Force Lodge, Big Horn Hotel, Cedar Lodge Motel, Cozy Nest B&B**. Full menu dine-in or take-out at **Kathy's Kitchen**.

Watson Lake has gas stations with unleaded, diesel and propane, automotive and tire repair. Stop by **Hougen's Department Store** for sporting goods, fishing licenses and souvenirs. The RCMP office is east of town centre on the Alaska Highway. There is 1 bank in Watson Lake, Canadian Imperial Bank of Commerce; it is open Monday through Thursday from 9:30 A.M. to

Black bear eating dandelions along the Alaska Highway. (©Sharon Nault)

WATSON LAKE
So Much More Than What You
See From The Highway

WELCOME TO WYE LAKE PARK

YUKON
LARGER THAN LIFE

TOWN OF WATSON LAKE
YUKON'S GATEWAY

Ph: (867) 536-8000
www.watsonlake.ca

NORTHERN LIGHTS CENTRE

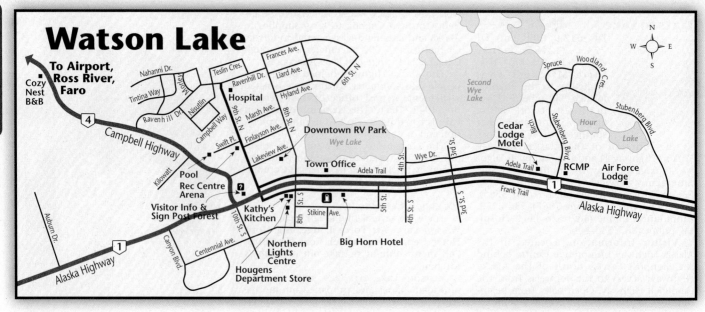

Watson Lake

4 P.M., Friday 9:30 A.M. to 5 P.M., closed holidays. ATM available 24 hours.

Check at the Visitor Information Centre for locations of local churches. Dennis Ball Memorial Swimming Pool is open in summer. Watson Lake also has a Recreation Centre and a skateboard park.

Air Force Lodge welcomes you to Watson Lake and invites you to stay at the historic 1942 pilots quarters, lovingly and completely restored. Custommade extra long beds. Rates: $79 single, $89 double. Value priced. Reservations recommended. From the guestbook: "We enjoyed a lovely and quiet sleep. Everything was so clean and comfortable."

"Golden Host Award Winner." A welcome and secure place for the traveler. Free WiFi. Phone/fax (867) 536-2890. Website www.airforcelodge.com. See display ad this page. [ADVERTISEMENT]

Big Horn Hotel. 29 beautiful rooms. Centrally located on the Alaska Highway in downtown Watson Lake. Our rooms are quiet, spacious, clean and boast queen-size beds; fridges; complimentary coffee; HD satellite TV. You get quality at a reasonable price. Available to you are honeymoon suite, Jacuzzi rooms, kitchenette suites. Wireless Internet. We know you'll enjoy staying with us. Book ahead. Pet friendly. Phone (867) 536-2020, fax (867) 536-2021. Email info@bighornhotel.ca. See display ad this page. [ADVERTISEMENT]

Cozy Nest B&B. Open year-round. Clean, quiet and cozy rooms. Continental breakfast. Lake activities at or nearby. Your hosts, Gord and Cindy, invite you to join us in the sauna or just sit and relax looking over the lake and rock gardens. Phone (867) 536-2204; email cozynest@northwestel.net; www.cozynestbandb.com. [ADVERTISEMENT]

Camping

Camping in Watson Lake at **Downtown R.V. Park**, on the access road to Wye Lake Park. Camping at Watson Lake Yukon Government Campground, located 2.4 miles/3.9 km west of the Signpost Forest (see **Milepost DC 615.3**).

Freshwater fillup and free dump station are located at Wye Lake Park.

Downtown R.V. Park (Good Sam), in the centre of town. 84 full-hookup stalls with 20/30/50, 26 with pull-through

WATSON LAKE ADVERTISERS

Air Force Lodge	Ph. (867) 536-2890
Big Horn Hotel	Ph. (867) 536-2020
Cedar Lodge Motel	Ph. (867) 536-7406
Cozy Nest B&B	Ph. (867) 536-2204
Downtown R.V. Park	Ph. (867) 536-2646
Hougen's Department Store	Ph. (867) 536-7475
Kathy's Kitchen	Ph. (867) 536-2400
Town of Watson Lake	Ph. (867) 536-8000
Yukon Heritage Attractions	Ph. (867) 667-4704

parking; showers; laundromat. Town water. RV wash available. Satellite TV. Free WiFi Hot Spot. Easy walking distance to town services. Just across the street from Wye Lake Park. Excellent hiking trails. Phone (867) 536-2646. See display ad this page. [ADVERTISEMENT]

Transportation

Air: No scheduled service. Helicopter charters available from Trans North Helicopters.

Bus: Scheduled service to Edmonton and Whitehorse via Greyhound.

Attractions

The **Alaska Highway Interpretive Centre**, operated by Tourism Yukon, is well worth a visit. Located behind the Signpost Forest, north of the Alaska Highway, the centre offers a video on Yukon history and the Alaska Highway. Excellent slide presentation and displays, including photographs taken in the mid-1940s showing the construction of the Alaska Highway in this area. The centre is open daily, May through September; free admission; phone (867) 536-7469.

Stop in and pick up your free **Yukon Gold Explorers Passport** at the visitor centre. Participants can use the passport as a guide to more than 30 Yukon museums and attractions. After getting your passport stamped at these locations, enter your name to win gold. The more exotic locations earn you more gold. The contest runs June 1 until August 31.

The **Watson Lake Signpost Forest**, seen at the north end of town at the junction of the Alaska and Robert Campbell highways, was started by Carl K. Lindley (1919–2002) of Danville, IL, a U.S. Army soldier in Company D, 341st Engineers, working on the construction of the Alaska Highway in 1942. Travelers are still adding signs to the collection, which numbers more than 75,000. Visitors are encouraged to add a sign to the Signpost Forest. **Historic Milepost 635** is located at the Signpost Forest.

The Watson Lake Sign Post Forest was designated a Yukon Historic Site in 2013; a formal ceremony recognizing the designation will take place some time in 2014.

Northern Lights Centre. The only planetarium in North America featuring the

myth and science of the northern lights. Using advanced video and laser technology, the centre offers presentations on the aurora borealis inside a 100-seat "Electric Sky" theatre environment. Interactive displays are also offered.

©Kris Valencia, staff

Afternoon and evening showings daily from May to September. Hours in 2013 were 1, 2, 3, 6:30, 7:30 and 8:30 P.M.. Admission charged (check with the Infocentre for coupon savings on admission fee). Located across from the Signpost Forest. Get your Yukon Explorer's Passport stamped here. Phone (867) 536-7827; website: www.northernlightscentre.ca.

Wye Lake Park offers a picnic area, a band shell and wheelchair-accessible restrooms. A 1.5-mile/2.5-km trail winds around First Wye Lake. Interpretive panels along the trail present information on Yukon wildflowers and local birds. The lake attracts both migrating birds (spring and fall) and resident species, such as nesting red-necked grebes. Also watch for tree swallows, violet-green swallows, mountain bluebirds and white-throated sparrows. The development of this park was initiated by a local citizens group.

St. John the Baptist Anglican Church

Add your sign to Watson Lake's Signpost Forest. (©Ankush Bharti)

has a memorial stained-glass window designed by Yukon artist Kathy Spalding. Titled "Our Land of Plenty," the window features a scene just north of Watson Lake off the Campbell Highway.

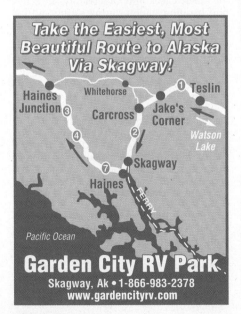

Lucky Lake, a few miles east of town on the Alaska Highway, is a popular local swimming hole for Watson Lake residents. Waterslide at the lake is open 1–4 P.M. on Sundays in summer. Very nice spot with picnic area, waterslide, ball diamond and 1.4-mile/2.2-km hiking trail through mature pine and spruce forest down to observation platform overlooking the Liard River.

Watson Lake Community Library offers public access to the Internet, email, photocopying and fax service. The library is open Tuesdays 10 A.M. to 8 P.M., Wednesdays and Thursdays 10 A.M. to 6 P.M., Fridays 10 A.M. to 5 P.M., and Saturdays 12:30–4:30 P.M. on Saturday. (Stop by and see the community quilt on display here.) Phone (867) 536-7517 for more information.

The **Watson Lake Airport Terminal Building**, located 8 miles/13 km north of town on the Campbell Highway, was built in 1942. This designated Heritage Building has an excellent display of historical photographs depicting the rich aviation history of this area, including early bush pilots and the WWII Lend Lease program.

Drive the Campbell Highway. This 362-mile/583-km Yukon highway connects Watson Lake to Ross River and Faro, junctioning with the Klondike Highway at Carmacks. Drive the first 51 miles/83 km of the highway north from Watson Lake to Simpson Lake for picnicking, fishing and camping. Or take an even shorter side trip out to Watson Lake Airport (8 miles/13 km out the Campbell) to see the historic terminal building. *NOTE: Motorists should check with the Visitor Centre in Watson Lake about current road conditions and road construction. The*

Campbell Highway to Ross River is a narrow gravel road with short stretches of improved and widened road. Weather and heavy truck traffic from mining activity may impact road surface. (Refer to CAMPBELL HIGHWAY section for highway log.)

Explore the area. Take time to fish, canoe a lake, take a wilderness trek or sightsee by helicopter. Outfitters in the area offer guided fishing trips to area lakes. Trips can be arranged by the day or by the week. Check with the visitor information centre.

AREA FISHING: Watson Lake has grayling, lake trout and pike. **Hour Lake**, in Bellview subdivision (follow signs at east end of town), is stocked with rainbow. **Lucky Lake**, south of town on the Alaska Highway, is stocked with rainbow; easily fished from shore. Fly-in lakes include **Toobally Lake** and **Stewart Lake**.

Alaska Highway Log
(continued)

Distance from Dawson Creek (DC)* is followed by distance from Delta Junction (DJ). Original mileposts are indicated in the text as Historical Mile.

*In the Canada portion of *The MILEPOST®* Alaska Highway log, mileages from Dawson Creek are based on actual driving distance and kilometres are based on physical kilometreposts. (Mileages from Delta Junction are based on actual driving distance, followed by the metric conversion.) See "Mileposts and Kilometreposts" in the introduction for more details.

Yukon Highway 1

Northbound: Good pavement with some easy

grades and curves. Slow for gravel breaks.

Southbound: Fair to good pavement. Some narrow winding road and irregular surfacing. Slow for gravel breaks.

DC 612.9 (980 km) **DJ 774.1** (1245.7 km) **Watson Lake Signpost Forest** at the **junction** of the Campbell Highway (Yukon Route 4) and Alaska Highway. The first 6 miles/9.7 km of the Campbell Highway is known locally as Airport Road; turn here for access to visitor information (in the Alaska Highway Interpretive Centre), airport, hospital and ski hill.

The Campbell Highway leads north to Ross River and Faro, and junctions with the Klondike Highway to Dawson City just north of Carmacks. Turn to the CAMPBELL HIGHWAY section on page 304 for log.

DC 615.3 (984 km) **DJ 771.7** (1241.9 km) Turnoff to north for side road to **Watson Lake Yukon government campground** and day-use area with boat launch, swimming and picnicking on Watson Lake. Drive in 3 miles/4.4 km via gravel access road (follow signs). There are 55 gravel sites, most level, 12 pull-through, drinking water, kitchen shelters, outhouses, firepits, firewood and litter barrels. Camping permit ($12/night).

🔺

DC 617.1 (986.9 km) **DJ 769.9** (1239 km) Watson Lake city limits.

DC 618.5 (989 km) **DJ 768.5** (1236.7 km) Watch for livestock.

DC 620 (991.3 km) **DJ 767** (1234.3 km) Upper Liard River bridge. The **Liard River** heads in the St. Cyr Range in southcentral Yukon Territory and flows southeast into British Columbia, then turns east and north to join the Mackenzie River at Fort Simpson, NWT. Fishing for grayling, lake trout, whitefish and northern pike.

DC 620.2 (991.7 km) **DJ 766.8** (1234 km) **Historical Mile 642.** UPPER LIARD VILLAGE, site of Our Lady of the Yukon Church.

NOTE: Slow for 50 kmph/30 mph speed zone through Upper Liard Village.

DC 620.8 (993 km) **DJ 766.2** (1233 km) Albert Creek bridge. Turnout with litter barrel to north at east end of bridge. Turnoff to south at west end of Albert Creek bridge for Albert Creek Bird Observatory, an active bird banding station during spring and fall migrations. The public is welcome. Follow gravel and dirt track 500m to station. Open daily from about third week in April to first week in June for spring migration. NOTE: No turnaround for RVs or large vehicles.

A sign near here marks the first tree planting project in the Yukon. Approximately 200,000 white spruce seedlings were planted in the Albert Creek area in 1993.

White spruce and lodgepole pine are the 2 principal trees of the Yukon, with white spruce the most common conifer. An average mature spruce can produce 8,000 cones in a good year and each cone has 140 seeds. The seed cones are about 2 inches/5 cm long and slender in shape. The pollen cones are small and pale red in colour. White spruce grow straight and fast wherever adequate water is available (mature trees reach 23 to 66 feet), and will grow to extreme old age without showing decay.

The lodgepole pine developed from the northern pine and can withstand extreme cold, grow at high elevations and take full

advantage of the almost 24-hour summer sunlight of a short growing season.

DC 623.9 (998 km) **DJ 763.1** (1228 km) *CAUTION: Watch for Little Rancheria caribou herd.*

DC 625.5 (1001.1 km) **DJ 761.5** (1225.5 km) **Historic Milepost 649** at turnoff to north for side road (Old Alaska Highway) to **Rantin Lake**; stocked with rainbow, good ice fishing.

DC 626.2 (1001.6 km) **DJ 760.8** (1224.3 km) **Historical Mile 649** at intersection of Alaska and Cassiar highways. Junction 37 Services; gas, diesel, RV park.

Junction with the Cassiar Highway, which leads south to Yellowhead Highway 16. Turn to end of CASSIAR HIGHWAY section on page 273 and read log back to front if you are headed south on the Cassiar.

DC 627 (1002.8 km) **DJ 760** (1223.1 km) **Historical Mile 650. The Northern Beaver Post/Nugget City** (open year-round) on the southwest side of the highway has a licensed restaurant; lodging in cottages; gift shop; 24-hour gas and diesel; tire repair, mechanic;

©Judy Nadon, staff

and an RV campground with pull-throughs for big rigs. Owners Linda and Scott Goodwin (pictured here) also host large groups in their group facility.

Nugget City/The Northern Beaver Post. See display ad this page.

DC 627.3 (1003.4 km) **DJ 759.7** (1222.6 km) Large double-ended gravel rest area with litter barrels, pit toilets and map to south. No overnight camping.

DC 630 (1009.7 km) **DJ 757** (1218.2 km) Look for rock messages that are spelled out along the highway here. The rock messages were started in summer 1990 by a Fort Nelson swim team. Along with the rock messages, travelers will probably see a number of inukshuks—originally rock cairns built by the Inuit as landmarks—left by travelers.

DC 633 (1014.5 km) **DJ 754** (1213.4 km) Gravel turnout to north.

DC 637.8 (1020.5 km) **DJ 749.2** (1205.7 km) Microwave tower access road to north. *CAUTION: Caribou next 25 km.*

DC 639.8 (1023.7 km) **DJ 747.2** (1202.5 km) *CAUTION: Hill and sharp curve.*

DC 647.4 (1035.9 km) **DJ 739.6** (1190.4 km) Little Rancheria Creek bridge.

DC 650.6 (1041.3 km) **DJ 736.4** (1185.1 km) Highway descends westbound to Big Creek.

DC 651.1 (1042 km) **DJ 735.9** (1184.3 km) Big Creek bridge, clearance 17.7 feet/ 5.4m. Turnout at east end of bridge.

DC 651.2 (1042.2 km) **DJ 735.8** (1184.1 km) Turnoff to north at west end of Big Creek bridge for **Big Creek Yukon government campground**, adjacent highway on

Big Creek; 15 sites (7 pull-through) on gravel loop road, outhouses, firewood, kitchen shelter, litter barrels, picnic tables, water pump. Camping permit ($12/night).

DC 651.3 (1042.4 km) **DJ 735.7** (1183.9 km) Watch for Little Rancheria Caribou herd southbound sign.

DC 658.5 (1059.8 km) **DJ 728.5** (1172.4 km) NorthwesTel microwave tower access road to north.

DC 664.1 (1062.7 km) **DJ 722.9** (1163.4 km) Transport Rest Area, a double-ended turnout with litter bins and outhouse to north on Lower Rancheria River.

DC 664.3 (1063.1 km) **DJ 722.7** (1163 km) Bridge over Lower Rancheria River. For northbound travelers, the highway closely follows the Rancheria River west from here to the Swift River. Northern bush pilot Les Cook was credited with helping find the best route for the Alaska Highway between Watson Lake and Whitehorse. Cook's Rancheria River route saved engineers hundreds of miles of highway construction.

Rancheria River, fishing for Dolly Varden and grayling.

DC 671.9 (1075.3 km) **DJ 715.1** (1150.8 km) Spencer Creek.

Stop and stretch your legs at Rancheria Falls Recreation Site. (©Sharon Nault)

DC 677 (1083.7 km) **DJ 710** (1142.6 km) Turnout with litter barrel to south overlooking the Rancheria River. Trail down to river.

According to R.C. Coutts, author of *Yukon: Places & Names*, the Rancheria River was named by Cassiar miners working Sayyea Creek in 1875, site of a minor gold rush at the time. Rancheria is an old Californian or Mexican miners' term in Spanish, meaning a native village or settlement. It is pronounced ran-che-REE-ah.

DC 678.5 (1086 km) **DJ 708.5** (1140.2 km) George's Gorge, culvert.

DC 683.2 (1093 km) **DJ 703.8** (1132.6 km) NorthwesTel microwave tower to south.

Improved highway northbound. Slow for loose gravel in construction areas!

DC 687.2 (1100 km) **DJ 699.8** (1126.2 km) **Historic Milepost 710. Rancheria Lodge** to south (description follows) has gas, diesel, propane, food, camping and lodging. Like other highway businesses that have to operate "off the grid," Rancheria Lodge runs diesel generators to power up their services. They are open year-round.

Historic highway lodge location: The Rancheria Hotel— described in the 1949 edition of The MILEPOST®—offered a "homelike atmosphere... emphasized by fine cookery served in a cozy rustic dining room." The lodge was owned by Bud and Doris Simpson for many years, then Bev Dinning. Today it is owned and operated by the Bouchard family, who have been renovating this classic Alaska Highway roadhouse, including a new restaurant in 2013. Historic sign and interpretive panel.

DC 689.2 (1103 km) **DJ 697.8** (1123 km) Canyon Creek.

DC 690 (1104.3 km) **DJ 697** (1121.7 km) Intermittent views of the Rancheria River, which parallels the Alaska Highway.

DC 692 (1107.5 km) **DJ 695** (1118.5 km) Culvert. Heavy rains washed out part of the Alaska Highway here in early summer 2012. Traffic was stopped on either side of the washout for about 48 hours while road crews stabilized the area. Traffic resumed via a shared stoplight-controlled single lane, while crews worked on rebuilding the second lane.

DC 692.5 (1108.2 km) **DJ 694.5** (1117.6 km) Young Creek. Named after Major Richard Henry Young of the Royal Canadian Engineers, Northwest Highway Systems.

DC 694.2 (1111.3 km) **DJ 692.8** (1114.9 km) **Historical Mile 717.5**. The old Message Post lodge, closed for many years, once offered food, gas, a beer garden and souvenirs. It operated from about 1976 until 1989.

DC 695.2 (1112.8 km) **DJ 691.8** (1113.3 km) **Rancheria Falls Recreation Site** has a good gravel and boardwalk trail through boreal forest to the picturesque falls; easy 10-minute walk. Large parking area with toilets and litter barrels at trailhead.

DC 696 (1114 km) **DJ 691** (1112 km) Porcupine Creek.

DC 697.4 (1116.6 km) **DJ 689.6** (1109.8 km) Beautiful views of the Cassiar Mountains.

DC 698.4 (1118 km) **DJ 688.6** (1108.2 km) **Historical Mile 721**. Continental Divide Lodge (current status unknown).

DC 698.7 (1118.6 km) **DJ 688.3** (1107.7 km) Upper Rancheria River bridge, clearance 17.7 feet/5.4m. For northbound travelers, the highway leaves the Rancheria River.

DC 699.3 (1119.6 km) **DJ 687.7** (1106.7 km) **Historic Milepost 722**. Turnoff for airstrip. **Private Aircraft**: Pine Lake airstrip 3 miles/4.8 km north; deserted WWII emergency airstrip; elev. 3,250 feet/991m; length 6,000 feet/1,829m; gravel, status unknown.

DC 699.4 (1120 km) **DJ 687.6** (1106.5 km) Large gravel turnout to north; outhouses, litter bins. Interpretive signs (excerpt follows) on the **Continental Divide**, which divides 2 of the largest drainage systems in North America—the Yukon River and Mackenzie River watersheds. Water draining west from this point forms the Swift River. This river drains into the Yukon River and continues a northwest journey of 3,680 kilome-

tres (2,300 miles) to the Bering Sea (Pacific Ocean). Water that drains to the east forms the Rancheria River which flows into the Liard River then the Mackenzie River. These waters flow northward and empty into the Beaufort Sea (Arctic Ocean) after a journey of 4,200 kilometres (2,650 miles). Sign reads:

"There is a distinct difference in traditional land use patterns corresponding with this separation of river drainages. Pacific salmon migrate up the Yukon River watershed providing a reliable and relatively abundant food resource. This resource could generally support a larger and less transient human population than lands to the east."

All rivers crossed by the Alaska Highway between here and Fairbanks, AK, drain into the Yukon River system, with the exception of the Aishihik River (**Milepost DC 965.7**) and the Jarvis River (**Milepost DC 1003.5**). These 2 Yukon rivers drain into the Dezadeash River, which flows to the Pacific.

DC 702 (1124 km) **DJ 685** (1102.4 km) Very large informal (not signed) gravel turnout with litter bins to south at east end of Swift River culvert; access to Swift River.

For northbound travelers, the highway now follows the Swift River west to the Morley River.

DC 705.6 (1130.4 km) **DJ 681.4** (1096,6 km) Very large turnout with gravel parking area and litter bins.

NOTE: Highway descends 6 to 7 percent grade next 1.1 miles/1.8 km northbound.

DC 709.1 (1136.2 km) **DJ 677.9** (1090.9 km) Seagull Creek, named by members of Company D, 29th Engineers Topographic Battalion, during construction of the Alaska Highway in 1942. According to Sgt. Jim West, all of the major streams and rivers— the Morley, Swan, Swift, Rancheria and Liard—were already named when the crews came through. "However, many smaller streams had no names, so we named them." In addition to Seagull Creek, these included Hazel Creek (Upper and Lower), Log Jam Creek and Friskie Creek.

DC 709.8 (1136.7 km) **DJ 677.2** (1089.8 km) **Historic Milepost 733, SWIFT RIVER**. The historic Swift River Lodge closed down in September 2009; current status unknown. The lodge was originally a "Clyde Wann station," offering gas, rooms, meals, a general store and trailer spaces. Clyde Wann, who was born in the U.S. in 1900, came North in the 1920s and co-founded Yukon Airways and Exploration Co. After the Alaska Highway was completed, Clyde Wann built and operated—along with his wife, Helen—several highway lodges, including Swift River Lodge, Morley River Lodge, Beaver Creek Lodge and Destruction Bay Lodge. Wann also had a Chrysler franchise.

There was a maintenance camp, repeater station, cafe, store and garage here in 1949.

CAUTION: Watch for moose northbound next 25 km.

DC 710.3 (1137.4 km) **DJ 676.7** (1089 km) **Historical Mile 733.5**. Welcome to British Columbia (northbound sign), Leaving British Columbia (southbound sign).

The highway re-enters British Columbia for approximately 42 miles/68 km northbound.

DC 712.7 (1140.9 km) **DJ 674.3** (1085.2 km) Partridge Creek.

DC 718.5 (1150.1 km) **DJ 668.5** (1075.8 km) Screw Creek.

DC 719.6 (1152 km) **DJ 667.4** (1074 km) **Historical Mile 743**. Swan Lake Rest Area to south; outhouse, litter bins and point-of-interest sign to south overlooking lake. The

pyramid-shaped mountain to south is Simpson Peak.

Access to **Swan Lake**; fishing for trout and whitefish.

DC 723.5 (1159 km) **DJ 663.5** (1067.8 km) Turnoff for Swan Lake business.

DC 726 (1162 km) **DJ 661** (1063.7 km) Distance marker southbound shows Watson Lake 182 km/113 miles.

DC 727.9 (1165 km) **DJ 659.1** (1060.7 km) Logjam Creek culvert.

DC 735.8 (1177.4 km) **DJ 651.2** (1048 km) Smart River bridge. Pull-outs at either end of bridge are posted "no camping." The **Smart River** flows south into the Cassiar Mountains in British Columbia. The river was originally called Smarch, after the Tlingit family of that name who lived and trapped in this area. The Smarch family currently includes world renowned carving artist Keith Wolfe Smarch.

DC 741.4 (1186.8 km) **DJ 645.6** (1039 km) Microwave tower access road to north.

DC 744.1 (1191 km) **DJ 642.9** (1034.6 km) Hazel Creek.

DC 745.2 (1192.9 km) **DJ 641.8** (1032.8 km) Lower Hazel Creek.

DC 746 (1194 km) **DJ 641** (1031.5 km) Rest area to north on lake; litter bins and outhouse.

DC 749 (1199.1 km) **DJ 638** (1026.7 km) Andrew Creek.

DC 750.8 (1202 km) **DJ 636.2** (1023.8 km) Morley Lake to north.

DC 751.2 (1202.7 km) **DJ 635.8** (1023.2 km) The Alaska Highway re-enters the Yukon Territory northbound. This is the last of 7 crossings of the YT–BC border.

DC 752 (1204 km) **DJ 635** (1021.9 km) Sharp turnoff on bermed access (*NOTE: RVs swing wide*) to north for Yukon government **Morley River Recreation Site**. This day-use area has a large gravel parking area (good for RVs), picnic sites with tables and firepits, firewood, kitchen shelter, water, litter bins and outhouses. Access to river; fishing.

DC 752.3 (1204.4 km) **DJ 634.7** (1021.4 km) Morley River bridge. The Morley River flows into the southeast corner of Teslin Lake. The river, lake and Morley Bay (on Teslin Lake) were named for W. Morley Ogilvie, assistant to Arthur St. Cyr on the 1897 survey of the Telegraph Creek–Teslin Lake route. Good fishing near mouth of **Morley River** for northern pike 6 to 8 lbs., best June to August, use small Red Devils; grayling 3 to 5 lbs., in May and August, use small spinner; lake trout 6 to 8 lbs., June to August, use large spoon.

DC 752.9 (1205.5 km) **DJ 634.1** (1020.4 km) **Historical Mile 777.7.** Morley River Lodge closed in 2005. This historic highway lodge was a Clyde Wann Station in the late 1950s called Morley River Auto Camp.

DC 754.8 (1209.5 km) **DJ 632.2** (1017.4 km) *CAUTION: Watch for livestock on highway.*

DC 757.9 (1212.2 km) **DJ 629.1** (1012.4 km) Memorial cairn to south (no turnout) commemorates Alaska Highway constuction worker: "In memory of Max Richardson 39163467, Corporal Co. F 340th Eng. Army of the United States; born Oct. 10, 1918, died Oct. 17, 1942. Faith is the victory."

DC 761.5 (1218.1 km) **DJ 625.5** (1006.6 km) Strawberry Creek.

DC 764.1 (1223.2 km) **DJ 622.9** (1002.4 km) Hays Creek.

DC 769.6 (1232 km) **DJ 617.4** (993.6 km) **Historical Mile 797.** Dawson Peaks Resort was closed in 2013; current status unknown.

DC 772.8 (1237.7 km) **DJ 614.2** (988.4 km) **Historic Milepost 800.** Demonstration Forestry Site to east via narrow, rutted, dirt road (no turn-around for large vehicles). Sign reads: "On this site, 8 forestry demonstration blocks were cut using variations of patch, shelterwood and selection, with machinery and horses. This was done to research alternative styles of sustainable harvesting in the North, harvesting that respects other traditional uses of the land, like trapping, fishing, or berrying and harvesting that reduces forest fire risk."

Report wildfires; phone 1-798-888-FIRE (3473).

DC 774.4 (1240 km) **DJ 612.6** (985.8 km) *Highway descends northbound* to Nisutlin Bay Bridge.

DC 774.8 (1240.6 km) **DJ 612.2** (985.2 km) Welcome to Teslin (northbound sign).

DC 775.5 (1242 km) **DJ 611.5** (984.1 km) Large double-ended rest area with litter barrels, information kiosk and view of Nisutlin Bay Bridge. Good photo-op.

NOTE: Begin 50 kmph/30 mph speed zone northbound (enforced).

DC 776 (1243 km) **DJ 611** (983.3 km) **Nisutlin Bay Bridge**, longest water span on the Alaska Highway at 1,917 feet/584m. *CAUTION: Metal grated bridge decking, slippery when wet.* The Nisutlin River forms the "bay" as it flows into Teslin Lake here. Put-in for canoeing the Nisutlin River is at Mile 42 on the South Canol Road. The Nisutlin Delta National Wildlife Area is an important waterfowl migration stop-over.

Teslin Lake straddles the BC–YT border; it is 86 miles/138 km long, averages 2 miles/3.2 km across, and has an average depth of 194 feet/59m. The name is taken from the Indian name for the lake—Teslintoo ("long, narrow water").

DC 776.3 (1243.5 km) **DJ 610.7** (982.8 km) **Historic Milepost 804. Yukon Motel & Lakeshore RV Park**; restaurant, gas station, lodging, RV park. Historic highway lodge location. Stop in and see their excellent Yukon Wildlife Gallery. The Teslin post office is also located here.

Viewpoint at Milepost DC 775.5 offers a good view of Nisutlin Bay Bridge and Teslin.
(©Kris Valencia, staff)

©Kris Valencia, staff

DC 776.4 (1243.7 km) **DJ 610.6** (982.6 km) Nisutlin Trading Post; gas, diesel, groceries, motel rooms.

Teslin

DC 776.5 (1244 km) **DJ 610.5** (982.5 km) **F 706.5** (1137 km) **Historic Milepost 804.** on the Alaska Highway. Teslin is 111 miles/179 km southeast of Whitehorse, and 163 miles/263 km northwest of Watson Lake. **Population:** 450. **Emergency Services:** RCMP, phone (867) 390-5555 (if no answer call 867/667-5555). **Fire Department**, phone (867) 390-2222. **Nurse**, phone (867) 390-4444.

Visitor Information: Local businesses are happy to help answer visitor questions. On the web, visit www.teslin.ca.

Elevation: 2,239 feet/682.4m. **Climate:** Average temperature in January, -7°F/-22°C, in July 57°F/14°C. Annual snowfall 66.2 inches/168.2 cm. Driest month April, wettest month July. Average date of last spring frost is June 19; first fall frost Aug. 19. **Radio:** CBC 940; CHONFM 90.5; CKRW 98.7. **Television:** Channel 13.

Situated at the confluence of the Nisutlin River and Teslin Lake, Teslin began as a trading post in 1903. Today the community consists of the original Nisutlin Trading Post (general store, motel and gas); the **Yukon Motel and Lakeshore RV Park** (restaurant, motel, RV park and gas station), a Catholic church, health centre, library (with Internet access) and post office. There is a 3-sheet regulation curling rink and a skating rink; a skateboard park, ballfield, Friendship Park and playground.

Teslin has one of the largest Native populations in Yukon Territory and much of the community's livelihood revolves around traditional hunting, trapping and fishing. In addition, some Tlingit (Klink-it) residents are involved in the development of Native woodworking crafts (canoes, snowshoes and sleds); traditional sewn art and craft items (moccasins, mitts, moose hair tufting, gun cases); and the tanning of moose hides. The Yukon Motel has an impressive display of Yukon wildlife.

The Teslin area has boat rentals, houseboat tours, charter fishing outfitters and an air charter service. Teslin Lake is famous for its lake trout fishing. Canoeists can fly into Wolf Lake for a 5- to 6-day trip down the Wolf River and Nisutlin River to Teslin Lake.

Don't miss the **George Johnston Museum**, located on the left side of the Alaska Highway heading north (see **Milepost DC 776.7**). A Tlingit Indian, the innovative George Johnston (1884–1972) was known for his trapping and his fine photography. His camera captured the lives of the inland Tlingit people of Teslin and Atlin between 1910 and 1940. Johnston brought the first car, a 1928 Chevrolet, by paddlewheeler to roadless Teslin 13 years before the Alaska Highway was built cutting a 3-mile track for his "Teslin taxi." In winter, he hunted by car on frozen Teslin Lake. The car is now on permanent display at the museum. Director Carol Geddes' beautiful short film tells his story.

Another highly recommended stop is the **Teslin Tlingit Heritage Centre**, located just north of town on the southwest side of the Alaska Highway. The centre's displays feature 200 years of Inland Tlingit history and culture. Five outdoor totems, carved by Keith Wolfe Smarch and other carvers, represent the Wolf, Eagle, Frog, Beaver and Raven clans. Narrated tours available. Ample parking and turnaround area for RVs. Watch for turnoff at **Milepost DC 779.1**.

AREA FISHING: Guided fishing trips

TESLIN ADVERTISERS

George Johnston Museum...........Ph. (867) 390-2550
Teslin Tlingit Heritage Centre....Ph. (867) 390-2526
Yukon Motel & Lakeshore
  RV Park...........................Ph. (867) 390-2575

available from Nisutlin Outfitting, located directly across from Nisutlin Trading Post. Day-use area with boat ramp at north end of Nisutlin Bay Bridge. **Teslin Lake's Nisutlin Bay** (at the confluence of the Nisutlin River and Teslin Lake), troll the mud line in May and June for lake trout up to 25 lbs.; **Eagle Bay**, casting close to shore for northern pike to 15 lbs.; **Morley Bay**, excellent fishing for lake trout at south end of the bay's mouth, good fishing at the bay's shallow east side for northern pike to 10 lbs. **Morley River**, excellent fly fishing for grayling to 4 lbs. near river mouth and upriver several miles (by boat), fish deep water.

Alaska Highway Log
(continued)

Distance from Dawson Creek (DC) is followed by distance from Delta Junction (DJ). Original mileposts are indicated in the text as Historical Mile.

In the Canada portion of *The MILEPOST®* Alaska Highway log, mileages from Dawson Creek are based on actual driving distance and kilometres are based on physical kilometreposts.

YUKON HIGHWAY 1 WEST

DC 776.7 (1244.2 km) **DJ 610.3** (982.2 km) **George Johnston Museum**, to west, displays Tlingit ceremonial robes and trade goods, a photo gallery of early Tlingit life, George Johnston's reconstructed general store and ice-highway car, and life-size subsistence trapping and hunting dioramas. Enter the rare 1942 Aeradio Range 'Beam' station on site. The Teslin Historical Museum Society (phone 867/390-2550), open the museum and film theatre daily, 9 A.M. to 5 P.M. in summer; admission charged, wheelchair accessible. Get your Yukon Explorer's Passport stamped here. Website: www.gjmuseum.yk.net. Email gjmuseum@hotmail.com.

DC 776.8 (1244.4 km) **DJ 610.2** (982 km) Distance marker northbound shows Whitehorse 181 km/112 miles.

DC 777 (1244.6 km) **DJ 610** (981.7 km) Airport and police. Historic Milepost 805. **Private Aircraft**: Teslin airstrip to east; elev. 2,313 feet/705m; length 5,500 feet/1,676m; gravel; fuel 100, jet. Runway may be unusable during spring breakup.

DC 777.3 (1245.2 km) **DJ 609.7** (981.1 km) Trailhead for George Johnson Trail to east.

DC 777.5 (1245.5 km) **DJ 609.5** (980.8 km) Begin 100 kmph northbound, begin 70 kmph southbound posted speed limits. *Slow for speed zones southbound.*

DC 778.1 (1246.5 km) **DJ 608.9** (979.9 km) Welcome to Teslin (southbound sign).

DC 778.3 (1246.8 km) **DJ 608.7** (979.6 km) Teslin Lake Viewing Platform at **Historic Milepost 806**, west side of highway, overlooks Teslin Lake. Interpretive panels, outhouses and parking.

DC 779.1 (1248 km) **DJ 607.9** (978.3 km) Turnoff (watch for sign) to southwest for **Tlingit Heritage Centre**, a highly recommended stop; www.tlingit.ca.

The centre (not visible from highway) highlights the last 200 years of Inland Tlingit history and includes displays on the lifestyles of the Tlingit people and "power of the mask." Includes Great Hall meeting place and gift shop. Ample parking and turnaround area for RVs. The 5 outdoor totems, carved by Keith Wolfe Smarch and other carvers, repre-

Tlingit Heritage Centre hosts First Nations events and offers cultural programs and displays. (©Judy Nadon, staff)

sent the Wolf, Eagle, Frog, Beaver and Raven clans. Our editor notes: "If you are lucky, you may get to sample some homemade bannock with wild berry jam."

Tlingit Heritage Centre. See display ad this page.

DC 779.5 (1248.7 km) **DJ 607.5** (977.6 km) Fox Creek.

DC 785.2 (1257.9 km) **DJ 601.8** (968.5 km) **Historical Mile 813.** Roadside rest area to west with outhouses and litter bins at entrance to **Teslin Lake Yukon government campground** to west; 27 sites (some level, 6 pull-through) in trees on Teslin Lake, water pump (water must be boiled for 2 minutes, minimum), litter bins, kitchen shelter, firewood, firepits, picnic tables. Camping permit ($12/night). Fishing. Boat launch 0.3 mile/0.5 km north of campground.

Ten Mile Creek.

DC 788.9 (1264 km) **DJ 598.1** (962.5 km) Lone Tree Creek.

DC 794.6 (1273.1 km) **DJ 592.4** (953.3 km) Deadman Creek.

DC 797.6 (1278 km) **DJ 589.4** (948.5 km) Timber Point Campground.

DC 800.8 (1283.5 km) **DJ 586.2** (943.4 km) Robertson Creek (not signed).

DC 801.6 (1284.4 km) **DJ 585.4** (942.1 km) Brooks' Brook at Historical Mile 829. According to R.C. Coutts in *Yukon: Places & Names*, this stream was named by black Army engineers, who completed this section of road in 1942, for their company officer, Lieutenant Brooks.

DC 807.6 (1294.4 km) **DJ 579.4** (932.4 km) Distance marker southbound shows Teslin 52 km/32 miles, Watson Lake 315 km/196 miles.

DC 808.2 (1295 km) **DJ 578.8** (931.5 km) **Junction** with the "South" Canol Road, a narrow, winding gravel road which leads north 137 miles/220 km to junction with the Campbell Highway near Ross River.

Rest area, parking, outhouses, litter bin

Teslin River Bridge is the third longest water span on the Alaska Highway.
(©Judy Nadon, staff)

and historic sign and interpretive panel about the Canol Project at junction. Several WWII vehicles from the Canol Project are on display here. (The old "graveyard" of WWII vehicles near here was significantly cannibalized and is no longer accessible.)

Junction with South Canol Road (Yukon Highway 6) which leads northeast to the Campbell Highway. See page 308 in the CAMPBELL HIGHWAY section for details.

The Canol (Canadian Oil) Road was built in 1942-44 to provide access to oil fields at Norman Wells, NWT. Today, it is a wilderness road, occasionally closed by washouts. *MILEPOST®* field editor Judy Nadon likes driving the South Canol for its "outrageously beautiful" scenery, but says it is slow going (she drives a Pontiac Grand AM). She suggests carrying 2 spare tires. "It's not for most RVs or big rigs," says Judy, "although locals—used to rough road conditions—take their campers and RVs up the South Canol when they hunt."

DC 808.6 (1295.6 km) **DJ 578.4** (930.8 km) **Teslin River Bridge** is the third longest water span on the highway (1,770 feet/539m). It was constructed with a very high clearance above the river to permit steamers of the British Yukon Navigation Co. to pass under it en route from Whitehorse to Teslin. River steamers ceased operation on the Teslin River in 1942. Before the construction of the Alaska Highway, all freight and supplies for Teslin traveled this water route from Whitehorse.

Distance marker northbound shows Whitehorse 130 km/81 miles.

DC 808.9 (1296.2 km) **DJ 578.1** (930.3 km) **Historic Milepost 836, JOHNSON'S CROSSING.** Johnson's Crossing Campground Services (to east at north end of bridge) was closed summer 2013; current status unknown.

The history of Johnson's Crossing is related in Ellen Davignon's *The Cinnamon Mine.* This is one of the original lodges on the Alaska Highway. They first advertised in the 1949 edition of *The MILEPOST®* as Porsild's Hotel, operated by "Robert Porsild,

old-timer of the North." The Porsilds later renamed it Johnson's Crossing, the local name for the Teslin River bridge.

Access to Teslin River; boat launch, no camping on riverbank. Canoeists report that the Teslin River is wide and slow, but with gravel, rocks and weeds. Adequate camping sites on numerous sand bars; boil drinking water. Abundant wildlife—muskrat, porcupine, moose, eagles and wolves—also bugs and rain. Watch for bear. The Teslin enters the Yukon River at Hootalinqua, an old steamboat landing and supply point (under restoration). Roaring Bull rapids: choppy water. Pullout at Carmacks. Inquire locally about river conditions before setting out.

Teslin River, excellent grayling fishing from spring to late fall, 10 to 15 inches, use spinner or red-and-white spoons for spinning or black gnat for fly-fishing. King salmon in August. 🎣

DC 809.1 (1296.4 km) **DJ 577.9** (930 km) Access road east to the Teslin River. The Big Salmon Range, also to the east, parallels the Teslin. For Alaska-bound travelers, the highway now swings north.

DC 810.3 (1298.4) **DJ 576.7** (928.1 km) Turnouts both sides, with litter bins.

DC 812.8 (1302.4 km) **DJ 574.2** (924.1 km) Little Teslin Lake on west side of highway.

DC 813.8 (1304.1 km) **DJ 573.2** (922.4 km) *CAUTION: Watch for caribou (Carcross herd) next 9 km/5.6 miles northbound.*

DC 814.5 (1305.3 km) **DJ 572.5** (921.3 km) Easy-to-miss unsigned turnoff on your right northbound (across from gated private drive on left northbound) at **Historic Milepost 843** to Squanga Lake flightstrip, another Alaska Highway airstrip that dates back to WWII and the Northwest Stating Route. There is an osprey nest on top of the old tower on your right as you approach the airstrip. Osprey feed on fish and may be observed perched on top of the poles along the highway here.

Private Aircraft: Squanga Lake airstrip, 1 N; elev. 2,630 feet/802m; length 6,000 feet/965m; gravel, summer only, current status unknown; no services.

DC 820.4 (1314.8 km) **DJ 566.6** (911.8

km) Seaforth Creek bridge. Gravel turnout to west at north end of bridge.

DC 821 (1315.9 km) **DJ 566** (910.9 km) Turnoff to **Squanga Lake Yukon government campground:** 16 sites, 4 pull-through, with kitchen shelter, drinking water, camping permit ($12/night). Small boat launch. Fishing for northern pike, grayling, whitefish, rainbow and burbot. 🎣 ▲

The Tagish name for Squanga Lake is Desgwaage Mene, "whitefish lake," referring to the rare Squanga Pygmy whitefish found in these waters.

DC 828.7 (1328.5 km) **DJ 558.3** (898.5 km) Rest area with large gravel parking area, litter bins and outhouses to northeast. Information panels.

DC 836.8 (1341.5 km) **DJ 550.2** (885.4 km) **Junction** with Tagish Road at **Historic Milepost 866, JAKE'S CORNER;** gas and diesel available. Turnoff for Tagish Road to Carcross and access to Atlin Road. Distance marker shows Tagish 21 km/13 miles, Carcross 55 km/34 miles, Atlin 100 km/62 miles. ⛽

Junction with Yukon Highway 8 (Tagish Road) to Carcross and Higway 7 (Atlin Road). See "Atlin–Tagish–Carcross Scenic Loop" log on pages 171-172.

The U.S. Army Corps of Engineers set up a construction camp here in 1942, under the command of Captain Jacobson, thus giving Jake's Corner its name. However, the name is also attributed to Jake Jackson, a Teslin Indian who camped in this area on his way to Carcross. Roman "Jake" Chaykowsky (1900–1995) operated Jake's Corner Service for many years. It was known locally as The Crystal Palace, after the first lodge Chaykowsky had owned at Judas Creek, just up the road.

Distance marker southbound shows Teslin 98 km/60 miles, Watson Lake 361 km/224 miles.

DC 837.5 (1342.5 km) **DJ 549.5** (884.3 km) Entering 911 service response area northbound.

View of White Mountain southeast, named by William Ogilvie during his 1887 survey, for Thomas White, then Minister of the Interior. The Yukon government introduced mountain goats to this area in 1981.

DC 843.2 (1351.8 km) **DJ 543.8** (875.1 km) Judas Creek bridge.

DC 850 (1362.5 km) **DJ 537** (864.2 km) Turnoff for resort marina on Marsh Lake; firehall and emergency service response centre; pay phone.

DC 852.2 (1366.7 km) **DJ 534.8** (860.6 km) Intermittent views of beautiful **Marsh Lake** to the west for the next several miles northbound. Marsh Lake, part of the Yukon River system, is approximately 20 miles/32 km long and was named in 1883 by Lt. Frederick Schwatka, U.S. Army, for Yale professor Othniel Charles Marsh. Marsh Lake and, in particular the sandy Army Beach, is a popular recreation area for Whitehorse residents.

DC 854.4 (1370 km) **DJ 532.6** (857.1 km) **Historic Milepost 883,** Marsh Lake/Camp 4F NWHS sign. Nolan Road. Boat launch to west.

DC 854.5 (1370.3 km) **DJ 532.5** (857 km) Nolan Road.

(Continues on page 173)

Atlin–Tagish–Carcross Scenic Loop

A popular side trip from the Alaska Highway is a visit to the village of Atlin, BC, a 59-mile/95-km drive south from Jake's Corner (**Milepost DC 836.8** Alaska Highway) via Atlin Road. Return to the Alaska Highway by taking the all-paved "Carcross Loop," a 66-mile/106-km drive via Tagish Road to Carcross and the South Klondike Highway back to the Alaska Highway at **Milepost DC 874.4**.

To reach Atlin Road, turn south at Jake's Corner onto Tagish Road and drive 1.1 miles/1.8 km to junction with Atlin Road (Highway 7). The 58-mile/93-km Atlin Road, built in 1949, is usually in good condition, with about 38 miles/61 km of paved road and 20 miles/32 km of gravel.

Sometimes called the Shangri-la of the North, Atlin overlooks the crystal clear water of 90-mile/145-km-long Atlin Lake, elev. 3,198 feet/975m. Surrounded by spectacular mountains, Atlin Lake covers 307 square miles/798 square km and is the largest natural lake in British Columbia.

Backtrack from Atlin and take the short but scenic Tagish Road to Carcross, where you will junction with the South Klondike Highway. Drive 32 miles/52 km up the South Klondike Highway and junction with the Alaska Highway just 12 miles/19 km south of Whitehorse, past the world's smallest desert and beautiful Emerald Lake. Stop by Caribou Crossing.

The Carcross Loop adds an extra 28 miles/46 km to the drive from Jake's Corner to Whitehorse. The Atlin side trip adds another 116 miles/187 km. Total driving distance is 182 miles/293 km.

Atlin Road Log

Distance from Tagish Road junction (J) is shown. *Physical kilometreposts show distance from Tagish Road junction.*

J 0 Junction of Tagish and Atlin roads, 1 mile/1.6 km south of Jake's Corner and the Alaska Highway. Distance marker shows Atlin 98 km/61 miles. Good chip seal road. No cell service.

J 2.4 (3.9 km) Large turnout to west on **Little Atlin Lake**; litter bin, toilets. Mount Minto (elev. 6,913 feet/2,107m) to the southwest.

J 3.7 (6 km) Turnoff at Kilometrepost 6 for **White Mountain Inn**. White Mountain Inn. See display ad this page.

J 4.8 (7.7 km) White Mountain (sign) to east. Look for sheep on White Mountain.

J 8 (12.9 km) Haunka Creek.

J 13.5 (21.7 km) *Pavement ends, gravel begins, southbound.*

J 15.5 (24.9 km) Snafu Creek. Snafu is an army acronym for Situation Normal All Fouled Up.

J 16.4 (26 km) Access road leads 0.7 mile/1.1 km to **Snafu Lake** Yukon government campground; 9 sites, camping permit ($12), outhouses, firewood, tables, boat ramp, grayling fishing.

J 18.4 (29.6 km) Tarfu Creek. Another army acronym: Things Are Really Fouled Up.

Begin improved wide gravel road southbound for 1.5 miles/2.4 km (2013). Expect continued construction and/or improved paved road in summer 2014.

J 19.8 (331.8 km) *Begin chip seal road with centerline southbound.*

J 20.1 (32.3 km) Side road leads 2.4 miles/3.8 km to **Tarfu Lake** Yukon government campground; 10 sites, camping permit ($12), boat launch, drinking water, outhouses, fishing. Not recommended for large RVs or trailers.

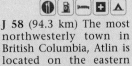

J 21.7 (34.9 km) View of Atlin Lake. The horizon is dominated by Mount Minto.

J 25.4 (42.4 km) Rest area with litter bin and outhouses.

J 25.6 (42.7 km) **BC–YT border.** *Road narrows, gravel begins, southbound.*

J 30.1 (50 km) *Narrow winding road continues southbound with 7 percent grades.*

J 32.5 (53.9 km) Double-ended gravel turnout to east. Hitchcock Creek, picnic area to west.

J 36 (59.4 km) Base Camp Creek (sign); turnout to west.

J 39.6 (65.1 km) Indian River.

J 39.7 (65.3 km) Turnout with litter bin. *Gravel ends, pavement begins, southbound.*

J 49.5 (80.8 km) Davie Hall Lake.

J 51.3 (83.6 km) MacDonald Lake BC Recreation Site.

J 52.6 (85.6 km) 4th of July Creek.

J 54.1 (87.1 km) Atlin Tlingit Fuels; self-serve gas, diesel.

J 54.9 (89.4 km) Como Lake BC Recreation Site.

J 56 (91.1 km) *Slow for 70 kmph/43 mph speed zone southbound.*

J 57.4 (93.4 km) *Slow for 50 kmph/31 mph speed zone southbound.*

J 57.7 (93.9 km) Turnout with litter bin at **junction** with Discovery Avenue. Turn west (right southbound) and follow Discovery Avenue into Atlin (description follows). Turn east (left southbound) on Discovery Avenue, which becomes Surprise Lake Road at its junction with Warm Bay Road. **Surprise Lake Road** leads 18 km/11 miles to Surprise Lake. Surprise Lake Road also leads to the Atlin airport, 1.1 miles; dump station 2.3 miles; Pine Creek falls, 3.5; public gold panning on Spruce Creek, 3.6 miles; and former townsite of Discovery, 5.4 miles.

Warm Bay Road leads 1.5 miles/2.4 km to Pine Creek campground (RVs and tent, fee posted, located on the south side of Pine Creek just past bridge); beach and Monarch Mountain trails, 3.5 km/2.2 miles; Palmer Lake recreation site, 18 km/11.2 miles; Warm Bay recreation site, 22 km/13.7 miles; and "The Grotto" recreation site, 25 km/15.5 miles.

J 57.8 (94 km) Pine Tree Restaurant, Shell gas, tire repairs.

Atlin

J 58 (94.3 km) The most northwesterly town in British Columbia, Atlin is located on the eastern shore of Atlin Lake, 60 miles/96 km south of the Alaska Highway, and 106 miles/171 km southeast of Whitehorse, YT (about a 2½-hour drive). **Population:** 350. **Emergency Services: RCMP**, phone (250) 651-7511. **Ambulance**, phone (250) 651-7700. **Red Cross outpost clinic**, phone (250) 651-7677.

Visitor Information: Atlin Historical Museum in 3rd Street; phone 250-651-7522. Atlin community website www.atlin.net. **Elevation:** 2,240 feet/683m.

Atlin was founded in 1898. The name was taken from the Indian dialect and means Big

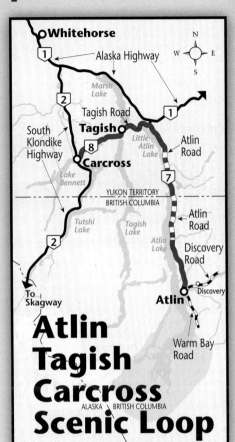

Atlin Tagish Carcross Scenic Loop
ALASKA ▪ BRITISH COLUMBIA

Atlin–Tagish–Carcross Scenic Loop (Continued)

Water. The Atlin Lake area was one of the richest gold strikes made during the great rush to the Klondike in 1897–98. The first claims were registered here on July 30, 1898, by Fritz Miller and Kenneth McLaren.

Lodging at **Brewery Bay Chalet** and the Atlin Inn. There are restaurants, laundromat (with showers), gas station (propane, diesel), auto repair, grocery, government liquor store and a post office. There are no banks in Atlin, but ATMs are available. Bus tours are welcome, but phone ahead so this small community can accommodate you.

The community-run Pine Creek Campground is located on Warm Bay Road. Some sites accommodate mid-sized RVs. Pine Creek Beach, 2 miles/3.5 km from town, has free tent camping.

The town fills up during the **Atlin Arts & Music Festival** (July 11-13, 2014). Last year more than 2,000 people flocked to Atlin to enjoy music, art and film in a family-friendly environment. During the festival, camping is available on the festival grounds (free with an advance ticket or purchase a festival wristband). For more information on this popular annual event, visit www.atlin festival.ca.

Attractions in Atlin include the **Atlin Historical Museum**, located in Atlin's original 1-room schoolhouse at 3rd Street and Trainor Avenue. The museum has mining artifacts and photo exhibits of the Atlin gold rush. Open 10 A.M. to 1 P.M. and 2–5 P.M. daily, May–Sept.; phone 250-651-7522. Admission charged. Historic walking tours by appointment.

Atlin Courthouse Gallery displays the work of internationally acclaimed local artists. Includes paintings, photography, art cards, collages, antler carvings, bead jewelry, stained glass, pottery, and wood boxes. Open 11 A.M. to 5 P.M. daily, May to September.

The MV *Tarahne* (Tah-ron) sits on the lakeshore in the middle of town. Built at Atlin in 1916 by White Pass & Yukon Route, she carried passengers and freight from Atlin to Scotia Bay until 1936.

The **Globe Theatre**, built in 1917, was restored by the Atlin Historical Society and re-opened in 1998. More information is available from the Atlin Historical Museum.

MV Tarahne on lakeshore at Atlin.
(©Earl L. Brown)

Fishing. The Atlin area is well known for its good fishing. Public boat launch on Atlin Lake, south of the MV *Tarahne*. Boat charters available. British Columbia fishing licenses are available from the government agent and at local outlets.

Tagish Road Log

After visiting Atlin, drive back out Atlin Road and follow Tagish Road to Carcross (log follows). The 34-mile/54-km paved Tagish Road connects the Alaska Highway and Atlin Road with the South Klondike Highway. It was built in 1942 to lay a gas pipeline during construction of the Alaska Highway.

Distance from junction with Alaska Highway (J) is shown. *Kilometreposts measure east to west from Alaska Highway junction to Carcross turnoff.*

J 1.1 (1.8 km) **Junction** with Atlin Road. Head west on Tagish Road.

J 8.8 (14.2 km) Jubilee Mountain (elev. 5,950 feet/1,814m) to the south; view from top of Little Atlin Lake and Tagish River. Jubilee Mountain was named by Dr. G.M. Dawson in 1887 in honor of Queen Victoria's Jubilee.

J 12.6 (20.2 km) **Tagish Yukon government campground** on **Six Mile River**. (Take Cottonwood Creek Road, slow for potholes.)

Fishing, boat launch, picnic area, playground, kitchen shelter, firewood, 28 campsites with firepits and tables, drinking water and toilets. Camping permit ($12). *CAUTION: Watch for black bears.*

J 12.8 (20.4 km) Gas, oil, minor repairs, snacks, groceries and post office. Marina on north side of road at east end of Tagish bridge has bait, tackle, fishing licenses, boat rental (posted hours are 8 A.M.–7 P.M.)

J 13 (21 km) **Tagish (Six Mile) River bridge.** West end of bridge has a day-use area with parking, 4 picnic sites and water. Good fishing from north side of bridge on anglers' walkway for lake trout, arctic grayling, northern pike, whitefish and cisco.

J 13.4 (21.5 km) Paved road leads to settlement of **TAGISH** (pop. 206) on the Tagish River (known locally as Six Mile River). Two miles/3.2 km south of Tagish on the Tagish River is **Tagish Post**, originally named Fort Sifton, the Canadian customs post established in 1897. Two of the original 5 buildings still stand. The North West Mounted Police and Canadian customs collected duties on thousands of tons of freight carried by stampeders on their way to the Klondike goldfields between September 1897 and February 1898.

J 13.6 (22 km) **Six Mile River Resort** to south (description follows) offers canoe and cabin rentals, restaurant/bakery. Tagish Stores (to north) has post office, cafe, motel, camping.

J 29.6 (48 km) Chootla Lake.

J 31 (49.9 km) First glimpse westbound of Montana Mountain (elev. 7,230 feet/2,204m) across narrows at Carcross.

J 33.8 (54 km) **C 0 Junction** with South Klondike Highway (Yukon Highway 2). Turn left for **CARCROSS**, a half-mile south; gas, food, souvenirs, visitor centre and historic sites. The WP&YR Warehouse (Koolseen Plac, including the little locomotive, the Duchess) has historical photographs.

Turn right (north) and continue 32 miles/51 km to junction with the Alaska Highway at **Milepost DC 874.4**. Scenic attractions along the way include **Carcross Desert** (1 mile north of this junction) and **Emerald Lake** (7 miles/11 km north). The **Yukon Rock Shop** is located on the right side of the highway driving northbound, just 0.4 mile/0.6 km west of the Alaska Highway junction.

Turn to SOUTH KLONDIKE HIGHWAY section for detailed log and description of attractions along the entire length of the South Klondike Highway.

Return to Milepost DC 874.4 Alaska Highway

(Continued from page 170)

DC 855.8 (1372.5 km) DJ 531.2 (854.9 km) Distance marker southbound shows Teslin 132 km/82 miles, Watson Lake 395 kmk/245 miles.

DC 857.8 (1375.9 km) DJ 529.2 (851.6 km) Paved shoulder parking east side of highway for commercial trucks only. Marsh Lake to west.

DC 859.9 (1379 km) DJ 527.1 (848.3 km) Historical Mile 890. Turnoff to west (watch for tent/camping sign) for **Marsh Lake Yukon government campground** via 0.4-mile/0.6-km gravel loop road: 41 sites, most level, some with lake views, 9 pull-through; outhouses, firewood, firepits, litter bins, picnic tables, kitchen shelter, water pump. Camping permit ($12). For group camping, follow signs near campground entrance. ▲

For group camping, follow signs near campground entrance. Day-use area includes sandy beach, change house, picnic area, playground, kitchen shelter and boat launch.

DC 860 (1379.1 km) DJ 527 (848.2 km) Turnoff to west on Army Beach Road for **Marsh Lake Recreation Site** (watch for picnicking sign). Day-use area includes sandy beach, change house, picnic area, playground, kitchen shelter.

DC 861.1 (1381.6 km) DJ 525.9 (846.1 km) McClintock River bridge. The river was named by Lieutenant Schwatka for Arctic explorer Sir Francis McClintock. Turnout to west at north end of bridge has boat ramp access, litter barrels and outhouse.

This boat launch is a popular put-in spot for canoe trips down the **McClintock River** to **McClintock Bay**, at the north end of Marsh Lake. The river is narrow, winding and silty, with thick brush along the shoreline, but it is a good river for boat trips, especially in late fall. McClintock Bay is a critical habitat for migrating waterfowl in spring. Good bird watching (Northern pintail, canvasback, American wigeon, common goldeneye, common merganser, American kestrels and bald eagles); best place to see mule deer in the Yukon; look for beaver lodges in sloughs. Fishing for grayling, jackfish and trout. ◀

DC 861.3 (1381.8 km) DJ 525.7 (846 km) Swan Haven Interpretive Centre (2 miles/3.2 km from highway via good gravel road) overlooks McClintock Bay and is open in April; guided walks. Outdoor displays open all year. Best time to see swans is during migration, from late March to early May. McClintock Bay's early open water hosts some 10,000 migrating trumpeter swans, as well as tundra swans, widgeons, Canada geese, northern pintails and other birds. The annual Celebration of Swans festival is held at the centre the third week of April; www.environmentyukon.gov.yk.ca/.

DC 864.3 (1388.1 km) DJ 522.7 (841.2 km) Kettley's Canyon.

DC 867.3 (1393 km) DJ 519.7 (836.4 km) Historic Milepost 897. Yukon River Bridge (elev. 2,150 feet/645m). Turnoff to north at east end of bridge for **Marsh Lake Dam Rest Area**; large gravel parking area, litter bins, outhouses and boat launch. Point of interest sign about Lewes Dam. Interpretive trail with signs about area history and wildlife. Viewing platform on hillside overlooks the beginning of the Yukon River (Lewes River Marsh).

Marsh Lake Dam Rest Area is located at the southeast end of the Yukon River Bridge.
(©Kris Valencia, staff)

Measuring nearly 2,000 miles/3,218 km, the Yukon River is the fourth or fifth longest river in North America (both the river's length and rank depend on the source). It is the principal river of both Yukon Territory and Alaska, draining three-quarters of Yukon Territory and a third of Alaska. It is also the "focal point of Yukon history," according to R. Coutts, in his book *Yukon: Places & Names*.

The Yukon River flows northwest from its headwaters near the Yukon Territory–British Columbia border to Fort Yukon in Alaska. From there it turns sharply southwest across Alaska to empty into the Bering Sea at Norton Sound. Major tributaries in Yukon include the Teslin, Pelly, White and Stewart rivers; in Alaska, the Porcupine, Charley, Tanana, Innoko and Koyukuk rivers.

Hudson's Bay Company traders first explored the upper Yukon River in the 1840s. Missionaries, fur trappers and prospectors soon followed. Some 50,000 prospectors (yet another number that changes with the source) followed the Yukon River from Lake Bennett to Dawson City during the Klondike Gold Rush of 1898-1899.

DC 868 (1394 km) DJ 519 (835.4 km) *Highway climb next 1.2 miles/1.9 km northbound.* Views of Yukon River to east.

DC 873.5 (1403 km) DJ 513.5 (826.4 km) Historical Mile 904. The Caribou RV Park with hookups, restrooms and showers, and RV/car wash. The campground includes the popular **Wolf's Den Restaurant** (try their spaetzle!); descriptions follow. ♿ ▲

The Caribou RV Park, 15 minutes from downtown. We are the little ones in town, your privacy and relaxation are important to us! Pets are welcome. Treed sites, walking trails, dump station, laundromat, car wash. Spacious pull-through sites (15/30-amp power and good drinking water) and the famous clean, private washrooms. From a guest: "From East to West, just the best!" (J. Thomson, WY). See it for yourself! Phone (867) 668-2961. See display ad this page. [ADVERTISEMENT]

©Kris Valencia, staff

The Wolf's Den Restaurant, conveniently located at the award-winning Caribou RV Park. We're not your ordinary eating spot ... come in, sit back and relax. Our meals are all prepared fresh, with Swiss and western cuisine. Daily specials, steaks and schnitzels, salads and pastas, fish and vegetarian dishes, too. Inquire about our special fondues. Be sure to check out our Wolf Den dessert selections. Open daily for breakfast, lunch and dinner. Licensed. Your hosts, Harry and Yvonne—We look forward to serving you. Wir sprechen Deutsch. (867) 393-3968. Email info@wolfsden.ca. Website www.wolfsden.ca. [ADVERTISEMENT]

DC 873.8 (1403.5 km) DJ 513.2 (825.9 km) Empress Road. *Speed zones northbound.*

DC 874.4 (1404.4 km) DJ 512.6 (824.9 km) Historical Mile 905. Junction with South Klondike Highway (Yukon Highway 2 South), which leads 98 miles/158 km to

historic Skagway, AK; 25 miles/40 km to scenic Emerald Lake; and 32 miles/52 km to Carcross. See also "Atlin–Tagish–Carcross Scenic Loop" on pages 171-172.

The **Yukon Rock Shop** is located 0.4 mile/0.6 km west of this junction in the lower level of a private home on the south side of the South Klondike Highway; worth a stop for rockhounds.

Yukon Rock Shop. See display ad this page.

Junction with South Klondike Highway which leads south 32 miles/52 km to Carcross and 98 miles/158 km to Skagway. See SOUTH KLONDIKE HIGHWAY section for log.

Distance marker southbound shows Teslin 161 km/100 miles, Watson Lake 424 km/682 km.

DC 874.5 (1404.6 km) DJ 512.5 (824.7 km) Distance marker northbound shows Whitehorse City Centre 22 km/14 miles, Dawson City 559 km/347 miles.

DC 874.9 (1405.2 km) DJ 512.1 (824.1 km) Welcome to Whitehorse (northbound sign). Incorporated June 1, 1950, Whitehorse expanded in 1974 from its original 3 square miles/8 square km to 162 square miles/420 square km.

DC 875.1 (1405.5 km) DJ 511.9 (823.8

km) Cowley Creek Subdivision, Salmon Trail.

DC 876.8 (1408.2 km) DJ 510.2 (821.1 km) **Historical Mile 906. Wolf Creek Yukon Government Campground** to east. An 0.8-mile/1.3-km gravel loop road leads through this campground: 40 sites, most level, 11 pull-through; kitchen shelters, water pumps, picnic tables, firepits, firewood, out-houses, litter barrels, playground; camping permit ($12). A 1.2-mile/2-km nature loop trail winds through boreal forest to an overlook of the Yukon River and returns along Wolf Creek. Interpretive brochure at trailhead and information panels at campground entrance. Fishing in Wolf Creek for grayling.

DC 878.3 (1410.6 km) DJ 508.7 (818.7 km) Meadow Lakes golf course to northeast.

DC 879.3 (1412.3 km) DJ 507.7 (817 km) Highway crosses abandoned railroad tracks of the **White Pass & Yukon Route** (WP&YR) narrow-gauge railroad. Although the WP&YR no longer serves Whitehorse by rail, it does offer scenic rail trips in summer out of Skagway, AK, to White Pass Summit, Lake Bennett and Carcross. (See Railroads in the TRAVEL PLANNING section for details. See also SOUTH KLONDIKE HIGHWAY section for map of rail route.)

Construction of the WP&YR began in May 1898 at the height of the Klondike Gold Rush. Completion of the railway in 1900 linked the port of Skagway, AK, with

Whitehorse, YT, providing passenger and freight service for thousands of gold seekers. The WP&YR ceased operation in 1982. In 1988, WP&YR started their sightseeing rail trips between Skagway and Fraser and are a very sought after tourist attraction.

DC 879.6 (1412.8 km) DJ 507.4 (816.6 km) 60° North Express commercial cardlock.

DC 879.7 (1413 km) DJ 507.3 (816.4 km) Petro Canada gas station with diesel to northeast.

DC 879.8 (1413.2 km) DJ 507.2 (816.2 km) **Historic Milepost 910.** Frasier Road/McCrae Business Park. Access to Fireweed RV Services.

McCrae originated in 1900 as a flag stop on the newly constructed White Pass & Yukon Railway. During WWII, this area served as a major service and supply depot, a major construction camp and a recreation centre.

DC 880 (1413.5 km) DJ 507 (815.9 km) **Historical Mile 910.5. Fireweed R.V. Services** to northeast, access via frontage road; repairs, parts and accessories.

Fireweed R.V. Services Ltd. See display ad this page.

DC 880.3 (1414 km) DJ 506.7 (815.4 km) Access via frontage road to Fireweed R.V. Services.

DC 880.8 (1414.7 km) DJ 506.2 (814.6 km) **Historic Milepost 911** (site of Utah Construction Co. Camp). **Pioneer R.V. Park** to east; treed campsites with hookups, WiFi, showers, laundry, store, gas/diesel/propane, dump station.

Pioneer RV Park. See display ad this page.

DC 881 (1415 km) DJ 506 (814.3 km) Turnoff for Mount Sima ski area. The Mount Sima complex, which includes a chairlift, day-lodge and observation tower (open in summer), was closed in 2013.

DC 881.3 (1415.7 km) DJ 505.7 (813.8 km) White Pass & Yukon Route's Utah siding to east. Also site of an Army camp where thousands of soldiers were stationed during construction of the Alaska Highway.

DC 881.7 (1416.2 km) DJ 505.3 (813.2 km) Sharp turnoff to northeast for **Miles Canyon** via Schwatka Lake Road (gated, closed Oct.–May). Drive down hill 0.3 mile and turn right for spur road to Miles Canyon; parking area is another 0.3 mile. RVs use turnout at turn or park up hill from parking area on curve by outhouses. *Parking area at Miles Canyon will not accommodate RVs.* (The parking area is only large enough for about a dozen cars; we parked our MILE-POST truck/camper there without much of a problem but if the lot had been full, turnaround space would have been tight.) Schwatka Lake Road continues another 2.7 miles from Miles Canyon spur to junction with Robert Service Way (the south access road into Whitehorse). Good viewpoint along the way of Miles Canyon and surrounding areas.

CAUTION: Watch for bicyclists, joggers and walkers on this winding, hilly side road.

Easy access from parking area to walking trails above canyon and pedestrian bridge across canyon. Popular spot with joggers, dog walkers and everyone else. *CAUTION: Steep dropoffs, supervise children and pets.*

Originally called "Grand Canyon" by early gold seekers, Miles Canyon was renamed in 1883 by Lt. Schwatka, U.S. Army, for Brigadier General Nelson A. Miles.

A 1.1-mile/1.7-km trail from the bridge leads to the historic site of **Canyon City**, a gold rush settlement that existed from 1897 to 1900 as a portage point around Miles Canyon and Whitehorse Rapids. Two tramways, each several miles long, transported goods along the east and west sides of the river. Completion of the White Pass & Yukon Route in 1900 made the trams obsolete, and the settlement was abandoned. Contact the Yukon Conservation Society about interpretive walks to **Canyon City** late June through August; (867) 668-5678, www.yukonconservation.org.

©Kris Valencia, staff

Miles Canyon was an imposing challenge for miners and stampeders on their way up the Yukon to the gold fields, mainly because the narrow channel through the canyon was followed by the more daunting Whitehorse Rapids. Both Whitehorse Rapids and Squaw Rapids were eliminated by construction of the hydro-electric power plant and dam on the Yukon River at Whitehorse in 1959, which created Schwatka Lake.

DC 882.7 (1417.8 km) **DJ 504.3** (811.5 km) **Philmar RV Service and Supply** to southwest; repairs, parts and welding.

Philmar RV Service and Supply. See display ad this page.

DC 882.9 (1418.1 km) **DJ 504.1** (811.2 km) Motel and RV park.

DC 883.1 (1418.5 km) **DJ 503.9** (810.9 km) Former Shell station (no gas!) to northeast houses popular highway grill.

DC 883.5 (1419 km) **DJ 503.5** (810.3 km) City of Whitehorse rest area to east is a large, double-ended turnout with litter barrels, outhouses and information signs.

DC 883.7 (1419.4 km) **DJ 503.3** (810 km) Traffic light at first Whitehorse exit northbound and access to **Hi Country RV Park: Junction** with Robert Service Way and Hamilton Blvd.; descriptions follow. *This is the first of 2 exits for Whitehorse northbound. Description of Whitehorse begins on page 176 at* **Milepost DC 887.4** *(Two Mile Hill), the second exit.*

Robert Service Way, the south access road to Whitehorse (righthand turn northbound), leads downhill to Schwatka Lake Road (Mile 1.1), Robert Service Campground (Mile 1.5), Welcome to Whitehorse turnout on Yukon River (Mile 1.8), then passes the entrance to the SS *Klondike* sternwheeler attraction to junction with 2nd Avenue in downtown Whitehorse (Mile 2.6).

Take Hamilton Blvd. (lefthand turn northbound) then first left-hand turn for Hi Country R.V. Park.

Hi Country R.V. Park. See display ad page this page.

DC 884.3 (1420.4 km) **DJ 502.7** (809 km) Historic Milepost 914. Whitehorse Weigh Station to southwest.

DC 885.5 (1422.1 km) **DJ 501.5** (807.1 km) First entrance northbound (for dropping off visitors only) to Yukon Beringia

Centre (see description next milepost). Centre frontdoor drop-off and handicap parking only.

DC 885.7 (1422.3 km) **DJ 501.3** (806.7 km) **Historical Mile 915**. Second entrance to public parking at **Yukon Beringia Interpretive Centre** accesses a frontage road that connects Yukon Beringia Centre, Yukon Transportation Museum and Whitehorse Airport.

The Yukon Berengia Centre traces the Ice Age in Yukon, which, unlike the rest of Canada, was for the most part ice-free. The Blue Fish Caves near Old Crow reputedly hold the earliest evidence of humans in the New World. Displays at the centre trace the science and myth of an Ice Age subcontinent inhabited by great woolly mammoths, giant short-faced bears and lions. Ice Age artifacts include a cast of the largest woolly mammoth skeleton ever recovered in North America. Open daily, mid-May to late September 9 A.M.–6 P.M. Phone (867) 667-8855; fax (867) 667-8844; email beringia@gov.yk.ca; www.beringia.com. Admission charged.

DC 885.8 (1422.6 km) **DJ 501.2** (806.6 km) **Skky Hotel** to southwest. Signed entrance to northeast for Whitehorse Airport (Erick Nielsen Whitehorse International Airport) as well as access to **DC-3 weathervane** and to **Yukon Transportation Museum** (descriptions follow) and also parking for to Yukon Beringia Interpretive Centre.

Skky Hotel. See display ad on page 176.

©Kris Valencia, staff

The **Yukon Transportation Museum** features exhibits about all forms of transportation in the North (see Attractions in following description of Whitehorse for more details). A mural on the front of the museum depicts the methods of transportation used in construction of the Alaska Highway in 1942. The 16-by-60-foot/5-by-19-m mural was painted by members of the Yukon Art Society. Open daily, from mid-May through August. Admission charged.

Cairns in front of the museum commemorate 18 years of service on the Alaska

Highway (1946–64) by the Corps of Royal Canadian Engineers. Near this site, the U.S. Army officially handed over the Alaska Highway to the Canadian Army on April 1, 1946.

The **Douglas DC–3 weathervane** here, mounted on a single pylon in a concrete base, was originally a C-47 that was built in 1942 and flew transport missions in Asia during the war. For more on the history of this unique weathervane, *see description on page 187 in Whitehorse Attractions.*

DC 886 (1423 km) **DJ 501** (806.3 km) FasGas and Airport Chalet to west. Turn-off to east for second entrance northbound to Erick Nielsen Whitehorse International Airport. The airport was built during WWII and used by both U.S. and Canadian forces. Mr. Nielsen was Yukon's longest standing member of Parliament.

DC 887.4 (1425.4 km) **DJ 499.6** (804 km) 4-lane highway with dedicated center turn lanes approaching traffic light at **Two Mile Hill/Hamilton Blvd. junction**. Turn to northeast (righthand turn northbound) and follow Two Mile Hill down to Whitehorse city centre via 4th avenue OR 2nd Avenue (requires left-hand turn). Access to Canadian Tire/Walmart/Starbucks/60° North via lefthand turn on Industrial Road (no turn light) and righthand turn on Quartz Road. Two Mile Hill is a busy road. Watch for Whitehorse Horse sculpture on right just past Range Road. *CAUTION: Easy to miss overhead traffic light at Range Road. Be alert for all overhead stoplights and pedestrian crosswalks in Whitehorse!*

The Whitehorse Horse on Two Mile Hill was created by artist Daphne Mennell with journeyman welder Roger Poole. (©Kris Valencia, staff)

This is the second (and last) exit northbound for Whitehorse.

Canada Games Centre/Centre Des Jeux Du Canada is up the hill to the west (lefthand turn northbound, righthand turn southbound).

Description of Whitehorse follows. *Alaska Highway log continues on page 189.*

Alaska Highway log continues on page 189.

Whitehorse

Historic Milepost 918. Located on the upper reaches of the Yukon River in Canada's subarctic at latitude 61°N. Whitehorse is 100 miles/160 km from Haines Junction; 109 miles/175 km from Skagway, AK; 250 miles/241 km from Haines, AK; and 396 miles/637 km from Tok, AK. **Population:** 26,418. **Emergency Services: RCMP, Fire Department, Ambulance,** phone 911. **Hospital,** phone (867) 393-8700.

Visitor Information: Yukon Visitor Information Centre is located next to the Yukon Territorial Government Building on 2nd Avenue. RV parking is available on the Lambert Avenue side of the Visitor Centre. The Centre offers a 15-minute film on the Yukon; daily updated information on accommodations, weather and road conditions; and printout information on attractions, restaurants and events in Whitehorse. The Centre is open daily, 8 A.M. to 8 P.M., from mid-May to mid-September. The rest of the year the Centre is open weekdays from 8:30 A.M. to 5 P.M. (closed for lunch). Phone (867) 667-3084, or contact a Travel Councilor with Tourism Yukon at Box 2703, Whitehorse, YT Y1A 2C6. Toll-free phone 1-800-661-0494; email vacation@gov.yk.ca; fax (867) 667-3546; Internet www.travel yukon.com.

The City of Whitehorse Tourism Dept. offers year-round visitor information (ask about their free CD-ROM; phone (867) 668-8687; email tourism@whitehorse.ca; or write the Tourism Department, City of Whitehorse, 2121 Second Ave., Whitehorse, YT Y1A 1C2. Access up-to-date information on events, accommodations and attractions at www.visitwhitehorse.com. Visitors are invited to stop by The Smith House (the little blue house at 3rd and Wood Street) to pick up a free city pin and a free 3-day Visitor Parking pass.

Elevation: 2,316 feet/706m. **Climate:** Wide variations are the theme here with no two winters alike. The lowest recorded temperature is -62°F/-52.2°C in January 1947 and the warmest 94°F/34.4°C in June 1969. Average daily temperature in January is 14°F/-17.7°C and for July 57°F/14°C. Annual precipitation is 10.3 inches, equal parts snow and rain. On June 21, Whitehorse enjoys 21 hours of daylight and on Dec. 21 only 5 hours, 37 minutes. **Radio:** CFWH 570, CBC network with repeaters throughout territory; CBC Whitehorse; CKRW 610, local; CHON-FM 98.1; 96.1-FM The Rush; CFET-FM 106.7. **Television:** CBC–TV live, colour via ANIK satellite, Canadian network; WHTV, NADR (First Nation issues), local cable; CanCom stations via satellite, many channels. **Newspapers:** *Whitehorse Star* (weekdays); *Yukon News* (3 times a week).

Private Aircraft: Whitehorse International Airport, 3 runways; has approach over city and an abrupt escarpment; elev. 2,305 feet/703m; main runway length 9,000 feet/2,743m; surfaced; fuel 80, 100, jet fuel available. Customs clearance available.

Floatplane base on Schwatka Lake above Whitehorse Dam (take the South Access Road from Alaska Highway and turn on Robert Service Way by the railroad tracks).

Description

Whitehorse has been the capital of Yukon Territory since 1953, and serves as the centre for transportation, communications and supplies for Yukon Territory and the Northwest Territories.

The downtown business section of Whitehorse lies on the west bank of the Yukon River. The Riverdale subdivision is on the east side. The low mountains rising behind Riverdale are dominated by Canyon Mountain, known locally as Grey Mountain. Wolf Creek, Hillcrest and Granger subdivisions lie south of the city; McIntyre subdivision is to the west; and Porter Creek, Takhini and Crestview subdivisions are north of the city. The Takhini area is the location of the Yukon College campus.

Downtown Whitehorse is flat and marked at its western limit by a rising escarpment dominated by the Whitehorse International Airport. Originally a woodcutter's lot, the airstrip was first cleared in 1920 to accommodate 4 U.S. Army planes on a test flight from New York to Nome. Access to the city is by Two-Mile Hill from the north and by Robert Service Way (South Access Road) from the south; both connect with the Alaska Highway.

In 1974, the city limits of Whitehorse were expanded from the original 2.7 square miles/6.9 square kilometres to 162 square miles/421 square kilometres, making Whitehorse at one time the largest metropolitan

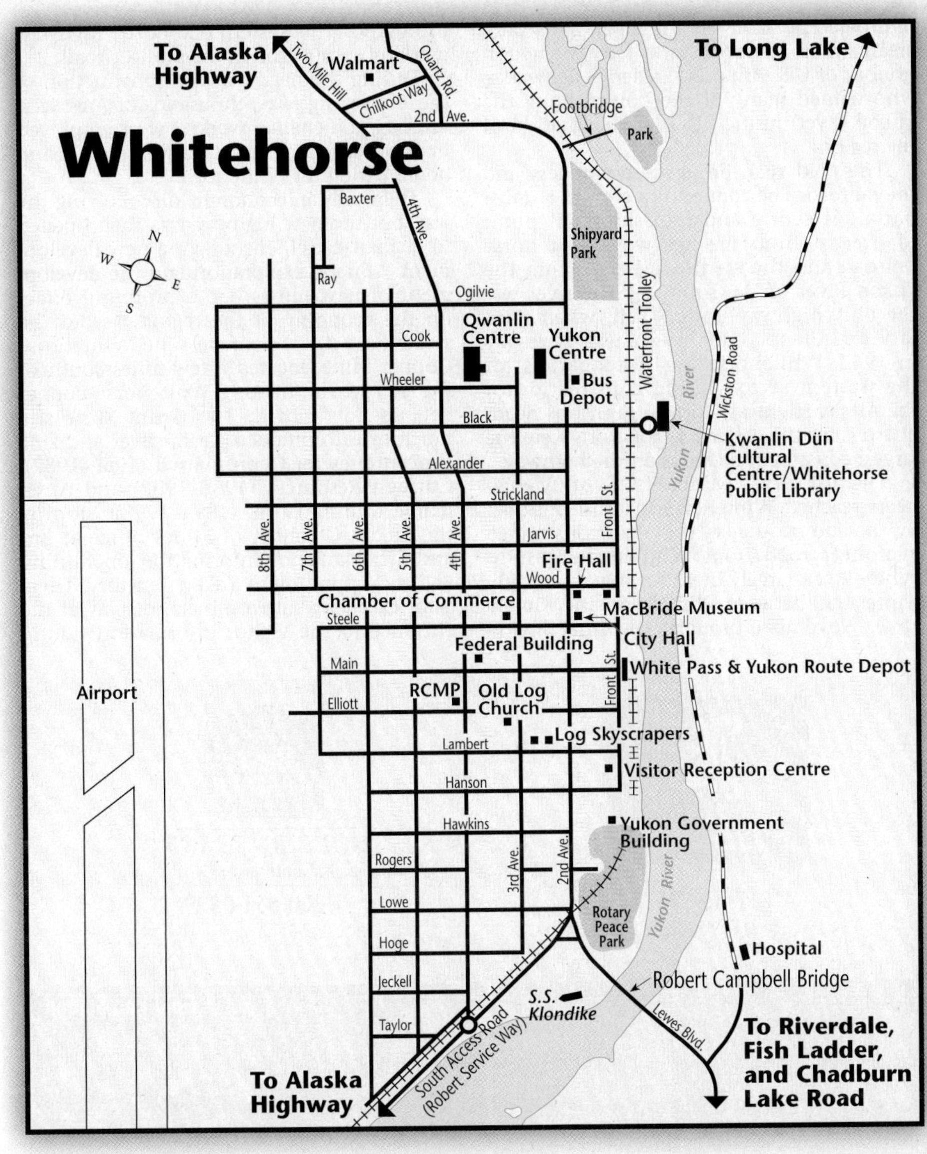
Whitehorse
To Alaska Highway
Walmart
Two-Mile Hill
Chilkoot Way
Quartz Rd.
2nd Ave.
Footbridge
Park
To Long Lake
Baxter
4th Ave.
Ray
Shipyard Park
Ogilvie
Cook
Qwanlin Centre
Yukon Centre
Wheeler
Bus Depot
Waterfront Trolley
Wickston Road
Black
Kwanlin Dün Cultural Centre/Whitehorse Public Library
Alexander
Yukon River
Strickland
Jarvis
Front St.
8th Ave.
7th Ave.
6th Ave.
5th Ave.
4th Ave.
Fire Hall
Wood
Chamber of Commerce
MacBride Museum
Steele
City Hall
Federal Building
Main
White Pass & Yukon Route Depot
Airport
RCMP
Old Log Church
Elliott
Log Skyscrapers
Lambert
Visitor Reception Centre
Hanson
Hawkins
Yukon Government Building
Rogers
3rd Ave.
2nd Ave.
Lowe
Rotary Peace Park
Hoge
Hospital
Jeckell
Robert Campbell Bridge
S.S. Klondike
Taylor
Lewes Blvd.
South Access Road (Robert Service Way)
To Alaska Highway
To Riverdale, Fish Ladder, and Chadburn Lake Road

WHITEHORSE ADVERTISERS

Accommodations

Best Western Gold Rush Inn .... Ph. 1-800-661-0539
Canadas Best Value Inn .... Ph. 1-866-949-7800
Coast High Country Inn .... Ph. 1-800-554-4471
Edgewater Hotel .... Ph. 1-877-484-3334
Hidden Valley B&B .... Ph. (867) 633-6482
Midnight Sun B&B .... Ph. 1-866-284-4448
Muktuk Adventures Ltd. .... Ph. 1-868-968-3647
Ramada Klondike Inn .... Ph. (867) 668-4747
Rivendell Farm .... Ph. 867-633-6178
Skyy Hotel .... Ph. 1-866-799-4933
Sundog Retreat .... Ph. (867) 633-4183
Takhini Hot Springs .... Ph. (867) 456-8000
Versleuce Meadows B&B .... Ph. (867) 633-6221
Westmark Whitehorse .... Ph. (867) 393-9700
Yukon Inn .... Ph. 1-800-661-0454

Attractions & Entertainment

Frantic Follies .... Ph. (867) 668-2042
Kwanlin Dun Cultural Centre .... Ph. (867) 456-5322
Takhini Hot Springs .... Ph. (867) 456-8000
Yukon Brewing Co. .... Ph. (867) 668-4183
Yukon Heritage Attractions .... Ph. (867) 667-4704
Yukon Wildlife Preserve .... Ph. (867) 456-7300

Campgrounds

Caribou RV Park .... Ph. (867) 668-2961
Hi Country R.V. Park .... Ph. (867) 667-7445
Pioneer RV Park .... Ph. (867) 668-5944
Takhini Hot Springs .... Ph. (867) 456-8000

Dining

High Country Inn .... Ph. 1-800-554-4471
Westmark Whitehorse Hotel .... Ph. (867) 393-9700
Wolf's Den .... Ph. (867) 393-3968
Yukon Inn .... Ph. 1-800-661-0454

RV & Auto Services & Supplies

Fireweed R.V. Services .... Ph. (867) 668-5082
Philmar RV Service & Supply .... Ph. (867) 668-6129

Shopping & Services

Bear's Paw Quilts .... Ph. (867) 393-2327
Mac's Fireweed Books .... Ph. 1-800-661-0508
Midnight Sun Emporium .... Ph. (867) 668-4350
Murdoch's .... Ph. (867) 667-7403
Yukon Rock Shop .... Ph. (867) 668-2772

Tours & Transportation

White Pass & Yukon Route Railway .... Ph. (867) 668-7245

Visitor Information

City of Whitehorse .... Ph. (867) 668-8687

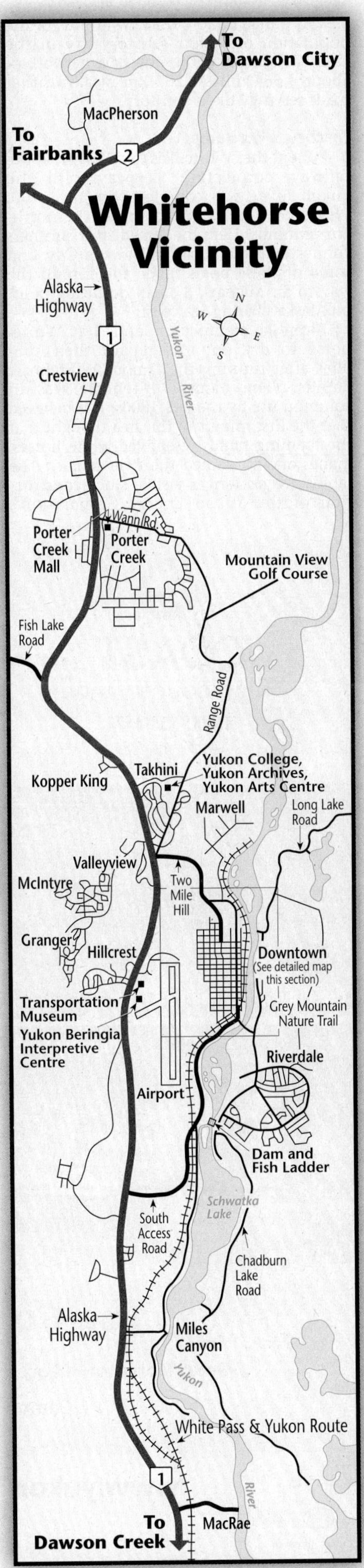
Whitehorse Vicinity
To Dawson City
MacPherson
To Fairbanks
2
Alaska Highway
1
Yukon River
Crestview
Wann Rd.
Porter Creek Mall
Porter Creek
Mountain View Golf Course
Fish Lake Road
Range Road
Takhini
Kopper King
Yukon College, Yukon Archives, Yukon Arts Centre
Marwell
Long Lake Road
Valleyview
McIntyre
Two Mile Hill
Granger
Hillcrest
Downtown
(See detailed map this section)
Grey Mountain Nature Trail
Transportation Museum
Yukon Beringia Interpretive Centre
Riverdale
Airport
Dam and Fish Ladder
South Access Road
Schwatka Lake
Chadburn Lake Road
Alaska Highway
Miles Canyon
Yukon
White Pass & Yukon Route
River
1
To Dawson Creek
MacRae

area in Canada. More than two-thirds of the population of Yukon Territory live in the city. Whitehorse is the hub of a network of about 2,664 miles/4,287 km of all-weather roads serving Yukon Territory.

History & Economy

When the White Pass & Yukon Route railway, connecting Skagway with the Yukon River, was completed in July 1900, Whitehorse came into being as the northern terminus. Here the famed river steamers connected the railhead to Dawson City, and some of these boats made the trip all the way to St. Michael, a small outfitting point on Alaska's Bering Sea coast.

Klondike stampeders landed at Whitehorse to dry out and repack their supplies after running the famous Whitehorse Rapids. (The name Whitehorse was in common use by the late 1800s; it is believed that the first miners in the area thought that the foaming rapids resembled white horses' manes and so named the river rapids.) The rapids are no longer visible since construction of the Yukon Energy Corporation's hydroelectric dam on the river. This dam created man-made Schwatka Lake, named in honour of U.S. Army Lt. Frederick Schwatka, who named many of the points along the Yukon River during his 1883 exploration of the region.

The gold rush brought stampeders and the railroad. The community grew as a transportation centre and transshipment point for freight from the Skagway–Whitehorse railroad and the stern-wheelers plying the Yukon River to Dawson City. The river was the only highway until WWII, when military expediency built the Alaska Highway in 1942. Whitehorse was headquarters for the western sector during construction of the Alaska Highway. Fort St. John was headquarters for the eastern sector. Both were the largest construction camps on the highway.

The first survey parties of U.S. Army engineers reached Whitehorse in April of 1942. By the end of August, they had constructed a pioneer road from Whitehorse west to White River, largely by following an existing winter trail between Whitehorse and Kluane Lake. November brought the final breakthrough on the western end of the highway, marking completion of the pioneer road.

During the height of the construction of the Alaska Highway, thousands of American military and civilian workers were employed in the Canadian North. It was the second boom period for Whitehorse.

There was an economic lull following the war, but the new highway was then opened to civilian travel, encouraging new development. Mineral exploration and the development of new mines had a profound effect on the economy of the region, as did the steady growth of tourism. The Whitehorse Copper Mine, located a few miles south of the city in the historic Whitehorse copper belt, is now closed. The Grum Mine site north of Faro produced lead, silver and zinc concentrates for Cyprus–Anvil (1969–1982), Curragh Resources (1986–1992) and Anvil Range Mining Corp. (1994–1998). Stop by the Yukon Chamber of Mines office at 3rd and Strickland for information on mining and rockhounding in Yukon Territory. There is an excellent Yukon mineral display at the entrance to the Visitor Information Centre

downtown.

Because of its accessibility, Whitehorse became capital of the Yukon Territory (replacing Dawson City in that role) on March 31, 1953.

Lodging & Services

Whitehorse has excellent accommodations, with many modern hotels and motels downtown and along the Alaska Highway, as well as several interesting bed-and-breakfast options (see ads this section). There are also a surprising number of dining choices, from barbecue to French and Swiss/German cuisine, from family dining to fine dining. Major chain fast-food outlets and restaurants are also available in Whitehorse.

Shopping downtown on Main Street. The Qwanlin Centre at 4th Ave. and Ogilvie has a supermarket and a variety of shops. The Yukon Centre Mall on 2nd Avenue has a government liquor store, clothing store, restaurants and a Western Union. Whitehorse also has "big box" stores like Walmart, Superstore, Canadian Tire and Staples. *Pedestrians and motorists note: Downtown Whitehorse is a busy place. Watch out for each other!*

In addition to supermarkets, banks, garages and service stations, there are churches, movie theaters and beauty salons. Whitehorse also has several banks with ATMs.

The Canada Games Centre/Centre Des Jeux Du Canada has an Aquatic Centre, walking/running track, 3 ice surfaces, drop-in programs and fitness classes. Visit www.canadagamescentre.whitehorse.ca; phone (867) 668-4836 for information.

Postal services in Whitehorse are pro-

Robert Service's Chair offers a photo-op in downtown Whitehorse. *(©Kris Valencia, staff)*

vided at the Shoppers' Drug Mart in the Qwanlin Centre (Ogilvie and 4th) and on Main Street at Third Avenue. The post office is located at the top of Two Mile Hill. Whitehorse area maps and Yukon maps are available at Mac's Fireweed Bookstore at 203 Main Street; phone (867) 668-2434.

Best Western Gold Rush Inn boasts a convenient Main Street location in the heart of downtown Whitehorse, seconds from shopping, sightseeing and the spectacular Yukon River waterfront. Our modern comfortable rooms offer the best night's sleep in the Yukon. Home to the famous Gold Pan Saloon and an Aveda spa. Free parking, free Internet and coin laundry. 1-800-661-0539. See display ad on page 178.
[ADVERTISEMENT]

Parks Canada offers tours of the SS Klondike sternwheeler, which sits beside the Yukon River near the Robert Campbell bridge in Whitehorse. (©Kris Valencia, staff)

Edgewater Hotel. Historic Front Street and Main location, across from White Pass Train Depot on the Yukon River. Cozy boutique hotel with modern rooms and a colourful history dating back to the Klondike Gold Rush! Home of The Cellar Chop House and Martini Bar and The Edge Bar & Grill. Free parking/Internet. A/C available. 1-877-484-3334. See display ad on page 178. [ADVERTISEMENT]

Coast High Country Inn. Famous for our 40-foot-tall wooden Mountie, we offer a great downtown Whitehorse location, steps away from the historic Yukon River and its scenic waterfront trails. We bring together modern comfortable rooms and uniquely Yukon character. Enjoy local favlour on "The Deck"—our colourful year-round patio, or a fine dining experience in Morels Restaurant. Free parking, free Internet and coin laundry. A/C available. 1-800-554-4471. See display ad on page 178. [ADVERTISEMENT]

Camping

RV and tent camping are available at several campgrounds south of Whitehorse on the Alaska Highway, including the following: **Hi Country RV Park (Milepost DC 884), Pioneer RV Park (Milepost DC**

880.8), Caribou RV Park (**Milepost DC 873.5**), and Wolf Creek Yukon government campground (**Milepost DC 876.8**). **Takhini Hot Springs** on the Klondike Loop is also a popular camping spot (half-hour drive from Whitehorse). Tent camping is available in Whitehorse at Robert Service Park on Robert Service Way.

Transportation

Air: Air Canada to Vancouver. Air North (www.flyairnorth.com) to Dawson City, Old Crow, Edmonton, Calgary, Ottawa, Vancouver, Yellowknife, seasonal service to Fairbanks, AK; phone 1-800-661-0407. WestJet to Calgary, Edmonton, Toronto, Vancouver. Condor (charter) connects Whitehorse, Fairbanks, AK, and Frankfurt, Germany, from May through October; phone 1-800-364-1667. Edelweiss Air flights weekly between Zurich, Switzerland, and Whitehorse from mid-May to mid-September; www.edelweis

sair.com. Whitehorse International Airport is reached from the Alaska Highway.

Seaplane dock on Schwatka Lake just above the Whitehorse Dam (take Robert Service Way from Alaska Highway and turn right on road by the railroad tracks to reach the base). Flightseeing tours available.

Bus: Whitehorse Transit offers downtown and rural service. Alaska/Yukon Trails offers scheduled service connecting Whitehorse to Alaska destinations. See Bus Lines in the TRAVEL PLANNING section.

Railroad: For White Pass & Yukon Route rail trips, phone WP&YR in Skagway at 1-800-343-7373, or contact Yukon Alaska Tourist Tours at the historic WP&YR station on Front Street, phone (867) 633-5710.

Car, **Truck**, **Motorhome** and **Camper Rentals**: Several local and national agencies are located in Whitehorse.

Attractions

S.S. Klondike National Historic Site. This grand old stern-wheeler sits beside

the Yukon River near the Robert Campbell bridge. There is an interpretive centre and public parking at the *S.S. Klondike* National Historic Site. The site is open from 9:30 A.M. to 5 P.M. and there are more than 7,000 artifacts on display. Self-guided tours in English and French are available throughout the day, and with entry for the last self-guided tour of the day at 4:30 P.M. The interpretive centre is open from mid-May to mid-September.

The *S.S. Klondike* was built in 1929 by the British Yukon Navigation Company (BYNC). The vessel was the largest on the Yukon, had a cargo capacity 50 percent greater than previous boats, and could carry over 300 tons. She ran aground in 1936 at the confluence of the Teslin and Yukon rivers in a section known as Thirty Mile. Salvaged parts were used to construct a new ship—the *S.S. Klondike II* (launched in 1937)—that was almost identical to the first.

The *S.S. Klondike* carried mail, general supplies, passengers and silver lead ore

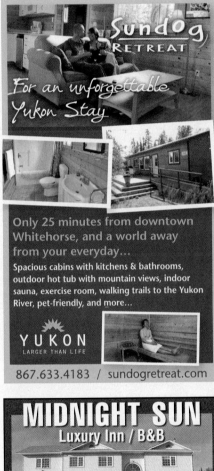

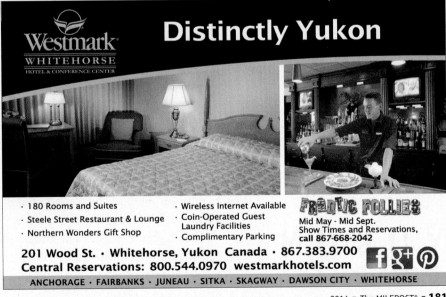

THE WILDERNESS CITY

Day Trips:
Skagway and the White Pass and Yukon Route railway, Kluane National Park, Takhini Hot Springs, Marsh Lake and Swan Haven Wildlife Viewing, Atlin, Fox Lake, Carcross and the world's smallest desert!

Travelling by RV.
The Alaska Highway is the trip of a lifetime but there are alternatives to driving the same route twice. You can arrive or return, via the Alaska Marine Highway at Skagway, a two hour scenic drive from Whitehorse.

Or choose the picturesque Highway 37, the Stewart-Cassiar route.

Or fly into Whitehorse – there are plenty of RV Rental agencies to choose from. Contact us and we'll help you with suggestions, tips, itineraries and community guides for your journey.

We're an RV friendly community. Parking can be found throughout the city core.

"Drop by the Yukon Visitor Information Centre at 2nd Avenue & Lambert Street or contact us for a free vacation planner."
www.travelyukon.com • 1-800-661-0494

Whitehorse

along the 460-mile route between White-horse and Dawson City until 1955 when she was retired. Donated to the Canadian government, the *S.S. Klondike* now rests on the west bank of the Yukon near the Robert Campbell Bridge in Whitehorse. Restoration work on the *S.S. Klondike* was completed in 2005.

Admission is charged to the *S.S. Klondike* National Historic Site. Telephone (867) 667-3910, toll free 1-800-661-0486, fax (867) 393-6701; website: parkscanada.gc.ca/ssklondike.aspx. A gift shop, picnic tables and plenty of parking for RVs and buses is available. Central to downtown and the *S.S. Klondike*, Rotary Peace Park is a popular picnic spot and the site of several White-horse special events. The Skateboard Park is located across the river from the *S.S. Klondike*. Walk or take the trolley to Shipyards Park, near the foot of Ogilvie and Second Avenue.

The MacBride Museum of Yukon History offers a comprehensive view of the colourful characters and groundbreaking events that built Canada's Yukon. Discover the truth behind the Robert Service legend at **Sam McGee's Original Cabin** (pictured below). See Engine 51, the locomotive that built the White Pass & Yukon Route Railway. Follow the Northwest Mounted Police as they establish law and order in the North. Come face to face with a 7-foot grizzly in the Wild World Gallery.

©Kris Valencia, staff

During the summer, the Museum offers daily tours, programs, and games. Visitors can also try their hand at gold panning. Winter activities include talks by local experts on geology, archaeology, anthropology and more.

The Museum gift shop features gold jewellery, works by local artists, historic photographs and books.

The MacBride Museum is located across from the Whitehorse waterfront on the corner of Front and Wood streets. The museum is open year-round: 9:30 A.M. to 5 P.M. daily from May to August; and 10 A.M. to 4 P.M. Tuesday–Saturday in winter. Admission is charged. Gift shop. For more information phone (867) 667-2709, or go to www.macbridemuseum.com.

The MacBride Museum has a North West Mounted Police Patrol Cabin. This re-creation of an early NWMP Patrol Cabin was built in 1995 as part of the 100th anniversary of the RCMP. Whitehorse became the territorial headquarters of the NWMP in 1900. The NWMP were bestowed the title "Royal" in 1904, and in 1920 became the Royal Canadian Mounted Police. The Patrol Cabin is dedicated each year to a famous figure in NWMP history. The distinctive red cloth tunic—or red serge—of the RCMP was first worn by the NWMP in 1897, but it is now worn only at formal occasions or for

special programs.

Kwanlin Dun Cultural Centre. This striking structure adjacent the Whitehorse Public Library on Front Street is a place to share First Nations history, traditions and culture through permanent and temporary exhibits. It is also one fo the largest meeting spaces in Whitehorse. www.kdcc.ca.

Whitehorse Public Library is right next-door to the Kwanlin Dun Cultural Centre, on Front Street and Black Street. Open 10 A.M. to 9 P.M. Monday to Thursday, 10 A.M. to 6 P.M. Friday to Sunday; closed holidays. Phone (867) 667-5239.

Special Events. Whitehorse has a number of festivals and special events throughout the year.

The **Kluane Mountain Bluegrass Festival** takes place in June at the Yukon Arts Centre in Whitehorse. For 2014 dates and schedule, check with the Yukon Bluegrass Music Society at www.yukonbluegrass.com.

The 26th annual **Yukon River Quest Canoe and Kayak Race** takes place June 25-29, 2014. The "Race to the Midnight Sun" begins in Whitehorse and ends in Dawson City, a 460-mile/740-km-long route that is the longest canoe and kayak race in the world. It attracts expert and novice paddlers from around the world. For more information: www.yukonriverquest.com.

July 1st is **Canada Day**, celebrated with events and entertainment for the whole family. July 11-20, 2014, is the **Junior Men's ISF World Softball Championship** (http://softballyukon.com) at the Pepsi Softball Centre. On July 21, 2014, the **Yukon 1000 Canoe and Kayak Races** take place; http://yukon1000.com.

The **Yukon River Trail Marathon** usually takes place in August, with last year's start/finish at Rotary Park. For 2014 event details, visit www.yukonmarathon.com.

The 31st annual running of the **Klondike Trail of '98 International Road Relay** takes place September 5-6, 2014. This is a 110-mile/175-km road relay from Skagway, AK, to Whitehorse, YT. For more information, visit www.klondikeroadrelay.com.

Whitehorse and Fairbanks are the 2 host cities for the **Yukon Quest 1,000 Mile International Sled Dog Race** in February, with each city alternating roles as the "start" and "finish" to this great endurance race. In 2014, the race started in Fairbanks and finished in Whitehorse. In summer you can visit the Yukon Quest office in the White Pass Depot at First and Main streets in downtown Whitehorse. (In Fairbanks, the Yukon Quest store and office are in the log cabin adjacent Golden Heart Plaza on First Avenue.) For more information, visit www.yukonquest.com.

Also in February is Whitehorse's big annual winter event: the **Yukon Sourdough Rendezvous Festival** at Shipyard's Park downtown (www.yukonrendezvous.com).

Frantic Follies Vaudeville Review. The long-running vaudeville stage show, Frantic Follies, is held nightly June through August at the Westmark Whitehorse Hotel. Now in its 45th year, this popular 1-½-hour show features cancan dancing, rousing music and hilarious skits from Robert W. Service ballads. Tickets are available at the box office in the Westmark or phone (867) 668-2042. Tickets are also available at some area RV parks. www.franticfollies.com.

©Kris Valencia, staff

Waterfront Walkway. A wonderful waterfront walking trail connects the city's major parks and provides a pleasant, easy way to see the Yukon River. This paved, wheelchair-accessible path passes many of the City's major attractions and crosses the Yukon River via the Rotary Centennial Bridge.

Visitors may also board the vintage **Waterfront Trolley** in front of the visitor centre for hop-on, hop-off services. This is a scenic route along the Yukon River from downtown to Walmart (fee charged).

Picnic at a park. Central to downtown and the S.S. *Klondike*, **Rotary Peace Park** is a popular picnic spot and the site of several Whitehorse special events. **Skateboard Park** is located across the river from the S.S. *Klondike*. Walk or take the trolley to **Shipyards Park**, near the foot of Ogilvie and Second Avenue.

Old Log Church Museum. Located in the heart of downtown Whitehorse, one block off Main on Elliott at 3rd, the Old Log Church Museum is one of the oldest buildings in Whitehorse, built in 1900 by Rev. R.J. Bowen for the Church of England. Director and Curator Taryn Parker calls it "a place of heart, soul and passion" and invites you to uncover the fascinating stories and hidden treasures of Yukon's early pioneers and missionaries. Open daily to the public from mid-May to early September. Phone (867) 668-2555; www.oldlogchurchmuseum.ca. Admission charged.

City tours. Historical walking tours of Whitehorse are conducted by the Yukon Historical & Museums Association. Tour guides wear period costumes for these walks that take in the city's heritage buildings. Meet at the Donnenworth House, 3126 3rd Ave.; phone (867) 667-4704. A $4 fee is charged. There are tours Monday through Saturday from June to the end of August. For self-guided tours, *Exploring Old Whitehorse* is available from local stores or from the Yukon Historical and Museums Assoc., 3126–3rd Ave., Whitehorse, YT Y1A 1E7.

Yukon Beringia Interpretive Centre traces the Ice Age in northern and central Yukon, which, unlike the rest of Canada, was ice-free. The Blue Fish Caves near Old Crow reputedly hold the earliest evidence of humans in the New World. Displays at the Centre present the science and myth of the Ice Age subcontinent of Beringia, inhabited by great woolly mammoths, giant short-faced bears and lions. Ice Age specimens include a well-preserved Ice Age Yukon horse hide and a reproduction of a scimitar cat, as well as other Ice Age mammals. Open daily, mid-May to late September. Open Sundays and Mondays, October to May. Phone (867) 667-8855; Fax (867) 667-8854; email beringia@gov.yk.ca; www.beringia.com. Admission fee charged.

Yukon Government Building, 2nd Avenue and Hawkins, open 9 A.M. to 5 P.M.

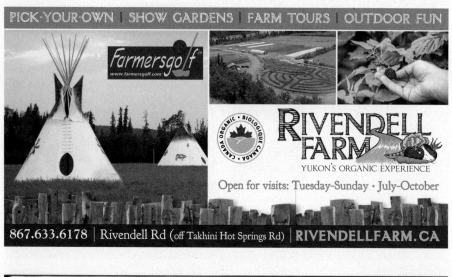

Administrative and Legislative headquarters of Yukon Territory, the building contains some notable artworks. On the main floor wall is an acrylic resin mural, 120 feet/37m long, which portrays the historical evolution of the Yukon. The 24 panels, each measuring 4 by 5 feet/1.2 by 1.5m, highlight events such as the arrival of Sir John Franklin at Herschel Island in 1825, the Klondike Gold Rush, and the coming of the automobile. The mural was created by Vancouver, BC artist David MacLagen.

In the Legislative Chamber, an 18-by-12-foot/5-by-4m tapestry is an abstraction of the fireweed plant, Yukon's floral emblem. The Yukon Women's Tapestry, 5 panels each 7 by 13 feet/2 by 4m, hangs in the legislative library lounge. The wool panels portray the role of women in the development of the territory, depicting the 5 seasons of the North; spring, summer, autumn, winter and "survival," the cold gray season between winter and spring and fall and winter. Begun by the Whitehorse Branch of the Canadian Federation of Business and Professional Women in 1976 to mark International Women's Year, the wall hangings were stitched by some 2,500 Yukoners.

The Yukon Transportation Museum, located on the Alaska Highway adjacent to the Whitehorse Airport (see **Milepost DC 885.8**), features exhibits of all forms of transportation in the North. Displays inside include the full-size replica of the *Queen of the Yukon* Ryan monoplane, sister ship to Lindbergh's *Spirit of St. Louis*; railway rolling stock; Alaska Highway vintage vehicles, dogsleds and stagecoaches. Also featured are the Chilkoot Trail, the Canol Highway and bush pilots of the North.

The museum includes video theatres and a gift shop with a selection of Northern books. Plenty of parking. Admission fee charged. Open daily mid-May to August 31. Phone (867) 668-4792; email ytm@northwestel.net; or visit www.yukontransportationmuseum.com.

World's largest weathervane. Located in front of the Transportation Museum on the Alaska Highway is the world's largest weathervane—a Douglas DC–3. According to Yukon pilot and aviation historian Bob Cameron, this vintage plane was originally a C-47 that was built in 1942 and flew transport missions in Asia during the war. Converted to civilian life as a DC-3 after the war (Canadian registration CF-CPY), she flew for Canadian Pacific Airlines, Connelly-Dawson Airways, Great Northern Airways and Northward Airlines from 1946 until 1970, when she blew an engine on takeoff and was then stripped for parts and parked at the Whitehorse airport.

An airlines maintenance engineer named Joe Muff orchestrated the donation of the historic plane to the Yukon Flying club in order to restore it for permanent display at the airport. It is now owned and managed by the Yukon Transportation Museum. The restored plane was mounted on a rotating pedestal in 1981, and acts as a weathervane, pointing its nose into the wind.

Whitehorse Rapids Fishway. Located at the end of Nisutlin Drive in the Riverdale suburb. The fish ladder was built in 1959 to provide access for chinook (king) salmon and other species above the Yukon Energy Corporation hydroelectric dam. It is the longest wooden fish ladder in the world. The fish ladder is flowing from mid-July to early September during salmon-spawning season.

Interpretive displays and viewing decks; open daily. Admission by donation.

Take a hike with the Yukon Conservation Society. From late June through August, the Yukon Conservation Society (YCS) offers free guided nature walks, ranging in difficulty from easy to strenuous. Trips are 2 to 6 hours in length and informative guides explain the local flora, fauna, geology and history along the trails. The YCS also conducts free interpretive walks to Canyon City (*see page 175*) twice daily, 7 days a week during July and August. Or pick up a copy of *Hikes & Bikes*, a guide to hiking and mountain biking trails in the Whitehorse area, produced by the Yukon Conservation Society. Contact Yukon Conservation Society at 302 Hawkins St.; phone (867) 668-5678; www.yukonconservation.org.

The Boreal Worlds Trail starts at the end of the student parking lot at Yukon College. The trail leads through an aspen grove, past a beaver pond, and through an area dense with lichen. Free interpretive brochure available at the bookstore.

Boat trip to Miles Canyon. Boat tours are offered on the Yukon River to scenic Miles Canyon. Originally called "Grand Canyon" by early gold seekers, the canyon was renamed in 1883 by Lt. Schwatka, U.S. Army, for Brigadier General Nelson A. Miles.

Miles Canyon, located on the Yukon River 2 miles south of Whitehorse, was an imposing challenge for miners and stampeders on their way up the Yukon to the gold fields, mainly because the narrow channel through the canyon was followed by the more daunting Whitehorse Rapids. Both Whitehorse Rapids and Squaw Rapids were eliminated by construction of the hydro-

electric power plant and dam on the Yukon River at Whitehorse in 1959, which created Schwatka Lake,

Miles Canyon is also accessible by road (closed in winter): take Schwatka Lake Road off Robert Service Way (South Access Road) into Whitehorse, or turn off the Alaska Highway (see **Milepost DC 881.7**) and follow signs.

Yukon Archives is located adjacent Yukon College at Yukon Place. The archives were established in 1972 to acquire, preserve and make available the documented history of the Yukon. The holdings, dating from 1845, include government records, private manuscripts, corporate records, photographs, maps, newspapers (most are on microfilm), sound recordings, university theses, books, pamphlets and periodicals. Visitors are welcome. Phone (867) 667-5321 for hours, or write Box 2703, Whitehorse, YT Y1A 2C6, for more information.

Tour the Yukon's only brewery. A popular stop in Whitehorse is the **Yukon Brewing Company**, located at 102 Copper Road. Yukon's only brewery, they have won national and international recognition for their beer as well as their distinctive labels. Yukon Brewing Company's flagship brands are: Yukon Red, Yukon Gold, and Chilkoot Lager. Open 11 A.M. to 6 P.M. daily year-round (closed major holidays). Tours daily in summer at noon, 2 P.M. and 4 P.M.; For more information, phone (867) 668-4183; www. yukonbeer.com.

Play Golf. Mountain View Public Golf Course is accessible via the Porter Creek exit off the Alaska Highway or from Range Road; 18 holes, grass greens; greens fees. Meadow Lakes Golf and Country Club, 5 minutes south of Whitehorse at **Milepost DC 878.3**, has a 9-hole par 36 course, clubhouse, cart and club rentals; phone (867) 668-4653.

Day trips from Whitehorse. Huge Marsh Lake is a popular recreation area for Whitehorse residents and visitors alike. Marsh Lake is located half-an-hour south of the city via the Alaska Highway. The nearby Swan Haven has a spring migration of swans; check them out from the viewing platform on the Yukon River Bridge. Marsh Lake Yukon government campground (turnoff at Milepost DC 859.9) offers camping, a sandy beach and picnicking.

For another popular local destination, drive north on the Alaska Highway to turn-off onto Klondike Highway 2 (the road to Dawson City) and drive just 3.6 miles/5.8 km from the junction to Takhini Hot Springs Road and access to Rivendell Farm, Takhini Hot Springs Resort and Yukon Wildlife Preserve. **Takhini Hot Springs Resort** (www. takhinihotsprings.com) offers a hot mineral pool, licensed restaurant, rental cabins, horseback riding, and camping. **Yukon Wildlife Preserve**, open daily in summer, offers interpretive bus tours and self-guided walking tours of their 750-acre wildlife park. **Rivendell Farm** offers tours, an organic show garden, raspberry labyrinth and more. (See page 278 in the KLONDIKE LOOP section for details on Takhini Hot Springs Road attractions.)

Longer day trips—which may be extended to an overnight to allow more sightseeing time—are to Atlin, about 2½ hours 1-way by car, and Skagway, 2 hours 1-way by car. Atlin is famous for its beau-

tiful setting. The Grotto, a natural hot springs, is also a popular destination in the Atlin area. Skagway is an old gold rush town and port of call for both the Alaska state ferries and cruise ships. Skagway is also home to the famed White Pass & Yukon Route railway, said to be the most scenic railway in the world as it climbs through beautiful mountain terrain to White Pass summit. Book ahead for the trip.

Scenery along the South Klondike Highway to Skagway is beautiful. Highlights include Carcross desert, the historic town of Carcross, and Emerald Lake. Tagish Road, another scenic route, connects Atlin Road with the South Klondike Highway and can be used to link these 2 side trips. See SOUTH KLONDIKE HIGHWAY section and "Atlin–Tagish–Carcross Scenic Loop" on pages 171-172.

Rockhounding and Mining. A wide variety of minerals can be found in the Whitehorse area. Sources of information for rock hounds and gold panners include the Yukon Rock Shop, on the South Klondike Highway just west of its junction with the Alaska Highway, which has mineral samples; and Murdoch's gem shop on Main Street, which displays gold nugget jewelry and gold rush artifacts and photos.

For a look at the area's copper mining history, visit the **Copperbelt Mining Railway and Museum**, an interpretive railway operating at the edge of the historic Whitehorse Copper Belt. For more information, contact The Miles Canyon Historic Railway Society, phone (867) 667-6198; website www.yukonrails.com.

Paddle the Yukon River. Despite its immensity—the Yukon River measures nearly 2,000 miles/3,218 km—and natural hazards, such as constantly changing weather, channels, islands, sweepers and sand and gravel bars, the Yukon is generally shallow and slow moving, and paddling is relaxing. There is a boat launch at Rotary Peace Park, behind the Yukon Government Building. You may also launch at Deep Creek Campground on Lake Laberge.

A highlight for river travelers on the Yukon is Fort Selkirk, at the confluence of the Yukon and Pelly rivers. Thirty Mile, referring to the stretch of river between Lake Laberge and Hootalinqua, is thought by some canoeists to be the most spectacular portion of the trip. A popular pull-out for paddlers is Coal Mine Campground at the Campbell Highway junction north of Carmacks on the Klondike Highway (see KLONDIKE LOOP section).

Going with a group and guide is recommended for those seeking a relaxing trip. From Whitehorse to Dawson City it is 467 miles/752 km by river and can take from 14 to 21 days to travel. Yukon River outfitters in Whitehorse are listed under Things To Do/Outdoor Activities/Canoeing & Kayaking at www.travelyukon.com. For information on Yukon River heritage sites, contact the Yukon government Heritage Branch in Whitehorse; phone 1-800-661-0408.

Chadburn Lake Recreation Area is accessed via a gravel side road just before reaching the Whitehorse Rapids and Fish Ladder at the end of Nisutlin Drive. Several small lakes with trails, picnic sites and boat launches make up the recreation area. Bird watching for yellow warblers, ruby-crowned kinglets, Northern waterthrush and Swainson's thrush.

Sportsmen can obtain complete informa-

Busy Two Mile Hill and Hamilton Blvd. intersection on the Alaska Highway. (©Kris Valencia, staff)

tion on fishing and hunting in the Whitehorse area by writing Tourism Yukon, Box 2703, Whitehorse, YT Y1A 2C6. List of guides and advice on licenses provided.

AREA FISHING: Fishing for rainbow, kokanee and king salmon in the following lakes: **Hidden Lakes** (1 and 3) and **Chadden Lake**, accessible from Chadburn Lake Road in the Riverdale subdivision; **Scout Lake**, access via Old Alaska Highway alignment from **Milepost DC 899.1** Alaska Highway; and **Long Lake**, accessible via Wickstrom Road. Nearby fly-in fishing lakes are accessible by charter plane.

Alaska Highway Log
(continued from page 176)
Distance from Dawson Creek (DC) is followed by distance from Delta Junction (DJ). Original mileposts are indicated in the text as Historical Mile.

In the Canada portion of *The MILEPOST®* Alaska Highway log, mileages from Dawson Creek are based on actual driving distance and kilometres are based on physical kilometreposts.

YUKON HIGHWAY 1 WEST
DC 887.4 (1425.4 km) **DJ 499.6** (804 km) 4-lane highway with dedicated center turn lanes approaching traffic light at **Two Mile Hill/Hamilton Blvd. junction.** Turn to northeast (lefthand turn southbound) and follow Two Mile Hill down to Whitehorse city centre. *This is the first exit southbound, second (and last) exit northbound for downtown Whitehorse.*
Southbound Alaska Highway log continues on page 175.
DC 888.3 (1426.9 km) **DJ 498.7** (802.5 km) Prospector Road. FasGas station and restaurant to southwest.

DC 888.7 (1427.4 km) **DJ 498.3** (801.9 km) Easy-to-miss gravel entrance to southwest for Copperbelt Mining and Railway Museum, a theme park built on the site of the early copper claims. A train ride through the park introduces visitors to the early mining and railway history of the area. Free parking. www.yukonrails.com.
DC 889.1 (1428.2 km) **DJ 497.9** (801.3 km) McIntyre Creek, Ravens Road.
DC 889.2 (1428.3 km) **DJ 497.8** (801.1

km) Fish Lake Road to west makes an interesting side trip; panoramic views from above tree line.
DC 890.1 (1429.3 km) **DJ 496.9** (799.7 km) Highway passes through Rabbit's Foot Canyon.
DC 890.3 (1429.7 km) **DJ 496.7** (799.3 km) Porter Creek subdivision.
DC 890.8 (1430.7 km) **DJ 496.2** (798.5 km) Tempo gas station and A grocery store. Last supermarket northbound on the Alaska Highway until Tok, Alaska, although there are several convenience stores attached to gas stations and campgrounds (such as Otter Falls Cutoff) along the highway.

DC 891.1 (1431.4 km) **DJ 495.9** (798.1 km) Wann Road; gas, convenience store, lodging.

DC 891.4 (1431.9 km) **DJ 495.6** (797.6 km) Motel, gas station, convenience store.

DC 894.1 (1436.3 km) **DJ 492.9** (793.2 km) Cousins airstrip road to northeast.
DC 894.2 (1436.5 km) **DJ 492.8** (793.1 km) Double-ended rest area to northeast with large gravel parking area, interpretive signs, litter bins and toilets.
DC 894.5 (1437 km) **DJ 492.5** (792.6 km) **Junction** with Klondike Highway 2 to Takhini Hot Springs/Yukon Wildlife Preserve,

Historic Klondike Loop Route

Just north of Whitehorse, the Alaska Highway junctions with Yukon Highway 2 with little fanfare: a mileage sign and highway marker the only indicators that Highway 2, the Klondike Highway, branches off the main route here, taking travelers north to Dawson City, first capital of the Yukon and home of the Klondike gold fields. Considering the significance of the Klondike in the history of the North, a billboard with flashing lights and a big arrow pointing to the turnoff might be more appropriate.

The Klondike Gold Rush was the largest gold rush of the century. Although it followed numerous earlier gold rushes to Alaska and British Columbia, George Carmack's 1896 discovery of gold on Rabbit Creek, a tributary of the Klondike River in Yukon Territory, was the richest gold strike ever in North America and it launched the most publicized era in the annals of gold fever.

It is estimated that more than 100,000 gold seekers headed for the Klondike when news of the gold strike reached the outside world in the spring of 1897. Almost none of them made it to Dawson City by the first winter of 1897; the few that did arrive early on faced starvation in the ill-supplied town. Founded in the early days of the gold strike, Dawson City was a tent-town in 1896, with less than 500 people. But it boomed explosively as the gold rush gained momentum: In its heyday in 1898, Dawson City—the "Queen City of the North"— boasted a population of 30,000 people.

Unlike those early stampeders to the Klondike, who climbed mountain passes, negotiated treacherous rivers and endured a host of other obstacles before reaching Dawson City, today's modern travelers can make the drive from Whitehorse in just under 6 hours on a paved highway.

Dawson City is a must stop for anyone interested in Northern history. The entire city is a national historic site, preserving many structures from the city's gold rush years, such as the Palace Grand Theatre, which opened in 1899. Visit the Dawson Museum for displays about the gold rush, or take in the Robert Service Show to recapture the spirit of the times. Service, sometimes referred to as the "bard of the Klondike," was born in England in 1874 and was working in a bank in Whitehorse, YT, when he began writing poetry, inspired by the vastness of the Yukon and the characters of the gold miners.

Travelers have a choice about how to visit this wonderfully preserved piece of the Klondike Gold Rush. They can either drive the 323 miles/520 km from the Alaska Highway to Dawson City and return the same way, or take the 498-mile/801-km Klondike Loop route to or from Alaska via Dawson City.

A description of the Klondike Highway and Klondike Loop begins on page 274, followed by mile-by-mile logs of these routes. The description of Dawson City begins on page 286.

10 miles/16 km; Dawson City, 323 miles/520 km; and the Top of the World Highway to Alaska. See "Historic Klondike Loop Route" above.

Junction with Klondike Highway 2 to Dawson City. See KLONDIKE LOOP section on page 274 for log of this route.

For Alaska-bound travelers, the highway now swings west.

DC 894.7 (1437.2 km) **DJ 492.3** (792.3 km) Distance marker northbound shows Haines Junction 144 km/89 miles, Fairbanks 946 km/588 miles.

Good highway northbound with occasional patched or damaged road surface. SLOW for loose gravel! Watch for horses on highway.

Distance marker southbound shows Whitehorse City Centre 12 km/7 miles, Teslin 194 km/121 miles.

DC 896.9 (1440.8 km) **DJ 490.1** (788.7 km) Whitehorse city limits.

DC 897.6 (1442 km) **DJ 489.4** (787.6 km) Gardner Road.

DC 897.8 (1442.3 km) **DJ 489.2** (787.3 km) Husky Trail. Access to **Muktuk Adventures Limited**; lodging, lunch and dinner (advance booking required), kennel tours.

Muktuk Adventures Limited. "Authentic!" "Unique!" Join our family, connect with over 100 Alaskan Huskies at the home of Yukon Quest legend Frank Turner. Located 20 minutes from downtown

Whitehorse, we offer year-round dog sled adventures, Yukon hospitality, and a northern dining experience like no other! Take a walk to the scenic Takhini River with a group of friendly huskies and learn about relationship dynamics in a team of sled dogs and its likeness to our human relationships.

Relax and enjoy Muktuk's Taste of Yukon lunch or dinner special featuring bison, caribou, elk, arctic char and more. Short on time? Stop by for a self-guided tour. Add our off-the-beaten-trail, dog-loving adventure to your journey. Phone (867) 668-3647; email info@muktuk.com, website www.muktuk.com; KM1443 Alaska Highway Whitehorse.

DC 899.1 (1443.8 km) **DJ 487.9** (785.2 km) South access to 3-mile/4.8-km loop drive on Old Alaska Highway (Mile 929 to Mile 934). Access to **Scout Lake** via unmaintained road which intersects Old Alaska Highway at gravel pit, according to Yukon Environment's angler's guide. Fishing from shore for rainbow and small king salmon.

DC 901.9 (1448.2 km) **DJ 485.1** (780.7 km) North access to 3-mile/4.8 km loop drive on Old Alaska Highway (Mile 934 to Mile 929).

DC 905.4 (1454.1 km) **DJ 481.6** (775 km) **Historic Milepost 937**. Viewpoint turnout to north with litter bins and point-of-interest sign about the old Dawson Trail. There were at least 50 stopping places along the old Dawson Trail winter stagecoach route between Whitehorse and Dawson City, and from 1 to 3 roadhouses at each stop. At this point, the stagecoach route crossed the Takhini River. This route was discontinued in 1950 when the Mayo–Dawson Road (now Klondike Highway 2) was constructed.

DC 907.2 (1457 km) **DJ 479.8** (772.1 km) *CAUTION: Slow for frost heaves next 1.2 miles/2 km northbound.*

DC 909.4 (1460.4 km) **DJ 477.6** (768.6 km) Wolf Ridge B&B Log Cabin Rentals.

DC 914 (1467.9 km) **DJ 473** (761.2 km) **Takhini Salt Flats**, a series of bowl-shaped depressions where salts form on the surface as water brought up from underground springs evaporates. Although alkaline flats are not uncommon in the Yukon, this one is notable for the size of its salt crystals as well as the variety of salt-loving plants that thrive here, such as the distinctive red sea asparagus.

DC 914.7 (1468.9 km) **DJ 472.3** (760.1 km) **Historic Milepost 946. Takhini River**

bridge. According to R. Coutts in *Yukon: Places & Names*, the name Takhini derives from the Tagish Indian *tahk*, meaning mosquito, and *heena*, meaning river.

DC 916.6 (1472 km) **DJ 470.4** (757 km) Distance marker southbound shows Whitehorse 50 km/30 miles, Watson Lake 496 km/308 miles.

DC 917 (1472.6 km) **DJ 470** (756.4 km) Distance marker northbound shows Haines Junction 109 km/67 miles, Fairbanks 910 km/565 miles.

CAUTION: Watch for elk (Takhini Valley Elk Herd) next 20 km/12 miles northbound. Also watch for horses and other livestock grazing on open range near highway. The elk were introduced in 1951–1954 from Elk Island National Park.

DC 923.9 (1481 km) **DJ 463.1** (745.3 km) Annie Ned Creek. Named for Yukon's revered native storyteller, the late Annie Ned. Ned was awarded the Order of Canada.

DC 924.5 (1484.8 km) **DJ 462.5** (744.3 km) Stoney Creek.

DC 924.7 (1485.2 km) **DJ 462.3** (744 km) View of Mount Bratnober, elev. 6,313 feet/1,924m. According to R. Coutts in *Yukon: Places & Names*, the mountain was named in 1897 by J.J. McArthur, Canadian government surveyor, for Henry Bratnober, who along with Jack Dalton was assisting in a cursory survey of the Dalton Trail.

DC 926 (1487 km) **DJ 461** (741.9 km) **Takhini Burn Rest Area**. Turnout to south with litter bins, outhouses and viewing platform with information panels on wildlife found in the Takhini River Valley. Point of interest sign about 1958 Takhini Burn. More than 1.5 million acres/629,058 hectares of Yukon forest lands were burned in 1958. Campfires were responsible for most of these fires.

DC 927.3 (1489.2 km) **DJ 459.7** (739.8 km) **Historic Milepost 960**. Turnoff to south for Kusawa Lake Road (winding, hard-packed dirt and gravel, fairly wide) that leads 14.7 miles/23 km to Kusawa Lake campground. This side road is slippery when wet. Short, steep stretch at Mile 8.7; watch for soft spots; and stay away from edge above river. Not recommended for large RVs or trailers.

Drive in 1.4 miles/3 km to Mendenhall Landing (historic sign, pull-out for canoeists and room to turn around for motorists who do not wish to continue). Mendenhall Landing was a freight transfer point in the early 1900s for goods shipped up the Yukon and Takhini rivers. From the landing, goods were loaded onto wagons headed for Kluane mining operations. Today the landing is a pull-out point for canoeists.

At Mile 9/15 km on the side road is **Takhini River Yukon government campground**, with 13 sites, and a put-in point for canoeists.

Continue to to end of road for access to **Kusawa Lake Yukon government campground** and boat launch at north end of lake. The campground has 48 sites, kitchen shelter, firepits and drinking water. Camping permit ($12). Fishing for lake trout to 20 lbs., good to excellent; also grayling and pike.

Stunning Kusawa Lake (pronounced KOO-sa-wa), located in the Coast Mountains, is 45 miles/72 km long and averages 2 miles/3.2 km wide, with a shoreline perimeter of 125 miles/200 km. The access road to the lake was first constructed by the U.S. Army in 1945 to obtain bridge timbers for Alaska Highway construction.

DC 931.5 (1495.7 km) **DJ 455.5** (733 km) Turnoff to northeast for **Mendenhall Malamute Bed & Breakfast, Cabin Rentals**; lodging.

Mendenhall Malamute Bed & Breakfast, Cabin Rentals. See display ad this page.

DC 935.9 (1502.2 km) **DJ 451.1** (726 km) End of 911 access area northbound.

DC 936.8 (1503.7 km) **DJ 450.2** (724.5 km) Mendenhall River culvert. A tributary of the Takhini River, the Mendenhall River—like the Mendenhall Glacier outside Juneau, AK—was named for Thomas Corwin Mendenhall (1841–1924), superintendent of the U.S. Coast & Geodetic Survey.

DC 937.2 (1504.4 km) **DJ 449.8** (723.9 km) Turnoff for south access to Indian community of Champagne.

Northbound, motorists are driving the Champagne Bypass, an 8.6-mile/13.9-km section of the Alaska Highway completed in 2002, which rerouted the Alaska Highway around **CHAMPAGNE**, formerly **Historical Mile 974** on the Alaska Highway. Originally a campsite on the Dalton Trail to Dawson City, established by Jack Dalton in the late 1800s, a roadhouse and trading post were built at Champagne in 1902. It became a supply centre for first the Bullion Creek gold rush and later the Burwash Creek gold rush in 1904. The origin of the name is uncertain, although one account is that Dalton's men—after successfully negotiating a herd of cattle through the first part of the trail—celebrated here with a bottle of French champagne.

DC 943 (1514.1 km) **DJ 444** (714.5 km) Small gravel turnout to north.

The Takhini River flows from beautiful Kusawa Lake, reached via a 15 mile/23 km side road.
(©Kris Valencia, staff)

DC 945.7 (1518.2 km) **DJ 441.3** (710.2 km) Turnoff for north access road to Champagne (see description at **Milepost DC 937.2**).

DC 951 (1527 km) **DJ 436** (701.6 km) Distance marker southbound shows Whitehorse 108 km/67 miles, Watson Lake 564 km/350 miles.

DC 955.8 (1532.8 km) **DJ 431.2** (693.9 km) First glimpse northbound of Kluane Range.

DC 957 (1534.8 km) **DJ 430** (692 km) **Historic Milepost 987**. Cracker Creek. Former roadhouse site on old stagecoach trail. Watch for Old Man Mountain on right northbound (the rocky crags look like a face, particularly in evening light).

DC 964.7 (1546 km) **DJ 422.3** (679.8 km) **Historical Mile 995**: Otter Falls Cutoff, **junction** with Aishihik Road; **Otter Falls Cutoff RV Park Campground**; restaurant, a surprisingly well-stocked little convenience store, gas, diesel, campground with laundry, showers. Open year-round, open 24-hours in summer

Otter Falls Cutoff RV Park Campground. See display ad this page.

Aishihik Road leads north 26.1 miles/42.2 km to Aishihik Lake campground and 73 miles/117 km to the old Indian village of Aishihik (pronounced ay-jhee-ack; means "high place"). This is a narrow, winding gravel road, maintained for summer travel only to the government campground at the lake. There are some steep hills and single-lane bridges. Aishihik Road is not recommended for large RVs or trailers. *CAUTION: Watch for bison on road. Be alert for bears in area.*

At Mile 17.4/28 km is **Otter Falls** viewpoint, a double-ended turnout with litter bins and point-of-interest sign, short steep path to water. Otter Falls was once pictured on the back of the Canadian $5 bill, but in 1975 the Aishihik Power Plant diverted water from the falls. The 32-megawatt dam was built by Northern Canada Power Commission to supply power principally to the mining industry. Water is still released over the falls during the summer; flow hours are

posted.

At Mile 17.5/28.2 km is Otter Falls Recreation Site, a day-use area on lake with large parking area, picnic tables, picnic shelter and outhouse.

At Mile 26.1/42.2 km is the turnoff for Aishihik Lake Yukon government campground, located at the south end of the

lake; 16 sites, drinking water, picnic tables, firepits, kitchen shelter and boat launch. Camping permit ($12).

Aishihik Lake, fishing for lake trout and grayling. As with most large Yukon lakes, ice is not out until late June. Low water levels may make boat launching difficult. *WARNING: Winds can come up suddenly on this lake.* **Pole Cat Lake**, just before the Aishihik weather station; fishing for pike.

DC 965.6 (1547.5 km) **DJ 421.4** (678.1 km) **Historic Milepost 996.** Turnoff to north at east end of Canyon Creek bridge for rest area; toilets. Interpretive signs (excerpt follows) about **Historic Canyon Creek Bridge**, a favorite photo-op.

©Kris Valencia, staff

"In 1903, a gold strike in the Alsek River drainage brought a stampede of miners to the area. A wagon road was built from Whitehorse in the next year and Sam McGee and Gilbert Skelly constructed a substantial bridge over Canyon Creek. This bridge survived heavy traffic and high springs floods until the 1920s, when the government contracted the Jacquot brothers from Burwash Landing to rebuilt it. In 1942, during construction of the Alaska Highway, the old bridge was dismantled and a new one built in 18 days. [Although most of the first American military bridges were of temporary pontoon and plank construction, the Canyon Creek bridge mimicked the original style.]"

The pioneer bridge was left in place when a permanent bridge was built just downriver. Restoration was done in 1986-87 and 2005.

Highway climbs northbound.

DC 965.7 (1547.7 km) **DJ 421.3** (678 km) Aishihik River bridge.

DC 966.3 (1548.7 km) **DJ 420.7** (677 km) View of impressive Kluane Range icefields straight ahead northbound between Kilometreposts 1550 and 1562.

DC 974.9 (1560.1 km) **DJ 412.1** (663.2 km) Turnout on Marshall Creek.

DC 976.9 (1566 km) **DJ 410.1** (660 km) Double-ended rest area to east with with interpretive signs, outhouses and litter bins to northeast.

View northbound of the rugged snow-capped peaks of the Kluane Icefield Ranges and the outer portion of the St. Elias Mountains to the west. The Kluane National Park Icefield Ranges are Canada's highest and the world's largest nonpolar alpine ice field, forming the interior wilderness of the park. In clear weather, Mount Kennedy and Mount Hubbard, 2 peaks that are twice as high as the front ranges seen before you, are visible from here.

DC 979.3 (1569.8 km) **DJ 407.7** (656.1 km) Between Kilometreposts 1570 and 1572, look for the NorthwesTel microwave repeater station on top of **Paint Mountain**. The station was installed with the aid of helicopters and supplied by a tramline.

DC 980.8 (1572.1 km) **DJ 406.2** (653.7 km) Turnoff to north for **Pine Lake Yukon government campground and recreation area.** Day-use area with gravel parking area, sandy beach, boat launch, dock, group

firepits, picnic tables, outhouses, playground and drinking water. The campground, on a 0.3-mile-loop road off the beach access road, has 42 treed sites, outhouses, firewood, litter bins, kitchen shelter, playground and drinking water. Camping permit ($12). Fishing is good for lake trout, northern pike and grayling. *CAUTION: Bears in area.*

A short nature trail winds through the boreal forest from the beach to the campground. Panels along the trail interpret the lake's aquatic habitats and marl formations. A 3.5-mile/6-km walking and biking trail begins at the campground entrance and ends at Haines Junction.

DC 980.9 (1572.4 km) **DJ 406.1** (653.5 km) Access road to floatplane dock.

DC 982.2 (1575 km) **DJ 404.8** (651.4 km) Turnoff to north for Haines Junction airport. **Private Aircraft**: Haines Junction airstrip; elev. 2,150 feet/655m; length 5,500 feet/ 1,676m; gravel; fuel (100L). Flightseeing tours of glaciers, fly-in fishing and air charters available; fixed-wing aircraft or helicopters.

Highway swings southwest approaching Haines Junction, offering a panoramic view of the Auriol Range ahead for northbound travelers.

DC 984.1 (1577.1 km) **DJ 402.9** (648.4 km) Welcome to Haines Junction sign northbound. *Slow for 31 mph/50 kmph speed zone northbound through Haines Junction.*

DC 984.7 (1578 km) **DJ 402.3** (647.4 km) **Fas Gas** gas station with diesel, convenience store and overnight RV parking to north, **Da Kų Cultural Centre** to south (description follows). The cultural centre also houses the Kluane National Park and Haines Junction vistor information desks; natural history displays, Native cultural displays. Plenty of parking, restrooms.

Fas Gas & RV Park. See display ad this page.

Da Kų Cultural Centre. Welcome to Da Kų (Our House). Learn about: *dan*–our people, *dan keyi*–our land, *dan ke*–our ways, and *Southern Tuchone*–our language. We are

proud to share our story with you. Please visit our retail store for local First Nations handiwork. Phone (867) 634-3300. daku@cafn.ca. www.cafn.ca/centre.html. [ADVERTISEMENT]

DC 985 (1578.5 km) **DJ 402** (647 km) **Historic Milepost 1016. Junction** of Alaska Highway and Haines Highway. Pay-n-Pump North 60 Express Petro gas station on northeast corner. Haines Junction wildlife monument to south.

IMPORTANT: This junction can be confusing; choose your route carefully! Fairbanks- and Anchorage-bound travelers turn right (north) at this junction for continuation of Alaska Highway (Yukon 1). Haines-bound motorists continue straight ahead. (Haines-bound motorists

note: It is a good idea to fill up with gas before leaving Haines Junction.)

Alaska Highway log continues on page 195.

Junction of Alaska Highway and Haines Highway (Haines Road). Head west on the Haines Highway (Yukon Highway 3) for port of Haines, AK. See HAINES HIGHWAY section.

Haines Junction

DC 985 (1578.5 km) **DJ 402** (646.9 km) **F 498** (801.4 km) **Historic Milepost 1016**, at the junction of the Alaska Highway (Yukon Highway 1) and the Haines Highway (Yukon Highway 3, also known as the Haines Road). Driving distance to Whitehorse, 100 miles/161 km; YT–AK border, 205 miles/330 km; Tok, 296 miles/ 476 km; and Haines, 151 miles/242 km. **Population:** 840. **Elevation:** 1,956 feet/ 596m. **Emergency Services: RCMP,** phone (867) 634-5555 or (867) 667-5555. **Fire Department,** phone (867) 634-2222. **Nursing Centre,** phone (867) 634-4444.

Visitor Information: Available at the Yukon Territory Government (YTG) Visitor Information Centre and at Kluane National Park and Reserve Visitor Centre, both relocated to the new Da Kų building alongside the Alaska Highway in Haines Junction. Tourism staff is on hand to provide Yukon wide travel information on events and activities, lodging and ferry information. The

Enjoy the mountain view at this rest area in Haines Junction. (©Sharon Nault)

centre features art by artisans throughout the territory and art from the Yukon Permanent Collection. Open mid-May to September, 8 A.M. to 8 P.M. daily (hours/days subject to change); 10 A.M.–6 P.M. during shoulder season. Phone Parks Canada at (867) 634-7207 or YTG at (867) 634-2345 for more information. Call with year round questions at 1-800-661-0494 or email: vic.hainesjunction@gov.yk.ca.

Private Aircraft: The airport is located on the Alaska Highway just east of town; see

description at **Milepost DC 982.2. Radio:** CBC North at 106.1 FM; 103.5 FM; CKRW 98.7 FM; CHON 90.5 FM.

Haines Junction is an important stop for travelers on the Alaska and Haines highways. Services are located along both highways, and clustered around the junction.

Haines Junction is on the eastern boundary of Kluane (pronounced kloo-WA-nee) National Park and Reserve. The park was first suggested in 1942, and in 1943 land was set aside and designated the Kluane

Game Sanctuary. A formal park region was established in 1972, and the national park and reserve boundaries were official in 1976. Kluane National Park and Reserve encompasses extensive ice fields, mountains and wilderness, and has become a world-class wilderness destination among outdoor recreation enthusiasts. Kluane National Park and Reserve, Tatshenshini–Alsek Wilderness Park, and Alaska's Glacier Bay National Park and Wrangell–St. Elias National Park, are a joint UNESCO World Heritage Site.

Haines Junction was established in 1942, during construction of the Alaska Highway, as an Army barracks for the U.S. Army Corps of Engineers. The engineers were to build a new branch road connecting the Alaska Highway with the port of Haines on Lynn Canal. The branch road—today's Haines

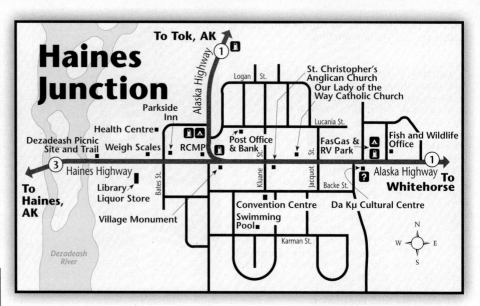

Haines Junction, Yukon
YUKON
LARGER THAN LIFE

"Gateway to Kluane"

Haines Junction is the ideal base for adventure travel in Kluane National Park & Tatshenshini-Alsek Park. You can go flightseeing, river rafting, mountain biking, horseback riding, hiking, fishing and hunting! Or bring your business and social gatherings to the new St. Elias Centre, overlooking spectacular mountains and glaciers. There is something for everyone in Haines Junction. Join us for these special events in 2014:

Saturday, June 21   Kluane to Chilkat International Bike Relay

On a team of eight, four, two, or one, cycle one of the most scenic mountain passes in the world. In 2013 over 1200 riders participated!   kcibr.org

Late June - August   Kluane National Park Interpretive Programs Begin

Join the experienced park staff for campfire talks and guided hikes.
634-7207

Tuesday, July 1   Canada Day

Celebrate Canada's 147th Birthday Haines Junction Style   634-7100

For more information about
Haines Junction *contact:*
Village of Haines Junction,
Box 5339, Haines Junction, YT Y0B 1L0

867-634-7100 or Fax 867-634-2008
Email: vhj@yknet.ca
www.hainesjunctionyukon.com

Highway—was completed in 1943.

Today, Haines Junction is also the southern end of the Shakwak Project, a massive reconstruction of approximately 300 miles/500 km of the Alaska Highway between Haines Junction and the Alaska border.

In the 1940s, civilian contractors were employed to reconstruct the Alaska Highway behind the U.S. military. Later, responsibility for the highway was passed to the Canadian Army, then Public Works Canada, and finally, Yukon Highways and Public Works.

By the 1970s, the southern sections of the Alaska Highway in Canada had been vastly improved, but the highway north of Haines Junction had received relatively little attention. Because about 85 percent of the traffic volume north of Haines Junction was of American origin, the U.S. agreed to fund reconstruction of this section of road, signing the Shakwak Agreement in 1977. The goal was to bring the road up to a modern 2-lane, 60-mph/100-kmph standard, but permafrost continues to be a major challenge for road maintenance north of Destruction Bay.

Lodging & Services

Haines Junction offers accommodations and also has a convention centre. Visitor services include motels/hotels (**Parkside Inn**, Alcan Motor Inn, the Raven), gas stations (**FasGas**, 60˚ Petro Express, Kluane RV), and garage services. Fast-food and fountain drinks at Frosty's. Fine dining at The Raven. Grocery items at **FasGas** and Kluane RV convenience stores. There is an indoor heated swimming pool with showers; open daily

from May to late-August, fee charged.

The James Smith Administration Building, at Kilometre 255.6 Haines Road, 0.2 mile/0.3 km south from the Alaska Highway junction, contains the government liquor store and public library. Outside the building is a dogsled sculpture—*Homeward Bound*—by local artist Bob Braun.

There are a post office, RCMP office, Lands and Forest District Office and health centre. The bank, adjacent the post office, is open weekday afternoons; extended hours on Fridays. Internet access available at the Yukon College library.

Camping

RV camping at **FasGas RV Park** (across from entrance to Da Ku Cultural Centre) and Kluane RV. Pine Lake Yukon government campground is located 4.2 miles/6.7 km east of junction on the Alaska Highway. Kluane National Park has one campground, Kathleen Lake, located 16 miles/27 km south of town on the Haines Highway. Dump stations and water are available at local service stations and at the campgrounds.

Attractions

St. Christopher's Anglican Church. Unique, quaint, and welcoming describes St. Christopher's octagonal log church situated in the heart of Haines Junction. The current church was constructed in the early 1990s

HAINES JUNCTION ADVERTISERS

Da Ku Cultural Centre...................Ph. (867) 634-3300
FasGas & RV Park.........................Ph. (867) 634-2840
Parkside Inn....................................Ph. (867) 634-2900
Village of Haines Junction............Ph. (867) 634-7100

by local volunteers, replacing the old church structure established after the completion of the Alaska Highway. Visitors are welcome to explore the interior of the church for a historic tour or stroll the prayer garden and labyrinth during the spring and summer months. St. Christopher's remains a mission parish supported by the Anglican Church of Canada welcoming all to join in Sunday worship at 10:30 A.M.

The Local Village Arts and Craft Guild displays and sells eclectic "art with soul" in the parish hall of St. Christopher's. One can find gifts of paintings, books, quilts, traditional beaded moccasins and mitts, jewellery, photographs, art cards, and knitted apparel all created by local Haines Junction artists and artisans. The gallery includes original paintings and limited edition prints by renowned artist Libby Dulac. Come peek or purchase. The gallery is open daily in June, July, and August, noon to 4 P.M. or whenever you see the church doors open. Also on the church grounds: a community market, every Wednesday from 3 to 6 P.M. during the summer months.

The Village Monument is probably the most photographed spot in Haines Junction. The 24-foot-high sculpture—nicknamed "The Muffin" or "Animal Cupcake"—is located at the junction of the Haines and Alaska highways. Area wildlife is depicted in close to life-size detail on a sculpted mountain.

The Da Ku "Our House" Cultural Centre features Champagne and Aishihik First Nations cultural exhibits reflecting the lifestyles and traditional identity of Southern Tutchone people. Guided tours, campfire talks, traditional artwork and cultural artifacts are also found at the centre.

The spectacular Da Ku Centre (across from FasGas) houses the Kluane National Park and Reserve Visitor Centre, which has an information desk, interpretive exhibits, displays and a 30-minute feature on bear safety. Check at the centre for details on the park's numerous hiking trails and for a schedule of guided hikes, walks and campfire talks. Kluane National Park activities also take place at Tachal Dhal Visitor Centre at Sheep Mountain on the Alaska Highway; see Milepost DC 1028.8 this section. (Kathleen Lake Campground on the Haines Highway, 16 miles/26 km west of Haines Junction, is the only established campground within Kluane National Park.) Nightly or annual wilderness permits may be purchased. Hikers note: You must register no later than 4:30 P.M. the day of departure for any overnight trip into the park. Parks Canada staff are available 9 A.M. to 5 P.M. (hours subject to change) daily in summer. Bear-resistant food canisters are mandatory on some overnight hikes; a $100 deposit is required.

Interpretive programs in Kluane National Park begin in June and continue through August. A fee is charged for guided walks

and hikes, but campfire programs are free. Contact Kluane National Park and Reserve at Box 5495, Haines Junction, YT Y0B 1L0, or phone (867) 634-7207, fax (867) 634-7208; www.parkscanada.gc.ca/kluane.

The St. Elias Convention Center houses a 3,000-square-foot Grand Hall, the municipal offices, a growing collection of artwork and a local history exhibit depicting significant events of the Kluane region since 1890.

Our Lady of the Way Catholic Mission is a local landmark and visitor attraction. Sign at the church reads:

"The church was built in 1954 by Father E. Morriset O.M.I., the first Catholic priest to preach the Gospel in the area. Resources were scarce and Father Morriset ingeniously converted an old quanset (sic) hut, which had been used by the American Army during construction of the Alaska Highway, into the distinctively beautiful church you see. It has the distinction of being the most photographed church in the Yukon."

Special events. Canada Day (the anniversary of Canada's confederation) is celebrated on July 1st with a parade, barbecue, afternoon sports activities and an evening movie.

The Kluane to Chilkat International Bike Relay is scheduled for June 21, 2014. This event draws more than 1,000 participants. Teams of 2, 4 and 8 bicyclists, as well as solo cyclists, ride in the 8-leg race, totaling 148 miles/238 km, from Haines Junction to Haines, AK. Watch for cyclists on the highway!

Flightseeing Kluane National Park by fixed-wing aircraft or helicopter from Haines Junction is a popular way to see the spectacular mountain scenery. Check with Sifton

Air at the airport.

Tatshenshini–Alsek Wilderness Park. Created in 1993, the park protects the magnificent Tatshenshini and Alsek rivers area in Canada, where the 2 rivers join and flow (as the Alsek) to the Gulf of Alaska at Dry Bay. Known to river runners as "the Tat," the Tatshenshini is famous for its whitewater rafting, stunning scenery and wildlife. Due to a dramatic increase in river traffic in recent years, permits are required from the park agencies (the National Park Service in Alaska and B.C. Parks in Canada). For more information about the park, contact BC Parks, Tatshenshini Office, Box 5544, Haines Junction, YT Y0B 1L0; phone (867) 634-4248, fax (867) 634-2108.

The Dezadeash River offers a relaxed rafting experience. Picnicking and hiking trail are available at a day-use area on the river at the west edge of town on the Haines Highway.

Alaska Highway Log
(continued from page 192)

YUKON HIGHWAY 1 NORTH

Distance from Dawson Creek (DC) is followed by distance from Delta Junction (DJ). Original mileposts are indicated in the text as Historical Mile.

In the Canada portion of The MILEPOST® Alaska Highway log, mileages from Dawson Creek are based on actual driving distance and kilometres are based on physical kilometreposts.

DC 985 (1578.5 km) DJ 402 (646.9 km) Junction of the Alaska Highway (Yukon Highway 1) and the Haines Highway (Yukon Highway 3); North 60° Petro Express.

Junction with the Haines Highway (Yukon Highway 3), which leads southwest 152 miles/246 km to Haines, AK. See the HAINES HIGHWAY section for log of that route.

NOTE: This junction can be confusing; choose your route carefully! Whitehorse-bound travelers turn east (left turn southbound) at

Northbound travelers on the Alaska Highway must make this right-hand turn to continue to Tok. If you drive straight ahead you will end up in Haines, AK. (©Kris Valencia)

These information signs are at the viewpoint overlooking Horseshoe Bay on Kluane Lake.
(©Kris Valencia, staff)

stop sign for continuation of Alaska Highway (Yukon Highway 1). Haines-bound motorists turn right southbound for the Haines Highway (Yukon Highway 3) to the port of Haines, AK, 152 miles/246 km from here. Haines-bound motorists note: It is a good idea to fill up with gas before leaving Haines Junction. Photo-op: Village Monument across the street.

DC 985.1 (1578.9 km) DJ 401.9 (646.8 km) Distance marker northbound shows Destruction Bay 108 kms/67 miles, Fairbanks 822 kms/510 miles. Beaver Creek is 295 kms/183 miles.

DC 985.3 (1579.3 km) DJ 401.7 (646.4 km) Kluane RV campground; gas.

DC 985.9 (1580 km) DJ 401.1 (645.5 km) Motel next door to Source Motors service station with 24-hour cardlock gas and diesel.

Distance marker northbound shows Destruction Bay 108 km/67 miles, Fairbanks 822 km/511 miles. The Highway follows the Kluane Ranges which are to the southwest.

DC 987.8 (1583.2 km) DJ 399.2 (642.4 km) Historical Mile 1019. Kluane National Park and Reserve resource, conservation and warden headquarters to northeast. (Visitor information available in Haines Junction inside the Da Ku Cultural Centre.)

DC 988.3 (1584 km) DJ 398.7 (641.6 km) Large paved rest area to west with litter bins and toilets.

DC 990.9 (1588 km) DJ 396.1 (637.4 km Beautiful views to southwest of the snow-covered Kluane Ranges as the Alaska Highway parallels the Kluane Ranges from Haines Junction to Koidern, presenting a nearly unbroken chain of mountains to 8,000 feet/2,438m interrupted by only a few large valleys cut by glacier-fed rivers and streams. West of the Kluane Ranges is the Duke Depression, a narrow trough separating the Kluane Ranges from the St. Elias Mountains. Major peaks in the St. Elias (not visible from the highway) are: Mount Logan, Canada's highest peak, at 19,545 feet/5,959m; Mount St. Elias, 18,008 feet/5,489m; Mount Lucania, 17,147 feet/5,226m; King Peak, 16,971 feet/5,173m; and Mounts Wood, Vancouver, Hubbard and Steele, all over 15,000 feet/

4,572m. Mount Steele (16,664 feet/5,079m) was named for Superintendent Sam Steele of the North West Mounted Police. As commanding officer of the NWMP in the Yukon in 1898, Steele established permanent detachments at the summits of the White and Chilkoot passes to ensure not only that gold stampeders obeyed Canadian laws, but also had sufficient supplies to carry them through to the gold fields.

DC 991.4 (1589 km) DJ 395.6 (636.6 km) Trailhead to west for Alsek Pass trail; 18 miles/29 km long, suitable for shorter day hikes, mountain bikes permitted.

DC 991.6 (1589.1 km) DJ 395.4 (636.3 km) Historic Milepost 1022, Mackintosh Trading Post historic sign. Bear Creek Lodge to east (closed 2012, current status unknown).

Highway makes gradual climb northbound to Bear Creek Summit.

DC 999 (1596.7 km) DJ 388 (624.4 km) Spruce Beetle Trail Interpretive Site to northeast; rest area with toilets, litter bins and interpretive trail. The 1-mile/1.7-km trail is an easy loop that examines the life of the spruce bark beetle and its effect on area forests. Allow 35 to 45 minutes for walk.

Millions of acres of northern spruce forests were infested by the spruce beetle (*Dendroctonus refipennis*) during the 1990s. Damage to the tree begins when the female spruce beetle bores through the spruce bark and lays eggs in the tree's tissue layer—called the phloem—on which the larvae and adult beetles feed. The tree attempts to fight back by exuding resin at the entrance site of the attacking beetle. Trees that are under attack can be identified by this resin, as well as by accumulations of reddish-brown dust on the bark and on the ground below the tree. Although the tree dies within weeks of the initial attack, the needles may not fall off or turn the tell-tale reddish-brown color of a beetle-killed tree for a year or more. Dead trees may continue to host beetles.

Spruce beetles do not attack any tree species other than spruce. Small colonies of these beetles are always present in spruce forests, but under certain conditions their numbers suddenly swell to epidemic, and destructive, proportions. Many scientists

relate the depredation of northern forests by spruce beetles in recent years to the influence of global warming.

DC 1000.1 (1598.6 km) DJ 386.9 (622.6 km) Bear Creek Summit (elev. 3,294 feet/1,004m), highest point on the Alaska Highway between Whitehorse and Fairbanks.

DC 1000.3 (1599 km) DJ 386.7 (622.3 km) Double-ended turnout to west.

DC 1003.5 (1608.3 km) DJ 383.5 (617.2 km) Jarvis River bridge.

DC 1003.6 (1608.5 km) DJ 383.4 (617 km) Historic Milepost 1035. Slow down for easy-to-miss turnout to west spur just north of crossing Jarvis River. Pretty spot for a picnic. Poor to fair fishing for grayling 8 to 16 inches all summer; Dolly Varden 8 to 10 inches, early summer.

DC 1007.2 (1614.2 km) DJ 379.8 (611.2 km) Turnoff on short dirt and gravel access road to northeast for Sulphur Lake; canoeing, birdwatching. Turnaround space at lake may be muddy and rutted in wet weather. Thousands of birds use the lake, mostly in late summer, for molting. Look for bald eagle nests along shore. Wolf pack in area.

DC 1015.7 (1628 km) DJ 371.3 (597.5 km) Double-ended turnout to southwest with view of Kluane Ranges.

DC 1017.2 (1630.4 km) DJ 369.8 (595.1 km) Christmas Creek.

Highway climbs northbound to Boutillier Summit.

DC 1019.5 (1633 km) DJ 367.5 (591.4 km) First glimpse of Kluane Lake for northbound travelers at Boutillier Summit (elev. 3,293 feet/1,003m), second highest point on the highway between Whitehorse and Fairbanks.

DC 1020 (1635 km) DJ 367 (590.6 km) Kluane Lake Viewpoint to east; double-ended turnout with litter bins, outhouse and interpretive signs on Kluane Lake and First Nations (excerpts follow).

Between 300 and 400 years ago, Kaskawulsh Glacier advanced across the Slims River and closed the drainage outlet of Kluane Lake. The water level rose more than 10m/30 feet and the lake's drainage reversed. Water that had flowed south to the Gulf of Alaska carved out a new channel at the northeast end of the lake to connect with the Yukon River system. Instead of travelling 225 km/140 miles south to the Pacific Ocean, Kluane Lake waters began a journey 10 times longer: north to the Bering Sea.

When the waters receded to their present level, the lake's drainage had been permanently altered. The highway crosses what is left of the Slims River at the south end of the lake. Looking across the lake from the highway, beaches from the former lake levels can be seen on grassy slopes up to 13m/40 feet above the present shoreline.

The Kluane Lake area was the site of a short-lived gold rush in the early 1900s. Tagish Charlie (of Klondike fame) staked the first claim on 4th of July Creek in the summer of 1903. The North West Mounted Police followed closely behind the prospectors, setting up summer detachments in canvas tents. A permanent NWMP post was established at Silver City (see Milepost DC 1020.5).

The Southern Tutchone people had a network of trails throughout the area, which became roads as the area developed. Silver City was the terminus of a trail between Whitehorse and Kluane Lake. The trail was upgraded to a wagon road in 1904 to serve area miners.

DC 1020.5 (1635.8 km) DJ 366.5 (589.8 km) Turnoff for Kluane Bed and Breakfast (3.1 miles/5 km east via unmarked dirt and gravel road). The ruins of Silver City, once the site of a trading post, roadhouse and North West Mounted Police barracks, begin about 2.1 miles/3.4 km in on this side road.

(Large RVs park at turnaround just before road narrows and walk to ruins.)

Silver City, located on private property, served traffic traveling the wagon road from Whitehorse to the placer goldfields of the Kluane Lake district from 1904 to 1924.

DC 1021 (1636.6 km) **DJ 366** (589 km) Silver Creek. *NOTE: Beginning northbound chipseal multi-use trail that parallels lakeshore for about 12 miles. Do not try to access this trail with vehicles. There are no turnarounds and it is not wide enough for vehicles.*

DC 1022.5 (1638.5 km) **DJ 364.5** (586.6 km) **Historical Mile 1055.** Turnoff for Kluane Lake Research Station and airstrip 0.9 mile/1.4 km east. The research station, sponsored by Arctic Institute of North America/University of Calgary, has a small interpretive room with information on area expeditions and research.

Private Aircraft: Silver City airstrip; elev. 2,570 feet/783m; length 3,000 feet/914m; gravel; no services.

DC 1023.7 (1641 km) **DJ 363.3** (584.6 km) **Historical Mile 1056** (**Historical milepost 1055**). Kluane Camp commemorative plaque. Kluane Lake Lodge (closed down about 1990).

DC 1024 (1642.1 km) **DJ 363** (584.2 km) Large gravel turnout on south shore of **Kluane Lake.** *CAUTION: Narrow approach with steep drop-off. Big rigs approach with care.*

Kluane Lake, largest lake in Yukon Territory, covering approximately 154 square miles/400 square km. The Ruby Range lies on the east side of the lake. Boat rentals are available at Destruction Bay and Burwash Landing. Excellent fishing for lake trout, northern pike and grayling.

Tachal Dhal (formerly known as Sheep Mountain) is directly ahead for northbound travelers. Tachal Dhal is Southern Tutchone and means "skin scraper mountain."

DC 1027.8 (1647.4 km) **DJ 359.2** (578.1 km) **Slims River Bridge.** The original Slims River bridge was built by the Canadian Army in 1955, and consisted of 2 steel through truss spans on reinforced concrete piers and abutments. Bridge was replaced in 2009-2010. Slim's River (A'ay Chu), which flows into Kluane Lake, was named for a packhorse that drowned here during the 1903 Kluane gold rush.

DC 1028.8 (1649.1 km) **DJ 358.2** (576.4 km) Turnoff for access road to **Tachal Dhal Visitor Centre.** Excellent interpretive programs, parking, outhouses and calling card phone available. Open mid-May to early September. Phone (867) 841-4500. Hours (subject to change) 9 A.M. to 4 P.M. daily in season. Stop here for information on Kluane National Park and Reserve's flora and fauna.

The southern slopes of Tachal Dhal (formerly known as Sheep Mountain) are the primary winter and spring range and lambing area of a Dall sheep population. A viewing telescope is set up to look for sheep. Rams migrate out of the area in May. Females with lambs may be seen from early May to early June. Sheep return from the alpine zone to the south-facing slopes of the mountain in late August. The face of the mountain has been designated a special preservation zone.

Check with the centre for hiking trail conditions for A'ay Chu East and A'ay Chu West trails. *Hikers must register for overnight hikes in Kluane National Park and Reserve at either Tachal Dhal Visitor Centre here or the Kluane National Park and Reserve*

Visitor Centre in Haines Junction. From the Visitor Centre, the A'ay Chu West trail is accessed via a 1.2-mile/2-km side road to trailhead parking (not recommended for motorhomes).

The small white cross on the side of Sheep Mountain marks the grave of Alexander Clark Fisher, a prospector who came into this area about 1906. The prospector's grave is accessible via the side road off the visitor centre access road.

DC 1029.7 (1650.8 km) **DJ 357.3** (574.8 km) Narrow, gated access (sharp turn, may be difficult for large RVs) to north to gravel parking area at trailhead to **Soldier's Summit**, **Historic Milepost 1061**; interpretive signs. Half-hour self-guided walk to Soldiers Summit. (Large vehicles may wish to park at the viewpoint; see next milepost.)

The Alaska Canada Military Highway was officially opened with a ribbon-cutting ceremony here on blizzardy Nov. 20, 1942. A plaque by the parking area was erected during the rededication ceremony held Nov. 20, 1992, commemorating the 50th anniversary of the highway.

DC 1029.8 (1650.8 km) **DJ 357.2** (574.8 km) Viewpoint to south with large parking area and interpretive signs overlooking Kluane Lake's Horseshoe Bay; good photo-op.

Interpretive signs at this turnout on the 1903 discovery of gold on Ruby Creek which caused a gold rush in the Kluane Lake area and led to the establishment of Silver City, at one time a sizable community with a NWMP post (see **Milepost DC 1020.5**); road building around Kluane Lake as a result of the gold rush; and the Southern Tutchone name for Kluane Lake (Lu'an Man or Whitefish Lake), which along with the English name is considered a variation of the Tlingit name, Luxhani or "whitefish country." Kluane Lake is a good place to fish for whitefish, trout and chum salmon but it can be quite dangerous when the wind picks up. The Kluane Lake peope travelled up A'ay (Slims River) to the Kaskawulsh River and Jarvis Creek on their seasonal travels to hunting and fishing grounds.

DC 1030.5 (1651.9 km) **DJ 356.5** (573.7 km) Boat launch (signed) via gravel side road down to lake. *CAUTION: The multi-use path along Kluane Lake north and south of here can be confusing, looking like a side road. Do not access this path in vehicles, as it is narrow and not intended for cars or RVs.*

DC 1034.2 (1657.8 km) **DJ 352.8** (567.8 km) Williscroft Creek culvert.

DC 1034.5 (1658.3 km) **DJ 352.5** (567.3 km) **Historical Mile 1067.** Turnoff on driveway towards lake for **Cottonwood RV Park and Campground** (description follows).

©Kris Valencia, staff

Cottonwood RV Park and Campground. Welcome to our "Wilderness Paradise." Park your RV by the lake or pitch a tent on the shore. Play mini-golf. View Dall sheep from your campsite or fish for trout and grayling. Birdwatching. Hiking trails nearby. Spectacular scenery! Just 3 hours from Whitehorse, 6 hours from Tok. "A place where people stop for a day and stay another." Free WiFi. Phone (867) 841-4066; email glen.brough@sympatico.ca; website www.yukonweb.com/tourism/cottonwood. See display ad on this page. [ADVERTISEMENT]

DC 1037.1 (1662.5 km) **DJ 349.9** (563.1 km) Double-ended gravel turnout to northeast.

DC 1039.3 (1666 km) **DJ 347.7** (559.5 km) **Historical Mile 1072.** Turnoff to east for **Congdon Creek** Yukon government campground on Kluane Lake. Double check at www.env.gov.yk.ca/camping to make sure this park has reopened. Clo-

sures possible due to bear activity. Drive in 0.4 mile/0.6 km via gravel loop road; tenting area, 81 level sites (some pull-through), outhouses, kitchen shelters, water pump, firewood, firepits, picnic tables, sandy beach, interpretive talks, playground, boat launch. Short, self-guiding interpretive trail follows shoreline of Kluane Lake. Camping permit ($12); self-registration.

DC 1039.7 (1666.6 km) DJ 347.3 (558.9 km) Congdon Creek. According to R. Coutts, *Yukon: Places & Names*, Congdon Creek is believed to have been named by a miner after Frederick Tennyson Congdon. A lawyer from Nova Scotia, Congdon came to the Yukon in 1898 and held various political posts until 1911.

DC 1046 (1676.8 km) DJ 341 (548.8 km)

Nines Creek.

DC 1046.4 (1677.5 km) DJ 340.6 (548.1 km) Mines Creek.

DC 1048.1 (1680.1 km) DJ 338.9 (545.4 km) Bock's Creek.

DC 1049.2 (1683 km) DJ 337.8 (542.6 km) *Slow for speed zones northbound from 70 kmph/43 mph to 50 kmph/31 mph.*

Destruction Bay

DC 1050.8 (1684.5 km) DJ 336.2 (541 km) F 432.2 (695.5 km) Talbot Arm Motel. Destruction Bay is located at **Historic Milepost 1083**, 66 miles/106 km north of Haines Junction and 116 miles/186 km south of

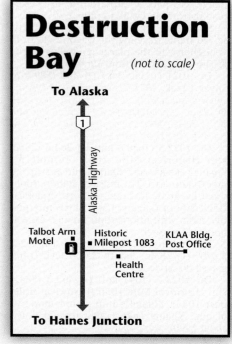

Beaver Creek. **Population:** 55. **Emergency Services: Health clinic,** phone (867) 841-4444; **Ambulance,** phone (867) 841-3333; **Fire Department,** phone (867) 841-3331.

Restaurant, gas, diesel, tire repair, souvenirs, convenience store, motel and RV park at **Talbot Arm Motel.** The Talbot Arm Motel, with its full-service dining room, began serving travelers in 1967. It was rebuilt in 1987.

Located on the shore of Kluane Lake, Destruction Bay is one of several towns that grew out of the building of the Alaska Highway. It earned its name when a storm destroyed buildings and materials here. Destruction Bay was one of the many relay stations spaced at 100-mile intervals to give truck drivers a break and a chance to repair their vehicles. A repeater station was also located here, providing telephone and telegraph service. Historic sign adjacent historic milepost. A highway maintenance camp is located here.

Destruction Bay Lodge has camping. Boat launch, boat rentals and guided fishing tours also available locally. The Kluane Lake Fishing Derby is in July.

Talbot Arm Motel. See display ad this page.

Alaska Highway Log
(continued)

DC 1051.2 (1685.1 km) DJ 335.8 (540.4 km) Rest area with litter bins and toilet.

DC 1051.3 (1685.3 km) DJ 335.7 (540.2 km) Cluett Creek.

DC 1051.5 (1685.6) DJ 335.5 (539.9 km) Distance marker northbound shows Burwash Landing 15 km/9 miles, Beaver Creek 190 km/118 miles, and Fairbanks 692 km/430 miles.

CAUTION: Watch for dips, frost heaves and gravel breaks north to Alaska border. Road crews had repaired much of this road by end of summer 2013, but be alert for possible damage. Damaged road is often but not always marked by signs or orange flags.

DC 1054.3 (1690.2 km) DJ 332.7 (535.4 km) Lewis Creek.

Burwash Landing

(not to scale)

Kluane Lake

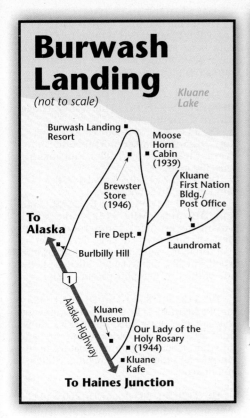

Burwash Landing Resort

Moose Horn Cabin (1939)

Kluane First Nation Bldg./ Post Office

Brewster Store (1946)

To Alaska

Fire Dept.

Burlbilly Hill

Laundromat

1

Alaska Highway

Kluane Museum

Our Lady of the Holy Rosary (1944)

Kluane Kafe

To Haines Junction

Kluane Museum of Natural History offers informative displays. (©David L. Ranta, staff)

DC 1057.5 (1695.3 km) DJ 329.5 (530.3 km) Copper Joe Creek.

DC 1058.4 (1696.7 km) DJ 328.6 (528.8 km) Memorial (on right northbound) is a family tribute to Douglas ("Dougie") Richard Twiss II, Dec. 13, 1982–June 3, 2005, a Southern Tutchone man from the Champagne and Aishihik First Nations: "Follow your dreams, be kind, and always remember to enjoy every day of your life."

DC 1060.4 (1700 km) DJ 326.6 (525.6 km) Welcome to Burwash Landing (sign northbound). Fireweed and charred trees are from June 1999 fire. The human-caused fire closed the Alaska Highway and Burwash Landing was evacuated. Some 8,000 acres were burned and 5 homes destroyed before fire crews contained the fire. Fireweed, as its name implies, is one of the first plants to reestablish itself in burn areas.

NOTE: Slow for speed zones 70 kmp/43 mph to 50 kmph/31 mph through Burwash Landing.

DC 1060.9 (1700.8 km) DJ 326.1 (524.8 km) Kluane Museum of Natural History and World's Largest Gold Pan to northeast.

Burwash Landing

DC 1061 (1701 km) DJ 326 (524.6 km) F 422 (679 km) **Historic Milepost 1093.** Located on Kluane Lake, 10 miles/16 km north of Destruction Bay, 76 miles/122 km north of Haines Junction, and 106 miles/170 km south of Beaver Creek. **Population:** 84. **Emergency Services: Ambulance**, phone (867) 841-3333; **Fire Department**, phone (867) 841-2221.

Visitor Information: Check at the Kluane Museum of Natural History, located on the east side of the Alaska Highway at the turnoff to Burwash Landing; Open 9 A.M. to 9 P.M. in summer; phone (867) 841-5561.

Burwash Landing has a post office, community hall, laundromat and church.

Visitor services include gas, diesel, dining (**Kluane Kafe** on highway), camping and lodging.

Flightseeing trips of Kluane National Park are also available out of Burwash Landing. For spectacular viewing of the world's largest non-polar icefields, contact **Rocking Star Adventures** (www.rockingstar.ca), an air charter service with a base at Burwash Landing Resort.

Burwash Landing Resort was one of the earliest lodges on the Alaska Highway. The original 2-story log lodge was built in 1944-45 and was owned and operated by Eugene Jacquot until his death in 1950.

Burwash Landing is one of the oldest settlements in the Yukon. The original trading post was established in 1904 by the Jacquot brothers, Louis and Eugene, as a supply centre for local miners. There are several historic structures in town, including Moose Horn Cabin (1939) and the Brewster Store (1946). The log Our Lady of the Holy Rosary Mission was built in 1944:

"This was the first church northwest of Whitehorse on the new Alcan Highway. Father Morrisset, then auxiliary chaplain to the U.S. Army at the road construction camps, was asked by the local residents to start a mission and day school. Land was donated by Eugene Jacquot, trading post owner. Building materials came from the Duke River camp site and included an unfinished U.S. Army mess hall and a log cabin, which form the 2 arms of the complex. The day school closed in 1952. The church opened with Christmas eve mass in 1944 and is still in use today."

The Kluane Museum of Natural History offers wildlife exhibits with dioramas depicting natural habitat. Also displayed are Native clothing, tools and weapons, and Yukon minerals. Northern videos shown. Gift shop with locally made crafts and Northern books. Pull-through parking area accommodates vehicles up to transport truck length. World's Largest Gold Pan is on display

in front of the museum; good photo-op. Phone (867) 841-5561 for more information. Admission charged.

Examples of burl bowls may be seen at local gift shops here, in Destruction Bay and elsewhere along the highway. Burls start as an irritation in the spruce. The tree sends extra sap as healant, which creates a growth or burl. Burls are either "green," harvested from live trees in the spring, or they are "dry burls," taken from dead burl trees. Burls are peeled of their bark and used in their natural form as fenceposts, for example, or they may be shaped and finished into a variety of objects, such as bowls.

Inquire locally about boat rentals and fishing on **Kluane Lake**. *CAUTION: Beware of high winds on Kluane Lake.*

Alaska Highway Log

(continued)

DC 1062 (1702.6 km) DJ 325 (523 km) Historic Milepost 1094. Private Air-

Enjoying the campfire at White River RV Park. (©Judy Nadon, staff)

craft: Burwash Airport to north; elev. 2,643 feet/806m; length 6,000 feet/1,829m; gravel, no fuel.

DC 1066.3 (1709.5 km) DJ 320.7 (516.1 km) **Duke River** bridge. The Duke River flows into Kluane Lake. It was named for George Duke, an early prospector. This bridge, completed in 2009, replaced the original Duke River bridge, which was built by the Canadian Army in 1955 and consisted of 2 steel through truss spans on reinforced concrete piers and abutments. The new bridge is built to resist the stress of earthquakes. Major bridge replacement projects along this stretch of the Alaska Highway are part of the Shakwak Project, a massive reconstruction of the Alaska Highway between Haines Junction and the Alaska border.

Slow for bumps, road damage, road repair and gravel breaks northbound.

DC 1071 (1717 km) DJ 316 (508.5 km) Narrow bridge crosses Burwash Creek, named for Lachlin Taylor Burwash, a mining recorder at Silver City in 1903.

DC 1075.7 (1724.6 km) DJ 311.3 (501 km) Sakiw Creek (not signed).

DC 1076.6 (1726 km) DJ 310.4 (499.5 km) **Kluane River Overlook Rest Area** to northeast; information panels and observation platform overlooking Kluane River. (This overlook is at a significant distance above the valley floor, use binoculars.) Interpretive panels describe the life cycle of the chum salmon that come to spawn in this river in August and September. Watch for grizzly bears and bald eagles feeding on salmon.

DC 1077.6 (1727.6 km) DJ 309.4 (497.9 km) Quill Creek Mine Road.

DC 1078.4 (1728.9 km) DJ 308.6 (496.6 km) Quill Creek.

DC 1079.9 (1731.4 km) DJ 307.1 (494.2 km) Glacier Creek.

DC 1083.4 (1737 km) DJ 303.6 (488.6 km) **Historical Mile 1118.** Kluane Wilderness Village (closed since fall 2006, current status unknown) began as Travellers Services (Yukon) Ltd., and was later known as Mount Kennedy Motel, in about 1964-65. By 1976 the business name appeared as Kluane Wilderness Village, owned and managed by John Trout and Joseph Frigon and later run

by John and his wife, Liz. View of Mount Kennedy, Mount Logan and Mount Lucania.

This is the halfway mark between Whitehorse and Tok.

DC 1085.1 (1739.7 km) DJ 301.9 (485.8 km) Swede Johnson Creek.

DC 1093.8 (1753.7 km) DJ 293.2 (471.8 km) Road to NorthwesTel microwave tower.

DC 1094.9 (1755.5 km) DJ 292.1 (470 km) Large turnout to west with view of Donjek River Valley and the Icefield Ranges of the St. Elias Mountains; litter bins, outhouses and interpretive sign (excerpt follows):

"The Icefield Ranges include the highest and youngest mountains in Canada. They form the main group of peaks in the St. Elias Mountains and include Canada's highest mountain, Mount Logan, at 5,959m (19,545 feet) plus 6 other peaks over 5,000m (16,000 feet).

"In 1896, the Duke of Abruzzi, an Italian nobleman, made the first successful ascent of Mount St. Elias—the second highest mountain in Canada at 5,489m. Between 1911 and 1913, the international boundary was surveyed through the Icefield Ranges.

"The largest non-polar icefield in North America extends over most of Kluane National Park and Reserve, sending long glacial fingers into the valleys between the peaks. The ice is more than 700m (2,200 feet) thick. This icefield is the remnant of previous glaciations. The latest was the Kluane Glaciation between 29,500 and 12,500 years ago. As the glaciers melted and retreated, wind-blown silt (called loess) blanketed the newly exposed rock. The new soil supported grasses that fed bison, moose and caribou."

DC 1098.7 (1761.6 km) DJ 288.3 (464 km) **Donjek River Bridge** (replaced in 2008) crosses the wide and silty Donjek River, a major tributary of the White River. According to R. Coutts, *Yukon: Places & Names*, the Donjek is was named by Charles Willard Hayes in 1891, from the Indian word for a peavine that grows in the area.

Observe No Hunting Zone Donjek River to Beaver Creek.

DC 1104.2 (1770.5 km) DJ 282.8 (455.1 km) Small gravel turnout to west. Beaver Creek Highway Maintenance sign northbound.

Since the Alaska Highway was first punched through the wilderness in 10 short months in 1942, this war-time road has been under reconstruction. There never seems to be a shortage of road to straighten, culverts to fix, bridges to replace, or surfaces to level out, especially along the stretch of bumpy road between the Donjek River and the Alaska border. From the 18th Co. Engineers' pioneer road building in 1943, to the modern engineering techniques of Yukon's Dept. of Highways, this section of the Alaska Highway has presented some unique challenges.

According to Public Works Yukon, much of the soil along the north Alaska Highway is of glacial origin and unsuitable for road embankments. "Anything that causes the permafrost to melt will cause the ice-rich soil to liquefy, and liquid soil has little strength and will settle or subside. Then if this soil refreezes during lower air temperatures, it will expand or heave." This process wreaks havoc on the drivability of the road surface by creating undulations and cracking.

Northbound travelers should watch for roadside flags indicating road damage, and slow down for bumps and dips in the highway. Short, improved sections of road alternate with damaged sections of road northbound. Expect ongoing road improvement projects in summer 2014. SLOW for gravel breaks and dips.

Watch for swans in lake to south (summer).

DC 1111.7 (1782.5 km) DJ 275.3 (443 km) Edith Creek bridge, turnout to west. Try your hand at gold panning here; "colours" have been found. Grayling fishing, June through September.

DC 1112 (1783.1 km) DJ 275 (442.5 km) **Historical Mile 1147.** Pine Valley Lodge; current status unknown.

DC 1112.8 (1784.3 km) DJ 274.2 (441.3 km) Distance marker northbound shows Beaver Creek 89 kms/55 miles, Fairbanks 612 kms/380 miles.

DC 1116.7 (1790.5 km) DJ 270.3 (435 km) Koidern River bridge No. 1.

DC 1117.1 (1791.1 km) DJ 269.9 (434.3 km) **Historical Mile 1152. Lake Creek** Yukon government campground southwest of highway; 28 large level sites (6 pull-through), water pump, litter barrels, firewood, firepits, picnic tables, kitchen shelter and outhouses. Camping permit ($12). ▲

DC 1123.9 (1802.1 km) DJ 263.1 (423.4 km) **Pickhandle Lake** rest area to southwest; toilets, tables, litter bins. Interpretive panels on Native trading routes, pond life and muskrats. Good fishing from boat for northern pike all summer; also grayling, whitefish and lingcod.

DC 1126.2 (1805.9 km) DJ 260.8 (419.7 km) Aptly named Reflection Lake to west mirrors the Kluane Range. The highway parallels this range between Koidern and Haines Junction.

DC 1128.8 (1810 km) DJ 258.2 (415.5 km) **Historical Mile 1164.** Jim and Dorothy Cook's Koidern River Lodge has been here since 1969. When they are open in the summer they sell souvenirs, snacks and pop; pay phone; and gas/diesel.

DC 1129 (1810.2 km) DJ 258 (415.2 km) Koidern River bridge No. 2.

DC 1132.1 (1815 km) DJ 254.9 (410.2 km) **Historic Milepost 1167.** Remains of Bear Flats Lodge at Koidern, which operated from 1973 until it closed in 1992. During the early days of the Alaska Highway, this was a highway maintenance camp and telephone and telegraph station. A number of businesses have operated here over the years: Rover's Inn in the 1950s; Northwest Trading Post 1960s; and Koidern Gulf Services, 1970.

Watch for grizzly bears along highway.

DC 1133.5 (1818 km) DJ 253.5 (408 km) **Historical Mile 1169.** Discovery Yukon Lodgings and White River RV Park (description follows). ▲

Discovery Yukon Lodging and White River RV Park is a relaxing oasis at Km 1818 on the historic Alaska Highway, just 50 kms south of Beaver Creek bordering Kluane Wildlife Sanctuary. Stay and enjoy the rugged natural beauty of the Yukon amid

landscaped grassy areas, spacious pull-through full-service RV sites, and clean, cozy cabins. Enjoy wildlife and historic military vehicle displays as well as our Northern botanical gardens. Take advantage of our many amenities such as hot showers, WiFi hotspot, museum, picnic areas and pet-friendly features. You'll love our exciting activities: guided nature tours aboard our WWII military vintage 6-wheeler, wildlife spotting, rockhounding on the White River, meeting new friends around our communal campfire. To book a cabin or RV or tent spot, call 867-862-7408 or email info@discovery yukon.com. We're a Good Sam member and Golden Host award recipient. www.dis-scoveryyukon.com. Our GPS coordinates are N61°59.096 by W140° 32.316. We look forward to meeting you! [ADVERTISEMENT]

DC 1134.1 (1818.6 km) **DJ 252.9** (407 km) **White River** bridge. The White River, a major tributary of the Yukon River, was named by Hudson's Bay Co. explorer Robert Campbell for its white colour, caused by the volcanic ash in the water. *NOTE: This river is considered very dangerous; not recommended for boating.*

CAUTION: Slow for frost-heaved road and gravel breaks northbound to Alaska border. Rough road is often signed or marked by orange flags, but not always. Expect improved highway in summer 2014.

DC 1140.4 (1828.5 km) **DJ 246.6** (396.8 km) **Moose Lake** to west, grayling to 18 inches, use dry flies and small spinners, midsummer. Boat needed for lake; look for moose.

DC 1141.9 (1831.1 km) **DJ 245.1** (394.4 km) Distance marker northbound shows Beaver Creek 39 km/24 miles, Fairbanks 562 km/349 miles.

DC 1142.7 (1832.4 km) **DJ 244.3** (393.2 km) Sanpete Creek, named by an early prospector after Sanpete County in Utah.

DC 1145.9 (1837.5 km) **DJ 241.1** (388 km) Dry Creek No. 1.

DC 1148 (1840.8 km) **DJ 239** (384.6 km) Rest area to southwest with dramatic mountain view; outhouses, litter bins.

DC 1148.7 (1841.8 km) **DJ 238.3** (383.5 km) **Historical Mile 1184.** Dry Creek No. 2. Gravel turnout to west at south end of bridge. Dry Creek Lodge was located in this area until it burned down in the fall of 1951. Travelers transferred from the Canadian operated B.Y.N. Lines to the Alaska Coachways buses here.

Highway climbs long hill northbound.

Distance marker southbound shows Haines Junction 268 km/166 miles.

DC 1153.3 (1849.3 km) **DJ 233.7** (376.1 km) Small Lake to east. Snag Road (dirt, passable for vehicles first mile only) connects the Alaska Highway here with the abandoned airfield and Indian village at **Snag** to the northeast.

In 1947, Snag functioned as an emergency airstrip for aircraft flying from Edmonton to Anchorage and Fairbanks. Snag's claim to fame is the lowest recorded temperature in Canada: -81.4°F/-63°C on Feb. 3, 1947. (Alaska's lowest recorded temperature was -80°F/-62.8°C on January 23, 1971, at Prospect Creek, a pipeline camp 25 miles southeast of Bettles.)

DC 1153.4 (1849.6 km) **DJ 233.6** (375.9 km) **Historical Mile 1188. Snag Junction Yukon government campground,** 0.4 mile/0.6 km north on gravel loop road. There are 15 tent and vehicle sites, 3 pull-through,

some overlooking lake, a kitchen shelter, outhouses, picnic tables, firewood, firepits and litter barrels. Camping permit ($12). Small-boat launch. Swimming in Small Lake.

There are several small lakes along the highway here. Watch for Trumpeter and Tundra swans resting and nesting in these ponds.

DC 1154.2 (1850.7 km) **DJ 232.8** (374.6 km) Dirt track northeast to lakes.

DC 1155.3 (1852.5 km) **DJ 231.7** (372.9 km) Dirt track north to lake.

DC 1159 (1858.4 km) **DJ 228** (366.9 km) Double-ended rest area to southwest with litter bins.

DC 1160.2 (1860.4 km) **DJ 226.8** (365 km) Enger Creek.

DC 1163 (1865) **DJ 224** (360.5 km) Vent-like structures alongside the highway here are part of the Alaska Highway Permafrost Research Project, which is testing specialized construction techniques. The techniques are designed to minimize melting of the permafrost by allowing cold air to penetrate the road embankment and increasing surface reflectivity. Permafrost temperatures will be monitored for the next several years to assess their effectiveness. If the designs prove to be practical and effective, they may be used more extensively along the highway. This is an international project involving Yukon Highways and Public Works, the U.S. Federal Highways Administration and other public agencies.

View of Nutzotin Mountains to northwest, Kluane Ranges to southwest. On a clear day you should be able to see the snow-clad Wrangell Mountains in the distance to the west.

DC 1165.3 (1868.6 km) **DJ 221.7** (356.8 km) Beaver Creek bridge.

Speed Zone: Slow to 70 kmph/43 mph and 50 kmph/30 mph northbound through Beaver Creek.

CAUTION: Slow for possible frost-heaved road and gravel breaks southbound to Burwash Landing. Rough road is often signed or marked by orange flags, but not always. Expect con-

tinued construction or improved highway in summer 2014.

NOTE: No cell phone service south to Burwash Landing.

Beaver Creek

DC 1166.5 (1870.6 km) **DJ 220.5** (354.8 km) **F 316.5** (509.3 km) Visitor Information Centre in Beaver Creek, **Historic Milepost 1202.** Driving distance to Tok, AK, 113 miles/182 km; to Haines Junction, YT, 184 miles/295 km; to Haines, AK, 334 miles/538. km; to Whitehorse 280 miles/450 km. **Population:** 112. **Emergency Services:** RCMP, phone (867) 862-5555. **Ambulance,** phone (867) 862-3333. **Nursing Station:** (867) 862-4444.

Visitor Information: Yukon government Visitor Information Centre is in the log building on the highway; open daily late May through September. Phone (867) 862-7321. The visitor centre has a book on display of dried Yukon wildflowers for those interested in the flora of the territory. The centre also has an Alaska Highway scrap-

BEAVER CREEK ADVERTISERS

Buckshot Betty's ....Ph. (867) 862-7111

Slow for road damage between the Donjek River and Alaska border. (©Kris Valencia, staff)

Southbound travelers on the Alaska Highway must stop at Canada Customs.
(©David L. Ranta, staff)

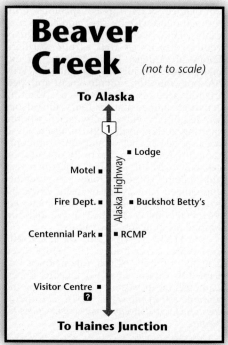

Beaver Creek *(not to scale)*

book with historical photos of lodges and life along the north Alaska Highway.

Private Aircraft: Beaver Creek Yukon government airstrip 1 NW; see description at **Milepost DC 1170.3**. **Radio**: CBC North at 93.1 FM, CHON 90.5 FM.

Lodging, camping and licensed restaurant and lounge at **Buckshot Betty's**. Gas stations with repair service, lodge with convenience and souvenir store located here. There is a post office; a bank, open 2 days a week, located in the post office building; ATMs; community library; and public swimming pool beside the community club.

Buckshot Betty's. Well, first we'd like to congratulate you on making it this far without breaking or losing anything! Stop and come on in! Have a coffee, some pie, sweet rolls or cookies. Browse our souvenirs: crazy Buckshot Betty T-shirts, sweat-pants or our great selection of Yukon and Alaska books. For lunch we offer our homemade soup, bread and great burgers. Or if you happen to arrive around supper-time you can order up some homemade pizza, steak, lasagna or our daily dinner special. Mosey up to the bar (handcrafted by Buckshot Betty) and have a drink—you might even

hear her having fun belting out karaoke. And you can lay your head down in one of our cozy cabins; we make a delicious breakfast, too. Thank you for being part of our day! (867) 862-7111 buckshotbetty@hotmail.com. See display ad this page. [ADVERTISEMENT]

Beaver Creek was the site of the old Canadian customs station. Local residents were pleased to see customs relocated north of town in 1983, having long endured the flashing lights and screaming sirens set off whenever a tourist forgot to stop.

Beaver Creek is 1 of 2 sites where Alaska Highway construction crews working from opposite directions connected the highway. In October 1942, Alaska Highway construction operations were being rushed to conclusion as winter set in. Eastern and western sector construction crews (the 97th and 18th Engineers) pushed through to meet at a junction on Beaver Creek on Oct. 28., thus making it possible for the first time for vehicles to travel the entire length of the highway. East–west crews had connected at Contact Creek on Sept. 15th or 24th (depending on your source), 1942.

Yukon Centennial Gold Rush figurines and displays are located just west of How Far

West Plaza (celebrating Beaver Creek's status as most westerly Canadian community) at town centre. The plaza features information on wildlife and a map of Beaver Creek.

Our Lady of Grace mission. Built in 1961 from a salvaged Quonset hut left over from highway construction days, it is 1 of 3 Catholic missions on the north Alaska Highway (the others are in Burwash Landing and Haines Junction). St. Columba's Anglican Church in Beaver Creek was prefabricated in Whitehorse and constructed in one week in 1975.

Alaska Highway Log
(continued)

DC 1167.9 (1872.8 km) **DJ 219.1** (352.6 km) Double-ended turnout to southwest with litter bins, picnic tables and outhouses.

Slow for 50 kmph/30 mph speed zone southbound through Beaver Creek.

DC 1168.4 (1873.6 km) **DJ 218.6** (351.8 km) **Private Aircraft**: Beaver Creek Airport, Yukon government airstrip; elev. 2,129 feet/ 649m; length 3,740 feet/1,140m; gravel; no fuel. Airport of entry for Canada customs.

Distance marker northbound shows U.S. Customs 30 kms/18 miles. Posted speed limit is 90 kmph/55 mph.

DC 1168.5 (1873.8 km) **DJ 218.5** (351.6 km) **Beaver Creek Canada Customs** station; phone (867) 862-7230. Open 24 hours a day year-round. All traffic entering Canada must stop here for clearance. Expect vigorous enforcement of customs requirements (see "Crossing the Border" in the TRAVEL PLANNING section for more details).

Extensive road construction was underway during the summer of 2013 to improve road conditions northbound to AK–YT border.

DC 1173.4 (1881.7 km) **DJ 213.6** (343.7 km) Snag Creek.

DC 1174.6 (1883.6 km) **DJ 212.4** (341.8 km) Mirror Creek.

Look for nesting swans in roadside lakes in summer.

DC 1175.1 (1884.4 km) **DJ 211.9** (341 km) Turnout to southwest with litter bin.

DC 1182.9 (1897 km) **DJ 204.1** (328.5 km) Little Scottie Creek.

DC 1186.3 (1902.5 km) **DJ 200.7** (323

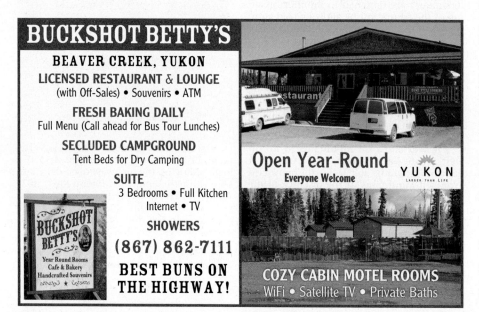

km) **Historic Milepost 1221. Canada–U.S. International Border.** Rest area to south with interpretive panels on the 141st Meridian and the challenges of northern road construction.

The international boundary marker here makes a good photo-op, as does the narrow clearing which marks the border. This is part of the 20-foot-/6-m-wide swath cut by surveyors from 1904 to 1920 along the 141st meridian (from Demarcation Point on the Arctic Ocean south 600 miles/966 km to Mount St. Elias in the Wrangell Mountains) to mark the Alaska–Canada border. This swath continues south to mark the boundary between southeastern Alaska and Canada. Portions of the swath are cleared periodically by the International Boundary Commission.

The boundary line between Alaska and Yukon was originally described in an 1825 treaty between Russia and England. The U.S. accepted this version of the boundary with its purchase of Alaska from Russia in 1867. But after gold was discovered in the Klondike in 1896, a dispute arose between the U.S. and Canada, with both claiming the seaports at the head of Lynn Canal. An international tribunal decided in favor of the U.S. in 1903.

TIME ZONE CHANGE: Alaska observes Alaska time, Yukon Territory observes Pacific time. Alaska time is 1 hour earlier than Pacific time.

Improved highway northbound next 14 miles. Highway from border to Tok was in fair to good condition in summer 2013.

Welcome to Alaska and Welcome to Yukon signs for northbound and southbound travelers respectively.

Distance marker northbound shows Tok 93 miles, Delta Junction 200 miles, Fairbanks 298 miles, Anchorage 421 miles.

ALASKA ROUTE 2

Distance from Dawson Creek (DC) is followed by distance from physical milepost (MP), distance from Delta Junction (DJ) and distance from Fairbanks (F).

NOTE: In the Alaska portion of The MILEPOST® Alaska Highway log, DC mileages from Dawson Creek are based on actual driving distance, and MP mileages are based on physical mileposts between Port Alcan and Delta Junction, AK, which reflect traditional distances from Dawson Creek, BC. There is a mileage difference of 35 miles between the historic mileposts and actual driving distance. Read the information on Mileposts and Kilometreposts in the introduction to the Alaska Highway for more on this subject.

DC 1186.8 MP 1221.8 **DJ 200.2 F 296.2 Port Alcan U.S. Customs and Border Protection** station, open 24 hours a day, 7 days a week, year-round; pay phone (credit card and collect calls only) and restrooms. Phone (907) 774-2252. *All traffic entering Alaska must stop for clearance. Do not get out of your vehicle unless instructed to do so by the border protection officer or until you have cleared customs. DO NOT TAKE PHOTOGRAPHS! Do not let pets out of vehicles.*

For details on customs requirements for returning residents and nonresidents entering the U.S., please read "Crossing the Border" in the TRAVEL PLANNING section.

Distance marker northbound shows Taylor Highway junction 77 miles, Fairbanks 297 miles, Anchorage 420 miles. Tok is 92 miles from here.

Distance marker southbound shows Canadian Customs 20 miles.

DC 1187.5 MP 1222.5 **DJ 199.5 F 295.5 Purple Heart Trail Honoring Veterans' Sacrifice** (northbound sign). The Alaska Highway from the border to Delta Junction was designated the "Purple Heart Trail" in May 2008, to honor veterans.

Distance marker northbound shows Tok 92 miles, Delta Junction 199 miles.

DC 1187.7 MP 1222.7 **DJ 199.3 F 295.3** Entering **Tetlin National Wildlife Refuge** northbound. Established in 1980, the 730,000-acre refuge stretches south from the Alaska Highway and west from the Canadian border. The major physical features include rolling hills, hundreds of small lakes and 2 glacial rivers (the Nabesna and Chisana), which combine to form the Tanana River. The complex association of lakes, ponds, marshes, streams, and rivers provide for a variety of habitat favorable to numerous species of waterfowl, and the refuge has been recognized internationally as an Important Bird Area because of its habitat for migrating sandhill crane and nesting trumpeter swans. The refuge provides habitat for 126 nesting species and more than 64 migrating species. 42 mammals including moose, black and grizzly bear, wolf, coyotes beaver, red fox, lynx and caribou are found on this refuge.

For more detailed information, contact the Refuge Manager, Tetlin National Wildlife Refuge, Box 779, Tok, AK 99780; phone (907) 883-5312. Refuge headquarters is located in Tok (take the Tok Cutoff to Borealis Avenue and drive 1.3 miles north). Information on the refuge is available seasonally at the Tetlin National Wildlife Refuge Visitor Center at **Milepost 1229** on the Alaska Highway.

DC 1188.2 MP 1223.2 **DJ 198.8 F 294.8** Distance marker northbound shows Tok 92 miles, Delta Junction 199 miles.

DC 1188.4 MP 1223.4 **DJ 198.6 F 294.6** Scottie Creek bridge. Old cabins to southwest.

DC 1189.6 MP 1224.6 **DJ 197.4 F 293.4** Scenic viewpoint overlooking Highway Lake. Look for beaver lodge in marshy area at north end of lake. Tetlin Refuge interpretive sign on migratory birds (excerpt follows):

"You are traveling along the route flown by hundreds of thousands of birds each spring. Some migrate from as far as South America. They return to Alaska to raise their next generation, surrounded by food, with long days for feasting. More than 126 species of birds find an ideal nursery in Tetlin National Wildlife Refuge.

"Trumpeter swans are nesting here in growing numbers, attracted by the refuge's many secluded ponds. They demand privacy for raising their cygnets and can chase away other nearby birds, including loons. About 30 species of birds live in this area all year."

DC 1190.4 MP 1225.4 **DJ 196.6 F 292.6** Parking area and canoe launch (not signed) for Desper Creek and access to Tetlin NWR on southwest side of highway. NOTE: This parking area is a small, overgrown dirt turn-out just south of Border City entrance and directly across the creek from their campground. It is used mostly by hunters in the fall.

NOTE: $1,000 fine for littering.

DC 1190.5 MP 1225.5 **DJ 196.5 F 292.5** Border City Lodge & RV Park west side of highway. This business usually offers food, gas, diesel, lodging and an RV park.

Historic highway lodge location: Border Trading Post advertised in the 1949 edition of *The MILEPOST®* as "your first opportunity to replenish your supply of American cigarettes and candy bars."

DC 1191 MP 1226 **DJ 196 F 292** Scottie Creek Services to east. This business usually offers gas and camping.

The old cabin adjacent Scottie Creek Services was identified in summer 1999 as the "Original Historic Canadian Customs Log Cabin (1946–1952)." It was built by Pete Ecklund and Bill Blair of Beaver Creek, YT. Originally it stood at Milepost 1220, but was moved to its present location in the early 1960s. *Watch for bears in area.*

DC 1193 MP 1228 **DJ 194 F 290** Large double-ended paved parking area to west. Good view to south of lakes in Chisana (Shu-SHAN-ah) River valley. The Nutzotin Mountains are to the west.

DC 1194 MP 1229 **DJ 193 F 289** Parking area to southwest for **Tetlin National**

Rest area at international boundary has interpretive panels on 141st Meridian and the challenge of northern road construction. (©Kris Valencia, staff)

Cache at Tetlin National Wildlife Refuge Visitor Center is a favorite photo-op.
(©Sharon Nault)

Wildlife Refuge Visitor Center adjacent highway. Great stop with viewing deck, telescopes and photo-op of a cache. The cache has had its legs first shortened then replaced in recent years to strengthen the structure. (The current cache is seen in the photo above.) Exhibits inside include spring migration, Athabascan culture, nesting swans, fish camp diorama, tracks box and signs tree, science on the refuge and a topographical map model.

Interpretive programs on and demonstrations of traditional Native Athabascan culture and crafts presented daily in summer. A selection of videos may be shown on request. Audio tour tape/CD available for travelers headed toward Tok (return tape to Public Lands Information Center or Mainstreet Visitor Center in Tok). Restrooms (wheelchair accessible) are located in the building adjacent the parking lot. The visitor center is open 8 A.M. to 4:30 P.M. May 15 to September 15. (The center extends its hours to 6:30 P.M. when staff is available.) *NOTE: No overnight camping here, but water is available for bikers and campers who are camping at Deadman Lake or Lakeview campgrounds.*

DC 1195 MP 1230 DJ 192 F 288 Sign reads: Dial 511 for travel information.

Cell service may not be available along the highway here. When you have Internet, you may also check road conditions for Alaska highways at http://511.alaska.gov/alaska511/mappingcomponent/index, the Alaska Dept. of Transportation & Public Facilities' Traveler Information website. Yukon Territory provides a similar service at http://www.511yukon.ca/.

DC 1195.7 MP 1230.7 DJ 191.3 F 287.3 View of Island Lake to northeast.

DC 1196 MP 1231 DJ 191 F 287 Long double-ended gravel turnout to northeast.

DC 1198.3 MP 1233.3 DJ 188.7 F 284.7 Long, narrow, double-ended paved turnout to northeast.

DC 1199.2 MP 1234.2 DJ 187.8 F 283.8 Sweetwater Creek.

DC 1199.5 MP 1234.5 DJ 187.5 F 283.5

Turnoff for **Seaton Roadhouse Interpretive Site and Trails** (Tetlin NWR), 0.4 to southwest via gravel road. This beautiful spot—recently developed—is a great place to get out and stretch your legs. There is a large parking area (good for big rigs, but no overnight RV parking); gravel hiking trails with observation decks; toilets; litter bins; and a large picnic pavilion with tables. Interpretive signs relate history of this area, the importance of Alaska roadhouses, and tell a bit about Irene and Bill Seaton, the owners of the roadhouse that was once located here.

Three primitive tent campsites with fire rings and benches near end of two spur trails (campers self-register).

Hikers watch for beaver, moose, wolf and bear. Old ridges of windblown glacial silt surround a small pond at site of former Seaton Roadhouse.

DC 1200 MP 1235 DJ 187 F 283 *End 14-mile stretch of improved highway northbound from border. Fair to good pavement to Tok.*

DC 1205 MP 1240 DJ 182 F 278 Small parking area to southwest; trailhead parking for 1-mile hike to **Hidden Lake** in Tetlin National Wildlife Refuge. Hidden Lake is stocked with rainbow trout; use spinners, wobbling spoons, or flies (streamers and bucktails with black and red in their patterns). No overnight camping.

Much of Hidden Lake trail is a narrow boardwalk through woods and marshes. *Bring mosquito repellent!* There are life jackets and a boat with homemade paddles at the lake. Interpretive signs on boreal forest and Tetlin Refuge. Beavers are active in this area. Beavers can swim underwater for 3 to 5 minutes and travel a half-mile before surfacing. They are most active from evening to early morning.

DC 1205.3 MP 1240.3 DJ 181.7 F 277.7 Waist-high vertical corrugated metal culverts topped with cone-shaped "hats" seen on either side of highway are an experiment to keep ground from thawing and thus prevent frost heaves.

DC 1208 MP 1243 DJ 179 F 275 Good

examples of sand dune road cut (and rock graffiti) typical along this stretch of highway. Westbound, the highway cuts through several of these sand dunes. The sand originally was part of the volcanic mountain range to the south. Prevailing winds moved the sand across the valley floor, forming crescent-shaped dunes now stabilized by plants. A distinct layer of volcanic ash is also found here and in the Yukon, evidence of a volcanic eruption in the St. Elias Range some 1,400 years ago.

DC 1208.7 MP 1243.7 DJ 178.3 F 274.3 Scenic viewpoint to south on loop road is a large, paved turnout with easy access. Short walking trail along ridge to west. Tetlin Refuge interpretive signs on fire ecology and boreal forest at turnout read:

"In a record year, more than 650 major wildfires burn across the state, half of them ignited by lightning. Although only 2 out of every 10 lightning bolts hit the ground, Interior Alaska can be struck 6,000 times daily. Without rain, lightning that strikes tinder dry fuels may ignite a wildfire.

"Quick drying, feathery mosses send fire racing along the ground in spruce forests. Fire can smolder beneath a mossy carpet several feet thick during wet weather and even throughout the winter. Where life or property is not at risk, lightning-caused fires are allowed to burn as part of the natural process of northern forest evolution.

"The Russian word *taiga* ('land of little sticks') best describes this boggy landscape of bottle brush trees. Black spruce grow so slowly that a tree 2 inches in diameter may be 100 years old. Where black spruce thrive, few other plants can survive. They spread their roots in the boggy, shallow soil above permanently frozen ground. Permafrost blocks water drainage and limits root growth and soil fertility.

"Black spruce invite fire. Drooping branches make a stepladder for flames to climb to the cone-laden crowns. The fire's heat opens the resin-sealed cones, spreading seeds of new life."

DC 1211.6 MP 1246.6 DJ 175.4 F 271.4 Gardiner Creek bridge.

DC 1212.6 MP 1247.6 DJ 174.4 F 270.4 Double-ended turnout to north.

DC 1214.3 MP 1249.3 DJ 172.7 F 268.7 **Historic Milepost 1254** at entrance to **Deadman Lake Campground** (sharp turn to southwest). This Tetlin Refuge campground is 1.2 miles in via a narrow, dirt and gravel access road. No camping fee, 15 sites in spruce forest along half-mile loop road; firepits, toilets, picnic tables, boat ramp, information board; no reservations taken. Interpretive pavilion for evening naturalist programs during the summer season. Self-guided Taiga Trail (wheelchair friendly) with interpretive signs ends at viewing deck on Deadman Lake. Maximum 14-day campground stay within a 28-day period. Scenic spot, swimming, fishing for northern pike. The lake was originally known as "Chuljuud Manh Choh," Athabascan for "Big Pike Lake."

DC 1215.3 MP 1250.3 DJ 171.7 F 267.7 Rest area to southwest is a double-ended paved parking area with picnic tables, concrete fireplaces and view. No water or toilets.

DC 1216.3 MP 1251.3 DJ 170.7 F 266.7 Distance marker southbound shows Canadian Border 30 miles, Haines Junction 235 miles.

DC 1217.2 MP 1252.2 DJ 169.8 F 265.8 Uphill double-ended gravel access to scenic viewpoint on hill to southwest with Tetlin Refuge interpretive sign on insects (excerpt follows).

"Those female mosquitoes biting you need a blood

meal before laying eggs. The first mosquitoes to bite in spring spent the winter as dormant adults. Others (about 30 kinds) hatch from eggs during summer. Until freeze-up, some type of mosquito is always hunting for blood. A moose may lose a pint a day to mosquitoes.

"If you see wiggly silver lines in leaves, another insect vampire is at work. Larval caterpillars of leaf miners are eating tissue used by trees to make food from sunlight. They leave behind silvery tunnels.

"Warmer winters are allowing more adult moths to survive and lay eggs on spring leaves, causing a population explosion. Several seasons of damage will stress the tree, but usually not kill it.

"Other biting insects include black flies (also called white sox), which cut a plug of skin and lick the blood; no-see-ums, silver-winged gnats that look like swarms of tiny mosquitoes; and deer flies, a bee-sized insect with a bite that packs a wallop. Even caribou run from them."

DC 1219 MP 1254 **DJ 168 F 264** Distance marker westbound shows Northway Junction 10 miles, Tok 60 miles.

Great view northbound from top of hill of lakes and muskeg in Chisana River valley.

DC 1221.3 MP 1256.3 **DJ 165.7 F 261.7** Northway Station (state highway maintenance) to south; no services.

DC 1221.7 MP 1256.7 **DJ 165.3 F 261.3** Turnoff to south for **Lakeview Campground** (Tetlin National Wildlife Refuge), 0.2 mile from highway via a narrow, gravel road to 11 sites on a loop road next to beautiful **Yarger Lake**; tables, firepits, wheelchair-accessible toilets, garbage container and a hand pump for drinking water (available late summer after ground thaws sufficiently). No camping fee. Kids Don't Float life-jackets. Short trail, marked by plastic ribbons, leads from back of spaces 6 and 7 to a photo blind; watch for loons. Interpretive signs about management of Tetlin National Wildlife Refuge. NOTE: *Not recommended for trailers, 5th wheels or RVs over 30 feet.*

Look for the Nutzotin Mountains to the south and Mentasta Mountains to the west. These 2 mountain masses form the eastern end of the Alaska Range.

DC 1228 MP 1263 **DJ 159 F 255** Former highway business, Old Wrangell View, to south (closed). Beautiful views for northbound travelers (weather permitting) of Wrangell Mountains and Chisana River to the southwest. This is the land of a thousand ponds, most unnamed. Good trapping country. In early June, travelers may note numerous cottony white seeds blowing in the wind; these seeds are from willow and poplars.

DC 1228.8 MP 1263.8 **DJ 158.2 F 254.2** Distance marker southbound shows Canadian Border 42 miles, Haines Junction 247 miles.

DC 1229 MP 1264 **DJ 158 F 254** **Northway Junction**: turnoff for 9-mile-long Northway Road (paved) south across Chisana River to Northway Airport and Village (descriptions follow). Naabia Niign (at turnoff) has crafts made by residents of Northway; gas, diesel, propane; groceries; campground; shower facilities (located in store); espresso; and picnic tables. **Alaska State Troopers** east side of highway.

NORTHWAY (pop. 136) consists of 3 dispersed settlements: Northway Junction at **Milepost 1264** on the Alaska Highway, where Naabia Niign is located; Northway at the airport, 6.5 miles south of Northway Junction; and the Native Village of Northway, 2 miles beyond the airport on the

Sylvia Pitka of Northway displays beadwork on gloves at Tetlin National Wildlife Refuge Visitor Center. (©Sharon Nault)

spur road. Northway has the post office (at 6650 Northway Road), which is across from the airport. According to the FAA website, "Northway is considered a gateway to Alaska for small aircraft following the Alaska Highway because that is where they must land to clear customs unless they have enough fuel to continue on to Fairbanks or Anchorage non-stop. Most pilots do not have enough range to do that, considering that no aviation fuel is available between Whitehorse, YT and Tok, AK.

"Northway has a Flight Service Station (FSS) on the airport which provides Local Airport Advisory (LAA) service to aircraft arriving and departing. This FSS is normally open seasonally May to September. There are very few services at Northway. The Lodge closed permanently July 1, 2010 so there is currently no lodging, food or fuel available. After clearing customs, most aircraft refuel at Tok Junction Airport which is 36 nautical miles further.

"If you are flying to or from Canada and are landing in Canada, make sure you file your arrival and departure information electronically in eAPIS (Electronic Advance Passenger Information System). Some pilots assume that they do not have to call on the phone since they are filing electronically and that is not true. You are still required to call the border station to coordinate your arrival at Northway in addition to filing electronically. Check the latest Supplement Alaska for the phone number and other details."

Pilots contact the Port of Alcan/Tok office at (907) 774-2252 two hours prior to landing at Northway in order to schedule an officer onsite. Customs and border protection agents are not on the field unless they are expecting an aircraft. They drive up from the border, which takes about 1 hour. Keep in mind that you are required to stay in the aircraft until they arrive.

Northway Village has a school and a Church of God. Historically occupied by Athabascan Indians, Northway was named to honor Chief Walter Northway. Chief Northway died in 1992; he was 117 years old.

DC 1229.4 MP 1264.4 **DJ 157.6 F 253.6** Distance marker westbound shows Tok 50 miles, Delta Junction 158 miles, Fairbanks 254 miles, Anchorage 371 miles.

DC 1232.3 MP 1267.3 **DJ 154.7 F 250.7** Wonderful view of the Tanana River at Beaver Slide. There is a tower at the top of Beaver Slide. The Tanana River is the largest tributary of the Yukon River.

DC 1233 MP 1268 **DJ 154 F 250** Beaver Creek. The tea-colored water flowing in the creek is the result of tannins absorbed by the water as it flows through muskeg. This phenomenon may be observed in other northern creeks.

DC 1234 MP 1269 **DJ 153 F 249 Historic Milepost 1271.** Scenic viewpoint to southwest is a large paved turnout with a Gold Rush Centennial sign about the short-lived Chisana Gold Rush and Tetlin Refuge interpretive signs on glacial rivers and whitefish (excerpts follow).

"The 1913 gold discovery on the north side of the Wrangell Mountains triggered the last major rush of the Gold Rush era. Some 2,000 stampeders reached the Chisana diggings, but most left disappointed: only a few creeks had gold and the area was remote and expensive to supply. The boom lasted little more than a year.

"As glaciers in the Wrangell Mountains melt, they wash their grindings into the headwaters of the Nabesna (Nah-BEZ-nah) and Chisana (Shu-SHAN-ah) rivers. These waters keep scooping up more sand and silt before converging near Northway to form the fifth longest river in Alaska, the Tanana (TAN-ah-nah). The murkiest river runs clear in winter when glacial melting stops. Fish adapt by laying eggs just before freeze-up so silt doesn't smother them before hatching.

"These murky rivers have long concealed the secrets of humpback whitefish from all but local Athabascan Indians, who learned their habits to survive.

"Related to salmon and trout, humpback whitefish can live 20 years or more. They first spawn around age 5 and many reproduce annually (unlike salmon that die after spawning). Whitefish fatten in large lakes in spring. By mid-summer they migrate into the river systems and swim farther up either the Nabesna or Chisana to spawn before freeze-up. Adults return downstream for the winter. Eggs hatch in spring. Spring floods sweep newly hatched whitefish downstream, far from this area. Where

Interpretive sign at viewpoint overlooking Midway Lake at physical Milepost 1289.5.
(©Kris Valencia, staff)

they grow up is unknown. Tetlin National Wildlife Refuge protects 2 of only a few known spawning sites for humpback whitefish in Alaska."

DC 1235 MP 1270 **DJ 152 F 248** *Begin 6 to 7 percent grades next 2 miles northbound.*

DC 1237.7 MP 1272.7 **DJ 149.3 F 245.3** Large paved turnout to southwest is a scenic viewpoint with Tetlin Refuge interpretive sign on local geology. To the northwest the Tanana River flows near the highway; beyond, the Kalukna River snakes its way through plain and marshland. Mentasta Mountains are visible to the southwest.

DC 1239 MP 1274 **DJ 148 F 244** Paved parking area to south (no view).

Distance marker southbound shows Northway 10 miles, Canadian Border 52 miles.

DC 1248 MP 1283 **DJ 139 F 235** Small, narrow, gravel turnout to north.

DC 1249 MP 1284 **DJ 138 F 234** Distance marker westbound shows Tok 30 miles, Fairbanks 235 miles.

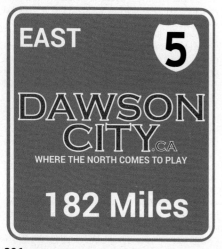

EAST 5
DAWSON CITY.CA
WHERE THE NORTH COMES TO PLAY
182 Miles

DC 1249.6 MP 1284.6 **DJ 137.4 F 233.4** Long double-ended paved turnout to north.

DC 1251 MP 1286 **DJ 136 F 232** View to southwest of 3.4-mile-long Midway Lake as Alaska Highway descends hill westbound.

DC 1254.1 MP 1289.1 **DJ 132.9 F 228.9** Large paved turnout to south overlooks Midway Lake.

DC 1254.5 MP 1289.5 **DJ 132.5 F 228.5** **Historic Milepost 1292.** Sharp turn on uphill road to north leads to paved parking area and scenic viewpoint; toilet, bear-proof litter bin. View of Midway Lake and Wrangell Mountains. Tetlin Refuge interpretive signs on caribou and winter (excerpts follow).

"Winter on Tetlin National Wildlife Refuge arrives in early October and departs by late April. On the shortest day of the year, the sun skims the horizon from about 10 A.M. to 2:45 P.M. Freezing temperatures of -40°F, down to a record of -72°, drive away memories of summer heat. This area often takes the prize as coldest in the state. Temperatures stay below freezing about 165 days of the year.

"After snow covers their summer calving and feeding area, caribou usually trek northward across this part of Tetlin National Wildlife Refuge. They're migrating up to 200 miles in search of lichens, their major winter food. Lichens are an ancient fusion of algae and fungi. They are loaded with carbohydrates. If caribou find areas with plentiful lichens, they can maintain their weight—rare for arctic animals in winter, the lean season. Wildfires in 2004 burned about a million acres in the caribou's winter range north of the Alaska Highway, removing large areas of lichens. If the caribou behave as in the past, they may avoid those burned areas for at least 60 years until lichens regain abundance.

"Wolf packs often shadow migrating caribou herds, targeting the slow and weak. Tetlin Refuge lands are also open for subsistence hunting by Upper Tanana Athabascans and other local residents."

DC 1255.2 MP 1290.2 **DJ 131.8 F 227.8** View of Midway Lake eastbound. Burn area from 1998 fire visible westbound.

DC 1256.5 MP 1291.5 **DJ 130.5 F 226.5** Distance marker eastbound shows Northway Junction 34 miles, Canadian Border 70 miles, Haines Junction 275 miles.

DC 1257.4 MP 1292.4 **DJ 129.6 F 225.6** Narrow entrance to large paved parking area to south; view obscured by trees.

DC 1258.7 MP 1293.7 **DJ 128.3 F 224.3** Paved parking to south.

DC 1259 MP 1294 **DJ 128 F 224** Distance marker westbound shows Tok 20 miles, Fairbanks 225 miles, Anchorage 355 miles.

DC 1266.6 MP 1301.6 **DJ 120.4 F 216.4** Distance marker eastbound shows Northway Junction 45 miles, Canadian Border 81 miles, Haines Junction 286 miles.

DC 1266.7 MP 1301.7 **DJ 120.3 F 216.3** **Historic Milepost 1306 Tetlin Junction**; Alaska Route 5 (Taylor Highway) leads 66 miles to Chicken, 160 miles to Eagle and 175 miles to Dawson City, YT. *NOTE: If you are traveling to Dawson City, keep in mind that both Canada's Little Gold Creek and the U.S. Poker Creek customs stations are closed at night; you CANNOT cross the border unless customs stations are open. Customs hours in summer 2013 were 8 A.M. to 8 P.M. Alaska time on the U.S. side, 9 A.M. to 9 P.M. Pacific time on the Canadian side. Customs stations are open daily in season, which is usually from about mid-May to mid-September (subject to change depending on road conditions). There are no phones at Poker Creek. Travelers are advised to check for current information at Alaska Public Lands Information Center in Tok or inquire at Port Alcan when crossing the border.*

Junction of the Alaska Highway with the Taylor Highway (Alaska Route 5) to Chicken and Eagle. The Taylor Highway junctions with Yukon Highway 9 (Top of the World Highway) to Dawson City. Turn to page 303 and read KLONDIKE LOOP section back to front for log of Highways 5, 9 and 2 to Dawson City and return to Alaska Highway See also "Side Trip to Eagle" feature on page 297.

In 1949, the Forty Mile Roadhouse located at this intersection served Alaska Highway travelers and motorists who were headed up the new Forty-Mile and Eagle Highway (now the Taylor Highway), which was still under construction with about 20 miles of road built. The roadhouse offered cabins, meals, a grocery store, and a garage with gas and oil. Ray and Mabel Scoby were listed as the proprietors of the roadhouse until 1975. The Native Village of Tetlin owned and operated the roadhouse until it closed in about 1985.

DC 1266.8 MP 1301.8 **DJ 120.2 F 216.2** Turnout to south.

Distance marker westbound shows Tok 12 miles, Fairbanks 217 miles, Anchorage 347 miles.

DC 1267.9 MP 1302.9 **DJ 119.1 F 215.1** Long paved turnout to south.

DC 1268 MP 1303 **DJ 119 F 215** Easy-to-miss turnoff to south for short access road to rest area at east end of Tanana River Bridge; paved parking, toilets, and excellent informative interpretive displays on construction of the old and new Tanana River bridges. Viewing platform is on former abutment of the old bridge; good view (and photo-op) of Tanana River and bridge. The old Tanana River bridge was a 3-span cantilevered subdivided Warren steel through truss bridge, built in 1943. It replaced a temporary wooden bridge built in 1942 by the U.S. Army. It was one of 133 bridges constructed on the Alcan Highway that were critical to the transport of troops and supplies to the North. It served highway traffic until it was replaced in 2010 by the concrete Girder-style bridge you see today. The new bridge allows for wider loads; has a shoulder for pedestrians and bicyclists; and has no overhead beams to limit vertical clearance.

DC 1268.6 MP 1303.6 **DJ 118.4 F 214.4** Crossing the **Tanana River Bridge**; access to large paved parking with toilets and boat ramp to north at west end of bridge. The original Tanana River Bridge was built in 1943 during construction of the Alaska Highway and was one of only 5 truss bridges built in Alaska during World War II still in use (see interpretive signs at rest area to south at east end of bridge; description at **Milepost DC 1268**). Tanana (TAN-uh-naw), an Indian name, was first reported by the Western Union Telegraph Expedition of 1886. According to William Henry Dall, chief scientist of the expedition, the name means "mountain river." The Tanana is formed by the confluence of the Chisana and Nabesna rivers and flows 440 miles northwest to the Yukon River.

Northbound, the highway parallels the Tanana River to Fairbanks. The Alaska Range is to the northwest.

DC 1269.6 MP 1304.6 **DJ 117.4 F 213.4** Evidence of 1990 burn from here to Tok. The Tok River fire in July 1990 burned more than 100,000 acres. The fire closed the Alaska Highway and Tok Cutoff. Tok

was evacuated as firefighters' efforts to stop the fire appeared to be in vain. A "miracle wind" diverted the fire from town at the last minute.

DC 1272.8 MP 1307.8 **DJ 114.2 F 210.2** Active sawmill to south. Some log cabin kits were manufactured here for Eagle, Alaska residents who lost their homes to the Yukon River during breakup in May 2009.

DC 1273.5 MP 1308.5 **DJ 113.5 F 209.5** Tok Weigh Station to southwest; phone.

Turnoff to northeast for U.S. Coast Guard Loran-C station and signal towers. This loran (Long Range Aids to Navigation) station is 1 of 7 in Alaska. It was constructed by the U.S. Coast Guard in 1976. A series of four 700-foot towers suspends a multi-element wire antenna used to transmit navigation signals. These signals may be used by air, land and sea navigators as an aid in determining their position. This station is located here as necessary for good geometry with 2 Gulf of Alaska loran transmitting stations.

DC 1274.2 MP 1309.2 **DJ 112.8 F 208.8** Turnoff to north just east of Tok River bridge for **Tok River State Recreation Site**; 27 campsites, some pull-through sites (vehicles to max. 60 feet).

Campsites are located along a good loop road beside the Tok River; campground host, tables, firepits, wheelchair-accessible toilets, litter barrels, nature trail, boat launch (can be very rough) and pay phone. Community firepits and covered picnic area. Check bulletin board for schedule of interpretive programs. Interpretive signs on WWII Lend-Lease Program, permafrost and other subjects. Camping fees posted. *CAUTION: Swift water.*

DC 1274.4 MP 1309.4 **DJ 112.6 F 208.6** Tok River bridge (clearance 15' 8"). The Tok River heads at Tok Glacier in the Alaska Range and flows 60 miles northeast into the Tanana River.

DC 1276 MP 1311 **DJ 111 F 207** Northbound travelers should have cell phone service starting here (we did).

DC 1277.2 MP 1312.2 **DJ 109.8 F 205.8** Purple Heart Trail Honoring Veterans' Sacrifice (southbound sign). The Alaska Highway from Delta Junction to the Canadian border was designated the "Purple Heart Trail" in May 2008, to honor veterans.

DC 1277.6 MP 1312.6 **DJ 109.4 F 205.4** Tok community limits. Sign southbound: "No studded tires May 1–Sept. 15." Speed limit is 35 mph (and closely watched).

DC 1277.7 MP 1312.7 **DJ 109.3 F 205.3** Tok Dog Mushers Assoc. track and buildings. Southeast end of paved bike trail.

DC 1278 MP 1313 **DJ 109 F 205** Entering Tok (northbound). Tok Junction airstrip (see Private Aircraft information in Tok). **Alaskan Stoves Campground** (adjacent 40-Mile Air); description follows.

Alaskan Stoves Campground. Milepost 1313 Alaska Highway in downtown Tok. Lowest prices in area. Real Alaskan-style camping. Small, family-run RV and tent park next to 40-Mile Air. Showers, laundry, hostel-style tent ($10 per bunk), community firepit, dump station. Biker and cyclist friendly. Jogging trail into Tok center. Phone (907) 883-5055. www.alaskanstovescamp ground.com. [ADVERTISEMENT]

Northbound travelers: *Slow for 35 mph/55 kmp speed zone (enforced) through Tok.*

Southbound travelers: Driving distance from Tok to Beaver Creek is 113 miles/182

km; Haines Junction 296 miles/476 km; Haines (departure point for Alaska state ferries) 446 miles/718 km; and Whitehorse 396 miles/637 km.

DC 1278.1 MP 1313.1 **DJ 108.9 F 204.9** **Gateway RV Park** (description follows) on right northbound.

Gateway RV Park. Relax in our cozy park. 43 level and wooded sites, 30–50 amp, water and electric, pull throughs, dump station, and a sparkling clean shower house. WiFi. Register at Fast Eddy's Restaurant next door. This is why you came to Alaska! [ADVERTISEMENT]

DC 1278.2 MP 1313.3 **DJ 108.8 F 204.8** **Young's Motel and Fast Eddy's Restaurant.** A touch of Alaskana in a modern setting. Affordable, clean and spacious. We

cater to the independent highway traveler. Open year-round with all the amenities: telephones, private baths, satellite TV, ample parking. Nonsmoking rooms. WiFi. Check in at Fast Eddy's full-service restaurant, open summer 6 A.M.

This beautiful log building houses the Tok Mainstreet Alaska Visitor Center.
(©Kris Valencia, staff)

to 11 P.M.; open winter 7 A.M. to 9 P.M. Reserve early! P.O. Box 482, Tok, AK 99780. (907) 883-4411; fax (907) 883-5023; email edyoung@aptalaska.net. See display ad previous page. [ADVERTISEMENT]

DC 1278.4 MP 1313.4 DJ 108.6 F 204.6 Tok RV Village on right northbound; Village Gas on left northbound.

Tok RV Village. See display ad this page.

DC 1279 MP 1314 DJ 108 F 204 Snowshoe Motel and Gifts (description follows),

Alaska Public Lands Information Center (see Visitor Information in Tok) and Blue Star Memorial Highway marker.

Snowshoe Motel and Fine Gifts invites you to come in and browse our selection of fine Alaskan arts and gifts. If you are staying the night with us, you will enjoy the spacious 2-room accommodations with a private bath, perfect for a family or couples traveling together. We offer satellite TV, phone, wireless Internet, coffee maker, microwave and refrigerator in every room for our guests' comfort and convenience. Phone

(907) 883-4511; website http://www.alaska-snowshoemotel.com; email snowshoe@apt alaska.net. See display page 209. [ADVERTISEMENT]

Distance marker eastbound shows Tetlin Junction 12 miles, Canadian Border 93 miles, Haines Junction 298 miles.

DC 1279.2 MP 1314.2 DJ 107.8 F 203.8 **Tok Junction.** Turn southwest on Tok Cutoff for Anchorage, continue straight ahead through intersection for continuation of Alaska Highway to Delta Junction and Richardson Highway to Fairbanks.

Junction of the Alaska Highway (Alaska Route 2) and the Tok Cutoff to the Glenn Highway (Alaska Route 1). It is 328 miles from Tok to Anchorage via Alaska Route 1. Turn to the GLENN HIGHWAY/TOK CUTOFF section on page 342 for log.

Tok post office (to your left northbound, adjacent **Burnt Paw Gift Shop & Cabins Outback**) and **Tok Mainstreet Visitor Center** (pictured on this page) and **Tok Memorial Park** (picnicking) on right northbound. **All Alaska Gifts** is located across from the Tok Visitor Center, adjacent the park.

All Alaska Gifts & Crafts. Located at Milepost 1314.2 Alaska Highway, next door to the Tok Visitor Center. Come in and enjoy free coffee with a sample of home-made fudge while looking at our life-size wildlife displays of moose, bears, sheep and wolves. We have hundreds of quality Alaska T-shirts, jewelry, Native crafts, gold nuggets and free WiFi. Chicken, Alaska RV/Cabin reservations here!www.allalaskagifts.com. See display ad page 210. [ADVERTISEMENT]

SOUTHBOUND ALASKA HIGHWAY TRAVELERS NOTE: In the Alaska portion of The MILEPOST® Alaska Highway log, DC mileages are based on actual driving distance from Dawson Creek, BC, and MP mileages are based on physical mileposts between Delta Junction and the Alaska-Canada border which reflect traditional distances from Dawson Creek, BC. There is a mileage difference of 35 miles between the traditional mileposts and actual driving distance.

Log continues on page 212.

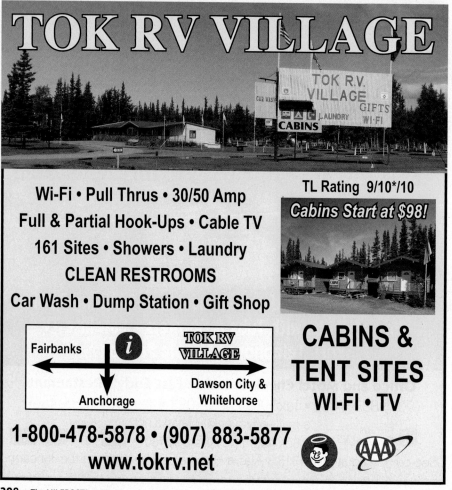
Tok

DC 1279.2 MP 1314.2 DJ 107.8 F 203.8 **Historical Milepost 1314** Alaska Highway, at the junction with the Tok Cutoff (Glenn Highway). Tok is 328 miles from Anchorage, 254 miles from Valdez, 108 miles from Delta Junction, 204 miles from Fairbanks, 113 miles from Beaver Creek, YT, 294 miles from Haines Junction, YT, and 445 miles from Haines, AK. **Population:** 1,435. **Emergency Services:** Phone 911 for emergency services. **Alaska State Troopers,** phone (907) 883-5111. **Fire Department,** phone (907) 883-5831. **Ambulance,** phone (907) 883-5111. EMT squad and air medivac available. **Community Clinic,** on the Tok Cutoff, phone (907) 883-5855.

Visitor Information: The **Alaska Public Lands Information Center** (APLIC), located in the Troopers Building just east of the junction at **Milepost 1314,** has public restrooms and information on the Alaska Marine Highway System state ferries, fishing and hunting regulations, and recreation

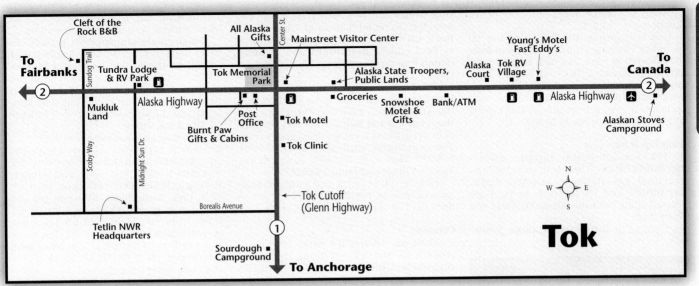

Tok

in state and national parks. Write P.O. Box 359, Tok, AK 99780; phone (907) 883-5666. The **Tok "Mainstreet Alaska" Visitors Center**, located at the junction of the Alaska Highway and Tok Cutoff, is open May through September. This beautiful log building houses the Tok Chamber of Commerce and the Tok Library. The visitor center offers trip planning help and complete travel information on the Alaska Highway, travel in and around Alaska, statewide brochures to most destinations and attractions, displays from communities around the state, as well as local information. The center also offers public telephones, restrooms, current road conditions and a message board. Phone (907) 883-5775; www.tokalaskainfo.com.

The Alaska Dept. of Fish and Game office is located on Center Street, across from Tok Mainstreet Visitor Center at **Milepost 1314.2**. Contact ADF&G, Box 355, Tok, AK 99780; phone (907) 883-2971; fax (907) 883-2970. Fishing licenses are available at local dealers.

Elevation: 1,635 feet. **Climate**: Mean monthly temperature in January is -19° F; average low is -32°F. Mean monthly temperature in July is 59°F; average high is 72°F. Record low was -71°F (January 1965); record high, 99°F. **Radio**: FM stations are 90.5, 91.1 (KUAC-FM, University of Alaska

Fairbanks) and 101.5. **Television**: Satellite channel 13. **Newspaper**: *Mukluk News* (twice monthly).

Private Aircraft: Tok Junction, 1 E; elev. 1,630 feet; length 2,510 feet; asphalt; fuel 100LL; unattended. Tok airstrip, on Tok Cutoff, 2 S; elev. 1,670 feet; length 3,000 feet; gravel; no fuel, unattended.

Description

Tok had its beginnings as a construction camp on the Alcan Highway in 1942. Highway engineer C.G. Polk was sent to Fairbanks in May of 1942 to take charge of Alaska construction and start work on the road between Tok Junction and Big Delta. Work was also under way on the Gulkana–Slana–Tok Junction road (now the Tok Cutoff on the Glenn Highway to Anchorage). But on June 7, 1942, a Japanese task force invaded Attu and Kiska islands in the Aleutians, and the Alcan took priority over the Slana cutoff.

A frequently-asked question is how Tok (pronounced to rhyme with poke) got its name. A couple of theories have been put forward over the years. One believed the name Tok was derived from Tokyo Camp, the name of an Alaska Highway road construction camp that was patriotically short-

ened to Tok in the 1940s. Another story was that Tok was named after a husky pup of that name, mascot to a U.S. Army's Corp battalion who were breaking trail north from Slana in 1942. Stop in at the Visitor Center for a handout on the latest historical research into Tok's name.

Because Tok is the major overland point of entry to Alaska, it is primarily a trade and service center for all types of transportation, especially for summer travelers coming up the Alaska Highway. A stopover here is a good opportunity to meet other travelers and swap experiences. Tok is the only town in Alaska that the highway traveler must pass through twice—once when arriving in the state and again on leaving the state. The governor proclaimed Tok "Mainstreet Alaska" in 1991. Townspeople are proud of this designation and work hard to make visitors happy.

Tok's central business district is at the junction of the Alaska Highway and Tok Cutoff. From the junction, homes and businesses spread out along both highways on flat terrain dotted with densely timbered stands of black spruce.

Tok has 8 churches, a public library, a K–12 school and University of Alaska extension center. Local clubs include the Lions,

Veterans of Foreign Wars and Chamber of Commerce.

Tok is known as the "Sled Dog Capital of Alaska" because so many of its residents are involved in some way with dogs and dog mushing, Alaska's official state sport. Judging by the number of Alaska Highway travelers cleaning their cars and RVs in Tok each summer, it may also qualify as the Vehicle Washing Capital of Alaska as well.

Lodging & Services

Tok has all visitor services including hotels, motels, bed and breakfast, restaurants, gas stations, auto/RV repair, car washes and laundromat. Services are located along both the Alaska Highway and Tok Cutoff.

Lodging at **Burnt Paw Cabins, Snow-**shoe Motel and **Tok Motel**, with bed and breakfast accommodations at **Cleft of the Rock B&B** (see ads this section). Dining at **Fast Eddy's Restaurant** and at **Sourdough Campground Cafe** (see ads this section).

The post office is located on the Alaska Highway just northwest of its junction with the Tok Cutoff, adjacent Burnt Paw gift shop. Fishing and hunting licenses and supplies available at local sporting goods store. Tok Liquor and Mini Mart at Tok Motel. Vehicle wash at Sourdough Campground, Tok RV Village and Tundra Lodge.

Parking, playground and picnic shelters are available at Tok Memorial Park, across from the Tok Mainstreet Visitor Center.

Camping

There are several RV parks and campgrounds in Tok located along the Alaska Highway and Tok Cutoff. See advertisements this section for **Alaskan Stoves Campground**, **Tok RV Village** and **Tundra Lodge RV Park** on the Alaska Highway; and **Sourdough Campground**, located on the Tok Cutoff.

Some RVers towing cars are using Tok as a jump-off point to visit Dawson City, YT, and other destinations, by leaving their big rigs at local campgrounds. Inquire locally about parking your RV at campgrounds.

Nearby state campgrounds include: Tok River State Recreation Site, 5 miles south of Tok on the Alaska Highway at **Milepost 1309.2**; Moon Lake State Recreation Site, 17.7 miles north of Tok at **Milepost 1331.9** Alaska Highway; and Eagle Trail State Recreation Site, 16 miles west of Tok at **Milepost GJ 109.3** Tok Cutoff.

Sourdough Campground and Cafe. Pre-season sites open mid-April with electric, shower, restroom and laundry. Free unlimited WiFi hot spot and showers included. Wide, level pull-thrus, great tent sites. Cafe, laundromat, RV wash, gift shop and 6-mile paved bike trail. Located 1.75 miles from Tok Mainstreet on Tok Cutoff (Glenn Highway). Home of the "Sourdough Pancake Toss." Compete to win a free breakfast. Phone (907) 883-5543. See display ad this page. [ADVERTISEMENT]

Tundra Lodge & RV Park. Spacious, naturally forested camping sites. Full and partial hookups; 20-, 30-, 50-amp power. Tent sites. Pull-throughs. Clean restrooms and showers included in price. Picnic tables, fire rings and wood. Dump station. Laundromat. Vehicle wash. Courtesy phone. Ice. Cocktail lounge and meeting room. Email/

Tok

Transportation

Air: Charter air service available; inquire at Tok state airstrip (**Milepost 1313**). Charter flightseeing and fly-in fishing trips available. Scheduled passenger and freight service between Tok, Delta Junction and Fairbanks.

Bus: See Bus Lines in the TRAVEL PLANNING section.

Highway: Tok is located at the junction of the Alaska Highway and Tok Cutoff (see GLENN HIGHWAY/TOK CUTOFF section). Tok has become a popular spot with RVers towing cars to park their big rigs here while they drive to Dawson City, YT, via the Taylor Highway, Boundary Spur Road and Top of the World Highway; see KLONDIKE LOOP section for details on these routes.

Attractions

The Alaska Public Lands Information Center (APLIC), located next door to the Tok Mainstreet Visitors Center, offers trip planning information and displays of beadwork and animal and fish mounts. The standing grizzly bear mount is an especially popular attraction at the Center. APLIC staff can help you with Alaska Marine Highway ferry reservations and provide details on recreation opportunities on state and federal lands in Alaska. Free State of Alaska map. Phone toll-free 1-888-256-6784.

Tok Mainstreet Visitors Center, located at the junction of the Alaska Highway and Tok Cutoff, houses the Tok Mainstreet Visitors Center and the Tok Community Public Library. Huge natural white spruce logs, brought in locally, support the open-beamed, cathedral ceiling of this 7,000-square-foot building. Seating and restrooms available to the public. Large picture windows frame the Alaska Range. Excellent displays of Alaska rocks, gems and fossils; gold rush history; Alaska wildlife and waterfowl; and Alaska Highway memorabilia. Picnic tables are located out in front. All Alaska Gifts is located next door to the Tok Visitor Center.

Tok Memorial Park, at the Alaska Highway and Tok Cutoff intersection (across from Tok Mainstreet Visitors Center), has day parking, a picnic shelter and playground.

The Upper Tanana Valley Migratory Bird Festival is held at Tok Memorial Park (and across the street at Tok Main Street Visitors Center) in May. The event includes bird banding demonstration and live bird presentations. Phone the Tetlin Refuge office for more information, (907) 883-5312.

Biking: A wide paved bike trail parallels the Alaska Highway and extends from Tok southeast to the Dog Mushers Assoc. track, and northwest to Tanacross Junction. Approximate length is 13 miles. There is also a 2.4-mile bike trail along the Tok-Cutoff west from Tok.

Flightseeing. 40-Mile Air offers passenger space on their twice weekly "milk run" to Chisana for $105. A good way to see the region from the air.

Local events. Check with the Tok Main Street Visitors Center about summer activities. For example, Tok RV Village offers live evening entertainment during the summer, and Sourdough Campground is the "home of the sourdough pancake toss."

Alaskan Crafts: Tok is a trade center for the Athabascan Native villages of Tanacross, Northway, Tetlin, Mentasta, Dot Lake and

Motorcyclists parked at All Alaska Gifts in Tok. (©Kris Valencia, staff)

Eagle. Several of the Native women make birch baskets, beaded moccasins, boots and beaded necklaces. The State of Alaska has a crafts identification program which authenticates Alaskan Native and Alaskan Craftsmen products. Examples of both may be seen at Burnt Paw, Snowshoe Fine Gifts and All Alaska Gifts in Tok.

Birch baskets were once used in the Native camps and villages. Traditionally, they had folded corners, held water, and were even used for cooking by dropping heated stones into the liquid in the baskets. The baskets are made by peeling the bark from the birch trees, usually in the early summer months. The bark is easiest to work with when moist and pliable. It is cut into shape and sewn together with strips of spruce root dug out of the ground and split. If the root is too dry it is soaked until it is manageable. Holes are put in the birch bark with a punch or screwdriver, and the spruce root is laced in and out. Native women dye the spruce root with food coloring, watercolors or berry juice. A few Natives also make model birch canoes and birch baby carriers.

Many of the moccasins and mukluks for sale in Tok are made with traditionally tanned moose hides. After scraping the hide clean, it is soaked in a soap solution. Then the moisture is taken out by constant scraping with a dull knife or scraper. The hide is then scraped again and rubbed together to soften it. Next it is often smoke-cured in rotted spruce wood smoke. The tanning process takes from a few days to a week.

Beading can be a slow and tedious process. Most women say if they work steadily all day they can put the beading on one moccasin, but usually they do their beadwork over a period of several days, alternating it with other activities.

Mukluk Land, at **Milepost 1317** Alaska Highway, has an indoor-outdoor museum, miniature golf, activities for kids, videos, educational displays. Open 2–8 P.M. daily, June through August. Phone (907) 883-2571; www.muklukland.net.

Sled Dog Trails and Races: Tok boasts a well-known and long-established dog mushing trail, which draws many world-class and

recreational mushers. The 20.5-mile/33-km trail begins at the rustic log Tok Dog Mushers Assoc. building at **Milepost 1312.8** on the Alaska Highway. The trail is a favorite with spectators because it affords many miles of viewing from along the Alaska Highway. Racing begins in late November and extends through the end of March.

The biggest race of the season in Tok is the Race of Champions, held in late March, which also has the largest entry of any sprint race in Alaska. Begun in 1954 as a bet between 2 roadhouse proprietors, today the Race of Champions includes over 100 teams in 3 classes competing for prize money and trophies. It is considered to be the third leg of sled dog racing's "triple crown," following the Fur Rendezvous in Anchorage and the Fairbanks North American Championship. Visitors are also welcome to attend the Tok Native Assoc.'s potlatch, held the same weekend as the race.

Also stop in at Burnt Paw gift shop and meet Bill Arpino. Bill was a finisher in the 1973 Iditarod. For many years the

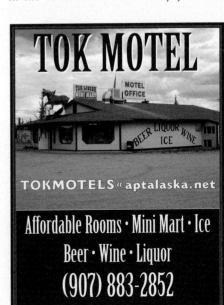

Tok is located at the junction of the Alaska Highway with the Tok Cutoff/Glenn Highway.
(©Sharon Nault)

Arpinos put on dog mushing demonstrations at their gift shop. Although the dog sled demos have ceased, Burnt Paw has a free outdoor dog team equipment display and often they have sled dog puppies in the kennel adjacent the display.

AREA FISHING: There are several walk-in fishing lakes along the Alaska Highway between Tok and Delta Junction, all stocked with rainbow trout. These include: **Robertson #2 Lake** at **Milepost 1348.1; Jan Lake** at **Milepost 1353.6; Lisa Lake** at **Milepost 1381; Craig Lake** at **Milepost 1383.8;** and **Donna Lake** and **Little Donna Lake** at **Milepost 1391.8.** Consult ADF&G offices in Tok (907/883-2971) and Delta Junction (907/895-4632) for details on fishing in these areas.

Alaska Highway Log
(continued from page 208)

ALASKA ROUTE 2
Distance from Dawson Creek (DC) is followed by distance from physical milepost (MP), distance from Delta Junction (DJ) and distance from Fairbanks (F).

NOTE: In the Alaska portion of The MILEPOST® Alaska Highway log, DC mileages from Dawson Creek are based on actual driving distance, and MP mileages are based on physical mileposts between Port Alcan and Delta Junction, AK, which reflect historic distances from Dawson Creek, BC. There is a mileage difference of 35 miles between the traditional mileposts and actual driving distance. Read the information on Mileposts and Kilometreposts in the introduction to the Alaska Highway for more on this subject.

DC 1279.2 MP 1314.2 DJ 107.8 F 203.8
Tok Junction. Tok Mainstreet Visitors Center and **All Alaska Gifts & Crafts.** *See description of Tok beginning on page 208.*

Junction of the Alaska Highway (Alaska Route 2) and the Tok Cutoff to the Glenn Highway (Alaska Route 1). It is 328 miles from Tok to Anchorage via Alaska Route 1. See GLENN HIGHWAY/TOK CUTOFF section on page 342 for log.

Improved bike trail next next 11.5 miles (to Tanacross Junction at **Milepost 1325.7**) westbound. ATV trails both sides of road to **Milepost 1323.**
DC 1279.3 MP 1314.3 DJ 107.7 F 203.7
Tok Post Office and **Burnt Paw Gifts and Cabins Outback** to southwest, Tok Memorial Park to northeast.
Burnt Paw Gift Shop & Cabins Outback. See display ad on this page.
Distance marker westbound shows Tanacross 12 miles, Delta Junction 109 miles, Fairbanks 205 miles. Sign: No studded tires May 1-Sept. 15.
DC 1279.6 MP 1314.6 DJ 107.4 F 203.4
Northbound sign: $1,000 fine for littering.
DC 1279.9 MP 1314.9 DJ 107.1 F 203.1
Tesoro gas station; diesel.

Slow for 35mph speed zone southbound through Tok.
DC 1280 MP 1315 DJ 107 F 203 Turnoff for **Tundra Lodge and RV Park;** hookups, dump station, vehicle wash; phone (907) 883-7875.

Tundra Lodge and RV Park. See display ad on page 210.
DC 1280.7 MP 1315.7 DJ 106.3 F 202.3
Midnight Sun Road. Sign: Tetlin Refuge Vistior Information 1.1 miles west. Tok city limits (northbound sign).
DC 1281.6 MP 1316.6 DJ 105.4 F 201.4
Access to **Cleft of the Rock Bed & Breakfast** to north; phone (907) 883-4219.
Cleft of the Rock Bed & Breakfast. See display ad on this page.
DC 1282 MP 1317 DJ 105 F 201
Mukluk Land. Don't miss Tok's highlight, Mukluk Land, the home of Santa's Rocket Ship. Memorable, enjoyable and affordable for all ages. Indoor-outdoor museum, entertainment center, unique collections, dollhouse, videos, mini-golf, and much more. Open 2–8 P.M. daily, June–August. Admission: $5 adults, $4.50 seniors, $2 kids 3-19. Mile 1317 Alaska Highway. Phone (907) 883-2571; www.muklukland.net. [ADVERTISEMENT]
DC 1289.6 MP 1324.6 DJ 97.4 F 193.4

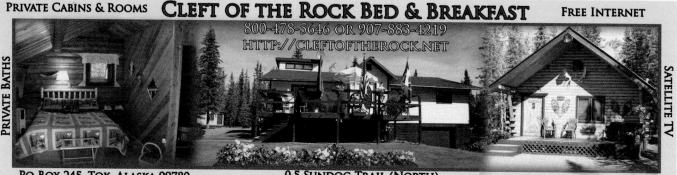

Gravel access road (Old Tanacross Road) leads northeast to Tanacross airstrip (0.5 mile), Alaska Dept. of Natural Resources (DNR) Tanacross Air Tanker Base 1 mile (description follows) and Tanacross Village and school 1.7 miles; or use main access at **Milepost 1325.7.** Distance marker southbound on the highway shows Tok 10 miles, Canada Border 103 miles.

The airfield at Tanacross was built in the 1930s, with assistance from local Natives, and was used by the U.S. Army in WWII as part of the Russia–America Lend Lease Program. (The Lend Lease Program sent war planes to Russia, a U.S. ally, to use in fighting Nazi Germany.) After WWII, the airfield was used for specialized arctic operations and maneuvers. The Tanacross Airfield was the sixth largest city in Alaska in 1962, housing more than 8,000 troops for "Operation Great Bear." In 1970, the Bureau of Land Management acquired the property because of the strategic location of its paved runway for refueling air tankers fighting forest fires. Alaska DNR now controls the air tanker operations at the airfield.

Private Aircraft: Tanacross airstrip; elev. 1,549 feet; 2 runways, length 5,000 feet and 5,100 feet; asphalt; unattended. *CAUTION: Forest fire aviation support may be in progress.*

DC 1289.8 MP 1324.8 **DJ 97.2 F 193.2** Distance marker westbound shows Dot Lake 37 miles, Delta Junction 99 miles, Fairbanks 195 miles.

DC 1290.6 MP 1325.6 **DJ 96.4 F 192.4 Historic Milepost 1328.** Burn area next 4 miles northbound

DC 1290.7 MP 1325.7 **DJ 96.3 F 192.3 Junction** with New Tanacross Road, the main access road north to Tanacross. Drive 1.2 miles on gravel road to "Y" intersection; turn right for airstrip (see **Milepost 1324.6**), turn left for loop road through the village of **TANACROSS** (pop. 144), a traditional Athabascan community; no visitor services.

End paved bike trail from Tok.

DC 1292.2 MP 1327.2 **DJ 94.8 F 190.8** Small informal turnout by small lake to southwest. Watch for swans in roadside ponds.

DC 1292.4 MP 1327.4 **DJ 94.6 F 190.6** Informal turnout to gravel parking area by pond (may be flooded in wet weather).

DC 1293 MP 1328 **DJ 94 F 190** *CAUTION: Slow for frost heaves westbound.*

DC 1295.6 MP 1330.6 **DJ 91.4 F 187.4** Paved parking to north.

DC 1296.9 MP 1331.9 **DJ 90.1 F 186.1 Moon Lake State Recreation Site**, 0.2 mile northeast via paved access road; 17 campsites, picnic area, toilets, tables, bear-proof litter bins, water, firepits, boat launch, sandy beach. Swimming area marked by buoys. Floatplanes use this lake. Motorized and non-motorized boating are popular activities on Moon Lake. This is also a good place to see loons. Camping fee $15/night.

DC 1297.2 MP 1332.2 **DJ 89.8 F 185.8** Turnout to south in large gravel pit.

DC 1298.6 MP 1333.6 **DJ 88.4 F 184.4 Historic Milepost 1339.** Yerrick Creek bridge. Turnout to south at west end of bridge.

DC 1302.6 MP 1337.6 **DJ 84.4 F 180.4** Distance marker southbound shows Tok 23 miles, Canadian border 116 miles.

DC 1303.2 MP 1338.2 **DJ 83.8 F 179.8** Highway crosses Cathedral Rapids #1 (signed).

DC 1303.5 MP 1338.5 **DJ 83.5 F 179.5** Turnoff to southwest for **Cathedral Creeks**

B&B and Campground (description follows).

Cathedral Creeks B&B and Campground. Historic site nestled between creeks in quiet mountain setting. Clean, cozy rooms with 2 twin beds; private cabin with queen bed and kitchenette. Delicious home-cooked breakfast. Scenic campground with firepit, free firewood, electricity. No pull-throughs. Free WiFi. Work crews welcome. Great rates. Wir sprechen deutsch. Phone (907) 883-4455, email cmbentele@yahoo.com. Website: www.cathedralcreeks.net. [ADVERTISEMENT]

DC 1303.7 MP 1338.7 **DJ 83.3 F 179.3** Highway crosses Cathedral Rapids #2 (signed).

DC 1304 MP 1339 **DJ 83 F 179** Highway crosses Cathedral Rapids #3 (signed).

DC 1307.2 MP 1342.2 **DJ 79.8 F 175.8** Sheep Creek culvert.

DC 1309.2 MP 1344.2 **DJ 77.8 F 173.8** Distance marker westbound shows Delta Junction 80 miles, Fairbanks 175 miles.

DC 1309.5 MP 1344.5 **DJ 77.5 F 173.5** Paved parking area to northeast with picnic tables, toilets, litter bin and viewpoint. Good photo stop with view of the Alaska Range. Wheel-chair-accessible path leads 300 feet to Tanana River viewpoint; interpretive panel on "Early Hunters of the Tanana." Interpretive panel on Alaska Highway and Slim Williams reads: "When Alaska Road Commissioner Donald MacDonald heard Clyde "Slim" Williams was mushing from Alaska to the Chicago World's Fair, he was delighted. It was perfect for promoting his idea for a highway linking Alaska with the Lower 48. He wired Slim at one of his stops asking him to place a banner on his sled and become a spokesman for the proposed road. Slim arrived at the Chicago World's Fair in September 1933, after 10 months en route. Slim Williams and his dogs gained immense popularity at the fair by giving rides to fairgoers. First Lady Eleanor Roosevelt was so impressed with her ride, she invited Slim to Washington DC to meet President Franklin D. Roosevelt."

Distance marker southbound shows Tok Junction 30 miles, Tetlin Junction 42 miles, Canada border 123 miles.

DC 1312 MP 1347 **DJ 75 F 171 Forest Lake** trailhead (not signed); 7.8-mile primitive ATV trail (not an easy access to this remote lake according to ADF&G). Stocked with rainbow trout in even years.

DC 1312.5 MP 1347.5 **DJ 74.5 F 170.5** Robertson River bridge. The river was named by Lt. Henry T. Allen for a member of his 1885 expedition. The Robertson River heads at the terminus of Robertson Glacier in the Alaska Range and flows 33 miles northeast to the Tanana River.

Good view of the Alaska Range to west on a clear day.

Entering Game Management Unit 20D westbound, Unit 12 eastbound.

DC 1313.1 MP 1348.1 **DJ 73.9 F 169.9** Side road west to public fishing access; parking. Hike in 0.3 mile for **Robertson No. 2 Lake**; rainbow trout fishing (stocked by ADF&G).

DC 1315.5 MP 1350.5 **DJ 71.5 F 167.5** Double-ended paved turnout to southwest.

DC 1317.5 MP 1352.5 **DJ 69.5 F 165.5** Distance marker westbound shows Delta Junction 70 miles, Fairbanks 165 miles.

Watch for moose.

DC 1318.6 MP 1353.6 **DJ 68.4 F 164.4** Jan Lake Road to south; public fishing access. Drive in 0.5 mile/0.8 km to parking area; no overnight camping, carry out garbage. **Jan Lake** is stocked by ADF&G with rainbow trout and silver (coho) salmon. Dot Lake Native Corp. land, limited public access.

DC 1319.2 MP 1354.2 **DJ 67.8 F 163.8** Distance marker eastbound shows Tanacross 32 miles, Tok Junction 40 miles.

DC 1321 MP 1356 **DJ 66 F 162** Large stands of aspen are seen on both sides of the highway here. Quaking aspen grow on well-drained benches, sunny south slopes and creek bottoms throughout interior Alaska. They can spread by sending up suckers from their root systems, thereby creating "clonal stands" of genetically identical trees that leaf at the same time in the spring and turn yellow at the same time in the fall.

DC 1322.3 MP 1357.3 **DJ 64.7 F 160.7** Bear Creek bridge. Paved shoulder parking to southside of highway at west end of bridge.

DC 1323.6 MP 1358.6 **DJ 63.4 F 159.4** Chief Creek bridge. Paved parking area to south at west end of bridge.

CAUTION: Watch for moose.

NOTE: Slow for 55 mph speed zone northbound through Dot Lake. Posted speed limit 65 mph southbound.

DC 1326 MP 1361 **DJ 61 F 157** Dot Lake School.

DC 1326.3 MP 1361.3 **DJ 60.7 F 156.7 DOT LAKE** (pop. 13), no services except post office here. Homesteaded in the 1940s, Dot Lake was originally a work camp called Sears City during construction of the Alaska Highway in 1942–1943. Former Dot Lake Lodge (now a private home) houses the Dot Lake Post Office; hours are 9 A.M. to 2 P.M., Monday–Saturday.

DC 1326.5 MP 1361.5 **DJ 60.5 F 156.5** Very large turnout on the shore of Dot Lake; a nice stopping spot, lots of birds on the lake in spring and summer. **Historic Milepost 1368** here commemorates the 50th anniversary of the Northwest Highway System (1942-1992). Nearby is Dot Lake Lakeside Community Chapel, built in 1949, a wonderful old-time Alaskan church.

Dot Lake was once an Athabascan hunting camp and a spot on an Indian freight trail to the Yukon River. **DOT LAKE VILLAGE** (pop. 62), separate from the highway community, is a traditional Upper Tanana Athabascan village. It is also headquarters for the Dot Lake Native Corp.

DC 1327 MP 1362 **DJ 60 F 156** *Posted speed limit 65 mph northbound.*

NOTE: Slow for 55 mph speed zone southbound through Dot Lake.

DC 1328.5 MP 1363.5 **DJ 58.5 F 154.5** Purple Heart Trail Honoring Veterans' Sacrifice signs. The Alaska Highway from Delta Junction to the Canadian border was designated the "Purple Heart Trail" in May 2008, to honor veterans.

DC 1329.3 MP 1364.3 **DJ 57.7 F 153.7** Distance marker southbound shows Tok Junction 50 miles, Tetlin Junction 62 miles.

DC 1335.2 MP 1370.2 **DJ 51.8 F 147.8** Double-ended paved turnout to north.

DC 1335.8 MP 1370.8 **DJ 51.2 F 147.2** Entering **Tanana Valley State Forest** westbound; managed by the Dept. of Natural Resources. Established as the first unit of Alaska's state forest system in 1983, Tanana Valley State Forest encompasses 1.81 million acres and lies almost entirely within the Tanana River Basin. The forest extends 265 miles from near the Canadian border to Manley Hot Springs. Almost 90 percent of

the state forest is forested, with the remainder mostly shrubland. Principal tree species are paper birch, quaking aspen, balsam poplar, black spruce, white spruce and tamarack.

DC 1336.4 MP 1371.4 **DJ 50.6 F 146.6** Berry Creek bridge. Parking area to south at west end of bridge.

DC 1336.9 MP 1371.9 **DJ 50.1 F 146.1** Distance marker westbound shows Delta Junction 50 miles, Fairbanks 145 miles.

DC 1339.3 MP 1374.3 **DJ 47.7 F 143.5** Sears Creek. Parking area to south at west end of crossing.

DC 1343 MP 1378 **DJ 44 F 140** Dry Creek culvert.

DC 1344 MP 1379 **DJ 43 F 139** Double-ended paved parking area with mountain views to south.

DC 1345.5 MP 1380.5 **DJ 41.5 F 137.5** Johnson River bridge (clearance 15' 6"). A tributary of the Tanana River, the Johnson River was named by Lt. Henry T. Allen in 1887 for Peder Johnson, a Swedish miner and member of his party.

DC 1346 MP 1381 **DJ 41 F 137** Paved double-ended parking area to south at trailhead for 0.7-mile hiking trail (muddy, ADF&G recommends not using an ATV) to **Lisa Lake**; stocked with rainbow trout.

DC 1348.8 MP 1383.8 **DJ 38.2 F 134.2** **Craig Lake** public fishing access (0.5-mile trail); stocked with rainbow trout by ADF&G.

DC 1350 MP 1385 **DJ 37 F 133** Double-ended paved parking area to north. Paved access road to Tanana River boat launch (4-wheel-drive required).

Distance marker westbound shows Delta Junction 37 miles, Fairbanks 135 miles.

Distance marker eastbound shows Tok 71 miles, Canada border 163 miles.

DC 1353.4 MP 1388.4 **DJ 33.6 F 129.6** Little Gerstle River bridge. Double-ended paved parking area at south end of bridge.

DC 1356.8 MP 1391.8 **DJ 30.2 F 126.2** Large double-ended paved turnout to south

at trailhead for public fishing access to **Donna Lake** (3.5 miles) and **Little Donna Lake** (4.5 miles); stocked with rainbow.

DC 1357.7 MP 1392.7 **DJ 29.3 F 125.3** Gerstle River Black Veterans Memorial Bridge; parking area and access to river both sides of bridge (see also **Milepost 1393**).

Built in 1944, the Gerstle River Bridge is 1 of 4 "steel through truss-style" bridge constructions on the Alaska Highway. It was renamed Black Veterans Memorial Bridge in 1993, to commemorate the 3,695 black soldiers of the 93rd, 94th, 95th, 97th and 388th U.S. Army Corps of Engineers for their contribution in constructing the Alcan Highway.

The Gerstle River was named for Lewis Gerstle, president of the Alaska Commercial Co., by Lt. Henry T. Allen, whose 1885 expedition explored the Copper, Tanana and Koyukuk river regions for the U.S. Army.

DC 1358 MP 1393 **DJ 29 F 125** Turnoff to south for rest area just west of Gerstle River bridge; covered picnic table, outhouses, garbage bin, short loop road to camping spots in trees. From the outhouses, drive towards the river where there is access to a large parking area. Also access via rough gravel road to a gravel bar with a good view of the bridge. CAUTION: Possible high water on gravel bars during spring melt and heavy rains in summer.

DC 1358.1 MP 1393.1 **DJ 28.9 F 124.9** Distance marker westbound shows Delta Junction 30 miles, Fairbanks 128 miles.

DC 1359 MP 1394 **DJ 28 F 124** Distance marker eastbound shows Tanacross 68 miles, Tok 80 miles.

DC 1366 MP 1401 **DJ 21 F 117** Double-ended paved parking area to northeast.

DC 1368.4 MP 1403.4 **DJ 18.6 F 114.6** Sawmill Creek Road to Delta barley fields. Planting is in May; harvesting in August or September. Turnout at Mile 0.6 Sawmill Creek Road (with a nice view of the Alaska Range on clear days); large RVs may have to search for turnaround space on this side

road. Look for buffalo and yaks at a wild game farm along this sideroad. One of our MILEPOST Facebook friends noted that tours of the farm are available in summer, and that "the mountain at the very end of Sawmill Creek Road, which the road seems to disappear into, is Panorama Peak."

View to west on a clear day of Granite Mountains, which are part of the Alaska Range.

DC 1368.7 MP 1403.7 **DJ 18.3 F 114.3** Sawmill Creek.

DC 1369.1 MP 1404.1 **DJ 17.9 F 113.9** Silver Fox Roadhouse; gas and diesel.

DC 1372 MP 1407 **DJ 15 F 111** Highway passes through area of permafrost, evidenced by the stunted black spruce, also called bog spruce or swamp spruce. As elsewhere in Interior Alaska, well-drained soil and south-facing slopes support tall, dense stands of white spruce, aspen and birch, while cold wet flats, muskeg and north-facing slopes are dominated by the stunted and crooked black spruce.

On the south side of the Alaska Highway approaching Delta Junction is the Bison Sanctuary, which provides the bison herd with autumn and winter grazing (not visible from highway). It was developed to reduce crop depredation by bison.

DC 1375 MP 1410 **DJ 12 F 108** Sign: Dial 511 for Travel Information.

DC 1376.5 MP 1411.5 **DJ 10.5 F 106.5** Paved double-ended turnout to south.

DC 1378 MP 1413 **DJ 9 F 105** Distance marker westbound shows Delta Junction 10 miles, Fairbanks 105 miles.

DC 1378.2 MP 1413.2 **DJ 8.8 F 104.8** Grain storage facility to south.

©Sharon Nault

DC 1378.4 MP 1413.4 **DJ 8.6 F 104.6** **Delta Meat & Sausage Co.** was a dream come true for Doug McCollum and his family, young and ambitious pioneers from Montana who one day longed to raise cattle again in Alaska. Today they are a successful family-run farm and own their USDA packing plant. Free sausage samples. Tourists welcome! 9 miles east of Delta Junction. Phone (907) 895-4006. See display ad this page.
[ADVERTISEMENT]

DC 1379.4 MP 1414.4 **DJ 7.6 F 103.6** Distance marker southbound shows Dot Lake 53 miles, Tok Junction 101 miles, Canada border 193 miles.

DC 1379.8 MP 1414.8 **DJ 7.2 F 103.2** Turnoff for Clearwater Road, which leads north past farmlands to **Clearwater State Recreation Site** state campground (directions follow) and also provides a "loop" drive back to the Alaska Highway northwest of Delta Junction (directions below). To reach the state campground, follow Clearwater Road 5.3 miles north to junction with Remington Road; turn right and drive 2.8 miles east for Clearwater state campground, situated on the bank of aptly-named Clear-

water Creek. There are 15 campsites, toilets, tables, firepits, water and boat ramp. Camping fee $8/night.

To drive the "loop" (which bypasses Delta Junction), follow Clearwater Road north and turn left on Remington Road; turn right on Souhrada; then left on Jack Warren Road, which junctions with the Richardson Highway at **Milepost V 268.3**.

The **Delta–Clearwater River** (local reference; stream is actually **Clearwater Creek**, which flows northwest to the Tanana River) is a premier arctic grayling (catch-and-release) stream. A boat is needed for best fishing; beautiful, clear, spring-fed stream; grayling and whitefish; silver salmon spawn. There is a fall (September) silver salmon run. **Goodpaster River**, accessible by boat via Delta–Clearwater and Tanana rivers; excellent grayling fishing.

DC 1380.2 MP 1415.2 DJ 6.8 F 102.8 Distance marker westbound shows Delta Junction 7 miles, Fairbanks 102 miles.

DC 1385.2 MP 1420.2 DJ 1.8 F 97.8 Welcome to Delta Junction (northbound sign).

DC 1385.7 MP 1420.7 DJ 1.3 F 97.3 Alaska State Troopers, Jarvis Office Center.

DC 1385.9 MP 1420.9 DJ 1.1 F 97.1 Private RV Park to north.

DC 1386 MP 1421 DJ 1 F 97 Purple Heart Trail Honoring Veterans' Sacrifice (southbound sign). The Alaska Highway from Delta Junction to the Canadian border was designated the "Purple Heart Trail" in May 2008, to honor veterans.

DC 1386.3 MP 1421.3 DJ 0.7 F 96.7 *NOTE: Slow for 35 mph speed zone westbound through Delta Junction.*

DC 1386.6 MP 1421.6 DJ 0.4 F 96.4 Diamond Willow Inn to south.

DC 1386.7 MP 1421.7 DJ 0.3 F 96.3 Distance marker eastbound shows Dot Lake 61 miles, Tok 108 miles, Canada Border 201 miles.

DC 1386.9 MP 1421.9 DJ 0.1 F 96.1 Turn on Grizzly Lane for access to Delta Junction Visitor Center parking, Sullivan Roadhouse and to connect with the Richardson Highway south to Paxson and Valdez.

DC 1387 MP 1422 DJ 0 F 96 **Junction** of the Alaska and Richardson highways, referred to locally as "The Triangle." The Alaska Highway merges with the Richardson Highway, which continues northwest to Fairbanks as Alaska Route 2.

> **Junction** of the Alaska Highway (Alaska Route 2) and the Richardson Highway (Alaska Route 4). Turn to **Milepost V 265.9** on page 496 in the RICHARDSON HIGHWAY section for log south to Paxson and Valdez; read log back to front.

NORTHBOUND TRAVELERS NOTE: Alaska Highway officially ends at Delta Junction, but we continue the Alaska Highway log to Fairbanks, beginning on page 219, via the Richardson Highway. This stretch is also logged in the RICHARDSON HIGHWAY section.

SOUTHBOUND ALASKA HIGHWAY TRAVELERS NOTE: In the Alaska portion of The MILEPOST® Alaska Highway log, DC mileages are based on actual driving distance from Dawson Creek, BC, and MP mileages are based on physical mileposts between Delta Junction and the Alaska-Canada border which reflect traditional distances from Dawson Creek,

Don't forget to take photos of the End of the Alaska Highway display in Delta Junction.
(©Kris Valencia, staff)

BC. There is a mileage difference of 35 miles between the traditional mileposts and actual driving distance.

Delta Junction

DC 1387 MP 1422 F 96 **Historical Milepost 1422** Alaska Highway, physical **Milepost V 266** Richardson Highway, located at **junction** of Alaska and Richardson highways. Delta Junction is 96 miles southeast of Fairbanks, 108 miles northwest of Tok, 266 miles north of Valdez and 80 miles north of Paxson and 151 miles north of Glennallen. **Population:** 984. **Emergency Services:** Phone 911 for all emergency services. **Alaska State Troopers**, in the Jarvis Office Center at **Milepost 1420.7**, phone (907) 895-4800. **Fire Department** and **Ambulance**, Delta Rescue Squad/EMS at 1328 Richardson Highway, emergency only phone 911. **Clinic**, Family Medical Center at **Milepost V 267.2**, phone (907) 895-5100. Dentist, Crossroads Family Dentistry, phone (907) 895-4274. **Chiropractor**, Arctic Chiropractic, phone (907) 895-5055.

Visitor Information: Visitor Center at junction of Alaska and Richardson highways, open daily 8 A.M. to 8 P.M., May to mid-September; phone (907) 895-5068, fax (907) 895-5141. The visitor center has historical and wildlife displays (for more details, see Attractions).

Highway information, phone (907) 451-2207. Dept. of Fish and Game at north edge of town; phone (907) 895-4484.

Elevation: 1,180 feet. **Climate:** Mean monthly temperature in January, -15° F; in July 58°F. Record low was -66°F in January 1989; record high was 88°F in August 1990. Mean monthly precipitation in July, 2.57 inches. **Radio:** KUAC-FM 91.7 and 89.9 FM (University of Alaska, Fairbanks). **Television:** Cable and Fairbanks channels KTVF-11, KFXF-7, KUAC-9, K13XD-13.

Private Aircraft: Delta Junction (former BLM) airstrip, 1 mile north; elev. 1,150 feet; length 2,400 feet, gravel; length 1,600 feet, dirt; no fuel; unattended.

Delta Junction is the official end of the

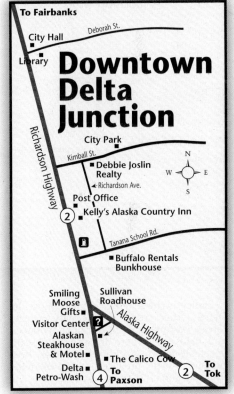

Alaska Highway. Here, the Alaska Highway (Alaska Route 2) seamlessly merges with the Richardson Highway to Fairbanks. The Richardson Highway (Alaska Route 4), connecting Valdez at tidewater with Fairbanks in the Interior, predates the Alaska Highway by 20 years.

Named after the nearby Delta River, Delta Junction began as a construction camp on the Richardson Highway in 1919. (It was first known as Buffalo Center because of the American bison that were transplanted here in the 1920s.) In the late 1970s, the state encouraged development of the agricultural industry in the Delta area by disposing of more than 100,000 acres of local land for farming purposes. Farms average around 500 acres, with a range of 20 to 3,000 acres.

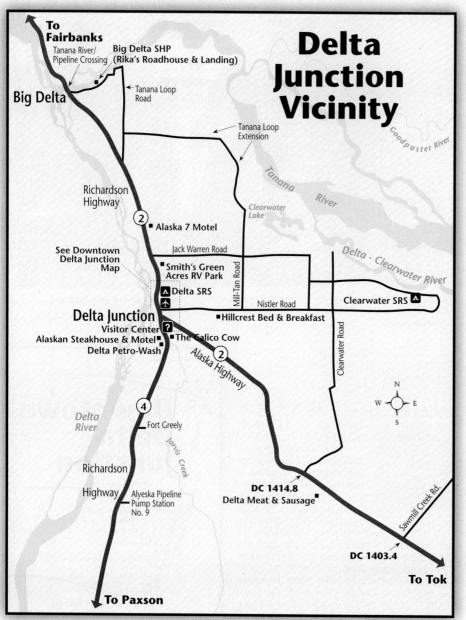

Delta Junction Vicinity

To Fairbanks

Tanana River/ Pipeline Crossing

Big Delta SHP (Rika's Roadhouse & Landing)

Big Delta

Tanana Loop Road

Tanana Loop Extension

Richardson Highway

Tanana River

Clearwater Lake

② Alaska 7 Motel

Jack Warren Road

See Downtown Delta Junction Map

Smith's Green Acres RV Park

Mill-Tan Road

Delta - Clearwater River

⛺ Delta SRS

Nistler Road

Clearwater SRS ⛺

Delta Junction

Visitor Center ❓ Alaskan Steakhouse & Motel ■ Delta Petro-Wash

■ Hillcrest Bed & Breakfast

■ The Calico Cow

② Alaska Highway

Clearwater Road

Goodpaster River

N W E S

④

Delta River

Fort Greely

Jarvis Creek

Richardson Highway

Alyeska Pipeline Pump Station No. 9

DC 1414.8 Delta Meat & Sausage ■

Sawmill Creek Rd.

DC 1403.4

To Tok

To Paxson

Barley is the major feed grain grown in Delta. Other crops include oats, wheat, forage, pasture, grass seed, canola, potatoes and field peas. There are also small-scale vegetable farms; greenhouses; dairies; beef producers; swine producers; bison, elk, reindeer, yak and musk-ox ranches.

American bison were transplanted into the Delta Junction area in the 1920s. Because the bison have become costly pests to many farmers in the Delta area, the 90,000-acre Delta Bison Sanctuary was cre-

DELTA JUNCTION ADVERTISERS

Alaska 7 Motel.................................Ph. (907) 895-4848
Buffalo Rentals Bunk House ......Ph. (907) 895-5422
Calico Cow, The.............................Ph. (907) 895-9895
Debbie Joslin Realty.....................Ph. (907) 895-9999
Delta Junction Chamber .... Ph. 1-877-895-5068
Delta Meat and Sausage Co.......Ph. (907) 895-4006
Hillcrest Bed & Breakfast...........Ph. (907) 895-6223
Kelly's Alaska Country Inn...........Ph. (907) 895-4667
Smiling Moose Gifts......................Ph. (907) 895-4428
Smith's Green Acres RV Park......Ph. (907) 895-4369

ated south of the Alaska Highway in 1980. However, keeping the bison on their refuge and out of the barley fields is a continuing problem. The herd contained 482 bison in 1992 when the last census was taken by the ADF&G.

About 40 percent of the area's working population is employed by the federal or state government or local school district.

Also contributing to Delta Junction's economy are the military and the trans-Alaska pipeline. Fort Greely is located 5 miles south of town on the Richardson Highway. Deactivated in 2000, Fort Greely was reactivated in 2002 as a Ground-based Midcourse Defense missile site. Alyeska Pipeline's Pump Station No. 9 is located 7 miles south of Delta Junction on the Richardson Highway.

Lodging & Services

Delta Junction offers lodging and dining (see ads this section), fast-food at local drive-in, gas stations, a car wash, a shopping center, post office. Smiling Moose Gifts is located between Pizza Bella and Granite View Sports, across from the visitor center. There are also RV parks, 2 banks with ATMs, a gro-

cery store and Debbie Joslin Realty. There are several churches.

Delta's Community Center and Senior Citizens Center (no meals for seniors at this time), library and City Hall are all located on Deborah Street. The library, school, City Hall and some local businesses are closed when winter temperatures drop below -50°F.

The Delta Community Library, at 2291 Deborah Street, 1 block off the Richardson Highway, has 24/7 wireless Internet and offers free 30-minute once-daily sessions on library computers (no charge, donations encouraged). Personal laptops and covered beverages are welcome in the library, but food and cell phones are not allowed. Public fax ($2/page) and copier (25 cents/page) available. The library has handicapped parking, a bike rack, clean restrooms and a picnic area. No overnight parking/camping. Free paperback, magazine and puzzle exchange; local and state newspapers; magazines; audio books; music CDs; videos and DVDs; public review documents, IRS tax forms, PFD forms; children's programs and evening events throughout the year. A community bulletin board featuring local meetings and for-sale items is in the lobby. Library hours (subject to change) are: Monday, Wednesday, Friday 10 A.M. to 6 P.M.; Tuesday and Thursday 10 A.M. to 8 P.M.; Saturday 10 A.M. to 5 P.M.; and Sunday noon to 5 P.M. Reference questions are welcome; phone (907) 895-4102. See the Delta Library online catalog and website for current information: deltalibrarylinks.org or connect on Facebook.

Delta Junction City Hall, located at Milepost V 266.5, has public restrooms, local maps, an Alaska Highway historical map display and a pleasant outdoor area with gazebo and benches. City employees are well practiced in giving directions to local businesses and attractions in both Delta and along the Richardson and Alaska Highways. A small conference room is available for a nominal fee for public meetings. Check with City Hall for reservations; phone (907) 895-4656. City Hall is open 8 A.M. to 5 P.M. weekdays. Notary Public service available at no charge; photocopies 25 cents each.

The Delta Junction Post Office (ZIP 99737) is located at Milepost V 266.2 Richardson Highway. The post office is open 9:30 A.M. to 5 P.M. weekdays, and 10:30 A.M. to noon on Saturday.

Camping

Smith's Green Acres RV Park is just west of town on the Richardson Highway, 2 miles from the visitor center at Milepost V 267.9 (see Milepost DC 1388.9 in continuation of highway log this section). A second RV park is located on the Alaska Highway east of the Triangle.

There are 3 public campgrounds in the area: Delta State Recreation Site campground, 1.1 miles north at Milepost V 267 Richardson Highway; Quartz Lake Recreation Area campground, 10.7 miles north via the Richardson Highway to Milepost V 277.7 and 2.5 miles east on a side road; and Clearwater State Recreation Site campground on Remington Road, accessible from Milepost 1414.8 Alaska Highway or Milepost V 268.3 Richardson Highway (see Delta Vicinity map this section).

Transportation

Air: Scheduled service from Tok to Fairbanks; Delta stop on request. Local air service available.

Attractions

Delta Junction Visitor Center. Have your picture taken with the monument in front of the visitor center that marks the highway's end or—another favorite—with the giant mosquito sculptures. The Chamber of Commerce visitor center has free brochures describing area businesses and attractions; restrooms; cold drinks for sale. Travelers may purchase certificates here, certifying that they have reached the end of the Alaska Highway, and shop for souvenirs in the Center's gift shop.

Indoor displays include Alaska wildlife, including a buffalo mount and trumpeter swans, and the history of area agriculture. Outside the visitor center, there is an interesting display of pipe used in 3 Alaska pipeline projects.

The center is open daily 8 A.M. to 8 P.M., May to mid-September; phone (907) 895-5068.

Enjoy free sausage samples at Delta Meat & Sausage, located 9 miles east of downtown (see **Milepost 1413.4**). The tasty meats and sauages for sale here are the product of a locally owned and operated family-farm. Open daily in summer, 8 A.M. to 5 P.M. weekdays and 10 A.M. to 3 P.M. Saturday and Sunday. Phone (907) 895-4006.

The **Sullivan Roadhouse Historical Museum**, located across from the visitor center on the Richardson Highway, is an original log roadhouse from 1905. It has been moved twice from its original location: once by horse and once by helicopter. It is one of the last surviving roadhouses from the Valdez to Fairbanks Trail and visitors shouldn't miss seeing the interior with its intricate log ceiling. Extensive historical displays and old photographs. It is open daily in summer. Sullivan Roadhouse is staffed by local residents who also help maintain the large summer garden, fashioned after those gardens that were a standard feature of early roadhouses. A display of equipment used during construction of the Alaska Highway is located between the Sullivan Roadhouse and the Visitor Center.

Delta Junction's Farmers' Market is held behind the Sullivan Roadhouse every Saturday and Wednesday in summer. A great spot for travelers to buy fresh local produce and locally-made crafts.

Rika's Roadhouse. Located 8 miles north of town on the Richardson Highway (see description at **Milepost V 275**). Rika's Roadhouse is now part of Big Delta State Historical Park. The Rika's Roadhouse complex contains a number of historic outbuildings, a garden, gift shop, telephone and restrooms. The parking area also accommodates overnight RV parking; camping fee $8 vehicle. Dump station ($3 fee) at nearby rest area. Big Delta State Historical Park and the Rika's Roadhouse complex are open daily in summer.

See the Pipeline Crossing. Delta Junction is the first view of the trans-Alaska pipeline for travelers coming up the Alaska Highway from Canada. A good spot to see and photograph the pipeline is at **Milepost V 275.4** Richardson Highway, 9.5 miles north of town, at the Tanana River crossing.

Special Events: Delta has an old-fashioned 4th of July celebration, and holds the Deltana Fair in late July. The fair includes a barbecue, Lions' pancake breakfast, local handicrafts, horse show, livestock display and show, games, concessions, contests and a parade. A highlight of the fair is the Great

Alaska Outhouse Race, held on Sunday, in which 4 pushers and 1 sitter compete for the coveted "Golden Throne" award.

The Festival of Lights is held in February; Friendly Frontier Days in May; and a Halloween Bash in October. Check with the Chamber of Commerce for dates; phone (907) 895-5068.

Tour the agriculture of the area. Take a drive on Sawmill Creek Road (turn off at **Milepost 1403.4** Alaska Highway) or Clearwater Road (see **Milepost 1414.8**) to see local agriculture and wild game ranches. Sawmill Creek Road goes through the heart of the grain-producing Delta Ag Project. Along Clearwater and Remington roads you may view the older farms, which produce forage crops and livestock. Tanana Loop Road (**Milepost V 271.7**), Tanana Loop Extension and Milltan Road also go past many farms.

Pick your own vegetables and strawberries at local farms.

Bird Watching. Delta's barley fields are a popular migration stop for 150,000 to 200,000 sandhill cranes. Delta-Clearwater Creek is a good place to see spring and fall migrations of sandhill cranes, geese and other waterfowl. Sandhill cranes have a distinctive gurgling call and are also easy to spot in the sky and on the ground because they are among the tallest birds in the world: They are about 4 feet tall and have a 6 to 7 foot wingspan!

AREA FISHING: Delta–Clearwater River (local name for Clearwater Creek), grayling and whitefish; silver salmon spawn here in October. Access via Clearwater Road or Jack Warren Road. **Goodpaster River,** accessible by boat via Delta–Clearwater and Tanana rivers; excellent grayling fishing.

There are 43 lakes in the Delta–Tok area that are stocked by the ADF&G. Lakes are stocked primarily with rainbow trout, and also with arctic grayling, lake trout, arctic char and king salmon. Lakes are located along the road or reached by trail. **Quartz Lake,** at **Milepost V 277.7** north of Delta Junction, one of the most popular fishing lakes in the Delta area, is also the largest and most easily accessed of area lakes; angler success is excellent. Consult ADF&G offices in Delta or Tok for other locations.

Richardson Highway Log
(continued from page 215)

ALASKA ROUTE 2
Distance from Dawson Creek (DC) is followed by distance from Valdez (V) and distance from Fairbanks (F). *NOTE: Physical mileposts between Delta Junction and Fairbanks reflect distance from Valdez on the Richardson Highway and are referenced in the log after the* V *mileage.*

DC 1387 V 266 F 96 Tesoro gas station; gas. diesel.

DC 1387.1 V 266.1 F 95.9 Buffalo Service Center (gas, diesel, propane, tire sales, convenience store, RV dump, 24-hour card fueling) at Nistler Road. Access to fairgrounds, ice arena, Delta schools, dental clinic and a pizza place.

DC 1387.2 V 266.2 F 95.8 Kelly's Alaska Country Inn to east.

DC 1387.3 V 266.3 F 95.7 Delta Junction post office and IGA Food Cache.

DC 1387.4 V 266.4 F 95.6 End 4-lane

Delta-Clearwater River offers fishing and boating opportunities. (©Sharon Nault)

highway, begin 2-lane highway, northbound.

DC 1387.5 V 266.5 F 95.5 Deborah Street; access east to Delta Junction City Hall, Community Center and Library. Veterinary clinic to west.

DC 1387.6 V 266.7 F 95.3 *Begin 35 mph speed zone southbound.*

Distance marker northbound shows North Pole 82 miles, Fairbanks 95 miles.

DC 1387.8 V 266.8 F 95.2 Alaska Dept. of Fish and Game office.

DC 1387.9 V 266.9 F 95.1 Rapids Road; turnoff for Delta Junction Airport.

DC 1388 V 267 F 95 Turnoff to northeast for **Delta State Recreation Site**; (across the highway from Delta River) 25 sites, water, tables, covered picnic shelter, toilets, $10 nightly fee. Campground host.

Just west of campground entrance on the Richardson Highway is a large parking area with access to a pleasant wooded picnic site. Excellent views of the Alaska Range.

DC 1388.1 V 267.1 F 94.9 Alaska Division of Forestry office.

DC 1388.2 V 267.2 F 94.8 Medical clinic to east.

©Kris Valencia, staff

DC 1388.9 V 267.9 F 94.1 Slow for turnoff to **Smith's Green Acres RV Park and Campground** on east side of highway, just before physical Milepost 268 westbound.

Smith's Green Acres RV Park and Campground. See display ad facing page.

DC 1389.3 V 268.3 F 93.7 Junction with Jack Warren Road (paved); see Delta Junction Vicinity map on page 216. Turnoff for **Clearwater State Recreation Site** (10.5 miles) which has 16 sites, 2 pull-throughs, toilets, tables, water and boat launch ($5 fee or annual pass); one of the state's pret-

tiest campsites: the spring-fed Clearwater River is crystal clear. Camping fee $10/night or resident pass. Good fishing. Laundromat nearby with showers. Nearby lodge has restaurant and nice large porch (fishing in front of lodge). Driving directions: follow Jack Warren Road 5.8 miles to a right turn where it becomes Souhrada Road; drive 1 mile then turn left on Remington Road and continue 3.7 miles to the state campground.

To make a "loop" drive through area farmland, bypassing Delta Junction and joining the Alaska Highway east of town, follow driving directions for state campground but drive only 1 mile up Remington Road, then turn right on Clearwater Road, which goes south 5.3 miles to the Alaska Highway (see **Milepost 1414.8**).

DC 1391.3 V 270.3 F 91.7 Alaska 7 Motel. See display ad facing page.

DC 1392.7 V 271.7 F 90.3 Tanana Loop Road (gravel). For an agricultural loop drive, follow Tanana Loop Road north 1.2 miles then turn east on Tanana Loop Extension and drive 9.1 miles to Jack Warren Road and follow Jack Warren Road 2.8 miles back to junction with the highway at **Milepost V 268.3**. There are seasonal U-pick farms along these side roads.

DC 1392.9 V 271.9 F 90.1 Big D Fire station at **BIG DELTA** (pop. 583). This unincorporated community at the junction of the Delta and Tanana rivers was originally a stop on the Valdez–Fairbanks trail. It was first known as Bates Landing, then Rika's Landing, McCarty, and finally Big Delta. Big Delta was the site of a WAMCATS telegraph station and also a work camp in 1919 during construction of the Richardson Highway. Today, agriculture, small business, and highway maintenance jobs provide employment.

DC 1395.6 V 274.6 F 87.4 Distance marker eastbound shows Delta Junction 8 miles, Tok 117 miles.

DC 1396 V 275 F 87 Tesoro gas station with diesel and Tanana Trading Post on southwest side of highway. Turnoff for **Rika's Roadhouse** to northeast. After turning, keep to left for Rika's Roadhouse parking lot, or drive straight ahead on the paved road for a small rest area with picnic table, potable water, outhouse and dump station ($5) on loop road. Day parking and over-

The History of the Alaska Highway

Construction of the "Alcan" Highway (ALCAN was the military acronym for the Alaska-Canada Highway) officially began on March 9, 1942. Army engineers were ordered to construct a road that would proceed in a northwesterly direction from the railhead at Dawson Creek, BC, and connect with the existing Richardson Highway at Delta Junction, AK. They punched a pioneer road through the wilderness in 8 months and 12 days.

An overland link between Alaska and the Lower 48 had been studied as early as 1930, under President Herbert Hoover, but with the bombing of Pearl Harbor in December 1941, it was deemed a military necessity. President Roosevelt authorized construction of the Alaska Highway on February 11, 1942. The U.S. secured rights-of-way through Canada in March. The formal agreement between the 2 countries stipulated that the U.S. pay for construction and turn over the Canadian portion of the highway to the Canadian government after the war ended. In turn, Canada furnished the right-of-way; waived import duties, sales tax, income tax and immigration regulations; and provided construction materials along the route.

A massive mobilization of men and equipment took place in that first month following the executive order to build a military road to Alaska. The Public Roads Administration tackled the task of organizing civilian engineers and equipment. Trucks, road-building equipment, office furniture, food, tents and other supplies all had to be located and then shipped north.

In Earl Brown's *Alcan Trail Blazers*, Harry Spiegel describes the scene upon arriving in the North in March 1942 with Company A, 648th Topographic Battalion, U.S. Army Corps of Engineers:

"We are now located on the last fringe of civilization; 60 miles from the nearest railroad and there are no roads save for one bush trail blazed about 300 miles north to Fort Nelson from here. Many convoys of heavy engineering and pontoon boat equipment are arriving every day. Even though I am in the midst of army activity all around me, all this impresses me as working on a huge, peacetime construction job, or being a member of a wilderness expedition. Very few wartime precautions are observed. Open fires burn at night, no camouflage is used and the trucks do not use their blackout lights."

By June, more than 10,000 American troops had poured into the Canadian North.

The general route of the Alcan Highway determined by the War Department was along a line of existing airfields from Edmonton, AB, to Fairbanks, AK, known as the Northwest Staging Route. (This chain of airfields was used to ferry more than 8,000 war planes to Russia as part of the Lend Lease Program.) But mapping out a general route for the Alaska Highway in Washington D.C., and actually surveying the route in the field, proved to be two very different things.

Some sections of the Alaska Highway followed existing winter roads, summer pack trails and winter trap lines. Where no trails existed, reconnaissance parties scouted through river valleys and mountain passes, often struggling through waist-deep snow and climbing over "boulders as big as

Sections of the Alcan became impassable during spring thaw. (© MILEPOST Archive Photo)

boxcars."

Recon parties often depended on local guides to help locate possible routes for the new road. And like the early-day explorers who preceded them, along with those who called this country home, the Alaska Highway construction crews often left their mark by naming the lakes, rivers and mountains they found along the way.

Once the route had been scouted, the survey crews would move in. "One man would set up with his compass on the staff and—utilizing the chosen bearing—locate a second man, who would proceed through the brush, waving a signal flag from the top of his staff as far as he could be seen," recalls Capt. Eschbach. "At that point, he would stick his staff in the ground, set up his compass, align it on the chosen bearing, and a third man would then move ahead of him... Leapfrogging in this manner, the unit could make as much as 8 or 10 miles on a good day."

For the soldiers and civilian workers building the Alaska Highway, it was a hard life. Working 7 days a week, they endured mosquitoes and black flies in summer and below zero temperatures in winter. And the farther away from base camp you were, the harder the living conditions. Weeks would pass with no communication between headquarters and field parties. According to one senior officer with the Public Roads Administration, "Equipment was always a critical problem. There never was enough."

In *Alcan Trail Blazers*, Sid Navratil describes the daily hardships for the troops. "We are working 16 hours a day, working like hell blazing a trail just ahead of the 'cats.' Our terrific chow shortage is getting everyone grumpy. The daily menu: breakfast, 3 pancakes, thin farina, coffee; lunch (when there is any), 2 biscuits size of a quarter each (and just as hard); supper, fish and potatoes... No cigarettes."

In June 1942, the Japanese invaded Attu and Kiska Islands in the Aleutians, adding a new sense of urgency to completion of the Alcan. Crews working from east and west connected at Contact Creek on September 15. Construction ended on Oct. 25, 1942, when it was possible for vehicles to travel the entire length of the highway. The official ribbon-cutting ceremony was held Nov.

20, 1942, on Soldier's Summit at Kluane Lake.

The Alaska Highway opened to the public in 1948. The highway was named an International Historical Engineering Landmark in 1996.

Song of the "Alcan" Pioneers

They gave us a job and we did it;
They said that it couldn't be done.
They figured that time would forbid it.
They licked us before we'd begun.

But there she is—eagles above her
The Road—see, she steams in the snow.
She's ours, and oh God, how we love her,
But now—marching orders—we go.

We started with nothing and won her,
We diced for her honor with death.
We starved, froze and died upon her
And damned her with agonized breath.

Blood-red ran the snow where we lay—
Blood-red rode the sun at her setting,
Cold white are the graves we're forgetting
Cold white are our ashes today.

We leveled the mountains to find her,
We climbed from the pit to the sky,
We conquered the forests to bind her,
We burrowed where mastodons lie.
Smooth, straight and true we have fashioned.
Clean she is, living, aglow.
The Road—feel her, vibrant, impassioned—
And now—marching orders—we go.

Go from the stardust of June night,
Go from the beauty we won.
Little lost lakes in the moonlight,
Snow-steepled spires in the sun.
We lend you the road—we who made it,
And bright may your victories burn.
We lend you The Road, we who laid it,
Until the day we return.

Attributed to "an unknown soldier," this poem appeared in the 1950 edition of The MILEPOST®.

night parking for Rika's Roadhouse (fees charged). 🅿️⛽♿🏕️

Rika's Roadhouse was built in 1910 by John Hajdukovich, who sold it in 1923 to Rika Wallen, a Swedish immigrant who had managed the roadhouse since 1917. Rika ran the roadhouse into the late 1940s and lived there until her death in 1969. It is now part of Big Delta State Historical Park and admission is free.

Pleasant walking paths with interpretive signs lead from the parking area through the park's grounds to the roadhouse. Historic structures open to the public include a small sod-roofed museum, a barn, blacksmith shop the old WAMCATS building and the roadhouse itself. Don't miss the colorful summer gardens at Rika's Roadhouse.

The Packhouse Restaurant and gift shop are located near the back of the property; current status unknown. The park grounds are open until 8 P.M. A must-stop and a good place to stretch your legs. Take a walk above the banks of the Tanana River.

DC 1396.5 V 275.5 F 86.5 Tanana River/ Big Delta Bridge. Turnoff to north at east end of bridge for large, rutted dirt parking area at Alyeska Pipeline Display about **Tanana River Pipeline Bridge**. Boat launch, boat trailer parking, litter barrels, portable outhouses, interpretive signs. *CAUTION: Fast-moving water, supervise small children and leash dogs.*

Spectacular view of the 1,200-foot-long section of pipeline suspended across the Tanana River between 2 towers. This is the second longest of the 13 major bridges along the pipeline's 800-mile length. Information panels give pipeline history and facts, as well as details on the suspension bridge.

DC 1398.7 V 277.7 F 84.3 Turn off to east on Quartz Lake Road for **Quartz Lake State Recreation Area**. Pass over the pipeline at 0.2 mile (good photo-op). Drive in 1.9 miles on narrow paved road with frost heaves to intersection: turn left for Lost Lake, continue straight ahead for Quartz Lake (another 0.4 mile); descriptions follow. Trailhead for the Bert Mount Overlook is along this road; it is a 1.7-mile hike (each way) to lovely views. At Mile 2.5 there is an ATV trail.

Quartz Lake has developed campsites on a good loop road. All sites are treed pull-ins only, with many long enough to accommodate large rigs. Firepits, water, tables, toilet and concrete boat launch (fee charged) available. Large dock and boat rental concession. Side-by-side pull-through overnight parking available in the parking lot.

Lost Lake has 12 pull-in or back-in campsites with picnic tables and a toilet. (Renovated sites can accommodate larger rigs; older sites are uneven and may require leveling blocks.) There is a large parking area with tables and litter bins. Small dock with bench at the end, nice picnic area with tables by the lake, beaver homes and water lilies.

Camping fee $10 at both campgrounds. Float planes sometimes land on Quartz Lake: Be sure to move out of their path if you are out fishing (they have the right-of-way). A trail connects Lost Lake and Quartz Lake camping areas. Quartz Lake SRA has 2 public-use cabins; 3-night maximum; visit www.dnr.alaska.gov/parks/cabins/index.htm for details. 🏕️

Quartz Lake covers 1,500 acres, more

Tanana River Pipeline Bridge is 1,200 feet long. *(©Kris Valencia, staff)*

than 80 percent of which are less than 15 feet deep. Maximum depth is 40 feet. There is a boat rental concession at the lake, making this a good spot to get out of your vehicle and on to the water. Popular fishing lake, stocked rainbow, arctic char and salmon (silver and king). Winter ice fishery; fishing huts for rent (go to www.dnr.alaska.gov/parks/cabins/icehuts .htm for details). **Lost Lake** is stocked with rainbows. 🎣

DC 1401.2 V 280.2 F 81.8 Gravel turnout to south.

DC 1401.3 V 280.3 F 81.7 *Begin 0.5-mile passing lane westbound.*

DC 1404 V 283 F 79 81-Mile Pond (stocked with rainbow trout by ADF&G); public fishing access to east. 🎣

DC 1405 V 284 F 78 Watch for moose in roadside ponds on both sides of highway. *CAUTION: Watch for moose on highway.*

DC 1407.5 V 286.5 F 75.5 Shaw Creek bridge. Popular boat launching area; gated parking area to north at east end of bridge. Shaw Creek road west side of bridge.

Good views westbound of Tanana River which parallels the highway.

DC 1408.1 V 287.1 F 74.9 Shaw Pond public fishing access to northeast. Good to excellent early spring and fall grayling fishing; subject to closure (check locally). Popular local informal camping spot. 🎣🏕️

DC 1409 V 288 F 74 Scenic viewpoint at parking area to west overlooking Tanana River with panoramic view (on clear days) to the south of 3 great peaks of the Alaska Range: Mount Hayes (elev. 13,832 feet) almost due south; Hess Mountain (11,940 feet) to the west or right of Mount Hayes; and Mount Deborah (12,339 feet) to the west or right of Hess Mountain.

Mount Hayes is named for Charles Hayes, an early member of the U.S. Geological Survey. Mount Deborah was named in 1907 by the famous Alaskan Judge Wickersham for his wife.

DC 1410.7 V 289.7 F 72.3 South entrance to long paved double-ended parking area to east in trees.

DC 1412.8 V 291.8 F 70.2 *Begin 0.7-mile passing lane westbound.*

DC 1413.8 V 292.8 F 69.2 *Highway descends next 1.4 miles westbound.*

Distance marker northbound shows North Pole 55 miles, Fairbanks 69 miles.

DC 1414.5 V 293.5 F 68.5 Tenderfoot Pottery on Ruby Road. Studio and gallery of artist Shellie Mathews; open daily.

Tenderfoot Pottery. See display ad this page.

DC 1414.9 V 293.9 F 68.1 Paved double-ended turnout to west with Gold Rush Centennial interpretive signs on "Getting the Gold" (placer mining) and "Gold in the Tenderfoot" (excerpt follows):

"Two miners from the Fortymile District found gold flakes on Tenderfoot Creek in 1888. This site was too far from a supply camp, so they abandoned it. 17 years later, after gold was discovered near Fairbanks, prospector E.H. Luce found gold on Tenderfoot Creek. News of his discovery attracted about a thousand people to the area. Between 1905 and 1995, the Tenderfoot Mining District produced 120,770 ounces (3.77 tons) of placer gold. Its most productive years were 1905 to 1916."

DC 1415 V 294 F 68 *CAUTION: Watch for road damage westbound.*

Begin 1.6-mile passing lane eastbound. Highway climbs miles eastbound.

DC 1415.6 V 294.6 F 67.4 Fairbanks North Star Borough boundary.

DC 1416.4 V 295.4 F 66.6 Banner Creek bridge; historic placer gold stream.

DC 1416.5 V 295.5 F 66.5 Distance

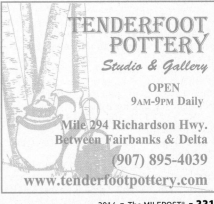

Birch Lake State Recreation Site has a grassy day-use area and beach. (©Sharon Nault)

marker southbound shows Delta Junction 28 miles, Tok 136 miles, Valdez 300 miles.

DC 1417.3 V 296.3 F 65.7 Paved scenic viewpoint to south with good view of the braided Tanana River.

DC 1419.2 V 298.2 F 63.8 Paved double-ended parking area to southwest in trees.

DC 1422 V 301 F 61 *Begin 0.4-mile passing lane westbound.*

DC 1422.5 V 301.5 F 60.5 East end of long double-ended turnout downhill north of highway.

DC 1422.8 V 301.8 F 60.2 West end of long double-ended turnout. East end at **Milepost V 301.5**.

DC 1423.5 V 302.5 F 59.5 *Begin 0.5-mile passing lane eastbound.*

DC 1425.2 V 304.2 F 57.8 Turnout to northeast.

DC 1426 V 305 F 57 Distance marker southbound shows Delta Junction 38 miles, Tok Junction 146 miles, Valdez 310 miles.

DC 1426.2 V 305.2 F 56.8 Signed turnoff to northeast on Birch Lake Road (0.2 mile) for loop road through **Birch Lake State Recreation Site**; swimming, picnicking, camping, boating, fishing, jetskiing. Lakeside picnic sites with tables, firepits, toilets and garbage on grassy day-use area. Overnight parking with campground host; 12 sites, some for tent campers; fee station; boat launch and fishing. Parking available for boat trailers. Overnight fee $10, day-use $5. Fish from shore in spring, from boat in summer. Stocked with silver salmon, grayling, arctic char and rainbow. "Kids Don't Float" program life jackets. Popular buoyed swimming area.

Birch Lake Military Recreation Site (USAF Recreation Camp) is located just beyond the state recreation site on the same access road.

DC 1427 V 306 F 56 Pleasant rest area northeast side of highway on the shore of Birch Lake; toilets, parking, dumpster, lakeside benches, day-use only.

DC 1427.1 V 306.1 F 55.9 Lost Lake Road to south.

DC 1428 V 307 F 55 *CAUTION: Watch for moose.*

DC 1428.1 V 307.1 F 54.9 Birch Lake DOT station to northeast.

DC 1428.2 V 307.2 F 54.8 Gravel parking

area at Koole Lake Trail (14.3 miles), public fishing access, to southwest.

DC 1430.3 V 309.3 F 52.7 *Begin 1.1-mile passing lane westbound.*

DC 1431 V 310 F 52 Large double-ended parking area to southwest.

DC 1431.7 V 310.7 F 51.3 *Begin 1-mile passing lane eastbound, uphill grade.*

DC 1434.1 V 313.1 F 48.9 Paved double-ended turnout to southwest on Tanana River. Gold Rush Centennial interpretive signs on "Alaska's Gold Rush Era" and "Tanana Valley Gold" (excerpts follow). This was also the site of Silver Fox Lodge, the Fox Farm and the Overland Roadhouse (circa 1910) at **Historic Milepost 1471** Alaska Highway.

Sign: "Prospectors made the first significant gold discovery in Alaska at Juneau in 1880. This discovery encouraged others to look throughout Alaska and the Yukon for gold. The first strike in Alaska's Interior was along the Fortymile River in 1886. It was followed by discoveries on other Yukon River tributaries and the Kenai Peninsula. On August 16, 1896, George Carmack, Skookum Jim and Tagish Charlie made the Klondike discovery in Canada's Yukon Territory.

"The Klondike discovery started a stampede to Dawson reminiscent of the California Gold Rush of 1849. Some of the stampeders prospected creeks in Alaska and made new strikes. The Nome, Fairbanks and Iditarod gold fields were the largest, but between 1896 and 1914 gold was found in hundreds of places around Alaska.

"The gold deposits found in 1902 north of present-day Fairbanks proved to be the richest in Alaska. Prospector Felix Pedro and trader E.T. Barnette played key roles in the discovery and initial rush.

"An Italian immigrant, Felix Pedro claimed to have found—and lost—a rich gold strike in the Tanana Valley foothills in 1898. Searching for the site in 1901, Pedro met Barnette, who was running a trading post on the Chena River, where he had been left by the riverboat captain he had hired to take him to the upper Tanana River.

"Pedro returned to Barnette's post on July 28, 1902, to announce a new gold discovery. Barnette sent word of the strike to nearby gold camps, exaggerating its richness. Hundreds of prospectors rushed into the area, only to find most creeks already staked, few claims being worked, and high prices for supplies at Barnette's trading post. Only after the disgruntled miners threatened to lynch the gold camp's promoters did Barnette lower his prices.

"In the fall of 1903, miners on Cleary, Fairbanks and Ester creeks in the Tanana foothills announced rich gold discoveries. Another rush occurred and 1,500 people

were mining in the area by Christmas. The camp Barnette named Fairbanks grew into a city of saloons and 2-story buildings. The amount of gold mined increased from $40,000 in 1903 to $9.6 million in 1909. The Tanana gold fields were Alaska's richest, and within a few years Fairbanks became the territory's largest city."

DC 1435.8 V 314.8 F 47.2 Midway Lodge.

DC 1436 V 315 F 47 "C" Lazy Moose RV Park & Gift Shop; full hookups, showers, laundry, free WiFi Phone (907) 488-8141; www.clazymooserv.com. [icon]

DC 1440.2 V 319.2 F 42.8 Harding Lake via Salcha Drive.

DC 1441.2 V 320.2 F 41.8 Distance marker northbound shows North Pole 30 miles, Fairbanks 44 miles.

DC 1442.5 V 321.5 F 40.5 Turnoff to east on Harding Drive for **Harding Lake State Recreation Area**; drive east 1.4 miles on paved road. A terrific stop for families with small children; bring beach shoes to enjoy wading on the very shallow, rocky bottom of Harding Lake. Fee station (or self-register), campground host and dump station at entrance. Grassy day-use area with picnic tables, grills, horseshoes, ballfields, There is a boat launch and a 1.4 mile nature trail; 80 campsites (plus large field for group camping). Camping ($10), day-use and launch fees charged. Quiet hours from 11 P.M.–6 A.M. Fishing for lake trout, arctic char, burbot, northern pike and salmon. Worth the drive! Bring your insect repellent, you may need it! Firewood from camp host or park ranger. Jet skis allowed. [icons]

DC 1443.2 V 322.2 F 39.8 SALCHA (pop. 953, unincorporated) extends along the highway for several miles. Post office (ZIP code 99714) open weekdays noon to 6 P.M., Saturday 10 A.M. to noon. Salchaket Roadhouse with food, gas, propane and lodging on east side of highway. The village was first reported in 1898 as "Salchaket," meaning "mouth of the Salcha." [icon]

DC 1444.1 V 323.1 F 38.9 Access to **Salcha River State Recreation Site** 0.2 miles to northeast (turn at Salcha Marine), a popular boat launch with a 130-site parking area for vehicles and boat trailers; a boat ramp; picnic area; a few developed campsites and some primitive campsites; toilets and water. There may be 300 or more people here on holidays. $10 launch fee and 10-minute launch limit. Camping fee ($10) charged. Fishing for king and dog salmon, grayling, sheefish, northern pike and burbot. Road at end of parking area by pit toilets leads to big area of sandbar parking and informal camping on Salcha River (beware soft sand areas). Winter-use cabin available; go to http://dnr.alaska.gov/parks/cabins/north.htm#salcha. [icons]

DC 1444.4 V 323.4 F 38.6 Salcha River bridge (50 mph).

DC 1445 V 324 F 38 Clear Creek bridge.

DC 1445.6 V 324.6 F 37.4 Double-ended gravel turnout to northeast.

DC 1445.8 V 324.8 F 37.2 Munsons Slough bridge; fishing; Monsons Slough Road. [icon]

DC 1446.4 V 325.4 F 36.6 Salcha Elementary School to northeast.

DC 1448.7 V 327.7 F 34.3 Little Salcha River bridge.

DC 1449.3 V 328.3 F 33.7 Salcha Store and Service (ice, gas) to northeast.

DC 1450.4 V 329.4 F 32.6 Tanana River flows next to highway.

DC 1451.1 V 330.1 F 31.9 Distance marker southbound shows Delta Junction 65 miles, Tok 173 miles.

DC 1451.3 V 330.3 F 31.7 Salcha Senior Center to northeast.

DC 1451.5 V 330.5 F 31.5 Salcha Rescue; phone (907) 488-5274. For emergencies dial 911.

DC 1452.7 V 331.7 F 30.3 Salcha Fairgrounds. Fair is held the last full weekend in June.

DC 1453.1 V 332.1 F 29.9 Access east to 31-Mile Pond; stocked with arctic char, rainbow.

DC 1453.2 V 332.2 F 29.8 The Knotty Shop to west has a large and interesting selection of gifts. Also of interest is their wildlife museum and display of ptarmigan. The burl creations out in front are popular photo ops *(but please DON'T climb on burl sculptures)*. There are also unusual and impressive burl railings on the front porch of the shop. Show them *THE MILEPOST®* advertisement for one free single scoop ice cream cone.

The Knotty Shop. See display ad this page.

DC 1455.7 V 334.7 F 27.3 Leaving Eielson AFB southbound. Entering Eielson AFB northbound (see description at **Milepost V 341.3**).

DC 1456.1 V 335.1 F 26.9 Access northeast to 28-Mile Pond; stocked with rainbow, arctic char.

DC 1458.5 V 337.5 F 24.5 View of Eielson AFB runway to northeast next 1.5 miles northbound. *NOTE: No stopping, no parking and no photography along this stretch of highway!* Watch for various military aircraft taking off and landing to the east.

DC 1461.5 V 340.5 F 21.5 *Begin 4-lane divided freeway, 55mph posted speed limit northbound.*

Begin 2-lane highway, 65mph posted speed limit, southbound.

CAUTION: Watch for heavy traffic southbound turning east into the base, 7–8 A.M., and merging northbound traffic, 3:45–5:30 P.M., weekdays. No parking, no stopping, no photography!

DC 1462.3 V 341.3 F 20.7 Main entrance to **EIELSON AIR FORCE BASE** (pop. 2,858). Eielson is the farthest north full-up fighter wing in the U.S. Air Force. The 345th Fighter Wing equips and trains the 18th Fighter Squadron of F-16s. Eielson has more than 60,000 square miles of military training airspace—the largest aerial range in the country. Military units from around the U.S. and the world come to hone their skills here.

Built in 1943 as a satellite base to Ladd Field (now Fort Wainwright) in Fairbanks, and called Mile 26 because of its location 26 miles from Fairbanks, Eielson served as a storage site for aircraft en route to the Soviet Union under the WWII Lend–Lease program. Closed after WWII, the base was reactivated in 1946 and renamed Eielson AFB, after Carl Ben Eielson, the first man to fly from Alaska over the North Pole to Greenland.

For current information on possible public tours of the base being available, phone the public affairs office at (907) 377-2116.

DC 1462.7 V 341.7 F 20.3 Exit to Eielson's main entrance is exit lane to north eastbound traffic.

DC 1463 V 342 F 20 North boundary of Eielson AFB.

DC 1463.7 V 242.7 F 19.3 Purple Heart Trail sign, eastbound.

DC 1464.6 V 343.6 F 18.4 Turnoff to north for Old Richardson Highway, Moose Creek Road and access to Moose Creek General Store; diesel, gas, propane. Turnoff to south for Eielson Farm Road to **Bathing Beauty Pond** and **Piledriver Slough.** Bathing Beauty Pond has a picnic area and is stocked with rainbow, arctic char and grayling. Piledriver Slough has outhouses, dumpster and boat launch on Chena River and is stocked with rainbow.

DC 1465.6 V 344.6 F 17.4 Moose Creek.

DC 1466.4 V 345.4 F 16.6 *CAUTION: Highway crosses Alaska Railroad tracks.*

DC 1466.7 V 345.7 F 16.3 Chena Flood Channel bridge. Upstream dam is part of flood control project initiated after the Chena River left its banks and flooded Fairbanks in 1967. A high water mark from this flood can be seen at the Pioneer Park train depot in Fairbanks.

DC 1467.3 V 346.3 F 15.7 Distance marker westbound shows North Pole exits: Dawson Road 1 mile, Mission Road, 2.5 miles, Badger Road 2.75 miles.

DC 1467.6 V 346.6 F 15.4 Exit north to Laurence Road (westbound traffic only) for Moose Creek Dam Bikeway and Chena Lake Recreation Area The 5-mile-long **Moose Creek Dam Bikeway** extends from the park-and-ride lot at Laurance and Nelson Roads

Diamond willow walking sticks on display at The Knotty Shop. (©Sharon Nault)

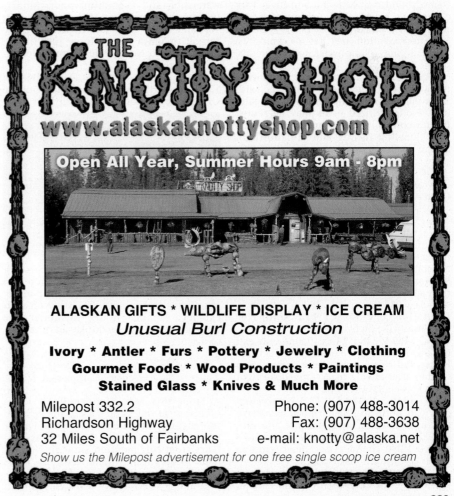

Visitors to Santa Claus House watch the reindeer feeding in outdoor enclosure.
(©Sharon Nault)

(0.8 mile from the highway) to the dam site on the Chena River.

Drive 2.5 miles to fee station at entrance to **Chena Lakes Recreation Area**. A map of the recreation area is displayed; open year-round, day-use and camping fees charged from Memorial Day to Labor Day. It is 5.5 miles from the highway to the visitor kiosk below the Moose Creek Dam on the Chena River at the end of Main Road. Constructed by the Army Corps of Engineers and run by Fairbanks North Star Borough. Lake Park Campground is at Mile 3.6 and River Park Campground at Mile 4.9. Camping fee $10/night tents, $12 campers/RVs. Day-use fee $5. The recreation area has 80 campsites, 92 picnic sites, pump water, toilets, firepits, picnic tables, trash bins and volleyball courts. There is a 250-acre lake with swimming beach. **Chena Lake** is stocked with silver salmon, arctic char, grayling and rainbow. Nonmotorized boats may be rented from a concessionaire. **Chena River** offers good grayling fishing and also northern pike, whitefish and burbot.

DC 1467.9 V 346.9 F 15.1 Eastbound exit for south Laurance Road (no access to Chena Lakes).

DC 1468.4 V 347.4 F 14.6 Westbound-only exit to Dawson and Buzby Roads. For Santa Claus House and North Pole Visitor Information Center, after exiting drive under the overpass and turn right on St. Nicholas Drive (frontage road). For Chena Recreation Area, turn right on Mistletoe, then left on Laurence Road; follow signs. See map page 226.

DC 1468.8 V 347.8 F 14.2 North Pole city limits (sign on overpass).

DC 1469 V 348 F 14 Eastbound-only exit to Dawson and Buzby Roads. For Santa Claus House and North Pole Visitor Information Center, after exiting make immediate right on to St Nicholas Drive.

DC 1469.5 V 348.5 F 13.5 Westbound-only exit north to Mission Road. Go north on Mission Road a short distance and turn west (left) in front of a big church for radio station KJNP complex (see description in North Pole attractions on page 225).

DC 1469.6 V 348.6 F 13.4 Eastbound traffic-only exit south to 5th Avenue and St.

Nicholas Drive in North Pole.

North Pole 5th Avenue Exit. See description of "North Pole" beginning on page 225.

DC 1470 V 349 F 13 Westbound traffic-only exit north to roundabout for access north to Badger Road and south to North Pole business district via Santa Claus Lane: fast food outlets, 24-hour gas/diesel, car and truck wash, supermarket, post office, police, city hall, banks, medical clinics, indoor waterslide and swimming pool, library, playgrounds, parks. Also access south via Santa Claus Lane to St. Nicholas Drive turnoff to **Santa Claus House** (description below) and to North Pole Visitor Information Center.

Santa Claus House. Established in 1952, the Santa Claus House is home of the Original Letter from Santa. Mail your cards

and letters here for an authentic North Pole postmark. Browse the gift shop and visit with Santa and his reindeer. Numerous photo opportunities. Open all year with extended summer hours, Memorial Day through Labor Day. See display ad next page.
[ADVERTISEMENT]

North Pole/Badger Road Exit. See description of "North Pole" beginning on page 225.

From this exit, **Badger Road** loops northwest 11 miles and back to the Richardson Highway at **Milepost V 356.6**. Badger Road provides access to the following (distance from this junction shown): Nordale Road (4.6 miles), which leads 5.6 miles north to Chena Hot Springs Road; gas station and **Riverview RV Park** (8.4 miles);

Fort Wainwright (10.1 miles); gas station (10.4 miles); and Old Richardson Highway (10.9 miles).

DC 1470.6 V 349.6 F 12.4 Eastbound traffic-only exit to to roundabout accesses North Pole business district to south (fast-food outlets, supermarket, etc.) and Badger Road to north (Tesoro station). Turn on St. Nicholas Road for **Santa Claus House** and North Pole Visitor Information Center.

DC 1471.1 V 350.1 F 11.9 Peridot Lane exiit to north and south (for east and westbound traffic).

DC 1471.5 V 350.5 F 11.5 Alaska Railroad crossing. Entering North Pole city limits (eastbound).

DC 1472.3 V 351.3 F 10.7 Distance marker westbound shows Fairbanks 11 miles, Fox 22 miles, Circle 169 miles.

DC 1476 V 355 F 7 $1,000 fine for littering (eastbound sign).

DC 1477.6 V 356.6 F 5.4 Badger Road interchange westbound. This 11-mile road loops back to the Richardson Highway at **Milepost V 349.5**, providing access to Old Richardson Highway (0.2 mile from this junction); gas station (0.7 mile); Fort Wainwright (1 mile); **Riverview RV Park** and gas station (2.7 miles); and Nordale Road (6.4 miles), which leads 5.6 miles north to Chena Hot Springs Road. At Mile 2.3 Nordale Road there is a boat launch on the Chena River with paved parking area, outhouses and dumpster.

DC 1478.6 V 357.6 F 4.4 Eastbound exit to Badger Road and **Riverview RV Park**.

DC 1480.2 V 359.2 F 2.8 Railroad crossing.

DC 1480.6 V 359.6 F 2.4 Westbound traffic use south lane to exit for Old Richardson Highway and South Cushman Street.

DC 1481.2 V 360.2 F 1.8 Distance marker eastbound shows North Pole 11 miles, Delta Junction 98 miles, Tok Junction 202 miles, Anchorage 440 miles.

DC 1481.5 V 360.5 F 1.5 Eastbound exit for Lakeview Drive. This area subject to fog (signed).

DC 1481.6 V 360.6 F 1.4 Westbound exit (next right northbound) for Mitchell Expressway, which **junctions** with Parks Highway (Alaska Route 3) to Denali Park and Nenana and Anchorage.

Begin 4-lane divided freeway eastbound (Alaska Route 2 South).

Turn to end of PARKS HIGHWAY section on page 442 and read log back to front for log of that highway from Fairbanks south to Anchorage.

DC 1482.2 V 361.2 F 0.8 Welcome to Fairbanks sign and flowers, westbound. Eastbound traffic exit to Mitchell Expressway to junction with Parks Highway (Alaska Route 3) to Denali Park and Nenana and Anchorage.

DC 1482.5 V 361.5 F 0.5 Eastbound traffic exit to South Cushman.

DC 1483 V 362 F 0 FAIRBANKS. **Junction** with Airport Way and Steese Expressway northbound; downtown Fairbanks to west (take Airport Way and turn north on Cushman Street for downtown); Fort Wainwright Main Gate (Gaffney Road) to east.

Turn to FAIRBANKS section beginning on page 443 for description of city and maps.

North Pole

North Pole

North Pole is on the Richardson Highway, approximately 14 miles southeast of Fairbanks. **Population:** 2,200. **Emergency Services:** Emergencies only phone 911. **Police**, phone (907) 488-6902. **Alaska State Troopers** (Fairbanks), phone (907) 451-5100. **Fire Dept./Ambulance**, phone (907) 488-2232.

Visitor Information: North Pole's Visitor Information Center is located just to the southeast of Santa Claus House behind the big Santa Claus. Open daily 10 A.M. to 6 P.M. late-May to early September and offers friendly traveler assistance, referrals, coffee, souvenirs, local handicrafts. Center is operated by the Chamber of Commerce. North Pole Chamber of Commerce, P.O. Box 55071, North Pole, AK 99705; phone (907) 488-2242, fax (907) 488-3002. Email: info@northpolechamber.us. City Hall (907) 488-2281; fax: (907) 488-3002; Website: www.northpolechamber.us.

Elevation: 483 feet. **Radio:** KJNP-AM 1170, KJNP-FM 100.3, TV Ch 4; also Fairbanks radio and television stations.

Private Aircraft: Bradley Sky Ranch, 1 NW; elev. 483 feet; length 4,100 feet; gravel; fuel 100.

North Pole has many services, including almost 20 restaurants with worldwide cuisines, gas stations, supermarkets, pharmacies and other services. The post office is on Santa Claus Lane. Lodging at **Beaver Lake Resort Motel** and **North Pole Cabins**. Camping at **Riverview RV Park** on Badger Road.

Full-service camping with hookups, showers and other amenities at **Riverview RV Park**, located on Badger Road (turnoff at **Milepost V 356.6** on the Richardson Highway). North Pole Public Park, on 5th Avenue, has tent sites in the trees along a narrow dirt road; no camping fee. Dump station available at North Pole Plaza.

North Pole Cabins. Located one mile from Santa Claus House, this lovely cabin retreat sits in quiet wooded waterfront privacy. Only 15 minutes from Fairbanks. Open year around. Private entrances. Private baths. Kitchenette. Queen beds. Therapeutic massage services available. www.northpolecabins.com, info@northpolecabins.com, P.O. Box 57194 North Pole, AK 99705. Phone (907) 490-6400. [ADVERTISEMENT]

North Pole is the home of many Fairbanks commuters but is also one of 2 energy production centers in Alaska. Almost half of Alaska Railroad's freight revenue comes from hauling petroleum products made in North Pole. The Flint Hills North Pole Refinery and the Petro Star Refinery produces heating fuel, jet fuel, asphalt and other petroleum products. Eielson AFB and Fort Wainwright military bases are nearby.

North Pole had its beginnings in 1944, when Bon V. and Bernice Davis homesteaded this area. Dahl and Gaske Development Co. bought the Davis homestead, subdivided it and named it North Pole, hoping to attract a toy manufacturer who could advertise products as being made in North Pole. The city incorporated in 1953 and developed as a theme city: "Where the spirit of Christmas lives year round." The city's light poles are painted to look like candy canes.

Local landmark and long-time visitor attraction **Santa Claus House** was started by Con and Nellie Miller in 1952. A merchant and fur buyer from Fairbanks, Con had been donning an old red Santa suit and entertaining village children at Christmas since arriving in the territory. Building the Santa Claus House in North Pole proved an inspired next step, as over the years it has garnered international attention.

Con Miller was the city's longest serving mayor (19 years), and Santa Claus House served as North Pole's post office for almost 20 years. The brightly decorated store is open year-round and visitors can shop for Christmas ornaments in July while their children tell Santa what they want for Christmas. Phone 1-800-588-4078 or (907) 488-2200; www.santaclaushouse.com.

Special Events: There's a big summer festival weekend celebration with carnival rides, food booths, arts and crafts booths, and a parade. Look for a Farmers' Market next to

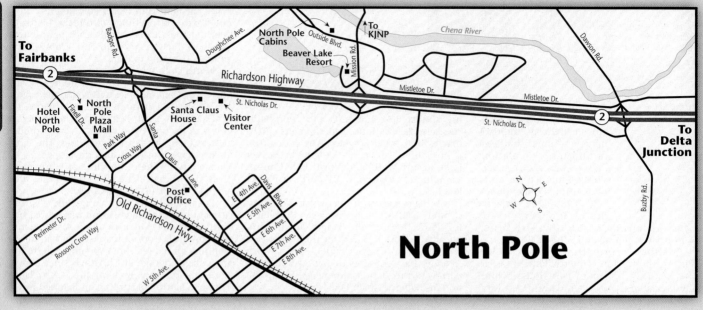

North Pole

Santa Claus House during the summer. Every third Friday of the month, celebrate local artists at the Third Friday Art Show at the North Pole Grange. North Pole has an annual Winter Carnival the first weekend of December with fireworks display, candle and tree lighting ceremonies, food and craft booths and other activities. Check out the www.christmasinice.org for an ice carving event in December.

Radio station KJNP (King Jesus North Pole), operated by Calvary's Northern Lights Mission, broadcasts music and religious programs on 1170 AM and 100.3 FM. The station was started in April 1956, by the late Don and Gen Nelson. The inspiration for the station came one Christmas when weather kept the couple from flying out to their ministry among rural villages. Instead, they broadcast their Christmas message from Fairbanks, and received such an overwhelming response that they started a regular program called "Far North Gospel Song and Hymn Time."

Visitors are welcome between 9 A.M. and 6 P.M.; large group tours may be arranged by calling (907) 488-2216. KJNP is located on Mission Road, about 0.6 mile northeast of the Richardson Highway (turn west in front of the large church). The missionary project includes a dozen hand-hewn, sod-roofed homes and other buildings constructed of spruce logs.

Return to Milepost V 348.5 or V 349 Richardson Highway

NORTH POLE ADVERTISERS

Yellowhead Highway 16

CONNECTS: Edmonton, AB to Prince Rupert, BC

Length: 902 miles   Road Surface: Paved   Season: Open all year

(See maps, page 228-230)

Scenic Yellowhead Highway 16 passes mountains, forest, rivers and farmland. (© Michael K. Robb)

Major Attractions:

Canadian Rockies/ Jasper National Park, 'Ksan, Mt. Robson, Fort St. James, North Pacific Cannery

Highest Summit:
Obed Summit 3,819 ft.

ellowhead Highway 16 is a paved trans-Canada highway that extends from Winnipeg, Manitoba, through Saskatchewan, Alberta and British Columbia to the coastal city of Prince Rupert. (The highway connecting Masset and Queen Charlotte on Graham Island is also designated Yellowhead Highway 16.) *The MILEPOST®* logs Yellowhead Highway 16 from Edmonton, AB, to Prince Rupert, BC, which is a distance of 902 miles/1,452 km. Prince Rupert is a port for BC Ferries and for the Alaska Marine Highway System to southeastern Alaska cities.

This is a major east–west route, providing access to a number of attractions in Alberta and British Columbia. Yellowhead Highway 16 is also a very scenic highway, passing through mountains, forest and farmland. Visitor services are readily available in towns along the way, and campsites may be found in towns and along the highway at both private and provincial park campgrounds. (It is unsafe and illegal to overnight in rest areas.)

Yellowhead Highway 16 Log

This section of the log shows distance from Edmonton (E) followed by distance from Prince George (PG).

Distance in miles	Edmonton	Jasper	Prince George	Prince Rupert	Terrace
Edmonton		220	454	902	810
Jasper	220		234	682	590
Prince George	454	234		448	356
Prince Rupert	902	682	448		92
Terrace	810	590	356	92	

The Yellowhead Highway log is divided into 2 sections: Edmonton to Prince George, and Prince George to Prince Rupert.

YELLOWHEAD HIGHWAY 16A WEST

E 0 PG 454 (730.6 km) **Junction** of Anthony Henday Drive North/Highway 216 with Highway 16A West/Stony Plain Road. *NOTE: Southbound travelers may bypass Edmonton city centre by taking Highway 216 south, skirting downtown but accessing businesses like the West Edmonton Mall. You will rejoin the East Access Route at* **Milepost CB 375.3;** *see page 68.*

E 3.9 (6.3 km) PG 450.1 (724.3 km)
(Continues on page 231)

Yellowhead Highway 16

Edmonton, AB to Prince George, BC (includes Bighorn Hwy.)

© 2014 The MILEPOST®

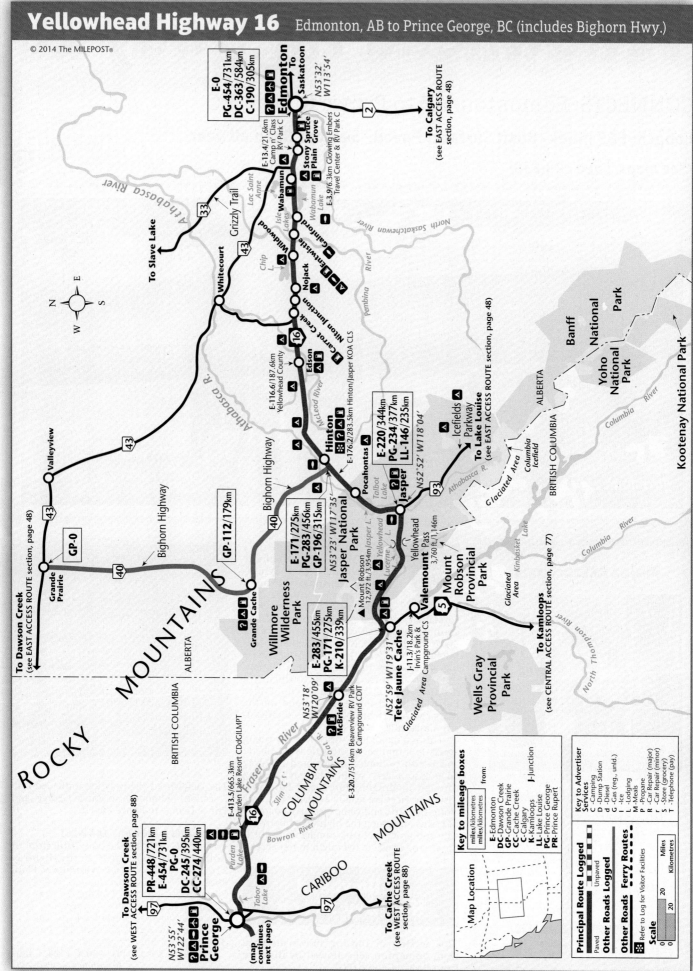

E-0
PG-454/731km
DC-363/584km
C-190/305km

E-13.4/21.6km
Camp n' Class
RV Park C

E-3.9/6.3km Glowing Embers
Travel Center & RV Park C

N53°32'
W113°54'

To Edmonton
To Saskatoon

To Calgary
(see EAST ACCESS ROUTE
section, page 48)

Stony Spruce
Plain Grove

Lac Saint
Anne

Athabasca River

Grizzly Trail

33

43

Whitecourt

To Slave Lake

Isle Wabamun
Lakes

Wabamun
Lake

North Saskatchewan River

Wildwood

Chip
L.

Entwistle

Nojack

Pembina River

Carrot Creek

Niton Junction

16

Edson

E-116.6/187.6km
Yellowhead County

Athabasca R.

McLeod River

E-171/275km
PG-283/456km
GP-196/315km

Bighorn Highway

40

Hinton

E-176.2/283.5km Hinton/Jasper KOA CLS

Pocahontas

E-220/344km
PG-234/377km
LL-146/235km

N53°23' W117°35'
Jasper National
Park

Talbot
Lake

Jasper

93

Icefields
Parkway

N52°52' W118°04'

To Lake Louise
(see EAST ACCESS ROUTE section, page 48)

Columbia
Icefield

Glaciated Area

Banff
National
Park

Yoho
National
Park

Kootenay National Park

ALBERTA

BRITISH COLUMBIA

Columbia River

Valleyview

43

GP-112/179km

Bighorn Highway

40

GP-0

43

To Dawson Creek
(see EAST ACCESS ROUTE section, page 48)

Grande
Prairie

40

Grande Cache

Willmore
Wilderness
Park

E-171/275km
PG-283/456km
GP-196/315km

ROCKY MOUNTAINS

ALBERTA

BRITISH COLUMBIA

▲ Mount Robson
12,972 ft./3,954m

Jasper L.

Lucerne
L.

Yellowhead
L.

Yellowhead
Pass
3,760 ft./1,146m

Mount
Robson
Provincial
Park

Valemount

5

Glaciated
Area

Kinbasket
Lake

Columbia River

North Thompson River

E-283/455km
PG-171/275km
K-210/339km

N53°78'
W120°09'

McBride

E-413.5/665.3km
Purden Lake Resort CDdGILMPT

E-320.7/516km Beaverview RV Park
& Campground CDIT

N52°59' W119°31'
Tete Jaune Cache

J-11.3/18.2km
Irvin's Park &
Campground CS

Glaciated Area

Wells Gray
Provincial
Park

To Kamloops

To Cache Creek
(see CENTRAL ACCESS ROUTE section, page 77)

Fraser River

Goat R.

Slim Cr.

COLUMBIA MOUNTAINS

CARIBOO MOUNTAINS

16

Bowron River

Purden
Lake

97

To Dawson Creek
(see WEST ACCESS ROUTE section, page 88)

PR-448/721km
E-454/731km
PG-0
DC-245/395km
CC-274/440km

N53°55'
W122°44'

Prince
George

97

To Cache Creek
(see WEST ACCESS ROUTE section, page 88)

Tabor
Lake

(map
continues
next page)

Key to mileage boxes

miles/kilometres
miles/kilometres   from:

E-Edmonton
DC-Dawson Creek
GP-Grande Prairie
C-Calgary
CC-Cache Creek
K-Kamloops
LL-Lake Louise
PG-Prince George
PR-Prince Rupert

J-Junction

Key to Advertiser Services

C –Camping
D –Dump Station
d –Diesel
G –Gas (reg., unld.)
I –Ice
L –Lodging
M–Meals
P –Propane
R –Car Repair (major)
r –Car Repair (minor)
S –Store (grocery)
T –Telephone (pay)

Map Location

Principal Route Logged

Paved
Unpaved

Other Roads Logged   Ferry Routes

Refer to Log for Visitor Facilities

Scale

0   20   Miles

0   20   Kilometres

www.themilepost.com

© 2014 The MILEPOST®

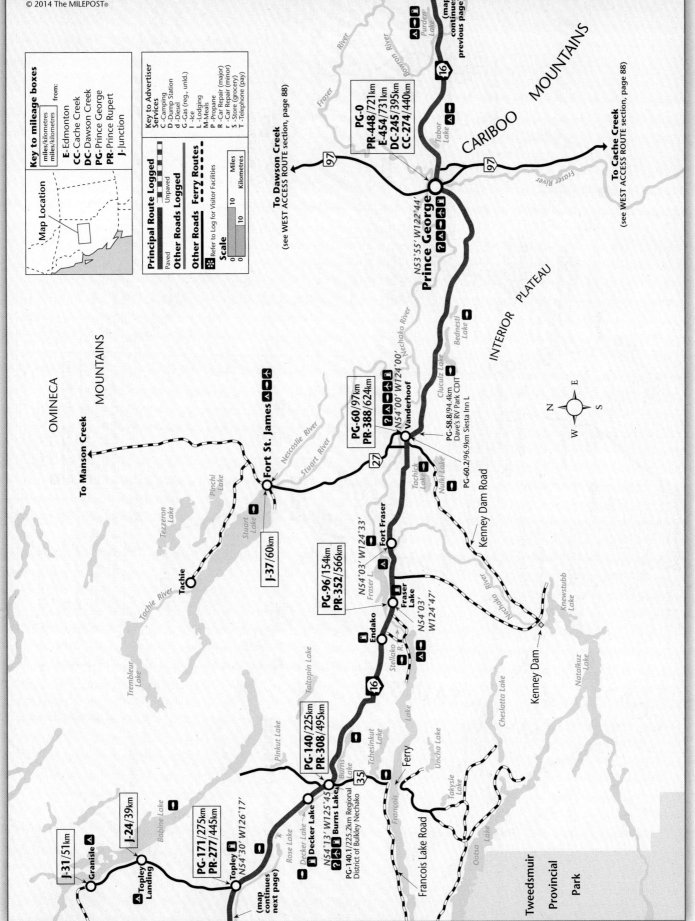

Key to mileage boxes

miles/kilometres
miles/kilometres
from:

E- Edmonton
CC- Cache Creek
DC- Dawson Creek
PG- Prince George
PR- Prince Rupert
J- Junction

Map Location

Key to Advertiser Services

C -Camping
D -Dump Station
d -Diesel
G -Gas (reg., unld.)
I -Ice
L -Lodging
M -Meals
P -Propane
R -Car Repair (major)
r -Car Repair (minor)
S -Store (grocery)
T -Telephone (pay)

Principal Route Logged
Paved
Unpaved

Other Roads Logged

Ferry Routes

Refer to Log for Visitor Facilities

Scale
Miles
0   10
0   10
Kilometres

CARIBOO MOUNTAINS

(map continues previous page)

16

PG-0
PR-448/721km
E-454/731km
DC-245/395km
CC-274/440km

To Dawson Creek
(see WEST ACCESS ROUTE section, page 88)

97

To Cache Creek
(see WEST ACCESS ROUTE section, page 88)

Prince George
N53°55' W12°44'

97

Fraser River

Tabor Lake

Purden Lake

Bowron River

Fraser River

INTERIOR PLATEAU

Bednesti Lake

Nechako River

OMINECA MOUNTAINS

To Manson Creek

Fort St. James

Nescoslie River

Stuart River

Pinchi Lake

Tezzeron Lake

Stuart Lake

J-37/60km

Tachie

Tachie River

Trembleur Lake

Babine Lake

PG-60/97km
PR-388/624km

Vanderhoof
N54°00' W124°00'

27

PG-58.8/94.4km Dave's RV Park CDIT
PG-60.2/96.9km Siesta Inn L

Cluculz Lake

Clucuiz Lake

Nulki Lake

Tachick Lake

Kenney Dam Road

Knewstubb Lake

Kenney Dam

Natalkuz Lake

PG-96/154km
PR-352/566km

Fort Fraser
N54°03' W124°33'

Fraser L.

Fraser Lake
N54°03' W124°47'

Endako
Stellako R.

Nechako River

Cheslatta Lake

16

Taltapin Lake

Tchesinkut Lake

Uncha Lake

Takysie Lake

Francois Lake Road

Ferry

Francois Lake

Oosa Lake

PG-140/225km
PR-308/495km

35

Pinkut Lake

Burns Lake

Burns Lake
N54°13' W125°45'

PG-140.1/225.2km Regional District of Bulkley Nechako

Decker Lake

Rose Lake

Decker Lake

J-31/51km

Granisle

J-24/39km

Topley Landing

PG-171/275km
PR-277/445km

Topley
N54°30' W126°17'

(map continues next page)

Tweedsmuir Provincial Park

Yellowhead Highway 16 Topley, BC, tp Prince Rupert, BC

© 2014 The MILEPOST®

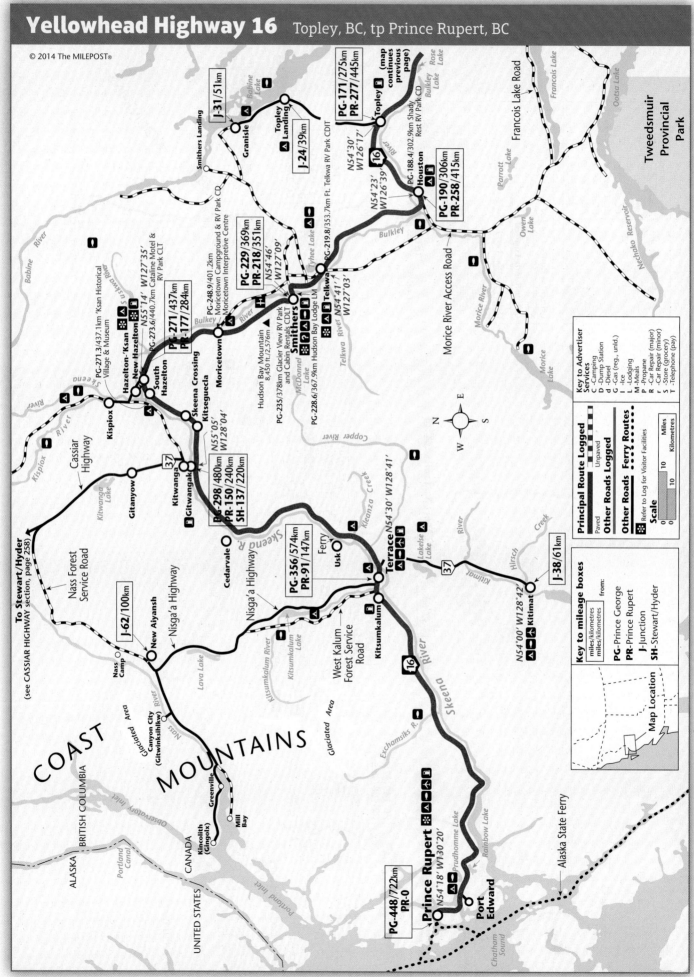

(Continued from page 227)
Exit to Devon Bypass/Highway 60. Access to Glowing Embers campground this exit.
Glowing Embers Travel Center & RV Park. See display ad page 67.

NOTE: Southbound travelers may bypass Edmonton by taking Highway 60 south, then Highway 19 east to Highway 2 (Devonian Way Bypass).

Junction with Highway 60 south to Highway 19 east and Edmonton Bypass route. See "Devonian Way Bypass" on page 65 and read log back to front.

E 6.4 (10.3 km) **PG 447.6** (720.3 km) Several U-pick locations near here.

E 9.2 (14.8 km) **PG 444.8** (715.8 km) **Spruce Grove Grain Elevator and Archives.** Tour the Spruce Grove Grain Elevator Museum, one of Alberta's last remaining wooden grain elevators and still in working condition, was built in 1958. To get here, go south on Golden Spike Road, then east on Railway Ave. Elevator is visible from Hwy 16A/Parkland Highway. Open Tuesday–Saturday 10 A.M.–3 P.M.; phone 780-960-4600 or visit the website at sprucegroveagsociety.com for more information. Events throughout the summer months.

E 10.2 (16.4 km) **PG 443.8** (714.2 km) Stoplight at Campsite Road in **SPRUCE GROVE** (pop. 23,326). All visitor facilities including hotels, motels, restaurants, fastfood, gas stations with diesel, shopping malls and all emergency services. Chamber of Commerce tourist information building at northwest edge of Rotary Park on Highway 16A, open year-round, weekends only; phone 780-962-2561. This is just to the west of Walmart, Subway, and other businesses. Nice picnic grounds here.

E 11.1 (17.9 km) **PG 442.9** (712.7 km) Distance marker westbound shows Stony Plain 6 km/4 miles, Edson 178 km/111 miles, Jasper 338 km/210 miles.

E 11.5 (18.5 km) **PG 442.5** (712.1 km) Rotary Park to south.

E 11.6 (18.7 km) **PG 442.4** (711.9 km) Turnout and Welcome to Spruce Grove sign for eastbound motorists. Spruce Grove visitor centre.

E 12.7 (20.4 km) **PG 441.3** (710.2 km) Entering Stony Plain westbound.

E 13.4 (21.6 km) **PG 440.6** (709 km) Turnoff for business park in **STONY PLAIN** (pop. 14,711). **Emergency Services:** RCMP, Fire Station and hospital dial 911. All visitor facilities including hotels, motels, restaurants, camping (**Camp n' Class** and Lions RV Park) supermarkets, shopping mall and gas stations with diesel and major repair service. Attractions in Stony Plain include 31 historic outdoor murals; Oppertshauser Art Gallery; and the Pioneer Museum. The Multicultural Heritage Centre here has historical archives, a craft shop and home-cooked meals.

Camp n' Class RV Park. Newly built RV park located on Hwy 16A and 50th St., in Stony Plain. Open year round. We have 77 sites, all big rig friendly, with full services including a patio and 50 amp power. Laundry, showers, WiFi and cable also available$. Gated park with managers on site. Easy access off Hwy 16A. Close to West Edmonton Mall, golf courses, and all town services. Reservations accepted. Call 855-455-2299 or

book online at www.campinclass.com. We accept Visa, MC, debit and cash. See display ad this page. [ADVERTISEMENT]

E 14.3 (23 km) **PG 439.7** (707.6 km) Exit on Secondary Road 779 for Stony Plain visitor centre (2 km/1.2 miles), housed in the **Dog Rump Creek railway station** at the Rotary Park rest area 4815 – 44th Ave. Open July and August 8:30 A.M. to 5:30 P.M. weekdays, 9:30 A.M. to 5:30 P.M. weekends; September and June weekdays only. Phone 780-963-4545.

E 17.3 (27.8 km) **PG 436.7** (702.8 km) Allan Beach Resort turnoff to north.

E 18 (29 km) **PG 436** (701.6 km) Turnoff for Hasse Lake Parkland County day-use area (10 km/6 miles south).

E 18.5 (29.8 km) **PG 435.5** (700.8 km) Turnoff for Hubbles Lake, 2 km/1.2 miles north; camping. Spring Lake to the south (shopping, gas).

E 20.1 (30.3 km) **PG 433.9** (698.3 km) Beach Corner, gas, diesel, auto repair, propane, cafe, store and liquor to north.

E 21.9 (35.2 km) **PG 432.1** (695.4 km)

Junction of Yellowhead Highway 16A with Highway 43 North. If you are continuing west for Prince George or Prince Rupert, BC, continue with this log. If you are heading north for Dawson Creek, BC, via Valleyview and Grande Prairie, turn to **Milepost E 21.9** on page 68 of the EAST ACCESS ROUTE section for log of Highway 43 North.

HIGHWAY 16

E 29.1 (46.8 km) **PG 424.9** (683.8 km) Gas station with diesel to south at Duffield turnoff.

E 31.8 (51.2 km) **PG 422.2** (679.4 km) **Wabamun Lake Provincial Park**, 1.8 miles/3 km east of Wabamun, then 1 mile/1.6 km south on access road; camping (276 sites), coin-op showers, hookups, public phones, sani-dump $3, picnicking, fishing, boating and swimming. Camping fees $21–$27. May–mid-October.

E 34 (54.7 km) **PG 420** (675.9 km) Overpass; exit for village of **WABAMUN** (pop. 662); **Emergencies:** dial 911. Services include gas, propane, hardware store, convenience store, car wash, laundromat, library, liquor store, groceries, bank, dump station, 3 hotels/motels, 1 bed and breakfast and post office. Wabamun Waterfront Park has a cooking area, shelter, water spray park, tables, boat launch, litter bins, washroom/changing rooms and flush toilets. Total of 6 city parks. World's largest dragonfly statue greets all visitors as they enter Wabamun.

E 37.9 (61 km) **PG 416.1** (669.6 km) Watch for evidence of strip mining for coal along the highway.

E 41.4 (66.6 km) **PG 412.6** (664 km) **FALLIS** (pop. 190); store.

E 45.1 (72.6 km) **PG 408.9** (658 km) Exit to Seba Beach, Isle Lake.

E 47.6 (76.6 km) **PG 406.4** (654 km) *NOTE: Slow for 80-kmph/50-mph speed zone*

Rotary Park picnic area at Stony Plain's Dog Rump Creek railway station visitor centre.
(©Claire Torgerson, staff)

Edson's Centennial Park and Galloway Station Museum. (©Brian Stein)

Edson

E 116.6 (187.6 km) **PG 337.4** (543 km) Highway 16 westbound and eastbound lanes form the main avenues of Edson, with services located along the highway and cross-streets. **Population:** 8,646. **Emergency Services: Hospital, Fire Department** and RCMP, dial 911.

Visitor Information: At Galloway Station Museum and Travel Centre, easily accessible from Yellowhead Highway 16; RV parking, coffee bar, free WiFi, restrooms. For more information on Edson, http://gallowaystationmuseum.com or www.edson.ca.

Edson is a large highway community with all services, including about a dozen motels, gas stations and truck stops, restaurants and major chain fast-food outlets. Edson's economy is based on coal mining, forestry, oil, natural gas and manufacturing. Active oil and gas exploration workers may fill up local hotel and motel rooms, so reserve ahead.

Recreatonal facilities include Kinsmen Spray Park, indoor pool, curling and ice rinks, 18-hole golf course, skageboard park, movie theatre and library. Camping at Lions Park Campground. Sani-dump on 1st Avenue between 56th and 57th streets.

Yellowhead County. See display ad facing page.

Yellowhead Highway 16 Log
(continued)

E 118.3 (190.3 km) **PG 335.7** (540.2 km) Edson airport.

E 118.7 (191 km) **PG 335.3** (539.6 km) Turnoff for Wilmore Park, 3.7 miles/6 km south; 41 campsites, self-register. Boat launch, fishing, hiking trails, day-use areas with picnic tables, camping fee $10.

E 120 (193.1 km) **PG 334** (537.5 km) *Begin 4-lane divided highway west. Resume 110 kmph/68 mph speed limit westbound.*

E 123.8 (199.2 km) **PG 330.2** (531.4 km) **Junction** with Highway 47 South.

E 126.2 (203.1 km) **PG 327.8** (527.5 km) Sundance Creek.

E 128.4 (206.6 km) **PG 325.6** (524 km) Hornbeck Creek Provincial Recreation Area to north; 33 campsites, picnic area, water pump. Open May 1–Oct. 12, camping fee $15.

E 141.3 (227.4 km) **PG 312.7** (503.2 km) Westbound-only roadside turnout with picnic tables, pit toilets and litter bins; generous, paved parking area.

E 143.4 (230.7 km) **PG 310.6** (499.8 km) Eastbound-only turnout with litter bins.

E 148.9 (239.6 km) **PG 305.1** (491 km) **Obed Lake Provincial Park** to north; 7 campsites, day-use area, firewood, pit toilets, boat launch, beach area. Open May 1–Nov. 30; camping fee $10. Fishing for brown trout, and eastern brook trout.

E 157.3 (253.1 km) **PG 296.7** (477.5 km) **Obed Summit**, highest elevation on the Yellowhead Highway at 3,819 feet/ 1,164m.

E 158.6 (255.2 km) **PG 295.4** (475.4 km) Westbound roadside turnout; generous parking area, picnic tables, toilets and litter bins. Good view of the Rockies from here.

E 161.7 (260.2 km) **PG 292.3** (470.4 km)

---

entering **GAINFORD** (pop. 205); cafe, hotel and post office. Public park with 8 campsites.

E 56.1 (90.3 km) **PG 397.9** (640.3 km) Overpass. Exit north for **ENTWISTLE** (pop. 453) town centre; food, lodging, store. Esso gas station to south. Camping at **Pembina River Provincial Park**, 1.9 miles/3.1 km north, near Pembina River gorge; 132 campsites, tables, showers, flush toilets, water and dump station. Camping fee charged. Open May 3–Oct. 11. Fishing, swimming, playground and phone. Fee $21–$27.

E 56.6 (91.1 km) **PG 397.4** (639.5 km) Pembina River bridge. Exit to **EVANSBURG** (pop. 879), gas station, restaurants, grocery store, lodging, recreation centre.

E 65.6 (105.6 km) **PG 388.4** (625 km) Exit to Chip Lake and **WILDWOOD** (pop. 277), the "Bingo Capital of Canada." Post office, hotel, gas station, restaurants and shops. Campground at **Chip Lake** (5.6 miles/9 km north, and 6.5 miles/10.5 km west of Wildwood) with 22 sites, $20 fee, tables, firewood, pull-throughs, pit toilets, water, fishing, swimming, boat launch.

E 67.9 (109.2 km) **PG 386.1** (621.3 km) Views of Chip Lake to north.

E 82.2 (132.3 km) **PG 371.8** (598.3 km) Nojack Recreation Area to north; day-use shelter, water/pump, camping (24 sites), open May 1–Oct. 31, camping fee $15.

E 88.4 (142.2 km) **PG 365.6** (588.4 km) Lobstick River.

E 89.1 (143.4 km) **PG 364.9** (587.2 km) **NITON JUNCTION.** Esso and Shell gas stations, restaurant and store to north.

E 92.8 (149.3 km) **PG 361.2** (581.3 km) **CARROT CREEK**; convenience store and gas station.

E 97.5 (156.9 km) **PG 356.5** (573.7 km) **Junction** with Highway 32 which leads 42 miles/67.6 km north to Peers, Whitecourt

---

and Highway 43.

E 99.2 (159.6 km) **PG 354.8** (571 km) Truck weigh scales, turnout with litter barrel.

E 101.9 (164 km) **PG 352.1** (566.6 km) Turnoff for Wolf Lake West Provincial Recreation Area, located 33 miles/53 km south on gravel road; 32 campsites, pit toilets, boat launch, water pumps, firewood. Open May–Oct. 13. Nightly fee $20.

E 104.9 (168.8 km) **PG 349.1** (561.8 km) Westbound turnoff for Edson rest area to south. Nice large facility off highway with flush toilets, water, tables, shelter, phone and sani-dump.

E 105.9 (170.4 km) **PG 348.1** (560.2 km) Rosevear Road; eastbound access to Edson rest area. Turn north on Rosevear Road to the Rosevear Ferry that departs from here. One of the few remaining Alberta ferries, it runs from May–October and has been in operation for more than 70 years.

E 107.9 (173.6 km) **PG 346.1** (557 km) Wild Rose Campground 3.1 miles/5 km north.

E 110.1 (177.2 km) **PG 343.9** (553.4 km) East of Edson RV Park to south.

E 113.2 (182.1 km) **PG 340.8** (548.4 km) McLeod River.

E 115 (185 km) **PG 339** (545.5 km) *Begin 80 kmph/50mph speed zone westbound entering Edson.*

E 115.6 (186 km) **PG 338.4** (544.6 km) Welcome to Edson sign westbound.

E 115.9 (186.5 km) **PG 338.1** (544.1 km) Edson RV Campground and 18-hole golf course and driving range to south.

E 116.6 (187.6 km) **PG 337.4** (543 km) Gas station, motel, fast-food and Lions Park Campground at east end of Edson.

Slow for 50 kmph/32 mph speed zone in town.

Highway 16 splits westbound, with 1-way westbound and eastbound lanes forming the main avenues of Edson.

Watch for elk and other wildlife along Yellowhead Highway 16.

(©Brian Stein)

Willowbrook Cabins RV Park to south.

E 167.7 (269.8 km) **PG 286.3** (460.7 km) Welcome to Hinton sign westbound.

E 168.8 (271.6 km) **PG 285.2** (459 km) Lakeview Inn & Suites and Esso gas station.

E 169.6 (272.9 km) **PG 284.4** (457.7 km) Turnoff for Day's Inn and Super 8 to north.

E 170.4 (274.2 km) **PG 283.6** (456.4 km) View of Hinton industrial area.

Begin 60 kmph/37 mph speed zone westbound.

Hinton

E 170.9 (275 km) **PG 283.1** (455.6 km) Stoplight in downtown Hinton. Hinton is a 3-hour drive from Edmonton and just east of the Bighorn Highway 40 junction. **Population:** 9,769. **Emergency services:** ambulance, fire, RCMP, dial 911. **Hospital, dentist** and **RCMP** post in town.

Visitor Information: Information Centre at **Milepost E 171**, phone 1-877-446-8666; Open daily Victoria Day to Canadian Thanksgiving 9 A.M. to 7 P.M.; winter hours Monday–Friday 9 A.M. to 5 P.M. Or contact Town of Hinton, phone 1-780-865-6000; www.tourhinton.ca.

A major service stop on Yellowhead Highway 16, Hinton has all visitor facilities, including major chain hotels/motels, restaurant and fast-food outlets; gas stations; RV parts and services; Safeway supermarket; shopping centres and shopping mall; bowling alley, curling rink, golf course and recreation complex with indoor pool. Big box stores include Walmart and Canadian Tire. Hinton is only 17.5 miles/28 km east of Jasper National Park gate, 4 miles/6.4 km east of the Bighorn Highway, 50 miles/80 km west of Edson and 178 miles/287 km west of Edmonton.

Camping at **Hinton/Jasper KOA**, located just west of the Bighorn Highway 40 North

junction; full hookups, pull-through sites, cabins, pets welcome. There are also several campgrounds within William A. Switzer Provincial Park along Highway 40 North (read through the "Bighorn Route" log this section).

East side of town, the Hinton Centre (Aboriginal Centre) has a city campground ($25 per night, no hook-ups, hot showers, fire pits, picnic tables, wooded sites). From west side, follow signs which lead through downtown.

Hinton began in the 1900s as a construction camp for railroad, coal mining and logging crews. The community grew dramatically after construction of the pulp mill in 1955. Major industry in community and surrounding area includes coal mining, forestry, oil and gas and tourism. Hinton's latest attraction is the 1.9 mile/3 km Beaver Boardwalk, winding through wetlands and offering views of an actively used beaver pond. The Hinton Mountain Bike Park and trails offer outdoor adventure and fun for all ages and skill levels. Ask for directions and a map at the Visitor Information Centre.

Yellowhead Highway 16 Log

(continued)

E 171.6 (276.1 km) **PG 282.4** (454.5 km) Second stoplight westbound in Hinton; access to Husky truck stop, Boston Pizza, Subway, Tim Hortons and other services.

E 172.3 (277.2 km) **PG 281.7** (453.3 km) The Hinton golf club has a new clubhouse with a spectacular view and Gateway RV Park turnoff.

E 172.6 (277.7 km) **PG 281.4** (452.9 km) Stoplight. Access to Parks West Mall; Walmart, Canadian Tire, Safeway, Best Western and McDonald's.

E 173.1 (278.5 km) **PG 280.9** (452 km) *Begin 100 kmph/62 mph speed limit westbound.*

E 173.8 (279.6 km) **PG 280.2** (450.9 km) **Junction** with Bighorn Highway 40 South.

E 175 (281.6 km) **PG 279** (449 km) **Junction** with Bighorn Highway 40 North

(paved) which leads 84 miles/135 km to Grande Cache and 196 miles/315 km to Grande Prairie.

Junction with Bighorn Highway 40 to Grande Cache and Grande Prairie. See "Bighorn Route" log beginning on facing page.

E 175.5 (282.4 km) **PG 278.5** (448.2 km) *End divided 4-lane highway, begin 2-lane highway with passing lanes westbound.*

E 176.2 (283.5 km) **PG 277.8** (447.1 km) **Hinton/Jasper KOA.** Highway 16 just 11 miles east of Jasper Park East Gate or 2.5 miles west of Hinton. Full hookups, 30–50 amps. Long pull-through sites. Big rigs and groups welcome. Kamping Kabins, Cabins, Deluxe Cabins, Lodges, Kamping Kitchen. Two laundries. Tent sites. Free wireless Internet. Free TV all sites. Convenience store, gift shop. Toddlers playroom. Handicap accessible. Pets welcome, on/off leash areas, pet playground. Central firepit building. Excellent base camp for touring Jasper National Park; half-mile off of Highway 40, "The scenic route to Alaska." Reservations phone 1-888-562-4714. Email brownkoa4@shaw.ca. N 53.35 W 117.65. See display ad page 233.

E 178.1 (286.6 km) **PG 275.9** (444 km) Jasper–Hinton airport.

E 179.5 (288.8 km) **PG 274.5** (441.8 km) Maskuta Creek. Private campground.

E 180.6 (290.6 km) **PG 273.4** (440 km) Weigh scales to south.

E 182 (292.8 km) **PG 272** (437.7 km) Turnoff for Wildhorse Lake Provincial Recreation Area, 3.1 miles/5 km north; camping (33 sites), water pump, firewood, hiking, fishing, boat launch. Open May 1–Oct. 31; camping fee $18/night.

E 184.4 (296.7 km) **PG 269.6** (433.9 km) Folding Mountain campground and cabins.

E 184.6 (297 km) **PG 269.4** (433.6 km) Eastbound roadside turnout with litter bin.

E 185.4 (298.3 km) **PG 268.6** (432.3 km) Westbound Folding Mountain rest area turnout with toilets, litter bins and point of interest sign about Yellowhead.

E 185.9 (299.1 km) **PG 268.1** (431.5 km) Food and lodging to north.

E 186.9 (300.7 km) **PG 267.1** (429.8 km) *CAUTION: Watch for bighorn sheep on and alongside the highway.*

E 187.6 (310.8 km) **PG 266.4** (428.7 km) **Jasper National Park, East Entrance.** Park fees are charged on a per-person basis and must be paid by all visitors using facilities in Rocky Mountain national parks. No charge for motorists passing through park on Highway 16. Public phones. RCMP phone number for Jasper 780-542-4848.

Alberta's Jasper National Park is part of the Canadian Rocky Mountains World Heritage Site. It is the largest of Canada's Rocky Mountain parks, covering 4,200 square miles/20,878 square kms. It adjoins Banff National Park to the south. Visitors can sightsee this spectacular mountain scenery from Highway 93 (Icefields Parkway).

Highway 16 has restricted speed zones through the park. Drive carefully and watch for wildlife. NOTE: It is illegal to feed, touch, disturb or hunt wildlife in the national park. All plants and natural objects are also protected and may not be removed or destroyed.

(Continues on page 237)

Bighorn Route

The Bighorn Highway (Alberta Highway 40) is a 202-mile/325-km route connecting Yellowhead Highway 16 and Highway 43. It is a 2-lane paved highway with moderate grades and curves and good mountain views. Watch for logging activity signs as well as signs noting reforestation projects within the first 45 miles/72.4 km of the road. Additional passing lanes are frequently provided for uphill stretches. Narrow shoulders, turnout only in designated locations. The 3 major communities along this route—Hinton (on Yellowhead 16), Grande Cache (on Highway 40), and Grande Prairie (on Highway 43)—have all visitor facilities. For emergencies along this route dial 911. Speed limit is 100 kmph/62 mph.

A cache welcomes visitors to Grande Cache on the Bighorn Highway.
(©Claire Torgerson, staff)

ALBERTA HIGHWAY 40

Distance from Yellowhead Highway 16 junction (Y) is followed by the distance from Grande Prairie (GP).

Y 0 GP 195.6 (314.8 km) Junction with Yellowhead Highway 16 at **Milepost E 175**, just west of Hinton.

Y 0.1 (0.2 km) GP 195.5 (314.6 km) Distance marker northbound shows Muskeg 113 km/70 miles, Grande Cache 142 km/88 miles, Grande Prairie 325 km/202 miles.

Y 2 (3.2 km) GP 193.6 (311.6 km) Community of **ENTRANCE** (pop. 15) to west. Railroad crossing overpass.

Y 3 (4.8 km) GP 192.6 (310 km) Athabasca River bridge.

Y 3.5 (5.6 km) GP 192.1 (309.2 km) Access road west to community of Brule (10 miles/16 km). Hinton airfield to east.

Y 4.6 (7.4 km) GP 191 (307.4 km) Entrance Ranch; trail rides.

Y 6.6 (10.6 km) GP 189 (304.2 km) *CAUTION: Logging trucks crossing* (sign).

Y 7.4 (11.9 km) GP 188.2 (302.8 km) Athabasca Lookout Nordic Centre (0.6 miles/1 km).

Y 7.9 (12.7 km) GP 187.7 (302 km) Turnout to east with litter bins and information sign about William A. Switzer Provincial Park.

Y 8.7 (14 km) GP 186.9 (300.7 km) Access road leads east to **Jarvis Lake** day-use area; water, phone, beach and boat launch.

Y 9 (14.5 km) GP 186.6 (300.2 km) Distance marker northbound shows Muskeg 90 km/56 miles, Grande Cache 119 km/74 miles, Grande Prairie 302 km/188 miles.

Y 11.3 (18.2 km) GP 184.3 (296.5km) Jarvis Creek.

Y 12.4 (20 km) GP 183.2 (294.8 km) William A. Switzer Provincial Park at **Kelley's Bathtub** to the west, offers a seasonal visitor centre (10 A.M.–4:15 P.M. or later, Thursdays to Sundays) and a day-use area to west; large easy-access parking area with toilets, public phone, swimming and hiking trail.

Y 13.9 (22.3 km) GP 181.7 (292.4 km) Winter Creek.

Y 14 (22.5 km) GP 181.6 (292.2 km) Side road to east leads 1.2 miles/2 km to Cache Lake and 2.4 miles/4 km to Graveyard Lake. **Cache Lake Campground** has 14 sites, sewer hookups, water pump, picnic tables, shelter, children's playground, camping fee $16. **Graveyard Lake Campground** has 12 sites, sewer hookups, water available at Cache Lake campground; fee $16.

Y 15.4 (24.8 km) GP 180.2 (289.9 km) Access road to east leads to **Gregg Lake** day-use area and campground; 164 sites, sewer hookups, tap water, picnic tables, shelter, playground, fish-cleaning stand, beach, hiking trails, boat launch, dock, public phone. Camping fee based on site chosen $18-$25.

Y 16.5 (26.5 km) GP 179.1 (288.2 km) Turnout to west with litter bins and information sign about **William A. Switzer Provincial Park** for southbound travelers.

Y 17.6 (28.3 km) GP 178 (286.5 km) Hay River Road. Distance marker northbound shows Muskeg 77 km/48 miles, Grande Cache 106 km/66 miles, Grande Prairie 289 km/180 miles.

Y 21.4 (34.4 km) GP 174.2 (280.3 km) Wild Hay River bridge.

Y 24.1 (38.8 km) GP 171.5 (276 km) Willmore Wilderness Park and side road to west leads 32 miles/51.5 km to **Rock Lake** Provincial Recreation Area and Campground on Rock Lake; 93 sites, sewer hookups, water pump, tables, shelter, trails, boat launch, camping fee of $15.

Y 32.3 (52 km) GP 163.3 (262.8 km) Distance marker northbound shows Muskeg 53 km/33 miles, Grande Cache 82 km/51 miles, Grande Prairie 265 km/165 miles.

Y 36.1 (58.1 km) GP 159.5 (256.7 km) *CAUTION: Railroad crossing* (sign).

Y 39.5 (63.6 km) GP 156.1 (261.5 km) Little Berland River bridge.

Y 41.2 (66.3 km) GP 154.4 (248.4 km) Fox Creek.

Y 42.1 (67.8 km) GP 153.5 (247 km) Damaged road surface with some bad potholes next 3 miles.

Y 45.9 (73.9 km) GP 149.7 (240.9 km) *CAUTION: Wild game on road next 32 kms/20 miles northbound.*

Y 46.9 (75.5 km) GP 148.7 (239.3 km) Wildlife sanctuary next 40 km/25 miles northbound. No hunting within 365m/400 yards of the road.

Y 47.3 (76.1 km) GP 148.3 (238.7 km) Berland River bridge. Big Berland Provincial Recreation Area's Big Berland Campground is at north end of bridge to west adjacent railroad tracks. It has 18 sites, sewer hookups, water pump, picnic tables, shelter, camping fee $20. Information boards on Cariboo Country.

Y 48.4 (77.9 km) GP 147.2 (236.9 km) Distance marker northbound shows Muskeg 27 km/17 miles, Grande Cache 56 km/35 miles, Grande Prairie 239 km/149 miles.

Y 48.6 (78.2 km) GP 147 (236.6 km) Cabin Creek.

Y 48.9 (78.7 km) GP 146.7 (236.1 km) Welcome to Yellowhead County, southbound.

Y 50.3 (80.9 km) GP 145.3 (233.8 km) Hendrickson Creek.

Y 51 (82.1 km) GP 144.6 (232.7 km) Welcome to the Municipal District of Greenview.

Y 54.4 (87.5 km) GP 141.2 (227.2 km) Wildlife Sanctuary.

Y 54.5 (87.7 km) GP 141.1 (227.1 km) Shand Creek.

Y 58.4 (94 km) GP 137.2 (220.8 km) Improved highway with wide shoulders next 5 miles/8 km northbound.

Y 59.7 (96.1 km) GP 135.9 (218.7 km) Burleigh Creek.

Y 62 (99.8 km) GP 133.6 (215 km) Pierre Grey's Lakes Provincial Recreation Area 3 km/1.8 miles to east; 83 campsites, pump water, picnic tables, shelter, fireplaces, firewood (for sale), hiking trails, boat launch, fishing, camping fee $20. Open May 1 to September 30.

Y 63.7 (102.5 km) GP 131.9 (212.2 km) Muskeg (pop. approximately 12).

Y 63.9 (102.8 km) GP 131.7 (212 km) Lone Teepee Creek.

Y 64 (103 km) GP 131.6 (211.7 km) Roadside turnout to east with Caribou Country signage.

Y 65.2 (104.9 km) GP 130.4 (209.8 km) Long paved turnout with litter bin.

Y 66.5 (107 km) GP 129.1 (207.7 km) Distance marker Grande Cache 27 km/16.7 miles, Grande Prairie 210 km/130.5 miles.

Bighorn Route
(continued)

Y **68.3** (109.9 km) **GP 127.3** (204.9 km) Veronique Creek.

Y **70.2** (113 km) **GP 125.4** (201.8 km) Findley Creek.

Y **71.2** (114.6 km) **GP 124.4** (200.2 km) User-maintained campground, no fee.

Y **71.4** (114.9 km) **GP 124.2** (199.9 km) Muskeg River bridge.

Y **72.2** (116.2 km) **GP 123.4** (198.6 km) Foothills Forest Products. *CAUTION: Logging trucks turning.*

Y **72.3** (116.4 km) **GP 123.3** (198.4 km) Mason Creek day–use area; picnic facilities and hiking trail to the Muskeg River.

Y **72.9** (117.3 km) **GP 122.7** (197.5 km) Access road to Grande Cache airport.

Y **74.3** (119.6 km) **GP 121.3** (195.2 km) Roadside turnout with litter bin to north with access to Muskeg Falls.

Y **76.2** (122.6 km) **GP 119.4** (192.2 km) *CAUTION: Use lower gear on narrowed road.*

Y **77.6** (124.9 km) **GP 118** (190 km) Susa Creek.

Y **78.3** (126 km) **GP 117.3** (188.8 km) Washy Creek Rough surface northbound 2 miles.

Y **80.1** (128.9 km) **GP 115.5** (185.9 km) Carconte Creek.

Y **80.8** (136 km) **GP 114.8** (184.7 km) **Grande Cache Lake** to south; picnic area, swimming, boat launch. Easy access for RVs.

Y **81.2** (130.7 km) **GP 114.4** (184.1 km) Allen Creek.

Y **82.3** (132.4 km) **GP 113.3** (182.3 km) *Slow for speed zone: 80 kmph/50 mph.*

Y **82.6** (132.9 km) **GP 113** (181.9 km) **Victor Lake** to south; canoeing, fishing. ⊷

Y **82.9** (133.4 km) **GP 112.7** (181.4 km) Northbound passing lane, ascending.

Grande Cache

Y **84.1** (135.3 km) **GP 111.5** (179.4 km) Entering Grande Cache northbound; visitor information and interpretive centre east side of highway. Grande Cache is 132 miles/212 km northwest of Jasper, Alberta. **Population**: 3,783. **Emergency services: RCMP, Ambulance, Fire department**, 911; **Hospital**, phone 780-827-3701.

Visitor Information: Grande Cache Tourism and Interpretive Centre is located at 9701 100th Street (Highway 40) at the south entrance into town. Summer hours from May 21–Oct. 10 daily open 9 A.M.–5 P.M. daily; winter (remaining dates) 9 A.M.–5 P.M. Monday–Saturday. Phone ahead to double check on hours: 780-827-3300 or 1-888-827-3790; email: tourism@grandecache.ca; www.grandecache.ca. They offer hiking guides, exhibits and displays spanning history from ice age to mining and trapping.

Elevation: 4,200 feet/1,280m. **Private Aircraft:** Grande Cache airport, 12 miles/19 km east on Highway 40; elev. 4,117 feet/1,255m; length 5,000 feet/1,524m; asphalt; no fuel available.

Grande Cache was established in 1969 in conjunction with resource development

Dramatic scenery at Sulphur Gates Provincial Park north of Grande Cache.
(©Brian Stein)

by McIntyre Porcupine Coal Ltd. In 1980 a sawmill was built by British Columbia Forest Products Ltd. and in 1984 a medium security correctional centre opened.

Historically, the location was used as a staging area for fur trappers and Natives prior to their departure to trap lines in the valleys and mountain ranges now known as Willmore Wilderness Park. Upon their return, they stored large caches of furs while waiting for transportation opportunities to trading posts. A "cache" is basically a cabin on stilts, and the origin of the city's name. Translated from French, it is pronounced "cash" and means "large storage place."

Visitor facilities include 4 motels, 3 hotels, several B & B's and lodging houses, restaurants, 2 banks and 2 credit unions, 3 real estate agencies, laundromats, 3 service stations (Petro-Can, Esso, Fas-Gas) and car washes. Shopping facilities include several small shopping centres, a supermarket, and 2 department stores. WiFi is available at Noelle's Cafe in the mall, and at the Tourism Centre. Public use computers available at municipal library and Far Side Convenience.

Grande Cache has been dubbed the "ATV Capital of Alberta," so inquire locally about trails. MILEPOST readers have commented on the great swimming pool available at the Akasaka Recreation Centre for a reasonable admission fee. The $26-million facility has the swimming pool (lap swim hours available), saunas, fitness rooms, a curling rink and skating rink.

Grande Cache Golf and Country Club, located in the northeast part of town, has 9 holes, clubhouse and pro shop.

Camping at municipal campground at the north end of town (take golf course turn-off); 77 serviced sites, full and partial hook-ups, washroom facilities, showers, public phone, laundromat, fee $20-25, open May 20 to October 12th.

No services northbound, next 184 km/114 miles.

Grande Cache Tourism Centre. See display ad on page 233.

Bighorn Route Log
(continued)

Y **84.5** (136 km) **GP 111.1** (178.8 km) Turnoff to east for golf course and Grande Cache Municipal Campground.

Y **87.3** (140.5 km) **GP 108.3** (174.3 km) Turnoff for **Smoky River** South Provincial Recreation Area; 22 sites in campground (fee $20), water pump, firewood, firepits, tables, pit toilets, boat launch. May–October. Fishing for arctic grayling, Dolly Varden, whitefish. ⊷ 🛶

Y **87.4** (140.7 km) **GP 108.2** (174.1 km) Smoky River bridge (wood deck).

Long, straight, uphill and downhill grades (to 7 percent) next 85 miles/137 km northbound.

Y **88.1** (141.8 km) **GP 107.5** (173 km) Distance marker northbound shows Grande Prairie 181 km/112 miles.

Y **88.2** (141.9 km) **GP 107.4** (172.8 km) Turnoff for Sulphur Gates Provincial Recreation Area (4 miles/6.4 km south); 11 sites, boil tap water for drinking, camping fee $20, May–October.

Y **88.3** (142.1 km) **GP 107.3** (172.7 km) Trail access to Willmore Wilderness Park. Horse staging area for entering Willmore Wilderness Park. May–October.

Y **90.5** (144.8 km) **GP 105.1** (169.1 km) User-maintained camping area both sides of highway. Wooded with picnic tables, firepits. No charge (signed).

Y **92.4** (148.7 km) **GP 103.2** (166.1 km) Posted speed limit is 80 kmph/50 mph.

Y **93.7** (150.8 km) **GP 101.9** (164 km) Beaverdam Road to Caw Ridge Wildlife Refuge.

Y **96** (154.5 km) **GP 99.6** (160.3 km) Northbound, the highway parallels the Northern Alberta Resource Railroad and the Smoky River.

Y **96.5** (155.3 km) **GP 99.1** (159.5 km) Alberta Power H.R. Milner Generating Station, Grande Cache Coal Corp. with smokestacks. Turnout to east for views. Litter bins.

Y **102.2** (164.5 km) **GP 93.4** (150.3 km) Turnoff east to Sheep Creek Provincial Recreation Area; 9 sites, camping fee $21, shaded picnic tables, water pump, firepits, firewood, litter bins, outhouses, hiking trails, equestrian trails and gravel parking. Smoky River boat launch. May–October.

Y **102.7** (165.3 km) **GP 92.9** (149.5 km) Sheep Creek.

Y **103.3** (166.2 km) **GP 92.3** (148.5 km) Sheep Creek Road.

Y **105.5** (169.8 km) **GP 90.1** (145 km) Wanyandie Road. *NOTE: Highway climbs series of uphill grades to 7 percent northbound.*

Y **111.2** (179 km) **GP 84.4** (135.8 km) Roadside turnout to east; litter bin.

Y **112** (180.2 km) **GP 83.6** (134.5 km) Roadside turnout to west; litter bin.

Y **114.5** (184.3 km) **GP 81.1** (130.5 km) Prairie Creek Road.

Y **120.2** (193.4 km) **GP 75.4** (121.3 km) Southview Provincial Recreation Area to east; parking area, 8 campsites edging a circle drive, picnic tables, litter bins, outhouses, seasonal highbush cranberries. Camping fee $20.

Y **123.8** (199.2 km) **GP 71.8** (115.6 km) *CAUTION: Logging trucks on roads next 60 km/37 miles.*

Y 125.5 (202 km) **GP 70.1** (112.8 km) 16th base line sign marks north–south hunting boundary.

Y 130.7 (210.3 km) **GP 64.9** (104.4 km) *CAUTION: Use lower gears, steep descent northbound.*

Y 135.4 (217.9 km) **GP 60.2** (96.9 km) Roadside turnout with litter bin to east.

Y 137.4 (221.1 km) **GP 58.2** (93.7 km) *CAUTION: Steep descent northbound.*

Y 140.4 (225.9 km) **GP 55.2** (88.8 km) Kakwa River bridge.

Y 140.6 (226.3 km) **GP 55** (88.5 km) **Kakwa River** Provincial Recreation Area has 14 campsites, picnic tables, firewood, firepits, water pump, litter bins, outhouses, parking area. User maintained, no fee. Open May–mid-September. Fish for arctic grayling.

Y 150.2 (241.7 km) **GP 45.4** (73 km) *CAUTION: Logging trucks entering road.*

Y 153.5 (247 km) **GP 42.1** (67.8 km) Access road leads east 3.6 miles/6 km to **Musreau Lake** Campground and day-use area; 50 picnic sites, 69 campsites, fee $20, picnic tables, firewood, firepits, water pump, litter bins, outhouses, equestrian trails, swimming, boat launch and fishing. Open mid-May–mid-October.

Y 157.1 (252.8 km) **GP 38.5** (62 km) *CAUTION: 7 percent descent, trucks use lower gears.*

Y 158.5 (255.1 km) **GP 37.1** (59.7 km) Cutbank River bridge. Camping both sides of the bridge for user-maintained campground, no fee. Current status unknown.

Y 159.8 (257.2 km) **GP 35.8** (57.6 km) Elk Creek.

Y 174.7 (281.2 km) **GP 20.9** (33.6 km) Big Mountain Creek.

Y 176.4 (283.9 km) **GP 19.2** (30.9 km) Bald Mountain Creek.

Y 182.5 (293.6 km) **GP 13.1** (21.1 km) Turnoff for Grovedale (11 km/7 miles).

Y 184.6 (297.1 km) **GP 11** (17.7 km) Bent Pipe Creek.

Y 187.7 (302.1 km) **GP 7.9** (12.7 km) Ainsworth O.S.B. Plant.

Y 192.7 (310.1 km) **GP 2.9** (4.7 km) Junction with Highway 666 which leads southwest to **O'Brien Provincial Park** day-use area; Dunes Golf and also access to **Nitehawk Ski Area** which has a full-service RV park in summer with dump station, showers, laundry.

Y 192.9 (310.4 km) **GP 2.7** (4.3 km) Wapiti River bridge.

Y 194.5 (313.1 km) **GP 1.1** (1.8 km) Turnoff for **Camp Tamarack RV Park**; full service sites, dump station, showers, laundry.

Y 194.6 (313.2 km) **GP 1** (1.6 km) Grande Prairie city limit.

Y 195.6 (314.8 km) **GP 0** Entering Grande Prairie northbound.

Junction with Highway 43. Turn to page 73 for description of Grande Prairie and page 75 for continuation of EAST ACCESS ROUTE log to Dawson Creek, BC, and Mile 0 of the Alaska Highway.

Turn to Milepost E 281
East Access Route or Milepost E 175
Yellowhead Highway

Dramatic mountain scenery and beautiful Athabasca River in Jasper National Park.
(©Michael K. Robb)

(Continued from page 234)

E 192 (308.9 km) **PG 262** (421.6 km) Pocahontas Cabins on highway; turnoff to south for **POCAHONTAS** (1.2 miles/2 km) and Miette Hot Springs Road to Pocahontas Campground, 0.6 mile/1 km, with 140 sites, open mid-May to mid-October, fee $22. Miette Hot Springs Pool is located 11 miles/17 km from the highway via this side road. There are 2 manmade pools fed by sulfur hot springs; bathing suit and towel rentals available. Beautiful setting. Open May to mid-October, fee charged; website www.pc.gc.ca/hotsprings.

E 195 (313.8 km) **PG 259** (416.8 km) Turnout to south with cairn, litter bin and pit toilet. Mineral lick here is frequented by goats and sheep. Watch for wildlife, especially at dawn and dusk.

E 195.4 (314.4 km) **PG 258.6** (416.1 km) Park area with litter bin by Rocky River. View of Pyramid Mountain.

E 195.9 (315.2 km) **PG 258.1** (415.4 km) First Rocky River crossing westbound.

E 197 (317 km) **PG 257** (413.6 km) Roadside turnout to north with litter bin.

E 197.3 (317.5 km) **PG 256.7** (413.1 km) Second Rocky River crossing westbound.

E 197.6 (317.9 km) **PG 256.4** (412.6 km) Roadside turnout to north with toilets and litter bin.

E 199.7 (321.3 km) **PG 254.3** (409.2 km) Roadside turnout to south by Talbot Lake; litter bin, pit toilet.

E 201.5 (324.2 km) **PG 252.5** (406.3 km) Roadside turnout to south with litter bin.

E 205.2 (330.2 km) **PG 248.8** (400.4 km) *CAUTION: Watch for elk westbound. Posted speed limit westbound 70 kmph/43 mph.*

E 205.5 (330.7 km) **PG 248.5** (399.9 km) Roadside turnout to south with litter bin.

E 205.8 (331.1 km) **PG 248.2** (399.4 km) Roadside turnout to south with litter bin.

E 206.2 (331.8 km) **PG 247.8** (398.8 km) Two bridges cross the Athabasca River.

E 207.1 (333.2 km) **PG 246.9** (397.3 km) View of "The Palisades" to north.

E 208.2 (335 km) **PG 245.8** (395.6 km) Snaring River bridge.

E 209.8 (337.6 km) **PG 244.2** (393 km) Jasper airfield to south.

E 211.4 (340.1 km) **PG 242.6** (390.4 km) Snaring River Campground (66 sites) and Palisades Centre to north, fee $16; primitive, open mid-May to mid-September.

E 212.1 (341.3 km) **PG 241.9** (389.3 km) Palisades picnic area.

E 213.2 (343 km) **PG 240.8** (387.4 km) Mount Edith Cavell and Colin Range viewpoint to south.

E 215.1 (346.1 km) **PG 238.9** (384.5 km) Roadside turnout to south with litter bin.

E 215.6 (346.9 km) **PG 238.4** (383.6 km) Turnout to north with information sign.

E 216.1 (347.7 km) **PG 237.9** (382.9 km) Access road south to Jasper Park Lodge (lodging, restaurant, golf), scenic Maligne Canyon (7 miles/11.5 km) and Maligne Lake (30 miles/48 km). Glacier-fed Maligne Lake is one of Jasper's premier attractions; scheduled boat tours, reserve ahead in Jasper, shuttles available. www.malignelake.com.

E 216.6 (348.6 km) **PG 237.4** (382 km) Turnout to south with litter barrel.

E 217.1 (349.4 km) **PG 236.9** (381.2 km) First turnoff westbound for Jasper.

E 217.3 (349.7 km) **PG 236.7** (380.9 km) Pine Bungalows to south.

E 218.6 (351.8 km) **PG 235.4** (378.8 km) Turnout to south with litter barrel; mountain viewpoint.

E 219.1 (352.6 km) **PG 234.9** (378 km) **Junction** with Highway 93A.

E 219.9 (353.9 km) **PG 234.1** (376.7 km) Stoplight at **junction** with Highway 93.

Turnoff to north for **JASPER** (pop. 4,643), townsite and park headquarters for Jasper National Park. **Emergencies:** dial 911. RCMP 780-542-4848.

Visitor Information: Jasper National Park Information Centre, housed in the historic 1914 building that originally housed park administration offices, offers maps, brochures, permits and visitor information. Open year-round, phone 780-852-6176, email pnj.jnp@pc.gc.ca.

Food, gas, diesel (at Petro Canada and Esso) and lodging available year-round, with

Rearguard Falls is an easy 5-minute downhill walk from the parking area along the highway. (©Linda Martin)

accommodations ranging from bungalows to luxury lodges like Jasper Park Lodge. A popular ski area in winter, Jasper also offers a variety of summer attractions, including fishing, hiking, horseback riding, rafting, boating, and boat tours on Maligne Lake.

Turnoff to south for scenic Highway 93 (Icefields Parkway) to Columbia Icefield, Lake Louise, Banff and Trans-Canada Highway 1 to Calgary.

Junction with Highway 93 (Icefields Parkway) south. Turn to the end of "Canadian Rockies Alternate Route" on page 62 and read log back to front.

NOTE: No fuel next 63 miles/101 km westbound on Highway 16 until Tete Jaune Cache.

E 220.4 (354.7 km) **PG 233.6** (375.9 km) Roadside turnout to south with information sign and litter bin and recycling.

E 220.5 (354.6 km) **PG 233.5** (375.8 km) Miette River.

E 221.7 (356.8 km) **PG 232.3** (373.8 km) Roadside turnout to north with litter bin.

E 222.3 (357.7 km) **PG 231.7** (372.9 km) Roadside turnout to north with litter bin.

E 225.6 (363 km) **PG 228.4** (367.6 km) Paved turnout to north on Miette River with pit toilet, litter bins and interpretive sign about Yellowhead Pass.

E 226.7 (364.8 km) **PG 227.3** (365.8 km) Meadow Creek bridge.

E 226.8 (364.9 km) **PG 227.2** (365.6 km) Trailhead parking to north for Virl Lake, Dorothy Lake and Christine Lake.

E 229.5 (369.3 km) **PG 224.5** (361.3 km) Clairvaux Creek.

E 232.6 (374.3 km) **PG 221.4** (356.3 km) *Slow to 60 kmph/37 mph speed limit on grade westbound.*

E 232.9 (374.7 km) **PG 221.1** (355.8 km) **Jasper National Park, West Entrance.** Park fee must be paid by all visitors using facilities in Rocky Mountain national parks. No charge for motorists passing through park on Highway 16. Pay phone.

E 235.4 (378.8 km) **PG 218.6** (351.8 km) **Yellowhead Pass** (elev. 3,760 feet/1,146m), Alberta–British Columbia border and east

entrance to **Mount Robson Provincial Park**. This park is designated a UNESCO World Heritage Site. Very nice rest area to north on picturesque Portal Lake; picnic tables, pit toilets, information board and hiking trail.

Named for an Iroquois trapper and guide who worked for the Hudson's Bay Co. in the early 1800s. His light-colored hair earned him the name Tete Jaune ("yellow head") from the French voyageurs.

TIME ZONE CHANGE: Alberta observes Mountain standard time. Most of British Columbia observes Pacific standard time. Both observe daylight saving time.

E 235.7 (379.2 km) **PG 218.3** (351.3 km) Large turnout to south with litter barrel.

E 238.8 (384.2 km) **PG 215.2** (346.3 km) Long narrow turnout to north with litter barrel and toilet.

E 239.2 (384.8 km) **PG 214.8** (345.6 km) Turnoff downhill to north for **Yellowhead Lake**; 2 picnic tables, litter bin, boat launch and fishing. Mount Fitzwilliam viewpoint.

E 241 (387.8 km) **PG 213** (342.7 km) **Mount Robson Provincial Park's Lucerne Campground** to north; 36 sites, picnic tables, hand water pump, pit toilets, firewood, swimming, horseshoe pits; camping fee $16.

E 242.8 (390.7 km) **PG 211.2** (339.9 km) Fraser Crossing rest area to south with litter bins and information sign.

E 242.9 (390.8 km) **PG 211.1** (339.8 km) Fraser River bridge No. 1.

E 244.7 (393.8 km) **PG 209.3** (336.8 km) Turnout to trail that goes to Mount Fitzwilliam. Litter bins and toilet.

E 244.8 (393.9 km) **PG 209.2** (336.7 km) Ghita Creek.

E 245.9 (395.7 km) **PG 208.1** (334.9 km) Fraser River bridge No. 2.

E 249.7 (401.8 km) **PG 204.3** (328.8 km) Grant Brook Creek.

E 252.6 (406.5 km) **PG 201.4** (324.1 km) Moose River bridge.

E 253 (407.1 km) **PG 201** (323.5 km) Mount George Graham view to north (sign).

E 254.7 (409.8 km) **PG 199.3** (320.7

km) Rest area to south at east end of **Moose Lake**; information sign, litter bin, pit toilet and boat launch, fishing.

E 256.2 (412.2 km) **PG 197.8** (318.3 km) The Comb view to south (sign).

E 257.8 (414.9 km) **PG 196.2** (315.7 km) Emerald Ridge view to south (sign).

E 259.3 (417.2 km) **PG 194.7** (313.3 km) Roadside turnouts both sides of highway; litter bin to north.

E 263.3 (423.6 km) **PG 190.7** (306.9 km) Large paved turnout to south with litter bins. Avalanche gates.

E 267.4 (430.2 km) **PG 186.6** (300.2 km) Turnout with litter bin to south.

E 268.1 (431.4 km) **PG 185.9** (299.1 km) *Begin long downhill grade westbound.*

E 270.3 (434.9 km) **PG 183.7** (295.6 km) Short turnout to south. Watch for falling rocks.

E 271.7 (437.2 km) **PG 182.3** (293.3 km) Avalanche gates.

E 271.8 (437.3 km) **PG 182.2** (293.2 km) **Overlander Falls** rest area to south; pit toilets, litter bins. Trail leads downhill to Overlander Falls viewpoint; allow about 20 minutes round-trip.

E 272.7 (438.8 km) **PG 181.3** (291.7 km) Viewpoint of **Mount Robson** (elev. 12,972 feet/3,954m), highest peak in the Canadian Rockies. The Visitor Infocentre (to north) is open daily in summer 8 A.M.–7 P.M.; gas, cafe, picnic tables, restrooms and litter bins. Berg Lake trailhead. **Mount Robson Provincial Park's Robson Meadows Campground** south of highway with 125 treed sites, sanistation, showers, pay phone, interpretive programs, tables, firewood, flush toilets, water and horseshoe pits; group camping; camping fee $21.

E 273.2 (439.6) **PG 180.8** (290.9 km) **Mount Robson Provincial Park's** Robson River Campground to north with 19 sites (some wheelchair-accessible), tables, firewood, pit toilets, showers, water and horseshoe pits; camping fee $21.

E 273.7 (440.4 km) **PG 180.3** (290.1 km) Robson River bridge. Look for Indian paintbrush June through August.

E 273.7 (440.4 km) **PG 180.3** (290.1 km) West entrance to **Mount Robson Provincial Park**. Turnout with litter bin and statue.

E 274.3 (441.3 km) **PG 179.7** (289.1 km) Turnout to south.

E 275.2 (442.8 km) **PG 178.8** (287.7 km) Swift Current Creek.

E 276 (444.2 km) **PG 178** (286.4 km) Gravel turnout to north.

E 277.3 (446.2 km) **PG 176.7** (284.3 km) Robson Shadows Campground.

E 278.3 (447.8 km) **PG 175.7** (282.7 km) **Mount Terry Fox rest area**; picnic tables, restrooms, phone and viewing telescope. The information board here points out the location of Mount Terry Fox in the Selwyn Range of the Rocky Mountains. The peak was named in 1981 to honour cancer victim Terry Fox, who, before his death from the disease, raised some $25 million for cancer research during his attempt to run across Canada.

E 279.3 (449.4 km) **PG 174.7** (281.1 km) Turnout to north with Yellowhead Highway information sign.

E 279.5 (449.7 km) **PG 174.5** (280.8 km) **Rearguard Falls Provincial Park** picnic area. Easy 5-minute walk downhill

to falls viewpoint. (CAUTION: Steep drop-offs, supervise children; pets on leash.) Upper limit of 800-mile/1,300-km migration of Pacific salmon; look for king salmon in late summer. Plan at least a half-hour to enjoy this amazing natural attraction.

E 280.8 (451.8 km) **PG 173.2** (278.7 km) Turnout with litter bin to south overlooking Fraser River. Avalanche gates.

E 282.2 (454.1 km) **PG 171.8** (276.4 km) Weigh scales. NOTE: 60 kmph/37 mph speed zone.

E 282.5 (454.5 km) **PG 171.5** (275.9 km) Tete Jaune Cache rest area; double-ended turnout with tables, litter bin and toilets.

E 282.9 (455.2 km) **PG 171.1** (275.3 km) **Junction** with Yellowhead Highway 5 south to **VALEMOUNT** (all services); camping at **Irvin's Park & Campground.** Web address: www.irvinsrvpark.com.

Irvin's Park & Campground. See display ad this page.

Junction with Yellowhead Highway 5 South to Valemount (12 miles/20 km), Wells Gray Provincial Park (134 miles/216 km) and Kamloops (210 miles/339 km). Southbound travelers turn to page 87 in the CENTRAL ACCESS ROUTE and read log back to front.

E 283.5 (456.2 km) **PG 170.5** (274.3 km) Lodge to south; food, gas, lodging, camping and rafting.

E 287.1 (461.9 km) **PG 166.9** (268.5 km) Spittal Creek Interpretive Forest to north; hiking trails, tables, litter bins and toilets.

E 292 (469.8 km) **PG 162** (260.7 km) Terracanna Resort to south; food, lodging.

E 292.9 (471.3 km) **PG 161.1** (259.2 km) Small River rest area to north by stream; picnic tables, toilets and litter bins.

E 297.5 (478.7 km) **PG 156.5** (251.8 km) Horsey Creek.

E 303.6 (488.5 km) **PG 150.4** (242 km) CAUTION: Watch for deer next 15 km/9 miles westbound; 80 kmph/50 mph speed limit.

E 304 (489.1 km) **PG 150** (241.4 km) Turnoff to south for settlement of Dunster; gas only, open until 5 P.M.

E 307.8 (495.3 km) **PG 146.2** (235.2 km) Holiday Creek.

E 308.3 (496.1 km) **PG 145.7** (234.4 km) Baker Creek rest area to south with tables, litter bin and toilets.

E 312.8 (503.3 km) **PG 141.2** (227.2 km) Golf course, cafe and camping to north.

E 315 (506.8 km) **PG 139** (223.7 km) Beaver Falls to north, hiking trail.

E 315.3 (507.3 km) **PG 138.7** (223.2 km) Holmes River.

E 320.7 (516 km) **PG 133.3** (214.5 km) **Beaverview RV Park & Campground;** grassy pull-through sites, hookups, laundry and sani-station. McBride Park, across from the RV park, has hiking trails.

Beaverview RV Park & Campground. See display ad this page.

E 321.2 (516.9 km) **PG 132.8** (213.7 km) Fraser River bridge. Regional park on west side of bridge; picnic tables, gazebos, toilets, litter bins.

E 321.6 (517.5 km) **PG 132.4** (213 km) Turnout to north with welcome sign, information boards and litter bin.

Historic train station houses McBride's Visitor Centre, a cafe and The Whistle Stop Gallery.
(©Michael K. Robb)

Entering McBride westbound. NOTE: Next gas westbound is 91 miles/146 km from here at Purden Lake Resort (summer only).

McBride

E 322.1 (518.3 km) **PG 131.9** (212.2 km) Turn off Highway 16 on Bridge Road to south for McBride town centre. **Population:** 740. **Elevation:** 2,350 feet/722m. **Visitor Information:** In the historic train station at the end of Main Street, 0.6 mile/1 km south of main highway; open daily, 9 A.M. to 5 P.M., June to September; 10 A.M. to 4 P.M., October to May. Phone 250-569-3366; toll-free 1-866-569-3366. The Beanery 2 Internet cafe, located in the train station, serves breakfast, homemade soup and sandwiches, and locally roasted coffee. Adjacent the cafe is **The Whistle Stop Gallery,** featuring local art.

Located in the Robson Valley by the Fraser River, the village of McBride was established in 1913 as a divisional point on the railroad and was named for Richard McBride, then premier of British Columbia. Forest products, agriculture and tourism are the mainstays of the local economy. **The Valley Museum and Archives,** at 241 Dominion St., displays local history as well as current artists.

McBride has all visitor facilities, including hotels/motels, bed and breakfasts, cabin rentals, supermarket, convenience/video stores, clothing stores, The Whistle Stop Gallery, several restaurants, a pharmacy, hospital and 2 gas/diesel stations (1 with

dump/transfer station, 1 co-op card lock, propane at JNR Auto Services). Full-service camping at **Beaverview RV Park & Campground**.

Yellowhead Highway 16 Log

(continued)

E 322.2 (518.4 km) **PG 131.8** (212.1 km) Food and lodging.

E 322.9 (519.5 km) **PG 131.1** (210.9 km) Roadside turnout to south with litter bin.

E 325.3 (523.4 km) **PG 128.7** (207.1 km) Dore River bridge.

E 330.8 (532.3 km) **PG 123.2** (198.2 km) Macintosh Creek.

E 332.2 (534.5 km) **PG 121.8** (196 km) Clyde Creek.

E 340.4 (547.7 km) **PG 113.6** (182.8 km) Highway crosses deep gorge of West Twin Creek.

E 347.3 (558.8 km) **PG 106.7** (171.7 km) Goat River bridge. Paved rest area to north with tables, toilets and litter bins.

E 351.2 (565.1 km) **PG 102.8** (165.4 km) Turnoff for Little LaSalle Recreation Area and BC Forest Service site to south.

Watch for bears browsing highway verge.

E 353.6 (568.9 km) **PG 100.4** (161.5 km) Snowshoe Creek.

E 364.5 (586.5 km) **PG 89.5** (144 km) Ptarmigan Creek.

E 367.6 (591.5 km) **PG 86.4** (139 km) Double-ended turnout to north with litter bin.

E 371.9 (598.4 km) **PG 82.1** (132.1 km) Winding 6 percent downgrade next mile westbound.

E 373 (600.2 km) **PG 81** (130.3 km) Dome Creek.

E 377.3 (607.1 km) **PG 76.7** (123.4 km)

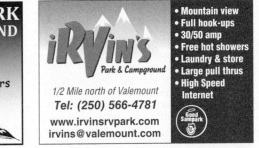

Sunday morning in Prince George means little traffic on Victoria Street. (© Kris Valencia, staff)

Slim Creek rest area to south with information kiosk, tables, playground, litter bins and wheelchair-accessible toilets. Watch for bears.

E 378.1 (608.4 km) **PG 75.9** (122.1 km) Slim Creek bridge.

E 382.1 (615 km) **PG 71.7** (115.5 km) **Ancient Rainforest Trail.** Trailhead parking to south at former gravel pit. Walk through a fascinating ancient forest.

E 389.7 (627 km) **PG 64.3** (103.5 km) Driscol Creek.

E 391.8 (630.4 km) **PG 62.2** (100.1 km) Roadside turnout to north with litter bin.

E 393 (632.3 km) **PG 61** (98.1 km) Lunate Creek.

E 396 (637.2 km) **PG 58** (93.3 km) Grizzly Den and Raven Lake Provincial Park Area. Grizzly hiking trail to south.

E 396.2 (637.5 km) **PG 57.8** (93 km) Hungary Creek. Sugarbowl Grizzly Den Provincial park boundary.

E 399.9 (643.4 km) **PG 54.1** (87 km) Sugarbowl Creek, gravel turnout to north.

E 403.4 (649.1 km) **PG 50.6** (81.4 km) Sugarbowl chain-up area eastbound, to the south.

E 404.3 (650.5 km) **PG 49.7** (80 km) Turnout to north with litter bin.

E 405.7 (652.8 km) **PG 48.3** (77.7 km) Kenneth Creek.

E 412.5 (663.7 km) **PG 41.5** (66.8 km) Purden Mountain ski resort.

E 413.1 (665.3 km) **PG 40.5** (65.2 km) **Purden Lake Resort** to north (description follows); cafe, fuel (May–September), phone, lodging and camping.

Purden Lake Resort. Lakefront RV park with marina and sandy beach; full hookups; sani-dump; hot coin shower; laundry; playground. Restaurant, fuel station (unleaded, diesel, propane) 60 kms/40 miles east of Prince George, 145 kms/90 miles west of McBride. P.O. Box 1239, Prince George, BC V2L 4V3. Phone 250-565-7777, www. purden.com. [ADVERTISEMENT]

NOTE: Next gas eastbound is 91 miles/146 km from here (McBride).

E 415.1 (667.9 km) **PG 38.9** (61.8 km) Turnoff for **Purden Lake Provincial Park**, 1.9 miles/3 km north; 78 campsites, day-use area with 48 picnic tables, water, dump station $5; firewood, litter and recycling bins, playground and horseshoe pits. Sandy beach,

change houses, swimming, walking trails, paddling, waterskiing and boat launch. Rainbow fishing to 4 lbs. Camping fee $16. No highway noise. Open May–Sept. 21.

E 417 (671 km) **PG 37** (59.5 km) Bowron River bridge.

E 417.1 (671.1 km) **PG 36.9** (59.4 km) Turnoff to north for rest area at west end of Bowron River bridge; toilets, tables and litter bins. Entrance on curve; use care.

E 424.2 (682.5 km) **PG 29.8** (47.9 km) Vama Vama Creek.

E 427.2 (687.4 km) **PG 26.8** (43.1 km) Wansa Creek.

E 430.3 (692.4 km) **PG 23.7** (38.1 km) Willow River bridge.

E 430.5 (692.7 km) **PG 23.5** (37.8 km) Willow River rest area to north at west end of bridge beside river; tables, litter bins, toilets and nature trail. The 1.2-mile-/1.9-km-long Willow River Forest Interpretation Trail is an easy 45-minute walk.

E 432.8 (696.4 km) **PG 21.2** (34.1 km) Bowes Creek.

E 432.9 (696.5 km) **PG 21.1** (33.9 km) Double-ended turnout to north with litter bins and information board on forest fire and moose habitat. Circle trail to moose observation site.

E 436.7 (702.7 km) **PG 17.3** (27.8 km) Large turnout to north with litter bin.

E 438.5 (705.5 km) **PG 15.5** (24.9 km) Tabor Mountain ski hill to south.

E 438.8 (706 km) **PG 15.2** (24.5 km) Turnout to north with litter bin.

E 439.5 (707.2 km) **PG 14.5** (23.3 km) *Begin 7 percent downgrade on curve westbound.*

E 440.9 (709.4 km) **PG 13.1** (21.1 km) **Tabor Lake** to south; good fishing for rainbow in spring.

E 448.1 (721 km) **PG 5.9** (9.5 km) **Junction** with bypass route to Highway 97 South. *(Southbound travelers using this bypass will join Highway 97 at **Milepost CC 266.4** in 6.2 miles; turn to page 109 in the WEST ACCESS ROUTE section and read log back to front.)* Reduce speed westbound.

E 448.7 (722 km) **PG 5.3** (8.5 km) Chevron gas station.

E 449.1 (722.6 km) **PG 4.9** (7.9 km) View of Prince George westbound from small turnout as Highway 16 descends to the

Fraser River.

E 450.7 (725.3 km) **PG 3.3** (5.3 km) Fraser River bridge.

E 451 (725.7 km) **PG 3** (4.8 km) Welcome to Prince George (westbound sign).

E 451.9 (727.1 km) **PG 2.1** (3.4 km) **Prince George Downtown Visitor Centre** (free WiFi) on First Avenue; phone 250-562-3700.

See map and description of Prince George beginning on page 110 in the WEST ACCESS ROUTE section.

E 452 (727.3 km) **PG 2** (3.2 km) Stoplight, turn left Highway 16 becomes Victoria Street westbound through downtown Prince George.

E 453 (728.9 km) **PG 1** (1.6 km) Highway 16/Victoria Street **junctions** with 20th Avenue in Prince George; gas stations. Turn west on 20th to continue on Highway 16 West. Turn east on 20th Avenue for Fort George Park.

E 454 (730.5 km) **PG 0 Junction** of Highway 16 and Highway 97. Continue west on Yellowhead Highway 16 for Prince Rupert (log follows).

Junction with Highway 97 south to Cache Creek and north to Dawson Creek and the beginning of the Alaska Highway. Turn to page 114 in the WEST ACCESS ROUTE section for the log of Highway 97 North. Turn to page 110 for Highway 97 South and read log back to front.

This section of the log shows distance from Prince George (PG) followed by distance from Prince Rupert (PR).

NOTE: Physical kilometreposts along Highway 16 between Prince George and Prince Rupert reflect distance from Prince Rupert.

PG 0 PR 447.7 (720.5 km) **Junction** of Highways 16 and 97 (20th Avenue/Central Avenue/Cariboo Highway) in Prince George.

From Prince George to Prince Rupert, Highway 16 is a 2-lane highway with 3-lane passing stretches. Fairly straight, with no high summits, the highway follows the valleys of the Nechako, Bulkley and Skeena rivers, paralleling the Canadian National Railway route. There are few services between towns.

PG 0.5 (0.8 km) **PR 447.2** (719.7 km) Stoplight. Ferry Avenue; access to Super Store and playfield.

PG 0.7 (1.1 km) **PR 447** (719.4 km) Stoplight. Vance Avenue; no services.

PG 1.1 (1.8 km) **PR 446.6** (718.7 km) Stoplight. Access to Costco, Boston Pizza, gas with diesel station and other services.

PG 2.1 (3.5 km) **PR 445.6** (717 km) Stoplight. Domano Boulevard; access south to gas, Home Depot, Walmart, Starbucks, Original Joe's, Shoppers Drugmart, Save-On supermarket and other shopping and services.

PG 2.4 (3.9 km) **PR 445.3** (716.6 km) Eastbound and westbound exits to Walmart, fast-food, Esso gas station with diesel, and Canadian Tire.

PG 3.1 (5 km) **PR 444.6** (715.5 km) Stoplight. Westgate Avenue.

PG 3.8 (6.1 km) **PR 443.9** (714.4 km) Bon Voyage Motor Inn and strip mall to south.

PG 4.7 (7.6 km) **PR 443** (712.9 km) Stoplight. Shell gas station with diesel and convenience store to north. Yellowhead Golf

Course to south.

Begin 4-lane highway eastbound.

Begin 2-lane highway westbound. Expect intermittent passing lanes and some 7 percent grades.

PG 5.7 (9.2 km) **PR 442** (711.3 km) **West Lake Provincial Park** 9 miles/14 km south; day-use area with picnic shelter, swimming beach, fishing and boat launch (above water exhaust motors prohibited).

PG 9.2 (14.8 km) **PR 438.5** (705.7 km) Petro-Canada gas, diesel, store to north.

PG 12.5 (20.1 km) **PR 435.2** (700.4 km) Chilako River.

PG 38.7 (62.3 km) **PR 409** (658.2 km) Cluculz rest area to south with flush toilets (summer only), picnic tables and litter bins.

PG 39.1 (62.9 km) **PR 408.56** (657.6 km) Brookside Resort to north; camping, gas, diesel.

PG 58.8 (94.4 km) **PR 388.9** (626.1 km) Derksen Road. Turnoff for **Dave's R.V. Park**, located 0.6-mile/1-km north on Derksen Road. This well-maintained RV park has full hookups, pull-throughs, showers and laundry, tent sites, and miniature golf.

Dave's R.V. Park. See display ad this page.

PG 58.9 (94.8 km) **PR 388.8** (626 km) At the "Welcome to Vanderhoof" sign, a pull-through rest stop with litter bins, picnic tables and area info map.

PG 59.9 (96.4 km) **PR 387.8** (624.1 km) Stoplight; no services.

PG 60.1 (96.7 km) **PR 387.6** (623.8 km) Stoplight. Tim Hortons restaurant, gas bar and supermarket to south.

PG 60.2 (96.9 km) **PR 387.5** (623.6 km) Stoplight at Burrard Avenue. Turn north to access the Visitor Centre and downtown businesses.

Vanderhoof

PG 60.2 (96.9 km) **PR 387.5** (623.6 km). Stoplight at A&W Husky and Chevron gas stations in Vanderhoof. **Population:** 4,049; area 12,000. **Elevation:** 2,225 feet/667.5m. **Emergency Services:** dial 911 (**Police**, phone 250-567-2222. **Fire Department**, phone 250-567-2345. **Ambulance**, phone 1-800-461-9911. **Hospital**, phone 250-567-2211).

Visitor Information: Visitor Centre is located downtown in the Chamber of Commerce building, at 2353 Burrard Ave., 1 block off Highway 16 (just north of the railroad tracks); phone 1-800-752-4094; www.vanderhoofchamber.com, www.vanderhoof.ca. Summer hours (June–Aug.), 9 A.M.–5 P.M. daily; winter hours (Sept.–May) 9 A.M.–5 P.M. weekdays, closed 12 P.M.–1 P.M.

Vanderhoof is the geographical centre of British Columbia on the Alaska Circle Route, and on your way to and from the northwest coast of B.C. The town was named

VANDERHOOF ADVERTISERS

for Chicago publisher Herbert Vanderhoof, who was associated with the Grand Trunk Railway. Today, Vanderhoof is the supply and distribution centre for area agriculture, forestry and mining and is a great stop for shopping, history, and beautiful scenery.

All visitor services are available in Vanderhoof, including food (Tim Horton's, Subway, A&W, etc.), WiFi, public library, pubs, gas/diesel and lodging (**Siesta Inn**, 1-800-914-3388).

Siesta Inn is centrally located on Highway 16 in Vanderhoof; very clean, quiet, queen and double beds, kitchens, fridges, microwave in every room, new bathrooms, 100% non-smoking, close to restaurants, in-room complimentary coffee, cable, DD phones, wireless internet, winter rates, extended stay rates available. Pets allowed, call for details. 14 units, $75-105. Toll-free 1-800-914-3388, siestainn@uniserve.com. www.siestainn.webs.com. [ADVERTISEMENT]

Summer recreation includes a tennis court, fishing lakes, an 18-hole golf course, outdoor running track, spray park, mountain bike park, hunting opportunities, farm tours. Hiking trails in the Vanderhoof area include Greer Creek Falls, Sinkut Mountain, Omineca Trail and Telegraph Trail. Pick up a trail map and area hiking guide at the visitor centre.

Camping is available at Riverside Park and Campground at the north end of Burrard Avenue (on the Nechako River. Camping at **Dave's RV Park** (see **Milepost PG 58.8**) with miniature golf, showers, laundry and full-service RV sites.

Vanderhoof Heritage Museum, on Highway 16, is a wonderful place to learn about the area's history. Relocated pioneer structures furnished with period artifacts recall the early days of the Nechako Valley.

The Hobson History Museum, at 2464 Burrard Ave., is a treasure trove of the history of one of the most famous families in the area. Rich Hobson's story starts in the United States and reaches across the world.

The **Migratory Bird Sanctuary**, located on the Nechako River, is a major migratory stopping place for thousands of Canada Geese. Other migratory species seen here include trumpeter swans, Northern pintails and sandpipers.

Yellowhead Highway 16 Log

(continued)

PG 60.4 (97.2 km) **PR 387.3** (623.3 km) **Junction** with Kenney Dam access road.

PG 60.6 (97.5 km) **PR 387.1** (623 km) Vanderhoof Museum to south; good photo stop.

Distance marker westbound shows Fort Fraser 37 km/23 miles, Terrace 477 km/296

miles, Prince Rupert 621 km/386 miles.

PG 64.7 (104.1 km) **PR 383** (616.4 km) **Junction** with Highway 27, which leads north 37 miles/60 km to the town and the historic site known as Fort St. James (description follows).

The community of **FORT ST. JAMES** (pop. 4,757) is located on 59-mile-/95-km-long Stuart Lake, southernmost in a 3-lake chain which provides hundreds of miles of boating and fishing. Fort St. James has several motels, lodges, B&B's, restaurants, a Subway, gas and repair stations, provincial and private campgrounds, dump stations and a variety of shopping options.

The Fort St. James Chamber of Commerce **Visitor Information Centre** has internet access, wheelchair access and picnic tables and is at the entrance to town on Douglas Avenue at Kwah Road and is open 9 A.M.–5 P.M. daily summers and 9 A.M.–5 P.M. weekdays in winter; website: http://fortstjames.ca.

Downtown offers a 1.2 mile/2 km self-guiding interpretive walk, exploring the community's past from fur trade post to a bastion of bush-plane aviation. It is about a 2-hour drive from Prince George and was the historic capital of New Caledonia.

The Murray Ridge Ski Area offers both down-hill and cross-country skiing, visiting golfers are welcomed at the Stuart Lake Golf Club and annual events include the Canada Day celebrations July 1, Stuart Lake Fishing Derby early July, Cottonwood Music Festival mid-July, Caledonia Classic Sled Dog Race held in late Feb./early March.

Fort St. James National Historic Site. This completely restored Hudson's Bay Company post, located on the shores of Stuart Lake, was an economic powerhouse of trade and commerce in the 19th Century. It is the largest group of original wooden buildings depicting the fur trade in Canada and portrays the relationship between the fur traders and the Carrier First Nations.

©*Michael K. Robb*

Costumed interpreters provide a first-hand look at how people lived, loved, ate, worked and died more than a century ago.

Check out the Daily Adventure programs, Sunday afternoon teas and varied special events during the operating summer season. The site is open 9 A.M. to 5 P.M. daily, mid-May to September 30, and by appointment the rest of the year. Admission is charged. On-site accommodations available. Phone 250-996-7191. Website: www.pc.gc.ca/eng/lhn-nhs/bc/stjames/index.aspx.

PG 83.1 (133.6 km) PR 364.6 (586.9 km) Turnout to south with litter bin and view of Nechako River. The Grand Trunk Pacific Railway was completed near this site in 1914. The railroad (later the Canadian National) linked Prince Rupert, a deep-water port, with interior British Columbia. Entering Lakes District. This high country has over 300 freshwater lakes.

PG 83.7 (134.6 km) PR 364 (585.9 km) NOTE: Slow for 50 kmph/31 mph speed zone through. FORT FRASER (pop. 950); 24-hour Petro-Canada truck stop with gas, diesel, propane, convenience store, restaurant, and hot showers; Subway; lodging; first-aid station.

Visitor Information: In railroad car to south. Named for Simon Fraser, who established a trading post here in 1806. Now a supply centre for surrounding farms and sawmills. The last spike of the Grand Trunk Railway was driven here, April 7, 1914.

PG 84.5 (135.9 km) PR 363.2 (584.6 km) Nechako River bridge. Turnout to south with parking, litter bins and access to Nechako River; fishing for rainbow and Dolly Varden, June to fall. At the east end of Fraser Lake, the Nautley River—less than a mile long—drains into the Nechako River.

PG 85.9 (138 km) PR 361.8 (582.5 km) Nautley Road. Beaumont Provincial Park, on Fraser Lake, north side of highway; site of original Fort Fraser. Boat launch, swimming, hiking, fishing, 49 campsites, picnic tables, firewood, flush toilets, water, playground, horseshoe pits, dump station. Fishing for rainbow and lake trout, burbot and Dolly Varden. Fee $15. May reserve in advance at www.discovercamping.ca.

PG 86.5 (138.8 km) PR 361.2 (581.7 km) CAUTION: Narrow bridge.

PG 88 (141.2 km) PR 359.7 (579.3 km) Piper's Glen Campground to north.

PG 89.5 (143.5 km) PR 358.2 (577 km) Dry William Lake rest area to south with picnic tables, toilets and litter bins.

PG 92.7 (148.6 km) PR 355 (571.9 km) Fraser Lake sawmill to north.

PG 93 (149.1 km) PR 354.7 (571.4 km) Cafe, gas and diesel to south.

Views of Fraser Lake (body of water) to north for westbound travelers.

PG 95.8 (153.7 km) PR 351.9 (566.8 km) Welcome to Fraser Lake (westbound sign).

PG 96.2 (154.3 km) PR 351.5 (566.2 km) NOTE: Slow for 50 kmph/31 mph speed zone through FRASER LAKE (pop. 1,354; elev. 2,200 feet/670m); visitor centre and police station to north. Visitor Information: Fraser Lake Museum and Visitor Centre in log building. Web address: www.fraserlake.ca. Small, lakeside community with all facilities. Known for white swans and great fishing opportunities. Created by Endako Mines Ltd. in 1964; named after the explorer Simon Fraser. Endako Mines Ltd. began operating in 1965 and was Canada's largest

St. John's Anglican Church on 1st Avenue in Burns Lake is a heritage building.
(©Michael K. Robb)

molybdenum mine until production slowed in 1982. Mining resumed in 1986.

PG 96.5 (154.7 km) PR 351.2 (565.8 km) Stoplight. Shopping center, Chevron gas station, motels and medical clinic.

PG 98.6 (158.1 km) PR 349.1 (562.4 km) Junction with main access road south to scenic Francois Lake; also accessible via roads from Burns Lake to Houston. Francois Lake Road (chip seal surfacing) leads south 7 miles/11 km to the east end of Francois Lake (where the Stellako River flows from the lake) and back to Highway 16 at Endako. (It does not link up to the Francois Lake Ferry, south of Burns Lake.) Golf course, Stellako Lodge, Nithi Resort, Francois Lake Resort and other resorts offering camping, cabins and boats, are located on this scenic rural road through the Glenannan area.

Francois Lake, good fishing for rainbow to 5 lbs., May to October; kokanee to ¾ lb., use flashers, willow leaf, flashers with worms, flatfish or spinners, August and September; char to 30 lbs., use large flatfish or spoon, June and July. Stellako River is considered one of British Columbia's better fly-fishing streams with rainbow over 2 lbs., all summer; whitefish averaging 1 lb., year-round.

PG 98.7 (158.3 km) PR 349 (562.2 km) Bridge over Stellako River.

PG 99.8 (160.1 km) PR 347.9 (560.4 km) Gas bar to north.

PG 104.8 (168.1 km) PR 342.9 (552.4 km) ENDAKO (pop. 150), a small highway community; roadhouse.

PG 107.4 (172.3 km) PR 340.3 (548.2 km) Endako River highway bridge and railroad bridge.

PG 111 (178.1 km) PR 336.7 (542.4 km) Savory rest area is a large double-ended turnout with picnic tables and litter bins to

north beside Watkins Creek.

PG 119.6 (191.8 km) PR 328.1 (528.7 km) Winding 7 percent downgrade next mile westbound. CAUTION: Watch for moose.

PG 123.2 (197.7 km) PR 324.5 (522.8 km) Double-ended paved turnout to south with litter bin and toilet.

PG 127.8 (205.2 km) PR 319.9 (515.3 km) Turnoff for Babine Forest Products to south.

PG 128.5 (206.5 km) PR 319.2 (514 km) Views of Burns Lake (body of water) to south.

PG 129.8 (208.5 km) PR 317.9 (512 km) Homeside Antique Place to south.

PG 132.1 (212.3 km) PR 315.6 (508.2 km) Rest area to south is a large double-ended turnout with toilet, tables, litter bins and Tintagel Cairn. The central stone in this cairn once formed part of the Norman walls of Tintagel Castle, reputed birthplace of King Arthur.

PG 135.8 (218 km) PR 312.9 (502.5 km) Private campground.

PG 139.5 (224 km) PR 308.2 (496.5 km) Stoplight at junction with Highway 35 South; lodging, fast-food, pub, shopping and supermarket at junction.

Scenic Highway 35 (paved) leads south 10 miles/16 km to campground on Tchesinkut Lake, and 18 miles/29 km to Francois Lake Ferry landing. This free ferry, with a capacity of 52 vehicles, makes at least one 15-minute crossings from the north and south shores each hour (see schedule at www.th.gov.bc.ca/marine/ferry_schedules.htm).

From the south shore of Francois Lake, Highway 35 continues to Takysie Lake and Ootsa Lake, with access to a number of other fishing lakes. Another of the Yellowhead's popular fishing areas with a variety of family-owned camping and cabin resorts.

PG 139.7 (224.3 km) PR 308 (496.2 km) Gas bar.

PG 139.8 (224.5 km) PR 307.9 (496 km) A&W/Chevron gas station at junction with Babine Lake Road, which leads north to provincial parks on Babine Lake (camping, fishing). Westbound, Highway 16 winds through the town of Burns Lake (description follows). Slow for speed zone through town.

Burns Lake

PG 140.1 (225.2 km) PR 307.6 (495.3 km) Burns Lake Heritage Centre and Museum. Population: 2,726; area 10,000. Elevation: 2,300 feet/707m. Emergency Information: Dial 911 (RCMP 250-692-7171; Lakes District Hospital and Health Centre 250-692-2400; Ambulance 1-800-461-9911).

Visitor Information: The Burns Lake Visitor Centre and Museum, housed in the Old Forestry Home, built in 1919 and located at 540 Highway 16. Open 8 A.M. to 8 P.M. daily in summer; 9 A.M. to 5 P.M. weekdays in winter. Free coffee for visitors. www.burnslakechamber.com or http://tourism.burnslake.ca/. Wireless internet is available inside or out of the centre; walking/biking trail takes off from parking lot. RVs are encouraged to use the larger parking area across the highway at the College. The

Lakes District Museum holds community artifacts since the turn of the century. Take the Heritage Buildings walking circle tour for standing history within the village. Farmer's Markets in summer, Saturdays 9 A.M.–3 P.M.

The village of Burns Lake had its modest beginnings in 1911, as the site of railway construction. Forestry is the mainstay of the economy, along with ranching and tourism.

Burns Lake has 4 motels, a hotel, a bed and breakfast (at Hospital Point on the south shore of Francois Lake), laundromat, library with internet access, food (Subway, A&W, etc.), a shopping centre and a golf course.

Burns Lake Bike Park has progressive dirt jumps, a 4-cross track and pump track. Boer Mountain Recreation Area draws skilled riders with numerous trails of all levels.

Camping is available at the municipal campground at Spirit Square Park, 2 blocks off Highway 16 on Highway 35; washrooms, playground, picnic tables and swimming area. Canoe, kayak and skateboard rental in summer. Skateboard park, playground and free outdoor exercise equipment nearby. Private lakeside campgrounds are located south of town.

From Burns Lake, a side road leads north to Babine Lake, the longest natural lake in the province and one of British Columbia's most important salmon-producing lakes.

Regional District of Bulkley Nechako. See display ad pages 244-245.

Yellowhead Highway 16 Log
(continued)

PG 140.6 (226 km) **PR 307.1** (494.5 km) Car wash, Napa Auto Parts.

PG 140.7 (226.2 km) **PR 307** (494.3 km) Sunshine Inn.

PG 141.1 (226.8 km) **PR 306.6** (493.7 km) Turnout with map and information sign to south.

PG 145 (233.3 km) **PR 302.7** (487.2 km) **DECKER LAKE Trading Post**; above-ground gas tank, ice, pop, fireworks. *Slow for 60 kmph/37 mph speed zone.*

PG 149.3 (240.2 km) **PR 298.4** (480.3 km) Golf course to north.

PG 150.9 (242.8 km) **PR 296.8** (477.7 km) Palling rest area to south is a large double-ended turnout with picnic tables, toilets, litter bins and a map.

PG 153.2 (246.5 km) **PR 294.5** (474 km) Baker airport to south.

PG 161.7 (260.2 km) **PR 286** (460.3 km) Duncan Lake gas station.

PG 164.7 (265.2 km) **PR 283** (455.3 km) Six Mile Summit (elev. 2,756 feet/840m) to west. China Nose Mountain, with steep west-facing cliff, is visible to the south.

PG 165 (265.4 km) **PR 282.7** (455.1 km) Turnout to north with brake check, toilet and litter bins. Turnout to south with litter bin.

Long 7 percent downgrade westbound.

PG 166.5 (267.9 km) **PR 281.2** (452.6 km) Turnout to south with litter bin. Chain-up area in winter.

Long 7 percent uphill grade eastbound.

PG 171 (275.1 km) **PR 276.7** (445.4 km) Turnout to north with map of **TOPLEY** (pop. 300); food, gas, lodging. Topley General Store has a grocery, take-out food.

PG 171.1 (275.3 km) **PR 276.6** (445.2 km) **Junction** with Highway 118 to Granisle and **Red Bluff Provincial Park** on **Babine Lake** the longest natural lake in B.C. From

its junction with the highway at Topley, mileages on this paved side road are as follows: Mile 24.4/39.3 km, turnoff to **TOPLEY LANDING** and access to Babine Lodge and Coopdogg's Fishing Lodge ; Mile 28.8/46.3 km, Fulton River spawning channel (red salmon run in August and September); Mile 28/45.1 km, Red Bluff Provincial Park with camping, picnicking, boat launch, swimming and fishing (with advanced reservations possible at www.discovercamping.ca); Mile 30.6/49 km, Lions Beach Park with camping, picnicking, playground, boat launch, swimming and fishing; Mile 31.4/50.5 km, **GRANISLE** (pop. 352); gas, restaurant, lodging, marina and Granisle Information Centre and Museum (www.granisle.ca). The annual Granisle Days is held the second weekend of August.

PG 171.8 (277.2 km) **PR 275.9** (444.3 km) Large double-ended rest area to south with map of Babine Lake, toilets and litter bins.

PG 179.7 (289.9 km) **PR 268.8** (431.6 km) Turnout to north with litter bin.

PG 188.4 (302.9 km) **PR 259.3** (417.6 km) Well-maintained **Shady Rest RV Park** to south has hookups, tent sites..

Shady Rest RV Park. See display ad this page.

PG 189.1 (304 km) **PR 258.6** (416.5 km) Houston Railway bridge. Bulkley River

bridge. *NOTE: Slow for 50 kmph/31 mph speed zone westbound through Houston.*

PG 189.7 (305 km) **PR 258** (415.5 km) A&W to south, Houston Visitor Centre to north. The Visitor Centre has a picnic area, parking, access to Houston Park walking trail and the World's Largest Fly Rod.

PG 189.8 (305.2 km) **PR 257.9** (415.3 km) Stoplight. Shopping mall to south.

Houston

PG 190 (305.5 km) **PR 257.7** (415 km) Stoplight: Esso gas station/7-11. Houston is located midway between Burns Lake and Smithers on Highway 16. **Population**: 3,163. **Emergency Services**: Dial 911 (**Police**, phone 250-845-2204. **Ambulance**, phone 250-845-2900. **Fire Department**, phone 250-845-2345).

Visitor Information: Visitor Information Centre in log building on Highway 16 across from the mall and next to Steelhead Park (look for the fish fountain); open year-round. Write Houston Visitor Infocentre, 3289 Highway 16, (P.O. Box 396) Houston, BC V0J 1Z0, or phone 250-845-7640. District of Houston at www.houston.ca or www.houstonchamber.ca; email manager@houstonchamber.ca or info@houstonchamber.ca. The Chamber has a large parking area for

Houston's Steelhead Park is a pleasant stop for motorists. (©Kris Valencia, staff)

WELCOME TO THE Bulkley-Nechako

- **ALL SEASON SPORTING ACTIVITIES**
- **SPECTACULAR NATURAL BEAUTY**
- **ABUNDANT WILDLIFE**
- **DIVERSE CULTURE**

Simply EXCEPTIONAL!

SMITHERS
TELKWA
GRANISLE
HOUSTON
BURNS LAKE

Alaska, USA

118

16

16

35

Southside

Smithers
www.TourismSmithers.com

- Follow the red brick sidewalks to great shopping & dining
- Walking, hiking & biking trails
- Lake & river fishing
- Rustic to full service camping
- RV servicing

🛈 1411 Court Street
Smithers, BC

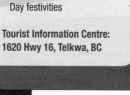

Where Rivers Meet and FRIENDS GATHER

Telkwa
www.telkwa.com

Visit our village at the confluence of the Telkwa and Bulkley Rivers.

- Telkwa Museum and Tourist Information
- River access and free boat launch
- Outdoor recreation trails
- Eddy Park: a riverside public park with gazebo and public washrooms
- Outdoor timber-framed stage

- Playgrounds
- All season activities
- Annual Telkwa BBQ Labour Day festivities

Tourist Information Centre:
1620 Hwy 16, Telkwa, BC

Where the Welcome is Warm and the WILDERNESS BECKONS...

Houston
www.houston.ca

- World's Largest Fly Rod
- 975lb Grizzly Bear display (24/7)
- Steelhead and Salmon fishing
- All season activities
- Extensive hiking trail system
- Community events such as the rodeo, chuck wagon races, drag races
- Boat launch to the Morice River
- Steelhead Park

🛈 3289 Hwy 16
Houston, BC

It's Only NATURAL

Burns Lake
Tourism.burnslake.ca

A small town full of big opportunities, Burns Lake is at the heart of the beautiful Lakes District.

- World-class mountain biking
- Fishing
- Hiking
- Spirit Square
- Free Lakeside campground
- Canoe & kayak rentals
- Cross-country skiing
- Friendly cafes

🛈 540 Hwy 16 W
Burns Lake, BC

Northern British Columbia
REGION

SUPER, NATURAL
BRITISH COLUMBIA®
CANADA

Granisle
www.granisle.ca

- An outdoor recreation destination
- Miles of trails for hiking, biking, snowmobiling, and cross country skiing
- Enjoy Water skiing or sailing

- Fishing for Rainbow Trout, Char, Kokanee, Burbot, and Salmon
- Visit the Fulton River Spawning Channel - the largest in the world!
- Camping at Red Bluff Provincial Park, Lions Beach and New Beach

Come and enjoy our year round hospitality!

On Beautiful BABINE LAKE

#3 Babine Drive Granisle, BC

Fort St. James
www.fortstjames.ca

You will love our:
- National Historic Site
- Interpretive walking trails
- Memorial to aviation legend, Russ Baker
- Scenic Stuart Lake, offering boating, fishing, Carrier pictographs and swimming

Enjoy Fort St. James, a playground for all seasons!
- Golf
- Camping
- Guided trail rides
- Alpine skiing
- Recreational vehicle trails

Historic and RESOURCEFUL

115 Douglas Ave Fort St. James, BC

FORT ST. JAMES

27

Prince George, BC

YELLOWHEAD 16 BC

FRASER LAKE

VANDERHOOF

Vanderhoof
www.vanderhoof.ca

For every season there is a reason… to visit us in Vanderhoof.

- Interpretive Community Trail Network
- Historical hiking trails
- Riverside Campground with Wi-Fi, outdoor fitness area, lit walking trail and playground
- Bird watching at the Migratory Bird Sanctuary
- Nechako White Sturgeon Conservation Centre
- Community Museum and historic OK Café
- Spray Park
- Mountain bike park

- Shopping and traveler services
- Events for the family: Concert in the Park, Pumpkin Walk, Parade of Lights, Airshow, Fall Fair, and much more!

The Heart OF IT ALL!

2353 Burrard Ave Vanderhoof, BC

www.vanderhoofchamber.com

Fraser Lake
www.fraserlake.ca

Your Recreation DESTINATION

- Fishing & Hunting
- Camping & Hiking
- ATVing & Snowmobiling
- Canoeing & Kayaking

Tourist Information Centre: 30 Carrier Cres., Fraser Lake, BC

Lakes, Rivers, Mountains, Trails & Wildlife abound!

PLAN YOUR ADVENTURE TODAY AT
VisitBulkleyNechako.ca

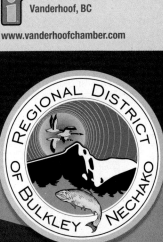

REGIONAL DISTRICT OF BULKLEY NECHAKO

View of Bulkley River from Eddy Park in Telkwa. (©Michael K. Robb)

RVs that is also bus friendly.

The World's Largest Fly Fishing Rod is on display at the Visitor Centre. The 60-foot-long anodized aluminum fly rod was designed by a local avid fly fisherman and built by local volunteers. (The 21-inch fly is a fluorescent "Skykomish Sunrise.") The Houston & District Chamber of Commerce, located on Highway 16, features the Hungry Hill Grizzly Bear. The park also has a steelhead fountain made by local artist, Frank Eberman.

Elevation: 1,926 feet/587m. **Climate**: Average temperature in summer, 71°F/21°C; in winter, 19°F/-7°C. **Radio**: The Peak CFBV 1450, The Mix CJFW-FM 105.5. **Newspaper**: *The Houston Today*. **Transportation**: Greyhound bus, VIA Rail.

Houston has all visitor facilities, including motels, campgrounds, restaurants, fast-food (Subway, A&W, etc.), gas stations, a shopping centre and golf courses. The Leisure Facility has a lap pool, leisure pool, fitness room, hot tub and steam room.

Established in the early 1900s, Houston was a tie-cutting centre during construction of the Grand Trunk Pacific Railway in 1912. It was named for Prince Rupert newspaperman John Houston, the former mayor of Nelson, BC. Logging continued to support the local economy with the rapid growth of mills and planer mills in the 1940s and 1950s. Houston was incorporated as a village in 1957.

The main industry in Houston today is still forest products. There are 2 large sawmills here, Houston Forest Products and Canadian Forest Products Ltd. Inquire at the Visitor Infocentre about mill tours available in July–August.

Mining is also an industry here. The Equity Silver Mine operated from 1980 to 1994. The Huckleberry Copper Mine, southwest of Houston, went into production in 1997. This open pit mine has an estimated life of 16 to 25 years, extracting copper as well as molybdenum, silver and gold.

Hunting, canoeing, snowmobiling and sportfishing are major attractions here. Special events include Pleasant Valley Days in May, Canada Day celebrations in July, a Trade Show in September and Light Up in December.

Yellowhead Highway 16 Log
(continued)

PG 190 (305.5 km) **PR 257.7** (415 km) Stoplight. Esso gas station/7-11; gas and convenience store.

PG 192.6 (310 km) **PR 255.1** (411.2 km) **Junction** with the Morice River access road which extends 52 miles/84 km south to Morice Lake. Approximately 20 miles/32 km along the Morice River Road you can turn east on a gravel road which leads past Owen Lake and Nadina River Road to Francois Lake. From Francois Lake ferry landing Highway 35 leads north to Burns Lake.

The 2 famous salmon and steelhead streams, **Morice** and **Bulkley**, unite near Houston, and it is possible to fish scores of pools all along the Morice River. Fishing for resident rainbow, cutthroat and Dolly Varden; steelhead and salmon (king, silver) in season.

NOTE: Special requirements apply to fishing

these streams; check with Fish and Game office.

PG 193 (310.7 km) **PR 254.7** (409.8 km) Bulkley River bridge; rest area to north at west end of bridge with tables, litter bins and toilets.

Highway climbs 8 percent hill next 1.5 miles/2.4 km westbound. Watch for moose.

PG 200.5 (322 km) **PR 247.2** (398.5 km) **Hungry Hill Summit** (elev. 2,769 feet/844m). To the north are the snow-capped peaks of the Babine Mountains, to the west is the Hudson Bay Range.

PG 203.3 (327.7 km) **PR 244.4** (393.8 km) Rest area to north with large paved parking area with picnic tables, toilets and litter bins.

PG 213.6 (343.4 km) **PR 234.1** (377.1 km) Round Lake Resort to north.

PG 217.1 (349.4 km) **PR 230.6** (371.1 km) Bulkley View roadside rest area to south; large double-ended turnout with picnic tables and litter bins overlooking the Bulkley River.

PG 219.8 (353.7 km) **PR 227.9** (366.8 km) **Ft. Telkwa RV Park** to south. ▲

Ft. Telkwa R.V. Park. See display ad this page.

Highway descends 7 percent winding downgrade westbound into Telkwa. Slow for 50-kmph/31-mph speed zone through town.

Telkwa

PG 220.4 (354.5 km) **PR 227.3** (366 km) Telkwa Museum to south; post office adjacent to the west of the museum. Telkwa (name means "meeting of the water") is located at the confluence of the Telkwa and Bulkley rivers.

Population: 1,400. **Visitor Information**: Visitor Infocentre at the Telkwa Museum and the Village of Telkwa office. Visit www.telkwa.com for more information.

Telkwa is a charming village with a convenience store, laundromat, post office, a service station that includes a laundromat and cafe, pottery store, Telkwa Museum, gift shop, ice cream parlour, furniture and clothing warehouse store and a coffee shop. Fishing and hunting information, licenses and supplies available at the general store. Riverside and lakeside lodging available. Camping at Fort Telkwa RV Park on the east edge of town and Tyhee Lake Provincial Campground, moments away from the village.

Eddy Park, on the western edge of town along the Bulkley River, is a good spot for picnicking (look for the wishing well). St. Stephen's Anglican Church (now Mount Zion Lutheran) was built in 1910 and the bell and English gate added in 1921. Other Heritage buildings date back to 1908. Historic walking tour brochures are available at the museum or village office or online at www.telkwa.com/html/history.htm. Walking trail to historic townsite of Aldermere and to Tyhee Lake Provincial Park.

The annual Kinsman Barbecue is held over Labour Day weekend. This event features a major northern baseball tournament, kids games, live music, contests, a demolition derby, and barbecue.

Yellowhead Highway 16 Log
(continued)

PG 220.7 (355 km) **PR 227** (365.5 km) Turnoff for **Tyhee Lake Provincial Park**, 0.6 mile/1 km north; 59 campsites, 26 day

use picnic tables, dump station, hiking trails, fishing, swimming, boat launch. Camping fee $25, sani-dump $5; reserve in advance at www.discovercamping.ca.

Also turnoff here on the Telkwa High Road, which intersects with Babine Lake access road (gravel), which leads 46 miles/74 km north to Smithers Landing (very, very rough road, not recommended for trailers or RVs) on Babine Lake and 56 miles/90 km to Granisle.

Tyhee Lake, rainbow and lake trout to 2 lbs., June through August; Kamloops trout to 2 lbs. **Babine River**, steelhead to 40 lbs., late fall. **Telkwa River**, spring and silver salmon to 24 lbs., summer to fall.

PG 221.1 (355.6 km) **PR 226.6** (364.9 km) Race Trac gas/diesel station to north.

PG 225.5 (362.7 km) **PR 222.2** (357.8 km) Second turnoff westbound to north for Babine Lake/Smithers Landing (very rough road not recommended for trailers or RVs).

PG 227.2 (366.1 km) **PR 220.5** (353.4 km) Riverside RV & Golf to south.

PG 227.5 (366.6 km) **PR 220.2** (353.9 km) Turnoff to north for Driftwood Canyon Provincial Park (11 km/6.8 miles); picnic area.

PG 227.6 (366.8 km) **PR 220.1** (353.7 km) Bridge over Bulkley River.

PG 227.8 (367 km) **PR 219.9** (354.5 km) Turnout to north with litter bin, picnic tables, area map and Welcome to Smithers sign.

PG 228 (367.3 km) **PR 219.7** (353.2 km) Stoplight. Forest District Office to north.

PG 228.6 (367.9 km) **PR 219.1** (352.6 km) Stoplight. Supermarket to north. Access to Canadian Tire, **Hudson Bay Lodge** and RCMP to south via frontage road.

Hudson Bay Lodge. See display ad on page 248.

PG 228.9 (368.8) **PR 218.8** (351.7 km) Stoplight. Access to RCMP and Chandler Park to south via frontage road.

PG 229.2 (368.3 km) **PR 218.5** (351.2 km) King Street stoplight in Smithers. Access to Safeway, Petro-Canada and Chevron gas stations.

Smithers

PG 229.3 (369 km) **PR 218.4** (350.5 km). Main Street stoplight in Smithers. Turn south for downtown shopping; turn north for Fire Department and Riverside Park. **Population**: 5,217; area 20,000. **Emergency Services**: Dial 911 (**Police**, phone 250-847-3233. **Hospital** and **Poison Centre**, 3950 8th Ave., phone 250-847-2611. **Ambulance**, phone 250-847-8808).

Visitor Information: The Visitor Centre and Chamber of Commerce are located behind the railcar, across from the Bulkley Valley Museum. The museum has developed a self-guided walking tour called the Smithers Culture Crawl and includes historic buildings and museum exhibits on display in downtown businesses. Open year-round, the Visitor Centre has detailed information and maps on area services and recreation. Contact P.O. Box 2379, Smithers, BC V0J 2N0; phone

1-800-542-6673; email info@tourism smithers.com; www.tourismsmithers.com and www.smitherschamber.com.

Elevation: 1,636 feet/496m. **Climate**: Relatively warmer and drier than mountainous areas to the west; average temperature in July is 58°F/14°C, in January 14°F/-10°C; annual precipitation, 13 inches. **Radio**: The Peak AM 870, CJFW-FM 92.9 or 105.5, CFNR FM-95.1, CBC-FM 97.5 and 88.1. **Television**: Channels 5, 13, satellite and cable. **Newspaper**: *Interior News* (weekly).

Transportation: **Air**—Scheduled service via Air Canada (Jazz), Hawkair and Central Mountain Air. **Railroad**—VIA Rail. **Bus**—Greyhound. **Car Rentals**—Available.

Sitting amidst rugged mountains, the downtown shopping area has alpine-themed storefronts and buildings murals. (There is even an alpenhorn statue at the helm of Main Street.) Main Street offers a wide array of unique boutiques, shops and restaurants.

Smithers celebrated its Centennial Year in 2013. Incorporated as a village in 1921, Smithers officially became a town in Canada's centennial year, 1967, but the original site was chosen in 1913 by construction crews working on the Grand Trunk Pacific Railway. The town was named for one-time chairman of the railway A.W. Smithers. Today it is a distribution and supply centre for farms, mills and mines in the area.

Smithers is the largest town in the Bulkley Valley and the site of Hudson Bay Mountain, a popular ski area in winter (skiing from November to mid-April); hiking and climbing in summer.

Smithers has 10 hotels and motels, 8 bed and breakfasts, 3 service stations (gas, diesel, propane), restaurants, laundromat, 2 car washes and unique shopping opportunities.

Barb's Bodacious Boutique in Smithers offers something very unique—they are the only store in North America to carry European fashion from ULLA POPKEN in sizes 12 to 32, shoes and accessories! Find them at 1176 Main Street; give them a call at 250-847-8789; check out their website www.barbsboutique.ca; or find them on Facebook.

Mention this ad to receive 15 percent discount! [ADVERTISEMENT]

The government liquor store is located on Queen Street at Broadway Avenue. There are two 18-hole golf courses with rentals and clubhouse. One is a par 3, with an RV park and the other is a championship course set at the base of Hudson Bay Mountain.

There is a municipal park and campground with security, free firewood, showers and flush toilets, water and electrical hookups, potable water, cookhouse and picnic area at Riverside Park on the Bulkley River; turn north on Main Street and watch for signs. There are private campgrounds located east and west of town; see highway log.

Special events include the Bulkley Valley Fall Fair—one of the largest agricultural exhibitions in the province—held the last weekend in August each year. The Midsummer Music Festival (first weekend in July) features local, regional and national artists and the Telkwa Barbecue and Demolition Derby is the longest running, consecutive event in B.C.

Smithers offers a number of scenic drives. Hudson Bay Mountain (elev. 8,700 feet/2,652m) is a 14-mile/23-km drive from Highway 16; the plateau above timberline at the ski area is a good spot for summer hikes. On the way up to the ski hill, visit a petting zoo at Double D Lux Ranch on Moncton Road.

Pedestrian-friendly Main Street of Smithers offers shopping and dining. (©Michael K. Robb)

I'm there.
Smithers
www.tourismsmithers.com

SMITHERS IS A FAVOURITE DESTINATION FOR TRAVELLERS ON BC'S YELLOWHEAD HIGHWAY 16.

Our inviting downtown shopping district welcomes your with red brick sidewalks and a mountain town atmosphere. You'll find clothing, artwork, unique gifts & jewelry, pastry shops, butcher shop with local products and so much more.

- Fishing licenses and fishing gear
- Cafés, restaurants, pubs

- Laundry, car washes (with RV bays)
- Fuel—gas, diesel, propane
- Mechanical & RV servicing
- Post Office, hospital and medical services
- Walking, hiking and biking trails
- Beaches, rivers and lakes within easy access
- 2 golf courses

Follow signs to the Visitor Centre. Conveniently located, the Visitor Centre provides RV parking and has a sani-dump on site. Here you can also browse for postcards, souvenirs and local art. The Visitor Centre has wireless internet and computer access for visitors.

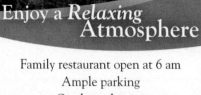

Fossil enthusiasts should drive to Driftwood Canyon Provincial Park; turn off Highway 16 just east of the Bulkley River bridge (travelers are advised to stop first at the Visitor Centre in town for a map and directions). A display at the park illustrates the fossils, such as metasequoia, a type of redwood which occurs in the shale formation. BC Parks asks visitors to refrain from removing any fossils.

A beautiful spot not to be missed is Twin Falls and Glacier Gulch. Drive west on Highway 16 1.9 miles/3 km, turning onto Lake Kathlyn Road to the south. Follow this to Glacier Gulch Road and turn left for 1.2 miles/2 km on pavement and 2.4 miles/3.8 km of gravel leads you to a day-use-only parking area. Hike along the creek to the right for 15 minutes for spectacular views. *CAUTION: Rocks are slippery when wet.*

In the winter months, Smithers boasts one of the largest ski hills in northern British Columbia at 6,000-foot/1,829-m. Hudson Bay Mountain's ski area's triple chair and 2 T-bars climb the 1,750-foot/533-m vertical, offering skiers dozens of runs. A list of lake and river fishing spots in the area, with information on boat launches and boat rentals, is available from the Visitor Centre, Box 2379, Smithers, BC V0J 2N0; phone 250-847-5072 or 1-800-542-6673.

Yellowhead Highway 16 Log
(continued)

PG 229.4 (369.6 km) **PR 218.3** (350.9 km) Stoplight at Queen Street in Smithers; access to Capri Motor Inn, Sandman Inn, Dairy Queen and Tim Horton's.

PG 229.9 (370.4 km) **PR 217.8** (350.1 km) Stoplight at Bulkley Drive and Toronto Street in Smithers; fast-food and lodging.

PG 230.5 (371.4 km) **PR 217.2** (349.1 km) Smithers Golf and Country Club.

PG 231.7 (373.2 km) **PR 216** (347.3 km) First turnoff westbound for Lake Kathlyn (Loop) Road, which leads south to Lake Kathlyn and junctions with Glacier Gulch Road. Municipal park with a small beach and boat launch located at Lake Kathlyn; powerboats not permitted. Glacier Gulch Road leads 4 miles/6.4 km (narrow, gravel) to **Twin Falls** and **Glacier Gulch**.

PG 232.7 (374.9 km) **PR 215** (345.6 km) Turnoff to north for Smithers airport.

PG 233.6 (376.3 km) **PR 214.1** (344.2 km) Lake Kathlyn Jct. Road, connects with Lake Kathlyn Road.

PG 234 (377 km) **PR 213.7** (343.5 km) Last turnoff westbound for Lake Kathlyn (Loop) Road to south, which junctions with Glacier Gulch Road (see **Milepost PG 231.7**).

PG 235 (378 km) **PR 212.7** (342.6 km)
Glacier View RV Park and Cabin Rentals. Panoramic view of glacier. P/w/s pull-throughs; p/w/s back-ins; tenting. Self-contained cabins and cottages with kitchen, bathroom with shower, open year-round. WiFi. Clean, relaxing showers; handicap-accessible shower; laundromat; dishwashing room; sani-station. 5 miles/8 kms west of Smithers off Highway 16, easy access. 1-877-847-3961. Search Glacier View RV Park on Facebook. See display ad this page. [ADVERTISEMENT]

PG 235.1 (378.4 km) **PR 212.6** (341.1 km) Hudson Bay rest area with picnic tables, litter bins and a wildlife museum. Beautiful view of Hudson Bay Mountain.

PG 243.1 (391.5 km) **PR 204.6** (329 km) Trout Creek bridge.

Moricetown Canyon west of Smithers is an aboriginal fishing spot. (©Chris Heitstuman)

PG 248.5 (400.7 km) **PR 199.2** (319.8 km) Pullout westbound with historic sign on Moricetown Canyon; litter bins.

PG 248.7 (400.9 km) **PR 199** (319.6 km) Turnout to north with view of Bulkley River and Moricetown Canyon; good photo stop.

PG 248.9 (401.2 km) **PR 198.8** (319.3 km) Telkwa High Road is a short side road on the north side of the highway leading to **Moricetown Canyon and Falls** on the Bulkley River, for centuries a famous First Nations' fishing spot. Aboriginal people may still be seen here netting salmon in July, August and September. A worthwhile stop. Continue across the bridge to **Moricetown Interpretive Centre** (description follows), adjacent **Moricetown Campground and RV Park**.

Moricetown Interpretive Centre. Located just off Highway 16: Turn at Telkwa High Road, cross the bridge and you will find

us at the RV park site overlooking Moricetown Canyon. Artifacts, old photos, historical information, local crafts, T-shirts and hats. See the replica traditional fish trap. Open seasonally, June–August. Phone 250-847-1471. Off-season call the Band Office at 1-800-821-1218. [ADVERTISEMENT]

Moricetown Campground and RV Park. See display ad this page.

PG 249.2 (401.5 km) **PR 198.5** (319 km) Esso gas station with diesel at junction with Beaver Road at **MORICETOWN** (pop. 815; elev. 1,341 feet/409m).

Moricetown is a First Nations reserve and village, and the oldest settlement in the province. Traditionally, the Native people (Wet'suwet'en) took advantage of the narrow canyon to trap salmon. The centuries-old settlement ('Kyah Wiget) is now named after Father A.G. Morice, a Roman Catholic missionary. Born in France, Father Morice came to British Columbia in 1880 and worked with the aboriginals of northern British Columbia from 1885 to 1904. He achieved world recognition for his writings in anthropology, ethnology and history.

PG 256 (412.5 km) **PR 191.7** (308 km) East Boulder Creek.

PG 259 (417.3 km) **PR 188.7** (303.2 km)

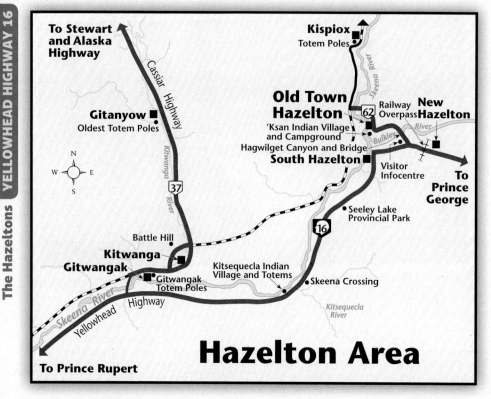

Hazelton Area

Paved turnout to north.

PG 259.9 (418.8 km) **PR 187.8** (301.7 km) Paved turnout with litter bin to north.

PG 260.8 (420.2 km) **PR 186.9** (300.3 km) Paved turnout to north with litter bin and view of Bulkley River.

PG 261.6 (421.5 km) **PR 186.1** (299 km) Paved parking to north.

PG 269.3 (433.9 km) **PR 178.4** (286.6 km) Turnoff for **Ross Lake Provincial Park**, 1.2 miles/2 km north; 25 picnic sites, boat launch (electric motors only), swimming. Fishing for rainbow to 4 lbs.

PG 270.7 (436.1 km) **PR 177** (284.4 km) Turnout to north with map of New Hazelton. Entering New Hazelton westbound (description follows). *Slow for 50-kmph/ 31-mph speed zone westbound through town.*

New Hazelton

PG 271 (436.5 km) **PR 176.7** (284 km) Stoplight. Food, gas and lodging along highway. **Population:** area 6,500. **Emergency Services:** Dial 911 for all emergencies. Police, phone 250-842-5244.

Visitor Information: Hazelton Area Visitor Centre in 2-story log building at the junction; museum, local artisan display, restrooms, free sani-dump, pota-

ble water, picnic tables.

Look for the 3 statues representing the gold rush packer Cataline, the Northwest miner, and the Upper Skeena logger. Phone 250-842-6071 in summer; 250-842-6571 Oct. to May; websites www.newhazelton.ca and www.hazeltonstourism.ca.

Elevation: 1,150 feet/351m. **Radio:** CBC 1170. **Transportation:** VIA Rail. Greyhound bus and regional transit system.

The first of 3 communities westbound sharing the name Hazelton (the others are Hazelton and South Hazelton), known collectively as The Hazeltons.

These 3 small highway communities offering lodging at **Bearclaw Lodge** (604-629-9578), **Bulkley Valley Motel** (888-988-1144), **Robber's Roost Motel & Lodge** (250-842-6916) and **Cataline Motel and RV Park** (250-842-5271). Camping at Cataline RV Park and at 'Ksan Campground (250-842-5940) on River Road. Dining at **The Historic BC Cafe** in Historic Old Hazelton. Other services include fast-food outlets (Subway), banks and credit unions, laundromat and service stations (Chevron, Esso). Shopping facilities include a bakery, a supermarket, sporting goods store and department store. ATMs located at the Chevron station in New Hazelton, at Bulkley Valley Credit Union in the mall on Highway 16 and at Royal Bank and Gitanmaax Food and Fuel gas station on Highway 62 leading to Old Hazelton.

Attractions here include Historic Old Hazelton, the Indian village of 'Ksan and sportfishing the Bulkley and Kispiox rivers (descriptions follow). The Rocher Deboule mountain range, which includes Hagwilget

Peak, elev. 8,000 feet/2,438m, towers behind the town.

From May through early fall, a Country Market is held Saturday and Sunday from 10 A.M. to 5 P.M. at the Travel Information Centre on Highway 16. A B.C. sanctioned Farmer's Market, held Saturdays June to Sept. at the ice arena, features locally grown produce and handmade goods.

The Hagwilget Canyon of the Bulkley River is one of the most photographed places in Canada. A 1-lane bridge spans the canyon on the road to Hazelton, one of the highest suspension bridges in Canada (spans 460 feet and is 262 feet above the river).

HAZELTON. Situated at the confluence of the Skeena and Bulkley rivers, Hazelton grew up at "The Forks" as a transshipping point at the head of navigation on the Skeena and a wintering place for miners and prospectors from the rigorous Interior. Thomas Hankin established a Hudson's Bay Co. trading post here in 1868. The name Hazelton comes from the numerous hazelnut bushes growing on the flats.

Cataline, famous pioneer packer and traveler, is buried near here in an unmarked grave at Pioneer Cemetery. Jean Caux (his real name) was a Basque who, from 1852 to 1912, with loaded mules, supplied mining and construction camps from Yale and Ashcroft northward through Hazelton, where he often wintered.

For some years, before the arrival of the railroad and highways, supplies for trading posts at Bear and Babine lakes and the Omineca goldfields moved by riverboat from the coast to Hazelton and from there over trails to the backcountry. Some of the Yukon gold rushers passed through Hazelton on their way to the Klondike, pack trains having made the trip from Hazelton to Telegraph Creek over the old Telegraph Trail as early as 1874.

OLD HAZELTON. Reconstructed to look much like it did in the 1890s, look for the antique machinery in downtown. The history of the Hazelton area can be traced by car on the Hand of History tour. Pick up a brochure from the Visitor Infocentre showing the location of the 19 historic sites on the driving tour. Also, in summer months, stop in Old Hazelton for a walking tour of the area (20 minutes to one hour in length). Pioneer Day is the second Saturday in August, celebrating the historic spirit.

'KSAN Historical Village and Museum, a replica Gitxsan Indian village, is 4.5 miles/7.2 km from Highway 16. It is a reconstruction of the traditional Gitxsan Village, which has stood at this site for centuries. It is located at the confluence of the Bulkley and Skeena rivers. There are 7 traditionally styled cedar longhouses, as well as various totem poles and dugout canoes.

For a nominal charge from May to September, you can join a guided tour of three longhouses. Performances of traditional song and dance are presented every Wednesday evening during July and August in the Wolf House. Admission to grounds is $5, children under 6 are free. Guided tours of the grounds run $10 for adults, $8.50 for students and seniors. Hours of operation: Open daily from April to October, hours are posted. In winter, hours are 10 A.M. to 4:30 P.M., Monday to Friday. Tours possible; phone 1-877-842-5518/www.ksan.org.

The **'Ksan Campground** adjacent to the museum, is a well-maintained full-service campground on the banks of the Skeena and

Don't miss 'Ksan Historical Village & Museum at Hazelton. (©Michael K. Robb)

Bulkley rivers operated by the Gitanmaax Band. Season runs June to October, contact 'Ksan Campground at 250-842-5940 or Gitanmaax Band. Season runs June–October; campground: 250-842-5297 or Gitanmaax Band: 250-842-5297. △

KISPIOX (pop. 825) Indian village and 3 fishing resorts are 20 miles/32 km north on a good paved road at the confluence of the Skeena and Kispiox rivers. Kispiox is noted for its stand of totems close to the river. There is a market garden (fresh vegetables) located approximately 7 miles/11 km north on the Kispiox Road (about 2 miles/ 3.2 km before the Kispiox totem poles). Camping, accommodations and fishing at various lodges and campgrounds located in the valley. Valley hosts the Kispiox Rodeo, an annual event since 1952, the first weekend of June. An annual music festival is held the last weekend in July

Bulkley River, Dolly Varden to 5 lbs.; spring salmon, mid-July to mid-August; silver salmon 4 to 12 lbs., Aug. 15 through September, flies, spoons and spinners; steelhead to 20 lbs., July through November, flies, Kitamats, weighted spoons and soft bobbers. **Kispiox River** is famous for its trophy-sized steelhead. Check on regulations with Fisheries and Oceans Canada and obtain a fishing license before your arrival. Fishing is done with single-hook only, with catch-release for steelhead in August and September. Season is mid-June to late September for salmon, trout and steelhead. Excellent fly-fishing waters: spring salmon, July to early August; silver salmon, late August to early September; steelhead from September until freezeup. Sizable Dolly Vardens and cutthroat. Steelhead average 20 lbs., with some catches over 30 lbs. 🎣

Yellowhead Highway 16 Log
(continued)

PG 271.2 (436.9 km) **PR 176.5** (283.6 km) Railroad bridge.

PG 271.3 (437.1 km) **PR 176.4** (283.4 km) Hazelton Visitor Centre at **junction** with Highway 62, which leads north to Old Historic Hazelton, 'Ksan Village, Museum and Campground and Kispiox Valley.

'Ksan Historical Village & Museum. See display ad page 251.

PG 271.8 (437.9 km) **PR 175.9** (282.6 km) Turnoff to south with Hazelton information sign and map (eastbound access).

PG 273.2 (440.1 km) **PR 174.5** (280.4 km) Mission Creek.

PG 273.6 (440.7 km) **PR 174.1** (279.8 km) Turnoff to north for **Cataline Motel & RV Park** (description follows). Side road continues through residential area of South Hazelton and loops back to the highway.

Cataline Motel & RV Park. Save $s. One block from highway. Reduced winter service. Quiet pets permitted. More details/ reservations: phone 250-842-5271; email poprightinn@telus.net. One-story motel: some kitchens, some dorm rooms. Green campground: RV hookups, boon-docking, tenting; flush toilets, showers, tables, etc.; laundromat, mini-store, fish freezer, public phone, WiFi. [ADVERTISEMENT] △

PG 277.3 (445.6 km) **PR 170.4** (273.9 km) Turnoff to south for **Seeley Lake Provincial Park**; 20 campsites, drinking water, pit toilets, firewood, day-use area with picnic tables, swimming, fishing, camping fee $16. 🎣 △

PG 287.2 (462.7 km) **PR 160.5** (257.8 km) River bridge.

PG 287.6 (463.2 km) **PR 161.1** (257.3 km) **KITSEGUECLA**, First Nation's village. Totem poles throughout village are classic examples, still in original locations.

PG 287.8 (463.6 km) **PR 160.9** (256.9 km) Turnoff to south with historical plaque about Skeena Crossing.

PG 295.8 (475.4 km) **PR 151.9** (244 km) Gravel turnout to north with litter bin. Shandilla Creek.

PG 298 (480.2 km) **PR 149.7** (240.3 km) Gas station at **junction** with Cassiar Highway. **GITWANGAK** (pop. 490), 0.2 mile/0.4 km north, has many fine old totems and St. Paul's church and bell tower.

> **Junction** with Cassiar Highway (BC Highway 37) north to the Alaska Highway, with access to Stewart, BC/Hyder, AK. See CASSIAR HIGHWAY section on page 258.

Westbound, the Yellowhead Highway offers good views of Seven Sisters peaks; the highest is 9,140 feet/2,786m.

PG 303.2 (488.6 km) **PR 144.5** (231.9 km) Boulder Creek bridge.

PG 303.5 (489.2 km) **PR 144.4** (231.4 km) Double-ended turnout with parking for large vehicles; toilets, litter bins and picnic tables.

PG 307.6 (495.6 km) **PR 140.1** (224.9 km) Paved turnout to north with litter bin.

PG 308 (496.3 km) **PR 139.7** (224.2 km) Gull Creek with hiking trail across from it.

PG 309.2 (498.2 km) **PR 138.5** (222.3 km) Hand of History sign about "Holy City."

Watch for black bears fishing the river for salmon in late July and early August.

PG 312.5 (503.5 km) **PR 135.2** (217 km) Paved turnout to north with litter bin overlooking the Skeena River.

PG 315.3 (507.9 km) **PR 132.4** (212.6 km) Flint Creek.

PG 318.5 (513 km) **PR 129.2** (207.5 km) Turnout to north with litter bin along river with historical plaque about Skeena River Boats:

From 1889, stern-wheelers and smaller craft fought their way through the Coast Mountains, churning past such awesome places as 'The Devil's Elbow' and 'The Hornet's Nest.' Men and supplies were freighted upstream, furs and gold downstream. A quarter century of colour and excitement began to fade in 1912, as the Grand Trunk Pacific neared completion.

PG 335.7 (540.2 km) **PR 112** (180.3 km) Large, very pleasant Sanderson Rest Area on Skeena River with double-ended access; water pump, picnic tables, toilets, recycling and litter bins. *Steep cliffs, supervise children.*

PG 342.8 (551.5 km) **PR 104.9** (169 km) Tiny chapel to south serves small community of **USK**. The nondenominational chapel is a replica of the pioneer church that stood in Usk on the other side of the river until 1936, when the Skeena River flooded, sweeping away the village and the church. The only item from the church to survive was the Bible, which was found floating atop a small pine table.

PG 345.2 (555.6 km) **PR 102.4** (165 km) Side road leads 0.5 mile/0.8 km south to **Kleanza Creek Provincial Park**; 32 campsites, 25 picnic sites, fishing, drinking water, toilets, firewood, wheelchair access. Camping fee $16. Gate closed between 11 P.M. and 7 A.M.; $6 firewood. No pets in day-use area. 🎣 △

PG 345.4 (555.9 km) **PR 102.3** (164.7 km) Kleanza Creek bridge. Salmon habitat.

PG 346.9 (558.3 km) **PR 100.8** (162.3 km) Paved turnout to north.

PG 350.5 (564.1 km) **PR 97.2** (156.4 km) **Copper (Zymoetz) River bridge**, can be fished from Highway 16 or follow local maps. Silver salmon to 10 lbs., use tee-spinners in July; steelhead to 20 lbs., check locally for season and restrictions. 🎣

PG 352 (566.5 km) **PR 95.7** (154 km) Double-ended turnout to north with tourist information sign and area map.

PG 352.2 (566.8 km) **PR 95.5** (153.7 km) Turnoff on frontage road for access to motel and RV park. △

PG 353.9 (569.6 km) **PR 93.8** (150.9 km) Chevron gas station and Northern Motor Inn to south. 🅱

PG 354.3 (570.2 km) **PR 93.4** (150.3 km) Esso and Petro-Canada gas/diesel and pro-

pane at Old Lakelse Lake Road south to Furlong Bay.

PG 354.7 (570.8 km) **PR 93** (149.7 km) 4-way stop at **junction** with Highway 37 South, which leads 38 miles/59 km to Kitimat (description follows). This side road is a good 2-lane paved highway with multiple passing lanes. Northwest Regional Airport is located at Mile 3/Km 4.8. **Lakelse Lake Provincial Park** recreation sites along the road are: Gruchy Beach unit and sockeye viewing trail at Mile 7.8/Km 12.5; picnic grounds at Mile 8.6/Km 13.8; and the Furlong Bay unit at Mile 11.3/Km 18, which has 156 vehicle and tent campsites, nature trails, swimming, sandy beach, flush toilets, showers, sani-dump, boat launch, drinking water, wheelchair access, firewood, interpretive programs, and fishing.

KITIMAT (pop. 8,780) is a major deep sea port and site of the Rio Tinto Alcan aluminum smelter. Originally planned and built in the early 1950s, when the B.C. government encouraged Alcan (Aluminum Co. of Canada) to establish a smelter here, the current plant is undergoing a $3.3 billion modernization to increase production capacity. Completion date for the project is 2014.

Visitor's Information: Visitor Centre at 2109 Forest Ave. Kitimat, BC V8C 2G7. Phone 250-632-6294 or 1-800-664-6554; www.tourismkitimat.ca.

Kitimat is a popular fishing spot. Fishermen line the banks of the Kitimat River in May for the steelhead run. The king salmon run follows in June and July and silvers fill the river in late August and into September.

Many scenic hiking trails are available. The Centennial Museum is located at city centre; phone 250-632-8950 for hours. Another attraction is Kitimat Village, the original aboriginal settlement area.

Camping at Radley Park; electrical hookups, showers, fishing, toilets, playground and dump station.

PG 354.9 (571.1 km) **PR 92.8** (149.4 km) First bridge westbound over the Skeena River. "Skeena" means "River of the mist" in First Nation's language.

PG 355.2 (571.7 km) **PR 92.5** (148.8 km) Ferry Island municipal campground; 90 sites, some electrical hookups; covered picnic shelters, barbecues, coin-op showers, Kids' Park, a fishing bar and walking trails with carvings in the trees done by local artists.

PG 355.3 (571.9 km) **PR 92.4** (148.6 km) Second bridge westbound over the Skeena River.

PG 355.6 (572.4 km) **PR 92.1** (148.1 km) Stoplight. Access to Walmart to south.

PG 355.7 (572.5 km) **PR 92** (148 km) Terrace Visitor Centre to south. Sani-dump behind Visitor Centre.

PG 355.8 (572.6 km) **PR 91.9** (147.9 km) Stoplight at Kalum Street. Tim Horton's to south, liquor store to north.

PG 355.9 (572.8 km) **PR 91.8** (147.7 km) A&W.

PG 356 (572.9 km) **PR 91.7** (147.6 km) Pedestrian stoplight. Esso station to north. Napa Auto Parts/Fountain Tire to south.

PG 356.2 (573.4 km) **PR 91.5** (147.1 km) Stoplight. Westbound (Prince Rupert-bound) travelers turn right and cross Sande Overpass. Eastbound (Prince George-bound) travelers turn left (no stoplight) and continue on Highway 16/Keith Street.

PG 356.4 (573.7 km) **PR 91.3** (146.8 km) Stoplight at Highway 16 and Sande. Westbound travelers turn left for continuation of Highway 16 to Prince Rupert, or turn right for Terrace city centre. Eastbound travelers turn right over Sande Overpass for continuation of Highway 16 to Prince George, or go straight ahead for downtown Terrace.

Terrace

PG 356.4 (573.7 km) **PR 91.3** (146.8 km) Located along Yellowhead Highway 16, a 1-1/2 hour's drive east of Prince Rupert. **Population:** 11,320; area 18,581. **Elevation:** 220 feet/67m. **Emergency Services:** Police, fire and ambulance located at intersection of Eby Street and Highway 16. **Police**, phone 250-635-4911. **Fire Department**, phone 250-638-8121. **Ambulance**, phone 250-638-1102. **Hospital**, located on south side off Highway 16; phone 250-635-2211.

Visitor Information: Visitor Centre located in the log Chamber of Commerce building on Highway 16. Open daily in summer, 8 A.M. to 5 P.M.; weekdays in winter, 8:30 A.M. to 4:30 P.M. www.visitterrace.com.

Logging was the major industry in Terrace for decades. For a time, the community was known as the "cedar pole capital of the world," and the world's largest cedar pole (162 feet/50 metres) was cut here. The economy has since diversified, and Terrace remains a commercial hub.

Terrace has major-chain motels, restaurants, fast-food outlets, and "big box" stores like Walmart. There are 15 motels/hotels and 2 shopping centres. The government liquor store is at 3250 Eby St. Secured RV storage can be found at Queensway Mini Storage; phone 250-638-0204 for more information.

The community has a library and art gallery, an aquatic centre with 2 saunas and full-sized and child-sized indoor swimming pools, tennis courts, a golf course, bingo parlour, bowling alley, fitness centres, skateboard park, Bike Skills Park, ice arena, racquetball court and theatre.

Terrace has several private campgrounds. There is a public campground located at Ferry Island (see **Milepost PG 355.2**). Lakelse Lake Provincial Park campground at Furlong Bay, located at Mile 11.3/Km 18 on Highway 37 South. Kleanza Creek Provincial Park campground is located on Highway 16 West at **Milepost PG 345.2**.

Heritage Park Museum, a collection of original log buildings chosen to represent both the different aspects of pioneer life as well as various log building techniques, is well worth a visit. The structures include the Kalum Hotel, Dix's Dance Hall, Hampton Barn, Johnstone Cabin, trapper's cabin, miner's cabin, lineman's cabin, Conroy Homestead cabin. These restored cabins house over 4,000 artifacts. Guided tours available, admission charged. http://heritageparkmuseum.com. To get to the park, follow Kalum St./Skeena View north.

Another historic building, the George Little House, was the homestead of the founder of Terrace. It is now home to the VIA Rail Depot downtown.

Special events in Terrace include the annual National Aboriginal Days celebration held June 21. In August, enjoy the Kermodei Cultural Crawl (month-long cultural site opportunities) and Riverboat Days, held the BC Day long weekend through to the following weekend to include the Riverside Music Festival.

Sportfishing in the **Skeena, Copper,**

Kalum Lake Hotel (1920) is one of the historic structures at Heritage Park in Terrace.
(©Kris Valencia, staff)

Heading up the Kalum River from the boat launch at Fishermen's Memorial Park.
(©Kris Valencia, staff)

Kalum, Nass, Tseax, Kitimat and **Lakelse rivers.** Cutthroat, Dolly Varden and rainbow are found in all lakes and streams; salmon (silver and king) from May to late autumn. Kings average 40 to 70 lbs.; silvers 14 to 20 lbs. Check locally for season and restrictions on steelhead. Information and fishing licenses are available from B.C. Government Access Centre, 3220 Eby St., Terrace; phone 250-638-6515, and at most sporting goods stores.

Yellowhead Highway 16 Log
(continued)

PG 356.5 (573.7 km) **PR 91.2** (146.7 km) Stoplight at Eby Street. Access north to Skeena Mall and Husky gas station.

PG 356.7 (574 km) **PR 91** (146.4 km) Sandman, Denny's.

PG 356.9 (574.4 km) **PR 90.8** (146.1 km) Shell gas station, Boston Pizza.

PG 357 (574.5 km) **PR 90.7** (146 km) Stoplight at Kenney Street. End 4-lane highway, begin 2-lane highway, westbound.

PG 357.2 (574.8 km) **PR 90.5** (145.6 km) Canadian Tire to north (2 entrances).

PG 357.5 (575.3 km) **PR 90.2** (145.2 km) **Junction** with the **Nisga'a Highway.** The Nisga'a Highway travels north providing access to the communities of New Aiyansh, Canyon City, Mill Bay, Greenville and Kincolith. This route is paved, with the exception of a few short gravel breaks north of Lava Lake. There are health centres in each community; call the RCMP for emergencies 250-633-2222.

The major attraction along the Nisga'a Highway is Anhluut'ukwsim Laxmihl Angwinga'asanskwhl (**Nisga'a Memorial Lava Beds Provincial Park**). There's an information kiosk on the Nisga'a lava beds at Mile 42.4, near the southern boundary of the park (at the south end of Lava Lake), and another at Mile 48.9, as the highway narrows and begins winding its way through the lava beds.

The Nisga'a Lava Beds and Area Visitor Centre is located approximately 59 miles/95 km north of the Yellowhead Highway junc-

tion. The Nisga'a Campground, adjacent the visitor centre, has 16 campsites, picnic tables, pump water, firepits, fishing and a $16 camping fee.

PG 358.4 (576.8 km) **PR 89.3** (143.7 km) Lodging with RV parks along highway here includes (from east to west) Evergreen Inn, Wild Duck Motel, Rainbow Inn, Reel Inn, and Kalum Motel.

PG 359 (577.7 km) **PR 88.7** (142.7 km) Entrance to Fishermen's Memorial Park and Boat Launch to south on Kalum River; parking for cars and boat trailers, outhouses, picnic table.

PG 359.1 (577.9 km) **PR 88.6** (142.6 km) Kalum River Bridge.

PG 359.2 (578.1 km) **PR 88.5** (142.4 km) Kitsumkalum Tempo gas station, convenience store and car wash to north. *(NOTE: last gas westbound until Prince Rupert.)* Kitsumkalum RV Park & Boat Launch to south; gravel lot, picnic tables, outhouse, firepits, camping fee $10.

PG 359.7 (578.9 km) **PR 88** (141.6 km) Wide shoulder parking south side of highway.

PG 360 (579.3 km) **PR 87.7** (141.1 km) Small paved turnout to south.

PG 360.2 (579.7 km) **PR 87.5** (140.8 km) Small double-ended turnout to south with litter bin and picnic tables. Good view of river.

PG 362.6 (583.4 km) **PR 85.1** (136.1 km) Zymacord River bridge.

PG 363.1 (584.1 km) **PR 84.6** (135.4 km) Begin 1.3-mile/2.1-km passing lane westbound.

PG 363.3 (584.4 km) **PR 84.4** (135.1 km) Yellow Cedar Lodge.

PG 363.6 (584.9 km) **PR 84.1** (134.6 km) Pioneer Fishing Lodge.

PG 365.7 (588.4 km) **PR 82** (132.1 km) Paved parking to south.

PG 370.9 (596.6 km) **PR 76.8** (123.9 km) Shames River, small gravel parking area to east.

PG 371.1 (597.1 km) **PR 76.6** (123.4 km) Shames Mountain Ski Area 13 km/8 miles north via good gravel road; summer hiking blueberry picking in August.

PG 374.1 (601.8 km) **PR 73.6** (118.7 km) Distance marker eastbound shows Terrace 29

km/18 miles, Kitimat 90 km/56 miles, Prince George 603 km/375 miles.

PG 375.6 (604.2 km) **PR 72.1** (116.3 km) Esker railroad overhead.

PG 376.9 (606.5 km) **PR 70.8** (114 km) Exstew Rest Area to south adjacent river; double-ended turnout with picnic tables, toilets.

PG 377.1 (606.9 km) **PR 70.6** (113.6 km) Avalanche gates.

PG 378 (608.1 km) **PR 69.7** (112.4 km) Exstew River highway and railroad bridges.

PG 382 (614.8 km) **PR 65.7** (105.7 km) Boat launch to south.

PG 382.7 (615.8 km) **PR 65** (104.7 km) *CAUTION: Slow for 40-kmph/25-mph curve as highway turns sharply across railroad tracks. Prepare to stop when lights flash.*

PG 384.1 (618 km) **PR 63.6** (102.5 km) Road narrows at "Carwash Rock."

PG 389.3 (626.5 km) **PR 58.4** (94 km) **Exchamsiks River Provincial Park** to north; day-use only with 20 picnic sites among old-growth Sitka spruce. Open May to October, water and pit toilets. Good salmon fishing in Exchamsiks River. Individual boat access to Gitnadoix River canoeing area across Skeena River.

PG 389.5 (626.8 km) **PR 58.2** (93.7 km) Exchamsiks River bridge.

PG 389.8 (627.3 km) **PR 57.9** (93.2 km) Turnoff to north for boat launch on Exchamsiks River; toilets, tables, litter bin.

PG 392.3 (631.1 km) **PR 55.4** (89.4 km) Kasiks Wilderness Resort to north; lodging, camping.

PG 394.3 (634.5 km) **PR 53.4** (85.9 km) Kasiks railway overhead.

PG 394.7 (636.2 km) **PR 53** (85.3 km) Kasiks River bridge.

PG 398.2 (640.8 km) **PR 49.5** (79.5 km) Small paved turnout to south. Short, steep, rocky access to gravel bars of Skeena River; *high clearance, 4WD vehicle only, drive at your own risk!*

PG 399.7 (643.2 km) **PR 48** (77.4 km) Snowbound Creek. Gravel turnout to south at west end of brige.

PG 401.4 (646 km) **PR 46.3** (74.7 km) Informal parking to south at west end of Kwinsta East Creek.

PG 404.6 (651.1 km) **PR 43.1** (69.4 km) Kwinsta River.

PG 409.1 (658.3 km) **PR 38.6** (62.2 km) Telegraph Point rest area to south on bank of Skeena River; small paved, double-ended turnout with outhouses, picnic tables, litter bins. Watch for seals and sea lions in spring and during salmon season.

PG 413.2 (664.9 km) **PR 34.5** (55.6 km) Paved turnout to south overlooking the Skeena River.

PG 415.4 (668.5 km) **PR 32.3** (52 km) Basalt Creek Rest Area to south just west of Basalt Creek bridge; picnic tables, toilet, litter bins, recycle, and good view of Skeena River. *Limited turnaround space for large RVs.*

PG 416.2 (669.6 km) **PR 31.5** (50.9 km) Khyex River bridge.

PG 418.7 (673.6 km) **PR 29** (46.9 km) Distance marker eastbound shows Terrace 100 km/62 miles, Kitimat 160 km/99 miles, Prince George 637 km/396.

PG 418.8 (674 km) **PR 28.9** (46.7 km) Inver River Bridge.

PG 420.1 (675.8 km) **PR 27.6** (44.7 km) Boat launch parking to south on Skeena River.

PG 422.5 (680 km) **PR 25.2** (39.8 km) Watch for pictograph, visible from the road for eastbound traffic only. It was rediscovered in the early 1950s by Dan Lippett of Prince Rupert. Look below 3 powerline poles at railway grade level; small white sign on rock face. There is no turnout here.

PG 423 (680.5 km) **PR 24.7** (40 km) Skeena River viewpoint (double-ended) to south with picnic tables, litter bins, historical plaque about the Skeena River:

"'K-Shian' The Skeena, 'river of mists', makes a major cleft through the Coast Mountains. To Coastal Tsimshian Indians and Interior tribes it was vital to trade and travel. In later years, Port Essington, near the river's mouth, became the main port on this swift, treacherous waterway—a route serving pioneers from the 1860s to 1914 when the railway was built."

Highway leaves Skeena River westbound.

Beautiful views of Skeena River eastbound.

PG 424.4 (682.8 km) **PR 23.3** (37.7 km) Large double-ended turnout with litter bin to north adjacent Green River Forest Road. Chain-up area in winter.

PG 424.6 (683 km) **PR 23.1** (37.5 km) McNeil River.

PG 424.9 (683.3 km) **PR 22.8** (37.2 km) Begin 0.8-mile/1.3-km passing lane westbound.

PG 427.6 (688 km) **PR 20.1** (32.5 km) Large turnout at top of **Rainbow Summit**, elev. 528 feet/161m.

PG 429.3 (690.7 km) **PR 18.4** (29.8 km) Large paved turnout to north.

PG 429.7 (691.5 km) **PR 18** (29 km) Viewpoint to south; gravel parking area.

PG 430 (692 km) **PR 17.7** (28.5 km) Boat launch (sign). Avalanche gates.

PG 431.9 (695 km) **PR 15.8** (25.5 km) Begin 0.5 mile/0.8 km passing lane eastbound.

PG 432.5 (696 km) **PR 15.2** (24.5 km) Turnoff for **Prudhomme Lake Provincial Park**; 24 campsites, well water, toilets, firewood, fishing, camping fee $16. May 15–Sept. 15. Gates are closed from 11 P.M. to 7 A.M. Kayak rentals are available in season. Gravel access road from highway to lake to north just east of park entrance.

PG 432.9 (696.5 km) **PR 14.8** (24 km) Paved turnout to north with litter bin.

PG 433.2 (697 km) **PR 14.5** (23.5 km) Diana Creek crossing.

PG 433.4 (697.3 km) **PR 14.3** (23.2 km) Turnoff for **Diana Lake Provincial Park**, 1.5 miles/2.4 km south via single-lane gravel road (use turnouts). Day-use facility, hiking trails. Grassy picnic area on lakeshore with picnic tables, kitchen shelter, firewood, grills, water (must be boiled for drinking), wheelchair access, outhouses and garbage cans. Parking for 229 vehicles. The only freshwater swimming beach in the Prince Rupert area. Fish viewing at Diana Creek on the way in to the lake. Fishing for all species of salmon.

PG 438.1 (705 km) **PR 9.6** (15.5 km) Turnout with litter bin to south. Distance marker eastbound shows Terrace 132 km/82 miles, Kitimat 194 km/121 miles, Prince George 703 km/437 miles.

PG 438.2 (705.2 km) **PR 9.5** (15.3 km) **Junction.** Turnoff to south for North Pacific Historic Fishing Village and Museum (6.3 miles). The historic North Pacific Cannery at **PORT EDWARD**, built in 1889, is the oldest cannery village on the north coast. It is a 6.3-mile drive from the main highway to

Colourful historic waterfront area of Prince Rupert near Atlin Terminal. (©Kris Valencia, staff)

the cannery via a paved road that narrows to no shoulders; surface is quite good but has rolling hills best taken slowly with RVs. *NOTE: There is a sharp downhill turn into the parking lot.* Join a guided tour or explore on your own. Admission charged. Phone 250-628-3538. Open May through September, please check in advance for hours of operation. For more information go to www.cannery.ca.

PG 438.3 (705.3 km) **PR 9.4** (15.2 km) Galloway Rapids bridge.

PG 438.6 (705.8 km) **PR 9.1** (14.7 km) Viewpoint to south is double-ended turnout with litter bins and picnic tables.

PG 440.4 (708.5 km) **PR 7.3** (12 km) Oliver Lake rest area to south adjacent highway; picnic tables, litter bins, grills. Oliver Lake Dwarf Forest Nature Walk.

PG 442.1 (711.5 km) **PR 5.6** (9 km) Welcome to Prince Rupert (westbound sign). Westbound turnoff for **Butze Rapids** viewpoint (1.9 km/1.2 miles) and trail. The current flowing over these rapids changes direction with the tide. The phenomenon is called a reversing tidal rapid, and the effect is most dramatic an hour after low tide. Easy, fairly level hiking on well-maintained, chip-covered interpretive trail (used as a loop it is 5.4 km/3.4 miles and takes about 1.5 hours).

PG 442.5 (712 km) **PR 5.2** (8.6 km) Distance marker eastbound shows Port Edward 11 km/7 miles, Terrace 139 km/86 miles, Stewart 710 km/441 miles.

PG 442.7 (712.4 km) **PR 5** (8.1 km) Turnoff for Prince Rupert industrial park. Petro-Canada gas station with propane and sani-dump.

Yellowhead Highway 16 becomes McBride Street as you enter the city centre.

PG 445.2 (716.1 km) **PR 2.5** (4.4 km) Stop sign on McBride at 5th Avenue.

PG 445.5 (717 km) **PR 2.2** (3.5 km) Stoplight on McBride and 3rd Avenue. Turnoff for Cow Bay.

PG 445.6 (717.1 km) **PR 2.1** (3.4 km) Westbound travelers turn onto 2nd Avenue from McBride and continue straight 2.1 miles/3.4 km for ferry terminal.

Eastbound travelers turn onto McBride from 2nd Avenue for continuation of Yel-

lowhead Highway 16E. Safeway supermarket (with Starbucks), gas stations, shopping and other services are located on 2nd Avenue West in downtown Prince Rupert.

PG 447 (719.4 km) **PR 0.7** (1.1 km) Entrance to Prince Rupert RV Campground on left eastbound, on right westbound.

PG 447.6 (720.3 km) **PR 0.1** (0.2 km) Welcome to Prince Rupert (eastbound sign). Posted 50 kmph/31 mph.

PG 447.7 (720.5 km) **PR 0** Ferry terminal for B.C. Ferries and Alaska state ferries. Airport ferry terminal. End of Highway 16 on mainland; Highway 16 continues on Graham Island in Haida Gwaii (formerly the Queen Charlotte Islands) west of Prince Rupert.

Prince Rupert

Located on Kaien Island near the mouth of the Skeena River, 90 miles/145 km by air or water (6-hour ferry ride) south of Ketchikan, AK. **Population**: 13,392; area 21,000. **Emergency Services**: Phone 911 for **Police**, **Ambulance** and **Fire Department**. RCMP, 6th Avenue and McBride Street, non-emergency phone 250-624-2136 (police). **Hospital**, Prince Rupert Regional, phone 250-624-2171.

Visitor Information: Visitor Centre located in the Museum of Northern British Columbia at 100 First Avenue West; open daily in summer, 9 A.M. to 5 P.M. (subject to change). Phone toll-free 1-800-667-1994 and 250-624-5637; www.visitprincerupert.com

Elevation: Sea level. **Climate**: Temperate with mild winters. Annual precipitation 95.4 inches. **Radio**: CHTK 99.1 FM, CBC 860 AM; CJFW 101.9 FM, CFNR 98.1 FM. **Television**: 64 channels, cable. **Newspaper**: *The Northern View* (published weekly).

Prince Rupert, "Gateway to Alaska," was surveyed prior to 1905 by the Grand Trunk

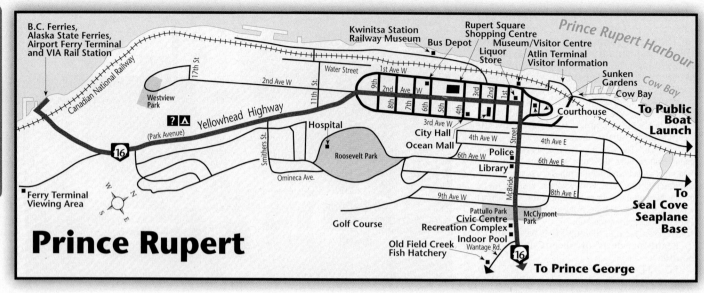

Prince Rupert

Pacific Railway (later Canadian National Railways) as the terminus for Canada's second transcontinental railroad.

Twelve thousand miles/19,300 km of survey lines were studied before a final route along the Skeena River was chosen. Some 833 miles/1,340 km had to be blasted from solid rock, 50 men drowned and costs rose to $105,000 a mile (the final cost of $300 million was comparable to Panama Canal construction) before the last spike was driven near Fraser Lake on April 7, 1914. Financial problems continued to plague the company, forcing it to amalgamate to become part of the Canadian National Rail-ways system in 1923.

Charles M. Hays, president of the company, was an enthusiastic promoter of the new terminus, which was named by competition from 12,000 entries. While "Port Rupert" had been submitted by two contestants, "Prince Rupert" (from Miss Eleanor M. Macdonald of Winnipeg) called to mind the dashing soldier–explorer, cousin to Charles II of England and first governor of the Hudson's Bay Co., who had traded on the coast rivers for years. Three first prizes of $250 were awarded and Prince Rupert was officially named in 1906.

Prince Rupert's proposed port and adja-cent waters were surveyed by G. Blanchard Dodge of the hydrographic branch of the Marine Dept. in 1906, and in May the little steamer *Constance* carried settlers from the village of Metlakatla to clear the first ground on Kaien Island. Its post office opened November 23, 1906, and Prince Rupert, with a tent-town population of 200, began an association with communities on the Queen Charlotte Islands, with Stewart, and with Hazelton, 200 miles/322 km up the Skeena River.

Incorporated as a city March 10, 1910, Prince Rupert attracted settlers responding to the enthusiasm of Hays, with his dreams of a population of 50,000 and world markets supplied by his railroad. Both the city and the railway suffered a great loss when Charles M. Hays went down with the *Titanic* in April 1912. Even so, work went ahead on the Grand Trunk Pacific. Two years later the first train arrived at Prince Rupert, linking the western port with the rest of Canada. Since then, the city has progressed through 2 world wars, economic ups and downs and periods of growth and expansion, not only as a busy port but also as a visitor centre.

During WWII, more than a million tons of freight and 73,000 people, both military and civilian, passed through Prince Rupert on their way to military operations in Alaska and the South Pacific.

In 1951, construction of wood processing facilities on Watson Island increased the eco-nomic and industrial potential of the area. The facilities, which included a pulp mill and a kraft mill, ceased operations in 2001.

With the start of the Alaska State Ferry System in 1963, and the British Columbia Ferry System in 1966, Prince Rupert's place as an important visitor centre and terminal point for highway, rail and marine transpor-tation was assured.

Prince Rupert is the second major deep-sea port on Canada's west coast, exporting grain, lumber and other resources to Europe and Asia. Prince Rupert has also become a major coal and grain port with facilities on Ridley Island. Other industries include fish-ing and fish processing, and the manufac-ture of forest products. Prince Rupert is underlaid by muskeg over solid rock.

Lodging & Services

More than a dozen hotels and motels accommodate the influx of ferry passengers each summer. Many restaurants feature fresh

PRINCE RUPERT
DISCOVER OUR NATURE

Northern British Columbia
REGION

SUPER, NATURAL
BRITISH COLUMBIA®
CANADA

www.visitprincerupert.com

local seafood in season.

Modern supermarkets and shopping centres are available. Government liquor store is at the corner of 2nd Avenue and Highway 16. There are 5 main banks and a laundromat.

The Jim Ciccone Civic Centre, located on McBride Street, has squash, basketball and badminton; ice skating and roller skating rinks (summer only); phone 250-624-6707 for more information. Earl Mah Aquatic Centre next door has an indoor swimming pool, tot pool, weight room, saunas, showers, whirlpool, slides and diving boards. Access for persons with disabilities. Phone 250-627-7946. Phone 250-624-9000 for 24-hour recorded information. Admission charged.

The golf course includes 18-hole course, resident pro, equipment rental, clubhouse and restaurant. Entrance on 9th Avenue West.

Camping

Prince Rupert RV Campground on Highway 16, between downtown and the ferry terminal, has 87 campsites with hookups, unserviced sites, restrooms, hot showers and laundry; phone 250-627-1000. Campground host meets late arrivals on BC Ferries run from Port Hardy.

There are 24 campsites at Prudhomme Lake Provincial Park, located 15.2 miles/24.5 km east from the ferry terminal at **Milepost PG 432.5** Yellowhead Highway 16. Open May 15–Sept. 15.

Transportation

Air: North Pacific Seaplanes and Inland Air Charter to outlying villages and Queen Charlotte Islands; Air Canada and Hawkair offer daily service to Vancouver.

Prince Rupert airport is located on Digby Island. A city-operated ferry/bus shuttle is provided for passengers with airline tickets. The airport shuttle leaves from the Highliner Plaza Hotel and Conference Centre. Please phone 250-622-2222 to find out what time you must catch your shuttle.

There is a seaplane base at Seal Cove with airline and helicopter charter services.

Ferries: British Columbia Ferry System (BC Ferries), Fairview dock, phone 1-888-223-3779, provides automobile and passenger service from Prince Rupert to Port Hardy, and between Prince Rupert and Skidegate in the Queen Charlotte Islands.

Alaska Marine Highway System, Fairview dock, phone 250-627-1744 or 1-800-642-0066, provides automobile and passenger service to southeastern Alaska.

Car Rentals: National Car Rental, phone 250-624-5318.

Taxi: Skeena Taxi, phone 250-624-2185. Prince Rupert taxi cabs are powered by LNG (liquefied natural gas).

Railroad: VIA Rail service to Prince George and Jasper. VIA Rail station is located at the B.C. Ferries terminal. Phone from Canada or the U.S. 1-888-842-7245; or www.viarail.ca.

Bus: City Transit System, phone 250-624-3343. Greyhound, phone 250-624-5090; www.greyhound.ca. Farwest Bus Lines, phone 250-624-6400. Charter sightseeing tours available.

RV Storage: Secured, covered storage at Queensway Mini Storage in Terrace; phone 250-638-0204.

Attractions

Totem Pole Tour. Scattered through-out the city are 18 large cedar totem poles, each with its own story. Most are reproductions by Native craftsmen of the original Tsimshian (SHIM-shian) poles from the mainland and the Haida (HI-duh) carvings from the Queen Charlotte Islands. The originals are now in the British Columbia Provincial Museum in Victoria. Several totem poles may be seen at Totem Park near the hospital. City maps and guidebooks are available at the Museum of Northern British Columbia.

City Parks. Mariner's Park, overlooking the harbour, has memorials to those who have been lost at sea. Roosevelt Park honours Prince Rupert's wartime history. Service Park overlooks downtown Prince Rupert. Sunken Gardens, located behind the Provincial Courthouse, is a public garden planted in the excavations for an earlier court building. City maps are available at the Visitor Centre, located in the Museum of Northern B.C.

The Museum of Northern British Columbia, is situated in an award-winning Chatham Village Longhouse, displays an outstanding collection of artifacts depicting the settlement history of British Columbia's north coast. Traveling art collections are displayed in the gallery. Located at 1st Avenue and McBride Street. Hours are 9 A.M. to 5 P.M. daily in summer and 9 A.M. to 5 P.M. Tuesday–Saturday in winter. Phone 250-624-3207. Admission charged.

Cow Bay. Located along the waterfront northeast of downtown, this revitalized area boasts numerous boutiques, cafes, a popular pub and a bed-and-breakfast. The ambience is historic (antique phone booths, old-fashioned lampposts), but the theme is bovine, with businesses and buildings bearing cow names or cow colors (the black and white Holstein pattern is popular).

Kwinitsa Station Railway Museum. Built in 1911, Kwinitsa Station is one of the few surviving stations of the nearly 400 built along the Grand Trunk Pacific Railway line. In 1985 the station was moved to the Prince Rupert waterfront park. Restored rooms, exhibits and videos tell the story of early Prince Rupert and the role the railroad played in the city's development. Phone for hours of operation: 250-624-3207, ext. 27.

Prince Rupert Fire Museum. This small museum is located at the fire hall on 1st Avenue, just south of the Museum of Northern British Columbia. The museum houses a rebuilt 1925 R.E.O. Speedwagon fire engine.

Special Events. Seafest is a 4-day celebration, held the second weekend in June, which includes a parade and water-jousting competition. June 21 is National Aboriginal Day and July 1 is Canada Day. The All Native Basketball Tournament, held in February, is the largest event of its kind in Canada.

North Pacific Cannery National Historic Site at Port Edward is located east of Prince Rupert on the Yellowhead Highway (turnoff at **Milepost PG 438.2**), then 6.3 mile south via paved road. Built in 1889, North Pacific Cannery is the oldest and most intact salmon cannery remaining on the West Coast of North America. Open May through September; www.northpacific cannery.ca.

Swim at Diana Lake. This provincial park, about 13 miles/21 km from downtown on Highway 16, offers the only freshwater swimming in the Prince Rupert area. Picnic tables, kitchen shelter, parking and beach.

Visit Haida Gwaii (formerly the Queen Charlotte Islands). Ferry service is available between Prince Rupert and Skidegate on Graham Island, largest of the 150 islands and islets that form the Haida Gwaii. More information at www.gohaidagwaii.ca.

Go Fishing. For information on bait, locations, regulations and licensing, contact local sporting goods stores or the Visitor Centre. This area abounds in all species of salmon, steelhead, crab and shrimp. Public boat launch facility is located at Rushbrook Public Floats at the north end of the waterfront. There is a parking fee. Public floats are also available at Fairview, past the Alaska Marine Highway terminal, near the breakwater.

Prince Rupert Visitor Centre and Museum of British Museum are inside this longhouse on 1st Avenue. (©Kris Valencia, staff)

Cassiar Highway

CONNECTS: Yellowhead Hwy. to Alaska Hwy.

Length: 450 miles   Road Surface: Paved   Season: Open all year

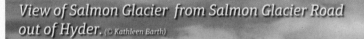

View of Salmon Glacier from Salmon Glacier Road out of Hyder. (© Kathleen Barth)

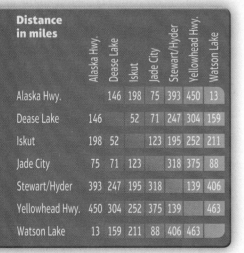

Distance in miles	Alaska Hwy.	Dease Lake	Iskut	Jade City	Stewart/Hyder	Yellowhead Hwy.	Watson Lake
Alaska Hwy.		146	198	75	393	450	13
Dease Lake	146		52	71	247	304	159
Iskut	198	52		123	195	252	211
Jade City	75	71	123		318	375	88
Stewart/Hyder	393	247	195	318		139	406
Yellowhead Hwy.	450	304	252	375	139		463
Watson Lake	13	159	211	88	406	463	

he Cassiar Highway (BC Highway 37), completed in 1972, is an all-season road connecting the Yellowhead Highway in British Columbia with the Alaska Highway in Yukon Territory, and also providing access to the communities of Stewart, BC, and Hyder, AK, via Highway 37A.

Dramatically improved in recent years

thanks to road reconstruction, the 450-mile-/724-km-long Cassiar Highway is a scenic route with sufficient fuel and service stops, outstanding scenery and good wildlife viewing. Watch for black bears with cubs along the highway (especially in spring); caribou at Gnat Pass (spring and fall); and Stone sheep south of Good Hope.

The Cassiar Highway junctions with Yellowhead Highway 16 at the Skeena River bridge (**Milepost PG 298** in the YELLOWHEAD HIGHWAY 16 section) and travels north to junction with the Alaska Highway 13.3 miles/21.4 km west of Watson Lake, YT (**Milepost DC 626.2** in the ALASKA HIGHWAY section). Total driving distance is 450.1 miles/723.7 km. (The Cassiar route offers a savings of about 130 miles/210 km over the all-Alaska Highway route.)

The Cassiar provides access to Hyder, AK, and Stewart, BC, via 40-mile-/64-km-long Highway 37A from Meziadin Junction at **Milepost J 97.5**; and to Telegraph Creek, via a 70-mile/113-km side road from Dease Lake junction at **Milepost J 303.9**. See detailed road logs and community descriptions this section.

The Cassiar Highway is generally narrower than most 2-lane highways, with little or no shoulder. It has easy curves and some long straight stretches. There are no pass-

(continues on page 260)

Major Attractions:

©Kris Valencia, staff

Hyder, AK/Stewart, BC, Salmon and Bear Glaciers, Grand Canyon of the Stikine River, Telegraph Creek, Jade City
Highest Summit:
Gnat Pass 4,072 ft.

Cassiar Highway

Yellowhead Highway Junction to Alaska Highway Junction (includes Stewart-Hyder Access Rd. and Telegraph Creek Rd.)

© 2014 The MILEPOST®

Key to mileage boxes

miles/kilometres
miles/kilometres from:
J-Yellowhead Hwy. Jct.
AH-Alaska Highway Jct.
M-Meziadin Lake Junction
D-Dease Lake Junction
PG-Prince George
PR-Prince Rupert
WL-Watson Lake
T-Teslin

Map Location

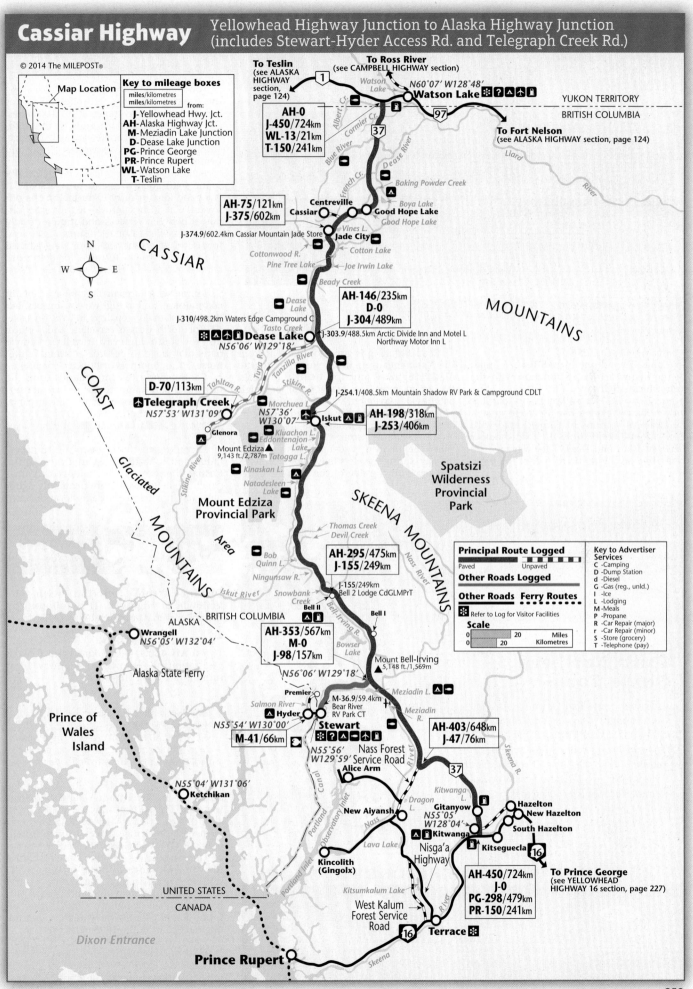

To Teslin (see ALASKA HIGHWAY section, page 124)

To Ross River (see CAMPBELL HIGHWAY section)

N60°07' W128°48'
Watson Lake

1

Watson Creek

Albert Cr.

Cormier Cr.

97

To Fort Nelson (see ALASKA HIGHWAY section, page 124)

YUKON TERRITORY
BRITISH COLUMBIA

Liard River

37

AH-0
J-450/724km
WL-13/21km
T-150/241km

Blue River

French Cr.

Dease River

Baking Powder Creek

CASSIAR

MOUNTAINS

AH-75/121km
J-375/602km

Centreville
Cassiar

Boya Lake

Good Hope Lake
Good Hope Lake

J-374.9/602.4km Cassiar Mountain Jade Store

Jade City

Vines L.

Cotton Lake

Cottonwood R.
Pine Tree Lake

Joe Irwin Lake

Beady Creek

AH-146/235km
D-0
J-304/489km

Dease Lake

J-310/498.2km Waters Edge Campground C
Tasto Creek

❄ ⛺ ✈ 🏨 **Dease Lake**
N56°06' W129°18'

J-303.9/488.5km Arctic Divide Inn and Motel L
Northway Motor Inn L

MOUNTAINS

Tuya River

Tanzilla River

Stikine R.

D-70/113km

✈ **Telegraph Creek**
N57°53' W131°09'

Tahltan R.

Morchuea L.
N57°36' W130°07'

J-254.1/408.5km Mountain Shadow RV Park & Campground CDLT

⛺ 🏨 **Iskut**

AH-198/318km
J-253/406km

COAST

Glaciated

Glenora

Kluachon L.
Eddontenajon Lake

Mount Edziza ▲
9,143 ft./2,787m

Tatogga L.

Spatsizi Wilderness Provincial Park

⛺ Kinaskan L.

Natadesleen Lake

Mount Edziza Provincial Park

Area

Stikine River

Thomas Creek
Devil Creek

SKEENA MOUNTAINS

⛺ Bob Quinn L.

Ningunsaw R.

AH-295/475km
J-155/249km

Iskut River

Snowbank Creek

J-155/249km
Bell 2 Lodge CdGLMPrT

Bell-Irving R.

Nass River

Bell I

MOUNTAINS

Principal Route Logged
Paved ▬▬▬ Unpaved ▬▬▬

Other Roads Logged

Other Roads ▬▬ **Ferry Routes** ▬▬

❄ Refer to Log for Visitor Facilities

Scale
0 ▬▬▬ 20 Miles
0 ▬▬▬ 20 Kilometres

Key to Advertiser Services
C -Camping
D -Dump Station
d -Diesel
G -Gas (reg., unld.)
I -Ice
L -Lodging
M -Meals
P -Propane
R -Car Repair (major)
r -Car Repair (minor)
S -Store (grocery)
T -Telephone (pay)

Bell II
⛺

ALASKA
BRITISH COLUMBIA

Wrangell
N56°05' W132°04'

AH-353/567km
M-0
J-98/157km
N56°06' W129°18'

Bowser Lake

Mount Bell-Irving ▲
5,148 ft./1,569m

Meziadin L. ⛺

Alaska State Ferry

Prince of Wales Island

Premier

Salmon River

⛺ Hyder
N55°54' W130°00'

M-36.9/59.4km
Bear River RV Park CT

Meziadin

Nass River

Stewart
❄ ? ⛺ ✈ 🏨

AH-403/648km
J-47/76km

N55°56' W129°59'

Ketchikan
N55°04' W131°06'

M-41/66km

Nass Forest Service Road

37

Alice Arm

New Aiyansh

Kitwanga L.

Dragon L.

Gitanyow
N55°05' W128°04'

Kitwanga

Hazelton
New Hazelton

South Hazelton

Kitseguecla

16

Portland Inlet

Observatory Inlet

Nass River

Nisga'a Highway

Kincolith (Gingolx)

Lava Lake

AH-450/724km
J-0
PG-298/479km
PR-150/241km

To Prince George (see YELLOWHEAD HIGHWAY 16 section, page 227)

UNITED STATES
CANADA

Kitsumkalum Lake

West Kalum Forest Service Road

Portland Canal

16

Terrace ❄

Skeena River

Prince Rupert

Dixon Entrance

There's good bear watching along the Cassiar. Look for both black bears and grizzly bears.
(©Kris Valencia, staff)

(continued from page 258)

ing lanes beyond one in the first few miles of the highway from its junction with the Yellowhead Highway. *Drive with your headlights on at all times.* Although not particularly hilly, there are a few 8 percent grades. Be aware of sections of bermed road with 2- to 5-foot dropoffs from the road shoulder between Iskut and Dease Lake. There is no centerline on the northern half of the highway.

Road surfacing is good to excellent from the Yellowhead Highway junction to the Alaska Highway junction, with the exception of an occasional gravel break or rough patches of pavement. Road improvement projects may be under way in summer: Slow down for construction flaggers.

Carry chains from October to April. While the highway is generally clear of snow by May, spring travelers may see ice on lakes and snow on the side of the road at higher elevations until June.

Watch for logging and freight trucks on the Cassiar Highway. *WARNING: Exercise extreme caution when passing or being passed by these trucks. Reduce speed and allow trucks adequate clearance.*

Food, gas and lodging are available along the Cassiar Highway, although distances between services averages 60 to 100 miles. Gas is available at both ends of the highway and at: Kitwanga, Stewart, Bell 2 Lodge, Tatogga Lake Resort (seasonal), Iskut and Dease Lake.

Be sure your vehicle is mechanically sound with good tires and carry a spare. It is a good idea to carry extra fuel in the off-season. Check the highway log for exact distances between services and inquire locally about possible seasonal closures of services. In case of emergency, motorists are advised to flag down trucks to radio for help since *cell phone service is generally not available on the Cassiar.*

Minor vehicle repair may be available in communities and at highway businesses, but the nearest major repair is in Watson Lake, YT, for north Cassiar travelers, and Terrace, BC, for south highway travelers. Vehicle parts may have to be ordered from Whitehorse, YT, or Smithers or Prince George, BC.

Camp at private campgrounds or in the provincial park campgrounds. There are several private campgrounds, provincial parks, and rustic recreation sites. *NOTE: It is unlawful to camp overnight in turnouts and rest areas unless otherwise posted.*

According to the Ministry of Transportation and Infrastructure, litter bins on the Cassiar Highway are often moved to areas which are being used more frequently. Litter bins may not be in the same location from season to season.

Cassiar Highway Log

Distance from junction with the Yellowhead Highway (J) is followed by distance from Alaska Highway (AH).

BC HIGHWAY 37 NORTH

J 0 AH 450.1 (723.7 km) Petro Canada gas station on Yellowhead Highway 16 at turnoff for Cassiar Highway.

Junction with the Yellowhead Highway, **Milepost PG 298**. Turn to page 252 in the YELLOWHEAD HIGHWAY section and continue with log to Prince Rupert or read log back to front to continue to Prince George.

J 0.1 (0.2 km) **AH 450** (723.5 km) Bridge across Skeena River from Yellowhead Highway 16 to Cassiar Highway.

J 0.2 (0.3 km) **AH 449.9** (723.4 km) Turn east on Bridge Street to view totem poles of **GITWANGAK**. The Native reserve of Gitwangak was renamed after sharing the name Kitwanga with the adjacent white settlement. Gitwangak has some of the finest authentic totem poles in the area. Also here is St. Paul's Anglican Church (the bell tower standing beside the church houses the original bell from the 1893 bell tower).

J 0.3 (0.5 km) **AH 449.8** (723.2 km) Distance marker northbound shows Stewart 217 km/134 miles, Dease Lake 489 km/303 miles, Alaska Highway junction 724 km/

450 miles.

J 1.7 (2.7 km) **AH 448.4** (721.6 km) Begin 0.4-mile/0.6-km passing lane northbound. This is the only truck lane on the Cassiar Highway.

J 2.5 (4 km) **AH 447.6** (719.7 km) Turnoff to west for RV park. Kitwanga River Salmon Enumeration floating fence, located near the river's mouth, directs fish through visual boxes, where they can be identified and counted. Good opportunity to watch the life cycle of the Pacific salmon. The Kitwanga River, a tributary of the Skeena River, supports ocean runs of steelhead and all 5 Pacific salmon, with pinks accounting for some 97 percent of the returning stock. Most of the salmon returning to the Kitwanga spawn during the late summer and early fall in the upper sections of the river.

J 2.7 (4.3 km) **AH 447.4** (719.4 km) South end of 1.5-mile/2.4-km Kitwanga Loop; post office, gas station about half-way around the loop. This access road leads to **KITWANGA** (pop. 481), Centennial Park and Kitwanga Fort Site (description follows).

Kitwanga is at the crossroads of the old upper Skeena "grease trail" trade. The "grease" was eulachon (candlefish) oil, which was a trading staple among tribes of the Coast and Interior. The grease trails are believed to have extended north to the Bering Sea.

A paved turnout with litter barrel and sign on the Kitwanga access road mark **Kitwanga Fort National Historic Site**, where a wooden fortress and palisade once crowned the large, rounded hill here. Seven interpretive panels along the stairway and boardwalk to Battle Hill explain the history of the site. Kitwanga Fort was the first major western Canadian Native site commemorated by Parks Canada.

J 4.4 (7 km) **AH 445.6** (717.1 km) North end of 1.5-mile/2.4-km loop access road (Kitwanga North Road) to Kitwanga; see description preceding milepost. Dollops gas station is located about halfway around the loop. At 0.7 km from this turnoff is the National Historic Site of Battle Hill. Also **junction** with alternate access route (signed Hazelton–Kitwanga Road) from Hazelton to the Cassiar Highway via the north side of the Skeena River.

J 5.5 (9 km) **AH 444.6** (714.7 km) Tea Lake Forest Service Road to east.

The mountain chain of Seven Sisters is visible to southwest (weather permitting) the next few miles northbound.

J 12.6 (20.3 km) **AH 437.5** (703.4 km) Turnout with litter barrels to west.

J 13.1 (21 km) **AH 437** (702.7 km) South access to **GITANYOW**, formerly Kitwancool (1.4 miles/2.3 km from highway), is a small Indian village; gas bar with convenience store (basic automotive supplies, groceries, snacks, fast-food style hot items). Gitanyow has one of the largest concentrations of standing totem poles in northwestern British Columbia. Guided tours of the totem poles may be available. Ask at gas bar if totem centre is open.

J 16.2 (26 km) **AH 433.9** (697.7 km) North access to Gitanyow.

J 18.9 (30.3 km) **AH 431.2** (693.4 km) Bridge over Moonlit Creek.

J 19.1 (30.6 km) **AH 431** (693.1 km)

Turnoff to east for rest area below highway; tables, toilets, litter barrels.

J 21.2 (34 km) **AH 428.9** (689.7 km) Distance marker northbound shows Meziadin Junction 121 km/75 miles, Stewart 183 km/114 miles, Dease Lake 454 km/282 miles.

J 26.4 (42.4 km) **AH 423.7** (681.3 km) Kitwancool Forest Service Road.

J 28.4 (45.6 km) **AH 421.7** (678.1 km) Entering Nass Wildlife Management Area northbound.

J 39.2 (63 km) **AH 410.9** (660.7 km) **Cranberry River** bridge No. 1. A favorite salmon stream in summer; consult fishing regulations.

J 42.3 (68 km) **AH 407.7** (656.1 km) Large, informal gravel turnout.

J 45.7 (73.4 km) **AH 404.4** (650.3 km) Distance marker northbound shows Meziadin Junction 83 km/52 miles, Stewart 144 km/89 miles, Dease Lake 415 km/258 miles.

J 45.9 (73.7 km) **AH 404.2** (650 km) Distance marker southbound shows Kitwanga 74 km/46 miles, Terrace 167 km/104 miles, Smithers 180 km/112 miles.

J 46.9 (74.7 km) **AH 403.2** (649 km) Turnout to west.

J 47.3 (76 km) **AH 402.8** (647.7 km) **Cranberry Junction**. Highway 37 junctions with Nass Forest Service Road, which leads west 30 miles/48 km to Nass Camp and beyond to **New Aiyansh** (pop. 806) and the Nisga'a Highway. Nass Road is rough and narrow; not recommended for low-clearance vehicles.

J 47.6 (76.5 km) **AH 402.5** (647.2 km) Cranberry River bridge No. 2. *Watch for bears.*

J 48.1 (77.3 km) **AH 402** (646.4 km) Mitten Forest Service Road.

J 50.6 (81.3 km) **AH 399.5** (642.4 km) Bonus Lake B.C. Forest Recreation Site to west has 3 campsites and dock for small boats and canoes.

J 50.7 (81.4 km) **AH 399.4** (642.3 km) Derrick Creek.

J 51.8 (83.2 km) **AH 398.3** (640.5 km) Derrick Lake B.C. Forest Recreation Site to south.

J 53.5 (86 km) **AH 396.6** (637.7 km) BC Hydro power line crosses and parallels highway. Completed in 1990, this line links Stewart to the BC Hydro power grid. Previously, Stewart's power was generated by diesel fuel.

J 55 (88.4 km) **AH 395.1** (635.3 km) Entering Kalum Forest District northbound. Watch for signs telling dates of logging activity, and observe patterns of regrowth.

J 56.1 (90 km) **AH 394** (633.7 km) Distance marker northbound shows Meziadin Junction 66 km/41 miles, Stewart 127 km/79 miles, Dease Lake 398 km/247 miles.

J 62.8 (100.8 km) **AH 387.3** (622.9 km) Grizzly culvert.

J 64.6 (103.7 km) **AH 385.5** (620 km) Paved turnout to west with litter bins.

J 66.9 (107.4 km) **AH 383.2** (616.3 km) Brown Bear Creek culvert.

J 68.3 (109.8 km) **AH 381.8** (614 km) Brown Bear Forest Service Road leads east 6 miles/10 km to Jigsaw Lake Recreation Site (MTCA) with 4 rustic campsites, canoeing, boating and fishing. Also access to Brown Bear Lake (9 miles/14 km) and Bonney Lakes (21 miles/34 km).

Views northbound (weather permitting) of the Coast Mountains to the northwest.

J 68.7 (110.3 km) **AH 381.4** (613.4 km) Van Dyke culvert.

J 70.8 (113.7 km) **AH 379.2** (610 km) Paved turnout with litter bin to west.

J 74 (118.7 km) **AH 376** (605 km) Distance marker northbound shows Meziadin Junction 38 km/24 miles, Stewart 99 km/62 miles, Dease Lake 370 km/230 miles.

J 75.4 (121 km) **AH 374.7** (602.7 km) Kitwankliks Creek.

J 77.5 (124.5 km) **AH 372.6** (599.2 km) Large paved parking area to west with litter bin.

Watch for black bears grazing alongside the highway.

Distance marker southbound shows Kitwanga 125 km/78 miles, Terrace 218 km/135 miles, Smithers 231 km/144 miles.

J 79.4 (127.5 km) **AH 370.7** (596.2 km) Paved turnout to west.

J 80.7 (129.7 km) **AH 369.4** (594 km) Wolverine Creek culvert.

J 82.6 (132.7 km) **AH 367.5** (591 km) Moore Creek.

J 85.8 (137.7 km) **AH 364.3** (586 km) Paved turnout to west.

J 86.1 (138.2 km) **AH 364** (585.5 km) Ellsworth culvert.

J 86.7 (139 km) **AH 363.4** (584.7 km) Van Dyke commercial camp to east; no public services.

J 88.4 (141.9 km) **AH 361.7** (581.8 km) *Slow for 50-kmph/31-mph curve as highway makes winding descent northbound to Nass River.*

J 88.7 (142.4 km) **AH 361.4** (581.3 km) Paved rest area with picnic tables, toilets and litter bins to east.

J 88.8 (142.6 km) **AH 361.3** (581.1 km) **Nass River Bridge**; *1-lane wood plank bridge, slippery when wet, yield to oncoming traffic.* The gorge is almost 400 feet/122m wide; main span of bridge is 187 feet/57m. Bridge decking is 130 feet/40m above the riverbed. Plaque at north end of bridge commemorates bridge opening in 1972 that joined roads to form Highway 37.

J 94.1 (151.1 km) **AH 356** (572.6 km) Tintina Creek bridge. Along with Hanna Creek, this stream produces 40 percent of the red salmon spawning in the Meziadin Lake watershed. Small parking areas on both sides.

J 95.2 (153.1 km) **AH 354.8** (570.6 km) Large informal gravel turnout to west.

J 95.5 (153.4 km) **AH 354.6** (570.3 km) Bridge over Hanna Creek South. Red salmon can be observed spawning here in autumn from a viewing platform. It is illegal to fish for or harass these fish. *CAUTION: Watch for bears.*

J 96.5 (155.3 km) **AH 353.4** (568.4 km) Turnoff for the lovely **Meziadin Lake Provincial Park** downhill to west; 66 campsites (many on lake), day-use area with picnic tables and shelter, small store (water pump adjacent), toilets, some wheelchair access, pay phone, WiFi, swimming, firewood, recycling, bear-proof garbage containers, boat launch. Camping fee $16, pay campground host. *CAUTION: Watch for bears. The hills around the lake are prime bear habitat.*

Meziadin Lake (pronounced Mezy-AD-in) has good fishing for rainbow trout, mountain whitefish and Dolly Varden. Best fishing at mouths of small streams draining into the lake. Four species of salmon spawn in the lake. This is one of only 3 areas in the province where salmon spawn in the bays and inlets of a lake.

J 97 (156.1 km) **AH 352.9** (567.9 km)
Check your fuel (northbound sign): Next gas northbound Stewart 65 km/40 miles, Bell II 93 km/58 miles.

J 97.5 (156.6 km) **AH 352.6** (567.1 km)
Meziadin Junction. This is the junction of Highway 37 (Cassiar) with Highway 37A (Stewart–Hyder Access Road). *Stop sign for traffic northbound on Highway 37. No stop for southbound traffic on Highway 37.* Highway 37A leads west 38 miles/61 km to Stewart, BC, and 41 miles/66 km west to Hyder, AK; food, gas, lodging and camping are available at these communities. Turnout with litter bin and map to north at start of Highway 37A.

> **Junction** with BC Highway 37A west to Stewart, BC, and Hyder, AK. See "Stewart, BC–Hyder, AK, Access Road" log beginning on facing page.

This junction can be confusing. Choose your route carefully. Turnoff for Highway 37A to Stewart and Hyder is a left turn northbound. Northbound travelers turn right to continue on Cassiar Highway to Alaska Highway. Southbound travelers go straight southbound to Stewart and Hyder or turn left to continue on Cassiar Highway to Yellowhead Highway 16.

J 97.7 (156.8 km) **AH 352.4** (566.9 km)
Distance marker northbound shows Iskut 260 km/162 miles, Dease Lake 333 km/207 miles, Alaska Highway 569 km/353 miles.

J 102.1 (164 km) **AH 348** (559.7 km)
Hanna Creek North *narrow, wood-decked bridge, slippery when wet.*

J 105.4 (169.3 km) **AH 344.7** (554.2 km)
Large double-ended turnout to west with litter bins. Southbound brake-check area with grade profile.

J 117.1 (187.7 km) **AH 333** (536 km)
Slow for 70 kmph/43 mph downhill curve northbound approaching Bell I Crossing.

J 117.3 (188 km) **AH 332.8** (535.7 km)
Bell I Crossing: Bell-Irving River Bridge #2 *(CAUTION: metal grating).*

J 117.4 (188.2 km) **AH 332.7** (535.3 km)
Double-ended paved turnout at north end of bridge to rest area with picnic tables, pit toilets and litter barrels.
Highway climbs long curve northbound to Kilometrepost 190.

J 119.4 (191.4 km) **AH 330.7** (532.3 km)
Spruce Creek bridge.

Northbound, watch for trucks turning at **Northwest Transmission Line (NTL)** service roads. Construction of the 287-kilovolt transmission line began in January 2012, with an in-service date of spring 2014. The line will eventually extend north to Dease Lake, providing power to the mining sector and local communities currently relying on diesel generators. The 344-km/214-mile transmission line extends from the Skeena Substation near Terrace to Bob Quinn Lake on the Cassiar.

J 120.8 (193.7 km) **AH 329.3** (530 km)
Distance marker northbound shows Dease Lake 294 km/183 miles, Alaska Highway 530 km/329 miles.

J 121.9 (195.3 km) **AH 328.2** (528.4 km)
Informal gravel turnout to west.

J 123.2 (197.4 km) **AH 326.9** (526.3 km)
Small gravel turnout to west.

J 124.8 (200 km) **AH 325.3** (523.7 km)
Bell-Irving River to west.

J 126.3 (202.6 km) **AH 323.8** (521.1 km)
Cousins Creek culvert. Turnout to east.

J 127.9 (205.2 km) **AH 322.2** (518.5 km) Ritchie Creek bridge. *Wood-decked bridge; slippery when wet.* Parking to west just beyond north end of bridge.

J 130.1 (209 km) **AH 320** (514.7 km)
Gravel turnout to west.

J 131.7 (211.3 km) **AH 318.4** (512.4 km) Taft Creek bridge. *Wood-decked bridge; slippery when wet.* Gravel turnout to west at north end of bridge.

J 133.4 (214 km) **AH 316.7** (509.7 km)
Signed pullout to west is a large gravel turnout with litter bin.

J 134.3 (215.5 km) **AH 315.8** (508.2 km)
Signed access to Brucejack Project (no trespassing), a high-grade gold excavation project in the Valley of the Kings.

J 137 (220 km) **AH 313.1** (503.7 km)
Distance marker southbound shows Meziadin Junction 64 km/40 miles, Stewart 126 km/78 miles, Kitwanga 221 km/137 miles.

Large gravel turnout to west.

J 137.3 (220.5 km) **AH 312.8** (503.2 km)
Deltaic Creek bridge. Entering Tahltan Territory northbound (sign).

J 138.1 (221.6 km) **AH 312** (502.1 km)
Distance marker northbound shows Iskut 197 km/122 miles, Dease Lake 270 km/168 miles, Alaska Highway 506 km/314 miles.

J 142.8 (229.2 km) **AH 307.3** (494.5 km)
Glacier Creek.

J 145 (232.7 km) **AH 305.1** (491 km)
Skowill Creek bridge.

J 149.5 (239.8 km) **AH 300.6** (483.9 km)
Oweegee Creek, with informal double-ended gravel turnout to east at south end.

J 153.6 (246.8 km) **AH 296.5** (476.9 km)
Mehan Lake Provincial Rest Area to east. Gravel parking area with information kiosk, picnic tables, litter bins, toilets, cartop boat launch. Fly or troll for small rainbows.

Mehan Lake to Burrage Seal Coating Project (northbound sign).

J 155 (249 km) **AH 295.1** (474.7 km)
Slow for 70-kmph/43-mph speed zone northbound at **Bell 2 Lodge**; food, gas, lodging and camping (description follows).

Bell 2 Lodge. Situated along the shores of the Bell Irving River. Once a basic service station, now a modern all-service lodge for travelers heading north or south. Enjoy the comforts of home in one of our log cha-

©Kris Valencia, staff

lets featuring separate entrances, satellite TV, ensuite bathrooms and wood-burning fireplaces. Full RV hookups (15-amp), tenting/camping facilities, with hot showers and laundry. Visit our fully licensed restaurant for excellent cuisine and a warm atmosphere. Bell 2 is open all year-round. Our amenities include: high-speed Internet access, telephone, coffee shop, minor tire repair and gas/diesel/propane. We accept all major credit cards. For reservations and information call 1-888-499-4354 or visit bell2lodge.com. In the winter monhs, Bell 2 Lodge is home to Last Frontier Heliskiing, 1-888-655-5566. Guided fly-fishing packages are offered in September and October. See display ad on this page. [ADVERTISEMENT]

NOTE: Next fuel northbound is 98 miles/ 157 km at Iskut. Next fuel southbound is in Stewart, 96 miles/154 km, or at the Yellowhead Highway junction, 155 miles/249 km.

J 155.2 (249.3 km) **AH 294.9** (474.4 km)
Bell II Crossing. Bridge crosses Bell-Irving River (metal grate decking).

J 158.3 (254 km) **AH 291.8** (469.7 km)
Informal gravel turnout to west by pond; watch for swans. Beautiful mountain views.

J 160.2 (257.2 km) **AH 289.9** (466.5 km)
Distance marker southbound shows Meziadin Junction 103 km/64 miles, Stewart 164 km/102 miles, Kitwanga 260 km/162 miles.

J 160.7 (257.9 km) **AH 289.4** (465.8 km)
Snowbank Creek bridge.

J 162.9 (261.6 km) **AH 287.2** (462.1 km) Double-ended turnout to rest area on east side of highway; picnic tables, toilets and avalanche information signs. Memorial plaque dedicated to highway avalanche technicians killed in a slide here. The avalanche chutes are clearly visible on mountain slopes to the west in summer.

CAUTION: Avalanche area northbound to Ningunsaw Pass; no stopping in winter or spring.

J 163.2 (262.1 km) **AH 286.9** (461.6 km)
(Continues on page 266)

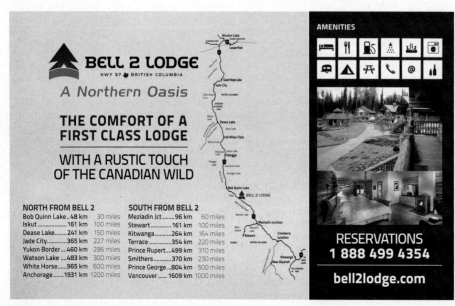

Stewart–Hyder Access Road (Highway 37A)

This 2-lane paved spur road (good surface with centerline, narrow to no shoulder) junctions with the Cassiar Highway at Milepost J 97.5 and leads west 40.4 miles/65 km to Stewart, BC, and on to Hyder, AK. Food, gas, lodging and camping are available at these 2 communities.

Highway 37A winds through scenic Bear Creek Canyon into the magnificent Coast Range mountains, snow-topped for much of the summer, with waterfalls cascading down the mountainsides.

Major attractions in the Stewart–Hyder area include Bear Glacier (along Highway 37A), Salmon Glacier and Fish Creek bear viewing area. There are several good places to eat. The road is now paved through Hyder all the way to the Fish Creek Observation Site.

Distance is measured from Meziadin Lake Junction (M) to the international border (B) at Hyder, AK.

Physical kilometreposts reflect distance from international border.

HIGHWAY 37A

M 0 B 40.4 (65 km) Junction of Highway 37A with Cassiar Highway (Highway 37) at **Meziadin Junction** (see **Milepost J 97.5**). Turnout to north with litter bin and signs.

M 1.3 (2.1 km) **B 39.1** (62.9 km) Turnout to south.

M 2.7 (4.3 km) **B 37.7** (60.6 km) Avalanche gates.

M 3.3 (5.3 km) **B 37.1** (59 km) Informal gravel turnout to south.

M 7.6 (12.2 km) **B 32.8** (52.8 km) Surprise Creek bridge.

M 8 (12.8 km) **B 32.4** (52.1 km) Large turnout to north. Chain up area for Windy Hill.

M 10.1 (16.2 km) **B 30.3** (48.8 km) Large turnout to south.

M 10.3 (16.6 km) **B 30.1** (48.4 km) Large turnout to north.

M 10.6 (17 km) **B 29.8** (48 km) Turnout to south.

M 11.3 (18.2 km) **B 29.1** (46.8 km) Windy Point bridge.

M 12 (19.3 km) **B 28.4** (45.8 km) Entrance bridge.

M 12.7 (20.4 km) **B 27.7** (44.6 km) Cornice Creek bridge.

M 13.3 (21.4 km) **B 27.1** (43.6 km) Strohn Creek bridge.

M 13.7 (22 km) **B 26.7** (43.2 km) Large gravel turnout to north.

M 15.2 (24.5 km) **B 25.2** (40.5 km) Multiple turnouts (CAUTION: No guardrails) along lake at the terminus of **Bear Glacier**. Morning light is best for photographing spectacular Bear Glacier. At one time the glacier reached this side of the valley. The old highway can be seen hundreds of feet above the present road.

Watch for falling rock from slopes above road next 2 km.

M 15.9 (25.6 km) **B 24.5** (39.4 km) Large gravel turnout to south with litter bin.

M 18.2 (29.3 km) **B 22.2** (35.7 km) Cullen River bridge.

M 20.5 (33 km) **B 19.9** (32 km) Rufus Creek culvert.

M 21.3 (34.4 km) **B 19.1** (30.8 km) Argyle Creek culvert. Turnout to south.

M 22.7 (36.5 km) **B 17.7** (28.5 km) Enter-ing narrow, scenic, steep-walled **Bear River Canyon** westbound. Leaving Bear River Canyon eastbound. *Watch for rocks on road.*

M 23.7 (38 km) **B 16.8** (26.9 km)Leaving Bear River Canyon westbound. Entering Bear River Canyon eastbound.

Distance marker eastbound shows Meziadin Junction 38 km/24 miles, Kitwanga 195 km/121 miles, Dease Lake 372 km/231 miles.

M 24.3 (39 km) **B 16.1** (26 km) Large gravel turnout with litter bin to north and American Creek Trailhead with parking.

The Stewart-Hyder Access Road is now paved through Hyder. Traffic must stop at Canadian Customs entering and leaving Hyder. (©Kris Valencia, staff)

Stewart–Hyder Access Road (Continued)

M 24.6 (39.6 km) **B 15.8** (25.6 km) Bear River bridge #2.

M 28.8 (46.3 km) **B 11.6** (19 km) Clements Creek bridge.

M 29.3 (47.2 km) **B 11.1** (17.8 km) Large gravel turnout to south. Avalanche gates.

M 29.7 (47.8 km) **B 10.7** (17.2 km) Forest Service Road to south leads 1 km to Clements Lake Recreation Site (MTCA); small rigs or tenting only, picnicking, canoeing, swimming and a floating dock.

M 29.9 (48 km) **B 10.5** (17 km) Bitter Creek bridge.

M 32.2 (51.8 km) **B 8.2** (13.2 km) Wards Pass cemetery. The straight stretch of road along here is the former railbed from Stewart.

M 36.4 (58.6 km) **B 4** (6.4 km) Avalanche gate for eastbound traffic.

Slow for 50-kmph/31-mph speed zone through Stewart. Speed limit eastbound on Highway 37A is 90 kmph/55 mph unless otherwise posted.

M 36.7 (59.1 km) **B 3.7** (6 km) Bear River bridge #1.

Distance marker eastbound shows Meziadin Junction 58 km/36 miles, Kitwanga 212 kmk/132 miles, Dease Lake 398 km/247 miles.

M 36.9 (59.4 km) **B 3.5** (5.6 km) Welcome to Stewart sign westbound; turnout to north. Turn south for **Bear River RV Park**.

Bear River RV Park. See display ad this page.

M 38 (61.2 km) **B 2.4** (3.9 km) RCMP, 8th Avenue. Rainy Creek Municipal Campground is 0.4 mile north.

M 38.2 (61.5 km) **B 2.2** (3.5 km) Stop sign for westbound traffic. Highway 37A/Conway Street joins main street (5th Avenue) of Stewart; description follows.

Petro-Canada gas station to left for westbound traffic.

M 38.5 (61.9 km) **B 1.9** (3.1 km) Visitor Info Centre, access to boardwalk nature trail, parking, toilets.

M 38.6 (62.1 km) **B 1.8** (2.9 km) Playground.

M 39.8 (64.1 km) **B 0.6** (1 km) Portland Canal Stewart Yacht Club.

M 39.9 (64.2 km) **B 0.5** (0.8 km) Salty Dog dock.

M 40.4 (65 km) **B 0** (0 km) **U.S.–Canada International Border.** Hyder (description follows). Canadian Customs at Hyder–Stewart Border Crossing is open 24 hours a day, 7 days a week. There is no U.S. Customs station here. You will need a passport to cross either direction.

NOTE: Stewart and Hyder observe Pacific time, although the post office in Hyder operates on Alaska time because it is a federal building.

Stewart, BC/Hyder, AK

Stewart is at the head of Portland Canal on the AK–BC border. **Hyder** is 2.3 miles/3.7 km beyond Stewart. **Population:** Stewart 699; Hyder 100. **Emergency Services:** Phone 911 for all emergencies. EMS personnel and Medivac helicopter available. *There is no hospital or pharmacy in Stewart/Hyder. Medical emergencies are sent to the hospital in Terrace.* **RCMP** (in Stewart), phone 250-636-2233. **Fire Department**, phone 250-636-2345.

©Kris Valencia, staff

Visitor Information: Stewart Visitor Infocentre (Box 306, Stewart, BC V0T 1W0), located in Chamber of Commerce Building on 5th Avenue; phone 250-636-9224, 1-888-366-5999, www.stewart–hyder.com. District of Stewart, phone 250-636-2251; www.districtofstewart.com.

The visitor centre is staffed with friendly representatives who can help you plan your time in Stewart/Hyder. This location is a good resource with a number of helpful brochures on sightseeing and recreational opportunities in the area, including one on local hiking trails.

Elevation: Sea level. Climate: Maritime, with warm winters and cool rainy summers. Summer temperatures range from 50°F/11°C to 68°F/20°C; winter temperatures range from 25°F/-4°C to 43°F/6°C. Average temperature in January is 27°F/-3°C; in July, 67°F/19°C. Reported record high 89°F/32°C, record low -18°F/-28°C. Slightly less summer rain than other Northwest communities, but heavy snowfall in winter. **Radio:** CBC 1415. **Television:** Cable, 15 channels.

Private Aircraft: Stewart airport, on 5th Street; elev. 10 feet/3m; length 3,900

STEWART-HYDER ADVERTISERS

feet/1,189m; asphalt; fuel 80, 100.

Description

Stewart and Hyder are on a spur of the Cassiar Highway, at the head of Portland Canal, a narrow saltwater fjord approximately 90 miles/145 km long. The fjord forms a natural boundary between Alaska and Canada. Stewart has a deep harbour and boasts of being Canada's most northerly ice-free port.

Prior to the coming of the white man, Nass River Indians knew the head of Portland Canal as *Skam-A-Kounst*, meaning safe place, probably referring to the place as a retreat from the harassment of the coastal Haidas. The Nass came here annually to hunt birds and pick berries. Little evidence of their presence remains.

In 1896, Captain D.D. Gaillard (after whom the Gaillard Cut in the Panama Canal was later named) explored Portland Canal for the U.S. Army Corps of Engineers. Two years after Gaillard's visit, the first prospectors and settlers arrived. Among them was D.J. Raine, for whom a creek and mountain in the area were named. The Stewart brothers arrived in 1902 and in 1905 Robert M. Stewart, the first postmaster, named the town Stewart. Hyder was first called Portland City. It was then renamed Hyder, after Canadian mining engineer Frederick B. Hyder, when the U.S. Postal Authority told residents there were already too many cities named Portland.

Gold and silver mining dominated the early economy. Hyder boomed with the discovery of rich silver veins in the upper Salmon River basin in 1917-18. Hundreds of pilings, which supported structures during this boom period, are visible on the tidal flats at Hyder.

Hyder became an access and supply point for the mines, while Stewart served as the centre for Canadian mining activity. Mining ceased in 1956, with the exception of the Granduc copper mine, which operated until 1984. Today the economy is driven by forestry, mining and tourism. Several movies and commercials have been filmed in the area. Films include "Bear Island" (1978), John Carpenter's "The Thing" (1981), "The Ice Man" (1982), "Leaving Normal" (1991) and "Insomnia" (2002).

Lodging & Services

Stewart: 2 hotels/motels, groceries at Arbourlight (free WiFi) and Luck Dollar Foods. There are: 3 churches, a Petro Canada station (gas, diesel, propane), post office, a BC liquor store, visitor information centre, museum, 2 gift shops and other shops. Camping at Bear River RV Park and Rainey Creek Municipal Campground. Dining at the King Edward Hotel/Motel, the Dash Bistro, Bitter Creek Cafe, a pizza place, and at the Rookery/Toaster Museum Cafe (breakfast only).

King Edward Hotel/Motel. Stewart's only full service hotel; located on the estuary and main street. We have hotel rooms to suit your every need and motel rooms that offer drive up comfort. All our rooms are air-conditioned; private bath; and DD phones. Kitchenettes, non-smoking and pet-friendly rooms available. All rooms equipped with high-speed Internet. Our incredible seafood meals—featuring Alaskan king crab—are served daily, and our "miner"-sized breakfast can satisfy even the largest of appetites. Casey's Place licensed

This storehouse, built in 1896, was Alaska's first masonry building. (©Kris Valencia, staff)

lounge and Prospector's liquor store located in hotel building. Phone 250-636-2244 or 1-800-663-3126; fax 250-636-9160; www.kingedwardhotel.com. See display ad on page 264. [ADVERTISEMENT]

Ripley Creek Inn. Stewart's finest accommodation, on the estuary, surrounded by mountain vistas. Located in lane behind 306 5th Avenue office. 32 unique rooms in lodge and adjoining historic buildings, furnished with antiques; spacious, quiet and private. Decks; common areas and sauna. Additional units available in our 1928 brothel and several self-contained prospector cabins. Pets on approval. Phone 250-636-2344; email ripleycreekinn@yahoo com; http://www.ripleycreekinn.com. [ADVERTISEMENT]

Hyder: A post office, 2 motels, 2 general stores and a Baptist church. Dining at Seafood Express, Glacier Inn and Grandview Inn. Camping at Camp Run-A-Muck RV Park.

Transportation

Private Boats: Public dock and boat launch available. A private dock in Stewart accommodates yachts.

Attractions

Stewart Historical Society Museum, in the Courthouse/Service BC building on Brightwell Street. Open 9 A.M. to 5 P.M., May to September. Galleries include the Mining Room and Movie Room. There are also early history and wildlife displays and exhibits. Guided group tours of historic buildings may be arranged in advance; phone the museum at 250-636-2229 or email stewart bcmuseum@gmail.com

Historic Buildings: In Stewart, the former fire hall at 6th and Columbia streets built in 1910; the Empress Hotel on 4th Street; and St. Mark's Church (built in 1910)

on 9th Street at Columbia.

On the border at Eagle Point is the stone storehouse built by Captain D.D. Gaillard of the U.S. Army Corps of Engineers in 1896. This is the oldest masonry building in Alaska. Originally 4 of these buildings were built to hold exploration supplies. This one was subsequently used as a cobbler shop and jail. Storehouses Nos. 3 and 4 are included on the (U.S.) National Register of Historic Places.

Estuary Boardwalk. Stroll down the boardwalk adjacent the visitor centre for a spectacular view of Portland Canal. Interpretive panels explain flora and fauna.

Special Events: Fourth of July begins July 1 as Stewart and Hyder celebrate Canada Day and Independence Day. Parade and fireworks.

The Bear Festival takes place the second weekend in August. Bear photos, craft tables and food.

Fish Creek Wildlife Observation Area. From the international border, follow paved road through Hyder (keep to right at T junction) and continue out Salmon River Road. The first parking area and pay station is about 4.3 miles/6.9 km from the border. RVs use second parking lot. This day-use recreation area, operated by the U.S. Forest Service, allows visitors to observe both brown (grizzly) and black bears as they fish for dog and pink salmon in the shallow waters of Fish Creek and Marx Creek. Best viewing times for bears are early morning and evenings, from mid-July through early September. Viewing is from a gated boardwalk that overlooks the creek; please observe rules posted at entrance. There was a $5 parking fee in effect in summer 2013; rate subject to change in 2014.

Salmon Glacier. Continue out Salmon River Road past the Fish Creek viewing area for views Salmon Glacier from Salmon Glacier Road. Pavement ends and gravel begins just past Fish Creek's second parking lot by Titan Trailhead. Salmon Glacier Road, built to connect Stewart with mining interests to the north, offers spectacular views of Salmon Glacier (weather permitting) and surrounding area. Premier Mines viewpoint at Mile 14 (distance measured from international border); Toe of Salmon Glacier viewpoint (Mile 16); Salmon Glacier Summit viewpoint (Mile 21.7). Road continues to Granduc Mine (private property). *CAUTION: Narrow, winding, steep gravel road with potholes and possible road construction. Dusty in dry weather, muddy in wet. Watch for mine traffic.* Pick up a brochure at the Visitor Information Centre on this side trip.

AREA FISHING: Portland Canal, salmon to 50 lbs., use herring, spring and late fall; coho to 12 lbs. in fall, fly-fishing. *(NOTE: Alaska or British Columbia fishing license required, depending on whether you fish U.S. or Canadian waters in Portland Canal.)* Excellent fishing for salmon and Dolly Varden at mouth of **Salmon River**. Up the Salmon River road from Hyder, Fish Creek has Dolly Varden 2 to 3 lbs., use salmon eggs and lures, best in summer. **Fish Creek** is a spawning ground for some of the world's largest dog salmon, mid-summer to fall; it is illegal to kill dog salmon in fresh water in British Columbia. It is legal to harvest them from both salt and fresh water in Alaska.

Return to Milepost J 97.5 on the Cassiar Highway

View of Burrage River canyon from bridge at Milepost J 207.
(©Kris Valencia, staff)

(Continued from page 262)
Redflat Creek.
J 165.7 (266.1 km) **AH 284.4** (457.6 km) Revision Creek.
J 166.7 (267.7 km) **AH 283.4** (456 km) Fan Creek.
J 168.2 (270 km) **AH 281.9** (453.7 km) Beaver Pond Avalanche Area next 2 km/1.2 miles northbound.
J 170.4 (273.5 km) **AH 279.7** (450.2 km) Gravel turnout to east.
J 171.2 (274.8 km) **AH 278.9** (448.9 km) **Ningunsaw Summit** (sign), elev. 1,530 feet/466m. Nass–Stikine water divide. Creeks northbound feed into the Ningunsaw River, which parallels the highway. The Ningunsaw is a tributary of the Stikine watershed.
J 171.3 (274.9 km) **AH 278.8** (448.8 km) Distance marker northbound shows Bob Quinn Lake 27 km/17 miles, Dease Lake 215 km/134 miles, Alaska Highway 451 km/280 miles.
J 171.5 (275.3 km) **AH 278.6** (448.4 km) Beaver Pond Creek bridge.
J 171.8 (275.8 km) **AH 278.3** (447.9 km) Liz Creek.
J 174.3 (280 km) **AH 275.8** (443.7 km) Alger Creek. Highway parallels Ninginsaw River northbound.
Avalanche chutes visible to west next 2 km south.
J 175.6 (282 km) **AH 274.5** (441.7 km) Gamma Avalanche Area. *Slow for curve.*
J 176.3 (283.1 km) **AH 273.8** (440.6 km) Bend Creek (sign).
J 177.2 (284.7 km) **AH 272.9** (439 km) Gamma Creek (sign).
J 177.4 (285 km) **AH 272.7** (438.7 km) Ningunsaw River (sign).
J 178.5 (286.8 km) **AH 271.6** (436.9 km) Ogilvie Creek.
J 179.4 (288 km) **AH 270.7** (435.7 km) Gravel turnout to west with point-of-interest sign about Yukon Telegraph line:
"Born of the Klondike Gold Rush of 1898, the 1,900-mile Dominion Telegraph Line linked Dawson City with Vancouver via the CPR wires through Ashcroft. Built in 1899–1901, the line blazed a route across the vast northern section of the Province but gave way to radio communications in the 1930s. Today, some of the trail and cabins used by the isolated telegraphers still serve wilderness travellers."

J 179.6 (288.4 km) **AH 270.5** (435.3 km) Echo Lake (signed) to west. Flooded telegraph cabins were once visible in the lake below. Good view of Coast Mountains to west. Spectacular cliffs seen to the east are part of the Skeena Mountains (Bowser Basin).
J 182.4 (292.9 km) **AH 267.7** (430.8 km) Avalanche gates.
J 182.6 (293.5 km) **AH 267.5** (430.2 km) Bob Quinn Forest Service Road. Turnoff to west for Northwest Projects AltaGas.
J 182.9 (293.8 km) **AH 267.2** (429.9 km) Distance marker southbound shows Meziadin Junction 147 km/91 miles, Stewart 209 km/130 miles, Kitwanga 304 km/189 miles.
J 183.2 (294.2 km) **AH 266.9** (429.5 km) **Little Bob Quinn Lake** (sign). Rainbow and Dolly Varden, summer and fall. Access to Bob Quinn Lake at **Milepost J 185.1.**

J 184 (295.5 km) **AH 266.1** (428.2 km) Paved rest area with litter bins, picnic tables and toilet next to Bob Quinn Lake airport (sign). This was once a staging site for supplies headed for the Stikine/Iskut goldfields. Today it is often used as a staging area for various highway and resource development projects along the Cassiar Highway.
J 185 (297.1 km) **AH 265.1** (426.6 km) Bob Quinn highway maintenance camp; helicopter base.
Distance marker northbound shows Iskut 109 km/68 miles, Dease Lake 192 km/119 miles, Alaska Highway 428 km/266 miles.
J 188.7 (303.2 km) **AH 261.4** (420.5 km) Turnouts with litter bins on both sides of highway.
J 192 (308.5 km) **AH 258.1** (415.2 km) Devil Creek bridge (metal grating). Large turnout to west at north end of bridge.
J 192.8 (309.8 km) **AH 257.3** (413.9 km) Large paved turnout to west.
J 195.4 (314 km) **AH 254.7** (409.7 km) Thomas Creek.
Highway passes through Iskut burn, where fire destroyed 78,000 acres in 1958. This is also British Columbia's largest huckleberry patch.
Northbound, the vegetation begins to change to northern boreal white and black spruce. This zone has cold, long winters and low forest productivity. Look for trembling

aspen and lodgepole pine.
Southbound, the vegetation changes to cedar–hemlock forest of the interior zone. Cool wet winters and long dry summers produce a variety of tree species including western hemlock and red cedar, hybrid white spruce and subalpine fir. Vegetation becomes more lush the farther south you drive on the highway.
Report wildfires; phone 1-800-663-5555.
J 198.1 (318.5 km) **AH 252** (405.2 km) Large paved turnout to west.
J 199.2 (320 km) **AH 250.9** (403.7 km) Slate Creek.
J 200 (321 km) **AH 250.1** (402.7 km) Distance marker southbound shows Meziadin Junction 166 km/103 miles, Stewart 228 km/142 miles, Kitwanga 323 km/201 miles.
J 200.3 (321.8 km) **AH 249.8** (401.9 km) Double-ended brake-check pullout to east for northbound trucks; litter barrel, information sign. *NOTE: 7 to 8 percent downgrades northbound.*
J 201.6 (323.9 km) **AH 248.5** (399.8 km) Durham Creek.
J 205.5 (330 km) **AH 244.6** (393.7 km) Double-ended turnout to east is brake-check area for northbound traffic. Double-ended turnout to west is chain-off area for southbound traffic. Litter bins.
Distance marker northbound shows Iskut 75 km/47 miles, Dease Lake 158 km/98 miles, Alaska Highway 394 km/245 miles.
J 207 (332.7 km) **AH 243.1** (391 km) *Downgrade to 8 percent and winding descent northbound* to **Burrage River** bridge. Note picturesque rock pinnacles upstream (to east) in Burrage River. Paved parking spot to west just north of bridge.
Begin 2.6-mile/4.2-km uphill grade to 8 percent northbound. Narrow, winding road, no shoulders, steep drop-offs.
J 207.5 (333.4 km) **AH 242.6** (390.3 km) Paved turnout to west with view of Iskut River as the highway winds along the hillside above the river; guardrails.
J 208.8 (335.2 km) **AH 241.3** (388.5 km) Paved turnout to west with view of Iskut River; good photo op (weather permitting).
J 209.8 (336.9 km) **AH 240.3** (386.8 km) Burrage Hill. Southbound brake-check area to west; litter bin, grade profile. Chain removal area for northbound traffic in winter.
J 212.3 (341.1 km) **AH 237.8** (382.6 km) Gravel turnout to west.
J 215 (345.5 km) **AH 235.1** (378.2 km) Rest area to west by Eastman Creek; picnic tables, outhouses, litter bins, and information sign with map and list of services in Iskut Lakes Recreation Area. The creek was named for George Eastman (of Eastman Kodak fame), who hunted big game in this area before the highway was built.
J 218 (350.2 km) **AH 232.1** (373.5 km) Rescue Creek bridge. *Narrow 2-lane wood-decked bridge; slippery when wet.*
J 220 (353.5 km) **AH 230.1** (370.2 km) Willow Creek bridge. *Narrow 2-lane wood-decked bridge; slippery when wet.*
J 220.6 (354.4 km) **AH 229.5** (369.3 km) Willow Creek Forest Service Road to west.
J 221.6 (356 km) **AH 228.5** (367.7 km) Gravel turnout to east.
J 222.4 (357.7 km) **AH 227.7** (366 km) Trailhead with pit toilet and parking area.
J 224.6 (360.8 km) **AH 225.5** (362.9 km) Unmaintained (soft spots, abrupt edge) double-ended gravel turnout to west.
Slow for patches of rough pavement northbound.

J 225 (361.8 km) **AH 225.1** (361.9 km) Halfway point on the Cassiar Highway.

J 227.1 (365 km) **AH 223** (358.7 km) Turnoff to west for **Kinaskan Provincial Park**. This park has a campground with 50 sites ($16 per site), outhouses, drinking water, and firewood. Picnic and day-use area with gravel parking for large vehicles, tables and firepits; some handicap-accessible facilities. Swimming, boat launch and rainbow trout fishing (July and August) on Kinaskan Lake. Trailhead for 15-mile/24-km hike to Mowdade Lake in Mount Edziza Provincial Park.

Distance marker southbound shows Meziadin Junction 214 km/133 miles, Stewart 276 km/172 miles, Kitwanga 371 km/231 miles.

J 229 (368.1 km) **AH 221.1** (355.6 km) Distance marker northbound shows Iskut 35 km/22 miles, Dease Lake 118 km/73 miles, Alaska Highway 354 km/220 miles.

J 230.2 (370 km) **AH 219.9** (353.7 km) First of 3 logged turnouts to west, some with views of Kinaskan Lake, the next 2 miles northbound.

J 231.2 (372.1 km) **AH 218.9** (352.3 km) Turnout with litter bin to west.

J 232.1 (373 km) **AH 218** (350.7 km) Turnout with litter bin to west. *Watch for bears.*

J 233.8 (375.8 km) **AH 216.3** (347.9 km) Pullout with litter bin to east.

J 234.4 (376.8 km) **AH 215.7** (346.9 km) Todagin Guest Ranch.

J 235.2 (378.1 km) **AH 214.9** (345.6 km) Gravel turnout to east.

J 235.5 (378.5 km) **AH 214.6** (345.2 km) Todagin River bridge.

J 240.5 (386.4 km) **AH 209.6** (337.3 km) Distance marker northbound shows Iskut 19 km/12 miles, Dease Lake 102 km/63 miles, Alaska Highway 338 km/210 miles.

Distance marker southbound shows Meziadin Junction 232 km/144 miles, Stewart 294 km/183 miles, Kitwanga 389 km/242 miles.

J 242.7 (390.3 km) **AH 207.4** (333.4 km) Tatogga Lake Resort; food, gas/diesel, camping, lodging (seasonal).

J 242.8 (390.5 km) **AH 207.3** (333.2 km) Jackson Creek.

J 243.1 (391 km) **AH 207** (332.7 km) Ealue Lake to Stikine Hill Sealcoating (sign).

J 243.3 (391.4 km) **AH 206.8** (332.3 km) Coyote Creek culvert.

J 244.6 (393.1 km) **AH 205.5** (330.6 km) *Highway narrows northbound. No centerline, no shoulders, bumpy road as highway winds along Eddontenajon Lake northbound. Guardrails.*

J 246.8 (396.8 km) **AH 203.3** (326.9 km) Rest area to west beside **Eddontenajon Lake** (Ed-don-TEN-ajon); picnic tables, litter bins and toilet. It is unlawful to camp overnight at turnouts. People drink from the lake; be careful not to contaminate it. Use dump stations. Spatsizi trailhead to east in Spatsizi Plateau Wilderness Park access. Trailhead for Didene Portage (128 km), Eaglenest Trail (49 km), McEwan Trail (28 km). Lake breaks up in late May; freezeup is early November. Rainbow fishing July and August.

J 250.4 (402.5 km) **AH 199.7** (321.1 km) Red Goat Lodge to west.

J 250.5 (402.7 km) **AH 199.6** (321 km) Iskut Motor Inn and Restaurant to east.

J 251.9 (404.5 km) **AH 198.2** (319.2 km) Iskut (unincorporated), northbound sign.

Slow for 60-kmph/37-mph speed zone northbound through Iskut.

J 252.2 (405.3 km) **AH 197.9** (318.4 km) Zetu Creek.

Iskut

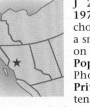

J 252.5 (406 km) **AH 197.6** (317.7 km) Kluachon Centre Store at Iskut, a small Native community on the Cassiar Highway. **Population:** 283. **Clinic:** Phone (250) 234-3511. **Private Aircraft:** Eddontenajon airstrip, 0.6 mile/1 km north of Iskut; elev. 3,100 feet/945m; length 3,000 feet/914m; gravel; fuel available.

Kluachon Centre Store on east side of highway houses the post office and has a grocery, hardware supplies, gas and diesel; open 7 days a week in summer. Camping and cabins at **Mountain Shadow RV Park** (www.mtshadowrvpark.com), which also offers seaplane sightseeing tours to Mount Edziza, Grand Canyon of the Stikine and Spatsizi Plateau; fishing, hiking, wildlife viewing.

Cassiar Highway Log
(continued)

J 253.1 (407 km) **AH 197** (316.7 km) Entering Iskut southbound. *Slow for 60-kmph/37-mph speed zone southbound.*

Check fuel sign northbound. Next gas 82 km/51 miles (Dease Lake).

Highway climbs northbound. No centerline, no shoulders.

J 254.1 (408.5 km) **AH 196** (315.2 km) **Mountain Shadow RV Park & Campground** 0.5-mile/0.8 km down hill to west. Cabins for rent. Short nature walk to Kluachon Lake with excellent fishing. Bird and wildlife viewing.

Mountain Shadow RV Park & Campground. See display ad this page.

J 257.6 (414 km) **AH 192.5** (309.7 km) Bear Paw Resort to west.

J 258.4 (415.5 km) **AH 191.7** (308.2 km) Trapper's Souvenirs.

J 260.1 (418.2 km) **AH 190** (305.5 km)

Tsaybahe Creek; private homestead.

J 263.1 (423 km) **AH 187** (300.7 km) Double-ended rest area on Morchuea Lake to west with toilets, picnic tables, litter bins, map and distance chart.

Panoramic views of Skeena and Cassiar mountains.

From here southbound, the dormant volcano of Mount Edziza (elev. 9,143 feet/2,787m) and its adjunct cinder cone can be seen to the southwest. The park, not accessible by road, is a rugged wilderness with a glacier, cinder cones, craters and lava flows.

J 264.3 (425 km) **AH 185.8** (298.7 km) Turnoffs to west for Morchuea Lake Recreation Site with 8 rustic campsites and boat launch.

J 266.5 (428.4 km) **AH 183.6** (295.3 km) Stikine River Provincial Park boundary (northbound sign).

J 267.3 (429.7 km) **AH 182.8** (294 km) South Stikine Hill brake-check area. Double-ended turnout to east for northbound trucks; litter bin and grade profile information sign. *Highway descends to Stikine River northbound. Long, winding, down-*

Enjoying a dip at Kinaskan Provincial Park south of Iskut. (©Chris Heitstuman)

Souvenir shop in Dease Lake acts as tourist information centre. (©Kris Valencia, staff)

grades to 8 percent. No centerline, no shoulders. *CAUTION: Abrupt dropoffs to 5 feet from road shoulder. Slow for gravel breaks and curves.*

J 270.8 (435.3 km) **AH 179.3** (288.4 km) *CAUTION: Slow for hairpin curve.*

J 271.7 (436.8 km) **AH 178.4** (286.9 km) Turnout to east with litter bin.

J 272.1 (437.4 km) **AH 178** (286.3 km) **Stikine River Bridge** (1-lane, metal decking). The Stikine River flows 330 miles northwest then south from British Columbia to the Eastern Passage in Alaska, 2 miles north of Wrangell. Stikine is a Tlingit Indian name meaning "Great River." The Stikine River was first reported in 1799 by Capt. Rowan, of the whaling ship *Eliza* out of Boston, Mass.

Long, winding upgrades to 8 percent next 4.6 miles/7.4 km southbound. Slow for gravel breaks.

Highway climbs northbound. Watch for livestock and wildlife and avalanche areas.

J 273.9 (440.3 km) **AH 176.2** (283.4 km) Distance marker northbound shows Dease Lake 49 km/30 miles, Alaska Highway 285 km/177 miles, Watson Lake 308 km/191 miles.

J 275.4 (442.6 km) **AH 174.7** (281.1 km) Distance marker southbound shows Meziadin 288 km/179 miles, Stewart 350 km/217 miles, Kitwanga 445 km/277 miles.

J 276 (443.7 km) **AH 174.1** (280 km) Brake check pullout to west for southbound traffic with litter bin and grade profile information sign. Stikine River Provincial Park boundary sign southbound.

CAUTION: Abrupt dropoffs to 5 feet from road shoulder.

Downhill grades to 7 percent next 3.8 miles southbound as highway descends to Stikine River.

J 281.7 (452.7 km) **AH 168.4** (271 km) Large gravel turnout with litter bin to east at Tees Creek.

J 284.7 (457.7 km) **AH 165.4** (266 km) Gravel turnout to east.

Long scar across Gnat Pass valley to east is grading preparation for B.C. Railway's proposed Dease Lake extension from Prince George. Construction was halted in 1977. Grade is visible for several miles northbound.

J 287 (461.4 km) **AH 163.1** (262.3 km) Narrow dirt access road east to **Upper Gnat Lake.**

J 288.6 (464 km) **AH 161.5** (259.7 km) Turnout to east with litter bin overlooking **Lower Gnat Lake.** Rainbow trout fishing.

J 290.6 (467.1 km) **AH 159.5** (255.6 km) Large turnout with litter bin to east.

J 291.2 (468.2 km) **AH 158.9** (255.5 km) Gravel turnout to west.

J 291.5 (468.5 km) **AH 158.6** (255.2 km) Gnat Pass Summit, elev. 4,072 feet/1,241m. Watch for caribou in spring.

J 294.5 (473.4 km) **AH 155.6** (250.3 km) Informal dirt turnout (watch for soft spots) to west. *Begin long downgrade to 6 percent northbound* as highway descends to the Tanzilla River.

J 298.1 (479.2 km) **AH 152** (244.5 km) **Tanzilla River** Bridge. Turnout to east at north end of bridge with picnic tables and outhouses. Entrance to Dease Lake Lions Campground at north end of narrow wooden bridge. Best for small rigs. Fishing for grayling, June and July; use flies.

J 298.7 (480.2 km) **AH 151.4** (243.5 km) Turnout with litter bin to west on Tanzilla River. Nice picnic spot.

J 299.3 (481.1 km) **AH 150.8** (242.6 km) Dalby Creek.

J 302.7 (486.6 km) **AH 147.4** (236.1 km) Welcome to Dease Lake (sign) northbound; see description at **Milepost J 303.9.**

Slow for speed zone northbound through Dease Lake.

J 303.3 (487.6 km) **AH 146.8** (236.1 km) Dease Lake RV Park.

J 303.5 (487.9 km) **AH 146.6** (235.8 km) Northern Bear Gifts and Souvenirs to west.

J 303.6 (488.1 km) **AH 146.5** (235.6 km) Ministry of Transportation to east; Northern Lights College campus.

J 303.8 (488.4 km) **AH 146.3** (235.3 km) Turnout to east at Arctic Pacific Crossroads sign, marking divide between Pacific and Arctic ocean watersheds.

Arctic Divide Inn and Motel to east. RCMP and restaurant to west. (**Northway Motor Inn** is behind the restaurant, next left northbound.)

J 303.9 (488.5 km) **AH 146.2** (235.2 km) Petro Canada station at junction with Telegraph Creek Road; gas, diesel, convenience store.

NOTE: Next fuel southbound 52 miles/82 km at Iskut. Next fuel northbound 146 miles/235 km at Alaska Highway junction.

Junction with Telegraph Creek Road. See "Telegraph Creek Road" log on page 270.

Dease Lake

J 303.9 (488.5 km) **AH 146.2** (235.2 km) Located at the **junction** of the Cassiar Highway and Telegraph Creek Road. **Population:** 450. **Emergency** Services: RCMP detachment; Volunteer Fire Dept.; Stikine Health Centre.

Private Aircraft: Dease Lake airstrip, 1.5 miles/2.4 km south; elev. 2,600 feet/792m; length 6,000 feet/1,829m; asphalt; fuel JP4, 100.

DEASE LAKE ADVERTISERS

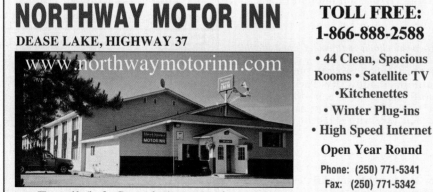

Visitor Information: Tourist information at Northern Bear Gifts & Souvenirs on Highway 37. Write Dease Lake and Tahltan District Chamber of Commerce, Box 338, Dease Lake, BC V0C 1L0; phone (250) 771-3900.

Dease Lake has all visitor services. Lodging at **Northway Motor Inn** and **Arctic Divide Inn and Motel** (description follows). Dining at Rumors Cafe, Tanzilla Pub and the restaurant that was formerly known as Mama Z's (and under improvement in summer 2013).

Arctic Divide Inn and Motel. Centrally located on Highway 37. Inn is log construction, nonsmoking, common kitchenette. Motel has drive-up rooms, 2 kitchenettes. All rooms clean, comfortable, spacious with ensuites, satellite TV, DD phones, wireless Internet, outside plug-ins. Open year-round. Accept VISA, AMEX, Mastercard. Box 219, Dease Lake, BC V0C 1L0. Phone (250) 771-3119; www.arcticdivide.ca. [ADVERTISEMENT]

Camping in town at Dease Lake RV, south of town at Dease Lake Lions Tanzilla River Campground; and north of town at **Water's Edge Campground.** Gas stations (with regular, unleaded, diesel, propane and minor repairs), hardware and food stores. Post office and laundromat. Internet access at Northway Motor Inn, Arctic Divide Inn and Motel, Rumors Cafe and other businesses.

A Hudson's Bay Co. post was established by Robert Campbell at Dease Lake in 1838, but abandoned a year later. The lake was named in 1834 by John McLeod of the Hudson's Bay Co. for Chief Factor Peter Warren Dease. Laketon, on the west side of the lake, was a centre for boat building during the Cassiar gold rush of 1872–80. In 1874, William Moore, following an old Indian trail, cut a trail from Telegraph Creek on the Stikine River to the gold rush settlement on Dease Lake. This trail became Telegraph Creek Road, which was used in 1941 to haul supplies for Alaska Highway construction and Watson Lake Airport to Dease Lake. The supplies were then ferried down the Dease River.

Today, Dease Lake is a government centre and supply point for the district. Northern Lights College (University of Northern British Columbia) has a campus here. It is also a popular point from which to fly-in, hike-in, or pack-in to Mount Edziza and Spatsizi wilderness parks.

Cassiar Highway Log
(continued)

J 303.9 (488.5 km) **AH 146.2** (235.2 km) Petro Canada station ; gas, diesel, convienence store. Turnoff to west for Telegraph Creek Road.

Junction with Telegraph Creek Road. See "Telegraph Creek Road" log on page 270.

NOTE: Next fuel northbound 146 miles/235 km at Alaska Highway junction. Next fuel southbound 52 miles/82 km at Iskut.

J 304 (488.7 km) **AH 146.1** (235 km) Post office, Rumors Cafe to west.

J 304.1 (488.9 km) **AH 146** (234.8 km) Distance marker northbound shows Good Hope Lake 137 km/85 miles, Alaska Highway 234 km/145 miles, Watson Lake, YT, 257 km/160 miles.

Distance marker southbound shows Meziadin Junction 334 km/208 miles, Stewart 399 km/248 miles, Kitwanga 491 km/305 miles.

J 304.2 (489.1 km) **AH 145.9** (234.6 km) Health Centre, Ambulance and Fire Department to west.

J 304.7 (489.7 km) **AH 145.4** (234 km) Hotel Creek.

J 304.9 (490 km) **AH 145.2** (233.7 km) *No centerline, road narrows, poor to fair surfacing northbound.*

J 306.7 (492.9 km) **AH 143.4** (230.8 km) Tahltan Floatplane Base to west.

J 307.1 (493.6 km) **AH 143** (230.1 km) Welcome to Dease Lake (sign) southbound. *Slow for speed zone southbound through Dease Lake.*

J 310 (498.2 km) **AH 140.1** (225.5 km) **Water's Edge Campground** (description follows) to west.

Water's Edge Campground. A beautiful wilderness campground situated on the shores of Dease Lake, 10 km/6 miles north of the townsite on Highway 37. RVs, campers, tents and cyclists welcome. Boat launch, firepits, picnic tables. Firewood available. Free WiFi. Fish from our boat launch. Your hosts: Chuck and Grace Phillips. Phone 250-771-3392. Email cwphillips99@hotmail.com; or website www.watersedgecampground.ca. [ADVERTISEMENT]

J 312 (501.3 km) **AH 138.1** (222.4 km) Turnout with litter bin to west. Views of Dease Lake to west.

J 312.7 (502.6 km) **AH 137.4** (221.1 km) Serpentine Creek.

J 313 (502.9 km) **AH 137.1** (220.8 km) Highway climbs northbound. *Slow for damaged road, gravel breaks, northbound.*

J 316.6 (508.7 km) **AH 133.5** (215 km) There are several informal gravel turnouts to west with some views of Dease Lake along this stretch of highway.

J 317.4 (510 km) **AH 132.7** (213.5 km) *Winding 8 percent downgrade northbound* (sign).

J 319 (512.4 km) **AH 131.1** (211.3 km) Large gravel turnout to west with litter bin. Foliage obscures view of Dease Lake.

CAUTION: Narrow winding road next 7 km/4.3 miles northbound (sign).

J 319.4 (513.4 km) **AH 130.7** (210.3 km) Halfmoon Creek.

J 320.5 (515 km) **AH 129.6** (208.6 km) *7 percent downgrade northbound* (sign).

J 322 (517.6 km) **AH 128.1** (206.1 km) **Rabid Grizzly Rest Area** to west with picnic tables, travel information signs, litter bins and toilets. View of Dease Lake.

Distance marker northbound shows Good Hope Lake 108 km/67 miles, Alaska Highway 205 km/127 miles, Watson Lake 228 km/142 miles.

J 322.6 (518.5 km) **AH 127.5** (205.2 km) The site of the ghost town Laketon lies across the lake. Laketon was the administrative centre for the district during the Cassiar gold rush (1872–80). Boat building was a major activity along the lake during the gold rush years, with miners heading up various creeks and rivers off the lake in search of gold.

J 323.5 (520 km) **AH 126.6** (203.7 km) Watch for black bear and moose along the highway.

J 325.4 (522.7 km) **AH 124.7** (201 km) Turnout to west with litter bin.

J 327.4 (526.6 km) **AH 122.7** (197.1 km) Black Creek.

J 329.6 (529.7 km) **AH 120.5** (194 km) Turnoff for Sawmill Point Recreation Site to west; 6 rustic campsites and boat launch access to **Dease Lake.** Fishing for lake trout to 30 lbs., use spoons, plugs, spinners, June–Oct., deep trolling in summer, spin casting in fall.

J 330.6 (531.4 km) **AH 119.5** (192.3 km) Dorothy Creek.

Road widens northbound.

J 331.3 (532.5 km) **AH 118.8** (191.2 km) Distance marker southbound shows Dease Lake 44 km/27 miles, Stewart 440 km/273 miles, Kitwanga 535 km/332 miles.

J 333.5 (536 km) **AH 116.6** (187.7 km) Beady Creek.

Entering the Cassiar Mountains northbound.

J 335 (538.4 km) **AH 115.1** (185.3 km) Turnout to west with litter bin overlooking the Dease River; pretty spot. The **Dease River** parallels the highway. Grayling, Dolly Varden and lake trout; northern pike, May through September.

Travelers fill up at the Petro-Canada station in Dease Lake. (©Sharon Nault)

Telegraph Creek Road

Telegraph Creek Road descends steeply to Tahltan River bridge. (©Kris Valencia, staff)

Built in 1922, Telegraph Creek Road was the first road into this remote area of northern British Columbia, long the domain of the Tahltan people. Robert Campbell was the first European in the area in 1838.

Settlement of the region grew with the discovery of gold on the Stikine River in 1861. Efforts to establish a transatlantic telegraph line also brought attention to the Telegraph Creek area in the 1860s. The Cassiar (1873–1876) and Klondike (1897–1898) gold rushes contributed to the growth of both Telegraph Creek and Glenora, 12 miles/20 km downriver, according to writer Rana Nelson.

The scenery along portions of this road is remarkable, with views of the Grand Canyon of the Stikine River and Mount Edziza. Historic Telegraph Creek at road's end has many turn-of-the-century buildings from the gold rush days.

Telegraph Creek Road is a narrow gravel road with several sets of steep switchbacks. Drive carefully and carry a spare tire. This road is not recommended for trailers or large RVs. Check road conditions at the highway maintenance camp or RCMP office in Dease Lake before starting the 70-mile/112.7-km drive to Telegraph Creek. Allow a minimum of 2 hours driving time with good conditions. Gas up in Dease Lake.

Distance from Dease Lake junction (D) on the Cassiar Highway is shown. *Kilometreposts show distance from Dease Lake.*

D 0 Dease Lake junction at **Milepost J 303.9** Cassiar Highway; Petro-Canada gas station. *Fill your gas tank in Dease Lake!*

D 0.9 (1.4 km) **T junction**: Turn left for Telegraph Creek, turn right for boat launch/floatplane base.

D 1.4 (2.3 km) Entrance to airport.

D 3.1 (5 km) *Pavement ends, gravel begins westbound.*

D 5 (8 km) Entering Tanzilla Plateau. *Road narrows, some winding 8 percent grades, some washboard.*

D 7.2 (11.6 km) Tatcho Creek (Eightmile) 1-lane bridge.

D 15.7 (25.3 km) 16 Mile Creek.

D 17 (27.3 km) Augustchilde Creek, 1-lane bridge.

D 18.8 (30 km) 19 Mile Creek.

D 18.9 (30.2 km) Turnout to south with litter bin.

D 20 (32.3 km) 22 Mile Creek.

D 20.5 (33 km) Turnout to north.

D 20.7 (33.3 km) Glimpse of Tanzilla River to south.

D 32 (51.3 km) Moose Horn swamp.

D 36.9 (58.9 km) Stikine River Provincial Park boundary.

D 37 (59 km) Turnout with toilet. Short walk uphill for good views and photographs.

D 38 (60.6 km) Turnout with litter bin to north. Excellent view of Mount Edziza on clear days.

D 42.5 (67.8 km) Sign reads: *Steep Mountain Highway next 70 km/43.5 miles. Grades to 20 percent.*

D 42.9 (68.4 km) Avalanche gate.

D 46.1 (74.2 km) Turnout with litter barrels to south.

Begin steep downgrades to 18 percent and 30-kmph/19-mph curves westbound.

D 47.7 (76 km) Tuya River 1-lane bridge.

D 47.9 (76.3 km) Turnout with litter bin.

D 49.4 (78.7 km) *Watch for horses on road!*

D 49.6 (79 km) Old section of Telegraph Creek Road intersects newer road.

D 50.8 (81 km) Old section of Telegraph Creek Road intersects newer road.

D 52.1 (82.9 km) Large turnout with litter bin and view.

CAUTION: 20 percent downhill grade for approximately 0.6 mile/1 km as narrow road switchbacks down hillside.

D 55.4 (89.7 km) Turnoff for short loop road through rest area with picnic tables, toilet, litter bin and view.

D 57.5 (91.3 km) Bottom of steep hill; point-of-interest sign reads:

"The Stikine River at the Tahltan has always been the lifeblood of the Tahltan Nation. Each year the Tahltan returned to the Stikine when the salmon were running as the fish it provided was a main food source. One fishing method involved using a gaff (long pole with a large hook at one end) to catch the salmon, which were dried in smokehouses. The Tahltan has been a main gathering place for meetings, potlatches and other ceremonial traditions."

D 57.6 (91.5 km) **Tahltan River** 1-lane bridge.

D 58 (92.1 km) *CAUTION: Begin section of very narrow road on ledge rising steeply up the wall of the Stikine Canyon next 3 miles/4.8 km, rising to 400 feet/122m above the river.*

D 58.6 (93 km) Turnout with view of the Grand Canyon of the Stikine and Tahltan Canyon. The Stikine River canyon is only 8 feet/2.4m wide at its narrowest point.

D 61.5 (98 km) Nine Mile Ranch.

D 64.3 (102.1 km) Turnout with view of the Grand Canyon of the Stikine. Good photo op.

D 69 (109.7 km) *Slow for 50-kmph/31-mph speed limit* entering **TELEGRAPH CREEK** (pop. 350; elev. 1,100 feet/335m). General store with groceries, gas, diesel and propane; nursing station; Catholic church; public school; and post office. Residents make their living working for the Tahltan First Nations; doing construction work, mining, logging and tourism.

D 70.3 (111.9 km) Keep left westbound for Telegraph Creek. *Steep, narrow winding descent* as road passes gold-rush era buildings to cross 1-lane bridge across Telegraph Creek.

D 70.4 (112.1 km) Y junction turnoff for Glenora Road (to left) and historic Telegraph Creek (to right). **Glenora Road** leads 12 miles/19.3-km to former townsite of Glenora, marked only by a couple of old foundations, a B.C. Forest Service campsite, hiking trail and boat launch. Glenora was the limit of larger riverboat navigation on the Stikine and the site of an attempted railroad route to the Yukon. There are 2 other B.C. Forest Service campsites on Glenora Road at Dodjatin Creek and Winter Creek.

D 70.9 (112.7 km) Vance Creek 1-lane bridge.

D 71 (112.9 km) T junction: turn right for Stikine Riversong Lodge in **Historic Telegraph Creek**, former head of navigation on the Stikine and once a telegraph communication terminal. An estimated 5,000 stampeders set off from Telegraph Creek to attempt the Stikine–Teslin Trail to the goldfields in Atlin and the Klondike. The scenic view along the main street bordering the river has scarcely changed since gold rush days. Historic St. Aidan's Anglican Church is located here.

D 71.1 (113 km) The 1898 Hudson's Bay Co. post, a Heritage Building, houses the Stikine RiverSong Lodge & Cafe, which is owned by the Tahltan Band. Open May through September; gifts, drinks, baked goods, rooms, shower. Phone 250-235-3004.

Return to Milepost J 303.9 Cassiar Highway

Free jade cutting demonstrations at Cassiar Mountain Jade Store make Jade City a popular stop. (©Kris Valencia, staff)

Marshy areas to west; good moose pasture. *CAUTION: Watch for wildlife on road, especially at dawn and dusk.*

J 336.7 (541.1 km) **AH 113.4** (182.6 km) Large gravel turnout to west with litter bins.

J 337.8 (542.9 km) **AH 112.3** (180.8 km) Packer Tom Creek, named for a well-known First Nations man who lived in this area.

J 339.4 (545.5 km) **AH 110.7** (178.2 km) Elbow Lake (signed) to west.

J 345.2 (554.8 km) **AH 104.9** (168.9 km) Pyramid Creek.

J 345.6 (555.3 km) **AH 104.5** (168.2 km) Dease River Crossing; closed sign up in summer 2013. Distance marker southbound shows Dease Lake 67 km/42 miles, Stewart 467 km/290 miles, Kitwanga 558 km/347 miles.

J 345.7 (555.5 km) **AH 104.4** (168 km) Dease River 2-lane concrete bridge.

J 346 (556 km) **AH 104.1** (167.7 km) Distance marker northbound shows Good Hope Lake 70 km/43 miles, Alaska Highway 167 km/104 miles, Watson Lake 190 km/118 miles.

J 347.3 (558.1 km) **AH 102.8** (165.6 km) Beale Creek.

J 348.5 (560 km) **AH 101.6** (163.7 km) Northbound, the highway travels in easy curves and straight stretches along a wide, flat valley floor.

Southbound, the highway begins a series of long, winding grades with some straightaways.

J 350.7 (563.5 km) **AH 99.4** (160.2 km) Turnout to east. Foilage blocks view of Pine Tree Lake.

J 351.3 (564.5 km) **AH 98.8** (159.2 km) Paved shoulder parking to east with litter barrel beside **Pine Tree Lake**. Good grayling and lake char fishing.

J 352.1 (566 km) **AH 98** (157.7 km) Kamlah Creek.

J 354.1 (569 km) **AH 96** (154.7 km) "13.6 Km Pipe" Creek.

Distance marker southbound shows Dease Lake 84 km/52 miles, Stewart 480 km/298 miles, Kitwanga 575 km/357 miles.

J 354.7 (572 km) **AH 95.4** (151.7 km) Evidence of old burn.

J 356.5 (572.9 km) **AH 93.6** (150.8 km) Cotton Lake (sign).

J 357.1 (573.9 km) **AH 93** (149.8 km) Gravel turnout with litter barrel to east.

J 359.9 (578.7 km) **AH 90.2** (145 km) Northbound rest area 0.4 mile/0.6 km west via old highway on south side of **Cottonwood River**. Fishing for grayling and whitefish. Early summer runs of Dolly Varden.

J 360.1 (579 km) **AH 90** (144.7 km) Cottonwood River bridge.

J 360.7 (580 km) **AH 89.4** (144 km) Southbound Cottonwood River rest area No. 2 is 0.5 mile/0.8 km west on old highway adjacent river; pit toilets, picnic tables, informal camping, litter bins. Slow for potholes on rest area access road.

J 367.2 (590 km) **AH 82.9** (133.7 km) Large turnout to west beside **Simmons Lake**; information kiosk and small beach. Fishing for lake trout.

J 368.7 (592.4 km) **AH 81.4** (131.3 km) Gravel turnout to west, access to Twin Lakes.

J 368.8 (592.6 km) **AH 81.3** (131.1 km) Road runs on causeway between Twin Lakes.

J 369.3 (593.4 km) **AH 80.8** (130.3 km) **Vines Lake**, named for bush pilot Lionel Vines; fishing for lake trout. Ice on lake to late May or early June.

J 370.5 (595.5 km) **AH 79.6** (128.2 km) Limestone Creek.

J 370.8 (596 km) **AH 79.3** (127.7 km) Lang Lake to east.

Views of Needlepoint Mountain southbound.

J 374.5 (601.8 km) **AH 75.6** (121.9 km) Trout Line Creek.

J 374.7 (602.1 km) **AH 75.4** (121.5 km) South entrance to Jade City on west side of highway (description follows).

Jade City

J 374.9 (602.4 km) **AH 75.2** (121.3 km) North entrance to Jade City on west side of highway. Jacde City is located 71 miles/114 km north of Dease Lake. **Population:** 50. **Visitor Information:** The store acts as the information centre for Cassiar Highway travelers.

Jade City is not a city but a highway community made up of one jade business: **Cassiar Mountain Jade Store.** They specialize in jade products—there is an extensive selection of gifts in their store—and offer free jade-cutting demonstrations. They also offer a 5-room hotel, free coffee, candy and cold drinks for sale, and free overnight RV parking (no services). A popular stop with travelers.

Jade City earned its name as a commercial outlet for jade mined from the nearby mountains. Cassiar Highway travelers have come to know this spot as the place to stop and buy jade. There are several major jade mines in the Cassiar region. The miners in the Cassiar Mountain Range, produce about 1 million pounds of jade each year, and half of that is exported.

Cassiar Mountain Jade Store. See display ad on page 271.

Cassiar Highway Log
(continued)

J 374.9 (602.4 km) **AH 75.2** (121.3 km) North entrance to Jade City on west side of highway.

J 375.7 (603.7 km) **AH 74.4** (120 km) Distance marker southbound shows Dease Lake 116 km/72 miles, Stewart 512 km/318 miles, Kitwanga 607 km/377 miles.

J 376 (604.2 km) **AH 74.1** (119.2 km) Distance marker northbound shows Good Hope Lake 21 km/13 miles, Alaska Highway 120 km/74 miles, Watson Lake 143 km/89 miles.

Junction with Cassiar Road, which leads west 6.2 miles/10 km to the former Cassiar Asbestos Mine and Cassiar townsite. Much of the world's high-grade chrysotile asbestos came from here. The mine closed in March 1992, and the townsite was dismantled and sold off then reclaimed by B.C. Chrysotile Corp. No services available. Former residents have created a virtual community at http://www.cassiar.ca/.

J 376.2 (604.5 km) **AH 73.9** (118.9 km) Large turnout to east with litter bin.

J 376.7 (605.3 km) **AH 73.4** (118.1 km) Gravel turnout to east.

J 377.1 (606.1 km) **AH 73** (117.6 km) McDame Creek.

J 380.5 (611.6 km) **AH 69.6** (112.1 km) No. 3 North Fork Creek.

J 380.7 (611.9 km) **AH 69.4** (111.8 km) Large gravel turnout to west at avalanche gates.

J 381.6 (613.5 km) **AH 68.5** (110.2 km) Turnout with litter bin to east overlooking Holloway Bar Project. Sign: 90m/295-foot drop to river. Danger!

J 381.9 (613.9 km) **AH 68.2** (109.8 km) No. 2 North Fork Creek.

J 382.6 (614.8 km) **AH 67.5** (108.9 km) Unmaintained double-ended gravel turnout to east.

J 384.6 (618 km) **AH 65.5** (105.7 km) Turnout to east with litter bin and historic plaque about Cassiar gold.

The gold rush town of Centreville was located in this area. Named for its central location between Sylvester's Landing (later McDame Post) at the junction of McDame Creek with the Dease River, and Quartzrock Creek, the upstream limit of pay gravel on McDame Creek, the town had a population of 3,000. A miner named Alfred Freeman washed out the biggest all-gold (no quartz) nugget ever found in British Columbia on a claim near Centreville in 1877; it weighed 72 ounces. Active mining in area.

J 384.7 (618.2 km) **AH 65.4** (105.5 km) No. 1 North Fork Creek.

J 387.7 (623.4 km) **AH 62.4** (100.3 km)

Distance marker southbound shows Dease Lake 137 km/85 miles, Stewart 537 km/334 miles, Kitwanga 628 km/390 miles.

J 388.9 (625.3 km) **AH 61.2** (98.4 km) Sign identifies Good Hope Lake.

J 389.5 (626.3 km) **AH 60.6** (97.4 km) **GOOD HOPE LAKE** (pop. 75). Store with gas (above-ground tank); current status unknown. *This is not a reliable source for gas. Slow for signed 60-kmph/37-mph speed zone.*

Road narrows, no centerline, winding road northbound.

J 390.3 (627.7 km) **AH 59.8** (96 km) Large turnout with litter bin to east on Aeroplane Lake (no access southbound).

J 391.2 (629 km) **AH 58.9** (94.7 km) Dry Creek.

J 393 (631.6 km) **AH 57.1** (92.1 km) Aptly named Mud Lake to east.

J 397.2 (638.7 km) **AH 52.9** (85 km) Turnout with litter bin to east at entrance to **Boya Lake Provincial Park**. This unusually beautiful provincial park is 1.2 miles/2 km east of highway via a good paved access road.

There are 42 campsites (some on lake, some in woods) along 2 loops, with picnic tables and grills. Litter bins, toilets, some wheelchair-accessible facilities, picnic area on lakeshore, boat launch, drinking water, firewood and swimming. A very scenic spot. Boya Lakeshore Trail, 1.5 km/0.9 mile. Campground attendant. Fishing for lake char, whitefish and burbot; $16 per site.

J 397.3 (638.9 km) **AH 52.8** (84.8 km) Distance marker northbound shows Alaska Highway 86 km/53 miles, Watson Lake 109 km/68 miles, Whitehorse 509 km/367 miles.

No centerline, no shoulders, easy curves, bumpy and rough pavement, gravel breaks, northbound

J 401.5 (645.5 km) **AH 48.6** (78.2 km) Charlie Chief Creek.

J 403 (647.9 km) **AH 47.1** (75.8 km) Beaver Dam Creek.

J 404.1 (649.3 km) **AH 46** (74.4 km) Beaver Dam Rest Area to west has a very large gravel parking area, toilets, information sign, picnic tables in trees, and litter bins.

Leaving Cassiar Mountains, entering Yukon Plateau, northbound. The Horseranch Range may be seen on the eastern horizon. These mountains date back to the Cambrian period, or earlier, and are the oldest in northern British Columbia.

J 406.1 (653.1 km) **AH 44** (70.7 km) Baking Powder Creek.

J 414.5 (666.4 km) **AH 35.6** (57.3 km) Turnoff for French Creek Recreation Site, which offers 4 rustic campsites and access to Dease River.

J 414.9 (667.1 km) **AH 35.2** (56.6 km) French Creek 2-lane concrete bridge.

Distance marker northbound shows Alaska Highway 57 km/35 miles, Watson Lake 80 km/50 miles, Whitehorse 561 km/348 miles.

J 416 (668.9 km) **AH 34.1** (54.8 km) Distance marker southbound shows Good Hope Lake 43 km/27 miles, Stewart 580 km/360 miles, Kitwanga 671 km/417 miles.

J 421.2 (677.3 km) **AH 28.9** (46.4 km) *Highway descends both directions to 28–Mile Creek. Cassiar Mountains to south.*

J 424 (681.8 km) **AH 26.1** (41.9 km) Wheeler Lake (signed) to west.

J 426.7 (686.1 km) **AH 23.4** (37.6 km) Blue River South Forest Service Road to east.

J 430.1 (691.4 km) **AH 20** (32.3 km) Blue River 2-lane concrete bridge.

J 430.6 (691.8 km) **AH 19.5** (31.9 km) Distance marker northbound shows Alaska Highway 33 km/20 miles, Watson Lake 56 km/35 miles, Whitehorse 537 km/333 miles.

Narrow winding road with some straight stretches, hilly with grades to 8 percent, no centerline, no shoulders, next 20 miles northbound. Keep to right on hills and blind corners.

J 433.6 (697.1 km) **AH 16.5** (26.6 km) Turnout with litter bin and picnic table on grassy point at **Blue Lakes**. Fishing for pike and grayling.

Evidence of 2010 burn. The forest fire, started by lightning on July 27, 2010, burned more than 30,000 hectares and closed this section of the Cassiar Highway to traffic for several days. A happy byproduct of the burn has been the abundance of mushrooms. Mushroom pickers may be camped along here in summer and mushrooms may be for sale depending on harvest.

J 435.4 (700 km) **AH 14.7** (23.7 km) Mud Hill Creek. *Highway climbs steeply, northbound.*

J 444.1 (714 km) **AH 6** (9.7 km) Cormier Creek.

Highway climbs northbound.

J 447.1 (718.7 km) **AH 3** (5 km) Dirt turnout at High Lakes to east. Pretty spot, informal campsite.

J 447.9 (720 km) **AH 2.2** (3.5 km) Leaving British Columbia (northbound sign).

J 448 (720.3 km) **AH 2.1** (3.4 km) **BC–YT Border**, 60th parallel. "Welcome to Yukon" (northbound sign), "Welcome to British Columbia" (southbound sign). Rest area with information sign, pit toilet and litter bin. *Seatbelt use required by law in Yukon Territory (northbound sign) and British Columbia (southbound sign). NOTE: Drive with headlights on at all times. Southbound travelers carry chains Oct. 1–April 30.*

Narrow winding road with some straight stretches, hilly with grades to 8 percent, no centerline, no shoulders, next 20 miles southbound. Keep to right on hills and blind corners.

Distance marker southbound shows Good Hope Lake 97 km/60 miles, Stewart 634 km/394 miles, Kitwanga 725 km/451 miles.

J 449.4 (722.4 km) **AH 0.7** (1.3 km) **Albert Creek**. Good grayling fishing. Yukon Territory fishing license required.

J 449.8 (723.2 km) **AH 0.3** (0.5 km) Distance marker southbound shows Dease Lake 235 km/146 miles, Kitwanga 723 km/449 miles.

J 450.1 (723.7 km) **AH 0 Junction** of Cassiar Highway with Alaska Highway. Junction 37 Services (gas, diesel). Watson Lake, 13.3 miles/21.4 km southeast, is the nearest major community. **Nugget City** (gas, accommodations, restaurant, gift shop, mechanic, camping) is located less than a mile west of here on the Alaska Highway.

Distance marker on the Alaska Highway shows Teslin 241 km/150 miles, Whitehorse 424 km/263 miles.

Turn to **Milepost DC 626.2** on page 165 in the ALASKA HIGHWAY section for log of Alaska Highway from this junction.

Blue-green waters of Good Hope Lake. (©Kris Valencia, staff)

Klondike Loop
Klondike, Top of the World and Taylor Highways
Includes Silver Trail

CONNECTS: Alaska Hwy. in YT to Alaska Hwy. in AK

Length: 498 miles   **Road Surface:** Pavement, Seal Coat & Gravel
Season: Hwy. 2 open all year, Hwys. 9 and 5 closed in winter

(See maps, pages 275-276)

An inukshuk and a top-of-the-world view on the Top of the World Highway near border. (©Earl L. Brown)

Distance in miles	AK Hwy YT Jct.	Carmacks	Chicken	Dawson City	Eagle	Tetlin Jct. AK	Whitehorse
AK Hwy YT Jct.		102	432	323	467	498	10
Carmacks	102		330	221	365	396	112
Chicken	432	330		109	95	66	442
Dawson City	323	221	109		144	175	333
Eagle	467	365	95	144		161	477
Tetlin Jct. AK	498	396	66	175	161		508
Whitehorse	10	112	442	333	477	508	

YT. Although about a hundred miles longer than taking the more direct all-Alaska Highway route between Whitehorse and Tok, the Klondike Loop is a popular choice for travelers because it takes them by way of historic Dawson City, the Top of the World Highway with its top-of-the-world views, and the Taylor Highway through Fortymile country to the colorful community of Chicken, AK.

The Klondike Loop is logged from its turnoff at **Milepost DC 894.8** Alaska Highway (just north of Whitehorse) to its junction at **Milepost DC 1301.7** Alaska Highway (just south of Tok).

The first section of the "loop" for motorists traveling northbound is the 323-mile/520-km-long stretch of Yukon Highway 2, the North Klondike Highway (also called the "Mayo Road"), from its junction with the Alaska Highway north of Whitehorse to Dawson City. The second stretch is the 79-mile/127-km Top of the World Highway (Yukon Highway 9 and Boundary Spur Road in Alaska), which connects Dawson City in the Yukon with the Taylor Highway at Jack Wade Junction

Together, the Klondike Highway, Top of the World Highway and Taylor Highway form the "Klondike Loop, a 498-mile/801-km route that takes Alaska Highway travelers through Dawson City,

Major Attractions:

Dawson City, Klondike Gold Fields, Gold Dredges, SS Keno, Keno Mining Museum

© David L. Ranta, staff

Klondike Loop Milepost J 0 to Milepost J 292 Klondike Hwy. (includes Silver Trail)

© 2014 The MILEPOST®

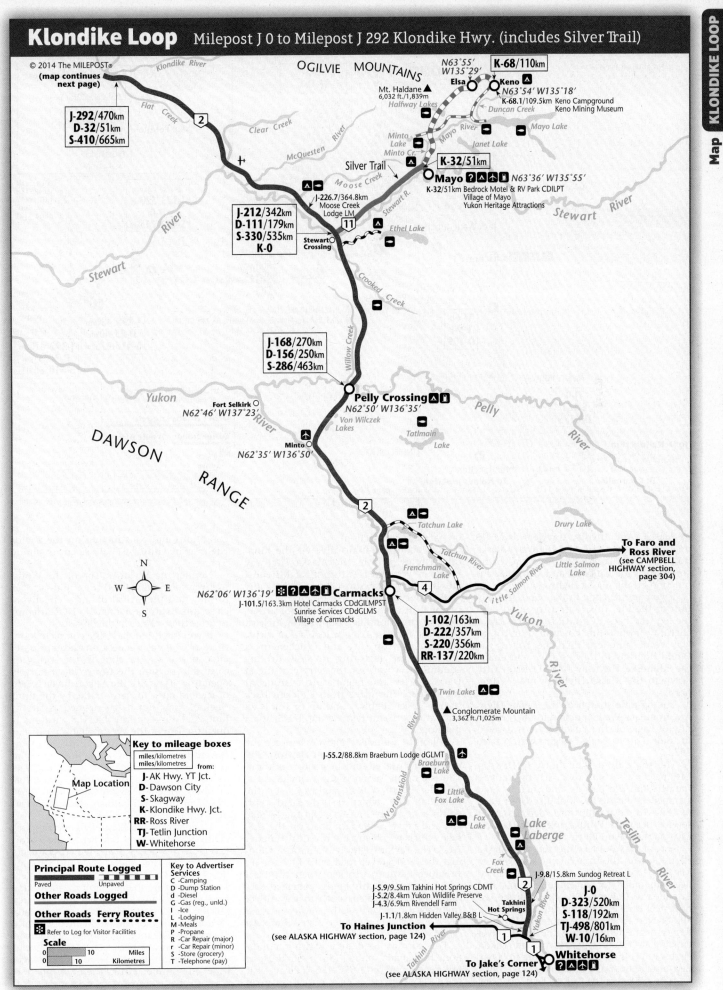

(map continues next page)

J-292/470km
D-32/51km
S-410/665km

OGILVIE MOUNTAINS

Klondike River

Flat Creek

Clear Creek

McQuesten River

Moose Creek

Silver Trail

J-226.7/364.8km
Moose Creek
Lodge LM

J-212/342km
D-111/179km
S-330/535km
K-0

Stewart Crossing

Mt. Haldane ▲
6,032 ft./1,839m
Halfway Lakes

N63°55'
W135°29'
Elsa

K-68/110km
Keno
N63°54' W135°18'
K-68.1/109.5km Keno Campground
Keno Mining Museum

Minta Lake
Minto Cr.
Duncan Creek

Mayo River

Janet Lake

Mayo Lake

K-32/51km
Mayo N63°36' W135°55'
K-32/51km Bedrock Motel & RV Park CDILPT
Village of Mayo
Yukon Heritage Attractions

Stewart R.

Ethel Lake

Stewart River

11

Crooked Creek

Stewart River

Willow Creek

J-168/270km
D-156/250km
S-286/463km

Fort Selkirk ○
N62°46' W137°23'

Yukon River

Pelly Crossing
N62°50' W136°35'

Von Wilczek Lakes

Tatlmain Lake

Pelly River

DAWSON

RANGE

Minto ○
N62°35' W136°50'

Tatchun Lake

Drury Lake

Tatchun River

2

Frenchman Lake

Little Salmon Lake

**To Faro and
Ross River**
(see CAMPBELL
HIGHWAY section,
page 304)

Little Salmon River

N62°06' W136°19' Carmacks
J-101.5/163.3km Hotel Carmacks CDdGILMPST
Sunrise Services CDdGLMS
Village of Carmacks

4

Yukon River

J-102/163km
D-222/357km
S-220/356km
RR-137/220km

Twin Lakes

▲ Conglomerate Mountain
3,362 ft./1,025m

River

Nordenskiold River

J-55.2/88.8km Braeburn Lodge dGLMT

Braeburn Lake

Little Fox Lake

Fox Lake

Lake Laberge

Teslin River

Fox Creek

J-9.8/15.8km Sundog Retreat L

J-5.9/9.5km Takhini Hot Springs CDMT
J-5.2/8.4km Yukon Wildlife Preserve
J-4.3/6.9km Rivendell Farm

J-1.1/1.8km Hidden Valley B&B L

To Haines Junction
(see ALASKA HIGHWAY section, page 124)

Takhini Hot Springs

2

Yukon River

J-0
D-323/520km
S-118/192km
TJ-498/801km
W-10/16km

1

1

Takhini River

To Jake's Corner
(see ALASKA HIGHWAY section, page 124)

Whitehorse

Key to mileage boxes

miles/kilometres
miles/kilometres
from:
J- AK Hwy. YT Jct.
D- Dawson City
S- Skagway
K- Klondike Hwy. Jct.
RR- Ross River
TJ- Tetlin Junction
W- Whitehorse

Map Location

Principal Route Logged
Paved   Unpaved

Other Roads Logged

Other Roads   Ferry Routes

▦ Refer to Log for Visitor Facilities

Scale
0   10   Miles
0   10   Kilometres

Key to Advertiser Services
C - Camping
D - Dump Station
d - Diesel
G - Gas (reg., unld.)
I - Ice
L - Lodging
M - Meals
P - Propane
R - Car Repair (major)
r - Car Repair (minor)
S - Store (grocery)
T - Telephone (pay)

www.themilepost.com

Klondike Loop
Milepost J 292 to Tetlin Junction, Alaska Highway (includes Top of the World and Taylor highways)

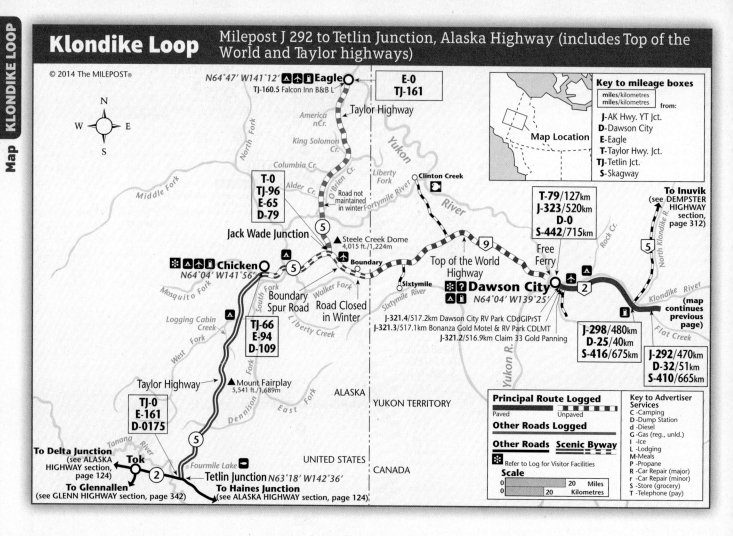

© 2014 The MILEPOST®

N64°47′ W141°12′ ▲✈🏠 Eagle
TJ-160.5 Falcon Inn B&B L

E-0
TJ-161

Taylor Highway

Key to mileage boxes

miles/kilometres miles/kilometres	from:
J-AK Hwy. YT Jct.
D-Dawson City
E-Eagle
T-Taylor Hwy. Jct.
TJ-Tetlin Jct.
S-Skagway

Map Location

AmericanCr.

King Solomon Cr.

Columbia Cr.

Middle Fork

North Fork

Alder Cr.

O'Brien Cr.

Liberty Fork

Fortymile River

Clinton Creek

Yukon

River

Rock Cr.

To Inuvik
(see DEMPSTER HIGHWAY section, page 312)

North Klondike R.

5

T-0
TJ-96
E-65
D-79

Road not maintained in winter

T-79/127km
J-323/520km
D-0
S-442/715km

Jack Wade Junction

5

▲ Steele Creek Dome
4,015 ft./1,224m

9

Free Ferry

Klondike River

(map continues previous page)

🌸▲✈🏠 Chicken
N64°04′ W141°56′

5

▲ Boundary

Boundary

Top of the World Highway

🌸🏠 Dawson City ✈
N64°04′ W139°25′

2

Flat Creek

Boundary Spur Road

Road Closed in Winter

Sixtymile

Sixtymile River

Walker Fork

South Fork

Liberty Creek

▲

Logging Cabin Creek

Mosquito Fork

TJ-66
E-94
D-109

J-321.4/517.2km Dawson City RV Park CDdGIPrST
J-321.3/517.1km Bonanza Gold Motel & RV Park CDLMT
J-321.2/516.9km Claim 33 Gold Panning

J-298/480km
D-25/40km
S-416/675km

J-292/470km
D-32/51km
S-410/665km

Taylor Highway

West Fork

▲ Mount Fairplay
5,541 ft./1,689m

East Fork

ALASKA

YUKON TERRITORY

TJ-0
E-161
D-0175

Dennison Fork

Principal Route Logged

Paved	Unpaved

Other Roads Logged

Other Roads   Scenic Byway

🌸 Refer to Log for Visitor Facilities

Scale

0 _____ 20 Miles
0 _____ 20 Kilometres

Key to Advertiser Services

C -Camping
D -Dump Station
d -Diesel
G -Gas (reg., unld.)
I -Ice
L -Lodging
M -Meals
P -Propane
R -Car Repair (major)
r -Car Repair (minor)
S -Store (grocery)
T -Telephone (pay)

5

Tanana River

To Delta Junction
(see ALASKA HIGHWAY section, page 124)

Tok

2

🏠 Fourmile Lake

UNITED STATES

CANADA

To Glennallen
(see GLENN HIGHWAY section, page 342)

◄ Tetlin Junction N63°18′ W142°36′

To Haines Junction
(see ALASKA HIGHWAY section, page 124)

in Alaska. And finally, travelers drive 96 miles/154 km of the Taylor Highway (Alaska Route 5) from Jack Wade Junction to the community of Chicken and on to Tetlin Junction on the Alaska Highway.

If you are traveling in the opposite direction of the log, this route is reversed (and the log read back to front): Drive the Taylor Highway from Tetlin Junction near Tok to Jack Wade Junction; then the Top of the World Highway to Dawson City; and finally the Klondike Highway from Dawson City down to the Alaska Highway near Whitehorse.

The 65-mile stretch of the Taylor Highway from Jack Wade Junction to the community of Eagle on the Yukon River is covered in "Side Trip to Eagle," beginning on page 297.

The route from Whitehorse to Dawson City began as a trail, used first by Natives, trappers and prospectors, and then by gold stampeders during the Klondike Gold Rush of 1897–98. Steamships provided passenger service between Whitehorse and Dawson City via the Yukon River.

A road was built connecting the Alaska Highway with the United Keno Hill Mine at Mayo in 1950. By 1955, the Mayo Road had been upgraded for automobile traffic and extended to Dawson City. In 1960, the last of 3 steel bridges, crossing the Yukon, Pelly and Stewart rivers, was completed. The only ferry crossing remaining is the Yukon River crossing at Dawson City. Mayo Road (Yukon Highway 11) from Stewart Crossing to Mayo, Elsa and Keno was redesignated the Silver Trail in 1985 (see the "Silver Trail" road log

on page 283 this section).

It is about a 6-hour drive via the Klondike Highway from the Alaska Highway north of Whitehorse (turnoff at **Milepost DC 894.8**) to Dawson City, a remarkably well-preserved gold rush town that is a national historic site and the major attraction on the Klondike Loop. Allow at least 5 hours for the 109-mile/175-km drive between Dawson City and Chicken (next service stop), factoring in slow driving conditions, a wait for the ferry crossing at Dawson City and negotiating customs at the border. The drive from Chicken back to the Alaska Highway and on to Tok is 78 miles/126 km and takes about 1-1/2 hours nonstop.

All of the Klondike Highway between the Alaska Highway junction and Dawson City is asphalt-surfaced and in good condition. The Top of the World Highway includes the 66-mile/106-km Yukon Highway 9 on the Canadian side, which is seal-coated (with potholes and gravel breaks), and the 13-mile dirt and gravel Boundary Road on the U.S. side, which was being improved in summer 2013. The Taylor Highway is a narrow, winding, dirt and gravel road with little or no shoulder south to Chicken, then chip seal and pavement (with many damaged sections) from Chicken south to the Alaska Highway. *Drive with your headlights on at all times and yield to oncoming large vehicles on curves.*

For current road and weather conditions in Canada, phone (867) 456-7623, or toll-free in Yukon 1-877-456-7623 or visit www.511yukon.ca. Check on current road

conditions and construction on the Taylor Highway by visiting 511.alaska.gov or phone 511.

Neither the Taylor or Top of the World highways are maintained from mid-October to May and the arrival of snow effectively closes the roads for winter. Do NOT attempt to drive these routes in the off-season.

If you intend to make the complete loop, there are 3 items to check on ahead of time. First, if you are traveling in the spring or early fall, be sure the *George Black* ferry is operating. Typically the Yukon River is free of ice and open for ferry traffic by the third week of May, but it has opened as late as June 22. Also, confirm that U.S. customs is open on Top of the World Highway so that you can cross into Alaska. Third, check on current road conditions along the Top of the World and Taylor highways. Good contacts for current information are the Visitor Information Centre in Dawson City, phone (867) 993-5566, and the Klondike Visitors Association, phone (867) 993-5575.

To complete the Klondike Loop requires taking the short ferry ride across the Yukon River on the *George Black* which connects the Klondike Highway at Dawson City with the Top of the World Highway. Travelers should be aware that in summer there may be a wait as long as 3 hours for the ferry during peak hours. Also, U.S. and Canada Customs on Top of the World are open daily in summer *only* (mid-May to late September, depending on weather). Hours were 9 A.M. to 9 P.M. (Pacific time), 8 A.M. to 8 P.M. (Alaska time) in summer 2013. There are no restrooms, services or currency exchanges avail-

able at the border and no phone.

Emergency Medical Services: On Yukon Highway 2 from **Milepost J 0** to **J 55.2** (Whitehorse to Braeburn Lodge), phone Whitehorse Ambulance at 911 or (867) 667-3333; RCMP at (867) 667-5555. From **Milepost J 55.2** to **J 167.7** (Braeburn Lodge to Pelly Crossing), phone Carmacks Medical Emergency (867) 863-4444 or RCMP (867) 863-5555. From **Milepost J 167.7** to **J 240** (Pelly Crossing to McQuesten River Lodge), phone Mayo Medical Emergency (867) 996-4444 or RCMP (867) 996-5555. From **Milepost J 240** to **J 323.4** and on Yukon Highway 9 from **Milepost D 0** to **D 66.1** (McQuesten River Lodge to Dawson City to Alaska border), phone Dawson City Medical Emergency (867) 993-4444 or RCMP (867) 993-5555. From **Milepost D 66.1** to **D 78.8** (Alaska border to Taylor Highway), phone Tok Area EMS at 911 or (907) 883-5111.

Klondike Loop Log

This section of the log shows distance from junction with the Alaska Highway (J) followed by distance from Dawson City (D) and distance from Skagway (S).

NOTE: Physical kilometreposts, on right hand side northbound, reflect distance from Skagway. In this log, distance from Skagway in miles reflects driving distance. Distance in kilometres reflects the physical kilometrepost and is not an accurate conversion of the mileage.

YUKON HIGHWAY 2

J 0 D 323.4 (520.3 km) **S 118.1** (191.7 km) Turnoff for Yukon Highway 2/Klondike Highway to Dawson City (323 miles/520 km) with continuation via Top of the World and Taylor highways to Chicken (432 miles/695 km from here) and junction with the Alaska Highway at **Milepost DC 1301.7** (498 miles/801 km from here).

> **Junction** with the Alaska Highway at **Milepost DC 894.8**; It is 7.4 miles/11.9 km southeast on the Alaska Highway from here to the Two Mile Hill exit to downtown Whitehorse. Turn to page 190 in the ALASKA HIGHWAY section.

J 0.5 (0.8 km) **D 322.9** (519.6 km) **S 118.6** (190.8 km) Distance marker northbound shows Carmacks 164 km/102 miles, Mayo 395 km/245 miles.

J 1.1 (1.8 km) **D 321.8** (517.8 km) **S 119.7** (192.6 km) Couch Road to the west provides access to **Hidden Valley Bed and Breakfast;** open year-round, phone (867) 633-6482.

Hidden Valley Bed and Breakfast. See display ad on page 181 in the ALASKA HIGHWAY section.

J 2.2 (3.5 km) **D 321.2** (516.9 km) **S 120.3** (195.5 km) Takhini River bridge. The Takhini flows into the Yukon River. The name is Tagish Indian, *tahk* meaning mosquito and *heena* meaning river, according to R. Coutts in *Yukon: Places & Names.*

Leaving Whitehorse city limits northbound.

J 3.6 (5.8 km) **D 319.8** (514.6 km) **S 121.7** (195.8 km) Gas bar and convenience store at **junction** with **Takhini Hot Springs Road** to Rivendell Farm, Yukon Wildlife Preserve, and Takhini Hot Springs.

A sunny day at Fox Lake, but boaters beware: Storms can blow up quickly on northern lakes.
(©Sharon Nault)

> See "Takhini Hot Springs Road" log on page 278

J 7.6 (12.2 km) **D 315.8** (508.2 km) **S 125.7** (202.3 km) Whitehorse rodeo grounds to west.

J 9.8 (15.8 km) **D 313.6** (504.6 km) **S**

127.9 (205.8 km) Turn off to the right on Policeman Point Road for **Sundog Retreat;** cabins, phone (867) 633-4183.

Sundog Retreat. See display ad on page 181 in the ALASKA HIGHWAY section.

J 10.4 (16.7 km) **D 313** (503.7 km) **S 128.5** (206.7 km) Shallow Bay Road.

J 12.5 (20.1 km) **D 310.9** (500.3 km) **S 130.6** (212 km) Horse Creek.

Takhini Hot Spring Road

Takhini Hot Springs resort is open year-round. (©Sharon Nault)

Takhini Hot Springs Road turns off the Klondike Highway/Yukon 2 just 3.6 miles/5.8 km northeast of the Alaska Highway. This straight, paved road, upgraded in 2013, leads west 6 miles/10 kms to Takhini Hot Springs, also providing access to 2 other interesting stops: the Yukon Wildlife Preserve and Rivendell Farm. Speed limit is 55 mph/90 kmph, but be alert for traffic from the many private residence driveways along the highway.

Distance is measured from the junction with Klondike Highway (K).

K 0 Junction with Klondike Hwy

K 1.1 (1.8 km) Boreal Road to east, access to Miner's Ridge residential subdivision.

K 1.3 (2.1 km) Spring Road to east, access to Pilot Mountain residential subdivision.

K 2.5 (4 km) Smith Road to west.

K 3.6 (5.8 km) Mile Road, access to Sir North Ranch.

K 4.3 (6.9 km) Rivendell Road to **Rivendell Farm** (description follows).

Rivendell Farm offers visitors an authentic farm escape and an opportunity to connect with local organic food. Visit this organic show garden to learn about

northern crops, sustainable farming, and life in the Yukon. Taste incredible local flavors, walk the raspberry labyrinth, play a game of farmers golf or rent a tipi picnic site. Yukon's Organic Experience! www.rivendellfarm.ca. See display ad on page 186 in the ALASKA HIGHWAY section. [ADVERTISEMENT]

K 4.9 (7.9 km) Kuhn Road to east.

K 5 (8 km) Ford Road to west.

K 5.2 (8.4 km) The **Yukon Wildlife Preserve** offers interpretive bus tours and self-guided walking tours on their 750-acre

wildlife park. Mountain goats, woodland caribou, moose, elk, wood bison, musk oxen, mule deer, and mountain sheep roam in their natural habitats. Phone (867) 456-7300; www.yukonwildlife.ca. Open daily May to early Sept.

The Yukon Wildlife Preserve. See display ad on page 184 in the ALASKA HIGHWAY section.

K 5.6 (9 km) Country Cabins B&B to east.

K 5.7 (9.2 km) Takhini River Road cutoff, access to Eldorado Elk Farm and Boarding Kennels (1.1 miles/1.7 km) and Takhini River Lodge (4.6 miles/7.4 km).

K 5.8 (9.3 km) Bean North Coffee Roasters café to east. Turnoff to east for Takhini Hot Springs RV park and campground. Tent and RV sites (30- and 50-amp).

K 5.9 (9.5 km) **Takhini Hot Springs**, open year-round; description follows.

Takhini Hot Springs. After a long drive there is nothing like a soak in our hot mineral pool and we're open year-round. Stay overnight in our beautiful wooded campground with pull-through sites, 30/50-amp power and tenting. There are 300 acres to hike and explore. We look forward to seeing you soon. Phone (867) 456-8000. www.takhinihotsprings.yk.ca. See display ad on page 184 in the ALASKA HIGHWAY section. [ADVERTISEMENT]

Return to Milepost J 3.6 Klondike Highway

J 20 (32.2 km) **D 303.4** (488.3 km) **S 138.1** (224 km) Deep Creek.

J 20.3 (32.7 km) **D 303.1** (487.8 km) **S 138.4** (224.6 km) Turnoff for Deep Creek Road to Lake Laberge Yukon Government Campground. Drive in 1.8 miles/2.9 km past residential area and Mom's Bakery; campground is on the shores of Lake Laberge next to Deep Creek. *NOTE: Unmarked roads in this area are residential driveways. Please do not park in front of these roads.*

Lake Laberge Yukon government campground has 16 sites, camping permit ($12), group camping area, kitchen shelter, water, boat launch, and fishing for lake trout, grayling and northern pike. Interpretive panels highlight the 30-mile Heritage River.

The Yukon River widens to form this 40-mile-/64-km-long lake. Lake Laberge was made famous by Robert W. Service with the lines: "The Northern Lights have seen queer sights. But the queerest they ever did see, was that night on the marge of Lake Lebarge I cremated Sam McGee," (from his poem "The Cremation of Sam McGee").

According to Yukon Renewable Resources, Lake Laberge is the only place in the Yukon where cormorants are seen. Loons and other water birds are commonly seen here.

CAUTION: Storms can blow up quickly and without warning on Lake Laberge, as on other northern lakes. Canoes and small craft stay to the west side of the lake, where the shoreline offers safe refuges. The east side of the lake is lined with high rocky bluffs, and there are few places to pull out. Small craft should not navigate the middle of the lake.

J 21.2 (34.1 km) **D 302.2** (486.3 km) **S 139.3** (226 km) Northbound the highway enters the Miners Range, plateau country of the Yukon, an immense wilderness of forested dome-shaped mountains and high ridges, dotted with lakes and traversed by tributaries of the Yukon River. To the west, Pilot Mountain in the Miners Range (elev. 6,739 feet/2,054m) is visible.

J 22.6 (36.4 km) **D 300.8** (484.1 km) **S 140.7** (228.4 km) **Fox Creek** bridge; grayling, excellent in June and July.

J 23.3 (37.5 km) **D 300.1** (483 km) **S 141.4** (229.5 km) Distance marker northbound shows Carmacks 125 km/78 miles, Dawson City 486 km/302 miles.

J 28.6 (46 km) **D 294.8** (474.4 km) **S 146.7** (238 km) Highway now follows the east shoreline of **Fox Lake** northbound. Fox Lake is a waterfowl stop during spring and fall migrations. Some waterfowl can be seen in spring (lake ice stays late), and large numbers of birds, especially swans, are present in fall. Muskrats also feed here: muskrat "push-ups" can be seen dotting the frozen surface of the lake in the winter and spring.

J 29.2 (47 km) **D 294.2** (473.5 km) **S 147.3** (239 km) Turnout to west on Fox Lake. Sign reads: "In 1883, U.S. Army Lt. Frederick Schwatka completed a survey of the entire length of the Yukon River. One of many geographical features that he named was Fox Lake, which he called Richthofen Lake, after geographer Freiherr Von Richthofen. Known locally as Fox Lake, the name was adopted in 1957. The Miners Range to the west was named by geologist/explorer George Mercer Dawson in 1887 'for the miners met by us along the river.'"

J 34.5 (55.5 km) **D 288.9** (464.9 km) **S 152.6** (247.7 km) Turnoff west for Fox

Lake Yukon government campground; 43 sites, camping permit ($12), kitchen shelter, playground drinking water and boat launch. Good fishing for lake trout and burbot from the shore at the campground; excellent grayling year-round.

J 38.4 (61.8 km) D 285 (458.6 km) S 156.5 (254 km) Burn area northbound is from a major forest fire in this area in summer 1998.

J 40.1 (64.5 km) D 283.3 (455.9 km) S 158.2 (256.6 km) 1998 Forest Fire (sign).

J 44.2 (71.1 km) D 279.2 (449.3 km) S 162.3 (263.2 km) Leaving 911 zone northbound.

J 44.6 (71.8 km) D 278.8 (448.6 km) S 162.7 (264 km) Little Fox Lake; lake trout 3 to 8 lbs., fish the islands. Watch for turnout with boat launch to west along lake.

J 49.5 (79.6 km) D 273.9 (440.8 km) S 167.6 (272 km) Boreal Fire Interpretive Site Rest Area is a large, double–ended parking area with outhouses, litter barrels and interpretive panels.

J 51.8 (83.4 km) D 271.6 (437.1 km) S 169.9 (275.5 km) CAUTION: Watch for elk along highway (northbound sign). According to Renewable Resources Wildlife Viewing Program, about 50 elk live here year-round. They are most commonly seen in winter and spring. Look for their distinctive white rumps on the exposed south-facing slopes. Elk are a protected species in the Yukon. Grizzly bears feed on roadside vegetation (and also elk) in this area in spring and summer.

J 55.2 (88.8 km) D 268.2 (431.6 km) S 173.3 (280.8 km) Braeburn Lodge to west; food, gas, diesel, lodging and minor car repairs. One Braeburn Lodge cinnamon bun will feed 4 people.

Braeburn Lodge. See display ad this page.

The lodge is also an official checkpoint for the 1,000-mile Yukon Quest International Sled Dog Race.

Private Aircraft: Braeburn airstrip to east, dubbed Cinnamon Bun Strip; elev. 2,350 feet/716m; length 3,000 feet/914m; dirt strip; wind sock.

J 65.6 (105.6 km) D 257.8 (414.9 km) S 183.7 (298 km) Paved pull-through turnout on east side of highway is a rest area and photo stop with information sign about Conglomerate Mountain (elev. 3,361 feet/1,024m). Sign reads:

"The Laberge Series was formed at the leading edge of volcanic mud flows some 185 million years ago (Early Jurassic). These flows solidified into sheets several kilometres long and about 1 km wide and 100m thick. This particular series of sheets stretches from Atlin, BC, to north of Carmacks, a distance of about 350 km. Other conglomerates of this series form Five Finger Rapids."

Several outcroppings of conglomerate may be found in the immediate area. Conglomerate, also called "Puddingstone" because of its appearance, consists of pebbles welded into solid masses of varying size by a natural cement. Composition of the cementing material varies, as does the size and composition of the pebbles.

J 71.3 (114.7 km) D 252.1 (405.7 km) S 189.4 (307 km) Turnouts on both sides of highway between Twin Lakes. These 2 small lakes, 1 on either side of the road, are known for their beauty and colour.

J 71.7 (115.4 km) D 251.7 (405.1 km) S 189.8 (307.7 km) Riser Lake to east.

J 71.9 (115.7 km) D 251.5 (404.7 km)

Montague House provided accommodations to weary travellers back in 1901. (©Sharon Nault)

S 190 (308 km) Turnoff to west for Twin Lakes Yukon government campground; 18 sites, camping permit ($12), drinking water, boat launch. Lake is stocked. Large parking area with informational panels on the Nordenskiold River. Enjoyable fishing for lake trout, grayling and pike. Good swimming for the hardy!

J 72.1 (116 km) D 251.3 (404.4 km) S 190.2 (308.4 km) Distance marker northbound shows Carmacks 48 km/30 miles, Mayo 280 km/174 miles, Dawson City 405 km/252 miles.

J 79.6 (128.1 km) D 243.8 (392.3 km) S 197.7 (320.5 km) Northbound motorist will note layers of volcanic ash in banks alongside highway. About 1,250 years ago a layer of white volcanic ash coated a third of the southern Yukon, or some 125,000 square miles/323,725 square km, and it is still quite visible along many roadcuts. This distinct line conveniently provides a division used by archaeologists for dating artifacts: Materials found below this major stratigraphic marker are considered to have been deposited before A.D. 700, while those found above the ash layer are postdated A.D. 700. It has been theorized that the ash may have been deposited during a single violent volcanic eruption from a source now buried under the Klutlan Glacier in the St. Elias Mountains in eastern Alaska.

J 80.6 (129.7 km) D 242.8 (390.7 km) S 198.7 (322.4 km) Rest area with picnic tables, litter barrel and outhouses to east at remains of Montague House, a typical early-day roadhouse which offered lodging and meals on the stagecoach route between Whitehorse and Dawson City. A total of 52 stopping places along this route were listed in the Jan. 16, 1901, edition of the Whitehorse Star under "On the Winter Trail between Whitehorse and Dawson Good Accommodations for Travellers." Montague House was listed at Mile 99. Good photo stop.

J 86 (138.4 km) D 237.4 (382 km) S 204.1 (330.8 km) CAUTION: Watch for rough road and loose gravel northbound.

J 93.3 (150.1 km) D 230.1 (370.3 km)

S 211.4 (345.4 km) Turnout to east, information sign about agate deposits.

J 95 (152.9 km) D 228.4 (367.6 km) S 213.1 (348.1 km) Wetlands to west are part of the Nordenskiold River system. Waterfowl stage here during spring and fall migrations. Watch for trumpeter swans and ruddy ducks. Other area wildlife include beaver, muskrat, moose, mink and fox.

The Nodenskiold River was named by Lt. Frederick Schwatka, U.S. Army, for Swedish arctic explorer Erik Nordenskiold. This river, which parallels the highway for several miles, flows into the Yukon River at Carmacks. Good grayling and pike fishing all summer.

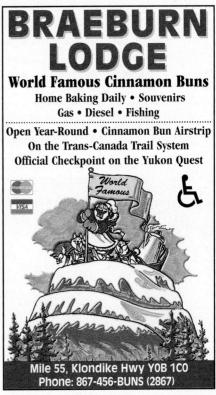

J 99.3 (159.8 km) D 224.1 (360.6 km) S 217.4 (352.3 km) Entering village of Carmacks (northbound sign).

J 100.6 (161.9 km) D 222.8 (358.6 km) S 218.7 (354.4 km) Very nice pull-through rest area to east with litter barrels and outhouses. The Carmacks Visitor Centre here has pamphlets, maps and information; open during the summer. Check here for local fishing tips.

The Welcome to Carmacks loon mosaic seen here was designed by artists Chris Schearbarth, Brian Tom and Clarence Washpan and constructed by members of Little Salmon First Natives.

Carmacks

J 101.5 (163.3 km) D 221.9 (357 km) S 219.6 (355.8 km). Located on the banks of the Yukon River, Carmacks is the only highway crossing of the Yukon River between Whitehorse and Dawson City. **Population: 444.**

Emergency Services: RCMP, phone (867) 863-5555. **Fire Department**, phone (867) 863-2222. **Ambulance**, phone (867) 863-4444. **Village Office**, phone (867) 863-6271. **Forest Fire Control**, phone (867) 863-5271.

Visitor Information: Located in the Old Telegraph Office, which also contains a mini-museum and a display of area geology. Phone the Visitor Information Centre at (867) 863-6330 (summers only). Or contact the Village of Carmacks, Box 113, Carmacks, YT Y0B 1C0; phone (867) 863-6271, fax (867) 863-6606.

Private Aircraft: Carmacks airstrip; elev. 1,770 feet/539m; length 5,200 feet/1,585m; gravel; no fuel.

Traveler facilities include lodging at the **Hotel Carmacks**, which also has RV parking with hookups and a restaurant. **Sunrise Services** has gas (unleaded, diesel), sani-dump, convenience store, a cafe, public phone, camping and a motel.

Carmacks was once an important stop for Yukon River steamers traveling between Dawson City and Whitehorse, and it continues as a supply point today for modern river travelers. Carmacks has survived—while other river ports have not—as a service centre for highway traffic and mining interests. Carmacks was also a major stopping point on the old Whitehorse to Dawson Trail. Restored pioneer structures in Carmacks include the Carmacks Roadhouse and the Hazel Brown cabin.

Carmacks was named for George Carmack, who established a trading post here in the 1890s. Carmack had come North in 1885, hoping to strike it rich. He spent the next 10 years prospecting without success. In 1896, when the trading post went bankrupt,

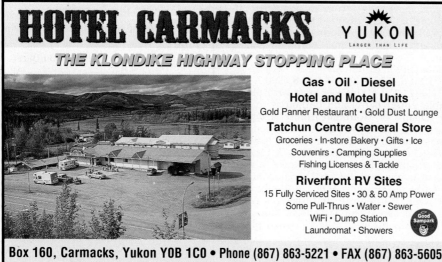
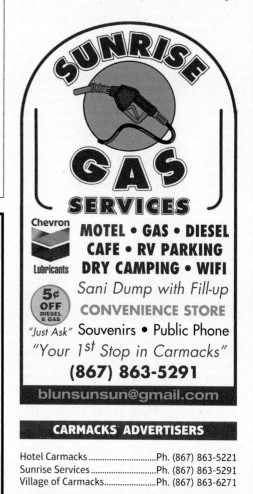

Carmack moved his family to Fortymile, where he could fish to eat and cut timber to sell. That summer, Carmack's remarkable persistence paid off—he unearthed a 5-dollar pan of coarse gold, during a time when a 10-cent pan was considered a good find. That same winter, he extracted more than a ton of gold from the creek, which he renamed Bonanza Creek, and its tributary, Eldorado. When word of Carmack's discovery reached the outside world the following spring, it set off the Klondike Gold Rush.

A 1.2-mile/2-km interpretive boardwalk makes it possible to enjoy a daytime stroll along the Yukon River; beautiful view of countryside and Tantalus Butte, gazebo and park at end of trail. Wheelchair accessible.

For rock hounds, there are 5 agate trails in the area, which can double as good, short hiking trails. Abundant fishing in area rivers and lakes: salmon, grayling, northern pike, lake and rainbow trout and whitefish. 🔚

Klondike Loop Log
(continued)

J 102.1 (164.3 km) **D 221.3** (356.1 km) **S 220.2** (356.8 km) **Yukon River bridge.** Turnout and parking area at south end of bridge; 2.3-mile-/3.7-km-long trail to Coal Mine Lake.

J 102.8 (165.4 km) **D 220.6** (355 km) **S 220.9** (358 km) Northern Tutchone Trading Post with post office at north end of Yukon River bridge. The Northern Tutchone First Nations **Tage Cho Hudan Interpretive Centre** features archaeological displays on Native life in a series of indoor and outdoor exhibits, and marked interpretive trails. The centre also features a mammoth snare diorama and has some arts and crafts.

J 103.5 (166.5 km) **D 219.9** (353.8 km) **S 221.6** (359.1 km) Turnoff to east for Campbell Highway, which leads south to Faro (110 miles/177 km), Ross River (144 miles/232 km) and Watson Lake (373 miles/600 km). The Coal Mine (campground, cabins, burgers) located at this junction, caters to river travelers; canoe rentals. 🅰

> **Junction** with Campbell Highway (Yukon Highway 4). Turn to end of CAMPBELL HIGHWAY section on page 311 and read log back to front.

Highway climbs northbound.

J 104.4 (168 km) **D 219** (352.4 km) **S 222.5** (360.6 km) Turnout to west with litter bins, information sign and view of Yukon River Valley.

J 116.3 (187.2 km) **D 207.1** (333.3 km) **S 234.4** (380 km) Large double-ended rest area to west with picnic table, hiking trails, toilets, litter bins and viewing platform for **Five Finger Rapids Recreation Site.** Five Finger Rapids named by early miners for the 5 channels, or fingers, formed by the rock pillars. They are a navigational hazard. The safest passage is through the nearest, or east, passage. Stairs (219 steps) and a 0.6-mile/1-km trail lead down to a closer view of the rapids. Area flora includes prairie crocus, kinnikinnick, common juniper and sage. Watch for white-crowned sparrows and American tree sparrows. Interpretive panels along stairway.

Information sign at turnout on the Wood Cutters Range, the low hills in front of you, which were named "to honor the wood cutters who, between 1898 and 1955,

Five Finger Rapids Recreation Site, at Milepost J 116.3, has a great view of the Yukon River.
(©Earl L. Brown)

worked tirelessly to stockpile wood for the fleet of sternwheelers on the Yukon River and its tributaries."

J 117.8 (189.6 km) **D 205.6** (330.9 km) **S 235.9** (382.2 km) Tatchun Creek bridge.

J 117.9 (189.7 km) **D 205.5** (330.7 km) **S 236** (382.4 km) Turnoff to east for **Tatchun Creek Yukon government campground**; 12 sites (4 pull-through), camping permit ($12), kitchen shelter and drinking water. Good fishing for grayling, June through September; salmon, July through August. 🔚🅰

Highway climbs; passing lane northbound.

J 118.5 (190.5 km) **D 205** (329.9 km) **S 236.5** (383.5 km) Turnoff to east for Frenchman Lake Road (narrow, gravel) which leads 5.2 miles/8.4 km to **Tatchun Lake Campground**; 20 campsites, $12 fee, boat launch.

If road conditions allow, this side road leads 20.7 miles/33.3 km to Nunatuk Campground and 26 miles/41.7 km to Frenchman Lake Campground (each have 10 campsites) before it junctions with the Campbell Highway. See **Milepost WL 337.5** in the CAMPBELL HIGHWAY section. 🔚🅰

J 125.5 (202 km) **D 197.9** (318.5 km) **S 243.6** (394.8 km) **Yukon Crossing Viewpoint** to west is a double-ended large gravel turnout with litter bins and toilets that overlooks the Yukon River. Good photo stop. Welcome to Beringa interpretive sign reads:

"Beringa is the land mass stretching from Eastern Siberia through Alaska to the Yukon. If you could stand here 15,000 years ago near the end of the last glaciation, the vista would be of a dusty, treeless steppe at the edge of the ice sheet."

J 130.8 (210.5 km) **D 192.6** (310 km) **S 248.9** (403.5 km) McGregor Creek.

J 133.6 (215 km) **D 189.8** (305.4 km) **S 251.7** (408 km) 1995 Forest Fire (northbound sign). The fire consumed 325,000 acres of forest.

J 134.7 (216.8 km) **D 188.7** (303.7 km) **S 252.8** (409.7 km) Distance marker northbound shows Pelly Crossing 55 km/34 miles, Dawson City 308 km/191 miles.

J 142.6 (229.5 km) **D 180.8** (291 km) **S 260.7** (422.5 km) McCabe Creek. Double-ended gravel turnout. *CAUTION: Watch for grizzly bears.*

J 146.6 (235.9 km) **D 176.8** (283.5 km) **S 264.7** (428.6 km) Access road to Minto Mine and Minto Resorts.

J 147.3 (237 km) **D 176.1** (283.4 km) **S 265.4** (429.9 km) Minto Road, a short loop road, leads west to location of the former riverboat landing and trading post of **MINTO. Private Aircraft**: Minto airstrip; elev. 1,550 feet/472m; length 5,000 feet/1,524m; gravel.

J 151.3 (243.5 km) **D 172.1** (277 km) **S 269.4** (436.3 km) *CAUTION: Slow for frost heaves and potholes northbound.*

J 154 (247.8 km) **D 169.4** (272.6 km) **S 272.1** (440.6 km) Side road east to L'hutsaw Lake (Von Wilczek Lakes), an important wetlands for duck staging, nesting and moulting.

J 158.8 (255.5 km) **D 164.6** (264.9 km) **S 276.9** (448.2 km) Narrow dirt side road leads east 0.2 mile/0.3 km to small turnaround at Rock Island Lake (Tthi Ndu Mun Lake). Water lilies and other seldom-seen aquatic wildflowers bloom in the shallow areas of the lake. American coots, rarely seen in the Yukon, nest in the area.

J 161.3 (259.6 km) **D 162.1** (260.9 km) **S 279.4** (449.7 km) Forest Fire 1969 (sign).

J 162 (260.7 km) **D 161.4** (260.7 km) **S 280.1** (453.5 km) Meadow Lake to west is an athalassic or inland salt lake; note white salt deposits along the lakeshore. Look for American coots and horned grebes.

J 163.1 (262.5 km) **D 160.3** (258 km) **S 281.2** (455.7 km) Distance marker northbound shows Pelly Crossing 8 km/5 miles, Mayo 136 km/85 miles, Dawson City 261 km/162 miles. Wild strawberries (in season) along the highway.

J 166 (267.1 km) **D 157.4** (253.3 km) **S 284.1** (460.4 km) Highway descends northbound to Pelly Crossing. *Reduce speed northbound entering Pelly Crossing.*

Distance marker southbound shows Carmacks 100 km/62 miles, Whitehorse 277 km/172 miles.

Interpretive signs and view of Pelly Crossing and river valley at Milepost J 168.8.
(©David L. Ranta, staff)

Pelly Crossing

J 167.8 (270 km) D 155.6 (250.4 km) S 285.9 (463.1 km) Located on the banks of the Pelly River. **Population**: 296. **Emergency Services**: RCMP phone (867) 537-5555 (in Whitehorse); **Ambulance**, phone (867) 537-4444. **Radio**: CBC North 106.1 FM. **Private Aircraft**: Pelly Airstrip, elev. 1,870 feet/570m; length 3,000 feet/914m; gravel; no services.

Gas, diesel, groceries, phone, lodging, camping and dump station at Selkirk Centre. The **Selkirk Heritage Centre** adjacent the grocery store is a replica of the Big Jonathon House at Fort Selkirk. The centre offers self-guided tours of First Nations heritage, including beadwork displays, and crafts are for sale. The large, inspiring murals here were painted by local artists. Open mid-May to mid-September, daily 9 A.M. to 7 P.M.

Pelly Crossing became a settlement when the Klondike Highway was put through in 1950. A ferry transported people and vehicles across the Pelly River, where the road eventually continued to Dawson City. Most inhabitants of Pelly Crossing came from historic Fort Selkirk, now a national historic site.

This Selkirk Indian community attracted residents from Minto when the highway to Dawson City was built. There is a school, curling rink, baseball field, swimming pool, church, youth centre and laundromat. The local economy is based on hunting, trapping, fishing and guiding. The Selkirk First Nation has erected signs near the bridge on the history and culture of the Selkirk people.

Klondike Loop Log

(continued)

J 168 (270.3 km) D 155.4 (250.1 km) S 286.1 (463.7 km) Pelly River bridge. Pelly River Crossing Yukon government campground to west at south end of bridge; covered tables, outhouses, grassy area. Camping permit $12.

Slow for frost heaves and rough pavement northbound.

J 168.8 (271.6 km) D 154.6 (248.8 km) S 286.9 (465 km) Turnout with litter bins to east. View of Pelly Crossing and river valley; monument and interpretive signs (excerpts follow).

"In the 1950s a road was constructed north from Whitehorse, and Pelly Crossing was established as a ferry crossing and highway construction camp. With the completion of the road, the paddlewheelers stopped running the rivers and Fort Selkirk was virtually abandoned. The Selkirk First Nation first moved to Minto and finally settled at Pelly Crossing. Their Final Claims and Self-Government Agreements were signed at Minto in 1997. The Selkirk First Nation Council administers the community of Pelly Crossing.

"Robert Campbell was a Hudson's Bay Co. clerk at Fort Halkett, on the Liard River, in May 1840. After receiving instructions to explore the upper Liard River, he and 7 travelling companions paddled north to Frances Lake, traveled overland past Finlayson Lake and, on reaching the Pelly River, built a raft and poled a short distance downstream. Pelly Banks Post was constructed at the head of the Pelly River in 1842-43 and Campbell spent the next 2 winters there.

"In the winter of 1847-48, Campbell established Fort Selkirk at the mouth of the Pelly River."

The Pelly River was named by Robert Campbell in 1840 for Sir John Henry Pelly, governor of the Hudson's Bay Co. The Pelly heads near the Northwest Territories border and flows approximately 375 miles/603 km to the Yukon River.

J 169.7 (273 km) D 153.7 (247.3 km) S 287.8 (466.5 km) **Private Aircraft**: Airstrip to east; elev. 1,870 feet/570m; length 3,000 feet/914m; gravel. No services.

J 172.1 (277 km) D 151.3 (243.5 km) S 290.2 (470.4 km) *Slow for frost heaves northbound.*

J 177.9 (286.3 km) D 145.5 (234.2 km) S 296 (479.5 km) Double-ended turnout to east.

J 182.2 (293.2 km) D 141.2 (227.2 km) S 300.3 (486.4 km) Willow (Du Dettho) Creek culvert.

J 193.2 (310.9 km) D 130.2 (209.5 km) S 311.3 (505.4 km) Distance marker northbound shows Stewart Crossing 30 km/48 miles, Mayo 85 km/53 miles, Dawson City 210 km/130 miles.

J 195.3 (314.3 km) D 128.1 (206.2 km) S 313.4 (508 km) Turnout with litter bins to east.

Winding descent begins for northbound

traffic.

Distance marker southbound shows Pelly Crossing 40 km/25 miles, Carmacks 146 km/91 miles, Whitehorse 322 km/200 miles.

J 203.7 (327.8 km) D 119.7 (192.6 km) S 321.8 (519.7 km) **Crooked Creek Bridge**. *(NOTE: Wood bridge decking can be slippery when wet.)* Large turnout with litter bin to west at north end of bridge. Pike; grayling, use flies, summer best.

Southern boundary of Ddhaw Gro Special Management Area (formerly McArthur Wildlife Sanctuary). Grey Hunter Peak and surrounding hillsides support many species of wildlife, including Fannin sheep.

J 205 (329.9 km) D 118.4 (190.5 km) S 323.1 (523.7 km) Pull-through turnout with litter barrel to east at turnoff for **Ethel Lake Yukon government campground**. Drive in 16.6 miles/26.7 km on narrow and winding side road (not recommended for large RVs) for campground; 12 sites, boat launch, fishing. Camping permit $12.

J 211.6 (340.5 km) D 111.8 (179.9 km) S 329.7 (534 km) Stewart Crossing; gas, diesel. Information sign west side of highway; Silver Trail information available; outhouses, litter bins. Highway maintenance camp.

In 1886 **STEWART CROSSING** was the site of a trading post established by Arthur Harper, Alfred Mayo and Jack McQuesten to support gold mining in the area. Later a roadhouse was built here as part of the Whitehorse to Dawson overland stage route. Stewart Crossing also functioned as a fuel stop for the riverboats and during the 1930s was a transfer point for the silver ore barges from Mayo. Harper, Mayo and McQuesten are 3 prominent names in Yukon history. Harper, an Irish immigrant, was one of the first white men to prospect in the Yukon, although he never struck it rich. He died in 1898 in Arizona. (His son, Walter Harper, was on the first complete ascent of Mount McKinley in 1913. Walter died in 1918 in the SS *Princess Sophia* disaster off Juneau.)

Mayo, a native of Maine, explored, prospected and traded in the Yukon until his death in 1924. McQuesten, like Harper, worked his way north from the California goldfields. Often referred to as the "Father of the Yukon" and a founding member of the Yukon order of Pioneers, Jack Leroy Napoleon McQuesten ended his trading and prospecting days in 1898 when he moved to California. He died in 1909 while in Seattle for the Alaska–Yukon–Pacific Exposition.

J 212.1 (341.3 km) D 111.3 (179.1 km) S 330.2 (535 km) Stewart River bridge. The Stewart River flows into the Yukon River upstream from Dawson City.

J 212.2 (341.5 km) D 111.2 (179 km) S 330.3 (535.2 km) Stop sign at north end of Stewart River bridge at **junction** with Yukon Highway 11 east to Mayo and Keno. (Northbound travelers turn right for Keno, left to continue to Dawson City.)

Junction with the Silver Trail (Yukon Highway 11) to Mayo, Elsa and Keno. See the "Silver Trail" log beginning on page 283.

View to southwest of Stewart River and mountains as highway climbs northbound.

J 218.5 (351.6 km) D 104.9 (168.8 km)
(continues on page 285)

Silver Trail

The Silver Trail leads northeast from **Milepost J 212.2** Klondike Highway to Mayo, Elsa and Keno City. It is approximately 140 miles/225 km round-trip to Keno City and an easy day trip for motorists. If you have a Yukon Explorer's Passport, the Binet House and the Keno Mining Museum in Keno are considered two of the most exclusive passport stamps.

The road is asphalt-surfaced to Mayo, and well-maintained gravel from Mayo to Keno City. *IMPORTANT: Gas is available only at Stewart Crossing and Mayo; there is no fuel in Keno.*

The Silver Trail to Mayo follows the Stewart River through what has been one of the richest silver mining regions in Canada. The Silver Trail region encompasses the traditional lands of the Na Cho N'y'ak Dun First Nations.

Yukon Highway 11
Distance is measured from the junction with the Klondike Highway (K).

K 0 Silver Trail (Stewart Crossing). The Silver Trail leads northeast from **Milepost J 212.2** on the Klondike Highway.

K 3 (4.8 km) Small turnout to south as road curves.

K 4 (6.4 km) View of Stewart River to the south. Highway follows river eastbound, view often obscured by trees.

K 6.4 (10.3 km) Devil's Elbow trail; parking and turnaround area at end of side road to south. Narrow interpretive trail leads back across Silver Trail and up steep bank to viewing platform; 30 minutes round-trip, bring mosquito repellent.

K 11.9 (19.1 km) Large double-ended turnout with litter barrels and information boards overlooking the Stewart River.

K 19.5 (31.3 km) Double-ended turnout and rescue shelter.

K 27.4 (44.1 km) Pull-through rest area; outhouses, litter barrel.

K 30.9 (49.7 km) McIntyre Park municipal campground (entrance prior to bridge westbound) on banks of the Mayo River west side of bridge; 9 picnic sites and a shelter; free camping and wood provided.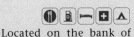

Mayo River bridge. Good fishing from bridge for grayling.

K 31.5 (50.7 km) **Junction** with access road to Mayo (description follows). Turn right (south) for Mayo, keep left (north) for road to Elsa and Keno City.

Mayo

Located on the bank of the Stewart River near its confluence with the Mayo River. **Population:** 470. **Emergency Services:** RCMP, phone (867) 996-5555. **Fire Dept.,** phone (867) 996-2222. **Nursing Station,** phone (867) 996-4444.

Visitor Information: At **Binet House Interpretive Centre/Museum,** open 10 A.M. to 6 P.M. daily mid-May to mid-September; phone (867) 996-2926; (867) 996-

2317; email mayo@northwestel.net; website: www.yukonweb.com/community/mayo. Visit the Binet House to see exhibits about the geology and history of the area plus an interesting display of early medical equipment, including the first iron lung ever made. Get your Yukon Explorer's Passport stamped here.

Elevation: 1,650 feet/503m. **Climate:** Residents claim it's the coldest and hottest spot in Yukon. Record low, -80°F/-62.2°C (February 1947); record high, 97°F/36.1°C (June 1969). **Radio:** CBC 1230, CHON-FM 98.5, CKRW 98-FM. **Television:** CBC Anik, Channel 7, TVNC. **Transportation:** Charter floatplane and helicopter service available.

Private Aircraft: Mayo airstrip, 4 miles/6.5 km north; elev. 1,653 feet/504m; length 4,850 feet/1,478m; gravel; fuel 100, Jet B.

Mayo has most traveler facilities. Gas, diesel, propane, snacks, restaurant and information available. Lodging and camping at **Bedrock Motel and RV Park.** Post office, liquor store and library located in the Territorial Building. Bank service available at

McIntyre Park municipal campground is located along the banks of the Mayo River.
(©David L. Ranta, staff)

old Village Office building Tuesday to Friday afternoons. Tire repair and minor vehicle repair are available. For recreation, Mayo has a tennis court/basketball court, a skateboard park, outdoor pool and baseball field.

Mayo began as a river settlement and port in 1902–03 after gold was discovered in the area. It was also known as Mayo Landing. River traffic increased with silver ore shipments from Keno Hill silver mines to Whitehorse. Today, Mayo is a service centre for mineral exploration in the area. Yukon Energy Corporation operates a hydroelectric project here.

Pick up a free copy of the excellent *Mayo Historical Buildings Walking Tour* booklet.

MAYO ADVERTISERS

Signpost monument is located on top of Keno Hill. (©David L. Ranta, staff)

There is a viewing deck with interpretive signs overlooking the Stewart River. Canoeists can put in at Mayo on the Stewart River for a paddle to Stewart Crossing or Dawson City. Mayo also has a swimming pool.

The Mayo Midnight Marathon takes place in June. The race includes a full marathon, half marathon and 10K events. Phone (867) 996-2368 for details. Arts in the Park is an annual event that coincides with Marathon weekend in summer.

Silver Trail Log

(continued)

K 31.5 (50.7 km) **Junction** with access road to Mayo.

K 32.1 (51.6 km) Bedrock Motel & RV Park. See display ad on page 283.

K 32.4 (52.1 km) Mayo airport, built in 1928 by the Treadwell Mining Co.

K 34.5 (55.5 km) Side road (closed to public) to Mayo hydro dam, built in 1951 and completed in 1952.

K 35.3 (56.8 km) Turnoff to west for **Five Mile Lake Yukon government campground**; 20 sites (camping fee $12), kitchen shelter, picnic tables, playground, hiking trails, firepits, swimming, boat launch.

K 35.5 (57.1 km) Five Mile Lake day-use area. *Pavement ends, gravel begins, northbound.*

K 37.2 (59.9 km) Wareham Lake to west, created by the Mayo River power project.

K 37.6 (60.5 km) Survival shelter to east.

K 39.8 (64 km) Minto Bridge; marshy area, good birdwatching. Parking to west with interpretive signs, toilets and garbage bins.

K 42.3 (68.5 km) **Junction** of Yukon Highway 11 with Minto Lake Road and Duncan Creek Road. Continue on Yukon Highway 11 for Keno City.

For **Minto Lake** drive 12 miles/19 km west on Minto Lake Road; good fishing for lake trout and grayling. Also access to Highet Creek.

The 25-mile/40-km Duncan Creek Road to east was the original Silver Trail used by Treadwell-Yukon during the 1930s to haul silver ore from Keno into Mayo. It is now a back road into Keno City. Inquire in Keno City about road conditions on this side road.

K 47.3 (76 km) Watch for turnoff for Mount Haldane trail; follow gravel road 2 miles/3.2 km to trailhead. This 4-mile-/6.4-km-long walking trail leads to the summit of **Mount Haldane**, elev. 6,023 feet/1,836m, and offers sweeping views of the McQuesten River valley and the Mines Site of Elsa and the Village of Mayo. Hikers in good physical condition can make the round-trip in approximately 6 hours. Inquire locally for current trail conditions. The switched-back trail is visible on the south face of Mount Haldane. The trail was cut by a mining company in the 1970s and brushed out in recent years.

K 47.5 (76.4 km) Turnout with information boards by Halfway Lake.

K 47.7 (76.7 km) Entrance to Silver Trail Inn.

K 48.4 (77.7 km) Mount Haldane Lions survival shelter.

K 53.8 (86.5 km) South McQuesten River Road.

K 59.3 (95.4 km) Main gate to **ELSA**. This is an active mining and reclamation site and there is no visitor access, although motorists buildings at Elsa are visible from the road and there are turnoffs to these structures. Information sign here reads:

"In 1924, prospector Charlie Brefalt staked a silver claim here on Galena Hill and named it after his sister, Elsa. It proved to be a major discovery and eventually produced millions of ounces of silver. Other properties in the area, such as the Silver King and Calumet, also developed into major mines. By the 1930s, the town of Elsa had taken shape and it gradually became the major community serving the mines. Since, 1948, Elsa has been home to United Keno Hill Mines, which at one time was the world's fourth largest producer of silver concentrates."

K 59.5 (95.7 km) Watch for a plaque commemorating American engineer Livingston Wernecke, who came to the Keno Hill area in 1919 to investigate the silver–lead ore discoveries for Treadwell– Yukon Mining Co.

K 63 (101.4 km) Side road leads north to Hanson Lakes and McQuesten Lake (9.2 miles/14.8 km). Galena Hill to east.

Keno City

K 68.1 (109.5 km) Historic frontier town nestled in the mountains at the end of the Silver Trail. **Population**: 20. **Visitor Information**: At the Keno Mining Museum; or visit www.kenocity.ca. Originally called Sheep Hill by the early miners, Keno City was renamed Keno—a gambling game—after the Keno mining claim that was staked by Louis Bouvette in July 1919. Enormously rich discoveries of silver made Keno City a boom town in the 1920s. Today it is home to an eclectic mix of oldtimers, miners, and artists.

Visitor services in Keno City include cabin accommodations, the Snack Bar (a favorite) and gift shops. Washers, dryers and showers are available for public use beside the recreation hall. **Keno Campground**, in town next to Lightning Creek, has secluded RV sites, water, firewood and firepits. There is free gold panning in the campground area. Other portions of Lightning Creek are private gold claims.

High-grade silver-lead veins were first discovered in the Keno Hill area in 1906. The first mill was constructed in 1925. Unique and informative displays at the **Keno City Museum** capture the area's rich gold and silver mining history. The museum has many new displays and outbuildings.

Displays include tools and equipment used in the early days of mining; a large photograph collection; and artifacts associated with everyday life in the Yukon's isolated mining communities. Also visit the Alpine Interpretive Centre, which houses information and displays on area fauna such as butterflies, marmots and pikas. Museum hours are 10 A.M. to 6 P.M. June–Sept. Have your Yukon Passport stamped here.

A network of good hiking and biking trails criss-cross the area, leading to historic mine sites, scenic valleys and alpine meadows. The trails vary in distance from a half-mile/1 km to 12 miles/20 kms, and range from easy to strenuous. There is also fishing and canoeing on area lakes.

A popular side trip is walking or driving the winding Keno Hill Road 6.5 miles/10.5 km to the signpost monument on top of **Keno Hill**, elev. 6,065 feet/1,849m. Panoramic views of the valley and mountain ranges.

NOTE: Inquire locally about road conditions before driving Keno Hill Road to the summit, or Duncan Creek Road back to Mayo.

Keno City Museum/Campground. See display ad this page.

**Return to Milepost J 212.2
Klondike Loop**

S 336.6 (545.4 km) Dry Creek.

J 222 (357.3 km) D 101.4 (163.2 km) S 340.1 (551 km) Double-ended dirt turnout to south is Stewart River viewpoint; outhouse, picnic tables, information signs. A major tributary of the Yukon River, the Stewart River was discovered in 1849 by James G. Stewart, an assistant to Robert Campbell of the Hudson's Bay Co.

J 224 (360.5 km) D 99.4 (160 km) S 342.1 (554.2 km) Distance marker northbound shows Dempster Highway 121 km/75 miles, Dawson City 161 km/100 miles.

J 226.7 (364.8 km) D 96.7 (155.6 km) S 344.8 (558.5 km) Moose Creek Lodge. A must for Yukon travellers! The historic log

building has a restaurant offering excellent food and legendary pastries; souvenir shop; and books. Cozy rustic guest cabins, operated as B&B with hearty breakfasts. Open daily 8 A.M. to 7 P.M., mid-May through mid-September. Groups, caravans, motorcycles welcome. Reservations recommended. www. moosecreek–lodge.com. Phone (867) 996-2550. [ADVERTISEMENT]

J 226.9 (365.1 km) D 96.5 (155.3 km) S 346 (556.8 km) Moose Creek bridge. Informal turnout to west at north end.

J 227.1 (365.5 km) D 96.3 (155 km) S 346.2 (559.3 km) Turnoff to west for **Moose Creek Yukon government campground** adjacent Moose Creek and Stewart River; good picnic spot (bring insect repellent); 30 RV sites (4 pull-throughs), 6 tent-only sites, kitchen shelter, playground, playfield. Camping $12. Short trail to **Stewart River** is a 30-minute walk through boreal forest along Moose Creek. Good fishing for grayling, 1 to 1¼ lbs. Listen for Northern waterthrush, Wilson's warbler and common yellow-throat.

Highway climbs northbound.

J 240.2 (386.6 km) D 83.2 (133.9 km) S 358.3 (580.2 km) Bridge over McQuesten River, a tributary of the Stewart River, named for Jack (Leroy Napoleon) McQuesten.

J 244.8 (394 km) D 78.6 (126.5 km) S 364.3 (587.8 km) Partridge Creek Farm.

J 246.6 (396.9 km) D 76.8 (123.6 km) S 364.7 (590.7 km) **Private Aircraft:** McQuesten airstrip 1.2 miles/1.9 km west; elev. 1,500 feet/457m; length 5,000 feet/1,524m; gravel and turf. No services.

J 248.6 (400.1 km) D 74.8 (120.4 km) S 366.7 (594 km) Clear Creek, access via side road west.

J 256.6 (412.9 km) D 66.8 (107.5 km) S 374.7 (607 km) Distance marker northbound shows Dempster Highway Jct. 71 km/44 miles, Dawson City 111 km/69 miles.

J 260.9 (419.9 km) D 62.5 (100.6 km) S 379 (614 km) Beaver Dam Creek.

J 263.2 (423.5 km) D 60.2 (96.9 km) S 381.3 (617.7 km) Willow Creek.

J 266.1 (428.2 km) D 57.3 (92.2 km) S 384.2 (621 km) Large rest area with information panels on **Gravel Lake**; litter barrels and outhouses. Gravel Lake is an important wetland for migratory birds in spring and fall. Because of its location on the Tintina Trench corridor, unusual birds are sometimes seen here, including ruddy ducks, black scoters and the most northerly sightings of American coots.

J 269.3 (433.4 km) D 54.1 (87.1 km) S 387.4 (626.1 km) Meadow Creek.

J 269.8 (434.2 km) D 53.6 (86.2 km) S 387.9 (626.9 km) 1953 Forest Fire (northbound sign).

J 276.2 (445.3 km) D 46.7 (75.2 km) S 394.8 (638 km) Stone Boat Swamp.

J 285.6 (459.6 km) D 37.8 (60.8 km) S 403.7 (652.4 km) Distance marker northbound shows Dempster Highway 21 km/13 miles, Dawson City 61 km/38 miles.

J 285.8 (459.9 km) D 37.6 (60.5 km) S 403.9 (654.3 km) Gravel turnout to west; flat parking area. *Begin 6 to 8 percent winding downhill grade northbound.*

J 286.3 (460.7 km) D 37.1 (59.7 km) S 404.4 (655.2 km) **Tintina Trench Rest Area** is a large gravel turnout to east with litter bins, toilets and information panels. The Tintina Trench, which extends hundreds of miles across Yukon and Alaska, is the largest fault in North America and 1 of 2 major bird migration corridors in the Yukon (the other is the Shakwak Trench).

J 291.9 (469.7 km) D 31.5 (50.7 km) S 410 (664.4 km) Flat Creek bridge.

J 294.4 (473.8 km) D 29 (46.7 km) S 412.5 (664.5 km) Viewpoint to east with historic sign about Klondike River and information sign on Dempster Highway.

Highway follows Klondike River northbound.

J 298.3 (480 km) D 25.1 (40.4 km) S 416.4 (674.6 km) **Dempster Corner.** The Dempster Highway leads northeast from here 456 miles/734 km to Inuvik, NWT. The only services on the Dempster are midway at Eagle Plains Hotel, and in Fort McPherson and Inuvik. Stop by the Dempster Highway and Northwest Territories Info Centre in the B.Y.N. Building on Front Street in Dawson City for more information.

Junction of Klondike Highway and the Dempster Highway (Yukon Highway 5), which leads northeast to Inuvik, NWT. See DEMPSTER HIGHWAY on page 312 for log of that road.

J 298.8 (480.9 km) D 24.6 (39.6 km) S 416.9 (675.5 km) Distance marker northbound shows Dawson City 40 km/25 miles.

J 304.1 (489.4 km) D 19.3 (31.1 km) S 422.2 (683.9 km) Goring Creek.

J 310.5 (499.7 km) D 12.9 (20.8 km) S 428.6 (694 km) Rock Creek.

J 311.7 (501.6 km) D 11.7 (18.8 km) S 429.8 (696.7 km) Turnoff to north for **Klondike River Yukon government campground**, located on Rock Creek next to the Klondike River; 38 sites (2 pull-through), kitchen shelter, drinking water, playground. Camping permit, $12. A nature trail leads to the river. Flora includes Labrador tea, highbush cranberry, prickly rose, Arctic bearberry and horsetails.

J 313.3 (504.2 km) D 10.1 (16.2 km) S 431.4 (697.5 km) **Dawson City airport** to southwest.

J 314 (505.3 km) D 9.4 (15.1 km) S 432.1 (700.2 km) Hunker Creek Road to west.

Hunker Creek Road (gravel) connects with Upper Bonanza Creek Road, which makes a 60-mile/96-km loop back to the Klondike Highway via Bonanza Creek Road. Upper Bonanza Creek Road is a narrow, gravel, mountain road that is *not suitable for RVs or trailers. The climb is a challenge, even for an average car.*

Albert Hunker staked the first claim on Hunker Creek Sept. 11, 1896. George Carmack made the big discovery on Bonanza Creek on Aug. 17, 1896. Hunker Creek is 16 miles/26 km long, of which 13 miles/21 km was dredged between 1906 and 1966.

J 315.6 (507.9 km) D 7.8 (12.5 km) S 433.9 (702.4 km) Bear Creek Road leads to subdivision.

J 315.9 (508.4 km) D 7.5 (12.1 km) S 434 (703 km) Distance marker northbound shows Dawson City 11 km/7 miles.

J 316.2 (508.9 km) D 7.2 (11.6 km) S 434.3 (703.8 km) Turnout to east with historic sign about the Yukon Ditch and tailings. The Yukon Ditch, built by Yukon Gold Co., was a ditch, flume and pipe system that carried water from the Ogilvie Mountains to the hydraulic mining operations on Bonanza Creek. It operated from 1909 until the 1930s. The tailings (mounds of gravel and rock) from these hydraulic mining operations line both sides of the Klondike Highway along here.

J 318.1 (511.9 km) D 5.3 (8.5 km) S 436.2 (706 km) Welcome to Dawson City kiosk.

J 319.5 (514.2 km) D 4.2 (6.7 km) S 437.6 (709.2 km) Callison subdivision. Environmental Refueling Services (ERS) 0.3 mile west: gas, diesel, propane.

J 321.2 (516.9 km) D 2.2 (3.5 km) S 439.3 (711.6 km) **Junction** with **Bonanza Creek Road.** Bonanza Creek Road provides access to Dredge No. 4 (7.8 miles/12.3 km) and Discovery Claim (9.3 miles/14.8 km); descriptions follow.

Claim 33 Gold Panning. Learn to pan for gold (guaranteed) at Historic Claim 33—one of the original claims staked on Bonanza Creek. Wander around

artifacts that will transport you back to the heyday of the Klondike Gold Rush. Souvenir shop and gold jewellery from the Klondike. Tours and groups welcome. Open mid-May–mid-Sept. Km 10/Mile 6 Bonanza Road. Phone (867) 993-6626. claim33@northwestel.net. [ADVERTISEMENT]

Dredge No. 4 is the largest wooden hull dredge in North America. There is an information kiosk at the site and tours may be available.

Marked by a plaque, **Discovery Claim** was the first gold claim on Bonanza Creek and the one that started the Klondike Stampede of 1898. Visitors are welcome to try gold panning for free at Klondike Visitor Association's **Claim No. 6**, located just beyond Discovery. You can pan for gold at anytime, but bring your own gold pan.

Bonanza Creek Road is maintained for 11 miles/18 km. It connects with Upper Bonanza Creek Road (narrow, winding, unmaintained gravel), which forms a

S.S. Keno and interpretive signs are on display along the waterfront in Dawson City.
(©David L. Ranta, staff)

60-mile/96-km loop that climbs to an elevation of 4,000 feet before descending back to the Klondike Highway at **Milepost J 314** via Hunker Creek Road. *Upper Bonanza Creek Road is not recommended for RVs or trailers.*

J 321.3 (517.1 km) **D 2.1** (3.4 km) **S 439.4** (711.9 km) Bonanza Gold Motel & RV Park. See display ad on this page.

J 321.4 (517.2 km) **D 2** (3.32 km) **S 439.5** (712 km) **Dawson City RV Park** and gas station (gas, diesel, propane).

Dawson City RV Park. See display ad on this page.

J 321.5 (517.4 km) **D 1.9** (3.1 km) **S 439.6** (712.4 km) Klondike River Bridge.

J 322 (518.2 km) **D 1.4** (2.3 km) **S 440.1** (713.4 km) Dome Road (chip-sealed) to north leads 4.5 miles/7.2 km to **Dome Mountain** (elev. 2,911 feet/887m), which

offers views of Dawson City, the Yukon and Klondike rivers, Bonanza Creek and the Ogilvie Mountains.

J 323.4 (520.4 km) **D 0 S 441.5** (715.4 km) Dawson City (description follows). Continue approximately 0.4 mile/0.6 km for Front Street and Yukon River crossing to Top of the World Highway. *Log of Klondike Loop continues on page 294.*

Dawson City

J 323.4 (520.3 km) **D 0 S 441.5** (715.4 km) Located 165 miles/266 km south of the Arctic Circle, 333 miles/536 km north of Whitehorse and 187 miles from Tok, AK. on the Yukon River at its confluence with the Klondike River. **Population:** 1,879. **Emergency Services:** RCMP, 1st Avenue S., phone (867)

993-5555. **Fire Department**, phone (867) 993-2222. **Nursing station**, phone (867) 993-4444. **Ambulance**, phone (867) 993-4444.

Visitor Information: Yukon Visitor Information Centre, operated by Tourism Yukon and Parks Canada at Front and King streets, is housed in a replica of the 1897 Alaska Commercial Co. store. Accommodation information, a Dawson City street map and a schedule of daily programs are offered by the Visitor Centre. Parks Canada walking tours are part of the daily schedule, either with a costumed guide or as a self-guided audio tour (fee charged). Films/videos on Dawson history are also shown at the centre. The visitor centre is open daily, 8 A.M. to 8 P.M. (hours may vary), from May to through September; phone (867) 993-5566; www.dawsoncity.ca. Tickets for Parks Canada tours may be purchased at the Parks Canada information desk at the visitor centre; phone (867) 993-7210. Also contact the **Klondike Visitors Association**; phone (867) 993-5575, fax (867) 993-6415. Dawson City has lots to do and see. If you want to take it all in, plan for 3 days or more to cover most of the attractions. Check out Dawson City on Facebook and Twitter (@dawsoncityyukon) for up-to-the-minute information and news.

The Dempster Highway and Northwest Territories Information Centre is located in the B.Y.N. (British Yukon Navigation) Building on Front Street, across from the Dawson City Visitor Information Centre; open daily 9 A.M. to 7 P.M. in summer. Information on Tombstone Territorial Park, the Northwest Territories and the Dempster Highway. Phone (867) 993-6167, fax (867) 993-6334.

The Government of Canada offers a website with extensive information on a variety of topics, from jobs and taxes to immigration and importing, for both residents and non-residents. Go to www.servicecanada.gc.ca, or visit the Dawson City Canada Service Community Office for in-person help at 902 Front St. next to Jimmy's Video. The centre is open weekday

mornings from 8:45 A.M. to 12:45 P.M.; phone (867) 993-5354.

Elevation: 1,050 feet/320m. **Climate**: There are 20.9 hours of daylight June 21, 3.8 hours of daylight on Dec. 21. Mean high in July, 72°F/22.2°C. Mean low in January, -30.5°F/ -34.7°C. First fall frost end of August, last spring frost end of May. Annual snowfall 59.8 inches. **Radio**: CBC 560 AM; local community radio broadcasts Thursday to Sunday at CFYT 106.9 FM. **Television**: Cable. **Newspaper**: *Klondike Sun* (semi-monthly).

Private Aircraft: 11 miles/17.7 km south. Runway 02-20; elev. 1,215 feet/370m; length 5,005 feet/1,526m; taxiway and apron are paved, airstrip is gravel; 100LL, Jet A. Customs available; call (867) 993-5338. Flightseeing trips and air charters available.

Description

For millennia, the Han-speaking Tr'ondek Hwech'in lived and travelled in a vast area extending from the Yukon River valley into the neighboring mountains. At the heart of their home was Tr'ochek, a large fish camp at the confluence of the Klondike and Yukon Rivers, adjacent to what is now Dawson City. With the discovery of gold on a Klondike River tributary (Rabbit Creek, renamed Bonanza Creek) in 1896, the Tr'ondek Hwech'in were displaced by the influx of gold seekers and the boom town built to serve them. The Tr'ondek Hwech'in moved their camp to Moosehide Village, downstream from Dawson City.

Most of the prospectors who staked claims on Klondike creeks were already in the North before the big strike, many working claims in the Fortymile area. The stampeders coming North in the great gold rush the following year found most of the gold-bearing streams already staked.

Dawson City was Yukon's first capital, when the Yukon became a separate territory in 1898. But by 1953, Whitehorse—on the railway and the highway, and with a large airport—was so much the hub of activity that the federal government moved the capital from Dawson City, along with 800 civil servants, and years of tradition and pride. Some recompense was offered in the form of a road linking Whitehorse with the mining at Mayo and Dawson City. With its completion, White Pass trucks replaced White Pass river steamers.

New government buildings were built in Dawson, including a fire hall. In 1962 the federal government reconstructed the Palace Grand Theatre for a gold rush festival that featured the Broadway musical *Foxy*, with Bert Lahr, who played the cowardly lion in the classic *Wizard of Oz*. A museum was established in the Administration Building and tours and entertainments were begun.

Dawson City was declared a national historic site in the early 1960s. Parks Canada is currently involved with 35 properties in Dawson City. Many buildings have been restored, some reconstructed and others stabilized. Parks Canada offers a range of interpretive programs for visitors to this historic town.

In 1998, 100 years after the gold rush, the Tr'ondek Hwech'in negotiated the return of self-governance. The Tr'ochek fish camp has been designated a Tr'ondek Hwech'in Heritage Site as well as a National Historic Site of Canada. (Visitors may explore the traditional and contemporary life of the Tr'ondek Hwech'in at the Danoja Zho

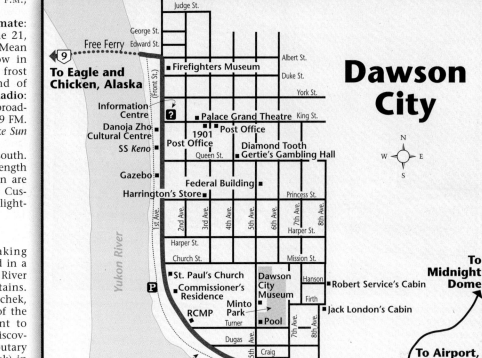

Cultural Center.)

Lodging & Services

Accustomed to a summer influx of visitors, Dawson has modern hotels and motels (rates average $125 and up), 2 bed and breakfasts and a hostel. The community has a bank, ATM, (credit card cash advances available through Diamond Tooth Gerties Casino), restaurants, 2 laundromats (with showers), grocery store with bakery, a deli/grocery store, general stores, souvenir shops, churches, art galleries, an art school, post office, government offices, government liquor store, nursing station and doctor services, information centres, hostel, swimming pool, tennis, basketball and plenty of entertainment. Many Dawson City merchants abide by the Fair Exchange Policy, offering travelers an exchange rate within 4 percent of the banks'. Dawson City's hotels, motels and the Dawson City River Hostel (867) 993-6823 (www.yukonhostels.com) fill up early in summer and for special events, so make

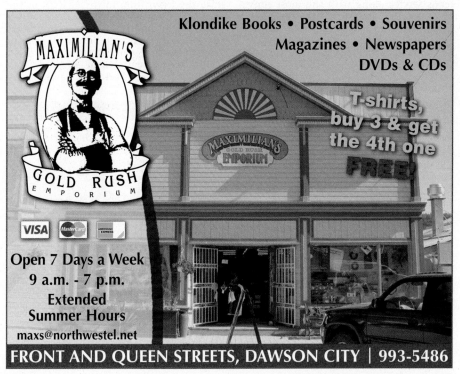

Dawson City's colourful buildings, many dating back to the gold rush era, make it a unique experience for visitors. (©Kris Valencia, staff)

reservations in advance.

5th Avenue Bed and Breakfast. Located adjacent to the museum overlooking Victory Gardens. Two air-conditioned buildings. Serving a full, hot breakfast. We

guarantee comfort, cleanliness and courteous service along with the most convenient location in town. We even have a room with 2 queen beds, private bath and balcony that can accommodate 4 adults. Credit cards accepted. Wireless Internet. Call Steve and Tracy, at (867) 993-5941; toll-free 1-866-631-5237. Website www.

5thavebandb.com. Dawson City, Yukon.

Bonanza Gold Motel & RV Park. 1 mile south of city centre at the entrance to Bonanza Creek Road. Motel with deluxe accommodations, Jacuzzis, kitchenettes, standard rooms with air conditioners or fans. Cable TV, WiFi. Bonanza Gold RV Park: full-service sites. RV/car wash. Laundromat. Toll-free 1-888-993-6789. Take advantage of our long-term-stay packages. Email bonanzagold.dawson@gmail.com; website www.bonanzagold.ca. See display ad on page 286.

Camping

There are 2 Yukon government (YTG) campgrounds in the Dawson area. Yukon River YTG campground is across the Yukon River (by ferry) from town, adjacent to the west-side ferry approach. Klondike River YTG campground is 15 minutes southeast of town near the airport. Private RV parks in Dawson include **Gold Rush Campground & RV Park**, downtown at 4th and York, **Bonanza Gold RV Park** and **Dawson City**

R.V. Park and Campground just east of downtown on the Klondike Highway.

Gold Rush Campground & RV Park. 4th Avenue and York Street. Dawson City's only downtown RV park. 82 sites: 23 with 15-amp/water, 7 with 15-amp/water/ sewer, 42 with 30-amp/water/sewer. 18 pull-throughs, 12 unserviced. Free WiFi. Public showers. Laundromat, dump station. Your hosts, Pat and Dianne Brooks. Discover Yukon hospitality. Toll-free 1-866-330-5006 (within Canada). Phone (867) 993-5247; Email goldrushcampground@shaw.ca. Fax (867) 993-6047. See display ad page 290.

Transportation

Air: Dawson City airport is 11.5 miles/ 18.5 km southeast of the city. Air North connects Dawson City with Whitehorse (daily service, except Saturday, in summer); with Inuvik, NWT, and Old Crow (3 times weekly in summer); and Fairbanks (4 times weekly in summer). Charter service from Alkan Air. Charter and flightseeing tours available.

Airport shuttle service available from downtown hotels and bed and breakfasts.

Ferry: The Yukon government operates a free ferry, the *George Black*, across the Yukon River from about mid-May to usually the second or third week in October. Season dates for the ferry depend on spring break-up and fall freeze-up.

The *George Black* makes the short (6 to 7 minutes on average) trip across the Yukon River 24 hours a day (except for Wednesdays, 5–7 A.M., when it is shut down for servicing), departing Dawson City on demand. It carries vehicles and passengers across to connect to the Top of the World Highway (Yukon Highway 9). To avoid long waits, don't cross during peak traffic times (7–11 A.M. and 4–7 P.M.) and ask the Visitor Centre about scheduled caravan departures. Shut off all propane appliances and follow directions from ferry personnel when loading/unloading. Tour bus traffic has priority 6–9 A.M. and 5–9 P.M.; fuel truck traffic has priority 7 P.M. to 6 A.M. Phone (867) 993-5441, fax (867) 993-5321 for more information.

Bus: Alaska/Yukon Trails offers daily Fairbanks–Dawson City–Whitehorse van service in summer; www.alaskashuttle.com.

Attractions

Take a Walking Tour. Town-core tours leave the Palace Grand Theatre daily in summer. The 1½-hour guided walk highlights the history of Dawson City. Audio tapes also available. Fee charged.

Visit the Palace Grand Theatre. This magnificently reconstructed theatre is part of the Dawson Historical Complex National Historic Site. Arizona Charlie Meadows opened the Palace Grand in 1899, and today's visitors, sitting in the curtained boxes around the balcony, will succumb to the charm of this beautiful theatre. Check the Klondike National Historic Sites' website for information on shows and programming in the Palace Grand Theatre. Tours of the building are offered daily by Parks Canada from mid-May through mid-September. There's also a dramatic program, the "Greatest Klondiker Contest," with colorful characters from the Klondike Gold Rush duking it out on stage. Admission charged or buy a Parks Pass. Check with the Visitor Centre for scheduling details.

DAWSON CITY ADVERTISERS

(continues on page 293)

YOU'VE NEVER SEEN
A TOWN LIKE THIS

Photos: CTC-Mueller, Simon Lucas, TH Archives

DAWSON
CITY.CA
WHERE THE NORTH COMES TO PLAY

Photo: Amanda Warren

YUKON
LARGER THAN LIFE

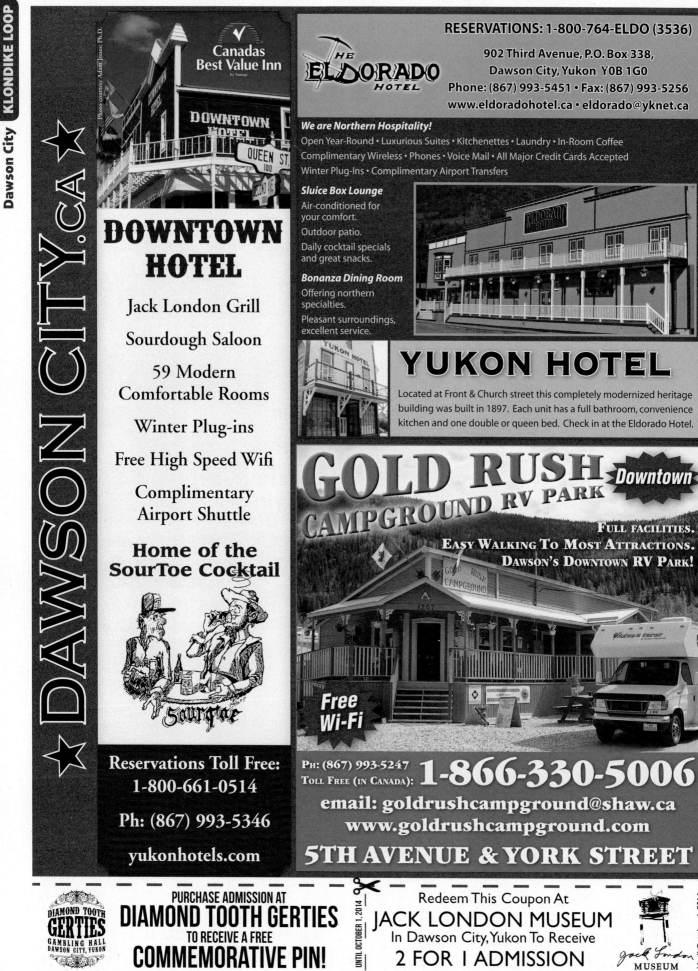

DAWSON CITY.CA

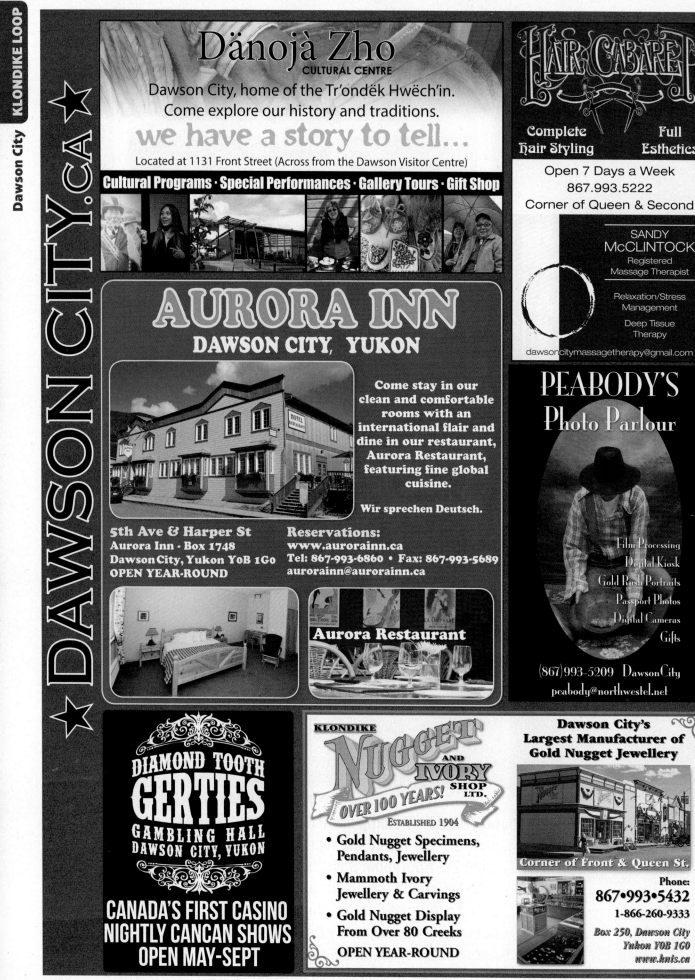

(continued from page 288)

Visit the Commissioner's Residence, located on Front Street and part of the Dawson Historical Complex National Historic Site. This was the official residence of the Yukon's federal government representative—the Commissioner of the Yukon—from 1900 to 1916. Throughout the decades it also served as a hospital and as the home of one of the Yukon's most intriguing and influential women, Martha Louise Black, who walked to Dawson City via the Trail of '98 and stayed to become the First Lady of the Yukon. Costumed guides are on hand to show visitors through the building; activities and videos are available. Open daily, admission fee charged or use your Parks Pass.

Danoja Zho Cultural Centre offers a relaxed and friendly atmosphere to explore the story of the original people of the Klondike: the Tr'ondek Hwech'in. There are 2 gallery exhibitions, guided tours, special events and film presentations. The gift shop boasts the largest selection of beaded moccasins in the Yukon and specializes in unique jewelry, First Nation gifts, art and books. Located on Front Street across from the Dawson City Visitor Centre. Open mid-May to September. Adult admission is $6; tickets are valid for 2 days.

Diamond Tooth Gerties Gambling Hall, open daily 7 P.M. to 2 A.M. early May to late Sept., with 3 shows nightly; early openings at 2 P.M. Saturdays and Sundays in summer (early June to Labour Day). Admission fee $10. The casino has Klondike gambling tables (specially licensed in Yukon), more than 60 slot machines, bar service and floor shows nightly. You may have a soft drink if you prefer, and still see the cancan girls present their floor show. Persons under 19 not admitted. Gerties hosts weekly Texas Hold 'Em poker tournaments.

SS *Keno* National Historic Site. The SS *Keno* was the last steamer to run the Yukon River when she sailed from Whitehorse in 1960 to her present berth on the riverbank next to the old CIBC bank. This 130-foot riverboat was built in Whitehorse in 1922 by the British Navigation Company. She was used to transport silver, lead and zinc ore from the Mayo District to Stewart. The SS *Keno* is one of only 2 old riverboats that survive in the Yukon (the other is the SS *Klondike* in Whitehorse). Open daily for visits, with costumed staff and an interpretive display by Parks Canada. Admission charged or use your Parks Pass.

Dawson City Museum is located on 5th Avenue in the Old Territorial Administration Building, now a National Historic Site. The museum features the Kings of the Klondike and City Life Galleries, First Nation and pre-gold rush exhibits. The film "City of Gold" is shown daily. Interesting demonstrations are scheduled throughout the day; check with the front desk.

The museum has a gift shop, wheelchair ramp, resource library, genealogy service and an extensive photograph collection. A building adjacent the Territorial Administration Building contains the museum's collection of narrow-gauge locomotives, including a Vauclain-type Baldwin engine, the last one in existence in Canada.

Dawson City Museum is open daily from 10 A.M. to 6 P.M., mid-May through early September; by appointment from October to May. Admission fees: $9 adults, $7 senior or youth, $18 family, $5/person in pre-booked groups. For more information write the museum at Box 303, Dawson City, YT Y0B 1G0; phone (867) 993-5291, fax (867) 993-5839; or email: info@dawsonmuseum.ca.

The Robert Service Cabin, part of the Dawson Historical Complex National Historic Site, sits on the hillside on 8th Avenue. The author–bank clerk's cabin has been restored by Parks Canada. Daily programs by a costumed guide include the recitation of some of Service's most memorable poems, including "The Shooting of Dan McGrew" and "The Cremation of Sam McGee." Open daily. Admission fee charged or use your Parks Pass. Robert Service's typewriter is on display at the Visitor's Information Centre.

Visit the Jack London Museum at the corner of 8th Avenue and Firth Street. Jack London was the author of *The Call of the Wild* and *White Fang*. The museum features a log cabin built with half of the original logs from the cabin where London stayed in 1897. (The other half of the original logs were used to build a second replica cabin located in Jack London Square in Oakland, CA.) Also at the site are a cache and a museum with a collection of photos tracing London's journey to the Klondike during the Gold Rush. Open daily, 11 A.M. to 6 P.M. in summer, with interpretive talks at 12:15 P.M. and 3:15 P.M. Admission fee $5.

Pierre Berton Residence, located on 8th Avenue, was the childhood home of the late Canadian author. Now used as a writers' retreat, tours of the home are not available, but you may visit the grounds and read the interpretive signs placed outside by the Klondike Visitors Association.

Special Events. Dawson City hosts a number of unique celebrations during the year. Following is a round-up of events. For more current information and 2014 dates inquire at the Visitor Centre or visit www.dawsoncity.ca.

Spring kicks off with the 28th Annual Dawson City **Gold Show** and Breakup Comedy Festival May 16-17, 2014.

Summer begins with the **Commissioner's Tea** at the Commissioner's Residence, and the **Commissioner's Ball** at the Palace Grand Theatre, both held the second Saturday in June. The **Top of the World Highland Games** are scheduled for June 13-15, 2014.

June's long days are celebrated with several other events as well. The **Midnight Sun Golf Tournament** is held at Top of the World Golf Course on or near summer solstice (June 21st); phone (867) 993-5888 for details. **Aboriginal Day Celebrations,** June 21, 2014, at the Danoja Zho Cultural Centre offers an incredible array of activities including live music, jigging contest, face painting for the kids and refreshments. The **Dust to Dawson Motorcycle Ride,** is a rally that begins wherever you are and culminates in Dawson City at the Downtown Hotel. Most riders come from Alaska over the Top of the World Highway, but others come from as far away as California and points east, to enjoy lively celebrations at the Sourdough Saloon. For more information contact stay@downtownhotel.ca. **Yukon River Quest** (www.yukonriverquest.com), a canoe and kayak race from Whitehorse to Dawson City, takes place June 25-29, 2014.

July begins with **Canada Day Celebrations** and the **Yukon Gold Panning Championship** on July 1st. Then it's the 36th annual **Dawson City Music Festival** (www.dcmf.com), held July 18–20, 2014, featuring entertainers and artists from Canada and around the world. The **International Dome Race** takes place the third in July, usually coinciding with the Music Festival. The **Mooseskin Gathering** is scheduled for July 31-August 3, 2014.

If you are in Dawson City Aug. 15–17, 2014, be sure to join the **Discovery Days Celebrations,** including a fun run, golf tournament, arts festival and other events. Discovery Day (third Monday in August) is a Yukon holiday commemorating the Klondike gold discovery of Aug. 17, 1896.

Labour Day Weekend is August 29 to Sept. 1, 2014, with the **Mixed Slowpitch Tournament** scheduled for Sept. 1. The **Great Klondike International Outhouse Race,** held in early September, is a race of decorated outhouses on wheels over a 3-km course through the streets of Dawson City. The **White Ram Poker Tournament,** held in Canada's oldest casino—Diamond Tooth Gertie's—on the weekend after Labour Day,

The Dawson City Music Festival in July draws an appreciative crowd. (©David L. Ranta, staff)

Explore the inner-workings of a gold dredge at Dredge No. 4 National Historic Site.
(©Larry Reiter)

the tournament offers a limit and no limit event.

Fire Fighters Museum, located at the fire hall on Front Street, features some rare turn-of-the-century firefighting equipment. The museum is open in summer, 11 A.M. to 5 P.M. Monday to Friday, 11 A.M. to 4 P.M. Saturdays. Admission by donation. Phone (867) 993-7407.

Harrington's Store, at Third Avenue and Princess Street, has a free interpretive exhibit entitled "Dawson As They Saw It." The store is open from 9:30 A.M. to 8 P.M. daily.

Dredge No. 4 National Historic Site, Built in 1912 for the Canadian Klondike Mining Co.'s claim on Bonanza Creek, the dredge was pulled from the muck in 1992, exactly as the last shift had left it 32 years before. It is the largest wooden hulled bucket line gold dredge in North America. This impressive machine represents the pinnacle of the insatiable quest for gold that transformed not just the landscape but Yukon society. There is also an information kiosk on site and tours may be available.

To reach the dredge, turnoff the Klondike Highway at 2.2 miles/3.5 km south of downtown (just south of Kilometrepost 712) and follow Bonanza Creek Road 7.8 miles/12.3 km up to Dredge No. 4. Continue up Bonanza Creek Road for Discovery Claim (description follows) and to see miles of gravel tailings worked over 2 and 3 times in the continuing search for gold.

Discovery Claim National Historic Site, just up the road past Dredge No. 4, was originally staked on August 17, 1896, and is the site of the gold discovery that sparked the Klondike Gold Rush. An 0.6-mile/1-km walking trail with interpretive panels describes the story of the discovery and the evolution of mining techniques. (An interpretive trail brochure is available for $1 at the Parks Canada information desk at the Visitor Centre in town.) This site is always open; free admission.

Pan for Gold. The chief attraction for many visitors is panning for gold. There are several mining operations set up to permit you to actually pan for your own "colours." Two on Bonanza Creek Road include Claim

33, at Mile 6/Km 10, and the Klondike Visitors Association's unsupervised public panning area at No. 6 above Discovery Claim, 13 miles/21 km from Dawson City on Bonanza Creek Road. (*Bonanza Creek Road continues up into the hills past private gold claims and connects with Hunker Creek Road; this portion of the road is not suitable for RVs or trailers.*) Check with the Visitor Information Centre or visit www.dawsoncity.ca.

See the Midnight Sun: If you are in Dawson City on June 21, be sure to make it to the top of the Dome by midnight, when the sun barely dips behind the 6,000-foot/1,829-m Ogilvie Mountains to the north—the picture of a lifetime. There's quite a local celebration on the Dome on June 21, so for those who don't like crowds, a visit before or after summer solstice will also afford fine views and photos.

Tour A Sled Dog Racing Kennel and Museum. Located 3.2 miles/5.1 km from **Milepost D 2.3** on the Top of the World Highway, Slow Rush Kennels is home to the Bouchard colleciton, the largest dog mushing and sled museum in the world. Dog racing demonstration, Yukon Quest film and talks on equipment and the sport of dog racing. No reservations necessary. Phone (867) 335-2036; www.slowrushkennels.com.

Klondike Loop Log
(continued from page 286)

TOP OF THE WORLD HIGHWAY

The **Top of the World Highway** (Yukon Highway 9 and Boundary Spur Road) connects Dawson City with the Taylor Highway (Alaska Route 5). Its top-of-the-world views make it a favorite with many travelers.

The *George Black* ferry crosses the Yukon River from Dawson City to Top of the World Highway daily from about mid-May to the second or third week in October. However, whether or not Customs is open at the border also determines the viability of this route and Customs has closed in September.

Yukon Highway 9 and Alaska Route 5 are not maintained from mid-October to April, and the arrival of snow effectively closes the roads for winter.

CAUTION: Allow plenty of time for this drive. This is a narrow, winding road with some steep grades and few guardrails. Watch for soft shoulders. Slow down on loose gravel and washboard. The maximum posted speed limit is 50 mph/80 kmph. DRIVE WITH YOUR HEADLIGHTS ON!

IMPORTANT: Driving time westbound to the international border is at least 1 hour and 30 minutes (or more, depending on road conditions). Alaska Customs closes at 8 P.M. Alaska Time (which is 9 P.M. Pacific Time). Make sure you allow enough time to arrive at the border when the Customs station is open.

The Canadian portion of Top of the World Highway (Yukon Highway 9) was seal-coated several years ago (and may be again), but approximately half of the surfacing has reverted to gravel. In summer 2013, there were a couple of long paved sections—one from the ferry landing and the other approaching the border—while the rest of the drive alternated brief pavement breaks interrupted by longer gravel breaks.

Top of the World Highway winds above timberline for many miles. The lack of fuel for warmth and shelter made this a perilous trip for the early sourdoughs.

On the Alaska side, Boundary Road remains all gravel from the international border to the junction with the Taylor Highway, although road improvement was underway in summer 2013. The Taylor Highway is winding gravel road to Chicken and to Eagle. For current road conditions visit 511.alaska.gov or phone 511. Also check with the Dawson City Visitor Information Centre for current road and weather conditions; phone (867) 993-5566.

The Alaska Highway is 175 miles/281 km from Dawson City via Yukon Highway 9 and Alaska Route 5.

NOTE: From Dawson City next gas stop westbound on the Klondike Loop is Chicken (108 miles/174 km) or Tok (187 miles/300 km).

YUKON HIGHWAY 9
This section of the log shows distance from Dawson City (D) followed by distance from Tetlin Junction on the Alaska Highway (TJ). *Physical kilometreposts show distance from Dawson City.*

©Kris Valencia, staff

D 0 TJ 175 (127.1 km) Ferry landing for free *George Black* ferry that carries passengers and vehicles across the Yukon River between Dawson City and Top of the World Highway from about mid-May to the third week in October (depending on break-up and freeze-up). The ferry wait can be as long as 3 hours during peak times. The ferry trip across the river is just a few minutes. *NOTE: The boarding process is not intuitive. Watch "Slow/Stop" signals from ferry personnel: If they point the Slow sign at your line, proceed to ferry. If they wave you back, it wasn't your turn. You do not necessarily board in the order you lined up!*

Driving distances for Alaska-bound trav-

elers on the Klondike Loop: Chicken 108 miles/174 km, Tok 187 miles/300 km.

D 0.2 (0.3 km) **TJ 174.8** (281.3 km) Turnoff to north for **Yukon River government campground** on riverbank opposite Dawson City. Very nice wooded campground with 74 RV sites, 24 tent-only sites, 18 pull-through sites, camping permit $12. 2 kitchen shelters, playground and drinking water. Free firewood available for use at campground only. Walk down to the river and head downstream, watching for remains of old stern-wheelers in the brush near shore. This campground is also a put-in and takeout spot for Yukon River travelers. Deck overlooks the Yukon River. A family of peregrine falcons nests in the cliffs across the river during the summer. ⛺

Highway climbs next 8.7 miles/14 km westbound. Views of Dawson City and the Yukon and Klondike rivers.

D 2.3 (3.7 km) **TJ 172.7** (277.9 km) Access via 3.2-mile/5.1-km Sunnydale Road (gravel) to Top of the World Golf Course and Slow Rush Kennels.

D 6.2 (10 km) **TJ 168.8** (271.6 km) *Begin variable road conditions westbound to international border with good chip seal surfacing, sections of potholes and damaged pavement, gravel breaks and washboard.*

D 8.9 (14.3 km) **TJ 166.1** (267.3 km) Double-ended turnout to large rest area with toilets, picnic tables, litter barrels. A short path leads to a viewing platform overlooking the Yukon River valley. Interpretive displays about the Fortymile caribou herd and the history of the people of this area. Welcome to Dawson City information kiosk.

D 11.6 (18.6 km) **TJ 163.4** (263 km) Large turnout to north with good view.

D 18.2 (29.3 km) **TJ 156.8** (252.3 km) Double-ended gravel turnout to south.

D 24.8 (40 km) **TJ 150.2** (241.7 km) Gravel turnout to north with view.

D 31.8 (51.2 km) **TJ 143.2** (230.5 km) Informal campsite to south near rock outcropping; large turnaround space, good views and hiking. Watch for grouse. ⛺

D 34.7 (56 km) **TJ 140.3** (225.8 km) Main outcropping of Castle Rock; lesser formations are also found along this stretch. Centuries of erosion have created these formations.

D 36.8 (59.2 km) **TJ 138.2** (222.4 km) Parking at turnoff for Clinton Creek Road, which leads north to the former settlement of Clinton Creek. Cassiar Asbestos Corp. Ltd. operated the Clinton Creek mine there from 1967 to 1978, when all of the available asbestos had been mined. Generally in fair condition for the first 33 miles/53 km to the Clinton Creek bridge. There are no facilities or services available along the road. The confluence of the Yukon and Fortymile rivers is 3 miles/4.8 km below the former townsite of Clinton Creek. Clinton Creek bridge is an access point on the Fortymile River National Wild, Scenic & Recreation River system. The Fortymile River offers intermediate and advanced canoeists over 100 miles/160 km of challenging water.

Yukon River, near Clinton Creek, grayling to 3 lbs. in April; chum salmon to 12 lbs. in August; king salmon to 40 lbs., July and August. **Fortymile River**, near Clinton Creek, grayling to 3 lbs. during spring breakup and fall freezeup; inconnu (sheefish) to 10 lbs. in July and August. 🚤

View from Davis Dome Wayside on the Boundary Spur Road . (©Kris Valencia, staff)

Distance marker shows U.S. border 43 km/27 miles.

D 38.1 (61.3 km) **TJ 136.9** (220.3 km) Large turnout to north with sweeping views.

D 53.6 (86.3 km) **TJ 121.4** (195.4 km) Rest stop with outhouses and litter bins to north adjacent old sod-roofed cabin. This was originally a supply and stopping place for the McCormick Transportation Co.

D 53.9 (86.7 km) **TJ 121.1** (194.9 km) Turnoff to south for 60 Mile Road to old mine workings at Sixtymile.

D 60.6 (98 km) **TJ 114.4** (184.1 km) Turnout to north. Gravel stockpile.

D 62.5 (100.6 km) **TJ 112.5** (181 km) Large gravel turnout with litter barrel to south. Information sign about Top of the World Highway viewpoint:

"Yukon Highway 9 began as a pack trail out of Dawson City shortly after the gold rush. It serviced Sixtymile and neighbouring gold creeks. The trail was gradually improved and came to be known as Ridge Road.

"In the 1930s, the road was extended to the border and from there to Jack Wade and Chicken, connecting these Alaskan communities to Dawson City in Canada. In the late 1940s, Alaska's Taylor Highway gave all these communities road access to the outside world by way of the newly completed Alaska Highway."

D 64 (103 km) **TJ 111** (178.6 km) Double-ended turnout to north.

Highway climbs westbound.

D 64.7 (104.5 km) **TJ 110.3** (177.5 km) Double-ended rest area to south, good view of Customs buildings. Just across the highway, short hike to cairn, excellent viewpoint. Highest point on Top of the World Highway (elev. 4,515 feet/1,376 m).

D 65.7 (105.7 km) **TJ 109.3** (175.9 km) **U.S.–Canada Border** (elev. 4,127 feet/ 1,258m). **U.S. Poker Creek and Canada Little Gold Creek Customs.** This joint facility opened in 2001-2002, replacing the construction trailer (now gone) that housed Canadian customs, and the log structure that housed U.S. customs, which you'll see on your right westbound after going through customs. *All traffic entering Alaska or Canada must stop here.* Road is gated after hours.

IMPORTANT: U.S. and Canada customs are open from about May 15 to late September

or October, depending on weather. In summer 2013, customs was open daily, 9 A.M. to 9 P.M. (Pacific time) on the Canadian side; 8 A.M. to 8 P.M. (Alaska time) on the U.S. side. Customs hours of operation subject to change; there is no phone at the border, so check with the RCMP or Visitor Information Centre in Dawson City. Serious fines are levied for crossing the border without clearing customs! There are no services or currency exchanges available here. See also "Crossing the Border" in the TRAVEL PLANNING section.

TIME ZONE CHANGE: Alaska observes Alaska time; Yukon Territory observes Pacific time. Alaska time is 1 hour earlier than Pacific time.

Downhill grade next 4 miles/6.4 km westbound.

BOUNDARY SPUR ROAD

D 65.9 TJ 109.1 Distance marker westbound shows Boundary 4 miles, Chicken 43 miles, Eagle 79 miles.

Westbound travelers watch for mining activity in the valley to south next 3 miles.

NOTE: Construction to widen and improve road to Jack Wade Junction was under way in summer 2013 and evening road closures were in effect. Expect continued road construction for 2014.

D 66.3 TJ 108.7 Davis Dome Wayside (BLM). Double-ended turnout to north with scenic viewing platform, toilets (not recommended). Beautiful views. Interpretive sign about Fortymile River Region. Welcome to Alaska sign.

D 67.1 TJ 107.9 Large, double-ended turnout to north with interpretive sign about the Fortymile caribou herd.

D 69.6 TJ 105.4 BOUNDARY. Boundary Roadhouse, which dates from about 1926, was one of the first roadhouses in Alaska. It served miners in the Walker Creek drainage, according to writer Ray Bonnell, who researched this area. The roadhouse dates from about 1926, while the mining camp was first established in the 1890s. A post office served the area from 1940 until 1956.

Jack Corbett owned and operated Boundary Roadhouse for many years, and more recently it has operated at various times

under various owners. It has been closed the last few years and the store burned down in 2012, although the original roadhouse was still standing in summer 2013.

D 69.7 TJ 105.3 Access road south to Boundary airstrip; elev. 2,940 feet/896m; length 2,100 feet/640m; earth and gravel; fuel 80; unattended.

D 74.6 TJ 100.4 Turnout to south.

D 78.5 TJ 96.5 Turnout to south.

D 79.3 TJ 95.7 Jack Wade Junction. First junction westbound: Keep right westbound at Y-junction for Eagle. Keep left westbound for Taylor Highway to Chicken (log continues). *CAUTION: "Y" intersection; watch for merging traffic.* The Taylor Highway extends 65 miles north from Jack Wade Junction to the community of Eagle on the Yukon River.

See "Side Trip to Eagle" log beginning on page 297.

Klondike Loop log continues on the Taylor Highway south to the Alaska Highway.

TAYLOR HIGHWAY
ALASKA ROUTE 5

This section of the log shows distance from Tetlin Junction on the Alaska Highway (TJ) followed by distance from Eagle (E) and distance from Dawson City (D).
Physical mileposts on the Taylor Highway (which are sporadic) reflect distance from Tetlin Junction. The few pysical mileposts left on Boundary Road reflect distance from Jack Wade Junction. Kilometreposts on the Top of the World Highway reflect distance from Dawson City and are erected on the north side of the highway for westbound travelers.

TJ 95.5 E 65 D 79.5 Jack Wade Junction (eastbound). First turnoff northbound at Y-junction. Keep to right for Top of the World Highway east to Dawson City, YT. Keep to left for continuation of Taylor Highway north to Eagle (see "Eagle Side Trip" this section).

Distance marker northbound shows Eagle 65 miles, Boundary 9 miles, Dawson City 75 miles. Distance marker southbound shows Tok 107 miles, Fairbanks 311 miles.

Southbound travelers NOTE: Sections of rough road, soft shoulders, hairpin curves, steep drop-offs and narrow road south to Chicken. Do not risk a tip over by putting a wheel into the soft shoulder! Stop for oncoming traffic at narrow spots.

TJ 92 E 68.5 D 83 Federal Subsistence Hunting Area boundary.

Highway straightens as the Taylor Highway follows Jack Wade Creek next 7 miles southbound. This stretch of road suffered washouts after heavy rains in summer 2011. Repairs included the addition of riprap along the riverbank to prevent future flooding.

Northbound travelers NOTE: Steep climb on narrow road northbound as highway ascends Jack Wade Hill. Limited passing room, soft shoulders and long drop-offs make this a dangerous stretch. If in doubt, STOP for oncoming traffic: Do not risk a tip over by putting a wheel into the soft shoulder!

TJ 91.3 E 69.2 D 83.7 Double ended turnout.

TJ 90 E 70.5 D 85 Double-ended dirt turnout.

TJ 89.7 E 70.8 D 85.3 Turnout to east.

TJ 89 E 71.5 D 86 Nice turnout to east above creek.

TJ 88.7 E 71.8 D 86.3 Gravel turnout to west. Highway climbs above creek north-

bound.

TJ 88.1 E 72.4 D 86.9 Nice gravel turnout to east by creek.

TJ 87.9 E 72.6 D 87.1 Large gravel turnout.

TJ 87.7 E 72.8 D 87.3 Gravel turnout.

TJ 87.3 E 73.2 D 87.7 Small turnout by creek. A private suction dredge was working this stretch of the creek in summer 2012 (with permission of the claim holder).

TJ 87 E 73.5 D 88 A major mining operation was underway here in summer 2013. *Do not trespass on mining claims.*

TJ 85.8 E 74.7 D 89.2 Informal camping here in summer 2013.

TJ 85.7 E 74.8 D 89.3 Access to Jack Wade Creek.

TJ 83.7 E 76.8 D 91.3 Turnout by Jack Wade Creek.

TJ 83.5 E 77 D 91.5 Turnout to west.

TJ 82 E 78.5 D 93 Crossing Walker Fork Bridge.

Turnoff to west at north end of bridge for Walker Fork BLM Campground; day-use area to east. Old road grader on display at campground entrance parking area, where there is an information board with BLM brochures on area attractions. The campground has 20 level sites (13 pull-throughs and 7 back-ins) on loop road; 2 tent platforms; 3 handicap sites with wheelchair accessible platforms; picnic tables; free firewood to paying campers; firepits, grills; litter bin; and the cleanest public outhouses we've ever seen on the road system. Campground hosts are Pat and Saundra White. Drinking water from water tank is hauled in from Fairbanks. Camping fee charged, discount with Federal Senior Pass and Access Lands Pass; 10-day limit. Hike up to see the Spirit Fence on limestone bluff above Walker Fork (ask Pat for directions). Walker Fork is a good gold panning stream. Check the campground information board or talk with the campground host about where you can gold pan on the river. You may not use motorized equipment including suction dredges, pumps, etc.

[A]

CAUTION: Expect stretches of narrow, winding road with hairpin curves and little or no road shoulder and no guardrails southbound. This is a very dangerous area to be passing and driving big rigs. Do NOT pull over too far or the soft shoulder may give way.

Highway straightens as the Taylor Highway follows Jack Wade Creek next 7 miles northbound. This stretch of road suffered washouts after heavy rains in summer 2011. Repairs included the addition of riprap along the riverbank to prevent future flooding.

TJ 80 E 80.5 D 95 *Highway descends next 2 miles northbound* to Walker Fork.

TJ 78 E 82.5 D 97 Views of South Fork and Walker Fork of the Fortymile River to west northbound between Mileposts TJ 78 and 82. *CAUTION: Approximately 1,000 foot drop-offs, no guardrails, soft shoulders.*

MILEPOST® field editor Sharon Nault says this stretch of road is "unique and spectacular!" Locals call it "the goat trail." Between the South Fork Fortymile River bridge and the Walker Fork bridge, the Taylor Highway winds along the side of the mountain like a narrow shelf, with vertical drops to the valley far, far below.

TJ 76.8 E 83.7 D 98.2 Small dirt turnout on curve. View of oxbow lakes in South Fork valley.

TJ 75.3 E 85.2 D 99.7 South Fortymile River Bridge.

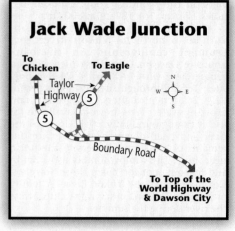

TJ 75.2 E 85.3 D 99.8 Turnoff to west for South Fork River Wayside. This BLM Wayside has a large turnaround area to the west on the south side of the bridge, for big rigs; outhouses; nice covered picnic area overlooking the river; cooking grills; dumpster; boat access; interpretive signs; and information board about the Fortymile Gold Rush. Life preservers available. Most popular river put-in and access point. Dirt road leads south to the launch then becomes a private road used by miners.

TJ 74.5 E 86 D 100.5 South Fork DOT/PF state highway maintenance station. Large level parking area (do not block gate). Access to South Fork Fortymile River across road from parking area.

TJ 72.3 E 88.2 D 102.7 Turnout by rock cut; muddy in wet weather.

TJ 72 E 88.5 D 103 Entering Federal Subsistence Hunting Area. Good views of South Fork Fortymile River.

TJ 70 E 90.5 D 105 Gravel pit parking to west.

CAUTION: Expect stretches of narrow, winding road with hairpin curves and little or no road shoulder and no guardrails northbound. This is a very dangerous area to be passing and driving big rigs. Do NOT pull over too far on the soft shoulder.

TJ 68.9 E 91.6 D 106.1 Lost Chicken Creek. Site of Lost Chicken Hill Mine, established in 1895. Mining was underway in this area several years before the Klondike Gold Rush of 1897–98. The first major placer gold strike was in 1886 at Franklin Gulch, a tributary of the Fortymile. Hydraulic mining operations in the creek. It is privately owned and mined.

TJ 68.1 E 92.4 D 106.9 BLM Chicken field station to west; information and emergency communications. Across the road from the field station, on the east side of the highway, is the trailhead for Mosquito Fork Dredge Hiking Trail.

Park at turnout on west side of road to hike this well-marked trail to an overlook with a bench and a view of the Mosquito Fork Dredge (also known as the Cowden Dredge, owned by the Alaska Gold Company). It is a 20- to 40-minute walk to the overlook; moderate downhill climb with a short, steep, stepped section near the end. Allow more time for uphill return. Well-maintained trail, but tree roots make for uneven walking surface. If you are short on time (or energy), it is only a 5-minute walk from the road to an overlook with a bench and a great view of the Chicken Creek area. *(Continues on page 299)*

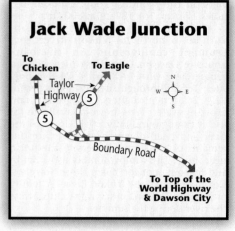

Jack Wade Junction

To Chicken

To Eagle

Taylor Highway 5

5

Boundary Road

N W E S

To Top of the World Highway & Dawson City

Side Trip to Eagle

At Jack Wade Junction, Klondike Loop travelers either veer east to Dawson City (if they are leaving Alaska) or turn south on the Taylor Highway (if they are entering Alaska). But Klondike Loop travelers have another option: They can head north on the Taylor Highway for a side trip to visit Eagle. Located at the end of the Taylor Highway on the Yukon River, Eagle has an impressive history for a small town at the end of a gravel road. Other highlights on the Taylor Highway to Eagle are the top-of-the-world views, the fireweed display at American Summit and the likelihood you'll see caribou along this road.

The Taylor Highway from Jack Wade Junction to Eagle is similar to the highway between Chicken and Jack Wade Junction: Narrow, winding, gravel, no shoulders or soft shoulders, steep dropoffs. There are numerous single-vehicle turnouts to allow traffic to pull over for oncoming vehicles on narrow road and approaching sharp curves. This section of the Taylor Highway is not recommended for large RVs. If you have a tow vehicle, consider leaving your big rig in Chicken.

It is 65 miles one-way from Jack Wade Junction to Eagle. Expect your highway speeds to be between 30 and 35 mph. Be alert for oncoming traffic on blind hills and curves! There are no services until you reach Eagle. Most Eagle businesses are open 9 A.M. to 5 P.M. daily in summer. Call ahead for lodging. Camping is available at the BLM campground, just past Fort Egbert.

The Taylor Highway is not maintained in winter, with seasonal maintenance ending about mid-October. Crews begin plowing snow and ice from the highway in early April. Current road conditions are available at 511.alaska.gov.

ALASKA ROUTE 5

Distance from Tetlin Junction (TJ) is followed by distance from Eagle (E).

Mileposts reflect distance from Tetlin Junction on the Alaska Highway.

TJ 95.7 E 64.8 Jack Wade Junction.

Continue north on the Taylor Highway (Alaska Route 5) for Eagle.

TJ 105 E 55.5 Downhill grade next 7 miles northbound (sign) as road begins spectacular descent from Polly Summit to the valley of the Fortymile River, so named because its mouth was 40 miles below Fort Reliance, an old trading post near the confluence of the Yukon and Klondike rivers.

TJ 112.5 E 48 BLM wayside at south end of Fortymile River Bridge *(wood decking, slippery when wet).* Information board, life jackets, handicap-accessible outhouse, picnic tables. No camping. Fortymile Mining District (sign); active mining in area.

Bumpy road to steep and difficult to access boat launch across road from wayside. Access to the Fortymile River National Wild, Scenic & Recreation River system.

TJ 113.1 E 47.4 O'Brien Creek DOT/PF state highway maintenance camp .

TJ 113.2 E 47.3 O'Brien Creek bridge. *CAUTION: Watch for small aircraft using road as runway.*

TJ 114.7 E 45.8 *Road narrows to 1-lane northbound for a short stretch. Watch for falling rock and steep drop-off next 1.5 miles northbound.* Highway parallels O'Brien Creek to Liberty Fork.

TJ 117.2 E 43.3 Alder Creek bridge, river access southwest side.

TJ 122 E 38.5 *CAUTION: Slow down for hairpin curves northbound.* Great view to south of Fortymile River Canyon.

TJ 124.5 E 36 Columbia Creek bridge.

TJ 125.5 E 35 Old O'Brien Creek Lodge (private property, closed).

TJ 131.5 E 29 King Solomon Creek bridge. (The creek has a tributary named Queen of Sheba.)

TJ 135.6 E 24.9 Large primitive camping area to west by landmark boulder, south of Solomon Creek.

TJ 135.7 E 24.8 North Fork King Solomon Creek bridge. *Road narrows northbound; watch for soft shoulders.*

TJ 138 E 22.5 Expansive view of fireweed and burn area *(see description of Taylor Complex fire at* **Milepost TJ 3.4** *on page 303).*

TJ 142.6 E 18 American Summit liquor store and snack shop (closed).

TJ 143.2 E 17.4 Turnout to east at **American Summit**. Top of the world views.

Highway begins winding descent northbound to Yukon River.

TJ 149.1 E 11.4 Discovery Fork Creek Bridge.

TJ 152.5 E 8 Bridge No. 2 over American Creek. Spacious turnout to east at south end of bridge. Turnout to west at north end of bridge.

TJ 153.2 E 7.3 Small turnout to east where spring water is piped to side of road.

TJ 159.3 E 1.2 Telegraph Hill Services; gas, diesel and tire repair. Telegraph Hill is visible from the road. Begin 15 mph.

TJ 159.6 E 0.9 Welcome to Eagle sign.

TJ 160.3 E 0.2 Turnoff for Eagle BLM campground and Fort Egbert.

TJ 160.4 E 0.1 Eagle Library.

Eagle

TJ 160.5 E 0 Front Street at the end of Taylor highway. **Population:** 86. **Emergency Services:** Alaska State Troopers (in Northway), phone (907) 778-2245; Eagle EMS/ Ambulance, phone (907) 547-2300; Eagle Village Health Clinic, phone (907) 547-2243.

Visitor Information: The **National Park Service and BLM Visitor Center**, located at the end of the grass airstrip, offers informal talks and interpretive programs; information on Yukon–Charley Rivers National Preserve; reference library; maps and books for sale; and public restrooms.

Visitor center hours are 8 A.M. to 5 P.M. daily in summer (Memorial Day weekend through Labor Day weekend) and the same hours on weekdays only in winter. Write Box 167, Eagle, AK 99738; phone (907) 547-2233.

Elevation: 820 feet. **Climate:** Mean monthly temperature in July 59°F; in January -13°F. Record low -71°F in January 1952; record high 95°F in July 1925. July also has the greatest mean number of days (21) with temperatures above 70°F. Mean precipitation in July, 1.94 inches; in December, 10.1 inches. Record snow depth 42 inches in April 1948. **Radio:** KEAA-LP 97.9 FM, Eagle's own radio station, is broadcast from

View of Well House and marker showing water line of 2009 flood. (©Kris Valencia, staff)

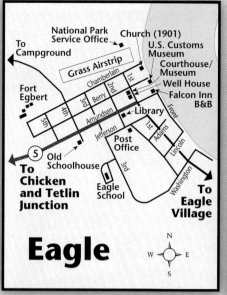

the school. Residents bring in their favorite tunes, which results in some interesting line-ups: a Hank Williams song followed by Led Zeplin followed by Tony Bennett.

Transportation: By road via the Taylor Highway (closed by snow October to April); air taxi, scheduled air service; dog team and snow machine in winter. U.S. customs available for persons entering Alaska via floating the Yukon River or by air in summer.

Private Aircraft: Eagle airstrip, 1.2 miles east on First Avenue, then 0.3 miles on airport access road; elev. 880 feet; length 4,500 feet; gravel; unattended. Float planes land on the Yukon River.

Eagle is located on the south bank of the Yukon River below Eagle Bluff (elev. 1000 feet/305m). This small community was once the supply and transportation center for miners working the upper Yukon and its tributaries. Francois Mercier established his Belle Isle trading post here in 1880. Eagle was founded in 1897 and became the commercial, military and judicial center for the Upper Yukon. By 1898, Eagle's population was 1,700.

Fort Egbert was established in 1899 adjacent to the city, and became a key communications center for Alaska when the 1,506-mile-long Washington-Alaska Military Cable and Telegraph System (WAMCATS) was completed in June 1903.

On July 15, 1900, Judge James Wickersham arrived to establish the first federal court in the Interior of Alaska. In 1901, Eagle became the first incorporated city in the Interior of Alaska.

View of the Yukon River at Front Street in Eagle. (©David L. Ranta, staff)

In 1905, Roald Amundsen trekked to Eagle to announce to the world the completion of the first successful Northwest Passage Sailing. A monument to him stands at the Amundsen Memorial Park at 1st and Amundsen Streets (with benches and covered pagoda). Flowers in summer.

By 1910, Eagle's population had dwindled to 178, as gold strikes in Fairbanks and Nome lured away many residents. With the conversion of telegraph communication to wireless, most of the U.S. Army left Fort Egbert in 1911.

Historic structures in town include: the Wickersham Courthouse, built in 1901 for Judge James Wickersham; the church (1901); the Waterfront Customs House (1900); the schoolhouse (1903); and the Improved Order of Red Men Lodge (1904).

Historically an important riverboat landing, today Eagle is a popular stop for Yukon River travelers. Breakup on the Yukon is in May; freeze-up in October.

During spring breakup in 2009, Eagle's waterfront suffered extensive damage when a Yukon River ice jam forced ice and water inland, moving some buildings off their foundations and destroying others. Signs around town show water levels from the 2009 flood. Although not as catastrophic, an ice jam during breakup in 2013 also caused damage and loss. As Pat Sanders of Eagle says, "The resiliency of Eagle's people is remarkable. So many have lost so much, yet they are always there to help a neighbor and lend a hand."

Eagle Village (pop. 67), a traditional Han Kutchin (Athabascan) community with a subsistence lifestyle, located about 3 miles east of Eagle (follow First Avenue out of town) overlooking the Yukon River; no visitor facilities. Village residents have relocated to housing near the road's end due to erosion and seasonal flooding on the Yukon River.

Lodging, Camping & Services

Groceries, gas, diesel, propane, ATM and laundromat/showers at Eagle River Trading Co. on First Avenue. Motel rooms are in high demand: Please reserve in advance of

your arrival at **Falcon Inn Bed and Breakfast.** Construction on a new hotel, restaurant and store on Front Street continued in summer 2013.

As in other small Northern communities, not all local businesses take credit cards and some food staples can be expensive here.

Eagle's well-house, hand-dug in 1903, provides water for about 70 percent of Eagle's residents. Three diesel generators provide the community's power: at 39 cents (2012 rate) a kilowatt, residents don't have a lot of extra appliances. Public phones are located in an old red telephone booth, across from the well-house. Satellite TV and Internet available.

Camping at the well-maintained **Eagle BLM Campground** just outside town (take 4th Avenue to Fort Egbert and follow signs). The BLM campground has 18 very nice sites in a beautiful forest setting; public drinking water, free firewood to paying campers, garbage containers, outhouses, $10 camping fee, $5 for Federal Senior or Access pass holders (cash or check).

Attractions

Eagle Historical Society Museum and Walking Tour. The Wickersham Courthouse houses the museum. Meet here for the Eagle Historical Society tour of Fort Egbert. The guided tours leave daily at 9 A.M. and 1 P.M. in summer except Sunday, when tours depart at 9 A.M. and 2:30 P.M. (hours may change). The museum and guided tour offer a wonderful look at Interior Alaska history, from early exploration and the military presence here to the lifestyle of gold miners and trappers. Contact Eagle Historical Society and Museums: phone/fax (907) 547-2325, 547-2244 or 547-2297; www.eaglehistorical society.com.

Eagle Library, on Amundsen and 2nd, is a unique place, with WiFi, a woodstove and an outhouse out back. Comfortable chairs and a homey atmosphere make this a fun place to visit. The library is staffed by volunteers and functions as an unofficial tourist information center. Check the visitor information board in front of the library for hours and for summer film schedule.

Fort Egbert, a National Historic Landmark, is comprised of 5 of the 45 original structures which were stabilized and restored by the BLM between 1974 and 1979. The BLM and Eagle Historical Society and Museums manage the Fort Egbert National Historic Landmark, which includes: the Quartermaster Storehouse (1899), the Mule Barn (1900), the Water Wagon Shed, the Granary (1903), and the NCO quarters (1900). The Storehouse has an interpretive exhibit and photo display showing the reconstruction. Check out the Jeffery (or Nash) Quad Truck built circa 1914, 1 of 2 still running in the U.S.

Yukon-Charley Rivers National Preserve (www.nps.gov/yuch). River runners float the 175 miles of the Yukon River between Eagle and Circle through the preserve. Eagle Bluff, the prominent rock to the west of the waterfront, is a landmark for Yukon River travelers. Its rusty color results from oxidation of iron in the greenstone. The Yukon River float trip takes from 5 to 10 days. It is suitable for canoes, kayaks or rafts (bring your own boat as rentals may not be available locally). River travelers are advised to file float plans and obtain bear proof containers (required for river travel) at the National Park Service visitor center in Eagle.

(Continued from page 296)
(There are 3 benches, including the one at the last overlook.)

TJ 67.1 E 93.4 D 107.9 Chicken Creek Bridge.

TJ 66.9 E 93.6 D 108.1 Turnoff to **The Goldpanner/Chicken Creek RV Park.**
Actual driving distance between physical Mileposts 67 and 66 is 0.6 mile.

TJ 66.4 E 94.1 D 108.6 Junction with Chicken Airport Road; access to **Beautiful Downtown Chicken** and **Chicken Gold Camp** east on Airport Road.

Chicken

Chicken is located 80 miles from Tok, AK, 94 miles from Eagle and 108 miles/174 km from Dawson City, YT. **Population**: 23 in summer, 7 in winter. **Private Aircraft**: Chicken airstrip, 0.8 mile east of highway (N 64° 04' W 141° 56'); elev. 1,640 feet; length 2,500 feet; gravel; maintained year-round. Use channel 122.8 Unicom when landing in Chicken; it is a surprisingly busy airport.

Commercial Chicken consists of 3 businesses, each with their own unique attraction for travelers, and each worth a visit: **Beautiful Downtown Chicken** and **Chicken Gold Camp & Outpost**, both just off the highway (turn on Chicken Airport Road), and **The Goldpanner/Chicken Creek RV Park**, located on the highway.

Although remote, Chicken is getting more and more traffic each year as the Klondike Loop continues to grow in popularity with motorists driving to and from Alaska. It is not unusual to see quite a diverse group of travelers enjoying this scenic little spot on the highway. For local businesses, it is something of a challenge to provide services to this growing number of travelers. There is no city water, sewer or electric service in Chicken. Generators and outhouses are utilized here, with residents providing their own water for drinking and showers, and generating their own electricity, including the 20- and 30-amp service for RVers at the RV parks. There is a dump station.

Chicken was supposedly named by early miners who wanted to name their camp ptarmigan, but were unable to spell it and settled instead for chicken, the common name in the North for ptarmigan. As the result of this choice, Chicken, Alaska is the place to find all manner of decor and trinkets with a "chicken" theme.

An active gold mining town, gold is often in local conversation. Chicken is also well-known as the home of the late Anne Hobbs Purdy, whose story is told in the book *Tisha* (by Anne Purdy and Robert Specht). This is a well-loved book about her experiences as a young schoolteacher in the Bush. *Tisha* and *Dark Boundaries* (also by Purdy) available locally.

Lodging, Camping & Services

The post office is located just off the highway at **Milepost TJ 66.3.** Travelers having mail forwarded to Chicken during their trip should factor in the twice-weekly mail service when planning their mail pickup and be sure to plan 10 days prior to the Tuesday or Friday that they would like to pick it up. Phone (via satellite or computer), internet (with WiFi), and email is available in Chicken.

Mining history is on display at the Chicken post office at Milepost TJ 66.3. Park at the post office, not on the highway. (©David L. Ranta, staff)

Services in Chicken are provided by the town's 3 major summer businesses (see map for locations). Alphabetically they are:

The unique **Beautiful Downtown Chicken** is owned by Susan Wiren, a pioneering-style woman with a cafe, saloon, cabins, gift shop and a business for 20-plus years. She likes to say "this is the REAL Alaska!"

The **Chicken Gold Camp and Outpost,** owned by 30-year residents Mike and Lou Busby and family, has an RV park, cabins, gift shop, cafe, gold panning, sani-station and offers tours of the historic Pedro Gold Dredge as well as more intense gold mining experiences out at mining claims. A few visitors have panned more than an ounce after going out on mining property and working

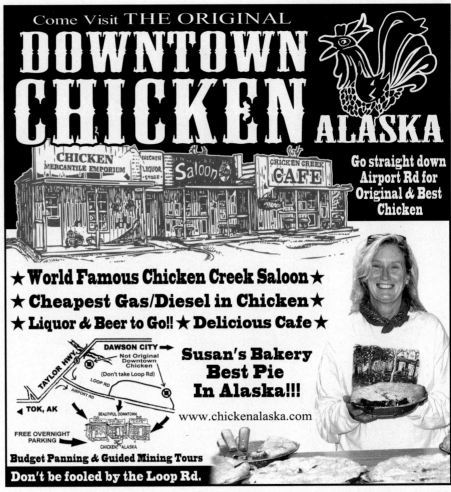

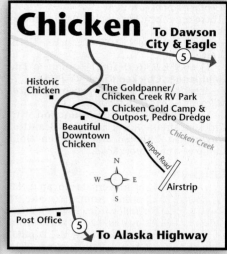

Pedro Dredge No. 4 is located at Chicken Gold Camp and Outpost on Airport Road.
(©David L. Ranta, staff)

CHICKEN ADVERTISERS

Downtown Chicken Mercantile Emporium,
    Cafe, Saloon and Gas................Chicken Airport Rd.
Chicken Gold Camp and
    Outpost ....Chicken Airport Rd.
The Gold Panner/
    Chicken Creek RV Park..............Ph. (907) 505-0231

hard at it.

The Gold Panner/Chicken Creek RV Park, owned by Bronk Jorgenson, is on the highway; gas, diesel, RV park, covered outdoor eating area, cabins, ATM, gift shop, tours of the original town of Chicken and dog sled rides.

Downtown Chicken Mercantile Emporium, Chicken Creek Cafe, Saloon and Chicken Liquor. Chicken is a rare treat for those with the courage to stray just

a few hundred yards from the beaten path. Turn on Airport Road and look for Downtown Chicken on the right. The Saloon and Cafe are some of the last remnants of the old frontier Alaska. Chicken Mercantile features a wealth of gifts, many designed by owner Susan Wiren. The cafe is well known for its fabulous homemade food, including wild Alaskan salmon and halibut. Homemade pies, cookies, blueberry muffins, cinnamon rolls and other delightful concoctions are made fresh from scratch daily. Downtown Chicken offers free camping, budget accommodations at $25, plus a private beautiful log cabin that sleeps 5 with a fabulous view! Free Internet access available for all and liquor to go.

E-mail Swiren@gci.net for reservations. See display ad on page 299. [ADVERTISEMENT]

Chicken Gold Camp & Outpost, a first class, rustic retreat including a well-maintained RV campground with 20/30 amp or dry sites, secluded tent sites, private cabins, showers, one of Alaska's finest gift stores showcasing Alaska/Yukon-made gifts and a café offering daily handmade gourmet treats. Mike, Lou and Josea Busby, who built and run the business, have lived in Chicken for over 30 years and are passionate about the area and its history. They give a fantastic tour of the historic Pedro Dredge, the most complete dredge open to the public on the road system. Interested in gold? The Camp provides access to their gold claims with guides, equipment and transportation if needed. Stake a mini-claim and keep the gold you find! The Camp has a growing membership in their "One Oz Club." The Roasted Rooster cafe is widely known for its fresh baked scones, pie squares and cookies; hearty homemade soups; delicious grilled Italian sandwiches; and Alaskan hand-roasted espresso. Enjoy micro-brewed beer, wine and ice cream on the picturesque deck. Free WiFi and firewood for campers. Take your picture with "Eggee," the huge metal chicken. Alaskan hospitality at its best! Located off the highway on the left side of Airport Road with big rig access and parking. ChickenRVpark@gmail.com. See display ad on facing page. [ADVERTISEMENT]

Town of Chicken/The Goldpanner. Welcome! We are at the Chicken Creek bridge. Stop in and get some World Famous Halibut and Burgers from the Cluck 'in Chicken Cafe. We have gold nuggets & 100's of T-shirts in the Goldpanner Gift Shop. You can fill your gas or diesel tank to get a free nights dry camping in the Chicken Creek RV Park. Stay in a cabin or in the only ensuite rooms in town. We have showers & the only flushing toilets on the Taylor Highway. RV park features 24-hour, 30 amp spaces, showers, free WiFi & goldpanning. Daily tours of Tisha's Schoolhouse and the historic town of Chicken from the 1890s. You will like our price and quality. www.townofchicken.com. See display ad this page. [ADVERTISEMENT]

Attractions

Tour Historic Chicken. The tin roofs of the old townsite may be seen from the road. The Historic Chicken tour includes the only remaining roadhouse (built in 1899) on the Taylor Highway, complete with a huge cookstove; Tisha's schoolhouse; the old John Powers Store, a former roadhouse; and a dozen or so other structures dating back to the early 1900s. This historic area—on the National Register of Historic Places—is located on private property; inquire at the Town of Chicken/The Goldpanner RV Park about guided tours.

Look for gold. A big attraction in Chicken is looking for gold, whether it's gold panning in a trough or in the creek, or going out on a real claim for some recreational gold mining. Both Town of Chicken/The Goldpanner and Chicken Gold Camp & Outpost offer gold panning. Chicken Gold Camp also offers recreational mining on a claim; bring your own sluices and highbankers or use what is there.

Gold Dredges. Mining dredges were used in Alaska and Yukon from the turn-of-the-century to the 1950s. The dredges were land-locked floating machines, digging ponds that allowed them to float across the area to be mined. The dredges operated 24 hours a day, from late April or early May and ending in November.

The floating dredge most commonly operated in the North was the California-type, also known as the bucket-line dredge. This type of dredge used a continuous line of buckets (called the "digging ladder") to scrape the bottom and edge of the pond. The buckets carried the mud and rock to a screening area, where the heavier metal particles were separated from the rest of the material. After the metal was captured, the waste rock—"tailings"— would be deposited out the back.

Parts of the old Jack Wade Dredge are on display across from the post office at **Milepost TJ 66.3**.

Views of the old Mosquito Fork Dredge from hiking trail at **Milepost TJ 68.1**.

Pedro Dredge No. 4 is located at Chicken Gold Camp and Outpost on Airport Road in Chicken. This dredge operated on Chicken Creek between 1959 and 1967, after mining Pedro Creek outside Fairbanks from 1938 until 1959. Mike Busby and Bernie Karl purchased the dredge and moved it and other mining equipment down to Chicken in 1998 as a tourist attraction. It was put on the National Register of Historic Places in 2006.

To reach Pedro Dredge (visible from the highway), turn on Chicken Airport Road at **Milepost TJ 66.4** then turn left on loop road for a large parking area with covered picnic tables adjacent the dredge. For more information on the dredge and/or tours, turn in at the Chicken Gold Camp off this road

The south half of the Taylor Highway has fair pavement and 9 percent grades at Mount Fairplay. (©Sharon Nault)

©David L. Ranta, staff

ground access road forks: Right fork leads to an open wooded camping area with 7 pull-throughs, firepits and grills, picnic tables, well maintained handicap-accessible outhouse, and picnic area with shelters and view; left fork leads to individual campsites on loop road.

Camping area on left fork has: 25 total level sites in trees (some pull-throughs, 18 back-in and 1 with an accessible tent platform; drinking water (hauled in from Fairbanks); litter bin, outstandingly clean, handicap-accessible outhouses (pictured above); tables, firepits; free firewood (for campground use only); and campground hosts. Some of the sites overlook Johna's Lake (named for former campground host Don Marshall's dog), where moose and beaver are often spotted. Watch for peregrine falcons, gray jays, snowshoe hare and lots of squirrels. Dumpster at campground entrance used for all trash. $10 camping fee charged (cash or check); $5 for Federal Senior Pass and Access Lands Pass (U.S. residents only). *Bring your mosquito repellent!*

TJ 48.3 E 112.2 D 126.7 Federal Subsistence Hunting Area boundary.

TJ 44.5 E 116 D 133.5 Federal Subsistence Hunting Area boundary.

TJ 43.5 E 117 D 134.5 View of Taylor Mountain, elev. 5,059 feet, straight ahead northbound.

TJ 43 E 117.5 D 135 Turnoff to west south side of bridge for gravel access road to **Logging Cabin Creek BLM Picnic Area.** *Slow for steep dip* at entrance to small parking area (no turnaround space for big rigs); pleasant picnic spot overlooking creek with a picnic table, cooking grill and information board. No overnight parking.

Logging Cabin Creek bridge. Logging Cabin Creek flows into the West Fork Dennison Fork.

TJ 39.3 E 121.2 D 135.7 Double-ended gravel turnout to west on curve with view of deep valley below.

TJ 37.6 E 122.9 D 137.4 View of Mount Fairplay southbound.

TJ 35.9 E 124.6 D 139.1 Unmaintained double-ended turnout to east.

TJ 35.1 E 125.4 D 139.9 Federal Subsistence Hunting Area boundary. In these areas, local residents have an expanded season for subsistence hunts of moose and caribou. There are several of these signs along the Taylor Highway.

TJ 35 E 125.5 D 140 South entrance to **Mount Fairplay Wayside,** a large double-ended turnout to east with interpretive signs on Taylor Highway, Fortymile River, caribou, moose. Viewing platform with good view of Mount Fairplay. Brochures regarding the 40 Mile Area are typically available at notice board; toilets (wheelchair accessible) and a picnic table. Look for the small root-covered trail that leads to open area with good views.

(www.chickengold.com).

The other notable landmark here is the **giant chicken statue** at Chicken Gold Camp. The 18-by-12 foot chicken was built of recycled high school lockers in Homer, AK, and transported to Chicken by truck (averaging 20 mph).

Annual Chickenstock music festival debuted in 2007, with the Last Frontier Bluegrass Band performing their greatest hits. For details on 2014 festival go to www.chickenstockmusicfestival.com.

Taylor Highway Log
(continued)

TJ 66.4 E 94.1 D 108.6 Junction with Chicken Airport Road; signs here point you in the direction of Chicken's 3 major businesses.

NOTE: Gas available in Chicken. Next gas for northbound travelers is in Eagle (94 miles) or Dawson City (108 miles). Next gas for southbound travelers is in Tok, 78 miles from here.

TJ 66.3 E 94.3 D 108.7 Chicken Post Office (Zip code 99732), and community hall, located up hill to west of road; large turnaround area for big rigs above the post office, do not park along the highway. A minor attraction in itself, the post office was established in 1903 along with the mining camp. The post office is open weekdays until 5 P.M.; the mail plane arrives twice a week (Tuesday's and Friday's; plan 10 days in advance for pick up of general delivery).

A few pieces of the Jack Wade Dredge are displayed here with interpretive signs and picnic tables. Formerly located near **Milepost 86** of the Taylor Highway, the dredge was dismantled by the BLM in September 2007. According to the *Fairbanks Daily News Miner,* BLM officials said the deteriorating condition of the old dredge made it a safety hazard. The Jack Wade Dredge was freighted up the Fortymile River from Dawson City, YT, in the winter of 1906-07. It was one of the first bucketline dredges in the Fortymile mining district and operated at this location from 1935 to 1941.

TJ 66 E 94.5 D 109 Chicken Community (northbound sign).

Actual driving distance between physical milepost 66 and 67 is 0.6 miles.

TJ 65.2 E 95.3 D 109.8 Federal Subsistence Hunting Area boundary. Small turnout to east with view of Mosquito Fork.

TJ 64.4 E 96.1 D 110.6 *Pavement ends, gravel begins northbound. Gravel ends, pavement begins southbound. Slow for areas of road damage (usually flagged) and gravel breaks southbound.*

TJ 64.3 E 96.2 D 110.7 Bridge over Mosquito Fork of the Fortymile River. **BLM Mosquito Fork Wayside** to west at north end of bridge.

The wayside is a day-use area with parking, 3 picnic tables, elevated cooking grill, handicap-accessible outhouse and information boards. This is a nice picnic spot overlooking the river.

The Mosquito Fork and Dennison Fork converge east of this bridge to form the 33-mile-long South Fork Fortymile River. The South Fork Fortymile crosses under the Taylor Highway at **Milepost TJ 75.3.**

TJ 63.7 E 96.6 D 111.3 Federal Subsistence Hunting Area boundary.

TJ 63 E 97.5 D 112 View of community of Chicken for northbound travelers.

TJ 58.9 E 101.6 D 116.1 Scenic viewpoint at turnout to east.

TJ 57 E 103.5 D 118 Rough gravel pit parking both sides of road with expansive views.

TJ 56.9 E 103.6 D 118.1 Large gravel turnout to east.

TJ 55.2 E 105.3 D 119.8 Highway descends northbound to Mosquito Fork of the Fortymile River.

TJ 55.1 E 105.4 D 119.9 Grassy turnouts to east and west.

TJ 52 E 108.5 D 123 Watch for moose.

TJ 50.4 E 110.1 D 124.6 Highway descends both directions to cross Taylor Creek bridge. Trail to Taylor and Kechumstuk mountains, used in hunting season.

NOTE: Slow for loose gravel and gravel breaks.

TJ 49.2 E 111.3 D 125.8 Bridge over **West Fork of the Dennison River.** Access point for Fortymile River National Wild, Scenic & Recreation River system; day-use area south of bridge. Fishing for grayling.

TJ 49 E 111.5 D 126 Turnoff to west for **West Fork BLM Campground,** a public campground and picnic area. The camp-

Entering **Fortymile Mining District** northbound. The second-oldest mining district in Alaska, it first yielded gold in 1886. Claims were filed in both Canada and Alaska due to boundary uncertainties.

This is the south end of the BLM's Fortymile River National Wild, Scenic & Recreation River, the second longest designated wild and scenic river in the nation.

TJ 34.5 E 126 D 140.5 *Highway begins 9 percent downgrade northbound.* Southbound, the highway begins long, winding 5 to 7 percent uphill and downhill grades for the next 25 miles as it descends from Mount Fairplay's summit.

TJ 34.4 E 126.1 D 140.6 Large double-ended gravel turnout to west with panoramic views of the Alaska Range and the many stream valleys that form the Fortymile River. Good photo-op.

TJ 32.9 E 127.7 D 142.1 Informal gravel turnout to west with view.

TJ 32.9 E 127.6 D 142.1 Informal gravel turnout to west with view.

TJ 28.4 E 132.1 D 146.6 Gravel turnout to west (across from gravel pit) with scenic views; Alaska Range visible on clear days.

TJ 27 E 133.5 D 148 Double-ended gravel to west. *Watch for soft spots and potholes.*

TJ 24.3 E 136.2 D 150.7 *Slow for loose gravel, 40 mph curve.*

TJ 22.2 E 138.3 D 152.8 Double-ended paved parking area to east with 3 information panels on Fortymile region, Mount Fairplay, the Taylor Highway, the Fortymile caribou herd, its history, status and their food supply (excerpt follows):

"*The Fortymile area is home range for the Fortymile caribou herd. Once a massive herd of 500,000 animals, the herd declined to a low of 6,000 in the mid-1970s. A 4-year recovery effort by the ADF&G using wolf control saw the herd grow from 22,500 to about 40,000. The herd moves east across the highway in late fall for the winter, and returns again in spring for calving. During the summer, small bands of caribou can sometimes be seen in the high country above timberline.*"

TJ 21 E 139.5 D 154 Very large, flat, gravel turnout to west.

TJ 19.4 E 141.1 D 155.6 Informal grassy turnouts along the Taylor are popular parking spots for berry pickers in August. Various plants, flowers and mushrooms flourish in burn areas along the Taylor Highway, including blueberries.

TJ 16 E 144.5 D 159 Watch for Northern hawk owls, one of the only owls to hunt during the day. These owls like to sit atop charred trees in the burn area.

TJ 15.6 E 144.9 D 159.4 Double-ended parking area to east with view.

View straight ahead northbound of Mount Fairplay, elev. 5,541 ft.

TJ 14 E 146.5 D 161 Highway travels through area ravaged by 2004 Taylor Complex fire.

Brilliant displays of fireweed (*Epilobium angustifolium*) in summer. A common wildflower along the roads of the North (it is the territorial flower of the Yukon), fireweed is named for its ability to flourish in burn areas. Another unique characteristic is its flower display. When it blooms in late June, the lowest flowers on the stem bloom first. As summer passes, it begins losing flowers from the top of the stem down. Fireweed can grow to 6 feet and is usually bright pink in color, although it also occurs in pale pink and white. In fall, leaves are a blaze of bright orange and reds.

TJ 12.4 E 148.1 D 162.6 Double-ended

Junction of the Taylor and Alaska highways, 12 miles southeast of Tok. *(©David L. Ranta, staff)*

parking area on viewpoint to east. Sign reads: $1,000 fine for littering.

Northbound, the Taylor Highway winds along ridges and over hills overlooking several streams that eventually converge to form the Fortymile River. To the west of the highway, Logging Cabin Creek flows into the West Fork Dennison Fork, which crosses under the Taylor Highway at **Milepost TJ 49.2** on its 53-mile journey northeast to join the Dennison Fork. The Dennison Fork, mostly out-of-sight to the east of the highway, flows 60 miles northeast to join Mosquito Fork and form the 33-mile-long South Fork Fortymile River. The North Fork Fortymile heads at Independence and Slate Creeks, flowing southeast 44 miles to join the South Fork and form the Fortymile River. The Fortymile River flows northeast 60 miles to the Yukon River in Canada.

TJ 10.7 E 149.8 D 164.3 Gravel stockpile to west, parking.

TJ 10.5 E 150 D 164.5 Entering Tok Management Area, Tanana State Forest, southbound.

TJ 10.1 E 150.4 D 164.9 Double-ended parking area to east on viewpoint. Views of valley and burn area.

TJ 9.4 E 151.1 D 165.6 Entering Game Management Subunit 20E northbound; entering GMU 12 southbound. Caribou hunting by permit only (sign).

TJ 8 E 152.5 D 167 *CAUTION: Slow for sections of frost heaves, soft spots, loose gravel and deteriorated pavement northbound. Most but not all are marked by orange flags.*

TJ 6 E 154.5 D 169 Gravel turnout to east.

Northbound, the highway begins long, winding 5 to 7 percent uphill and downhill grades for the next 25 miles as it ascends to Mount Fairplay's summit.

TJ 5.7 E 154.8 D 169.3 Entering Tok Management Area, Tanana Valley State Forest, northbound.

TJ 4.9 E 155.6 D 1670.1 *Highway descends 7 percent grade northbound.*

TJ 4.4 E 156.1 D 170.6 Large double-ended parking area to east.

A 0.7-mile trail leads to **Four Mile Lake**; rainbows, sheefish.

TJ 3.4 E 157.1 D 171.6 The Taylor Complex Fires in summer 2004 burned 1.3 mil-

lion acres. There is still some evidence of the fire damage along the Taylor Highway here, particularly in the spectacular displays of fireweed in the summer. Wildfires are common in Alaska from April or May through the summer months (depending on rainfall), with lightning the most common cause. The total number of fires in 2004 was 707, a not unusually high number in what was a very hot and dry summer for most of the state. What was high was the total acreage burned: 6,385,496 acres, making it the largest in recorded Alaska history. In areas recently destroyed by fire, vegetation like willows and birch may flourish.

TJ 2.6 E 157.9 D 172.4 Double-ended paved parking area to west.

TJ 2.5 E 158 D 172.5 Highway descends 5 percent grade northbound.

TJ 1 E 159.5 D 174 Note stabilized sand dunes (and rock graffiti) next several miles northbound.

TJ 0.8 E 159.7 D 174.2 Double-ended turnout to east. Sign for caribou hunters.

TJ 0.2 E 160.3 D 174.8 Next services (food, gas, camping) northbound 67 miles (sign) at Chicken. Nearest service to this junction are in Tok, 12 miles northwest on the Alaska Highway.

TJ 0 E 160.5 D 175 **Tetlin Junction.** Forty Mile Roadhouse, closed since about 1985 (see page 206 in the ALASKA HIGHWAY section for more information on this old roadhouse).

Junction with the Alaska Highway, 12 miles southeast of Tok. Turn to **Milepost DC 1266.7** on page 206 in the ALASKA HIGHWAY section for log of that route.

For those traveling north from the Alaska Highway here, the Taylor Highway begins a long, winding climb (up and down grades, 5 to 7 percent) out of the Tanana River valley. Speed limit is 50 mph unless otherwise posted.

Distance marker northbound shows Chicken 66 miles, Boundary 104 miles, Customs 109 miles, Eagle 160 miles. *Dawson City-bound motorists cross international border. U.S. and Canada Customs open mid-May to mid-September; hours in summer 2013 were 8 A.M. to 8 P.M. Alaska Time, 9 A.M. to 9 P.M. Pacific Time.*

Campbell Highway

CONNECTS: Watson Lake, YT, to Klondike Hwy.

Length: 362 miles   Road Surface: 40% Paved, 60% Gravel   Season: Open all year **4**

Lapie River Canyon near Ross River. The Lapie River flows into the Pelly River from Lapie Lakes. (©Kris Valencia, staff)

Distance in miles	Carmacks	Dawson City	Faro	Ross River	Watson Lake
Carmacks		221	111	145	364
Dawson City	221		330	364	582
Faro	111	330		45	258
Ross River	145	364	45		225
Watson Lake	364	582	258	225	

Named for Robert Campbell, the first white man to penetrate what is now known as Yukon Territory, this all-weather road leads 362 miles/583 km northwest from the Alaska Highway at Watson Lake,

to junction with the Klondike Highway just north of Carmacks. The Campbell Highway is both gravel and pavement, with road improvement ongoing. This road can be rough and slippery in winter.

The Campbell Highway is an alternative route to Dawson City. It is about 20 miles/32 km shorter than driving the Alaska Highway through to Whitehorse, then driving up the Klondike Highway to Dawson City, but it is a significantly rougher (and slower) road.

Between Watson Lake and the turnoff for Ross River, a distance of 225 miles/363 km, the Campbell Highway is a mostly narrow, winding gravel road with occasional short stretches of seal-coat or improved wide gravel road. There is very little traffic and there are no services on this stretch of highway outside of Watson Lake and Ross River.

On the 137-mile/220-km stretch of the Campbell Highway between Ross River and its junction with the Klondike Highway, the road is mostly paved, with *frequent* gravel breaks. This portion of the highway is generally wider, straighter and more heavily traveled.

The Campbell Highway junctions with the South Canol Road to the Alaska High-

way and with the Nahanni Range Road to the Tungsten mine site (not recommended for tourist travel).

The speed limit posted on gravel sections of the Campbell Highway is 70 kmph/43 mph. Gas is available at Watson Lake, Ross River, Faro and Carmacks. *Watch your gas tank. (Motorcyclists carry auxiliary tanks.)*

You have a good chance of seeing black bears along this road as well as some lake scenery (although many views are obscured by trees and brush). This is a wilderness drive with long distances between services. *NOTE: Drive with your headlights on at all times. Keep to right on corners and hills. Be prepared for rough road in construction and mining areas. Check current road conditions in Watson Lake at the visitor centre and at http://511yukon.ca.*

The Robert Campbell Highway was completed in 1968 and closely follows sections of the fur trade route established by Robert Campbell. Campbell was a Hudson's Bay Co. trader who was sent into the region in the 1840s to find a route west into the unexplored regions of central Yukon. He followed the Liard and Frances rivers, building a chain of posts along the way. His major discovery came in 1843, when he reached the

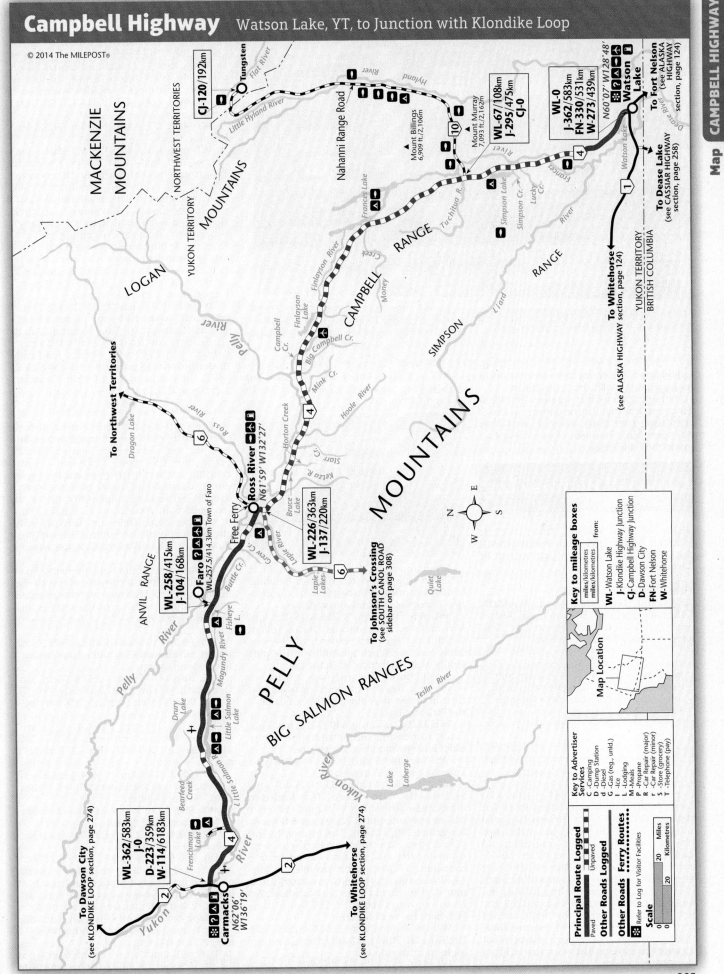

Campbell Highway
Watson Lake, YT, to Junction with Klondike Loop

© 2014 The MILEPOST®

Stop by the Watson Lake Visitor Information Centre for Campbell Highway road reports.
(©Kris Valencia, staff)

Yukon River, which was to become the major transportation route within the Yukon.

Emergency medical services: For emergency services dial 911 or phone the RCMP at: Watson Lake (867) 563-5555; Ross River (867) 969-5555; Faro (867) 994-5555 or Carmacks (867) 863-5555.

Campbell Highway Log

Distance from Watson Lake (WL) is followed by distance from junction with the Klondike Highway just north of Carmacks (J).

YUKON HIGHWAY 4 WEST

WL 0 J 362.2 (582.9 km) **WATSON LAKE;** all services. Watson Lake Visitor Information Centre and Watson Lake Signforest are located at this junction.

Junction of the Campbell Highway with the Alaska Highway. Turn to description of Watson Lake beginning on page 161 in the ALASKA HIGHWAY section.

Watch for soft spots, rutted road, washboard and road construction northbound. Check current road conditions at 511yukon.ca or with the Watson Lake Visitor information Centre.

WL 4.3 (6.9 km) **J 357.9** (576 km) Access road on right northbound to Mount Maichen ski hill; 2 lifts, 9 runs, a partial half pipe, and a full service ski chalet with viewing and eating areas; a concession and lounge; a ski shop offering rental services for skiers and snowboarders. The U.S. Air Force based at the Watson Lake airport between 1943 and 1952, cleared the land for a ski run and built a small warm-up shed. In 1968, the area was turned over to the newly formed Watson Lake Ski Club whose members "dedicated their time, energy and personal resources to develop the ski area's facilities into what it is today."

WL 6.3 (10.1 km) **J 355.9** (572.7 km) Airport Road leads west 1.7 miles/2.7 km to Watson Lake Airport.

The terminal at the airport was built in 1942 and is a designated Heritage Building. Inside, historical photographs on the aviation history of this area are on display.

WL 6.6 (10.6 km) **J 355.6** (572.3 km) Watson Creek. Tamarack is rare in Yukon, but this northern type of larch can be seen along here. Although a member of the pine family, it sheds its needles in the fall.

Northbound, the highway begins to climb to a heavily timbered plateau and then heads north following the east bank of the Frances River.

WL 22.2 (35.7 km) **J 340** (547.2 km) Tom Creek, named after an Indian trapper whose cabin is at the mouth of the stream.

WL 24.9 (40.1 km) **J 337.3** (542.8 km) Turnout and access to lake.

WL 29.1 (46.9 km) **J 333.1** (536.1 km) Sa Dena Hes Mine access. This lead-zinc mine began production in August 1991, but due to low zinc prices ceased operations in November 1992. During the 14 months the project was in operation, the mine produced approximately 607,500 tons of concentrate containing 374,400 tons of payable zinc and 290,200 tons lead. The mine is currently in a state of permanent closure. Reclamation and closure activities started in 2013 with completion of the work in 2015.

WL 35.2 (56.6 km) **J 327** (526.2 km) Tuchitua Highway Maintenance section begins northbound.

WL 35.6 (57.3 km) **J 326.6** (525.6 km)

Frances River bridge. Named by Robert Campbell for the wife of Sir George Simpson, governor of the Hudson's Bay Co. for 40 years, the Frances River is a tributary of the Liard River. The Frances River was part of Hudson's Bay Co.'s route into central Yukon for many years before being abandoned because of its dangerous rapids and canyons.

WL 46.1 (74.2 km) **J 316.1** (508.7 km) Lucky Creek.

WL 48.3 (77.8 km) **J 313.9** (505.2 km) Simpson Creek.

WL 50.5 (81.3 km) **J 311.7** (501.6 km) Access road leads west 1 mile/1.6 km to Yukon government **Simpson Lake Campground:** 10 campsites (2 pull-throughs), tables, firewood, toilets, boat launch, dock, swimming beach, playground, kitchen shelter and water (boil water for drinking). Wheelchair accessible. Camping fee $12. Excellent fishing for lake trout, arctic grayling and northern pike.

WL 57.6 (92.7 km) **J 304.6** (490.2 km) Large turnout with litter barrels.

WL 67 (107.8 km) **J 295.2** (475.1 km) **Junction** with Nahanni Range Road/Yukon Highway 10. The Nahanni Range (Tungsten) Road leads 120 miles/192 km to deadend at a barricade, where a road continues on private property to **TUNGSTEN,** NWT, the company town for the Canadian Tungsten (CanTung) mine. *The Yukon government does not recommend this road for tourist travel.*

The CanTung deposit was first discovered in 1954. Production began in November 1962, and at its height Tungsten had 600 people, an RCMP post, 2 schools, a medical clinic and a jail. The mine has been shut down a number of times over the years, usually because of commodity prices. It reopened with production beginning again in October 2010. There are currently only about 140 people per shift. Cantung produces more than 4 percent of the world's tungsten.

Construction of the Nahanni Range Road was begun in 1961 to provide access to the mining property. The road was completed in 1963 with the bridging of the Frances and Hyland rivers. *There are no services along Nahanni Range Road.*

WL 68.7 (110.5 km) **J 293.5** (472.3 km) Yukon government Tuchitua River maintenance camp to east.

WL 68.8 (110.7 km) **J 293.4** (472.2 km) One-lane bridge over Tuchitua River.

WL 90 (144.8 km) **J 272.2** (438 km) Jules Creek.

WL 97.8 (157 km) **J 264.4** (425.5 km) Distance marker northbound shows Ross River 221 km/137 miles, Faro 275 km/171 miles.

WL 98.2 (158 km) **J 264** (424.8 km) Distance marker southbound shows Watson Lake 160 km/99 miles.

WL 98.8 (159 km) **J 263.4** (423.9 km) 99 Mile Creek (not signed).

WL 104.6 (168.3 km) **J 257.6** (414.6 km) Caesar Creek (not signed).

WL 106.5 (171.4 km) **J 255.7** (411.5 km) Access road east leads to Yukon government **Frances Lake Campground** and boat launch. From highway, drive 0.6 mile/1 km east then turn left and drive 0.4 mile/0.6 km to campground. For boat launch, continue straight ahead instead of turning (it is 0.7 mile/1.1 km from highway).

The well-maintained campground has 24 sites (some on lake), firewood, litter

bins, picnic tables, firepits, kitchen shelter, water (boil water for drinking) and out-houses. Camping permit ($12). The solitary peak between the two arms of **Frances Lake** is called Simpson Tower (elev. 5,500 feet/1,676m), named by Robert Campbell for Hudson's Bay Co. Governor Sir George Simpson.

Fishing for lake trout, grayling and northern pike.

WL 106.6 (171.5 km) **J 255.6** (411.3 km) Money Creek, named for Anton Money, a mining engineer and prospector who mined placer gold in this area between 1929 and 1946. Money later operated "The Village" service station at Mile 442 on the Alaska Highway.

Highway climbs 8 percent grade northbound.
WL 106.9 (172.1 km) **J 255.3** (410.8 km) View of Frances Lake.

WL 108.2 (174 km) **J 254** (408.8 km) *Road narrows northbound, gravel continues.*

WL 111.1 (178.8 km) **J 251.1** (404.1 km) Dick Creek (not signed).

WL 118 (190 km) **J 244.2** (393 km) Wolverine Mine Site access road. Yukon Zinc's Wolverine Mine is a high grade zinc-silver-copper-lead-gold underground mine, with on-site milling capabilities. Operations started in 2011. The majority of the concentrate from Wolverine is trucked south to the British Columbia port at Stewart.

WL 120.9 (194.6 km) **J 241.3** (388.3 km) Highway descends Finlayson River valley northbound. Mountains to the west are part of the Campbell Range.

WL 123.6 (198.9 km) **J 238.6** (384 km) Light Creek (not signed).

WL 126.2 (203.1 km) **J 236** (379.8 km) Van Bibber Creek (not signed).

WL 129.7 (208.6 km) **J 232.5** (374.2 km) Entering Tatchun Fire Management Zone northbound.

WL 133.4 (214.5 km) **J 228.8** (368.2 km) Distance marker northbound shows Ross River 171 km/106 miles, Faro 225 km/140 miles.

WL 143 (230.1 km) **J 219.2** (352.7 km) Finlayson Creek (not signed).

The creek was named by Robert Campbell in 1840 for Chief Factor Duncan Finlayson, who later became director of the Hudson's Bay Co. Placer gold mined at the mouth of Finlayson River in 1875 is believed to be some of the first gold mined in the territory. Finlayson Lake (elev. 3,100 feet/945m), on the Continental Divide, separates watersheds of Mackenzie and Yukon rivers.

WL 143.4 (230.8 km) **J 218.8** (352.1 km) Access road east to Finlayson Lake Floatplane base.

Highway climbs 8 percent grade northbound.
WL 144.1 (231.9 km) **J 218.1** (351 km) Private side road to mineral exploration at Kudz Ze Kayah. Part of the R15 Project, located in the Yukon Tanana Terrane (YTT) of southeastern Yukon Territory that hosts numerous other volcanic-hosted massive sulphide deposits including the high-grade, poly-metallic Wolverine deposit, the GP4F deposit, and the Kudz Ze Kayah deposit.

WL 144.8 (233.1 km) **J 217.4** (349.9 km) Turnout to east is **Finlayson Lake Viewpoint** with observation platform and information panels on Finlayson caribou herd. The herd population was just over 3,000 animals in 2007, the most recent survey available online. The caribou's winter range is east of Ross River in lowland forest.

WL 146.6 (235.9 km) **J 215.6** (347 km)

A 7-mile/11.2-km access road connects Campbell Highway with Ross River. (©Kris Valencia, staff)

Watch for moose next 20 kms/12 miles northbound (sign).

WL 153 (246.2 km) **J 209.2** (336.7 km) **Private Aircraft**: Finlayson Lake airstrip to south; elev. 3,300 feet/1,006m; length 2,100 feet/640m; gravel. No services.

WL 157 (252.6 km) **J 205.2** (330.2 km) Distance marker northbound shows Ross River 121 km/75 miles, Faro 175 km/109 miles.

WL 160.4 (258.2 km) **J 201.8** (324.7 km) Campbell Creek. Robert Campbell followed this creek to the Pelly River in 1840.

WL 166.3 (267.7 km) **J 195.9** (315.3 km) Bridge over Big Campbell Creek, which flows into Pelly River at Pelly Banks. Robert Campbell named the river and banks after Hudson's Bay Co. Governor Sir John Henry Pelly. Campbell built a trading post here in 1846; never successful, it burned down in 1849. Isaac Taylor and William S. Drury later operated a trading post at Pelly Banks, one of a string of successful posts established by their firm in remote spots throughout the Yukon from 1899 on.

The highway follows the Pelly River for the next 90 miles/145 km. *Highway climbs steeply northbound.*

WL 173.9 (279.9 km) **J 188.3** (303 km) Mink Creek culvert.

WL 187.3 (301.4 km) **J 174.9** (281.5 km) Distance marker northbound shows Ross River 71 km/44 miles, Faro 125 km/78 km.

WL 188.2 (302.8 km) **J 174** (280 km) Bridge over Hoole River; turnout to north at west end of bridge. Confluence of the Hoole and Pelly rivers. Dig out your gold pan—this river once yielded gold. A walking trail leads into Hoole Canyon, which has interesting volcanic rock formations.

WL 194.1 (312.4 km) **J 168.1** (270.5 km) Star Creek culvert.

WL 200.8 (322.9 km) **J 161.4** (259.7 km) Horton Creek.

WL 201.1 (323.4 km) **J 161.1** (259.2 km) Private side road (not maintained) leads south 27 miles/44 km through the Ketza River Valley to the Ketza River Property. The first gold bar was poured at Ketza River mine in April 1988, and the mine operated from July 1988 until October 1990. The property

has been dormant since 1998. The Ketza River hard-rock gold deposit was first discovered in 1947. No visitor facilities.

The Ketza is a scenic river/mountain valley and a good area for canoeing, kayaking, hiking, climbing, mountain biking and gold panning. The valley has 3 formerly active gold mines and an old silver mine.

WL 211.7 (340.7 km) **J 150.5** (242.2 km) Ketza River. St. Cyr Range to southwest.

WL 212.9 (342.6 km) **J 149.3** (240.3 km) Little Ketza Creek.

WL 215 (345.7 km) **J 147.2** (236.8 km) Beautiful Creek culvert.

WL 218.4 (351.5 km) **J 143.8** (231.4 km) **Coffee Lake** to south; local swimming hole, trout fishing (stocked).

WL 220.5 (354.5 km) **J 141.7** (228 km) **Junction** with South Canol Road. Floatplane base on Jackfish Lake here.

> **Junction** with South Canol Road, which leads south 129 miles/207 km to Johnson's Crossing on the Alaska Highway. See "South Canol Road" log on page 308.

WL 225.4 (362.7 km) **J 136.8** (220.2 km) Main access road leads 7 miles/11.2 km to Ross River (description follows).

Ross River

Located on the Pelly River. **Population**: 352. **Emergency Services**: RCMP, phone (867) 969-5555. **Health Centre**, 24-hour nurse on call and ambulance, phone (867) 969-4444. **Visitor Information**: In Faro at the Campbell Region Interpretive Centre.

Radio: CBC 990 (local AM station), CHON 90.5 FM (road reports and weather), CKRW-FM (Faro). **Transportation**: There is no scheduled air service. **Private Aircraft**: Ross River airstrip; elev. 2,408 feet/734m; length 5,500 feet/1,676m; gravel; fuel 40.

Ross River is a supply and communica-
(Continues on page 309)

South Canol Road

The Canol Road between Johnson's Crossing on the Alaska Highway and Ross River on the Campbell Highway is referred to as the South Canol Road, while the road between Ross River and the YT–NWT border is referred to as the North Canol Road (not logged in The MILEPOST®).

The 137-mile/220-km South Canol Road is a narrow winding road which threads its way above Lapie Canyon via a difficult but scenic stretch of road then crests the Big Salmon Range (elev. about 4,000 feet/1,219m). It is maintained to minimum standards in summer and is closed to traffic and not maintained in winter.

There are some 1-lane wooden bridges and the road can be rough, with occasional road closures due to washouts. Driving time is about 4 hours one way. Use caution on steep hills and bad corners. There are no facilities along the South Canol Road, and it is not suitable for RVs or trailers. Not recommended for any vehicle in wet weather. *WARNING: The only facilities on the Canol Road are at Ross River. Be sure to check your gas supply before you go.*

The Canol Road (Yukon Highway 6) was built in 1942-44 as part of the Canol (Canadian Oil) Project to provide access to oil fields at Norman Wells, NWT, on the Mackenzie River and to facilitate construction and maintenance of a 4-inch-diameter pipeline. Construction costs ballooned from an initial estimate of $30 million to more than $134 million, and production costs for the Canol oil was 4 times higher than the world price for oil, plus it was cheaper to ship oil from Skagway. Only about a million barrels of oil were pumped before the project was shut down in 1944. (Today, Norman Wells is still a major supplier of oil with a pipeline to Zama, AB, built in 1985. It was the first ever buried pipeline built in the Canadian north.)

South Canol Road

Distance from the Campbell Highway junction (C) is followed by distance from the junction with the Alaska Highway (J). *Kilometre figures in the log from the Alaska Highway junction reflect the location of physical kilometreposts when they occur.*

YUKON HIGHWAY 6

C 0 J 136.8 (220 km) Campbell Highway junction.

C 1.2 (1.9 km) **J 135.6** (218.2 km) Jackfish Lake to west; floatplane dock.

C 3.8 (6.1 km) **J 133** (214 km) Erosional features called hoodoos can be seen in the clay banks rising above the road.

C 4.5 (7.2 km) **J 132.3** (212.9 km) Narrow 1-lane bridge over Lapie River No. 2. Point of interest sign on north end of bridge about the **Lapie River Canyon**. Lapie Canyon walking trail.

Road climbs southbound to an elevation of about 500 feet/152m above the river.

Rest area just off the Alaska Highway at south end of South Canol Road.
(©Kris Valencia, staff)

CAUTION: Narrow road, watch for rocks

C 10.5 (16.9 km) **J 126.3** (203.2 km) Turnouts overlooks Lapie River Canyon. Toilets, litter bins.

C 13.5 (21.7 km) **J 123.3** (198.4 km) Kilometrepost 200. Distance marker northbound shows Ross River 26 km/16 miles. Lapie River to east.

C 16.1 (25.9 km) **J 120.7** (194.2 km) Road climbs northbound through Lapie River Canyon.

C 29.4 (47.3 km) **J 107.4** (172.8 km) Lapie River No. 1 culverts. Ponds reported good for grayling fishing. *NOTE: Watch for horses on the road.*

C 31.5 (50.7 km) **J 105.3** (169.5 km) Short walking trail to Ian H. Thomson Falls. Old gold exploration trails in the area are great for hiking and mountain biking.

C 34.3 (55.2 km) **J 102.5** (165 km) Access road west to **Lapie Lakes**. Good place to camp; excellent lake trout fishing. There is also a gravel road between the lakes that leads east to the Groundhog Creek area. The creek leads to **Seagull Lakes**, which have excellent grayling fishing.

C 35.7 (57.4 km) **J 101.1** (162.7 km) Lakes to west are part of **Lapie Lakes** chain, headwaters of the Lapie River. These features were named by Dr. George M. Dawson of the Geological Survey of Canada in 1887 for Lapie, an Iroquois Indian who accompanied explorer Robert Campbell. A short dirt road provides access to the lakeshore. Watch for moose and nesting waterfowl. Unmaintained camping area and boat launch.

C 39.3 (63.2 km) **J 97.5** (156.9 km) Pony Creek. Caribou Mountain (elev. 6,905 feet/2,105m) to west.

C 39.7 (63.9 km) **J 97.1** (156.2 km) Rose Lake to east.

C 40.4 (65 km) **J 96.4** (155.1 km) Rose River No. 6.

C 41.7 (67.1 km) **J 95.1** (153 km) Upper Sheep Creek joins the Rose River here. To the east is Pass Peak (elev. 7,194 feet/2,193m).

C 42.7 (68.7 km) **J 94.1** (151.4 km) Distance marker northbound shows Ross River 76 km/47 miles.

C 43 (69.2 km) **J 93.8** (151 km) Rose River No. 5 culverts.

C 45.3 (72.9 km) **J 91.5** (147.2 km) Rose River No. 4 culverts.

C 47.1 (75.8 km) **J 89.7** (144.3 km) Rose River No. 3 culverts.

C 49.7 (80 km) **J 87.1** (140 km) Rose River No. 2 culvert.

C 53.1 (85.4 km) **J 83.7** (134 km) Dodge Creek culvert.

C 55.7 (89.6 km) **J 81.1** (130 km) Road crosses creek (unsigned) in culvert.

C 61.1 (98.3 km) **J 75.7** (121.8 km) Gravel Creek culvert.

C 64.9 (104.4 km) **J 71.9** (115.7 km) Deer Creek.

C 66.4 (106.8 km) **J 70.4** (113.3 km) Canol Creek culvert.

C 71.3 (114.7 km) **J 65.5** (105.4 km) One-lane Bailey bridge across Rose River No. 1. According to R.C. Coutts in *Yukon: Places and Names*, Oliver Rose prospected extensively in this area in the early 1900s. He came to the Yukon from Quebec.

C 74.2 (119.4 km) **J 62.6** (100.7 km) Distance marker northbound shows Ross River 126 km.

C 75.3 (121.2 km) **J 61.5** (99 km) Yukon government Quiet Lake maintenance camp on left northbound. A vintage Canol Project dump truck and pull grader is on display in front of the camp. There are no traveler services here, but the crew at the station has a satellite phone for emergency use only.

C 75.6 (121.6 km) **J 61.2** (98.5 km) Turn-off west for **Quiet Lake North Yukon government campground;**, 10 sites, camping fee $12, kitchen shelter, day-use area with picnic sites, water, boat launch and fishing. Entry point for canoeists on the Big Salmon River.

C 80.8 (130 km) J 56 (90.1 km) Turnout with litter barrels and point-of-interest sign overlooking Quiet Lake. This is the largest of 3 lakes that form the headwaters of the Big Salmon River system. The 17-mile-/28-km-long lake was named in 1887 by John McCormack, 1 of 4 miners who prospected the Big Salmon River from its mouth on the Yukon River to its source.

C 82.1 (132.1 km) J 54.7 (88 km) Lake Creek. **Quiet Lake** to west; good fishing for lake trout, northern pike and arctic grayling.

C 89 (143.2 km) J 47.8 (76.9 km) **Quiet Lake South Yukon government campground**; 20 sites (3 pull–throughs), camping fee $12, boat launch, picnic tables, kitchen shelter, firewood.

C 94.8 (152.5 km) J 42 (67.6 km) Access road east 0.4 mile/0.6 km to Nisutlin River Recreation Site, viewpoint and unmaintained camping area, boat launch, day-use area; tables, litter bins and outhouse. Look for wildlife.

C 97.7 (157.2 km) J 39.1 (62.9 km) Road crosses Cottonwood Creek.

C 105.9 (170.4 km) J 30.9 (49.7 km) Turnout with litter barrel to east.

C 106.2 (170.9 km) J 30.6 (49.2 km) Access road east to Sidney Lake. Nice little lake and good place to camp.

C 108.1 (174 km) J 28.7 (46.2 km) Sidney Creek culvert.

C 109.8 (176.7 km) J 27 (43.4 km) Evelyn Creek 1-lane wooden bridge.

C 117.4 (188.9 km) J 19.4 (31.2 km) Murphy Creek.

C 119.5 (192.3 km) J 17.3 (27.8 km) 17 Mile Creek.

C 122.9 (197.8 km) J 13.9 (22.4 km) Moose Creek. Small gravel turnout with litter barrels.

C 132.9 (213.8 km) J 3.9 (6.2 km) Four-mile Creek.

C 133.1 (214 km) J 3.7 (6 km) Short, rough access road leads to **Haircut Lake**; trout fishing. Difficult access and limited parking.

C 136.7 (220 km) J 0.1 (0.2 km) Distance marker northbound shows Ross Rive 226 km/140 miles.

C 136.8 (220.2 km) J 0 Rest area with toilets and interpretive signs at **junction** with Alaska Highway. A few old vehicles from the Canol Project days are on display here. Signs may be posted here indicating current status of Canol Road. Road is gated during off-season.

Information signs relate the history of the Canol Pipeline Project, which was funded by the American military; the Canol Road; the U.S. Army Black Engineers of the 388th Engineers; and the Teslin River Bridge, which is located on the Alaska Highway less than a half-mile from this junction.

Nearest food, gas and lodging in summer 2013 was in Teslin, 32 miles/51 km southeast of here. Whitehorse is about 75 miles/121 km northwest.

Junction of the Canol Road (Yukon Highway 6) with the Alaska Highway (Yukon Highway 1). Turn to **Milepost DC 808.2** on page 169 in the ALASKA HIGHWAY section for log.

Check locally for barge schedule. The pedestrian bridge across the Pelly River was scheduled to be torn down, rehabilitated or replaced at our presstime. (©Kris Valencia, staff)

(Continued from page 307) tion base for prospectors testing and mining mineral bodies in this region. It was named by Robert Campbell in 1843 for Chief Trader Donald Ross of the Hudson's Bay Co. Ross River is one of 2 Kaska Dena communities in the Yukon.

With the building of the Canol pipeline service road in WWII and the completion of the Robert Campbell Highway in 1968, Ross River was linked to the rest of the territory by road. Originally situated on the north side of the Pelly River, the town has been in its present location on the southwest bank of the river since 1964.

Accommodations at T&D hotel (seasonal), which has a restaurant. The Dene General Store has a gas station with diesel, groceries and some merchandise (open Monday to Friday 9 A.M. to 6 P.M., noon to 5 P.M. weekends), phone (867) 969-2280. There is a Toronto–Dominion bank (no ATM, hours are Monday and Wednesday–Friday noon–3 P.M.) and a post office (open 11 A.M.–2 P.M. Monday–Friday). Internet access is available at the Community Campus of Yukon College and at the public library.

The nearest campground is Lapie Canyon (see **Milepost WL 226.5**).

Ross River, located in the heart of the Tintina Trench, is a jumping-off point for big game hunters and canoeists. Canoeists traveling the Pelly River can launch just downriver from the ferry crossing. Experienced canoeists recommend camping on the Pelly's many gravel bars and islets to avoid bears, bugs and the danger of accidentally setting tundra fires. The Pelly has many sweepers, sleepers and gravel shallows, some gravel shoals, and extensive channeling. There are 2 sets of rapids between Ross River and the mouth of the Pelly: Fish Hook and Granite Canyon. Water is potable (boil first), firewood available and wildlife plentiful. Inquire locally about river conditions before setting out.

Wildlife viewing is very popular around Ross River and along the Campbell Highway. Species include moose, black and grizzly bears, wolves, lynx, Fannin sheep, Finlayson woodland caribou and a variety of waterfowl and migratory birds.

Rock hounds check Pelly River gravels for jaspers and the occasional agate, and plant lovers keep your eye out for the numerous Yukon endemic plants in the area.

The footbridge across the Pelly River at Ross River was closed by the Yukon government in fall 2013. The 70-year-old suspension bridge was found to be in imminent danger of collapse. Service on the the government-operated Pelly Barge across the Pelly River was restricted to vehicles only. The ferry runs almost underneath the bridge on an underwater cable and was in danger of being hit by debris if the bridge fell. Normal daily schedule in season (May to mid–October) has been from 8 A.M.–5 P.M.

Across the river, the **North Canol Road** leads 144 miles/232 km to Macmillan Pass at the Northwest Territories border. The North Canol Road is a narrow, winding, rough road which some motorists have compared to a roller coaster. All bridges on the North Canol are 1-lane. Road surface can be very slippery when wet. Not recommended during wet weather and not recommended for RVs or trailers. Subject to closure due to washouts.

Inquiries on the current status of the North Canol Road, Pelly Barge and pedestrian bridge should be made locally or visit www.511yukon.ca. *Drive with headlights on at all times! Make sure your tires are in good shape and carry a spare. WARNING: There are no facilities on the North Canol Road beyond Ross River.*

Campbell Highway Log
(continued)

WL 225.4 (362.7 km) J 136.8 (220.2 km) Main access road leads 7 miles/11 km to Ross River (see preceding description).

WL 225.5 (362.9 km) J 136.7 (220 km) Double-ended rest area; toilets, litter bins.

WL 226.4 (364.4 km) J 135.8 (218.5 km) Lapie River bridge and picturesque **Lapie River Canyon**. Turnout to north at west end of bridge. The Lapie River flows into the Pelly River from Lapie Lakes on the South Canol Road. There is a walking trail to the

Both the Campbell Region Interpretive Centre and Faro town office have displays and visitor information. (©Judy Nadon, staff)

river and canyon from Lapie Canyon Yukon government campground (see next entry).

WL 226.5 (364.5 km) **J 135.7** (218.4 km) Turnoff to south for **Lapie Canyon Campground** (description follows); drive downhill 0.3 mile/0.5 km (keep left at fork).

This Yukon government campground has 18 campsites (5 pull–throughs), firewood, tables, firepits, a group picnic area, kitchen shelters, walk-in tent sites and water (boil water for drinking). Camping permit ($12) required. Short scenic trails to the Lapie River. Mountain biking. Fishing for lake trout; access to other lakes and streams with grayling fishing.

WL 229.1 (368.5 km) **J 133.1** (214.2 km) Danger Creek.

WL 233.3 (375.4 km) **J 128.9** (207.4 km) Double-ended turnout.

WL 235 (378.1 km) **J 127.2** (204.8 km) Small turnout beside pond to west.

WL 252.3 (406 km) **J 109.9** (176.9 km) Buttle Creek, named for Roy Buttle, a trapper, prospector and trader who lived here in the early 1900s and at one time owned a trading post at Ross River.

WL 257.5 (414.3 km) **J 104.7** (168.5 km) Paved access road leads 5.6 miles/9 km northeast to Faro (description follows); point of interest sign about Faro at intersection. Road to Faro also accesses airport and Johnson Lake Campground, 3.5 km/2.2 miles on Faro Road, with 15 sites (6 pull-throughs), boat launch, firewood and kitchen shelter. Camping fee is $12.

Faro

Located in east-central Yukon Territory, 220 road miles/354 km from Whitehorse. **Population**: 380. **Emergency Services**: RCMP, phone (867) 994-5555. **Fire Department**, phone (867) 994-2222. **Nursing Station/Ambulance**, phone (867) 994-4444.

Visitor Information: Campbell Region Interpretive Centre, located across from John Connolly RV Park. Open daily 10 A.M. to 6 P.M. June–August; off season tours may be arranged by contacting the Town Office. The centre is a must-stop, with historical displays, local and regional information. Brochure of area hiking trails available. Contact Faro Town Office, P.O. Box 580, Faro, YT Y0B 1K0; phone (867) 994-2728, or (867) 994-2288 first weekend in May to end of September; www.faroyukon.ca; email cao-faro@faro yukon.ca.

Climate: Temperatures range from -51°F/-46°C in winter to a summer maximum of 84°F/29°C. **Radio**: CBC-FM 105.1 (weather alerts), CKRW-FM 98.7, CHON-FM 90.5 (road reports and weather). **Television**: CBC and satellite channels.

Private Aircraft: Faro airport; 1.5 miles/2.4 km south; elev. 2,351 feet/717m; length 4,000 feet/1,219m; gravel.

A former mining town, named after a card game, Faro lies on the northern escarpment of the Tintina Trench. Many places in town offer a commanding view of the Pelly River. The Anvil lead-silver and zinc mine, one of the largest open-pit mines in the world operated off and on from 1969 until 1998.

©Judy Nadon, staff

The Faro Studio Hotel has a lounge, restaurant (breakfast, lunch, dinner) and rooms for rent. There are bed and breakfasts in Faro.

The cardlock gas station has gas and diesel and takes cash or major credit cards but not debit cards. For questions, contact

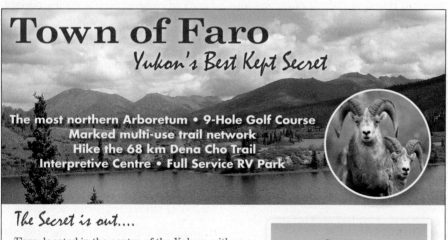

the town office at (867) 994-2728.

Other services in town include a grocery/hardware store, liquor store, post office and recreation centre with indoor swimming pool and squash courts. Catholic and Protestant churches are located here.

Faro has the John Connolly municipal campground and RV park with electrical hookups, water, showers, laundromat and free sani-dump. Camping fees begin at $15.

Attractions include an all-season observation cabin and isolated photographer's blind for wildlife viewing. Viewing areas are accessible via a gravel road skirting the Fannin sheep grazing area and are within 4 miles/6.4 km of town. A public boat ramp is available for exploring the Pelly River or Fisheye Lake.

Faro has a unique, "urban," 9-hole golf course that plays through the town's "green spaces." Off of Mitchell Road, look for the Faro Arboretum, which has viewing decks, interpretive panels and walking trails showcasing native plants and animals.

The Dena Cho Trail is a 42-mile/68-km trail that follows the original First Nations route between Ross River and Faro. For more information, contact the Town of Faro Municipal Office at (867) 994-2728.

Faro hosts a variety of events throughout the year, including the annual Crane & Sheep Viewing Festival in May and the Fireweed Festival in August.

Town of Faro. See display ad on facing page.

Campbell Highway Log
(continued)

WL 257.5 (414.3 km) **J 104.7** (168.5 km) Paved access road leads 5.6 miles/9 km northeast to Faro (see preceding description).

WL 257.6 (414.5 km) **J 104.6** (168.3 km) Large rest area with toilets and litter barrels just west of this junction.

WL 259.3 (419.5 km) **J 102.9** (165.6 km) Short access road to parking area on **Fisheye Lake**; boating, rainbow trout fishing.

WL 269.6 (433.9 km) **J 92.6** (149 km) Large turnout to south.

WL 290 (466.7 km) **J 72.2** (116.2 km) Good view westbound of **Little Salmon Lake.** The Campbell Highway follows the north shore of this large, deep, fjord-like lake. Fishing for northern pike, grayling, lake trout.

WL 290.9 (468.1 km) **J 71.3** (114.7 km) Short access road south to **Drury Creek Campground.** This Yukon government campground, situated on the creek at the east end of **Little Salmon Lake**, has a boat launch, fish filleting table, kitchen shelter, group firepit, water, 15 campsites (5 pull–throughs), $12 camping fee. Good fishing for northern pike, grayling, whitefish, lake trout 2 to 5 lbs., June 15 through July.

WL 291.1 (468.5 km) **J 71.1** (114.4 km) Drury Creek bridge. Yukon government maintenance camp to north.

WL 291.3 (468.8 km) **J 70.9** (114.1 km) Distance marker northbound shows Carmacks 111 km/69 miles, Whitehorse 294 km/183 miles, Dawson City 469 km/291 miles.

WL 292.1 (470 km) **J 70.1** (112.8 km) Turnout with litter bin to south.

Highway winds along above Little Salmon Lake.

WL 311.8 (501.9 km) **J 50.4** (81.1 km) Steep, narrow, winding access road south

to Yukon government **Little Salmon Lake Campground**; boat launch, fishing, 15 campsites (7 pull–throughs), $12 fee, water, picnic tables, outhouses, firepits and kitchen shelter.

WL 315.1 (506.9 km) **J 47.1** (75.8 km) Bearfeed Creek, a tributary of Little Salmon River. Access to creek to north at west end of bridge.

Highway follows Little Salmon River westbound.

WL 333.8 (537.2 km) **J 28.4** (45.7 km) Picnic spot on Little Salmon River, which flows into the Yukon River.

WL 337.5 (543.3 km) **J 24.7** (39.7 km) Frenchman Lake Road (narrow, gravel) to north accesses Yukon government campgrounds. Follow road 2.8 miles/4.5 km for

Frenchman Lake Campground; 10 sites (4 pull-throughs), boat launch, $12 fee, fishing for trout, pike and grayling. Follow road 5 miles/8 km on Frenchman Road from this junction for **Nunatak Campground**; 10 sites (2 pull-throughs), $12 fee, boat launch.

This side road loops around to Tatchun Lake Campground another 4.3 miles/7 km, and then continues 5.2 miles/8.4 km to junction with the Klondike Highway 17 miles/27 km north of Carmacks (see **Milepost J 118.5** in the KLONDIKE LOOP section). Total driving distance on Frenchman Lake Road is 28.7 miles/46.2 km. The stretch between Nunatuk and Tatchun Lake can be quite rutted.

WL 345.6 (555.7 km) **J 16.6** (26.7 km)

Turnout with litter bins and toilets to north. **Columbian Disaster Rest Area** to south overlooks Yukon River; sign reads:

"The worst accident in the history of the territory's riverboat travel occurred here at Eagle Rock, on the Yukon River. In September 1906, the sternwheeler *Columbian* exploded and burned, killing 5 men and badly burning another. The steamer was carrying a crew of 25 men and a full cargo, including cattle and 3 tons of blasting powder destined for the Tantalus Butte coal mine, 30 miles downriver.

"The fire started when Phil Murray, the deckhand, showed his loaded gun to Edward Morgan. Morgan, ironically the fireman on watch, accidentally fired the weapon into a load of blasting powder stored on deck. The powder exploded and a sheet of flame swept the boat.

"Captain J.O. Williams was protected in the wheelhouse, but could not work the steering or communicate with the engine room. He raced down to the freight deck and told the engineer to stop the engines. As they headed into a bend in the river, he ordered the engines started again to ram the bank. After the bow hit, the stern swung round in the current and Williams ordered full astern to back the vessel up on the shore. His quick thinking allowed the crew to jump ashore and prevented the disaster from being even worse."

WL 359.3 (578.3 km) **J 2.9** (4.6 km) **Private Aircraft**: Carmacks airstrip to south; elev. 1,770 feet/539m; length 5,200 feet/1,585m; gravel.

WL 360 (579.4) **J 2.2** (3.5 km) View of Tantalus Butte, named by U.S. Army Lt. Frederick Schwatka in 1883, because of its tantalizing appearance around many bends of the river before it was reached.

WL 362.2 (582.9 km) **J 0** Turn south on the Klondike Highway for Carmacks (2 miles/3.2 km), the nearest gas stop; turn north for Dawson City (220 miles/354 km). Coal Mine Campground is located at this junction.

Junction with the North Klondike Highway (Yukon Highway 2). Turn to **Milepost J 103.5** on page 281 in the KLONDIKE LOOP section for highway log.

Little Salmon Lake has 2 Yukon government campgrounds. (©Judy Nadon, staff)

Dempster Highway

CONNECTS: Klondike Highway to Inuvik, NWT

Length: 456 miles   Road Surface: Gravel   Season: Open all year

The Dempster Highway offers breathtaking vistas. (©Sharon Nault)

Distance in miles	Dawson City	Ft. McPherson	Inuvik	Klondike Hwy.
Dawson City		367	481	25
Ft. McPherson	367		114	342
Inuvik	481	114		456
Klondike Hwy.	25	342	456	

Construction of the Dempster Highway began in 1959 and was finally completed in 1978, although it did not officially open until Discovery Day weekend in 1979. It was named for Inspector William John Duncan Dempster of the RCMP.

The first 5 miles/8 km of the Dempster are seal-coated, and the last 6 miles/10 km are paved, but the rest of the road is gravel. Although in relatively good condition, this highway requires drivers pay attention at all times for sudden changes in road surface, including frost heaves, potholes, boggy or slick stretches, crushed shale (hard on tires) and other drivers. Drivers should pull-over (if space allows) for oncoming trucks or to allow trucks to pass. *Drive with your headlights on at all times.*

The posted speed limit is 90 kmph/55 mph unless otherwise posted. Calcium chloride is used to reduce dust and as a bonding agent; wash your vehicle as soon as practical. Some stretches of this highway can be very slippery in wet weather.

It is strongly advised that Dempster motorists carry a full-sized spare tire—or 2 spare tires if they are an unusual size—as well as extra water and gas.

Facilities are still few and far between on the Dempster. Full visitor services are available in Dawson City, 25 miles/40 km north of the Dempster Highway turnoff (Dempster Corner) on the Klondike Highway. Gas,

The Dempster Highway (Yukon Highway 5, NWT Highway 8) begins about 25 miles/40 km east of Dawson City, YT, at its junction with the Klondike Highway (see the KLONDIKE LOOP section page 274) and leads 456 miles/734 km northeast to Inuvik, NWT. The highway can be driven in 10 to 14 hours, but it is strongly recommended that motorists slow down and enjoy the trip, allowing extra time for hiking, camping, fishing, wildlife viewing (especially birds) and the spectacular photo opportunities this remote road affords.

Major Attractions:

© Sharon Nault

Lost Patrol Gravesite, Mackenzie River Delta, Arctic Circle Crossing

Highest Summit:
North Fork Pass 4,265 ft.

Dempster Highway Klondike Highway Junction to Inuvik, NWT

© 2014 The MILEPOST®

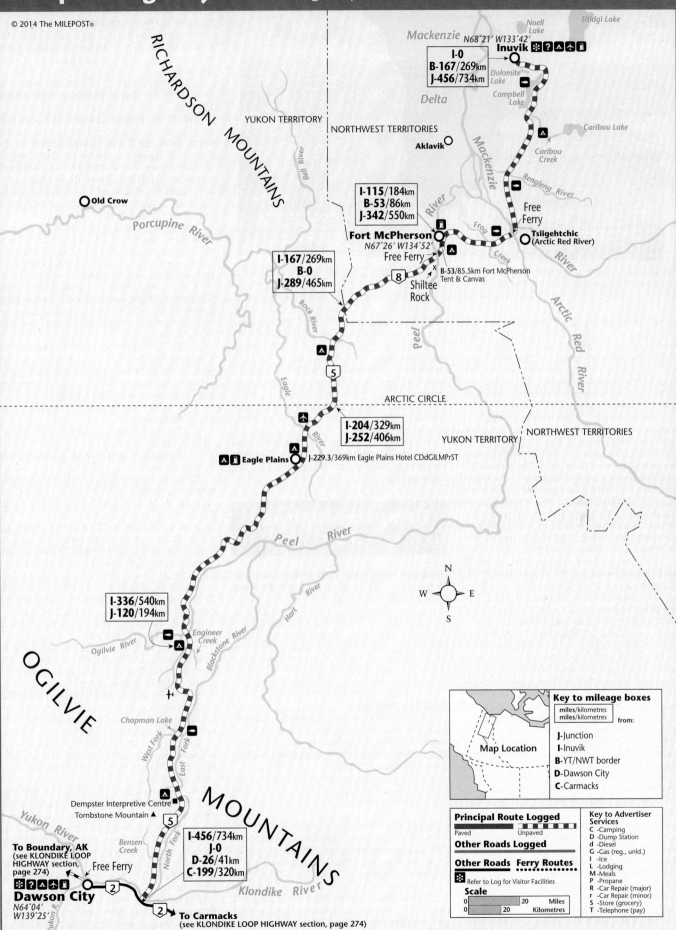

Mackenzie

Noell Lake

Sitidgi Lake

N68°21' W133°42'

Inuvik

I-0
B-167/269km
J-456/734km

Delta

Dolomite Lake

Campbell Lake

YUKON TERRITORY

NORTHWEST TERRITORIES

● **Aklavik**

Caribou Lake

Caribou Creek

Rengleng River

○ **Old Crow**

Porcupine River

RICHARDSON MOUNTAINS

Bell River

I-115/184km
B-53/86km
J-342/550km

Fort McPherson
N67°26' W134°52'

Free Ferry

River

Free Ferry

Frog

Tsiigehtchic
(Arctic Red River)

Creek

Arctic Red River

I-167/269km
B-0
J-289/465km

Rock River

8

Shiltee Rock

× B-53/85.5km Fort McPherson
Tent & Canvas

Peel

Eagle River

5

ARCTIC CIRCLE

I-204/329km
J-252/406km

YUKON TERRITORY   NORTHWEST TERRITORIES

Eagle Plains   J-229.3/369km Eagle Plains Hotel CDdGILMPrST

Peel River

River

Hart River

I-336/540km
J-120/194km

Engineer Creek

Ogilvie River

Blackstone River

OGILVIE

Chapman Lake

West Fork

East Fork

5

Dempster Interpretive Centre
Tombstone Mountain ▲

MOUNTAINS

Bensen Creek

North Fork

To Boundary, AK
(see KLONDIKE LOOP
HIGHWAY section,
page 274)

Free Ferry

I-456/734km
J-0
D-26/41km
C-199/320km

2

Dawson City
N64°04'
W139°25'

Yukon River

Klondike River

2

To Carmacks
(see KLONDIKE LOOP HIGHWAY section, page 274)

N
W · E
S

Key to mileage boxes

miles/kilometres
miles/kilometres   from:

Map Location

J-Junction
I-Inuvik
B-YT/NWT border
D-Dawson City
C-Carmacks

Principal Route Logged

Paved   Unpaved

Other Roads Logged

Other Roads   Ferry Routes

❉ Refer to Log for Visitor Facilities

Scale
0   20   Miles
0   20   Kilometres

Key to Advertiser Services

C -Camping
D -Dump Station
d -Diesel
G -Gas (reg., unld.)
I -Ice
L -Lodging
M -Meals
P -Propane
R -Car Repair (major)
r -Car Repair (minor)
S -Store (grocery)
T -Telephone (pay)

There are 2 free ferry crossings on the Dempster Highway. (©Sharon Nault)

diesel, propane, food, lodging, and car and tire repair are also available at **Eagle Plains Hotel** (phone 867/993-2453), located at about the halfway point on the Dempster. Gas, food and lodging are also available in Fort McPherson. Inuvik has all visitor services. Gas up whenever possible. Also fill water containers whenever possible.

The Dempster is open year-round, but summer travel gives visitors long hours of daylight for recreation. The highway is well-traveled in summer: A driver may not see another car for an hour, and then pass 4 cars in a row. Locals say the highway is smoother and easier to drive in winter, but precautions should be taken against cold weather, high winds and poor visibility; check road conditions before proceeding in winter. Watch for herds of caribou mid-September to late October and in March and April.

Free government ferry service is available approximately 15 hours a day in summer at each of the 2 river crossings on the Dempster: At **Milepost J 334.9** the *Abraham Francis* crosses the Peel River near Fort McPherson (normal hours are 9 A.M to 1 A.M.); and at **Milepost J 377.9** the *Louis Cardinal* crosses the Mackenzie River (8:15 A.M. to 11:35 P.M.). Ferries operate June to mid-October or early November. Crossing is by ice bridge in winter. No crossing during freeze–up and break–up. *"Ferries in the NWT can close with little or no notice due to low water levels, ice conditions, or other factors. Caution should be used on landings and approaches. Always check road bulletins before travelling to ensure ferries on your route are operating normal hours."*

Visit www.dot.gov.nt.ca and click on Highway/Ferry Conditions in the pull-down menu under Drivers/Vehicles for open and close dates for the ferry system, ice bridges and winter roads. For recorded messages on current ferry service, road and weather conditions, phone 1-800-661-0750. Road conditions may also be found by calling (867) 456-7623 or 1-877-456-7623.

General information on Northwest Territories is available by calling the Arctic Hotline at 1-800-661-0750. If you are in Dawson City, visit the Dempster Highway and Northwest Territories Information Centre, located in the B.Y.N. Building on Front Street, across from the Yukon Visitor Centre. It is open daily 9 A.M. to 7 P.M., May 15 to Sept. 15; phone (867) 777-7237. Or visit the following sites for more information: www.inuvik.ca or www.spectacularnwt.com.

And don't forget the bug spray: mosquitoes and black flies can be fierce at times during the summer.

The MILEPOST® expresses its appreciation to Northwest Territories and Yukon Territory for their assistance with information in this highway log.

Dempster Highway Log

Distance from junction with Klondike Highway 2 (J) is followed by distance from Inuvik (I).

NOTE: The kilometre figure following (J) in the highway log reflects the nearest physical kilometrepost along the road. Kilometreposts are green with white lettering and are located on the right-hand side of the highway, northbound. Kilometres are converted to miles in this log to help determine distance for motorists used to miles.

YUKON HIGHWAY 5

J 0 I 456.1 (734 km) **Dempster Corner,** 25 miles/40 km southeast of Dawson City. Klondike River Lodge, which was on the east side of highway just north of here, burned down in January 2013.

NOTE: Fill your tank in Dawson City. Next gas northbound is at Eagle Plains, 229 miles/369 km from here.

Junction of Klondike Highway (Yukon Highway 2) and Dempster Highway (Yukon Highway 5). Turn to **Milepost J 298.3** on page 285 in the KLONDIKE LOOP section for log of Klondike Highway.

J 0.1 (0.2 km) **I 456** (733.8 km) Dempster Highway Gateway Interpretive Display with information panels on history and culture, wildlife, ecology and driving tips. Worth a stop.

J 0.2 (0.3 km) **I 455.9** (733.7 km) One-lane wood-planked bridge over Klondike River. The road follows the wooded (spruce and poplar) North Klondike River valley.

J 0.9 (1.4 km) **I 455.2** (732.6 km) Distance marker northbound shows Eagle Plains 363 km/226 miles, Inuvik 735 km/457 miles.

J 3.4 (5 km) **I 452.7** (728.5 km) Burn area from 1991 fire that burned 5,189 acres/2,100 hectares.

J 4 (6 km) **I 452.1** (727.6 km) North Fork Ditch (now obscured by brush) channeled water from the North Klondike River to the Granville Power Co. (built in 1909), which provided power and water for gold-dredging operations farther down the valley. Later owned and operated by Yukon Consolidated Gold Co., dredging and the power plant shut down in the 1960s.

J 4.8 (8 km) **I 451.3** (726.3 km) North Fork Road leads east across the North Klondike River to the Viceroy heap-leach gold mine, which operated until 2002. Reclamation was completed in 2005.

J 6.5 (10.5 km) **I 449.6** (723.5 km) Antimony Mountain (elev. 6,693 feet/2,040m), about 18.5 miles/30 km away, is one peak of the Ogilvie Mountains and part of the Snowy Range.

J 12.4 (20 km) **I 443.7** (714 km) North Klondike Range, Ogilvie Mountains to the west of the highway lead toward the rugged, interior Tombstone Range. These mountains were glaciated during the Ice Age.

J 14.3 (23.1 km) **I 441.8** (711 km) Large, well-used turnout.

J 15.2 (24.4 km) **I 440.9** (709.5 km) Glacier Creek.

J 17.8 (28.6 km) **I 438.3** (705.4 km) Bensen Creek.

J 20.5 (33 km) **I 435.6** (701 km) Spacious turnout to west.

J 28.6 (46 km) **I 427.5** (688 km) Scout Car Creek. Watch for grouse.

J 31.3 (50.3 km) **I 424.8** (683.6 km) Wolf Creek. Private cabin beside creek.

J 31.4 (50.5 km) **I 424.7** (683.5 km) Tombstone Territorial Park boundary (unsigned).

J 33.1 (53.2 km) **I 423** (680.7 km) View of microwave tower. There are more than a dozen of these towers along the highway.

J 34.1 (54.8 km) **I 422** (679.1 km) View of North Fork Klondike River.

J 36.4 (58.5 km) **I 419.7** (675.4 km) Grizzly Creek. Mount Robert Service on right northbound. Grizzly Ridge Trail to west to overlook (2- to 3-hour hike).

J 40.4 (65 km) **I 415.7** (669 km) Klondike Camp Yukon government highway maintenance station. No visitor services but may provide help in an emergency.

J 41.4 (66.6 km) **I 414.7** (667.4 km) First crossing northbound of the North Fork Klondike River, which flows under the road in huge culverts.

The highway now moves above tree line and on to tundra northbound, crossing the watershed between the Yukon and Mackenzie basins at an elevation of approximately 4,003 feet/1,220m. Sign reads: No motorized vehicles except on authorized trails.

J 43 (69.2 km) **I 413.1** (664.8 km) Spectacular first view of Tombstone Range northbound.

J 44.4 (71.5 km) **I 411.7** (662.5 km) **Dempster Interpretive Centre** to west; large parking area, outhouses, litter bins. Open daily from mid-June to early September. This

"green" designed building offers natural history and cultural displays, a resource library, campfire talks, nature walks and a self-guiding trail. Pick up a copy of *The Dempster Highway Travelogue* here; this free booklet has detailed descriptions of the geographical regions along the road.

Just north of the Interpretive Centre is the turnoff for **Tombstone Territorial Park Yukon Government Campground** (elev. 3,392 feet/1,034m); 36 sites, camping fee $12, shelter, fireplaces (firewood included in fee), water from the river, tables, pit toilets, group shelter. Designated cyclist camping area. A short hiking trail connects the campground with the Interpretive Centre. *CAUTION: Hikers should inquire about recent bear activity in the area before setting off.* ▲

J 46 (74 km) **I 410.1** (660 km) **Tombstone Range Viewpoint**; large double-ended parking area. Good views of North Fork Pass and river. To the southwest is the needle-like peak of Tombstone Mountain (elev. 7,195 feet/2,193m), which forms the centrepoint in a panorama of ragged ridges and lush green tundra slopes. To the north is the East Fork Blackstone River valley; on each side are the Ogilvie Mountains, which rise to elevations of 6,890 feet/2,100m. Watch for Dall sheep, grizzlies, hoary marmots and ptarmigan. The Tombstone, Cloudy and Blackstone mountain ranges are identified as a Special Management Area by the Yukon government. Look for Northern Wheatear nesting in nearby cliffs.

Day hikes up the North Klondike River valley and 4-day wilderness hikes to Tombstone Mountain are popular. (There are no established trails.) The staff at the Dempster Interpretive Centre can provide maps and suggest itineraries. Hikers should be well prepared for rough terrain, drastic weather changes and potential wildlife encounters, as well as practicing "leave-no-trace" camping. For more information on the Tombstone region, call Yukon Parks at (867) 667-5648 or (inside Yukon) 1-800-661-0408. Heli-hiking is also growing in popularity; inquire in Dawson City about fly-in/hike-out packages as well as flightseeing trips.

J 46.2 (74.4 km) **I 409.9** (659.7 km) Side road east to microwave tower accesses Goldensides Mountain, reportedly a good hiking area (inquire at Dempster Interpretive Centre).

J 48.2 (76.9 km) **I 407.9** (656.4 km) Blackstone River culvert. This is the first river on the Dempster that drains into the Arctic watershed.

J 48.6 (78.2 km) **I 407.5** (655.8 km) Hart River winter road. Good place for viewing caribou.

J 49.3 (79.3 km) **I 406.8** (654.7 km) **North Fork Pass Summit**, elev. 4,593 feet/1,400m, is the highest point on the Dempster Highway and the continental divide between the Yukon River watershed, where rivers flow west to the Bering Sea, and the Mackenzie River system, where rivers flow north into the Beaufort Sea.

J 50 (80.4 km) **I 406.1** (653.5 km) Double-ended turnout to east. Wildflowers abundant in late June, early July. Good bird-watching area. A hike up the mountain slopes increases the chance of seeing pika, marmots, ptarmigan and golden eagles. Also watch for gyrfalcon, which feed on ptarmigan. *NOTE: Do not hike here during lambing season in May and June to avoid disturbing the sheep.*

J 52 (83.5 km) **I 404.1** (650.3 km) Anglecomb Peak (also called Sheep Mountain) is a lambing and nursery habitat for Dall sheep during May and June. This is also a frequent nesting area for a pair of golden eagles.

J 53.3 (85.8 km) **I 402.8** (648.2 km) First crossing of East Fork Blackstone River.

J 54.6 (87.9 km) **I 401.5** (646.1 km) White fireweed in summer.

J 56.4 (90.8 km) **I 399.7** (643.2 km) Guide and outfitters camp to east.

CAUTION: Watch for horses on road.

The Blackstone Uplands, stretching from North Fork Pass to Chapman Lake, are a rich area for birdlife (long-tailed jaegers, gyrfalcons, peregrine falcons, red-throated loons, whimbrels, upland sandpipers and long-tailed ducks) and big game hunting for Dall sheep and grizzly bear. The open tundra vegetation here is similar to high arctic tundra.

J 62.6 (100.7 km) **I 393.5** (633.2 km) Distance marker northbound shows Eagle Plains 261 km/162 miles, Inuvik 633 km/393 miles.

Distance marker southbound shows Dawson 142 km/88 miles, Whitehorse 600 km/373 miles.

J 63.7 (102.5 km) **I 392.4** (631.5 km) **Two Moose Lake**; turnout with information panels and viewing platform. A good spot to see moose, which are relatively scarce in the Blackstone Uplands. Bird watching here includes waterfowl: Northern pintail, scaup, American wigeon, Northern shoveller, harlequin ducks.

J 66.9 (107.6 km) **I 389.2** (626.3 km) Large gravel pullout to east with dumpster and outhouse. Access to Blackstone River.

J 69.6 (112 km) **I 386.5** (622 km) Parking area to east with memorial to local residents Joseph and Annie Henry.

J 71.3 (114.8 km) **I 384.8** (619.3 km) First crossing of **West Fork Blackstone River**. Watch for arctic terns. Good fishing for Dolly Varden and grayling a short distance downstream where the west and east forks of the Blackstone join to form the Blackstone River, which the road now follows. After the river crossing, 2 low, cone-shaped mounds called pingos are visible upriver about 5 miles/8 km. ✏

J 72.1 (116 km) **I 384** (618 km) Turnout to west with litter bins. View over **Chapman Lake**, one of the few lakes close to the highway that is large enough to permit floatplane operations. The lake is named for Ernest Chapman, a local trader, trapper and prospector. Common loons nest on island. Commemorative road sign about sled dog patrols of the Royal North West Mounted Police.

Porcupine caribou herd sometimes crosses the highway in this area in mid-October.

J 74.8 (120.3 km) **I 381.3** (613.6 km) Northern boundary of Tombstone Territorial Park.

J 77.3 (124.4 km) **I 378.8** (609.6 km) **Private Aircraft**: Government airstrip (road is part of the strip); elev. 3,100 feet/945m; length 3,000 feet/914m.

J 87 (140 km) **I 369.1** (594 km) Note black or reddish hematite in the pale limestone to the west. When cut and polished, black hematite is known as Alaskan black diamond.

J 95 (153 km) **I 361.1** (581.1 km) Northbound, highway crosses Windy Pass Summit at the start of the Northern Ogilvie Mountains. This is part of eastern Beringia, which escaped glaciation during the Ice Age and allowed refuge for plant and animal species, such as a certain moth species not found anywhere else.

J 99.1 (159.6 km) **I 357** (574.5 km) Highway crosses Engineer Creek. (Engineer Creek Campground is 21.4 miles north of here.)

J 104.4 (168 km) **I 351.7** (566 km) Northbound, the highway travels through a highly mineralized area for the next several miles. Water percolates through limestone, gypsum, salt- and sulfide-bearing sediments, which when dissolved color the water and earth in reds and orange-brown hues. The distinctive smell is from the aptly-named Sulfur Springs nearby. *Do not drink creek water!*

Watch for wildlife at Tombstone Range Viewpoint, Milepost J 46. (©Sharon Nault)

Erosional features like these rock outcroppings are found along the Dempster. *(©Sharon Nault)*

Note the red shale on the hillsides. The color is a result of iron oxide in the rock.

J 120.4 (193.8 km) **I 335.7** (540.2 km) **Engineer Creek Yukon Government Campground**; 15 sites, camping fee $12, fireplaces, firewood, water, picnic tables, pit toilets, screened kitchen shelter with stove and tables. Grayling fishing.

Sapper Hill rises to the west, across Engineer Creek from the campground. It is a massive hill of dolomite exhibiting huge and interesting rock formations. It was named in 1971 in honour of the 3rd Royal Canadian Engineers who built the Ogilvie River bridge. "Sapper" is a nickname for an army engineer.

J 121.2 (195 km) **I 334.9** (539 km) Engineer Creek bridge. Look for fossil coral in limestone outcrops northeast of bridge.

J 121.5 (195.5 km) **I 334.6** (538.5 km) The 360-foot/110-m Ogilvie River Bridge (metal decking), also called Jeckell Bridge. Built by the Canadian Armed Forces Engi-

neers as a training exercise, it is named in honour of Allan Jeckell, controller of the Yukon from 1932 to 1946. The Ogilvie River and Ogilvie Mountains were named in honour of William Ogilvie, a highly respected Dominion land surveyor and commissioner of the Yukon during the Klondike Gold Rush.

For the next 25 miles/40 km northbound, the highway follows the narrow valley of the Ogilvie River. Good views of unglaciated, castlelike outcroppings of rock, known as tors, on mountain to north. Also watch for bird nests in the shale embankments along the highway.

J 137.5 (221.2 km) **I 318.6** (512.7 km) Elephant Rock turnout to east with litter barrels. Elephant Rock is on distant mountain ridge—use binoculars. Easy access to **Ogilvie River**; good grayling fishing.

J 137.6 (221.5 km) **I 318.5** (512.6 km) Davies Creek.

J 138.9 (223.6 km) **I 317.2** (510.5 km) Begin avalanche area northbound.

J 139.2 (224 km) **I 316.9** (510 km) Churchwood Hill. Fascinating mountain—last of the Ogilvie Mountains northbound—of broken rock and shale. The Gwich'in call this Beaver House Mountain because they say a giant beaver occupied this mountain during Beringia. (Beringia refers to a large, ice-free land area that occurred during the last ice age in northern Yukon and Alaska.)

Dolomite cliff faces along road. Look for peregrine falcon nests.

J 140 (225.3 km) **I 316.1** (508.7 km) End avalanche area northbound.

J 147.3 (237 km) **I 308.8** (497 km) Ogilvie airstrip. The great gray owl, one of Canada's largest owls, is known to nest as far north as this area. These impressive birds may be seen hunting during the day.

J 151.4 (243.6 km) **I 304.7** (490.4 km) Northbound sign reads: "Welcome, you are now entering Vuntut Gwitchin Settlement Lands."

J 152 (244.6 km) **I 304.1** (489.4 km) Highway climbs Seven Mile Hill, the escarpment of the Eagle Plain plateau. The road

continues to follow a high ridge (elev. 1,969 feet/600m), with broad sweeps and easy grades, crossing the continental divide for a second time northbound. Waters on the southeast side of the road flow to the Beaufort Sea; waters on the northwest side of the road flow to the Bering Sea.

This is one of the few unglaciated areas in Canada, with a landscape shaped by wind and water erosion rather than by ice. Views of Mount Cronkhite and Mount McCullum to the east.

Overgrown seismic lines next 62 miles/100 km are a reminder that this was the major area of oil and gas exploration activity for which the road was originally built.

J 160.9 (259 km) **I 295.2** (475 km) Panoramic **Ogilvie Ridge/Gwazhal Kak Viewpoint** is a large double-ended turnout with interpretive panels on the geology of the area; outhouse, litter barrels. Lowbush cranberries in August.

J 168.9 (271.8 km) **I 287.2** (462.2 km) Large turnout and microwave tower to west. Highway begins descent northbound and crosses fabulous high rolling country above tree line. In season, fields of cotton grass and varieties of tundra plants make good photo subjects.

J 187.7 (302 km) **I 268.4** (431.9 km) Evidence of forest fire which burned more than 5,500 hectares/13,590 acres in July 1991.

J 192.6 (310 km) **I 263.5** (424 km) Distance marker southbound shows Dawson City 346 km/215 miles, Whitehorse 804 km/500 miles.

J 201.6 (324.5 km) **I 254.5** (409.6 km) Double-ended turnout with litter barrels and outhouses. Road widens to become part of an airstrip.

J 215.6 (347 km) **I 240.5** (387 km) Richardson Mountains, to the northeast, extend to the Arctic coast on the west side of the Mackenzie Delta.

The thick blanket of rock and gravel that makes up the roadbed ahead is designed to prevent the underlying permafrost from melting. The roadbed conducts heat more than the surrounding vegetation does and must be extra thick to compensate. Much of the highway was built in winter.

J 224.8 (361.8 km) **I 231.3** (372.2 km) Distance marker northbound shows Eagle Plains Lodge 7 km/4 miles, Inuvik 379 km/236 miles.

J 229.3 (369 km) **I 226.8** (365 km) **Mile 231. EAGLE PLAINS** (pop. approx. 8); **Eagle Plains Hotel** and large parking area. Eagle Plains Hotel offers food, bar, gas, diesel, propane, tire repair, lodging, camping. Open year-round. See the collection of historical photographs in the hotel. Full caribou mount in bar area. An interesting and cozy stop for travelers.

Eagle Plains Hotel. Located midway on the Dempster, this year-round facil-

ity is an oasis in the wilderness. Modern hotel rooms, plus restaurant and lounge. Full camper services including electrical hookups, laundry, store, dump station, minor repairs, tires, propane and road and area information. Check out our historical photos. (867) 993-2453. Email: eagleplains@ northwestel.net. See display ad previous page. [ADVERTISEMENT]

Built in 1978, just before completion of the Dempster Highway, construction of the hotel was an engineering challenge. Engineers considered the permafrost in the area and found a place where the bedrock was at the surface. The hotel was built on this natural pad, thus avoiding the costly process of building on pilings.

J 234.9 (378 km) **I 221.2** (356 km) Eagle River bridge. Like the Ogilvie bridge, it was built by the Dept. of National Defense as a training exercise. In contrast to the other rivers seen from the Dempster, the Eagle is a more sluggish, silt-laden stream with unstable banks. It is the main drainage channel for the western slopes of the Richardson Mountains. The **Eagle River** and its tributaries provide good grayling fishing. Canoeists leave here bound for Alaska via the Porcupine and Yukon rivers.

J 239.4 (385.3 km) **I 216.7** (348.7 km) Views of the unglaciated Richardson Mountains (elev. 3,937 feet/1,200m) ahead. Named for Sir John Richardson, surgeon and naturalist on both of Sir John Franklin's overland expeditions to the Arctic Ocean.

J 241.7 (389 km) **I 214.4** (345 km) **Private Aircraft:** Emergency airstrip; elev. 2,365 feet/721m; length 2,500 feet/762m; gravel. Used regularly by aircraft hauling freight to Old Crow, a Vuntut Gwich'in settlement on the Porcupine River and Yukon's most northerly community.

J 252 (405.5 km) **I 204.1** (328.5 km) Large double-ended turnout at **Arctic Circle Crossing**, N 66°33'; interpretive sign, picnic tables, litter barrels, outhouses.

On June 21, the sun does not fall below the horizon for 6 weeks at this latitude.

Highway crosses arctic tundra on an elevated berm beside the Richardson Mountains; sweeping views.

J 257.3 (414 km) **I 198.8** (319.9 km) Highway passes through large open areas of tundra intermixed with islands of spruce forest. Stunning views.

Microwave tower to west.

J 257.8 (414.8 km) **I 198.3** (319.1 km) Glacier Creek.

J 261.5 (420.8 km) **I 194.6** (313.2 km) Vadzaih Kan Njik Creek (culvert), meaning "creek of the caribou den" in Gwich'in, is a favorite Native hunting site.

J 262.2 (422 km) **I 193.9** (312 km) Beaver Creek.

J 264.7 (426 km) **I 191.4** (308 km) *CAUTION: Slow for shale road surfacing.* Save your tires by not stopping too fast on sharp-edge shale. Potholes and frost heaves northbound as highway passes through soggy tundra.

J 269 (432.9 km) **I 187.1** (301.1 km) Sheep Creek.

J 276.6 (445.2 km) **I 179.5** (288.9 km) Large building to east with turnout. Interpretive boards about Porcupine caribou herd.

J 277 (445.8 km) **I 179.1** (288.2 km) **Rock River Yukon Government Campground**; 20 sites (3 pull–throughs), camping fee $12, tables, kitchen shelter, water, firepits, outhouses. *NOTE: Black flies and*

Sharon Nault and J.V. Teague at the Arctic Circle Crossing turnout, Milepost J 252.
(©Sharon Nault)

mosquitoes can be fierce; bring repellent.

J 277.4 (446.4 km) **I 178.7** (287.6 km) Highway crosses Rock River (culvert).

J 280.1 (452 km) **I 176** (283.2 km) Turnout. Highway descends northbound toward the Richardson Mountains. Good hiking area and excellent photo possibilities.

J 287.9 (463.2 km) **I 168.2** (270.7 km) Plaque about Wright Pass, named for Al Wright, a highway engineer with Public Works Canada who was responsible for the routing of the Dempster Highway.

J 288 (463.4 km) **I 168.1** (270.5 km) Turnout; good overnight spot for self-contained vehicles. View of highway to north as it climbs towards George's Gap in the Richardson Mountains near the YT–NWT border.

J 288.9 (465 km) **I 167.2** (269.1 km) **YT-NWT Border**. Historical marker. Continental Divide in the Richardson Mountains: West of here, water flows to the Pacific Ocean. East of here, water flows to the Arctic Ocean. Good photo spot. Day-use area open June 1–Sept. 1.

TIME ZONE CHANGE: Yukon Territory observes Pacific standard time; Northwest Territories is on Mountain time. Advance your clocks 1 hour.

Highway descends, road narrows, northbound.

NWT HIGHWAY 8

Distance from YT-NWT border (B) is followed by distance from junction with Klondike Highway 2 (J) and distance from Inuvik (I). *Kilometreposts northbound (white numerals on a blue background) now indicate distance from YT–NWT border.*

NOTE: The kilometre figure following the (B) in the highway log reflects the nearest physical kilometrepost along this section of the highway.

B 0 J 288.9 (465 km) **I 167.2** (269.1 km) **YT-NWT Border**. Mount Sittichinli, elev. 5,164 feet/1,574m, is 7.5 miles/12 km to the north and is the highest peak in the Richardson Mountains.

B 3.7 (6.2 km) **J 292.6** (470.9 km) **I 163.5** (263.1 km) Very large turnout to west.

Northbound, between Kilometreposts 10 and 20, the highway winds in and out of mountains characterized by massive "folds." The Vittrekwa Valley is named for a well-known Fort McPherson family.

B 8.7 (14.2 km) **J 297.6** (478.9 km) **I 158.5** (255.1 km) **James Creek**; good grayling fishing; good drinking water. Highway maintenance camp. Good spot to park overnight.

B 11.8 (19 km) **J 300.7** (483.9 km) **I 155.4** (250.1 km) Sign advises no passing next 4.3 miles/7 km; climb to Wright Pass summit.

B 14.6 (23.6 km) J 303.5 (488.4 km) **I 152.6** (245.6 km) **Wright Pass Summit**. From here northbound, the Dempster Highway descends 2,300 feet/853m to the Peel River crossing, 31 miles/50 km away.

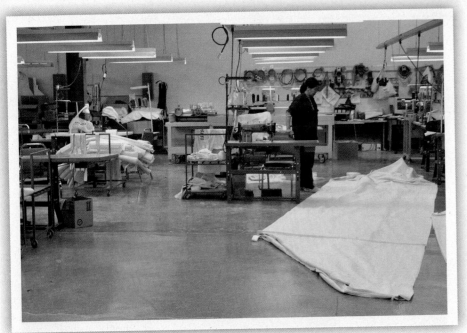

Fort McPherson Tent and Canvas factory produces wall tents, tipis, bags, backpacks and other items . *(©Sharon Nault)*

B 27.3 (44 km) **J 316.2** (508.9 km) **I 139.9** (225.1 km) Side road leads down to **Midway Lake**, site of the annual Midway Lake Music Festival held the long weekend in August.

B 29.8 (48 km) **J 318.7** (512.9 km) **I 137.4** (221.1 km) **Private Aircraft**: Highway widens to form Midway airstrip; length 3,000 feet/914m.

B 40.5 (65.2 km) **J 329.4** (530.1 km) **I 126.7** (203.9 km) **Tetlit Gwinjik Wayside** Park for Peel River Plateau viewpoint. Short walk up to viewing platform. Magnificent views of Richardson Mountains, Mackenzie Delta, Peel River Valley and Fort McPherson. Interpretive panels and litter barrels.

B 43.5 (70 km) **J 332.4** (534.9 km) **I 123.7** (199.1 km) Highway begins descent northbound to Peel River.

B 46 (74 km) **J 334.9** (539 km) **I 121.2** (195 km) **Peel River Crossing**, locally called Eight Mile because it is situated 8 miles/12.8 km south of Fort McPherson. Free government ferry (CF *Abraham Francis*) operates approximately 15 hours a day (9 A.M.–1 A.M.) from late May or early June to mid-October or first week in November. The *Abraham Francis* is a double-ended cable ferry: Drive on, drive off. Light vehicles cross by ice bridge in late November; heavier vehicles cross as ice thickens. *No crossing possible during freezeup or breakup.* Phone toll free

1-800-661-0750 for information on ferry crossings, road conditions and weather. Historically, opening dates have ranged from May 22 to June 10, while closing dates have ranged from October 20 to November 5.

The level of the Peel River changes rapidly in spring and summer in response to meltwater from the mountains and ice jams on the Mackenzie River. *Extreme high and low water level fluctuations may cause delays in ferry service.*

Natives from Fort McPherson have summer tent camps on the Peel River. The Indians net whitefish and sheefish (inconnu) then dry them on racks or in smokehouses for the winter. The alluvial flood plain is covered by muskeg on the flats, and scrubby alder and stunted black spruce on the valley sides.

About 4 miles/6.4 km south upstream is a trail leading to Shiltee (or Shildee) Rock, which gives excellent views of the Peel River and the southern end of the Mackenzie.

B 47.1 (75.8 km) **J 336** (540.7 km) **I 120.1** (193.3 km) **Nitainlaii Territorial Park Interpretive Centre** to west, open 12 hours a day from June 1 to September 1. Exhibits and displays show Gwich'in traditional ways of life. Name is from the Gwich'in term *Noo-til-ee*, meaning "water flowing out in all directions."

Nitainlaii Territorical Park Camp-

ground adjacent with 23 campsites. Camping permits, potable water, firewood, pit toilets, shower building and kitchen shelter available. For reservations visit www.camp ingnwt.ca.

B 51.7 (83.4 km) **J 340.6** (548.1 km) **I 115.5** (185.9 km) Access road right to Fort McPherson airport.

B 53 (85.5 km) **J 341.9** (550.2 km) **I 114.2** (183.8 km) **Junction** with access road to Fort McPherson (Tetl'it Zheh); description follows.

Fort McPherson

Located on a flat-topped hill about 100 feet/30m above the Peel River, 24 miles/38 km from its junction with the Mackenzie River; 100 miles/160 km southwest of Aklavik by boat along Peel Channel, 31 miles/50 km directly east of the Richardson Mountains. **Population**: 791. **Emergency Services**: RCMP, phone (867) 952-1111. **Health Centre**, phone (867) 952-2586.

Visitor Information: Contact Hamlet of Fort McPherson at Box 57, Fort McPherson, NT Canada X0E 0J0; phone (867) 952-2428; fax (867) 952-2725. Or visit www.spectacu larnwt.com. **Radio**: CBC 680.

Transportation: Air—Aklak Air provides scheduled air service from Inuvik during breakup and freezeup.

Private Aircraft: Fort McPherson airstrip; N 67°24', W 134°51'; elev. 142 feet/43m; length 3,500 feet/1,067m; gravel.

This Dene Indian settlement has a public phone, cafe; 2 general stores and 2 service stations with gas and diesel; craft store; a tent and canvas factory (tours are possible, phone ahead 867/952-2179) and a tire repair shop. A co-op hotel here offers 8 rooms. **Fort McPherson Tent and Canvas** factory produces a variety of "Arctic tough" canvas items.

Fort McPherson was named in 1848 for Murdoch McPherson, chief trader of the Hudson's Bay Co., which had established its first posts in the area 8 years before. Between 1849 and 1859 there were frequent feuds with neighboring Inuit, who later moved farther north to the Aklavik area, where they established a fur-trading post.

In addition to subsistence fishing and hunting, income is earned from trapping (mostly muskrat and mink), handicrafts, government employment, and commercial enterprises.

Photos and artifacts depicting the history and way of life of the community are displayed in the Chief Julius School. **The Lost Patrol Gravesite** is in the cemetery outside the Anglican church. Buried there are Inspector Francis J. Fitzgerald and 3 men from the ill-fated North West Mounted Police patrol of 1910–1911 between Fort McPherson and Dawson. A plaque inside the church commemorates the Lost Patrol. The original church, St. Matthew's, was built in 1860. It was replaced about 100 years later by the present-day church.

Inspector Fitzgerald and the men had left Fort McPherson on Dec. 21, 1910, carrying mail and dispatches to Dawson City. By Feb. 20, 1911, the men had not yet arrived in Dawson, nearly a month overdue. A search party led by Corporal W.J.D. Dempster was sent to look for the missing patrol. On

March 22, 1911, Dempster discovered their frozen bodies only 26 miles from where they had started. Lack of knowledge of the trail, coupled with too few rations, had doomed the 4-man patrol. One of the last entries in Fitzgerald's diary, quoted in Dick North's *The Lost Patrol*, an account of their journey, read: "We have now only 10 pounds of flour and 8 pounds of bacon and some dried fish. My last hope is gone. ... We have been a week looking for a river to take us over the divide, but there are dozens of rivers, and I am at a loss."

Fort McPherson Tent and Canvas. See display ad on facing page.

Dempster Highway Log
(continued)

B 66.4 (106.8 km) **J 355.3** (571.8 km) **I 100.8** (162.2 km) Microwave tower to west.

B 68.4 (110 km) **J 357.3** (575 km) **I 98.8** (159 km) Highway passes through area of numerous lakes and densely forested terrain, a change due to the more productive conditions provided by the lower elevation, nutrient-rich soil and warmer climate of the Mackenzie River Delta.

B 76.1 (122.5 km) **J 365** (587.4 km) **I 91.1** (146.6 km) **Frog Creek.** Grayling and pike. Road on right northbound leads to picnic area.

B 88.2 (142 km) **J 377.1** (606.8 km) **I 79** (127.1 km) View of the confluence of the Arctic Red and Mackenzie rivers.

B 89 (143.2 km) **J 377.9** (608.2 km) **I 78.2** (125.8 km) **Mackenzie River Crossing.** Free government ferry (MV *Louis Cardinal*) operates approximately 15 hours a day (8:15 A.M. to 11:15 P.M.) from early June to late October. Double-ended ferry: Drive on, drive off. Light vehicles may cross by ice bridge in late November; heavier vehicles can cross as ice thickens.

No crossing possible during freezeup and breakup. Motorcycles should be especially careful in this area due to dust and gravel (low visibility). Always drive with headlights on!

The ferry travels between landings on either side of the Mackenzie River and also provides access to **TSIIGEHTCHIC**, formerly **ARCTIC RED RIVER**, a small Gwichya Gwich'in community (pop. about 200) located at the confluence of the Mackenzie and Arctic Red rivers (visible from ferry landing). Tsiigehtchic has a grocery store, post office and pay phone.

The Arctic Red River (Tsiigehnjik) was declared a Canadian Heritage River in 1993. Tsiigehnjik, the Gwich'in name for the river, winds its way out of the Mackenzie Mountains and flows into the Mackenzie River at Tsiigehtchic. The Gwichya Gwich'in have long used and traveled the river for fishing, hunting and trapping.

B 110.7 (178.1 km) **J 399.6** (643 km) **I 56.5** (90.9 km) **Rengling River**, picnic area with good grayling fishing.

B 114 (183.5 km) **J 402.9** (648.4 km) **I 53.2** (85.6 km) Microwave tower to east.

B 115.3 (185.5 km) **J 404.2** (650.4 km) **I 51.9** (83.5 km) Begin of 13-mile/21-km stretch of straight highway northbound.

B 118.3 (190.3 km) **J 407.2** (655.2 km) **I 48.9** (78.7 km) Highway crosses Neilo Creek.

B 119.5 (192.3 km) **J 408.4** (657.2 km) **I 47.7** (76.8 km) Lynx Creek.

B 120.7 (194.3 km) **J 409.6** (659.2 km) **I 46.5** (74.8 km) Distance marker north-

The MV Louis Cardinal carries passengers and vehicles across the Mackenzie River.
(©Sharon Nault)

bound shows Inuvik 75 km/47 miles.

B 137.1 (220.7 km) **J 426** (685.6 km) **I 30.1** (48.4 km) **Vadzaih Van Tsik Campground**; tables, 11 campsites, firewood, firepits, barbecue pits and toilets. Adjacent to Caribou Creek. ▲

B 137.3 (220.9 km) **J 426.2** (685.8 km) **I 29.9** (48.1 km) Caribou Creek bridge. Day-use area to east at north end of bridge.

B 143.9 (231.5 km) **J 432.8** (696.4 km) **I 23.3** (37.5 km) Benoit Lake (sign).

B 144.3 (232.3 km) **J 433.2** (697.2 km) **I 22.9** (36.9 km) **Titheqehchii Vitail Lookout** to west; parking. Very scenic 10-minute walk to viewing platform with information signs overlooking Campbell Lake.

B 145 (233.4 km) **J 433.9** (698.3 km) **I 22.2** (35.7 km) View of Campbell Lake to west.

B 145.6 (234.3 km) **J 434.5** (699.2 km) **I 21.6** (34.8 km) **Gwich'in Territorial Campground**; 15 non-powered RV sites and 4 tent sites. firepits, kitchen shelter and toilets. Beach access to Campbell Lake. ▲

B 151.6 (244 km) **J 440.5** (708.9 km) **I 15.6** (25.1 km) **Ehjuu Njik Wayside Park**; picnic tables, firepits, firewood, pit toilets. Arctic grayling fishing in Cabin Creek.

B 153.5 (247 km) **J 442.4** (711.9 km) **I 13.7** (22 km) **Nihtak Wayside** on north side of road by Campbell Creek; 8 picnic sites with firewood, tables, firepits and toilets. Boat launch on south side of highway. Creek flows a short distance to **Campbell Lake**. *Bring mosquito repellent.* Good fishing for pike and whitefish, some sheefish (inconnu).

B 161 (259.2 km) **J 450** (724.1 km) **I 6.1** (9.8 km) Airport Road turnoff.
Pavement begins northbound.

B 164.9 (265.4 km) **J 453.8** (730.3 km) **I 2.3** (3.7 km) **Jak Territorial Park**; 36 campsites, 6 pull-through, 24-hour reception and security, kitchen shelter, playground, fire-

wood, water, showers, nightly fee (reservations at www.campingnwt.ca); canoe launch and walking trails. Lookout tower for views of Mackenzie River Delta and the Richardson Mountains. Interpretive information available. Area offers good bird watching and berry picking. Jak is the Gwich'in word for "berry." ▲

B 167.2 (269.1 km) **J 456.1** (734 km) **I 0** Turn left northbound for Inuvik town centre via Mackenzie Road (description follows). Nova Inn at junction.

Inuvik

Situated on a flat wooded plateau on the east channel of the Mackenzie River, some 60 air miles/96 km south of the Beaufort Sea, 36 air miles/58 km and 70 water miles/113 km from Aklavik on the western edge of the delta. **Population**: 3,430, Dene, White and Inuvialuit. **Emergency Services**: RCMP, phone (867) 777-1111. **Hospital**, Inuvik Regional, phone (867) 777-8000. **Ambulance**, (867) 777-4444. **Fire Department**, (867) 777-2222.

Visitor Information: Western Arctic Regional Visitors Centre is located on Mackenzie Road across from the hospital; phone (867) 777-7237. The centre is open mid-May to mid-September, 9 A.M.–7 P.M. daily, and features interactive displays, excellent wildlife displays, clean restrooms and knowledgeable staff.

Stop by to sign the guest book and pick up a certificate of the Arctic Circle "Order of Arctic Adventurers." Also ask about Inuvik's "Tourist of the Week" program, or check it out at www.inuvik.ca/tourism. Look for the large log signs at entrance (as you come into town). Contact the Town of Inuvik, #2 Firth St., Box 1160, Inuvik, Northwest Territories X0E 0T0;

phone (867) 777-8600; fax (867) 777-8601. Or visit www.inuvik.ca or www.inuvikinfo.com. Email info@town.inuvik.nt.ca.

Elevation: 224 feet/68m. **Climate:** May 24 marks 57 days of midnight sun. The sun begins to set on July 19; on Dec. 6, the sun sets and does not rise until Jan. 6. Average annual precipitation 4 inches rainfall, 69 inches snowfall. July mean high 67°F/19°C, mean low 45°F/7°C. January mean high is -11°F/-24°C, mean low is -30°F/-35°C. **Radio and Television:** CBC and local. **Newspaper:** *The Drum* (weekly).

Private Aircraft: Mike Zubko Airport (daily jet service) 8 miles/ 14 km from city; elev. 220 feet/67m; length 6,000 feet/1,829m; asphalt; fuel 80, 100.

Inuvik, meaning "The Place of Man," is the largest Canadian community north of the Arctic Circle, and the major government, transportation and communication centre for Canada's western Arctic. Construction of the town began in 1955 and was completed in 1961.

Inuvik is constructed on permafrost, so a unique utilidor system carries water, sewage and heating systems between buildings. Inquire at the Visitor Centre about utilidor and permafrost exhibits.

Inuvik was the main supply base for the petrochemical exploration of the delta until Tuktoyaktuk took over that role as activity centered in the Beaufort Sea. In Inuvik, some hunting, fishing and trapping is done, but most people earn wages in government and private enterprises, particularly in transportation, tourism and construction. As the delta is one of the richest muskrat areas in the world, Inuvik is the western centre for shipping furs south.

The town's official monument says, in part, that Inuvik was "the first community north of the Arctic Circle built to provide the normal facilities of a Canadian town." There is a post office, territorial liquor store, a library, a bank (CIBC) and churches. Inuvik also has one of the most northerly mosques in the world, brought here by road and river from Manitoba. There are 2 gas stations with gas, diesel and car wash; propane, auto repair and towing are available. The town has a hardware, grocery, general stores, gift shops and a pharmacy.

Recreation includes a community driving range and an indoor pool with water slide. The pool is attached to the Midnight Sun Complex, which includes a fitness centre and hockey and curling rinks.

Transportation

Air: Inuvik Airport is a transportation hub for the western Arctic. Licensed operators provide scheduled services between Inuvik and Tuktoyaktuk, Sachs Harbour, Paulatuk and Ulukhaktok (formerly Holman). Regional carriers are Canadian North and First Air North from Edmonton and Calgary, AB and Yellowknife, NWT. Air North provides scheduled service to and from Whitehorse, Dawson City and Old Crow, YT and Fairbanks, AK. Several air charter services operate out of Inuvik, offering flights to delta communities and charter service for hunting, fishing and camping trips.

Highways: Dempster Highway, open all year. Winter roads to Aklavik (73 miles/117 km) and Tuktoyaktuk (121 miles/194 km).

24-hr. emergency roadside assistance, phone (867) 777-4747 or 678-5410 after hours.

Bus: MGM Services offers on-demand bus service to and from Inuvik; call (867) 777-4295 for information.

Taxi: United Taxi at (867) 777-5050; Delta Cabs at (867) 777-5100.

Lodging & Services

Accommodations at **Capital Suites** (1-877-669-9444), **Mackenzie Hotel** (867/777-2861), **Arctic Chalet** (800-685-9417) and Nova Inn. Mackenzie Hotel has a restaurant and lounge. There are also fast-food outlets (at the North Mart), a burger place, 2 Chinese take-outs, a cafe, and dining at the hospital cafeteria, the Royal Canadian Legion (lunch), the Midnight Sun Recreation Complex and the Inuvik airport.

Arctic Chalet and Arctic Adventure Tours. Experience something uniquely Northern. Charming log home and full-service cabins and 1 honeymoon cabin in a beautiful lakeside setting on the edge of Inuvik. Wireless Internet, telephone and satellite TV; kitchenettes with breakfast foods. Walking trails. Specializing in tours to Tuktoyaktuk and Herschel Island and much more. www.arcticchalet.com; Phone (867) 777-3535; 1-800-685-9417. [ADVERTISEMENT]

Mackenzie Hotel, centrally located in Inuvik. After roaming the Dempster, you'll enjoy our special touch of Northern hospitality in Inuvik's only full-service hotel. Telephone, cable, Internet, laundry service, in-house movies, fitness centre, business centre, Jacuzzi suites, licensed dining, lounge, banquet rooms. 185 Mackenzie

Road. Email: mackenziehotel@northwestel. net. Phone (867) 777-2861; Fax (867) 777-3317. [ADVERTISEMENT]

Camping

Happy Valley Territorial Campground overlooking the east channel of the Mackenzie River is named for the mood of the place when it was a tent camp during the construction of Inuvik in the 1950s. Services include 24-hour reception and security; 36 sites, some with electrical hookups and some overlooking the Mackenzie River; hot showers, laundromat, firewood, water; fee charged. Located at the terminus of the Dempster Highway and open June 1–Sept. 1. Phone (867) 777-3652.

Attractions

Swim above the Arctic Circle (indoors) at the Inuvik Family Centre. A favorite stop for our field editors after the long drive. The facility includes a leisure pool, lane pool, hot tub, steam room, sauna, squash courts, kids' play zone, and the Arctic's only waterslide (190 feet long). Adult swims scheduled. Phone (867) 777-8640; http://inuvik.ca/ living-in-inuvik/recreation-facilities/inuvik-family-centre/.

The **Mackenzie River Delta**, second largest delta in North America (one of the tenth largest in the world) and an important wildlife corridor to the Arctic, is 40 miles/64 km wide and 60 miles/97 km long. A maze of lakes, channels and islands, the delta supports a variety of bird life, fish and muskrats. Boat tours of the Mackenzie River are available.

Igloo Church, The most photographed landmark in Inuvik, Our Lady of Victory Roman Catholic Church or "the Igloo Church" owes its distinctive architecture and construction to a community effort over the course of 2 years. Completed in 1958, the Igloo Church's interior is decorated with stations of the cross painted by one of the Delta's most famous Inuvialuit artists, Mona Thrasher. Visitors are welcome and tours are offered in the summer months. 174 Mackenzie Rd., phone (867) 777-2236.

Inuvik Community Greenhouse is the most northerly greenhouse in Canada and serves as a model for other northern communities. Created by the Community Gardening Society of Inuvik as a focus point for community development, the greenhouse allows for production of a greater variety of crops in an area where fresh (and affordable) produce is often unavailable. Open from June to September, check at the visitor center for tour times.

Great Northern Arts Festival. More than 100 artists and performers—Inuit, Inuvialuit, Gwich'in, Dene, Metis and non-Native—gather for 10 days every summer for a festival under the midnight sun. Carvers, print-makers, painters, jewellers and sewers create works of art as visitors look on. Meet the artists, enjoy scheduled art workshops or choose from works of art in the gallery. Eve-

Inuvik's most photographed landmark is Our Lady of Victory church. (©Sharon Nault)

nings are full of music, dance, story-telling and fashion shows showcasing the diverse cultures of the North. Scheduled for July 11-20, 2014. For more information contact the Great Northern Arts Festival, Box 2921, Inuvik, NT X0E 0T0; phone (867) 777-8638; email gnaf@inuvik.ca; www.gnaf.org.

Ingamo Hall Friendship Centre is a 2-story log community hall that serves the social and recreational needs of Native families. Visitors are welcome. The hall was built by Allan Crich over a 3-year period, using some 850 logs that were cut from white spruce trees in the southern part of the Mackenzie River valley and floated down the river to Inuvik. Phone (867) 777-2166.

Go for a hike on one of the area's walking trails. Jimmy Adams Peace Trail follows a loop around Boot Lake. Hiking is also available on local ski trails and at Jak Park. Pick up a map at the Visitor Centre.

Take a Tour. Fly out to one of the following destinations with a local tour operator:

TUKTOYAKTUK (pop. 956), or "Tuk," is an Inuit village on the Arctic coast and site of oil development (also accessible by ice road in winter). Tuk boasts a Pingo boardwalk so visitors can get a good look at those odd conical hills that push up out of the Arctic tundra.

AKLAVIK (pop. 629), located 36 miles/58 km west of Inuvik by air, is an important centre for muskrat harvesting and is also the final restiing place of Albert Johnson, "The Mad Trapper of Rat River." Something of a mystery man, Johnson killed one mounted policeman and wounded another in 2 separate incidents involving complaints that Johnson was tampering with Native trap lines. The ensuing manhunt became famous in the North, as Johnson eluded Mounties for 48 days during the winter of 1931–32. Johnson was killed in a shoot-out on Feb. 17, 1932.

Ivvavik National Park. According to Parks Canada, Ivvavik—which means "a place for giving birth, a nursery"—is the first national park in Canada to be created as a result of an aboriginal land claim agreement. The park protects a portion of the calving grounds of the Porcupine caribou herd and represents the Northern Yukon and Mackenzie Delta natural regions. Popular visitor destinations within the park, which offers a unique Arctic landscape, include the Firth River and Babbage Falls. Phone 867-777-8800 about a guided 4-day visit.

Deh Cho Route

CONNECTS: Grimshaw, AB, to the Alaska Highway via Northwest Territories

Length: 795 miles   **Road Surface: 60% Paved, 40% Gravel**   **Season: Open all year**

35 49 2 1 2 3 4 5 6 7 77

Completed in 2013, the Mackenzie River Bridge replaced the summer ferry and winter ice bridge on Highway 3 to Yellowknife. (©William Helms)

Distance in miles	Alaska Hwy.	Ft. Resolution	Ft. Simpson	Ft. Smith	Grimshaw	Yellowknife
Alaska Hwy.		563	282	636	795	596
Ft. Resolution	563		357	185	459	389
Ft. Simpson	282	357		430	588	390
Ft. Smith	636	185	430		532	462
Grimshaw	795	459	588	532		620
Yellowknife	596	389	390	462	620	

Named after the Mackenzie River—Deh Cho is Slavey Dene for "big river"— the Deh Cho route is a 795-mile/1,279-km wilderness loop connecting Grimshaw in the Peace River region of northern Alberta with the Alaska Highway in British Columbia by way of the Mackenzie River region of Northwest Territories. The Deh Cho also provides access to an additional 700 miles/1,127 km of Northwest Territories' road system.

Pick up a Deh Cho Travel Connection Passport and collect stamps when you travel this route. For more information, visit www. DehChoTravel.ca or phone 1-800-661-0788.

This route begins for northbound travelers on the EAST ACCESS ROUTE in either Grande Prairie or Valleyview. The Grande Prairie route (via Alberta Highway 2) leads 108 miles/174 km north via historic Dunvegan to Grimshaw and Alberta Highway 35 (the Mackenzie Highway) to Northwest Territories. The Valleyview route (via Alberta Highways 49 and 2) leads 101 miles/163 km north to connect with Alberta Highway 35/ Mackenzie Highway. (The official Deh Cho route offers a loop route that includes the distance between Grande Prairie to Dawson Creek; if you choose to follow that portion, turn to the EAST ACCESS ROUTE for a log of those miles.)

From the Alberta/NWT border, the Deh Cho Route continues north and west as NWT Highway 1 (the Waterfalls Route) to Checkpoint and the junction with the Liard Trail (NWT Highway 7/BC Highway 77). The Deh Cho "loop" is completed as the

Major Attractions:

© Judy Nadon, staff

Waterfalls, Fort Vermilion/La Crete, Nahanni & Wood Buffalo National Parks, Great Slave Lake, Mackenzie River

Deh Cho Route Grimshaw, AB, to Alaska Hwy, BC via NWT Highways

© 2014 The MILEPOST®

Principal Route Logged
Paved · · · Unpaved

Other Roads Logged

Other Roads · · · **Ferry Routes**

Key to Advertiser Services
C -Camping
D -Dump Station
d -Diesel
G -Gas (reg., unld.)
I -Ice
L -Lodging
M -Meals
P -Propane
R -Car Repair (major)
r -Car Repair (minor)
S -Store (grocery)
T -Telephone (pay)

Scale
0 — 20 Miles
0 — 20 Kilometres

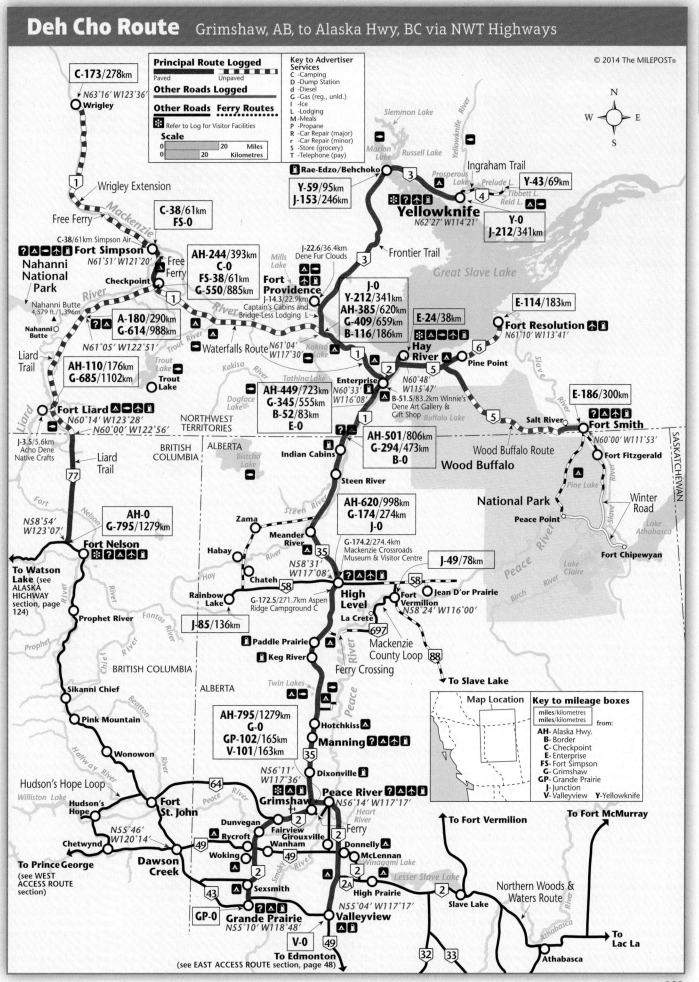

C-173/278km
N63°16' W123°36'
Wrigley

1
Wrigley Extension
Free Ferry
Mackenzie

C-38/61km
FS-0

C-38/61km Simpson Air
Fort Simpson
N61°51' W121°20'
Free Ferry

AH-244/393km
C-0
FS-38/61km
G-550/885km

Nahanni National Park
Nahanni Butte 4,579 ft./1,396m

Checkpoint
1

Fort Providence
Captain's Cabins and Bridge-Less Lodging L
J-14.3/22.9km

J-22.6/36.4km Dene Fur Clouds

Mills Lake

Slemmon Lake
Russell Lake
Marion Lake

3
Prosperous Lake
Ingraham Trail
Prelude L.
4
Tibbett L.
Reid L.

Y-43/69km

Y-59/95km
J-153/246km

Yellowknife
N62°27' W114°21'

Y-0
J-212/341km

Frontier Trail

Great Slave Lake

A-180/290km
G-614/988km
N61°05' W122°51'

Liard Trail
River

Nahanni Butte

AH-110/176km
G-685/1102km

Trout Lake

Kakisa River
Tathlina Lake

Dogface Lake

Kakisa Lake
N61°04' W117°30'
Waterfalls Route

1

J-0
Y-212/341km
AH-385/620km
G-409/659km
B-116/186km

E-24/38km

Hay River
N60°48' W115°47'
2

E-114/183km
Fort Resolution
N61°10' W113°41'

6
Pine Point
5

Slave River

E-186/300km

Enterprise
N60°33' W116°08'

B-51.5/83.2km Winnie's Dene Art Gallery & Gift Shop

Buffalo Lake

5
Salt River
Fort Smith
N60°00' W111°53'

AH-449/723km
G-345/555km
B-52/83km
E-0

AH-501/806km
G-294/473km
B-0

Wood Buffalo Route
Wood Buffalo
National Park

Fort Fitzgerald

Winter Road

Peace Point
Pine Lake
Lake Athabasca

Fort Liard
N60°14' W123°28'
N60°00' W122°56'

NORTHWEST TERRITORIES
ALBERTA
BRITISH COLUMBIA

Indian Cabins

Steen River

Bistcho Lake

77

J-3.5/5.6km Acho Dene Native Crafts
Liard Trail

Liard

Fort Nelson
N58°54' W123°07'

AH-0
G-795/1279km

To Watson Lake (see ALASKA HIGHWAY section, page 124)

Prophet River

Sikanni Chief

Pink Mountain

Wonowon

Hudson's Hope Loop
Williston Lake

Hudson's Hope
N55°46' W120°14'
64

Chetwynd
To Prince George (see WEST ACCESS ROUTE section)

Fort St. John

Dawson Creek

49
43
2

Zama

AH-620/998km
G-174/274km
J-0

Meander River
35
N58°31' W117°08'
G-174.2/274.4km Mackenzie Crossroads Museum & Visitor Centre

Habay

Chateh
58

Rainbow Lake

J-85/136km

G-172.5/271.7km Aspen Ridge Campground C

High Level

La Crete

Paddle Prairie
Keg River

Ferry Crossing

Twin Lakes

AH-795/1279km
G-0
GP-102/165km
V-101/163km

Hotchkiss
Manning

35

Dixonville
N56°11' W117°36'

Grimshaw
Peace River
N56°14' W117°17'

Dunvegan
Rycroft
2
Fairview
Girouxville
Wanham

Woking
49
Sexsmith
2
43
GP-0
Grande Prairie
N55°10' W118°48'

V-0
49
To Edmonton
(see EAST ACCESS ROUTE section, page 48)

Ferry
Donnelly
McLennan
2
Winagami Lake
High Prairie
2A
N55°04' W117°17'
Valleyview

J-49/78km

Fort Vermilion
N58°24' W116°00'
Jean D'or Prairie
58

697
Mackenzie County Loop
88
To Slave Lake

Peace River
Birch River
Lake Claire

Fort Chipewyan

Slave Lake
Northern Woods & Waters Route
Athabasca River
2

32
33
Athabasca
To Lac La

To Fort Vermilion
To Fort McMurray

Lesser Slave Lake

Map Location

Key to mileage boxes
miles/kilometres
miles/kilometres from:
AH - Alaska Hwy.
B - Border
C - Checkpoint
E - Enterprise
FS - Fort Simpson
G - Grimshaw
GP - Grande Prairie
J - Junction
V - Valleyview
Y - Yellowknife

A free ferry crosses the Liard River on Highway 1 to Fort Simpson.
(©Judy Nadon, staff)

Liard Trail junctions with the Alaska Highway about 17 miles/27 km north of Fort Nelson, BC.

Connecting routes in Northwest Territories logged in this section (and considered Deh Cho sidetrips) include the Heritage Route (Highway 1) from Checkpoint to Fort Simpson and Wrigley; Great Slave Route (Highways 2 and 6) from Enterprise to Hay River and Fort Resolution; Wood Buffalo Route (Highway 5) from its junction with Highway 6 south to Fort Smith; and the Frontier Trail (Highway 3) from its junction with Highway 1 to Yellowknife.

Road conditions range from 2-lane paved highway in Alberta and on NWT Highways 1 and 3 to Yellowknife to mostly gravel with some paved sections on NWT Highway 1 to Wrigley, NWT Highways 2 and 5 to Fort Smith, and NWT Highway 6 to Fort Resolution. An asphalt paving program is under way on the remaining gravel portions of Northwest Territories highways. The Liard Trail, a relatively straight 2-lane road, is gravel in Northwest Territories and chipseal/pavement in British Columbia.

Gravel road can be muddy when wet and dusty when dry. "Dust-free zones" on gravel roads are treated with calcium chloride; wash your vehicle when possible. Watch for moose, black bear, wood bison and grouse along the road.

The NWT government provides free summer ferry service for cars and passengers across the Liard River to Fort Simpson and across the Mackenzie River to Wrigley. In winter, traffic crosses on the ice. For current crossing information and road conditions, phone 1-800-661-0750 or visit www.dot.gov.nt.ca. For visitor information on travel in Northwest Territories, phone 1-800-661-0788 or visit www.spectacularnwt.com. For camping information, locations and reservations, go to www.campingnwt.ca.

Deh Cho Route: From Valleyview

Distance from Valleyview (V) is shown.

ALBERTA HIGHWAY 49

V 0 Visitor Centre on Highway 43 in **VALLEYVIEW** (pop. 1,884). See description of Valleyview beginning on page 71 in the EAST ACCESS ROUTE section.

V 2 (3.2 km) **Junction** of Highways 43 and 49. Continue north on Highway 49.

V 4.1 (6.6 km) **Junction** with Highway 669. Turnoff to east for Sunset House (16 miles/26 km).

V 6.1 (9.8 km) Sturgeon Creek.

V 18.3 (29.4 km) New Fish Creek Road.

V 20.2 (32.5 km) **East Dollar Lake** to west; picnic tables, litter bins, toilets, boat launch. Stocked with rainbows and popular with locals for fishing.

V 26.6 (42.8 km) **Junction** with Highway 686 West.

V 28.5 (45.9 km) Little Smokey River Ski Area to west. A common sight along the road are small rectangular water ponds, called "dugouts," that are used to water stock.

V 31.3 (50.4 km) Distance marker southbound shows Valleyview 47 km/29 miles, Grande Prairie 156 km/97 miles, Edmonton 385 km/239 miles.

V 31.6 (50.8 km) **Junction** with Highway 2A east to High Prairie (32 km).

V 32.6 (54.4 km) Turnout with litter bins to east. Information board on Alberta history.

V 38.8 (62.4 km) Community of **GUY** (pop. 40), pronounced Gee, to east. Access road leads west 7 miles/11 km to Five Star Golf Course. The primary industry here is honey production.

V 44 (70.8 km) **Junction** with Highway 679 East which leads 12.4 miles/20 km to Highway 2.

V 52 (83.7 km) **Junction** of Highway 49 and 2 (**Donnelly Corners**). Continue north on Highway 2 for Peace River. Go east 3 miles/5 km for camping. Turn west for **Fahler**, Alberta's largest honey producer (an estimated 5 million lbs. annually).

The community of **DONNELLY** (pop. 177) has a restaurant, store, a library and a museum. 15 campsites west side of village (follow signs, 1.5 km via gravel road).

ALBERTA HIGHWAY 2

V 61.9 (99.6 km) Side road leads 7 miles/11 km west to **JEAN COTE** (pop. approx. 65), and 18 miles/28 km on gravel to Rainbow Trout Park and Campground; 55 sites, hookups, picnic tables, shelter, firewood, playground, rentals cabins, mini-golf, horseshoe pits. Camping fee.

V 68.1 (109.6 km) ACC Road leads east 5.6 miles/9 km to Reno.

V 71.7 (115.4 km) **NAMPA** (pop. 372) visitor centre and museum to west (open June–September daily, 10 A.M.–5 P.M., donations appreciated); phone 780-322-3852, www.nampa.ca. Nampa was founded in 1917 when the East Dunvegan and BC Railway Company built a line through the area. Today, grain is shipped from the Great

Northern Grain terminals, located at the north side of town, south to Fahler. Visitor facilities include an inn, a motel, restaurants, grocery and retails stores; service stations with repair facilities; a library, curling rink, ball diamonds and tennis courts. Camping at Mill Brown Memorial Park, 6 sites, power hookups, walking trails.

V 72.1 (116 km) **Junction** with Highway 683 West to Highway 744 (6 miles/10 km).

V 72.7 (117 km) North Heart River bridge.

V 83.6 (134.5 km) Turnoff for Highway 688 East to St. Isadore (4.3 miles/7 km) and to junction with Highway 986 (15 miles/24 km), the main east-west route connecting Peace River to Highway 88/Red Earth Creek).

V 84.4 (135.8 km) Cecil Thompson Park; picnic area. Peace River Equestrian Centre and Fairgrounds.

V 87.6 (141 km) Turnout to east with information sign about Peace River. Rendez-Vous RV Park & Storage with 60 fully serviced sites used by crews but also open to the travelling public; phone (780) 618-1345.

Peace River

V 88.4 (142.3 km) Located on the banks of the Peace River, 15 miles/24 km northeast of Grimshaw (Mile 0 of the Mackenzie Highway), in Northern Sunrise County. **Population**: 6,240. **Emergency Services**: RCMP, Peace River Detachment, phone (780) 624-6611. **Hospital**, Peace River Community Health Care Centre (www.pchr.ca), phone (780) 624-7500. **Ambulance** and **Fire Department**, phone 911.

Visitor Information: In the NAR station at the east entrance to downtown, open mid-May to mid-September; (780) 624-4166. Online visit www.mightypeace.com.

Elevation: 1,066 feet/325m. **Private Aircraft**: Peace River airport, 6 miles/10 km west; elev. 1,873 feet/571m; length 5,000 feet/1,524m; asphalt; fuel; terminal.

An important transportation centre on the Peace River, the town of Peace River was incorporated in 1919. Today, Peace River is a centre for government services in the region. Area industry includes a pulp mill, gas and oil and farming.

Visitor facilities include 8 hotels/motels and many restaurants. Visitors will find WiFi available throughout downtown Peace River. Peace River has a Super Walmart. Camping at Lions Club Campground, phone (780) 624-4166, and at Citadel Ridge RV Park, phone (780) 618-5585, both on the west side of the river south of Highway 2.

The **Peace River Museum** on the south side of town along the river (10302–99th St.), houses archives and exhibits on Sir Alexander Mackenzie, the fur trade and local history. Open Monday to Saturday 10 A.M. to 4:30 P.M., year-round; phone (780) 624-4261. Admission fee. Website: www.peaceriver.ca; email museum@peaceriver.net.

Visitors can take a historic walking tour to various points of interest around town. The tour includes the statue of **Twelve-Foot Davis**, a gold miner who struck it rich on a 12-foot strip of land between 2 larger claims in the Cariboo gold fields.

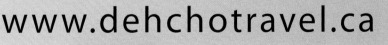

View of Dunvegan Bridge and Peace River Valley on Alberta Highway 2. (©Michael K. Robb)

Deh Cho via Valleyview Log
(continued)

V 89.2 (143.5 km) Peace River bridge.

V 90.1 (145 km) Highway 684 south to Peace River Lions Campground and to Citadel Ridge RV Park on Shaftesbury Trail.

V 91.6 (147.4 km) Turnout to south with information sign about Peace River.

V 92.9 (149.5 km) Highway descends 7 percent grade northbound.

V 94.7 (152.4 km) Peace River airport to south.

V 96 (154.5 km) Roma Junction with Highway 2A to Grimshaw (7miles/12 km southwest).

V 97.1 (156.3 km) Turnoff for Mighty Peace Golf Course (1.2 miles/2 km); 18 holes, licensed dining room, pro shop.

V 99.1 (159.5) Turnoff to south for Wilderness Park; picnic tables, outhouses, hiking trails, fishing (1 km on gravel).

V 101.1 (162.7 km) **Junction** with Highway 35 (Mackenzie Highway) to Northwest Territories.

Turn to Milepost G 2.8 in the Deh Cho Route: Mackenzie Highway, facing page.

Deh Cho Route: From Grande Prairie

Distance from Grande Prairie (GP) is shown.

ALBERTA HIGHWAY 2

GP 0 Junction of Highways 43 East and Highway 2 North. **GRANDE PRAIRIE** (pop. 50,227) city centre 4.5 miles south; all services. See description beginning on page 73 in the EAST ACCESS ROUTE section.

GP 1 (1.6 km) Stoplight at 84th Street (Business Route).

GP 2.3 (10.9 km) Exit to Clairmont.

GP 2.9 (4.7 km) Exit to Clairmont; camping.

GP 4 (6.4 km) Private RV park.

GP 6.1 (9.8 km) **Junction** with Highway 672 West to Hythe on Highway 43 (32 miles/52 km).

GP 8.7 (14 km) Exit to **SEXSMITH** (pop. 2,255), sometimes called the "Grain Capital of Alberta." Heritage Park Campground at the south entrance to city.

GP 9.1 (14.6 km) Husky gas station, Tags Foods.

GP 10.3 (16.6 km) **Junction** with Highway 59 West to La Grace (39 miles/63 km) on Highway 43, and **junction** with Highway 674 East to Teepee Creek and Highway 733 (15 miles/24 km).

GP 11.5 (18.5 km) End 4-lane divided freeway northbound, begin 2-lane undivided highway.

GP 13.3 (21.4 km) Spruce Meadows Golf Course and Campground to east.

GP 20 (32.2 km) Saddle Hills County (northbound sign).

GP 27.3 (43.9 km) Exit to Woking (5 km), Chinook Valley Golf Resort; camping.

GP 28.3 (45.5 km) **Junction** with Highway 677 East to Peoria and Highway 833 (16 miles/26 km).

GP 30.9 (49.7 km) Saddle River.

GP 36.7 (59.1 km) Sylvan Meadows Golf Course (9 holes) and campground. Phone (780) 765-2088.

GP 37.5 (60.4 km) Vehicle inspection station to east with litter bins.

GP 38.2 (61.5 km) **Junction** with Highway 49. Town of Rycroft to west (pop. 5,500). Gas, propane, diesel and lodging. Town website: www.rycroft.ca, (780) 765-3652.

GP 41.1 (66.1 km) Spirit River.

GP 46.9 (75.5 km) Double-ended paved turnout with litter bins.

GP 47.9 (77.1 km) Highway descends northbound to **Dunvegan Bridge** across the Peace River.

GP 51 (82.1 km) Dunvegan Bridge crosses Peace River. This is Alberta's only motor vehicle suspension bridge.

GP 51.5 (82.9 km) Entrance to **Dunvegan Provincial Park & Historic Site**. Visitor Centre open daily 10 A.M. to 6 P.M., mid-May to Labour Day; summer phone (780) 835-7150, or visit http://www.albertaparks.ca. Admission $3 adults, $2 seniors; camping fees charged. "The Maples" is a beautiful picnic area with playground, horseshoe pits and chemical toilets. Adjacent campground has 67 sites (28 with electrical hookups, 3 handicap accessible), firewood, table, pit toilets, sani-dump and phone. Phone (780) 538-5350.

Historic Dunvegan is the site of one of Alberta's earliest Hudson's Bay posts and Oblate missions. Several of the 19th century log buildings have been restored and furnished in meticulous detail, including the Rectory, St. Charles Mission Church and the Hudson's Bay Factor's House. Visit the nearby market gardens, which are still farmed as they were a hundred years ago.

Highway climbs steep grade next 2.2 miles northbound.

GP 56 (90.1 km) Turnout to west (southbound) with litter bins, recycling, information on Peace River.

GP 59.3 (95.4 km) **Junction** with Highway 64 for Hines Creek and Fort St. John.

GP 62.6 (100.7 km) Turnout with Alberta's history.

GP 66 (106.2 km) Visitor information centre at south edge of Fairview (description follows), an agriculture centre for the northwest Peace River region.

Fairview

GP 67 (107.8 km) **Junction** with Highway 732. Highway forks: turn right northbound for continuation of Highway 2; go straight for access to downtown Fairview. **Population:** 3,250. **Emergency Services: RCMP**, phone (780) 835-2211, and **Hospital**.

Fairview has hotels/motels, fastfood outlets, restaurants, museums. The RCMP Centennial Celebration Museum is at 103 Ave. East of Providence building. Open late May to early September, Tuesday–Saturday, 1–5 P.M. The Fairview Pioneer Museum (1 km north of Fairview) is open May to September, Tuesday to Saturday, 9 A.M. to 5 P.M.

Fine Arts Centre for northern art and the Information Centre are at the south end of town and open May–Sept. (780) 835-5999; www.fairview.ca. City phone number (780) 835-5461.

Cummings Park Recreation Area 2 km north of Fairview on Highway 732 has a day-use area, ball parks and a campground with showers and powered sites; camping fee $18/night with electric hookup. Good perch fishing. Trail circles lake for a 11 km loop walk. Phone (780) 835-5461.

The George Lake Campground is 1.9 miles/3 km south of Hines Creek on Highway 64. Open May 1 to October, with 30 sites, hiking trails, a lake, free firewood, pad-

dle-wheeler rides, and washroom with showers. Phone (780) 494-2419.

Deh Cho via Grande Prairie
(continued)

GP 72.5 (116.6 km) Blue Sky, picnic and skiing to west.

GP 75.5 (121.5 km) Leith River.

GP 80 (128.7 km) Whitelaw and Highway 735 North.

GP 88.4 (142.2 km) Brownvale. **Junction** with 737N. Picnicking, North Peace Museum.

GP 95.4 (153.5 km) Berwyn to west. Library, cafe, camping.

GP 95.6 (153.8 km) Distance marker northbound shows Grimshaw 11 km/7 miles, Peace River 37 km/23 miles.

GP 100.1 (160.9) Turnoff for Shaftsbury Road to Shaftsbury Ferry and Highway 684 (10 miles/16 km).

GP 101.7 (163.7) Welcome to Grimshaw.

Grimshaw

GP 102.2 (165 km) **G 0 AH 794.5** (1278.5 km) Mile 0 of the Mackenzie Highway, monument at Grimshaw Visitor Centre; turnoff for City Centre. **Population:** 2,435. **Emergency Services:** 911. Non-Emergencies **RCMP**, phone (780) 332-4666. **Hospital and Ambulance**, phone (780) 332-6500.

Visitor Information: In the NAR railway car adjacent the centennial monument marking Mile 0 of the Mackenzie Highway. Get your Deh Cho Travel Connection Passport stamped here. Online visit www.grimshaw.ca.

Named for pioneer doctor M.E. Grimshaw, the community developed as a shipping centre for surrounding farms with the arrival of the railroad in 1921. Grimshaw gained town status in February 1953. Local resources are wheat and grains, livestock, gravel, lumber, gas and oil.

Grimshaw has 2 motels including the **Dee-Jay Motel**, a hotel, restaurants, service stations, car washes, a laundromat, a recreation park and other shops and other services. Camping at Queen Elizabeth Provincial Park 1.9 miles north of town. The Lac Cardinal Pioneer Village Museum is adjacent the provincial park.

Dee-Jay Motel. See display ad on this page.

Town of Grimshaw. See display ad on this page.

Deh Cho Route: Mackenzie Highway

Distance from Grimshaw (G) is followed by distance from Alaska Highway (AH) via Northwest Territories.

ALBERTA HIGHWAY 35

G 0 AH 794.5 (1278.5 km) **GRIMSHAW**, Mile 0 of the Mackenzie Highway; see preceding description. Southbound travelers going to Peace River go east 2 miles on Highway 35 to junction with Highway 2, then turn south to follow Highway 2 to Peace River, then Valleyview.

G 1.9 (3 km) **AH 792.6** (1275.5 km)

Grimshaw's Mile 0 of the Mackenzie Highway monument. *(©Michael K. Robb)*

Queen Elizabeth Provincial Park, 3 miles/5 km west on Lac Cardinal via side road; day-use area with boat launch; 36 unserviced sites and 20 powered campsites, picnic shelter, firewood, firepits, toilets, playground, swimming, trails, sanidump. Phone (780) 624-6486. Nightly fee $24/unserviced and $30/power (Canadian cash or cheques). Group camping available. Lac Cardinal is only 6 feet deep. [△]

Adjacent the park is **Lac Cardinal Pioneer Village Museum** (donation), open mid-May to mid-September, 11 A.M. to 5 P.M. daily. Annual Pioneer Days the second weekend of August with horse and wagon rides, and demonstrations. Beyond the entrance to the museum there are dry campsites in a field, camping fee $10/night.

G 2.8 (4.6 km) **AH 791.7** (1274 km) **Junction** of Highways 35 and 2 East.

G 4.1 (6.6 km) **AH 790.4** (1272 km) Turnout to east with litter barrels. Pine Bluff information boards and McKenzie River.

G 6.9 (11.1 km) **AH 787.6** (1267.5 km) Vehicle inspection station; pay phone, recycle bin, litter bin.

G 7.7 (12.4 km) **AH 786.8** (1266.2 km) Bear Creek Drive and the Creek Golf Course & Campground, 1 mile to west. [△]

G 8.6 (13.8 km) **AH 785.9** (1264.7 km) **Junction** with SR 737 which leads west 12.4 miles/20 km to **Figure 8 Lake Provincial Recreation Area**; 20 campsites (no hookups), firepits, firewood$, water, tables, outhouses, boat launch, hiking trails. Lake stocked with rainbow; no gas motors. [⬅][△]

G 12.3 (19.7 km) **AH 782.2** (1258.7 km) *Road widens to 4-lane divided highway northbound.*

G 12.5 (20.1 km) **Junction** with High-

way 986 East to Peace River (19 miles/30 km) and Highway 88/Red Earth Creek (101 miles/162 km).

G 13 (20.9 km) **AH 781.5** (1257.6 km) *Road narrows to 2 lanes northbound. Pass with care.*

G 23 (37 km) **AH 771.5** (1241.5 km) Whitemud River bridge.

G 24.8 (39.9 km) **AH 769.7** (1238.7 km) **Junction** with Highway 689 west at **DIXONVILLE** (pop. 100, surrounding area 300); gas station, general store. Dixonville Museum is housed in a 100-year-old building that was formerly a trading post. Shady Lane Campground has 22 treed campsites. [▯][△]

G 26.9 (43.3 km) **AH 767.6** (1235.2 km) Sulphur Lake Road (dirt and gravel) leads west to junction with Highway 689. **Sulphur Lake Provincial Campground** is 34 miles/55 km west via 689. 11 sites, boat launch, fishing, swimming. [⬅][△]

CAUTION: Watch for deer northbound.

G 39.1 (62.9 km) **AH 755.4** (1215.7 km) **Junction** with SR 690 east to hamlet of Deadwood (7 miles/11 km). Private exotic

Look for the mighty moose to find Manning Visitor Centre. (©Judy Nadon, staff)

bird farm located 2 miles/3.2 km east then 1 mile/1.6 km south.

G 45.1 (72.5 km) **AH 749.4** (1206 km) Buchanan Creek.

G 47.5 (76.4 km) North Star to east.

G 49.6 (79.8 km) **AH 744.9** (1198.8 km) RV park to west; 15 sites with power, tables, firepits, outhouses. [▲]

G 51.4 (82.7 km) **AH 743.1** (1195.9 km) **Junction** with Highway 691. Turnoff for Battle River Pioneer Museum (1 km). Buildings open 1-6 P.M. daily, May and September, 10 A.M. to 6 P.M. July and August. Donations appreciated. Phone (780) 836-2374.

CAUTION: Slow for speed zone and pedestrians northbound through Manning.

Manning

[🍴][⛽][🛏][➕][▲]

G 52 (83.7 km) **AH 742.5** (1194.9 km) Located 122 miles/196 km south of High Level; an hour's drive north of Grimshaw. **Population:** 1,493. **Emergency Services:** Phone 911 for all emergency services. **Visitor Information:** Visitors Information Centre is located on the main street; look for the mighty moose. Get your Deh Cho Travel Connection Passport stamped here. A campground and sani-dump are just north of the visitor centre. For more information, go to www.manning.ca or phone (780) 836-3606.

Manning has motels/hotels, restaurants, a municipal campground, a pharmacy and drug mart, gas stations (diesel). *NOTE: Fuel pumps have green handles for regular and plain handles for diesel.* There is a grocery store and other shops and services.

Named for an Alberta premier, Manning was established in 1947. The railway from Roma, AB, to Pine Point, NWT, reached Manning in September 1962. Today, Manning is a service centre and jumping-off point for hunters and fishermen, emphasized by the large moose statue in the city.

Attractions include the Old Hospital Gallery & Museum in city centre. See what life was like for an early missionary nurse. Open May to September, Monday through Friday, 10 A.M. to 5 P.M. Donations appreciated. Phone (780) 836-3606.

Mackenzie Highway Log
(continued)

G 52.1 (83.8 km) Notikewin River.

G 53.8 (86.6 km) **AH 740.7** (1192 km) Manning airport to west.

G 54.2 (87.2 km) **AH 740.3** (1191.4 km) Truck stop, gas. [⛽]

G 55.5 (89.3 km) **AH739** (1189.3 km) Community of Notikewin to west. Historically known as "Big Prairie."

G 59.9 (96.4 km) Railroad Crossing.

G 60.6 (97.5 km) Turnout to west with litter bin.

G 61.6 (99.1 km) **AH 732.9** (1179.5 km) Hotchkiss River bridge. Historically known as the "Second Battle."

G 61.7 (99.3 km) **AH 732.8** (1179.3 km) Hotchkiss Community Club Park to east in the **Hotchkiss River** valley; 10 sites, picnic shelter, tables, firepits, fishing, outhouses and water pump. [🎣][▲]

©Judy Nadon, staff

G 62.2 (100.1 km) **AH 732.3** (1178.5 km) Condy Meadows golf course and campground to east. [▲]

G 66 (106.2 km) *CAUTION: Steep, sharp bends, rough pavement.*

G 66.5 (107 km) Chinchaga Forestry Road to west.

G 67.8 (109.1 km) **AH 726.7** (1169.5 km) Meikle River bridge. Historically known as the "Third Battle." *CAUTION: Steep, sharp bends northbound.*

G 68.8 (110.7 km) **AH 725.7** (1167.9 km) Hawk Hills Road to east. Railroad crossing.

G 72 (115.9 km) **AH 722.5** (1162.7 km) Roadside turnout with litter bins to west.

G 75 (120.7 km) **AH 719.5** (1157.9 km) **Junction** with Highway 692 and access to **Notikewin Provincial Park** (18.6 miles/30 km), with camping (19 sites), no services, water pump $17 per night; free firewood, day-use area, hiking trails, good wildlife viewing, picnicking and fishing for walleye and pike on the Notikewin and Peace rivers. Narrow portions of the access road make this unsuitable for large 5th wheelers or long trailers. Phone (780) 624-6486. [🎣][▲]

G 89.4 (143.9 km) **AH 705.1** (1134.7 km) Twin Lakes Lodge to east; they are the caretakers for the Twin Lakes Campground—if they appear closed, knock for service.

G 89.8 (144.5 km) **AH 704.7** (1134.1 km) **Twin Lakes Campground**, 0.5 mile west; 49 shaded campsites, $17 fee ($2 senior discount), firewood$, picnic shelter, firepits, firewood, tables, outhouses, water pump, beach, boat launch (no gas motors), playground, hiking trails; small store and office at entrance. Fish for stocked rainbow from June–Sept. Phone (780) 624-6486. [🎣][▲]

G 96.4 (155.1 km) **AH 698.1** (1123.5 km) Roadside turnout to west with litter bins.

G 96.6 (155.5 km) Railroad crossing.

G 104 (167.4 km) **AH 690.5** (1111.2 km) Kemp Creek.

G 112.2 (180.6 km) **AH 682.3** (1098 km) **Junction** with Highway 695 East to Carcajou.

G 113.4 (176.6 km) **AH 681.1** (1096.1 km) Keg River bridge. The community of **KEG RIVER** (pop. approx. 400). Keg River Cabins; food, gas, diesel, convenience store, liquor store, post office, Greyhound bus station, lodging. There are some bison ranches in the area. [⛽]

G 116.5 (181.4 km) **AH 678** (1091.1 km) **Junction** with Secondary Road 695 West. This paved road leads 9 miles/14.5 km to Keg River Post. A spot once rich in fur trade history, the post has Peace River Constituency's first MLA, "Allie" Brick, buried in its cemetery.

G 130.3 (203.9 km) **AH 664.2** (1068.9 km) **PADDLE PRAIRIE** (pop. approx. 164) has a gas bar, school and store. Paddle Prairie is a Metis settlement. The Metis culture, a combination of French and Amerindian, played a key role in the fur trade and development of northwestern Canada. [⛽]

G 135.1 (211.5 km) **AH 659.4** (1061.2 km) Roadside turnout to west with litter bins and recycle bins.

G 137 (218.6 km) **AH 657.5** (1058.1 km) **Junction** with Highway 697, a 2-lane paved highway that helps form the "Mackenzie County Loop" drive through La Crete, Tomkin's Landing and Fort Vermilion back to Highway 35 at High Level.

Junction with Highway 697 east to La Crete and Fort Vermilion. See "Mackenzie County Loop" on page 330.

G 141.8 (222.2 km) **AH 652.7** (1050.4 km) Entering Municipal District of Mackenzie (northbound sign).

G 145.5 (234.2 km) Turnout to east with

litter bins and recycling.

G 147.2 (231 km) AH 647.3 (1041.7 km) Chuckegg Creek.

G 154.2 (242.4 km) AH 640.3 (1030.4 km) Roadside turnout with litter bins and recycle bins to west. Watch for waterfowl in small lakes along highway.

G 161 (253.3 km) AH 633.5 (1019.5 km) Road dips at Bede Creek.

G 161.7 (254.4 km) AH 632.8 (1018.4 km) Road dips at Parma Creek.

G 166.1 (261.4 km) AH 628.4 (1011.3 km) Melito Creek.

G 168.1 (264.6 km) AH 626.4 (1008.1 km) Railroad crossing.

G 168.4 (265.1 km) AH 626.1 (1007.6 km) Footner OSB Plant to east.

G 171.2 (269.8 km) AH 623.3 (1003.1 km) Truck weigh station. Interpretive sign about Fort Vermilion.

G 172.5 (271.7 km) AH 622 (1001 km) Aspen Ridge Campground. See display ad this page.

G 174 (274 km) AH 620.5 (998.6 km) Junction with Highway 58 West, which leads 85 miles/136 km to **RAINBOW LAKE** (pop. 1,186), a service community for oil and natural gas development in the region.

High Level

G 174.2 (274.4 km) AH 620.3 (998.2 km) Tourist Information Center and service road. High Level is located at the junction of Highways 35 and 58. **Population:** 3,887. **Emergency Services:** Phone 911. RCMP, 911. **Northwest Health Centre,** phone (780) 841-3200 **Ambulance,** phone 911. **Fire Department,** phone 911.

Visitor Information: Southeast edge of town at **Mackenzie Crossroads Museum & Visitors Centre,** 10803–96th Street.

The centre has extensive local and regional information for Alberta and the Northwest Territories; museum displays; free Internet access; road and weather reports; pay phone; and gift shop. Fishing licenses for the Northwest Territories are sold here. Rest area with picnic tables. Open year-round, 9 A.M. to 8 P.M. daily in summer. Phone (780) 926-4811; www.highlevel.ca.

Private Aircraft: Scheduled air service

Mackenzie Crossroads Musuem features Alberta's pioneer history. (©Judy Nadon, staff)

to High Level airport, 7.5 miles/12 km north; elev. 1,110 feet/338m; length 5,000 feet/1,524m; asphalt; fuel 80, 100, Jet B. Footner Lake floatplane base, 0.6 mile/1 km west.

In 1786 fur traders arrived in the area but it wasn't until 1947 that the first settlers arrived. High Level began as a small settlement on the Mackenzie Highway after WWII. It grew with the oil boom of the 1960s and completion of the railroad to Pine Point. High Level has a strong agricultural economy (and the most northerly grain elevators in North America); 2 major forestry companies; and serves as a transportation centre for the northwestern Peace River region. The community offers a hospital, banks, schools, churches and a library.

Visitor facilities include major motels, a guest ranch, a bed-and-breakfast, fast-food outlets and restaurants; 24-hour gas station;

grocery stores, hardware store, laundromats and car washes.

Camping 1.7 miles/2.7 km south of town at **Aspen Ridge Campground.** Treed sites, full hookups, laundry facilities and fresh garden produce.

Dump station and freshwater fill-up are located at the corner of 94th Street and 105th Avenue, just northeast of the Visitors Centre.

Recreation includes a golf course, indoor swimming pool, skateboard park, playgrounds, tennis courts, ball diamonds, hiking trails, cycling, boating, canoeing, snowmobile trails, ice arena and curling rinks, hunting (moose, caribou, deer, bear) and fishing for northern pike, perch, walleye, whitefish, goldeye and grayling.

Mackenzie Crossroads Museum & Visitors Centre. See display ad this page.

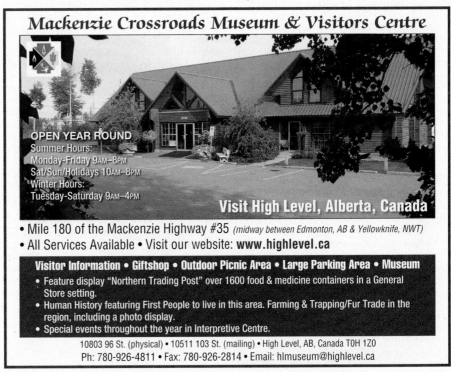

The Mackenzie County Loop

La Crete Ferry campground near Tompkin's Landing has spacious sites.
(© Judy Nadon, staff)

Mackenzie County is larger than Prince Edward Island and makes up more than 12 percent of Alberta's land. Explore just part of this huge area by taking this 125-mile/200-km loop off the Mackenzie Highway to La Crete and Fort Vermilion.

Highway 697 leads 11 miles/18 km east from **Milepost G 137** on the Mackenzie Highway (Alberta 35) to cross the Peace River at **Tompkin's Landing**, via a free ferry which operates 24 hours a day, except in heavy fog, and carries 4–6 vehicles. Campground nearby has spacious campsites (some overlook river) and electrical hookups; phone 780-841-2705.

Highway 697 continues east through Buffalo Head Prairie, which has a small store and gas, to **LA CRETE** (pop. 2,000), 54 miles/87 km northeast of Highway 35. La Crete serves an area of 7,000 but continues to have the charm of the Mennonite settlers that founded it. Established in the

early 1900s by Mennonite settlers, LaCrete celebrates Farmer's Day in June and Pioneer Days in September. A rodeo takes place in July.

La Crete Mennonite Heritage Village has unique buildings and farming artifacts. It is open May to September and is 1 mile/3 km southwest of town; phone (780) 928-4447.

The majority of the town speaks Plattdeutsch, or "low German," while "high German" is mainly reserved for church services. English is spoken at the town businesses, which include restaurants and a motel with 60 rooms. The motel also offers electrical hookups for RVs. Reinland Park in town has a day-use area, sani-dump, playground and picnic shelter. Woodland Park, 3.1 mile/5 km south of LaCrete, has 50 sites, water and sani-dump; phone (780) 926-1107.

Stop in at the Chamber of Commerce at 10406–100 St. (park in Co-op parking lot). They have maps and brochures, the sought-after Green Deh Cho Passports and stamps, historical items and many souvenirs and gifts. Phone for more information (780) 928-2278; www.lacretechamber.com.

From La Crete, drive northeast 25 miles/40 km via Highway 697 to junction with Highway 88 and access to the hamlet of **FORT VERMILION** (pop. 871), the oldest settlement in Alberta, established in 1788. Visitor facilities include hotels, restaurants, grocery and liquor stores. Fort Vermilion has a 36-bed hospital (phone 780/927-3761) and a Provincial Court. The community library on River Drive is open Tuesday to Saturday, from 12:30 P.M. to 5:30 P.M. or later.

Stop in at the Visitor Centre and Museum, June–August; phone (780) 927-3216. It is housed in a historic building dating back to 1923, one of 25 historic sites in Fort Vermilion. Visit the **Fort Vermilion Heritage Centre Museum** and old log house for a look at First Nations and fur trade history. A walk through the site includes the Trappers Shack. Built in 1912-1916, it is 1 of 3 dove-tailed log buildings in the community. Other historic buildings include an old Hudson's Bay store, Kratzs' Clinic, a Catholic mission site and St. Luke's Anglican Cemetery. Open from June to August; phone (780) 927-4603.

Camping at Fort Vermilion's Fantasy North Park, located at the 9-hole golf course; phone (780) 927-3227. Heritage Bicentennial Park has campsites, day-use facilities, boat launch and fishing; phone (780) 927-4222. Fort Vermilion Provincial Recreation Area, located 6.2 miles/10 km west of town on Highway 88, has 10 campsites.

Highway 88/Bicentennial Highway continues south 255 miles/410 km (unpaved) to Slave Lake. No services on Highway 88 between Fort Vermilion and Slave Lake.

When you leave Fort Vermilion you are only 49 miles/79 km west of High Level via Highway 58. Along the way is the **Machesis Lake Forest Provincial Recreation Area** (drive 16 miles/30 km east on 58 then 9 miles/17 km south); 20 campsites, boat launch and fishing for rainbows.

Mackenzie County. See display ad this page.

Return to Milepost G 137 or Milepost G 174.9

Mackenzie Highway Log
(continued)

G 174.9 (275.5 km) **AH 619.6** (997.1 km) **Junction** with Highway 58 East to Jean D'Or Prairie (77 miles/125 km, paved/gravel). Highway 58 leads 49 miles/78 km east (paved) to Fort Vermilion, the oldest settlement in Alberta, and junctions with Highway 697 to La Crete, forming the "Mackenzie County Loop" for travelers.

See "Mackenzie County Loop" log on this page.

G 177.1 (279 km) **AH 617.4** (993.6 km) Golf and country club to east; clubhouse, grass greens 18 holes, pro shop, power carts and camping facilities. ▲

G 181.7 (286.5 km) **AH 612.8** (986.2 km) Turnoff to west for High Level Airport. *Watch for deer northbound.*

G 194.4 (306.9 km) **AH 600.1** (965.7 km) Turnoff to west for Hutch Lake recreation area. ➤ ▲

G 196.5 (310.3 km) **AH 598** (962.4 km) Roadside turnouts with litter bins both sides of highway.

G 206.8 (327 km) **AH 587.7** (945.8 km) Wooden railway bridge to east.

G 218.7 (346.2 km) **AH 575.8** (926.6 km) **MEANDER RIVER** (pop. 289); no highway services. Fish the Meander River where it meets Hay River for pike and walleye. ➤

G 224.9 (356.3 km) **AH 569.6** (916.6 km) Roadside turnout to west with litter bins.

G 227 (359.5 km) **AH 567.5** (913.3 km) The Mackenzie Highway crosses the Hay River here and follows it north into Northwest Territories. Great Slave Lake Railway bridge over Hay River to east. This railway line extends 377 miles/607 km from Roma Junction near Peace River, AB, to Hay River, NWT, on the shore of Great Slave Lake. (A 54-mile/87-km branch line extended the line to the now-defunct lead–zinc mine at Pine Point, NWT.) Opened in 1964, the line carries mining shipments south and fuel and supplies north to Hay River.

G 227.5 (360.3 km) **AH 567** (912.5 km) Gravel road leads west 39 miles/63 km to ZAMA (pop. 250), an oilfield community. Drilling and related operations take place at Zama, which is the southern terminal of the interprovincial pipeline, carrying Norman Wells crude to Edmonton refineries.

Zama has a full-service campground and Cardlocks grocery store (phone 780/683-2215 for more information). The Zama Library doubles as a visitor center and has Internet access. It is open Sundays 1–4 P.M., Tuesdays and Thursdays 7–9 P.M. Zama Community Park has a fish pond. It is adjacent the hamlet's RV park offering full services, picnic area, sani-dump, firepits and playground.

Many fishing lakes are in this area; local air charters are available to take you to them. Ask at the library or plan ahead by calling in advance of your arrival.

G 232.3 (368 km) **AH 562.2** (904.7 km) Slavey Creek.

G 241 (382 km) **AH 553.5** (890.7 km) Railroad crossing.

G 242.8 (384.8 km) **AH 551.7** (887.8 km) Paved turnout with litter bins to west.

G 249.5 (395.4 km) **AH 545** (877.1 km) Lutose Creek.

G 262.2 (416 km) **AH 532.3** (856.6 km) Steen River bridge.

G 263.2 (417.6 km) **AH 531.3** (855 km) Access road west to Steen River Gas Plant (8 miles/13 km).

G 265.6 (421.5 km) **AH 528.9** (851.2 km) **STEEN RIVER** (pop. approx. 25) to east; no services.

G 265.8 (421.8 km) **AH 528.7** (850.8 km) Steen River Forestry Tanker Base to west. Grass airstrip.

G 270 (428.6 km) **AH 524.5** (844.1 km) Jackpot Creek.

G 276.2 (438.6 km) **AH 518.3** (834.1 km) Road crosses creek. Improved road, northbound to border.

G 284 (450.7 km) **AH 510.5** (821.5 km) **INDIAN CABINS** (pop. 10); gas, diesel, cafe, lodging, showers, liquor, pay phone and native crafts. The old Indian cabins that gave this settlement its name are gone, but nearby is an Indian cemetery with spirit houses. Historic log church.

G 285.3 (452.5 km) **AH 509.2** (819.5 km) Delphine Creek.

G 287.3 (455.7 km) **AH 507.2** (816.2 km) Microwave tower to east.

G 293.5 (465.8 km) **AH 501** (806.3 km) 60th parallel. Border between Alberta and Northwest Territories. The Mackenzie Highway now changes from Alberta Highway 35 to NWT Highway 1, the Waterfalls Route.

Deh Cho Route: Waterfalls Route

Distance from AB–NWT border (B) is followed by distance from Grimshaw (G) and distance from the Alaska Highway (AH).
Kilometreposts on Highway 1 reflect distance from AB–NWT border. You need Canadian cash to pay for camping in territorial parks. They do not accept credit cards, cheques or U.S. cash.

NWT HIGHWAY 1

B 0 G 293.5 AH 501 (806.3 km) AB–NWT border, 60th Parallel. **Sixtieth Parallel Territorial Park and Visitor Centre** with brochures, maps, fishing licenses, camping permits, litter bins, pay phone, free WiFi when satellite works, drinking water and free coffee. Dene (Indian) arts and crafts are on display. Check here on road and ferry conditions before proceeding. Visitor centre hours are May 15 to Sept. 15 from 8:30 A.M. to 8:30 P.M. daily.

©Judy Nadon, staff

NOTE: For details on Northwest Territories campgrounds visit http://nwtparks.ca/; reserve at https://www.campingnwt.ca/.

Campground and picnic area adjacent visitor centre; 12 dry, level, non-powered campsites on treed loop. Dump station, showers, washrooms, picnic sites, kitchen shelter and toilet at end of campground road overlooks Hay River; unmaintained boat launch, fishing. A short walking trail

around a pond leads to the 60th Parallel Monument.

Distance marker northbound shows Hay River 75 miles/120 km; Fort Simpson 295 miles/474 km; Wrigley 432 miles/695 km; Fort Providence 138 miles/222 km; Yellowknife 331 miles/532 km; Fort Smith 236 miles/380 km.

NOTE: Fines are double for drivers speeding through school or construction zones and triple for those driving without a valid license. Driving without insurance is a $1,700 fine plus a victim surcharge that totals $1,955.

B 1.7 (2.9 km) **G 295.2 AH 499.3** (803.5 km) **Reindeer Creek**; pike, pickerel.

B 25.5 (40.9 km) **G 319 AH 475.5** (765.2 km) Swede Creek.

B 26.1 (42 km) **G 319.6 AH 474.9** (764.3 km) Large dirt turnout, toilets and gravel stockpile to west.

B 40.4 (65.1 km) **G 333.9 AH 460.6** (741.2 km) Mink Creek.

B 45 (72 km) **G 338.5 AH 456** (733.8 km) Turnoff to east for **Twin Falls Gorge Territorial Park**, **Alexandra Falls picnic area**; toilets, litter bins, picnic shelters and interpretive signs. Paved parking area and gravel walkway to falls viewpoint, overlooking the Hay River, which plunges 109 feet/33m to form **Alexandra Falls**. Excellent photo opportunities; walk down stairs to top of falls. A 1.9-mile/3-km trail through mixed boreal forest (with good canyon views) connects with Louise Falls.

B 46.4 (74.6 km) **G 339.9 AH 454.6** (731.6 km) Turnoff to east for **Twin Falls Gorge Territorial Park**, **Louise Falls Campground**; nice reception area just off of road. Small building nearby is where you register before turning into the campground loops. Camping fee $28CN; 18 powered campsites, tables, toilets, firepits, firewood,Tent pads, water at site. Drive in 0.3 mile for picnic area with kitchen shelter, playground. Showers are in Loop B (8 A.M.–8 P.M.). Pleasant walking trail to viewpoint overlooking 3-tiered **Louise Falls**, which drops 50 feet/15m. Walk down spiral stairs to top of falls. Look for fossils at edge of falls. A 1.9-mile/3-km trails connects with Alexandra Falls.

B 48.2 (77.5 km) **G 341.7 AH 452.8** (728.7 km) **Escarpment Creek** picnic and group camping area; tables, shelter, toilets, firepits, garbage container, water. Spectacular series of waterfalls on Escarpment Creek; access from north side of creek. A 2.6-mile/4.4-km trail connects to Louise Falls.

B 51.5 (83.2 km) **G 345 AH 449.5** (723.4 km) **ENTERPRISE** (pop. 90), a highway community with food, gas, diesel, motel/cafe and B&B, grocery store, pay phone. Enterprise Regional Tourist Info Centre in old weigh station; open daily in summer; phone (867) 984-3017. Native crafts at **Winnie's Dene Art Gallery & Gift Shop**. Food at **Sandra's Restaurant**. Lodging at motel and B&B. Minor vehicle repair available. View of Hay River Gorge just east of the highway. Look for sandhill cranes in this area. *Slow for 50 kmph/31 mph speed zone.*

Winnie's Dene Art Gallery & Gift Shop offers a wide variety of unique northern art and services: birchbark baskets, tuftings, quill and beadwork, traditional tanned moosehide items, Northern books/music/

NWT Visitor Centre at border on Highway 1.
(©Judy Nadon, staff)

quilt patterns and crafting materials. Gas is available here too. Step next door for delicious homestyle meals from Sandra's Restaurant. Email winniesdeneartgallery@yahoo.ca. Phone toll-free Canada/USA 1-877-267-9196.
[ADVERTISEMENT]

B 51.6 (83.3 km) **G 345.1 AH 449.4** (723.2 km) "Y" intersection of Highways 1 and 2. Northbound travelers keep left for Yellowknife, right for Hay River. (Kilometreposts are white, on the right side of road.)

Junction of Highway 1 with Highway 2 to Hay River; see "Great Slave Route" on page 331 for log.

Great Slave Route: Highways 2 & 6

The Great Slave Lake Route begins at the junction of Highways 1 and 2 at Enterprise. Highway 2 leads north 24 miles/38 km to the community of Hay River, the largest shipping centre in the north. Highway 2 also junctions with Highway 5, which connects with Highway 6 to the historic town of Fort Resolution on the south shore of Great Slave Lake.

Distance from Enterprise (E) is shown.

Highway 2 is paved from Enterprise to Hay River. Kilometreposts along the highway reflect distance from Enterprise. There are no services between Hay River and Fort Resolution.

NWT HIGHWAY 2

E 0 **Junction** with Highway 1 at Enterprise, **Milepost B 51.6.**

E 8.5 (13.6 km) Paradise Gardens.

E 15.7 (25.3 km) Hay River Golf Course; large log clubhouse, driving range, 9 holes (par 36), artificial greens. 10 powered RV sites available, $22.50/night.

E 19.8 (31.9 km) **Junction** with Highway 5, which connects with Highway 6 to Fort Resolution.

Hay River

E 23.6 (38 km) **H 0** Located on the south shore of Great Slave Lake at the mouth of the Hay River. **Population**: 3,825 **Emergency Services**: RCMP, phone (867) 874-1111. **Fire Department**, phone (867) 874-2222. **Ambulance**, phone (867) 874-9333. **Hospital**, phone (867) 874-7100.

Visitor Information: Visitor Information Centre, just east of the highway; phone (867) 874-3180. Open daily, 9 A.M. to 9 P.M., late May to early September. There is a dump station located here. Also visit www.hayriver.com or www.hayrivercham ber.com; email: tourism@northwestel.net. Sani-dump available at the Hay River Centre.

Transportation: Air—Scheduled service. **Bus**—Frontier Coachlines (affiliated with Greyhound for this area) (867) 874-2566. **Rental cars**—Available.

Private Aircraft: Hay River airport; elev. 543 feet/165m; length 6,000 feet/1,830m, paved; 4,000 feet/1,219m, gravel; fuel 100, Jet B.

Hay River was established in 1868 with the building of a Hudson's Bay Co. post. Today, the community is the transfer point from highway and rail to barges on Great Slave Lake bound for arctic and subarctic communities. Hay River harbour is also home port of the Mackenzie River barge fleet that plies the river in summer.

The airstrip was built in 1942 on Vale Island by the U.S. Army Corps of Engineers. Vale Island was the townsite until floods in 1951 and 1963 forced evacuation of

the population to the mainland townsite, where most of the community is now concentrated. Vale Island, referred to as "Old Town," is bounded by Great Slave Lake and the west and east channels of the Hay River.

Hay River has schools, churches, a civic centre with a swimming pool (1 of only 2 year-round swimming pools in Northwest Territories), bowling alley, curling sheets, hockey arena and dance hall. The Hay River Speedway has car racing. Northwest Territories Centennial Library headquarters is located here. There is a public boat launch at Porritt Landing on Vale Island.

Visitor services include food, gas and lodging (**North Country Inn**). There are supermarkets, shopping, banks and other services.

Hay River Territorial Park and Campground on Vale Island on Great Slave Lake (follow signs; it's about 6 miles/10 km past the information centre); 35 sites all with power, some pull-throughs, hookups, showers, firewood, toilets, dump station and firepits, camping fee, open mid-May to mid-September. The beach park offers picnic sites. Also camping at 2 Seasons Adventures in Hay River.

Great Slave Lake, northern pike up to 40 lbs.; Inconnu (sheefish); grayling; good pickerel fishing in Hay River from bank.

Hay River fisherman with his catch.
(©Judy Nadon, staff)

NWT HIGHWAY 5

E 19.8 (31.9 km) **Junction** with Highway 5, which connects with Highway 6 to Fort Resolution.

E 21.1 (34 km) Railroad and auto bridge crosses Hay River.

E 21.3 (34.3 km) Access road leads north 3.7 miles/5.9 km to Hay River Reserve and Dene Cultural Centre.

E 50.1 (80.6 km) Good gravel road leads 1 mile/1.6 km north to **Polar Lake**; no motorboats allowed. Day-use fee $5; camping $10/night. Good bird watching.

E 54 (86.9 km) Buffalo River bridge.

E 54.4 (87.5 km) Turnout to north with outhouse, litter barrel and map.

E 57.6 (92.7 km) **Junction** with Highway 5 to Fort Smith. *See "Wood Buffalo Route" log on page 340. Continue on Highway 6.*

NWT HIGHWAY 6

E 70.8 (113.9 km) Main access road north to **PINE POINT** (abandoned); no services. Pine Point was built in the 1960s by Cominco Ltd. The open-pit lead–zinc mine shut down in 1987. Once a community of almost 2,000 residents, most people moved out in 1988, and houses and structures have been moved or destroyed. The Great Slave Lake Railway, constructed in 1961 from Roma, AB, to Pine Point to transport the lead-zinc ore to market, is no longer in operation.

E 72.2 (116.2 km) *Pavement ends, gravel begins, eastbound.*

E 89.9 (144.7 km) Turnoff to north for Dawson Landing viewpoint on Great Slave Lake, accessible via a 25-mile/40-km bush road (not recommended in wet weather).

E 94 (151.3 km) Turnout to north with litter barrel.

E 99.4 (160 km) **Little Buffalo River Crossing Territorial Park** to south; 12 non-powered campsites, picnic tables, kitchen shelter, firewood, toilets, litter barrels, boat launch.

E 99.5 (160.1 km) Bridge over **Little Buffalo River**. Good fishing for northern pike and walleye.

E 113.5 (182.7 km) **FORT RESOLUTION** (pop. 580), located on the south shore of Great Slave Lake on Resolution Bay. **Emergency Services**: RCMP, phone (867) 394-1111. **Visitor Information**: Stop in at the Dene Noo Community Council.

The earliest fur trading post on Great Slave Lake, the Hudson's Bay Co. post was established here in 1786. Missionaries settled in the area in 1852, establishing a school and hospital to serve the largely Chipewyan population. The road connecting Fort Resolution with Pine Point was built in the 1960s.

Today's economy is based on trapping, fishing, and a logging and sawmill operation. Visitor services include food, gas and groceries and a service station. Canada Post outlet located in Northern Store.

B 51.9 (83.8 km) **G 345.4 AH 449.1** (722.7 km) Weigh station.

B 56.4 (90.7 km) **G 349.9 AH 444.6** (715.5 km) Microwave tower to north.

B 74.7 (120.2 km) **G 368.2 AH 426.3** (686 km) Paved double-ended turnout north to **McNallie Creek Territorial Park**, a day-use picnic site with outhouses, litter bins, viewing platform and short trail to an interesting waterwall. While not as massive as Alexandra or Lady Evelyn Falls, field editor Judy Nadon calls it "spectacular, a must stop." Plaque explains origin of name.

B 74.8 (120.4 km) **G 368.3 AH 426.2** (685 km) McNallie Creek.

B 76.5 (122.9 km) **G 370 AH 424.5** (683.1 km) Double-ended paved turnout to north with picnic tables, litter bins and no toilets. *CAUTION: Failing edge. Supervise children and dogs.*

B 104 (167.1 km) **G 397.5 AH 397** (638.9 km) Access road leads south 4.2 miles/6.8 km to **Lady Evelyn Falls Territorial Campground** and continues another 4 miles/7.4 km to the Slavey village of **KAKISA** (pop. 40) and **Kakisa Lake**.

The Kakisa River drops 49 feet/15m over an escarpment to form **Lady Evelyn Falls**. Staircase down to viewing platform. Hiking trail to base of falls; swimming, fishing and wading. Ample parking, interpretive display, territorial campground with 23 sites with power, camping fee $28CN, 7 picnic sites, group picnic site, showers, toilets, tables, firepits, firewood, garbage containers, water pump, kitchen shelters, visitor centre.

B 104.9 (168.5 km) **G 398.4 AH 396.1** (637.4 km) Kakisa River bridge.

B 105.1 (168.8 km) **G 398.6 AH 395.9** (637.1 km) **Kakisa River Territorial Park**; day-use only picnic area with tables, toilets, fireplaces and firewood. Hiking trail to Lady Evelyn Falls. Good fishing in **Kakisa River** for grayling.

B 115.5 (185.6 km) **G 409 AH 385.5** (620.4 km) Double-ended turnout to east with litter bins, toilet. Informational boards here about the Deh Cho route.

B 115.7 (186 km) **G 409.2 AH 385.3** (620 km) Turnoff to north for Highway 3 to Yellowknife.

> **Junction** of Highway 1 with Highway 3, which leads 211 miles/340 km north to Yellowknife. See "Frontier Trail" log on page 334.

B 116 (186 km) **G 409.5 AH 385** (619.6 km) *Pavement ends, gravel begins, westbound.*

B 116.8 (188 km) Double-ended turnout.

B 144.1 (233 km) **G 437.6 AH 356.9** (574.4 km) Turnout with litter bins and outhouse to south.

B 158.6 (255 km) **G 452.1 AH 342.4** (551 km) Double-ended turnout to north with litter bins.

B 160.8 (258.5 km) **G 454.3 AH 340.2** (547.5 km) Microwave tower to north.

B 162 (260.7 km) **G 455.5 AH 339** (545.5 km) **Axe Handle Creek**; fishing.

B 172.5 (277.4 km) **G 466 AH 328.5** (528.7 km) **Bouvier Creek**; good fishing in spring.

B 173.5 (279 km) **G 467 AH 327.5** (527 km) Turnout with litter bins to south.

B 180.1 (289.4 km) **G 473.6 AH 320.9** (516.4 km) Double-ended turnout with litter bins, toilet east side of Wallace Creek. Scenic canyon to north; trail access on west side of creek; 15-minute walk to waterfall.

B 183.8 (295.2 km) **G 476.6** (AH 317.9 (511.6 km) Gravel access to north at east end of **Redknife River** bridge; local fishing spot for pickerel and grayling.

B 195 (313.5 km) **G 488.5 AH 306** (492.4 km) Morrisey Creek.

B 200.1 (321.3 km) **G 493.6 AH 300.9** (484.2 km) Winter ice road leads south 78 miles/126 km to **TROUT LAKE** (pop. 82), a Dene settlement known for its big fish (lake trout and pickerel/walleye), sandy beaches and traditional lifestyles. Fly-in, no road access, in summer

B 202 (324.3 km) **G 494.7 AH 299.8** (482.5 km) Turnoff to **Sambaa Deh Falls Territorial Park** just east of Trout River bridge. Beautiful information centre with brochures and visitor guides regarding area attractions. Well-maintained campground with 20 large, non-powered, wooded campsites, picnic tables, litter barrels, immaculate showers, kitchen shelter, firepits, firewood, water; $22.50CN. *Emergency phone.* RCMP, phone (867) 695-1111. Visitor centre, parking and picnic area. Sambaa Deh Falls can be seen from the highway bridge. From the campground's Loop B, hike 0.6 mile/1 km south to **Coral Falls**. Good trout fishing.

B 202.1 (324.5 km) **G 495.6 AH 298.9** (481 km) Trout River Bridge. View of Sambaa Deh Falls to north from bridge. You can walk down to the falls for a better look, but you'll have to park at the Territorial Park. Good fishing hole below the falls north of the bridge. Hike 0.6 mile/1 km north on west side of river to access to **Trout River Canyon**. Fossils are embedded in the rocks along the Trout River.

B 202.7 (326.2 km) **G 496.3 AH 298.2** (479.9 km) Trailhead parking for Trout River Canyon trails to see fossils embedded in rocks along the river.

B 206.5 (331.6 km) **G 500 AH 294.5** (474 km) Emergency survival cabin and turnout

with litter bins to north.

B 234 (375.4 km) **G 527.5 AH 267** (429.7 km) Double-ended turnout to north with litter barrel and information sign on Jean Marie River.

B 234.1 (375.5 km) **G 527.6 AH 266.9** (429.5 km) **Junction** with an all-weather, gravel road leading 17 miles/27 km to community of **JEAN MARIE RIVER** (pop. 69), located on the south shore of the Mackenzie River at the confluence with the Jean Marie River. A very traditional community known for its native crafts. Visitors are welcome to visit traditional camps along the road. *Please respect private property.*

Visitor Information: Available from friendly staff at the Band Office in the large brown building in front of the central playground. If the office is closed, ask anyone you see in the community.

Services here include an undeveloped camping area (located near airport); picnic site on the river; Lucy's Bed & Breakfast and gas. Arts and crafts available; inquire at the Band Office. There is a co-op store, territorial government offices and nursing station here. Local crafts include beaded moose hide and moose hair tuftings. The historic tugboat *Jean Marie River* rests up shore, retired from shipping lumber down the Mackenzie to Arctic communities. Good photo opportunity. Ask about guided boat tours.

B 234.4 (376 km) **G 527.9 AH 266.6** (429 km) Sign here says to phone (867) 695-1111 for RCMP Emergency in this area.

B 236.2 (379 km) **G 529.7 AH 264.8** (426.1 km) Emergency survival cabin and turnout to north with outhouse and litter bins.

B 242 (388 km) **G 535.5 AH 259** (416.8 km) Pipeline camp and pump station to north. Highway crosses pipeline. Microwave tower visible to south.

B 256 (410.5 km) **G 549.5 AH 245** (394.3 km) *Gravel ends, pavement begins, westbound. Pavement ends, gravel begins, eastbound.*

B 256.5 (412 km) **G 550 AH 244.5** (393.5 km) Jean Marie River bridge.

B 256.7 (412.3 km) **G 550.2 AH 244.3** (393.1 km) "Checkpoint" at **junction** with

(Continues on page 337)

Small but beautiful McNallie Creek falls on Highway 1. (©Judy Nadon, staff)

Frontier Trail: Highway 3 to Yellowknife

Watch for wood buffalo along Northwest Territories highways. *(©Judy Nadon, staff)*

Highway 3 is a wide, paved, all-weather road in good condition leading 211 miles/341 km from its junction with Highway 1 to Yellowknife. There is a ferry crossing in summer/ice road crossing in winter of the Mackenzie River. Gas is available at Fort Providence, Behchoko and in Yellowknife.

Distance from junction of Highways 1 and 3 (J) is shown.

NWT HIGHWAY 3

J 0 Highway 3 leads north 211 miles/341 km to Yellowknife from **Milepost B 115.5** on Highway 1.

J 12.7 (20.4 km) **Dory Point Territorial Park** (day-use only); picnic area to east with 5 sites and screened in kitchen shelter with large center fire pit for cooking, no drinking water; overlooking Mackenzie River with view of passing riverboats.

J 14.3 (23 km) **Captain's Cabins and Bridge-Less Lodging.** Peaceful setting on the Mackenzie River, fishing with buddies or romantic getaway. Cozy cabins or Lodge House. Enjoy access to fully-equipped kitchen, BBQ, WiFi, satellite TV. Great fishing and boat launch close by. Awesome views, sunrise/sunsets, Deh Cho Bridge,

Northern Lights. April–September. Message (250) 483-5866, ginajula@yahoo.ca. Like us on Facebook! [ADVERTISEMENT]

J 14.8 (23.8 km) South bank of the Mackenzie River and approach to Deh Cho Bridge. Construction of the $185-million cablestay bridge across the Mackenzie River took 4 years. It officially opened Nov. 30, 2012. This bridge marks the end to a long history of ferry and ice road transport only across the Mackenzie River. It is the longest joint-less bridge in North America with a total length of 1,045m/3,428ft. For project details, go to www.dehcho bridge.info.

J 15.6 (25.1 km) North bank of the Mackenzie River.

J 16.2 (26 km) Mackenzie Bison Sanctuary next 50 miles (92.6 km). "Watch for Bison" sign. *Use EXTREME CAUTION driving Highway 3: Slow down and watch for bison on highway north from the river crossing!*

J 16.3 (26.2 km) Turnout to west with litter bins and information boards.

J 19.5 (31.4 km) Big River Service Center has gas, diesel, propane; a boat launch; motel and lounge; full-service restaurant (overlooking the Mackenzie RIver) and groceries. *NOTE: Next gas available northbound*

is in Rae (Behchoko) 140 miles/228 km. For southbound travelers, no gas until Enterprise or Fort Simpson.

J 20.9 (33.6 km) **Fort Providence Territorial Park** 1.2 miles/2 km west. 21 powered sites for $28 per night, showers, information centre, screened in kitchen, sani dump, located in a poplar forest. Good fishing.

J 22.6 (36.4 km) **Junction** with access road which leads 3.1 miles/5 km west to **FORT PROVIDENCE** (approx. pop. 748); food and lodging at Snow Shoe Inn; medical clinic.

A Roman Catholic mission was established at Fort Providence in 1861. (Our Lady of Fort Providence church is a major landmark.) Although noted for its early agricultural endeavors, Fort Providence is traditionally a trapping community.

Moose hair embroidery is found in local gift shops and local craftswomen are also noted for their porcupine quill work. Hand knit fur garments and accessories found at **Dene Fur Clouds**.

Dene Fur Clouds. See display ad this page.

Historical monument, boat launch and picnic sites on the **Mackenzie River**. Spectacular photo opportunities here for sunsets on the river. Also good bird watching for eagles, sandhill cranes and other birds. Guides, cabins, boats and air charters available locally. Good to excellent fishing. Northern pike to 30 lbs., May 30 to September, use large Red Devils; grayling and pickerel from 1 to 6 lbs., June–September, use anything (small Red Devils will do).

NOTE: No services on highway from here to Yellowknife (193 miles/310 km). You can find gas/fuel at **J 152.9** by turning off at junction for Rae-Edzo/Behchoko (130 miles north of Fort Providence).

J 32.5 (52.3 km) Occasional loose gravel northbound.

NOTE: Use EXTREME CAUTION driving in this area; slow down and watch for bison on highway! A local from Yellowknife offered the tip that if you see a bison on a rise pointing downhill with his head down, he's likely getting ready to charge. Use caution if you stop to take photographs; stay in your vehicle and maintain a safe distance.

J 42.5 (68.4 km) Double-ended turnout to east with litter bin.

J 44 (70.8 km) Watch for herds of bison alongside or standing in the middle of the road.

J 51.7 (83.2 km) Double-ended turnout to west with litter bins, toilets. Information boards on wood bison are here and at several additional turnouts northbound.

J 64.5 (103.8 km) Gravel breaks northbound.

J 75.8 (122 km) **Chan Lake Territorial Park** (day-use only) to east. Double-ended parking area with picnic tables, picnic shelter, litter bins and outhouse. Watch for waterfowl.

J 77.5 (124.7 km) Turnout to east with litter bin.

J 86.4 (139 km) Double-ended turnout to

east with litter bins.

J 90.5 (145.6 km) Double-ended turnout to west.

J 100.7 (162.1 km) Double-ended turnout with litter bin to east.

J 130.4 (209.8 km) Double-ended turnout with litter bins to east. Northbound travelers may notice the trees are getting shorter as you move farther north.

J 141.9 (228.4 km) Highway descends northbound to **Mosquito Creek**. Fishing for pickerel and whitefish; closed May and June, open season July thru April.

J 144.8 (233 km) **North Arm Territorial Park** on the shores of Great Slave Lake to east; picnic area, tables, toilets, firewood and firepits. Lowbush cranberries and other berries in area. Boat launch. *Beware of bears.*

J 148.1 (236 km) Access road west to Behchoko airport. Rolling frost heaves begin here, northbound to Yellowknife.

J 148.9 (239.6 km) **Junction** with winter ice road north to communities of Wha Ti (formerly Lac La Marte) and Rae Lakes (Gameti).

J 149.5 (240.6 km) **Junction** with access road west to community of Edzo, no services (see description at **Milepost J 152.2**).

Watch for frost heaves and gravel breaks north to Yellowknife. Highway turns east for northbound travelers.

J 148.8 (239.5 km) Pickerel fishing in **West Channel**.

J 152.2 (245 km) Bridge over **Frank Channel**, which extends from the head of the North Arm of Great Slave Lake to the Aboriginal village of Rae. Boating and fishing for whitefish.

J 152.9 (246 km) **Junction** with road which leads west 6.2 miles/10 km to **BEHCHOKO**, which includes the 2 hamlets of Rae–Edzo (descriptions follow). **Population:** 1,500. **Emergency Services:** RCMP, in Rae, phone (867) 392-1111. **Nursing station (Emergencies)**, in Rae, phone (867) 392-6075.

Rae, located on Marion Lake, is the largest Dogrib community in the territory. Rae has a large general store, a post office, 2 motels, a restaurant and gas stations (one with deli/inside seating). The mission church at Rae has a tipi-style entrance. Inquire locally about buying local crafts (beaded jackets, slippers, etc.) and a traditional Dene camp and wilderness spa.

Edzo is a residential community a few kilometres away from Rae. Edzo was developed in 1965 by the government to provide schools and a sanitation system.

J 159.9 (257.3 km) Turnout to west with litter bins.

J 160.1 (257.6 km) Stagg River bridge. After crossing the North Arm of Great Slave Lake, the highway swings southeast toward Yellowknife. Winding road to Yellowknife, good opportunities to see waterfowl in the many small lakes.

J 175 (280.1 km) Double-ended turnout to south with litter bins.

J 189.7 (305.3 km) Double-ended turnout to west with litter bin.

J 207.5 (334 km) Yellowknife Golf Club to north; 18 holes, sand fairways, artificial greens, pro shop, licensed clubhouse. Built on the Canadian Pre-Cambrian Shield, the course is mostly sand and bedrock. Each player gets a small piece of carpet to

Camping is available at Fred Henne Territorial Park. (©Judy Nadon, staff)

take along on the round as their own portable turf. Site of the June 21 Midnight Tournament. Some modified rules have been adopted by this Far North golf course, among them: "No penalty assessed when ball carried off by raven."

J 208.5 (335.5 km) Yellowknife airport to south.

J 208.7 (335.9 km) Turnoff to north for **Fred Henne Territorial Park** day-use area Long Lake Beach at **Long Lake** with picnic sites, boat launch, snack bar, sandy beach and swimming.

J 209.2 (336.7 km) Old Airport Road access to Yellowknife; 2.2 miles/3.5 km to Walmart, 2.8 miles/4.5 km to Franklin Ave. Wardair Bristol freighter to the south. A plaque commemorates the Bristol freighter, which was the first wheel-equipped aircraft to land at the North Pole.

J 209.4 (337 km) Turnoff to north for **Fred Henne Territorial Park**. Well-maintained public campground with 115 sites: 64 powered $32; 39 non-powered RV sites $22.50; 12 tent pads $15. Canadian cash only for camping fees. Generators are permitted. There is water, electrical hookups, kitchen shelters, dump station, playground, firewood, firepits, showers, laundromat and pay phone. Daily and seasonal rates available. Open from mid-May to mid-September. Campground gates close at 10:30 P.M.

J 210 (338 km) Small turnout overlooking Jack Fish Lake south, litter bin.

J 210.4 (338.6 km) **Junction** with Highway 4/Ingraham Trail; *see log on page 336.* Turn south for Yellowknife (*description follows*).

Yellowknife

J 211.6 (340.5 km) Intersection of Highway 3 and Franklin Avenue in downtown Yellowknife. Yellowknife is located on the north shore of Great Slave Lake, approximately 940 miles/1,513 km from Edmonton, AB. **Population:** 19,429. **Emergency Services:** RCMP, phone (867) 669-1111. **Fire Department** and **Ambulance**, phone (867) 873-2222.

Hospital, Stanton Yellowknife, phone (867) 669-4111.

Visitor Information: At Northern Frontier Regional Visitors Centre, 4807 49th Street. Experienced and friendly staff ready to assist all visitors; interpretive displays. See the diamond display showcasing the diamond industry of the NWT, Canada. Open daily year-round; weekdays June to August 8:30 A.M. to 6 P.M., September to May 9 A.M. to 5 P.M.; noon to 4 P.M. weekends and holidays. Phone (867) 873-4262, toll free (877) 881-4262, fax (867) 873-3654; email info@ northernfrontier.com; web site: www.north ernfrontier.com.

Or contact Northwest Territories Tourism, P.O. Box 610, Yellowknife, NT X1A 2N5. Phone 1-800-661-0788 or (867) 873-7200, fax (867) 873-4059; web site www. explorenwt.com.

Private Aircraft: Yellowknife airport; elev. 674 feet/205m; length 7,500 feet/ 2,286m; asphalt; fuel 100/130, Jet B. Floatplane bases located at East Bay and West Bay of Latham Island.

Transportation: Air—Scheduled air service to Edmonton and Calgary aboard First Air Canadian North, Air Canada Jazz, WestJet. Several carriers serve Yellowknife and Arctic communities. Charter service available. **Bus**—Available via Frontier Coachlines Tuesday–Sunday with connections to Greyhound in Enterprise. **Taxi**—2 taxi companies. **Rentals**—Several major car rental agencies; boat, canoe and houseboat rentals.

No trip to the Northwest Territories would be complete without a stay in the Diamond Capital of North America™. Set in the wondrous natural surroundings of Great Slave Lake, Yellowknife is a modern city where you can experience rustic nature and traditional culture without missing out on urban amenities.

Whether you are driving an ice road; dancing under the aurora borealis; enjoying

Yellowknife has all the amenities of a major city, including a good bookstore.

(©Claire Torgerson, staff)

a dogsled ride; golfing under the midnight sun; fishing for world class trophies; watching the creation of a brilliant northern diamond, the unique character and warmth of Northern hospitality shines through.

Yellowknife became capital of the Northwest Territories in 1967, developing as a mining, transportation and government administrative centre for the territories. The Northwest Territories Legislative Assembly building is located on Frame Lake (tours are available).

European settlers arrived in the 1930s with the discovery of gold in the area and radium at Great Bear Lake. Cominco poured its first gold brick in 1938. WWII intervened and gold mining was halted until Giant Yellowknife Mines began milling on May 12, 1948. The road connecting the city with the provinces was completed in 1960.

The discovery of diamonds north of Yellowknife at Lac de Gras in 1992, set off a rush of claim stakers, and Yellowknife is now the service centre for several diamond mines. An estimated 150 companies have staked claims in an area stretching from north of Yellowknife to the Arctic coast, and east from the North Arm of Great Slave Lake to Hudson Bay. In winter, the Ingraham Trail (NWT Highway 4) is used as part of the 380-mile/612-km ice road to Lupin gold mine, which now extends to Lac de Gras, heart of the diamond rush, and Contwoyto Lake.

Lodging & Services

Accommodations at **Super 8** and other hotels, motels, inns, and B&Bs. There are many restaurants to choose from. There are major-chain retail stores such as Walmart here. Northern books downtown at **The Book Cellar**; gas stations and all other visitor services available.

Attractions

The Prince of Wales Northern Heritage Centre, built to collect, preserve, document, exhibit, study and interpret the North's natural and cultural history, is located on Frame Lake, accessible via 48th Street or by way of a pedestrian causeway behind City Hall. Do not miss the moose-skin boat or the video about the construction of this craft. The narrative and old photos about missionaries making their way North is also excellent. Good overview of aviation history in NWT.

Walking tour. Pick up a free copy of *Historical Walking Tours of Yellowknife* and explore Old Town—"The Rock"—the area surrounding Bush Pilot's Monument. Ragged Ass Road is found in Old Town. Have a meal at the **Wildcat Cafe**, which first opened in 1937. It reopened in 2013 after a 2-year renovation. Walk around Latham Island to see historic structures dating back to the 1930s, and modern buildings with very innovative architectural solutions to the problem of building on solid rock. .

Downtown, stop in at the **Diavik Diamond Display** in Diavik Diamond Mines main lobby.

Walk along the popular **Frame Lake Trail** (8 km loop) with its views of Yellowknife's skyline, including the Legislative Assembly buildings. "Will and Kate" visited and planted bushes near the "Hope Garden" on their visit in summer 2011.

Summer events. Various special events mark June 21, the longest day of the year and also Aboriginal Day, a territorial holiday. Canada Day (July 1) is a national holiday celebrated with a parade, music and games.

Take a tour by boat or van, enjoy fish fry dinners on the lake, take a flightseeing tour by float plane, or explore the waters along the Ingraham Trail by canoe or Great Slave Lake by cruiseboat.

Ingraham Trail, NT Highway 4, is a 43-mile/69-km road leading northeast of Yellowknife to picnicking, camping, fishing, canoeing and bird watching opportunities along a string of lakes and rivers. Pick up an Ingraham Trail map at Northern Frontier Visitors Centre. Log follows.

Ingraham Trail

Distance from Yellowknife (Y) is shown.

Y 0 Junction of Highways 3 and 4.

Y 2.9 (4.7 km) Side road leads north 3 miles/5 km to Vee Lake.

Y 4.7 (7.5 km) Yellowknife River bridge.

Y 4.8 (7.7 km) **Yellowknife River Day Use Area** with boat launch, 6 picnic sites, firewood, firepits and toilets. Good fishing for northern pike and grayling.

Y 12.2 (19.7 km) **Prosperous Lake** boat launch to north with toilets; fishing.

Y 14.9 (24 km) **Madeline Lake Park** to north with Boat launch, picnic sites, firewood, firepits and toilets. Fishing.

Y 16.4 (26.4 km) **Pontoon Lake** picnic area to south with picnic sites, firewood, firepits, toilets and boat launch. Fishing for northern pike, whitefish, cisco and suckers.

Y 17.4 (28 km) Side road leads north 1 mile/1.6 km to **Prelude Lake Territorial Campground**; 41 campsites, 20 picnic sites, firewood, water, showers, dump station, toilets, marina, boat launch, swimming. Prelude Wildlife hiking trail. Fishing for lake trout, grayling, whitefish, cisco, burbot, suckers, northern pike.

Y 17.5 (28.2 km) *Pavement ends, gravel begins, eastbound.*

Y 27.3 (44 km) **Powder Point Park** on Prelude Lake to north; parking area and toilets. Boat launch for canoeists doing the route into Hidden Lake Territorial Park, Lower Cameron River, or 4-day trip to Yellowknife River bridge.

Y 28.4 (45.8 km) **Hidden Lake Day-use Area** and **Cameron River Falls** trailhead to north; parking and toilets. A 0.6-mile/1-km trail leads to cliffs overlooking Cameron River Falls. Pedestrian bridge over river.

Y 33.5 (53.9 km) Bridge across Cameron River; parking area, toilets, picnicking, canoeing, hiking and swimming.

Y 34.4 (55.3 km) Informal campsites on sand esker overlooking Cameron River next 0.3 km eastbound.

Y 36.7 (59 km) **Reid Lake Territorial Campground** with 56 campsites, 10 picnic sites, kitchen shelter, swimming, hiking trail, playground, boat launch and fishing. Canoe launch point for Upper Cameron River and Jennejohn Lake routes. *CAUTION: Watch for bears.*

Y 42.8 (68.9 km) **Tibbitt Lake**. End of road. Launch point for Pensive Lakes canoe route (advanced canoeists only).

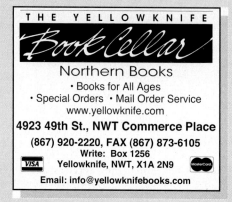

(Continued from page 333)
the Liard Highway. No visitor's services.

Junction of Highway 1 with the Liard Trail (Highway 7). Continue with this log for the Liard Trail to Fort Liard and junction with the Alaska Highway. See "Heritage Route" on page 338 for continuation of Highway 1 to Fort Simpson and Wrigley.

Deh Cho Route: Liard Trail

Distance from Grimshaw (G) is followed by distance from junction with Highway 1 (J) and distance from the Alaska Highway (AH).
Kilometreposts southbound on Highway 7 reflect distance from BC–NWT border. Kilometreposts eastbound on Highway 1 reflect distance from NWT–Alberta border. You need Canadian cash to pay for camping in territorial parks. They do not accept credit cards, cheques or U.S. cash.

HIGHWAY 7

G 550.2 J 0 AH 244.3 (393.2 km) Junction of Highways 1 and 7 at Checkpoint; no services. The Liard Trail is named for the Liard River Valley through which it runs for most of its length. In French, Liard means "black poplar," and this wilderness highway (officially opened in June 1984) is a corridor through a forest of white and black spruce, trembling aspen and balsam poplar.

G 550.3 J 0.1 (0.2 km) **AH 244.2** (393 km) *Pavement ends, gravel begins, southbound on Liard Trail.* **Emergency services:** RCMP, phone (867) 770-1111.

G 550.8 J 0.6 (1 km) **AH 243.7** (392.1 km) Double-ended turnout with litter bins and interpretive signs about the Liard Highway.

G 566.4 J 15.9 (25.6 km) **AH 228.1** (367.1 km) NorthwesTel Microwave tower to east. Vegetation changes northbound to muskeg with black spruce, tamarack and jack pine.

G 561.3 J 21 (33.8 km) **AH 223.3** Southbound, begin 40 km of rough frost heaves.

G 571.7 J 21.5 (34.6 km) **AH 223.4** (359.5 km) *Slow for one-lane metal-decked bridge* over **Poplar River.** Good grayling and pike fishing in Poplar River culverts.

G 582.7 J 32.5 (52.3 km) **AH 209** (387 km) Highway descends both directions to Birch River bridge (elev. 840 feet/256m).

G 585.1 J 34.9 (56.2 km) **AH 205** (379.7 km) Double-ended turnout with litter bins, outhouse. Informal campsite.

G 593.5 J 43.3 (69.7 km) **AH 201** (323.5 km) Microwave tower to east.

G 612.6 J 62.4 (100.4 km) **AH 181.9** (292.7 km) Entrance to Lindberg Landing; guest cabins, reservations required.

G 614.2 J 64 (103 km) **AH 180.3** (290.2 km) Entrance to **Blackstone Territorial Park and Campground.** The visitor information building, built with local logs, is located on the bank of the Liard River with superb views of Nahanni Butte (elev. 4,579 feet/1,396m). The centre is staffed and open from mid-May to mid-September.

There are 19 non-powered campsites with tables and firepits; firewood, hand-pump water and garbage containers, boat dock and state-of-the-art restroom and shower facility. Camping fee $22.50CN. The boat launch is

usable only in high water early in the season; use boat launch at Cadillac Landing or Lindberg's Landing during low water. The area offers wildlife and bird viewing, great scenery, river canoeing and other activities. ▲

G 616.7 J 66.5 (107) **AH 177.8** (286.1 km) Blackstone River bridge.

G 617 J 66.8 (107.5 km) **AH 177.5** (285.7 km) Blackstone River Park to west; picnic area with litter bins and outhouse.

G 617.1 J 66.9 (107.7 km) **AH 177.4** (285.5 km) Upper Blackstone River bridge.

G 618 J 67.8 (109.1 km) **AH 176.5** (284 km) Microwave tower to east.

G 627.3 J 77.1 (124 km) **AH 167.2** (269.1 km) Turnoff to west for winter ice road that leads 13.8 miles/22.3 km to the Dene settlement of **NAHANNI BUTTE** (pop. 116), at the confluence of the South Nahanni and Liard rivers. Summer access by boat, floatplane or by wheeled plane using the village's all-weather runway. Boats to Nahanni Butte can be arranged at Blackstone Territorial Park.

This is a busy outfitting area in season for deer, elk, grizzly and wood bison.

G 629.7 J 79.5 (127.9 km) **AH 164.8** (265.2 km) Road widens for an emergency airstrip; elev. 512 feet/156m.

G 635.7 J 85.5 (137.6 km) **AH 158.8** (255.6 km) Netla River bridge. The Netla River Delta is an important waterfowl breeding habitat, and Native fishing and hunting area.

G 644.6 J 94.4 (152 km) **AH 149.9** (241.2 km) Views of Mackenzie Mountains southbound. Road widens for an emergency airstrip; elev. 981 feet/299m.

G 646.3 J 96.1 (154.7 km) **AH 148.2** (238.5 km) *Limited visibility southbound* as road crests hill.

G 660 J 109.8 (176.7 km) **AH 134.5** (216.5 km) Double-ended turnout to west with interpretive panels, litter bins and outhouse.

G 668.1 J 117.9 (189.7 km) **AH 126.4** (203.4 km) Big Island Creek bridge (elev. 827 feet/252m). Good views of Liard Range to the west and northwest for the next 13 miles/21 km northbound.

G 671 J 120.8 (194.4 km) **AH 123.5** (198.7 km) Rabbit Creek.

G 679.5 J 129.3 (208 km) **AH 115** (185.1 km) **Muskeg River** bridge (elev. 814 feet/248m). River access and interpretive sign to west at north end of bridge. Gravel bars on the river make a good rest area, small rigs only. Swimming; fishing for pike, pickerel and freshwater clams.

G 685 J 134.8 (216.9 km) **AH 109.5** (176.2 km) **Junction** with Fort Liard Access Road. From this junction it is 1.7 miles/2.7

Acho Dene offers authentic Native crafts.
(©Judy Nadon, staff)

km to Hay Lakes Campground and 3.5 miles/5.6 km to Acho Dene craft store and a gas station. Double-ended turnout with interpretive signs west of junction on access road.

Views from road into Fort Liard across the Liard River of Mount Coty (elev. 2,715 feet/830m) and Pointed Mountain (elev. 4,610 feet/1,405m) at the southern tip of the Liard Range.

NOTE: Slow for 19 mph/30 kmph speed zone through town.

Fort Liard

Located on the south bank of the Liard River near its confluence with the Petitot River (known locally as Black River because of its colour), about 50 miles/80 km south of Nahanni Butte. **Population:** 591. **Emergency Services:** RCMP, phone (867) 770-1111. **Fire Department,** phone (867) 770-2222. **Health Centre,** phone (867) 770-4301. **Radio:** CBC 107.1 FM, CKLB 101.9.

Visitor Information: Visitor Information Centre/**Acho Dene Native Crafts** (closed Sundays), phone (867)
(Continues on page 339)

Heritage Route: Fort Simpson & Wrigley

National Aboriginal Day celebration June 21 in Fort Simpson. (©Judy Nadon, staff)

Highway 1 continues northwest from Checkpoint to Fort Simpson as the Heritage Route. Driving distance from the junction of Highway 1 with the Liard Trail at Checkpoint is 38 miles/61 km. This route crosses the Liard River via ferry in summer, ice road in winter. Fort Simpson is jump-off point for Nahanni National Park Reserve.

From the Fort Simpson turnoff, Highway 1 continues 137 miles/221 km to Wrigley. The "Wrigley extension," completed in 1994, made this small community the northernmost all-season access point along Highway 1.

Distance from Checkpoint (C) is shown. *Physical kilometreposts reflect distance from Alberta border.*

NWT HIGHWAY 1

C 0 **Junction** of Highway 1 with the Liard Trail (Highway 7) at Checkpoint. *Turn to Deh Cho Route log on page 337 for description of the Liard Trail to Fort Liard and the Alaska Highway. Continue with this log for Fort Simpson and Wrigley.*

A popular stop at one time, Checkpoint no longer offers visitor services.

C 26.6 (42.8 km) Free government-operated **Liard River** (South Mackenzie) ferry, the *Lafferty*, operates daily late May through October from 8 A.M. to 11:30 P.M., 7 days a week; on demand until 11:45 P.M. Crossing time is 6 minutes. Capacity is 8 cars or 2 trucks, with a maximum total weight of 130,269 lbs./59,090 kg. An ice bridge opens for light vehicles (to 6,614 lbs./3,000 kg) usually by late November; heavier vehicles can cross as ice thickens. *NOTE: This crossing is subject to extreme high and low water level fluctuations which may cause delays. No crossing possible during breakup (about mid-April to mid-May) and freezeup (mid-October to mid-November).* For crossing information, phone 1-800-661-0750.

C 35.7 (57.5 km) **Junction** of NWT Highway 1 with Fort Simpson access road. NWT Highway 1 turns and continues to Wrigley (*see Wrigley Extension log on page 339*). Fort Simpson access road leads 2.3 miles/3.8 km to Fort Simpson (description follows).

Fort Simpson

C 38 (61 km) Located on an island at the confluence of the Mackenzie and Liard rivers. **Population:** 1,233. **Emergency Services: RCMP,** phone (867) 695-3111. **Health Centre** with 1 doctor, daytime phone (867) 695-7000 or (867) 695-3232 for after hours emergencies. **Fire Department** (volunteer), phone (867) 695-2222.

Visitor Information: Very nice Visitor Information Centre with a wealth of old photos and historical displays. A movie theatre shows films. The visitor centre is open 9 A.M. to 8 P.M. weekdays, noon–8 P.M. weekends, from May to September. Winter hours are 1–4 P.M. weekdays only. Ask for Historical Walking Tours booklet and guide. Also visit www.fortsimpson.com. Phone (867) 695-3182.

Nahanni National Park Reserve office is open daily June 15–September 15, 8 A.M. to noon and 1–5 P.M.; weekdays the rest of the year, 8:30 A.M.–noon and 1–5 P.M. Phone (867) 695-3151; summer phone for duty officer (867) 695-3732.

Transportation: Air—Scheduled service to Yellowknife and Whitehorse, YT. Charter services available. **Rental cars**—Available. **Taxi service**—Available.

Private Aircraft: Fort Simpson airport; elev. 554 feet/169m; length 6,000 feet/1,829m; asphalt; fuel 100, Jet B. Fort Simpson Island; elev. 405 feet/123m; length 3,000 feet/914m; gravel; fuel 100, Jet B.

Fort Simpson or Liidlii Kue (South Slavey for "the place where the rivers come together") is the administrative headquarters for the Deh Cho (Big River) region. It is the oldest continuously occupied site on the Mackenzie River, dating from 1804 when the North West Co. established its Fort of the Forks. There is a National Historic Site plaque on the bank of the Mackenzie overlooking the confluence.

The Hudson's Bay Co. began its post here in 1822. At that time the fort was renamed after Sir George Simpson, one of the first governors of the combined North West Co. and Hudson's Bay Co. Fort Simpson served as the Mackenzie District headquarters for the Hudson's Bay Co. fur-trading operation. Its key location on the Mackenzie River also made Fort Simpson an important transportation centre. Anglican and Catholic missions were established here in 1858 and 1894.

Fort Simpson continues to be an important centre for the Northwest Territories water transport system. Visitors may walk along the high banks of the Mackenzie River and watch the boat traffic and floatplanes.

Lodging & Services

Fort Simpson is a full-service community. Accommodations at motels and bed-and-breakfasts.

There are 2 restaurants; 2 gas stations one with repair service (unleaded and propane available); 2 grocery stores, department store, hardware store, a bank, laundromat, post office, and 1 craft shop. Small engine repair shop and mechanics available. Diesel

available at Imperial Oil bulk plant Monday through Friday.

Recreational facilities include an arena, curling rink, gym, ball diamond, tennis, small indoor pool, a 9-hole golf course (longest hole is 475 yards) with clubhouse and gear rental ($15 day pass) and a boat launch at government wharf.

Camping at **Fort Simpson Territorial Park** on village access road; 21 powered campsites, 11 non-powered campsites, 4 picnic sites, kitchen shelter; showers (867) 695-7232.

Attractions

Shopping. Fort Simpson features Dene crafts, such as birch-bark baskets, beadwork, moose hide crafts, northern carvings and other hand made crafts.

One of the easiest places to get down to the water is by Albert Faille's cabin on Mackenzie Drive. Faille was a well-known Fort Simpson pioneer and prospector.

Fort Simpson Heritage Park, overlooking the National Historic Site Ehdaa, also known as the Papal Grounds where Pope John Paul II landed in 1987, features the McPherson House, built in 1936 and home to local pioneers George and Lucy McPherson and "Doc" Marion. Contact the Fort Simpson Historical Society, through the Fort Simpson Visitor Centre, phone (867) 695-2543 for tours. Some old structures are from the Experimental Farm, or Research Station, which operated at Fort Simpson for more than 20 years.

Fort Simpson is also a jumping-off point for fly-in trips with **Simpson Air** to **Nahanni National Park Reserve**, listed as a unique geological area on the UNESCO World Heritage Site list. The park is accessible only by nonpowered boat or aircraft. Located southwest of Fort Simpson near the Yukon border, air charter companies operate day-trip flightseeing tours to Little Doctor and Glacier lakes, Ram Plateau, Cirque of the Unclimbables, the Ragged Range and Virginia Falls on the South Nahanni River. Virginia Falls in Nahanni National Park Reserve are 300 feet/90m high, twice as high as Niagara Falls. One of the most popular attractions in the park for experienced river paddlers is running the South Nahanni River or its tributary, the Flat River.

The park has a mandatory reservation, registration and de-registration system for overnight use and charges a day use fee for Virginia Falls. For details contact Nahanni National Park Reserve, Box 348, Fort Simpson, NT X0E 0N0; phone (867) 695-7750; email nahanni.info@pc.gc.ca; website www.pc.gc.ca/nahanni.

Simpson Air. See display ad on page 338.

NWT HIGHWAY 1
WRIGLEY EXTENSION
(continued)

Distance from Checkpoint (C) is followed by distance from Fort Simpson access (FS). *NOTE: Availability of services in Wrigley is not certain.*

C 35.7 (61 km) **FS 0 Junction** with Fort Simpson access road. Driving time to Wrigley, 137 miles/221 km north from here, is approximately 3 hours. Allow at least 2 hours from Wrigley to the N'Dulee Crossing on the MV *Johnny Berens* ferry crossing.

C 46.6 (75 km) **FS 10.9** (16.3 km) Martin River Bridge. Turnout at north end of bridge. *CAUTION: Reduce speed for bridge crossing.*

C 71.2 (114.6 km) **FS 35.5** (57.2 km) Shale Creek 1-lane bridge. *CAUTION: Reduce speed for bridge crossing.*

C 84 (135.3 km) **FS 48.3** (77.7 km) N'Dulee/Camsell Bend ferry/ice crossing of the Mackenzie River on MV *Johnny Berens.*

©Judy Nadon, staff

Ferry operates daily, late May through October, 9 to 11 A.M. and 2 to 8 P.M. on demand. Capacity is 6 cars or 4 trucks. Call 1-800-661-0750 or 1-800-661-0751 for information. *NOTE: There are no overnight facilities for anyone missing the ferry. Ferry does not operate in fog. Be prepared to wait.* Ice crossing in winter.

C 131.9 (212.3 km) **FS 96.2** (154.8 km) Willowlake River bridge, longest bridge in the Northwest Territories. *Slow to 26 kmph/14 mph, single-lane.*

C 135.6 (218.2 km) **FS 99.9** (160.8 km) Turnout to west at top of hill with litter barrels and scenic view of the Mackenzie Valley and River with Mackenzie Mountains in the background.

C 148.6 (239 km) **FS 112.9** (181.7 km) Single-lane wooden bridge over the "River Between Two Mountains."

C 172.7 (278 km) **FS 137** (220.5 km) **WRIGLEY** (pop. 182; 90 percent Dene ancestry). **Emergency Services: RCMP,** station manned intermittently. **Nursing Station,** with full-time nurse, phone (867) 581-3441. **Visitor Information:** The Pehdzeh Ki Dene Band Complex has information for visitors. **Private Aircraft:** Wrigley airport, 4 miles/7 km south of town; elev. 493 feet/142m; length 3,500 feet/1,148m; gravel; fuel 80.

The Hudson's Bay Co. built a trading post here in 1870 called Fort Wrigley. The fort was abandoned in 1910 due to disease and famine, and the inhabitants moved down-river to Old Fort Wrigley near Roche-qui-trempe-a'-l'eau (the rock that plunges into the water), a well-known land form. Although a church and school were built at that site in 1957, the community decided to move to higher ground in 1965. Wrigley is the home of the Pehdzeh Ki First Nation. Log-cabin-style homes often have teepees to dry and store fish and game in traditional ways.

Signs inform motorists when winter roads and ice crossings are open. Winter roads in Northwest Territories provide access to bush camps and communities and remote mining sites otherwise serviced by air. Winter roads are either snow roads built over land, or ice roads built over water. Winter roads status and load limits are posted online at www.dot.gov.nt.ca. *(Driving a public winter or ice road or ice crossing when it is closed or before its official opening carries a significant fine.)*

Wrigley provides a stopover for vehicles driving north to Fort Norman (148 miles/238 km), Norman Wells (198 miles/318 km), Fort Franklin (266 miles/428 km), Fort Good Hope (289 miles/465 km), and Colville Lake. Ice crossings north of Wrigley are at Deline and Tulita.

(continued from page 337) 770-4161; email adnc@ntsympatico.ca. Visitor information also available from Hamlet of Fort Liard. Write: General Delivery, Fort Liard, NT Canada X0G 0A0; phone (867) 770-4104; Fax (867) 770-4004; www.fortliard.com.

Elevation: 686 feet/209m. **Climate:** Comparatively mild considering Fort Liard's geographical location. Fort Liard is known as the "tropics of the north." **Radio** and **Television:** CBC radio (microwave) and CKLB 101.9 from Yellowknife; CBC Television (Anik), APTN and private satellite receivers. Bell cellular service available.

Private Aircraft: Liard airstrip; elev. 700 feet/213m; length 2,950 feet/899m; gravel.

Transportation: Air—Charter service year-round via Villars Air. **Barge**—Non-scheduled barge service in summer.

This small, well-laid-out settlement of both traditional log homes and new modern housing is located among tall poplar, spruce and birch trees on the south bank of the Liard River. Oil and gas exploration, forestry and tourism support the economy. Fort Liard residents are well known for the high quality of their birch-bark baskets and porcupine quill workmanship

The North West Co. established a trading post near here at the confluence of the Liard and Petitot rivers called Riviere aux Liards in 1805. The post was abandoned after the massacre of more than a dozen residents by Indians. It was taken over by the Hudson's Bay Co. in 1821 and re-established in 1822 when the 2 companies merged. The well-known geologist Charles Camsell was born at Fort Liard in 1876.

Lodging, groceries, hardware and sundries available at Liard Valley General Store and Motel. Gas, diesel, propane and fishing and hunting licenses available here at the Fort Liard Fuel Centre (which includes Johnnie's Cafe, crafts and groceries). Post office at the Northern Store. There is the modern Echo Dene School and a Roman Catholic mission (not open for tours). There is no bank in Fort Liard. ATMs in the Northern Store and the Liard Fuel Centre.

Stop in at **Acho Dene Native Crafts** store to shop for quill-decorated birchbark berry baskets and bowls (a Fort Liard specialty), beaded moccasins and mukluks, moose-hair tufting, miniature birchbark canoes and many other traditional native handicrafts.

Community-run **Hay Lake Campground** has 12 campsites (no power or hook-ups), sani-dump, potable water, picnic tables, cooking shelter, toilets and a hiking trail around the lake. Bring insect repellent. There is no charge for these sites.

Recreation and sightseeing in the area include fishing (for pike, pickerel, goldeye and spring grayling) at the confluence of the Liard and Petitot rivers and Liard River canoe and boat tours.

Acho Dene Native Crafts. See display ad on page 337.

Deh Cho Route Log
(continued)

G 685 J 134.8 (216.9 km) **AH 109.5** (176.2 km) **Junction** with Fort Liard Access Road: Hay Lakes Campground 1.7 miles/2.7 km west; gas station 3.5 miles/5.6 km west.

G 686 J 135.8 (218.5 km) **AH 108.5** (174.6 km) Vehicle inspection station to east (closed in summer 2011). Parking.

G 708.2 J 158 (254.3 km) **AH 86.3**
(continues on page 341)

Wood Buffalo Route: Highway 5

Viewpoint of Salt Plains, a unique environment where only plants adapted to high salinity can grow. (©Judy Nadon, staff)

Highway 5 leads 166 miles/267 km from its junction with Highway 2 to the community of Fort Smith.

Distance from Enterprise (E) is shown.

There are no services between Hay River and Fort Smith.

NWT HIGHWAY 5

E 19.8 (31.9 km) **Junction** with Highway 2 to Hay River and Enterprise.

E 21.1 (34 km) Railroad and auto bridge crosses Hay River.

E 21.3 (34.3 km) Access road leads north 3.7 miles/5.9 km to Hay River Reserve and Dene Cultural Centre.

E 50.1 (80.6 km) Good gravel road leads 1 mile/1.6 km north to **Polar Lake**; no motorboats allowed. Day-use fee $5; camping $10/night. Good bird watching.

E 54 (86.9 km) Buffalo River bridge.

E 54.4 (87.5 km) Turnout to north with outhouse, litter barrel and map.

E 57.6 (92.7 km) **Junction** with Highway 6 to Fort Resolution; see "Great Slave Lake Route" log on page 332. Continue on Highway 5 south for Fort Smith.

E 74.3 (119.6 km) Turnoff for **Sandy Lake**, 8 miles/13 km south; swimming, sandy beach, fishing for northern pike.

E 79.8 (128.4 km) Entrance to Wood Buffalo National Park. Established in 1922 to protect Canada's largest free roaming herd of wood bison (more than 5,000), **Wood Buffalo National Park** (a UNESCO World Heritage Site) is a vast wilderness area larger than the size of Switzerland with 44,800 square kilometres and the greater portion located in the northeast corner of Alberta. Park headquarters and Visitor Reception Centre are located in Fort Smith and Fort Chipewyan. The park is open all year and numerous hiking trails and outdoor activities draw visitors from around the world. For more information, contact Wood Buffalo

National Park, Box 750, Fort Smith, NT X0E 0P0; phone (867) 872-7960. Website: www.parkscanada.gc.ca/woodbuffalo.

E 82 (132 km) Picnic area with tables, toilets and playground to north at Angus Fire Tower. Giant sinkhole here is typical of karst topography.

E 85.8 (138 km) *Pavement ends, gravel begins, eastbound.*

E 94 (151.2 km) Turnout to south with litter barrel, toilets and interpretive signs on bison and the Nyarling River. *Watch for wood bison.*

E 119 (192.2 km) Grader station and last restroom stop until Fort Smith.

E 130 (209.2 km) Highway crosses Sass River. Shallow lakes from here south to Preble Creek provide nesting areas for whooping cranes.

E 135.3 (217.7 km) Highway crosses Preble Creek.

E 143.6 (231.1 km) Turnout with litter barrel, walking trail and interpretive signs on wetlands habitat.

E 150.3 (241.9 km) Little Buffalo River bridge.

E 153.5 (247 km) Access road leads 0.6 mile/1 km to **Little Buffalo River Falls Campground** with shelter, firewood, firepits, picnic tables, toilets, tent platforms, interpretive trail and boat/canoe launch. Park is open mid-May to mid-September.

Gravel ends, pavement begins, southbound.

E 163.5 (263.1 km) Turnoff for Parsons Lake Road (narrow gravel) which leads south 8 miles/13 km to **Salt Plains Overlook**; interpretive exhibit and viewing telescope. Gravel parking area with tables, firepits and toilets at overlook. A hiking trail down to Salt Plains (bring boots).

Springs at the edge of a high escarpment bring salt to the surface and spread it across the huge flat plain; only plants adapted to high salinity can grow here. Fine view of a unique environment. Some 227 species

of birds are known to travel through here. More information on the Salt Plains is available at the Park office in town.

CAUTION: Parsons Lake Road beyond the overlook is a narrow bush road that may be impassable in wet weather and/or blocked by fallen trees.

E 166.6 (268.1 km) Salt River bridge.

E 170.8 (274.9 km) Good gravel side road leads 10 miles/16 km north to settlement of **SALT RIVER**; campground, small-boat launch, and fishing for pike, walleye, inconnu and goldeye.

E 176.3 (283.7 km) Access road north to old Bell Rock, where goods portaged from Fort Fitzgerald were loaded on boats bound for Great Slave Lake and the Mackenzie River.

E 181.9 (292.8 km) Turnoff to north for Fort Smith airport and **Queen Elizabeth Park Campground** with 17 campsites with electrical hookups, 15 picnic sites, toilets, water, kitchen shelter, showers, dump station, firewood, firepits, fishing and playground.

Short hike from campground to bluff overlooking Rapids of the Drowned on the Slave River; look for pelicans feeding here.

Fort Smith

E 186.4 (300 km) Located on the Slave River. **Population**: 2,400. **Emergency Services**: RCMP, phone (867) 872-1111. **Fire Department**, phone (867) 872-2222. **Ambulance**, phone (867) 872-3111. **Health Centre**, phone (867) 872-6200. **Visitor Information**: At Wood Buffalo National Park visitor centre; open year-round, daily in summer, 9 A.M.–6 P.M., and weekdays in off season, 9 A.M.–5

P.M. (closed for lunch). Phone (867) 872-3065. Pick up *A Walking Tour Guide to Historic Trails* brochure here. Online information at www.fortsmith.ca. Or contact the Town of Fort Smith, P.O. Box 147, Fort Smith, NT X0E 0P0; phone (867) 872-8400.

Transportation: Air—Scheduled and charter service available. **Bus**—Available. **Rental cars**—Available.

Private Aircraft: Fort Smith airport; elev. 666 feet/203m; length, 6,000 feet/1,829m; asphalt; fuel 80, 100.

Fort Smith began as a trading post at a favorite campsite of the portagers traveling the 1,600-mile/2575-km water passage from Fort McMurray to the Arctic Ocean. The 4 sets of rapids, named (south to north) Cassette, Pelican, Mountain and the Rapids of the Drowned, separate the Northwest Territories from Alberta. In 1872, Hudson's Bay Co. established a permanent post, and the Roman Catholic mission was built here in 1876. By 1911 the settlement had become a major trading post for the area.

There is a hotel/motel, multiple bed and breakfasts, 2 grocery stores, post office, 1 bookstore, 3 gift shops, several restaurants and a take-out place, 3 bars, 3 convenience stores, 3 gas stations and several repair services locations.

Attractions include the multi-image presentation at **Wood Buffalo National Park visitor reception centre** at 149 McDougal Rd., Fort Smith, NT X0E 0P0. Wood Buffalo National Park was established in 1922 to protect the last remaining herd of bison in northern Canada. It also serves to protect the Canada Northern Boreal Plains. Phone (867) 872-7960; www.parkscanada.gc.ca/woodbuffalo.

The excellent **Northern Life Museum & Cultural Centre** showcases Native basketry, the fur trade and birdlife, especially the miraculous comeback of the Whooping Crane. Open Mon.–Sat., 10 A.M. to 5 P.M., June thru August; weekdays only, Sept. thru May.

Fort Smith Mission Park historic site is open May 15–Sept. 15. Inquire locally about interpretive tours.

A lookout with viewing telescope is located at the north edge of town. Enjoy **Slave River beach** and the network of walking trails along the riverbank.

Walk down to **Rapids of the Drowned** to watch white pelicans fishing for walleyes, eels and suckers; interpretive sign at overlook. Fort Smith has the northernmost colony of nesting white pelicans.

Drive out to Pine Lake Road in Wood Buffalo National Park. There are several hiking trails off the road. There are 25 non-powered sites at **Pine Lake Campground** for tenting or RV campers. Day-use and overnight. Beautiful beach. Must boil water for drinking here. Located 38 miles/61 km south of Fort Smith. Groups contact the park office at (867) 872-7960.

View of Nahanni Butte and Liard River from Blackstone Territorial Park. (©Judy Nadon, staff)

(Continued from page 339)
(138.9 km) Double-ended turnout to east with litter bins.

BC HIGHWAY 77

G 708.5 J 158.3 (254.7 km) **AH 86** (138.4 km) **BC–NWT border.** *TIME ZONE CHANGE: British Columbia observes Pacific time, Northwest Territories observes Mountain time.*

Gravel ends, pavement begins, southbound. Gravel road may be slippery when wet.

G 710.6 J 160.4 (258.1 km) **AH 83.9** (135 km) Highway descends in both directions to **Petitot River** bridge. The Petitot River was named for Father Petitot, an Oblate missionary who came to this area from France in the 1860s. It is reputed to have the warmest swimming water in British Columbia (70°F/21°C). Good bird-watching area. Also freshwater clams, pike and pickerel; short grayling run in spring.

The Petitot River bridge was the site of the official opening of the Liard Highway on June 23, 1984. The Liard Highway replaced the old Fort Simpson winter road that joined Fort Nelson and Fort Simpson. The original Simpson Trail was first blazed in November 1942 by Alaska Highway engineers, including the 648th, Company A detachment.

G 712 J 161.8 (260.4 km) **AH 82.5** (132.8 km) Crest of Petitot River hill; *10 percent grades.*

G 721 J 170.8 (274.9 km) **AH 73.5** (45.7 km) Gravel turnout to west.

G 724.4 J 174.2 (280.3 km) **AH 70.1** (112.8 km) Bridge over Deasum Creek (elev. 1,608 feet/490m). Good bird-watching area. *Slow gravel breaks southbound.*

G 724.9 J 174.7 (281.1 km) **AH 69.6** (112 km) There are several roads in this area used by the forest, oil and gas industries.

G 730.6 J 180.4 (290.3 km) **AH 63.9** (102.8 km) Long paved turnout to north.

G 740.1 J 189.9 (305.6 km) **AH 54.4** (87.5 km) *Improved pavement from here south to the Alaska Highway.*

G 753.8 J 203.6 (327.7 km) **AH 40.7** (65.5 km) Tsiana Creek.

G 757.7 J 207.5 (333.9 km) **AH 36.8** (59.2 km) Paved turnout to east.

G 767.9 J 217.7 (350.3 km) **AH 26.6** (42.8 km) Turnout to west at north end of bridge with pit toilet, table and litter bins.

G 768 J 217.8 (350.5 km) **AH 26.5** (42.6 km) *Slow for 1-lane wood-decked bridge* across

©Judy Nadon, staff

Fort Nelson River (elev. 978 feet/298m). The Nelson bridge is the longest Acrow bridge in the world at 1,410 feet/430m. It is 14 feet/4m wide, with a span of 230 feet/70m from pier to pier. The Acrow bridge, formerly called the Bailey bridge after its designer, Sir Donald Bailey, is designed of interchangeable steel panels coupled with pins for rapid construction.

G 771.2 J 221 (355.7 km) **AH 23.3** (37.5 km) Long chip-sealed turnout to east.

G 780 J 229.8 (369.8 km) **AH 14.5** (23.3 km) Stanolind Creek. Beaver dams to west.

G 786.7 J 236.5 (380.7 km) **AH 7.8** (12.5 km) Beaver Lake Recreation Site to east. Narrow, bumpy dirt road access to user maintained camping area (not appropriate for mid- to large-size rigs); 6 small sites, dumpster, outhouse.

G 794.5 J 244.3 (393.2 km) **AH 0** **Junction** of Liard Trail and the Alaska Highway. From this junction it is 18 miles/29 km to Fort Nelson, BC; 113 miles/182 km to Fort Liard, NWT; 282 miles/454 km to Fort Simpson; 405 miles/651 km to Fort Providence; and 596 miles/960 km to Yellowknife. *NOTE: Next gas stops northbound: Fort Liard, Fort Simpson and Fort Providence.*

Junction with the Alaska Highway. Turn to **Milepost DC 301** on page 152 in the ALASKA HIGHWAY section.

Glenn Highway Tok Cutoff

CONNECTS: Tok to Anchorage, AK

Length: 328 miles   **Road Surface:** Paved   **Season:** Open all year

(See maps, page 343-344)

1 **4**

The scenic Glenn Highway offers spectacular mountain views. *(©Sharon Nault)*

Distance in miles	Anchorage	Glennallen	Palmer	Tok	Valdez
Anchorage		189	42	328	304
Glennallen	189		147	139	115
Palmer	42	147		286	262
Tok	328	139	286		254
Valdez	304	115	262	254	

The Glenn Highway/Tok Cutoff (Alaska Route 1) is the principal access route from the Alaska Highway west to Anchorage, a distance of 328 miles. This paved all-weather route includes the 125-mile Tok Cutoff, between Tok and the Richardson Highway junction; a 14-mile link via the Richardson Highway; and the 189-mile Glenn Highway, between the Richardson Highway and Anchorage. The 139-mile stretch of the Glenn Highway between Anchorage and Eureka Summit was declared a National Scenic Byway in 2002.

It is a full day's drive between Tok and Anchorage, although there are enough attractions along the way to recommend making this a 2- or 3-day drive. The speed limit varies, from 35-mph through communities to 65-mph on the relatively straight stretch of improved road between **Mileposts A 91** and **A 185** along the Glenn Highway. Current road conditions and weather at http://511.alaska.gov.

Road conditions are generally good along the Tok Cutoff and Glenn Highway, with a number of improved sections of highway that have been realigned and/or widened. Motorists can expect about 25 miles of winding road and future road improvement projects on the stretch of highway from **Milepost A 91** (Purinton Creek) to **Milepost A 66** (near Sutton), where the Glenn makes its way through the Talkeetna and Chugach mountains.

Four side roads are logged in this section: the Nabesna Road, which also pro-

© Meghan Mackey, staff

Major Attractions:

National Scenic Byway, Matanuska Glacier, Alaska State Fair, Independence Mine

Highest Summit:
Eureka Summit 3,322 ft.

www.themilepost.com

Glenn Highway   Tok Cutoff (GJ-125 to GJ-0) to Milepost A 160

© 2014 The MILEPOST®

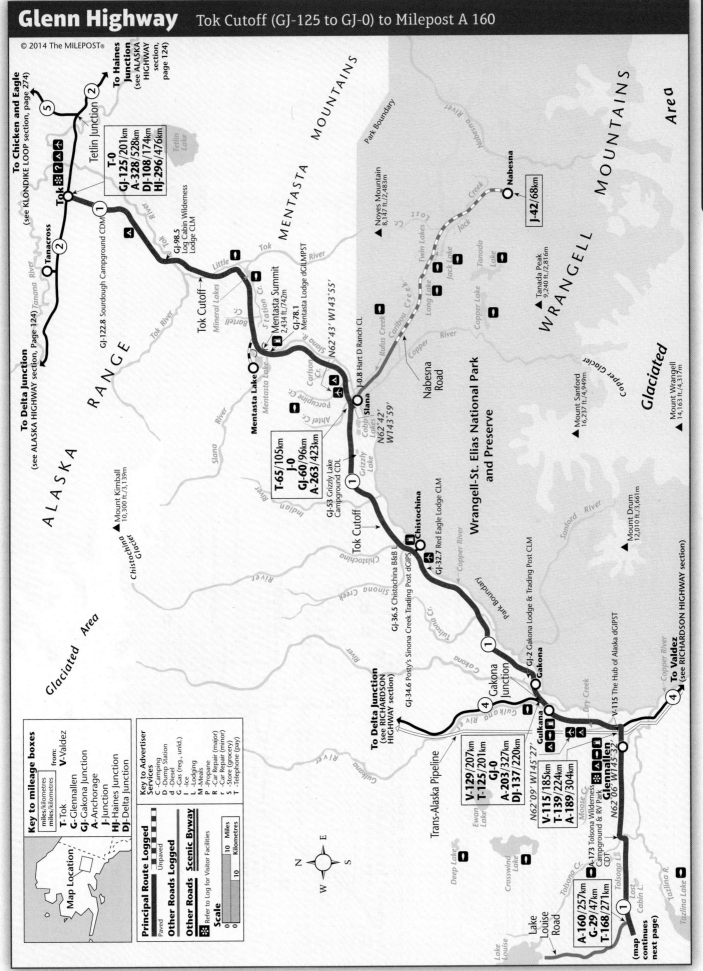

To Haines Junction
(see ALASKA HIGHWAY section, page 124)

Tetlin Junction

T-0
GJ-125/201km
A-328/528km
DJ-108/174km
HJ-296/476km

To Chicken and Eagle
(see KLONDIKE LOOP section, page 274)

To Delta Junction
(see ALASKA HIGHWAY section, Page 124)

Tanacross

Tok

GJ-122.8 Sourdough Campground CDM

GJ-98.5
Log Cabin Wilderness
Lodge CLM

Tok Cutoff

MENTASTA MOUNTAINS

Mentasta Summit
2,434 ft./742m

GJ-78.1
Mentasta Lodge dGILMPST
N62°43' W143°55'

J-0.8 Hart D Ranch CL

Mentasta Lake

**T-65/105km
J-0
GJ-60/96km
A-263/423km**

GJ-53 Grizzly Lake
Campground CDL

Cobb
Lakes

Slana
N62°42'
W143°59'

Grizzly
Lake

Noyes Mountain
8,147 ft./2,483m

Nabesna

J-42/68km

Nabesna
Road

Tanada Peak
9,240 ft./2,816m

WRANGELL MOUNTAINS

Glaciated Area

Mount Sanford
16,237 ft./4,949m

Mount Drum
12,010 ft./3,661m

Mount Wrangell
14,163 ft./4,317m

**Wrangell-St. Elias National Park
and Preserve**

Copper Glacier

ALASKA RANGE

Mount Kimball
10,300 ft./3,139m

Chistochina
Glacier

Glaciated Area

Tok Cutoff

GJ-34.6 Posty's Sinona Creek Trading Post dGIPST

GJ-36.5 Chistochina B&B L

Chistochina

GJ-32.7 Red Eagle Lodge CLM

Park Boundary

GJ-2 Cakona Lodge & Trading Post CLM

Gakona

Gakona
Junction

To Delta Junction
(see RICHARDSON
HIGHWAY section)

Trans-Alaska Pipeline

Gulkana

V-115 The Hub of Alaska dGIPST

To Valdez
(see RICHARDSON HIGHWAY section)

**V-129/207km
T-125/201km
GJ-0
A-203/327km
DJ-137/220km**

N62°09' W145°27'

**V-115/185km
T-139/224km
A-189/304km**

Glennallen
N62°06' W145°32'

A-173 Tolsona Wilderness
Campground & RV Park
CDT

Lake
Louise Road

**A-160/257km
G-29/47km
T-168/271km**

(map
continues
next page)

Key to mileage boxes
miles/kilometres

from: **V-Valdez**
T-Tok
G-Glennallen
GJ-Gakona Junction
A-Anchorage
J-Junction
HJ-Haines Junction
DJ-Delta Junction

Map Location

Key to Advertiser Services
C -Camping
D -Dump Station
d -Diesel
G -Gas (reg., unld.)
I -Ice
L -Lodging
M -Meals
P -Propane
R -Car Repair (major)
r -Car Repair (minor)
S -Store (grocery)
T -Telephone (pay)

Principal Route Logged
Paved
Unpaved

Other Roads Logged   **Scenic Byway**

Other Roads

Refer to Log for Visitor Facilities

Scale
0   10 Miles
0   10 Kilometres

Glenn Highway Milepost A 160 to Anchorage, AK

© 2014 The MILEPOST®

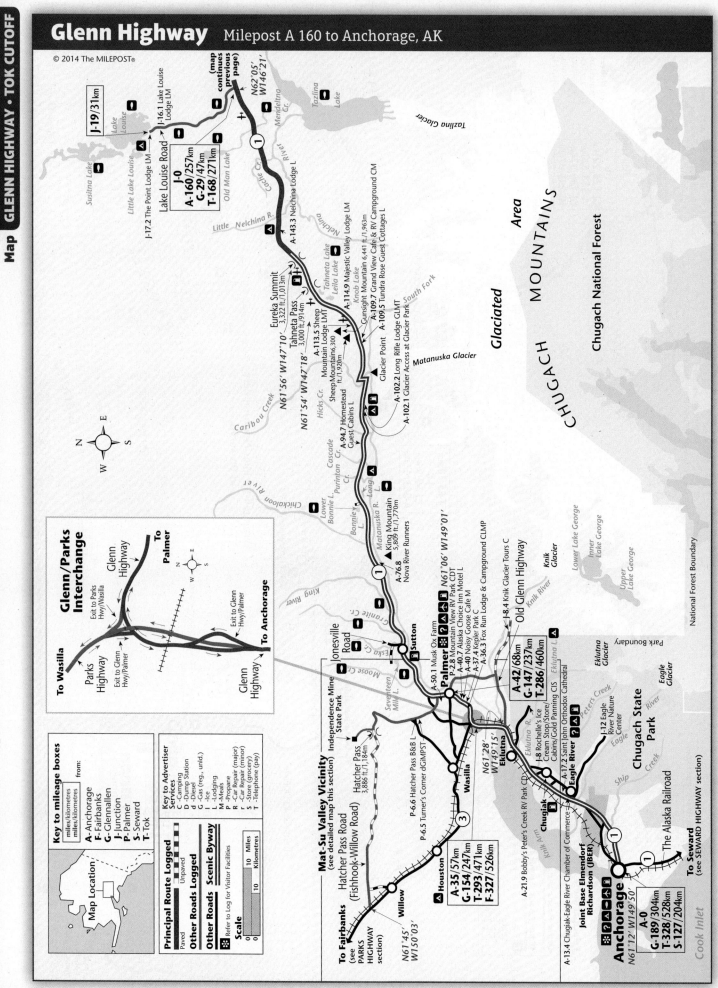

(map continues previous page)

N62°05'
W146°21'

J-19/31km

J-16.1 Lake Louise Lodge LM

J-17.2 The Point Lodge LM

Lake Louise Road

J-0
A-160/257km
G-29/47km
T-168/271km

A-143.3 Nelchina Lodge L

Eureka Summit 3,322 ft./1,013m
N61°56' W147°10'

Tahneta Pass 3,000 ft./914m
N61°54' W147°18'

A-113.5 Sheep Mountain Lodge LMT

Sheep Mountain 6,300 ft./1,920m
A-114.9 Majestic Valley Lodge LM

Tahneta Lake
Leila Lake
Gunsight Mountain 6,441 ft./1,963m
Knob Lake

A-109.7 Grand View Cafe & RV Campground CM
A-109.5 Tundra Rose Guest Cottages L
A-102.2 Long Rifle Lodge GLMT
Glacier Point
A-102.1 Glacier Access at Glacier Park Matanuska Glacier

A-94.7 Homestead Guest Cabins L

King Mountain 5,809 ft./1,770m

A-76.8
Nova River Runners

Glenn/Parks Interchange

To Palmer

Glenn Highway

Exit to Parks Hwy/Wasilla

Exit to Glenn Hwy/Palmer

Exit to Glenn Hwy/Palmer

Parks Highway

To Wasilla

Glenn Highway

To Anchorage

Sutton

Jonesville Road

A-50.1 Musk Ox Farm

Palmer N61°06' W149°01'
P-2.8 Mountain View RV Park CDT
A-40.7 Alaska Choice Inn Motel L
A-40 Noisy Goose Cafe M
A-37.4 Kepler Park C
A-36.3 Fox Run Lodge & Campground CLMP
A-42/68km
G-147/237km
T-286/460km

Old Glenn Highway

Knik Glacier

I-8.4 Knik Glacier Tours C

Eklutna N61°28' W149°15'
I-8 Rochelle's Ice Cream Stop/Store/Cabins/Gold Panning CIS
A-17.2 Saint John Orthodox Cathedral
Eagle River
I-12 Eagle River Nature Center

A-21.9 Bobby's Peter's Creek RV Park CD

A-13.4 Chugiak-Eagle River Chamber of Commerce

Chugach State Park

Eklutna Glacier
Eagle Glacier

Peters Creek
Ship Creek

The Alaska Railroad

To Seward (see SEWARD HIGHWAY section)

Joint Base Elmendorf Richardson (JBER)

Anchorage N61°12' W149°50'
A-0
G-189/304km
T-328/528km
S-127/204km

Cook Inlet

Mat-Su Valley Vicinity
(see detailed map this section)

Independence Mine State Park

Hatcher Pass 3,886 ft./1,184m

Hatcher Pass Road (Fishhook-Willow Road)

P-6.6 Hatcher Pass B&B L
P-6.5 Turner's Corner dGiMPST

Wasilla N61°34' W149°28'
Chugiak

Houston
A-35/57km
G-154/247km
T-293/471km
F-327/526km

Willow
N61°45' W150°03'

To Fairbanks (see PARKS HIGHWAY section)

Key to mileage boxes

miles/kilometres from:

A- Anchorage
F- Fairbanks
G- Glennallen
J- Junction
P- Palmer
S- Seward
T- Tok

Map Location

Key to Advertiser Services

C - Camping
D - Dump Station
d - Diesel
G - Gas (reg., unld.)
I - Ice
L - Lodging
M - Meals
P - Propane
R - Car Repair (major)
r - Car Repair (minor)
S - Store (grocery)
T - Telephone (pay)

? Refer to Log for Visitor Facilities

Principal Route Logged

Paved
Unpaved

Other Roads Logged

Other Roads
Scenic Byway

Scale

0   10 Miles
0   10 Kilometres

Glaciated Area

CHUGACH MOUNTAINS

Chugach National Forest

National Forest Boundary

Park Boundary

Lower Lake George
Inner Lake George
Upper Lake George

Lake Louise
Little Lake Louise
Susitna Lake
Lake Louise LM

Cache Cr.
Mendeltna Cr.
Old Man Lake
Tazlina Lake
Tazlina Glacier
Tazlina River

Little Nelchina R.
Nelchina R.
Caribou Creek

Hicks Cr.
Cascade Cr.
Purinton Cr.
Lower Bonnie L.
Bonnie L.
Long L.

Matanuska R.
Chickaloon River
King River
Granite Cr.
Eska Cr.
Moose Cr.
Seventeen Mile L.
Sixteen Mile L.

Knik River
Knik Arm
Eklutna L.
Eklutna R.

vides access to Wrangell–St. Elias National Park and Preserve; Lake Louise Road to Lake Louise Recreation Area; the Hatcher Pass Road, connecting the Glenn and Parks highways to Independence Mine State Historical Park; and the Old Glenn Highway, an alternate route between Palmer and Anchorage that offers camping, fishing and Knik Glacier access via airboat.

Emergency medical services: Phone 911 or EMS/Alaska State Troopers dispatch Tok, (907) 883-5111; Cross Road Medical Center Glennallen, (907) 822-3203; Alaska State Troopers Glennallen, (907) 822-3263; Mat-Su Borough EMS (Palmer/Wasilla), (907) 745-4811; Alaska State Troopers Palmer, (907) 745-2131; Chugiak Fire & Rescue dispatch, (907) 622-9111; Alaska State Troopers Anchorage, (907) 269-5511.

Tok Cutoff Log

Distance from junction with the Richardson Highway at Gakona Junction (GJ) is followed by distance from Anchorage (A) and distance from Tok (T).

Physical mileposts (located on the southeast side of the highway) show distance from Gakona Junction.

ALASKA ROUTE 1

GJ 125 A 328 T 0 TOK; Junction of Alaska Highway and Tok Cutoff. Distance marker eastbound shows Fairbanks 208 miles, Canadian border 90 miles. Westmark Inn at northwest corner of this intersection; Tok's visitor center at southeast corner. (See Tok map page 209.) Paved bike path begins south side of highway. *Improved highway westbound to Milepost GJ 109.*

> **Junction** of the Tok Cutoff (Alaska Route 1) and the Alaska Highway (Alaska Route 2) in Tok. Turn to page 208 in the ALASKA HIGHWAY section for description of Tok and log of the Alaska Highway southeast to the Canadian border or northwest to Delta Junction.

Distance marker westbound shows Glennallen 141 miles, Valdez 254 miles, Anchorage 328 miles.

GJ 124 A 327 T 1 *Actual driving distance between Milepost 124 and 125 at Tok junction is 0.5 miles.*

GJ 123.5 A 326.5 T 1.5 Turnoff to north on Borealis Avenue for **Tetlin National Wildlife Refuge Headquarters** (1.3 miles northwest). The Tetlin NWR office is open weekdays 8 A.M. to 4 P.M., year-round; parking, information boards, a good display of Alaska's owls, brochures on the refuge, information on campgrounds, and import/export permits for hunters. (The visitor center for Tetlin National Wildlife Refuge is located at **Milepost DC 1229** Alaska Highway.)

Begin 55 mph speed limit westbound. Slow for 35 mph speed zone eastbound.

GJ 122.8 A 325.8 T 2.2 Sourdough Campground to west; thickly treed, full-service campground with cafe serving pancake breakfast.

GJ 122.6 A 325.6 T 2.4 Private Aircraft: Tok airstrip to southeast; elev. 1,670 feet; length 1,700 feet; gravel; unattended. No services. Private airfield across the highway.

GJ 118 A 321 T 7 Flashing lights to north

are from U.S. Coast Guard loran station at **Milepost DC 1308.5** on the Alaska Highway.

GJ 116.6 A 319.6 T 8.4 Paved turnout at westbound boundary sign for Tok Management Area, **Tanana Valley State Forest.** End of the paved bike trail coming from Tok.

Established as the first unit of Alaska's state forest system in 1983, **Tanana Valley State Forest** encompasses 1.81 million acres and lies almost entirely within the Tanana River Basin. The forest extends 265 miles from near the Canadian border to Manley Hot Springs. Almost 90 percent of the state forest is forested. Principal tree species are paper birch, quaking aspen, balsam poplar, black spruce, white spruce and tamarack. Almost 7 percent of the forest is shrubland, chiefly willow. The forest is managed by the Dept. of Natural Resources.

GJ 114 A 317 T 11 Distance marker eastbound shows Tok 10 miles, Canadian Border 100 miles.

GJ 112 A 315 T 13 Large paved parking area to southeast.

GJ 111 A 314 T 14 Distance marker westbound shows Nabesna Junction 53 miles, Glennallen 128 miles, Anchorage 315 miles.

GJ 110 A 313 T 15 Highway straightens eastbound.

GJ 109.3 A 312.3 T 15.7 Clearwater Creek bridge.

GJ 109.2 A 312.2 T 15.8 Turnoff to north for **Eagle Trail State Recreation Site** at west end of Clearwater Creek bridge. Gravel access to creek to south.

Eagle Trail SRS has 35 campsites in nicely wooded area, 15-day limit, 4 picnic sites, water, toilets, firepits, pay phone (located at left of entrance off highway), picnic pavilion. Camping fee $15/night. After entering campground, big rigs should take second right for pull-throughs and park-alongs. Information boards at trailhead for Valdez to Eagle Trail (Old Slana Highway and WAMCATS); 1-mile nature trail or 2.5-mile trail to overview of Tok River Valley.

Report wildfires at (907) 883-FIRE.

GJ 106 A 309 T 19 Mountain views westbound as the highway passes through the Alaska Range. The Mentasta Mountains are to the southeast.

GJ 104.4 A 307.4 T 20.6 Paved shoulder parking to north. **Tok Overflow** runs under highway in culvert; fishing for grayling and Dolly Varden.

GJ 104 A 307 T 21 *Actual driving distance between Milepost 103 and 104 is 1.4 miles. CAUTION: Watch for moose.*

GJ 103.8 A 306.8 T 21.2 Bridge over **Tok River**, side road north to riverbank and boat

launch. The Tok River heads at Tok Glacier in the Alaska Range and flows northeast 60 miles to the Tanana River. Tok-bound travelers are in the Tok River Valley, although the river is out of sight to the southeast most of the time.

GJ 103.5 A 306.5 T 21.5 Paved shoulder parking to north. Tok Overflow; fishing for grayling and Dolly Varden.

GJ 99.5 A 302.5 T 25.5 Turnout to north. Wild rose hips in season.

GJ 98.5 A 301.5 T 26.5 Turnoff to southeast on Old Tok Cutoff Road (wide paved and gravel, some bumps), which leads 2 miles southeast to **Log Cabin Wilderness Lodge.** The owners have restored 3 original cabins from the 1940s, as well as constructing new cabins. A favorite with visitors: the wood boiler used to heat the house and shop. RV parking available.

Log Cabin Wilderness Lodge. See display ad this page.

GJ 98.2 A 301.2 T 26.8 Bridge over **Little Tok River,** which parallels highway. Narrow, sloping access road to south at west end of bridge. The Little Tok River heads in the Mentasta Mountains to the south and flows north 32 miles to the Tok River.

Slow for gravel breaks, mild frost heaves, bumps and patched road westbound.

GJ 95.4 A 298.4 T 29.6 Paved rest area to southeast; surrounded by mountains on the edge of a deep valley. Views to north and northeast.

GJ 91 A 294 T 34 Little Tok River bridge (weight limit 20 tons); good fishing for grayling, 12 to 14 inches, use small spinner. Large turnout.

Distance marker shows Slana 34 miles, Glennallen 109 miles.

GJ 90.1 A 293.1 T 34.9 Paved turnout.

GJ 89 A 292 T 36 Between **Milepost GJ 89** and **GJ 86** watch for moose and trumpeter swans (see **Milepost GJ 77.9**) in wetlands along Lower Station Creek to the southeast. The creek provides excellent moose habitat and a breeding place for waterfowl. The creek flows into Mineral Lake and makes a pleasant canoe trip. Fishing is good for northern pike and grayling.

GJ 88.2 A 291.2 T 36.8 Large informal gravel turnout to northwest.

GJ 85.7 A 288.7 T 39.3 Small turnout to north.

GJ 83.2 A 286.2 T 41.8 Bridge over Bartell Creek. Just beyond is the divide between the drainage of the Tanana River, tributary of the Yukon River system flowing into the Bering Sea, and the Copper River system, emptying into the North Pacific near Cordova.

Tok Cutoff has both straight and winding road with both good pavement and gravel breaks.
(©Kris Valencia, staff)

GJ 82.9 A 285.9 T 42.1 Distance marker eastbound shows Tok Junction 40 miles, Canada Border 136 miles.

GJ 81.5 A 284.5 T 43.5 Gravel turnout to south.

GJ 81 A 284 T 44 Access road leads north 6 miles to **MENTASTA LAKE** (pop. 112), unincorporated. This is a primarily Athabascan community with a subsistence-based lifestyle; no visitor services.

The Mentasta area was particularly hard hit by a 7.9 earthquake that jolted the Interior and Southcentral regions of the state at 1:12 P.M. on Nov. 3, 2002. Centered about 80 miles south of Fairbanks, it was the strongest quake ever recorded along the Denali Fault. (The Denali Fault runs in a great arc from Southeast Alaska through Canada, then re-enters Alaska, slicing Denali National Park in half.) The Tok Cut-Off, Richardson and Glenn highways all sustained damage.

GJ 79.2 A 282.2 T 45.8 Mentasta Summit (elev. 2,434 feet). The U.S. Army Signal Corps established a telegraph station here in 1902. The Mentasta Mountains rise to about 6,000 feet on either side of the highway. The 40-mile-long, 25-mile-wide Mentasta Range is bounded on the north by the Alaska Range. Watch for Dall sheep on mountainsides.

Boundary between Game Management Units 12 and 13C and Sportfish Management Units 8 and 2.

GJ 78.1 A 281.1 T 46.9 Mentasta Lodge to southeast. This long-time Alaskan lodge has a cafe, motel, gas, diesel, propane, laundromat, showers, bar, liquor store, car, RV and truck parking.

Mentasta Lodge. See display ad this page.
NOTE: Next gas westbound is at Posty's in Chistochina, 43 miles from here. There is no gas available on the Nabesna Road.

GJ 77.9 A 280.9 T 47.1 Large gravel turnout to northwest by large pond; watch for waterfowl.

Watch for **trumpeter swans** in the spring and fall in bodies of water along northern highways. Eighty percent of the world's population of trumpeter swans (the largest of the 7 types of swans found worldwide) nest in Alaska, although they are far outnumbered by the smaller tundra swans. Other than the size difference, the 2 swans are similar in appearance, although tundra swans have a bright yellow mark on their otherwise black bills, while trumpeter swans have all-black bills.

From here west to Gakona Junction, the highway becomes a patchwork of good highway going bad (frost heaves, damaged pavement), and improved sections of highway. Watch for and slow down for frost heaves and gravel breaks!

GJ 76.3 A 279.3 T 48.7 Bridge over Mable Creek. Mastodon flowers (marsh fleabane) in late July; very large (to 4 feet) with showy seed heads.

GJ 75.8 A 278.8 T 49.2 Bridge over Slana Slough.

CAUTION: Watch for moose.

GJ 75.5 A 278.5 T 49.5 Bridge over **Slana River**. Double-ended rest area with picnic table and outhouse to south just west of bridge. This river flows from its source glaciers some 55 miles to the Copper River.

GJ 73.9 A 276.9 T 51.1 Large gravel turnout to south is scenic viewpoint of Mentasta Mountains, with view of Slana River.

GJ 72.3 A 275.3 T 52.7 Distance marker westbound shows Nabesna Junction 13 miles, Glennallen 88 miles.

GJ 69 A 272 T 56 Large gravel turnout to north. Views westbound (weather permitting) of snow-covered **Mount Sanford**, elev. 16,237 feet, to south. Mount Sanford is in the Wrangell Mountains and it is 1 of Alaska's 10 highest peaks.

GJ 68 A 271 T 57 Small gravel pullout to south.

GJ 67.9 A 270.9 T 57.1 Carlson Creek bridge.

GJ 65.5 A 268.5 T 59.5 Paved turnout overlooking Slana River to south (by mail boxes) is a scenic viewpoint; road leads down to riverbank. Magnificent views (weather permitting) of the Wrangell mountains. Dominant peak is snow-covered Mount Sanford.

Highway parallels Slana River westbound.

GJ 64.2 A 267.2 T 60.8 Sharp turn to north at east end of Porcupine Creek bridge for **Porcupine Creek State Recreation Site**, 0.2 mile from highway. Thickly forested area with 12 campsites on loop road, 15-day limit, $15 nightly fee per vehicle, water pump (boil water), firepits, outhouses, picnic tables and good fishing for Dolly Varden and arctic grayling. Hiking trails up Porcupine Creek to Carlson Lake and Bear Valley (trails are poorly marked, carry topo map). Lowbush cranberries in fall. Watch for moose.

GJ 64.1 A 267.1 T 60.9 Bridge over Porcupine Creek.

GJ 63 A 266 T 62 Scenic viewpoint to southeast with view of Wrangell Mountains. The dominant peak to the southwest is Mount Sanford, a dormant volcano; the pinnacles of Capital Mountain can be seen against its lower slopes to the west. Mount Jarvis (elev. 13,421 feet) is visible due south, with the jagged buttresses of Tanada Peak (elev. 9,240 feet) to its left.

Sign here about Noyes Mountain, elev. 8,147 feet (view obscured by brush), which was named for U.S. Army Brig. Gen. John Rutherford Noyes, a one-time commissioner of roads in the Territory of Alaska. Appointed adjutant general of the Alaska National Guard in 1953, he died in 1956 from injuries and frostbite after his plane crashed near Nome.

GJ 62.7 A 265.7 T 62.3 Duffy's Roadhouse (closed for many years). **Private Aircraft:** Duffy's Tavern/Slana (private) airstrip, N62°43.48' W143°55.23'; elev. 2420 feet; 1,200 feet, gravel; unattended.

GJ 62 A 265 T 63 *Begin 7 percent downhill grade next 1.7 miles westbound.*

GJ 61 A 264 T 64 Midway Service to northwest; grocery store, cabins rentals, tent camping.

Begin 7 percent uphill grade next 1.7 miles eastbound. Slow for damaged road.

GJ 60.8 A 263.8 T 64.2 Bridge over **Ahtell Creek**; grayling fishing allowed. Watch for salmon spawning late June

through July. (*This stream is closed to king salmon fishing*). Gravel parking area at end of bridge across from midway service. This stream drains a mountain area of igneous rock, where several gold and silver-lead claims are located.

GJ 60 A 263 T 65 Distance marker eastbound shows Tok 66 miles, Tetlin Junction 78 miles, Canada Border 158 miles.

GJ 59.9 A 262.9 T 65.1 Turnoff to east for Nabesna Road; post office, pay phone, private camping and lodging (open year-round) at **Hart D Ranch**, Mile 0.5 Nabesna Road. Wrangell-St. Elias National Park ranger station is located just 0.1 miles south of here. *There is no gas available on Nabesna Road. Nearest gas is at Mentasta Lodge (18 miles east) or Posty's (25 miles west).*

Hart D Ranch See display ad on page 348.

Junction with Nabesna Road. See the "Nabesna Road" log beginning on page 348.

Begin long 6 percent uphill grade westbound.

GJ 59.4 A 262.4 T 65.6 Distance marker southwestbound shows Glennallen 76 miles; Valdez 189 miles; Anchorage 263 miles.

GJ 58.7 A 261.7 T 66.3 *Begin long 6 percent down grade eastbound.*

GJ 56.5 A 259.5 T 68.5 Double-ended turnout to south is a scenic viewpoint overlooking Cobb Lakes, a chain of 3 lakes. Red raspberries in season. Watch for moose in ponds. View to the south and southwest of Tanada Peak (9,240 feet); Mount Sanford (16,237 feet), center; Mount Blackburn (16,390 feet); and Mount Drum (12,010 feet). Gold Rush Centennial sign reads:

In 1885, Lieutenant Henry T. Allen led one of America's epic journeys of exploration. In 5 months, his expedition crossed 1,500 miles of largely unexplored territory including this valley. Ordered to investigate the unmapped Copper and Tanana river valleys, Allen started up the Copper River in March 1885 and passed this point 2 months later, reaching the headwaters of the Copper River and entering the Tanana Valley. Allen descended the Tanana River and trekked from the Yukon to the headwaters of the Koyukuk River.

Begin long 6 percent downgrade northeastbound toward Tok.

GJ 55.2 A 258.2 T 69.8 Tanada Peak viewpoint; long, large double-ended paved turnout to south.

CAUTION: Watch for horses on road.

GJ 53 A 256 T 72 Turnoff to south for **Grizzly Lake Campground**; lodging, RV park, trail rides. Owned by long-time Alaskans Doc and Phoebe Taylor, and by their daughter, Cathy, and her husband Jim Knighten. Grizzly Lake Campground is situated in a beautiful wilderness setting with wonderful views.

Grizzly Lake Campground. See display ad this page.

GJ 46 A 249 T 79 Southwestbound, Mount Drum (12,010 feet) is directly ahead; Mount Sanford (16,237 feet) is to the left of Mount Drum.

GJ 43.8 A 246.8 T 81.2 Bridge over Indian River. Watch for salmon spawning in late-June through July. (*This river is closed to king salmon fishing.*)

GJ 43.7 A 246.7 T 81.3 Rest area to south at west end of Indian River bridge; toilet, garbage bins, access to gravel bars in river, canoe launch.

GJ 40.1 A 243.1 T 84.9 Gravel turnout

to south.

GJ 39 A 242 T 86 Views of the Copper River valley and Wrangell Mountains. Looking south, peak on left is Mount Sanford and on right is Mount Drum (elev. 12,010 feet).

GJ 38.7 A 241.7 T 86.3 Gravel shoulder parking to north.

GJ 37 A 240 T 88 Chistochina (sign westbound).

GJ 36.5 A 239.5 T 88.5 Chistochina Bed and Breakfast on north side of highway welcomes drop-ins.

Chistochina Bed and Breakfast See display ad this page.

GJ 35.5 A 238.5 T 89.5 Chistochina River bridge.

GJ 35.2 A 238.2 T 89.8 Turnoff to north at west end of bridge for 0.1-mile drive in to a very spacious, flat, paved, parking area with outhouse. Access to Chistochina River trailhead allows access to approximately 40 miles of trails in hills north of the highway, according to the BLM. Used during hunting season by ATV and large track vehicles; trails may be muddy in wet weather. For permits or more information, phone Ahtna in Glennallen at (907) 822-3476. Sign reads:

"This is a 50-foot-wide easement owned by the Village of Cheesh'Na. Please respect the private property you have the privilege of driving through. Travel off this easement is considered trespassing. Markers appear every half-mile. Allowed: Foot traffic, dog sleds, animals, snowmachines, 2- and 3-wheeled vehicles, track vehicles, 4-wheel-drive vehicles. Prohibited: Camping on easement, hunting on easement, travel off easement, fishing from easement, blocking easement."

The **Chistochina River** heads in the Chistochina Glacier in the Alaska Range and flows south 48 miles to the Copper River, which is just south of the highway

here. The Tok Cut-Off parallels the Copper River from here southeast to the Richardson Highway.

GJ 34.6 A 237.6 T 90.4 Posty's Sinona Creek Trading Post to north is open daily year-round; food, gas diesel, gifts, laundry and showers, fishing/hunting licenses.

Posty's Sinona Creek Trading Post. See display ad this page.

NOTE: Next gas eastbound is at Mentasta Lodge, 43 miles from here.

GJ 34.5 A 237.5 T 90.5 Bridge over Sinona Creek. Sinona is said to mean "place of the many burls," and there are indeed many burls on area spruce trees. Paved bike path begins and extends 1.6 miles westbound alongside highway.

(Continues on page 350)

Posty's at Chistochina is a long-time Alaska business. (©Kris Valencia, staff)

Nabesna Road

The Nabesna Road provides a scenic side trip for Tok Cutoff travelers. (©David L. Ranta, staff)

The 42-mile Nabesna Road leads southeast from **Milepost GJ 59.9** on the Tok Cutoff to the northern area of Wrangell–St. Elias National Park and Preserve and is 1 of only 2 road accesses to the park (the other is McCarthy Road). Take time to drive out to Dead Dog Hill Wayside at Mile 17.8 or Rock Lake Wayside at Mile 21.8: The scenery is worth the trip.

Stop at the ranger station at **Milepost J 0.2** for details on activities within the park, off-road vehicle permits (required), cabin permits and current road conditions.

Visitor services available on Nabesna Road include lodging and camping at **Hart D Ranch** (**Milepost J 0.5**), owned and operated by artist and sculptor Mary Frances DeHart. Gas, groceries and food are not available on this road. The nearest gas and food are on the Tok Cutoff at either Mentasta Lodge 18 miles east at **Milepost GJ 78.1**, or Posty's, 25 miles west at **Milepost GJ 34.6**. Midway Service at **Milepost GJ 61** has groceries.

There are several developed waysides with outhouses, picnic tables, firepits and litter bins as well as primitive campsites and established campgrounds on Nabesna Road. The area offers good fishing and hunting in season. Horses are permitted on all trails. Wildlife to watch for: black and brown bears, wolves, caribou, moose, ptarmigan, trumpeter swans and other birds.

The first 16 miles of road are paved/chip sealed, the remainder is dirt and gravel. Carry a good spare tire. Culverts and gravel fill have replaced almost all creek crossings south from **Milepost J 29**. *Sudden changes in creek water levels possible in spring or during heavy rains, requiring high clearance or 4-wheel-drive vehicle.* The dirt and gravel portion of the road can be slick in wet weather: Watch for soft shoulders and soft spots in turnouts. Cell phone service is sporadic on Nabesna Road.

This is not a road for big rigs; smaller RVs are fine. If you have a tow vehicle, you can drop your RV or trailer at Hart D Ranch, drive the road, then return for an overnight.

Distance is measured from the junction with the Tok Cutoff (J).

Driving distance is based on physical mileposts on the Nabesna Road.

J 0 Junction with the Tok Cutoff at **Milepost GJ 59.9**.

J 0.2 Turnoff to right southbound for access to Slana Ranger Station (parking, visitor information, restrooms) and Slana DOT Maintenance Station. Not a through road, limited parking (big rigs can usually turn around just beyond the station). The ranger station has information on road conditions and activities in Wrangell–St. Elias National Park and Preserve; issues ATV permits; provides backcountry trip planning assistance and bear-proof containers (free with deposit); and has hunting information and subsistence permits available. Ask about summer ranger programs for visitors. USGS maps and natural history books for sale. Open 8 A.M. to 5 P.M daily, Memorial Day through September; by appointment rest of year. Phone (907) 822-7401.

J 0.8 Slana post office (with antique glass-fronted boxes), open Monday, Wednesday, Friday, 8:30 A.M. to 1 P.M. Pay phone station at entrance to **Hart D Ranch** complex; lodging (year-round) and RV park. This picturesque ranch is the home and studio of sculptor Mary Frances DeHart. DeHart also raises Affenpinscher dogs. Call ahead in winter months.

Hart D Ranch. See display ad this page.

J 1.1 Slana elementary school. **SLANA** (pop. 94; unincorporated), once an Indian village on the north bank of the Slana River, now refers to this general area, much of which was homesteaded in the 1980s. Slana once boasted a popular road-house, now a private home.

J 1.6 Slana River Bridge. Boundary between Game Management Units 11 and 13C. Private property, no roadside parking, next few miles southbound.

J 3.8 Entering Wrangell–St. Elias National Park & Preserve ahead southbound, National Preserve boundary.

J 3.9 Four Mile Road. Huck's Hobbit Hostel B&B (phone ahead, 907/822-3196).

J 4.6 Double-ended gravel turnout.

J 5.4 Signs mark Wrangell–St. Elias National Park lands to southwest, National Preserve lands to northeast.

J 6.1 Pleasant primitive campsite to east with picnic table and firepit on bank of **Rufus Creek**. Fishing for Dolly Varden to 8 inches, June to October. Watch for bears, especially during berry season.

J 7 Road crosses Rufus Creek culvert; small turnout. Private homes.

J 7.9 Large rough turnout to west, can be

muddy in wet weather.

J 8.8 Rough gravel turnout to south.

J 8.9 Large open parking area to south; informal camping.

J 9.2 Dirt turnout to east.

J 10.2 Lowbush cranberries along road.

J 11 Suslota Lake trail to east; trailhead parking at **Milepost 11.1**. This trail can be very wet. It is used primarily by ATVs and is not recommended for hiking. Blueberries, cranberries and Labrador tea.

J 11.1 Large gravel parking area to west.

J 11.9 Creek culvert. Watch for owls (great horned, northern hawk, short-eared and boreal) in tall trees in this area.

CAUTION: Watch for gravel breaks and patched roadway.

J 12.2 Parking to west at **Copper Lake trailhead**; picnic table, primitive campsite.

©David L. Ranta, staff

Good trail for short day hikes, with recent gravel work done on first 3 miles of trail, to Tanada Creek Bridge. Plan on 2-day strenuous hike (stream crossings) to reach Copper Lake (16.7 miles). Fishing for lake trout, grayling, burbot.

J 12.8 Large informal dirt and gravel parking area with sloping approach to east. Watch for moose.

J 13.4 Dirt turnout to east.

J 16 *Pavement/chip seal ends, gravel begins, southbound.*

J 16.6 Primitive campsite to south; picnic table, firepit. Unusual and no doubt often photographed sign southbound stating "Toilet 1 mile." Beautiful views of Kettle Lake, Mount Sanford, Capital Mountain, Mount Wrangell, Mount Zanetti and Tanada Peak in the Wrangell Mountains to the southwest.

J 17.8 Dead Dog Hill Wayside; camping, picnic table, vaulted toilet, litter bin. Look for trumpeter swans on lake just east of this rest area. Great view of Noyes Mountain (elev. 8,235 feet) in the highly mineralized Mentasta Mountains to the north.

J 18.3 Caribou Creek culvert.

J 18.8 Signed gravel parking area to east for Caribou Creek trail, which is 1,500-feet up the road (see next milepost).

J 19.1 Caribou Creek trail; park at **Milepost J 18.8**. This is a multi-use trail for first 3 miles to Caribou Creek public-use cabin (reservation required, phone Slana Ranger Station at 907/822-7401). Good hiking with views of the Wrangell Mountains and the Copper River valley.

J 20.6 Large, primitive, double-ended parking area to east.

J 21.1 Rock Creek culvert.

J 21.8 Rock Lake Wayside to west; camping, picnic table, vaulted toilet, litter bin. Great views of Mount Sanford and Tanada Peak to the south.

Trail to east for Viking Lodge public-use

cabin (reservation required, phone Slana Ranger Station at 907/822-7401). No ATVs allowed on trail.

J 22.4 Long Lake (signed); grayling fishing.

J 22.8 Small turnout at dip in road is protected from the wind.

J 23.4 Single-vehicle turnout to east.

J 23.9 Tanada Lake trailhead parking to west. Trail can be very wet; not recommended for hiking. Fishing for grayling and lake trout.

J 24.6 Watershed divide (elev. 3,320 feet) between streams draining into the Copper River watershed and into the Gulf of Alaska, and those entering the Yukon River watershed which drains into the Bering Sea. Boundary between Sportfish Areas C and K, and Game Management Areas 11 and 12.

J 24.9 Local homes and lodge. Glimpse of Tanada Lake beneath Tanada Peak to the south.

J 25.3 Little Jack Creek culvert.

©David L. Ranta, staff

J 27.8 Kendesnii Campground gravel loop road to 10 campsites; picnic tables, interpretive signs, vaulted toilet, litter bin. Twin Lakes is a good place to observe waterfowl (this is a major gathering place for swans in the fall). Fishing for lake trout and grayling 10 to 18 inches, mid-May to October, flies or small spinner. Wildflowers in June include Lapland rosebay, lupine and mountain avens.

J 28 Sportsmen Paradise Lodge (Doug and Judy Fredericks are the owners); bar, liquor store, firewood (fee), cold sodas and chips. There are many wilderness hiking and fishing opportunities in the area.

Watch for a small resident caribou herd on Sugarloaf Mountain to the south. The larger Nelchina caribou herd migrates through here in October, according to the Fredericks, who say the caribou usually stay until April and are a popular attraction, with sightseers coming in by snowmachine to see the herd.

J 29 Trail Creek culvert.

J 29.2 Trail Creek trailhead.

J 30.7 Lost Creek crossing: split into 2 streams between high gravel banks. Culverts may be installed here, making the crossing easier.

J 30.9 Lost Creek trailhead, a multi-use trail with access to Big Grayling Lake, Soda Creek, Platinum Creek, Mineral Springs and Soda Lake. Inquire at Slana Ranger Station for ATV permits and private property boundaries in area.

J 31 Small creek crossing.

J 31.6 Chalk Creek culvert.

J 33.3 Radiator Creek culvert.

J 35.3 Jack Creek 1-lane bridge and a small rest area (big rigs check turnaround space before entering) to west. Pretty spot for camping with vaulted toilet, litter bin.

1-lane bridge crosses Jack Creek at Mile 35.3.
(©David L. Ranta, staff)

Grayling fishing.

J 36 *Road narrows and gravel surface begins southbound, soft spots in road after rain.* Timbers from old corduroy road visible in roadbed.

J 36.2 Skookum Volcano trail (hiking only).

J 36.4 Rock and gravel cover former creek crossing. *These crossings can be rough, with large rocks.*

J 37.9 Rock and gravel cover former creek crossing.

J 39.6 Rock and gravel cover former creek crossing.

J 40 Reeve's Field trailhead. This trail was constructed during WWII to connect Nabesna Road with a large airstrip near the Nabesna River. The airstrip (which has washed out) and trail were named for aviation pioneer Bob Reeve.

J 40.2 *Begin long uphill climb southbound.*

J 40.6 State maintenance ends. Begin 10 mph speed limit.

J 40.8 Leaving Wrangell-St. Elias National Park and Preserve southbound.

J 42 Road ends just beyond Devils Mountain Lodge (www.devilsmountainlodge. com); flyout hiking, backpacking, flightseeing, camping and lodging at End of the Road B&B. Coffee and desserts available at the lodge in summer. Active airstrip with fishing, hunting and hiking fly-outs. Kirk Ellis of Ellis Guiding & Outfitting advises visitors not to park at the airstrip. There is parking past the Ellis property around the corner from the airstrip.

Hiking trail to Rambler Mine (owned by the National Park Service) begins a half-mile past the parking area. Signs point to trailhead. Trail climbs about a mile up the mountainside: Beautiful views of the Nabesna River and valley. Areas above the mine are very steep: Traverse with caution!

A private unmaintained road continues 3 miles to the Nabesna Gold Mine. The mine operated from 1923 until the late 1940s; it is on the National Register of Historic Sites. The buildings, mill and mine adits are privately owned. Inquire about mine tours at Devil's Mountain Lodge.

Return to Milepost GJ 59.9
Tok Cutoff

Good view of Mount Sanford from the Tok Cutoff. (©Sharon Nault)

(Continued from page 347)

GJ 33 A 236 T 92 Distance marker westbound shows Glennallen 49 miles, Valdez 155 miles, Anchorage 227 miles.

Distance marker eastbound shows Tok 90 miles, Canadian border 180 miles.

GJ 32.9 A 235.9 T 92.1 Chistochina school. Road access to **CHISTOCHINA** (pop. 103, unincorporated), a traditional Copper River Athabascan Indian village.

Private Aircraft: Chistochina airstrip, adjacent south; elev. 1,850 feet; length 2,060 feet; turf and gravel; unmaintained, unattended.

GJ 32.8 A 235.8 T 92.2 Site of old Chistochina Lodge to southeast which burned down in November 1999. Built in the early 1900s, the original roadhouse served sled traffic on the Valdez to Eagle Trail.

Paved bike path ends.

Begin improved highway westbound.

GJ 32.7 A 235.7 T 92.3 Red Eagle Lodge. Fly-in or drive-in. Experience "Real Alaska" at a 1920s Roadhouse site along the old Valdez to Eagle Trail. Themed authentic homestead cabins feature rustic luxury. The historic cabins' ambience is enhanced with queen beds (down bedding), woodburning stoves, braided rugs, handcrafted quilts, antiques. For RVers and campers there is a newly scribed 30x50-foot log bathhouse equipped with washers/dryers. Red Eagle offers relaxation and adventure. Experience "glamourous camping" in a platform wall tent. Try a float trip or fish for Copper River salmon. Watch wildlife in comfort from a porch swing/rocker. Read, play table games, horseshoes, etc. Enjoy spectacular views of Mount Sanford on the bike path (bicycles provided). In the evening, relax in the warmth of a campfire cookout. Start your day with a special breakfast served by owners at the lodge, Richard and Judy Dennis. www.redeaglelodge.net. Phone (907) 822-5299. See display ad this page.

GJ 31.4 A 234.4 T 93.6 Paved parking to north.

GJ 31 A 234 T 94 Chistochina (eastbound sign).

GJ 30.1 A 233.1 T 94.9 Small paved turnouts both sides of highway.

End improved highway westbound.

GJ 28.2 A 231.2 T 96.8 Long double-ended paved parking area to south (no view) with a marker on the Alaska Road Commission. The ARC was established in 1905, the same year the first automobile arrived in Alaska at Skagway. The ARC operated for 51 years, building roads, airfields, trails and other transportation facilities. It was replaced in 1956 by the Bureau of Public Roads (referred to by some Alaskans at the time as the Bureau of Parallel Ruts). In 1960, the Bureau of Public Roads was replaced by the Dept. of Public Works.

GJ 24 A 227 T 101 Turnoff to south at physical Milepost 24 for a large rest area with paved double-ended parking area, toilets and litter bins. Picnic tables and firepits in treed area. The Copper River—out of sight to the south—heads on the north side of the Wrangell Mountains and flows 250 miles to the Gulf of Alaska. Gold Rush Centennial sign in woods near parking area reads:

In San Francisco, 'Captain' I.N. West told a story of finding gold in Alaska years before. He was 72 years old when he returned to Alaska in the spring of 1898, intent on staking claims. He became ill while crossing the Valdez Glacier trail and left Alaska, but not before telling his story to several stampeders.

George Hazelet and Andrew Meals were 2 prospectors who heard West's story. Later that summer, an Athabaskan called "Indian Charlie" led Hazelet and Meals to the Chistochina River, where they found a few flakes of gold. Hazelet and Meals staked claims and began mining the following summer.

After leaving Alaska to obtain financing and equipment, Hazelet and Meals returned in 1900 to find other miners working their claims. While victorious in the ensuing legal battle for ownership, Hazelet and Meals lost their claims when they failed to produce enough gold to pay their creditors. Other area miners had better luck: Over the years, some 5.5 tons of gold were recovered from the Chistochina District.

Placer gold can be dust, flakes or nuggets found mixed with gravel in river bars, streambeds and hillside benches. Prospectors wash gravels in water with a pan, hoping to find a paystreak where gold is heavily concentrated.

Miners dug pits ("open cuts") to extract the pay dirt that had settled just above bedrock. They shoveled the pay dirt into rockers or sluice boxes, using water to separate the gold from the gravel.

Hydraulic mining—using water under pressure to thaw gravel and push it through sluice boxes—and dredges replaced hand mining.

Deeply buried placer gold is extracted by underground mining. Shafts were sunk into the frozen ground using fires or boiler-heated water to thaw the ground. If gold was found, miners dug horizontal tunnels or "drifts" to get at the pay streak. Pay dirt was hoisted to the surface and piled in dumps, which were sluiced in summer when running water was available.

GJ 22.9 A 225.9 T 102.1 Small pull-in parking space (no turn-around) above

Copper River; view of river and mountains.

GJ 22 A 225 T 103 *Highway climbs 7 percent grade between* **Milepost GJ 22 and 21.**

Views to southeast of the Wrangell Mountains: Mount Sanford on the left, Mount Drum on the right.

GJ 21 A 224 T 104 *Highway descends 7 percent grade between* **Milepost GJ 21 and 22** *eastbound.*

GJ 20.9 A 223.9 T 104.1 Shoulder parking to southeast.

GJ 20 A 223 T 105 Concentrations of black spruce occur in several areas along the Tok Cutoff/Glenn Highway. Note the black spruce in this area, recognizable by their stunted size and often crooked shape, topped by fat, shrubby clusters of branches. Look for thick, ball-shaped tangles of spruce branches, twigs and needles close to the trunk of the tree which are called Witch's broom. Witch's broom is caused by a fungus. Black spruce are generally found in poorly drained areas, such as wetlands and permafrost, where white spruce will not grow.

Gray jays are abundant in this area. Of the family *Corvidae*, gray jays are also called "camp robbers" for their propensity to make off with any food left out on picnic tables or elsewhere in camp.

GJ 18.2 A 221.2 T 106.8 Large informal gravel turnout to northwest.

GJ 17.6 A 220.6 T 107.4 Tulsona Creek bridge. Good grayling fishing. Walk down the old Tok Cutoff here for access to the creek away from the road.

GJ 14.2 A 217.2 T 110.8 *Highway descends long grade eastbound.* Views of river and mountains (Mount Sanford and Mount Drum).

GJ 13 A 216 T 112 Gravel shoulder parking to north.

GJ 12.1 A 215.1 T 112.9 Distance marker westbound shows Glennallen 28 miles, Anchorage 215 miles.

GJ 11.7 A 214.7 T 113.3 Gravel shoulder parking to southeast. Look for yellow pond lily (*Nuphar polysepalum*) in pond north side of highway.

GJ 11.3 A 214.3 T 113.7 HAARP (High Frequency Active Auroral Research Program) to north of highway. The HAARP program, begun in 1990 and jointly managed by research arms of the Air Force and Navy, studies the physical and electrical properties of the Earth's ionosphere, which can affect military and civilian communication and navigation systems. Principal elements include an HF transmitter and antenna array and UHF ionospheric radar. An annual open house is held for the public, generally over 2 days at the end of the summer season. Dates and times are announced in advance on the HAARP home page (www.haarp.alaska.edu/).

GJ 6.5 A 209.5 T 118.5 Small paved turnout to south. Views (weather permitting) to south of Mount Sanford and Mount Drum as highway descends westbound to Gakona River.

Begin uphill grade eastbound.

GJ 4.6 A 207.6 T 120.4 Red Igloo Cabins to south.

GJ 4.2 A 207.2 T 120.8 Gakona Alaska RV Park and Cabins to south.

GJ 2.6 A 205.6 T 122.4 Post office to south serves GAKONA (pop. 234). Originally a Native wood and fish camp, and then a permanent village of the Ahtna Indians, this unincorporated community is located at the confluence of the Gakona and Copper rivers.

Interpretive sign at viewpoint overlooking Gakona and Copper rivers at Milepost GJ 1.
(©Kris Valencia, staff)

(Gakona is Athabascan for rabbit.) The community has a commercial district, a non-Native residential area, and a Native village with approximately 90 houses.

GJ 2 A 205 T 123 Historic **Gakona Lodge & Trading Post**, open May–October, with camping and lodging, and a restaurant (open for dinner only, June through August). Gakona Lodge was built in 1929. It replaced an earlier roadhouse built in 1904 known as Doyle's. Located at the junction of the Valdez to Eagle and Valdez to Fairbanks trails, this was an essential stopping point for travelers. Eleven structures here are listed on the National Register of Historic Places. Read a more detailed history of this beautiful old lodge at the main building.

Gakona Lodge & Trading Post. See display ad this page.

GJ 1.8 A 204.8 T 123.2 Gakona River bridge. The river flows 64 miles south from Gakona Glacier in the Alaska Range to join the Copper River here.

Entering Game Management Unit 13B westbound and 13C eastbound.

GJ 1 A 204 T 124 Paved viewpoint to south overlooks the valley of the Gakona and Copper rivers, picnic table near edge of bluff offers fine view of the many channels where the Gakona and Copper rivers join. View of Mount Drum and Mount Sanford. Good photo stop. Gold Rush Centennial sign about Alaska's first telegraph.

Known as the Washington-Alaska Military Cable and Telegraph System (WAMCATS), the line was built to assist communication between U.S. Army posts during the Gold Rush. Crews completed the 1,506-mile line in 1903. Although a military line, WAMCATS carried more civilian than military messages, as it assisted commerce and safe travel between gold camps and brought in news of the outside world. By the late 1920s, radio technology made WAMCATS obsolete.

NOTE: Highway descends eastbound.

GJ 0.2 A 203.2 T 124.8 Gakona (sign eastbound); see description at **Milepost GJ 2.7.**

GJ 0.1 A 203.1 T 124.9 Distance marker eastbound shows Tok Junction 125 miles; Tetlin Junction 137 miles; Canadian border 213 miles.

From here east to Tok, the highway is a patchwork of new, improved highway and good highway going bad (frost heaves, damaged pavement).

GJ 0 A 203 T 125 Gakona Junction; drive-thru espresso stand. Stop sign westbound at **junction** of Tok Cutoff (Alaska Route 1) with Richardson Highway (Alaska Route 4). The 2 roads share a common alignment for the next 14 miles south. Westbound travelers: Turn north here on the Richardson Highway for Delta Junction; turn south on the Richardson Highway for Glennallen and Valdez.

NOTE: This junction can be confusing; see map on page 352.

Paxson- or Delta Junction-bound travelers turn to **Milepost V 128.5** on page 490 in the RICHARDSON HIGHWAY section for log of Alaska Route 4 North.

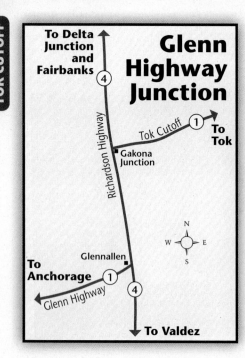

Glenn Highway Junction

To Delta Junction and Fairbanks

Richardson Highway

Tok Cutoff

To Tok

Gakona Junction

To Anchorage

Glennallen

Glenn Highway

To Valdez

Distance from Valdez (V) is followed by distance from Anchorage (A) and distance from Tok (T). *Because physical mileposts for the next 14 miles southbound give distance from Valdez, distance from Valdez is given first.*

ALASKA ROUTE 4

V 129 A 203 T 125 Gakona Junction; Gakona ECO gas station and grocery/con-venience store. Check-in for **Copper River Salmon Charters** (www.copperriversalmon charters.com).

Northbound travelers: Turn east on Tok Cutoff (Alaska Route 1) for Tok and junction with the Alaska Highway to the Canadian border (continue with this log); continue north on the Richardson Highway for Paxson and Delta Junction. *See map this page.*

Distance marker southbound shows Glennallen 16 miles, Valdez 129 miles, Anchorage 196 miles. Improved highway southbound.

Distance marker northbound shows Paxson 56 miles, Delta Junction 137 miles; Fairbanks 235 miles.

V 128 A 202 T 126 *Highway descends long hill next 1.2 miles southbound to Gulkana River.*

V 126.9 A 200.9 T 127.1 Access road east to village of **GULKANA** (pop. 177) on the east bank of the Gulkana River at its confluence with the Copper River. Established as a telegraph station in 1903 and named "Kulkana" after the river.

Most of the Gulkana River frontage in this area is owned by Gulkana Village and managed by Ahtna, Inc. Ahtna lands are closed to the public for hunting and trapping. However, land use permits may be purchased from the Gulkana Village Tribal Office for fishing and boating access on Ahtna lands. The sale, importation and possession of alcohol is prohibited.

V 126.8 A 200.8 T 127.2 Gulkana River Bridge. Very popular fishing spot in season. *Watch for pedestrians.* Public access to river south of bridge; see **Milepost V 126.5.** *No*

public access to river at north end of bridge. The Gulkana River flows more than 90 miles to the Copper River. Entering Game Management Unit 13B northbound, 13A southbound.

Highway climbs next 1.2 miles northbound.

V 126.5 A 200.5 T 127.5 Gravel access road east to large parking area and further access (use right fork) via rough gravel/paved road to second large parking area and boat launch on **Gulkana River**; day-use. This is a very busy area when the fish are in. *NOTE: Access roads can be in rough shape, with big potholes and steep drop-offs.*

Fishing in the Gulkana River for grayling all year; kings June to mid-July; red salmon late July to late August. Click "Fishing Reports" at www.sf.adfg. state.ak.us/statewide/sf_home.cfm and go to Interior region then Upper Copper/Upper Susitna Management Area. Be familiar with current fishing regulations and closures.

V 126.4 A 200.4 T 127.6 Gravel road east to parking; poor river access. Alyeska pipeline access road to west.

V 126.2 A 200.2 T 127.8 Gravel road to east; no river access. Gravel pit to west.

V 126 A 200 T 128 Paved turnout to west.

V 118.1 A 192.1 T 135.9 Private Aircraft: Gulkana Airport to east; elev. 1,579 feet; length 5,000 feet; asphalt; fuel 100LL.

V 118 A 192 T 136 Dry Creek State Recreation Site (to west); 50 wooded campsites, drive-in, pull-through or walk-in. Open May 15–Sept. 15. Clean pit toilets, potable water, fire rings, tent pads. Quiet hours strictly enforced. Camping fee $15 (self-registration); day-use fee $5. Pets on leash are welcome.

V 116.9 A 190.9 T 137.1 MBC Automotive and Towing Service to west; phone (907) 822-5900.

V 115.4 A 189.4 T 138.6 Ace Hardware Store to west.

V 115.2 A 189.2 T 138.8 Distance marker northbound shows Paxson 71 miles, Tok 139 miles, Fairbanks 251 miles, Canada Border 256 miles.

Slow for frost heaves northbound.

V 115 A 189 T 139 Junction of Glenn and Richardson highways; 24-hour gas, diesel, and convenience grocery at **The Hub** (open year-round). **Copper River Valley Visitor Center**, open daily in summer, and The aptly name The Hub of Alaska is on the northwest corner of this intersection; a busy place in summer. Ahtna Building is on the east side of the Richardson Highway at this intersection.

The Hub of Alaska. See display ad this page.

Junction of the Richardson Highway (Alaska Route 4) and Glenn Highway (Alaska Route 1). Turn to **Milepost V 115** on page 488 in the RICHARDSON HIGHWAY section for log of highway south to Valdez.

ALASKA ROUTE 1

Distance from Anchorage (A) is followed by distance from Glenn–Richardson highway junction (G) and distance from Tok (T). *Distance is calculated in relation to the locations of physical mileposts between Glennallen and Anchorage. Physical mileposts reflect distance from Anchorage.*

A 189 G 0 T 139 Junction of the Glenn and Richardson Highways; 24-hour gas, diesel, and convenience grocery at **The Hub** (open year-round). Copper River Valley Visitor Center, open daily in summer.

Distance marker westbound shows Glennallen 2 miles, Palmer 141 miles, Anchorage 189 miles.

Slow for 40-mph speed zone westbound through Glennallen. Improved highway (2013) westbound.

A 188.9 G 0.1 T 139.1 Sign westbound for "Bruce A. Heck Memorial Corridor." A plaque also memorializes this slain Alaska State Trooper at **Milepost A 120.2.**

A 188.8 G 0.2 T 139.2 Gas station to south.

A 188.7 G 0.3 T 139.3 Convenient camping on levels sites in trees at **Northern Nights RV Campground** to north.

A 188.5 G 0.5 T 139.5 Glennallen Community Chapel to north.

A 188.1 G 0.9 T 139.9 Prince William Sound Community College to south.

A 188 G 1 T 140 Westbound sign for Glennallen.

A 187.5 G 1.5 T 140.5 Wells Fargo Bank to north, cafe to south.

A 187.3 G 1.7 T 140.7 Alaska Wildlife Museum with over 50 animals on display.

A 187.1 G 1.9 T 140.9 Copper Valley IGA to north is an impressively well-stocked supermarket.

Glennallen

A 187 G 2 T 141 Downtown Glennallen (post office); located 2 miles west of the junction of the Glenn and Richardson highways. Distance marker shows Palmer 138 miles, Wasilla 151 miles, Anchorage 187 miles, Valdez 117 miles. **Population:** 454. **Emergency Services: Alaska State Troopers, Milepost A 189,** phone (907) 822-3263. **Fire Department,** phone 911. **Ambulance, Copper River EMS,** phone (907) 822-3203 or 911. **Clinic,** and pharmacy, Cross Road Medical Center at **Milepost A 186.6;** urgent care available; phone (907) 822-3203.

Visitor Information: The Greater Copper Valley Chamber of Commerce Visitor Information Center is located at the junction of the Glenn and Richardson highways, **Milepost A 189;** open daily in summer, phone (907) 822-5555 or write Box 469, Glennallen, AK 99588. The Alaska Dept. of Fish and Game office is located at **Milepost A 186.3** on the Glenn Highway, open weekdays 8 A.M. to 5 P.M.; phone (907) 822-3309.

Elevation: 1,460 feet. **Climate**: Mean monthly temperature in January, -10°F; in July, 56°F. Record low was -61°F in January 1975; record high, 90°F in June 1969. Mean precipitation in July, 1.53 inches. Mean precipitation (snow/sleet) in December, 11.4 inches. **Radio**: KCAM 790, KOOL 107.1, KUAC-FM 92.1, KXGA-FM 90.5 (community public radio.) **Television**: KYUK (Bethel) and Wrangell Mountain TV Club via satellite; Public Broadcasting System.

Private Aircraft: Gulkana airstrip, northeast of Glennallen at **Milepost A 192.1;** elev. 1,579 feet; length 5,000 feet; asphalt; fuel 100LL. Parking with tie downs.

The name Glennallen is derived from the combined last names of Capt. Edwin F. Glenn and Lt. Henry T. Allen, both leaders in the early exploration of the Copper River region.

Four prominent peaks of the majestic Wrangell Mountains are to the east; from left they are Mounts Sanford, Drum, Wrangell and Blackburn. The best views are on crisp winter days at sunset. The rest of the countryside is relatively flat.

Towering above the town is an AT&T Alascom microwave tower. AT&T Alascom owns and operates more than 350 microwave and satellite communication sites statewide. The towers are also located along the Alaska, Parks, Richardson, Dalton and Sterling highways, as well as on mountaintops in Southeast Alaska and in remote locations such as Nome. With heights ranging from 100 to more than 300 feet, they are often used as landmarks, but their primary purpose is to carry digital or analog microwave signals for the transmission of long-distance voice and data messages and, in

View of Mount Drum eastbound on the Glenn Highway approaching Richardson Highway junction. (©Kris Valencia, staff)

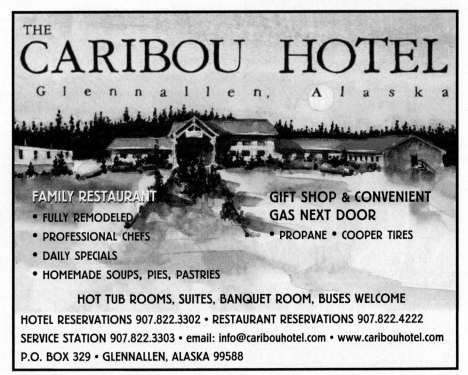

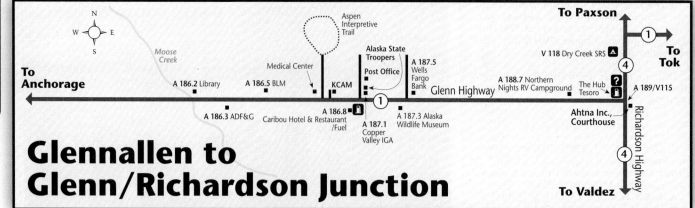

Glennallen to Glenn/Richardson Junction

some cases, 2-way radio communications.

Glennallen businesses are located for several miles along the Glenn Highway west from the junction of the Glenn and Richardson highways. About two-thirds of the area's residents are employed by trade/service firms; the balance hold various government positions.

Offices for the Bureau of Land Management, the Alaska State Troopers and Dept. of Fish and Game are located here. Glennal-

len is also home to the state's only accredited resident 4-year Bible college. There are several small farms in the area. There is a substantial Native population in the area, and the Native-owned Ahtna Corp. has its headquarters in Glennallen at the junction of the Glenn and Richardson highways. Also headquartered here is KCAM radio, which broadcasts area road condition reports and also airs personal messages during the popular "Caribou Clatters."

Glennallen is a fly-in base for several guides and outfitters. Recreation in Glennallen includes flightseeing, hunting, fishing and river rafting in summer; snow-machining and dog sledding in winter. ATVs are popular here and rentals are available locally.

Transportation

Air: Gulkana airport, northeast of Glennallen at **Milepost V 118.1** on the Richardson Highway.

Bus/Van: Service to McCarthy in summer with Kennicott Shuttle (www.kennicottshuttle.com); phone (907) 822-5292. Soaring Eagle Transit (www.gulkanacouncil.org) serves the Copper River area and offers service to Valdez and Anchorage; phone (907) 822-4545.

Lodging & Services

Glennallen has all visitor services. Accommodations and dining at **New Caribou Hotel and Restaurant**. Groceries, espresso, deli and bakery at **Copper Valley IGA**. Auto parts, gifts, clothing, pro-

Welcome to Ahtna Country

We welcome you to the traditional homeland of the Ahtna Athabascan People. The Ahtna People's historic use of wildlife, fish, plants, trails, land and surrounding rivers is well documented. Please visit the Ahtna Cultural Center for more in-depth Ahtna history.

There is so much to do whether it's fishing for our world famous Copper River Salmon, driving on one of several roads that connects urban to rural Alaska, or taking in our glorious mountains, with their breathtaking scenic vistas; you will have ample opportunity for hiking, camping, ATV riding, and snow machining!

And don't worry about running out of daylight. The midnight sun is guaranteed to keep up with you, no matter what you decide to do.

Please remember Ahtna lands are private lands. While we welcome visitors and have developed visitor use areas, we ask visitors to be respectful and follow our rules regarding use of our lands. Permits are issued for land crossing, access, fishing, predator control, camping, and bison hunting. Hunting is not allowed on Ahtna lands, except for predator control and bison hunting.

Permits can be purchased online at http://permits.ahtna-inc.com, in person at MP-115 Richardson Highway, or by mail at PO Box 649 Glennallen, AK 99588.

Learn more at:
http://www.ahtna-inc.com/ldp.html

Or give us a call at:
(907) 822-3476

*Ahtna, Incorporated is an Alaska Native Regional Corporation based out of Glennallen, Alaska, that was established by Congress under terms of the Alaska Native Claims Settlement Act of 1971. Our shareholders are the Ahtna Athabascan people of the Cantwell and Copper River regions, and we currently own and manage more than 1.5 million acres of land within the Ahtna Region.

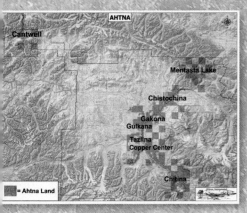

Learn more about Ahtna, Inc. at
www.ahtna-inc.com

Fireweed marks the passage of summer.
(©Kristin Wilkinson, staff)

pane, sporting goods and other supplies are available at local stores. Services include a Wells Fargo Bank with ATM, First National Bank Alaska with ATM, a dentist, several churches, a chiropractic center, a laundromat, gas stations and major auto repair. WiFi access at the Hub of Alaska, the Caribou Hotel and Copper Valley Community Library.

Camping

Northern Nights Campground & RV Park is near the Glenn–Rich Highway junction, on the north side of the Glenn Highway, at Milepost A 188.7. The Caribou Hotel offers RV camping as well. **Dry Creek State Recreation Site** is 3 miles north of the Glenn-Rich Junction on the Richardson Highway. West of Glennallen there's camping at **Tolsona Wilderness Campground and RV Park**, Milepost A 173.

Northern Nights Campground & RV Park. A very well-maintained, beautifully landscaped RV campground offering large, level, spruce tree-lined pull-through sites. "Ultimate Tow" vehicles with triple/quads slide rigs will have no problem parking here. The friendly and knowledgeable operators enjoy making their guests relaxed and comfortable. An always hot, private, large individual shower facility with flush toilets is available to help guests unwind after a long day of sightseeing and fishing. Free WiFi. Free "Dessert Nights" are offered to guests on Monday and Friday nights from mid-June to mid-August. Located only 900 yards from the Richardson and Glenn Highway junction on the Glenn Highway. This park is open from May 15 to September 15 (weather permitting). See display ad on page 354. [ADVERTISEMENT]

Attractions

Alaska Wildlife Museum. Located on the Glenn Highway in downtown Glennallen, across from the bank, this small but unique museum has over 50 realistic anatomical displays of predators and their prey, including grizzly and black bears, wolves, wolverine, moose, caribou, Dall sheep, mountain goat, marten, lynx, fox and coyote. Hand-painted murals create a realistic feeling of mountains, woods and riverbank. Admission charged.

Aspen Interpretive Trail is a 1-mile walk through 3 boreal forest ecosystems: aspen/white spruce forest, black spruce forest and sedge meadow. Information signs about area plants and animals were developed by local students. Trailhead parking is on Co-op Road (turn north off the Glenn Highway just east of the BLM office).

Glennallen is the service center for the Copper River Basin. It is also the starting point and finish line for the **Copper Basin 300 Dog Sled Race.** Called by some "the toughest 300 miles in Alaska," the race is held the second Saturday in January. One of the first races of the season, the Copper Basin is a qualifier for the Iditarod, attracting a variety of participants, from top mushers to first-time rookies. The race travels through Chistochina, over to Paxson, down to Sourdough, Lake Louise and Tolsona before returning to Glennallen. Spectators can watch from a number of lodges along the course. Race information and memorabilia is available at the visitor center or at www.cb300.com.

Summer special events include a parade and salmon bake on the **4th of July** and an arts and crafts fair on the July 4th weekend.

Glennallen is the gateway to the Wrangell Mountains. The **Wrangell-St. Elias National Park Visitor Center** is about 10 miles from Glennallen on the Richardson Highway and well worth a visit. The National Park visitor center offers interpretive programs during the summer.

Lake Louise, 27 miles west on the Glenn Highway and 16 miles north on Lake Louise Road, is a popular recreation area for fishing (grayling, lake trout and burbot) in summer and snowmobiling in winter. Lakeside resorts offer food, lodging and boat rentals. **Lake Louise State Recreation Area** offers camping and a boat launch.

FISHING: Grayling fishing and good king and red salmon fishing (June and July) in the **Gulkana River** at the Gulkana River bridge on the Richardson Highway, a 14-mile drive from Glennallen.

According to the ADF&G, 28 lakes in the Glennallen area are stocked with grayling, rainbow and silver salmon. A complete list of lakes, locations and species is available at the visitor center at the Glenn-Rich junction, or from the ADF&G office at Milepost A 186.3. Locally, there is good grayling fishing in **Moose Creek**; **Tolsona Creek** to the east at Milepost GJ 17.6; and west on the Glenn Highway at **Tolsona Creek**, Milepost A 172.8, and at **Lake Louise**.

Fly-in lakes include: **Crosswind Lake**, large lake trout, whitefish and grayling, early June to early July; **Deep Lake**, all summer for lake trout to 30 inches; **High Lake**, lake trout to 22 inches, June and early July; **Tebay Lakes** and **Summit Lake**, excellent rainbow fishing, 12 to 15 inches, all summer; **Jan Lake**, 12- to 14-inch silver salmon, June, spinners; also rainbow; **Hanagita Lake**, excellent grayling fishing all summer; and **Minnesota Lake**, lake trout to 30 inches, all summer.

Glenn Highway Log
(continued)

Distance from Anchorage (A) is followed by distance from Glenn–Richardson highways junction (G) and distance from Tok (T).

A 186.9 G 2.1 T 141.1 KCAM radio station to north. Distance marker westbound shows Palmer 138 miles, Anchorage 187 miles. Aspen Hiking trailhead to north.

A 186.7 G 2.3 T 141.3 Cross Road Medical Center clinic (EMS, 24-hour emergency room) to north has a pharmacy and clinic. Phone (907) 822-3203.

A 186.5 G 2.5 T 141.5 Bureau of Land Management Glennallen Field Office; phone (907) 822-3217.

A 186.4 G 2.6 T 141.6 AT&T microwave tower.

A 186.3 G 2.7 T 141.7 Alaska State Dept. of Fish and Game to south; phone (907) 822-3309.

A 186.2 G 2.8 T 141.8 Copper Valley Library to north.

A 186.1 G 2.9 T 141.9 Moose Creek culvert; good grayling fishing.

A 185.4 G 3.6 T 142.6 NOTE: *Begin 40 mph speed zone, improved highway, eastbound through Glennallen. Improved highway, posted 55-mph speed limit, westbound. Watch for continued road construction westbound on the Glenn Highway in summer 2014.*

A 185 G 4 T 143 True Value Hardware store.

A 182.2 G 6.8 T 145.8 Liquor store to south has some interesting topiary done in native shrubs like willow and birch.

A 177 G 12 T 151 Distance marker westbound shows Palmer 129 miles, Anchorage 177 miles.

A 176.7 G 12.3 T 151.3 Paved historical viewpoint to south with view southeast across the Copper River valley to Mount Drum. Northeast of Mount Drum is Mount Sanford, and southeast is Mount Wrangell (elev. 14,163 feet), the only active volcano in the Wrangell Mountains. Portable outhouse available in summer 2013.

Tolsona (westbound sign), an unincorporated community located along about a 16-mile stretch of the Glenn Highway.

A 176.5 G 12.5 T 151.5 Distance marker eastbound shows Glennallen 10 miles, Tok 152 miles.

A 174.8 G 14.2 T 153.2 Double-ended paved turnout to south.

Great views (on clear days) of Mount Drum directly ahead for eastbound travelers.

A 173 G 16 T 155 Turnoff to north for **Tolsona Wilderness Campground and RV Park** (see description following), a beautiful spot.

Tolsona Wilderness Campground & RV Park. AAA approved, Good Sam Park. This beautiful campground, located three-quarters of a mile north of the highway, is surrounded on 3 sides by untouched wilderness. All 80 campsites are situated beside sparkling Tolsona Creek and are complete with table and fireplace. It is a full-service campground with tent sites, restrooms, dump station, hot showers, laundromat, water and electric hookups for RVs. Free Wi-Fi. Browse through the extensive turn-of-the-century antique display. Hiking trail and public phone. Open from May 20 through September 10. Phone (907) 822-3865. Email: camp@tolsona.com. See display ad on facing page. [ADVERTISEMENT]

Ask about visiting the Tolsona Mud Vol-

cano (1-mile trail). Sherry Simpson wrote about the mud volcanoes in the Oct. 2009 issue of *Alaska magazine*: "...our curiosity increased as we followed the path from the Tolsona Wilderness Campground, helpfully marked with CDs nailed to spruce trees. The authors of *True Secrets of Alaska Revealed!* describe the volcano as, 'kind of like the one in Close Encounters of the Third Kind, but bigger and not built by Richard Dreyfuss.' The campground owners more modestly refer to Tolsona 'mud spring.'"

A 172.8 G 16.2 T 155.2 Turnout to south at east end of **Tolsona Creek** bridge (new bridge under construction summer 2013); parking for walk-in use (no overnight camping). Fishing for grayling to 16 inches, use mosquito flies in still, clear pools behind obstructions, June, July and August. Best fishing 1.5 miles upstream from highway. ⬅

Highway climbs westbound.

A 170.5 G 18.5 T 157.5 Turnoff to north for Tolsona Lake Resort; air taxi, lodging and meals. Public parking and boat launch available. Fishing for grayling and stocked rainbow trout. ⬅

Good views eastbound on the Glenn Highway (weather permitting) of Mount Drum (center peak); Mount Sanford (to left of Drum); and Mount Wrangell (to right of Drum).

A 170 G 19 T 158 Crosswind Lake trail (sign missing in summer 2013). This is a 14-mile winter snowmachine trail for access to the lake. According to the ADF&G, the lake supports arctic grayling, burbot, lake trout, sockeye (red) salmon and whitefish.

The trail is too boggy for summer use.

A 169.5 G 19.5 T 158.5 *Slow for frost heaves and damaged pavement.*

A 169.3 G 19.7 T 158.7 Paved double-ended parking area to south. Long narrow **Mae West Lake**, fed by Little Woods Creek, is less than a mile from the highway. Grayling fishing. ⬅

A 168 G 21 T 160 Soup Lake to north (view obscured by trees). Trumpeter swans can sometimes be seen in lakes and ponds along this section of highway. Watch for moose. In June and July look for wildflowers such as sweet pea, fireweed, lupine, cinquefoil, oxytrope, Jacob's ladder and milk-vetch.

A 166.9 G 22.1 T 161.1 Distance marker westbound shows Lake Louise Junction 7 miles, Sutton 106 miles, Palmer 119 miles.

A 165.9 G 23.1 T 162.1 Paved double-ended turnout to south and hiking trail to **Lost Cabin Lake** to north; fishing for grayling and burbot. ⬅

Tolsona Mountain (elev. 2,974 feet), a prominent ridge just north of highway, is a landmark for miles in both directions. This area is popular with berry pickers in late summer and early fall. Varieties of wild berries include blueberries, lowbush cranberries and raspberries.

A 164 G 25 T 164 Halfway point between Tok and Anchorage. Glimpse of Tazlina Glacier and lake in the distance to south as you drive westbound.

A 162.3 G 26.7 T 165.7 Paved turnout to south.

A 162 G 27 T 166 Gravel turnout to north for signed public fishing access to **Tex**

Smith Lake; stocked with rainbow. ⬅

A 161 G 28 T 167 *Slow for road damage.* Westbound travelers may note changes in vegetation as the highway passes through various transition zones. Well-drained soil and south-facing slopes support tall, dense stands of white spruce, aspen and birch, while cold wet flats, muskeg and north-facing slopes are dominated by the stunted and crooked black spruce.

A 160 G 29 T 168 Eastbound sign for TOLSONA (area pop. 64), an unincorporated community located along about a 16-mile stretch of the Glenn Highway.

A 159.8 G 29.2 T 168.2 Turnoff to north for **Lake Louise Road** (see description this section).

Junction with 19.3-mile Lake Louise Road (paved) to lodges and State Recreation Area on Lake Louise. See "Lake Louise Road" log on page 358.

A 159.6 G 29.4 T 168.4 **Little Junction Lake** signed public fishing access to south (0.5-mile hike) grayling. ⬅

A 157.9 G 31.1 T 170.1 *SLOW for dips and damaged road.*

A 157 G 32 T 171 Distance marker westbound shows Palmer 109 miles, Anchorage 157 miles. Public fishing access trails to south to **DJ Lake** 0.5 mile (landlocked silver, rainbow) and **Sucker Lake** 4 miles (grayling, burbot). ⬅

Distance marker eastbound shows Glenn-
(Continues on page 359)

Lake Louise Road

This paved road leads north 19.3 miles from **Milepost A 159.8** Glenn Highway to **LAKE LOUISE** (pop. 84), known for its fishing (lake trout and grayling) and its lakeside lodges and campgrounds. Dining, boat rentals and fishing charters are available at the lodges. Excellent cross-country skiing and snowmobiling in winter. Good views of Tazlina Glacier and berry picking (in season) along Lake Louise Road. Posted speed limit is 45 mph; maintained year-round.

Distance is measured from the junction with the Glenn Highway (J).

J 0 Junction with Glenn Highway at **Milepost A 159.8.** *Slow for frost heaves and damaged pavement. Posted speed limit 45 mph. Watch for caribou next 20 miles. Watch for snow machines in winter.*

J 0.2 Junction Lake to east; grayling fishing.

J 1 Large gravel turnout to west.

J 1.2 Double-ended turnout to west with view of Tazlina Glacier. Just north is the road west to **Little Crater Lake** and **Crater Lake**, stocked with rainbow trout by ADF&G.

J 5.1 Old Road Lake and Round Lake to east (.25 mile via narrow, potholed road); stocked with rainbow trout.

J 6.7 Mendeltna Creek to west 5 miles via rough road (4-wheel-drive access only); grayling fishing.

J 7 Gravel parking area across from 0.1-mile trail east to **Forgotten Lake**; grayling fishing.

J 9.4 Signed shoulder parking to west. First view of Lake Louise northbound.

J 10 View of pothole lakes.

J 10.5 Highway descends hill northbound. Good view on clear days of the Alaska Range and Susitna River valley.

J 11.5 Dirt parking. Side road leads west then north to **Caribou Lake**; grayling fishing. Turnout to east by **Elbow Lake**; grayling fishing.

J 13.9 Gravel parking area to east.

Watch for caribou along Lake Louise Road.
(©Sharon Nault)

J 14 Boundary of Matanuska–Susitna Borough. Welcome to Lake Louise (sign). Eureka trailhead (signed).

J 14.9 Turnout to east.

J 15.3 Waste transfer site.

J 15.8 Signed gravel shoulder parking to east.

J 15.9 North and **South Jans Lakes** to east (7 miles; trail access); rainbows.

J 16.1 Turnoff for **Lake Louise Lodge** on Lake Louise (0.8 miles); lodging and dining. Lake Louise Lodge. See display ad this page.

J 16.5 Turnoff for Evergreen and Wolverine lodges.

J 16.8 Conner Lake public access; grayling fishing.

J 17 Snowmachine Crossing.

J 17.2 Gravel side road leads northeast to **The Point Lodge** (0.8 miles) and **Lake Louise State Recreation Area**. Drive 0.3 miles to "T"; turn left and continue 0.5 mile for **The Point Lodge** and another 0.3 mile for Lake Louise Campground; turn right at "T" for Army Point Campground (0.7 mile). The Point Lodge. See display ad this page.

©David L Ranta, staff

Army Point Campground and **Lake Louise Campground** (Lake Louise State Recreation Area) have 60 campsites on loop roads, firepits, water pumps (boil water), toilets (wheelchair accessible), covered picnic tables, picnic shelter, walking trail. Camping fee $15/night; walk-in sites $5/night; boat launch $10; daily parking $5. Swimming in Lake Louise. Popular winter ski trail access.

J 18 *Slow for gravel breaks northbound.*

J 18.3 Private Aircraft: Lake Louise airport, N62°17.62' W146°34.77'; elev. 2,450 feet; length 7,000 feet; gravel; unattended. Lake Louise seaplane base, N62°16.97', W146°31.13'. Attended daylight hours in summer.

J 19.3 Road ends. Large parking area to west and boat launch to **Dinty Lake** (west) and **Lake Louise** (east). Lake Louise rest area to east at road end has picnic tables, fireplaces, toilets.

Grayling and lake trout fishing good year-round, best spring through July, then again in the fall; early season use herring or whitefish bait, cast from boat; later (warmer water) troll with #16 red-and-white spoon, silver Alaskan plug or large silver flatfish; for grayling, casting flies or small spinners, June, July and August; in winter jig for lake trout. Check ADF&G regulations. **Susitna Lake** can be reached by boat across Lake Louise (narrow channel; watch for signs); burbot, lake trout and grayling fishing. *Both lakes can be rough; under-powered boats not recommended.*

Return to Milepost A 159.8 Glenn Highway

(Continued from page 357)
allen 31 miles, Tok 173 miles.

A 156.4 G 32.6 T 171.6 Good view (weather permitting) to south of **Tazlina Glacier**, which feeds into 20-mile-long Tazlina Lake, at the head of the Tazlina River. The Tazlina River is a tributary of the Copper River.

A 156.3 G 32.7 T 171.7 Gravel turnout. **Buffalo Lake** public fishing access to north; stocked with rainbow.

A 156 G 33 T 172 Tazlina airstrip to north; elev. 2,450 feet; length 1,200 feet; gravel. Not recommended for use.

A 155.8 G 33.2 T 172.2 Arizona Lake public fishing access to south; arctic grayling.

A 155.6 G 33.4 T 172.4 Turnout to south.

A 155.4 G 33.6 T 172.6 *Begin long downhill grade westbound.*

A 155.3 G 33.7 T 172.7 Gergie Lake public fishing access to south (1¼ mile); fishing for rainbow (stocked).

A 154 G 35 T 174 Westbound sign for **MENDELTNA** (pop. 70). This unincorporated community includes the historic Mendeltna Creek Lodge. The area was originally a stop used by Natives traveling from Lake Tyone to Tazlina Lake. Gold brought prospectors into the area in the late 1800s.

A 153.5 G 35.5 T 174.5 Mendeltna Community chapel to south.

A 153 G 36 T 175 Mendeltna Creek Lodge to south.

A 152.7 G 36.3 T 175.3 Mendeltna Creek bridge; spawning salmon in August. Fishing for grayling and whitefish, May to November, use spinners and flies. This creek is closed to all salmon fishing. Good fishing north to **Old Man Lake**; watch for bears.

A 152.6 G 36.6 T 175.4 Paved double-ended rest area to north with toilet, litter bin and picnic table.

A 151.4 G 37.6 T 176.6 "Mendeltna" sign eastbound; see description at **Milepost A 154**.

A 151 G 38 T 177 Distance marker eastbound shows Glennallen 37 miles, Tok 179 miles.

A 150.4 G 38.6 T 177.6 Westbound sign for **NELCHINA** (pop. 55). This unincorporated community consists of approximately 33 homes.

A 150 G 39 T 178 Distance marker westbound shows Sutton 89 miles, Palmer 103 miles. Eastbound view of Mount Sanford and Mount Drum straight ahead.

A 149 G 40 T 179 Grizzly Country Store and Towing. **Ryan Lake** public fishing access to south; rainbow.

A 143.3 G 45.7 T 184.7 Nelchina Lodge.

A 142.6 G 46.4 T 185.4 Distance marker eastbound shows Lake Louise Junction 17 miles, Glennallen 47 miles, Tok 189 miles.

A 141.2 G 47.8 T 186.8 Nelchina state highway maintenance station.

A 140 G 49 T 188 Gravel turnout to north.

A 139.5 G 49.5 T 188.5 Espresso and smoothies shop to south.

A 139 G 50 T 189 Scenic Byway sign westbound. "Nelchina" sign (missing summer 2013) eastbound (see description at **Milepost A 150.4**).

Glimpse of Nelchina Glacier in distance from turnout at Milepost A 129.4. (©Kris Valencia, staff)

A 138.5 G 50.5 T 189.5 Highway descends to Little Nelchina River westbound. *Trucks use low gear on downhill westbound.*

A 137.6 G 51.4 T 190.4 Former Little Nelchina State Recreation Site (no sign) 0.3 mile north from highway; unmaintained campsites on pot-holed loop road, no fee, no drinking water, firepits, outhouse, boat launch. No ATVs. Watch for moose and bear. Fishing for grayling.

A 137.5 G 51.5 T 190.5 Little Nelchina River bridge.

NOTE: Eastbound, highway curves uphill from bridge. Westbound to summit it is good paved straightaway with passing lanes.

A 137.5 G 51.5 T 190.5 Boundary of Matanuska–Susitna Borough (sign). A borough is a unit of regional government in Alaska, much like counties in the rest of the U.S. Boroughs are either first- or second-class and have the power to mandate education, land use and taxes. There are currently 16 boroughs in the state, but they do not represent all of the state. There are several areas outside the existing boroughs. Ranked in terms of population, the Matanuska–Susitna Borough is probably one of the fastest growing, thanks to recent rapid growth in "the valley" (mainly Palmer and Wasilla).

A 135.9 G 53.1 T 192.1 Paved turnout to north.

A 135.1 G 53.9 T 192.9 Slide Mountain Cabins and RV Park to north

A 134.1 G 54.9 T 193.9 *Truck lane begins westbound.*

A 133 G 56 T 195 Double-ended paved turnout to north. John Lake trailhead (unsigned).

Truck lane ends westbound. Highway descends eastbound.

Watch for caribou.

A 132 G 57 T 196 Great views (weather permitting) to southwest of Nelchina Glacier. View of snow-covered Mount Drum eastbound.

Bent poles along highway are snow poles to guide snow plows during winter.

A 130.5 G 58.5 T 197.5 Large gravel parking area to north used by hunters, ATVers

and hikers. Old Man Creek trailhead (Old Man Creek 2 miles; Crooked Creek 9 miles; Nelchina Town 14.5 miles). Established trails west from here to Palmer are part of the Chickaloon–Knik–Nelchina trail system.

A 129.5 G 59.5 T 198.5 Eureka Summit (elev. 3,322 feet), highest point on the Glenn Highway. Unobstructed views to south of the Chugach Mountains. Nelchina Glacier winds downward through a cleft in the mountains. To the northwest are the peaks of the Talkeetnas, and to the west the highway descends through river valleys which separate these 2 mountain ranges. This is the divide of 3 major river systems: Susitna, Matanuska and Copper.

A 129.4 G 59.6 T 198.6 Double-ended turnout to south with Gold Rush Centennial sign about Captain Edwin F. Glenn, who passed near here on his way from Cook Inlet to the Tanana River in 1898. Glenn led one of 3 teams, the Cook Inlet Exploring Expedition. His orders were to locate the most practical route from Prince William Sound through Cook Inlet to the Tanana River. The Glenn Highway is named in his honor.

A 128.5 G 60.5 T 199.5 Distance marker eastbound shows Glennallen 58 miles, Valdez 179 miles, Tok 198 miles.

A 128.3 G 60.7 T 199.7 Food, gas, diesel, lodging, bar and liquor store at the Eureka Lodge. The first lodge on the Glenn Highway, opened by Paul Waverly in 1937.

Private Aircraft: Eureka (Skelton) airstrip, one of the highest in the state; elev. 3,289 feet; length 2,400 feet; gravel; fuel autogas; unattended. Runway narrows to 15 feet.

A 128 G 61 T 200 Gunsight Mountain (elev. 6,441 feet) is visible to the west for the next few miles to those approaching from Glennallen. The notch or "gunsight" is plain if one looks closely. Eastbound views (weather permitting) of snow-covered Mount Sanford, Mount Drum, Mount Wrangell and Mount Blackburn.

Bruce A. Heck Memorial Corridor (sign); see **Milepost A 120.2**.

A 127 G 62 T 201 *CAUTION: Watch for caribou.* Caribou crossing. The Nelchina

Landmarks along the Glenn Highway between Tahneta Pass and Sheep Mountain include Gunsight Mountain, the notched peak seen here. (©Kris Valencia, staff)

caribou herd travels through here October through November.

A 126.4 G 62.6 T 201.6 Watch for turn-off to south to Chickaloon-Knik-Nelchina Trail System. (Eureka Creek 1.5 miles, Goober Lake 8 miles, Nelchina River 9 miles), trailhead parking.

A 123.4 G 65.6 T 204.6 Belanger Pass trailhead to north via Marten Road. Marten Road (rutted dirt) leads north 1.5 miles through private homesteads and then forks: keep to left at fork for Belanger Pass trail. According to the DOT, this 8-mile trail terminates at Caribou Creek Trail. It is part of a network of ATV trails and mining roads around Syncline Mountain in the Talkeetna Mountains to the north.

A 122.7 G 66.3 T 205.3 Tahneta Lake to south has "good spring fishing" according to the ADF&G.

A 122.5 G 66.5 T 205.5 Boundary of Sportfish Management Area 2 and Sheep Mountain Closed Area.

A 122 G 67 T 206 Tahneta Pass (elev. 3,000 feet).

A 121.4 G 67.6 T 206.6 Signed trailhead to north; small parking area. According to

DOT, this 1-mile-long trail loops around a small lake north of Leila Lake. Leila Lake: grayling 8 to 14 inches abundant through summer, best fishing June and July; burbot, success spotty for 12 to 18 inches in fall and winter; whitefish.

NOTE: Improved highway westbound.

A 120.3 G 68.7 T 207.7 Gravel pit parking to north. Gunsight Mountain Ski Hill (abandoned). The hexagonal Chalet St. Christopher and a rope tow were built here in the 1960s.

A 120.2 G 68.8 T 207.8 Scenic viewpoint to south (double-ended paved turnout). The largest lake is Leila Lake; in the distance is Tahneta Lake. A monument here honoring Trooper Bruce A. Heck reads:

"On a cold winter night, on January 10, 1997, Alaska State Trooper Bruce Heck gave his life in the line of duty near this location. While on duty in the area of Mile 157.9 of the Glenn Highway, Trooper Heck attempted to arrest a suspect who had run into the woods after wrecking a stolen taxicab. In sub-zero temperatures and deep snow, a struggle ensued where the suspect overpowered Trooper Heck and took his life. The suspect, who was arrested by other officers who arrived on scene shortly thereafter, was convicted and sentenced to life in

prison. In 1999, the Alaska State Legislature designated the Glenn Highway from Mile 128 to Mile 189 as the Trooper Bruce A. Heck Memorial Corridor so that his sacrifice will not be forgotten. This monument is placed in remembrance of Trooper Heck's selfless act of giving his life while protecting the citizens of Alaska."

A 118.8 G 70.2 T 209.2 Double-ended turnout to south with beautiful view of Chugach Mountains (weather permitting) and Knob Lake. The landmark "knob" (elev. 3,000 feet), topped by microwave tower, marks entrance to Chickaloon Pass for small planes.

This turnout is a popular birder gathering spot in the spring, when raptors pass through on their way to western Alaska nesting sites. The migration of golden eagles, gyrfalcons, kestrels, hawks and other raptors usually takes place during a 2- to 4-week window beginning in early April. The Anchorage Audubon Society holds an annual Raptor Tailgate Party and Census during April.

A 118.5 G 70.5 T 209.5 Trailhead Road rest area to north; large parking area with outhouses, picnic tables, viewing telescope and Gold Rush Centennial signs. Nice stop, good views.

Access to 4-mile section of Old Glenn Highway from parking area (abandoned road; ditches across road). See also **Milepost A 115**. Trailhead for the Chickaloon-Knik-Nelchina Trail System.

A 118.4 G 70.6 T 209.6 Alascom Road leads 3.3 miles south to a microwave tower visible on hill. Narrow gravel road in fair condition. There are no turnarounds for large vehicles and small turnouts along the road are used as informal campsites. Public access to **North** and **South Knob Lakes**; stocked with rainbow trout. Road up to tower is steep and narrow (single-vehicle only) with small turnaround at stop; signed No Trespassing.

A 118.3 G 70.7 T 209.7 Trail Creek.

A 118.2 G 70.8 T 209.8 *Truck lane begins westbound.*

A 118 G 71 T 210 *Truck lane ends eastbound. Truck lane ends westbound.*

A 117.4 G 71.6 T 210.6 *Truck lane begins eastbound.*

A 117.3 G 71.7 T 210.7 Paved double-ended turnout to south with view of Chugach Mountains. Signed Camp Creek Trailhead.

CAUTION: Slow for frost heaves and damaged road.

A 117.1 G 71.9 T 210.9 Camp Creek.

A 116.9 G 72.1 T 211.1 *Truck lane ends eastbound.*

A 116 G 73 T 212 *Truck lane begins eastbound. CAUTION: Frost heaves.*

A 115.5 G 73.5 T 212.5 Paved double-ended turnout to south with view.

A 115 G 74 T 213 Double-ended paved turnout to north. Access to 4-mile section of Old Glenn Highway alignment (abandoned road; ditches across road). See also **Milepost A 118.5**.

Truck lane ends eastbound.

A 114.9 G 74.1 T 213.1 Turnoff to south for **Majestic Valley Lodge** (description follows), a lodge offering rooms, cabins and fine dining with advance reservations.

Majestic Valley Lodge is a handcrafted log lodge offering rooms and cabins with private baths. 100-person capacity dining room and lounge with spectacular mountain views serves unforgettable meals (*advance reservation required*). Relax on the

Gypsum and iron oxide color the slopes of Sheep Mountain, photographed from the viewpoint at Milepost A 112.8. (©Kris Valencia, staff)

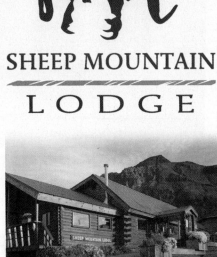

SHEEP MOUNTAIN LODGE

covered porch with a cup of coffee or a glass of wine. Miles of hiking, skiing or snowmobiling trails make this a pristine destination. Hike in the Dall Sheep Reserve, just steps out your door, or view wildlife, take a glacier trek, or go river rafting. Wireless Internet access and TV in lodge rooms. Phone (907) 746-2930; fax (907) 746-2931; website www.majesticvalleylodge.com. See display ad on page 360. [ADVERTISEMENT]

A 114.8 G 74.2 T 213.2 *Highway descends westbound.*

For Anchorage-bound travelers a vista of incomparable beauty as the road descends in a long straightaway toward Glacier Point, also known as the **Lions Head**, an oddly formed rocky dome.

A 114.2 G 74.8 T 213.8 Shoulder parking to north.

A 113.6 G 75.4 T 214.4 *Truck lane begins eastbound.*

A 113.5 G 75.5 T 214.5 Turnoff for **Sheep Mountain Lodge** (description follows), located on the north side of the highway; restaurant, lodging, camping, pay phone. The lodge also maintains a hiking trail system.

The **Fireweed 400** round-trip bike race to Valdez, scheduled for July 11-12, 2014, is the largest and longest event of its kind in Alaska and it begins and ends at Sheep Mountain Lodge. There are also 50-, 100-, 200- and 300-mile races starting at the lodge the same time. For details and registration, visit www.fireweed400.com.

Sheep Mountain Lodge. Our charming log lodge, established in 1946, has been serving travelers for half a century. We're famous for our wholesome homemade food, fresh baked breads, pastries and desserts. Our comfortable guest cabins, all with private bathrooms, boast spectacular mountain views. We also have RV hookups, full bar, and Alaskan gifts. Stretch your legs on our well-marked trail system, offering easy strolls and challenging ascents. Trail maps available at the lodge. You can watch Dall Sheep through our telescope and relax in the hot tub or sauna after a day of traveling or hiking. Toll-free phone 1-877-645-5121. Phone (907) 745-

5121. Internet: www.sheepmountain.com. See display ad this page. [ADVERTISEMENT]

Wonderful views to north of **Sheep Mountain** (elev. 6,300 feet). Sheep are often seen high up these slopes. In the 1930s trapper Ed Ueeck, known as the man from Sheep Mountain, was concerned that construction of the Glenn Highway would lead to overhunting of area sheep. His efforts led to the designation of the Sheep Mountain Closed Area, where sheep hunting is illegal. As the highway descends westbound into the valley of the Matanuska River, there is a view of the great glacier which is the main headwater source and gives the water its milky color.

A 113 G 76 T 215 Turnoff for Sheep Mountain airstrip to north. **Private Aircraft:** Sheep Mountain airstrip; elev. 2,750 feet; length 2,300 feet; gravel/dirt; unattended.

A 112.8 G 76.2 T 215.2 Double-ended paved turnout to south; good camera viewpoint for Sheep Mountain to north and Chugach Mountains to south. Interpretive signs on Sheep Mountain gypsum and Dall sheep (excerpt):

"Current theories indicate Dall sheep use licks each spring to replenish depleted supplies of calcium and magnesium. In this area, the Dall sheep may be getting calcium by eating gypsum (a form of calcium sulfate).

"Gypsum is a clear to white mineral, but here it is stained with small amounts of iron oxide. The same hydrothermal system that created the gypsum also oxidized (rusted) the iron underground, by exposing it to hot water and sulfuric acid."

A 112.7 G 76.3 T 215.3 *Truck lane ends eastbound.*

A 112.1 G 76.9 T 215.9 Gypsum Creek (sign).

A 111.6 G 77.4 T 216.4 *Truck lane begins eastbound.*

A 111 G 78 T 217 *Truck lane ends eastbound.* Distance marker westbound shows Palmer 63 miles, Anchorage 104 miles.

A 110.5 G 78.5 T 217.5 *Truck lane begins eastbound.*

A 110.1 G 78.9 T 217.9 Jackass Creek.

A 109.7 G 79.3 T 218.3 Aptly named **Grand View Cafe and RV Campground** (description follows) to south has home-

Matanuska Glacier from viewpoint at Milepost A 101. The glacier's average width is 2 miles; at its terminus it is 4 miles wide. Glacier meltwater drains into a stream that flows into the Matanuska River. (© Kris Valencia, staff)

style dining in log lodge, pull-through RV sites.

Grand View Cafe & RV Park. Matanuska Glacier, Dall sheep, an ancient volcano; spectacular sights surrounding this scenic stop. Log cafe serves home-style meals, brick oven pizza, espresso, beer and wine. Repeatedly praised for cleanliness and friendliness, and centrally located between Palmer and Glennallen. Full service pull-thru RV sites include free WiFi, TV and cell reception; the only park providing these amenities on the Glenn Highway. Breakfast Special for RV guests. Summer only (907) 746-4480. Winter email: info@grandviewrv.com; www.grandviewrv.com. See display ad this page. [ADVERTISEMENT]

Good views westbound of Matanuska Glacier.

A 109.5 G 79.5 T 218.5 Turnoff to south for **Tundra Rose Guest Cottages** overnight accommodations (description follows) with Matanuska Glacier view.

Tundra Rose Guest Cottages. Affordable, quality log cottages with fireplaces, kitchenettes, TV, decks with mountain/glacier views in a quiet setting. Birds, Dall sheep and other wildlife viewing. Casual dining, laundry and free WiFi within walking distance. Complimentary coffee/tea and discounted breakfast special. Our guests repeatedly state that we are the cleanest, most scenic find during their travels. Reserve online www.tundrarosecabins.com. Phone (907) 745-5865. See display ad this page. [ADVERTISEMENT]

A 109 G 80 T 219 *Begin 6 to 8 percent downgrade westbound.*

A 108.1 G 80.9 T 219.9 Paved shoulder parking on north side of highway.

A 107.7 G 81.3 T 220.3 Large paved scenic viewpoint to south. Fortress Ridge (elev. 5,000 feet) to the north.

A 106.9 G 82.1 T 221.1 **Caribou Creek Bridge.** Caribou Creek is a Recreational Gold Mining Area. Recreational gold panning, mineral prospecting or mining using light portable field equipment (e.g. hand-operated pick, backpack power drill, etc.) is allowed in these designated areas on state lands without mining claims. Contact the Dept. of Natural Resources Public Information Center in Anchorage for more information; phone (907) 269-8400. See the Division Fact Sheet at www.dnr.state.ak.us/mlw/factsht/; click on Caribou Creek Recreational Mining.

There are 26 creeks named Caribou Creek in the *Dictionary of Alaska Place Names*. This Caribou Creek heads at a glacier terminus in the Talkeetna Mountains and flows 35 miles southeast to the Matanuska River.

Sheep Mountain reserve boundary.

A 106.2 G 82.8 T 221.8 *Begin passing lane westbound. Highway climbs 7 percent uphill grade westbound.*

A 106 G 83 T 222 Caribou Creek Recreation Area (signed); watch for sharp turnoff to a *small* gravel parking area on hillside. According to the DNR, a steep trail leads down to the creek from the parking lot. Only pedestrian traffic is permitted on the trail (sorry, no all-terrain vehicles). "Physical fitness, health, and age should be considered due to the steepness of the trail."

A 105.5 G 83.5 T 222.5 *End passing lane westbound. End passing lane eastbound.*

A 104.7 G 84.3 T 223.3 *Begin passing lane eastbound.*

A 104.4 G 84.6 T 223.6 Paved shoulder parking both sides of highway.

A 104 G 85 T 224 Access to Glacier View Elementary School, which overlooks Matanuska Glacier.

A 103.3 G 85.7 T 224.7 Shoulder parking to south with view of Matanuska Glacier.

A 102.5 G 86.5 T 225.5 Turnoff to south for MICA Guides; 1 hour to half-day trips on Matanuska Glacier.

A 102.2 G 86.8 T 225.8 **Long Rifle Lodge** to south; open year-round, offers breakfast, lunch and dinner, gas, gifts and lodging overlooking Matanuska Glacier. 🅿

Long Rifle Lodge. See display ad this page.

A 102.1 G 86.9 T 225.9 Access to Matanuska Glacier to south via steep side road to **Glacier Park** (description follows); admission charged. Camping available. 🅰

Glacier Access at Glacier Park. Join us for a great, fun-filled day exploring Matanuska Glacier, the largest glacier accessible by personal vehicle. We offer a recommended guided hike with Matanuska Glacier Adventures to take you onto the white ice. This is a real Alaskan, real world experience and lots of adventure. No reservations required May through September. Gift shop and snacks. Access at Mile 102 Glenn Highway (66500 Park Road, Sutton, AK 99674). Two hour drive from Anchorage. Attention: From Anchorage, you must drive through Palmer NOT Wasilla. Confusing interchange at Mile 34 Glenn Highway: You must exit the Glenn Highway at Mile 34 to stay on the Glenn Highway. 1-888-253-4480; www.bestglacier.com. See display ad this page.
[ADVERTISEMENT]

A 101.5 G 87.5 T 226.5 Paved shoulder parking to south with good view of Matanuska Glacier across from a popular rock message wall on the roadcut.

A 101 G 88 T 227 **Matanuska Glacier State Recreation Site** to south; campground and rest area with scenic viewpoint. Campground (to right after turning off the Glenn Highway) has 12 campsites on a gravel loop road, water pump, toilets, $15 nightly fee with self-registration, $18 if attendant collected; 15-day limit. Log cabin available for nightly rental, phone (907) 745-5151. Access road continues straight ahead and loops through rest area.

The rest area has a large paved parking area (will accommodate large RVs), toilets, litter bin, interpretive shelter and scenic viewpoint with excellent views of Matanuska Glacier. Overnight parking in rest area, $10 fee charged (pay at campground). Edge Nature Trail, a 20-minute walk through boreal forest to glacier viewing platforms with interpretive signs. This fairly easy trail is a good place to stretch your legs (and walk your pet) but it does have moderate inclines and an uneven walking surface. ♿ 🅰

Matanuska Glacier heads in the Chugach Mountains and trends northwest 27 miles. Some 18,000 years ago the glacier reached all the way to the Palmer area.

The glacier's average width is 2 miles; at its terminus it is 4 miles wide. The glacier has remained fairly stable the past 400 years. At the glacier terminus meltwater drains into a stream that flows into the Matanuska River.

Distance marker westbound shows Sutton 42 miles, Palmer 53 miles, Anchorage 94 miles.

A 100 G 89 T 228 *CAUTION: Watch for moose.*

A 99.6 G 89.4 T 228.4 Paved double-ended turnout to north is a scenic viewpoint with view of Matanuska Glacier.

A 98.6 G 90.4 T 229.4 *Begin passing lane westbound. End passing lane eastbound.*

A 98.5 G 90.5 T 229.5 Glacier View Bible Church to north.

A 98.3 G 90.7 T 229.7 Shoulder parking to south, view.

A 98 G 91 T 230 *Passing lane ends westbound.*

A 97.5 G 91.5 T 230.5 Pinochle Circle. Distance marker eastbound shows Glennallen 90 miles, Valdez 207 miles, Tok 226 miles.

A 97 G 92 T 231 *Begin passing lane eastbound.*

A 96.6 G 92.4 T 231.4 Glenn Highway alignment passes through an enormous road cut. Crews moved over 2.4 million cubic yards of material and finished blasting through this solid rock hill in 2008 as part of the Hicks Creek Road Project, which rerouted this stretch of the Glenn Highway.

A 96.4 G 92.6 T 231.6 Trailhead Road to north, paved turnout to south. Trailhead Road is entrance for **Nova River Runners** staging facility for their Matanuska River rafting and glacier hiking. (Nova's primary office is in Chickaloon, across from King Mountain Lodge.)

A 96.3 G 92.7 T 231.7 Bridge over Hicks Creek. Hicks Creek was named by Captain Glenn in 1898 for H.H. Hicks, the guide of his expedition. Anthracite Ridge to the north.

A 96.2 G 92.8 T 231.8 Larged paved turnout to north. *Begin passing lane westbound.*

A 96.1 G 92.9 T 231.9 Matanuska Road to south.

A 95 G 94 T 233 Large paved turnout southwest of this milepost.

Distance marker eastbound shows Glennallen 92 miles, Valdez 209 miles, Tok 243 miles.

A 94.8 G 94.2 T 233.2 Enormous paved parking area to south; scenic viewpoint overlooking Matanuska River.

A 94.7 G 94.3 T 233.3 Victory Way to north; access to **Homestead Guest Cabins** (description follows).

Homestead Guest Cabins. Cozy hand-crafted log cabins available year-round; located off the highway in a quiet, peaceful setting, just minutes away from the Matanuska Glacier and close to hiking, 4-wheeler and snowmachine trails. Cabins are furnished with full kitchens and private baths. Owners are friendly, helpful and long-time Alaskans. Phone (907) 745-4514; www.homesteadcabinsak.com. [ADVERTISEMENT]

A 93.8 G 95.2 T 234.2 *End passing lane eastbound.*

A 93.6 G 95.4 T 234.4 Distance marker westbound shows Palmer 46 miles, Anchorage 87 miles.

A 92 G 97 T 236 *End passing lane westbound. Begin passing lane eastbound. Begin improved highway eastbound.*

A 90.8 G 98.2 T 237.2 **Purinton Creek Trailhead** (sign); large gravel parking area to north.

CAUTION: Narrow, winding road westbound next 25 miles; no passing lanes, very few turnouts, 7 percent grades, slow for 35 mph curves. For current road construction projects underway, go to http://511.alaska.gov.

A 89 G 100 T 239 Puritan Creek bridge (sign); small turnout to north at west end of bridge. Stream heads on Anthracite Ridge and flows into the Matanuska River.

CAUTION: Watch for moose.

A 88.7 G 100.3 T 239.3 Small gravel turnout to south.

A 88.2 G 100.8 T 239.8 Gravel turnout to south.

A 88 G 101 T 240 Small gravel turnout to south.

A 87.8 G 101.2 T 240.2 Small gravel turnout to south.

A 87.6 G 101.4 T 240.4 Single-vehicle access to south at west end of **Weiner Lake** (stocked); public fishing access. Fishing for rainbow and grayling. 🐟

A 87.4 G 101.6 T 240.6 Gravel turnout to north.

A 87.2 G 101.8 T 240.8 End slide area eastbound. Begin slide area westbound. *CAUTION: Winding road as highway descends hillside next 1.7 miles westbound; soft dirt shoulder to south with steep dropoffs and no guardrails.* Views of Long Lake.

A 85.5 G 103.5 T 242.5 Begin slide area eastbound.

A 85.4 G 103.6 T 242.6 **Long Lake State Recreation Site**; parking. **Long Lake** is a

Pinnacle Mountain rises above roadside cottonwoods and aspen. (©Sharon Nault)

favorite fishing spot for Anchorage residents. Stocked with rainbow trout and arctic char. Fair for grayling to 18 inches, and native lake trout, spring through fall; fish deeper as the water warms in summer. Fair ice fishing in winter for burbot, average 12 inches.

CAUTION: Highway winds up hillside next 1.7 miles eastbound. Falling rock, soft dirt shoulder to south with steep dropoffs and no guardrails.

A 84.4 G 104.6 T 243.6 Gravel turnout. End slide area westbound. Begin slide area eastbound.

A 84.1 G 104.9 T 243.9 Large gravel parking area to south.

Great views of Matanuska River and Chugach Mountains to south as highway makes winding descent eastbound.

A 83.3 G 105.7 T 244.7 Narrow gravel road leads north to **Ravine Lake** and **Lower Bonnie Lake**. *(This steep and winding side road is signed as unsafe and closed to motorhomes, large vehicles or trailers; not recommended for any vehicle during rainy season.)* Drive in 0.8 mile on side road to reach Ravine Lake; fishing from shore for rainbow trout. Lower Bonnie Lake is a 2-mile drive from the highway. ADF&G public access at Lower Bonnie Lake; good fishing for native rainbow trout and grayling. No camping or fires.

A 83 G 106 T 245 Views westbound of distinctive pyramid shape of **King Moun-**

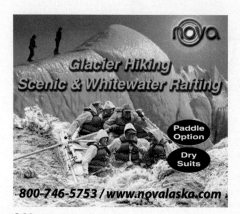
tain (elev. 5,809 feet) to the southeast.

Distance marker westbound shows Chickaloon 5 miles.

A 80.8 G 108.2 T 247.2 Eastern boundary of Matanuska Valley Moose Range. Small turnout to south.

CAUTION: Watch for moose.

A 80.1 G 108.9 T 247.9 Distance marker eastbound shows Glennallen 107 miles, Tok 224 miles, Valdez 243 miles.

Expansive views of King Mountain and Matanuska River.

A 78.5 G 110.5 T 249.5 Small gravel turnout to south.

A 78.3 G 110.7 T 249.7 Signed parking to south.

A 78.1 G 110.9 T 249.9 Gravel turnout to south at east end of **Chickaloon River Bridge**. Boundary between Game Management Units 13 and 14. Entering Subunit 14A westbound.

A 78 G 111 T 250 Turnoff to north for Chickaloon River Road at west end of Chickaloon River bridge. No trespassing and private property signs are posted along this road (state road maintenance ends 1.2 miles from highway).

A 77.5 G 111.5 T 250.5 Signed shoulder parking to south.

The Glenn Highway closely parallels the Matanuska River westbound to Palmer. Nova River Runners offers scenic floats and whitewater trips on the river. The **Matanuska River** is formed by its East and South forks and flows southwest 75 miles to the Knik Arm of Cook Inlet.

A 77.3 G 111.7 T 250.7 Small gravel turnout to north.

A 77.2 G 111.8 T 250.8 Signed gravel parking to south.

A 76.8 G 112.2 T 251.2 King Mountain Lodge to south, Nova River Runners main office to north; phone (907) 745-5753. **CHICKALOON** (pop. 249) is an unincorporated community, established around 1916 as the terminus of an Alaska Railroad spur. It currently serves as a stop for river rafters. Store/gas station closed in 2013, current status unknown.

Nova River Runners. See display ad this page.

A 76.6 G 112.4 T 251.4 Distance marker westbound shows Palmer 29 miles, Anchor-

age 70 miles.

End slide area eastbound. View of King Mountain to the southeast.

A 76.2 G 112.8 T 251.8 King Mountain State Recreation Site. Pleasant campground on the banks of the Matanuska River *(Danger: Swift current)*; 22 campsites, picnic shelter, campground host, fireplaces, picnic tables, water, toilets. Camping fee $15/night; 7-day limit. Daily parking fee $5.

A 76 G 113 T 252 Single-vehicle gravel turnouts to south on Matanuska River. *Driving distance between physical Mileposts 76 and 75 is 0.5 mile.*

A 74.5 G 114.5 T 253.5 Signed parking areas to south along Matanuska River.

A 73.2 G 115.8 T 254.8 Small paved parking to north.

A 72.9 G 116.1 T 255.1 Fish Lake Road leads north 3 miles through rural residential area; views of Castle Mountain. Limited public fishing access to **Ida Lake** via Gronvold Drive (0.2 mile north from highway, then left on Ida to Oline Circle); steep walk down to narrow shoreline.

A 71 G 118 T 257 Signed parking areas to south along Matanuska River.

A 70 G 119 T 258 RV park and cafe to north with antique tractors.

A 68.4 G 120.6 T 259.6 Paved and gravel shoulder parking (signed) to south along Matanuska River next 0.5 mile westbound.

A 68 G 121 T 260 Begin slide area eastbound (sign). **Pinnacle Mountain** (elev. 4,541 feet) rises directly southeast of the highway, easy to identify by its unusual top. Cottonwoods and aspen along the highway. Talkeetna Mountains to the north.

A 66.6 G 122.4 T 261.4 Gravel turnout to south on river.

A 66.5 G 122.5 T 261.5 Gravel turnout to north and access to river at east end of **King River** bridge. Fishing for Dolly Varden char, early summer best, use eggs.

A 66.3 G 122.7 T 261.7 Turnoff to north just west of King River bridge for paved access road to river (no turnaround) and access to **King River Trail** (multi-use public access; ATVs 15 mph) with parking on loop road.

Turnoff to south for improved gravel access road to King River at confluence with Matanuska River; informal camping.

Begin passing lane and improved highway westbound.

CAUTION: Narrow, winding road eastbound next 25 miles; no passing lanes, very few turnouts, 7 percent grades, 35-mph curves. For current road construction projects go to http://511.alaska.gov.

A 65.4 G 123.6 T 262.6 *End passing lane eastbound.*

A 64.3 G 124.7 T 263.7 Distance marker eastbound shows Glennallen 123 miles, Valdez 240 miles, Tok 259 miles.

A 64.1 G 124.9 T 263.9 *End passing lane westbound.*

Begin passing lane eastbound.

A 62.7 G 126.3 T 265.3 Large double-ended parking area along Matanuska River. Dwarf fireweed and sweet pea in June.

A 62.4 G 126.6 T 265.6 Granite Creek bridge; beautiful stream. Fishing for small Dolly Varden, spring or early summer, use flies or single eggs.

Paved bike path begins westbound on

the north side of the highway and extends to Sutton.

Begin 45 mph speed zone westbound.

A 61.6 G 127.4 T 266.4 Turnoff on Chickaloon Way to north for Sutton post office (Zip 99674), library and entrance to historical park (description follows).

Alpine Historical Park, an open-air museum featuring the concrete foundation of the Sutton Coal Washery (1920–22) and historic mining equipment from the Wishbone Hill Coal Mining Company. Admission is free, but donations are greatly appreciated. The park is open Memorial Day through Labor Day, from 9 A.M. to 7 P.M. The 6-acre site contains several historical buildings; an Athabascan winter lodge built by local Athabascans from Chickaloon; coal mining relics and local fossils; perennial gardens, picnic area, restrooms and parking (tour bus access). The park is home to the Coal Miner's Hall of Fame, with photos and biographies of the inductees (in the yellow building). There is an indoor Road Builders exhibit of photographs and narrative recalling construction of the Glenn Highway.

A 61 G 128 T 267 SUTTON-ALPINE (area pop. 1,310). This small highway community has a fire station with emergency phone, a bar, library, general store and cafe. Sutton was established as a railroad siding in about 1918 for the once-flourishing coal industry at Jonesville Mine, which operated on and off from 1920 until 1959. A post office was established at Sutton in 1948. Underground and surface coal mining in the Jonesville area on Wishbone Hill north of Sutton dates back to the early 1900s. The Sutton General Store has photos of the old mine.

Jonesville Road leads north to Sutton residential area; access to Sutton library. Pavement ends at Mile 1.3. Access to **Slipper Lake** west from Mile 1.5 stocked with rainbows (just before physical Milepost 2). State maintenance ends and road deteriorates at Mile 1.9. Road (in very poor condition) continues to Coyote Lake and access to Granite Peak; 4-wheel-drive, high-clearance recommended. **Coyote Lake** has some fair rainbow trout fishing and is also a popular spot to hunt fossils.

A 60.8 G 128.2 T 267.2 Eska Creek bridge.

A 60.7 G 128.3 T 267.3 Distance marker westbound shows Palmer 13 miles, Anchorage 54 miles.

A 60.6 G 128.4 T 267.4 *Begin 45 mph speed zone eastbound.*

Begin truck lane westbound.

A 60.4 G 128.6 T 267.6 Long, narrow, double-ended turnout to south.

A 59.9 G 129.1 T 268.1 Long double-ended turnout to south.

A 59.6 G 129.4 T 268.4 Gas station to south.

A 58.5 G 130.5 T 269.5 Scenic viewpoint to south with view of Matanuska River.

A 58 G 131 T 270 *Truck lane ends eastbound.*

A 57.8 G 131.2 T 270.2 58–Mile Road leads north 1 mile to Palmer Correctional Center. Also access to **Seventeenmile Lake** stocked with rainbows and char.

Drive 0.5 mile north and turn east; continue 2.4 miles through rural residential area, keeping to right at forks, to reach lake. Seventeenmile Lake day-use area provides parking (no camping) for boaters and public access to lake. Private property in area. Fish-

ing for small grayling, early spring; trout, early spring.

Truck lane ends westbound.

A 56.8 G 132.2 T 271.2 Western boundary of Matanuska Valley Moose Range.

A 55.9 G 133.1 T 272.1 *Truck lane begins eastbound. Begin improved highway eastbound to* Milepost A 66.4.

Fair pavement and some winding road westbound to Milepost A 50.1.

A 54.6 G 134.4 T 273.4 Bridge over **Moose Creek**. Fishing for Dolly Varden, summer, use eggs.

A 54.5 G 134.5 T 273.5 Turnout to north and 0.3-mile gravel loop through former campground (no facilities).

A 54 G 135 T 274 *Begin 0.6-mile truck lane westbound.*

A 53 G 136 T 275 Buffalo Mine Road to north. Access to Wishbone Lake 4-wheel-drive trail.

A 50.9 G 138.1 T 277.1 Harold Stephan Fire Station.

A 50.7 G 138.3 T 277.3 Farm Loop Road, a 3-mile loop road connecting with Fishhook–Willow Road.

A 50.4 G 138.6 T 277.6 Distance marker eastbound shows Glennallen 137 miles, Valdez 254 miles, Tok 273 miles.

A 50.1 G 138.9 T 277.9 Sharp turn north on Archie Road (watch for signs before turnoff) for the **Musk Ox Farm** (just 0.2 miles north) a great place to see these magnificent animals.

The Musk Ox Farm. Experience this unique agricultural project where prehistoric musk oxen are raised for their fine underwool, *qiviut*. The *qiviut* is collected by combing in the spring, and knit into garments by Native Alaskans to supplement their subsistence lifestyles. Visit these shaggy Ice Age survivors romping in beautiful pastures at an original 1930s Colony Farm, with Pioneer Peak as a backdrop. Open daily, starting Mother's Day in May, 10 A.M.–6 P.M. Winter tours by appointment. Museum, *qiviut* garments, gifts, picnic area. 12850 East Archie Road, Palmer. www.muskoxfarm.org. See display ad this page. [ADVERTISEMENT]

Begin 3-lane highway westbound. Begin 2-lane highway eastbound.

Winding road next 5.7 miles eastbound.

A 50 G 139 T 278 Double-ended turnout to south is a Matanuska River viewpoint. A short pedestrian walkway leads up to a fenced viewing area *CAUTION: Steep, eroding cliffs.* Good photo op. Gold Rush interpretive sign about Hatcher Pass.

A 49.5 G 139.5 T 278.5 Junction with Palmer-Fishhook Road; access to Fishhook Golf Course and Hatcher Pass Road to **Independence Mine State Historical Park** (17 miles).

Junction with Hatcher Pass (Palmer-Fishhook) Road which connects with the Parks Highway at **Milepost A 71.2** north of Willow. See "Hatcher Pass Road" log beginning on page 366.

A 49.1 G 139.9 T 278.9 Cedar Hills subdivision to north. Entering Palmer, which extends to **Milepost A 41**. (*Actual driving distance between Milepost 49 and 42 is 1 mile.*) Good view westbound of the farms and homes of one of Alaska's major agricultural areas.

NOTE: Begin 45 mph speed zone westbound. Begin 55 mph posted speed limit eastbound.

A 42 G 147 T 286 Traffic light at West Arctic Avenue/Old Glenn Highway; Tesoro and Fred Meyer gas stations. First of several turnoffs south to downtown Palmer for westbound travelers. West Arctic becomes the **Old Glenn Highway**. Access to Palmer

(Continues on page 367)

The Musk Ox Farm is a favorite destination for Mat-Su Valley visitors. (©Kris Valencia, staff)

Hatcher Pass Road

There are sweeping views from the bluff near Summit Lake recreation site, Milepost P 19.3 Hatcher Pass Road. (©Meghan Mackey, staff)

A highly recommended summer side trip to scenic alpine country and the historic Independence Mine, this 49-mile-long road loops over Hatcher Pass (elev. 3,886 feet) between the Glenn Highway and the Parks Highway (see Mat-Su Valley Vicinity map on page 368). Independence Mine opens for visitors the first Saturday in June (depending on snow) and closes after Labor Day.

Hatcher Pass Road is both an old-time Alaska road—narrow, bumpy, dirt and gravel—and a modern paved route complete with scenic turnouts for the tourists. It is improved paved road to **Milepost P 17.2** from the Palmer side, and for the first 10 miles from the Willow side. Much of the gravel stretch is steep, narrow, switch-backed road with potholes and washboards.

Popular summer activities along this road include hiking, biking, paragliding, gold panning and berry picking.

Hatcher Pass is a popular winter sports area for snowmobiling and cross-country skiing. Both Gold Mint and Fishhook trailheads are used by snowmobiles in winter. Hatcher Pass Road is maintained in winter from the Palmer side to the historical park and Hatcher Pass Lodge. However, Gold Cord Road (to historical park) is not plowed and the 15.2-mile stretch of Hatcher Pass Road from **Milepost P 17.2** to **P 32.4** is not maintained in winter and may be closed and gated from October to June, depending on snow.

Distance from junction with the Glenn Highway at Palmer (P) is followed by distance from junction with the Parks Highway at Willow (W).

P 0 W 49.1 Junction of Hatcher Pass Road/Palmer-Fishhook Road with the Glenn Highway at **Milepost A 49.5.**

P 0.1 W 49 Palmer Fishhook Golf Course.

P 1.4 W 47.7 Junction with Farm Loop Road.

P 2.4 W 46.7 Junction with Trunk Road.

P 3.2 W 45.9 Wasilla Creek.

P 6.5 W 42.6 Turner's Corner. Gateway to Hatcher Pass. Jim Turner welcomes you to scenic Hatcher Pass. We have 3 grades of gasoline, diesel and propane. Also grocery store, liquor store, cafe, soft-serve ice cream, ice, showers, laundromat, ATM, air and water. Stop by the Yellow Store—Turner's Corner. VISA, MasterCard, Discover accepted. [ADVERTISEMENT]

P 6.6 W 42.5 Hatcher Pass Bed & Breakfast. Experience our authentic Alaskan log cabins and chalets located at the base of beautiful Hatcher Pass. Comfortable, sparkling clean, private, and equipped with all the modern conveniences. Breakfast is included in the privacy of your own cabin. Come enjoy a peaceful getaway! Phone (907) 745-6788, fax (907) 745-6787. Website www.hatcherpassbb.com. [ADVERTISEMENT]

P 6.8 W 42.3 Junction with Wasilla–Fishhook Road (Wasilla 11 miles); continue on Willow-Fishhook Road for Hatcher Pass.

P 7.8 W 41.3 Hatcher Pass Management Area boundary northbound. Recreational activities allowed within this public use area include (unless posted as prohibited): hiking, picnicking, berry picking, camping, skiing, snowmachining, snow boarding, fishing, grazing, hunting and trapping. ATVs and dirt bikes are prohibited on roadway. No discharge of weapons within ¼ mile of roadway. Recreational mining is allowed within the boundaries of the public use area except on land with valid active mining claims. The Dept. of Natural Resources suggests recreational miners use the parking areas along the Little Susitna River or the Gold Mint Trail, which runs north along the Little Susitna River from the trailhead parking lot. Gold panning is also allowed in the Independence Mine State Historical Park, but consult with park personnel before panning.

P 8.5 W 40.6 Little Susitna River bridge. Large double-ended paved scenic overlook at north end of bridge; interpretive signs.

Road parallels river northbound. This scenic mountain stream heads at Mint Glacier in the Talkeetna Mountains and flows 110 miles to Cook Inlet. This is a gold-bearing stream.

P 8.6 W 40.5 Avalanche gate. Winding road climbs northbound.

P 8.9 W 40.1 Scenic viewpoint of river, across from rock cut; parking on loop turnout.

P 9.3 W 39.8 Shoulder parking along Little Susitna River.

P 9.5 W 39.6 Shoulder parking area.

P 10.3 W 38.8 Gravel parking area to east.

P 10.8 W 38.3 Government Peak riverside picnic and camping area; outhouse, tables; $5 day-use fee, $10 camping fee. ▲

P 11.3 W 37.8 Parking area.

P 11.9 W 37.2 Parking area. Popular sledding hill in winter.

P 12.6 W 36.5 Parking area.

P 13 W 36.1 Small parking area.

P 13.3 W 35.8 Small parking area.

P 13.8 W 35.3 Milepost 14. Motherlode Lodge (closed in 2013, current status unknown). **Gold Mint Trailhead**; parking, restrooms, picnicking, car camping. Day-use fee $5; camping fee $10. Gold Mint is a very popular trail with hikers and mountain bikers in summer. It is 8 miles one-way to Mint Glacier. Gold Mint Trail is 1 of 2 snowmobile trailheads on the east side of the pass in winter (the other is Fishhook Trailhead). ▲

Avalanche gate. *Hatcher Pass Road makes a sharp turn and begins climb to Hatcher Pass via a series of switchbacks. Posted speed limit 35 mph.*

P 14.1 W 35 Double-ended gravel turnout to northwest.

P 14.6 W 34.5 Parking area to southeast and turnoff for Archangel Valley Road (extremely rough in 2013), which leads 4 miles up Archangel Valley and ends at Fern Mine (private property, do not trespass). Access to **Reed Lakes Trail** (9-mile hike roundtrip) from this side road. Not recommended for RVs. Archangel Road is a groomed, multi-use trail in winter.

P 14.9 W 34.2 Gravel turnouts next 2 miles northbound.

P 15.9 W 33.2 Large paved parking area with sweeping view.

P 16.4 W 32.7 Fishhook Trailhead; paved parking fee, outhouse. Popular with paragliders in summer. Snowmobile access to Marmot Mountain, Gold Mint Trailhead/Archangel Road Trail, and 18-mile Hatcher Pass Trail, which follows unplowed road up and over the pass toward Willow.

P 17.2 W 31.9 Hatcher Pass Road makes a *sharp* turn southwest. For **Independence Mine State Historical Park** (description follows) turn north on Gold Cord Road (paved). Hatcher Pass Lodge (lodging, dining) is just north of the junction, adjacent the park's lower parking lot (public toilets) and fee station. The upper parking lot for Independence Mine is 1.2 miles from turnoff and has public toilets. Fee is $5 per vehicle for day-use parking at historical park.

The 271-acre **Independence Mine State Historical Park** includes several buildings and old mining machinery. Restoration of the buildings is on-going. Park visitor center (wheelchair accessible) is housed in what was originally the mine manager's home, built in 1939. Alaska Pacific Consolidated

Mine Co., one of the largest gold producers in the Willow Creek mining district, operated here from 1938 through 1941. The Gold Cord Mine buildings (private property)

©Meghan Mackey, staff

are visible on the hill above and to the north of Independence Mine. **Gold Cord Lake Trail** (1.7 miles round-trip) is a good hike for families and all fitness levels.

The park usually opens the second Saturday in June (depending on snow), with guided tours ($6 fee charged) of the building complex beginning later in the month. Visitors can take a free self-guided tour of the park at any time. The park's visitor center is open in summer, Wed.–Sun. 11 A.M.–6 P.M.. For current season dates, visitor center hours and guided tour times, phone (907) 745-2827 in summer.

P 17.2 W 31.9 Gates. Winter road closure for westbound traffic from October to July.
Pavement ends, steep, winding gravel begins westbound.

P 18.3 W 30.8 Summit Lake State Recreation Site boundary westbound; no camping or ground fires permitted. Turnout.

P 18.9 W 30.2 Hatcher Pass Summit (elev. 3,886 feet); parking area, April Bowl Trailhead (2.2 miles round-trip).
Steep, winding descent eastbound.

P 19.3 W 29.8 Parking area at **Summit Lake State Recreation Site**. Summit Lake is the headwaters of Willow Creek. Visitors can walk around the lake or up to bluff for scenic views to west. Good view to northeast of "Nixon's Nose," a launch point for paragliders. Elevation about 3,800 feet.

Westbound, the road descends following Willow Creek from here to the Parks Highway. *CAUTION: Steep, narrow, winding road westbound as highway descends.*

P 20.5 W 28.6 Summit Lake State Recreation Site boundary eastbound; no camping or ground fires permitted.

Gates. Winter road closure for eastbound traffic from October to July.

P 20.6 W 28.5 Junction with Upper Willow Creek Valley Road (road deadends).

P 23.1 W 25.9 Pullout above valley.

P 23.2 W 25.8 Lucky Shot Gold Mine road to north, rough.

P 23.8 W 25.3 Craigie Creek Road (rough) leads to old mine sites. Remains of historic Lucky Shot (on left) and War Baby (on right) mines visible on hillside to north.

P 25.5 W 23.6 Large gravel pullouts both sides for ATV's and informal campsites.

P 26.2 W 22.9 *Road narrows and begins more steep grades eastbound; watch for potholes and rough road.*

P 27.2 W 21.9 Small turnout; good view of beaver ponds and terraced beaver dams. Watch for more beaver dams and lodges along here.

P 28.2 W 20.9 Pullout above creek.

P 30.3 W 18.8 Leaving Hatcher Pass Management Area westbound.

P 30.5 W 18.6 Pullout by river.

New boardwalk paths access old mine structures at Independence Mine.
(©Meghan Mackey, staff)

P 31.9 W 17.2 Dave Churchill Memorial Trail; popular snowmobile trail in winter. Access to informal camping on gravel bars.

P 32.4 W 16.7 No winter maintenance beyond this point (eastbound sign).

P 33.5 W 15.6 Informal turnouts along road eastbound allow access to scenic Willow Creek.

P 34.2 W 14.9 Little Willow Creek bridge. Turnout to north at east end of bridge; snowmobile access to Willow Mountain trail in winter.

P 34.5 W 14.6 Turnout to north with view of Willow Creek.

P 35.7 W 13.4 Twelvemile Lake (no public access).

P 36.4 W 12.6 North Star Bible Camp.

P 38.9 W 10.2 *Gravel ends, pavement begins, westbound.*
Pavement ends, narrow gravel road begins eastbound. Watch for potholes.

P 39.2 W 9.9 Public Safety Building to north; *Emergency Phone 911.*

P 41.7 W 7.4 Coyote Gardens (private). The gardens at this private home are open one weekend a year in July as a fund-raiser for the Willow Garden Club and the Alaska Botanical Garden in Anchorage.

P 42.8 W 6.3 Albino Hare Gallery and Garden.

P 47.7 W 1.4 Deception Creek public fishing access.

P 47.8 W 1.3 Deception Creek bridge; turnout at east end.

P 47.9 W 1.2 Junction with Willow Station Road south to Willow to rejoin the Parks Highway at **Milepost A 69.6.**

P 48.5 W 0.6 Road crosses railroad tracks. Turnoff to south for North Country RV Park.

P 49.1 W 0 Junction of Fishhook-Willow Road (Hatcher Pass Road) with the Parks Highway at **Milepost A 71.2.** *(Turn to page 422 the PARKS HIGHWAY section for log of that road.)*

Return to
Milepost A 49.5 Glenn Highway
or Milepost A 71.2 Parks Highway

High School to north at this junction. 🚻

Junction with Old Glenn Highway, an alternate route that rejoins the Glenn Highway at **Milepost A 29.6.** Turn to the end of the Old Glenn Highway log on page 374 and read log back to front if you are heading south on the Old Glenn Highway from this junction.

A 41.6 G 147.4 T 286.4 Traffic light at Dogwood Avenue to south. Access to Palmer Post Office, Fred Meyer and downtown.

A 41.5 G 147.5 T 286.5 Traffic light at **junction** with Palmer–Wasilla Highway and West Evergreen Avenue; Urgent Care clinic, chiropractor, Chevron gas station and fastfood to south; Safeway/Carrs and fast-food to north. The 10-mile Palmer-Wasilla Highway connects Palmer on the Glenn Highway with Wasilla on the Parks Highway. It is a busy road with a number of businesses and residential subdivisions. 🚻

Palmer

A 42 G 147 T 286 In the Matanuska Valley northeast of Anchorage. **Population:** 5,559. **Emergency Services: Ambulance, Fire and Rescue, Police** (emergency only), phone 911. **Alaska State Troopers,** phone (907) 745-2131. **City Police,** phone (907) 745-4811. **Fire Department,** phone (907) 745-3709. **Hospital,** Mat-Su Regional Medical Center, phone (907) 861-6000. **Chiropractic,** Arctic Chiropractic, phone (907) 746-7842.

Visitor Information: The **Palmer Visitors Center & Museum** are located in the log cabin at 723 South Valley Way at East Fireweed Avenue. A great place to pick up brochures, get a cup of coffee, chat with local tour guides and learn about local history. Pick up a walking tour map of historic Palmer, and check the outdoor kiosk for visitor information. Open daily 9 A.M. to 6 P.M. May 1 to September 30. Restrooms and pay phone. Website: www.palmermuseum.org.

Be sure to visit the Matanuska Valley Agricultural Showcase Gardens, adjacent the visitor center, featuring exotic flowers and giant vegetables. Or contact the Palmer Visitors Center and Museum, 723 S. Valley Way, Palmer, AK 99645; phone (907) 746-7668.

Elevation: 240 feet. **Climate:** Temperatures range from 4° to 21°F in January and December, with a mean monthly snowfall of 8 to 10 inches. Record low was -40°F in January 1975. Temperatures range from 44° to 68°F in June and July, with a mean monthly precipitation of 2 inches. Record high was 89°F in June 1969. Mean annual rainfall is 15.5 inches, with 50.7 inches of snow. **Radio:** KJLP 88.9; Anchorage stations; KMBQ 99.7 (Wasilla). **Television:** Anchorage channels and cable. **Newspaper:** *The Frontiersman* (3 times weekly).

Private Aircraft: Palmer Municipal Airport, 1 nm SE; elev. 232 feet; length 6,000 feet and 3,616 feet; asphalt; fuel 100LL, Jet. FSS and full services.

Description

This appealing community is both a bit of pioneer Alaska as well as a modern-day commercial center for the Matanuska and Susitna valleys (collectively referred to as

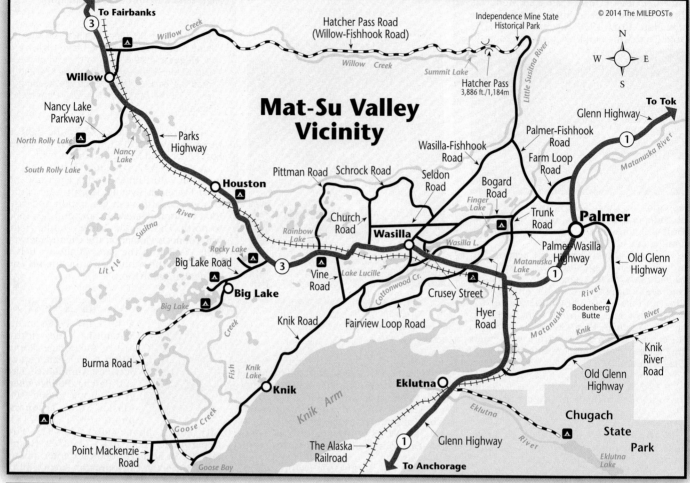

Mat-Su Valley Vicinity

© 2014 The MILEPOST®

the Mat–Su Valley). Take time to explore the small downtown area off the highway.

Palmer was established about 1916 as a railway station on the Matanuska branch of the Alaska Railroad. Before that, the area had long been used by Athabascan Indians and, starting in 1890, the site of a trading post run by George Palmer.

In 1935, Palmer became the site of one of the most unusual experiments in American history: the Matanuska Valley Colony. The Federal Emergency Relief Administration, one of the many New Deal relief agencies created during Franklin Roosevelt's first year in office, planned an agricultural colony in Alaska to utilize the great agricultural potential in the Matanuska Valley, and to get some American farm families—struck by first the dust bowl, then the Great Depression—off the dole. Social workers picked 203 families, mostly from the northern counties of Michigan, Wisconsin and Minnesota, to join the colony, because it was thought that the many hardy farmers of Scandinavian descent in those 3 states would have a natural advantage over other ethnic groups.

The colonists arrived in Palmer in the early summer of 1935, and though the failure rate was high, many of their descendants

still live in the Matanuska Valley. Palmer gradually became the unofficial capital of the Matanuska Valley, acting as headquarters for a farmers' cooperative marketing organization and as the business and social center for the state's most productive farming region.

Palmer is Alaska's only community that developed primarily from an agricultural economy. The growing season averages 100 to 118 days annually, and the unique micro-climate produces amazing giant vegetables, many of which are displayed at the annual Alaska State Fair in Palmer. Fresh vegetables from Valley farms are popular with Anchorage residents, many of whom drive out to pick up fresh seasonal produce. Locally-grown produce is available at farmers' markets and in local stores.

The University of Alaska Fairbanks has a district Cooperative Extension Service Office at 809 S. Chugach Street. According to District Agriculture Agent Stephen C. Brown, many local Mat-Su farmers are using GPS to automate their tractors, making planting more efficient. An expert on GPS and geo-caching, Brown maintains the geocache at the Extension office.

The community has the Mat–Su College (University of Alaska), banks, the

Mat–Su Borough offices, borough school district, state and federal agency offices and churches. The United Protestant Church in Palmer, the Church of a Thousand Logs, dates from Matanuska Colony days and is one of the oldest churches in Alaska still holding services. It is included in the National Register of Historic Places.

Lodging & Services

Accommodations (see ads this section) in Palmer include 2 historic properties, the **Colony Inn** and the **Historic Valley Hotel**; as well as the **Peak Inn Motel** on West Evergreen/Palmer-Wasilla Highway, and **Alaska Choice Motel** and on the Glenn Highway. Take Hatcher Pass/Palmer-Fishhook Road (see "Hatcher Pass Road" log this section) for **Hatcher Pass B&B**.

There are several good restaurants in Palmer, including **Peking Gardens Mandarin Cuisine**, **Turkey Red**, **Noisy Goose Cafe** and the **Valley Hotel Cafe**.

Palmer has all visitor services, including a Fred Meyer and Carrs/Safeway, gas stations, fast-food outlets, laundromat, auto repair and parts. Public restrooms are located next to the Visitor Center, across the street from the library. Post office is located at 500 S. Cobb Street.

Palmer is extremely pedestrian friendly, with a downtown core for shopping that includes everything from original art to used books, all within walking distance of the Visitor Center. Local artist **Shane Lamb** has a studio in Palmer featuring his Alaska scenes. Also check out **Fireside Books** and **Just Sew**, to name just a few of Palmer's downtown businesses.

Camping

Mountain View RV Park is located 3 miles from downtown Palmer via the Old Glenn Highway. The Mat–Su Borough operates the 86-site Matanuska River Park, located 1 mile from town on the Old Glenn Highway; *see log of Old Glenn on page 373 this section*. Finger Lake State Recreation Site campground is accessible from **Milepost P 4** Palmer-Wasilla Highway. There are 2 campgrounds west of Palmer on the Glenn Highway, going towards Anchorage: **Kepler Park** at **Milepost A 37.4**, and **Fox Run Lodge & Campground**.

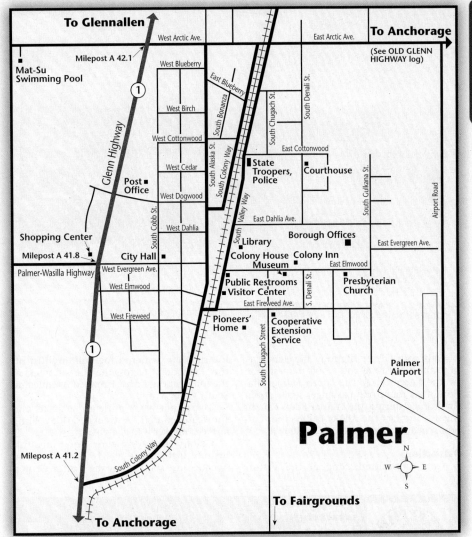

PALMER ADVERTISERS

Alaska Choice Inn Motel...............Ph. (907) 745-1505
City of Palmer................................Ph. (907) 745-3271
Colony House Museum.................Ph. (907) 745-1935
Colony Inn.....................................Ph. (907) 745-3330
Fireside Books ....Ph. (907) 745-2665
Fox Run Lodge
  and Campground.......................Ph. (907) 745-6120
Hatcher Pass B&B.........................Ph. (907) 745-6788
Historic Valley Hotel & Cafe ....Ph. (907) 745-3330
Just Sew...Ph. (907) 745-3649
Kepler Park ....Mile 37.4 Glenn Hwy.
Knik Glacier Tours........................Ph. (907) 745-1577
Mountain View RV Park...............Ph. (907) 745-5747
Musk Ox Farm ....Ph. (907) 745-4151
Noisy Goose Cafe ....Ph. (907) 746-4600
Peak Inn Motel..............................Ph. (907) 746-5757
Shane Lamb Gallery......................Ph. (907) 746-3343
Turkey Red.....................................Ph. (907) 746-5544
Turner's Corner.................Mile 6.5 Hatcher Pass Rd.

Transportation

Air: No scheduled service, but the local airport has a number of charter operators.

Bus: Mat-Su Community Transit connects Palmer, Wasilla, Eagle River and Anchorage.

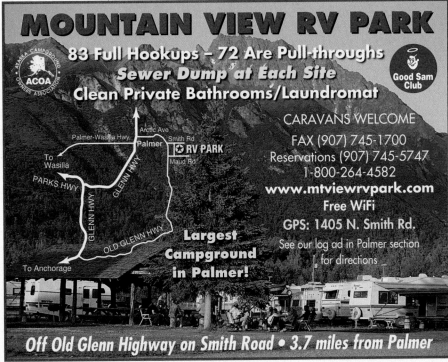

Vendors line the street outside Palmer Visitor Center during Colony Days in June.
(© Kris Valencia, staff)

Railroad: Glenn Highway travelers may note the tidy stone and wood train station by the fairgrounds. The South Palmer Station offers round-trip passenger service from Anchorage during the Alaska State Fair in August. Contact the Alaska Railroad for current schedule; phone (907) 265-2494.

Attractions

Get Acquainted: Stop at the Visitor Information Center, a log building just off the "main drag" (across the railroad tracks at the intersection of East Fireweed Avenue and South Valley Way).

The center has a museum, artifacts and showcase garden. A weekly Friday Fling farmers' market is held across the street.

Colony House Museum. Don't miss this historic little house at 316 East Elmwood Avenue, just south from the Visitor Center.

Built in the 1930s, the house represents modification of one of 4 basic house plans available to Matanuska Valley Colonists. The Colony House was moved to its present location and restored and furnished by members of Palmer's pioneer community. Open 10 A.M. to 4 P.M. May 1 to August 31.

The restored **Colony Inn**, at 325 East Elmwood, which now serves as a hotel, was built as a teacher's dormitory for the Matanuska Colony project.

Drive the Old Glenn Highway. An alternate route bypassing part of the Glenn Highway, the Old Glenn Highway also accesses recreation sites and businesses. **Knik Glacier Tours**, 10 miles south via the Old Glenn then 8.4 miles up Knik River Road, transports visitors to the face of Knik Glacier. *See the "Old Glenn Highway" log on pages 373-374 this section.*

Play Golf. Known for its scenery and one-of-a-kind setting, Palmer Golf Course has 18 holes (par 72, USGA rated), gas golf carts and clubs, driving range, pro shop, practice green and bar, RV parking and a snack bar. A favorite for locals and visitors alike, it is one of the first Alaska courses to open in spring (as early as mid-April some years). Located across the street from the airport off the Old Glenn Highway. Phone (907) 745-4653.

The unique Fishhook Golf Course on Palmer-Fishhook Road (see Hatcher Pass Road log this section), is a 9-hole course set in a former horse pasture. Though it's a short course, it's more challenging than it looks. Cart rentals, a driving range and a small pro shop with snacks. Phone (907) 745-7274.

Go to a Mat-Su Miners Game. The Mat-Su Miners, based in Palmer, are one of six teams in the Alaska Baseball League. The ABL is a premiere summer collegiate baseball league with players from major colleges. The other league teams are the Fairbanks Alaska Goldpanners, the Anchorage Bucs, the Anchorage Glacier Pilots, the Peninsula Oilers and Chugiak-Eagle River Chinooks. Miners home games are at Hermon Bros. Field: turn off the Glenn Highway at the Alaska State Fairgrounds main parking lot and continue to the far end of the lot to the ballpark's main gate. Baseball schedules are published in the local newspapers or visit www.matsuminers.org.

The excellent local library, located at 655 S. Valley Way, has a paperback and magazine exchange. Open Monday through Saturday; wheelchair accessible. The monument in front of the library is dedicated to the families of the Matanuska Colony.

Don't miss the Musk Ox Farm. Located east of Palmer (turnoff the Glenn Highway at **Milepost A 50.1; see page 341**), this is a great place to learn about and see the shaggy

prehistoric musk oxen up-close. A native cooperative uses the fine wool (qiviut) to knit beautiful and warm wares. Hunted to near extinction in Alaska in 1865, the species was reintroduced in the 1930s. May to September; fee charged, gift shop onsite.

Hike or bike area trails. Hiking trails south of Palmer on the Old Glenn Highway (see log this section) include: Matanuska Peak, turnoff 3 miles south of Palmer (**Milepost J 15.6**); Lazy Mountain, 2.4 miles from Palmer (**Milepost J 16.1**); Bodenburg Butte, 6.9 miles from Palmer (**Milepost J 11.5**); and **Pioneer Ridge-Austin Helmers Trail** from Knik River Road, 10 miles south of Palmer (**Milepost J 8.6**).

The Crevasse Moraine trail system is accessible from **Milepost P 1.9** Palmer-Wasilla Highway.

Trail descriptions and maps are available online at www.matsugov.us/community development/recservices/trails/trail-guides.

Go Swimming: The 80-foot swimming pool is open to the public weekdays (closed weekends). Fees charged, showers available. The pool is located at Palmer High School on West Arctic Avenue; phone (907) 745-5091.

Enjoy Water Sports. Fishing, boating, waterskiing, and other water sports are popular in summer at Finger Lake. Drive west on Palmer-Wasilla Highway 4 miles, then go north on Trunk Road 1 mile to Bogard Road; turn west and drive 0.7 mile to **Finger Lake State Recreation Site**. A scenic spot with camping, picnic tables, water and boat launch. Life jackets provided.

On the Glenn Highway, visit Kepler-Bradley Lakes, accessible from the family-run **Kepler Park** at **Milepost A 37.4**, which offers camping, day use, boat rentals and a small store. Kepler-Brakley Lakes is also accessible from the state recreation area at **Milepost A 36.4**.

Special events. Friday Flings, a weekly Farmers' Market, is held in downtown Palmer across from the visitors center every Friday, 11 A.M. to 6 P.M. from about mid-May to mid-August. Purchase Alaska-grown produce, flowers and crafts from local vendors.

Annual events include **Palmer Colony Days** in June, a festival commemorating the colonists of the Matanuska farming community; craft fair, farmer's market, carnival rides, fun run, parade, etc. The **Palmer Pride Picnic**, held the fourth Friday in July, is a free picnic hosted by the City of Palmer and Greater Palmer Chamber of Commerce. **Colony Christmas**, the second weekend in December, is an old-fashioned, family-oriented Christmas celebration. Various community events taking place from Friday to Sunday include: the Parade of Lights, a fireworks display, craft fairs, cookie contest, sleigh rides, reindeer petting, and a gingerbread house competition. For more information on events in Palmer, phone The Greater Palmer Chamber of Commerce at (907) 745-2880.

The **Alaska State Fair**, Alaska's largest event, takes place Aug. 21–Sept. 1 in 2014. It is 12 days of giant vegetables, entertainment, food booths, midway rides, farm animals, pony rides, pig races and more. This is a very popular event: Be prepared for lots of traffic! Visit www.alaskastatefair.org or phone (907) 745-4827 for more information.

Visit Scenic Hatcher Pass. From **Milepost A 49.5** near Palmer, Hatcher Pass Road/Palmer-Fishhook Road provides access to the beautiful Hatcher Pass Recreation Area

and Independence Mine State Historical Park. Well worth the 20-mile drive. (*See "Hatcher Pass Road" log on pages 366-367.*)

See the Matanuska Glacier: Drive 60 miles east on the Glenn Highway from Palmer to visit this spectacular 27-mile-long glacier, one of the few you can drive to and explore on foot. Access to the foot of the glacier is through Glacier Park at **Milepost A 102**; admission charged. If you're not interested in getting close, you can see the glacier from the highway or from Matanuska Glacier State Recreation Site at **Milepost A 101**.

Glenn Highway Log
(continued)

A 41.5 G 147.5 T 286.5 Traffic light at **junction** with Palmer–Wasilla Highway and West Evergreen Avenue; gas, clinic, supermarket. Access to Peking Motel.

A 41.3 G 147.7 T 286.7 Tesoro gas station/Taco Bell fast-food, oil/lube shop and auto parts store on south side of highway.

A 41.2 G 147.8 T 286.8 First access eastbound to Palmer business district via South Colony Way.

A 41.1 G 147.9 T 286.9 Commercial Drive.

A 40.9 G 148.1 T 287.1 Inner Springer Loop.

A 40.7 G 148.3 T 287.3 Alaska Choice Inn Motel to north.

Alaska Choice Inn Motel. See display ad this page.

A 40.2 G 148.8 T 287.8 Main entrance to Fairgrounds (site of **Alaska State Fair**) and Hermon Bros. Field (home of the Mat–Su Miners baseball team). The Alaska State Fair is held the end of August through the first week in September (August 21 to September 1, 2014). *Slow for special traffic patterns during fair and obey speed limits!* Check Alaska Railroad schedule for train service to the **South Palmer Train Station**, south side of highway, during the fair. There are 6 Glenn Highway National Scenic Byway interpretive panels at the South Palmer Station.

A 40 G 149 T 288 Noisy Goose Cafe. See display ad this section.

A 39.8 G 149.2 T 288.2 Inner Springer Loop Road.

A 39.2 G 149.8 T 288.8 Outer Springer Loop. Short, steep trail to **Meiers Lake**; grayling and rainbow trout fishing.

A 37.4 G 151.6 T 290.6 Slow down for Kepler Drive turnoff on north side of highway for access to **Kepler Park** (description follows); camping, boat rentals, fishing and store. Scenic spot.

Prize-winning quilts at the Alaska State Fair in Palmer, Aug. 21–Sept. 1, in 2014.
(©Sharon Nault)

Kepler Park. Family-owned and operated with a family atmosphere. Camping, day-use, boating, fishing on 2 beautiful lakes stocked annually. Pedal boat, rowboat, canoe rentals. Small store with concessions, bait, tackle. Short distance to local conveniences and other attractions. Open May 1 to September 30. Phone (907) 745-3053. Website www.keplerpark.com.
[ADVERTISEMENT]

Enjoying a sunny summer's day on Matanuska Lakes at Kepler Park, Milepost A 37.4.
(©Ankush Bharti)

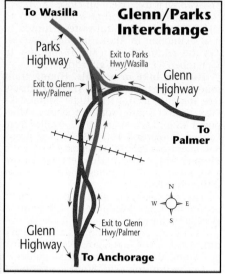

Glenn/Parks Interchange

To Wasilla

Parks Highway

Exit to Parks Hwy/Wasilla

Exit to Glenn Hwy/Palmer

Glenn Highway

To Palmer

Exit to Glenn Hwy/Palmer

Glenn Highway

To Anchorage

N W E S

A 37.2 G 151.8 T 290.8 Echo Lake public parking and fishing access to south; 4-vehicle parking and short trail to lake (visible from parking area). Fishing for land-locked salmon and rainbow (stocked).

A 36.4 G 152.6 T 291.6 Entrance to **Matanuska Lakes** (formerly called **Kepler–Bradley Lakes**) **State Recreation Area** to north; day-use area on Matanuska Lake; water, toilets, parking, picnic tables, hiking trails and fishing. Small tent camping area. ADF&G stocks lakes (Kepler, Bradley, Matanuska, Canoe, Irene, Long, Claire and Victor lakes) with rainbow trout, grayling and silver salmon. Wheelchair-accessible trail to lake.

Distance marker eastbound shows Palmer 5 miles, Glennallen 145 miles, Tok 281 miles.

A 36.3 G 152.7 T 291.7 Fox Run Lodge & Campground (description follows) to north; full-hookup sites in woods.

Fox Run Lodge features a variety of services for travelers, including take-out daily specials in our restaurat. Also, RV and tent sites, private lakefront hotel rooms, efficiencies, dorm-style cabins, WiFi, laundry, showers, swimming, hiking, fishing, boat rentals, massage for the weary muscles, and oil changes for motorhomes. See display ad this page. [ADVERTISEMENT]

A 35.8 G 153.2 T 292.2 Glenn–Parks Interchange (see illustration above). Westbound exit for Wasilla/Parks Highway (Alaska Route 3). Also access this exit to Matanuska-Susitna Visitor Center and Mat-Su Regional Medical Center (use Trunk Road exit off the Parks Highway).

Junction of the Glenn Highway (Alaska Route 1) with the Parks Highway (Alaska Route 3) to Denali Park and Fairbanks. See the PARKS HIGHWAY section on page 407 for log.

A 34 G 155 T 294 Palmer/Glenn Highway exit for northbound traffic continuing east on the Glenn Highway (Alaska Route 1). Wasilla/Parks Highway traffic continues straight ahead.

Anchorage-bound Glenn Highway traffic merges with southbound traffic from Parks Highway.

A 33.7 G 155.3 T 294.3 Distance marker westbound shows Anchorage 35 miles.

A 33.5 G 155.5 T 294.5 Palmer Hay Flats State Game Refuge (southbound sign) supports migrating waterfowl and shorebirds, plus a variety of other wildlife. In winter, large numbers of moose congregate on the flats. The refuge can be accessed at the Knik River Access/Reflections Lake trail (see **Milepost A 30.6**).

CAUTION: Watch for moose.

A 31.5 G 157.5 T 296.5 Bridge over the Matanuska River, which is fed by the Matanuska Glacier.

A 30.8 G 158.2 T 297.2 Sgt. James Bondsteel Bridge of Honor crosses Knik River. The **Knik River** comes down from the Knik Glacier to the east and splits into several branches as it approaches Knik Arm. Knik Arm is a 3-mile-wide estuary that extends 40 miles southwest to Cook Inlet.

Matanuska–Susitna Borough boundary.

A 30.6 G 158.4 T 297.4 Knik River Access. *NOTE: Knik River Access is subject to seasonal closure Nov. 1–April 30.* Access to Reflections Lake trail. The 1-mile loop trail around Reflections Lake is now ADA accessible, with boardwalk over the wetlands, benches and scenic overlooks, a kiosk with interpretive panels, and permanent restrooms. Wildflowers, nesting waterfowl, beaver activity and other wildlife are abundant. Free Family Fun Days are held here in January and July; contact Alaskans for Palmer Hay Flats for more information, 907-357-8711 or www.palmerhayflats.org.

A 30.3 G 158.7 T 297.7 Knik River bridge.

A 29.6 G 159.4 T 298.4 Exit to the Old Glenn Highway to Eklutna Tailrace day-use area (3.7 miles), Knik River, Knik Glacier Tours, Alaska Backcountry ATV tours, Mountain View RV Park and Palmer (see log).

Junction with Old Glenn Highway. See "Old Glenn Highway" log beginning on facing page.

A 27.3 G 161.7 T 300.7 The highway crosses a swampy area known locally as Eklutna Flats. These flats are a protected wildflower area (picking flowers is strictly prohibited). Look for wild iris, shooting star, chocolate lily and wild rose in early June.

A 26.5 G 162.5 T 301.5 Eklutna exit. Exit for **Eklutna Lake Road** and Eklutna Historical Park (descriptions follow).

Exit west for **Eklutna Historical Park** and **EKLUTNA** (pop. 377), a residential community and Athabascan village. The small historical park, just west of the highway, includes the Eklutna Heritage Museum, St. Nicholas Russian Orthodox Church, a hand-built Siberian prayer chapel and traditional spirit houses or grave houses. Admission fee charged. Open mid-May to mid-September. *The parking area at Eklutna Historical Park may not afford enough turn-around space for big rigs.*

From the overpass, follow signs east about a half-mile to Eklutna Lake Road (paved)

Old Glenn Highway

which leads 9.5 miles to **Eklutna Lake Recreation Area** in Chugach State Park. (The last 7 miles of Eklutna Lake Road are narrow and winding with no shoulders.) **Rochelle's Ice Cream Stop** is at Mile 8.

The road deadends at the recreation area day-use parking lot ($5 to park), adjacent the beach and lakeside trail. You will pass the turnoff for the campground before reaching the day-use area.

There are 50 campsites in the trees; 23 picnic sites, also in the trees; water pumps, picnic tables, firepits, outhouses; campground host in residence; ranger station; overflow camping area. Camping fee charged; 15-day limit. A public-use cabin and hut are available for rent. Reservations may be made online; go to www.dnr.state.ak.us/ parks/cabins/howto.htm; or phone the Dept. of Natural Resources Public at (907) 269-8400.

Eklutna Lake is the largest lake in Chugach State Park, measuring approximately 7 miles long by a mile wide. The lake is used to generate power at the Eklutna Plant, and is also a water source for Anchorage. Fed by Eklutna Glacier, Eklutna Lake offers fair fishing for Dolly Varden. *CAUTION: High winds can make this lake dangerous for boaters.* Interpretive displays on wildlife and a viewing telescope are located at the trailhead.

The Lakeside trailhead parking lot at Eklutna Lake accommodates 80 cars and offers easy access to the lake. It also acts as a boat launch for hand-carried boats. The Lakeside trail—popular with hikers and bicyclists—follows Eklutna Lake shoreline and gives access to Eklutna Glacier (12.7 miles). The Eklutna Lake Challenge, a duathlon held in May, uses the Lakeside Trail for its 3-mile run and 15-mile mountain biking stages. An optional kayaking stage was added to the race in 2013.

A 25.2 G 163.8 T 302.8 Thunderbird Falls exit for northbound traffic only. From exit drive 0.4 mile (follow signs) to small trailhead parking lot just before Eklutna River bridge (bridge closed to motor vehicles).

Thunderbird Falls is a 2-mile round-trip hike from the trailhead. This easy family walk is along a wide, scenic trail, but supervise children because there are steep cliffs just off the trail. The trail forks, with the right fork leading to a viewing platform, and the left fork leading down a steep path to Thunderbird Creek. The falls are just upstream. $5 parking fee. *CAUTION: Do NOT venture beyond the end of the trail to climb the steep cliffs overhanging the falls!*

A 24.5 G 164.5 T 303.5 Southbound-only exit to Edmonds Lake residential area and **Mirror Lake Municipal Park**; boating, swimming, fishing, picnic shelters, picnic tables, grills, outhouses, volleyball court, play field, beach, swings. Mirror Lake, located at the foot of Mount Eklutna, is stocked with rainbow and king salmon.

Fishing at Eklutna Tailrace on the Old Glenn Highway. (©Meghan Mackey, staff)

The Old Glenn Highway is a moderately busy 18.4-mile paved 2-lane road with 45-mph curves. It is used by local residential traffic and as an alternate route to the Glenn Highway, with which it junctions at **Milepost A 29.6** and **Milepost A 42.1** (in Palmer). This road also provides access to campgrounds, the Knik River and businesses offering ATV and boat tours to Knik Glacier. The Bodenburg Butte area—accessible via a loop road—has original Matanuska Colony farms and 2 popular local attractions: the Reindeer Farm and a hiking trail up Bodenburg Butte itself.

Distance from south junction with the Glenn Highway (J) is followed by distance from Palmer (P).

J 0 P 18.4 Exit from Glenn Highway at **Milepost A 29.6**.

J 0.4 P 18 Small parking area by rock-cut, short trail to popular bouldering/climbing knob.

J 0.5 P 17.9 Bridge over railroad tracks.

J 1.6 P 16.8 Turnout.

J 3.7 P 14.7 Eklutna Tailrace ADF&G day-use area and public fishing access. Open May to October 1; good spring and early summer fishing for silver and king salmon (stocked).

Large gravel parking area *(drive slowly; access road and parking area may be potholed)* with portable toilets and dumpster; fish-cleaning table; bridge/walkway (extends from here to paved turnout at **Milepost J 4** by power plant). No fee.

J 4 P 14.4 Small paved parking area to west for walk-in only access to Eklutna Tailrace fishing (connects with main area at Milepost 3.7). Across the road is the Eklutna Power Plant (Alaska Power Administration), which uses water from Eklutna Lake to provide power to Anchorage and the Mat-Su Valley.

J 6 P 12.4 Goat Creek Bridge.

J 6.9 P 11.5 *Winter avalanche area next 1.5 miles, do not stop.*

Road parallels Knik River.

J 7.4 P 11 Small turnouts to west. Views of Bodenburg Butte across Knik River.

J 7.7 P 10.7 Turnout for views to east.

J 8.5 P 9.9 Paved turnout to west.

J 8.6 P 9.8 Junction with **Knik River Road**, an11-mile-long road that is bordered by private property. The first 9.7 miles are paved. **Pioneer Falls** (a waterfall) at Mile 1.2 *(CAUTION: Black bears)*; public access to Knik River at Mile 1.4; Pioneer Ridge-Austin Helmers trailhead at Mile 3.9 (4.5-mile-hike 1-way, difficult, great views); and a view of Knik Glacier at about Mile 7.2 (the glacier is best viewed from the river). **Knik Glacier Tours** at Mile 8.7 (description follows) offers camping and daily airboat trips to Knik Glacier. Knik River Road deadends 11.1 miles east of the Old Glenn Highway at Knik River Lodge.

J 8.7 P 9.7 Knik River bridge. Entering Game Management Subunit 14A northbound. Pedestrian bridge adjacent highway bridge (formerly the old highway).

J 9 P 9.4 Access to river and pedestrian bridge at east end of Knik River bridge.

J 10 P 8.4 Pioneer Peak dominates the skyline for southbound travelers.

J 10.4 P 8 Sullivan Avenue. Turnoff for Alaska Raceway Park (0.8 mile).

J 11.5 P 6.9 Gas station/grocery at **junction** of Bodenburg Loop Road and Plumley Road; access to the Reindeer Farm, Bodenburg Butte and Jim Creek (descriptions follow).

Old Glenn Highway (Continued)

Bodenburg Butte is a popular family hike. (©Meghan Mackey, staff)

The 5.8-mile Bodenburg Butte Road rejoins the Old Glenn Highway opposite Back Acres Road (**Milepost J 12.6**). From this junction it is 0.6 mile to **Bodenburg Butte** trailhead and 0.7 mile to the Reindeer Farm. The Bodenburg Butte area has original Matanuska Colony farms.

For **Jim Creek**, follow Plumley Road to Caudill Road and take a right. After about a mile you will come to a large parking area on the left; continue on rough gravel road for about 2 miles to the mouth of Jim Creek. Jim Creek provides the latest fishable run of silvers in the Mat-Su Valley, with fish available from late July through freeze-up in Oct.–Nov. This popular fishing area is making something of a comeback thanks to Alaska State Troopers enforcing regulations to control vandalism, litter and other unlawful activities.

J 11.8 P 6.6 BUTTE (pop. 3,246); fire and ambulance service station #21; emergency phone 911. Fire permits May 1 to Sept. 30.

J 12 P 6.4 Junction with Marilyn Road.

J 12.6 P 5.8 Junction with Back Acres Road, north end of Bodenburg Butte Loop Road (see **Milepost J 11.5**).

J 13.1 P 5.3 Small paved turnouts to west.

J 15.6 P 2.8 Junction with Smith Road. Access to **Mountain View RV Park**, 0.8 mile (description follows).

Mountain View RV Park offers breathtaking views of the Matanuska mountains. Watch wildlife from your door. Full hookups, hot showers included. New bathrooms and laundromat, sewer dump at each site. Good Sam Park. Espresso. WiFi. Hiking trails and salmon fishing nearby. From Mile A 42.1 Glenn Highway (Arctic), follow Old Glenn Highway 2.8 miles. Turn east on Smith Road, drive 0.6 mile, turn right (0.3 mile). We're 3.7 miles from the Glenn Highway. www.mtviewrvpark.com; email starr1@mtaonline.net. GPS N 61° 35′ 40.8″ W 149° 01′ 29.8″. See display ad on page 369. [ADVERTISEMENT]

Smith Road also accesses Matanuska Peak Trail; drive in 1.5 miles for trailhead. Matanuska Peak Trail climbs 5,670 feet in 4.1 miles. It is rated moderate to difficult.

J 16 P 2.4 Clark–Wolverine Road; access to several garden nurseries and to **Lazy Mountain Recreation Area**. For recreation area, drive east 0.8 mile to "T"; turn right on Huntley Road at T and drive 0.9 mile; then take right fork downhill 0.2 mile to trailhead parking for popular 2.5-mile hike to summit of Lazy Mountain (elev. 3,720 feet); steep and strenuous. Outhouse at trailhead.

J 16.6 P 1.8 Paved loop road down to Matanuska River photo viewpoint and gravel riverbank, a popular gathering spot.

J 16.8 P 1.6 George Palmer Memorial Bridge crosses the Matanuska River. Photo viewpoint to east at north end of bridge on old alignment; access to pedestrian bridge and trail.

J 17.4 P 1 Turnoff for **Matanuska River Park** (Mat-Su Borough Parks & Recreation) camping and day-use areas; 80 level tent/RV sites with picnic tables on gravel loop road. Day-use area has playground and picnic pavilions. Facilities include some pull-through sites, water, fireplaces, dump station, flush toilets, hot showers and hiking trails. Camping, shower and dump station fees charged. Phone (907) 745-9631 for more information.

J 17.6 P 0.8 Airport Road leads west to Palmer municipal airport and to Palmer Golf Course.

J 17.9 P 0.5 *Slow for 35 mph speed zone entering downtown Palmer.*

J 18.2 P 0.2 Valley Way; go west for Palmer city center.

J 18.3 P 0.1 Traffic light at Alaska Street; go west for Palmer city center.

J 18.4 P 0 Junction of Old Glenn Highway (West Arctic Avenue) with **Milepost A 42.1** Glenn Highway at Palmer. *Description of Palmer begins on page 367.* Fred Meyer and Tesoro gas stations (diesel).

Return to Milepost A 42 or A 29.6 Glenn Highway

A 23.6 G 165.4 T 304.4 Northbound-only exit to **Mirror Lake Municipal Park** (see description above), located immediately off this exit; frontage road deadends at parking area on lake (ice fishing in winter). Return to freeway via access to Edmonds Lake.

A 23 G 166 T 305 Exit to North Peters Creek Business Loop (use next exit at **Milepost A 21.9** for more direct access to services).

A 21.9 G 167.1 T 306.1 Southbound exit to **PETERS CREEK**. Take Voyles Blvd. west to Old Glenn Highway/Bill Stephens Drive for access to local businesses. Services this exit include gas stations, grocery, body repair shop and restaurant and **Bobby's Peter's Creek RV Park**.

Bobby's Peter's Creek RV Park. See display ad this page.

A 21.5 G 167.5 T 306.5 Northbound exit to Peters Creek; (see description of businesses previous milepost).

A 20.9 G 168.1 T 306.9 North Birchwood Loop Road exits both sides of highway. Turn east for community of **CHUGIAK** (pop. 11,000) on the Old Glenn Highway. Chugiak has a post office, senior center, convenience store with gas, diesel, showers and laundromat. Loretta French Municipal Park offers ballfields, an equestrian center, and an archery range and model airplane field for club members. It is also home to the Chugiak-Eagle River Chinooks ABL baseball team (www.cerchinooks.com).

Bicycles and pedestrians may use the multi-use path alongside the Glenn Highway between Chugiak and East Anchorage. Pedestrians are not allowed on the Glenn Highway between Chugiak and the Parks Highway junction, although bicyclists may use the shoulders along this segment.

A 17.2 G 171.8 T 310.8 South Birchwood Loop Road exits both sides of highway. Access west to Chugiak High School (indoor swimming pool, public hours); Park and Ride Lot; and summer hiking trails/winter ski trails from Beach Lake Chalet. Also access to Beach Lake Municipal Park (0.8 mile west, turn left and follow narrow, winding, mostly gravel road 2 miles); fishing, swimming and canoeing in summer at Beach Lake; dog mushing trails in winter (Chugiak Dog Mushing Assoc. is headquartered here).

Private Aircraft: Birchwood Airport; elev. sea level; 2 runways, paved and gravel.

Exit east for **St. John Orthodox Cathedral** (description follows); drive 0.6 mile east on Birchwood Loop; turn right on Old Glenn Highway and drive 0.2 mile; turn on Monastery Drive and drive 0.3 mile to cathedral.

Saint John Orthodox Cathedral.
Take a peaceful break from your travels.
Visit this unique, geodesic-dome cathedral

with birch ceiling and beautiful icons.
Or hike to St. Sergius Chapel. Visitors are
welcome at our services: Saturday Vespers,
7:15 P.M.; Sunday Divine Liturgy, 10 A.M.
Bookstore. Monastery Drive off Old Glenn.
(907) 696-2002. www.stjohnalaska.org.

[ADVERTISEMENT]

A 15.5 G 173.5 T 312.5 Exit to North
Eagle River, Terrace Lane. Follow signs to
Old Glenn Highway junction (0.2 mile) for
Providence Health & Services, Fred Meyer/
gas and Spenard Builders Supply. Turn right
at light on Old Glenn Highway for downtown Eagle River (you'll rejoin the Glenn
Highway at **Milepost A 13.4**); turn left on
Old Glenn Highway and drive 0.5 mile
north and turn off on to Harry McDonald
Road for the Harry J. McDonald Memorial
Center (0.4 mile uphill). This recreation
facility offers an Olympic sized ice rink,
multi-use turf, indoor jogging track and
meeting rooms.

A 13.4 G 175.6 T 314.6 Eagle River exit
east to community of Eagle River via Artillery Road; all visitor services (description
follows). Also access to Eagle River Road to
Eagle River Nature Center in Chugach State
Park (*see Eagle River Road description page
376*).

Eagle River

A 13.4 G 175.6 T 314.6
Population: 24,000; area
35,000. **Emergency Ser-
vices: Police,** Anchorage
Police Dept., phone (907)
786-8500. **Alaska State
Troopers,** phone (907)
269-5711. **Ambulance,**
phone 911. **Fire Depart-
ment,** phone 911.

Visitor Information: Contact the Chu-
giak-Eagle River Chamber of Commerce,
P.O. Box 770353, Eagle River, AK 99577;
phone (907) 694-4702; or visit www.cer.org.
You can also visit the Chamber office in the
Eagle River Town Center, 12001 Business
Blvd., Suite 108. Newspaper: *Chugiak-Eagle
River Star* (www.alaskastar.com), 11401 Old
Glenn Highway, Suite 105.

The Chugiak–Eagle River area was homesteaded after WWII when the new Glenn
Highway opened this rural area northeast
of Anchorage. Today, Eagle River is a fast-
growing residential area with a full range
of businesses, most located along the Old
Glenn Highway east off the Glenn Highway.

The Chugiak-Eagle River area has more
than 20 churches, including the very
unique **Saint John Orthodox Cathedral**
(see **Milepost A 17.2**) with its geodesic
dome.

Visitor services include fast-food restaurants, supermarkets, banks, laundromat,
post office, gas stations and shopping centers. Ice skating, hockey and speed skating
at the Harry J. McDonald Memorial Center
located a half-mile north of the Fred Meyer
store via the Old Glenn Highway and 0.4

mile uphill on Harry McDonald Road. The
nearest public campground is Eagle River
Campground; take Hiland exit, then follow
signs on frontage road (see **Milepost A
11.6**).

There is a summer **Farmer's Market** on
Tuesdays at the VFW Post parking lot.

The annual **Alaska Highland Games
and Gathering of the Clans** takes place
the last Saturday in June at Lion's Club Park
in Eagle River. This annual event features
Scottish music, dancing, food and events
(hammer toss, caber and stone throw). For
details and dates, visit their website at www.
alaskascottish.org.

The 29th annual **Bear Paw Festival** is
scheduled for July 9-13, 2014. The Festival
features the Teddy Bear Picnic and Family
Fun Day, the Bear Paw Royalty Pageant and
Running with the Bears, a 300-yard fun
run—"because after 300 yards it isn't fun
anymore." There's also a classic car show
and, of course, the Grand Parade. Phone
(907) 694-4702 or visit www.bearpawfestival.

org for more information.

Eagle River Nature Center at Mile 12.5
Eagle River Road has natural history displays
and self-guiding nature trails. Guided nature
hikes are offered in summer and there are
nature programs scheduled year-round. Visit
www.ernc.org or phone (907) 694-2108 for
current information. *See "Eagle River Road"
log on page 376 for details.*

Eagle River Nature Center is also the
finish line for the **Crow Pass Crossing**, an
annual 24-mile marathon held the third Saturday in July. This mountain race follows
the Crow Pass trail from Girdwood to Eagle
River. Visit www.alaskamountainrunners.org
for registration information.

Mile 12 Eagle River Road
Eagle River
Alaska

907-694-2108
Trails, programs,
& hike-to yurts
& cabin.

www.ernc.org

**CHUGIAK-EAGLE RIVER
CHAMBER OF COMMERCE**
**VISITOR
INFORMATION**
CER TOWN CENTER
12001 BUSINESS BLVD., STE 108
P.O. BOX 770353, EAGLE RIVER, ALASKA 99577
www.bearpawfestival.org   www.cer.org
(907) 694-4702
July 3 – Fireworks and Festivities at Lions Park
July 4 – Chugiak Community Parade
Mid-July – Bear Paw Festival and Parade

Eagle River Road

Enjoying a picnic in the back deck area of Eagle River Nature Center. (©Kris Valencia, staff)

Eagle River Road leads 12.6 miles east from downtown Eagle River to Eagle River Nature Center in Chugach State Park. It is a paved 2-lane road, with local traffic, accessible from the Glenn Highway via Artillery Road from the Eagle River exit at **Milepost A 13.4**, or from Eagle River Loop road, which exits at **Milepost A 11.6**.

Beyond Mile 6 Eagle River Road becomes narrow and winding, with potholes and no shoulders. Posted speed limit is 40 to 55 mph. *NOTE: Watch for driveway traffic, school bus stops, pedestrians and moose. Slow vehicles use turnouts.*

Distance from junction (J) with Old Glenn Highway is shown.

J 0 Junction with Old Glenn Highway.

J 0.2 Fire station to west, police station to east.

J 1.6 Junction with Eagle River Loop Road.

J 1.7 Walmart.

J 2.3 End bike route from Eagle River.

J 3.3 P&M Gardens greenhouses.

J 7.8 Mile 7.4 North Fork Put-In. Short, bumpy, gravel road south to **North Fork Eagle River** access for kayaks, rafts and canoes; large gravel parking area, outhouse. Day-use area only, no camping. No fires; carry out trash. Hiking trail from parking area to main stem of river. The Eagle River offers class II, III and IV float trips. Fishing for rainbow trout, Dolly Varden and a limited king salmon fishery. Cross-country skiing and snow machining in winter. Check with Chugach State Park ranger (907/345-5014) for information on river conditions. ☛

J 9 Mile 9 Moose Pond Put-In; small gravel parking area at boat access for Eagle River floats. Fill site for Fire Department.

J 10.5 Chugach State Park (sign).

J 11.6 Rough gravel turnout to south; abrupt pavement edge.

J 12.6 Eagle River Nature Center; parking ($5 fee), outside pay phone. Operated by the nonprofit Friends of Eagle River Nature Center to provide educational and interpre-

tive opportunities for Chugach State Park visitors. The Nature Center has restrooms, brochures, natural history displays and year-round nature programs. Beautiful views of the Chugach Mountains, particularly from the viewing decks on the Rodak Nature Trail. Walk the nature trails at your own pace, or join one of the free guided nature walks offered 1:30–2:30 P.M. Wednesday–Sunday from June 1 to August 31. Pets must be on leash on the Rodak and Albert Loop trails.

The center is open year-round from 10 A.M. to 5 P.M.; Wednesday through Sunday (May–Sept.) and Friday through Sunday (Oct.–April). Trails are always accessible, but check for bear and wildlife warnings posted at building and trailhead. A rustic cabin

©Meghan Mackey, staff

and 3 **yurts** (pictured above)—each located within 2.5 miles of the Nature Center—are available for rent ($65/night) and may be reserved up to a year in advance online. Contact the center for current activities schedule and trail conditions. Phone (907) 694-2108, or visit their website at www.ernc.org.

This is also the trailhead for the Historic Iditarod–Crow Pass Trail and the finish line for the Crow Pass Crossing, an annual 24-mile marathon held the third Saturday in July. This mountain race follows the Crow Pass trail from Girdwood to Eagle River. Visit www.alaskamountainrunners.org for more information.

Eagle River Nature Center. See display ad on page 375.

**Return to Milepost A 13.4
Glenn Highway**

The 4.5-mile Eagle River Loop (see map page 375) provides access to Eagle River residential and business areas. Alaska State Parks maintains a day-use area and river access at Mile 1.5 Eagle River Loop (eastbound access only). Boaters are advised that a permit is required for boating the Eagle River on Fort Richardson Military Reservation.

Chugiak-Eagle River Chamber of Commerce. See display ad on page 375.

Glenn Highway Log
(continued)

A 12.8 G 176.2 T 315.2 Eagle River Bridge.

A 11.6 G 177.4 T 316.4 Exit to Hiland Drive/Eagle River Loop; access to Anchorage Municipal Landfill, state correctional center (follow signs) and state campground (description follows). Hiland Drive accesses the **South Fork Valley trailhead** in Chugach State Park; 6-mile trail to Eagle and Symphony lakes, spectacular view of surrounding peaks.

The 4.5-mile Eagle River Loop/Veterans Memorial Highway provides access to Alaska State Parks Eagle River Access (1.5 miles from exit, eastbound access only); junctions with Eagle River Road 2.5 miles from exit (*see Eagle River Road log this page*); and connects to Old Glenn Highway in downtown Eagle River.

For Eagle River Campground (Chugach State Park) follow signs 1.4 miles from the highway; 57 campsites, walk-in tent camping, 4-day camping limit, picnic shelter (may be reserved in advance), dump station, pay phones, flush toilets and drinking water. Camping fee is $15/night. Day-use fee $5. Dump station $5. Operated by concessionaire; phone (907) 694-7982. ▲

Highway narrows from 3 to 2 northbound lanes. Highway widens to 3 southbound lanes.

A 10.6 G 178.4 T 317.4 Truck weigh stations on both sides of highway; pay phones. Trooper Hans Roelle Memorial Station eastbound only.

The last 9 miles of the Glenn Highway into Anchorage has been designated the **Veterans' Memorial Parkway.**

A 7.5 G 181.5 T 320.5 D Street Gate to **Joint Base Elmendorf-Richardson** (JBER— pronounced "J-Bear"). Visitor Control Center at this gate is open 24 hours a day, 7 days a week. *Visitor and vehicle passes required to get on base. Visitors must have current vehicle registration or rental car agreement; current driver's license; name, location and phone number of sponsor on base. Other restrictions may apply; check with gate personnel.*

JBER is home to Air Force, Army, Alaska Army and Air National Guard, and Marine Corps Reserve units. **FORT RICHARDSON** was first established as the home of "America's Arctic Warriors," a name originating in 1867 when Brevet Major General Jefferson C. Davis assumed command of the Military District of Alaska and instituted the motto Arctic Tough and the salute Arctic Warriors. The major units under USARAK (U.S. Army Alaska) are the 1st Stryker Brigade Combat Team. The 4th Brigade Combat Team (Airborne), 25th Infantry Division, is at Fort Richardson. There is a National Cemetery at Fort Richardson, however getting on base is difficult and generally not an opportunity available to the general public.

CAUTION: Watch for moose next 7 miles northbound.

A 6.1 G 182.9 T 321.9 Northbound only exit to Arctic Valley Road (description follows) and access to JBER D Street Gate (north 1 mile via frontage road, follow signs). Follow Arctic Valley Road 1 mile for **Moose Run Golf Course**; 36-holes (Hill Course and Creek Course), driving range, rental carts and clubs, clubhouse. This military course is open to the public. Phone (907) 428-0056 for tee times; www.mooserungolfcourse .com. Season is about May to October, depending on snow.

Arctic Valley Road/Ski Bowl Road leads 7 miles from junction with frontage road to Arctic Valley Alpenglow in Chugach State Park; hiking, alpine wildflowers and berry picking in summer, weekend skiing in winter. (The Anchorage Ski Club operates a T-bar and 2 chairlifts.) Pavement ends at Mile 1.6; wide gravel road to end; some steep grades and washboard; posted 25 to 30 mph. Military gate at Mile 1.7 is closed from 10 P.M. to 6 A.M. (Much of the land along the road is part of Fort Richardson and there are often training exercises going on in the area.) Best view of Fort Richardson and Anchorage from turnout at Mile 4.2. Emergency phones at Mile 3.7 and 6.3. Trailhead for Arctic to Indian trail (Chugach State Park) at Mile 6.3. Views of Arctic Valley from road are obscured by foliage. Fee parking, toilets and summer hiking at Arctic Valley Alpenglow ski area, Mile 7. Trailhead for Rendezvous Peak Trail: "The hike to the saddle (elev. 3,468 feet) is a relatively gentle climb, and the added push to Rendezvous Peak (elev. 4,050 feet) is well worth the spectacular scenery that awaits." Allow 2 to 5 hours for the 3.5-mile round trip.

A 5 G 184 T 323 *Actual driving distance between physical Mileposts 5 and 6 is only 0.5 mile.*

A 4.2 G 184.8 T 323.8 Muldoon Road overpass; exit north for **Alaska Native Heritage Center** (description follows), Tikahtnu Commons Shopping Center (includes **Regal Stadium 16 & IMAX** the-

atre, pictured above), Target, U.S. Air Force Hospital and Bartlett High School. Entrance (Muldoon Gate) to Joint Base Elmendorf-Richardson (JBER) is on Provider Drive; hours of operation are 0500–1800 hours Monday through Thursday, 0500-2400 hours Friday, and 0900-2400 hours Saturday and Sunday.

Exit south on Muldoon for food, gas, shopping, lodging and Centennial Park municipal campground (description follows). Muldoon connects with the New Seward Highway via Tudor Road. There is a bicycle trail alongside the Glenn Highway from Muldoon Road to Mirror Lake at **Milepost A 23.6.**

Alaska Native Heritage Center is a premier cultural center sharing the rich heritage of Alaska's 11 major cultural groups. Six

One of 6 traditional village sites at the Alaska Native Heritage Center. Take Muldoon Road North exit and turn right on signed access road for center. (©Kris Valencia, staff)

traditional village sites are along a walking path around a 2-acre lake. Cultural presentations, food and crafts inside the Welcoming House. Open daily in summer, 9 A.M. to 5 P.M. Admission fee. www.alaskanative.net.

Alaska Native Heritage Center. See display ad on page 391.

Centennial Park is open mid-May to October 1. It is recommended for large RVs and has 100 RV/campsites, 2 group sites, and 6 pull-through sites. To reach Centennial Park, take Muldoon Road south to first left onto Boundary, take the next left and follow the signs. For more details, phone (907) 343-6986 May–October.

A 3.4 G 185.6 T 324.6 Turpin Road (eastbound exit only).

A 3.3 G 185.7 T 324.7 Distance marker eastbound shows Eagle River 10 miles, Palmer 38 miles, Wasilla 39 miles.

A 3 G 186 T 325 Boniface Parkway overpass. Exit south for services (food, gas, shopping) and Russian Jack Springs City Park on Boniface Parkway just north of DeBarr. Exit north for JBER (description follows).

Exit north and drive 0.5 mile on Vandenberg Avenue for Boniface Gate entrance to **Joint Base Elmendorf-Richardson (JBER)**; Visitor Control Center at this gate is open 24 hours a day, 7 days a week. *NOTE: Visitor and vehicle passes required to get on base. Visitors must have current vehicle registration or rental car agreement; current driver's license; name, location and phone number of sponsor on base. Other restrictions may apply; check with gate personnel.* On July 30, 2010, the 673d Air Base Wing activated as the host wing combining installation management functions of **ELMENDORF AIR FORCE BASE's** 3rd Wing and U.S. Army Garrison Fort Richardson. It is headquarters for the U.S. Alaskan Command, 11th Air Force, U.S. Army Alaska, and the Alaskan North American Aerospace Defense

Command Region. Go to http://www.jber. af.mil/library/history/index.asp.

A 1.7 G 187.3 T 326.3 Bragaw Street overpass. Exit north on Bragaw for Alaska Museum of Science & Nature.

A 1.2 G 187.8 T 326.8 Traffic light. Turn south on Airport Heights Drive for access to Northway Mall, Merrill Field and Alaska Regional Hospital. Turn north on Mountain View Drive and take first or second right for access to Glenn Square Shopping Center (visible from freeway just east of exit).

NOTE: Begin 40 mph speed zone westbound. Begin 65 mph speed limit eastbound.

A 1 G 188 T 327 Traffic light at Reeve Blvd. intersection; access to Merrill Field.

A 0.6 G 188.4 T 327.4 Traffic light at Concrete and Wilbur intersection.

A 0.4 G 188.6 T 327.6 Welcome to Anchorage sign for westbound travelers.

A 0.2 G 188.8 T 327.8 Glenn Highway forks and becomes 5th Avenue one-way westbound to downtown Anchorage. Coming from downtown Anchorage, 6th Avenue (one-way eastbound) ends here. A Blue Star Memorial Highway marker is located at this 'Y.' The Blue Star Memorial Highway program began in 1945 in cooperation with the National Council of State Garden Clubs as a way to honor the armed forces of the United States. Blue Star Memorials are found on highways in every state, each marker sponsored and maintained by a local garden club. A 0.1 G 188.9 T 327.9 Traffic light at Karluk Street intersection.

A 0 G 189 T 328 **Junction** with Ingra Street (one-way northbound) is followed by **junction** with Gambell Street (one-way southbound) for westbound drivers. For the Seward Highway to the Kenai Peninsula (see SEWARD HIGHWAY section), turn south on Gambell Street, which becomes the New Seward Highway. See ANCHORAGE section following for description of city.

Alaska's state motto, "North to the Future," was chosen in 1967 during the Alaska Purchase Centennial.

Anchorage

(See maps, pages 382, 384 and 388)

Bull moose on Powerline Pass trail, with Anchorage in the background.
(©Michael F. Jones)

Alaska's largest city, Anchorage is in the heart of the state's southcentral gulf coast. Located on the upper shores of Cook Inlet, at 61° north latitude and 150° west longitude, the Anchorage bowl is on a low-lying alluvial plain bordered by mountains, water and dense forests of spruce, birch and aspen. Cook Inlet's Turnagain Arm and Knik Arm define the broad peninsula that is the city's home, and the rugged Chugach Mountains form a striking backdrop. More than half the state's pop-

ulation lives in Anchorage and the neighboring Matanuska-Susitna borough, which includes Palmer and Wasilla. Anchorage is situated 362 miles south of Fairbanks via the Parks Highway; 328 miles from Tok via the Glenn Highway/Tok Cutoff; 304 miles from Valdez, southern terminus of the trans-Alaska pipeline, via the Glenn and Richardson highways; 2,459 driving miles via the West Access Route, Alaska Highway and Glenn Highway/Tok Cutoff from Seattle; 1,644 nautical miles, and approximately 3–3.5 hours flying time from Seattle. Prior to the opening of Russia's Far East to air traffic and refueling, Anchorage was named the "Air Crossroads of the World," and today is still a major air logistics center and cargo carrier for Asia, Europe and North America. In terms of nonstop air mileages, Anchorage is the following distance from each of these cities: Amsterdam, 4,475; Chicago, 2,839; Copenhagen, 4,313; Hamburg, 4,430; Honolulu, 2,780; London, 4,487; Paris, 4,683; San Francisco, 2,015; Seattle, 1,445; Tokyo, 3,460.

Population: 295,570 (U.S. Census July 2011). **Emergency Services: Police, Fire Department, Ambulance** and **Search & Rescue**, phone 911. **Anchorage Police Department (APD)** Headquarters, 4501 Elmore Road, Anchorage, AK 99507; main phone (907) 786-8500. **Emergency Information** recording, (907) 343-4701. **Alaska State Troopers**, phone (907) 248-7200/ www.dps.alaska.gov/ast. **Alaska Mountain Rescue Group**, (907) 566-2674 or (907) 428-

7200. **Search and Rescue Civil Air Patrol**, (call State Troopers who do the dispatch for this) (907) 248-7200; **Emergency Coast Guard**, 1-800-478-5555 or VHS Channel 16. **Hospitals:** Alaska Regional Hospital, (907) 276-1131; Alaska Native Medical Center, (907) 563-2662; Providence Alaska Medical Center, (907) 562-2211; Elmendorf Air Force Base emergency room, (907) 580-5555; Fort Richardson U.S. Army Medical Clinic, (907) 384-0600. **Emergency Management**, (907) 343-1400. **Suicide and Crisis and Psych Intervention**, (907) 563-3200 (24-hour service). **Rape and Assault**, (907) 276-7273 (24-hour service). **Child Abuse**, (907) 269-4000. **Abused Women's Aid in Crisis**, (907) 272-0100 (24-hour service). **Pet Emergency**, (907) 274-5636. **Poison Control**, 1-800-222-1222. **Road Conditions**, statewide, phone 511, outside Alaska 1-866-282-7577; or visit http://511.alaska.gov.

Visitor Information: Visit Anchorage (formerly the Anchorage Convention & Visitors Bureau) operates 2 information centers at the corner of 4th Avenue and F Street: The Log Cabin Visitor Information Center, which fronts 4th Avenue, and directly behind it—and part of the old City Hall building—a modern walk-in Visitor Information Center. Both offer free brochures and maps. The centers are open daily, year-round (except for major holidays); phone (907) 257-2363. Hours mid-May to mid-September are 8 A.M. to 7 P.M.; from mid-September to mid-May, hours are 9 A.M. to 4 P.M..

A third visitor information center is

Distances in miles	Anchorage	Denali NP	Fairbanks	Homer	Seward	Tok	Valdez
Anchorage		237	362	233	127	328	304
Denali NP	237		125	470	364	565	541
Fairbanks	362	125		595	489	206	366
Homer	233	470	595		180	561	537
Seward	127	364	489	180		455	431
Tok	328	565	206	561	455		254
Valdez	304	541	366	537	431	254	

Busy 4th Avenue today in downtown Anchorage. See photo facing page of 4th Avenue after the 1964 earthquake. (©Kris Valencia, staff)

located in the South Terminal of Ted Stevens Anchorage International Airport. For current and upcoming events, things to do and other travel planning help, and to order a free guide to Anchorage, visit www.anchorage.net/.

The **Alaska Public Lands Information Center (APLIC)**, 605 W. 4th Ave., Suite 105 in the historic Old Federal Building, has extensive displays and information on outdoor recreation lands in Alaska *(see detailed description on page 391)*. APLIC phone is (907) 644-3661.

The Dept. of Natural Resources Public Information Center, 550 W. 7th Avenue, Suite 1260, is open weekdays from 10 A.M. to 5 P.M. with information on state parks and recreational mining.

Other contacts for information about the city include the Municipality of Anchorage at www.muni.org, Anchorage Downtown Partnership at www.anchorage.downtown.org, or the Anchorage Chamber of Commerce at www.anchoragechamber.org.

Elevation: Sea level. **Climate**: Anchorage has a climate resembling that of the Rocky Mountains area, tempered by proximity to the Pacific Ocean. Shielded from excess ocean moisture by the Kenai Mountains to the south, the city has an annual average of only 15.9 inches of precipitation. Winter snowfall averages about 69 inches per year, with snow on the ground typically from October to April.

Anchorage is in a transition zone between the moderating influence of the Pacific and the extreme temperatures of Interior Alaska. The average temperature in January (coldest month) is 14°F; in July (warmest month), 58°F. A record 41 days of 70°F temperatures or higher was set in 2004. The record high was 86°F in June 1953. The record low was -38°F in February 1947.

The 100–120 day growing season extends from late May to early September. Anchorage has a daily maximum of 19 hours, 22 minutes of daylight in summer, and a minimum of 5 hours, 28 minutes in winter.

Radio: AM stations: KTZN 550 (The Zone, Sports Radio); KHAR 590 (Easy Listening); KENI 650 (News, Talk, Sports); KBYR 700 (News, Talk, Sports); KFQD 750 (News, Talk); KUDO 1080 (Business, News, Talk). FM stations: KRUA 88.1 (The Edge, UAA); KAKL 88.5 (KLOV Christian Radio); KATB 89.3 (Christian Radio); KNBA 90.3 (Public Radio, Native-owned); KSKA 91.1 (National Public Radio); KAFC 93.7 (Christian Radio); KFAT 92.9 (Hip-hop and R&B); KZND 94.7 (Rock); KEAG 97.3 (KOOL FM, Oldies); KLEF 98.1 (Classical Music); KYMG 98.9 (Magic, Adult Contemporary); KBFX 100.5 (The Fox, Pure Rock); KGOT 101.3 (The Mix, 80s, 90s, Top 40); KDBZ 102.1 (The Buzz, Hot Adult Contemporary); KMXS 103.1 (Contemporary); KBRJ 104.1 (KBEAR, Country Favorites); KNIK 105.7 (The Breeze, Smooth Jazz); KWHL 106.5 (Modern Rock); KASH 107.5 (New Country). **Television**: Broadcast channels are Channel 2 KTUU (NBC); Channel 4 KTBY (Fox); Channel 5 KYES (Anchorage's only locally-owned TV station, a UPN affiliate); Channel 7 KAKM (PBS); Channel 11 KTVA (CBS); and Channel 13 KIMO (ABC). Cable channels available by satellite and pay cable television service.

ANCHORAGE ADVERTISERS

Newspapers: *Anchorage Daily News* (daily); *Alaska Journal of Commerce* (weekly); *Anchorage Press* (weekly); *Alaska Military Weekly* (weekly); *Alaska Star* (weekly).

Private Aircraft: Anchorage airports provide facilities and services to accommodate all types of aircraft. Consult *Supplement Alaska*, and related aviation guides and charts for Ted Stevens Anchorage International, Merrill Field and Lake Hood seaplane and airstrip.

History & Economy

In 1914, Congress authorized the building of a railroad linking an ocean port with the interior river shipping routes. The anchorage at the mouth of Ship Creek became the construction camp and headquarters for the Alaskan Engineering Commission. By the summer of 1915, the population, housed mainly in tents, had grown to about 2,000.

Among the names suggested for the settlement were Ship Creek, Spenard, Woodrow and Knik Anchorage, and the name Anchorage was selected by the federal government when the first post office opened in May 1915. Later that year, the bluff south of Ship Creek was cleared and surveyed, and 655 lots, on 347 acres, were auctioned off by the General Land Office for $148,000. The center of the business district was the 4th Avenue and C Street intersection. Anchorage prospered and was incorporated in 1920. Anchorage's growth has been in spurts, spurred by: (1) construction of the Alaska Railroad and the transfer of its headquarters from Seward to Anchorage in 1917; (2) colonization of the Matanuska Valley, a farming region 45 miles to the north, in 1935; (3) construction of Fort Richardson and Elmendorf Field in 1940; (4) discovery of oil in Cook Inlet between 1957 and 1961; and (5) the development of North Slope/Prudhoe Bay oil fields and the construction of the trans-Alaska pipeline—all since 1968.

The current population includes diverse racial and cultural groups, with about 66 percent white, 7.9 percent Alaska Native or part Native, 5.6 percent African-American, 10 percent Asian-Pacific Islander, 8 percent Hispanic groups and 2.5 percent 3 or more races.

Government jobs, including the military, account for about one-quarter of the employment picture. The military is a visible presence in Anchorage, with military aircraft taking off and landing from JBER (Joint Base Elmendorf–Richardson). Military personnel are also a visible presence in town when in uniform, and are also a welcome presence here in Anchorage whether in uniform or civilian clothes. Many local businesses, such as movie theaters, offer special military discounts.

Service industries make up about a quarter of available jobs in Anchorage. The oil, gas and mining industries employ roughly 3 percent. Other fields of work are similar to those in other American cities of this size.

The Good Friday earthquake of March 27, 1964, the most powerful quake (8.6 on the Richter scale, Magnitude/Mw 9.2) ever recorded in North America, caused more than $300 million in damages throughout southcentral Alaska. In Anchorage, most losses resulted from landslides caused by changes in the composition of the clay underlying much of the city. Government Hill, downtown neighborhoods and the Turnagain area, now known as Earthquake

Photograph of 4th Avenue 50 years ago after the Good Friday earthquake of March 27, 1964. (©Wide World Photos)

Park, suffered the most extensive damage, losing many homes and other buildings. Considering the severity of the disaster, the number of casualties in Alaska (115) was miraculously low. Relief funds in the form of federal Small Business Administration loans

helped many rebuild, and from the devastation, a distinctly new Anchorage emerged.

In the 1970s and 1980s, Anchorage experienced a population and construction boom related to oil production. Major oil companies set up corporate headquarters, and

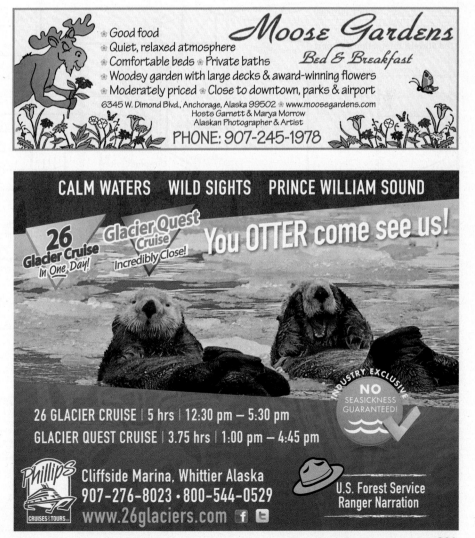

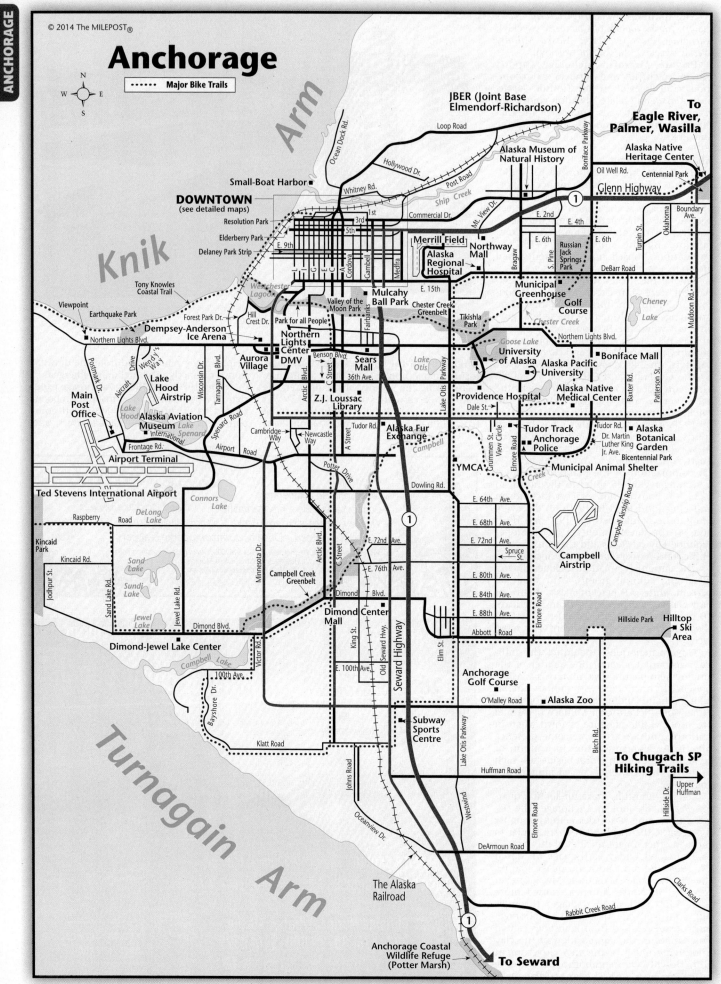

Anchorage

····· Major Bike Trails

N W E S

© 2014 The MILEPOST®

Knik Arm

Turnagain Arm

JBER (Joint Base Elmendorf-Richardson)

Loop Road
O'Cean Dock Rd.
Hollywood Dr.
Whitney Rd.
Post Road
Ship Creek

To Eagle River, Palmer, Wasilla

Alaska Native Heritage Center

Oil Well Rd.
Centennial Park

Alaska Museum of Natural History

Boniface Parkway

Glenn Highway

Boundary Ave.

Small-Boat Harbor

DOWNTOWN
(see detailed maps)

Resolution Park
Elderberry Park
Delaney Park Strip

Commercial Dr.
Mt. View Dr.
E. 2nd
E. 4th
E. 6th
E. 6th

Turpin St.
Oklahoma
DeBarr Road

1st
3rd
5th
E. 9th

Merrill Field
Alaska Regional Hospital

Northway Mall

Bragaw
S. Pine

Russian Jack Springs Park

Tony Knowles Coastal Trail

Westchester Lagoon

Park for all People

Valley of the Moon Park

Cordova
Cambell
Medfra
Fairbanks

Mulcahy Ball Park

E. 15th

Chester Creek Greenbelt

Tikishla Park

Municipal Greenhouse

Golf Course

Cheney Lake

Muldoon Rd.

Viewpoint
Earthquake Park

Northern Lights Blvd.

Forest Park Dr.
Hill Crest Dr.

Chester Creek

Goose Lake

Northern Lights Blvd.

Dempsey-Anderson Ice Arena

Northern Lights Center DMV

Benson Blvd.

Sears Mall
36th Ave.

Lake Otis

University of Alaska

Alaska Pacific University

Boniface Mall

Aurora Village

Aircraft
Wendy's Way

C Street

Z.J. Loussac Library

Lake Otis Parkway

Providence Hospital

Alaska Native Medical Center

Baxter Rd.
Patterson St.

Lake Hood Airstrip

Wisconsin Dr.
Tarnagain Dr.
Spenard Road

Arctic Blvd.

Dale St.

Main Post Office

Alaska Aviation Museum

Lake Spenard
Lake Hood
International

Cambridge Way
Newcastle Way

A Street

Tudor Rd.

Alaska Fur Exchange

Campbell Creek

View Circle
Grummen St.

Tudor Track
Anchorage Police

Elmore Road

Tudor Rd.
Dr. Martin Luther King Jr. Ave.

Alaska Botanical Garden
Bicentennial Park

Frontage Rd.

Airport

Airport Road

Potter Drive

YMCA

Municipal Animal Shelter

Airport Terminal

Ted Stevens International Airport

Connors Lake

Dowling Rd.

E. 64th Ave.
E. 68th Ave.
E. 72nd Ave.

Campbell Airstrip Road

Raspberry Road

DeLong Lake

Arctic Blvd.

E. 72nd Ave.
Spruce St.

Campbell Airstrip

Kincaid Park

Kincaid Rd.

Sand Lake
Sundi Lake

C Street

E. 76th Ave.

E. 80th Ave.

Jodhpur St.

Minnesota Dr.

Campbell Creek Greenbelt

Dimond Blvd.

E. 84th Ave.
E. 88th Ave.

Hillside Park

Hilltop Ski Area

Sand Lake Rd.

Jewel Lake Rd.

Jewel Lake

Dimond Blvd.

Dimond Center Mall

Abbott Road

Elmore Road

Dimond-Jewel Lake Center

Campbell Lake

Victor Rd.

100th Ave.

King St.

Dimond Center Mall

Seward Highway

Elim St.

Anchorage Golf Course

O'Malley Road

Alaska Zoo

Bayshore Dr.

E. 100th Ave.

Old Seward Hwy.

Klatt Road

Subway Sports Centre

Johns Road

Lake Otis Parkway

Birch Rd.

To Chugach SP Hiking Trails

Huffman Road

Westwind

Elmore Road

Hillside Dr.

Upper Huffman

Oceanview Dr.

The Alaska Railroad

DeArmoun Road

Clarks Road

Rabbit Creek Road

1

Anchorage Coastal Wildlife Refuge
(Potter Marsh)

To Seward

Anchorage's first 20-story buildings punctuated the skyline. Declining oil prices in the 1980s and 1990s triggered a slowdown in the economic climate, but business prospects are upbeat today, and the number of new building starts is high. As in the Lower 48, mergers, malls and megastores are the order of the day here.

With its strategic location and modern facilities, Anchorage plays a key role as the center of commerce and distribution for the rest of Alaska. Some 90 percent of the merchandise goods for 85 percent of Alaska's population come through the Port of Anchorage (www.portofalaska.com). One of only 19 Dept. of Defense National Strategic Seaports, the Port of Anchorage is a major source of gasoline, diesel, heating oil and aviation gas, providing 100 percent of Elmendorf AFB's jet fuel and most of the jet fuel used by airplanes at Ted Stevens International Airport. Nearly 100 million pounds of goods bound for more than 250 villages in the state pass through the Port of Anchorage. *See "Downtown Anchorage" on page 388 for additional information on the port.*

The city's growth now supports 2 convention centers: Egan Convention Center on 5th Avenue, and the newer Dena'ina Civic and Convention Center (completed in 2008), which occupies an entire city block on 7th Avenue, between F and G streets. At 200,000-square-feet, Dena'ina is the largest civic center in Alaska.

Description

Covering 1,961 square miles (1,697 square miles of land and 264 of water), Anchorage lies between the Chugach Mountains on the east and Knik Arm of Cook Inlet on the west. The surrounding mountain ranges—the Chugach, the Kenais, the Talkeetnas, the icy peaks of the Tordrillo Mountains across Cook Inlet, and the dramatic peaks of the Alaska Range (with Mount McKinley visible on the northern horizon, weather permitting) surround the city in scenic splendor. Perched within the edge of Alaska's vast, varied expanse of forests, mountains, rivers, taiga and tundra, the city offers abundant wilderness experiences in every direction. Combining cosmopolitan amenities with the creative enthusiasm of a young, progressive city gives Anchorage its appeal as an excitingly unique destination.

Alaska Center for the Performing Arts is the performance venue for Anchorage opera and symphony. *(©Kris Valencia, staff)*

Anchorage is one of only 11 cities to have been voted an All-American City 4 or more times. Sponsored by the National Civic League and awarded to only 10 cities each year, this award recognizes the cities' citizens, governments, businesses and non-profit organizations and their ability to successfully address local issues and produce positive results. Anchorage is also a 4-time winner in the "100 Best Communities for Young People" list, most recently in 2010.

One common way by which residents and visitors describe Alaska, is that it is big! Only here in Anchorage do winter Olympians such as Kikkan Randall, Holly Brooks, James Southam and Lars Flora practice for the upcoming ski season in their own backyard training facilities such as Kincaid Park. Anchorage's extensive award-winning trail system is one of the best in the country, encompassing 135 miles (217 km) of paved trails and 300 miles (482 km) of unpaved and wilderness trails, offering endless opportunities for activities such as running,

walking, rollerblading, biking, hiking, horseback riding and rollerskiing. Within the city limits of Anchorage there are an estimated 1,000 moose, nearly 250 black bears and almost 60 brown bears. With all that Anchorage has to offer, and its wild attractions, it is no wonder that the city brand is Big Wild Life™, encompassing the components of work, life and play.

Anchorage is noted for the profusion of flowers and hanging baskets that decorate homes and businesses during summer months: parks, street medians and lampposts are vibrantly colored with millions of flower blossoms, dubbing it the City of

Anchorage City Center

Old Federal Building (Alaska Public Lands Info Center)

Alaska Railroad Depot

Ship Creek Salmon Viewing

Whitney Rd.

Ship Creek

Post Road

E. Ship Creek Ave.

The Alaska Railroad

Nesbitt Courthouse

Christensen Dr.

W. 1st — E. 1st — E. 1st

W. 2nd — E. 2nd Ct. — E. 2nd

Oscar Anderson House

Resolution Park

W. 3rd — E. 3rd

Knik Arm

Elderberry Park

W. 4th — Sunshine Plaza — 4th Avenue Market — Pioneer Schoolhouse — E. 4th — Mile 0 Glenn Highway

State Court Bldg. — Log Cabin Visitor Center — Old City Hall — Egan Center — Fire — W. 5th — E. 5th

5th Ave. Mall — Center for the Performing Arts — W. 6th — E. 6th

Bus Accommodation Center — City Hall — Anchorage Museum — W. 7th — E. 7th — City Cemetery

Hostel — W. 8th — Federal Bldg. — E. 8th

W. 9th — E. 9th

W. 10th — Delaney Park Strip — E. 10th

W. 11th — E. 11th

W. 12th — E. 12th

W. 13th — E. 13th

W. 14th — E. 14th

W. 15th — E. 15th

W. 15th Ter. — E. 15th Ter. — George M. Sullivan Sports Arena — Begin/End New Seward Highway

W. 16th — Avenues West — Avenues East — E. 16th — Mulcahy Ball Park — Ben Boeke Arena — McHugh Ln. — E. 16th Ter.

Virginia Ct. — Coffey Ln. — Inlet Pl.

Street labels (vertical): P Street, O Street, N Street, M Street, L Street, K Street, I Street, H Street, G Street, F Street, E Street, D Street, C Street, B Street, A Street, Barrow St., Cordova St., Denali St., Eagle St., Fairbanks St., Gambell St., Ingra St., Hyder St., Juneau St., Karluk St., Latouche St., Medfra St., Nelchina St., Orca St., Denali St., Eagle St., Medfra St.

Creekwood Inn

A Budget Motel with a First Class Heart

Motel & RV Park in Anchorage, Alaska

Next to beautiful walking and bike paths, Sears mall, restaurants, grocery stores and theaters. In mid-town, minutes from every place in Anchorage you might want to visit.

Motel
- Comfortable, clean rooms
- Queen beds in each room
- Large fully-equipped kitchenettes & suites
- Microwave, refrigerator, FREE coffee, hairdryers in all rooms
- Wi-Fi
- FREE cable TV with HBO

RV Park
- 67 spaces — 58 full hookups
- Cable TV available
- FREE showers for RV guests
- Fish freezer available
- Propane
- Laundry facility
- Daily/weekly rates

Connects to map above

Sullivan Sports Arena

Creekwood Inn

Gambell St. — Ingra St. — 15th Ave. — 22nd Ave. — Fireweed Lane

A Warm and Happy Welcome!

FREE coffee in the lobby 24 hours

2150 Seward Hwy., Anchorage, AK 99503
Tel: 907 258-6006
Fax: 907 279-8972
1-800-478-6008 (Reservations Only)

www.creekwoodinn-alaska.com

Flowers. In winter, Anchorage is transformed into the City of Lights. Residents are encouraged to follow the lead of municipal agencies in displaying strings of miniature white lights on homes, trees and office buildings, to brighten the entire city.

Remember: You are in bear and moose country! Anchorage shares its streets, yards, greenbelts and trails with these wild animals, and it is not uncommon to see either a bear or moose crossing the road or foraging along a trail.

While most people know to give bears a wide berth, they may not realize that moose can be extremely dangerous if they are startled or feel threatened. And they are particularly agitated by dogs. *Do not approach or intercept moose at any time, whether for purposes of photography or to satisfy curiosity.* The ADF&G advises: "Give moose an extremely wide berth if you have a dog with you and don't let your dog chase a moose."

Two premier convention facilities (www.anchorageconventioncenters.com) form the downtown Anchorage convention district: The William A. Egan Civic & Convention Center on 5th Avenue and the Dena'ina Civic and Convention Center on 7th Avenue. The Dena'ina, named after the Athabascan people that first populated southcentral Alaska, features works of art from local and national artists, all incorporating the relationship between Alaska's indigenous peoples and the land.

Heated sidewalks and covered walkways connect the 2 convention centers and a third public building—the Alaska Center for the Performing Arts ("the PAC")—a 176,000-square-foot structure with 4 theaters that host the city's symphony, opera, an extensive concert schedule and other events. The PAC (www.myalaskacenter.com) is located on beautiful Town Square Park between 5th and 6th avenues.

The Anchorage Museum on C Street, between 6th and 7th avenues, is another

Anchorage has metered on-street parking as well as pay parking lots of all sizes.
(©Kris Valencia, staff)

important public building that is both a major visitor attraction and an integral part of the city's cultural life. *See page 390 in "Downtown Anchorage" section for detailed information on the museum.*

Lodging & Services

There are more than 8,000 motel and hotel rooms in the Anchorage area, with prices for a double room ranging from $50 to $300 and up. Reservations are a must. Bed-and-breakfast and hostel accommodations are also available in more than 250 private residences; prices range from about $60–$200 for bed-and-breakfasts.

Courtyard by Marriott Anchorage Airport. Redesigned lobby with coffee and cocktail bar and media pods make the Courtyard a place to relax and recharge.

For breakfast and dinner, you'll find a satisfying selection at The Bistro–Courtyard's newest way to make the most of your stay. In-room microwave, mini-fridge and coffee-maker, plus pool, whirlpool and exercise room. Phone toll-free 1-877-729-0197 or www.marriott.com/anccy. [ADVERTISEMENT]

SpringHill Suites by Marriott Anchorage Midtown. Located in midtown, near shopping and entertainment. Each spacious suite is stylishly furnished and smartly designed with a pull-out sofa bed, LCD TVs, mini-refrigerator, coffee maker, microwave and wet bar. Also enjoy our complimentary breakfast buffet, heated pool and whirlpool, exercise room and wireless. Phone toll-free 1-877-729-0197 or www.marriott.com/ancsh. [ADVERTISEMENT]

Residents and visitors alike appreciate the summer displays of flowers in downtown Anchorage. (©Donna Dewhurst)

SpringHill Suites by Marriott Anchorage University Lake. Nestled at the base of the Chugach Mountain Range, this lakefront lodging provides easy access to nature and the city, plus you'll find the space you need to relax and reconnect. Enjoy in-room microwave and fridge, plus indoor pool, whirlpool, exercise room, wireless and complimentary breakfast buffet. Phone toll free 1-877-729-0197 or www.marriott.com/ancum. [ADVERTISEMENT]

Residence Inn by Marriott Anchorage Midtown. Newly redesigned lobby, spacious studios, suites and eating areas. Fully equipped kitchens with microwave, dishwasher, fridge, desk, wireless and pull-out sofa. Enjoy complimentary breakfast buffet and guest receptions Monday through Thursday, heated pool, whirlpool, exercise room, newspaper, complimentary grocery shopping services, guest laundry and valet service. Pets accepted. Phone toll-free 1-877-729-0197 or www.marriott.com/ancri. [ADVERTISEMENT]

Comfortable, low-cost hostel accommodations at **Alaska Backpackers Inn**, 409 Eagle Street, from May to September (rooming house accommodations Oct.–April); phone (907) 277-2770, www.alaskabackpackers.com.

Camping

Anchorage has several private campgrounds (see advertisers listed under "Campgrounds" on page 380). Anchorage has one public campground: **Centennial Campground**, open mid-May to early September, and recommended for large RVs. It is operated by the Municipality of Anchorage and has showers, flush toilets, water, dump stations, no hookups, 100 sites, 2 group sites, and 6 drive-through sites. To reach Centennial Park, take the Muldoon Road exit south off the Glenn Highway, take the first left onto Boundary, take the next left on frontage and follow the signs. For more details, phone (907) 343-6986 May–September; (907) 343-6992 off-season or visit the website at www.muni.org/Departments/parks/Pages/Camping.aspx.

Chugach State Park campgrounds located near Anchorage on the Glenn Highway are Eagle River at **Milepost A 11.6** and Eklutna Lake, access via Eklutna Lake Road from **Milepost A 25.2** or **A 26.5**. Campground maps are available from the Dept. of Natural Resources Public Information Center at 550 W. 7th Ave., Suite 1260, or the Alaska Public Lands Information Center on 4th Avenue.

Transportation

Air: More than 25 international and domestic air carriers and numerous intrastate airlines serve Ted Stevens Anchorage International Airport, located west of Minnesota Drive (take L Street south from downtown and follow signs). More than 280 flights arrive daily, with over 5 million passengers using the airport each year. A new, state of the art rental car center at the airport makes renting and returning a car safe, easy and warm.

Cruise Ship: Cruise ships do not dock in Anchorage. The nearest ports are Whittier and Seward, with passengers traveling to Anchorage either by rail or by motorcoach. See "Cruising" in the TRAVEL PLANNING section.

Ferry: The nearest ferry port to Anchor-

age is Whittier on Prince William Sound, served by the Alaska state ferry system with service to Cordova and Valdez. Whittier is accessible from Anchorage via the Seward Highway and Whittier Access Road (see SEWARD HIGHWAY section). See "Ferry Travel" in the TRAVEL PLANNING section and also the ALASKA MARINE HIGHWAY section.

Railroad: The Alaska Railroad offers daily passenger service aboard 3 trains during the summer. Service includes daily round-trip service between Anchorage and Seward; northbound service to Talkeetna, Denali National Park and Fairbanks; and service from Anchorage to Whittier, where passengers can connect to Prince William Sound cruises, Spencer Whistlestop and scenic Grandview Valley. Reduced service in winter, when weekend passenger service between Anchorage and Fairbanks is available. Contact Passenger Services Dept., 411 W. First Ave., 99501; toll free 1-800-544-0552 or (907) 265-2494, fax (907) 265-2323; email reservations@akrr.com; www.Alaska Railroad.com. The Alaska Railroad Depot is located on First Avenue, within easy walking distance of downtown.

Bus: Local service via People Mover, serving most of the Anchorage bowl from Peters Creek to Oceanview. Passes, schedules and tokens available at the 6th Avenue and H Street and the Dimond Transit Centers. For bus route information, phone the Ride-Line at (907) 343-6543, or visit www.people mover.org.

Alaska Bus Guy. Alaskan economy scheduled service: Anchorage, Talkeetna, Denali National Park. Departs Anchorage Egan Center (5th and F) 7 A.M. Anchorage return (5:30 P.M.) from Denali. Custom group tours: 1–12 day packages. www.alaskabusguy.com. Scenic and wildlife photo stops. Why pay more? Reservations strongly suggested: $74 one-way, round-trip $145. Phone (907) 720-6541. [ADVERTISEMENT]

For more options in bus service to other communities, see "Bus Lines" in TRAVEL PLANNING section.

Anchorage Trolley Tours, (907) 276-5603, offers sightseeing service; departs from Log Cabin Visitor Center. Shuttle service also

Raven whispers to the bear: "I really enjoy watching you fish for salmon in Ship Creek," at Bear Square on 4th Avenue. (©Kris Valencia, staff)

available to Alaska Native Heritage Center, Alaska Zoo, Ulu Factory and airport.

The Bear Square, (907) 277-4545, offers both Anchorage City Trolley Tours and Segway tours.

Taxi: Alaska Cab Company, (907) 562-6805; Alaska Yellow Cab, (907) 222-2222; Anchorage Checker Cab, (907) 274-3333.

Car and Camper Rentals: There are dozens of car rental agencies located at the airport and downtown, as well as several *(Continues on page 392)*

4731 O'Malley Road   Anchorage, AK 99507   907-346-3242   www.alaskazoo.org

the Alaska ZOO

Open Daily Year Round
Summer Shuttle From Downtown

Alaska Zoo

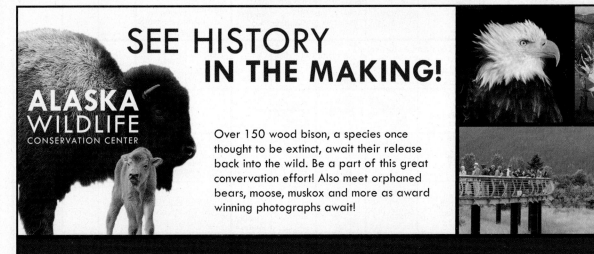

SEE HISTORY IN THE MAKING!

ALASKA WILDLIFE CONSERVATION CENTER

Over 150 wood bison, a species once thought to be extinct, await their release back into the wild. Be a part of this great conversation effort! Also meet orphaned bears, moose, muskox and more as award winning photographs await!

OPEN YEAR-ROUND!
Just 45 minutes south of Anchorage on the scenic Seward Highway! AWCC is a non-profit wildlife refuge located on a scenic 200 acre preserve dedicated to wildlife conservation and education.

Mile 79 Seward Highway
Portage, AK 99587
907.783.2025
alaskawildlife.org

Downtown Anchorage

Colorful banks of flowers mark entrances to Town Square from 5th and 6th avenues. (©Kris Valencia, staff)

Knik Arm

The Alaska Railroad

Tony Knowles Coastal Trail

↑ To Port of Anchorage
The Ulu Factory

Ship Creek Ave.

W. 1st

Alaska Railroad Depot

Elevated roadway to Government Hill only

Statehood Monument

W. 2nd

Anchorage (weekend) Market & Festival

Resolution Park

W. 3rd

Hilton

State Court Bldg.

Nesbitt Courthouse

Old Federal Bldg.

Bear Square Trolley Tours

Post Office

4th Ave Market Place

Alaska Veterans Museum

Downtown Bicycle Rental

Oscar Anderson House

W. 4th

Sunshine Plaza

RV Parking

Hotel Captain Cook

Log Cabin Visitor Center

Rondy HQ

David Green

Fire Dept.

Elderberry Park

Historic City Hall/ACVB

Westmark Hotel

Egan Convention Center

W. 5th

Rodeway Inn

People Mover

Center for the Performing Arts

Town Square

5th Ave. Mall

W. 6th

Oomingmak

City Hall

Anchorage Museum at Rasmuson Center

W. 7th

Hostel

Conoco Phillips Bldg.

Dena'ina Convention Center

Federal Bldg./ U.S. Courthouse

Quality Suites

W. 8th

N St.

M St.

L Street

K Street

I Street

H Street

G Street

F Street

E Street

D Street

C Street

B Street

A Street

Barrow St.

Cordova St.

Denali St.

Christensen Dr.

Clarion Suites

W. 9th

W. 9th

Delaney Park Strip

The best way to begin your exploration of downtown Anchorage is with a stop at the **Log Cabin Visitor Information Center** and adjacent **Downtown Visitor Information Center**, located on 4th Avenue and F Street. The picturesque Log Cabin visitor center is a favorite meeting place and popular photo subject with its sod roof and flowers. The Downtown visitor center (through the arch behind the Log Cabin) is housed in a modern addition to the city's historic City Hall. Pick up brochures and a copy of the Anchorage Convention and Visitors Bureau's *Official Guide to Anchorage* here. Phone (907) 257-2363; www.anchorage.net.

Visit the Ulu Factory. The ulu, or Eskimo woman's knife, is an all-purpose, traditional tool with a flat, fan-shaped blade that is used for cutting and scraping. A very popular and useful souvenir. At the Ulu Factory on West Ship Creek Avenue, visitors can learn the history of the ulu knife and see a demonstration. Free trolley rides to and from the factory from the Log Cabin Visitor Center downtown. Phone (907) 276-3119 or 1-800-488-5592; www.theULUfactory.com.

Enjoy the Flowers. Numerous hanging baskets transform the core area of downtown Anchorage, and thematic arrangements highlight the well-maintained flower

Visitor Information Center and Log Cabin visitor center on 4th Ave. and F Street.
(© Kris Valencia, staff)

beds lining the city's walkways. The Centennial Rose Garden is the centerpiece of the Delaney Park Strip at 9th and N streets, and the downtown area at the **Town Square** municipal park, located between 5th and 6th avenues along E Street, next door to the **Performing Arts Center**, offers the city's most spectacular flower displays in summer.

On the west wall of the J.C. Penney store is the "**Whaling Wall**," a 400-foot-long air-brushed mural of beluga whales, bowhead whales and seals by artist Wyland.

Oscar Anderson House Museum is located at the west end of 5th Avenue, 420 M St., in Elderberry Park. It is one of the city's first privately built wood-frame houses and Anchorage's only historic house museum. Built in 1915, it was home to Oscar Anderson, a Swedish immigrant and early Anchorage pioneer and businessman

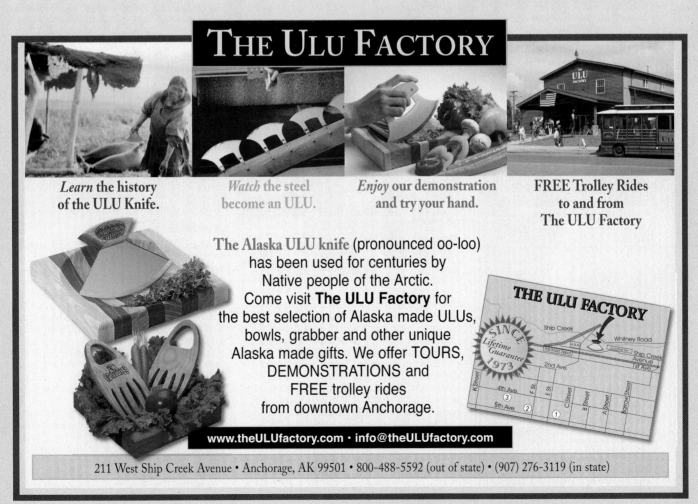

The Old Federal Building houses the Alaska Public Lands Information Center.
(©Kris Valencia, staff)

Court and main post office until the 1970s, when Federal courts and offices moved to the new federal building on West 7th and C Street, although, the refurbished court room in the west wing has been home to the federal bankruptcy court since 1988. When court is not in session—look for the "Open to the Public" sign displayed by the front door facing 4th Avenue—visitors are welcome in the Historic Court Room, which has a Depression-era mural by artist Arthur Kerrick, and visit the small conference room across the hall with its displays of old photos and a history of bankruptcy information panel.

Oomingmak, Musk Ox Producers' Co-operative, is a Native-owned co-operative specializing in knitted masterpieces. Using Qiviut, the soft and rare fiber from the arctic Musk Oxen, our 250 Native Alaskan knitters create hats and scarves in a variety of traditional patterns from their culture. Since 1969, this co-operative organization has provided the opportunity for Native women to earn a supplementary

income while still pursuing their subsistence lifestyle. For over 40 years, the exquisite items the co-op members make on their knitting needles have been worn with pride and enjoyment by satisfied customers from around the world. We invite you to visit us in downtown Anchorage at the little brown house with the Musk Ox mural on the corner of 6th and H streets. (907) 272-9225, 604 H St., Anchorage, AK 99501. www.qiviut.com. qiviut@gci.net. See display ad this section. [ADVERTISEMENT]

The Anchorage Museum, located at the corner of 7th Avenue and C Street, has something for the whole family. The place to start for adults with kids is the Imaginarium Discovery Center, which offers a hands-on Alaska science center with live animals in marine touch tanks. For very young children (5 and under), there is the TOTE KidSpace, which offers a variety of tactile experiences.

The 48-seat Thomas Planetarium is also part of the Imaginarium Discovery Center. Educational and entertaining films and presentations that explore the night sky and the solar system are offered.

On Level 2 of the Museum is the world-class Smithsonian Arctic Studies Center, with some 600 objects (on loan for 7 years). This is a marvel of exhibits and interactive touch screens with close-ups of displayed artifacts and videos of Native stories.

Also in the 2nd floor west wing is the ConocoPhillips gallery, with its contempo-

(the 18th person to arrive in what became Anchorage). Now on the National Register of Historic Places, it has been beautifully restored and is well worth a visit. Swedish Christmas tours, first 2 weekends in December. Tours (maximum 10 participants per group) may be possible if arranged in advance. Phone (907) 274-2336 for hours and fees.

Downtown City Parks. Peratrovich Park at 4th Avenue and E Street hosts the popular "Music in the Park" series on summer afternoons. The concerts, featuring local groups playing everything from jazz to country, take place from noon to 1 P.M. on Wednesdays, Thursdays and Fridays in

summer; check locally for a current schedule or online at website: www.AnchorageDowntown.org.

Elderberry Park, at the west end of 5th Avenue, faces Knik Arm and accesses the popular Coastal Trail, which begins at the end of West 2nd Avenue. Resolution Park, at 3rd Avenue and L Street (no parking adjacent to this park, it is directly off of L Street), displays a statue of Capt. James Cook overlooking the Knik Arm of the inlet which bears his name.

Delaney Park Strip, from A to P streets between 9th and 10th avenues, has ball fields, tennis courts and Engine No. 556 at 9th and E Street, a historic locomotive for children to explore. Delaney Park Strip also plays host to a number of special events throughout the year.

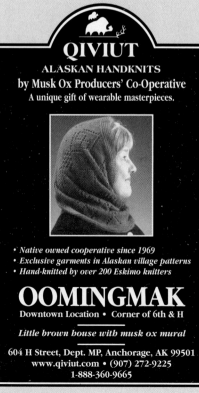

Anchorage Trolley Tours. Make the most of your stay in Anchorage by hopping aboard Anchorage's favorite trolley. Visit historic spots, watch floatplanes depart from Lake Hood, view the breathtaking mountains, and don't forget the camera for the many photo opportunities. Learn about Anchorage's past and present with tips on the best places for shopping, dining and entertainment. Phone (907) 276-5603; Cyrus Aldeman. www.Alaskatrolley.com. [ADVERTISEMENT]

The Old Federal Building at 605 West 4th Avenue (at F Street) is listed on the National Register of Historic Places and currently houses the Alaska Public Lands Information Center (see description on page 391) in the east wing. Built in 1940, this Federal Building served as the city's Federal

rary Alaska Native art exhibit featuring both traditional and non-traditional works.

Additional floors house rotating exhibits, while the Alaska History Gallery, a favorite with visitors for its artifacts, photos, maps, full-scale displays and detailed miniature dioramas depict Alaska Native cultures, the Russian occupation, the gold rush, WWII and statehood.

Walk down the stairs to the main level of the Atrium and take a break: sandwiches and coffee at the Atrium Cafe or full-service restaurant at Muse, just off the foyer. Also on this level are the Lower Atrium Gallery (rotating exhibits) and the Art of the North Gallery, with paintings by such Alaskan luminaries as Sydney Laurence.

The museum offers 4 docent guided 1-hour tours daily (included as part of the general admission). The themed tours take in the Alaska History Gallery, Art of the North Gallery and Smithsonian Arctic Studies Center. History tour at 11 A.M. and 1 P.M.; Art of the North tour at noon; and First Peoples of Alaska tour at 2 P.M. Current schedule at www.anchoragemuseum.org/visit/tours.aspx.

Regular museum admission is $12 for adults; $9 seniors/students/military; and $7 for ages 3–12; infants to 2 year-olds are free. The Culture Pass gets you admission to both the Anchorage Museum and Alaska Native Heritage Center for $29.95.

Summer museum hours (May 1 through Sept. 30) are 9 A.M. to 6 P.M. daily. Winter hours are 10 A.M.–6 P.M. Tuesday through Saturday and noon–6 P.M. Sunday; closed Mondays, and major holidays. Wheelchair accessible. Lockers are available. Phone (907) 929-9200 for recorded information; www.anchoragemuseum.org.

Anchorage Alaska Public Lands Information Center (AAPLIC), located in the historic Old Federal Building (see description above) on 4th Avenue at F Street, offers a wide variety of exhibits, movies, special programs and information on all of Alaska's state and federal parks, forests, wildlife refuges and other public lands. Natural history and cultural exhibits, interactive GIS stations and a self-help trip-planning area are available. Center staff provides additional

Alaska Territorial Guard statue stands in front of the Alaska Veterans Museum at 333 West 4th Avenue. *(©Kris Valencia, staff)*

assistance, maps, brochures and current travel information. Federal passes (annual, senior and access) and state park day-use passes are available.

Rangers, authors and other special speakers present programs at 2 P.M. daily in the summer; call for current schedule. A walking tour at 11 A.M. and 2:30 P.M. daily during the summer, delves into Captain Cook's exploration of Alaska. Museum scavenger hunts are a popular activity enjoyed by young and old alike. The center is open year-round. Summer hours (Memorial Day to Labor Day) are 9 A.M. to 5:30 P.M. daily (building doors close at 5 P.M.); winter hours are 10 A.M. to 5 P.M. Monday through Friday; closed weekends and holidays. Hours may change; please call ahead. For information, phone (907) 644-3661 or 1-866-869-6887; write the center at 605 W. 4th Ave., Suite 105, Anchorage, AK 99501; or visit the website at alaska centers.gov.

Alaska Veterans Museum, 333 W. 4th Ave., Ste. 227, was created to honor the memory and sacrifices of our veterans. A small museum that packs "a wallop for all 5 Armed Services and the Merchant Marine," they are open Monday through Saturday, 10 A.M. to 6 P.M., in summer. Phone (907) 677-8802; www.alaskaveterans.com.

Alaska State Trooper Museum. This unique museum presents the history of law enforcement in the Territory and State of Alaska, with displays of photos and exhibits of historic police equipment. Gifts and memorabilia are available for purchase. Admission free. Hours are 10 A.M. to 4 P.M. weekdays and noon to 4 P.M. Saturdays. 245 W. 5th Ave., between B and C streets. Phone (907) 279-5050 or (800) 770-5050; foast@gci.net; www.alaskatroopermuseum.com.

Visit the Anchorage Market & Festival. This popular outdoor market operates

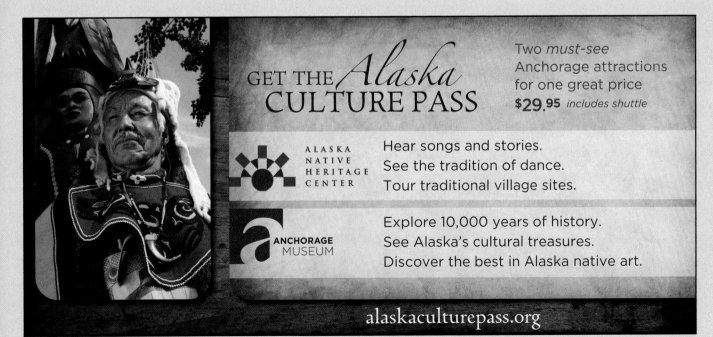

Alaska Statehood Monument includes a bust of President Eisenhower.
(©Kris Valencia, staff)

10 A.M. to 6 P.M, Saturday and Sunday, from mid-May through mid-September. Held in the parking lot at 3rd Avenue between C and E streets, there is no admission fee. About 300 booths sell a variety of Alaskan-made and Alaska-grown products as well as handmade and imported home and novelty items of all types. Plenty of food booths and live entertainment. It's a great family event. Phone (907) 272-5634, or visit www.anchoragemarkets.com.

Alaska Statehood Monument. Located at the corner of 2nd Avenue and E Street (just a block downhill from the Hilton) at the Ship Creek Overlook. A plaque and bronze bust of President Eisenhower commemorate the Alaska Statehood Act that made Alaska the 49th state on January 3, 1959.

First Fridays. Anchorage's numerous art galleries offer special exhibits and honor the artists at late afternoon/evening receptions on the first Friday of each month. For detailed information about the artists and locations of the galleries, consult the entertainment and arts sections of the local newspapers or www.anchoragedowntown.org.

Anchorage Fire Department Museum, located in the headquarters building at 4th Avenue and A Street, has a vintage 1921 American LaFrance pumper, the department's first fire truck. Check out the equipment and technology and learn about the history of the Anchorage Fire Department. Hours are Monday–Friday 7:30 A.M. to 4:30 P.M. For more information, call (907) 267-4936.

Port of Anchorage. A fascinating look behind the scenes of cargo carrying in Anchorage, AK, this port is also designated as a National Strategic Port by the Department of Defense. Stop by in summer for a tour. Please check in advance for tour times and availability at www.portofalaska.com.

See an Old Schoolhouse: The Pioneer Schoolhouse at 3rd Avenue and Eagle Street is a 2-story memorial to the late Ben Crawford, an Anchorage banker. On the National Register of Historic Places, this was the first school in Anchorage. The interior is not open to the public.

Ship Creek Salmon Viewing. From downtown, either walk down the hill from the Hilton toward the train station, or stroll down Christensen Street (with its fish fence and fine views of the inlet) past the train station, to reach the Ship Creek area. There is a paved path that begins adjacent the Bridge coffee house/gift shop (behind the Ulu Factory and Comfort Inn) that follows Ship Creek to a pedestrian bridge across the creek. Visitors can watch the salmon—as well as the fishermen—from spots along either bank, from the viewing platform or from the dam. Watch for kings from early June until mid-July, silvers in August.

(Continued from page 387)
RV rental agencies (see advertisements this section).

Parking (cars and RVs): Diamond Parking Service (www.diamondparking.com) manages 33 surface lots in Anchorage with daily and monthly parking; fees average $5 for 0-2 hours. EasyPark (Anchorage Community Development Authority) manages all on-street metered parking for downtown Anchorage as well as more than a dozen lots and garages. For location and rates of parking, visit www.easyparkalaska.com/. EasyPark office located at 440 B Street; phone (907) 276-PARK (7275). After Hours or Security (907)297-4471; Email info@easyparkalaska.com

Highway: Anchorage can be reached via the Glenn Highway and the Seward Highway. See GLENN HIGHWAY and SEWARD HIGHWAY sections for details.

Attractions
(See also Downtown section beginning on page 388.)

Enjoy the Parks. Anchorage parks are rich in the range of activities they offer, with something for everyone's taste, from small "pocket parks" perfect for relaxing or picnicking to vast tracts set aside for skiing, hiking and bicycling. According to the Parks & Recreation website (www.muni.org/departments/parks/pages/default.aspx) they have "10,946 acres of municipal parkland; 223 parks with 82 playgrounds; 250 miles of trails and greenbelts linking neighborhoods with surrounding natural open spaces and wildlife habitat (135 miles of paved trails); 110 athletic fields; 5 pools; and 11 recreation facilities." For information on park facilities and group reservations to use municipal park picnic facilities, phone (907) 343-4355 or email parks@muni.org.

Parks & Recreation also offers 2 facilities to rent for indoor functions such as meetings, parties, weddings, receptions, seminars and special events: Lidia Selkregg Chalet (in Russian Jack Springs Park) and Kincaid Outdoor Center in Kinkaid Park.

Following we highlight just a few of Anchorage's parks and trails.

Kincaid Park: It is not unusual to run into a moose or see a bear at 1,400-acre Kincaid Park. Located southwest of the airport, this park's rugged trails are popular in summer with mountain bikers, runners and disc golfers. In winter, the trails are groomed for cross-country skiers. To reach the Kincaid Outdoor Center, follow Raspberry Road west from Minnesota Drive to the park entrance. The park road winds uphill (past trailheads) to end at a large parking area in front of the Center, which houses an information desk, tables, restrooms and vending machines. The Center has limited hours; park gates lock at 10 P.M. daily. Kincaid is also accessible via the Tony Knowles Coastal Trail, which follows the shoreline from West 2nd Avenue, downtown, to the Kincaid Outdoor Center.

Russian Jack Springs: One of the city's oldest parks, with land transferred from the BLM in 1948, Russian Jack Springs has a lot going on. Facilities at the park include Selkregg Chalet, the Mann Leiser Memorial Greenhouse within the Municipal Greenhouse Complex, Cartee and RJS Softball Complexes, soccer fields, the Girl Scouts Day Camp, tennis courts, picnic/playground areas, the 9-hole Russian Jack Springs golf course and 9 miles of bike/ski trails.

Valley of the Moon Park: The best park for parents looking for a playground to keep their children entertained, Valley of the Moon Park is located on Arctic Boulevard/ E Street in the Chester Creek Greenbelt. This park, voted best playground by *Anchorage Daily News* readers, has parking, restrooms, a large grassy area and picnic tables.

Earthquake Park: Set aside to commemorate the 1964 Good Friday Earthquake, Earthquake Park offers views as well as interpretive displays about the quake (evidence of the 9.2 earthquake has been obscured by time). A paved path leads from the parking lot to the earthquake exhibit and Knik Arm overlook. From the New Seward Highway, drive west (toward the water) on Northern Lights Boulevard for 3.5 miles to reach Earthquake Park.

Point Woronzof: The best park views of Cook Inlet (Knik Arm) and the Alaska Range are at Point Woronzof. Drive west on Northern Lights Boulevard, which becomes Point Woronzof Road at Postmark Drive. (Postmark Drive leads one mile south to Anchorage's airport post office.) A viewpoint at this intersection offers parking and view of downtown Anchorage, Cook Inlet, and Denali and Foraker (on clear days). Follow Point Woronzof Road 1 mile to Point Woronzof, a favorite spot to watch the sunset, with fine views of the inlet and mountains. Point Woronzof can also be reached via the Tony Knowles Coastal Trail.

Off Leash Dog Parks. Designated areas of University Lake Park, Far North Bicentennial Park (North Gasline Trail), Russian Jack Park, Connors Bog and South Anchorage Sports Park are off-leash dog parks. Areas are marked, and dog owners may let their dogs play unleashed, as long as Parks & Recreation and Animal Control regulations are followed. For information and maps, visit http://www.muni.org/Departments/parks/Pages/DogParks.aspx.

Take in a Free Film. The Alaska Public Lands Information Center, located in the historic Old Federal Building on 4th Avenue and F Street, offers a schedule of films about Alaska in their theatre. (907) 644-3661 or www.nps.gov/anch.

Sea Services Veterans Memorial Park, at the mouth of Ship Creek, is a good place to see the Anchorage waterfront, with its huge cargo cranes off-loading supplies from container ships. The park is dedicated to veterans of the Navy, Marine Corps, Coast Guard and Merchant Marine. The monument consists of a huge anchor and chain weighing 22,500 pounds upon a raised mound. The park also offers good whale watching when belugas are in the inlet. From downtown, take E Street and West 2nd down the hill to merge with North C Street. Continue across the second set of railroad tracks and turn left. The access road follows Ship Creek out to the small-boat dry dock harbor and the park.

Tour Anchorage by Bicycle or On Foot: The municipality has an impressive and ever-expanding pedestrian and bike trail system (135 miles of paved trails). The 11-mile-long **Tony Knowles Coastal Trail** begins downtown, runs through Earthquake Park, then wraps around the airport (it is not uncommon to encounter moose in the narrow strip of woods between the ocean and the fenced runways). The Tony Knowles trail ends at Kincaid Park, with its roller-coaster terrain that serves cross-country skiers in winter and mountain bikers in

Alaska Railroad's Historic Anchorage Depot on First Avenue serves passenger trains to Seward, Denali Park and Anchorage. (©Kris Valencia, staff)

summer.

Tony Knowles Coastal Trail also connects with the **Ship Creek Trail**, which parallels Ship Creek from North C Street 2.5-miles East to William Tyson Elementary School. The western trailhead is located at the intersection of North C Street and Ship Creek by near the Alaska Railroad Corporate Building.

For cyclists and joggers looking for a pleasant ride or run through the trees, the **Lanie Fleischer Chester Creek Trail** fills the bill. The 4-mile trail stretches from Westchester Lagoon, at 15th Avenue and U Street, to Goose Lake, a favorite summer swimming beach (accessible from UAA Drive). Chester Creek trail is accessible from all of the parks along its length, including Tikishla (in the Airport Heights area), Valley of the Moon Park (Arctic Boulevard/E Street) and Westchester Lagoon, where it junctions with the Coastal bike trail.

Campbell Creek Greenbelt paved trail system begins at Dimond Boulevard, between Minnesota Drive and Jewel Lake Road, and follows Campbell Creek to the Old Seward. Taku Lake/Campbell Park, located off King Street, offers fishing access (stocked) and picnic tables.

Peter Roberts of Downtown Bicycle Rental says that bicyclists can combine the Coastal Trail, Ship Creek, Chester Creek and Campbell Creek greenbelt trails, creating a 36-mile circuit with "very little road riding." Their website's Trails/Routes drop-down menu at www.alaska-bike-rentals.com/Home.aspx has information on the city's major bike trails as well as Kincaid Park.

Chugach State Park also offers a multi-

Anchorage boasts an extensive bike trail system and a number of small lakes for fishing and swimming. (© Kris Valencia, staff)

tude of options for bicyclists (and even more for hikers)—from leisurely rides on easy gravel roads to gnarly mountainside single track. A few of the most popular area bike trails include Bird to Gird, a paved 7-mile trail that parallels the Seward Highway along Turnagain Arm; Eklutna Lakeside Trail, a 13.5-mile dirt trail along Eklutna Lake; and the Powerline Trail, an 11-mile dirt trail in Chugach State Park. Chugach Parks trail maps are available at the Alaska Public Lands Information Center downtown.

Free Anchorage bike maps are available at the Anchorage Convention and Visitors Bureau's Visitor Center on 4th Avenue and F Street and at Downtown Bicycle Rental (W. 4th Avenue and C Street). See also www.trailsofanchorage.com/map.htm.

The **Tour of Anchorage** bike race takes place in summer. For more information on this event and other local bike races, visit www.arcticbike.org, the website for the non-profit Arctic Bicycle Club, which promotes bicycling safety, education and sporting activities in Anchorage.

Visit the Alaska Native Heritage Center:

Located just 10 minutes east of downtown, the Heritage Center allows visitors the opportunity to experience a sample of Alaska's Native cultures in one facility. Located on 26 wooded acres on Heritage Center Drive (take the North Muldoon Road exit off the Glenn Highway), the center includes the 26,000-square-foot Welcome House, 6 traditional village settings, a 2-acre lake and walking trails.

Many of the programs and exhibits celebrating Alaska Native culture take place indoors in the Welcome House. Visitors experience Alaska Native culture first-hand through engaging storytelling, authentic Native song and dance, artist demonstrations, and Native Games demonstration in the Gathering Place. A 95-seat theater offers a film introduction to Native history and culture.

Heritage Gifts provides a wonderful shopping opportunity for Native arts and crafts. An outdoor walk around Tiulana Lake takes visitors to 6 different regions, each representing one of Alaska's 6 Native cultures: Athabascan, Yupik/Cupik, Inupiaq,

Unangax, Alutiiq and Tlingit/Haida/Eyak/Tsimshian. Demonstrations of traditional techniques for fishing, hunting, building kayaks and constructing dwellings take place in summer.

Heritage Center hours are from 9 A.M. to 5 P.M. daily mid-May through September; 10 A.M. to 5 P.M. Saturdays only in winter. Summer rates: adults, $24.95 (Alaskans pay $9.95); children (7-16), $16.95; military/seniors (62 or older), $21.15. Only open for special events in winter (October–April), reduced rates. Phone (907) 330-8000; toll free 1-800-315-6608; www.alaskanative.net.

The Alaska Culture Pass (alaskaculturepass.net) gives you admission to the Alaska Native Heritage Center and the Anchorage Museum for $28.95, a 20 percent discount. This includes shuttle service between the two locations. Group rates available for 20 or more people.

Running events. Anchorage also has its share of 5Ks, 10Ks, marathons and triathlons. The Heart Run, held at the end of April, kicks off the summer running season. Two popular women's runs are the Alaska Run for Women in June and the Women's Gold Nugget Triathlon in mid-May. Many Anchorage residents celebrate Summer Solstice by running in the Mayor's Marathon, half-marathon or 5-miler (June 21, 2014). Mid-August there is also the Big Wild Life Run which features a children's run, 5K race, half and full marathons as well as a team marathon relay.

Information on running events can be found at www.anchoragerunningclub.org. Anchorage Parks & Recreation's complete schedule of city and statewide running events is at www.muni.org/Departments/parks/Pages/RunnersCalendar.aspx.

Watch Small Planes: Drive out to Merrill Field, Lake Hood or Lake Spenard for an afternoon of airplane watching.

While at Merrill Field, named for early Alaska aviator, Russell Hyde Merrill, you can see more than 1,100 takeoffs and landings on a summer day. Follow 15th Avenue East to light at Lake Otis Parkway, and turn north on Merrill Field Drive. This route takes you under the approach to one of the runways. Merrill Field is also accessible off the Glenn Highway and from Airport Heights Drive (across from Northway Mall). For more information, visit http://www.muni.org/departments/merrill_field/pages/default.aspx.

Lake Hood is the world's largest and busiest seaplane base, with approximately 500 takeoffs and landings on a peak summer day. Easy access to lakes Hood and Spenard off International Airport Road: Heading west

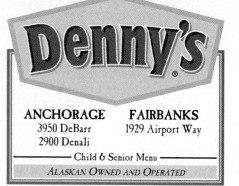

from Minnesota, turn right on Spenard then left on Aviation Drive, which follows the shore of Lake Spenard and dead-ends at the Dept. of Transportation parking lot. From here you are looking at the channel connecting lakes Hood and Spenard, which is used by floatplanes shuttling between the two lakes or for take-offs and landings. From the DOT building, get back onto International Airport way going west (towards the airport) then exit for the Aviation Museum on Lake Hood (see description following).

Alaska Aviation Museum, 4721 Aircraft Dr. is on the south shore of Lake Hood in Anchorage, the busiest seaplane base in the world. The museum preserves and displays Alaska's aviation heritage in 5 hangars. Observe rare aircraft being restored or pilot the on site flight simulator.

The museum features over 25 Alaskan aircraft, bush pilot photo exhibits, 2 theaters and a unique gift store. RV parking. Open in summer (May 15–Sept. 15), 9 A.M. to 5 P.M. daily. Winter hours (Sept. 16–May 14), 9 A.M. to 5 P.M. Wednesday–Saturday, Sunday noon–5 P.M. (closed Monday–Tuesday). Phone (907) 248-5325. Admission fees (subject to change): Adults $10, with 20 percent discount for active military and veterans; seniors and students (age 12–18), $8; children 5 to 12; $6; children under 5 free. Group rates available. Wheelchair accessible. Web address is: www.alaskaairmuseum.org.

Enjoy a stroll through the Alaska Botanical Garden, located at 4601 Campbell Airstrip Road. A non-profit public garden dedicated to education, research, conservation and recreation, the Alaska Botanical Garden showcases native Alaskan plants and hardy perennials (standouts include Himalayan blue poppies and the Gold Medal peony collection), as well as wildflowers, herbs and alpine plants. Explore on your own (open year-round) or join a guided tour (offered daily at 1 P.M. or by appointment, June through August).

A paved loop trail provides easy walking through the boreal spruce and birch forest to visit the various gardens. Signs identify plants in the garden areas. There are a retail nursery and a gift shop near the garden entrance. A 1.1-mile nature trail offers views of Campbell Creek and the Chugach Mountains. Open year-round during daylight hours. Entrance fee payable at gate. Food allowed only in the entrance area due to the high concentration of wildlife in area, including moose and bears. Popular special events here include the Annual Plant Sale in May. Call for information on hours, special events and guided tours; phone (907) 770-3692; email garden@alaskabg.org; www.alaskabg.org.

From the Seward Highway, drive east (toward the mountains) 3.2 miles on Tudor and turn right (south) on Campbell Airstrip Road (across from Baxter), and continue 0.2 mile past the fire station and turn left into the Botanical Garden/Benny Benson School Parking lot. From the Glenn Highway go south on Muldoon Road, which becomes Tudor, and turn left (south) on Campbell Airstrip Road. Free parking.

Alaska Heritage Museum at Wells Fargo, on Northern Lights Boulevard and C Street, has an excellent collection of over 900 Alaska Native artifacts and fine art by Alaskan artists. Started and maintained by the prominent Rasmuson family of Alaska, the collection continues to keep Alaska art in the state and to share Alaska history and culture

Watch floatplanes take-off and land on Lakes Hood and Spenard.
(©Kris Valencia, staff)

with residents and visitors. The collection includes prehistoric artifacts, carved ivory pieces, a large basket collection and examples of traditional Native clothing.

Sydney Laurence, Eustace Ziegler and Fred Machetanz are among featured artists. A 46 oz. gold nugget found near Ruby, AK, is part of the Alaskan mining history collection.

Free admission. Open weekdays year-round: noon–5 P.M. summer; noon–4 P.M. winter. Phone (907) 265-2834; www.wellsfargohistory.com. Wheelchair accessible.

Other Native art displays and gift shops are located at the Alaska Native Medical Center and the Anchorage Museum at Rasmuson Center.

Carl Nesjar Memorial Fountain at Z.J. Loussac Library. Cuddy Family Park is to the south of the library. (©Kris Valencia, staff)

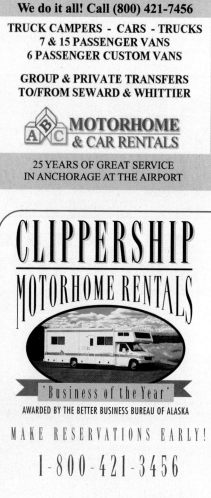
Z. J. Loussac Public Library, located at 36th Avenue and Denali Street (3600 Denali St.), is headquarters for the Anchorage Public Library system. Its unique architecture also makes it a local landmark, as does its Carl Nesjar Memorial Fountain, dedicated to Mrs. Jack M. (Kay) Linton, and statue of William H. Seward. The library hosts various events throughout the year, from "Live at the Library" and summer reading programs for kids, teens, and adults. Loussac Library has an extensive collection of books related to Alaska history and culture. Hours are Monday–Thursday 10 A.M. to 9 P.M., Friday and Saturday 10 A.M. to 6 P.M. and Sunday 1 P.M. to 5 P.M. For information, phone (907) 343-2975 or visit www.anchoragelibrary.org.

Adjacent to the library is **Cuddy Family Park**, with picnic tables, benches, paths, a pond and a large open field used for kite flying and other summer fun. An ice-skating oval is available at Cuddy Park in winter.

Science and Nature Museum (formerly Museum of Natural History) is located at 201 N. Bragaw St., 2 blocks north off the Glenn Highway. The museum houses interpretive collections of polar dinosaur fossils, minerals, Ice Age life and mammals, whales, puffins and other birds, Alaskan artifacts and interactive, touchable displays and wildlife mounts, and more. It has a children's play area with a library and several activity areas. Special activities for the family every week in the summer and special events throughout the year. Admission fee: Adults $5; children over the age of 2, $3; senior/military discounts. Special events take place throughout the year. For information, call (907) 274-2400, or visit www.alaskamuseum.org.

Take a Tour: Tour operators offer local and area sightseeing tours. These range from a 1-hour narrated trolley tour of Anchorage to full-day tours of area attractions such as Portage Glacier and Alyeska Resort. Flightseeing tours provide an up-close view of Mount McKinley and a bird's-eye view of bears and other wildlife. Two-day or longer excursions by motorcoach, rail, ferry and air to nearby attractions such as Prince William Sound or remote areas are also available. See advertisers listed under Tours & Transportation on page 380.

Alaska Heritage Tours. Customize your self-drive adventure by adding lodging or activities with just one call. We make it easy to book your adventure while you travel along the scenic byways. Visit Kenai Fjords National Park to photograph wildlife; cruise near 10,000-year-old glacier ice in Prince William Sound; and explore Denali National Park. We package the best of Alaska. 1-877-258-6877; www.Alaska HeritageTours.com/mpl. [ADVERTISEMENT]

Portage Glacier Cruise. See Alaska's most popular attractions, up close from the deck of the MV *Ptarmigan*. This Gray Line of Alaska cruise takes you right to the face of the imposing 10-story-high Portage Glacier. An incredible experience. Tours depart Anchorage twice daily or you may drive to Portage Glacier and board the MV *Ptarmigan* for the cruise-only portion. Tour price is $79 per person; cruise-only price is $29 per person. Prices subject to change. Phone 1-800-544-2206. [ADVERTISEMENT]

Tour a Campus: Two colleges are located in Anchorage: the University of Alaska Anchorage at 3211 Providence Dr., Anchorage, AK 99508, and Alaska Pacific (formerly Alaska Methodist) University at 4101 University Dr., Anchorage, AK 99508.

Alaska Pacific University (APU) was dedicated June 29, 1959, the same year that Alaska became the 49th state, and is now the state's largest private 4-year university. APU's first students were enrolled in the fall of 1960. The university offers liberal-arts-based educational programs for all ages. The APU campus is located on 170 forested acres, featuring the 3-tiered Atwood Fountain, Waldron Carillon Bell Tower and the Jim Mahaffey Trail System for skiers, runners, hikers and mountain bikers. Phone (907) 561-1266 or (800) 252-7528 for tours or information about university programs, or visit www.alaskapacific.edu.

The University of Alaska Anchorage

(UAA) is the largest branch of the University of Alaska, with a main campus in the heart of Anchorage, satellite campuses in Kenai, Palmer, Soldotna and Valdez and extension centers in many other communities around the state. Founded as Anchorage Community College in 1952, it has undergone explosive growth in recent years. Expansion and development continue as UAA attracts a larger and more diverse student base. To meet the needs of Alaska's far-flung population, it has become a world leader in distance education. Fully accredited, the university offers more than 120 graduate and undergraduate degree programs, plus many associate degrees and professional certificates. For more information, call (907) 786-1800 or visit www.uaa.alaska.edu or www.alaska.edu.

Joint Base Elmendorf-Richardson (JBER, pronounced j-bear), formerly Elmendorf Air Force Base and Fort Richardson, is reached via the Boniface Gate or the D Stret Gate off the Glenn Highway. Visitors must go to the Visitor's Center at either of these gates for base access. Visit their website at www.jber.af.mil. Tours are possible if arranged in advance. See link at website or contact public relations.

Visit the Alaska Zoo, located on 20 wooded acres along O'Malley Road in South Anchorage, 2 miles east of the Seward Highway. The zoo provides homes for more than 130 orphaned and injured animals from both arctic and subarctic climates, making it the most complete collection of animals in the state of Alaska. Resident zoo species include brown bears, moose, Dall sheep, river otters, black bears, fox, muskoxen, bald eagles, wolverines, wolves and more. The polar bear exhibit is home to an orphaned female polar bear named Ahpun, and her male polar bear roommate, Lyutyik (or "Louie"). The polar bear exhibit features an underwater viewing area and waterfalls. The zoo is also home to many non-native species, including Bactrian camels, Amur tigers, snow leopards, and Tibetan yaks.

Services include a gift shop, coffee shop and shuttle service (summers only) from downtown Anchorage. Summer zoo hours are from 9 A.M. to 6 P.M. daily, May 1 through Labor Day, with extended hours until 9 P.M. on Tuesdays and Fridays. Tuesday evenings in the summer include educational programs beginning at 7 P.M. and musical acts at 7 P.M. on Friday evenings in summer. Daily, behind-the-scenes naturalist tours are also offered during summer months. Winter hours are from 10 A.M. to 4:30 P.M. (or dusk) daily (except for Thanksgiving and Christmas). Educational camps and programs for children and families are also offered year-round. "Zoo Lights," a fun display of lighted animal silhouettes with movement and sound, takes place during the Christmas holidays and Fur Rondy with evening hours Thursday-Sunday from Thanksgiving. Entrance fee of $7.

Zoo admission is $12 adults, $9 seniors and military with ID, $6 children 3–17. For more information and details on special events visit www.alaskazoo.org. Phone (907) 346-3242. The zoo is wheelchair accessible.

Hike Chugach Park. Chugach State Park's 500,000-acre wonderland borders the edge of the Anchorage bowl. Whether it is a leisurely afternoon stroll or a strenuous, weekend-long backpack trip, the Chugach Mountains offer wilderness opportunities for everyone.

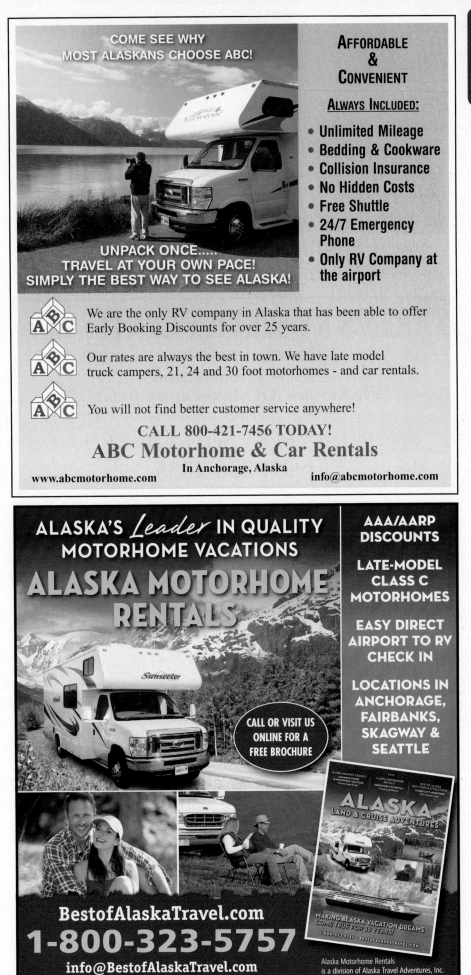

View from Flattop hiking trail, part of Chugach State Park's Hillside Trail System. This is Alaska's most popular hiking trail. (©Kris Valencia, staff)

The park is open year-round and there are a number of easy-to-access trailheads from Girdwood to Eagle River. A park trail map is available. To see the map online go to www.dnr.alaska.gov/parks/aspunits/index.htm and click link to access park map. For the printed version, visit Chugach State Park headquarters in the Potter Section House, 11.8 miles south of downtown Anchorage on the Seward Highway, or contact Chugach State Park, H.C. 52, Box 8999, Indian, AK 99540; (907) 345-5014. For hiking trail information you may also stop by the Alaska Public Lands Information Center on 4th Avenue in downtown Anchorage (phone 907/644-3661) or phone the Department of Natural Resources at (907) 269-8400.

The most popular and accessible day hikes in Anchorage are located in the park's Hillside Trail System with its 3 trailheads—Glen Alps, Prospect Heights and Upper Huffman—all accessed via residential areas on the Anchorage Hillside. All trailhead parking lots have a $5/day parking fee. Weather conditions can change rapidly in Chugach Park—always bring extra clothing, water and proper footwear. Bears and moose frequent the area, so make noise.

Hillside trails, known for their panoramic views of the city and surrounding mountains and valleys, include Powerline, Wolverine Peak, Near Point, and—the most popular hiking trail in the state—Flattop. On a sunny summer day, it sometimes seems that half of Anchorage is out hiking to the top of Flattop Mountain. The 3.5-mile (round trip) trail takes anywhere from 2 to 5 hours and offers spectacular views of the Anchorage bowl, Cook Inlet and the Alaska Range. As popular as it is, it is imperative to be cautious while climbing. Accidents and rescues are not uncommon. Above all, stay on the path.

Flattop Mountain (elev. 3, 510 feet), and Powerline trail are accessed from the Glen Alps trailhead. From the New Seward Highway, turn east on O'Malley Road. At Hillside Drive go right (south) for 1 mile, then turn left (east) at Upper Huffman Road. Go uphill 0.7 mile and turn right (south) on Toilsome Hill Drive (4-wheel drive vehicles and chains are advised in winter). Toilsome will switchback uphill for another 1.3 miles, becoming Glen Alps Road. Look for the Glen Alps parking lot on the left.

There is a Flattop Shuttle from downtown (fee charged) that brings hikers to the trailhead; phone (907) 279-3334; www.hike-anchorage-alaska.com.

Powerline trail is an old gravel roadway that heads up the South Fork Campbell Creek Valley from Glen Alps parking lot. Hikers and bikers enjoy the 12-mile trail for its rolling terrain and relatively flat surface. A number of trails branch off from the Powerline trail to access surrounding peaks.

To the north of the Glen Alps trailhead is Prospect Heights trailhead for Near Point and Wolverine Peak trails. From the New Seward Highway, turn east on O'Malley Road and follow it approximately 4 miles. After a sharp left (north) turn, take a right (east) on Upper O'Malley and go uphill approximately 0.5 mile. At the T-intersection, take a left (north) on Prospect Drive and follow it for 1 mile to the Prospect Heights parking lot.

Visit the Greenhouses: The municipality maintains the extensive Mann Leiser greenhouses and horticulture complex at Russian Jack Park, 1321 Lidia Selkregg Lane, where myriad plantings supply local parks—like downtown's Town Square—with flowers. The horticulture section of Anchorage Parks & Recreation is resonsible for planting and maintaining the city's 461 flower beds and baskets with more than 76,000 annual flowers at 81 sites, as well as trees and shrubs and turf throughout Anchorage.

Visitors to the greenhouse enjoy the displays of tropical plants, the fish pond and the aviary where finches, cockatiels and tropical birds enliven an attractive area popular for small weddings and volunteer-guided educational tours. Open daily year-round, 8 A.M. to 3 P.M., (closed holidays). Phone (907) 343-4717; www.muni.org/Departments/parks/Pages/Greenhouse.aspx.

Watch the Tide Come In: With frequent tidal ranges of 30 feet within 6 hours, and some approaching 40 feet, one of Anchorage's best nature shows is the action of the tides in both the Knik and Turnagain arms of upper Cook Inlet. Vantage points along Knik Arm are Earthquake Park, Elderberry Park (west end of 5th Avenue), Resolution Park (near corner of 3rd Avenue and L Street) and the Anchorage small-boat harbor.

Turnagain Arm has one of the highest tides in North America, rising to a maximum

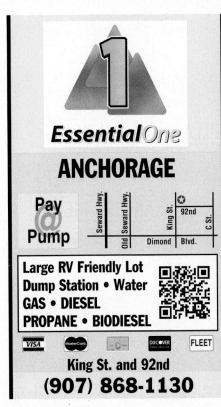

height of 42 feet. There are good views of Turnagain Arm from the Seward Highway, starting about 12 miles south of Anchorage. Good overlooks for Turnagain tides are Beluga Point at **Milepost S 110.4** Seward Highway, 16.6 miles south of Anchorage; and Bird Point at **Milepost S 96.5**, 30.5 miles south of Anchorage. With careful timing you might see a bore tide, an interesting phenomenon rarely seen elsewhere. A bore tide is a foaming wall of tidal water, up to 6 feet in height, formed by a flood tide surging into the constricted inlet of Knik and Turnagain arms.

CAUTION: In most places, the mud flats of Knik and Turnagain arms are like quicksand. Do not go wading!

Play Golf: What better way to enjoy the midnight sun than on a golf course? Anchorage offers unique opportunities for golfing enthusiasts, from short, par-3 courses to 36-hole links.

The Russian Jack Springs Golf Course, located in Russian Jack Springs Park, is run by Anchorage Parks & Recreation. It is a 9-hole course that features artificial greens, wooded fairways, beautiful scenery and is just a 15 minute drive from downtown Anchorage. For additional information or tee-times call (907) 343-6992.

The Anchorage Golf Course is an 18-hole, par 72 course located about 15 minutes from downtown Anchorage. Tee times begin as early as 4:30 A.M., and golfers can play until after midnight on long summer days. It offers a pro shop, lessons, a driving range and putting green, snack bar, pull carts, electric carts and club rentals. Open May–October depending on weather. For more information, call the pro shop at (907) 522-3363 or visit http://anchoragegolfcourse.com.

Moose Run is a 36-hole, military-run facility accessed via Arctic Valley Road off of the Glenn Highway. Moose Run has a driving range, clubhouse, and plenty of wildlife viewing opportunities on its Hill and Creek Courses. In 2007, the Creek Course was ranked #49 in a list of America's 50 Toughest Golf Courses. Its Hill Course was named in *Golf Digest's* 2008-2009 "Best Places to Play."

Tanglewood Lakes Golf Club maintains an 9-hole, par-3 course with a chalet for parties at 11801 Brayton Dr.; phone (907) 345-4600 for greens fees. Tanglewood also has a golf "dome" with an indoor driving range. Located on the east side of the New Seward Highway between Huffman and O'Malley exits (use 1-way frontage road north from the Huffman exit).

Alaska's golf season lasts from May to September, depending on the weather.

Play Disc Golf: Disc golf is played with a plastic flying disc instead of clubs and a ball, and the "hole" is a metal basket mounted on a pole. Players throw their discs into the baskets and the low score wins. A round of disc golf takes only 1 to 2 hours, can be played year-round and is usually free. Anchorage has many established courses. Two of the most popular are at Kincaid Park and Westchester Lagoon. Kincaid is a grass/dirt, 18-basket, par 54 course that begins near the park's chalet. Westchester Lagoon is a par 54 grass/dirt course with 9 baskets that begins near the parking lot. Visit www.alaskadiscgolf.com for a list of all courses and dates of local tournaments and other events.

Play Tennis: The municipality of Anchorage maintains almost 50 tennis courts. In addition, private clubs offer year-round indoor courts. Parks & Recreation offers tennis lessons in June through mid-August; phone (907) 343-4121 for details.

Watch Birds: Excellent bird-watching opportunities are abundant within the city limits. Westchester Lagoon and lakes Hood and Spenard, for example, are teeming with seaplanes but also, during the summer, are nesting areas for grebes and arctic loons. Also seen are sandhill cranes, widgeons, arctic terns, mew gulls, green-winged teals and sandpipers.

Large flocks of Canada geese nest and raise their young here during the summer. It

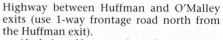
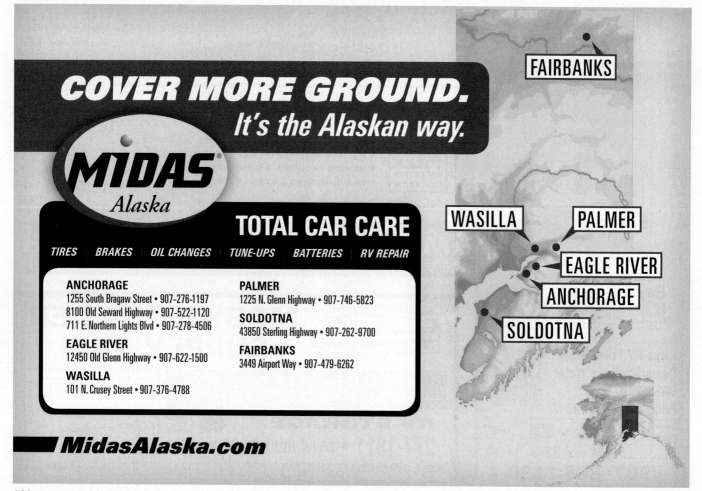

is not unusual to see traffic at a standstill as a pair of geese, followed by a tandem procession of goslings, cross the street.

Another great spot is the **Potter Point State Game Refuge** (also known as Potter Marsh or the Anchorage Coastal Wildlife Refuge), south of downtown on the Seward Highway at **Milepost S 117.6**. Viewing boardwalks extend over the marshland offering close-up photo opportunities. Early July evenings are best, according to local bird watchers. Forests surrounding Anchorage also are good for warblers, juncos, robins, white-crowned sparrows, varied thrushes and other species.

At the Park for All People on W. 19th Avenue and Spenard Road in the Chester Creek Greenbelt, a nature trail winds through a bird-nesting area.

See a Baseball Game: Every summer the Alaska Baseball League hosts some of the nation's top college players (among past notables are Tom Seaver and 1998 home-run king Mark McGwire). They play for the Anchorage Glacier Pilots, Anchorage Bucs, Peninsula Oilers, Mat–Su Miners and the Fairbanks Goldpanners. Anchorage games are played at Mulcahy Stadium, Cordova Street and E. 16th Avenue. Check local newspapers for schedules or phone the Anchorage Bucs, (907) 561-BUCS (2827), www.anchoragebucs. com; or the Glacier Pilots, (907) 274-3627, www.glacierpilots.com.

See a Hockey Game: Anchorage has its own professional hockey team, the Anchorage Aces, playing at Sullivan Arena Oct.– April; phone (907) 258-2237, www.alaska aces.com. Hockey fans can also watch the University of Alaska Anchorage Seawolves (www.goseawolves.com) play teams from around the country. The new UAA sports arena (Alaska Airlines Center) on Providence Drive, adjacent the hospital, is scheduled to open August 2014.

Go Berry Picking. There are nearly 50 types of berries (most of which are edible) found all over Alaska. These berries and other native fruit have been major sources of food for Native peoples for centuries.

Berries in the greater Anchorage area include blueberries, mossberries, crowberries and highbush cranberries. There are numer-

Potter Point State Game Refuge is a great spot for bird photographers. (©Donna Dewhurst)

ous places to pick berries (and mushrooms) around the area. The most popular spots include Hatcher Pass off the Glenn Highway; Mount Alyeska off the Seward Highway in Girdwood; along the Flattop Mountain Trail; Rendezvous Peak Trail, adjacent to Alpenglow Ski Area; South Fork Valley Trail; Mile 7.5 Hiland Road off Eagle River Loop exit from the Glenn Highway; Peters Creek Trail on Mount Eklutna; and Bear Mountain and Eklutna Lakeside Trail off Eklutna Lake Road.

Watch Salmon: King, silver, pink and a few chum salmon swim up Ship Creek and can be seen at the Ship Creek Viewing Area

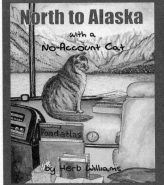

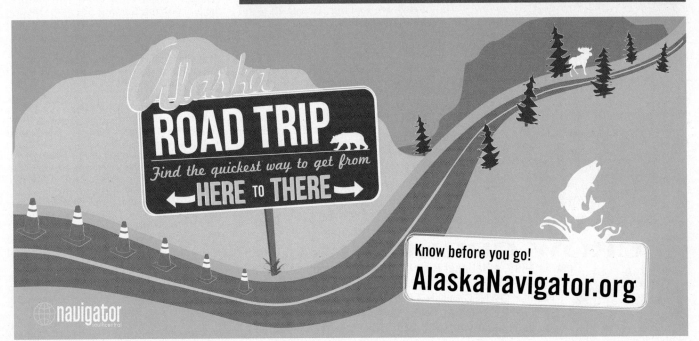

Day Trips from Anchorage

Historic Crow Creek Mine, located off the Alyeska Highway, offers gold panning and tours.
(©Kris Valencia, staff)

Anchorage is the hub for southcentral Alaska: You can get anywhere in the state from here, traveling by car, plane or train. Here are just a few driving trips you can take, ranging from a few hours to all day.

Eklutna Lake/Thunderbird Falls

Drive north on the Glenn Highway to the Eklutna exit at **Milepost A 26.5** for **Eklutna Lake Recreation Area**, located 10 miles from the highway. Located within Chugach State Park, Eklutna Lake offers camping, picnicking and hiking. The 13-mile Lakeside Trail is especially popular with local hikers and mountain bikers.

Another hiking trail accessible from this exit is **Thunderbird Falls**. This easy family trail is only 2 miles round trip from the parking lot to the viewing platform of the falls.

Eklutna Lake is an easy 72-mile round-trip drive from downtown Anchorage. If you have more time than that, turn off at the Eagle River Exit at **Milepost A 13.4** and drive 12.6 miles to the **Eagle River Nature Center** or take the **Old Glenn Highway** to Knik River Road and arrange for a trip out to see **Knik Glacier**.

See pages 372-377 in the GLENN HIGHWAY section.

Hope

From downtown Anchorage, take the Seward Highway south to the Hope Cutoff at **Milepost S 56.3**, then drive 16.5 miles northwest to the town of Hope. Hope's historic district, just off the paved Hope Highway, includes the 1896 store (now a cafe) and the 1902 log Social Hall, which still hosts community events. The popular 5-mile Gull Rock Trail ends at Gull Rock overlooking Turnagain Arm. Another popular hiking trail accessible from the Hope Highway is the 38-mile-long Resurrection Pass Trail.

This is a 177-mile round-trip drive from downtown Anchorage, offering many fine views of Turnagain Arm. There are outfitters located on the Hope Highway offering rafting trips on Sixmile Creek. For those wishing to make this a 2-day trip, Hope offers both food and accommodations (reserve rooms well in advance as space is limited).

See "Hope Highway" in the SEWARD HIGHWAY section.

Alyeska

Drive south on the Seward Highway to **Milepost S 90** (37 miles from Anchorage) and turn off on the Alyeska Highway. About 2 miles up this road is the small town of Girdwood, where the Girdwood Forest Fair takes place in July. Drive another 2 miles up the Alyeska Highway to reach the Hotel Alyeska. Located at the base of Mount Alyeska, **Alyeska Resort** is Alaska's largest ski resort. The 60-passenger **Alyeska Aerial Tramway** carries summer sightseers (and winter skiers) from the hotel to a mountaintop complex featuring the Seven Glaciers and Glacier Express restaurants. The tram ride offers wonderful views of Turnagain Arm.

The Crow Creek Mine Road, off of the Alyeska Highway, accesses the **Crow Creek Mine** historic site. Today visitors can view historic buildings dating to 1898 and go gold panning.

This is an 82-mile round-trip drive from downtown Anchorage. See "Alyeska Highway" in the SEWARD HIGHWAY section.

Whittier Tunnel/Portage Glacier

Drive south on the Seward Highway to **Milepost S 78.9** (48.1 miles from Anchorage) to junction with the access road east to Portage Glacier (5.4 miles from the highway) and Whittier (11.4 miles from the highway). Total driving miles round-trip from downtown Anchorage is 119 miles.

At Portage Glacier, the **Begich, Boggs Visitor Center** offers interactive interpretive displays, films and other programs on the natural history of this area, regular showings of films of interest and Forest Service naturalists are available to answer your questions. Portage Glacier Cruises offers daily sightseeing trips on Portage Lake from mid-May to mid-September.

Continue east to Whittier. At Mile 7, traffic enters the Anton Anderson Memorial Tunnel, at 13,300 feet the longest highway tunnel in North America. It takes a vehicle 6.5 minutes to travel through this tunnel which was formerly dedicated to train travel. There is a toll charged and travel is one-way in the tunnel. Openings are for 15 minutes each hour from either side. Vehicles must wait in the staging area before entering the tunnel.

Returning to the Seward Highway for the drive back to Anchorage, stop by the **Alaska Wildlife Conservation Center**, just north of the junction (on the west side of the road) at **Milepost S 79**, for a walk/drive-through tour of this wildlife park. The non-profit center is home to moose, bears, caribou, bison, elk, Sitka black-tailed deer and other wildlife.

See "Whittier/Portage Glacier Road" in the SEWARD HIGHWAY section.

Hatcher Pass

Drive out on the Glenn Highway from Anchorage through Palmer to **Milepost A 49.5** and turn on to Palmer–Fishhook Road for Hatcher Pass. Hatcher Pass Road is paved from the Palmer end up to Mile 17.2, entrance to **Independence Mine State Historical Park**. This is a beautiful drive along the Little Susitna River into the Hatcher Pass area. Great views and the old mine ruins are well worth the drive.

If you are prepared to drive an old-time Alaska road—narrow, winding dirt and gravel (check with car rental agency to see if this is permitted in your contract)—continue on Hatcher Pass Road 2 miles further to beautiful Summit Lake State Recreation Area. You can either turn around here, returning the way you came (137 miles roundtrip) or continue on this road another

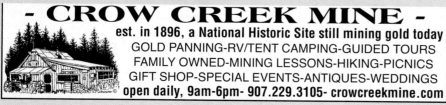

30 miles to Willow and return to Anchorage via the Parks and Glenn highways (215 miles roundtrip). See pages 366-367 in the GLENN HIGHWAY section.

Mat-Su Valley

Wasilla and Palmer are the portals to Alaska's famous Mat-Su Valley. For a day-long circle tour of this area, drive north on the Glenn Highway to **Milepost A 29.6** and take the Old Glenn Highway to downtown Palmer for lunch and shopping. Visit the **Colony House Museum**, a restored 1930s home originally occupied by Matanuska Valley colonists. Down the street is the **Colony Inn**, a teacher's dormitory in the 1930s, and now a hotel.

Head back down the Glenn to the Glenn/Parks Interchange and turn northwest on the Parks Highway for Wasilla. Local history is also featured at Wasilla's **Dorothy Page Museum and Historical Townsite** in downtown Wasilla. Follow Main Street across the Parks Highway to Knik Road and drive west 2.2 miles for the **Iditarod Trail Sled Dog Race™ Headquarters and Visitor Center**. The center has displays of race memorabilia, films on dog mushing and Iditarod souvenirs. Continue down Knik Road to Mile 13.9 for the **Knik Museum Mushers' Hall of Fame** for more Iditarod Race history.

This itinerary is approximately 130 miles round-trip from Anchorage. Other Mat-Su attractions that may be added include the **Museum of Alaska Transportation and Industry**, northwest of downtown Wasilla at **Milepost A 47** Parks Highway, and the **Musk Ox Farm**, northeast of Palmer at **Milepost A 50.1** Glenn Highway. Big Lake, 10.1 miles from Wasilla, is also a popular year-round recreation area.

See pages 407-419 in the PARKS HIGHWAY section and pages 365-374 in the GLENN HIGHWAY section.

Rail Trip to Talkeetna

Reserve a seat on the Alaska Railroad's *Denali Star* train for a morning trip to Talkeetna. Enjoy a few hours of sightseeing, dining and shopping in this charming Alaska village. Visit unique museums and historic sites, take a boat trip on the Susitna River or enjoy spectacular views of Denali (Mount McKinley) on a flightseeing trip around North America's highest mountain before returning to Anchorage by train in the late afternoon.

For premium service and views, book your trip on the railroad's GoldStar cars. Call the Alaska Railroad, (907) 265-2494 or (800) 544-0552 for reservations.

Spencer Glacier and Grandview

A scenic day trip on the Alaska Railroad's *Glacier Discovery* heads out of Anchorage on summer and fall mornings. Destination: Grandview, 50 miles southeast along scenic Turnagain Arm to the Kenai Peninsula, with a side trip to Whittier on Prince William Sound.

You may choose to detrain at Spencer Glacier for a 2 ½-hour float or canoe tour on the Placer River, or you may opt to stay on the train for the stunning alpine views of Grandview and the historic Loop District. You will be back in Anchorage by evening. Or take the whistle-stop service to Spencer Lake for a day or overnight trip.

For additional information on the Alaska Railroad, see "Railroads" in the TRAVEL PLANNING section.

Spectacular mountain scenery along Turnagain Arm near Hope on the Kenai Peninsula. (©Tim Grams)

(see description in Downtown Anchorage attractions) and near the Alaska Department of Fish and Game's William Jack Hernandez Sport Fish Hatchery on Reeve Boulevard. Watch for kings from early June until mid-July and for other species from mid-August until September. Salmon can also be viewed in Campbell Creek, which runs through the middle of Anchorage. Watch for spawning kings in late July and silvers in August from the boardwalks at Folker Street off Tudor Road. Another excellent viewing spot is the Potter Marsh Nature Trail, June through August.

Watch an Equestrian Event. The William Clark Chamberlin Equestrian Center in 530-acre Ruth Arcand Park (1.8 miles east of Dimond exit off the New Seward Highway on Abbott Road) hosts a variety of equestrian events every weekend from late May through late September. This public facility is open from 10 A.M. to 10 P.M. daily. Phone (907) 522-1552. The Eaton Equestrian Centre at 5801 Moose Meadow Lane on the hillside offers riding lessons and special events. Phone (907) 346-3745 for more information.

Charter a Plane: Dozens of air taxi operators are based in Anchorage. Fixed-wheel planes or floatplanes (skis in winter) may be chartered for flightseeing trips to Mount McKinley and Prince William Sound, for fly-in hunting and fishing, wildlife and glacier viewing, photo safaris or just for transportation. Scheduled flightseeing trips by helicopter are also available. See advertisements in this section, and inquire locally. Weather is a factor when traveling by aircraft in Alaska. Be prepared to change plans if the weather is bad. Check the FAA website at http://akweathercams.faa.gov for weather conditions and flight information.

River Running: Guided rafting tours in the region include the Matanuska near Palmer, Sixmile near Hope, and the Kenai River on the Kenai Peninsula. Also on the Kenai Peninsula are the Swanson River and Swan Lake canoe trails, located within Kenai National Wildlife Refuge.

Nancy Lake State Recreation Area, 67 miles north of Anchorage, offers a popular canoe trail system which includes public-use cabins and camping for overnight trips.

Closer to Anchorage, Kepler-Bradley Lakes State Recreation Area, at **Milepost A 36.4** Glenn Highway, also offers canoeing.

Check with advertisers in *The MILEPOST®* about guided river trips: Nova River Runners at www.novalaska.com, and Alaska Rivers Company at www.alaskarivers.com, are good examples of what's available.

Boating: Cook Inlet waters around Anchorage are only for the experienced because of powerful bore tides, unpredictable weather, dangerous mud flats and icy, silt-filled waters.

Sailing in the Anchorage area is limited to small boats in freshwater lakes and lagoons (usually ice-free by May). Big Lake, 52.3 miles north of Anchorage off the Parks Highway, is used by small sailboats but is more popular with jet skiers and power boats. Lake Lucille along the Parks Highway in Wasilla is also popular with jet skiers and other boaters.

Sailing and sea kayaking Prince William Sound out of Whittier and Resurrection Bay out of Seward are also popular.

Canoeing is allowed on Mirror Lake, 24.5 miles north of Anchorage on the Glenn Highway, and Beach Lake (take South Birchwood Loop off the Glenn Highway). Contact Eagle River Parks and Recreation at (907) 343-1500 for more information.

Boating Alaska's rivers is usually done with skiff and outboard or by jet boat. Popular destinations within about an hour's drive of Anchorage include the Little Susitna River (boat launch off Knik Road); the Susitna and Deshka rivers (boat launch at Deshka Landing west of **Milepost A 70.8** Parks Highway); Susitna Landing **Milepost A 82.5** Parks Highway; and the Twentymile River from **Milepost S 80.7** Seward Highway. The nearest public boat launch to Anchorage for the Kenai River is the Cooper Landing facility at **Milepost S 48** Sterling Highway, 101 miles from Anchorage.

Cruises on larger boats are available from Whittier into Prince William Sound, from the Homer Spit into Kachemak Bay and Cook Inlet, and from Seward into Resurrection Bay and Kenai Fjords National Park.

Swimming: Anchorage has an indoor waterpark, located east off the O'Malley exit on the New Seward Highway. The

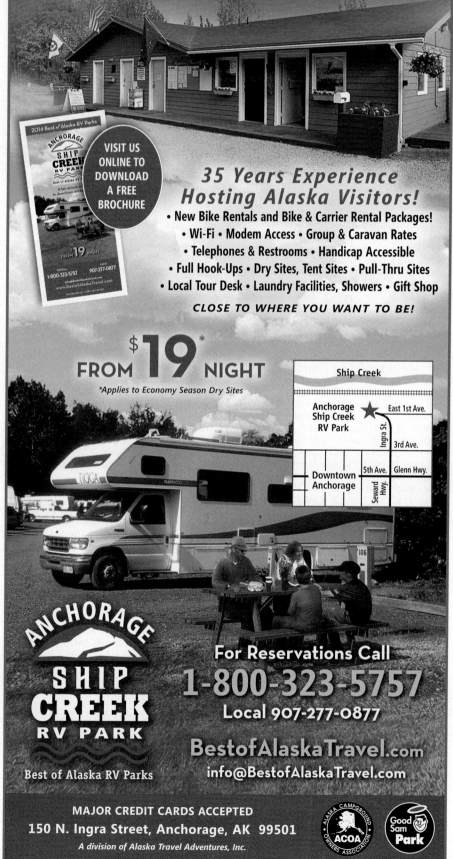

This angler holds a pink salmon caught in downtown's Ship Creek. (©Donna Dewhurst)

YMCA, at 5353 Lake Otis Pkwy., has a swimming pool; phone (907) 563-3211; www.ymcaalaska.org. The University of Alaska pool is located on Providence Drive; phone (907) 786-1231.

The municipality operates 6 swimming pools located in local high schools; public hours vary: Service Pool on Abbott Road; Bartlett Pool on Muldoon Road; West High Pool (pool and water slide) on Hillcrest Drive; East High Pool at Northern Lights Boulevard and East 24th Avenue; Dimond High Pool at 2909 W. 88th Ave.; and Chugiak Pool at 16525 S. Birchwood Loop.

For more information on aquatics at Anchorage pools, contact the Anchorage Parks & Recreation Dept.; phone (907) 343-4355 or visit their www.muni.org/Departments/parks/Pages/Pools.aspx.

There are 2 municipal beaches in Anchorage, located at Jewel Lake and Goose Lake, with supervised swim areas. Lifeguards are on duty from May 18 to August 21, noon to 9 P.M. daily. The lakes are prone to "swimmer's itch" in the mid to late summer months. For more information on Anchorage lake, go to www.muni.org/Departments/parks/Pages/Lakes.aspx.

Goose Lake has basketball courts, softball field (available for rental), playground equipment, covered picnic shelter, picnic tables, swimming area, beach, paved parking, bike trail access and non-motorized small craft area. No sail craft allowed due to low power lines. Building restrooms open daily during summer months, noon to 9 P.M. Goose Lake is located 2 miles east of the Seward Highway (take Benson to 3220 East Northern Lights Blvd.) at UAA Drive.

Jewel Lake, 6.5 miles from downtown Anchorage on W. 88th Avenue and Gloralee off Jewel Lake Road, has covered picnic shelter, softball field, volleyball sand lot, playground equipment, picnic tables, swimming area, beach, paved parking, restrooms, bike

Iditarod mushers follow a race course through Anchorage. (©Tim Grams)

trail access and non-motorized small craft area. Fishing permitted 50 feet from swim area.

CAUTION: Do not even consider swimming in Cook Inlet! Quicksand-like mud, swift tides and icy water make these waters extremely dangerous!

Saltwater Charter Boats: Sightseeing and fishing charters are available on the Kenai Peninsula at Whittier, Seward, Ninilchik and Homer. Peak times for saltwater fishing for salmon and halibut are June and July. May

and August can also be excellent fishing, depending on the weather.

Freshwater Charter Boats: There are a wide variety of river and lake fishing charters available throughout Southcentral, from Cantwell to Homer such as Angle 45 Adventures at www.angle45.com. River seasons run from the May king salmon fishery through the September silver salmon fishery. Some lake charters run year-round for ice fishing.

Winter Attractions. The major event of the winter season is "Rondy," more formally known as **Anchorage Fur Rendezvous** (Feb. 21–March 2, 2014). This 10-day-long celebration dates from 1935, when it began primarily as a winter sports tournament and fur auction. Today there are more than 120 events, including arts and crafts exhibits, a parade, dances, a carnival, and an ice and snow sculpturing contest along with a fur auction. Highlights include the annual World Championship Dog Weight Pulling Contest and the World Championship Sled Dog Race, which begins and ends on 4th Avenue in downtown Anchorage. The Rondy festival includes a sanctioned, organized snowball fight called Yukigassen. Women's and junior world championship sled dog races are held at Tozier Track. Visit Rondy headquarters at 4th Avenue and D Street. For event dates, visit their website www.furrondy.net.

The **Iditarod Trail Sled Dog Race™** has a ceremonial start on 4th Avenue in downtown Anchorage on the first Saturday in March (March 1, 2014). Mushers can be seen on the trail along the Glenn Highway to Eagle River. The racers then pack up and head to Willow, 70 miles north of Anchorage on the Parks Highway, for the official start of the race the following day (Sunday March 2, 2014). For more information, phone (907) 376-5155; www.iditarod.com.

Anchorage accommodates a wide range of winter activities, from outdoor ice skating to downhill skiing. Alyeska Resort, Alaska's largest ski area, with an international reputation for its facilities, is a 45-mile drive south from Anchorage. Closer to home, Hilltop Ski Area, on the hillside in south Anchorage, offers lighted slopes for beginner to intermediate as does Arctic Valley Ski Area off the Arctic Valley exit from the Glenn Highway.

Cross-country skiing is big in Anchorage, with a network of trails at Kincaid, Russian Jack and Hillside Park. The Tour of Anchorage ski marathon (March 2, 2014), North

America's longest running and largest citizen's racing and touring series, offers a 50k, 40k, or 25k route across town. The Tour is part of the American Ski Marathon Series. For more information, visit www.anchoragenordicski.com/tour_of_anchorage.html

Fishing: The Alaska Dept. of Fish and Game annually stocks more than 20 lakes and 3 streams in the Anchorage area with rainbow trout, landlocked and anadromous king (chinook) salmon, anadromous silver (coho) salmon, grayling and arctic char. All stocked lakes are open to the public. In addition, salmon-viewing areas and limited salmon fishing are available in the immediate Anchorage area. For specific information, check the Alaska Sport Fishing Regulations Summary booklet; contact the agency for Sport Fish Information Center, at (907) 267-2218; 333 Raspberry Road, Anchorage, AK 99518; www.adfg.alaska.gov. Urban salmon fisheries have been developed by the Alaska Department of Fish and Game in 3 Anchorage-area streams. King, silver and pink salmon can be caught in Ship Creek in downtown Anchorage; silver, pink and chum salmon are available in Bird Creek from July 14–August. Silver salmon fisheries are found in Campbell Creek in Anchorage and also at Bird Creek just north of Girdwood on the Seward Highway.

The Ship Creek King Salmon Derby takes place in early June. Many excellent fishing spots are within a day's drive of Anchorage. The Kenai Peninsula offers streams where king, red, silver, pink and chum salmon may be caught during the summer. Dolly Varden, steelhead and rainbow trout also run in Peninsula streams. Many lakes contain rainbow, lake trout and Dolly Varden. In-season saltwater fishing for halibut, rockfish and several species of salmon is excellent at many spots along the Peninsula and out of Whittier, Homer and Seward. For specific fishing spots both north and south of Anchorage, see the SEWARD, STERLING, GLENN and PARKS HIGHWAY sections. Because of the importance of fishing to Alaska, both commercially and for sport, regulations are strictly enforced. Regulations are updated yearly by the state, often after *The MILEPOST®* deadline, so it is wise to obtain a current regulations book. Check the ADF&G Sport Fish Division home page at www.adfg.alaska.gov. You can also find information on fishing at the local sporting goods stores or at www.adfg.alaska.gov/index.cfm?adfg=fishingSportFishingInfo.SouthcentralPublications.

Parks Highway

CONNECTS: Anchorage to Fairbanks, AK

Length: 362 miles   **Road Surface:** Paved   **Season:** Open all year

(See maps, pages 408-409)

① ③

View of Nenana River and fall colors from the Moody Bridge, George Parks Highway. (©Linda Martin)

Major Attractions:

©Kris Valencia, staff

Alaska Veterans Memorial, Denali National Park, Mat-Su Valley

Highest Summit:

Broad Pass 2,400 ft.

The Parks Highway was called the Anchorage–Fairbanks Highway after its completion in 1971, then renamed the George Parks Highway in July 1975, in honor of George A. Parks (1883–1984), the territorial governor from 1925 to 1933. Still officially the George Parks Highway, it is more commonly referred to as the "Parks" Highway. Designated Alaska Route 3, the Parks Highway junctions with the Glenn Highway (Alaska Route 1) 35 miles from Anchorage and leads 327 miles north to Fairbanks. Together, these highways connect Alaska's largest population centers.

Designated a National Scenic Byway in 2009, the George Parks Highway passes through some of the grandest scenery that Alaska has to offer. Highest summit on the Parks Highway is at Broad Pass (see **Milepost A 195**), at approximately 2,400 feet. Motorists can see current weather conditions at Broad Pass by checking the FAA videocam at Summit airport at http://akweathercams.faa.gov/sitelist.php. The Parks Highway between **Milepost A 132** and Fairbanks is an Alaska Scenic Byway.

Distance in miles	Anchorage	Denali Park	Fairbanks	Talkeetna	Wasilla
Anchorage		237	362	113	42
Denali Park	237		125	153	195
Fairbanks	362	125		278	320
Talkeetna	113	153	278		71
Wasilla	42	195	320	71	

The Parks Highway junctions with the Denali Highway (Alaska Route 8) at Cantwell at **Milepost A 210**. The entrance to Denali National Park is located at **Milepost A 237.4** on the Parks Highway, approximately 27 miles north of Cantwell and 125 miles south of Fairbanks.

Parks Highway Anchorage, AK, to Milepost A 169

© 2014 The MILEPOST®

Denali National Park and Preserve

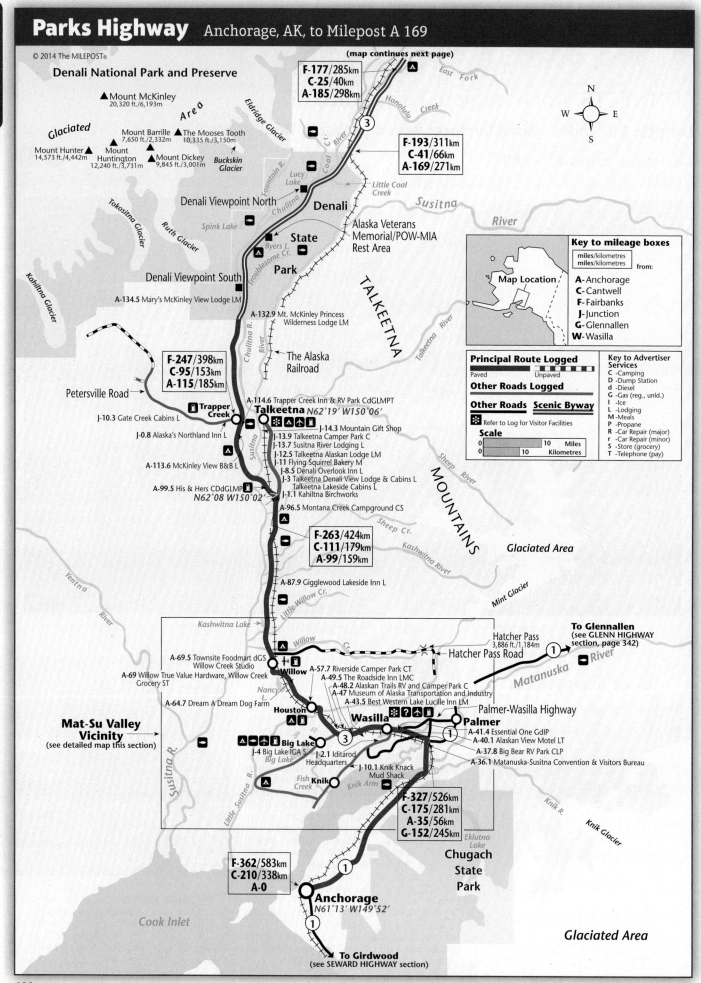

(map continues next page)

F-177/285km
C-25/40km
A-185/298km

▲ Mount McKinley
20,320 ft./6,193m

Glaciated

Mount Barrille
7,650 ft./2,332m

▲ The Mooses Tooth
10,335 ft./3,150m

Mount Hunter
14,573 ft./4,442m

Mount Huntington
12,240 ft./3,731m

▲ Mount Dickey
9,845 ft./3,001m

Buckskin Glacier

Area

Eldridge Glacier

Tokositna Glacier

Ruth Glacier

Kahiltna Glacier

Lucy Lake

Fountain R.

Chulitna R.

Denali Viewpoint North

Spink Lake

Byers L.

Troublesome Cr.

Denali Viewpoint South

A-134.5 Mary's McKinley View Lodge LM

A-132.9 Mt. McKinley Princess Wilderness Lodge LM

Denali

State

Park

Coal Cr.

Little Coal Creek

Alaska Veterans Memorial/POW-MIA Rest Area

Susitna

River

F-193/311km
C-41/66km
A-169/271km

East Fork

Honolulu Creek

TALKEETNA

F-247/398km
C-95/153km
A-115/185km

The Alaska Railroad

Chulitna River

Petersville Road

Trapper Creek

A-114.6 Trapper Creek Inn & RV Park CdGLMPT

J-10.3 Gate Creek Cabins L

Talkeetna N62°19' W150°06'

J-0.8 Alaska's Northland Inn L

J-14.3 Mountain Gift Shop

J-13.9 Talkeetna Camper Park C

J-13.7 Susitna River Lodging L

J-12.5 Talkeetna Alaskan Lodge LM

J-11 Flying Squirrel Bakery M

J-8.5 Denali Overlook Inn L

J-3 Talkeetna Denali View Lodge & Cabins L
Talkeetna Lakeside Cabins L

J-1.1 Kahiltna Birchworks

A-113.6 McKinley View B&B L

A-99.5 His & Hers CDdGLMP
N62°08 W150°02'

A-96.5 Montana Creek Campground CS

Sheep Cr.

Kashwitna River

Talkeetna River

MOUNTAINS

Sheep River

Glaciated Area

F-263/424km
C-111/179km
A-99/159km

A-87.9 Gigglewood Lakeside Inn L

Little Willow Cr.

Yentna River

Mint Glacier

Kashwitna Lake

Willow

A-69.5 Townsite Foodmart dGS
Willow Creek Studio

A-69 Willow True Value Hardware, Willow Creek Grocery ST

A-64.7 Dream A Dream Dog Farm

Willow

Houston

Nancy L.

A-57.7 Riverside Camper Park CT
A-49.5 The Roadside Inn LMC
A-48.2 Alaskan Trails RV and Camper Park C
A-47 Museum of Alaska Transportation and Industry
A-43.5 Best Western Lake Lucille Inn LM

Hatcher Pass
3,886 ft./1,184m

Hatcher Pass Road

To Glennallen
(see GLENN HIGHWAY section, page 342)

Matanuska River

Wasilla

Palmer-Wasilla Highway

Palmer

A-41.4 Essential One GdIP
A-40.1 Alaskan View Motel LT
A-37.8 Big Bear RV Park CLP
A-36.1 Matanuska-Susitna Convention & Visitors Bureau

Mat-Su Valley Vicinity
(see detailed map this section)

Big Lake

J-4 Big Lake IGA S

Big Lake

J-2.1 Iditarod Headquarters

Susitna R.

Little Susitna R.

Knik

Fish Creek

J-10.1 Knik Knack Mud Shack

Knik Arm

F-327/526km
C-175/281km
A-35/56km
G-152/245km

Eklutna Lake

Knik R.

Knik Glacier

Chugach
State
Park

F-362/583km
C-210/338km
A-0

Cook Inlet

Anchorage
N61°13' W149°52'

To Girdwood
(see SEWARD HIGHWAY section)

Glaciated Area

Key to mileage boxes

miles/kilometres
miles/kilometres   from:

A - Anchorage
C - Cantwell
F - Fairbanks
J - Junction
G - Glennallen
W - Wasilla

Map Location

Principal Route Logged

Paved   Unpaved

Other Roads Logged

Other Roads   Scenic Byway

Refer to Log for Visitor Facilities

Scale

0 _____ 10 Miles
0 _____ 10 Kilometres

Key to Advertiser Services

C - Camping
D - Dump Station
d - Diesel
G - Gas (reg., unld.)
I - Ice
L - Lodging
M - Meals
P - Propane
R - Car Repair (major)
r - Car Repair (minor)
S - Store (grocery)
T - Telephone (pay)

Parks Highway Milepost A 169 to Fairbanks, AK

© 2014 The MILEPOST®

Key to mileage boxes

miles/kilometres
miles/kilometres from:

A-Anchorage
C-Cantwell
J-Junction
F-Fairbanks
P-Paxson

Map Location

Principal Route Logged

Paved   Unpaved

Other Roads Logged

Other Roads   Scenic Byway

✿ Refer to Log for Visitor Facilities

Scale

0 ——— 10 Miles
0 ——— 10 Kilometres

Key to Advertiser Services
C -Camping
D -Dump Station
d -Diesel
G -Gas (reg., unld.)
I -Ice
L -Lodging
M -Meals
P -Propane
R -Car Repair (major)
r -Car Repair (minor)
S -Store (grocery)
T -Telephone (pay)

To Manley Hot Springs
(see ELLIOTT HIGHWAY section)

To Circle
(see STEESE HIGHWAY section)

F-0
A-358/576km

Murphy Dome
2,930 ft./893m ▲

A-353.4 Gold Hill Imported Beer & Fine Wine

N64°50′ W148°01′ ✿ Ester

A-351.2 Judie Gumm Designs

The Alaska Railroad

To Chena Hot Springs

Fairbanks
N64°50′ W147°43′

F-10/16km
C-142/228km
A-352/566km

To Delta Junction
(see RICHARDSON HIGHWAY section, page 481)

A-313.6 Parks Highway Towing

N64°34′ W149°05′
✿?⛺🍴 **Nenana**

F-58/93km
C-95/152km
A-305/490km

J-6 City of Anderson CD
Anderson
✈ **Clear**

F-79/126km
C-74/118km
A-284/456km

A-280 Clear Sky Lodge IMPT
A-276 Tatlanika Trading Co. and RV Park CD

Rex Dome ▲
4,155 ft./1,266m

Jumbo Dome ▲
4,493 ft./1,369m

Walker Dome ▲
3,942 ft./1,202m

A-251.1 Denali's Faith Hill Lodge L

N63°51′ W148°58′

A-245.1 Denali RV Park & Motel CDLT

Stampede Road

A-249.5 Motel Nord Haven L

A-247 Denali Outdoor Center CL

✿🍴 **Healy**
⛺ **Suntrana**
✈ **Usibelli**

Dora Peak ▲
5,572 ft./1,698m

Sugarloaf Mountain ▲
4,450 ft./1,356m

Mount Healy ▲
5,716 ft./1,742m

⛺ **Park Entrance**

Mount Fellow ▲
4,476 ft./1,364m

A-238.9 Denali Outdoor Center
A-238.7 Denali Rainbow Village RV Park & Motel CL
A-238.6 Denali ATV & Denali Jeep Excursions
        Denali Raft Adventures, Inc.
A-238.5 Denali Princess Wilderness Lodge LM
A-238.4 Denali Bluffs Hotel LM
A-238.1 Grande Denali Lodge L
A-238 Cabins at Denali L
      ERA Helicopters
      Nenana Raft Adventures

A-231 Denali Grizzly Bear Resort CILPST

Park Road
(see DENALI NATIONAL PARK section)

F-125/201km
C-27/44km
A-237/382km

Denali National Park and Preserve

Kantishna

A-210.8 BluesBerry Inn LM

N63°23′W148°56′ ⛺✈🍴 **Cantwell**

A-210 Atkins Guiding & Flying Service L
      Backwoods Lodge
      Cantwell RV Park C

N63°523′ W148°54′

RANGE

To Paxson
(see DENALI HIGHWAY section)

Broad Pass
2,300 ft./701m

F-152/245km
C-0
A-210/338km
P-136/218km

ALASKA

Mount McKinley ▲
20,320 ft./6,194m

Mount Huntington ▲
12,240 ft./3,731m

The Mooses Tooth ▲
10,335 ft./3,150m

Mount Barrille ▲
7,650 ft./2,332m

Mount Dickey ▲
9,845 ft./3,001m

Buckskin Glacier

Glaciated Area

Eldridge Glacier

Coal Cr.

West Fork

Chulitna River

Middle Fork

East Fork

Chulitna R.

Honolulu Creek

F-193/311km
C-41/66km
A-169/271km

(map continues previous page)

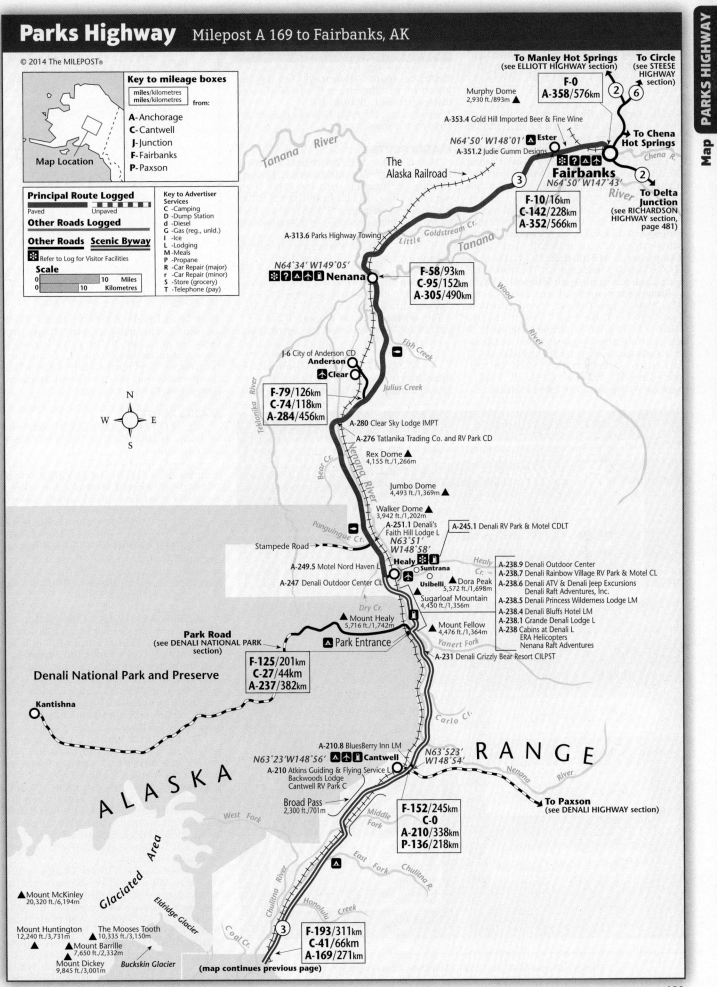

The Parks Highway is a good 2-lane paved road, with passing lanes on improved sections. Several sections of moderate S-curves and heavy foliage may reduce sight distance: Pass with care. *CAUTION: Drive with headlights on at all times. Watch for moose. Watch for local cross traffic. Check highway conditions in winter.*

The Parks Highway provides the most direct highway access to Denali National Park and Preserve (formerly Mount McKinley National Park) from either Anchorage or Fairbanks. Mount McKinley—also called Denali—(elev. 20,320 feet) is visible from the highway, weather permitting. Some of the best Denali viewpoints along the highway are within Denali State Park. Formal mountain viewpoints are: Denali Viewpoint South, **Milepost A 134.8**; Denali Viewpoint North, **Milepost A 162.4**; and Denali View North Campground, **Milepost A 162.7**. There is also a Denali viewpoint on the Talkeetna Spur Road, 12.9 miles from **Milepost A 98.7**.

Emergency medical services: Phone 911. Alaska State Trooper posts in Anchorage, Wasilla, Talkeetna, Cantwell, Healy, Nenana and Fairbanks. Hospitals in Anchorage and Fairbanks and at junction of Glenn and Parks Highway (Mat-Su Regional Medical Center). Ambulance/Fire/EMS in Anchorage, Chugiak, Wasilla, Cantwell, Healy, Nenana, Anderson/Clear, Ester, Fairbanks.

Parks Highway Log

Distance from Anchorage (A) is followed by distance from Cantwell (C) and distance from Fairbanks (F).
Mileposts along the Parks Highway indicate distance from Anchorage.

ALASKA ROUTE 1

A 0 C 210 F 362 ANCHORAGE. Follow the Glenn Highway (Alaska Route 1) north 35 miles to junction with the Parks Highway. (Turn to the end of the GLENN HIGHWAY section on page 377 and read log back to front from Anchorage to junction with the Parks Highway).

A 34 C 176 F 328 Exit east to Palmer via Glenn Highway for northbound traffic.

> **Junction** of the Parks Highway (Alaska Route 3) with the Glenn Highway (Alaska Route 1) to Glennallen and the Tok Cutoff. Turn to **Milepost A 34** on page 372 in the GLENN HIGHWAY section for log of that route.

A 35 C 175 F 327 Glenn-Parks Interchange: Northbound sign on overpass indicates Glenn Highway (Alaska Route

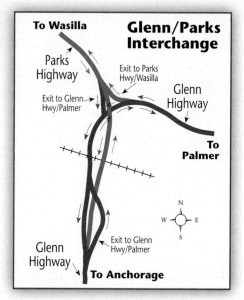

1) ends and Parks Highway (Alaska Route 3) begins. This massive interchange has obscured the start of the Parks Highway, since the interchange provides 2 lanes for continuous flow north–south traffic while those eastbound on the Glenn Highway (Route 1) to Palmer must exit.

ALASKA ROUTE 3

A 35.4 C 174.6 F 326.6 Southbound exit for Glenn Highway (Route 1) east to Palmer and Glennallen.

A 35.5 C 174.5 F 326.5 Trunk Road exit northbound; access to Mat-Su Visitor Center and Mat–Su Regional Medical Center (both are visible from the highway on hill to east); see description at **Milepost A 36.1**.

A 36.1 C 173.9 F 325.9 Trunk Road overpass; use north- and southbound exits to access **Mat-Su Visitor Center** and **Mat-Su Regional Medical Center** to east. Exit west and follow frontage road north to Church Street for access to **Big Bear RV Park** (see description at **Milepost A 37.8**).

Matanuska–Susitna Convention & Visitors Bureau. See display ad this page.

Trunk Road leads northeast 0.7 mile to University of Alaska Fairbanks' Matanuska agricultural research farm; no tours, but you can walk through the display gardens. Also access via Trunk Road to Mat-Su College (1.8 miles); Palmer-Wasilla Highway (3.1 miles); Bogard Road (4.2 miles); and Palmer-Fishhook Road (6.5 miles).

Mat–Su Visitor Center is open May to September, 8:30 A.M. to 6:30 P.M. daily. This large center offers a wide variety of displays and information on the Mat–Su Valley; free WiFi access, pay phone, gift shop. The visitor center offers real-time vacancy reports for accommodations and activities (after business hours, this is posted at the door); for additional information phone (907) 746-5000; email info@alaskavisit.com or visit www.alaskavisit.com.

Adjacent to the Visitors Center is the Veterans Monument, a 20-ton granite boulder with a bronze plaque and inscription, which honors all veterans of the U.S. armed forces. The Veterans Wall of Honor—intended to resemble the Vietnam Wall in Washington D.C.—consists of black granite panels inscribed with the names of veterans, living or deceased, who have either received an honorable discharge or are pres-

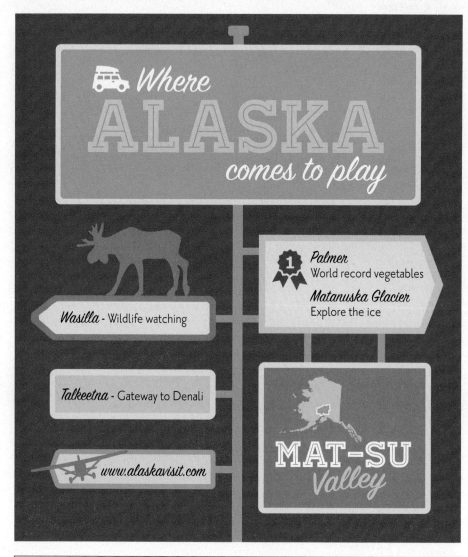

Drive with your headlights on at all times on Alaska highways.

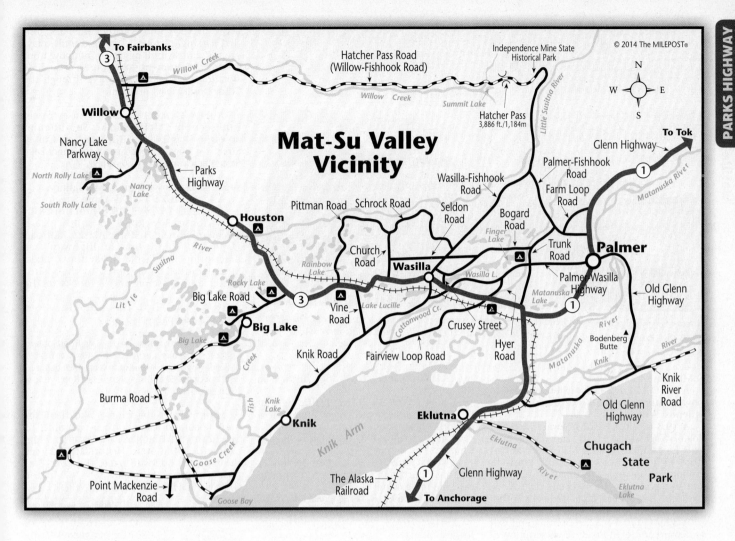

Mat-Su Valley Vicinity

© 2014 The MILEPOST®

ently serving in the military. The names of the only 2 Alaskan MIAs (Marine E4 Thomas E. Anderson and Navy E3 Howard M. Koslosky) from the Vietnam War appear on the Wasilla Wall of Honor, in view of Mount POW/MIA, which is the flat-topped mountain to the right of Twin Peaks. Inspiration for designating the peak in honor of American prisoners of war and soldiers missing in action came from Vietnam veteran John J. Morrissey, who spent 20 years climbing mountains in various states trying to get one named Mount POW/MIA. "It is easier to climb the mountains than to go through all the paperwork of getting a mountain named," Morrissey said. He climbed the formerly unnamed mountain in 1999, planting a POW/MIA flag at the summit. With the help of Leo Kaye, who along with others helped initiate the Veterans' Wall here, the state Board of Geographic Names adopted the new name.

A 36.4 C 173.6 F 325.6 Trunk Road southbound exit; access to Mat-Su Visitor Center and Mat–Su Regional Medical Center (both are visible from the highway on hill to east); see description at **Milepost A 36.1**.

A 36.9 C 173.1 F 325.1 Distance marker northbound shows Wasilla 7 miles, Denali National Park 201 miles, Fairbanks 319 miles.

A 37.5 C 172.5 F 324.5 Fairview Loop/ Hyer Road northbound exit. See description at **Milepost A 37.8**.

A 37.8 C 172.2 F 324.2 Fairview Loop/ Hyer Road underpass: use north- and southbound exits to access gas station/foodmart. Denali Harley–Davidson Shop east off exit.

Exit west and follow frontage road south to Church Street for access to **Big Bear RV Park**.

Big Bear RV Park. See display ad this page.

Also use this exit to Palmer Hay Flats State Game Refuge from Fairview Loop (see description at **Milepost J 4.1** Knik–Goose Bay Road log this section).

A 38.2 C 171.8.5 F 323.8 Fairview Loop/ Hyer Road southbound exit. See description

Veterans' Monument is adjacent the Mat-Su Visitor Center off Trunk Road in Wasilla.

(©Kris Valencia, staff)

at **Milepost A 37.8.**

A 39 C 171 F 323 Northbound exit to Seward Meridian Road; see description at **Milepost A 39.3.**

A 39.3 C 170.7 F 322.7 Seward Meridian Road overpass: use north- and southbound exits for Meridian Center Mall and Walmart store to south, Sears to north. Wasilla's Walmart is the largest Walmart in the state and, as reported by the *Anchorage Daily News*, has sold more duct tape than any other Walmart in the world.

A 39.6 C 170.4 F 322.4 Southbound exit to Seward Meridian Road; see description at **Milepost A 39.3.**

A 40 C 170 F 322 Grand View; lodging.

A 40.1 C 169.9 F 321.9 Alaskan View Motel to west; lodging.

Alaskan View Motel. See display ad this page.

A 40.4 C 169.6 F 321.6 Traffic light at Hermon Road; access to Lowes, liquor store and other businesses.

A 40.5 C 169.5 F 321.5 Pilgrims Baptist Church.

A 40.7 C 169.3 F 321.3 Sun Mountain Avenue. Sportsman's Warehouse to northeast, shopping center.

A 40.8 C 169.2 F 321.2 Creekside Plaza; UPS store.

A 41 C 169 F 321 Wasilla Police, fast-food, shipping.

A 41.1 C 168.9 F 320.9 Traffic light at **junction** with Palmer-Wasilla Highway; access to Target, Fred Meyer, Tesoro and **Essential One** gas stations.

Essential One. See display ad this page.
The 10-mile Palmer-Wasilla Highway connects Wasilla on the Parks Highway with Palmer on the Glenn Highway. The highway accesses several business parks and residential subdivisions, and acts as a shortcut between the 2 communities for local traffic. It is a very busy road. The **Essential One** at 2858 E Palmer-Wasilla Highway is RV friendly with gas, diesel, biodiesel, propane, ice and food.

Palmer–Wasilla Highway extension to west connects with Glenwood Avenue to Knik–Goose Bay Road.

A 41.8 C 168.2 F 320.2 Northbound

access to **Newcomb Wasilla Lake Park**; limited parking, picnic shelter, restrooms, playground and swimming beach, rainbow trout fishing. Monument to George Parks. Kids flotation devices available here through the "Kids Don't Float" program.

A 41.9 C 168.1 F 320.1 Crusey Street intersection; McDonald's. Southbound access to Wasilla Lake. Turn east on Crusey Street for Bogard Road access to Finger Lake State Recreation Site (6.6 miles).

A 42 C 168 F 320 Carr's Mall to east; supermarket, **Town Square Art Gallery**.

A 42.1 C 167.9 F 319.9 Yenlo Street.

A 42.2 C 167.8 F 319.8 Junction with Knik-Goose Bay Road to south, Main Street to north. Historic Alaska Railroad Depot on south side of highway (see description in Wasilla Attractions). Main Street leads 1 block north to the visitor center and museum and 2 blocks to the post office.

Iditarod Trail Headquarters. See display ad on page 414.

Junction with Knik-Goose Bay Road and access to Lake Lucille Park, Iditarod Trail Sled Dog Race Headquarters and other attractions. See "Knik-Goose Bay Road" log on page 414.

Main Street becomes Wasilla–Fishhook Road and leads northeast 10 miles to junction with Hatcher Pass Road to Independence Mine State Historical Park; see the map on opposite page. (Hatcher Pass Road is logged on pages 366–367 in the GLENN HIGHWAY section.)

Wasilla

A 42.2 C 167.8 F 319.8 Located between Wasilla and Lucille lakes in the Susitna Valley, about an hour's drive from Anchorage. **Population**: 7,831. **Emergency Services**: Phone 911 for Police, Fire and Ambulance. **Alaska State Troopers**, (907) 373-8300. **City Police**, Milepost A 41, phone (907) 352-5401. **Hospital**, Mat-Su Regional Medical Center, 2500 South Woodworth Loop, Palmer; phone (907) 861-6000.

Visitor Information: At the Dorothy Page Museum and Historic Town Site on Main Street just off the Parks Highway, phone (907) 373-9071, fax 373-9072. Or contact Greater Wasilla Chamber of Commerce, 415 E. Railroad Ave., Wasilla, AK; website: www.visitwasilla.org. The GWCC is open year-round, Monday–Friday 1 P.M. to

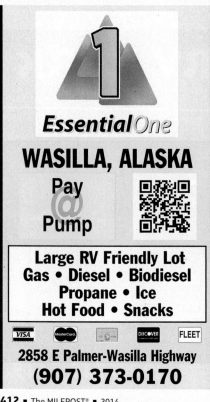

5 P.M., phone (907) 376-1299. Exit at Trunk Road and follow signs to Mat–Su Visitors Center. Write Mat–Su Convention & Visitors Bureau, 7744 E. Visitors View Ct., Palmer, AK 99645; phone (907) 746-5000, www.alaska visit.com.

Radio and **Television** via Anchorage stations; KMBQ 99.7, Country Legends 100.9, Hometown radio 1430. **Newspapers:** *The Valley Sun* (weekly); *The Frontiersman* (tri-weekly). **Transportation: Air**—Charter service available. **Railroad**—Alaska Railroad stops at the historic depot (visible on south side of Parks Highway), located at 415 E. Railroad Avenue. The depot is not staffed by the Alaska Railroad and "is often closed and locked at train arrival/departure times." **Bus**—Mat-Su Community Transit, service between Mat-Su locations and Anchorage; phone (907) 376-5000. **Rental Cars**—Enterprise Rent–A–Car (907) 373-2080; Valley Car Rental (907) 775-2880. **Taxis**—Available.

Private Aircraft: Wasilla municipal airport, 4.8 miles north on Museum Drive; elev. 348 feet; length 3,700 feet; asphalt; unattended. Wasilla Lake seaplane base, 0.9 mile east; elev. 330 feet. Numerous private airstrips and lakes in vicinity.

One of the Matanuska–Susitna Valley's pioneer communities, Wasilla began as a station on the Alaska Railroad about 1917. With the railroad, and a government land auction bringing in new settlement, Wasilla became a supply staging point for gold mines in the Willow Creek Mining District.

With the advent of a farm-based economy in the 1930s and 40s—precipitated by the Matanuska Valley Colony project—Palmer replaced Wasilla as the regional service and supply center. Palmer remained the commercial hub of the Mat-Su Valley until the 1970s, when the new Glenn Highway bypassed downtown Palmer, and the Anchorage–Fairbanks Highway (now Parks Highway) was completed. The new highway, coupled with the pipeline boom, brought both people and traffic to Wasilla.

Today, major chain retail stores, small businesses, fast-food restaurants and auto dealerships line the Parks Highway in Wasilla. New residential subdivisions have sprung up along Wasilla's back roads in this fastest-growing area in the state. Wasilla has also become the focus of national attention as the hometown of former Alaska governor

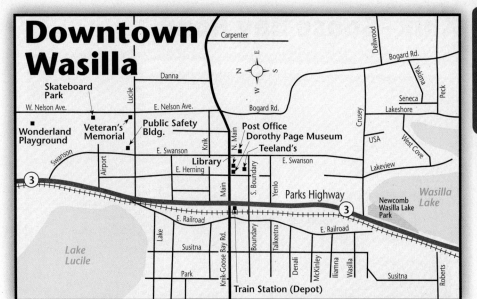

and vice presidential candidate, Sarah Palin.

Lodging & Services

All visitor facilities available, including accommodations at **Alaskan View Motel**, **Best Western Lake Lucille**, **Hillside Cabins**, and other hotels/motels. Wasilla has banks, post office, gas stations, major-chain retail stores, supermarkets, tire and RV repair, laundromats and other services.

Iditapark, featuring Wonderland playground, a skateboard park, BMX track as well as basketball, volleyball and tennis courts, is located at 500 W. Nelson Ave.; it is a great stop for families traveling with active children. The Brett Memorial Ice Arena, at Bogard Road and Crusey Street, has ice skating and fitness court. The City's Curtis C. Menard Sports Complex, at 1001 S. Mack Drive, is a premier indoor sports facility with NHL-size ice arena and indoor artificial turf courts; phone (907) 357-9100.

Best Western Lake Lucille Inn: Conveniently located on the way to Denali, only 45 miles from Anchorage. The Valley's premier hotel has a superb location on beautiful Lake Lucille with breathtaking views of the Chugach Mountains. Amenities: Deluxe continental breakfast, wireless Internet, laundry, fitness room, hot tub and sauna. 1-800-897-1776; www.BestWesternLake LucilleInn.com. See display ad on this page.
[ADVERTISEMENT]

Camping

There are several RV parks on the Parks Highway, including **Big Bear RV Park** and

Alaskan Trails RV & Camper Park. Public campgrounds in the Wasilla area include Lake Lucille Park on Knik Road; Little Susitna River public-use facility off Point Mackenzie Road; and Finger Lake State Recreation Site on Bogard Road (descriptions follow).

For **Lake Lucille Park** (Mat-Su Borough), take Knik-Goose Bay Road 2.3 miles southwest and turn on Endeavor Street (just beyond Iditarod headquarters parking lot), then drive 0.6 mile on a gravel access road. There are 59 campsites and 2 RV sites in a heavily wooded area on a gravel loop road; picnic pavilions; campground host; firewood, firepits, restrooms. Camping fee of $10 (2 tent/2 vehicle limit per site). *See Milepost J 2.2 "Knik–Goose Bay Road" log page 414.*

Little Susitna River public use facility is *(Continues on page 416)*

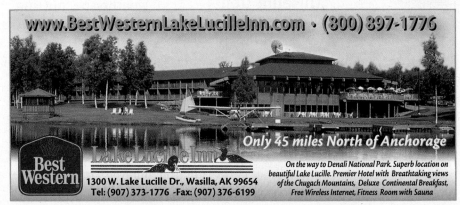

WASILLA ADVERTISERS

Alaskan Trails RV &
Camper Park ....Ph. (907) 376-5504
Alaskan View Motel .....Ph. (907) 376-6787
Best Western Lake Lucille Inn..Ph. 1-800-897-1776
Big Bear RV Park ....Ph. (907) 745-7445
Essential One................Ph. (907) 373-0170
Gold Rush Jewelers .....Ph. 1-800-770-3650
Hillside Cabins.............Ph. 1-800-770-3650
Iditarod Trail Headquarters ....Ph. (907) 376-5155
Knik Knack Mud Shack ...Ph. (907) 376-5793
Last Frontier Brewing Co., The ..Ph. (907) 357-7200
Mat-Su Convention & Visitors
Bureau ....Ph. (907) 746-5000
Museum of Alaska Transportation
and Industry.................Ph. (907) 376-1211
Roadside Inn, The.........Ph. (907) 373-4646
Sylvia's Quilt Depot......Ph. (907) 376-6468
Town Square Art Gallery............Ph. (907) 376-0123

Knik–Goose Bay Road

Little Susitna River public-use facility is a popular boat launch site. (©Kris Valencia, staff)

Knik-Goose Bay Road leads southwest from the Parks Highway in Wasilla, providing access to Goose Bay State Game Refuge and to Point Mackenzie Road. Point Mackenzie Road accesses the popular Little Susitna River Public-use Facility in Susitna Flats State Game Refuge. *CAUTION: Drive carefully! This road is a Highway Safety Corridor due to* *its high accident rate.* Posted speed limit is 55 mph. There are quite a few subdivisions along this road; expect heavy traffic during commuting hours.

The first 15 miles of Knik-Goose Bay Road have been designated the Joe Redington Sr. Memorial Trail, who was instrumental in organizing the Iditarod Trail Sled Dog Race. (Stop by the Iditarod Trail headquarters at **Milepost J 2.1** for more on the history of this major Alaskan sporting event.)

KNIK-GOOSE BAY ROAD
Distance from the junction (J) with Parks Highway.

J 0 Junction with Parks Highway at **Milepost A 42.2**, Main Street, Wasilla.

J 0.1 Wasilla Chamber of Commerce in old Railroad Depot. *CAUTION: Road crosses railroad tracks.*

J 0.5 Benteh Nuutah Valley Native Primary Care Center.

J 0.7 Traffic light at **junction** with the Palmer-Wasilla Highway which connects with the Parks Highway at **Milepost A 41**.

J 1.2 Entering Wasilla (sign).

J 1.5 Gas station, tire store, Subway.

J 1.9 Smith Ballfields.

J 2.1 Main entrance for **Iditarod Trail Sled Dog Race™ Headquarters** and visitor center. The center has historical displays and films on sled dog racing and mushers, as well as a souvenir shop with Iditarod memorabilia. Dog cart rides in summer. Sled

dog puppies. Open 8 A.M. to 7 P.M., daily in summer, weekdays 8 A.M. until 5 P.M. the rest of the year.

Iditarod Trail Headquarters. See display ad facing page.

J 2.2 Turnoff on Endeavor Street (also access to Iditarod headquarters parking lot) for **Lake Lucille Park** (Mat–Su Borough) campground and day-use area, located 0.6 mile north via gravel road. There are 57 campsites and 2 pull-throughs in a heavily wooded area on a gravel loop road; picnic pavilions; campground host; water; firewood, firepits, restrooms. Camping fee $10. Fishing for landlocked silver salmon. Short boardwalk walking trail to lake. Open May 15-September 30, weather permitting.

J 4.1 Tesoro gas station, liquor and grocery at junction with Fairview Loop Road, which leads 11 miles to junction with the Parks Highway.

Palmer Hay Flats State Game Refuge is a 45-square-mile area of forests, wetlands, lakes, creeks and tidal sloughs that supports tens-of-thousands of migrating waterfowl and shorebirds plus a variety of other wildlife. Accessed by driving 1.9 miles on Fairview Loop from this junction to where the road makes a 90-degree turn and intersects with Hayfield Road. Follow Hayfield Road 1.3 miles to the signed turnoff for Palmer Hay Flats refuge. Improved gravel access road leads from Hayfield Road 0.3 miles to Scout Ridge trailhead with covered observation deck with panoramic views, and forested walking trail. Another 0.3 miles along the access road leads to second trailhead at Cottonwood Creek with restrooms and wetlands trail. This site is popular for salmon fishing (open weekends only 6 A.M. to 6 P.M.), fall waterfowl hunting (limited ATV trail use generally allowed), bird watching (especially during spring migration), photography, hiking, trapping, cross-country skiing and snow machining. Annual Run For The Refuge (5K, 10K and kids dash) held here in August. More information at www.adfg.state.ak.us and www.palmerhayflats.org.

Grocery store location to the north with liquor and outdoor gear.

J 6 Three Bears Alaska warehouse-style shopping. Shell Gas.

J 6.8 Traffic light at **junction** with Vine Road, which leads 3.4 miles to the Parks Highway. Vine Road also junctions with Hollywood Road, which leads 6.5 miles to connect with Big Lake Road.

J 7 Central Mat-Su Fire Department Station No. 62; *emergency phone.*

J 7.9 Gas station at turnoff for Settlers Bay residential area; post office, restaurant. Access to 18-hole Settlers Bay golf course (follow signs). Paved bike path ends.

J 10.1 Turnoff for **Knik Knack Mud Shack**, featuring Native Clay giftware.

Knik Knack Mud Shack. See display ad this page.

J 12.6 Joe Redington Sr. Memorial Trail (sign)

J 13 Knik Historic District (sign). **KNIK–FAIRVIEW**, formerly known as Knik (pop. 14,923) has a bar, pay phone, liquor store, gas station and private campground on Knik Lake. Knik is a checkpoint on the Iditarod Trail Sled Dog Race™ route. It's been called the "Dog Mushing Center of the World" in reference to the many dog mushers that

have lived in this area.

J 13.9 Double ended turnout to northwest (watch for "Old Knik" sign); museum and public fishing access to **Knik Lake** (stocked with rainbow; 5 hp motors only). Short, steep, narrow gravel access road to museum and lake. Interpretive signs.

A traditional Athabascan graveyard with fenced graves and spirit houses is located behind Knik Museum. The graveyard is on sacred ground; visitors may view it from a section of the Iditarod Trail.

Knik Museum and Sled Dog Mushers' Hall of Fame is housed in 1 of 2 buildings remaining from Knik's gold rush era (1897–1917). Regional memorabilia, artifacts, archives, dog mushing equipment, mushers' portraits and historical displays on the Iditarod Trail. The museum is open from June 1 to August 31, Thursday to Sunday, 1–6 P.M. Admission $3. Phone (907) 376-7755 or (907) 376-2005 in summer. Open for tours in winter, by appointment call (907) 376-5679 in advance.

Annual Picnic Social held in July.

J 14.5 Double-ended scenic overlook to south.

J 16 Fish Creek bridge.

J 17.1 Point Mackenzie Road junction. *Turn here for access to Little Susitna River Public-Use Site (Point Mackenzie Road log follows). Continue straight ahead for Goose Bay.*

J 18.4 Tug Bar and Goose Bay Inn; liquor store, ATM, camping, cabin and snow machine rentals.

J 19.5 Turnoff northwest leads 1.2 miles (keep to left at "Y") via very steep, deeply rutted, winding access road *(recommended for 4WD only)* to **Goose Bay State Game Refuge** boat launch. Good waterfowl hunting in the fall; no developed public-use facilities.

J 19.7 Goose Bay airport. Popular area for target shooting.

POINT MACKENZIE ROAD

Distance from Mile J 17.2 Knik-Goose Bay Road (K) is followed by distance from Parks Highway junction (J).

K 0 J 17.2 Junction with Knik Goose Bay Road.

K 3.4 J 20.6 Central Mat-Su Fire Department Station 64, Mat-Su EMS; *emergency phone.*

K 7.4 J 24.6 'T' **junction**: turn left on paved road for Goose Creek Correctional Center (4 miles) and Point Mackenzie (13.5 miles), proposed site of Knik Arm bridge to Anchorage. Turn right at this junction for Susitna Flats State Game Refuge, 5.2 miles (continue with this road log).

K 7.5 J 24.7 *Pavement ends, gravel begins.*

K 7.6 J 24.8 Junction with Burma Road, (gravel) which leads 8.5 miles to Big Lake Road.

K 8.6 J 25.8 Dirt side road leads 0.5 mile to **Carpenter Lake** public fishing access.

K 9.5 J 26.7 Guernsey Road; access to Point Mackenzie Rehabilitation Farm (0.6 mile), Farmer and Barley lakes.

K 10 J 27 Little Susitna River trailhead.

K 10.2 J 27.4 Road forks; keep to right for Little Susitna.

K 12 J 29.2 Entering Susitna Flats state Game Refuge (sign).

Statue at Iditarod Headquarters honors race founder Joe Redington Sr.
(© Kris Valencia, staff)

K 12.7 J 29.9 My Creek Trailhead. Day-use area. Parking $5.

K 13.1 J 30.3 Entrance/fee station for **Little Susitna River Public-use Facility** at River Mile 28.5 in the Susitna Flats State Game Refuge (N 61°26.229' W 150°10.453'). Continue on access road for Little Susitna River campground and boat launch; 83 parking spaces, 40 campsites, picnic tables, litter bins, outhouses, firewood $5, boat ramps, dump station $3, water, tables, toilets. Daily parking $5; boat launch, $10 (includes parking); overnight camping, $10. Popular boat launch site for fishermen after salmon on the Little Susitna. Phone (907) 745-3975.

Return to Milepost A 42.2
Parks Highway

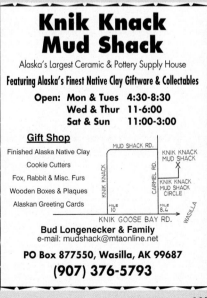

Enjoy the Farmer's Market every Wednesday in summer at Wasilla's Historic Town Site.
(© Kris Valencia, staff)

(Continued from page 413)
located off Point Mackenzie Road, 29.8 miles from the Parks Highway. There are 83 parking spaces, 65 campsites, campsite host, boat ramps, dump station, water, tables, toilets. Daily parking, $5; boat launch, $10 (includes parking); overnight camping, $10. *See Milepost K 13.1 in "Knik–Goose Bay Road" log on page 414.*

Finger Lake State Recreation Site is located at Mile 6.6 Bogard Road from the Crusey Street intersection on the Parks Highway. Scenic spot with 39 campsites, wheelchair-accessible toilets, picnic tables, water and boat launch, $15 camping fee, 7-day limit. Life preservers available for children through the "Kids Don't Float" program. *(Bogard Road is also accessible from Trunk Road off the Palmer–Wasilla Highway; see map on page 411.)*

Attractions

Dorothy G. Page Museum and Historic Town Site at 323 N. Main St., next to the library, is where visitors come to see exciting traveling exhibits, learn local history and walk through historic homes and buildings. The museum, housed in what was originally the community hall, was established in 1967 as Wasilla's first museum. The museum building and 1917 schoolhouse are listed on the National Register of Historic Places. The historic town, located behind the museum, has 8 preserved buildings. The museum is open year-round, Tuesday–Saturday, from 9 A.M. to 5 P.M.. Admission charged. For more information, visit their website at www.cityofwasilla.com/museum.

Town Square Art Gallery. Voted "Best Art Gallery" in the Valley. Representing the finest Alaskan artists—prints and originals distinctively custom framed. Jewelry, pottery, unique gifts, sculptures and cards. Open Monday–Friday 10 A.M. to 6 P.M., Saturdays 10 A.M. to 5 P.M. Carrs Mall. 591 E. Parks Highway, #406. Phone (907) 376-0123. www.townsquareartgallery.com. [ADVERTISEMENT]

A **Farmers Market** is held at the Old Wasilla Town Site every Wednesday during the summer from 11 A.M. to 7 P.M. A great place to buy fresh, Mat-Su Valley vegetables. The museum and library share a small parking lot. RVs should park on the street where permitted.

Iditarod Trail Sled Dog Race™ headquarters is located just west of the Parks Highway in Wasilla at 2100 S. Knik-Goose Bay Road. The internationally known 1,049-mile Iditarod Trail Sled Dog Race™ to Nome takes place the first Saturday in March with the start in Anchorage, followed by the re-start in Willow. The headquarters, open year-round, has historical displays on the Iditarod, videos, summer cart rides with an Iditarod musher and dog team, and a gift shop with unique souvenirs. Open daily in summer 8 A.M.–7 P.M., weekdays in winter 8 A.M.–5 P.M.. Large tours are welcome (calls in advance appreciated), phone (907) 376-5155, ext. 108. Circular drive for buses and motorhomes. No fee for museum or film. Fee charged for rides on wheeled cart pulled by dogs.

In 2012, Dallas Seavey, age 25, became the youngest musher to win the Iditarod, and in 2013 his father, 53-year-old Mitch Seavey, became the oldest musher to win the race. John Baker, the 2011 winner, holds the fastest winning time at 8 days, 18 hours, 46 minutes and 39 seconds—3 hours less than the previous record. Find out more about "The Last Great Race on Earth®" at www.iditarod.com.

Tour an Iditarod sled dog kennel. Iditarod racer **Vern Halter's Dream A Dream Iditarod Tours** on the Parks Highway (see **Milepost A 64.7**) offers daily tours of his kennels in summer; www.vernhalter.com, phone (907) 495-1197.

Knik Museum and Sled Dog Mushers' Hall of Fame, at Mile 13.9 Knik-Goose Bay Road, has dog mushing equipment, musher's portraits and historical displays of the Iditarod Trail. The museum is open June 1–August 31, Thursday–Sunday, noon–6 P.M. Admission $3. Phone (907) 376-7755 or (907) 376-2005 in summer. Open for tours in winter, by appointment call (907) 376-5679 in advance of your desired tour date.

Wasilla's 1917 Alaska Railroad Depot is also on the National Register of Historic Places. Restored by the local Lions Clubs and the Wasilla Chamber of Commerce, the depot is located on the south side of the Parks Highway at Main Street. A sign there reads: "Construction of the depot began 1916 as part of a national goal for the Alaska Railroad to open access to the interior of Alaska. This site marks the R.R. junction with the important Carle Trail (now known as Knik Rd./Main St./Fishhook Rd.) that was the main supply route between the tidewater trade center of Knik and the gold mines of the Willow Creek (Hatcher Pass) area. By drastically improving the lines of supply to miners and settlers in this region, this junction both created the new town of Wasilla and hastened the demise of Knik. For many years this depot was the major 'Outside' communication point for the surrounding district, via trains, the telegraph, and later one railroad system telephone. (On a regional basis, electricity did not become available to local farms and homes until 1942, and telephone until 1957.)"

Museum of Alaska Transportation and Industry, located a few miles west of Wasilla at **Milepost A 47**, has 20 acres of historic aircraft, railroad equipment, old farm machinery, heavy equipment and 1937 Colony Barn. Gift shop, clean restrooms and gallery for your enjoyment. New exhibits and events are being added all the time. www.museumofalaska.org.

The restored **Herning-Teeland-Mead Building**, which now houses a cafe, was built in 1918. Located on Herning Avenue adja-

cent the historical park, it is on the National Register of Historic Sites.

Special Events. Iditarod Days is held in conjunction with the Iditarod Race in March. Check with the Mat-Su Visitors Bureau for details on other winter and summer events.

Play Golf. The well-maintained, 18-hole Settlers Bay Golf Course, located off Knik-Goose Bay Road (see log this section), offers stunning views of the Mat-Su Valley and Chugach mountains. The course has several challenging holes. Cart rentals, driving range, putting green, pro shop and dining are also available. Visit www.settlersbay.org or phone (907) 376-5466 for information.

Sleepy Hollow Golf Course, a 9-hole, par 27 course, is located 7 miles north of Wasilla. Driving range, putting green, pull carts, rental clubs. The longest hole is 200 yards. Hours are 9 A.M. to 9 P.M. daily, May–Sept. For more information and driving directions, phone (907) 376-5948.

AREA FISHING: Check the ADF&G website for sport fishing updates for Mat-Su Valley (Palmer/Matanuska-Susitna Valley) lakes and streams at www.sf.adfg.state.ak.us. Also check with local fishing guides.

Mat-Su Valley lakes are stocked with rainbow trout, landlocked salmon, arctic grayling, lake trout, arctic char, or some combination of these fish. A list of stocked lakes is available from ADF&G at www.sf.adfg.state.ak.us/statewide/lakedata/.

King salmon begin to move into the clear water streams of the **Susitna River** drainage in early June. Highest catch rates in early June are usually from **Deshka River** and the **Little Susitna River**. The Little Susitna River produces fair to good catches of king salmon through June, with most of the fishing occurring from the Little Susitna Public-Use Facility *(see "Knik Goose Bay Road" log pages 414-415)* upstream to the Parks Highway. By late June, fishing is good near the Parks Highway bridge. As June wears on, king fishing improves in the Parks Highway streams. **Willow Creek** and the other Parks Highway roadside streams are open to king fishing from Jan. 1 through June 20, and then on weekends only until the season closes on July 13. A weekend is Saturday, Sunday, and Monday. *NOTE: Check fishing regulations carefully for seasons and restrictions.*

Parks Highway Log
(continued)

A 42.5 C 167.5 F 319.5 Stoplight at Lucille Street. View of Lake Lucille to south.

A 42.7 C 167.3 F 319.3 Frontier Mall to north.

A 42.8 C 167.2 F 319.2 Wasilla Shopping Center to north.

A 43 C 167 F 319 Stoplight at Weber Dr. Access to Iditapark.

A 43.1 C 166.9 F 318.9 B & J Mall.

A 43.2 C 166.8 F 318.8 Westside Center.

A 43.5 C 166.5 F 318.5 Lucus Road; Hallea Lane access to Lake Lucille; access to **Best Western Lake Lucille Inn** to south. Bike route begins northbound.

Best Western Lake Lucille Inn. See display ad on page 413.

A 44 C 166 F 318 *Begin 2-lane highway northbound. Begin 4-lane highway southbound.* Welcome to Wasilla (southbound sign).

A 44.5 C 165.5 F 317.5 Church Road/S. Mack Drive. Access north to Bumpus ball fields. Take Mack Drive 1/4 mile to **Curtis C.**

Wasilla's Dorothy G. Page Museum and visitor center on Main Street. (©Kris Valencia, staff)

Menard Sports Complex; ice rink, turf court and running track. Open to public.

CAUTION: Moose Danger Zone. Watch for moose next 12.7 miles northbound.

A 44.6 C 165.4 F 317.4 *CAUTION: Begin* **Highway Traffic Safety Corridor** *northbound to* **Milepost 53***: Traffic fines double. Drive carefully! This is considered a dangerous section of road because of the high number of head-on collisions and accidents with fatalities. This section of highway is targeted for major redesign with stoplights and additional lanes added for increased safety.*

A 45.2 C 164.8 F 316.8 Distance marker northbound shows Cantwell 164 miles, Denali National Park 192 miles, Fairbanks 309 miles.

A 45.4 C 164.6 F 316.6 Wasilla city limits.

A 47 C 163 F 315 3800 Turnoff to south on West Museum Drive for Wasilla municipal airport and the **Museum of Alaska Transportation and Industry.** The museum, located approximately 1 mile from the highway (follow signs), makes a nice stop for travelers. Historic aircraft, railroad equipment, old farm machinery and heavy equipment are displayed in a 20-acre park-like setting. Meander among the airplanes and trains, or have a picnic on the grounds. RV parking and turnaround. Open daily, 10 A.M. to 5 P.M., from May 11 to September 1, 2014.

Museum of Alaska Transportation and Industry. See display ad this page.

A 47.3 C 162.7 F 314.7 Distance marker northbound shows Big Lake Junction 5 miles, Houston 10 miles.

A 47.7 C 162.3 F 314.3 Stoplight at Vine Road. Shell Gas Station with diesel to south. (Vine Road connects with Knik-Goose

Bay Road.)

[b]

A 48.2 C 161.8 F 313.8 Alaska Trails RV and Camp Park to south offers super-sized pull through sites for large RVs.

[A]

Alaskan Trails RV and Camper Park. See display ad this page.

A 48.6 C 161.4 F 313.4 Stoplight at junction with Sylvan Road and Pittman Road to Rainbow Lake. Tesoro/7-Eleven, cafe and access to Meadow Lakes City Center to south. Alaska State Troopers/Mat-Su West Post is to the north at 527 Pittman Road, visible from the Parks Highway, next to Three

Always be alert for wildlife crossing Alaska roads and highways. (©Laurie Gerber)

Bears. Hours are 8 A.M. to 4:30 P.M.; phone (907) 373-8300. If you require assistance after hours, phone (907) 352-5401 (Mat-Com Dispatch).

A 48.7 C 161.3 F 313.3 Holiday gas station with diesel/Subway to north; Meadow Lakes Road access to Seymour, Lalen Visnaw lakes.

A 49.5 C 160.5 F 312.5 **The Roadside Inn** to west; home-style food, lounge, motel. **The Roadside Inn.** See display ad on this page.

A 50.2 C 159.8 F 311.8 Private RV park.

A 51 C 159 F 311 Veterinary hospital.
A 51.5 C 158.5 F 310.5 Fishers Fuel Inc. Tesoro gas station with diesel to west.

Highway Safety Corridor, 55 mph speed zone southbound.

A 52.2 C 157.8 F 309.8 Southbound distance marker indicates Wasilla 10

miles, Anchorage 52 miles.

A 52.3 C 157.7 F 309.7 **Junction** with Big Lake Road; Meadowood Mall. Big Lake Road leads west to Big Lake recreation area (camping, boating). East Lake Mall at Mile 4 on Big Lake Road has **Big Lake IGA** (voted "best grocery in the Valley") .

Junction with Big Lake Road. See "Big Lake Road" log on facing page.

Houston city limits. Houston is the only place in the Mat-Su Borough where it is legal to sell fireworks, so there are usually several fireworks outlets near the Big Lake Road junction. Fireworks are illegal in Anchorage.
Begin bike route southbound.
Passing lane southbound. CAUTION: High traffic area. Drive carefully!
A 52.7 C 157.3 F 309.3 Distance marker northbound indicates Cantwell 157 miles, Denali National Park 184 miles, Fairbanks 302 miles.
A 53.2 C 156.8 F 308.8 Turnoff for Houston High School and Mid-Valley Senior Center (visitors welcome).
A 54 C 156 F 308 *Begin passing lane northbound.*
A 54.8 C 155.2 F 307.2 Bike Route begins northbound, east side of highway.
A 55.4 C 154.6 F 306.6 *End passing lane northbound.*
A 56.1 C 153.9 F 305.9 Miller's Reach Road. Alaska's most destructive wildfire began here in June 1996. The Big Lake wildfire burned some 37,500 acres and 433 buildings and homes.
A 56.3 C 153.7 F 305.7 Alaska Railroad overpass.
A 56.6 C 153.4 F 305.4 King Arthur Drive; public access to Bear Paw, Prator and Loon lakes to east (no camping).
Views of Pioneer Peak southbound.
A 56.8 C 153.2 F 305.2 *CAUTION: Moose Danger Zone. Watch for moose next 12.7 miles southbound.*
Improved highway northbound.
A 57 C 153 F 305 Highway bridge and pedestrian bridge cross the Little Susitna River; a very popular fishing and camping area. Parking areas both sides of highway

with pedestrian access to Little Susitna River.
The **Little Susitna River** has a tremendous king salmon run and one of the largest silver salmon runs in southcentral Alaska. King salmon to 30 lbs., mid-May through late June on lower river, mid-June through season close in mid-July on upper river; use large red spinners or salmon eggs. Silvers to 15 lbs., mid-July through mid-August on lower river, early August through early September on upper river. Also red salmon to 10 lbs., mid-July through early August. Charter boats nearby. This river heads in the Talkeetna Mountains to the northeast and flows 110 miles into Upper Cook Inlet.

A 57.3 C 152.7 F 304.7 Turnoff to east on Armstrong Road for Houston City Hall, William A. Philo Public Safety Bldg. *(emergency phone)* and city-operated **Little Susitna River Campground** (follow signs). Dump station ($5) at entrance to campground is open May through October. The campground has 86 sites (many wide, level gravel sites); picnic tables, firepits; restrooms, water pump, playground, large picnic pavilion; 10-day limit, $10 camping fee charged.

A 57.4 C 152.6 F 304.6 HOUSTON (pop. 1,588) has a grocery store, laundromat, gift shop, food, lodging, pay phone, campground and gas station. Post office located in the grocery store.

Houston is a popular fishing center for anglers on the Little Susitna River. Fishing charter operators and marine service are located here. Emergency phone at Houston fire station. Originally Houston siding on the Alaska Railroad, the area was homesteaded in the 1950s and incorporated as a city in 1966. A Founder's Day celebration is held in August. This annual event features a barbecue dinner, fireworks and entertainment.
A 57.5 C 152.5 F 304.5 Miller's Place; groceries, soft ice cream, food, post office.
A 57.7 C 152.3 F 304.3 **Riverside Camper Park.** RV Park on the Little Susitna River. 56 full-service hookups (water, sewer and electric on each site). Showers, laundromat, free WiFi. Excellent bank fishing area in RV park. Center lawn with pavilion for group activities. Phone (907) 892-9020. P.O. Box 940087, Houston, AK 99694. Email: aksalmon@mtaonline.net.
[ADVERTISEMENT]

A 58.3 C 151.7 F 303.7 *Begin passing lane northbound.*
A 60.1 C 149.9 F 301.9 Gold Miners Lodge; motel, cafe to east.
A 60.7 C 149.3 F 301.3 *End passing lanes northbound and southbound. Watch for moose.*
A 61 C 149 F 301 Houston city limits northbound.
A 61.1 C 148.9 F 300.9 Welcome to Willow northbound.
A 61.3 C 148.7 F 300.7 Family Health Clinic to west.
A 62.1 C 147.9 F 299.9 *Begin passing lane southbound.*
A 62.4 C 147.6 F 299.6 *Begin passing lane northbound.*
A 63.9 C 146.1 F 298.1 *End passing lane northbound.*
A 64.7 C 145.3 F 297.3 Allen Road. Turnoff to east and drive 1.5 miles for Iditarod racer Vern Halter's **Dream A Dream Dog Farm** (description follows); lodging and tours. Go to www.vernhalter.com for details.

(Continues on page 420)

Big Lake Road

Big Lake Road is a paved 2-lane road providing access to homes and recreation areas on Big Lake. It is an extremely busy road. Posted speed limit is 45 to 55 mph; slow for curves and speed zones. *Pass with care!* There is a bike trail along Big Lake Road.

Big Lake has been a resort destination for Alaskans since the 1940s. The area has grown in recent years—along with the rest of the Mat-Su Valley—and now has a number of residential subdivisions and the traffic that accompanies population growth. Watch for ATVs in summer and snowmachines in winter along Big Lake Road.

Summer recreation at Big Lake includes swimming, camping, boating, fishing and jet skiing. Public access to the lake is provided by 2 state recreation sites: Big Lake North and Big Lake South. Winter sports include snowmachining, cross-country skiing and ice fishing.

For more information on state recreation sites, phone the regional Alaska State Parks office at (907) 269-8400; or visit their web site at www.dnr.state.ak.us/parks.

BIG LAKE ROAD

Distance is measured from the junction (J) with the Parks Highway, Milepost A 52.3

J 0 Junction with Parks Highway.

J 0.1 Meadowood Mall; auto parts store.

J 0.2 Begin bike route westbound.

J 1.3 Turnoff to north for Houston High School and senior center.

Willow, birch and aspen trees have replaced the spruce forest that fueled the June 1996 Miller's Reach Fire, which burned more than 37,0000 acres and destroyed 433 buildings and homes.

J 3.3 Junction with Beaver Lake Road; access to Rocky Lake SRS and Martin Buser's Happy Trails Kennel. Drive 0.5 mile north (follow signs) for **Rocky Lake State Recreation Site**; 12 campsites ($15 fee) on a bumpy, gravel loop road, outhouses, canoe rentals, firepits, water pump and boat launch (lake is closed to jet skis, jet boats and airboats). Life preservers available for children through the "Kids Don't Float" program. Not recommended for large RVs.

Drive 0.9 mile north on Beaver Lake Road then 4.3 miles west on West Lakes Blvd. for Happy Trails Kennel; for kennel tour times phone (907) 892-7899 or visit www.buserdog.com.

J 3.5 Tesoro 24-hour gas station, store, ATM. Welcome to Alaska's Year-Round Playground sign here has map of Big Lake. Big Lake is connected with smaller lakes by dredged waterways. It is possible to boat for several miles. Fish in Big Lake include Dolly Varden, rainbow trout, red and silver salmon, burbot and arctic char.

J 3.6 Fisher's Y; junction with North Shore Drive. **BIG LAKE** (pop. 3,350) post office at 'Y' (ZIP code 99652); liquor store, laundromat. **Visitor information:** Big Lake Chamber of Commerce, P.O. Box 520067, Big Lake, AK 99652; phone (907) 892-6109, www.biglakechamber.org.

Take North Shore Drive (paved) 1.5 miles to end at **Big Lake North State Recreation Site**; 60 overnight parking spaces ($15 fee),

walk-in tent sites, campground host, pay phone, picnicking, shelters, water, outhouses, dumpsters, snack shop, day-use fee $5, boat launch $10. Located on the lake; good views of the Alaska Range and Denali on a clear day. Life preservers are available for children to use through the statewide "Kids Don't Float" program.

Keep left at 'Y' westbound to continue on South Lake Road.

SOUTH LAKE ROAD

J 3.6 Post office.

J 3.8 Edward "Bud" Beech Firehall/West Lake Fire Dept. *Emergency phone.*

J 3.9 Big Lake Library to north.

J 4 East Lake Mall; **Big Lake IGA** grocery, 2 restaurants, liquor store, credit union, gift shop, espresso and other businesses. Big Lake Chamber of Commerce Visitor Center is located in a cabin at the corner of this parking lot. Junction with Hollywood Road, which connects to Knik Road via Vine.

Big Lake IGA. See display ad this page.

J 4.2 Laundromat, showers.

J 4.5 Big Lake Elementary school.

J 4.6 Private Aircraft: Big Lake airport; elev. 150 feet; length 2,400 feet; gravel; fuel 100LL.

J 4.8 Big Lake Motel to north.

J 4.9 Fish Creek Park (Mat-Su Borough), a popular day-use area with access to Fish Creek, salmon spawning observation deck, picnic area, swimming, pavilion, restroom, playground, parking and open lawn area. End bike lane. Bridge over Fish Creek.

J 5.2 Big Lake South State Recreation Site; gravel parking area (watch for potholes); day-use and overnight camping with 20 campsites ($15 fee), firepits, outhouses, water, dumpsters, parking, fishing and boat ramp. "Kids Don't Float" life preservers. Day-use $5 feet, boat launch $10.

J 5.4 Turnoff for South Port Marina; phone, rentals, sales and repair, boat launch, gas, propane.

J 5.5 Sunset View Resort and Boathouse Restaurant.

J 6 Road narrows, tight curves, speed limit 25 mph.

J 7.9 State road maintenance ends (sign); turnout.

J 8.2 Access road to north for day-use area, paved parking (fee charged), boat launch $10, restrooms.

J 9 Stop sign at "Four Corners" inter-

Big Lake is popular for boating and jet skis as well as swimming, camping and fishing.
(©Kris Valencia, staff)

section of South Lake Road with Marion, Susitna and Burma roads. Continue straight ahead 3.5 miles to junction of Burma Road and Bryant; turn right on to Burma Road (follow signs). Burma Road is a winding dirt road that leads 8.5 miles south to junction with Point Mackenzie Road.

Marion Road leads 0.5 mile east to public fishing access, then continues past private lakefront homes through a rural residential area.

Turn north on Susitna Parkway for access to Flat Lake and Mud Lake. Continue north on Susitna Parkway for Diamond Lake public fishing access (3.2 miles from Four Corners junction) and Crooked Lake public fishing access (3.6 miles from junction). Susitna Parkway junctions with Timberline Drive in a rural residential area.

**Return to Milepost A 52.3
Parks Highway**

The Alaska Railroad parallels and crosses the Parks Highway between Anchorage and Fairbanks. (©Sharon Nault)

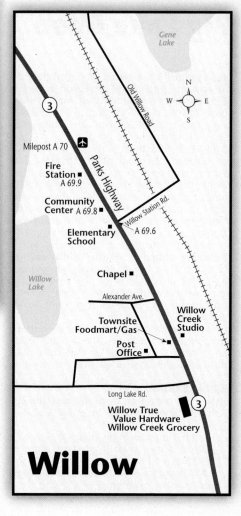

Willow

(Continued from page 418)

Dream A Dream Dog Farm is a fantastic place to visit or stay. People rave about our great Iditarod presentation, our nature hikes with the pups, and that our rides are inspirational and fun. We have raced 26 Iditarod and Yukon Quest races. Plan on your visit being personal, exclusive and fun! Plan on learning about and enjoying our dogs and pups. Stay overnight too! Call for appointment, (907) 495-1197. Dream a Dream Dog Farm, P.O. Box 389, Willow, AK 99688; vhalter@mtaonline.net; www.vernhalter.com. See display ad this page. [ADVERTISEMENT]

A 66.3 C 143.7 F 295.7 White's Crossing highway bridge crosses railroad tracks.

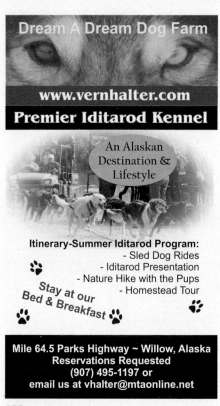
A 66.5 C 143.5 F 295.5 Turnoff to west for **Nancy Lake State Recreation Site**; turn left (south) on Buckingham Palace Road and drive 0.3 miles; 30 campsites, 30 picnic sites, toilets, boat launch, horseshoe pits, camping fee $10/night. This is the easiest public access to Nancy Lake, which offers 4 public-use cabins accessible by land or canoe (see also Nancy Lake Parkway access at **Milepost A 67.3**).

A 67 C 143 F 295 Distance marker southbound shows Wasilla 25 miles, Anchorage 67 miles.

A 67.1 C 142.9 F 294.9 Sunshine Community Health Center's Willow Clinic to west; phone (907) 495-4100.

A 67.2 C 142.8 F 294.8 St. Christopher's Catholic Church.

A 67.3 C 142.7 F 294.7 Turnoff to west on Nancy Lake Parkway (paved) for Nancy Lake State Recreation Area; very popular canoeing area with canoe trails, public-use cabins, hiking trails, fishing, picnicking and camping. Access to lakes, cabins and canoe trails from trailheads along Parkway (description follows). Ice is usually off area lakes by mid-May.

Nancy Lake Parkway mileages: **Mile 0.7** Lynne Lake Road; **Mile 1.3** entrance station and park ranger; **Mile 1.6** trail to Nancy Lake canoe launch; **Mile 1.8** trailhead parking and summer trail to Nancy Lake public-use cabins 1, 2, 3 and 4; **Mile 2.1** trailhead parking and winter gates (gate closes in October, date determined by snowfall, as it is unmaintained); Access allowed beyond this gate closure for skiers, dog mushers, snow-machines as a multi-use trail; **Mile 2.6** Bald Lake trailhead; **Mile 4.8** Tanaina Lake, canoe trailhead; **Mile 5.1** Rhein Lake trailhead; **Mile 5.9** North Rolly Lake trailhead; **Mile 6.1** South Rolly Overlook (picnic area); **Mile 6.5** road ends at Red Shirt Lake trailhead parking and entrance to South Rolly Lake Campground. The campground has 98 sites, firepits, toilets, water, canoe rental and boat launch (trolling motors only); firewood for sale. Camping fee $10/night. Canoe rentals

at Tippecanoe Rentals office at South Rolly Lake; phone (907) 495-6688, www.paddle alaska.com. **South Rolly Lake** has a small population of rainbow that average 12 to 14 inches.

To help you plan a multi-lake/multi-cabin canoe trip, download a cabin fact sheet at http://dnr.alaska.gov/parks/cabins/nancylkfs.pdf and general information brochure at http://dnr.alaska.gov/parks/brochures/nancylake.pdf

The public-use cabins are $45–$60 a night, and they sleep 4–8. Make sure to bring sleeping pads (the wood sleeping platforms are hard) and bug spray (lots of mosquitoes). Also consider a sleeping mask in the summer: There are no shades on the windows and it stays light until quite late on summer nights.

A 67.5 C 142.5 F 294.5 Mormon Church and Camp LaDaSa to east.

A 67.6 C 142.4 F 294.4 United Methodist Church to west.

End passing lane southbound.

NOTE: Driving distance between Mileposts 68 and 70 is 1.8 miles.

A 68.5 C 141.5 F 293.5 Newman's Hilltop Tesoro west side of highway. Weekly Willow Farmers Market on Fridays in summer, east side of highway.

Begin passing lane southbound.

A 68.6 C 141.4 F 293.4 Entering Willow, northbound. *Begin 45 mph speed zone northbound. Begin 55 mph speed limit southbound.*

A 69 C 141 F 293 Willow Creek Grocery and **Willow Creek True Value Hardware** store on west side

of highway. Willow extends about 2.5 miles north along the Parks Highway.

Willow True Value Hardware and Willow Creek Grocery. See display ad this page.

A 69.2 C 140.8 F 292.8 Long Lake Road. Burger Bus at junction.

A 69.3 C 140.7 F 292.7 Beluga Road access to Willow medical clinic and minimall. Roni's Chinook Deli.

A 69.5 C 140.5 F 292.5 Townsite Foodmart to west, open 24 hours, has gas, diesel, deli, liquor store, fishing licenses and supplies, pay phone. Alexander Avenue; access west to Willow Post Office. **Willow Creek Studio** on the east side of the road makes an interesting stop.

Townsite Foodmart. See display ad this page.

Willow Creek Studio. See display ad this page.

WILLOW (pop. 2,102) had its start about 1897, when gold was discovered in the area. In the early 1940s, mining in the nearby Talkeetna Mountains slacked off, leaving Willow a virtual ghost town. The community made a comeback upon completion of the Parks Highway in 1972. In 1976, Alaska voters selected the Willow area for their new capital site. However, funding for the capital move from Juneau to Willow was defeated in the November 1982 election. **Radio:** KTNA 88.5-FM.

The Willow civic organization sponsors an annual Winter Carnival in January and the Iditarod in early March. The **Iditarod Restart** takes place on Willow Lake (access from **Milepost A 69.8** Parks Highway) on Sunday, following the ceremonial start of the race in Anchorage on the first Saturday in March. There is very limited parking in Willow for the Iditarod Restart, so park at one of the organized sights offering shuttle bus service. For the 2013 Iditarod, there was parking/shuttle service at Wasilla High School, Houston High School and Curtis D. Menard Memorial Sports Center on Mack Road. (If you go to the Iditarod Restart, get an early start: Even with the shuttle buses, traffic on the Parks Highway can be at a standstill.)

The Iditarod starting chute stretches along Willow Lake and it is an exciting place to be, with thousands of race fans lined up, cheering on their favorites. The first musher was out of the gate at 2 P.M. in 2013, followed by more than 60 other racers at fixed intervals. Between Willow and Nome, they are on the trail for 1,049 miles.

Willow has a well-established winter trail system, popular with snowmobiles and recreational mushers.

The Big Susitna River and Deshka River on the west and the Willow Creek tributaries flowing from the east make for fantastic area fishing. All 4 species of salmon, along with rainbow and grayling fishing, are found here.

A 69.6 C 140.4 F 292.4 Willow Elementary School to west. Willow Station Road (paved) leads east to Willow Trading Post (restaurant) and continues north to junction with the Willow-Fishhook Road to Hatcher Pass or return to Parks Highway (see **Milepost A 71.2**).

On a clear day, views northbound of Denali down the center of the road.

A 69.8 C 140.2 F 292.2 Access road west to **Willow Library and Willow Community Center.** Library hours vary; phone (907)

Iditarod Sled Dog Race Restart enthralls crowds lined up to watch on Willow Lake.
(©Kris Valenica, staff)

495-7323. The community center has a large parking area, commercial kitchen, covered picnic pavilion, grills, ball court, boat launch and pay phone. Available for rent to groups, 500-person capacity; phone (907) 495-6633. Site of Iditarod Restart on Willow Lake in March.

A 69.9 C 140.1 F 292.1 Fire station to west. *Emergency phone.*

A 70 C 140 F 292 Willow Airport Road to east. **Private Aircraft:** Willow airport; elev. 221 feet; length 4,400 feet; gravel; fuel 100LL. Unattended.

A 70.1 C 139.9 F 291.9 *Begin 45 mph speed zone southbound. Resume 55 mph northbound.*

A 70.8 C 139.2 F 291.2 Junction with Willow Creek Parkway (paved); access to Susitna River from Willow Creek SRA and Deshka Landing (descriptions follow).

Follow Willow Creek Parkway west 3.7

Willow-Fishhook Road leads east off the Parks Highway along Willow Creek then up to Hatcher Pass. (©Meghan Mackey, staff)

miles to **Willow Creek State Recreation Area** entrance/fee station; camping $10 per night, parking $5 per day. Paved parking for side-by-side camping with firepits and tables, litter bins, water and toilets. Day-use parking area is potholed gravel. Campground host, walking paths, interpretive displays, walk to creek. Fishing for silvers, pinks, chum and king salmon. It is ¼-mile to confluence with the Susitna River. Willow Creek is the 4th busiest king salmon fishing area in the state. Current fishing conditions posted at fee station.

Access to **Deshka Landing** boat launch facility: At Mile 1.8 Willow Creek Parkway; turn on Crystal Lake Road and continue 5.2 miles on paved road (Crystal Lake to Mishap Avenue to Gomer Lane to Deshka Landing Road). Concessionaire-operated facility at Deshka Landing is open daily 5 A.M. to midnight in summer; phone (907) 495-3374 for winter hours. Fees charged for boat launch and parking; season pass available. Fishing for king and silver salmon, rainbow. www.deshkalanding.com.

The **Susitna River** begins at Susitna Glacier in the Alaska Range to the northeast and flows west then south for 260 miles to Cook Inlet. The **Deshka River**, a tributary of the Susitna River about 6 miles downstream from Deshka Landing, is one of southcentral Alaska's best king salmon fisheries. According to the ADF&G, the king salmon run is from late May through late June on the lower river, and early June through season close in mid-July on the upper river; peak fishing at the mouth of the Deshka River is usually June 13–20. The Deshka River is open to the retention of king salmon for the first 19 miles, which is indicated by a marker at Chijuk Creek. Silver salmon run from mid-July through early August on the lower river, and late July through early September on the upper river.

Also signed public fishing access to **Little Lonely Lake** on Crystal Lake Road and to **Vera Lake** on Deshka Landing Road.

A 71.2 C 138.8 F 290.8 Willow–Fishhook (Hatcher Pass) Road. This 49-mile side road connects with the Glenn Highway at Palmer. Independence Mine State Historical Park is 32 miles from here on the east side of Hatcher Pass, which is usually snow-free by mid-June.

Junction with Willow–Fishhook (Hatcher Pass) Road. See "Hatcher Pass Road" log on in the GLENN HIGHWAY section. Turn to page 367 and read log back to front.

Distance marker northbound shows Cantwell 138 miles, Denali National Park 166 miles, Fairbanks 283 miles.

Bike trail ends northbound, begins southbound.

A 71.4 C 138.6 F 290.6 Willow Creek Bridge. Resort to west at north end of bridge. Excellent king salmon fishing in **Willow Creek**; also silvers, rainbow. Inquire at resort for information. Entering Game Management Subunit 14B northbound, 14A southbound.

A 72 C 137 F 290 *Speed limit 65 mph northbound; 55 mph speed zone southbound.*

A 74.5 C 135.5 F 287.5 *Improved highway with passing lanes next 9 miles northbound.*

A 74.7 C 135.3 F 287.3 Bridge over **Little Willow Creek**. Parking to west, pedestrian access to east. Fishing for salmon and trout; *check regulations booklet carefully!*

A 75.2 C 134.8 F 286.8 Capital City Speedway to west.

A 76.4 C 133.6 F 285.6 Turnout to west by **Kashwitna Lake**. Signed public fishing access to Kashwitna Lake, which is stocked with rainbow trout. Small planes land on lake. Private floatplane base on east shore. Good camera viewpoints of lake and Mount McKinley.

A 81.3 C 128.7 F 280.7 Turnout to west. **Grey's Creek**; fishing.

A 82.4 C 127.6 F 279.6 Distance marker southbound shows Wasilla 40 miles, Anchorage 83 miles.

A 82.5 C 127.5 F 279.5 Susitna Landing **Access Facility**, Public Boat Launch; 1 mile west via gravel road. Concessionaire **Susitna Landing** operates an RV park, campground, cabin rentals and boat launch on ADF&G land. The boat launch is on the **Kashwitna River**, just upstream of the **Susitna River**, and provides access to both rivers. Fees charged for camping, boat launch, daily parking and firewood. Wheelchair-accessible restrooms, showers, espresso and bank fishing. Winter snowmobile access.

A 82.6 C 127.4 F 279.4 *Road construction next 7 miles (summer 2013). Expect continued construction and/or improved highway in summer 2014.*

A 83.2 C 126.8 F 278.8 Bridge over the Kashwitna River. A pedestrian bridge also crosses this river. The Kashwitna River heads in the Talkeetna Mountains and flows westward to the Susitna River.

Views of Denali northbound (weather permitting).

A 84 C 126 F 278 Turnoff for Susitna Shores. Public access (walk-in) for fishing at **Caswell Creek**; kings, silvers, pinks and rainbow.

A 85.1 C 124.9 F 276.9 Caswell Creek.

A 86 C 124 F 276 Resolute Drive. Turnoff to west for **Sheep Creek Slough** public fishing access. Drive 1 mile west to large gravel parking area, toilets, dumpster and wheelchair-accessible trail to mouth of creek. Fishing for kings, silvers, pinks and rainbow.

A 87.9 C 122.1 F 274.1 Hidden Hills Road to east; turnoff for **Gigglewood Lakeside Inn**.

Gigglewood Lakeside Inn. See display ad this page.

A 88 C 122 F 274 Sheep Creek Lodge, in a picturesque Swedish-scribed log building on the east side of the highway. Current status unknown.

A 88.5 C 121.5 F 273.5 Bridge over **Sheep Creek.** Vehicle access to creek to west at north end of bridge. Pedestrian bridge crosses creek; pedestrian tunnel under highway. Fishing for salmon and trout.

A 89 C 121 F 273 Large gravel turnout to west; small gravel turnout to east.

A 90.8 C 119.2 F 271.2 Mat-Su Valley RV Park 0.1 mile east.

A 91.6 C 118.4 F 270.4 *CAUTION: Railroad crossing. Slow for bumpy road.*

A 92.2 C 117.8 F 269.8 Gravel shoulder parking to east.

A 93 C 117 F 269 Gravel turnout to west.

A 93.4 C 116.6 F 268.6 **Goose Creek** culvert (unsigned); gravel turnouts to east and west. Fishing.

A 93.5 C 116.5 F 268.5 Distance marker northbound shows Talkeetna Road Junction 5 miles.

A 94.2 C 115.8 F 267.8 Upper Susitna shooting range to east.

A 94.7 C 115.3 F 267.33 Gravel turnout to west.

A 96 C 114 F 266 Gravel turnouts to east and west.

A 96.1 C 113.9 F 265.9 Montana Creek shoulder parking to west.

A 96.2 C 113.8 F 265.8 Montana Creek Road. **MONTANA CREEK** (pop. about 500) was settled by homesteaders in the 1950s. Radio: KTNA 88.5-FM.

A 96.5 C 113.5 F 265.5 **Montana Creek Campground,** east side of highway, has camping, short-term parking for fishermen ($10), general store with fishing supplies, rental gear, snacks, beverages; firewood available for campers. Montana Creek State Recreation Site west side of highway; camping. Pedestrian tunnel under highway and pedestrian bridge adjacent highway bridge across Montana Creek. Public access trail to mouth of Montana Creek on the Susitna River. Excellent king salmon fishing, also silvers, pinks (even-numbered years), grayling, rainbow and Dolly Varden.

Montana Creek Campground. See display ad this page.

A 96.6 C 113.4 F 265.4 Montana Creek Bridge.

A 97.4 C 112.6 F 264.6 Large gravel turnout to east.

A 97.7 C 112.3 F 264.3 *Begin 55 mph speed zone northbound.*

A 98.4 C 111.6 F 263.6 Turnoff to west for Senior Center and for Su Valley Jr/Sr High School, which burned down in 2007. The new School, completed in 2010, is the first high school in Alaska to receive certification as a LEED (Leadership in Energy and Environmental Design) building. A 3.1-mile trail for running in summer, cross-country skiing in winter. Baptist church to east.

Distance marker southbound shows Wasilla 56 miles, Anchorage 98 miles.

A 98.6 C 111.4 F 263.4 Cubby's Marketplace to east; groceries, deli, liquor store.

A 98.7 C 111.3 F 263.3 **Talkeetna Y.** Turn east on paved spur road for Talkeetna. Talkeetna/Denali Visitor Center at junction with information on area attractions and lodging; restrooms, picnic area. Tesoro gas station just north of junction.

Montana Creek pedestrian bridge provides safe passage. (©Kris Valencia, staff)

Junction with Talkeetna Spur Road, which leads 14 miles northeast to Talkeetna. See "Talkeetna Spur Road" beginning on page 424 for log of road and description of Talkeetna.

A 98.8 C 111.2 F 263.2 Public Safety Building on west side of highway; *emergency phone.* Tesoro gas station with store, Subway, ATM, gas, diesel, propane, pay phone and showers (for a fee), east side of Parks Highway, north of Talkeetna "Y."

A 99.3 C 110.7 F 262.7 Montana Lake to east, **Little Montana Lake** to west. Public access to Little Montana Lake (stocked with rainbow) from parking area to west.

Distance marker northbound shows Cantwell 111 miles, Denali National Park 138 miles, Fairbanks 256 miles.

A 99.5 C 110.5 F 262.5 **His & Hers Lakeview Lounge & Restaurant**; food, gas station with diesel, cabins, RV park to east overlooking lake (description follows).

His & Hers. Restaurant, lounge, RV sites. Enjoy lakeview dining; lunch and dinner. "Our bread pudding is famous statewide." Lakeside camping; pull-throughs, 30-amp RV sites, RV dump, laundry, showers. Caravans and tours welcome (please call in advance, 48-hour notice). Phone (907) 733-2415. [ADVERTISEMENT]

A 100.4 C 109.6 F 261.6 *CAUTION: Railroad crossing.*

A 101.3 C 108.7 F 260.7 *Begin 55 mph speed zone southbound. Posted speed limit is 65 mph northbound.*

A 102.2 C 107.8 F 259.8 Large, paved turnout to east.

A 102.6 C 107.4 F 259.4 Sunshine Creek Road to east; transfer station. Access east to **Sunshine Creek** via 0.6-mile narrow, dirt road to Sunshine Creek Stream Access (Mat-Su Borough; phone (907) 745-4801); public

parking. Fishing for rainbow trout.

A 103.9 C 106.1 F 258.1 Distance marker southbound shows Talkeetna Road Junction 5 miles.

(Continues on page 429)

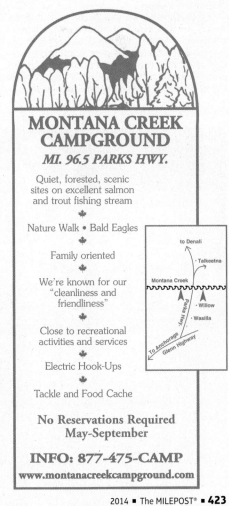

Talkeetna Spur Road

Viewpoint at Milepost J 12.9 on the Talkeenta Spur offers view of Denali on a clear day.
(©Rebecca Barker Permar, staff)

The Talkeetna Spur Road turns off the Parks Highway at **Milepost A 98.7** and leads north 14 miles to dead end at the community of Talkeetna. This is a good, paved side road with a non-motorized trail along the west side of the road.

Talkeetna is a unique blend of old-time Alaska small town and modern tourist destination. It is an aviation and supply base for Denali/Mount McKinley climbing expeditions. Talkeetna has restaurants, lodging, shops, excellent museums, sled dog kennel tours, fishing, flightseeing and river tours.

Distance from Parks Highway junction (J) at Milepost A 98.7 is shown.

J 0 Junction with the Parks Highway at **Milepost A 98.7.**

J 0.1 Talkeetna/Denali Visitor Center has information on area activities, lodging and reservation services; WiFi spot, phone 1-800-660-2688 or (907) 733-2688. Next door is Cubby's Marketplace for liquor, and groceries; fast-food outlet.

J 0.2 State Troopers to the north. True Value Hardware.

J 1.1 Kahiltna Birchworks (Alaska Wild Harvest) offers tastings and tours.
Kahiltna Birchworks. See display ad this page.
J 3 Talkeetna Denali View Lodge & Cabins and Talkeetna Lakeside Cabins.
Talkeetna Denali View Lodge & Cabins. See display ad this page.
Talkeetna Lakeside Cabins. See display ad this page.
J 3.1 E. Yoder Road (gravel). Go south 0.5 mile then left on Lakeview Street 0.7 mile for public fishing access to **Benka Lake** (stocked with rainbow). Go south 2.6 miles on Yoder Road for informal access to gravel bars at **Montana Creek** bridge. Yoder Road junctions with Montana Creek Road.

J 3.5 Talkeetna baptist church.
J 4.2 Sunshine Community Health Center to west; phone (907) 733-2273.
J. 5.2 Answer Creek.
J 7.6 Birch Creek Road east.
J 8.5 Turnoff for the **Denali Overlook Inn.**
Denali Overlook Inn. See display ad facing page.
J 9 Alaska Bush Floatplane base on Fish Lake, very picturesque.
J 10.4 Kwik Kard gas, diesel.
J 10.5 Wildlife North Art Gallery to west.
J 10.8 Whigmi Road. **Tigger Lake** public fishing access via 0.3-mile dirt road to short trail to lake. Stocked with rainbow.

J 11 Flying Squirrel Bakery Cafe to east (description follows).
Flying Squirrel Bakery Cafe. Visit this unique cafe with creative deli-style menu and artisan breads baked in a wood-fired brick oven. Something for everyone: Vegetarian, vegan, gluten-free and meat-lovers too. Organic Alaska-roasted espresso, WiFi. 3 miles from Talkeetna—no tour bus crowds; trees out the windows; open year-round. (907) 733-6887. www.

flyingsquirrelcafe.com. See display ad on this page. [ADVERTISEMENT]

J 12 Comsat Road (paved) leads east 0.6 mile to X-Y Lakes trailhead and 3 miles (via Comsat, Madison/Freedom Dr.) to **Grace & Bill's Freedom Hills B&B**. Christiansen Lake Road off Comsat Road has public fishing access.

J 12.3 Double-ended gravel turnout to the north.

J 12.5 Talkeetna Alaskan Lodge; accommodations, restaurant, viewing deck, geocache course.

Speed zone reduce to 45 mph northbound.

J 12.9 Large paved double-ended turnout with interpretive sign and viewpoint to west. Splendid views of Mount McKinley, Mount Foraker and the Alaska Range above the Susitna River. A must photo stop. *Watch for bicyclists; do not park on bike trail!*

J 13.4 *CAUTION: Alaska Railroad crossing. Speed zone, reduce to 35 mph.*

J 13.6 Talkeetna Public Library open Monday–Saturday 11 A.M.-6 P.M. Excellent Alaska section and free Internet/Wi-Fi.

J 13.7 Susitna River Lodging; cabins, private suites.

Susitna River Lodging. See display ad on this page.

J 13.9 Talkeetna Camper Park full-service RV park.

Talkeetna Camper Park. See display ad on this page.

J 14.1 Second Street leads to state airport (K2 Aviation, **Talkeetna Air Taxi**), **Talkeetna Hostel**, St. Bernard's Catholic Church, Climbers' Memorial (at cemetery), **Swiss Alaska Inn**, Talkeetna RV Park and Campground, **Mahay's Jetboat Adventures** and public boat launch.

J 14.2 Museum of Northern Adventure features 24 dioramas highlighting Alaska history. Includes exhibits on railroad construction, homesteading, prospecting and wildlife. Open daily year-round. Gift shop. Admission charged (see more information under attractions).

J 14.3 Talkeetna Post Office (ZIP code 99676).

Mountain Gift Shop. Come shop this fun place with Mount McKinley, railroad and moose theme items. Moose "nugget" novelties our specialty. Also handcrafted antler buckles, Bolos and jewelry; kids' plush moose/bear toys; wind chimes; numerous sale T-shirts, hats; Alaskan snacks and candy. Open May–September. (907) 733-1686/2710. [ADVERTISEMENT]

J 14.4 Main Street, Talkeetna. "Welcome to Beautiful Downtown Talkeetna" sign and Talkeetna's Village Park. Public parking available.

Talkeetna

Located on a spur road, 14 miles north of Milepost A 98.7 Parks Highway, at the confluence of the Talkeetna, Susitna and Chulitna rivers. **Population: 876. Emergency Services: Alaska State Troopers, Fire Department** and **Ambulance**, phone 911 or (907) 733-2256. Sunshine Community Health Center, at Mile 4.4 Talkeetna Spur Road, phone (907) 733-2273.

Visitor Information: Stop by the **Talkeetna/Denali Visitors Center**: office on Main Street adjacent to Nagley's General

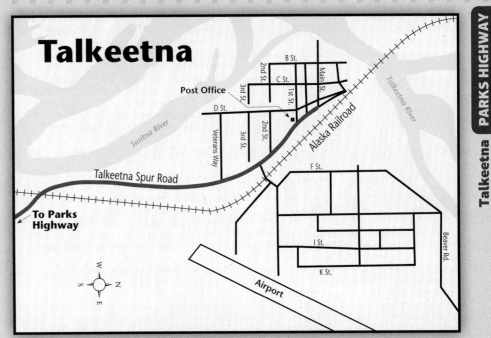

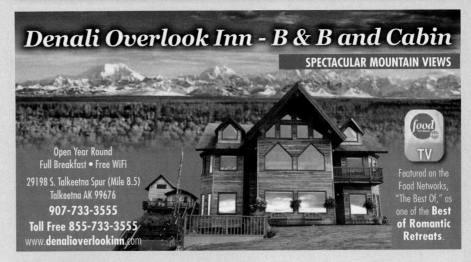

Store, for information, reservations, brochures, maps. The Talkeetna Chamber of Commerce may be contacted by mail, P.O. Box 334, Talkeetna, AK 99676; www.talkeetnachamber.org; info@talkeetnachamber.org.

Walter Harper Talkeetna Ranger Station on B Street is open all year. Information on Denali National Park and climbing in the Alaska Range; reference library, mountaineering orientation program for climbers and a free film throughout the day. Mountaineering regulations and information may be obtained from Talkeetna Ranger Station, P.O. Box 588, Talkeetna, AK 99676; phone (907) 733-2231; or at www.nps.gov/dena/.

Elevation: 346 feet. **Radio:** KSKA-FM (PBS) and local station KTNA 88.9-FM, which broadcasts to communities through-

out the Upper Susitna Valley. **Television:** Channels 2, 4, 5, 7, 13. **Newspaper:** *Talkeetna Good Times* (biweekly).

Private Aircraft: Talkeetna State Airport, adjacent east; elev. 358 feet; length 3,500 feet; paved; fuel 100LL, Jet B (call out).

Talkeetna began as a trading post in 1896, and grew as a riverboat supply base following the Susitna River gold rush in 1910. The population boomed during construction of the Alaska Railroad, when Talkeetna was headquarters for the Alaska Engineering Commission in charge of railroad construction, but declined following completion of the project. Talkeetna has several historic buildings and is on the National Register of Historic Places.

Few other locations are blessed with such fortunate geography, with breathtaking views of Denali and the Alaska Range. This spectacular setting combines with a highly creative citizenry, imaginative shops and businesses, and the mystique of the mountain-climbing community.

Talkeetna is the jumping-off point for most climbing expeditions to Mount McKinley (Denali). Most expeditions use the West Buttress route, pioneered by Bradford Washburn. Specially equipped ski-wheel aircraft fly climbers to Kahiltna Glacier to start the climb from about 7,200 feet to the summit of the South Peak (elev. 20,320 feet). Several air services based in Talkeetna specialize in the glacier landings necessary to ferry climbers and their equipment

to and from the mountain. The climb via the West Buttress route usually takes 18 to 20 days. Flightseeing the mountain is also popular.

Lodging & Services

Talkeetna has 4 motels/hotels, 2 hostels, many bed and breakfasts, cabins, and rooms at the roadhouse; see ads this section. Talkeetna also has several restaurants. Gas is available at Mile 10.4 on the Spur Road. Bike rentals available at south edge of town. The general store carries groceries, deli items, beer and wine and other items. There are a number of locally owned and operated gift shops and galleries; descriptions follow.

Talkeetna Alaskan Lodge. Denali is our backyard! Relax by a 46-foot river-rock fireplace or on the spacious deck. Take in the view of Mount McKinley and the Alaska Range from our deck, our great room, our dining rooms, or your hotel room! Explore the geocache course. Dine on delicious entrees and desserts. Free parking. Complimentary shuttle. Alaska Native owned. Mile 12.5 Talkeetna Spur Road, (23601 S. Talkeetna Spur Road), Talkeetna. 1-888-959-9590. www.TalkeetnaLodge.com/mpl. [ADVERTISEMENT]

Talkeetna Roadhouse. Located on Main Street in "beautiful downtown Talkeetna" the Frank Lee cabin, circa 1917, has been in operation as a full-service roadhouse since 1944. Now famous for breakfasts—featuring a 1902 sourdough starter—as well as cinnamon rolls, daily breads, pies, cookies, savory pasties, reindeer chili and a simple menu of meals all made from scratch, served at big tables where folks sit family-style. Overnight accommodations in co-ed hostel-style Bunk Room ($21), private rooms ($68.25–$89.25), cabins ($110.25–$136.50) and the Museum Apart-

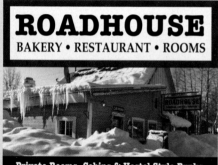
TALKEETNA ADVERTISERS

ment ($157.50). Open year-round. Phone (907) 733-1351. See display ad on previous page. [ADVERTISEMENT]

Gift Shop at Museum of Northern Adventure. Artistic gift shop featuring Eskimo dolls, carved totems, handmade knives, Alaskan yarn, ivory jewelry, Native masks, baskets, pottery and CDs. Carved grizzly outside to greet you. Phone (907) 733-3999. [ADVERTISEMENT]

Bears & Beyond Gift Shop (located behind Mostly Moose Gift Shop). This fun store has figurines, jewelry, baskets, kids' books, Christmas ornaments, pottery, quality shirts and jackets, throws, Alaskan-made treasures, knives and more. Open daily, May–September, 10 A.M.–6 P.M.. Just off Main Street Talkeetna. (907) 733-7100 or 2710. [ADVERTISEMENT]

Mostly Moose Gift Shop. In the historic downtown Dahl cabin. Featuring Alaskan pottery, jewelry, antler-handled knives and moose mugs. Men's corner with outfitter hats, denim shirts and belts. Rustic home decor, pet nook, moose rubber stamps and fun T-shirts. Daily May–September, 10 A.M.–6 P.M. daily. Main Street, Talkeetna. (907) 733-3722/2710. [ADVERTISEMENT]

Talkeetna Gifts & Collectables. "One of the nicest and most complete gift shops in Alaska," with handmade keepsakes, souvenirs, jewelry, books, Alaskana, quilts, fabric and kuspuk patterns. Sweatshirts, plush toys, puppets and huggable Eskimo dolls. Alaskan foods, cookie cutters and sourdough. Gallery with artwork, birch boxes, antler crafts, fur slippers/accessories. Quality merchandise, friendly service. We ship. Open daily year-round. Downtown Talkeetna. (907) 733-2710. [ADVERTISEMENT]

Camping

RV camping at **Talkeetna Camper Park** at Mile 13.9 Talkeetna Spur Road. Tent camping only at Talkeetna River Park at the end of Main Street; fee charged. Camping is also available at the ADF&G concessionaire-operated public boat launch in East Talkeetna near the Swiss Alaska Inn. Turn off at airport and follow posted signs for directions to private campground.

Transportation

Air: There are several air taxi services in Talkeetna. Charter service, flightseeing and glacier landings are available. See ads this section.

Talkeetna state airport has a 3,500-foot paved runway. Local flying services have offices downtown and at the airport.

Railroad: The Alaska Railroad provides daily passenger service on its Anchorage–Denali Park–Fairbanks service. Flag-stop ser-

Talkeetna is a pedestrian-friendly town with shops and restaurants to entertain.
(©Kris Valencia, staff)

The first ascent of the true summit of Mount McKinley was made in June 1913 by the Rev. Hudson Stuck, Walter Harper, Harry Karstens and Robert Tatum.

vice between Talkeetna and Hurricane (see Attractions this section). Railroad Depot is located at Mile 13.5 Talkeetna Spur Road; open daily 9:30 A.M. to 6 P.M., mid-May to mid-September.

Highway: At the end of a 14-mile-long spur road off the Parks Highway.

Van service: Sunshine Transit operates a van between downtown and the Talkeetna Y on weekdays from 8 A.M. to 6 P.M., with stops along the way; $1 one-way.

Taxi: Talkeetna Taxi.

Attractions

Museum of Northern Adventure has 24 realistic dioramas with life-sized figures and sounds. This educational stop focuses on homesteading, prospecting, wildlife, famous characters and more.

The Talkeetna Historical Society Museum is located 1 block off Main Street opposite the Fairview Inn. The original 1-room schoolhouse, built in 1936, exhibits historical items, local art and a display on the late Don Sheldon, famous Alaskan bush pilot. In the Railroad Section House see the impressive 12-foot-by-12-foot scale model of Mount McKinley (Denali) with photographs by Bradford Washburn. A mountaineering display features pioneer and recent climbs of Mount McKinley. The Ole Dahl cabin, an early trapper/miner's cabin located on the museum grounds, is furnished with period items. Admission: $3 adult, under 16 free. Pick up a free walking tour map of Talkeetna's historic sites here. Museum buildings open 10 A.M. to 6 P.M. daily, early May to mid-September. Reduced hours other seasons; P.O. Box 76, Talkeetna, AK 99676. Phone (907) 733-2487.

Jetboat tours up Susitna River, Talkeetna River, Devils Canyon, and Chulitna River are available. Several guides also offer riverboat fishing trips from Talkeetna. Commercial float trips and raft tours offer another popular way of exploring the roadless wilderness. Talkeetna is located at the confluence of the Susitna, Talkeetna and Chulitna Rivers. Inquire locally and see ads this section.

Ride "The Hurricane Turn" Train. The Alaska Railroad's flag-stop train between the Talkeetna depot and Hurricane makes an interesting trip. Used by people who live in the Bush, as well as hunters, hikers, and fishermen, the 115-mile route parallels the Susitna River and traverses Indian River Canyon. The train stops for anyone wanting to be picked up for a ride into town or to be dropped off in the wilderness between Talkeetna and Hurricane, so it may run late depending on the number of stops. The train runs Thursday through Sunday in summer; www.alaskarailroad.com. Tickets may be purchased onboard, at the depot or call 1-800-544-0552 or (907) 265-2494.

Special Events. 4th of July barbecue and parade. Winterfest in December features a month of special events and competitions, of which the best known are the Wilderness Women's Contest and the Bachelor Auction, both held the first Saturday in December. The Talkeetna Bachelor Auction raises funds for local charities by auctioning off bachelors for cash. For more information, www.bachelorsoftalkeetna.org.

Fishing. The **Susitna River** basin offers many top fishing streams and lakes, either accessible by road, plane or riverboat.

Return to Milepost A 98.7 Parks Highway

(Continued from page 423)

A 104 C 106 F 258 Big Su Lodge (closed 2013, current status unknown).

A 104.2 C 105.8 F 257.8 Bridge over Susitna River. Entering Game Management Unit 16A, northbound, Unit 14B southbound.

A 104.6 C 105.4 F 257.4 Unsigned gravel road to west at north end of bridge accesses gravel bars on Susitna River.

A 104.8 C 105.2 F 257.2 Large gravel turnout to west.

A 105.7 C 104.3 F 256.3 Rabideux Creek (northbound sign); watch for signed public fishing access.

A 107.8 C 102.2 F 254.2 View of Mount McKinley (weather permitting) for northbound travelers.

A 108 C 102 F 254 *CAUTION: Watch for moose.*

A 109.9 C 100.1 F 252.1 Distance marker northbound shows Trapper Creek 5 miles.

A 113.2 C 96.8 F 248.8 Trapper Creek Welcomes You (sign)

A 113.6 C 96.4 F 248.4 McKinley View Bed and Breakfast to west.

McKinley View B&B. See display ad this page.

A 114 C 96 F 248 *Begin 55 mph speed zone northbound. Speed limit is 65 mph southbound.*

A 114.6 C 95.4 F 247.4 Trapper Creek Inn & RV Park on east side of highway; gas and diesel, cafe, store, camping and lodging. *NOTE: Next gas northbound is in Cantwell, 95 miles from here.*

Trapper Creek Inn & RV Park. Rich in history, Trapper Creek welcomes you to explore! A complete travelers destination! Gateway to South Denali! We take pride in our clean establishment, and hope you enjoy your stay. Lodging, 50-amp RV park, food, convenience store, ATM, espresso, ice cream, laundromat, showers, RV dump, propane and fuel. Tour buses welcome. (907) 733-2302. See display ad this page.

A 114.8 C 95.2 F 247.2 TRAPPER CREEK (pop. 426) is located at the **junction** of the Parks Highway and Petersville Road; food, gas and lodging at Trapper Creek Inn & RV Park and **Alaska's Northland Inn. Emergency services: Ambulance,** phone 911. Trapper Creek has a post office (zip code 99683) and a library. The library, located at 8901 E. Devonshire Dr., is open Mondays, Wednesdays, Thursdays and Saturdays; free Internet and computer stations (time limit may apply), Alaskana section and book exchange for travelers. The community holds a Fireweed Festival in July.

Alaska's Northland Inn. Enjoy the Northern Wilderness and our downhome hospitality! Offering spacious, private lodging with fully equipped kitchens, bath, queen beds, satellite T.V. and WiFi. Family friendly, groomed trails. Outdoor Gazebo and fire with a BBQ. Great room with pool table. www.alaskasnorthlandinn.com. Phone (907) 733-7377. See display ad on

Homemade "last gas" signs are often used to alert travelers in the North. *(©Kris Valencia, staff)*

page 430. [ADVERTISEMENT]

A 114.9 C 95.1 F 247.1 Petersville Road turnoff to west. Miners built the Petersville Road in the 1920s, and federal homesteading began here in 1948. Today, a cluster of businesses around this junction serve Parks Highway travelers and make up the community of Trapper Creek. Accommodations along Petersville Road at **Alaska's Northland Inn** and **Gate Creek Cabins.**

Junction with Petersville Road, which leads west 18.7 miles. See "Petersville Road" log on page 430.

A 115.4 C 94.6 F 246.6 Distance marker northbound indicates Cantwell 94 miles, Denali National Park 122 miles, Fairbanks 239 miles.

A 115.5 C 94.5 F 246.5 Trapper Creek Trading Post east side of highway.

A 115.6 C 94.4 F 246.4 Highway crosses Trapper Creek.

Excellent views of Mount McKinley (weather permitting) northbound.

A 115.7 C 94.3 F 246.3 Trapper Creek Pizza Pub—Angela's Heaven; homemade pizza, German beer bread. Seasonal hours; phone (907) 733-3344.

A 116.2 C 93.8 F 245.8 *Begin 55 mph speed zone southbound, 65 mph northbound.*

A 118 C 92 F 244 View of Denali northbound (weather permitting).

A 119.6 C 90.4 F 242.4 Distance marker southbound shows Trapper Creek 5 miles, Wasilla 78 miles, Anchorage 120 miles.

A 121.1 C 88.9 F 240.9 Chulitna high-
(Continues on page 434)

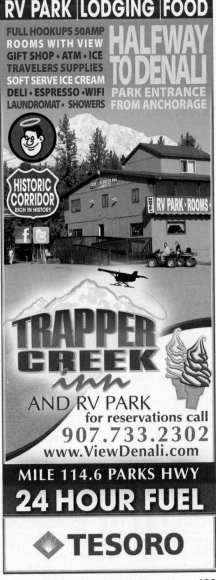

Petersville Road

On clear days, Petersville Road offers vistas of Mount McKinley. (©Monte Budahl)

Petersville Road leads west and north from Trapper Creek at **Milepost A 114.9** on the Parks Highway through a homestead area notable for its mountain views and its bed and breakfasts. The Trapper Creek/Petersville Road area is a logical and convenient stop for travelers, particularly those headed for Denali National Park.

Built as a mining road, today Petersville Road is very popular with 4-wheelers in summer and snow machines in winter (*please respect private property*). *The MILE-POST®* logs the first 18.7 miles of Petersville Road to Peters Creek access. Inquire locally for current road conditions beyond Forks.

Distance from junction with the Parks Highway (J) is shown.

J 0 Junction with Parks Highway at **Milepost A 114.9**, Trapper Creek (see description on page 429).

J 0.1 Distance marker shows Moose Creek 7 miles, Peters Creek 19 miles.

J 0.6 Historic Donaldson 59er Cabin to south. Gold Rush Centennial sign:

"In 1906, prospectors ascended the Susitna River and discovered gold in several creeks in the Cache Creek–Dutch Hills area. News of the discoveries set off a rush the following year. Miners later developed an easier route to their claims that included travel by boat from Cook Inlet up the Susitna and Yentna rivers to a supply point called McDougall. Hiking and using pack-horses, they continued up the McDougall Trail crossing rushing streams, swampy bogs and rugged mountains. In winter, travel was easier over firm, frozen ground with the use of dog and hand sleds.

"Miners improved the 50-mile McDougall Trail, but in places it was hard to follow. In 1917, packer Richard Feltham lost his way in the swamps near Hungryman Camp. After 6 days, a search party found him near his horse. 'Evidences of the struggle of the man to find his way were pitiful to see,' according to one of his rescuers. Feltham had blazed marks on trees in a futile effort to find what other miners considered 'a most obscure trail.' Feltham died several hours after he was found.

"Miners in the area petitioned the government for help in the construction of a 'dirt road that will guarantee to get us home in safety ... and won't leave us somewhere to perish, as it did Dick Feltham.' After crews started building a railroad through the area, miner Henry Bamburg blazed a trail from the mines to the new railstop called Talkeetna. In 1918, the Alaska Road Commission began improving the trail, which is now the Petersville Road that passes in front of the Trapper Creek Museum."

J 0.8 Alaska's Northland Inn. See display ad this page.

J 2 Grocery store, ATM, propane, gifts.

J 2.6 Trapper Creek elementary school to south.

J 6.3 Oil Well Road.

J 7 Moose Creek.

J 8.8 Small turnout to north.

J 9.3 Large turnout. *Pavement ends westbound; gravel begins, 30 mph speed limit. Watch for potholes.*

J 10.3 Gate Creek Cabins. Alaska's Best Lodging Value...is a one-of-a-kind property that delivers the "Alaska Experience" you've been looking for. Clean, comfortable, inviting...family-sized cabins are completely self-contained, full kitchens, private baths, linens, decks/grills. Property features two small lakes nearby with vistas of Mount McKinley. Fish-ing, mountain biking, hiking, photography, wildlife viewing. Snowmobile rentals and tours. Romantic, friendly and affordable. (907) 733-1393. www.gatecreekcabins.com. [ADVERTISEMENT]

J 10.4 Gate Lake.

J 11.6 Turnouts on both sides of road.

J 11.8 Downhill grade westbound. Turnout to south.

J 12.4 Turnouts on both sides of road.

J 12.9 Turnouts both sides of road.

J 13.7 Large gravel parking area is staging area for snow machines in winter. *Begin steep downhill westbound; slow for sharp curve.*

J 13.9 Kroto Creek. *Road narrows westbound. Slow for rough road (washboard and potholes). Muddy road in spring or during heavy rains.*

J 15.7 Parking at ORV trailhead.

J 17.2 Parking at Shulin Lake ORV trailhead.

J 17.4 Parking at Kenay Lake ORV trailhead.

J 18.7 (30.1 km) Petersville Road forks: Right fork is continuation of Petersville Road (*high clearance 4-wheel drive vehicles only beyond Forks Roadhouse*) and leads to Petersville Recreational Mining Area. Left fork leads 0.2 mile to Peters Creek (descriptions follow).

This site was a supply depot for gold miners in the Petersville Hills and Susitna Valley in the early 1900s. In the early 1930s, the Forks Roadhouse was constructed here; it carried mining supplies and had a saloon. The roadhouse operated for some 80 years until it burned down in April 2012.

Take the left fork for informal camping (no facilities) on Mat-Su Borough public land at **Peters Creek**. Beautiful spot. Fishing for salmon and trout; bridge across Peters Creek is Dollar Creek Trailhead: ORVs only, no cars on bridge or trail.

Take right fork for Petersville Road to former mining camp of Petersville and downstream boundary of Petersville Recreational Mining Area (about 11 miles). Peters Creek must be forded to reach the upper end of the Recreational Mining Area. Petersville Road ends about 18 miles beyond the Forks. This stretch of road is usually not passable until late June.

Recreational gold panning, mineral prospecting and mining using light portable field equipment are allowed without any permit from the Dept. of Natural Resources (DNR). Mining in fish-bearing bodies of water using suction dredges requires a permit from Dept. of Fish & Game Division of Habitat; phone (907) 267-2821. Or phone the Division of Mining, Land & Water in Anchorage at (907) 269-8600. Visit http://dnr.alaska.gov/mlw/ and click on Fact Sheets then Petersville Recreational Mining Area.

Return to Milepost A 114.9 Parks Highway

way maintenance camp to west.

A 121.5 C 88.5 F 240.5 South end of paved loop which leads east to parking areas and outhouses; access to Chulitna Bluffs and East-West Express winter trails.

A 123.8 C 86.2 F 238.2 Large gravel turnout to west.

A 126.6 C 83.4 F 235.4 Large paved parking area to east.

A 127.1 C 82.9 F 234.9 Large gravel turnout to west.

A 132.2 C 77.8 F 229.8 South boundary of **Denali State Park**. Adjacent to the southern border of Denali National Park and Preserve, this 324,420-acre parkland borders the Parks Highway between the Talkeetna Mountains and the Alaska Range. The park's 3 campgrounds, 4 viewpoints and 5 trailheads are located along the Parks Highway between here and **Milepost A 168.5**.

The park's outstanding features are the 30-mile spines of Curry and Kesugi ridges. Small lakes and unspoiled tundra cover the ridge lands, whose heights overlook the heart of the Alaska Range, the spires of the Tokosha Mountains, glaciers, gorges and the vast, braided Chulitna River. The Kesugi Ridge hike has been rated a "must do" trail by national backpacking magazines. Hardwood forests along the highway and alpine tundra above tree line are home to myriad wildlife, including brown/grizzly and black bears.

A 132.8 C 77.2 F 229.2 Middle of the **Chulitna River** bridge. Fishing for grayling, rainbow.

Entering Game Management Subunit 13-E, leaving unit 16A, northbound.

Slow for 45mph curve, turning traffic.

A 132.9 C 77.1 F 229.1 Intersection with Mt. McKinley View Drive at north end of bridge. Turn east uphill and follow paved road 0.4 mile for turnout with view and 1 mile for **Mt. McKinley Princess Wilderness Lodge**; restaurants (open to public), lodging, packaged tours, beautiful view from deck of Alaska Range.

Mt. McKinley Princess Wilderness Lodge. See display ad on this page.

A 133 C 77 F 229 Narrow dirt double ended turnout to west.

A 134.5 C 75.5 F 227.5 Longtime restaurant and accommodations located on Mary Carey's original homestead. Spectacular view

Denali Viewpoint South is always a great place to stop, especially on a clear day.
(©Kris Valencia, staff)

of Denali/Mount McKinley.

Mary's McKinley View Lodge. See display ad this page.

A 134.8 C 75.2 F 227.2 Double-ended entrance west to **Denali Viewpoint South (Denali State Park)**; paved and landscaped day-use parking area; scenic viewpoint, viewing scopes, interpretive boards; 9 campsites ($10/night); toilets, water pump; and 800-foot-long uphill trail to overlook. Parking area accommodates large vehicles. [A]

A 135 C 75 F 227 Construction is underway west of here for the South Denali Visitor Center Complex, scheduled to open in 2015. The ground-breaking ceremony for the project took place August 16, 2013. Links for project description and status updates at http://www.southdenali.alaska.gov/.

A 135.2 C 74.8 F 226.8 Troublesome Creek rest area. From here northbound for many miles there are views (weather permitting) of glaciers on the southern slopes of the Alaska Range to the west. Ruth, Buckskin and Eldridge glaciers are the most conspicuous. Flightseeing trips offer close-up views of Mount McKinley, Don Sheldon Amphitheater, Ruth Glacier, the Great Gorge and

Moose's Tooth.

Ruth Glacier extends 31 miles southeast through the Great Gorge, nicknamed the Grand Canyon of Alaska for its towering

Best view of Ruth Glacier? From a plane. Take a sightseeing flight from one of the flying services in Talkeetna, Denali Park or along the highway. (©Earl L. Brown)

5,000-foot peaks that rise up on both sides of the glacier. The gorge opens into Don Sheldon Amphitheater at the head of Ruth Glacier, where the Don Sheldon mountain house sits. Donald E. Sheldon (1921–75) was a well-known bush pilot who helped map, patrol, and aid search and rescue efforts in this area.

View of 20,320-foot Mount McKinley on a clear day. Peaks to be sighted, south to north, along the next 20 miles to the west are: Mount Hunter (elev. 14,573 feet); Mount Huntington (12,240 feet); Mount Barrille (7,650 feet); and Mount Dickey (9,845 feet).

A 137.2 C 72.8 F 224.8 Lower Troublesome Creek (Denali State Park) **campground** and trailhead to west. There are 10 campsites in trees with tables and firepits and 32 overnight parking spaces (for camper use between 6 P.M. and 9 A.M.); $10 camping fee per vehicle/night. Day-use area with sheltered picnic sites, toilets, water and litter barrels. There is a 0.6-mile trail to the Chulitna River from the parking lot. [A]

A 137.4 C 76.6 F 224.6 Troublesome Creek bridge. **Troublesome Creek** is usually a clear runoff stream, not silted by glacial flour. The stream heads in a lake and flows 14 miles to the Chulitna River. Fishing for rainbow, grayling and salmon (king salmon fishing prohibited), June–September. [fish]

A 137.7 C 72.3 F 224.3 Upper Troublesome Creek Trailhead is a 15.2-mile trail to Byers Lake Campground (see **Milepost A 147**). The trail, rated as difficult, climbs to the Kesugi Ridge; expansive views. Check for postings on current trail conditions before heading out. *CAUTION: Watch for bears.*

A 139.8 C 70.2 F 222.2 Small paved turnout to west.

Distance marker southbound shows Wasilla 98 miles, Anchorage 140 miles.

A 143.9 C 66.1 F 218.1 Bridge over Byers Creek.

A 144 C 66 F 218 Byer's Creek Lodge to west (closed summer 2013, status unknown)

A 145.6 C 64.4 F 216.4 Paved turnout to west.

A 147 C 63 F 215 Turnoff for **Byers Lake Campground** (Denali State Park) to east via paved road. Drive downhill 0.3 miles for day-use parking area with picnic tables and firewood. Access road continues east to additional parking (0.4 miles from highway), water pump, boat launch, and campground loop road (0.6 mile from highway). Byers Lake Cabin #1 is also located on this access road. It is one of 3 public-use cabins available for rent in Denali State Park. Byers Lake Cabins #2 and #3 are a half-mile walk from the campground or 1.7 miles from the road in winter. For details on the cabins and availability, go to the Dept. of Natural Resources website at http://dnr.alaska.gov/parks/cabins/matsu.htm.

The campground has 73 sites, dump station, campground host, camping fee $10 per night, $5 sani-dump fee, picnic tables, firepits, water, toilets (wheelchair accessible). Walking trails connect campground with Veterans Memorial (see **Milepost A 147.1**). **Byers Lake** (electric motors permitted) has fishing for grayling, burbot, rainbow, lake trout and whitefish. *CAUTION: Bears frequent campground. Keep a clean camp.*

Byers Lake Trailhead is on campground loop road. Hiking distances are: Byers Creek Bridge 1 mile; Cascade 1.6 mile; Lakeshore Campground (a remote campsite) 1.8 miles; Tarn Point 4.2 miles; Troublesome Creek Trailhead 15 miles (closed for repairs). [fish] [A]

A 147.1 C 62.9 F 214.9 South end of **Medal of Honor Loop to Alaska Veterans Memorial/POW–MIA** rest area to east; large parking areas for vehicles and big rigs; picnic tables, drinking water; visitor information center, interpretive kiosk, viewing scopes; toilets, garbage containers; pet walk. Wheelchair accessible. A popular picnic stop. Stretch your legs on the short trail down to Byers Lake Campground that begins at the upper (big rig) parking area. The visitor center/store is open daily in summer. Camping is permitted at this rest area only "after 8 P.M. if Byers Lake Campground is full. You must pay the $10 camping fee at the campground."

The **Alaska Veterans Memorial** adja-

cent the rest area, consists of an alcove and a semicircle of five 20-foot-tall concrete panels, one for each branch of service and each with a large star on the upper part and inscriptions on the lower part.

Panels and plaques also memorialize the Alaska National Guard; the Merchant Marine; the Submariners, victims of the Air Force C-47 crash on nearby Kesugi Ridge in February 1954, and other memorials. Three flag poles stand at the site: the center pole flying the American flag; the pole to the right the Alaska flag, and the pole to the left the flags of the POW-MIA.

The memorial was erected in 1983 and dedicated in 1984 by Governor Bill Sheffield, a veteran, and other civilian and military leaders. The Byers Lake site was selected because it was centrally located between Alaska's 2 largest cities, Anchorage and Fairbanks, and there is a wonderful view of Mount McKinley/Denali from the entrance to the memorial.

The memorial reads: "We dedicate this quiet place to the remembrance of the veterans of Alaska who have served their country at home and throughout the world. We honor their heroism and dedication."

A 147.5 C 62.5 F 214.5 North end of Medal of Honor Loop to Alaska Veterans Memorial/POW–MIA Rest Area to east (see description preceding milepost).

A 156 C 54 F 206 Distance marker northbound indicates Cantwell 54 miles, Denali National Park 81 miles, Fairbanks 199 miles.

A 156.2 C 53.8 F 205.8 Small gravel turnout to west.

A 156.5 C 53.5 F 205.5 Ermine Hill Trailhead (Denali State Park) to east, 3 miles one-way; parking ($5 parking fee).

A 157.7 C 52.3 F 204.3 Small paved turnout to west.

A 159.3 C 50.7 F 202.7 Double-ended paved turnout to west.

A 159.8 C 50.2 F 202.2 Distance marker southbound shows Wasilla 118 miles, Anchorage 160 miles.

A 161 C 49 F 201 Long, gravel, downhill turnout northbound.

A 162.4 C 47.6 F 199.6 Denali Viewpoint (Denali State Park); large paved turnout to west with a view of Mount McKinley.

A 162.7 C 47.3 F 199.3 Denali View North Campground (Denali State Park) to west. Large, open, paved parking area with day-use parking and 20 side-by-side spaces for overnight parking with firepits and picnic tables; also long pull-through sites for large RV rigs with pull-cars. Camping fee is $10/night. Campground host. Outhouse (wheelchair accessible), water, interpretive kiosks, spotting scope, nature trail (wheelchair accessible). Overlooks Chulitna River. Views (weather permitting) of Denali, Moose's Tooth, Mount Huntington and Alaska Range peaks above Hidden River valley. [A]

A 163.1 C 46.9 F 198.9 Large double-ended paved turnout to west.

A 163.2 C 46.8 F 198.8 Little Coal Creek. Rainbow, grayling and salmon, July through September. [fish]

A 163.8 C 46.2 F 198.2 Turnoff to east for Little Coal Creek Trailhead (Denali State Park); parking area ($5 parking fee). According to park rangers, this trail offers easy access (1½-hour hike) to alpine country. It is a 27-mile hike to Byers Lake via Kesugi Ridge.

A 165.5 C 44.5 F 196.5 Paved turnouts on both sides of highway by creek. Good berry picking in the fall.

A 168.5 C 41.5 F 193.5 Denali State Park boundary (leaving park northbound, entering park southbound). See park description at **Milepost A 132.2**.

CAUTION: Winding hilly road northbound, foliage obscures sight line, pass with care.

A 169 C 41 F 193 *CAUTION: Railroad crossing.* A solar collector here helps power the warning signals.

A 170 C 40 F 192 Long paved parking area on west side of highway.

A 173 C 37 F 189 Paved turnout to west.

A 173.9 C 36.1 F 188.1 Shoulder parking west side of highway, just south of bridge.

A 174 C 36 F 188 **Hurricane Gulch Bridge.** Parking area to west at north end of bridge. The 550-foot deck of the bridge is 260 feet above Hurricane Creek, not as high as the railroad bridge that spans the gulch near the Chulitna River. Construction cost for the bridge was approx. $1.2 million.

Highway begins a gradual descent northbound to Honolulu Creek.

A 176 C 34 F 186 Small paved turnout to east.

NOTE: Slow for curves as highway descends long grade northbound to Honolulu Creek.

A 176.5 C 33.5 F 185.5 Narrow, double-ended turnout on curve to west with uphill grade.

A 177.8 C 32.2 F 184.2 Small paved parking area to east.

A 178.1 C 31.9 F 183.9 Honolulu Creek Bridge. Gravel access to creek to west at north end of bridge.

Highway begins ascent northbound to Broad Pass, the gap in the Alaska Range crossed by both the railroad and highway.

A 179.5 C 30.5 F 182.5 Paved turnout to west by **Mile 180 Lake**; public fishing access (stocked with grayling).

A 180 C 30 F 182 Double-ended turnout to west by Mile 180 Lake

A 180.5 C 29.5 F 181.5 Radio tower to west.

A 183.2 C 26.8 F 178.8 Double-ended paved turnout to west of highway. Look to the west across the Chulitna River for dramatic view of the Alaska Range (weather permitting).

A 184.5 C 25.5 F 177.5 Paved turnout to west.

A 185 C 25 F 177 Bridge over East Fork Chulitna River.

A 185.6 C 24.4 F 176.4 **East Fork Chulitna Wayside** to east; 0.5-mile paved loop to rest area and overnight parking with picnic tables, concrete fireplaces, picnic shelter, toilets. Popular stop for RVers.

This wayside is located in a bend of the East Fork Chulitna River amid a healthy growth of Alaskan spruce and birch.

A 186.3 C 23.7 F 175.7 Single-vehicle turnout to east. View from highway of eroded bluffs to east.

Winding upgrade northbound, slow for 50-mph curve.

A 187.5 C 22.5 F 175.5 Paved double-ended turnout to west; single-vehicle paved turnout east side of highway.

Solar powered microwave tower site to west.

A 188.7 C 21.3 F 174.3 Igloo City (still closed in 2013).

A 191.1 C 18.9 F 170.9 Large paved parking area to west. Look for cotton grass. There are 14 species of cotton grass in Alaska.

A 192 C 18 F 170 *NOTE: Ahtna Inc. lands border much of the Parks Highway northbound to Milepost A 230. Ahtna lands are open to entry by permit only; for more information and links to online permits go to http://permits. ahtna-inc.com.*

A 194.4 C 15.6 F 167.6 *CAUTION: Highway curves and crosses railroad tracks.*

No passing zone northbound.

A 194.6 C 15.4 F 167.4 Bridge over Middle Fork Chulitna River. Gravel access to river at south end of bridge; informal parking.

CAUTION: Highway curves, windy area through Broad Pass.

A 195 C 15 F 167 Entering **Broad Pass** northbound. Broad Pass is one of the most beautiful areas on the Parks Highway. A mountain valley, bare in some places, dotted with scrub spruce in others, and surrounded by mountain peaks, it provides a top-of-the-world feeling for the traveler, although it is one of the lowest summits along the North American mountain system. Named in 1898 by George Eldridge and Robert Muldrow, the 2,400-foot pass, sometimes called Caribou Pass, marks the divide between the drainage of rivers and streams that empty into Cook Inlet and those that empty into the Yukon River.

A 195.8 C 14.2 F 166.2 Large paved turnout to east; mountain views.

A 199 C 11 F 163 Summit Lake (1.3 miles long) to east.

A 201 C 9 F 161 Large paved parking area to east with mountain view. Mount McKinley/Denali is visible to the southwest on clear days.

A 201.3 C 8.7 F 160.7 **Broad Pass summit** (not signed), 2,409 feet. Summit airport (sign) and abandoned weather service station to west. An FAA Flight Service Station was commissioned here in May 1940 and closed in 1972. Currently the FAA maintains a remote weather reporting service and video camera here (go to http://akweathercams.faa.gov/sitelist.php and click on Summit).

Private Aircraft: Summit state airport; elev. 2,409 feet; length 3,800 feet; gravel; unmaintained.

A 202 C 8 F 160 Small green-roofed white cabins at south end of Mirror Lake to east are privately owned; no road access.

A 202.1 C 7.9 F 159.9 Boundary of Matanuska–Susitna and Denali boroughs. Alaska is unique among the 50 states in that much of the state (but not all of it) is organized into local forms of government called boroughs, similar to counties in other states. There are 16 boroughs in Alaska.

A 203.2 C 6.8 F 158.8 *Railroad overpass.*

A 203.5 C 6.5 F 158.5 Large paved parking area to east with view of Mount McKinley/Denali (weather permitting).

A 206.8 C 3.2 F 155.2 Watch for caribou.

A 208 C 2 F 154 Paved viewpoint to west at south end of Pass Creek bridge. *Slow for frost heaves next 1 mile northbound.*

A 208.7 C 1.3 F 153.3 *Begin 55 mph speed zone northbound.*

A 209 C 1 F 153 Distance marker northbound shows Denali Highway 1 mile.

A 209.3 C 0.7 F 152.7 *Begin 45 mph speed zone northbound.*

A 209.4 C 0.6 F 152.6 Welcome to Cantwell (northbound sign).

A 209.6 C 0.4 F 152.4 Bridge over Jack River. Cleared area on southeast side is Private Property. Do not enter.

A 210 C 0 F 152 **Junction** of Parks and Denali highways at Cantwell. **Backwoods Lodge** is located just east of this intersection (0.2 mile) on the Denali Highway. Turn west for **Cantwell RV Park** (0.3 miles), tire repair (0.5 miles), the Alaska Railroad and **Atkins Guiding & Flying Service** (1.9 miles). Turn east for Denali Highway to Paxson (134 miles east). ▲

Junction of the Parks Highway (Alaska Route 3) and the Denali Highway (Alaska Route 8). Turn west for the rest of Cantwell; see description of Cantwell this section. If eastbound on the Denali Highway, turn to the end of the DENALI HIGHWAY section on page 516 and read log back to front.

Cantwell

A 210 C 0 F 152 Located at **junction** with the Denali Highway, 21 miles south of entrance to Denali National Park. **Population:** 183. **Emergency Services:** Phone 911 for all emergency ser-

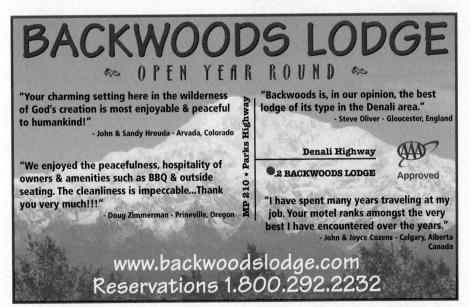

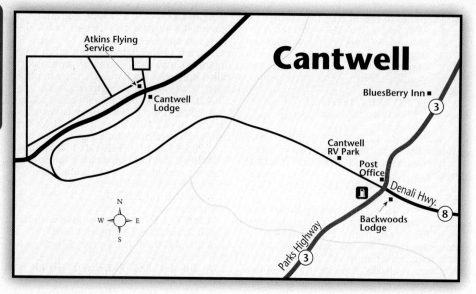

Cantwell

vices. **Alaska State Troopers**, business phone (907) 768-2202. **Fire Department**, Cantwell VFD, phone (907) 768-2162. **Clinic**, Cantwell Clinic, phone (907) 768-2122.

Elevation: 2,190 feet. **Private Aircraft**: Cantwell airport, adjacent north; elev. 2,190 feet; length 2,100 feet; gravel; fuel 100LL.

Cantwell began as an Alaskan Railroad flag stop and continues as a work station for the railroad. The village was named for the Cantwell River, the original name of the Nenana River, named by Lt. Allen in 1885 for Lt. John C. Cantwell of the Revenue-Cutter Service, Kobuk River area explorer.

Cantwell visitor services include a gas station; **Backwoods Lodge**, **Cantwell RV Park**, **BluesBerry Inn** and **Atkins Guiding & Flying Service**. Tire repair and some groceries are available. Cantwell businesses are located both at the intersection of the Denali and Parks highways and west of the Parks Highway on the access road to downtown Cantwell.

NOTE: Next gas southbound on the Parks Highway is at Trapper Creek, 95 miles from here. First gas stop eastbound on the Denali Highway is Tangle River Inn, 114 miles from Cantwell. (First food service eastbound on the Denali Highway is not until Maclaren River Lodge, 92 miles from Cantwell; see the DENALI HIGHWAY section for details.)

Cantwell caters to both Parks Highway travelers, Denali Highway travelers as well as visitors to Denali National Park. A good view of Denali (weather permitting) in the Cantwell area is from a turnout 1 mile east on the Denali Highway.

Berry pickers, hikers, hunters and other oudoor recreationists visiting the Cantwell area should inquire locally about land status before venturing off-road. Ahtna Inc. lands border much of the Parks Highway between **Milepost A 192** and **A 230**, including Cantwell and permits are required. For more information and links go to www.ahtna-inc.com/ldp.html.

Parks Highway Log
(continued)

A 210.1 C 0.1 F 151.9 Cantwell post office (ZIP 99729), west side of highway; open 8 A.M. to 4 P.M., Monday–Friday, and 9:30 A.M. to 1:30 P.M. on Saturdays.

Distance marker northbound indicates Denali National Park 21 miles, Healy 40 miles, Fairbanks 149 miles.

A 210.3 C 0.3 F 151.7 Chevron gas sta- tion (rebuilt and open for gas and snacks summer 2013 after burning down in 2011) to east. *Begin 55 mph speed zone northbound. Begin 45 mph speed zone southbound.*

A 210.8 C 0.8 F 151.2 BluesBerry Inn. Family-friendly log cabin motel in beautiful Cantwell. 18 affordable rooms; most rooms have private bath/shower and TV, all have WiFi (from $65+T dry cabins, $85+T rooms with bath or shower). Wild blueberry country! MP 210.8, west on (unmarked) Matlock Drive 0.1 mile. GPS: Intersection Matlock Drive and Gore Lane, Cantwell 99729 or coordinates N63.40052 W 148.89336. Reservations (907) 768-2415; www.bluesberryinn.com. [ADVERTISEMENT]

A 211.6 C 1.6 F 150.4 Double-ended parking area to west. *Begin 55 mph speed zone southbound. Resume 65 mph speed limit northbound.*

A 212 C 2 F 150 Highway parallels the Nenana River northbound. Slide area northbound.

A 213.1 C 3.1 F 148.9 Denali Borough Transfer Station to west.

A 213.8 C 3.8 F 148.2 Paved double-ended parking area to west among tall white spruce and fireweed.

A 215 C 5 F 147 View of Limestone Mine at base of mountain northbound. The mine supplied the Healy Clean Coal Project until that facility was shut down in 1999.

A 215.4 C 5.4 F 146.6 Gravel access road on west side of highway leads 0.4 mile to parking area at Nenana River; jet boat tours.

A 215.8 C 5.8 F 146.2 Nenana River bridge. This is the first crossing of the Nenana River northbound. The Nenana River heads at Nenana Glacier in the Alaska Range and flows north 140 miles to the Tanana River at the town of Nenana. Guided

rafting trips on the Nenana are popular; see river raft operators in the Denali Park commercial area at **Milepost A 238**.

Highway narrows northbound.

A 216 C 6 F 146 Paved double-ended parking area on rise to west. Good spot for photos of Panorama Mountain (elev. 5,778 feet), the prominent peak in the Alaska Range visible to the east.

Entering Game Management Unit 20A and leaving unit 13E northbound.

A 218.5 C 8.5 F 143.5 Paved double-ended parking area to west with beautiful view of Nenana River.

A 218.9 C 8.9 F 143.1 Begin slide area northbound.

A 219.3 C 9.3 F 142.7 End slide area northbound.

A 219.8 C 9.8 F 142.2 Double-ended parking area to west.

A 220.5 C 10.5 F 141.5 South end of long, paved, double-ended parking area to west on old highway alignment along the Nenana River. North end at **Milepost A 220.8**. Good place to view rafters.

A 222 C 12 F 140 Snow poles beside roadway guide snowplows in winter.

A 222.2 C 12.2 F 139.8 Paved double-ended turnout to west beside Nenana River.

A 223.9 C 13.9 F 138.1 Carlo Creek Lodge to west.

A 224 C 14 F 138 Bridge over Carlo Creek. The Perch Restaurant and Panorama Pizza Pub uphill to east at south side of Carlo Creek bridge. McKinley Creekside Cabins and Cafe to east at north end of Carlo Creek bridge. Denali Mountain Morning Hostel to west.

A 224.9 C 14.9 F 137.1 Large informal gravel parking area to west; posted No Overnight Camping. Beautiful mountain views southbound.

A 226 C 16 F 136 Fang Mountain (elev. 6,736 feet) to west. Erosion pillars on hillside ahead northbound.

A 229 C 19 F 133 Denali Cabins to east.

A 229.1 C 19.1 F 132.8 Denali Air.

A 229.4 C 19.4 F 132.6 229 Parks Restaurant and tavern to west,

A 229.7 C 19.7 F 132.3 Double-ended paved parking area to west.

A 230 C 20 F 132 NOTE: *Ahtna Inc. lands border much of the Parks Highway southbound to Milepost A 192. Ahtna lands are open to entry by permit only; for more information and links to online permits go to http://permits. ahtna-inc.com.*

A 230.5 C 20.5 F 131.5 *Highway descends 6 percent grade northbound.*

A 231 C 21 F 131 Turnoff for **Denali Grizzly Bear Resort** to west; description follows. Denali River Cabins/Cedars Lodge and McKinley Village Lodge to east.

Denali Grizzly Bear. Toll-free 1-866-583-2696. Denali Park. Variety of Alaskan accommodations, pioneer family owned and operated. New Cedar hotel, rooms with private decks on river, TV, WiFi$ and other amenities. Charming, affordable cabins, private, with spectacular views. For camping, wooded RV sites and riverside tent. Only AAA-approved campground in Denali area. See display ad page 472 in the DENALI NATIONAL PARK section.

[ADVERTISEMENT]

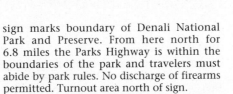

A 231.1 C 21.1 F 130.9 Nenana River Bridge. This is the second bridge over the Nenana River northbound (first crossing is at **Milepost A 215.8**).

A 231.3 C 21.3 F 130.7 Northbound

Mile 238 Rest Area offers a good place to park and enjoy views of the Nenana River. (©Kris Valencia, staff)

sign marks boundary of Denali National Park and Preserve. From here north for 6.8 miles the Parks Highway is within the boundaries of the park and travelers must abide by park rules. No discharge of firearms permitted. Turnout area north of sign.

A 231.4 C 21.4 F 130.6 Gravel parking area east side of highway; posted no overnight camping. No Hunting (sign). View of Mount Fellows and Pyramid Peak.

A 233.1 C 23.1 F 128.9 Small gravel turnout to east.

A 234.1 C 24.1 F 127.9 Double-ended scenic viewpoint up hill to east; litter barrels, no camping. Mount Fellows (elev. 4,476 feet), to the east, makes an excellent camera subject with its constantly changing shadows. Exceptionally beautiful in the evening. To the southeast stands Pyramid Peak (elev. 5,201 feet).

Travel information tune to 1610 radio (sign).

A 235 C 25 F 127 *CAUTION: Railroad crossing.* Solar panels and wind generators provide power for crossing signals.

Slow for rough road next 1 mile northbound (summer 2013).

A 236 C 26 F 126 *Begin 55 mph speed zone northbound. Resume 65 mph southbound.*

A 236.7 C 26.7 F 125.3 Alaska Railroad crosses over highway. *Highway begins 6 percent downgrade northbound.*

A 237 C 27 F 125 *Slow for 45 mph speed zone northbound.*

A 237.3 C 27.3 F 124.7 Riley Creek bridge. Distance marker southbound shows Cantwell 27 miles, Wasilla 196 miles, Anchorage 237 miles.

A 237.4 C 27.4 F 124.6 Denali National Park and Preserve entrance. Turnoff to west on Park Road for access to Denali National Park and Preserve. There is a double-ended parking area by the Denali Park sign, located just west of the turnoff here, that is a popular stop for photos.

Drive 0.3 mile west on Park Road for turnoff to Riley Creek Mercantile (open 7 A.M. to 11 P.M. in summer; you may register for campsites at the store) and Riley Creek Campground. Drive 0.5 mile west for turnoff to Wilderness Access Center (hub for

park buses and camping permits). Drive 1.2 miles west for access to Denali Visitor Center Complex and Alaska Railroad Depot.

Junction 92-mile-long Park Road, which provides access to visitor services and attractions in Denali National Park. See DENALI NATIONAL PARK section on page 469 for Park Road log and details on park entrance fee, campgrounds, transportation and activities in the park.

Begin paved pedestrian path on west side of Parks Highway, which leads north along the highway to Denali Park commercial area.

Begin 45 mph speed zone northbound.

A 237.7 C 27.7 F 124.4 Turnout by Denali National Park sign southbound.

A 238 C 28 F 124 Third bridge northbound over the Nenana River. Access to west Glacier Way. Access to west for double-ended Mile 238 Rest Area (description follows). *CAUTION: Supervise children; pets must be on a leash. It is a long drop to the river from the rest area.* Access to east for **Era Helicopters Denali Flightseeing**.

Mile 238 Rest Area offers parking, toilets, tables and access to the pedestrian path. It is also the access point for Nenana River rafting companies and a great spot to watch riverrunners start down the Class III and IV whitewater section of the Nenana. The pedestrian path and pedestrian bridge across the Nenana River are used by walkers and bicyclists heading south to the park or north to the commercial area.

Begin Denali Park commercial area northbound. This mile-long strip of seasonal services is called the Nenana River Canyon, and it is where most park visitors and many highway travelers stop in summer. For residents, **DENALI PARK** (pop. 145 in summer) refers to the area along the Parks Highway from about Carlo Creek, 13 miles south of the Park entrance, to the Nenana River Canyon, 3 miles north of the Park entrance. A variety of services is offered, including river-running trips and ATV bookings; gift shops, accommodations, restaurants; groceries/liquor store; and a gas station. Most businesses are open in summer only.

Commercial area for Denali National Park is found along the Parks Highway at the head of Nenana Canyon. (©Kris Valencia, staff)

Cabins at Denali. See display ad page 473 in the DENALI NATIONAL PARK section.

Nenana Raft Adventures. See display ad page 477 in the DENALI NATIONAL PARK section.

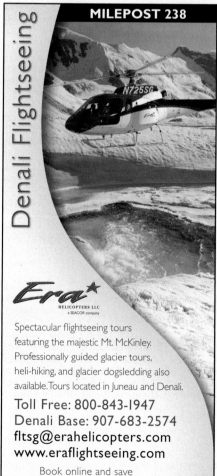
Era Helicopters Denali Flightseeing. See display ad this page.

Distance marker northbound indicates Healy 11 miles, Nenana 67 miles, Fairbanks 117 miles.

A 238.1 C 28.1 F 123.9 Kingfisher Creek. North entrance to Mile 238 Rest Area (see description at **Milepost A 238**) to west. Grande Drive to east to Grande Denali Lodge.

Grande Denali Lodge. Authentically Alaskan. Extraordinary views of the Denali Park wilderness. Located just north of the Denali National Park entrance, perched high atop Sugarloaf Mountain. Featuring timbered greatroom with stone fireplace, Alpenglow Restaurant, Peak Spirits Lounge, espresso bar, tour desk, shuttle, laundry and gift shop. Phone toll-free 1-866-683-8500 or www.denali alaska.com. [ADVERTISEMENT]

A 238.4 C 28.4 F 123.6 Bluffs Road to east to **Denali Bluffs Hotel**; description follows. Market and liquor store.

Denali Bluffs Hotel. Authentically Alaskan. Nestled into Sugarloaf Mountain, next to Denali National Park, the hotel offers warm and cozy guestrooms in a wilderness setting, just steps from adventure. Featuring a log-beamed lobby with stone fireplace, Mountaineer Grill & Bar, Perky Moose Espresso, tour desk, shuttle, laundry and gift shop. Phone toll-free 1-866-683-8500 or www.denalialaska.com. [ADVERTISEMENT]

A 238.5 C 28.5 F 123.5 The huge **Denali Princess Wilderness Lodge** complex begins on the west side of the highway; description follows. Parking to east for restaurant.

Denali Princess Wilderness Lodge. Riverside accommodations overlooking Nenana River and Denali National Park.

One mile from park entrance and Visitors Center. On-site dining: dinner theatre, bistro, espresso, pizza and upscale. Hot tubs, tour desk; gifts, Internet access and shuttle service to Park and rail depot. Rail packages from Anchorage or Fairbanks. Reservations/information 1-800-426-0500; Princesslodges.com. See display ad on page 474 in the DENALI NATIONAL PARK section. [ADVERTISEMENT]

A 238.6 C 28.6 F 123.4 Traffic light at Denali Drive. More of **Denali Princess Wilderness Lodge** to west. Park Mart gas and convenience store to east. South entrance to **Denali Rainbow Village RV Park and Motel.** Local and seasonal businesses are housed in the row of log cabins that make up a mall on the east side of the highway here; see map facing page.

Denali ATV and Denali Jeep Excursions. Denali's two must-do activities: Four unique, fully guided 2½–4 hour ATV tours on single or 2–6 person side-by-side units or a spectacular 5-hour guided Jeep trip along National Geographic's #2 "Drive of a Lifetime" on the Denali Highway. See wildlife or

even Denali! On the Boardwalk near Tesoro Gas. (907) 683-4ATV or 683-JEEP. www.DenaliATV.com or www.DenaliJeep.com. See display ad on page 477 in the DENALI NATIONAL PARK section. [ADVERTISEMENT]

Denali Raft Adventures, Inc., established in 1974, is the original Nenana River rafting company at the entrance to Denali National Park. Try a raft trip for fun, choose from guided scenic or whitewater trips in an oar raft or paddle raft. Trip lengths vary from 2 hours to all day. Currently the only company to offer Goretex drysuits. Ages 5 and up welcome. Call toll-free 1-888-683-2234, local (907) 683-2234; www.denaliraft.com. [ADVERTISEMENT]

A 238.7 C 28.7 F 123.3 Sourdough Road. Access east to **Denali Rainbow Village RV Park**, located behind the row of businesses that make up the mall (see map). Urgent Care to west.

Denali Rainbow Village RV Park and Motel. See display ad on page 476 in the DENALI NATIONAL PARK section.

A 238.9 C 28.9 F 123.1 Traffic light at Canyon Drive. Turnoff to west for McKinley Chalet Resort (lodging, dining, tour desk), which hosts the popular Cabin Nite Theater; turnoff to east for several local businesses, including **Denali Outdoor Center** (rafting outfitter, description follows) and Prospectors Historic Pizzeria. Also access east to DOT Nenana Canyon Viewpoint, which is also the end of the pedestrian/bike path that extends into Denali Park.

Denali Outdoor Center. Denali's most diversified river outfitter! Oar rafts, paddle

rafts, inflatable kayak tours and mountain bike rentals. 2-hour, 4-hour, and half-day guided whitewater and scenic wilderness river trips. Custom "drysuits," professional guides and exceptional equipment provided. Ages 5 and up. Call for reservations (888) 303-1925 or (907) 683-1925. Major credit cards accepted. See display ad on page 475 in the DENALI NATIONAL PARK section. [ADVERTISEMENT]

A 239 C 29 F 123 Entering Nenana River Canyon northbound. Slide area northbound.

A 239.8 C 29.8 F 122.2 Slide area southbound.

A 240 C 30 F 122 Bridge over Iceworm Gulch. Iceworm Creek.

CAUTION: Sharp curves, rock slide area, northbound. Park only at turnouts. High winds in the Nenana Canyon can make this stretch of road dangerous for camper vehicles.

A 240.1 C 30.1 F 121.9 Hornet Creek.

A 240.2 C 30.2 F 121.8 Double-ended parking area to west; no camping.

A 240.7 C 30.7 F 121.3 Parking area to west; no camping.

A 240.9 C 30.9 F 121.1 Double-ended parking area to west; no camping.

A 241 C 31 F 121 Fox Creek.

A 241.6 C 31.6 F 120.4 Large, gravel turnout to west; posted no camping, south

entrance to turnout is steep.

A 242.2 C 32.2 F 119.8 Paved double-ended parking area to west.

A 242.3 C 32.3 F 119.7 Dragonfly Creek.

A 242.8 C 32.8 F 119.2 Paved double-ended turnout to west. Moody Bridge across Nenana River. *CAUTION: Windy area next mile northbound.* This 4th bridge northbound over the Nenana River measures 174 feet from its deck to the bottom of the canyon.

A 243.5 C 33.5 F 118.5 Bridge over Bison Gulch. Sharp turn at north end to east for paved viewpoint; no camping. Hiking trail across highway goes up mountain to west.

A 244 C 34 F 118 Large gravel turnout to east, no camping.

NOTE: Watch for bumpy, patched pavement and frost heaves northbound.

A 244.6 C 34.6 F 117.4 Bridge over Antler Creek. Creek access to west at south end of bridge.

A 245.1 C 35.1 F 116.9 Denali RV

Park and Motel. Full hookups $44. Full hookup pull thru $49. Ten percent Good Sam, Senior and Military discounts on RV rates. Room with double, single beds $84. Four-bed room with kitchen $149. Free WiFi and cable TV. Laundry, gift shop. www.denaliRVparkandmotel.com. Located 8 miles north of park entrance (245.1 George Parks Highway). (907) 683-1500. See display ad on page 473 in the DENALI NATIONAL PARK section. [ADVERTISEMENT]

CAUTION: Frost heaves northbound.

A 246.8 C 36.8 F 115.2 Paved turnout to east. *End passing lane southbound.*

A 247 C 37 F 115 Junction with **Otto Lake Road,** to the west. This area is a fast-growing tourist destination of its own, providing food, lodging, activities and entertainment just outside the bustle of the park. Log of this side road is as follows:

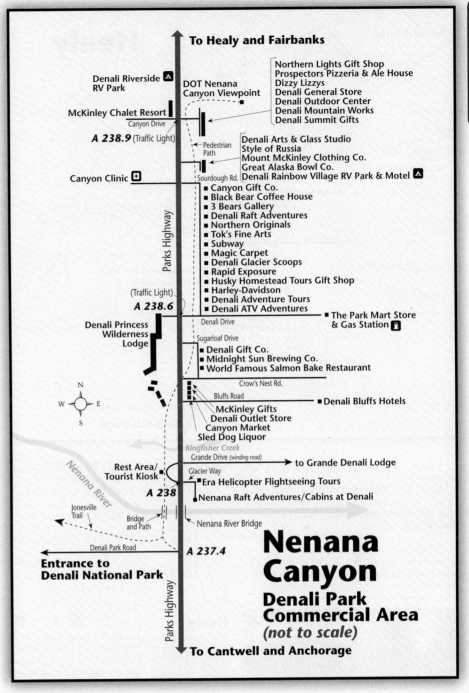

To Healy and Fairbanks

Denali Riverside RV Park

DOT Nenana Canyon Viewpoint

Northern Lights Gift Shop
Prospectors Pizzeria & Ale House
Dizzy Lizzys
Denali General Store
Denali Outdoor Center
Denali Mountain Works
Denali Summit Gifts

McKinley Chalet Resort
Canyon Drive

A 238.9 (Traffic Light)

Pedestrian Path

Denali Arts & Glass Studio
Style of Russia
Mount McKinley Clothing Co.
Great Alaska Bowl Co.
Denali Rainbow Village RV Park & Motel

Canyon Clinic

Sourdough Rd.

Canyon Gift Co.
Black Bear Coffee House
3 Bears Gallery
Denali Raft Adventures
Northern Originals
Tok's Fine Arts
Subway
Magic Carpet
Denali Glacier Scoops
Rapid Exposure
Husky Homestead Tours Gift Shop
Harley-Davidson
Denali Adventure Tours
Denali ATV Adventures

Parks Highway

(Traffic Light)
A 238.6

Denali Princess Wilderness Lodge

Denali Drive

The Park Mart Store & Gas Station

Sugarloaf Drive

Denali Gift Co.
Midnight Sun Brewing Co.
World Famous Salmon Bake Restaurant

Crow's Nest Rd.

Bluffs Road

Denali Bluffs Hotels

McKinley Gifts
Denali Outlet Store
Canyon Market
Sled Dog Liquor

N
W E
S

Kingfisher Creek

Grande Drive (winding road) → to Grande Denali Lodge

Nenana River

Rest Area/ Tourist Kiosk

Glacier Way
Era Helicopter Flightseeing Tours
A 238
Nenana Raft Adventures/Cabins at Denali

Jonesville Trail

Bridge and Path
Nenana River Bridge

Denali Park Road

A 237.4

Entrance to Denali National Park

Parks Highway

Nenana Canyon
Denali Park
Commercial Area
(not to scale)

To Cantwell and Anchorage

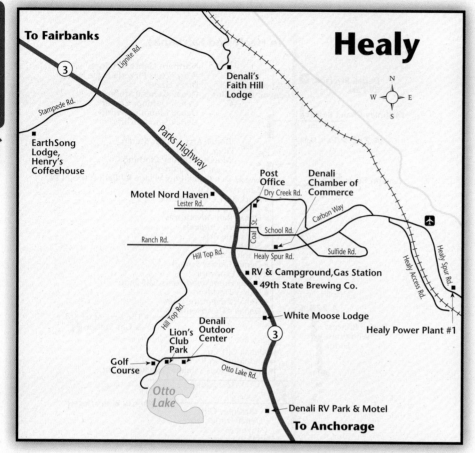

Healy

To Fairbanks

To Anchorage

Mile 0.1 Turnoff to north for Denali Park Hotel.

Mile 0.6 **Denali Outdoor Center** to south rents bikes, canoes and kayaks, and offers camping, cabins and river trips (description follows). 🏕

Denali Outdoor Center. Located ½ mile west on Otto Lake Road. Enjoy the peace and tranquility of our private setting on the lake. We offer canoe, kayak and bike rentals, whitewater and scenic rafting

adventures, camping and cabin rentals. Just 10 minutes from the Denali Park entrance. Open May to September. www.denaliout doorcenter.com. See display ad on page 475 in the DENALI NATIONAL PARK section.
[ADVERTISEMENT]

Mile 0.7 Lion's Club Park to south on Otto Lake offers swimming area, playground, firepits, picnic tables, outhouses.

Mile 0.8 Black Diamond Golf Course, 9-holes, clubhouse.

A 247.3 C 37.3 F 114.7 *Highway descends long downhill grade to Healy northbound.*

A 247.9 C 37.9 F 114.1 *Begin truck lane southbound.*

A 248 C 38 F 114 Large, paved turnout to east. **White Moose Lodge** to west; lodging.

White Moose Lodge. See display ad on

page 471 in the DENALI NATIONAL PARK section.

A 248.2 C 38.2 F 113.8 *Begin 45 mph speed zone northbound.*

A 248.4 C 38.4 F 113.6 49th State Brewing Co. to east.

A 248.5 C 38.5 F 113.5 McKinley RV Park, gas, market and deli. ⛽🏕

A 248.7 C 38.7 F 113.3 **Junction** with Healy Spur Road to Healy (description follows).

Healy 🍴⛽🛏➕

Located along the Parks Highway at Healy Road. **Population:** 1,027. **Emergency Services: Alaska State Troopers**, phone (907) 683-2232. **Fire Department**, Tri–Valley Volunteer Fire Dept., phone 911 or (907) 683-2223/2222. **Clinic**, Interior Community Health Clinic, located on 2nd floor of Tri–Valley Community Center at Mile 0.5 Healy Road, phone (907) 683-2211 (weekdays 9–5) or 911 (available 24 hours).

Visitor Information: Available at the Chamber of Commerce log building at Mile 0.4 Healy Spur Road from 10 A.M. to 6 P.M. June 1–Labor Day. Phone (907) 683-4636; www.denalichamber.com. Stop in and get the scoop on the area from friendly and knowledgeable volunteers.

Elevation: 1,294 feet. **Radio**: KUAC-FM 101.7 (from Fairbanks). **Private Aircraft**: Healy River airstrip 2.1 miles east of Parks Highway via Healy Road; length 2,920 feet; asphalt; unattended. 8 tie-downs available. A commercial air taxi operates here in summer.

Visitor services in Healy include several choices for lodging: in town at **Motel Nord**

Haven; **White Moose Lodge** at **Milepost A 248** Parks Highway; and **Denali's Faith Hill Lodge** just north of town. Gas, deli/market and campsites at McKinley RV & Campground. Healy post office is located on Coal Street (left off Suntrana).

The 49th State Brewing Company at **Milepost 248.4** has an indoor restaurant/bar and an outdoor beer garden where the bus from the movie *Into the Wild* is on display. The bus is an exact replica of the Fairbanks City Transit System Bus 142 that Christopher McCandless used as his wilderness home until his death. Inside are photos from the movie.

Healy has the state's only commercial coal mine. Emil Usibelli started mining coal at Healy in 1943, and Usibelli Coal Mines Inc. now supplies coal to 3 military power plants (Fort Wainwright, Eielson AFB and Clear Air Station) and 3 non-military power plants. From 1984 until 2002, Usibelli exported some 750,000 tons of coal annually to South Korea through the port of Seward.

Healy coal is sub-bituminous with relatively low BTUs per pound. Its low sulfur and nitrogen content make it a clean-burning fuel. Coal is mined from seams near the surface using open-pit mining methods. Mined coal is trucked to 2 sets of crushers, where it is reduced to smaller pieces then loaded into Alaska Railroad coal trains.

The 25-megawatt Healy Power Plant and adjacent 50-megawatt Healy Clean Coal Project (built in 1997) are located 3.3 miles east of the Parks Highway at the end of Healy Road. The power plant is part of the Golden Valley Electric Assoc., which furnishes electric power for Fairbanks and vicinity. The Fairbanks–Tanana Valley area uses primarily coal and also oil to meet its electrical needs. The newer Clean Coal plant has been idle since 1999, following a dispute over the operating efficiency of the $297 million facility. Tours are available free of charge with *advance reservation* at 10 A.M. and 2 P.M. weekdays; phone (907) 683-2226. Pick-up will be at the mine gate. Tours are given weekdays, June 1 to August 22.

Parks Highway Log
(continued)

A 249 C 39 F 113 Suntrana Road to east; access to Tri–Valley School. Healy post office is located on Coal Street (left off Suntrana).

A 249.2 C 39.2 F 112.8 Fuel, gas, diesel, propane. ⛽

A 249.3 C 39.3 F 112.7 Dry Creek Bridge No. 1.

A 249.5 C 39.5 F 112.5 Motel Nord Haven to west. Description follows.

Motel Nord Haven. Meticulously kept family-owned inn. 28 large rooms, all non-smoking, feature queen beds, private baths, wireless DSL, TVs, phones and homey Alaskan decor. We serve breakfast and pack lunches ($12) for our summer guests. Our peaceful location is a 15-minute drive from Denali Park entrance. Phone 1-800-683-4501 from U.S. or (907) 683-4500 from Canada.

A 249.6 C 39.6 F 112.4 Roses Cafe to west. Large turnout to west just beyond cafe. *Begin 55 mph northbound.*

A 249.8 C 39.8 F 112.2 Dry Creek Bridge No. 2. Good berry picking area first part of August. Evans Industries to east (sand, gravel, construction).

A 250 C 40 F 112 *Begin 65 mph northbound and 55 mph speed zone southbound.*

A 251.1 C 41.1 F 110.9 **Junction** with Lignite Road to east and Stampede Road to west. **Denali's Faith Hill Lodge** is located at Mile 1.9 Lignite Road. Description of Denali's Faith Hill Lodge below, followed by log of Stampede Road.

Denali's Faith Hill Lodge. Open year-round. Just minutes from the main entrance of Denali National Park and only 2 miles from the highway. 3000-sq.-ft. lodge with viewing decks, B&B-style comfortable lodging in 8-plex facility, access to full kitchen, WiFi and laundry. Full cooked-to-order breakfast! www.faithhilllodge.com. (907) 683-2921. [ADVERTISEMENT]

Stampede Road (paved/gravel) leads west 8 miles and accesses some beautiful, treeless, highland country on the north side of Denali. Camping, hunting and shooting prohibited. *Please drive slowly.*

Mile 4 **EarthSong Lodge** and Henry's Coffeehouse (open 7–9 A.M. and 6–9 P.M."usually"; slide show was shown at 8 P.M. summer 2013).

Earthsong Lodge. See display ad on page 474 in the DENALI NATIONAL PARK section.

Mile 4.1 Pavement ends, gravel begins, eastbound. Horse outfitter (hunting trips).

Mile 5.2 Large gravel turnout to north.

Mile 8 Stampede Road ends for vehicle traffic; large turnaround. Narrow gravel ATV road continues.

If you've read *Into the Wild*, locals advise it is a long hike in from the end of Stampede Road and you have to cross the Savage and Teklanika Rivers. *River crossings can be dangerous during high water and drownings have occurred.* Inquire locally for more information on the current status of the bus, the trail and the rivers before proceeding. (The bus from the movie is located at the 49th State Brewing Co. in Healy. For details on the McCandless Foundation visit http://www.chrisspurpose.org/.)

A 251.5 C 41.5 F 110.5 *Road work was underway the next 11 miles northbound in summer 2013. Expect continued construction and/or improved highway in summer 2014.*

A 252.5 C 42.5 F 109.5 Bridge over Panguingue Creek. Gravel turnout to west at south end of bridge. Moderate success fishing for grayling. This stream, which flows 8 miles to the Nenana River, was named for a Philippine card game.

A 259.3 C 49.3 F 102.7 Large paved turnout to east just north of Ferry Road. Views of Rex Dome to the northeast. Walker Dome, Jumbo Dome and Liberty Bell mining area to the east.

Distance marker southbound shows Denali Park 22 miles, Cantwell 52 miles, Anchorage 262 miles.

A 260.7 C 50.7 F 101.3 Slide area next 0.3 miles northbound.

A 260.9 C 50.9 F 101.1 Rough gravel turnout to east.

A 261 C 51 F 101 **Parks 261 Pond** public fishing access; rainbow.

Tatlanika Trading Co. and RV Park has many historical and educational displays.
(©Sharon Nault)

Long upgrade northbound.

A 262 C 52 F 100 Improved highway northbound.

A 262.7 C 52.7 F 99.3 Large paved turnout to east.

A 263.5 C 53.5 F 98.5 Large wind generators to east at top of ridge.

A 264.3 C 54.3 F 97.7 Paved turnout to west.

A 269 C 59 F 93 June Creek rest area and picnic spot to east with tables, bear-proof trash cans and toilets.

A 269.4 C 59.4 F 92.6 Bridge over Bear Creek.

A 269.8 C 59.8 F 92.2 Distance marker northbound indicates Nenana 34 miles, Fairbanks 85 miles.

A 271.4 C 61.4 F 90.6 Paved turnout to west.

A 275.6 C 65.6 F 86.4 Entering Game Management Unit 20A northbound, 20C southbound.

A 275.8 C 65.8 F 86.2 Jack Coghill/Nenana River Bridge. Scenic spot; northbound travelers can see Tatlanika Trading Co. RV Park campsites above the river.

Begin improved stretch of highway north of bridge.

A 276 C 66 F 86 **Tatlanika Trading Co. and RV Park.** Wilderness setting along the Nenana River. Tent sites and riverfront RV parking, 20- and 30-amp hookups, dump station, clean restrooms, showers, laundry and potable water. 10 acres of grass for walking dogs, and trails. 39 miles from Denali National Park on the Nenana River. Our gift shop features a gathering of handmade art/crafts/artifacts from various villages. See over 50 mounts including world-class polar bear, along with relics and antiques from Alaska's colorful past in a museum atmosphere. Many historical and educational displays. Visitor information. Refreshments, snacks, ice cream and free coffee. This is a must stop. See display ad on page 479 in the DENALI NATIONAL PARK section. [ADVERTISEMENT]

A 280 C 70 F 82 Clear Sky Lodge to west, open year-round; dining (known for its steaks), WiFi, liquor store, propane, ice.

Clear Sky Lodge. See display ad this page.

A 280.1 C 70.1 F 81.9 Rochester Lodge to east.

A 282.5 C 72.5 F 79.5 *CAUTION: Moose Danger Zone next 22 miles northbound. Watch for moose!*

A 283.5 C 73.5 F 78.5 **Junction** with paved access road west 1.9 miles to **Clear Air Force Station** gate and 6 miles to Anderson Riverside Park and the town of Anderson (description follows). Clear is a military installation (ballistic missile early warning site); sign at turnoff states it is unlawful to enter without permission. However, you can drive into Anderson without permission. The turnoff for Anderson is 1.2 miles west of the Parks Highway before you get to Clear AFS.

ANDERSON (pop. 536), named for homesteader Arthur Anderson, was settled in the late 1950s and was incorporated in 1962.

Nenana Visitor Center has a picnic area, replica tripod and Taku Chief tug boat.

(©Kris Valencia, staff)

Visitor Information: Contact the city office at (907) 582-2500. **Emergency Services**: Anderson Fire Dept./EMS Ambulance, phone 911 or (907) 582-6432. The community has a medical clinic, city hall/post office, store, churches, a restaurant, softball fields and shooting range.

Anderson's **Riverside City Park** campground (a 6.3-mile drive from the highway) has 40 sites on the Nenana River. A real "getaway from it all" area it is especially good for travelers with pets. Lots of wide open spaces for game playing. Rustic camping is $12, electric hookups $15 and sani-dump $5. Host, restrooms/shower, phone and pavilion. Drive straight through Anderson toward the river to reach the park.

City of Anderson. See display ad this

page.

A 283.6 C 73.6 F 78.4 Distance marker northbound indicates Nenana 20 miles, Fairbanks 71 miles.

A 285.7 C 75.7 F 76.3 Julius Creek.

A 286.3 C 76.3 F 75.7 View (weather permitting) of Denali/Mount McKinley southbound.

A 286.8 C 76.8 F 75.2 Double-ended paved turnout to east.

Improved road northbound to Nenana.

A 288.2 C 78.2 F 73.8 Denali Borough boundary: leaving borough northbound.

A 288.5 C 78.5 F 73.5 Fireweed Roadhouse. *CAUTION Watch for moose.*

A 296.7 C 86.7 F 65.3 Bridge over **Fish Creek.** Gravel access to creek at south end of bridge; grayling fishing.

A 298 C 88 F 64 Tamarack Inn (closed in 2013).

A 301.5 C 91.5 F 60.5 Nenana city limits.

A 303 C 93 F 59 *Begin 55 mph speed zone northbound.*

Begin 65 mph speed limit southbound.

A 303.7 C 93.7 F 58.3 Nenana Airport Road.

A 304 C 94 F 58 *Begin 45 mph speed zone northbound.*

Begin 55 mph speed zone southbound.

A 304.3 C 94.3 F 57.7 Alaska State Troopers and courthouse to west.

A 304.4 C 94.4 F 57.6 Chevron gas station and food mart to west; gas, diesel.

A 304.5 C 94.5 F 57.5 Entering Nenana (description follows) northbound at **junction** with A Street access to downtown. The Nenana Visitor Center sits at the "V" fork between the Parks Highway and A Street; visitor information, Nenana Ice Classic tickets, restrooms.

CAUTION: Moose Danger Zone next 22 miles southbound. Watch for moose!

Nenana

A 304.5 C 94.5 F 57.5 Located at the confluence of the Tanana and Nenana rivers. **Population:** 553. **Emergency Services:** Phone 911 for all emergency services. **Fire Department,** VFD/EMS, phone (907) 832-5632.

Clinic, Nenana Native Clinic, phone (907) 832-5247, or Fairbanks hospitals. **Police,** Alaska State Troopers (907) 832-5554.

Visitor Information: In the sod-roofed log cabin at the junction of the highway and A Street. Open 8 A.M. to 6 P.M., 7 days a week, Memorial Day to Labor Day; phone (907) 832-5435; www.nenana.org. Ice Classic tickets may be purchased here. Picnic tables and restrooms are beside the restored *Taku Chief*, located behind the visitor information center. This little tugboat plied the waters of the Tanana, Yukon and Koyukuk rivers for many years.

Elevation: 400 feet. **Climate:** Nenana has an extreme temperature range, with an average daily maximum in summer of 65 to 70° F; daily minimum in winter is well below 0° F. **Radio:** KIAM 630–AM, KUAC–FM 91.1. **Transportation: Air**—Nenana maintains an FAA-approved airport. **Railroad**—The Alaska Railroad.

Private Aircraft: Nenana Municipal Airport, 0.9 mile south; elev. 362 feet; length 4,600 feet; asphalt; fuel 100LL, Jet B. Floatplane and ski-plane strip.

Nenana has food, gas, lodging, an RV park, auto repair shop, radio station, several churches, a library, restaurants, a cultural center, a laundromat, a seniors' social center and senior housing units. Coghill's General Merchandise built in 1916 has served the community for more than 90 years. The **Rough Woods Inn & Cafe** (food and lodging) reflects the woodworking skill of Larry Coy and the cooking talent of Ruth Coy, both pioneer Alaskan homesteaders. Camping at **Nenana RV Park and Campground.**

The town was first known as Tortella, a white man's interpretation of the Athabascan word *Toghottele*. A 1902 map indicates a village spelled Tortilli on the north bank of the Tanana River, on the side of the hill still known as Tortella. In the same year Jim Duke built a roadhouse and trading post, supplying river travelers with goods and lodging. The settlement became known as Nenana, an Athabascan word meaning, "a good place to camp between the rivers." The town thrived as a trading center for Natives of the region and travelers on the vast network of interior rivers.

Nenana boomed during the early 1920s as a construction base for the Alaska Railroad. On July 15, 1923, Pres. Warren G. Harding drove the golden spike at Nenana signifying the completion of the railroad.

Today, Nenana is the hub for the tug boat/barge shipping industry that traverses the rivers of the Interior, providing goods to numerous villages. Tons of fuel, freight and supplies move from the docks at Nenana from late May through September each year. Because the rivers are shallow and silt-laden, the barges move about 12 mph downstream and 5 mph upstream.

Nenana is perhaps best known for the **Nenana Ice Classic,** an annual event that awards cash prizes to the lucky winners who guess the exact minute of the ice breakup on the Tanana River. The contest has been a spring highlight since 1917.

Ice Classic tickets are sold throughout Alaska from February 1st through April 5th. In Nenana, tickets may be purchased at the Ice Classic Office on Main Street and at various local businesses. In other Alaska communities, try the local general store or supermarket (e.g. Carrs/Safeway), VFW and American Legion posts, bars, restau-

rants and other businesses. (For a complete list of ticket sale locations in Alaska, go to www.nenanaakiceclassic.com.) Completed tickets with name, address, date, and time sections filled out, are then deposited into Nenana Ice Classic cans located at the ticket sales location. (*NOTE: Mailing tickets to the Ice Classic is restricted to participants living in areas where tickets are not available. The Ice Classic is unable to mail tickets due to U.S. Postal regulations.*)

Ice Classic festivities begin the last weekend in February with the Tripod Raising Festival and culminate at breakup time in late April or May. When the surging ice on the Tanana River dislodges the tripod, a line attached to the tripod trips a clock located in a tower atop the Ice Classic office, thus recording the official breakup time. Summer visitors can see the clock tower and this year's winning time at the Ice Classic office on Front Street. The tripod for the next Ice Classic is displayed next to the office during River Daze, held the first weekend in June.

The **Alaska Railroad Depot**, located at the end of Main Street, is on the National Register of Historic Places. Built in 1923 and renovated in 1988, the depot houses the state's Alaska Railroad Museum, open 8:30 A.M. to 6 P.M. daily.

One block from the railroad depot is **St. Mark's Episcopal Church**. This little log building, built in 1905, is always open to the public. It is graced with hand-hewn pews and a raised altar decorated with Native beaded moosehide frontal and dossal hangings.

The **Nenana Cultural Center and Gift Shop** is located near the end of C Street and open daily May until mid-September. Learn about the history of the natives in Nenana and the surrounding area as well as the city's early history. Come in and see the many historical items on display as well as a large selection of exceptional Native crafts and other hand-crafted items that on for sale. View the Tanana River and bridges from front porch.

The **Nenana Public Library** offers the highway traveler computers and Internet access, fax and copy machines (Wednesday–Thursday 11 A.M.–7 P.M.; Friday 9 A.M.–5 P.M.; Saturday 12 P.M.–8 P.M.) 2nd Avenue and Market Street. Phone (907) 832-5812.

Parks Highway Log
(continued)

A **305 C 95 F 57** The north end of the **Alaska Native Veterans' Honor Bridge**

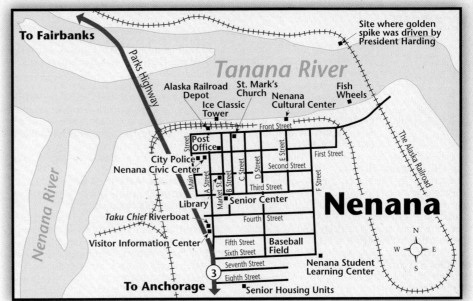

across the Tanana River. Sharp turn to west at north end of bridge through narrow entrance for turnout *(not recommended for RVs or trailers).*

This steel through-truss style bridge was built in 1966-67. It was dedicated on Aug. 5, 2000, to commemorate Alaska Natives who have served in U.S. Armed Forces. The bridge spans the Tanana River just upstream of the confluence of the Nenana River. There is no other bridge downstream of this one all the way to the mouth of the Yukon River in Norton Sound.

Second, smaller bridge northbound is the Shirley Demientieff Memorial Bridge. Shoulder parking to west at north end.

The Tanana is formed by the joining of the Chisana and the Nabesna rivers near Northway and flows 440 miles westward to the Yukon River. From the bridge, watch for freight-laden river barges bound for the Yukon River. North of this bridge, fish wheels may sometimes be seen in action and occasionally fish may be purchased from the owners of the wheels.

Entering Game Management Unit 20B northbound, 20A southbound.

A **305.9 C 95.9 F 56.1** Large double-ended gravel turnout to east, small turnout to west.

A **306 C 96 F 56** *Begin 65 mph speed limit northbound.*
Begin 55 mph speed zone southbound.

A **308 C 98 F 54** *Driving distance between Mileposts 308 and 309 is 0.7 mile.*

A **308.3 C 98.3 F 53.7** Highway overpass

passes over the railroad tracks.

A **308.9 C 98.9 F 53.1** Double-ended turnout to west. View obstructed by foliage.

A **309.1 C 99.1 F 52.9** Turnoff to west and down side road for Monderosa Restaurant, a local favorite for its big burgers.

A **311.2 C 101.2 F 52.8** Reindeer and tree farm to west.

A **312 C 102 F 52** Distance marker northbound shows Ester 39 miles, Fairbanks 44 miles.

Highway begins a series of long winding grades with intermittent passing lanes next 38 miles northbound. Patched pavement.

A **313.6 C 103.6 E 48.4 Parks Highway Towing** to west; 24-hour towing, jump starts, tire changes, phone 1-800-478-8697.

Parks Highway Towing. See display ad on this page.

A **314.6 C 104.6 F 47.4** Narrow, paved double-ended turnout to northwest.

A **314.7 C 104.7 F 47.3** Bridge over Little Goldstream Creek.

A **318.7 C 108.7 F 43.3** Paved double-ended scenic viewpoint to north. Beautiful view looking out over Minto Flats, mostly bogs, small lakes, and creeks with names like at former gold mining claims called Hard Luck and Fortune. The Tanana River is on both sides of the highway here. It follows a horseshoe-shaped course, the top of the closed end being the bridge at Nenana.

Ester

Located 0.6 mile west of **Milepost A 351.2** Parks Highway via Old Nenana Highway to Village Road. **Population:** 2,041. **Emergency Services:** Emergency only, phone 911. **Fire Department**, phone (907) 479-6858. **Radio:** KCBF 820-AM. Post office is on Village Road at Old Nenana Highway. Nearest Visitor Center is in Fairbanks. **Newspaper:** *Ester Republic* www.esterrepublic.com.

Ester is an appealing combination of historic and contemporary Alaska, with its old buildings and mining artifacts, and its cutting edge artists, all located in a beautiful setting.

A tent camp of miners in 1906, the Fairbanks Exploration Company built Ester Camp 30 years later to support a large-scale gold dredge operation. After 20 years of operation, the mine was shutdown, but it reopened in 1958 as a summer visitor attraction. The Ester Gold Camp complex, which includes the Malemute Saloon and historic Bunkhouseg, has been closed since 2009.

Ester Community Park, located just past the turnoff from the Parks Highway onto the Old Nenana Highway, has a children's playground. Fresh produce may be available for purchase at the park in summer.

As you turn into Ester, across from the Post Office in the woods is a small gazebo, perfect for a picnic or to watch the world go by. And check out the facade of the Golden Eagle Saloon. The Post Office is open weekdays, 10 A.M. to 1 P.M. and 1:30–5 P.M., and Saturdays, 10 to 11 A.M.

Several artists make their home in Ester. **Judie Gumm Designs** is on Main Street (follow signs to her house/shop).

Judie Gumm Designs. Noted for her silver sculptural interpretations of Northern images, Judie Gumm's work has been featured in many national publications. Priced moderately, easy to pack, her jewelry makes a perfect remembrance of your adventure North. Ester turnoff (Mile 351.2). In Ester, just follow her studio signs. Weekdays 10-6 and Saturday 12-5. RV parking available across from the Golden Eagle Saloon. [ADVERTISEMENT]

**Return to Milepost A 351.2
Parks Highway**

A 322 C 112 F 40 Distance marker southbound shows Nenana 17 miles, Clear 43 miles, Anchorage 322 miles.

A 324.5 C 114.5 F 37.5 South end of 0.2-mile-long double-ended access road to scenic viewpoint (**Purvis Lookout**) on old highway alignment. North end at **Milepost A 324.7**.

A 325.6 C 115.6 F 36.4 Entering Fairbanks North Star Borough northbound.

A 328 C 118 F 34 Longtime lodging provider to west.

A 331.6 C 121.6 F 30.4 South end of 0.3-mile-long double-ended parking area to east along old highway alignment. North end at **Milepost A 331.9**.

A 335.6 C 125.6 F 26.4 South end of 0.4-mile-long double-ended gravel parking area to west along old highway alignment. North end at **Milepost A 336**.

A 338.5 C 128.5 F 23.5 Expansive views to southeast of Tanana River. Look for Murphy Dome (elev. 2,930 feet), with white communication installations on summit, to northeast.

This stretch of highway is often called Skyline Drive; views to west.

A 341 C 131 F 21 South end of long double-ended gravel scenic viewpoint to west. North end at **Milepost A 341.2**.

A 342.5 C 132.5 F 19.5 Old Nenana Highway to west.

A 344.3 C 134.3 F 17.7 Viewpoint to southeast with view of Tanana River; good photo opportunity. Monument in honor of George Alexander Parks (1883-1984) the territorial governor of Alaska from 1925 to 1933, for whom the Parks Highway is named. On a clear day, the Alaska Range is visible from this viewpoint.

A 349 C 139 F 13 Cripple Creek Road to south, Parks Ridge Road to north.

A 349.2 C 139.2 F 12.8 *Highway climbs southbound. This is the first in a series of long winding grades with intermittent passing lanes next 38 miles southbound.*

A 349.8 C 139.8 F 12.2 Alder Creek.

A 351.2 C 141.2 F 10.8 Turnoff to west for Ester via Old Nenana Highway to Village Road (first right). Ester Post Office on Village Road and Old Nenana Highway. Fire station at Parks Highway junction. Ester Community Park adjacent, with playground, hosts a weekly open-air market June through August; farm produce, food, local arts and crafts for sale.

Junction with side road west to Ester; see "Ester" description this page.

A 352.2 C 142.2 F 9.8 Gold Hill Road. The U.S. Smelting, Refining and Mining Co. mined some 126,000 ounces of gold from Gold Hill between 1953 and 1957.

Bike path begins northbound.

A 353.4 C 143.4 F 8.6 North side of highway has **Gold Hill Imported Beer and Fine Wine** and a Tesoro gas station.

Gold Hill Imported Beer and Wine. See display ad this page.

A 355.7 C 145.7 F 6.3 Turnoff to north for Sheep Creek Road to Ester Dome Road and access to Ester Dome single-track bike trail. Contact Goldstream Sports Shop (907/455-6520) for details or visit www.happytrailsak.com/esterdome.php.

A 356 C 146 F 6 Distance marker southbound shows Ester 5 miles, Nenana 53 miles, Anchorage 357 miles.

Begin 4-lane divided highway eastbound.
Begin 2-lane highway westbound.

A 356.8 C 146.8 F 5.2 Geist Road/Chena Pump Road Exit. Access to **University of Alaska Museum of the North** (2.5 miles north from highway via Geist Road and Fairbanks Street).

A 357.7 C 147.7 F 4.3 Bridge over Chena River.

A 357.8 C 147.8 F 4.2 West Airport Way exit to Fairbanks International Airport and access to **Riverboat Discovery**.

A 358 C 148 F 4 East Airport Way exit to **River's Edge RV Park** and **River's Edge Resort** (lodging, camping, dining), Fred Meyer store, and University Avenue to **Chena River State Recreation Site**. Also access to Johansen Expressway.

Parks Highway (Alaska Route 3) continues through Fairbanks as the Mitchell Expressway.

A 359 C 149 F 3 Stoplight at University Avenue.

A 360 C 150 F 2 Peger Road South exit for eastbound traffic.

A 360.3 C 150.3 F 1.7 Stoplight at intersection with Peger Road; access to North Peger Road. North for access to **Pioneer Park**, Alaska's only Pioneer Theme Park.

A 361.2 C 151.2 F 0.8 Stoplight at Lathrop Street intersection.

A 362 C 152 F 0 First visible milepost westbound, last milepost eastbound. Exit to Cushman Street to Fairbanks City Centre. See FAIRBANKS section beginning on facing page for description of city.

The Parks Highway divides eastbound about 0.3 miles from here, merging with the Steese Expressway (Alaska Route 2 North) and the Richardson Highway (Alaska Route 2 South).

Junction with Richardson Highway (Alaska Route 2 South) and Steese Highway (Alaska Route 2 North). Turn to end of the ALASKA HIGHWAY section on page 224 and read log back to front for log of Alaska Route 2 South. Turn to the STEESE HIGHWAY section on page 517 for log of Alaska Route 2 .

Fairbanks

(See maps, pages 450 and 452)

Cruising the Chena River on a Discovery stern-wheeler is a top attraction in Fairbanks. (©Kris Valencia, staff)

Located in the heart of Alaska's Interior, Fairbanks is approximately 1,488 driving miles north of Dawson Creek, BC, the start of the Alaska Highway (traditional milepost distance is 1,523 miles); 98 miles from Delta Junction (official end of the Alaska Highway); 358 miles from Anchorage via the Parks Highway; and 2,305 miles from Seattle.

Population: Fairbanks city, 32,506; Fairbanks–North Star Borough, 98,660. **Emergency Services: Alaska State Troopers**, 1979 Peger Road, emergency phone 911; for non-emergencies, (907) 451-5100, and for TTY service, (907) 451-5344. **Fairbanks Police**, 911 Cushman St., emergency phone 911 or, for non-emergencies, phone (907) 450-6500. **Fire Department** and **Ambulance** Service, phone 911. **Hospitals**, Fairbanks Memorial, 1650 Cowles St., phone (907) 452-8181; Chief Andrew Isaac Health Center (907) 451-6682; Bassett Army Hospital, Fort Wainwright, phone (907) 361-5172, emergency room (907) 361-5144; Eielson Clinic, Eielson AFB, phone (907) 377-1847. **Chiropractic**, Arctic Chiropractic, phone (907) 451-7246. **Pet Emergency** (907) 479-2700, 8 Bonnie Ave., open 24-hours.

Visitor Information: The Fairbanks Convention and Visitors Bureau (www.explorefairbanks.com) Visitor Center is located at 101 Dunkel St., inside the **Morris Thompson Cultural and Visitors Center**. This facility is truly a marvelous place, with visitor information and trip-planning help

from a knowledgeable staff, and an interpretive exhibit gallery featuring displays on the land, seasons and people of Fairbanks, Interior Alaska and the Arctic. There is also a theatre, public restrooms, and ample visitor parking. Open 7 days a week, 8 A.M. to 9 P.M. in summer, 8 A.M. to 5 P.M. in winter. Closed Thanksgiving Day, Christmas Day and New Year's Day. Phone (907) 456-5774 or 1-800-327-5774. Inquire about driving and walking tours and various city attractions. Audiotapes are available in English and German for self-guided walking tours. Free Internet access (no printer available) for 10-minute periods, first-come/first-served basis.

Special events occur year-round in Fairbanks, from the 1-day Harley Davidson Motorcycle Spring Run to the multi-day Midnight Sun Intertribal Powwow. For a listing of current events and activities, phone (907) 456-4636 or visit the CVB website at www.explorefairbanks.com/events.

Visitor information is also available at the Fairbanks International Airport in the baggage claim area, Pioneer Park and the Alaska Railroad depot.

For information on Alaska's state parks, national parks, national forests, wildlife refuges and other outdoor recreational sites, visit the **Alaska Public Lands Information Center**, located at 101 Dunkel St., in the Morris Thompson Cultural and Visitors Center, downtown. The APLIC offers free trip-planning assistance, free films on Alaska, interpretive programs, lectures, exhibits, artifacts, photographs and short

video programs on each region in the state. The center also houses the Alaska Geographic bookstore. The exhibit area and information desk are open daily in summer, 8 A.M. to 9 P.M.; daily in winter, 9 A.M. to 5 P.M. Phone (907) 459-3730 or toll-free 1-866-869-6887; www.alaskacenters.gov/fairbanks.cfm.

Elevation: 439 feet at Fairbanks International Airport. Climate: January temperatures range from 18°F to -22°F. The lowest temperature ever recorded was -66°F in December 1961. July temperatures aver-

(Continues on page 448)

Distances in miles	Fairbanks	Anchorage	Denali NP	Homer	Seward	Tok	Valdez
Fairbanks		362	125	595	489	204	366
Anchorage	362		237	233	127	328	304
Denali NP	125	237		470	364	565	541
Homer	595	233	470		180	561	537
Seward	489	127	364	180		455	431
Tok	204	328	565	561	455		254
Valdez	366	304	541	537	431	254	

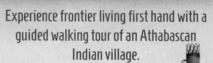

Riverboat Adventure

Your three hour cruise will take you into the heart of Alaska with a family who has made the rivers of Alaska a way of life for five generations. You will see a bush floatplane taking off from the river, visit the home and kennels of the late four-time Iditarod Champion Susan Butcher, and learn about the ancient Athabascan Indian culture. Alaskan Native guides who have worked and lived in Alaska will take you on a personalized tour of the Chena Indian Village. Definetely one of the most unique ways to explore Alaska.

Take our Athabascan Indian and Pioneer tour through a Native village and Mining era Cabin. Learn about local Native Alaskan culture and what it took to live in the last frontier during the gold rush.

One of the toughest, most grueling traditions in Alaska is the Iditarod. A 1,100 mile race from Anchorage to Nome. During your experience you will visit the home of the late Iditarod four-time Champion Susan Butcher and get to meet her champion team.

Visit Steamboat Landing, Alaska's largest and most well known gift shop. Here you can grab a snack or pick up that perfect keepsake for yourself or someone special. This is a truly memorable stop along your adventure.

Most definetely the COOLEST experience in Fairbanks... "Alaska at 40° Below" is a quick trip into a special cooling chamber that drops your environment to 40 degrees below zero where you will learn first hand about life in subzero temperatures.

Gold Mining Experience

Join us for a trip through Alaska's gold mining history. Ride a replica of the Tanana Valley Railroad for an adventure into the gold fields of the Interior. A two-hour guided tour takes you out to Gold Dredge 8, a National Historic site. Enjoy a walking tour of our mining camp. Meet and talk with Alaska miners as you learn about present day placer mining methods. After a short course in gold mining, grab your own "poke" filled with pay dirt right out of a sluice box and try your hand at panning for gold. Everyone finds gold. We guarantee it!

Earl, your train's Conductor, will guide you along the rail tour through the Tanana Valley with lively music and lots of educational and humorous tidbits. A great way to explore the wildlife and terrain of the interior.

Get ready to explore "Gold Dredge 8", a historic gold mining facility in Alaska. See how machinery helped push forward the mining era and compare it to your hand panning experience.

Visit the famous TransAlaska Pipeline, a marvel of modern engineering and part of the largest industry in Alaska. Many who live in Alaska have never seen it up close so this will be a real treat to see.

Authentic gold nugget jewelry and lockets available in our gift shop to take home the gold you panned. Show off your pioneer adventure in The Last Frontier!

BOOK THESE ADVENTURES TODAY! 866-479-6673

RIVER'S EDGE
RV PARK & CAMPGROUND
Located in the heart of Fairbanks

4140 Boat St, 99709 • (907) 474-0286

www.riversedge.net
book on-line

1-800-770-3343

"River's Edge is RV heaven!"
Dr. Helen Stover of Richmond, VA

Home of
Rosehip Gifts
featuring Alaskan made gifts

**50 & 30 Amp Electric • Wireless Internet • Cable TV
Full & Partial Hook-Ups • Gift Shop • Tour Sales
180 Sites • Pull Throughs • Car Wash • Laundry
Tent Sites • Dump Station
Walking distance to shopping & groceries**

Showers for registered guests

GPS: N 64.83 W 147.83

**Chena's
Alaskan Grill**
*featuring Fresh
Alaska Seafood*

**River's Edge daily tours
Historical Fairbanks City Tours
Riverboat Discovery
Arctic Circle and
Point Barrow Tours**

From Anchorage/
Denali, AK3: take East
Airport Way exit, left
on Sportsmans Way,
left on Boat Street.
From Tok/Richardson
Hwy., AK2: left on
Airport Way, cross
University Ave., right
on Sportsmans Way,
left on Boat Street.

River's Edge Resort
Chena's Fine
Dining & Deck
River's Edge RV Park
Chena River
SPORTSMANS WAY
UNIVERSITY AVE.
PARKS HWY.
BOAT STREET
AIRPORT WAY
Fred Meyer West
From AK 3
From AK 2
N
EAST AIRPORT WAY EXIT

Good Sampark

**4140 Boat Street (off Airport Way),
Fairbanks, Alaska 99709**

Fairbanks has its share of big box chain stores, like these on Johansen Expressway, west of the Steese Expressway. (©Sharon Nault)

(Continued from page 444)
age 62°F, with a record high of 99°F in July 1919. In June and early July daylight lasts more than 21 hours—and the nights are really only twilight. Annual precipitation is 8.4 inches, with an annual average snowfall of 58.5 inches. The record for snowfall is 147.3 inches, set the winter of 1991. **Radio**: CHET-FM, KFAR-AM, KCBF-AM, KAKQ-FM, KFBX-AM, KIAK-FM, KJNP-AM/FM (North Pole), KKED-FM, KSUA-FM, KUWL-FM, KXLR-FM, KWLF-FM, KYSC-FM, KUAC-FM

89.9. **Television**: Channels 2, 4, 7, 9, 11, 13 and cable. **Newspapers**: *Fairbanks Daily News–Miner*.

Private Aircraft: Consult the *Alaska Supplement* for information on Eielson AFB, Fairbanks International, Fairbanks International Seaplane, Chena Marina Air Field and Fort Wainwright Army Base. Or phone the Fairbanks Flight Service Station at (907) 474-0137. For recorded information on special use airspace for central Alaska, phone 1-800-758-8723.

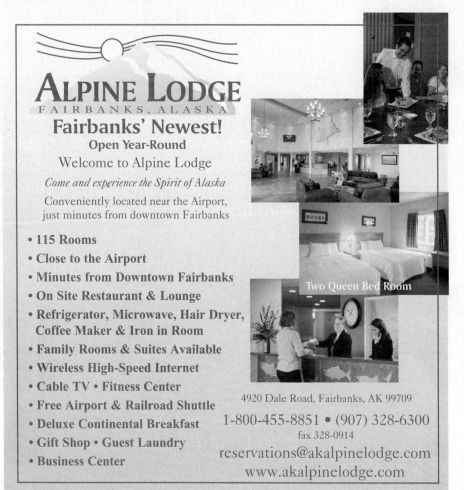
History & Economy

In 1901, Captain E.T. Barnette set out from St. Michael on the stern-wheeler *Lavelle Young*, traveling up the Yukon River with supplies for his trading post, which he proposed to set up at Tanana Crossing (Tanacross), the halfway point on the Valdez–Eagle trail. But the stern-wheeler could not navigate the fast-moving, shallow Tanana River beyond the mouth of the Chena River. The stern-wheeler's captain dropped off Barnette on the Chena near the present site of First Avenue and Cushman Street. A year later, Felix Pedro, an Italian prospector, discovered gold about 16 miles north of Barnette's temporary trading post, and, alert to the possibilities, Barnette abandoned his original plan to continue on to Tanana Crossing.

In September 1902, Barnette convinced the 25 or so miners in the area to use the name "Fairbanks" for the town that he expected would grow up around his trading post. The name had been suggested that summer by District Court Judge James Wickersham, who admired Charles W. Fairbanks, the senior senator from Indiana. The senator later became vice president of the United States under Theodore Roosevelt.

The town grew, largely due to Barnette's promotion of gold prospects and discoveries in the area, and in 1903 Judge Wickersham moved the headquarters of his Third Judicial District Court (a district which encompassed 300,000 square miles) from Eagle to Fairbanks.

Thanks to Wickersham, the town gained government offices and a jail. Thanks to Barnette, it gained a post office and a branch of the Northern Commercial Company, a large Alaska trading firm based in San Francisco. In addition, after Barnette became the first mayor of Fairbanks in 1903, the town acquired telephone service, set up fire protection, passed sanitation ordinances and contracted for electric light and steam heat. In 1904, Barnette started a bank. The town of "Fairbanks" first appeared in the U.S. Census in 1910 with a population of 3,541.

Today, the city's economy is linked to its role as a service and supply point for Interior and Arctic industrial activities. Fairbanks played a key role during construction of the Trans-Alaska Oil Pipeline in the 1970s. The Dalton Highway (formerly the North Slope Haul Road) to Prudhoe Bay begins about 84 miles north of town. Extractive industries such as oil and mining continue to play a major role in the economy.

Government employment contributes significantly to the Fairbanks economy. Including military jobs, more than 30 percent of employment in Fairbanks is through the government.

Fort Wainwright (www.wainwright.army.mil/sites/local/) was the first Army airfield in Alaska, established in 1938, and named Ladd Field, in honor of Maj. Arthur Ladd, an Air Corps pilot killed in a crash in 1935. The first Air Corps detachment arrived April 1940. The men tested clothing and equipment during the bitter cold winters until World War II. Ladd Field became a transfer point for the Lend Lease Program, in which the U. S. delivered nearly 8,000 aircraft to Russia.

The Army assumed control of Ladd Air Force Base in January 1961, renaming it Fort Jonathan M. Wainwright, in honor of the WWII general who led forces on Bataan and Corregidor. The fort currently employs about 6,650 soldiers and 1,375 civilians. Fort Wain-

GO BEYOND
YOUR
EXPECTATIONS

Go deep inside Alaska, where the unparalleled meets the unexpected ... in Fairbanks. The Morris Thompson Cultural and Visitors Center exceeds your expectations for a visitors center. Here you will discover the warmth of knowledgeable and friendly information services staff. Take advantage of free options such as: brochures, world-class exhibits, daily films, WiFi and Internet access. Be enlightened by cultural programs and much more. Let the Center be your first stop to experiencing the energy of Fairbanks, Denali, Interior and Arctic Alaska. Located in downtown Fairbanks at 101 Dunkel Street. Call (907) 456-5774 for more information.

FAIRBANKS
ALASKA

WWW.EXPLOREFAIRBANKS.COM

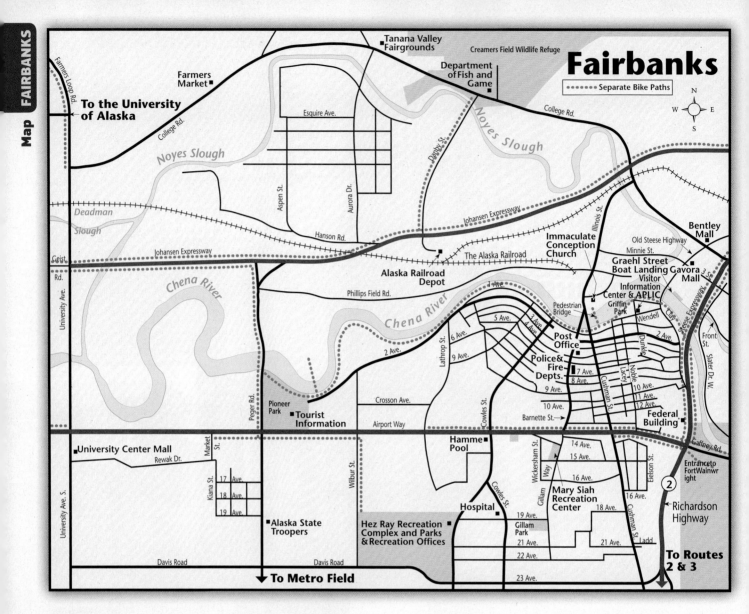

Fairbanks

········· Separate Bike Paths

Tanana Valley Fairgrounds

Creamers Field Wildlife Refuge

Department of Fish and Game

Farmers Market ■

To the University of Alaska

College Rd.

Esquire Ave.

Noyes Slough

College Rd.

Farmers Loop Rd.

Aspen St.

Darby St.

Aurora Dr.

Johansen Expressway

Noyes Slough

Deadman Slough

Johansen Expressway

Hanson Rd.

Geist Rd.

University Ave.

Chena River

Phillips Field Rd.

Alaska Railroad Depot

The Alaska Railroad

Chena River

Illinois St.

Bentley Mall

Old Steese Highway   Minnie St.

Immaculate Conception Church

Graehl Street Boat Landing   Gavora Mall

Visitor Information Center & APLIC

Griffin Park

Pedestrian Bridge

Ave.

5 Ave.

2 Ave.
4 Ave.

6 Ave.

Lathrop St.

9 Ave.

2 Ave.

Wendell

Post Office

Police & Fire Depts.

Dunkle

2 Ave.

Steese Expressway

3 St.

Front St.

Slater Dr. W.

Pioneer Park

Tourist Information

Peger Rd.

Crosson Ave.

Airport Way

Cowles St.

7 Ave.

8 Ave.

9 Ave.

10 Ave.

Barnette St.

Cushman St.

Noble
Lacey

10 Ave.

11 Ave.

12 Ave.

Federal Building

Gaffney Rd.

University Center Mall ■

Rewak Dr.

Market St.

Hamme Pool ■

Wilbur St.

Wickersham St.

14 Ave.

15 Ave.

16 Ave.

Way

Gillam

16 Ave.

Eielson St.

Entrance to Fort Wainwright

2

Richardson Highway

17 Ave.

18 Ave.

19 Ave.

Kiana St.

University Ave. S.

Alaska State Troopers ■

Cowles St.

Hospital ■

Gillam Park

19 Ave.

Mary Siah Recreation Center

18 Ave.

Cushman St.

Ladd

To Routes 2 & 3

Hez Ray Recreation Complex and Parks & Recreation Offices

21 Ave.

22 Ave.

23 Ave.

21 Ave.

Davis Road

Davis Road

↓ To Metro Field

wright is home to a Stryker brigade combat team and an aviation brigade.

Eielson Air Force Base (www.eielson. af.mil), located 25 miles southeast of Fairbanks on the Richardson Highway, also has a strong economic impact on the city. The 354th Fighter Wing is the host unit at Eielson Air Force Base and is assigned to 11th Air Force, headquartered at JBER in Anchorage.

Construction on Eielson Air Force Base was completed in 1944. Originally a satellite base to Ladd Army Air Field (now Fort Wainwright) and called Mile 26, it served as a storage site for aircraft on their way to the Soviet Union under the WWII Lend–Lease program. (A statue honoring this program is located in Griffin Park.) Closed after WWII, the base reopened in 1946. In 1948, it was renamed Eielson Air Force Base after Carl Ben Eielson, the first pilot to fly from Alaska over the North Pole to Greenland. Eielson AFB is the farthest-north fighter wing in the U.S. Air Force, and at 60,000 square miles of military training space, it has the largest aerial range in the country.

Also boosting the Fairbanks economy are the University of Alaska Fairbanks, and trade and service industries such as retail sales and tourism.

Description

Alaska's second largest city and the administrative center of the Interior, Fairbanks lies on the forested valley floor of the Tanana River on the banks of the Chena River. Good views of the valley are available from Chena Ridge Road to the west and Farmers Loop Road to the north.

The city is a blend of old and new: Modern full-service hotels, shopping centers and malls stand beside log cabins and historic wooden buildings.

Fairbanks is bounded on the north, east

and west by low rolling hills of birch and white spruce. To the south are the Alaska Range and Denali National Park, about a 2 ½-hour drive via the Parks Highway. The Steese and Elliott highways lead north to the White Mountains.

Lodging & Services

Fairbanks has all visitor services. Reservations are suggested for all Fairbanks accommodations during summer. Shopping ranges from unique Northern art galleries to major chain retail stores like Walmart. (The University Avenue Fred Meyer is the largest Fred Meyer store in the U.S.) There are more than 100 restaurants, including favorites like **The Cookie Jar** and **The Turtle Club**. Several of the more than 2 dozen hotels and motels in Fairbanks also offer fine dining experiences, like **Chena's Alaskan Grill** at River's Edge, the **Golden Nugget**, Zach's at Sophie Station, the **Red Lantern** at the Westmark.

AAA-7 Gables Inn & Suites. Located centrally to major attractions, lodging includes rooms, condos and apartments. Most have private Jacuzzis, and many have fireplaces and kitchens. All come with TV/DVDs, free wireless Internet and free breakfasts. Laundry facilities. Rates range $60 and up. www.7gablesinn.com. 4312 Birch Lane, Fairbanks. Phone (907) 479-0751. [ADVERTISEMENT]

AAAA Care B&B/Inn. It's the 4-A place to stay. Hospitality of an Alaskan log home. Clean quality rooms, private and shared baths, full breakfast, kitchen with beautiful decks. Conveniently located near airport, train, downtown, UAF. Open year-round. (907) 479-2447. 557 Fairbanks Street (off Geist Rd.), Fairbanks, AK 99709. www.aaaacare.com. [ADVERTISEMENT]

Ah, Rose Marie Downtown Bed and Breakfast. Wow! Two quaint, cozy 1930's homes near old downtown restaurants, shops, galleries & Visitors Center. Full breakfasts. Families, groups welcomed. Extraordinary hospitality. Hosts John, son Chris. Friendly cat, dog. Guide-

book recommended. (Est. 1989.) Year round, $65–$110. 302 Cowles St., Fairbanks, AK 99701. Phone (907) 456-2040; ahrosemarie@yahoo.com; www.akpub.com/akbbrv/ahrose.html. [ADVERTISEMENT]

Bridgewater Hotel. Alaska's genuine northern hospitality can be found here—located in the heart of downtown, overlooking the Chena River. Offering exceptional guest service, fresh breakfast buffet, laundry facility, clean cozy guestrooms and easy walk to shopping, restaurants and visitors center. Scheduled complimentary Around Town Express. Reservations: Fountainhead Hotels 1-800-528-4916. [ADVERTISEMENT]

Fairbanks International Hostel with 3 locations in Fairbanks near the University.

$25/single bed, $60–75/private arrangements, $10 tent space. Nearby bus stop. Full kitchens, free wireless Internet, bike rentals, free canoes and kayaks, free storage, coin-op laundry. Office located at 4316 Birch Lane, Fairbanks, Alaska. Phone (907) 479-7300. www.fairbankshostel.com. [ADVERTISEMENT]

Sophie Station Suites. Where you want to stay in Fairbanks! Constantly creating an atmosphere where guest service is the ultimate amenity. Offering expansive one bedroom suites with kitchens, free internet, a 24-hour fitness room and convenient laundry facilities. Exceptional food at Zach's and a lounge with 80" HDTV. Reservations: Fountainhead Hotels 1-800-528-4916. [ADVERTISEMENT]

University of Alaska Museum of the North is one of the state's most distinctive architectural landmarks. (©Meghan Mackey, staff)

FAIRBANKS ADVERTISERS

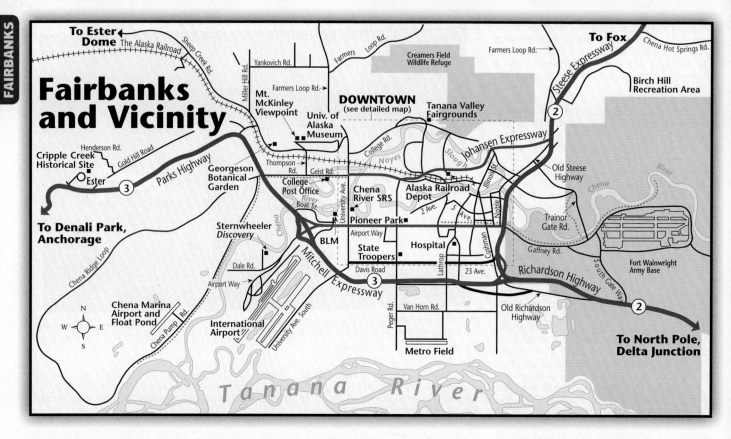

Fairbanks and Vicinity

To Ester Dome The Alaska Railroad
To Fox
Chena Hot Springs Rd.
Creamers Field Wildlife Refuge
Farmers Loop Rd.
Steese Expressway
Birch Hill Recreation Area
Yankovich Rd.
Sheep Creek Rd.
Miller Hill Rd.
Farmers Loop Rd.
Mt. McKinley Viewpoint
DOWNTOWN (see detailed map)
Univ. of Alaska Museum
Tanana Valley Fairgrounds
Johansen Expressway
Henderson Rd.
Cripple Creek Historical Site
Gold Hill Road
Parks Highway
Georgeson Botanical Garden
College Rd.
Noyes
Slough
Old Steese Highway
Chena
River
Ester
Thompson Rd.
Geist Rd.
College Post Office
University Ave.
Chena River SRS
Alaska Railroad Depot
2 Ave.
Illinois St.
Trainor Gate Rd.
To Denali Park, Anchorage
Chena Ridge Loop
Sternwheeler Discovery
Chena Boat St.
Pioneer Park
BLM
Airport Way
State Troopers
S Ave.
Noble
Hospital
Cushman
Gaffney Rd.
Fort Wainwright Army Base
Dale Rd.
Airport Way
Davis Road
Lathrop
23 Ave.
Richardson Highway
South Gate Way
Chena Marina Airport and Float Pond
Chena Pump Rd.
N W E S
International Airport
University Ave. South
Peger Rd.
Van Horn Rd.
Old Richardson Highway
To North Pole, Delta Junction
Metro Field

T a n a n a   R i v e r

SpringHill Suites by Marriott Fairbanks. Located in the heart of downtown on the Chena River, SpringHill Suites is the perfect place to take a break from road travel. Each spacious suite has a pull-out sofa bed, mini-refrigerator, microwave, coffee maker, and wet bar. Also enjoy a complimentary continental breakfast buffet, indoor pool and exercise room. Phone toll-free 1-877-729-0197 or www.marriott.com/faish.
[ADVERTISEMENT]

Wedgewood Resort. The spacious residential-style suites & guestrooms at the resort are nestled between two wildlife refuges. Walk the nature trails leading to Wander Lake, connect to the free internet and dine at Bear Lodge morning to

night. On-site Antique Auto Museum—a must see family attraction! Reservations: Fountainhead Hotels 1-800-528-4916. [ADVERTISEMENT]

Camping

There are several excellent RV parks in the Fairbanks area: **River's Edge RV Park** (off East Airport Way), **Fairbanks RV Park and Campground** at **Chena River State Recreation Site** (north on Washington Drive to Geraghty Ave. from Airport Way; follow signs) in Fairbanks; and **Riverview RV Park**, east of the city on Badger Road. **Northern Moosed RV Park** is 12 miles north of Fairbanks on the Elliott Highway near Fox.

There is overnight camping at Pioneer Park parking lot for self-contained RVs only, with a 4-night limit, nightly fee charged. For more information, call (907) 459-1087.

Public campgrounds are also located on Chena Hot Springs Road northeast of the city *(see log on pages 466-468 for details)*.

River's Edge RV Park. Located in the heart of Fairbanks! 15 acre wooded landscaped riverfront park. 190 sites. 50 & 30 amp electric. Wireless Internet. Cable TV. Full & partial hook-ups. Pull-throughs. Laundry, car wash, gift shop. Tour shuttles. Historical city tour, Point Barrow & Arctic Circle tours. Full-service riverfront restaurant "Chena's Alaskan Grill" serving Alaska seafood. Check out our Resort Cottages! See display ad page 447. [ADVERTISEMENT]

Northern Moosed RV Park & Campground. Easy access, full hookups, water, 30 Amp electricity, sewer; dump station, bathrooms, laundry, showers. Base your travel through Alaska here. Close to general store, gas, restaurants. From Fairbanks follow Alaska Route 2 north 12 miles to Fox. Located at 0.2 mile on Elliott Highway just past the weigh station. Open June–Sept. Phone (907) 451-0984. [ADVERTISEMENT]

Transportation

Air: International, interstate and intra-Alaska carriers serve Fairbanks International Airport, accessible via the West Airport Way exit off the Parks Highway (Alaska Route 3). Frontier Airlines offer several times weekly, nonstop flights from Denver on the shoulder season with an expected increase of flights offered during peak season. Additional airlines include Alaska, Delta, United and many others.

Fairbanks' aurora borealis monument is located on the road leaving Fairbanks International Airport. The *Solar Borealis* sculpture is faced with material which disperses sunlight into a rainbow of colors as you drive by.

Air charter services are available in Fairbanks for flightseeing; fly-in fishing, hunting and hiking, and trips to bush villages; see ads this section.

Railroad: Alaska Railroad passenger depot at 1745 Johansen Expressway and Danby Road, 2 miles from downtown. Depot is open daily 6:30 A.M. to 3 P.M. from mid-May to mid-September. Open limited hours for arrival/departure days only in winter. Daily passenger service in summer between Fairbanks and Anchorage with stopovers at Denali National Park. Weekend service only in winter. Phone (907) 265-2494; 1-800-544-0552; or go to www.alaskarailroad.com.

Bus: Local bus service is provided by the Metropolitan Area Commuter System (MACS), Monday through Saturday (limited scheduled on Saturdays); no service on Sundays and 6 major holidays. Drivers do not carry change so exact change or tokens must be used. Purchase a day pass and ride all day. Seniors ride free. MACS serves most major hotels, tourist attractions and shopping

Unknown First Family bronze dominates Golden Heart Park. (©Kris Valencia, staff)

Morris Thompson Cultural and Visitors Center. Take the walking path from here through the Antler Arch and along the Chena River to Golden Heart Park. (©Kris Valencia, staff)

and tips on what to see and how to get there. Information and audio tapes for self-guided walking tours. Free Internet access for 10-minute periods. Phone (907) 456-5774 or 1-800-327-5774. For a recording of current daily events phone (907) 456-4636, email info@explorefairbanks.com or go to www.explorefairbanks.com.

Meet a Real Alaskan–Schedule a Golden Heart Greeter. Golden Heart Greeter is a free service where visitors are matched, based on interests, with friendly, helpful, local Fairbanks, Alaskan residents who want to share their insights and enthusiasm for Fairbanks. Greeters, who are not commercial tour guides but volunteers from different walks of life, welcome travelers and help them get more from their stay. A typical visit is 1–2 hours in a public place such as a coffee house, hotel lobby or some other agreed-upon location. Schedule a greeter by email at: goldenheartgreeter@explorefairbanks.com or by calling (907) 456-5774. A minimum of 1 week's notice is needed.

Golden Heart Park, is the site of the 18-foot bronze monument, "Unknown First Family." The statue, by sculptor Malcolm Alexander, and park were dedicated in July 1986 to celebrate Fairbanks' history and heritage.

The park is a venue for free summer (June and July) concerts; Tuesday and Fridays at noon or Wednesday evenings enjoy an hour-long concert by varied performers. Phone (907) 456-1984 or visit www.festivalfairbanks.org for more information.

A pedestrian bridge crosses the Chena River at Golden Heart Park, providing safe, scenic access for foot traffic to a wonderful riverwalk that connects to the Morris S. Thompson Cultural and Visitors Center via an antler arch. The riverwalk provides convenient benches and fine views of river activities.

Visit the Fountainhead Antique Auto Museum, one of the top attractions in Fairbanks, located at Wedgewood Resort. This collection showcases more than 70 historically significant automobiles produced in the United States prior to World War II, including the first car in the Territory of Alaska, built in 1905, a rare 1921 Heine-Velox Sporting Victoria, and an unusual Fordson Snow Devil. For a complete list, go to www.fountainheadmuseum.com.

venues. Information Transit Park located at 601 Cushman St.; (907) 459-1196 or go to www.fnsb.us/transportation.

Dalton Highway Express van service between Fairbanks and Deadhorse from June through August; phone (907) 474-3555.

Tours: Local and area sightseeing tours are available from several companies. **Northern Alaska Tour Company** offers Arctic Circle tours, Barrow Adventure Tours and Arctic Ocean Adventure tours, phone 1-800-474-1986. **Marina Air** offers fly-in fishing, phone (907) 479-5683. **Warbelow's Air Ventures** offers Arctic Journey tours, phone 1-800-478-0812.

Taxi: More than 20 cab companies.

Car and Camper Rentals: Several companies rent cars, campers and trailers.

Attractions

Get Acquainted: A good place to start is the **Fairbanks Visitor Information Center** at 101 Dunkel St., (downtown Fairbanks), inside the **Morris Thompson Cultural and Visitors Center**, adjacent to Griffin Park, where you will find free brochures, maps

Approximately 70 vehicles are on display, each illustrating an important development in early American automotive history, from early steam, electric and hybrid cars, to the first American production car with front-wheel drive. Almost every car displayed at the museum is maintained in operating condition. Historical Alaskan photographs line the walls and a fabulous vintage fashion collection follows the cars through time. Wedgewood Resort is located at 212 Wedgewood Drive; phone (907) 456-3642.

Tour the University of Alaska Fairbanks. Situated on a 2,250-acre ridge overlooking Fairbanks and the Alaska Range, UAF has the best view in town. With all the amenities of a small town, including a fire station, post office, radio and TV stations, medical clinic, museum and a concert hall, it boasts a world-class faculty and a unique blend of students from around the world.

UAF is a Land, Sea and Space Grant Institution. It serves 170 communities statewide through in-person and distance delivery of instruction, public service and research activities. With an enrollment of nearly 11,000 students each year, it is America's only arctic university as well as an international arctic research center, playing center stage for researching global climate change and arctic phenomena.

The Alaska Volcano Observatory, on-site and working in conjunction with the Alaska Geophysical Institute, the U.S. Geological Survey and the Alaska Division of Geological and Geophysical Surveys, has served the state since 1988. University of Alaska Fairbanks graduate students work in tandem with scientists to monitor all volcanoes in

Fountainhead Antique Auto Museum has some 70 classic vehicles on display. *(©Sharon Nault)*

the North Pacific region daily. Information on current volcanic activity in Alaska and North Pacific is available at their website: www.avo.alaska.edu/.

Free guided walking tours of campus are offered in summer. Tours begin at the Signers Hall and last about an hour. For information on any university-related tour, phone (907) 474-7500; or visit www.uaf.edu/admissions/visit/. Guided tours of campus

for prospective students can be arranged throughout the year by calling the Admissions Office, (907) 474-7500 or 1-800-478-1823; email admissions@uaf.edu.

Summer Sessions and Lifelong Learning hosts many events throughout the summer, including special guest lectures, free movies and concerts. Visit www.uaf.edu/summer or phone (907) 474-7021 for details.

Public Parks. Fairbanks has more than

The WWII Lend-Lease Monument commemorates Alaska's critical role during the war.

(©Kris Valencia, staff))

100 public parks that make good stops for a picnic. Graehl Park has a boat launch and is a good place to watch river traffic.

Griffin Park, also on the river, has the **WWII Lend–Lease Monument**, a memorial erected in 2006. This statue honors WWII Russian and American pilots as well as Women Airline Service Pilots. The monument commemorates Alaska's importance as a strategic location and staging ground in fighting this war.

Parks and Recreation also offers a number of scenic trails around town, and unless otherwise posted, pet owners may run their dogs as long as the animals are on leashes and under control at all times. Owners are responsible for cleaning up after their pets. A fenced park area where dogs can run freely is located on Second Avenue across from the National Guard Armory. The Fairbanks North Star Borough Parks & Recreation office at (907) 459-1070 can provide directions and more information.

For more information on all Fairbanks City and Borough parks, email parks@co.fairbanks.ak.us or visit www.co.fairbanks.ak.us/ParksandRecreation.

The University of Alaska Museum of the North is Alaska's most distinctive architectural landmark and a "must-see" for Fairbanks visitors. From its modest beginning in 1929, with the collection of amateur naturalist Otto Geist, the museum has evolved into a world-class facility. The museum exhibits are the best introduction to Alaska's diverse wildlife, people and land.

Highlights from the Gallery of Alaska include the state's largest public display of gold; Blue Babe, a 36,000-year-old steppe bison mummy; and extensive displays of Alaska wildlife and Alaska Native culture. The Rose Berry Alaska Art Gallery presents 2,000 years of Alaskan art, with ancient ivory carvings, coiled grass baskets and other Alaska Native works displayed side by side with both historical and contemporary paintings and sculptures. The Living Room offers a sitting area with art books and artwork, designed to give visitors a place to relax and absorb their gallery experience

while enjoying the architecture in the new wing. The permanent installation called "The Place Where You Go to Listen" draws on cycles of day and night, seismic activity and the electromagnetic activity of the aurora to create an ever-changing sound and light experience.

An audio guide complements the material on display with soundscapes of the natural world, samples of Alaska Native languages and historic footage, including radio reports from the 1964 Good Friday earthquake and 1989 *Exxon Valdez* oil spill. The museum also presents several special exhibits each year.

The museum store offers a wide variety of Alaska Native artwork, jewelry, books and other fine gifts. All items relate to the museum's collections and all proceeds support the educational and research mission of the museum. The café (open in summer only) offers gourmet sandwiches, salads and desserts, as well as espresso drinks and other beverages.

The museum is situated on the west ridge of the UAF campus, overlooking Geist Road, a major artery from the Parks Highway into Fairbanks. Summer hours (May 15–Sept. 15) are 9 A.M. to 7 P.M. daily. Winter hours (Sept. 16–May 14) are 9 A.M. to 5 P.M. Monday–Saturday, closed Sundays, Thanksgiving, Christmas and New Year's Day. Admission is charged; children 6 and under free. For more information, phone (907) 474-7505; email museum@uaf.edu; or visit www.uaf.edu/museum/.

Georgeson Botanical Garden on the UAF campus is open to the public from May to September, 9 A.M.–8 P.M. daily. Originally part of a USDA Agricultural Experiment Station established in 1906, today the Experiment Farm is part of the 300-acre Agricultural & Forestry Experiment Station in the university's School of Natural Resources & Agricultural Sciences. It serves as a demonstration garden for annual and perennial horticulture plants and is part of the Fairbanks Experiment Farm. There are colorful displays of many varieties of flowers in season and the kiosk at the site offers information on horticulture in northern climes. Admission is $5; children under 6 are free. *Note: No pets please, in the garden or on nearby lawn.* Located on Tanana Drive, just below the campus. Phone (907) 474-7222 or

visit www.georgesonbg.org for more details.

Originally part of a USDA Agricultural Experiment Station established in 1906, today the Experiment Farm is part of the 300-acre Agricultural & Forestry Experiment Station in the University's School of Natural Resources & Agricultural Sciences.

The **Alaska Public Lands Information Center**, downtown at 101 Dunkel St., in the Morris Thompson Cultural and Visitor Center, offers free information and trip-planning assistance for recreational opportunities in the state. The center also offers films, lectures, an Alaska Geographic bookstore and free brochures and pamphlets on natural history, cultural artifacts and public lands in Alaska. The exhibit area and information desk are open daily in summer, 8 A.M. to 9 P.M.; 8 A.M. to 5 P.M. daily in winter. Phone (907) 459-3730 or toll-free 1-866-869-6887. Or visit their website at www.alaskacenters.gov.

Celebrate Summer Solstice: Downtown fun under the midnight sun is scheduled for Saturday, June 21st. Music, food and vendors occupy the city's streets on the longest day of the year. Event website: www.downtownfairbanks.com.

Baseball. Summer visitors can take in a semi-pro baseball game at Growden Park where the Alaska Goldpanners take on other Alaska league teams several times each week, typically at 7 P.M. in the summer months. Check the local newspaper for game schedule, phone (907) 451-0095 or visit their website at www.goldpanners.com.

The annual **Midnight Sun Baseball Game** begins at 10:30 P.M. on June 21st and is played without artificial lights.

In summer, the Chena River in Fairbanks is busy with motorboats, rafts, canoes and jet skis from morning until night. (©Kris Valencia, staff)

World Eskimo-Indian Olympics. Since 1961 this annual event pits athletes against each other in unique sporting events. The ear-pull, one-legged jump and other competitions continue the Native tradition of competing for athletic prowess as well as preparing for occasions of extremes. Each event is significant to Native life and tradition. July 16–19, 2014. www.weio.org or phone the Carlson Center at (907) 451-7800.

Golden Days, when Fairbanksans turn out in turn-of-the-century dress and celebrate the gold rush, is scheduled for July 16–20, 2014. Golden Days starts off with a Felix Pedro look-alike taking his gold to the bank and includes a parade and rededication of the Pedro Monument at **Milepost 16.6** of the Steese Highway (Alaska Route 6), honoring the man who started it all when he discovered gold in the Tanana Hills. Other events include canoe and raft races, and a rubber ducky race on the

The Chena Village stop on the Riverboat Discovery Cruise highlights the Interior's Native culture. (©Kris Valencia, staff)

Chena River. The Red Green Regatta winds up the festivities on Sunday July 21. This regatta consists of wildly decorated flotation devices carrying people in a non-race, race and is an eye opener for revealing local humor. For additional information, phone (907) 452-1105 or visit www.fairbankschamber.org.

Fairbanks Summer Arts Festival. Join us and awaken your inner artist! Taught by internationally acclaimed artists, Festival provides workshops and performances for all levels in music, dance, theatre, culinary, literary, healing and visual arts. Held July 13-27, 2014, in Fairbanks and outreach locations in Alaska. Share your talents and explore your creativity. Phone (907) 474-8869; www.fsaf.org. [ADVERTISEMENT]

The Tanana Valley State Fair, began in 1924, making it Alaska's oldest fair. It takes place August 2–10, in 2014, and features agricultural exhibits, arts and crafts, food booths, carnival rides, more than 300 vendors, and lots of entertainment. For more information, phone (907) 452-3750; website www.tananavalleystatefair.org.

Enjoy the Chena River from shore. From the Morris Thompson Cultural and Visitors Center, walk through the world's "Farthest North Antler Arch" (made up of over 100 caribou and moose antlers collected from all over Interior Alaska) and take the River Walk along the Chena River to Golden Heart Park. From Cushman Street the River Walk extends more than 1.5 miles to Pioneer Park.

Chena River State Recreation Site has a day-use area by the boat launch with picnic tables and great river views. From Airport Way take Washington Drive north to Gerarghty and follow signs to the park.

Cruise the Chena River. Fairbanks is situated on the Chena River, near its confluence with the Tanana River, and the river is a popular form of transportation for both residents and visitors alike. Most visitors explore the river aboard the Riverboat *Discovery* (see description following), but you can do it on your own.

Alaska Outdoor Rentals, located at "Paddler's Cove" on Peger Road (behind Pioneer Park), has canoes and kayaks for rent and both pick-up and drop-off service available. For more information and reservations, phone (907) 457-2453. Paddlers may launch from "Paddler's Cove" and travel downstream to the Chena Pump House, or they can launch from Nordale Road *(see Milepost J 6.3 in "Chena Hot Springs Road" log on page 466)* for a longer trip.

Take the Riverboat Discovery Cruise. This family-owned, Fairbanks attraction began in 1950 and today is justifiably one of the city's most popular destinations, both with visitors and Alaskans. Cruises depart daily at 8:45 A.M. and 2 P.M., mid-May to mid-September, on a half-day cruise on the Chena and Tanana rivers. Enjoy informative narration about Native culture; view Susan Butcher's Iditarod dogs in action; see a bush pilot demonstration; walk through the Old Chena Indian Village; and just enjoy a pleasant few hours on the water. Snacks onboard, plus complimentary donuts and coffee.

To get to the dock, exit south off the Parks Highway on Airport Way to Dale Road and follow signs. For information on rates, additional cruise times, etc., contact Riverboat Discovery, 1975 Discovery Dr., Fairbanks, AK 99709; email reservations@riverboatdiscovery.com; phone (907) 479-6673 or 1-866-479-6673; or visit their website at www.riverboatdiscovery.com.

Visit Historic Churches. Saint Matthew's Episcopal Church, 1029 1st Ave., was originally built in 1904, but burned in 1947 and was rebuilt the following year. Of special interest is the church's intricately carved altar, made in 1906 of Interior Alaska birch and saved from the fire, and the church's 12 stained glass windows, 9 of which trace the historical events of the church and Fairbanks. Immaculate Conception Church, on the Chena River at the new Barnette Street bridge, was drawn by horses to its present location in the winter of 1911 from its original site at 1st Avenue and Dunkel Street.

The Robert G. White Large Animal Research Station (LARS), operated by UAF, allows visitors a close-up view of muskoxen,

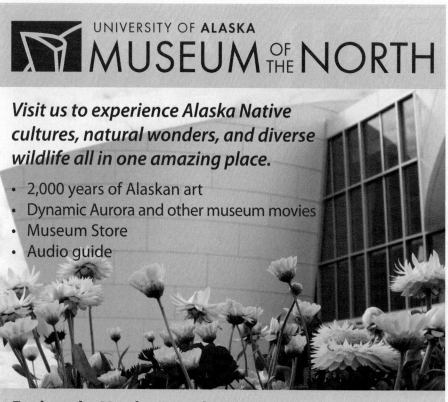

MUSEUM OF THE NORTH

Visit us to experience Alaska Native cultures, natural wonders, and diverse wildlife all in one amazing place.

- 2,000 years of Alaskan art
- Dynamic Aurora and other museum movies
- Museum Store
- Audio guide

Explore the North – Tour the Museum
Summer Hours: 9 AM – 7 PM Daily
Winter Hours: 9 AM – 5 PM Monday – Saturday
907 Yukon Drive • Fairbanks, AK 99775 • museum.uaf.edu • 907.474.7505

UNIVERSITY OF ALASKA FAIRBANKS
UAF is an AA/EO employer and educational institution.

458 ■ The MILEPOST® ■ 2014

www.themilepost.com

caribou and reindeer. Public tours are offered June through August (closed 4th of July weekend). Tour times are posted in the parking lot at LARS and also on the LARS website at www.muskoxuaf.org or phone (907) 474-5724 for information.

Outdoor walking of 0.25 mile for tour. Admission is $10 for adults, $6 for students, $9 for senior citizens (over 65) and for military, with children 6 and under free. To reach LARS from Geist Road, drive north 2 miles on University Avenue (it becomes Farmers Loop Road north of College), turn left on Ballaine Road, then make a left-hand turn on Yankovich Road and drive 1.2 miles west to LARS, which will be on your right.

Watch Birds at Creamer's Field. Follow the flocks of waterfowl to Creamer's Field Migratory Waterfowl Refuge at 1300 College Road. Located 1 mile from downtown Fairbanks, on the site of the historic Creamer's Dairy Farm, this 2,000-acre refuge managed by the Alaska Dept. of Fish and Game offers opportunities to observe large concentrations of ducks, swans, geese, shorebirds, sandhill cranes and other birds during the spring and fall migrations, and resident wildlife throughout the year. Explore over 5 miles of trails including the 1.5-mile self-guided Boreal Forest Trail which features winding boardwalks through a boreal forest. Entrance to the Refuge is free and trails are always open. Stop by the renovated historic farmhouse that serves as a visitor center and gift shop to find the trail and viewing area information, maps and brochures on Creamer's Field and get information about the historic dairy buildings.

Creamer's Field migratory bird refuge occupies a historic dairy farm. *(©Meghan Mackey, staff)*

The visitor center is open daily 9:30 A.M. to 5 P.M. mid-May to mid-September, and Saturdays noon to 4 P.M. the rest of the year. The non-profit Friends of Creamer's Field offers Guided Nature Walks weekdays at 10 A.M. and Wednesday evenings at 7 P.M. during June, July and August.

Friends of Creamer's Field also sponsors refuge events and activities throughout the year. The Tanana Valley Sandhill Crane Festival is scheduled for August 22-24, 2014. For additional information and a full calendar of events at Creamer's Field, phone (907) 452-5162 or visit www.creamersfield.org.

Farmhouse Visitor Center, Creamer's Field Migratory Waterfowl Refuge. 1300 College Road. Visitor Center hours 9:30 A.M. to 5 P.M., May 14–Sept. 15, noon–4 P.M. Saturdays, Sept. 17–May 12. Trails open year-round. Free guided nature walks in the summer and events throughout the year. Call for schedule. Phone (907) 452-5162; programs@creamersfield.org or visit www.creamersfield.org. [ADVERTISEMENT]

Wedgewood Wildlife Sanctuary is a 75-acre private preserve providing habitat for wildlife of Interior Alaska. Two trails stretch through boreal forest with access to views of beaver lodges, interpretive signs, benches that line the trails, and an observation deck. These trails go through grounds adjacent the Creamer's Field refuge area and are accessed by entering the Wedgewood parking area between the McKinley and Laurel buildings.

Ride Bikes. Pick up a "Bikeways" map for Fairbanks and vicinity in the Morris Thompson Cultural and Visitor Center or go to www.akbike.com/summerbiking.html for online suggestions. The city is developing an extensive network of bike trails (multi-use paths). Best choices for day touring around Fairbanks include the bike trail from Pioneer

Pioneer Park's Mining Valley displays gold mining equipment. (©Kris Valencia, staff)

Visit Pioneer Park. Visitors will find a relaxed atmosphere at Pioneer Park. It is a pleasant stop especially for those with children, with its historic buildings, small shops, food, entertainment, picnicking, playgrounds, miniature golf and train rides. The park is open year-round, although most attractions within the park are open only from Memorial Day to Labor Day. Admission to the park is free, with a nominal charge for some activities. There is free WiFi throughout the park. For more information about Pioneer Park, phone (907) 459-1087.

To drive to Pioneer Park (at Airport Way and Peger Road), take Airport Way to Wilbur, turn north onto Wilbur, then immediately west onto access road, which leads into the Pioneer Park parking lot.

The 44-acre historic park was created in 1967 as the Alaska Centennial Park to commemorate the 100th anniversary of U.S. territorial status and provide a taste of Alaska history. Visitors may begin their visit at the information center, located just inside the park's main gate. Walk through Gold Rush Town, a narrow, winding street of authentic old buildings that once graced downtown Fairbanks: the Kitty Hensley and Judge Wickersham houses, furnished with turn-of-the-century items; the First Presbyterian Church, constructed in 1904; and the Pioneers of Alaska Museum, dedicated to those who braved frontier life to establish Fairbanks. Free guided historical walking tours take place daily in summer.

Most of the pioneer buildings house shops selling food and crafts. There is an old-time portrait photographer—a fun way to remember your trip to Fairbanks.

The top level of the Alaska Centennial Center for the Arts houses an art gallery featuring rotating contemporary exhibits and paintings; open noon to 8 P.M. daily, Memorial Day through Labor Day; noon–6 P.M. Monday–Saturday the rest of the year.

The Pioneer Air Museum, located behind the Alaska Centennial Center for the Arts, displays aircraft in Alaska from 1913 to present day. This is a favorite with aviation buffs. Open daily noon to 8 P.M. Admission is charged. Phone (907) 451-0037 for details.

Pioneer Park is home to the renovated SS *Nenana*, a national historic landmark. The *Nenana*, known as the "Last Lady of the River," is the largest stern-wheeler ever

Park to 1st Avenue downtown, and Airport Way/Boat Street west to Chena Pump Road or Geist Road.

Bicycle rentals are available from Alaska Outdoor Rentals at Pioneer Park. For more information on summer bicycle rentals and bicycling in the Fairbanks area, or for reservations, call (907) 457-2453, or visit www.akbike.com.

For year-round organized rides, there's the Fairbanks Cycle Club. Membership information and a monthly calendar of rides at www.fairbankscycleclub.org.

For information on the Ester Dome Singletrack Loops, accessed via Sheep Creek Road to Ester Dome Road west of Fairbanks, check with the Fairbanks Cycle Club or http://goldstreamsports.com.

built west of the Mississippi, and the second largest wooden vessel in existence. Also on display is a 300-foot diorama of life along the Tanana and Yukon rivers in the early 1900s. Explore the old stern-wheeler on your own, or take a formal tour, offered daily in summer from noon to 8 P.M.

At the rear of the park is Mining Valley, with displays of gold mining equipment. The popular Alaska Salmon Bake, with both outdoor and heated indoor seating areas, is also part of Mining Valley. The Alaska Salmon Bake is open daily for dinner, 5–9 P.M., from late May to mid-September. Salmon, halibut and prime rib are served, rain or shine.

The show season at Pioneer Park runs from mid-May through mid-September. The Palace Theatre & Saloon features the musical comedy review, "Golden Heart Revue," about life in Fairbanks. Performances daily at 8:15 P.M.

The Big Stampede show in Gold Rush Town is a theater in the round, presenting the paintings of Rusty Heurlin, depicting the trail of '98, with a narrative by Ruben Gaines.

The Crooked Creek & Whiskey Island Railroad, a narrow-gauge train, takes passengers for a 12-minute ride around the park; adults $2, children under 12 $1.

The Tanana Valley Railroad Museum holds displays of Interior Alaskan railroad history as well as the historic Engine #1, a 8.5 ton, 36" gauge, H.K. Porter, coal fired and built in 1899. The first locomotive to this area, it is today, the farthest north operating steam engine. Volunteers restored and operate the engine and museum. Museum hours noon to 8 P.M. daily, Memorial Day–Labor Day. For more information, contact Friends of the Tanana Valley Railroad (http://ftvrr.org). The engine operates for various special occasions; see website for schedule.

Other recreational activities available at Pioneer Park include miniature golf, an antique carousel and picnicking in covered shelters. A public dock is located on the Chena River at the rear of the park, and visitors can rent canoes, kayaks and bicycles at Alaska Outdoor Rentals located near the boat dock.

Visitors are welcome to take part in square, round and contra dances year-round at the Farthest North Square and Round Dance Center. Phone (907) 452-5699 evenings for calendar of events.

Running Reindeer Ranch. See reindeer in their pen or walk with the reindeer through their boreal forest. Jane Atkinson and daughter Robin offer tours to help support the feeding and care of the reindeer. An

Pioneer Park is home to the historic stern-wheeler SS Nenana. (©Meghan Mackey, staff)

opportunity for to get up-close to reindeer. www.RunningReindeer.com.

Take a Day Trip to Chena Hot Springs (125 miles round trip). Drive 5 miles north from Fairbanks via the Steese Expressway and exit east on Chena Hot Springs Road. This good all-weather paved road leads 57 miles east to Chena Hot Springs,

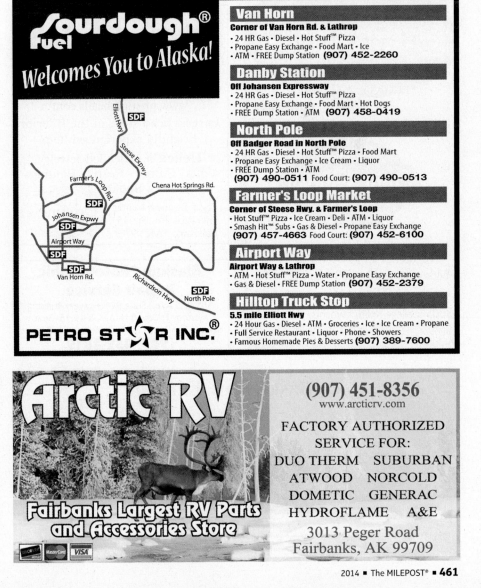

Chena Hot Springs Resort, a little more than an hour's drive northwest of Fairbanks, is a popular side trip with its hot spring pools, horseback riding, dog kennels, and dozens of other activities. (©Linda Martin)

a private resort (open daily year-round) offering indoor and outdoor natural mineral hot springs pools; the **Aurora Ice Museum**, the world's only year-round ice museum and ice bar; a restaurant; lodging; camping; trails rides; and other recreational activities. *(See "Chena Hot Springs Road" log on pages 466-468.)*

Visit North Pole, Chena Lake Recre- ation Area and Eielson AFB. Head down Highway 2 (Richardson Highway) to North Pole, 13 miles from downtown Fairbanks, and get a head start on your Christmas shopping *(see description of North Pole on pages 225-226)*. Drive another 2 miles east of North Pole for Chena Lake Recreation Area. Operated by the Fairbanks North Star Borough Parks and Recreation Department, this recreation area is built around the Chena Flood Control Project constructed by the Army Corps of Engineers. Drive 5.5 miles from the highway on the main road along Moose Creek Dike to the visitor kiosk below the dam site. You can also bike out to the dam on the 5-mile-long Moose Creek Dam Bikeway. From the Main Road, turn on Lake Park Road for 250-acre Chena Lake. There are campsites, walking trails, a swimming beach, play area, picnic tables, shelters, kayak and canoe rentals, fishing dock and boat ramp. Chena Lake Bike Trail begins at Chena Lake swim beach and intersects with the Moose Creek Dam Bikeway. Camping fees and a per vehicle day-use fee are charged between Memorial Day and Labor Day. For more information about Chena Lake Recreation Area, phone (907) 488-1655.

Eielson Air Force Base, 25 miles southeast of Fairbanks on the Richardson Highway, offers free 1-hour guided tours of the base at 10 A.M. every Friday between Memorial Day and Labor Day, federal holidays or wing-down days (tours must be reserved in advance or you will not be allowed entry). Foreign visitors must submit their reservation request 2 weeks in advance. The tour includes a stop at the Lady of the Lake—an abandoned WB-29 airframe—and concludes with a photo stop at Heritage Park. Phone the public affairs office at (907) 377-2116; email community. relations@eielson.af.mil; website www.eielson.af.mil.

View Peaks of the Alaska Range: Enjoy Fairbanks' best views of the Tanana Valley and the high peaks the Alaska Range through the Alaska Range Viewing Window in the UAF Museum of the North. Weather permitting, you may see: Mount Hayes (elev. 13,832 feet); Hess Mountain (elev. 11,940 feet); Mount Deborah (elev. 12,339 feet); and Mount McKinley/Denali (elev. 20,320 feet).

Visit a Gold Mine. Head out the Steese Expressway to **Milepost F 9.5**, turn on Goldstream Road and then turn left onto Old Steese Highway North to see the historic **Gold Dredge 8**, a 5-deck, 250-foot dredge built in 1928. Tours of the dredge and gold panning are available, and it is reported that 40,000 prospectors/tourists visit the dredge each year. For more information, call (907) 479-6673, email info@golddredge8.com or visit www.golddredge8.com.

After these stops, you can either return to Fairbanks to make this an easy 50-mile round trip, or extend your drive 100 miles to see more of gold mining history. At **Milepost F 28.6** on the Steese Highway, across from Chatanika Lodge, there's an old gold dredge that operated from the 1920s until 1962. It is the second largest stacker dredge in Alaska. The dredge is on private land, but is easily viewed from the highway; do not trespass.

Farther out on the Steese Highway, at **Milepost F 57.3**, is the Davidson Ditch Historical Site. This large pipe was built in 1925 by the Fairbanks Exploration Co. to carry

water to float gold dredges. The 83-mile-long ditch begins at **Milepost F 64** Steese Highway and ends near Fox. If you are feeling adventurous, U.S. Creek Road (steep, gravel) winds up and over the hills from the Davidson Ditch site 7 miles to Nome Creek Gold Panning Area in the White Mountains National Recreation Area.

See the STEESE HIGHWAY section for a detailed log of this road.

Gold Dredge 8. Your adventure at Gold Dredge 8 begins with a ride on a replica of the Tanana Valley Railroad through the gold fields of Interior Alaska. Before you board our train, enjoy a close-up view

Gold Dredge 8 introduces visitors to Interior Alaska mining history with a close-up look at a real gold dredge. (©Kris Valencia, staff)

of the TransAlaska pipeline and informational displays about the pipeline. Aboard the train our conductor and local miners provide lively commentary about the history of mining in Alaska. The train ride takes you to Gold Dredge 8 where you will see first hand how the dredge worked the gold fields. Once the train arrives at the camp, you will receive a poke sack filled with pay dirt, and get a chance to pan for gold. You will find gold—we guarantee it! After you pan for gold, explore the dredge and feel the history come alive. This tour is interesting and entertaining for the whole family. Travel professionals describe this tour as "the best 2 hours you will spend in the State." Tours depart daily and reservations are recommended. Contact Gold Dredge 8 at (907) 479-6673, reservations@golddredge8.com, www.golddredge8.com. 1803 Old Steese Highway North, Fairbanks, AK 99712. See display ad on page 445. [ADVERTISEMENT]

See the Pipeline. For a good look at the Trans-Alaska Oil Pipeline System (TAPS)—the oil pipeline—and a taste of the Dalton Highway, consider this long day trip. Drive out the Steese Expressway from Fairbanks, stopping first at the TAPS viewpoint just outside Fairbanks at **Milepost F 8.4.** You can walk along a portion of the pipeline and see a "pig"—a device used to collect data and clean the pipeline walls. Excellent opportunity for pipeline photos.

Drive north a few more miles to the end of the Steese Expressway and then continue north on the Elliott Highway 73 miles to the junction with the Dalton Highway. The Elliott Highway is paved to the Dalton Highway junction. Turn off onto the Dalton Highway and drive 55.6 miles north to the Yukon River bridge. The pipeline parallels the route much of the way, although there is no public access, so you'll get good views but no close-ups until you reach the BLM visitor center at Yukon River Crossing.

From the Yukon River Crossing it is

Sunbathing at Chena River State Recreation Site. (©Kris Valencia, staff)

Go Swimming. Fairbanks North Star Borough Parks and Recreation Dept. offers 3 pools that are open to the public. Mary Siah Recreation Center, at 805 14th Ave., also offers a sauna, whirlpool and fitness equipment; phone (907) 459-1082 or (907) 459-1081 for recorded information. Robert Hamme Memorial Pool, at 901 Airport Way, also offers diving boards and lap lanes; phone (907) 459-1085. Robert Wescott Memorial Pool, at 300 E. 8th in North Pole, offers lap lanes and a water slide; phone (907) 488-9401.

Play Golf: The 18-hole Chena Bend Golf Course is located on Fort Wainwright, open to the public; phone (907) 353-6223. North Star Golf Club, located 10 minutes north of downtown on the Old Steese Highway, offers a regulation 18-hole course, open to the public; phone (907) 457-4653; website www.northstargolf.com.

Go Fishing: There are several streams and lakes within driving distance of Fairbanks, and local fishing guides are available. Chena Lake, about 20 miles southeast of the city via the Richardson Highway at Chena Lake Recreation Area, is stocked with rainbow, king, silver salmon and arctic grayling and arctic char. The Chena River and its tributaries offer fishing for arctic grayling, whitefish, northern pike and burbot. The Chena River flows through Fairbanks. Arctic grayling fishing in the upper Chena is very good, with some large fish. Grayling fishing in the Chena is restricted to catch-and-release year-round. Chena Hot Springs Road off the Steese Highway provides access to fisheries in the Chena River State Recreation Area *(see log of "Chena Hot Springs Road" on pages 466-468)*. The Steese Highway also offers access to the Chatanika River. Special regulations apply in these waters for grayling and salmon fishing. ADF&G Division of Sport Fish office phone (907) 459-7228.

Air taxi operators and guides in Fairbanks offer short trips from the city for rainbow,

another 60 miles to the Arctic Circle BLM Wayside, adding 120 miles to the already 280-mile trip. The Arctic Circle wayside has an interpretive display and picnic area, at N 66°33' W 150°48'. At this latitude, the sun does not set on summer solstice (June 20 or 21) and it does not rise on winter solstice (December 21 or 22).

See the ELLIOTT HIGHWAY and the DALTON HIGHWAY sections for details.

Play Tennis: There are 6 outdoor asphalt courts at the Dan Ramras Community Tennis Courts off Airport Way on Schaible Street (due east of Lathrop High School). No fees or reservations. For more information, phone the Fairbanks Tennis Association at (907) 455-4301.

Birch Hill Recreation Area, located in the hills of Fairbanks, is a world class multi-use recreational facility. More than 30 kilometers of trails are great for hiking, biking, and running, but it's also a quiet, peaceful place for a picnic. One of its most popular summer attractions is its 18-hole Disc Golf course, free of charge. Birch Hill trails are popular with cross-country skiers in winter.

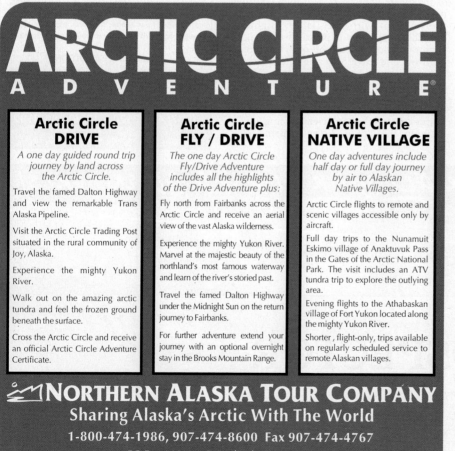

grayling, northern pike, lake trout and in lakes and streams of the Tanana and Yukon river drainages. Some operators have camps set up for overnight trips while others specialize in day trips. The air taxi operators usually provide a boat and motor for their angling visitors. Rates are reasonable and vary according to the distance from town and type of facilities offered.

Winter in Fairbanks. Although winter temperatures in Fairbanks can dip well below zero, the city has a number of big attractions that draw thousands of visitors and residents alike outdoors, even on the coldest days.

The **BP World Ice Art Championships** (www.icealaska.com), scheduled for Feb. 24–March 30, 2014, hosts an international field of artists who come to sculpt art from ice. And not just any ice. Harvested from a pond in Fairbanks the ice has been called "the purest ice in the world," so clear you can read through it. The event begins with huge blocks of ice, known as "Arctic diamonds." Skilled competitors transform these blocks into life-sized reindeer, dragons, airplanes, chariots, knights on horseback and other imaginative works of art. When completed, the colossal sculptures are exhibited at the Ice Park and may be viewed during the day or at night, when colorful illumination adds a magical quality to the creations.

Aurora Borealis. Another major winter event that brings visitors from the States as well as from overseas to Fairbanks is the opportunity to experience the aurora borealis or northern lights. The best time to see the northern lights is August–April after dark, when skies are clear. In Fairbanks, the aurora is seen on at least 8 out of 10 clear, dark nights in winter. While the mystery of the aurora has been solved by science, its beauty continues to amaze and entrance viewers.

Great viewing opportunities can be found at nearly any high viewpoint in Fairbanks at night or out at the Chena Hot

Cold winters in Fairbanks are perfect for ice art. This dental office on 3rd Street features an ice angel carving every winter. (©Michael K. Robb)

Springs Resort. Far from the city lights, natural viewing is possible by just stepping outside or even while enjoying the hot springs from this location.

The University of Alaska Fairbanks Museum of the North shows a 30-minute "Dynamic Aurora" film in summer. Daily forecasts of auroral activity over Alaska are available from the Geophysical Institute at UAF at www.gi.alaska.edu/AuroraForecast.

Sled Dog Racing. A big winter attraction in Fairbanks is sled dog racing. The Alaska Dog Mushers Assoc. (www.sleddog.org) holds a series of sprint races from December through March. Championship races in March include the Limited North American, with 1, 2, 3-dog skijor and 4-, 6- and 8-dog races over various distances. The 8-mile Jeff Studdert Passenger Race—number of dogs on teams based on 1 dog per 40 lbs. combined weight of musher and passenger—takes places March 18, 2014. The race season is crowned by the Open North American Championship Sled Dog Race (20/20/27.6 miles), March 21–23, 2014, in downtown Fairbanks. First run in 1946, the Open is the oldest continuously run sled dog race of any kind in the world.

The Mushers Hall and Jeff Studdert Racegrounds are located at 925 Farmers Loop Road, where visitors can watch dog teams train and race. For more information and a complete schedule of races and events, visit www.sleddog.org or call (907) 457-6874.

Fairbanks also hosts the 1,000–mile **Yukon Quest Sled Dog Race** (distance race) between Whitehorse, YT, and Fairbanks, AK with the start alternating between the two cities each year. The 2014 race starts in Fairbanks and finishes in Whitehorse. For more information, visit the Yukon Quest online at www.yukonquest.com. In summer, visit the Yukon Quest store located in the log cabin adjacent the Golden Heart Plaza on 1st Avenue.

The annual **Iron Dog** race is February 16–22, 2014. Two-man snowmachine teams race from Big Lake to Nome with a finish in Fairbanks on the Chena River. This popular event is the world's longest and toughest snowmobile race in which racers cross 2,000 miles of Alaska wilderness.

Chena Hot Springs Road

A beautiful day on the Chena River at Tors Trailhead Day-Use Area, Milepost J 39.4. (©Sharon Nault)

Head out the Steese Expressway from Fairbanks to **Milepost F 4.9** to junction with Chena Hot Springs Road. This good, all-weather paved road (posted 55 mph) leads east through Chena River State Recreation Area, an exceptional year-round recreation area for picnicking and camping (at Rosehip, Tors and Red Squirrel); hiking the popular Granite Tors Trail and others); canoeing the river from various put-in points; fishing the popular arctic grayling fishery (river is catch-and-release only); and wildlife viewing, particularly moose.

There are numerous unsigned, narrow dirt tracts leading off Chena Hot Springs Road, some to public-use river access and others to private property. Watch for posted private property signs before exploring these side roads.

For links to maps and other information on the recreation area, visit http://dnr.alaska.gov/parks/units/chena/index.htm.

The road ends at Chena Hot Springs Resort, a major Fairbanks attraction known for its innovative uses of geothermal energy and for its famous Aurora Ice Museum. Chena Hot Springs Resort is open daily year-round with modern accommodations, hotsprings pools (indoor and outdoor), RV parking, and camping, dining, horseback riding and many other activities in summer and winter.

NOTE: Picnicking and camping on the gravel bars of the Chena River is one of the great pleasures of this side trip. However, in spring or during heavy rains, be aware that flooding can occur on the Chena River and plan accordingly when choosing your recreation sites.

Distance is measured from junction with the Old Steese Highway (J).

J 0 Junction of Chena Hot Springs Road

with Old Steese Highway at Curry's Corner (groceries and gas to the north, post office to south), 0.2 mile west of the Steese Expressway. Access to **North Star Golf Club** (0.8 mile) via Old Steese Highway north to Golf Club Road.

J 0.1 Junction of Chena Hot Springs Road with the Steese Expressway, **Milepost F 4.9** (see STEESE HIGHWAY section). Chena River Recreation Area begins 26 miles from here. Four-lane highway travels up and down hills through busy rural residential area next 4 miles. *CAUTION: Watch for frost heaves here to* **Milepost 20.8***.*

J 1.6 *CAUTION: Watch for moose.*

J 3 Hot Springs Gas station to south.

J 3.7 Steele Creek Road.

J 4 *Road narrows eastbound to 2 lanes. Eastbound travelers note: Numerous private drives and local roads cross Chena Hot Springs Road. Pass with care! Begin 4-lane highway westbound.*

J 6.3 Junction with Nordale Road, which leads south 5.7 miles to Badger Road, which junctions with the Richardson Highway. From this turnoff it is 3.2 miles south to the Chena River public boat launch on Nordale Road.

J 8.4 Paved double-ended turnout to south. *NOTE: No shooting area (posted along the road in several places).*

J 11.8 Bridge over Little Chena River. Water gauging station in middle of bridge. This Army Corps of Engineers flood control project, completed in 1979, was designed to prevent floods such as the one which devastated Fairbanks in 1967.

J 12 *CAUTION: Slow for frost heaves and cracks in pavement.*

J 13 Road climbs hills next 1.5 miles

eastbound.

J 15.9 Two Rivers Lodge restaurant to north.

J 16 *CAUTION: Slow for dips.*

J 17.4 Trail Crossing (signed).

J 18.3 Junction with Two Rivers Road to elementary school and Two Rivers Recreation Area (skiing, hiking, transfer site and nature trails).

J 20 Highway crosses Jenny M. Creek. Watch for moose.

J 20.1 Double-ended paved parking area to south.

J 20.5 Watch for horses.

J 23.3 Pizza place to north.

J 23.4 Pleasant Valley Store to south; gas (last chance to buy gas), diesel, groceries, liquor, firewood and ice, and **TWO RIVERS** post office (ZIP 99716).

This unincorporated community (pop. 663) is home to a number of dog mushers, including 5-time Iditarod champ Rick Swenson. There is an extensive system of mushing trails in the area (motorists will notice the "trail crossing" signs along the road), and the Yukon Quest trail runs through the middle of Two Rivers. Mushers often camp in the big field near store. Picnic tables here for use.

Mail drop at east end of store and Post Office.

J 23.9 Laundromat and showers, beauty shop. Propane. Long grassy strip with picnic tables for the public.

J 25 Large gravel parking area to north.

J 26.1 Entering the 254,000-acre **Chena River State Recreation Area**. No shooting except at target range at **Milepost J 36.4**. For more information on Chena River State Recreation Area contact the Alaska State Parks in Fairbanks, phone (907) 451-2695, or visit

the Alaska Public Lands Information Center in downtown Fairbanks. Reservations are required, and fees are charged for public-use cabins within Chena River SRA. There are many single-vehicle turnouts along the road within the recreation area. Grayling are catch-and-release only.

J 26.4 Dog Crossing.

J 26.5 Flat Creek. Large paved parking area with ATV ramp to north; no overnight parking, Chena Hot Springs Trail winter trail for snowmachines.

J 26.7 Flat Creek Slough. Large parking area with loop road to boat launch ($5 fee).

J 27 Turnoff to south for **Rosehip State Campground**. Rest area on paved shoulder by campground entrance; toilets, bear-proof litter bins and informational signs. Campground has 36 level, shaded sites, picnic tables, firepits, toilets, water. Nightly camping fee. Large gravel pads are pull-in or back-in, no pull-throughs. Some hold 2 units. An easy 0.7-mile loop road make this a good campground for large RVs and trailers. Also tent camping area for hand launched boats. Firewood available, $5. Campground host. Maps and information on the Chena River State Recreation Area, fishing, area wildlife and canoe and hiking trails. Beautifully situated on the Chena River. Drive back into park for a well-marked nature trail, which starts by the river.

Also access to **Mile 27 River Access**, a canoe and rafting exit point. The Chena is popular with paddlers, but should not be underestimated: The river is cold and the current very strong. Watch for river-wide logjams and sweepers. Secure your gear in waterproof containers. Suggested paddles are **Milepost J 37.9** to **J 27** (First Bridge to Rosehip Campground); **J 39.4** to **J 37.9** (Second Bridge to First Bridge); **J 44** to **J 39.4** (Third Bridge to Second Bridge); and **J 48.9** to **J 44** (Fourth Bridge to Third Bridge). Allow about an hour on the river for each road mile traveled.

J 27.5 Gravel turnout to south.

J 27.8 Mile 28 River Access to south 0.6 mile. *NOTE: This river access is too steep for large RVs. Many vehicles were prevented from using it in summer 2013 due to a washout.* Large parking area turnaround. Canoe and raft exit point. Two adequate primitive camping spots on the road. Access to gravel bar parking at end. Popular sunbathing spot. Outhouse. Speed limit 10 mph.

J 28 Watch for moose in Slough Lake next 0.6 mile.

J 28.5 River Access (signed Gravel Bar River Access; requires high-clearance vehicle) leads south 0.7 mile to canoe launch, outhouse, parking.

J 29.5 Compeau trailhead parking to north; multi-use year-round trail provides access to Colorado public-use cabin and views of Chena River Valley, Alaska Range and White Mountains. Hodgins Slough (unsigned) turnout to south.

J 30 Twin Bears Camp (available for rent by groups). Public access to lake when camp is not in use. Stocked with grayling, arctic char and rainbow.

J 31.4 Mile 31.4 River Access, 0.2 mile to loop turnaround and canoe launch; undeveloped, no sandbar access. Also trailhead for South Fork winter trail to Nugget Fork Cabin.

Moose are commonly spotted along Chena Hot Springs Road. (©Kris Valencia, staff)

J 31.7 Turnoff to north for gravel parking at Colorado Creek trailhead for winter trail to Colorado Creek public-use cabin (summer access via Compeau Trailhead) and for Lower Stiles Creek. Bring mosquito repellent. Water pump (handle missing in summer 2013) and outhouse. Bear-proof trash cans, ATV ramp and good turnaround area.

J 32.2 Gated access road to Chena River Cabin (public-use) to south; by reservation only.

J 33.9 Highway crosses Four Mile Creek. Watch for moose grazing here.

J 35.8 Scenic viewpoint to south; paved parking, interpretive signs about tamaracks (excerpt follows) and tors (see **Milepost J 39.4**).

"Tamarack, also called larch, is a distinctive tree found in bogs of the Chena Recreation Area. Tamarack is one of the few trees capable of tolerating the bog's wet, acidic soil. This suits the tamarack, since the bog's soil condition prevents the growth of competitors, and the tamarack cannot grow in the shade of other trees. If moss covers the tamarack's lower branches, those branches sprout roots and become individual trees, allowing tamaracks to reproduce asexually.

"The tamarack has needles and cones like an evergreen, but like a deciduous tree it sheds its foliage every fall. Alaska's Interior winters are extremely cold and tend to dehydrate plants, since cold air holds less moisture. Tamaracks conserve water by dropping their needles, dramatically lowering the amount of surface area exposed to winter's dry air.

"The tamarack is also challenged by wildlife. Porcupines feed on the inner bark, snowshoe hares browse on seedlings, and red squirrels eat its seeds and needles. It's the attack of the larch sawfly which is often most obvious. The larvae eat the tamarack's needles, leaving bare curved shoots at the ends of the branches. Although sawfly larvae can denude a tamarack in a few weeks, it takes several years of constant attack to kill a tree."

J 36.4 Turnoff to north for Stiles Creek Trailhead and shooting range (follow signs); large gravel parking area with outhouse; weapons discharge notice posted; informal camping around pond. Designated areas for ATV use. Take road to right for shooting range, road to left for pond campsites.

Mist Creek trailhead south of highway;

6-mile hike, experienced hikers only, provides year-round access to Nugget Creek cabin.

J 37.7 Mile 37.7 River Access. Turnoff to south on dirt road, turn left and continue past outhouse for access to river, launch area and informal camping on gravel bar. NOTE: Small turnaround area on dirt road, larger turnaround on gravel bar (watch for soft spots), water level permitting. *Be aware of changing water levels due to snowmelt in spring or heavy rainfall in summer when camping on gravel bars!*

J 37.9 First Bridge over the North Fork Chena River.

J 38.2 Mile 38.2 River Access. Side road to spacious gravel parking area along river. Primitive camping. Plenty of turnaround space. Room for many units. Also, wide road on top of levee between pond and river.

J 39.1 Paved turnout to south.

J 39.4 Second Bridge over North Fork Chena River.

Turnoff to north just east of bridge for double-ended loop road through **Tors Trailhead State Campground and Day-Use Area** (loop road exits back on to Chena Hot Springs Road at Mile 39.7). Campground has 24 large sites (good for large RVs) among tall birch and spruce trees, water, toilets, tables, firepits, litter bins, nightly camping fee, firewood$; campground host, fee station.

Beautiful riverside picnic area, restrooms and large paved parking area for day-use adjacent camping area. Day-use fee charged. This is the parking area for the **Granite Tors Trail** which begins at the west end of the bridge and to the south across Chena Hot Springs Road on west side of bridge. Interpretive signs at kiosk about Granite Tors Trail and tors, climbing and hiking safety. Trail sign reads:

"An able-bodied hiker should plan 6–10 hours roundtrip for this 15-mile loop trail. Trailhead sign warns hikers of sudden and extreme weather changes in the vicinity of the tors. Sometimes visibility gets very low. Carry a compass, GPS and pay attention to landmarks. Dress for the unexpected. Tors are isolated pinnacles of granite jut-

Chena Hot Springs Road (Continued)

Sip an appletini in the Aurora Ice Museum at Chena Hot Springs Resort. (©Sharon Nault)

ting up from the tundra. Originally part of a granite mass called a pluton, tors were first exposed by erosion and then shaped and sculpted by "frost wedging." This is a process in which water seeps into cracks, freezes and expands, fracturing the rock. The portions of granite with the most cracks erode more quickly (selective weathering), resulting in the "characteristically-shaped tors."

J 39.6 Mile 39.6 River Access; good 0.2-mile side road leads south to Chena River primitive camping and picnic area with pit toilets and a riverbank of flat rocks ideal for sunbathing. Easy small boat launch.

J 39.7 Parking and toilet at Tors Trailhead Campground Road exit.

J 41.6 Long gravel parking area to south by stream.

J 42 Double-ended paved parking area to south. Watch for muskrats and beaver in ponds here.

J 42.6 Gated access to Hunt Memorial Cabin to south. Reservation only access.

J 42.8 Red Squirrel Campground; good gravel road leads north to pleasant picnic area on lawn, good campground for tenters, 12 sites; 2 covered picnic areas, firepits, outhouses and water. Camping fee. Located on pond stocked with grayling, arctic char and rainbow. Good turnaround to west after entering. Reservations taken for picnic shelter, (907) 451-2695. No motorized boats. Watch for moose.

J 42.9 Gravel turnout to south overlooking river. Primitive camping spot.

J 43 Side road leads south to **Mile 43 River Access**.

J 44 Third Bridge over North Fork Chena River. **Mile 44 River Access**. Gravel parking area with toilets to north, outhouse, canoe and raft launch, primitive camping near river. Canoe launch. Sign here lists approximate times for float trips to different loca-

tions down the river.

J 45.5 Mile 45.5 Pond. Public fishing access to south via good gravel road (watch for potholes). Firepit grill, picnic table, primitive camping, turnaround space. Pond is stocked with arctic grayling. Beavers may be active in pond.

J 45.7 Bridge across south of North Fork Chena River (signed).

J 46 Small paved turnout to south.

J 46.7 Double-ended paved turnout to south.

J 47.7 North Fork public-use cabin to north. By reservation only, gated road.

J 47.8 Public fishing access to **48-Mile Pond** 0.1 mile south via good gravel road. Pond is stocked with grayling, arctic char and rainbow; picnic tables, outhouse, informal campsites around pond. Bring your own firewood, carry out your trash..

J 48.9 Fourth Bridge over **North Fork Chena River**. Turnoff to south at west end of bridge for Angel Rocks trail (description follows).

Loop road leads south through parking and picnic area for **Angel Rocks Trailhead**, one of the best developed public-use sites on Chena Hot Springs Road. (Good place for a picnic, even if you don't intent to hike the trail!) There is a large cement pad with picnic tables, firepits and grills, outhouse, bear-proof garbage cans. Angel Rocks trail is a 3.5-mile loop trail to spectacular rock outcroppings; moderately difficult hike (elevation gain of 900 ft.). Details regarding an additional 8.5-mile-hike on Chena Hot Springs Trail are at the trailhead. Day-use fee charged. Fishing. Information boards about wildfires, trails and rock formations. Parking

fee $5 (fine for not paying this is $60). No overnight camping.

J 49.1 Good gravel side road leads 0.2 mile north and loops through **Lower Chena Dome Trailhead**; parking, water (no handle on pump summer 2013) and toilets. This 30-mile loop trail is a strenuous hike that circles the Angel Creek drainage. Bring mosquito repellent!

J 49.7 Angel Creek Lodge to north. *Watch for horses along road.*

J 49.9 Bridge over Angel Creek. Small turnout to north.

J 50.5 Turnoff to north for **Upper Chena Dome and Angel Creek Trailhead**; parking loop to north adjacent road; toilets, bear-proof garbage cans. Bring mosquito repellent!

J 50.6 Leaving Chena River SRA eastbound.

J 51 Evidence of 2002 wildfire between here and just beyond **Milepost J 54**.

J 52.3 Bridge over West Fork Chena River. Access to riverbank for camping to south at west end of bridge.

J 53.3 Large, paved double-ended turnout in burn area; loading ramp for ATVs.

J 55.4 North Fork Chena River bridge. Double-ended turnout to south at east end of bridge.

J 56 Welcome to Chena Hot Springs (sign).

J 56.6 Entrance to **Chena Hot Springs Resort** (description follows); home of the **Aurora Ice Museum** and ice-carved appletini glasses (between 12,000 and 15,000 of these unique glasses are carved each year). Chena Hot Springs Resort offers camping, lodging, indoor and outdoor hot springs pools, and *many* activities year-round. Wonderful flower displays in summer, internationally known aurora watching site in winter.

Chena Hot Springs Resort. Rustic Alaskan year-round 100+ year old hot springs resort. Only 60 scenic miles from Fairbanks. 440 pristine acres of wilderness, 80 lodge rooms, full service restaurant and

lounge, natural outdoor hot springs adult (ages 18+) rock lake and indoor family pool, RV park, summer and winter activities. Feel the chill of 25 degrees in our year-round Aurora Ice Museum. Sip your very own appletini in an ice carved martini glass, your souvenir to take with you! Daily tours: 11 A.M., 1 P.M., 3 P.M., 5 P.M. and 7 P.M. Free daily 2 P.M. Geothermal Energy Tours showcasing Chena's renewable energy projects. Winter aurora viewing and summer packages too! (907) 451-8104. Website: www.chenahotsprings.com. See display ad on page 453. [ADVERTISEMENT]

Denali National Park

Includes log of Park Road

(See map, page 470)

View of Mt. McKinley/Denali, North America's highest mountain at 20,320 feet. (©Michael F. Jones)

Denali National Park and Preserve was established in 1917 as Mount McKinley National Park. It was designated a park and preserve—and renamed Denali—in 1980. The park lies on both sides of the Alaska Range, 250 miles south of the Arctic Circle. The park road entrance is 237 highway miles north of Anchorage and 125 miles south of Fairbanks via the Parks Highway.

The park is open all year, although visitor access varies with the change of seasons. Opening and closing dates for the Park Road are dependent on the weather (specifically, the snow).

The park road is open to the public to Mile 30 (Teklanika Rest Area from mid-April until shuttle buses start running on May 20th. From late May to mid-September, the Visitor Transportation System (comprised of shuttle buses and tour buses) provides transportation into the park beyond Mile 15. (The first 15 miles of the park road are open to all vehicles during the summer.) The park road is also open to the public to Mile 30 from mid-September until the first major snowstorm (usually in October). From October through April, the park road is maintained only to park headquarters at Mile 3. Beyond Mile 3, the road is unplowed and access to the park is by skis, snowshoes or dog sleds, depending on snow cover. In mid-February 2014, the road will be open to Mile 12.7 (Mountain Vista Rest Area) on a trial basis for 3–5 years to provide increased access for winter visitors.

NOTE: Each September, after the shuttle buses stop running for the season, a 4-day lottery allows 400 lucky winners to drive their private vehicles along the length of the Park Road (or as far as it is passable) per day. For more information on the Denali Park Road Lottery, refer to "Special Permits" on page 474.

Most campgrounds, as well as food and shuttle bus service within the park, are available only from late May to mid-September. (Riley Creek Campground, near the park entrance area, is open year-round; no running water in winter.) Opening dates for facilities and activities for the summer season are announced in the spring by the Park Service and depend mainly on snow conditions in May.

General rules and regulations affecting visitors are mentioned here. For specific regulations governing the use of aircraft, firearms, snowmachines and motorboats in the park additions and in the national preserve units, and for all other questions, write Denali National Park and Preserve, P.O. Box 9, Denali Park, AK 99755; phone (907) 683-2294, website: www.nps.gov/dena.

At approximately 6 million acres, most visitors will see only a fraction of the park from the 92-mile Park Road. The crown jewel of the park is Mount McKinley, North America's highest mountain at 20,320 feet.

On a clear day, Mount McKinley is visible from Anchorage and many points along the Parks Highway. However, summer's often overcast or rainy weather frequently obscures the mountain, allowing summertime visitors only about a 30 to 40 percent chance of seeing "the mountain" even inside the park boundaries.

First mention of "the mountain" was in 1794, when English explorer Capt. George Vancouver spotted "a stupendous snow mountain" from Cook Inlet. Early Russian explorers and traders called the peak *Bolshaia Gora*, or "Big Mountain." The Athabascan Indians of the region called it Denali, "the High One." In 1896 a prospector, William A. Dickey, named the mountain for presidential nominee William McKinley of Ohio, although McKinley had no connection with Alaska. Protests that the moun-

Distances in miles	Denali NP	Anchorage	Fairbanks	Homer	Seward	Tok	Valdez
Denali NP		237	125	470	364	565	541
Anchorage	237		362	233	127	328	304
Fairbanks	125	362		595	489	206	366
Homer	470	233	595		180	561	537
Seward	364	127	489	180		455	431
Tok	565	328	206	561	455		254
Valdez	541	304	366	537	431	254	

Denali National Park and Preserve

© 2014 The MILEPOST®

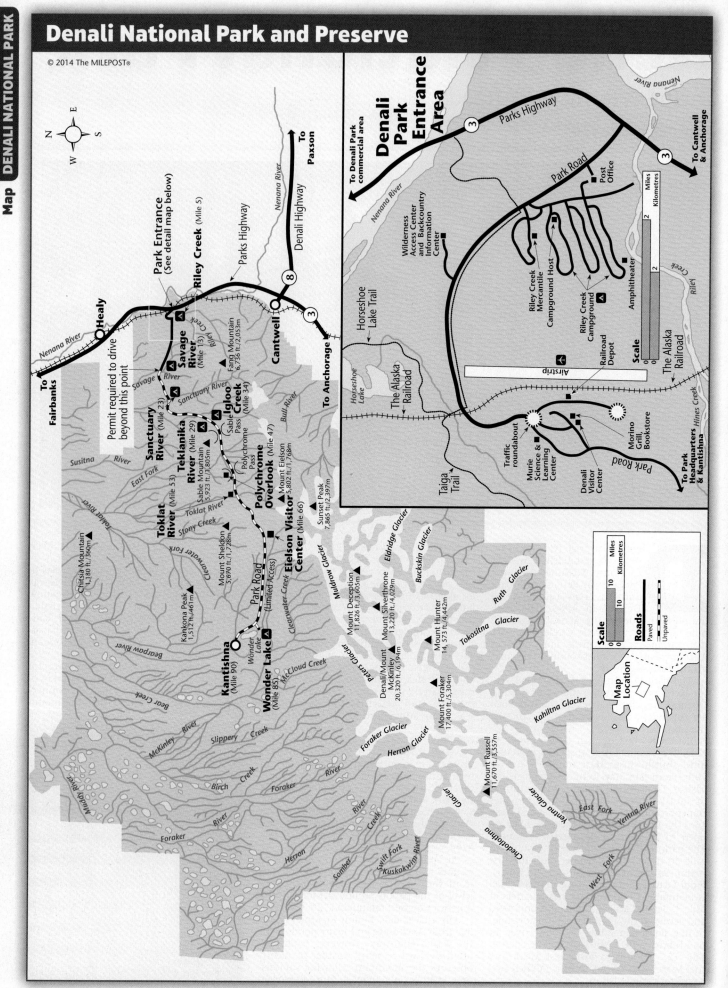

Denali Park Entrance Area

To Denali Park commercial area

Parks Highway

3

To Cantwell & Anchorage

3

Park Road

Post Office

Miles
Kilometres

Wilderness Access Center and Backcountry Information Center

Horseshoe Lake Trail

Riley Creek Mercantile

Campground Host

Riley Creek Campground

Amphitheater

Riley Creek

Scale

Railroad Depot

The Alaska Railroad

Airstrip

Horseshoe Lake

The Alaska Railroad

Morino Grill, Bookstore

Hines Creek

Taiga Trail

Traffic roundabout

Murie Science & Learning Center

Denali Visitor Center

Park Road

To Park Headquarters & Kantishna

N
W E S

To Paxson

Park Entrance (See detail map below)

Riley Creek (Mile 5)

Parks Highway

Nenana River

Denali Highway

8

Cantwell

3

Healy

Nenana River

To Fairbanks

Permit required to drive beyond this point

Savage River (Mile 13)

Fang Mountain 6,736 ft./2,053m

Riley Creek

To Anchorage

Sanctuary River (Mile 23)

Sanctuary River

Savage River

Igloo Creek (Mile 34)

Sable Pass

Teklanika River (Mile 29)

Sable Mountain 5,923 ft./1,805m

Polychrome Pass

Polychrome Overlook (Mile 47)

Mount Eielson 5,802 ft./1,768m

Bull River

Susitna River

East Fork

Toklat River (Mile 53)

Clearwater Fork

Toklat River

Stony Creek

Mount Sheldon 5,670 ft./1,728m

Eielson Visitor Center (Mile 66)

Sunset Peak 7,865 ft./2,397m

Muldrow Glacier

Teklanika River

Chitsia Mountain 1,180 ft./360m

Kankona Peak 1,512 ft./461m

Bearpaw River

Park Road (Limited Access)

Clearwater Creek

McCloud Creek

Mount Deception 11,826 ft./3,605m

Peters Glacier

Mount Silverthrone 13,220 ft./4,029m

Eldridge Glacier

Buckskin Glacier

Ruth Glacier

Kantishna (Mile 90)

Wonder Lake

Wonder Lake (Mile 85)

Mount Hunter 14,573 ft./4,442m

Denali/Mount McKinley 20,320 ft./6,194m

Tokositna Glacier

Moose River

Slippery Creek

McKinley River

Birch Creek

Foraker River

Bear Creek

Foraker Glacier

Peters Glacier

Mount Foraker 17,400 ft./5,304m

Herron Glacier

Herron

Somber Creek

Swift Fork

Kuskokwim River

Mount Russell 11,670 ft./3,557m

Chedotlothna Glacier

Glacier

Kahiltna Glacier

Yentna River

Yentna Glacier

East Fork

West Fork

Scale

Miles
Kilometres

10

10

Roads

Paved

Unpaved

Map Location

tain be returned to its original name, Denali, ensued almost at once. But it was not until the Alaska National Interest Lands Conservation Act of 1980 changed the park's status and name that the Alaska Board of Geographic Names changed the mountain's name back to Denali. (The U.S. Board of Geographic Names, however, still shows the mountain as McKinley.) The 1980 legislation also enlarged the park from 2 million acres to its present 6 million acres to protect Mount McKinley on all sides and to preserve the habitat of area wildlife.

The history of climbs on McKinley is as intriguing as its names. In 1903, Judge James Wickersham and party climbed to an estimated 10,000 feet, while the Dr. Frederick A. Cook party reached the 11,000-foot level in 1903. Cook returned to the mountain 3 years later and claimed to have reached the summit. Cook's vague description of his ascent route and a questionable summit photo led many to doubt his claim. (The exhaustive research of McKinley expert Bradford Washburn has proven the exaggeration of Cook's claim.)

The 1910 Sourdough Party, which included Tom Lloyd, Charles McGonagall, Pete Anderson and Billy Taylor, claimed they had reached both summits (north and south peaks), but could not provide any photographic evidence. However, the spruce pole they left behind on the north peak was witnessed in 1913.

The first ascent of the true summit of Mount McKinley was made in June 1913 by the Rev. Hudson Stuck, Episcopal archdeacon of Yukon, Walter Harper, Harry Karstens (co-leader) and Robert Tatum. Harper, a Native Athabascan, was the first person to set foot on the higher south peak. (Harper drowned in 1918, along with more than 300 other passengers and crew, when the SS *Princess Sophia* sank near Juneau.) Harry Karstens went on to become the first superintendent of Mount McKinley National Park.

Out of respect for the Native people, Stuck refused to refer to the mountain as McKinley. He recorded the story of their achievement in his book, *The Ascent of Denali*.

Today, more than a thousand people attempt to climb McKinley each year between April and mid-July, most flying in to base camp at 7,200 feet on Kahiltna Glacier. In a typical season, slightly more than

Park shuttle bus negotiates winding section of the Park Road. (©Tim Grams)

half the climbers attempting to summit Denali succeed.

Geographic features in the park bear the names of early explorers: Eldridge and Muldrow glaciers, after George Eldridge and Robert Muldrow of the U.S. Geographic Service who determined the peak's altitude in 1898; Wickersham Wall; Karsten Ridge; Harper Icefall; and Mount Carpe and Mount Koven, named for Allen Carpe and Theodore Koven, both killed in a 1932 climb.

Climate and Landscape: Typical summer weather in the park is cool, wet and windy. Visitors should bring clothing for temperatures that range from 40°F to 80°F. Rain gear, a light coat, sturdy walking shoes or boots and insect repellent are essential. Winter weather is cold and clear, with temperatures sometimes dropping to -50°F at park headquarters. In the lowlands, snow seldom accumulates to more than 3 feet.

Timberline in the park is at 2,700 feet. Below timberline are vast areas of taiga, a term of Russian origin that describes scant tree growth. Together with the subarctic tundra, the landscape of Denali National Park and Preserve supports more than 750 species of trees, shrubs, herbs and flowering

plants. Major species of the taiga are white spruce in dry areas; dry tundra covers the upper ridges and rocky slopes above the tree line from about 3,500 to 7,500 feet. In the wet tundra black spruce is common, intermingled with aspen, paper birch and balsam poplar. Wet tundra features willow and dwarf birch, often with horsetails, sedges and grasses along pothole ponds.

Denali's subarctic ecosystem helped it gain International Biosphere Reserve

DENALI PARK AREA ADVERTISERS

status in 1976. Outstanding features of the park include the Outer Range, Savage River Canyon, Wonder Lake, Sanctuary River, Muldrow Glacier and the Kantishna Hills. The Outer Range, located just north of the central Alaska Range, is composed of some of Alaska's oldest rocks, called Bison Gulch schist, which can be clearly seen in the Savage River Canyon.

Caribou calving grounds are located near the headwaters of the Sanctuary River, which passes through the Outer Range between Mount Wright and Primrose Ridge. Muldrow Glacier, the largest glacier on the north side of the Alaska Range, is 32 miles long and descends 16,000 feet from near Denali's summit.

Wonder Lake, 2.6 miles long and 280 feet deep, hosts many migrating species and is a summer home for loons, arctic terns and other birds. It also offers a peerless reflection of Denali. Wonder Lake is at Mile 84.6 on the Park Road.

The Kantishna Hills were first mined in 1905 when the town of Eureka boomed with gold seekers. In 1980 the Kantishna area was included in the park. From the park entrance at **Milepost A 237.4** of the Parks Highway, the 92-mile Park Road traverses the national park to private land holdings in Kantishna.

Visitor Information

Visitor Centers: The visitor centers are your source for on-site information about camping, backcountry travel, the park shuttle bus system and daily ranger-led hikes, walks and interpretive programs.

The **Denali Visitor Center** is accessed from the roundabout at Mile 1.2 Park Road. It is open 8 A.M. to 6 P.M. from mid-May to mid-September. *NOTE: Budget cuts may lead to decreased open hours in National Park Service facilities in 2014.* At the Denali Visitor Center you can chat with a Denali Park ranger, watch a film at the Karstens Theatre or learn

more about natural history in the exhibit hall. This is the main visitor center for the park, and the complex includes the Denali Bookstore (operated by Alaska Geographic) and the Morino Grill.

The **Murie Science & Learning Center**, at Mile 1.3 of the Park Road, is used as a winter visitor center from mid-September until mid-May.

The turnoff for the **Wilderness Access Center** (WAC), is at Mile 0.5 Park Road. The WAC acts as the park's transportation hub, where visitors can make reservations for shuttle or bus tours and reserve or check-in for campsites in the park. The Backcountry Information Center is located in the WAC parking lot. The WAC is open from mid-May to mid-September. Hours are 5 A.M. to 8 P.M. for bus loading, 7 A.M. to 7 P.M. for the reservation desk; phone (907) 683-9278.

Eielson Visitor Center, at Mile 66 on the Park Road, is an excellent Mount McKinley viewpoint. Eielson is open daily from 9 A.M. to 7 P.M., June 1 until mid-September.

For more information, contact Denali National Park and Preserve, P.O. Box 9, Denali Park, AK 99755; phone (907) 683-9532, web site: www.nps.gov/dena.

Entrance Fees: Visitors camping in the park or riding a shuttle bus (green bus) or tour bus (tan bus) will pay a park entrance fee of $10 per person for visitors 16 years of age and older. *(NOTE: Fees are subject to change.)* The National Parks Pass, the America the Beautiful Interagency Passes and Denali Annual Passes can be applied to the fee; information about these passes may be obtained at the visitor center. In addition to entrance and camping fees, there is a nonrefundable $4 processing fee for each campground reservation.

Advance Reservations: Park shuttle bus tickets and park campsites may be reserved by fax, phone, online, mail or in person. Reservations for 2014 began December 1, 2013. You may make 2014 reservations for shuttles and campgrounds until September 11, 2014. Reservations may be made by phone or in person up to 2 days in advance (1 day by phone or internet) of your visit. Mail-in reservations must be received 30 days in advance.

For online reservations and information, visit www.reservedenali.com. For reservations by phone, call toll-free 1-800-622-7275 (nationwide), or for international calls, phone 1-(907) 272-7275. Address mail-in requests to: Doyon/ARAMARK Joint Venture, VTS/Campground Reservations, 2445 W. Dunlop Ave., Phoenix, AZ 85021. Mail-in requests are processed in the order received.

When mailing reservation requests, include ages of each passenger, as youth discounts do apply. It is helpful to include alternative dates of travel. Include credit card numbers (VISA, MasterCard or Discover), and their expiration dates. Other payment options are personal check (received 10 working days in advance) or money order. Cancellation fees ($4 for each seat or campsite) apply.

Sixty-five percent of the park's shuttle bus seats, and 100 percent of Riley Creek, Savage River, Teklanika River and Wonder Lake campsites, are available for advance reservations. Online, there are several parts to a campground reservations: under rate type is first the abbreviation for the campground, followed by the kind of site. For example, your fee includes a campground abbrevia-

tion (ex: RC for Riley Creek Campground). The fee also notes what size of site you have chosen starting from "A," 30'-40' or "B," for less than 30' RVs. The walk-in tent-only sites are listed as "C" sites. Your reservation rate type can thereby look like: RC NPS PASS "B" which demonstrates that you have a reservation at Riley Creek for a smaller than 30' RV site at $22 per night (rates are $28 for greater than 30' and $14 for tent/walk-in only).

There are discounts for AAA, seniors (55+) and government/military. Prepaid, reserved shuttle bus tickets may be picked up at the Wilderness Access Center shuttle desk. Any unclaimed, prepaid tickets for buses departing before 7 A.M. will be in the possession of the bus driver; however, the drivers do not sell tickets.

Riley Creek Mercantile, at Mile 0.3 Park Road, has shuttle bus and tour ticket sales and campground reservations and check-in. The Mercantile is open 7 A.M. to 11 P.M. in summer; phone (907) 683-9246.

Backcountry Permits: Backpackers must obtain a backcountry permit and carry Bear-Resistant Food Containers (BRFCs). BRFCs are available for pick-up at the Backcountry Information Center or park headquarters, and must be returned at the end of your trip. These containers may also be purchased at the Denali Bookstore.

Backcountry permits are available at the Backcountry Information Center in summer, and at the Murie Science and Learning Center in the winter. Backcountry permits are issued 1 day in advance and reservations are not accepted. The Backcountry Information Center (BIC), located adjacent to the Wilderness Access Center, is open daily from 9 A.M. to 6 P.M. during the summer. (The permitting process takes about an hour, so arrive no later than 5 P.M.) Information on obtaining a backcountry permit is also available on the park website at www.nps.gov/dena/planyourvisit/bcper mits.htm.

Before obtaining permits, backpackers must: 1) Watch the Backcountry Simulator program, available at the Backcountry Information Center, with its information on bear safety, minimum-impact camping, river crossing tips, wildlife and safety emergencies; 2) Denali's backcountry consists of 85 units, in which a limited number of visitors are allowed per night (see www.nps.gov/dena/planyourvisit/ unitsys.htm). Check the Quota Board at the Backcountry Information Center for unit availability. Backpackers must confirm that their desired unit is not closed. *NOTE: Large groups may be divided if units are too full.* 3) Read Backcountry Description Guides available from the Backcountry Information Center or the Denali Bookstore or online links from www.nps.gov/dena/planyour visit/unitsys.htm; 4) Consult topographic maps to plan your trip and routes through the park; 5) Consult the backcountry gear checklist provided by the Park Service.

Camping gear should include a gasoline or propane stove, rain gear and a tent or waterproof shelter. Water should be boiled or treated. A camper bus pass ($34.50) must be purchased in order to reach most backcountry camping units.

Day hikers do not need a special permit.

Pets: Pets are not allowed in the backcountry. They are allowed in parking lots and on roads, or in campsites.

Mountaineering: Whether you call it McKinley or Denali, climbing "the moun-

Bring your telephoto lens for photographing Denali Park wildlife, like this caribou.
(©Tim Grams)

DENALI NATIONAL PARK

Grizzly sow and 2 cubs on the Park Road. Shuttle bus passengers may see bears along the road. Hikers must maintain a mandatory minimum distance of 1/4 mile from bears.

(©Michael F. Jones)

tain" requires extensive planning. Registration is mandatory for all climbs on McKinley and Foraker. Mountaineers are required to purchase a permit ($360/person age 25 or older, $260 age 24 or younger) before climbing McKinley or Foraker. An unknown amount of increase will occur Jan. 1, 2014. *Permit applications must be received at least 60 days prior to the start of the expedition.*

The National Park Service maintains a ranger station in Talkeetna that is staffed full-time year-round. Rangers there can provide all necessary information on climbing McKinley, Foraker and other peaks of the Alaska Range. Contact the Talkeetna Ranger Station at P.O. Box 588, Talkeetna, AK 99676; phone (907) 733-2231; or see www.nps.gov/dena/planyourvisit/mountaineering.htm.

Special Permits: Each year the park issues permits to a limited number of individuals, selected by lottery, to drive their vehicles through the park on the Friday through Monday of the second weekend after Labor Day (Sept. 12–Sept. 15, 2014). It is not unusual for these late-season visitors to have their tour curtailed by early snows within the park. Road lottery applications are accepted online during the month of May. A $10 fee is required for each entry application and each entry must be received at the park (or completed online) before the end of the month. If selected, an additional $25 fee will be charged. Website: www.nps.gov/dena/planyourvisit/road-lottery.htm.

For more details on the road lottery, visit the park web site at www.nps.gov/dena or by phone (907) 683-9532.

Also log on to the park website (www.nps.gov/dena) for information concerning special permits for the Professional Photographer Program, the Artist-in-Residence Program and Commercial Filming.

Fishing Licenses: Not required in the wilderness area; state law is applicable on all other lands. Specified limits for each person per day should be carefully observed. Fishing is poor because most rivers are silty and ponds are shallow.

Emergency Services: Call 911, or contact state troopers at (907) 683-2232, or (907) 768-2202. For healthcare, go to Canyon Clinic, an Urgent Care Clinic on the Sourdough Road, just north of Princess Lodge.

Lodging & Services

North of the park entrance about a mile on the Parks Highway is a commercial district with numerous hotels, restaurants, RV parks, a gas station with convenience store, assorted shops and commercial outfitters. Lodges, cabins, campgrounds and restaurants are also found along the Parks Highway south and north of the park entrance, from Cantwell to Healy; see pages 433-439 in the PARKS HIGHWAY section. (See also "Denali's Front Country" feature on page 478.) There are 4 wilderness lodges inside the Park in the Kantishna area, at the far western edge of the park.

The Riley Creek Mercantile at Riley Creek Campground is stocked with a limited selection of groceries. Firewood, showers and laundry facilities are also available at the Mercantile. If the Mercantile doesn't have what you need, there are stores with grocery items and sundries located in the Nenana River Canyon commercial area on the Parks Highway.

No food/drink service is available in the park past the Denali Visitor Center complex at Mile 1.2 on the Park Road.

Denali Rainbow Village. Good Sam RV Park, 1 mile north of Denali Park entrance. Large motel rooms with kitchens and queen beds and Suite (sleeps up to 8) are available. 55 RV sites with full or partial hook-up, pull-thrus, WiFi, cable TV, showers, laundry and dump station. Mall with services and activities. (907) 683-7777. See display ad on page 476. [ADVERTISEMENT]

Transportation

Highway: Access via the Parks Highway from Anchorage or Fairbanks. The entrance to Denali National Park is at **Milepost A 237.4** Parks Highway, 237 miles north of Anchorage; 28 miles north of Cantwell and 125 miles south of Fairbanks. See PARKS HIGHWAY section.

The 92-mile Park Road (log begins on page 479) provides access to Denali National Park's campgrounds and the Kantishna area, where some privately owned, backcountry lodges are located. The Park Road is closed to private vehicles beyond Mile 14.8 (Savage River checkpoint). The exception is for campers with vehicles overnighting at Teklanika Campground at Mile 29.1. You must have camping reservations for Teklanika (also accessed by bus) and there is a 3-night minimum stay requirement. The other 3 campgrounds beyond the checkpoint are tents only and accessible only via the shuttle bus system.

Air: Charter flights are available from many nearby locations, and flightseeing tours are offered by operators from the park area or out of Talkeetna, Anchorage or Fairbanks. A round-trip air tour of the park from Anchorage takes 3-4 hours.

Private Aircraft: McKinley Park airstrip; elev. 1,720 feet; length 3,000 feet; gravel; unattended.

Aviation information for private pilots available at www.nps.gov/dena/planyourvisit/pilotinformation.htm.

Talkeetna Air Taxi. Explore Denali National Park and Mount McKinley with Talkeetna Air Taxi as your flightseeing guide. Experience an ice age world

among sculpted peaks and land on amazing glaciers with our spectacular tours. Call 1-800-533-2219 for a free brochure and see our web cam at www.talkeetnaair.com for live views of Denali. See display ad on page 428 in the PARKS HIGHWAY section. [ADVERTISEMENT]

Railroad: The Alaska Railroad offers daily service between Anchorage, Denali Park and Fairbanks during the summer. The Denali Park Depot is located 1.2 miles west of the Parks Highway via the Park Road, within walking distance of the Denali Visitor Center Complex. The depot is open daily, 9:30 A.M. to 5:30 P.M., from mid-May to mid-September. Bag-

The Alaska Railroad includes a stop in Denali from both Anchorage and Fairbanks.
(©Kris Valencia, staff)

gage storage is available at the Denali Visitor Center. Phone Reservations at (907) 265-2494 or toll-free at 1-800-544-0552 or visit www.alaskarailroad.com for more information.

Princess (www.princess.com) and Holland America (www.hollandamerica.com) cruise tour options include overland itineraries with rail travel to Denali National Park. Holland America's McKinley Explorer® and Princess's Direct-to-the-Wilderness® rail service both feature luxurious domed rail cars that are pulled by the Alaska Railroad train.

Bus: Daily bus service to the park is available from Anchorage and Fairbanks (see "Bus Lines" in the TRAVEL PLANNING section). See also Tour and Shuttle Buses following.

Shuttle Buses and Bus Tours: Visitors have the choice of taking the park shuttle buses or one of the 5 formal, narrated bus tours offered by the park concessionaire in summer. Both tour buses and shuttle buses use the Park Road. For reservations for shuttle buses and bus tours, phone 1-800-622-7275; email denalireservations@aramark.com; or visit www.reservedenali.com.

Bicyclists may ride the length of the Park Road. (©Michael F. Jones)

The Visitor Transportation System (VTS) was established in 1972 to protect the natural resources of Denali National Park. The green VTS buses depart the Wilderness Access Center (WAC) throughout the day between 5:15 A.M. and 3 P.M. for Toklat River (3 hours), Eielson Visitor Center (4 hours), and Wonder Lake (5-½ hours). Some shuttle buses operate exclusively in the entrance area, shuttling visitors between the WAC, Riley Creek Campground, railroad depot, Denali Visitor Center Complex, Horseshoe Lake Trailhead, Park Headquarters, the sled dog demonstrations and out to the Savage River area at Mile 15.

Travelers accessing park campgrounds or hiking trails, or looking for a no-frills sightseeing trip, use the shuttle buses. The VTS buses are school bus-style; they are not luxurious. You must bring your own food and beverages. There are rest stops no more than 2 hours apart which allow you to stretch your legs, use the restrooms and photograph the view (weather permitting). You can disembark the shuttle bus to hike, photograph or spend time in an area of interest by asking the bus driver to let you off. When you are ready to re-board, flag down the next bus that comes by and—if space is available—you can continue along the bus route.

The 6-, 8- and 11-hour round-trip shuttle bus trips can be exhilarating and exhausting at the same time. Consider carefully your ability to endure narrow, cliffside roads (no guardrails, buses passing each other on a narrow road); endless searching of a terrain that may be empty of wildlife that day; and a ground-speed of 35 mph or less. Children may become bored on these tours, since the wildlife viewing is uncertain, infrequent and typically at quite a distance, at the best of times. Planning ahead to get off the bus and do your own hike, then catch a bus on its return route, is a great way to maximize the VTS-style travel experience. (NOTE: Do *not* wait until the last bus of the day to catch a return ride or you may be disappointed. If you are in a group, be willing to split up.)

The VTS shuttle buses do not offer narration, although many of the park bus drivers are long-term navigators of the Park Road, quite knowledgeable about the area, and happy to answer questions. The shuttle buses do stop for wildlife viewing and photography (from inside the bus, telephoto lens and binoculars are helpful). Brown bears, wolves, foxes and moose sometimes walk the road. Wheelchair-accessible buses are available.

The concessionaire-operated bus tours are: the Tundra Wilderness Tour (7 to 8 hours); the Denali Natural History Tour (4 ½- to 5 hours); the Windows in Wilderness Tour to Mile 30 (6 hours with snack, water and guided .75 mile walk); and the Kantishna Experience (11 to 12 hours). The Teklanika Tundra Wilderness Tour (4 to 5 hours) is offered May 15-19 and September 14-21 only.

The bus tours use an upgraded bus, similar in style to a coach, are narrated by the driver/naturalist, and include a boxed lunch, snacks and beverages, and pick-up/drop-off at area hotels. Wheelchair-accessible buses are available on request when you make your reservation, and all stops are wheelchair accessible.

There are morning and afternoon departures for the Tundra Wilderness Tour, which travels 53 miles into the Park to the Toklat River rest area, and the Denali Natural History Tour, which goes to Primrose Ridge at Mile 17 on the Park Road. The Kantishna Experience, which travels 92 miles to the end of the Park Road, departs once daily at 7 A.M. and returns around 7 P.M.

Bicycles: There is no policy restricting bicycle access on the Park Road, although bicyclists must stay on the road. Bicyclists wishing to camp in the park must either camp in one of the campgrounds or, if they are camping in the backcountry, must park their bikes in one of the campgrounds. Some Eielson buses have bike racks—make a reservation. Only 2 bikes can be accommodated

on camper buses, so reserve ahead.

Camping

Denali National Park has 6 campgrounds located along the Park Road: Riley Creek (**Mile J 0.3**), Savage River (**Mile J 12.8**), Sanctuary River (**Mile J 22**), Teklanika River (**Mile J 29.1**), Igloo Creek (**Mile J 34.2**) and Wonder Lake (**Mile J 84.6**). Campgrounds along the paved portion of the road—Riley Creek and Savage River—are accessible by personal vehicle at any time. Wonder Lake, Igloo Creek and Sanctuary River are tents only (no vehicles) and access is by shuttle bus. Teklanika River Campground is for both tents and RVs.

Riley Creek Campground is the largest campground in the park, with 146 tent/vehicle sites located along 3 gravel loops. Campsite assignment at Riley Creek is based on vehicle size. It is the campground most convenient to services, located in the park entrance area adjacent the Mercantile, which carries grocery items and firewood and also has laundry and shower facilities.

Teklanika River (or Tek) Campground is open to tent and RV camping with a minimum 3-night stay. Access is by shuttle bus or by personal vehicle (restricted to one round-trip only). The Tek shuttle bus pass is for campers based at Teklanika Campground and ensures a bus seat farther into the park. On the first complete day of a visitor's stay, the Tek Pass is good for a confirmed space on any available shuttle (green) bus. During the remainder of the stay, the pass allows space available seating on any shuttle bus.

Camping fees range from $9 to $28 a night, not including reservations fees. Group camping is available at Savage Group Campground for $40 a night.

There are no RV hookups in park campgrounds. Visitors may camp a total of 14 days per year. Riley Creek is the only park campground open year-round (no running water in winter). The other campgrounds are open from late May–early June to mid-September, depending on the weather. *NOTE: Campgrounds may be closed to tent camping or all camping due to bear activity.* You can reserve campsites ahead of time (see "Reservations" this section) or check with the Wilderness Access Center (WAC) upon arrival for current campsite availability. The WAC is open 7 A.M. to 7 P.M. in summer; phone (907) 683-9278. You can also register for campground sites at the Riley Creek Mercantile, which is open from 7 A.M. to 11 P.M. in summer; phone (907) 683-9246.

Also keep in mind that private campgrounds are located outside the park along the Parks Highway. The nearest to the park entrance is **Denali Rainbow Village** in the

Rangers are on hand at Denali Park Kennels to answer questions from visitors.
(©Kris Valencia, staff)

Nenana Canyon area. See "Denali 's Front Country" on page 478 for more Parks Highway campgrounds, from Cantwell to Healy.

Attractions

Free Sled Dog Demonstrations are held at the Park Kennels. Board the free dog demo bus and catch the morning program or one of the afternoon demonstrations (check schedule at the visitor center for bus and demonstration times). Kennel visitors can photograph and pet the sled dogs before attending the formal demonstration at the adjacent viewing platform. The dog sled demonstration includes a talk by park rangers about the dogs, their role in the park and the history of the kennel. Donations are accepted to help support the kennel.

Wildlife viewing is probably second only to mountain viewing as the goal for visitors in Denali. The park is home to one amphibian (the wood frog) and 39 species of mammals which, among many others, include: caribou, grizzly bear, wolf, wolverine, moose, Dall sheep, red fox, lynx, ground squirrel, snowshoe hare and vole. About 169 species of birds have been recorded in the park. Year-round residents include the great horned owl, raven, and white-tailed, rock and willow ptarmigan. The majority of species, however, visit the park only during summer. Some of these summer visitors include: sandhill cranes, long-tailed ducks, sandpipers, plovers, gulls, buffleheads and

goldeneyes. Golden eagles are a common sight throughout the park. Feeding of any wildlife is prohibited.

Hiking in Denali National Park is cross-country: There are few established trails in the backcountry. For the day-hiker or the visitor with only a short amount of time, however, there are several trails in the front-country/entrance area from Mile 1 to Mile 15 (Savage River) that are acces-

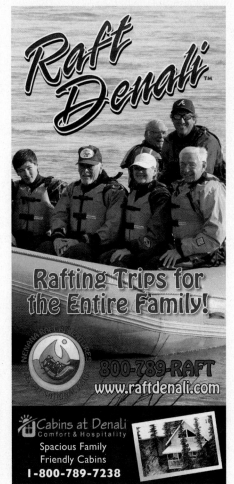

Denali Park's "Front Country"

Businesses serving Park visitors are found along the Parks Highway.
(©Meghan Mackey, staff)

Businesses along the 40-mile stretch of the Parks Highway between Cantwell and Healy—known as Denali Park's "Front Country"—provide Park visitors with a wide range of accommodations and services not available on park lands. Here's a look at what's available:

Accommodations run from the rustic to the luxurious. In the Cantwell area, **Milepost A 210**, about 27 miles south of the park entrance, **Backwoods Lodge** (www.back woodslodge.com), on the Denali Highway just east of the junction with the Parks Highway, offers 11 units in secluded woodlands. Less than a mile further north, **BluesBerry Inn** (www.bluesberryinn.com) is family friendly and affordable log cabin motel with sourdough pancakes for breakfast and open-mic and gospel blues on some Friday and Saturday nights.

Continuing north, you'll see a cluster of businesses at **Milepost A 231**. West of the highway is the **Denali Grizzly Bear** (www.denaligrizzlybear.com) owned and operated by a pioneer Alaska family, provide cabins, a hotel, gift shop, grocery/liquor store, tour desk and campground. The Cedar Hotel at Grizzly Bear has rooms with private decks overlooking the Nenana River.

Just beyond the bridge over the river, you will enter the southern boundary of Denali National Park and reach the park road entrance at **Milepost A 237.4**. At **Milepost A 238**, just past the Nenana River bridge, begins the concentration of hotels, restaurants, gift shops, retail and recreational outfitters that serve visitors to the national park. **Cabins at Denali** www.cabinsatdenali.com), **Nenana Raft** (www.raftdenali.com) and **Era Helicopters** (www.eraflightseeing.com) are across from the Mile 238 Rest Area. At **Milepost 238.1**, drive east up the hill to the **Grande Denali Lodge** (www.denali alaska.com) with its sweeping views and fine dining at the Alpenglow Restaurant. **Denali Bluffs Hotel** (www.denalialaska.com), at **Milepost 238.4**, has the Mountaineer Grills

& Bar and espresso.

At **Milepost A 238.5**, the **Denali Princess Wilderness Lodge** complex features river view rooms, a dinner theatre, several dining choices, a tour desk, gift shop, and shuttle service. At **Milepost A 238.9**, on the west side across from the Nenana Canyon viewpoint is McKinley Chalet Resort, now owned by Holland America, offers lodging, dining and dinner theatre. Across the highway is Prospectors Pizzeria and Ale House.

Head north through the narrow canyon of the Nenana River, across the 174-foot-high Moody bridge, to **Denali RV Park & Motel** (www.denalirvparkandmotel.com) at **Milepost A 245.1**. A little farther up the highway at **Milepost A 247** is the turnoff for Otto Lake Road, where a number of lodges are located. **Denali Outdoor Center** (www.denalioutdoorcenter.com) on Otto Lake Road offers rafting adventures, camping and cabin rentals. **White Moose Lodge** (www.whitemooselodge.com), on the west side of the Parks Highway at **Milepost A 248**, is situated in a peaceful wooded location. The **Motel Nord Haven** (www.motelnordhaven.com), on the west side of the Parks Highway, provides comfortable accommodations in a gracious setting.

Just north of Healy at **Milepost A 251.1**, the Parks Highway junctions with Stampede Road (leading west) and Lignite Road (leading east). Head west to Mile 4 Stampede Road for **EarthSong Lodge** www.earthsong lodge.com); 10 log cabins and evening programs at Henry's coffee house. Head east 1.9 miles on Lignite Road for **Denali's Faith Hill Lodge** (www.faithhilllodge.com).

RVers also have a generous selection of stopping-places, starting at Cantwell to the south with **Cantwell RV Park**, located just west of the Parks–Denali highways junction at **Milepost A 210**; good fishing sites are within walking distance of this popular RV park. **Milepost 231** has RV sites and riverside tenting at the **Denali Grizzly Bear** with groceries and gifts on site. At **Milepost**

A 238.7 Parks Highway, **Denali Rainbow Village RV Park** (www.denalirv.com) is in the heart of the commercial area at the head of Nenana Canyon. **Denali RV Park and Motel** (www.denalirvparkandmotel.com) at **Milepost A 245.1** is located in the dramatic Nenana Canyon and the latter provides motel rooms in addition to RV sites. **Tatlanika Trading Co. and RV Park**, located just 39 miles north of the park at **Milepost 276**, is a wonderful Alaskan destination, with pioneer artifacts and campsites overlooking the Nenana River.

Denali Rainbow Village mall at **Milepost A 238.6** (Denali Drive), includes gift shops, a coffee house, a sandwich shop, booking offices for **Denali ATV Tours**, **Denali Jeep Excursions**, **Denali Raft Adventures** and various other businesses. A gas station and convenience store are also located here.

Interested in river rafting? Contact **Nenana Raft Adventures** (www.raft denali.com) at **Milepost A 238**; **Denali Raft Adventures** (www.denaliraft.com) at **Milepost A 238.6**; the **Denali Outdoor Center** (www.denalioutdoorcenter.com) at **Milepost A 238.9** in the Park commercial area and also on Otto Lake Road, turnoff at **Milepost A 247**. Each offers whitewater rafting, scenic floats or kayak tours.

Is flightseeing on your list? Try **Atkins Flying and Guiding Service** in Cantwell (phone 907/768-2143); **Sheldon Air Service** (www.sheldonairservice.com), Talkeetna Air Taxi (www.talkeetnaair.com) and K2 Aviation (www.flyk2.com) in Talkeetna; and **Era Helicopters** (www.eraflightseeing.com) at **Milepost 238**, offer trips with dramatic up-close views of Denali and the national park.

Would you rather see the country from an ATV? **Denali ATV Tours** (www.denali atv.com) at **Milepost A 238.6** has fully guided 2 ½- to 4-hour ATV tours .

Car problems? **Parks Highway Towing** is available for this area at 1-800-478-8697.

Campground	Spaces	Tent	RVs	Pit toilets	Flush toilets	Tap water	Fee
Igloo Creek	7	•	•				$9
Riley Creek	147	•	•	•	•	•	$22-28
Savage River	33	•	•		•	•	$22-28
Sanctuary River	7	•		•			$9
Teklanika River	53	•	•	•		•	$16
Wonder Lake	28	•		•		•	$16

sible by car, shuttle bus, on foot or by bike. These trails range from easy to strenuous and provide opportunities to experience the wildlife and grandeur of Denali. Also check the Daily Ranger Program Schedule at the visitor center for time and location of ranger-guided hikes. A board is at the entrance each day with updated information offered on it. The Explore Denali guided hiking service offers 3 additional guided hiking adventures for $35–$55. For more information contact www.denalipark resorts.com or call toll-free 1-800-276-7234.

Murie Science and Learning Center specializes in educational programs that foster stewardship for national parks. These programs include field seminars, teacher trainings and youth camps. Visitors can stop by the Center's main building and explore an array of exhibits on science and research, purchase books and enjoy comfortable seating and views. The Center is open year-round. For more information on educational programs, visit www.murieslc.org. For general inquiries, phone (907) 683-6432.

Planning park activities. How much you can see and enjoy in Denali depends a lot on your schedule. A half-day visit might include watching the 18-minute film "Heartbeats of Denali" at the Denali Visitor Center or riding the Savage River shuttle bus to Mile 15. You can get off the bus at any location, do a short hike, then reboard the Savage River shuttle bus coming out of the park, all for free. (The visitor center will have suggestions on short hikes you can take.) Mount McKinley is visible in the distance, weather permitting, from about Mile 10 on the Park Road.

If you have a full day, take a bus farther out into the park; get off and hike or just sit and enjoy the wilderness; join a ranger for Discovery Hike or Guided Walk (schedules and locations at visitor center); plan your own hike (topo maps, guide books and knowledgeable staff can assist you with trip planning).

If you have a few days, visit Wonder Lake and hike the McKinley Bar Trail or do another Discovery Hike; attend a ranger-led program; experience adventure activities outside the park such as river-rafting, flight-seeing and horseback riding.

During Denali summers when there are between 18 and 21 hours of daylight, recreational opportunities such as hiking, gold panning and other activities extend into late evening hours. Evenings are ideal for flight-seeing adventures or for an easy hike around Horseshoe Lake near the DVC. Visitors staying in the Nenana Canyon commercial area just north of the park entrance will enjoy a fun and energetic show—along with fam-

Campers can register for overnight sites at Riley Creek Mercantile.
(©Kris Valencia, staff)

ily-style dining—at the Cabin Nite Dinner Theatre, with 2 shows presented nightly at McKinley Chalet Resort.

Winter visits. The park is accessible in winter beyond Mile 3.1 Park Road by skis, snowshoes, skijor or dog sled. Winter attractions include observing wildlife, viewing the aurora borealis and seeing the park's impressive wintertime landscape. Beginning mid-February 2014, the Park Service will plow the Park Road to Mile 12 (Mountain Vista Rest Area) for a trial period of 3–5 years to enhance winter recreational opportunities

The annual Winterfest Celebration, held in late February, is a 3-day community-wide celebration offering snowshoe walks, sled dog rides, ski and skijoring events, avalanche safety awareness clinics, stargazing, winter ecology programs and more. Information available at park headquarters, phone (907) 683-9532.

Park Road Log

Distance from the junction (J) with Parks Highway is shown.

J 0 Junction with the Parks Highway (Alaska Route 3) at **Milepost A 237.4**; turn west onto the Park Road. The Park Road is paved to the Savage River bridge.

NOTE: The park was designed for scenic enjoyment, not for high speed. Maximum speed is 35 mph and lower limits are posted. There is a gravel walking trail along the Park Road to Mile 1.2.

J 0.2 Turnoff for **post office**, long-term parking and access to Riley Creek Campground (see description next milepost).

J 0.3 Turnoff for **Riley Creek Mercantile** and **Riley Creek Campground**. The Mercantile is open 7 A.M. to 11 P.M. in summer; phone (907) 683-9246. The Mercantile has shuttle bus and tour ticket sales and campground reservations and check-in; carries convenience foods and other merchandise; and has a public phone, showers, laundry facilities and firewood for sale. Make sure you get all necessary supplies before proceeding to campgrounds west of here on the Park Road. Riley Creek Campground has 146 sites along 3 gravel loops. ("Bear" loop is open year-round for camping.) Walking trails to the Mercantile and to an amphitheatre. A campground host, flush toilets

Green camper bus stops at Igloo Creek Campground on the Park Road. (©Linda Martin)

and water pumps are available in summer at Riley Creek. (During the off-season, a vault toilet is provided and water may be obtained at the Murie Science and Learning Center.)

J 0.5 Turnoff for **Wilderness Access Center (WAC)**, 0.2 mile to parking area. The WAC is the transportation hub of the park and has shuttle bus tickets, camping permits and restrooms. The WAC is open from mid-May to mid-September. Hours are 5 A.M. to 8 P.M. for bus loading, 7 A.M. to 7 P.M. for the reservation desk; phone (907) 683-9278.

Overnight hiking permits are available from the Backcountry Information Center (BIC), which is housed in the renovated trailer in the WAC parking lot. The BIC is open daily from 9 A.M. to 6 P.M. during the summer.

J 0.9 Alaska Railroad crossing. Horseshoe Lake Trailhead parking; trail length, 1.5 miles round trip, allow about 1 hour.

J 1.2 Traffic roundabout provides access to **Denali Visitor Center Complex**, the **Alaska Railroad Depot** and continuation of Park Road. *NOTE: No commercial traffic allowed without permit beyond this point.*

J 1.3 Murie Science and Learning Center dedicated to ongoing scientific park research, and science-based education programs.

J 3.5 The **Park Kennels** are located here; sled dog demonstrations are given at 10 A.M., 2 P.M. and 4 P.M.; access is via shuttle bus from Denali Visitor Center. (Check schedule at the visitor center for bus and demonstration times.) Visitors can tour the kennels before attending the formal program, which includes a demonstration and explanation of the role of sled dogs in the park. The demonstration is free but donations are accepted to help support the kennel. A fun stop and perfect for visitors of all ages.

Park Headquarters: Denali National Park and Preserve administration. Report emergencies to the rangers. *NOTE: There are no public phones west of this point.*

J 5.5 Paved viewpoint. There are numerous small turnouts along the Park Road. Mount McKinley/Denali is first visible about Mile 10 (weather permitting).

J 7.3 Paved turnout to south.

J 10.2 Paved turnout to north.

J 10.5 Paved turnout to south, wild lupine edge road (in season).

J 12.7 Mountain Vista Rest Area and Trailhead. Vault toilets, picnic tables and short interpretive trail. This will eventually tie into the Savage Alpine Trail.

J 12.8 Savage River Campground (elev. 2,780 feet); 33 campsites (8-person maximum/site); 3 group tent sites (9–20 people/site); reservations required.

J 13 Savage Cabin Interpretive Trail.

J 14.7 Bridge over the Savage River. Blacktop pavement ends. Access to river, toilet and picnic tables at east end of bridge.

J 14.8 Savage River check station. *Permit or shuttle bus ticket required beyond this point. Road travel permits for access are issued at the Denali Visitor Center only under special conditions. In early May and late September, the road may be open to all vehicles to Mile 30 (weather permitting).*

J 17.3 Primrose Ridge. Viewpoint of the Alaska Range with restrooms.

J 21.3 Hogan Creek bridge (unmarked)

J 22 Sanctuary River ranger station and **Sanctuary River Campground** (tents only). Sanctuary available by shuttle bus only. No advance reservations accepted.

J 22.1 Teklanika River bridge. Elev. 2,940. Wolves may be spotted crossing riverbed.

J 29.1 Teklanika River Campground, elev. 2,580 feet. Tent camping and RVs; no trailers or towed vehicles except for 5th wheels. There is a water filling station. Private vehicles to this point must have camping reservations and there is a 3-night minimum requirement. Look for grizzly bears on gravel bars nearby.

J 30.7 Rest area with vault toilets and viewing deck overlooking Teklanika River.

J 31.3 Bridge over Teklanika River. Wolves may be seen crossing this riverbed.

J 34.2 Igloo Creek Campground (tent camping only), vault toilets, water taken from creek. Reserve 2 days in advance only at the WAC or Riley Creek Mercantile. $9 per night.

J 37 Igloo Creek bridge. Grizzlies are often seen in the area.

J 37.2 Views of Cathedral Mountain to left, Igloo Mountain to right.

NOTE: The area within 1 mile of each side of the Park Road from **Milepost J 38.3** *to* **J 42.9** *is closed to all off-road foot travel as a special wildlife protection area. These closures vary from year to year, place to place. Watch for signs.*

J 39.1 Sable Pass (elev. 3,900 feet).

J 43.4 Bridge over East Fork Toklat River. Views of Polychrome Mountain, the Alaska Range and several glaciers are visible along the East Fork from open country south of the road. Elev. 3,061.

J 45.9 Summit of **Polychrome Pass** (elev. 3,700 feet); rest stop with toilets. The broad valley of the Toklat River is visible below to the south. Good hiking in alpine tundra above the road.

J 47 Wide valley views.

J 53.1 Bridge over the Toklat River. The Toklat and all other streams crossed by the Park Road drain into the Tanana River, a tributary of the Yukon River.

J 53.7 Toklat River Contact Station; bookstore, vault toilets, viewing telescopes.

J 58.3 Summit of **Highway Pass** (elev. 3,980 feet). This is the highest highway pass on the Park Road.

J 61 Stony Hill Lookout (elev. 4,508 feet). A good view of Mount McKinley and the Alaska Range on clear days.

J 62 Viewpoint.

J 64.5 Thorofare Pass (elev. 3,900 feet).

J 66 Eielson Visitor Center has an energy efficient design, with solar panels and microhydroelectric generator. Excellent Mount McKinley viewpoint. On clear days the north and south peaks of Mount McKinley are visible to the southwest. The impressive glacier, which drops from the mountain and spreads out over the valley floor at this point, is the Muldrow.

For several miles beyond the visitor center the road cut drops about 300 feet to the valley, paralleling the McKinley River.

J 84.6 Access road leads left, westbound, to **Wonder Lake Campground** (elev. 2,090 feet). Tents only; campground access by shuttle bus only. An excellent Denali/ Mount McKinley viewpoint.

J 85.6 Reflection Pond, a kettle lake formed by a glacier.

J 86.6 Wonder Lake ranger station.

J 87.7 Moose Creek bridge.

J 88 North Face Lodge; accommodations, meals and activities.

J 88.2 Camp Denali; accommodations, meals and activities.

J 91 KANTISHNA (pop. 110 in summer, 0 in winter; elev. 1,750 feet). Established in 1905 as a mining camp at the junction of Eureka and Moose creeks. Some of the area around Kantishna is private property and there may be active mining on area creeks in summer. Kantishna Roadhouse, consisting of a lodge, dining room and guest log cabins, comprises the mining district of Kantishna.

Private Aircraft: Kantishna airstrip, 1.3 miles northwest; elev. 1,575 feet; length 1,850 feet; gravel; unattended, no regular maintenance.

J 92 Denali Backcountry Lodge, at end of Park Road; accommodations, meals and activities.

Richardson Highway

CONNECTS: Valdez to Fairbanks, AK

Length: 366 miles   Road Surface: Paved   Season: Open all year

(See maps, pages 482-483)

4

View of Worthington Glacier
from the Richardson Highway.
(©Sharon Nault)

Major Attractions:

© Kris Valencia, staff

Trans-Alaska Pipeline, Worthington & Gulkana Glaciers, Rika's Roadhouse

Highest Summit:
Isabel Pass 3,280 ft.

The Richardson Highway extends 366 miles from Valdez on Prince William Sound to Fairbanks in the Interior of Alaska. This is a very scenic route—much of the highway is designated an Alaska Scenic Byway—with magnificent views of the Chugach Mountains and Alaska Range, and some of the best glacier viewing in Alaska, with drive-up access to Worthington Glacier. The Richardson is a wide, paved, mostly 2-lane highway in fair to good condition, with some sections of frost heaves and patched pavement. Updated road conditions are available online at 511.alaska.gov or by dialing 511.

The Richardson Highway (Alaska Route 4) junctions with 7 other highways: the Edgerton Highway (Alaska Route 10) at **Milepost V 82.5**; the Glenn Highway (Alaska Route 1) at **Milepost V 115** at Glennallen; the Tok Cut-Off (Alaska Route 1) at **Milepost V 128.5** Gakona Junction; the Denali Highway (Alaska Route 8) at **Milepost V 185.5** at Paxson; the Alaska Highway (Alaska Route 2) at **Milepost V 266**, Delta Junction (where the Richardson Highway becomes Alaska Route 2 between Delta Junction and Fairbanks); and with the Parks Highway (Alaska Route 3) and the Steese Expressway/Steese Highway (Alaska Route 2/6) at its end in Fairbanks.

In Valdez, the Richardson Highway junctions with the Alaska Marine Highway's Southcentral ferry system. Ferry service to Cordova and Whittier is available from Valdez; see the ALASKA MARINE HIGHWAY section.

The Richardson Highway offers good views of the trans-Alaska pipeline. The trans-Alaska pipeline carries oil 800 miles from Prudhoe Bay on the Arctic Ocean to the pipeline terminus at Port Valdez. There are formal viewpoints with interpretive signs at **Milepost V 216** (Denali Fault), **Milepost V 243.5**, and the Tanana River Pipeline Crossing at **Milepost V 275.4**.

The Richardson Highway was Alaska's first road, known to gold seekers in 1898 as the Valdez to Eagle trail. Gold stampeders started up the trail again in 1902, this time headed for Fairbanks, site of a big gold

Distance in miles	Delta Jct.	Fairbanks	Glennallen	Paxson	Valdez
Delta Jct.		96	151	80	270
Fairbanks	96		247	177	366
Glennallen	151	247		71	119
Paxson	80	177	71		190
Valdez	270	366	119	190	

Richardson Highway
Valdez, AK, to Delta Junction, AK

© 2014 The MILEPOST®

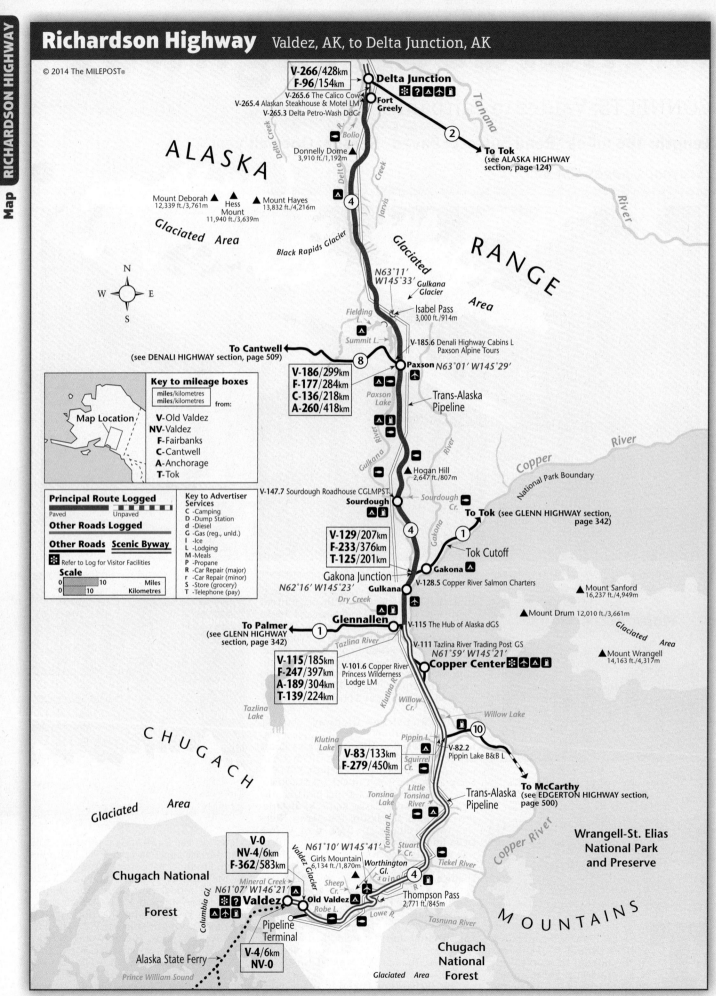

V-266/428km
F-96/154km Delta Junction

V-265.6 The Calico Cow
V-265.4 Alaskan Steakhouse & Motel LM
V-265.3 Delta Petro-Wash DdGr

Fort Greely

To Tok
(see ALASKA HIGHWAY section, page 124)

ALASKA

Bolio L.

Donnelly Dome
3,910 ft./1,192m

Mount Deborah ▲
12,339 ft./3,761m

Hess Mount ▲
11,940 ft./3,639m

Mount Hayes ▲
13,832 ft./4,216m

Glaciated   Area

Black Rapids Glacier

Glaciated

RANGE

N63°11'
W145°33'   Gulkana Glacier

Fielding L.

Isabel Pass
3,000 ft./914m

Area

Summit L.

To Cantwell
(see DENALI HIGHWAY section, page 509)

V-185.6 Denali Highway Cabins L
Paxson Alpine Tours

Paxson   N63°01' W145°29'

V-186/299km
F-177/284km
C-136/218km
A-260/418km

Paxson Lake

Trans-Alaska Pipeline

Key to mileage boxes
miles/kilometres
miles/kilometres   from:

V-Old Valdez
NV-Valdez
F-Fairbanks
C-Cantwell
A-Anchorage
T-Tok

Map Location

Hogan Hill ▲
2,647 ft./807m

Copper

River

National Park Boundary

Principal Route Logged
Paved   Unpaved

Other Roads Logged

Other Roads   Scenic Byway

✻ Refer to Log for Visitor Facilities

Key to Advertiser Services
C -Camping
D -Dump Station
d -Diesel
G -Gas (reg., unld.)
I -Ice
L -Lodging
M -Meals
P -Propane
R -Car Repair (major)
r -Car Repair (minor)
S -Store (grocery)
T -Telephone (pay)

V-147.7 Sourdough Roadhouse CGLMPST

Sourdough

Sourdough Cr.

To Tok (see GLENN HIGHWAY section, page 342)

V-129/207km
F-233/376km
T-125/201km

Tok Cutoff

Scale
0   10   Miles
0   10   Kilometres

Gakona Junction
N62°16' W145°23'

Gakona

V-128.5 Copper River Salmon Charters

Gulkana

Dry Creek

Mount Sanford ▲
16,237 ft./4,949m

Mount Drum ▲ 12,010 ft./3,661m

To Palmer
(see GLENN HIGHWAY section, page 342)

Glennallen

V-115 The Hub of Alaska dGS

V-111 Tazlina River Trading Post GS
N61°59' W145°21'

Tazlina River

V-115/185km
F-247/397km
A-189/304km
T-139/224km

V-101.6 Copper River Princess Wilderness Lodge LM

Copper Center

Mount Wrangell ▲
14,163 ft./4,317m

Glaciated   Area

Tazlina Lake

Klutina R.

Willow Cr.

Willow Lake

Klutina Lake

Pippin L.

V-83/133km
F-279/450km

Squirrel Cr.

V-82.2 Pippin Lake B&B L

To McCarthy
(see EDGERTON HIGHWAY section, page 500)

CHUGACH

Tonsina Lake

Little Tonsina River

Trans-Alaska Pipeline

Area

Glaciated

Tonsina R.

Wrangell-St. Elias National Park and Preserve

V-0
NV-4/6km
F-362/583km

Girls Mountain
6,134 ft./1,870m
N61°10' W145°41'

Stuart Cr.

Tiekel River

Copper River

Chugach National Forest

Mineral Creek

Worthington Gl.

Valdez Glacier

N61°07' W146°21'

Sheep Cr.

Thompson Pass
2,771 ft./845m

Old Valdez

Valdez

Robe L.

Lowe R.

Tasnuna River

MOUNTAINS

Pipeline Terminal

Alaska State Ferry

V-4/6km
NV-0

Prince William Sound

Chugach National Forest

Glaciated   Area

Richardson Highway   Delta Junction, AK to Fairbanks, AK

© 2014 The MILEPOST®

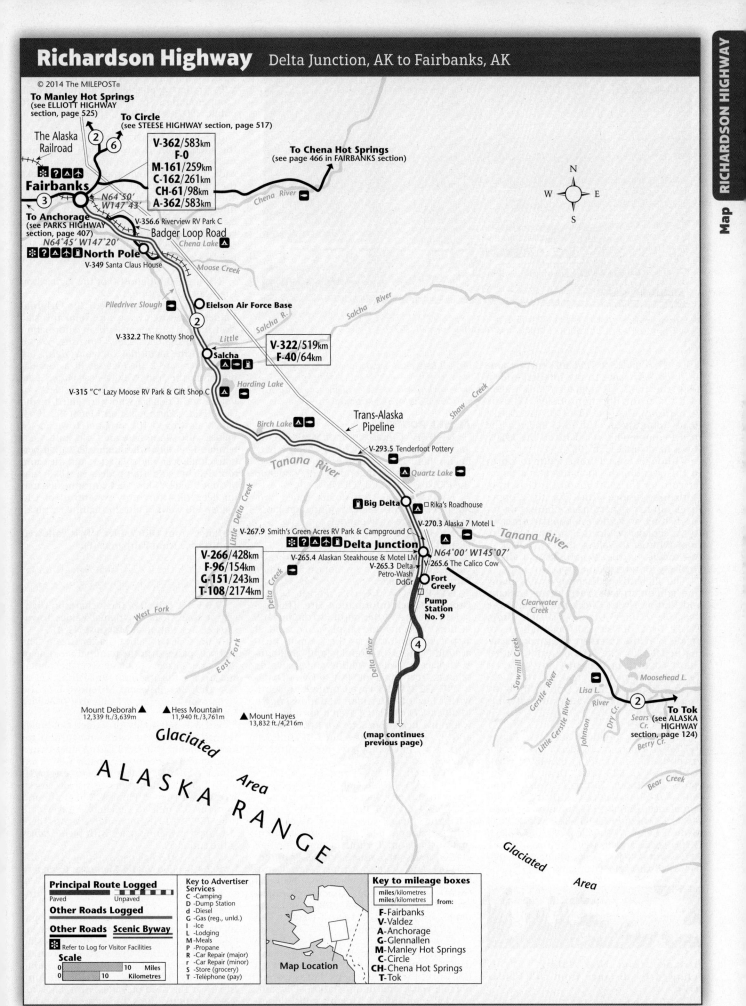

To Manley Hot Springs
(see ELLIOTT HIGHWAY
section, page 525)

To Circle
(see STEESE HIGHWAY section, page 517)

The Alaska
Railroad

To Chena Hot Springs
(see page 466 in FAIRBANKS section)

V-362/583km
F-0
M-161/259km
C-162/261km
CH-61/98km
A-362/583km

Fairbanks

N64°50'
W147°43'

Chena River

To Anchorage
(see PARKS HIGHWAY
section, page 407)

V-356.6 Riverview RV Park C

Badger Loop Road

N64°45' W147°20'

Chena Lake

North Pole

Moose Creek

V-349 Santa Claus House

Piledriver Slough

Eielson Air Force Base

Salcha R.

Little

Salcha River

Shaw Creek

V-332.2 The Knotty Shop

V-322/519km
F-40/64km

Salcha

V-315 "C" Lazy Moose RV Park & Gift Shop C

Harding Lake

**Trans-Alaska
Pipeline**

Birch Lake

V-293.5 Tenderfoot Pottery

Tanana River

Quartz Lake

Little Delta Creek

Big Delta

Rika's Roadhouse

V-270.3 Alaska 7 Motel L

Tanana River

V-267.9 Smith's Green Acres RV Park & Campground C

Delta Junction

V-266/428km
F-96/154km
G-151/243km
T-108/2174km

V-265.4 Alaskan Steakhouse & Motel LM
V-265.3 Delta-
Petro-Wash
DdGr

N64°00' W145°07'

V-265.6 The Calico Cow

Clearwater
Creek

**Fort
Greely**

**Pump
Station
No. 9**

Delta Creek

West Fork

Delta River

East Fork

Sawmill Creek

Gerstle River

Little Gerstle River

Johnson River

Dry Cr.

Lisa L.

Moosehead L.

2

To Tok
(see ALASKA
HIGHWAY
section, page 124)

Sears
Cr.

Berry Cr.

Bear Creek

**(map continues
previous page)**

Mount Deborah ▲
12,339 ft./3,639m

▲ Hess Mountain
11,940 ft./3,761m

▲ Mount Hayes
13,832 ft./4,216m

Glaciated   Area

A L A S K A   R A N G E

*Glaciated
Area*

Principal Route Logged

Paved   Unpaved

Other Roads Logged

Other Roads   Scenic Byway

❄ Refer to Log for Visitor Facilities

Scale

0   10   Miles
0   10   Kilometres

**Key to Advertiser
Services**
C -Camping
D -Dump Station
d -Diesel
G -Gas (reg., unld.)
I -Ice
L -Lodging
M -Meals
P -Propane
R -Car Repair (major)
r -Car Repair (minor)
S -Store (grocery)
T -Telephone (pay)

Map Location

Key to mileage boxes

miles/kilometres
miles/kilometres   from:

F-Fairbanks
V-Valdez
A-Anchorage
G-Glennallen
M-Manley Hot Springs
C-Circle
CH-Chena Hot Springs
T-Tok

View from Valdez public dock of pipeline terminal at end of Dayville Road. (©Sharon Nault)

strike. The Valdez to Fairbanks trail became an important route to the Interior, and in 1910 the trail was upgraded to a wagon road under the direction of Gen. Wilds P. Richardson, first president of the Alaska Road Commission. The ARC updated the road to automobile standards in the 1920s. It was hard-surfaced in 1957.

Although logged from south to north in this section, the Richardson is a popular corridor for southbound travelers from Fairbanks, headed either for the Copper River dip-net fishery near Chitina, or for the fishing at Valdez. A popular itinerary for Anchorage residents is to take the ferry from Whittier to Valdez, then drive back to Anchorage via the Richardson and Glenn Highway (or reverse itinerary).

The Richardson Highway passes many fine salmon streams, such as the Gulkana and Klutina rivers. Check the *Copper Basin Roadside Fishing Guide*, available from Alaska Dept. of Fish and Game offices, for details. On the Internet, check sport fishing updates for the Interior region (either Upper Copper/Upper Susitna Area or Lower Tanana management areas for the Richardson Highway) under Information By Area at www.sf.adfg.state.ak.us/statewide /sf_home.cfm.

Emergency medical services: Phone 911 for all emergencies. Alaska State Troopers posts in Valdez, (907) 835-4307; Glennallen, (907) 822-3263; Delta Junction, (907) 895-4800; Fairbanks/North Pole, (907) 451-5100. Valdez Fire Dept./EMS and ambulance, phone 911; Providence Valdez Medical Center, (907) 835-2249; Cross Road Medical Center Glennallen, (907) 822-3263; Delta Rescue Squad, Delta Junction, phone 911; North Pole Fire Dept., phone (907) 488-0444; Fairbanks Fire Dept., phone 911.

Richardson Highway Log

Distance from New Valdez (NV) is followed by distance from Old Valdez (OV).

Mileposts on the Richardson Highway were erected before the 1964 Good Friday earthquake and therefore begin 4 miles from present-day downtown Valdez near the Old Valdez townsite (destroyed during the earthquake).

ALASKA ROUTE 4

NV 0 OV 4 Intersection of Meals Avenue and the Richardson Highway. A bike path begins here and continues to the end of Dayville Road. See description of Valdez in the PRINCE WILLIAM SOUND section.

NV 0.4 OV 3.6 Paved double-ended turnout to north with Valdez information kiosk, maps, brochures, pay phones.

NV 0.5 OV 3.5 DOT/PF Southcentral District Office.

Distance marker northbound indicates Glennallen 117 miles, Anchorage 306 miles, Fairbanks 355 miles.

NV 0.9 OV 3.1 U.S. Forest Service **Crooked Creek Information Site.** This spacious structure to the north, accommodates visitors, exhibits and displays. Located at a spot known locally as the "salmon turnaround," this is a popular and well-situated place to watch wildlife and spawning salmon. Open Memorial Day to Labor Day.

NV 1.2 OV 2.8 Paved turnout to south with view of intertidal wetlands known locally as "Duck Flats." Watch for migrating waterfowl here from late April to mid-May and in October. Nesting birds in summer. This is a game sanctuary; no shooting is allowed.

NV 1.9 OV 2.1 Paved turnout to south.

NV 2.1 OV 1.9 Mineral Creek Loop Road; access to Port of Valdez container terminal.

NV 3.4 OV 0.6 Junction with Airport Road and Mineral Creek Loop; **Acres Kwik Trip** gas station, deli, market and laundromat at junction. Turnoff to north for heli glacier tours (0.6 mile); **Valdez Pioneer Airport** and Valdez Airport Man Camp (0.9 mile); hardware store, saloon, National Guard Armory, **Valdez Glacier (Kimberlin's) Campground** (2.3 miles); shooting range (2.6 miles); and **Valdez Glacier** (3.6 miles). Descriptions follow.

Valdez Glacier Campground has 87 standard sites and 21 RV pads with 20/30 amp hookups. Facility provides hot showers, potable water and dump station. Pleasant, wooded campground. Firepits, grills, dump-

sters, covered picnic areas and tent camping. Firewood available. Campground host. Tent sites $15, for military $10; RV hookups $35, military $30. RVs with no hookups $20. Trailers available for military rental. Campground run by Fort Greely but open to public. (907) 803-3695. *CAUTION: Beware of bears, but watch for eagles!*

For Valdez Glacier, drive 3.6 miles from the Richardson Highway until you come to the end of the pavement. Continue on wide, but often rough gravel road and take the right fork; gravel parking area next to grassy area with picnic tables, trash cans and interpretive signs at glacial lake in the glacial moraine. Interesting views of icebergs in lake and the tops of 2 glaciers in the mountains to the west. The Valdez glacier is across the lake and hidden behind a corner to the south.

NV 4 OV 0 Milepost 0 of the Richardson Highway (log continues).

Turnoff to south (signed) for **Original Valdez Townsite** as you turn onto this side road there is a turnout with an information sign about the Old Valdez Townsite. Watch for townsite memorial on your right, 0.4 mile. There are 2 plaques set in a foundation from the "old" Valdez Post Office. One plaque lists the names of those residents of Valdez and Chenega who were killed in the Good Friday Earthquake on March 27, 1964, which destroyed the original townsite of Valdez. Also along here are Gold Rush Centennial signs about the stampeders, their perilous climb over Valdez Glacier, and the camp founded by gold stampeders in 1897 that became Valdez. Side road continues (watch for deep ruts) to empty waterfront of Old Valdez and views of pipeline marine terminal.

Distance from Old Valdez (V) is followed by distance from Fairbanks (F).
Physical mileposts begin northbound showing distance from Old Valdez. (Southbound travelers note: Physical mileposts end here; it is 4 miles to downtown Valdez.)

V 0 F 362 Mile 0 of the Richardson Highway at access road to Original Valdez Townsite (see description at **Milepost NV 4**).

V 0.9 F 361.1 Valdez Glacier stream. The highway passes over the terminal moraine of the Valdez Glacier, bridging several channels and streams flowing from the melting ice.

V 1 F 361 Physical Milepost 1 of the Richardson Highway, 0.1 mile east of Valdez Glacier bridge.

V 1.6 F 360.4 City of Valdez Goldfields Softball Complex to south and turnoff for local swimming hole and Early Valdez Cemetery (signed). For cemetery, follow well-maintained Walter Day Memorial Drive (gravel) south 0.6 mile; turn right on narrow, rocky access road (signed Pioneer Cemetery) and continue 0.2 mile to cemetery. Graves date from 1897 to 1916; interpretive signs. There is a firepit gathering place with picnic tables at the entrance.

V 1.7 F 360.3 Ball parks and playground.

V 2.4 F 359.6 Valdez Memorial Cemetery to south along a loop road.

V 2.6 F 359.4 Double-ended paved turnout to south.

V 2.8 F 359.2 Turnoff to south for popular **Dayville Road**, an excellent option for RVers. This is a wide, paved, improved side road (with bike trail) that leads to shoreside camping, picnicking, fishing and scenic views along Port Valdez, the 13-mile-long estuary at the head of Valdez Arm. Look for seals, sea lions, birds and bears (especially

when salmon are spawning). Berry picking in season; *watch for bears.*

Dayville Road is open to the public to Mile 5.4, where a guardhouse restricts public access to the Alyeska Pipeline Terminal complex. *NOTE: There is NO public access to the marine terminal and there are NO public tours of the terminal.* The Solomon Gulch Fish Hatchery and large parking area are located at Mile 3.8. There are some dramatic views and photo opportunities from the bridge here of the Solomon Gulch Falls and dam site (Copper Valley Electric co-generation project). Walkways at the fish hatchery go to a viewing platform and along the ponds and hatchery building, more information signs. Mile 4.5 marks the beginning of camping areas (with water, dumpsters, outhouses, pay phone). There is a wonderful array of wildlife viewing opportunities, steps away from your campsite. Camping and day-use fees charged. (Main campground registration area is at Mile 5.1.)

At Mile 4.7 is the head of the Solomon Gulch hiking trail. Trail begins with steep hill to the east of the road. Pink and silver salmon fishing from shore in season at **Allison Point**. Handicapped fishing platform is located at Mile 4.8.

V 3 F 359 Weigh station (closed).

V 3.3 F 358.7 Paved side road leads 0.5 mile north to **Robe Lake**; private floatplane dock and small public recreation area with toilet, parking and launch area at lake. Robe Lake is popular with jet skiers. *Watch for bears!*

V 4 F 358 Long gravel turnout to southeast along **Lowe River**; Dolly Varden, red salmon (fly-fishing only, mid-May to mid-June).

V 6 F 356 Turnoff to north for Robe Lake.
V 8 F 354 Watch for horses on the road.
V 9.3 F 352.7 Noted as mail carrier Emil Wegner Memorial Corridor.
V 11.6 F 350.4 Paved turnout to southeast, with road closure bars.
V 11.8 F 350.2 Turnoff to west for Pack Trail of 1899. Paved 0.7-mile loop road to access trail. Loop road leads 0.4 mile to trailhead; parking best at north end of loop at **Milepost V 12.4.**
V 12.8 F 349.2 Lowe River emerges from **Keystone Canyon.** The canyon was named by Captain William Ralph Abercrombie, presumably for Pennsylvania, the Keystone State. In 1884, Abercrombie had been selected to lead an exploring expedition up the Copper River to the Yukon River. Although unsuccessful in his attempt to ascend the Copper River, he did survey the Copper River Delta and a route to Port Valdez. He returned in 1898 and again in 1899, carrying out further explorations of the area (see **Milepost V 13.7**). The Lowe River is named for Lt. Percival Lowe, a member of his expedition. Glacier melt imparts the slate-gray color to the river.
V 13.5 F 348.5 **Horsetail Falls**; large paved turnout to west.
CAUTION: Watch for pedestrians.
V 13.9 F 348.1 Large paved turnout to west across from **Bridal Veil Falls.**
This is also the trailhead for the **Valdez Goat Trail** (begins near the south end of turnout to west); hike to scenic overlook (¼ mile), trail end 2 miles. This is a restored section of the Trans-Alaska Military Packtrain Trail through Keystone Canyon that led to the first glacier-free land route

Beautiful Blueberry Lake in the state recreation site in Thompson Pass area.
(©Sharon Nault)

from Valdez to the Interior. The first gold rush trail led over the treacherous Valdez Glacier, then northeast to Eagle and the Yukon River route to the Klondike goldfields. Captain W.R. Abercrombie and the U.S. Army Copper River Exploring Expedition of 1899 rerouted the trail through Keystone Canyon and over Thompson Pass, thus avoiding the glacier. As the Klondike Gold Rush waned, the military kept the trail open to connect Fort Liscum in Valdez with Fort Egbert in Eagle. In 1903, the U.S. Army Signal Corps laid the trans-Alaska telegraph line along this route.
V 14.9 F 347.1 Lowe River Bridge No. 1 (first of 3 bridges northbound); turnout to east at north end of bridge. View of Huddleston Falls.
V 15 F 347 Large paved turnout at **Old Railroad Tunnel** with sign that reads:
"This tunnel was hand cut into the solid rock of Keystone Canyon and is all that is left of the railroad era when 9 companies fought to take advantage of the short route from the coast to the copper country. However, a feud interrupted progress. A gun battle was fought and the tunnel was never finished. The Iron Trail by Rex Beach describes these events and this area."
NOTE: You can walk into this tunnel.
V 15.3 F 346.7 Turnout to east at south end of Lowe River Bridge No. 2. Horse and Sled Trail (sign) reads:
"On the far side, just above the water, are the remains of the old sled trail used in the early days. It was cut out of the rock, just wide enough for 2 horses abreast. 200 feet above can be seen the old goat trail. This road was used until 1945."
V 15.4 F 346.6 Two bridges make up what is called Lowe River Bridges No. 2, built in 1980, replaced previous highway route through the long tunnel visible beside highway.
V 15.6 F 346.4 Sloping entrance to informal gravel turnout to east.
V 15.7 F 346.3 Leaving Keystone Canyon northbound, entering Keystone Canyon southbound.
V 16 F 346 Turnout down off the road to rock quarry to east.
V 16.3 F 345.7 Lowe River Bridge No. 3.
V 16.6 F 345.4 Double ended gravel turnout to east.
V 18.1 F 343.9 Large paved turnouts both sides of highway; *emergency phone* and

trailhead at turnout to west. Good stop for northbound travelers before heading up the long grade to Thompson Pass.
V 18.6 F 343.4 Sheep Creek bridge.
V 18.8 F 343.2 *Gates here for road closure. Truck lane begins northbound as highway climbs next 7.5 miles to Thompson Pass; few turnouts, steep grade. Narrow outside lane northbound, hemmed in by guardrail, makes for a really tight squeeze when big rigs are passing. Large vehicles USE CAUTION when passing.*
This was one of the most difficult sections of pipeline construction, requiring heavy blasting of solid rock for several miles. The pipeline runs underground beside the road.
V 18.9 F 343.1 Paved turnout to east at Heiden View. Beautiful mountain view. Do not block pipeline road access.
V 21.5 F 340.5 Large paved turnout to east with scenic view.
V 22.3 F 339.7 Snow poles along highway guide snow plows in winter.
V 23 F 339 Large wide gravel parking area east side of highway.
V 23.4 F 338.6 Paved turnout to east. Photo-op of mountains and glaciers.
V 23.5 F 338.5 Access to **Thompson Lake** (formerly Summit Lake No. 1) to west makes a nice stop; parking area and lake access, grayling and rainbow fishing.

V 23.7 F 338.3 Paved turnout to east.
V 24.1 F 337.9 Paved road leads south to **Blueberry Lake State Recreation Site**; 15 campsites (2 lakeshore area with covered picnic tables), toilets, firepits, water, camping fee $15/night, campground host. Firewood is sometimes available. Tucked into an alpine setting between tall mountain peaks, this is one of Alaska's most beautifully situated campgrounds. Access trail beside campsite #9 for a hike up above the brush to alpine terrain; beautiful 360° views. Berry picking in season. **Blueberry Lake** offers grayling and rainbow fishing.

V 24.4 F 337.6 Large paved turnout to west.
V 25.5 F 336.5 Large paved turnout to west. Rough access road out to promontory; terrific view of Lowe River far in the valley below. Great place to stretch your legs and

View of the Chugach Range near Thompson Pass. (©Sharon Nault)

get top-of-the-world views. Bare-bone peaks of the Chugach Mountains rise above the highway. Thompson Pass ahead northbound.

Marshall Pass is to the east. During the winter of 1907, the A.J. Meals Co. freighted the 70-ton river steamer *Chitina* (or *Chittyna*) from Valdez over Marshall Pass and down the Tasnuna River to the Copper River. The ship was moved piece by piece on huge horse-drawn freight sleds and assembled at the mouth of the Tasnuna. The 110-foot-long ship navigated 170 miles of the Copper and Chitina rivers above Abercrombie Rapids, moving supplies for construction crews of the Copper River & Northwestern Railway. Much of the equipment for the Kennicott mill and tram was moved by this vessel.

V 25.7 F 336.3 Excellent 2-level view parking area to south. Lower level has very steep entrance. You can walk down to the lower level for a great view of the mountains and lower river valley far below. Painters often come here to paint this scene.

V 25.9 F 336.1 Thompson Pass (elev. 2,678 feet) at head of Ptarmigan Creek. Beautiful alpine area.

End northbound truck lane.

Begin 7.5-mile steep descent southbound.

Thompson Pass, named by Captain Abercrombie in 1899, is comparatively low elevation but above timberline. Wildflower lovers will be well repaid for rambling over the rocks in this area: tiny alpine plants may be in bloom, such as Aleutian heather and mountain harebell.

The National Climatic Center credits snowfall extremes in Alaska to the Thompson Pass station, where record measurements are: 974.5 inches for season (1952–53); 298 inches for month (February 1953); and 62 inches for 24-hour period (December 1955). Snow poles along the highway mark the road edge for snow plows.

Private Aircraft: Thompson Pass airstrip; elev. 2,080 feet; length 2,500 feet; turf, gravel; unattended.

V 26 F 336 Paved turnout to east. Good views of 27 Mile Glacier to north.

Slow for damaged road.

V 26.8 F 335.2 Thompson Pass highway maintenance station.

V 27.5 F 334.5 Entrance to parking area to east overlooking **Worthington Lake**; rainbow fishing.

V 28.2 F 333.8 Parking to north by stream.

V 29 F 333 Worthington Glacier State Recreation Site. The entrance to the glacier is about 0.3 miles before physical milepost 29. Paved access road leads 0.4 mile up hill to large paved parking area (pull-through sites for large vehicles), shelter, viewing telescopes, interpretive displays, restrooms. (Pay phone at a rest area with information boards, located near highway entrance.) No camping. Pets on leash. Gold Rush Centennial sign about Thompson Pass at bottom of hill near highway.

According to state park rangers, this is the most visited site in the Copper River Basin. Views of Worthington Glacier, which heads on Girls Mountain (elev. 6,134 feet), from the parking area and from paved path which leads to glacier viewpoints with benches and interpretive signs. This is a National Natural Landmark. *WARNING: Do not approach any glacier from below due to falling ice. Do not walk on any glacier unless you are experienced in and equipped for crevasse rescues. Trail closures may occur due to unstable glacial ice.*

V 29.1 F 332.9 Paved parking area to west; good photo-op of Worthington Glacier. Great blueberry picking in the fall.

V 29.4 F 332.6 Gravel parking to north.

V 30.1 F 331.9 Large paved turnouts both sides of highway. Excellent spot for photos of Worthington Glacier.

V 32.4 F 329.6 Highway parallels Tsaina River northbound. Long climb up to Thompson Pass for southbound motorists; views of Worthington Glacier.

V 34.5 F 327.5 Double-ended turnout to west. Tsaina Lodge to east.

The mountains in this area are the site for many winter activities like extreme skiing. Helicopter businesses are offering back-country adventures and tours.

V 37 F 325 Entering BLM public lands northbound, leaving BLM public lands southbound.

V 37.3 F 324.7 Tsaina River bridge at scenic Devil's Elbow. Large paved turnout to east at south end of bridge. Deep gorge visible from each side of bridge.

V 37.8 F 324.2 *Begin avalanche area northbound: Do not stop (in winter).*

V 40.5 F 322.5 Large turnout to west at crest of hill with beautiful mountain views. *Highway descends next 1.5 miles northbound.*

V 42.1 F 319.9 Small gravel turnout to west.

V 43 F 319 Large double-ended turnout to west, sheltered by brush.

V 45.5 F 316.5 Stuart Creek bridge. Paved, large turnout north end of bridge.

V 45.6 F 316.4 Lodge and tavern, heli-camp for winter sports (usually open Feb.–March for heli-tours).

V 45.7 F 316.3 Welcome to Copper River Valley (northbound sign).

V 46.8 F 315.2 Tiekel River bridge; small Dolly Varden. Small turnout to west at north end of bridge.

V 47.8 F 314.2 Entrance to large rest area to west. Drive to end of access road for loop road through treed area near Tiekel River with outhouses, 4 covered picnic sites with room to pitch tents under and rock fire rings, dumpsters but no water. Historical sign about Mount Billy Mitchell. View of Mount Billy Mitchell to south. There is an old log cabin near this entrance.

Lieutenant William "Billy" Mitchell (1879-1936) was a member of the U.S. Army Signal Corps, which in 1903 was completing the trans-Alaska telegraph line (Washington–Alaska Military Cable and Telegraph System) to connect all the military posts in Alaska. The 2,000 miles/3,200 km of telegraph wire included the main line between Fort Egbert in Eagle and Fort Liscum at Valdez, and a branch line down the Tanana River to Fort Gibson and on to Fort St. Michael near the mouth of the Yukon and then to Nome. Mitchell was years later to become the "prophet of American military air power" with his idea that "He who holds Alaska will hold the world as far as defending the North American continent." He received the Medal of Honor posthumously for his foresight.

V 50.6 F 311.4 Bridge over Tiekel River. Look for lupine in June, dwarf fireweed along the Tiekel River in July. Dead spruce trees in this area were killed by beetles. The old Tiekel River Lodge was northeast of here. There are private cabins in this area.

V 54.1 F 307.9 Large, paved turnout to east.

V 54.5 F 307.5 *CAUTION: Watch for moose.*

V 55.1 F 306.9 Large paved turnout to east.

V 56 F 306 Lodge with camping and gas.

V 56.2 F 305.8 Large paved turnout to east alongside Tiekel River.

V 57 F 305 Southbound sign identifying the Memorial Corridor named for long-time mail carrier, Emil Wegner. Watch for beaver dams.

V 58 F 304 Wagon Point Creek culvert.

V 60 F 302 Paved turnout to east; access to Tiekel River. Highway parallels **Tiekel River**, visible to the east southbound; fishing for small Dolly Varden is especially fun with a fly rod.

V 61.6 F 300.4 This area used to be cov-

ered with moose ponds that were also home to numerous beavers. Heavy rainfall in 2009 flooded the area. Placer mining to the east.

V 62 F 300 Ernestine Station (DOT/PF highway maintenance) to west.

V 62.2 F 299.8 Entering Upper Copper/Upper Susitna Sport Fish Management Area northbound.

V 63.6 F 298.4 Views of pipeline from highway; no turnouts.

V 64.6 F 297.4 Pump Station 12 to east; no public access. Begun in March 1975 and completed in 1977, pipeline construction employed some 30,000 workers at its peak and was the largest and most expensive privately funded construction project ever undertaken. These boom years, known as "pipeline days," also brought lasting changes to Alaska's landscape and economy.

Today, the pipeline is owned and operated by Alyeska Pipeline Service Company, a consortium of oil companies that includes BP, ConocoPhillips, Exxon/Mobil, Unocal, and Koch Alaska.

The 48-inch-diameter pipeline winds through 3 major mountain ranges, with its highest point (4,739 feet) at Atigun Pass in the Brooks Range, 170 miles south of Prudhoe Bay. Along the Richardson Highway, the pipeline crests the Alaska Range at 3,420 foot at Isabel Pass, before descending into the Copper River basin. It crosses the Chugach Mountains at Thompson Pass and descends through the Keystone Canyon to Valdez, where it is fed by gravity into tanks or directly into waiting oil tankers at the marine terminal.

V 65 F 297 Little Tonsina River; fishing for Dolly Varden and Arctic grayling (bait and treble hooks allowed). Closed to king salmon fishing.

V 65.1 F 296.9 Unmarked road to the west just after Milepost 65 for northbound traffic. Former Little Tonsina River State Recreation Site to west on short loop road through pleasant wooded area; no services or facilities. Pull-in parking areas, good picnic spots. Day-use only. Good berry picking in fall.

V 65.3 F 296.7 For weather information, turn to 790 on your radio.

V 70 F 292 *CAUTION: Slow for rough road.*

V 71 F 291 Double-ended turnout to east.

V 72 F 290 Double-ended paved turnout to west with view across valley of trans-Alaska pipeline following base of mountains.

Leaving BLM public lands northbound. Entering BLM public lands southbound.

CAUTION: Slow for expansion joints and frost heaves in highway north and southbound.

V 73 F 289 Tonsina Controlled Use Area (sign): Closed to motorized vehicles and pack animals, July 26 to Sept. 30.

V 74.4 F 287.6 Double-ended dirt turnout to west. According to our ADF&G source: "There is a side pipeline access road here, just past the turnout that allows access to the Little Tonsina River and its confluence with the Tonsina River. There is a great campsite along the river and some good fishing for Dolly Varden, grayling, red salmon and silver salmon (mid-Sept.–Oct.) Fishing for king salmon is prohibited."

V 76.3 F 285.7 Watch for moose in pond to west.

V 79 F 283 Tonsina River Lodge to east. Distance marker northbound shows Copper Center 21 miles, Glennallen 36 miles.

V 79.2 F 282.8 Bridge over Tonsina River, which rises in Tonsina Lake to the southwest.

V 79.3 F 282.7 Gravel turnout to east.

V 79.5 F 282.5 Squirrel Creek State Recreation Site to east at south end of Squirrel Creek bridge; 27 treed, pleasant, shaded campsites with tables and firepits on the bank of Squirrel Creek and near a pond. Some pull-through spaces; camping fee $12/night; bear-proof trash cans, outhouses, potable water and firepits. Pets on leash. Day-use fee $7. Close to Tonsina River Lodge and the Tonsina River. Turnaround for big rigs at the end of campground road. Fishing for rainbow and grayling in pond, and grayling in creek. Fishing for reds and king salmon in Tonsina River (bait and treble hooks allowed). Open May 15–Sept. 30.

V 79.7 F 282.3 Highway climbs Tonsina Hill northbound. *Begin 1.2-mile passing lane and 8 percent upgrade northbound. Watch for frost heaves. Turnout to east at top of hill*

V 81 F 281 *End passing lane northbound. Begin 8 percent downgrade southbound.*

V 82.2 F 279.8 Turnoff for **Pippin Lake Bed and Breakfast.**

Pippin Lake Bed and Breakfast. See display ad this page.

V 82.5 F 279.5 Junction with the Edgerton Highway to Chitina (33 miles) and end of McCarthy Road (92 miles) with access to Kennicott/McCarthy.

Junction with the Edgerton Highway (Alaska Route 10) east to Chitina and McCarthy Road to Kennicott/McCarthy area. See EDGERTON HIGHWAY section on page 500 for log of that route.

V 82.6 F 279.4 Gift shop to west with snacks, fishing licenses and other items.

V 83 F 279 Paved turnout to west; public fishing access to **Pippin Lake.** Stocked with rainbow.

V 83.7 F 278.3 Highway descends hill next 3 miles northbound.

V 87.7 F 274.3 Large, paved double-ended turnout to east at scenic **Willow Lake Viewpoint**; viewing platforms with telescopes; information sign identifies peaks in the Wrangell Mountains to east. (There is no public access to this lake and it is barren of fish.)

On a clear day this lake mirrors the Wrangell Mountains to the east, which lie within Wrangell–St. Elias National Park and Preserve. From left to right they are: Mount Drum, with the smaller Snider Peak on its south flank; Mount Sanford; Mount Wrangell, with the pyramid-shaped Mount Zanetti on its northwest flank; and Mount Blackburn. Gold Rush Centennial interpretive sign at turnout about copper mining in the Wrangell Mountains (excerpt follows):

"In 1899, Chief Nicolai of the lower Copper River people directed several prospectors to copper deposits in the Chitina River valley. This set off a copper rush. The next year on Bonanza Ridge, two prospectors

stumbled across the highest-grade commercial copper deposit ever found. Entrepreneur and mining engineer Stephen Birch quickly purchased the Bonanza Ridge claims. Birch formed the Alaska Syndicate with investments from J.P. Morgan and Daniel Guggenheim to extract, process and sell the copper. To get the ore out of Alaska, the Syndicate (later Kennecott Copper Co.) built a $23 million railroad and operated a steamship company. Between 1911 and 1938, the company made $100 million in profits by processing 4.6 million tons of copper ore."

V 90.8 F 271.2 Paved turnout to west by Willow Creek culvert.

V 91 F 271 Old Edgerton Highway access to Kenny Lake, east.

V 96 F 265 *Slow for rough patches and frost heaves.*

V 100.2 F 261.8 South junction with **Old Richardson Highway** loop road through Copper Center; well worth a stop. Access to camping, fishing charters and groceries and gas at 0.5 mile. From 0.5 mile, take the loop road 0.4 miles to Copper Center Lodge (under construction), restaurant and museum.

See "Copper Center Loop" beginning on page 489 for description of Copper Center and attractions along the Old Richardson Highway.

V 100.6 F 261.4 Gravel side road (Slemsec Way) east to private RV park.

V 101.1 F 260.9 Klutina River bridge. Access to river to the southeast of bridge, *poor turnaround area for big rigs.* Excellent fishing in the **Klutina River** for red and king salmon. Also grayling and Dolly Varden. Kings to 65 lbs., average 35-45 lbs.; from June 15 to Aug. 10, peaking in mid-July. Reds' peak run is from late June to early August. Check sportfishing conditions online under Information By Area at www.sf.adfg.state.ak.us/statewide/sf_home.cfm; go to Interior region, Upper Copper/Upper Susitna Management Area. Be familiar with current fishing regulations and closures. *NOTE: Most riverfront property is privately owned. Inquire locally about river access.*

©Kris Valencia, staff

V 101.6 F 260.4 Turnoff to west for **Copper River Princess Wilderness Lodge**; drive 0.9 mile uphill and turn left at Princess sign, just before end of pavement. For access to Klutina Lake Road, continue straight on gravel to T junction, then turn left 1.4 miles

from highway. Turn east off highway to access Old Richardson Highway and Copper Center via Brenwick–Craig Road.

Good views of Copper Center, the Klutina River and the Wrangell Mountains from the Copper River Princess Wilderness Lodge. The casual visitor can park at the Princess Lodge and walk out along Klutina Lake Road for bird's-eye views of the Klutina River.

Klutina Lake Road is a 24-mile-long narrow dirt road to Klutina Lake. Visitors planning to drive Klutina Lake Road can contact the BLM office and/or Ahtna Inc. in Glennallen for current road conditions. Primitive campsites along the road with fee boxes are maintained by the Copper River Native Corp.

Copper River Princess Wilderness Lodge. See display ad on page 489.

V 106.1 F 255.9 North junction with Old Richardson Highway loop road 5.6 miles through Copper Center (for fastest access to main business area, turn off at **Milepost V 100.2**, 5 miles south of here). Copper Center is well worth a stop. From this junction it is 1.9 miles to the Copper River Native Association's Headquarters; 4.5 miles to the post office; and 4.7 miles to the loop road that takes you to the George I. Ashby Museum adjacent the **Copper Center Lodge**. Access to Klutina River charter services and food, gas and lodging in Copper Center.

See "Copper Center Loop" beginning on facing page for description of Copper Center and attractions along the Old Richardson Highway.

V 106.8 F 255.2 Turnoff to east for 0.2 mile access road to **Wrangell-St. Elias National Park and Preserve Visitor Center**; parking and information panels at entrance.

Field editor Sharon Paul Nault says this is "a great facility and a 'must stop' for travelers." Take the half-mile Boreal Forest Valdez Trail Loop through the balsam poplar, quaking aspen and paper birch trees; interpretive programs usually available in summer. *Crown of the Continent* is a 22 minute movie about the park shown in the theatre building on the hour from 10 A.M.–5 P.M. There is also a Junior Ranger Program for kids.

The visitor center has a large parking area that accommodates buses and RVs; indoor restrooms; drinking water, benches, picnic tables, phone with free local calls and pop machines. Hot drinks available (for a donation) at the Visitor Center. Interpretive displays, a bookstore/gift shop (topographic maps are available for sale here), fireplace with comfortable couch and chairs, and park staff to answer questions on the park and the Copper River Valley region are housed in one building. Beautiful view of the Wrangell Mountains from a short interpretive trail behind the center.

The Visitor Center is open year-round, 9 A.M. to 6 P.M. daily in late May to mid-September, weekdays in winter (call for hours). Phone (907) 822-5234; website http://www.nps.gov/wrst/index.htm.

The Trans-Alaska Pipeline parallels the Richardson Highway. (©Kris Valencia, staff)

Also stop by the Ahtna Cultural Center, located in the visitor center complex. The center has a big fish wheel on display outside and Native history and culture on display inside. Open daily in summer.

V 109.2 F 252.8 Long downhill northbound.

V 110 F 252 Tazlina DOT station and Dept. of Natural Resources office. Report forest fires here or phone (907) 822-5534.

Begin long uphill southbound.

V 110.6 F 251.4 Rest area to east at south end of Tazlina River Bridge; large paved parking area, 2 covered picnic tables, handicap accessible toilets, dumpster. Short road leads down to boat launch area on Tazlina River. *Riverbank may be hazardous during high water. Watch for hazard signs and barricades.*

V 110.8 F 251.2 Tazlina River bridge. *Tazlina* is Athabascan for "swift water." The river flows east from Tazlina Glacier into the Copper River. Fishing for reds, rainbow and burbot (no bait, single hook only except for burbot sets).

V 110.9 F 251.1 Old School Road leads to a former Catholic boarding school, now destroyed, but once attended by many who live in the **TAZLINA** (pop. 207) area.

V 111 F 251 Tazlina River Trading Post to east; groceries and gas. *MILEPOST®* readers have commented that this store has an amazing variety and selection of items.

Tazlina River Trading Post. See display ad this page.

Begin 0.7-mile bike path northbound.

V 111.7 F 250.3 Copperville Road. Developed during pipeline construction, this area has a church, private homes and Glennallen fire station. Bike path ends northbound.

Highway climbs Simpson Hill northbound; views to east of Wrangell Mountains. Mount Drum dominates the skyline to east.

V 112.3 F 249.7 Steep grade southbound

to Tazlina River.

V 112.6 F 249.4 Long paved parking area east side of highway (muddy when wet but has a large opening in brush that offers good views) and short frost-heaved access road to scenic viewpoint and large turnaround that proceeds to the south. There is a diagram of the Wrangell Mountains (hidden in a brushy alcove with view): Mount Sanford (elev. 16,237 feet); Mount Drum (12,010 feet); Mount Wrangell (14,163 feet); and Mount Blackburn (16,390 feet). Sign at viewpoint reads:

"Across the Copper River rise the peaks of the Wrangell Mountains. The 4 major peaks of the range can be seen from this point, with Mount Drum directly in front of you. The Wrangell Mountains, along with the St. Elias Mountains to the east, contain the most spectacular array of glaciers and ice fields outside polar regions. The Wrangell Mountains are part of Wrangell–St. Elias National Park and Preserve, the nation's largest national park."

Visitor information for Wrangell–St. Elias National Park is available at **Milepost V 106.8** Richardson Highway. From Glennallen it appears as if Mount Drum is the highest! It is actually 4,000 ft. less than Mount Sanford.

V 115 F 247 Junction of Richardson and Glenn highways. **The Hub of Alaska** and **Copper Valley Visitor Information** are located at the northwest corner of the intersection; 24-hour gas and diesel, convenience grocery, pay phones. Courthouse and Ahtna building on east side of highway. The town of **GLENNALLEN** extends west along the Glenn Highway from here; **Cross Road Medical Center** located 2.3 miles west on Glenn Highway; phone (907) 822-3203. **Alaska State Troopers** (phone 907/822-3263) (See description of Glennallen on pages 353-356 in the GLENN HIGHWAY section.)

The Hub of Alaska. See display ad on page 352 in the GLENN HIGHWAY section.

Junction of the Richardson Highway (Alaska Route 4) with the Glenn Highway (Alaska Route 1) to Anchorage (189 miles west from here). Anchorage-bound travelers turn to **Milepost A 189** on page 352 in the GLENN HIGHWAY section for log of that route.

Valdez- or Fairbanks-bound travelers continue with this log. For the next 14 miles northbound the Richardson and Glenn highways share a common alignment. They split at **Milepost V 128.5**. The Copper Valley visitor information center is a large facility with friendly staff, many exhibits (including a full-sized bear mount), telephone and gift shop. Open 9 A.M.–7 P.M. Local hiking trails, fishing and other pertinent information found here.

Distance marker southbound indicates Copper Center 14 miles, Valdez 115 miles.

Distance marker northbound shows Paxson 71 miles, Tok 139 miles, Fairbanks 251 miles, Canada Border 256 miles.

Slow for sections of frost heaves northbound to Paxson.

V 115.4 F 246.6 Ace Hardware store to west.

V 116.8 F 245.2 Ice/beer/liquor store to east.

V 116.9 F 245.1 MBC Automotive and Towing Service to west; phone (907) 822-5900.

V 118 F 244 Dry Creek State Recre-
(Continues on page 490)

Copper Center Loop

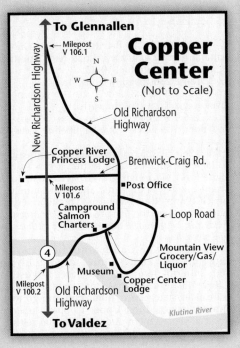

Fishing the Klutina River attracts many visitors to Copper Center. (©Kris Valencia, staff)

Copper Center

Located on the Old Richardson Highway; 105 miles north of Valdez via the Richardson Highway; 200 miles from Anchorage. **Population**: 297. **Emergency Services**: Phone 911. Ambulance in Glennallen, phone 911.

Elevation: 1,000 feet.

Private Aircraft: Copper Center NR 2 airstrip, 1 S; elev. 1,150 feet; length 2,200 feet; gravel; unattended.

A historical marker at **Milepost V 101.9** Old Richardson Highway reads: "Founded in 1896 as a government agriculture experiment station, Copper Center was the first white settlement in this area. The Trail of '98 from Valdez over the glaciers came down from the mountains and joined here with the Eagle Trail to Forty Mile and Dawson. 300 miners, destitute and lonely, spent the winter here. Many suffered with scurvy and died. Soon after the turn of the century, the Washington–Alaska Military Cable and Telegraph System, known as WAMCATS, the forerunner of the Alaska communications system, operated telegraph service here between Valdez and Fairbanks."

A post office was established here in 1901, the same year as the telegraph station. Copper Center became the principal settlement and supply center in the Nelchina–Susitna region.

Originally occupied by the Ahtna Native people, Copper Center's first and other name is Kluti-Kaah.

Copper Center has a post office. Dining and lodging at the **Copper River Princess Wilderness Lodge** (access via side road west from **Milepost V 101.6**. Dining at Copper Center Lodge (see description following paragraph). Mountain View Grocery, Gas & Liquor is open daily; unleaded gas, propane available. The nearest public campground is Squirrel Creek State Recreation Site, located on the Richardson Highway at **Milepost V 79.5**. Try local fishing charter services in Copper Center for campsites as well.

The landmark Copper Center Roadhouse, located on the inner loop road, burned down on May 20, 2012. The roadhouse had its beginning as the Holman Hotel and was known as the Blix Roadhouse during the gold rush days of 1897–98. It was the first lodging place in the Copper River Valley and was replaced by the Copper Center Lodge in 1932. Rebuilding of the Copper Center Roadhouse was in progress in summer 2013; the restaurant was operating and a few new rooms had been built in adjacent buildings.

Visitor information available at the George I. Ashby Memorial Museum and Trail of '98 Museum, housed in historical cabins located beside the Copper Center Lodge which were spared by the fire. Operated by the Copper Valley Historical Society, the

George I. Ashby Memorial Museum in historical cabin survived the Copper Center Lodge fire.
(©Kris Valencia, staff)

museum was open daily, June 1 to September 15, in summer 2013 (museum hours may vary). Early Russian religious articles, Athabascan baskets, telegraph equipment and minerals, copper and gold mining memorabilia, and trapping articles from early-day Copper Valley are on display. The gift shop has locally made items available. Free admission, but donations are appreciated! Interpretive boards outside the museum reveal local history.

For a good viewpoint of Copper Center, the Klutina River and the Wrangell Mountains, drive up the hill to the Copper River Princess Wilderness Lodge. The view from the observation point in front of the lodge offers fine views on a clear day of the surrounding area and mountains.

Copper Center is located on the **Klutina River**, 1 mile from its confluence with the **Copper River**. Fishing charters, tackle, riverboat service, jet-boat adventure tours, hunting and fishing guides are available locally;

try **Alaska River Wrangellers** and **Full Curl Outdoors** (see display ads this page).

There is a short trail to the Klutina behind Copper Center Lodge; ask permission at museum. The Klutina River is popular for its red (sockeye) salmon run from June to early August, and its king salmon run, which peaks in mid-July. Check current fishing regulations.

A favorite photo subject is the Copper Center City Hall, an outbuilding located near the post office. Businessman Bill Wyatt of Valdez tacked the sign on this structure years ago as a joke, and owners Bob and Jeanie Sunder let it stay.

The first church in the Copper River region, the Chapel on the Hill, was built here in 1942 by Vince Joy and U.S. Army volunteers stationed in the area. Mr. Joy built other churches and a Bible college in the area over the years. A former visitor attraction in Copper Center, the log Chapel on the Hill, was disassembled in 2010-11 and was reassembled on private property visible from the road.

Return to Milepost V 100.2 or V 106
Richardson Highway

(Continued from page 488)

ation Site to west via short, potholed access road offers 50 wooded campsites, drive-in, long pull-throughs, walk-ins, picnic tables, firepits, dumpster, toilets, water, room for big rigs, no ATVs. Pets on leash. Camping fee $15 per night; day-use fee $5. Open May 15–September 15. ▲

V 118.1 F 243.9 Private Aircraft: Gulkana airport to east; elev. 1,579 feet; length 5,000 feet; asphalt; fuel 100LL.

V 126 F 236 Paved turnout to west.

V 126.2 F 235.8 Gravel road to east; no river access. Gravel pit to west.

V 126.4 F 235.6 Gravel road east to parking; poor river access. Alyeska pipeline access road to west.

V 126.5 F 235.5 Gravel access road east to large parking area and further access (use right fork) via rough gravel/paved road to second large parking area and boat launch on **Gulkana River**; day-use. This is a very busy area when the fish are in. *NOTE: Access roads can be in rough shape, with big potholes and steep drop-offs.*

Fishing in the Gulkana River for grayling all year; kings June to mid-July; red salmon late July to late August. Click "Fishing Reports" at www.sf.adfg.state.ak.us/statewide/sf_home.cfm and go to Interior region then Upper Copper/Upper Susitna Management Area. Be familiar with current fishing regulations and closures. ➥

V 126.8 F 235.2 Gulkana River Bridge. Very popular fishing spot in season for reds, kings and grayling. *Watch for pedestrians.* Public access to river south of bridge; see **Milepost V 126.5.** *No public access to river at north end of bridge.* The Gulkana River flows 60 miles from Gulkana Glacier in the Alaska Range to the Copper River. Entering Game Management Unit 13B northbound, 13A southbound. ➥

Highway climbs next 1.2 miles northbound.

V 126.9 F 235.1 Access road east to village of **GULKANA** (pop. 177) on the east bank of the Gulkana River at its confluence with the Copper River. Established as a telegraph station in 1903 and named "Kulkana" after the river.

Most of the Gulkana River frontage in this area is owned by Gulkana Village and managed by Ahtna, Inc. Ahtna lands are closed to the public for hunting and trapping. However, land use permits may be purchased from the Gulkana Village Tribal Office for fishing and boating access on Ahtna lands. The sale, importation and possession of alcohol are prohibited.

V 128 F 234 *Highway descends long hill next 1.2 miles southbound to Gulkana River.*

V 128.5 F 233.5 Gakona Junction; Gakona ECO gas station and Stop 'n Shop Grocery/convenience store; check-in for **Copper River Salmon Charters.** ⓑ

Copper River Salmon Charters. See display ad this page.

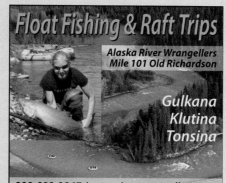

This is the **junction** of Richardson Highway (Alaska Route 4) and Tok Cutoff (Alaska Route 1). The 2 roads share a common alignment for the next 14 miles southbound. Turn east on Alaska Route 1 for Tok. Continue north on Alaska Route 4 for Paxson and Delta Junction. Continue south on Route 4 for Valdez and turnoff for Glennallen and Alaska Route 1 (Glenn Highway) to Anchorage. Gakona Lodge, a National Historic Site, is 2 miles northeast on the Tok Cut-Off Highway from this junction.

Junction of the Richardson Highway with Tok Cutoff to Tok (125 miles east from here). Tok-bound travelers turn to **Milepost GJ 0** on page 351 in the GLENN HIGHWAY/TOK CUTOFF section and read log back to front.

Distance marker northbound shows Paxson 56 miles, Delta Junction 137 miles; Fairbanks 235 miles. Distance marker southbound shows Glennallen 16 miles, Valdez 129 miles, Anchorage 196 miles. Improved highway southbound.

Valdez- or Fairbanks-bound travelers continue with this log.

V 128.9 F 233.1 Gulkana River Ranch.

V 129.4 F 232.6 Easy-to-miss turnoff to west for **Sailor's Pit** BLM public easement and Ahtna Inc. primitive campground and Gulkana River access. BLM trail at highway turnoff: access to public lands for foot traffic, dog sleds, animals, snowmobiles, 2 or 3-wheel vehicles, ATVs less than 3,000 lbs. GVW. Wide, gravel road goes straight downhill 0.4 mile to Ahtna Inc. river access; sign lists all permits and fees, payable in a box, here. Fees (subject to change) $10/day-use, $20/camping near river in forested area. Keep to the right to get up the ridge to the campground, self-register using recreation fee permit envelopes. *(NOTE: The Gulkana River is open to the public, but much of the land along the river here is owned by Ahtna Inc. and recreation permits are required to use or cross Ahtna lands.)*

Gulkana River; fishing for rainbow, grayling, king and red salmon. *Check fishing regulations carefully before fishing.*

V 130 F 232 Paved parking area to west.

V 132 F 230 Gulkana River Fishing and Camping Park.

V 132.2 F 229.8 Gravel parking area to west.

V 135.8 F 226.2 Paved parking to east.

V 136.4 F 225.6 Coleman Creek.

V 136.8 F 225.2 Turnoff with steep access to west (signed "BLM Gulkana River Trail") is a gravel side road that leads 0.3 mile to Ahtna Inc.'s **Poplar Grove/Gulkana River** public fishing access trail (portage boat to launch over narrow trail to river) and informal camping in dirt parking lot area. Recreation fee box is at entrance to access road with signs about Ahtna fees and regulations; $15/day-use (individual), $25/camping per group or vehicle (summer 2013 rates); seasonal passes for individuals and families available, go to https://permits.ahtna-inc.com/. Also access to BLM Gulkana River trail.

V 138.1 F 223.9 Poplar Grove Creek (sign). Turnout to west.

V 139.4 F 222.6 Paved parking to west.

V 140.6 F 221.4 Paved parking to east. Glimpse of the Alaska Range northbound on a clear day. Southbound view of the Wrangell Mountains, dominated by—from

east to west—Mount Sanford (16,237 feet), Mount Wrangell (14,163 feet) and Mount Drum (12,010 feet).

V 141.4 F 220.6 Paved double-ended scenic viewpoint to west. BLM trail (1-mile) to Gulkana River.

V 141.7 F 220.3 Sign: Rough road next 2 miles (northbound).

CAUTION: Slow for frost heaves to Milepost V 145.

V 145 F 217 Distance marker northbound shows Paxson 40 miles, Delta Junction 120 miles. More frost heaves southbound.

Watch for roadside ponds with water lilies. The Yellow Pond Lily (*Nuphar polysepalum*) is common in shallow ponds in Alaska: large floating leaves, bright yellow blooms.

V 146.4 F 215.6 Entering Federal Subsistence Hunting Area northbound, leaving southbound.

V 147 F 215 Double-ended scenic viewpoint to west. Limited views of Alaska Range and pipeline northbound, weather and foliage permitting.

Road construction underway next 11 miles northbound in summer 2013. Expect continued construction and/or improved highway in summer 2014.

V 147.5 F 214.5 Sourdough Creek BLM Campground to west across Sourdough Creek bridge. Follow signs for boat launch and grassy day-use area or camping area. There are 42 level sites on a gravel loop with raised tent platforms (designated handicapped sites) and covered picnic tables, (a trail with information boards is near here and takes you to Sourdough Creek and around the campground), grills, outhouses; information boards; firewood $5; campground host. Camping fee $12 in summer 2013, current fees posted; $6 for walk-in camping. Golden Age Passport senior pass gives a ½-price discount. Walk-in tenting areas with outhouse and bear-proof cans and food storage.

For boaters, there is the "Kids Don't Float" life jacket program in effect at **Gulkana River** boat launch. Large parking area, grills, benches, outhouse, picnic area. Guided fishing trips available. Dump station

for boaters is behind the outhouse (there is no RV sani-dump), recycling for aluminum. *Beware of bears.*

The Gulkana River is part of the National Wild and Scenic Rivers System managed by the BLM. A popular float trip for experienced canoeists begins at Paxson Lake and ends at Sourdough Campground. See description at **Milepost V 175.**

Gulkana River above Sourdough Creek, grayling 9 to 21 inches (same as Sourdough Creek below), rainbow 10 to 24 inches, spinners, June through September; red salmon 8 to 25 lbs. and king salmon up to 62 lbs., use streamer flies or spinners, mid-June through mid-July. **Sourdough Creek**, grayling 10 to 20 inches, use single yellow eggs or corn, fish deep early May through first week in June, use spinners or flies mid-June until freezeup. This can be a very productive creek.

V 147.6 F 214.4 Sourdough Creek.

V 147.7 F 214.3 Historic **Sourdough Roadhouse** (description follows); food, gas, lodging, camping. Try their homemade bread and pies!

©Sharon Nault

Sourdough Roadhouse, established in 1903, destroyed by fire in 1992, reopened in 1994. Services: gasoline, propane, rustic cabins, showers, groceries, fishing tackle and licenses, shuttles, RV plug-ins, salmon charters, restaurant with home cooking and baking, featuring our 1896 sourdough starter. Summer (907) 822-3636, or winter (208) 596-6116. Email: patty–denton@yahoo.com. [ADVERTISEMENT]

V 148.5 F 213.5 Improved highway. Several large turnouts to the west over the next two miles.

V 153.9 F 208.1 Distance marker northbound shows Paxson 32, Delta Junction 112, Fairbanks 206.

V 156.8 F 204.2 Large, new turnout to west with great views.

V 157 F 204 As the highway winds through the thickly treed and brush covered foothills of the Alaska Range, over a crest called Hogan Hill (elev. 2,647 feet), there are magnificent views of 3 mountain ranges (on a clear day): the Alaska Range through which the highway leads, the Wrangell Mountains to the southeast and the Chugach Mountains to the southwest.

Good views of pothole lakes to west. The headwaters of the Susitna River converge on the platform to the west. The Susitna empties into Cook Inlet west of Anchorage.

Good long-range viewpoints from highway. Moose and other game may be spotted from here (use binoculars).

V 158.8 F 202.2 Road narrows.

V 159 F 202 Northbound highway travels through wilderness, with few good turnouts. Plan ahead to stop at Mile 169.4 gravel pit if you need a large area to stop. Do not block APL access roads.

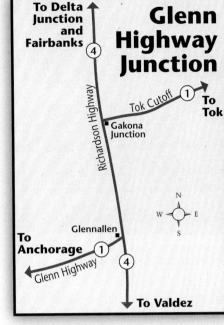

To Delta Junction and Fairbanks

Glenn Highway Junction

Richardson Highway

Tok Cutoff

To Tok

Gakona Junction

N / W / E / S

Glennallen

To Anchorage

Glenn Highway

To Valdez

The Richardson Highway between Glennallen and Delta Junction. (© Sharon Nault)

V 160.3 F 201.6 Big wilderness views descending northbound.

V 160.6 F 201.4 Haggard Creek BLM trailhead parking to west (can be muddy); grayling fishing. Access to Gulkana River 7 miles to west.

V 160.9 F 201.1 Haggard Creek.
Slow for rough road.

V 161.5 F 200.5 Wilderness views as road descends southbound.

V 162.2 F 199.8 Long, narrow, sloping, double-ended gravel turnout to east (muddy in wet weather), very uneven.

V 166.4 F 195.6 June and **Nita Lakes** BLM trail; 1 mile to west, take trail west for 0.5 miles to first fishing access.

V 168.1 F 193.9 Gillespie Lake BLM trailhead and small (bumpy) parking area to west. Walk up creek 0.4 mile to lake; grayling fishing.

V 169.4 F 192.6 Large gravel pit. Turnout to west. Gravel road to Middle Fork BLM trail to **Meier's Lake** and Middle Fork Gulkana River at north corner of gravel pit turnout. Meier's Lake offers good grayling fishing.

V 170 F 192 Meier's Lake Roadhouse to west; gas, bar, restaurant, bunkhouse, phone and dry camping. Russian and German are spoken here. Historic church on east side of road holds non-denominational services at 7:30 P.M. Sundays in summer; all are welcome.

There is a long, narrow, gravel parking area just north of the lodge on the west side of the highway, one of the few turnouts along Meirs Lake. Good place to spot trumpeter swans, lesser scaups and other waterfowl. Watch for resident bald eagles. Birds are especially abundant in fall (and the fall colors are beautiful). Also watch for otters in the lake. Watch for caribou in the fall.

There are a few rough roads down to the shore between here and the end of the lake northbound but they are really only appropriate for 4-wheel drive vehicles.

V 171.6 F 190.4 Gravel turnout to west with sloping entrance.

V 171.7 F 190.3 Large gravel turnout to west.

V 172.9 F 189.1 Access to Dick Lake to east. Big gravel park and turnaround area, primitive road leads down to lake, no turnaround on this road. Good grayling fishing in summer. View of trans-Alaska pipeline across the lake. Good spot for photos. Primitive camping.

V 173 F 189 Dick Lake access by steep turn east up hill. (Long units will drag.) Nice primitive parking camping area. 2 trails down to lake. Small, carryable boats may be launched here. Turnaround area. View of Alaska Range from lake.

V 174 F 188 New paved section of highway begins northbound.

V 175 F 187 Turnoff to west for **Paxson Lake BLM Campground** and Gulkana Wild River boat launch. Wide gravel access road (with great views of Paxson Lake) leads downhill 1.4 miles for access to camping and boat launch. Child-sized life jackets here as part of the "Kids Don't Float" program. Large camping area near lakeshore has 50 campsites (40 RV, some pull-throughs, 10 walk-in tenting sites), 14-day limit, outhouses, water, tables, firepits, and free dump station, recycling bins, information boards about river travel. Camping fee $12 ($6 for walk-in campsites, bear-proof food locker storage for tenters and walk-in sites) in summer 2013, check current fees posted. Concrete boat launch and parking area for 80 vehicles. View of Alaska Range on a clear day. Bring mosquito repellent. Fishing in **Paxson Lake** for lake trout, grayling and red salmon. New boater registration cabin uphill from boat launch. Boaters are required to register before launching; registration box is located outside cabin and offers information for boaters. *CAUTION: Watch for bears*

This is the launch site for floating the Gulkana River to Sourdough Creek Campground at **Milepost V 147.5**. Total distance is about 50 miles and 4 days travel, according to the BLM, which manages this national wild river. While portions of the river are placid, the Gulkana does have Class II and III rapids, with a gradient of 38 feet/mile in one section. Canyon Rapids may be Class IV depending on water levels (there is a portage). Recommended for experienced boaters only. For further information on floating the Gulkana, contact the BLM at P.O. Box 147, Glennallen, AK 99588, or phone (907) 822-3217; or visit www.blm.

gov/ak/st/en/fo/gdo.html and click on Gulkana River.

V 177 F 185 Two turnouts, just south of the physical milepost to the east and 1 to the west.

V 178.5 F 183.5 Turnout to west.

V 178.7 F 183.3 Long turnout to west with view of Paxon Lake.

V 179 F 183 Hufman Creek. Double ended turnout to east.

V 180.1 F 181.9 Large paved turnout to west by lake.

V 180.2 F 181.8 Double-ended gravel turnout to west near lake.

V 182.2 F 179.8 Large gravel turnout. Sign here reads: No bait allowed, only unbaited single hook, artificial lures are permitted in Paxson and Summit lakes. Southbound views of Paxson Lake.

V 183.1 F 178.9 Paved turnout to west.

V 184 F 178 Good view of Gulkana River. Old highway alignment east beyond this milepost, provides a good turnout for informal camping.

V 184.3 F 177.7 *Improved widened highway next 1.7 miles northbound; slow for dips.*

V 184.7 F 177.3 One Mile Creek bridge. Paxson Mountain to west; good example of a lateral moraine created by Gulkana Glacier (visible).

V 185.2 F 176.8 AT&T building to east.

V 185.4 F 176.6 Entering Paxson Closed Area southbound (see description at **Milepost V 182.2**). Distance marker southbound.

V 185.5 F 176.5 PAXSON (pop. 16) at the **junction** of the Richardson Highway (Alaska Route 4) and the Denali Highway (Alaska Route 8). Paxson began in 1906 when Alvin Paxson established a roadhouse at Mile 192. He later built a larger roadhouse at Mile 191. The current Paxson Lodge, a local landmark, was reported as closing its doors in December 2013; current status unknown. Huffman airstrip is across highway from the lodge.

Lodging at **Denali Highway Cabins**, wildlife-viewing raft trips, birding trips and other local tours available in Paxson from **Paxson Alpine Tours** (see descriptions at **Milepost V 185.6**).

Gas may be found at Meirs Lake Roadhouse (south of here at **Milepost V 170**) or at Tangle River Inn (20 miles west on the Denali Highway).

Distance marker southbound shows Glennallen 74 miles, Valdez 186 miles.

Private Aircraft: Paxson airstrip, adjacent south; elev. 2,653 feet; length 2,800 feet; gravel; emergency fuel; attended.

Junction with Denali Highway (Alaska Route 8) to Cantwell and the Parks Highway. See DENALI HIGHWAY section on page 509 for log.

V 185.6 F 176.4 Access west to **Denali Highway Cabins** and **Paxson Alpine Tours**; lodging, Gulkana River float trips and local tours.

Denali Highway Cabins and Paxson Alpine Tours. See display ad facing page.

V 185.8 F 176.2 Ruins of old Paxson Roadhouse (private property) east side of highway. Paxson Station DOT highway maintenance to west. Speed limit 65 mph.

V 188 F 174 Gulkana Hatchery to west (not open to public). Bank erosion threatened the hatchery and construction was underway in summer 2013 to prevent it

from falling in the river.

V 188.4 F 173.6 Long paved double-ended rest area with outhouse and litter bin to east across from Gulkana River. Sign commemorates Alvin J. Paxson's Timberline Tent Roadhouse established near here in 1906. The Gulkana River flows south to the Copper River.

V 189.5 F 172.5 Long, very narrow paved double-ended turnout to west.

V 190.4 F 171.6 Paved parking area by **Gulkana River Salmon Spawning Viewpoint** to west; views of pipeline, picnic table, toilets, viewing platform and interpretive sign about spawning red salmon. Large screen box protects dumpster from bears attracted by spawning salmon. Good photo op. *Fishing for salmon prohibited.* Public fishing access to **Fish Lake** (2 miles); trailhead across highway from turnout. Fish Lake offers grayling fishing.

V 191 F 171 Welcome to Copper River Valley sign southbound. Snow poles along highway.

NOTE: There is only 0.5 mile between physical mileposts 191 and 192.

V 191.1 F 170.9 Beautiful Summit Lake; cottages and camping at Water's Edge.

V 192.2 F 169.8 Gravel turnout on **Summit Lake** with public access boat launch. Posted fishing regulations: "no bait, single-hook artificial lures only on Paxson and Summit lakes April 16 to Oct. 31." Fishing for lake trout, grayling, burbot and red salmon.

Summit Lake, 7 miles long, is named for its location near the water divide between the Delta and Gulkana rivers. The Gulkana River flows into the Copper River, which flows into Prince William Sound. The Delta River is part of the Yukon River drainage.

V 192.6 F 169.4 Large gravel turnout to west on Summit Lake. Highway winds along shore of Summit Lake.

V 193 F 169 Small informal turnouts along Summit Lake next few miles northbound.

V 195 F 167 SUMMIT LAKE; elev. 3,210 feet (above the timber line). There are a number of homes in this alpine valley on the east side of Summit Lake. Magnificent Gulkana Glacier comes into view for northbound travelers.

Summit Lake hosts the Annual **Arctic Man Ski & Sno–Go Classic, scheduled for** April 7-13, 2014. The main event involves 2-member teams—a downhill skier and a snowmachine and driver. The skiers start at 5,800 feet elevation and drop 1,700 feet in less than 2 miles to the bottom of a narrow canyon, where they must catch the tow rope from their partner on the snowmachine, who then tows them 2-¼ miles uphill (at speeds up to 86 mph), before they separate and the skier finishes the race by going over the side of a second mountain and dropping 1,200 feet to the finish line. Entry forms and details on the event are found at www.arctic man.com.

The Arctic Man is a major winter event held in the Alaska wilderness. Arctic Man draws many thousands of spectators. Camping at designated parking area off the Richardson Highway.

V 196 F 166 North end of Summit Lake.

V 196.7 F 165.3 Access to Gunn Creek to west.

V 196.8 F 165.2 Gunn Creek bridge.

V 197 F 165 View of pingo to south.

Pingos are dome-shaped, ice-cored hills that form in areas of permafrost.

V 197.5 F 164.5 Large gravel turnout to east. Wide gravel road to east leads past old Isabel Pipeline camp site (no evidence remains of the camp) toward the base of **Gulkana Glacier**. Primitive camping begins at Mile 1.2. Best glacier views are at first campsites. If any areas look as if they could be used as airstrips, they might! Park on the edges. Remarkable scenery and photo op.

V 197.7 F 164.3 Summit of **Isabel Pass** (elev. 3,280 feet). View of Gulkana Glacier to the northeast. Gravel parking area to east. This glacier, perched on 8,000-foot Icefall Peak, feeds streams that drain into both Prince William Sound and the Yukon River.

Gold Rush Centennial interpretive sign about women in the gold rush, including Isabelle Barnette, for whom Isabel Pass is named. This is a moose wintering area.

Memorial monument honoring Gen. Wilds P. Richardson, for whom the highway is named. Sign here reads:

"Captain Wilds P. Richardson presented the need for roads to Congress in 1903. His familiarity with Alaska impressed Congress with his knowledge of the country and his ability as an engineer. When the Act of 1905 became a law, he was placed at the head of the Alaska Road Commission, a position he served for more than a decade. The Richardson Highway, from Valdez to Fairbanks, is a fitting monument to the first great road builder of Alaska."

Entering Sport Fish Management Area C southbound.

V 198.2 F 163.8 Gravel turnout to west.

V 198.5 F 163.5 Gravel parking area to west with view.

V 199.9 F 162.1 Large gravel parking area to east.

V 200.4 F 161.6 Wide, rough and sometimes rocky gravel side road (*drive slowly!*) leads west 1.4 miles to **Fielding Lake State Recreation Area**. Several primitive campsites on the way in. Well used ATV trail at 0.7 mile entering the area. 0.1 mile further, another, grassy ATV trail goes off to the south. State campground is situated in a pleasant area above tree line; berry picking; 17 campsites, no water, no camping fee, picnic tables, bear proof garbage cans, pit toilets, large parking areas and boat launch. (No overnight parking allowed at boat launch.) Loop turnaround. *(Hunting camps and private cabins adjacent recreation area; respect private property signs.)* Fielding Lake public-use cabin available for rent; sleeps 6, 3-night maximum; visit www.dnr. alaska.gov/parks/cabins/index.htm. Fishing for lake trout, grayling, burbot.

V 201 F 161 Snow poles along highway help plow drivers identify the roadbed in bad snowstorms.

V 201.4 F 160.6 Phelan Creek bridge. Gulkana Glacier is the headwaters of Phelan Creek and flows 16 miles to the Delta River.

V 202.4 F 159.6 McCallum Creek bridge, highway follows Phelan Creek northbound. Gulkana Glacier is the headwaters for Phelan Creek, which flows northwest to the Delta River. Turnout down road to south on east side. Historically, the glacial-colored stream emptied into Summit Lake but was diverted into Phelan Creek, which makes Summit Lake a clear water lake today. There is a turnout to the east, south of the McCallum bridge.

Rainbow Ridge is a colorful landmark along the Richardson Highway. (©Sharon Nault)

Views northbound of Rainbow Ridge and Rainbow Mountain (see description at **Milepost V 206**).

V 203.1 F 158.9 Entering Federal Subsistence Lands northbound, leaving subsistence lands southbound.

V 203.9 F 158.1 Double-ended paved area to east. Water piped from hillside is potable (reportedly).

V 204.6 F 157.4 Large gravel parking area to west. Good photo op northbound of pipeline going up overhill.

V 206 F 156 Double-ended paved scenic viewpoint. Good photo-op. Good view southbound of **Rainbow Ridge** and **Rainbow Mountain**. This 6,000-foot-high ridge extends northwest 8 miles from McCallum Creek. The highest point on the ridge is 6,700-foot Rainbow Mountain.

The last mountain of Rainbow Ridge, Mount Naidine, was named for Naidine Johnson, owner/operator of Tangle River Inn at **Milepost P 20** on the Denali Highway. Popular photo subjects, the mountain and ridge were named for their varicolored talus slopes. The reds and greens are volcanic rock; the yellows and pastels are siltstone and sandstone. Snow poles along highway guide snowplows in winter.

Improved highway northbound.

V 206.3 F 155.7 Distance marker northbound shows Delta Junction 60 miles, Fairbanks 155 miles.

V 207 F 155 Large gravel turnout to west.

V 207.2 F 154.8 Begin rock slide and avalanche area next 5 miles northbound, end slide area southbound.

V 208.1 F 153.9 Gravel turnout to west overlooking creek.

V 208.5 F 153.5 Large gravel parking area to west overlooking creek.

V 209 F 153 Gravel shoulder parking to east. Leaving Federal Subsistence Lands northbound, entering subsistence lands southbound.

V 209.6 F 152.4 Shoulder parking, sharp dropoff to river; views.

CAUTION: Falling rock. Watch for rough patches of road northbound to **Milepost V 220**.

V 210 F 152 Good view southbound of aptly named Rainbow Ridge and Mountain (see description at **Milepost V 206**).

V 210.3 F 151.7 Turnout down to gravel bar, west.

V 211.5 F 150.5 Huge gravel parking area to west. Dikes in place for flood control.

V 212.3 F 149.7 Wide gravel shoulders and turnouts to west beside Phelan Creek are found along the highway north and south of here. Road to the west leads to a take-out point for Delta River float that begins at Tangle Lakes Campground on the Denali Highway and is marked for river travelers along this stretch of the Richardson Highway. Take-out point changes due to river channeling. A pull off here takes you to parking down by the river.

Experienced kayakers or whitewater rafters may also float 18 miles downstream from here past Black Rapids Glacier. See "Lower Delta, Black Rapids Section" at www.blm.gov/ak/st/en/prog/nlcs/delta_nwsr/lowerdelta.print.html.

V 213.2 F 148.8 Gravel shoulder parking to west.

V 213.6 F 148.4 Rock slide and avalanche area ends northbound, begins southbound.

V 214 F 148 Double-ended paved turnout to east.

V 214.3 F 147.7 Entering Federal Subsistence Lands northbound, leaving subsistence lands southbound.

V 215.2 F 146.8 Miller Creek bridge; turnouts both sides of bridge. Pipeline crosses creek next to bridge.

V 215.9 F 146.1 Large gravel parking area to west with interpretive sign is **Denali Fault/Pipeline Visitor Viewing Area**; good stop for pipeline photos. Interpretive signs at viewing area give pipeline history and facts, and detail design solutions used to make the pipeline earthquake-proof. The zigzag pattern often seen in the above-ground sections allows for pipe expansion or contraction due to temperature changes or movement caused by other forces, such as earthquakes. *Do not climb on pipe.*

The pipeline has an earthquake detection system. Ground accelerometers at pump stations measure earth movement, and computers identify critical supports, valves and other items to check after a quake.

The pipeline's design was tested in November 2002 by the tremendous 7.9 earthquake. For more on the earthquake and the Denali Fault, see **Milepost V 262.5**.

V 216.2 F 145.7 Leaving Federal Subsistence Lands northbound, entering subsistence lands southbound.

Distance marker northbound shows Delta Junction 50 miles, Fairbanks 149 miles.

V 216.7 F 145.3 Lower Miller Creek bridge. Gravel turnout to west at south end. Pipeline crosses the river above ground alongside the bridge to the west.

V 217 F 145 Gravel turnout. Do not block pipeline access road. Good view of pipeline from turnout.

V 217.2 F 144.8 Castner Creek; turnout to west at south end of bridge.

V 218.2 F 143.8 Trims Camp. Trims Station (DOT/PF highway maintenance) to west.

V 218.8 F 143.2 Bridge over Trims Creek. Wildflowers in the area include lupine, sweet pea and fireweed. Watch for caribou on slopes. Parking to the northwest.

V 219.1 F 142.9 Access road west to Pump Station No. 10.

V 219.8 F 142.2 Michael Creek bridge; turnout to east at north end.

Southbound drivers have a spectacular view of Pump Station No. 10 and the surrounding mountains.

V 220.6 F 141.7 Gravel viewpoint to west with view to the south of pump station 10, mountains and glaciers.

V 220.7 F 141.3 Flood Creek bridge; parking to east at north end of bridge.

V 222.5 F 139.5 Gravel turnout to west, view of flood control dikes on river. Several narrow tracts leads to the river dike along here.

V 223 F 139 Whistler Creek bridge. Turnout to east at north end of bridge.

V 223.8 F 138.2 Boulder Creek bridge. Parking to east at north end of bridge.

V 224.5 F 137.5 Lower Suzy Q Creek bridge; parking to east, both ends of bridge.

V 224.7 F 137.3 Entering Federal Subsistence Lands southbound. Leaving Federal Subsistence Lands northbound.

V 224.8 F 137.2 Upper Suzy Q Creek bridge. Gravel turnout to east at north end of bridge.

V 225.2 F 136.8 Large gravel turnout to east. Watch for lush growths of cow parsnip along roadside in summer.

V 225.4 F 136.6 Double-ended scenic paved viewpoint with picnic table to west. Interpretive sign on area bison (excerpt follows):

"Each year, from April to August, the Delta bison herd is visible from this spot. During the summer months, the herd forages along the Delta River Flood Plain, moving to the Delta area in the winter. At the closest, they are 2 miles distant. Binoculars or spotting scopes are helpful. Alaska's present day herds are from a 1928 transplant from Montana."

Glass the high slopes to the east of this scenic viewpoint: They often have Dall sheep on them.

Historical marker here identifies the terminal moraine of Black Rapids Glacier to the west. Currently a retreating glacier with little ice visible, this glacier was nicknamed the Galloping Glacier when it advanced more than 3 miles during the winter of 1936–37. Rapids Lake Trail begins across the highway from the historical sign (0.3 mile to lake). Look for river beauty and wild sweet pea blooming in June. Rapids Lake is stocked with rainbow by the ADF&G.

V 226.2 F 135.8 Gravel shoulder parking.

V 226.4 F 135.6 Falls Creek bridge.

V 226.5 F 135.5 Camp Terry Creek. Boundary between Game Management Units 20D and 13.

V 226.7 F 135.3 Black Rapids U.S. Army

training site at Fall Creek.

V 226.9 F 135.1 Gunny Sack Creek.

V 227 F 135 Gravel shoulder parking to west.

V 227.4 F 134.6 The Black Rapids Roadhouse, on the east side of the highway, was established about 1902 and is one of the last remaining roadhouses on the historic Valdez–Fairbanks Trail (today's Richardson Highway). Restoration efforts have stabilized the old roadhouse. The new lodge offers lodging and meals.

V 228.3 F 133.7 One Mile Creek bridge.

V 229.7 F 132.3 Paved shoulder parking west side of highway, access to river. *CAUTION: Be aware of possible steep sloping shoulders when pulling over to use roadside parking.*

V 230.3 F 131.7 Paved turnout to west.

Good view from highway south of this turnout of Delta River. The Delta River heads at Tangle Lakes and flows 80 miles north to the Tanana River.

V 230.9 F 131.1 Turnout to west.

V 231 F 131 Darling Creek. View of braided Delta River to west. The wind can really whip up the dust along the riverbed.

V 231.6 F 130.4 Gravel parking area to west, nice mountain views.

V 232.1 F 129.9 Gravel turnout to west.

V 233.3 F 128.7 Bear Creek bridge. Small gravel turnout with access to creek to west south of bridge. Wildflowers in season include pale oxytrope, yellow arnica, fireweed, wild rhubarb and cow parsnip. Fiber optic cable laid here by AT&T, beneath visible orange stakes.

V 234.2 F 127.8 Gravel turnout to east, pipeline access road.

V 234.5 F 127.5 Large paved turnout to west.

V 234.7 F 127.3 Ruby Creek bridge; parking both sides of highway at north end of bridge.

V 236 F 126 Distance marker southbound shows Paxson 51 miles, Glennallen 121 miles, Valdez 236 miles.

V 237.9 F 124.1 Distance marker southbound shows Paxson 53 miles, Glennallen 127 miles.

V 238 F 124 Narrow, gravel loop road leads west through **Donnelly Creek State Recreation Site**, a lushly forested scenic spot with mountain views, 12 treed campsites, tables, firepits, outhouses, water pump and garbage containers. Big rigs can park in a wide parking area at the entrance (fee required). At least 1 pull-through campsite and the rest are pull-in. Some very long campsites for extra-big rigs and some campsites have a tenting area. Camping fee $10/night. A large dike built to keep the river from flooding here, provides a good place to walk. Blueberries in season.

Highway makes long winding ascent northbound to **Milepost V 241.3***.*

V 238.2 F 122.8 Gravel parking to east above pond.

V 239.2 F 122.8 Gravel turnout to east.

V 240.3 F 121.7 Gravel turnout to west.

V 241.3 F 120.7 Large paved turnout to west at top of hill; good photo-op of Delta River to west, top of Donnelly Dome to east. Southbound views of braided Delta River.

Highway makes long winding descent southbound to **Milepost V 238***.*

V 242.1 F 119.9 Easy-to-miss turnoff for Coal Mine Road to east, not well marked, and a good parking area (road is 4-wheel-drive vehicles only) which leads east to 8 small fishing lakes, most stocked with rainbow trout, some with arctic char and grayling as well. Lakes are **Coal Mine #5** and **Backdown** lakes (trailhead at Mile 1.6); **Last Lake** (Mile 1.9) **Brodie Lake** (Mile 2.1); **Paul's Pond** (Mile 2.6); **Rangeview Lake** (Mile 2.7); **Dick's Pond** (Mile 4.1); and **Ken's Pond** (Mile 4.7).

The ADF&G says: "A nice place to try on a bright sunny day with little or no wind, offering a beautiful vista of hanging glaciers and snow-capped mountains. Fishing from shore is tricky due to alders, but a float tube or small canoe or even just wading out from shore will increase your effectiveness. Try dry flies or Mepps spinners (0 to 1) for best luck."

V 242.8 F 119.2 Public fishing access to west for **Weasel Lake**; stocked with rainbows. Recreation Access Permit (RAP) required.

V 243.5 F 118.5 Pipeline Viewpoint to east with interpretive signs with pipeline facts and an overview of Alaska animals. Good photo stop. The trans-Alaska pipeline snakes along the ground and over the horizon. Because of varying soil conditions along its route, the pipeline is both above and below ground. Where the warm oil would cause icy soil to thaw and erode, the pipeline goes above ground. Where the frozen ground is mostly well-drained gravel or solid rock, and thawing is not a problem, the line is underground.

V 243.8 F 118.2 Gravel side road to lake.

V 243.9 F 118.1 Paved double-ended scenic viewpoint to east. A spectacular view (on a clear day) to the southwest of 3 of the highest peaks of the Alaska Range. From west to south they are: Mount Deborah (elev. 12,339 feet); Hess Mountain (11,940 feet), center foreground; and Mount Hayes (13,832 feet).

V 244.3 F 117.7 Rough informal dirt turnout (dips from road).

V 244.4 F 117.6 Public fishing access to east to **Donnelly Lake**; king and silver salmon; stocked with rainbows and arctic char. 3 turnouts next mile, northbound.

V 244.6 F 117.4 Double-ended rough gravel turnout to east.

V 245.6 F 116.4 Informal gravel turnout to east.

V 245.9 F 116.1 Distance marker northbound shows Delta Junction 20 miles, Fairbanks 118 miles.

V 247.3 F 114.7 From here northbound the road extends straight as an arrow for 4.8 miles. Good view southbound of Donnelly Dome. *NOTE: No shoulders, drive carefully.*

Donnelly Dome to west (elev. 3,910 feet), was first named Delta Dome. For years the mountain has been used to predict the weather: "The first snow on the top of the Donnelly Dome means snow in Delta Junction within 2 weeks." Great view southbound of the Alaska Range.

CAUTION: Watch for moose and caribou (especially in August).

V 247.5 F 114.5 Bumpy gravel track leads east to informal camping. Walk road before driving in.

V 248.7 F 113.3 U.S. Army Donnelly Training Area.

V 249.5 F 112.5 Distance marker southbound shows Paxson 65 miles, Glennallen 139 miles.

V 249.6 F 112.4 Turnoff to west for **Dome Road**, which crosses U.S. Army Military Reservation Donnelly Training Area. This is a restricted access area: "When flag is flying, military training is being conducted in this area and this area is off limits. For entry at other times, contact Range Control, Monday–Friday, 7:30 A.M.–4:30 P.M.) at 873-4714. Recorded Range Information dial 873-3181."

V 252.8 F 109.2 Paved, double-ended turnout to west.

V 256 F 106 Fort Greely Ridge Road and old Richardson Highway to west. Access to Ghost, Nickel, "J" and Chet lakes; Recreation Access Permit (RAP) required.

V 257.6 F 104.4 Meadows Road to west; access to 10 fishing lakes, Army permit required to enter this area. Sign on a memorial rock here reads:

"Named in honor of Benjamin Earl Meadows Lieutenant Colonel Corps of Army Engineers US Army, Alaska "Whose personal initiative was largely responsible for the construction of the road. Born Oct. 20, 1904 killed in an

View of Donnelly Dome southbound on the Richardson Highway. (©*Kris Valencia, staff*)

Giant mosquitoes are a favorite photo-op at Delta Junction Visitor Center. (©Kris Valencia, staff)

airplane crash at Summit Lake, Alaska, August 22, 1951."

V 258.3 F 103.7 Alyeska Pipeline (Delta Region Raw Maintenance and Oil Spill Response Base) Pump Station No. 9 to east; no tours. This station is at Pipeline Mile 548.71, with the Prudhoe Bay station being Mile 0. The pipeline was designed with 12 pump stations, although Pump Station 11 was never built. Interpretive sign at pump station entrance reads:

"Construction of this facility was completed May 16, 1977. As oil was introduced into the line during a 39 day period in 1977, the oil front passed through this station at 10:37 A.M., July 20, 1977. The travel time of the oil from Prudhoe Bay to this site under normal operating conditions is 98.06 hours. Another 44.97 hours is required to move the oil to the Valdez Terminal. The oil travels at about 5.59 miles per hour. The mainline pumps at the station move 22,000 gallons of oil a minute, which is 754,285 barrels a day. Hot gas provided by aircraft-type jet engines drives a turbine wheel to power each of the pumps. Each engine can produce 17,300 horsepower."

V 258.7 F 103.3 South boundary of Fort Greely.

V 260.9 F 101.1 Distance marker southbound shows Paxson 76 miles, Glennallen 150 miles.

V 261.1 F 100.9 FORT GREELY (restricted area) main gate to east flanked by 2 tanks on exhibit. Fort Greely was established in 1941 by the Civil Aeronautics Administration as one of a chain of strategic defense airfields. It was an alternate landing field between 1942–45 for aircraft en route to Russia during the Lend–Lease program.

In 1948, Fort Greely was activated as a staging area for the U.S. Army's first post-WWII cold weather training maneuver—"Exercise Yukon"—which led to the establishment of the Northern Warfare Training Center here. Cold weather field tests of Army equipment began at Fort Greely's Cold Regions Test Center in 1949. The Fort Greely area has temperature extremes ranging from –69°F to 91°F. Fort Greely was named for A.W. Greely, arctic explorer and author of *Three Years of Arctic Service*. Scheduled for closure in 2001, Fort Greely was reactivated as a ballistic missile defense site in 2002. It is operated by the Alaska National Guard, which maintains 20 interceptors, or antiballistic missiles, in ground silos. The 65-foot-long, 3-stage missiles

travel 17,000 mph.

Watch for heavier traffic between Fort Greely and Delta Junction.

Distance marker northbound, Delta Junction, 5 miles.

V 261.6 F 100.4 Wills Range Road to west.

V 262.1 F 99.9 An ATV trail begins near Delta and comes out at Fort Greely.

V 262.5 F 99.5 Double-ended paved rest area to west with litter bins, toilets, picnic tables, scenic view. Gold Rush Centennial sign about the Richardson Highway and interpretive sign on the Denali Fault. Area subject to high winds.

"The Denali Fault runs in a great arc from Southeast Alaska through Canada, then re-enters Alaska, slicing Denali National Park in half. The great fault passes just south of here, allowing the spectacular Alaska Range to tower above its surroundings."

The Denali Fault became a little more real to Alaskans on November 3, 2002, when a 7.9 earthquake jolted the Interior and South-central regions. The quake struck at 1:12 P.M. and was centered about 80 miles south of Fairbanks. The Richardson Highway, Tok Cut-off and Glenn Highway all sustained damage.

V 264.8 F 97.2 Jarvis Creek.

V 264.9 F 97.1 Leaving Fort Greely Military Reservation northbound, entering Fort Greely Military Reservation and Donnelly Training Center southbound.

V 265.1 F 96.9 "Welcome to Delta Junction" sign northbound. *NOTE: Begin 35 mph speed zone northbound. Resume 65 mph speed limit southbound. CAUTION: High wind area.*

V 265.2 F 96.8 Taste of Europe restaurant.

V 265.3 F 96.7 Delta Petro-Wash. 24-hour gas station and convenience store with free RV dump station, potable water

and air for tires. Clear away the road dust at their carwash with RV and automatic bays. Coin-op laundry. A deli-style restaurant serves hot breakfasts and espresso, specialty

salads and sandwiches, fresh pizza, baked goods and soft-serve ice cream (6 A.M.–8 P.M.). Ice, ATM, DVD rentals, automotive supplies, and free WiFi. More information at www.DeltaPetroWash.com or by calling (907) 895-5073. [ADVERTISEMENT]

V 265.4 F 96.6 Alaskan Steakhouse & Motel. See display ad on page 217 in the ALASKA HIGHWAY section.

V 265.6 F 96.4 The Calico Cow quilting shop to east; Alaskan fabrics, classes, patterns, books.

The Calico Cow. See display ad on page 217 in the ALASKA HIGHWAY section.

V 265.7 F 96.3 Buffalo Center Drive-in adjacent **Sullivan Roadhouse Museum,** which is across Grizzly Lane from the Visitor Center on the east side of Richardson Highway. Open daily in the summer, this original 1906 Roadhouse has an extensive garden and displays Alaska Highway road-building equipment. A Farmers' Market is held behind the Roadhouse on Saturdays, 10 A.M. to 6 P.M., from June to September.

Pizzabella restaurant to west.

NOTE: Turn east on Grizzly Lane for access to Alaska Highway eastbound (to Tok) and for Delta Junction visitor center parking. Continue straight ahead northbound for access to Alaska Highway westbound (to Fairbanks); see next entry at Milepost V 265.9.

V 265.8 F 96.2 Delta Junction Visitor Information Center, on the east side of the Richardson Highway and south side of the Alaska Highway, sits at what is locally referred to as The Triangle. The visitor center, open 8 A.M.-8 P.M. in summer, has information on area agriculture, local sights and services. Drinking water, brochures and restrooms. Delta Junction Visitor Center's End of Alaska Highway monument and pipeline display. **Smiling Moose Gifts** adjacent Granite View Sports & Gifts to west.

Smiling Moose Gifts. See display ad on page 217 in the ALASKA HIGHWAY section.

ALASKA ROUTE 2

V 265.9 F 96.1 Stop sign northbound marks end of Alaska Route 4 and continuation of Alaska Route 2 to Fairbanks. *CAUTION: Northbound traffic crosses oncoming traffic traveling eastbound on Highway 2, and must merge with westbound Alaska Highway traffic.*

Junction of the Richardson and Alaska highways in DELTA JUNCTION. Turn to page 215 in the ALASKA HIGHWAY section for description of Delta Junction and log of Alaska Highway to Tok.

For northbound travelers, the Richardson Highway continues north to Fairbanks as Alaska Route 2.

V 266 F 96 Tesoro gas station; gas, diesel.

V 266.1 F 95.9 Buffalo Service Center (gas, diesel, propane, convenience store, RV dump, 24-hour card fueling) at Nistler Road. Access to fairgrounds, ice arena, Delta schools, dental clinic and a pizza place.

V 266.2 F 95.8 Kelly's Alaska Country Inn. See display ad on page 218 in ALASKA HIGHWAY section.

V 266.3 F 95.7 Delta Junction post office and IGA Food Cache.

V 266.4 F 95.6 End 4-lane highway, begin 2-lane highway, northbound.

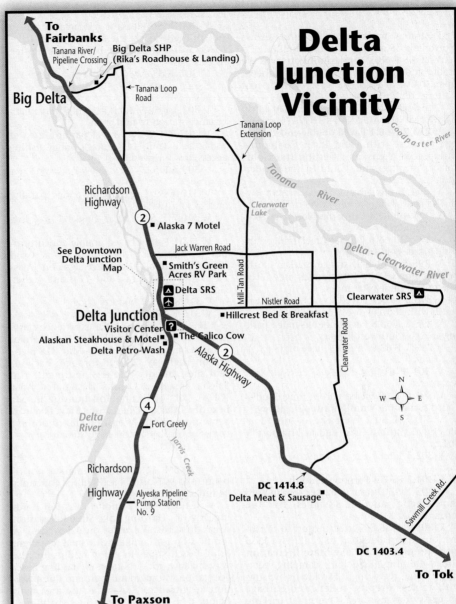

Delta Junction Vicinity

To Fairbanks

Tanana River/Pipeline Crossing

Big Delta SHP (Rika's Roadhouse & Landing)

Big Delta

Tanana Loop Road

Tanana Loop Extension

Goodpaster River

Tanana River

Richardson Highway

Clearwater Lake

Delta - Clearwater River

Alaska 7 Motel

Jack Warren Road

See Downtown Delta Junction Map

Smith's Green Acres RV Park

Mill-Tan Road

Nistler Road

Clearwater SRS

Delta SRS

Hillcrest Bed & Breakfast

Delta Junction

Visitor Center

Alaskan Steakhouse & Motel

The Calico Cow

Delta Petro-Wash

Alaska Highway

Clearwater Road

N W E S

Delta River

Jarvis Creek

Fort Greely

DC 1414.8 Delta Meat & Sausage

Richardson Highway

Alyeska Pipeline Pump Station No. 9

Sawmill Creek Rd.

DC 1403.4

To Tok

To Paxson

V 266.5 F 95.5 Deborah Street; access to Delta Junction City Hall; Community Center and Library; veterinary clinic across street

V 266.7 F 95.4 *Begin 35 mph speed zone southbound.* Distance marker northbound shows North Pole 82 miles, Fairbanks 95 miles.

V 266.8 F 95.2 Alaska Dept. of Fish and Game office.

V 266.9 F 95.1 Rapids Street; turnoff for Delta Junction Airport.

V 267 F 95 Turnoff to northeast for **Delta State Recreation Site** (across the highway from Delta River); 25 sites, water, tables, covered picnic shelter, toilets, $10 nightly fee. Campground host.

V 267.2 F 94.8 Medical clinic to east.

V 267.9 F 94.1 Smith's Green Acres RV Park and Campground.

Smith's Green Acres RV Park and Campground. See display ad on page 218 in ALASKA HIGHWAY section.

V 268.3 F 93.7 Junction with Jack Warren Road (paved); see Delta Vicinity map this section. Turnoff for **Clearwater State Recreation Site** (10.5 miles).

V 270.3 F 91.7 *Alaska 7 Motel,* 16 large, clean, comfortable rooms with private bath. Satellite TV, WiFi, microwaves, small refrigerators and phones in all rooms. Comfort at a comfortable price. Major credit cards accepted. **Milepost V 270.3** Richardson Highway. Phone (907) 895-4848. Email: manager@alaska7motel.com. Internet: www.alaska7motel.com. See display ad on page 218 in the ALASKA HIGHWAY section.
[ADVERTISEMENT]

V 270.6 F 91.4 Welcome to Delta Junction sign for southbound travelers.

V 271.7 F 90.3 Tanana Loop Road (gravel).

V 272 F 90 BIG DELTA (pop. 583) Big D Fire station. This unincorporated community at the junction of the Delta and Tanana rivers was originally a stop on the Valdez–Fairbanks trail. It was first known as Bates Landing, then Rika's Landing, McCarty, and finally Big Delta. Big Delta was the site of a WAMCATS telegraph station and also a work camp in 1919 during construction of the Richardson Highway. Today, agriculture, small business, and highway maintenance jobs provide employment.

V 275 F 87 Tesoro gas station with diesel and Tanana Trading Post on southwest side of highway. Turnoff for **Rika's Roadhouse** to northeast. After turning, keep to left for Rika's Roadhouse parking lot, or drive straight ahead for a small rest area with picnic table, outhouse and dump station ($5) on loop road. Day parking and overnight parking for Rika's Roadhouse (fees charged).

Rika's Roadhouse was built in 1910 by John Hajdukovich, who sold it in 1923 to Rika Wallen, a Swedish immigrant who had managed the roadhouse since 1917. Rika ran the roadhouse into the late 1940s and lived there until her death in 1969. It is now part of Big Delta State Historical Park and admission is free.

Pleasant walking paths with interpretive signs lead from the parking area through the park's grounds to the roadhouse. Historic structures open to the public include a small sod-roofed museum, a barn, black-smith shop, the old WAMCATS building and the roadhouse itself. Don't miss the colorful summer gardens at Rika's Roadhouse.

The Packhouse Restaurant and gift shop are located near the back of the property (current status unknown). The park grounds are open until 8 P.M. A must-stop and a good place to stretch your legs. Take a walk above the banks of the Tanana River.

V 275.4 F 86.6 Big Delta Bridge; **Tanana River/Pipeline Crossing.** Spectacular view of pipeline suspended across river and river boat traffic. *Slow down* for parking area to east at south end of bridge; litter barrels, interpretive signs.

V 277.7 F 84.3 Turn off to east on Quartz Lake Road for **Quartz Lake State Recreation Area.** Quartz Lake has developed campsites on a good loop road. Lost Lake has 12 pull-in or back-in campsites with picnic tables, toilet, and a large parking area with tables and litter bins. A trail connects Lost Lake and Quartz Lake camping areas. Quartz Lake SRA has 2 public-use cabins; 3-night maximum; visit www.dnr.alaska.gov/parks/cabins/index.htm for details.

V 280.2 F 81.8 Gravel turnout to south.

V 280.3 F 81.7 *Begin 0.5-mile passing lane westbound.*

V 283 F 79 81-Mile Pond (stocked with rainbow trout by ADF&G); public fishing access to east.

V 286.5 F 75.5 Shaw Creek bridge. Popular boat launching area; gated parking area to north at east end of bridge.

V 287.1 F 74.9 Shaw Pond public fishing access to northeast. Good to excellent early spring and fall grayling fishing; subject to closure (check locally). Informal camping.

V 288 F 74 Scenic viewpoint at parking area to west overlooking Tanana River with panoramic view (on clear days) to the south of 3 great peaks of the Alaska Range: Mount Hayes (elev. 13,832 feet) almost due south; Hess Mountain (11,940 feet) to the west or right of Mount Hayes; and Mount Deborah (12,339 feet) to the west or right of Hess Mountain.

V 289.7 F 72.3 South end of long paved double-ended parking area to east in trees.

V 291.8 F 70.2 *Begin 0.7-mile passing lane westbound.*

V 292.8 F 69.2 *Highway descends next 1.4 miles westbound.*

Distance marker northbound shows North Pole 55 miles, Fairbanks 69 miles.

V 293.5 F 68.5 Tenderfoot Pottery is the studio and gallery of artist Shellie Mathews; open 9 A.M. to 9 P.M. daily; www.tenderfoot pottery.com or phone (907) 895-4039.

Tenderfoot Pottery. See display ad on page 221 in the ALASKA HIGHWAY section.

V 293.9 F 68.1 Paved double-ended turnout to west with Gold Rush Centennial interpretive signs on "Getting the Gold" (placer mining) and "Gold in the Tenderfoot."

V 294 F 68 *Begin 1.6-mile passing lane eastbound. Highway climbs miles eastbound.*

V 294.6 F 67.4 Fairbanks North Star Borough boundary.

V 295.4 F 66.6 Banner Creek bridge; historic placer gold stream.

V 295.5 F 66.5 Distance marker southbound shows Delta Junction 28 miles, Tok 136 miles, Valdez 300 miles.

V 296.3 F 65.7 Paved scenic viewpoint to south with good view of Tanana River.

V 298.2 F 63.8 Paved double-ended parking area to southwest in trees.

V 299.1 F 62.9 *Begin 0.4-mile passing lane eastbound.*

V 301 F 61 *Begin 0.4-mile passing lane westbound.*

V 301.5 F 60.5 East end of long double-ended turnout downhill north of highway.

V 301.8 F 60.2 West end of long double-ended turnout. East end at **Milepost V 301.5.**

V 302.5 F 59.5 *Begin 0.5-mile passing lane eastbound.*

V 304.2 F 57.8 Turnout to north.

V 305 F 57 Distance marker southbound shows Delta Junction 38 miles, Tok 146 miles, Valdez 310 miles.

V 305.2 F 56.8 Signed turnoff to northeast on Birch Lake Road (0.2 mile) for loop road through **Birch Lake State Recreation Site**; swimming, picnicking, camping, boating, fishing, jet skiing. Lakeside picnic sites with tables, firepits, toilets and garbage on grassy day-use area. Overnight parking with campground host; 12 sites, some for tent campers; fee station; boat launch and fishing. Parking available for boat trailers. Overnight fee $10, day-use $5. Fish from shore in spring, from boat in summer. Stocked with silver salmon, grayling, arctic char and rainbow. "Kids Don't Float" program life jackets. Popular buoyed swimming area.

Birch Lake Military Recreation Site (USAF Recreation Camp) is located just beyond the state recreation site on the same access road.

V 306 F 56 Pleasant rest area northeast side of highway on the shore of Birch Lake; toilets, parking, lakeside benches, dumpster, day-use only.

V 307 F 55 *CAUTION: Watch for moose. Field editor Sharon Nault saw a huge moose here one summer.*

V 307.1 F 54.9 Birch Lake highway maintenance station to northeast.

V 307.2 F 54.8 Gravel parking area at Koole Lake Trail (14.3 miles), public fishing access, to southwest.

V 309.3 F 52.7 *Begin 1.1-mile passing lane westbound.*

V 310 F 52 Large double-ended parking area to southwest.

V 310.7 F 51.3 *Begin 1-mile passing lane eastbound, uphill grade.*

V 313.1 F 48.9 Paved double-ended turnout to southwest on Tanana River. Gold Rush Centennial interpretive signs on "Alaska's Gold Rush Era" and "Tanana Valley Gold."

V 314.8 F 47.2 Midway Lodge.

V 315 F 47 **"C" Lazy Moose RV Park & Gift Shop.** Your Alaska experience starts at the "C" Lazy Moose RV Park & Gift Shop. Located on the Tanana River, Mile 315 Richardson Highway. 28 pull-through, back-in, tent sites, laundry, showers, restrooms. The Salcha area is a Census Designated Area (CDA). Lots of fishing and hunting in our beautiful Alaska. Open from May 1st until September 30th. Website: clazymooserv.com. See display ad this page. [ADVERTISEMENT]

V 320.2 F 41.8 Distance marker northbound shows North Pole 30 miles, Fairbanks 44 miles.

V 321.5 F 40.5 Turnoff to east on Harding Drive for **Harding Lake State Recreation Area**; drive east 1.4 miles on paved road. A terrific stop for families with small children; bring beach shoes to enjoy wading on the very shallow, rocky bottom of Harding Lake. Fee station, campground host and dump station at entrance. Grassy day-use area with picnic tables, grills, horseshoes, ballfields. There is a boat launch and a 1.4 mile nature trail; 80 campsites (plus large field for group camping). Camping ($10), day-use and launch fees charged. Quiet hours from 11 P.M.–6 A.M. Fishing for lake trout, arctic char, burbot, northern pike and salmon. Worth the drive! Bring your insect repellent, you may need it! Firewood from camp host or park ranger. Jet skis allowed.

V 322.2 F 39.8 SALCHA (pop. 953, unincorporated) extends along the highway for several miles. Post office (ZIP code 99714)

open weekdays noon to 6 P.M., Saturday 10 A.M. to noon. Salchaket Roadhouse with food, gas, propane and lodging on east side of highway. The village was first reported in 1898 as "Salchaket," meaning "mouth of the Salcha." There have been grizzly bear sightings in this area in summer.

V 323.1 F 38.9 Access to **Salcha River State Recreation Site** 0.2 miles to northeast (turn at Salcha Marine). This is a very popular boat launch with a 130-site parking area for vehicles and boat trailers; a boat ramp; picnic area; a few developed campsites and some primitive campsites; toilets and water. There may be 300 or more people here on holidays. $10 launch fee and 10-minute launch limit. Camping fee ($10) charged. Fishing for king and dog salmon, grayling, sheefish, northern pike and burbot. Road at end of parking area leads to big area of sandbar parking and informal camping on Salcha River (beware soft sand areas). Winter-use cabin available; go to http://dnr.alaska.gov/parks/cabins/north.htm#salcha.

V 323.4 F 38.6 Salcha River bridge *(slow to 50 mph).*

V 324.6 F 37.4 Double-ended gravel turnout to northeast.

V 324.8 F 37.2 Munsons Slough bridge; fishing; Munsons Slough Road.

V 328.3 F 33.7 Salcha Store and Service (gas) to east.

V 332.1 F 29.9 Access east to **31-Mile Pond**; stocked with arctic char, rainbow.

V 332.2 F 29.8 The Knotty Shop to west; gifts and wildlife museum. The burl creations out in front are popular photo ops (please DON'T climb on these).

The Knotty Shop. Stop and be impressed by a truly unique Alaskan gift shop and wildlife museum. From the unusual burl construction to the Alaskan wildlife displayed in a natural setting to the handcrafted Alaskan gifts. Don't miss the opportunity to stop and browse. Show us *THE MILEPOST*® advertisement for one free single scoop ice cream cone. See display ad in the ALASKA HIGHWAY section page 223. [ADVERTISEMENT]

V 335.1 F 26.9 Access east to **28-Mile Pond**; stocked with rainbow, arctic char.

V 340.5 F 21.5 *Begin divided 4-lane highway northbound. Begin 2-lane highway southbound.*

CAUTION: Watch for heavy traffic southbound turning east into the base, 7–8 A.M., and merging northbound traffic, 3:45–5:30 P.M., weekdays. No parking, no stopping, no photography!

V 341.3 F 20.7 Main entrance to **EIELSON AIR FORCE BASE** (pop. 2,858). Eielson is the farthest north full-up fighter wing in the U.S. Air Force. The 345th Fighter Wing equips and trains the 18th Fighter Squadron of F-16s. Eielson has more than 60,000 square miles of military training airspace—the largest aerial range in the country. Military units from around the U.S. and the world come to hone their skills here.

Built in 1943 as a satellite base to Ladd Field (now Fort Wainwright) in Fairbanks, and called Mile 26 because of its location 26 miles from Fairbanks, Eielson served as a storage site for aircraft en route to the Soviet

Union under the WWII Lend–Lease program. Closed after WWII, the base was reactivated in 1946 and renamed Eielson AFB, after Carl Ben Eielson, the first man to fly from Alaska over the North Pole to Greenland. For more information, phone the public affairs office at (907) 377-2116.

V 343.6 F 18.4 Turnoff to north for Old Richardson Highway, Moose Creek Road and access to Moose Creek General Store; diesel, gas, propane. Turnoff to south for Eielson Farm Road to **Bathing Beauty Pond** and **Piledriver Slough**. Bathing Beauty Pond has a picnic area and is stocked with rainbow, arctic char and grayling. Piledriver Slough has outhouses, dumpster and boat launch on Chena River and is stocked with rainbow.

V 344.6 F 17.4 Moose Creek.

V 345.4 F 16.6 *CAUTION: Highway crosses Alaska Railroad tracks.*

V 345.7 F 16.3 Chena Flood Channel bridge. Upstream dam is part of flood control project initiated after the Chena River left its banks and flooded Fairbanks in 1967. A high water mark from this flood can be seen at the Pioneer Park train depot in Fairbanks.

V 346.6 F 15.4 Exit north to Laurence Road (westbound traffic only) for Moose Creek Dam Bikeway and Chena Lake Recreation Area. The 5-mile-long **Moose Creek Dam Bikeway** extends from the park-and-ride lot at Laurance and Nelson Roads (0.8 mile from the highway) to the dam site on the Chena River.

Drive 2.5 miles to fee station at entrance to **Chena Lakes Recreation Area**. A map of the recreation area is displayed; open year-round, day-use and camping fees charged from Memorial Day to Labor Day. It is 5.5 miles from the highway to the visitor kiosk below the Moose Creek Dam on the Chena River at the end of Main Road. This park was constructed by the Army Corps of Engineers and is run by the Fairbanks North Star Borough. Lake Park Campground is at Mile 3.6 and River Park Campground at Mile 4.9. Camping fee $10/night tents, $12 campers/RVs. Day-use fee $5. The recreation area has 80 campsites, 92 picnic sites, pump water, toilets, firepits, picnic tables, trash bins and volleyball courts. There is a 250-acre lake with swimming beach. **Chena Lake** is stocked with silver salmon, arctic char, grayling and rainbow. Nonmotorized boats may be rented from a concessionaire. **Chena River** offers good fishing for grayling, northern pike, whitefish and also for burbot.

V 347.4 F 14.6 Westbound-only exit to Dawson and Buzby Roads. For Santa Claus House and North Pole Visitor Information Center, after exiting drive under the overpass and turn right on St. Nicholas Drive (frontage road). For Chena Recreation Area, turn right on Mistletoe, then left on Laurence Road; follow signs. See map page 226.

V 347.8 F 14.2 North Pole city limits (sign on overpass).

V 348 F 14 Eastbound-only exit to Dawson and Buzby Roads. For Santa Claus House and North Pole Visitor Information Center, after exiting make immediate right on to St. Nicholas Drive.

V 348.5 F 13.5 Westbound-only exit north to Mission Road. Continue north on Mission Road a short distance and turn west (left) in front of a big church for **radio station KJNP** complex (see description in North Pole on page 226).

V 348.6 F 13.4 Eastbound traffic-only exit south to 5th Avenue and St. Nicholas Drive in North Pole.

For a complete description of North Pole businesses and attractions, see "North Pole" on pages 225-226 in the ALASKA HIGHWAY section.

V 349 F 13 Westbound traffic-only exit north to roundabout for access north to Badger Road and south to **NORTH POLE** (pop. 2,200) business district via Santa Claus Lane: fast-food outlets, 24-hour gas/diesel, car and truck wash, supermarket, post office, police, city hall, banks, medical clinics, indoor waterslide and swimming pool, library, playgrounds, parks.

Also access south via Santa Claus Lane to St. Nicholas Drive turnoff to famous **Santa Claus House**. Established in 1952, this is a favorite stop for many visitors, who can't resist the photographing the reindeer outside or buying Christmas ornaments in the gift shop. Visits with Santa for children or order a Letter from Santa (fee charged). **North Pole Visitor Information Center** is located just to the southeast of Santa Claus House behind the big Santa Claus.

Santa Claus House. See display ad on page 225 in the ALASKA HIGHWAY section.

From this exit, **Badger Road** loops northwest 11 miles and back to the Richardson Highway at **Milepost V 356.6**. Badger Road provides access to the following (distance from this junction shown): Nordale Road (4.6 miles), which leads 5.6 miles north to Chena Hot Springs Road; gas station and **Riverview RV Park** (8.4 miles); Fort Wainwright (10.1 miles); gas station (10.4 miles); and Old Richardson Highway (10.9 miles).

V 349.6 F 12.4 Eastbound traffic-only exit south to roundabout for access north to Badger Road and south to North Pole (see description above at westbound exit **Milepost V 349**).

V 350.1 F 11.9 Peridot Lane exit to north and south (for east and westbound traffic).

V 350.5 F 11.5 Alaska Railroad crossing. Entering North Pole city limits (eastbound).

V 356.6 F 5.4 Exit for westbound traffic for Badger Road interchange. This 11-mile road loops back to the Richardson Highway at **Milepost V 349.6**, providing access to Old Richardson Highway (0.2 mile from this junction); gas station (0.7 mile); Fort Wainwright (1 mile); Nordale Road, boat launch for Chena River, parking, outhouse and dumpster at (2.3 mile); **Riverview RV Park** and gas station (2.7 mile); Nordale Road (6.4 mile), which extends 5.6 miles north to Chena Hot Springs Road.

V 357.6 F 4.4 Exit for eastbound traffic for Badger Road interchange (see description previous mileost); access to **Riverview RV Park**.

V 359.6 F 2.4 Westbound traffic use south lane to exit for Old Richardson Highway and South Cushman Street.

V 360.6 F 1.4 Westbound exit (next right northbound) for Mitchell Expressway which **junctions** with Alaska Route 3 (Parks Highway to Denali Park, Nenana and Anchorage).

Turn to end of PARKS HIGHWAY section on page 442 and read log back to front for log of that highway from Fairbanks south to Anchorage.

V 361.2 F 0.8 Welcome to Fairbanks sign and flowers, westbound. Eastbound traffic exit to Mitchell Expressway which **junctions** with Route 3, Parks Highway to Nenana, Denali National Park and Anchorage.

V 361.5 F 0.5 Eastbound traffic exit to South Cushman.

V 362 F 0 FAIRBANKS. Junction with Airport Way and Steese Expressway northbound; downtown Fairbanks to west (take Airport Way and turn north on Cushman Street for downtown); Fort Wainwright Main Gate (Gaffney Road) to east.

Turn to FAIRBANKS section beginning on page 443 for description of city and maps.

Quartz, Birch, Harding and Chena Lake recreation areas along the Richardson Highway offer water sports, picnicking, camping and fishing. (©Sharon Nault)

Edgerton Highway McCarthy Road

CONNECTS: Richardson Highway Junction to McCarthy, AK

Length: 93 miles   **Road Surface:** 40% Paved, 60% Gravel

Season: McCarthy Road not maintained in winter

Early evening on the McCarthy Road (©Meghan Mackey, staff)

Distances in miles	Anchorage	Chitina	Fairbanks	Glennallen	McCarthy	Valdez
Anchorage		255	362	187	314	308
Chitina	255		313	67	60	120
Fairbanks	362	313		249	372	366
Glennallen	187	67	249		127	119
McCarthy	314	60	372	127		179
Valdez	308	120	366	119	179	

gateway to the McCarthy Road. The gravel McCarthy Road leads 58.8 miles east from Chitina, across the Copper River, and dead-ends at the Kennicott River. From the end of the road, travelers must walk or take a shuttle to McCarthy (0.6 mile from footbridge) and Kennicott (5 miles from footbridge). Total driving distance from the Richardson Highway turnoff to the end of the McCarthy Road is 93 miles. The McCarthy Road is not recommended for large RVs or trailers beyond the Chitina–McCarthy Bridge across the Copper River.

NOTE: Gas and diesel are available at Kenny Lake Mercantile at Milepost J 7.2 Edgerton Highway. The last gas stop eastbound is at Chitina. There is NO gas for sale in McCarthy.

This corner of Alaska is drawing an increasing number of visitors each year, and with good reason. Chitina has several picturesque old buildings and a growing number of services. The town of McCarthy retains many of its original structures and all of its original flavor. Nearby Kennicott offers solitude and scenery, including the massive moraine of Kennicott and Root glaciers and the historic Kennecott Mine mill and concentrator. All of this is surrounded by the

Major Attractions:

©Meghan Mackey, staff

Copper River, Kennicott/McCarthy, Wrangell-St. Elias National Park & Preserve

The Edgerton Highway (Alaska Route 10) is a scenic paved road leading 33.6 miles east from its junction with the Richardson Highway (Alaska Route 4) to the small town of Chitina,

Edgerton Highway/McCarthy Road — Richardson Highway to McCarthy, AK

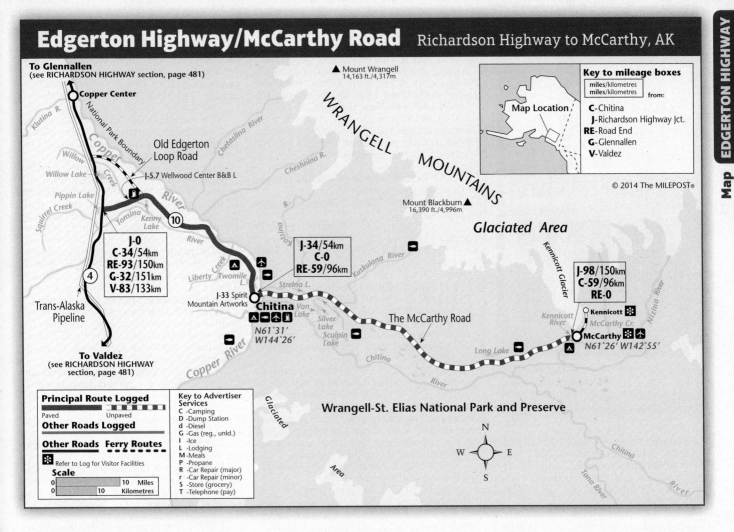

© 2014 The MILEPOST®

Key to mileage boxes

miles/kilometres
miles/kilometres from:

C-Chitina
J-Richardson Highway Jct.
RE-Road End
G-Glennallen
V-Valdez

Map Location

To Glennallen (see RICHARDSON HIGHWAY section, page 481)

Copper Center

Mount Wrangell 14,163 ft./4,317m

WRANGELL MOUNTAINS

Mount Blackburn 16,390 ft./4,996m

Glaciated Area

Kennicott Glacier

Old Edgerton Loop Road

J-5.7 Wellwood Center B&B L

J-0
C-34/54km
RE-93/150km
G-32/151km
V-83/133km

Trans-Alaska Pipeline

To Valdez (see RICHARDSON HIGHWAY section, page 481)

J-34/54km
C-0
RE-59/96km

J-33 Spirit Mountain Artworks

Chitina
N61°31' W144°26'

The McCarthy Road

J-98/150km
C-59/96km
RE-0

Kennicott
McCarthy Cr.
McCarthy
N61°26' W142°55'

Kennicott River
Long Lake

Wrangell–St. Elias National Park and Preserve

Principal Route Logged
Paved   Unpaved

Other Roads Logged

Other Roads   Ferry Routes

Refer to Log for Visitor Facilities

Scale
0   10 Miles
0   10 Kilometres

Key to Advertiser Services
C -Camping
D -Dump Station
d -Diesel
G -Gas (reg., unld.)
I -Ice
L -Lodging
M -Meals
P -Propane
R -Car Repair (major)
r -Car Repair (minor)
S -Store (grocery)
T -Telephone (pay)

N W E S

---

wilderness of Wrangell–St. Elias National Park and Preserve.

Food, gas, lodging and 2 full-service RV parks are available along the Edgerton Highway to Chitina. There is paid parking and camping at the end of the McCarthy Road. Food and lodging are available in the McCarthy/Kennicott area. *(NOTE: Some businesses do not take credit cards.)* See the road logs this section for more detailed information.

Named for U.S. Army Major Glenn Edgerton of the Alaska Territorial Road Commission, the Edgerton Highway—known locally as the Edgerton Cutoff—provides access to homesteads in the Kenny Lake area and to the salmon dip-net fishery on the Copper River at Chitina. A popular seasonal activity for many Alaskans, details on the Copper River personal use dip-net fishery are posted at the ADF&G website (www.adfg.state.ak.us). Updates are also available by phone in summer at (907) 267-2511 in Anchorage; 459-7382 in Fairbanks; or 822-5224 in Glennallen.

The McCarthy Road follows the right-of-way of the old Copper River & Northwestern Railway. Begun in 1907, the CR&NW (also referred to as the "can't run and never will") was built to carry copper ore from the Kennecott Mines to Cordova. It took 4 years to complete the railway. The railway and mine ceased operation in 1938. The McCarthy-Kennicott Historical Museum, housed in the historic railway depot, has historical artifacts and photos.

The McCarthy Road is recommended for those who like adventurous driving. Passenger cars, pickups, vans, campers and a few smaller RVs regularly traverse the McCarthy Road in the summer and early fall. For those who don't like adventurous driving, Wrangell Mountain Air provides twice daily air service to McCarthy/Kennicott from Chitina. Or let Kennicott Shuttle (www.kennicottshuttle.com) or Wrangell St. Elias Tours (www.alaskayukontravel.com) do the driving for you.

Take your time on the McCarthy Road. We recommend slow speeds (5 to 10 mph) on sections of rough road, and no more than the posted speed limit—35 mph—on improved gravel. Watch for sharp rocks, railroad spikes, no shoulders, narrow sections of road, soft spots, washboard, potholes and a few "roller coaster" curves. Motorists with large vehicles or trailers should exercise caution, especially in wet weather.

Flat tires are not uncommon on the McCarthy Road: Carry a spare. Tire repair is available in Chitina and McCarthy.

The National Park Service ranger station in Chitina has information on current road conditions and also on backcountry travel in Wrangell–St. Elias National Park and Preserve. The station is open daily from noon to 4 P.M.

There is no vehicle access to McCarthy/Kennicott for visitors from the Kennicott River footbridge at the end of the McCarthy Road. Motorists must park and cross the Kennicott River via a pedestrian bridge that also accommodates bicycles and possibly 4-wheelers (inquire locally). It is a little more than a half-mile walk from the footbridge to the town of McCarthy. It is 5 miles from the footbridge to Kennicott.

Local businesses offer shuttle van service between the footbridge, McCarthy and Kennicott. If you arrive after shuttles have quit for the day, try calling local businesses from the free phone at the end of the bridge to ask about a ride.

Emergency medical services: Between the junction of the Richardson and Edgerton highways and McCarthy, contact the Cross Road Medical Center in Glennallen, phone 911 or (907) 822-3203. Nearest Alaska State Troopers are in Glennallen, phone (907) 822-3263.

Edgerton Highway Log

Distance from junction with Richardson Highway (J) is followed by distance from McCarthy Road junction at Chitina (C).

ALASKA ROUTE 10 EAST

J 0 C 33.6 The Edgerton Highway leads east from the Richardson Highway. *Downhill grade next 4 miles eastbound. View from the top of this hill is of 7.2 miles of straight highway going east. Fine for littering, $1000.*

Junction of the Edgerton Highway (Alaska Route 10) and the Richardson Highway (Alaska Route 4). Turn to **Milepost V 82.5** on page 487 in the Richardson HIGHWAY section for log of Route 4.

Distance marker eastbound shows Chitina 33 miles, McCarthy 94 miles.

False-fronted Spirit Mountain Artworks building in Chitina was restored by owner Art Koeninger. (©Kris Valencia, staff)

Excellent views of Wrangell Mountains as highway descends eastbound. Most prominent are Mount Drum (elev. 12,010 feet) to the northeast, and Mount Wrangell (14,163 feet) and Mount Blackburn (16,390 feet), straight ahead.

J 4.5 C 29.1 Begin bike path eastbound. Do not park on this path even though it resembles a parking area at this point.

J 5.1 C 28.5 Kenny Lake Fire Station to south on Alpine Way.

J 5.2 C 28.4 Kenny Lake School, to south, has about 109 students in grades K–12. Access here for the Kenny Lake Interpretive Trail (panels on flora and fauna). Easy walking 15-20 minutes each way through pristine woods. Trail begins at the back of the school at the west end of the football field (southwest corner of the field).

J 5.7 C 27.9 Wellwood Center Bed and Breakfast, phone (907) 822-3418, www.wellwoodcenter.com.

Wellwood Center Bed & Breakfast. See display ad this page.

J 7.2 C 26.4 Kenny Lake Mercantile & RV Park to north with grocery store, hunting and fishing licenses, cafe, gas, diesel, propane, laundromat, showers, hotel room, camping and dump station.

J 7.3 C 26.3 Intersection with old Edgerton Highway. End bike path eastbound. Begin bike path westbound.

J 7.4 C 26.2 Kenny Lake Community League Hall and fairgrounds. **KENNY LAKE** (pop. 412) is an unincorporated agricul-

tural community located along the Edgerton Highway between about Mile 1 and Mile 17. **Radio**: KCAM (Glennallen).

The Kenny Lake Fair, held on a Friday evening and Saturday in August, is an enjoyable family event with games, food and crafts booths and local entertainment. The Kenny Lake Fair was first held in 1973 as part of the school carnival. Proceeds from the fair benefit the local school scholarship fund. The fairgrounds also host a musical festival, "Music Between the Ranges," in mid-July.

J 7.7 C 25.9 Long double-ended turnout to south in trees beside lake.

J 9.2 C 24.4 Kenny Lake Community Chapel to south.

J 9.5 C 24.1 Golden Spruce Cabins to north.

J 10.3 C 23.3 Wengers Country Store to south. Groceries, propane, ATM, dipnet permits.

J 11 C 22.6 Libby's Farm to south.

J 12.3 C 21.3 Paved parking area to south for **Tonsina River Trail**. Well-marked 2-mile (round trip) BLM trail leads south through woods to a picnic site overlooking the Tonsina River. Rated easy. Private property borders this trail.

J 12.5 C 21.1 Paved parking area to north; **Copper River** trailhead at west end of turnout. This BLM trail is 7 miles round-trip and recommended as a good trail for bird watchers. The trail is fairly flat and marshy, winding through dense vegetation to end at the Copper River. Use caution along the Copper River: it is very swift and cold.

J 12.9 C 20.7 Turnoff to south for access to Tonsina Native Arts & Crafts.

J 13 C 20.6 In summer, fresh produce and homemade baked goods may be available at a roadside stand to the north (operated by SAPA, a Pentecostal Christian community of about 70 people). SAPA runs a successful local sawmill.

J 14.9 C 18.7 Farming area; most fields are planted in hay. Also watch for Tibetan yaks grazing in a field south of the road along here. Herd belongs to Circle F Ranch (www.alaskayaks.com); tours.

J 15 C 18 Small gravel pullout, great for viewing yaks.

J 17.6 C 16 *Steep (8 percent) downhill grade next 1 mile eastbound.* Views of the Copper River and bluffs to north.

CAUTION: Watch for falling rock on road from cliffs.

J 19.3 C 14.3 Tonsina River bridge.

Both black and grizzly bears—difficult to see in the dense brush below the road along the Copper River—pass under this bridge. Tonsina River Retreat is to the east at the end of this bridge.

J 20.5 C 13.1 *Highway climbs steep 1.3-mile hill eastbound. Watch for fallen rock and rough road.*

J 21.5 C 12.1 Paved viewpoint to north with sweeping view of Copper River. View of Wrangell Mountains to north on clear day (Mount Blackburn and Mount Wrangell are nearest). Bison roam above the bluffs across the river. *Begin steep 1.3-mile downhill grade westbound.*

J 21.8 C 11.8 Begin long gradual descent eastbound with winding downhill (and uphill) grades.

J 23.3 C 10.3 Liberty Falls Creek BLM trailhead to south. This trail does not provide views of falls, go to the campground 0.3 miles north for best views.

J 23.6 C 10 Liberty Creek bridge (8-ton

load limit). Entrance to **Liberty Falls State Recreation Site**, just south of the highway on the banks of rushing Liberty Creek; camping fee $15. Best for vehicles and smaller RVs. *(Big rigs check out access road before driving in: road is steep, narrow and brushy. Of the 2 access roads, the one to the east is better.)*

This recreation site has picnic tables and tent platforms. Great view of this picturesque waterfall from the bridge across Liberty Creek. Hiking trail to falls.

J 28.4 C 5.2 Wide side road leads 0.1 mile to Chitina Tribal Community Health Clinic (open to public) and an RV park (current status unknown); 0.2 mile to Chitina DOT/PF maintenance station; and 0.4 mile north to busy Chitina Airport. **Private Aircraft**: Chitina airport, elev. 556 feet; length 2,800 feet; gravel; unattended. Parking area with outhouse located at top of hill overlooking airport. Good parking for big rigs and for overnight.

Wrangell Mountain Air provides daily commuter service to McCarthy from here for those who prefer flying to driving to McCarthy; phone 1-800-478-1160, www.WrangellMountainAir.com.

Watch for community fish wheels on the Copper River in the airport area. Interesting to watch and photograph, but ADF&G reminds us that it is illegal to walk on the fish wheel platforms or touch the fish if you don't have a permit for the wheel.

J 29.5 C 4.1 Small pot-holed gravel turnout by Three Mile Lake to north.

J 29.7 C 3.9 Paved turnout to north by **Three Mile Lake**; good grayling and rainbow fishing (stocked by ADF&G). Frequented by moose.

J 30.7 C 2.9 Large paved parking area to south at east end of **Two Mile Lake**; good grayling and rainbow fishing (stocked by ADF&G).

J 31.7 C 1.9 One Mile Lake (also called First Lake). Access road at east end of lake. One Mile Lake cabin rentals (nightly or long term). Paid RV parking avaialble with toilet, no hookups.

J 32 C 1.6 Begin 1.5-mile bike path eastbound.

Slow for frost heaves next mile eastbound.

J 32.1 C 1.5 "Welcome to Chitina" sign eastbound; hostel to north.

J 33 C 0.6 Chitina Post Office.

Chitna

J 33 C 0.6 Chitina is located 120 miles northeast of Valdez, and 66 miles southeast of Glennallen. **Population**: 105. **Emergency Services**: Phone 911 for all emergency services. **Copper River EMS**, phone (907) 822-3671; **Chitina Clinic**, phone (907) 823-2213; **Copper Center Clinic**, phone (907) 822-3541; **Cross Road Medical Center** in Glennallen, phone (907) 822-3203; **Chitina Volunteer Fire Department**, phone (907) 823-2263 or 823-2250; **Alaska State Troopers** in Glennallen, phone (907) 822-3263.

Visitor Information: The Wrangell–St. Elias National Park and Preserve Chitina Ranger Station is housed in the cozy, historic Ed S. Orr Cabin (1910). It is operated

by Park Rangers. The Alaska Geographic Bookstore is also here. Stop here for road conditions, and information about local trails, nearby fish wheels and fishing Copper River; phone (907) 823-2205. Visitors may stop by the Park's main visitor center/park headquarters at **Milepost V 106.8** Richardson Highway, 9 miles south of Glennallen, which is open year-round; phone (907) 822-7250; website www.nps.gov/wrst.

Climate: Temperature extremes from -58°F to 91°F; average snowfall 52 inches, annual precipitation 12 inches. **Newspaper**: *Copper Valley* Bi-Weekly.

Chitina (pronounced CHIT-na) sprang to life almost overnight with the arrival of the Copper River & Northwestern Railway on September 11, 1910. The railroad was built to haul ore from Kennecott Copper Mines at McCarthy to Cordova for shipment south to Seattle, and Chitina became a supply town for both the railway and mine. Chitina's population numbered in the thousands at a time when Anchorage was just a tent city.

Chitina also became the main freight route for goods and materials moving into the Interior via the Richardson trail, (now the Richardson Highway) and a tourist stop. Tourists would arrive in Chitina by rail from Cordova or by stagecoach and later motorcar shuttle from Valdez and Fairbanks via the Richardson Trail.

When the mine closed in 1938, Chitina became a ghost town almost overnight. In the 1950s and 1970s, ghosts were painted on several of the abandoned buildings.

Today, several original buildings remain and some have been restored. The false-fronted, picturesque building that houses **Spirit Mountain Artworks** was restored by owner Art Koeninger. The historic 1914 building next door, Gilpatrick's Hotel Chitina, has also been restored and renovated.

Chitina is the gateway to the McCarthy Road and Wrangell–St. Elias National Park and it is also Alaska's "Dip-Netting Capital." Alaskans come by the hundreds to participate in the seasonal dip-net salmon fishery on the Copper River, and almost as many non-Alaskans come to watch. Motorists stop in Chitina to eat, rest, hike, bike, fish, picnic or spend the night. And it's only going to get more popular as more people discover this scenic corner of Alaska.

Gilpatrick's Hotel Chitina, open daily May 1 to Oct. 1, offers rooms with private baths, a full-service restaurant and small pub; phone (907) 823-2244 in summer, or www.hotelchitina.com. Uncle Tom's Tavern (check out their antiques) is open year-round. A gas station is planned for summer 2014. Wrangell View Store (open daily year-round) has groceries, an ATM and fishing and hunting licenses. Mechanic and tire repair services available locally.

Fresh drinking water is available for 50 cents at the hard-to-find city well. From Main Street, turn at the Chitina Emporium and watch for right turn at "Chitina Public Well" sign (across from the fire station). Continue to rear of red building.

The big attraction—the **Copper River** dip-net salmon fishery—coincides with the seasonal salmon run (reds, kings or silvers).

Road cut marks start of McCarthy Road. (©Meghan Mackey, staff)

(*NOTE: This fishery is open to Alaska residents only.*) Fishermen are allowed to dipnet between O'Brien Creek and Haley Creek, with Wood Canyon offering the best results. Vehicle access to Copper River via O'Brien Creek Road (see **Milepost J 33.4**). Charter operations in Chitina ferry fishermen from a site upstream of O'Brien Creek to fishing spots on the river. The dip-net fishery for salmon runs June through September (depending on harvest levels), with scheduled opening dates and hours announced throughout the season. *CAUTION: The Copper River is a cold, swift and powerful river; exercise extreme caution.* Special regulations and permits apply. Check with ADF&G recorded information line in Anchorage at (907) 267-2511; in Fairbanks at (907) 459-7382; and in the Glennallen area at (907) 822-5224. Local residents ask that you clean your fish in the river, not in the lake.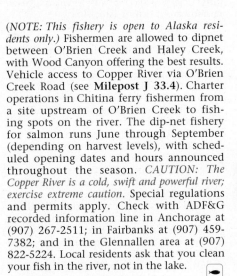

Edgerton Highway Log
(continued)

J 33.4 C 0.2 Junction with **O'Brien Creek Road**, a wide gravel road leading 2.8 miles to a large parking area at O'Brien Creek bridge; access to gravel bars and the Copper River. (Sign says" "End of the Copper River Highway.") This side road provides access to the Chitina subdistrict personal use dip-net salmon fishery on the Copper River between O'Brien Creek and Haley Creek. (Check with ADF&G for season, regulations, public access points and other permit details.) *WARNING: Copper River is extremely swift and can be hazardous; fishermen have been swept away.* Good view of Copper River at Mile 2.1.

Steep descent to the O'Brien Creek parking area begins at Mile 2.6. Also access to 10 Mile (RT) trail, easy to moderate, from O'Brien to Haley Creek. Trail follows railbed

of 1911 CR & NW railway. Stay on trail, privately-owned land all around.

J 33.5 C 0.1 Chitina Wayside; day-use only state-maintained rest area with large paved parking lot, public restrooms, phone, covered picnic table. Across the road is Chitina Lake (also called Town Lake). End 1.5-mile bike path eastbound.

J 33.6 C 0 Junction with McCarthy Road (log follows).

McCarthy Road Log

The McCarthy Road is a gravel road built along the old Copper River & Northwestern railway bed. Watch for old rails and railroad ties embedded in the road or lying along the roadside. The McCarthy Road ends at the Kennicott River, 58.8 miles east of Chitina and a little over half-a-mile west of the town of McCarthy.

Field editor Sharon Paul Nault encourages McCarthy Road motorists to "drive slowly over potholed and washboard sections and watch for sharp rocks. Don't power around corners because there's a chance you might meet someone on the curve." Remember, flying rocks damage windshields and cars! Posted speed limit is 35 mph.

Be sure to carry a fully inflated spare, *not a doughnut tire!* Flats are more apt to happen after recent road grading, when small nails and spikes are churned up. You may spot these hazards if you drive slowly and watch for them.

Keep in mind that much of the land along the McCarthy Road is privately held. Use only signed public access points for off-road activities. Local residents have

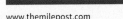

asked that visitors please help protect water sources from contamination and that they carry out their garbage. From here on, physical milepost markers may be seen on either side of the road.

Cell phone coverage has been sporadic on the McCarthy Road, but may improve with the construction of a microwave network by a local provider. Verizon, AT&T and ACS have worked in the Kennicott/McCarthy area for our field editors.

NOTE: There is no gas or diesel available on the McCarthy Road. Last gas stop eastbound is Chitina (station planned for 2014) or Kenny Lake Mercantile (which has diesel). Tire repair is available in Chitina and McCarthy.

Distance from Chitina (C) is followed by distance from road end (RE).

ALASKA ROUTE 10 EAST

C 0 RE 58.8 McCarthy Road begins. Trains used to travel on the very high narrow rock cut where the pavement ends and the road continues. No road maintenance east of here between October 15 and May 15.

C 1.1 RE 57.7 Copper River (Chitina–McCarthy) Bridge. Construction of this 1,378-foot steel span, designed for year-round use, cost $3.5 million. It re-established access across the river into the McCarthy–Kennicott area when it was completed in 1971.

View from bridge of fishwheels on the Copper River. Dip netting and fishwheels are permitted upstream of the bridge as part of the Glennallen subdistrict subsistence salmon fishery permit. Fishwheels are not allowed downstream of the bridge in the Chitina permit area. Watch for bears and eagles.

C 1.5 RE 57.3 Turnoff to southeast for campground with more than 17 campsites in trees, some picnic tables, firepits and toilets. (Fresh water available in Chitina at city well; dump station at Wrangell View RV park on Chitina airport road). Turnoff to northwest for well-marked easement across Ahtna land which leads to informal camping and vehicle parking on gravel bars alongside Copper River; portable toilets, no camping fee on public land. The state has posted a large map showing the public easement. Camping fee is $20 for camping on Ahtna lands. 🔺

Copper River fishing for red and king salmon, tag return box located here. Watch for bears. Popular spot to park and camp. This is a very interesting location: When dipnetting and the fishwheels are in full swing, there is *a lot* of activity. Look for both bald and golden eagles. 🔄

NOTE: Hunting, fishing and trapping for any purpose is strictly forbidden on property of Ahtna Inc. Fees are posted for day-use, for camping and seasonal use on Native lands.

Signs on road read: "Entering Wrangell-St. Elias National Park Preserve Boundary 21.5 miles," and "Much of the land along the road is privately owned. For land ownership information, contact Ahtna at (907/822-3476), Chitina Village Corp. Inc. (907/823-2223), or the National Park Service (907/822-7250)."

Pavement ends, gravel begins eastbound. CAUTION: Slow for frost heaves, potholes, washboard and loose rocks. Watch for soft spots in road. Narrow winding road with steep drop-offs, falling rock, no guardrails and small turnouts.

Expansive views as road climbs above Copper River eastbound.

C 1.6 RE 57.2 Entering Game Management Unit 11 eastbound, GMU 13D westbound.

C 2.9 RE 55.9 Ahtna Hilltop Campground under development but not finished summer 2013 to east. Drive 0.2 mile up to small hilltop to check on current status. 🔺

C 5 RE 53.8 Gravel turnouts next mile eastbound. Expansive view of Chitina River.

C 6.9 RE 51.9 Large gravel turnout.

C 10.1 RE 48.7 Public fishing access via 0.3 mile trail north to **Strelna Lake**; rainbow trout and silver salmon. *(Please respect private property adjacent trail.)* 🔄

C 10.8 RE 48 Turnout to north for parking and signed pedestrian public fishing access (walk-in only) to **Silver Lake** and **Van Lake** to the south; good rainbow trout fishing. Please stay inside the 10-foot easement; ADF&G phone (907) 822-3309. 🔄

C 12 RE 46.8 Sculpin Lake signed public fishing access to south; pedestrian access only. *Please respect private property.* Good rainbow trout fishing (stocked). 🔄

C 12.5 RE 46.3 Beaver house to the north of the road. Marshy areas with ponds; watch for beaver and swans.

C 14.3 RE 44.5 Airstrip.

C 14.4 RE 44.4 Gravel road to north; signs read "Access to Nugget Creek Trailhead and Dixie Pass Trailhead."

C 14.8 RE 44 Strelna Creek in culvert.

C 16.9 RE 41.9 Turnouts (one small, one large) with views of Kuskulana River and bridge; good photo op.

C 17.2 RE 41.6 Kuskulana Bridge, mid-span. *NOTE: 1-lane bridge, yield to oncoming traffic.* This former railroad bridge (built in 1910) is approximately 525 feet long and 238 feet above the river. It is a narrow 3-span steel railway bridge with new wood decking and guardrails.

Wayside at southeast end of Kuskulana Bridge has a picnic table, bear-proof litter bins, an outhouse and interpretive signs. Additional parking at gravel pit (adjacent east). As you approach the bridge going to McCarthy a steep access road leads down to parking and primitive camping near the river. *CAUTION: Underneath the bridge, the banks above the canyon are unstable and extremely dangerous. DO NOT STAND TOO CLOSE TO THE EDGE!*

C 20 RE 38.8 View opens up eastbound as road crosses large, marshy meadow.

Posted speed limit is 35mph.

C 23.7 RE 35.1 Large gravel turnout to northeast.

C 25 RE 33.8 Lou's Lake to north; silver salmon and grayling fishing. Watch for swans. Beaver lodge at end of lake. 🔄

Look for mastodon flowers, also called marsh fleabane, along here.

C 25.6 RE 33.2 Preserve/Park signs.

C 26.5 RE 32.3 Alaska Halfway House B&B and Chokosna Trading Post.

C 26.7 RE 32.1 Private property to west, airstrip entrance to east.

C 26.8 RE 32 Chokosna River bridge.

C 28.8 RE 30 Wilderness/Preserve signs.

C 29 RE 29.8 *Steep grades both directions down to* Gilahina River bridge (1-lane); large gravel parking area to south at west end of bridge with tables. A National Park Service footpath on the other side of the road leads a short ways up and under the old wooden **Gilahina Trestle**, which can be seen from the road.

C 29.5 RE 29.3 Large gravel turnout to east.

C 30.3 RE 28.5 Turnout to south.

C 30.5 RE 28.3 Turnout to south.

C 33.1 RE 25.7 Turnout to north.

C 34.6 RE 24.2 Turnout toward high mountains for Crystalline Hills trailhead. Beautiful mountain views in this area. Trail is moderate, 2-3 hours, 2.5 mile loop. Stays mostly in forest but you can leave the trail for views of Moose Lake and the Chitina River Valley.

C 34.8 RE 24 Entering Wrangell-St. Elias National Park & Preserve (westbound sign).

C 35.3 RE 23.5 Access south to lake; primitive camping.

C 35.6 RE 23.2 Leaving Wrangell-St. Elias National Park & Preserve (westbound sign). Marshy lowland area prone to potholes and flooding.

C 41.2 RE 17.6 Culvert crossing; *slow for roller coaster dip in road.*

C 41.4 RE 17.4 TJ's Rock and Roll Camping (current status unknown).

C 42.8 RE 16 Small turnout with view (beyond the brush).

C 43 RE 15.8 Road follows high ridge; steep drop-off to south and no shoulder. Small turnouts.

C 44.1 RE 14.7 Lakina (pronounced "lack-in-aw") River 1-lane bridge; maximum height 13'2". Access to river from turnout to north at west end of bridge.

C 44.3 RE 14.5 Espresso, ice cream, gift stand (summer 2013).

C 44.5 RE 14.3 Long Lake Wildlife Refuge; shooting prohibited (eastbound sign).

Road narrows eastbound as it follows shoreline of Long Lake.

C 45.1 RE 13.7 Sign identifies entrance to Collins Estate (1961), a well-known wilderness home. Private property extends along the roadside.

C 45.3 RE 13.5 Turnout with access to **Long Lake**; a beautiful spot. Fishing for lake trout, silver salmon, grayling, Dolly Varden, burbot. Salmon spawning lake; 10 hp boat motor restriction. 🔄

C 47.6 RE 11.2 Large gravel turnout overlooking lake.

C 48.5 RE 10.3 Small turnout to south.

C 50.8 RE 8 Large gravel turnouts both sides of road at physical milepost 51. Man-made rock structures, similar to the "inukshuks" or cairns made by the Inuit, sometimes show up here in summer.

C 52.2 RE 6.6 Turnout to south.

C 53.5 RE 5.3 Culvert crossing; *slow for dip in road.*

CC 55 RE 3.8 Alaska State Forestry Wayside; large rest area with outhouses, covered picnic area, 2 tables, firepits, bear-proof litter bins and information boards. Day-use only, no camping.

CC 56 RE 2.8 Swift Creek. *Roller coaster section of road.*

C 56.7 RE 2.1 Currant Ridge Cabins offers very nice cabins and private guest house with full bath.

C 57.3 RE 1.5 Small turnout. Road travels along Fireweed Mountain. *Road narrows eastbound. Steep drop-off, slow speeds advised.*

C 57.7 RE 1.1 Damaged road (washout) summer 2013.

C 58.4 RE 0.4 Turnoff to north for

National Park Service McCarthy Ranger Station, an information kiosk with personnel available at posted hours. Public phone on side of building (free local calls). Public toilets near kiosk. Trailhead for West Kennicott Glacier Trail (signed).

Tire repair business to south.

C 58.5 RE 0.3 McCarthy B&B, Glacier View Campground; camping. Glacier View is also the first of 3 paid parking areas available eastbound. Note signs and posted fees indicating paid day-use and long-term parking areas. Visiting motorists use one of the posted parking areas along here unless you are certain you can legally park in a "free" spot (unlikely).

🏕

C 58.6 RE 0.2 Visitor Information cabin and second of 3 paid parking areas to north.

C 58.7 RE 0.1 Kennicott River Lodge cabins and hostel.

C 58.8 RE 0 Entrance to Base Camp, last paid parking area; camping (fee charged) available; potable water. (There's no garbage service; please carry out your trash.) The McCarthy Road ends here, at the Kennicott River; a pedestrian bridge spans the river's main channel to provide access to the road on the other side of the river that leads to the town of McCarthy (0.6 mile) and the old mining town of Kennicott (5 miles). Pedestrians, bicycles and possibly 4-wheelers (inquire locally) can cross the footbridge. Luggage carts are usually available at the pedestrian bridge.

🏕

Before the state constructed the footbridge across the Kennicott River in 1997, travelers had to haul themselves across the river on a hand-pulled, open-platform cable tram. *CAUTION: Do not attempt to wade across this glacial river; strong currents and cold water make it extremely treacherous.*

The Kennicott River flows from Kennicott Glacier to the Nizina River. *There is no vehicle access for visitors across the river.* (Residents pay an annual fee to use a restricted service bridge downstream.)

Walk or bicycle 0.6 mile to the town of McCarthy. The historic mining area of Kennicott is 5 miles from the footbridge. The lodges and flying services run shuttles throughout the day between the bridge, McCarthy and Kennicott; cost is $5 one-way.

Use the courtesy phones by the bridge to call businesses in McCarthy and Kennicott (if you are staying at one of the lodges, they will provide van service).

Public phones are located at both ends of the footbridge; on the front of McCarthy Lodge; on the road below Kennicott Glacier Lodge (behind menu); and at the National Park Service Ranger Station. Local calls are free. For long-distance use a credit card, phone card or call collect.

If you bring your dog, be aware there are *many* loose local dogs in the McCarthy/Kennicott area.

McCarthy/Kennicott

Located 314 miles from Anchorage. McCarthy is 0.6 mile by road from the Kennicott River pedestrian bridge at the end of the McCarthy Road; Kennicott is 5 miles by road from the pedestrian bridge. **Population**: 51. **Emergency Services**: Chitina Health Clinic, phone (907) 823-2213; Copper Center

Pedestrian bridge at the Kennicott River spans the main channel. (©Kris Valencia, staff)

Clinic, phone (907) 822-3541; Cross Road Medical Center in Glennallen, phone (907) 822-3205; Alaska State Troopers in Glennallen, phone (907) 822-3263.

Elevation: 1,531 feet. **Climate**: Temperature extremes from -58°F to 91°F; average snowfall 52 inches; annual precipitation 12 inches. **Radio**: KSKO AM 870, KXKM FM 89.7 (community public radio,) IAM 95.3 (local).

Private Aircraft: McCarthy NR 2, 1 NE; elev. 1,531 feet; length 3,500 feet; gravel; unattended, unmaintained. This is a busy airstrip in summer.

The 2 settlements in this area, McCarthy and Kennicott, both originated with the establishment of the Kennecott Mines Company in 1906. (An early day misspelling made the mining company Kennecott, while the glacier and river are Kennicott.)

The mining town of Kennicott, perched on the side of Bonanza Ridge above the wide and rocky Kennicott Glacier moraine, housed the mine offices, homes, a hospital, school and a movie theatre. Today, the 14-story Kennecott Mine mill and concentrator building towers over the narrow gravel road through "town," which includes historic structures like the old hospital and assay office, the restored recreation center, some private buildings and Kennicott Glacier Lodge. Restoration of several buildings ongoing.

McCarthy, 5 miles away, sprang up to provide the miners with more housing, saloons, a newspaper, stores, hotels, restaurants and a red-light district. A number of these pioneer structures have been restored or rebuilt and now house a variety of businesses that serve the influx of summer visitors and the small year-round population of

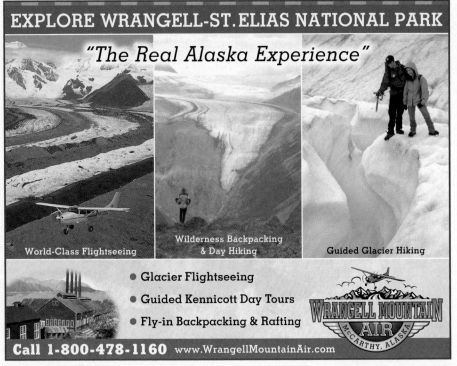

homesteaders.

There are no central water, sewer or electrical systems in McCarthy/Kennicott. Generators provide power and water is pumped from wells or hauled by hand. Outhouses and septic systems are in use. There are no state schools or health clinics (the nearest clinic is in Chitina). The mail plane arrives year-round, although the local population drops in winter.

The area's remoteness, historic buildings and magnificent scenery are what draw an increasing number of visitors every year. Food, lodging and guide and flying services are provided by the local businesses that operate here in summer (see ads this section). Tire service was available in 2013.

Lodging & Services

McCarthy has the **McCarthy Lodge** (with fine dining), the **New Golden Saloon** (casual dining) and **Ma Johnson's Hotel** (description follows), as well as McCarthy Mercantile (a grocery store that also serves ice cream), the Roadside Potatohead (food and espresso) and other small businesses. McCarthy public restrooms are near the museum.

Accommodations and services in Kennicott are more limited, with the well-known **Kennicott Glacier Lodge** offering lodging

and dining (ask about their daily meal specials and Labor Day barbecue); description follows. There is a pizza parlour in Kennicott. The restored General Store, operated by the National Park Service, sells books, souvenirs and some outdoor gear.

McCarthy Lodge & Ma Johnson's Hotel. Our "Living Museum Hotel" won a coveted spot in National Geographic's "129 Hotels We Love To Stay At." New York Magazine's Grubstreet.com rated us the #1 destination restaurant in Alaska. Featured in Sunset magazine's Food Lovers issue. Food & Wine rated us "one of 5 new summer destinations." Outstanding wine list. Visit www.McCarthyLodge.com. (907) 554-4402. See display ad on this page. [ADVERTISEMENT]

Kennicott Glacier Lodge, in the middle of Wrangell-St. Elias National Park, offers the area's finest accommodations and dining. Family owned and operated for 25 years, Kennicott Glacier Lodge provides 35 clean, comfortable guest rooms, 3 family rooms, and a spacious dining room. From the 180-foot front porch you get a panoramic view of the Wrangell Mountains, Chugach Mountains and Kennicott Glacier. The new South Wing features 10 guest rooms, each with private bathrooms: a unique luxury in a remote lodge. The

homemade food, served family-style, has been called "wilderness gourmet." Activities at this destination lodge include alpine and glacier hiking, flightseeing, historical and nature tours, and rafting. Open May 24 to Sept. 13, 2014. Phone 1-800-582-5128. www.KennicottLodge.com. See display ad facing page. [ADVERTISEMENT]

Camping

Camping is available on the west side of the pedestrian bridge at Base Camp parking lot and Glacier View Campground. There is no free camping on the parking area side of the footbridge at the end of the McCarthy Road. A fee of $20 (subject to change) is charged for camping on private land in this area.

There are no designated campgrounds within the surrounding national park and preserve; wilderness camping only, the nearest being a 1.5-mile hike out of Kennicott. Check with the National Park Service about camping in the Kennicott area. Mandatory bear-resistant containers are loaned with deposit. (Earth Sacks do not meet the requirements here and are illegal.)

Transportation

Transportation: Air—Charter service to and from airstrip near McCarthy. **Wrangell Mountain Air** also offers 3 scheduled flights daily between Chitina and McCarthy, phone (907) 554-4411. The airstrip is reached via a wide road south from McCarthy. Shuttle service available. Good photo opportunities for shots of surrounding mountains from the airstrip.

Van—Shuttle service between McCarthy and Kennicott via Wrangell Mountain Bus

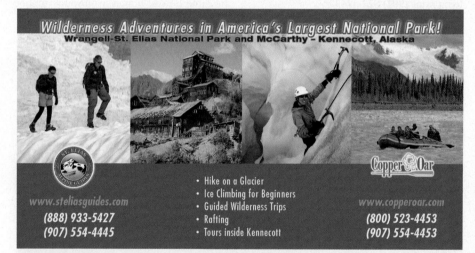

MCCARTHY/KENNICOTT ADVERTISERS

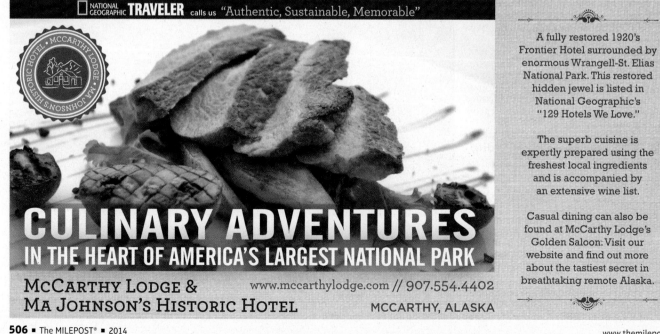

from Wrangell Mountain Air office; 1-way fare $5/adults, $2/dogs; phone (907) 554-4411. The McCarthy–Kennicott shuttle runs on the half-hour. Local lodges also run shuttles for guests.

Attractions

The **McCarthy–Kennicott Historical Museum** is located in the historic railway depot and has historical artifacts and photos

©David L. Ranta, staff

Root Glacier Trail is a popular day hike from Kennicott. (©Meghan Mackey, staff)

from the early mining days. It is open 11:30 A.M. to 7 P.M. daily, staffed by volunteers. A self-guided Historical Walking Tour of McCarthy is on sale at the museum. A short walking trail takes off across from the museum to an old railroad turnaround.

Join a guided tour of Kennicott and the mine buildings. The tours offer a fascinating look at this area's history. National Park Service tours are free and tour the more accessible mine buildings. The mill tour with St. Elias Alpine Guides is more strenuous and there is a fee. Do not miss these tours!

Slide presentations, a film, and other programs are presented by the National Park Service at Kennicott in summer. Inquire at the park visitor center in the restored General Store (built in 1917).

A popular day hike from Kennicott is the **Root Glacier Trail**. The easy to moderate 3-mile round trip takes you from Kennecott Mill Town along the lateral moraine of the Kennicott and Root Glaciers to the toe of the glacier. Allow 2 to 6 hours to hike. Also makes a good mountain bike trip, according to the Park Service. The Bonanza Mine hike is a longer and more strenuous hike (9 miles round-trip with 3,800-foot elevation gain) that splits off of the Root Glacier trail

about 0.5 mile from Visitor Center. Another that splits off the same trail is the Jumbo Mine trail. It is a 10-mile, 3,300-foot elevation gain route to Jumbo Mine. Check with Park personnel about other area hikes.

Guided hikes, flightseeing, ice climbing, river rafting, fly-in and/or hike-in backpacking, mountaineering, ziplines and other outdoor activites are offered by area outfitters. Outfitters usually offer scheduled trips to accommodate independent travelers and small tour groups, but also customize both dates and trips to satisfy individual needs. Contact: **St. Elias Alpine Guides** (www.steliasguides.com); **Wrangell Mountain Air** (www.WrangellMountainAir.com); and **Copper Oar** (www.copperoar.com). Alaska Boreal Canopy, headquartered in McCarthy, has a canopy course with 6 zip lines.

St. Elias Alpine Guides offers full and half day hikes on nearby glaciers with professional guides. Those looking for unique Alaskan adventure can try ice climbing with a full day beginner lesson. Historic tours inside the Kennecott mill building available daily. Call for information and reservations.

Phone (888) 933-5427 or (907) 554-4445. www.steliasguides.com. See display ad on facing page. [ADVERTISEMENT]

Wrangell Mountain Air provides 3 scheduled flights daily between Chitina and McCarthy–Kennicott as an alternative to driving the McCarthy Road. Just park your car or RV at the Chitina Airport and enjoy a spectacular flight with world-class vistas of 16,000-foot peaks, 25-mile-long glaciers and massive icefalls. Day trips and overnight lodging available. Guided Kennicott Tours, glacier hikes, ice climbing and river rafting are just some of the unique experiences you will find in the area. Wrangell Mountain Air specializes in flightseeing tours of the Park, fly-in backpacking and rafting trips as well as day hiking. Aircraft are high wing for unobstructed viewing and equipped with intercoms and individual headsets for each passenger. Call toll-free for reservations and information, 1-800-478-1160 or (907) 554-4411. Email: info@WrangellMountainAir.com. Visit our website at www.WrangellMountainAir.com. See display ad on page 505. [ADVERTISEMENT]

Wrangell–St. Elias National Park and Preserve

Explore Kennecott on your own or take a guided tour. (©Meghan Mackey, staff)

Wrangell-St. Elias National Park and Preserve is the largest unit in the National Park system, encompassing 13.2 million acres of wild lands and 9.7 million acres of designated Wilderness. Formed by the Wrangell, St. Elias, Chugach and Alaska mountain ranges, the park contains the greatest collection of peaks over 16,000 feet on the continent, including Mount St. Elias (18,029 feet), the second tallest peak in the United States. Major peaks in the park include Mount Wrangell (14,163 feet, an active volcano), Mount Blackburn (16,390 feet), Mount Sanford (16,237 feet) and Mount Drum (12,010 feet).

The park also contains the largest concentration of glaciers on the continent. One of these, Malaspina Glacier, is North America's largest piedmont glacier, a type formed when 2 or more glaciers flow from confined valleys to form a broad fan- or lobe-shaped ice mass. Malaspina Glacier covers an area of about 1,500 square miles—larger than the state of Rhode Island. It has been designated a National Natural Landmark. Hubbard Glacier, which flows out of the St. Elias Mountains into Disenchantment Bay, is one of the most active glaciers in North America. It is presently advancing in spite of global climate change.

Also located in the park are Chitistone and Nizina canyons. Both have been described as exceeding the scale of Yosemite Valley in California, with an even greater variety of geological wonders. There is a spectacular, 300-foot waterfall in upper Chitistone Canyon, and the lower canyon has sheer walls rising 4,000 feet above the river.

Although the scale of the park seems overwhelming, for motorists the choices of how to visit Wrangell-St. Elias are relatively few. Road access to the northern section of the park and preserve is from Slana on the Tok Cutoff via the 43-mile Nabesna Road. The major road access to the west side of Wrangell-St. Elias is via the Edgerton Highway/McCarthy Road.

The Kennecott area is one of the major centers of activity in the park, perhaps because it contains one of the park's best known attractions: the huge complex of barn-red buildings that make up the Kennecott mill town, now a National Historic Landmark. The mill was built in 1907 by Kennecott Copper Corporation (an early day misspelling made the mining company Kennecott, while the glacier and river are Kennicott).

The National Park Service purchased many of the mill structures (although several are still privately owned), and work is under way to rehabilitate and stabilize the site. There is variable access to the buildings: not all structures are open due to concerns for visitor safety. Narrated tours of the mill are available from St. Elias Alpine Guides. The National Park Service conducts daily summer ranger programs at the Kennecott Visitor Center and offers daily programs in the recreation hall in Kennecott.

The Kennecott mines, including 70 miles of subterranean tunnels, are up near the ridge top (behind present-day Kennicott Glacier Lodge), and were connected to the mill by aerial trams. The mine operated from 1911 until 1938. *WARNING: Do not enter or attempt to enter any mine in the park.*

While copper mining inspired some of the early prospectors to travel to the land that is now Wrangell-St. Elias National Park and Preserve, it was the discovery of gold in Chisana (pronounced Shooshana) that began the last great gold rush in Alaska. In 1913, thousands of stampeders made the treacherous journey through rugged country by whatever means possible to reach the newfound mining district. Chisana soon became known as "the largest log cabin town in the world." It was a short boom, lasting only a few years, but an important part of the history of this area.

Recreational opportunities in Wrangell-St. Elias include hunting, fishing, expedition mountaineering, backpacking/hiking, cross-country skiing, rafting/kayaking and wildlife observation. All hunting, fishing and trapping must be done in accordance with state and federal laws and regulations.

Navigable rivers in the park include the Copper and Chitina rivers. It is also possible to float several other streams in the park, such as the Nabesna and Kennicott rivers. Several guides and outfitters offer a variety of trips in the park and preserve.

Other than a handful of improved trails, hikers follow unimproved backcountry routes consisting of mining trails, historic routes, streambeds, shorelines, game trails and open country. For many hikers, hiring the services of a local guide will make the trip safer and more enjoyable. In general, the areas above tree line afford the easiest hiking and best views. These areas are often accessed by charter plane to one of the many "bush" landing strips in the park. Contact the park for current information on summer and winter use of ATVs on park and preserve lands.

The Park Service cautions that visitors to the Wrangell-St. Elias backcountry must be self-sufficient; sources of assistance are frequently many miles away. Wilderness travel and survival skills are essential.

There are 14 public-use cabins located within Wrangell-St. Elias. All cabins are in remote locations and require hikers/campers to make appropriate plans for backcountry travel. Most cabins are available on a first-come, first-served basis, however there are currently 5 cabins that require advance reservations. Go to the park's public-use cabin page at www.nps.gov/wrst/planyourvisit/backcountry-cabins.htm to learn more about these cabins and to make a reservation.

There are a few designated campgrounds within the park/preserve; most opportunities are wilderness camping. No permits are necessary for camping or backpacking although voluntary registration is requested.

Visitor Information: The Kennecott Visitor Center is located at the restored General Store in Kennecott, built in 1917. Open daily in summer; books, souvenirs and other items for sale. Slide presentations, a film, and other programs are presented here by the National Park Service.

The main Wrangell-St. Elias National Park and Preserve Visitor Center complex is located at **Milepost V 106.8** on the Richardson Highway. The visitor center, theater and exhibit hall are open daily in summer. Call ahead for winter schedule.

Park information is available intermittently at the historic Chitina Ranger Station in Chitina, and at the McCarthy Ranger information station kiosk at **Milepost C 58.4** McCarthy Road.

At the northern end of the park, information is available daily during the summer and weekdays during the winter at the Slana Ranger Station at Mile 0.2 Nabesna Road off the Tok Cutoff.

For more information, contact Wrangell St. Elias National Park and Preserve, Park Headquarters, P.O. Box 439, Copper Center, AK 99573; phone (907) 822-7250, fax (907) 822-7216; visit www.nps.gov/wrst; email wrst_interpretation@nps.gov.park. Or phone the ranger stations at Slana (907/822-7401), Chitina (907/823-2205), Kennecott (907/554-1105) and in Yakutat (907/784-3295).

Denali Highway

CONNECTS: Paxson to Cantwell, AK

Length: 134 miles   **Road Surface:** 15% Paved, 85% Gravel   **Season:** Closed in winter

(See map, page 510)

(See map, page 510)

⑧

The Denali Highway's spectacular scenery makes it a favorite destination for Alaskans and visitors.
(© Sharon Nault)

Major Attractions:

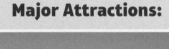

Tangle Lakes–Delta River Canoe Trail, Maclaren Summit Trail, Susitna River, Alaska Range

Highest Summit:
Maclaren Summit 4,086 ft.

The 134-mile-long Denali Highway links Paxson at **Milepost V 185.5** on the Richardson Highway to Cantwell at **Milepost A 210** on the Parks Highway. When the Denali Highway opened in 1957, it was the only road link to Denali National Park and Preserve (then Mount McKinley National Park) until the completion of the Parks Highway in 1972. This is a very scenic route and motorists have a good chance of seeing wildlife.

The first 21 miles of the Denali Highway from Paxson and the first 3 miles from Cantwell are paved. The remaining 110 miles are gravel.

Summer road conditions on the gravel portion of the Denali Highway vary, depending on highway maintenance, weather and the opinion of the driver. Trenching along the highway makes for rough access to many of the turnouts.

Road surfacing beyond the paved sections normally ranges from good gravel to rough and rocky. Washboard and potholes can develop quickly after days of rain. You must be prepared to go slowly on this route, if necessary. This can be a dusty drive for motorists—and a very dusty ride for bicyclists—in dry weather. All types of vehicles and bicyclists share this road. The recommended speed of travel is 30 mph on gravel portions of the road (with slower speeds in areas with sharp rocks, remember to decrease speed with approaching traffic so rocks do not get thrown into the oncoming car or its windshield). For updated road information, phone 511 in state, toll-free 1-866-282-7577 out of state, or http://511.alaska.gov.

The highway becomes narrower and more winding west of Maclaren Summit (elev. 4,086 feet). This is the second highest highway pass in the state, and represents the only significant grade on the highway.

The Denali Highway is closed in winter. Seasonal maintenance ends October 15. The Alaska Dept. of Transportation & Public Facilities reminds drivers that travel on a non-maintained highway during the winter

Distance in miles	Cantwell	Delta Junction	Denali Park	Paxson
Cantwell		214	27	134
Delta Junction	214		241	80
Denali Park	27	241		161
Paxson	134	80	161	

Denali Highway
Paxson, AK, to Cantwell, AK

© 2014 The MILEPOST®

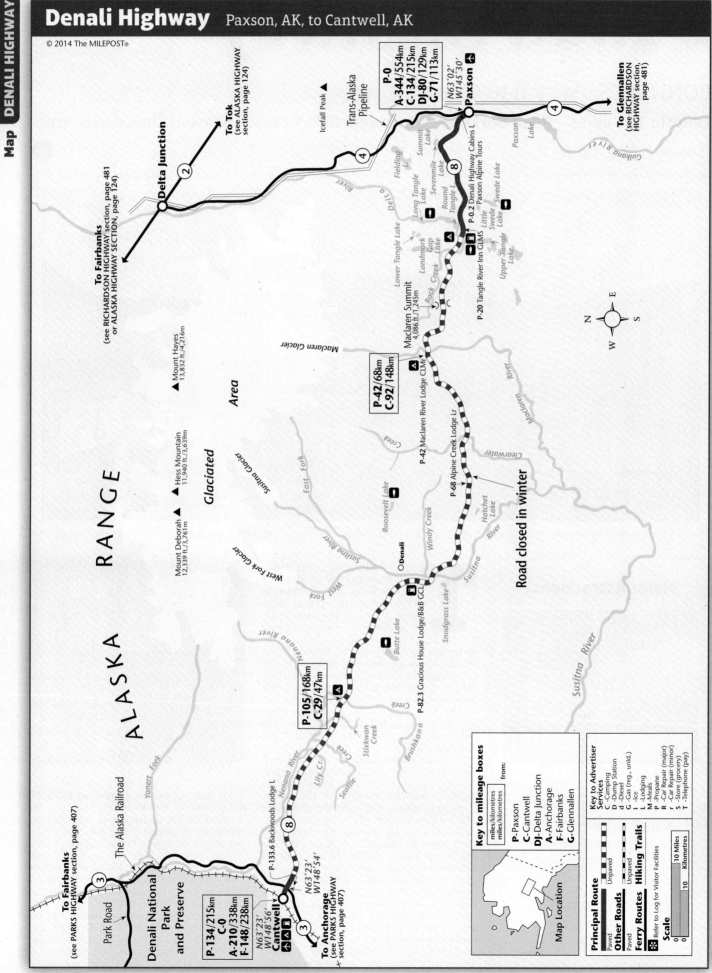

To Tok
(see ALASKA HIGHWAY
section, page 124)

Icefall Peak ▲

Trans-Alaska
Pipeline

P-0
A-344/554km
C-134/215km
DJ-80/129km
G-71/113km

N63°02'
W145°30'
Paxson

To Glennallen
(see RICHARDSON
HIGHWAY section,
page 481)

To Fairbanks
To Fairbanks
(see RICHARDSON HIGHWAY section, page 481
or ALASKA HIGHWAY SECTION, page 124)

Delta Junction

Summit
Lake

Fielding
Lake

Denali Highway Cabins L
Paxson Alpine Tours

P-0.2

Sevenmile
Lake

Long Tangle
Lake

Round
Tangle L

Little
Swede
Lake

Swede Lake

Paxson
Lake

Guikana River

P-20 Tangle River Inn GLMS

Upper Tangle
Lake

▲ Mount Hayes
13,832 ft./4,216m

Lower Tangle Lake

Landmark
Gap
Lake

Rock Creek

Maclaren Summit
4,086 ft./1,245m

Maclaren Glacier

N   E
W   S

Glaciated
Area

Mount Deborah ▲
12,339 ft./3,761m

▲ Hess Mountain
11,940 ft./3,639m

Susitna Glacier

P-42/68km
C-92/148km

P-42 Maclaren River Lodge CLM

Maclaren
River

Clearwater

ALASKA
RANGE

West Fork Glacier

East Fork

Susitna River

Creek

Roosevelt Lake

Windy Creek

Denali

P-68 Alpine Creek Lodge Lr

Hatchet
Lake

Susitna River

Road closed in winter

Susitna River

P-82.3 Gracious House Lodge/B&B GCL

Snodgrass Lake

Brushkana

Nenana River

Butte Lake

P-105/168km
C-29/47km

Creek

Stikiwan Creek

To Fairbanks
(see PARKS HIGHWAY section, page 407)

Park Road

The Alaska Railroad

Denali National
Park
and Preserve

P-133.6 Backwoods Lodge L

Lily Cr.

Scottie

Nenana River

N63°23'
W148°54'

P-134/215km
C-0
A-210/338km
F-148/238km

N63°23',
W148°56'

Cantwell

To Anchorage
(see PARKS HIGHWAY
section, page 407)

Yanert Fork

Creek

Key to mileage boxes
miles/kilometres
miles/kilometres

from:

P-Paxson
C-Cantwell
DJ-Delta Junction
A-Anchorage
F-Fairbanks
G-Glennallen

Key to Advertiser Services
C -Camping
D -Dump Station
d -Diesel
G -Gas (reg., unld.)
I -Ice
L -Lodging
M -Meals
P -Propane
R -Car Repair (major)
r -Car Repair (minor)
S -Store (grocery)
T -Telephone (pay)

Refer to Log for Visitor Facilities

Map Location

Principal Route
Paved
Unpaved

Other Roads
Paved
Unpaved

Ferry Routes Hiking Trails

Scale
0   10 Miles
0   10 Kilometres

is extremely risky. Crews begin opening the highway in early May, which involves 8 personnel working for 3 weeks from both Cantwell and Paxon. When snow covered, the Denali Highway is regularly used by snowmachines traveling out to the different lodges, but drifts can claim a vehicle.

The Denali Highway has been a favorite destination for many Alaskans over the years. Long-standing businesses and newer businesses along the highway attest to this road's enduring popularity with travelers: Audie and Jenny's Denali Highway Cabins at Paxson; Tangle River Inn at **Milepost P 20**; MacClaren River Lodge at **Milepost 42**; Gracious House at **Milepost 82**; and Alpine Creek Lodge at **Milepost 68**.

The Denali Highway provides access to the Delta River canoe trail at Tangle Lakes, headwaters of the Delta National Wild and Scenic River. For detailed information on ORV (off road vehicle) use on public lands or canoeing the Delta River, contact the Bureau of Land Management office in Glennallen, phone (907) 822-3217, or visit www.blm .gov/ak/st/en/prog/recreation/denali_high way.html for more information.

Birders will find Smith's Longspur, harlequin ducks, gyrfalcons, arctic warblers and more than 100 other species along the Denali Highway. Birders might want to stop in at Paxson Alpine Tours or at Denali Highway Cabins (www.denalihwy.com) at **Milepost P 0.2** to talk to Dr. Audubon L. Bakewell IV and view his resident nesting merlins. Dr. Bakewell is co-author of the *ABA Bird Finding Guide to Alaska*.

Emergency medical services: Alaska State Troopers at Cantwell, phone (907) 768-2202. Cantwell Volunteer Ambulance, dispatch (907) 768-2982. NOTE: *Cell phone service is spotty on the Denali Highway to* **Milepost P 31**, *and then no service on the highway until* **Milepost P 128.2**, *just a few miles from the Parks Highway. Calling from lodges can be expensive via radio phone.*

Stunning view of Alaska Range from rest area at Milepost P 7. (©Meghan Mackey, staff)

Denali Highway Log

Distance from Paxson (P) is followed by distance from junction with the Parks Highway at Cantwell (C).

ALASKA ROUTE 8

P 0 C 133.8 PAXSON (pop. 16; elev. 2,650 feet) began in 1906 when Alvin Paxson established a roadhouse at Mile 192. He later built a larger roadhouse at Mile 191; the ruins can be seen on the east side of the highway at **Milepost V 185.8** Richardson Highway. The current Paxson Lodge, a local landmark, was reported as closing its doors in December 2013; current status unknown. Lodging is available at **Denali Highway Cabins**, which also operates **Paxson Alpine Tours**; see description at **Milepost P 0.2**.

> **Junction** of the Richardson Highway (Alaska Route 4) with the Denali Highway (Alaska Route 8). Turn to **Milepost V 185.5** on page 492 in the RICHARDSON HIGHWAY section for log.

Private Aircraft: Paxson airstrip, adjacent south; elev. 2,653 feet; length 2,800 feet; gravel; emergency fuel; attended.
Posted speed limit 50 mph westbound.

P 0.2 C 133.6 Gulkana River bridge.

Side road north to **Denali Highway Cabins**; very nice cabins, communal kitchen, gift shop. Gulkana River float trips and nature tours offered by hosts Dr. Audubon Bakewell and Denali Jenny. Stop by and meet Aurora and Borealis (the dogs).

Denali Highway Cabins & Paxson Alpine Tours. See display ad on page 493 in RICHARDSON HIGHWAY section.

P 0.3 C 133.5 Active gravel pit to south; informal camping. Spawning red salmon in season. (This portion of the Gulkana River is closed to salmon fishing.) Look for "harleys" (harlequin ducks), arctic terns and other birds. Trail to Mud Lake.

Distance marker shows Tangle Lakes 21 miles, Cantwell 136 miles, Denali Park 164 miles.

P 0.4 C 133.4 There are several long upgrades and many turnouts the next 21 miles westbound. Wildflowers carpet the tundra in the spring and summer. Watch for nesting swans and brilliant fall colors. This is an Alaskan favorite road for beauty, hiking, ORV trails, hunting and fishing.

Entering Paxson Closed Area (sign) westbound. The area south of the Denali Highway and east of the Richardson Highway is closed to the taking of all big game.

P 0.7 C 133.1 Large paved turnout to south.

P 1.5 C 132.3 Large paved turnout to south.

P 2.1 C 131.7 Large paved turnout on hilltop to south. Westbound travelers may note the change in vegetation from spruce forest to alpine tundra.

P 3.4 C 130.4 Paved turnout to south. Several more turnouts next 3 miles westbound with views of Summit Lake to the north, Gakona Glacier to the northeast, Icefall Peak and Gulkana Glacier west of Icefall Peak, all in the **Alaska Range**. The 650-mile-long range, which extends across southcentral Alaska from the Canadian border southwest to Iliamna Lake, also contains Mount McKinley (Denali), the highest peak in North America.

Good views of trans-Alaska pipeline for Paxson-bound travelers.

P 4 C 129.8 Paved turnout to north. Views to east next 3 miles westbound of

Mounts Sanford, Wrangell and Drum in the Wrangell Mountains; see viewpoint at **Milepost P 12.7**.

P 4.4 C 129.4 Paved viewpoint to the north.

P 5 C 128.8 Large paved turnout to north.

P 5.7 C 128.1 Paved turnout to north.

P 6.2 C 127.6 Turnout to south.

P 6.4 C 127.4 Side road to north leads to small lake and down to Sevenmile Lake to limited parking and informal camping.

Small boats can be launched here for good lake trout fishing. 🐟

P 6.7 C 127.1 Paved turnout to south.

P 7 C 126.8 Paved rest area to the north. Vehicle, bus and RV parking. Viewing benches, picnic tables, outhouse, bearproof garbage cans.

Stunning view of Alaska Range and 7 Mile Lake to northeast of Summit Lake and Gulkana Glacier. Information board with diagram showing the Alaska Range being pushed up by the North American plate. Another board shows a diagram of the mountains and their names. Other boards show a map of the highway and illuminate topics like "Fish on the Denali" and "Trauma Under the Ice." A visually appealing and informative stop.

P 7.2 C 126.6 Paved turnout to north. Highway climbs westbound.

P 7.8 C 126 Paved turnout to north.

P 8.3 C 125.5 Federal Subsistence area boundary. Paved turnout to north.

P 9.5 C 124.3 Paved turnout overlooking Ten Mile Lake. Primitive camping area.

P 10 C 123.8 Sloping, paved turnout to south overlooking **Ten Mile Lake**.

P 10.5 C 123.3 Paved turnout overlooking **Ten Mile Lake** to south at the top of an extensive glacial outwash plain dotted with kettle ponds; known locally as Hungry Hollow. These are examples of kettle lakes, formed by melting chunks of buried glacier. Highway begins to climb hill westbound. 🐟

P 10.6 C 123.2 Rough, narrow, gravel road leads 0.3 mile south to **Octopus Lake**; limited parking, fishing for lake trout, grayling, whitefish. 🐟

P 11 C 122.8 Federal Subsistence Hunting area (westbound sign).

P 11.1 C 122.7 Paved turnout to south. Look for blueberries in season. This is an area of treeless tundra.

NOTE: Watch for frost heaves next 5.2 miles westbound.

P 11.5 C 122.3 Paved turnout to south. Views of Hungry Hollow continue westbound.

P 12.1 C 121.7 Paved turnout to south with sweeping views of the tundra and lakes below.

P 12.5 C 121.3 Large gravel turnout at top of hill to south with panoramic views and a primitive campsite.

P 12.7 C 121.1 Paved turnout to south is Wrangell Mountain viewpoint. BLM information sign on Denali Highway campgrounds, trailheads, points of interest and services. BLM brochures on the area are usually available at a box next to the sign.

The Wrangell Mountains are about 78 air miles southeast of here. The prominent peak on the left is Mount Sanford (16,237 feet); Mount Drum (12,010 feet) is on the right; and Mount Wrangell (14,163 feet) is in the center. Mount Wrangell is the northernmost active volcano on the Pacific Rim.

CAUTION: Slow for frost heaves and potholes to MP P 16.

P 13.6 C 120.2 Lake locally referred to as Cottongrass Lake; masses of cotton grass grow in this area.

P 14 C 119.8 Turnout to **14 Mile Lake**. Area offers primitive camping and fishing for rainbow trout (ADF&G stocked lake). A trail across the highway starting at the top of the cut bank, travels north along the top of ridge and offers good views of the area. The lake is 2.5 miles north of the highway and is in the valley to the west of Ridge Trail. It is stocked with rainbow and lake trout. There are many trails in this area. Ask Jack Johnson at the Tangle River Inn for details as he and his father and friends pioneered the local trails.

P 14.1 C 119.7 Paved turnout; small visible lakes to north. Hikers often begin the 14 Mile Lake hike from here.

P 14.6 C. 119.2 Paved turnout to north. Highway begins descent westbound to Tangle Lakes area. Frost heaves. Rough road, both sides of the turnout.

P 15.4 C 118.4 Paved turnout to south with view of Swede lakes area to southwest.

P 16.1 C 117.7 Swede Lake Trail to south; Little Swede Lake 3 miles (take right fork), Big Swede Lake 4 miles. Access via signed primitive gravel loop road. This trail connects with the Middle Fork Gulkana River branch trail (access to Dickey Lake and Meier Lake trail) and the Alphabet Hills trail. **Big Swede Lake** has excellent fishing for lake trout, grayling, whitefish and burbot. **Little Swede Lake** is excellent for lake trout. Inquire at Tangle River Inn for directions and trail information.

P 16.2 C 117.6 Entering **BLM Tangle Lakes Archaeological District** (sign to south) westbound. Within this 226,000-acre area, more than 500 archaeological sites chronicle man's seasonal reliance on the local natural resources. For more than 10,000 years, hunter-gatherers have dug roots, picked berries, fished and hunted big game (primarily caribou) in this area. You may hike along the same high, gravel ridges once used by prehistoric people and used today by modern hunters, anglers and berry pickers. To protect cultural resources, ORV travel is restricted to designated trails from this point to **Milepost P 38.**

P 16.7 C 117.1 Gravel pit and paved turnout to south. Trucks entering the roadway here. Long gravel turnout to north is referred to by locals as "the one with the big rock in it," a landmark because of area fishing lakes. At the east end of the turnout, a trail leads to an unnamed but good fishing lake. At the west end of the turnout, alongside the road, is a shallow lake that has fish when water levels are high. For fishing questions and local lakes, ask Jack Johnson at Tangle River Inn. He and his father pioneered most of this area's trails.

P 17.1 C 116.7 Paved turnout to north. Trailhead for **Rusty Lake** ¾ mile to lake. Registration box at head of the trail. Fish for lake trout and grayling.

P 17.6 C 116.2 Paved turnouts both sides of highway.

P 18.1 C 115.7 Gravel turnouts by small lakes both sides of highway.

P 18.3 C 115.5 Entrance to private hunting camp to south.

P 18.6 C 115.2 Paved view turnout to north.

P 19.3 C 114.5 Paved turnout to south. A hiking trail is located here and provides access to Swede Mountain and views of the Tangle Lakes and Alaska Range. Federal Subsistence area boundary. Delta U.S. Department of Interior Wild and Scenic River (sign).

P 20 C 113.8 Tangle River Inn to south; food, gas, lodging. Jack Johnson homesteaded this area in 1953. The BLM honored his wife, Naidine Johnson, by naming a mountain after her in 2003. Stop in and see the plaque and the map showing the location of Mount Naidine.

Tangle River Inn. See display ad this page.

P 20.2 C 113.6 Large paved turnout to north just west of the Tangle River Inn overlooks **Round Tangle Lake**. This lake is one of a series of long, narrow lakes connected by the Tangle River that form the headwaters of the Delta River. The name Tangle is a descriptive term for the maze of lakes and feeder streams contained in this drainage system. Canoe rentals available at Tangle River Inn.

View to north of Alaska Range.

P 21 C 112.8 The Nelchina caribou herd travels through this area, usually around the end of August or early in September, and hundreds have been spotted in this area as early as late July.

P 21.1 C 112.7 *NOTE: Pavement ends, gravel begins westbound. Watch for potholes, washboard and washouts westbound. Slow for frost heaves in pavement eastbound.*

P 21.3 C 112.5 One-lane bridge over Tangle River. Turnoff to north for access to **Tangle Lakes BLM Campground**, 0.7 mile north from highway. Campground fee $12/night in 2013, rates subject to change. There are 45 sites; toilets, tables, firepits, potable water, aluminum-can recycling, bear-proof garbage cans, numerous hiking trails, cement boat launch, personal flotation devices (free to use for children and return), volunteer campground host. Firewood available for $5. Information board gives instructions on what to do if you catch a tagged fish. This is a favorite place to camp for many Alaskans. Good berry picking in season. Walk the high ridges for wonderful views. Watch for mink, squirrels, ptarmigan, eagles, swans, caribou and moose along the Tangle River. Popular fishing spot for grayling, lake trout.

Easy access to boat launch for **Delta River Canoe Trail**, which goes north through Tangle Lakes to the Delta River. Self-register for river trips. The 2- to 3-day float to the takeout point on the Richardson Highway requires 1 portage. The Delta River Canoe Trail is managed by the BLM.

P 21.5 C 112.3 Delta National Wild and Scenic River BLM Wayside and Boat Launch to south, day-use only; picnic tables, fire grills, garbage cans, toilets, potable water, boat launch area, no fee. 2 turnaround loops for easy-flow traffic in narrowed areas. Launch point for Upper Tangle Lakes canoe trail, which goes south through Tangle Lakes (portages required) to Dickey Lake, then follows the Middle Fork to the main Gulkana River. For details, contact the BLM, Box 147, Glennallen, AK 99588; phone (907) 822-3217. Register here for river trips. Area has life jackets and sign for Kids Don't

Float program. Info boards on water, wildlife and willows.

Watershed divide. The Gulkana River joins the Copper River, which flows into Prince William Sound. The Delta River joins the Tanana River, which flows into the Yukon River. The Yukon flows into the Bering Sea.

The Tangle Lakes system north and south of the highway (**Long Tangle, Round Tangle, Upper Tangle and Lower Tangle Lake**) offers good grayling and lake trout fishing. Fishing begins as soon as the ice goes out, usually in early June, and continues into September. Troll shelf edges for lake trout.

P 22 C 111.8 Tangle Lakes Lodge (closed in 2013; current status unknown).

P 22.3 C 111.5 Federal Subsistence area boundary.

P 24.4 C 109.4 Turnout to south. Landmark Gap Trailhead visible to north, Rock Creek Bridge to west.

Distance marker shows Cantwell 110.

P 24.5 C 109.3 Landmark Gap, the cut in the mountains to the north, is visible from the highway. It is used by caribou during migration. This is a favorite trail for hikers too. A side road leads north to well-marked, improved **Landmark Gap Trailhead**. Primitive camping up rocky road onto a hill to the north. The trail leads 4 miles north to the south end of **Landmark Gap Lake**; grayling and lake trout fishing. According to the State of Alaska, Department of Natural Resources, this trail is suitable for mountain bikes and hiking.

P 24.7 C 109.1 Rock Creek 1-lane bridge; turnout and informal camping to north at west end of bridge. Grayling fishing. Parking and creek access to north at both ends of bridge.

P 24.8 C 109 Landmark Gap South ORV Trail is well signed to the southwest of highway; parking. The trail leads to the Oscar Lake area (11 miles).

Double-ended gravel parking to south just west of trailhead.

P 25.4 C 108.4 Rough gravel turnout to south for informal campsite and expansive views.

P 25.5 C 108.3 Gravel turnout to the south.

P 26 C 107.8 Side road to north.

P 28.1 C 105.7 Gravel turnout to north, overlooking lake and ponds.

P 29.3 C 104.5 Informal campsite beside small lake to south. Watch for grouse and caribou. Unmarked primitive roads to north and south.

P 30 C 103.8 Downhill access to north to primitive camping area.

P 30.5 C 103.3 Glacier Lake Trailhead to north; well-marked with signs. Primitive camping uphill.

Turnout to north on high, sometimes windy, overlook for **Glacier Lake ORV Trail**, which leads north 3 miles to Glacier Lake; lake trout and grayling fishing. 360 degree views of Alaska Range. Rock Creek to the north runs parallel to the highway in valley below.

Highway winds along steep-sided esker westbound. An esker is a ridge made of silt, sand, gravel, rocks and boulders carried by a stream beneath a glacier in those areas. When the glacier melts, an elongated rise of these substances, remains. The Denali High-

way has some of the best examples of eskers, found in North America.

P 30.7 C 103.1 Gravel turnout to north overlooking lake and ponds.

P 31 C 102.8 Short, rough, steep road to north, up small knoll with big views, called the "knob."

P 31.4 C 102.4 Very rough, rock turnout to north. In spite of this, people camp here for the view (primitive). Cell phone, via AT&T, worked here in 2013.

P 32.1 C 101.7 Gravel turnout to south and turnout to north (can have a pond in wet weather) with dramatic view of Amphitheater Mountains above High Valley. Glacier Lake is visible in the gap in these mountains. Glacier Gap trailhead; multipurpose trail. East side of parking lot runs to Glacier Gap Lake and out to 7 Mile lake. Trail to 7 Mile Lake is 9 miles (local trailbuilder labeled the lake "spectacular").

Sporadic cell phone reception.

P 33.6 C 100.2 Parking area and informal camping to south. Small turnout to north. Locals claim that there are 20 to 30 caribou that range near here, year-round.

P 34.5 C 99.3 Dramatic high peaks of the Alaska Range visible to north, weather permitting.

P 35.2 C 98.6 Turnout to north. Views to the northwest of lakes on the western rim of "High Valley." Below the plunging rim to the west is the valley of the Maclaren River. The Amphitheatre Mountains parallel the highway to the northwest. Wildflowers here include various heaths, frigid shooting star, dwarf fireweed.

P 36 C 97.8 36 Mile Lake 0.5-mile hike north; lake trout and grayling.

P 36.3 C 97.5 Small rough turnout to south (turns down steeply to south). This area gets muddy in wet weather.

P 36.4 C 97.4 Huge views at turnout to north.

P 36.7 C 97.1 Oscar Lake ORV Trail to south leads approximately 7 miles to Oscar Lake. Good parking area to south for both this and the **Maclaren Summit ORV Trailhead** on north side of road. The trailhead sign says it is about 2 miles; it is 1.5 miles to

a fork, bear left for best views. Trail continues if you are looking for a longer hike.

The Alaska Dept. of Natural Resources recommends this 3-mile trail for mountain biking and hiking. Black currant berries and blueberries in season. Good views of the Alaska Range. Watch for swans, moose and other wildlife here. Registration boards with map.

Maclaren Summit (elev. 4,086 feet). Second highest highway pass in Alaska (after 4,800-foot Atigun Pass on the Dalton Highway). From here you can look to the west where the Denali Highway enters the notch at **Milepost P 45.1.** For westbound travelers the highway drops down beneath the rim of the High Valley Mesa to the Maclaren River.

P 36.8 C 97 Maclaren Summit elevation sign (elevation noted above). Small turnout to west with view of river valley, Mount Hayes (13,382 feet) and the Alaska Range. (There are several good view turnouts around Maclaren Summit.) As you descend your view is of Mount Hayes with Maclaren Glacier beneath, Eureka Glacier is to the east of Maclaren.

P 37 C 96.8 Turnout with view of valley to west. Northbound traffic watch for soft muddy section west side of road.

P 37.6 C 96.2 Leaving Tangle Lakes Archaeological District westbound; see description at **Milepost P 16.2.** Turnout to south.

P 38.4 C 95.4 Small turnout to west, views.

P 39.7 C 94.1 Sevenmile Lake ORV Trail to north (watch for sign about 200 feet from road); 6.5-miles-long, brushy, parallels Boulder Creek, crosses peat bog. This is often very muddy in summer. See cow parsnips along the highway

P 40.2 C 93.6 Gravel turnout to west.

P 40.5 C 93.3 Entering Mat-Su Bourough (westbound sign)

P 40.6 C 93.2 Tangle Lakes Archaeological District (eastbound sign)

P 40.8 C 93 Pond with sloughing bank to the south with marshy bottom. Areas here have been carbon dated to 10,500 years ago.

P 41.2 C 92.6 Turnout and parking to

The Tangle Lakes system incudes Long, Round, Upper and Lower Tangle Lake. (©Sharon Nault)

Maclaren Summit trailhead at Milepost P 36.7. (© Sharon Nault)

south. Entrance to airstrip that serves this area.

P 41.3 C 92.5 Double-ended turnout and dirt track to south.

P 41.4 C 92.4 Rough turnout to north.

P 41.5 C 92.3 Turnout with view to north above river.

P 42 C 91.8 Maclaren River Bridge, a 364-foot multiple span crossing this tributary of the Susitna River; parking. Turnout with picnic area and fire-ring to north at east end of bridge; great views of Maclaren Glacier. *CAUTION: Large, deep pothole possible at east approach to bridge.*

Maclaren River Lodge to south on west side of bridge; food, cabins, camping, tire repair, boat launch, boat trips. Maclaren River Lodge is a popular snowmachine destination in winter and provides a rustic, real-Alaska experience. It is surrounded by 100 miles of groomed snowmachine trails extending out from the lodge. New Year's Eve is a major celebration here with fireworks display. Dog mushers come, even from overseas, to celebrate Christmas. Groups book in advance for this charming location. Ask about remote camps in summer, especially the one at Maclaren Glacier (overnight near the glacier, great for families, accessed by boat).

Maclaren River Lodge. See display ad this page.

Denali Highway Tours and Cabins to south on east side of bridge.

P 43.3 C 90.5 Maclaren River Road to north leads 14 miles to Maclaren Glacier; mountain biking. Small parking area near entrance. It is 4 miles to river crossing which can be deep and treacherous.

The **Maclaren River** rises in the glaciers surrounding Mount Hayes. For the next 60 miles westbound, the highest peaks of this portion of the mighty Alaska Range are visible, weather permitting, to the north. From east to west: Mount Hayes, Hess Mountain (11,940 feet) and Mount Deborah (12,339 feet). Mount Hayes, first climbed in August 1941, is named after Charles Hayes, an early member of the U.S. Geological Survey. Mount Deborah, first climbed in August 1954, was named in 1907 by Judge Wickersham after his wife.

Clearwater Creek Controlled Use Area to north (sign).

P 44.1 C 89.7 Look for old, grass-covered beaver lodge in pond to south.

P 44.4 C 89.4 Distance marker westbound shows Cantwell 90 miles.

P 44.5 C 89.3 Turnout to south. Side road leads to gravel pit.

P 44.8 C 89 Westbound, the highway enters **Crazy Notch**, a long gap in the glacial moraine cut by a glacial stream that geologists state is 12,000-13,000 years old. From Crazy Notch to **Milepost 56** there are many primitive campsites and side roads.

P 46 C 88.8 Eastbound, highway enters Crazy Notch (see description above).

P 46.1 P 87.7 Long gravel turnout to north.

P 46.4 C 87.4 Unsigned roads in this area lead to lake north of the highway. Watch for swans, hawks and redpoles. Fishing for grayling in lake and outlet stream.

P 46.6 C 87.2 Side road to informal camping above lake to north.

P 47.1 C 86.7 Side road to north.

P 47.8 C 86 Very small turnout to north with view.

P 48 C 85.8 Excellent grayling fishing in **Crooked Creek**, which parallels the highway.

P 48.5 C 85.3 Informal campsite by small lake to south. Turnouts both sides of road. Trail leads to mountain to the south. Beaver house and new dam, below road to the north.

P 49 C 84.8 The highway follows an esker between 4 lakes. Watch for ducks, geese, grebes and shorebirds in lakes, as well as bald eagles, moose, caribou, beaver and fox in the vicinity. Look for a pingo (earth-covered ice hill) at lakeshore.

P 49.3 C 84.5 Turnout to north. Good views of lakes and mountains.

P 49.4 C 84.4 Turnout to north overlooks 50 Mile Lake. Interpretive plaque on glacial topography and wildlife:

Pools of Life: Hundreds of small lakes and ponds along the Denali Highway are reminders of ancient glaciers passing. As these glaciers receded they left behind blocks of slower melting ice that formed depressions called kettle holes or kettle lakes. The kettle lakes are home to beaver, loons, lesser yellowlegs, arctic terns and migrating trumpeter swans.

Watch for moose to south.

P 49.6 C 84.2 Primitive road to north leads down to lake and informal camping. Used in fall by hunters.

P 50.9 C 82.9 Small turnout to southwest with view.

P 51.3 C 82.5 Esker ahead for eastbound traffic; northbound traffic leaves esker. Eskers are ridges of silt, sand and gravel carried by inner glacial streams and left behind when the glacier receded. The eskers along Denali Highway are some of the best examples in North America.

P 51.5 C 82.3 Road to north to informal campsites. Private hunting camp to south. Trail and overlook to north. Beaver house in pond to south.

P 53.2 C 80.6 Gravel road to north.

P 53.6 C 80.2 Gravel track to south.

P 55.3 C 78.5 Large primitive camping area to south.

P 55.7 C 78.1 Clearwater Creek 1-lane bridge. Wayside with toilet east side of bridge; informal camping, 2 firepits, 2 picnic tables, grayling fishing. Large turnouts both sides of bridge. One with launch area. Clearwater Creek Trail South begins here. See map at Registration booth. Caribou have been seen in this area in early August.

P 57.5 C 76.3 Clearwater Creek Controlled Use Area, walk-in (no motorized vehicles) hunting area north of highway. Gravel turnout to north.

P 58 C 75.8 Road winds atop an esker flanked by kames and kettle lakes; great views below. Watch for moose, birds, other wildlife.

P 59 C 74.8 Narrow turnout to north with view.

P 59.1 C 74.7 Long turnout to north. Look for patches of blueberries in season on top of esker.

P 59.7 C 74.1 Begin climb up esker for westbound traffic. Leave esker for southbound traffic.

P 60 C 73.8 Large, primitive campsite to south with ATV trail.

P 61 C 72.8 Jagged mountain peaks are close to road to the north.

P 61.9 C 71.9 Narrow side road to south leads ¼ mile to informal camping.

P 62.6 C 70.2 Rough informal camping

with fire rings to south.

P 63 C 70.8 Turnout to north by small lake.

P 63.7 C 70.1 Rough double-ended turnout to south.

P 64 C 69.8 Road descends westbound into Susitna River valley; good view of river ahead as you drive down the hill to the west. Small turnout to south.

P 64.4 C 69.4 Small turnout to south. Distance marker shows Cantwell 70 miles for westbound traffic.

P 65.4 C 68.4 A rough road up to a primitive campsite to the north, has great views.

Many small, view turnouts next mile westbound.

P 67.7 C 66.1 Turnout to south.

P 68 C 65.8 Alpine Creek Lodge (description follows) offers free coffee and has tire repair, espresso and many other amenities. There are 2 entrances to the north: Use the western entrance for best access. Park at the first level and walk up, or drive all the way up and use the large parking area in back of the lodge.

Alpine Creek Lodge is the "Best Place in Alaska!" We are open year-round. Fishing, hunting, ATVing, hiking, snow machining, photography, etc. Coffee is always free, so stop in and enjoy a cup! Check us out at www.alpinecreeklodge.com or call (907) 743-0565. See display ad this page. [ADVERTISEMENT]

P 69.5 C 65.3 Road winds around Clearwater Mountains westbound.

P 69.8 C 64 Small turnout to south with view.

P 71 C 62.8 Road winds through brush on side of mountain. Watch for caribou.

P 72.7 C 61.1 There are 2 lakes to the north. Eastbound views of Clearwater Mountains.

P 73.6 C 60.2 Road travels along the lake to north. Good turnaround area, primitive campsites on the hill above large lake. Brushy trail to water.

P 74.7 C 59.1 Small turnout with view to south. Informal camping.

P 77.3 C 56.5 Airfield to north.

P 77.7 C 56.1 Old Susitna Lodge sits next to lake northeast of highway and has been closed for years; no services. For northbound traffic, old mining trails are visible to the side of the 5,556-foot mountain straight ahead, part of the Alaska Range, near Windy Creek.

P 78.2 C 55.6 Road to north into gravel pit.

P 78.4 C 55.4 Narrow road to south goes to end of esker. Walk out to view.

P 78.5 C 55.3 Expansive view of Susitna River and bridge.

P 79.1 C 54.8 Valdez Creek Road leads 11.5 miles north to the former mining camp of Denali. *NOTE: The first few miles of this side road have several informal camping areas that have been used as primitive mining camps. Travel may not be recommended due to road damage and washouts.* Denali was first established in 1907 after the 1903 discovery of gold in the Clearwater Mountains. The Valdez Creek Mine operated at this site until closing in 1995, producing 495,000 ozs. of gold. Area mining equipment was donated to the Museum of Transportation and Industry, located at **Milepost A 47** Parks Highway. *Do not trespass on private mining claims.*

Fair fishing reported in **Roosevelt Lake** and area creeks. Watch for bears.

Clearwater Creek Controlled Use Area (sign).

P 79.4 C 54.4 Susitna River boat launch at northeast end of bridge. May be rough due to earlier flooding. The bank can drop off steeply depending on water levels. It is possible to launch with a boat trailer but advisable to have some help with you. Very limited parking, with most available space needed for launching. Parking available at **Milepost 78.8**, Valdez Creek Road, **Milepost 80** and 80.3–heavily used in busy season.

P 79.5 C 54.3 Susitna River Bridge (1-lane), a combination multiple span and deck truss, 1,036 feet long. Butte Creek trailhead.

CAUTION: Bridge is slippery when wet.

The Susitna River heads at Susitna Glacier in the Alaska Range (between Mounts Hess and Hayes) and flows southwest 260 miles to Cook Inlet. Downstream through Devil's Canyon, it is considered unfloatable. The river's Tanaina Indian name, said to mean "sandy river," first appeared in 1847 on a Russian chart. Blueberry picking west end of bridge in fall.

Entering Game Management Unit 13E westbound, leaving unit 13B eastbound.

P 80 C 53.8 Gravel pit; parking to south. Distance marker eastbound shows Paxson 80.

P 80.3 C 53.5 Parking areas both sides of highway (used by hunters in season; watch for ATVs on road). There are some good, level places.

P 80.4 C 53.4 Double-ended turnout to south.

P 81.1 C 52.7 Road north to lake is private property. Please do not trespass.

P 82.3 C 51.5 Historical Milepost 82. Gracious House Lodge to south; bar, snacks, homebaked pies, gas, tire repair, gift shop, lodging. Blow your horn for service if no one is around.

Gracious House Lodge/B & B. See display ad this page.

P 84 C 49.8 Large Lake 0.5 mile south; grayling fishing. Watch for moose here (especially on autumn mornings).

P 84.4 C 49.4 Distance marker westbound shows Cantwell 50 miles.

P 84.6 C 49.2 View of lake (0.5 miles) and the Alaska Range westbound. Blueberries in season along highway.

P 85.2 C 48.6 Turnout to north. There are numerous informal campsites heavily used by hunters and campers the next 10 miles westbound. Lake to south very close to road.

P 87 C 46.8 Turnout to north. Primitive gravel camping area to north. Pothole-type lake to south. View of Valdez Creek mining area across Susitna River to south.

P 87.6 C 46.2 Turnout and side road to south.

P 87.9 C 45.9 Side road to south leads to primitive parking and trail that goes up and over mountain to south. (Trail can be used by ORVs.)

P 88.2 C 45.6 Turnout to south, primitive camping with firepit ring. Good view of Alaska Range.

P 88.4 C 45.4 Turnout to north with sweeping view of mountains.

P 88.5 C 45.3 Lake next to highway to north.

P 89.2 C 44.6 Double ended turnout to north with beautiful mountain views.

P 89.9 C 43.9 Good turnout with views to north.

P 90.1 C 43.7 Steep, rough road turnout overlooking lake to south.

P 90.5 C 43.3 Pond to south fed by small stream. A major water drainage divide occurs near here. East of the divide, the tributary river system of the Susitna flows south to Cook Inlet. West of the divide, the Nenana River system flows north to the Yukon River, which empties into the Bering Sea.

P 92.7 C 41.1 Rough road to north leads to informal camping, firepit.

P 93.4 C 40.4 Primitive campsite to north. ORV trail to south.

P 93.7 C 40.1 Very small turnout to north with views and informal campsite. Caution: deep dip at entrance.

P 94 C 39.8 Butte Lake ORV Trail leads 5 miles south to lake; well-used road to trailhead. Best fishing June through September. Lake trout, troll with red-and-white spoons or grayling remains; grayling, small flies or spinners.

P 94.1 C 39.7 Rough turnout with big view to north.

P 94.5 C 39.3 Short road north leads to parking areas above pond with expansive views, primitive camping. Interpretive plaque on earthquakes and schematic identifying peaks of Alaska Range. Beautiful view of Monahan Flat and Alaska Range to the north. This is a favorite viewpoint of many Alaskans. The ORV trail below this parking area travels 12 miles north to the West Fork Glacier, below Mount Deborah. Okay for hiking but can be rough and muddy. Look for caribou here late in July.

Begin steep downhill westbound.

P 94.9 C 38.9 Bridge over Canyon Creek.

Turnout to north at west end of bridge has a great "sitting rock" with a view of Mount Deborah and Mount Hess.

P 95.5 C 38.3 Turnout to north with view.

P 96 C 37.8 Turnout and overlook to north. Primitive firepit and fairly level parking. Looking north up the face of this glacier, Mount Deborah is the peak on the left; Mount Hess is the peak nearest it.

P 96.5 C 37.3 Parking both sides of highway and access to "the Knob" viewpoint; expansive views of valley, mountains and West Fork Glacier. A favorite spot for hunters, hikers and photographers, just a short walk from the road (may be accessible with 4-wheel-drive vehicles). This viewpoint is surrounded by an amphitheater of mountains. A trail leads south across the road from the viewpoint and goes up over the top of the hill to the south.

P 97.2 C 36.6 Side road leads south to viewless, sheltered parking area. From the highway, the Alaska Range is to the north, Mount Deborah, is to the right and behind it is Hess Mountain. Further to the right, the highest, with 2 knobs is Mount Hayes; to the left are the lower peaks of the Alaska Range and Nenana Mountain.

P 97.8 C 35 Narrow, short road to campsite to the north, view of Alaska Range.

P 98 C 35.8 Road to north leads to large uneven forested viewpoint of Alaska Range. Transition zone westbound between alpine and forested terrain as spruce trees begin to appear.

P 99 C 33.8 Sloping turnout to south.

P 99.5 C 33.3 Private lodge to south (status unknown).

P 100.8 C 33 Primitive camping area with view of the Alaska Range to north.

P 101.6 C 32.2 Steep road up to viewpoint, primitive camping to north.

P 102.2 C 31.6 Turnout to north.

P 102.9 C 30.9 Several small turnouts with terrific views on a clear day from atop an esker. Blueberries in season. Good view of Alaska Range, weather permitting. Watch for caribou and swans. Nice place for a walk, bird watching, views to spot wildlife.

P 103.3 C 30.5 Long narrow turnout north on top of esker; 360° view. Look for moose, caribou and marmot.

P 104 C 29.8 Dirt turnout; also road leading south.

P 104.4 C 29.4 Area of private homes.

P 104.6 C 29.2 Brushkana River bridge (narrow). Brushkana Creek Campground to north. River access on both sides of bridge. Well-maintained BLM campground to north at west end of bridge. Sign with map of campground is at entrance. Turnaround area at fee box. Camping fee was $12/night in summer 2013, fee subject to change. There are 22 sites for both tent and RVs (tent sites with some raised, grass-covered, accessible platforms) beside river, most sites are in trees; tables, picnic shelter, firepits, toilets, vendor-provided firewood (fee), bear-proof litterbins, aluminum-can recycling, and potable water. Campground hosts. Nice day-use area with covered picnic area and tables, right on the river. Very good fishing for grayling. Access to BLM Brushkana Creek trail (2 miles).

P 105.5 C 28.3 Dirt road to south.

P 106.9 C 26.8 Canyon Creek, grayling fishing. Side road to north.

P 107.4 C 26.4 Stixkwan Creek flows under highway in culvert. Small level turn-out to north above creek.

P 108.2 C 25.6 Stream runs through culvert under highway.

P 109.3 C 24.5 Parking area both sides of highway.

P 110.4 C 23.4 Road to gravel pit to north.

P 110.6 C 23.2 CAUTION: Steep downgrade westbound next 0.7 mile to Seattle Creek; trucks use low gear.

P 111.3 C 22.5 Seattle Creek 1-lane bridge. Fishing for grayling and Dolly Varden. Boat access to north on east side of bridge, as well as a camping spot. Watch for moose and porcupine.

P 111.4 C 22.4 Turnout to south.

P 111.7 C 22.1 Turnout to north with nice view. Trail to south.

P 112.2 C 21.6 Lily Creek. Side road to north leads out along bluff and then down to informal camping area on Lily Creek.

P 113.5 C 20.3 Matanuska–Susitna Borough boundary eastbound and Denali Borough, westbound.

P 113.6 C 20.2 Turnout with view to north; trail to south. View to east of the Alaska Range and extensive rolling hills and valleys grazed by caribou.

P 115 C 18.8 Side road to south.

P 116 C 17.8 Small turnout to north, view of Nenana River obscured by brush.

Large turnout to north with BLM interpretive sign about the Denali Highway and view of Nenana River.

Steep downgrade westbound. The Denali Highway parallels the Nenana River westbound. The Nenana River heads in Nenana Glacier and flows into the Tanana River, a tributary of the Yukon River. The Nenana is popular with professional river rafters—particularly the stretch of river along the Parks Highway near the Denali Park entrance—but it is not good for fishing, due to heavy glacial silt.

P 116.8 C 17 Begin steep grade up hill next 0.8 mile eastbound.

P 117 C 16.8 Section may be dusty.

P 117.7 C 16.1 Informal campsite in a small hollow to the north of the highway. There is river access here (in disrepair), but respect posted private property near this area. Westbound motorists are leaving BLM public lands.

P 118 C 15.8 Ahtna Inc. lands border highway to Parks Highway junction. Ahtna lands are open to entry by permit only; for more information and links to online permits go to http://permits.ahtna-inc.com.

P 118.3 C 15.5 Turnout to north on Nenana River at Mile 16 Put-In for Nenana River Users. A small boat can be put over the bank here. Caution: Fast flowing waters! Difficult to put trailers with wheels in. There is a very narrow parking area and a steep, narrow boat launch. NOTE: The boat launch access has been in poor shape in the past due to flooding. Sign here reads: "The Upper Nenana River float runs approximately 18 river miles from Mile 16 of the Denali Highway to takeout at Nenana River One Bridge at Parks Highway Mile 215.7. The river along this stretch is rated Class I to II. Warning: Below the Nenana River One Bridge the river rating changes to Class II, III and IV white-water. The Nenana River is about 45°F; an unprotected person will survive 6–10 minutes."

P 118.5 C 15.3 Gravel parking area to south.

P 118.7 C 15.1 Large stream runs through culvert under highway. Parking area and gravel pit to south.

P 120 C 13.8 Watch for moose. Distance marker eastbound shows Paxson 120.

P 121.2 C 12.6 Large gravel turnout to south.

P 121.5 C 12.3 Turnout at gravel pit to north.

P 121.8 C 12 Large stream runs under road in culvert.

P 122.9 C 10.9 Large level turnout to north. Views westbound of Mount McKinley/Denali (weather permitting).

P 124.3 C 9.5 Parking area to north. Turnout overlooking pond to south.

P 125.5 C 8.3 Primitive road south to parking and informal camping area.

P 126.2 C 7.6 Turnout to south with parking and lake access. Joe Lake, about 0.5 mile long, is south of highway and is used by a local air service. Jerry Lake is about 0.2 mile north of the highway; grayling.

P 126.5 C 7.3 Turnout to south on Joe Lake (can flood).

P 127.2 C 6.6 Turnout to north.

P 128.2 C 5.6 Fish Creek. Access to creek and turnout to south at east end of bridge. We had cell phone service from here westbound in 2013.

Beautiful view (weather permitting) of Talkeetna Mountains and Mount McKinley to the south.

P 130.5 C 3.3 Turnout and informal camping to south.

P 130.8 C 3 Very large turnout to north. Popular parking spot for snowmachiners in winter.

P 131 C 2.8 No parking zone! Large, inviting turnout is a turnaround for school buses, snow plows and road graders.

P 131.1 C 2.7 Gravel ends, pavement begins, westbound. Pavement ends, gravel begins, eastbound. Watch for potholes, washboard and washouts on highway east from here.

P 132.5 C 1.3 Large gravel turnout to north.

P 132.7 C 1.1 Large gravel turnout to north.

P 132.8 C 1 Small paved turnout to south.

P 133.0 C 0.8 Power station to north.

Turnouts (2) close together to the south, one of the best photo ops of Denali on clear days.

P 133.4 C 0.4 Cantwell Station DOT highway maintenance camp.

P 133.6 C 0.2 Alaska State Troopers to north.

P 133.7 C 0.1 Backwoods Lodge, open year-round; overnight lodging.

Backwoods Lodge. See display ad on page 433 in the PARKS HIGHWAY section.

P 133.8 C 0 CANTWELL at junction of the Denali Highway (Route 8) and the Parks Highway (Route 3); food, gas, RV park and lodging straight ahead; see description beginning on page 433. Turn north on Parks Highway for post office, lodge, Denali Park and Fairbanks. Turn south on highway for gas station, Wasilla and Anchorage. There is a large, cleared area here that is PRIVATE PROPERTY. Do not enter this lot. NOTE: Ahtna Inc. lands border highway to MILEPOST P 118, permit required; http://permits.ahtna-inc.com.

Junction of Denali Highway and Parks Highway at Cantwell. Turn to Milepost A 210 on page 433 in the PARKS HIGHWAY section for log.

Steese Highway

CONNECTS: Fairbanks to Circle, AK

Length: 161 miles   **Road Surface:** 50% Paved, 50% Gravel   **Season:** Open all year

(See map, page 518)   **2** **6**

Eagle Summit viewpoint on the Steese Highway.
(© Sharon Nault)

Major Attractions:

©Kris Valencia, staff

*Davidson Ditch,
Gold Dredge No. 8,
Pipeline Viewpoint,
Nome Creek Valley,
Yukon River*

Highest Summit:

*Eagle Summit
3,685 ft.*

The Steese Highway was completed in 1927 and named for Gen. James G. Steese, U.S. Army, former president of the Alaska Road Commission. It connects Fairbanks to Central and ends at Circle. Circle is a small settlement 161 miles to the northeast with a boat launch for the Yukon River 50 miles south of the Arctic Circle. At 2,000 miles, this river is Alaska's largest and heads in Canada then flows west into Norton Sound on the Bering Sea. The Steese Highway is designated a Scenic Byway and the scenery alone makes this a worthwhile drive. It is especially colorful in late August and early September when the leaves turn. Acres of fireweed have filled up burned areas and offer bright splashes of color in the summer and fall.

The first 81 miles of the Steese Highway are paved. From the end of the pavement it is a wide gravel road into Central at **Milepost F 127.7**, where there is a short stretch of paved road. From Central to Circle, the highway is a narrow, winding gravel road: This road can be slow and difficult in places, with miles of teeth-chattering washboards, tight curves and soft spots. However, it is quite drivable and usually has little traffic. The condition of the gravel surfacing varies based on grading schedules.

The highway is open year-round; check with the Dept. of Transportation in Fairbanks regarding winter road conditions; the road may be closed by weather. Phone 511 in Alaska; online go to 511.Alaska.gov.

Gas and diesel are available at the Tesoro at **Fox General Store** (also with propane), **Milepost F 11** Steese Expressway; in Central, **Milepost F 127.7**, at **Gold Country Services and Energy** at Mile 0.5 Circle Hot Springs Road; and at the **H.C. Company Store** at the end of the highway in Circle, **Milepost F 161.**

The Steese Highway is a highway of summits and spectacular views. Eagle Summit

Distance in miles	Central	Chena Hot Springs	Circle	Fairbanks
Central		180	34	128
Chena Hot Springs	180		213	61
Circle	34	213		161
Fairbanks	128	61	161	

Steese Highway Fairbanks, AK to Circle, AK

© 2014 The MILEPOST®

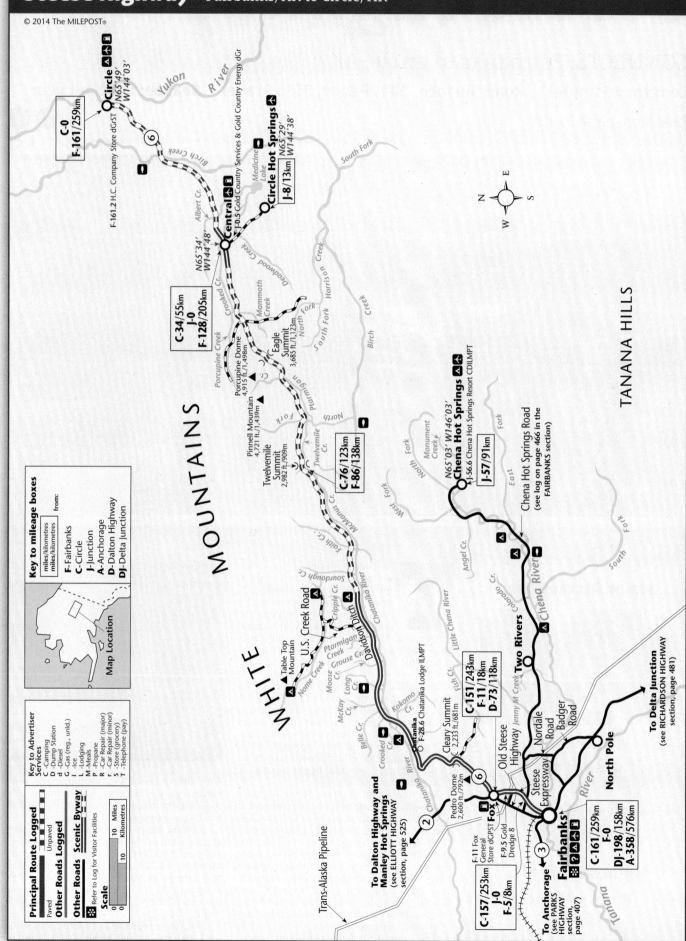

Key to mileage boxes
from:
miles/kilometres
miles/kilometres

F- Fairbanks
C- Circle
J- Junction
A- Anchorage
D- Dalton Highway
DJ- Delta Junction

Map Location

Principal Route Logged
Paved
Unpaved
Other Roads Logged
Scenic Byway
Refer to Log for Visitor Facilities

Key to Advertiser Services
C - Camping
D - Dump Station
d - Diesel
G - Gas (reg., unld.)
I - Ice
L - Lodging
M - Meals
P - Propane
R - Car Repair (major)
r - Car Repair (minor)
s - Store (grocery)
T - Telephone (pay)

Scale
0   10   Miles
0   10   Kilometres

C-0
F-161/259km

Circle
N65°49',
W144°03'

F-161.2 H.C. Company Store dGrST

Yukon   River

Birch   Creek

Medicine Lake

Circle Hot Springs
J-8/13km   N65°29',
W144°38'

0.5 Gold Country Services & Gold Country Energy dGr

Central
N65°34',
W144°48'

Albert Cr.

Deadwood Creek

South Fork

Mammoth Creek

Harrison Creek

Birch   Creek

South Fork

C-34/55km
J-0
F-128/205km

Crooked Cr.

North Fork

Porcupine Creek

Eagle Summit
3,685 ft./1,498m

Porcupine Dome
4,915 ft./1,498m

Pinnell Mountain
4,721 ft./1,439m

Ptarmigan   Creek

North   Fork

Twelvemile Summit
2,982 ft./909m

Twelvemile Cr.

C-76/123km
F-86/138km

TANANA HILLS

Chena Hot Springs
N65°03' W146°03'
J-56.6 Chena Hot Springs Resort CDILMPT

J-57/91km

Chena Hot Springs Road
(see log on page 466 in the FAIRBANKS section)

North Fork

Monument Creek

West   Fork

East   Fork

South   Fork

Chena   River

Little Chena River

McManus Cr.

Faith Cr.

Sourdough Cr.

Davidson Ditch

Chatanika River

Cripple Cr.

Angel Cr.

Colorado Cr.

WHITE   MOUNTAINS

U.S. Creek Road

Table Top Mountain

Nome Creek

Moose Cr.

Long Cr.

Grouse Cr.

Ptarmigan Creek

McKay Cr.

Belle Cr.

Crooked Cr.

Kokomo Cr.

Chatanika
F-28.6 Chatanika Lodge ILMPT

Cleary Summit
2,233 ft./681m

C-151/243km
F-11/18km
D-73/118km

Two Rivers

Jenny M Creek

Fish Cr.

Nordale Road

Badger Road

Chena River

To Delta Junction
(see RICHARDSON HIGHWAY section, page 481)

Old Steese Highway

Steese Expressway

North Pole

C-161/259km
F-0
DJ-198/158km
A-358/576km

Fairbanks

To Anchorage
(see PARKS HIGHWAY section, page 407)

C-157/253km
J-0
F-5/8km

To Dalton Highway and Manley Hot Springs
(see ELLIOTT HIGHWAY section, page 525)

Chatanika River

Pedro Dome
2,600 ft./792m

Fox
F-9.5 Gold Dredge 8

F-11 Fox General Store dGrST

Trans-Alaska Pipeline

Tanana   River

at **Milepost F 107.1** is the highest, and has unobstructed views of the midnight sun at solstice as well as wildflowers in summer. Twelvemile Summit at **Milepost F 85.5** offers biking opportunities, views and access to Pinnell Mountain Trail with viewing platform and Circle–Fairbanks Historic Trail. Caribou are often spotted at Eagle and Twelvemile summits in the fall, a favorite place for hunters. Cleary Summit at **Milepost F 20.5**, is the first summit on the route but has obstructed views. Turn off at **Milepost F 57.4** for the U.S. Creek Road and drive 3.5 miles for 360 degree views from platform and blueberry picking in season.

The Steese Expressway junctions with Chena Hot Springs Road at **Milepost F 4.6**. This 56-mile side road provides access to the Chena River Recreation Area and to **Chena Hot Springs Resort**. (See "Chena Hot Springs Road" log on pages 466-468 in the FAIRBANKS section.)

The Steese Highway also provides access to the richest gold mining district in Alaska. Higher gold prices have led to renewed interest in mining along this highway. As a sign along the highway puts it: "the old Gold Rush days are not over yet!" Watch for mining operations along the highway.

Artifacts from the region's early mining days include dredges (at **Mileposts F 9.5** and **F 28.6**) and the Davidson Ditch (at **Milepost F 57.3**). Gold Dredge 8 also offers gold panning along with a tour of the dredge. Recreational gold panning is allowed at Pedro Creek, across from the Pedro Monument at **Milepost F 16.6**, at Nome Creek Valley, accessible from **Milepost F 57.4** and at Cripple Creek Campground. For information on Nome Creek gold panning, check with the Alaska Public Lands Information Center in Fairbanks, or visit Bureau of Land Management (BLM) website at www.blm.gov/ak/st/en/prog/nlcs/white_mtns/summer_recreation/gold_panning.html.

Emergency medical services: Phone 911. Alaska State Troopers in Fairbanks, phone (907) 451-5100.

Steese Highway Log

Distance from Fairbanks (F) is followed by distance from Circle (C).

Physical mileposts on the Steese Highway show distance from Fairbanks. Several of these posts have the mileage obscured due to bullet holes.

ALASKA ROUTE 2

F 0 C 161.3 Stoplight at junction of Steese Highway with the Richardson Highway at Airport Way in Fairbanks. Begin 4-lane Steese Expressway northbound. Note: Physical mileposts along this route are often spaced less than 1 full mile apart.

Turn to end of RICHARDSON HIGHWAY section on page 499 and read log back to front for log of that highway from Fairbanks south to Delta Junction, Paxson and Valdez.

F 0.3 C 161 Stoplight at Tenth Avenue intersection; city center access, Regency Hotel.

F 0.6 C 160.7 Expressway crosses Chena River.

F 0.8 C 160.5 Stoplight at Third Street

intersection; Joann Fabrics, VFW, FedEx and small shops.

F 1 C 160.3 Stoplight at College Road exit to west and access to Bentley Mall; shopping, fast food, restaurants, laundromat, carwash, Office Max and Cornerstone Mall.

F 1.3 C 160 Stoplight. Trainor Gate Road; access west to Fort Wainwright and Fred Meyers. Expressway crosses railroad tracks.

F 2 C 159.3 Stoplight. Johansen Expressway west to College Road (for Fountainhead Auto Museum, Peger Road and University Avenue; access to Home Depot, Lowes, Walmart and other "big box" stores. City Lights Blvd. to east.

F 2.1 C 159.2 Distance marker northbound shows Fox 8 miles, Livengood 76 miles, Circle 156 miles.

F 2.7 C 158.6 Stoplight at **junction** with Farmers Loop Road (to west) and Fairhill Road (to east); **Sourdough Fuel** (diesel, unleaded) with foodmart to west.

Exit east for **Birch Hill Recreation Area**. Drive 1.8 miles to 'T' and turn right; continue 0.3 mile on gravel access road for this Fairbanks North Star Borough recreation area. Nordic skiing only (no dogs, sleds or foot traffic) Oct. 15–April 15; chalet.

F 4 C 157.3 Distance marker southbound shows Fairbanks 2 miles, North Pole 17 miles, Delta Junction 100 miles.

F 4.6 C 156.7 Northbound exit for Chena Hot Springs Road. Exit west for Curry's Corner (gas pump, grocery) and access to **North Star Golf Club** on Old Steese Highway (0.7 mile north from Curry's Corner). Exit east for Chena Hot Springs Road, which leads to Chena Hot Springs Resort (56.6 miles). Access to Chena River Recreation Area via Chena Hot Springs Road.

See "Chena Hot Springs Road" log on pages 466-468 in the FAIRBANKS section.

F 5 C 156.3 Southbound exit for Chena Hot Springs Road. Dial 511 for travel information.

F 5.7 C 155.6 Distance marker northbound shows Fox 5 miles, Livengood 72 miles, Circle 153 miles.

F 6.3 C 155 Steele Creek Road. Exit for Bennett Road, Hagelbarger Avenue, Old Steese Highway and Gilmore Trail. Speed limit is 55 mph.

F 8 C 153.3 *CAUTION: Watch for moose.*

F 8.4 C 152.9 Trans–Alaska Oil Pipeline Viewpoint with interpretive displays. Excellent opportunity for pipeline photos. This is Mile 449.6 on the 800-mile-long pipeline that begins at Prudhoe Bay.

Monument here remembers pipeline designer James A. Maple. There are 2 "pigs" on display here. "Pigs" are tools used for maintenance of pipes.

F 9.5 C 151.8 Exit west and take Goldstream Road to Old Steese Hwy. N., turn left and continue to **Gold Dredge 8 National Historic Site**; daily tours of the dredge include gold panning, gold rush history, train ride and gift shop. Call ahead for tour times, phone (907) 479-6673; www.golddredgeno8.com/.

Gold Dredge 8. See display ad on page 445 in the FAIRBANKS section.

The dredge, built in 1928, was added to the list of national historic sites in 1984 and designated a National Historical Mechanical Engineering Landmark in 1986. The 5-deck, 250-foot-long dredge operated until 1959; it is now privately owned and open to the public for tours daily during summer. (Admission fee).

F 11 C 150.3 Steese Expressway from Fairbanks ends at **junction** of Steese and Elliott Highways (Alaska Routes 6 and 2); **Fox General Store** (gas, diesel, propane, groceries, liquor store, ATM) to southwest, weigh station to northeast.

Fox General Store. See display ad this page.

Access west to **FOX** (pop. 435), established as a mining camp before 1905 and named for nearby Fox Creek, has **Fox General Store**; Silver Gulch Brewery, Fox Gar-

dens, the Howling Dog Saloon, and the **Turtle Club** restaurant, at Mile 0.5 Old Steese Highway North, for great prime rib.

The Turtle Club. See display ad on page 454 in the FAIRBANKS section.

Turn east for continuation of Steese Highway, now Alaska Route 6 (log follows). Distance marker shows Chatanika 17 miles; Central 118 miles; Circle 152 miles. Turn onto the Old Steese Highway and go 1.3 miles north here to the Gold Dredge 8.

Junction with Elliott Highway (Alaska Route 2) which continues northwest to the Dalton Highway and Manley Hot Springs. See ELLIOTT HIGHWAY section on page 525 for log.

ALASKA ROUTE 6

F 11.1 C 150.2 Distance marker eastbound shows Chatanika 17 miles, Central 118 miles, Circle 152 miles. *NOTE: Next gas on Steese Highway is 117 miles from here.*

F 11.9 C 149.4 Tailings (gravel and boulders of dredged streambeds alongside highway) from early mining activity which yielded millions of dollars in gold.

F 13.5 C 147.8 Gated entrance to NOAA/NESDIS Command and Data Acquisition Station at Gilmore Creek to east. This facility tracks and commands multiple NOAA polar orbiting, environmental satellites (circle earth at 520 miles above its surface). Tours are not available.

A log cabin visitor's center with handicapped access is conveniently located at the entrance. Visitors may view artifacts and a video presentation of the station's mission and history. No restrooms are available.

Frost heaves in area in 2013.

F 14.2 C 147.1 Some homes in this area are built on or between old tailing piles.

F 16.4 C 144.9 West entrance, south to the **Felix Pedro Creek**, with large parking area. *Use caution as you exit highway into parking lot due to uneven surfaces (noted in summer 2013).*

Recreational gold panning is allowed on the Creek, across from the monument. This is the **Discovery Claim**, owned by Igloo No. 4, Pioneers of Alaska. Recreational gold panning only (no mechanical devices). A sign here reads: "Good Panning and Good Luck!" Pedro and Gilmore creeks join just down-

stream of the panning area to form Goldstream.

F 16.6 C 144.7 Felix Pedro Monument and Wayside. Large, paved parking area with pedestrian ramp (wheelchair-accessible) to monument; picnic shelter over benches, and (wheelchair-accessible) toilet. Nice place for a walk with paved walkway lined by information boards, an overlook of the Steese Highway and free gold panning. This loop trail ends at the lower parking lot.

Felix Pedro was the prospector who discovered gold in July 1902 and started the rush that resulted in the founding of Fairbanks. Information signs here provide interesting facts, figures and photographs about gold discoveries in this area. Approximately $1.8 million in gold was taken from the Fairbanks mining district 1903–1910. Gold at that time was $17.73 an ounce.

Winding ascent (6 to 8 percent grades) northbound next 3.5 miles to Cleary Summit.

F 17.5 C 143.8 Large paved parking area to east.

F 19.6 C 141.7 Large paved turnout to southeast.

F 19.7 C 141.6 Twin Creek Road. Signed: No public access.

F 20 C 141.3 Twin Creeks Road, Fort Knox Gold Mine to east (no public access) is Alaska's largest operating gold mine. It has produced nearly 3.5 million ounces of gold since beginning production late in 1996.

True North Road is to the north.

F 20.5 C 140.8 Cleary Summit (elev. 2,233 feet). The summit was named for early prospector Frank Cleary. Fairbanks Creek Road. Turn south and then east for large, elevated, double ended parking area close to the highway. Viewpoint of valley to east was obscured by brush in 2013. Side road leads east 0.1 mile to Skiland Road (ski area is 0.8 mile up access road). Circle to Fairbanks Historic Trail is 3.4 miles from Steese Highway. Turnaround area and sign at trailhead. Fish Creek Road has good views of area.

Highway descends steep winding 7 percent grade northbound.

F 20.9 C 140.4 Long double-ended turnout to east. Venturing beyond the parking surface is considered trespassing.

F 21.5 C 139.8 View through brush from highway of current mining activity and old buildings from early mining and dredging on Cleary Creek below and to the east.

F 23.8 C 137.5 Gravel turnout to the south.

F 28 C 133.3 Sharp turn up hill to southeast for historical Chatanika Gold Camp, the Old F.E. (Fairbanks Exploration Co.) Camp; current status unknown. The camp was built in 1925 to support gold dredging operations in the valley. Between 1926 and 1957, the F.E. Co. removed an estimated $70 million in gold. The gold camp is on the National Register of Historic Places.

F 28.6 C 132.7 Chatanika Lodge to east; food and lodging. Old gold dredge behind tailing piles to west: No trespassing. There was a fire on the dredge in 2013, but it is still there and an interesting site.

Originally a trading post for miners beginning in the late 1930s, Chatanika Lodge burned down in 1974 and was then rebuilt and expanded to offer food, lodging and entertainment. Owners Ron and Shirley Franklin have decorated the lodge with Alaskan artifacts, including a 1955 T-Bird inside the lodge. Also look for Paul Potvin's diamond willow art, including lamps, at Chatanika Lodge. Locals consider this a favorite

meeting place.

Chatanika Lodge. See display ad this page.

The old gold dredge across the highway from Chatanika Lodge operated from the 1920s until 1962. It is the second largest stacker dredge in Alaska. *(Dredge is private property; a short walk on a rocky path across from lodge lends better viewing but you must not get on the dredge itself.)*

F 29.5 C 131.8 Access south to **29.5 Mile Pond** to the north (stocked) public fishing access; rainbow and grayling.

Turnoff to south for Neal Brown Road to **Poker Flat Research Range**, operated by the Geophysical Institute, University of Alaska Fairbanks. It is the largest land-based rocket research range in the world and the only high-latitude rocket range in the United States. Poker Flat launches scientific sounding rockets, performs satellite tracking and is home to a growing fleet of unmanned aircraft. Visit www.pfrr.alaska.edu/.

F 31 C 130.3 Imaging Riometer Antenna Array, a joint 10-year study of polar middle and upper atmosphere by CRL of Japan and UAF's Geophysical Institute. Sign posted states "The Aurora Borealis makes the atmosphere opaque to radio noise from our galaxy at altitudes of 60–100 km, reducing the intensity of the noise received at the ground. The imaging riometer works like a camera, taking a picture of the radio noise once a second."

F 31.6 C 129.7 Public fishing access to **31.6 Mile Pond** to west; pond very close to road is stocked with rainbow, grayling.

F 32.3 C 129 Captain Creek bridge, no turnouts.

F 33 C 128.3 Old cabin on pond to north.

F 33.5 C 127.8 Access to 33.5 Mile Pond to north. Double ended turnout. Stocked with rainbow and grayling.

F 34.6 C 126.7 Pleasant parking area by **Mile 34.6 Pond** public fishing access to south (stocked); rainbow, grayling.

F 34.8 C 126.5 Double-ended paved turnout to north. River makes big horseshoe bend by turnout.

Highway parallels the Chatanika River northbound.

F 35.8 C 125.5 Mile 35.8 Pond public fishing access to south; rainbow, grayling.

F 36.3 C 125 Paved turnout to south.

F 36.4 C 124.9 Mile 36.6 Pond public fishing access to west; stocked with grayling; 3 good primitive campsites by pond.

F 37.3 C 124 Kokomo Creek bridge.

F 39 C 122.3 Chatanika River bridge. **Upper Chatanika River State Recreation Site**, just north of the bridge, is a beautiful state campground with river access and rocky beach. Access was rut-filled in 2013. Registration at entrance to campground. There are 24 wooded sites with firepits and a gravel parking area with toilets and a water pump at the entrance. Leveling blocks needed for some sites. Camping fee $10/night. Firewood may be available for sale. Plentiful wild roses in June. **Chatanika River**, grayling 8 to 20 inches, use flies or spinners, May to September. Canoes and small boats can be launched on the gravel

bars by the river. Bring your mosquito repellent and suntan lotion. This is an access point to the Chatanika River canoe trail. See **Milepost F 60** for more information on canoeing this river.

F 40.4 C 120.9 Bridge over Crooked Creek.

F 41.4 C 119.9 Bridge over Belle Creek. Private homes in area.

F 42.5 C 118.8 Double-ended gravel turnout to north; sled dog unloading area. **McKay Creek Trailhead.** McKay Creek Trail is 17.5 miles long. It climbs steeply for 5.5 miles to ridge top at boundary of White Mountains National Recreation Area. The first 8 miles are suitable for summer use, (hiking, 4-wheeling and ORV) according to the BLM. Winter use from November to April. This trail intersects with the Lower Nome Creek Trail. Information sign boards. Groomed trails for dog mushing, skiing, snowshoes and snowmachining in winter. Do not block private road.

F 42.6 C 118.7 Bridge over McKay Creek.

F 43 C 118.3 Highway travels through burn area.

F 43.9 C 117.4 Double-ended paved turnout to north.

F 45.5 C 115.8 Long Creek bridge. Long Creek Trading Post to west at north end of bridge; current status unknown. This area began as a hunting camp, and it continues to be a very popular hunting destination. Fishing (and gold panning) in **Long Creek**; grayling 8 to 14 inches, use spinners or flies, May to September.

F 48.2 C 113.1 Large double-ended turnout to southeast. View of Chatanika River valley from turnout (foliage has obscured river valley views from highway). Evidence of 2004 Taylor Complex fires. The fires came very close to buildings at Long Creek and fire damaged parts of the Davidson Ditch.

F 50.2 C 111.1 Long narrow, loose gravel parking area with views of burn.

F 52.6 F 109.7 Steep descent northbound.

F 55.9 C 105.4 Paved turnout to south and access to road that leads to valley floor.

F 57.3 C 104 Entering **BLM White Mountains National Recreation Area** northbound. Access to this area's trails and cabins along highway.

Turn north and drive 0.1 mile to large turnaround area and the close-up views of the **Davidson Ditch** historical site. There are information signs here about the large pipe was built in 1925 by the Fairbanks Exploration Co. to carry water to float gold dredges. The 83-mile-long ditch, designed and engineered by J.B. Lippincott, begins near **Milepost F 64** on the Steese Highway and ends near Fox. A system of ditches and inverted siphons, the pipeline was capable of carrying 56,100 gallons per minute. After the dredges closed, the water was used for power until 1967, when a flood destroyed a bridge and flattened almost 1,000 feet of pipe.

F 57.4 C 103.9 Spacious, level wayside with outhouses, paved parking, loading ramp for ATVs and litter bins at turnoff for **U.S. Creek Road** (steep wide gravel), which winds up and over the hills to the north for 7 miles to junction with Nome Creek Road (descriptions follow). *NOTE: For status on road conditions and more information on area, check with BLM in Fairbanks, phone (907) 474-2200.*

The summit of U.S. Creek Road is at Mile

The Davidson Ditch was built in 1925 to carry water to float gold dredges. (©Sharon Nault)

3.5; 360 degree views from a large viewing platform, picnic area and information boards about the area. Good blueberry picking in fall. Nome Creek Bridge Wayside at Mile 6.8 has bear-proof trash cans, outhouse, and information boards with map of Nome Creek Valley and instructions of where it is legal to pan for gold.

From junction with U.S. Creek Road, Nome Creek Road (narrow in places and can be very rough) branches off to either end of Nome Creek Valley. Follow Nome Creek Road to Mile 3.3 for Quartz Creek Trailhead and on to Mile 4 (rough, potholes) at the upper end of Nome Creek Valley for **Mt. Prindle Campground**; 13 sites, well water, picnic tables, firepits, outhouse, bear proof garbage cans, $6 per night. This campground is close to Nome Creek and favored by miners. Gold panning is limited to the designated area and non-motorized tools, such as gold pans, rocker boxes, sluice boxes, picks and shovels. This area has more than 200 maintained miles of trail in winter.

From U.S. Creek Road, follow Nome Creek Road to the lower end of the valley 8.3 miles for Tabletop Mountain Trailhead parking; sign-in, trail map. Continue to Mile 12 for **Ophir Creek Campground**; 19 sites, picnic tables, well water, firepits, some grills, $6 per night. Catch-and-release grayling. Beaver Creek National Wild River put-in. The road to Ophir crosses Moose Creek culverts at Mile 3.3. There may be water crossings at Mile 5.6 and Mile 6.2 depending on rain. Recreational gold panning ends below the road to the south, where Moose Creek enters Nome Creek.

F 58 C 103.3 Large, paved, double-ended turnout to south overlooking river.

F 58.2 C 103.1 Sign: Alaska Highway 6 East.

F 59 C 102.3 Very large double-ended paved parking area to south, flat and wide.

F 60 C 101.3 Turnoff to east for **Cripple Creek BLM Campground, day-use area and boat launch.** Drive straight in for campground which has 6 tent-only sites

and 12 regular campsites; 7-day limit; crank water pumps, firepits, outhouses, bear-proof dumpsters, picnic tables; nature trail and information boards. Camping fee $6 (half off for America the Beautiful senior pass holders); $3 for walk-ins.

Take gravel road to left at entrance for forested day-use area with outhouses, trash cans and launch. Nature trail leads to old trapper's cabin. The road from this day-use area to the river is 4-wheel-drive only. Recreational gold panning permitted. The Chatanika River winds around this campground. Bring mosquito repellent!

Access to Cripple Creek BLM recreation cabin. Pre-register and pay $20-25 fee at BLM office, 1150 University Ave., Fairbanks, AK 99709; or phone (907) 474-2251 or 1-800-437-7021 and use a credit card.

Cripple Creek bridge is the uppermost access point to the Chatanika River canoe trail. Follow 0.2 mile side road near campground entrance to canoe launch site; parking area, outhouses. *CAUTION: This canoe trail may not be navigable at low water.* The Chatanika River is a clear-water Class II stream. The Steese Highway parallels the river for approximately 28 miles and there are many access points to the highway downstream from the Cripple Creek bridge. No major obstacles on this canoe trail, but watch for overhanging trees. Downstream pullout points are Perhaps Creek, Long Creek and Chatanika Campground.

F 60.2 C 101.1 North to Old Steese Highway with evidence of old burn.

F 62.2 C 99.1 Sloping, double-ended gravel turnout to south, poorly maintained in 2013. Watch for moose.

F 62.5 C 98.8 Improved highway eastbound.

F 63 C 98.3 Small dirt turnout to south.

F 63.3 C 98 View of historic Davidson Ditch pipeline to north (see **Milepost F 57.3**). Highway continues through burn area.

F 63.8 C 97.5 Old Steese Highway to north.

Migrating caribou may be seen on the Steese Highway from late July through mid-September. (©Sharon Nault)

F 64.8 C 96.5 View of Davidson Ditch to south below the road is accessed via a dead-end, limited turnaround road.

F 65 C 96.3 Large parking area on hill with good view to south (partially obscured by brush) of Chatanika River valley, Davidson Ditch pipe and extensive burn area from 2004 Taylor Complex fire.

Southbound highway sign: Alaska 6 S.W.

F 65.5 C 95.8 Sourdough Creek bridge, private home.

F 65.8 C 95.7 Sourdough Creek Road; sign states "use this road at your own risk."

F 66.6 C 94.7 Watch for moose.

F 67.8 C 93.5 Very nice large turnout to southeast below highway.

F 68 C 93.3 Long gravel turnout to south.

F 68.5 C 92.8 Gated gravel pit road.

F 69 C 92.3 Faith Creek bridge. Active mining near here in 2013.

Highway climbs 6 to 7 percent grade next 2 miles northbound.

F 70 C 91.3 Distance marker southbound shows Fox 70 miles, Fairbanks 79.

F 71.6 C 90.7 Large gravel turnout to south.

F 75.1 C 86.2 Distance marker northbound shows Central 50 miles, Circle 84 miles.

F 79.1 C 82.2 Road widens with long narrow gravel parking area next 500 feet. View down to McManus Creek.

F 80.1 C 81.2 Montana Creek state highway maintenance station to northeast. Long double-ended turnout to south. Montana Creek runs under road and into McManus Creek to the east. McManus Dome (elev. 4,184 feet) to west.

F 81.2 C 80.1 Road closure gates (for avalanches).

F 81.3 C 80 *Pavement ends, gravel begins, northbound.*

Highway begins ascent to Twelvemile Summit. Speed limit is 50 mph.

F 81.6 C 79.7 Steep entrance to gravel

parking, south below road.

F 83 C 78.3 *CAUTION: Slow down for 30 mph hairpin curve.*

F 84.4 C 76.9 Guardrails and yellow poles are for additional safety and navigation in winter for snowplows.

F 84.5 C 76.8 Small dirt turnout to southeast.

F 84.7 C 76.6 Highway rises above tree line northbound.

F 85 C 76.3 *CAUTION: Slow down for 35 mph curve.*

F 85.5 C 75.8 Parking area to south with outhouse, trash cans and viewing platform. The registry for Pinnell Mountain Trail (see description below) is at this parking area. The trailhead is across the Steese Highway and to the north.

An access road leads 0.5 mile south to **Twelvemile Summit** (elev. 3,190 feet), which is on the divide of the Yukon and Tanana river drainages. The Circle Fairbanks Historic Trail begins 0.3 mile in on this side road. There is a large viewpoint area at the end of the access road with turnaround space and room for informal camping. This is a favorite parking area for hunters. Blueberry picking in season. Caribou in the fall. Sweeping views in every direction.

Pinnell Mountain National Recreation Trail, also accessible from Eagle Summit at **Milepost F 107.1**, was named in honor of Robert Pinnell, who was fatally injured in 1952 while climbing nearby Porcupine Dome. This 27-mile-long hiking trail—marked by rock cairns—winds through alpine terrain, along mountain ridges and through high passes. Highest elevation is 4,721 feet. Shelter cabins at Mile 10.7 and Mile 17.7. Views of the White Mountains, Tanana Hills, Brooks Range and Alaska Range from vantage points along the trail. Wildlife includes willow ptarmigan, hoary marmot, rock pika, moose, wolf and caribou. Mid-May through July is the prime time for wildflowers, with flowers peaking in mid-June. Carry drinking water and insect repellent at all times. Contact the Bureau of Land Management, 1150 University Ave., Fairbanks, AK 99708-3844; phone (907) 474-2200; www.blm.gov/ak/st/en/prog/recreation/pinnell_mtn_rec.html.

This is caribou country; from here to beyond Eagle Summit (**Milepost F 108**), watch for migrating herds of caribou from late July through mid-September. Wildflowers carpet the alpine tundra slopes.

The boundary between Game Management Units 25C and 20B, and marks Fairbanks–North Star Borough limits.

Distance marker northbound shows Central 40 miles, Circle 74 miles.

Highway descends 6 percent grade next 2.5 miles northbound.

F 86.6 C 74.7 Small dirt turnout to southeast.

F 88.6 C 72.7 Bridge over Reed Creek.

F 90.6 C 70.7 Double-ended gravel turnout to southeast. Lichen-covered slopes (much loved by caribou) to the south.

F 92 C 69.3 Highway parallels Twelvemile Creek in valley below.

F 93.4 C 67.9 Bridge over the North Fork Twelve Mile Creek. Nice picnic spot to the north on the east side of the bridge.

F 94 C 67.3 Unmarked gravel road leads 0.2 miles down to Twelve Mile Creek access and 0.2 miles further down to **Birch Creek** access on north fork of Birch Creek, a Wild and Scenic River; very large, level parking area near creek; information boards with

maps; outhouses, garbage cans; registration kiosk; canoe launch. This is the main put-in point for Birch Creek canoe trail. Informal campsite by creek. Extensive mining in area. **Birch Creek**, grayling to 12 inches; use flies, June to October.

F 95.1 C 66.2 Evidence of active gold mining operations to south below this stretch of highway in summer 2013. *IMPORTANT: Do not trespass. Do not approach mining equipment without permission.*

F 95.8 C 65.5 Bridge over Willow Creek. Cotton grass grows along roadside.

F 97.6 C 63.7 Bridge over Bear Creek. Private home to south. Turnout is west of bridge.

F 98.8 C 62.5 Butte Creek comes out of the mountains and down to the valley near the road.

F 99 C 62.3 Highway travels along Fish Creek to the south. Active mining below road.

F 99.3 C 62 Bridge over Fish Creek; cabins and mining road.

F 100.8 C 60.5 Informal gravel parking along Ptarmigan Creek.

F 101.4 C 59.9 Site of old 101 Lodge. This is a checkpoint on the Yukon Quest International Sled Dog Race, which follows the Steese Highway between Circle and Milepost 94. Read about the trail at www.yukonquest.com/site/trail/.

Weather gates. May be closed if road conditions are hazardous over the summit.

Bridge over Ptarmigan Creek (elev. 2,398 feet). Highway climbs to summit northbound. Alpine meadows carpeted with wildflowers in spring and summer for next 9 miles. Good view to east of mining activity down in valleys.

F 102 C 59.3 Road ascends towards Eagle Summit eastbound.

F 103.5 C 57.8 Highway travels above tree line for eastbound traffic. Active mining in the valley below to the south.

F 103.6 C 57.6 Mining road to south, drops over side and down to active mining claims.

F 104.5 C 56.8 Old mining buildings below to south.

F 105 C 56.3 Snow poles mark road edge.

F 105.4 C 55.9 Large gravel turnout to north of the highway. Ptarmigan in area.

F 107.1 C 54.2 Eagle Summit Wayside; large parking area 0.2 mile west with wheelchair-accessible toilet, bear-proof litter container, emergency shelter, information boards. Pinnell Mountain Trail access (Eagle Summit trailhead) is well marked and starts here; see description at **Milepost F 85.5**. A short loop trail is also provided at the trailhead and has interesting information boards and a viewing platform. The tundra here is covered with lichen and small flowers. A sign board says lichen are some of the world's oldest living things. They can live for thousands of years and even break down rocks. They are prime food for caribou. Weather station.

Favorite spot for local residents to observe summer solstice (weather permitting) on June 21. This area also has some of the best wildflower viewing on Alaska's highway system. Wildflowers found here include: dwarf forget-me-nots, alpine rhododendron or rosebay, rock jasmine, alpine azalea, arctic bell heather, mountain avens, Jacob's ladder, anemones, wallflowers, Labrador tea, lupine, oxytropes, gentians and louseworts. The museum in Central has a

photographic display of Eagle Summit alpine flowers to help highway travelers identify the wildflowers of this area.

F 107.3 C 54 Eagle Summit sign eastbound (elev. 3,685 feet). This is the third and highest of 3 summits (including Cleary and Twelvemile) along the Steese Highway.

F 108 C 53.3 Westbound Eagle Summit sign.

F 109.5 C 51.8 Large parking area to south. *Highway begins 7-mile-long descent northbound edges treeline.*

F 111.4 C 50.9 Parking area on curve to east. Acres of fireweed cover forest fire burned areas along Steese Highway.

F 113.7 C 48.6 Views (some obscured by brush) of "Gold Rich" Mastodon, Mammoth and Independence creeks all flowing into narrow valley below the road.

F 114.2 C 47.1 Avalanche gates. Parking area to east above the Mastodon, Mammoth, Miller and Independence creeks area (view is somewhat obscured by foliage). Prospectors were finding gold on these creeks 2 years before the Klondike gold rush. Active mining still takes place in this area.

The historic Miller House, which began in 1896 as a cabin built by prospector Fritz Miller, was located near here. Miller House was originally a stopover on the sled trail between Circle City and Fairbanks. With the completion of the Steese Highway, it became a year-round roadhouse, offering meals, gas, groceries, a post office and rental cabins, operating until 1970. Items taken from here are now in Central's Museum. The Miller House burned down some years ago.

F 114.3 C 47 Mining road to the south leads down to the creeks and passes close to the location of the old Miller House. No state maintenance on this road, not recommended for travel.

F 116 C 45.3 Loose gravel in 2013.

F 116.3 C 45 Bridge over Mammoth Creek, flowing from Independence and Mastodon creeks. Near here, fossil remains of many species of pre-glacial Alaska mammals have been excavated and may be seen at the University of Alaska museum in Fairbanks and at the museum in Central.

F 117 C 44.3 Highway crosses over Stack Pup Creek. From here the highway gradually descends to Central.

F 117.5 C 43.8 Parking area to north.

F 119.1 C 42.2 Bedrock Creek. Access to creek that flows into Crooked Creek.

F 120.8 C 40.5 Partial views of mining operations through trees to north obscured by foliage; old tailing piles in the Crooked Creek/Albert Creek area.

F 121 C 40.3 Bridge over Sawpit Creek.

F 122.5 C 38.8 Road north has pond-side parking.

F 125.3 C 36 Bridge over Boulder Creek.

F 126 C 35.3 Lupine and wild roses bloom along the road in June.

F 126.7 C 34.6 *Begin 1.5-mile stretch of paved highway northbound. Begin 30 mph speed zone northbound.*

F 127.2 C 34.1 Mitze's Restaurant.

F 127.5 C 33.8 Central post office (ZIP code 99730), postcards for sale.

F 127.6 C 33.7 The **Circle District Historical Society Museum**, open during the summer months, has displays covering the history of the Circle Mining District and its people. Also here are a photo display of wildflowers, fossilized remains of pre-glacial mammals, a minerals display, library and archives, gift shop and visitor information. A large barn beside the museum (which also

Central District Historical Society Museum has a variety of interesting displays. (©Sharon Nault)

serves as a community center) has displays of mining equipment, household items, antique toys and dogsleds. A large covered wagon offers photo-op.

A Farmers' Market is held here Saturday mornings during the summer.

Public restrooms are located beyond the museum building on the left side and are open 7 days a week. $1 donation requested; members free. Open Friday to Monday, noon to 5 P.M., Memorial Day–Labor Day.

F 127.7 C 33.6 Junction of Steese Highway and Circle Hot Springs Road at **CENTRAL** (pop. 92; elev. 965 feet); gas, propane, food, lodging, WiFi and bar at Central Corner; open all year. Gas, diesel, snacks and small gift shop with locally made crafts available at **Gold Country Services and Gold Country Energy** at Mile 0.3 Circle Hot Springs Road (see log below).

Central, formerly called Central House, is situated on Crooked Creek and is the central point in the huge Circle Mining District, one of the oldest and still one of the most active districts in the state. The annual Circle Mining District Picnic for local miners and their families is held in August in the museum's display barn. The caribou migration sometimes travels right through town.

Circle Hot Springs Road accesses local businesses and Circle Hot Springs Lodge (closed: for sale in 2013). Road log follows.

Mile 0.3 **Gold Country Services and Gold Country Energy.** Gas, diesel, oil products, tire and minor repairs, hunting and fishing licenses, copying and faxing, cold drinks, snacks and local crafts. We accept MasterCard, Visa, Discover and American Express. We're also the electric utility for Central, so we're open every day all year. Stop in and say hi! Rick and Sheila Symons, proprietors. (907) 520-5681. [ADVERTISEMENT]

Mile 2.7 Deadwood Creek.

Mile 4.7 Ketchem Creek Road, a 1-lane dirt and gravel road which leads to private mining claims and rock formations (keep right at forks in road) continues 3+ miles.

Mile 5.7 Ketchum Creek, former BLM campground; unmaintained, condition unknown. Access is on southwest side of bridge.

Mile 7.3 Dave's tire repair.

Mile 8.2 Circle Hot Springs Resort (no trespassing, closed to public for many years). The hot springs were used as a gathering place by area Athabascans before the gold rush. Local prospectors used the springs as early as the 1890s. Cassius Monohan homesteaded the site in 1905, selling out to Frank Leach in 1909. Leach built the airstrip, on which Noel Wien landed in 1924. (Wien pioneered many flight routes between Alaska communities.) Leach also built a 3-story hotel, which formed the core of the resort complex.

F 127.8 C 33.5 Bridge (1-lane) over Crooked Creek. Remains of Central House roadhouse on north side of bridge is covered in brush.

Distance marker northbound shows Circle 33 miles.

F 128.1 C 33.2 Central DOT/PF highway maintenance station.

F 128.2 C 33.1 *Pavement ends, gravel begins, northbound. Use caution while traveling the portion of road from here to Circle due to curves, narrow sections and soft shoulders with soft spots and sloughing tendencies. Subject to rough and rocky surfacing with washboard between gradings.*

F 128.4 C 32.9 Private Aircraft: Road to south leads to Central Airport; state-maintained airstrip, adjacent north; elev. 932 feet; length 2,700 feet; gravel; unattended.

F 130.5 C 30.8 Pond frequented by a variety of ducks and lots of cattails. Road proceeds east through miles of burned trees.

F 131 C 29.3 Albert Creek bridge, creek access to north at east end of bridge.

F 138 C 23.3 Limited view through trees to faraway old homestead and primitive road to Crazy Hills area to north.

F 139.4 C 21.9 *Washboard road conditions northbound in summer 2013.*

F 140.4 C 20.9 Lower Birch Creek Wayside (BLM) to east. Drive in 0.1 mile via wide gravel road to a very large parking area

Circle is located on one channel of the Yukon River. Off-duty fire fighters enjoy the view.
(©Sharon Nault)

with outhouse, bear-proof garbage containers and boaters' registration kiosk. Area is suitable for tent camping and RV parking. Boaters can put in here and float down to Birch Creek bridge at **Milepost 147.2**. Much of the bedrock along this waterway consists of Birch Creek schist, one of the oldest rocks in Alaska. Area wildlife includes marten, red fox, wolves, peregrine falcons, sandhill cranes, bald eagles and waterfowl. Information board with maps. Fishing for northern pike and grayling. You can see trees stunted by permafrost on the way in and old growth trees at the Wayside.

F 141 C 20.3 CAUTION: Road narrows; some blind curves next few miles northbound. Drive carefully!

F 141.2 C 20.1 Small turnout to south. Gravel pit parking to north.

F 141.7 C 19.6 Taller trees in area, indicates absence of permafrost.

F 142.8 C 18.5 Gravel turnout to south.

F 144.4 C 16.9 Road travels through large, very open, burned area.

F 145.1 C 16.2 Birch Creek to south.

F 146.3 C 15 Note: Highway kept from erosion here by built-up large rock bank along Birch Creek. Wide parking space to north with good open view of Birch Creek.

F 147.2 C 14.1 One-lane bridge over Birch Creek; clearance 13 feet, 11 inches. Spur roads at south and north ends of bridge lead to turnouts. Creek (muddy in wet weather; check before driving in). Primitive camping at turnouts. Access to takeout point for the **Birch Creek Canoe Trail** is 0.1 mile east at south end of bridge.

F 147.6 C 13.7 Large, weed-covered turnout to south. Watch for mud.

Narrow road becomes wider going toward Circle. Many widened corners and small passing areas.

F 147.8 C 13.5 July 2009 brought major fire damage followed by extensive tree cutting to prevent windfalls from closing road in winter. Speed limit 20 mph, next 11 miles.

F 148.6 C 12.7 Turnout in gravel pit to east. Varying road conditions next 0.5 mile.

F 150.6 C 11.7 Narrow, dangerous curve around pond. Drive cautiously.

F 154 C 7.3 Beautiful displays of fireweed in burn areas and cottongrass in season.

F 155.5 C 5.8 CAUTION: Hairpin curve. No shoulder and sloping road.

F 156 C 5.3 Improved section of road in 2013 with high bare banks. Can be muddy on the sides.

F 156.6 C 4.7 Gravel pit, turnout north.

F 157.5 C 3.8 Turnout to south on curve.

F 158.4 C 2.9 Speed limit 30 mph, watch for children.

This area is seemingly a graveyard to cars that go in, but never come back out.

F 159.5 C 1.8 Old Indian cemetery to east. (Private, do not stop.)

F 161 C 0.3 Circle post office (ZIP code 99733). Speed limit 20 mph.

F 161.1 C 0.2 Private Aircraft: Circle City state-maintained airstrip, adjacent west; elev. 610 feet; length 3,000 feet; gravel; fuel 100LL.

Warbelow Air Service flies 5 times weekly.

F 161.2 C 0.1 H.C. Company Store has unleaded and diesel, tire repair, groceries, snacks; open year-round. Phone booth in front of store. Washeteria to east.

H.C. Company Store. See display ad this page.

F 161.3 C 0 Road ends at a large parking area on Yukon River. Boat launch, picnic tables, trash cans, overnight parking allowed. This is a good place to sit and watch traffic. Information boards on the Yukon National Wildlife Refuge.

Circle

F 161.3 C 0 "Welcome to Circle City" sign. From here you are looking at one channel of the mighty Yukon River and are centrally located in this small town. **Population:** 113. **Emergency Services:** Central Rescue Squad, phone (907) 520-5451 or 520-5228. **Clinic,** Circle Health Clinic, phone (907) 773-7425. **Elevation:** 596 feet. **Climate:** Mean monthly temperature in July 61.4°F, in January -10.6°F. Record high 91°F July 1977, record low -69°F in February 1991. Snow from October through April. Monthly precipitation in summer averages 1.45 inches.

Located on the banks of the Yukon River, 50 miles south of the Arctic Circle, Circle City was the largest gold mining town on the Yukon River, before the Klondike Gold Rush of 1898 created Dawson City, YT. The town began as a supply point to the new gold diggings on Birch Creek in 1893, and grew as a hub for Interior gold camps.

The town was named Circle City because the early miners thought it was located on the Arctic Circle. Today, Circle serves a small local population and visitors coming in by highway or by river. The school had about 22 students enrolled in 2013. A large hotel in Circle remains unfinished and for sale. There's a lot of summer river traffic here. Inquire locally about guided river trips and air service.

Gas, diesel, groceries, snacks and sundries are available at the **H.C. Company Store**. Free camping at unmaintained parking area/boat launch on the banks of the Yukon at the end of the Steese Highway.

When the Yukon River flooded most recently on May 18, 2013, 45 inches of water covered the H.C. Company Store. Depth and date marks for various floods are found inside the store. During the Interior's summer fires in 2009, some 300 firefighters camped out in Circle.

The old Pioneer Cemetery, with its markers dating back to the 1800s, is an interesting spot to visit. To get there, walk west to the gravel road that goes to the right just before the Yukon River parking lot. Keep to the left fork by private homes. To the right, behind some trees, you can see the old Army Wireless Building built in 1908. Continuing on to the cemetery you will have to cross through a private front yard (please be respectful of property) to get to the trail. Walk straight ahead on the trail, which goes through densely wooded trees (many mosquitoes), for about 10 minutes. The path is to the left of the graves, which are scattered among the trees.

Elliott Highway

CONNECTS: Fox to Manley Hot Springs, AK

Length: 150 miles   **Road Surface:** 50% Paved, 50% Gravel   **Season:** Open all year

(See map, page 526)

2

Elliott Highway near its junction with the Dalton Highway. (©Sharon Nault)

Major Attractions:

©Sharon Nault

Manley Roadhouse, Minto Lakes

The Elliott Highway leads 150 miles from its junction with the Steese Highway at Fox (11 miles north of Fairbanks) to Manley Hot Springs, a small settlement with a natural hot springs near the Tanana River. The Elliott Highway provides access to the village of Minto, which accounts for much of the traffic on the road, and to the Dalton Highway to Prudhoe Bay, which along with Livengood creates most of the truck traffic on the Elliott. The highway was named for Malcolm Elliott, president of the Alaska Road Commission from 1927 to 1932.

This is a great drive to a pocket of pioneer Alaska. West from its junction with the Dalton Highway—where the pavement ends—the gravel portion of the Elliott Highway travels the ridges and hills to Manley Hot Springs, with "top of the world" views along the way.

The paved section of the Elliott Highway —the first 73.1 miles of the highway—was in fair to good condition in summer 2013. Despite improvements made in previous summers, this is *not* a highway for relaxed driving. Be alert for frost heaves, uneven grooves and cracks in the pavement, and sloughing shoulders. *Drive with care!*

The remaining 77.9 miles—from the Dalton Highway junction to Manley—are mostly gravel, with a couple of sections of improved and/or chip-sealed road and—in summer 2013—many sections of rocky gravel with sharp rocks embedded in the surface, making it hard on tires. Road conditions depend on weather and maintenance. It can get very slick when wet. The gravel portion of the highway is subject to potholes and ruts in wet weather. Be sure to carry a good spare that is mounted on a rim and prepare to travel at slow speeds in these conditions. Gravel road may be treated with calcium chloride for dust control in dry weather; wash your vehicle after travel to prevent corrosion.

Distance in miles	Dalton Hwy	Fairbanks	Manley	Minto
Dalton Hwy		84	77	47
Fairbanks	84		161	131
Manley	77	161		51
Minto	47	131	51	

Despite the sometimes challenging road conditions, the panoramic views make this a worthwhile drive.

From Fox to the Dalton Highway junction, the Elliott Highway is a series of long upgrades and downgrades, as the road winds through the White Mountains. From the Dalton Highway junction to Manley, the road is narrow and winding, with some steep grades, blind hills, curves and hard rocky stretches.

Fresh spring water is available on the Elliott Highway at **Milepost FX 0.3**. Gas, diesel and propane are available at Fox General Store, Hilltop Truckstop at **Milepost FX**

Elliott Highway   Fox, AK, to Manley Hot Springs, AK

© 2014 The MILEPOST®

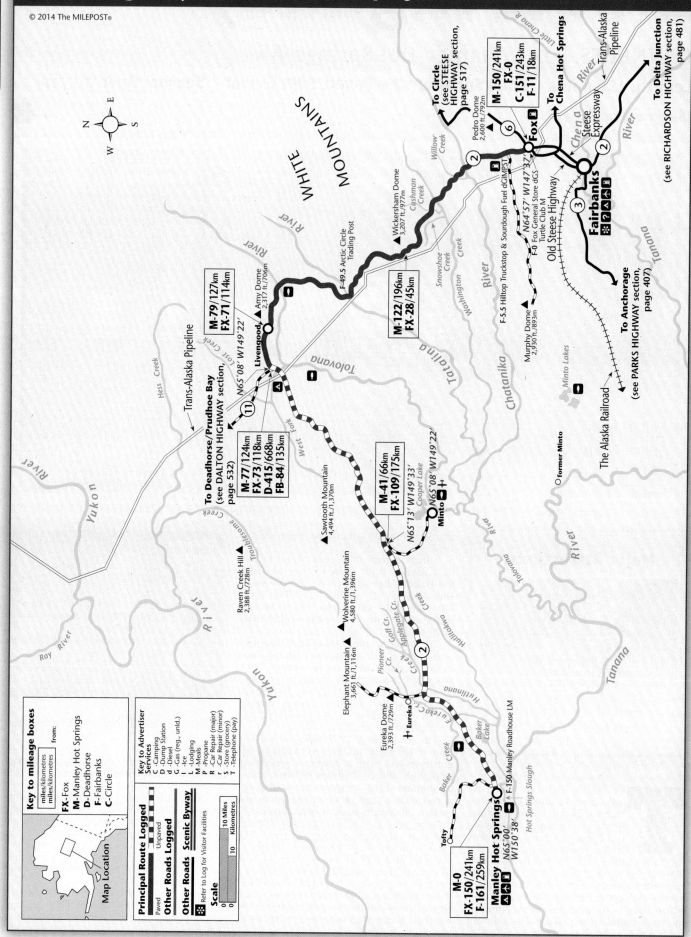

WHITE MOUNTAINS

To Circle
(see STEESE
HIGHWAY section,
page 517)

M-150/241km
FX-0
C-151/243km
F-11/18km

To Chena Hot Springs

Trans-Alaska Pipeline

Pedro Dome
2,600 ft./792m

Wickersham Dome
3,207 ft./977m

6   Fox

To Delta Junction
(see RICHARDSON HIGHWAY section,
page 481)

F-5.5 Hilltop Truckstop & Sourdough Fuel dGIMPST
F-0 Fox General Store dGS
Turtle Club M
Old Steese Highway

2

Steese Expressway

Fairbanks

3

To Anchorage
(see PARKS HIGHWAY section,
page 407)

F-49.5 Arctic Circle
Trading Post

Amy Dome
2,317 ft./706m

M-79/127km
FX-71/114km

Livengood

N65°08' W149°22'

M-122/196km
FX-28/45km

Snowshoe Creek
Washington Creek
Murphy Dome
2,930 ft./893m

Minto Lakes

The Alaska Railroad

Trans-Alaska Pipeline

To Deadhorse/Prudhoe Bay
(see DALTON HIGHWAY section,
page 532)

11

M-77/124km
FX-73/118km
D-415/668km
FB-84/135km

West Fork

Sawtooth Mountain
4,494 ft./1,370m

M-41/66km
FX-109/175km

N65°13' W149°33'
Cooper Lake

N65°08' W149°22'
Minto

former Minto

Raven Creek Hill
2,388 ft./728m

Wolverine Mountain
4,580 ft./1,396m

Goff Cr.
Applegate Cr.

2

Pioneer Cr.

Elephant Mountain
3,661 ft./1,116m

Eureka

Eureka Dome
2,393 ft./729m

Eureka Cr.

Baker Lake

Baker Creek

F-150 Manley Roadhouse LM

Tofty

Manley Hot Springs

N65°00'
W150°38'

Hot Springs Slough

M-0
FX-150/241km
F-161/259km

Key to mileage boxes

miles/kilometres
miles/kilometres   from:

FX- Fox
M- Manley Hot Springs
D- Deadhorse
F- Fairbanks
C- Circle

Key to Advertiser Services

C - Camping
D - Dump Station
d - Diesel
G - Gas (reg., unld.)
I - Ice
L - Lodging
M - Meals
P - Propane
R - Car Repair (major)
r - Car Repair (minor)
S - Store (grocery)
T - Telephone (pay)

Map Location

Principal Route Logged
Paved
Unpaved

Other Roads Logged
Other Roads   Scenic Byway

Refer to Log for Visitor Facilities

Scale
0   10 Miles
0   10   Kilometres

5.5 and in Manley, **Milepost FX 151**. If you are headed up the Dalton Highway, the first gas/diesel and propane stop on that highway is at the Yukon River crossing, **Milepost J 56** (56 miles north of junction with the Elliott Highway, 129 miles from Fox or 140 miles from Fairbanks).

Watch for large trucks on the Elliott Highway between Fairbanks and the Dalton Highway junction. The Elliott Highway is open year-round.

The Elliott Highway provides access to 4 trailheads in the White Mountains National Recreation Area. These trails (most are for winter use) lead to recreation cabins. For more information and cabin registration, stop by the BLM office at 1150 University Ave., Fairbanks, AK 99707, phone (907) 474-2200 or 1-800-437-7021; or the Alaska Public Lands Information Center, 101 Dunkel St., Ste. 101, Fairbanks, AK 99701; Phone (907) 439-3730; or visit www.blm.gov/ak/st/en/prog/nlcs/white_mtns.html and follow links.

Emergency medical services: Between Fox and Manley Hot Springs, phone the state troopers at 911 or (907) 451-5100. Use CB channels 19.

Elliott Highway Log

Distance from Fox (FX) is followed by distance from Manley Hot Springs (M).
NOTE: To determine distance from Fairbanks, just add 11 miles to the distance from Fox figure given in the log.
The Elliott Highway ends at physical milepost 153 on the banks of the Tanana River, just beyond the settlement of Manley Hot Springs.

ALASKA ROUTE 2

FX 0 M 150 Steese Expressway from Fairbanks ends at **junction** of Steese and Elliott Highways (Alaska Routes 6 and 2); the convenient **Fox General Store** to west is a great travel stop with gas, diesel, propane, groceries, liquor store, and ATM. Weigh station at northeast corner of intersection.

> **Junction** with Steese Highway (Alaska Route 6) which leads 161 miles to Circle. Turn to **Milepost F 11** in the STEESE HIGHWAY section on page 519 for log of that route.

Access west to **FOX** (pop. 417), which was established as a mining camp before 1905 and named for nearby Fox Creek. Silver Gulch Brewery is 0.1 mile to the west (restaurant, tours); the Howling Dog Saloon is across the road from Silver Gulch; and the local favorite for great prime rib, the **Turtle Club** restaurant, is located at Mile 0.5 Old Steese Highway North. Turn right just past Silver Gulch Brewery for Fox Gardens.

Fox General Store. See display ad on page 519 in STEESE HIGHWAY section.

Turtle Club. See display ad on page 454 in the FAIRBANKS section.

FX 0.1 M 149.9 Distance marker northbound shows Livengood 67 miles, Manley 154 miles. Watch for frost heaves next 12 miles northbound.

FX 0.2 M 149.8 Northern Moosed RV Park & Campground offers full hookups and easy access.

Begin climb northbound toward hilltop.
FX 0.3 M 149.7 Fox Spring double-ended

paved turnout to west. Fresh spring water tap popular with local residents. Good place to fill up water bottles. Water content is posted. Sign (missing in 2013): $1,000 fine for littering.

FX 1.3 M 148.7 Eldorado Gold Mine Road.

FX 3.3 M 146.7 Old Murphy Dome Road (current status unknown) leads west around Murphy Dome to Murphy Dome Road.

FX 3.4 M 146.6 Silver Fox Mine Road.

FX 5.5 M 144.5 Hilltop Truckstop (3 entrances); 24-hour gas, diesel, propane, restaurant, phone, ATM and groceries. Homemade pies, a favorite with locals and visitors, are a Hilltop specialty.

Hilltop Truckstop. See display ad on page 459 in the FAIRBANKS section.

Next services northbound are at Yukon Crossing on the Dalton Highway, 118 miles, or at Manley, 145 miles.

FX 7.4 M 142.6 Views to northeast of Pedro Dome and Dome Creek. Buildings of Dome and Eldorado camps are in the valley below to the east (best view is southbound). 55 mph speed limit posted.
CAUTION: Lots of truck traffic here.

FX 9.2 M 140.8 Sign reads "Entering Olnes City (pop. 1)." Olnes was a railroad station on the Tanana Valley Railroad and a mining camp. Old tailings and abandoned cabins.

FX 10.6 M 139.4 Turnoff for **Lower Chatanika River State Recreation Site at Olnes Pond**, 1 mile southwest of highway via wide gravel side road; fishing, camping, firepits, dumpster, outhouses; campground host; 15-day limit, no fee in summer 2013. Very popular with ATVers (speed limit enforced), local families and campers visiting Fairbanks. Campsites are in the trees and in open grassy areas around the large pond, which is stocked with rainbow and grayling by the ADF&G. Camper rules posted and enforced. No motorized watercraft on pond. Access to Chatanika River.

FX 11 M 139 Chatanika River bridge. Access to **Lower Chatanika River Whitefish Campground** to southwest at north end of bridge. Parking area by river below bridge. Access road continues to parking areas on small loop and entrance to picnic area with covered tables and a firepit surrounded by benches located in a grassy opening. Also access to small campsites along the river; picnic tables, firepits, toilets, dumpster. Boat launch area with pit toilet at back of campground.

FX 11.4 M 138.6 Haystack Drive to north.

FX 13.1 M 136.9 Willow Creek bridge.
CAUTION: Slow for frost heaves and pavement cracks next 4 miles northbound.

FX 15 M 135 Himalaya Road.

FX 17.2 M 132.8 Begin long sweeping downgrade westbound into deep valley.

FX 18.4 M 131.6 Washington Creek bridge. Access to creek at east end of bridge.

FX 18.9 M 131.1 Small turnout to south with sign that reads:

"Located here is an experimental trenching site that is part of a project studying the feasibility to construct a natural gas pipeline to transport gas from Alaska's North Slope to market. The technical trenching trials were conducted here to determine the efficiency and economics of various methods of trenching in permafrost. This site, which is 1 of 3, was chosen because it is composed of discontinuous permafrost in silt. The other sites, which

contain continuous permafrost, are located in the Prudhoe Bay area. The trenching trial was completed in spring 2002. The site will be monitored for 10 years to evaluate the amount of fill subsidence and to study the success of several methods of revegetation."

FX 19 M 131 *Patched pavement and frost heaves in this area.*

FX 20.1 M 129.9 Paved double-ended parking area to northeast near gravel pit.

FX 23.4 M 126.6 Large double-ended parking area on 40-mph curve to southwest.

FX 24.2 M 125.8 Long double-ended turnout on Old Elliott Highway alignment to northeast at 40-mph curve.

NOTE: Although these old highway alignments make good pullouts for rest stops or overnights, motorists are reminded that they are not maintained. These sections of old highway can be narrow and rough, with potholes, bumps, or overgrown brush; you may not be able to drive completely around the loop. MILEPOST® staff have NOT driven all of these old alignments.

FX 25 M 125 Long double-ended turnout on Old Elliott Highway alignment to northeast at 35 mph-curve.

FX 27.6 M 122.4 Entering **BLM's White Mountains National Recreation Area** northbound. Large double-ended parking area to south on curve. (Cell phones sometimes work here, depending on provider.) Turnoff to north for large parking area with outhouse, bear-proof garbage cans, ATV loading/unloading dock and access to 2 trailheads (descriptions follow).

Wickersham Creek Trail (winter-use) is 20 miles long, ATVs permitted as far as Lee's Cabin. White Mountain Summit Trail (year-round) is 20 miles long and accesses Borealis–LeFevre BLM cabin (ski loop trail junction 2 miles, Beaver Creek and Borealis/LeFevre Cabin 20 miles). Be sure to register before hiking; sign-up sheets in metal boxes at trailheads. Blueberries in season; no ATVs allowed on this trail.

White Mountains NRA is primarily a winter-use area. There is good summer hiking on upper trails, but lower trails are often very wet.

The Elliott Highway winds around the base of Wickersham Dome (elev. 3,207 feet). Views of the White Mountains, a range of white limestone mountains (elev. 5,000 feet).

Entering Livengood/Tolovana Mining District northbound, Fairbanks Mining District southbound. Begin long descent to Washington and Willow Creeks.

FX 28 M 122 Distance marker northbound shows Manley 125 miles, Dalton Highway 46 miles. Distance marker southbound shows Fox 26 miles, Fairbanks 36 miles.

FX 28.8 M 121.2 Paved double-ended parking area to south.

FX 29.3 M 120.7 Long double-ended turnout on Old Elliott Highway alignment to northeast. *(Rough spot at south end; not recommended for large vehicles.)*

FX 29.6 M 120.4 Paved turnout to south. Spring water piped to road. (A sign here warns that the spring water is not tested for purity and it should be boiled or chemically disinfected before drinking.)

FX 30.4 M 119.6 Paved double-ended parking area to southwest. Fairbanks–North Star Borough boundary.

Watch for Sled Dog Rocks on horizon northbound. Southbound traffic gets a good view of these rocks between Mileposts 32 and 31.

FX 31 M 119 Long double-ended road, Old Elliott Highway alignment to northeast

Arctic Circle Trading Post is an interesting stop along the Elliott Highway. (©Sharon Nault)

on 40-mph curve.

FX 32 M 118 Large turnout to southwest; partial view.

FX 32.6 M 117.4 *Begin long 6 percent downgrade next 2.2 miles northbound to Globe Creek.* First good view northbound of trans-Alaska pipeline as it emerges from hillside.

FX 34.4 M 115.6 Good view of pipeline to west.

FX 35 M 115 *CAUTION: Slow for frost heaves and breaks in road between Mileposts 35 and 36.*

FX 36.4 M 113.6 Large paved double-ended turnout to north with mountain views.

FX 36.8 M 113.2 Small gravel turnout to north.

FX 37 M 113 Globe Creek bridge. Small parking area at west end of bridge with sloping access. **Grapefruit Rocks**—2 large outcrops—are visible ahead, northbound. Grapefruit Rocks is a popular rock-climbing spot; hike in from turnout at **Milepost F 39.**

Slow for frost heaves west of bridge.

FX 38 M 112 Highway climbs west-bound.

FX 39 M 111 Side road to northeast deadends at a small turnaround. According to APLIC, access to Upper Grapefruit Rocks is from here; follow trail leading up above road. Beautiful views. Trail is steep and exposed to hot sun; bring water, insect repellent and sunscreen. Highway descends southbound. View of Globe Creek canyon. Rocks are visible to southbound traffic.

FX 39.3 M 110.7 Double-ended turnout to south. According to APLIC, Lower Grapefruit Rocks is accessible from this turnout by following the 4-wheel drive trail leading west from the turnout to a clearing with a firepit. Hike is an easy ¼ mile, but trail can be muddy and mosquitoes can be bad.

FX 40.5 M 109.5 Double-ended paved turnout to north, scenic view. *Caution: Large lowered drain imbedded in part of parking area.*

FX 41.1 M 108.9 Double-ended parking area on Old Elliott Highway alignment to north.

FX 41.6 M 108.4 Small paved turnouts both sides of highway.

FX 41.9 M 108.1 Small paved turnouts both sides of highway.

FX 42.8 M 107.2 Pipeline pump station No. 7 to west (not visible from road). No services.

FX 43 M 107 *Begin long downgrade northbound.*

FX 44.4 M 105.6 Views of trans-Alaska pipeline to northwest. Ascending long grade southbound.

FX 44.7 M 105.3 Paved and gravel parking area to east at **Tatalina River** bridge. Walk to old bridge upstream from parking area beside river. Primitive campsite above river. The Tatalina is a tributary of the Chatanika. Tatalina is the Athabascan name for this 60-mile-long stream.

FX 47.1 M 102.9 Gravel turnout to east. View of valley below.

FX 47.4 M 102.6 Turnout to west into active gravel pit.

FX 48 M 102 Unmaintained turnout to south.

CAUTION: Slow for frost heaves northbound.

FX 49.5 M 100.5 "Welcome to Joy,

AK" (sign). According to local resident Joe Carlson, **JOY** has a population of about 30 people and quite a few dogs. Joy was named for the late Joy Griffin, who homesteaded this land with her husband, Norman "Dick" Griffin. Joy wrote a popular book (now out-of-print), *Home Sweet Homestead*, about her experiences.

Arctic Circle Trading Post to east was built by the Carlson's, who settled here with their 23 children (18 of whom were adopted). Books by Nancy Carlson (*Joy Abounds*) and daughter Cherie Carlson Curtis (*The Homestead Kid*) are for sale at the Arctic Circle Trading Post. The sign may still read Wildwood General Store, but it has been Arctic Circle Trading Post since 1997. The trading post has free coffee and Arctic Circle Crossing certificates, as well as gifts, snacks and Arctic Circle memorabilia for sale. Posted by the door is a sign that reads: "Not a single mosquito at Joy ... they are all married with large families."

The Arctic Circle Trading Post. See display ad this page.

FX 51.4 M 98.6 Snack shack to east down side road with interesting signs.

FX 51.9 M 98.1 Large parking area to north on curve at top of hill.

Glimpses—through thick brush—of White Mountains to northeast and the Elliott Highway descending slopes of Bridge Creek valley ahead. Bridge Creek flows into the Tolovana River. Steep winding downgrades northbound.

FX 52 M 98 *CAUTION: Slow for dangerous frost heaves between Mileposts 52 and 55.*

FX 56.9 M 93.1 Distance marker northbound shows Dalton Highway 14 miles, Manley 93 miles.

FX 57 M 93 *Slow for frost heaves between Mileposts 57 and 58.*

FX 57.1 M 92.9 Colorado Creek Trailhead to east at south end of **Tolovana River** bridge; large paved parking, wheelchair-accessible outhouse with ramp, bear-proof litter container, registration kiosk, information board about local gold, the Dalton Highway and Walter Roman—he discovered the prehistoric "Blue Ox" on display at the UAF Museum (Blue Ox is 36,000 years old). Colorado Creek trail (recommended for winter use) leads 15 miles to Colorado Creek Cabin and connects with Windy Creek Trail; for current trail conditions, phone (907) 474-2372.

If access road to old wayside across highway is signed "closed," do NOT stay there. A local referred to this area by saying "People who come to Alaska think that bears are the danger when really it is the creeks and rivers." Do not park on the sandbars or low areas near water in wet weather, flooding can happen quickly. Fishing for grayling to 11 inches; whitefish 12 to 18 inches; northern pike. ➥

Slow for frost heaves between Mileposts 54 and 58.

FX 58 M 92 Northbound highway winds around Amy Dome (elev. 2,317 feet) to east. The Tolovana River flows in the valley to the southwest, paralleling the road.

FX 59.4 M 91.6 Parking area on sloping road to small primitive camping area near riverbank; not recommended for large RVs.

FX 60 M 90 Parking area with view to south. Grouse have been seen here.

Slow for frost heaves and patched pavement between Mileposts 60 and 61.

FX 61 M 89 *Begin long upgrade westbound.*

FX 62.3 M 87.7 Watch for gravel road to northeast which winds uphill 0.3 mile to the Fred Blixt BLM public use cabin. Pre-register to use the cabin with the BLM office in Fairbanks.

According to the BLM, the original cabin was built in 1935 by Fred Blixt, a Swedish trapper and prospector who built several such cabins in the Livengood area. The original cabin burned down in 1991 and was replaced in 1992. The cabin is 12-by-16 feet and constructed with 2-sided logs.

FX 65.5 M 84.5 North Country Mercantile (closed to general public).

FX 65.8 M 84.2 Good eastbound view of highway unspooling in 3 long folds across the hills ahead.

FX 68.5 M 81.5 Highway begins descent westbound to Livengood.

FX 70 M 80 *Slow for frost heaves and rough road westbound.*

FX 70.1 M 79.9 Livengood Creek bridge. Money Knob to northeast. Rough road from here to Livengood.

FX 71 M 79 Gravel access road (can be rough) leads 2 miles to Livengood state highway maintenance station; no visitor services. One-lane bridge at Mile 0.8. Yield to trucks and heavy equipment on all Livengood roads. Overnight parking beside Elliott Highway at double-ended turnout near this intersection. Blueberries in season.

LIVENGOOD (pop. 24), unincorporated, consists of 31 homes on 265 square miles of land. Nathaniel R. Hudson and Jay Livengood discovered gold on Livengood Creek in July 1914, and by 1915 there was a mining camp and a post office. Between 1915 and 1920, the claim yielded some $9.5 million in gold. Large-scale mining attempts in the late 1930s and in the 1940s failed. The post office was discontinued in 1957. A mining corporation acquired much of the gold-rich Livengood Bench. Active mining may be underway. *No trespassing on mining claims.*

FX 71.1 M 78.9 Large paved double-ended turnout to south. Overnight parking allowed (big rigs often stop here, so pull over far enough to allow them to drive through turnout). Practice "Leave no trace" camping and take your trash with you. △

FX 71.3 M 78.7 Large gravel pit/storage area to north.

FX 73 M 77 Distance marker westbound shows Minto 40 miles, Manley 80 miles, Yukon River 56 miles.

FX 73.1 M 76.9 Road forks at **junction** of Elliott and Dalton Highways. This is a popular photo-op for the Dalton HIghway sign, but there is very little parking, so watch out for each other. (There is a new sign at Milepost 1.1 Dalton Highway.)

TURN SOUTHWEST HERE to continue on Elliott Highway to Minto and Manley Hot Springs (log follows). Turn north for Dalton Highway for Yukon River Bridge, Coldfoot, Arctic Circle and Deadhorse/Prudhoe Bay.

Junction with Dalton Highway (Alaska Route 11). See DALTON HIGHWAY section on page 532 for log.

NOTE: Pavement ends, gravel begins, westbound to Manley. Watch for sharp rocks embedded in road. Road narrows (no shoulders). Gravel is treated with calcium chloride to control dust.

FX 74.3 M 75.7 Former Livengood pipeline camp to north.

There's good blueberry picking in season along the Elliott Highway. (© Sharon Nault)

FX 74.7 M 75.3 West Fork Tolovana River bridge. River access at both ends of bridge; grayling to 15 inches, use spinners or flies. Small boat launch west of bridge with long parking area (subject to flooding); picnicking, overnight parking. ⛵

Travelers may notice an abundance of dragonflies along the Elliott Highway. Their main food is mosquitoes. The Four-Spot Skimmer Dragonfly was adopted as the state insect in 1995.

FX 78.6 M 71.4 Double-ended turnout on old road alignment.

FX 79.1 M 70.9 Turnout to south; level parking in former gravel pit.

FX 79.4 M 70.6 Low hills to north form Cascaden Ridge.

FX 79.9 M 70.1 Sloping access to parking area to south.

FX 82.5 M 67.5 *Slow for steep, blind hill.* Large turnout to south at top of hill.

Rough road westbound with few turnouts.

FX 83 M 67 The burned areas both sides of the road are from the Applegate fire of June 1, 2010. Evidence of this fire continues on towards Manley.

FX 85.4 M 64.6 Turnouts on both sides of road. Highway crosses unnamed stream.

FX 86.4 M 63.6 Small turnout to southwest with view. Highway climbs westbound; no guard rails through this burned area.

FX 88.5 M 61.5 Looking south through dense trees toward the Tolovana River valley, travelers may glimpse Tolovana Hot Springs Dome (elev. 2,386 feet).

FX 89.6 M 60.4 *CAUTION: Road is slippery in wet weather.* Road begins a long ascent of Ptarmigan Hill westbound.

FX 91.2 M 58.8 Turnout. Distance marker westbound shows Minto 29 miles, Manley 61 miles.

Bird watchers note: Local resident Frank Gertler relayed to field editor Sharon Nault that there are 4 kinds of grouse in this area in addition to ptarmigan: spruce hens, willow grouse, sharp-tailed and blue grouse.

FX 92 M 58 Sweeping views to southeast and northwest as highway straddles a ridge westbound.

FX 92.6 M 57.4 Turnout to south.

FX 93 M 57 Large viewpoint turnout to south with loading platform. Trailhead for Tolovana Hot Springs. The moderate to strenuous 10-mile hike crosses over Tolovana Hot Springs Dome (spectacular views). The trail continues past the springs to the Tolovana River Valley, where canoeing and fishing are available. Tolovana Hot Springs may also be reached by air taxi from Fairbanks. The Hot Springs has 3 hot tubs and cabins. For reservations (required), phone (907) 455-6706 or visit their website at www.tolovana hotsprings.com. The trail and cabins are heavily used in winter by locals traveling on skis, snowshoes and by snow machine.

MILEPOST® field editors Sharon Nault and J.V. Teague had cell phone service at this viewpoint last summer.

FX 93.5 M 56.5 Beautiful view of Minto Flats.

FX 94 M 56 Long narrow turnout with great view near top of Ptarmigan Hill. Good vantage point to view Minto Flats, Tanana River and foothills of the Alaska Range to south. The White Mountains are to the northeast and Sawtooth Mountain is to the northwest.

Between about Milepost 93 and 108, the Elliott Highway is subject to high winds in winter and drifting snow often causes temporary road closures. Summer drivers may notice that the roadside brush is cleared far from the road shouders along here; Road maintenance workers do this to minimize winter snow drifts.

FX 96.3 M 53.7 Eastbound traffic climbs Ptarmigan Hill; turnout. Alaska cotton in June. *Rough road. Watch for moose.*

FX 97.8 M 52.2 Small turnout to south with panoramic view. The mountains to the north are (from east to west): Sawtooth (elev. 4,494 feet); Wolverine (4,580 feet); and Elephant (3,661 feet). To the south are Tolovana River flats and Cooper Lake.

FX 98.3 M 51.7 Small gravel turnout to south with view. Start looking for blueberries in season along the highway westbound.

FX 100.1 M 49.9 The highway along here can be muddy in wet weather as potholes fill with rain.

FX 101.3 M 48.7 Large turnout to north.

Minto Lakes refers to all lakes in the Minto Flats area, a popular duck hunting spot.
(©Sharon Nault)

FX 102 M 48 *CAUTION: Watch for sharp rocks in road, especially between Mileposts 102 and 103.*

FX 104 M 46 This area can be a paradise for blueberry pickers in August.

FX 105.8 M 44.2 Highway climbs to summit westbound.

FX 106.4 M 43.6 Turnout with view of Sawtooth Mountains to north; information board with map.

FX 109.2 M 40.8 Distance marker westbound shows Minto 11 miles, Manley 43 miles.

FX 109.3 M 40.7 Junction with 10.5-mile access road to village of **MINTO** (pop. 191). Minto Road is wide pavement with some breaks; turnout areas at Mile 4.6, Mile 7.4 (Sam's Creek) and Mile 8.1 (cemetery); airport at Mile 9.6. *10 mph speed limit through village.* Minto is located on the west bank of the Tolovana River. Enjoy sweeping views of Tolovana River, creeks, ponds, lakes and the huge area that is Minto Flats. Groceries, gas, diesel, propane and lodging are available. Minto has a health clinic, a senior center and a school. Village Express twice-weekly van service to Manley Hot Springs and Fairbanks, departing Minto View Lodge. Minto is a "dry" village: The sale or importation of alcohol is banned. There are hefty fines and possible jail time for offenders.

Minto residents are mainly Tanana Athabascans. The Minto Band originally built permanent cabins at Old Minto on the Tanana River. The village was relocated to its present location, 40 miles north of the old site, in 1969 due to repeated flooding and erosion. The present site had been used as a fall and winter camp since the early 1900s.

The climate here is extreme: the average daily maximum temperature during July is in the low 70s; the average daily minimum in January is well below zero, with extended periods of −40°F and very strong wind chill factors. Average annual precipitation is 12 inches, with 50 inches of snowfall.

Most of the year-round employment is with the school, clinic or village council. Many residents work during summers, fire fighting for the BLM. Some residents trap or make birch-bark baskets and beaded skin

and fur items. Subsistence is an important part of the local economy. Salmon, whitefish, moose, bear, small game, waterfowl and berries are utilized. Several families have seasonal fishing/hunting camps and trapping areas on the Tanana River.

Minto Flats is one of the most popular duck hunting spots in Alaska, according to the ADF&G. **Minto Lakes** refers to all lakes in this lowland area. Accessible only by plane or boat; best to fly in. Pike to 36 inches; use wobblers, bait, red-and-white spoons, good all summer. Also grayling, sheefish and whitefish.

Private Aircraft: Minto airstrip 1 mile east; elev. 460 feet; length 2,000 feet; gravel; unattended. Recently upgraded and renamed the "Minto Al Wright Airport."

FX 110.1 M 39.9 Small gravel turnout to south.

FX 110.2 M 39.8 Large gravel turnout to south.

FX 110.4 M 39.6 Culvert under road. *CAUTION: Watch for soft shoulder.*

FX 111.3 M 38.7 Turnout north to gravel pit. Watch for grouse.

FX 112 M 38 *CAUTION: Watch for sharp rocks in road, especially between Mileposts 112 and 115.*

FX 114.1 M 35.9 *CAUTION: Narrow, winding, roller-coaster road westbound for next 6 miles. Slow for blind hills and corners. Speed limit is 25 mph.*

FX 115.1 M 34.9 Gravel turnout. Steep road at the turnout leads up to a small primitive turnout with great views and some privacy.

FX 116.4 M 33.6 Turnout at top of blind hill; good view.

FX 117.5 M 32.6 Improved road begins steep climb westbound up North Hill. Good views.

FX 118.6 M 31.4 Turnout.

FX 119 M 31 Small turnout to south. Narrow road proceeds west on high ledge with good views to the north.

FX 119.5 M 30.5 Turnout at top of hill with view (if not obscured by brush) of Eureka Dome (elev. 2,393 feet) to north.

FX 120 M 30 Turnout to north and some views through brush from turnout to the

south.

FX 120.1 M 29.9 *Begin improved road surface westbound to **Milepost 137.5**, but watch for frost heaves, potholes and gravel breaks.*

FX 121.5 M 28.5 *Watch for moose.*

FX 122.7 M 27.3 Large parking area to north with view of Elephant Mountain and the Applegate burn area (2010).

Highway makes long curve and begins descent of 6 Mile Hill westbound.

FX 123.4 M 26.6 Long crack in surface of southbound lane (summer 2013).

FX 127.6 M 22.4 *Begin pavement westbound.*

FX 128.8 M 21.2 Hutlinana Creek bridge. Small turnouts both sides of road.

FX 129.1 M 20.9 Long, weed-covered turnout to south.

F X 130.5 M 19.5 Junction with Eureka and Rampart Road (11.8 miles); unmaintained. Active mining claims in area: *NO TRESPASSING*. A trail leads to the former mining camp of Eureka, at the junction of Pioneer and Eureka creeks, 3 miles south of Eureka Dome. Manley 19 miles (signed).

CAUTION: Winter dog and snow machine trails cross highway ahead; 50 mph posted speed limit.

FX 131.3 M 18.7 Junction with Old Elliott Highway loop. The 2010 Applegate fire jumped back and forth across the highway along here.

FX 132.1 M 17.9 Junction with Old Elliott Highway loop. Sign: "Watch for children at play."

FX 136.1 M 13.9 Bridge over **Baker Creek**. Fishing for grayling 5 to 20 inches, use flies, black gnats, mosquitoes, May-September.

CAUTION: Watch for moose.

FX 136.7 M 13.3 *Pavement ends westbound, begin narrow rocky gravel road. This long 13.5-mile stretch of highway into Manley winds through extremely dense trees and brush.*

FX 142 M 8 First good, large, dirt turnout to the south.

FX 146.5 M 3.5 Sign reads: "No Shooting in Residential Areas."

FX 148.1 M 1.9 Sanitary landfill with sani-dump for RVs. Dumping RVs here is legal; call (907) 672-3412 if there are any problems. *CAUTION: Negotiate this area with care and do not drive too close to edge of pit.*

FX 148.3 M 1.7 Walter Woods Park and Hall. This is a tribal hall used for potlatches and meetings. Washeteria to north; laundromat, restrooms, showers (well-marked with signage).

FX 149 M 1 *Pavement begins, gravel ends, westbound.* Clinic, community well house to north (move silver-colored switch to activate potable water). Please do not take more than 100 gallons.

"Welcome to Manley Hot Springs" sign.

FX 149.1 M 0.9 DOT station to south.

FX 149.2 M 0.8 Junction with Tofty Road, which leads 15 miles to gold mining area of Tofty, founded in 1908 by pioneer prospector A.F. Tofty. Road deteriorates at Mile 5. A new road alignment from the end of Tofty Road to the Yukon River across from the Village of Tanana is under consideration by the ADOT&PF. There is active placer mining in the area; do not trespass.

Iditarod Kennels, owned by Joee and Pam Redington, is on Tofty Road; inquire about tours at Manley Roadhouse.

FX 149.7 M 0.3 Turn uphill for private hot springs, owned by long-time resident

Gladys Dart.

The hot springs—contained in 4 concrete baths inside the Dart greenhouse—are used by locals and visitors alike. No changing rooms; donations welcome, 1-hour limit. Instructions for reservations are sometimes posted at greenhouse entrance (or call ahead from the Manley Roadhouse–call is free 907-672-3231).

Gladys Dart School, a National Historic Site, is located on the road to the hot springs. Established in 1958, it was named for Gladys (owner of the hot springs), who taught there until her retirement in 1986. *NOTE: Do NOT drive big rigs up to the greenhouse. Park along highway (or in Manley) and walk up. Or you may park in front of the old school near the greenhouse.*

FX 150 M 0 One-lane bridge over Hot Springs Slough (yield to oncoming traffic). Manley Roadhouse is on your left after you cross the bridge. Campground is to your right, across from the roadhouse; pay $5 camping fee at the roadhouse. ▲

The airport, grocery, post office and gas station with propane are located a short drive beyond Manley Roadhouse. Continue on road (Elliott Highway) around long curve for these services. The dirt road ends at Milepost 153 on the banks of the Tanana River.

Manley Hot Springs

FX 150 M 0 Manley Hot Springs is located on Hot Springs Slough, 3 miles north of the Tanana River and 161 miles from Fairbanks via the Elliott Highway. **Population**: 81. **Emergency Services**: Volunteer Fire Dept.; **Clinic**, phone (907) 672-3333; **Alaska State Troopers**, in Fairbanks, phone (907) 451-5100. **Elevation**: 330 feet.

Climate: Mean temperature in July is 59°F, in January -10.4°F. Record high 93°F in June 1969, record low -70°F in January 1934. Precipitation in summer averages 2.53 inches a month. Snow from October through April, with traces in September and May. Greatest mean monthly snowfall in January (11.1 inches). Record snowfall 49 inches in January 1937. **Transportation**: Air taxi service.

Private Aircraft: Manley Hot Springs civil airstrip (open year-round), adjacent southwest; elev. 270 feet; 3,400-feet long, 60-feet wide; gravel; fuel avgas. This new runway opened in August 2013; the old runway has been converted into a taxiway leading to an aircraft parking area

A pocket of "Pioneer Alaska." J.F. Karshner homesteaded here in 1902, about the same time the U.S. Army Signal Corps established a telegraph station nearby. The location soon became known as Baker Hot Springs, after nearby Baker Creek, and later was known simply as Hot Springs. Frank Manley built the 4-story Resort Hotel here in 1907. The population peaked at about 1000 in 1910, as the village became a trading center for nearby Eureka and Tofty mining districts. In 1913, the hotel burned down. By 1950, the population was down to 29 as mining waned. The settlement's name was changed to Manley Hot Springs in 1957.

Today, Manley Hot Springs is a quiet settlement with gardening, hunting and fishing helping to sustain many residents. There

are now about 50 private phones in Manley. The post office, gas station with propane, diesel, phone and grocery are at the trading post. Meals, a bar and overnight accommodations are available at the Manley Roadhouse, which dates back to 1903. Its great room is a flashback in history with cozy furniture, original piano, local artifacts and pictures as well as a large mammoth bone hanging near the dining room. The abandoned Northern Commercial Co. is down the road from Manley Roadhouse.

Residents have long been taking baths in the square cement tubs at the hot springs (see **Milepost F 150.8**), thanks to the generosity of Gladys Dart. The hot springs water is soft, containing some chloride and carbonate but no sulfur. Visitors are asked to be respectful of the pools and greenhouse plants. Call ahead for specific times to go (stays are limited to 1 hour).

Manley Roadhouse. Come visit one of Alaska's oldest original roadhouses from the gold rush era. See the many prehistoric and Alaskana artifacts on display. New rooms with private baths added 1997. Private cabins. The Manley Roadhouse is a great place to meet local miners, dog mushers, trappers or fishermen. We specialize in traditional Alaska home-style hospitality, fresh-baked pies, giant cinnamon rolls and good food. Largest liquor selection in Alaska. Stop by and see us. See display ad this page. [ADVERTISEMENT]

There is a big annual 4th of July celebration here, featuring a community feed and boat races on the slough. Manley Hot Springs hosts the Stanley Dayo Championship Sled Dog Race in winter. Iditarod musher Charlie Boulding is from Manley Hot Springs.

Manley is also the home of Mr. and Mrs. Joe Redington Jr., who have **Iditarod Kennels** just outside town where they raise sprint dogs for racing. Tours of their kennel are a special Alaskan experience and your only opportunity to see pictures of Joe Redington Sr. (father of the Iditarod Sled Dog Race) and Susan Butcher (multi-year winner of the race) as they climbed Mount McKinley with their sled dog teams. Joe is a tal-

ented and well-known carver of bone and a basket maker. His work is displayed at the kennel along with a large and unique collection of Eskimo dolls. Inquire locally about availability or call (907) 672-3412.

There is a picnic area, playground and tent camping at park on the slough at the Manley Roadhouse. Two tent and vehicle camping locations here in a picturesque grove of birches across the street; one is managed by the Manley Park Association and the other by the Roadhouse. Pay camping fees as applicable to your campground (fees have been $5). Showers are available at the roadhouse for a fee. The washeteria just outside town has showers and a laundry (see **Milepost F 148.3**). Also a boat launch here.

Hot Springs Slough flows into the Tanana River. Fishing for pike 18 to 36 inches, use spinning and trolling lures, May through September. Follow the dirt road (Elliott Highway) 3 miles beyond the Hot Springs Slough bridge to reach the **Tanana River**; 2 benches available for relaxing and a new (2013) toilet in the parking area. A fish wheel is often pulled up on the bank here.

CAUTION: Areas of this bluff are sloughing off into the river.

King, silver and dog salmon from 7 to 40 lbs., June 15 to Sept. 30. Fish wheels and nets are used. Fishing charter services are available locally. ↩

Interior of Manley Roadhouse recalls pioneer Alaska. A great place to visit. (©Sharon Nault)

Dalton Highway

CONNECTS: Elliott Hwy. to Deadhorse/Prudhoe Bay, AK

Length: 415 miles   **Road Surface: 25% Paved, 75% Gravel**

Season: Open all year   **Steepest Grade: 12 percent**

The Dalton Highway rolls across the North Slope (© Sharon Nault)

Distance in miles	Coldfoot	Deadhorse	Fairbanks
Coldfoot		240	259
Deadhorse	240		499
Fairbanks	259	499	

he 415-mile Dalton Highway (also known as the "Haul Road") begins at **Milepost FX 73.1** on the Elliott Highway, 84 miles from Fairbanks, and ends at Deadhorse/Prudhoe Bay on the Beaufort Sea coast. The highway follows the Trans-Alaska pipeline, up hills and down, through forested valleys, over the Brooks Range at Atigun Pass, and across the treeless North Slope.

The Dalton Highway is unique in its scenic beauty, wildlife and recreational opportunities, but it is also one of Alaska's most remote, dangerous and challenging roads. Driving distance (round-trip) between Fairbanks and Deadhorse is approximately 1,000 miles. Allow at least 3 days for the trip. The Dalton is open all year and can be driven in winter.

The Dalton is still called "the Haul Road" by many, a name that harkens back to its days as an access road during construction of the Trans-Alaska Pipeline System (TAPS). Today, all different types of vehicles—from motorcycles to passenger cars to freight haulers—drive the Dalton Highway each year. Not everyone, however, is meant for this drive. We encourage you to read the entire log of this highway before you decide to set out on this adventure so you are prepared for Dalton Highway road conditions.

The Dalton is a favorite drive of *MILEPOST®* field editor Sharon Nault: "The wide empty vistas thrill me and the animals are awesome!" But she is realistic about its challenges: "Hit a pothole or frost heave going too fast and you may end your trip sooner than you planned on. Caution and slower than normal speeds are the way to assure you have a wonderful adventure. Fortunately, there are a lot of people driving the Dalton who will stop and help if you run into trouble." At the same time, keep in mind the Bureau of Land Management's (BLM) advice on driving the Dalton: "Expect and prepare for all conditions. Prepare to be self-sufficient."

Despite recent improvements, the Dalton

Major Attractions:

© Sharon Nault

Trans-Alaska Pipeline, Arctic Circle, Arctic Ocean, Yukon River Crossing

Highest Summit:
Atigun Pass 4,800 ft.

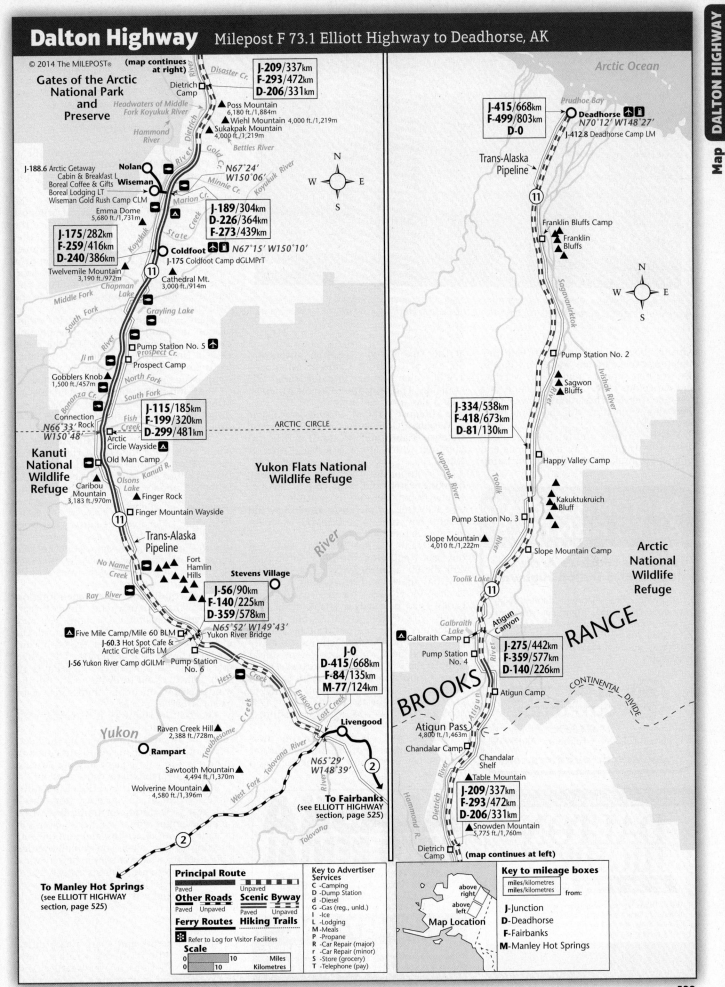

Watch for flaggers at road construction along the Dalton Highway in summer. (©Sharon Nault)

remains about 75 percent gravel, with tire-puncturing rocks, bumpy washboard, dust in dry weather, slippery mud in wet weather, and dangerous curves. Reconstruction of a 7-½-mile stretch of hazardous highway from the Dalton's junction with the Elliott Highway is under study.

Services are few and far between along the Dalton Highway. Gas, food, phone and lodging are available at **Yukon River Camp** at the Yukon River crossing, **Milepost J 56**, and at **Coldfoot Camp** at **Milepost J 174.8**, which also has ultra-low sulfur fuel available. **The Hot Spot Cafe at Milepost J 60.3** has food and lodging. In Wiseman (see **Milepost J 188.6**), lodging is available at **Wiseman Gold Rush Camp B&B**, **Arctic Getaway Cabin and Breakfast** and **Boreal Lodging**, which also has **Boreal Coffee & Gifts**.

It is important that you bring along drinking water, and refill your water jugs whenever potable water is available. This is especially true for bicyclists: Water may add weight, but there is no drinking water for *long* stretches of road.

At Deadhorse/Prudhoe Bay you can buy gas (including ultra-low sulfur fuel and diesel) and there is a general store that has snacks and drinks, but it is best to shop for groceries before departing Fairbanks. Food is usually available at oil field hotels with dining facilities, but accommodations may not be available to the general public: These facilities normally cater to oil field workers, so phone ahead 3 to 10 days in advance of arrival. **Deadhorse Camp** at **Milepost J 412.8** caters to tourists and offers rooms and dining to pre-registered guests; phone (907) 474-3565 or 1-888-474-3565, www.deadhorse camp.com.

IMPORTANT: If you plan on driving the Dalton Highway to Deadhorse/Prudhoe Bay in summer 2014, phone ahead for overnight accommodations to assure that space is available. See Lodging & Services in Prudhoe Bay on page 549.

Access to the Arctic Ocean is possible only through the authorized tour operator: Northern Alaska Tour Co./Deadhorse Camp, phone 1-888-474-3565. Photo I.D. and 24-hour advance reservations are required for this tour. Stop and check with Arctic Interagency Visitor Center in Coldfoot for current details on Arctic Ocean tours.

The Bureau of Land Management (BLM) has one developed campground along the Dalton Highway (Marion Creek) and 3 undeveloped no fee sites: At Milepost 60 BLM Campground, located just north of the Hot Spot Cafe (see description at **Milepost J 60.5**); Arctic Circle, on the hill above the picnic area at Arctic Circle Wayside (**Milepost J 115.5**); and Galbraith Lake, 2.5 miles west of **Milepost J 274.7**. Camping on BLM lands is limited to 14 days at any one location. Coldfoot Camp has RV hookups and tent sites. Informal campsites alongside the road are noted in the log.

There is no formal overnight RV campground in Prudhoe Bay, but generally you can find an overnight space. Try the Arctic Oilfield Hotel or Tesoro station. Tent camping is discouraged due to bears. Many people camp along the Sag River at informal sites.

Sani-dump stations are available at **Milepost J 60.5** (no fee) and at Deadhorse (inquire at NANA office). *Please do NOT dump holding tanks along the road.*

The BLM manages 2.1 million acres of public land along the Dalton Highway. For information, contact the BLM's Fairbanks District Office at 1150 University Avenue in Fairbanks; phone (907) 474-2200; www.blm. gov/ak/dalton.

NOTE: There is no cell phone service, public Internet or WiFi from just outside Fairbanks until you reach Deadhorse. Land lines are available at Yukon River Camp, in Coldfoot and Wiseman, but have a calling card or credit card with you or plan to call collect (calls between Coldfoot and Wiseman are free).

Road conditions vary depending on weather, maintenance and time of year. On recently rehabilitated sections, you may find good pavement or chip-sealed road. On some gravel sections of road, the washboard can be so severe your teeth rattle. The posted speed limit for most of the highway is 50 mph, but, to avoid throwing rocks into the windshields of oncoming traffic, *slow down when passing other vehicles!*

The Dalton Highway is a narrow road with some stretches built up 6 to 15 feet above the ground, with little or no shoulder, soft shoulders, and no guardrails, making roll-overs a not infrequent mishap. Driving the Dalton demands extra concentration!

NEVER STOP YOUR VEHICLE on hills, curves or bridges. If you must stop, check your rear-view mirror for traffic first, then pull to the right only if you have a clear line of sight in both directions, and turn on your direction signals. When you do pull over for a photo or for whatever reason, be very wary of soft shoulders; use turnouts instead. There are several steep (10 to 12 percent) grades on the Dalton Highway. *Drive with your headlights on at all times. Keep headlights and taillights clean so that you are visible in dust, fog and snow.*

Watch for ruts and sharp rocks; dusty driving conditions in dry weather; potholes and soft spots in wet weather; and trucks and road maintenance equipment at

all times. The volume of truck traffic hauling materials between Fairbanks and Prudhoe Bay varies, but *always watch for trucks and give them the right-of-way.* Pull off at the nearest turnout and let faster-moving trucks pass. Slow down and pull over to the side of the road when meeting oncoming trucks. *Use caution when pulling over to the side of the road. Soft shoulders and abrupt drop-offs at the edge of the roadway have caused tipovers.*

IMPORTANT: CB radios are strongly recommended to monitor road conditions and truck traffic. Use channel 19.

Check for current road construction projects at http://511.alaska.gov or call the Alaska Dept. of Transportation's construction department at (907) 456-7623.

Flat tires are a common occurrence on this road. The BLM recommends that travelers carry at least 2 full-sized spare tires mounted on rims. *MILEPOST®* field editors Sharon Nault and J.V. Teague have helped many people with flat tires along Alaska's roads, and suggest a tire-changing run-through before leaving home to test out your jack. They also recommend carrying an extra set of lugs and nuts.

Towing fees by private wrecker service can be costly. If you belong to an auto or RV club with road service, inquire about coverage on the Dalton Highway before you depart. Alaska Dept. of Transportation maintenance stations along the highway do *not* provide vehicle services or gas. Calcium chloride is used on unpaved sections of road to control dust; it is corrosive to vehicles and slippery when wet.

Rental car agencies, such as **Arctic Outfitters** and **Alaska Auto Rental** in Fairbanks, may offer a limited number of vehicles that are allowed for travel on the Dalton Highway. Renters are responsible for towing and vehicle damage while traveling on this and other gravel roads.

For those who don't want to drive themselves, commercial tours are available from **Dalton Highway Express** (www.daltonhighwayexpress.com) and **Northern Alaska Tour Company's Arctic Ocean Adventure** (www.northernalaska.com). See display ads this section for details.

The highway is named for James William Dalton, an arctic engineer involved in early oil exploration efforts on the North Slope. It was built as a haul road between the Yukon River and Prudhoe Bay during construction of the trans-Alaska pipeline, and was originally called the North Slope Haul Road. Construction of the road began April 29, 1974, and was completed 5 months later. The road is 28 feet wide with 3 to 6 feet of gravel surfacing. Some sections of road are underlain with plastic foam insulation to prevent thawing of the permafrost.

Construction of the 800-mile-long pipeline between Prudhoe Bay and Valdez began April 29, 1974, and ended June 20, 1977. It cost $8 billion to build. The 48-inch-diameter pipeline, of which slightly more than half is above ground, has 6 operating pump stations. The operations control center is in Valdez. Design, construction and operation of the pipeline are managed by Alyeska Pipeline Service Company. For more information, contact Alyeska Pipeline Service Co., 900 E. Benson Blvd., Anchorage, AK 99519-6660; phone (907) 830-9548.

Alyeska pump stations do not provide any public services. Although former pipeline camp names are noted on our strip map, these camps have been removed.

Truckers take advantage of long summer days by making long hauls. (©Sharon Nault)

Commonly spotted wildlife along the Dalton Highway include grizzly bear, moose, caribou, Dall sheep, musk ox and the ubiquitous arctic ground squirrel. Some 158 bird species have been recorded in the diverse habitats along this road, from northern boreal forest to the tundra of the North Slope and Arctic coastal plain. The checklist *Birds Along the Dalton Highway* is available at the Alaska Public Lands Information Center in Fairbanks, the Yukon Crossing Visitor Contact Station, and the Arctic Interagency Visitor Center in Coldfoot.

Mosquitoes are also prevalent along the Dalton Highway, so bring along mosquito nets and/or spray!

All waters between the Yukon River bridge and Dietrich River are part of the Yukon River system, and most are tributaries of the Koyukuk River. Fishing for arctic grayling is especially good in rivers accessible by foot from the highway. The large rivers also support burbot, salmon, pike and whitefish. Small Dolly Varden are at higher elevations in streams north of Coldfoot. Fishing for salmon is closed within 5 miles either side of the highway in the trans-Alaska pipeline corridor. According to the Dept. of Fish and Game, anglers should expect high, turbid water conditions throughout much of June as the snowpack melts in the Brooks Range, with the best fishing occurring during July and August.

Fishing regulations are available online or at ADF&G offices or from the Arctic Interagency Visitor Center, Yukon Crossing Visitor Contact Station or any license vendors.

Report wildlife violations to Fish & Wildlife or the State Trooper at Coldfoot.

Bicyclist from Argentina poses for a photo at Deadhorse/Prudhoe Bay. (© Sharon Nault)

Emergency services: Contact the Alaska State Troopers Fairbanks dispatch office at (907) 451-5333, the Troopers statewide line at 1-800-811-0911, via CB radio, Channel 19, or contact any state highway maintenance camp along the highway. DOT maintenance camp personnel are not medically trained, but they will assist travelers in contacting the proper authorities to get medical attention in the event of an accident or medical emergency.

Dalton Highway Log

Distance from junction with Elliott Highway (J) is followed by distance from Fairbanks (F) and Deadhorse/Prudhoe Bay (D).

ALASKA ROUTE 11

J 0 F 84 D 415 Dalton Highway begins at Elliott Highway junction (N65°29', W148°39'). Sign at start of Dalton Highway: "Heavy Industrial Traffic. All vehicles drive with headlights on. Speed 50 mph next 416 miles."

CAUTION: Steep grades and frequent narrow road northbound. Watch for trucks and road construction! Use your rear-view mirrors continuously. The first few miles of the Dalton Highway require extra driver alertness. Give oncoming trucks plenty of room.

Junction with Elliott Highway to Fairbanks and Manley Hot Springs. Turn to **Milepost FX 73.1** on page 529 in the ELLIOTT HIGHWAY section for log of that route.

Distance marker southbound shows Fairbanks 81 miles, Minto 48 miles, Manley 80 miles.

J 0.1 F 84.1 D 414.9 *Gravel begins, pavement ends, northbound. Road climbs through permafrost stunted trees.*

J 1.1 F 85.1 D 413.9 Large gravel turnout at ADOT&PF Dalton Highway sign; good photo-op.

Distance marker northbound shows Yukon River 56 miles, Coldfoot 175 miles, Deadhorse 414 miles.

J 1.4 F 85.4 D 413.6 *Steep downhill grade next 1.5 miles northbound.*

J 3 F 87 D 412 Turnout to west.

J 3.2 F 87.2 D 411.8 Top of short, steep grade, steep downhill ahead northbound.

J 4 F 88 D 411 Small turnout to south as highway descends "Five Mile Hill" into the Lost Creek valley. *CAUTION: This is a steep, curving stretch of road; there have been accidents here. Shift to low gears and remember to watch out for big trucks and stay out of their way.*

Pipeline is visible stretching across the ridge of the distant hill.

J 5.6 F 89.6 D 409.4 Turnout to west on south side with access to Lost Creek which flows under the highway in culverts and on into the west fork of the Tolovana River. Physical mileposts may be obscured by brush.

J 5.7 F 89.7 D 409.3 APL (Alyeska pipeline) access road; no public admittance. There are many of these pipeline access roads along the highway; most are signed with the milepost on the pipeline. Because they are so numerous, most APL pipeline access roads are not included in *The MILEPOST®* log unless they occur along with another feature. Most of these access roads are closed to the public for security and safety concerns. Do not block APL access roads.

J 6.1 F 90.1 D 408.9 Large gravel turnout to west is on a curve and top of hill.

J 6.6 F 90.6 D 408.4 Small dirt turnout to west. Muddy when wet.

J 7.7 F 91.7 D 407.3 Turnout to east; muddy when wet.

J 8.3 F 92.5 D 406.7 Large turnout at side road. Some side roads along the Dalton lead to private mining claims.

J 8.4 F 92.4 D 406.6 Entering Game Management Unit 20F northbound.

J 9.3 F 93.3 D 405.7 Good view of pipeline as highway descends northbound.

Steep and winding 9 percent downgrades next 3 miles northbound. Some soft shoulders and narrowed shoulders.

J 11 F 95 D 404 Turnout to west.

J 12 F 96 D 403 Large turnouts near huge culvert.

Highway climbs northbound next 3 miles.

J 13.7 F 97.7 D 401.3 Small turnout to west.

J 15 F 99 D 400 Evidence northbound of the July 2003 Erickson Creek Fire, which was caused by lightning. The lightning touched down many times in this area, setting off fires that then jumped the road, ultimately burning 120,606 acres.

J 15.9 F 99.9 D 399.1 Turnouts both sides of highway.

J 17.4 F 101.4 D 397.6 Turnout to west

J 18.5 F 102.5 D 396.5 *Begin 4.5 miles of paved road northbound.* Panoramic views. Well-used side road to west.

J 19.4 F 103.4 D 395.6 *CAUTION: Slow for frequent gravel breaks next 1.2 miles northbound (summer 2013).*

J 20.6 F 104.6 D 394.4 Long parking area west side of road with sweeping view of mountains and the valley where Hess Creek is flowing en route to the Yukon River. Interpretive panels on the Erickson Creek Fire and the 1991 Hess Creek Fire, which burned 120,600 acres. Views of old Dalton Highway below.

J 21.3 F 105.3 D 393.7 Active gravel pit to east.

Steep downhill grade next 2.4 miles northbound as highway descends to Hess Creek.

J 23 F 107 D 392 *Pavement ends, gravel begins and road narrows, northbound.*

J 23.7 F 107.7 D 391.3 Hess Creek bridge; turnouts at both ends. Whitefish and grayling fishing at bridge. *Bring your mosquito repellent!* Hess Creek, known for its colorful mining history, is the largest stream between the Elliott Highway junction and the Yukon River bridge.

J 23.9 F 107.9 D 391.1 Dirt side road leads west to small primitive campsite in tall trees. Side road ends 0.2 mile from highway at large pond in grassy meadow (*caution: boggy in wet weather*).

J 24.5 F 108.5 D 390.5 Turnout to west by rock face.

J 25.1 F 109.1 D 389.9 Double-ended gravel turnout to east.

J 25.5 F 109.5 D 389.5 Small turnout. Pipeline and remote-operated valve site nearby. Highway descends southbound to Hess Creek and valley. Evidence of lightning-caused forest fires. Distance marker northbound shows Yukon River 31 miles, Coldfoot 150 miles, Deadhorse 389 miles.

J 26.4 F 110.4 D 388.6 Turnout at side road to west.

J 26.6 F 110.6 D 388.4 Pipeline parallels highway about 250 feet away; good photo op. APL access. There is room to park, but do not block the road.

J 27.5 F 111.5 D 387.5 Highway passes lush open spaces, dotted with dead trees from old burn and, in season, covered with fireweed.

J 28.2 F 112.2 D 386.8 Large turnout to west. State monitors CB Channel 9 (sign).

CAUTION: Downgrade northbound, slow for 35-mph curves next 1.5 miles. Drive with headlights on at all times.

J 28.6 F 112.6 D 386.4 Pipeline parallels road.

J 29.8 F 113.8 D 385.2 Double-ended gravel turnout to east (do not use in wet weather).

J 31 F 115 D 384 Small turnout to west.

J 32.6 F 116.6 D 382.4 Double-ended turnout to east.

J 33.5 F 117.5 D 381.5 Turnouts both sides of road, gravel pit.

Crosses along the highway are memorials to those who have died in accidents on this road.

J 33.8 F 117.8 D 381.2 APL pipeline access road. Goalpost-like structures, called "headache bars," guard against vehicles large enough to run into and damage the pipeline.

J 35.5 F 119.5 D 379.5 Turnout to east is muddy when wet.

J 36.6 F 120.6 D 378.4 *Begin 12.5-mile stretch of improved wide paved road northbound. CAUTION: Slow for sections of patched pavement and frost heaves next 9.4 miles northbound.*

J 37 F 121 D 378 Small turnout to west.

J 38.1 F 122.1 D 376.9 Mile 38 Dalton Highway Crossing: Pipeline goes under road. Good photo opportunity. APL access road.

J 40.7 F 124.7 D 374.3 Spacious paved parking area to east with view of highway.

J 42 F 126 D 373 View of Dalton Highway as it snakes up a hillside northbound provides a good photo op.

J 46 F 130 D 369 "Top of the world" scenery comes into view for northbound travelers.

CAUTION: Slow for sections of patched pavement and frost heaves next 9.4 miles southbound.

J 46.6 F 130.6 D 368.4 Small paved turnouts both sides of highway.

J 47.3 F 131.3 D 367.7 Paved turnout to west.

J 49.2 F 133.2 D 365.8 *End 12.5-mile stretch of paved road, begin narrow, calcium-chloride treated road, northbound.* Very small gravel turnouts both sides of road.

J 50.4 F 134.4 D 364.6 Side road to east with access to pond.

J 51.1 F 135.1 D 363.9 Private side road with two entrances leads east 5.4 miles to Yukon River. Closed to the public.

J 53 F 137 D 362 Views of the Yukon River and Yukon River Bridge as road descends next mile northbound. The Yukon River is the longest river in Alaska; it flows 1,979 miles from Canada to the Bering Sea. Fort Hamlin Hills are beyond the river.

Steep downhill grade next mile northbound.

J 53.8 F 137.8 D 361.2 Pump Station No. 6 (also an "oil spill response base") to west. Alyeska pump stations monitor the pipeline's oil flow on its journey from Prudhoe Bay to Valdez. No public facilities.

J 54.2 F 138.2 D 360.8 Highway passes over pipeline. *CAUTION: Do NOT stop or park here.*

J 54.5 F 138.5 D 360.5 Turnout to west at side road to small knoll. APL access to east.

J 55.1 F 139.1 D 359.9 Distance marker northbound shows Arctic Circle 60 miles, Coldfoot 120 miles, Deadhorse 360 miles.

J 55.3 F 139.3 D 359.7 *Gravel ends, pavement begins, northbound.*

J 55.4 F 139.4 D 359.6 Very small turnout to west just before bridge. APL access to east. **Yukon River Bridge** (formally the E.L. Patton Bridge, named for the president of the Alyeska Pipeline Service Co. after his death in 1982). This wood-decked bridge, completed in 1975 (upgraded in 1999), is 2,290 feet long and has a 6 percent grade. This is the largest privately funded construction project in U.S. history. Edward L. Patton led the (approximately) 7,000 men and women who constructed it.

J 56 F 140 D 359 Turnoff to east and drive under pipeline for **BLM Yukon Crossing Visitor Contact Station**; parking, pit toilets, observation decks, interpretive

View of Yukon River Camp from Yukon River Bridge. (©Sharon Nault)

panels. The center, staffed by volunteers, is open from 9 A.M. to 6 P.M. daily in summer. Information on road conditions and Arctic Circle Crossing certificates available here. Short trail to Yukon River observation decks with information boards: Excellent view of Yukon River Bridge.

Exit west for **Yukon River Camp** (see description following); gas, diesel, propane, restaurant, lodging, gift shop and phone. Phone works with phone card, credit card or collect calls only. Cards sold at the Camp. Check out the boarded up window at the Camp with a picture of a bear on it. The window was broken one winter by a bear. (There's a handout on the incident at the front desk.) In the parking lot, local resident Dorothy Towson often sells crafts from a shed during summer.

Yukon River Camp. Your base camp for enjoying the Yukon River. Rustic lodging, fuel and Arctic Circle Gifts. Extensive menu with great Alaskan salmon burgers, seafood and homemade dessert. Packages available including transportation, tours and lodging. Convenient location just on the north side of the Yukon River Bridge. (907) 474-3557. See display ad this page.
[ADVERTISEMENT]

Follow the access road between Yukon River Camp buildings and the river west for public boat launch, trailer parking and wayside with picnic tables, pit toilets and garbage containers.

IMPORTANT: Travelers headed for Deadhorse/Prudhoe Bay call ahead to confirm availability of accommodations; see Lodging & Services on page 549 or check with the Visitor Contact Station here. And remember that 24-hour advance reservations are required for the Arctic Ocean tour; phone 907/474-3565 or 1-888-474-3565.

NOTE: Next gas stop northbound is at Coldfoot, 119 miles from here.

J 56.1 F 140.1 D 358.9 Double-ended turnout to west with bear-proof garbage cans and toilet. Also second turnoff to west northbound for Yukon River Camp. (Inquire at Yukon River Camp about overnight parking options in their large parking areas.)

State law prohibits the use of motor-

ized vehicles (including ATVs) within 5 miles of either side of the Dalton Highway from the Yukon River north to Deadhorse/Prudhoe Bay. Only persons with valid mining claims may use ORVs on certain trails to access their claims.

Hunters note: The Alaska Dept. of Fish & Game allows bow hunting only (NO firearms) within the 5-mile corridor from the Yukon River north to Deadhorse/Prudhoe Bay.

J 59.5 F 143.5 D 355.5 Note the change in vegetation northbound, as the highway passes through boreal forests, boggy lowlands and tundra. Tall, dense forests of white spruce and birch, like these, are found in well-drained soil without permafrost, usually on south-facing slopes.

J 60.1 F 144.1 D 354.9 Northbound sign indicates "Next services 120 miles" (Coldfoot). A good reminder for travelers to stop for gas at Yukon River Camp and to get drinking water at the Milepost 60 BLM campground stand pipe.

J 60.3 F 144.3 D 354.7 Turnoff to west is first of 2 entrances northbound to the **Hot Spot Cafe**, open 10 A.M. to about 11 P.M.

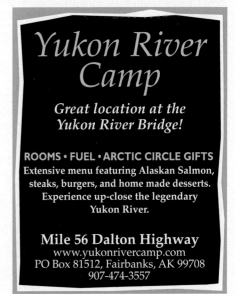

Watch for wildlife along the Dalton Highway. This moose was photographed at Grayling Lake, Milepost J 150.2. (©Sharon Nault)

(depending on daylight) in summer; good food, gifts, rooms (description follows). Mammoth remains were discovered near the Hot Spot Cafe during highway construction. The beautiful gardens at the Hot Spot make it a fun stop for photos. Also access to Milepost 60 BLM Campground via a loop road; see description at **Milepost J 60.5.**

Hot Spot Cafe and Arctic Circle Gifts. "A stop you don't want to miss on the Dalton Highway." Since 1996 a truly Alaskan experience: Dine with the local celebrity and Ice Road Truckers; get the latest Haul Road news and gossip. Best food on the road, maybe even the state. Try our famous big burgers or BBQ. Best in Alaska! Ice cream, homemade desserts, trucker-style. The biggest selection of Arctic Circle souvenirs. Ice Road trucking gifts can be found in their gift shop, along with local Native arts and crafts. It will be the best food and gift shopping stop along the road. The cleanest and most comfortable motel rooms for rent at the best prices. No reservation needed. Call, email or just show up! HotSpotCafe@gci.net or (907) 378-9161. [ADVERTISEMENT]

J 60.5 F 144.5 D 354.5 Second entrance northbound to the **Hot Spot Cafe** (see description above) and **Milepost 60 BLM Campground** (description follows) via loop road.

Drive west of highway to 2 artesian wells. The BLM campground is located across from the artesian wells. It is a flat, bare gravel parking area with picnic tables, firepits, firewood (for campground-use ony), an upgraded pit toilet, bear-proof trash containers, interpretive panels and campground host. *CAUTION: Watch for bears.* The dump station was out of order and there was no public water fill-up for campers at the artesian wells in summer 2013. (The truckers could fill up with from a large high-pressure water hose.) Both the dump station and potable water fill-up are expected to be available in summer 2014. Next potable water fill-up is at **Milepost J 174.8** (Coldfoot). Campers should have their own hose to use. Bicyclists should bring a filtration system with them. Do not wash vehicles here, it contaminates the ground water. *(Water at dump station is NOT potable; no vehicle washing.)*

J 60.7 F 144.7 D 354.3 Highway crosses pipeline. Old Five Mile Airstrip (not in use).

J 61.8 F 145.8 D 353.2 Seven Mile Station DOT highway maintenance to east; no services. APL access road to west.

J 62.1 F 146.1 D 352.9 Watch for thaw pipes along the road here. They are used to infuse steam heat into culverts during winter.

J 63.6 F 147.6 D 351.4 Turnout to west near creek below road. Creek is often used by DOT to fill water truck.

J 66.8 F 150.8 D 348.2 Long, double-ended turnout to west at bottom of hill; muddy when wet, use caution.

Highway climbs northbound and southbound.

J 67.6 F 151.6 D 347.4 Turnouts both sides of road. *Highway descends steeply northbound with sharp curve at bottom of hill.* Thaw pipe to east on curve.

J 69.1 F 153.1 D 345.9 Long, double-ended turnout to west.

J 69.4 F 153.4 D 345.6 Good view northbound of buried pipeline going up hill.

J 70.1 F 154.1 D 344.9 Turnout to west.

J 70.7 F 154.7 D 344.3 *Steep descent northbound.*

J 72.5 F 156.5 D 342.5 Sloping turnouts both sides of highway at south end of Fort Hamlin Hills Creek bridge. Water trucks often use the sloping turnout to east.

J 73.3 F 157.3 D 341.7 Turnout to west; muddy when wet.

J 73.4 F 157.4 D 341.6 *Begin steep 0.5-mile ascent of Sand Hill (signed) northbound.*

J 74.9 F 158.9 D 340.1 Large turnouts both sides of highway at top of hill; muddy when wet. This is a brake check area.

Begin steep descent northbound followed by steep ascent, dubbed the "Roller Coaster."

J 75.7 F 159.7 D 339.3 *"Roller Coaster" begins southbound.*

J 77 F 161 D 338 Stunted, low-growing black spruce in this area indicate permafrost (permanently frozen soil) near the surface, or poorly drained soil.

J 79 F 163 D 336 Narrow bridge over **No Name Creek** (signed), also called North Fork of the Ray River. Small turnout to east near creek; fishing for burbot, grayling and whitefish.

Steep descent southbound.

J 81.6 F 165.6 D 333.4 Fort Hamlin Hills are visible to the southeast. Tree line on surrounding hills is about 2,000 feet. Highway travels through old burn area.

J 82 F 166 D 333 Views of Castle Mountain to northeast.

J 85.3 F 169.3 D 329.7 This section of the highway passes close to the pipeline.

J 86.6 F 170.6 D 328.4 Side road (will accommodate most rigs, but drive slowly) leads west 1 mile to scenic **86-Mile Overlook** located in an interesting mountainside gravel pit: Observation deck provides expansive views of pipeline and sweeping views to the south. Interpretive panels about the 8.6-million-acre Yukon Flats National Wildlife Refuge. Nice view of tors to northeast, Yukon Flats Wildlife Refuge to east and Fort Hamlin Hills to southeast. Loop turnaround through pit.

Tors are high, isolated pinnacles of jointed granite jutting up from the tundra and are a residual feature of erosion.

APL access road to east.

J 87.2 F 171.2 D 327.8 *Begin long, steep ascent up imposing Mackey Hill next 1.5 miles northbound; slippery in wet weather. Drive defensively.*

J 88.5 F 172.5 D 326.5 It is possible to pull over here, but do not block pipeline access road. *Begin steep 0.5-mile descent of Mackey Hill northbound.*

Entering Game Management Unit 25D northbound, Unit 20F southbound.

J 89.3 F 173.3 D 325.7 Narrow pullout to east. *CAUTION: Severe cracks in road surface (summer 2013).*

J 90.1 F 174.1 D 324.9 *Begin paved road northbound, begin gravel road southbound. (Pavement continues to Coldfoot turnoff at* **Milepost J 175.)**

J 90.2 F 174.2 D 324.8 Long paved parking areas on both sides of highway at crest of hill. These are used by truckers for rest or to check on their loads so give them lots of room to pull in if you stop here. Good photo-op of road and pipeline to the north. Note the zigzag design which allows the pipeline to flex, accommodating temperature changes. The small green structure over the buried pipe is a radio-controlled valve used to shut down oil flow when necessary.

Highway descends northbound to Dall Creek. Drive with headlights on at all times (sign). *CAUTION: Slow for frost heaves and bumps.*

J 91.1 F 175.1 D 323.9 Dall Creek. Sloping access to creek on east side of highway, used by water trucks.

Highway climbs steeply next mile northbound near pipeline.

J 91.3 F 175.3 D 323.7 *Northbound traffic slow for frost heaves, potholes and a variety of damaged pavement northbound to* **Milepost J 98.1.**

J 94.1 F 178.1 D 320.9 Turnout to west at side road to former gravel pit road. Sweeping view of portion of highway and pipeline.

J 95 F 179 D 320 The vegetation changes noticeably northbound as the highway crosses an area of alpine tundra for about the next 5 miles. Lichens and white mountain avens dominate the well-drained rocky ridges, while the more saturated soils alongside the road are covered by dense stands of dwarf shrubs. Beautiful views. Finger Rock (elev. 1,875 feet) stands out on horizon ahead for northbound traffic.

J 96 F 180 D 319 Good view northbound of **Finger Rock**, a tor, east of the road. Tors are visible for the next several miles north-

bound and date back to the cretaceous period nearly 110 million years ago. Prehistoric hunting sites are also numerous in this region. *Please do not collect or disturb artifacts.*

J 97 F 181 D 318 Pull-in/back-out parking pad to east.

J 97.9 F 181.9 D 317.1 Distance marker southbound on Finger Mountain shows Yukon River 42 miles, Fox 166 miles, Fairbanks 176 miles.

J 98.1 F 182.1 D 316.9 Turnoff to east at crest of hill for **Finger Mountain BLM Wayside**. Rest area with 2 pit toilets, parking, interpretive trail. No camping. Excellent interpretive panels on the area. Interpretive trail leads to nearby rock formations. Hiking out to **Finger Rock** requires walking over rough terrain.

This wayside offers good opportunities for picnicking, photography, berry picking (blueberries, low-bush cranberries) in season, wildflower viewing and hiking. Also great for bird watching and seeing arctic ground squirrels.

Olsens Lake, Kanuti Flats, Kanuti River drainage and site of former Old Man Camp are visible ahead northbound as the road descends and passes through several miles of valley bottom. Excellent mountain views.

Highway descends steeply next 1.7 miles northbound.

J 98.3 F 182.3 D 316.7 Large roadside turnout parallel to and just above the wayside offers expansive views in all directions. Steep descent northbound, posted speed limit 50 mph.

J 99.5 F 183.5 D 315.5 Pipeline access road to east. Room to park (do not block access road); walk to nearby rock formations. Steep descent for northbound traffic to **Milepost J 100**.

J 100.6 F 184.6 D 314.4 Buried pipeline passes under road. Highway offers sweeping 360 degree views northbound.

CAUTION: Challenging road surface northbound, summer 2013. Watch for potholes, pavement breaks, frost heaves and eroding shoulders as detailed in log.

J 102.3 F 186.3 D 312.7 Cluster of buildings (private property).

J 103.5 F 187.5 D 311.5 **View of** Caribou Mountain to west.

J 104.1 F 188.1 D 310.9 Distance marker northbound shows Coldfoot 71 miles, Deadhorse 311 miles.

J 105.7 F 189.7 D 309.3 Large parking area to east at south end of **Kanuti River** bridge; cement ramp to river, fishing for burbot, whitefish, northern pike and grayling. The size of the area draining into this river is that of Delaware state. Good pipeline photo op. 🔁

J 107 F 191 D 308 Level parking area below road to east at site of Old Man Camp, a former pipeline construction camp; no structures remain. Big views.

J 107.4 F 191.4 D 307.6 Sloping turnout to east. *Watch for bears. A fed bear is a dead bear. Do not feed bears!*

J 108.3 F 192.3 D 306.7 Buried pipeline passes under highway. APL access road.

J 109.8 F 193.8 D 193.8 D 305.2 Beaver Slide sign. *Highway descends 9 percent gravel grade next 2 miles northbound. CAUTION: Calcium-chloride treated surface may be slippery when wet.*

J 111 F 195 D 304 *CAUTION: Rough, patched pavement next 17 miles northbound.*

J 112.2 F 196.2 D 302.8 Turnout at pipeline access road. Moose and bear frequent

Hike to distinctive Finger Rock, a tor, from Finger Mountain BLM Wayside. (©Sharon Nault)

willow thickets here.

J 114 F 198 D 301 Turnouts at both ends of Fish Creek bridge. Bumpy, sandy access down to creek to west at north end of bridge. Fishing for grayling 12 to 18 inches. Nice spot. 🔁

J 115.5 F 199.5 D 299.5 Well-signed turnoff to east for loop road to **Arctic Circle BLM Wayside** with picnic tables scattered through pristine woods, grills, pit toilets, litter barrels and interpretive display on observation deck. The road to campground is at the north end of wayside. (No camping allowed at wayside area.)

The Arctic Circle sign, with a big blue earth and Latitude 66°33' on it, is a popular photo op with travelers. At this latitude (N 66°dd' W 150° 48'), the sun does not set on summer solstice (June 20 or 21) and it does not rise on winter solstice (December 21 or 22). A third of Alaska lies within the Arctic Circle, the only true polar region in the state.

For overnight camping, follow a good gravel side road at the north end of the wayside, 0.5 mile uphill for the camping area (if you reach the red Alyeska access gate, you have driven too far). This pleasant camping area is on a loop road, located on higher ground and still under development. It has some picnic tables, a pit toilet and bear-proof garbage containers in an area thick with birch trees. No camping fee. Many people enjoy staying here so they can say "we spent the night on the Arctic Circle!" 🔺

Distance marker northbound shows Coldfoot 60 miles, Deadhorse 300 miles.

Distance marker southbound shows Arctic Circle 1 mile, Yukon 60 miles, Fairbanks 194 miles.

J 115.6 F 199.6 D 299.4 North entrance to Arctic Circle BLM Wayside and camping area (0.5 mile). Long turnout with pit toilet and garbage container on highway.

NOTE: Remember to drive with headlights on and keep checking your rearview mirror. Northbound traffic begins steep and winding 0.7-mile descent followed by 2-mile upgrade.

J 118 F 202 D 297 Wide pipeline access road to the east is closed to the public. Please do NOT block this road.

J 120.7 F 204.7 D 294.3 **Connection Rock** is marked by a sign (but there's no

place to park). North and south road-building crews linked up here.

Steep descent northbound (9 percent grade).

J 121.1 F 205.1 D 293.9 Side road to west leads down to creek.

J 122.3 F 206.3 D 292.7 Long double-ended turnout at APL access road to east.

J 124.7 F 208.7 D 290.3 **South Fork Bonanza Creek** bridge; burbot, grayling, whitefish. *Extremely steep* access south to small area near creek. Gold panning is permitted downstream on Bonanaza Creek or upstream for 2.5 miles. Suction dredging is prohibited on federal lands along the highway. For more information, pick up the BLM brochure "Panning for Gold Along the Dalton Highway." 🔁

J 125.7 F 209.7 D 289.3 **North Fork Bonanza Creek** bridge (narrow). Access to creek to east at south end of bridge; small, informal campsite. Fishing for burbot, grayling, whitefish. 🔁

J 126.5 F 210.5 D 288.5 Northbound, the highway climbs steep curve up Paradise Hill; "Oh Sh-t Corner" (sign). Many truckers have lost their loads coming around this sloping curve too fast. Blueberries and lowbush cranberries in season on hillside. Rock tors to the east.

J 127.7 F 211.7 D 287.3 Large turnout to east. This area is lush with lichens and the small plants that dominate the alpine tundra.

J 129 F 213 D 286 *Begin long, steep, ascent next 2 miles northbound.*

J 130 F 214 D 285 Highway travels through burned area.

J 131.5 F 215.5 D 283.5 Stunning view of wide vistas and Pump Station No. 5 to north. Best photo op at **Milepost J 132.1**.

J 132.1 F 216.1 D 282.9 **Gobblers Knob Wayside** (elev. 1,500 feet). Large turnout with bear-proof litter barrels and pit toilet. Observation deck with interpretive panels about Haul Road construction ("the last 358 miles of road were completed in just 154 days"), includes an old photo of the first treacherous road built over Atigun Pass.

A map here helps travelers name the mountains seen from here: the Jack White Range, Pope Creek Dome (the dominant peak to the northwest), Prospect Creek

Coldfoot Camp offers gas, lodging, tire repair, a post office and dining at the famous Trucker's Cafe. (©Sharon Nault)

drainage, Pump Station No. 5, Jim River drainage, South Fork Koyukuk drainage and the Brooks Range on the northern horizon.

Truckers often overnight at the very large gravel pit parking area across the road from wayside. Blueberry picking in early June.

Begin long, steep descents northbound and southbound.

J 135 F 219 D 280 Narrow bridge over **Prospect Creek**; grayling, whitefish and pike. Active gold mining area. Gold panning is permitted downstream on Prospect Creek or upstream for 1.5 miles. Further access via materials site access road to south. Good informal campsite by pond here.

CAUTION: Steep uphill grade northbound; watch for trucks on blind hill.

J 135.7 F 219.7 D 279.3 Turnout to west. Panoramic view to north of Pump Station No. 5. Access to site of **PROSPECT CAMP**, which holds the record for lowest officially recorded temperature in Alaska (-80°F/-62°C, Jan. 23, 1971). Motorized vehicles prohibited beyond the old camp.

J 136 F 220 D 278 *CAUTION: Slow for more bumps and frost heaves and grooved pavement next 40 miles northbound. Particularly bad sections in summer 2013 are noted in log.*

J 137.1 F 221.1 D 277.9 APL access road at Mile 274.7 on the pipeline at **Pump Station No. 5** to east. Pump station No. 5 is not actually a pump station, but a "drain down" or pressure relief station to slow the gravity-fed flow of oil descending from Atigun Pass in the Brooks Range. Glacial moraine marks the southern boundary of Brooks Range glaciers during the most recent ice age.

Private Aircraft: Airstrip sign; length 5,000 feet; lighted runway. This airstrip is used as a BLM fire fighting staging area.

J 138.1 F 222.1 D 276.9 Jim River Station (DOT/PF highway maintenance) to west; no services.

NOTE: Drive with headlights on at all times. Speed limit is 50 mph unless otherwise posted.

J 140.1 F 224.1 D 274.9 Small turnout (single-vehicle campsite) to east at south end of **Jim River No. 1** bridge. Stand of unusually large spruce trees for this far north. Fishing for burbot, grayling, pike, whitefish. Fish-

ing for salmon is prohibited within 5 miles of highway from the Yukon River north. *CAUTION: Bears here for fall salmon run.*

J 141 F 225 D 274 Small turnout to west at south end of **Jim River No. 2** bridge; fishing.

J 141.8 F 225.8 D 273.2 Douglas Creek crossing. Good view of pipeline as it parallels highway. Active beaver pond below highway to west; beaver dams and lodges are visible.

J 144.1 F 228.1 D 270.9 Large parking area at APL access road to east at south end of **Jim River No. 3** bridge crossing the river's main channel. Room for primitive camping. Fishing. Interpretive display states how kings and chum salmon swim from the Bering Sea, 1,040 miles against swift currents to arrive at the Jim River to spawn. Parking area and river access at north end of bridge. APL access.

J 145.5 F 229.5 D 269.5 Small vehicle turnout. Pipeline passes under road.

J 148.6 F 232.6 D 266.4 *CAUTION: Slow for rough road and frost heaves northbound to Milepost J 150.2.*

J 150.2 F 234.2 D 264.8 Grayling Lake Wayside to east; parking, pit toilet and bear-proof garbage cans. Pleasant gravel walking path. Beautiful view of pipeline, highway and lake. Interpretive display on early hunters who used the area. Ducks, loons, bears and moose may be seen here.

J 150.8 F 234.8 D 264.2 Turnout to east. Access to Grayling Lake. Place to launch canoe or small, light boats. *CAUTION: Floatplanes use lake.* Small primitive camping area.

J 151.4 F 235.4 D 263.6 *CAUTION: Slow for breaks and grooves in road surface northbound.*

J 153.3 F 237.3 D 261.7 Northbound, the highway traverses a scenic pass (elev. approximately 1,340 feet) that is used by wildlife. Watch for moose.

J 154.1 F 238.1 D 260.9 Access road uphill to gravel pit visible from highway.

J 155.1 F239.1 D 259.9 Turnouts both sides of road. Good photo op for vistas of South Fork Koyukuk River, pipeline and highway.

Sign: Bow hunting only area.

J 156.1 F 240.1 D 258.9 Large parking area with pit toilet and litter barrels to east at south end of **South Fork Koyukuk River** bridge. This large river flows past the villages of Allakaket, Hughes and Huslia before draining into the Yukon River near Koyukuk. Primitive campsite to west at south end of bridge. Fishing for grayling, whitefish. Fishing for salmon prohibited within 5 miles of the highway from the Yukon River north.

North from this bridge, the highway sweeps uphill in a steep curve. You are passing through the foothills of the Brooks Range. There is active gold mining beyond the hills to the west. Many side roads off the Dalton Highway lead to these private claims (motorized vehicle access restricted to claim holders).

J 157.4 F 241.4 D 257.6 Large gravel turnout to east.

J 158.8 F 242.8 D 256.2 Turnout to east. An abundance of Alaska cotton here in summer.

J 159.1 F 243.1 D 255.9 Bridge over pipeline; large-animal crossing over pipeline to the west.

Pipeline parallels highway northbound.

J 159.4 F 243.4 D 255.6 Gravel pit access road. Large turnout area to west below highway.

J 160 F 244 D 255 Good view of Chapman Lake west of road as highway descends steeply northbound. Side road visible to west leads to active mining claims, motorized access restricted to claim holders.

J 161.1 F 245.1 D 253.9 Long gravel turnout to west, parking.

J 164.6 F 248.6 D 250.4 Example of sag bend to east. This is a short section of buried pipeline that allows large animals to cross.

J 165.2 F 249.2 D 249.8 Two turnouts to west, one is on lake. Good view/photo-op of pipeline which is close to the road here.

J 165.7 F 249.7 D 249.3 Large gravel turnout at scenic overlook to west.

J 166.4 F 250.4 D 248.6 Large double-ended turnout to west. Pipeline goes under road.

J 168 F 252 D 247 View of Cathedral Mountain to northeast, Twelvemile Mountain to east.

J 168.6 F 252.6 D 246.4 Large turnout to west.

J 168.8 F 252.8 D 246.2 Watch for light-green thaw pipes in the culverts here that can be filled with steam to thaw culverts when needed.

J 169.5 F 253.5 D 245.5 Begin steep 0.5-mile descent northbound, followed by ascent of steep hill, northbound.

J 170.7 F 254.7 D 244.3 Distance marker northbound shows Deadhorse 244 miles.

J 171.7 F 255.7 D 243.3 View northbound of pipeline and Coldfoot Airport in the distance below the road next to the Middle Fork Koyukuk River.

J 172.6 F 256.6 D 242.4 Large, flat turnout to west. Side road to east.

Steep downgrade northbound.

J 173 F 257 D 242 Entering public lands (signed) northbound. Steep descent, southbound. Road to west is a pipeline road which goes along the lake.

J 173.7 F 257.7 D 241.3 Turnout to west.

J 174.3 F 258.3 D 240.7 *Slow for 35 mph speed zone northbound. Watch for moose.*

J 174.8 F 258.8 D 240.2 First signed turnoff northbound for half-mile loop road

which leads east to **COLDFOOT** (pop. 12; elev. approximately 1,086 feet); food, gas, lodging, camping, tire and minor vehicle repair, post office (open 1:30–6 P.M., Monday, Wednesday, Friday), airport and phone. (Accommodations also available in Wiseman, 13 miles north.) **Emergency Services**: Alaska State Troopers, phone (907) 678-5211. (Phone at Coldfoot Camp.) Also signed turnoff for the **Arctic Interagency Visitor Center** to west. See descriptions following.

Visitor Information: The award-winning **Arctic Interagency Visitor Center**, operated by the BLM, USF&WS and National Park Service, is a "must stop" for visitors, providing travel information, topographic maps, natural history exhibits, a bookstore, evening programs (8 P.M. daily) about the region, hunting and fishing information, bear-proof container loans, helpful staff, trip-planning assistance, backcountry registration and clean restrooms. Impressive boulder display of native rocks at entrance. You can listen to recorded oral history given by area residents or watch the film *Arctic Visions and Voices.* Interesting short trails near here—listed in *Trail Map and Guide* pamphlet—offer scenic viewpoints and an opportunity to stretch your legs or walk the dog. Field editor Sharon Nault calls this location "a haven for weary travelers." It is open late May through the first week of September; phone (907) 678-5209 (summer only). Access the Visitor Center website at www.blm.gov/ak/dalton, then click on "Visitor Centers."

Coldfoot Camp (local phone 907/678-3500 or 1-866-474-3400) offers food, lodging and 24-hour fuel. The "trucker's table" at the restaurant is a good place to get news on the highway. This is also one of the few places to get potable water along the highway, so fill your water jugs. There are also a gift shop, bar, pay phone (takes phone cards, sold here if you need one; calls to Wiseman are free), laundromat with showers, fuel facility with gas and diesel (pay at restaurant before you pump and remember your pump number); 24-hour clerk (food service ends at midnight); tire repair, minor vehicle repair; and RV park with hookups. Post office is adjacent to restaurant.

Coldfoot is the jump-off point for flights into the Brooks Range. There is a 4,000-foot runway maintained by the state (see Private Aircraft at **Milepost J 175**). Area tours include a Koyukuk River float trip and fly-in visit to the village of Anaktuvuk Pass.

Coldfoot is a former mining camp, located at the mouth of Slate Creek on the east bank of the Middle Fork Koyukuk River. A post office was first established here in 1902, when Coldfoot consisted of "one gambling hole, 2 roadhouses, 2 stores and 7 saloons."

The name Coldfoot was first reported in 1933 by Robert Marshall, a forester who made a reconnaissance map of the northern Koyukuk Region. "In the summer of 1900, one of the waves of green stampeders got as far up the Koyukuk as this point, then got cold feet, turned around, and departed. This incident was enough to change the first, unromantic appellation of the settlement to Coldfoot." Mining activity later moved upstream to Nolan and Wiseman creeks.

Coldfoot experienced another short boom during the 1970s, when it became a construction camp for the trans-Alaska pipeline. In 1995, when the highway opened to the public, all the way to Deadhorse, Coldfoot became an important service stop for travelers and a gateway to the Brooks Range wilderness.

Coldfoot Camp. See display ad this page.

NOTE: Travelers headed to Deadhorse/Prudhoe Bay should call ahead about the availability of hotel rooms (3 or more days in advance) and for space on the Arctic Ocean tours (requires 24-hour advance security clearance with ID required). Phone Northern Alaska Tour Company at (907) 474-8600 or 1-800-474-1986; tours depart from **Deadhorse Camp** *at Milepost J 412.8.*

IMPORTANT: Next gas/diesel northbound is 240 miles from here at Deadhorse/Prudhoe Bay. Drive with headlights on at all times!

J 175 F 259 D 240 Coldfoot Airport, Alaska State Troopers and Dept. of Transportation to west. Second turnoff (for northbound traffic) to east for loop road to Coldfoot; post office, food, gas, lodging, RV hookups, potable water and tire repair at Coldfoot Camp (see preceding description).

Begin 21.8 miles of improved pavement northbound.

Private Aircraft: Coldfoot airport to west, N67°15.13', W150°12.23'; elev. 1,042 feet; length 4,000 feet; gravel; runway surface soft and muddy after rain, packed snow on runway during winter. Unattended.

J 175.1 F 259.1 D 239.9 Narrow bridge over Slate Creek. Gold bearing gravel was discovered here in 1899. A 23 oz. nugget came from here in 1940.

J 175.5 F 259.5 D 239.5 *Resume 50 mph speed limit northbound. Slow for speed zone*

COLDFOOT CAMP

Legendary hospitality above the Arctic Circle in Alaska's Brooks Mountain Range.

The Inn at Coldfoot

It all happens at Coldfoot Camp. Come spend a night (or two or three) with us. Not your typical inn. Our 52-room inn, which once housed pipeline workers, is still rustic yet now feature rooms with private restrooms and showers.

Trucker's Café

It is the place to be. The Trucker's Café is known for miles around for its great home-style cooking and old-fashioned guest service. Built by the world's greatest truckers, the Trucker's Café has become the region's hometown restaurant where both locals and visitors alike stop-by around the clock to get the latest on what's happening along the Dalton Highway.

Adventure At Coldfoot

You can do it all at Coldfoot. North of the Arctic Circle. Gateway to the Gates of the Arctic National Park. Surrounded by millions of acres of Brooks Mountain Range wilderness. Coldfoot is the perfect place to realize your dreams of Alaska adventure. Float the Koyukuk River, visit the Nunamiut Eskimo village of Anaktuvuk Pass by air, fish for the world-renowned Arctic Circle Grayling, rent a mountain bike, or enjoy a hike. We invite you to spend a few adventurous days with us. Plan to do it all at Coldfoot.

Frozen Foot Saloon

Coldfoot is so cool they named a beer after it. Relax and unwind from an exciting day of arctic adventure over a Coldfoot Pilsner or a glass of wine at the Frozen Foot Saloon, the furthest north watering hole in the United States.

DON'T TURN AROUND UNTIL YOU REACH COLDFOOT!!!
Mile 175 Dalton Highway.
Just 60 paved miles north of the Arctic Circle.

24-HOUR FUEL • POST OFFICE • TIRE REPAIR

PO Box 81512
Fairbanks, AK 99708

www.coldfootcamp.com

907-474-3500
866-474-3400

Wiseman is a historic mining town on the Koyukuk River with a population of about 16.
(©Sharon Nault)

southbound.

J 179.7 F 263.7 D 235.3 Turnoff to east for **Marion Creek BLM Campground**; 26 sites on gravel loop road, $8 camping fee (half price with Golden Age/Access Pass), tables, grills, firepits, toilets, bear-proof litter and food containers, information kiosk, 3 raised tent pads and 11 pull-through RV sites. Wheelchair-accessible. A campground host ("meet the farthest north public campground host in America") is present from Memorial Day to Labor Day. No satellite TV or cell phone reception available and no hookups. Potable water may not be available at this campground. △

This is a popular spot to park RVs and drive tow vehicles to Prudhoe Bay. *It is strongly recommended that you have overnight accommodations arranged before you get to Prudhoe Bay (see Lodging & Services on page 549).*

Marion Creek Falls trailhead (signed) is a 1- to 2-hour 2-mile hike upstream to waterfall (much of it follows a mining road). *CAUTION: Bears in area, store food safely.* Bearproof locker at trailhead at back of campground. Good berry picking (blueberries, lowbush cranberries) in season. Inquire with campground host for more details.

J 179.8 F 263.8 D 235.2 Marion Creek bridge.

J 185 F 269 D 230 Kalhabuk Mountain to west.

J 186.2 F 270.2 D 228.8 Large paved parking area to east.

J 186.7 F 270.7 D 228.3 Paved parking areas both sides of highway.

J 187.2 F 271.2 D 227.8 Parking areas at south end of **Minnie Creek** bridge (narrow); fishing for grayling. Placer gold creek. ⬱

J 188.3 F 272.3 D 226.7 Distance marker southbound shows Coldfoot 13 miles, Fairbanks 267 miles.

J 188.4 F 272.4 D 226.6 Distance marker northbound shows Wiseman 3 miles, Dietrich 22 miles, Deadhorse 227 miles.

J 188.5 F 272.5 D 226.5 Middle Fork Koyukuk River No. 1 crossing (narrow bridge); turnout. Grayling, burbot. ⬱

J 188.6 F 272.6 D 226.4 Turnoff for Wiseman, (2.3 miles to Wiseman) access Road (improved, narrow in spots), which leads 1.5 miles south to **junction** with road to Nolan and 0.8 mile beyond Nolan intersection south along the Koyukuk River to Wiseman (description follows); good photo op of pipeline.

The road to **Nolan** is narrow dirt and gravel, ranging from good to very poor (obey road signs). It leads 5.5 miles west to Nolan Creek Gold placer mine. There is a signed turnaround area before you reach the mine: *Do not proceed on to mine property without permission.* The mine is owned by Silverado Gold Mines Ltd. of Canada.

WISEMAN (pop. 16), 2.3 miles south of the highway, is a historic mining town on the Koyukuk River established in 1905. The heyday of Wiseman came in about 1910, after gold seekers abandoned Coldfoot. This is still an active mining area. A 150 oz. gold nugget was found in the Hammond River.

Visitor services are limited. Accommodations at **Arctic Getaway**, **Boreal Lodging** and **Wiseman Gold Rush Camp B&B** (directions follows). Wiseman Gold Rush Camp B&B is located near the museum; office is in the little green house. Continue on access road across bridge past the old Wiseman Co. Trading Post for Arctic Getaway Cabin & Breakfast (in the historic Pioneer Hall Igloo No. 8). Road continues to the antler decorated entrance to Boreal Lodging and Boreal Coffee and GIfts. There is a good-sized turnaround area at the entrance to Boreal Lodging.

There is no formal campground here, but camping in turnouts is accepted off of Wiseman Road. There is river access and informal camping off Wiseman Road near the Middle Fork of the Koyukuk River bridge. *CAUTION: Be aware that sand bars do flood at high water.*

Public phone located by the Community Center. For public phone, pass the green house, go to south side of road and it is in dense trees. Coldfoot calls are free, outside calls require a calling card. Pay phone number is (907) 389-1012.

A limited supply of groceries may now be purchased at Boreal Lodging. They have coffee and snacks, and homemade soap, candles and gifts.

The non-denominational **Kalhabuk Memorial Chapel** (on access road past the lodges) is a small, cozy log cabin, always open and a favorite stop for visitors. Sunday services are at 11 A.M., public welcome. Access road continues to airstrip.

Several interesting historic buildings are found in Wiseman. Visitors can park by the post office (not in service), located in an original log cabin, and walk around this picturesque settlement. (*All the structures are privately owned and most are residences; be respectful while taking photos!*)

The **Wiseman Historical Museum**, located in the historic Carl Frank Cabin (behind the small green house), contains old miner's journals, hotel registers and historical photos. It is open only for guided tours; contact Northern Alaska Tour Company (see ad this section or inquire at Coldfoot Camp). The **Koyukuk Miners Museum** is located on the road surrounded by mining equipment and across from the green house. The old Pingel Roadhouse sits near the river to the east of the museum and is privately owned. Inquire locally about access to the museum. (If there is someone in the little green house with the flags, ask if "Clutch" Lounsbury is available to let you into his

WISEMAN ADVERTISERS

Arctic Getaway Cabin
   & Breakfast..................................Ph. (907) 678-4456
Boreal Coffee & Gifts ....Ph. (907) 678-4566
Boreal Lodging..............................Ph. (907) 678-4566
Wiseman Gold Rush Camp
   Bed & Breakfast.......................Ph. ((907) 678-3213

miners' museum.)

Near the mining museum and east of the old post office a weathered gray board on the north side of the road marks the trail to the old Wiseman cemetery. It is about a 20-minute walk to the cemetery; bring mosquito repellent! Along the way you'll see a "white man's totem pole" constructed of cans in memory of a former resident.

The American Legion Arctic Post #9, the farthest north post in the world, sponsors the **Miners Picnic on 4th of July**; music, food and miners; public welcome.

This is one of the best areas to watch the aurora borealis with near guaranteed, exceptional viewing on or around March 21 and September 21 each year.

J 189 F 273 D 226 The improved stretch of highway along here is built on a high gravel base above the river; *no shoulders, drive carefully!* Spur (finger) dikes keep the river away from the highway and pipeline during high water. Some dikes may be parked on but there is no room to turn around so you must back out.

J 190.6 F 274.6 D 224.4 Narrow bridge over Hammond River *(CAUTION: Rough bridge decking in summer 2013)*. Gold mining area upstream. No turnout here.

J 190.9 F 274.9 D 224.1 Middle Fork Koyukuk River No. 2 crossing *(CAUTION: Narrow bridge; rough bridge decking in summer 2013)*. View of "guide banks," another example of river training structures.

J 192.7 F 276.7 D 222.3 Link Up (signed), where 2 sections of road constructed by different crews were joined when the Dalton Highway was completed in 1974.

J 194 F 278 D 221 First view northbound of **Sukakpak Mountain** (elev. 4,000 feet) to north, it rises 3,000 feet above road. Sukakpak Mountain is sometimes said to mark a traditional boundary between Eskimo and Athabascan Indian territories. Wiehl Mountain (5,765 feet) is east of Sukakpak.

J 195 F 279 D 220 Wide side road leads to large, level, open space; primitive camping. Grassy hills are result of reseeding project.

J 196 F 280 D 219 Pipeline close to road is mounted on sliding shoes to allow flexing. It takes about a week for oil in pipeline to travel from Prudhoe Bay to Valdez.

196.8 F 280.8 D 218.2 *Begin 21.8 miles of improved pavement southbound.*

J 197 F 281 D 218 Gold Creek bridge. From 1900–1970 more than 330,000 oz. of placer gold was produced in the upper Koyukuk and Chandalar mining districts. Many miners and active mines in area. Do not trespass on private claims.

J 197.5 F 281.5 D 217.5 Linda Creek in culvert. Private mining claims on creek.

J 197.6 F 281.6 D 217.4 Large paved turnout to east and view of Wiehl Mountain. Side road to gold mining area; motorized vehicle access restricted except for holders of valid mining claims.

J 199 F 283 D 216 Pipeline to west closely parallels highway next 0.3 mile northbound.

J 200 F 284 D 215 View of the Middle Fork Koyukuk River, a typical braided river exhibiting frequent changes of the streambed during high water.

J 203.1 F 287.1 D 211.9 Paved parking area to east. View of ponds and Sukakpak Mountain.

J 203.4 F 287.4 D 211.6 Paved parking area to west.

J 203.7 F 287.7 D 211.3 Large parking area to east by pond. Turnouts next 0.6 mile northbound with view of palsas, the short mounds of earth visible between the road and Sukakpak Mountain, which are formed by ice beneath the soil pushing the vegetative mat and soil upward.

J 204 F 288 D 211 Paved parking area to west.

J 204.3 F 288.3 D 210.7 Middle Fork Koyukuk River No. 3 bridge. Large parking area with toilets to east at north end of bridge offers good access to riverbank. Primitive camping. Beautiful views of imposing Sukakpak Mountain. The pressures on the limestone have changed much of the mountain into marble. Note veins of copper, quartz, crystalline and cinnabar in mountain face.

J 204.5 F 288.5 D 210.5 Middle Fork Koyukuk River No. 4 crossing (narrow bridge); parking to east at south end of bridge, river access.

J 204.7 F 288.7 D 210.3 Paved turnout to west.

J 205.2 F 289.2 D 209.8 Long, paved turnout to west (do not block pipeline access road). Good view of north side of Sukakpak Mountain.

J 206 F 290 D 209 View of Dillon Mountain (elev. 4,820 feet) just east of highway.

J 207 F 291 D 208 Dietrich River bridge. Half-way mark on the Dalton Highway. Turnouts at both ends of bridge. Fishing for burbot, grayling, whitefish and Dolly Varden. The Dietrich River flows south to join Bettles River, forming the Middle Fork Koyukuk River.

The dominant mountain nearest the highway looking south is Dillon Mountain. This mostly limestone mountain was named for JT Dillon, an Alaskan geologist who spent his life studying the Brooks Range. 🕮

J 208.5 F 292.5 D 206.5 $1,000 fine for littering (sign).

J 209.2 F 293.2 D 205.8 Distance marker northbound shows Dietrich 1 mile (to west), Deadhorse 205 miles. Dietrich is a former pipeline construction camp (dismantled, no public access).

J 209.3 F 293.3 D 205.7 Turnout to east. *Pavement ends, gravel begins, northbound. Gravel surfacing ranges from poor to good (if recently graded).*

J 209.4 F 293.4 D 205.6 Distance marker southbound shows Coldfoot 35 miles, Fairbanks 289 miles.

J 210.9 F 294.9 D 204.1 Very large turnout to east with old loading dock at back of parking area. Former Disaster Creek checkpoint when travel on the highway north of here was restricted to permit holders.

J 211.8 F 295.8 D 203.2 Pipeline goes under road twice between here and just north of **Milepost J 212.** In 1985 a 270-foot-long section of pipe here had to be raised up after the ice-ledge it was on, settled 15 feet.

J 213 F 297 D 202 Many large and small streams flow under the highway the next 14 miles northbound. Some of these streams continue to flow during winter below a frozen surface. Tall piping on some creek culverts are "thaw pipes," which help keep ice from blocking culverts in winter.

This is an area of wilderness vistas: river views, quiet valleys, spectacular mountains.

J 213.5 F 297.5 D 201.5 Creek flows under road in culvert.

J 216.2 F 300.2 D 198.8 Snowden Creek culvert. Panorama of Dietrich River valley and Brooks Range north and west of the road. View of mountain spires to east.

J 217.5 F 301.5 D 197.5 Small primitive parking area to east down by creek. Unusual mountain formations above. Rock spire to east is part of **Snowden Mountain** (elev. 6,240 feet). *NOTE: There are no established hiking trails off the Dalton Highway within the Brooks Range.*

J 218 F 302 D 197 Good view of Snowden Mountain to north.

J 219.8 F 303.8 D 195.2 Gravel pit access road to west.

J 219.9 F 303.9 D 195.1 Highway crosses creek in culvert; turnout. Pipeline goes underground in valley to west. There can be large white patches of snow in creeks even in July and August.

J 221.1 F 305.1 D 193.9 Highway crosses large stream; parking area.

J 221.7 F 305.7 D 193.3 Quarry to east has black marble with white calcite veins. The rock is used as rip-rap on road and river embankments.

J 222.2 F 306.2 D 192.8 Parking to west

The pipeline crosses the Central Arctic caribou herd's range on the North Slope. (©Sharon Nault)

A truck makes its way through the Brooks Range near Atigun Pass. (©Sharon Nault)

below road. Near river.

J 222.6 F 306.6 D 192.4 Large gravel stockpile to west on the Dietrich River. Castellated mountains to east.

J 223 F 307 D 192 North of Snowden Mountain there are several distinctive peaks that are unnamed. Watch for grizzly bears.

J 224 F 308 D 191 Turnout at gravel pit to east.

J 224.3 F 308.4 D 190.7 Turnouts both sides of highway. Creek runs under highway in culvert.

J 225.4 F 309.4 D 189.6 Narrow, double-ended turnout to west on wide braided section of Dietrich River. Also turnout to east.

J 225.7 F 309.7 D 189.3 Turnouts on both sides of highway.

J 225.9 F 309.9 D 189.1 Room to park at APL access road (do NOT block road). Pipeline remote valve just west of road. The arch-shaped concrete "saddle weights" keep pipeline buried in areas of possible flooding. They may be stored here until needed.

J 226.7 F 310.7 D 188.3 Turnout to west.

J 227.3 F 311.3 D 187.7 Narrow wooden bridge over **Nutirwik Creek**, a tributary of the Dietrich River. Narrow shoulder parking on west side of highway. View of Table Mountain to northeast.

J 228 F 312 D 187 Highway parallels Dietrich River. Physical milepost here is on the west, all others have been to the east.

J 228.9 F 312.9 D 186.1 Double-ended turnout to east; view of pipeline valve to east.

J 229.5 F 313.5 D 185.5 Turnout to east.

J 230.2 F 314.2 D 184.8 Turnout below the road to west.

J 230.8 F 314.8 D 184.2 Stream flows under road in culvert.

J 230.9 F 314.9 D 184.1 Turnout to west overlooking Dietrich River, which can be a vivid glacial blue depending on the light; good photo op.

J 231.3 F 315.3 D 183.7 Small turnouts both sides of highway.

J 232.5 F 316.5 D 182.5 Turnout to the east near creek which flows through a culvert beneath the highway.

J 232.7 F 316.7 D 182.3 Gravel turnout to west.

J 234.4 F 318.4 D 180.6 View to east of pipeline emerging from under ground

J 234.8 F 318.8 D 180.2 Northbound sign reads: Entering North Slope Borough—the world's largest municipality (in land area). Unlike the rest of the United States, which is organized into counties, Alaska's unit of regional government is the borough. Each borough has independent, incorporated communities within its boundaries. Approximately 6,807 people live in this borough which makes up about 15 percent of Alaska. 73 percent of these people are Alaska Native or part Native, according to the Alaska Community Database. North Slope Borough offices are located in Barrow.

J 235.1 F 319.1 D 179.9 Turnout to east.

J 235.2 F 319.2 D 179.8 Before it was killed by vandals, the spruce tree here (still standing in summer 2013) was the farthest north spruce tree along the Dalton. There are now at least 3 other spruce trees growing to the north of here.

J 235.4 F 319.4 D 179.6 Very large turnout with bear-proof litter barrel, interpretive panels on northern treeline and tundra, and a pit toilet. Truck chain-up area in winter. NOTE: Turnouts along here can be *very* muddy in wet weather; bring your mud boots!

Road climbs to Chandalar Shelf. Treeline here is at 2,500 feet (in contrast, Alberta's treeline is at 7,500 feet, Colorado is at 12,000 feet and Ecuador, near the equator is 19,000 feet).

Begin 2-mile-long 10 percent uphill grade northbound. Give trucks plenty of room. Do not stop on road. Dirt road surface can be slippery in wet weather, be sure to slow down. Watch for soft spots.

J 236.8 F 320.8 D 178.2 Turnout to west up steep hill to flat area; great informal campsite and photo-op, but poor choice for big rigs because of small turnaround space.

CAUTION: Steep descent southbound.

J 237.1 F 321.1 D 177.9 Turnoff to east for large parking area at summit of **Chandalar Shelf**, spectacular views. Headwaters of the Chandalar River are to the east. Table Mountain (elev. 5,042 feet) is 5 miles south. Dietrich River valley to west. Evidence of a

glacial moraine lies on the shelf left by a glacier that extended over the side and down into the Dietrich Valley.

J 238.8 F 322.8 D 176.2 *SLOW (sign).* Aircraft control gate.

J 239.3 F 323.3 D 175.7 *SLOW DOWN* (northbound sign) alerts motorists to intersection with access roads west to Chandalar Station (DOT/PF highway maintenance); no visitor services are available at the station. Use CB Channel 19 for emergencies.

Chandalar Camp, the former pipeline construction camp, was located just south of here.

J 239.5 F 323.5 D 175.5 Airstrip entrance. Bridge over river to east, primitive camping. No camping near runway.

J 239.9 F 323.9 D 175.1 Distance marker northbound shows Galbraith 34 miles, Deadhorse 173 miles.

Distance marker southbound shows Dietrich 32 miles, Coldfoot 67 miles, Fairbanks 321 miles. Speed limit 50 mph (signed).

J 240.6 F 324.6 D 174.4 Turnout to east. Watch for arctic ground squirrels, a food staple of foxes, golden eagles, wolves, weasels, wolverines and grizzly bears. These squirrels dig extensive burrows and are at home on well-drained tundra. They are most abundant in mountainous terrain.

J 242.1 F 326.1 D 172.9 Small turnout to east. Atigun Pass (sign). Avalanche gun emplacement. *CAUTION: Watch for open metal covers on the ground.*

J 242.2 F 326.2 D 172.8 West Fork of the North Fork Chandalar River bridge. Turnout by bridge. The scalloped waves of soil seen to the north on the hillside are formed when meltwater saturates the thawed surface soil then flows down the hill. These are called solifluction lobes.

Begin long, steep (12 percent), winding, uphill grade northbound to Atigun Pass. Winter avalanche area. Slide area next 5 miles northbound.

The pipeline is to the east in a buried, insulated concrete cribbing to protect it from rock slides and avalanches, and to keep the ground from thawing. Construction in this area was extremely complex, difficult and dangerous.

J 242.6 F 326.6 D 172.4 Rough gravel turnout overlooks valley below; spectacular views.

J 243.4 F 327.4 D 171.6 Turnout with great view of Slide Path 11 (signed), one of several areas where rock and debris have crashed down and across the road. These slide paths are signed and numbered on Atigun Pass.

J 244.1 F 328.1 D 170.9 Turnout to east. Look for Dall sheep on rocky slopes below. The pipeline is buried in the narrow deep valley far below the highway. *CAUTION: Watch for falling rock.*

J 244.3 F 328.3 D 170.7 Evidence of a 2012 slide at Slide Path 25 in summer 2013.

J 244.5 F 328.5 D 170.5 Long, narrow turnout to east.

J 244.7 F 328.7 D 170.3 "Avalanche Safety Zone" (sign). Turnout at top of **Atigun Pass**, elev. 4,800 feet, in the Brooks Range, highest highway pass in Alaska; Continental Divide. A Wyoming Gauge to measure precipitation is located here. Nice example of a cirque, an amphitheater-shaped bowl or depression caused by glacial erosion, in mountain east of road. Endicott Mountains are to the west, Philip Smith Mountains to the east. James Dalton Moun-

tain is ahead and to the left, northbound. Avalanche safety area (sign) to east.

CAUTION: Watch for Dall sheep. The sheep congregate on and near the highway to lick the calcium chloride put on the roads for dust reduction. Dall sheep range throughout Alaska's major mountain ranges. The only white, wild sheep in the world, Dall sheep have honey-colored or dark brown horns. Rams have heavy, curled horns. Ewes and immature sheep of both sexes have thinner, almost straight horns, which causes some viewers to mistake them for mountain goats. The white-coated mountain goats have a black muzzle, a long beard, slender black horns and a more squarish body than Dall sheep. Mountain goats are generally confined to Southeast and southcentral Alaska.

J 245 F 329 D 170 Many mountains in this area exceed 7,000 feet in elevation.

J 245.4 F 329.4 D 169.6 Gravel turnouts. *CAUTION: Sloping parking area to west may be too difficult to access. Do not block work areas.* Best access is to large parking area to east. Two avalanche gun emplacements.

J 245.6 F 329.6 D 169.4 Very long parking area to west, but difficult due to deep drainage furrows. Best chance to access turnout is at the north end. View down the north side of Atigun Pass.

J 246.8 F 330.8 D 168.2 Very large, fairly flat, turnout to east. Avalanche gun emplacement. Pipeline is under road.

Begin long, steep (12 percent), winding, uphill grade southbound to Atigun Pass. Winter avalanche area. Slide area next 5 miles southbound.

J 247.7 F 331.7 D 167.3 Very small gravel turnout to east.

J 248.4 F 332.4 D 166.6 Large gravel turnouts both sides of highway. Big views of valley below.

J 249.4 F 333.4 D 165.6 Gravel turnout to west. Creek runs through culvert.

Permafrost to the north of Atigun Pass is called continuous and is found everywhere. Its thickness increases on the north side of the pass. Permafrost to south is discontinuous (spotty, decreases in thickness).

J 249.7 F 333.7 D 165.3 Road closure gates used to stop traffic in extreme weather or emergency conditions. Very small parking area by APL access road (do not block) that leads east to staging area.

J 250 F 334 D 165 Long gravel turnout to east, large sloping gravel turnout to west. Large cleared area below road used for various kinds of camps.

NOTE: There are 2 physical Milepost 250's here. The MILEPOST® measures distance from the one farthest south.

J 251.5 F 335.5 D 163.5 Several turnouts next 0.2 mile northbound provide opportunities for photos.

J 252.9 F 336.9 D 163.1 Large parking area to west below road just south of Atigun River Bridge No. 1.

J 253 F 337 D 162 Atigun River Bridge No. 1. Gravel pit to east at north end of bridge.

CAUTION: Watch for oncoming truck traffic in rearview mirrors and pull over when possible.

J 256 F 340 D 159 Great photo opportunity of pipeline, mountains and highway. Long straight section with pipeline beside it. Calcium chloride on highway, northbound. From Atigun Valley northward, you may see some unusual songbirds such as the Northern wheatear, yellow wagtail, Smith's longspur and bluethroat. Some of these birds winter as far away as Africa and Asia.

Galbraith Camp, like Toolik Lake, is a former pipeline camp. (©Sharon Nault)

J 257.5 F 341.5 D 157.5 "Check valves" on pipeline keep oil from flowing backwards in the event of a leak. Expansive views of pipeline, valley and James Dalton Mountain to south.

J 258.5 F 342.5 D 156.5 Trevor Creek bridge. Turnout to west at south end of bridge.

Gravel ends, pavement begins, northbound.

J 258.6 F 342.6 D 156.4 Turnout to west. Good spot to park and hike up to rocks. *CAUTION: Grizzly bears in area.*

J 260.7 F 344.7 D 154.3 Gravel pit access road to east up hill.

J 260.8 F 344.8 D 154.2 Large turnout to west.; view of check valve. *Slow for rough pavement.*

J 261.4 F 345.4 D 153.6 Turnout close to the pipeline.

J 262 F 346 D 153 View northbound of Pump Station No. 4 in the distance; see description at **Milepost J 269.2.**

J 263.2 F 347.2 D 151.8 Small turnout to east and APL access to west. View to east of interesting rock formations on mountains.

J 264 F 348 D 151 Views of pipeline in the distance as it zigzags toward Pump Station 4. Lots of arctic ground squirrels in this area. Bears like arctic ground squirrels.

J 265.1 F 349.1 D 149.9 Roche Moutonee [sic] Creek bridge. (Correct spelling is Roche Moutonnee, French for a glacially scoured rock ridge in the shape of a sheep's back. The formation is located several miles upstream.) Turnout to west at north end of bridge.

Pavement ends gravel begins, northbound.

J 266.8 F 350.8 D 148.2 Very small turnout to west.

J 267.1 F 351.1 D 147.9 Turnout to west.

J 267.5 F 351.5 D 147.5 Bridge over Holden Creek. Creek access both sides of bridge.

J 269.2 F 353.2 D 145.8 Entrance to **Pump Station No. 4.** This station has the highest elevation of all the pipeline stations (2,760 feet), and is also a launching and receiving station for special measuring and cleaning devices called "pigs." A scraper pig consists of spring-mounted scraper blades and/or brushes on a central body which

moves through the pipe, cleaning accumulated wax from interior walls and monitoring conditions inside the pipe. There are "dumb" pigs and "smart" pigs. Dumb pigs clean out wax deposits in the line. Smart pigs scan the pipeline to check welds, wall thickness and other properties to help insure the integrity of the piping and identify maintenance needs. **Tea Lake** off road; fishing for grayling and burbot.

J 269.3 F 353.3 D 145.7 Road narrows northbound.

J 269.4 F 353.4 D 145.6 Highway bridge over pipeline. Tea Lake Outfall culvert (signed).

J 270 F 354 D 145 Second signed Tea Lake Outfall culvert northbound.

J 270.4 F 354.4 D 144.6 Bowhunting Only (sign).

J 270.9 F 354.9 D 144.1 Atigun River Bridge No. 2. Large parking area to west, south of bridge, with large cement boat launch ramps to the north, west side of bridge.

J 271 F 355 D 144 View of Galbraith Lake and Galbraith camp. Galbraith Lake is a remnant of a huge glacial lake that filled the valley in the last ice age. It was named by USGS geologists in 1951 for Bart Galbraith, a bush pilot who was lost while flying in the area.

J 273.6 F 357.6 D 141.4 *Road construction underway next 17 miles northbound in summer 2013. Expect continued construction and/or improved highway in summer 2014.*

J 274.6 F 358.6 D 140.4 Distance marker northbound shows Galbraith 1 mile, Deadhorse 139 miles.

J 274.7 F 358.7 D 140.3 Improved gravel road leads 4.3 miles west to **GALBRAITH CAMP.** This access road passes an active airstrip, several buildings and the Arctic National Wildlife Refuge Administrative Cabin (at Mile 2.1), which is open to the public *only in an emergency.* Continue 2.2 miles beyond the cabin, past huge active gravel pit, for Galbraith Campground. The campground sits in a wide tundra-covered valley ringed by mountains. The clear waters of Camp Creek run down its

Caribou hunters camp alongside the Dalton Highway. (©Sharon Nault)

south boundary. It is a large campground with well-spaced, unimproved sites, some picnic tables, a pit toilet, litter barrels and bear-proof containers for tent campers. A road leads to many primitive camping areas in the brush. Nice wildflower display in season, good bird watching, interesting fossils and lots of arctic ground squirrels. Interpretive panels on Galbraith's archaeological sites, survival skills of plants, arctic butterflies, mosquitoes and much more. A favorite spot for many Alaskans. Plenty of hiking/walking opportunities. *CAUTION: Watch for gravel trucks on Galbraith access road.* The gravel pit opened in 2011 and is used for nearby road construction. Huge amounts of gravel are required for road construction on the Dalton and other roads in Alaska. ▲

J 274.9 F 358.9 D 140.1 Distance marker southbound shows Galbraith 7 miles, Coldfoot 92 miles, Fairbanks 346 miles.

J 276.5 F 360.5 D 138.5 Island Lake to west.

J 278.4 F 362.4 D 137.6 Turnout to west; large parking area.

J 281.7 F 365.7 D 133.3 View of Toolik Field Station (see next milepost). Watch for caribou.

J 282.7 F 366.7 D 132.3 Large turnout to east.

J 284.3 F 368.3 D 130.7 Side road west to Toolik Lake, originally a pipeline construction camp, now the site of **Toolik Field Station**. Run by the Institute of Arctic Biology of the University of Alaska Fairbanks, the field station conducts research on Arctic ecology and the effects of climate change. No public facilities or services available. Scientists from around the world come here to study an intact arctic ecosystem. Closed to public.

This area is designated as a Research Natural Area (RNA) by the BLM. The public may fish and hunt on this land but overnight camping is not permitted anywhere in the RNA including the highway between **Mileposts J 278 and J 293.**

J 286.2 F 370.2 D 128.8 Turnout to east at high point in road. Excellent photo stop; 360° view. View of Toolik Lake and Field Station. View of Brooks Range south and east. Philip Smith Mountains to west. Panoramic views of incredible beauty.

Bow hunting only area (sign).

J 288.4 F 372.4 D 126.6 Highway descends northbound to Kuparuk Creek bridge.

J 288.9 F 372.9 D 126.1 Kuparuk Creek bridge. Access east to creek at both ends of bridge. Informal camping at turnout; do not block pipeline access road. Watch for caribou here.

J 289.3 F 373.3 D 125.7 Small parking on east side. Highway crosses over pipeline. Short buried section of pipeline to west is called a sag bend and allows for wildlife crossing. Watch for caribou northbound.

J 290.3 F 374.3 D 124.7 Turnout to east with 360 degree view. Steep downgrade followed by long upgrade northbound. APL access.

J 290.6 F 374.6 D 124.4 Imnavait Creek culvert.

J 291.3 F 375.3 D 123.7 Toolik River culvert.

J 294.3 F 378.3 D 120.7 Sag bend in pipeline to west.

J 294.5 F 378.5 D 120.5 We saw our first caribou northbound here in August 2013. *Watch for caribou crossing the highway.*

J 297 F 381 D 118 Pullout used by hunters in caribou season. *NOTE: There are dozens of these single-vehicle pullouts along the highway from here to Deadhorse. Be sure to use them rather than stop in the middle of or on the side of the road.*

J 297.5 F 381.5 D 117.5 Snow poles ("delineators") mark roadway for truckers during whiteouts from blowing snow or during dense fog. Metal brackets in ground from broken poles can be a tire buster.

J 297.8 F 381.8 D 117.2 Oksrukukuyik (or locally "Oks," pronounced *ox*) Creek culvert. Two large sloping turnouts to the east at both south and north end of bridge.

J 298.2 F 382.2 D 116.8 Small turnouts both sides of highway at top of hill. First view northbound of Sagavanirktok ("the Sag") River valley. **Slope Mountain** (elev. 4,010 feet) to west. Watch for Dall sheep. Many blind hills, keep to right.

J 300 F 384 D 115 Northern boundary of BLM-managed land (sign missing summer 2013). Land north of here is managed by the Alaska Dept. of Natural Resources.

J 301 F 385 D 114 Slope Mountain to west, good place to glass for Dall sheep and birds. Parking to west by APL access road (do not block traffic).

Northbound traffic sign "Only state hunting regulations apply." Entering public lands.

J 305.5 F 389.5 D 109.5 Distance marker northbound shows Slope Mountain Camp 1 mile, Deadhorse 110 miles. Pipeline goes underground.

J 305.6 F 389.6 D 109.4 Sag River Station DOT highway maintenance. Slope Mountain Camp No. 1, a former pipeline construction camp, (now dismantled) 1 mile east. APL access.

J 305.7 F 389.7 D 109.3 Distance marker southbound shows Coldfoot 131 miles, Fairbanks 385 miles.

J 306.3 F 390.3 D 108.7 Small turnout to west.

J 307 F 391 D 108 A long stretch of exceptionally brilliant fireweed seen to the west (in season) along 2.5-mile stretch of highway. Posted speed limit 50 mph.

J 309 F 393 D 106 Highway parallels Sagavanirktok River northbound.

J 309.3 F 393.3 D 105.7 Turnout to east.

J 311.9 F 395.9 D 103.1 Entrance to **Pump Station No. 3**; mobile construction camp facility.

Road widens northbound.

J 312 F 396 D 103 Watch for caribou.

J 313.8 F 397.8 D 101.2 Sam Schuyler Memorial Bridge crosses Oksrukukuyik Creek.

CAUTION: Highway northbound built on high gravel base; no shoulders, abrupt drop-offs to tundra and few turnouts.

J 314.3 F 398.3 D 100.7 Narrow gravel side road to east is a popular informal campsite for hunters during bowhunting season.

J 318.1 F 402.1 D 96.9 Side road east toward river (do not block); primitive campsites, no turnaround areas for big rigs.

CAUTION: Steep, blind hills northbound. Watch for oncoming traffic on hills. Trucks will need to gather speed to crest hills. NOTE: Oil Spill Hill (coming up) and Ice Cut at **Milepost J 325** are 2 dangerous spots where CB radio users should call out ahead of the curve: "northbound 4-wheeler" or "southbound 4-wheeler" at "[name the curve]." (To truckers, anything not a big rig—such as cars, pickup trucks, vans, campers—is a "4-wheeler." Large RVs should identify themselves as "large RV.")

J 319.6 F 403.6 D 95.4 Turnout to east at Oil Spill Hill.

Steep downhill grade.

J 320 F 404 D 95 The long range of hills east of the road are the Kakutukruich Bluffs. Nice views northbound of Sagavanirktok River.

J 320.6 F 404.6 D 94.4 Gustafson Gulch culvert.

J 320.8 F 404.8 D 94.2 Short side road east to Sag River; primitive campsite, limited turnaround space, do not block road.

J 322.7 F 406.7 D 92.3 Small single-vehicle pullout to east.

J 323 F 407 D 92 *Due to heavy truck traffic, the road is heavily treated with calcium chloride north to Deadhorse.*

J 323.3 F 407.3 D 91.7 Short side road east to Sag River; primitive campsite.

J 234.9 F 408.9 D 90.1 Side road east to popular primitive campsite.

"Ice Cut" (sign) signals steep grade northbound.

J 325.5 F 409.5 D 89.5 Turnout on steep

and rocky "Ice Cut" grade. *NOTE: Stay out of the way of northbound trucks accelerating for the steep climb.* Popular in season with bow hunters after caribou because of its view. There are also turnouts at the bottom and at the top of this grade. Pipeline road access to large gravel area near river.

J 325.8 F 409.8 D 89.2 Large flat turnout to east with big views of pipeline to west and Sag River to east.

J 326.2 F 410.2 D 88.8 Pipeline crosses under bridge. APL access.

J 327 F 411 D 87 Watch for grizzly bears digging for roots and other food around the pipeline supports.

J 328.8 F 412.8 D 86.2 Turnout by creek to west.

J 330.7 F 414,7 D 84.3 Steep downhill (both directions) to Dan Creek bridge. Small sloping turnout to east at north end of bridge. Happy Valley buildings can be seen in the distance to the north.

J 332.9 F 416.9 D 82.1 Turnout to east.

J 334.4 F 418.4 D 80.6 Happy Valley, a former pipeline construction camp, now used by road crews, a private guiding operator and the Alaska State Troopers. Huge, active gravel pit. The airstrip is busy in summer and during hunting season. Additional parking on west side of Dalton Highway in large gravel area.

Watch for caribou northbound.

J 334.8 F 418.8 D 80.2 *Begin short section of gravel with calcium chloride northbound.*

J 339.8 F 423.8 D 75.2 Distance marker northbound shows Deadhorse 74 miles.

Distance marker southbound shows Slope Mountain Camp 36 miles, Coldfoot 166 miles, Fairbanks 420 miles.

J 344 F 428 D 71 Peregrine falcons, gyrfalcons and rough-legged hawks are often sighted here. They often hunt near bluffs along the river in the distance. Area thick with wildflowers.

J 345.6 F 429.6 D 79.4 Long gravel break in pavement.

Pavement ends, gravel begins, northbound.

J 346.5 F 430.5 D 68.5 Ungated gravel road leads east to river.

J 347.8 F 431.8 D 67.2 Sag River Overlook. Long, narrow, sloping parking area to west. Gravel path beside road leads up to observation deck with interpretive displays. Watch for falcons hunting along the bluffs.

J 350.5 F 434.5 D 64.5 View of Sagwon Bluffs to the east.

J 352 F 436 D 63 Steeep down grade to creek crossing followed by slow rolling ascent northbound.

J 353.2 F 437.2 D 62.8 Side road west to gravel pit.

J 354.6 F 438.6 D 60.4 Last Chance Wayside to west at crest of hill. Large gravel parking area *(CAUTION: Avoid holes along backside of this wayside)*, pit toilet and garbage container. Panoramic views (weather permitting) of Arctic coastal plain; look for musk-oxen. Follow short dirt road uphill from wayside for primitive campsites. *HUNTERS PLEASE NOTE: Do not dump gut piles in trash containers. State hunting regulations require game be field dressed out of sight of roads and trails. And the seasonal workers who haul out the trash will appreciate it!*

Porcupine and Central Arctic caribou herds migrate through this area on their way to and from their calving grounds.

Migratory birds from around the world nest and breed on the Arctic coastal plain. Bird watchers come to view the king eiders, spectacled eiders, Canada geese, snow geese,

tundra swans, jaegers, snowy owls and a variety of other species seen here in the spring.

Road widens as highway descends northbound.

J 355 F 439 D 60 Long, narrow turnout to east with expansive panoramic view. A favorite stop for truckers.

Highway widens northbound

J 356.5 F 440.5 D 58.5 Metal poles mark road edge, a great help in winter when blowing snow obscures road.

The small brown object far out on the tundra to the west draws lots of attention each year, but it's a barrel, not a bear!

J 357.2 F 441.2 D 57.8 *Gravel ends, pavement begins, northbound.*

J 359 F 443 D 56 Entrance to **Pump Station No. 2** to the east. Begin long, straight stretch northbound.

J 360.2 F 444.2 D 54.8 Small gravel turnout to east.

J 362 F 446 D 53 *CAUTION: The worst winter weather conditions on the Dalton Highway are experienced the next 38 miles northbound. Blowing snow may obscure visibility and block road.*

Pavement ends, pot-holed gravel begins, northbound.

J 365.1 F 449.1 D 49.9 Large level turnout to west. Watch for waterfowl, especially swans, geese and ducks, in large lakes along highway.

J 366.6 F 450.6 D 48.4 Gravel side road to primitive campsites. Used by commercial hunting guide during caribou season; do not block road.

J 367.8 F 451.8 D 47.2 Lake Desiree turnout to the west. Floatplanes sometimes land at this lake.

J 369.6 F 453.6 D 45.4 Distance marker southbound shows Coldfoot 196 miles, Fairbanks 450 miles.

J 370.9 F 454.9 D 44.1 Narrow side road to primitive campsite; do not block road.

J 375 F 459 D 40 To the east (not visible from road), the Ivishak River empties into the Sagavanirktok River on its journey to the Arctic Ocean.

J 376 F 460 D 39 The small hill seen on the horizon, about 3 miles west of the road, is a pingo (this one is named "Percy Pingo"). Pingos often form from the bed of a spring-

fed lake that has been covered by vegetation. Freezing of the water can raise the surface several hundred feet above the surrounding terrain.

J 377.3 F 461.3 D 37.7 Large, extra nice turnout to east is viewpoint for distant Franklin Bluffs. Oxidized iron minerals give these bluffs their colors. The white patches are usually snow. There is a large, flat, storage area at this turnout.

J 383 F 467 D 32 Buried pipeline and Franklin Bluffs to the east, and a pingo to the west.

J 384 F 468 D 31 Dalton Highway snakes its way northbound across the flat coastal plain. Watch for golden eagles, ducks, arctic fox, snowy owl, jaegers, swans, bears and caribou.

J 386.1 F 470.1 D 28.9 Large gravel turnout to east; good spot for photos of Franklin Bluffs.

J 387.1 F 471.1 D 27.9 Public access to east. Primitive parking and camping. Sag River.

J 388.6 F 472.6 D 26.4 Turnout to east. Musk-oxen are often seen along here between the road and the river.

J 394.7 F 478.7 D 20.3 Distance marker northbound shows Deadhorse 20 miles. Southbound sign shows Coldfoot 220 miles, Fairbanks 474 miles.

J 395.3 F 479.3 D 19.7 Turnout to east, Caren Pond to west.

J 395.9 F 479.9 D 19.1 Watch for musk-oxen along the Sagavanirktok ("Sag") River.

J 399.4 F 483.4 D 15.6 Side road east toward river. Bird-watching area near water.

J 400.9 F 484.9 D 14.1 Turnout to east.

J 403.3 F 487.3 D 11.7 Turnout to east; access to Sagavanirktok ("Sag") River. Watch for caribou.

J 405 F 489 D 10 Large gravel turnout to east; look for caribou and other wildlife.

J 406.3 F 490.3 D 8.7 Gravel access road leads east toward Sag River.

J 407 F 491 D 8 Popular local fishing spot and informal camping area used by travelers (tents and RVs) along the Sag River. There are primitive firepits; carry out your trash.

J 408 F 492 D 7 Small turnout to east.

J 408.7 F 492.7 D 6.3 Turnout to west.

Watch for musk-oxen along the Sagavanirktok ("Sag") River. (©Sharon Nault)

End of the Dalton Highway. View of Lake Colleen and beyond it the distinctive outline of Deadhorse/Prudhoe Bay on the horizon. (©Sharon Nault)

J 411.1 F 495.1 D 3.9 Narrow gravel side road to east.

J 411.5 F 495.5 D 3.5 Access road to large gravel pit. Bill Meyer Lake.

J 412.1 F 496.1 D 2.9 Gravel turnout to west.

J 412.8 F 496.8 D 2.2 Deadhorse Camp (www.deadhorsecamp.com) offers rooms and dining for overnight guests; phone ahead for reservations, (907) 474-3565 or 1-888-474-3565. Gift shop. The Arctic Ocean Shuttle leaves from Deadhorse Camp; make reservations at least 24-hours in advance with them.

Deadhorse Camp. See display ad this page.

J 413.1 F 497.1 D 1.9 Gravel side road.

J 413.3 F 497.3 D 1.7 Southbound distance marker shows Coldfoot 240 miles, Fairbanks 494 miles; next services 240 miles. Drive with lights on, buckle up for safety, speed limit 50 mph.

J 413.8 F 497.8 D 1.2 Double-ended turnout by Sag River.

J 414.1 F 498.1 D 0.9 Large turnout on curve. Free maps of Deadhorse are usually available in a box here (please secure lid after taking a map). Be sure to pick one up, they are very useful. Lake Colleen is north of the highway as you drive into town. Watch for birds, bears and caribou.

Deadhorse/Prudhoe Bay

J 415 F 499 D 0 Stop sign: End of Dalton Highway. Business signs will point you in the direction of various services in Deadhorse/ Prudhoe Bay. Behind the signs is Lake Colleen, an important body of water in Prudhoe Bay because it provides water for the camps. What look like small cabins across the lake are actually oil wells. Since Deadhorse/Prudhoe Bay in no way resembles a traditional town, it is hard to know where you are within it especially when it is foggy. Best bet is to follow signs to any of the businesses mentioned in *The MILEPOST®*, since they serve the traveling public. You may not drive to the Arctic Ocean: It is reached via a secured area and unavailable to the public except on tours (inquire about a tour *before* arriving and allow 24 hours for security clearance).

Population: 4 permanent; 3,000 to 6,000 or more part-time depending on oil production (this is why hotels often run 100 percent capacity). *NOTE: Cell phone service is available in Deadhorse/Prudhoe Bay and for about the first 14 miles south on the Dalton Highway, then there is no service until near Fairbanks. Radio station to 1610 AM for weather information.*

Visitor Information: You can try local businesses (see Lodging & Services). Deadhorse Camp at Milepost 412.8 runs the Arctic Ocean Shuttle; phone (907) 474-3565.

Private Aircraft: Deadhorse Airport, N70°11.69' W148°27.91'; elev. 65 feet; length 6,500 feet, asphalt; fuel NC-100, B, mogas. A 5,000 foot private gravel airstrip is owned and maintained by ConocoPhillips Alaska, Inc. A state-owned heliport is located here.

Climate: Arctic, with temperatures ranging from -56°F in winter to 78°F in summer. Precipitation averages 5 inches; snowfall 20 inches. **Radio**: KCDS 88.1 FM. **Transportation**: Scheduled jet service to Deadhorse/ Prudhoe Bay from Anchorage, Fairbanks and Barrow. (Flying time from Anchorage is 1 hour, 35 minutes.) Packaged tours of the North Slope area are available from Anchorage and Fairbanks. Air taxi service is available at Deadhorse Airport.

Deadhorse is located on Prudhoe Bay, on the Beaufort Sea Coast, Arctic Ocean. Prudhoe Bay is the largest oil field in the United States and the 18th largest in the world. Prudhoe Bay oil fields provide about 2 to 3 percent of the nation's domestic oil supply, according to the Alaska Dept. of Commerce. A number of oil fields make up the Prudhoe Bay industrial area: Kuparuk, Milne Point, Point McIntyre, Prudhoe Bay, Niakuk, Endicott, Alpine Field and North Star Field.

Most buildings are modular, pre-fab-type

construction. Some are set on refrigerated concrete slabs that do not melt the permafrost. Other buildings are constructed on pilings. Virtually all the businesses here are engaged in oil field or pipeline support activities, such as drilling, construction, maintenance, telecommunications, warehousing and transportation. Oil field employees work a rotation, such as 2 weeks on the job, then 2 weeks off. Workers typically work 7 days a week, 10 to 12 hours each day. The 4 major oil companies here are Shell, BP, ConocoPhillips and Standard Oil.

According to Deborah Bernard in an article in the *Prudhoe Bay Journal*, there is more than one version of how Deadhorse got its name, but basically it was named after Deadhorse Haulers, a company hired to do the gravel work at the Prudhoe Bay airstrip. (How the company came to be called Deadhorse Haulers is another story.) Everybody began calling the airstrip "Deadhorse," and the name stuck—too well for those who prefer the name Prudhoe Bay. Some people were surprised when Prudhoe Bay got its own ZIP code on June 3, 1982, and was listed as "Deadhorse, AK 99734," rather than Prudhoe Bay. It was later changed to Prudhoe Bay, AK 99734.

Transportation

Air: Alaska Airlines.

Bus: Scheduled van service between Fairbanks and Deadhorse via Dalton Highway Express. Phone (907) 474-3555.

Lodging & Services

Visitor accommodations and meals (call ahead) are available for Northern Alaska Tour Co. guests at **Deadhorse Camp**, located south of Deadhorse at **Milepost 412.8**, phone (907) 474-3565, toll-free 1-888-474-3565, www.deadhorsecamp.com. Prudhoe Bay Hotel (907/659-2449), Arctic Oilfield Hotel (907/659-2614) and Aurora Hotel & Suites (907/670-0600) cater primarily to oil field workers. You can't count on rooms being available at these hotels, so call ahead anywhere from 3 to 10 days in advance. Also ask about purchasing meals at their cafeterias. Cafeteria hours are generally: Breakfast 5:30–8 A.M., lunch noon–1 P.M., dinner 5–8 P.M., with self-serve snacks available for purchase in-between.

Many of the visitor services available in Deadhorse are found at Brooks Range Supply (phone 907/670-5100). They are located in the building with the "Welcome to Deadhorse, Alaska, end of the Dalton Highway" sign, which houses the Napa Store, Prudhoe Bay General Store and the post office (open 1–3:30 P.M. and 6:30–9 P.M. daily). Check out the post office bulletin board, which is covered with interesting photos of local happenings. The "Colville Mini-Mall" carries industrial supplies and sundries, everything from postcards and snacks to propane in portable bottles, and Arctic survival gear. Alcohol, ammunition and weapons are not available in Deadhorse. They may be able to refill your propane bottles if they have the right fitting.

Dump station is behind the Nenana Oil Service Building. Public restrooms at the Tesoro station.

There is no bank in Deadhorse, but ATMs are available. Credit cards and traveler's checks are generally accepted, but Fish and Game licenses and postage must be paid for in cash.

Regular unleaded gasoline and No. 1

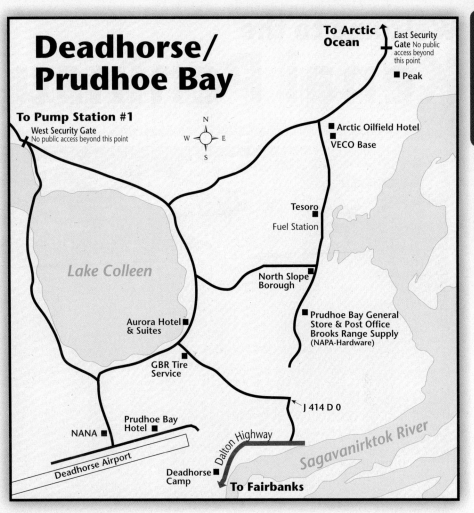

diesel are available at NANA (Chevron) or the Deadhorse/Prudhoe Bay Tesoro Station. Tesoro is a 24-hour self-serve station; an attendant is available and cash accepted from 7 A.M. until 6 P.M. After hours, you can pump gas yourself as long as you have a credit card.

Gas pumps here are probably not what travelers are used to. Pumps at Tesoro are located on the side of the building. Patrons must pay prior to pumping (pay with credit card at machine inside building). At NANA, the pumps are kept in barrels, and you can pay at a machine inside. Both fueling places have instructions inside to help you figure out their pumping stations. Tire and vehicle repairs are available at Prudhoe Bay Fleet Service, Veco (CH2M Hill) Base Fleet Services, NANA and at GBR (located at Milepost 415). Local auto parts and hardware store has an assortment of supplies. Warranty work is available in Deadhorse for Ford and Dodge vehicles.

Public access beyond Deadhorse is restricted. For security reasons, travel north of Deadhorse, including visits to the Arctic Ocean, is limited to commercial tours. Tour information is available at the hotels or call Northern Alaska Tour Company at (907) 474-8600 or 1-800-474-1986.

CAUTION: Beware of bears in the area.

Camping

There is no formal overnight RV campground but usually you can find an overnight space. Try the Arctic Oilfield Hotel or Tesoro station. Tent camping is generally discouraged due to bears. Many people camp just

outside town on the Dalton Highway at turnouts along the Sag River.

CAUTION: The Prudhoe Bay/Deadhorse area has been overrun with grizzly bears in summers past. Polar bears have been known to wander into town (though infrequently). Use caution when camping or walking around.

Attractions

Take the Arctic Ocean Shuttle from Deadhorse Camp on an oil field tour. The tour takes you by the largest natural gas processing plant in the world and the largest drilling rig tower in the world (named "Liberty"). Take a dip in the Arctic Ocean and become a part of the Polar Bear Club; certificates are available for those who go into the water (limited entry—no deeper than your knees—due to liability concerns). Tour bus drivers bring towels and blankets. *You must reserve space on this tour 24-hours in advance and carry identification. Inquire about additional restrictions.* For tour information and reservations, phone (907) 474-3565 or 1-888-474-3565.

Wildlife watching is always an attraction here. It is not unusual to see a number of caribou in Prudhoe Bay. Caribou congregate on the coast after calving in late June and July.

Birders will enjoy a unique opportunity to see breeding colors on species that are in normally only in remote areas, such as the king, common and spectacled eider, pomarine, parasitic jaeger, Sabine's gull and many more. Drive around Deadhorse roads slowly and scan ponds and wetlands from late May to late June.

Welcome to the
Kenai Peninsula

Homer Spit is a favorite destination on the Kenai Peninsula. (©Sharon Nault)

The Kenai Peninsula, south of Anchorage, has been labeled the playground of southcentral Alaska. It is a favorite destination for Alaskans and visitors from Outside, who are drawn by its incomparable scenery and world-class fishing on the Kenai, Russian and Kasilof rivers, and in Resurrection Bay, Kachemak Bay and Cook Inlet.

The Seward Highway provides access to the Kenai Peninsula from Anchorage. Completed in 1951, the Seward Highway (Alaska Routes 1 and 9) winds along the north shore of Turnagain Arm, crossing the isthmus that separates the Kenai Peninsula from the rest of southcentral Alaska some 52 miles south of Anchorage. Without the "Welcome to the Kenai Peninsula" sign at **Milepost S 75**, motorists probably would never notice they had crossed onto a peninsula, having left behind the urban setting of Anchorage just 45 miles up the Seward Highway.

Along that 52-mile stretch of the Seward Highway between Anchorage and the Kenai Peninsula, motorists enjoy panoramic vistas of the Chugach and Kenai mountain ranges and Turnagain Arm.

Turnagain Arm is a 48-mile-long estuary stretching from the mouth of the Placer River to the head of Cook Inlet. It was named "River Turnagain" by Captain James Cook in 1778, when he discovered it had no eastern outlet. The name was adopted by Captain George Vancouver, who surveyed the area in 1794, as Turnagain Arm.

That stretch of the Seward Highway also junctions with the Alyeska Highway to Mount Alyeska recreation area, and with the Portage Glacier/Whittier Access Road. The Alyeska Highway leads to Girdwood, a community of nearly 2,000, and home of the world-class ski resort at Mount Alyeska. The Portage Glacier/Whittier Access Road leads to the Anton Anderson tunnel, originally a railroad tunnel now doubles as road access to the formerly isolated port of Whittier. Portage Glacier, a popular tourist destination, has the Begich-Boggs Visitor Center and boat trip to view Portage Glacier.

Once the Seward Highway crosses on to the Kenai Peninsula, it first climbs to Turnagain Pass, a stunning alpine area that is a favorite winter recreation area as well as a summer viewpoint. Beyond Turnagain Pass at **Milepost S 56.3**, the Seward Highway junctions with the 18-mile Hope Highway, which leads to the historic mining town of Hope on the south shore of Turnagain Arm.

The Seward Highway ends at the picturesque town of Seward on Resurrection Bay, gateway to Kenai Fjords National Park.

The Sterling Highway is the other major highway on the Kenai Peninsula. The Sterling Highway begins at its junction with the Seward Highway at **Milepost S 37**, Tern Lake Junction, 90 miles south of Anchorage. (It is at this junction that the Seward Highway becomes Alaska Route 9.) From here, the Sterling Highway (Alaska Route 1) travels 57 miles west to Cook Inlet, before turning south and following the west coast of the Kenai Peninsula 85 miles to the scenic town of Homer on Kachemak Bay. (This stretch of highway offers magnificent views across Cook Inlet of 3 active volcanoes: Redoubt, Iliamna and Augustine.) Across from Homer are the settlements of Halibut Cove and Seldovia, both accessible by boat.

The Sterling Highway provides access to the communities of Cooper Landing, Soldotna, Kenai (via the Kenai Spur Road), Kasilof, Clam Gulch, Ninilchik and Anchor Point. The Sterling Highway also provides access to the world-famous Kenai River and Russian River, Kasilof River and Anchor River, considered to be some of the most popular fishing rivers.

Hiking and canoeing are 2 equally well known pursuits on the Kenai Peninsula, and the Sterling Highway provides access to the popular Resurrection North Pass Trail and to canoe trails in the Kenai National Wildlife Refuge.

Detailed information about the attractions of the Kenai Peninsula, including the geography, history, communities, wildlife, fishing, camping and other recreation will be found in the SEWARD HIGHWAY section beginning on page 551, and in the STERLING HIGHWAY section beginning on page 581.

Seward Highway

CONNECTS: Anchorage to Seward, AK

Length: 127 miles   **Road Surface: Paved**   **Season: Open all year**

(See map, page 552)

(1) (9)

The Seward Highway is an Alaska Scenic Byway. (©Kathleen Barth)

Major Attractions:

©Meghan Mackey

Portage and Exit Glaciers, Mount Alyeska, Kenai Fjords National Park

Highest Summit:
Turnagain Pass 988 ft.

The 127-mile-long Seward Highway connects Anchorage with the community of Seward on the east coast of the Kenai Peninsula (driving time about 3 hours). The Seward Highway's outstanding scenic, historic and recreational resources have given it a triple designation: National Forest Scenic Byway, All-American Road and Alaska Scenic Byway.

The Seward Highway also provides access to Girdwood and Alyeska ski resort via the Alyeska Highway from **Milepost S 90**; to Whittier and to Portage Glacier via the Whittier/Portage Road from **Milepost S 78.9**; to Hope via the Hope Highway from **Milepost S 56.3**; and to the Sterling Highway from **Milepost S 37** (Tern Lake Junction), 90 miles south of Anchorage. The Sterling Highway leads to Soldotna, Kenai and Homer (see log of that route beginning on page 581).

The Seward Highway is open all year. Physical mileposts along this route reflect distance from Seward (Mile 0). There are no gas stations on the Seward Highway between **Milepost S 90** (Girdwood turnoff) and Seward.

The first 9 miles of the highway are referred to as the "New" Seward Highway, a major Anchorage thoroughfare (4-lane divided freeway) connecting South Anchorage with downtown. South of Anchorage, the Seward Highway is a paved, 2-lane highway with passing lanes.

Leaving Anchorage, the Seward Highway follows the north shore of Turnagain Arm through Chugach State Park and Chugach National Forest, permitting a panoramic view of the south shore and the Kenai Mountains on the Kenai Peninsula. The Kenai Peninsula is just that—a peninsula, measuring 150 miles long and 70 miles wide, extending southwest from Turnagain

Distance in miles	Alyeska	Anchorage	Hope	Seward	Whittier
Alyeska		42	56	95	28
Anchorage	42		88	127	60
Hope	56	88		75	52
Seward	95	127	75		91
Whittier	28	60	52	91	

Seward Highway Anchorage, AK, to Seward, AK

© 2014 The MILEPOST®

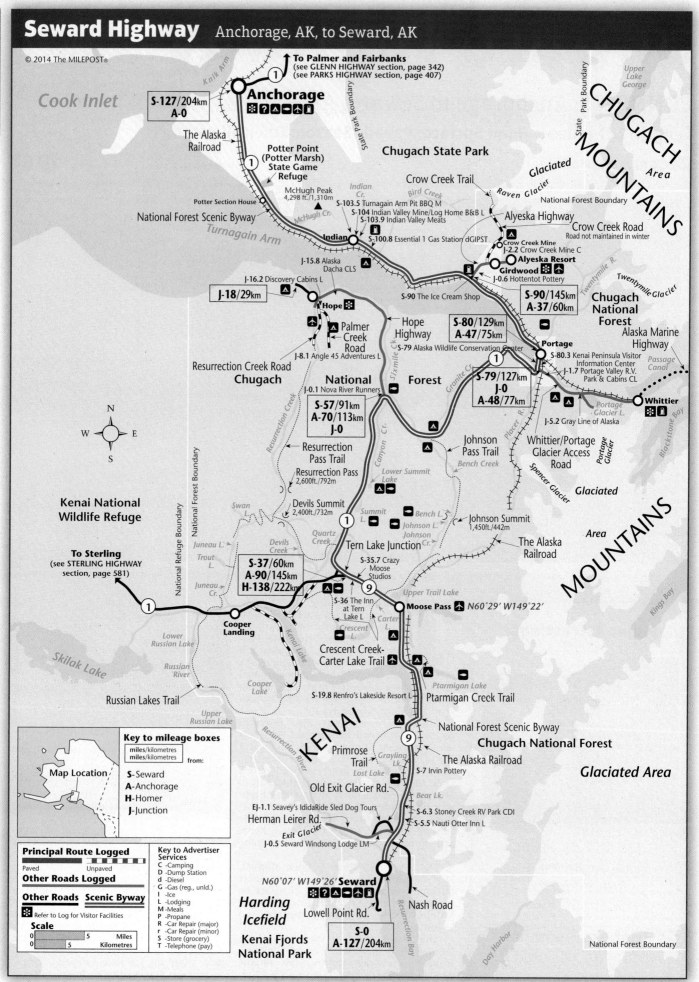

Cook Inlet

S-127/204km
A-0

To Palmer and Fairbanks
(see GLENN HIGHWAY section, page 342)
(see PARKS HIGHWAY section, page 407)

Anchorage

The Alaska Railroad

Potter Point
(Potter Marsh)
State Game
Refuge

Chugach State Park

McHugh Peak
4,298 ft./1,310m

Potter Section House

National Forest Scenic Byway

Turnagain Arm

Crow Creek Trail

Glaciated

Raven Glacier

National Forest Boundary

CHUGACH
MOUNTAINS Area

Upper
Lake
George

State Park Boundary

Indian
Cr.

Bird Creek

S-103.5 Turnagain Arm Pit BBQ M
S-104 Indian Valley Mine/Log Home B&B L
S-103.9 Indian Valley Meats

Indian

S-100.8 Essential 1 Gas Station dGIPST

McHugh Cr.

Alyeska Highway

Crow Creek Road
Road not maintained in winter

Crow Creek Mine
J-2.2 Crow Creek Mine C

Alyeska Resort

Girdwood
J-0.6 Hottentot Pottery

S-90 The Ice Cream Shop

S-90/145km
A-37/60km

Twentymile R.

Twentymile Glacier

Chugach
National
Forest

Alaska Marine
Highway

J-15.8 Alaska
Dacha CLS

J-16.2 Discovery Cabins L

J-18/29km

Hope

Palmer
Creek
Road

Hope
Highway

S-80/129km
A-47/75km

S-79 Alaska Wildlife Conservation Center

Portage

S-80.3 Kenai Peninsula Visitor
Information Center
J-1.7 Portage Valley R.V.
Park & Cabins CL

Passage
Canal

Resurrection Creek Road

J-8.1 Angle 45 Adventures L

Chugach

National

Forest

J-0.1 Nova River Runners

S-57/91km
A-70/113km
J-0

Resurrection
Pass Trail

Resurrection Pass
2,600ft./792m

Devils Summit
2,400ft./732m

Fix mile Ck.

Canyon Cr.

Lower Summit
Lake

Granite Cr.

Placer R.

S-79/127km
J-0
A-48/77km

J-5.2 Gray Line of Alaska

Whittier/Portage
Glacier Access
Road

Johnson
Pass Trail

Bench Creek

Johnson Summit
1,450ft./442m

Spencer Glacier

Portage
Glacier L.

Portage
Glacier

Whittier

Blackstone Bay

Glaciated

Area

Kenai National
Wildlife Refuge

National Refuge Boundary

National Forest Boundary

Swan
L.

Devils
Creek

Quartz
Creek

Juneau L.

Trout
L.

Juneau
Cr.

Summit
L.

Bench L.

Johnson L.
Johnson
Cr.

The Alaska
Railroad

MOUNTAINS

Kings Bay

To Sterling
(see STERLING HIGHWAY
section, page 581)

Tern Lake Junction

S-35.7 Crazy
Moose Studios

S-37/60km
A-90/145km
H-138/222km

S-36 The Inn
at Tern
Lake L

Upper Trail Lake

Moose Pass N60°29' W149°22'

Lower
Russian Lake

Russian
River

Cooper
Landing

Kenai Lake

Crescent
L.

Carter
L.

Crescent Creek-
Carter Lake Trail

Skilak Lake

Cooper
Lake

Upper
Russian Lake

Russian Lakes Trail

Resurrection River

KENAI

S-19.8 Renfro's Lakeside Resort L

Ptarmigan Lake

Ptarmigan Creek Trail

National Forest Scenic Byway

Chugach National Forest

Glaciated Area

Primrose
Trail

Grayling
Lk.

Lost Lake

S-7 Irvin Pottery

The Alaska Railroad

Old Exit Glacier Rd.

EJ-1.1 Seavey's IdidaRide Sled Dog Tours

Herman Leirer Rd.

Exit Glacier

J-0.5 Seward Windsong Lodge LM

Bear Lk.

S-6.3 Stoney Creek RV Park CDI

S-5.5 Nauti Otter Inn L

N60°07' W149°26' Seward

Harding
Icefield

Kenai Fjords
National Park

Lowell Point Rd.

S-0
A-127/204km

Nash Road

Day Harbor

National Forest Boundary

Key to mileage boxes

miles/kilometres
miles/kilometres   from:

S - Seward
A - Anchorage
H - Homer
J - Junction

Map Location

Key to Advertiser Services

C - Camping
D - Dump Station
d - Diesel
G - Gas (reg., unld.)
I - Ice
L - Lodging
M - Meals
P - Propane
R - Car Repair (major)
r - Car Repair (minor)
S - Store (grocery)
T - Telephone (pay)

Principal Route Logged

Paved   Unpaved

Other Roads Logged

Other Roads   Scenic Byway

Refer to Log for Visitor Facilities

Scale

0   5 Miles
0   5 Kilometres

Arm and Passage Canal. It is bounded to the east by the Gulf of Alaska, and to the west by Cook Inlet. The Seward Highway crosses the isthmus that separates the Kenai Peninsula from the rest of southcentral Alaska at **Milepost S 75**, 52 miles south of Anchorage.

Bike trails along the Seward Highway include a 3-mile trail between Indian and Bird; a 6-mile trail between Girdwood and Bird Point; and an 8-mile bike trail (the Six-mile Trail) between the Hope Highway junction and the Johnson Pass Trailhead.

There are also a number of trailheads along the Seward Highway for both Chugach State Park and Chugach National Forest hiking trails.

Emergency medical services: Phone 911. Hospitals in Anchorage and Seward, and in Soldotna (on the Sterling Highway). Alaska State Trooperes in Girdwood, phone (907) 783-0972; Crown Point (Moose Pass), (907) 288-3346; and Cooper Landing (on the Sterling Highway), (907) 595-1233. Emergency call boxes are located at Turnagain Pass (**Milepost S 68.5**); at **Milepost J 0.2** on the Hope Highway near junction (**S 56.3**), Summit Lake Lodge (**S 45.8**) and at the Sterling Highway junction. *NOTE: Cell phone service is sporadic between Anchorage and Seward.*

Seward Highway Log

Distance from Seward (S) is followed by distance from Anchorage (A).
Physical mileposts show distance from Seward. Many mileposts were missing in summer 2013.

ALASKA ROUTE 1

S 127 A 0 Gambell Street and 10th Avenue in Anchorage. The New Seward Highway (Gambell Street southbound, Ingra northbound) connects with the Glenn Highway in Anchorage via 5th Avenue (westbound) and 6th Avenue (eastbound). (See map on page 382 in the ANCHORAGE section.) Follow Gambell Street south.

S 126.8 A 0.2 Traffic light at 13th. Carr's/Safeway supermarket.

S 126.7 A 0.3 Traffic light at 15th Avenue. Access east to Merrill Field, Alaska Regional Hospital.

S 126.6 A 0.4 Access southbound to Sullivan sports arena, Ben Boeke ice rinks and baseball stadium.

Begin divided 4-lane highway southbound.

S 126 A 1 Traffic light at Fireweed Lane. Gas, shopping and services to west.

S 125.8 A 1.2 Traffic light at Northern Lights Boulevard (one-way westbound). Access west to Walgreens (open 24 hours) at northwest corner, and Sears Mall (southwest corner). Sears Mall was the first shopping mall in Anchorage. Fred Meyer and gas stations east side of highway (southbound traffic use Benson Blvd. for access).

S 125.7 A 1.3 Traffic light at Benson Boulevard (one-way eastbound). Fred Meyer access southbound.

S 125.4 A 1.6 Southbound access only to Old Seward Highway and 36th Ave. businesses; popular Moose's Tooth Pizza to west.

S 125.3 A 1.7 Traffic light at 36th Avenue. Providence Hospital and UAA campus are 2 miles east. Z.J. Loussac Library, Midtown post office, Century 16 Cinema,

fast-food and other services to the west.

Begin 4- to 6-lane freeway and 65 mph speed limit southbound. Begin 4-lane divided highway and 45 mph speed limit northbound.

S 124.7 A 2.3 Tudor Road overpass. Exit west for gas station, Dairy Queen, Home Depot, IHOP, Lowes and other businesses. Exit east for Anchorage Police, Municipal Animal Shelter, shopping and services.

S 124.4 A 2.6 Highway crosses Campbell Creek; Campbell Creek Greenbelt. Chugach Mountains are to the east.

S 123.7 A 3.3 Dowling Road underpass; exits east and west to businesses. Roundabouts at both Dowling off ramps: Exiting motorists are reminded to yield to traffic already in the circle; to follow the counter-clockwise traffic pattern in the circle without stopping; and to use turn signals when exiting the circle. Access to Anchorage recycling center to west.

S 123 A 4 76th Avenue exit (southbound traffic only) intersects Dimond Boulevard.

S 122.2 A 4.8 Dimond Boulevard overpass; exits on both sides of highway. Access west to **Sportsman's Warehouse**, Dimond Center Mall, 24-hour gas stations, fast-food and major shopping area. Gas stations and supermarkets to east.

S 120.7 A 6.3 O'Malley Road underpass; exits north and southbound. Turn east on O'Malley Road and drive 2 miles to reach the **Alaska Zoo**. Continue east on O'Malley for Chugach State Park Upper Hillside hiking trails (follow signs), which include the popular **Flattop Mountain** trail. Large structure visible on east side of this exit is Alaska's only indoor waterpark.

Turn west for Minnesota Drive to Ted Stevens Anchorage International Airport.

S 119.7 A 7.3 Huffman Road underpass; exits both sides of highway to roundabouts. Exit west for gas station, 24-hour supermarket, pharmacy, fast-food outlets and other services. South Anchorage residential area. The large inflated dome on the east side of the highway near this exit is an indoor golf driving range with 9-hole outdoor course; access via 1-way frontage road north on east side of freeway.

S 118.8 A 8.2 DeArmoun Road southbound exit only. (Northbound access to DeArmoun is via Rabbit Creek exit, then north on Old Seward Highway.)

S 118.1 A 8.9 Exit to Rabbit Creek Road (east), Old Seward Highway (west); access to South Anchorage subdivisions. The picturesque Chapel by the Sea overlooks Turnagain Arm. The church is often photographed because of its unique setting.

View of Turnagain Arm and Mount Spurr southbound. Seward Highway Scenic Byway sign southbound.

S 117.6 A 9.4 Turnoff to east at 154th for **Potter Marsh** access road to large parking area with restroom and access to a great place to take a walk and see wildlife (description follows). Turnoff to west for **Rabbit Creek Rifle Range** (ADF&G); description follows.

Potter Marsh (Anchorage Coastal Wildlife Refuge) is a very popular spot for bird watching. From the parking lot, an extensive boardwalk with interpretive signs crosses the marsh, a refuge and nesting area for waterfowl, including arctic terns, Canada geese, trumpeter swans, gulls and many small birds. Muskrats, foxes and other small animals are often seen here. Bring binoculars. The 564-acre marsh was created during construction of the Alaska Railroad when an embankment was built to support the railroad tracks and the resulting pond was filled with fresh water by area creeks.

Rabbit Creek Rifle Range is open to the public; summer and winter hours posted on gate or phone (907) 566-0130 for recorded information. Closed state holidays and all of December. Center-fire range, hand-gun range, rim-fire range, and archery range. Visit www.adfg.alaska.gov/index. cfm?adfg=anchoragerange.main.

Begin 2-lane highway southbound. Pass with care! Drive with headlights on at all times.

Begin 4-lane highway northbound.

CAUTION: High accident rate on Seward Highway southbound due to heavy traffic, variable weather conditions, speeding and unsafe passing. Be alert to shared passing lanes. Delay of 5 vehicles or more is illegal; use slow vehicle turnouts. Drive with headlights on at all times.

NOTE: Designated Highway Safety Corridor next 30.5 miles southbound. This des-

Watch for dall sheep along the Seward Highway. (©Kathleen Barth)

View of Turnagain Arm from Bird Ridge. Trailhead is at Milepost S 102.1. (©Kathleen Barth)

ignation is given to provide extra enforcement of speed limits and passing zones and discourage aggressive driving behavior in high accident areas. Traffic fines double in these zones. Highway Traffic Safety Corridor ends at Milepost S 90.

For avalanche conditions along the Seward Highway in winter, phone 511 or visit http://511.alaska.gov.

S 117.3 A 9.7 Distance marker southbound shows Girdwood 27 miles, Seward 115 miles, Homer 211 miles.

S 116 A 11 Potter Marsh pullout east side of highway.

S 115.4 A 11.6 Junction with Old Seward Highway; access to Potter Valley Road east to subdivision. Old Johnson trail begins 0.5 mile up Potter Valley Road; parking at trailhead. Only the first 10 miles of this state park trail are cleared. Moderate to difficult hike; watch for bears.

The natural gas pipeline from the Kenai Peninsula emerges from beneath Turnagain Arm here and follows the roadway to Anchorage.

WARNING: When the tide is out, the sand in Turnagain Arm might look inviting. DO NOT go out on it. Some of it is quicksand. You could become trapped in the mud and not be rescued before the tide comes in.

S 115.2 A 11.8 Entering Chugach State Park southbound. Turnoff to west for **Chugach State Park Headquarters**, housed in the Potter Section House. The historic structure was once home to a small crew of Alaska Railroad workers who maintained the tracks between Seward and Anchorage in the days of coal- and steam-powered locomotives.

Chugach State Park offers exceptional outdoor recreational opportunities year-round, including hiking, biking, fishing, camping, kayaking, rafting, climbing, ATV and snow machine riding, skiing, hunting and trapping.

Maps and information on Chugach State Park, as well as park parking passes, are available in the headquarters building. Open Mon.–Fri. 10 A.M.–4:30 P.M. (closed for lunch noon to 1 P.M.); phone (907) 345-5014 or visit http://dnr.alaska.gov/parks/units/chugach/.

S 115.1 A 11.9 Turnoff to east for **Potter Creek Viewpoint and Trail** (Chugach State Park). Small parking area overlooking marsh with interpretive signs about wetlands and the railroad's role in creating these accidental marshes. Also an interpretive sign about the feeding habits of moose, who eat in marshes like these as well as in the backyards of Anchorage residents. Moose can eat the equivalent in twigs of a 50-lb. sack of dog food a day. They munch twigs and strip bark from willow, birch and aspen trees.

Drive up the hill via 2-lane paved road for large parking area (fee area), viewing platform with telescopes, interpretive signs and hiking trails. The 0.4-mile nature trail examines the natural history of the surrounding forest, a blending of 2 climates: the continental climate (the boreal forest of Interior Alaska) and the wetter coastal climate (Sitka spruce, hemlock).

This is the Potter Creek Trailhead for **Turnagain Arm Trail**. From here to McHugh Creek Picnic Area (at **Milepost S 111.9** on the Seward Highway) it is 3.3 miles, making it a good choice for a family hike. One-way walking time is about 1½ hours. Turnagain Arm trail continues to Rainbow (7.5 miles) and to Windy Corner (9.4 miles) at **Milepost S 106.7** Seward Highway; see trail information signs. Turnagain Arm Trail parallels the Seward Highway and offers good views of Turnagain Arm. Rated as easy, with 250- to 700-foot elevation gains from the parking areas to the generally level trail on the hillside above the 4 trailheads.

S 114.7 A 12.3 Weigh stationto east.

S 114.5 A 12.5 Double-ended gravel turnout to east (posted no camping).

S 113.4 A 13.6 Gravel turnout to east.

S 113.3 A 13.7 Slow vehicle turnout to west for southbound traffic. *Delay of 5 vehicles illegal; must use turnouts.*

S 113.1 A 13.9 The first of several informal gravel turnouts used by rock climbers on the east side of the highway. Watch for rock climbers practicing on rock walls alongside the highway for about the next 6 miles southbound.

S 113 A 14 Informal gravel turnout to east at McHugh boulder area. The cliffs are part of the base of McHugh Peak (elev. 4,298 feet).

S 111.9 A 15.1 Easy-to-miss turnoff to east for **McHugh Creek Picnic Area**, uphill via paved side road. (Access road not recommended for vehicles over 24-feet.) This state wayside on the flank of McHugh Peak has 3 parking levels, each with outhouses. There is a $5 day-use fee (after a 30-minute grace period). Exceptional picnic overlook on second level with tables, grills and viewing platform with telescopes. Good view of Turnagain Arm. Access to McHugh Creek trailhead from third parking level. McHugh Creek trail connects to Turnagain Arm Trail. *Beware of bears.*

S 111.6 A 15.4 Informal turnout to east used by rock climbers.

S 110.3 A 16.7 Beluga Point scenic viewpoint and photo stop to west is a large paved double-ended turnout with a commanding view of Turnagain Arm. A good place to see bore tides and beluga whales. (The only all-white whales, belugas are easy to identify.) Tables, benches, telescopes and interpretive signs on orcas, bore tides, mountain goats, and Captain Cook.

Turnagain Arm is known for having one of the world's remarkably high tides, with a diurnal range of more than 33 feet. A bore tide is an abrupt rise of tidal water just after low tide, moving rapidly landward, formed by a flood tide surging into a constricted inlet such as Turnagain Arm. This foaming wall of water may reach a height of 6 feet and is very dangerous to small craft. To see a bore tide, check the Anchorage-area tide tables for low tide, then add approximately 2 hours and 15 minutes to the Anchorage low tide for the bore to reach points between 32 miles and 37 miles south of Anchorage on the Seward Highway. Visitors should watch for bore tides from Beluga Point south to Girdwood.

An easterly extension of Cook Inlet, Turnagain Arm was called Return by the Russians. Captain Cook, seeking the fabled Northwest Passage in 1778, called it Turnagain River, and Captain Vancouver, doing a more thorough job of surveying in 1794, gave it the present name of Turnagain Arm.

WARNING: Do not go out on the mud flats at low tide. The glacial silt and water can create a dangerous quicksand.

S 110.1 A 16.9 Gravel turnout to east used by rock climbers.

S 109.8 A 17.2 Slow vehicle turnout to west for southbound traffic. Watch for falling rocks.

S 109.2 A 17.8 Small paved turnout to west. Fresh water spigot out of rock wall across highway. (*A dangerous spot to cross the highway on foot: lots of fast-moving traffic.*)

S 108.7 A 18.3 Paved double-ended viewpoint to west; view of Kenai Mountains, Turnagain Arm.

S 108.3 A 18.7 Rainbow trailhead (Turnagain Arm Trail) parking east side of highway; posted no camping.

S 108.2 A 18.8 Paved turnout to west.

S 108.1 A 18.9 Parking east side of highway.

S 107.7 A 19.3 Turnout to west with Gold Rush Centennial signs "Hope Survives Gold Fever" and "Stampeders Flood the Arm" (excerpt follows):

Alexander King discovered gold in about 1890 on Resurrection Creek, across the Arm from here. Prospectors set up camp at the mouth of the creek, where supply boats could land, and named it—legend has it—after Percy Hope, a 17 year-old stampeder. By spring of 1896, Hope City was overrun by 700 gold seekers. Hope was

one of the largest towns in Alaska during its 1895-98 heyday. Many left Hope City for Sunrise City, the supply camp for prospectors working new gold discoveries at the mouth of Sixmile Creek, 8 miles east of Hope. While mining declined at Sunrise, commercial gold mining and new settlement kept Hope alive. Early residents like Robert Mathison and George Roll stayed after the stampede, making a life mining, hunting and subsistence gardening. Little mining is done around Hope these days, but the town's historic district retains the appearance and feel of its gold rush past.

S 106.9 A 20.1 Scenic viewpoint to west; popular rock climbing face, Goat's Head Soup begins here. Trail begins left of the big tree. Double-ended paved turnout. Popular spot to watch for Dall sheep on steep hillsides above highway (bring binoculars). *Do not feed wildlife. CAUTION: Watch for slowing traffic and watch for pedestrians on highway.*

S 106.7 A 20.3 Windy Corner Trail. Trailhead to Turnagain Arm Trail east side of highway; parking.

S 106.6 A 20.4 Shoulder parking to west.

S 105.7 A 21.3 Falls Creek Trailhead parking east side of highway. Moderate 1.5-mile hike along creek.

S 104.9 A 22.1 Very small single-vehicle turnout to east under rock overhang by small waterfall.

S 104.1 A 22.9 Very small, gravel, single-vehicle turnout to east.

S 104 A 23 Indian Valley Mine National Historic Site and **Log Home B&B** (description follows); gold panning, lodging.

©Kris Valencia, staff

Indian Valley Gold Mine/Log Home B&B. Alaskan family owned and operated National Historic Site. Hear true accounts of Peter Strong while touring miners' cabins as well as tall tales for plenty of laughs! Learn to pan here with guaranteed gold bearing paydirt. indianvalleymine.com; moorecreek.com. Phone (907) 653-1120. [ADVERTISEMENT]

S 103.9 A 23.1 Indian Road (paved) leads east up hill 0.3 mile to Forget-Me-Not Nursery and 0.4 mile to **Indian Valley Meats** (description follows).

Indian Valley Meats. Reindeer sausage and much more from this federally inspected processor of exotic game and fish. Fish boxes ready for shipping, gift packs with game jerky, smoked salmon and much more. Come visit our gift shop. Great buys! In business 34 years. Tour the stunning grounds, featuring flowers, rock walls, B&B. Just ½ mile up Indian Road. See display ad this page. [ADVERTISEMENT]

S 103.8 A 23.2 INDIAN (sign). Indian was first listed as a flag stop on the timetables of The Alaska Railroad in 1922. Its name is derived from the nearby creek.

S 103.5 A 23.5 Turnagain Arm Pit BBQ; drive-thru, hours posted.

Turnagain Arm Pit BBQ. Milepost 103.5. Open 7 days 12–9 P.M. Authentic southern "Q" on the shores of Turnagain Arm with the 'most stellar view of ANY BBQ place in the world.' Low'n'slow pit smoked brisket, pulled pork, ribs, beans'n'slaw, fried okra, real sweet tea and more! Beer'n'wine. Find us on Facebook and UrbanSpoon. www.turnagainarmpit.com. (907) 653-1953. Dine-in, take-out, drive-thru. We cater. 'Northern Exposure to Southern Smoke.' [ADVERTISEMENT]

S 103.4 A 23.6 Indian House restaurant (Current status unknown)

S 103.2 A 23.8 Ocean View Road. Access to Indian Valley trailhead (1.4 miles), a 6-mile moderately steep hike to Indian Pass. Turnagain House restaurant.

S 103.1 A 23.9 Bridge over **Indian Creek;** parking to west with outhouse, interpretive signs and telescope. Begin 3-mile-long Indian to Bird bike trail south to Bird Creek campground. Indian Creek is heavily fished for pink salmon, sea-run Dolly Varden, few silver salmon and rainbow.

S 103 A 24 Bar and motel to east; pay phone.

S 102.8 A 24.2 Valley Bible Chalet.

S 102.1 A 24.9 Bird Ridge Trailhead parking (fee) east side of highway. This steep 2.5-mile hike (moderate to difficult) is the first snow-free spring hike in Chugach State Park, according to rangers. Hike offers exceptional views of Turnagain Arm.

S 101.6 A 25.4 Bird Creek Access (Chugach State Park) to east. Large parking area with vault toilets just north of Bird Creek; $5 day-use fee. **Bird Creek** is a very popular fishing spot. Silver salmon run from late July through mid-August. Pink salmon (even-numbered years), from early July through mid-August. Check with ADF&G for current information on salmon runs and fishing regulations.

S 101.4 A 25.6 Highway crosses Bird Creek.

S 101.2 A 25.8 Bird Creek Campground and Day-Use Area, Chugach State Park. Parking area to east for day-use has interpretive signs, view telescope, picnic tables, toilet, firepits, and 20 overflow campsites. Campground on west side of highway has 28 campsites, firepits, pay phone, covered picnic tables, toilets and water. Firewood is sometimes available. Camping $15 per night and day-use fee $5. Paved 3-mile Indian to Bird bike trail goes through campground.

WARNING: Do not go out on the mud flats at low tide. The glacial silt and water can create a dangerous quicksand.

Bird Creek is a popular fishing spot for pink and silver salmon. Access from parking areas at Milepost S 101.6 and S 101.2. (©Kathleen Barth)

Viewpoints along the busy Seward Highway allow motorists a safe way to enjoy the scenery of Turnagain Arm. (©Sharon Nault)

S 100.8 A 26.2 Essential 1 Gas Station (diesel, propane and grocery).

Essential 1 Gas Station. See display ad this page.

S 100.7 A 26.3 Bird Ridge Motel & RV Park to east; lodging and RV park.

S 100.5 A 26.5 Bird House Garage.

S 100 A 27 Paved parking area adjacent bike trail to west.

S 99.9 A 27.1 Avalanche gates.

S 99.3 A 27.7 Paved parking area to west with view across Bird Flats on Turnagain Arm to the cut in the mountains where Sixmile Creek drains into the arm (the old mining settlement of Sunrise was located there). The town of Hope is to the south-

west. The peak visible across Turnagain Arm between here and Girdwood is Mount Alpenglow in the Kenai mountain range.

S 99.1 A 27.9 Double-ended paved turnout to west with plaque reads:

"This monument is dedicated to Mr. Brookman and the men and women of the Alaska Railroad and Alaska Dept. of Transportation who work on the front line each winter keeping Alaska's railroad and highways safe for the traveling public. While working to clear 2 avalanches that had closed the railroad and highway east of this site, Mr. Brookman from the Alaska Railroad and 2 co-workers from the Dept. of Transportation were engulfed by a third avalanche. Mr. Brookman died on Feb. 1, 2000, from injuries sustained in this tragic incident. His co-workers survived."

Prior to highway reconstruction in 2004-2005, the 9-mile corridor from here south to the Girdwood turnoff was known as "avalanche alley."

S 98.8 A 28.2 *Begin passing lane, begin 65 mph speed limit, southbound.*

End passing lane, begin 55 mph speed limit, northbound.

S 97.7 A 29.3 *End passing lane southbound.*

S 97.2 A 29.8 *Begin passing lane northbound.*

S 96.5 A 30.5 Southbound turn lane for **Bird Point Scenic Overlook** (Chugach State Park) to west. Very nice rest area with restrooms and a large parking lot. Day-use fee $5 after 30-minute grace period. Wheelchair-friendly walkway to sheltered viewpoint; benches, telescopes, information boards and an excellent view of Turnagain Arm. This is one of the best places along the arm to stop for a breather and enjoy the scenery. (Also a popular spot with local residents for weddings.)

Beluga whales are often spotted from Bird Point. Look for the sculptures of these white whales half buried at the end of the parking area. The sculptures are deliberately designed to reflect how belugas appear when swimming in the water.

Access from overlook parking area to the Bird Point to Girdwood ("Bird to Gird") Trail. This 6-mile bike trail goes over Bird Hill on the old Seward Highway alignment. The trail has information displays, viewpoints and telescopes along the way.

S 95.6 A 31.4 *Begin passing lane south-*

bound. CAUTION: Watch for 2 directional passing lanes.

S 95.3 A 31.7 Double-ended scenic turnout to west overlooking Turnagain Arm. Gold Rush Centennial signs about Sunrise City, a gold rush camp established in 1895 at the mouth of Sixmile Creek, and the Crow Creek Boys, a partnership of stampeders formed in 1896 to mine gold on Crow Creek near present-day Girdwood. ("The boys" sold out to 2 Nome mining engineers in the early 1900s, and Crow Creek mine went on to become one of the largest gold producing mines on Turnagain Arm.) Interpretive signs on Turnagain Arm (excerpt follows):

"The terrain surrounding Turnagain Arm varies widely, from flat-bottomed valleys to high, rocky peaks. Mountains around Turnagain Arm rise sharply from the shoreline to heights approaching 4,000 feet. Treeline occurs at about 1,500 feet here—much lower than in mountains of the Lower 48 states."

S 94.1 A 32.9 Scenic turnout to west with interpretive signs on belugas, hooligan and whales (excerpts follow):

"Five different populations of beluga whales live in Alaska. While 4 of these populations have overlapping ranges in the winter, the belugas living in Cook Inlet remain geographically separate and have grown genetically distinct. More than half of the Cook Inlet belugas disappeared in the 1990s, and they were declared 'depleted' under the Marine Mammal Protection Act. Belugas have very low birthrates—one pregnancy every 2 to 3 years. The isolated Cook Inlet belugas must recover to about 60 percent of its optimum population in order to survive. It is estimated this will take until at least 2025.

"Belugas feed on hooligan and salmon. Hooligan—small, oily members of the smelt family—are the first fish species to appear in Turnagain Arm in the spring, usually in late April or early May. They are followed a few weeks later by salmon. The fish are gone by late October or early November. The belugas are believed to winter over in southern Cook Inlet."

S 93.6 A 33.4 *End passing lane southbound.*

S 93.3 A 33.7 Double-ended scenic turnout to west overlooking Turnagain Arm with interpretive signs on beluga whales, tides, mudflats and bore tides.

S 92.7 A 34.3 *End passing lane northbound.*

S 92.5 A 34.5 Double-ended scenic turnout to west overlooking Turnagain Arm with interpretive signs on the 1964 earthquake, Portage Pass and Trails, Rails and Blacktop.

S 92.2 A 34.8 Large double-ended paved turnout to east. Watch for Dall sheep.

S 91.5 A 35.5 Double-ended scenic turnout to west overlooking Turnagain Arm with interpretive signs on glaciers (excerpt follows):

"Look at the mountains surrounding Turnagain Arm and you can see V- and U-shaped valleys. These valleys are formed by streams and glaciers eroding away their banks and beds. The V-shaped valleys began with a mere trickle of water following an irregularity in the ground's surface. U-shaped valleys start as stream valleys but are carved into wide-bottom valleys by glaciers. Sometimes a V-shaped notch forms in the bottom of a U-shaped valley. This happens when a stream erodes a channel in the bottom of a glacier-carved valley after the glacier has receded."

S 91 A 36 Distance marker shows Anchorage 36 miles.

S 90.5 A 36.5 Bridge crosses Tidewater Slough.

S 90.4 A 36.6 Leaving Chugach State Park southbound, entering the state park northbound.

Begin 55 mph speed zone southbound. Resume 65 mph speed limit northbound.

The 1964 Good Friday earthquake caused land to sink in the Turnagain Arm area, particularly apparent from here to **Milepost S**

74. As a result, many trees had their root systems invaded by salt water, as seen by the stands of dead spruce trees along here. Good bird watching, including bald eagles, arctic terns and sandhill cranes.

S 90.2 A 36.8 Toadstool Drive. Welcome to Girdwood sign southbound. Turnoff for Girdwood Railroad Station to east. Girdwood DOT maintenance station; parking, access to Bird to Gird bike trail.

End avalanche area southbound.

Begin passing lane northbound. Watch for 2-directional passing lanes.

S 90 A 37 Girdwood Junction. Girdwood Station Mall here has a 24-hour Tesoro station (dump station and water) with a convenience store and The Ice Cream Shop (ice cream cones, shakes, sundaes, espresso). Alaska State Troopers are located here: phone (907) 783-0972.

The Ice Cream Shop. See display ad this page.

This intersection of the Seward Highway and Alyeska Highway is "old" Girdwood. After the 1964 earthquake, Girdwood moved up the access road 2.1 miles to the New Girdwood townsite (see "Alyeska Highway" log on page 558).

Junction with 3-mile Alyeska Highway to Crow Creek mine, Girdwood and Alyeska Recreation Area. Worth the drive! See "Alyeska Highway" log beginning on page 558.

NOTE: Next gas available southbound on the Seward Highway is at Milepost S 1.7 (approximately 88 miles); next gas available northbound at Milepost S 100.8 (10.8 miles from here); next gas available westbound on Sterling Highway is at Milepost S 45, Sunrise (approximately 60 miles).

S 89.8 A 37.2 Glacier Creek bridge.

Wonderful views southbound of the glaciated Kenai Mountains

S 89.5 A 37.5 *Resume 65 mph speed limit southbound. Begin 55 mph speed zone northbound.*

S 89.1 A 37.9 Virgin Creek bridge. View of 3 hanging glaciers to east.

S 88.8 A 38.2 Distance marker southbound shows Seward 87 miles, Homer 183 miles.

S 88.2 A 38.8 Gravel road leads east to pond.

S 87.4 A 39.6 Abrupt turn west to rough gravel turnout at avalanche gun emplacement. Turnout to east.

Distance marker southbound shows Portage Glacier Road Junction 9 miles, Whittier 20 miles.

S 87 A 40 *IMPORTANT NOTE: Highway Safety Corridor next 30.5 miles northbound. This designation is given to provide extra enforcement of speed limits, passing zones and discourage aggressive driving behavior in high accident areas. Traffic fines double in these zones.*

S 86 A 41 Small parking area with Chugach National Forest boundary sign.

Watch for belugas on incoming tides and bald eagles on mud flats at low tide.

S 84.1 A 42.9 Peterson Creek. View of Blueberry Mountain. Watch for waterfalls on mountainsides east of the highway between Mileposts 84 and 83.

S 82 A 45 Good view of Spencer Glacier, directly ahead southbound. The Alaska Railroad offers excursions to Spencer Glacier in summer. Bartlett and Trail glaciers to the south of Spencer Glacier (Discovery Glacier

The Alyeska Aerial Tramway serves the resort's extensive mountain-top complex.
(©Kathleen Barth)

train trip). Pavement has rough surfaced areas next few miles.

S 81.1 A 45.9 *Begin 55 mph speed zone southbound. Slow for pedestrians and parked cars along this stretch of highway during hooligan fishing.*

S 81 A 46 Turnoff to east for gravel side road leading 0.3 mile to dead end at Twentymile River between railroad and highway bridges.

Distance marker northbound shows Girdwood 9 miles, Anchorage 46 miles.

S 80.7 A 46.3 Parking and boat launch to west at north end of Twentymile River Bridge (rough surface) Watch for dip-netters in the spring fishing for hooligan (also known as eulachon or candlefish), a species of smelt.

The Twentymile River flows out of Twentymile Glacier and other glaciers through a long green valley. Twentymile Glacier can be seen at the end of the valley to the northeast. Good hooligan fishing in May. These smelt are taken with long-handled dip nets. Pink, red and silver salmon 4 to 10 lbs., use attraction lures, best in August. Dolly Varden 4–10 lbs., eggs best, good all summer in clear-water tributaries.

S 80.5 A 46.5 Parking to east.

S 80.3 A 46.7 First turnoff southbound to Alaska Railroad parking area and visitor information center on east side of highway. This is the former Whittier shuttle vehicle loading area. Prior to the completion of the road to Whittier, the shuttle was the only means of overland transportation to Whittier. The Alaska Railroad currently offers day trips on the *Glacier Discovery Train* to Grand-

view and Spencer Glacier from their Portage facility. Kenai Peninsula Information Center (description follows) is located here.

Kenai Peninsula Visitor Information Center. First turnoff southbound to gift shop and reservation service for lodging,

tours and other activities. Discounts on glacier and wildlife cruises. Open 7 days a week from 9 A.M. to 6 P.M., Memorial Day through Labor Day. Phone (907) 783-3001. Alaska Railroad tickets available, daily departures from Portage. [ADVERTISEMENT]

S 80.1 A 46.9 Deteriorating buildings and rusting truck barely visible through overgrowth on the west side of the highway are all that remain of PORTAGE, once a flag stop on the Alaska Railroad. An estimated 50 to 100 residents of Portage were forced to move after the 1964 earthquake caused the land to drop between 6 and 12 feet along Turnagain Arm. High tides then flooded the area with salt water. (The dead trees you see along the highway here were killed by salt water.)

Leaving Game Management Unit 14C, entering unit 7, southbound.

S 80 A 47 Second turnoff southbound to former railroad loading area and Kenai Peninsula Visitor Information Center (reser-

(Continues on page 561)

Alyeska Highway

Historic Crow Creek Mine on Crow Creek Road. (©Kris Valencia, staff)

The 3-mile Alyeska Highway provides access to Crow Creek Road and the historic Crow Creek Mine, Girdwood, Mount Alyeska ski area, the Hotel Alyeska and Alyeska Resort. There are many restaurants, gift shops and accommodations in the Girdwood/Alyeska area. Major attractions include the Alyeska Aerial Tramway and rain forest hiking trails. Well worth the drive.

There is a bike trail along this highway. **Distance is measured from junction with Seward Highway (J).**

J 0 Girdwood Junction. Girdwood Station Mall here has a 24-hour Tesoro station (dump station and water) with a convenience store and **The Ice Cream Shop** (ice cream cones, shakes, sundaes, espresso). **Alaska State Troopers** are located here: phone (907) 783-0972.

The Ice Cream Shop. See display ad on page 557.

J 0.2 Bridge over Alaska Railroad tracks.

Paved bike trail to Alyeska Resort begins. This is also the south end of the Bird to Gird bike trail from Bird Point at **Milepost S 96.5** on the Seward Highway.

J 0.3 Forest Station Road. **Chugach National Forest Glacier Ranger District** office (P.O. Box 129, Girdwood, AK 99587;

phone 907/783-3242). Open 8 A.M. to 5 P.M. weekdays in summer; closed holidays. Maps and information available here.

J 0.6 Hottentot Pottery. Turn past the Candle Factory onto Hottentot Mine Road to #293. Beautiful, functional, porcelain pottery by award-winning potter Kathy Peters. Kathy has been creating magnificent casseroles, plates, goblets, bowls, mugs and other pieces for table and home since 1983. View and purchase pottery from the gallery. Phone (907) 783-2276. jbraham@alaska.net.
[ADVERTISEMENT]

J 0.7 Local transfer station to left. Access to fishing on **Glacier Creek.**

J 1.4 The Bike Shop; bike rentals in summer, ski and snowboard equipment in winter.

J 1.9 Junction with **Crow Creek Road** (not maintained in winter) which leads to: the Double Musky Inn (dining) at Mile 0.3; Iditarod Trail parking at Mile 1.4 and at Mile 2.5; parking for Glacier Creek handtram/Winner Creek Trail at Mile 2.7; and **Crow Creek Mine National Historic Site** at Mile 3. Crow Creek Mine is open May to September daily, gold panning, RV and tent campground.

Crow Creek Mine. See display ad this page.

Beyond Crow Creek Mine, the road narrows and continues to the trailhead for Crow Pass Trail at Mile 6. (Winner Creek and Crow Pass trails are part of the Iditarod National Historic Trail.) There is a vehicle turnaround area at the Crow Pass trailhead, but this road is not recommended for large RVs beyond Crow Creek Mine at Mile 3. Stop at Glacier Ranger District office at Mile-

post J 0.3 on the Alyeska Highway for more detailed information on area hiking trails.

J 2 California Creek bridge.

Girdwood

J 2.1 "New Girdwood Townsite" (sign) is located at the **junction** of Alyeska Highway, Hightower Road and Egloff Drive. **Population:** about 2,000. **Emergency Services: Alaska State Troopers,** Ph. (907) 783-0972. **EMS** and **Fire Dept.,** phone 911 or (907) 783-2511 or (907) 269-5711. **Medical Clinic: Girdwood Clinic,** across from the post office at the corner of Hightower and Lindblad, has a family nurse practitioner and is open Tuesday–Saturday, 10 A.M. to 6 P.M.; phone (907) 783-1355.

Visitor Information: There is no visitor center in Girdwood, but the Girdwood Chamber of Commerce publishes a free map of local businesses, or visit www.girdwoodchamber.com for more information. **Radio:** KEUL 88.9.

Newspaper: *Turnagain Times,* bimonthly.

The town was named after Col. James Girdwood, who established a mining operation near here in 1901.

Today, Girdwood has a substantial year-round community and a flourishing seasonal population, thanks to its appeal as both a winter and summer resort destination. Recent (2012) construction in the downtown area created paved streets, sidewalks and a lovely town park with beautiful landscaping, lights and seating.

Lodging & Services

Girdwood offers bed-and-breakfast accommodations (see ads this section) as well as home and condo rentals. The nearest major hotel is the Hotel Alyeska, a 2-mile drive from downtown Girdwood. Girdwood's Alyeska Hostel, located at 227 Alta Dr., has dormitory bunks, private rooms and cabins; phone (907) 783-2222 or visit www.alyeskahostel.com. There are several restaurants in the Girdwood area. Girdwood has a grocery, laundromat, vacation rental offices, a school (K thru 8), library and fire hall. Girdwood Post Office is located at 118 Lindblad Avenue; open weekdays 9 A.M. to 12 P.M. and 1 P.M. to 5 P.M., Saturdays 10 A.M. to noon. Flightseeing services at Girdwood airport.

Alyeska Accommodations. "Has-it-all" for lodging in Girdwood. Offering affordable rooms, efficient condos with private baths and kitchens, cozy cabins with hot tubs, and luxury mountain homes with

glacier views and romantic fireplaces. With Girdwood's largest inventory of nightly vacation rentals, we have accommodations for every budget. Only 35 minutes from Anchorage along scenic Turnagain Arm. Stop by our office on Olympic Mountain

Loop for your key and helpful information. Open year-round, 7 days a week, with after hours courtesy phone available; phone (907) 783-2000, 1-888-783-2001. www.alyeska accommodations.com; info@alyeskaaccommodations.com. See display ad this page. [ADVERTISEMENT]

Bud & Carol's Bed & Breakfast is a custom-built home at the base of Mount Alyeska. Two beautiful guest rooms and fully equipped kitchen on ground level. No stairs! Each guest room has queen bed, free WiFi, cable TV/VCR/DVD, private bath, double vanities and jacuzzi. Mountain views! Families welcome. Non-smoking, no pets. Summer vacationers' paradise. Skiers/boarders winter dream home. Open year-round. Located at 211 Brighton Road. Phone (907) 783-3182. Email: budcarolbb@gmail. com. www.budandcarolsbandb.com. See display ad this page. [ADVERTISEMENT]

Chair Five Restaurant. A favorite of locals and travelers since 1983. One of Alaska's original roadhouses, Chair 5 is a must stop for fabulous dining and drinking. Daily offerings include fresh Alaskan halibut, salmon, and our famous gourmet burgers, ground fresh in Alaska at Mr. Prime Beef and Indian Valley Meats, or enjoy one of our homemade gourmet, fresh dough pizzas that get rave reviews. Also the home of Alaska's original "Deep Dish Square Pizza." Or order a huge, fresh, (never frozen), hand-cut rib-eye steak. Offering one of the largest selections of single malt scotches in Alaska with over 60 microbrews and 45 small batch tequilas. So stop in, say hi to Spike, enjoy the jukebox and join us in the bar for a game of pool. "The road goes on forever but the party never ends." Open daily 11 A.M.–1 P.M. Located at 5 Lindblad Avenue in the "New Girdwood Town Square." AMEX/MC/Visa/Diners/Discover. Phone (907) 783-2500. www.chairfive.com. [ADVERTISEMENT]

Camping

The only RV and tent campground in the Girdwood area is at Crow Creek Mine on Crow Creek Road Mile 3. However, tent camping (20 walk-in sites) is available next to Girdwood Lions Park (turn on Egloff Drive). Overnight RV parking is available at the Alyeska Resort Daylodge parking area (turn off at **Milepost J 2.9** Alyeska Highway). Fee is $10/night, no hookups.

Attractions

Crow Creek Mine. A historic site dating to 1896 that offers a glimpse into the Alaska Gold Rush past as well as a chance to pan for gold. Call ahead for privately guided tours. Open daily May–September. Call for winter activities. RVs and tenters welcomed; WiFi available. Phone (907) 229-3105.

Girdwood Lions Park, known locally as Forest Fairgrounds, is at the corner of Hightower Road, Egloff Drive and Alyeska Highway. The park hosts the big annual **Girdwood Forest Fair**. This popular summer crafts fair, which draws thousands of visitors, will be held July 4–6, 2014, and features crafts, food and entertainment. There is a playground, baseball field and 18-hole disc golf course.

The Alyeska Blueberry Festival takes place in August at the Hotel Alyeska. The outdoor festival celebrates blueberry season and features live music and food vendors.

Local artists are also on display at the Girdwood Center of Visual Arts. This artists' co-op studio, located on Olympic Mountain Loop, adjacent The Bake Shop, is open daily in summer and free to the public.

Hiking trails in the area include Winner Creek Gorge Trail and Upper Winner Creek Trail. Both of these Chugach National Forest trails begin near the Alyeska Aerial Tramway ticket office. The Winner Creek trail is a good one to experience Girdwood's rain forest and a good day hike for the entire family. The 2.5-mile-long trail is a pleasant hike with no severe ups or downs and a maximum elevation gain of only 260 feet. Wooden planking keeps hikers above most soggy spots. The trail leads through a tall spruce and hemlock forest to the picturesque

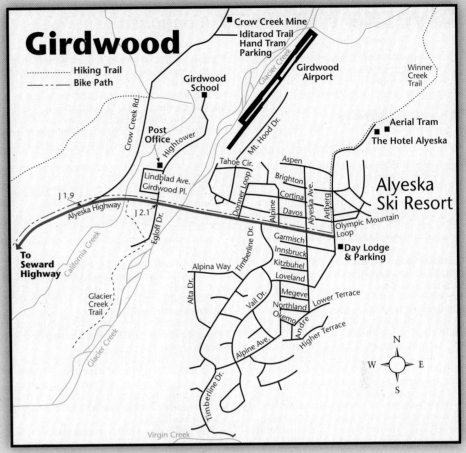

Alyeska Highway *(Continued)*

gorge where Winner Creek cascades through a small cleft in the rocks. Upper Winner Creek Trail climbs 5.5 miles beyond Winner Creek gorge and is a good overnight hike.

Alyeska Highway
(continued)

J 2.2 Glacier Creek bridge.

J 2.5 Donner Drive access to Girdwood airstrip (follow signs); flightseeing.

Private Aircraft: Girdwood airstrip; elev. 150 feet; length 2,100 feet; gravel; unattended.

J 2.6 Timberline Drive to residential area of Girdwood. Trailhead parking at end of road for **Virgin Creek Falls** hike.

J 2.9 Alyeska Highway ends at **junction** with Arlberg Avenue, which forks; turn south (right) for Alyeska Daylodge; overnight RV parking in summer, ski school and rentals in winter. Turn north (left) and continue with this log for the Hotel Alyeska and tram at **Milepost J 4.1**. Bike and walking path continues to hotel.

Alyeska Resort, Alaska's largest ski area, is a popular year-round destination that includes The Hotel Alyeska and the mountaintop Seven Glaciers restaurant, as well as the ski area and its facilities.

Ski season is generally from mid-Nov.–April. Facilities include the 60-passenger aerial tramway, which operates year-round and departs from The Hotel Alyeska (see description at **Milepost J 4.1**); 2 high-speed detachable quads, 2 fixed-grip quads, 2 double chair lifts and 2 Magic Carpets. Night skiing is available during holiday periods in December, and Thursday through Saturday, January through March. Ski school, ski rental shop and sports shops are available. Phone (907) 754-7669 for information. A popular skiing event at Alyeska in April is the **Spring Carnival and Slush Cup**, known as the "biggest beach party this side of

Hawaii." Skiers in costume ski downhill then try to jump across a 100-foot-long pond of ice cold water.

Summer activities include sightseeing, hiking, mountain biking, paragliding, berry picking and flightseeing. The Alyeska Mountain Run is held in August, the final stop for the Alaska Mountain Runners Grand Prix series.

Alyeska Resort. See display ad this page.

J 3 Olympic Circle; access to **Alyeska Accommodations** and The Bake Shop.

Alyeska Accommodations. See display ad on page 559.

J 3.1 Bud & Carol's Bed & Breakfast. See display ad on page 559.

J 3.2 Gravel turnout by Moose Meadows; watch for moose, bears and other wildlife. Access to bike trail which extends to Hotel Alyeska and connects with the Bird to Gird trail from Bird Creek.

J 3.9 Entrance to the Hotel Alyeska; follow signs for parking and shuttle bus to hotel and tram.

J 4.1 "T" **junction**: turn left for parking and shuttle to **The Hotel Alyeska** and Aerial Tramway Terminal; turn right for passenger drop-off only (no parking) at tramway terminal. Our Lady of the Snows church is located near the parking area.

The 304-room deluxe chateau-style Hotel Alyeska features 5 dining venues including a coffee bar cafe, sushi bar, plus a full service spa and 3 retail shops and a fitness center with indoor swimming pool, sauna, whirlpool and exercise room. For information phone (907) 754-1111 or 1-800-880-3880; www.alyeskaresort.com.

The **Alyeska Aerial Tramway** transports visitors to the 2,300-foot level of Mount Alyeska (the mountain's summit is at 3,939 feet) and a mountaintop complex featuring fine dining at Seven Glaciers Restaurant and casual dining at the Glacier Express

Upper Virgin Creek Trail from end of Timberline Drive leads 0.2 mile to view of Virgin Creek Falls. (©Kathleen Barth)

(check for food service hours before departing base). The 60-passenger enclosed tram is a great sightseeing choice for anyone, especially those who have difficulty walking or negotiating stairs. There is a passenger drop-off right in front of the tram, and there is elevator access to the tram level at both the bottom of the mountain and the top. Panoramic views from the top of surrounding glaciers, Turnagain Arm and the Chugach Mountains. The Roundhouse Museum here features Alyeska history; open daily in summer, 10 A.M. to 7 P.M.

Hikers can use the **North Face Trail** to reach the top of Mount Alyeska. The scenic, winding, 2.2-mile trail takes 1 to 1 ½ hours to hike, climbing 2,300 feet. Stop to catch your breath and enjoy the stunning views above tree line. The trail begins near the tram terminal at the resort. Hikers can get a free tram ride back down the mountain.

The tram operates daily in summer (beginning late May) from 9:30 A.M. to 9:30 P.M. Tram cars depart every 10 to 15 minutes. Purchase tickets at the ticket windows at the foot of the tram. Check current schedule and rates by phoning (907) 754-2275. It is closed for 2 weeks in May and mid-Oct.–mid-Nov. for annual maintenance.

Winner Creek Trail for hikers and bikers (cyclists walk bikes first 0.3 mile) begins directly above the tram's lower terminal. Continue 1.2 miles to junction with the Upper Winner Creek Trail. Stay on Lower Winner Creek Trail until you reach the hand-tram across Glacier Creek. Hikers can make the 7.7-mile Girdwood Valley Loop rail by crossing Glacier Creek via the hand-tram to Crow Creek Road, walking down Crow Creek Road to the Alyeska Highway and returning via the bike path back to the resort parking lot. Check bulletin board at Winner Creek trailhead for bear alerts.

5K Nordic Loop trail system begins at the end of Arlberg Ave. close to Hotel Alyeska. Multi-use in summer, ski-only, winter.

**Return to Milepost S 90
Seward Highway**

(Continued from page 557)

vation service for lodging, tours and other activities).

S 79.4 A 47.6 Portage Creek No. 2 bridge. Parking to west at south end of bridge. This gray-colored creek carries the silt-laden glacial meltwater from Portage Glacier and Portage Lake to Turnagain Arm. Mud flats in Turnagain Arm are created by silt from the creek settling close to shore.

S 79 A 48 Turnoff to west just north of Portage Creek No. 1 bridge for **Alaska Wildlife Conservation Center**. This 140-acre drive-through animal park is a major attraction and well worth the stop. Dedicated to the rehabilitation of orphaned and injured animals, AWCC works year-round with state and federal agencies, providing wildlife emergency treatment, rescue and care. Bear viewing is particularly popular here, with up-close looks at both adult and juvenile brown bears. A new bear enclosure with an elevated walkway (completed in 2013) provides a unique viewing experience.

Along with bears, the center features eagles, owls, caribou, moose, musk-oxen, elk, Sitka black-tailed deer, and bison. The bison has been extinct in Alaska for more than 100 years. AWCC is involved with the state's wood bison reintroduction program.

A log lodge houses the AWCC gift shop and a snackbar operates on the lodge deck during the summer months. Admission and gift store purchases contribute to the animal care program. Open year-round, daily in summer. Admission fee per person with a $30 maximum per vehicle. Phone (907) 783-2025 for current hours and fees.

Alaska Wildlife Conservation Center. See display ad on page 387 in the ANCHORAGE section.

Portage Creek No. 1 bridge.

S 78.9 A 48.1 Turnoff for Whittier and Portage Glacier. Access to **Portage Valley R.V. Park & Cabins** at Mile 1.7 Whittier/Portage Glacier Road. Large gravel turnout to east. △

Junction with Whittier/Portage Glacier Access Road, which leads 5.4 miles to Portage Glacier and 11.4 miles to Whittier. See "Whittier/Portage Glacier Access Road" log beginning on page 562.

S 78.4 A 48.6 **Placer River** bridge (rough surface); parking and access east side of highway at south end of bridge.

The Placer River has good hooligan fishing in May. These smelt are taken with long-handled dip nets. Silver salmon may be taken in August and September.

Between Placer River and Ingram Creek, there is an excellent view on clear days of Skookum Glacier to the northeast. To the north across Turnagain Arm is Twentymile Glacier. Arctic terns and waterfowl are often seen in the slough here.

S 77.9 A 49.1 Placer River overflow bridge has rough surface. Paved turnout to east at south end of bridge.
Begin 55 mph speed zone northbound.
S 77.8 A 49.2 Distance marker southbound shows Seward 76 miles, Homer 172 miles.
S 76 A 51 *Road work next 10 miles (summer 2013). Expect continued construction and/or improved highway in 2014.*
S 75.6 A 51.4 Distance marker northbound shows Portage 4 miles, Whittier 15 miles.
S 75.5 A 51.5 Paved double-ended Scenic Byway turnouts both sides of highway.
Road access to **Ingram Creek** from eastside turnout; fishing. 🐟
S 75.2 A 51.8 Bridge over Ingram Creek.
CAUTION: The Seward Highway from Ingram Creek through Turnagain Pass to Summit Lake has a high number of traffic accidents due to speeding and unsafe passing. DRIVE CAREFULLY!
S 75 A 52 Paved turnout to west; Welcome to the Kenai Peninsula sign. The Seward Highway has now crossed the isthmus that separates the Kenai Peninsula from the rest of southcentral Alaska.
Highway climbs next 6.5 miles southbound to Turnagain Pass.
S 74.9 A 52.1 *Passing lane begins southbound and extends 5.7 miles.*
S 74.5 A 52.5 Long paved double-ended turnout to east for northbound traffic.
S 72.5 A 54.5 Double-ended paved turnout to east for northbound traffic.
S 71.4 A 55.6 Long paved double-ended turnout to west for southbound traffic.
S 71.2 A 55.8 Double-ended paved turnout to west for southbound traffic.
S 70.9 A 56.1 Large paved turnout to east for northbound traffic.
S 68.8 A 58.2 *Passing lane ends southbound. Begin 1.4-mile divided highway southbound. End divided highway northbound.*
Wide shoulder to east next 0.2 mile northbound for slow vehicles.
S 68.5 A 58.5 **Turnagain Pass Recreation Area** (elev. 988 feet). Parking area west side of highway with restrooms (southbound lane). Paved loop walking path. *Emergency phone.* U-turn lane.

Turnagain Pass Recreation Area is a favorite winter recreation area for snowmobilers (west side of highway) and cross-country skiers (east side of highway). Snow depths here frequently exceed 12 feet. Patches of snow here into June.
S 68 A 59 Parking area east side of highway with restrooms and picnic tables for northbound traffic. A 1/4-mile trail crosses Lyon Creek and ends at a remote picnic site; a ski trail (not developed for summer use) continues up to Center Ridge. U-turn lane.
S 67.7 A 59.3 Bridge over Lyon Creek.

The highway traverses an area of mountain meadows and park like stands of spruce, hemlock, birch and aspen interlaced with glacier-fed streams. The many flowers seen in surrounding alpine meadows here include lupine, wild geranium, yellow and purple violets, mountain heliotrope, lousewort and paintbrush.
S 67.5 A 59.5 *End divided highway southbound, begin 1.4-mile divided highway northbound.*
S 67.4 A 59.6 Gravel access to west to informal camping.
S 66.8 A 60.2 Paved double-ended turnout to east. Beaver dam north of turnout.
(Continues on page 567)

Meeting some moose at the Alaska Wildlife Conservation Center. *(©Kris Valencia, staff)*

Whittier/Portage Glacier Access Road

The MV Ptarmigan cruises past Begich, Boggs Visitor Center on Portage Lake.
(©Meghan Mackey, staff)

As its name suggests, this side road allows access to Portage Glacier, 5.4 miles from the Seward Highway, which along with the Begich, Boggs Visitor Center is a major attraction for visitors, and to Whittier (11.4 miles), gateway to Prince William Sound.

The stretch of road between Portage Glacier and Whittier was the culmination of a 3-year project to connect that community to the road system. Opened in June 2000, the road branches off the older Portage Glacier Highway. Prior to construction of the Whittier spur road, Whittier was accessible overland only by train.

The Whittier vehicle access spur required the modification of the 2.5-mile-long Anton Anderson Memorial Tunnel to handle both railroad and vehicle traffic. The Anton Anderson tunnel is 1-lane, and cars and trains take turns travel-ing through it. In summer, the tunnel is open daily 5:30 A.M. to 11:15 P.M., allow-ing 15-minute alternating directional use for vehicle traffic every half-hour except during scheduled passenger trains. Vehicles must wait in the staging areas on either end of the tunnel when the train is using the tunnel. It is recommended that motor-ists arrive at least 5 minutes before the scheduled tunnel opening. *NOTE: It is espe-cially important that motorists with ferry res-ervations out of Whittier time their arrival to allow for the tunnel opening as well as for ferry check-in.*

Tunnel tolls are charged according to vehicle class and are round-trip. Tolls are as follows: Motorcycles and passenger vehicles and RVs (less than 28 feet) not pulling trail-ers, $12; RVs 28 feet or greater not pulling trailers/towing vehicles, or less than 28 feet pulling a trailer, $20; RVs 28 feet or greater pulling a trailer/towing vehicles, $35. Tolls are paid by eastbound motorists at the Bear Valley staging area. Tolls are not charged for vehicles traveling westbound from Whittier to Portage. *NOTE: Bicycles and pedestrians are NOT permitted in the tunnel.*

For current tolls and more tunnel infor-mation phone (907) 566-2244 from Anchor-age; toll-free (877) 611-2586; or visit www.tunnel.alaska.gov.

Distance is measured from junction with the Seward Highway (J).

J 0 Junction with Seward Highway at **Milepost S 78.9.** *CAUTION: Alaska Railroad crossing.*

J 1.2 Moose Flats Day-use Area; picnic tables, hiking trails, beautiful glacier-fed ponds with accessible docks and outhouses. RV pull-throughs and litter bins. The "Wet-land Walk" is a ¼-mile gravel and boardwalk trail with interpretive displays. The longer Trail of Blue Ice extends 5 miles to Portage Lake and the Begich, Boggs Visitor Center. The trail is level and perfect for easy hiking, biking and cross-country skiing. Non-motor-ized use only.

J 1.4 Alder Pond Day-use Area to south; parking, picnic tables, out-house, garbage bin. Hiking trails to fishing docks; trout fishing.

J 1.7 Portage Valley R.V. Park & Cabins. See display ad this page.

J 2.4 Explorer Glacier Viewing Area; dou-ble-ended paved turnout. Access to Trail of Blue Ice, picnic tables, interpretive kiosk.

J 3.2 Tangle Pond access to east. Trout fishing.

J 3.6 Turnout to north with creek access.

J 3.7 Black Bear USFS Campground; 13 sites designed for tents and pop-up camp-ers (no RVs). First-come, first-served only. Campfire rings, bear-proof dumpster, bear-proof food containers, water pump, picnic tables and outhouses. No hookups, no dump station. Camping fee $14. Pleasant spruce tree wooded area.

J 4.1 Williwaw Fish Viewing Platform. Spawning reds, chum and pink salmon can be viewed from late July to mid-September. Trailhead for the Williwaw Nature Trail is located to the right of the platform. This trail connects to the Trail of Blue Ice and connects back to the Fish Viewing Platform to create a 2-mile loop. Williwaw Creek is closed to all salmon fishing.

J 4.3 Williwaw USFS Campground, beautiful campground south of road below Middle Glacier; 59 fully accessible paved campsites designed for RV and tent camp-ing; some pull-throughs; campground host; campfire rings, bear-proof dumpster, bear-proof food containers, water pump, picnic tables and outhouses. No hookups, no dump station. Camping fee $18 single, $28 double. Some sites may be reserved, the rest are first-come, first served. (For reserva-tions, phone 1-877-444-6777 or visit www.recreation.gov; $9 online reservation fee, $10 for call center reservation.)

CAUTION: Unexploded artillery shells from avalanche mitigation may be found in various locations in Portage Valley. While extremely rare, if you do find one, mark its location 10 feet away with a rock pile or bright cloth. Report it to the Alaska State Troopers in Girdwood; (907) 783-0972.

J 4.5 Parking near river, picnic table.

J 5.2 Road forks: right fork leads to Por-tage Glacier Day Lodge; 0.2 mile to Begich, Boggs Visitor Center at Portage Lake; 1.2 miles to Byron Glacier trailhead and 1.5 miles to Portage Glacier Cruises (descriptions follow). Left fork leads to Whittier (continue with this log).

Begich, Boggs Visitor Center at Por-tage Lake focuses on the Chugach National Forest and its rich natural and cultural his-tory. U.S. Forest Service interpreters are available to answer questions and present programs. Main exhibit rooms are arranged so visitors have a sense of walking up Por-tage Valley, through Portage Pass and down into Prince William Sound. Visitors may also enter the "Alaskans and Their Stories" room, where they can read or listen to stories about real people who lived in this area. The "Wild

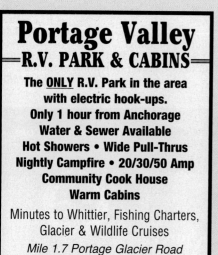

Side" room focuses on animals that live in the Chugach National Forest. Displays include a life-size moose and calf as well as a life-sized model of Smokey Bear.

The Visitor Center includes a 200-seat theater that shows the award-winning "Voices from the Ice" and the Portage Valley Learning Center, a 100-seat classroom facility. The center is named for congressmen Nick Begich of Alaska and Hale Boggs of Louisiana, both of whom died in a plane crash in 1972.

The Visitor Center is open daily, 9 A.M. to 6 P.M., from Memorial Day weekend to mid-September, and also for the last 2 weekends in September. For more information visit http://www.fs.usda.gov/detail/chugach/home?cid=stelprdb5251094 or phone the visitor center at (907) 783-2326 (May–Sept.) or (907) 783-3242 (Oct.–April). Fee $5 for adults 16 and older to access the exhibit hall and movie. Season passes are available. Interagency Federal Lands Passes, including the Annual, Senior and Access Passes, are sold and honored; all provide free entry for pass holder and 3 others.

At lakefront parking lot of Portage Lake, look for the trailhead for the "Trail of Blue Ice" which leads 5 miles, semi-paralleling the road, back to the Moose Flats Day-Use area. It is for non-motorized use only and is a lovely walk or bike ride.

Just past the Portage Glacier Day Lodge is Byron Glacier Road which leads to **Byron Glacier Trail**. Trailhead is 0.6 mile down the road, second parking lot on the right. This 0.8-mile trail makes a good family outing, according to the Forest Service, with a flat, well-maintained path to the glacier viewpoint, followed by a rocky path with small stream crossings to the snowfields below Byron Glacier. Avalanche danger can exist in the early part of the summer.

Drive past the trailhead 0.3 mile for **M/V Ptarmigan** boat dock and passenger waiting area. Portage Glacier Cruises offers daily sightseeing trips on Portage Lake at 10:30 A.M., noon, 1:30, 3 and 4:30 P.M., from mid-May to mid-September. Portage Glacier has retreated dramatically in recent years. Up until the early 1990s, the glacier was within view of the visitor center, but in recent years it has retreated around the corner of Byron Peak's northeast ridge. This cruise is the only way to get an up-close view of Portage Glacier. A U.S. Forest interpreter is onboard the vessel.

Gray Line of Alaska Portage Glacier Cruise. See display ad this page.

J **5.3** Whittier Road crosses Portage Creek and enters 450-foot tunnel under Begich Peak.

J **6** Placer Creek.

J **6.1** Large paved parking area provides views of Begich, Bogg Visitor Center, Portage Lake, Byron Glacier and part of the receding Portage Glacier. Sign about tunnel tolls.

There are several excellent spots in the area to observe salmon spawning (August and September) in Portage Creek and its tributaries.

J **6.7** Toll booths at **Bear Valley staging area.** The 8-lane staging area controls vehicle traffic entering the **Anton Anderson Memorial Tunnel.** The tunnel uses a computerized traffic-control system that regulates both rail and highway traffic. Each vehicle class is metered into the tunnel at different time intervals, with commercial trucks entering the tunnel last. The speed limit in the tunnel is 25 mph. It takes 6.5 minutes for a vehicle

to travel through the tunnel. The tunnel's ventilation system combines jet and portal fans. It is the longest highway tunnel and longest combined highway/railroad tunnel in North America at 13,200 feet.

NOTE: Motorcycles need to be particularly cautious of the slick surface inside the tunnel and avoid getting near or crossing the steel railways.

The Anton Anderson Memorial Tunnel through Maynard Mountain was built in 1941–43 as part of the Whittier Cutoff, a 12.4-mile-long railway line constructed to safeguard the flow of military supplies from the port of Whittier. The tunnel was named in 1976 for the chief engineer of that project—Anton Anderson. The railway line includes a second tunnel between Bear Valley and Portage that is 4,910 feet long.

J **6.8** Entering Anton Anderson Memorial Tunnel eastbound.

J **9.6** Exiting Anton Anderson Memorial Tunnel eastbound.

J **10** Whittier staging area for westbound tunnel traffic.

J **10.1** Rest area, pay phone and interpretive signs.

J **10.2** Shakespeare Creek.

Chugach National Forest access road to Portage Pass trailhead. This trail has a 750-foot elevation gain.

J **11.1** Whittier Street. Access to paid parking lot, camping and Whittier businesses.

J **11.2** Whittier Boat Harbor.

J **11.3** Whittier Creek.

J **11.4** Alaska State Ferry terminal.

Whittier

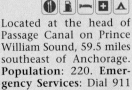

Located at the head of Passage Canal on Prince William Sound, 59.5 miles southeast of Anchorage. **Population:** 220. **Emergency Services:** Dial 911 or City Police, Fire Dept. and Ambulance, phone (907) 472-2340. **Clinic:** Whittier Health Clinic, phone (907) 472-2303. Alaska State Troopers: In Girdwood, phone (907) 783-0972. **Harbormaster:**

phone (907) 472-2330.

Visitor Information: Stop by the Harbormaster's office or ask at local businesses. Visit the Greater Whittier Chamber of Commerce website at www.whittieralaskachamber.org or the City of Whittier website at www.whittieralaska.gov. The U.S. Forest Service yurt, located at the West Boat

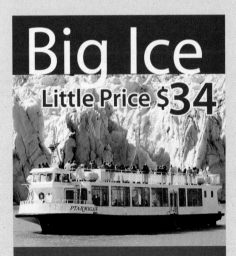

Whittier is a great place to enjoy waterfront sightseeing, fishing, shopping and dining.
(©Kris Valencia, staff)

Whittier/Portage Glacier Access Road (Continued)

Launch Ramp, has information on kayaking and camping in Prince William Sound.

Elevation: 30 feet. **Climate**: Normal daily temperature for July is 56°F; for January, 25°F. Maximum temperature is 84°F and minimum is -29°F. Mean annual precipitation is 174 inches, including 260 inches of snow. Winter winds can reach speeds of 60mph and greater.

Private Aircraft: Airstrip adjacent northwest; elev. 30 feet; length 1,100 feet; gravel; no fuel; unattended. *CAUTION: Bird activity in area.* Runway condition not monitored, visual inspection recommended prior to landing. No winter maintenance.

Named after the poet John Greenleaf Whittier, the community of Whittier is nestled at the base of mountains that line Passage Canal, a fjord that extends eastward into Prince William Sound. Passage Canal (also known as Portage Bay, Passage Arm and Passage Channel) leads to a portage between Prince William Sound and Cook Inlet. It was named by Capt. Vancouver in 1794.

Whittier was created by the U.S. Army during WWII as a port and petroleum delivery center tied to bases farther north by the Alaska Railroad and later a pipeline. The railroad spur from Portage was completed in 1943, and Whittier became the primary debarkation point for cargo, troops and dependents of the Alaska Command. Construction of the huge buildings that dominate Whittier began in 1948, and the Port of Whittier, strategically valuable for its ice-free deepwater port, remained activated until 1960, at which time the population was 1,200. The city of Whittier was incorporated in 1969.

The 14-story Begich Towers, formerly the Hodge Building, houses more than half of Whittier's population and the City Offices. Now a condominium, the building was used by the U.S. Army for family housing and civilian bachelor quarters. The building was renamed in honor of U.S. Rep. Nick Begich of Alaska, who, along with Rep. Hale Boggs of Louisiana, disappeared in a small plane in this area in 1972.

The Buckner Building, completed in 1953, once the largest building in Alaska, was called the "city under one roof."

Whittier Manor was built in the early 1950s by private developers as rental units for civilian employees and soldiers who were ineligible for family housing elsewhere. In early 1964, the building was bought by another group of developers and became a condominium, which now houses the remainder of Whittier's population.

Since military and government activities ceased, the economy of Whittier rests largely on the fishing industry (commercial and sportfishing), the port and increasingly on tourism. The Alaska State Ferry docks here as do Prince William Sound tour boats and cruise ships. Whittier is also a popular harbor with Anchorage boat-owners.

Lodging & Services

Lodging at **Glacier View Suites**, **Anchor Inn** and The Inn at Whittier. Dining at hotels and on the Triangle. **Lazy Otter Charters** offers a cafe serving espresso, ice cream, snacks and boxed lunches. Anchor Inn has a laundromat. Check the Chamber of Commerce website for more information at www.whittieralaskachamber.org.

Many of the waterfront businesses—restaurants, shops and tours—located along Harbor View Drive and "the Triangle," are

seasonal, operating only during the summer months.

NOTE: Parking is at a premium in Whittier in the summer. Look for signed 2-hour free public parking. 24-hour parking permits are required for the long-term lot; purchase permit from the Harbormaster or at the boat launch kiosk at the east end of the harbor. RVs park at campground and walk.

The Harbormaster's office is located about mid-harbor and has showers and a public restroom.

Gas and diesel are available in Whittier at Shoreside Petroleum on Harbor Loop Road.

Whittier also has a marine services and repairs, marine supply store, boat launch and lift, freight services, dry storage and self-storage units. The Harbor Store (907/440-2847) has groceries, fishing supplies and an ATM (open May–September, only). Card gas available at harbor.

Camping

There is camping in a gravel lot in the trees behind the boat trailer parking; outhouse. Tent camping is allowed. Self-pay fee box for overnighters.

Transportation

Ferry: Cross-Sound service to Valdez and Cordova via Alaska Marine Highway. Whittier Terminal, phone (907) 472-2378. See ALASKA MARINE HIGHWAY section for details.

Railroad: Alaska Railroad passenger service from Anchorage. There is no Alaska Railroad depot in Whittier. The *Glacier Discovery Train* loads and off-loads passengers in the white tented area across from the cruise ship terminal and the marina. Visit www.alaskarailroad.com.

Cruise Ship: Princess Cruises and Norwegian Cruiseline call at Whittier.

Highway: Accessible via an 11-mile side road from Seward Highway.

Boat Charters: Available.

Bus: There is no scheduled bus or shut-tle van service operating out of Whittier, although the Magic Bus offers on-demand to/from service; phone (907) 230-6773. Cruise ship and tour boat operators may also arrange bus transportation for clients.

Rental Cars: Avis car rentals available at the Harbor Store seasonally (May to September), phone (907) 440-2847.

Attractions

The major attraction in Whittier is Prince William Sound, whether you come to Whittier to take a cruise ship, tour boat or ferry across the Sound, launch a motorboat or paddle a kayak into the Sound. The second biggest attraction has to be watching all this activity in Whittier's harbor. Sightseeing cruises departing from Whittier include the **26 Glacier Cruises** and **Major Marine Tours** cruise.

26 Glacier Cruise. Voted "Best Glacier & Wildlife Cruise" by residents. See tidewater glaciers, otters and kittiwakes! Our 26 Glacier Cruise and Glacier Quest Cruise explore glacier cared fjords, view magnificent glaciers and watch for playful wildlife.

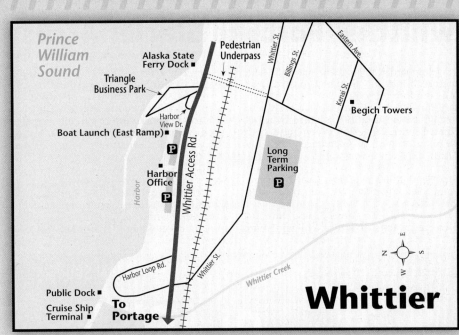

Whittier

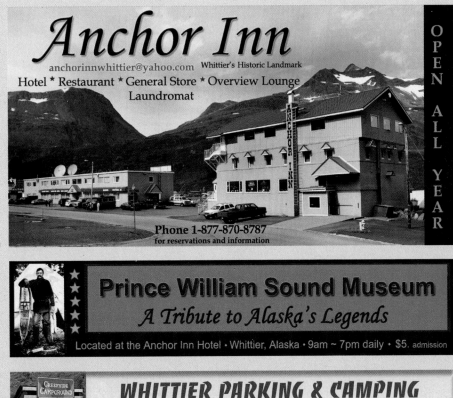

Whittier/Portage Glacier Access Road *(Continued)*

Travel aboard stable catamarans with large picture windows, assigned heated seating, outdoor viewing decks, complimentary hot lunch and full service bar/snacks for purchase. Narration provided by a U.S. Forest Service Ranger on every cruise. Only 75 minutes south of Anchorage, this is one Alaska experience you won't want to miss! Sharing the Sound for 50+ years. Daily May–Sept. 1-800-544-0529. www.26glaciers. com. See display ad on this page. [ADVERTISEMENT]

Major Marine Tours. Cruise the calm, protected waters of Prince William Sound with a Chugach Forest Ranger. By high-speed catamaran visit Surprise Glacier and pass by a working salmon hatchery, or take a leisurely trip to Blackstone and Beliot tidewater glaciers. Cruises feature a freshly prepared Alaska salmon and prime rib meal served onboard. Daily departures from Whittier, May through September. Call 800-764-7300 or 907-274-7300; www.majormarine.com. See display ad this page. [ADVERTISEMENT]

Area hiking trails. Follow Whittier Street 0.5 mile to Eastern Avenue; cross Eastern and drive 0.3 mile up Blackstone Road, then turn right on Salmon Run Road just past the Buckner Building. Salmon Run Road (narrow, dirt) leads 0.4 mile to **Horsetail Falls Trail**, a 1-mile planked trail to a viewing platform overlooking Whittier and Passage Canal. Or follow Salmon Run Road 0.2 mile and turn left on a second narrow dirt road for 0.4 mile to Smitty's Cove, Cove Creek picnic area and Salmon Run (Shotgun Cove) hiking trail along coastline.

For the 1.75-mile-long **Portage Pass Trail**, turnoff on the Chugach National Forest access road just east of the tunnel. The first 0.75 miles of this trail—to the pass at 750 feet elevation—is well maintained. It continues another mile as a primitive route to Portage Lake.

A Tribute to Alaska's Legends/Prince William Sound Museum, located at the Anchor Inn in downtown Whittier, has many exhibits and new ones debuting every year. Some highligh the town's history. Other exhibits cover the Anton Anderson Memorial Tunnel, the Alaska Railroad, the Alaska Steamship Co., the battle of Attu and Kiska in the Aleutians, Cold War military

©Sharon Nault

flights—"The Eagle and the Bear"—guarding Alaska's coastline, and heroic rescue and survival stories, including the sinking of the S.S. *Yukon* in 1946. An outstanding museum experience. Open 9 A.M. to 10 P.M. in summer; admission fee $5.

Annual events in Whittier include an old-fashioned **Fourth of July Celebration** with a parade and barbecue. Fireworks at midnight on July 3rd. **Whittier Fish Derby,** for halibut and salmon, takes place May 1 to Sept. 15. For more details visit www.whittieralaska fishderby.org. Check with the Chamber for current status of the annual Tunnel Walk to Whittier. This event opens the Anton Anderson tunnel to walkers for 2 hours on a day in June. Registration required; helmet required; no bicycles, inline skates or dogs. (This event did not take place in 2013.)

Return to Milepost S 78.9
Seward Highway

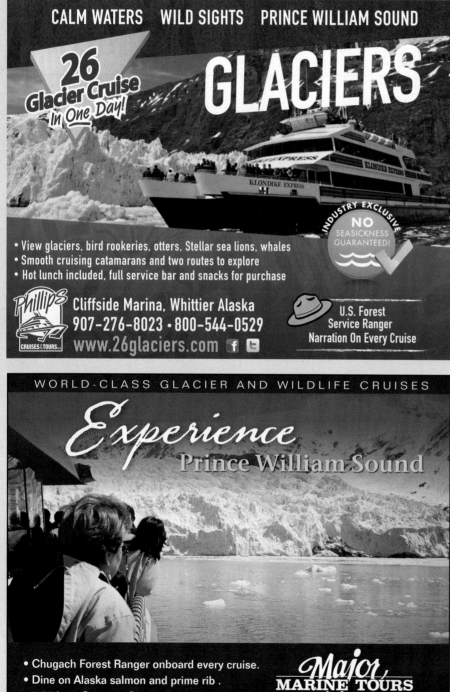

(Continued from page 561)

S 66 A 61 Gravel turnout to east.

S 65.4 A 61.6 Bertha Creek (signed). Turnoff to west for **Bertha Creek USFS Campground**; 12 sites in nicely wooded area by creek; hand-pumped water, toilets, firepits, tables, garbage containers, firewood $5; camping fee $14. Waterfall across from site #6. Small bear-proof food lockers are located at the campground. ⛺

S 65.3 A 61.7 Paved turnout to west.

S 65.1 A 61.9 *Begin passing lane southbound. End passing lane northbound.*

S 64.7 A 62.3 Spokane Creek (signed).

S 64 A 63 Pete's Creek. *End passing lane southbound.*

S 63.9 A 63.1 *Begin passing lane northbound.*

S 63.7 A 63.3 Access road to large parking area with toilets at **Johnson Pass Trailhead**. This is the north trailhead of the 23-mile-long Chugach National Forest trail. Rated easy, this is a good, fairly level trail which follows a portion of the Old Iditarod trail which went from Seward to Nome (see **Milepost S 32.6**). Johnson Pass trail leads to **Bench Lake**, which has arctic grayling, and **Johnson Lake**, which has rainbow trout. Both lakes are about halfway in on trail. 🎣

North end of **Sixmile Trail**, an 8-mile-long paved bike trail along Sixmile Creek's east fork to the Hope Highway Cutoff at **Milepost S 56.3**.

CAUTION: Watch for moose next 4 miles southbound.

S 63.3 A 63.7 Bridge over Granite Creek. Halfway point on highway between Anchorage and Seward. Begin bike trail on east side of highway.

S 62.7 A 64.3 *Begin passing lane southbound. End passing lane northbound.*

S 62.6 A 64.4 Granite Creek USFS Campground, 0.8 mile east of highway via narrow, winding dirt road *(expect potholes)*, keep right at fork. There are 19 back-in sites located on a loop road; some sites are beside creek and some sites will accommodate large RVs. This campground has water, toilets, dumpsters, tables, firepits, firewood (fee charged), campground host, $14 camping fee. Campsite reservations at www.recreation.gov or phone 1-877-444-6777. Scenic setting (meadow and spruce forest) with mountain views. Fishing for small Dolly Varden. Interpretive sign about how beetles kill spruce trees. 🎣⛺

S 62.2 A 64.8 Granite Creek recreation area to east; gated, undeveloped, closed to public.

S 61.8 A 65.2 *Begin passing lane northbound. End passing lane southbound.*

S 61.5 A 65.5 Bridge over East Fork Sixmile Creek.

S 61.3 A 65.7 Watch for moose next 4 miles southbound (sign).

S 61.1 A 65.9 Silvertip Creek (sign).

S 61 A 66 *Begin passing lane southbound. End passing lane northbound.*

S 60.4 A 66.6 *End passing lane southbound. Begin passing lane northbound.*

S 59 A 68 Paved parking area to west with interpretive sign about moose. Staging area for raft trips on **Sixmile Creek** to take-out near Sunrise on the Hope Highway. *CAUTION: Sixmile Creek has Class IV and V rapids; consult with local river runner outfitters (several are located on the Hope Highway) before*

Beautiful Summit Lake from Summit Lake Lodge access at Milepost S 45.8.
(©Meghan Mackey, staff)

attempting to paddle this creek.

Excellent place to photograph this glacial stream. The Sixmile bike trail and walking path leads south to the Hope Highway junction and north to Johnson Pass trailhead.

S 58.5 A 68.5 North end of double-ended turnout on old highway alignment to west.

S 58.3 A 68.7 South end of double-ended turnout on old highway alignment to west.

S 57.7 A 69.3 Scenic viewpoint to west; parking area. Steep climb down through trees overlooks Sixmile Creek canyon. Access to Sixmile Trail (bike trail).

S 56.8 A 70.2 Parking and trailhead to east. Bike trail on west side of highway.

Distance marker southbound shows Seward 54 miles, Homer 150 miles.

Distance marker northbound shows Whittier 33 miles, Girdwood 33 miles, Anchorage 70 miles.

S 56.7 A 70.3 Canyon Creek Rest Area to west with large paved parking area and restrooms overlooks confluence of Canyon and Sixmile creeks; interpretive signs, access to Sixmile Trail (bike trail).

S 56.5 A 70.5 Canyon Creek bridge; view of old Canyon Creek bridge.

S 56.3 A 70.7 Hope Cutoff. Southbound turn lane for Hope Highway. Rest area and access to Sixmile Trail (bike trail) at Mile 0.1 Hope Highway. *Emergency phone at Mile 0.2 Hope Highway.*

Junction with Hope Highway to historic community of Hope. See "Hope Highway" log beginning on page 568.

Begin passing lane southbound.

S 56.2 A 70.8 Distance marker southbound shows Seward 54 miles, Homer 150 miles.

S 55.3 A 71.7 Scenic viewpoint (narrow shoulder parking) east side of highway. Distance marker northbound shows Hope Junction 1 mile.

S 54.7 A 72.3 Double-ended paved parking area to east.

S 53.5 A 73.5 Parking area to east with Gold Rush Centennial signs about hydraulic mining and Wible's mining camp

on Canyon Creek (excerpt follows):

"California engineer and banker Simon Wible had a relapse of gold fever and came to Alaska in 1898 when he was 67 years old. He introduced hydraulic mining in this area. His largest mine was just across Canyon Creek from this spot. "Hydraulic mining used water under pressure to blast away entire hills and push gold-bearing gravel into sluice boxes that trapped the gold. The technology of hydraulics created an efficient but high impact method of mining."

S 53.3 A 73.7 *End passing lane southbound.*

S 52.6 A 74.4 Slow vehicle turnout to east.

S 52.4 A 74.6 Sign northbound reads: Delay of 5 vehicles illegal, must use turnouts.

Begin passing lane southbound as highway climbs 7 percent grade.

S 51.4 A 75.6 Double-ended scenic viewpoint to east.

Begin 7 percent downgrade northbound.

S 51.2 A 75.8 Distance marker northbound shows Hope Junction 5 miles.

S 50.6 A 76.4 Scenic viewpoint to east.

S 50.3 A 76.7 *End passing lane southbound.*

S 48.7 A 78.3 *Begin passing lane southbound.*

S 48.5 A 78.5 *End passing land southbound.*

S 47.9 A 79.1 Large paved parking area to east.

S 47.7 A 79.3 Double-ended parking area to east at north end of Lower Summit Lake with access to path and footbridge.

S 47.3 A 79.7 Double-ended turnout to east is a slow vehicle turnout for northbound traffic at the south end of Lower Summit Lake. A favorite photo stop. Extremely picturesque with lush growth of wildflowers in summer.

Upper and Lower Summit lakes, good spring and fall fishing for landlocked Dolly Varden (goldenfins) and rainbow. 🎣

S 46 A 81 Colorado Creek bridge. Turnoff to east at south end of bridge for **Tenderfoot Creek USFS Campground**, located 0.6 mile from highway via gravel access road. There are 35 sites (some pull-throughs, no hookups) located along a loop road. Beauti-
(continues on page 569)

Hope Highway

Hope is a picturesque community and well worth the drive. (©Sharon Nault)

The paved 17.8-mile Hope Highway leads northwest from **Milepost S 56.3** on the Seward Highway to the historic community of Hope on the south side of Turnagain Arm and provides access to the Resurrection Creek area. This is a good 2-lane road with a posted speed limit of 50 mph and some 35- to 40-mph curves.

There are a number of scenic highlights along this road, including glimpses of (and access to) Turnagain Arm; the picturesque town of Hope; the spectacular high country off Palmer Creek Road; and Resurrection Pass Trail. Angle 45 Adventures and Nova Riverrunners have operations along the Hope Highway, and offer various wilderness trips.

Hope makes a good 1- or 2-day trip from Anchorage.

Distance is measured from junction with the Seward Highway (J).

J 0 Junction with Seward Highway at Milepost S 56.3.

J 0.1 Rest area with outhouse, parking and access to Canyon Creek pedestrian bridge. River runner departure point for **Sixmile Creek** trips. *CAUTION: Sixmile Creek has Class IV and V rapids; consult with local river runner outfitters before attempting to paddle this creek.* Rafting outfitters generally require participants have the ability to swim across the river before signing on for this trip.

This is also the south end of the Sixmile Trail, an 8-mile-long bike trail along Sixmile Creek's east fork to the Johnson Pass trailhead at **Milepost S 63.7** Seward Highway.

J 0.2 Silvertip highway maintenance station. *Emergency phone.*

J 0.7 Narrow double-ended turnout to east.

J 2.2 Turnout to east with mountain view.

J 3.3 Paved turnout to east. Narrow, bumpy, dirt track leads to informal campsite.

J 3.5 Small gravel turnout to east.

J 3.9 Paved turnout to east.

J 4.4 Paved double-ended turnout to east.

J 4.9 Small gravel turnout to east.

J 5.8 Small gravel turnout to east.

J 6.4 Single-vehicle turnout to west by stream.

J 7.6 Chugach Outdoor Center.

J 8.1 Angle 45 Adventures. See display ad this page.

J 10 Paved turnout to east with view of Turnagain Arm.

J 11.1 Large paved turnout to east with view of Turnagain Arm.

J 11.7 Paved turnout to east overlooking Turnagain Arm.

J 13 Very narrow dirt track loops down to scenic cove on Turnagain Arm.

J 15 *Begin 35 mph speed zone: Slow down for access to Hope businesses and pedestrians.*

J 15.1 Waste transfer station to west.

J 15.6 Fire Department to west.

J 15.7 Bear Creek Road to west.

J 15.8 Alaska Dacha; grocery, laundry, showers, cabins and RV park. ▲

Alaska Dacha, on the right, coming into Hope. Groceries, fresh/fruits/vegetables, frozen meats, camping supplies. Full service laundry and private hot showers, towels furnished. ATM. WiFi. Lovely motel rooms, private baths, sleeps 2–4. New cabins with private baths. Reserve early as Hope has few cabin rentals. RV park has grassy, level sites. Full hookups, 50 amps. www.alaskadacha.com. (907) 782-3223. [ADVERTISEMENT]

J 15.9 Bear Creek Lodge.

J 16 Bear Creek.

J 16.2 Junction with **Resurrection Creek Road** (see description below). Access to Hope School, post office and Discovery Cabins. Take first left on Nearhouse Lane, then right on Discovery Drive for **Discovery Cabins** (handcrafted log cabins); description follows. Post office is across from Discovery Cabins.

Discovery Cabins. 5 individual log cabins overhanging rushing Bear Creek. Great rates! Each privately set in the trees, there is also a creekside fire ring. Come hike, bike or just plain relax in the tranquility of historic Hope. Phone 1-800-365-7057; (907) 782-3730; email cabins@AdventureAlaskaTours.com; website www.AdventureAlaskaTours.com/cabins.htm. [ADVERTISEMENT]

Resurrection Creek Road continues to Hope airport (0.9 miles from highway), the USFS trailhead (4 miles from highway) for **Resurrection Pass North Trailhead** and to a recreational mining area (with several primitive camping spots). The 38-mile-long Resurrection Pass Trail climbs from an elevation of 400 feet at the north trailhead to Resurrection Pass at 2,600 feet, before descending to the south trailhead at **Milepost S 53.2** on the Sterling Highway.

Palmer Creek Road junctions with Resurrection Creek Road 0.6 mile south of the Hope Highway. Palmer Creek Road provides access into Chugach National Forest. The road is winding and gravel, not recommended for RVs or vehicles with trailers, and leads 7 miles to Coeur d'Alene USFS Campground (6 walk-in tent sites, primitive). No fee. *CAUTION: Watch for bears.* ▲

J 16.5 First turnoff northbound for Hope via gravel loop road (description follows; also see map on page 569). Cafe on this corner. Public restrooms are just beyond the Hope Social Hall.

Hope

Located at the end of the Hope Highway on Turnagain Arm, 87 miles from Anchorage. **Population**: 151. **Visitor Information**: Hope Chamber of Commerce, P.O. Box 89, Hope, AK 99605; visit their web site at www.hopealaska.info. The staff at the Hope and Sunrise Community Library and the Hope and Sunrise Historical and Mining Museum—both open every afternoon in the summer—may also be able provide visitor information.

Hope has a post office, library (bear-proof trash cans here) and museum, 2 cafes, lodging and campground. Visitor services are found along the highway from **Milepost J 15.5** to road end, and along the loop road through "downtown" Hope. Check for gas availability with Pioneer Liquor & Gas at **Milepost J 17.7**; phone (907) 782-3418.

Private aircraft: Hope airstrip 1 mile SE; elev. 200 feet; length 2,000 feet; gravel.

This picturesque community was a frenzy of gold rush activity in 1896. Miners named their mining camp on Resurrection Creek Hope City, after 17-year-old prospec-

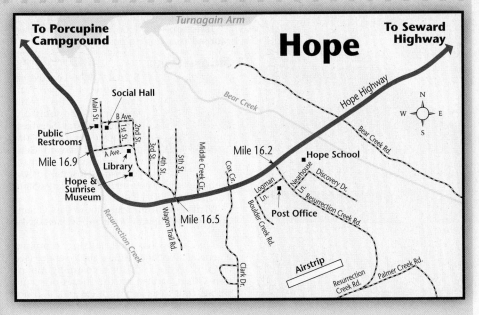

To Porcupine Campground

Turnagain Arm

Hope

To Seward Highway

Social Hall

Bear Creek

Main St.

Hope Highway

Bear Creek Rd.

B Ave.

2nd St.

1st St.

Public Restrooms

A Ave.

3rd St.

Mile 16.9

Library

4th St.

5th St.

Middle Creek Cir.

Mile 16.2

Hope School

Cox Cir.

Hope & Sunrise Museum

Nearhouse Ln.

Discovery Dr.

Logman Ln.

Mile 16.5

Wagon Trail Rd.

Boulder Creek Rd.

Post Office

Resurrection Creek Rd.

Resurrection Creek

Clark Dr.

Airstrip

Resurrection Creek Rd.

Palmer Creek Rd.

N W E S

---

tor Percy Hope. But the gold rush here was short-lived. By 1899, many of the miners had joined the gold rush to the Klondike. Hope City persisted, and it is now the best preserved gold rush community in south-central Alaska.

Hope's historic district includes the 1896 store (now the Seaview Cafe) and the 1902 log Social Hall, which still hosts community events. The **Hope and Sunrise Historical and Mining Museum** has an extensive collection of gold mining equipment, displayed both indoors and outside on the museum grounds.

Today, Hope is a quiet, friendly oasis, popular with hikers, campers, bicyclists, fishermen, bird watchers and recreational gold miners. Special events here include the annual 2-day **Wagon Trail Festival** (3rd weekend in July), which features a 5K run, pancake breakfast and cake walk at the Hope Social Hall.

At the end of the Hope Highway, Porcupine USFS Campground offers very pleasant campsites—some with views of Turnagain Arm—surrounded by lush foliage. Porcupine is also the trailhead for Gull Rock Trail, a 5-mile hike out to a rocky viewpoint overlooking Turnagain Arm.

Turnoff the Hope Highway at **Milepost J 16.2** and follow Resurrection Creek Road 3.4 miles to reach the trailhead for **Resurrection Pass North National Recreation Trail**. This 38-mile-long trail climbs to Resurrection Pass (elev. 2,600 feet) then down to the south trailhead at **Milepost S 53.1** on the Sterling Highway. There are 8 public-use cabins along the trail (reserve cabins in advance).

Resurrection Creek Road also provides access to **Palmer Creek Road**, which leads 6 miles to Coeur d'Alene USFS Campground. Palmer Creek Road continues past the campground to alpine country above 1,500 feet elevation; great views and wildflowers in summer (although snow can remain at

higher elevations through June). The road past the campground is subject to closure and recommended only for mountain bikes.

Hope Highway Log
(continued)

J 16.9 Second turnoff northbound for Hope via dirt loop road. Access to Seaview Cafe and Bar and campground.

Continue 35 mph speed zone on highway.

J 17 Resurrection Creek bridge.

J 17.7 Pioneer Liquor & Gas, call ahead to see if they have gas; (907) 782-3418.

J 17.8 Hope Highway ends. An 0.8-mile loop road leads through **Porcupine USFS Campground** providing access to campsites, 2 overlooks with picnic tables, and 2 trail-heads. This is a very pleasant campground set in lush vegetation with a few sites overlooking Turnagain Arm. There are 24 paved sites, tables, tent spaces, campground host, outhouses, firewood, firepits, dumpster, drinking water. Camping fee $14; fee for firewood. Hope Point Trailhead is located near campground entrance.

Trailhead parking for the 5-mile **Gull Rock Trail** on campground loop road. Rated easy, this is a relatively flat trail through lush vegetation that ends at Gull Rock overlooking Turnagain Arm. Allow 2- to 3-hours to hike one way. Trail has lots of tree roots and some muddy spots.

Return to Milepost S 56.3 Seward Highway

(Continued from page 567)

ful setting on the east side of **Upper Summit Lake**; great for canoes, kayaks and small fishing boats. A favorite campground for many Alaskans. There are tables, firepits, bear-proof dumpsters, water, toilets (wheelchair accessible), and a boat launch. Firewood available (fee charged). Campground host. Camping fee $14. Campsite reservations at www.recreation.gov or phone 1-877-444-6777. Lake fishing for Dolly Varden and stocked rainbow. Also access to Colorado Creek at back of campground.

S 45.8 A 81.2 Summit Lake Lodge east side of highway; food and lodging. Closed in winter. Emergency phone located on pole next to lodge sign.

S 45.7 A 81.3 Winter avalanche area begins southbound. Avalanche gates. *Emergency phone.*

S 45.4 A 81.6 Turnout to east overlooking Upper Summit Lake.

S 44.5 A 82.5 Double-ended turnout to east at south end of Upper Summit Lake.

S 43.9 A 83.1 Gravel turnout to east.

S 43.8 A 83.2 Winter avalanche area begins northbound. Avalanche gates.

S 43.7 A 83.3 Double-ended parking to east.

S 42.4 A 84.6 *End passing lane northbound.*

S 42.2 A 84.8 Quartz Creek.

S 41.5 A 85.5 *Begin passing lane northbound.*

S 39.6 A 87.4 Avalanche gates.

S 39.5 A 87.5 Devils Creek Trail; trailhead parking to west; toilet. This 10-mile (one-way) USFS trail (rated more difficult) starts at an elevation of 1,000 feet and follows Devils Creek to Devils Pass (elev. 2,400 feet), continuing on to Devils Pass Lake and Resurrection Pass North and South trails. Hiking time to Devils Pass is about 5 to 6 hours.

Camping options are at Mile 2.3 the Beaver Pond tent site, or at Mile 5.3 for a campsite or the Devils Pass public-use cabin (must be reserved in advance). Avalanche danger begins at Mile 3 in winter and winter use is not recommended beyond this point. Not open to snowmachine use. Closed to horses April–June.

S 39.4 A 87.6 Distance marker northbound (missing in 2013) shows Anchorage 88 miles; Whittier 50 miles, Girdwood 50 miles.

S 39.2 A 87.8 *End passing lane northbound.*

S 39 A 88 *Begin passing lane northbound.*

S 38.5 A 88.5 Small paved turnout overlooking Jerome Lake.

S 38.4 A 88.6 Paved double-ended Scenic Byway turnout to west adjacent **Jerome Lake**; interpretive signs and public fishing access. Lake is stocked; rainbow and Dolly Varden to 22 inches, use salmon egg clusters, year-round, still-fish.

S 38.1 A 88.9 *End passing lane northbound.*

S 37.7 A 89.3 First exit (southbound-traffic only) to west for Sterling Highway (Alaska Route 1). Continue straight ahead on Alaska Route 9 for second Sterling Highway exit at Tern Lake and for continuation of Seward Highway.

First **junction** southbound with Sterling Highway to Soldotna, Homer and other Sterling Highway communities. Turn to the STERLING HIGHWAY on page 581 for log.

S 37.2 A 89.8 Paved double-ended turn-

Tern Lake wildlife viewing area on the Sterling Highway is just west of Milepost S 37 on the Seward Highway. (©Sharon Nault)

out to west overlooks Tern Lake. Access to Tern Lake is from the Sterling Highway; use Tern Lake Junction turnoff (next turnoff southbound).

S 37 A 90 Tern Lake Junction. Main junction of Seward and Sterling highways. Turn off to west (2-way traffic) on Sterling Highway for access to Tern Lake and **Tern Lake USFS Wildlife Viewing Area.** This is a good spot to see nesting birds, mountain goats, sheep and occasionally moose and bear. Tern Lake is a prime bird-watching area in summer.

Tern Lake Junction: Second turnoff southbound and first northbound of the Seward Highway with the Sterling Highway (Alaska Route 1) to Soldotna, Kenai and Homer. Turn to **Milepost S 37** on page 584 in the STERLING HIGHWAY section for log.

Seward-bound travelers continue straight ahead southbound on Alaska Route 9 for Seward (continue with this log).
Begin 1-mile passing lane northbound.

ALASKA ROUTE 9

S 36.5 A 90.5 Distance marker southbound shows Moose Pass 7 miles, Seward 34 miles.

S 36.4 A 90.6 Avalanche gates.

S 36 A 91 The Inn at Tern Lake is located centrally near the junction of Routes 1 and 9 and provides access to many activities from Seward to western Kenai Peninsula. 4 spacious, distinctively appointed rooms, satellite TV, wireless, private baths and balconies overlooking several ponds; guest kitchen, spacious sitting area and large BBQ deck. Fishing guide available! Open year-round. www.ternlakeinn.com. (907) 288-3667. [ADVERTISEMENT]

S 35.7 A 91.3 Crazy Moose Studios to east (on left southbound); description follows.

Crazy Moose Studios. Wide circle driveway for motorhomes. Bring your camera for a souvenir photo with "The Moose!" Like no other shop in Alaska. Two artists, husband and wife, inspired by Alaska, creating heirlooms on site. Russ and Melis-

sa's creations, once sold in fine art galleries and shops around the state, are now available exclusively at Crazy Moose Studios. If coming from Seward, get ready to turn after Milepost 35. www.crazymoosestudios.com. [ADVERTISEMENT]

S 33.1 A 93.9 Carter Lake USFS trailhead No. 4 to west; parking and a toilet. Trail starts at an elevation of 500 feet and climbs 986 feet to **Carter Lake** (stocked with rainbow). Trail is 2 miles long, good, but steep; rated more difficult with a hiking time of 2 hours. Good access to sheep and mountain goat country. Excellent snowmobiling area in winter.

S 32.6 A 94.4 Johnson Pass USFS south trailhead with parking area, toilet. North trailhead at **Milepost S 63.7.**

S 32.4 A 94.6 Turnout to west; short trail to stream where spawning salmon may be seen in August.
Caution: Be very bear aware. This is a high-use area for bears in salmon spawning season.

S 32.1 A 94.9 Cook Inlet Aquaculture Association. **Trail Lake Fish Hatchery** on Moose Creek; this hatchery raises reds and silver salmon and has juveniles and smaller (no adults). Display room (in winter, if this is locked, just come to the office and they will open it for you). Open 8 A.M. to 5 P.M. daily, year-round; phone (907) 288-3688.
NOTE: There is no public restroom here but there is an outhouse at the Johnson Pass South trailhead, 0.5 mile north of here.

S 31.7 A 95.3 Double-ended turnout to east on **Upper Trail Lake**; picnic table.

S 30.3 A 96.7 *Begin 45 mph speed zone southbound. Resume 55 mph speed limit northbound.*

S 29.7 A 97.3 Turnout east side of highway with view of **Trail Lake.**

S 29.6 A 97.4 *Begin 35 mph speed zone southbound. PLEASE DRIVE SLOWLY THROUGH TOWN!*
Begin 45 mph speed zone northbound.

S 29.5 A 97.5 Moose Pass DOT Highway maintenance station. Avalanche phone (907) 478-7675.

S 29.4 A 97.6 Groceries and waterwheel west side of highway and Trail Lake Lodge

motel and restaurant to east at turnoff.
Junction with loop road leads east past Moose Pass school to post office.

Moose Pass

S 29.4 A 97.6 Located on the shore of Upper Trail Lake, 98 miles from Anchorage. **Population:** 189. **Emergency Services:** Volunteer Fire Dept./EMS, phone 911; Seward General Hospital or Central Peninsula Hospital in Soldotna by highway or helicopter. Alaska State Trooper Post (907) 288-3346.

Visitor Information: Moose Pass Chamber of Commerce, www.moosepassalaska.com.

Moose Pass has food, lodging, camping, a general store and fishing guide service (see ads this section). This is a charming mountain village located on the shores of scenic Upper Trail Lake. A post office and highway maintenance station are located here.

Moose Pass began as a construction camp on the Alaska Railroad in 1912. Local resident Ed Estes attributed the name Moose Pass to a 1904 observation by Nate White of the first moose recorded in this area. Another version holds that "in 1903, a mail carrier driving a team of dogs had considerable trouble gaining the right-of-way from a giant moose." A post office was established in 1928 and first postmistress Leora (Estes) Roycroft officially named the town Moose Pass.

Moose Pass has a 1.3-mile-long paved bike trail which winds along Trail Lake from the Moose Pass ball diamond to the McFadden house on the south. Gravel turnout by lake.

The main street of town is the site of the Annual Moose Pass Summer Festival, a community-sponsored event which takes place the weekend nearest summer solstice (June 21). The festival features a triathlon, arts and crafts booths, a barbecue and other events.

The large waterwheel on the west side of the road is a local landmark, as is the sign posted there for so many years: "Moose Pass is a peaceful little town. If you have an ax to grind, do it here." This is a third generation waterwheel, rebuilt by Jeff Estes with the help of local craftsmen in 2003, in memory of his father, Ed Estes. This waterwheel replaces one built by Ed Estes in 1976, which in turn was a replica of a waterwheel built by his stepfather, Frank Roycroft, that was used to cut lumber for the family's homestead.

Seward Highway Log
(Continued)

S 28.5 A 98.5 *Begin 35 mph speed zone northbound. Begin 45 mph speed zone southbound.*

S 28.3 A 98.7 Moose Pass (sign) northbound.

S 27.5 A 99.5 *Begin 45 mph speed zone northbound. Resume 55 mph speed limit southbound.*

S 25.8 A 101.2 Gravel turnout to west. The timbered slopes of Madson Mountain (elev. 5,269 feet) to the west. Crescent Lake lies just west of Madson. Lower Trail Lake is on the east side of the highway. Grant Lake lies just east of Lower Trail Lake.

S 25.4 A 101.6 One-lane bridge over Trail River.

Trail to east at south end of bridge leads 1.5 miles to **Vagt Lake**; stocked with

rainbow trout.

S 25 A 102 New bridge constructed in 2013 crosses Falls Creek.

S 24.2 A 102.8 Side road leads 1.2 miles to **Trail River USFS Campground**; 91 campsites, some pull-throughs, good for all size rigs. Campground host. Group camping available; large covered pavilion. Park and walk to picnic tables on shore of Kenai Lake. Camping fee $14 single, $18 double. Campsite reservations at www.recreation.gov or phone 1-877-444-6777. Shelter, volleyball net, playground. Good spot for mushrooming and berry picking in August.

Lower Trail River, lake trout, rainbow and Dolly Varden, July, August and September, small spinners. Access via Lower Trail River campground road. **Trail River**, Dolly Varden and rainbow. Closed to fishing mid-April to mid-June; use of bait prohibited year-round.

S 23.5 A 103.5 *CAUTION: Railroad crossing.* USFS Kenai Lake work center (no information services available). Report forest fires here. Alaska State Troopers to west.

Private Aircraft: Lawing landing strip; elev. 475 feet; length 2,200 feet; gravel; unattended.

S 23.3 A 103.7 Gravel turnout to west. Turnoff for **Ptarmigan Creek USFS Campground**; 16 back-in sites, water, toilets, tables, firepits and dumpsters. Campground host. Camping fee $14. Campsite reservations at www.recreation.gov or phone 1-877-444-6777. Fair to good fishing in creek and in **Ptarmigan Lake** (hike-in, see trail information following) for Dolly Varden. Viewing platform to watch for spawning salmon in Ptarmigan Creek, best in August and September.

Water and picnic area at trailhead for Ptarmigan Creek USFS trail, which begins at the campground (elev. 500 feet) and leads 3.5 miles to Ptarmigan Lake (elev. 755 feet). Trail is steep in spots; round-trip hiking time 5 hours. Good chance of seeing sheep, goats, moose and bears. Carry insect repellent. Trail is poor for winter use due to avalanche hazard.

S 23.1 A 103.9 Ptarmigan Creek bridge; *narrow bridge, slow for curves on approach.*

S 22.7 A 104.3 Gravel turnout to east. Paved shoulder parking west side of highway provides scenic viewpoint overlooking Kenai Lake. This lake (elev. 436 feet) extends 24 miles from the head of the Kenai River on the west to the mouth of Snow River on the east. A sign here explains how glacier meltwater gives the lake its distinctive color.

Winter avalanche area next 3 miles southbound.

S 21.8 A 105.2 Gravel turnout to west with view of Kenai Lake.

S 21.4 A 105.6 Gravel turnout to west overlooking Kenai Lake (view obscured by brush).

S 20 A 107 Victor Creek bridge. Victor Creek USFS trail No. 23 on north side of bridge is a 2.25-mile hike with good view of mountains. Elevation gain of 1,100 ft.

S 19.8 A 107.2 Renfro's Lakeside Retreat to west has an RV park with full hookups and lakeside guest cabins (description follows). *Turnoff is between 0.1 and 0.2 mile south of Victor Creek bridge and physical Milepost 20, and 1.3 miles north of physical Milepost 18.*

Boardwalk viewpoint overlooks aptly named Lily Pad Lake. (©Meghan Mackey, staff)

S 18 A 109 *Driving distance between physical Mileposts 18 and 20 is 1.2 miles.*

S 17.5 A 109.5 Bridge over center channel of Snow River. This river has 2 forks that flow into Kenai Lake.

S 17 A 110 Distance marker northbound shows Kenai 68 miles, Homer 151 miles, Anchorage 110 miles.

S 16.9 A 110.1 Bridge over south channel of Snow River. Easy-to-miss turnoff for Primrose Spur Road at south end of bridge which leads west 1 mile to **Primrose USFS Campground**. *(Campground access road leads past private homes: Drive carefully!)* The campground, overlooking Kenai Lake, has 8 sites best suited for small rigs and tents. There are toilets, bear-proof food storage containers, dumpsters, tables, firepits, boat ramp, water, $14 camping fee.

Primrose trail (6.5 miles long) starts from the campground and connects with Lost Creek trail (7 miles). High alpine hike to **Lost Lake**, rainbow (stocked).

S 16.8 A 110.2 *Begin 1.1-mile passing lane southbound.*

S 16.6 A 110.4 Distance marker southbound shows Seward 17 miles.

S 15.8 A 111.2 Snow River Hostel. (907) 440-1907 (call between 6 P.M. and 10 P.M. Alaska Time). http://www.snowriverhostel.org/.

S 15.7 A 111.3 *End passing lane southbound.*

S 15.5 A 111.5 Large gravel turnout to east.

S 14.7 A 112.3 Paved parking at boardwalk viewpoint overlooking **Lily Pad Lake** to east. Watch for moose in lake and swans nesting nearby.

S 14 A 113 View to east of railroad bridge.

S 13.3 A 113.7 *Begin passing lane southbound.*

S 13.2 A 113.8 Large paved parking area to east. **Grayling Lake USFS trailhead** parking to west. Grayling Lake trail is rated easy. Allow 1 hour each way for the 1.6-mile hike. It connects with trails to Meridian, Long and Leech lakes. Good spot for photos of Snow River valley. Watch for moose. **Grayling Lake**, 6- to 12-inch grayling, use flies, May to October. **Meridian and Long lakes** are stocked with rainbow.

S 12.3 A 114.7 Scenic viewpoint to east is a very large paved parking area with interpretive signs on Chugach culture and the Native Claims Settlement Act (excerpts follow):

In 1971 the U.S. Congress found and declared: "There is an immediate need for a fair and just settlement of all claims by natives and native groups of Alaska, based on aboriginal land claims." The resulting legislation, known as the Alaska Native Claims Settlement Act, was a comprehensive and complete law involving cash and land settlements and the establishment of regional and village corporations. Forty-four million acres and nearly a billion dollars were involved in the settlement. The intent of the "corporate" structuring was to create a revenue producing entity that would assure a financial future for all Alaskan Natives.

In additional to the (12) regional corporations the Alaskan Native Claims Settlement Act created a system of local village corporations. These smaller organizations were awarded lands in the immediate vicinity of the village. The population of the village (according to the 1970 census) determined the amount of land the village was entitled to.

S 12 A 115 *End passing lane northbound.*

S 11.3 A 115.7 Golden Fin Lake trailhead parking to west. This is a 0.6-mile hike on a very wet trail: wear rubber footwear. Fishing at Golden Fin Lake for Dolly Varden averaging 8 inches. Ski trails in winter.

S 10.6 A 116.4 Large paved turnout to east.

S 10 A 117 *Driving distance between physical mileposts 10 and 11 is 0.8 mile.*

S 8.8 A 118.2 *Begin 3.2-mile passing lane as highway climbs next 3 miles northbound.*

S 8.2 A 118.8 Large paved turnout to east. Entering Chugach National Forest (sign) northbound.

Black bear on Harding Icefield trail. Watch for bears and moose on Exit Glacier and Harding Icefield trails. (©Michael F. Jones)

S 7 A 120 Turnoff to west on Timber Lane for **Irvin Pottery**. Description follows.

Irvin Pottery, just outside Seward, is a delightfully unique home pottery, operated by Tom and Sharon Irvin. They offer fine, hand-crafted, functional, wheel-thrown and hand-built stoneware pottery with original and colorful hand painted glaze designs. Dishwasher safe and non-toxic. Turn on Timber Lane, follow signs to pottery. 14527 Rain Forest Circle, Seward, AK 99664; irvpots@gmail.com; www.irvinpottery.com; (907) 224-3534. [ADVERTISEMENT]

S 6.6 A 120.4 Junction with Bear Lake Road to **Bear Creek Weir** (0.6 miles west), a popular viewing spot for red salmon in late spring/early summer and silver salmon in late summer/fall. There is also a resident population of dipper birds. The salmon pass through the weir on their 7-mile journey from Resurrection Bay to their spawning grounds in nearby Bear Lake. Cook Inlet Hatchery releases smolt here increasing the potential of productive return salmon runs. The weir is operated by Cook Inlet Aquaculture Assoc. (www.ciaanet.org). *Be bear aware. Where there are salmon, there are bears.*

S 6.5 A 120.5 Bear Creek.

S 6.3 A 120.7 Stoney Creek Avenue, crosses railroad tracks. Access to **Stoney Creek RV Park** (description follows).

Stoney Creek RV Park. Seward's only luxury RV park, located on 15 acres of pristine creekside property, and built to accommodate travelers who enjoy cleanliness, friendliness, and full utility services at their individual sites, including water, power, sewer, satellite TV. We also have clean hot showers and laundry facilities. Phone, DSL and WiFi, and shuttle to town available. Please see our display ad map (Mile 6.3) for directions. You may email us at info@stoneycreekrvpark.com. Phone toll free 1-877-437-6366. See display ad this page. [ADVERTISEMENT]

S 5.9 A 121.1 Salmon Creek. Good fishing in stream begins Aug. 1st for sea-run Dolly Varden averaging 10 inches; use of bait prohibited Sept. 16–Dec. 31.

S 5.5 A 121.5 Lodging at the **Nauti Otter Inn, Cabins and Hostel.**

Nauti Otter Inn, Cabins and Hostel. See display ad this page.

Seward Highway Scenic Byway (northbound sign).

S 5.2 A 121.8 Turnoff to west for Lost Lake subdivision and access to **Lost Lake USFS Trail**. For trailhead, drive west 0.2 mile and turn left on Heather Lee Lane; drive 0.2 mile and turn right on Hayden Berlin Road; rough and narrow road winds uphill and deadends at trailhead.

S 5.1 A 121.9 Bear Creek volunteer fire department to west. *Emergency phone.*

S 5 A 122 Large double-ended turnout to west.

A 4.1 A 122.9 Distance marker northbound shows Soldotna 91 miles, Anchorage 123 miles, Homer 165 miles.

S 3.8 A 123.2 Clear Creek bridge.

S 3.7 A 123.3 Turnoff to west for Exit Glacier in Kenai Fjords National Park, located 8.4 miles west via Herman Leirer Road. Lodging and attractions are located on Exit Glacier Road and Old Exit Glacier Road. A scenic drive.

Junction with Herman Leirer Road to Exit Glacier. See "Exit Glacier" on facing page.

S 3.2 A 123.8 Turnoff for Nash Road. At Mile 2 Nash Road crosses Salmon Creek. At Mile 2.1 is the trailhead for the multiple-use

Exit Glacier

Turn west on Herman Leirer Road (paved, 45 mph posted speed limit) at **Milepost S 3.7** Seward Highway and drive 8.4 miles to reach Exit Glacier in Kenai Fjords National Park. Close-up views of Exit Glacier and Resurrection River, as well as access to local attractions, make this a worthwhile side trip.

Lodging, dining and camping are located along Herman Leirer Road and on Old Exit Glacier Road (gravel), which loops off the main access road just west of the Seward Highway (logs for both these roads follow).

HERMAN LEIRER ROAD LOG
Distance from junction (J) with the Seward Highway is shown.

J 0 Junction with the Seward Highway at **Milepost S 3.7.**

J 0.1 Junction with Old Exit Glacier Road loop (see log following).

J 0.5 Seward Windsong Lodge. See display ad in Seward on page 576.

J 1.2 Large paved parking area to south.

J 1.3 Junction with Old Exit Glacier Road loop (see log following).

J 1.4 Kenai Fjords National Park (sign). Winter gates; no road maintenance beyond this point generally Nov. to mid-May. Exact closure dates based on snow and ice conditions. In winter, the road is open only to skiers, snowmachines and mushers.

Entering **Exit Glacier Road Special Use Area** (Alaska Dept. of Natural Resources) westbound; recreational tent and small RV camping at designated off-road pullouts next 2.2 miles westbound; 8-day limit, outhouses, pack out garbage.

J 3.1 Small paved pullout to south overlooking river.

J 3.6 Chugach National Forest (sign). Large turnouts both sides of road. (Speed limit increases to 45 mph.)

J 4.6 Bridge.

J 4.7 Shoulder parking area.

J 6.3 Small turnouts both sides of road.

J 6.7 Parking area and scenic viewpoint of Exit Glacier; good photo op.

J 6.9 Trailhead parking with toilet for **Resurrection River Trail** (Chugach National Forest). This 16-mile trail ties in with the Russian Lakes trail and is part of the 75-mile Hope-to-Seward route. *CAUTION: Black and brown bears also use this trail.*

J 7 Resurrection River bridge. *Slow for sharp edges at bridge approaches.*

J 7.2 Welcome to Kenai Fjords National Park's Exit Glacier (sign).

J 8.1 Turnoff for walk-in tent campground with 12 sites (no fee, reservations).

J 8.4 Parking area. Easy walk on paved path to Exit Glacier Nature Center; adjacent handicap-accessible restrooms and picnic area. *NOTE: Pets must be on leash in parking lot and are not allowed outside the parking lot area. Overnight parking is prohibited in the parking area, but there is free camping at pullouts along Herman Leirer Road (see* **Milepost J 1.4**).

Exit Glacier Nature Center is open seasonally, with displays, Alaska Geographic bookstore, and park information. Exit Glacier is 2.4 miles long and descends some 3,500 feet from the Harding Icefield. Continue on paved path 0.4 mile past Nature Center to fork: Harding Icefield Trail (4.1-

Visitors can enjoy close-up views of Exit Glacier. *(©Kathleen Barth)*

miles, strenuous) heads uphill; Edge of the Glacier Trail (moderate uphill on dirt, gravel and rock) leads another 0.6 mile to the edge of Exit Glacier (worth the effort). You can see the glacier midway on the 1-mile-long Glacier View Trail, which loops back to the Exit Glacier Nature Center. *CAUTION: Falling ice possible at face of glacier; stay behind warning signs. Watch for moose and bears on trails.*

Summer activities include: Ranger-led nature walks to the Harding Icefield; daily ranger-led walks; and daily talks in the pavilion. A public-use cabin is available in winter. Phone the park office in Seward at (907) 422-0500; for recorded information phone (907) 422-0573; or visit www.nps.gov/kefj.

OLD EXIT GLACIER ROAD
Distance is measured from the east junction (EJ) and west junction (WJ) with Exit Glacier Road.

EJ 0 WJ 1.6 Junction with Exit Glacier Road at Mile 0.1.

EJ 0.5 WJ 1.1 Clear Creek

EJ 1.1 WJ 0.5 IdidaRide Sled Dog Tours. Mitch Seavey, the 2013 and 2004 Iditarod winner, and his family introduce visitors to their sled dog business on Old Exit Glacier Road homestead. Guests can take a dog sled ride on a wheeled sled; pet irresistible sled dog puppies, check out the arctic gear worn at 50 below temperatures, and hear fascinating stories about dogs and dog mushing. **Seavey's IdidaRide Sled Dog Tours.** See display ad this page.

EJ 1.5 WJ 0.1 Entering Glacier Road Special Use Area; 8-day camping limit.

EJ 1.6 WJ 0 Junction with Exit Glacier Road at Mile 1.3.

Return to Milepost S 3.7
Seward Highway

Scenic Seward Boat Harbor is a must-stop for visitors. (©Anela Apostadiro)

(hike, bike, ATV, horse, ski, snow machine) Iditarod Trail, which begins in downtown Seward: Hike to Bear Lake, trail continues from lake to Mile 12 on the Seward Highway. Paved turnouts and excellent views of Resurrection Bay and Seward after Mile 3. At Mile 5.1 turn west for **Spring Creek Campground**; beach parking, outhouse, dumpster, fish from shore. Nash Road continues beyond campground to Polar Seafood, Marine Electronics and Wards Shipyard and Dry Dock.

S 3 A 124 Resurrection River bridge; first of 3 bridges southbound crossing 3 channels of the river. This river flows from the Harding Icefield into Resurrection Bay just northeast of Seward.

Seward city limits.

S 2.9 A 124.1 Resurrection River bridge No. 2.

S 2.8 A 124.2 Resurrection River bridge No. 3.

S 2.7 A 124.3 Turnoff to east just south of bridge for Seward airport.

S 2.5 A 124.5 Hemlock Street. Turnoff for **Forest Acres Municipal Campground** just off highway; wooded sites on gravel loop; flush toilets, firepits, picnic tables, 14-day limit. Camping fee: $10/tent, $15/RV, no power or water hookups available here.

Begin 45 mph speed zone entering Seward.

S 2.3 A 124.7 Sea Lion Avenue. Access to a vacation facility for active and retired military.

S 2 A 125 Seward Chamber of Commerce and Convention and Visitors Bureau Visitor Center west side of highway. Stop in with questions and see their 11-foot, 1,400-lb. Alaska brown bear mount. Open Monday through Saturday.

S 1.9 A 125.1 Safeway supermarket, Starbucks.

S 1.7 A 125.3 Grocery and **Essential 1 gas station** to west; gas, diesel, propane, car/boat/RV wash, convenience store; phone (907) 224-8041.

S 1.4 A 125.6 Phoenix Road to west. Port Avenue to east, access to cruise ship dock. Train station to east (access is from **Milepost S 2**).

Slow for 35 mph speed zone southbound.

S 1.3 A 125.7 Dairy Hill Lane to west. Large parking area to west at **Benny Benson Memorial**. In 1926, as a seventh-grader, Benny Benson entered a contest to design the Alaska flag. His winning design—8 gold stars (representing the Big Dipper and the North Star) on a field of blue—earned him a $1,000 scholarship.

S 1.2 A 125.8 North Harbor Street; Chevron gas station.

S 1.1 A 125.9 South Harbor Street; Breeze Inn. Access to Seward Boat Harbor, Harbormaster office, Kenai Fjords National Park Visitor Center and boardwalk (see details in Seward Lodging & Services and Attractions).

S 1 A 126. Van Buren Street.

S 0.6 A 126.4 Monroe Street.

S 0.4 A 126.6 Madison Street. Post office 2 blocks east. Hostel.

S 0.3 A 126.7 Jefferson Street. Seward Senior Center. Hospital at Jefferson and First. City Hall is one block east. Mount Marathon Trail is at the end of Jefferson; continue past hospital and one block up Lowell Canyon Road.

S 0.2 A 126.8 Adams Street.

S 0 A 127 Mile 0 of the Seward Highway (3rd Avenue) at Railway Avenue, which becomes Lowell Point Road. Alaska SeaLife Center is located on the bay at the end of 4th Avenue (one block south of here on Railway Avenue).

Seward

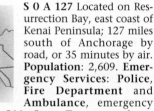

S 0 A 127 Located on Resurrection Bay, east coast of Kenai Peninsula; 127 miles south of Anchorage by road, or 35 minutes by air. **Population:** 2,609. **Emergency Services: Police, Fire Department** and **Ambulance,** emergency only, phone 911. **State Troopers,** phone (907) 288-3346. **Hospital,** Providence Seward

Medical Center, 1st Avenue and Jefferson Street, phone (907) 224-5205. **Maritime Search and Rescue**, phone (800) 478-5555.

Visitor Information: Available at the Seward Chamber of Commerce–Convention and Visitors Bureau Visitor Center at **Milepost S 2** Seward Highway. Open daily Memorial Day through Labor Day, weekdays the rest of the year; phone (907) 224-8051; www.seward.com.

Kenai Fjords National Park Visitor Center, 1212 4th Ave. (in the Small Boat Harbor), is open 8:30 A.M. to 7 P.M. daily in summer. Information on the park, videos, and a bookstore. Phone the park office at (907) 442-0500 or the Visitor Information recorded message at (907) 422-0573. Or write P.O. Box 1727, Seward, AK 99664; web site www.nps.gov/kefj.

Chugach National Forest, Seward Ranger District office, is located at 334 4th Ave. USFS personnel can provide information on hiking, camping and fishing opportunities on national forest lands. Open weekdays, 8 A.M. to 5 P.M. Mailing address: P.O. Box 390, Seward, AK 99664. Phone (907) 224-3374; www.fs.fed.us/r10/chugach.

Elevation: Sea level. **Climate**: Average daily maximum temperature in July, 62°F; average daily minimum in January, 18°F. Average annual precipitation, 67 inches; average snowfall, 80 inches. **Radio**: KSKA-FM 88.1, KPEN 102.3, KPFN 105.9, KSWD 950, KWVE 104.9. **Television**: Several channels by cable. **Newspaper**: *Seward City News* (eNews: sewardcitynews.com). **Private Aircraft**: Seward airport, 2 NE; elev. 22 feet; length 4,200 feet; asphalt; fuel 100LL, jet.

Seward—known as the "Gateway to Kenai Fjords National Park" and voted an All-America City for the third time in 2005—is a picturesque community nestled between high mountain ranges on a small rise stretching from Resurrection Bay to the foot of Mount Marathon. Thick groves of cottonwood and scattered spruce groves are found in the immediate vicinity of the city, with stands of spruce and alder growing on the surrounding mountainsides.

Historically, Seward was an important transportation hub for Alaska's mining, exploration, fishing and trapping indus-

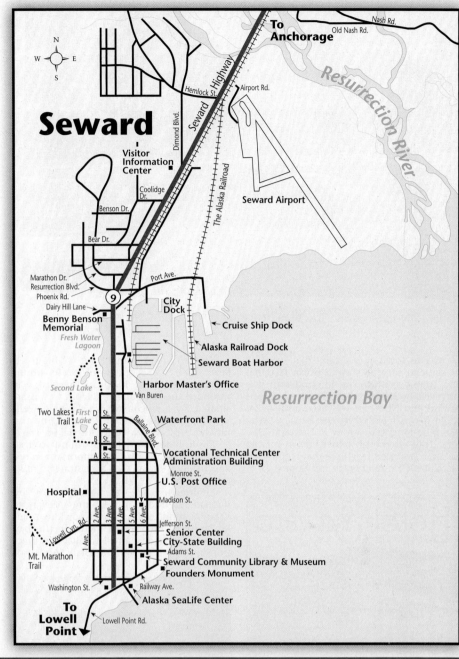

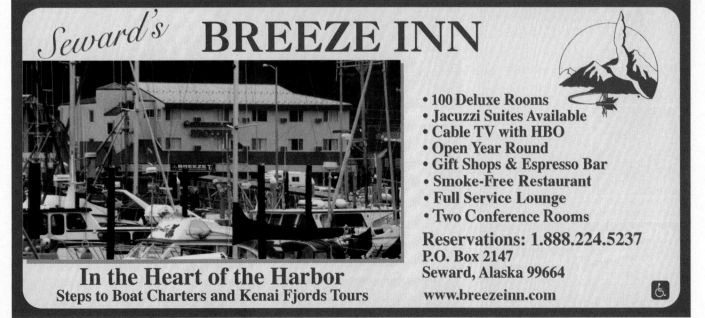

Seward offers a pedestrian-friendly downtown shopping district. *(©Sharon Nault)*

the Resurrection (Easter).

Seward's economic base includes tourism, a coal terminal, marine research, fisheries and government offices. The Alaska Vocational Technical Center is located here. The Alaska SeaLife Center, a marine educational center, is located here (see Attractions this section for more details).

Lodging & Services

Seward has all visitor facilities, including hotels, motels, hostels, bed and breakfasts, cafes and restaurants, post office, grocery stores, drugstore (inside the Safeway grocery store), a library/museum (see Attractions this section), travel agencies, gift shops, gas stations, bars, laundromats, churches, and a theater.

The Harbor Master Building has public restrooms, pay showers, drinking water fill-up, mailbox and pay phones. Weather information is available here during the summer. Phone the Harbormaster at (907) 224-3138.

Public restrooms and pay showers on Ballaine Boulevard along the ocean between the boat harbor and town. There are well-marked day-use picnic areas with ocean views and covered tables along Ballaine Blvd., just south of the harbor, and at Adams Street. The Moby Dick Hostel is at 432 3rd Ave., phone (907) 224-7072; website: www.mobydickhostel.com.

Breeze Inn, Restaurant, Motel, Lounge & Gift Shops. In the heart of the harbor. Two conference rooms, 100 exceptionally clean deluxe rooms, including accessible units, Jacuzzi® suites, smoking/non-smoking rooms. Free local calls. Friendly, courteous staff. The Breeze Inn Restaurant is open 6 A.M.–9 P.M. daily. Guests say: "The best breakfast in town." Phone (907) 224-5238 or 1-888-224-5237. www.breezeinn.com. See display ad page 575.

Hotel Seward, Restaurant, Lounge and Book a Wes's Fishing Adventure! Charming boutique hotel, Alaskan Victorian theme, in the heart of downtown.

Great History and Wildlife display! Spacious rooms, pillow-top beds, flat screen TV, HBO,

tries. The town was established in 1903 by railroad surveyors as an ocean terminal and supply center. The Iditarod trail was surveyed in 1910 as a mail route between Seward and Nome. It was used until 1924, when it was replaced by the airplane. (The 938-mile-long trail—now a National Historic Trail—is probably best known for the Iditarod Trail Sled Dog Race that is run each March between Anchorage and Nome.)

The city was named for William H. Seward, U.S. Secretary of State under president Andrew Johnson. Seward was wounded the same night Lincoln was assassinated, by a co-conspirator, Lewis Powell. Seward was instrumental in arranging the purchase of Alaska from Russia in 1867.

Resurrection Bay, a year-round ice-free harbor, made Seward an important cargo and fishing port as well as a strategic military post during WWII.

Resurrection Bay was named in 1792 by Russian fur trader and explorer Alexander Baranof. While sailing from Kodiak to Yakutat he found unexpected shelter in this bay from a storm and named the bay Resurrection because it was the Russian Sunday of

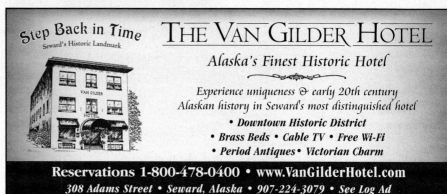

microwave, refrigerator, and free WiFi. Our friendly staff is available 24 hours! www.hotelsewardalaska.com. 1-800-440-2444 or (907) 224-8001. See display ad page 576. [ADVERTISEMENT]

Taroka Motel. Clean, comfortable, convenient and affordable. Family-owned, operated and oriented. We offer kitchen units with private bathrooms, in-room phones and 2 (cable) TVs in each suite. Couples traveling together have a little more privacy. One queen bed in the bedroom and another in the living room (not a foldout). Our larger units accommodate up to 9 people. Great for a family on a budget! Located on the corner of 3rd and Adams. Near shops, museum. Two blocks to Alaska SeaLife Center. ¾ mile to Small Boat Harbor. Free WiFi. Pets on approval. tarokainn@gci.net. Phone (907) 224-8975. www.alaskaone.com/taroka. [ADVERTISEMENT]

The Van Gilder Hotel. Step back in time, enjoy Alaska's finest historic hotel. Long time favorite of tourists and Alaskans, built in 1916 and placed on the National Register of Historical Places. Period antiques, Victorian charm, located in downtown Seward, it's a short walk to waterfront, shopping, SeaLife Center, museums, dining and nightlife. 1-800-478-0400. See display ad page 576. [ADVERTISEMENT]

Camping

Waterfront Park Municipal Campground (City of Seward) provides designated tent and RV camping areas along the waterfront between the Seward Boat Harbor and downtown. Camping fee charged, no reservations. Restrooms with coin-operated showers; water and electric hookups available at some sites; dump station. Contact Seward Parks & Recreation, phone (907) 224-4055. Camping fee: $10/tent, $15 RV, $30/RV with electric and water hookup.

RV parks on the Seward Highway near town are **Stoney Creek RV Park** at **Milepost S 6.3** and Forest Acres Municipal Campground at Milepost S 2.5.

Seward is the Mural Capital of Alaska. (©Sharon Nault)

Transportation

Air: Seward airport is reached by turning east on Airport Road at **Milepost S 2.7** on the Seward Highway. There is no scheduled service into Anchorage. Flightseeing, fly-in fishing and backcountry drop-offs are available, ask locally or at the visitor's center.

Railroad: Seward is Mile 0 of the Alaska Railroad. The Alaska Railroad connects Seward to Anchorage and Fairbanks. Depot at 410 Port Avenue, open daily 10 A.M. to 6 P.M. from mid-May to mid-Sept.

Bus: Scheduled service to Anchorage.

Taxi: Service available.

Car Rental: Hertz, phone (907) 224-4378.

Highway: Seward is Mile 0 of the Seward Highway. The 127-mile Seward Highway (Alaska Routes 9 and 1) connects Seward with Anchorage.

Cruise Ships: Seward is port of call for several cruiselines, including Holland America, Celebrity, Royal Caribbean, Silversea and

SEWARD ADVERTISERS

Alaska SeaLife Center offers close encounters with marine life. (©Sharon Nault)

Regent Seven Seas.

Charter Boats: Check at the Seward Boat Harbor and see advertisements this section.

Private Boats: Contact the Harbormaster office, phone (907) 224-3138.

Attractions

Walking Tour of Seward encompasses more than 30 attractions including homes and businesses that date back to the early 1900s; some are still being used, while others have been restored as historic sites. A brochure containing details on all the attractions of the tour is available at the visitor center or online at www.seward.com. The complete tour covers about 2 miles and takes about 1 to 2 hours, depending upon how much time you wish to spend browsing.

Walking the bike path along the water is your best bet at spotting sea otters in the bay.

The Alaska SeaLife Center is a non-profit, world-class, cold water marine research facility that opened to the public in May of 1998. Today it stands as Alaska's premier public aquarium and marine wildlife rescue and rehabilitation center situated on the shores of Resurrection Bay in Seward, Alaska. Visitors to this "window to the sea" can have close encounters with puffins, octopus, sea lions and other marine life while learning from our staff of educators and studying Alaska's rich seas and diverse sealife. The Alaska SeaLife Center has nearly 2,000 invertebrates, fish, seabirds, and marine mammals on exhibit—approximately 177 different species—and offers a variety of tours and encounters for all ages.

Capital funding for the $56-million facility was made possible through the *Exxon Valdez* Oil Spill Settlement, the City of Seward revenue bonds, and private/corporate fundraising.

Behind the scenes tours, puffin, octopus, and marine mammal encounters and Discovery Labs are a few of the options for enhancing visitors' experiences. Call ahead or ask the ticketing staff for schedules, pricing and details. Open year-round. Admission fee charged. Age restrictions apply on some tours. Call toll-free 1-888-378-2525 or log on to www.alaskasealife.org.

Murals. Seward was named the "Mural Capital of Alaska" in 2008 by Gov. Sarah Palin at the completion of the town's 12th colorful outdoor mural. Don't miss these outdoor artworks created by the Seward Mural Society. The murals are designed by Alaskan artists, including Jon Van Zyle, Tom Missel, Gail Niebrugge, Susan Swiderski, Dot Bardarson and Barbara LaVallee.

Each artist's design is projected on to sheets of Alumalite and traced with pens, then each outlined shape is assigned a number corresponding to a paint color. Society members and volunteers fill in the colors.

Visit the Seward Boat Harbor. This busy municipal harbor, built after the 1964 earthquake, is home port to fishing boats, charter boats and sightseeing boats. Stop by around 7 P.M. on a summer evening and watch charter boats bring in their fish to clean and display. The harbor is also home to sea otters—watch for them! Visitors may notice the great number of sailboats moored here: many are members of the William H. Seward Yacht Club, which sponsors an annual sailboat and yacht show.

St. Peter's Episcopal Church, at the corner of 2nd Avenue and Adams Street, was built in 1906. It is considered the oldest Protestant church on the Kenai Peninsula.

In 1925, Dutch artist Jan Van Emple was commissioned to paint the Resurrection, for which Alaskans were used as models and Resurrection Bay as the background. Obtain key to church from the Seward Museum.

Seward Community Library & Museum combines the 2 formerly separate entities in a strikingly modern new building at 239 6th Ave., on the corner of Sixth and Adams. Dedicated January 12, 2013, "The Seward Community Library & Museum is a community center with the facilities and resources to provide its users with the opportunity for continuing education, community enrichment and preservation of Seward's heritage."

The library offers more than 30,000 volumes, including recorded books, music, computer CDs and DVDs, and digital content for download. Free WiFi, 4 public access computers and 5 laptops for use in the building. The museum contains thousands of objects, photographs and archives that represent the history of Seward. Special programs are offered for visitors and local residents. The community rooms are available for scheduled use. For current hours and other information, phone (907) 224-4082.

Mount Marathon Race®. Good things rarely come out of a bar bet, but when 2 Sourdoughs wagered over whether Seward's Mount Marathon could be climbed in under an hour, a legend was born. Seward's annual Fourth of July endurance race to the top of Mount Marathon (elev. 3,022 feet) and back down is a grueling test for athletes. The descent is so steep that it's part run, part jump and part slide. The race attracts competitors from all over, and thousands of spectators line the route each year.

The race is said to have begun in 1909 with a wager between 2 sourdoughs as to how long it would take to run up and down Mount Marathon. The first year of the official race is uncertain: records indicate either 1912 or 1915. Eric Strabel set a course record in 2013, completing the race in 42 minutes, 55 seconds. The previous record of 43 minutes, 23 seconds held by Bill Spencer had stood since 1981.

Seward's annual Mount Marathon Race takes place on July 4th. (©Sharon Nault)

The race start is in downtown Seward at 4th and Adams. Spectators congregate along 4th Avenue, where there is always food, music and lots of excitement. The crowd then follows the racers as they make their way up 4th Avenue then to the end of Jefferson and up Lowell Canyon Road. The race finish at 4th and Washington is marked by medics standing by to bandage cuts, scrapes and bruises. This race shares the claim as the second oldest footrace in America; entries are limited and fill up months in advance.

Grazing Moose Summer Market and Artists' Co-op. Where happy people come to buy art, crafts, earth friendly goods, and fresh baked bread/rolls/sweets (inside). Outside, organic produce every Thursday. Open Thursday–Sunday 10 A.M.–4 P.M. May–Sept. and for the holidays. 312 5th Ave. between Jeferson & Adams. contact@thegrazingmoose.com. [ADVERTISEMENT]

Kayak Adventures Worldwide and Bear Paw Lodge. We specialize in environmentally friendly, educational guided kayak trips in Resurrection Bay and Kenai Fjords National Park. No experience necessary! Our kayak shop is located right in downtown Seward, on 3rd Avenue. We offer visitor lodging in our hand-built log home. Personal attention, a gorgeous rustic setting

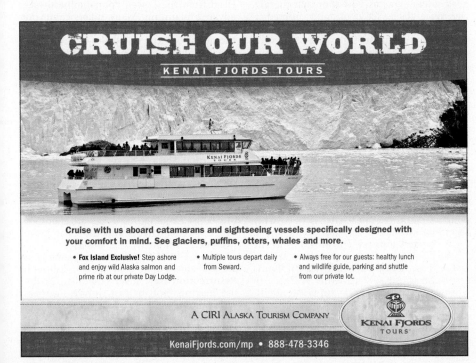

Kenai Fjords National Park

View of Exit Glacier, accessible by road and trail. Narrated boat tours and guided kayak trips to Kenai Fjords' scenic coastline are also available in Seward. (©Michael F. Jones)

Kenai Fjords National Park was formed when glaciers flowed down to the sea from the Harding Icefield and then retreated, leaving behind fjords, the deeply carved glacial valleys filled with sea water. These fjords characterize the park's coastline.

Substantial populations of marine mammals inhabit or migrate through the park's coastal waters, including sea otters, Steller sea lions, Dall porpoises and whales. Icebergs from calving glaciers provide ideal refuge for harbor seals, and the rugged coastline provides habitat for more than 100,000 nesting birds.

The park's scenic coastline and coastal wildlife is most commonly viewed by private tour and charter boats that depart from Seward's Small Boat Harbor daily in summer (see advertisements this section).

Two public-use cabins are located in the park at Holgate Arm and Aialik Bay. The cabins are available for use in summer (Memorial Day through Labor Day) by reservation only. Reservations are accepted starting January 1st; they are often booked for the summer by April. Phone the Alaska Public Lands Information Center (APLIC) at (907) 271-2737. The park's web site has descriptions of the cabins; go to www.nps.gov/kefj/planyourvisit/lodging.htm.

Kayakers and boaters may camp on the beaches but must be aware ahead of time of land status. Some 42,000 acres of coastline are owned by Native corporations. Public camping is available by permit only from the Native corporations. For more information about Native lands and permits, phone (907) 284-2212. Maps indicating land ownership are available from the park visitor center.

NOTE: Private boaters should consult with the Harbormaster in Seward for detailed information on boating conditions.

Another dominant feature of the 607,805-acre Kenai Fjords National Park is the Harding Icefield, a 714-square-mile vestige of the last ice age. Harding Icefield can be reached by a strenuous all-day hike (8.2 miles round trip, 3,500-foot elevation gain) from the base of Exit Glacier or by a charter flightseeing trip out of Seward.

Exit Glacier is the most accessible of the park's glaciers. Turn at **Milepost S 3.7** on the Seward Highway and follow Herman Leirer Road to the Nature Center parking area. Exit Glacier Nature Center is open daily from Memorial Day weekend through Labor Day, from 9 A.M. to 8 P.M. The center offers interpretive programs, exhibits and has an Alaska Geographic bookstore.

There are several trails in the Exit Glacier area that afford excellent views of the ice and surrounding mountains. A 1-mile trail leads from the parking lot to the glacier. The 8.2-mile round trip Harding Icefield Trail is a spectacular day hike. Make sure to heed safety signs as you approach the glacier, since glacier ice is unstable, unpredictable and *very dangerous*. Ranger-led nature walks are available in summer at 10 A.M., 2 P.M. and 4 P.M. There is also a picnic area and 12 walk-in campsites at Exit Glacier. Visitor information is available at the Exit Glacier Nature Center; open summer only. Exit Glacier is accessible in winter by skis, dogsled or snow machine. One public-use cabin is available in winter by permit. Call (907) 422-0500 for additional information on Exit Glacier's winter-only Willow Cabin.

Videos, exhibits and information on Kenai Fjords National Park and organized activities at the park are available at the park visitor center on 4th Avenue in the Seward Boat Harbor area next to the Harbormaster's office. The center is open daily Memorial Day–Labor Day from 8:30 A.M. to 7 P.M. Rangers also present programs at the Alaska SeaLife Center on marine related research projects. Shoulder season hours are 9 A.M. to 5 P.M. The center is closed in winter. Write the park superintendent, Box 1727, Seward, AK 99664, or phone the park office at (907) 442-0500 or the Visitor Information recorded message at (907) 422-0573; or visit their website at www.nps.gov/kefj.

and the true feeling of home: All at a reasonable price. Hot tub and grill. (907) 224-3960. www.kayakak.com; fun@KayakAK.com. [ADVERTISEMENT]

Visit a brewery. Seward Brewing Co. (www.sewardbrewingcompany.com), located 1 block north of the SeaLife Center at 4th Avenue and Washington.

Major Marine Tours. Wildlife and glacier cruises into the Kenai Fjords National Park and Prince William Sound. All cruises are hosted by park rangers and offer junior ranger programs for kids. Large tour boats feature reserved table seating inside a heated cabin. Enjoy our freshly prepared all-you-can-eat salmon and prime rib meal. Daily departures from Seward and Whittier, May through September. 1-800-764-7300 or (907) 274-7300; www.majormarine.com. See display ad page 578. [ADVERTISEMENT]

Sunny Cove Sea Kayaking Company. Experience the beauty and wildlife of Resurrection Bay and Kenai Fjords National Park. Paddle through bergy bits while watching glaciers calve. Have a chance to observe sea otters, seals and even whales from water level. Check out tour details and pictures of the area at www.sunnycove.com or call us at 1-800-770-9119. [ADVERTISEMENT]

Drive Lowell Point Road. This gravel road, narrow in places, hugs the shore of Resurrection Bay on its way to Lowell Point, a geographical feature just 3 miles from downtown Seward that encompasses a small rural residential community and a recreation area. Beachcombing, hiking, camping, boating and access to historical sites comprise the opportunities on this side road. Many visitors just walk out the first 0.2 mile to see the gushing Lowell Creek waterfall cascade down under a bridge.

At Mile 2.2 turn right on Pinnacle View Road and follow signs for **Lowell Point State Recreation Site**. The Tonsina Trail and Caines Head State Park trails leave from here. (Beyond this is the Lowell Point State Recreation Area beach parking lot with a narrow stretch of rocky beach shore enjoyed for beachcombing.) Caines Head was the sentry for Resurrection Bay in WWII.

Hiking the 4.5-miles (1-way) to Caines Head from the Lowell Point trailhead takes advance planning. Many hikers camp out, but remember that the hike is dependant on the tides, so check tide tables before you go. The shorter hike to Tonsina Point (1.5 miles) is easier, and should be considered a good choice for any average hiker. For up-to-date information on these trails, phone the Kenai/PWS office at (907) 262-5581. Visit http://dnr.alaska.gov/parks/units/caineshd.htm.

Large vehicles and RVs use extra care when meeting oncoming traffic on Lowell Point Road. Watch for fallen rocks on road.

Annual Seward Silver Salmon Derby® in August is one of the largest sporting events in Alaska. 2014 will be the derby's 59th year. Record derby catch to date is a 22.24-lb. salmon caught by Shirley Baysinger of Cooper Landing, AK. Prizes are sponsored by various merchants and the Chamber of Commerce. Phone (907) 224-8051.

AREA FISHING: Charter and rental boats are available. Public boat launch. Fishing in **Resurrection Bay**, silver salmon to 22 lbs., use herring, troll or cast, July to October; king salmon to 45 lbs., May to August; also bottom fish, flounder, halibut to 300 lbs. and cod, jig weighted spoons and large red spinners, year-round.

Sterling Highway

CONNECTS: Seward Highway to Homer, AK

Length: 142 miles   **Road Surface:** Paved   **Season:** Open all year

(See maps, page 582-583)

(See maps, page 582-583)

1

Fall colors along the Kenai
River at Cooper Landing.
(© William J. Rome)

Major Attractions:

©Kris Valencia, staff

*Kenai National
Wildlife Refuge,
Kenai River,
Russian Orthodox
Churches,
Homer Spit*

The Sterling Highway (Alaska Route 1) begins 90 miles south of Anchorage at its junction with the Seward Highway at Tern Lake and ends 142 driving miles later at the end of Homer Spit in Homer. Several major Kenai Peninsula side roads junction with the Sterling Highway, including Skilak Lake (loop) Road, Swanson River Road, Kenai Spur Highway, Kalifornsky Beach Road, Funny River Road, Cohoe Loop Road and Anchor River Beach Road.

The Sterling Highway, open year-round, is a paved, mostly 2-lane highway, with few passing lanes and some short sections of 4-lane highway. The Sterling Highway passes through Chugach National Forest and Kenai National Wildlife Refuge. The Kenai Mountains are home to Dall sheep, mountain goats, black and brown bears, and caribou. The many lakes, rivers and streams of the Kenai Peninsula are famous for their sportfishing.

From Soldotna south, the Sterling Highway follows the west coast of the Peninsula along Cook Inlet. There are beautiful views of volcanic peaks of the Chigmit Mountains across Cook Inlet.

Distance in miles	Anchorage	Homer	Kenai	Seward	Soldotna
Anchorage		226	158	127	147
Homer	226		90	173	79
Kenai	158	90		105	11
Seward	127	173	105		94
Soldotna	147	79	11	94	

The Sterling Highway opened in the fall of 1950, connecting the small communities and scattered homesteads on the west side of the Kenai Peninsula with the road to Seward on the east side. The Sterling Highway was named in honor of Hawley Sterling, an engineer of the Alaska Road Commission.

(Continues on page 584)

Sterling Highway   Tern Lake Junction to Soldotna, AK

© 2014 The MILEPOST®

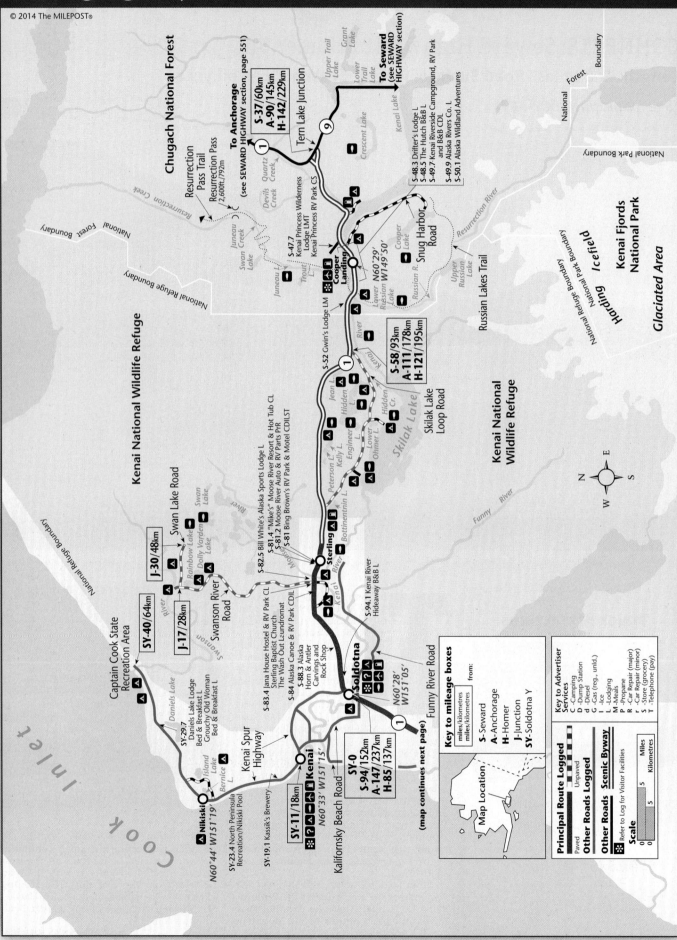

Chugach National Forest

Upper Trail Lake

Grant Lake

Lower Trail Lake

National Forest

Boundary

To Anchorage
(see SEWARD HIGHWAY section, page 551)

**S-37/60km
A-90/145km
H-142/229km**

Tern Lake Junction

To Seward
(see SEWARD
HIGHWAY section)

Resurrection
Pass Trail

Resurrection Pass
2,600ft./792m

Crescent Lake

Kenai Lake

National Park Boundary

Juneau Creek

Devils Quartz Creek

S-48.3 Drifter's Lodge L
S-48.5 The Hutch B&B L
S-49.7 Kenai Riverside Campground, RV Park and B&B CDL
S-49.9 Alaska Rivers Co. L
S-50.1 Alaska Wildland Adventures

S-47.7
Kenai Princess Wilderness Lodge LMT
Kenai Princess RV Park CS

Swan Lake

Trout L

Juneau L

Cooper Landing

N60°29'
W149°50'

Lower Russian Lake

Cooper Lake

Russian R.

Snug Harbor Road

Resurrection River

Upper Russian Lake

Russian Lakes Trail

National Refuge Boundary

Kenai National Wildlife Refuge

Kenai Fjords National Park

Harding Icefield

Glaciated Area

S-52 Gwin's Lodge LM

Kenai River

**S-58/93km
A-111/178km
H-121/195km**

Skilak Lake Loop Road

Jean L

Hidden L

Hidden Cr.

Skilak Lake

Peterson L

Kelly L

Engineer L

Lower Ohmer L

Lower Russian L

Kenai National Wildlife Refuge

Funny River

N
W   E
S

Swan Lake Road

J-30/48km

Rainbow Lake

Dolly Varden Lake

Swan Lake

Swanson River Road

SY-40/64km

J-17/28km

River

Swanson River

S-81.4 "Mike's" Moose River Resort & Hot Tub CL
S-81.2 Moose River Auto & RV Parts PrR
S-81 Bing Brown's RV Park & Motel CDILST

S-82.5 Bill White's Alaska Sports Lodge L

Moose River

Sterling

S-83.4 Jana House Hostel & RV Park CL
Sterling Baptist Church
The Wash Out Laundromat
S-84 Alaska Canoe & RV Park CDIL

Bottinentnin L

Kenai River

S-88.3 Alaska Horn & Antler Carvings and Rock Shop

S-94.1 Kenai River Hideaway B&B L

Daniels Lake

Captain Cook State Recreation Area

SY-29.7
Daniels Lake Lodge
Bed & Breakfast L
Grouchy Old Woman
Bed & Breakfast L

SY-23.4 North Peninsula Recreation/Nikiski Pool

Kenai Spur Highway

Island Lake

Bernice L

SY-19.1 Kassik's Brewery

SY-11/18km

Kenai

N60°33' W151°15'

Kalifornsky Beach Road

**SY-0
S-94/152km
A-147/237km
H-85/137km**

Soldotna

N60°28'
W151°05'

Funny River Road

(map continues next page)

▲ Nikiski
N60°44' W151°19'

Cook Inlet

Key to mileage boxes
S-/kilometres
miles/kilometres   from:

S- Seward
A- Anchorage
H- Homer
J- Junction
SY- Soldotna Y

Key to Advertiser Services
C -Camping
D -Dump Station
d -Diesel
G -Gas (reg., unld.)
I -Ice
L -Lodging
M -Meals
P -Propane
R -Car Repair (major)
r -Car Repair (minor)
S -Store (grocery)
T -Telephone (pay)

Map Location

Principal Route Logged
Paved
Unpaved
Other Roads Logged
Scenic Byway

♿ Refer to Log for Visitor Facilities

Scale
0   5   Miles
0   5   Kilometres

Sterling Highway Soldotna, AK, to Homer, AK

© 2014 The MILEPOST®

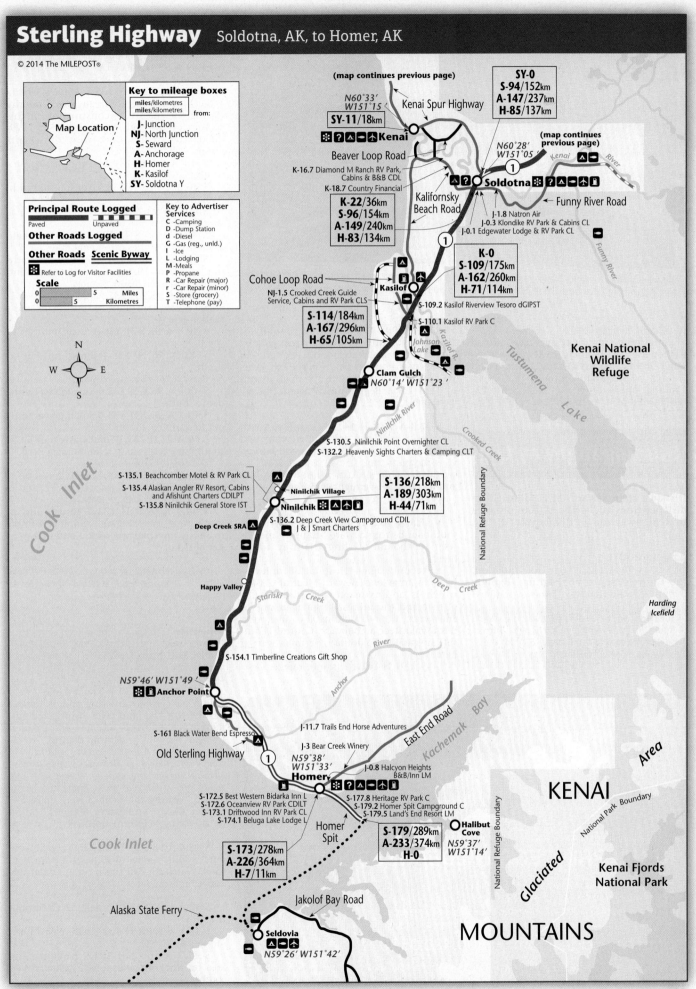

Key to mileage boxes

miles/kilometres
miles/kilometres

from:

J- Junction
NJ- North Junction
S- Seward
A- Anchorage
H- Homer
K- Kasilof
SY- Soldotna Y

Map Location

Principal Route Logged
Paved   Unpaved

Other Roads Logged

Other Roads   **Scenic Byway**

❄ Refer to Log for Visitor Facilities

Scale
0 _____ 5 Miles
0 _____ 5 Kilometres

Key to Advertiser Services
C -Camping
D -Dump Station
d -Diesel
G -Gas (reg., unld.)
I -Ice
L -Lodging
M -Meals
P -Propane
R -Car Repair (major)
r -Car Repair (minor)
S -Store (grocery)
T -Telephone (pay)

(map continues previous page)

SY-0
S-94/152km
A-147/237km
H-85/137km

N60°33'
W151°15'

Kenai Spur Highway

SY-11/18km

❄?⛺▭⛵✈ **Kenai**

(map continues previous page)

N60°28'
W151°05'

Beaver Loop Road

K-16.7 Diamond M Ranch RV Park, Cabins & B&B CDL
K-18.7 Country Financial

Kalifornsky Beach Road

⛺? **Soldotna** ❄?⛺▭✈🛏

Funny River Road

J-1.8 Natron Air
J-0.3 Klondike RV Park & Cabins CL
J-0.1 Edgewater Lodge & RV Park CL

K-22/36km
S-96/154km
A-149/240km
H-83/134km

K-0
S-109/175km
A-162/260km
H-71/114km

Cohoe Loop Road

⛺
🛏
Kasilof ⛺✈

NJ-1.5 Crooked Creek Guide Service, Cabins and RV Park CLS

▭
S-109.2 Kasilof Riverview Tesoro dGIPST

S-114/184km
A-167/296km
H-65/105km

S-110.1 Kasilof RV Park C

Johnson Lake

⛺

Clam Gulch ⛺
N60°14' W151°23'

▭

▭

S-130.5 Ninilchik Point Overnighter CL
S-132.2 Heavenly Sights Charters & Camping CLT

S-135.1 Beachcomber Motel & RV Park CL
S-135.4 Alaskan Angler RV Resort, Cabins and Afishunt Charters CDILPT
S-135.8 Ninilchik General Store IST

⛺
▭ **Ninilchik Village**
❄⛺✈🛏 **Ninilchik**

S-136/218km
A-189/303km
H-44/71km

S-136.2 Deep Creek View Campground CDIL
J & J Smart Charters

Deep Creek SRA ⛺

▭

▭

Happy Valley ▭

⛺

▭

S-154.1 Timberline Creations Gift Shop

▭

N59°46' W151°49'
❄🛏 **Anchor Point**

⛺

▭

S-161 Black Water Bend Espresso

Old Sterling Highway

⛺

J-11.7 Trails End Horse Adventures

East End Road

J-3 Bear Creek Winery

N59°38'
W151°33'
Homer

J-0.8 Halcyon Heights B&B/Inn LM

S-172.5 Best Western Bidarka Inn L
S-172.6 Oceanview RV Park CDILT
S-173.1 Driftwood Inn RV Park CL
S-174.1 Beluga Lake Lodge L

❄▭⛺▭🛏

S-177.8 Heritage RV Park C
S-179.2 Homer Spit Campground C
S-179.5 Land's End Resort LM

Homer Spit

S-179/289km
A-233/374km
H-0

○ **Halibut Cove**
N59°37'
W151°14'

S-173/278km
A-226/364km
H-7/11km

Cook Inlet

Cook Inlet

Kenai River

Funny River

Kenai National Wildlife Refuge

Tustumena Lake

Crooked Creek

National Refuge Boundary

Ninilchik River

Stariski Creek

Anchor River

Deep Creek

Harding Icefield

National Refuge Boundary

KENAI

National Park Boundary

Kenai Fjords National Park

Kachemak Bay

Area

Glaciated

MOUNTAINS

Alaska State Ferry

Jakolof Bay Road

▭ ○
Seldovia ⛺▭✈
▭
N59°26' W151°42'

Cooper Landing Boat Launch at Milepost S 48 is a popular launch spot. (©Terry Sheely)

(Continued from page 581)

Emergency medical services: phone 911 or use CB channels 9, 11 or 19. Hospitals are located in Seward, Soldotna and Homer. Alaska State Troopers in Cooper Landing, phone (907) 595-1233; Soldotna, (907) 262-4453; Anchor Point, (907) 235-8239; Ninilchik, (907) 567-3660.

Sterling Highway Log

Distance from Seward (S) is followed by distance from Anchorage (A) and distance from highway end on Homer Spit (H).
Physical mileposts show distance from Seward.

ALASKA ROUTE 1

S 37 A 90 H 142.1 Tern Lake Junction, the T-intersection of the Sterling Highway with the Seward Highway. Two-way traffic.

Junction with Seward Highway (Alaska Route 9) to Seward and Anchorage. Turn to **Milepost S 37** on page 570 in the SEWARD HIGHWAY section for log.

S 37.1 A 90.1 H 142 Turnout to south for **Tern Lake Wildlife Viewing Area**; parking areas along lake. Watch for arctic terns in spring and trumpeter swans in the fall. Bears are occasionally spotted on the small islands in Tern Lake. Begin Alaska Scenic Byway westbound.

S 37.3 A 90.3 H 141.8 Turnoff to south for USFS Tern Lake salmon viewing and picnic area. Rest area with toilet and salmon viewing platform. Gravel travel leads to secluded picnic sites in forest with tables and firepits (no overnight camping).
Begin passing lane westbound.
Watch for moose and bear.

S 37.5 A 90.5 H 141.6 One-way traffic southbound from Seward Highway merges with westbound Sterling Highway traffic here.

Eastbound sign—"Hospital 38 miles"—refers to Providence Seward Medical Center, which is approximately 38 miles south of here and the nearest hospital in case of emergency. Cooper Landing, 11 miles west, has a volunteer ambulance. Central Peninsula Hospital in Soldotna is 58 miles west of here.

S 38 A 91 H 141.1 Distance marker west-bound shows Soldotna 57 miles, Kenai 60 miles, Homer 131 miles.

S 38.5 A 91.5 H 140.6 Distance marker westbound shows Cooper Landing 6 miles.

S 39 A 92 H 140.1 *End passing lane westbound at Milepost 39.*

S 39.6 A 92.6 H 139.5 Dave's Creek. Protecting this scenic stream was a priority during the massive reconstruction of this section of the Sterling Highway in 1999-2000. Dave's Creek flows west into Quartz Creek.

S 40 A 93 H 139.1 *Begin passing lane westbound.*

S 40.2 A 93.2 H 138.9 Turnout to north. Avalanche gates.

S 40.7 A 93.7 H 138.4 *End passing lane westbound.*

S 40.8 A 93.8 H 138.3 Quartz Creek. This stream empties into Kenai Lake.

S 41.9 A 94.9 H 137.2 Small paved turnout to south. Distance marker eastbound shows Seward Highway 5 miles.

S 42.5 A 95.1 H 137 Large paved double-ended scenic viewpoint to south with information boards.

S 42.8 A 95.8 H 136.3 Small turnout to south.

S 43 A 96 H 136.1 Small turnout to south.
Begin passing lane westbound.

S 43.5 A 96.5 H 135.6 Small gravel turnout to south.

S 43.7 A 96.7 H 135.4 Small gravel turnout to south.

S 44 A 97 H 135.1 Solid waste transfer to south; easy access loop road, hours posted.
End passing lane westbound.

S 44.5 A 97.5 H 134.4 Small gravel turnout to north.
CAUTION: Watch for horses.

S 44.9 A 97.9 H 134.2 Sunrise Inn to south; food, gas, lodging, camping. Turnoff to south for **Quartz Creek Road** access to **Kenai Lake**

CAUTION: Slow for turning traffic. Highway narrows, winding road, westbound. Begin 45 mph speed zone westbound.

Junction with Quartz Creek Road south to Kenai Lake and Quartz Creek Recreation Area. See "Quartz Creek Road" log on facing page.

S 45 A 98 H 134.1 Kenai Lake. Westbound travelers are entering one of Alaska's best-known lake and river fishing regions. Kenai Lake drainage—all lakes and tributaries—are closed to salmon fishing. *NOTE: The diversity of fishing conditions and frequent regulation changes on all Kenai waters make it advisable to consult locally for fishing news and regulations or online at www.sf.adfg.state.ak.us.*

See "Fishing the Kenai River," page 588 (Upper Kenai) and pages 600-601 (Lower Kenai) for more information.

S 45.6 A 98.6 H 133.5 Large paved turnout to south; view of Kenai Lake through trees. Watch for dall sheep on mountainside above highway.

S 47 A 100 H 132.1 Small, paved turnout to south.

S 47.1 A 100.1 H 132 Small, paved turnout to south.

S 47.2 A 100.2 H 131.9 Large parking area overlooking lake; toilet. Restaurant to south.

S 47.6 A 100.6 H 131.5 Turnoff to north, just west of Wildman's convenience store, for **Cooper Landing Chamber of Commerce Visitor Cabin**; small log cabin, limited parking in front.

S 47.7 A 100.7 H 131.4 Turnoff to north on paved access road and drive 2 miles for **Kenai Princess Wilderness Lodge** and **Kenai Princess RV Park** (description follows). Paved turnout with good view of Kenai River at Mile 1.1.

Kenai Princess Lodge. See display ad on facing page.

Kenai Princess RV Park. A stunning wilderness setting on the Kenai River. Premier RV accommodations with water, septic, TV hookup and power at each site. General store, laundry, showers. Dining, lounge and free wireless at Kenai Princess Lodge. Mile 47.7 Sterling Highway, 17225 Frontier Circle, Cooper Landing, AK 99572. Mid-May through mid-September. $40 per night. (907) 595-1425. [ADVERTISEMENT]

©Kris Valencia, staff

S 47.8 A 100.8 H 131.3 Bridge over Kenai River at mouth of **Kenai Lake**. Kenai Lake serves as the headwaters of the Kenai River Special Management Area, established in 1984 to protect this unique resource. The 105-mile-long KRSMA stretches from Kenai Lake almost to the city of Kenai. The Kenai River flows directly alongside the highway for the next 10 miles westbound.

S 47.9 A 100.9 H 131.2 Junction with **Snug Harbor Road** (description follows), which leads 12.1 miles south to Cooper Lake. Volunteer fire department to north. Alaska State Trooper station.

From the Sterling Highway, Snug Harbor Road leads 0.1 mile south to the post office and continues past St. John Neumann Catholic Church to pavement end at Mile 1.1. (Road conditions on the gravel portion of Snug Harbor Road depend on grading.) *Watch for children at Mile 4.* Primitive road leads to shore of Kenai Lake (check before driving) at Mile 5.7. Gravel road continues along Kenai Lake to Mile 8.2, then begins a long ascent to a mountain valley. At Mile 8.9 is a winter recreation parking area for snowmachine access to Chugach National Forest; outhouse. At Mile 10.8 is the **Rainbow Lake** trailhead; ¼-mile hike to lake stocked with rainbow. The road reaches the **Russian Lakes** trailhead at Mile 11.3. (*NOTE: Large vehicles use trailhead turnouts to turn around; there is limited to no room at end of road.*) The 23-mile-long Russian Lakes trail is open to hikers and mountain bikes in summer, cross-country skiers in winter (check seasons for horses and snowmachines); permits required for public-use cabins on trail. Contact Chugach National Forest's Seward office, phone (907) 224-3374. Primitive ATV trail to Cooper Lake at Mile 11.8.

Snug Harbor Road ends at a gate at Mile

Quartz Creek Road

Quartz Creek Road junctions with the Sterling Highway at **Milepost S 44.9**, next to the Sunrise Inn and leads south along Kenai Lake to Quartz and Crescent creeks and Chugach National Forest recreation facilities. **Distance from junction with the Sterling Highway (J) is shown.**

J 0 Junction with Sterling Highway at **Milepost S 44.9** at Sunrise Inn; cafe, bar, motel, gas, RV sites.

J 0.1 Horse outfitter.

J 0.2 Turnoff for **Quartz Creek Day-use Area**; parking, life jackets for kids, boat ramp on Kenai Lake. Paved loop road accesses picnic sites, toilets, and campsites.

J 0.5 Quartz Creek USFS Campground; well-groomed, spacious sites on paved loop road; 45 campsites (will accommodate large RVs), some pull-throughs, tables, firepits, flush toilets, campground host. Camping fee $18 single, $28 double; Golden Age discounts. Dump station $8. Open mid-May to mid-Sept. Reservations, phone 1-877-444-6777 or www.recreation.gov.

J 0.6 *Pavement ends, gravel begins.*

J 0.8 One-lane bridge over **Quartz Creek**;

12.1 by Cooper Lake. Beautiful Cooper Lake offers informal camping, but there is very limited turnaround space and the short access road to the lake may be in poor condition.

S 48 A 101 H 131.1 Turnoff to north for access road to **Cooper Landing State Recreation Site Boat Launch Facility**, adjacent to the Kenai River Bridge. Pleasant rest area/day-use facility adjacent boat launch has toilets, walkways along Kenai River, information boards and telescopes. $5 parking fee after 30-minute grace period. The state boat launch has a concrete boat ramp. $5 launching fee.

A log cabin construction business is located near the rest area which attracts sightseers in summer.

Upper Kenai River, from **Kenai Lake** to **Skilak Lake**, including Skilak Lake within a half mile of the Kenai River inlet, special regulations apply. For current recorded fishing forecast, phone (907) 267-2502 Anchorage or (907) 262-2737 Soldotna; Silver salmon 5 to 15 lbs., July 1–Oct. 31; pink salmon 3 to 7 lbs., July–August; red salmon 3 to 12 lbs., June 11–mid-August; rainbow and Dolly Varden, arctic grayling, lake trout June 11–October. *IMPORTANT: Be familiar with current regulations and closures. Dates given here are subject to change!*

S 48.2 A 101.2 H 130.9 Grocery, hardware and tackle shop.

Slow for 35 mph speed zone westbound.

S 48.3 A 101.3 H 130.8 **Drifters Lodge.** On the Kenai River in spectacular Cooper Landing. Riverfront cabin rentals, nightly campfire, breakfast and riverfront sauna. Guided fishing—15 half- and full-day trips, beginners to experts. Trophy trout, salmon

fishing for rainbow, midsummer; Dolly Varden to 25 inches, late May through June.

J 1.1 Road forks: Keep left for Crescent Creek Campground and Crescent Lake Trailhead. For day-use area on Kenai Lake (parking only, no toilets or tables), keep right at this fork and drive 0.3 mile to second fork; keep right again and continue 0.2 mile past area of private homes to road end at Kenai Lake.

Road narrows.

J 2.7 Crescent Creek 1-lane bridge.

J 2.8 Entrance to **Crescent Creek USFS Campground**; 9 level sites (a few will accommodate large RVs) on gravel loop in heavily wooded area, toilet, firepits, tables, water pump, bear-proof food box. Campground host. Camping fee $14.

J 3.3 Maintained road ends at **Crescent Creek Trailhead**; large parking area, toilets and registration box. Crescent Creek USFS Trail leads 6.2 miles to **Crescent Lake**; stocked with grayling. *Watch for bears.* Public-use cabin at lake; permit required.

Return to Milepost S 44.9 Sterling Highway

(sockeye, king and silver). Scenic floats—easy, good for all ages; 2 hour, 3 hour and 5 hour. Call today (907) 595-5555. www.drifters lodge.com. [ADVERTISEMENT]

Cooper Landing

S 48.4 A 101.4 H 130.7 Cooper Landing is located at the west end of Kenai Lake. **Population:** 293. **Emergency services:** Cooper Landing Volunteer Ambulance/Rescue, phone 911. Nearest hospital is Central Peninsula in Soldotna (50 miles) or Providence Seward Medical Center in Seward (48 miles).

Visitor Information: Cooper Landing Chamber of Commerce operates a log cabin visitor center at **Milepost S 47.6**, adjacent Wildman's convenience store and towing service. Open daily in summer; phone (907) 595-8888.

Private Aircraft: State-owned Quartz Creek airstrip, 3 W; elev. 450 feet; length 2,200 feet; gravel; unattended. Floatplanes land at Cooper Lake.

Cooper Landing stretches along several miles of the Sterling Highway (see map). The post office is located on Snug Harbor Road, **Milepost S 47.9** Sterling Highway. The Cooper Landing Library is located at Mile 0.8 Bean Creek Road. All visitor facilities are available in Cooper Landing; see advertised accommodations and services this section. Gas at Sunrise Inn (**Milepost S 44.9**) and at Hamilton's (**Milepost S 48.5**).

Cooper Landing was named for Joseph Cooper, a miner who discovered gold here in 1894. A school and post office opened in the 1920s to serve the miners and their families living in the area. Cooper Landing was

Cooper Landing

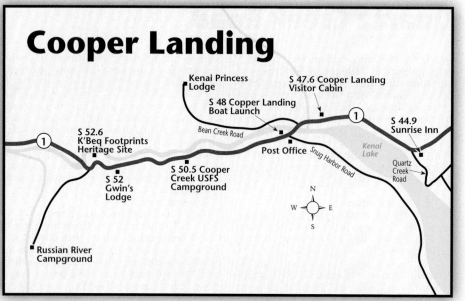

connected to Kenai by road in 1948, and to Anchorage in 1951. According to the Alaska Dept. of Community and Regional Affairs, the population of the area nearly doubles each summer to support tourism businesses and activities.

Cooper Landing Museum is located at Milepost S 48.7. The museum features a fully articulated brown bear skeleton. Look for the museum complex on the north side of the highway, housed in the pioneer school and post office buildings.

Sterling Highway Log
(continued)

S 48.4 A 101.4 H 130.7 CAUTION: Speed limit 35 mph westbound. Heavily congested area next 4 miles, with many driveways fronting the highway. Watch for sloughing pavement on highway shoulders. Narrow road, no turnouts. Drive with care.

S 48.5 A 101.5 H 130.6 Lodging at **The Hutch Bed and Breakfast** (description follows). Hamilton's Place; gas.

The Hutch B&B. 12 clean, smoke-free rooms with private baths at very reasonable rates. Plus new 2-bedroom cabin. Continental breakfast served until 10 A.M. WiFi. Common area TV/VCR. View mountain goats, Dall sheep and Kenai River from our covered decks. Our parking area accommodates boat trailers and large vehicles. Look for the "Bunny Trail" sign. Phone (907) 595-1270, fax (907) 595-1829. See display ad this page. [ADVERTISEMENT]

S 48.7 A 101.7 H 130.4 Cooper Landing Museum complex on the north side of the highway, housed in the pioneer school and post office buildings. The museum features a fully articulated brown bear skeleton.

S 49.4 A 102.4 H 129.7 Large gravel turnout to south on busy curve by Kenai River. The highway winds along the Kenai River.

S 49.7 A 102.7 H 129.4 Kenai Riverside Campground, RV Park and B&B. On the banks of the Kenai River, in Cooper Landing. 30 open, level RV sites; 18 partial hookups; 2 pull-throughs; 20/30 amps plus water. 10 dry sites. B&B rooms; riverside campsites; showers; fish cleaning area; dump station. Guest discounts on guided fishing and rafting trips. Visa/MasterCard; phone 1-888-KENAIRV [888-536-2478]; info@kenai RV.com; www.kenaiRV.com/mp. See display ad this page. [ADVERTISEMENT] ▲

S 49.9 A 102.9 H 129.2 Alaska Rivers Co., right side westbound. Rafting daily on the beautiful Kenai River. Half-day scenic

float, or full-day canyon trip with exhilarating rapids. Trips include snack and/or picnic lunch; excellent opportunity for wildlife viewing; professional guides; and all equipment. All ages welcome. Guided drift boat fishing for all species of fish. Riverfront cabins on private grounds. Family-owned and operated by Cooper Landing residents. (907) 595-1226. Email: info@ alaskariverscompany.com. www.alaska riverscompany.com. See display ad this page. [ADVERTISEMENT]

S 50.1 A 103.1 H 129 Alaska Wildland Adventures offers Kenai River trips.

Kenai River Trips with Alaska Wildland Adventures (AWA). Rafting and fishing day trips on the Kenai River since 1977. Join a scenic natural history float, a full-day Kenai Canyon raft trip, or fish with our friendly, professional guides for the Kenai River's world-famous salmon and rainbow trout. Gear provided; four raft departures daily. Located in Cooper Landing; look for the blue sign! Overnight cabin rentals with private bath available. Save $5 with this ad! 1-800-478-4100; info@alaska rivertrips.com; www.alaskarivertrips.com/ mp. See display ad on facing page. [ADVERTISEMENT]

S 50.3 A 103.3 H 128.8 Slow for 35-mph speed zone eastbound through Cooper Landing.

S 50.5 A 103.5 H 128.6 Bridge over Cooper Creek.

Cooper Creek USFS Campground (South). Huge cottonwood trees mark the entrance to wooded camping area to south (Loop B): 23 large, level sites on good gravel

COOPER LANDING ADVERTISERS

road; tables, water, firepits, firewood, out-houses; campground host. Camping fee is $18 single, $28 double. Campsites may be reserved, phone 1-877-444-6777 or visit www.recreation.gov. ▲

S 50.6 A 103.6 H 128.5 Cooper Creek USFS Campground (North). Turnoff to north for narrow 0.2-mile 1-way gravel road through Loop A camping area; 7 small sites (2 riverside sites), tables, firepits, outhouse, bear-proof food locker. Camping fee $18/night. Walk-in tent camping area. ▲

Sackett's restaurant to south.

S 50.7 A 103.7 H 128.4 Double-ended turnout to south.

S 51 A 104 H 128.1 *Begin 55-mph speed zone westbound; slow for curves.*

Begin 45-mph speed zone eastbound.

S 52 A 105 H 127.1 Gwin's Lodge to south is a historic log roadhouse and long-time local landmark; restaurant, cabins, tackle, general store; phone (907) 595-1266.

Gwin's Lodge. See display ad this page.

S 52.6 A 105.6 H 126.5 U.S. Forest Service K'Beq Footprints Heritage Site north side of highway, Russian River USFS Campground to south. Descriptions follow.

K'Beq Heritage Site, operated by Kenaitze Indian Tribe, has a large parking area and outhouse, information center and gift shop. Walk paths on guided tour or just stop for a short walk and pick up a brochure about local plants and Native history.

USFS Russian River Campground access road to south (*CAUTION: Slow for bumps and dips in road*). Fee station at Mile 0.2 and parking area; Upper Russian Lake and Russian Falls trailhead parking at Mile 1.1 (see trail descriptions following); dump station at Mile 1.3; Park Manager at Mile 1.6; camping and day-use sites to Mile 1.9; Lower Russian Lake trailhead parking at Mile 2.6. The Russian River Campground is often full during the summer, particularly during the Russian River red salmon runs. Arrive early! There are 84 sites, toilets, water, tables, firepits and firewood. *CAUTION: Bears are frequent visitors to this campground and may be on trails and at river. Please do not clean fish at the river or in the campground; use Kenai River cleaning stations.*

Camping fees (subject to change): $18 single RV occupancy, $28 double RV occupancy, $11 12-hour day-use parking, $8 dump station. Concessionaire-operated. Reserve campsites by phoning 1-877-444-NRRS or visit www.recreation.gov. ▲

The **Russian River**: Closed to all fishing April 15 through June 15. Bait prohibited at all times in Russian River drainage. Check regulations for limits and other restrictions. Red salmon run starts mid-June. Second run begins July 20–25 and lasts about 3 weeks. Must use flies prior to Aug. 21. Silver salmon to 15 lbs., run begins mid-August. Catch-and-release only for rainbows in lower part of river at all times that season is open. *NOTE*: Please do not clean fish at the river or in the campground; use Kenai River cleaning stations located near the ferry crossing. *CAUTION: Bears in this area will get into belongings. Keep your backpack on or near. Do not leave food in your pack. Do not leave your cleaned fish lying around. Do NOT approach bears. There have been attacks in this area.* 🐟

Lower Russian Lakes Trail: elev. 500

"Stop, Chop and Throw" sign reminds fishermen to properly dispose of fish carcasses after cleaning their catch. (©Sharon Nault)

feet; hiking time 1½ hours; good trail first 3 miles; spur trail to Russian River Falls viewing platform. A good place to view jumping salmon from mid-June–end of July, and a nice family hike. Handicap accessible trail. There are pathways and metal stairways to

Fishing the Upper Kenai River

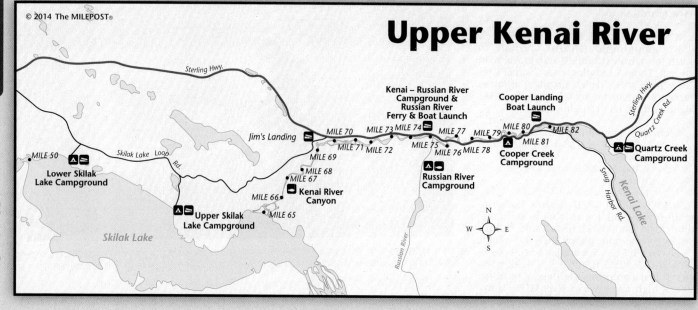

© 2014 The MILEPOST®

Upper Kenai River

The Kenai River originates in Kenai Lake, about 100 road miles south of Anchorage, and flows 85 river miles west to Cook Inlet. For anglers, the river divides itself into 2 rivers: the "upper" and the "lower" Kenai River. The first 17.3 miles of the river—from Kenai Lake to Skilak Lake—constitutes the Upper Kenai River. The Upper Kenai River is closed to motorized boats from approximately 1 mile downstream of the Cooper Landing Boat Launch (River Mile 80.7) to Skilak Lake.

Following is a log of campgrounds, recreation areas and river access points on the Upper Kenai River. See pages 600-601 for access points on the Lower Kenai River. If it is a road-accessible river access, the milepost and road are given first.

Upper Kenai River Access

Most of the following locations offer either camping or fishing, or both. No symbols are being used here to define these items as they apply in nearly all entries.

Milepost 0.2 Quartz Creek Road/River Mile 85.5. Quartz Creek Recreation Area; boat launch, day-use area and campground on Kenai Lake, just south of **Milepost 44.9** Sterling Highway.

Milepost 48 Sterling Highway/River Mile 82. Cooper Landing Boat Launch at Kenai Lake Outlet. This public access point is near the Kenai River Bridge. Concrete boat launch adjacent Kenai River Bridge; restrooms, day-use parking, viewing decks, telescopes and informational panels. Fees charged for parking and boat launch.

Milepost 50.5 Sterling Highway/River Mile 79.1. Cooper Creek Campground North; the campground loop on the north side of the highway is on the south bank of the river. (Cooper Creek Campground South is on the south side of the highway and parallels Cooper Creek.)

Milepost 52.6 Sterling Highway/River Mile 75. Russian River Campground. Fishing access to Russian River. Good fishing for red salmon. Popular during the salmon runs. *Watch for bears!*

Milepost 54.9 Sterling Highway/River Mile 73.5. Russian River Ferry. The ferry crosses the Kenai River to the mouth of the Russian River. This recreation site is popular and heavily used during salmon runs. Fee charged for ferry transport.

Milepost 55.5 to 56.8. 3 parking areas with river access.

Milepost 0.1 Skilak Lake (loop) Road/River Mile 70.4. Jim's Landing; accessed via a 0.2-mile road to the west bank of the river. Experienced boaters only.

Milepost 57.9 Sterling Highway/River Mile 69.9. Kenai National Wildlife Refuge Visitor Information Center.

River Mile 65 Skilak Lake Inlet. Hike the 1.3-mile Hidden Creek Trail from Milepost 4.5 Skilak Lake Road for view of Skilak Lake and Kenai Mountains. *CAUTION: Skilak Lake Road travels through prime brown bear habitat. Hikers should be aware of the possibility of encountering a bear and plan accordingly.*

Milepost 8.4 Skilak Lake Road/River Mile 58. Upper Skilak Lake Campground.

Milepost 13.7 Skilak Lake Road/River Mile 51.1. Lower Skilak Lake Campground.

River Mile 50.2 Skilak Lake Outlet. Boat access only. Good fishing opportunities in this area.

access the river's edge. Stay out of the green fenced areas. This area is under bank restoration. **Upper Russian Lake:** elev. 690 feet, 12 miles. Trail continues to Cooper Lake at end of Snug Harbor Road (see **Milepost S 47.9**). Public-use cabins along trail. Winter use: good snowmobiling to lower lake only, avalanche danger beyond.

S 53 A 106 H 126.1 Bridge over Kenai River. Cooper Landing (eastbound sign). Watch for bears and moose from bridge.

S 53.2 A 106.2 H 125.9 Wide shoulder parking to north. Gravel road leads north to **Resurrection Pass Trailhead**, large parking area with toilet and registration kiosk. This 38-mile-long USFS trail climbs to Resurrection Pass (elev. 2,600 feet) and descends to the north with trailhead near Hope on Turnagain Arm.

S 53.6 A 106.6 H 125.5 Turnout to south with 1,100-foot-long woodchip trail along Kenai River was established in 1992 to preserve, protect and interpret Kenaitze Indian Tribe cultural and natural resources in this area. Fishing access and parking (no RVs or trailers).

S 53.7 A 106.7 H 125.4 Resurrection Pass trailhead to north.

S 53.8 A 106.8 H 125.3 Turnout to south connects with Kenaitze woodchip trail along Kenai River.

Distance marker westbound shows Soldotna 41 miles, Kenai 44 miles, Homer 115 miles.

S 54.6 A 107.6 H 124.5 Small gravel parking area to south at Chugach National Forest boundary sign.

S 54.8 A 107.8 H 124.3 Small parking area to south is used by motorists who do not want to pay the daily fee at Sportsman's Landing.

S 54.9 A 107.9 H 124.2 Kenai-

Russian River Access/Sportsman's Access Site (ADF&G)/Kenai-Russian River Ferry entrance to south; 180-space parking lot *(minimum 24-hour parking fee charged)*, scenic overlook, picnic tables, boat launch, toilets and access to bank fishing and ferry. Privately operated 26-person **Russian River Ferry** crosses the Kenai River to opposite bank and to the mouth of the Russian River for fishermen. Early red salmon run usually arrives by June 15 on the Russian River. The second run usually arrives in mid-July and is the larger of the 2 runs. *CAUTION: Bears frequently walk the riverbanks. Call out if you see a bear.*

Fees (subject to change): 24-hour parking, vehicle under 20 feet, $10.25; vehicle over 20 feet, $13.25; ferry $9.25 adults, $4.50 children 3-11 years; boat launch $10.25. America the Beautiful Annual Pass and

Senior Pass discounts. During salmon season this recreation area is heavily used; parking area fills up quickly.

S 55 A 108 H 124.1 Entering **Kenai National Wildlife Refuge** westbound, administered by the USF&WS; contains more than 1.97 million acres of land set aside to preserve the moose, bear, sheep and other wildlife found here. Leaving Game Management Unit 7, entering Unit 15 westbound.

Distance marker eastbound shows Cooper Landing 7 miles, Seward 54 miles, Anchorage 108 miles.

NOTE: Actual driving distance between physical mileposts 55 and 58 is 3.6 miles.

S 55.5 A 108.5 H 123.6 Parking area to south; Kenai River access.

S 56.4 A 109.4 H 122.7 Parking area to south; Kenai River access.

S 56.8 A 109.8 H 122.3 Double-ended parking area to south; Kenai River access.

S 57.2 A 110.2 H 121.9 Fuller Lakes trailhead (well marked); parking to north. Steep hike with scenic views. No camping at trailhead. **Lower Fuller Lake**, arctic grayling; **Upper Fuller Lake**, Dolly Varden.

S 57.9 A 110.9 H 121.2 Large gravel parking area for Jim's Landing boat trailer overflow parking, toilets.

S 58 A 111 H 121.1 East junction with Skilak Lake Road which loops southwest past Kenai National Wildlife Refuge recreation sites to rejoin the Sterling Highway at **Milepost S 75.3**.

> **Junction** with Skilak Lake Road. See "Skilak Lake Road" log on page 590.

CAUTION: Moose Danger Zone next 21 miles westbound to Milepost 79. This stretch of highway crosses the Kenai National Wildlife Refuge and has one of the highest moose-vehicle collision rates in the state.

Actual driving distance between physical mileposts 58 and 59 is 1.2 miles.

S 60 A 113 H 119.1 Large double-ended turnout to north *(abrupt pavement edge)*. Easy-to-miss turnoff (not signed) down hill to south leads to **Jean Lake Campground**; 3 sites, picnic area; boat launch, rainbow fishing. *(Big rigs: Check access before driving down to Jean Lake.)*

S 60.6 A 113.6 H 118.5 Gravel turnout to south overlooking lake (view obscured).

S 61.4 A 114.4 H 117.7 Skyline Trail: double-ended parking area to south, trailhead to north. Skyline Trail leads north into the Mystery Hills, steep climb, good views.

S 62.6 A 115.6 H 116.5 Large gravel turnout to north. Hideout Hill to the south.

Highway straightens westbound and descends into old Kenai Burn. *CAUTION: High speed traffic on straightaway westbound; pass with care.*

Eastbound traffic descends toward Kenai River.

S 64 A 117 H 115.1 Mystery Creek Access Road (gated) to north. This road provides access to the Mystery Hills area; ATVs prohibited. For seasonal opening dates, contact Kenai NWR at (907) 262-7021.

S 68.8 A 121.8 H 110.3 Turnoff to south for Petersen Lake (0.4 mile, turn right at fork) and Kelly Lake (0.6 mile, go straight) public campgrounds. Both sites have lakeside gravel parking with picnic tables, firepits, toilets, water and a boat launch. **Kelly** and **Petersen lakes** have

rainbow population. Access to Seven Lakes trail.

S 70.7 A 123.7 H 108.4 Egumen Lake trailhead parking area to south (trailhead is east of parking area). Half-mile marshy trail to **Egumen Lake** (lake not visible from highway); good rainbow population.

S 71.3 A 124.3 H 107.8 Parking areas both sides of highway. Entrance to Watson Lake public campground; 0.4-mile drive from highway to small campground with 3 sites, toilets, picnic tables, fire grates, water, and steep boat launch (suitable for canoes or hand-carried boats). East Fork Moose River trailhead. **Watson Lake**, rainbow.

S 72.9 A 125.9 H 106.2 Paved double-ended turnout to south, lake to north.

S 75 A 128 H 104.1 End of Scenic Byway designation.

S 75.3 A 128.3 H 103.8 West junction with Skilak Lake Road, which loops southeast past Kenai National Wildlife Refuge recreation sites to rejoin the Sterling Highway at **Milepost S 58**.

> **Junction** with Skilak Lake Road. See "Skilak Lake Road" log on page 590.

S 76 A 129 H 103.1 Entering Kenai National Wildlife Refuge lands eastbound.

S 76.3 A 129.3 H 102.8 Distance marker westbound shows Sterling 5 miles.

S 79 A 132 H 100.1 *CAUTION: Moose Danger Zone next 21 miles eastbound to Milepost 58.*

S 79.5 A 132.5 H 99.6 Kenai Keys Road. *Begin 4-lane divided highway westbound. Begin 2-lane undivided highway eastbound.*

S 80.3 A 133.3 H 98.8 Turnoff for lodging, camping, fishing packages, boat rentals, Kenai River access and Bing's Landing State Recreation Site (description follows).

Bing's Landing State Recreation Site (0.5 mile from highway to campground turnoff) is a large campground in a forest setting, accommodating rigs of all sizes. There are has 36 tent/RV campsites, tables, water, firepits, toilets (wheelchair accessible),

dumpster. Firewood available. Campground host. Picnic area, boat launch. Naptown Rapids Trail begins at campground. Camping fee $10/night, 7-day limit June 1–Aug. 15, 15-day limit all other times; boat launch $10. Access to Kenai River. A busy place when the fish are in. Parking ($5 fee) in launch area; toilets and fee boxes.

S 80.5 A 133.5 H 98.6 Welcome to Sterling (westbound sign). *Slow for 45 mph speed zone westbound.*

S 80.6 A 133.6 H 98.5 Very large double-ended paved parking area to south.

S 80.8 A 133.8 H 98.3 June Drive.

Sterling

S 81 A 134 H 98.1 Located on the Sterling Highway at the confluence of the Moose and Kenai rivers. **Population:** 5,690. **Emergency services:** Central Emergency Services, **Milepost S 83.7**, phone 911. **Hospital**, Central Peninsula in Soldotna, phone (907) 714-4404. **Elevation:** 150 feet. **Climate:** Average winter temperatures from 4°F to 22°F; summer temperatures from 46°F to 65°F. Annual precipitation 20 inches.

This unincorporated community serves the summer influx of Kenai River sportfishermen, campers and canoeists paddling the Moose and Swanson rivers. Businesses with a Sterling mailing address extend from the Bing's Landing turnoff at **Milepost S 80.3** west to **Milepost S 84.9** on the Sterling Highway.

Traveler services include food, gas, diesel; the **Wash Out Laundromat** (on Swanson River Road); gift and hardware/automotive supply stores; and several campgrounds and places to stay. Accommodations/camping at: **Bing Brown's RV Park & Motel** (Milepost S 81), "Mike's" Moose River Resort (Milepost S 81.4), Bill White's Alaska Sports Lodge (Milepost S 82.5); Jana House Hostel & RV Park (Milepost S 83.4), and Alaska Canoe & RV Park (Milepost S 84). Bing's Landing State Recreation Site at **Milepost S 80.3** has

Bing's Landing State Recreation Site at Milepost S 80.3 is a busy place when the fish are in.
(©Sharon Nault)

Skilak Lake Road

Skilak Lake Road offers camping, boating and fishing at 4 lakes. (©Sharon Nault)

Originally part of the first Sterling Highway that opened in 1950, the 19-mile Skilak Lake Road is a good gravel road that loops off the Sterling Highway at **Milepost S 58**, traveling through the Skilak Wildlife Recreation Area to campgrounds, trails and fishing spots before rejoining the Sterling Highway at **Milepost S 75.3**. NOTE: Do not leave valuables in unattended boats or vehicles.

CAUTION: Skilak Lake Road travels through prime brown bear habitat. The Kenai National Wildlife Refuge cautions hikers to be aware of the possibility of encountering a bear and plan accordingly.

Distance from east junction (EJ) with Sterling Highway at Milepost S 58 is followed by distance from west junction (WJ) with Sterling Highway at Milepost S 75.3.

EJ 0 WJ 19 Junction with Sterling Highway at **Milepost S 58**.

EJ 0.1 WJ 18.9 Double-ended turnout to west across from turnoff to Jim's Landing day-use area, 0.2 mile from road on Kenai River; toilets, tables, firepits, water, boat launch, parking area.

Pavement ends westbound.

NOTE: The Kenai River downstream from Jim's Landing is considered Class II and Class III white water and for experienced boaters only. Wear a personal flotation device. The Kenai River is non-motorized to Skilak Lake. Motors may be used on Skilak Lake to travel to Upper Skilak Lake Campground boat ramp. There is no road access to the Kenai River between Jim's Landing and Upper Skilak Lake Campground; be prepared to travel the entire distance by boat. Use caution when crossing Skilak Lake, as winds from Skilak Glacier frequently create dangerous boating conditions. Be prepared to wait overnight at river mouth until winds abate.

EJ 0.6 WJ 17.9 East entrance to Upper Kenai River Trail; trailhead parking, map and trail chart. Hike in 0.5 mile for scenic view of Kenai Canyon. Oversized vehicle parking.

EJ 1.9 WJ 17.1 Hideout trailhead; parking.

EJ 2.3 WJ 16.7 West entrance to Lower Kenai River Trail; trailhead parking. Hike in 0.3 mile to see regrowth from 1991 Pothole Lake Fire.

EJ 2.4 WJ 16.6 Pothole Lake Overlook; gravel parking area overlooks scene of Pothole Lake forest fire of 1991. Interpretive sign on fire. Brush obscures view.

EJ 3.5 WJ 15.5 Hidden Lake Campground, 0.5 mile down paved road, is an exceptionally nice lakeshore camping area with 44 sites on paved loop roads. It has picnic pavilions, a dump station, wheelchair-accessible toilets, tables, water, firepits, firewood, dump station, non-potable water and boat launch. Campground host. Campfire programs Fri.–Sat. evenings in summer at amphitheater. Observation deck for viewing wildlife. Camping fee $10 for vehicles. Trailer parking area, interpretive exhibits and kitchen shelter with barbecue. Access to "Burnies Trail." Good place for swimming near launch. ♿ ⛺

Hidden Lake, lake trout average 16 inches and kokanee 9 inches, year-round, best from May 15 to July 1, use spoon, red-and-white or weighted, by trolling, casting and jigging. This lake is a favorite among local ice fishermen from late December through March. ⟡

EJ 4.5 WJ 14.5 Parking area and information sign at Hidden Creek trailhead; 3 mile round-trip hike to beach on Skilak Lake.

©Sharon Nault

EJ 5.1 WJ 13.9 Scenic overlook with sweeping view of one arm of Skilak Lake. Evidence of 1996 Hidden Creek Fire is visible.

EJ 5.4 WJ 13.6 Gravel parking area (no facilities) at Skilak Lookout trailhead; 5 mile round-trip hike.

EJ 6 WJ 13 Parking for Bear Mountain trailhead; 2 mile round-trip hike (moderate, steep) to view of Skilak Lake and probable wildlife sightings.

EJ 6.8 WJ 12.2 Turnout with overlook (steep drop-off, no guardrails).

EJ 7.6 WJ 11.4 Upper Ohmer Lake public-use cabin parking. Located a short walk from here, this popular cabin must be reserved in advance. Cost is $45 per night. Phone (907) 262-7021.

EJ 8.4 WJ 10.6 Upper Skilak Lake Campground, drive 1.8 miles along Lower Ohmer Lake; wide, paved 0.2-mile loop road through well-maintained campground (good for big rigs). There are 25 campsites (some sites on lakeshore), tables, toilets, firepits, water, and boat launch with boat trailer parking. Campground host. Large day-use picnic area with covered tables. Camping fee $10/vehicle, $5/tent site (walk-in). Access to 1.5-mile-long Vista Trail from campground. ⛺

EJ 8.6 WJ 10.4 Lower Ohmer Lake Campground side road to parking area on lake; 5 campsites, toilet, boat launch, firepits, tables. ⛺

Lower Ohmer Lake, rainbow 14 to 16 inches, year-round. **Skilak Lake** offers rainbow and Dolly Varden. Red salmon enter lake in mid-July. ⟡

EJ 9.3 WJ 9.7 Turnout overlooking Engineer Lake.

EJ 9.4 WJ 9.6 A 0.4-mile side road (narrow in places) leads to **Engineer Lake**; boat launch and Seven Lakes trailhead (4.4-mile hike to campground at Kelly Lake). Turnaround and parking area with firepits at Engineer Lake.

EJ 11.7 WJ 7.3 Large, paved, double-ended parking area to south with dump stations and toilets.

EJ 13.7 WJ 5.3 Wide gravel 1-mile side road leads south to **Lower Skilak Lake Campground**; 14 campsites, tables, toilets, firepits, picnic areas and boat launch for Skilak Lake and Kenai River fishing. CAUTION: Skilak Lake is cold; winds are fierce and unpredictable. Wear life jackets! ⛺

Kenai River from Skilak Lake to Soldotna. Consult regulations for legal tackle, limits and seasons. King salmon 20 to 80 lbs., use spinners, excellent fishing June to August; red salmon 6 to 12 lbs., many, but hard to catch, use flies, best from July 15 to Aug. 10; pink salmon 4 to 8 lbs., abundant fish on even years Aug. 1 to Sept. 1, spoons; silver salmon 6 to 15 lbs., use spoons, Aug. 15 to Nov. 1; rainbow, Dolly Varden 15 to 20 inches, June through September, use spinners, winged bobber, small-weighted spoon. ⟡

EJ 18.5 WJ 0.5 Bottenintnin Lake; well-marked side road leads 0.3 mile to large parking area (good turnaround) on lakeshore; no facilities, carry out trash. This is a shallow lake: No sport fish, but nice for recreational canoeing. Watch for loons and grebes.

EJ 18.9 WJ 0.1 Turnout with hunting information sign. Pavement ends eastbound.

EJ 19 WJ 0 Junction with Sterling Highway at **Milepost S 75.3**.

Return to Milepost S 58 or S 75.3 Sterling Highway

36 tent/RV campsites.

The name Sterling was formalized in 1954 when a post office was established. The Sterling post office is at **Milepost S 81.4**. Sterling has one school. **Sterling Baptist Church** at **Milepost S 83.4** (Swanson River Road). Moose River Raft Race and Sterling Days are held in July.

Sterling Highway Log
(continued)

S 81 A 134 H 98.1 Bing Brown's RV Park & Motel. Jim and Debbie just flat take care of you. Quiet, wooded setting, full hookups, park dump station, guest showers and laundry. Campground fish cleaning station. Daily social hour around the fire-pit. Easy double access off the highway. Spacious motel kitchenette rooms are fully outfitted, private baths, satellite TV, parking by your door. Liquor store (check out Jim's willow wine rack) stocks favorite brands, excellent wine selection. Ice. Fishing tackle and new convenience store with groceries, ice cream, travel items. Large, year-round storage area for boat/RV/trailer/etc. Reasonable rates. www.bingbrowns.com; (907) 262-4780. See display ad this page. [ADVERTISEMENT]

S 81.2 A 134.2 H 97.9 Moose River Auto & RV Parts. See display ad this page.

S 81.4 A 134.4 H 97.7 "Mike's" Moose River Resort & Hot Tub, Riverfront Chalet & RV Sites. See display ad this page.

S 81.5 A 134.5 H 97.6 Sterling post office (ZIP code 99672) to south.

S 81.7 A 134.7 H 97.4 Gas, diesel, ATM, food.

S 81.9 A 134.9 H 97.2 Turnoff to south at east end of bridge for **Izaak Walton State Recreation Site**, located at the confluence of the Kenai and Moose rivers. Turn on access road by picturesque sod-roofed log cabin. Day-use parking areas and campground with 31 campsites; tables, toilets, water, dumpster, boat launch. Firewood available for $5. Campground host. Camping fee $10/night, 7-day limit; day-use parking $5 after 30-minute grace period; boat launch $10. Good access to Kenai River; fly fishing only.

S 82 A 135 H 97.1 Bridge over **Moose River**; 0.3 mile of fishing down to confluence with Kenai River. *CAUTION: Drive carefully during fishing season when fishermen walk along bridge and highway.* Reds here in June. Big summer run of reds follows into August; silvers into October. **Kenai** and **Moose rivers** (confluence), Dolly Varden and rainbows, salmon (king, red, pink,

silver). June 15 through October for trout; year-round for Dolly Varden. King salmon from May through July, pink salmon in August and silver salmon from August through October. This is a fly-fishing-only area from May 15 through Aug. 15; closed to fishing from boats, May 15 until the end of the king salmon season or July 31, whichever is later. Always check ADF&G regulation booklet or call (907) 262-9368 Soldotna, for updates.

This is one terminus of the Swan Lake canoe trail *(see "Swanson River Road" log on page 593 for information on canoe trail).*

S 82.5 A 135.5 H 96.6 Access to **Bill White's Alaska Sports Lodge** (description follows).

Bill White's Alaska Sports Lodge. Where fishing and comfort come together in beautiful new riverfront chalets (sleeps up to 5) with full kitchen and bath. Lodge rooms for 2 with private bath, lounging deck. The best professional guides on the Kenai River assure a great experience for the seasoned angler and novice alike. This is where Alaskans come to play! Make your reservations now to ensure your preferred dates for fishing, lodging and Alaska tours. Military discounts. Toll-free 1-800-662-9672. In Alaska, phone (907) 260-8454, Mail: Bill White, P.O. Box

Be alert for moose: They cross the road without warning. (©Sharon Nault)

Swanson River Road leads to campsites and canoe trails. (©Sharon Nault)

1201, Sterling, AK 99672. Email wbw@ alaskasportslodge.com; www.AlaskaSports Lodge.com. [ADVERTISEMENT]

S 82.7 A 135.7 H 96.4 Truck weigh station; senior center to south.

Highway narrows to 2 lanes westbound. Begin divided 4-lane highway eastbound.

S 83.4 A 136.4 H 95.7 Junction with Scout Lake Loop Road south to Morgan's Landing State Recreation Site (see details at **Milepost S 84.9**) and **junction** with **Swanson River Road** to north. **Sterling Baptist Church** (Sunday worship 11 A.M. and 6 P.M.) at Swanson River Road junction. Access via Swanson River Road north to **The Wash Out Laundromat** (0.1 mile), **Jana House Hostel & RV Park** (0.4 mile; see description following), and Swan Lake Road (Mile 17). Access to popular canoe trails.

Junction with Swanson River Road. See "Swanson River Road" on page 593.

Jana House Hostel & RV Park. New! Easy access for big rigs. Full-service 60 amp

pull-through RV and tent sites. Fish cleaning station. Private/dorm-style rooms. Bathroom/shower/kitchen privileges. Satellite TV. Large parties welcome. Easy access to Moose and Kenai rivers. Turn north on Swanson River Road, Mile 83.4 Sterling Highway (0.4 mile in, off highway). 38670 Swanson River Road. Reservations phone (907) 260-4151. Fax (907) 562-9982. Email: janamae@hot mail.com; spenardpawnshop@yahoo.com. [ADVERTISEMENT]

Sterling Baptist Church. See display ad this page.

The Wash Out Laundromat. See display ad this page.

S 83.5 A 136.5 H 95.6 Central Emergency Services to north.

S 84 A 137 H 95.1 Alaska Canoe & RV Park. Wooded setting, full service RV hookups, including 30-amp. New deluxe cabins with private baths. Hot showers and laundry. Free WiFi. Big rigs welcome. The park store has tackle, gear and equipment rental including rafts and river or sea kayaks. Ready to enjoy a stunning Alaska adventure? Book half-day to multi-day Swanson River canoe trip. Any experience level can enjoy this amazing river system's pristine wilderness. See wildlife, catch fish, enjoy bird viewing (swans, geese, loons, osprey, and more). This is the trip you'll talk about and remember. And the best part is the dependable shuttle service to/from pickup and drop-off points, at your convenience! Look for the signs and canoes. www.alaskacanoetrips.com; email alas kacanoe@yahoo.com. (907) 262-2331. See display ad this page. [ADVERTISEMENT]

S 84.9 A 137.9 H 94.2 Turnoff to south for Scout Lake Loop Road (4.3-mile paved road) which leads to Scout Lake day-use area and Morgan's Landing State Recreation Area and Campground (descriptions follow) before rejoining the Sterling Highway at **Milepost S 83.4.** *Begin 55 mph Highway Safety Corridor westbound to Soldotna for Sterling Highway traffic. Fines double in these zones.*

Scout Lake State Recreation Site (0.1 mile south) has water, toilets and a covered picnic shelter. Scout Lake has good fishing for stocked rainbows and grayling.

Drive 1.5 miles south on Scout Lake Loop Road and turn right on Lou Morgan Road (paved, winding road; use caution), then drive 2.4 miles for **Morgan's Landing State Recreation Area**; day-use parking area, 41 campsites, 10 pull-through sites, some double sites in park-like setting, picnic tables; gravel paths down to Kenai River; toilets and water; $10 camping fees, $5 day-use fee. 7-day limit.

Morgan's Landing SRA is one of the few public areas offering good access to bank fishing on the **Kenai River.** Fishing for king salmon, mid-June through July, average 30 lbs. Red salmon average 8 lbs., use flies in July–Aug.; silver salmon to 15 lbs., Aug.–Sept., use lure; pink salmon average 4 lbs. with lure, best in July, mainly even-numbered years; rainbow and Dolly Varden, use lure, June–Aug. Alaska State Parks Special Management Area Headquarters is located at Morgan's Landing.

S 85.4 A 138.4 H 92.7 Solid waste transfer station.

S 87.7 A 140.7 H 91.4 Robinson Loop Road to north, Tustumena Loop Road to south.

Swanson River Road: World-Class Canoe Trails

Swanson River Road leads north from **Milepost S 83.4** to what *Alaska* magazine calls "a world-class canoe trail system." Located within the David Spencer Wilderness Unit of Kenai National Wildlife Refuge, the system consists of 2 canoe trails: the 60-mile Swan Lake route, connecting 30 lakes; and the 80-mile Swanson River route, linking 40 lakes. Trips can range anywhere from 1 to 7 days.

Swanson River Road connects canoeists with the Swanson River route at 2 places: Swanson River Landing, 17.5 miles north of the Sterling Highway, and Paddle Lake at Mile 12 Swan Lake Road, entrance to the Swan Lake canoe trail.

Basic canoe skills are required to successfully negotiate these canoe trails. Sudden winds pose the greatest danger on lake crossings, so it is recommended that canoeists stick to the shoreline rather than cutting straight across the lakes. The most physically demanding part of a canoe trip on these trails are the portages, from short watery canals to one-mile long portage trails, though none are too grueling if you pack light as you would for backpacking.

In *Alaska* magazine's "Peaceful Paddling on the Kenai Canoe Trails," author Andy Hall reveals an insiders perspective.

"The Kenai Canoe Trails afford the quintessential Alaska wilderness adventure. Visitors and locals alike can find something on this trip to suit their tastes.

"These trails are broken into two systems: Swan Lake and Swanson River. Both are located within the Kenai National Wildlife Refuge and are equally breathtaking and equally adventurous. Swanson River is the road less traveled and has a few more long portages, but both are well worth a side trip.

"The options for itineraries are almost limitless. Canoe Lake #1 and #2 as well as some of the other lakes close to the Swan Lake trailhead are great for day trips to fishing and paddling areas. For the weekend traveler, just a day's paddle gets you to the heart of the trail system on more isolated Gavia Lake, with camping and other recreation. Those who have a little more time (five days) can do the popular loop trail from the put in on Swan Lake Road to the Moose River bridge outside of Sterling.

"Even for the novice canoeist, the Kenai Canoe Trails are feasible and fun. In just a few hours of steady but leisurely paddling (and some hiking over portages), you can be deep in the wilderness enjoying the serenity of the lakes.

"There are numerous established campsites along the lakeshores though travelers must keep in mind that this is wilderness camping, and the sites are primitive. Minimal-impact camping and recreation are also the rules, and you should leave all areas just as you found them.

"But the trip isn't just about paddling. There's plenty of fishing, hiking, sightseeing, canoeing, kayaking, wildlife viewing & bird watching (200 species in this area). Be sure to take your binoculars and camera.

"For comprehensive information on the trails and everything you need to know to have a great trip, *The Kenai Canoe Trails* by Daniel Quick (www.northlite.biz/canoe) is a must-read and must-carry."

Locally, canoe rentals, shuttle service and

Swanson River Road visitor brought bike and bug net. (©Sharon Nault)

information are available at **Alaska Canoe & RV Park, Milepost S 84** Sterling Highway; www.alaskacanoetrips.com, email alaska canoe@yahoo.com or phone (907) 262-2331. Also contact Kenai National Wildlife Refuge, Ski Hill Road, Box 2139, Soldotna, AK 99669, for more information.

CAUTION: Do not leave valuables in vehicles at canoe trailheads. Drive with headlights on at all times. Watch for truck traffic at all times.

SWANSON RIVER ROAD LOG

Swanson River Road is a fairly wide and level winding gravel road. Although well-maintained, be prepared for washboard. Posted speed limited is 35 mph.

Distance from junction with the Sterling Highway (J) is shown.

J 0 Junction with Sterling Highway at **Milepost S 83.4. Sterling Baptist Church.**
  J 0.1 The Wash Out Laundromat.
  J 0.4 Jana House Hostel & RV Park. 🏕

  J 0.6 Robinson Loop Road; rejoins Sterling Highway at **Milepost S 87.5.**
  Pavement ends, gravel begins, northbound.
  J 3.5 Turnout.
  J 4.4 Entering Kenai National Wildlife Refuge. Turnout with interpretive display.
  J 7.8 Mosquito Lake, turnout; 0.5-mile trail to lake. Rainbows. 🎣

  J 8.6 Turnout.
  J 9 Silver Lake trailhead parking; 1-mile hike to lake. Rainbow and arctic char. Arctic char are most easily caught in spring when the surface water is still cool. Once summer temperatures warm the surface, the char descend to deeper waters and are much harder to catch. 🎣

  J 10.4 Forest Lakes parking; 0.3-mile trail to lake. Rainbows; best fished from canoe or raft. 🎣

  J 12.8 Small turnout by **Weed Lake** trail; rainbow. 🎣

  J 13 Drake and **Skookum** lakes trail-head parking (not signed), registration kiosk; 2-mile trail. Rainbows and arctic char (spring). 🎣

  J 13.7 Parking and access to Breeze Lake.
  J 13.9 Dolly Varden Lake Campground; 15 sites, water, toilets, boat launch. Large RVs and trailers note: 0.5-mile loop road to campground is narrow and very bumpy; check turnaround space before driving in. Beautiful camping area. Some campsites overlook lake. Fishing for Dolly Varden and rainbow; best in late August and September. 🎣 🏕

  J 14.5 Continue straight ahead north-bound for Swanson River Landing. Southbound stop sign at oil field access road to west (gated; closed to private vehicles). The Swanson River Road was originally built as an access road to the Swanson River oil field. Richfield Oil Co. and Standard Oil established the first oil well—Swanson River Unit No. 1—in September 1957. Because the well was located on Kenai National Moose Range land administered by the U.S. Fish & Wildlife Service, the well was capped as soon as it was completed. It was not until late 1958 that then Interior Secretary Fred Seaton opened the northern half of the range to oil drilling and production. (Kenai National Moose Range became Kenai National Wildlife Refuge in 1980.) Other companies also began drilling in the area, and in 1959, Unocal discovered a major natural gas field near the Swanson River oil field. Current oil and gas fields operator is Hilcorp, Alaska.

  J 15.4 Rainbow Lake Campground; small 3-unit camping area on lakeshore with outhouse, water pump and boat launch. Pack out garbage. Fishing for Dolly Varden and rainbow. *CAUTION: Steep road; difficult turnaround. Large RVs check visually before driving in.* 🎣 🏕

  J 17 Junction with **Swan Lake Road**, which leads east 12 miles and deadends at Paddle Lake access. Driving distance from this junction to facilities and lakes on Swan Lake Road are as follows: Mile 3 Fish Lake Campground (2 campsites, outhouse, tables); Mile 3.5 Canoe Lake (Swan Lake Canoe Route west entrance); Mile 6.1 Merganser Lakes, parking, outhouse, picnic table; Mile 8 Nest Lake parking area; Mile 9.5 Portage Lake (Swan Lake Canoe Route east entrance), 15-minute parking only, outhouse, registration kiosk; Mile 10.1 double-ended pullout with parking; Mile 11.5 gravel turnout; Mile 12 End Swan Lake Road, begin 0.5-mile access road to Paddle Lake (entrance to Swanson River Canoe Route), parking, outhouse, registration kiosk.
  J 17.3 Swanson River Landing Campground; 4 sites, tables, firepits, outhouse and water. 14-day limit. Carry out trash. 🏕

  J 17.5 Swanson River Landing at end of Swanson River Road; gravel parking area, boat launch, fishing. This is the terminus of the Swanson River canoe route, which begins at Paddle Lake at the end of Swan Lake Road. 🎣

Return to Milepost S 83.4
Sterling Highway

Extensive fishwalk along the Kenai River at Soldotna Creek Park. (©Sharon Nault)

S 88 A 141 H 91.1 St. Theresa Drive.

S 88.3 A 141.3 H 90.8 Alaska Horn & Antler Carvings and Rock Shop. Free Mammoth Ivory! That's right! Stop in! Receive one piece of mammoth ivory when you visit us. Horn antlers, bone, stone, ivory, raw products, gift items, jewelry and fine art. Watch Tom carve. Large pull-through driveway, Mile 88.3 Sterling Highway. Phone (907) 262-9759. [ADVERTISEMENT]

S 88.7 A 141.7 H 90.4 West Drive to south. Public fishing access and boat launch on **Longmere Lake**; stocked with rainbows and silver salmon.

Gas station. *CAUTION: Moose Danger Zone next 6 miles westbound.*

S 89.8 A 142.8 H 89.3 Jim Dahler Road.

S 91.3 A 144.3 H 87.8 Gas and diesel station, grocery and liquor store to south.

S 91.4 A 144.4 H 87.7 Pan for gold. Ice cream.

S 91.8 A 144.8 H 87.3 Harley Davidson to south. Soldotna city limits (sign).

S 92 A 145 H 87.1 Birch Ridge public golf course.

S 92.2 A 145.2 H 86.9 Car wash, laundry and showers to south. State Division of Forest, Land and Water Management. Fire danger indicator sign. Soldotna Animal Hospital; phone (907) 260-7851.

S 93.7 A 146.7 H 85.4 Brewery to south (just to the east of Fred Meyer); turn on side street. This is a very popular eatery serving pizza, soups, sandwiches, salads and, of course, beer.

Begin 4-lane highway and 35-mph speed zone westbound through Soldotna.

NOTE: Begin 55-mph Highway Safety Corridor eastbound to **Milepost S 84.9**. *Fines double in these zones.*

S 94 A 147 H 85.1 Traffic light at Devin Drive; turnoff to Fred Meyer to south. Overnight RV parking permitted in parking lot. Also access to fast food and gas station from Fred Meyer parking lot. Bucket's Sports Grill to north.

This is also the easiest access for westbound traffic to East Redoubt Avenue and Swiftwater Park Campground (see description next milepost).

S 94.1 A 147.1 H 85 East Redoubt Avenue; access to **Swiftwater Park Municipal Campground** (0.4 mile from highway), **Kenai River Hideaway B&B** (3.1 miles from highway) and Moose Range Meadows Fishing Access (3. 7 miles); descriptions follow.

Follow East Redoubt 0.4 miles south to turnoff for **Swiftwater Park Municipal Campground**, then another 0.4 mile west to park entrance. This municipal campground has 42 campsites (some pull-throughs) along a loop road above the Kenai River; tables, firepits, firewood, phone, dump station, 2-week limit, litter barrels, toilets, boat launch. Camping and day-use fees posted. No camping Sept. 30 to May 1. Excellent fishing access to Kenai River.

Kenai River Hideaway B&B. See display ad on page 601.

For **Moose Range Meadows Public Fishing Access**, continue on East Redoubt Avenue—which turns into Keystone Drive—3.7 miles to the fishing access on the north bank of the Kenai. This Kenai NWR Kenai River public fishing access is open July 1 to Sept. 30; gravel parking area, toilets, no camping. Fishing platforms and boardwalks along a 3-mile stretch of river in this area. Moose Range Meadows is subject to fishing closures.

S 94.2 A 147.2 H 84.9 Traffic light at **Soldotna Y.** Westbound travelers continue straight on Sterling Highway for Soldotna businesses (about 1.5 mile stretch) and continuation of highway to Homer. There is a book store and several casual eateries here at the Y.

Turn north on Kenai Spur Highway for more Soldotna businesses, the city of Kenai, Nikiski and Captain Cook State Park.

Junction with Kenai Spur Highway to city of Kenai. See "Kenai Spur Highway" log beginning on page 602.

CAUTION: Moose Danger Zone next 6 miles eastbound.

S 94.4 A 147.4 H 84.7 Gas station. Access to **Soldotna Creek Park** (day-use only); follow road behind Mexican restaurant. The park has benches overlooking the river, a playground, picnic tables and restrooms. It is also the site of the annual Kenai River Festival and Progress Days.

Follow trail down hill to extensive fishwalks along the Kenai River. Massive ice flows sometimes devastate these fishwalks in winter, and they have to be repaired or rebuilt in spring for summer use.

S 95 A 148 H 84.1 *Actual driving distance between physical Mileposts 94 and 95 is 0.6 mile.*

S 95.1 A 148.1 H 84 Traffic light at Binkley Street; access to fire station, police station and post office. Peninsula Center Mall: 24-hour Safeway.

Sterling Highway log to Homer continues on page 608.

Soldotna

S 95.2 A 148.2 H 83.9 On the western Kenai Peninsula, the city stretches over a mile southwest along the Sterling Highway and northwest along the Kenai Spur Highway. **Population:** 4,299; Kenai Peninsula Borough 56,756. **Emergency Services:** Phone 911 for all emergency services. **Alaska State Troopers** at Mile 22 Kalifornsky Beach Road just off Sterling Highway, phone (907) 262-4453. **City Police**, phone (907) 262-4455. **Fire Department**, phone (907) 262-4792. **Ambulance**, phone (907) 714-4444. **Hospital**, Central Peninsula at 250 Hospital Place, phone (907) 714-4404. **Veterinarians:** Soldotna Animal Hospital (907) 260-7851, Twin Cities Veterinary (907) 262-4581.

Visitor Information: The Soldotna Visitor Information Center is located in downtown Soldotna on the Sterling Highway south of Kenai River's David Douthit–Veterans Memorial bridge. Fish walk access to Kenai River. The center is open daily 9 A.M. to 7 P.M. mid-May to mid-September; 9 A.M. to 5 P.M. Monday–Friday mid-September to mid-May. Write: Greater Soldotna Chamber of Commerce, 44790 Sterling Highway, Soldotna, AK 99669; phone (907) 262-1337 or 262-9814, fax (907) 262-3566. For a free Soldotna recreation guide, phone (907) 262-9814; email info@soldotnachamber.com; or visit www.soldotnachamber.com.

Elevation: 115 feet. **Climate:** Average daily temperature in July, 63°F to 68°F; January, 19°F to 23°F. Annual precipitation, approximately 18 inches. **Radio:** KSRM 920, KSLD 1140, KDLL-FM 91.9, KKIS-FM 96.5, KPEN-FM 101.7. **Television:** Network channels 2 (NBC), 4 (FOX), 7 (PBS), 11 (CBS), and 13 (ABC) from Anchorage, and cable channels. **Newspapers:** *Peninsula Clarion* (daily); *The Redoubt Reporter* (weekly).

Private Aircraft: Soldotna airstrip 1 SE on Funny River Road; elev. 107 feet; length 5,000 feet; asphalt; fuel 100LL; unattended.

The town of Soldotna was established in the 1940s because of its strategic location at the Sterling–Kenai Spur Highway junction. (Visitors may see the homestead cabin, which became Soldotna's first post office in

1949, at its original location on the Kenai Spur Highway at Corral Avenue.)

Soldotna was incorporated as a first-class city in 1967. It has become the retail, governmental and medical hub of the Peninsula. Kenai Peninsula Borough headquarters and state offices of the Departments of Highways, Public Safety, Fish and Game, and Forest, Land and Water Management are located here.

Central Peninsula Hospital in Soldotna serves the Soldotna and Kenai areas. Soldotna is also headquarters for the Kenai Peninsula Borough school district. University of Alaska–Kenai Peninsula College is also located in Soldotna.

While the best unobstructed views of the volcanic mountains across Cook Inlet are from either the Kenai Spur Highway north of Soldotna or the Sterling Highway south of Soldotna, there are frequent views of Mount Redoubt from Soldotna city streets. Mount Redoubt (elev. 10,197 feet) erupted in March 2009, after a 20-year nap. For the current status of the volcano, visit the Alaska Volcano Observatory at www.avo.alaska.edu/index.php.

Soldotna gets very busy during fishing season. Popular fishing rivers in the area include the Kasilof River and the Kenai River. For those fishermen who want a more remote fishing spot—or for visitors who want to see wildlife and glaciers—local outfitters offer fly-in fishing trips for rainbow, grayling, salmon and Dolly Varden.

Lodging & Services

All facilities are available, including supermarkets, banks, hotels/motels, bed-and-breakfasts, cabin rentals and lodges restaurants and drive-ins, medical and dental clinics, golf courses, veterinarians, pet supply/

David Douthit-Veterans Memorial Bridge across the Kenai River. (©Sharon Nault)

dog wash, UPS shipping services and churches. Two shopping malls are located on the Sterling Highway in town, including **Sweeney's Clothing Store** and **Trust Worthy Hardware & Fishing** can help you with those items you forgot to bring.

Joyce Carver Memorial Library offers temporary cards for visitors; Internet access, large sunlit reading areas for both adults and children; Alaska videos on summer Saturday afternoons; call ahead for schedule. Open 10 A.M. to 6 P.M. Mon., Wed., Fri., and Sat., and 10 A.M. to 8 P.M. Tue., and Thurs. 235 N. Binkley St., Soldotna, phone (907) 262-4227.

Soldotna Regional Sports Complex, on Kalifornsky Beach (K-Beach) Road, has an Olympic-sized hockey rink, a jogging track, 2 racquetball/volleyball courts, a weight and exercise room, dressing rooms and showers. The

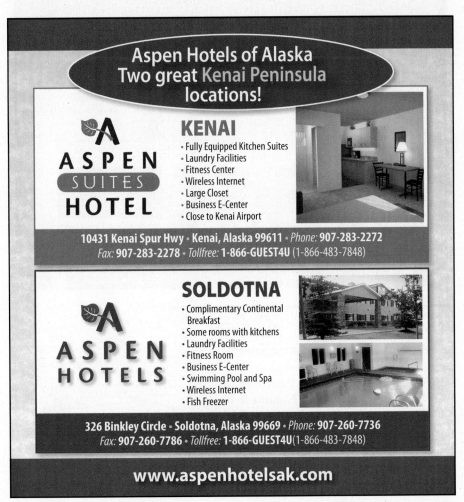

Sports Center also has convention facilities and meeting rooms. Phone (907) 262-3151 for more information.

Edgewater Lodge & RV Park, located right on the Kenai River, across from the Soldotna Visitor Center. 15 spacious riverfront rooms with private baths, 60 full and partial hookups, WiFi, laundry, showers, grassy sites, guide services, bank fishing and fish cleaning facilities. Walk to stores and restaurants. Reservations and information: Phone (907) 262-7733; website www. sunriseresorts.com. P.O. Box 976, Soldotna, AK 99669. See display ad on page 601.
[ADVERTISEMENT]

Camping

There are several private campgrounds located in and near Soldotna; see ads this section. The Fred Meyer at the "Y" allows overnight RV parking (use signed areas).

There are 2 **City of Soldotna** campgrounds: Swiftwater and Centennial. Campsites for both tents and RVs (no hookups). These campgrounds are heavily used; check in early.

For Swiftwater Campground, turn off the Sterling Highway on East Redoubt Street, between Driven Auto Body and the Holiday gas station by the "Y" (**Milepost S 94.1** Sterling Highway), and drive 0.4 mile to campground turnoff; 40-plus campsites (some pull-throughs) along a loop road above the Kenai River; tables, firepits, firewood, phone, dump station, 2-week limit, litter barrels, toilets, boat launch. Camping fee; day-use fee. No camping Sept. 30–May 1. Steep stairway down to Kenai River.

Centennial Park Campground is 0.1 mile from the Sterling Highway just south of the Kenai River bridge on Kalifornsky Beach Road (turn west at **Milepost S 96.1**) on the banks of the Kenai River; 176 campsites (some on river), tables, firepits, firewood provided, water, restrooms, dump station, pay phone, 2-week limit. Register at entrance. Boat launch and fishing site from fishwalk.

Transportation

Air: Soldotna airport is south of Soldotna at Mile 2 Funny River Road. Turn off the Sterling Highway at **Milepost S 96.1**, just after crossing Kenai River bridge. Charters available from Natron Air, phone 1-877-520-8440 or (907) 262-8440.

Local: Taxi service; motorhome, auto, van and pickup rentals; vehicle leasing; and boat rentals and charters are available.

Highway: Accessible via the Sterling and Seward highways (Alaska Routes 9 and 1), 148 miles from Anchorage.

Attractions

Fishwalks. Several public fishwalks have been constructed in the Soldotna area in order to make the popular Kenai River more accessible to the public. Although this beautiful river cuts right through the center of town, public access is limited by private land ownership along the riverbank, as well as the nature of the river itself. The wide, swift Kenai River does not have an easily accessible, gently sloping riverbank. The fishwalks allow the city to put people on the riverbank without degrading the environment.

Check out the fishwalks located at the city's 2 campgrounds (Centennial and Swiftwater); at the Soldotna Visitor Center (by the Kenai River bridge); behind the Donald E. Gilman River Center on Funny River Road; and at Soldotna Creek Park, located off the Sterling Highway in the center of town (access road is behind the Mexican restaurant); and the 2 off of East Redoubt Street approximately 3.5 & 6 miles (these are USFWS fishwalks called Upper & Lower Moose Range Meadows). Swiftwater Park, the Soldotna city campground down East Redoubt Street (turn by the Fred Meyer) has the most extensive fishwalk, with 200 feet of riverfront fishwalk. Swiftwater Rotary park and the Soldotna Visitor Center have handicap accessible river access with assistance. There are handicap-only fishing platforms at East Redoubt, Centennial, Swiftwater and Soldotna Creek parks.

Soldotna's Homestead Museum, located

off K-Beach Road on Centennial Park Road, features a wildlife display and some of the area's early homestead cabins. Soldotna's first homesteaders arrived in 1947. How they lived is revealed in a collection of handmade utensils and pioneer artifacts on display in the former Chamber of Commerce log tourist center. Slikok Valley School, the last of the Territorial log schools, built in 1958, is maintained in its original state. Damon Hall, a large building constructed for the Alaska Centennial, features an outstanding display of wildlife mounts. An interesting display of Alaska Native artifacts are also displayed in Damon Hall. Fishing has been a mainstay, beginning with the first settlers, and boats are part of the museum's collection as well. A profusion of Alaska wildflowers lines the pathways between the historic log buildings. The museum is open May 15–Sept. 15, 10 A.M. to 4 P.M., Tuesday through Saturday; Sunday noon to 4 P.M.; closed the remainder of the year.

Birch Tree Gallery. Unique gifts. Large selection of pottery, original art, jewelry, stained glass, hand-carved birds and note cards by Alaskan artists. Hand-knit wool hats, vests, scarves, socks and designer baby garments. Beautiful quality yarn, knitting supplies and porcelain buttons. Located ¼ mile Funny River Road. (907) 262-4048.

[ADVERTISEMENT]

Natron Air. How about an unforgettable flight over breathtaking sights for the most lasting memory of your Alaskan experience? Natron Air is the charter for you. If you're an avid fisherman, you know the success of fly-out fishing trips generally exceeds that of road accessible waters. The Kustatan

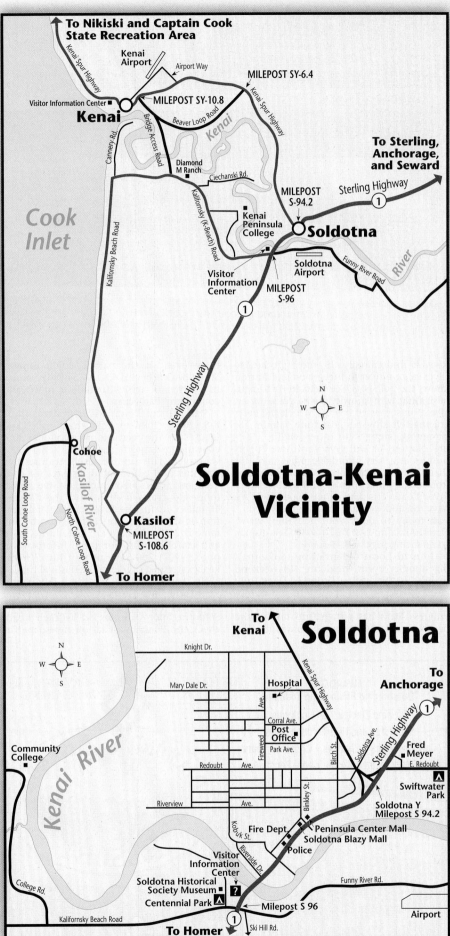

Soldotna-Kenai Vicinity

To Nikiski and Captain Cook State Recreation Area
Kenai Airport
Airport Way
MILEPOST SY-6.4
Kenai Spur Highway
Visitor Information Center
MILEPOST SY-10.8
Kenai
Beaver Loop Road
Kenai
Cannery Rd.
Bridge Access Road
Diamond M Ranch
Ciechanski Rd.
Kalifornsky (K-Beach) Road
Kenai Peninsula College
MILEPOST S-94.2
Sterling Highway
To Sterling, Anchorage, and Seward
1
Soldotna
Visitor Information Center
Soldotna Airport
Funny River Road
River
MILEPOST S-96
Cook Inlet
Kalifornsky Beach Road
1
Sterling Highway
N
W E
S
Cohoe
South Cohoe Loop Road
North Cohoe Loop Road
Kasilof River
Kasilof
MILEPOST S-108.6
To Homer

Soldotna

To Kenai
Knight Dr.
N
W E
S
Mary Dale Dr.
Kenai Spur Highway
Hospital
Corral Ave.
Ave.
Post Office
Park Ave.
Birch St.
Soldotna Ave.
Sterling Highway
To Anchorage
1
Fred Meyer
E. Redoubt
Community College
Fireweed
Redoubt Ave.
Swiftwater Park
Soldotna Y Milepost S 94.2
Kenai River
Riverview Ave.
Binkley St.
Kobuk St.
Fire Dept.
Riverside Dr.
Police
Peninsula Center Mall
Soldotna Blazy Mall
Visitor Information Center
Soldotna Historical Society Museum
Centennial Park
?
Milepost S 96
Funny River Rd.
Airport
College Rd.
Kalifornsky Beach Road
To Homer
1
Ski Hill Rd.

Mount Redoubt, visible from Soldotna, last erupted in March 2009.

Stop by the Soldotna Visitor Information Center, just south of the Kenai River bridge on the Sterling Highway in Soldotna. Fish walk access and travel help available. (©Kris Valencia, staff)

River is undoubtedly the most productive silver salmon river in this region and Natron knows the hot spots. See bears in their natural habitat with knowledgeable guides in an area of unsurpassed beauty. Watch the bears grazing, chasing and catching salmon, or clamming, along with other wildlife viewing. Natron Air will give you these opportunities at a very affordable price. Look for their sign at the Soldotna Airport, 1.8 miles from the Sterling Highway bridge on Funny River Road. Tim and Janet Pope say: "We have fun and we want to share it with you." Call today to book your activities! www. NatronAir.com. 1-877-520-8440. See display ad on facing page. [ADVERTISEMENT]

Join in Local Celebrations. Soldotna's big summer event, held the 4th weekend in July, is the annual **Progress Days** (July 26-27, 2014). Started in 1960 to commemorate the completion of the natural gas line, Progress Days has grown into one of the peninsula's biggest annual attractions. The main event is the parade down Binkley Street, which begins 11 A.M. Saturday morning. Other activities include a rodeo and community barbecues.

The annual **Kenai River Festival** (June 6-8, 2014), held at Soldotna Creek Park, focuses on the recreational, economic and educational importance of the Kenai River watershed. This summer event features free activities and educational displays for children and adults alike, including live music, food and crafts booths, and the 5K and 10-mile Run for the River. A special attraction is the Salmon on Parade, led by the famous 20-foot "Skuq'a." Live music, food and crafts booths. For more information, phone (907) 260-5449 or visit http://www. kenaiwatershed.org/kenairiverfestival.html.

In August, watch for the 1-day **Kenai Peninsula Beer Festival**. The third annual event was held last year on Saturday at the Soldotna Sports Center on K-Beach Road; check the Peninsula Clarion newspaper or

with the visitor center about 2014 dates. Local brewers include St. Elias Brewing Company (their restaurant is on the Sterling Highway just east of the Fred Meyer) and **Kassik's Brewery** (see description on page 606), located at **Milepost SY 19.1** on the Kenai Spur Highway.

In January, the Peninsula Winter Games take place in Soldotna. Activities include an ice sculpture contest, ice bowling, and the Native Youth Olympics. Games, booths, concessions and demonstrations are held throughout the weekend. For more information visit http://soldotnachamber.com.

The first Saturday in February is also the start of the Tustumena 200 Sled Dog Race. The T-200 is a qualifier for the Iditarod and Yukon Quest, so mushers from around the world head to the Kenai Peninsula to particiapte. The race starts in Kasilof, heads into the Caribou Hills to Homer, and ends back in Kasilof. There are several accessible checkpoints from which to view the race. For more information visit www.tustumena200.com.

Kenai National Wildlife Refuge Visitor Center, located at the top of Ski Hill Road (south turnoff at **Milepost S 97.9**) and also accessible from Funny River Road, hosts some 25,000 visitors annually. This modern center has dioramas containing lifelike mounts of area wildlife in simulated natural settings. Free wildlife films are shown on the hour daily from noon to 4 P.M., June–August. Information available here on canoeing, hiking and camping. There is a ¾-mile-long nature trail with an observation platform on Headquarters Lake. For those looking for a longer hike, try the 3-mile (round-trip) Centennial Trail. In winter, 8 miles of cross-country ski trails are available, accessed from the visitor center. The Alaska Geographic bookstore has books, posters and videos. Open weekdays 8 A.M. to 4:30 P.M year-round; weekends June–August, Saturdays 9 A.M. to 5 P.M. and Sundays noon–5 P.M. September–May Saturday only 10 A.M. to 5 P.M. No admission fee.

The refuge was created in 1941 when President Franklin D. Roosevelt set aside 1.73 million acres of land (then designated the Kenai National Moose Range) to assure

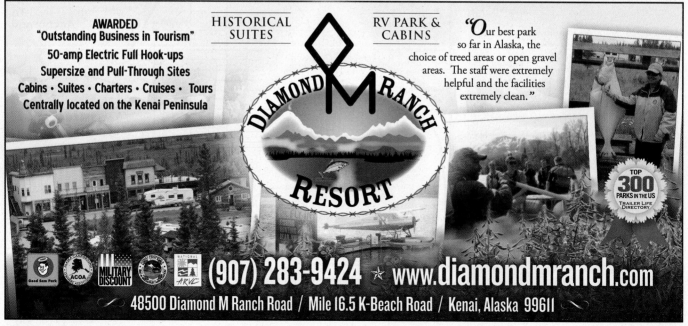

that the large numbers of moose, Dall sheep and other wild game would remain for people to enjoy. With the passage of the Alaska National Interest Lands Conservation Act in 1980, the acreage was increased to 1.92 million acres and redesignated Kenai National Wildlife Refuge. Write: Refuge Manager, Kenai National Wildlife Refuge, P.O. Box 2139, Soldotna, AK 99669; phone (907) 262-7021; www.kenai.fws.gov.

Take a canoe trip in the Kenai National Wildlife Refuge on established canoe trails: the Swanson River route (80 miles) and Swan Lake route (60 miles). Complete information on Kenai Peninsula canoe trails is available at the Kenai National Wildlife Refuge visitor center in Soldotna.

Visit Soldotna Municipal Airport. Located on Funny River Road, 1.8 miles east of its intersection with the Sterling Highway, the airport is home to flying services like **Natron Air**; (1-877-520-8440), which offer bear viewing, fly-out hunting and fishing, and flightseeing.

©Kris Valencia, staff

Up on a pedestal by the airport entrance gate is a Starduster SA 100 single-engine, single seat, open cockpit biplane. Built by local residents in the early 1960s, the plane was used for aerobatics at Alaska air shows until the 1990s. It was retired to this spot in 2001 as a remembrance of early Soldotna area aviators.

Fish the Kenai River. Soldotna is one of Alaska's best-known sportfishing headquarters (see ads this section). The largest king salmon ever caught here was in 1985, at 97 lbs., 4 oz. hooked by Les Anderson, a local (see the skin mount of Les's fish and the carving of Les and his fish at the

Soldotna Visitor Center). The early run of kings begins about May 15, with the peak of the run typically occurring between June 12 and 20. The late run enters the river about July 1, peaking between July 23 and 31; season closes July 31. Always check ADF&G regulation booklet or call (907) 262-9368 Soldotna, for updates. The first run of reds enter the river during early June and is present in small numbers through the month; the second run enters about July 15 and is present through early August. In even years pinks are present from early through mid-August. The early silver run arrives in early August, peaks in mid-August, and is over by the end of the month. Late run silvers enter the Kenai in early September, peak in mid-to late September, and continue to enter the river through October. Dolly Varden and trophy rainbows can be caught all summer.

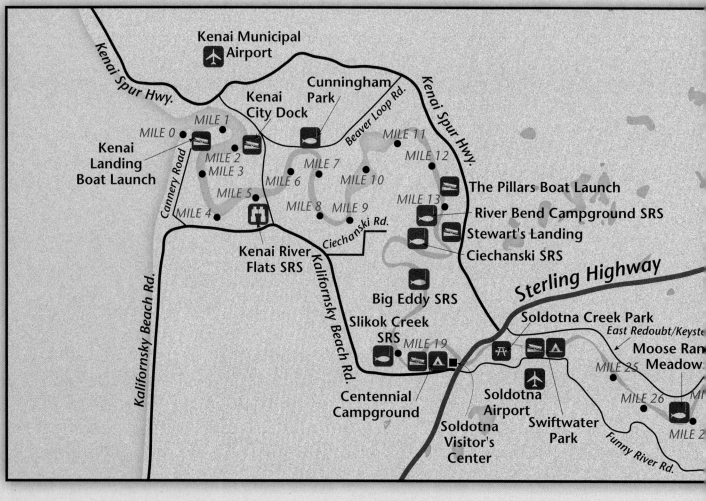

Fishing the Lower Kenai River

The Kenai River is one of Alaska's great treasures. Often referred to as the world's greatest sportfishing river, its turquoise waters have produced the world record king salmon (just over 97 lbs.). The Kenai offers anglers 4 species of Pacific salmon (king, red, silver, pink), as well as rainbow and Dolly Varden.

The watershed of the Kenai River covers approximately 2,200 square miles, or 1.4 million acres, across the central region of the Kenai Peninsula. Driving south from Anchorage, you will enter the Kenai River watershed at Summit Lake and remain in this vast drainage basin almost to Seward on the Seward Highway, and through Soldotna on the Sterling Highway.

Several groups have organized to help maintain the Kenai River. Two of the most active are the Kenai Watershed Forum (www.kenaiwatershed.org) and the Kenai River Sportfishing Assoc. (www.krsa.com).

There are many special regulations regarding boats, motors and fishing on the Kenai River. Please check with Alaska Department of Fish and Game and Alaska State Parks for closures and restrictions, and obtain the current fishing regulations before beginning your visit to the Kenai River.

Use extreme caution while fishing and boating on the Kenai River as it is deep, swift, cold and presents many obstacles throughout its course. This area is also very heavily used, so be courteous of other visitors.

Following is a list of public access points along the lower Kenai River, beginning at Kenai Keys and ending at Cook Inlet. Many charter services are offered in this area; inquire at your campground or hotel about local fishing guide services.

Lower Kenai River Access

River Mile 44.5–46 Kenai Keys State Recreation Site, an undeveloped site accessible by boat on the north bank of the river. There are no facilities. Red salmon fishing can be good from the gravel bars near the site.

Milepost 80.3 Sterling Highway/River Mile 39.5. Bing's Landing State Recreation Site is on the north side of the Kenai and has a 36-site campground and boat launch.

Milepost 81.9 Sterling Highway/River Mile 36.5 Izaak Walton State Recreation Site, located at the confluence of the Kenai and Moose rivers. It is on the north bank of the Kenai and has a 31-site campground and boat launch with good river access. Great salmon fishing but closed to boat fishing during king salmon season. Also check for bank closures.

Milepost 84.9 Scout Lake Loop Road/River Mile 31. Morgan's Landing State Recreation Area offers a 41-site campground and good bank fishing in the Kenai River for trout and salmon throughout the summer. This is one of the few public parks with Kenai River bank fishing.

Mile 11.2 Funny River Road/River Mile 30.5. Funny River State Recreation Site, located on the south bank of the Kenai River, just upstream from the confluence of the Kenai and Funny rivers. It has 10 small campsites and a short trail to a fish-walk and stairs to the Kenai River. Fills up quickly mid-July when fishing season starts.

Milepost 94.1 Sterling Highway/River Miles 23 and 27. East Redoubt Avenue to **Swiftwater Park Municipal Campground** and **Moose Range Meadows Fishing Access.** Swiftwater Park has a fishwalk and boat launch. Site also provides handicap access to riverbank.

For Moose Range Meadows, stay on East Redoubt Avenue until it turns into Keystone Drive; it is 3.7 miles to the fishing access on the north bank of the Kenai. Fishing platforms and boardwalks along a 3-mile stretch in this area. Moose Range Meadows is subject to fishing closures.

Milepost 94.4 Sterling Highway/River Mile 22. Soldotna Creek Park. Fishwalk on the north bank of the Kenai River.

Milepost 95.7 Sterling Highway/River Mile 21. Soldotna Visitor Information Center. The visitor center is located just south of the 5-lane David Douthit–Veterans Memorial Bridge in Soldotna on the west side of the highway. Fishwalk on the south bank of the Kenai River.

Milepost 95.8 Sterling Highway/River Mile 20.3. Centennial Park Municipal Campground, located off Kalifornsky Beach Road on the south bank of the Kenai River; popular bank fishing site. Also handicap fishing platform available. Area closed to boat fishing during king salmon season.

Lower Kenai River

© 2014 The MILEPOST®

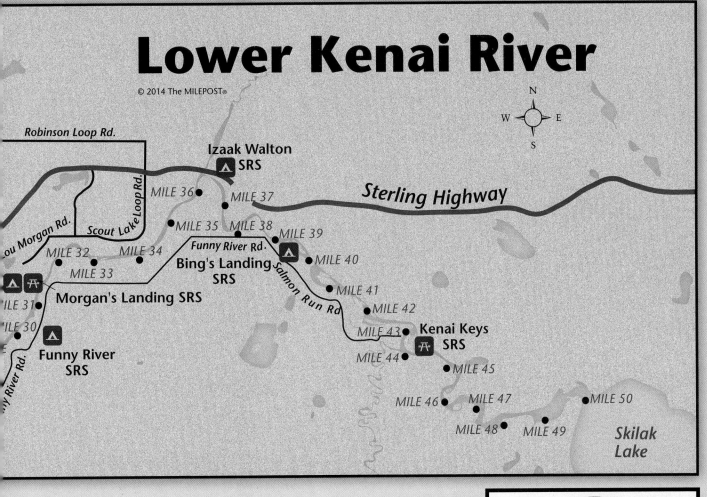

Robinson Loop Rd.

Izaak Walton SRS

MILE 36 · MILE 37 · Sterling Highway

MILE 35 · MILE 38 · MILE 39

Scout Lake Loop Rd.

Lou Morgan Rd.

MILE 32 · MILE 34 · Funny River Rd. · MILE 40

MILE 33 · Bing's Landing SRS

Morgan's Landing SRS

MILE 31 · Salmon Run Rd · MILE 41

MILE 30 · MILE 42

Funny River SRS · MILE 43 · Kenai Keys SRS

MILE 44

MILE 45

MILE 46 · MILE 47 · MILE 50

MILE 48 · MILE 49 · Skilak Lake

Funny River Rd.

Milepost 20.5 Kalifornsky Beach Road/ River Mile 19. Slikok Creek State Recreation Site, accessible from Chugach Drive or from Endicott Drive. The Slikok Creek unit offers trail access to fishing access along the Kenai River on the upstream and downstream sides of Slikok Creek. Good red salmon fishing on south side of Slikok Creek. $5 day use fee or annual pass, $40.

Milepost 17.5 Kalifornsky Beach Road/ River Mile 15.3. From K-Beach Road, Ciechanski Road to Porter Road leads 2.4 miles to private RV parks and Ciechanski State Recreation Site on the Kenai River. This small state recreation site is easy to overlook, as it's tucked in the corner across from Kenai River Quest RV Park. Its primary purpose is to provide restroom access for boaters. There is 12-hour public parking (no camping), a picnic table, outhouse and dock walk (no fishing from dock).

Milepost 4.2 Kenai Spur Highway/ River Mile 12.4. Follow Silver Salmon Drive (paved and gravel) 0.5 mile west for The Pillars Boat Launch (managed by Alaska State Parks) on the Kenai River. Open May 1. Bank fishing is prohibited.

Milepost 1.9 Kenai Spur Highway/ River Mile 14. Big Eddy Road leads west to 12-hour public parking and latrine at Mile 1.4. Road ends at Mile 1.8 (end of Fish Trap Court); access to fishing guides and private boat launch, Big Eddy Jetty.

Milepost 6.4 Kenai Spur Highway/ River Mile 6.5. From Kenai Spur follow Beaver Loop Road 2.7 miles to Cunningham Park public access to Kenai River. The park, which has a trail, fishwalk and restrooms, is one of the more popular area bank fishing

spots during peak salmon runs.

Milepost 10.8 Kenai Spur Highway/ River Mile 1.6. Bridge Access Road leads west 1.6 miles to City of Kenai public dock and boat ramp. Boat launch fees start at $15.

Kenai Spur Highway

Dipnetters crowd the beach off Kenai Spur Highway at Milepost SY 11.9 when the fish are in.
(©Sharon Nault)

The Kenai Spur Highway junctions with the Sterling Highway at the Soldotna Y and leads north through Soldotna 10 miles to the city of Kenai. It ends at Captain Cook State Recreation Area, 39 miles north of Soldotna. This is an excellent 2- to 4-lane paved highway with posted speed limits from 35- to 55-mph.
Distance from Soldotna Y (SY) is shown.

SY 0 Junction with Sterling Highway at Milepost S 94.2 (see page 594).

SY 0.6 Soldotna City Hall.

SY 0.7 Soldotna elementary school to east on E. Park Avenue; playground. Post office is on N. Binkley.

SY 1 Marydale Avenue. Central Peninsula General Hospital 0.4 mile west. 24-hour gas station east side of highway.

SY 1.9 Big Eddy Road to west; 6-hour public parking (1.4 miles); access to fishing guides and private boat launches (1.8 miles).

SY 2.1 Cheechako Drive. Access to Stewart's Landing off Fish Trap Court (¼

mile); private parking and boat launch on Kenai River.

SY 2.3 Sport Lake Road, access to public fishing.

SY 2.8 Distance marker northbound shows Kenai 1 mile, Nikiski 24 miles.

SY 3.3 Small chapel to east is privately owned and rented out for receptions.

SY 4.2 Silver Salmon Drive (paved and gravel) leads 0.5 mile west to **The Pillars Boat Launch** closed October–May (Alaska State Park) on the Kenai River; large gravel parking area, water, toilets, boat ramp, fee station. Bank angling not permitted. Fees: $10/launch, $5/day-use.

SY 6.4 Twin City Raceway to east, a popular venue for motocross races. This intersection is also the south **junction** with **Beaver Loop Road** to west, which provides access to the Bridge Access Road (3.7 miles; see description at **Milepost SY 10.8**). Also access via Beaver Loop Road to **Cunningham Park** (2.7 miles), which has public access to the **Kenai River**, a trail, fishwalk and restrooms;

one of the more popular bank fishing spots during peak salmon runs.

SY 8 *Begin divided 4-lane highway, 45 mph speed zone, northbound. Begin 2-lane highway southbound.*

SY 9.4 Traffic light at Tinker Lane. Access to Peninsula Oilers baseball park, **Kenai Golf Course** (18 holes, open 7 A.M. to 10 P.M., daylight permitting, May–Oct., 907/283-7500) and Kenai Eagle Disc Golf Course.

SY 9.7 Kenai Central High School.

SY 9.8 Challenger Learning Center of Alaska, a science, math and technology space center for Alaska youth; day programs for youth and residential camps. Visit www. akchallenger.org.

SY 10.1 Welcome to Kenai sign.
Begin 35 mph speed zone northbound.

SY 10.2 Traffic light and access east to Walmart and Daubenspeck Family Park. The community park has a small beach, restrooms and parking. The lake is used for ice skating in winter.

SY 10.4 Traffic light at **junction** with Airport Way and Walker Lane. Access east to Home Depot and Kenai airport, access west to Aspen Suites.

SY 10.6 Kenai Plaza shopping; Home Depot, Carrs/Safeway.

SY 10.8 Traffic light at **junction** with south end of Main Street Loop in Kenai to east and Bridge Access Road to west (description follows); Holiday gas station, Arby's. Continue straight ahead on Kenai Spur Highway for Kenai Visitor and Cultural Center.

Bridge Access Road leads to **junction** with Beaver Loop Road (1.3 miles); City of Kenai public dock and boat ramp (1.6 miles west, 0.4 mile north; parking, outhouse, views of Kenai waterfront, $15 launch fee); Kenai Flats boardwalk viewing telescope (2.2 miles); Warren Ames Bridge (2.6 miles); **Kenai Flats State Recreation Site** (2.8 miles); 6-hour parking, picnic tables, information signs, bird watching); and **junction** with Kalifornsky Road (3.3 miles). See **Milepost S 6** in "Kalifornsky Beach Road" log on page 610 (see also area map on page 597).

SY 11 Leif Hansen Memorial Park. The Kenai City Clock and Merchant Marine Memorial are located in the park. The memorial is dedicated to "American WWII Merchant Marine Veterans, all Mariners, present and future."

SY 11.2 Junction with Willow Street. Turn southwest to Frontage Road, then Spur View Drive to Senior Court for Kenai Senior Center (www.ci.kenai.ak.us/senior center.html), located in a large building on the bluff. Turn northeast for post office (on corner of Fidalgo and Bidarka), library and city offices.

SY 11.5 Traffic light at **junction** with north end of Main Street Loop. **Kenai Visitor and Cultural Center** to west (see description in Kenai under Visitor Information and under Attractions). Turn west here and continue toward ocean for Holy Assumption of Virgin Mary Russian Orthodox Church and the St. Nicholas Chapel. This is Kenai's Old Town, a great place to take a walk among interesting historical buildings (see descriptions under Attractions in Kenai).

CAUTION: Lefthand turn for northbound traffic wishing to access the Visitor Center and Old Town crosses 2 busy southbound lanes. Watch for oncoming cars!

Kenai

SY 11.5 Junction of the Kenai Spur Highway with Kenai's Main Street. Kenai is 159 driving miles from Anchorage (about a 3-hour drive) and 89 miles from Homer. **Population:** 7,132. **Emergency Services:** Phone 911 for all emergency services. **Alaska State Troopers** (in Soldotna), phone (907) 262-4453. **Kenai City Police,** phone (907) 283-7879 or 283-7980. **Fire Department and Ambulance,** phone 911. **Hospital** (in Soldotna) Central Peninsula Hospital, phone (907) 714-4404. **Health Center,** phone (907) 335-2022. **Maritime Search and Rescue,** dial 0 for Zenith 5555, toll free. **Veterinarian,** phone (907) 283-4148.

Visitor Information: The Kenai Visitor and Cultural Center, located at Main Street and Kenai Spur Highway, provides brochures, free WiFi, reservation assistance, directions, recommendations, maps and other visitor information. Very nice restrooms. The Visitor Center, managed by the Kenai Chamber of Commerce & Visitor Center, offers year-round art shows, wildlife displays, excellent cultural exhibits, special visitor programs and, during the summer months, an outdoor Saturday market.

Write the Kenai Chamber of Commerce & Visitor Center, 11471 Kenai Spur Highway, Kenai, AK 99611; phone (907) 283-1991, email info@visitkenai.com; www.visitkenai.com.

The historic Moose Meat John's Cabin is located across the parking lot from the Kenai & Cultural Center.

Elevation: 93 feet. **Climate:** Average daily maximum temperature in July, 61°F; January temperatures range from 11° to -19°F. Lowest recorded temperature in Kenai was -48°F. Average annual precipitation, 19.9 inches (68.7 inches of snowfall). **Radio:** KDLL-FM 91.9, KBAY-FM 93.3, KKIS-FM 96.5, KWHQ-FM 100.1, KPEN-FM 102, K-WAVE-FM 105, KGTL 620, KSRM 920, KSLD 1140. **Television:** Several channels and cable. **Newspaper:** *Peninsula Clarion* (daily).

Private Aircraft: Kenai Municipal Airport is the principal airport on the Kenai Peninsula. It is accessible from Willow Street or Airport Way. There is a terminal building with ticket counter and baggage handling for commuter airlines, and a large parking lot. Elev. 92 feet; length 7,575 feet; grooved

KENAI ADVERTISERS

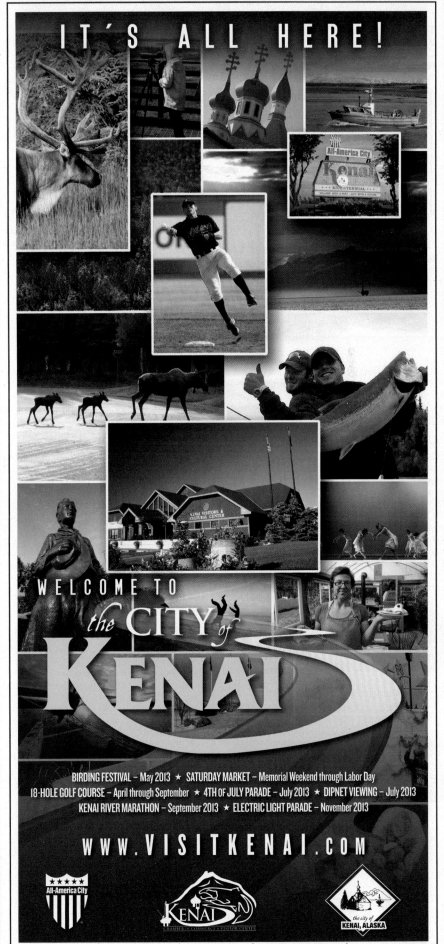

IT´S ALL HERE!

WELCOME TO
the CITY of
KENAI

BIRDING FESTIVAL – May 2013 ★ SATURDAY MARKET – Memorial Weekend through Labor Day
18-HOLE GOLF COURSE – April through September ★ 4TH OF JULY PARADE – July 2013 ★ DIPNET VIEWING – July 2013
KENAI RIVER MARATHON – September 2013 ★ ELECTRIC LIGHT PARADE – November 2013

WWW.VISITKENAI.COM

All-America City

KENAI
CHAMBER OF COMMERCE & VISITOR CENTER

the city of
KENAI, ALASKA

11471 Kenai Spur Hwy | Kenai, Alaska 99611 | (907) 283-1991 | www.kenaichamber.org | info@visitkenai.com

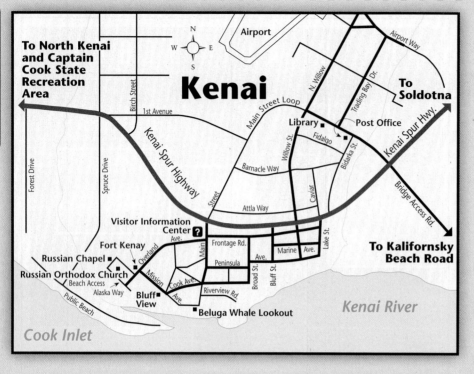

To North Kenai and Captain Cook State Recreation Area

Kenai

Airport

Airport Way

To Soldotna

To Kalifornsky Beach Road

Cook Inlet

Kenai River

Library · Post Office · Visitor Information Center · Fort Kenay · Russian Chapel · Russian Orthodox Church · Beach Access · Bluff View · Beluga Whale Lookout · Public Beach

---

and paved; fuel 100LL and Jet A; attended. A 2,000-foot gravel runway is also available. There is an adjacent floatplane basin with a 4,600-foot water runway; camping spots and slips are available.

Kenai is situated on a low rise overlooking the mouth of the Kenai River where it empties into Cook Inlet. The area affords majestic views across Cook Inlet of 3 major volcanic peaks in the Alaska Range: Mount Spurr (elev. 11,100 feet), the largest, which last erupted in 1992; Mount Iliamna (elev. 10,016 feet), identified by the 3 smaller peaks on its left; and Mount Redoubt (elev. 10,197 feet), which was identified by its very regular cone shape until it erupted in December 1989. Mount Redoubt erupted again in 2009. Both eruptions had significant impact on the aviation and oil industries, as well as the people, of the Kenai Peninsula.

There are good views of Spurr, Iliamna and Redoubt from various points along the Kenai Spur Highway. In Kenai, walk out to the bluff viewpoints on Mission Avenue in Historic Old Town Kenai. There is a public beach access at the end of Spruce Drive, turnoff at **Milepost SY 11.7** Kenai Spur Highway, or try the scenic viewpoint 0.4 mile west on South Forest Drive from **Milepost SY 11.9** Kenai Spur Highway.

Kenai is the largest city on the Kenai Peninsula. Prior to Russian Alaska, Kenai was a Dena'ina Native community. The Dena'ina people fished, hunted, trapped, farmed and traded with neighboring tribes here. In 1791 it became the second permanent settlement established by the Russians in Alaska, when a fortified post called Fort St. Nicholas, or St. Nicholas Redoubt, was built near here by Russian fur traders. In 1797, at the Battle of Kenai, the Dena'ina defeated the Russian settlement of 150 men. In subsequent years, the post remained a minor trading post. In 1848, the first Alaska gold discovery was made on the Russian River. In 1869 the U.S. Army established Fort Kenai (Kenay). The first fish canneries were established in the 1880s. A post office was authorized in 1899.

Oil exploration began in the mid-1950s, with the first major discovery in this area, the Swanson River oil reserves, 20 miles/32.2 km northeast of Kenai in 1957. Two years later, natural gas was discovered in the Kali-

fornsky Beach area 6 miles/9.6 km south of the city of Kenai. Extensive exploration offshore in upper Cook Inlet has established that Cook Inlet's middle-ground shoals contain one of the major oil and gas fields in the world.

The industrial complex on the North Kenai Road is the site of Agrium, which produces ammonia and urea for fertilizer. ConocoPhillips operates an LNG plant and Tesoro has a refinery there.

Offshore in Cook Inlet are 15 drilling platforms, all with underwater pipelines bringing the oil to the shipping docks on both sides of Cook Inlet for loading onto tankers.

Federal and state agencies based in and around Kenai contribute to the local economy. Next to oil, tourism, fishing and fish processing are the leading industries.

Kenai has 2 elementary schools, a middle school and Kenai Central High School.

Kenai is the home of Challenger Learning Center of Alaska (www.akchallenger.org), a science, math and technology space center for Alaska youth, grades 4–12. Students from all over Alaska take part in simulated missions at the facility.

Lodging & Services

Kenai has all shopping facilities and conveniences. Several motels and hotels and about a dozen restaurants and drive-ins are located in Kenai. Medical and dental clinics, banks, laundromats, theaters, pharmacies, supermarkets, and numerous gift and specialty shops are located on and off the highway and in the shopping malls. Local artists are featured at the Kenai Fine Arts Center on Cook Street.

Charlotte's Restaurant. Everyone loves Charlotte's and the contemporary home-style breakfasts and lunches. Unique, original salads and sandwiches. Order the favorite—chicken Caesar sandwich—served on delicious homemade sourdough hoagie. All soups, breads and desserts, such as the local's favorite, black-bottom coconut cream pie, made in-house daily. Reservations for groups suggested 'cause everyone loves Charlotte's! "A truly delightful atmosphere." (907) 283-2777. See display ad this page. [ADVERTISEMENT]

Tanglewood Bed & Breakfast. Fish king salmon from our backyard, on lower Kenai River. View moose, caribou, bears, wolves, eagles, ducks, seals, beluga whales on regular basis. Rooms $100. Common room with fireplace. Fully equipped private suite with Jacuzzi, $150. Full breakfast. Laundry facilities. (907) 283-6771. Open year-round. Life-long Alaskans. See display ad this page. [ADVERTISEMENT]

Kenai Recreation Center on Caviar Street has showers, sauna, weight room, racquetball courts and gym; phone (907) 283-3855 for hours. Indoor swimming and a waterslide are available at the Nikiski Pool (see **Mile SY 23.4** Kenai Spur Highway); phone (907) 776-8800.

The Unity Bike Trail along the Kenai Spur Highway is popular with runners and bicyclists. The mile markers along the Unity trail were put up by local resident Terrence Carlson as part of an Eagle Scout project with help from family, friends and other scouts.

The Kenai Senior Center, accessible from **Milepost SY 11.2** Kenai Spur Highway, is located on the bluff overlooking the Kenai River flats. The center provides a variety of

services to seniors, including a computer room, Internet access, arts and crafts classes, exercise program, quilting, sewing, no-host dinners and an active community outreach program. Visitors are welcome.

Camping

Private RV parks are available in Kenai; see ads this section. Public campgrounds are also available north of Kenai on the Kenai Spur Highway in Captain Cook State Recreation Area (see highway log). Dump stations located at several local service stations and city dock.

Beluga Lookout Lodge & RV Park, 3 blocks from Visitors Center in Historic Old Town Kenai. Overlooking the mouth of the Kenai River, spectacular views of Cook Inlet and Kenai beach, Mount Redoubt, Beluga whales. Book bear viewing and fishing charters. Historic Russian Orthodox Church next door. Lodge rooms, gift shop, private showers, private bathrooms, laundry. 65 full hookups, free WiFi, free TV, pull-throughs, 20-30-50-amps. Caravans welcome. Phone (907) 283-5999; Fax (907) 283-4939; reservations at www.belugalookout.com. Email belugarv@belugalookout.com. See display ad on page 602. [ADVERTISEMENT]

Diamond M Ranch Resort RV Park, Cabins, Suites & B&B. Small working ranch overlooking the magnificent Kenai River, Cook Inlet and the Alaska Mountain Range. Lodging includes historical suites, cabins, B&B. Full hookup, new super-size sites, pull-throughs, free WiFi. Laundromat, showers, fish cleaning facility. The Martin family—long time year-round Alaskans—offer free fun-filled activities: Clam digging, commercial fish-site tours, weekly socials, wildlife viewing, hiking/biking. Secluded setting near towns. www.diamondmranch.com. (907) 283-9424. See display ad on page 598. [ADVERTISEMENT]

Transportation

Air: Kenai Municipal Airport is served by Ravn Aviation (www.flyeravn.com) and Grant Aviation (www.flygrant.com), both of which offer scheduled passenger service to Ted Stevens International Airport in Anchorage and numerous other destinations throughout Alaska. It is a 25-minute flight from Kenai to Anchorage (about 60 miles) and there are more than a dozen flights a day to choose from.

Local: Limousine and taxi service is available as well as car rentals, vehicle leasing, boat rentals and charters.

Highway: On the Kenai Spur Highway, 11 miles north of Soldotna.

Attractions

The Kenai Visitor and Cultural Center, located at Main Street and Kenai Spur Highway, features excellent cultural and wildlife displays, seasonal art shows, Alaska-themed movies, books and reference materials, maps, and apparel. The Visitor Center is headquarters for the annual Kenai Birding Festival, held each May. The Kenai Visitor and Cultural Center also sponsors a Saturday market from May through September that features Alaskan products, crafts and gift items. For more information and a calendar of events, visit www.visitkenai.com.

Watch A Baseball Game. Kenai is the home of the **Kenai Peninsula Oilers**. It is one of 6 teams that make up the Alaska

The Kenai Visitor and Cultural Center is a must-stop for its cultural and wildlife displays, trip planning help and art shows. (©Kris Valencia, staff)

Baseball League. The other teams are the Fairbanks Goldpanners, Anchorage Bucs, Anchorage Glacier Pilots, Matsu Miners and an Athletes in Action (AIA) Baseball franchise. Some fine semipro baseball is played at Coral Seymour Memorial Ball Park in Kenai. For current game schedule, phone (907) 283-7133 or visit their website at www.oilersbaseball.com.

Already Read Books/C Cups Cafe, Explore our melange of already read books, Kenai's Epicenter for the bibliophile or casual reader, while enjoying the intrinsic flair of our cafe. Features specialty coffees, gourmet cupcakes, quiche and delectable pastries. Use the exchange policy to replenish your books for the trip "home." 506 Attla, Kenai, 99611 Purple Building (907) 335-2665. [ADVERTISEMENT]

Kenai Community Library is centrally located at 163 Main Street Loop, adjacent the Fire Station and City Hall. The library has a large collection of Alaskana for history buffs, as well as books, periodicals, CDs, DVDs and audio books. A non-resident library card is available to visitors and summer residents with a local mailing address. WiFi hot spot with free Internet access. Mini laptops may be checked out for use in the library. Phone (907) 283-4378 or go to www.kenailibrary.org for library hours, programs and other information.

Old Town Kenai self-guided walking tour takes in Fort Kenay, the Russian Parish House Rectory, Russian Orthodox church and chapel (see descriptions following). Pick up a walking tour brochure at Kenai Visitors and Cultural Center and walk down Overland Street toward Cook Inlet.

Fort Kenay was the first American military installation in the area, established in 1868. More than 100 men were stationed here in the 1½ years it officially served to protect American citizens in the area. A replica of the fort's barracks building was constructed as an Alaskan Purchase Centennial project by Kenai residents in 1967. This was the site of the original Russian schoolhouse which was torn down in 1956.

Parish House Rectory, constructed in 1881, directly east of Fort Kenay, is considered to be the oldest building on the Kenai Peninsula. Of the 4 rectories contracted by

the Russian Orthodox Church in Alaska it is the only one still remaining. Restored in 1998–99, the rectory continues to be the

Mount Spurr erupted once in 1953, and 3 times in 1992, depositing ash as far away as Anchorage.

Holy Assumption of the Virgin Mary Russian Orthodox Church in Kenai. (©Sharon Nault)

residence of priests who serve the church. Hand-hewn logs, joined with square-notched corners, are covered by wood shingle siding and painted the original colors.

Holy Assumption of the Virgin Mary Russian Orthodox Church, across from the rectory, is one of the oldest Russian Orthodox churches in Alaska and a National Historic Landmark. The original church was founded in 1846 by a Russian monk, Father Nicholai. The present church was built with a $400 grant from the Russian Synod some 50 years after the original, and with its 3 onion-shaped domes is considered one of the finest examples of a Russian Orthodox church built on a vessel or quadrilateral floor plan. Icons from Russia and an 1847 Russian edition of the Holy Gospel—with enameled icons of Matthew, Mark, Luke and John on the cover—are displayed. Regular church services are held here. Please call ahead for tours. Phone (907) 283-4122. Donations are welcomed.

St. Nicholas Chapel was built in 1906 as a memorial to Father Nicholai and his helper, Makary Ivanov, on the site of the original church, which was inside the northwest corner of the Russian trading post of Fort St. Nicholas. The 2 men were honored for their distribution of the first smallpox vaccine in the territory.

Play Golf. Golfers will enjoy the Kenai Golf Course; 18 holes, pro shop, driving range, cart and club rentals. From Kenai Spur Highway, turn on Tinker, then make a left on Lawton. Phone (907) 283-7500.

Volcano and Whale Watching. The Kenai River beach at the west end of Spruce Street and Erick Hansen Scout Park at the end of Kenai's fish-processing industry and Cook Inlet volcanoes, including Mount Redoubt, which last erupted in 2009. Also look for beluga whales, the only all-white whale, in the spring and fall.

Visit a local brewery. Kassik's Brew Stop in North Kenai features 10 quality ales on tap, including their signature brews, Moose Point Porter and Caribou Kilt Scotch Ale. Samples and tours available. From Mile 19.1 Kenai Spur Highway, turn right on Miller Loop, right

on Holt-Lamplight, then left on Spruce Haven. Phone (907) 776-4055; www.kassiks brew.com.

Kenai Parks and Recreation maintain facilities popular with both visitors and residents. Leif Hansen Memorial Park in downtown Kenai on the highway is perhaps the premier location in town for viewing flowers. The park also has a gazebo, water fountain, benches and drinking fountain. Erik Hansen Scout Park, at the end of Upland Street in Old Towne Kenai, features benches and a great view of Cook Inlet. The Kenai Eagle 18-hole Disc Golf Course on Tinker Lane, behind the Peninsula Oilers baseball field, is free and open year-round. Kenai Skate Board Park, located on Coral Street, is designed for skaters and BMX riders.

North Peninsula Recreation. Don't miss the waterslide at the indoor **Nikiski Pool**, located 12 miles north of downtown Kenai at **Milepost SY 23.4** on the Kenai Spur Highway.

Kenai River Flats is a must stop for birdwatchers. Siberian snow geese and other waterfowl stop to feed on this saltwater marsh in the spring. Kenai Flats State Recreation Site on the Bridge Access Road at the west end of Warren Ames Bridge; parking, picnic tables, outhouse and interpretive signs. A boardwalk and viewing telescope for wildlife-watchers is located on the Bridge Access Road east of the Warren Ames Bridge.

The **Kenai Birding Festival** is a natural for this bird–filled area. This annual event is scheduled for May 15-18, 2014. Visit www.kenaibirdfest.com for more information.

Kenai City Dock. Take the Bridge Access Road west from Kenai Spur Highway 1.6 miles then turn off for the City of Kenai public dock and boat launch. A busy and fascinating place in summer, the port has 2 boat launches, a 170-foot concrete dock with floats, 3 cranes, gas and diesel fuel, restrooms and parking. Trailered boats may be launched from May to September. Parking and launch fees charged.

Kenai Spur Highway Log
(Continued)

SY 11.9 Spruce Drive. Follow Spruce Drive west for huge parking area on flat

area near beach; restrooms. A very busy spot during dip netting season. An access road for cars and trucks only from the parking lot to a drop-off/pick-up area on the beach is used to transport fishing and camping gear.

SY 12.1 Traffic light at Forest Drive. Access west to Handicapable Park; playground, toilets. This large forested park has trails and picnic tables (some covered).

Scenic viewpoint with parking at end of Forest Drive overlooks Cook Inlet and has stairway access to beach.

End 4-lane highway, begin 2-lane highway, northbound.

SY 12.8 Kenai Sports Complex; ball fields.

SY 13 Mount Spurr is directly ahead northbound.

SY 17.8 Nikiski Fire Station No. 1.

SY 19 Views through trees of Mount Redoubt to west and Mount Spurr to north.

SY 19.1 South Miller Loop. **Kassik's Brewery** (description follows), a 1.6-mile drive through rural North Kenai, was established in 2004 and has won 4 World Beer Championships and a World Beer Cup. Open daily in summer (May–Aug.) and 6 days a week the rest of the year.

SY 20.5 Tesoro gas station and 2Go Store to west.

SY 21 Agrium Kenai Nitrogen Operations plant. This petrochemical facility produced nitrogen-based agriculture products urea and ammonia. This plant closed September 2007 due to natural gas shortage in Cook Inlet.

SY 21.4 ConocoPhillips 66 LNG Plant.

SY 22.2 Tesoro Road to Tesoro Refinery. The Tesoro Kenai Refinery was built in 1969 and refines about 72,000 barrels of oil a day. The crude oil—of which 67 percent comes from Alaska's North Slope, 20 percent from Cook Inlet, and 13 percent from foreign sources—is turned into propane, gasoline, jet fuel, diesel fuel and fuel oil, among other products.

SY 23.4 Turnoff to west on Poolside Avenue and drive 0.3 mile for **North Peninsula Recreation's Nikiski Pool**, housed in the copper-domed building seen from the highway.

This is a great place to take a break from driving and get in some laps. Kids love the 136' water slide. The Nikiski Pool has lap lanes, kiddie swim area with "Rainbrella" and "Bubble Beach," a hot tub, restrooms with showers and lockers, visitor observation area, weight room, racquetball and volleyball courts, outdoor picnic area and playground, skateboard park and hiking trails (3-mile handicap accessible, fitness stations along the way). The Jason Peterson Memorial Ice Rink is located in the large building behind the pool facility. Courtesy RV parking (must be self–contained). Recently updated playground. Phone (907) 776-8800 for pool hours. Website: www.northpenrec.com.

SY 25.8 Island Lake Road. Senior Center

to east.

SY 26.7 NIKISKI (pop. 4,345). **Emergency Services**, phone 911 for fire and paramedics. **Radio:** KXBA 93.3. Grocery, Chevron gas station, 2 restaurants, bar, liquor store, post office and water-fill station.

Nikiski, also known as "North Kenai" or "The North Road," was homesteaded in the 1940s and grew with the discovery of oil on the Kenai Peninsula in 1957. By 1964, oil-related industries here included Unocal Chemical, Phillips LNG, Chevron and Tesoro. Oil docks serving offshore drilling platforms today include Rigtenders, ConocoPhillips, offshore systems–Kenai (OSK dock). Commercial fishing is still a source of income for some residents.

SY 26.8 Nikiski Fire Station No. 2 at turnoff for Nikishka Beach Road. Access west to Nikiski High School (0.3 mile) and OSK Heliport (0.5 mile). Drive to road end (0.8 mile) for good view of Nikishka Bay and oil platforms in Cook Inlet; Arness Dock, built on a base of WWII Liberty ships (still visible); and scenic view of Mount Spurr and Alaska Range.

SY 29.7 Halbouty Road; access to **Daniels Lake Lodge** (2.1 miles) and **Grouchy Old Woman B&B**.

Daniels Lake Lodge Bed & Breakfast. Secluded along peaceful lakeshore. Forested acreage away from the hustle and bustle but close to activities. Trout fishing. Boats. Hot tub. Moose, loons, eagles, birding. Log cabins or guest-rooms with whirlpool baths. Kitchens. Near hiking, beachcombing, salmon fishing, restaurants, pool with waterslide. Smoke-free. Family friendly. Christian hosts. (907) 776-5578, www.Daniels LakeLodge.com. See display ad this page. [ADVERTISEMENT]

Grouchy Old Woman B&B. See display ad this page.

SY 32.3 Turnout west opposite Twin Lakes.

SY 35.6 Entering **Captain Cook State Recreation Area** northbound. No hunting with firearms (sign).

SY 35.9 Bishop Creek (Captain Cook SRA) Discovery Campground 0.1 mile to west; parking ($5 fee), water, picnic tables, firepits. A 0.2-mile walk through lush forest to beach and creek access, viewpoint and outhouses. A great walk. Spawning red salmon in creek in July and August, silvers August to September. Closed to all salmon fishing.

SY 36.5 Stormy Lake (Captain Cook SRA) day-use area located 0.5 mile east via gravel road (downhill grade); large parking

area, wading area (not much beach), change house, picnic shelter, toilet, water. Dolly Varden, longnose suckers, rainbows, silvers and stocked with arctic char. *Restrictions on boating and fishing may be in effect here in 2014 due to chemical treatment of the lake.*

SY 36.7 Stormy Lake Overlook, a large paved turnout to east, offers a panoramic view.

SY 36.9 One-way 0.3-mile loop road provides access to 2 covered picnic tables located on brushy bluff with view of Stormy Lake.

SY 37.8 Stormy Lake boat launch 0.2 mile. Day-use area with water pump/drinking fountain, toilets, parking and turn-around area. No fires. Popular shore fishing. Day-use fee $5, boat launch $5.

SY 38.6 Turnoff on wide gravel road for Swanson River canoe landing area; 0.6 mile east to parking, picnic tables and toilets, river access. *No turnaround area at river access for vehicles over 35-feet long.* End of the Swanson River canoe trail system.

SY 38.7 Clint Starnes Memorial Bridge crosses **Swanson River**; parking next to bridge. *Watch for fishermen on bridge.* View of Mount Spurr. Fishing for silver and red salmon, and rainbow.

SY 39 Highway ends. Turn left for **Discovery Campground** (0.4 mile) and picnic area (0.5 mile) via gravel access road. Campground has 53 campsites, Maggie Yurick Memorial hiking trail, water, scheduled fireside programs in season. Camping fee $10/night.

Day-use picnic area (keep to right at second fork) has gravel parking area, tables

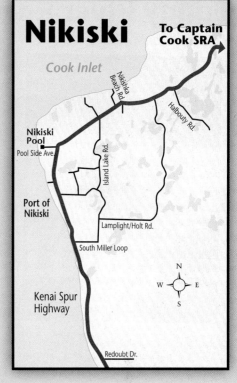

and toilets on bluff overlooking ocean. Stupendous views of Mount Spurr across Cook Inlet. *CAUTION: Steep, high cliffs; no guardrails. Supervise children and pets!* Spur access road to beach (4-wheel drive vehicles only); signed as "unsafe due to high tides and loose sand." Parking area. ATVs are allowed in designated areas only.

Funny River Road

Fishing the Kenai River off Funny River SRS on Funny River Road. (©Kris Valencia, staff)

Funny River Road branches east off the Sterling Highway at **Milepost S 96**, providing access to rural residential areas, lodges and a state recreation site. There is no Kenai River crossing on this road. It is paved with little or no shoulder to Mile 17 and deadends at private property. Speed limit is 45 mph with 30-mph curves.

Distance from junction with the Sterling Highway is shown (J).

J 0 Junction with Sterling Highway. Immediate right turn (in front of Spenard Builders Supply) is to Ski Hill Road, which leads 0.8 mile to access to Kenai National Wildlife Refuge visitor center.

J 0.1 Edgewater Lodge & RV Park to north; phone (907) 262-7733.

Edgewater Lodge & RV Park. See display ad on page 601.

J 0.3 Birch Tree Gallery has pottery, art, jewelry, stained glass and knitting supplies. Access to **Klondike RV Park & Cottages** (description follows).

Klondike RV Park & Cottages. 35 sites with full hookups, rigs to 60-feet. Most sites are 25 feet wide. Free WiFi, showers, restrooms. Laundromat on site. Located 1 block off the Kenai River in Soldotna, Alaska. We have cottages for rent. Four W Woodall rating. (907) 262-6035 or 1-800-980-6035. See display ad on page 597. [ADVERTISEMENT]

J 1.6 Donald E. Gilman River Center to north is a major resource center for information on the Kenai River and other fish waters within the Kenai Peninsula Borough; library, educational displays, meeting rooms, stained glass window by local glass artist Joyce Getchell. Access to Kenai River is behind the center on the south bank and near to the Soldotna Airport. Visitors may access the river utilizing 5 staircases and a handicap accessible ramp. Use the gravel walkway on the east side of the center to access the staircases. Staircases are open for public use from May 15–October 1. It may be closed till June 1, 2014 for construction. Toilets, garbage cans and fish-cleaning facilities provided. This area has been engineered to provide access for both able-bodied and disabled anglers while protecting the riverbank and fish habitat.

J 1.8 Entrance to Soldotna Municipal Airport (electronic gate) and access to **Natron Air**; bear viewing, fly-out hunting and fishing, phone 1-877-520-8440.

Natron Air. See display ad shown on page 599.

Private Aircraft: Soldotna airstrip 1 SE on Funny River Road; elev. 107 feet; length 5,000 feet; asphalt; fuel 100LL, Jet A; unattended. Privately-operated hangar facilities and fuel service. Temporary tie down spaces available.

Up on a pedestal by the entrance gate is a Starduster SA 100 single-engine, single seat, open cockpit biplane. Built by local residents in the early 1960s, the plane was used for aerobatics at Alaska air shows until the 1990s. It was retired to this spot in 2001 as a remembrance of early Soldotna area aviators.

J 2.9 Entering Kenai National Wildlife Refuge lands eastbound. Small paved pullout to north.

J 3.9 Small paved turnout to south.
Slow for 30 mph curves.

J 6.5 Paved turnout to south.

J 6.7 Paved parking to south; marked trailhead for horse trail.

J 8.8 Paved turnout to south.

J 9.4 Gravel turnout to north.

J 9.9 Solid waste facility; dumpsters.

J 10.1 Scenic viewpoint on curve to north; view of Kenai River through trees.

J 11.1 Funny River bridge.

J 11.2 Funny River State Recreation Site 0.2 mile to north; access road deadends at small turnaround area. This state park accommodates about 6 RVs and also has tent sites; $10 camping fee; outhouse, drinking water, tables; pack out trash; campground host. Open May to September, 7-day camping limit. Day-use parking on one side of access road (signed). Fills up quickly mid-July when fishing season starts. Short trail to **Kenai River** fishwalk.

J 11.7 Funny River Store; groceries, laundry, showers. Access road south to Bird Homestead 9-hole golf course.

J 12.5 Turnoff for Funny River Community Center (0.1 mile) via Pioneer Access Road. The community center has an annual festival the weekend after Soldotna's Progress Days.

J 16.9 Central Emergency Services, Funny River Station.

J 17 Large turnaround with many mailboxes.

Road forks; pavement ends, gravel begins. Moonshine Road to southeast. Salmon Run Road continues to the right.

J 19.6 Junction of Salmon Run Road with Fisherman's Court Road and Ashermans Road. Fisherman's Court Road continues to right 1.4 miles to a fork: left fork leads to private property, right fork is Kiley Road, which leads 0.2 mile to lodges.

Return to Milepost S 96 Sterling Highway

Sterling Highway Log
(Continued from page 594)

S 95.1 A 148.1 H 84 Traffic light at Binkley Street; access to fire station, police station, post office. Peninsula Center Mall; 24-hour Safeway.

S 95.4 A 148.4 H 83.7 Traffic light at Kobuk Street, Lovers Lane; access to Kaladi Brothers (coffee shop), Soldotna High School.

S 95.6 A 148.6 H 83.5 David Douthit–Veterans Memorial Bridge across the Kenai River. Entering Game Management Unit 15B, southbound.

S 95.9 A 148.9 H 83.2 Soldotna Visitor Center and Soldotna Chamber of Commerce to west at south end of Kenai River bridge; visitor information, displays including the record 97 lb. king salmon and rainbow trout. Restrooms, good parking, good turnaround. Access to Homestead Museum by walking/bike path. Access to fishwalk on Kenai River.

Entering Game Management Unit 15A northbound.

S 96 A 149 H 83.1 Traffic light at **junction** with Funny River Road to east (Soldotna businesses, airport and state recreation site) and Kalifornsky (K-Beach) Road to west; access to **Centennial Park** campground (description follows) and Soldotna Homestead Museum (see "Kalifornsky Beach Road" log); also access to Alaska State Troopers, ADF&G, **Diamond M Ranch** and other businesses. K-Beach Road also provides access to Kenai River Flats SRS and to Kenai via the Warren Ames Bridge.

Junction with Kalifornsky (K-Beach) Road and with Funny River Road. See "Funny River Road" log on this page; see "Kalifornsky Beach Road" log on page 610.

Centennial Park Campground and Homestead Museum, 0.1 mile west, on the banks of the Kenai River; 126 campsites (some on river), day-use areas, tables, firepits, firewood provided, water, restrooms, dump station, pay phone, 2-week limit. Register at entrance. Large parking area at boat launch. This is a popular riverbank fishing site.

S 97.2 A 150.2 H 81.9 Distance marker southbound shows Kasilof 12 miles, Homer 73 miles.

S 98 A 151 H 81.1 Skyview High School to west. Ski Hill Road to east *(turnoff is easy to miss)* leads 1 mile to **Kenai National Wildlife Refuge Visitor Center**. This popular center has wildlife exhibits, free wildlife films, and rangers on hand to answer questions on canoeing, hiking and camping in the refuge. There is a nature trail down to an observation platform on Headquarters Lake. Open weekdays 8 A.M. to 4:30 P.M; June–August weekend (Saturday 9 A.M.–5 P.M.& Sundays noon–5 P.M.). September through May weekend are Saturday only, 10 A.M. to 5 P.M. Inquire here about the 15 public-use cabins available to rent within the refuge, or go to kenai.fws.gov/cabin.htm for details. Ski Hill Road loops 0.8 mile back to Funny River Road.

Skyview High School has the popular **Tsalteshi Trails System** (built by volunteers), with nearly 9 miles of loop trails for walking, running and skiing. (The first 3.5 miles of trail are lit during evening hours in winter.) Park near the hockey rink at the rear of the school; trails start behind the rink. The

West Cook Inlet

Motorists driving down the west coast of the Kenai Peninsula may not realize it, but there is an equally spectacular destination just across the water that also offers great scenery and fishing, along with bear viewing and bird watching—West Cook Inlet. Most of these activities take place at the 2 lodges located on a 160-acre parcel of private land within Lake Clark National Park on the west coast of Cook Inlet. Sport fishermen and wildlife photographers stay overnight or do a day trip with one of the lodges—Silver Salmon Creek Lodge or Homestead Lodge—flying in from Soldotna, Kenai, Homer or Anchorage.

Silver Salmon Creek, a short walk from the lodge, is a big draw for visitors. Its late July to September silver salmon run attracts visiting fishermen, as well as bears.

Bears are a major attraction here. The brown bears may be seen fishing Silver Salmon Creek; prowling the tide line, looking for anything edible that might have washed up onshore; and foraging or sleeping in the huge grassy meadow that lies between the beach and the lodges. And bears occasionally wander around the lodges.

The lodges accommodate both overnight guests and day trippers. For day visitors, excursions are typically 4-hours or full day tours. They can accommodate large groups, but generally like to focus on smaller groups, with 2–6 guests with one guide for bear watching from mid-June through mid-September.

For being remote, these lodges offer wonderfully comfortable rooms and dining experiences for visitors choosing to stay overnight. For maximum relaxation in this unique wilderness, the lodges recommend a 3–5 day package. Rates and details at: www.silversalmoncreek.com and http://alaska homesteadlodge.com.

Other activities offered by the lodges for full-service guests include a boat trip up the coast to view colonies of kittiwakes, puffins, cormorants and murres; canoeing Silver Salmon Lake; clam digging; photography; and hiking.

Transportation to West Cook Inlet lodges from Soldotna is via a 30-minute flight with **Natron Air**; stop by their office at the Soldotna Airport on Funny River Road or phone (907) 262-8440; www.natronair.com.

Johnson Lake on Tustumena Road allows non-motorized boats. (©Sharon Nault)

State Cross Country Running Championship, Arctic Winter Games events and Junior Olympic qualifying events are held here.

S 98.1 A 151.1 H 81 Alaska Dept. of Transportation to east.

S 98.3 A 151.3 H 80.8 Arc Lake to east; dirt and gravel parking area, picnic table, unmaintained. Easy boat launch for canoes, kayaks.

S 98.5 A 151.5 H 80.6 Landfill to east.

CAUTION: Moose Danger Zone next 10 miles southbound.

S 99 A 152 H 80.1 Kenai Peninsula Archers Range to east.

S 100 A 153 H 79.1 Three Guys No Wood.

S 102 A 155 H 77.1 Gas, diesel, propane; convenience store.

S 105.6 A 158.6 H 73.5 Large paved pull-out to east.

S 107 A 160 H 72.1 Rogue Lake public fishing access to east. Decanter Inn restaurant, motel.

S 108.6 A 161.6 H 70.5 South junction with Kalifornsky Beach (K-Beach) Road. *(Actual driving distance between physical Mileposts 108 and 109 is 0.7 miles.)*

K-Beach Road is a 22-mile loop road that rejoins the Sterling Highway at **Milepost S 95.8.** Kasilof post office is 0.1 mile west of here on K-Beach Road; Kasilof Regional Historical Museum is 0.5 miles west; and beach access is 4.8 miles (via Kasilof Beach Road).

Junction with Kalifornsky (K-Beach) Road. See "Kalifornsky Beach Road" log on page 610.

S 109 A 162 H 70.1 Kasilof Mercantile east side of road. **KASILOF** (pop. 560) was originally a settlement established in 1786 by the Russians as St. George. A Kenaitze Indian village grew up around the site, but no longer exists. The current population of Kasilof is spread out over a 90-square-mile area. Income is derived from fishing and fish processing.

S 109.2 A 162.2 H 69.9 Kasilof Riverview Tesoro to west with gas, diesel, groceries, liquor store, espresso and tackle.

Gravel parking area east side of highway; pedestrian-only access to Kasilof River.

Kasilof Riverview Tesoro. See display ad this page.

S 109.3 A 162.3 H 69.8 Bridge over Kasilof River, which drains Tustumena Lake. Entering Game Management Subunit 15C southbound, 15B northbound.

S 109.5 A 162.5 H 69.6 Turnoff for **Kasilof River State Recreation Site** (to east) on Spetz Road; day-use area on a knoll above the river. Picnic tables and firepits in forested area above parking; wheelchair-accessible toilets, water and interpretive trails. This is a popular boat launch for drift boaters fishing for king salmon late May through July. Parking $5 after 30-minute grace period. Boat launch fee $5. The **Kasilof River** red salmon dip-net fishery here is open by special order for Alaska residents only; check with the ADF&G for current regulations. See "Kasilof River/Crooked Creek and Cohoe Loop Road" on pages 612-613.

S 110 A 163 H 69.1 Tustumena Elementary School to east.

Distance marker northbound shows Soldotna 14 miles, Kenai 25 miles and Anchorage 162 miles.

S 110.1 A 163.1 H 69 Central Emergency Services, Kasilof Station, west side of highway;

S 110.2 A 163.2 H 68.9 Abram Avenue. Turn east on Abram for access to **Johnson Lake Recreation Area, Tustumena Lake** and **Kasilof RV Park**; directions follow.

Drive 0.1 mile on Abram then turn right and drive 0.3 mile on Johnson Lake Road for Johnson Lake Recreation Area day-use site; toilets, picnic tables and trash container in a pleasant woodsy setting.

Continue to the left past the day-use area to the big metal "T" which marks the beginning of Tustumena Lake Road. Johnson Lake Recreation Area Campground is at Mile 0.1 of Tustumena Lake Road (descriptions follow).

Turn to the right at the day-use area and drive 0.1 mile, then turn on Crooked Creek Road and continue 0.5 for **Kasilof RV Park**.

Kasilof RV Park offers true park-like setting, modern clean facilities with quiet, relaxing atmosphere making this Kenai's favorite. We offer a peaceful retreat central to all Peninsula activities, including salmon and halibut fishing, dip-netting, clamming or trout fishing on Johnson Lake. Expect visits by moose and babies, eagles, loons, and see

Kalifornsky Beach Road

Mouth of Kasilof River, accessed via Kasilof Beach Road, is a happening place in summer.
(©Sharon Nault)

Also called K–Beach Road, Kalifornsky Beach Road is a paved 45 mph road (the speed limit changes to 55 mph near Ciechanski Road, southbound) which leads west from the Sterling Highway at Soldotna, following the shore of Cook Inlet south to Kasilof. K-Beach Road also provides access to Kenai via the Bridge Access Road. The first 5.6 miles has many Soldotna businesses.

Distance from the Sterling Highway junction at Milepost S 96 at Soldotna (S) is followed by distance from Sterling Highway junction at Milepost S 108.6 at Kasilof (K). *Mileposts run south to north and reflect mileage from Kasilof.*

S 0 K 22.2 Junction with Sterling Highway at Milepost S 96.
S 0.1 K 22.1 Turnoff for **Centennial Park Municipal Campground** and **Homestead Museum** (0.1 mile). This huge municipal campground, located on the banks of the Kenai River, is a popular spot for day-use fishing, and the parking lot fills up fast when the fish are in. Within walking distance of Soldotna shopping. Campground has 126 campsites (some on river), tables, firepits, firewood, water, restrooms, dump station, pay phones, newspaper kiosk (in summer), boat launch and fishwalk. No campsite reservations, first-come, first-served. Fees are $14.70/night for camping, $6.30 parking/day-use, $10.50 boat launch, $5.50 firewood and $10.50 dump station. Access to Angler's Trail (signed), a footpath for fishermen. Seasonal day-use and boat launch passes available.

At the Soldotna Historic Society's **Homestead Museum**, visitors will find many interesting displays, both outside and inside, including examples of different kinds of authentic Alaska cabins, an Alaskan "cache," a double-ended Bristol Bay fishing boat, and a Cook Inlet dory built in the mid-1950s. There is an 0.2 mile walking path that loops through timber and along the riverbank. Large parking area with turnaround space.
S 0.2 K 22 Alaska State Troopers.
S 0.4 K 21.8 Gehrke Field, rodeo grounds.
S 0.6 K 21.6 Soldotna Sports Center on Sports Center Road; phone (907) 262-3151. The Center welcomes visitors with showers available for $3 in summer months from noon to 4 P.M., Tuesday–Friday and a small number of camping spots for rent near the center.
S 0.8 K 21.4 West Endicott Drive access ½ mile to the Slikok Creek unit of the Kenai River Special Management Area. Parking and trail access to mouth of **Slikok Creek**, Kenai River public fishing access. Day-use fee charged. Public toilets available.
S 1.6 K 20.6 College Loop Road to Kenai Peninsula College (1.3 miles north).
S 2.7 K 19.5 Harvard Avenue. K–Beach center. ADF&G office, wildlife troopers; stop in here for current sportfishing information.
S 2.9 K 19.3 Poppy Lane intersection; Gas station, espresso.

Access to Kenai Peninsula College (1.3 mile north). At the college, the Boyd Shaffer nature trail begins directly behind the Clayton Brockel building. Trail access to **Slikok**

Creek State Recreation Area, a Kenai River public fishing access; watch for sign marking trailhead. Day-use fee charged.
S 3.5 K 18.7 Red Diamond Center; theatre, gas, restaurants, motel, grocery and other stores. **Country Financial** (insurance and financial planning).

Country Financial. See display ad this page.
S 4.7 K 17.5 Ciechanski Road; access to **Ciechanski State Recreation Site** (2.4 miles) on the Kenai River (River Mile 15.5). This small site's primary purpose is to provide restroom access for boaters. There is a small, 12-hour public parking area (no camping), outhouse and dock walk, which offers a good view of the river, but no bank access to river and no fishing from the dock.
S 5.5 K 16.5 Turnoff for **Diamond M Ranch RV Park, Cabins & B&B**. Large RV park with lodging and many activities. A popular destination, Diamond M is also the site of the annual Summer Solstice Music Festival held in June. Visit www.diamondm ranch.com for more information.
Diamond M Ranch RV Park, Cabins & B&B. See display ad on page 598 this section.

S 6 K 16.2 Traffic light at **junction** with Bridge Access Road. Turn here for access to **Kenai River Flats State Recreation Site** (0.5 mile), 6-hour parking, picnic tables, information signs, bird watching; **Warren Ames Bridge** (0.7 mile); Kenai Flats boardwalk viewing telescope (1.1 miles); City of Kenai public dock (1.6 miles); Beaver Loop Road junction (1.9 miles); and Kenai Spur Highway (3.3 miles) at city of Kenai.
Bike route ends, road narrows, northbound.
S 8.3 K 13.7 Cannery Road leads 1.2 miles to public beach access at the mouth of the Kenai River.
S 10 K 12.2 Central Emergency Services (fire station).
S 17.4 K 4.8 Kasilof Beach Road leads 0.9 mile to unimproved grassy dunes bordering mud flats at mouth of Kasilof River; pleasant, primitive and busy day-use and overnight area during salmon runs. No public access beyond cannery gate. Respect private property.
S 20.1 K 2.1 Private aircraft; Kasilof airstrip, 2N; elev. 125 feet; length 2,100 feet; gravel; unattended.
S 21.8 K 0.4 Kasilof Regional Historical Museum is housed in the McLane Building, a fish cannery hospital in 1890s, which was moved here from the mouth of the Kasilof River. The building was used as the Kasilof Territorial School from 1937 until the 1950s. Museum displays and photos highlight early Native culture, fox farming, trapping, homesteading and fishing history of the area. Open 1–4 P.M., Tuesday–Sunday, Memorial Day through Labor Day; the rest of the year by appointment. Very pleasant grounds with log structures dating from 1891, open for viewing. Dogsled used to deliver mail to Seward also on display. Museum is staffed by a friendly and knowledgeable group of volunteers. Paved parking, free admission. Picnic table and outhouse on grounds. For information, phone (907) 262-2999.
S 22.1 K 0.1 Kasilof Post Office.
S 22.2 K 0 Junction with Sterling Highway at Kasilof, **Milepost S 108.6**.

Return to Milepost S 96 or S 108.6
Sterling Highway

beautiful wildflowers. Facilities include clean restrooms, free showers, WiFi, laundry, full/ partial hookups and pull-through. Boats or camper storage available. Memorial weekend to Labor Day. www.kasilofrvpark.com. See display ad this page. [ADVERTISEMENT]

Tustumena Lake Road is a 6-mile paved and gravel road (gravel portion can be rough) that begins at the large metal T on Johnson Lake Road and ends at the Kasilof River. Road log is as follows:

Mile 0.1 **Johnson Lake State Recreation Area Campground**; 50 sites (some pull-throughs) in forested area on lake; tables, firepits, toilets, water, dumpster, launch for non-motorized boats. **Johnson Lake** is stocked with rainbow trout. Swimming. Campground host. Camping fee $10 (subject to change).

Mile 2.9 Pavement ends, dirt and gravel begins.

Mile 3.8 Access to **Centennial Lake** public fishing access; large parking area, no facilities (carry out garbage). Swimming, canoeing, and fishing for landlocked salmon and rainbow (stocked).

Mile 6 Road ends at a boat launch on the Kasilof River which provides access to Tustumena Lake (description follows). Large parking area and toilets, primitive campsites (no fees in 2013).

Tustumena Lake, which is upriver from the boat launch, is 6 miles wide and 25 miles long, accounting for more than 60,000 acres of Kenai National Wildlife Refuge. For fishing regulations, refer to the ADF&G regulations booklet or go online for statewide and regional regulations at www. sf.adfg.state.ak.us. *WARNING: Tustumena Lake is subject to sudden and severe winds. Water temperatures rarely exceed 45˚F. Be prepared.* Strong winds coming off Tustumena Glacier and the Harding Icefield can change boating conditions from calm water to 3–6-foot waves without warning. The silty waters create zero visibility obscuring submerged rocks and logs. Weather systems in Cook Inlet and the Gulf of Alaska can also bring high winds. Boaters unfamiliar with operating in these conditions should not venture out on lake.

S 110.5 A 163.5 H 68.6 Double-ended paved turnout to west.

S 110.6 A 163.6 H 68.5 Tustumena Lodge to west.

S 111 A 164 H 68.1 Junction with Cohoe Loop Road to west; paved parking to east. (*Actual driving distance is 0.8 mile between Mileposts 111 and 112 and between Mileposts 112 and 113.*)

Junction with North Cohoe Loop. See "Kasilof River/Crooked Creek and Cohoe Loop Road" log on page 611-612.

This is the north junction with 15.6-mile **Cohoe Loop Road**, which rejoins the Sterling Highway at **Milepost S 114.3.** Use this turnoff for most direct access to **Crooked Creek State Recreation Site.**

S 113.3 A 166.3 H 65.8 Distance marker southbound shows Clam Gulch 5 miles, Homer 57 miles.

S 114.3 A 167.3 H 64.8 South junction with 15.6-mile Cohoe Loop Road which loops back to the Sterling Highway at **Milepost S 111.**

Kasilof River/Crooked Creek and Cohoe Loop Road

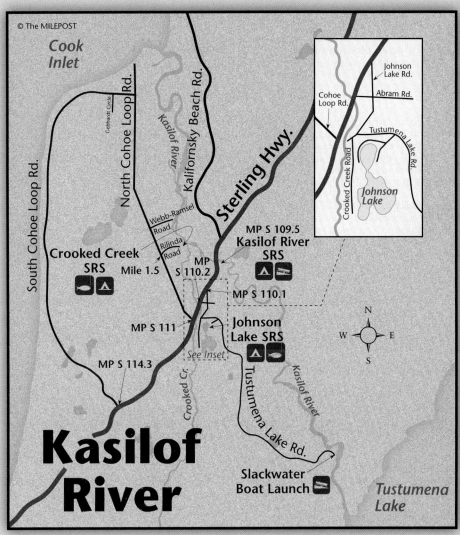

© The MILEPOST

The Kasilof River is a powerful glacial river draining Tustumena Lake, the Kenai Peninsula's largest lake, and flowing 17 miles northwest to Cook Inlet. Although silty, very rocky and shallow in places, the Kasilof River is popular for its sportfishing, white-water kayaking, canoeing and wildlife viewing opportunities.

Most of the sportfishing on the Kasilof River takes place between the Sterling Highway bridge at **Milepost S 109.3** and the river's confluence with Crooked Creek. The Kasilof supports an early king salmon run, peaking in mid-June; a late king salmon run in July; a silver salmon return, peaking in mid-August; and a major red salmon return from late June until early August. Shore anglers have good success, although some anglers fish from drift boats.

The most popular section for anglers fishing from drift boats is downstream from the Sterling Highway bridge, where the river

Kasilof River/Crooked Creek and Cohoe Loop Road (continued)

is characterized by fewer rocks and obstacles. Most drift boats launch at the **Kasilof River State Recreation Site** at Milepost S 109.5 to access downstream fishing.

Other anglers choose to access the bank fishing at the Kasilof River's confluence with Crooked Creek from the public and private campgrounds on Cohoe Loop Road. The Crooked Creek area is one of the most productive bank fishing spots on the Kenai Peninsula for king salmon fishing, and is popular late in the season for silver salmon fishing.

For the most direct access to campgrounds near the Crooked Creek confluence, turn off the Sterling Highway at **Milepost S 111** at the north end of Cohoe Loop Road (see road log following).

The section of the Kasilof River between its outlet from Tustumena Lake and the Sterling Highway bridge at **Milepost S 109.3** is the wildest and least used section of the river. Several sections of Class II white-water rapids make this section of river exciting for kayaking or canoeing by experienced boaters. Access to the upper river and Tustumena Lake is from the Slackwater Boat Launch on Tustumena Lake Road. See description at **Milepost S 110.2** Sterling Highway.

One note of caution should be made for persons boating any part of the Kasilof River. This is a very cold and powerful river. Rocks are plentiful in this river. The silty nature of the glacial water makes it difficult to see underwater obstacles. During periods of low water, navigating the river in a power boat is nearly impossible due to the rocky, shallow conditions. During high water, the swift current makes boating conditions hazardous. Recreational boaters should have moderate levels of experience with white water if boating this river. All boaters should plan for a safe trip by always wearing proper personal flotation devices and filing trip plans with friends or other responsible parties.

Special restrictions apply to both boating and fishing on the Kasilof River, so check the ADF&G regulation booklet carefully.

Cohoe Loop Road

The 15.3-mile Cohoe Loop Road (see map) accesses the popular Crooked Creek fishing and camping area, the Cohoe area, scattered businesses and private homes. Distance from north junction (NJ) with Sterling Highway is followed by distance from south junction (SJ).

NJ 0 SJ 15.3 North junction with the Sterling Highway at **Milepost S 111.**

NJ 1.5 SJ 13.8 Turnoff on Rilinda Road and continue straight (keep to left) 0.4 miles on access road to "Y" intersection: **Crooked Creek State Recreation Site** entrance is to your left, **Crooked Creek Guide Service, Cabins and RV Park** entrance is to your right. Descriptions follow.

Crooked Creek Guide Service, Cabins and RV Park. Centrally located on the Kenai Peninsula at the confluence of the Kasilof River and Crooked Creek with the best bank fishing on the peninsula. Full service salmon and halibut charters. New cabins with private bathrooms, wooded RV sites, full/partial hookups, showers, laundry, fishing-cleaning station, and free WiFi. Our store sells fishing licenses, tackle, bait, snacks and goods. Open May 1–September 15. (907) 262-1299; www.CrookedCreek FishAlaska.com. See display ad this page. [ADVERTISEMENT]

Crooked Creek State Recreation Site has a large parking lot which accommodates 79 vehicles with side-by-side overnight parking; 36 day-use sites; toilets, well water, pay phones; tent sites; campground host; and trails along the Kasilof River for fishermen. Mike Heinicke memorial bench here is named for a long-time park host. Camping fee $10/night, day-use fee $5/vehicle, boat launch fee $15.

NJ 5.3 SJ 10 Old settlement of Cohoe 0.2 mile north of here, then west on Ness; now private homes.

NJ 5.6 SJ 9.7 Access west 0.7 mile to beach; parking area with outhouses and dumpsters. Beach access for 4-wheel-drive vehicles only. Watch for eagles. Clam digging and set-netting in season.

NJ 11.2 SJ 4.1 Beach access. Drive by gas facility to limited parking on bluff; 4-wheel drive advised.

NJ 13.6 SJ 1.7 Double-ended turnout to west.

NJ 15.3 SJ 0 Junction with Sterling Highway at **Milepost S 114.3.**

Return to Milepost S 111 or S 114.3 Sterling Highway

Junction with South Cohoe Loop. See "Kasilof River/Crooked Creek and Cohoe Loop Road" log beginning on page 611.

S 117.3 A 170.3 H 61.8 Parking area to east.

S 117.4 A 170.4 H 61.7 Clam Gulch State Recreation Area, 0.5 mile west from highway via dirt access road; picnic tables, picnic shelter, toilets, water, 116 side-by-side overnight parking spaces, campground host, $10 nightly camping fee, $5 day-use fee. Long stairway leads from mid-campground down to beach. *CAUTION: High ocean bluffs are dangerous.* Short, steep access road to beach (recommended for 4-wheel-drive vehicles only); deep, loose sand at beach.

Clam digging for razor clams on most of the sandy beaches of the western Kenai Peninsula from Kasilof to Anchor Point can be rewarding. Many thousands of clams are dug each year at **Clam Gulch.** You must have a sportfishing license to dig, and these are available at most sporting goods stores. The bag limit is 25 clams regardless of size and you must keep the first 25 you dig (always check current regulations). There is no legally closed season, but quality of the clams varies with month; check locally. Good clamming and fewer people in March and April, although there may still be ice on the beach. Any tide lower than minus 1-foot is enough to dig clams; minus 4- to 5-foot tides are best. The panoramic view of Mount Redoubt, Mount Iliamna and Mount Spurr across Cook Inlet and the expanse of beach are well worth the short side trip even during the off-season.

S 118.2 A 171.2 H 61 CLAM GULCH (pop. 175); post office, established in 1950, and Bakers Clam Shell Lodge

S 119 A 172 H 60.1 AT&T Alascom microwave tower to east.

S 119.2 A 172.2 H 59.9 Double-ended turnout to east.

S 119.6 A 172.6 H 59.5 Clam Gulch Lodge.

S 121 A 174 H 58.1 Double-ended turnout to west.

S 122.9 A 175.9 H 56.2 Paved parking area to west (no view).

S 124.9 A 177.9 H 54.2 Double-ended paved scenic viewpoint to west.

S 126.8 A 179.8 H 52.3 Double-ended paved parking to west (no view).

S 127 A 180 H 52.1 Double-ended paved scenic viewpoint to west with access to Scenic View RV Park. Interpretive sign at viewpoint about the "ring of fire": Mount Iliamna, elev. 10,016 feet, 52 miles away; Mount Redoubt, elev. 10,197 feet, 54 miles away; Mount Augustine, elev. 4,025 feet, 83 miles to the south; and Mount Spurr, elev. 11,100 feet, 85 miles to the north. Mount Augustine has erupted several times, most recently in 2006. Mount Spurr last erupted on March 22, 2009, resulting in ash fall as far away as Anchorage. Visit the Alaska Volcano Observatory at www.avo.alaska.edu/index.php for details on Alaska's volcanoes.

S 130.5 A 183.5 H 49 Ninilchik Point Overnighter. See display ad this page.

S 130.6 A 183.6 H 48.5 Distance marker southbound shows Ninilchik 5 miles, Homer 40 miles.

S 132.2 A 185.2 H 46.9 Heavenly Sights Charters and Campground. Dan and the crew invite you to Heavenly Sights, named for the dramatic view of the Inlet and 4 volcanoes. If you want to catch fish and stay at a friendly campground, with reasonable rates, this is it. Fish with the best Cook Inlet guides for halibut, salmon in their clean, 28-ft. boats with enclosed cabins and marine heads. Fish filleting included and vac/pac/freeze arrangements can be made. Clam digging and great eagle photo-op nearby. RV sites have electric, water and sewage hookups. Fishermen's cabins can accommodate 6. Laundry and bathroom facilities. Book early for the best dates. Military, senior discounts. Convenient location. www.heavenlysights.com. 1-800-479-7371.

Turnoff on Orthodox Avenue at Milepost S 134.6 to visit Holy Transfiguration of Our Lord, Russian Orthodox Church. (©Sharon Nault)

See display ad on facing page. [ADVERTISEMENT]

S 133.4 A 186.4 H 45.7 Distance marker northbound shows Soldotna 36 miles, Kenai 48 miles, Anchorage 184 miles.

S 134 A 187 H 45.1 Ninilchik (southbound sign).

S 134.2 A 187.2 H 44.9 *Begin 45 mph speed zone southbound.*
Begin 55 mph speed limit northbound.

S 134.5 A 187.5 H 44.6 Turnoff to east for Ninilchik River State Recreation Site Campground; 39 campsites set among birch and spruce trees on 2 gravel loop roads (upper and lower loops); campground host; picnic tables, grills, water, outhouses; $10 camping fee. Firewood available. Trail to Ninilchik River; fishing for king and silver salmon, steelhead and Dolly Varden (seasonal restrictions apply, consult

ADF&G booklet).

134.6 A 187.6 H 44.5 *CAUTION: Slow for 35 mph curve (southbound sign).* Turnoff to west on gravel Orthodox Avenue which leads 0.4 mile west to Holy Transfiguration of Our Lord Russian Orthodox Church (not visible from highway), one of the most popular tourist sites on the Kenai Peninsula.

Parking and turnaround space in front of church. (Big rigs park at flag display.) Beautiful views and photo-ops of Cook Inlet, Ninilchik Village and church cemetery (especially when fireweed is in bloom). A small American Legion cemetery and Leo Steik Veterans Memorial Wall are also located here. *(NOTE: This is an active church. Please respect church services and activities.)*

S 134.9 A 187.9 H 44.2 Ninilchik River Scenic Overlook (Ninilchik SRA) to east. This is a 2-tiered paved parking area with

The Ninilchik River snakes through Ninilchik Village. A trail leads up to the Russian Orthodox Church visible on the hillside. (©Sharon Nault)

walking trail (hike or to fish) above river; toilets, picnic tables, interpretive signs, barbecues, garbage, water pump; $10 camping fee, $5 day-use fee.

S 135.1 A 188.1 H 44 Ninilchik River bridge. At south end of bridge there is a large parking area and the turnoff to west for Mission Avenue to **Ninilchik Village** and Ninilchik State Recreation Area Beach (0.5 mile). Drive west on Mission Avenue 0.2 mile to Y: Turn right for Ninilchik Village, continue straight ahead for beach. **Beachcomber Motel & RV Park** is on the Beach Road; description follows.

There is a large parking area above the Ninilchik River by the old blue fishing boat (signed the "Bob Chenier Fishermen's Memorial"). This is a popular fishing spot on the river and good beach walking area. Continue on beach road for private RV park, cabins, cannery, boat harbor and turnaround area. Crowded when the fish are in.

Beachcomber Motel & RV Park. Located on the Beach & River in Old Ninilchik Village. Long-time Alaskan's Phil & Dee welcome you. Rooms with two queen beds, private bath, 360 view of inlet and volcanoes. RV Park has full hook-ups, 30 amp service, view of inlet and river from all spaces. Fish for salmon right behind your RV spaces and rooms. Clam digging out in front on an minus tide. Shovel and buckets available for guests. Looking forward to making your stay a memorable one. www.beachcombermotelrvpark.com. Winter: (480) 802-8544, Summer: (907) 567-3417. [ADVERTISEMENT]

NINILCHIK VILLAGE, at the mouth of the Ninilchik River, was settled at the turn of the 19th century and is the "old" village. (The "new" Ninilchik is located on the Sterling Highway.) The village has several old dovetailed log buildings. A trail leads up to the green and white Russian Orthodox Church on the hill (please do not walk through private property) or drive to the church via Orthodox Avenue from Mile-

post **S 134.6** Sterling Highway. A popular beach for razor clamming is reached by driving through the old village and taking the primitive road under the bluff (4-wheel-drive only). Access to clamming beds during minus tides. *CAUTION: Drownings have occurred here. Be aware of tide changes when clam digging. Incoming tides can quickly cut you off from the beach.*

S 135.4 A 188.4 H 43.7 Turnoff for Kingsley Road; access to Ninilchik post office (0.2 mile), medical clinic and senior citizens center (0.3 mile), full-service RV parks, lodging and charter services at **Alaskan Angler RV Resort, Cabins and Afishunt Charters** (description follows). Kingsley Road leads east to junction with Oilwell Road.

Alaskan Angler RV Resort, Cabins and Afishunt Charters is Ninilchik's largest, friendliest, best equipped, Good Sam RV park, cabins and charters. Enjoy modern amenities in our easily accessed, large, flat sites or furnished cabins with full kitchens and baths. Free high-speed WiFi at your site,

satellite TV, 30-50 amp service, new laundry and clean, private showers. Experience Alaska's best halibut and king salmon fishing with Afishunt Charters on site. Charter discounts for campers. Walk to river salmon fishing or the beach for razor clamming and use our private fish cleaning tables. We can vacuum pack, freeze, box and ship your prized catch home. 15640 Kingsley Road. Reservations 1-800-347-4114, (907) 567-3393. Email: aarvresort@yahoo.com. www. alaskabestrvpark.com. See display ad on this page. [ADVERTISEMENT]

DOT/PF road maintenance station to east.

S 135.5 A 188.5 H 43.6 Inlet View Lodge. **Ninilchik View State Campground** to west has dump station ($5 fee) by entrance; 12 campsites with tables on narrow gravel loop road; toilets, drinking water fill-up and litter disposal available. Best for smaller camping units. Camping fee $10/night. View of Ninilchik Village from bluff at campground. Long stepped path leads down to beach and village. Watch for eagles.

S 135.7 A 188.7 H 43.4 Ninilchik High School to west.

S 135.8 A 188.8 H 43.3 First of several entrances southbound to a cluster of businesses on west side of highway which include **Afishunt Charters** and **Ninilchik General Store**.

Ninilchik General Store. A clean, friendly atmosphere where everyone is ready to help. Offers wide variety of goods including, groceries, bait, licenses, clothing, hardware, firewood, ice, and a large gift section of unique items. They have everything you need for your clamming or fishing trip. You can get a steaming hot cup of chocolate or espresso, a fresh deli sandwich, or try one of the eight different flavors of the hand-dipped ice creams. ATM machine. Copy and fax service. This is where the locals shop year-round! Phone (907) 567-3378. [ADVERTISEMENT]

Ninilchik

S 135.9 A 187.9 H 44.2 Junction with **Oilwell Road**; gas station at southeast corner. Ninilchik (pronounced Ni-NILL-chick) is located between **Mileposts S 119** and **S 144** on the Sterling Highway, with a number of businesses located between the Ninilchik River (at **Milepost S 135.1**) and Deep Creek (at **Milepost S 137.3**). **Population:** 842. **Emergency services:** Phone 911. **Medical Clinic,** Ninilchik Health Clinic on Kingsley Road, phone (907) 567-3970.

Visitor Information: Local businesses are very helpful.

Private Aircraft: Ninilchik airstrip, 3 SE; elev. 276 feet; length 2,400 feet; dirt and gravel; unattended.

Ninilchik is a destination for fishermen after salmon and halibut in Cook Inlet. The community's many services—including grocery stores, gas stations, lodging, dining, fishing charters and campgrounds—are located along several miles of the Sterling Highway or just off the highway on Oilwell Road. See the advertisements along the highway and in town to see what is available for lodging, camping and other visitors services,

especially fishing charters. There is a hostel, the Eagle Watch, on Oilwell Road. Ninilchik has an active senior center, a library and swimming at Ninilchik High School pool.

The original village of Ninilchik (signed Ninilchik Village) is reached via Mission Avenue (see description at **Milepost S 135.1**), which follows the Ninilchik River to Cook Inlet.

On Memorial Day weekend, Ninilchik is referred to as the third biggest city in Alaska, as thousands of Alaskans arrive for the fishing (see Area Fishing description).

The **Kenai Peninsula Fair** is held at Ninilchik the third weekend in August. Dubbed the "biggest little fair in Alaska," it features the Peninsula Rodeo, a parade, horse show, livestock competition and exhibits ranging from produce to arts and crafts. Pancake breakfasts, bingo and other events, such as the derby fish fry, are held at the fairgrounds throughout the year. A halibut derby, sponsored by the Ninilchik Chamber of Commerce, runs from Father's Day through Labor Day.

AREA FISHING: Well-known area for saltwater king salmon fishing and record halibut fishing. Charter services available. (Combination king salmon and halibut charters are popular.) Salt water south of the mouth of **Deep Creek** has produced top king salmon fishing in late May, June and July. Kings 50 lbs. and over are frequently caught. "Lunker" king salmon are available 1 mile south of Deep Creek in **Cook Inlet**, late May through July. Trolling a spinner or a spoon from a boat is the preferred method. Silver, red and pink salmon are available in salt water between Deep Creek and the Ninilchik River during July. A major halibut fishery off Ninilchik has produced some of the largest trophy halibut found in Cook Inlet, including a 466-lb. unofficial world record sport-caught halibut.

Sterling Highway Log
(Continued)

S 135.9 A 188.9 H 43.2 Junction with **Oilwell Road**; Tesoro gas station at southeast corner. Oilwell Road is a busy paved road with lots of charter businesses, B&Bs and a bakery in the first mile. Fishing charters at Mile 1 (description follows). There is an RV park and restaurant at Mile 3.1. Pavement ends at Mile 5.8 on Oilwell Road.

S 136 A 189 H 43.1 Access west side of highway to cluster of Ninilchik businesses.

S 136.2 A 189.2 H 42.9 Peninsula Fairgrounds to east, site of the Kenai Peninsula Fair (August) and 4th of July Rodeo. Deep Creek View Campground/J&J Smart

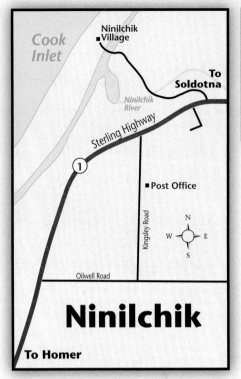

Charters to west; description follows.

J&J Smart Charters. See display ad on this page.

Deep Creek View Campground. Million dollar view! Family-owned campground located on the bluff overlooking Cook Inlet, with an incredible view of snow-covered volcanoes, eagles soaring, and spectacular sunsets. Grassy tent camping areas; electrical hookups, dump station, shower building, and new cabins with private baths. Book Alaska halibut fishing charters available now with J&J Smart Charters. Fish safely in the 28-foot Alumaweld and new 30-foot ABC boat with hard-top cabins and marine head. Professional vacuum sealing, freezing, and shipping of your catch. Don't miss your Alaskan experience! Call now, toll-free number 1-888-HALIBUT (1-888-425-4288) www.smartcharters.com. See display ad on this page. [ADVERTISEMENT]

S 136.7 A 189.7 H 42.4 Bridge over Deep Creek. Recreation sites to the east on either side of Deep Creek: **Deep Creek North** and **Deep Creek South**. Deep Creek North offers camping. Deep Creek South is day-use only. Both have restrooms, water, interpretive kiosks, tables and fireplaces. $10 camping fee; $5 day-use fee.

Walking the beach at Deep Creek Recreation Area. This is a good place to watch the tractor boat launch; see bald eagles; camp and fish . (©Sharon Nault)

Freshwater fishing in **Deep Creek** for king salmon up to 40 lbs., use spinners with red bead lures, Memorial Day weekend and the 3 weekends following; Dolly Varden in July and August; silver salmon to 15 lbs., August and September; steelhead to 15 lbs., late September through October. No bait fishing permitted after Aug. 31. Mouth of Deep Creek access from **Deep Creek State Recreation Area** turnoff at **Milepost S 137.3**. NOTE: *Sportfishing openings/closings can change based on Emergency Order.*

S 137.3 A 190.3 H 41.8 Turnoff to west for Deep Creek State Recreation Area access road. Drive 0.3 miles down paved road for **Deep Creek State Recreation Area** on the beach at the mouth of Deep Creek. A favorite with Alaskans and tourists alike. Drive by busy boat launch area to large day-use parking area adjacent: $5 fee after 30-minute grace period. Additional gravel parking area adjacent day-use parking has 100 overnight campsites, some by the beach, others in a flat camping area surrounded by beach grasses; water, tables, dumpsters, restrooms, firepits, campground host. Firewood is sometimes available. Camping fee $10/night per vehicle.

Anglers try to intercept king salmon in the saltwater before the salmon reach their spawning rivers. A private tractor-launch service here gets boats from the beach into Cook Inlet. There are only a few hours on either side of a high tide to float them without use of the tractor-launch. The cost of putting in and retrieving a boat is about $55.

Good bird watching in wetlands behind beach. Watch for bald eagles. Good clamming at low tide. The beaches here are lined with coal, which falls from the exposed seams of high cliffs.

Most visitors enjoy watching boats coming and going with their catches. Park in designated areas and keep yourself and your rig out of the busy launching area.

CAUTION: Extreme tides, cold water and bad weather can make boating here hazardous. Carry all required and recommended USCG safety equipment. There are seasonal checks by U.S. Coast Guard for personal flotation devices, boating safety. Although the mouth of Deep Creek affords boaters good protection, low tides may prevent return; check tide tables.

S 137.6 A 190.6 H 41.5 *Begin 45 mph speed zone northbound.*

Begin 55 mph speed limit southbound.

S 138.5 A 191.5 H 40.6 Solid waste transfer station; dumpsters to west.

S 149 A 193 G 39.1 NOTE: *Watch for ruts and cracks in surfacing and patched pavement southbound to **Milepost S 156**.*

S 142.5 A 195.5 H 36.6 Double-ended paved turnout to west is one of the best photo viewpoints of Mount Iliamna; hayfield and fireweed in the foreground. Sign (currently missing) read:

"Looking westerly across Cook Inlet, Mt. Iliamna and Mt. Redoubt in the Chigmit Mountains of the Aleutian Range can be seen rising over 10,000 feet above sea level. This begins a chain of mountains and islands known as the Aleutian Chain extending west over 1,700 miles to Attu beyond the International Date Line to the Bering Sea, separating the Pacific and Arctic oceans. Mt. Redoubt on the right, and Iliamna on the left, were recorded as active volcanoes in the mid-18th century. Mt. Redoubt had a minor eruption in 1966."

Mount Redoubt had a major eruption in December 1989. The eruptions continued through April 1990, then subsided to steam plumes. Beginning again in early 2009 Mount Redoubt was quite active on and off during the spring and summer, shutting down air traffic multiple times due to volcanic activity or the imminent threat of another eruption. Late September of 2009 the mountain was finally given the all-clear that it was no longer actively perking.

S 143.7 A 196.7 H 35.4 Happy Valley Creek (sign).

S 145.2 A 198.2 H 33.9 Happy Valley Store to west.

S 148 A 201 H 31.1 Double-ended paved turnout to west with good view of Mount Iliamna.

S 150.8 A 203.8 H 28.3 Stariski Creek Bridge. Parking to west at north end of bridge. Access to **Stariski Creek** fishwalk; public fishing access. Reminder here about cleaning off boats to avoid spreading invasive species.

Begin Scenic Byway southbound, which extends to Homer Spit.

S 151.5 A 204.5 H 27.6 Distance marker southbound shows Anchor Point 5 miles, Homer 20 miles.

S 151.9 A 204.9 H 27.2 Turnoff to west for **Stariski State Recreation Site**; 16 campsites in tall trees on gravel loop road; $12 nightly fee; toilets (wheelchair accessible) and well water. Small campground with outstanding views of Iliamna and Redoubt. This is a good place to stop for a picnic or to take a break. *CAUTION: Eroding bluff; supervise children.*

S 152.6 A 205.6 H 26.5 Short (0.4 mile) but *extremely* steep road access west to **Whiskey Gulch Beach**. At the bottom of this side road there is a small camping area to the right and a larger camping area to the left. There is an outhouse, but carry out your trash. *Do not trespass on private land.* Sign reads: "Whiskey Gulch Access Road is narrow and has a blind 90 degree turn at the top of the hill. The road is maintained as a 4-wheel drive vehicle access road only. The road to the beach is very steep and difficult to climb, even in 4-wheel drive. Two-week camping limit."

S 154.1 A 207.1 H 25 Timberline Creations Gift Shop specializes in unique antler, fossil ivory and scrimshaw gifts and jewelry created by the Lettis family in their workshop. A must-stop for the traveler that enjoys quality craftsmanship. Call (907) 235-8288. Email: tcalaska@xyz.net. Website www.timberlinecreations.com. See display ad this page. [ADVERTISEMENT]

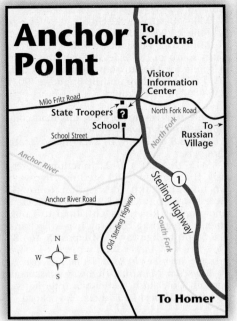

Anchor Point

To Soldotna

Milo Fritz Road
State Troopers
School
School Street
Anchor River
Anchor River Road

Visitor Information Center
North Fork Road
To Russian Village
North Fork
Sterling Highway
Old Sterling Highway
South Fork

N
W E
S

To Homer

Anchor River Road ends at most westerly point on the Northern American continent accessible by continuous road system. (©Sharon Nault)

S 155.7 A 208.7 H 23.4 Anchor Point welcome sign southbound.

Watch for black bears and watch for moose.

Distance marker northbound shows Soldotna 58 miles, Kenai 69 miles, Anchorage 206 miles.

S 156 A 209 H 23.1 *Begin 45 mph speed zone southbound.*

S 156.3 A 209.3 H 22.8 Grocery to west; 24-hour gas station to east.

Anchor Point

S 156.6 A 209.6 H 22.5 Anchor Point post office. Anchor Point is located on the Sterling Highway, 61 miles south of Soldotna. **Population:** 2,007. **Emergency services:** Phone 911. Alaska State Troopers, phone (907) 235-8239. SVT Medical Clinic on the Anchor River Inn property, phone (907) 226-2238.

Visitor Information: Anchor Point Chamber of Commerce, P.O. Box 610, Anchor Point, AK 99556; phone (907) 235-2600; www.anchorpointchamber.org; info@ anchorpointchamber.org. Located in the small brown building on west side of highway between school and Troopers office.

Anchor Point is a full-service community with a Chamber of Commerce, post office and a variety of businesses. Lodging, restaurants, gas stations, fishing charters, seafood processors, RV parks, groceries, laundries and gift shops can be found along the highway and area roads. Churches, a library, senior citizen center and VFW are among the many organizations here.

Anchor Point was originally named

"Laida" by Captain James Cook in the summer of 1778, when the *Resolution* and *Discovery* sailed into Cook Inlet looking for the Northwest Passage. It was later renamed Anchor Point by early homesteaders to commemorate the loss of an anchor off the point by Captain Cook. A post office was established here in 1949.

Anchor Point is the home of the "Most Westerly Highway in North America." Take your photo with the sign located at the end of Anchor River (Beach) Road; *see log on page 618.*

In addition to fishing, local attractions include beachcombing, golf and hiking. The Russian village of Nikolaevsk is located 9 miles from downtown Anchor Point and has a picturesque Russian church and cafe, gift shop, B&B.

Special events in Anchor Point include Snow Rondi (last weekend in February); Saltwater King Tournament (Mother's Day weekend); Memorial Weekend Family Fun Festival; Kids All-American Fishing Derby (June); and 4th of July celebration.

The Anchor Point area is noted for its excellent seasonal king and silver salmon, steelhead and rainbow fishing opportunities. There is bank fishing along the Anchor River for king and silver salmon, rainbow and steelhead and Dolly Varden, or fishermen can access salt water by using the tractor launch on the beach. Fishing begins the weekend prior to Memorial Day weekend in Anchor Point on the Anchor River for king salmon and continues for the next 5 weekends. July 1, the Anchor River reopens with Dolly Varden, followed by silver salmon, which runs into the steelhead fishery that continues until freezeup. The Cook Inlet fishery consists of all 5 species of salmon, halibut and a variety of rockfish.

Sterling Highway Log

(continued)

S 156.7 A 209.7 H 22.4 Junction with Milo Fritz Avenue to west and North Fork Road to east (description follows). Milo Fritz Avenue leads the Fire station at Mile 0.1; the VFW and library at Mile 0.2; the senior center at Mile 0.3; Anchor River Lodge at Mile 0.7; and continues to private homes (no turnaround areas).

North Fork Road to east is a 10.2-mile paved road as follows:

Mile 0.1 mile **Sleepy Bear Cabins.**

Mile 0.5 Anchor River.

Mile 8.3 Entering **NIKOLAEVSK** (pop. 312), a settlement of "Russian Old Believers," whose ancestors originally settled in Woodburn, OR, after the Bolshevik Revolution of 1917. The first Old Believer settlers purchased land here in 1967. According to the Dept. of Community & Economic Development: "The community includes Russian Orthodox, Russian Old Believers (Old Right Believers) and some non-Russians, living in 3 distinct settlements. The Old Believers in this area lead a family-oriented, self-sufficient life-style. They use modern utilities, and food sources are from gardening, small livestock, fishing and hunting. Families are typically very large (8 to 12 children). Traditional clothing is worn, Russian is the first language, and the church dictates that males do not shave."

Mile 9.4 Anchor Point Vounteer Fire Sta-

Anchor River (Beach) Road

The Anchor River is a popular fishing stream. (©Kris Valencia, staff)

Turn off the Sterling Highway at **Milepost S 157.1** on to the Old Sterling Highway and continue past the Anchor River Inn and across the Anchor River bridge. Just beyond the bridge, turn on Anchor River (Beach) Road, a 1.2-mile spur road providing access to the popular Anchor River Recreation Area for camping and fishing. Anchor River Road ends at the most westerly point on the North American continent accessible by continuous road system.

According to the Alaska Dept. of Fish and Game, the king salmon run on the Anchor River is late May to mid-June; silver salmon, late July through mid-September; and steelhead (catch-and-release only) from mid-August to early November. Check current fishing regulations for the Anchor River. Special restrictions apply to king salmon.

Distance from junction (J) is shown.

J 0 Junction of Old Sterling Highway and Sterling Highway in Anchor Point at **Milepost S 157.1**. Liquor store, groceries, dentist, charter services, medical clinic and lodging.

J 0.3 Anchor River Bridge, also known as "the erector set bridge." Clearance 13' 2".

J 0.4 Road forks: Turn right (west) for Anchor River (Beach) Road. Left fork is Old Sterling Highway, which continues south through rural residential area and rejoins Sterling Highway at **Milepost S 164.8**.

At this junction—on Anchor River Road—is the first of 5 recreation sites in Anchor River State Recreation Area: **Silver-King Day-Use Area** (**Anchor River State Recreation Area**) on river; parking area, toilets, dumpster, $5 day-use fee.

J 0.6 Coho Campground (Anchor River SRA); parking, toilets, $10 camping fee, $5 day-use fee. Side-by-side parking.

J 0.8 Steelhead Campground (Anchor River SRA); gravel side-by-side day-use parking area and grassy tent camping area in trees. Picnic tables and toilets but no water; $10 camping fee, $5 day-use fee.

J 1.1 Slidehole Campground (Anchor River SRA); 30 campsites on loop road, day-use parking area, $10 camping fee, $5 day-use fee, tables, water, toilets, special senior/wheelchair camping area, large day-use parking lot, trail access to river. Camp host may sell firewood.

J 1.5 Halibut Campground (Anchor River SRA); day-use parking area and picnic sites, 20 campsites on gravel loop, toilets, water. $10 camping fee, $5 day-use fee.

Access to beach. Covered viewing area inside campground entrance. Benches, telescopes. Views of seals and birds. Display boards. Beautiful view of Aleutian Range from parking area. Gold Rush Centennial sign here reads (excerpt): "The first mining of gold on a commercial scale in Southcentral Alaska occurred along this beach. Miners sluiced gravel at the base of the bluff throughout the 1890s. They recovered small amounts of gold, but a bonanza eluded them."

Sign here marks the most westerly point on the North American continent accessible by continuous road system. N 59°46' W 151°52'.

J 1.6 Road dead-ends on shore of Cook Inlet; viewing deck, telescopes, beach access, 12-hour parking ($5 fee). Private tractor boat launch service. Tractor assistance has revolutionized sportfish access to Cook Inlet by allowing boats to launch at just about any tide, rather than having to wait for high tide. Drive on beach at your own risk (soft sand).

Return to Milepost S 157.1 Sterling Highway

tion No. 2.

Mile 9.8 Nikolaevsk School.

Mile 9.9 Post Office.

Mile 10.1 Russian Orthodox Church. Turn south on Nikolaevsk Road and drive 0.3 mile for **The Russian "Samovar" Café, RV Park, Gift Shop and B&B**; phone (907) 235-6867 for reservations.

Mile 10.2 Pavement ends, dirt road continues through private property.

S 156.8 A 209.8 H 22.3 Alaska State Troopers.

S 157.1 A 210.1 H 22 Junction of Sterling Highway and Old Sterling Highway; Anchor River Inn (description follows). Access west to Anchor Point Visitor Center, and **Anchor River (Beach) Road** to Cook Inlet. Old Sterling Highway (paved) rejoins the Sterling Highway at **Milepost S 164.8**. *Description of Anchor Point on page 617. See "Anchor River (Beach) Road" log on this page.*

Blue Star Memorial Highway marker at turnoff. Gold Rush Centennial interpretive sign is at **Milepost J 1.5** Anchor River Road.

Junction with Old Sterling Highway and access to Anchor River (Beach) Road. See "Anchor River (Beach) Road" log on this page.

S 157.2 A 210.2 H 21.9 Anchor River Bridge.

S 157.5 A 210.5 H 21.6 Welcome to Anchor Point (northbound) sign.

S 158.5 A 211.5 H 20.6 Distance marker southbound shows Homer 14 miles.

S 161 A 214 H 18.1 Black Water Bend Espresso to west, Norman Lowell Road to east; descriptions follow.

Black Water Bend Espresso. Not your average drip! Double entrances, easy access for big rigs to get your favorite coffee, latte, decaf, smoothie, tea, juice, sugar-free drink, goodies. Something for everyone, treats for your dog. Look for big sign and pink barn. 3:30 A.M.-10 P.M. Call ahead for faster service. blackwaterbend@horizonsatellite.com; phone (907) 235-6884. [ADVERTISEMENT]

Norman Lowell Road to east, across from Black Water Bend Espresso, leads to the spacious gallery of longtime Alaskan homesteader Norman Lowell, a well-known Alaska artist. His gallery is filled with paintings of glaciers, volcanoes and the local area. You may also walk through his gardens and his original homesteaded cabin. Plenty of turn-around parking.

S 161 A 214 H 18.1 Anchor River bridge.

S 161.4 A 214.4 H 17.7 Double-ended turnout to east by Anchor River.

S 161.9 A 214.9 H 17.2 Distance marker northbound shows Anchor Point 5 miles.

S 162.3 A 215.3 H 16.8 Narrow track access to river.

S 164.3 A 217.3 H 14.8 North Fork (Loop) Road.

S 164.8 A 217.8 H 14.3 Junction with Old Sterling Highway (paved) which leads 8 miles northwest to connect with Anchor River (Beach) Road.

S 165.5 A 218.5 H 13.6 Narrow, gravel, unmaintained turnout to west, no view.

S 167.1 A 220.1 H 12 Diamond Ridge Road to residential area.

S 168.2 A 221.2 H 10.9 *Begin 45 mph speed zone southbound a curve.*

S 169 A 222 H 10.1 24-hour gas, groceries, snacks, soft-serve ice cream, supplies, and campground. Homer DOT/PF highway maintenance station on east side of

highway.

Begin 4-lane highway southbound. Begin 2-lane highway northbound.

Distance marker northbound shows Soldotna 71 miles, Kenai 82 miles, and Anchorage 219 miles.

S 169.6 A 222.6 H 9.5 Popular rest area at top of Homer Hill has a large paved parking area, container gardens, and a spectacular view of Kachemak Bay, Homer Spit, glaciers, mountains and the oceans. Telescopes, wheel-chair accessible restrooms, litter barrels and benches.

A great photo stop and favorite photo-op on a clear day. Gold Rush Centennial interpretive sign: "A party of 50 prospectors from Kings County (Brooklyn), New York, sailed to Alaska in 1898, bound for the Turnagain Arm gold fields. Their schooner reached Cook Inlet late in the fall and encountered ice. The captain offloaded the stampeders at Kachemak Bay. The party, calling themselves the Kings County Mining Company, set off overland with their belongings in wheelbarrows. The quantity and weight of their gear, not to mention the mode of transportation, was a serious impediment to traversing the rough terrain buried in deep snow. Add the penetrating cold of Alaska's winters and their journey quickly turned into an arduous trek. The exhausted party finally reached Skilak Lake and built a cabin. Discouraged by weather, sickness, squabbling and other hardships, the company disbanded the next spring. Most of the party returned to their homes, although 3 stayed to search for gold. Some artifacts from this ill-fated expedition are displayed at Pratt Museum in Homer."

Begin 6 percent downgrade southbound.

S 170.3 A 223.3 H 8.8 Expansive views of Homer Spit and Kachemak Bay as highway descends "Homer Hill."

Posted 45 mph speed zone southbound.

S 171.9 A 224.9 H 7.2 West Hill Road; connects to Skyline Drive and East Hill Road for scenic drive along Homer Bluff.

S 172 A 225 H 7.1 Last physical milepost southbound on Sterling Highway is attached to the streetlight.

S 172.1 A 225.1 H 7 West Homer Elementary School to east.

S 172.5 A 225.5 H 6.6 Best Western Bidarka Inn, Fireside Lounge and Otter Room Grill to west. Homer Middle School to east.

S 172.6 A 225.6 H 6.5 Turnoff to west for **Oceanview RV Park**; big rigs welcome.

S 172.8 A 225.8 H 6.3 Pioneer Avenue; turn here for downtown **HOMER** (description follows). Drive 0.2 mile on Pioneer Avenue and turn left on Bartlett Avenue for the **Pratt Museum** (see description on page 626), the hospital and for access to Karen Hornaday Park Campground. Pioneer Avenue continues to Homer businesses, the police and fire department, before connecting with East End Road.

S 173 A 226 H 6.1 Homer Chamber of Commerce Visitor Center on right side of highway going into Homer.

S 173.1 A 226.1 H 6 Sterling Highway intersects with Main Street. Turn east (left southbound) to connect with Pioneer Avenue to downtown Homer.

Turn west (right southbound), towards water, for access to **Driftwood Inn RV Park**. Turn left on E. Bunnell Avenue and right on Beluga Avenue for **Bishop's Beach Park**; public beach access, parking, picnic tables and Beluga Slough trailhead.

S 173.2 A 226.2 H 5.9 Alaska Islands

& Ocean Visitor Center. The center is open daily from 9 A.M. to 6 P.M., Memorial Day through Labor Day; Tuesday through Saturday from 10 A.M. to 5 P.M. the rest of the year. Admission is free. This facility allows visitors to "virtually visit" Alaska Maritime National Wildlife Refuge, which encompasses the remote Alaska coastline and the Kachemak Bay Research Reserve. Interactive exhibits capture the islands, rocky coastline, seabirds and marine mammals in fiberglass and through audio-visual aids. Ample parking, restrooms, bookstore, wheelchair accessible. **Beluga Slough Trail** access. Inquire inside about naturalist-led walks.

S 173.4 A 226.4 H 5.7 Safeway Center; open 5 A.M. to midnight, daily, supermarket. *NOTE: Homer's banned the use of disposable plastic shopping bags effective in January 1st, 2013.*

S 173.5 A 226.5 H 5.6 Heath Street. Homer Post Office (ZIP code 99603) northeast side of highway. Homer Animal Shelter is down side street to west.

S 173.6 A 226.6 H 5.5 Entrance to dump station. Fee required.

S 173.7 A 226.7 H 5.4 Traffic light at Lake Street; McDonalds. Access to Pioneer Avenue business area and Lakeside Center, Ulmers True Value Hardware and pharmacy.

S 174 A 227 H 5.1 Beluga Lake; floatplane bases.

S 174.1 A 227.1 H 5 Turnoff for **Beluga Lake Lodge** (dining, lodging).

S 174.2 A 227.2 H 4.9 Farmer's Market takes place here Wednesday and Saturday in summer.

S 174.4 A 227.4 H 4.7 Douglas Place. Access to Alaska Dept. of Fish and Game office at 3298 Douglas Place (behind Alaska Tire Co.). Stop by for a current copy of area fishing regulations.

S 174.6 A 227.6 H 4.5 Airport (FAA) Road to Homer Airport terminal and Beluga Wetlands Wildlife Observation deck across from airport.

S 174.8 A 227.8 H 4.3 Junction with Kachemak Drive; access to air charter services. Begin pedestrian/bike trail along Homer Spit; trailhead parking. Sterling Highway crosses onto Homer Spit (see description

in Homer Attractions). Lighthouse Village and pizza restaurant.

S 174.9 A 227.9 H 4.2 First of 2 viewing platforms overlooking Mud Bay on pedestrian/bike path along Homer Spit; telescopes, bike stands, trash bins and information boards.

S 175.3 A 228.3 H 3.8 Mariner Beach Park; public parking and camping; picnic tables, firepits, outhouse, fee charged. Public camping on Homer Spit requires a permit, available at the Fee Office across from the Fishing Lagoon. Mariner Beach is a favorite for kite flying.

S 176.4 A 229.4 H 2.7 Highway passes weathered, beached vessel that resembles a pirate ship and serves as a private home. Good view of old boats and buoys from pedestrian/bike path.

S 176.9 A 229.9 H 2.2 Kevin Bell Arena (Homer ice rink). Ice hockey is very popular in Homer (and in Alaska!).

S 177.7 A 230.7 H 1.4 Heritage RV Park with 24-hour office, private beach.

S 177.9 A 230.9 H 1.2 The Fishing Lagoon; public parking, restrooms. Fee Office to north for Homer Spit public camping permits. Camping Office phone (907) 235-1583.

S 178 A 231 H 1.1 The Fishing Lagoon public campground; restrooms, dump station, picnic tables. Fish cleaning station. Homer's Pier One Theatre.

S 178 A 231 H 1.1 Freight Dock Road. Access to public boat ramp, boat trailer parking, deep-water dock and **Sportsman's Supply & RV Park**. The *Time Bandit* fishing vessel from the *Deadliest Catch* TV series may be docked here.

S 178.2 A 231.2 H 0.9 Fishing Village Boardwalk, public parking.

From here to end of spit Homer Spit Road can get pretty congested, with vehicles and pedestrians. Boat Harbor parking area has 7-day limit, no camping. *Posted speed limit 25 mph.*

S 178.3 A 231.3 H 0.8 Homer Jackpot

Great view of Kachemak Bay and Homer Spit from rest area at Milepost S 169.6. (©Sharon Nault)

The pedestrian and bike path on Homer Spit is popular with both residents and visitors.

(©Sharon Nault)

Halibut Derby; maps, information, restrooms, fee parking at ramps to boat harbor. The city of Homer provides spaces for beach camping and limited RV parking (no hookups); stop here and find out where these areas are located. ⛺

S 178.5 A 231.5 H 0.6 Harbormaster building, public restrooms. Fee parking for Ramp 2 to boat harbor adjacent.

S 178.6 A 231.6 H 0.5 Famous Salty Dawg Saloon & Lighthouse, built in 1898.

S 178.7 A 231.7 H 0.4 Often photographed **Seafarer's Memorial**, a monument to those who have been lost at sea. Memorial Bell, picnic tables and benches.

S 178.8 A 231.8 H 0.3 Homer Spit Campground has beachside campsites with power hookup, showers and laundry. ⛺

S 178.9 A 231.9 H 0.2 U.S. Coast Guard dock, storage and private parking area.

S 179 A 232 H 0.1 Alaska State Ferry Homer Terminal.

S 179.1 A 232.1 H 0 Sterling Highway ends at **Land's End Resort** at the tip of Homer Spit. Parking area by beach. Beach fishing. Walk on beach around the front of the Land's End Resort to see memorial bench dedicated to Jean Keene (see below).

NOTE: It is illegal to feed eagles on the Spit or anywhere else in Homer. This ordinance went into effect in March 2009, ending a tradition started by the late Jean Keene more than 20 years before. Ms. Keene, also known as "the Eagle Lady," fed fish scraps to eagles near her former home at the end of Homer Spit. Keene fed the eagles over the winter months and also monitored injured and sick birds until her death in January 2009. The current law also prohibits the feeding of crows, gulls and ravens.

Homer

Located on the southwestern Kenai Peninsula on the north shore of Kachemak Bay; 226 miles by highway or 40 minutes by jet aircraft from Anchorage. **Population:** 5,153 **Emergency Services:** Phone 911 for all emergency services. **City Police**, phone (907) 235-3150. **Fire Department** and **Ambulance**, phone (907) 235-3155. **Animal Control**, phone (907) 235-3141. **Port/Harbor**, phone (907) 235-3160. **Coast Guard**, phone (907) 235-4288. **Hospital**, South Peninsula Hospital, phone (907) 235-8101. **Veterinary Clinic**, phone (907) 235-8960.

Visitor Information: Chamber of Commerce Visitor Center is located on the Sterling Highway (Homer Bypass) between Pioneer and Main Street as you drive into town. The center offers free maps, a phone for local calls, restrooms and information on activities and lodging. Open year-round, daily in summer. Contact the Homer Chamber of Commerce, 201 Sterling Highway, Homer 99603; phone during business hours (907) 235-7740; website www.homer alaska.org. To find out about local concerts, art shows and other arts events in Homer, phone the Homer Council of the Arts at (907) 235-4288; or check out the **Homer News**, published each Thursday (see display ad on page 628).

The **Wildlife Refuge Visitor Center:** The **Alaska Islands & Ocean Visitor Center** is on the Sterling Highway just past the Chamber of Commerce. The Visitor Center offers information on area wildlife watching tours, family nature programs, and wildlife watching hotspots and recent sightings. During the summer months the Visitor Center is open daily from 9 A.M. to 6 P.M., with free admission, and Ranger-led walks, talks, and hands-on marine labs. Winter hours are noon-5 P.M. Tuesday–Saturday. For more information, call (907) 235-6961, email: info@IslandsAndOcean.org or visit their website at www.IslandsAndOcean.org.

The **Pratt Museum** is open daily 10 A.M. to 6 P.M. from mid-May to mid-September; open noon to 5 P.M. Tuesday through Sunday from mid-September to mid-May; closed in January. Contact the Pratt Museum, 3779 Bartlett St., Homer 99603. Phone (907) 235-8635; email info@prattmuseum.org; website www.prattmuseum.org.

Elevation: Sea level to 800 feet. **Climate:** Winter temperatures occasionally fall below

zero, but seldom colder. The Kenai Mountains north and east protect Homer from severe cold, and Cook Inlet provides warming air currents. The highest temperature recorded is 81°F. Average annual precipitation is 27.9 inches. Prevailing winds are from the northeast, averaging 6.5 mph/10.5 kmph.

Radio: KGTL-AM 620, KWVV 103.5/104.9/106.3, MBN-FM 107.1/96.7/95.3, KBBI-AM 890, KMJG-FM 88.9; KPEN-FM 99.3/100.9/102.3, KWHQ-FM 98.3. **Television:** KTUU, KTBY, KTVA, KAKM, KIMO. **Newspaper:** *Homer News* (weekly), *Homer Tribune* (weekly).

Private Aircraft: Homer airport on Airport Road; elev. 78 feet; length 7,400 feet; asphalt; fuel 100LL, Jet A; attended. Terminal building.

Homer was established on the north shore of Kachemak Bay at Homer Spit in 1895, and named for local prospector Homer Pennock. A post office was established here in 1896.

Kachemak, the Russian name for the bay, means "high cliffs on the water." Another interpretation of the name suggests it means "smoky bay" and is derived from the smoke which once rose from the smoldering coal seams jutting from the clay bluffs of the upper north shore of Kachemak Bay and the cliffs near Anchor Point.

In the early days many of the exposed coal seams were slowly burning from causes unknown. Today the erosion of these bluffs drops huge fragments of lignite and bituminous coal on the beaches, creating a plentiful supply of winter fuel for the residents. There are an estimated 400,000,000 tons of coal deposit in the immediate vicinity of Homer.

A coal mine was operating at Homer's Bluff Point in the late 1800s, and a railroad carried the coal out to the end of Homer Spit. (The railroad was abandoned in 1907.) Gold seekers debarked at Homer, bound for the goldfields at Hope and Sunrise.

Coal mining operations ceased around the time of WWI, but settlers continued to trickle into the area, some to homestead, others to work in the canneries built to process Cook Inlet fish.

Jutting out for 4.3 miles from the Homer shore is the **Homer Spit**, a long, narrow bar of gravel. The road along the backbone of the Spit is part of the Sterling Highway, which is the main road through Homer. The Spit has had quite a history, and it continues to be a center of activity for the town. In 1964, after the earthquake, the Spit sank 4 to 6 feet, requiring several buildings to be moved to higher ground.

Today, Homer Spit is the site of a major dock facility for boat loading, unloading, servicing and refrigerating. The deep-water dock can accommodate 340-foot vessels and 30-foot drafts, making it accessible to cruise and cargo ships. The Pioneer Dock can accommodate ships up to 800 feet. Homer is home port to the Alaska Marine Highway ferry MV *Tustumena* and U.S. Coast Guard vessels. The small-boat harbor on the Spit has a 5-lane load/launch ramp. Also in the small-boat harbor area are the harbormaster's office, canneries, parking/camping areas, charter services, small shops, live theatre, galleries, restaurants, motels and bed and breakfasts.

Rising behind downtown are bluffs which level off at about 1,200 feet to form the southern rim of the western plateau of the Kenai Peninsula. These slopes provide a colorful backdrop from the bay, tinted in green and pastel shades by wildflowers from June to September, and in golds and yellows in the fall. The slopes are also prime residential real estate, thanks to their view of magnificent Kachemak Bay.

Homer's picturesque setting, mild cli-

Homer Harbor is a major dock facility for commercial and recreational vessels. (©Sharon Nault)

Shops and businesses are located on Homer Spit (pictured here) and in downtown Homer. (©Sharon Nault)

mate and great fishing (especially for halibut) attract thousands of visitors each year. In addition to its tourist industry and role as a trade center, Homer's commercial fishing industry is an important part of its economy. Homer calls itself the "Halibut Fishing Capital of the World." Manufacturing and seafood processing, government offices, trades and construction are other key industries.

Homer is host to a large artist community. Potters, sculptors, painters and jewelers practice their crafts and sell their goods in local shops, weekend markets and galleries. The local theater group provides live performances year-round.

Homer has 8 schools. The modern Homer High School has the complete skeleton of a sperm whale hanging from the ceiling of the school's lobby. A local fisherman found the dead whale washed up on Chugach Island in 1998. It was recovered and the skeleton preserved through the efforts of the U.S. Coast Guard, the Pratt Museum and the high school students.

Lodging & Services

Budget Travel chose Homer as 1 of the "top 10 coolest small towns" in 2006 and we think you will agree. Homer has hundreds of small businesses offering a wide variety of goods and services. Accommodations available at a number of hotels, motels, and bed and breakfasts. There are 2 hostels. Camping at private and municipal campgrounds (reservations advised in summer). Dozens of restaurants offer everything from fast food to fine dining.

Homer has a post office, library, museum, laundromats, gas stations with propane and dump stations, banks, churches, a hospital and airport terminal. There are many fishing charter services, boat repair and storage facilities, marine fuel at Homer marina; bait, tackle and sporting goods stores; and also art galleries, gift shops and groceries. Homer Spit has long-term parking and camping.

The recent addition of day-use parking lots for large RV's make getting around Homer, even easier. From the Sterling Highway, turn onto Ohlson Lane and take a left into the Homer Chamber of Commerce and Visitor's Center lot. For the second option, turn uphill onto Pioneer Avenue from the Sterling Highway, and take the first left onto Woodside. The parking lot for an older, two-story, tan building is the old middle school and functions as the second day use lot. Both of these lots are free, convenient for walking to shopping and sights and available from 8 A.M. to 9 P.M. mid-May–Labor Day. Look for signage.

Beluga Lake Lodge. This impressive lodge, is located on the edge of Beluga Lake and slough where thousands of birds and abundant wildlife gather and float-planes take off in the distance. The Lodge proudly announces new owners and management, who are going the extra mile to create a newly refurbished, fresh, clean environment, with all new beds and mattresses, new carpeting and brand new deck to comfortably enjoy the fabulous views. All 35 rooms are non–smoking, have Free WiFi, private baths, phones, cable–TV. Affordable rates. Some 4 bed and 2 bed kitchenettes with refrigerators and microwaves. Guests can enjoy the Beluga Bar & Grills, with deck overlooking the lake and beyond. The Lodge is just 1 mile to the Spit and walk-

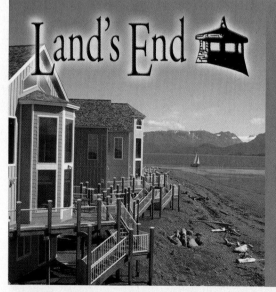

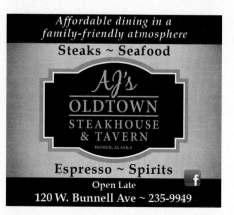

ing distance to Bishops Beach, nearby fishing or bear viewing charters, restaurants and shopping. www.belugalakelodging.com. 204 Ocean Drive Loop. Phone (907) 235-5995. [ADVERTISEMENT]

Best Western Bidarka Inn, on the right coming into Homer, is 1 block from the visitor center, 2 blocks from the Islands and Ocean Visitor Center, downtown shopping, museum, galleries and just a 15 minute drive to the famous Homer Spit. The AAA approved, Bidarka offers 74 rooms including several view rooms, two very special hot-tub suites and free hot breakfast. All rooms are equipped with queen or king beds and for your convenience; coffee maker, hair dryer, iron/board, micro/fridge, HBO, cable-TV, free high-speed internet access and free local phone calls. Do you want to tour Homer's many wonderful sights, go on a memorable bear-viewing trip, watch whales, go halibut fishing, visit unique Halibut Cove or historic Seldovia? Tour information at our front desk. Guest's fish packaging, freezing and shipping available. Check your email or use the Business Center's guest computer. Stay in shape at the Fitness Center! 575 Sterling Highway. Reservations 1-866-685-5000. Phone: (907) 235-8148. Fax (907) 235-8140. info@bidarkainn.com. www.bidarkainn.com. See display ad on page 621. [ADVERTISEMENT]

Best Western Bidarka Inn, Fireside Lounge and Otter Room Grill. Start your day by treating yourself to our free hot breakfast while enjoying a spectacular view of the mountains and glaciers surrounding Kachemak Bay. In the evening, savor the best steaks in town and fresh Alaska seafood at the Otter Room Grill. Visit the inviting, friendly full service Fireside Lounge where stories of the day's adventures are often heard and told. Big screen TV's bring you the latest sporting events. info@bidarkainn.com; www.bidarkainn.com. (907) 235-8148. See display ad on page 621. [ADVERTISEMENT]

Driftwood Inn, Charters and RV Park. Offering rooms with king-size beds. Charming, newly refurbished, historic beachfront inn, lodge and cottage with 27 rooms and full-hookup RV park. Both have spectacular views overlooking beautiful Kachemak Bay, mountains, glaciers. Quiet in-town location. Immaculately clean, charming rooms. Free coffee, tea, local information. Comfortable common areas with TV, fireplace, library, microwave, refrigerator, barbecue, shellfish cooker, fish cleaning area, freezer, picnic and laundry facilities. Central highspeed Internet access, WiFi free. Economy breakfast available in lobby. We are a smoke-free facility. Halibut and salmon charters available year round with experienced captains and

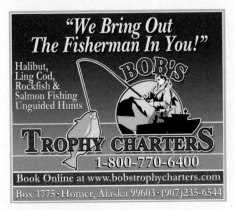

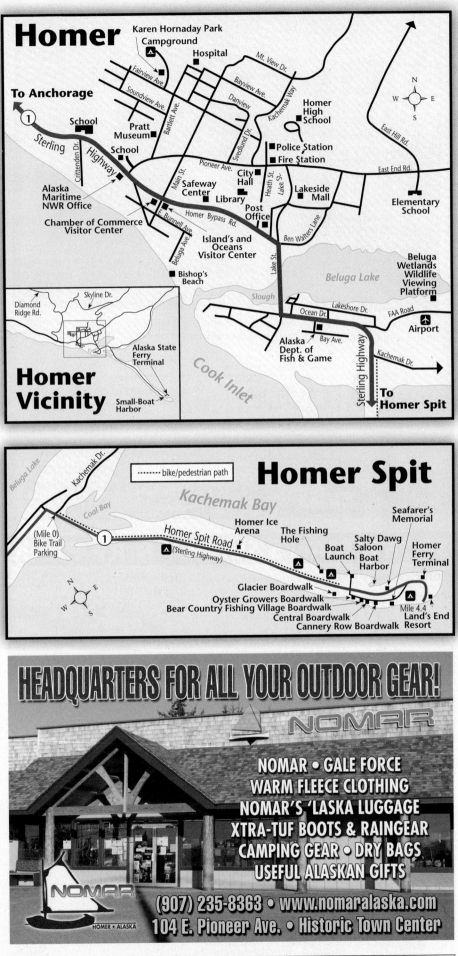

Alaska averages more than 2 volcanic eruptions a year.

Both full-service campgrounds and primitive beach camping are available on Homer Spit.
(©Sharon Nault)

lifelong Alaskans. The RV park has 20-/30-/50-amp electric, water, sewer, clean, comfortable laundry and shower room for RV guests. Friendly, knowledgeable staff, specializes in helping make your stay in Homer the best possible. Reasonable, seasonal rates. Pet friendly. Open year-round. Owned by 5th generation Alaskans. Write, call for brochure. 135 W. Bunnell Ave., MP, Homer, AK 99603. (907) 235-8019. Email: driftwoodinn@alaska.com. Website: www.thedriftwoodinn.com. See display ad page 622. [ADVERTISEMENT]

Land's End Resort. Alaska's premier oceanfront resort at the tip of the Homer Spit, surrounded by majestic views of Kachemak Bay. Homer's full service year-round resort with restaurant, bar, catering, group and event sales and luxury beachfront lodges. Tour Desk books charters, tours, excursions, adventures and our own Raven's Nest Spa. Phone 1-800-478-0400. See display ad on page 622. [ADVERTISEMENT]

Camping

Homer is popular with campers, so there are a number of private RV parks (see ads this section). There is public camping on the Homer Spit. Daily camping fees are $15/day for RVs, $8 for tents. No reservations; no hookups; pets on leash. There is a 14-day limit. Restrooms, water and garbage are available. Check in with the Fee Office across from the Fishing Lagoon; phone (907) 235-1583.

The city campground is Karen Hornaday Hillside Park, accessed via Bartlett and Fairview avenues (follow signs). Located behind the ballfields, in a densely treed and brushy hillside, the park has 31 campsites, restrooms, water, picnic tables, firepits, trash cans and a playground, but no campground host. Camping fee is $15/day for RVs, $8 for tents. No reservations, no hookups; only small RVs. Information available at visitor center. Weekly rates, 2–week limit.

Homer offers 2 municipal RV dump sites: on the Spit near the lagoon, and across from the post office along the Sterling Highway.

A Fisherman's Resort–Homer's newest RV Park. On the Sterling Highway just walking distance to the famous Homer Spit (⅛ mile.) Full hookups 30/50 amps, free WiFi, cable TV. Large landscaped lots with patio slabs and picnic tables. Full service fish pro-

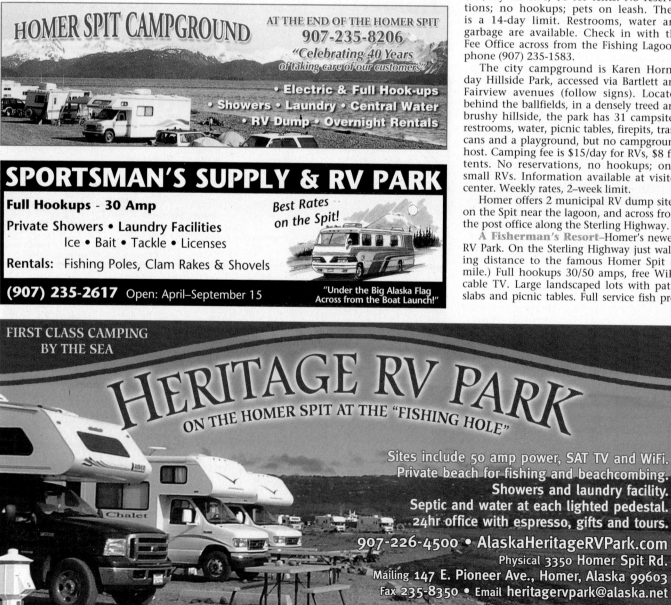

cessing and FedEx shipping. Private, large lake-view rooms with full kitchens. Reserve early. Phone: (907) 235-1997. 1302 Ocean Drive, Homer, Alaska 99603. www.Afisher mansResort.com. [ADVERTISEMENT]

Heritage RV Park. Homer's only full-service RV park located on the Homer Spit, adjacent to the "Fishing Hole." All spacious sites include hookups; 50 amp electric, septic, city water, Satellite TV and free WiFi. Laundry room with free showers for guests. Beachfront sites are directly on the water for wonderful beachcombing, clamming, eagle-watching and fishing. Local Alaskan art store and coffee café in the common building. Enjoy the bike trail, charters and all of Homer's recreation opportunities on the Homer Spit! See display ad on facing page. [ADVERTISEMENT]

Homer Spit Campground, where the land ends and the sea begins, on beautiful Kachemak Bay. RV camping on the beach at the end of the Spit. Showers, electric, pull-throughs, dump station, laundromat, overnight rentals and gift shop. Book halibut charters and recreational activities. Satisfying our customers for 40 years. (907) 235-8206. stay@homerspit campground.com. See display ad on facing page. [ADVERTISEMENT]

Oceanview RV Park (Good Sam), 455 Sterling Highway, past Best Western Bidarka Inn on right coming into Homer. Big rigs welcome. Spectacular view of Kachemak Bay, beachfront setting. 85 large pull-through spaces in a terraced park. WiFi available at site. Full/partial hookups, heated super-clean restrooms, free showers, laundry, TV, picnic area. Best gift shop, best prices. Free T-shirt with $100 purchases. Easy walking distance to downtown Homer. Discounted halibut charter rates for park guests and local booking reservations assistance. www.ocean view-rv.com. Phone (907) 235-3951. Email: camp4fun@gci.net. See display ad on this page. [ADVERTISEMENT]

Transportation

Air: Regularly scheduled air service to Anchorage. Several charter services also operate out of Homer; inquire locally.

Ferry: The Alaska State ferry system connects Homer with Seldovia and Kodiak. The Alaska Marine Highway System ferry terminal is located at the Pioneer Dock on Homer Spit; phone (907) 235-8449. See the ALASKA MARINE HIGHWAY section. Information, reservations and ticketing, phone 1-800-642-0066, (907) 235-8449; www.ferryalaska.com.

Water taxis, catamarans and day-tour boats offer passenger service to Seldovia and to Halibut Cove from Homer Spit. Crossing time to Seldovia is anywhere from a half-hour direct to 3 hours on sightseeing cruises. Catamaran service in summer aboard the 150-passenger, 83-foot, fast ferry *Kachemak Voyager*, departing Homer Spit for Seldovia twice daily.

Rental cars and Taxis: Available.
Charter boats: See ads this section.

Attractions

Shopping. Homer is well known as an artists colony and galleries line the streets to prove it. There is the downtown shopping district in the Pioneer Avenue area and there are Homer Spit's boardwalk shops.

Alaska Islands & Ocean Visitor Center, located at **Milepost S 173.2** Sterling Highway, is a state-of-the-art interpretive and educational facility for

Bench is dedicated to the late Jean Keene, the "Eagle Lady," who fed eagles on Homer Spit for 20 some years. It is now illegal to feed eagles, crows, gulls and ravens. (©Sharon Nault)

the Alaska Maritime National Wildlife Refuge and the Kachemak Bay Research Reserve. This facility allows visitors to "virtually visit" the remote Alaska coastline through interactive exhibits that capture the islands, rocky coastline, seabirds and marine mammals in fiberglass and through audio-visual aids. Informative movies are shown throughout the day.

Ample parking, restrooms, bookstore, wheelchair accessible. Access to Beluga Slough trail. In 2014 the center will unveil a new series of signs using poems to interpret the slough. Also ask about naturalist-led walks and tours. The center is open daily from 9 A.M. to 5 P.M., Memorial Day through Labor Day; Tuesday through Saturday from noon to 5 P.M. the rest of the year. Admission is free.

View of Seafarer's Memorial across a rocky stretch of beach on the Homer Spit.
(©Kris Valencia, staff)

Pratt Museum, located off Pioneer Avenue at 3779 Bartlett St., is a must-stop for visitors interested in the arts, science and culture of the area. "Kachemak Bay, an Exploration of People and Place," displays artifacts from the first Native people here, thousands of years ago, to those of homesteaders of the 1930s and 1940s. Audio exhibits, films, lectures and interactive exhibits also introduce visitors to the region.

Excellent aquariums and a tide pool tank display live Kachemak Bay sea creatures. Fish feedings are Tuesdays and Fridays at 4 P.M. throughout the year. Alaskan birds and land and sea mammals, including the complete skeletons of a Bering Sea beaked whale and a beluga whale, are on display.

A popular attraction at the museum is the Sea Bird Cam, showing live images via remote video camera of the seabird rookery at Gull Island, located 8 miles away in Kachemak Bay. Between May and September, visitors may manipulate the camera for a close-up view of common murres, kittiwakes, puffins, cormorants and glaucous-winged gulls in their natural habitat. The Pratt Museum's live BearCam is located at Katmai National Park across Cook Inlet with broadcasts viewable in the museum gallery and on the web.

Summer visitors may take a self-guided tour through the outdoor Botanical Garden and on the Forest Ecology Trail. The Forest Trail includes an annual exhibit by local artists on the theme "*Facing the Elements.*"

The Museum Store features a variety of books, Alaskan gifts and jewelry, and Alaskan Native arts and crafts, as well as a large selection of educational toys and games.

Admission is charged. Summer hours (mid-May to mid-September) are 10 A.M. to 6 P.M. daily. Winter hours noon to 5 P.M., Tuesday through Sunday. The museum is closed in January. Phone (907) 235-8635; website www.prattmuseum.org.

Homer Trolley. $12 all-day pass. Visit the Homer Spit, Old Town, Pratt Museum, Islands & Oceans Visitors Center, galleries

and more! (907) 235-2228. www.HomerTrolley.com. [ADVERTISEMENT]

NOMAR® (Northern Marine Canvas Products) began business the summer of 1978 in a yellow school bus! Today, visit our manufacturing facility and retail store at 104 E. Pioneer Ave., downtown Homer. NOMAR® manufactures a wide variety of products for our Alaskan lifestyles. Warm NOMAR® fleece clothing to keep you warm, no matter what the adventure. Soft-sided 'Laska Luggage that's stuffable and float-plane friendly. Watertight bags and camping essentials for kayak tours or off-road camping. Plus, well-made, Homer-made, packable, mailable, useful gifts. "The ultimate Alaskan souvenir." Park in our spacious, paved parking lot and walk around our town, it's a nice stroll. Easy access for RV'ers. We'll gladly ship your purchases for you. (907) 235-8363. See display ad on page 623. [ADVERTISEMENT]

Homer Spit. Visitors and residents naturally gravitate toward this bustling strip of land jutting out into Kachemak Bay. Highlights include a 3-mile biking/walking trail from the parking area at Kachemak Drive. Watch for eagles on the mud flats from the trail's viewing platforms.

A Spit landmark is the **Seafarer's Memorial** at **Milepost S 179**, dedicated to those who have lost their lives at sea. There is a parking area adjacent the memorial. Another Spit landmark and favorite photo subject is the Salty Dawg Saloon's lighthouse.

Fishing charter services and a variety of shops and restaurants are housed in the Spit's unique boardwalk structures. The Spit also offers camping and accommodations. The Homer Boat Harbor and State Ferry Terminal are located on the Spit.

The Homer Farmer's Market is held on Ocean Drive (Sterling Highway, between Beluga Lake and the Spit) across from the Washboard, every Saturday beginning the last weekend in May from 10 A.M. to 3 P.M., and Wednesdays beginning first week in July 3–6 P.M., until September. Locally grown produce, seafood, prepared foods, and hand crafted items. No pets or smoking. For information, visit www.homerfarmersmarket.org.

The Kachemak Bay Shorebird Festival celebrates the arrival of 100,000 migrating shorebirds to the tidal flats of Kachemak Bay. The 22nd annual festival is scheduled for May 8–11, 2014. The event promotes

East End Road

East End Road begins at Pioneer Avenue and Lake Street in Homer and ends for the public at Mile for 19.7 east of downtown. Paved the first 19 miles, East End Road affords breathtaking views of Kachemak Bay, but local traffic and a lack of scenic turnouts make it difficult to enjoy the bird's-eye view of the Spit. Homes and businesses, including several bed-and-breakfasts, are found along East End Road.

Distance from junction with Pioneer Avenue and Lake Street (J) is shown.

J 0 Junction of East End Road begins at the stop-lighted intersection of Pioneer Avenue and Lake Street. Pioneer Avenue becomes East End Road for eastbound traffic. *Speed limit is 25 mph.*

J 0.8 East Hill Road to north. Access to **Halcyon Heights B & B** (phone 907/235-2148) via East Hill Road to Mission Road, across from Alaska Bible Institute. Continue up East Hill road to Skyline Drive for Carl E. Wynn Nature Center (1.5 miles); guided 1-hour walks twice daily.

J 1.1 Mariner Drive; drive 0.2 mile via dirt road through residential area to dead-end at small parking area for Calvin & Coyle Nature Trail, a Kachemak Bay Birding Hot Spot.

J 2.1 American Legion Post 16.

J 2.5 Bear Creek Road.

J 2.7 Home Run Oil to east.

J 2.9 Liquor store, Down East Saloon, laundry.

J 3 Turnoff on to East Bear Creek Drive to north for **Bear Creek Winery**; tours, tasting, gift shop and lodging. Phone (907) 235-8484; www.bearcreekwinery.com.

Bear Creek Winery. See display ad this page.

J 3.4 Kachemak gearshed, East Village mini-storage, and drive-thru espresso.

J 3.6 Junction with Kachemak Drive, a 3.6 mile road that ends at Lake Street at the base of the Homer Spit.

J 4.1 Glacier View Cabins.

J 4.5 Wasabi's Restaurant.

J 6.4 Golf course to north.

J 8.1 Unincorporated community of FRITZ CREEK (pop. 1,809); Fritz Creek General Store, Tesoro gas, liquor store, deli and post office. Homestead Restaurant.

J 8.2 Fritz Creek Gardens, a nursery with

View of beach from end of East End Road. Trails End Horse Adventures offers half-day rides to the head of the bay. (©Sharon Nault)

theme gardens and outdoor art.

J 10 Middleton. Turnoff for **Moose Creek Cabins**.

J 11.7 Trails End Horse Adventures; half-day rides to head of Kachemak Bay, phone (907) 235-6393.

J 12.3 Old East End Road to south.

J 12.4 Fire Station.

J 12.5 McNeil Canyon School to north.

From here, the road traverses south along the edge of a bluff high above Kachemak Bay. Stunning views on a clear day.

J 13.8 Alpine Meadow Road to north; 0.3 miles to **Eveline State Recreation Site**. Large monument to east just before parking area displays Eveline's picture. Two well-marked trails start from this parking area: Alpine Meadows (loop to right) and Glacier View Loop (to left); small parking area and outhouse.

J 14 *Road narrows.*

J 14.5 Timber Bay B&B.

J 15.4 *Slow for 15- to 20-mph curves.*

J 17.1 Snow machine club parking area.

J 18 *CAUTION: Pavement breaks and cracks, no shoulder, extreme curves.*

J 19.5 Voznesenka Water Utility.

J 19.7 Pavement ends; small turnaround

area. Road continues through Russian farm community (private property) to another turnaround parking area on top of a very high bluff near an old cemetery; 4-wheel-drive only access down to beach. This road is used to access a Russian village and is also used by hunters and others going to the head of the bay. It is a steep, difficult, gravel road to the beach. Watch for ATV, vehicle and pedestrian traffic on the steep section in summer.

awareness of this critical shorebird habitat that provides a feeding and resting place for at least 20 species of shorebirds on the last leg of their journey from Central and South America to breeding grounds in western and northern Alaska. Festival highlights include guided bird walks, classes for beginning and advanced birders, children's activities and more. Sponsored by the Homer Chamber of Commerce and U.S. Fish & Wildlife Service; phone (907) 235-7740 for more details. The Homer Bird Hotline is (907) 235-7337.

Attend the Theatre. Homer's community theatre—Pier One Theatre—presents weekend performances of plays, dance concerts and a variety of other shows, from Memorial Day to Labor Day (typical playnights are Thursdays–Sunday). Pier One,

which started in 1973, is located in a converted city warehouse on Homer Spit. Phone (907) 235-7333.

Attend a Concert. The **Kenai Peninsula Orchestra** puts on its 2-week Summer Music Festival featuring classical music concerts, free lunch-time concerts and a gala. Phone (907) 235-4899 for more information.

Concert on the Lawn, an annual rite of summer in Homer, benefits KBBI Public Radio. Daily admission charged. Please no pets. Held at Karen Hornaday Park; food vendors. The 35th annual concert is scheduled for July 12-13, 2014. Check out their website at http://www.kbbi.org for more information.

Visit a Winery. Alaska has 11 licensed wineries, and one of them is right here in

Homer. Bear Creek Winery, off East End Road *(see log above)*, features Alaska berry wines, which retain the natural sweetness of the berries without being syrupy. Some of Bear Creek's most popular flavors include their Blu Zin, Rhubarb and Wild Berry. Summer hours are daily, 10 A.M. to 6 P.M. (May–Sept.); Winter (Oct.–April) hours are noon to 6 P.M. Monday to Saturday, and noon to 4 P.M. Sunday. Phone (907) 235-8484; www.bearcreekwinery.com.

Charter Boats, operating out of the boat harbor on Homer Spit, offer sightseeing and fishing trips and drop-off service for kayakers and wilderness hikers. Homer is one of Alaska's largest charter fishing areas (most charters are for halibut fishing). Charter operators provide gear, bait and expert

Beluga Slough trail can be accessed from Bishop's Beach or Alaska Islands and Ocean Visitor Center parking lot. (©Kris Valencia, staff)

knowledge of the area. Several sightseeing boats operate off the Homer Spit, taking visitors to view the bird rookery on Gull Island, and providing transportation to Halibut Cove and to Seldovia. (Sightseeing trips are generally available from Memorial Day to Labor Day.) Out on the water, watch for whales, puffins, sea otters, seals and other marine wildlife.

Bishop's Beach is accessible by car from the Sterling Highway (Homer Bypass) at Main Street. Parking, public access to the beach, picnic tables and the trailhead for the award-winning Beluga Slough Pedestrian Trail are located at Bishop's Beach. It is possible to walk several miles along the coastline in either direction from Bishop's Beach. *CAUTION: Check tide tables.* (A walking path connects the beach with the Alaska Islands and Ocean Visitor Center.)

Take a scenic drive. The glaciers that spill down from the Harding Icefield straddling the Kenai Mountains across the bay create an ever-changing panorama visible from most points in Homer, particularly from the Skyline Drive. The most spectacular and largest of these glaciers is Grewingk Glacier in Kachemak Bay State Park, visible to the east directly across Kachemak Bay from Homer. The glacier was named by Alaska explorer William H. Dall in 1880 for Constantin Grewingk, a German geologist who had published a work on the geology and volcanism of Alaska. The Grewingk Glacier has a long gravel bar at its terminal moraine, called Glacier Spit, which is a popular excursion spot, and may be visited by charter plane or boat.

Motorists can follow East Hill Road to intersect with the Sterling Highway down West Hill Road at **Milepost S 171.9.** Or motorists may continue out East End Road,

which accesses many Homer businesses. Drive out to Mile 11.2 East End Road and take a half-day trail ride to the head of Kachemak Bay with Trails End Horse Adventures.

Trails End Horse Adventures. Horses, cattle and Alaska are my life. Join me, Homer's working cowboy, in my 29th season offering trail rides in the Homer area, featuring half-day rides to the head of Kachemak Bay, or overnight camp at Mark's rustic ranch homestead. View mountains, glaciers, Fox River flats. Gentle Alaskan horses. All experience levels welcome. Mile 11.2 East End Road. Mark Marette, 53435 East End Road, Homer, AK 99603. Phone (907) 235-6393. [ADVERTISEMENT]

Bear Viewing. Homer is often referred to as the "bear viewing capital of Alaska." It is the main base for visitors flying across Cook Inlet to bear viewing areas at McNeil River State Game Sanctuary and Katmai National Park, as well as areas within Lake Clark National Park. Local air services offer bear viewing, as well as custom charters, flightseeing, fly-in fishing and hiking.

Visits to the **McNeil River** game sanctuary are on a permit basis; a drawing is held in March each year. (Permits are not required for Katmai or Lake Clark visits.) Applications for McNeil River permits are available from the Alaska Dept. of Fish and Game, Attn: McNeil River, 333 Raspberry Road, Anchorage 99518; phone (907) 267-2100.

Visit Halibut Cove and Seldovia. These 2 communities on Kachemak Bay are accessible by ferry from Homer boat harbor. See descriptions of these appealing destinations on pages 629 and 630.

The Center for Alaskan Coastal Studies The Center for Alaskan Coastal Studies is a Homer-based nonprofit organization that offers summer tours at 3 of their educational sites (descriptions follow). Phone (907) 235-6667 or visit www.akcoastalstudies.org for more information on the Center's programs.

Carl E. Wynn Nature Center is located at Mile 1.5 East Skyline Drive, overlooking Homer. From downtown Homer, follow East End Road to East Hill Road, drive up hill and turn on East Skyline Drive, continue straight 1.5 miles; the Center will be on your left. The Center offers guided 1-hour walks twice daily (at 10 A.M. and 2 P.M.) through forest and wildflower meadow, focusing on medicinal and Native uses of plants. Self-guided tours and evening and children's programs are also available. No reservations necessary. There's also 800 feet of handicap-accessible boardwalk trail plus a trail for the visually impaired. Carl E. Wynn Nature Center is open daily, 10 A.M. to 6 P.M., Fridays until 8 P.M., from June 15 to Labor Day.

The Peterson Bay trips include a 15-minute boat ride across Kachemak Bay, viewing the Gull Island seabird rookery; exploring the rich intertidal life on remote beaches (tide dependent) and in live tanks on the decks of their **Peterson Bay Field Station**; and hiking in the coastal forest around Peterson Bay. Hiking/kayaking combination tours also offered. These tours are offered daily from Memorial Day to Labor Day, departing Homer Spit at 8 A.M. and returning at 4 P.M. Reservations are advised.

The Center for Alaskan Coastal Studies yurt on the Homer Spit offers a Creatures of the Dock Tour twice a day from mid-June to mid-August. The yurt (a circular canvas structure) is located across from the harbormaster's office on the Homer Spit.

Kachemak Bay State Park is located on

the south shore of the bay and accessible by float plane or private water taxis from Homer. It is one of Alaska's most popular parks for sea kayaking, hiking, fishing and beachcombing. The park's coves, bay, valleys and mountains provide a great variety of recreational opportunities, including: more than 80 miles of trails (see website for trail descriptions: www.dnr.state.ak.us/parks/units/kbay/kbaytrs.htm); campsites at Glacier Spit, Halibut Cove Lagoon, China Poot Lake and additional backcountry locations; 5 public-use cabins; and excellent kayaking, clamming, tide pooling and beachcombing opportunities. For cabin information and reservations, visit www.alaskastateparks.org or phone (907) 262-5581. For more information, phone the district office at (907) 235-7024 or visit the Chamber of Commerce Visitor Center.

Fish the Annual Homer Halibut Derby, sponsored by the Homer Chamber of Commerce, runs from May 1 to Sept. 30. The state's largest cash halibut derby (over $190,000 in cash prizes) provides 5 monthly cash prizes, 100 tagged fish, lady angler prizes and final jackpot prize. The derby also offers a $10,000 cash prize drawing for a lucky angler releasing a fish over 60 pounds, plus final cash drawings for all ticket buyers. The 2013 winner was Gene Jones of Bellevue, WA, with a 263.2-lb. halibut. Tickets are available at the Jackpot Halibut Derby headquarters on Homer Spit, at the visitor center and from some local businesses. Phone (907) 235-7740; www.homerhalibutderby.com.

AREA FISHING: The Kachemak Bay and Cook Inlet area is one of Alaska's most popular spots for halibut fishing, with catches often weighing 100 to 200 lbs. (though typically caught in the 20-30 lb. range). Guides and charters are available locally. Halibut up to 350 lbs. are fished from June through September; fish the bottom with herring. Year-round trolling for king salmon is popular; use small herring or artificial lures. King salmon may also be taken during late May and June in area streams. Pink salmon (4 to 5 lbs.) may be caught in July and August; use winged bobbers, small weighted spoons and spinners. Similar tackle or fresh roe will catch silver salmon weighing 6 to 8 lbs. in August and September. Dolly Varden are taken throughout the area April to October; try single eggs, small spinners or spoons or wet flies. Steelhead/rainbow are available in local streams, but for conservation purposes must be immediately released unharmed.

Fishermen have had great success in recent years casting from the shore of Homer Spit for king salmon. **The Nick Dudiak Fishing Lagoon** (named by the City of Homer for a state fisheries biologist who resided in Homer from 1977-2005, and also referred to as the Fishing Lagoon or Spit Lagoon) on the Homer Spit supports a large run of hatchery-produced kings and silvers beginning in late May and continuing to September. Kings range from 20 to 40 lbs. The fishery is open 7 days a week in season.

The city allows overnight parking in some areas next to the lagoon, for a fee. This area has fish cleaning tables nearby and can be a good place to view eagles as fishermen clean their catches.

Regulations vary depending on species and area fished, and anglers are cautioned to consult their charter service or the Alaska Department of Fish and Game regulations before fishing. 🢖

Halibut Cove

Halibut Cove, on the east shore of Kachemak Bay, has no roads and is reached by boat. (©Sharon Nault)

Located 7 miles southeast of Homer on the east shore of Kachemak Bay. **Population**: 23. **Emergency Services**: South Peninsula Hospital in Homer (907) 235-8101, Halibut Cove Ranger Station VHF 16 or (907) 235-6999 (summer only), Coast Guard VHF 16. **Elevation**: 10 feet. **Climate**: Summer temperatures from 45° to 65°F; winter temperatures from 14° to 27°F; average annual precipitation, 24 inches.

Visitor Information: Welcome and information shack at the top of the ramp at the main dock. Local businesses, or visit website: www.halibutcove.com.

Transportation: Air—Floatplane. **Boat**—Private 29-passenger Kachemak Bay Ferry, M/V *Danny J*, departs Homer twice daily in summer, cruising Gull Island on the way to Halibut Cove; for reservations and tickets, phone (907) 296-2223.

The community of Halibut Cove is nestled along a 3-mile-wide bay on the east shore of Kachemak Bay. The bay was named Halibut Cove by W.H. Dall of the U.S. Coast & Geodetic Survey in 1880.

Between 1911 and 1928, Halibut Cove had 42 herring salteries and a population of about 1,000. Today, the community of Halibut Cove is made up of self-employed artists, commercial fishermen and craftsmen. There are no state schools in the community.

Overnight guests in Halibut Cove can stay in several lodges, cabins or bed-and-breakfasts. There is one restaurant, the Saltry Restaurant; reservations are required; email thesaltery@gmail.com. There is a post office. Banks, grocery stores and similar services are not available in Halibut Cove.

There are no roads in Halibut Cove, but some 12 blocks of boardwalk run along the water's edge and provide a scenic and relaxing way to explore this charming community. Stroll the boardwalks for spectacular views of Kachemak Bay, access to the Saltry Restaurant and to galleries displaying the work of more than a dozen local artists.

Walk to the end of the main boardwalk in Halibut Cove to reach the beach. Beachcomb, look at tide pools or have a picnic lunch at the tables provided. During salmon season, visitors may see seiners set out their nets.

Visitors can also walk down to the floats to see several historic wooden boats.

Besides its scenic location and local art, attractions here include bird watching, which is excellent, and hiking trails. Kachemak Bay State Park hiking trails are accessible from Halibut Cove Lagoon. The China Poot Lake Trail (2.6 miles) begins at Halibut Cove Lagoon near the Ranger Station. The Lagoon Trail winds along Halibut Cove to intersect with the China Poot Lake trail (total 5.5 miles). Several other trails begin in this same area (all lengths and abilities). Campgrounds also line the lagoon, near the station. There are also 5 public use cabins in the area which may be reserved online at www.dnr.state.ak.us/cabins (go to "Kenai Area" for the Halibut Cove cabins).

The bay shoreline offers excellent kayaking, clamming, tide pooling and beach combing opportunities. Keep in mind that Kachemak Bay's tides are among the largest in the world and tidal currents can be substantial. A tide book is essential. Phone the district Alaska State Parks office at (907) 235-7024 for more information on hiking Kachemak Bay State Park.

Outer Kachemak Bay is one of Alaska's most popular spots for halibut fishing, with catches often weighing 100 to 200 lbs. Halibut up to 350 lbs. are fished from June through September. 🢖

Seldovia

Scenic Seldovia is reached by boat and ferry.
(©Kris Valencia, staff)

Located in Seldovia Bay, on the southwestern arm of Kachemak Bay and within the Kenai Peninsula; 16 miles by water from Homer. **Population:** 284. **Emergency Services:** **City Police, Ambulance, Fire and Rescue,** emergency only, phone 911, monitor CB Channel 9. **Medical Clinic,** Seldovia Medical Clinic, phone (907) 234-7825; SVT Health & Wellness, phone (907) 234-7898, ext. 237. Seldovia has a resident doctor, visiting practitioners, and a seasonal dentist. **Harbor/Port,** phone (907) 234-7886. **City Police,** phone (907) 234-7640.

Visitor Information: Seldovia Chamber of Commerce, P.O. Drawer F, Seldovia, AK 99663; phone (907) 234-7612; www.seldoviachamber.org and www.seldovia.com. **Newspaper:** *Seldovia Gazette* (www.seldoviagazette.com).

Transportation: Air—Scheduled service from Homer via Homer Air and Smokey Bay Air (15 minute flight). **Ferry**—Alaska state ferry service from Homer. **Water Taxis, Catamarans and Tour Boats**—Service between Homer and Seldovia small boat harbors via catamaran in summer aboard the 150-passenger *Kachemak Voyager*, departing Homer Spit for Seldovia twice daily, phone 1-877-703-3779, www.seldoviabayferry.com; MV *Discovery*, phone (907) 235-7847; and MV *Rainbow Connection*, phone (907) 235-7272. Service between Homer and Jakolof Bay via Mako's Water Taxi,

phone (907) 235-9055, or Red Mountain Marine, phone (907) 399-8320. *Passengers arriving by water taxi at the Jakolof Bay dock must taxi 11 miles into town.* **Taxi**—Halo Cab, phone (907) 399-4229.

Private Aircraft: Seldovia airport, 1 E; elev. 29 feet; length 1,850 feet; gravel; unattended; no fuel.

Seldovia is a small community accessible by air or by boat. Seldovia has a modern and conveniently accessible small boat harbor and is surrounded by the bay and the slough. Seldovia is connected to Homer by the Alaska Marine Highway ferry system. The only road of significant length is Jakolof Bay Road to Red Mountain (11.4 miles long).

Because it is removed from Kenai Peninsula highways, Seldovia has retained much of its old Alaska charm and traditions (the historic boardwalk dates from 1931).

The name Seldovia is derived from Russian *Seldevoy,* meaning "herring bay." Between 1869 and 1882, a trading station was located here. The St. Nicholas Russian Orthodox Church was built in 1891. It is now a national historic site. A post office was established in Nov. 1898. Seldovia holds the distinction of being 1 of 2 Alaskan cities with an ice free harbor in the winter.

Seldovia has 2 active churches, a non-denominational church and a Lutheran church. Seldovia's icon is the St. Nicholas Russian Orthodox Church. It has stood on the hill welcoming returning sailors to port since 1891. The bell tower was installed in 1906 and the church was restored and consecrated in 1981. At times a visiting Russian Orthodox Priest will hold a service.

The only school, Susan B. English School, offers grades K through 12.

Lodging, Services & Camping

Seldovia has most visitor facilities, including 2 hotels, bed and breakfasts, a general store, a whole-foods store, a restaurant, 2 coffee shops and 2 gift stores. The post office is in the center of town. Public restrooms are found at the Harbormaster's Office, the City Offices, the Library/Multipurpose Room (when open), and at the Seldovia Village Tribe Visitor Center. There is 24-hour WiFi from the library parking lot.

City campground with RV/tent sites, firepits, restrooms and water; fee charged. Located at Mile 1.2 Jakolof Bay Road; look for "Wilderness RV Park" sign on left-hand side of road. Maximum stay 14 days. Pay at city offices during office hours or at the Harbormaster's Office weekends and evenings. Dump station next to boat storage area.

Attractions

Taking a stroll around this picturesque town, doing some shopping, taking a hike, going fishing, riding a rented ATV or bicycle, enjoying a meal or ice cream cone, bird watching or just having a cup of coffee and looking at the great scenery are all favorite activities here.

The Seldovia Village Tribe Visitor Center/Museum is located directly across the street from the small boat harbor on

Main Street. The museum features Native culture, history and local artifacts. Phone (907) 234-7898; www.svt.org.

Hiking trails. The Otterbahn Trail is a 1.2-mile trail from town to Outside Beach, a beautiful spot and popular destination for beachcombing and surf fishing. View from Outside Beach of Kachemak Bay and the volcanoes St. Augustine, Mount Iliamna and Mount Redoubt. Also watch for sea otters, seals, eagles and other wildlife. The trailhead is located behind the school. Check the tidal charts before you go; access to the Outside Beach is cut off at high tide.

Tutka Bay Trail is described as a moderately easy trail to Tutka Bay Salmon Hatchery. Look for trailhead signs at Mile 11.4 Jakolof Bay Road.

The challenging Rocky Ridge Trail, which begins on the road to the landfill site (Rocky Street), offers spectacular scenery but is not recommended for small children.

Bikers, hikers and visitors are reminded that permits are required for crossing Seldovia Native Association corporate land in the Seldovia–Red Mountain area. Stop by the SNA office at 206 Main Street during business hours for permits.

Jakolof Bay Road offers panoramic views of Kachemak Bay, McDonald's Spit, Jakolof Bay and Kasitsna Bay. At Mile 6.2 Jakolof Bay Road, look for trail (unmarked) that leads down by private homes to 1.5-mile-long **McDonald Spit**, a favorite spot for seabirds and marine life. Great place to explore but be aware of tides. Beach is bordered by private property. At Mile 8.1 Jakolof Bay Road, there is a public dock and outhouse.

Bird Watching. A diverse number of species may be seen in Seldovia, along area hiking trails and at Jakolof Bay, ranging from the American crow to the yellow warbler. Visitors traveling to Seldovia by boat will see a number of pelagic birds.

Kayaking. Seldovia's sheltered bay is ideal for kayaking. Kayaking tours are available at TreeTops Lodge. Kayak rentals are available from Kayak'Atak in Seldovia, and may be arranged with Mako's Water Taxi in Homer.

Special Events. The annual Craft Invitational Chainsaw Carving Exhibition on Labor Day Weekend attracts carvers and spectators alike. Take the "View the Carvings Walk" and locate the carvings donated to the Seldovia Chamber of Commerce and positioned throughout the city for public enjoyment. The Human-Powered Fishing Derby takes place Memorial Day weekend.

The Seldovia Summer Solstice Folk Music Festival, held in June, features a number of national recording artists as well as Alaskan musicians. The Seldovia Arts Council also offers concerts throughout the summer.

Just about the whole town participates in Seldovia's old-fashioned Fourth of July celebration. The holiday includes food booths, parade, rubber ducky race, canoe jousting, kayak races, and a baseball game.

Fishing: Kachemak Bay, king salmon Jan.–Aug.; halibut May–Oct.; Dolly Varden June–Sept.; silver salmon in Aug.–Sept.; red salmon July–August. **Seldovia Bay,** king, silver and red salmon, also halibut, May–Sept. Excellent bottom fishing. The Seldovia Slough has a king salmon and silver salmon run much-enjoyed by fishermen. There is a fish cleaning station located near the boat ramp in the harbor.

Kodiak

(See map, page 633)

Kodiak's 87 miles of road lead to fishing streams and beautiful beaches. (©Sharon Nault)

The Kodiak Island Archipelago lies in the Gulf of Alaska, southwest of Cook Inlet and the Kenai Peninsula. The city of Kodiak is located near the northeastern tip of Kodiak Island, at the north end of Chiniak Bay. By air it is 55 minutes from Anchorage. By ferry from Homer it is 9 to 10 hours. **Population:** 6,431 (city), 14,041 (Kodiak Island Borough). **Emergency Services in Kodiak:** Dial 911 for emergencies. **Alaska State Troopers**, phone (907) 486-4121. **Police**, phone (907) 486-8000. **Fire Department**, phone (907) 486-8040. **Harbor:** phone (907) 486-8080. **Hospital**, Providence Kodiak Island Medical Center, Rezanof Drive, phone (907) 486-3281. **Coast Guard**, phone (907) 487-5760. **Crime Stoppers**, phone (907) 486-3113.

Visitor Information: Located at 100 E. Marine Way, Suite 200, Kodiak, AK 99615. Hours are 8 A.M. to 5 P.M. Monday through Friday year-round, with extended weekday hours and additional weekend hours in summer. A very helpful place to stop: Knowledgeable staff will answer questions, help arrange tours and charters, and make sure you don't miss anything on Kodiak Island. Free maps, brochures, and hunting/fishing information available here. Good view from visitor center of *The Starr of Kodiak*, a WWII Liberty ship now used as a cannery.

Contact the Kodiak Island Convention & Visitors Bureau: phone (907) 486-4782 or 1-800-789-4782; email: visit@kodiak.org; www.kodiak.org.

Elevation: Sea level. **Climate**: Average daily temperature in July is 57°F; in January 30°F. September, October and January are the wettest months in Kodiak, with each month averaging more than 6 inches of precipitation. **Radio**: KVOK-AM 560, KMXT-FM 100.1 (public station, website: www.KMXT.org), KRXX-FM 101.1 (Jack FM), KPEN-FM 102.7 (country), KWAV 104.9 (rock). **Television**: Local channel KMXT 9, and via cable and satellite. **Newspapers**: *The Kodiak Daily Mirror* (weekdays only).

Private Aircraft: Kodiak state airport, 4.8 miles southwest; elev. 73 feet; length 7,500 feet; asphalt; fuel 100LL, Jet A-1. Kodiak Municipal Airport, 2 miles northeast; elev. 139 feet; length 2,500 feet; paved; unattended. Trident Basin seaplane base, on east side of Near Island, unattended, floats for 14 aircraft; fuel. Trident Basin has AVgas, (credit card or prepay).

Gravel airstrips at Akhiok, length 3,320 feet; Karluk, length 2,000 feet; Larsen Bay, length 2,700 feet; Old Harbor, length 2,750 feet; Ouzinkie, length 3,300 feet; and Port Lions, length 2,200 feet.

Kodiak Island, home of the oldest permanent European settlement in Alaska, is known as Alaska's Emerald Island. It is the largest island in Alaska and the second largest island in the United States (after Hawaii), with an area of 3,588 square miles and about 87 miles of road (see logs this section). The Kodiak Island Borough includes some 200 islands, the largest being Kodiak (about 100 miles long), followed in size by Afognak, Sitkalidak, Sitkinak, Raspberry, Tugi-dak, Shuyak, Uganik, Chirikof, Marmot and Spruce islands. The borough has two unincorporated townsites, **KARLUK** (pop. 41), on the west coast of Kodiak Island, 75 air miles from Kodiak, and **ALENEVA** (pop. 37) on Afognak Island.

The 6 incorporated cities in the Kodiak Island Borough are: **KODIAK** (pop. 6,431), with all visitor services (see Visitor Services, Transportation and Attractions this section); **AKHIOK** (pop. 87) at Alitak Bay on the south side of Kodiak Island, 80 miles southwest of Kodiak; **LARSEN BAY** (pop. 93) on the northwest coast of Kodiak Island, 62 miles southwest of Kodiak; **OLD HARBOR**

Major Attractions:

The Baranov Museum, Fort Abercrombie SHP, Kodiak NWR

© Sharon Nault

Kodiak is one of the largest commercial fishing ports in the U.S. (©Sharon Nault)

(pop. 206) on the southeast side of Kodiak Island, 54 miles from Kodiak; **OUZINKIE** (pop. 178) on the west coast of Spruce Island; and **PORT LIONS** (pop. 201) on Settler's Cove on the northeast coast of Kodiak Island, served by state ferry to/from Kodiak and Homer. The **KODIAK COAST GUARD STATION** (pop. 1,301) is on the west side of Kodiak Island, south of Kodiak.

Kodiak Island was originally inhabited by the Alutiiq people, who were maritime hunters and fishermen. More than 7,000 years later, the Alutiiq people still call Kodiak home.

In 1763, the island was discovered by Stephen Glotov, a Russian explorer. The name Kodiak, of which there are several variations, was first used in English by Captain Cook in 1778. It is derived from the Alutiiq word for island, *qikertaq*. Kodiak was Russian Alaska's first capital city, until the capital was moved to Sitka in 1804.

Kodiak's turbulent past includes natural disasters such as the 1912 eruption of Novarupta Volcano, on the nearby Alaska Peninsula, and tsunamis resulting from the 1964 earthquake. The Novarupta eruption covered northern parts of the archipelago with a black cloud of ash. When the cloud dissipated, Kodiak was buried under 18 inches of drifting ash.

On Good Friday in 1964, the greatest earthquake ever recorded in North America

(8.6 on the Richter scale, Mw 9.2) shook the Kodiak area. The tsunami that followed virtually leveled downtown Kodiak, destroying the fishing fleet, processing plants, canneries and 158 homes. Giant waves also destroyed 3 Alutiiq villages.

Because of Kodiak's strategic location for defense, military facilities were constructed on the island in 1939. Fort Abercrombie, now a state park and a national historic landmark, was one of the first secret radar installations in Alaska. Cement bunkers still remain for exploration by the curious.

The Coast Guard occupies the old Kodiak Naval Station. Coast Guard Base Kodiak is the largest Coast Guard base in the country. The base is overseen by Integrated Support Command Kodiak, which supports several tenant commands in Kodiak and remote units throughout western Alaska.

The base is home to Air Station Kodiak, which operates HC-130 Hercules airplanes, MH-60 Jayhawk and HH-65 Dolphin helicopters. Cutters that call Kodiak home are the 378-foot Coast Guard Cutter *Munro* (WHEC-724), 270-foot Cutter *Alex Haley* (WMEC-39) and the 225-foot Cutter *SPAR* (WLB-206). Cutters are designed as multimission platforms to carry out the Coast Guard's many safety, security and stewardship roles, some of which include enforcing federal laws at sea, conducting search and rescue operations and protecting homeland security.

A 12-foot star, situated halfway up the side of Old Woman Mountain overlooking the base, was rebuilt and rededicated in 1981 in memory of military personnel who have lost their lives while engaged in operations from Kodiak. Originally erected in the 1950s, the star is lit every year between

Thanksgiving and Christmas.

St. Paul and St. Herman harbors are homeports to 800 local fishing boats and serve several hundred outside vessels each year.

Commercial fishing is the backbone of Kodiak's economy. Kodiak is one of the largest commercial fishing ports in the U.S. Some 1,000 commercial fishing vessels use the harbor each year, delivering salmon, shrimp, herring, halibut and whitefish, plus king, tanner and Dungeness crab to the 11 processing companies in Kodiak. Cannery tours are available with pre-scheduling. Kodiak's famous seafood is pre-marketed, with almost all of the commercially caught seafood exported. Kodiak is also an important cargo port and transshipment center. Container ships stop twice weekly.

Lodging & Services

There are hotels, motels and bed-and-breakfast accommodations available. Contact the Visitor Center for names. A variety of restaurants offers a wide range of menus and prices. Shopping is readily available for gifts, general merchandise and sporting goods. There is a movie theater and 750-seat performing arts center.

There are more than 30 remote fly-in hunting and fishing lodges in the Kodiak area; several roadhouses on the island road system; public-use cabins available within Kodiak National Wildlife Refuge, Shuyak Island and Afognak Island state parks; and private wilderness camps and cabin rentals available throughout the Kodiak area.

Camping

There are 3 state campgrounds: Fort Abercrombie, north of town (see "Rezanof–Monashka Bay Road" this section); Buskin River state recreation site, south of town is a good choice for big rigs (see "Chiniak Road" this section); and Pasagshak River state recreation site at the end of Pasagshak Bay Road (see log this section). There is also Leave No Trace free camping along rivers, on beaches above high-tide line, and beside roads (be sure to park so that you do not interfere with traffic). Inquire locally about permits from the Leisnoi Native Corp.

Dump stations are located at the Petro Express station on Mill Bay Road and St. Paul Harbor spit in front of Alaska Fresh Seafoods (contact the harbormaster's office at 403 Marine Way phone 907/486-8080).

Transportation

Air: Scheduled service to Kodiak via Era Aviation and Alaska Airlines. On island, there is charter service for flightseeing, bear viewing, fishing and hunting or transportation, available from: **Andrew Airways**, phone (907) 487-2566; and **Sea Hawk Air**, phone 1-800-770-4295.

Ferry: The Alaska Marine Highway System serves Kodiak from Homer (9½-hour ferry ride). Kodiak is also the port of departure for Aleutian Chain trips in summer. The Kodiak ferry terminal is downtown; phone

KODIAK ADVERTISERS

Alutiiq Museum ....Ph. (907) 486-7004
Andrew Airways............................Ph. (907) 487-2566
Budget Rent-a-Car ....Ph. (907) 487-2220
Sea Hawk Air ....Ph. 1-800-770-4295

(907) 486-3800. See Southwest and Aleutian Chain schedules; www.ferryalaska.com. See ALASKA MARINE HIGHWAY section.

Cruise Ships: Cruise ships planning to make Kodiak a port of call in 2014 include Holland America's *Volendam* and *Amsterdam*, Oceania Cruises *Regatta*, Silversea Cruises *Silver Shadow* and Crystal Cruises MV *Serenity* and *Symphony*.

Highways: There are 4 roads on Kodiak Island (see logs this section). The 11-mile Rezanof–Monashka Bay Road leads from downtown Kodiak north to Fort Abercrombie and Monashka Bay. Chiniak Highway leads 42.8 miles south from Kodiak along the island's eastern shore to Chiniak Point and Chiniak Creek. Anton Larsen Bay Road leads 11.7 miles from junction with Chiniak Road near Kodiak airport to Anton Larsen Bay. Pasagshak Bay Road branches off Chiniak Road and leads 16.4 miles to Fossil Beach at Pasagshak Point.

Car Rental: Available from **Budget Rent-A-Car** at the airport, phone (907) 487-2220, and downtown, phone (907) 486-8550.

Taxi: Kodiak Island Taxi (907) 486-2515.

Attractions

The Baranov Museum (Erskine House), maintained by the Kodiak Historical Society at 101 Marine Way, Kodiak 99615; phone (907) 486-5920, is open in summer, 10 A.M. to 4 P.M. Monday through Saturday; Labor Day–late May, 10 A.M. to 3 P.M. Tuesday–Saturday. Special openings upon request. The building was originally a fur warehouse built in 1806-08 by Aleksandr Baranov. It is the oldest Russian-built structure in Alaska. Purchased by the Alaska Commercial Co. around 1867, it was sold to W.J. Erskine in 1911, who converted it into a residence. It was then referred to as the Erskine House. In 1962, it was declared a National Historic Landmark.

Many items from the Alutiiq, Russian and American eras are on display, in the three exhibit rooms. In the gift shop, work by local artists and crafters and Russian art and handiwork including nesting dolls are for sale. Donations accepted, $5 per adult, children under 12 free; email: baranov@ak.net; or visit their website at www.baranovmuseum.org.

Kodiak National Wildlife Refuge Visitor Center, at 402 Center Street, is a U.S. Fish & Wildlife visitor center that features unique and detailed life-size carvings of Alaskan animals, including huge Kodiak bears and a fully articulated gray whale skeleton. This is a very interesting stop. Stop by and see "A Bear's Supermarket." Exhibits, hands-on interactive displays, a bookstore, public talks and films on Kodiak's wildlife and Kodiak National Wildlife Refuge. The center is open 10 A.M. to 5 P.M. Tuesday–Saturday, all year. Phone (907) 487-2626 or 1-888-592-6942 for more information or go to their website at www.kodiakwildliferefuge.org.

Kodiak Tribal Council with the **Kodiak Alutiiq Dancers** perform dances in the summer. They have been recreated from stories passed down through generations of the Alutiiq people, who have inhabited Kodiak Island for more than 7,000 years. Dance performances are held at 312 W. Marine Way. The dances are not regularly scheduled. For more information contact the visitors center, call (907) 486-4449, or email: kodiakdancers@gci.net.

The Alutiiq Museum and Archaeological Repository in downtown Kodiak interprets the history of Kodiak's Native people. The museum houses and displays artifacts from archaeological sites around Kodiak Island as well as historic items, Native clothing and contemporary Alutiiq artwork. Located at 215 Mission Road, Suite 101; phone (907) 486-7004; website www.alutiiqmuseum.org; email info@alutiiqmuseum.org. From June through August, museum hours are 9 A.M. to 5 P.M. Monday–Friday; 10 A.M. to 5 P.M. Saturday. From September to May, hours are 9 A.M. to 5 P.M.,

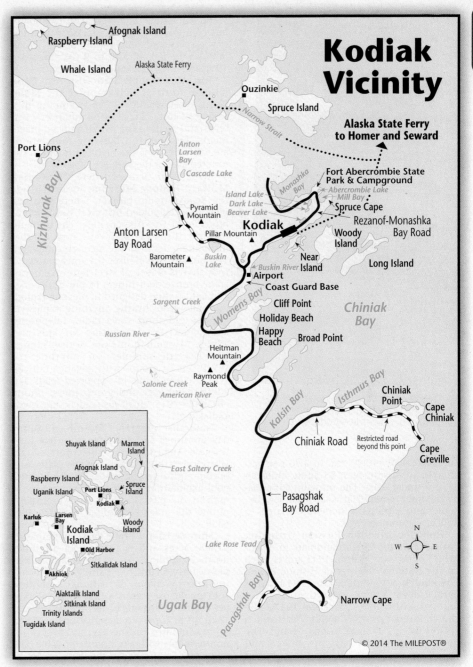

Kodiak Vicinity

© 2014 The MILEPOST®

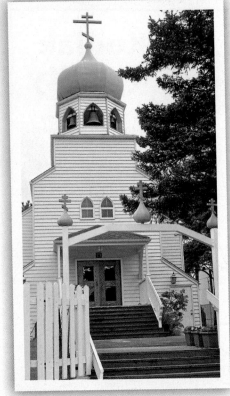

Holy Resurrection Russian Orthodox Cathedral in downtown Kodiak. (©Sharon Nault)

Tuesday–Friday; 10:30 A.M. to 4:30 P.M. Saturdays. Admission fees: $5 adult, children 16 and under, free. The museum store features contemporary Native artwork, jewelry, books and children's items all related to Kodiak cultural heritage.

Holy Resurrection Russian Orthodox Cathedral, a prominent landmark in downtown Kodiak, was built in 1945 and is listed on the National Register of Historic Places. The church was founded in 1794 but has burned down 3 times since then. The current structure dates back to 1947. The church interior provides a visual feast which visitors are encouraged to photograph. The public is invited to visit the church and attend services. Vespers is held Saturdays at 6 P.M. and Sunday services at 9 A.M. Phone (907) 486-3854. Donations are appreciated.

The All Saints of Alaska log chapel, a scale replica of the original Holy Resurrection church building, is located nearby on the grounds of St. Herman Theological Seminary on Mission Road.

Visit Kodiak's Harbors. Kodiak offers a full range of dockage, boat yard and marine services for commercial fishing, cargo, passenger, and recreational vessels. The City of Kodiak's Harbor Department operates 2 marinas: St. Paul Harbor downtown and St. Herman Harbor on Near Island.

The 2 harbors provide protected moorage for 650 vessels up to 150 feet in length. Large vessels, including the state ferry, cruise ships and cargo vessels are moored at the 3 deepwater piers. Call or visit the Harbormaster's office for more information. Harbor staff may be reached 24 hours per day, 7 days per week on VHF channel 12 or 16. The office is open 8 A.M. to 5 P.M. Monday through Friday in the winter. During the summer months, the office is open 7 days per week.

Holmes Johnson Memorial Library at 319 Lower Mill Bay Road is a good spot to spend some time on a rainy day. The library has computers, Internet access, magazines, newspapers and 68,000-plus books. Open Monday–Friday, 10 A.M. to 9 P.M., Saturday 10 A.M. to 5 P.M., and Sunday 1–5 P.M.

Fort Abercrombie State Historical Park, located north of Kodiak on scenic Miller Point, offers picnicking and camping in a setting of lush rain forest, wildflowers, seabirds and eagles. The WWII gun emplacements, bunkers and building foundations are scattered along the high bluffs and in the forested area of the park.

Make your first stop here the **Kodiak Military History Museum**, located inside the Ready Ammo bunker, where you can pick up a self-guided historical walking tour brochure of Fort Abercrombie. The museum features displays of WWII memorabilia, including relics from the Aleutian campaign. The bunker that houses the museum has a roof that is 5 feet of steel reinforced concrete; bronze door hinges to prevent sparks; and light fixture designed to prevent exploding bulbs from hitting anything explosive. Try the old short wave radio, telephones and typewriter. Interesting for kids and adults. Museum hours are Friday–Sunday 1–4 P.M. in summer (or anytime for WWII vets or groups with advance notice). Winter closures due to unplowed roads. For additional hours and group tours, phone (907) 486-7015; email jbs@kadiak.org; www.kadiak.org.

Naturalist programs are offered Saturday mornings and evenings from late June through August at Fort Abercrombie State Historical Park. Programs include plant lore, outdoor photography, sea kayaking, tidepool exploration and more. For more information on park facilities and programs, phone the State Park office at (907) 486-6339.

Shuyak Island State Park encompasses 47,000 acres and is located 54 air miles north of Kodiak. Access by boat or float plane only. Hunting, fishing and kayaking are the major recreational activities. Four public-use cabins available at $60–$75 per night. Cabins are 12 feet by 20 feet and sleep up to 8 people. Reservations accepted up to 6 months (to the day) in advance for non-residents with a full nonrefundable payment and 7 months (to the day) for Alaska residents. Call (907) 486-6339 or www.dnr.state.ak.us/parks/units/kodiak/shuyak.htm.

Go for a Hike. Hiking trails around the Kodiak area provide access to alpine areas, lakes, coastal rain forests and beaches. Waterproof hiking/birding trail guides available for $12 at the visitors center, phone (907) 486-4782, and at other locations around the city. Pay attention to notes regarding footwear and clothing, tides, bears, trailhead access and weather conditions.

Picnic and camp on the beach. There are some outstandingly beautiful, unpopulated beaches along Chiniak Road (see log this section). Excellent beachcombing. Watch for Sitka black-tailed deer and foxes.

Kodiak Fisheries Research Center houses the National Marine Fisheries Service and Alaska Dept. of Fish and Game. Dedicated to enriching public knowledge of the Kodiak Island Archipelago ecosystems, the Aquarium and Touch Tank are open to the public; beaked whale skeleton on display. Admission is free. Open 8 A.M. to 4:30 P.M. year-round, Monday–Saturday from Memorial Day to Labor Day, weekdays only the rest of the year. To get there, cross the Fred Zharoff Bridge to Near Island, turn on Trident Way, then take second left to science building. Phone (907) 481-1800.

Go Mountain Biking. Kodiak is fast becoming known for its premier mountain biking, attracting racers and enthusiasts from around the country. Bicycle rentals are available from local vendors.

Visit a brewery. Visitors may taste test local beer at the Kodiak Island Brewing Co., located at 338 Shelikof Avenue. Phone (907) 486-2537 for tour information or visit www.kodiakbrewery.com.

Bear Valley Golf Course. The 9-hole Bear Valley Golf Course is located on Anton Larsen Bay Road. Owned and operated by the U.S. Coast Guard, the course has a driving range, putting green and pro shop. The course is open to the public from June until October, depending on weather. The pro shop carries golf clothing, items and rental equipment, and serves food and beer. Hours of operation vary according to weather and daylight hours. Phone (907) 487-5323.

Special Events. ComFish Alaska, the nation's largest commercial fishing trade show, takes place April 17-19, 2014. The Whalefest Kodiak, in April also, celebrates the return of migrating whales. Whale sightings are reported daily and arts performances are scheduled throughout the festival; visit www.whalefestkodiak.org.

The Kodiak King Crab Festival, held each May, celebrates the history of Kodiak's crab industry with parades, carnival booths and midway, races and tournaments, blessing of the fleet, Kodiak Seafood Cook-off, concerts and art shows; visit www.kodiak.org/crabfest.html.

The Pillar Mountain Running Race is a 9.2-mile mountain race from the Harbormaster Building; phone (907) 486-8665 for dates. The Kodiak Kids' Pink Salmon Jamboree takes place in mid-August. And Kodiak's State Fair and Rodeo are held Labor Day weekend at the fairgrounds in Women's Bay.

During St. Herman's Pilgrimage, which takes place in early August, pilgrims travel to Monk's Lagoon at Spruce Island where St. Herman lived and originally was buried. Father Herman, the first saint of the Russian Orthodox Church in North America, was canonized in Kodiak in 1970. Father Herman arrived in Kodiak in 1794. A schedule of services during the Pilgrimage is available upon request; phone (907) 486-3854 or visit www.dioceseofalaska.org.

See Kodiak by Kayak. One of the best ways to experience Kodiak's beautiful coastline, and view marine mammals and seabirds, is from a kayak. Day kayak tours around the nearby islands are available for all skill levels, or schedule an extended tour.

Guided tours. There are several charter and guide services in Kodiak. Arrange a boat or air charter for guided fishing or hunting, sightseeing or photography

Kodiak National Wildlife Refuge encompasses 2,812 square miles on Kodiak Island, Uganik Island, Afognak Island and Ban Island. The refuge was established in 1941 to preserve the natural habitat of the famed Kodiak brown bear and other wildlife. Biologists estimate that more than 3,000 bears inhabit Kodiak Island. Most bears enter dens by November and remain there until April. Bears are readily observable on the refuge in June through August, when they congregate along streams to feed on salmon. Visitors to the refuge typically go to fish,

observe and photograph wildlife, backpack, kayak, camp and hunt. There are primitive public-use cabins available (reservations must be made in advance through refuge headquarters). *NOTE: The refuge is accessible only by floatplane or boat. Using Kodiak National Wildlife Refuge land requires a permit (free). Public-use cabins are available for rent; phone for more information 1-888-408-3514. For Koniag Tribe land use permit, phone 1-877-355-2327 (Karluk Wilderness Adventures) or call (907) 481-4132.*

More information is available at the Kodiak Refuge Visitor Center located downtown at the corner of Center and Mission. Or contact Kodiak National Wildlife Refuge at 1390 Buskin River Road, Kodiak, AK 99615; phone 1-888-408-3514; kodiak@fws.gov; http://kodiak.fws.gov.

AREA FISHING: Kodiak Island is in the center of a fine marine and freshwater fishery and possesses some excellent fishing for rainbow, steelhead, halibut, Dolly Varden and 5 species of Pacific salmon. Visiting fishermen will have to charter a boat or aircraft to reach remote lakes, rivers and bays, but the island road system offers many good salmon streams in season. Roads access red salmon fisheries in the Buskin and Pasagshak rivers. Introduced king salmon runs are available at the American and Olds rivers plus in lower Monashka Creek. Pink and silver salmon are found in virtually all road accessible streams including the **Buskin, Saltery,** and **Pasagshak rivers,** and **Monashka, Pillar, Russian, Salonie, American, Olds, Roslyn, Sargent** and **Chiniak creeks.**

Afognak and Raspberry islands, both approximately 30 air miles northeast of Kodiak, offer excellent remote hunting and fishing. Both islands are brown bear country. Hikers and fishermen should make noise and stay in the open, use bear-proof food containers, and discard fish waste in rivers. If you take a dog, make sure it is under control. Dogs can create dangerous situations with bears.

CAUTION: A paralytic-shellfish-poisoning alert is in effect for all Kodiak Island beaches. This toxin is extremely poisonous. There are no approved beaches for clamming on Kodiak Island. For more current information, call the Dept. of Environmental Conservation in Anchorage at (907) 269-7501.

Rezanof–Monashka Bay Road Log

Distance is measured from the junction of Rezanof Drive and Marine Way in downtown Kodiak (K).

K 0.1 Mill Bay Road access to library, post office and Kodiak businesses.

K 0.2 Entrance to Near Island bridge and North End Park (trails, picnic areas); St. Herman Harbor (boat launch); Rotary Park. Access to Trident Basin seaplane base.

K 0.5 Kodiak High School, Home of the Bears.

K 1.4 Providence Kodiak Island Medical Center.

K 1.8 Benny Benson Drive. Turn left to Kodiak College and beginning of paved bicycle trail, which parallels main road to Fort Abercrombie State Historic Park. Excellent

Free-ranging bison can be a road hazard on Kodiak Island. (©Terry Sheely)

for walking, jogging and bicycling.

K 3.3 Turnout and parking area for Mill Bay Park. Scenic picnic spot with picnic tables, barbecue grates. Good ocean fishing for silvers from beach.

K 3.5 Bayside Fire Department.

K 3.7 Drive in 0.2 mile to **Fort Abercrombie State Historical Park**; large parking lot, unmaintained beach access road (small turnaround). Follow signs for campground (0.5 mile from Rezanof Drive to fee box); 13 small, unlevel campsites; overflow parking area accommodates larger RVs; 7-night limit; $10 per night; water, toilets; campground host; stocked rainbow fishing, swimming and picnic shelter at Lake Gertrude; view of bay and beach.

A big attraction at Fort Abercrombie State Historical Park is the **Kodiak Military History Museum**, housed in the Ready Ammo bunker *(see detailed description of park and museum on facing page).* The park also has an extensive system of scenic hiking trails. Trailhead for Lake Gertrude is at Mile 0.4 on the access road. No off-road biking. Saturday evening naturalist programs June through August. Just beyond the campground entrance is the Alaska State Parks ranger station, (907) 486-6339, open Sunday–Monday 1 P.M. to 4 P.M.; pay phone, public restrooms, park information; www.dnr.state.ak.us/parks/units/kodiak/ftaber.htm.

K 4.3 Monashka Bay Park at junction with Otmeloi Way; playground, picnic area.

K 6.1 Kodiak Island Borough baler/landfill facility. Recycling center.

K 6.8 Turnoff for VFW RV park with electrical hookups, scenic views, restaurant and lounge, phone (907) 486-3195. Access to Sportsman Assoc. indoor shooting range, (907) 486-8566, www.kisaorg.com.

K 7.5 Pillar Creek bridge and Pillar Creek Hatchery.

K 7.9 Turnoff (unsigned) for Pillar Beach, a beautiful black-sand beach at mouth of creek. Scenic picnic area, but access road is narrow and steep with large potholes; not

recommended for vehicles with low clearance. Dolly Varden pink and silver salmon; fishing allowed downstream from Monashka Bay Road.

K 9 Scenic overlook and panoramic views of Monashka Bay and Monashka Mountain.

K 10.2 Turnout and parking; North Sister trailhead.

K 10.9 Bridge over Monashka Creek.

K 11 Road ends; large turnaround parking area. Paths lead through narrow band of trees to secluded **Monashka Bay** beach. Large, sweeping sandy beach. Excellent for picnics. Picnic tables, restrooms, improved beach access. Fishing off beach for Dolly Varden, pinks, silvers, kings.

To the north of parking area is trailhead for **Termination Point Trail**, a beautiful 5-mile hike on a loop trail along meadows, ocean bluffs and dense Sitka spruce forest. *NOTE: Leisnoi Tribal Corp. user permit required to hike Termination Point Trail.*

Chiniak Highway Log

Distance from Kodiak's U.S. post office building (K).

K 0 Kodiak U.S. post office building on Mill Bay Road.

K 0.2 Rezanof Center.

K 0.3 Marine Way.

K 2.2 Gibson Cove. Large, double-ended turnout with telescopes and benches at Deadman's Curve; panoramic view of Kodiak, Chiniak Bay and nearby islands.

K 2.7 Small pullout.

K 3.3 Steep access to small pullout.

K 3.6 Boy Scout Lake, paved turnout and parking to left.

K 3.7 Paved turnout.

K 4.1 Kodiak National Wildlife Refuge headquarters (modern building with sod roof); open weekdays, 8 A.M. to 4:30 P.M. Access to **Buskin River State Recreation**

Kodiak offers both road-accessible and fly-in fishing opportunities. This is the Saltery River.
(©Terry Sheely)

Site (Alaska State Parks) campground, overflow parking and day-use area near beach (1-mile drive from Chiniak Highway).

The campground has 15 RV campsites with a 14-night limit at $15/night, picnic tables, firepits with grills, covered picnic area, bear-proof food containers, toilets, drinking water, trails and beach access. Campground host. Fishing along Buskin River and on beach area at river's mouth for red, silver and pinks, Dolly Varden and trout. Parking; handicap accessible fishing platform. For details contact Alaska State Parks.

K 4.8 Turnoff for Anton Larsen Bay Road before crossing the Buskin River Bridge (see log this section).

K 4.9 Kodiak airport.

K 6.3 Entrance to U.S. Coast Guard station.

K 6.6 Turnout on Women's Bay with picnic tables and information boards. USCG aircraft and helicopters may be seen on apron.

K 6.9 Road continues around Women's Bay. USCG cutters tie up at pier across the bay. The drive out to Chiniak affords excellent views of the extremely rugged coastline of the island.

K 7.2 Large shipping and container operation and log storage area.

K 9 Turnoff to Kodiak Island Fairgrounds and Kodiak Island Raceway. Excellent bird watching on tideflats; park at entrance to gravel road across from fairgrounds on tidal flats.

K 9.8 **Sargent Creek** bridge. Good fishing for pink salmon in August.

K 10 Russian River Bridge; parking area. Good fishing for pinks, Dolly Varden in August, silvers in September. Access to Sergeant Creek and Bell's Flats roads.

K 10.4 Grocery and liquor store, diesel and unleaded gas.

K 10.5 Java Flats restaurant and Russian River Roadhouse.

K 10.8 Rendezvous Bar and Grill.

K 11.3 Small pullout.

K 11.4 Four-wheeler trail and trailhead to 2,300-foot Kashevaroff Mountain. Gradual incline, great views in alpine country, low-bush cranberries in fall. *Watch for bears.*

K 11.5 Small pullout.

K 11.7 Salonie Creek; small parking area. Pinks (early August), chums, silvers, Dolly Varden.

K 12.1 Salonie Creek Rifle Range turnoff.

K 12.2 Large turnout with bay access.

K 12.5 Begin climb up Marine Hill. Kashevaroff trailhead; wildflowers, cranberries in fall. *NOTE: Very hazardous section of road in winter when icy.*

K 13.3 Turnout with panoramic view of Mary Island, Women's Bay, Bell's Flats, Kodiak. Mountain goats visible with binoculars in spring and fall in mountains behind Bell's Flats.

K 14.1 Pullout at **Heitman Lake** trailhead. Beautiful views. Lake is stocked with rainbow.

K 14.3 Turnout to Dragon Fly Lake. View of Long Island and Cliff Point.

K 14.9 Dirt road and trailhead to Horseshoe Lake. Trail continues past second grove of spruce trees down to lake.

K 15.6 Turnout at top of hill on ocean side of highway.

K 16.7 USCG communications facility; emergency phone.

K 18.7 Undeveloped picnic area in grove of trees along beach of Middle Bay; easy access to beach. Watch for livestock.

K 19.2 Small Creek bridge.

K 19.7 Salt Creek bridge. Excellent bird watching on tideflats to left.

K 20.5 American River bridge. Turnout at **American River**. **Saltery River** access road (very rugged, recommended for 4WD only); excellent fishing for pinks, chums, silvers, stocked kings and Dolly Varden; Saltery fished for reds, pinks, chums, silvers, steelhead/rainbows and Dolly Varden.

K 20.6 Unimproved road (barely passable even for 4-wheel-drive) to Saltery Cove. Primitive camping.

K 20.7 Felton Creek Bridge.

K 22.8 Foot access to gravel beach; nice picnic site.

K 23.7 *CAUTION: Steep switchbacks. Slow to 10 mph.*

K 24.2 Pullout and access to Mayflower Lake; stocked with silver salmon.

K 24.3 Pullout for Mayflower Beach. Beachcombing, picnicking, hiking.

K 25.1 Double-ended pullout with view of beach.

K 25.2 Double-ended pullout with view of beach.

K 27.4 Turnout with spectacular view of Kalsin Bay and highway winding along coastline.

K 27.8 Improved pullout.

K 27.9 Improved pullout. Steep road drops down to head of Kalsin Bay.

K 28.2 Improved pullout.

K 28.6 Kalsin Bay Inn; food, bar, laundromat, showers, tire repair; open year-round. Goats often seen in hills in fall and spring.

K 29 Deadman Creek Bridge.

K 29.7 Turnout at Olds River. Excellent fishing for pinks, chums, silvers and Dolly Varden.

K 30.2 Kalsin River (creek) bridge.

K 30.4 **Junction:** Turn left for Chiniak, right for Pasagshak Bay and Olds River Inn. *See Pasagshak Bay Road log this section.*

Cattle range freely in this area. *CAUTION: Watch for cattle on road.*

K 30.7 **Kalsin Pond;** excellent silver salmon fishing in fall.

K 30.9 Turnoff for access to mouth of Olds River and beach.

K 31.3 Highway maintenance station.

K 31.4 *Pavement ends, gravel begins.*

K 31.5 Karl Armstrong Campground.

K 31.8 Picnic area beside Kalsin Bay. Nice beach.

K 32.1 Road to unimproved picnic area. Gravel beach. Fishing for pinks.

K 32.9 Myrtle Creek bridge just past turnoff; picnic site.

K 33 Access to Myrtle Beach.

K 34.6 Thumbs Up Cove; old pier.

K 34.7 Chiniak post office. Window hours Tuesday and Thursday 4–6 P.M., Saturday noon to 2 P.M. Hunting and fishing licenses sold here. Visitor information.

K 35.6 Brookers Lagoon. Access to gravel beach. Excellent birding for waterfowl, eagles and shorebirds.

K 36.9 Roslyn River Bridge.

K 37.4 Access to mouth of Roslyn River.

K 39.3 Access to a beautiful point overlooking the sea; site of WWII installations. Good place for photos. Sea otters in kelp beds year-round.

K 39.5 Twin Creeks Beach, dark sand and rolling breakers. Good place for beach walking, tide pooling. Watch for sea otters in kelp beds. Look for 3 WWII bunkers on the cliffs above the beach.

K 40.1 **Twin Creeks.** Good silver fishing in fall.

K 40.5 Silver Beach.

K 40.6 Pony Lake.

K 40.7 Small turnout by beach.

K 40.8 Beach access road.

K 41.1 Chiniak wayside, a borough park; benches, beautiful setting.

Chiniak school, playground and ballfield. Baseball diamond, play area, picnic tables.

K 41.2 Turnoff onto King Crab Way. Location of Tsunami Evacuation Center and public library.

K 41.9 Roads End Restaurant. Excellent whale watching for gray whales in April just beyond restaurant.

Beyond this point the cliff is eroded right to the edge of the road. Exercise extreme caution while driving this stretch.

K 42.1 Chiniak Point, seen in the distance, is also known as Cape Chiniak. It is the southernmost point of land at the entrance to Chiniak Bay. (Capt. Cook named the point Cape Greville in 1778, but that name is now applied to the point of land 2 miles southeast of here.) Watch for unmaintained roads leading toward the point. Hike up the bluff to WWII bunker. Fantastic views from here. Watch for whales, sea lions, seals and puffins. Wonderful secluded beach; primitive camping.

State road maintenance ends here. Unmaintained road continues as public easement across Leisnoi Native Corp. land. Public access is limited beyond Chiniak Creek.

K 42.6 Public road ends at **Chiniak Creek** culvert. Pink salmon fishing in midsummer; excellent silver salmon fishing in fall. View of Chiniak Point. Turnaround point.

WWII bunker at Chiniak Point. Fantastic views from here. (©Sharon Nault)

Anton Larsen Bay Road Log

Distance is measured from the turnoff (T) at Milepost K 4.8 Chiniak Road.
NOTE: Road may be closed in winter.

T 0 Turnoff for Anton Larsen Bay Road at **Milepost K 4.8** on Chiniak Road immediately before crossing the Buskin River bridge.

T 0.6 Buskin River bridge No. 6. Parking area accesses fishing along river. (There are several turnouts along the road in this area.) Side road leads to good fishing holes.

T 0.9 Enter posted restricted-access area in USCG antenna field. Do not leave road for approximately next 2 miles.

T 1.5 Buskin River bridge No. 7. Turnoff before crossing bridge to access river and outlet of Buskin Lake. Good fishing for Dolly Varden, steelhead and salmon.

T 1.6 Paved road leads to USCG communications site. Paved side road leads to Anton Larsen Bay and to golf course. Scenic drive, berry picking, mountain views, wildflowers, boat launch ramp. Excellent kayaking in bay and around outer islands.

T 2 Pyramid Mountain (elev. 2,420 feet).

T 2.3 End restricted access area.

T 2.9 Bear Valley Golf Course (USCG); driving range, 9-holes, open to the public April–October, weather permitting; (907) 487-5323.

Pavement ends, gravel begins.

T 3.5 Begin slow ascent northbound.

T 3.8 Bridge across creek.

T 4.1 Steep switchback. *Road narrows; slow down.*

T 5.7 Buskin Valley Winter Recreation Area. Excellent spot for sledding, skiing, snowboarding; great for kids. Summer trailhead to top of 2,400-foot Pyramid Mountain. Trail follows ridgeline. Great vistas from top.

T 6.6 Gradual descent with switchbacks northbound. Slow down. View of valley and mountains to west.

T 6.8 First view of Anton Larsen Bay.

T 7.2 *CAUTION: Switchback with no guardrail northbound. Slow!*

T 7.5 Red Cloud River bridge. Small,

unimproved campsite adjacent river.

T 9.3 Head of Anton Larsen Bay. Fox, land otters and deer can be seen in this area. Good bird watching along tidal flats.

T 10.3 Public small-boat launch adjacent to narrow parking area.

T 10.4 Anton Larsen Bay public dock. Departure point for sea kayakers and residents traveling to villages.

T 10.7 Small pullout with view overlooking Anton Larsen Bay.

T 11.6 Turnaround with parking and beach access.

T 11.7 Road ends at turnaround; parking. A footpath continues beyond this point to access beach.

Pasagshak Bay Road Log

Distance is measured from junction with Chiniak Road (J).

J 0 Turn at **Milepost K 30.4** Chiniak Road for Pasagshak Bay. Olds River Inn.

J 3.7 Turnout to picnic area in trees.

J 4.7 Turnouts at top of Pasagshak Pass; scenic views.

J 5.3 Turnout.

J 5.8 Large gravel turnout.

J 6.8 Road crosses Lake Rose Tead on causeway. Good fishing in Lake Rose Tead for silvers and in river from here to ocean. Good place to view spawning salmon and eagles late summer through fall.

J 7 Combined barn and single aircraft hangar to right. Remnant of Joe Zentner Ranch, established in the 1940s.

J 7.9 Turnout with dumpster.

J 8.7 Entering Pasagshak River State Recreation Site.

J 8.8 Begin **Pasagshak River State Recreation Site** next half-mile to mouth of Pasagshak River: 10 tent sites (park on right side of road and walk down to sites on river); 2 pullouts on road for RV parking. This recreation site has some picnic tables, firepits, well water, dumpster, out-

house; campground host. No fee. Fishing and beach access.

J 9.3 End Pasagshak River SRS camping area. Turnout at Boat Bay, traditional gravel boat launch ramp and mooring area. Four-wheel-drive vehicles required to use launch ramp.

J 9.9 Turnoff to Pasagshak Point, access to Bull Lakes; stocked rainbow, nice vistas.

J 10.3 Cattle Guard crossing and beginning of Kodiak Cattle Co. grazing lease. Public land—hunting, fishing, hiking, but keep vehicle on road.

CAUTION: Watch for free-roaming cattle and bison. Bison sometimes block the road. Stop and wait; they will eventually move. Sounding your horn is not advised. Do not approach bison on foot.

J 11.3 Road to beach access.

J 11.6 Bear Paw Ranch Youth Camp.

J 12.1 Road access to beach; big breakers when surf is up. Primitive camping, carry out trash.

J 13.1 Access to Kodiak Launch Complex, a 3,100-acre, low-earth-orbit launch facility of the Alaska Aerospace Development Corporation (AADC). The complex is the nation's first commercial aerospace launch facility on non-federally-funded land. Site includes support, payload and processing facilities and launch pad. There are no visitor facilities.

J 15.1 Gravel access road to **Fossil Beach**; beachcombing, whale watching and hiking along the bluffs.

J 15.4 Steep road in poor condition descends to Fossil Beach; parking available at top of road, walk down.

CAUTION: Be certain of your ability to drive back up before descending the hill. Cliffs are extremely unstable. Watch for falling rocks.

J 16.2 Twin Lakes to east; stocked rainbow.

J 16.4 Road ends at Fossil Cliffs; parking area. Fossils embedded in cliffs are visible along Fossil Beach to left and right (low tide only). Beautiful vistas and views of WWII observation bunkers on Narrow Cape to the left.

Prince William Sound

Includes communities of Valdez and Cordova and the Copper River Highway

College Fiord in beautiful Prince William Sound. (©William J. Rome)

Major Attractions:

*Columbia Glacier,
Childs Glacier,
Million Dollar Bridge,
Copper River*

Southcentral Alaska's Prince William Sound is an area famous for its scenery and wildlife. Dotted with islands, this 70-mile-wide gulf extends 30 miles north and west from the Gulf of Alaska to the Kenai Peninsula. It is bounded to the southeast by Montague and Hinchinbrook islands, which form Hinchinbrook Entrance, the 10-mile-long water passage from the Gulf of Alaska to Prince William Sound. To the north: a rugged, glaciated coastline and the Chugach Mountains.

Whether you take the almost 7-hour-long ferry ride or the 3-hour fast ferry ride between Whittier and Valdez or Cordova, you can't fail to be impressed by the sheer size and natural beauty of Prince William Sound. The crossing is spectacular, particularly on a clear day, when you are surrounded by a pristine wilderness of snow-capped mountains and emerald isles, watching whales and dolphins cut through the dark blue water.

The star attraction of Prince William Sound is Columbia Glacier, one of the largest and most magnificent of the tidewater glaciers along the Alaska coast. (The Hubbard Glacier, southeast of here near Yakutat, is the largest tidewater glacier in Alaska.)

Columbia Glacier is also the second fastest moving glacier in the world. It travels about 80 ft. per day and discharges 2 cubic miles of ice into the Sound annually. It has receded more than 9 miles since 1980. The glacier is currently 34 miles in length, 3 miles wide and more than 3,000 feet thick in some places. It is the biggest North American glacial contributor to increasing sea levels. Visitors to Prince William Sound see its tidewater terminus 6 miles away. How close you get to the glacier's face depends on iceberg production: the more icebergs, the greater the danger and the less chance boats have to get close.

The glacier was named by the Harriman Alaska expedition in 1899 for Columbia University in New York City. The glacier's source is Mount Einstein (elev. 11,552 feet) in the Chugach Mountains.

There are several ways to explore Prince William Sound. From Anchorage, drive south on the Seward Highway 47 miles and take the Whittier/Portage Glacier Access Road 11.4 miles to Whittier at the head of Passage Canal on Prince William Sound. From Whittier, you may take the state ferry across the Sound to Valdez or Cordova. (For a description of Whittier and a log of the access road, see pages 562-566 in the SEWARD HIGHWAY section.)

Or you may start your trip across Prince William Sound from Valdez, by driving 304 miles from Anchorage to Valdez via the Glenn and Richardson highways (see GLENN HIGHWAY and RICHARDSON HIGHWAY sections). From Valdez, the state ferry system serves both Cordova and Whittier.

From Whittier, Valdez or Cordova, take the state ferry or one of the privately operated excursion or charter boats to tour Prince William Sound. Flightseeing trips are also available. All-inclusive tours of Prince William Sound are available out of Anchorage. Depending on itinerary and transportation, you may return to Anchorage the same day or overnight along the way.

Captain Fred shares his knowledge and enthusiasm aboard the *"Limousine of Prince William Sound"* on the most entertaining glacier/wildlife cruise in Alaska...
...it's simply the BEST!

Lu-Lu Belle
Glacier Wildlife Cruises

For more information:
P. O. Box 1832
Valdez, AK 99686
(907) 835-5141

Reservations Hotline
1-800-411-0090
www.lulubelletours.com

Glacier Wildlife Cruises/Lu-Lu Belle. The motor yacht Lu-Lu Belle is probably the cleanest, plushest tour vessel you will ever see! This is an adult oriented cruise, and yes they will allow quitet, well behaved kids; however unruly unattended children will be sold to pirates. When you come aboard and see all the teak, mahogany and oriental rugs, you will understand why Captain Fred Rodolf asks you not to smoke and to wipe your feet before boarding. The Lu-Lu Belle has wide walk-around decks, thus assuring everyone ample opportunity for unobstructed viewing and photography.

Captain Fred is a born entertainer; he will personally guide and narrate every cruise. He has logged over 4,496 Columbia Glacier Cruises since 1979—that is more than anyone in Alaska. He is also known to be a "bit of a character".

The Columbia Glacier Wildlife Cruise of Prince William Sound is awesome! Wildlife seen on the cruises will vary throughout the season as the Lu-Lu Belle cruises from Valdez to the Columbia glacier on the calm protected waters of the Sound.

Boarding time is 10:45am each day from May 24 thru August. The length of the cruise can vary from 7 to ? hours. Please don't watch the clock because the crew does not. In this world of mass merchandising what a refreshing experience to enjoy a day aboard the wonderfully unique Lu-Lu Belle with Alaska's ever popular and entertaining Captain Rodolf. This up close and personal tour is event oriented not schedule oriented. The iceberg conditions at the Columbia Glacier are always changing. There is no way to predict how long it will take to get to the glacier face, but if any boat can make it all the way to the face, it will be the Lu-Lu Belle! Experience spectacular calving events, see for yourself as the ice falls into the sea causing thunderous explosions and massive plumes of spray. They will stay at the glacier for at least 1 hour to make sure you have a chance to record some of those amazing events.

The cost is $125.00 per person (with a cash discount price of $120.00)*. On Sunday mornings from 8:00 to 9:00am, the Lu-Lu Belle becomes the "Chapel of the Sea"—everyone is welcome, no charge.

On the cruises the crew prepares fresh baked goodies in the galley, all at reasonable prices. Gracious hospitality on a beautiful yacht are reasons why people refer to the Lu-Lu Belle as the "Limousine of Prince William Sound".

Join Captain and crew for an extra-special day and find out why Captain Fred refers to Switzerland as the "Valdez of Europe". They know that the best advertisement is their happy guests. They honor any and all competitors' coupons and discounts on a space-available basis. Phone (800) 411-0090 or (907) 835-5141.

Pre-season bookings will be locked in at this price. During the season, a fuel surcharge may be added.

"A different church service" Cruise the Port of Valdez each Sunday morning, 8:00-9:00am aboard the **Lu-Lu Belle**

Sponsored by Valdez First Baptist Church

www.lulubelletours.com   *Everyone Welcome*

Valdez

Kayakers paddle out of Valdez Harbor. Partial view of Trans-Alaska Pipeline terminal on Dayville Road. (©Sharon Nault)

Located on Port Valdez (pronounced val-DEEZ), an estuary off Valdez Arm in Prince William Sound. Valdez is 115 air miles and 304 highway miles from Anchorage, 366 highway miles from Fairbanks. Valdez is the southern terminus of the Richardson Highway and the trans-Alaska pipeline. **Population:** 3,976.

Emergency Services: City Police, Fire Department and **Ambulance,** emergency only phone 911. **Hospital,** Providence Valdez Medical Center, phone (907) 835-2249. **U.S. Coast Guard Search and Rescue,** (907) 835-7206. **Oil Spills,** 1-800-478-9300. **Harbormaster,** phone (907) 835-4981; www. ci.valdez.ak.us/harbor/. **Police Department** (907) 835-4560; **Alaska State Troopers,** phone (907) 835-4307.

Visitor Information: The visitor information center is located at 104 Chenega Street. It has speed dial set up for local B & B's and other businesses. Open 8 A.M. to 7 P.M. daily in summer. Phone (907) 835-2984. Write: **Valdez Convention and Visitors Bureau,** P.O. Box 1603, Valdez, AK 99686; phone (907) 835-2984; fax (907) 835-4845; email info@valdezalaska.org; website www.valdezalaska.org. Or visit the City of Valdez website at www.ci.valdez. ak.us. Visitors may also check the community calendar at the Valdez Civic Center by phoning the hotline at (907) 835-3200. Local calls are free from multiple phones around Valdez (provided by Copper Valley Telephone).

Elevation: Sea level. **Climate:** Record high was 90°F in June 2013; record low -23°F in February 1968. Normal daily maximum in January, 27°F; daily minimum 17°F. Normal daily maximum in July, 62°F; daily minimum 48°F. Average snowfall in Valdez from October to May is 326.3 inches, or about 27 feet. (By comparison, Anchorage averages about 6 feet in that period.) New snowfall records were set in January 1990, with snowfall for one day at 47½ inches. Record monthly snowfall is 180 inches in February 1996. Record rainfall in one day on Oct. 8th, 2013, 1.81 inches. Windy (often to 40 mph) in late fall. **Radio:** KCHU AM 770, KVAK AM 1230 and KVAK-FM 93.3. **Television:** Many channels via cable and satellite. **Newspaper:** *Valdez Star* (weekly).

Private Aircraft: Valdez, 3 miles east; elev. 120 feet; length 6,500 feet; asphalt; fuel 100LL, Jet B; attended. The airport terminal building has the Puddle Jumpers Saloon (beer, grill, coffee, hamburgers).

Situated in a majestic fjord, where the 5,000-foot-tall Chugach Mountains rise from Prince William Sound, Valdez is often called Alaska's "Little Switzerland." The city lies on the north shore of Port Valdez, an estuary named in 1790 by Spanish explorer Don Salvador Fidalgo for Antonio Valdes y Basan, a Spanish naval officer.

Valdez was established in 1897–98 as a port of entry for gold seekers bound for the Klondike goldfields. Thousands of stampeders arrived in Valdez to follow the All American Route to the Eagle mining district in Alaska's Interior, and from there up the Yukon River to Dawson City and the Klondike. The Valdez trail was an especially dangerous route, the first part of it leading over Valdez Glacier, where the early stampeders faced dangerous crevasses, snowblindness and exhaustion.

Copper discoveries in the Wrangell Mountains north of Valdez in the early 1900s brought more conflict and development to Valdez. A proposed railroad from tidewater to the rich Kennicott copper mines near McCarthy began a bitter rivalry between Valdez and Cordova for the railway line. The Copper River & Northwestern Railway eventually went to Cordova, but not before Valdez had started its own railroad north. The Valdez railroad did not get very far: The only trace of its existence is an old hand-drilled railway tunnel at **Milepost V 15** on the Richardson Highway.

The old gold rush trail out of Valdez was developed into a sled and wagon road in the early 1900s. It was routed through Thompson Pass (rather than over the Valdez Glacier) by Captain Abercrombie of the U.S. Army, who was commissioned to connect Fort Liscum (a military post established in 1900 near the present-day location of the Alyeska Marine Pipeline Terminal) with Fort Egbert in Eagle. Colonel Wilds P. Richardson of the Alaska Road Commission further developed the wagon road, building the first automobile road from Valdez to Fairbanks which was completed in the early 1920s.

Until 1964, Valdez was located about 4 miles east of its present location, closer to Valdez Glacier. The 1964 Good Friday earthquake, the most destructive earthquake ever to hit southcentral Alaska, virtually destroyed Valdez. The quake measured 9.2 on the Richter scale and was centered in Prince William Sound. A series of local waves caused by massive underwater landslides swept over and engulfed the Valdez wharf, taking 33 people with it. Seismic action shook the downtown and residential areas. Though much damage was sustained, only the waterfront was destroyed. After the quake the Army Corps of Engineers deter-

mined the town should be relocated. By late August 1964, relocation was under way. The last residents remaining at "old" Valdez moved to the new town in 1968.

Since its days as a port of entry for gold seekers, Valdez has been an important gateway to Interior Alaska. As the most northerly ice-free port in the Western Hemisphere, and connected by the Richardson Highway to the Alaska Highway system, Valdez offers the shortest link to much of interior Alaska for seaborne cargo.

Construction of the trans-Alaska pipeline began in 1974 and was completed in 1977. The 800-mile-long pipeline begins at Prudhoe Bay on the Arctic Ocean and ends at the marine terminal at Port Valdez, where it is fed by gravity into tanks or directly into waiting oil tankers. The first tanker load of oil shipped out of Valdez on August 1, 1977. National attention was focused on Valdez and the pipeline when the oil tanker *Exxon Valdez* ran aground on Bligh Reef (some 30 miles from Valdez) in March 1989, causing an 11-million-gallon oil spill.

Valdez's economy depends on the oil industry, the Prince William Sound fishery, government and tourism. The city limits of Valdez comprise an area of 274 square miles and include all surrounding mountains to timberline. Valdez has long been known for its beautiful setting, with the Chugach Mountains rising behind the city and the small-boat harbor in front. There are wide streets and open spaces, with the central res-

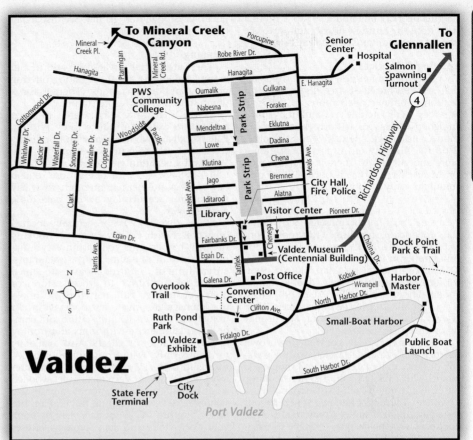

The record snowfall for Valdez, 560.7 inches, was recorded in the winter of 1989-1990.
Read more here: http://www.adn.com/2012/01/06/2249330/snow-keeps-piling-up-in-valdez.html#storylink=cpy

idential district built around a park strip that runs from the business district almost to the base of the mountains behind the town.

Lodging & Services

Valdez has motel/hotel facilities and several bed and breakfasts (see display ads this section). Summer reservations are advised. Services here include restaurants, sporting goods stores, gas stations (1 in town on Pioneer near Eagle's Rest RV Park, the other 2 on the highway on Airport Road), liquor store and gift shops. There is a supermarket on Meals Avenue that is open 4:30 A.M. to midnight, daily in summer.

Downtown B & B Inn. Motel accommodations, 113 Galena Dr. Centrally located near small boat harbor, museum, ferry terminal, downtown shopping. View rooms, private and shared baths, coin-op laundry, TV and phones in rooms. Wheelchair accessible. Deluxe continental breakfast May 15–Sept. 15. Reasonable rates. Single, double, family rooms. Phone 1-800-478-2791 or (907) 835-2791. Email: 1n2rs@alaska.net. Free WiFi. www.valdezdowntowninn.com. See display ad on this page. [ADVERTISEMENT]

Keystone Hotel. Located downtown (corner of Egan and Hazelet) within walking distance to ferry terminal and shops. 100 rooms with cable TV, phones, nonsmoking, accessible, coin-op laundry. Complimentary continental breakfast and free Wi-Fi. Try our spacious king bed suites. Comfortable, clean rooms at reasonable rates. 1-888-835-0665.

Email: keystonehotel@gci.net. See display ad this page. [ADVERTISEMENT]

Camping

There are several private RV parks in and around Valdez (see ads this section), offering hookups and dump stations. (There is also a dump station at the Tesoro station.)

Bayside RV Park is located in town and within walking distance to everything. Full, partial and no hookups with hot unmetered showers, laundromat, cable TV, free WiFi and a beautiful view of the mountains. Call 1-888-835-4425 for reservations. email: bayside1@cvinternet.net Internet: www.baysiderv.com. See display ad on page 645. [ADVERTISEMENT]

Bear Paw R.V. Park, centrally located on scenic North Harbor Drive overlooking the boat harbor, puts you within easy walking distance of museum, shops, restaurants, entertainment, charter boats—no need to unhook and drive to grocery stores or points of interest. Full, partial or no hookups; immaculate private restrooms with hot, unmetered showers. Dump station and coin-operated launderette with irons and ironing boards available for guests. Also available, for adults only: waterfront full-hookup RV sites with cable TV, guest lounge, computer modem access line. Very nice, quiet wooded adult tent sites, some platforms, among the salmonberries on Porcupine Hill. Tables, fire pits. Campfire wood for sale. Let us book your glacier tour with Stan Stephens Cruises

at the reservations desk in our spacious office lounge. Don't miss the Bear Paw Trading Post Gift Shop. Advance reservations recommended: (907) 835-2530. (Bear Paw does fill up!) The coffee pot is always on at Bear Paw. Let us know if you're coming in on the evening ferry and we'll be there to help you get parked. Email: bearpaw@valdezak. net. Internet: www.bearpawrvpark.com. See display ad on page 644. [ADVERTISEMENT]

Eagle's Rest RV Park, the friendliest RV park in downtown Valdez, offers you Good Sam Park service with a smile. Let our helpful staff take care of all your bookings on cruises, tours and charters. Enjoy the beautiful panoramic view of our mountains and glaciers right off our front porch! We also can let you know where the hottest fishing spots are or the quietest walking trails! Fish-cleaning table available. Self-contained rental cabins available. Capt'n Joe's Tesoro next door offers a convenience store, gas, diesel, propane, potable water, sewer dump. Parking with us puts you within walking distance of our museum, gift shops, touchless car wash and RV/truck wand wash, banks. Shuttle service

for glacier cruises. No charge to wash your RV at your site. Phone us for reservations, 1-800-553-7275 or (907) 835-2373. Fax (907) 835-KAMP (835-5267). Email: rvpark@ alaska.net. Internet: www.eaglesrestrv.com. Stay with us and leave feeling like family. See display ad on page 643. [ADVERTISEMENT]

Valdez Glacier Campground has 87 standard sites and 21 RV pads with 20/30 amp hookups. This facility provides hot showers, potable water and dump station. Pleasant wooded campground. Firepits, grills, dumpsters, covered picnic areas and tent camping. Firewood available. Campground host. Tent sites $15, for military $10; RV hookups $25, military $20. RVs with no hookups $15. Trailers available for military rental. Campground run by Fort Greely but open to public. (907) 803-3695. *CAUTION:*

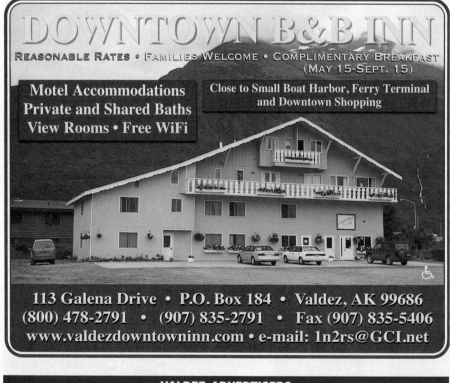
VALDEZ ADVERTISERS

Beware of bears. Watch for eagles here!

There is also RV and tent camping at **Allison Point**, a favorite fishing spot, between Mile 4.3 and 5.3 on Dayville Road. Use signed overnight RV parking areas. Day-use only parking is also available (there is a fee charged). Bears are prevalent on Dayville Road. Never get near or feed bears. Visit the Valdez Visitor's Bureau for bear awareness information and safety tips.

Transportation

Air: Daily scheduled service via Era Aviation and Grant Aviation. Several air taxi services operate out of Valdez. There are no scheduled flights to Cordova. Helicopter services available both for summer flightseeing as well as winter package tours for extreme sports.

Ferry: Scheduled state ferry from Whittier and Cordova. Phone 1-800-642-0067 (Juneau office). Reservations are a must! See Southcentral/ Prince William Sound schedules in the ALASKA MARINE HIGHWAY section or visit www.ferryalaska.com.

Taxi: One local taxi service, Valdez Yellow Cab (907) 835-2500.

Car Rental: One company offers car rentals; available at airport terminal: Valdez U-Drive (907) 835-4402.

Highway: The Richardson Highway extends north from Valdez to the Glenn Highway and the Alaska Highway. See the RICHARDSON HIGHWAY section.

Attractions

Exploring the Valdez waterfront. The waterfront in Valdez is set up to accommodate fishermen as well as visitors out for a stroll. Restaurants, shops boat and kayak rentals line one side of North Harbor Drive, while across the street the public promenade offers fine views of—and access to—the Small Boat Harbor. Public fish-cleaning stations are located at the small boat harbor.

Walk east along the promenade (which has picnic tables and public restrooms) to Dock Point Park, located past the boat launch where Kobuk Drive curves around the harbor. Dock Point Park has covered picnic tables, a restroom and a 1-mile trail with scenic overlooks of the Port of Valdez. The combination gravel and boardwalk trail provides easy access for people of all ability levels. Note: Kobuk Drive curves around the harbor and passes the PeterPan cannery and its fresh seafood market.

Walk the promenade along Valdez harbor, a lively spot in summer with fishermen, kayakers, fishing boats and tour boats. (©Sharon Nault)

Walk west on North Harbor Drive to Fidalgo Drive and continue to **Ruth Pond Park** on the corner of Hazelet Avenue and Fidalgo Drive. There are picnic tables and a trail at Ruth Pond. Across the street is the Valdez Museum Annex, which houses the Remembering Old Valdez Exhibit (see description this section). A memorial bench by a standing plaque here commemorates the Copper River Gold Rush History at the corner of Hazelet and Meals.

Walk up Hazelet Avenue and turn up the hill on Clifton Avenue (towards the Valdez Convention & Civic Center). **Overlook Trail** branches off this street, affording fine views of downtown Valdez. Continue on Clifton Avenue to return to North Harbor Drive.

Visit the **Valdez Museum & Historical Archive**, located in downtown Valdez at 2 locations. At 217 Egan Dr. the museum exhibits artifacts and tells stories originating in 1898 to the present. Interpretive exhibits explain the impact of the gold rush, the 1907 railroad speculation boom, and the construction of the trans-Alaska oil pipeline. "A Moving Experience" commemorates the 1964 earthquake. Learn about the cultural heritage of the region's Native peoples, the Ahtna, Alutiiq and Eyak. Not to be missed are the exhibit about the 1989 Exxon Valdez Oil Spill and a fully restored 1907 Ahrens steam fire engine. Also see regional art here. Open daily, 9 A.M. to 5 P.M. May–Sept.; 12–5 P.M. Tuesday–Sunday in winter.

At 436 South Hazelet Ave., near the waterfront, the **Remembering Old Valdez Exhibit**, commemorates the devastating 1964 Good Friday Earthquake, and marks the transition from the Historic Old Town Valdez to the Valdez of today. The original town site is remembered in a 1:20 scale replica as it appeared in 1963. This detailed model includes over 400 buildings and 60 city blocks, recalling the thriving community that existed before the 9.2 quake. Efforts are underway to reinterpret Old Town.

Visit the original Valdez town site. Located 4 miles from downtown via the Richardson Highway. Watch for information sign about Old Valdez town site 0.1 mile south of highway turnoff. A memorial is located 0.4 mile south of the highway turnoff consisting of 2 plaques set in a foundation from "old" Valdez. One plaque lists the names of those residents of Valdez and Chenega who were killed in the 9.2 Good Friday earthquake March 27, 1964 which destroyed the original town site of Valdez.

The Remembering Old Valdez Exhibit is open daily, 9 A.M. to 5 P.M., May to September in summer; by appointment only in

winter. Phone (907) 835-2764, or visit www. valdezmuseum.org.

The Maxine and Jesse Whitney Museum at Prince William Sound Community College, 303 Lowe St., (go north down Hazelet, right at the first community college sign) is well worth a visit. This huge collection in a state-of-the-art facility, features an extensive array of Alaskan animal mounts, including 2 full-sized polar bears, black bear and grizzly bears, musk ox, moose and more, Native dolls, an Eskimo kayak, prehistoric artifacts (check out the arrowheads in drawers) and a unique collection of Native carved ivory, including the Paul Kulik Transportation Collection. Admission fee is by donation. For more information and details on summer hours and programs, phone (907) 834-1690; www. MJWhitneymuseum.org.

Valdez Consortium Library, located on Fairbanks Street, has an extensive Alaska Historical & Archive section, as well as many Alaska videos which can be viewed at the library. It also features a paperback exchange for travelers and a variety of current newspapers; a trade is appreciated but not required. The library has music listening booths, public computers, WiFi available, typewriters and a photocopier. Wheelchair accessible. Drinking fountains, restrooms, telephone with 3 minute limit. Open Monday and Friday 10 A.M. to 6 P.M., Tuesday through Thursday 10 A.M. to 8 P.M., Saturday noon to 5 P.M. and Sunday 1–5 P.M. Website: www. ci.valdez.ak.us/library.

Take a boat tour to see Columbia Glacier, second largest tidewater glacier in North America, Shoup Glacier and other Prince William Sound attractions. Meares Glacier and other Prince William Sound attractions. See ads in this section.

Stan Stephens Glacier & Wildlife Cruises. Explore the fjords and passageways of Prince William Sound with Stan Stephens Glacier and Wildlife Cruises. Stan and his family invite you to travel the calm waters of the Sound to Columbia Glacier and/or Meares Glaciers. Stan Stephens Cruises—the only Valdez-based cruise company operated by Alaskans—has shared the wonders of Prince William Sound with travelers since 1971. A day spent on the water with Stan Stephens is a complete Alaskan experience! They will take the time to let you experience all of the Sound, from magnificent icebergs at Columbia Glacier; calving at Meares Glacier; orca or humpback whales, sea lions, sea otters, seals, puffins, bald eagles, kittiwakes, cormorants, porpoise, goats or bears. You will also learn about the history of the Sound including commercial fishing, oil shipping, gold and copper mining and early explorers. Unique to Stan Stephens Cruises is their all Alaskan staff. Stan Stephens Cruises offers 2 departures daily ranging in length from 6.5 to 9 hours. Travelers of all ages, families and special groups are welcome and encouraged. Staying in an RV park? We offer complimentary park to dock transfers. For more information please contact Stan Stephens Cruises toll free at 1-866-867-1297 or online at www.stanstephenscruises.com. See display ad on page 641. [ADVERTISEMENT]

Go fishing. Fish from the wharf for salmon. (Remember to reel in if a boat or ferry get close.) Or show up and watch salmon being caught. The parking area is across from the "Remembering Old Valdez" exhibit. Photo-op spot for Valdez pipeline terminal just across from here. Fish at the edge of the ocean from Allison Point.

Valdez Gold Rush Days, this early August celebration is an annual event that includes a parade, contests, game night and town fish fry. During Gold Rush Days, cancan girls peruse local establishments and a jail is pulled through town by "deputies" who arrest citizens without beards.

Other Special Events: The **Mayday Fly-in & Air Show**, which takes place over Mother's Day weekend in May and celebrates the history of bush flying in Alaska with bush pilot competitions, aerial acrobatics and airplane exhibits.

The **Fireweed 400** bicycle race is scheduled for July 11–12, 2014. This annual race begins at Sheep Mountain Lodge on the Glenn Highway and culminates in Valdez

with plenty of bike oriented festivities for the avid cyclist.

The Last Frontier Theatre Conference, sponsored by Prince William Sound Community College, takes place at the Valdez Convention and Civic Center June 8–14, 2014. Details at www.theatreconference.org.

Go sea kayaking. There are sea kayak rentals and guided tours available from outfitters such as **Pangaea Adventures** at the Small Boat Harbor. This is an ideal way to explore Prince William Sound. Guided trips range from an afternoon paddle around Port Valdez to glacier day tours and camping tours. Trips suitable for beginners to experts.

Visit Crooked Creek Science Center/ Salmon Spawning Viewing Area. Drive out the Richardson Highway about a mile from downtown to see salmon spawning in Crooked Creek. A viewing platform offers a close-up look at spawning pink and chum salmon mid-July to early September.

This spacious structure accommodates visitors, exhibits and displays. Located at a spot known locally as the "salmon turnaround," this is a popular and well-situated place to watch wildlife and spawning salmon. Open Memorial Day to Labor Day.

Across the highway from the viewing area are intertidal wetlands known locally as "Duck Flats." Watch for migrating waterfowl here from late April to mid-May and in October. Nesting birds in summer. This is a game sanctuary; no shooting is allowed. Good spot for photos.

Visit the Original Valdez Townsite, located 4 miles from downtown Valdez via the Richardson Highway. Watch for information sign about Old Valdez townsite 0.1 mile south of highway turnoff. A memorial is located 0.4 mile south of the highway turnoff consisting of 2 plaques set in a foundation from "old" Valdez. One plaque lists the names of those residents of Valdez and Chenega who were killed in the 9.2 Good Friday Earthquake on March 27, 1964, which destroyed the original townsite of Valdez.

Drive Dayville Road. Dayville Road is 6.8 miles from Valdez via the Richardson Highway. Turnoff on this 5.4-mile-long side road for opportunities to enjoy wild Alaska without venturing far from your vehicle. This is a wide, paved, improved side road (with bike trail) that leads to shoreside

camping, picnicking, fishing and scenic views along Port Valdez, the 13-mile-long estuary at the head of Valdez Arm. There are many roadside benches. Look for seals, sea lions, birds, bears (especially when salmon are spawning or afterward, at the end of the bay, in the fall). Berry picking in season.

Dayville Road is open to the public to Mile 5.4, where a guardhouse restricts public access to the Alyeska Pipeline Terminal complex. *NOTE: There is NO public access to the marine terminal and there are NO public tours of the terminal.*

Prince William Sound Community College is located at 303 Lowe St. (The school's student housing is located on Pioneer Street.) Access from the college parking lot to park strip and Barney Meyring Park, with children's play area and picnic tables.

©Meghan Mackey, staff

Also look for the 2 huge wooden carvings by artist Peter Toth on campus. One is at the college proper on Lowe Street and the other is in front of the student housing on Pioneer Street. Both are dedicated to the Native Americans. Toth has carved 67 statues honoring Native Americans and donated them to towns in each of the 50 states. Referred to as "Whispering Giants," the 20- to 40-foot-high monuments are found on the grounds of museums, parks, libraries and other public places throughout North America.

The **Solomon Gulch Fish Hatchery** and large parking area are located at Mile 3.8. There are some dramatic views and photo opportunities from the bridge here of the Solomon Gulch Falls and dam site (Copper Valley Electric co-generation project). Walkways at the fish hatchery go to a viewing platform and along the ponds and hatchery building, more information signs. Mile 4.5 marks the beginning of camping areas (with water, dumpsters, outhouses, pay phone). There is a wonderful array of wildlife viewing opportunities, steps away from your campsite. Camping fee is $12; day-use fee $3. (The main campground registration area is at Mile 5.1.) Mile 4.7 is the head of the Solomon Gulch hiking trail. Trail begins with steep hill to the east of the road. Pink

and silver salmon fishing from shore in season at **Allison Point**. Handicapped fishing platform is located at Mile 4.8.

See Waterfalls. From downtown Valdez, drive out the Richardson Highway 17.5 miles to see **Horsetail Falls**. A short distance beyond Horsetail Falls is **Bridal Veil Falls**. Both are favorite photo stops. There are also waterfalls visible from town.

Go Hiking. A popular short day hike is to Gold Creek, 3.5 miles from Valdez. Other area hikes include Keystone Canyon (2.6 miles), Dock Point Trail (1 mile) and Solomon Gulch Trail (3.8 miles). A 10-mile hike along Valdez Arm to Shoup Bay State Marine Park starts at the Mineral Creek trailhead in town.

State marine parks in the Valdez area include Shoup Bay, Jack Bay and Sawmill Bay. Accessible mainly or only by water, these parks offer camping on tent platforms, fire rings and latrines. They are popular with fishermen and sea kayakers. For more information, visit www.alaskastateparks.org.

Public-use Cabins. McAllister Creek and Kittiwake public-use cabins are located within Shoup Bay State Marine Park. Check the fact sheet at http://dnr.alaska.gov/parks/cabins/shoupbaycabin.pdf. Jack Bay USFS cabin is located at the east end of Jack Bay off of Valdez Narrows. Access is by float plane (15 minutes from Valdez) or boat (20 miles from Valdez). Cabin reservations can be made by calling 1-877-444-6777 or visit www.recreation.gov.

Winter Sports. Valdez's proximity to Thompson Pass has made it a desirable winter destination for adventurous back-country skiers, snowmachiners and snowboarders and various snowboarding championship competitions take place here. Three Heliski operators take people out for backcountry adventures. Tailgate Alaska takes place in March. Check with the Valdez Convention and Visitors Bureau for a list of winter events and outfitters by going online at www.valdezalaska.org.

Fish a Derby. The Halibut Derby takes place May 17 to August 29, 2014. James Culley won the 2013 Halibut Derby and $15,000 for his 325 pound halibut.

Other annual fishing derbies include the Silver Salmon Derby, the Women's Silver Salmon Derby and The Kids' Pink Salmon Derby. Silver Big Prize Fridays are July 25 and August 29, 2014. Cash and prizes are awarded to the winners. Buy a derby ticket ($10/daily or $50/season) and read the rules to qualify. For further information, contact Valdez Fish Derbies: phone (907) 835-5680; email info@valdezfishderbies.com; or visit www.valdezfishderbies.com.

AREA FISHING: Valdez Arm supports the largest sport fishery in Prince William Sound. Important species include pink salmon, silver salmon, halibut, rockfish and Dolly Varden. Charter boats are available in Valdez. Favorite shoreside public fishing spots are Valdez city dock and Allison Point. Allison Point is located on Dayville Road; turnoff is 4.8 miles east of downtown via the Richardson Highway. The **Allison Point** fishery, created by the Solomon Gulch Hatchery, has one of the largest pink salmon fisheries in the state and also produces a major silver salmon return annually. Pinks from mid-June through late July; silvers from mid-July through late August.

Cordova

First Street in downtown Cordova offers shopping, a visitor center and the museum and library. (©Sharon Nault)

Located on the southeast shore of Orca Inlet on the east side of Prince William Sound. Cordova is accessible only by plane, boat and ferry. **Population:** 2,290. **Emergency Services:** dial 911. **Alaska State Troopers,** phone (907) 424-3184, **emergency** phone 911. **Police, Fire Department, Ambulance,** emergency only phone 911; police department business calls, phone (907) 424-6100. **Hospital,** phone (907) 424-8000. Ilanka Health Center, phone (907) 424-3622.

Visitor Information: Chamber of Commerce, 404 1st St.; stop in and chat with a Chamber representative: They will know where to send you for what you need, and will have information regarding room availability. It can be a challenge to find a room if you haven't reserved in advance. Phone (907) 424-7260 or write Box 99, Cordova, AK 99574; email visit cordova@ak.net; or visit www.cordovachamber.com. Visitors may also get information at the Museum/Library, City Hall and at the Forest Service.

Chugach National Forest Cordova Ranger District office is located at 612 2nd St. in the original federal building for the town of Cordova, built in 1925, which once housed the post office, jail and courthouse. Natural history displays on the 2nd and 3rd floors. USFS personnel can provide information on trails, cabins and other activities on national forest lands. Open weekdays from 8 A.M. to 5 P.M. Write P.O. Box 280, Cordova, AK 99574, or phone (907) 424-7661; www.fs.fed.us/r10/chugach/cordova.

Elevation: Sea level to 400 feet. **Climate:** Average temperature in July is 65°F, in January 21°F. Average annual precipitation is 167 inches. During the winter of 2011–2012, Cordova had over 220 inches of snow, the largest amount since the record-breaking winter of 1998–1999, when almost 200 inches fell. Prevailing winds are easterly at about 4 knots. **Radio:** KLAM-AM 1450 (country), KCHU-FM 88.1 (Community Public Radio), KCDV-FM 100.9 (The Eagle). **Television:** Cable. **Newspaper:** The *Cordova Times* (weekly).

Private Aircraft: Merle K. "Mudhole" Smith Airport, Mile 12.1 Copper River Highway; elev. 42 feet; length 7,500 feet; asphalt; attended. It has an EMAS arrestor bed safety feature made of crushable, lightweight concrete and is 1 of 47 airports nation-wide to feature this technology. Aircraft that overrun the runway sink into this bed and stop. Cordova Municipal (city airfield), 0.9 mile east; elev. 12 feet; length 1,900 feet; gravel; fuel 100, 100LL; available for private sales when Cordova Air is open. Eyak Lake seaplane base, 0.9 mile east, adjacent to city field.

The Cordova area was first inhabited by the Eyak tribe. European fishermen came to ply the surrounding fish-rich waters, and by 1889 there was a busy fish camp and cannery site on Odiak Pond.

The town had its origin as the railroad terminus and ocean shipping port for the copper ore shipped by rail from the Kennecott mine up the Copper River. The town was named Cordova by Michael J. Heney, builder of the Copper River & Northwestern Railway. The name of the town was derived from the adjacent water—Puerto Cordova—so named by Spanish explorer Don Salvador Fidalgo in 1790. A post office was established here in 1906. The townsite was moved from Eyak Lake to the shore of Orca Inlet in 1908. The first trainload of copper ore from Kennicott arrived on April 8, 1911.

Cordova was incorporated in 1909. The mines closed in 1938 but the town continued to prosper due to the fishing industry.

Commercial fishing in Cordova supplanted mining as the basis of the town's economy. The fishing industry boomed as the verdant waters of the gulf and sound held amazing quantities in multiple fisheries. The *Exxon Valdez* oil spill in 1989 devastated the herring fishery and other fisheries in the area. The recovery has been long and slow. The city now has 5 processing plants in operation, staffed by locals, college students and workers from Romania, Russia and other countries. The fishing fleet can be seen at Cordova harbor, also the home port of the USCG cutter *Sycamore*. The season for salmon runs from early May to September, with king, red and silver salmon taken from the Copper River area, red, chum and pink salmon from Prince William Sound. Black cod, halibut and shrimp seasons run during the winter months.

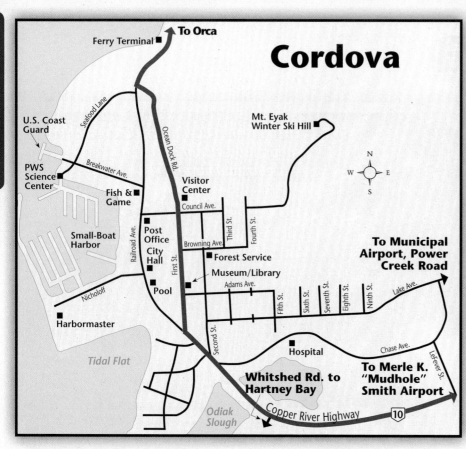

Cordova

- To Orca
- Ferry Terminal
- U.S. Coast Guard
- Seafood Lane
- Ocean Dock Rd.
- Mt. Eyak Winter Ski Hill
- PWS Science Center
- Breakwater Ave.
- Fish & Game
- Visitor Center
- Council Ave.
- Third St.
- Fourth St.
- Small-Boat Harbor
- Railroad Ave.
- Post Office City Hall
- Browning Ave.
- First St.
- Forest Service
- Museum/Library
- Pool
- Adams Ave.
- Nicholoff
- Harbormaster
- Fifth St.
- Sixth St.
- Seventh St.
- Eighth St.
- Ninth St.
- Lake Ave.
- To Municipal Airport, Power Creek Road
- Tidal Flat
- Second St.
- Hospital
- Chase Ave.
- Lefever St.
- To Merle K. "Mudhole" Smith Airport
- Whitshed Rd. to Hartney Bay
- Odiak Slough
- Copper River Highway — 10

A favorite photo-op at Cordova harbor is "The Southeasterly," by sculptor Joan Bugbee Jackson. (©Sharon Nault)

Since 1989, the Prince William Sound Science Center has facilitated and conducted research and education programs to contribute to the preservation and ecological understanding of Prince William Sound, the Copper River Delta and Gulf of Alaska. The Center, located at the entrance of the Cordova harbor, provides educational opportunities for students and volunteers. For more information on camps, events and natural science information on the area, visit www. pwssc.org or phone (907) 424-5800.

Lodging & Services

Accommodations at **The Reluctant Fisherman Inn** (40 rooms) and **Prince William Motel** (16 rooms). It is highly recommended that you reserve rooms via phone or internet before arriving.

Cordova has several eating spots, a laundromat, 2 supermarkets, several other stores and gift shops. There are 2 banks in town: First National Bank of Anchorage and Wells Fargo.

Short-term and long-term parking available in designated areas in the harbor area. For information phone (907) 424-6200. *NOTE: If you are parking streetside, do NOT park within 20 feet of a cross-walk: You may receive a ticket.*

The small boat harbor has 727 slips. Contact the Harbormaster for reservation information prior to arrival. The Harbormaster's office on Nicholoff Way has free tide books and other information. Pay phone, book swap, restrooms, showers, drinking fountains also available here. The office is open 8 A.M. to 5 P.M. weekdays; phone (907) 424-6400 or visit their website at www.city ofcordova.net/harbor.htm. A dump station for RVers is right behind this building. Follow the signs. There are also used oil receptacles.

Cordova Library, located adjacent the museum in the Centennial Building on 1st Street, is open in summer, Tuesday through Friday, from 10 A.M. to 8 P.M. and 10 A.M. to 5 P.M. ON Saturday; closed Sunday and Monday. The library offers free Internet access via PC computers and WiFi, phone (907) 424-6667; website www.cordovalibrary.org.

The Bidarki Recreation Center has a weight room, showers, sauna and exercise facility. It is located at 2nd and Council. Open 6 A.M. to 9:30 P.M., Monday–Friday, 9 A.M. to 9:30 P.M. on Saturday. Rent Skater's Cabin, on Eyak Lake for $25/night, through the Recreation Center. Phone (907) 424-7282.

Bob Korn Memorial Swimming Pool is located on Railroad Avenue, next to the police station at the head of Nicholoff. The heated indoor Olympic-sized pool offers

lap swim, family swim, exercise classes and lessons. Open year-round. Phone (907) 424-7200 for pool hours and programs. Admission is $10/adults, $3/youth or senior. Showers available with paid admission.

The U.S. Forest Service maintains 17 public-use cabins in the Cordova district. Phone 1-877-444-6777, or visit www.recreation.gov, for details.

Public phones and toilets are at the Visitor Center & Chamber of Commerce, the Harbormaster's Office, the Ferry Office, the A/C Market (on Nicholoff Way), the Museum/Library and at the Airport.

Camping

Cordova has 2 formal campgrounds. Odiak Camper Park on Whitshed Road is a flat gravel site with toilets and 24 RV spaces that have electric hookups; reserve sites at Bidarki Recreation Center, phone (907) 424-7282. Shelter Cove tent camping and overnight RV parking is 0.6 mile out Orca Road (flat gravel area for RVs). Tent platforms in woods, fish cleaning area on the bay. RV parking $11.20, tents $5.60. If you arrive after hours, you may park at the Shelter Cove overflow area and pay the following morning at Bidarki Recreation Center.

NOTE: The Childs Glacier Recreation Area, an 11-site campground 48 miles out the Copper River Highway, is closed to vehicle access indefinitely due to the bridge failure on the Copper River Highway. However, the recreation area is open to the public. Phone the Cordova Ranger District for details at (907) 424-7661.

Transportation

Air: Scheduled service via Alaska Airlines and Era Alaska. Local charter service with Cordova Air Service at (907) 424-3289 and Alaska Wilderness Outfitters at (907) 424-5552.

Ferry: The Alaska Marine Highway system connects Cordova with Valdez and Whittier. Phone (907) 424-7333 or 1-800-642-0066. See the ALASKA MARINE HIGHWAY section.

Taxis: Cordova Taxi (907) 253-5151. For airport shuttle, call Chinook Auto Rentals (907) 424-5279 ($10 per person shuttle pickup at the airport).

Car Rentals: Available.

Highways: The Alaska state highway system does not connect to Cordova. The 49-mile Copper River Highway leads east from Cordova and ends just beyond the Million Dollar Bridge, although currently the highway remains closed indefinitely at Mile 36 due to bridge Bridge No. 339 failure. This closure will remain in effect until the bridge is replaced, estimated for 2015.

Private Boats: Cordova has a 727-slip boat harbor serving recreational boaters as well as the commercial fishing fleet. Contact the harbormaster's office at (907) 424-6400 or on VHF Channel 16.

Attractions

Take a walking tour. A self-guided walking tour map of Cordova historic sites, prepared by the Cordova Historical Society, is available at the Visitor Center as well as the Cordova Museum. Although much of early Cordova was destroyed by fire, several picturesque old structures and historic sites remain.

Cordova Fishermen's Memorial, *The Southeasterly*, is located on Nicholoff overlooking the "new harbor." Created by local sculptor Joan Bugbee Jackson, this is a favorite photo subject for visitors and is a reminder of the dangers this fishing fleet encounters.

Ilanka Cultural Center, located across from the Fishermen's Memorial, features contemporary artwork as well as artifacts of the local Eyak tribe. Demonstrations by local artists occur throughout the week; call ahead for schedule. On site gift shop has authentic handicrafts and unique and beautiful items for purchase. Open 10 A.M. to 5 P.M., Tuesday through Friday. Phone (907) 424-7903.

Cordova Historical Museum, located on First Street, offers an excellent overview of

©Sharon Nault

the area's history, tracing "the tracks of Cordova's past through industrial and cultural exhibits, displays and interpretation."

The museum also displays original work by Alaskan artists Sydney Laurence, Eustace Ziegler and Jules Dahlager. Donations suggested for those 12 and older. Open 10 A.M. to 6 P.M. Monday through Friday, 10 A.M. to 5 P.M. Saturday, and 1–5 P.M. Sundays, from Memorial Day to Labor Day. Winter hours (Labor Day to Memorial Day) are 10 A.M. to 5 P.M. Tuesday through Friday and 1–5 P.M. Saturday. Tours can be arranged. Write P.O. Box 391, Cordova 99574; phone (907) 424-6665 or visit www.cordovamuseum.org. The Cordova Historical Society operates a gift shop at the museum featuring books of local interest and Alaskan crafts.

Watch Birds. The Copper River Delta is one of the most important stopover places in the Western Hemisphere for one of the largest shorebird migration in the world. As many as 5 million shorebirds rest and feed here during spring migration. Birders can view up to 31 different species. Birders planning to visit in the spring should consider timing their arrival to coincide with the Copper River Delta Shorebird Festival in early May.

Hartney Bay and Alaganik Slough are the most popular of several bird-watching areas. Drive out Whitshed Road 5.5 miles to road end to reach Hartney Bay, part of the 300,000-acre Copper River Delta mudflats and a great place to see shorebirds. The USFS recreation area at Alaganik Slough is a 20-mile drive from downtown, but worth the drive to see trumpeter swans up-close. There's a boardwalk with viewing blind at the slough for bird watchers.

Special Events. The Copper River Delta Shorebird Festival is scheduled for May 9–11, 2014. Many birder activities, speakers, workshops and community events are scheduled throughout the festival.

An Old Time Downtown 4th of July Party draws hundreds of residents and visitors to First Street each year to enjoy and participate in activities, like the Kelp box derby—always popular with young and old alike—a race of homemade soapbox-style racers. Moose Kids games for children ages 3 to 12 includes races, an egg toss, and other competitions for prizes. The highlight of the day is the free red salmon barbeque potluck feast served up hot from the grills by volunteers. Community members provide side dishes and desserts and the local seafood processors such as Trident Seafoods and Copper River Seafoods generously donate fresh Copper River wild red salmon for everyone's enjoyment.

Cordova's Copper River Wild Salmon Festival July 18–19, 2014, features food, the Salmon Jam Music Festival and the Alaska Salmon Runs, sponsored by the Cordova Running Club. The King Salmon Marathon starts at the Mile 27 Bridge on the Copper River Highway and ends in Cordova. There's also the Sockeye Half Marathon, Coho 10k and Humpy 5k and the Smolt 1k kids run.

The Alaska State ferry MV Chenega serves Cordova, Valdez and Whittier in summer.
(©Sharon Nault)

Cordova boat harbor serves recreational boaters and a commercial fishing fleet.
(©Sharon Nault)

In 1961, a few Cordovans created the Ice-worm Festival as a way to break the winter blues. The first full weekend of every February is set aside for the major winter, the Ice-worm Festival, the highlight of which is the 100-foot-long "iceworm" that winds its way through the streets of Cordova during the parade. Other activities include the survival suit race, variety show, a talent show, food and craft fairs, and the selection of Miss Ice-worm who then represents Cordova at the Fur Rondy festival in Anchorage.

Visit the USCGC *Sycamore*. While there are no formal tours of the *Sycamore*, if the cutter is in port and the crew is not busy, you may be able to get on board. Inquire at the Quarterdeck shack on the North Fill Dock, just off of Seafood Lane or the "T" Pier.

Walk or drive Orca Bay Road. Pleasant evenings bring local walkers out Orca Bay Road. It is also a favorite with dog-walkers. Orca Bay Road is 2.1 miles long, with access to beaches at Mile 0.6. This beautiful road offers wildlife viewing (otters, seals, birds) and photo-ops of boats on Orca Bay. There is an active lodge at the end of the road.

Drive Power Creek Road. This is a scenic drive out along the shore of Lake Eyak and through some massive, moss covered trees, to the trailhead for the Power Creek USFS Trail (description follows). Check with the USFS office in town for trail status, (907) 424-7661. Enjoy the berry picking, fish viewing and fishing along this road.

From 2nd Avenue in downtown Cordova, drive out Lake Street 0.6 mile to Nirvana Park on Lake Eyak. Built in 1930-35, the park once contained whimsical sculptures (photographs of them are at the museum in town). Continue out past the municipal airport. An old airplane hangar here is thought to be the oldest in Alaska. The pavement ends and wide gravel road begins at Mile 1.2. At Mile 1.7 is Crater Lake USFS Trail and City of Cordova's Skaters Cabin (rent from Bidarki Recreation Center). The 2.4-mile trail climbs to 1,500 feet. Excellent views, alpine lake with fishing for rainbow. *Watch for bears.*

At Mile 2.5 a sign notes: "road narrows next 4 miles" as it winds toward the head of the lake at Mile 5.7. The road ends at Mile 7.3 at the Power Creek Trail trailhead and a turn around area. This trail accesses both the USFS public-use cabin in Power Creek Basin and a ridge that connects with the Crater Lake trail, creating a 12-mile loop. Power Creek trail (4.2 miles long) offers spectacular scenery, with waterfalls, hanging glaciers and views of Power Creek Basin (called "surprise valley" by locals), the Chugach Range and Prince William Sound. Excellent berry picking. *CAUTION: Watch for bears.*

Drive the Copper River Highway. The first 36 miles of the highway are open, allowing access to wildlife viewing (Hartney Bay, Alagnik Slough), hiking trails (Sheridan Mountain, Haystack, Pipeline Lakes and McKinley Lake) and views of the Copper River Delta.

The Copper River Highway is closed to vehicle traffic beyond the Mile 36 bridge. The closure will last until the bridge is replaced: Current estimate is 2015 at the earliest. Two of the highway's major attractions—the Million Dollar Bridge and Childs Glacier, both at road's end—are not accessible by vehicle. There are private carriers that offer river transportation service to the other side of the bridge, and the USFS camping site at Childs Glacier.

Childs Glacier, at **Milepost C 48.3** Copper River Highway, is famous for its calving icebergs. The U.S. Forest Service recreation area across from the glacier has a wonderful viewing area, interpretive signs, nature trails, campsites and picnic tables. Because of the bridge closure, Childs Glacier is closed to vehicles but open to the public and permitees.

Orca Adventure Lodge (www.orcaadventurelodge.com/rates.html) offers boat access to the Childs Glacier viewing area via a 36-foot 660 hp vessel sheathed for running in heavy ice. They offer the trip both as transportation only or as a full tour. On the full tour they pick up clients in town and drive them to the vessel; transport-only customers meet them at their departure point

at Flag Point, **Milepost C 26.5** Copper River Highway. They land at the Million Dollar Bridge and walk the 1 mile to the viewing area. It is about a 6 hour trip from start to return.

Take a hike. A popular family hike for local residents and visitors is the **Haystack Trail** at Mile 19.1 Copper River Highway. This easy 0.8-mile trail leads up stairs and along boardwalk through a lush spruce-hemlock forest to a spot overlooking the Copper River Delta. Wonderful view and a good chance of seeing moose.

Another popular hike is the **Heney Ridge Trail** at Mile 5.1 Whitshed Road. A 3.5-mile-long hike, the first 2 miles are rated easy and offer good views of Hartney Bay. The last mile is a steep climb up to the ridge, where you are treated to spectacular views of Prince William Sound on a clear day. *Watch for bears.*

Stop by the USFS office on 2nd for current conditions and more details on area hiking trails. Phone (907) 424-7661.

Go Boating. Cordova is ideally situated for exploring Prince William Sound. Visit the harbor area, where you may charter a jet boat for fishing or sightseeing.

Mount Eyak Ski Area. Ski Hill is usually open for skiing early December to the end of April, depending on snow conditions. Winter schedule is Wednesday, Saturday, Sunday and holidays, 9 A.M. to dusk. Phone (907) 424-7766 for further information. To reach the historic single-chair lift take 1st Avenue and turn on Browning, then left on 4th Avenue, right on Council, left on 6th up to the ski area (about 1 mile from Main Street).

Brought here from Sun Valley, Idaho, the single chair lift rises 800 feet/244m up Mount Eyak and overlooks the town and harbor from 1,200 feet. Walk up, take the tour bus or drive your own vehicle. A hiking trail from the base of the mountain to the top of the chair lift and beyond connects with the Forest Service Crater Lake trail.

AREA FISHING: According to the ADF&G, "Saltwater fishing in **Orca Inlet** and adjacent eastern Prince William Sound is readily accessible from Cordova. Species include halibut, rockfish and 5 species of salmon. Trolling for salmon is best for kings in the winter and spring, and silvers in the summer and fall. Boat charters are available locally. Road-accessible fishing opportunities exist for salmon in salt water at **Fleming Spit/Lagoon**, near the ferry terminal off Orca Bay Road. Strong runs of hatchery-enhanced kings (in the spring) and silvers (August and September) return to this terminal fishery.

"Road-accessible freshwater fishing is also good in the Cordova Area. **Eyak River** supports strong returns of reds during June and July and silvers in August and September. The area at the outlet of the lake, where the road crosses, is fly-fishing only. Several streams along the **Copper River** Highway between Eyak Lake and the Million Dollar Bridge also support runs of reds and silvers. These streams include **Clear Creek, Alaganik Slough, Eighteen-mile Creek, Ibeck Creek and Twenty-mile Creek.** In addition, cutthroat trout and Dolly Varden are present in most of these streams. Lake fishing for reds, Dolly Varden and cutthroat trout is available in **McKinley Lake, Power Creek** and the **Pipeline Lake** system. Fly-out fishing from Cordova is also popular for salmon, Dolly Varden and cutthroat trout. Charter operators are available locally."

Copper River Highway

The Million Dollar Bridge at the end of the Copper River Highway. (©Sharon Nault)

Designated a Scenic Byway in 2011, the Copper River Highway crosses 584 square miles of Copper River Delta and supports the Copper River salmon fishery.

This highway begins where the Ferry Terminal road intersects with Orca Road and leads 48.6 miles northeast from Cordova to the Childs Glacier Recreation Area and the Million Dollar Bridge across the Copper River. This is a good gravel road with several U.S. Forest Service hiking trails and interpretive stops. Stop at the USFS office in Cordova for current road/trail conditions. The highway is not maintained in winter beyond Mile 12.3. Snow may prevent access to many points along the highway well into spring. Conditions vary tremendously from year to year. *NOTE: The highway is closed at Mile 36 until the bridge there is replaced (earliest estimate 2015). Orca Adventure Lodge offers boat trips to Childs Glacier/Million Dollar Bridge. Check with the US Forest Service or Chamber of Commerce for other permitted outfitters offering access to Childs Glacier.*

Construction of the Copper River Highway began in 1945. The highway was to extend to Chitina (on the Edgerton Highway), thus linking Cordova to the Richardson Highway. Construction was halted by the 1964 Good Friday earthquake, which severely damaged the highway's roadbed and bridges. The quake also knocked the north span of the historic Million Dollar Bridge into the Copper River and distorted the remaining spans. The bridge was officially re-opened to traffic in 2005 after a year-long rebuilding process.

The highway is built along the abandoned railbed of the Copper River & Northwestern Railway, although there is no evidence visible of the old railway line. Begun in 1907 and completed in 1911, the CR&NW railway connected the port of Cordova with the Kennecott Copper Mines near Kennicott and McCarthy. The mine and railway ceased operation in 1938.

ALASKA ROUTE 10
Distance is measured from Cordova (C).

C 0 CORDOVA. *See description beginning on page 647.* The mileage begins at junction of the short Ferry Terminal road and Orca Road.

C 0.3 Road to west, access boat harbor through cannery area.

C 0.7 Council Avenue to west. Access post office and boat harbor.

C 1.0 Railroad Avenue to Cordova Harbor.

C 1.1 School to south.

C 1.3 Turn south for **Whitshed Road**. At Mile 0.5 is Odiak municipal camper park (24 sites, tenting area). After passing physical milepost 5, watch for trailhead. Parking by bridge in boat launch area. At Mile 5.1 is **Heney Ridge USFS Trail** (3.5-miles); watch for bears. At Mile 5.6 (road end) is **Hartney Bay**, a popular birdwatching spot for the spring shore bird migration. Fishing from Hartney Bay bridge for Dolly Varden from May; pink and chum salmon, mid-July and August; closed for salmon upstream of bridge. Use small weighted spoons, spinners and eggs. Clam digging at low tide (license required). 🔭 🎣 ⛺

C 2.1 **Powder House Restaurant**, a popular local spot overlooking Eyak Lake. Site of CR&NW railway powder house.

C 2.2 Paved turnout to north by **Eyak Lake**. This Y-shaped lake has two 3-mile-long arms.

Heney Range to the south. Mount Eccles (elev. 2,357 feet) is the first large peak. Pointed peak beyond is Heney Peak (elev. 3,151 feet).

C 3.5 Large paved turnout overlooking Eyak Lake.

C 4.1 Low cement marker here notes those who lost their lives during construction of CR&NW railway.

For the next 2 miles, watch for bears during early morning and late evening (most often seen in June). *CAUTION: Avalanche area.*

C 5.6 Paved turnout at Eyak Lake to north. Bridge over Eyak River; access to **Eyak River USFS Trail**. The 2.2-mile trail, much of which is boardwalk over muskeg, is popular with fishermen. Fly-fishing regulations posted. Go over guardrail to the north at the east end of the bridge to access trail.

This is a good spot to see waterfowl feeding near the outlet of Eyak Lake. Watch for trumpeter swans. Although most trumpeter swans fly south for the winter, as many as 100 will winter at the outlet to Eyak Lake where the water remains ice-free.

C 5.9 **Eyak River USFS Boating Site**. Toilet and boat launch. Dolly Varden; red salmon, June–July; silvers, Aug.–Sept. Also pinks and chums. Use Vibrax spoon, spinner or salmon eggs. Fly-fishing only for salmon from 200 yards upstream of Eyak Lake dam to 200 yards downstream from the bridge at the outlet of Eyak Lake. Parking limited to 24 hours; no overnight parking allowed. 🚣

C 6.5 *CAUTION: Road narrows eastbound, no shoulders.*

C 7.3 Paved turnout to south. *CAUTION: High winds for next 4 miles. In January and February, these winds sweep across this flat with such velocity it is safer to pull off and stop.*

C 7.5 Bridge over slough.

C 7.6 First bridge across Scott River. Large, wide parking shoulder at east end of bridge to the south. Late August, silver salmon are everywhere. No fishing from bridge.

C 8 Bridge over slough waters. Gravel turnout; access to slough.

C 8.4 Scott River bridge. Between here and **Milepost 10** there are several bridges across the Scott River and the slough. Sloughs along here are from the runoff of the Scott Glacier, visible to the northeast. Bear and moose are often seen, especially in July and August. This is the only nesting area of dusky Canada geese, which winter in Oregon's Willamette Valley. Watch for them in May and August.

Moose feed in the willow groves on either side of the highway. Moose are not native to Cordova; the mountains and glaciers prevent them from entering the delta country. Today's herd stems from a transplant of 26 animals made between 1949 and 1959.

C 9.2 Bridge over slough.

C 9.5 Bridge over large river, gravel pit to south at the east end.

C 9.7 Bridge over Scott River.

C 10.5 Small turnout. Watch for beaver dams and lodges beside the highway.

C 10.7 Large paved turnout with bear-proof litter barrel to south. U.S. Forest Service Dept. of Agriculture covered pavilion with 8 interpretive plaques about Copper River Delta/Chugach National Forest areas. View of slough to south, Sheridan and Scott Glacier to north. The Copper River Delta is the largest continuous wetland on the west coast of North America. Continue over bridge. Beaver lodge to the north.

C 11 Elsner River bridge. Long gravel turnout to east of bridge.

C 11.7 State of Alaska Cordova highway maintenance station to northeast. U.S. Coast Guard station to south.

C 12 **Cordova Airport** to south; it is the Merle K. "Mudhole" Smith Airport with Alaska Airlines Terminal and Era Aviation (regional carrier). Merle K. "Mudhole" Smith was a legendary Alaska bush pilot who flew for Cordova Air Service for many years. He later served as president of the air service, which merged with Alaska Airlines in 1968.

Access north 2.5 miles via narrow road (no directional signs) to **Lake Elsner USFS Trailhead**; toilet and bear-proof litter barrel at Cabin Lake; cutthroat fishing (check current regulations for bag limits and length restrictions). 🚣

Copper River Highway (Continued)

C 12.3 *Pavement ends, gravel begins.* No road maintenance after Nov. 1.

NOTE: RV parking allowed for 1-night only in all pull-outs between Mile 13 and Mile 26.

C 13.6 Access road leads 4 miles to the terminus of **Sheridan Glacier** and trailhead for **Sheridan Mountain USFS Trail** (2.9 miles long; difficult). The glacier was named by U.S. Army explorer Capt. Abercrombie for Gen. Philip H. Sheridan of Civil War fame. Easy walking trail to good views of glacier. Outhouses, bear proof cans. Watch for bears.

C 14.5 WWII era building to the south. Troops stationed at Cordova.

C 14.8 Bridge over Sheridan River. Large gravel turnout to north at west end, raft takeout point is to the east, south side of the bridge. View of Sheridan Glacier. To the east of Sheridan Glacier is Sherman Glacier.

C 15.7 One Eye Pond informal picnic area to north.

C 16 Beautiful views of Sheridan Glacier to the northeast. Walking access to the Sheridan Glacier is available from the end of Sheridan Glacier Road.

C 16.3 Bridge over slough. Turnouts both sides, west end. Municipal landfill and quarry access.

C 16.8 Turnoff for Alaganik Slough Road (narrow, maintained gravel) to **Alaganik Slough Chugach National Forest Recreation Area**. Drive in 3 miles for fishing line recycle box, interpretive sign and trailhead for 1-mile trail for anglers. At Mile 3.2 there are picnic tables, firepits, wheelchair-accessible toilets, bear-proof garbage, aluminum can recycling, information kiosk and boat launch. Tent sites and RV parking. Interpretive boardwalk passes a viewing blind for watching birds and wildlife and ends at an elevated viewing platform. No water. Fishing for Dolly Varden, reds (July) and silver salmon (Aug.–Sept.). *Bring mosquito repellent!*

Trumpeter swans, one of the largest of all North American waterfowl (6- to 8-foot wingspan), may be seen in ponds. Alaska harbors more than 80 percent of breeding trumpeters, and more than 7 percent of the world's trumpeter population breeds in the Copper River Delta. Interpretive plaque on side road reads: "Why are Delta moose the largest and healthiest? This moose herd, first introduced in 1949, maintains its vitality primarily due to its abundant willow supply. As part of a normal cycle, accelerated by the 1964 earthquake, much of the willow is becoming unavailable to moose. As the willow grows tall, the moose can no longer reach the tender new shoots. In the future this could cause a decrease in the numbers of moose on the delta. To slow the cycle down, the Forest Service is experimenting in this area, cutting back the shrubs. This should increase the amount of available willow browse. Biologists will evaluate the response of moose to new willow growth."

C 18.1 U.S. Forest Service indicates tent sites to south at Eighteen Mile and One-eyed Pond (also RV parking).

C 18.7 Turnout to north access to **Muskeg Meander USFS Ski Trail**; length 3.1 miles. This trail offers a beautiful view of the Copper River Delta. Recommended for winter use only. This is the only cross-country ski trail in the district.

C 19.1 Haystack USFS Trail and trailhead parking to south. Easy 0.8-mile board-walk trail (lots of stairs) leads to delta overlook with interpretive signs. The overlook is an excellent place to see moose and bear. Popular family hike through lush spruce-hemlock forest; allow 45 minutes round-trip.

Several small turnouts next mile.

C 20 Large gravel turnout to south. Fishing. Beaver dam.

C 21.3 Pipeline Lakes USFS Trail to north, trailhead parking to south. The 1.8-mile trail was originally built as a water pipeline route to supply locomotives on the CR&NW railway. Segments of the pipeline are still visible. Fishing for cutthroat; bait is not allowed April 15–June 14. Trail joins McKinley Lake Trail.

C 21.5 McKinley Lake USFS Trail to north; easy 2.2-mile hike with excellent fishing for sockeye, Dolly Varden and cutthroat. Access to USFS public-use cabins: McKinley Trail cabin (100 yards from highway) and McKinley Lake cabin (45-minute walk in from highway; also accessible by boat via Alaganik Slough). Trail is a local favorite, orginally built in 1917. It has toilets, easy access and is family-friendly.

C 22.1 Entrance to **Alaganik Slough** with emerald-colored water, boat ramp, picnic tables, firepits, toilets, bear-proof garbage, covered tables, wildflowers, interpretive signs on the origin of the Eyak people and fishing access to south at west side of bridge. Red and silver salmon, July to September. Also boat access to McKinley Lake, well-loved by locals.

Alaganik Slough river bridge.

C 23.8 Salmon Creek.

C 24.8 Channel to beaver pond for spawning salmon. Beaver dam at lake outlet to north. Plaque to south reads: "Pathway to salmon rearing grounds. Channel provides access to beaver pond (north side of road) for silver salmon fry. Beaver pond can support up to 25,400 young salmon. Fallen trees and brush provide cover from predators."

Side road leads north 1 mile to **Saddlebag Glacier USFS Trail** and trailhead parking area. Tent camping and RV parking. This is an easy 3-mile trail to Saddlebag Lake and the best trail in the district for mountain biking. View of Saddlebag Glacier and icebergs; look for goats on surrounding mountains. *CAUTION: Watch for bears.*

C 26.5 Flag Point. Turnout with view of the Copper River. Side road north to boat launch. Orca Adventure Lodge customers meet here for boat ride to Childs Glacier.

Monument on the riverbank is dedicated to the men who built these bridges and "especially to the crane crew who lost their lives on July 21, 1971." Park on the south side of road to access monument.

CAUTION: Extreme high winds next 10 miles in fall and winter. Stay in your vehicle.

Two bridges cross the Copper River to Round Island, a small island with sand dunes. Some people picnic here. Check sand conditions before driving down.

In midsummer, the Copper River has half-a-million or more red and king salmon migrating 300 miles upstream to spawn in the river's clear tributaries. There is no sport-fishing in this stretch of the Copper River because of glacial silt.

Candlefish (eulachon) also spawn in the Copper River. Candlefish oil was once a significant trade item of the Coastal Indians. These fish are so oily that when dried they can be burned like candles.

C 27.5 Copper River Bridge No. 3 from Round Island to Long Island. The 6.2 miles/10 km of road on Long Island pass through a sandy landscape dotted with dunes. Long Island is in the middle of the Copper River.

C 30.8 Watch for nesting swans, other birds and beaver in slough to south of road.

C 33 View of 2 glaciers to the northwest; nearest is Goodwin, the other is Childs.

C 33.2 First bridge leaving Long Island. View to south down Hotcake Channel to Heart Island. Road built on top of a long dike which stretches across the Copper River Delta. From here to **Milepost C 37.6** there are 8 more bridges across the delta. The Copper River channels have changed and many bridges now cross almost dry gulches. *NOTE: Watch for large potholes before and after bridges through this section.*

C 34.1 Large gravel turnout to north, watch for loose sand.

C 34.3 Copper River bridge.

C 35.7 Large gravel turnout to north.

C 35.9 Bridge No. 4 crossing main flow of the Copper River. Access to river at east end of bridge. Watch for seals that follow the salmon runs up the Copper River.

C 36.1 Bridge No. 339. *NOTE: Highway closed to all traffic at this bridge.* According to the Alaska DOT: Bridge No. 339 is one of 11 bridges crossing the Copper River Delta. Naturally occurring changes to the flow of water between channels across the delta led to a dramatic increase in the amount of water running under the bridge. Due to the increased amount of water, 50 feet of 'scour', or erosion, was observed at the bridge in 2011. The scour resulted in a lowering of the channel bottom that compromised the structure of the bridge and necessitated the closure. Bridge No. 339 was constructed in 1977. Based upon the channel configurations at that time, bridge designers estimated that water under the bridge would flow at 18,500 cubic feet per second (cfs). During the summer of 2011, U.S. Geological Survey (USGS) hydrologists measured the water flow to exceed 85,000 cfs. The bridge was closed in August 2011.

C 48.3 U.S. Forest Service **Childs Glacier Recreation Area** has a large covered viewing platform for watching the 300-foot face of Childs Glacier as it calves into the Copper River. There are information boards, Copper River hiking trail, 11 large campsites, picnic tables, litter bins, toilets, and water pump. *Closed to vehicle access indefinitely due to the bridge failure on the Copper River Highway. Open to the public and permitees. Contact Cordova Ranger District at (907) 424-7661.*

C 48.6 The Million Dollar Bridge. Constructed from 1909 to 1910 for $1.4 million, the 1,550-foot-long steel truss bridge spans the Copper River. It was the longest steel bridge on the 196-mile-long Copper River and Northwestern Railway. The north span of the bridge collapsed during the 1964 earthquake. The bridge was added to the National Register of Historic Places in 2000. The bridge was officially reopened to vehicle traffic in 2005. Signed weight limit is 6,600 lbs.

Southeast Alaska

LeConte Glacier with floating icebergs is Alaska's southernmost glacier ending in saltwater. (©Sharon Nault)

Southeast Alaska, known simply as "Southeast," stretches from Dixon Entrance at the U.S.–Canada border south of Ketchikan to Icy Bay northwest of Yakutat. It is Alaska's Panhandle: A unique region where industry, transportation, recreation and community planning are dictated by spectacular topography. Its narrow strip of mainland backs up against the Coast Mountains and Canada and together with hundreds of islands it forms the Inside Passage.

Attractions include Russian and Tlingit dance performances, museums, totem poles, colorful saloons and fine dining; sportfishing, hiking trails and wilderness adventure tours by kayak, canoe and raft; glaciers and icefield flightseeing; sightseeing cruises of Glacier Bay, Misty Fiords, LeConte Glacier, the Stikine River and Tracy Arm. Bear viewing at Anan and Pack creeks, and whale watching are also top attractions.

The region is accessible by air, land or sea. Jet service is available to Juneau, Ketchikan, Wrangell, Petersburg, Sitka and Gustavus. Smaller communities are served by local commuter aircraft. The port communities of Haines and Skagway offer road connections to the Alaska Highway system via the Haines Highway and Klondike Highway 2, and there is fast ferry passenger service between the 2 cities.

Cruise ships are a popular way to visit Southeast, with hundreds of sailings and varied itineraries to choose between. See "Cruising to Alaska" in the TRAVEL PLANNING section for details.

The Alaska Marine Highway ferry system is used by both residents and visitors to get around. These ferries move people and vehicles between water locked ports and connect Southeast Alaska/Inside Passage with Prince Rupert, BC, and Bellingham, WA, and to southcentral Alaska via Cross-Gulf sailings between Juneau and Whittier. The Inter-Island Ferry Authority offers daily, year round passenger and vehicle service between Ketchikan and Hollis on Prince of Wales Island. See "Ferry Travel" in the TRAVEL PLANNING section for details.

Southeast Alaska lies between 54°40' and 60° north latitude, the same as Scotland and southern Sweden. The region measures about 125 by 400 miles, with 60 percent consisting of thousands of islands covered with dense forests of spruce, hemlock and cedar, a result of the mild, moist coastal climate. These islands make up the Alexander Archipelago and include Prince of Wales Island, the third largest island in the United States (the Big Island of Hawaii is first, followed by Kodiak).

The majority of Southeast Alaska lies within Tongass National Forest, the largest national forest in the United States. Southeast Alaska has over 5.8 million acres of designated wilderness.

Some 69,000 people live along the Inside Passage. Slightly less than 20 percent of the region's population is Native. Mostly Tlingit (KLINK-it) Indian, Haida (HI-duh) and Tsimshian (SHIM-shian). Alaska's Natives occupied this region long before Vitus Bering arrived in Alaska in 1741.

Russia controlled Alaska from the turn of the 19th century until October 18, 1867, when Alaska was transferred to the U.S. As the Russian capital of Alaska, Sitka was the center of Russia's fur-trading empire and a port of international trade, controlling trading posts from California to the Aleutians.

In 1867, the United States, under President Andrew Johnson, purchased Alaska from Russia for $7.2 million. The American flag was raised at Sitka on Oct. 18, 1867. As the Russian population moved out, and the fur trade declined, so did interest in Southeast Alaska. But it was rekindled by the salmon industry as canneries were established, the first at Klawock in 1878. Salmon canning peaked in the late 1930s then declined from overfishing.

The first significant white populations arrived because of gold. Thousands of gold seekers traveled through the Inside Passage in 1898 to Skagway and on to Canada's Klondike (sparking interest in the rest of Alaska). The largest gold ore mine of its day, the Treadwell near Juneau, began operation in 1884.

Juneau became Alaska's capital in 1906, and Southeast remained Alaska's dominant region until WWII, when military activity and the Alaska Highway shifted emphasis to Anchorage and Fairbanks.

Additional population growth came to Southeast with new timber harvesting in the 1950s. Increased government activities, as a result of Alaska statehood in 1959, brought even more people. Fishing is an ongoing industry in Southeast, with well-managed and sustainable fisheries.

The Inside Passage is the last stronghold of the American bald eagle. More than 20,000 eagles reside in the region, and sightings are frequent. Humpback and killer whales, porpoises, sea lions and seals are often observed from ferries, cruise ships and charter boats. Bear viewing opportunities are offered at Pack Creek on Admiralty Island, Anan Creek near Wrangell, Fish Creek near Hyder and Herring Cove near Ketchikan.

Ketchikan

Once the "red light" district, Creek Street is now a shopping area and visitor attraction. (©Sharon Nault)

Major Attractions:

©Sharon Nault

Saxman Totem Park, Totem Bight, Creek Street, Misty Fiords National Monument

Located on the southwest coast of Revillagigedo Island, Ketchikan is 235 miles south of Juneau and 90 miles north of Prince Rupert, BC. Ketchikan and Saxman are the only communities on Revillagigedo Island. **Population:** 8,291 (Ketchikan Gateway Borough population, which includes the city of Ketchikan, is 13,938).

Emergency Services: Phone 911 for all emergency services. **Alaska State Troopers**, at **Milepost K 7.3** North Tongass Highway, phone (907) 225-5118. **City Police**, phone (907) 225-6631. **Coast Guard**, Base Ketchikan, 1300 Stedman St., phone (907) 228-0340; or Juneau, phone (907) 463-2000. **Veterinarian:** Ketchikan Veterinary, phone (907) 225-6051. **Hospital**, Ketchikan General at 3100 Tongass Ave., phone (907) 225-5171.

Visitor Information: The Ketchikan Visitors Bureau operates the **Ketchikan Visitor Information Center**, located downtown at Berth 2. Open daily during business hours, May through September, and 8 A.M. to 5 P.M. weekdays from October through April. Public restrooms. Write them at 50 Front St., Suite 203, Ketchikan 99901; phone (907) 225-6166 or 1-800-770-3300; fax (907) 225-4250; email: info@visit-ketchikan.com; www.visit-ketchikan.com. There is also a seasonal sub-station located on the docks at Berth 3 and open daily May–Sept.

Revillagigedo Island is located in Tongass National Forest. Maps, brochures, trip planning assistance and general information on recreational opportunities in Tongass National Forest and other federal lands in Alaska are available at the **Southeast Alaska Discovery Center**, 50 Main St., Ketchikan, AK 99901; phone (907) 228-6220, fax (907) 228-6234; www.alaskacenters.gov/ketchikan.cfm.

The Ketchikan-Misty Fiords U.S. Forest Service Ranger District encompasses 3.2 million acres of Tongass National Forest land in Southeast Alaska, maintaining 60 miles of trails, 2 campgrounds, and 30 public-use cabins (most accessible by floatplane or boat). The district office is located at 3031 Tongass Ave.; open 8 A.M. to 4:30 P.M. weekdays; phone (907) 225-2148; www.fs.usda.gov/tongass/. Cabins and campsites can be reserved through the National Recreation Reservation Service (NRRS); phone toll-free 1-877-444-6777 or visit www.recreation.gov.

Elevation: Sea level. **Climate:** Rainy. Yearly average rainfall is 162 inches and snowfall is 36.9 inches. Average summer temperature if 55°F and average winter temperature is 31°F. **Radio:** KTKN-AM 930, KRBD-FM 105.9, KGTW-FM 106.7, KFMJ-FM 99.9. **Television:** KUBD, KTOO (Ketchikan) and 43 cable channels. *Ketchikan Daily News* (daily); *The Local Paper* (weekly).

Private Aircraft: Ketchikan International Airport on Gravina Island; elev. 88 feet; length 7,500 feet; asphalt; fuel 100LL, A. Ketchikan Harbor seaplane base downtown; fuel 80, 100, A.

Ketchikan is located on the southwest side of Revillagigedo (ruh-vee-uh-guh-GAY-doh) Island, on Tongass Narrows opposite Gravina Island. One interpretation of the name Ketchikan is derived from a Tlingit name, Kitschk-Hin, which translates to "spread wings of a prostrate eagle." Ketchikan Creek flows through the town, emptying into Tongass Narrows. Before Ketchikan was settled, the area at the mouth of the creek was a Tlingit Indian fish camp. Settlement began with interest in both mining and fishing. The first salmon cannery moved here in 1886, operating under the name of Tongass Packing Co. It burned down in August 1889. Gold was discovered nearby in 1898. Ketchikan was incorporated in 1900.

As mining waned, the fishing industry began to grow. By the 1930s, more

than a dozen salmon canneries had been built. During the peak years of the canned salmon industry, Ketchikan earned the title of "Salmon Capital of the World." But overfishing caused a drastic decline in salmon by the 1940s. Today, Southeast Alaska accounts for slightly more than half the pink salmon harvested in Alaska. Trident Seafood Corporation, a shore-based cannery in Ketchikan, produces canned salmon, operating from early July through September.

As fishing reached a low point, the timber industry expanded. The first sawmill was originally built in 1898 at Dolomi on Prince of Wales Island to cut timber for the Dolomi Mine. It was dismantled and moved to Ketchikan and rebuilt in 1903. A large pulp mill was constructed a few miles northwest of town in 1953 at Ward Cove. It closed in 1997.

Tourism is an extremely important industry here. Ketchikan is Alaska's seventh largest city. The closest city in British Columbia is Prince Rupert. Ketchikan is Alaska's first city and the first port of call on the Alaska Marine Highway's northbound Inside Passage sailings from Bellingham, WA, and Prince Rupert, BC. The Inter-Island Ferry Authority's MV *Stikine* connects Ketchikan with Prince of Wales Island.

Ketchikan is a linear waterfront city, with much of its 3-mile-long business district suspended above water on pilings driven into the bottom of Tongass Narrows. Its homes cling to the steep wooded hillside, many reached by "staircase streets"—lengths of wooden stairs rather than paved road. All of Ketchikan's original streets and walkways were built as wooden trestles because of the steep and rocky terrain.

Ketchikan is an easy town to explore on foot or by tour bus. The waterfront is the center of the city, and most attractions are within walking distance of where the cruise ships dock. Pick up walking tour map at the Visitors Bureau on this dock. Highlights of the walking tour include: St. John's Episcopal Church; the Grant Street Trestle, on the National Register of Historic Places; the Ketchikan Creek Fish Ladder; and other landmarks. You may also arrange for tours by booking them while at the Visitors Bureau.

The area supports 5 public grade schools, 4 parochial grade schools, a junior high school, 2 high schools and the University of Alaska Southeast campus.

Lodging & Services

Accommodations at **Super 8 Motel** (1-800-800-8000; www.super8.com), Best Western Plus Landing Hotel (907/225-5166; www.landinghotel.com), Cape Fox Lodge (907/225-8001; www.capefoxlodge.com), the historic Gilmore Hotel (907/225-9423; www.gilmorehotel.com), and Inn at Creek Street & New York Hotel (907/225-0246; www.thenewyorkhotel.com). There are also several bed-and-breakfasts in Ketchikan.

Ketchikan Hostel is located downtown in the United Methodist Church at Grant and Main Streets. The hostel accommodates 19; separate male and female dorms for sleeping, floor mattresses provided (bring sleeping bags or there is bedding for rent); showers and kitchen facilities. Open June 1 to August 31. Check-in time is 7–9 A.M. and 5–11 P.M. (will open for late ferry arrivals; phone from terminal as soon as you arrive). Reservations recommended. Phone (907) 225-3319 (summer); email ketchikanhostel@gmail.com.

Shopping and restaurants are located downtown and at Plaza Mall on Tongass Avenue (North Tongass Highway). There is a laundromat (with showers). Ketchikan also has a Walmart, located 4 miles north of downtown off the Tongass Highway.

There is a bookstore on Stedman Street, with a good selection of Alaska titles as well as current bestsellers and other fiction and non-fiction titles.

The new Ketchikan Library offers free WiFi, restrooms, plug-ins for personal computers, public computers available for 30 minute intervals (with I.D.). Here, mountain views and comfortable chairs make a comfortable time-out from travel. Hours are Mon.–Wed. 10 A.M. to 8 P.M. and Thurs.–Sat. 10 A.M. to 6 P.M. Located at 1110 Copper Ridge Lane. Acceess the Library at the south end of Berth 4 (along the waterfront promenade). Phone (907) 225-3331.

Ketchikan's 35,000-square-foot Gateway Aquatic Center connects to the existing Recreation Center and offers visitors a place to swim laps, take a sauna and work out, all for the price of a $6 admission fee. The Aquatic Center has an 8-lane main competition pool; 1-meter and 3-meter diving boards; a separate warm-water pool with walk-in entry; 2 slides, including a twisty one called the "Tongass Tornado"; sauna; locker rooms and family changing rooms with showers; fitness and weight room. Located at 601 Schoenbar Road; phone (907) 228-6650; www.borough.ketchikan.ak.us/parks_and_rec/parks.htm.

Camping

There are 3 public campgrounds in the Ketchikan vicinity: Signal Creek and Last Chance, U.S. Forest Service campgrounds at Ward Lake Recreation Area, approximately 10 miles north of downtown; and Settlers

Cove State Recreation Site, 18 miles north of the city via North Tongass Highway (see highway log this section). Advance reservations can be made for designated sites at the Forest Service campgrounds through the NRRS; phone toll-free 1-877-444-6777 or visit www.recreation.gov.

The only private RV park with hookups is Clover Pass Resort at **Milepost K 14.2** North Tongass Highway, phone 1-800-410-2234.

The Walmart at Mile 4 North Tongass Highway may allow overnight camping in their parking lot for self-contained RVs; check with store.

A dump station is located at Ketchikan

KETCHIKAN ADVERTISERS

Super 8 Motel................................Ph. (907) 225-9088

Filled with exhibits, the Southeast Alaska Discovery Center also offers Ketchikan visitors trip planning assistance. (©Sharon Nault)

Street Department Warehouse Mile 2.5 Tongass Highway. It is available weekdays from 8 A.M. to 4:30 P.M. Ask inside the building to have the potable water turned on; you must bring your own hose.

Transportation

Air: Daily scheduled jet service is provided from the Ketchikan International Airport by Alaska Airlines to other Southeast cities, Anchorage and Seattle, WA. Commuter and charter service is available to other Southeast communities via Pacific Airways, Promech Air, Southeast Aviation and Taquan Air.

Airport terminal, across Tongass Narrows on Gravina Island, is reached via shuttle ferry (5-minute ride one way) departing at half-hour intervals from the airport parking area on Tongass Avenue (North Tongass Highway), 2.8 miles from downtown.

Ferry: Two ferry systems operate out of Ketchikan—the Alaska Marine Highway System and the Inter-Island Ferry Authority.

Alaska Marine Highway vessels connect Ketchikan with all mainline southeastern Alaska port cities, Prince Rupert, BC, and Bellingham, WA, and the Cross Gulf ferry. There are also daily Alaska state ferry connections between Ketchikan and Metlakatla (1 hr. 15 min.). For schedules, fares and information, turn to the ALASKA MARINE HIGHWAY section.

The Alaska Marine Highway Terminal is located 2.3 miles north of downtown Ketchikan on Tongass Avenue (North Tongass Highway). The terminal building has a large waiting room, vending machines, restrooms, public phones and brochure racks; phone (907) 225-6182 or toll-free 1-800-642-0066. Taxicabs meet most ferry arrivals. Bus schedules are available in the terminal building and there is a bus stop nearby.

The Inter-Island Ferry Authority's MV *Stikine* or MV *Prince of Wales* provide daily passenger and vehicle service of 3 hours between Ketchikan and Hollis/Clark Bay on Prince of Wales Island. It departs Ketchikan at 3:30 P.M. for Hollis/Clark Bay from the IFA dock adjacent the Alaska Marine Highway terminal. Return trip departs Hollis/Clark Bay at 8:00 A.M. Check with the IFA reservation desk located inside the Alaska

Marine Highway terminal building; phone (907) 225-4838. For current information and reservations visit www.interisland ferry.com.

See also "Ferry Travel" in the TRAVEL PLANNING section.

Bus: The free, downtown loop, Salmon Run shuttle service has a decorated bus which travels a 20-minute circuit between popular destinations from May to September. The silver bus line provides service from the ferry terminal and airport south to downtown and north to Walmart. The silver line bus also serves Saxman totem park south of the city and north of the city to to Totem Bight State Park. Regular fares $1 per ride or $.50 senior/student. Contact Ketchikan Gateway Borough Transportation Services with questions, phone (907) 225-8726; www.borough.ketchikan.ak.us/bus/info.htm.

Parking: There is 2-hour on-street parking available. When *The MILEPOST®* visited Ketchikan last summer, we had no problem parking our camper on the street, but there are no parking lots downtown to accommodate large RVs. It is best to find large-rig parking away from the downtown and ride the buses or rent a car.

Car Rental: Available from Alaska Car Rental on Tongass Avenue, phone (907) 225-5000 or toll-free 1-800-662-0007; First City Rental, phone (907) 225-7368; Budget Rent-a-Car, phone (907) 225-6003; Alaska Smart Rentals, phone (907) 225-1753.

Taxi: Sourdough Taxi Co., Alaska Cab and Yellow Taxi, phone (907) 225-5555. Taxicabs meet ferry arrivals and meet airport arrivals at the Ketchikan-side terminal areas.

Highways: North Tongass and South Tongass highways (see logs this section).

Cruise Ships: Ketchikan is first port-of-call for many cruise ships to Alaska. There are anywhere from 1 to 5 ships docked at Ketchikan on any given day in summer. See "Cruising to Alaska" in the TRAVEL PLANNING section.

Tour Boats: Harbor cruises and day cruises to Misty Fiords available. Contact Alaska Coastal Quest, phone (907) 225-3498; www.smallshipalaskacruises.com.

Private Boats: Two public docks downtown, Thomas Basin and Casey Moran Harbor (City Float), provide transient moorage. In the West End District, 1 mile from

downtown, Bar Harbor has restrooms, moorage, showers. No gas available. Permits required. Moorage space in Ketchikan is limited; all private boats should contact the harbormaster's office at (907) 228-5632 prior to arrival to secure a spot.

Attractions

Enjoy the Waterfront Promenade. This unique walkway provides a pedestrian path along Ketchikan's busy shoreline, with plenty of photo viewpoints, helpful signage, historical markers, unique benches for sitting and enjoy the view, and colorful art. The completed section of the Waterfront Promenade starts at Tongass Avenue near cruise ship Berth 4, and continues past Casey Moran Harbor, Berth 3, and the Ketchikan Visitor Bureau's Visitor Annex (with public restrooms) down past "The Rock Statues" to the Downtown Visitors Bureau on the concrete docks at Berth 2. The promenade continues past the Salmon Landing market, behind the Great Alaskan Lumberjack Show, to the Federal Building. Additional platforms extend out into Thomas Basin for scenic views and fishing.

Cape Fox Hill Funicular. Constructed in 1990, this automated cable car traverses a 70 percent incline, rising 130 vertical feet from Creek Street to the top of Cape Fox Hill and the lobby of the Cape Fox Lodge. The hotel has an extensive collection of Native art. Cape Fox Lodge is also accessible by road.

The funicular operates very much like an elevator. From Creek Street, press the call button for the funicular. When the doors open, get inside and push the Up button to go up or the Down button to go down. During the summer months, a fee is charged to ride the funicular.

Return to Creek Street by following Married Man's Trail (boardwalk and stairs) back down the hill through the trees. Great views and good photo ops of downtown from this trail.

Southeast Alaska Discovery Center, located at 50 Main Street, is 1 of 4 Alaska Public Lands Information Centers (APLICs) in the state (the others are located in Fairbanks, Anchorage and Tok). The Discovery Center, like the other APLICs, offers trip planning assistance, information on Alaska public lands, and a well-stocked Alaska Geographic Association bookstore and a gift shop. In addition, the Discovery Center has interpretive exhibits on Native Traditions, Rain Forest, Eco-system, Wildlife, Natural Resources and Art. The 200-seat theatre presents a multi-media program for visitors.

The Discovery Center is open 8 A.M to 3 P.M. daily, May to September, and noon to 8 P.M. on Fridays in winter. Admission fee $5, 15 years and under free. Phone (907) 228-6220 or www.alaska centers.gov/ketchikan.cfm.

City Park is a beautiful park offering a pleasant and convenient rest stop for walking tourists and a popular outdoor area for Ketchikan residents. The park's small ponds were once used as holding ponds for Ketchikan's first hatchery. The generically named City Park is located along Park Avenue. Hiking access to the park is via a footbridge from Totem Heritage Center.

Whale Park, conveniently located between the cruise ship docks and Creek Street on Mill Street, is shaped like a whale. A very small park, it is a popular rest stop and has the Chief Kyan Totem Pole (carved by Israel Shotridge) and the historic Knox

Brothers Clock.

Tours, tours, and more tours. From narrated trolley rides and historical sightseeing cruises to tours by airplane and amphibious boat, Ketchikan has an abundance of tour opportunities, many tailored for the thousands of cruise ship passengers spending the day here. Stop by Ketchikan Visitors Bureau's tour center, located on the cruise ship docks at 131 Front Street, where a couple of dozen vendors are on hand, offering everything from fishing charters to zipline tours.

The zipline tours are a popular attraction in Alaska. Also called "canopy tours," they offer visitors the opportunity to glide through the treetops, or forest canopy, hanging from cables strung between platforms high up in the trees. Alaska Canopy Tours, located at the Alaska Rainforest Sanctuary (see South Tongass Highway log this section), is one such tour operator. Independent travelers should phone (907) 225-5503 to inquire about availability.

Totem poles, a major attraction in Ketchikan, are scattered around the city. Major collections are found at the Totem Heritage Center, Saxman and Totem Bight (see detailed descriptions this section).

Saxman Totem Park, located 2.3 miles south of downtown via South Tongass Highway, is included on the itineraries of most local sightseeing companies. The totem park, open year-round, has 21 totems and a clan house. Guided tours May through September include demonstrations at the Carving Center and performances by the Cape Fox Dance group at the Beaver Clanhouse. For more information email the Cape Fox Tours office at info@capefoxtours.com, www.capefoxtours.com.

Totem Heritage Center, at 601 Deermount St., houses 33 totem poles and fragments retrieved from deserted Tlingit and Haida Indian villages. This national landmark collection comprises the largest exhibit of original totems in the United States. Facilities include craft exhibits, a full range of classes (a few for children) and the formal Native Arts Study Program and reference library. Outside the center are 2 poles by Tlingit carver (and National Living Treasure), Nathan Jackson.

Guided tours during summer months. Admission fee charged. Summer hours are 8 A.M. to 5 P.M. daily. Winter hours (October to April) are 1–5 P.M. Monday through Friday. Phone (907) 225-5900.

Totem Bight State Historical Park, located at **Milepost 9.9** North Tongass Highway, contains an excellent model of a Tlingit community house and 14 totems in a beautiful wooded setting. The park began as a Civilian Conservation Corps (CCC) project in 1938, when a U.S. Forest Service program aimed at salvaging abandoned totem poles by using older skilled Native carvers and young, unskilled apprentices to reconstruct or copy the poles. Alaskan architect Linn Forrest designed the model Native village, which was originally called Mud Bight. The name was changed to Totem Bight and title to the land transferred to the state in 1959 and added to the National Register of Historic Places in 1970.

The community house, or clanhouse, is representative of those found in many early 19th century Indian villages. The totems reflect Haida and Tlingit cultures.

Potlatch Park, adjacent Totem Bight, has

South Tongass Highway

The Saxman area around these totems was founded in the late 19th century. (©Sharon Nault)

The 12-mile-long South Tongass Highway provides access to Saxman Totem Park, Rotary Beach Park, Mountain Point and George Inlet.

Distance from downtown Ketchikan (K) is shown.

K 0 Stedman Street and Totem Way intersection.

K 0.1 Ketchikan Creek Bridge. Walking access to Creek Street and area businesses. Bike path begins on the south side with uneven sidewalks. It extends to Saxman Village. It begins again about 0.2 mile north of Rotary Park and extends to Milepost 5.

K 0.3 Deermount Avenue. Totem Heritage Center is 0.2 mile up this road. Access City Park by walking across bridge in front of the center.

K 0.9 U.S. Coast Guard Station Ketchikan, established in 1989, provides search and rescue, maritime law enforcement and environmental protection.

K 2.3 Turnoff for Totem Row Road. Good view of Saxment Totem Park by looking up this road. On foot, this is where you can access the park, or, continue on Tongess Highway for vehicle access, 0.1 mile.

K 2.4 Vehicles turn on Bear Clan Street for **Saxman Totem Park**. Access for large parking lot with short footpath by restrooms, carving house, tribal house and gift shop. This is an easy attraction to enjoy for an independent traveler. Not all cultural events occur daily. If you are arriving in Ketchikan by cruise ship, make tour reservations through the shore excursion office aboard ship. Tour may include: a short video introducing the culture and history of Saxman, a visit to the Beaver Clan House, where visitors are welcomed by song and dance by the Cape Fox Dance group and possible demonstrations. If you are visiting Ketchikan and not arriving by cruise ship, email info@capefoxtours.com for information on how to join one of the tour groups. **SAXMAN** (pop. 434) was founded in 1896 by Tlingit Alaska Natives and named after a Presbyterian missionary who served the Tlin-

git people.

K 2.6 Petro Express gas station and convenience store to west.

K 3.4 Large parking area.

K 3.5 Rotary Beach Recreation Area; Large parking area. Shelter and tables, swimming in warm weather.

K 5 Parking area. Mountain Point, a point of land at the south coast of Revillagigedo Island, was named in 1883 by Lt. Comdr. H.E. Nichols, USN. Access to good salmon fishing from shore in July and August.

K 5.6 Public boat launch, toilets.

K 5.7 South Tongass Fire Dept.

K 6 Several small turnouts along coast.

K 8 Turnoff on Wood Road for **Alaska Rainforest Sanctuary** (0.2 mile) and Alaska Canopy Tours. Alaska Rainforest Sanctuary consists of a network of boardwalk and gravel paths that take visitors past Herring Cove, a former logging camp, then through dense hemlock and spruce rainforest. Admission fee charged; inquire at the gift shop. The canopy (zipline) tours are offered as daily shore excursions for Ketchikan cruise ship passengers. Independent travelers should phone (907) 225-5503 regarding availability.

K 8.2 Herring Cove bridge. Private hatchery for chum, king and silver salmon. Road at the south end of bridge leads to small parking and viewing area just prior to a private hatchery road. There is bear watching from here and the bridge when salmon are running.

K 8.4 *Pavement ends, gravel begins.*

K 8.7 Whitman Creek and bridge.

K 10.2 Scenic waterfall.

K 10.9 Another scenic waterfall.

K 11.2 Large gravel turnout.

K 11.5 Hole in the Wall bar and boat dock (lots of stairs).

K 12.9 Road ends. According to the U.S. Forest Service, it is a 1-mile walk up John Mountain Trail from the trailhead parking at Beaver Falls Power House to Lower Silvis Lake picnic area. Large turnaround area. Multiple hiking trails starting from this area.

North Tongass Highway

From downtown Ketchikan, North Tongass Highway follows the shoreline of Revillagigedo Island northwest along Tongass Narrows, then north along Clover Passage to deadend at Settlers Cove State Recreation Site. The 18.4-mile-long North Tongass Highway is paved but in need of resurfacing. The work was begun in 2009.

Distance from downtown Ketchikan (K) is shown.

K 0 Ketchikan Visitors Bureau on the cruise ship docks at Front and Mission streets. Follow Front Street north.

© Sharon Nault

K 0.3 To the west is tiny Eagle Park, dominated by the massive **"Thundering Wings"** carving by Tlingit master Nathan Jackson. Front Street becomes Tongass Avenue northbound after passing through the Tunnel (built in 1954).

K 1.2 Traffic light at Washington Street. The Plaza shopping mall and McDonald's to west. Safeway; gas station. Also access to Super 8 motel. This is the West End commercial zone, much of which was built on fill in the late 1960s and early 1970s.

K 1.7 Bar Harbor boat basin to west.

K 2 Ketchikan Ranger Station/Misty Fiords National Monument to west.

K 2.2 Carlanna Lake Road. Access east to Ketchikan General Hospital.

K 2.3 Entrance to **Ketchikan Ferry Terminal** for the Alaska Marine Highway to west; Best Western on east side of highway. Ferry terminal building has seating area, restrooms, vending machines and brochure racks.

The Inter-Island Ferry Authority (IFA) ticket desk for MV *Stikine* service to Hollis is located inside the ferry terminal. The *Stikine* ferry loading dock is to the south of the terminal building. Once daily departures from Ketchikan at 3:30 P.M. arrive in Hollis at 6:30 P.M.

Tongass Avenue becomes North Tongass Highway northbound.

K 2.4 Main branch U.S. post office.

K 2.6 Carlanna Creek and bridge.

K 2.7 Texaco gas station.

K 2.8 Entrance to Ketchikan International Airport parking and airport ferry shuttle service.

K 3.1 Viewpoint to west. Airport terminal is visible across Tongass Narrows on Gravina Island.

K 4 Don King Road; Wells Fargo bank to east and access to Walmart.

K 5.5 Small, double-ended, viewpoint to west overlooking Tongass Narrows. Floatplane dock.

K 5.7 Ketchikan city limits.

K 6 Cannery Creek and bridge.

K 6.6 Large dirt turnout with unobstructed view of Ward Cove Cannery and Ketchikan Pulp Mill.

The cannery was built in 1912 and purchased in 1928 by Wards Cove Packing Co. The pulp mill was built in 1953 and closed in 1997.

K 6.7 Ward Lake Road (open to hikers and bikers only); access to Ward Lake Recreation Area (see description at **Milepost 7**).

K 6.9 Ward Creek and bridge. Ketchikan sawmill, owned by Ketchikan Pulp Co.

K 7 Junction with 6.7-mile Revilla Road to **USFS Ward Lake Recreation Area**, Harriet Hunt Road and Brown Mountain Road (log of road follows).

Mile 1.3 Revilla Road: Turn off for paved access road to Ward Lake day-use area (0.6 mile) and Signal Creek campground (1 mile). **Ward Lake day-use area** has 3 picnic shelters, paved parking and a nature trail. The easy 1.3-mile Ward Lake Trail circles Ward Lake through spruce-hemlock forest. Single-vehicle picnic sites and access to the walk-in Grassy Point picnic area located along access road between the day-use area and road end at Signal Creek Campground. Also on this stretch of road is parking for Perseverance Lake Trail; a 2.2-mile gravel and boardwalk trail to Perseverance Lake (elev. 518 feet). *Watch for black bears.* Three C's Group Campground, adjacent Perseverance Lake Trail, open for overflow camping only. **Signal Creek Campground** has 24 gravel sites (2 are drive-in) with tables, firepits, campground host; water and pit toilets; and a $10 camping fee. Phone 1-877-444-6777 for reservations. Access to Ward Lake Trail.

Mile 2.3 Revilla Road: Turn off for **Last Chance Campground**, with 19 gravel sites, drive-in camping units, 17 are wheelchair accessible, tables, pit toilets, water, $10 camping fee. Phone 1-877-444-6777 for reservations.

Mile 2.4 Revilla Road: Pavement ends and gravel begins. Turn on Connell Lake Road for trailhead to 2-mile Connell Lake Trail.

Mile 6.5 Revilla Road: Turnoff for Harriett Hunt Road, which leads 2.4 miles to Harriet Hunt Lake Recreation Area; parking, pit toilets and fishing.

Mile 6.6 Revilla Road: Road dead ends just past turnoff for Brown Mountain Road (gravel). Brown Mountain Road ends at Dude Mountain Trail, which is a 1-mile ascent to the 2,848-foot peak.

K 7.2 WARD COVE. Post office, gas station and Ward Cove Market.

K 7.3 Alaska State Troopers Ketchikan Post, phone (907) 225-5118.

K 8.7 Refuge Cove State Recreation Site to west; 14 picnic sites.

K 9.9 Totem Bight State Historical Park; parking area, restrooms, bookstore and phones. A short trail leads through the woods to Totem Bight community house and totem park. A striking setting. Don't miss this!

The park's totems are either restored originals or duplicates carved by Natives as part of a U.S. Forest Service program begun in 1938 using Civilian Conservation Corps (CCC) funds.

© Sharon Nault

The park's clanhouse or community house is representative of those found in many early 19th century Indian villages in Southeast.

K 10 Paved turnout with viewpoint.

K 10.8 Grocery store and Tesoro gas station.

K 11.7 Whipple Creek.

K 11.9 Gas station and convenience store. Pond Reef Road.

K 12.2 South Higgins Point Road winds 1.2 miles west through residential area to deadend at Higgins Point.

K 12.9 Scenic viewpoint overlooking **Guard Islands lighthouse**. This light marks the easterly entrance to Tongass Narrows/Clarence Strait. It was established in 1904; first lit in 1924; and automated in 1969. Present optic is solar powered. It is an active navigation aid.

K 14.2 Junction with 0.9-mile-long North Point Higgins Road. Turnoff on Knudson Cove Road, just west of highway, and drive 0.5 mile for Knudson Cove Marina and public boat launch. (Knudson Cove Road rejoins North Tongass Highway at **Milepost K 14.7.**) North Point Higgins Road provides access to Clover Pass Resort, 0.6 mile west.

K 14.7 Knudson Cove Road west to public boat launch (0.3 mile from highway).

K 15.4 Paved turnout.

K 15.7 Gravel turnout.

K 16 Watch for Deer.

K 16.1 First Waterfall Creek.

K 16.6 Turnoff for Salmon Falls Resort; phone (907) 225-2752.

K 16.7 Second Waterfall Creek.

K 18.2 Settlers Cove Road leads to **Settlers Cove State Recreation Site**, which has a 14-site campground ($10 camping fee) and a day-use parking area; picnic area with tables, water, picnic shelters, pit toilets, campround host, hiking trails (descriptions follow). Access to good gravel beach. Open May 1–Sept. 30. Campers register at fee station. Site is gated from 10 P.M. to 6 A.M.

The Lower Lunch Falls Loop Trail (¼ mile) is a scenic boardwalk hike through spruce-hemlock forest with access to rocky beach. This trail is wheelchair accessible only to the bridge over Lunch Creek, where you may see spawning pink salmon in August. The upper trail follows Lunch Creek for 3.5 miles and provides additional wildlife viewing opportunities for black bears and Sitka black-tailed deer.

K 18.4 Road ends. Trailhead parking.

24 totem poles and a recreated Native village which includes a clan house. For more information go to their website: www.potlatch park.com.

Creek Street, a boardwalk street on pilings that spans Ketchikan Creek near the Stedman Street bridge, was once Ketchikan's "red-light district," where Black Mary, Dolly, Frenchie and others plied their trade for over half a century until 1954. At one time nearly 20 houses lined the far side of Ketchikan Creek. Today, the remaining old houses have been restored and along with newer structures house a variety of shops. Dolly's House, a former brothel, is open during the summer (admission $5 charged).

In late July, watch for salmon in Ketchikan Creek. Besides shopping and seeing the creek, visitors can take a ride on the Cape Fox Hill Funicular.

Misty Fiords National Monument. Located east of Ketchikan, Misty Fiords National Monument encompasses 2.3 million acres of wilderness and is known for its spectacular scenery. Taking its name from the almost constant precipitation characteristic of the area, Misty Fiords is covered with dense forests of Sitka spruce, western hemlock and cedar, which grow on nearly vertical slopes from sea level to mountain tops. Dramatic waterfalls cascade into glacially carved fjords. The monument is bisected by the 100-mile-long Behm Canal, extraordinary among natural canals for its length and depth. New Eddystone Rock, a 237-foot volcanic plug, rises straight out of Behm Canal and is visible for miles.

The monument is accessible by boat or by floatplane from Ketchikan. Tours of Misty Fiords by floatplane and by boat are available out of Ketchikan. Some cruise ships include Behm Canal and Rudyerd Bay in their itineraries. Rudyerd Bay is also a popular destination for sea kayakers.

For more information on the monument, stop by the Southeast Alaska Discovery Center on Main Street in Ketchikan, phone (907) 228-6220, or the U.S. Forest Service office at 3031 Tongass Ave., phone (907) 225-2148; www.fs.usda.gov/tongass/.

Tongass Historical Museum, located in the Centennial Building on Dock Street. The museum features photos and artifacts of early-day Ketchikan and its development from Native fish camp to Alaska's "First City." The museum is open in summer (May 1 to Sept. 30) from 8 A.M. to 5 P.M. daily. Winter (October 1 to April 30) hours are 1–5 P.M. Tue.–Fri., 10 A.M.–4 P.M. Sat. and closed on Sun.–Mon. The Raven Stealing the Sun totem stands at the entrance. Salmon viewing platforms. Ketchikan's Centennial Building, which was built to commemorate the purchase of Alaska from Russia in 1867. Phone (907) 225-5600 for more information. Admission fee $3 for 13 and older.

Charter a boat. About 120 vessels operate out of Ketchikan for half-day, all-day or overnight sightseeing or fishing trips and transport to USFS public-use cabins and outlying communities. Outfits like Alaska Coastal Quest (www.smallship alaskacruises.com) offer sightseeing cruises aboard their 60-foot yacht *Misty Fjord* to see whales, glaciers, birds and other wildlife. Stop by the Visitor Information Centers on the cruise ship docks.

Go sea kayaking. Ketchikan is located on Revillagigedo Island. Circumnavigation of the island is about a 150-mile trip. The east coast of Revillagigedo Island lies within Misty Fiords National Monument Wilderness. Popular kayaking destinations within the monument include Rudyerd Bay, Punchbowl Cove and Walker Cove.

For trip planning help, stop by the Southeast Alaska Discovery Center on Main Street, phone (907) 228-6220, or the U.S. Forest Service office at 3031 Tongass Avenue, phone (907) 225-2148; www.fs.usda.gov/tongass/.

Charter planes operate from the airport and from the waterfront on floats and are available for fly-in fishing, bear viewing, service to lodges and smaller communities and flightseeing, including Misty Fiords.

Great Alaskan Lumberjack Show, featuring events such as buck sawing, axe throwing, power sawing, springboard chop, logrolling duels, and a 50-foot tree climb. Covered grandstand seating. Located 1 block off cruise ship docks near Salmon Landing Market. Shows performed daily, May through September. Phone toll-free 1-888-320-9049 or (907) 225-9050; www.lumberjack sports.com or www.capefoxtours.com.

Arts and entertainment. The Main Street Gallery is a community art gallery committed to community artist development. The gallery hosts exhibits year-round and displays a wide variety of mediums from local and national artists, as well as traveling exhibits. The Main Street Gallery is home to the Ketchikan Area Arts & Humanities Council, phone (907) 225-2211; www.Ket chikanarts.org.

Across the street from the Main Street Gallery are the First City Players, located in the old Fireside/Elks Building at 335 Main Street (destined to become Ketchikan's Performing Arts Center and home to both the First City Players and Ketchikan Theatre Ballet).

First City Players lineup for summer 2014 begins in June. Check the website for scheduled attractions. The 16th annual Gigglefeet Dance Festival takes place at Ketchikan High School Auditorium, in early August. Celebrating the joy and diversity of dance, Gigglefeet performances feature choreographers and dancers of many different schools of training, varied ages and cultures. For more information, contact First City Players box office at (907) 225-4792; email info@firstcityplayers.org; www.first cityplayers.org.

Special Events. The Alaska Hummingbird Festival takes place in the spring. Local parade and vending booths with food, games and crafts for the 4th of July. The Blueberry Festival and the Gigglefest Dance Festival are held in August. For details, go to www.visit–ketchikan.com.

Hiking trails, for all levels of ability, are accessible by road in the Ketchikan area. Three U.S. Forest Service trails are accessible from Revilla Road north of Ketchikan (see **Milepost 7** North Tongass Highway). Ward Lake Nature Trail is an easy 1.3-mile path around Ward Lake that connects facilities within Ward Lake Recreation Area and has interpretive signs on old-growth forests. The 2.3-mile Perseverance Lake Trail begins near Grassy Point picnic area in the Ward Lake Recreation Area providing access to fishing in Perseverance Lake. Past Ward Lake Recreation Area is the 2-mile Connell Lake Trail.

An easy and accessible hike is the Rainbird Trail. Just 0.5 mile from downtown on the 3rd Avenue Bypass, this trail offers spectacular views of the Ketchikan Waterfront

Professional loggers demonstrate their trade in the Great Alaskan Lumberjack Show. (©Sharon Nault)

without a lot of effort.

A strenuous hike but offering spectacular views as a reward is the Deer Mountain Trail, which begins at the corner of Fair and Deermount streets. The 3-mile, 3,001-foot ascent gives trekkers an excellent vantage of downtown Ketchikan and Tongass Narrows. Also access to Deer Mountain cabin, the only USFS public-use cabin accessible by trail from Ketchikan. (The cabin is being managed as a shelter, and is therefore available on a first-come, first-served basis with no fee.)

Picnic areas. Drive out to Settlers Cove State Recreation Site at **Milepost 18.2** North Tongass Highway. **Settlers Cove** has a day-use area with picnic tables. From the picnic area take the Lower Lunch Falls Loop, a ¼ mile boardwalk trail through lush forest that also provides access to the rocky beach.

Other picnic areas accessible from the North Tongass Highway are Refuge Cove State Recreation Site at **Milepost 8.7**, and picnic facilities along Ward Lake, accessible from Mile 1.3 Revilla Road.

Views of Tongass Narrows from **Rotary Beach Recreation Area**, south of downtown at **Milepost 3.5** South Tongass Highway.

Annual King Salmon Derby is held in May and June. For derby dates, rules and past derby winners, visit http://ketchikan kingsalmonderby.com.

Fishing lodges and resorts in the area offer sportfishing for steelhead, salmon, halibut, trout, lingcod and red snapper. Resorts near Ketchikan include Yes Bay Lodge. There are also several fishing lodges on nearby Prince of Wales Island. For details, go to www.visit–ketchikan.com for details.

AREA FISHING: Check with the Alaska Dept. of Fish and Game at 2030 Sea Level Dr., Suite 205, or phone (907) 225-5195 for details on fishing in the Ketchikan area. Good fishing spots range from Mountain Point, a 5-mile drive from Ketchikan on South Tongass Highway, to streams, lakes, bays, and inlets 50 miles away by boat or by air. Half-day and longer charters and skiff rentals available out of Ketchikan. Fish include salmon, halibut, steelhead, Dolly Varden, cutthroat and rainbow, arctic grayling, eastern brook trout, lingcod and rockfish; shellfish include Dungeness crab and shrimp.

Prince of Wales Island

Local fishing vessels cover the Craig, Alaska harbor. (©Sharon Nault)

Major Attractions:

© Terry Sheely

*El Capitan Cave,
Totem Parks,
Sportfishing*

Visitor Information: Prince of Wales Chamber of Commerce, P.O. Box 490, Klawock, AK 99925; phone (907) 755-2626, fax (907) 755-2627; email info@princeofwales coc.org; www.princeofwalescoc.org. The **U.S. Forest Service** has offices in Craig, phone (907) 826-3271, and in Thorne Bay, phone (907) 828-3304; www.fs.fed.us/r10/tongass/districts/pow/index.shtml.

Prince of Wales Island is the third largest island under the American flag (Kodiak is second, the Big Island of Hawaii is first), measuring roughly 135 miles north to south by 45 miles east to west. A mountainous, heavily forested island with a cool, moist, maritime climate, the island is best known for its fishing and for having the most extensive road system in Southeast Alaska.

Designated a State Scenic Byway in 2010, the island road system offers visitors a unique driving experience. Although narrow, winding and about half gravel, the roads have good surfacing and very little traffic. And the scenery is anything but repetitive, as the roads travel through old-growth forest and clear-cut areas, with mountain views and views of coastline and offshore islands.

Wildlife viewing opportunities abound—from bald eagles to bears. It is not uncommon to have to brake for black bears or Sitka black-tailed deer crossing the road.

The road system also accesses hiking trails; roadside fishing streams (red, pink and silver salmon, cutthroat, rainbow and Dolly Varden); and some unique geological attractions.

Most of the island is within **Tongass National Forest**. Tongass National Forest comprises 16.9 million acres, 13.7 million acres of which are either wilderness or National Monuments. Timber harvest is allowed on less than one half of one percent per year. On Prince of Wales Island, the Forest Service manages 5 designated wilderness areas, as well as public-use cabins, campgrounds, hiking trails and canoe trails.

It is estimated that there are thousands of caves on the island. The major geological attraction on the island is **El Capitan Cave**, located 75 miles from Craig via the North Prince of Wales Road.

With more than 13,000 feet of passageways, El Capitan Cave is the largest known cave in Alaska. A steep staircase trail (more than 365 steps) leads up to the cave entrance. The cave is accessible only by guided tour offered by the Forest Service. These tours are offered daily from Memorial Day to Labor Day. To book a tour, phone the Thorne Bay Ranger District at (907) 828-3304 at least 2 days in advance. Tours last about 2 hours and tour groups are limited to 6 people. For safety reasons, no children under age 7 are allowed on the tour. Wear warm clothes and boots. The Forest Service provides flashlight and safety helmet with headlamp.

Four miles south of the turnoff for El Capitan is the Beaver Falls Karst Trail. This 1-mile boardwalk trail crosses ancient muskegs and cathedral forests, and displays many karst features, such as sinkholes, deep vertical pits, lost rivers and collapsed channels.

Historically, salmon and timber have been the economic mainstays of Prince of Wales Island. One of Alaska's first canneries was built at Klawock in 1878, and some 25 more canneries were eventually built on the island to process salmon.

Annual events on the island include the International Marathon in May. The 26.2-mile marathon begins in Hollis and ends in Craig. This annual event takes place the Saturday preceding Memorial Day. For fishermen there are salmon derbies in Thorne Bay (May–July) and Craig–Klawock (June–August).

Many of the island's communities began as logging camps. Today, timber harvests

Prince of Wales Island

© 2014 The MILEPOST®

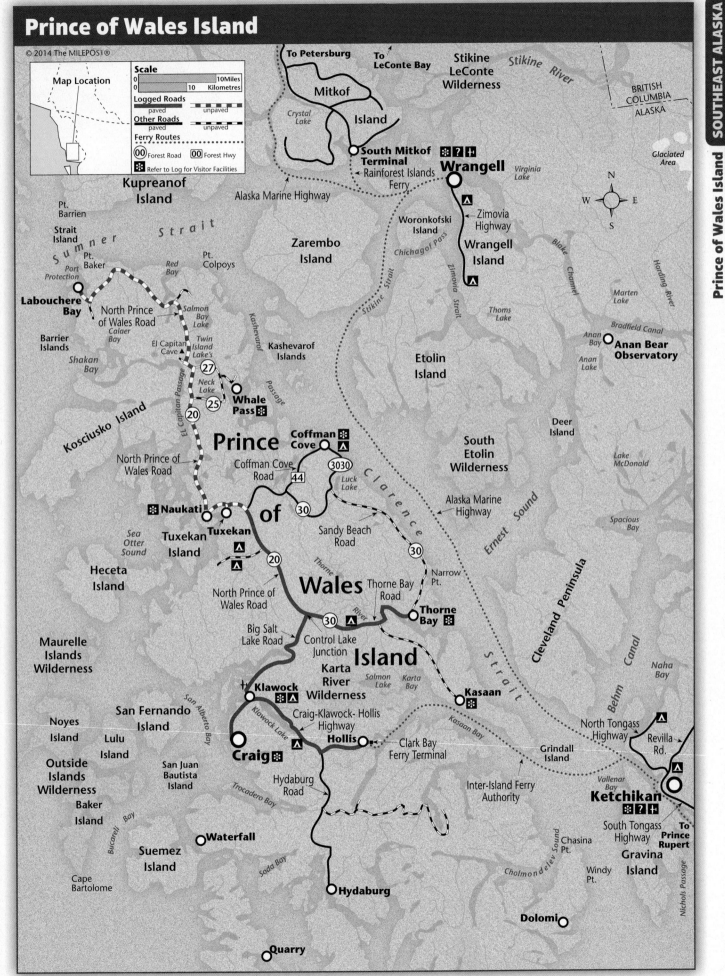

Scale
0   10 Miles
0   10   Kilometres

Logged Roads
paved   unpaved
Other Roads
paved   unpaved
Ferry Routes

00 Forest Road   00 Forest Hwy
✳ Refer to Log for Visitor Facilities

Map Location

To Petersburg
To LeConte Bay

Stikine LeConte Wilderness

Stikine River

BRITISH COLUMBIA
ALASKA

Mitkof Island

Crystal Lake

Kupreanof Island

South Mitkof Terminal
Rainforest Islands Ferry

Wrangell

Alaska Marine Highway

Woronkofski Island

Virginia Lake

Zimovia Highway

Wrangell Island

Glaciated Area

Pt. Barrien

Strait Island

Sumner Strait

Zarembo Island

Chichagof Pass

Port Protection
Pt. Baker

Labouchere Bay

North Prince of Wales Road
Calaer Bay

Red Bay

Pt. Colpoys

Salmon Bay Lake

Kashevarof

Kashevarof Islands

Stikine Strait

Zimovia Strait

Blake Channel

Harding River

Marten Lake

Thoms Lake

Bradfield Canal

Anan Bay
Anan Bear Observatory

Barrier Islands

Shakan Bay

Twin Island Lake's
El Capitan Cave

El Capitan Passage

27

Neck Lake

20 25

Whale Pass

Passage

Etolin Island

Anan Lake

Deer Island

Kosciusko Island

North Prince of Wales Road

Coffman Cove

Prince

of

Wales

Coffman Cove Road
44

3030

Luck Lake

30

South Etolin Wilderness

Clarence

Lake McDonald

Naukati

Tuxekan Island
Tuxekan

Sea Otter Sound

20

Sandy Beach Road

Thorne

Narrow Pt.

30

Alaska Marine Highway

Ernest Sound

Spacious Bay

Heceta Island

North Prince of Wales Road

Thorne Bay Road

Thorne Bay

Island

River

Maurelle Islands Wilderness

Big Salt Lake Road

30

Control Lake Junction

Karta River Wilderness

Salmon Lake

Karta Bay

Kasaan

Cleveland Peninsula

Strait

Behm Canal

Naha Bay

San Fernando Island

Klawock

Craig-Klawock-Hollis Highway

Kasaan Bay

North Tongass Highway

San Alberto Bay

Klawock Lake

Hollis

Clark Bay Ferry Terminal

Grindall Island

Revilla Rd.

Noyes Island

Lulu Island

Craig

Outside Islands Wilderness

San Juan Bautista Island

Hydaburg Road

Inter-Island Ferry Authority

Vallenar Bay

Baker Island

Waterfall

Trocadero Bay

Bucareli Bay

Suemez Island

Soda Bay

Ketchikan

South Tongass Highway

To Prince Rupert

Chasina Pt.

Gravina Island

Cholmondeley Sound

Windy Pt.

Nichols Passage

Cape Bartolome

Hydaburg

Dolomi

Quarry

Catching crab is child's play in Southeast Alaska. (©Sharon Nault)

on the island are only a fraction of what they once were. Motorists get a close-up look at the effects of logging as they drive the island's roads. Clear-cut areas, in various stages of regrowth, alternate with old-growth forest as you travel from one end of the island to the other.

A major attraction here is the world-class saltwater sportfishing that abounds immediately offshore and throughout the many smaller islands surrounding Prince of Wales Island. Most communities have boat ramps. Visiting fishermen may also charter out with a local operator. Fireweed Lodge provides lodging and guided fishing charters and packages. Log Cabin Resort offers self-guided fishing packages and charters along with cabin accommodations and an RV park. Shelter Cove Lodge offers guided fishing and oceanfront lodging.

Several hatcheries on the Island offer up-close (non-fishing) opportunities to see salmon via a Visitor Center/Hatchery, as well as possibly providing fresh fish buying opportunities in season.

Ocean fishing for salmon is best in July and early August for kings (chinook), August and September for silver, July, August and September for pinks, and August and September for chum. Halibut to 100 lbs., 50-lb. king salmon and 15-lb. silver salmon are not considered uncommon in the sport season, usually May through August due to the weather and fish migration patterns. Abundant bottom fish, including lingcod, halibut and red snapper, reside throughout these waters year-round.

Communities

Of the 9 communities connected by the island road system, Craig, Klawock, Thorne Bay, Hydaburg, Coffman Cove and Kasaan have city status and are described in more detail in this section beginning on page 663. The smaller communities of Hollis, Naukati and Whale Pass are described in the road

logs in this section.

PORT PROTECTION (pop. 42) and POINT BAKER (pop. 16) are 2 communities not on the island road system. Located on the northern tip of Prince of Wales Island, these 2 small fishing villages are accessible by floatplane and skiff.

Lodging & Services

Accommodations on the island range from lodges, cabins and bed-and-breakfasts to guest houses and apartments. If you are dining out, Craig has the widest selection of restaurants, from pizza places to hotel dining rooms. Shopping and other services are also found mainly in Craig and in neighboring Klawock. WiFi can be found in multiple locations: At the Chamber of Commerce office in the Klawock-Heenya Mall in Klawock; at libraries in Craig, Coffman Cove, Thorne Bay and Whale Pass; and at the North Cove Harbor in Craig and the Main Harbor in Thorne Bay.

Fireweed Lodge in Klawock and Shelter Cove Lodge in Craig are major lodging facilities with dining rooms. Like most lodges on Prince of Wales Island, Fireweed and Shelter Cove also provide fishing charter services. Log Cabin RV Park & Resort in Klawock has cabins for rent with easy access to Saltwater Beach and boat dock. McFarland's Floatel in Thorne Bay is 2 miles by water from town. On Whiskey Creek in Hollis offers a private beachfront cabin for do-it-yourself adventurers.

Camping

Log Cabin RV Park & Resort in Klawock has waterside camping. Oceanview RV Park and Campground is on the beach in Coffman Cove. Also Rain Country RV on JS Drive in Craig and Klawock RV Park in Klawock. There is a municipal RV park in Thorne Bay; phone City Hall at (907) 828-3380.

There are 2 developed U.S. Forest Service campgrounds on the island—Eagle's Nest on Thorne Bay Road and Harris River on the Craig–Klawock–Hollis Highway. Camping fee at both is $8 (Golden Age card is honored at both of these for half-price camping). Campsites may be reserved by phoning toll-free 1-877-444-6777; a reservation fee is charged. Several undeveloped dispersed campsites are accessible via the island road system; see www.fs.usda.gov/tongass/.

There are 20 USFS cabins (accessible by plane, boat or on foot) available for public use; reservations and a fee are required ($20-45 a night, per cabin). Online reservations are available; visit www.fs.usda.gov/tongass/.

Transportation

Air: All communities on the island are served by floatplane. Wheel planes land at Klawock Airport. Daily scheduled service from Ketchikan. Taquan Air (www.fly taquan.com); phone 1-800-770-8800. Island Air Express, phone 1-888-387-8989. Pacific Airways, phone 1-877-360-3500. Harris Aircraft Services (www.harrisair.com), phone (907) 966-3050. Promech Air (www.prome chair), phone 1-800-860-3845.

Ferry: Inter–Island Ferry Authority MV *Stikine* or MV *Prince of Wales* from Ketchikan to Hollis/Clark Bay; crossing time about 3 hours, daily trips. For reservations, phone 1-866-308-4848; Hollis terminal, phone (907) 530-4848; online at www.inter islandferry.com. In Ketchikan, stop by the IFA ticket counter inside the Alaska Marine

Coffman Cove sportfishermen clean their day's catch of halibut. (©Sharon Nault)

Highway terminal, or phone (907) 225-4838.

If you are planning to catch the early morning ferry from Hollis to Ketchikan, you may be able to park in the terminal log, overnight (for self-contained campers). Ask for permission at Terminal Building.

Shuttle van service connects with all IFA ferry arrivals and departures at Clark Bay/Hollis. Inquire locally or onboard.

Car rentals: Rainforest Auto Rentals, phone (907) 826-2277; www.rainforestauto rentals.com.

Highways: Four of the island's main roads are logged in this section: the Craig–Klawock–Hollis Highway (paved); Big Salt Lake Road (paved); Thorne Bay Road (paved); and the North Prince of Wales Road (15 miles of pavement, 63 miles gravel). *NOTE: Many of the island's roads are narrow, winding, paved and/or gravel roads. Paving and upgrading have improved several roads on the south end of the island, but extensive construction continues on the north island road until 2015, with some especially difficult stretches for anything more than a small 4x4 vehicle. Road conditions vary dramatically depending on construction and weather. Inquire locally for current conditions and recommendations based on your particular vehicle. Be alert for oncoming traffic on hills and corners, and watch for logging trucks, deer and bears.*

Taxi: Island Ride (907) 401-1414.

PRINCE OF WALES ADVERTISERS

A Bed and Breakfast	Ph. (907) 401-3131
City of Coffman Cove	Ph. (907) 329-2233
City of Thorne Bay	Ph. (907) 828-3380
Fireweed Lodge	Ph. (907) 755-2930
Inter-Island Ferry Authority	Ph. 1-866-308-4848
Log Cabin RV Park & Resort	Ph. 1-800-544-2205
McFarland's Floatel, Beachfront Log Cabins	Ph. 1-888-828-3335
On Whiskey Creek	(907) 530-7081
Prince of Wales Island Chamber of Commerce	Ph. (907) 755-2626
Rainforest Auto Rentals	(907) 826-2277
Shelter Cove Lodge	Ph. (907) 826-2939

Coffman Cove

Located 55 miles north of Klawock, a 2-hour drive from Hollis/ferry terminal. **Population:** 198. **Emergency Services:** Coffman Cove Fire/EMS, phone 911. **Coffman Cove Clinic:** Part-time hours, call (907) 329-2051. See wildlife including black bears, Sitka blacktail deer, whales, herons, Steller's sea lions and incredible bird watching while you enjoy hiking, kaya-

Totems flank the Hydaburg Public School. (©Sharon Nault)

king, fishing or boating. Stay in a fully furnished lodge, a bed-and-breakfast, one of the local cabins, or the RV campground. Additional camping available at Oceanview RV Park & Lodgings.

Coffman Cove has a public library with WiFi. Other tourist services available include: the Riggin Shack, a small general merchandise and grocery store; the Doghouse Saloon and Liquor store; and the Bait Box Take-Out, which serves hamburgers and sandwiches. R&R Fuels has gas, diesel and propane.

The scenic Seaside Park with telescopes and covered tables is a perfect picnic spot. Guided ocean charters are available locally. Coffman Cove is the only community on the north end of Prince of Wales Island that is accessible by paved road. It is also connected to Thorne Bay by the narrow, scenic Sandy Beach Road.

Coffman Cove is the site of a large archaeological project where researchers in partnership with the Stikine Tlingit Tribe are excavating the site of a principal village of the Stikine Tlingit people with settlement dating from 9,000 BC. The Canoe Lagoon Oyster Co. here is the state's oldest and largest oyster producer; fresh oysters available locally at the Riggin Shack and the Doghouse Saloon and Liquor Store. Please see city website for more information on floatplane services, ferry and water taxi and links to local businesses.

Coffman Cove has a post office on the corner of Loggers Lane and Kodiak Drive (open 1–3:30 P.M. weekdays except Tuesdays when it is open from 5–7:30 P.M.). Oceanview RV Park/Campground, on the beach, which also offers full-hookup RV sites and bunkhouse accommodations. There is a public dock, fish cleaning tables, boat launch, public phone and restrooms here. The Harbormaster's phone is (907) 329-2233.

Special Events. The second annual Halibut Derby is scheduled for June 1 through August 31, 2014. The Silver Salmon Tournament is held July 3rd. The fourth annual "By the Sea" Arts & Seafood Festival will be held on August 9–10, 2014. For more information on these events, contact the City of Coffman Cove, phone (907) 329-2233; email artsfestival@ccalaska.com; www.ccalaska.com.

Craig

Located 31 miles from Clark Bay ferry terminal and 7 miles from Klawock, on the western shore of Prince of Wales Island. **Population:** 1,241. **Emergency Services:** Craig EMS, phone 911. **Police,** phone 911 or (907) 826-3330. **Clinic,** PeaceHealth Medical Group, phone (907) 826-3257; Craig Public Health Center, phone (907) 826-3433. **Dentist,** Southeast Dental Centers, phone (907) 826-2273. **Hospital,** transport to Ketchikan General.

Visitor Information: www.craigak.com. There is an RV dump station located downtown. It is just off of Cold Storage Road behind the business building to the right. Named for founder Craig Millar, who established a saltery and cold storage facility here in the early 1900s, Craig was incorporated in 1922. Today, it is the largest city on the island and offers most services. There are a half-dozen places to eat, from pizza places to restaurants, cafe, sandwich shop and pastry eatery; 2 banks and a Credit Union; supermarket and liquor stores; gas stations, propane, towing and auto repair; and several gift shops. If you're shopping for something specific, ask a local. Many businesses are tucked away in hard-to-find places. Nearest campground is in Klawock.

Accommodations are available at **Shelter Cove Lodge** (phone 907/826-2939), Ruth Ann's Hotel, Shaan-Seet Hotel, and **A Bed and Breakfast** (907/401-3131).

Craig has 2 modern boat harbors, North Cove and South Cove, located on either side of the causeway crossed by the Craig–Klawock–Hollis Highway where it merges with Water Street. The harbor is a nice place for visitors to stroll and take in the local atmosphere. Bald eagles are common here and along the waterfront. Craig also has a seaplane float, fuel dock, city dock and float, 2 fish-buying docks and an old cannery dock. The Craig harbormaster's office, with public showers and restrooms, is located on the corner close to South Cove; phone (907) 826-3404, VHF

Channel 16.

Craig is the home port of many commercial fishing and charter sportfishing boats. Halibut, silver and king salmon, lingcod and red snapper (yelloweye) are the primary target species.

Hydaburg

Located 36 miles from Hollis, 45 miles from Craig. **Population:** 367. **Emergency Services:** Phone 911. **Alaska State Troopers,** in Klawock, phone (907) 755-2918. **Clinic,** Hydaburg Health Center, phone (907) 285-3462; EMS (907) 285-3375.

Hydaburg was founded in 1911, and combined the populations of 3 Haida villages: Sukkwan, Howkan and Klinkwan. President William Howard Taft established an Indian reservation on the surrounding land in 1912, but, at the residents' request, most of the land was restored to its former status as part of Tongass National Forest in 1926. Hydaburg was incorporated in 1927, 3 years after its people became citizens of the United States.

Most of the residents are commercial fishermen, although there are some jobs in construction and the timber industry. Subsistence is also a traditional and necessary part of life here. There is also good salmon fishing here in the fall.

Hydaburg has an excellent, large collection of restored Haida totems. A totem park is in front of the Hydaburg School. Native carvers restored and replicated totems brought in from the traditional Haida villages on southern Prince of Wales Island. The totem restoration project was founded in the late 1930s by the Civilian Conservation Corps and managed by the Tongass National Forest.

Two boardinghouses provide rooms and meals for visitors. Groceries and sundry items available locally. B & T Cafe is the local eatery. There is no fuel or gas available. Cable television is available.

Klawock

Located 23 miles from Hollis. **Population:** 799. **Emergency Services:** Phone 911 for all emergencies. **City Police,** phone (907) 755-2777; **Alaska State Troopers,** phone (907) 755-2291. **Clinic,** Alicia Roberts Medical Center, phone (907) 755-4800. **Private Aircraft:** Klawock airstrip, 2 miles northeast; elev. 50 feet; length 5,000 feet; lighted and paved. The **Prince of Wales Chamber of Commerce and Visitor Center** is located in the Klawock-Heena Mall (907) 755-2626.

Klawock originally was a Tlingit Indian summer fishing village; a trading post and salmon saltery were established here in 1868. Ten years later, a salmon cannery was built, one of several cannery operations in the area. Over the years, the population of Klawock, like other Southeast communities, grew and then declined with the salmon harvest. The local economy is still dependent on fishing, along with timber cutting and sawmilling. A fish hatchery operated by

Craig–Klawock–Hollis Highway

This paved highway begins at the ferry terminal at Clark Bay near Hollis and leads 31 miles west through Klawock then south to Craig, taking motorists through the temperate rainforest environment typical of Southeast Alaska. It is a 2-lane road with good surface and narrow shoulders. Posted speed is 50 mph with some 35 to 40 mph curves and speed zones through communities.

Distance from Craig (C) is followed by distance from Clark Bay ferry terminal (F). *Physical mileposts reflect distance from Craig.*

©Sharon Nault

C 31 F 0 Entrance to **Inter-Island Ferry Authority Hollis terminal** at Clark Bay; phone (907) 530-4848. There is a lot of paved turnout area. If you're catching an early ferry, you may ask permission at the Terminal to stay here, in your self-contained rig.

Distance marker shows Craig 30 miles, Klawock 23 miles, Thorne Bay 51 miles, Hollis 2 miles.

C 29.6 F 1.3 Turnoff south 0.3 mile to **HOLLIS** (pop. 109). Access to Hollis Boat Launch Ramp, view turnout and harbor. A former Ketchikan Pulp Co. logging camp that served as the base for timber operations on Prince of Wales Island until 1962, when the camp was moved to Thorne Bay.

C 28.5 F 2.3 Maybeso Creek bridge. Parking area to side of bridge. Fish include cutthroat; Dolly Varden; pink and silver salmon; steelhead run begins in mid-April. Pools offer the best fishing. Walking good along streambed but poor along bank. *Watch for bears.*

C 26.6 F 4.4 Large paved turnout with picnic tables. Welcome to Hollis sign.

C 24.3 F 6.7 Turnout.

C 22.7 F 8.3 Tongass National Forest boundary.

C 22.6 F 8.4 USFS hiking trail to **Harris River** fishing: cutthroat; steelhead run mid-April; salmon and Dolly Varden run beginning in mid-July. Easy walking on the gravel bars in the middle of 1.3-mile-long river.

C 20.5 F 10.5 Junction with Hydaburg Road (chip sealed) which leads south 23 miles to the community of Hydaburg (see description this section). Mileage along this road is distance from Hydaburg, not from this junction.

Hydaburg Road also provides access to One Dutch Trailhead (Mile 20), Cable Creek with fish viewing (Mile 13.3), side road to access 12 Mile Cabin, Dog Salmon Fishpass and Polk Inlet with Estuary (Mile 12.5). This side road is very narrow and not meant for large RVs. **Dog Salmon Fish Pass** provides an excellent opportunity to watch Alaska's salmon climb up the foaming waterfall or use the alternate fish ladder route. Bear viewing is excellent during the salmon run

from mid-July through mid-September. Facilities at the site include a table, firepit, viewing platform and interpretive signs illustrating the ecological web of creatures that utilize the stream and its resources.

C 20 F 11 USFS trailhead for 3-mile-long Twenty Mile Spur Trail to north.

C 19.7 F 11.3 Turnoff to southwest for **Harris River USFS Campground and Picnic Area**. 14 campsites on gravel loop road (best suited for small to medium RV's); firepits, tables, campground host, outhouse, bear-proof garbage and water (water was potable in 2013). Camping fee $8. Muskeg nature trail. Very nice walk-in picnic area with tables, water, firepits, firewood, toilets and group shelter, walkway overlooking Harris River (terrific salmon fishing!). Park at campground entrance and follow gravel path to picnic area. Reserve at www.recreation.gov.

C 19.6 F 11.4 Harris River bridge. Access north of bridge to open area, restrooms, covered picnic tables. Walkway over beautiful Harris River. Trail access to campground.

C 18.6 F 12.4 Large turnout.

C 18.4 F 12.6 Tongass National Forest boundary.

C 16 F 15 Glimpses through the trees of 7-mile-long Klawock Lake.

C 14.9 F 16.1 Paved turnout and access to Klawock Lake.

C 9.1 F 21.9 Turnout.

C 9 F 22 Prince of Wales Hatchery, operated by the Prince of Wales Hatchery Assoc., produces silver salmon. Calling ahead is appreciated; visitors are always welcome. Visitor center has gift shop with local items and maps, an aquarium, public restrooms and a focus on outreach education. Daily guided tours provided by volunteers 9 A.M.–4 P.M. weekdays or by appointment for large groups, phone (907) 755-2231. Donations are appreciated. Fresh silvers may be for sale, August–September. Ask about the Port St. Nick Hatchery, a 30 minute drive from here which raises king salmon.

C 8.9 F 22.1 Large turnout.

C 8.3 F 22.7 Klawock city limit. (See description of Klawock this section.)

C 7.4 F 23.5 Entrance to Klawock-Heenya mall at Boundary Road; large supermarket, with liquor store and deli, U. S. Post Office, eye clinic, Western Union, beauty salon. Cafe nearby. **Prince of Wales Island Chamber of Commerce** office inside mall has visitor information. **Tlingit Longhouse** to the east with new carving shed (built in 2013).

Distance marker southbound shows Hollis 21 miles, Clark Bay Ferry 27 miles.

A short distance up Boundary Road is a gas station with propane and diesel.

Junction with Boundary Road (which quickly becomes Big Salt Lake Road); leads 16.2 miles to Control Lake Junction, where it intersects with Thorne Bay Road and North Prince of Wales Road. See "Big Salt Lake Road" log on page 666.

C 7.3 F 23.7 Junction with Big Salt Lake Road. Petro Express gas station. Black Bear Grocery Store with tackle, hunting and fishing license. Turn here to access **Log**

Cabin RV Park & Resort, a popular resort with RV sites and cabins on Saltwater Beach.

Log Cabin RV Park & Resort. See display ad page 662.

C 7.2 F 23.8 Office of Alaska State Troopers and **Klawock Police Station** phone (907) 755-2918. Hemlock Street.

C 7.1 F 23.9 Turnoff for **Fireweed Lodge**; motel rooms, family-style dining and fishing charters available.

Fireweed Lodge. See display ad on page 662.

Across the street from Fireweed Lodge is St. John's by the Sea Catholic Church. It was designed and built with local lumber and materials by the local church community. The stained-glass windows were designed and built by local artists. Visitors are welcome to view the church.

C 7 F 24 Turn west on Anchorage Street to access Dan Snider Park with picnic area, the city boat ramp and harbor. Continue on loop road to Bayview Boulevard

©Sharon Nault

and Church street to see **Klawock Totem Park**. Large collection of totems located on hillside overlooking Klawock; good photo op. Also access via Klawock Street to city park, ballfields and boat launch.

C 6.8 F 24.2 Bayview Boulevard loops west to Klawock Totem Park (turn on Union).

C 6.6 F 24.4 Klawock River bridge spans tidal estuary where river meets salt water; no fishing. Good eagle viewing in Klawock River estuary during salmon season.

Alicia Roberts Medical Center. *Begin 25 mph speed zone entering Klawock.*

C 6 F 25 Viking sawmill.

C 4.2 F 26.8 Turnout with scenic view of Klawock Inlet and San Alberto Bay.

C 4 F 27 Craig city limit.

C 1.5 F 29.5 Craig High School and Crab Creek.

C 1 F 30 Point St. Nicholas Road, scenic views along water, turnouts. Begin bike path northbound, extends 0.8 mile.

Begin speed zone entering Craig.

C 0.6 F 30.4 Napa Auto Parts. Port Bagial Boulevard access to large hardware store/lumber yard.

C 0.5 F 30.5 Craig post office (ZIP 99921), Wells Fargo bank and very large supermarket.

C 0.4 F 30.6 Cold Storage Road. Annie Betty's Restaurants, Papa's Pizza, gift shop and dump station in vacant lot behind buildings at intersection.

C 0.3 F 30.7 Hamilton Drive. North and South Cove harbors, operated by the city of Craig. Harbormaster's Office, restrooms, public showers, pay phone. Highway becomes Water Street. Turn on 9th Street for USFS Craig Ranger District office.

C 0 F 31 Intersection of Third, Front and Water streets in Craig. Ruth Ann's Hotel with restaurant and bar located here. Cafe and general store nearby.

Big Salt Lake Road

Prince of Wales Island roads offer prolific views of wildlife. (©Sharon Nault)

Big Salt Lake Road (SR 929) begins as Boundary Road at **Milepost C 7.5** on the Craig–Klawock–Hollis Highway and extends 16.2 miles to junction with Thorne Bay Road and North Prince of Wales Road at Control Lake Junction. It is an improved paved road with posted speed limits to 50 mph.

Distance from junction with Craig–Klawock–Hollis Highway at Klawock (K) is followed by distance from Thorne Bay (T). *Physical mileposts reflect distance from Klawock.*

K 0 T 33 Junction with Craig–Klawock–Hollis Highway at Klawock. Shopping mall with supermarket, liquor store, post office and visitor information.

Junction with "Craig–Klawock–Hollis Highway" (SR 924) at **Milepost C 7.4** on that highway; see log on page 665.

K 0.5 T 32.5 Boundary Road becomes Big Salt Lake Road at junction with old Big Salt Lake Road.

Turnoff for **Log Cabin RV Park & Resort**: lodging, camping, boat rentals.

K 0.7 T 32.3 Klawock city limit.

K 1.4 T 31.6 Bennett Creek.

K 2.3 T 30.7 Turnoff for Klawock Airport (0.6 mile).

Private Aircraft: Klawock airstrip; elev. 50 feet; length 5,000 feet; lighted and paved.

K 3.7 T 29.3 Little Salt Creek. Big Salt Lake Road climbs eastbound. Beautiful views of islands and inlets. Evidence of clear cutting.

K 5.3 T 27.7 Duke Creek (sign).

K 8.3 T 24.7 Large paved turnout and gravel access to **Big Salt Lake**. An estuary, Big Salt Lake extends northeast 8 miles off Klawak and Shinaku inlets on the west coast of Prince of Wales Island. This saltwater body is protected by small islands that are visible from several spots along Big Salt Lake Road. If boating on this tidal lake, be aware of strong currents.

K 9.3 T 23.7 Turnout at west end of **Black Bear Creek** bridge. Fishing for cutthroat, Dolly Varden, red, pink, chum and silver salmon.

K 9.7 T 23.3 Paved turnout.

K 10.2 T 22.8 Paved turnout. Second growth forest management (signed), trail.

K 10.5 T 22.5 Paved turnout with views of Big Salt Lake (many views available along this good paved, winding road).

K 12 T 21 Steelhead Creek bridge. Fishing for cutthroat, Dolly Varden, steelhead, pink, chum and silver salmon.

K 13 T 20 Entering Tongass National Forest land eastbound; paved shoulder parking.

K 13.2 T 19.8 Road into large gravel parking area.

K 16 T 17 Control Lake; shoulder parking. Fish available: rainbow and cutthroat trout; Dolly Varden; steelhead (spring and fall run); pink and silver salmon; good red salmon stream in August. USFS public-use cabin with skiff at lake.

K 16.1 T 16.9 Distance marker westbound shows Klawock 17 miles, Craig 23 miles, Hollis 42 miles.

K 16.2 T 16.8 Control Lake Junction. Large parking areas both sides of highway.

Junction of Big Salt Lake Road (SR 929) with Thorne Bay Road (FH 42/30) and North Prince of Wales Road (FH 43/20). See road logs this section.

Distance marker for northbound traffic shows Naukati 26 miles, Coffman Cove 30 miles, Whale Pass 48 miles, Labouchere Bay 81 miles.

Distance marker for eastbound traffic shows Thorne Bay 18 miles, Kasaan 28 miles.

Prince of Wales Hatchery Assoc. is located on Klawock Lake, very near the site of a salmon hatchery that operated from 1897 until 1917. Visitors are welcome. Read more about the hatchery and visitor center at Milepost 9, Craig-Klawock-Hollis Highway. Klawock Lake offers canoeing and boating.

A major attraction in Klawock is the **Totem Park**, which contains many totems. The poles were originally part of the old village of Tuxekan and relocated here in 1938–40 as a Civilian Conservation Corps project. The Long House named Gaani Ax Adi is located along the main highway in downtown Klawock near the new carving shed.

A large grocery store with deli and liquor, eye clinic, beauty salon, western union, and many other businesses are here. Gas, diesel and propane is available. Black Bear Grocery and Tackle is on Big Salt Lake Road. Accommodations and family-style dining at **Fireweed Lodge**, located along the main highway, near the Big Salt Road junction; phone (907) 755-2930. Cabins and full-hookup RV sites at **Log Cabin RV Park & Resort**, phone 1-800-544-2205.

Recreation here includes good fishing for salmon and steelhead in Klawock River, saltwater halibut fishing.

Thorne Bay

Located 57 miles from the Inter-Island ferry terminal at Hollis; 34 miles from Klawock. **Population**: 508. **Emergency Services**: Phone 911. **Village Public Safety Officer**, phone (907) 828-3905. **Alaska State Troopers**, in Klawock, phone (907) 755-2918. **Clinic**, Thorne Bay Clinic, phone (907) 828-8848. **Visitor Information**: www.thornebayalaska.net.

Thorne Bay has a grocery store and liquor store; general merchandise, boat fuel, convenience store, gas, diesel and post office at The Port. The Tackle Shack has fishing/hunting licenses and supplies. City RV dump station on Shoreline Drive.

Camping at Thorne Bay RV Park on Sandy Beach Road, across the street from the Thorne Bay Ranger Station.

Thorne Bay was incorporated in 1982, making it one of Alaska's newest cities. The current community of Thorne Bay began as a logging camp in 1962, when Ketchikan Pulp Co. (KPC) moved its operations from Hollis to here, building a shop, barge terminal and Log Sort Yard. Thorne Bay was connected to the island road system in 1974. Camp residents created the community, which gained second-class city status from the state. This was made possible under the Alaska Statehood Act.

When timber was big in the 1960s and 1970s, Thorne Bay was the largest logging camp in North America, with more than 600 residents. The population has fluctuated with the lumber industry. Ketchikan Pulp Co. completed its final timber sales in 2001 and closed down operations here.

Winding, gravel Sandy Beach Road leads north from Thorne Bay to Coffman Cove, a driving distance of 37 miles. There are a number of ocean views along the way to beautiful **Sandy Beach USFS Picnic Ground** at Mile 7. It has a great driftwood beach.

Thorne Bay Road

Thorne Bay Road is a paved road with easy curves, no steep grades and posted speed limits to 50 mph. It extends 16.8 miles from Control Lake Junction to the community of Thorne Bay.

Distance from Control Lake Junction (CJ) is followed by distance from Thorne Bay (T). *Physical mileposts reflect distance from Thorne Bay.*

CJ 0 T 16.9 Control Lake Junction. Paved turnout at junction.

> **Junction** with Big Salt Lake Road at **Milepost K 16.2** from Klawock, **Milepost 16.8** from Thorne Bay, and Milepost 0 of the North Prince of Wales Road. See Big Salt Lake Road log on facing page and North Prince of Wales Road log on page 668.

CJ 1.3 T 16.6 Control Creek.

CJ 1.8 T 15.1 Eagle's Nest USFS campground on a 0.6-mile paved road; 12 sites on level, gravel pads; some sites can accommodate very long RVs; $8 camping fee; walk-in tent sites; potable water, tables, firepits, garbage, outhouses. Campground host. A wheelchair-accessible **boardwalk trail** (pictured above) offers views of spawning salmon. Also watch for waterfowl in spring and summer, bald eagles year-round. Trail to **Balls Lake** picnic area. Access to **Control Creek**; fishing for cutthroat, Dolly Varden, red, pink and silver salmon. Advance reservations available through the National Recreation Reservation Service; phone toll-free 1-877-444-6777 or see www.recreation.gov.

CJ 2.1 T 14.8 Balls Lake USFS picnic area and trail; paved parking area for 10 cars, vault toilet, no potable water, litter bin. Follow gravel trail about 150 feet from parking area to picnic shelter with 2 tables and fire ring. Trailhead for Balls Lake Trail by picnic shelter; trail is 2.2 miles around lake, 0.5 mile to Eagle's Nest Campground.

CJ 4.7 T 12.2 Rio Roberts Creek bridge; cutthroat, pink and silver salmon fishing. A 0.7-mile cedar-chip and boardwalk trail leads to a viewing deck overlooking falls and Rio Roberts Fish Pass.

CJ 5.1 T 11.8 Newlunberry Creek (narrow bridge).

CJ 6.8 T 10.1 Rio Beaver Creek (narrow bridge).

CJ 6.3 T 9.6 Several paved turnouts next 3 miles.

CJ 10.7 T 6.2 Goose Creek bridge (narrow bridge); turnout at east end. Excellent spawning stream. Pink salmon run mid-August; cutthroat and silver salmon.

CJ 10.9 T 6 Junction with Kasaan Highway. This rough, washboarded, narrow gravel road leads 16 miles southeast to **KASAAN** (pop. 69). Located at the head of Kasaan Bay, Kasaan was connected to the road system in 1996. It has a post office, school and boat docks. The main visitor attraction here is the totem park (access via dirt trail, about a half-mile

©Sharon Nault

hike). The last remaining Haida long house left in the United States is here; under repair in 2013.

CJ 11 T 5.9 Double-ended paved turnout.

CJ 12 T 4.9 Paved turnout.

CJ 12.4 T 4.5 Thorne River (narrow bridge). Fishing in **Thorne River** for cutthroat, Dolly Varden, steelhead, rainbow, red, pink, chum and silver salmon.

Slow for 30 mph curve.

CJ 12.7 T 4.2 Paved turnout.

CJ 12.9 T 4 Paved turnout.

CJ 13 T 3.9 Falls Creek bridge; parking.

CJ 13.1 T 3.8 Gravelly Creek USFS picnic area; walk in to picnic area on the bank of Thorne River at the mouth of Gravelly Creek; 3 tables, fire rings, vault toilet and open-sided shelter. Pink salmon run in August and September. Watch for bears, Sitka black-tailed deer, bald eagles, red-breasted sapsuckers and songbirds. This site was logged in 1918. Notches in stumps were used by old-time loggers for spring boards to stand on while sawing or chopping.

CJ 13.4 T 3.5 Gravelly Creek bridge.

CJ 16 T 0.9 Former Ketchikan Pulp Co. (KPC) Log Sort Yard.

CJ 16.1 T 0.8 Welcome to Thorne Bay (sign) at paved turnout with picnic table and litter bin. See description of Thorne Bay this section.

CJ 16.9 T 0 Junction of Thorne Bay

Road (to the right) and Sandy Beach Road (straight ahead). Description follows. Thorne Bay Ranger Station and the **Municipal RV Park** are located 0.1 mile from Sandy Beach Road.

Sandy Beach USFS Picnic Ground, at Mile 7 Sandy Beach Road, has picnic tables, firepits, toilets and shelters; wildlife watching; tidepooling; and beautiful driftwood beach setting. Camping is allowed in designated area at Sandy Beach.

© Sharon Nault

Sandy Beach Road (FR 30) follows the east coast of Prince of Wales Island 28 miles north from Thorne Bay to Luck Lake Junction, where FR 3030 leads 9 miles north to Coffman Cove and FH 30 leads 10 miles to junction with FH 23/44. Driving distance from Thorne Bay to Coffman Cove via FH 30/FR 3030 is 37 miles. It is a scenic drive with mountain views and views of Clarence Strait (water views begin about Mile 6.1 from Thorne Bay). *CAUTION: Sandy Beach Road is a 1-lane, sometimes narrow, winding gravel road with steep grades (not suited for large RVs). There are no services or facilities along the road. Mileposts reflect distance from Control Lake Junction.*

Thorne Bay Road continues as Shoreline Drive through Thorne Bay. Access to The Port (store, gas and diesel), Post Office, grocery, boat ramp, cafe, tackle shop, city hall, harbor, RV dump station. *See description of Thorne Bay on page 666.*

Enjoy the Gravelly Creek USFS area for your picnic location. (©Sharon Nault)

North Prince of Wales Road

North Prince of Wales Road (Forest Highways/FHs 43/20), the "island highway," leads north 78 miles from Control Lake Junction to Labouchere Bay on the northwest corner of the island. This road provides paved access to Coffman Cove, Naukati, Whale Pass, Cavern Lake, El Capitan Cave and Beaver Falls Karst Trail. This is an interesting drive through old-growth forest and clear-cut areas, with a good chance of seeing deer and black bear.

Distance from Control Lake Junction (CJ) is followed by the physical milepost (MP). *Physical mileposts reflect distance from Thorne Bay on the 15 miles of improved road to the Coffman Cove turnoff. Beyond that, physical mileposts reflect distance from Hydaburg.*

CJ 0 MP 16.9 Control Lake Junction. Large paved turnout on left northbound. *Improved wide paved road next 15.4 miles northbound.*

Junction with Big Salt Lake Road and Thorne Bay Road; see logs this section.

CJ 3.5 MP 20.5 Turnout at 787-foot summit on highway.

CJ 9.2 MP 26.4 Double-ended turnout to west.

CJ 10.5 MP 27.7 Distance marker northbound shows Naukati 15 miles, Coffman Cove 26 miles, Whale Pass 37 miles.

CJ 10.6 MP 27.6 Turnoff on FR 2054 to west which leads 5 miles to **Staney Creek Cabin.** Nightly fee of $25–45. www.fs.fed.us/r10/tongass/districts/pow/recreation/cabins/shtml. Small salmon run in September. Watch for bald eagles, loons and other waterfowl; Sitka black-tailed deer; black bears; harbor seals and river otters.

CJ 13.5 MP 30.7 Gravel pit turnout.

CJ 14.6 MP 31.6 Large gravel turnout.

CJ 15 MP 68.8 Distance marker northbound shows Naukati 10 miles, Whale Pass 28 miles, El Capitan 38 miles, Coffman Cove 21 miles.

CJ 15.1 MP 68.7 Junction with **Coffman Cove Road** which leads 19.7 miles northeast via FH 44/FR 23/30/3030 to the community of **COFFMAN COVE** *(see description on pages 663–664).* Paved, widened and improved with moderate grades and curves. *Watch for deer!* This road also provides access to Log Jam Creek (Mile 4.6) and Honker Divide Canoe Trail (Mile 9). At Mile 9.7, Coffman Cove Road **junctions** with FR 30 to Luck Lake (19 miles) and Thorne Bay (37 miles) via Sandy Beach Road. *(Milepost marker 55 at this junction reflects distance from Control Lake Junction via FR 30.)* Sweetwater Lake Cabin access, trailhead and parking at Mile 13.

Note: Road improvements and paving under way northbound through 2015.

Distance marker southbound shows Thorne Bay 33 miles, Hollis 55 miles.

CJ 17.9 MP 71.8 Naukati Creek.

CJ 20.4 MP 74.5 FR 2058. Distance marker southbound shows Naukati 5 miles, Thorne Bay 39 miles.

CJ 20.8 MP 74.9 Yatuk Creek.

CJ 22.5 MP 76.7 Distance marker northbound shows Naukati 3 miles, Whale Pass 25 miles, El Capitan 27 miles.

CJ 22.6 MP 76.8 Junction with FR 2059 to east and FR 2060 to west. Turnoff to west for Naukati (pronounced KNOCK-eh-tee). Drive west 2 miles and follow signs for Naukati's store. Drive west 2.5 miles from the highway and take middle road at wrecker yard to reach boat launch.

NAUKATI BAY (pop. 115) was established as a mining camp and then a logging camp for Ketchikan Pulp Co. Today, it has a number of single-family homes located along a labyrinthian road system with many children playing and loose dogs. Naukati's post office, liquor, groceries, gas, propane and diesel available at the Naukati Connection; free RV parking on the waterfront. The boat ramp at Naukati provides access to Tuxekan Narrows and Sea Otter Sound. There is a school and a floatplane dock. In summer, Naukati hosts the popular "mud bogs," a competition involving large trucks and lots of mud. For more information, go to www.naukatibay.com.

CJ 25.2 MP 79.4 Clam Creek.

CJ 25.6 MP 79.8 Clam Creek No. 2.

CJ 25.7 MP 79.9 Sarkar Lake to east; parking, outhouses, boat launch, fishing for cutthroat, Dolly Varden and salmon. Wildlife watching: Sitka black-tailed deer, black bear, otter, mink, beaver and marten. This scenic lake is part of the Sarkar Lake Canoe Loop, a 15-mile trail covering 7 lakes, with Sarkar Lake as the terminus. USFS public-use cabin at east end of lake. Skiff here is for registered cabin users only. For cabin reservations phone toll-free 1-877-444-6777 or go to www.recreation.gov.

CJ 26.2 MP 80.5 Road forks; keep to right northbound on FH 20.

CJ 27.2 MP 81.6 Bridge over "Sarkar Rapids" (Sarkar Lake outlet to salt water); red salmon in July. Small gravel pullout. Watch for bears.

CJ 27.5 MP 81.9 Deweyville Trail.

CJ 33 MP 87.7 Bridge over creek (unsigned).

CJ 36.3 MP 91 Gravel pit turnout.

CJ 38.7 MP 93.5 Distance marker northbound shows El Capitan 13 miles, Labouchere Bay 40 miles, Neck Lake 1 mile, Whale Pass 8 miles.

CJ 38.8 MP 93.6 Junction with FR 25 which leads east 8 miles to the community of Whale Pass and connects with FR 27, which loops back to the island highway at **Milepost CJ 47.5.** About 1 mile east of here, FR crosses **Neck Lake.** This beautiful 3-mile-long lake is also visible from the highway.

WHALE PASS (pop. 39) was the site of a floating logging camp on Whale Passage. The camp moved out in the early 1980s, but new residents moved in with a state land sale. There is a small grocery store and gas pump (no diesel, irregular hours). Accommodations at Alaska's Fish Tales Lodge. There is also a school, post office and floatplane dock. WiFi available at community library.

CJ 45.5 MP 100.6 Beaver Falls Karst Trail to east; parking, toilets. This 1-mile boardwalk trail crosses ancient muskegs and cathedral forests, and displays many karst features, such as sinkholes, deep vertical pits, lost rivers and collapsed channels.

CJ 45.7 MP 100.8 *Begin winding downgrade next 2 miles northbound.*

CJ 47.5 MP 102.6 Junction with FR 27 which leads east past **Twin Island Lake** to **Whale Pass** (7 miles) and **Exchange Cove** (16 miles). FR 27 junctions with FR 25, which loops back to the island highway at **Milepost CJ 38.8.** There is a parking area and short trail down to **Cavern Lake Cave** overlook 3.4 miles east of here on FR 27. This unusual geological feature is at the lake outlet, where Cavern Lake drains first into a cave, then exits out of a cavern several hundred feet downstream.

Distance marker northbound shows El Capitan 4 miles, Whale Pass 7 miles, Exchange Cove 15 miles, Memorial Beach 24 miles.

CJ 49.8 MP 104.9 Distance marker northbound shows Red Bay 8 miles, Labouchere 31 miles, El Capitan 1 mile.

CJ 49.9 MP 105 Junction with FR 15 which leads west 1 mile to **El Capitan Cave.** A steep staircase trail (more than 365 steps) leads up to the cave entrance. The Forest Service offers guided cave tours throughout the summer; phone the Thorne Bay ranger district (907) 828-3304 for tour times, reservations and other information (must reserve 2 days in advance). Because of prior damage to cave formations, a gate was installed to regulate visitation. Open visitation only to the locked gate a short distance within the cave; guided tours only beyond the gate.

CJ 54.4 MP 109.6 Summit of the North Island Road (elev. 907 feet).

CJ 58.8 MP 114.1 Red Bay Lake Trail.

CJ 59.5 MP 115 Red Creek 1-lane bridge.

CJ 60.4 MP 115.9 Big Creek 1-lane bridge.

CJ 60.5 MP 116 Distance marker northbound shows Labouchere Bay 18 miles.

CJ 61.8 MP 117.3 Little Creek (signed).

CJ 62.5 MP 118 Duck Creek (signed).

CJ 64.1 MP 119.6 Distance marker northbound shows Labouchere Bay 14 miles.

CJ 64.8 MP 120.4 *Winding downhill northbound.*

CJ 66.2 MP 121.9 Buster Creek 1-lane bridge.

CJ 66.8 MP 122.5 Shine Creek.

CJ 68.7 MP 124.4 East Alder Creek 1-lane bridge.

CJ 68.8 MP 124.5 Alder Creek 1-lane bridge.

CJ 70.5 MP 126.4 Flicker Creek 1-lane bridge.

CJ 70.6 MP 126.5 Memorial Beach picnic area 1.7 miles north via FR 2086; follow signs to parking area. A short trail leads to picnic tables, pit toilet, memorial plaque and beach. Camping is allowed at the trailhead and on the beach.

This site is a memorial to 12 victims of a 1978 air crash. Good view of Sumner Strait and Kupreanof Island. According to the ADF&G, Memorial Beach is a good spot to look for humpback and killer whales in the strait, harbor seals and Steller sea lions closer to shore. Summer birds include pelagic cormorants, rhinoceros auklets, buffleheads, storm petrels and pigeon guillemots.

CJ 71.8 MP 127.7 Distance marker northbound shows Labouchere Bay 6 miles.

CJ 75.4 MP 131.4 FR 2090; Calder Mountain

CJ 77.6 MP 133.8 Labouchere Bay (sign). Wide sand and rock area covered with debris from the sea. Road circles to right for skiff launch to Port Protection (very rough access).

Wrangell

With a population of about 2,500, Wrangell is a friendly, full-service, small town.
(©Sharon Nault)

Located at northwest tip of Wrangell Island on Zimovia Strait; 6 miles southwest of the mouth of the Stikine River delta; 3 hours by ferry or 32 air miles southeast of Petersburg, the closest major community; and 6 hours by ferry or 85 air miles north of Ketchikan. **Population**: 2,448. **Emergency Services**: Phone 911 for all emergencies. **Police**, phone (907) 874-3304. **Alaska State Troopers**, phone (907) 874-3215. **Fire Department** and **Ambulance**, phone (907) 874-2000. **Maritime Search and Rescue**, contact the Coast Guard at (800) 478-5555. **Hospital**, Wrangell Medical Center, 310 Bennett St. just off Zimovia Highway, phone (907) 874-7000.

Visitor Information: Stop by the visitor information desk at the James and Elsie Nolan Center on Campbell Drive. The Nolan Center also houses the Wrangell Museum. Short videos are shown on request at the small theatre in the Nolan Center (inquire at visitor information counter or in the museum gift shop). Phone 1-800-367-9745 or (907) 874-3699; www.wrangell.com; wrangell@wrangell.com.

Visitor information is also available at a kiosk in the Stikine Inn (run by the Chamber of Commerce, seasonally).

The U.S. Forest Service maintains several recreation sites and trails along the Wrangell Island road system, as well as remote public-use cabins. Contact the USFS office in Wrangell, 525 Bennett St., phone (907) 874-2323; www.fs.usda.gov/tongass/.

Elevation: Sea level. **Climate**: Mild and moist with slightly less rain than other Southeast communities. Mean annual precipitation is 79.2 inches, with 63.9 inches of snow. Record monthly precipitation, 20.43 inches in October 1961. Average daily maximum temperature in June is 61°F; in July 64°F. Daily minimum in January is 23°F. **Radio**: KSTK-FM 101.7. **Television**: Cable and satellite. **Newspaper**: *Wrangell Sentinel* (weekly).

Private Aircraft: Wrangell airport, adjacent northeast; elev. 44 feet; length 6,000 feet; paved; fuel 100LL, A.

Wrangell is the only Alaska city to have existed under 4 nations and 3 flags—the Stikine Tlingits, the Russians, Great Britain and the United States. Wrangell began in 1834 as a Russian stockade called Redoubt St. Dionysius, built to prevent the Hudson's Bay Co. from fur trading up the rich Stikine River to the northeast. The Russians leased Wrangell Island and the mainland of southeastern Alaska to Hudson's Bay Co. in 1840. Under the British the stockade was called Fort Stikine.

The post remained under the British flag until Alaska was purchased by the United States in 1867. A year later, the Americans established a military post here, naming it Fort Wrangell after the island, which was named by the Russians after Baron von Wrangel, a governor of the Russian–American Co.

Its strategic location near the mouth of the Stikine River made Wrangell an important supply point not only for fur traders but also for gold seekers following the river route to the goldfields. Today, Wrangell serves as a hub for goods, services and transportation for outlying fishing villages, remote settlement areas and logging camps. The town depended largely on fishing until Japanese interests arrived in the mid-1950s and established a mill (now Silver Bay Logging). Fishing remains one of Wrangell's largest industries and active seafood processing operations are on the waterfront.

Major Attractions:

©Sharon Nault

Chief Shakes Island, Nemo Point, Anan bears, Stikine River

Lodging & Services

Accommodations at **Alaskan Sourdough Lodge** (1-800-874-3613; www.akgetaway.com), and the **Stikine Inn** (1-888-874-3388; www.stikineinnak.com); see ads on facing page. The Wrangell Hostel, open June–Aug, is located in the Presbyterian church; phone (907) 874-3534.

Meals at the Stikine Inn, Marine Pizza, and 2 cafes. Wrangell has 2 supermarkets and a small discount grocery; gas stations; hardware, marine, sporting goods and auto parts stores; banks; a laundromat; clothing stores and gift shops. The Nolan Center serves as the local movie theatre, showing current feature films on most weekends.

Breakaway Adventures (1-888-385-2488; www.breakawayadventures.com), **Alaska Waters Inc. Wrangell Tours** (1-800-347-4462; www.alaskawaters.com) and other tour operators offer trips to the Anan Bear and Wildlife Observatory as well as to the Stikine River; *see ads on this page*.

Irene Ingle Public Library, just up from the ferry terminal on Second Street, has Internet, computers, a copy machine, paperback exchange and public restrooms. Open Mon. & Fri. 10 A.M. to noon and 1-5 P.M.; Tues.–Thurs. 1-5 P.M. and 7-9 P.M.; Sat. 9 A.M.–5 P.M. Closed Sun. Access free public WiFi outside the library, 24/7.

Camping

The city-owned **Shoemaker RV Park and Campground** provides tent and RV camping at Shoemaker Bay Recreation Area, **Milepost 4.5** Zimovia Highway. Tent sites are located adjacent to the creek and park area. RV sites are located in the harbor with some overflow sites in the harbor parking lot. There are a total of 25 RV spaces: 16 with electricity, and the harbor parking lot sites with no hookups. Shoreline campsites, many with views, have picnic tables. Camping fees are $15/night without hookups, $25/night with hookups. Phone (907) 874-2444 or email aal-haddad@wrangell.com. Dump stations located at Shoemaker Bay and downtown. **Wrangell Tours** has an RV Park with full hookups and WiFi. *See ads on this page.*

Tent camping only at City Park, **Milepost 1.7** Zimovia Highway; restrooms, tables and firepits. Tent camping is restricted to 24 hours; no tents in picnic shelters. Because overnight parking is prohibited at the city park, tent sites are restricted to bicyclists or walk-ins. Nice views during the day off of this park's loop for travelers.

Nemo Point USFS Recreation Area, 13.6 miles south of town via the Zimovia Highway, has 4 recreation sites for tent campers and RVs with dramatic views of Zimovia Strait. No fees, no reservations. Steep and narrow gravel access road to sites; NOT good for large RVs. Stop and check with campground hosts at Mile 0.5 on the access road about site accessibility, summer weekly interpretive programs and other campground activities.

Another option is staying at Wrangell's USFS public-use cabin. The Middle Ridge Cabin is located 19 miles from Wrangell. Cabin is at 1500 feet elevation and access may be limited seasonally because of snow. For details, contact the Forest Service office in Wrangell or visit www.fs.fed.us/r10/tongass.

Transportation

Air: Daily scheduled jet service is provided by Alaska Airlines to other Southeast cities with through service to Seattle and Anchorage. Charter services available.

The airport terminal is 1.1 miles from the ferry terminal via Evergreen Avenue or 1.1 miles from Zimovia Highway via Bennett Street. Taxi to town or check with locals hotels about courtesy van service.

Ferry: Alaska Marine Highway vessels connect Wrangell with all Southeastern Alaska ports plus Prince Rupert, BC, and Bellingham, WA. Ferry terminal is at the end of Second/Church streets. Walk or take a taxi from terminal to town. Terminal facilities include ticket office, waiting room and vehicle waiting area. Phone (907) 874-3711. See also ALASKA MARINE HIGHWAY section.

Car Rental: Available at the airport from Practical Rent-A-Car (907) 874-3975.

Taxi: Northern Lights, phone (907) 874-4646.

Highways: Zimovia Highway (see log this section). Logging roads have opened up most of Wrangell Island to motorists. Check with the USFS office at 525 Bennett St. for a copy of the Motor Vehicles Use Map which may be useful. Write USDA Forest Service, Wrangell Ranger District, Box 51, Wrangell, AK 99929; phone (907) 874-2323.

Private Boats: Transient moorage downtown on Reliance Float near Shakes Tribal House, and at Mile 1.4 Zimovia Highway at Heritage Harbor. If you are traveling to Wrangell by boat, radio ahead to the harbor master for tie-up space. Or phone (907) 874-3736 or 874-3051. VHF Ch. 16 is monitored throughout this area.

Attractions

Chief Shakes Island and Tribal House, in the middle of Wrangell Harbor, is reached by boardwalk. Constructed in 1940 by the Civilian Conservation Corp as a replica of the original 19th century Tribal House. In 2012 the Tribal House was reconstructed using local carvers and laborers working just like they did more than 70 years ago.

WRANGELL ADVERTISERS

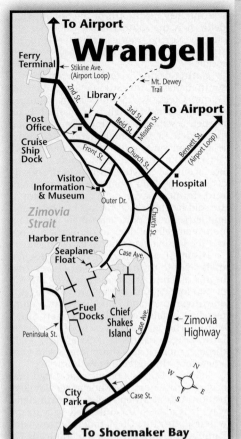

Wrangell map. To Airport. Ferry Terminal. Stikine Ave. (Airport Loop). Mt. Dewey Trail. Library. 2nd St. 3rd St. To Airport. Post Office. Reid St. Mission St. Cruise Ship Dock. Front St. Church St. Bennett St. (Airport Loop). Visitor Information & Museum. Outer Dr. Hospital. *Zimovia Strait*. Harbor Entrance. Seaplane Float. Case Ave. Church St. Zimovia Highway. Fuel Docks. Chief Shakes Island. Case Ave. Peninsula St. City Park. Case St. To Shoemaker Bay. N W E S

The Tribal House renovation project culminated with the re-dedication of Chief Shakes Island in 2013. The Tribal House is normally open irregular hours when cruise ships are in port during the summer or by appointment. Call (907) 874-3097 for details. Admission is charged.

Wrangell Museum, in the **Nolan Center**, features exhibits highlighting Wrangell's diverse history. Exhibit areas focus on Native culture; fur trade and exploration; the military; mining, fishing, timber; and 20th century topics. The oldest known Tlingit houseposts in Southeast Alaska are on display, along with a spruce root and cedar bark basket collection. Museum hours are 10 A.M. to 5 P.M. Monday–Saturday from May 1 to Sept. 30; 1-5 P.M. Tuesday–Saturday in winter. Phone (907) 874-3770, fax (907) 874-3785. Email museum@wrangell.com. Admission charged (children 6 and under free). Current movies are shown Friday–Sunday at the theatre in Nolan Center if other events are not scheduled.

St. Rose of Lima Catholic Church is a 0.2-mile walk from the Ferry Terminal up Second/Church streets. This picturesque church is the oldest Roman Catholic parish in Alaska, founded May 2, 1879.

Just beyond is the First Presbyterian Church, which has a red neon cross, 1 of 2 in the world that serve as navigational aids. This was the first church in Wrangell and is one of the oldest Protestant churches in Alaska (founded in 1877 and built in 1879). In the summer months it doubles as the Wrangell Hostel.

Muskeg Meadows Golf Course is a USGA regulation 9-hole golf course with a 250-yard driving range. The annual opening tournament in April coincides with the Stikine River Birding Festival. Muskeg Meadows

Zimovia Highway

Zimovia Highway leads 13.8 miles south of the ferry terminal where it connects with the island's Forest Service road system. A paved walking and biking path parallels the Zimovia Highway to Mile 5.2. **Distance from ferry terminal is shown.**

0 Alaska Marine Highway ferry terminal at end of Second Street, which becomes Church Street then Zimovia Highway. Paved bike path to Mile 5.2 Zimovia Highway.

0.1 Wrangell Public Library.

0.2 Rose of Lima Catholic Church

0.3 The Wrangell Hostel is housed here at the First Presbyterian Church (summer months only). Cross serves as navigational beacon.

0.4 Wrangell High School/Middle School.

0.5 Church Street/Wrangell Ave. junctions with Bennett Street and Zimovia Highway. Access to Wrangell Medical Center. Bennett Street (Airport Loop) leads north to the airport and back around to the ferry terminal.

0.6 Public Safety Building, fire station.

1.2 Alaska Waters RV Park. See display ad on page 670.

1.4 **Heritage Harbor**; transient moorage and commercial fishing vessels. Nearby cemetery.

1.5 Cemetery.

1.7 Loop road along shore accesses **City Park**; picnic area with shelters, firepits, restrooms, litter barrels. Tent camping only; 24-hour limit.

2 Turnout with public parking and beach access to west. Watch for bald eagles, shorebirds and great blue herons in Zimovia Strait.

3.3 Gravel turnouts.

4.6 **Shoemaker Bay Recreation Area** has two areas next to each other that make up the **Shoemaker RV Park & Campground**. 16 sites with electric hook-ups. Sites are along shoreline, some with views. Very few level sites. Restrooms are over in the Shoemaker Harbor Parking Lot. Pay area is small green box near big white sign. Envelopes are in green box, fill them out and put into brown tube with slit for registration (all unmarked in 2013); $25/night camping fee. While staying in the RV Park portion of the Recreation Area, you have free use of the city recreation facility with swimming pool, gym and showers.

Shoemaker RV Park & Campgrounds. See display ad on page 670.

4.7 **Shoemaker Harbor Parking Lot.** $15 per night, no hook-ups. Pull in grassy area between painted log stumps. Pay area is small green box near big white sign. Envelopes are in a green box, fill them out and put into brown tube with slit for registration. Parking tip: be watchful of sinking in grassy areas if it's wet. Restrooms, dump station.

Trailhead for **Rainbow Falls/Institute Creek/High Country Trails** on east side of Zimovia Highway across from harbor entrance.

4.8 Tennis court, horseshoe pits and children's playground.

4.9 Institute Creek. Watch for spawning

chum salmon in July.

5 Paved turnout with beach access.

5.2 Shoemaker Bay Loop road. Bike path ends.

5.8 Shoemaker Bay Loop road. Bike path ends.

6.7 Scenic turnout.

7.6 Turnout.

8.2 Turnout; access to **8 Mile Beach** (aka Agate Beach) tide permitting. This undeveloped recreation area has a beautiful beach.

8.8 Small paved turnout.

10.6 Turnoff to FR 6259 which leads 0.4 mile to **Pat's Lake**; watch for migrating trumpeter swans in early spring. One-mile trail from lake to estuary at mouth of Pat's Creek. Picnic and camping areas on short spur at turnoff.

11 Pat's Creek. The estuary at the mouth of Pat's Creek is a good place to watch spawning pink salmon, late July to early August. A 1-mile trail follows the creek from the estuary to Pat's Lake. Watch for American dippers, Sitka black-tailed deer and the occasional black bear along the trail.

13.3 McCormack Creek bridge. Small, active sawmill east side of road.

©Sharon Nault

13.6 Turnoff for **Nemo Point Recreation Area** via FR 6267. Narrow, gravel road with steep grades not suitable for large rigs, leads half-mile to the campground host campsite. In summer, stop here and check with hosts about campsite availability, road conditions and weekly campfire programs. Access road continues to Yunshookuh Campsite (Mile 0.7), 3 Sisters Overlook/Campsite (Mile 1.5), Anita Bay Overlook/Campsite (Mile 2.3) and Highline Campsite (Mile 3.5). Fantastic views of Zimovia Strait and north Etolin Island. Picnic tables, firewood, fire grills and outhouses each site. Access road continues for miles to remote campsites (no fee sites available) and lakes along the Wrangell Island forest road system. Highbush Lake, Thoms Lake and Long Lake have skiffs for public use. Check with USFS office in Wrangell for more information.

13.8 Two-lane paved road ends just beyond Tongass National Forest sign. *Large vehicles use turnaround at "Road Narrows" sign.* One-lane gravel FR 6265 begins and connects with other Forest Roads. A map showing island roads with recreation sites and trails is available from the USFS office in Wrangell.

Watch for logging trucks and other heavy equipment.

Nemo Point Recreation Area provides sensational views for campers. (©Sharon Nault)

LeConte Bay, just north of the Stikine River delta. It is the southernmost tidewater glacier in North America. Charter trips for sightseeing LeConte Glacier are available locally.

Garnet Ledge, a rocky outcrop on the south bank of the Stikine River delta at Garnet Creek, is 7.5 miles from Wrangell Harbor, reached at high tide by small boat. Garnet, a semiprecious stone, can be found embedded in the ledge here. The garnet ledge is on land deeded to the Presbytery of Alaska from the Southeast Council of the Boy Scouts of America (who had previously acquired the land from the late Fred Hanford, former mayor of Wrangell). Garnets are sold by children at the docks when ships and ferries are in port. Permits are needed for non-Wrangell children to dig garnets. Contact the Presbyterian Church in Wrangell.

Hiking Trails. There are several popular trails close to town. The Mount Dewey Trail begins at Third Street and leads to the top of 400-foot Mount Dewey, overlooking the downtown area and Zimovia Strait. Volunteer Park Trails, located off Bennett Street behind the elementary school, near the Little League ballfields. It is an easy walk through muskeg and shrub forests and with a new loop through old growth forest.

Rainbow Falls is a popular local trail that begins across from the Shoemaker Bay Recreation Area at **Milepost 4.6** Zimovia Highway. It is a steep 0.7-mile trail to a scenic waterfall. Institute Creek trail intersects with Rainbow Falls trail at Mile 0.6 and leads 2.7 miles to viewpoint and shelter overlooking Shoemaker Bay and Zimovia Strait. Institute Creek Trail also intersects with Wrangell High Country trail, which leads to 2 high-elevation shelters.

Nemo Point USFS Recreation Area, 13.6 miles south of town via the Zimovia Highway, offers dramatic views of Zimovia Strait from campsites and overlooks. From the end of the Zimovia Highway and from the Nemo Point road there is access to the island's extensive forest road system. These logging roads are very narrow provide access to lakes, trails and campsites. Favorite destinations for locals include Earl West Cove recreation site; Highbush Lake; and Thoms and Long lakes (both walk-in). **USFS cabins** in the surrounding area are a major attraction here. There are 22 USFS public-use cabins scattered throughout the region that are accessible by air or by boat. The U.S. Forest Service office is open 8 A.M. to 4:30 P.M. weekdays; 525 Bennett St., phone (907) 874-2323; or visit www.fs.usda.gov/tongass/.

AREA FISHING: Pats Lake and **Highbush Lake** are accessible by road. **Thoms Lake** and **Long Lake** are accessible via road and trail. Fly in to **Kunk Lake, Anan Lake, Marten Lake, Salmon Bay, Virginia Lake** and **Eagle Lake**. **Stikine River** near Wrangell (closed to non-resident king salmon fishing), Dolly Varden to 22 inches, and cutthroat to 18 inches, best in midsummer to fall; steelhead to 12 lbs., silver salmon 10 to 15 lbs., September and October. Saltwater fishing near Wrangell for king salmon, 20 to 40 lbs., best in May and June. There are bait, minimum size and other restrictions (see current sportfishing regulations). Stop by the Dept. of Fish and Game at 215 Front St. for details. Wrangell Salmon Derby runs from mid-May to mid-June; kings to more than 50 lbs. are not unusual.

hosts tournaments almost every weekend during the summer. For information, phone (907) 874-4653; www.wrangellalaskagolf.com.

©Sharon Nault

Petroglyph Beach State Historic Park is located a half-mile from the ferry terminal via Stikine Avenue (watch for sign; limited parking). The park has some 40 petroglyphs (ancient designs carved into rock faces) that may be found between low and high tide marks. These are thought to be Tlingit in origin. A boardwalk provides access from cul-de-sac to an observation deck with interpretive signs overlooking the beach. Stairs lead from the deck to the beach. The petroglyphs are protected by state and federal antiquities laws: Visitors may only photograph the real petroglyphs. Make rubbings using the replica petroglyphs displayed on the observation deck.

Anan Wildlife Observatory is located 30 miles southeast of Wrangell. During July and August, visitors can watch black and brown bears catch pink salmon headed for the salmon spawning grounds. Anan (pronounced an-an) is accessible by boat or plane only. It is managed by the U.S. Forest Service, which maintains the covered deck/observation platform overlooking the creek and falls, and the trail leading to it.

Visitors to Anan, arriving by plane or boat, are dropped off at the "lagoon entrance" and must walk in on the half-mile boardwalk trail (some stairs). No food or beverages (except water) are allowed at the observatory.

The observatory is open from 8 A.M. to 6 P.M. A day-pass is required to visit Anan between July 5 and August 25; cost is $10 per person per day (non-refundable). The permit system limits visitors to 60 per day. If you visit the observatory with a guide or outfitter, the permit may be included in the cost of the trip. The Forest Service office in Wrangell has more information about the permit system and a list of guides and outfitters permitted to transport visitors to Anan; phone (907) 874-2323. Visitors may register online at www.fs.usda.gov/tongass/.

The Stikine River delta lies north of Wrangell within the Stikine–LeConte Wilderness and is accessible only by boat or plane. The Stikine is the fastest free flowing, navigable river in North America, and can be rafted, canoed or run by skiff or jetboat. Air and jetboat charters for both sightseeing and drop-offs at put-in sites for river runners are available in Wrangell.

The Stikine River plays host to stunning numbers of birds each spring, according to the Alaska Dept. of Fish and Game. The second highest concentration of bald eagles in the world occurs on the Stikine during the annual spring run of eulachon. Grasses and sedges on the Stikine Flats at the mouth of the river attract up to 10,000 snow geese each year. The Stikine Delta is a critical refueling stop for thousands of shorebirds during their annual migration. These birds feed on tiny invertebrates and small fish before continuing on to their arctic breeding grounds. Great bird watching, but like all migratory bird watching, timing is everything and the birds have their own schedule. The **Stikine River Birding Festival** celebrates spring and the arrival of the birds in April. Check with the local visitor's bureau or Forest Service office when planning a birding trip.

LeConte Glacier, also within the Stikine-LeConte Wilderness, is at the head of

Petersburg

Sons of Norway Hall as viewed across the Hammer Slough. (©Sharon Nault)

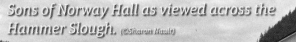

Located on the northern tip of Mitkof Island at the northern end of Wrangell Narrows, midway between Juneau and Ketchikan. **Population:** 3,200. **Emergency Services: Borough Police, Fire Department** and **Ambulance**, phone 911. **Alaska State Troopers**, phone (907) 772-3983. **Police**, phone (907) 772-3838. **Search and Rescue/ Petersburg Police**, phone (907) 772-3838. **Hospital** and **Clinic**, Petersburg Medical Center, 2nd and Fram St., phone (907) 772-4291. **Poison Control** (statewide), phone 1-800-222-1222. **Maritime Search and Rescue:** Contact the Coast Guard at (800) 478-5555. Harbormaster, phone (907) 772-4688, CB Channel 9 or VHF Channel 16.

Visitor Information: The Petersburg Visitor Information Center is located in the historic old ranger station at 1st and Fram streets. The 24-foot by 28-foot wooden structure holds a surprising amount of information. The center is open Monday–Saturday from 9 A.M. to 5 P.M., Sundays noon to 4 P.M., May through Labor Day in September; Monday–Friday from 10 A.M. to 2 P.M., October through April. Write Petersburg Visitor Information Center, Box 649, Petersburg 99833; phone (907) 772-4636 or toll-free 1-866-484-4700; www.petersburg. org.

Clausen Museum, 2nd and Fram streets, phone (907) 772-3598. Alaska Dept. of Fish and Game, State Office Building, Sing Lee Alley; open 8 A.M. to 4:30 P.M., Monday through Friday, phone (907) 772-3801. Area maps and general information on U.S. Forest Service lands available at the Petersburg Ranger District office in the Federal Building downtown, open weekdays 8 A.M. to 5 P.M. and at the Visitor Center.

Elevation: Sea level. **Climate:** Average daily maximum temperature in July, 64°F; daily minimum in January, 20°F. All-time high, 84°F in 1933; record low, -19°F in 1947. Mean annual precipitation, 110 inches; mostly as rain. **Radio:** KFSK-FM 100.9. **Television:** Alaska Rural Communication Service, Channel 15; KTOO (PBS) Channel 9 and cable channels. **Newspaper:** *Petersburg Pilot* (weekly).

Private Aircraft: James A. Johnson Airport (PSG), 1 mile southeast; elev. 107 feet; length 6,000 feet; asphalt; fuel 100, A. Seaplane base 0.5 mile from downtown.

Petersburg boasts the largest home-based fishing fleet in Alaska and is also well known for its shrimp, crab, salmon, herring and other fish products. Many families depend on the fishing industry for livelihood.

Petersburg was named for Peter Buschmann, who selected the present townsite for a salmon cannery and sawmill in 1897. The sawmill and dock were built in 1899, and the cannery was completed in 1900. He was followed by other Norwegian immigrants who came to fish and work in the cannery and sawmill. Since then the cannery has operated continuously (with rebuilding, expansion and different owners) and is now known as Petersburg Fisheries Inc., a division of Icicle Seafoods Inc. Petersburg Fisheries shares the waterfront with two other canneries, other cold storage plants and several other fish processing facilities.

The Borough Hall and the Federal Building are both located downtown. Petersburg's 2 healing totem poles, one commemorating the Eagle Clan and one the Raven Clan, are located at the corner of Nordic and Haugen

Major Attractions:

Whale watching, Le Conte Glacier, Little Norway Festival

adjacent the Federal Building. The poles were carved by Sitka carver Tommy Joseph.

Lodging & Services

Readers of *Yachting Magazine* chose Petersburg as the best yachting location for 2013. This "Little Norway" mixes atmosphere and amazing natural beauty with sufficient amenities to stand out among port cities. Lodging downtown at 2 hotels/motels and several bed-and-breakfasts; visit www.petersburg.org for listings. Dining downtown at Coastal Cold Storage and Deli, Papa Bear's, Inga's Galley, Helse, and El Rincon. The 5-block-long downtown commercial area on Main Street (Nordic Drive) has

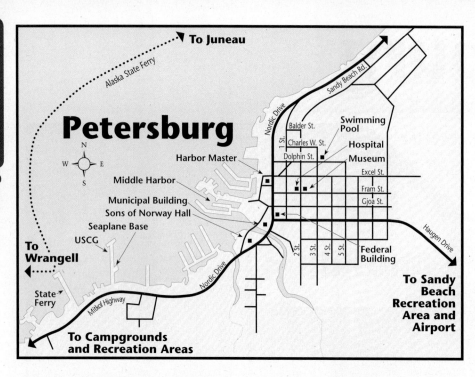

Petersburg

a grocery store; 2 coffee shops, 2 hardwares, marine and fishing supply stores; drugstore; bookstore and fabric store, a travel agency (**Viking Travel Inc.**); banks (Wells Fargo, First Bank); a liquor store, 2 bars; several gift shops and art galleries; and clothing stores specializing in both Alaskan and Norwegian items. Auto repair, towing, gas and diesel at the corner of 2nd and Haugen.

The post office, 13 churches and the spacious Hammer and Wikan grocery/deli are located a half-mile from downtown on Haugen Drive.

A community gym with racquetball courts, climbing wall and weight room is located between the high school and ele-mentary school on Charles W. Street off 3rd street. The Petersburg Aquatic Center, also located at the school, offers daily open swims with 2 pools and water slide. Phone Petersburg Parks and Recreation at (907) 772-3392.

Camping

RV campsites with hookups and a gen-eral store at **The Trees RV Park**, Mile 10.2 Mitkof Highway. The nearest public camp-ground is Ohmer Creek USFS Campground, at Mile 21.7 Mitkof Highway, with 10 sites (can accommodate RVs to 35 feet). There are 20 campsites at Green's Camp Campground on Sumner Strait, Mile 26.1 Mitkof High-way. *(See Mitkof Highway log on facing page for details.)*

Transportation

Air: Daily scheduled jet service by Alaska Airlines, (907) 772-4255, to major Southeast cities and Seattle, WA, with connections to Anchorage and Fairbanks. A scheduled regional carrier and several local carrier and charter services also serve the area, including Pacific Wing and Nordic Air.

The airport is located 1 mile from the Federal Building on Haugen Drive. It has a ticket counter and waiting room. Hotel cour-tesy van and taxi service available.

Ferry: Alaska Marine Highway vessels connect Petersburg with all Southeastern Alaska cities plus Prince Rupert, BC, and Bellingham, WA. (See ALASKA MARINE HIGHWAY section.) State ferries dock at the ferry terminal near town, at **Milepost 0.8** Mitkof Highway; phone (907) 772-3855. It is not a long walk to downtown from the ferry terminal, unless you arrive late at night and it's raining or you have a lot of luggage.

See also "Ferry Travel" in the TRAVEL PLANNING section.

Car Rental: Available from Scandia House Hotel and Avis at Tides Inn.

Taxi: Island Cab (907) 518-1279; City Cab (907) 518-1225.

Highways: The 34-mile Mitkof Highway (see log this section); 21-mile Three Lakes Loop Road; and Sandy Beach Road.

Cruise Ships: Smaller cruise ships dock at Petersburg's South Harbor and Petro dock.

Private Boats: There are 3 boat harbors that can accommodate up to a 200 ft vessel. Transient vessels check in with harbor-master; VHF Channel 16, CB Channel 9 or phone (907) 772-4688.

Attractions

Clausen Memorial Museum, 203 Fram St., features Petersburg area history. On display are artifacts representing the cannery and fisheries, a world-record 126.5-lb. king salmon, the Cape Decision light station lens, a Tlingit canoe and the wall piece "Land, Sea, Sky." The museum has a store with local and regional art, books and gifts. **The Fisk** (Norwegian for fish), a 10-foot bronze sculpture commemorating Petersburg's fish-ing tradition, stands in a working fountain in front of the museum. It was completed during the Alaska centennial year of 1967 by sculptor Carson Boysen.

The museum is open 10 A.M.–5 P.M., Monday–Saturday in summer; 10 A.M.–2 P.M., Tuesday–Saturday Sept. 5–Dec. 23.; Phone (907) 772-3598 for more information.

Little Norway Festival, held May 15–18, 2014, is an annual event celebrating Nor-wegian Constitution Day. Pageantry, old-country dress, contests, Vikings & Valkyries, a Viking ship, dancing, Norwegian pastries, a parade and a Norwegian "fish feed" for locals and visitors are featured.

Sons of Norway Hall, on the National Register of Historic Places, was built in 1912. Situated on pilings over Hammer Slough (a favorite photography subject), its window shutters are decorated with rosema-ling (Norwegian tole painting). **Fisherman's Memorial Park**, next to the Sons of Norway Hall, commemorates those townspeople lost at sea. The Viking ship *Valhalla*, next to the memorial, is another favorite photo subject.

Viking Travel, Inc. 101 N. Nordic, phone (800) 327-2571, (907) 772-3818. Great selection of cruises, tours and activities all over Alaska. Whale-watching, sea kayak-ing, LeConte Glacier Bay, fishing charters, black and brown bear viewing, river rafting, Glacier Bay tours. Independent travel pack-ages for all Alaska. Instant ferry and airline reservations and ticketing. www.AlaskaFerry. com. [ADVERTISEMENT]

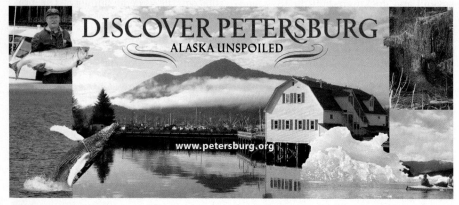

Mitkof Highway

The major road on Mitkof Island, Mitkof Highway leads 33.8 miles south from downtown Petersburg to the Stikine River delta at the south end of the island. The highway is paved to **Milepost 25**; wide gravel to road end. Walking/biking path along waterfront to Mile 1.8, paved shoulder to Mile 2.8. *Watch for deer.*

Distance from downtown Petersburg is shown.

0 Federal Building and totem poles at Nordic Drive and Haugen.

0.1 Bridge over Hammer Slough, an intertidal estuary.

0.4 South Harbor parking with a small viewing area, benches and information boards about humpback whales.

0.8 Alaska Marine Highway ferry terminal, office and waiting area on right.

1 Bike path next 1.7 miles southbound.

2.9 RV campground on Scowbay Loop Road; hookups.

5 Three small turnouts between Mile 5 and 6.

6.1 Large paved turnout with view.

7.4 Twin Creek.

7.5 Twin Creek RV Park campground. △

8.7 Petersburg city limits.

10.2 The Trees RV Park and General Store; open year-round, hookups, rental cabins, laundry, store.

The Trees RV Park and General Store. See display ad on page 674. △

10.6 Junction with **Three Lakes Loop Road**. This 21-mile-long, hilly, narrow, winding gravel road (not recommended for RVs) loops from **Milepost 10.2** to **Milepost 20.6** Mitkof Highway. (Locals use the entrance at **Milepost 20.6** to reach hiking trails on this side road.) There are no services available along the road, but there are boardwalk hiking trails to 3 lakes: Sand, Hill and Crane. Rowboats available for public-use at the lakes.

Distance marker at junction shows Sand Lake Trail 13.9 miles, Hill Lake Trail 14.3 miles, Crane Lake Trail 14.7 miles. The turnoff for LeConte Glacier Overlook, a picnic site with a spectacular view of the mainland, is located 12.1 miles from this junction on Three Lakes Loop Road.

10.7 Falls Creek and 3 new viewing platforms that overlook the fish ladder. "This is a fantastically beautiful place, well-worth the stop, even if there are no fish present" according to our contributing editor, Sharon Nault. See steelhead, April and May; pink salmon below falls in August; silver salmon, August and September; Dolly Varden and cutthroat late summer and fall. No fishing within 300 feet of fish ladder. *CAUTION: Watch for bears.* ☛

10.9 Turnoff for Papke's Landing boat launch (0.5 mile).

14 Entering Tongass National Forest.

14.2 Blind River Rapids very large parking area and ¼-mile trail; outhouse. Boardwalk trail through muskeg meadow to Blind River Rapids fishing area. Wheelchair-accessible boardwalk loop. Hatchery steelhead, mid-April to mid-May; king salmon, June to late July; pink salmon, July and August; silver salmon, mid-August to October. Also Dolly Varden and cutthroat trout. Be sure to check applicable regulations prior to fishing. ☛

Wildlife viewing on Blind River Rapids trail includes: Sitka black-tailed deer, bald eagles, moose, black bears, red-breasted sapsuckers, Steller's jays, chickadees, belted kingfishers and winter wrens.

16.1 Blind Slough Trumpeter Swan Observatory. Covered platform with interpretive signs; bring binoculars or spotting scope for best viewing. Hundreds of trumpeter swans stop to feed and rest here between mid-October and December before resuming their southern migration. Up to 75 swans spend the winter here each year. Also watch for mergansers, mallards, geese and bald eagles in summer.

17.2 Turnoff for short road to **Blind Slough Picnic Area** and fish hatchery. A large picnic area with many nice tables, large shelter and pit toilets; no overnight camping. This is a very popular place for locals. Swimming and grassy areas, short walk over bridge to hatchery. Area is closed at 10 P.M. **Crystal Lake Fish Hatchery** is open for visiting, but no tours (907) 650-7077. Fishing in **Blind Slough** for cutthroat and Dolly Varden in summer; silver salmon, mid-August to mid-September; king salmon, June and July. Check with ADF&G for current regulations; phone (907) 772-3801. ☛

19.7 Turnoff on short loop road for **Man-Made Hole Picnic Area** with tables, firepits, toilets, swimming and trail. Beautiful spot. Fishing for cutthroat and Dolly Varden year-round; best summer/fall. ☛

20.4 Junction with 21-mile-long **Three Lakes Loop Road** (see description at **Milepost 10.2**). Distance marker at junction shows Crane Lake Trail 6.3 miles, Hill Lake Trail 6.7 miles, Sand Lake Trail 7.2 miles. The turnoff for LeConte Glacier Overlook, a picnic site with a spectacular view of the mainland, is 8.3 miles from this junction.

21.2 Ohmer Creek nature trail, 1.5 mile loop; first 0.3 mile is barrier-free.

21.4 Katelyn Ohmer Markley Bridge crosses Ohmer Creek. **Ohmer Creek USFS Campground**, 10 sites in trees on half-mile loop road; toilets, garbage containers, tables, drinking water, firepits, camping fee of $6 charged. Open spring to fall. Accommodates RVs to 35 feet. Trout fishing July and August; pink salmon August to September. ☛ △

22.7 Leaving Tongass National Forest.

24.2 Site of Blind Slough USFS Log Transfer Facility, huge parking area. Fishing from skiff for silver salmon, mid-August to mid-September. Fishing from shore for kings. ☛

26.1 Access to Green's Camp campground on Sumner Strait; 20 campsites. △

28 Wilson Creek recreation area (not signed); picnic table, grills, toilet, parking. Beautiful level parking area with picnic sites along Sumner Straight.

28.6 Banana Point Boat Launch Ramp; narrow 0.2-mile access road to concrete boat ramp, outhouse, gravel loop, parking.

29.3 Pavement ends, highway continues along Sumner Straight.

31 Stikine River mud flats, visible at low tide. Part of the Stikine River delta, where Dry Strait meets Sumner Strait.

32.9 Stikine Wilderness Boat Launch (City of Petersburg/U.S. Forest Service); steep gravel drive to rocky water access (improvements to this boat launch are planned).

33.8 Road ends with turnaround.

Whale Watching. Of the estimated 6,000 humpback whales in the North Pacific, approximately 2,000 feed in Southeast Alaska during the summer, and nearly half of those enter Frederick Sound.

A whale watching cruise tour out of Petersburg provides consistent and often spectacular whale viewing. These whale watching trips start in May and continue through the summer, with July and August the prime viewing time for humpbacks. Hundreds of humpbacks congregate in Frederick Sound and lower Stephen's Passage. Other large marine mammals to see are killer whales, Dall's porpoises, harbor seals and Steller sea lions. Bird watching on these trips includes marbled murrelets, scoters and pigeon guillemots. Charters generally take 6–14 people per trip; advance booking is strongly recommended. Contact Viking Travel, Inc., phone (907) 772-3818.

LeConte Glacier, a major area attraction, lies 25 miles east of Petersburg in LeConte Bay. It is the continent's southernmost active tidewater glacier and the fastest flowing glacier in the world. The glacier continually "calves," creating icefalls from its face into the bay. Seals are common and killer whales are sometimes seen. Helicopters, small aircraft and boats may be chartered in Petersburg (or Wrangell) to see LeConte Glacier. Tongass Kayak Adventures offers guided kayak trips to LeConte Glacier; www.tongasskayak.com. Contact Viking Trail at 101 N. Nordic in town; phone (907) 772-3818.

Sandy Beach Road. Make a 4.5-mile loop drive beginning downtown on Nordic Drive, which quickly turns into Sandy Beach Road. First stop (and also an easy 0.1-mile walk from downtown) is **Eagle's Roost Park**, which has picnic tables and usually a couple of eagles sitting in the trees.

Continue on Sandy Beach Road 1.4 miles to **Outlook Park**, a small, easy-to-miss park tucked in between waterfront homes. Outlook has a small parking area, shelter and 2 spotting scopes. Look for humpback whales in Frederick Sound from June through September.

Continue 1.1 miles beyond Outlook Park to **Sandy Beach Park**, which offers picnic tables, 3 shelters, firepits, playground, volleyball court and a sandy beach. Parking is a little more generous at Sandy Beach Park, where there are roadside spaces and a gravel parking lot (not recommended for RVs). This park is located at the junction with Haugen Drive, which takes you 1.7 miles back to downtown Petersburg.

U.S. Forest Service public-use cabins, canoe/kayaking routes and hiking trails may be accessed from Petersburg, which is the administrative center for the Stikine Area of Tongass National Forest. For information, stop by the USFS office in the Federal Building, or write the Petersburg Ranger District, P.O. Box 1328, Petersburg, AK 99833; phone (907) 772-3871; www.fs.usda.gov/tongass/.

The Visitor Center also has a kiosk with information on forest service cabins, trails and other recreating in the Tongass.

Take a drive. The 34-mile-long Mitkof Highway and 21-mile Three Lakes Loop Road may only add up to 55 miles of road system, but there are quite a few interesting spots to stop along these routes. *(See detailed road log page 675.)*

Watch for Sitka black-tailed deer along the road system, especially in June and July when does bring their fawns to feed on lush roadside plants. Fawns sometimes bed down right on the road, so be alert while driving. Also, deer almost always travel in pairs, so if you see one, slow down for the second one.

The boardwalk trail (handicap-accessible) at Blind River Rapids, **Milepost 14.2** Mitkof Highway, is not only a popular destination for fishermen, it also offers a close-up view of muskeg. Muskeg—a wet and acidic mix of plant life in various stages of decomposition—covers 10 percent of Alaska.

Salmon migration and spawning may be observed July through September at Falls Creek bridge and fish ladder, see **Milepost 10.7** Mitkof Highway.

Three Lakes Loop Road makes a nice side trip and an opportunity to experience a temperate rain forest. This narrow, winding, hilly road loops off the Mitkof Highway between **Mileposts 10.2** and **20.6**, providing access to 3 lakes—Sand, Hill and Crane—via boardwalk trails. Spectacular view of the mainland from LeConte Glacier Overlook.

And make sure to stop for a picnic at one of Mitkof Highway's 2 scenic picnic sites. Man-Made Hole at **Milepost 20** is a beautiful spot, with a handicap-accessible boardwalk trail, picnic tables and shelter. Blind Slough, at **Milepost 17.3**, another picturesque setting, is adjacent the Crystal Lake Fish Hatchery.

The Crystal Lake Fish Hatchery produces silver and king salmon for local waters. No tours, but hatchery personnel will answer questions. Visitors welcome Monday through Friday from 8 A.M. to 4 P.M., and Saturday and Sunday from 8 A.M. to 2 P.M.

AREA FISHING: Salmon, steelhead, cutthroat and Dolly Varden fishing at **Falls Creek, Blind Slough and Blind River Rapids** (see log of Mitkof Highway this section). Salmon can be caught in the harbor area and **Scow Bay** area. (Rapid tidal currents in front of the town necessitate the use of an outboard motor.) Dolly Varden can be caught from the beach north of town and from downtown docks. **Petersburg Creek**, directly across Wrangell Narrows from downtown within Petersburg Creek–Duncan Salt Chuck Wilderness Area, also offers good fishing. Contact the Sport Fish Division of the Alaska Dept. of Fish and Game in Petersburg at (907) 772-3801 for more information. **Petersburg King Salmon Derby** takes place Memorial Day weekend. Check with the visitor information center for details.

Sitka

Even on an overcast day (not uncommon in Southeast), Sitka is a beautiful city.
(©Sharon Nault)

Major Attractions:

©Sharon Nault

Sitka National Historic Park, Baranof Castle Hill State Historic Site, Sitka Summer Music Festival

Located on the west side of Baranof Island, 95 air miles southwest of Juneau, 185 air miles northwest of Ketchikan; 2.5 hours flying time from Seattle, WA. **Population:** 9,084. **Emergency Services: Alaska State Troopers, City Police, Fire Department,** and **Ambulance,** phone 911. **Hospitals:** Sitka Community, 209 Moller Ave., phone (907) 747-3241; SEARHC

Mount Edgecumbe, 222 Tongass Dr., phone (907) 966-2411. **Maritime Search and Rescue,** phone the Coast Guard at (907) 463-2000 or the Operations Center for Sitka at 966-5447.

Visitor Information: Contact the Sitka Convention and Visitors Bureau at 303 Lincoln St. Ste. 4/Box 1226-MP, Sitka, AK 99835; phone (907) 747-5940; www.sitka.org. Summer information desk at Harrigan Centennial Hall, 330 Harbor Dr. For USDA Forest Service information write the Sitka Ranger District, 204 Siginaka Way, Sitka, AK 99835; phone (907) 747-6671; email r10_sitka_rd@fs.fed.us; www.fs.usda.gov/tongass/. For information on Sitka National Historical Park, write 106 Metlakatla St., Sitka, AK 99835; phone (907) 747-0110; website: www.nps.gov/sitk.

Elevation: Sea level. **Climate:** Average daily temperature in July, 56°F; in January, 34°F. Annual precipitation, 86 inches. **Radio:** KIFW-AM 1230, KAQU-FM (Whale Radio) 88.1, KSBZ-FM 103.1, KCAW-FM 104.7/90.1. **Television:** Cable channels and KTNL-CBS. **Newspaper:** *Daily Sitka Sentinel.*

Private Aircraft: Sitka's "Rocky Guitierrez" airport on Japonski Island; elev. 21 feet; length 6,500 feet; asphalt; A1. Sitka Seaplane base adjacent to the west.

Facing the Pacific Ocean, Sitka is protected by smaller islands like Kruzof Island, where 3,201-foot Mount Edgecumbe, a dormant volcano, is situated. O'Connell Bridge connects Sitka with Japonski Island. The 1,255-foot-long bridge was the first cable-stayed, girder-span bridge in the United States, dedicated Aug. 19, 1972.

Originally occupied by Tlingit Indians, Alexander Baranof, chief manager of the Russian–American Co. (headquartered in Kodiak) built a trading post and fort (Redoubt St. Michael's) north of Sitka in 1799. Indians burned down the fort in 1802, but Baranof returned in 1804, and by 1808,

Sitka was capital of Russian Alaska. Baranof was governor from 1799 to 1818.

Salmon was the mainstay of the economy from the late 1800s until the 1950s, when the salmon population decreased. A pulp mill operated at nearby Silver Bay from 1960 to 1993. History-rich Sitka has many important historic sites, meaninful in Alaska's history. The first flag raised in Alaska, was here at Halibut Point State Recreation site. Castle Hill is the site where the US purchased Alaska from the Russians. There is also wide-spread evidence of the Tlingit Alaska Native tribe throughout Sitka.

Sitka's beauty is renown, and in part because of that its economy is supported by tourism. Sitka has also attracted the attention of Hollywood: it was named as the hometown of a character in the movie "The Proposal." However, Sitka's location was too remote for the producers to actually film here (the movie was filmed in Rockport, MA, instead), but there is some beautiful footage—shot without actors—of the Sitka area included in the movie.

Healthcare, government and commercial fishing continue to be economic mainstays here. Herring eggs, or roe, are a major fishery in Sitka. Between late February and early April, thousands of herring move into the waters of Sitka Sound to spawn along the beaches. The fish lay sticky eggs that cluster on rocks, pilings and kelp.

Lodging & Services

Accommodations in Sitka at **Alaska Ocean View Bed & Breakfast Inn** (description follows), phone (907) 747-8310; Sitka Super 8 (907) 747-8804; and others. Sitka's hostel is downtown, phone (907) 747-8661 for information. There are over 15 bed and breakfasts, numerous lodges and vacation rentals.

Alaska Ocean View Bed & Breakfast Inn. You'll enjoy casual elegance at affordable rates at this superior B&B, where guests experience exceptional personal comfort, privacy and friendly hosts. Open your day with the tantalizing aroma of fresh bread baking, freshly ground coffee brewing and a sumptuous organic breakfast. Close your day with a refreshing soak in the bubbling outdoors hot-tub spa. Open year-round, smoke-free. Central location, view, concierge, WiFi. "Delighted beyond our expectations!" Brochure and reservations: 1101 Edgecumbe Drive, Sitka, AK 99835; (907) 747-8310. Email: www.sitka-alaska-lodging.com. [ADVERTISEMENT]

Services in Sitka's downtown area include restaurants, drugstore, clothing and grocery stores (grocery store at Mile 0.6 Halibut Point Road), and gift shops. Laundry may be done at the Super 8 as they allow the public to use their facilities. There are 2 additional laundromats: one 1 mile and the second 1.5 miles from downtown. Shopping and services are also available along Sawmill and Halibut Point roads. Dump stations are located at the Wastewater Treatment Plant on Japonski Island.

The Sitka Library is conveniently located near Harrigan Centennial Hall at the waterfront. Tables with plug-ins for electronics, nice views, restrooms and helpful staff make this a good stop for visitors.

Camping

RV camping in the Sitka area at the **Sitka Sportsman's RV Park**, located a block from the ferry terminal on Halibut Point Road. It

is open year-round with 16 full-service ocean front sites; phone 1-800-750-4712; www.rvsitka.com. The municipal campground, Sealing Cove Campground, is adjacent to Sealing Cove Boat Harbor on Japonski Island, and open April 1–Sept. 30. Phone (907) 747-3439.

The U.S. Forest Service operates Starrigavan Recreation Area at Mile 7.1 Halibut Point Road (see description in the Halibut Point Road log on page 678). This campground is gated at night. Arrangements can be made for gates to be left open for late arrivals. Campground manager can be reached at (907) 747-4216. Reservations for Starrigavan campsites may be made by phoning 1-877-444-6777 or online at www.recreation.gov.

Transportation

Air: Scheduled jet service by Alaska Airlines. Charter service also available. The airport is on Japonski Island, across O'Connell Bridge, 1.7 miles from downtown. Van and taxi service available to downtown hotels and accommodations.

Ferry: The MV *Fairweather* serves Sitka from Juneau in summer. Sitka is also a mainline port on select sailings from Prince Rupert, BC, and Bellingham, WA. See ALASKA MARINE HIGHWAY section. The Alaska Marine Highway ferry terminal is

located at **Milepost 7** Halibut Point Road; local phone (907) 747-8737 when ferry is in port or 1-800-642-0066. Bus meets all arrival ferries or phone for taxi.

Bus: The Ride (http://publictransit.sitkatribe.org) offers weekday service from 6:30 A.M. to 7:30 P.M. in town. Purchase tickets on the bus or at Sitka Tribal Enterprises (204 Katlian St.), Old Harbor Books (201 Lincoln St.), Bear Country Gifts (401 Lincoln St.) or Sea Mart Grocery (1867 Halibut Point Rd.); phone The Ride Hotline at (907) 747-7103.

Airport shuttle to accommodations and downtown area, May–Sept. Visitor Shuttle Bus to attractions operates when cruise ships are in port; phone (907) 747-7290.

Car Rental: Avis and North Star Rent-a-Car at the airport.

Taxi: Baranof Taxi and Sitka Cabs.

Highways: The 7.1-miles-long Halibut Point Road provides access to many businesses, the Alaska Marine Highway ferry

Halibut Point Road

Halibut Point Road (paved) leads northwest from Lake Street to dead end just beyond the entrance to Starrigavan recreation area. **Distance from Lake Street is shown.**

0 Traffic circle for Lake Street, Erler Street and Sawmill Road.

0.6 Stoplight at Katlian; Lakeside Center, NC Company.

0.7 Beachfront Turnaround Park, has a skatepark, dog park, large paved parking area (below road) and beach access.

0.8 Emergency entrance to Sitka Community Hospital McDonalds, laundromat, dollar store and True Value Hardware.

1.6 Seamart Grocery to west.

1.7 Pioneer Park to west with picnic area; parking, beach access via trails.

1.8 Paved turnout; picnic shelter, beach access via trails.

2 Cascade Creek bridge.

2.2 Sandy Beach; good swimming (cold water), parking, restrooms. View of Mount Edgecumbe.

2.7 Gravel turnout overlooking water.

3.1 Turnoff for Harbor Mountain Bypass/Kramer Avenue; wide and paved for 0.25 mile, then wide gravel road to Mile 1 where road narrows at gate; steep, narrow, winding gravel road 5 miles to picnic area and viewpoint, (from here it is not suitable for RVs motorhomes, travel trailers or pick-up campers as per Sitka Ranger District); 5.6 miles to **Harbor Mountain Ridge Trailhead.**

4.2 Halibut Point State Recreation Site; parking areas, swimming beach, picnic shelters, tables, fireplaces and toilets. Golf course across road.

5.4 Halibut Point Services, container storage.

5.6 Cove Marina next to Alaska Wildlife Protection Troopers Office and Dock.

6.4 Sportsmans RV Park. See display ad page 677.

6.5 Alaska Marine Highway ferry terminal. Turn right when leaving Ferry Dock for Sportsmans RV and Sitka, or left to Starrigaven USPS Recreation Area.

6.8 Old Sitka State Recreation Site; boat launch, parking. Trailhead: forest and muskeg trail ¾-mile, barrier free.

6.9 Old Sitka State Historic Site; commemorative plaque. This was the site of Fort Archangel Michael, the first Russian settlement in the area in 1799. In 1802, in a surprise attack, the Tlingit Indians of the area destroyed the fort and killed most of its occupants, driving the Russians out until Baranof's successful return in 1804.

7 Starrigavan Creek. Spawning pink salmon in August and September. Estuary Life trailhead north side of creek; parking. The **Estuary Life Trail** is a barrier-free ¼-mile boardwalk trail around the estuary where the saltwater Starrigavan Bay meets the freshwater Starrigavan Creek. Excellent birding for great blue herons, bald eagles, common mergansers, belted kingfishers, canvasbacks, mallards, buffleheads and many other birds.

7.1 Starrigavan USFS Recreation Area. Popular year-round recreation area includes 23 individual campsites, 2 double family sites and Starrigavan Creek Cabin in the "Estuary Loop"; 3 hike-in campsites overlooking Starrigavan Bay in the "Bayside Loop" (parking in service area); and 6 hike-in campsites in the "Backpacker Loop" (hikers and bikers only).

Camp host, ADA accessible sites, garbage service, message board, picnic tables, toilets. Camping fees $12–$16 for individual sites, $30 for double family sites, $50 for Starrigavan Creek Cabin. Some campsites are first-come, first-served, other campsites and cabins may be reserved up to 4 days in advance by phoning 1-877-444-6777 or online at www.recreation.gov.

The Estuary Loop has an artesian well, a popular source of water for local residents and visitors. Bring your water bottles.

Bayside Loop to west leads to Starrigavan Picnic Area, with 4 picnic sites and 2 group shelters; access to and views of Starrigavan Bay. Also access to Mosquito Cove Trail, a 1.3-mile loop that passes through 'spruce-hemlock forest and along shoreline.

Recreation area gates are closed and locked from 10 P.M. to 7 A.M. daily, May 1 through Labor Day. (Off-season vehicle access restricted when there is snow or ice on roadway.) There is a year-round host at the entrance to the Bayside Loop. For further information, contact the Sitka Ranger District at (907) 747-6671 or the recreation area manager at (907) 747-4216; email r10_sitka_rd@fed.us.

Halibut Point Road ends just beyond the entrances to Starrigavan Recreation Area.

---

terminal and Starrigavan Recreation Area *(see log above)*. Sawmill Creek Road leads 5.5 miles south from Lake Street to Sawmill Cove Industrial Park.

Cruise Ships: Cruise ships either anchor in Sitka Sound, and passengers are lightered to shore to the Crescent Harbor visitors' dock and O'Connell Bridge visitors' dock, or +at the Old Sitka Dock, located 5 miles from downtown near the ferry terminal

Private Boats: Transient moorage available at Thomsen Harbor, Katlian Street, 0.6 mile from city center. Contact Harbormaster (907) 747-3439 or Channel 16 VHS.

Attractions

The **Sitka Summer Music Festival**, is an annual event featuring the best in chamber music performed by world-famous artists. Scheduled for June 6 through July 5, 2014, premiere chamber music concerts are presented Friday and Saturday evenings in Harrigan Centennial Hall, with additional concerts and special events taking place during the festival. Advance tickets are a good idea; the concerts are popular. *Children under 6 years not admitted.* Contact Sitka Summer Music Festival, P.O. Box 3333, Sitka, AK 99835; phone (907) 747-6774; www.sitkamusicfestival.org.

The **Harrigan Centennial Hall**, built in 1967, hosts the Summer Music Festival and houses the Sitka Historical Museum (description follows). It is located on Harbor Drive along the waterfront. This location has a summer information desk run by the Sitka Convention and Visitors Bureau (open only when cruise ships are docked) and it provides free maps and visitor information.

Sitka Historical Museum provides a great overview of Sitka's rich Tlingit, Russian and American past through displays, photographs and artifacts and is a great first-stop to orient visitors to Sitka. A unique diorama model of Sitka in 1867, at the time of the transfer from Russia to the United States, is popular with children and adults alike. The museum gift shop features a selection of historical books about Sitka, locally created Tlingit art and a other gifts, including handmade wooden Russian Matryoshka nesting dolls. Free maps available at the museum guide visitors to Sitka's Historic Sites.

The museum is located at 330 Harbor Drive, inside Harrigan Centennial Hall. Open daily from 9 A.M. to 4 P.M. most days in summer; call for winter hours. Phone (907) 747-6455; www.sitkahistory.org.

The **New Archangel Dancers** are a group of local women who perform authentic Russian dances in authentic costumes. For dance performances, check the schedule board at Harrigan Centennial Hall or call the Russian Dance Hotline at (907) 747-5516.

Alaska Day, October 18, commemorates the transfer of Alaska from Russia to the United States. An Alaska Day Festival takes place in Sitka October 11-18, 2014.

Walking tour of Sitka. Historic landmarks and contemporary shops are all within walking distance in downtown Sitka. One of the city's most noticeable landmarks, **St. Michael's Cathedral**, is located in the center of Lincoln Street downtown. Originally built in 1844–48, then rebuilt after it burned down in 1966, this is the focal point of Sitka's history as the capital of Russian Alaska and a favorite photo-op. Another favorite is the Russian Bishops house across from Crescent Harbor, built in 1743. Tours are available of both of these buildings.

©Sharon Nault

The **Sitka Pioneers' Home** at Lincoln and Katlian streets was built in 1934 on the old Russian Parade Ground. Pioneers' Homes are also located in Fairbanks, Palmer, Anchorage, Ketchikan and Juneau. These state-supported homes offer housing and care for Alaskans who are at least 65 years old. The Sitka Pioneers' Home has a gift shop on the first floor featuring handicrafts made by residents. **The Prospector**, a 13½-foot clay and bronze statue in front of the Pioneers' Home, was sculpted by Alonzo Victor Lewis and dedicated on Alaska Day in 1949. The model for the statue was real pioneer William "Skagway Bill" Fonda.

Building 29 (Tilson Bldg.), at 206 Lincoln Street, is a National Historic Landmark. Built in 1835 of spruce logs, with sawdust insulation, it is one of the only surviving structures from Alaska's Russian era.

The **Alaska Native Brotherhood (ANB) Hall** on Katlian Street is another landmark. Built in 1914, it serves as a Tlingit

community center and houses Sitka's farmers market.

Castle Hill (Baranof Castle Hill State Historic Site) is where Alaska changed hands from Russia to the United States on Oct. 18, 1867. Walkway is located on south side by the bridge (look for sign) or on north side off of Lincoln Street. Good photo-op of the harbor and town.

Totem Square, has a newly (fall 2011) reinstalled and restored double-headed eagle totem that reflects Sitka's Russian heritage. Master carver Tommy Joseph did the restoration. This park is a grassy, open area with benches. The **Russian Blockhouse**, located behind the Pioneers' Home, is a replica of the blockhouse that was part of the stockade wall that separated Russian and Tlingit sections of Sitka after the Tlingits moved back to the area approximately 20 years after the 1804 battle.

Sitka Lutheran Church contains artifacts from the original 1843 Finnish Lutheran Church. Free tours by volunteers on limited days from mid-May to mid-September. Princess Maksoutoff, first wife of Alaska's last Russian governor, Dimitri Maksoutoff, is buried in the Lutheran cemetery.

Sheet'ka Kwaan Naa Kahidi Tribal Community House on 200 Katlian St., is a modern rendition of a northwest coast tribal clan house. Constructed in traditional Naa Kahidi design and aimed at preserving the Tlingit culture, the Community House offers Native culture exhibits and summer Tlingit dance performances.

Crescent Harbor Park runs between Lincoln Street and Crescent Harbor. The park strip offers benches, picnic shelters, basketball and tennis courts, a playground and views of Crescent Harbor. The largest picnic shelter is often the location of many of Sitka's special events. Ramps below the shelter are often used for special tour boat pick-ups.

There are 5 harbors in Sitka, fun for exploring and watching the commercial fishing fleet come and go.

Sheldon Jackson Museum, 104 College Drive, on the Sheldon Jackson College campus. The museum contains some of the fines Native arts and crafts found in Alaska. Built in 1897 and occupied since, it is the first concrete building built in Alaska. The majority of artifacts were collected between 1888 and 1900. Museum shop specializes in Alaska Native arts and crafts. Summer admission is $5/adults, $4/seniors (65 years and older), free for under 18 years. Open in summer, 9 A.M. to 5 P.M. daily. Winter admission is $3. Winter hours are 10 A.M. to 4 P.M. Tuesday through Saturday. Phone (907) 747-8981, or visit www.museums.alaska.gov.

After walking around the museum, enjoy the old Sheldon Jackson Campus. This Historic Landmark is being revitalized by new owners, the Sitka Fine Arts Camps. They are involved in almost every aspect of the arts on the campus and in Sitka. Check their office for various entertainment events.

Sitka Sound Science Center, at 834 Lincoln Street, is located on the waterfront on the way to the Sitka National Historic Park. The Science Center operates an educational fish hatchery and the Molly Ahlgren Aquarium, where touch tanks provide an up-close view of the organisms found in an outer coast tide pool. A special fish tank features an observation bubble for children to crawl into and enjoy a different view of fish.

The Science Center welcomes visitors in the summer; hours are 9 A.M. to 4 P.M.

Sheet'ka Kwaan Naa Kahidi Tribal House houses Alaska Native dance performances.
(©Sharon Nault)

Tours of the hatchery are available; call for tour times. Admission is $5 per person. The Center also offers regular natural history lectures on topics such as commercial fisheries, fish, wildlife and forest ecology. SSSC is open in summer 9 A.M. to 4 P.M. Winter hours are 10 A.M. to 4 P.M. Phone (907) 747-8878, or visit www.sitkascience.org

Visit the Alaska Raptor Center, located on Raptor Way, 0.7 mile south on Sawmill Creek Road from downtown. This unique facility treats injured eagles, hawks, owls and other birds. The Raptor Center is open daily in summer. Tour the outside displays and enjoy views of eagles inside the building through one-way glass. Informative guides are on site. Large group tours may be possible with advanced notice. Summer hours are typically 8 A.M.–4 P.M. daily; call for winter hours. Phone (907) 747-8662; www.alaskaraptor.org. Admission $12 for adults, $6 for children.

Sitka National Historical Park reflects both the community's rich Southeast Alaska Native heritage and its Russian-American past. Its Visitor Center is open daily in summer 8 A.M. to 5 P.M. The 113-acre park consists of 2 units—the Fort Site, located at the end of Lincoln Street, a half-mile from town, and the **Russian Bishop's House**, located on Lincoln Street near Crescent Harbor. Built by the Russian–American Co. in 1843 for the first Russian Orthodox bishop to reside in Alaska, the house was occupied by the church until 1969, and was added to Sitka National Historical Park in 1972. It is open 9 A.M. to 5 P.M. in summer. Russian Bishop's House tours are available on request in winter.

A free self-guiding trail leads through the park to the fort site. The National Park Service conducts guided walks in summer; check for schedule. The park's totem pole collection includes original pieces collected in 1901–03, and copies of originals lost to time and the elements. The park grounds and trails are open daily, 6 A.M. to 10 P.M., in summer; 6 A.M. to 8 P.M. in winter. Hiking through the rainforest in this park is an experience considered to be one of the most memorable, when visiting Sitka.

The park's Visitor Center houses an exhibit of Tlingit and Russian artifacts. The building is open 8 A.M. to 5 P.M. daily in summer. Phone (907) 747-0110 for more information.

Fortress of the Bear, at Mile 5.5 Sawmill Creek Road in the Sawmill Cove Industrial Park, is a non-profit education and rescue center for orphaned brown bear cubs. Open 9 A.M. to 6 P.M. daily mid-April through September; weekends 10 A.M. to 4 P.M. from October to mid-April; admission charged; phone (907) 747-3032; http://fortressofthebear.org/.

Drive Sawmill Creek Road. From its junction at Lake anf Erler Street traffic circle, Sawmill Creek Road leads 0.4 mile on to Sitka National Cemetery and 0.6 mile to Indian River. At Mile 0.7, Raptor Way provides access to the Alaska Raptor Center. At Mile 0.9 is the parking lot for Sitka National Historic Park trails and for the Visitor Center. At Mile 3.3 is parking for the 1.8-mile Thimbleberry Lake-Heart Lake trail. Whale Park Wayside at Mile 3.7 has covered picnic tables and viewing platform overlooking Silver Bay. The road ends at the Fortress of the Bears at Mile 5.3.

Sitka Whalefest, scheduled for Oct. 30–Nov. 2, 2014, focuses on marine mammal research and offers a unique opportunity to anyone interested in whales to broaden their knowledge and appreciation of these creatures. Local, national and international speakers, whale watching cruises, art and music are all part of the event. Visit www.sitkascience.org/sitka-whalefest/ or phone (907) 747-8878 for more information.

AREA FISHING: Sitka holds an annual salmon derby Memorial Day weekend and the weekend following. Contact the Sitka Sportsman's Assoc.; phone (907) 747-6790. Saltwater fishing charters available locally. There are also many lakes and rivers on Baranof Island with good fishing; these range from **Katlian River**, 11 miles northeast of Sitka by boat, to more remote waters such as **Rezanof Lake**, which is 40 air miles southeast of Sitka. USFS public-use cabins at some lakes. Stop by the Dept. of Fish and Game office at 304 Lake St. for details; phone (907) 747-5355.

Juneau

The Mendenhall Glacier wows visitors from around the world. (©Sharon Nault)

Major Attractions:

©Sharon Nault

Mendenhall Glacier, Mt. Roberts Tramway, Tracy Arm

Located on Gastineau Channel, 95 miles northeast of Sitka. **Population:** Borough 32,832. **Emergency Services:** Phone 911 for all emergencies. **Police**, phone (907) 586-0600. **Fire Department**, phone (907) 586-5322. **Alaska State Troopers**, phone (907) 465-4000. **Hospital**, Bartlett Regional, 3260 Hospital Dr., phone (907) 796-8900. **Maritime Search and Rescue**, Coast Guard, phone (907) 463-2000 or 1-800-478-5555.

Visitor Information: Juneau Convention & Visitors Bureau, phone (907) 586-2201 or 1-888-581-2201; www.traveljuneau.com; Email: info@traveljuneau.com. Visitor information centers are operated year-round, in the Juneau airport lower terminal and at the Auke Bay ferry terminal. The seasonal visitor center downtown is open from May through September 8 A.M. to 5 P.M. at Marine Park near the library, from mid-May to mid-Sept. Visitor information is also available at the cruise ship terminal on S. Franklin Street when cruise ships are in port, and at the Auke Bay ferry terminal. For convention and business meeting needs, contact the Centennial Hall Business Office (907) 586-5283 in advance for special assistance.

U.S. Forest Service information on camping, trails and cabins is available from the Juneau Ranger District, 8510 Mendenhall Loop Road, Juneau, AK 99801; phone (907) 586-8800. For Tongass National Forest information online: www.fs.usda.gov/tongass/.

The Alaska Dept. of Fish and Game website is an excellent resource for information on fishing, wildlife viewing, hunting and birding. Visit their home page at www.adfg.state.ak.us and follow links.

Elevation: Sea level. **Climate**: Mild and wet. Juneau averages 222 days of precipitation a year, with September and October the wettest months and April through June the driest. The monthly rainfall record for July is 10.36 inches (1997). Average daily maximum temperature in July, 64°F; daily minimum in January, 19°F. Highest recorded temperature, 90°F in July 1975; the lowest was 22°F in January 1968 and 1972. Average annual precipitation, 56.5 inches (airport), 92 inches (downtown); 103 inches of snow annually. Snow on ground intermittently from mid-November to mid-April. Prevailing winds are east-southeasterly. **Radio:** KBJZ-FM 94.1, KJNO-AM 630, KINY-AM 800, KXLL-FM 100.7, KRNN-FM 102.7, KTOO-FM 104.3, KTKU-FM 105.1, KSUP-FM 106.3, KVIM-FM 92.7. **Television:** KJUD Channel 8 (ABC); KATH Channel 15 (NBC); KTNL Channel 14 (CBS); KTOO Channel 10 (PBS). **Newspapers**: *Juneau Empire* and *Capital City Weekly*.

Private Aircraft: Juneau International Airport, 9 miles northwest; elev. 18 feet; length 8,456 feet; asphalt; fuel 100LL, Jet A. Juneau harbor seaplane base, due east; restricted use, no fuel. International seaplane base, 7 miles northwest; 5,000 feet by 450 feet, avgas, Jet A. For more information, phone the Juneau Flight Service Station at (907) 586-7382.

History and Economy

In 1880, nearly 20 years before the great gold rushes to the Klondike and to Nome, 2 prospectors named Joe Juneau and Dick Harris found "color" in what is now called Gold Creek, a small, clear stream that runs through the center of present-day Juneau. Local history states that it was a Tlingit, Chief Kowee, who showed Joe Juneau where to find gold in Gold Creek. What the prospectors found led to the discovery of one of the largest lodes of gold quartz in the world. Juneau (called Harrisburg the first year) quickly boomed into a gold rush town as claims and mines sprang up in the area.

In 1881, Pierre "French Pete" Erussard discovered gold on Douglas Island, across Gastineau Channel from Juneau. A year later, John Treadwell bought the claims and in 1887 he formed Alaska Treadwell Gold

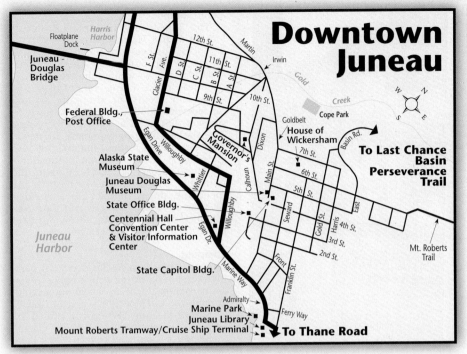

Downtown Juneau

Mining Company. In 36 years of operation, Treadwell produced an estimated $66 million in gold. A cave-in and flood closed the mine in 1917. The Alaska–Gastineau Mine, operated by Bart Thane in 1911, had a 2-mile shaft through Mount Roberts to the Perseverance Mine near Gold Creek. The Alaska–Juneau (A–J) Mine was constructed on a mountain slope south of Juneau and back into the heart of Mount Roberts. It operated until 1944, when it was declared a nonessential wartime activity after producing over $80 million in gold. Post–WWII wage and price inflation and the fixed price of gold prevented its reopening.

Congress first provided civil government for Alaska in 1884. Alaska was governed by a succession of presidential appointees, first as the District of Alaska, then as the Territory of Alaska. Between 1867 (when the United States purchased Alaska from Russia) and 1884, the military had jurisdiction over the District of Alaska, except for a 3-year period (1877–79) when Alaska was put under control of the U.S. Treasury Dept. and governed by U.S. Collector of Customs.

By 1900, Juneau had eclipsed Sitka—capital of Russian Alaska and then the Territory of Alaska—as the center of power in Southeast. A Civil Code for Alaska, passed by Congress under the Carter Act in 1900, provided the Territory with 3 judicial districts, one of which was Juneau, and moved the seat of government from Sitka to Juneau.

In 1974, Alaskans voted to move the capital from Juneau to a site closer to Anchorage. In 1976, Alaska voters selected a new capital site near Willow, but funding for the capital move—an estimated $2.8 billion—was defeated in November 1982.

Prior to the arrival of the Russians, explorers, prospectors, miners and other settlers, this was Tlingit land. Described as having one of the most sophisticated social structures and intricate societies of any indigenous people in the world, the Tlingit are 1 of the 2 major Indian people in Southeast Alaska. The other major group, the Haidas, have a different language although their lifestyle, history and tradition are similar to the Tlingit, as is the lifestyle of the Tsimshians, a neighboring Indian group from Canada that settled on Annette Island.

It was a Tlingit, William Paul Sr., who was instrumental in bringing about the Alaska Native Claims Settlement Act of 1971. One of the first Tlingits to receive a college degree and the first Native Alaskan to win a seat in the territorial legislature, Paul originally brought suit against the U.S. government in the 1930s for lands taken from the Tlingits and Haidas. Forty-four million acres and nearly a billion dollars were involved in the Alaska Native Claims Settlement Act. In addition to cash and land

JUNEAU ADVERTISERS

Adventure Bound Alaska
  Cruises ....Ph. 1-800-228-3875
Alaskan Brewing Co.......................Ph. (907) 780-5866
Goldbelt Hotel.............................Ph. 1-888-478-6909
Mount Roberts Tramway...........Ph. 1-888-461-8726
Spruce Meadow RV Park..............Ph. (907) 789-1990
Super 8..Ph. (907) 789-4858
Tracy Arm Fjord–
  Adventure Bound.....................Ph. 1-800-228-3875

settlements, the act established 12 regional corporations and a system of local village corporations. The intent of the corporate structuring was to create a revenue-producing entity that would assure a financial future for all Alaska Natives.

The local corporation formed for the Juneau area was Goldbelt, Inc. Currently, Goldbelt, Inc. has some 3,300 Tlingit and Haida shareholders. Many shareholders are employed in Goldbelt's tourism businesses, which include the Mount Roberts Tramway and the Goldbelt Hotel Juneau.

Education, health services and tourism and mining are the largest employers in Juneau's private sector, while government (federal, state and local) comprises an estimated half of the total basic industry.

Description

Juneau, often called "a little San Francisco," is nestled at the foot of Mount Juneau (elev. 3,576 feet) with Mount Roberts (elev. 3,819 feet) rising immediately to the east on the approach up Gastineau Channel. The residential community of Douglas, on Douglas Island, is south of Juneau and connected by a bridge. Neighboring residential areas around the airport, Mendenhall Valley and Auke Bay lie north of Juneau on the mainland.

Shopping is in the downtown area and at suburban malls in the airport and Mendenhall Valley areas.

Juneau's skyline is dominated by several government buildings, including the Federal Building (1962), the massive State Office Building (1974), the State Court Building (1975) and the older brick and marble-columned Capitol Building (1931). The modern Sealaska Plaza is headquarters for Sealaska Corp., 1 of the 13 regional Native corporations formed after congressional passage of the Alaska Native Claims Settlement Act in 1971.

The Juneau area supports 35 churches, 2 high schools, 2 middle schools, 7 elementary schools, 2 charter/community schools and a University of Alaska Southeast campus at Auke Lake. There are 3 municipal libraries and the state library.

ANCHORAGE
36 Ave. & Minnesota Dr.
907-276-8884

FAIRBANKS
Airport & Wilbur Way
907-451-8888

JUNEAU
Across from Nugget Mall
907-789-4858

KETCHIKAN
Next to Plaza Mall
907-225-9088

Super 8
FREE
* Airport Shuttle
* Healthy SuperStart® Breakfast
* Wireless Internet
1.800.800.8000
super8.com

Goldbelt MOUNT ROBERTS TRAMWAY
Hiking Trails
Bear Viewing Platforms
Birding • Culture
Crab Feed (in season)
Raven Eagle Gifts

JUNEAU, ALASKA
888-461-8726
MountRobertsTramway.com

Downtown Juneau is nestled against a mountainside. (©Sharon Nault)

The area is governed by the unified city and borough of Juneau, which encompasses 3,108 square miles. It is the first unified government in the state, combining the former separate and overlapping jurisdictions of the cities of Douglas and Juneau and the greater Juneau borough.

Lodging & Services

Juneau has several hotels and motels downtown and in the airport area. The recently renovated **Gold Belt Hotel** (1-888-478-6909) is downtown. **Super 8** (907/789-4858) is across from Nugget Mall by the airport turnoff..

The Juneau International Hostel is located at 614 Harris St. (Juneau 99801), 4 blocks northeast of the Capitol Bldg. Phone (907) 586-9559; email juneau hostel@gci.net; www.juneauhostel.net.

Juneau offers a wide variety of dining spots and plenty of shopping. Watch for sidewalk food vendors downtown in summer. Juneau also has a microbrewery, **The Alaskan Brewing Company**, located at 5429 Shaune Dr. in the Lemon Creek area; phone (907) 780-5866 for tour information.

Juneau Library, at South Franklin and Admiralty Way, between Marine Park and the cruise ship terminal, has a wonderful view of Juneau, Douglas and Gastineau Channel. Take the elevator to the 5th floor above the public parking garage.

Camping

Juneau has no place for overnight parking except at organized campgrounds. If you are parked overnight anywhere but a campground, you will probably be asked to move.

Spruce Meadow RV Park is located 2.2 miles east of the Glacier Highway via the Mendenhall Loop Road (signed "Back Loop Road"; turnoff at **Milepost 12.1**); phone (907) 789-1990; www.juneaurv.com.

Spruce Meadow RV Park. 49 level full-service sites in 12.5 acres of spruce and alder. 30-amp, free WiFi and cable TV, clean restrooms and showers, handicap access, laundromat, tour information, and located on city bus route. 4 miles to Mendenhall Glacier, 3.7 miles from ferry terminal, 14 miles to downtown Juneau. Outstanding service. MC/VISA. Reservations *strongly* recommended. 10200 Mendenhall Loop Road, Juneau, AK 99801. Phone (907) 789-1990; website www.juneaurv.com. [ADVERTISEMENT]

Savikko Park, owned by the City & Borough of Juneau, in Douglas has 4 sites for fully self-contained RVs. No hookups or other services are available. $10 camping fee, 3-day limit; obtain permit and directions on weekdays at Harbormaster's office at 1600 Harbor Way, phone (907) 586-5255.

There are 2 USFS campgrounds north of Juneau accessible from the Glacier Highway/ Juneau Veterans' Memorial Highway (see log on pages 686-687): Mendenhall Lake Campground and Auke Village Campground. Both are first-come, first-served and both have 14-day limits.

Mendenhall Lake Campground has a total of 69 sites; 9 sites have electric, water and sewer; 9 sites have electric and water; and 7 sites are located in a separate walk-in area for backpackers. RVs to 45 feet. Picnic tables, firepits, water, flush toilets and hot showers available. There is a dump station. Campground host on site. Camping fees are $10 to $29 per night. To reach Mendenhall Lake Campground from the Ferry Terminal, turn off at **Milepost 12.1** Glacier Highway and take the Back Loop Road across from DeHarts grocery. Drive 2.5 miles to Montana Creek Road and turn onto it; continue 0.7 mile (keep to right when Mountain Creek Road becomes Skaters Cabin Road) to the fancy rock faced entry to campground. To go to Skaters Cabin, continue past the campground entrance and there is a stone picnic shelter with a spectacular view of the glacier. Skater's Cabin is available first-come, first-served or by reservation for group picnics. From the city, you take the Glacier Highway to Mile 9.3

Auke Village Campground is located in the Auke Village Recreation Area (see **Milepost 14.7** Glacier Highway). It has 11 campsites, $10 camping fee, toilets, water, tables and fire rings. RVs to 24 feet. Open May 1 to September 30.

Eagle Beach State Recreation Area, at **Milepost 27.6** Juneau Veteran's Memorial highway, has overnight parking for vehicles and gravel pads for tenters. Park host on site, $10 camping fee, 7-day limit. An extensive trail system here accesses the beach and river.

The City and Borough of Juneau operates a 24-hour dump station at Jackie Renninger Park, 2400 Mendenhall Loop Road, next to

the skateboard park; phone (907) 790-2525.

Transportation

Air: Juneau International Airport is northwest of downtown via Glacier Highway. Airport terminal contains ticket counters, waiting area, gift shop, rental cars, restaurant, lounge and visitor information center. Phone (907) 789-7821.

The city express bus inbound, stops at the airport weekdays from 7:11 A.M. to 6:11 P.M. Taxi service to downtown is also available. Courtesy vans to some hotels.

Alaska Airlines serves Juneau daily from Anchorage (90-minute flight) and other Alaska cities, and from Seattle, WA (2-hour flight). Scheduled commuter service to Haines, Skagway, Sitka, Angoon and other points via various air services.

Charter air service is available for hunting, fishing, flightseeing and transportation to other communities. Flightseeing by helicopter is very popular in Juneau, and several helicopter services operate here.

Ferry: Juneau is served by Alaska Marine Highway ferries (see the ALASKA MARINE HIGHWAY section for schedules, fares and information). The state ferries dock at the Auke Bay Terminal at **Milepost 13.8** Glacier Highway; phone (907) 465-8853; or go to www.ferryalaska.com. The main reservation center is located at 6858 Glacier Highway (7 miles from downtown Juneau) and is open Monday–Friday, 8 A.M.–5 P.M.; phone (907) 465-3941 or 1-800-642-0066. There is a ticket counter at the Auke Bay terminal. It is open only when a vessel is arriving or departing.

Taxi: Service is available from Auke Bay terminal to downtown Juneau. There is also a bus stop 1.5 miles toward town from the ferry terminal.

Bus: Capital Transit, (907) 789-6901, www.juneau.org/capitaltransit/index.php. Route map and schedule available at the visitor information center or can be downloaded from their website. Use exact fare ($2 adult, $1 ages 6-18); drivers do not make change.

Parking: Parking in the core downtown area is metered and is closely monitored. On-street parking available with 2 hours (consecutive) free parking with registration; follow instructions at pay stations. Public parking garages at Downtown Library (Marine Park Garage), Downtown Transportation Center on Main Street and adjacent Shopper's Lot; and North Franklin Lot at corner of Franklin Street and Second Street.

Juneau streets are narrow and it is difficult—if not impossible—to find a legal spot to park a large RV. Leave RV at campground and use tow vehicle, arrange for a rental car or park outside city and bus or taxi in to town.

Highways: Glacier Highway begins in downtown Juneau and leads 39.7 miles north to Echo Cove; see "Glacier Highway/Juneau Veterans' Memorial Highway" this section. Other major roads are Douglas and North Douglas highways.

Cruise Ships: Juneau is southeast Alaska's most frequent port of call. There are more than 640 port calls by cruise ships annually.

Car Rental: Car rental agencies located at the airport (reserve ahead of time because of the great demand for cars). Avis (907) 789-9450; Hertz (907) 789-9494; Budget, (907) 790-1086; National/Alamo (907) 789-9814; and Juneau Rental Car (will drop-off vehicle), phone (907) 957-7530.

For spectacular city views, ride the Mount Roberts Tramway. (©Sharon Nault)

Boats: Charter boats are available for fishing, sightseeing and transportation. Kayak rentals available. The visitor information center can provide a list of charter operators. Transient moorage is available downtown at Harris and Douglas floats and at Auke Bay. Most boaters use Auke Bay. For more information, call the Juneau harbormaster at (907) 586-5255.

Bicycles: Bike rentals available downtown. Designated bike routes to Douglas, Mendenhall Glacier and Auke Bay. The Mendenhall Glacier route starts at the intersection of 12th Street and Glacier Avenue; total biking distance is 15 miles. Bike-route map and information available at visitor information centers.

Attractions

Juneau walking tour. It is easy to explore downtown Juneau on foot, and preferable to driving. The streets are narrow and congested with pedestrians and traffic. Walking tour maps of Juneau are available at all visitor information centers. Descriptive signs are posted at many locations, identifying significant sites in the downtown historic district.

Downtown landmarks to look for include the Ed Way bronze sculpture, "Hard Rock Miners," located at Marine Park. Marine Park is located at the foot of Seward Street, and has tables, benches, an information kiosk and a small public dock. Another bronze sculpture commemorates "Patsy Ann," a bull terrier that during the 1930s and 1940s would meet arriving vessels at Juneau's dock.

USS *Juneau* Memorial, located on the waterfront, immediately north of the S. Franklin Dock, commemorates the sinking of the USS *Juneau* during WWII. All but 10 of the crew of 700 lost their lives (including the 5 Sullivan brothers) when the ship was torpedoed the night of Nov. 13, 1942.

Mount Roberts Tramway. One of Juneau's top attractions, the Mount Roberts Tramway brings spectacular views within easy reach of visitors. Two 60-passenger aerial trams transport visitors from Juneau's downtown waterfront to a modern mountaintop complex at the 1,800-foot level of Mount Roberts. Observation platform with

panoramic view of the city, harbor and surrounding mountains. The mountaintop complex includes a theater, restaurant, bar, gift shop, and access to alpine walking trails. The tram ticket and a hand stamp allow you to ride the tram all day long if you wish. The tram operates daily, 9 A.M. to 9 P.M., from May through September; (907) 463-3412.

The Alaskan Brewing Company. Crafting some of the country's best beers in one of the most beautiful settings on earth.

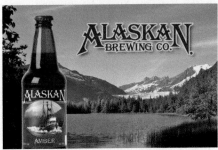

Find Alaskan beers throughout Alaska and the Western states. While in Juneau, enjoy a tutored tasting at the Alaskan Brewery at 5429 Shaune Dr., or visit our retail store downtown, the Alaskan Brewing Depot at 219 S. Franklin for clothing, glassware and a virtual tour. Visit www.alaskan-beer.com for hours or call (907) 780-5866.

State Capitol Building. 120 E. 4th St. Congress authorized construction of the Federal and Territorial Building in 1911, but the $1 million structure was not started until 1929, after local citizens and businesses pitched in by buying some of the lots needed for the building site and deeding them over to the federal government. Completed in 1931, the brick-faced reinforced concrete structure, with its limestone and marble portico and lobby, once contained the Legislature, Governor, the post office, Courts, and other federal and territorial agencies.

Under the Alaska Statehood Act of July 7, 1958, the building became the property of the State of Alaska and the state capitol. Today, the Capitol building houses the offices of the State Legislature, the Governor,

One of the stops along the Alaska State Capitol Building tour. (©Sharon Nault)

and the Lieutenant Governor. Because it was originally designed as an office building for the Territory, Alaska's Capitol building is one of the few capitols in the U.S. that does not have a dome.

Free tours are available from the capitol lobby daily in summer every half-hour from 9 A.M. to 5:30 P.M. The State Office Building, one block west, houses the State Historical Library and Kimball theater organ.

Juneau–Douglas City Museum, located in the Veterans Memorial Building across from the State Capitol Building at Fourth and Main streets, exhibits history, art and culture of the Juneau-Douglas area. Special exhibits change seasonally. A 500- to 700-year-old basketry-style fish trap, interactive kiosks, a relief map of Juneau's topography and a video, *Juneau: City Built on Gold*, are other attractions. Two authentic totem poles are displayed on the museum grounds. The museum gift shop features gifts, books and trail guides by local craftsmen and authors. Guided historic downtown walking tours are available May to September.

Pick up a copy of *Historic Juneau: Places & Faces* ($3.50), a self-guided tour of historic downtown Juneau, here.

The museum's summer hours are 9 A.M. to 6 P.M. weekdays, 10 A.M. to 5 P.M. weekends; admission is $6/adults, $5/seniors, 12 and under free. Winter hours are 10 A.M. to 4 P.M. Tuesday–Saturday and admission is free thanks to community sponsors. For more information, phone (907) 586-3572 or visit www.juneau.org/parksrec/museum/.

Alaska State Museum has been a major highlight of Juneau at 395 Whittier St. It is slated to close its doors in February 2014 for construction of a newly combined Alaska State Library Archives and Museum Building. It will reopen summer 2016.

St. Nicholas Orthodox Church, 5th and Gold streets, a tiny structure built in 1894, is now the oldest original Russian Orthodox church in southeast Alaska. Visitors are welcome to Sunday services; open daily for summer tours. Phone (907) 586-1023.

Wickersham State Historic Site. A steep climb up to Seventh Street takes visitors to the historic home of Alaska's Judge James Wickersham. Wickersham was the first judge of the Third Judicial District of Alaska, arriving in Eagle, AK, from Tacoma, WA, in 1900. Wickersham House contains the judge's collection of artifacts gathered during his extensive travels throughout his 300,000-square-mile district. Phone (907) 586-9001 for current information.

The Governor's House at 716 Calhoun Ave., has been home to Alaska's chief executives since it was completed in 1913. The 2½-story structure, containing 12,900 square feet of floor space, took nearly a year to build. Tours may be possible by advance arrangement. Phone (907) 465-3500.

Glacier Gardens Rainforest Adventure. Access to Gardens at Fred Meyer exit on Glacier Highway Mile 7.9, then right on old Glacier Highway. What was once a landslide-scarred hillside has been transformed into a fantastic garden featuring hundreds of plants. Huge hanging baskets of flowers dominate the greenhouse, which also houses a gift shop and cafe. Outside, upside-down tree stumps act as whimsical flower pots. The tour includes a trip by motorized golf cart through the rainforest of Thunder Mountain. Open 9 A.M. to 6 P.M. daily, tours available May 1–Sept. 30. Phone (907) 790-3377; website www.glaciergardens.com. *RVers NOTE: Use bus entrance. The parking lot is not suitable for large RVs and there is no on-street parking.*

Mendenhall Glacier and Visitor Center. Located about 13 miles from downtown Juneau, spectacular Mendenhall Glacier and the adjacent U.S. Forest Service visitor center are a major attraction in Juneau. The visitor center offers a hands-on exhibit hall, a theater, an observatory and short interpretive presentations during the summer season. Remote cams offer live viewing of a salmon stream and beaver den.

From downtown Juneau, drive out Glacier Highway/Egan Drive and turn right at **Milepost 9.3** (Mendenhall Loop Road), then drive straight 3.4 miles to Mendenhall Glacier parking area. From the Alaska Marine Highway ferry terminal in Auke Bay, drive toward downtown Juneau on Glacier Highway and turn left at Milepost 9.3. There are 2 public parking areas; one can accommodate motorhomes. (Charter and tour buses use assigned parking area.) Paved walking paths lead uphill to the visitor center (elevator available) and out to glacier viewpoints. There are also short trails down to the lake, along a salmon stream and newly constructed trail around the lake to Nugget Falls. Trailheads for 2 longer trails—East Glacier and Nugget Creek—originate from the visitor center.

The visitor center is open from 8 A.M. to 7:30 P.M., May–September; admission fee $5 (15 and under free). From October to April no fee is charged and the visitor center is open Thursday–Sunday, 10 A.M. to 4 P.M. Special programs and facility rental are available. For more information, phone (907) 789-0097 or visit www.fs.fed.us/r10/tongass/districts/mendenhall/index/.

Take a Tour. Tours of Juneau and area attractions—by boat, bus, plane, helicopter or kayak—are available locally. These tours range from whale-watching boat trips and day cruises to Tracy Arm to helicopter flightseeing trips of the 1,500-square-mile Juneau Icefield.

Tracy Arm. Located 50 miles southeast of Juneau, Tracy Arm and adjoining Endicott Arm are the major features of the Tracy Arm–Fords Terror Wilderness Area. Both Tracy and Endicott arms are long, deep and narrow fjords that extend more than 30 miles into the heavily glaciated Coast Mountain Range. Active tidewater glaciers at the head of these fjords calve icebergs into the fjords.

Fords Terror, off of Endicott Arm, is an area of sheer rock walls enclosing a narrow entrance into a small fjord. The fjord was named in 1889 for a crew member of a naval vessel who rowed into the narrow canyon at slack tide and was caught in turbulent icy currents for 6 terrifying hours when the tide changed.

Access to this wilderness area is primarily by boat or floatplane from Juneau. Some large and small cruise ships and charter boats include Tracy Arm and Endicott Arm in their itineraries. It is also a popular destination for sea kayakers.

Tracy Arm Fjord–*Adventure Bound*, Alaska's greatest combination of mountains, wildlife, icebergs and tidewater glaciers. Tracy Arm could be called "cascade fjord" because of its many waterfalls or "icy fjord" because it is the home of Alaska's largest icebergs. Best viewed from the *Adventure Bound*. Juneau's favorite because the Weber family doesn't overcrowd and they take the time to enjoy it all. For comfort, viewing time, elbow room and personal attention, this is the quality cruise that you are looking for. Street address: 76 Egan Drive (the *Adventure Bound* office is across from the Goldbelt Hotel). Mailing address: P.O. Box 23013, Juneau, AK 99802. Reservations: Phone (907) 463-2509, 1-800-228-3875; www.adventureboundalaska.com. See display ad on page 682. [ADVERTISEMENT]

Mount Roberts Trail is "the closest Juneau has to a designated wildlife viewing area," according to the ADF&G. Access to Mount Roberts Trail is from the mountaintop complex at the tramway or from the trailhead at Mile 0.4 Basin Road. Hike all the way to the 3,819-foot summit. For a less strenuous hike, there is an excellent observation point above Juneau reached by a 20-minute hike from the trailhead.

Mount Roberts hikers may purchase down-only tram tickets in the shop or bar at the **Mount Roberts Tramway** mountaintop

complex at the 1,800 foot level. Or spend $10 or more in the restaurant or gift shop and use their receipt as a ticket.

Last Chance Mining Museum is the only historic mining building open to the public from Juneau's Gold Rush era. On display are historic mining tools and equipment and the world's largest Ingersoll-Rand air compressor. Drive or walk to the end of **Basin Road** to reach the museum, which is located in the Compressor Building of the historic Alaska–Juneau Mine. Basin Road ends 1 mile from East Street; park at Perseverance Trailhead and follow trail uphill to the museum. The museum is open daily, 9:30 A.M. to 12:30 P.M. and 3:30–6:30 P.M.; $5 admission. Open from mid-May to mid-September. The museum is operated by the non-profit Gastineau Channel Historical Society; phone (907) 586-5338. Renee Hughes can answer any questions you may have. Basin Road offers good views of Mount Juneau waterfall and also accesses the Perseverance Trail. *NOTE: Basin Road is very narrow in spots and popular with joggers, walkers and dogs. Drive carefully.*

Hike the Perseverance Trail. This scenic and popular trail, which begins at the end of Basin Road, is a wonderful hike and popular with local walkers and joggers. It follows what is said to be the first road in Alaska. Originally called the Johnson Road, it provided access to gold mining operations in the Gold Creek Valley, including Perseverance Mine and the Alaska-Juneau mine. Ruins and artifacts from the old mining operations are still scattered throughout the valley. Beautiful scenery, wide rocky trail that doesn't get muddy in wet weather, 3.5 miles long, junctions with several other trails.

Macaulay Salmon Hatchery. See more than 100 species of Southeast Alaska sealife in one of Alaska's largest saltwater aquarium displays inside the Macaulay visitor Center. Outside, visitors get a chance to see adult salmon up-close and personal on an educational tour of the hatchery, which incubates, rears and releases 3 species of Pacific salmon (king, chum and silver). Watch salmon make their way up a 450-foot fish ladder. Open weekdays 10 A.M. to 6 P.M., weekdays and 10 A.M. to 5 P.M. in summer; by appointment in winter. Admission is charged. operated by Douglas Island Pink and Chum, Inc. (DIPAC), is located at 2697 Channel Drive, 2½ miles from downtown. Phone (907) 463-4810 or 1-877-463-2486; www.dipac.net.

Take a Drive. Glacier Highway/Juneau Veterans' Memorial Highway provides access to a number of attractions, including: Mendenhall Glacier; Auke Village and Lena Beach picnic areas; Eagle Beach recreation areas; the **Shrine of St. Therese**, a complex that includes the famous stone chapel and the stations of the cross; and numerous hiking trails. (See Mile 22.5 in the "Glacier Highway/Juneau Veterans' Memorial Highway" log on facing page for details.)

Thane Road begins just south of downtown Juneau and extends 5.8 miles along Gastineau Channel. Sheep Creek Trailhead is at Mile 4.

Visit University of Alaska Southeast/ Juneau Campus. Thanks to its beautiful lakeshore setting and Alaska Native art, the campus can be a rewarding site for Juneau visitors. The entrance to the campus is located 0.1 mile from **Milepost 12.1** Glacier Highway on Mendenhall (Back Loop) Road. On campus there are 2 towering authentic totem poles honoring the Eagle and Raven

Shopping and services delight visitors in pedestrian-friendly downtown Juneau. *(©Sharon Nault)*

clans; an enormous black metal raven sculpture honoring *Loki*, "The Trickster" of Tlingit history; and a much-photographed wall mural by Alaska artist Ray Troll. The university boasts an extensive collection of Authentic Tlingit Native art inside the William A. Egan Library, including totemic carvings, wall posts and weavings.

Douglas Island offers some fine scenery and sights for motorists. Take the Juneau-Douglas Bridge across Gastineau Channel. South Douglas Highway leads 2.3 miles to the city of Douglas and accesses the popular Sandy Beach recreation area. The scenic North Douglas Highway follows the island's shoreline 11.4 miles to False Outer Point. This is access to the Eagle Crest Ski Area, North Douglas Boat Harbor, Rainforest Trail and Outer Loop Trail.

Douglas Island also offers 6,000 feet of dual ziplines, suspension bridges, and a ground-based trail network through the rainforest at the Alaska Canopy Adventures site near historic Treadwell Mine. For details, phone (907) 523-2920 or visit www. akzipline.com.

Bear Watching at Pack Creek. The Stan Price State Wildlife Sanctuary at the mouth of Pack Creek, on the east side of Admiralty Island, 28 air miles south of Juneau, is a well-known bear-viewing area in Southeast. Pack Creek is a 30-minute flight from Juneau via charter floatplane. Visitors typically arrive via floatplane "drop-off" service or by floatplace as part of a guided tour. Permits, required both peak and shoulder season visits, become available each year, February 1st and are issued on a first-come, first served basis. Between June 1 and Sept. 10, permits allow visitation between 9-9 on permit day.

Peak season—July 5 through August 25—when only 24 people are allowed per day. These permits are ONLY available by advanced reservation at www.recreation.gov or 1-877-444-6777. Peak season permits are $50 a day for adults, $25 a day for seniors and children.

Shoulder seasons are June 1–July 4 and Aug. 26–Sept. 10, and the cost is $20 per day for adults, $10 for seniors and children.

It may be possible to get a last minute reservation during those dates. Visitors should have exact change or check (U.S. Currency), credit card and an application filled out for each individual in the group. Access to Pack Creek is only by plane, boat or kayak. No camping is allowed at the creek but is allowed on nearby Windfall Island.

Glacier Bay National Park contains some of the most impressive tidewater glaciers in the world. Juneau is located about 50 miles east of the bay and is the main jumping-off point for many Glacier Bay visitors. Check locally for 1- and 2-day or longer boat and air packages to the park. The Alaska Marine Highway System operates ferry service three times weekly in summer, from Juneau to Gustavus, entry point to Glacier Bay. (See GLACIER BAY NATIONAL PARK and ALASKA MARINE HIGHWAY sections.)

Golden North Salmon Derby takes place August 8–10, 2014. Begun in 1947 and sponsored by the Territorial Sportsmen, this is the oldest salmon derby in Alaska. The event provides scholarships for students. Large cash prizes are awarded. Derby activity is centered around the docks at Amalga, Douglas and Auke Bay. The 2013 winner was Jody Haas with a 29.2-lb. king. To confirm derby dates and details, visit www.golden northsalmonderby.org.

AREA FISHING: Good Dolly Varden fishing available along most saltwater shorelines in Juneau area especially from mid-May through June; king salmon best from mid-May to mid-June, pink salmon available about mid-July through August, silver salmon best August to mid-September. Good fishing by boat from Juneau, Auke Bay or Tee Harbor in **Favorite** and **Saginaw channels**, **Chatham Strait** and near mouth of **Taku Inlet** for salmon and halibut. USFS public-use cabins available. For up-to-date angling data in the Juneau area, phone (907) 465-4116 for recorded ADF&G message (April–October). For specific angling information, contact the ADF&G, Division of Sport Fish, Area Management Biologist, P.O. Box 240020, Douglas 99824; phone (907) 465-4270; www.state.ak.us/adfg.

Glacier Highway/Juneau Veterans' Memorial Highway

Juneau Vicinity (map)

Point Bridget
Berners Bay
Echo Cove
Juneau Veterans' Memorial Highway
Eagle Glacier
Eagle River
Eagle Beach USFS Picnic Area
Eagle Beach SRA
Shrine of St. Therese
Herbert Glacier
Windfall Lake
Juneau Veterans' Memorial Highway
Shelter Island
Favorite Channel
Lynn Canal
Tee Harbor
Peterson Lake
Lena Cove
Mendenhall Lake Campground
Mendenhall Glacier
Lena Beach USFS Picnic Area
Montana Creek Rd.
Mendenhall Lake
Auke Bay Ferry Terminal
Auke L.
Auke Village Recreation Area
Auke Bay
Glacier Hwy.
Mendenhall Glacier Visitor Center
Mendenhall Loop Rd.
Mendenhall Peninsula
Mendenhall River
Fritz Cove
Airport
Old Glacier Highway
North Douglas Highway
Egan Dr.
Salmon Creek Reservoir
Hospital
Macaulay Salmon Hatchery
Tongass National Forest
Juneau-Douglas Bridge
Downtown Juneau
Eaglecrest Ski Area
Douglas Bridge
Douglas Highway
Cruise Ship Docks
Stephens Passage
Douglas Island
Douglas
Thane Rd.
Sandy Beach Recreation Area

From the cruiseship terminal on South Franklin Street in downtown Juneau, head northwest along the waterfront. South Franklin Street becomes Marine Way, then Egan Drive, named for William A. Egan (1914–84), first governor of the State of Alaska. Egan Drive becomes Glacier Highway at **Milepost 9.4**, then Juneau Veterans' Memorial Highway from **Milepost 12.1** to road end, 40 miles north of Juneau at Echo Cove on Berners Bay. This is a very scenic drive along Favorite Channel.
Distance from downtown Juneau cruiseship terminal is shown.

0 Cruise ship terminal, Mount Roberts Tramway terminal; South Franklin Street.

1.1 Stoplight at **junction** with Tenth Street to east and Douglas Highway west

to Douglas Island via the Juneau–Douglas Bridge. Access to Sandy Beach Recreation Area and North and South Douglas Highways.

1.2 Turnoff for Harris boat harbor.

1.4 Harbormaster's office.

1.6 Turnoff for Aurora boat harbor.

2.8 Northbound access east to Glacier Highway, which loops south through residential area.

3.8 Stoplight. Intersection of Glacier Highway and Channel Drive. Turnoff to east for Bartlett Memorial Hospital, Alaska Native Health Center and access via Glacier Highway north to Twin Lakes Picnic Area. Turnoff to west for Channel Drive and access to Ladd Macaulay Visitor Center.

4 View of Twin Lakes picnic area to east; use Glacier Highway access at **Milepost 3.8**.

5.3 Stoplight. Vanderbilt Hill Road; police.

6 Mendenhall Wetlands State Game Refuge. Great place to see eagles and waterfowl. Viewpoint, southbound only.

6.2 Northbound exit east to Glacier Highway, Walmart (no overnight parking) and Switzer Creek.

7.9 Exit east to Fred Meyer shopping center and access east to Glacier Gardens Rainforest Adventure (see description in Juneau Attractions), located less than a half-mile from Fred Meyer via Glacier Highway. Also access east to bike trail.

8.5 Stoplight at **junction** with Glacier Highway; access to commercial area and Juneau International Airport, a **Super 8**, McDonald's, Nugget shopping mall with Office Max and JoAnn Fabrics, gas and a grocery store. The 1-mile Glacier Highway Loop to east rejoins Egan Drive at **Milepost 9.3**.

9.3 Stoplight. Glacier Highway becomes Eagan Drive, **South junction** with **Mendenhall Loop Road**. Turn west for airport. Turn east for Mendenhall Mall and post office (just east of junction).

To reach Mendenhall Glacier from this junction, drive east 3.4 miles to parking area. **Mendenhall Glacier Visitor Center**, a short walk uphill from the parking lot, is open daily in summer (*see description page 684*).

Mendenhall Loop Road is a paved 6-mile loop that rejoins Glacier Highway at **Milepost 12.1**. To reach **Mendenhall Lake USFS Campground**, drive east 2.1 miles to where road makes a 90 degree turn. Turn on Montana Creek Road and continue 0.4 mile, keeping to right where road then becomes Skater Cabin Road. Look for large rock at campground entrance. (Total driving distance from downtown Juneau is 13.7 miles; distance from Ferry Terminal is 4.1 miles.) Also access to West Glacier and Montana Creek trailheads on this loop. ▲

9.5 Stoplight. Riverside Drive; access to Mendenhall Mall.

9.6 Vintage Blvd. (northbound exit only); access to post office, Safeway (open 5 A.M. to midnight in summer), gas station and Mendenhall Mall. 🛢

9.7 *Begin 2-lane highway northbound. Begin 4-lane highway southbound.*

9.8 Mendenhall River and Brotherhood Bridge. The bridge was named in honor of the Alaska Native Brotherhood; bronze plaques symbolize the Raven and Eagle clans.

10 Industrial Blvd. to west; access to Hardware and Building Supply, and 9-hole Mendenhall Golf Course. Mendenhall Glacier viewpoint to east; parking area and trailhead for Kaxdegoowu Heen Dei/Clear Water Creek Trail (Mendenhall River Greenbelt). This popular paved trail extends 0.9 mile to Montana Creek, 2.1 miles to River Road parking lot. Wheelchair-accessible.

10.4 Alaska State Troopers to west.

10.6 Engineer's Cutoff to west through residential area. Mendenhall Peninsula Road branches south off Engineer's Cutoff; signed public access to Mendenhall Wetlands State Game Refuge (2.1 miles).

11.3 Small turnout with access to Auke Lake; bus stop, trail. The **Auke Lake Trail** has has been renovated and expanded to 3-miles. Easily accessed and scenic, it offers forest and water views. A popular choice for hikers of all abilities, it also offers viewing opportunities of wildlife and birds. Wheelchair friendly. ♿

11.4 Large gravel parking area to east with toilet and boat launch on Auke Lake. Good view of Mendenhall Glacier reflected in the lake. This is one of the most photographed spots in Alaska. Red, pink and silver salmon spawn in Auke Lake system July to September.

11.5 Fritz Cove Road to west leads 2.6 miles through residential area and deadends at Smuggler's Cove; weekend parking for kayakers.

Turnoff to east for **Chapel-by-the-Lake**, a Presbyterian congregation with 2 sanctuaries. The smaller log structure perched above Auke Lake is one of the most photographed churches in Southeast Alaska.

11.8 Short road west to Alaska Fisheries Science Center's Auke Bay Laboratory. ABL conducts research programs on fishery management problems for the National Marine Fisheries Service.

12.1 North junction with **Mendenhall Loop Road** (signed **Back Loop Road**); DeHart's Store here has a gas station, convenience store, liquor store and deli. Auke Bay small-boat harbor to west.

CAUTION: Merging traffic. NOTE: A roundabout is proposed for this busy intersection and may be under construction in summer 2014.

The 6-mile Mendenhall Loop Road rejoins Glacier Highway at **Milepost 9.3**. From this junction it is: 0.1 mile to **University of Alaska Southeast** campus entrance; 2.1 miles to **Spruce Meadow RV Park**; 2.5 miles to Montana Creek Road where you turn and travel 0.4 more miles to access **Mendenhall Lake USFS Campground**, West Glacier trailhead and Montana Creek trailhead; and 5.4 miles to Mendenhall Glacier visitor center. Also access to USFS Juneau Ranger District office. *See Juneau Vicinity map this page.* ▲

Glacier Highway becomes Juneau Veterans' Memorial Highway northbound.

12.4 AUKE BAY; post office (99821), pay phone, gas, RV park, marina, bait, fuel. 🛢

12.6 Spaulding trailhead to east; 3-mile hike through muskeg meadow (5 to 6 hours round trip). Popular cross-country ski route in winter. Also access to **Auke Nu Trail**; junction is 0.8 mile up then 2.5 miles to

John Muir USFS cabin.

12.8 Waydelich Creek and bridge.

13.4 Stabler's Point Rock Quarry (no stopping).

13.8 Alaska State Ferry Auke Bay Terminal. Follow signs for parking area. Check-in at ticket counter *before* entering loading lanes. Restrooms, vending machines, pay phones and visitor information inside terminal.

NOTE: If you are arriving in Juneau by ferry, you will turn right onto the highway upon leaving the ferry terminal for Mendenhall Glacier or downtown Juneau (read this road log backwards from here). Mendenhall Loop Road that leads to the Mendenhall Lake USFS Campground is signed "Back Loop Road" here and exits the Glacier Highway across from DeHarts Store at Milepost 12.1. (Additional directions at 12.1 Glacier Highway.) You will turn left on the highway if you are headed for Auke Village recreation area or other destinations northwest of here along Juneau Veterans' Memorial Highway (continue with this road log).

14.7 Exit west for 2-mile loop road through **Auke Village Recreation Area**. Located along this side road are trails to beachside picnic shelters and Auke Village USFS campground, with 11 campsites, tables, firepits, water, flush and pit toilets; camping fee $10, Golden Age and Golden Access cardholder discounts. ▲

15.8 Aant'Iyeik Park uphill to east.

16.2 South end of Point Lena Loop Road and north end of Auke Village Loop Road (0.1 mile west) to Auke Village Recreation Area (see description at **Milepost 14.7**).

Lena Loop ballpark at turnoff.

16.8 North end of Point Lena Loop Road.

16.9 Lena Beach Picnic Area.

17 Turnoff to west for **Lena Beach USFS Picnic Area** (toilets, picnic shelters, tables, firepits).

18 Tee Harbor–Point Stevens turnoff. Paved road leads 0.3 mile west to public parking area and a private marina.

18.8 Inspiration Point. Turnouts to west here and at **Milepost 19** with views of the Chilkat Range, Tee Harbor and Shelter Island across Favorite Channel. Once a bread-and-butter commercial fishing area, hence the name "The Breadline" for this stretch of shoreline, it is now a popular sportfishing area.

20.5 Cohen Drive.

21.8 Breadline Bluff Trail; paved parking area to west. This is an old cannery trail that leads 3 miles from Amalga to Tee Harbor, following a bluff above the rocky shore of Favorite Channel. The south trailhead is located off Cohen Drive.

22.5 Turnoff for **Shrine of St. Therese**, a complex that includes gardens, Stations of the Cross, a labyrinth, lodge, cabins, a gift shop, restrooms and the famous stone chapel. Park at first or "upper" lot and follow signs downhill to the complex. (There is handicap parking and passenger off-loading at the bottom of the hill for anyone with physical challenges.) Or park at lower lot overlooking channel and follow signed gravel path to the complex. *Pets on leash.*

The Shrine of St. Therese, built in honor of St. Therese of Lisieux ("The Little Flower"), Patron Saint of Alaska, began with construction of a retreat house in 1933. It was to be followed by construction of a log chapel on Crow Island (later renamed Shrine Island), a tiny island located about 400 feet from the mainland shore. A cause-

The Shrine of St. Therese was constructed using natural stone. (©Kris Valencia, staff)

way was built out to the island. The chapel is located in a quiet glade. It was built in 1938 using natural stone.

The lodge and cabins can be rented by "groups or persons who respect the spirit of the shrine." Phone (907) 780-6112 for more information. The complex is open 8:30 A.M. to 10 P.M., April to September and provides beautiful, secluded views and walks through quiet forest gardens along the bay.

22.6 Gravel turnout to west.

22.8 Large paved turnout to west with view of channel. The small island on which the Shrine of St. Therese is situated is directly in front of you to the south.

23.2 Jensen-Olsen Arboretum open Wed.–Sun, year-round. Small parking area is also Point Caroline trailhead parking.

23.5 Paved trailhead parking area east side of highway for Peterson Lake trail; 4.2-mile hike through muskeg (planked) and forest to Peterson Lake cabin. Rated more difficult; estimated round-trip 5 to 7 hours.

23.8 Peterson Creek bridge. View spawning salmon here in late summer and early fall. Trout fishing. Bears in area. 🕊

24.4 Turnoff to west for Amalga Harbor; boat launch (permit required to launch). Access to Ernest Gruening State Historical Park.

26.5 Paved trailhead parking area to east. A gravel road here also leads east 0.7 mile to Windfall Lake trailhead and large parking area alongside Herbert River. Windfall Lake is a 3.2-mile easy hike, 4 hours round-trip.

26.8 Herbert River bridge.

26.9 Paved trailhead parking area on east side of highway for Herbert Glacier trail; 4.6-mile hike to views of glacier. Rated easy; 5 to 6 hours round-trip.

27.1 Entering Eagle Beach State Recreation Area northbound.

27.2 Eagle River bridge. Paved parking east at north end of bridge for Eagle Glacier trailhead to east; Eagle River Trail to west. The 5.6-mile trail Eagle Glacier trail leads to Eagle Glacier USFS cabin and continues another 2 miles to Eagle Glacier. Rated most difficult; round-trip 10 to 12 hours; rubber boots recommended.

The Eagle River trail connects with network of walking trails from Eagle Beach SRA.

27.6 Roadside parking west side of highway at entrance to **Eagle Beach State Recreation Area**; large paved parking area, restrooms, extensive trail system accesses beach and river; picnic sites; interpretive signs; viewing scopes; campsites; handicap accessible. Three rentable cabins on site. Open all year; cross-country skiing in winter. Day-use and camping fee charged. Park host in summer. ▲

Yankee Basin trailhead is located on the east side of the highway across from Eagle Beach SRA entrance. This is a 6-mile trail, rated difficult, that follows an old mining route.

28.2 Entrance to **Eagle Beach USFS Picnic Area** (day-use only); picnic shelter, picnic tables, toilets, park host. View of Chilkat Range across Lynn Canal. Good bird watching, parasailing.

28.3 Two scenic viewpoints next 0.5 mile to west.

29 Road down to Kayak launch.

30.2 Large gravel turnout above ocean,

30.5 Waterfall beside highway.

31.4 Turnout on ocean side with view.

32.2 Turnout to west with view of Benjamin Island to southwest; just beyond it is Sentinel Island lighthouse. Visible to the northwest is North Island and northwest of it is Vanderbilt Reef, site of a great sea disaster. The SS *Princess Sophia*, carrying 288 passengers and 61 crew, ran aground on Vanderbilt Reef early in the morning of Oct. 24, 1918. All aboard perished when a combination of stormy seas and a high tide forced the *Princess Sophia* off the reef and she sank early in the evening of Oct. 25. Walter Harper, in 1913 was the first person to stand on the summit of Mount McKinley, and was among the *Princess Sophia's* casualties. Vanderbilt Reef is now marked by a navigation light.

Some pavement breaks and construction under way next 0.8 northbound (summer 2013).

33.2 Kensington Mine Dock Road. Access to a wilderness lodge.

33.9 Scenic viewpoint to west. Northbound, watch for unsigned, small turnouts next mile with access to beach.

35.1 Sunshine Cove public beach access (signed); parking, toilets.

36.5 Unsigned shoulder parking to west; with beach access.

37 Parking to west, North Bridget Cove, beach access.

38 Point Bridget trailhead to west; 3.5-mile hike to Point Bridget (7 hours round-trip); panoramic view of Lynn Canal and Chilkat Mountains from point. The 2,850-acre Point Bridget State Park offers meadows, forests, rocky beaches, salmon streams and a trail system. Popular area for cross-country skiing in winter. Fires allowed on beach with fire ring.

Highway descends 6 percent grade northbound.

38.8 Kowee Creek bridge; fishing. Large parking area to west at north end of bridge.

39.7 Turn west on spur road 0.2 mile for Echo Cove city boat launch ramp on Berners Bay; outhouse, parking, camping. Berners Bay is a popular destination for Juneau paddlers. It is 3 miles across and 34 miles northwest of Juneau by water. ▲

Road ends at gate. Large turnaround area.

You don't have to fish to enjoy Glacier Bay. Whale viewing is prevalant. (©Mike Halbert)

Glacier Bay

One of southeastern Alaska's most dramatic attractions, Glacier Bay has been called "a picture of icy wildness unspeakably pure and sublime" (John Muir, 1879). A national park and preserve, Glacier Bay is most often viewed from the water, from a cruise ship, a tour boat or charter out of Gustavus—the nearest community. The only land route to Glacier Bay National Park is a 10-mile road connecting the small community of Gustavus to Bartlett Cove, site of the park's ranger station, walk-in campground (no vehicle parking or RV services), visitor center, Glacier Bay Lodge and the concessionaire-operated tour boat. There are no entrance fees or user fees at Glacier Bay and no vehicle campgrounds or recreational vehicle services (no sani-dump, no hook-ups, no parking) available.

Visitor Information: Glacier Bay National Park and Preserve, P.O. Box 140, Gustavus, AK 99826; phone (907) 697-2230, fax (907) 697-2654; www.nps.gov/glba.

Glacier Bay Visitor Center, located on the second floor of Glacier Bay Lodge has exhibits, an information desk, bookstore and auditorium. Open daily from late May through early Sept. Park rangers present evening programs, show educational videos and lead walks and hikes. Junior Ranger program for kids.

Emergency services: In Gustavus dial 911. Inside park, phone (907) 697-2651. KWM20 Bartlett Cove on marine band 16.

With passage of the Alaska National Interest Lands Conservation Act in December 1980, Glacier Bay National Monument, established in 1925 by Pres. Calvin Coolidge, became a national park. More than a half-million acres were added to the park/preserve to protect fish and wildlife habitat and wilderness. The 3.3 million acre park includes Mount Fairweather, the highest peak in Southeast Alaska, located in the Fairweather Range of the St. Elias Mountains.

When the English naval explorer Capt. George Vancouver sailed through the ice-choked waters of Icy Strait in 1794, Glacier Bay was little more than a dent in the coastline. Across the head of this seemingly minor inlet stood a towering wall of ice marking the seaward terminus of an immense glacier that completely filled the broad, deep basin of what is now Glacier Bay. To the north, ice extended more than 100 miles into the St. Elias Mountains, covering the intervening valleys with a 4,000-foot-deep mantle of ice.

During the century following Vancouver's explorations, the glacier retreated some 40 miles back into the bay, permitting a spruce–hemlock forest to gradually fill the land. By 1916, the Grand Pacific Glacier, which once occupied the entire bay, had receded some 65 miles from the position observed by Vancouver in 1794. Nowhere else in the world have glaciers been observed to recede at such a rapid pace.

Today, few of the many tributary glaciers that once supplied the huge ice sheet extend to the sea. Glacier Bay National Park encloses 9 active tidewater glaciers, including several on the remote and seldom-visited western edge of the park along the Gulf of Alaska and Lituya Bay. Icebergs, cracked off from near-vertical ice cliffs, dot the waters of upper Glacier Bay.

Glacier Bay's rich marine waters are a sanctuary for endangered humpback whales. Special vessel regulations apply and the National Park Service limits the number of vessels from June to August. Check with the National Park Service for current regulations.

Glacier Bay is a seasonal home to a wide variety of wildlife both marine and terrestrial. Look for mountain goats on steep cliffs in the mid- to upper bay. Moose are common in Gustavus, Bartlett Cove and the lower bay where they browse the grasses and willows around the bay, but they are relative newcomers: moose weren't seen here until the late 1960s. Small mammals include porcupine, coyotes, river otters and red squirrels. Boaters may see harbor seals, sea lions, harbor porpoise and sea otters.

The park is also home to brown/grizzly bears and black bears. One unique variation specific to this area is the "glacier" bear. It is a black bear that has adapted to a blue-gray color with long guard hairs that are yellow or white and blend in with a backdrop of glaciers. Visitors are cautioned to practice bear safety, especially when fishing or hiking and camping in the backcountry. Bear spray is recommended.

Fishing in Glacier Bay and Icy Straits for silver and pink salmon, Dolly Varden and halibut. Charter fishing trips are available from Gustavus.

Lodging & Services

Glacier Bay Lodge, located at Bartlett Cove, is the only accommodation within the national park, although nearby Gustavus *(description on page 690)* has a number of lodges, inns, and bed and breakfasts. For information on Glacier Bay Lodge and excursion boat cruises offered from the lodge, phone 1-888-229-8687, or visit www.visitglacierbay.com.

Glacier Bay Lodge & Tours. See display ad page 690.

There is a Visitor Information Station for Boaters and Campers with restrooms and picnic shelter located near the lodge by the public-use dock (pictured above) in Bartlett Cove. Open May through September; phone (907) 697-2627.

Camping

There is walk-in only campground at Bartlett Cove with 33 tent sites, 14-day limit, firewood, and warming hut may be available; open year-round. No RV services of any kind— such as dump stations or hook-ups—are available anywhere in Gustavus or Glacier Bay National Park and there is no overnight parking allowed.

Wilderness camping available throughout the park; many campers/kayakers use the drop-off service from the park's concession-operated tour boat. Campers must obtain a free permit and attend a camper orientation (presented daily at the Visitor Information Station). Bear-resistant food canisters, available at no charge, are required for back-country camping.

Transportation

Air: Scheduled Alaska Airlines and Juneau-based charter air service to Gla-

Glacier Bay National Park and Preserve

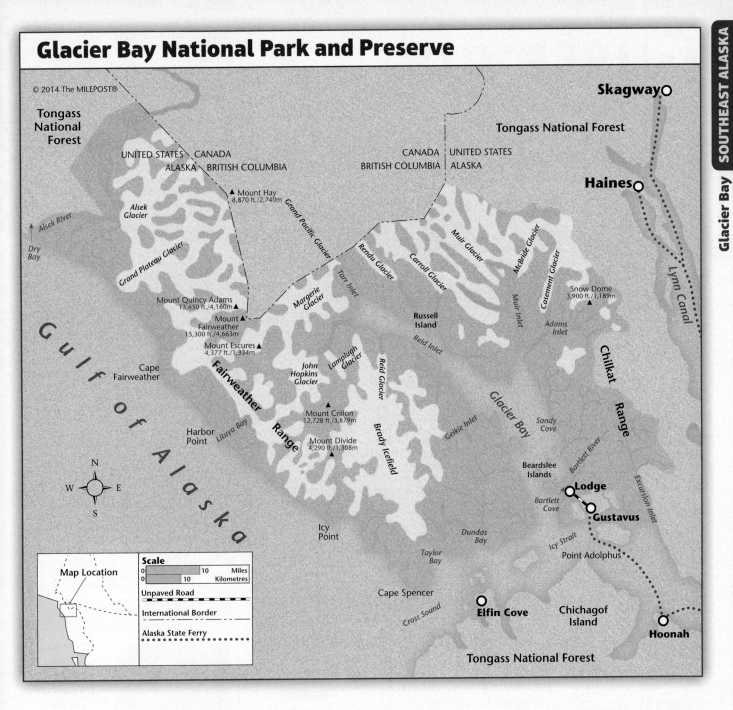

© 2014 The MILEPOST®

cier Bay lands at Gustavus airport. Landing within the park is restricted to salt water. All wilderness/non-motorized waters are closed to aircraft landing between May 1 to September 15. For air service information, go to www.gustavusak.com.

Ferry: Alaska Marine Highway MV *Le Conte* has regularly scheduled sailings between Juneau and Gustavus in summer. *NOTE: There are no vehicle friendly camp-grounds or services for recreational vehicles in Gustavus or Glacier Bay National Park and Gustavus has less than 20 miles of paved roads. Please review the park website at www.nps.gov/glba prior to booking ferry travel or review the city website at www.gustavusak.com.*

Boat Service: Excursion boats oper-ated by Glacier Bay Lodge concession-aire depart from Bartlett Cove. Charter boats are available in Gustavus for sight-seeing, whale watching or fishing. Over-night cruise tours and scheduled day trips by catamaran are available from Juneau.

Cruise Ships: Thousands of park visitors experience the beauty of Glacier Bay from the decks of cruise ships and a number of cruise lines visit Glacier Bay as part of longer itineraries.

Private Boats: Glacier Bay National Park is approximately 100 miles from Juneau by boat. Park rangers at Bartlett Cove are available to assist in advising visi-tors who wish to tour Glacier Bay in private boats or by kayak. Kayak rentals and daily guided kayak trips from Glacier Bay Sea Kayaks (907) 697-2257, www.glacierbaysea kayaks.com. Multi-day guided kayak trips are available through Spirit Walker Expeditions Gustavus, phone 1-800-529-2537; Alaska Discovery in Juneau, phone 1-800-586-1911, www.akdiscovery.com; and Alaska Mountain Guides in Haines, phone 1-800-766-3396.

Permits are required for private marine motorized vessels from June 1 through August 31; permits are free and good for 7 consecutive days. Permits must be obtained prior to entry into Glacier Bay and Bartlett

Cove. Phone (907) 697-2627 or call KWM20 Bartlett Cove on marine band 16 to confirm permits are available. Advance application is strongly advised. Permit applications are available online at www.nps.gov/glba (go to "Permits") or request an application by mail, phone or fax *(see Visitor Information on facing page)*. Boat permit applications may be made no more than 60 days in advance of the pro-posed date of entry.

Fuel dock at Bartlett Cove (phone lodge or contact on marine band 16 for hours). Vessels may dock at Bartlett Cove Dock for no more than 3 hours in a 24-hour period. Anchor out in designated areas at Bartlett Cove. The Park Service identifies possible anchorages on their website and during the boater orientation. *CAUTION BOATERS: No attempt should be made to navigate Glacier Bay without appropriate charts, tide tables and local knowledge. Floating ice is a special hazard. Because of the danger from waves caused by fall-ing ice, small craft should not approach closer than 0.25 mile from tidewater glacier fronts.*

Gustavus

Gateway to Glacier Bay National Park and Preserve, the small community of Gustavus is located at the mouth of the Salmon River, on the north shore of Icy Strait, 48 miles northwest of Juneau. It is 10 miles by road from Gustavus to Bartlett Cove within the park. **Population**: 492. **Emergency Services**: Phone 911. **Clinic**: Gustavus Community Clinic, phone (907) 697-3008.

Visitor Information: Gustavus Visitors Assoc., phone (907) 697-2354; website www.gustavusak.com. And http://www.nps.gov/glba/planyourvisit/index.htm.

Private Aircraft: Gustavus airport, adjacent northeast; elev. 36 feet; length 6,700 feet; asphalt.

Surrounded by Glacier Bay National Park, Gustavus has a panoramic view of the majestic Fairweather Mountains and the Chilkat Range. Gustavus offers expansive sandy beaches, open land and forest. It is a small community with fishing, whale watching, kayaking, hiking, golfing and flightseeing opportunities.

Homesteaded in 1914 as a small agricultural community, the area was once named Strawberry Point because of its abundant wild strawberries.

Today, residents work in seasonal tourism, create and sell arts and crafts, work for the National Park Service, fish (commercial

©Jona Brent

and subsistence) and in various other local trades.

Gustavus was incorporated as a city on April 1, 2004, but it retains the charm of a small and remote settlement where people wave at strangers, ride bikes to get around, volunteer within the community and appreciate the wildlife and natural beauty of the area.

Lodging & Services

Accommodations in Gustavus include full-service inns and lodges, such as Annie Mae Lodge, vacation homes and bed-and-breakfasts. The lodges and inns serve meals for guests and often feature local seafood. (Drop-in customers check for space-available meal reservations.)

Shop for locally made treasures created by an amazing number of talented local artists, painters, potters, sculptors, jewelers and woodcarvers fill the galleries, studios and shops with unique items.

Gustavus has a post office; library with Internet access; 4 churches; a K–12 school; 1 general store with groceries and hardware; cafe; liquor store; 3 coffee shops; natural foods store (with sandwiches); and fish-processing/retail store. Fishing supplies and licenses may be purchased locally.

Glacier Bay Lodge, located at Bartlett Cove, has a restaurant and lounge, also operates the day boat trip up into Glacier Bay! (Bartlett Cove offers one of two campgrounds in the Gustavus area—walk-in, tenting only.) A second campground is at the Mount Fairweather Golf Course.

Annie Mae Lodge in Gustavus at Glacier Bay. Beautiful full service lodge on the Good River. Boasting gourmet food and wine, Glacier Bay tours, fishing, whale watching, kayaking, courtesy van, bikes and much more. We offer an experience of a lifetime while carrying on the tradition of country hospitality in frontier Alaska. Your true Alaskan experience is waiting for you here. Box 55, Gustavus, AK 99826. Phone 1-800-478-2346 or (907) 697-2346, fax (907) 697-2211. Email: reservations@anniemae.com. www.anniemae.com. See display ad on this page. [ADVERTISEMENT]

Growley Bear Lodge. Located in Gustavus. Affordable and modern luxury lodging, with views of the Fairweather Mountain Range and ocean. Home to Fish Alaska Charters and close to hiking trails and other Alaskan adventures, the lodge is 0.8 miles from the Ferry Dock and minutes from the airport. Each room has satellite television and a private bathroom. www.growleybear.com. Phone 1-888-878-8610. [ADVERTISEMENT]

Transportation

Ferry: Alaska Marine Highway ferry service year-round. Check current schedules at www.ferryalaska.com.

Air: Alaska Airlines daily jet flights from Juneau to Gustavus airport in summer. 3 year-round air taxis. Scheduled and charter service from Juneau, Sitka, Haines and Skagway to the Gustavus airport. Bus service between the airport and Bartlett Cove is available for arriving jet flights as is taxi ser-

vice. Courtesy van service is available from many of the local accommodations.

Roads: Gustavus has less than 20 miles of paved roads.

Taxi: TLC Taxi, (907) 697-2239.

Rental Cars: Bud's Rent-A-Car, phone (907) 697-2403.

Boat Service: A catamaran day-boat tour of Glacier Bay National Park, operated by the park concession, departs from Bartlett Cove daily in summer. Saltwater charter boats are available in Gustavus for sightseeing/whale watching or fishing.

Attractions

Besides its proximity to the national park, Gustavus offers a truly unique Southeast Alaska experience. Cruise ships do not stop here, so independent travelers can experience Alaska without the crowds. Guests and locals alike enjoy exploring Icy Strait, Point Adolphus, the Outer Coast, Glacier Bay and Pleasant Island.

The Glacier Bay National Park Visitor Center is open daily in Bartlett Cove. Exhibits, park information, films and trip planning. Join a park ranger for daily guided walks, hikes and evening presentations. Check the schedules posted in town and at the Glacier Bay Lodge.

Sea kayaking companies provide kayak rentals and guided tours. These tours range in length from a few hours to many weeks.

Local **charter boats**—sometimes called "6 packs" because they carry about 6 passengers—are available for sportfishing (salmon, halibut), sightseeing Icy Strait and Glacier Bay, and whale watching. Whale sightings are almost guaranteed at nearby Point Adolphus.

©Mike Halbert

The Gustavus area is very flat and **bike riding** is a popular way to get around. (There's a paved road in town.) Most inns offer bicycles for use by guests.

The gas station is a local attraction: the **Gustavus Dray**, a pre-WWII replica of a Mobil gas station that has a working 1937 Wayne 60 gas pump, a gift shop and a petroleum museum.

Mount Fairweather Golf Course is a 9-hole, par 36, 3,000-yard facility in an amphitheater of mountains and inland waterways.

The Gustavus shoreline offers 18 miles of wild sandy beach, ideal for **beachwalking**. There are several trails and hikes highlighted in "Gustavus Wildlife Viewing Trails" at www.nps.gov/glba/naturescience/animals.htm.

Haines

View of historic Fort Seward and Haines waterfront. (©Sharon Nault)

Located on Portage Cove, Chilkoot Inlet, on the upper arm of Lynn Canal, 80 air miles northwest of Juneau; 150 road miles southeast of Haines Junction, YT, via the Haines Highway. *NOTE: Haines is only 15 miles by water from Skagway, but it is 359 miles by road (Alaska Marine Highway ferries and more frequent passenger-only fast ferry, available)!* **Population:** Haines Borough 2,620. **Emergency Services: Alaska State Troopers**, phone (907) 766-2552. **Police**, phone (907) 766-2121. **Fire Department** and **Ambulance**, emergency only phone 911; business phone: (907) 766-2115. **SEARHC Haines Medical Clinic**, phone (907) 766-6300. **Maritime Search and Rescue**, contact the Coast Guard at 1-800-478-5555.

Visitor Information: Haines Convention and Visitors Bureau, 122 Second Ave. S., Box 530, Haines, AK 99827; phone (907) 766-2234; toll free 1-800-458-3579; www.haines.ak.us; email hcvb@haines.ak.us. Open 8 A.M. to 5 P.M. weekdays, 9 A.M. to 4 P.M. weekends, June–Sept. Open 8 A.M. to 5 P.M. weekdays, Oct.–May. Free brochures for all of Alaska and the Yukon. The Visitors Guide has WiFi spots (citywide) noted on a map inside of it.

Elevation: Sea level. Climate: Average daily maximum temperature in July, 66°F; average daily minimum in January, 16°F. Extreme high summer temperature, 98°F; extreme winter low, -18°F; average annual precipitation, 59 inches. **Radio:** KHNS-FM 102.3. **Television:** 35 cable channels. **Newspaper:** *Chilkat Valley News* (weekly).

Major Attractions:

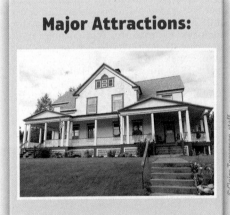
©Claire Torgerson, staff

*Fort Seward,
Welcome Totems,
Alaska Chilkat Bald Eagle
Preserve*

Private Aircraft: Haines airport, 4 miles west; elev. 16 feet; length 3,000 feet; asphalt; fuel 100; unattended.

Haines is a small town that plays host to a large number of visitors each summer. As a gateway to the Alaska Highway for Inside Passage travelers, Haines has become an important service stop. Its spectacular scenery, outdoor recreation and laid-back lifestyle have also made Haines a popular destination. At least part of the community's appeal lies in its small town friendliness, captured in local writer Heather Lende's book, *If You Lived Here, I'd Know Your Name:*

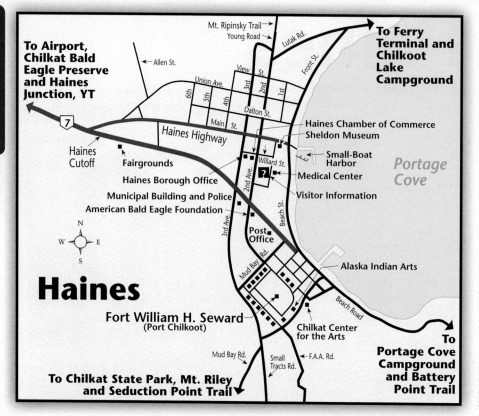

Haines

Fort William H. Seward
(Port Chilkoot)

News from Small-Town Alaska.

The original Indian name for Haines was *Dtehshuh,* meaning "end of the trail," referring to where Chilkat and Chilkoot Indians met and traded with Russian and American ships at the end of the peninsula. It was also their portage route for transporting canoes from the Chilkat River to Portage Cove and Lynn Canal.

In 1879 missionary S. Hall Young and naturalist John Muir came to the village of Yandustuky (near today's airport) to determine the location of a Presbyterian mission and school. The site chosen was on the narrow portage between the Chilkat River and Lynn Canal. The following year, George Dickinson established a trading post for the Northwest Trading Company, next to the mission site. His wife Sarah began a school for Tlingit children. By 1881, Eugene and Caroline Willard arrived to establish Chilkat Mission. The mission and town were named for Francina E. Haines, secretary of the Presbyterian Women's Executive Society of Home Missions, who raised funds for the new mission.

In 1882 the Haines post office was established. The Dalton Trail, which crossed the Chilkat mountain pass to the Klondike goldfields in the Yukon, started at Pyramid Harbor Cannery across the Chilkat River from Haines. The town became an important outlet for the Porcupine Mining District, producing thousands of dollars' worth of placer gold at the turn of the century.

Just to the south of Haines city center is Fort Seward on Portage Cove. Named Fort William H. Seward, in honor of the secretary of state who negotiated the purchase of Alaska from Russia in 1867, this was established as the first permanent Army post in the territory. The first troops arrived in 1904 from Camp Skagway. In 1922, the fort was renamed Chilkoot Barracks, after the mountain pass and the Indian tribe on the Chilkoot River. (There are 2 tribes in this area: the Chilkat and the Chilkoot.)

Chilkoot Barracks was deactivated in 1946 and sold in 1947 to a group of enterprising U.S. veterans who had designs of creating a business cooperative on the site. Their original plans were never fully realized, but most stayed on, creating the city of Port Chilkoot by converting some of the buildings into homes and businesses.

In 1970, Port Chilkoot merged with Haines to become a single municipality, the City of Haines. Two years later, the post was designated a national historic site and became officially known, again, as Fort William H. Seward (although the underlying land is still owned by the Chilkoot Company). In 2002, the City of Haines was consolidated with the Borough of Haines to form Haines Borough.

Fishing and gold mining were the initial industries of the Haines area. The Porcupine Gold Mine in this area is featured on *Discovery Channel's* reality show *"Gold Rush Alaska"* which began in 2010. Haines is also remembered for its famous strawberries, developed by Charles Anway about 1900. His Alaskan hybrid strawberry, *Burbank,* was a prize winner at the 1909 Alaska–Yukon–Pacific Exposition in Seattle, WA. A strawberry festival was held annually in Haines for many years, and this local event grew into the Southeast Alaska State Fair, which each summer draws thousands of visitors. Today, halibut and gill-net salmon fishing and tourism are the basis of the economy. Haines is an important port on the Alaska Marine Highway System as the southern terminus of the Haines Highway, 1 of the 2 year-round roads linking southeastern Alaska with the Alaska Highway in Canada.

Lodging & Services

For a small town, Haines is very much a full-service community *(see listing of services on pages 694-695).* Haines has hardware stores, grocery stores (Howser's IGA Supermarket, Olerud's Market Center); restau-

rants, cafes and taverns; automotive repair, a car wash; laundries, a post office and First National Bank, Alaska. The bank, Howser's IGA Supermarket and the Fogcutter Bar all have ATMs. There are several gift shops and galleries, many featuring the work of local artisans. The Haines Senior Center invites seniors to come and have lunch. They are open 8 A.M.–3 P.M. weekdays. Call in advance (907) 766-2383. The award-winning Haines public library offers Internet access. Swimming available at Haines Pool adjacent the high school.

Accommodations at **Captain's Choice Motel** (phone 1-800-478-2345), **Eagle's Nest Motel** (907) 766-2891, and historic **Hotel Halsingland** (1-800-542-6363). Bed and breakfast accommodations at **The Summer Inn**, phone (907) 766-2970. See ads and descriptions this section.

Camping

There are several private RV parks in Haines include **Haines Hitch-up RV Park**, and **Oceanside RV Park**. See ads and descriptions this section.

Haines Hitch-Up RV Park offers easy access to 92 full hookups, spacious, grassy, level sites. Cable TV & 50 AMP sites available. Laundromat and free immaculate restrooms and WiFi for our guests. Gift shop. Tour tickets and information. Located at the junction of the Haines Highway and Main Street. GPS 59°13'26"N 135°26'48"W. P.O. Box 383, Haines, AK 99827. Phone (907) 766-2882. www.hitch uprv.com. See display ad on page 696. [ADVERTISEMENT]

There are 4 state campgrounds in the Haines area: Portage Cove State Recreation Site on the waterfront, with 9 walk-in tent sites; Chilkat State Park, located 7 miles south of Haines on Mud Bay Road (then another 2 miles on the Chilkat State Park Road). It has 32 tent/RV sites, 3 waterfront tent sites; Chilkoot Lake State Recreation Site, 10 miles from downtown Haines via Lutak Road, has 32 sites; and at **Milepost H 27.3, the** Mosquito Lake State Recreation Site has 5 sites.

Transportation

Air: Haines airport is 3.5 miles from downtown. Alaska Seaplanes (www.flyalas

Alaska Native blanket weaving demonstration held outside the Haines Museum. (©Sharon Nault)

kaseaplanes.com and Wings of Alaska (www. wingsofalaska.com) offers daily scheduled service to and from Juneau, Skagway and other southeast Alaska communities. There are also 2 charter services. Some motels offer courtesy car pickup from the airport.

Car Rental: At Captain's Choice Motel, phone (907) 766-3111 and Avis Car Rental at Hotel Halsingland (907) 766-2000.

Highways: The Haines Highway connects Haines, AK, with Haines Junction, YT. It is maintained year-round. U.S. Customs is open 8 A.M. to midnight (Alaska Time). See HAINES HIGHWAY section.

The 10-mile Lutak Road leads to the Alaska Marine Highway terminal and Chilkoot Lake SRS. The 7-mile Mud Bay

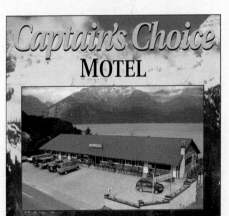

Photo by Jason Allgood

Photo by Fred Bretthauer, Haines Hitch-Up RV Park

Photo by Jason Allgood

experience...

HAINES, ALASKA

unspoiled & unhurried

Photo by Ron Horn

Come for the **SERENITY**, Stay for the **ADVENTURE**.

- Native Tlingit Culture
- Watchable Wildlife
- Local Artisans
- Valley of the Eagles
- Fisherman's Dream Land

HAINES CHAMBER OF COMMERCE BUSINESS DIRECTORY

(See map for business locations)

ATTRACTIONS/TOURS

1. CHILKAT RIVER ADVENTURES
Adventurers on a river boat tour to the remote wilderness of the Chilkat Valley and the Bald Eagle Preserve • PO Box 556 • Haines, AK 99827 • 907-766-2050 • 907-766-2051 Fax • riveradventures@aptalaska.net • www.jetboat alaska.com

2. SOCKEYE CYCLE
Bicycle Tours, Rentals, Sales and Service. Fully Supported Tours from 3hrs -10 days! The most spectacular Bike Tours in the World! • 24 Portage St. • PO Box 829 • Haines, AK 99827 • 907-766-2869 • 877-292-4154 • 907-766-2851 Fax • sockeye@cyclealaska.com • www.cycle alaska.com

GALLERIES/GIFTS/SHOPPING

3. ALASKA ROD'S
Quality handmade products: fudge, custom knives, healing salves, devils club products, photography, jewelry, leather, carvings, sculptures and more. Open year round. 126 Main Street • PO Box 253 • Haines, AK 99827 • 907-766-2352 • store@alaskarods.com • www. alaskarods.com

GROCERY/BEVERAGE STORES

4. MOUNTAIN MARKET & CAFÉ / RIPINKSY ROASTERS
Natural & organic groceries; fresh produce; beer & wine spirits; homemade soups, baked goods & salads; sandwiches; wraps; a full espresso bar featuring our own coffee roasted in-house. Open year-round • Corner of 3rd Ave. & Haines Highway • PO Box 1509 • Haines, AK 99827 •

907-766-3340 • mountain_market@yahoo.com • www.mountain-market.com

LODGING

5. THE SUMMER INN BED & BREAKFAST
Open year-round, this Inn is the perfect getaway. Built 100 years ago by a member of Skagway's notorious Soapy Smith gang. Excellent views of the Lynn Canal. Big enough for privacy, small enough for conversation. • 117 Second Avenue • PO Box 1198 • Haines, AK 99827 • 907-766-2970 • innkeeper@summerinnbnb.com • www. summerinnbnb.com

6. CAPTAIN'S CHOICE MOTEL
Best view in town overlooking the Lynn Canal, AAA Approved, pet friendly, free Wi-Fi, complimentary continental breakfast, conveniently

Alaska. We operate a fleet of 11 float and wheel equipped aircraft. Please call one of our friendly and knowledgeable customer service agents in Haines. • 907-766-3800 Haines • 907-983-2479 Skagway • 907-789-3331 Juneau • www.flyalaskaseaplanes.com

10. ALASKA FJORDLINES
Fjord Express to Juneau. Whale watching on every trip! See the Eldred Rock Lighthouse, Mendenhall Glacier, State capitol and downtown Juneau • PO Box 246 • Haines, AK 99827 • 907-766-3395 • 1-800-320-0146 • 866-279-8206 Fax • info@alaskafjordlines.com • www.alaska fjordlines.com

SERVICES

11. CANAL MARINE CO. & AUTO SERVICE
Parts/Service Outboard Marine, Auto & Small Engine Repair Shop. Open Year-Round. Certified Full Service Mechanic on Duty 6 days a week. Welding. "If Man Made It, We Can Fix It!" Locally Owned and Operated • 10 Front Street • PO Box 1569 • Haines, AK 99827 • 907-766-2437 • canalmarine@aptalaska.net

12. PARTS PLACE
Auto-RV-Marine. If you need it and we don't have it, we will get it! • 104 3rd Avenue St. • PO Box 9 • Haines, AK 99827 • 907-766-294

located downtown, Lounge with ocean view, guest Laundromat and rental cars with unlimited miles. • 108 Second Avenue • PO Box 392 • Haines, AK 99827 • 907-766-3111 • Fax: 907-766-3332 • 1-800-478-2345 • captain@aptalaska.net • www.capchoice.com

7. HAINES HITCH-UP RV PARK
Ninety-two spacious sites. Cable TV & 50 AMP Sites available. Gift Shop Laundromat. Free Spotless Showers & Wi-Fi for our Guests. Tour Information & Ticket Sales • 851 Main Street • PO Box 383 • Haines, AK 99827 • 907-766-2882 • www.hitchuprv.com

8. OCEANSIDE RV PARK
Panoramic View of Lynn Canal. Open Year-Round. 23 Full hook-ups. Clean restrooms. Shower ($) Laundry ($) Wi-Fi ($). One block from town. Good Sam Park. Reservations recommended. Home Away from Home Atmosphere. • 10 Front Street • PO Box 1569 • Haines, AK 99827 • 907-766-2437 greatview@oceansiderv.com • www.oceansiderv.com

TRANSPORTATION

9. ALASKA SEAPLANES
Full Service Air Transportation offering scheduled flights from Haines to Juneau, Skagway, Gustavus, Hoonah, Kake, Angoon, Tenakee, Pelican, Elfin Cove and Excursion Inlet on a year-round basis. Charters, sightseeing and cargo flights also available throughout Southeast

*experience...***Haines, Alaska**

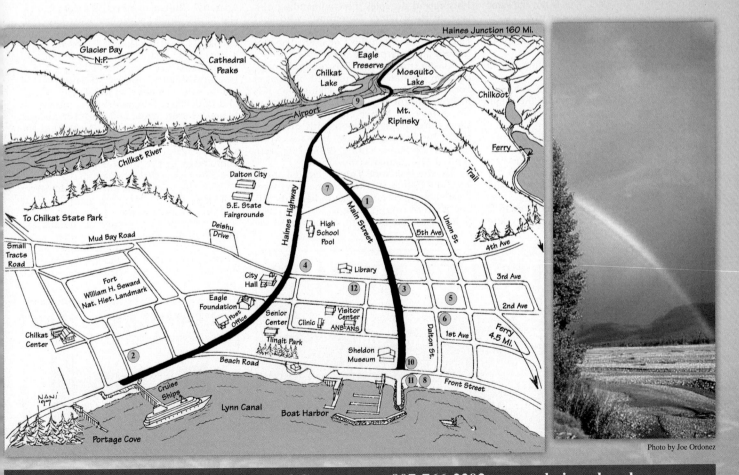

Photo by Joe Ordonez

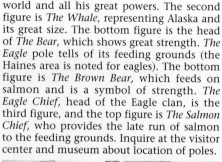

This tongue-in-cheek "electric hammer" is on display at The Hammer Museum. *(©Sharon Nault)*

world and all his great powers. The second figure is *The Whale*, representing Alaska and its great size. The bottom figure is the head of *The Bear*, which shows great strength. *The Eagle* pole tells of its feeding grounds (the Haines area is noted for eagles). The bottom figure is *The Brown Bear*, which feeds on salmon and is a symbol of strength. *The Eagle Chief*, head of the Eagle clan, is the third figure, and the top figure is *The Salmon Chief*, who provides the late run of salmon to the feeding grounds. Inquire at the visitor center and museum about location of poles.

Road accesses Chilkat State Park.

Bus: Visitor Shuttle Bus when cruise ships are in port offer inexpensive, loop rides around city on regular intervals (approximately every half hour).

Ferries: Alaska Marine Highway vessels provide year-round service to Haines; see ALASKA MARINE HIGHWAY section. Ferry terminal on Lutak Road, 4.5 miles from downtown Haines; phone (907) 766-2111.

Haines–Skagway Fast Ferry provides passenger-only service between Skagway and Haines 1-888-766-2103. This is not the same as the Alaska Marine Highway ferries.

Alaska Fjordlines offers a day cruise to Juneau in summer; phone 1-800-320-0146 or (907) 766-3395.

Cruise Ships: Several cruise ships call in Haines.

Private Boats: Transient moorage is available at Letnikof Cove and at the small-boat harbor downtown. Contact the harbormaster, phone (907) 766-2448.

Attractions

Take **the walking tour** of historic Fort William H. Seward; details and map are available at the visitor information center and at other businesses.

Historic buildings of the post include the former cable office; warehouses and barracks; fire hall; the guard house (jail); the contractor's office; plumber's quarters; the post exchange (now a lodge); gymnasium; movie house; the mule stables; and "Soapsuds Alley," the housing for noncommissioned officers whose wives did laundry for the soldiers. The former headquarters building, fronted by a cannon and a totem depicting a bear and an eagle, is now a private residence.

Officers' Row at the "Top O' the Hill" is now restored homes and apartments. Hotel Halsingland occupies the commanding officers quarters. Elinor Dusenbury, who later wrote the music for the state song—"Alaska's Flag"—once lived in these quarters. Look for historic and interpretive signs.

Alaska Indian Arts. This nonprofit organization, located in the restored hospital at Fort Seward, is part of the walking tour. It is dedicated to the revival of Tlingit Indian art. See displays of Native art. Local craftsmen carve totem poles and work with silver and stone. Visitors hours 9 A.M. to 5 P.M. weekdays, year-round. Phone (907) 766-2160; www.alaskaindianarts.com.

See the Welcome Totems located at the Y on the Haines Highway. These poles were created by carvers of Alaska Indian Arts Inc. and are read from bottom to top. *The Raven* pole is symbolic of Raven, as founder of the

Sheldon Museum and Cultural Center is located on the old Haines Mission property at the end of Main Street by the boat harbor. The museum was named after Steve Sheldon (1885–1960), a multi-talented resident of Haines who, with his wife Bess, collected many things for the museum. He once owned and operated a hardware store, a drugstore, a trading post, a hotel, a grocery and a steam laundry. He even made his own set of false teeth which are on display at the museum. Exhibits present the pioneer history of the Chilkat Valley, the history of Fort William H. Seward, the culture of the Tlingit Native people and the works of local artisans. Chilkat blankets, Russian trunks, the Eldred Rock Lighthouse lens, Jack Dalton's sawed-off shotgun, and photographs of Haines and the Haines Highway, make a fascinating history lesson. Open daily in summer, 10 A.M.–5 P.M. weekdays, 1–4 P.M. weekends. Open Monday to Saturday 1–4 P.M. in winter. Admission fee $5; children 12 and under free. Museum store is upstairs. It features locally made and Alaska items and a selection of Alaska books. Prints from the museums valuable photo collection are for sale and feature pictures of many unusual shipwrecks in the southeast. Phone (907) 766-2366; www.sheldonmuseum.org.

The Hammer Museum on Main Street can't be missed: There's a giant hammer in front, created by Dave Pahl, who is also responsible for the collection of hammers on display inside. The outdoor hammer, modeled after a Maydole hammer manufactured in 1923, consists of a 19-foot-long, 26-inch-diameter spruce log shaped to form the

handle and a foam-and-fiberglass hammer head.

Inside the museum, there are more than 1,800 hammers to see, from blacksmith hammers to an 800-year-old Tlingit hammer. The hammers are grouped by purpose and age, revealing the many uses of this familiar tool. Don't miss the table of "joke" hammers which includes the one with electric plug-in and switch. Open May–Sept., 10 A.M. to 5 P.M. Admission fee $3, kids under 12 free. Web address: www.hammer museum.org.

American Bald Eagle Foundation Natural History Museum and Live Raptor Center, located on the Haines Highway at 2nd Avenue, shows visitors how the bald eagle interacts with its environment. In addition, the facility allows the foundation to house up to 11 raptors providing live bird presentations daily. Call for the eagles daily feeding schedule. Admission fee $10. Phone (907) 766-3094; www.baldeagles.org.

Alaska Chilkat Bald Eagle Preserve is the annual gathering site of more than 3,500 bald eagles from mid-October through December with the Bald Eagle Festival in November each year (www. baldeaglefestival.org). The 48,000-acre preserve was established in 1982 to protect and perpetuate one of the world's greatest concentration of bald eagles and their critical habitat. The main eagle viewing area lies along the Chilkat River flats between **Milepost H 18** and **H 24** of the Haines Highway. There is a walkway and viewing platform system that spans between the parking lots at Mile 19 and 21 and includes interpretive displays. The eagles are drawn here by the late run of salmon, mostly chum and some silver. For more information, contact Alaska State Parks, phone (907) 766-2292, or www.dnr.state. ak.us/parks/units/eagleprv.htm.

Special Events. The 22nd annual Great Alaska Craft Beer and Home Brew Festival, held at Dalton City May 23–24, 2014, features a gourmet beer banquet and a microbrew tasting. The 22nd Kluane to Chilkat Bike Relay (June 21st, 2014) starts in Haines Junction, YT, and finishes 152 miles later in downtown Haines, AK. The free Community King Salmon Barbecue follows the bike race at "Dalton City" in the Haines Fairgrounds. The Southeast Alaska State Fair, July 31–Aug. 3, 2014, features 4 fun-filled days of live music, food and crafts booths, exhibits, a 5K Adventure Run, wearable art show regional talent show, childrens carnival, kids' stage, a beer garden horseshoe tournament, fishermen's rodeo, volleyball tournament, logging show, rides and games and a grand parade. The Alaska Bald Eagle Festival, Nov. 10–16, 2014, celebrates the winter gathering of eagles near Haines.

Dalton City is a replica of the gold rush town and was built for the "White Fang" Disney film set. It is located at the Haines fairgrounds. The former movie set houses a microbrewery, pizzeria and several shops, and hosts special events like the Homebrew Festival, festivities surrounding the annual Kluane to Chilkat Bike Relay, as well as the Southeast Alaska State Fair.

Drive out Mud Bay Road. This scenic side road is logged as follows: Mile 2.4, Mount Riley Trail and parking area; Mile 3.4, roadside spring water; Mile 3.7, large paved view turnout along water; Mile 4.5, large parking area, boat harbor, launch, outhouse and views of Haines Packing Co.; Mile

Glacier views await those who drive Mud Bay Road. (©Sharon Nault)

4.8, entrance to Haines Packing Co.; Mile 6.1, turnoff on gravel road which leads to **Chilkat State Park and Campground**. For the state park, turn right and continue 1.2 miles to park entrance, then a half-mile further for fee station. The campground has 35 campsites, picnic sites, beach access, a boat launch and a 7-mile (one-way) hiking trail to Seduction Point at the southern tip of the Chilkat Peninsula. For more information, contact Alaska State Parks, phone (907) 766-2292, or go to http://dnr.alaska.gov/parks/ units/haines.htm.

If you don't turn off of Mud Bay Road at Mile 6.1 for the campground, you can continue a half-mile to a shoreline picnic area with spectacular views, grill-style firepits, tables, shelters and pit toilets. This is a favorite picnic spot for local residents. There are beautiful views of Rainbow and Davidson glaciers across Chilkat Inlet.

Drive out Lutak Road. This road begins at the intersection of Dalton and Second Avenue (which becomes Lutak Road). At Mile 3.1 there is a popular, large picnic area overlooking Lutak Inlet. Level parking, tables, grill-style firepits, bear-proof trash bins, pit toilets. The Alaska Marine Highway terminal is located at Mile 4 Lutak Road. Continue north past the ferry terminal to road end at Chilkoot Lake Road and turn left. The road parallels the Chilkoot River for about a mile before it ends at a parking area on beautiful Chilkoot Lake. It is a total of about 10 miles from downtown Haines to **Chilkoot Lake State Recreation Site**, which has a picnic area and 80-site campground. For more information, contact Alaska State Parks, phone (907) 766-2292, or go to http:// dnr.alaska.gov/parks/units/haines.htm.

The ADF&G operates a fish weir on the Chilkoot River between June and September to count the red salmon returning to Chilkoot Lake and the river. This area is good for fish and wildlife viewing. En route along this road there are areas that restrict drivers from stopping and getting out of their cars, because of bear activity during the salmon run season.

Wildlife Viewing at Center. The Kroschel Films Wildlife Center at Mile 29 north of Haines off the Haines Highway, provides access to wildlife viewing. Take Mosquito

Lake Road to Mile 1.8. Shows are approximately 2 hours and include a guided walk on an easy trail. The Center provides access to over 15 species of Alaska wildlife, some of which may be petted or fed. Open May 15–Sept. 15 for scheduled, organized tours. For more information, call (907) 767-5464 or visit www.kroschelfilms.com.

Go Flightseeing. Local air charter operators offer flightseeing trips for spectacular close-up views of glaciers, ice fields, mountain peaks and bald eagles. The heart of Glacier Bay is just west of Haines.

Take a Tour. Charter boat operators in Haines offer fishing, sightseeing and photography trips. Local tour companies offer bicycle tours, guided hiking, bus tours and nature walks.

Hike Area Trails. Stop at the visitor information center for a free copy of the pamphlet, *Haines is for Hikers*, which contains trail descriptions and maps.

Mount Ripinsky trail is a strenuous all-day hike—recommended for experienced hikers only—with spectacular views from the summit of mountains and tidal waters. Battery Point trail leads about 1.2 miles to Kelgaya Point overlooking Lynn Canal along relatively flat ground. Mount Riley (elev. 1,760 feet) has 3 routes to the summit. The steepest and most widely used trail starts at Mile 3 Mud Bay Road and climbs 2.8 miles to the summit and, according to our trusty Park Ranger source, Preston Kroes, this trail may also be accessed from 0.9 mile of the Battery Point Trail.

AREA FISHING: Good fishing May–June for king salmon in **Chilkat Inlet**. Halibut best June–Sept. in **Chilkat**, **Lutak** and **Chilkoot inlets**. Dolly Varden fishing good in all lakes and clear water rivers, and along marine shorelines from early spring to late fall. Great pink salmon fishing in August along the marine shoreline of **Lutak Inlet** and in the **Chilkoot River**. Red salmon in the **Chilkoot River**, late June through August. Silver salmon in the **Chilkoot** and **Chilkat rivers**, mid-September through October. Cutthroat trout year-round at **Chilkoot** and **Mosquito lakes**. Contact the Alaska Dept. of Fish and Game at (907) 766-2625.

Skagway

Skagway is a great little town for pedestrians, with many Gold Rush era buildings.

(© Sharon Nault)

Major Attractions:

©Sharon Nault

Klondike Gold Rush National Historical Park, White Pass & Yukon Route Railway

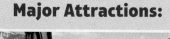

Located on the north end of Taiya Inlet on Lynn Canal, 90 air miles northwest of Juneau; 108 road miles south of Whitehorse, YT. The northern terminus of the Alaska Marine Highway Southeast ferry system and southern terminus of the South Klondike Highway, which connects with the Alaska Highway. *NOTE: Although Skagway is only 15 miles by water from Haines, it is 359 miles by road (Alaska*

Marine Highway ferries and more frequent passenger-only fast ferry available)! **Population:** 968. **Emergency Services**: Phone 911 for all emergencies. **Police**, phone (907) 983-2232. **Fire Department** and **Ambulance**, phone (907) 983-2450. **Dahl Memorial Clinic**, phone (907) 983-2255. **Maritime Search and Rescue**, contact the Coast Guard at 1-800-478-5555. **U.S. Customs** located at Mile 6.8 Klondike Highway 2; phone (907) 983-2325.

Visitor Information: The Visitor Center is located in Arctic Brotherhood Hall between 2nd and 3rd on Broadway. Open daily early May–late Sept; only Mon.–Fri. during winter. They offer information on area attractions and accommodations, walking and trail maps. Write the Skagway Convention and Visitors Bureau, Box 1029, Skagway, AK 99840; phone (907) 983-2854, www.skagway.com.

Klondike Gold Rush National Historical Park Visitor Center, located in the restored railroad depot at 2nd Avenue and Broadway. Open daily in summer; exhibits and films on the history of the area and information on hiking the Chilkoot Trail. Write Klondike Gold Rush NHP, Box 517, Skagway, AK 99840; phone (907) 983-9200; web site www.nps.gov/klgo. Public restrooms are located in a small building at the east end of 6th Street. The Klondike Gold Rush National Historic Park and the Railroad Depot provide public restrooms as well as many other buildings and businesses throughout town.

Elevation: Sea level. **Climate**: Average daily temperature in summer, 57°F; in winter, 23°F. Average annual precipitation is 29.9 inches. **Radio**: KHNS-FM 91.9. **Television**: KTOO and ARCS. **Newspaper**: *Skagway News* (bimonthly).

Private Aircraft: Skagway airport, adjacent west; elev. 44 feet; length 3,550 feet;

asphalt; fuel 100LL; attended.

The name Skagway (originally spelled Skaguay) is said to mean "stiffly wind rippled water" in Tlingit. It is the oldest incorporated city in Alaska (incorporated in 1900). Skagway is also a year-round port and 1 of the 2 gateway cities to the Alaska Highway in Southeast Alaska: Klondike Highway 2 connects Skagway with the Alaska Highway. (The other is Haines, connected to the Alaska Highway via the Haines Highway.)

Skagway owes its birth to the Klondike Gold Rush. Skagway, and its nearby neighbor, Dyea boomed as thousands of gold seekers arrived to follow the White Pass and Chilkoot trails to the Yukon goldfields.

In July 1897, the first boatloads of stampeders bound for the Klondike landed at Skagway and Dyea. By October 1897, according to a North West Mounted Police report, Skagway had grown "from a concourse of tents to a fair-sized town, with well-laid-out streets and numerous frame buildings, stores, saloons, gambling houses, dance houses and a population of about 20,000." Less than a year later it was reported that "Skagway was little better than a hell on earth." Customs office records for 1898 show that in the month of February alone 5,000 people landed at Skagway and Dyea.

By the summer of 1899 the stampede was all but over. The newly built White Pass & Yukon Route railway reached Lake Bennett, supplanting the Chilkoot Trail from Dyea. Dyea became a ghost town. Its post office closed in 1902, and by 1903 its population consisted of 1 settler. Skagway's population dwindled to 500. But Skagway persisted, both as a port and as terminus of the White Pass & Yukon Route railway, which connected the town to Whitehorse, YT, in 1900. Throughout most of the twentieth century the railroad transported regular shipments of ore and freight to and from Skagway's port. Cruise ships, and later the Alaska State Ferry System, brought tourism and business to Skagway. Scheduled state ferry service to southeastern Alaska began in 1963.

Today, tourism is Skagway's main economic base, with Klondike Gold Rush National Historical Park, and the White Pass and Yukon Route railway, Skagway's major visitor attractions. Within Skagway's downtown historical district, false-fronted buildings and boardwalks dating from gold rush days line the streets. The National Park Service, the city and local residents have succeeded in preserving Skagway's gold rush atmosphere.

Lodging & Services

For a small historic town, Skagway has an impressive number of modern visitor services, just like it did when the gold seekers arrived in '98. There are several restaurants, cafes and bars serving beer, local salmon and halibut, burgers, pasta, sandwiches, wraps, soups and baked goods. Don't miss the famous **Red Onion Saloon & Brothel Museum** and the award-winning **Olivia's Restaurant** at the Skagway Inn downtown, or lunch at **Poppies Restaurant** at Jewell Gardens at Mile 2 South Klondike Highway.

Skagway has a grocery; hardware store, the **Klothes Rush** clothing store; and many gift and novelty shops offering Alaska and gold rush souvenirs, photos, books, furs and ivory. The **Skaguay News Depot** on Broadway carries a great selection of local books and out-of-town newspapers. Skagway has a post office, gas stations (with diesel) and

several churches. There is 1 bank in town (Wells Fargo) with an ATM.

Skagway offers a variety of accommodations from hotels to bed and breakfasts, including **At The White House**, phone (907) 983-9000, and the **Historic Skagway Inn**, (description below) phone 1-888-752-4929.

The Historic Skagway Inn B & B. You will enjoy snowy white sheets, cozy rooms, period antiques, and a full hot breakfast here. The Inn began within the red-light district, and to honor our past, the ten guest rooms are named for the ladies who worked here. Turn-of-the-century ambiance helps you soak in the history, mystery and magic of the Klondike Gold Rush. Located in historic downtown Skagway and walking distance to all services and attractions. Complimentary van pick up, WiFi and luggage storage. Within the Inn, Olivia's fully licensed restaurant and bistro features Alaskan seafood and bounty from our own award-winning, culinary garden. Toll free 1-888-SKAGWAY; local phone (907) 983-2289; www.skagwayinn.com. See display ad on page 700. [ADVERTISEMENT]

Red Onion Saloon & Brothel Museum. Don't miss a visit to Skagway's World Famous Red Onion Saloon & Brothel Museum, located on 2nd and Broadway. Enjoy cold Alaskan beers, hot pizza, chili, nachos, sandwiches, gifts, cocktails, live music and great atmosphere in this historic Gold Rush building. Complete your trip with an informative and entertaining tour of our Brothel Museum with one of the fun-loving Red Onion Madams. Open daily 10 A.M. to close. www.redonion1898.com. See display ad page 700. [ADVERTISEMENT]

Camping

RV camping at **Garden City RV Park** (see ad this section) at 15th and 17th on State Street in town is a Good Sam Park; phone (907) 983-2378; www.gardencityrv.com. Dyea Campground at the Chilkoot Trail trailhead has 22 campsites but the narrow winding road is not recommended for vehicles over 25 feet.

There is one public campground along the 98-mile Klondike Highway out of Skagway, although there are several campgrounds from the junction with the Alaska Highway on in to Whitehorse.

Transportation

Air: Daily scheduled service between Skagway and Haines and Juneau via Wings of Alaska, phone (907) 983-2442; www.

wingsofalaska.com. Charter service also available between towns and for flightseeing. Flightseeing also offered by **Temsco Helicopters**, phone (907) 983-2900, www.temscoair.com. Transportation to and from the airport is provided by the flight services and local hotels.

Bus: Bus/van service to Anchorage, Fairbanks and Whitehorse, YT (summer only). The S.M.A.R.T. Bus provides shuttle service in town and to/from the ferry and cruise ship pier, (907) 983-2743.

Car Rental: Avis; Sourdough Rentals.

Highway: Klondike Highway 2 was completed in 1978 and connects Skagway to the Alaska Highway. It is open year-round. See

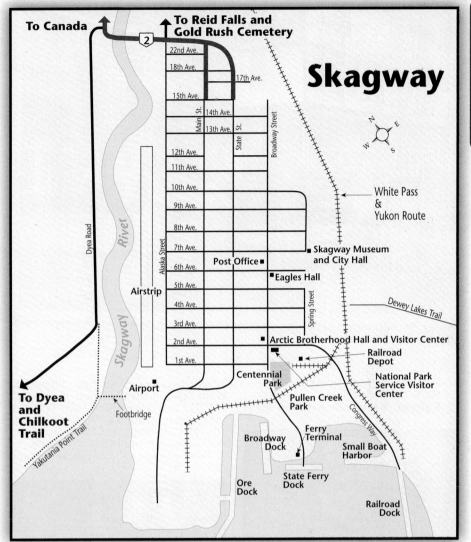

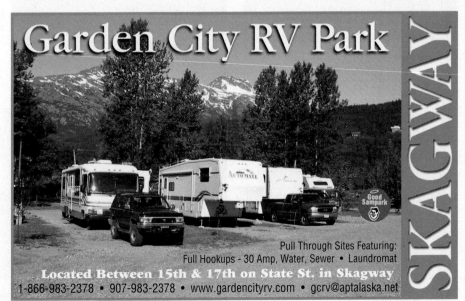

Garden City RV Park

SKAGWAY

Pull Through Sites Featuring:
Full Hookups - 30 Amp, Water, Sewer • Laundromat

Located Between 15th & 17th on State St. in Skagway
1-866-983-2378 • 907-983-2378 • www.gardencityrv.com • gcrv@aptalaska.net

Skagway's air of history is amplified by a ride in a horse & buggy. *(©Sharon Nault)*

SOUTH KLONDIKE HIGHWAY section.
NOTE: *Gas up in Skagway.*
Railroad: White Pass & Yukon Route

offers 3-hour excursions from Skagway to White Pass Summit and return. Phone (907) 983-2217 or toll-free phone 1-800-343-7373; www.wpyr.com. See also "Railroads" in the TRAVEL PLANNING section for details on WP&YR packages available out of Skagway.

Ferries: Skagway is the northern termi-nus of the Alaska Marine Highway Southeast ferry system; see the ALASKA MARINE HIGHWAY section. The ferry terminal is at the end of Broadway on the waterfront (see city map this section); restrooms and pay phone. Ferry terminal office hours vary and are usually posted on the front door. Phone (907) 983-2941 or 983-2229. It is an easy walk into town, but some hotel and motel vans do meet ferries.

Private passenger ferry service is available. **Alaska Fjordlines Express** service between Skagway and Juneau; phone (907) 766-3395 or 1-800-320-0146, or visit www. alaskafjordlines.com.

Haines–Skagway Fast Ferry provides passenger-only service between Skagway and Haines 1-888-766-2103. This is not the same as the Alaska Marine Highway ferries.

Cruise Ships: Skagway is a regular port of call for cruise ships from Princess, Holland America, Norwegian Cruise Lines, Regent Seven Seas, Silversea, Oceania, Celebrity Cruises and Royal Caribbean.

Private Boats: Transient moorage is available at the Skagway small-boat harbor. Contact the harbormaster at (907) 983-2628. Space for cruisers up to 100 feet; gas, diesel fuel and water available.

Attractions

The Arctic Brotherhood Hall, located on Broadway between 2nd and 3rd avenues, houses the Skagway Visitor Center. The Arctic Brotherhood Hall's facade has more than 8,833 pieces of driftwood sticks arranged in a mosaic pattern, with the Brotherhood's AB letters and symbols, a gold pan with nuggets.

Klondike Gold Rush National Historical Park was established by Congress in 1976 to preserve and interpret the history of the Klondike Gold Rush of 1897–98. In 1998 this became the nation's only International Historical Park, with units in Seattle, Skagway, British Columbia and the Yukon. The United States section of the park, managed by the National Park Service, consists of 4 units: a 6-block historic district in Skagway's business area; a 1-mile-wide, 17-mile-long corridor of land comprising the Chilkoot Trail and Dyea; a 1-mile-wide, 5-mile-long corridor of land comprising the White Pass Trail; and a visitor center in Seattle, WA. The Skagway unit is the most-visited national park in Alaska. For information, phone (907) 983-9200; www.nps.gov/klgo/index.htm.

A variety of free programs is available at the park in summer. There are daily guided walking tours of the downtown Skagway historic district and ranger talks on a variety of topics. Films are also shown. Check with the Park Service's visitor center in the restored

SKAGWAY

(You should see us in the summer!)

www.skagway.com
1-888-762-1898

railroad depot on 2nd Avenue and Broadway. Visitor center hours: 7:30 A.M. to 7 P.M., Mon.–Fri. and 8 A.M. to 6 P.M. Sat.–Sun., from May through Sept.

Hike the Chilkoot Trail. This 33-mile trail begins on the Dyea Road and climbs over Chilkoot Pass (elev. 3,739 feet) to Lake Bennett, following the historic route of the gold seekers of 1897–98. The original stampeders took an average of 3 months to transport the required "ton of goods" (a year's worth of supplies and equipment) over the Pass. Today's adventurers take 3 to 5 days to hike the Chilkoot Trail.

Information on permits and fees, customs requirements, regulations, camping, weather, equipment and trail conditions available from the Chilkoot Trail Center in Skagway. The center is open 8 A.M. to 5 P.M. daily, June to September; phone (907) 983-9234. Information is also available online at www.nps.gov/klgo. This site links to the Parks Canada website for information and reservations on the Canadian side, or phone (867) 667-3910, toll-free 1-800-661-0486; www.pc.gc.ca/chilkoot.

Jewell Gardens & Glassworks, at the historic Clark Farm at Milepost 2 on the South Klondike Highway, is Skagway's showcase garden. An easy drive or bike ride from town, Jewell Gardens also has a glass-

©Sharon Nault

blowing studio where glass blowing is demonstrated for visitors; a gift shop; G-scale railroad; and a restaurant that serves lunches (daily) featuring local produce. Phone (907) 983-2111.

Skagway parks. Centennial Park, at the foot of Broadway, has the Rotary Snowplow #1 on display, the city's Centennial Statue, benches, and native flora. Nearby Pullen Creek Park has a covered picnic shelter, a footbridge and a small dock. Watch for pink salmon in August, silver salmon in September (Pullen Creek and pond are closed to fishing Sept. 15–Nov. 30). The Mollie Walsh Park is at the end of 6th Street and has an elaborate children's playing area (picnic tables nearby for adults).

The Days of '98 Show, the longest running show in the North, is held in Alaska's oldest Eagles aerie, F.O.E. #25 (established 1899), at 6th Avenue and Broadway. This lively 1-hour musical/drama is based on historical records and centers on con man Soapy Smith's reign over Skagway during the days of the Klondike Gold Rush. Shows are performed up to 4 times daily. Phone (907) 983-2545.

McCabe College Building/City Hall is the first granite building constructed in Alaska. It was built by the Methodist Church as a school in 1899–1900 to be known as McCabe College, but public-school laws were passed that made the enterprise impractical, and it was sold to the federal government. Today it houses City Hall and

the Skagway Museum.

The **Skagway Museum,** in the McCabe College Building (also City Hall), is one block east of Broadway on 7th Avenue; The museum's primary interest is to help preserve Alaskan historical material and to display Alaskan pioneer life. On display is a Tlingit canoe, a Portland Cutter sleigh, kayaks and an Alaska Native Heritage collection of baskets, beadwork and carvings. Also exhibited are tools, supplies and gambling equipment used in the Klondike Gold Rush of 1898. The museum is open daily, May through September, from 9 A.M. to 5 P.M. weekdays; 10 A.M. to 5 P.M. Saturday; and 10 A.M. to 4 P.M. Sunday. Call for winter hours. Phone (907) 983-2420; www.skagwaymuseum.org; email info@skagwaymuseum.org.

Corrington Museum of Alaska History, 5th and Broadway, offers 40 exhibits featuring scenes from Alaska history, each hand-engraved (scrimshawed) on a walrus tusk. Open in summer; free admission.

Drive Dyea Road. This narrow, winding, gravel road offers spectacular scenery for those driving appropriate vehicles. Read through the log on facing page, for more information on its condition. The road begins at **Milepost S 2.5** South Klondike Highway and leads southwest to the trailhead for Yakutania Point, then northwest past Long Bay and the Taiya River to the old Dyea Townsite. The National Park Service offers daily walking tours of this historic site in summer. There are fine views of Skagway, Taiya Inlet and the Skagway River from Dyea Road. *(See "Dyea Road" log on facing page.)*

Tour by train, helicopter, bike, jeep, ferry or car. Ride mountain bikes down from White Pass Summit to Skagway, or drive up the Klondike Highway. See glaciers from the air or fly out to dog sled camp. Take a ride on the historic White Pass & Yukon Route railway. Take the fast ferry over to Haines and explore Lynn Canal.

Gold Rush Cemetery is 1.9 miles from downtown and makes a nice walk. Go

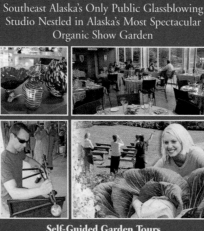
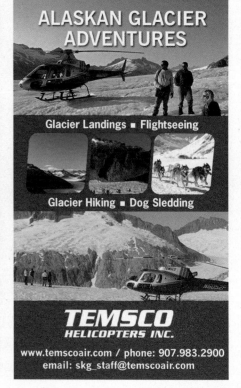

Dyea Road

The Dyea Road begins at **Milepost S 2.5** on the South Klondike Highway and leads approximately 7 miles to the old Dyea townsite. This road accesses the Skagway overlook (Mile 1.4), the head of the Chilkoot Trail and two campgrounds. During the Klondike Gold Rush of 1898-1899, Dyea housed thousands of people, many if not most bound for the Klondike gold fields via Chilkoot Pass.

Dyea Road is a narrow, winding, gravel road beyond the Mile 1.4 overlook and is not recommended for motorhomes more than 25 feet in length.

Distance from junction (J) with the South Klondike Highway is shown.

J 0 **Junction** with the South Klondike Highway, 2.5 miles from Skagway.

J 0.6 Turnout at old cemetery.

J 1.4 Scenic overlook with view of Skagway, Taiya Inlet and the Skagway River; new outhouse.

J 1.7 Steep, primitive road leads 0.4 mile to Skagway River; view of Skagway and Taiya Inlet; access to Yakutania Point and hiking trail to Skagway.

J 1.8 Road narrows, pavement ends. Watch for blind curves.

J 1.9 Skyline trailhead, parking south side of road. This trail leads to top of AB Mountain (elev. 5,000 feet).

J 2.1 Long Bay.

J 3.3 Mathews Creek.

J 3.4 Turnout with view.

J 4 Area of former Skagway brothel.

J 4.3 Good view of Taiya Inlet as road curves away from Long Bay.

J 4.8 Road narrows and winds along flats.

J 5.1 View of the old pilings in Taiya Inlet and interpretive signs. The docks of Dyea used to stretch from the trees to beyond the piling to reach deep water. The road is very narrow at points and there are many small turnouts.

J 5.7 Taiya River; hooligan (smelt) run in May and June.

J 6.2 Pavement begins.

J 6.4 Turnout with interpretive signs, riverside.

J 6.7 Dyea Campground and Ranger Station and Chilkoot Trail trailhead campground; 22 campsites, pit toilets, picnic tables, grills, bear proof trash cans and food containers at each site; campground host; $10 camping fee. Golden Age Pass accepted for half-price camping. △

J 6.8 **Chilkoot Trail Outpost**, open May–September, offers lodging. Phone (907) 983-3799; www.chilkoottrailoutpost.com.

J 7.2 Chilkoot Trail trailhead. Taiya River bridge.

J 7.7 Turn left for **Klondike Gold Rush National Park's Dyea Historic Town Site and Slide Cemetery**. Go 0.7 mile to a 0.3 mile access road to cemetery parking lot. The cemetery contains the graves of men killed in the Palm Sunday avalanche, April 3, 1898, on the Chilkoot Trail.

Continue 0.7 to intersection and right for Historic Dyea Town Site parking and restrooms. Ranger-led walking tours of the Dyea Town Site leave the parking area daily from June through August at 10 A.M. and 2 P.M. daily (*confirm tour schedule with the National Park Service visitor center in Skagway before arrival*). Self-guided walking tours may be done using pamphlets located near path. Rest area facilities near parking lot.

Now covered with wild iris, fireweed and lupine in summer, hardly a trace remains of the buildings that housed up to 8,000 people and 150 businesses—from attorneys to undertakers—at the height of the gold rush in 1898. Fewer than 500 people remained after the summer of 1898, and by 1903 only a half dozen were still here. Time, weather and the shifting Taiya River have obliterated most of the buildings.

J 8.2 State-maintained road ends at West Creek bridge. Large gravel turnaround area. Signage for Chilkoot Trail.

Return to Milepost S 2.5 South Klondike Highway

©Sharon Nault

north on State Street a short drive. Then follow posted direction signs to the cemetery. "Bad guy" Soapy Smith and "good guy" Frank Reid are buried here (both men died in a gunfight in July 1898). It is a short hike from Reid's grave to scenic **Lower Reid Falls** (pictured above).

Special Events: The Buckwheat Cross-Country Ski Classic is held in March. The International Mini Folk Festival is held in April. A big Independence Day Celebration takes place every 4th of July. For the Flower & Garden Show, plan to be in Skagway in August. The Klondike International Road Relay is scheduled for September.

AREA FISHING: Obtain a fishing license through local charter operators or at the Skagway Hardware store on Fourth and Broadway. Local charter boat operators offer king salmon fishing trips. The Pat Moore Memorial Game Fish Derby is held two weekends in July. The Alaska Dept. of Fish and Game, Sport Fish Division, recommends the following areas and species:

Fish the shore of **Skagway Harbor**, **Long Bay** and **Taiya Inlet**, May through August, for Dolly Varden. Also try the **Taiya River** by the steel bridge in Dyea when the water is clear in early spring or fall; use red and white spoons or salmon eggs. Hatchery-produced king salmon have been returning to the area in good numbers in recent years. Try fishing in salt water, downtown Skagway, June–August. Pink salmon are plentiful at **Pullen Creek** in August. Silver, pink and chum salmon near the steel bridge on the **Taiya River**, mid-July through September. Trolling in the marine areas is good but high winds are often dangerous for small boats. A steep trail near town will take you to Dewey lakes, which were stocked with Colorado brook trout in the 1920s. **Lower Dewey Lake**, ½-hour to 1-hour hike; heavily wooded shoreline. The brook trout are plentiful and grow to 16 inches but are well fed, so fishing can be frustrating. **Upper Dewey Lake**, a steep 2½-hour to 4-hour hike to above tree line, is full of hungry brook trout to 11 inches. Use salmon eggs or size #10 or #12 artificial flies. **Lost Lake** is reached via a rough trail near Dyea (ask locals for directions). The lake lies at about elev. 1,300 feet and has a good population of rainbow trout. Use small spinners or spoons. For more information contact the Alaska Dept. of Fish and Game office in Haines; phone (907) 766-2625. ☛

SOUTHEAST ALASKA

Skagway

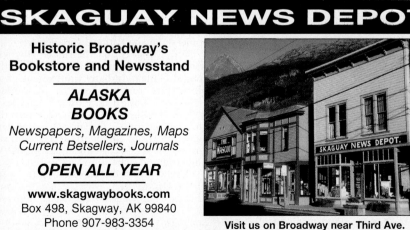

Haines Highway

CONNECTS: Haines, AK, to Haines Junction, YT

Length: 146 miles   **Road Surface:** Paved   **Season:** Open all year

The Haines Highway is noted for the variety of its scenery. (©Sharon Nault)

Distance in miles	Beaver Creek	Haines	Haines Jct.	Tok	Whitehorse
Beaver Creek		329	184	113	283
Haines	329		146	443	246
Haines Jct.	184	146		297	100
Tok	113	443	297		396
Whitehorse	283	246	100	396	

The 146-mile/235-km Haines Highway connects Haines, AK, at the head of Lynn Canal, with Haines Junction, YT, on the Alaska Highway. Open year-round, and usually snow-free by late May, it is a good, 2-lane paved highway. Driving time is approximately 4 hours.

Noted for its grand views of glaciated mountains and the variety of its scenery—from coastal forests to alpine tundra—the Haines Highway was awarded National Scenic Byway status in 2009.

The Haines Highway winds through the Chilkat River flats outside Haines before beginning a long climb up to Chilkat Pass (elev. 3,510 feet), where it meanders through a wide alpine valley before descending to Haines Junction via a series of long, easy grades. It accesses the Chilkat Bald Eagle Preserve; skirts Tatshenshini–Alsek Wilderness Provincial Park; and follows the eastern border of Kluane National Park Reserve.

Part of what is now the Haines Highway was originally a "grease trail" used by the coastal Chilkat Indians trading eulachon oil for furs from the Interior. In the late 1880s, Jack Dalton developed a packhorse trail to the Klondike goldfields along the old trading route. The present road was built in 1943 as a military access highway during WWII to provide an alternative route from tidewater into Yukon Territory.

IMPORTANT: U.S. customs is open 7 A.M.–11 P.M. (Alaska time), while Canada customs is open the same hours, but due to the time zone difference, from 8 A.M. to midnight (Pacific time). This means you cannot drive south to Haines or north of the U.S. border at any time between 11 P.M. and 7 A.M. (Alaska time). Phone (907) 767-5511 for changes in U.S. and Canadian customs hours in 2014. Fill up your gas tank in Haines, AK, or in Haines Junction, YT.

A valid Alaska fishing license is required for fishing along the highway between Haines and the international border at **Milepost H 40.4**. The highway then crosses the northern tip of British Columbia into Yukon Territory. You must have valid fishing licenses for both British Columbia and Yukon Territory if you fish these areas, and a national park fishing license if you fish waters in Kluane National Park.

Check road conditions by phoning (867) 456-7623 for daily recorded report or visit http://511Yukon.ca or http://511.alaska.gov. Note that flashing lights at the Haines Junction weigh scales indicate hazardous winter road conditions (travel not recommended). In Haines Junction, the maintenance station (867/634-2227) or weigh scale station may also have details on driving conditions.

Emergency medical services: Between Haines and the U.S.–Canada border, phone 911 or Alaska State Troopers in Haines at (907) 766-2552. Between the U.S.–Canada border and Haines Junction, phone the RCMP at (867) 634-5555.

Haines Highway Haines, AK, to Haines Junction, YT

© 2014 The MILEPOST®

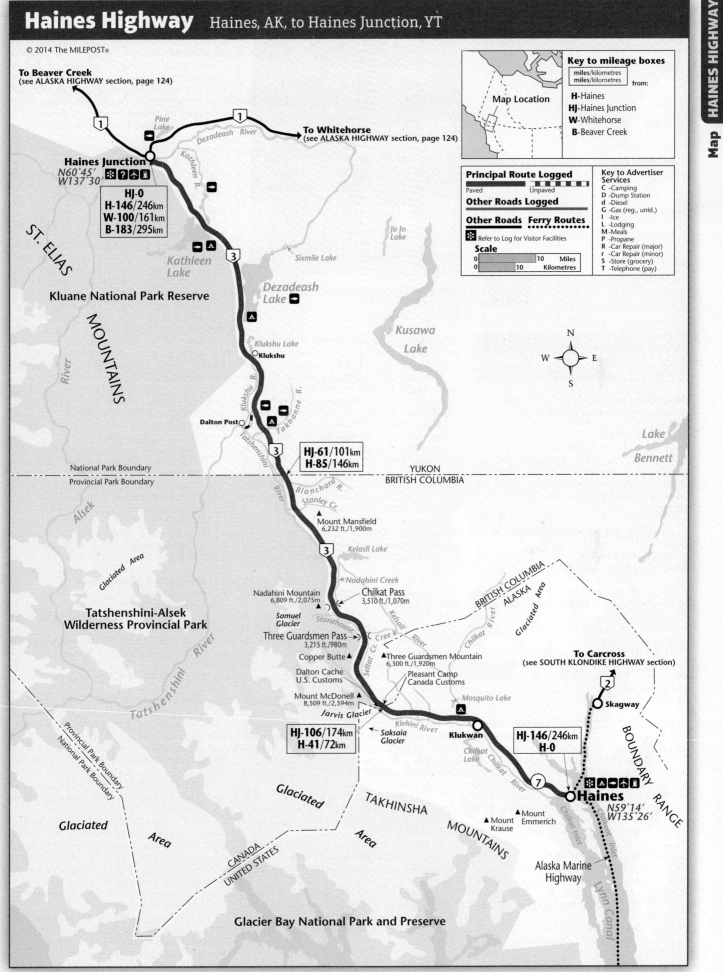

To Beaver Creek
(see ALASKA HIGHWAY section, page 124)

Pine Lake

To Whitehorse
(see ALASKA HIGHWAY section, page 124)

Dezadeash River

Kathleen R.

Haines Junction
N60°45'
W137°30'

**HJ-0
H-146/246km
W-100/161km
B-183/295km**

ST. ELIAS

Kathleen Lake

Kluane National Park Reserve

Jo Jo Lake

Sixmile Lake

Dezadeash Lake

Kusawa Lake

Klukshu Lake

Klukshu

Kluksu R.

Takhanne R.

Dalton Post

Tatshenshini R.

**HJ-61/101km
H-85/146km**

YUKON
BRITISH COLUMBIA

Lake Bennett

National Park Boundary
Provincial Park Boundary

Alsek River

Blanchard R.
Stanley Cr.

Mount Mansfield
6,232 ft./1,900m

Kelasll Lake

Glaciated Area

Nadahini Creek

Tatshenshini-Alsek
Wilderness Provincial Park

Nadahini Mountain
6,809 ft./2,075m

Chilkat Pass
3,510 ft./1,070m

BRITISH COLUMBIA
ALASKA

Glaciated Area

Samuel Glacier

Stonehouse

Three Guardsmen Pass
3,215 ft./980m

Seltat Cr.

Ketcall River

Chilkat River

Copper Butte

Three Guardsmen Mountain
6,300 ft./1,920m

To Carcross
(see SOUTH KLONDIKE HIGHWAY section)

Dalton Cache
U.S. Customs

Pleasant Camp
Canada Customs

Mount McDonell
8,509 ft./2,594m

Skagway

Jarvis Glacier

Mosquito Lake

BOUNDARY RANGE

**HJ-106/174km
H-41/72km**

Saksaia Glacier

Klehini River

Klukwan

**HJ-146/246km
H-0**

Tatshenshini River

Provincial Park Boundary
National Park Boundary

Glaciated Area

Glaciated

Glaciated Area

CANADA
UNITED STATES

TAKHINSHA MOUNTAINS

Chilkat Lake

Chilkat River

Haines
N59°14'
W135°26'

Mount Krause

Mount Emmerich

Alaska Marine Highway

Lynn Canal

Chilkoot Inlet

Chilkat Inlet

Glacier Bay National Park and Preserve

Key to mileage boxes

miles/kilometres
miles/kilometres from:

H-Haines
HJ-Haines Junction
W-Whitehorse
B-Beaver Creek

Map Location

Principal Route Logged
Paved   Unpaved

Other Roads Logged

Other Roads   Ferry Routes

❄ Refer to Log for Visitor Facilities

Scale
0   10 Miles
0   10 Kilometres

Key to Advertiser Services
C -Camping
D -Dump Station
d -Diesel
G -Gas (reg., unld.)
I -Ice
L -Lodging
M -Meals
P -Propane
R -Car Repair (major)
r -Car Repair (minor)
S -Store (grocery)
T -Telephone (pay)

N W E S

HAINES HIGHWAY Map

www.themilepost.com

2014 ■ The MILEPOST® ■ **705**

The Haines Highway (Main Street) in downtown Haines. (©Sharon Nault)

Haines Highway Log

Distance from Haines (H) is followed by distance from Haines Junction (HJ).

ALASKA ROUTE 7

H 0 HJ 146.2 HAINES *(see description beginning on page 691)*; food, gas, lodging and camping. **Junction** of Haines Highway (Main Street) and Beach/Front Road (in front of Harbor Bar and near the Sheldon Museum).

H 0.2 HJ 146 Second Avenue to Visitor Center

H 0.5 HJ 145.7 Haines Hitch-Up RV Park; full-service sites, laundromat.

H 0.7 HJ 145.5 Junction of Old Haines Highway (Haines Cutoff) and Main Street (Haines Highway), a "Y" intersection for southbound motorists and location of 2 welcome totem poles.

H 0.9 HJ 145.3 Eagle's Nest Motel.

H 1.9 HJ 144.3 Milepost 2. Mile 0 of the Haines Highway was originally measured from Fort Seward. *Driving distances northbound are now measured against physical mileposts.*

H 3.5 HJ 142.7 Private Aircraft: Haines airport; elev. 16 feet; length 4,000 feet; asphalt; fuel 100; unattended.

H 4.3 HJ 141.9 Informal gravel turnout by river. There are several of these turnouts along the Chilkat River the next 10 miles northbound that are used for camping, picnicking and fishing. Watch for fish wheels on river.

The Haines Highway winds through the Chilkat River Valley for the next 18 miles northbound. The Chilkat River heads at Chilkat Glacier in British Columbia's Coast Mountains and flows 52 miles to Chilkat Inlet on Lynn Canal.

H 6.9 HJ 139.3 7-Mile trailhead (Mount Ripinski).

Magnificent views to the southwest of Takhinsha Mountains across Chilkat River. This range extends north from the Chilkat Range. Glacier Bay is on the other side.

Prominent peaks are Mount Krause (elev. 6,183 feet) and Mount Emmerich (elev. 6,405 feet) in the Chilkat Range.

H 8.3 HJ 137.9 Entering **Alaska Chilkat Bald Eagle Preserve** northbound. *NOTE: Please use pullouts.* Established in 1982, the 48,000-acre preserve is the seasonal home to more than 3,000 bald eagles, which gather each year to feed on the late run of chum salmon. Eagle-viewing area begins at **Milepost H 19**; best viewing is mid-October to January. Of the more than 40,000 bald eagles in Alaska, most are found in Southeast. Eagles build nests in trees along the shoreline. Nests are added to each year and can be up to 7 feet across. (Nests the size of pickup trucks have fallen out of trees.) Nesting eagles have a second backup nest. Eagles lay their eggs in April; the eaglets fledge in August.

Look for fishwheels—in operation, 2013. Also watch for trumpeter swans along the Haines Highway.

H 14.3 HJ 131.9 Double-ended, narrow gravel turnout with outhouse by Chilkat River. There are several informal turnouts along the Chilkat River next 10 miles southbound that are used for camping, picnicking and fishing. Watch for **fish wheels** on river.

H 19.3 HJ 126.9 Council Grounds Chilkat Bald Eagle Preserve viewing area; parking, interpretive panels, restrooms. Access to paved pedestrian path along river. Begin eagle viewing area (northbound) on Chilkat River flats. Best viewing is mid-October to January. *CAUTION: No stopping on highway; use turnouts!*

H 19.7 HJ 126.5 Paved parking area and access to paved pedestrian path to Council Grounds viewpoints.

H 20.1 HJ 126.1 Paved turnout by river; access to paved pedestrian path to viewpoints. Another small turnout is 0.3 miles beyond.

H 20.6 HJ 125.6 Council Grounds Chilkat Bald Eagle Preserve viewing area; paved parking area with toilet and interpretive panel. Access to paved pedestrian path to viewpoints.

H 21.5 HJ 124.7 Turnoff via paved access

road for Chilkat Indian village of **KLUK-WAN** (pop. 72). The name Klukwan is taken from the Tlingit phrase *Tlakw Aan* which means "Eternal Village." Klukwan was originally settled many years ago by a group of Gaanaxteidi (Raven Clan) men and their Kaagwaantaan (Eagle Clan) wives. The Village site was chosen because of its rich natural environment. Today, the village offers tours and an introduction to its Native Heritage at the **Jilkaat Kwaan Cultural Center**, Hospitality House and Bentwood Box Gift Shop; http://chilkatindianvillage.org/

H 23.8 HJ 122.4 Chilkat River bridge. Highway now follows Klehini River northbound. *CAUTION: Watch for moose.*

H 24.6 HJ 121.6 Phone booth to west, signed "last call."

H 26.2 HJ 120 Porcupine Crossing; side road leads west across Klehini River.

H 26.7 HJ 119.5 Klehini River scenic viewpoint; paved parking area, picnic shelter/tables, interpretive signs, viewing scopes.

H 27.2 HJ 119 Turnoff on Mosquito Lake Road for the Kroschel Films Wildlife Center at Mile 1.8 and **Mosquito Lake State Recreation Site**, at Mile 2.4 east of highway; keep to right at road fork (Mile 2.1), then watch for easy-to-miss, narrow, gravel road leading down to lake. There is a dock and boat launch. The recreation site has a small day-use area and 5 campsites in the trees along a narrow road (best for small RVs or vans); firepits, tables, toilets, $10 camping fee. Beautiful spot. Be sure to pack out your own garbage and bring insect repellent. There is a large turnaround area here.

The Wildlife Center provides access to over 15 species of Alaska wildlife, some of which may be petted or fed. Open May 15–Sept. 15 for scheduled, organized tours. For more information, call (907) 767-5464.

H 28.8 HJ 117.4 Muncaster Creek bridge.

H 31 HJ 115.2 Scenic viewpoint; double-ended parking area to west overlooking the **Klehini River**. The Klehini heads in a glacier on Nadahini Mountain in Canada and flows 42 miles to the Chilkat River.

Leaving Alaska Chilkat Bald Eagle Preserve northbound.

H 31.6 HJ 114.6 Bridge over Little Boulder Creek.

H 33.1 HJ 113.1 33 Mile Roadhouse; food, gas, diesel, laundromat, beer.

H 33.8 HJ 112.4 Bridge over Big Boulder Creek.

Begin improved highway northbound; 55 mph speed limit.

H 35.5 HJ 110.7 Paved, level turnout to east with interpretive signs about wetlands and a good view of the Saksaia Glacier. Note finger dikes along the river, which help prevent erosion.

H 35.6 HJ 110.6 Paved parking area to west with interpretive signs about gold seekers and Tlingits. View of Saksaia Glacier.

H 40.2 HJ 106 Port of Entry: Dalton Cache U.S. Customs and Border Protection. All travelers entering the United States MUST STOP. *U.S. customs is open daily from 7 A.M. to 11 P.M. (Alaska time). You cannot drive south to Haines if the customs station is closed.* Phone (907) 767-5511. Restrooms, large parking area.

Old Dalton Cache, on the National Register of Historic Places, is located behind the customs building. View of Jarvis Glacier moraine from here.

H 40.4 HJ 105.8 U.S.–Canada border.

Million Dollar Falls is accessible by boardwalk trail from the campground at Milepost H 93.5.
(©Judy Nadon, staff)

TIME ZONE CHANGE: Alaska observes Alaska time, Canada observes Pacific time. Alaska time is 1 hour earlier than Pacific time.

BC HIGHWAY 3

H 40.6 (72 km) **HJ 105.6** (174 km) **Pleasant Camp Canada Customs and Immigration office.** All travelers entering Canada MUST STOP here. *Canada customs is open daily from 8 A.M. to midnight (Pacific time). You cannot drive north into Canada if the customs station is closed.* Phone (907) 767-5540. No public facilities. *NOTE: $500 fine for littering.*

H 40.8 (72.3 km) **HJ 105.4** (173.7 km) Marinka's Hill.

H 41.9 (74 km) **HJ 104.3** (172 km) Kilometrepost 74; first kilometrepost northbound, last kilometrepost southbound. *Kilometres logged on the Canadian portion of this highway reflect physical kilometreposts and are not a metric conversion of the mileage figure. Driving distances from Haines are based on driving distance between physical mileposts.*

H 42.5 (75 km) **HJ 103.7** (171 km) Large gravel turnout to west. Distance marker southbound shows U.S. Customs 3 kms.

H 43.6 (76.9) **HJ 102.6** (169.1 km) Tatshenshini-Alsek Park (northbound sign).

H 44.5 (78.2 km) **HJ 101.7** (167.8 km) Five Mile Creek.

H 46.8 (82.2 km) **HJ 99.4** (163.8 km) Distance marker northbound shows Haines Junction 174 km/108 miles.

H 48.4 (84.8 km) **HJ 97.8** (161.2 km) Fuchs Creek.

H 49 (85.4 km) **HJ 97.2** (160.6 km) Gravel turnout to west.

H 49.9 (87.3 km) **HJ 96.3** (158.7 km) Double-ended turnout to west with interpretive sign about Haines Road and **Historic Milepost 48.** Beautiful views of glaciated mountains as highway descends southbound.

H 50 (87.5 km) **HJ 96.2** (158.5 km) Highway crosses Seltat Creek. Three Guardsmen Mountain (elev. 6,300 feet/1,920m) to east.

H 50.6 (88.4 km) **HJ 95.6** (157.6 km) Marinka's Hill.

H 51.3 (89.2 km) **HJ 94.9** (156.8 km) Gravel turnout to west.

H 51.5 (89.8 km) **HJ 94.7** (156.2 km) Steep hill next 18 kms southbound; check brakes.

H 52.6 (91.6 km) **HJ 93.6** (154.4 km) South end of Three Guardsmen Lake. Glave Peak (elev. 6,325 feet/1,928m), part of Three Guardsmen Mountain, rises directly behind the lake.

H 55.1 (96 km) **HJ 91.1** (150 km) Stonehouse Creek. The tall poles along the highway indicate the edge of the road for snowplows.

H 55.4 (96.5 km) **HJ 90.8** (149.5 km) Clear Creek.

H 56 (97.6 km) **HJ 90.2** (148.4 km) Distance marker northbound shows Haines Junction 149 km/93 miles, Whitehorse 308 km/191 miles, Fairbanks 981 km/610 miles.

H 59 (102.4 km) **HJ 87.2** (144 km) Double-ended paved viewpoint to west at **Haines Highway Summit** (elev. 3,510 feet/1,070m), **Chilkat Pass.** The wind blows almost constantly on the summit and causes drifting snow and road closures in winter. Snow until late May. This is avalanche terrain and fatal accidents have occurred here.

The Chilkat Pass was one of the few mountain passes offering access into the Yukon from the coast. The Chilkat and the Chilkoot passes were tenaciously guarded by Tlingit Indians. These southern Yukon Indi-ans did not want their lucrative fur-trading business with the coastal Indians and Russians jeopardized by white strangers. But the gold rush of 1898, which brought thousands of white people inland, finally opened Chilkat Pass, forever altering the lifestyle of the Interior Natives.

H 59.7 (103.5 km) **HJ 86.5** (142.5 km) Large gravel viewpoint to west with entrance to gravel road.

H 61.2 (106 km) **HJ 85** (140 km) Distance marker southbound shows U.S. Customs 35 kms/22 miles, Haines 100 kms/62 miles.

H 61.7 (106 km) **HJ 84.5** (140 km) Large gravel turnout with outhouse to west.

H 62.5 (108 km) **HJ 84** (135.2 km) Outhouse and warming shelter.

H 63.2 (109.3 km) **HJ 83** (136.7 km) Nadahini River.

H 66.8 (115 km) **HJ 79.4** (131 km) Wind sock at airstrip.

Private Aircraft: Mule Creek airstrip, elev. 2,900 feet/884m; length 4,000 feet/1,219m; gravel/turf. No services.

H 67.8 (116.5 km) **HJ 78.4** (129.5 km) Mule Creek. **Historical Mile 75.** Mule Creek Highway Maintenance Station, with outhouse.

H 72.2 (124 km) **HJ 74** (122 km) Goat Creek bridge.

H 74.2 (127.2 km) **HJ 72** (118.8 km) Holum Creek.

H 76.3 (130.9 km) **HJ 69.9** (115.1 km) Twin Lakes (northbound sign). Watch for trumpeter swans.

H 76.6 (131.3 km) **HJ 69.6** (114.7 km) Twin Lakes (southbound sign).

H 78.2 (134 km) **HJ 68** (112 km) Very large gravel parking area to west is viewpoint for Tatshenshini–Alsek Wilderness Provincial Park. The Tatshenshini and Alsek rivers are famous for their river rafting opportunities.

H 78.6 (134.5 km) **HJ 67.6** (111.5 km) Mansfield Creek.

H 79.8 (136.5 km) **HJ 66.4** (109.5 km) Stanley Creek.

H 84.3 (144 km) **HJ 61.9** (102.1 km) Turnout to west, by pond. Beautiful mountain scenery opens up for southbound travelers as the highway crosses a wide alpine valley.

H 84.8 (144.8 km) **HJ 61.4** (101.2 km) Blanchard River bridge. This is the put-in point for whitewater rafting on the Blanchard River. (Turnoff for rafting outfitter to west just north of bridge.) The Blanchard River crosses the Yukon–BC boundary and joins the Tatshenshini River near Dalton Post.

H 85.2 (145.5 km) **HJ 61** (100.5 km) Welcome to Kluane Country/Welcome to Yukon (northbound signs). Welcome to British Columbia (southbound sign); small turnout with litter bin to east. BC–YT border. Drive with headlights on.

In Yukon, maximum speed is 50 km wherever equipment is working and using radar detection is illegal.

YUKON HIGHWAY 3

H 85.9 (146.6 km) **HJ 60.3** (99.4 km) Distance marker northbound shows Haines Junction 100 km/62 miles, Whitehorse 259 km/161 miles, Fairbanks 922 km/573 miles.

H 88.3 (150.6 km) **HJ 57.9** (95.4 km) Large gravel viewpoint to west.

H 93.5 (159 km) **HJ 52.7** (87 km) Turnoff for Yukon government **Million Dollar Falls Campground** (0.7 mile/1.1 km west); 33 campsites (many level), kitchen shelters, firewood, camping permit ($12), playground, drinking water (boil water), hiking trails, wheelchair accessible. Boardwalk trail with many steep stairways leading to viewing platform of scenic falls and rapids.

Good fishing below **Takhanne Falls** for grayling, Dolly Varden, rainbow and salmon. **Takhanne River**, excellent king salmon fishing in early July. *CAUTION: The Takhanne, Blanchard, Tatshenshini and Klukshu rivers are grizzly feeding areas. Exercise extreme caution when fishing or exploring in these areas.*

H 93.6 (159.2 km) **HJ 52.6** (86.8 km) Takhanne River bridge.

H 93.7 (159.4 km) **HJ 52.5** (86.6 km) Short gravel access road west to informal turnout by Takhanne River. Nice spot.

Highway climbs next 1.7 miles/2.7 km

Kluane Range viewpoint at the rest area at Milepost H 95.4. (©Sharon Nault)

northbound.

H 95.4 (162 km) **HJ 50.8** (84 km) Large paved rest area; photo viewpoint of Kluane Range with viewing platform, litter barrels, outhouse. Interpretive panels reveal details of early exploration in this area. Communications tower is across highway.

Highway descends steep grade next 1.7 miles/2.7 km southbound.

H 96.7 (164.1 km) **HJ 49.5** (81.9 km) Turnoff to west (not signed) for Dalton Post. Narrow, winding, dirt and gravel road with some washboard, deep ruts and a short but very steep downhill section. *Not suitable for RVs.* Road forks at Mile 3.2; follow right fork 0.2 mile for Shawshee/Dalton Post day-use area; large gravel parking area, toilets, garbage containers. The **Klukshu River** system hosts seasonal runs of king, red and silver salmon. Information signs on salmon. Fishing restrictions posted. *CAUTION: Watch for bears.*

H 101 (171 km) **HJ 45.2** (75 km) Motheral Creek.

H 102.1 (173 km) **HJ 44.1** (73 km) Large turnout to west.

H 102.7 (174.2 km) **HJ 43.5** (71.8 km) Vand Creek.

Begin improved highway northbound.

H 107.3 (181.9 km) **HJ 38.9** (64.1 km) Klukshu Creek. Paved turnout to east at south end of creek crossing. *CAUTION: Watch for bears.*

H 108.1 (183.2 km) **HJ 38.1** (62.8 km) **Historic Milepost 118** at turnoff for **KLUKSHU**, an Indian village, located 0.6 mile/1 km off the highway via a good gravel road. This summer fish camp and village on the banks of the Klukshu River is a handful of log cabins, meat caches and traditional fish traps and fish drying racks.

Klukshu is on the old Dalton Trail and offers good photo possibilities. Information panels on First Nations heritage and traditional fish drying and fishing techniques. Crafts for sale at small shop (if locked, inquire locally).

H 109.2 (185 km) **HJ 37** (59.5 km) Gribbles Gulch.

H 110.3 (186.8 km) **HJ 35.9** (57.7 km) Parking and interpretive boards at **St. Elias Lake trailhead** (Kluane National Park trail). Trail winds through subalpine meadow; 4.5 miles/7.2 km round-trip.

H 112.7 (190.7 km) **HJ 33.5** (53.9 km) Flying Squirrel Creek.

H 113.4 (192 km) **HJ 32.8** (52.8 km) Hay Ranch; hostel. Phone 1-867-634-2666.

H 113.8 (192.6 km) **HJ 32.4** (52.1 km) **Historic Milepost 125.** Old Dezadeash Lodge; interpretive sign. Mush Lake Road behind lodge is an old mining road; ski trail in winter.

H 114.5 (194 km) **HJ 31.7** (52 km) Turnout along **Dezadeash Lake.** There are good views of this large lake for several miles along the highway. Dezadeash Lake (pronounced DEZ-dee-ash) offers good trolling, also fly-fishing along shore at feeder streams, for northern pike, lake trout and grayling. *CAUTION: Storms come up quickly on this lake.*

H 115.6 (195.7 km) **HJ 30.6** (50.3 km) Entrance to a sometimes rut-filled loop road for Yukon government **Dezadeash Lake Campground,** a very scenic spot on the lake is down below the highway; 20 campsites (no pull-throughs), camping permit ($12), kitchen shelter, picnic area, boat launch, no drinking water, pit toilets.

H 117.7 (199 km) **HJ 28.5** (47 km) Distance marker northbound shows Haines Junction 47 km/29 miles, Whitehorse 206 km/128 miles, Fairbanks 819 km/509 miles.

H 119.6 (202.3 km) **HJ 26.6** (43.7 km) **Rock Glacier Trail** to west; short 0.5-mile/0.8-km self-guiding trail, partially boardwalk. Interesting walk, some steep sections. Parking area and viewpoint.

H 122.5 (207 km) **HJ 23.7** (39 km) Dalton Trail Lodge.

H 130.2 (219.7 km) **HJ 16** (26.3 km) Turnoff to west and drive downhill 0.7 mile/1.1 km via good gravel road to picnic area on glacier-fed, turquoise-blue Kathleen Lake; parking, outhouses, picnic tables. Beau-

tiful spot. The 53-mile/85-km Cottonwood Loop and Kings Throne trailhead nearby.

Access at Mile 0.5 on this side road to **Kathleen Lake Campground,** the only established campground within Kluane National Park; 39 campsites and a kitchen area; day-use area with picnic tables, restrooms, water; boat launch at lake; campfire programs by park staff. 2 group sites can be reserved in advance, other sites are first come, first served. Camping fee $15.70. Firewood $8.80 per site.

Kathleen Lake, nearly 400 feet/122m deep, offers fishing for lake trout in June and July; kokanee, and grayling June to September. *NOTE: National Park fishing license required. Road to lake kept open year round, 4–6 sites are kept open throughout the winter.*

H 130.5 (220.2 km) **HJ 15.7** (25.8 km) **Historic Milepost 142.** Kathleen Cabins at Kathleen Lake Lodge; motel, B&B, campground, showers. Call for season and reservations in 2014; phone (867) 634-2888 or visit www.kathleenlakelodge.com.

H 131.1 (221 km) **HJ 15.1** (25 km) Kathleen River bridge. Gravel turnout to east has information boards and provides access to the Kathleen River. Easy half-day paddle to Lower Kathleen and Rainbow lakes. Fishing for rainbow, June to September; grayling, July and August; lake trout in September.

H 134.4 (226.5 km) **HJ 11.8** (19.5 km) Turnout to west with view of Kathleen Lake; good photo op. Information plaque.

H 138.4 (233.2 km) **HJ 7.8** (12.8 km) Quill Creek. *Watch for moose and bears.*

H 142 (239 km) **HJ 4.2** (7 km) Parking area and interpretive sign to west at **Auriol Trailhead** (4.5 mile/15 km loop trail); skiing/hiking.

H 143.7 (242 km) **HJ 2.5** (4 km) Paved turnout to southeast; litter bins, toilets. Welcome to Haines Junction (sign) and view of Haines Junction and Shakwak Valley for northbound travelers.

H 145.4 (244.7) **HJ 0.8** (1.3 km) *Slow for 70 to 50 kmph/45 to 30 mph speed zones northbound into Haines Junction.*

H 145.8 (245.4 km) **HJ 0.4** (0.6 km) Dezadeash River bridges. Dezadeash Trail to north at east side of bridge; easy walk along river's edge (2.2 miles/3.5 km).

H 145.9 (245.6 km) **HJ 0.3** (0.4 km) Truck weigh scales. Watch for a large unsigned parking area behind the weigh scales building. Pit toilets, trash bins, river access for canoes and rafts, picnic table and river trailhead.

H 146.2 (246 km) **HJ 0 HAINES JUNCTION;** food, gas, lodging, camping, and RCMP. Visitor Center is 0.8 miles north on the Alaska Highway. *See description on pages 193-195.*

Haines Highway travelers fill your gas tank in Haines Junction. Next gas stop southbound is Haines, AK.

Junction of the Haines Highway (Yukon Highway 3) and Alaska Highway (Yukon Highway 1) at Haines Junction. Turn to **Milepost DC 985** on page 193 in the ALASKA HIGHWAY section for highway log. Whitehorse-bound travelers read log back to front, Alaska-bound travelers read log front to back.

South Klondike Highway

CONNECTS: Skagway, AK, to Alaska Hwy., YT

Length: 98 miles **Road Surface:** Paved **Season:** Open all year

Highest Summit: White Pass 3,292 feet

(See map, page 710)

2 **98**

The Yukon's Emerald Lake at Milepost S 72.7. (© Sharon Nault)

he 98-mile/158-km South Klondike Highway (also known as the Skagway–Carcross Road) connects Skagway, AK, with the Alaska Highway at **Milepost 874.4**, 12 miles/19 km south of downtown Whitehorse. The highway between Skagway and Carcross (referred to locally as the Skagway Road) was built in 1978, and formally dedicated on May 23, 1981. The highway connecting Carcross with the Alaska Highway (referred to locally as the Carcross Road) was built by the U.S. Army in late 1942 to lay a gas pipeline from Skagway to Whitehorse. (The North Klondike Highway turns off the Alaska Highway north of Whitehorse and leads to Dawson City. See the KLONDIKE LOOP section for log of this road.)

The South Klondike Highway offers some spectacular scenery and adds only about 60 miles/100 km to the trip for Alaska-bound motorists compared to the Haines Highway route. (Driving distance from Haines to Tok,

AK, is approximately 415 miles/670 km; driving distance from Skagway to Tok is about 475 miles/760 km. Add 328 miles/528 km for distance to Anchorage; 206 miles/332 km for distance to Fairbanks.)

The South Klondike Highway is a 2-lane, asphalt-surfaced road, open year-round. There is a steep (11 percent grade) 11.5-mile/18.5-km stretch between Skagway and White Pass. For daily recorded road condition report, phone Skagway Maintenance Station at (907) 983-2333 or Yukon 511 road reporting system at (867) 456-7623; or visit http://511Yukon.ca and http://511.alaska.gov.

*IMPORTANT: U.S. and Canada border crossings are open 24-hours daily in summer (April 1 to Oct. 31). In winter (Nov. 1–March 31) the U.S. Customs station is open daily from 7 A.M. to 11 P.M. (Alaska time); the Canadian Customs station is open 8 A.M. to midnight (Pacific time). This means that **during the winter** you cannot drive to Skagway or north of the U.S. border between 11 P.M. and 7 A.M. (Alaska time). Check* locally for changes in U.S. and Canadian customs hours in 2014. For U.S. border information, phone (907) 983-2325. For Canada border

Distance in miles	Alaska Hwy. Jct.	Atlin	Carcross	Skagway	Whitehorse
Alaska Hwy. Jct.		125	32	98	12
Atlin	125		92	158	81
Carcross	32	92		65	45
Skagway	98	158	65		110
Whitehorse	12	81	45	110	

South Klondike Highway

Skagway, AK, to Alaska Highway Jct. (includes Tagish and Atlin Roads)

© 2014 The MILEPOST®

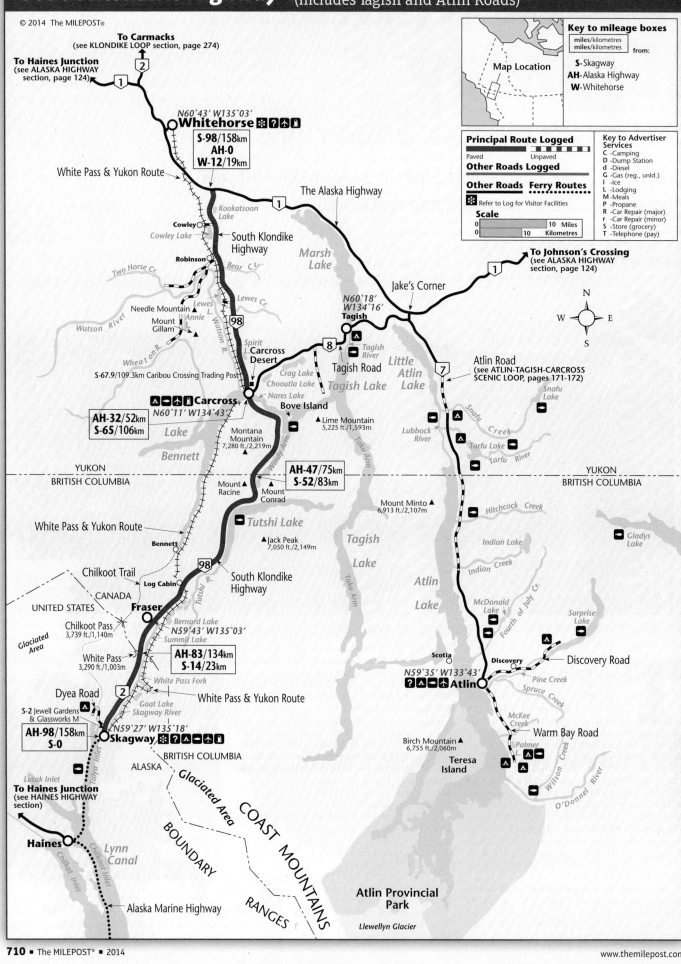

To Carmacks
(see KLONDIKE LOOP section, page 274)

To Haines Junction
(see ALASKA HIGHWAY section, page 124)

Key to mileage boxes

miles/kilometres
miles/kilometres   from:

S-Skagway
AH-Alaska Highway
W-Whitehorse

Map Location

N60°43' W135°03'
Whitehorse
S-98/158km
AH-0
W-12/19km

White Pass & Yukon Route

Kookatsoon Lake

Cowley

Cowley Lake

South Klondike Highway

Robinson

Two Horse Cr.

Bear Cr.

Lewes Cr.

The Alaska Highway

Marsh Lake

Jake's Corner

To Johnson's Crossing
(see ALASKA HIGHWAY section, page 124)

Principal Route Logged
Paved   Unpaved

Other Roads Logged

Other Roads   Ferry Routes

❄ Refer to Log for Visitor Facilities

Scale
0 _____ 10 Miles
0 _____ 10 Kilometres

Key to Advertiser Services
C -Camping
D -Dump Station
d -Diesel
G -Gas (reg., unld.)
I -Ice
L -Lodging
M -Meals
P -Propane
R -Car Repair (major)
r -Car Repair (minor)
S -Store (grocery)
T -Telephone (pay)

Needle Mountain

Mount Gillam

Lewes L.

Annie

Watson River

Watson R.

Wheaton R.

Spirit L.

Carcross Desert

N60°18' W134°16'
Tagish

Tagish River

Tagish Road

Little Atlin Lake

Atlin Road
(see ATLIN-TAGISH-CARCROSS SCENIC LOOP, pages 171-172)

Snafu Lake

S-67.9/109.3km Caribou Crossing Trading Post

Crag Lake

Chooutla Lake

Nares Lake

Bove Island

Lime Mountain
5,225 ft./1,593m

Carcross
N60°11' W134°43'
AH-32/52km
S-65/106km

Lake Bennett

Montana Mountain
7,280 ft./2,219m

YUKON
BRITISH COLUMBIA

Mount Racine

Mount Conrad

AH-47/75km
S-52/83km

Windy Arm

Taku Arm

Lubbock River

Snafu Creek

Tarfu Lake

Tarfu River

YUKON
BRITISH COLUMBIA

Mount Minto
6,913 ft./2,107m

Hitchcock Creek

Gladys Lake

White Pass & Yukon Route

Tutshi Lake

Jack Peak
7,050 ft./2,149m

Bennett

Tagish Lake

Indian Lake

Indian Creek

Atlin Lake

Chilkoot Trail

Log Cabin

CANADA
UNITED STATES

Fraser

Chilkoot Pass
3,739 ft./1,140m

Glaciated Area

White Pass
3,290 ft./1,003m

Dyea Road

S-2 Jewell Gardens & Glassworks M

AH-98/158km
S-0

Tutshi R.

South Klondike Highway

Bernard Lake
N59°43' W135°03'
Summit Lake

AH-83/134km
S-14/23km

White Pass Fork

White Pass & Yukon Route

Goat Lake
Skagway River

N59°27' W135°18'
Skagway

BRITISH COLUMBIA
ALASKA

Lutak Inlet

To Haines Junction
(see HAINES HIGHWAY section)

Taiya Inlet

Haines

Chilkat Inlet

Lynn Canal

Alaska Marine Highway

McDonald Lake

Fourth of July Cr.

Surprise Lake

Scotia

N59°35' W133°43'
Atlin

Discovery

Discovery Road

Pine Creek

Spruce Creek

McKee Creek

Warm Bay Road

Birch Mountain
6,755 ft./2,060m

Teresa Island

Palmer

Wilson Creek

O'Donnel River

COAST MOUNTAINS RANGES

BOUNDARY

Atlin Provincial Park

Llewellyn Glacier

N   W   E   S

information, phone (867) 821-4111.

The South Klondike Highway is 1 of 2 highways connecting ferry travelers with the Alaska Highway; the other is the Haines Highway out of Haines (see HAINES HIGHWAY section). The South Klondike Highway, like the Haines Highway, crosses from Alaska into British Columbia, then into Yukon.

Emergency medical services: Between Skagway and Log Cabin at **Milepost S 27.3,** phone 911 or the Skagway Fire Department at (907) 983-2450. Between Log Cabin and Annie Lake Road at **Milepost S 87.5,** phone the RCMP at (867) 821-5555 or the Carcross Ambulance at (867) 821-4444. Between Annie Lake Road and the junction with the Alaska Highway, phone 911 for the Whitehorse ambulance.

South Klondike Highway Log

Distance from Skagway (S) is followed by distance from Alaska Highway (AH).

Mileposts in Alaska and kilometreposts in Canada reflect distance from Skagway. Kilometre distance from Skagway in the Canadian portion of the log reflects physical kilometreposts and is not necessarily a metric conversion of the mileage figure.

ALASKA ROUTE 2

S 0 AH 97.7 Alaska Marine Highway System ferry terminal at the foot of Broadway Street in downtown **SKAGWAY** *(see description of Skagway beginning on page 698).*

Distance marker northbound shows US–Canada border 15 miles/24 km, Carcross 66 miles/106 km, Whitehorse 113 miles/180 km.

Northbound access to private RV park, railroad dock and small boat harbor. [A]

S 0.1 AH 97.6 White Pass & Yukon Route (WP&YR) railroad tracks. The WP&YR dates back to the Klondike Gold Rush. For more railroad history and the current WP&YR schedule, see "Railroads" in the TRAVEL PLANNING section.

S 0.3 AH 97.4 Centennial Park; rotary snowplow #1 and sculpture of Chilkoot packers.

S 0.4 AH 97.3 Access to Ferry Terminal: Turn at the corner of First and State. Follow signage.

S 0.5 AH 97.2 Gas station located behind the IGA store. [fuel]

S 0.9 AH 96.6 Turn on 12th Ave. for dump station (signage).

S 1.2 AH 96.5 Garden City RV Park at 16th Street and State Street; pull-throughs, full hookups; phone (907) 983-2378. [A]

S 1.7 AH 96 Welcome to Skagway sign southbound. WP&YR railway maintenance shops. Turnoff on signed gravel side road for **Gold Rush Cemetery** (0.6 mile), the final resting place of Skagway's first citizens. "Bad guy" Soapy Smith and "good guy" Frank Reid are buried here (both men died in a gunfight in July 1898). It is only a short hike from Frank Reid's grave to Reid Falls.

S 1.8 AH 95.9 Skagway River highway bridges. Pat Moore bridge for bicyclists and pedestrians.

S 2 AH 95.7 Jewell Gardens & Glassworks. Skagway's showcase garden. Glass-

blowing studio; a gift shop; G-scale railroad; and a restaurant. Open for lunch daily; call ahead for dinner availability. Phone (907) 983-2111. A highly recommended stop.

S 2.2 AH 95.5 Klondike Gold Fields; gold dredge, gold panning, restaurant and brewery.

S 2.5 AH 95.2 Junction with Dyea Road. This is a narrow, winding, gravel road is about 7 miles in length and beyond the Mile 1.4 overlook, is not recommended for motorhomes more than 25 feet. There are fine views of Skagway, Taiya Inlet and the Skagway River from this road. *(See "Dyea Road" log on page 703 for details.)*

During the Klondike Gold Rush, some 8,000 people lived at Dyea. **Slide Cemetery** at Dyea contains the graves of those killed in the Palm Sunday avalanche (April 3, 1898) on the Chilkoot Trail.

This road accesses the Skagway overlook (Mile 1.4), the head of the Chilkoot Trail and two campgrounds. During the Klondike Gold Rush of 1898-1899, Dyea housed thousands of people, many if not most bound for the Klondike gold fields via Chilkoot Pass. The National Park Service offers daily walking tours of this historic site in summer.

S 2.8 AH 94.9 Highway maintenance camp and avalanche gate.

S 3 AH 94.7 *Highway begins steep 11.5-mile/18.5-km ascent northbound from sea level to 3,290 feet/1,003m at White Pass; 11 percent grade.*

There are interpretive viewpoints (logged) and several pullouts with amazing waterfall views along this stretch of road.

S 5 AH 92.7 Turnout to east with view across canyon of White Pass & Yukon Route railway tracks and bridge. The narrow-gauge WP&YR railway was completed in 1900.

S 5.5 AH 92.2 Turnout to west with historical information signs about Brackett Wagon Road and WP&YR (excerpts follow):

"Construction of the Brackett Wagon Road began on Nov. 8, 1897. By the following March the toll road was open to White Pass City, 10 miles up the valley. Built by George A. Brackett, it proved to be a tremendous improvement over the miserable Trail of 1897. The road was popular with packers and proved to be immensely

helpful during railroad construction. However, many chafed at the fees Brackett charged and toll gate wars ensued over payment. Bracket sold the road to the railroad for $100,000 in June 1898."

"The White Pass and Yukon Route is one of the last narrow-gauge railroads built in North America. Construction began on May 28, 1898, with rails reaching the summit by February 18, 1899, and completed to Whitehorse by July 29, 1900. British investors supplied contractor Michael J. Heney with the money to complete the 110-mile lifeline to the Yukon. More than 2,000 workers labored with hand tools to build the railroad that claimed 35 lives."

S 6 AH 91.7 Solid waste facility.

S 6.8 AH 90.9 Port of Entry Skagway: U.S. Customs and Border Protection, open 24 hours daily in summer (April 1 to October 31); 7 A.M.–11 P.M. daily in winter (November 1 to March 31). Phone (907) 983-3144 for border crossing (immigration); phone (907) 983-2325 for customs in Skagway. All travelers entering the United States must stop. Have identification ready. See "Crossing the Border" in the TRAVEL PLANNING section.

Southbound view of glacier above customs station.

S 7.4 AH 90.3 Turnouts and shoulder parking areas along side of highway.

S 7.7 AH 90 Viewpoint with interpretive sign about Goat Lake project; good photo stop for **Pitchfork Falls,** visible across the canyon.

The 4,000 kilowatt Goat Lake hydroelectric project was licensed on July 15, 1996, to provide electricity to Skagway. A 15-mile-long underwater cable connected Haines to the grid in 1998. Water is piped from Goat Lake reservoir down to the powerhouse next to the Skagway River.

S 7.8 AH 89.9 Turnouts and parking along highway next 0.9 mile northbound.

S 8.2 AH 89.5 Avalanche gate. Snow poles along the highway guide snow plows and traffic over White Pass in winter.

S 9.1 AH 88.6 Paved turnout to east with historical interest signs about White Pass City and Deadhorse Trail (excerpts follow):

"Hidden from view is the site of the abandoned gold rush settlement of White Pass City. It evolved quickly in

South Klondike Highway starts on the waterfront in downtown Skagway. *(©Sharon Nault)*

1897 as a good place to rest before making the grueling climb to the summit. A mass of 1,500 to 2,000 eager stampeders congregated here in tents, log cabins and makeshift shanties. The 'city' grew with the influx of teamsters, packers, and railroad workers busily constructing the White Pass and Yukon Route. The completion of the railroad marked the swift end to this boom-to-bust town.

"At first considered a lower-elevation alternative to the nearby Chilkoot Trail, White Pass Trail never reached its potential. Instead, rains in the fall of 1897 and the influx of hundreds of inexperienced stampeders transformed the trail into a quagmire. The carcasses of over 3,000 pack animals soon turned White Pass into Deadhorse Trail. Although the trail is no longer visible, the entrance to part of it, Dead Horse Gulch, can be seen below the railroad in the far left distance."

S 9.8 AH 87.9 Truck emergency runout ramp to west for large transport units that may lose air brakes on steep descent southbound. *It is illegal to park here.*

S 10 AH 87.7 Parking area and Bridal Veil Waterfall. View of WP&YR railway across valley.

S 10.6 AH 87.1 Gravel turnout to east.

S 11.1 AH 86.6 William Moore Bridge. This unique suspension bridge spans a 110-foot-wide gorge over Moore Creek, 180 feet below. Just north of the bridge to the west is a large waterfall. The bridge is named for Capt. William Moore, a riverboat captain and pilot, prospector, packer and trader, who played an important role in settling the town of Skagway. Moore helped pioneer this route over White Pass into Yukon and was among the first to realize the potential of a railroad across the pass.

S 11.5 AH 86.2 Large paved parking areas to east with interpretive signs and view of Skagway River gorge, William Moore Bridge and waterfalls.

S 12 AH 85.7 Truck emergency runout ramp to west. There are vehicle turnouts on both sides of the highway as you approach White Pass northbound.

S 13 AH 84.7 Gravel turnout to west with view (weather permitting) toward summit of White Pass.

S 14.3 AH 83.4 White Pass Summit (elev. 3,292 feet/1,003m). Turnout to west with interpretive signs. Skagway cycling firms start their downhill trips from here.

CAUTION: Southbound traffic begins steep 11.5-mile/18.5-km descent to Skagway; 11 percent grade.

Thousands of gold seekers poured into Canada over the Chilkoot and White passes on their way to Dawson City. An initial contingent of North West Mounted Police, led by Inspector Charles Constantine, had come over the Chilkoot Pass in 1894—well before the gold rush—to establish law among the miners at Dawson City. But in 1898, the Canadian government sent reinforcements, led by Superintendent Samuel Steele.

Upon his arrival at the foot of Chilkoot Pass in February of 1898, Steele found thousands of men waiting to pack their supplies over the pass. He immediately stationed permanent detachments at the summits of Chilkoot and White passes, both to maintain law and order and to assert Canadian sovereignty at these 2 international borders.

After witnessing the desperate condition of many men arriving in the Klondike, Steele set a minimum requirement of a year's supply of food and equipment—"one ton of goods"—for any miner entering Canada.

S 14.5 AH 83.2 Paved turnout to west offers good photo op of Welcome to Alaska

sign and inukshuk erected by the Kiwanis.

S 14.7 (24 km) AH 83 (133.6 km) U.S.–Canada (AK–BC) border. Welcome to Canada (northbound sign) and Welcome to USA (southbound sign). Avalanche gate. Turnout to west offers view of International Boundary Monument, located atop the rock wall to the southeast (across from avalanche gate). Plaque reads:

"This unfortified boundary line between the Dominion of Canada and the United States of America should quicken the remembrance of the more than century old friendship between these countries, a lesson of peace to all nations."

TIME ZONE CHANGE: Alaska observes Alaska time; British Columbia and Yukon observe Pacific time.

NOTE: Drive with headlights on at all times.

WINTER DRIVERS NOTE: Snow plows working when lights flashing.

BC HIGHWAY 98

S 14.9 (24.2 km) AH 82.8 (133.3 km) Distance marker northbound shows Canada Customs 12 km/7 miles, Whitehorse 156 km/97 miles.

S 15 (24.5 km) AH 82.7 (133.1 km) Turnout to west offers best view of International Border Falls, on rocky hillside to west.

S 15.4 (25 km) AH 82.3 (132.4 km) Large gravel turnout to east with toilets and litter bins. Signs in this area about avalanche danger and an avalanche gate to stop traffic when road is closed due to avalanches.

Northbound, the highway winds through the rocky valley of Summit Lake (visible to east). The subalpine landscape of stunted trees and lakes between the U.S. border and Log Cabin, often referred to as a "moonscape," represents a transition zone between the treed lower elevations and the true alpine above tree line. The small, twisted alpine firs (also known as "mopheads") are shaped by a combination of heavy snow burying their lower branches and icy winds sculpting their upper branches.

S 16 (26 km) AH 81.7 (131.5 km) Gravel turnout overlooking Summit Lake at "Seat belt use required by law in Yukon" sign.

S 21.6 (35 km) AH 76.1 (122.2 km) Gravel turnout to east.

S 21.9 (35.2 km) AH 75.8 (122 km) Signage regarding upcoming border crossing (1 km).

S 22 (36 km) AH 75.7 (121.8 km) Large turnout.

S 22.5 (36.5 km) AH 75.2 (121 km) Canada Border Services at FRASER (elev. 2,400 feet/732m). Open 24 hours daily in summer (April 1 to October 31); open 8 A.M. to midnight daily in winter (November 1 to March 31). Phone (867) 821-4111. All travelers entering Canada must stop. *Have proper ID for all travelers, including children. Review border crossing information in the TRAVEL PLANNING section.*

The red building to the east is the last water tower remaining from the WP&YR railway's steam locomotive era. Highway maintenance camp to west. Average annual snowfall at Fraser is 721 cm/24 feet.

S 22.7 (36.9 km) AH 75 (120.7 km) Fraser Rest Area to east is a large double-ended gravel turnout with viewing platform overlooking beautiful deep-green Bernard Lake; benches, litter bins. Interpretive signs about Fraser (excerpt follows):

"The present-day location of Canadian Customs is also the site of one of the WP&YR railway stations. The station was named Fraser, probably to honour a politician from eastern Canada who had helped the railway

company in its early days. Fraser is located on the stretch of track between the Summit, site of the International border, and Bennett, at the south end of Bennett Lake. This section of track was built during the winter of 1898-99, a winter that saw exceptionally heavy snowfall and cold temperatures. It also involved cutting a railway roadbed through solid rock. Rock debris had to be hauled by hand or by horse-drawn wagons."

Distance marker northbound shows Carcross 70 km/44 miles, Whitehorse 144 km/90 miles.

S 24.5 (40 km) AH 73.2 (117.8 km) Shallow Lake to east.

S 26.2 (42.7 km) AH 71.5 (115.1 km) There are several large gravel turnouts to the east in this area. Beautiful views of Tormented Valley, a rocky desolate "moonscape" of stunted trees and small lakes east of the highway.

S 27 (43.9 km) AH 70.7 (113.8 km) LOG CABIN (Chilkoot Trail National Historic Site); parking, historic information panels. With completion of the railway in 1900, the North West Mounted Police moved their customs checkpoint from the summit to Log Cabin. Highway crosses tracks of the White Pass & Yukon Route.

S 27.1 (44 km) AH 70.6 (113.6 km) Distance marker northbound shows Carcross 61 km/38 miles, Tagish 95 km/59 miles, Whitehorse 135 km/84 miles.

S 28.3 (45.9 km) AH 69.4 (111.7 km) Narrow double-ended gravel turnout to west.

S 29.4 (47.2 km) AH 68.3 (109.9 km) Yukon Suspension Bridge. Man-made suspension bridge offers bird's eye view of Tutshi River; cafe, gift shop and historical display. Admission charged. (Current status unknown, closed in 2013.)

S 35.2 (57.1 km) AH 62.5 (100.7 km) Large turnout; highway parallels **Tutshi Lake** for several miles northbound. This large lake in the Tagish Highland supports lake trout and grayling. *Be sure you have a British Columbia fishing license.*

S 35.6 (57.9 km) AH 62.1 (99.9 km) Large gravel turnout overlooking Tutshi Lake.

S 38.2 (62 km) AH 59.5 (95.8 km) Large gravel turnouts overlooking Tutshi Lake next 0.6 mile/1 km northbound.

S 39.6 (64.5 km) AH 58.1 (93.5 km) Gravel access road to scenic picnic area on Tutshi Lake; outhouse, boat launch. *Large vehicles check turnaround space before driving in.*

S 42.4 (68.8 km) AH 55.3 (89 km) Distance marker northbound shows Carcross 37 km/23 miles.

S 43 (70 km) AH 54.7 (87.9 km) Gravel turnout overlooking Tutshi Lake. Good photo op.

S 44 (71.3 km) AH 53.7 (86.4 km) *Begin 1.8-mile passing lane northbound.*

S 45.8 (74.3 km) AH 51.9 (83.5 km) *End passing lane northbound.*

S 46 (74.6 km) AH 51.7 (83.2 km) To the east is the site of the Venus Mines concentrator (private property), which had a capacity of 150 tons per day. A drop in silver prices caused the Venus mill's closure in October 1981. It was being developed by owner in 2013.

S 48.1 (78 km) AH 49.6 (79.8 km) South end of spectacular Windy Arm, an extension of Tagish Lake.

S 49.2 (79.7 km) AH 48.5 (78 km) Dall Creek. Watch for Dall sheep and mountain goats on Dall Peak to west.

S 49.5 (80.3 km) AH 48.2 (77.6 km) Large gravel turnout to east overlooking Windy Arm at Welcome to the Yukon (sign). BC–

YT border. Look for mountain goats and Dall sheep in summer on Montana Mountain to the northwest, and Racine Mountain to the southwest.

YUKON HIGHWAY 98

S 51.5 (83.4 km) **AH 46.2** (74.4 km) Remnants of mine to west up hill.

S 52.2 (84.5 km) **AH 45.5** (73.2 km) Pooly Creek canyon, named for J.M. Pooly, who staked the first Venus claims in 1901. Watch for rocks on the road.

S 52.5 (85.2 km) **AH 45.2** (72.6 km) Gravel turnout to east overlooks Windy Arm.

Slow for frost heaves.

S 53.5 (86.7 km) **AH 44.2** (71.1 km) Old Venus Mill, built in 1908 to serve Venus mines. The first claim on Montana Mountain was staked by W.R. Young in 1899. New York financier Col. Joseph H. Conrad acquired most of the Montana Mountain claims and formed Conrad Consolidated Mines, which began gold exploration and mining in 1905. A town of about 300 people—Conrad City—sprang up along Windy Arm and an aerial tramway was built from the town up the side of Montana Mountain. Venus Mill proved uneconomical and was closed by 1911.

Small mining operations continued over the years, with unsuccessful startups by various mining interests. United Keno Hill Mines acquired the mining claims and their Venus Mines division saw limited production of high-grade gold/silver veins from 1969 to 1970 and again in 1980-81.

S 55 (89 km) **AH 42.7** (68.7 km) Old tramline support east side of highway.

S 56.9 (92.2 km) **AH 40.8** (65.6 km) Small gravel turnout to east.

S 58.7 (95 km) **AH 39** (62.8 km) Rest area and Bove Island Viewpoint; litter bin. Lt. F. Schwatka, US Army, renamed Tagish Lake in 1883 after Lt. Bove of the Italian navy, who had served with the Austro-Hungarian Expedition of 1872-74. Dr. G.M. Dawson, GSC, gave Tagish Lake its original name in 1887, after the First Nations people who lived there and it was originally spelled Ta-Gish-Ai. He left Bove's name on the island.

Magnificent views along here of Windy Arm and its islands (Bove is the larger island). Windy Arm is an extension of Tagish Lake. Lime Mountain (elev. 5,225 feet/1,593m) rises to the east beyond Bove Island.

S 60.7 (98.2 km) **AH 37** (59.5 km) Avalanche gates; large gravel turnout.

S 61.4 (99.5 km) **AH 36.3** (58.4 km) *End southbound passing lane.*

S 61.8 (99.8 km) **AH 35.9** (57.8 km) Highway descends northbound; trucks use low gear (sign).

S 62.2 (100.8 km) **AH 35.5** (57.1 km) *Begin 0.8-mile/1.3-km passing lane southbound.*

S 64.3 (104 km) **AH 33.4** (53.7 km) *NOTE: Slow for 50 kmph/31 mph speed zone northbound entering Carcross.*

Highway climbs next 2.5 miles/4 km southbound.

S 64.4 (104.2 km) **AH 33.3** (53.5 km) Nares Lake (sign). Waterfront Drive turnoff to public dock and boat launch.

S 64.7 (104.7 km) **AH 33** (53.1 km) Natasheeni Village turnoff.

Caribou Mountain (elev. 5,645 feet/ 1,721m) is visible to the east.

S 65 (105.2 km) **AH 32.7** (52.6 km) Nares Bridge crosses the narrows between Lake Bennett and Nares Lake. Larger lakes freeze to an ice depth of more than 3 feet/1m in winter, when air temperatures drop well below -40°F/-40°C. In spring and fall look for swans, teal, pintail, goldeneye and wigeon on Nares Lake. Fishing in **Lake Bennett** for lake trout, northern pike, arctic grayling, whitefish and cisco.

S 65.8 (105.9 km) **AH 32.9** (52.1 km) Turnoff west on Carcross Road for historic Carcross town centre (description follows). The Visitor Center is in the first building after you cross the railroad tracks.

Distance marker northbound shows Whitehorse 74 km/46 miles, Dawson City 612 km/380 miles.

S 65.8 (105.8 km) **AH 32.7** (52 km) Montana Services gas, convenience store, liquor sales, and full-service RV park to west. Government offices, covered pavilion on shore of Nares Lake to east.

Carcross

On the shore of Lake Bennett, 44 miles/71 km southeast of Whitehorse. **Population**: 399. **Emergency Services**: RCMP, phone (867) 821-5555. **Fire Department**, phone (867) 821-2222. **Ambulance**, phone (867) 821-4444. **Health Centre**, phone (867) 821-4444.

Visitor Information: Carcross Visitor Reception Centre (first building to your left when you cross the railroad tracks southbound). This new (2013) complex of small buildings is called the Carcross Commons. The colorful crests on the fronts of these buildings are representative of First Nations' clans. The Center is painted with the "welcoming" crest and is operated by Tourism Yukon. Open daily from 8 A.M. to 8 P.M., from early May to late September; phone (867) 821-4431. The visitor centre has both Yukon and Alaska travel information.

Elevation: 2,175 feet/663m. **Climate**: Average temperature in January, -4.2°F/- 20.1°C; in July, 55.4°F/13°C. Annual rainfall 11 inches, snowfall 2 to 3 feet. Driest month is April, wettest month August. **Radio**: 590-AM, CIKO-FM 97.5, CHON-FM 90.5, CKRW.

Television: CBC, APTN.

Transportation: White Pass & Yukon Route offers train service to Skagway, with a stop at Lake Bennett, Sundays through Fridays in summer; reservations and passports required. WP&YR also offers motorcoach service to Whitehorse and Skagway from Carcross (can be combined with 1-way train excursions).

Private Aircraft: Carcross airstrip, 0.3 mile/0.5 km north via highway; elev. 2,161 feet/659m; length 2,000 feet/610m.

Carcross has several gift shops, a post office open Mondays, Wednesdays and Fridays 8 A.M.–noon and 1:00 P.M.–3:45 P.M.; Tuesday and Thursday from 10:00 A.M.–11:45 A.M.; it has distinctive cancellations.

The local Isabelle Pringle library is open Monday–Thursday with varied hours. Carcross' community pool is open late June through August (867) 821-3211.

The Riverboat Warehouse displays historical photographs and artifacts including the royal mail carriage. It is open for retail.

Several totems in downtown were carved by Native carver, Keith Smarch who also runs the carving studio in Carcross.

Lodging in Carcross located in **Chilkoot Cabins** (description follows).

Chilkoot Cabins. Open year-round, our 4 cabins have a queen bed, private bathroom, TV/Internet. Laundry, firepit/ barbeque available. Breakfast is included for guests by stepping across the street to our Chilkoot Trail Authentic Sourdough Bakery. Contact (867) 821-6004 for cabins; (867) 821-3330 for bakery (open 8 A.M.–4:30 P.M. in summer months; www.chilkoot bakery.com). All currencies except AMEX.

The Caribou Hotel, established in 1901, is a Yukon Heritage Site and has an expected renovation completion date of 2014.

Camping is available at Carcross government campground near the airstrip.

Historic Carcross was formerly known as

A beautiful day on Lake Bennett at Carcross. (©Sharon Nault)

Caribou Crossing because of the large numbers of caribou that traversed the narrows here between Bennett and Nares lakes. In 1904 Bishop Bompas, who had established a school here for Native children in 1901, petitioned the government to change the name of the community to Carcross because of confusion in mail services due to duplicate names in Alaska, British Columbia and the Klondike.

Carcross became a stopping place for gold stampeders on their way to the Klondike goldfields. It was a major stop on the White Pass & Yukon Route railroad from 1900 until 1982, when the railroad ceased through train service. In the early days, passengers and freight transferred from rail to stern-wheelers at Carcross. The partially rebuilt hull of the old stern-wheeler SS *Tutshi* (too-shy) makes up the **SS Tutshi Memorial**. The *Tustshi* burned town in July 1990.

A cairn beside the railroad station marks the site where construction crews laying track for the White Pass & Yukon Route from Skagway met the crew from Whitehorse. The golden spike was set in place when the last rail was laid at Carcross on July 29, 1900. The construction project had begun May 27, 1898, during the height of the Klondike Gold Rush.

The White Pass & Yukon Route runs a popular trip down to Skagway from Carcross. See details under "Railroads" in the TRAVEL PLANNING section. Their ticket office is located in the train depot with a gift shop area and historical displays.

Walk down to the **Bennett Lake Viewing Platform** on the shore of Bennett Lake. The footpath begins adjacent the post office. This scenic overlook on the Carcross waterfront has picnic tables, an interpretive sign on the Klondike Gold Rush, 2 toilets and access to the beach.

Other visitor attractions include **St. Saviour's Anglican Church**, built in 1902; the Royal Mail Carriage; and the little locomotive **Duchess**, which operated on the 2.5-mile portage between Taku Landing on Tagish Lake and Scotia Bay on Atlin Lake until 1921.

Carcross is also becoming known as a **mountain biking** destination. Carcross Tagish First Nations has constructed singletrack bike trails on 7,233-foot Montana Mountain with worldwide bicyclists coming to ride.

South Klondike Highway Log
(continued)

S 65.7 (106.2 km) **AH 32** (51.5 km) Carcross airstrip to east. Also access via side road to **Carcross Tagish First Nation's** campground; 12 campsites, picnic tables, firewood, no water provided, outhouses, camping permit ($12).

S 65.8 (106.4 km) **AH 31.9** (51.3 km)

Junction with paved Tagish Road, which leads east to Tagish (20 miles/33 km), Atlin Road (33 miles/53 km) and the Alaska Highway at Jake's Corner (34 miles/55 km). See "Atlin–Tagish–Carcross Scenic Loop" on pages 171-172.

S 66.6 (107.7 km) **AH 31.1** (50 km) Turnout with litter bin and point of interest sign about **Carcross Desert**.

©Sharon Nault

This unusual desert area of sand dunes, east of the highway between Kilometreposts 108 and 110, is the world's smallest desert and an International Biophysical Programme site for ecological studies. The desert is composed of sandy lake-bottom material left behind by a large glacial lake. Strong winds off Lake Bennett make it difficult for vegetation to take hold here and yet it has an enormous variety of plants, including kinnikinnick, a low trailing evergreen with small leathery leaves that are used for brewing tea.

S 67.9 (109.3 km) **AH 29.8** (47.9 km) **Caribou Crossing Trading Post** (description follows), another highly recommended stop, has a life-size woolly mammoth.

Caribou Crossing Trading Post offers several activities under one roof: wildlife gallery with the world's largest polar bear and life-size woolly mammoth, a new historical Mountie Museum, drop-in scenic dog cart rides with Iditarod teams, and cozy cafe with sandwiches, soups and local coffees. Affordable admission rates ($8.50) gain admission to the museum, a visit with their adorable husky puppies, and also a stroll through the petting farm. Open 9 A.M.–4:30 P.M. www.cariboucrossing.ca; (867) 821-4055. See display ad on this page. [ADVERTISEMENT]

S 71.3 (115.4 km) **AH 26.4** (42.5 km) Spirit Lake Wilderness Resort.

S 72.7 (117.6 km) **AH 25** (40.2 km) Large turnout with litter bin and information signs overlooking beautiful **Emerald Lake**, also called **Rainbow Lake** by Yukoners, to west. (Good view of lake by climbing the hill across from the turnout.)

The rainbow-like colors of the lake result from blue-green light waves reflecting off the white sediment of the lake bottom. This white sediment, called marl, consists of fragments of decomposed shell mixed with clay; it is usually found in shallow, freshwater lakes that have low oxygen levels during the summer months.

S 75.4 (122 km) **AH 22.3** (35.9 km) Highway follows base of **Caribou Mountain** (elev. 5,645 feet/1,721m). View of Montana Mountain to south, Caribou Mountain to east and Gray Ridge Range to the west between Kilometreposts 122 and 128. Flora consists of jack and lodgepole pine.

S 78.9 (127.5 km) **AH 18.8** (30.2 km) Highway crosses Lewes Creek.

S 79.5 (128.6 km) **AH 18.2** (29.3 km) Access road west leads 1 mile/1.6 km to Lewes Lake.

S 84.6 (136.6 km) **AH 13.1** (21.1 km) Rat Lake to west.

S 85.7 (138.5 km) **AH 12** (19.3 km) Bear Creek.

S 86.4 (139.6 km) **AH 11.3** (18.2 km) Access road west to large gravel parking area with litter bin, toilets, information signs and short trail to view **Robinson** and **Robinson Roadhouse**. In 1899, the White Pass & Yukon Route built a railroad siding at Robinson (named for Stikine Bill Robinson). Gold was discovered nearby in the early 1900s and a townsite was surveyed. A few buildings were constructed and a post office, manned by Charlie McConnell, operated from 1909 to 1915. Low mineral yields caused Robinson to be abandoned, but postmaster McConnell stayed and established one of the first ranches in the Yukon.

S 86.6 (139.9 km) **AH 11.1** (17.9 km) Annie Lake Road; access to Annie Lake golf course (0.8 mile/1.4 km). Large gravel turnout to north of road entrance on west side.

S 92.3 (148.4 km) **AH 5.4** (8.7 km) Truck pullout to east.

S 94.3 (152.3 km) **AH 3.4** (5.5 km) Turnoff to east for **Kookatsoon Lake Yukon Government Recreation Site** (day-use only, no camping, gate locked at 10 P.M daily); picnic tables, playground, firepits, pit toilets, canoe launch. Kookatsoon Lake has a nice sandy beach and is shallow and usually warm enough for swimming in summer. Look for Bonaparte's gulls and arctic terns nesting at the south end of the lake.

S 97 (156.5 km) **AH 0.7** (1.1 km) *Speed zones northbound: Slow to 70 kmph/43 mph then 50 kmph/31 mph approaching Alaska Highway.*

S 97.2 (156.9 km) **AH 0.5** (0.8 km) Auto repair shop.

S 97.3 (157 km) **AH 0.4** (0.6 km) **Yukon Rock Shop** is located in residence on southeast side of highway.

S 97.7 (157.8 km) **AH 0 Junction** with the Alaska Highway. Turn left/northwest for Whitehorse (downtown is about 12 miles/19 km from here); turn right/southeast for Watson Lake (262 miles/422 km).

Junction with the Alaska Highway. Turn to **Milepost DC 874.4** on page 173 in the ALASKA HIGHWAY section: Whitehorse-bound travelers continue with that log; travelers heading south down the Alaska Highway read that log back to front.

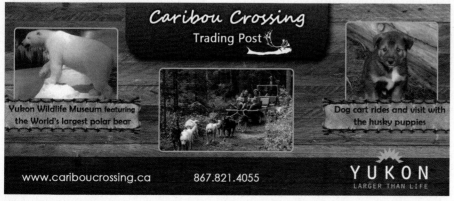

Alaska Marine Highway

Schedules & Tariffs

(See maps, pages 716-718)

MV Malaspina docked next to a cruise ship in Skagway. (©Sharon Nault)

The Alaska Marine Highway System provides passenger/vehicle ferry service in 3 regions: Southeast, Southcentral/Prince William Sound and Southwest. There is also Cross-Gulf service in the summer connecting Juneau in Southeast Alaska and Whittier in Southcentral. The ferry system stretches more than 3,500 miles from Bellingham, WA, to Dutch Harbor, AK, with service to and from Prince Rupert, BC, to Inside Passage communities and connecting ferry service across the Gulf of Alaska to Prince William Sound. Ferries also connect the Kenai Peninsula to Kodiak Island and the Aleutian Chain.

The Alaska ferry system has 2 seasons: May 1 to Sept. 30 (summer), when sailings are most frequent; and Oct. 1 to April 30 (fall/winter/spring), when service is less frequent. Alaska Marine Highway System summer 2014 schedules and tariffs available at our press time are included in this section. For updates to the summer schedules, fare specials and to make reservations online, go to the Alaska Marine Highway System website at www.ferryalaska.com. For questions not answered here or on the website, email the Alaska Marine Highway

System at dot.ask.amhs@alaska.gov or phone the central reservations office in Juneau at 1-800-642-0066.

The reservation office of the Alaska Marine Highway System is in Juneau. Write 6858 Glacier Highway, or P.O. Box 112505, Juneau, AK 99811-2505; local phone (907) 465-3941; phone toll-free 1-800-642-0066; fax (907) 465-8824; TDD 1-800-764-3779; website www.ferryalaska.com. For updates on vessel information you may now also dial 511 to access the Department of Transportation's Information System or visit www.dot.state.ak.us/amhs/map.shtml and click on a ship's icon.

Vessels are indicated in all schedules by a 3-letter abbreviation. See vessel descriptions on page 720 this section.

Southeast Alaska summer schedules for Inside Passage north- and southbound sailings are on pages 723-730. For additional service within Southeast, see the MV *Kennicott* Cross-Gulf schedule on page 722, and the Dayboat schedules on pages 734-741. (For MV *Lituya* summer service between Ketchikan and the new Annette Bay ferry terminal at Metlakatla go to www.ferryalaska.com.)

Southeast Alaska tariffs for passengers,

vehicles and cabins are on pages 731-732. Cross-Gulf summer tariffs for passengers, vehicles and cabins appear on page 733.

The Southwest/Aleutian Chain sailings of the MV *Tustumena*, and MV *Kennicott* with service to/from Homer, Seldovia, Kodiak and Aleutian Chain ports, appear on pages 743-744. Tariffs are on pages 745-746.

Prince William Sound summer service between Whittier, Valdez, Tatitlek and Cordova is on page 742. Passenger and vehicle fares for Prince William Sound sailings are on page 745.

NOTE: Schedules and fares provided here are courtesy of the Alaska Marine Highway System. The state reserves the right to revise or cancel schedules and rates without prior notice and assumes no responsibility for delays and/or expenses due to such modifications.

Reservations: The Alaska state ferries are very popular in the summer. Walk-on traffic is usually accommodated, but reservations are strongly recommended, especially for those traveling with a vehicle or wanting a cabin. You can make reservations online at www.ferryalaska.com (www.dot.state.ak.us/amhs/index.shtml); with travel agents/booking agents or with

(Continues on page 718)

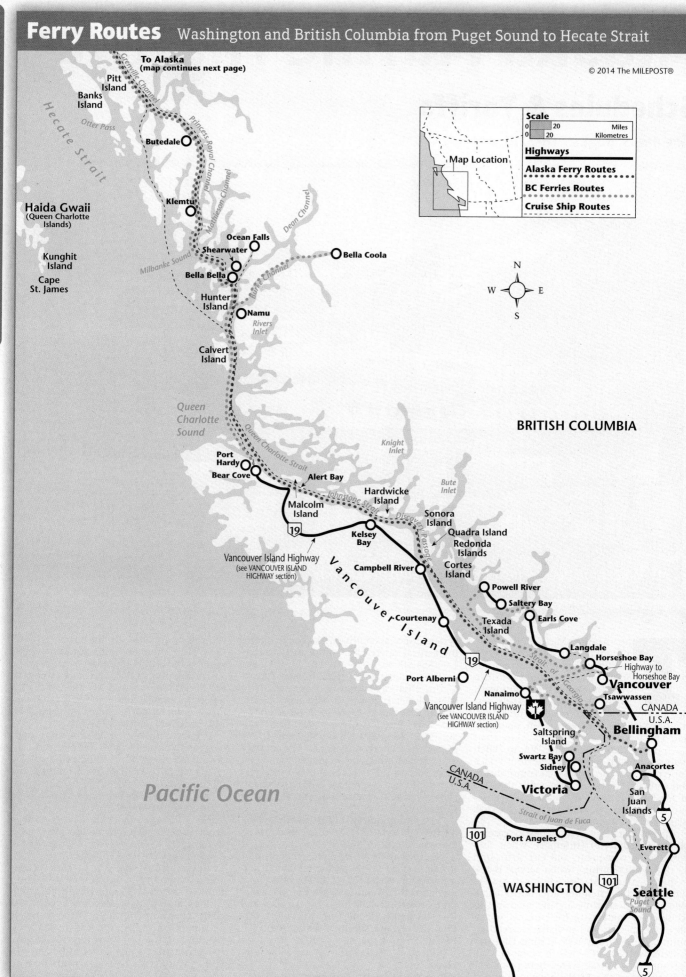

Ferry Routes Washington and British Columbia from Puget Sound to Hecate Strait

© 2014 The MILEPOST®

To Alaska
(map continues next page)

Pitt Island

Banks Island

Otter Pass

Butedale

Grenville Channel

Princess Royal Channel

Klemtu

Mathieson Channel

Hecate Strait

Haida Gwaii
(Queen Charlotte Islands)

Kunghit Island

Cape St. James

Ocean Falls

Shearwater

Bella Bella

Milbanke Sound

Hunter Island

Namu

Rivers Inlet

Calvert Island

Dean Channel

Bella Coola

Burke Channel

BRITISH COLUMBIA

Scale
0 20 Miles
0 20 Kilometres
Map Location
Highways
Alaska Ferry Routes
BC Ferries Routes
Cruise Ship Routes

N W E S

Queen Charlotte Sound

Knight Inlet

Queen Charlotte Strait

Port Hardy

Bear Cove

Alert Bay

Bute Inlet

Johnstone Strait

Malcolm Island

Hardwicke Island

Sonora Island

Quadra Island

Redonda Islands

Cortes Island

Discovery Passage

19

Kelsey Bay

Vancouver Island Highway
(see VANCOUVER ISLAND HIGHWAY section)

Campbell River

Powell River

Saltery Bay

Earls Cove

Courtenay

Texada Island

Langdale

Horseshoe Bay

Highway to Horseshoe Bay

Vancouver Island

19

Port Alberni

Nanaimo

Strait of Georgia

Vancouver

Tsawwassen

CANADA U.S.A.

Bellingham

Vancouver Island Highway
(see VANCOUVER ISLAND HIGHWAY section)

Saltspring Island

Swartz Bay

Sidney

Anacortes

San Juan Islands

5

CANADA U.S.A.

Victoria

Pacific Ocean

Strait of Juan de Fuca

101

Port Angeles

Everett

101

WASHINGTON

Seattle
Puget Sound

5

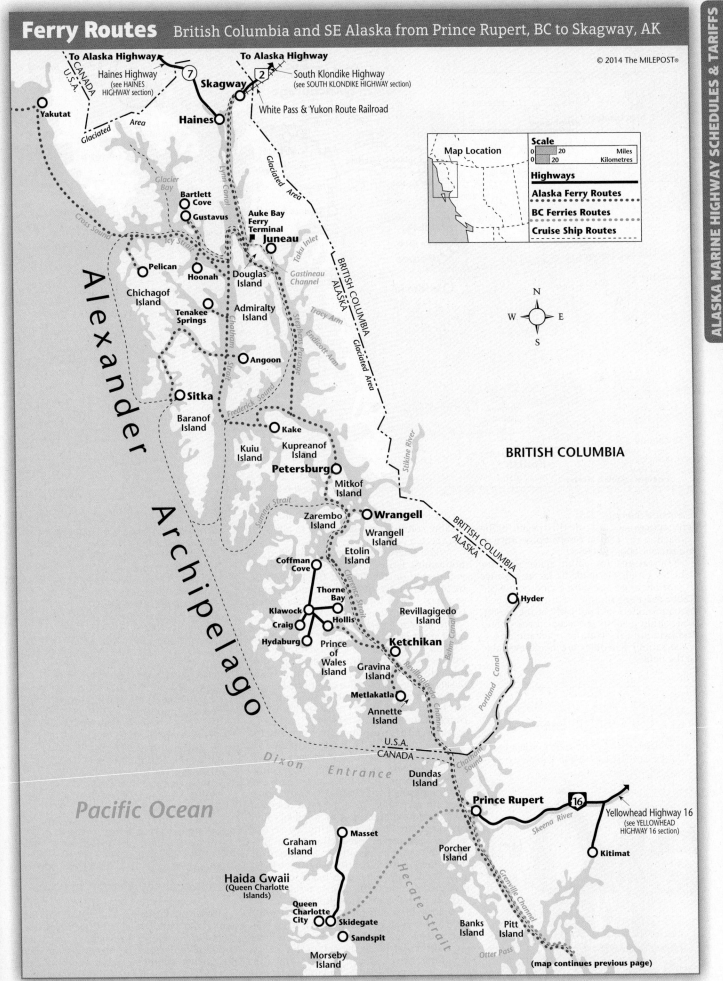

Ferry Routes British Columbia and SE Alaska from Prince Rupert, BC to Skagway, AK

© 2014 The MILEPOST®

To Alaska Highway
To Alaska Highway

Haines Highway
(see HAINES
HIGHWAY section)

7

Skagway

South Klondike Highway
(see SOUTH KLONDIKE HIGHWAY section)

2

Haines

White Pass & Yukon Route Railroad

Yakutat

CANADA
U.S.A.

Glaciated Area

Glacier Bay

Glaciated Area

Cross Sound

Bartlett Cove

Gustavus

Auke Bay Ferry Terminal

Juneau

BRITISH COLUMBIA
ALASKA

Lynn Canal

Pelican

Hoonah

Douglas Island

Taku Inlet

Gastineau Channel

Chichagof Island

Icy Strait

Tenakee Springs

Admiralty Island

Tracy Arm

Endicott Arm

Angoon

Chatham Strait

Stephens Passage

Glaciated Area

Sitka

Baranof Island

Frederick Sound

Stikine River

Kake

Kuiu Island

Kupreanof Island

BRITISH COLUMBIA

Petersburg

Mitkof Island

Sumner Strait

Zarembo Island

Wrangell

Wrangell Island

Etolin Island

Coffman Cove

Thorne Bay

Klawock

Hollis

Craig

Hydaburg

Prince of Wales Island

Clarence Strait

Revillagigedo Island

Hyder

BRITISH COLUMBIA
ALASKA

Ketchikan

Behm Canal

Gravina Island

Revillagigedo Channel

Metlakatla

Annette Island

Portland Canal

U.S.A.
CANADA

Chatham Sound

Dundas Island

Dixon   Entrance

Pacific Ocean

Prince Rupert

16

Yellowhead Highway 16
(see YELLOWHEAD HIGHWAY 16 section)

Skeena River

Porcher Island

Kitimat

Masset

Graham Island

Grenville Channel

Haida Gwaii
(Queen Charlotte Islands)

Hecate Strait

Queen Charlotte City

Skidegate

Sandspit

Banks Island

Pitt Island

Morseby Island

Otter Pass

(map continues previous page)

Map Location

Scale
| 0 | 20 | Miles |
| 0 | 20 | Kilometres |

Highways
- Alaska Ferry Routes
- BC Ferries Routes
- Cruise Ship Routes

N
W   E
S

Alexander Archipelago

ALASKA MARINE HIGHWAY SCHEDULES & TARIFFS

Southcentral/Southwest Ferry Routes

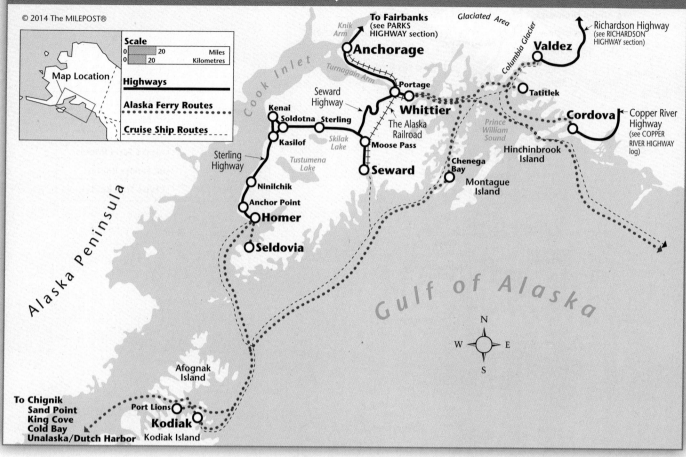

© 2014 The MILEPOST®

Map Location

Scale
0 — 20 Miles
0 — 20 Kilometres

Highways ———
Alaska Ferry Routes ———
Cruise Ship Routes ·········

To Fairbanks
(see PARKS
HIGHWAY section)

Knik Arm

Glaciated Area

Columbia Glacier

Richardson Highway
(see RICHARDSON
HIGHWAY section)

Valdez

Anchorage

Cook Inlet

Turnagain Arm

Portage

Tatitlek

Seward Highway

Whittier

Copper River
Highway
(see COPPER
RIVER HIGHWAY
log)

Cordova

Kenai

Soldotna   Sterling

The Alaska
Railroad

Prince
William
Sound

Kasilof

Skilak Lake

Moose Pass

Sterling
Highway

Tustumena
Lake

Seward

Chenega
Bay

Hinchinbrook
Island

Montague
Island

Ninilchik

Anchor Point

Homer

Seldovia

Alaska Peninsula

Gulf of Alaska

N
W   E
S

Afognak
Island

To Chignik
Sand Point
King Cove
Cold Bay
Unalaska/Dutch Harbor

Port Lions

Kodiak

Kodiak Island

(Continued from page 715)
ferry offices (see list on this page); or by contacting the central reservations office in Juneau at 1-800-642-0066.

Reservations for cabin space and for vehicles should be made as far in advance as possible to get the sailing dates you wish. Cabin space on summer sailings from Bellingham is often sold out early in the season. Reservation requests are accepted year-round and held until reservations open and/or seasonal sailing schedules are made available to the public.

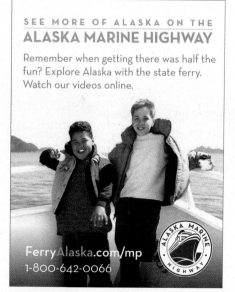

Always factor in enough time when making connecting reservations to allow for unexpected delays.

While reservations are recommended, do not assume ferries are sailing at capacity. If you decide on the spur of the moment to include the ferry in your itinerary, phone or check online to see if the Alaska Marine Highway System has space available.

In order to guarantee a reservation, payment must be received by the payment due date on the reservation confirmation. Reservations not paid for by this date are automatically cancelled. You can pick up your tickets at any AMHS office or terminal.

To change a reservation, contact the central reservation office at 1-800-642-0066, or contact your local ferry terminal.

Fares and fare payment: Payment for reserved space may be made by phone or online with a credit card or by mail with a cashier's check, money order or personal check drawn on an Alaska bank. There is a small additional fee charged if you change your itinerary once space has been reserved. Cancellation charges will be applied when any cancellation is made within 14 days of sailing, resulting in a reduction in the prepaid amount. The penalty is 15 percent of the unused portion. A $10 change fee will be applied when any change is made to a vehicle itinerary, unless the change results in an increase of the value of the itinerary.

Vehicle fares depend on the size of vehicle. You are charged by how much space you take up, so a car with trailer is measured from the front of the car to the end of the trailer, including hitch space. Charges are also applied to bicycles, kayaks and inflatables.

Terminal/Ticket Office Phone #s
Toll-Free 1-800-642-0066
Angoon, phone (907) 788-3653
Bellingham, (360) 676-8445 or (360) 676-0212 (24-hour recorded)
Cordova, phone (907) 424-7333
Haines, phone (907) 766-2113
Homer, phone (907) 235-8449
Hoonah, phone (907) 945-3292
Juneau/Auke Bay, phone (907) 465-3940
Juneau, central reservations, toll-free 1-800-642-0066
  TDD/TDY 1-800-764-3779
Kake, phone (907) 785-3804
Ketchikan, phone (907) 225-6181
Kodiak, phone (907) 486-3800
Petersburg, phone (907) 772-3855
Prince Rupert, phone (250) 627-1744
Seldovia, phone (907) 234-7868
Sitka, phone (907) 747-3300
Skagway, phone (907) 983-2229
Valdez, phone (907) 835-4436
Whittier, phone (907) 472-2378
Wrangell, phone (907) 874-3711

Reservation Agent Phone #s
Alaska Ferry Adventures & Tours, phone 1-800-382-9229
Viking Travel, phone 1-800-327-2571

Passenger tariffs are charged as follows: adults and children 12 and over, full fare; children 6 to 11, approximately half fare; children under 6, free. Passenger fares do not include cabins or meals. Senior citizen (over 65) may qualify for a discount between

Alaska ports only; restrictions may apply. Special passes are also available to persons with disabilities. Contact the Alaska Marine Highway System for more on these fares and restrictions.

Vessels: The fast ferries are the newest vessels on the Alaska Marine Highway and travel at 35 knots. Traditional Marine Highway vessels travel at between 12 and 18 knots. Descriptions of all 11 Alaska Marine Highway vessels appear on page 720.

In-port time: In-port time on all vessels is usually only long enough to unload and load. You may go ashore while the ferry is in port *but you must be back onboard at least 20 minutes prior to departure. Make sure you have your ticket receipt and I.D. with you when you debark, as you will need them to reboard.* Keep in mind that ferry terminals are often some distance from city center, and you may not have enough time to sightsee, depending on how long and at what hour you are in port (some port calls are late at night or in the very early hours of the morning). If your schedule allows, you may want to make a "stopover."

Ferry terminals on the Southcentral/Southwest system are located within a half-mile of city centers. In Southeast, ferry terminals close to city center include Wrangell and Skagway. Terminals more distant from city center (from nearest to farthest) are: Petersburg (0.9 mile); Ketchikan (2.5 miles); Haines (5 miles); Sitka (7.1 miles); and Juneau (14 miles). Check with the purser about bus service from the terminals.

Running times between ports are listed on this page.

Stopovers: A stopover is getting off at

Approximate Running Times
(* indicates "fast ferry" times)

SOUTHEAST/INSIDE PASSAGE
Bellingham–Ketchikan	37 hrs.
Haines–Skagway	1 hr.
Juneau–Haines	4 hrs. 30 min.
Juneau–Haines	2 hrs. 15 min.*
Juneau–Skagway	2 hrs. 30 min.*
Ketchikan–Metlakatla	1 hr. 30 min.
Ketchikan–Wrangell	6 hrs.
Petersburg–Juneau	8 hrs.
Petersburg–Sitka	10 hrs.
Prince Rupert–Ketchikan	6 hrs.
Sitka–Juneau	8 hrs. 45 min.
Sitka–Juneau	4 hrs. 30 min.*
Wrangell–Petersburg	3 hrs.

SOUTHEAST FEEDER ROUTES
Petersburg–Kake	4 hrs.
Kake–Sitka	8 hrs.
Kake–Angoon	4 hrs.
Sitka–Angoon	5 hrs. 30 min.
Angoon–Hoonah	4 hrs.
Angoon–Tenakee	2 hrs. 30 min.
Tenakee–Hoonah	3 hrs. 15 min.
Hoonah–Juneau	3 hrs. 15 min.
Hoonah–Pelican	4 hrs. 15 min.
Juneau–Pelican	6 hrs. 30 min.

SOUTHCENTRAL
Cordova–Tatitlek	3 hrs. 30 min.
Cordova–Valdez	3 hrs.*
Cordova–Valdez	5 hrs. 30 min.
Cordova–Whittier	3 hrs. 15 min.*
Cordova–Whittier	7 hrs.
Valdez–Cordova	5 hrs. 30 min.
Valdez–Cordova	3 hrs.*
Valdez–Whittier	6 hrs. 45 min.
Valdez–Whittier	3 hrs.*
Whittier–Chenega Bay	4 hrs. 30 min.
Whittier–Cordova	3 hrs. 15 min.*
Whittier–Valdez	6 hrs. 45 min.
Whittier–Valdez	3 hrs.*

SOUTHCENTRAL/SOUTHWEST
Chenega Bay–Whittier	4 hrs. 30 min.
Homer–Kodiak	9 hrs. 30 min.
Homer–Port Lions	10 hrs.
Homer–Seldovia	1 hr. 30 min.
Kodiak–Homer	9 hrs. 30 min.
Kodiak–Port Lions	2 hrs. 30 min.
Whittier–Kodiak	13 hrs. 15 min.

CROSS-GULF
Juneau–Yakutat	17 hrs. 15 min.
Yakutat–Whittier	22 hrs.

SOUTHWEST
Akutan–False Pass	10 hrs. 30 min.
Akutan–Unalaska	3 hrs. 30 min.
Chignik–Kodiak	18 hrs. 30 min.
Chignik–Sand Point	9 hrs. 15 min.
Cold Bay–False Pass	4 hrs. 15 min.
Cold Bay–King Cove	2 hrs.
False Pass–Akutan	10 hrs. 30 min.
False Pass–Cold Bay	4 hrs. 15 min.
King Cove–Cold Bay	2 hrs.
Kodiak–Chignik	18 hrs. 30 min.
Kodiak–Unalaska	59 hrs. 30 min.
Sand Point–Chignik	9 hrs. 15 min.
Sand Point–King Cove	6 hrs. 30 min.
Unalaska–Akutan	3 hrs. 30 min.
Unalaska–Kodiak	59 hrs. 30 min.

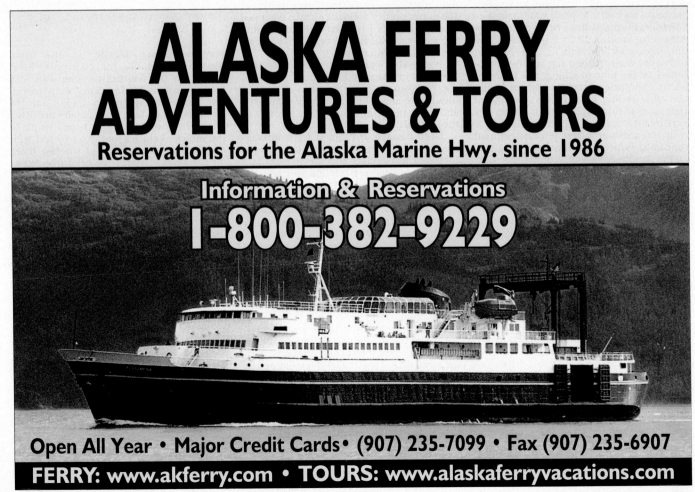

Motorcyclists wait to board the ferry. Motorcycles usually board ahead of vehicles.
(©Sharon Nault)

VESSELS

Aurora (AUR), began service 1977; carries 300 passengers, 34 vehicles; food service, solarium.

Chenega (CHE) Fast Ferry, began service 2005; carries 250 passengers, 36 vehicles; food service.

Columbia (COL), began service 1974; carries 600 passengers, 134 vehicles, 103 cabins; dining room, cafeteria, gift shop, cocktail lounge, solarium.

Fairweather (FWX) Fast Ferry, began service 2004; carries 250 passengers, 36 vehicles; cafeteria.

Kennicott (KEN), began service 1998; carries 499 passengers, 80 vehicles, 109 cabins; food service, heated solarium.

LeConte (LEC), began service 1974; carries 300 passengers, 34 vehicles; food service, cocktail lounge, solarium.

Lituya (LIT), began service 2004; carries 149 passengers, 18 vehicles.

Malaspina (MAL), began service 1963, renovated 1972; carries 499 passengers, 88 vehicles, 73 cabins; cafeteria, gift shop, cocktail lounge, solarium.

Matanuska (MAT), began service 1963, renovated 1968; carries 499 passengers, 88 vehicles, 108 cabins; cafeteria, gift shop, cocktail lounge, solarium.

Taku (TAK), began service 1963, renovated 1981; carries 370 passengers, 69 vehicles, 44 cabins; cafeteria, gift shop, cocktail lounge, solarium.

Tustumena (TUS), began service 1964, renovated 1969; carries 174 passengers, 36 vehicles, 26 cabins; cafeteria, cocktail lounge, solarium.

any port between your point of origin and final destination and taking another vessel at a later time. For travelers with vehicles and/or cabins this can be done as long as reservations to do so have been made in advance. Passenger, vehicle and cabin fares are charged on a point-to-point basis, and stopovers may increase the total ticket cost.

Waitlisted and Standby Travel: If the desired space is not available, reservation personnel may offer to place your request on a waitlist. If cancellations occur, you will be notified of confirmation of space, at which time payment will be due.

If your cabin request has not been confirmed by the time of sailing, you may sign up on the purser's standby list on board. Once the sailing is underway, the purser assigns available cabins to those on the standby list.

If you arrive at a ferry terminal without confirmed vehicle space, you must sign up on the standby list at the terminal.

Check-in times: Summer check-in times for reserved vehicles prior to departure are: Bellingham and Prince Rupert, 3 hours; Ketchikan, Juneau, Haines, Skagway, Homer, Kodiak, and Whittier 2 hours; Petersburg, 1½ hours; all other ports, 1 hour. Passengers without vehicles must check in 1 hour prior to departure at all ports except Bellingham, where check-in is 2 hours prior to departure. You must check-in at the above listed times even if you already have a reservation and a ticket. When you check in you will be assigned a lane for boarding and you will be recorded on the manifest.

NOTE: It is especially important that motorists with ferry reservations out of Whittier time their arrival to allow for the tunnel opening as well as for ferry check-in. (See Whittier Access Road on page 562.)

Cabins: If you are traveling on one of the longer ferry runs, such as the 37-hour trip between Bellingham, WA, and Ketchikan, AK, you should reserve a cabin well in advance. Cabin space is limited and sells out very quickly. Due to U.S. Coast Guard regulations, passengers cannot sleep in their vehicles.

Cabins are outfitted with single or double bunk bed-style berths and vary in size and availability. Most cabins have a toilet, shower and linens (towels, sheets, blankets). Pick up cabin keys from the purser's office when you board. Cabins are sold as a unit, not on a per-berth basis. In other words, the cost of the cabin is the same whether 1 or more passengers occupy it. If cabins are sold out on a sailing, you can get on a waitlist at the purser's office onboard. Cabins equipped to accommodate passengers with disabilities are also available, and all vessels have elevator access to cabin decks.

Besides distributing cabin keys, the purser also rents blankets, pillows and towels for a fee. The purser's office is manned 30 minutes before and 30 minutes after port arrivals. If the purser is unavailable, ask one of the stewards.

Deck Passage: If cabin space is unavailable on your overnight sailing, or you wish to save a few dollars and travel without a cabin, the inside recliner lounges and the covered solariums located on the upper decks serve as sleeping areas. There is space to roll out a sleeping bag on the floor of the recliner lounges and on the plastic lounge chairs on the solarium deck. If you choose this route, a sleeping pad greatly increases the comfort of reclining chairs or floor. Overhead heaters keep the solarium deck pretty toasty, although a sleeping bag is necessary (the blankets available for rent from the purser's office are NOT warm enough for the solarium deck).

Small, free-standing tents are also permitted on the solarium deck (but not under the heated covered area) and on the stern of the cabin deck if space allows (except on the *Kennicott*). Beware of wind; it is advisable for campers to duct-tape their tents to the deck. Pillows and blankets are available for rent from the purser on most sailings. Public restrooms are available on all vessels and public showers are available on most vessels.

Smoking is allowed on the outside decks only; specific locations vary by vessel.

Vehicles: Reservations are strongly recommended. Any vehicle that

may be driven legally on the highway is acceptable for transport. Most vessels on the Southeast system can load vehicles up to 70 feet long with special arrangements. Maximum length on the *Tustumena* is 40 feet. Vehicle fares are determined by the overall length and width of the vehicle. Vehicles from 8½ to 9 feet wide are charged 125 percent of the fare listed for the vehicle length. Vehicles over 9 feet in width are charged 150 percent of the fare listed for vehicle length.

On the vehicle deck, a crew member will direct you to your parking location. Park, set your hand brake, lock your vehicle, take the personal possessions you will need and proceed to a passageway leading to the passenger areas. If the vehicle you are putting onboard will not be accompanied, lock the vehicle and leave the keys with the loading officer.

Hazardous materials may not be transported on the ferries. The valves on propane or similar type tanks must be turned off and sealed by a ferry system employee. If this has not been done by the time you board, notify the purser when surrendering your ticket for boarding. Portable containers of fuel are permitted but must be stored with vessel personnel while en route.

Although it is possible to ship a vehicle unattended, keep in mind that the state assumes no responsibility for the loading and unloading of unattended vehicles. You must make your own arrangements to have your vehicle loaded and unloaded from the ferry.

Food Service: Food service varies from vessel to vessel. Hot meals, snacks, and beverages are available in cafeteria or snack bar style on all vessels, except the *Lituya*. The *Columbia* and *Tustumena* also have full-service sit-down dining rooms. Food service hours vary based on sailing departure times, so keep in mind that if you board at night, you might miss the meal service. An example of cafeteria hours (from the *Taku*) are: Breakfast 7–10:30 A.M., Lunch noon–4:30 P.M., Dinner 6–9 P.M. The cost of meals is not included in passenger, cabin or vehicle fares. Tipping is prohibited.

Alcoholic beverages are served on the *Columbia, Kennicott, Malaspina, Matanuska, Taku* and *Tustumena*. Beer and wine are served on the *Fairweather* and *Chenega*. Alcohol may be consumed only in cabins or cocktail lounges by persons 21 years of age or older, and may not be consumed in public areas of the ship. The cocktail lounges are open from noon to midnight.

You can bring your own food and beverages, but keep in mind that refrigeration is not available on board; however, microwaves are available on all vessels. Coin-op ice, soft drink and candy machines are available on mainline vessels.

Luggage: You are responsible for your own luggage! Foot passengers may bring up to 100 lbs. of hand luggage. There is no limit on luggage carried in a vehicle. Coin-operated storage lockers are available aboard most ships. Baggage carts for carry-on luggage are driven between the terminals and the car deck. Baggage handling is *NOT* provided and the Alaska Marine Highway System is not responsible for lost, stolen or damaged luggage.

Vehicle deck restrictions: Due to Coast Guard regulations, passengers are not allowed on the car deck while the ship is underway, unless they are accompanied by an AMHS employee. Periodic "car deck calls" are made 3 times a day between Bellingham and Ketchikan and on Cross-Gulf trips. These are announced over the loudspeaker and allow passengers approximately 15 minutes to visit the car deck and walk pets, retrieve items from cars, etc. Otherwise car deck visits are allowed only when the ferry is in port.

Pet policy: For a pet to be transported via ferry between Bellingham, WA, or Prince Rupert, BC, and Alaska ports, they must have a valid rabies certificate and a health certificate, issued within the past 30 days. Both must clearly identify your animal and be presented at check–in. (Also check "Crossing the Border" in the TRAVEL PLANNING section for requirements for pets.)

A certificate of health is not required for travel between Alaska ports.

Dogs and other pets are not allowed in cabins and must be transported on the vehicle deck only, the exception being animals aiding disabled passengers when prior approval has been obtained. Pets are to be transported inside a vehicle or in suitable containers furnished by the passenger. (Keep in mind that the car decks can be cool in the winter.) Animals and pets must be cared for by the owner. On long sailings, you may feed, water and/or walk your pet on the car deck during one of the 15-minute announced car deck calls. You may also walk your pet at port stops. Keep in mind that some port stops are very brief and that sailing time between some ports will be as long as 37 hours (Bellingham to Ketchikan).

History of the AMHS

The Alaska Marine Highway System's inaugural year was 1963, when the State of Alaska's expanded ferry system connected Prince Rupert, BC, to Haines and Skagway, AK, with 3 new vessels: the *Malaspina* (pictured above), the *Taku* and the *Matanuska*. These ferries—along with the original *Chilkat*—provided 6-days-a-week service through the Inside Passage. The cover of the 1963 edition of *The MILEPOST®* announced: "Now there are TWO Alaska Highways— Interior Route, or Coastal Route via the State of Alaska's new auto-passenger ferries."

The dream of providing Alaskans in remote or road-less coastal communities with reliable marine transportation began in 1948, with a private enterprise. Steve Homer and Ray and Gustav Gelotte of Haines created Chilkoot Motorship Lines to provide ferry service between Haines and Juneau. They purchased a former U.S. Navy Landing craft, the MV *Chilkoot*: 121 feet in length, a 33-foot beam, and drawing 3.5 feet when loaded. Although passenger services were limited, the vessel could carry up to 14 vehicles. The ferry's first customers were Simon Hellenthal, a Juneau attorney, and Ernest Gruening, the governor of the Territory of Alaska.

The new company faced financial hardships after only a couple years of service when weather related issues prevented them from operating year-round. Seeing the potential value of the ferry service, the Territorial Government purchased Chilkoot Motorship Lines from its 3 founders in June 1951.

Demand for the ferry service soon outgrew the available resources, and in 1957 the *Chilkoot* was replaced by the MV *Chilkat*. The 99-foot-long *Chilkat* was capable of carrying 59 passengers and 15 vehicles, and could load from either the beach or a dock. Daily auto and passenger service began between Juneau and Haines, which was connected to the Alaska Highway via the Haines High-

way, and Skagway, where the White Pass & Yukon Route Railway connected travelers to Whitehorse on the Alaska Highway. (The highway between Skagway and the Alaska Highway was not completed until 1978.) In 1959, when Alaska became the 49th state in the union, the MV *Chilkat* became the first state-owned ferry in what would soon be a small fleet.

In 1963, the Alaska Marine Highway System (AMHS) was born, its mission to "provide transportation of people, goods and vehicles between Alaska communities, Canada and the 'Lower 48.'"

"A new easy way to visit the fabulous 49th State," touted the 1963 edition of *The MILEPOST®*. "Now you can take one of Alaska's large new ferries from Prince Rupert, BC, through the calm waters of the beautiful 'Inside Passage' to Skagway, Alaska. Each ferry carries 500 passengers and 108 autos— and has a dining room, snack bar, cocktail lounge, 14 staterooms, and airplane-type reclining chairs."

The ferries stopped at the same mainline ports they call at today: Ketchikan, Wrangell, Petersburg, Sitka, Juneau, Haines and Skagway. In its first year of operation, the fleet transported 16,000 vehicles and 83,000 passengers.

Today, the AMHS connects 35 port communities from Alaska to British Columbia and Washington, with a ferry system spanning 3,500 miles. The fleet now consists of 11 vessels *(see list on facing page)* carrying on average 330,000 passengers and 110,000 vehicles annually.

The Alaska Marine Highway offers a unique mode of travel, providing not only transportation but also the chance to soak in the unchanging beauty of Alaska's coastal scenery. The Alaska Marine Highway was named a National Scenic Byway in 2002, and designated an All-American Road a few years later by the Federal Highway Administration.

Car deck calls are dependent on weather conditions and other variables.

Cross-Gulf Ferry Travel: Cross-Gulf ferry trips connect Whittier, Yakutat and Juneau, with through-service to and from Ketchikan and Bellingham on the MV *Kennicott*. The

real distinction of the Cross-Gulf trips is that you sail across the Gulf of Alaska, less protected waters than the Inside Passage, and you may encounter white caps and some significant rolling motion. Conditions in the Gulf may prohibit regular car deck calls.

Ketchikan ferry terminal at Milepost 2.3 North Tongass Highway. (©Sharon Nault)

Summer 2014, MV *Kennicott*
Cross Gulf Northbound

For updated schedules and fares,
go to www.ferryalaska.com

	Bellingham	Ketchikan	Juneau	Yakutat	Whittier	Chenega Bay	Kodiak	Homer
MAY			T29 12:00P	W30 8:00A	Th1 10:30A	Th1 4:00P	F2 12:00P	F2 9:00P
	S10 6:00P	M12 11:00A	T13 12:00P	W14 8:00A	Th15 10:30A	Th15 4:00P	F16 12:00P	F16 9:00P
	S24 6:00P	M26 11:00A	T27 12:00P	W28 8:00A	Th29 10:30A	Th29 4:00P	F30 12:00P	F30 9:00P
JUNE	S7 6:00P	M9 11:00A	T10 12:00P	W11 8:00A	Th12 10:30A	Th12 4:00P	F13 12:00P	F13 9:00P
	S21 6:00P	M23 11:00A	T24 12:00P	W25 8:00A	Th26 10:30A	Th26 4:00P	F27 12:00P	F27 9:00P
JULY	S5 6:00P	M7 11:00A	T8 12:00P	W9 8:00A	Th10 10:30A	Th10 4:00P	F11 12:00P	F11 9:00P
	S19 6:00P	M21 11:00A	T22 12:00P	W23 8:00A	Th24 10:30A	Th24 4:00P	F25 12:00P	F25 9:00P
AUGUST	S2 6:00P	M4 11:00A	T5 12:00P	W6 8:00A	Th7 10:30A	Th7 4:00P	F8 12:00P	F8 9:00P
	S16 6:00P	M18 11:00A	T19 12:00P	W20 8:00A	Th21 10:30A	Th21 4:00P	F22 11:00A	F22 8:00P
SEPTEMBER	S30 6:00P	M1 11:00A	T2 12:00P	W3 8:00A	Th4 10:30A	Th4 4:00P	F5 11:00A	F5 8:00P
	S13 6:00P	M15 11:00A	T16 12:00P	W17 8:00A	Th18 10:30A	Th18 4:00P	F19 11:00A	F19 8:00P

Summer 2014, MV *Kennicott*
Cross Gulf Southbound

	Homer	Kodiak	Chenega Bay	Whittier	Yakutat	Juneau	Ketchikan	Bellingham
MAY	Su4 10:45A	Su4 10:45P	M5 1:15P	M5 11:45P	T6 9:00P	W7 4:00P	Th8 3:00P	S10 8:00A
	Su18 10:45A	Su18 10:45P	M19 1:15P	M19 11:45P	T20 9:00P	W21 4:00P	Th22 3:00P	S24 8:00A
JUNE	Su1 10:45A	Su1 10:45P	M2 1:15P	M2 11:45P	T3 9:00P	W4 4:00P	Th5 3:00P	S7 8:00A
	Su15 10:45A	Su15 10:45P	M16 1:15P	M16 11:45P	T17 9:00P	W18 4:00P	Th19 3:00P	S21 8:00A
JULY	Su29 10:45A	Su29 10:45P	M30 1:15P	M30 11:45P	T1 9:00P	W2 4:00P	Th3 3:00P	S5 8:00A
	Su13 10:45A	Su13 10:45P	M14 1:15P	M14 11:45P	T15 9:00P	W16 4:00P	Th17 3:00P	S19 8:00A
AUGUST	Su27 10:45A	Su27 10:45P	M28 1:15P	M28 11:45P	T29 9:00P	W30 4:00P	Th31 3:00P	S2 8:00A
	Su10 10:45A	Su10 10:45P	M11 1:15P	M11 11:45P	T12 9:00P	W13 4:00P	Th14 3:00P	S16 8:00A
	Su24 10:45A	Su24 10:45P	M25 1:15P	M25 11:45P	T26 9:00P	W27 4:00P	Th28 3:00P	S30 8:00A
SEPTEMBER	Su7 9:45A	Su7 10:45P	M8 1:15P	M8 11:45P	T9 9:00P	W10 4:00P	Th11 3:00P	S13 8:00A
	Su21 10:45A	Su21 10:45P	M22 1:15P	M22 11:45P	T23 9:00P	W24 4:00P	Th25 3:00P	S27 8:00A

See also pages 743-744 Southwest and Aleutian Chain for MV *Kennicott* service.

Vessel key (for facing page): Columbia (COL); Malaspina (MAL); Matanuska (MAT); Taku (TAK)
See pages 734-741 for additional ferry service between Petersburg, Sitka, Pelican, Angoon, Gustavus, Tenakee, Hoonah, Juneau, Haines, Skagway.
The State of Alaska reserves the right to alter, revise or cancel schedules and rates without prior notice, and assumes no responsibility for delays and/or expenses due to such modifications.

MAY 2014
Southeast Alaska/Inside Passage Northbound

	Bellingham	Prince Rupert	Ketchikan	Wrangell	Petersburg	Kake	Sitka	Juneau	Haines	Skagway
TAK		T29 7:00A	T29 3:15P	T29 10:00P	W30 1:45A	W30 6:30A	W30 5:00P	Th1 7:30A	Th1 12:00P	
MAT		S3 4:15A	S3 11:30A	S3 6:15P	S3 10:00P	Su4 2:45A	Su4 1:15P	Su4 10:30P		
MAL								S3 7:00A	S3 12:30P	S3 1:30P
COL	F2 6:00P		Su4 10:00A	Su4 4:30P	Su4 8:30P			M5 6:45A	M5 1:15P	M5 2:15P
MAL								Su4 7:00A	Su4 12:30P	Su4 1:30P
MAL								T6 7:00A	T6 12:30P	T6 1:30P
MAT		T6 3:00P	W7 12:45A	W7 7:30A	W7 11:15A			W7 9:00P	Th8 3:30A	Th8 4:30A
MAL								W7 7:00A	W7 12:30P	W7 1:30P
MAL								Th8 8:00A	Th8 1:30P	Th8 2:30P
MAL								F9 7:00A	F9 12:30P	F9 1:30P
MAT		S10 6:00A	S10 12:45P	S10 7:30P	S10 11:15P	Su11 4:00A	Su11 2:30P	Su11 11:45P		
MAL								S10 7:00A	S10 12:30P	S10 1:30P
COL	F9 6:00P		Su11 11:30A	Su11 6:30P	Su11 10:30P			M12 8:45A	M12 3:15P	M12 4:15P
MAL								Su11 7:00A	Su11 12:30P	Su11 1:30P
MAL								T13 7:00A	T13 12:30P	T13 1:30P
MAT		T13 3:00P	W14 12:45A	W14 7:30A	W14 11:45A			W14 9:45P	Th15 4:15A	Th15 5:15A
MAL								W14 7:00A	W14 12:30P	W14 1:30P
MAL								Th15 8:00A	Th15 1:30P	Th15 2:30P
MAL								F16 7:00A	F16 12:30P	F16 1:30P
MAL								S17 7:00A	S17 12:30P	S17 1:30P
MAT		S17 10:00A	S17 5:15P	Su18 12:30A	Su18 4:15A	Su18 9:00A	Su18 7:30P	M19 6:15A		
COL	F16 6:00P		Su18 9:00A	Su18 3:30P	Su18 7:30P			M19 5:45A	M19 12:15P	M19 1:15P
MAL								Su18 7:00A	Su18 12:30P	Su18 1:30P
MAL								T20 7:00A	T20 12:30P	T20 1:30P
MAT		T20 4:15P	W21 12:30A	W21 7:30A	W21 11:15A			W21 9:30P	Th22 4:00A	Th22 5:00A
MAL								W21 7:00A	W21 12:30P	W21 1:30P
MAL								Th22 8:00A	Th22 1:30P	Th22 2:30P
MAL								F23 7:00A	F23 12:30P	F23 1:30P
MAT		S24 5:30A	S24 12:45P	S24 7:30P	S24 11:15P	Su25 3:45A	Su25 2:15P	Su25 11:30P		
MAL								S24 7:00A	S24 12:30P	S24 1:30P
COL	F23 6:00P		Su25 11:30A	Su25 6:30P	Su25 10:30P			M26 8:45A	M26 3:15P	M26 4:15P
MAL								Su25 7:00A	Su25 12:30P	Su25 1:30P
MAL								T27 7:00A	T27 12:30P	T27 1:30P
MAT		T27 11:30A	T27 6:45P	W28 1:30A	W28 5:15A			W28 4:45P	W28 11:15P	Th29 12:15A
MAL								W28 7:00A	W28 12:30P	W28 1:30P
MAL								Th29 8:00A	Th29 1:30P	Th29 2:30P
MAL								F30 7:00A	F30 12:30P	F30 1:30P
MAT		S31 6:15A	S31 3:30P	S31 10:45P	Su1 2:30A	Su1 7:15A	Su1 5:45P	M2 3:00A		
MAL								S31 7:00A	S31 12:30P	S31 1:30P
COL	F30 6:00P		Su1 10:30A	Su1 5:00P	Su1 9:00P			M2 8:45A	M2 3:15P	M2 4:15P

MAY 2014
Southeast Alaska/Inside Passage Southbound

	Skagway	Haines	Juneau	Sitka	Kake	Petersburg	Wrangell	Ketchikan	Prince Rupert	Bellingham
TAK		Th1 2:00P	Th1 8:30P			F2 5:00A	F2 8:45A	F2 2:45P		
MAT								F2 4:45P	S3 12:15A	
MAL	S3 3:00P	S3 5:00P	S3 9:30P							
MAL	Su4 3:00P	Su4 5:00P	Su4 9:30P							
MAT			M5 4:00A			M5 2:15P	M5 6:15P	T6 3:30A	T6 11:00A	
COL	M5 5:15P	M5 8:15P	T6 4:15A	T6 4:15P		W7 2:30A	W7 6:30A	W7 5:00P		F9 8:00A
MAL	T6 3:00P	T6 5:00P	T6 9:30P							
MAL	W7 3:00P	W7 5:00P	W7 9:30P							
MAT	Th8 7:30A	Th8 10:30A	Th8 6:15P		F9 2:45A	F9 7:30A	F9 11:30A	F9 6:45P	S10 2:00A	
MAL	Th8 4:00P	Th8 6:00P	Th8 10:30P							
MAL	F9 3:00P	F9 5:00P	F9 9:30P							
MAL	S10 3:00P	S10 5:00P	S10 9:30P							
MAL	Su11 3:00P	Su11 5:00P	Su11 9:30P							
MAT			M12 2:45A			M12 11:45A	M12 3:45P	T13 3:30A	T13 11:00A	
COL	M12 6:45P	M12 9:30P	T13 4:15A	T13 4:00P		W14 2:15A	W14 6:15A	W14 5:00P		F16 8:00A
MAL	T13 3:00P	T13 5:00P	T13 9:30P							
MAL	W14 3:00P	W14 5:00P	W14 9:30P							
MAT	Th15 8:15A	Th15 11:15A	Th15 8:15P		F16 5:45A	F16 11:15A	F16 3:15P	F16 10:30P	S17 6:00A	
MAL	Th15 4:00P	Th15 6:00P	Th15 10:30P							
MAL	F16 3:00P	F16 5:00P	F16 9:30P							
MAL	S17 3:00P	S17 5:00P	S17 9:30P							
MAL	Su18 3:00P	Su18 5:00P	Su18 9:30P							
MAT			M19 8:15A			M19 5:15P	M19 9:15P	T20 4:45A	T20 12:15P	
COL	M19 4:15P	M19 7:15P	T20 3:00A	T20 3:30P		W21 2:45A	W21 6:45A	W21 5:00P		F23 8:00A
MAL	T20 3:00P	T20 5:00P	T20 9:30P							
MAL	W21 3:00P	W21 5:00P	W21 9:30P							
MAT	Th22 8:00A	Th22 11:00A	Th22 5:30P		F23 2:00A	F23 6:45A	F23 10:45A	F23 6:15P	S24 1:45A	
MAL	Th22 4:00P	Th22 6:00P	Th22 10:30P							
MAL	F23 3:00P	F23 5:00P	F23 9:30P							
MAL	S24 3:00P	S24 5:00P	S24 9:30P							
MAL	Su25 3:00P	Su25 5:00P	Su25 9:30P							
MAT			M26 2:30A			M26 11:30A	M26 3:30P	T27 12:00A	T27 7:30A	
COL	M26 6:15P	M26 9:15P	T27 4:00A	T27 3:45P		W28 2:00A	W28 6:00A	W28 5:00P		F30 8:00A
MAL	T27 3:00P	T27 5:00P	T27 9:30P							
MAL	W28 3:00P	W28 5:00P	W28 9:30P							
MAT	Th29 3:15A	Th29 6:15A	Th29 2:45P		Th29 11:15P	F30 4:00A	F30 8:00A	F30 6:45P	S31 2:15A	
MAL	Th29 4:00P	Th29 6:00P	Th29 10:30P							
MAL	F30 3:00P	F30 5:00P	F30 9:30P							
MAL	S31 3:00P	S31 5:00P	S31 9:30P							

June 2014

For updated schedules and fares, go to www.ferryalaska.com

Southeast Alaska/Inside Passage Northbound

	Bellingham	Prince Rupert	Ketchikan	Wrangell	Petersburg	Kake	Sitka	Juneau	Haines	Skagway
MAT		S31 6:15A	S31 3:30P	S31 10:45P	Su1 2:30A	Su1 7:15A	Su1 5:45P	M2 3:00A		
MAL								S31 7:00A	S31 12:30P	S31 1:30P
COL	F30 6:00P		Su1 10:30A	Su1 5:00P	Su1 9:00P			M2 8:45A	M2 3:15P	M2 4:15P
MAL								Su1 7:00A	Su1 12:30P	Su1 1:30P
MAL								T3 7:00A	T3 12:30P	T3 1:30P
MAT		T3 3:00P	T3 11:45P	W4 6:30A	W4 10:15A			W4 8:45P	Th5 3:15P	Th5 4:15A
MAL								W4 7:00A	W4 12:30P	W4 1:30P
MAL								Th5 8:00A	Th5 1:30P	Th5 2:30P
MAL								F6 7:00A	F6 12:30P	F6 1:30P
MAT		S7 6:15A	S7 2:30P	S7 9:45P	Su8 1:30A			Su8 9:30A		
MAL								S7 7:00A	S7 12:30P	S7 1:30P
COL	F6 6:00P		Su8 10:00A	Su8 4:30P	Su8 8:30P			M9 6:45A	M9 1:15P	M9 2:15P
MAL								Su8 7:00A	Su8 12:30P	Su8 1:30P
MAT		M9 11:00P	T10 8:45A	T10 4:30P	T10 8:30P	W11 1:15A		W11 1:45P	W11 8:15P	W11 9:15P
MAL								T10 7:00A	T10 12:30P	T10 1:30P
MAL								W11 7:00A	W11 12:30P	W11 1:30P
MAL								Th12 8:00A	Th12 1:30P	Th12 2:30P
MAL								F13 7:00A	F13 12:30P	F13 1:30P
MAT		S14 5:15A	S14 1:30P	S14 8:15P	Su15 12:00A			Su15 8:00A		
MAL								S14 7:00A	S14 12:30P	S14 1:30P
COL	F13 6:00P		Su15 9:00A	Su15 3:30P	Su15 7:30P			M16 5:45A	M16 12:15P	M16 1:15P
MAL								Su15 7:00A	Su15 12:30P	Su15 1:30P
MAL								T17 7:00A	T17 12:30P	T17 1:30P
MAT		T17 3:30P	T17 10:45P	W18 5:30A	W18 9:15A			W18 8:45P	Th19 3:15A	Th19 4:15A
MAL								W18 7:00A	W18 12:30P	W18 1:30P
MAL								Th19 8:00A	Th19 1:30P	Th19 2:30P
MAL								F20 7:00A	F20 12:30P	F20 1:30P
MAT		S21 6:15A	S21 3:00P	S21 9:45P	Su22 1:30A	Su22 6:15A	Su22 6:30P	M23 3:45A		
MAL								S21 7:00A	S21 12:30P	S21 1:30P
COL	F20 6:00P		Su22 10:00A	Su22 5:00P	Su22 9:00P			M23 7:15A	M23 1:45P	M23 2:45P
MAL								Su22 7:00A	Su22 12:30P	Su22 1:30P
MAL								T24 7:00A	T24 12:30P	T24 1:30P
MAT		T24 3:00P	W25 12:00A	W25 7:15A	W25 11:00A			W25 10:30P	Th26 5:00A	Th26 6:00A
MAL								W25 7:00A	W25 12:30P	W25 1:30P
MAL								Th26 8:00A	Th26 1:30P	Th26 2:30P
MAL								F27 7:00A	F27 12:30P	F27 1:30P
MAL								S28 7:00A	S28 12:30P	S28 1:30P
MAT		S28 9:00A	S28 4:15P	S28 11:00P	Su29 2:45A			Su29 10:45A		
COL	F27 6:00P		Su29 9:00A	Su29 3:30P	Su29 7:30P			M30 6:45A	M30 1:15P	M30 2:15P
MAL								Su29 7:00A	Su29 12:30P	Su29 1:30P
TAK		Su29 6:15P	M30 4:00A	M30 10:45A	M30 2:30P	M30 7:15P	T1 5:45A	T1 2:45P		

Vessel key: Columbia (COL); Malaspina (MAL); Matanuska (MAT); Taku (TAK)
See pages 734-741 for additional ferry service between Petersburg, Sitka, Pelican, Angoon, Gustavus, Tenakee, Hoonah, Juneau, Haines, Skagway. See also Kennicott service, page 722.
The State of Alaska reserves the right to alter, revise or cancel schedules and rates without prior notice, and assumes no responsibility for delays and/or expenses due to such modifications.

For updated schedules and fares, go to www.ferryalaska.com

JUNE 2014
Southeast Alaska/Inside Passage Southbound

	Skagway	Haines	Juneau	Sitka	Kake	Petersburg	Wrangell	Ketchikan	Prince Rupert	Bellingham
MAL	Su1 3:00P	Su1 5:00P	Su1 9:30P							
MAT			M2 5:00A			M2 2:00P	M2 6:00P	T3 3:30A	T3 11:00A	
COL	M2 7:15P	M2 10:15P	T3 8:15A	T3 8:15P		W4 6:30A	W4 10:30A	W4 5:00P		F6 8:00A
MAL	T3 3:00P	T3 5:00P	T3 9:30P							
MAL	W4 3:00P	W4 5:00P	W4 9:30P							
MAT	Th5 7:15A	Th5 10:15A	Th5 6:15P		F6 2:45A	F6 7:30A	F6 11:30A	F6 6:45P	S7 2:15A	
MAL	Th5 4:00P	Th5 6:00P	Th5 10:30P							
MAL	F6 3:00P	F6 5:00P	F6 9:30P							
MAL	S7 3:00P	S7 5:00P	S7 9:30P							
MAT			Su8 1:00P			Su8 10:00P	M9 2:00A	M9 11:30A	M9 7:00P	
MAL	Su8 3:00P	Su8 5:00P	Su8 9:30P							
COL	M9 5:15P	M9 8:15P	T10 2:45A	T10 2:45P		W11 1:45A	W11 5:45A	W11 5:00P		F13 8:00A
MAL	T10 3:00P	T10 5:00P	T10 9:30P							
MAL	W11 3:00P	W11 5:00P	W11 9:30P							
MAT	Th12 12:15A	Th12 3:15A	Th12 11:45A		Th12 8:45P	F13 2:00A	F13 5:45A	F13 5:45P	S14 1:15A	
MAL	Th12 4:00P	Th12 6:00P	Th12 10:30P							
MAL	F13 3:00P	F13 5:00P	F13 9:30P							
MAL	S14 3:00P	S14 5:00P	S14 9:30P							
MAT			Su15 12:00P	M16 12:15A	M16 12:15P	M16 5:30P	M16 9:30P	T17 5:00A	T17 12:30P	
MAL	Su15 3:00P	Su15 5:00P	Su15 9:30P							
COL	M16 4:15P	M16 7:15P	T17 2:15A	T17 2:15P		W18 2:45A	W18 6:45A	W18 5:00P		F20 8:00A
MAL	T17 3:00P	T17 5:00P	T17 9:30P							
MAL	W18 3:00P	W18 5:00P	W18 9:30P							
MAT	Th19 7:15A	Th19 10:15A	Th19 5:15P		F20 1:45A	F20 6:30A	F20 10:30A	F20 6:45P	S21 2:15A	
MAL	Th19 4:00P	Th19 6:00P	Th19 10:30P							
MAL	F20 3:00P	F20 5:00P	F20 9:30P							
MAL	S21 3:00P	S21 5:00P	S21 9:30P							
MAL	Su22 3:00P	Su22 5:00P	Su22 9:30P							
MAT			M23 5:15A			M23 2:15P	M23 6:15P	T24 3:30A	T24 11:00A	
COL	M23 5:45P	M23 8:45P	T24 2:45A	T24 2:30P		W25 12:45A	W25 4:45A	W25 5:00P		F27 8:00A
MAL	T24 3:00P	T24 5:00P	T24 9:30P							
MAL	W25 3:00P	W25 5:00P	W25 9:30P							
MAT	Th26 9:00A	Th26 12:00P	Th26 8:00P		F27 5:30A	F27 10:30A	F27 2:15P	F27 9:30P	S28 5:00A	
MAL	Th26 4:00P	Th26 6:00P	Th26 10:30P							
MAL	F27 3:00P	F27 5:00P	F27 9:30P							
MAL	S28 3:00P	S28 5:00P	S28 9:30P							
TAK								Su29 7:45A	Su29 3:15P	
MAT			Su29 12:15P	M30 12:30A		M30 12:45P	M30 4:45P	T1 2:30A	T1 10:00A	
MAL	Su29 3:00P	Su29 5:00P	Su29 9:30P							
COL	M30 5:15P	M30 8:15P	T1 7:15A	T1 7:15P		W2 5:30A	W2 9:30A	W2 5:00P		F4 8:00A

Vessel key: Columbia (COL); Malaspina (MAL); Matanuska (MAT); Taku (TAK)
See pages 734-741 for additional ferry service between Petersburg, Sitka, Pelican, Angoon, Gustavus, Tenakee, Hoonah, Juneau, Haines, Skagway. See also Kennicott service, page 722.
The State of Alaska reserves the right to alter, revise or cancel schedules and rates without prior notice, and assumes no responsibility for delays and/or expenses due to such modifications.

JULY 2014

For updated schedules and fares, go to www.ferryalaska.com

Southeast Alaska/Inside Passage Northbound

	Bellingham	Prince Rupert	Ketchikan	Wrangell	Petersburg	Kake	Sitka	Juneau	Haines	Skagway
MAL								T1 7:00A	T1 12:30P	T1 1:30P
MAT		T1 2:00P	T1 9:45P	W2 4:30A	W2 8:15A			W2 7:45P	Th3 2:15A	Th3 3:15A
MAL								W2 7:00A	W2 12:30P	W2 1:30P
TAK		Th3 6:30A	Th3 1:45P	Th3 8:30P	F4 12:15A	F4 5:00A		F4 12:30P		
MAL								Th3 8:00A	Th3 1:30P	Th3 2:30P
MAL								F4 7:00A	F4 12:30P	F4 1:30P
MAT		S5 4:45A	S5 1:00P	S5 7:45P	S5 11:30P			Su6 7:30A		
MAL								S5 7:00A	S5 12:30P	S5 1:30P
COL	F4 6:00P		Su6 9:00A	Su6 3:30P	Su6 7:30P			M7 5:45A	M7 12:15P	M7 1:15P
MAL								Su6 7:00A	Su6 12:30P	Su6 1:30P
TAK		Su6 6:00P	M7 4:15A	M7 11:00A	M7 2:45P	M7 7:30P	T8 6:00A	T8 3:00P		
MAL								T8 7:00A	T8 12:30P	T8 1:30P
MAT		T8 2:00P	T8 10:45P	W9 6:00A	W9 9:45A			W9 9:15P	Th10 3:45A	Th10 4:45A
MAL								W9 7:00A	W9 12:30P	W9 1:30P
MAL								Th10 8:00A	Th10 1:30P	Th10 2:30P
TAK		Th10 8:30A	Th10 4:45P	Th10 11:30P	F11 3:15A	F11 8:00A		F11 3:30P		
MAL								F11 7:00A	F11 12:30P	F11 1:30P
MAT		S12 6:15A	S12 2:30P	S12 9:15P	Su13 1:00A			Su13 9:00A		
MAL								S12 7:00A	S12 12:30P	S12 1:30P
COL	F11 6:00P		Su13 2:00P	Su13 9:30P	M14 1:30A			M14 11:45A	M14 6:15P	M14 7:15P
MAL								Su13 7:00A	Su13 12:30P	Su13 1:30P
TAK		Su13 9:15P	M14 4:30A	M14 11:15A	M14 3:00P	M14 7:45P	T15 6:15A	T15 3:15P		
MAL								T15 7:00A	T15 12:30P	T15 1:30P
MAT		T15 2:00P	T15 9:45P	W16 4:30A	W16 8:15A			W16 7:45P	Th17 2:15A	Th17 3:15A
MAL								W16 7:00A	W16 12:30P	W16 1:30P
TAK		Th17 4:45A	Th17 12:00P	Th17 6:45P	Th17 10:30P	F18 3:15A		F18 10:45A		
MAL								Th17 8:00A	Th17 1:30P	Th17 2:30P
MAL								F18 7:00A	F18 12:30P	F18 1:30P
MAT		S19 6:15A	S19 1:30P	S19 8:15P	Su20 12:00A			Su20 8:00A		
MAL								S19 7:00A	S19 12:30P	S19 1:30P
COL	F18 6:00P		Su20 9:00A	Su20 3:30P	Su20 7:30P			M21 5:45A	M21 12:15P	M21 1:15P
MAL								Su20 7:00A	Su20 12:30P	Su20 1:30P
TAK		Su20 4:00P	Su20 11:15P	M21 6:00A	M21 9:45A	M21 2:30P	T22 1:00A	T22 10:00A		
MAL								T22 7:00A	T22 12:30P	T22 1:30P
MAT		T22 2:00P	T22 10:45P	W23 6:00A	W23 9:45A			W23 9:15P	Th24 3:45A	Th24 4:45A
MAL								W23 7:00A	W23 12:30P	W23 1:30P
TAK		Th24 7:00A	Th24 2:15P	Th24 9:00P	F25 12:45A	F25 5:30A		F25 1:00P		
MAL								Th24 8:00A	Th24 1:30P	Th24 2:30P
MAL								F25 7:00A	F25 1:00P	F25 2:00P
MAT		S26 5:45A	S26 1:00P	S26 7:45P	S26 11:30P			Su27 7:30A		
MAL								S26 7:00A	S26 12:30P	S26 1:30P
COL	F25 6:00P		Su27 8:00A	Su27 2:30P	Su27 6:30P			M28 4:45A	M28 11:15A	M28 12:15P
MAL								Su27 7:00A	Su27 12:30P	Su27 1:30P
TAK		Su27 9:15P	M28 4:00A	M28 10:45A	M28 2:30P	M28 7:15P	T29 5:45A	T29 2:45P		
MAL								T29 7:00A	T29 12:30P	T29 1:30P
MAT		T29 1:00P	T29 8:45P	W30 3:30A	W30 7:15A			W30 6:45P	Th31 1:15A	Th31 2:15A
MAL								W30 7:00A	W30 12:30P	W30 1:30P
MAL								Th31 8:00A	Th31 1:30P	Th31 2:30P

Vessel key: Columbia (COL); Malaspina (MAL); Matanuska (MAT); Taku (TAK)
See pages 734-741 for additional ferry service between Petersburg, Sitka, Pelican, Angoon, Gustavus, Tenakee, Hoonah, Juneau, Haines, Skagway. See also Kennicott service, page 722.
The State of Alaska reserves the right to alter, revise or cancel schedules and rates without prior notice, and assumes no responsibility for delays and/or expenses due to such modifications.

JULY 2014
Southeast Alaska/Inside Passage Southbound

ALASKA MARINE HIGHWAY SCHEDULES & TARIFFS

	Skagway	Haines	Juneau	Sitka	Kake	Petersburg	Wrangell	Ketchikan	Prince Rupert	Bellingham
MAL	T1 3:00P	T1 5:00P	T1 9:30P							
TAK			T1 5:45P		W2 2:00A	W2 6:45A	W2 10:45A	W2 8:00P	Th3 3:30A	
MAL	W2 3:00P	W2 5:00P	W2 9:30P							
MAT	Th3 6:15A	Th3 9:15A	Th3 5:15P			F4 2:15A	F4 7:15A	F4 5:15P	S5 12:45A	
MAL	Th3 4:00P	Th3 6:00P	Th3 10:30P							
MAL	F4 3:00P	F4 5:00P	F4 9:30P							
TAK			F4 3:30P	S5 3:45A	S5 12:30P	S5 5:15P	S5 9:15P	Su6 7:30A	Su6 3:00P	
MAL	S5 3:00P	S5 5:00P	S5 9:30P							
MAT			Su6 11:30A	Su6 11:45P		M7 11:45A	M7 3:45P	T8 2:30A	T8 10:00A	
MAL	Su6 3:00P	Su6 5:00P	Su6 9:30P							
COL	M7 4:15P	M7 7:15P	T8 1:30A	T8 1:15P		T8 11:30P	W9 3:30A	W9 5:00P		F11 8:00A
MAL	T8 3:00P	T8 5:00P	T8 9:30P							
TAK			T8 8:00P		W9 4:15A	W9 9:00A	W9 1:00P	W9 10:00P	Th10 5:30A	
MAL	W9 3:00P	W9 5:00P	W9 9:30P							
MAT	Th10 7:45A	Th10 10:45A	Th10 5:30P			F11 2:30A	F11 7:30A	F11 6:45P	S12 2:15A	
MAL	Th10 4:00P	Th10 6:00P	Th10 10:30P							
MAL	F11 3:00P	F11 5:00P	F11 9:30P							
TAK			F11 9:00P	S12 9:30A	S12 6:15P	S12 11:00P	Su13 3:00A	Su13 10:45A	Su13 6:15P	
MAL	S12 3:00P	S12 5:00P	S12 9:30P							
MAT			Su13 11:30A	Su13 11:45P		M14 12:45P	M14 4:45P	T15 2:30A	T15 10:00A	
MAL	Su13 3:00P	Su13 5:00P	Su13 9:30P							
COL	M14 9:45P	T15 12:45A	T15 6:45A	T15 6:45P		W16 5:00A	W16 9:00A	W16 5:00P		F18 8:00A
MAL	T15 3:00P	T15 5:00P	T15 9:30P							
TAK			T15 5:15P		W16 1:30A	W16 6:15A	W16 10:15A	W16 6:15P	Th17 1:45A	
MAL	W16 3:00P	W16 5:00P	W16 9:30P							
MAT	Th17 6:15A	Th17 9:15A	Th17 5:45P			F18 2:45A	F18 7:45A	F18 6:45P	S19 2:15A	
MAL	Th17 4:00P	Th17 6:00P	Th17 10:30P							
MAL	F18 3:00P	F18 5:00P	F18 9:30P							
TAK			F18 3:45P	S19 4:00A	S19 12:45P	S19 5:30P	S19 9:30P	Su20 5:30A	Su20 1:00P	
MAL	S19 3:00P	S19 5:00P	S19 9:30P							
MAT			Su20 11:30A	Su20 11:45P		M21 11:45A	M21 3:45P	T22 2:30A	T22 10:00A	
MAL	Su20 3:00P	Su20 5:00P	Su20 9:30P							
COL	M21 4:15P	M21 7:15P	T22 1:30A	T22 1:30P		T22 11:45P	W23 3:45A	W23 5:00P		F25 8:00A
MAL	T22 3:00P	T22 5:00P	T22 9:30P							
TAK			T22 6:30P		W23 3:45A	W23 8:30A	W23 12:30P	W23 8:30P	Th24 4:00A	
MAL	W23 3:00P	W23 5:00P	W23 9:30P							
MAT	Th24 7:45A	Th24 10:45A	Th24 5:45P			F25 2:45A	F25 7:45A	F25 6:15P	S26 1:45A	
MAL	Th24 4:00P	Th24 6:00P	Th24 10:30P							
TAK			F25 2:45P	S26 2:45A	S26 6:00P	S26 10:45P	Su27 2:45A	Su27 10:45A	Su27 6:15P	
MAL	F25 3:00P	F25 5:00P	F25 9:30P							
MAL	S26 3:00P	S26 5:00P	S26 9:30P							
MAT			Su27 11:00A	Su27 11:15P		M28 11:30A	M28 3:30P	T29 1:30A	T29 9:00A	
MAL	Su27 3:00P	Su27 5:00P	Su27 10:00P							
COL	M28 3:15P	M28 6:15P	T29 5:45A	T29 5:45P		W30 4:00A	W30 8:00A	W30 5:00P		F1 8:00A
MAL	T29 3:00P	T29 5:00P	T29 9:30P							
TAK			T29 8:45P		W30 7:15A	W30 12:15P	W30 4:15P	W30 11:30P	Th31 7:00A	
MAL	W30 3:00P	W30 5:00P	W30 9:30P							
MAT	Th31 5:15A	Th31 8:15A	Th31 4:15P			F1 1:15A	F1 6:15A	F1 4:45P	S2 12:15A	
MAL	Th31 4:00P	Th31 6:00P	Th31 10:30P							

Vessel key: Columbia (COL); Malaspina (MAL); Matanuska (MAT); Taku (TAK)
See pages 734-741 for additional ferry service between Petersburg, Sitka, Pelican, Angoon, Gustavus, Tenakee, Hoonah, Juneau, Haines, Skagway. See also Kennicott service, page 722.
The State of Alaska reserves the right to alter, revise or cancel schedules and rates without prior notice, and assumes no responsibility for delays and/or expenses due to such modifications.

AUGUST 2014

For updated schedules and fares, go to www.ferryalaska.com

Southeast Alaska/Inside Passage Northbound

	Bellingham	Prince Rupert	Ketchikan	Wrangell	Petersburg	Kake	Sitka	Juneau	Haines	Skagway
TAK		Th31 10:00A	Th31 5:15P	F1 12:00A	F1 3:45A	F1 8:30A		F1 4:00P		
MAL								F1 7:00A	F1 12:30P	F1 1:30P
MAT		S2 4:15A	S2 12:30P	S2 7:15P	S2 11:00P			Su3 7:15A		
MAL								S2 7:00A	S2 12:30P	S2 1:30P
COL	F1 6:00P		Su3 10:00A	Su3 4:30P	Su3 8:30P			M4 6:45A	M4 1:15P	M4 2:15P
MAL								Su3 7:00A	Su3 12:30P	Su3 1:30P
TAK		Su3 7:00P	M4 3:15A	M4 10:00A	M4 1:45P	M4 6:30P	T5 5:00A	T5 2:00P		
MAL								T5 7:00A	T5 12:30P	T5 1:30P
MAT		T5 2:00P	T5 10:15P	W6 5:00A	W6 8:45A			W6 8:15P	Th7 2:45A	Th7 3:45A
MAL								W6 7:00A	W6 12:30P	W6 1:30P
TAK		Th7 7:30A	Th7 2:30P	Th7 9:15P	F8 1:00A	F8 5:45A		F8 1:30P		
MAL								Th7 8:00A	Th7 1:30P	Th7 2:30P
MAL								F8 7:00A	F8 12:30P	F8 1:30P
MAT		S9 5:15A	S9 12:30P	S9 7:15P	S9 11:15P			Su10 7:30A		
MAL								S9 7:00A	S9 12:30P	S9 1:30P
COL	F8 6:00P		Su10 1:00P	Su10 8:00P	M11 12:15A			M11 10:30A	M11 5:00P	M11 6:00P
MAL								Su10 7:00A	Su10 12:30P	Su10 1:30P
TAK		Su10 10:00P	M11 7:30A	M11 2:15P	M11 6:00P	M11 11:00P	T12 10:45A	T12 7:45P		
MAL								T12 7:00A	T12 12:30P	T12 1:30P
MAT		T12 12:30P	T12 8:15P	W13 3:00A	W13 7:00A			W13 7:30P	Th14 2:00A	Th14 3:00A
MAL								W13 7:00A	W13 12:30P	W13 1:30P
MAL								Th14 8:00A	Th14 1:30P	Th14 2:30P
TAK		Th14 9:30A	Th14 4:45P	Th14 11:30P	F15 3:15A	F15 8:00A		F15 3:30P		
MAL								F15 7:00A	F15 12:30P	F15 1:30P
MAT		S16 4:15A	S16 12:00P	S16 6:45P	S16 10:45P			Su17 7:15A		
MAL								S16 7:00A	S16 12:30P	S16 1:30P
COL	F15 6:00P		Su17 9:00A	Su17 3:30P	Su17 7:15P			M18 5:30A	M18 12:00P	M18 1:00P
MAL								Su17 7:00A	Su17 12:30P	Su17 1:30P
TAK		Su17 6:45P	M18 3:00A	M18 9:45A	M18 1:30P	M18 6:15P	T19 4:45A	T19 1:45P		
MAL								T19 7:00A	T19 12:30P	T19 1:30P
MAT		T19 2:00P	T19 10:45P	W20 5:30A	W20 9:15A			W20 8:15P	Th21 2:45A	Th21 3:45A
MAL								W20 7:00A	W20 12:30P	W20 1:30P
TAK		Th21 7:45A	Th21 2:45P	Th21 9:30P	F22 1:15A	F22 6:00A		F22 1:30P		
MAL								Th21 8:00A	Th21 1:30P	Th21 2:30P
MAL								F22 7:00A	F22 12:30P	F22 1:30P
MAT		S23 3:45A	S23 12:00P	S23 6:45P	S23 10:30P			Su24 7:30A		
MAL								S23 7:00A	S23 12:30P	S23 1:30P
COL	F22 6:00P		Su24 1:00P	Su24 8:00P	M25 12:00A			M25 10:15A	M25 4:45P	M25 5:45P
MAL								Su24 7:00A	Su24 12:30P	Su24 1:30P
TAK		Su24 9:15P	M25 8:00A	M25 2:45P	M25 6:30P	M25 11:15P	T26 9:45A	T26 6:45P		
MAL								T26 7:00A	T26 12:30P	T26 1:30P
MAT		T26 12:00P	T26 8:15P	W27 3:00A	W27 6:45A			W27 7:00P	Th28 1:30A	Th28 2:30A
MAL								W27 7:00A	W27 12:30P	W27 1:30P
MAL								Th28 8:00A	Th28 1:30P	Th28 2:30P
TAK		Th28 9:15A	Th28 4:30P	Th28 11:15P	F29 3:00A	F29 7:45A		F29 3:15P		
MAL								F29 7:00A	F29 12:30P	F29 1:30P
MAT		S30 6:15A	S30 3:00P	S30 10:15P	Su31 2:30A			Su31 10:30A		
MAL								S30 7:00A	S30 12:30P	S30 1:30P
COL	F29 6:00P		Su31 10:00A	Su31 4:30P	Su31 8:30P			M1 6:45A	M1 1:15P	M1 2:15P

Vessel key: Columbia (COL); Malaspina (MAL); Matanuska (MAT); Taku (TAK)
See pages 734-741 for additional ferry service between Petersburg, Sitka, Pelican, Angoon, Gustavus, Tenakee, Hoonah, Juneau, Haines, Skagway. See also Kennicott service, page 722.
The State of Alaska reserves the right to alter, revise or cancel schedules and rates without prior notice, and assumes no responsibility for delays and/or expenses due to such modifications.

AUGUST 2014
Southeast Alaska/Inside Passage Southbound

ALASKA MARINE HIGHWAY SCHEDULES & TARIFFS

	Skagway	Haines	Juneau	Sitka	Kake	Petersburg	Wrangell	Ketchikan	Prince Rupert	Bellingham
MAL	F1 3:00P	F1 5:00P	F1 9:30P							
TAK			F1 7:30P	S2 7:45A	S2 4:30P	S2 9:15P	Su3 1:15A	Su3 8:30A	Su3 4:00P	
MAL	S2 3:00P	S2 5:00P	S2 9:30P							
MAT			Su3 9:30A	Su3 9:45P		M4 9:45A	M4 1:45P	T5 2:30A	T5 10:00A	
MAL	Su3 3:00P	Su3 5:00P	Su3 9:30P							
COL	M4 5:15P	M4 8:15P	T5 5:15A	T5 6:00P		W6 6:30P	W6 10:30A	W6 5:00P		F8 8:00A
MAL	T5 3:00P	T5 5:00P	T5 9:30P							
TAK			T5 8:45P		W6 5:30A	W6 10:15A	W6 2:15P	W6 9:15P	Th7 4:30A	
MAL	W6 3:00P	W6 5:00P	W6 9:30P							
MAT	Th7 6:45A	Th7 9:45A	Th7 4:45P			F8 1:45A	F8 5:45A	F8 5:45P	S9 1:15A	
MAL	Th7 4:00P	Th7 6:00P	Th7 10:30P							
MAL	F8 3:00P	F8 5:00P	F8 9:30P							
TAK			F8 9:00P	S9 9:15A	S9 6:15P	Su10 12:30A	Su10 4:30A	Su10 11:45A	Su10 7:00P	
MAL	S9 3:00P	S9 5:00P	S9 9:30P							
MAT			Su10 10:00A	Su10 10:15P		M11 11:30A	M11 3:30P	T12 1:00A	T12 8:30A	
MAL	Su10 3:00P	Su10 5:00P	Su10 9:30P							
COL	M11 9:00P	T12 12:00A	T12 6:00A	T12 6:00P		W13 4:15A	W13 8:15A	W13 5:00P		F15 8:00A
MAL	T12 3:00P	T12 5:00P	T12 9:30P							
TAK			T12 9:30P		W13 7:45A	W13 12:30P	W13 4:30P	W13 11:30P	Th14 6:30A	
MAL	W13 3:00P	W13 5:00P	W13 9:30P							
MAT	Th14 6:00A	Th14 9:00A	Th14 5:15P			F15 2:15A	F15 7:15A	F15 4:45P	S16 12:15A	
MAL	Th14 4:00P	Th14 6:00P	Th14 10:30P							
MAL	F15 3:00P	F15 5:00P	F15 9:30P							
TAK			F15 7:30P	S16 7:45A	S16 4:15P	S16 9:00P	Su17 1:00A	Su17 8:15A	Su17 3:45P	
MAL	S16 3:00P	S16 5:00P	S16 9:30P							
MAT			Su17 10:00A	Su17 10:15P		M18 10:15A	M18 2:15P	T19 2:30A	T19 10:00A	
MAL	Su17 3:00P	Su17 5:00P	Su17 9:30P							
COL	M18 3:30P	M18 6:30P	T19 12:30A	T19 12:15P		T19 11:15P	W20 3:15A	W20 5:00P		F22 8:00A
MAL	T19 3:00P	T19 5:00P	T19 9:30P							
TAK			T19 8:45P		W20 5:30A	W20 10:15A	W20 2:15P	W20 9:30P	Th21 4:45A	
MAL	W20 3:00P	W20 5:00P	W20 9:30P							
MAT	Th21 6:45A	Th21 9:45A	Th21 5:15P			F22 2:15A	F22 7:15A	F22 4:15P	F22 11:45P	
MAL	Th21 4:00P	Th21 6:00P	Th21 10:30P							
MAL	F22 3:00P	F22 5:00P	F22 9:30P							
TAK			F22 8:30P	S23 8:45A	S23 6:45P	S23 11:30P	Su24 3:30A	Su24 10:45A	Su24 6:15P	
MAL	S23 3:00P	S23 5:00P	S23 9:30P							
MAT			Su24 10:00A	Su24 10:00P		M25 10:00A	M25 1:45P	T26 12:30A	T26 8:00A	
MAL	Su24 3:00P	Su24 5:00P	Su24 9:30P							
COL	M25 8:45P	M25 11:45P	T26 5:45A	T26 5:30P		W27 3:45A	W27 7:45A	W27 5:00P		F29 8:00A
MAL	T26 3:00P	T26 5:00P	T26 9:30P							
TAK			T26 9:00P		W27 6:15A	W27 11:30A	W27 3:30P	W27 10:45P	Th28 6:15A	
MAL	W27 3:00P	W27 5:00P	W27 9:30P							
MAT	Th28 5:30A	Th28 8:30A	Th28 4:45P			F29 1:45A	F29 6:45A	F29 6:45P	S30 2:15A	
MAL	Th28 4:00P	Th28 6:00P	Th28 10:30P							

Vessel key: Columbia (COL); Malaspina (MAL); Matanuska (MAT); Taku (TAK)
See pages 734-741 for additional ferry service between Petersburg, Sitka, Pelican, Angoon, Gustavus, Tenakee, Hoonah, Juneau, Haines, Skagway. See also Kennicott service, page 722.
The State of Alaska reserves the right to alter, revise or cancel schedules and rates without prior notice, and assumes no responsibility for delays and/or expenses due to such modifications.

SEPTEMBER 2014

For updated schedules and fares, go to www.ferryalaska.com

Southeast Alaska/Inside Passage Northbound

	Bellingham	Prince Rupert	Ketchikan	Wrangell	Petersburg	Kake	Sitka	Juneau	Haines	Skagway
COL	F29 6:00P		Su31 10:00A	Su31 4:30P	Su31 8:30P			M1 6:45A	M1 1:15P	M1 2:15P
MAL								Su31 7:00A	Su31 12:30P	Su31 1:30P
TAK		Su31 6:00P	M1 1:15A	M1 8:00A	M1 11:45A	M1 4:30P	T2 3:00A	T2 12:00P		
MAL								T2 7:00A	T2 12:30P	T2 1:30P
MAT		T2 2:00P	T2 10:15P	W3 5:00A	W3 8:45A			W3 7:15P	Th4 1:45A	Th4 2:45A
MAL								W3 7:00A	W3 12:30P	W3 1:30P
TAK		Th4 5:30A	Th4 2:45P	Th4 9:30P	F5 1:15A	F5 6:00A		F5 1:30P		
MAL								Th4 8:00A	Th4 1:30P	Th4 2:30P
MAL								F5 7:00A	F5 12:30P	F5 1:30P
MAT		S6 6:15A	S6 2:30P	S6 9:15P	Su7 1:00A			Su7 9:00A		
MAL								S6 7:00A	S6 12:30P	S6 1:30P
COL	F5 6:00P		Su7 12:15P	Su7 7:15P	Su7 11:15P			M8 9:30A	M8 4:00P	M8 5:00P
MAL								Su7 7:00A	Su7 12:30P	Su7 1:30P
TAK		Su7 7:00P	M8 2:15A	M8 9:00A	M8 12:45P	M8 5:30P	T9 4:00A	T9 1:00P		
MAL								T9 7:00A	T9 12:30P	T9 1:30P
MAT		T9 3:45P	W10 1:30A	W10 8:45A	W10 12:30P			W10 10:00P	Th11 4:30A	Th11 5:30A
MAL								W10 7:00A	W10 12:30P	W10 1:30P
MAL								Th11 8:00A	Th11 1:30P	Th11 2:30P
TAK		Th11 8:45A	Th11 4:00P	Th11 10:45P	F12 2:30A	F12 7:15A		F12 2:45P		
MAL								F12 7:00A	F12 12:30P	F12 1:30P
MAT		S13 6:15A	S13 5:30P	Su14 12:15A	Su14 4:00A			Su14 12:00P		
MAL								S13 7:00A	S13 12:30P	S13 1:30P
COL	F12 6:00P		Su14 10:00A	Su14 4:30P	Su14 8:30P			M15 6:45A	M15 1:15P	M15 2:15P
MAL								Su14 7:00A	Su14 12:30P	Su14 1:30P
TAK		Su14 6:00P	M15 2:15A	M15 9:00A	M15 12:45P	M15 5:30P		T16 1:00A		
MAL								T16 7:00A	T16 12:30P	T16 1:30P
MAT		T16 2:00P	T16 7:15P							
TAK			T16 11:45P	W17 6:30A	W17 10:15A			W17 9:45P	Th18 4:15A	Th18 5:15A
MAL								W17 7:00A	W17 12:30P	W17 1:30P
MAL								Th18 8:00A	Th18 1:30P	Th18 2:30P
MAL								F19 7:00A	F19 12:30P	F19 1:30P
TAK		S20 5:15A	S20 12:00P	S20 6:45P	S20 10:30P	Su21 3:15A	Su21 1:45P	Su21 11:00P		
MAL								S20 7:00A	S20 12:30P	S20 1:30P
COL	F19 6:00P		Su21 12:00P	Su21 7:00P	Su21 11:00P			M22 9:15A	M22 3:45P	M22 4:45P
MAL								Su21 7:00A	Su21 12:30P	Su21 1:30P
MAL								Su21 7:00A	Su21 12:30P	Su21 1:30P
MAL								T23 7:00A	T23 12:30P	T23 1:30P
TAK		T23 12:00P	T23 7:15P	W24 2:00A	W24 5:45A			W24 5:15P	W24 11:45P	Th25 12:45A
MAL								W24 7:00A	W24 12:30P	W24 1:30P
MAL								Th25 8:00A	Th25 1:30P	Th25 2:30P
MAL								F26 7:00A	F26 12:30P	F26 1:30P
TAK		S27 6:15A	S27 3:30P	S27 10:45P	Su28 2:30A	Su28 7:15A	Su28 5:45P	M29 3:00A		
MAL								S27 7:00A	S27 12:30P	S27 1:30P
COL	F26 6:00P		Su28 9:00A	Su28 3:30P	Su28 7:30P			M29 5:45A	M29 12:15P	M29 1:15P
MAL								Su28 7:00A	Su28 12:30P	Su28 1:30P
KEN	S27 6:00P		M29 8:00A							
TAK		T30 3:00P	T30 11:45P	W1 6:30A	W1 10:15A			W1 9:45P	Th2 4:15P	Th2 5:15A

SEPTEMBER 2014

Southeast Alaska/Inside Passage Southbound

	Skagway	Haines	Juneau	Sitka	Kake	Petersburg	Wrangell	Ketchikan	Prince Rupert	Bellingham
COL	M1 5:15P	M1 8:15P	T2 4:15A	T2 4:15A		W3 4:45A	W3 8:45A	W3 5:00P		F5 8:00A
MAL	T2 3:00P	T2 5:00P	T2 9:30P							
TAK			T2 5:00P		W3 1:15A	W3 6:00A	W3 10:00A	W3 7:00P	Th4 2:30A	
MAL	W3 3:00P	W3 5:00P	W3 9:30P							
MAT	Th4 5:45A	Th4 8:45A	Th4 3:15P			F5 12:15A	F5 5:15A	F5 6:45A	S6 2:15A	
MAL	Th4 4:00P	Th4 6:00P	Th4 10:30P							
MAL	F5 3:00P	F5 5:00P	F5 9:30P							
TAK			F5 7:30P	S6 7:45A	S6 4:30P	S6 9:15P	Su7 1:15A	Su7 8:30A	Su7 4:00P	
MAL	S6 3:00P	S6 5:00P	S6 9:30P							
MAL	Su7 3:00P	Su7 5:00P	Su7 9:30P							
MAT			Su7 3:00P	M8 3:15A		M8 3:15P	M8 7:15P	T9 4:15A	T9 11:45A	
COL	M8 8:00P	M8 11:00P	T9 5:00A	T9 5:00A		W10 3:15A	W10 7:15A	W10 5:00P		F12 8:00A
MAL	T9 3:00P	T9 5:00P	T9 9:30P							
TAK			T9 9:00P		W10 6:30A	W10 11:15A	W10 3:15P	W10 10:15P	Th11 5:45A	
MAL	W10 3:00P	W10 5:00P	W10 9:30P							
MAT	Th11 8:30A	Th11 11:30A	Th11 8:00P			F12 5:00A	F12 9:00A	F12 6:45P	S13 2:15A	
MAL	Th11 4:00P	Th11 6:00P	Th11 10:30P							

Southeast Alaska
Passenger & Vehicle Fares Summer 2014, May 1-Sept. 30

ADULTS 12 YEARS OR OLDER (Meals and berth not included)
Children under 6 travel free. Children 6 thru 11 years approximately 1/2 adult fare. Senior rates may be available on some sailings.

	BEL	YPR	KTN	WRG	PSG	KKE	SIT	PEL	ANG	GUS	TKE	HNH	JNU	HNS
KTN	239	54												
WRG	260	78	37											
PSG	279	89	60	33										
KKE	293	108	74	54	35									
SIT	301	115	83	60	45	37								
PEL	359	186	144	118	97	80	64							
ANG	320	149	99	80	64	47	35	60						
GUS		174	140					31						
TKE	326	157	107	87	66	50	35	50	31					
HNH	326	157	107	87	66	60	37	35	33	32	31			
JNU	326	141	107	87	66	66	45	50	37	33	35	33		
HNS	353	160	134	107	89	89	66	76	66		60	60	37	
SGY	363	171	147	122	101	101	76	91	74		72	72	50	31
YAK	411	241	186							85			85	

Bicycles (No Trailers)

	BEL	YPR	KTN	WRG	PSG	KKE	SIT	PEL	ANG	GUS	TKE	HNH	JNU	HNS
KTN	38	14												
WRG	44	18	14											
PSG	45	19	18	12										
KKE	47	20	19	15	12									
SIT	49	22	20	18	14	12								
PEL	57	33	27	24	22	20	18							
ANG	52	27	22	20	18	14	11	15						
GUS		40	34					12						
TKE	53	31	22	21	19	15	12	15	11					
HNH	53	31	22	21	19	18	12	12	12	12	11			
JNU	53	28	22	21	19	19	14	15	14	12	14	12		
HNS	57	31	29	25	22	22	20	21	19		19	19	15	
SGY	58	32	31	27	24	24	21	22	20		20	20	18	12
YAK	67	46	33							14			14	

Kayaks/Inflatables

	BEL	YPR	KTN	WRG	PSG	KKE	SIT	PEL	ANG	GUS	TKE	HNH	JNU	HNS
KTN	57	22												
WRG	65	28	22											
PSG	68	29	27	19										
KKE	72	31	29	24	19									
SIT	74	32	31	27	22	19								
PEL	88	49	38	35	34	31	27							
ANG	77	38	34	31	27	22	15	24						
GUS		60	53					19						
TKE	80	45	34	32	29	24	19	24	15					
HNH	80	45	34	32	29	27	19	19	19	19	15			
JNU	80	41	34	32	29	29	22	24	22	19	22	19		
HNS	88	45	41	37	34	34	31	32	29		29	29	24	
SGY	89	48	45	38	35	35	32	34	31		31	31	27	19
YAK	102	70	49							22			22	

VEHICLES UP TO 10 FEET (Driver not included)

	BEL	YPR	KTN	WRG	PSG	KKE	SIT	PEL	ANG	GUS	HNH	JNU	HNS
KTN	305	61											
WRG	340	95	49										
PSG	362	115	75	37									
KKE	383	136	97	65	44								
SIT	397	146	106	75	52	47							
PEL	469	240	184	150	124	101	80						
ANG	421	189	132	102	80	55	41	75					
GUS		219	182					38					
HNH	431	199	142	109	88	75	47	46	40	35			
JNU	431	179	142	109	88	88	52	65	47	40	38		
HNS	462	212	176	143	120	120	86	102	83		75	49	
SGY	478	222	189	156	134	134	99	114	94		88	63	31
YAK	548	328	261							117		117	

VEHICLES UP TO 15 FEET (Driver not included)

	BEL	YPR	KTN	WRG	PSG	KKE	SIT	PEL	ANG	GUS	HNH	JNU	HNS
KTN	515	98											
WRG	558	150	77										
PSG	601	184	115	54									
KKE	637	221	156	103	66								
SIT	655	237	173	115	79	75							
PEL	786	398	308	247	211	162	124						
ANG	701	308	220	166	124	89	63	115					
GUS		360	296					57					
HNH	739	336	238	179	139	120	75	70	58	49			
JNU	739	302	238	179	139	139	79	103	70	58	57		
HNS	797	356	294	238	195	195	136	162	129		118	75	
SGY	820	374	317	260	222	222	159	188	152		139	98	41
YAK	932	555	442							193		193	

VEHICLES UP TO 19 FEET (Driver not included)

	BEL	YPR	KTN	WRG	PSG	KKE	SIT	PEL	ANG	GUS	HNH	JNU	HNS
KTN	617	116											
WRG	667	176	91										
PSG	712	217	136	64									
KKE	759	262	185	121	79								
SIT	780	302	204	137	93	87							
PEL	937	465	364	294	246	192	149						
ANG	833	364	259	195	149	104	75	136					
GUS		430	350					68					
HNH	877	400	280	214	167	138	87	84	70	59			
JNU	877	360	280	214	167	167	92	121	84	70	68		
HNS	949	416	350	280	233	233	159	191	152		136	86	
SGY	976	440	376	308	262	262	188	222	181		166	111	49
YAK	1105	658	525							228		228	

VEHICLES UP TO 21 FEET (Driver not included)

	BEL	YPR	KTN	WRG	PSG	KKE	SIT	PEL	ANG	GUS	HNH	JNU	HNS
KTN	770	143											
WRG	862	225	111										
PSG	918	280	173	80									
KKE	976	336	237	152	99								
SIT	1003	360	263	174	115	108							
PEL	1210	605	463	377	316	246	188						
ANG	1071	463	330	248	188	132	93	173					
GUS		547	449					86					
HNH	1133	509	360	271	214	178	108	104	89	72			
JNU	1133	458	360	271	214	214	114	152	105	89	86		
HNS	1223	542	444	360	297	297	204	245	194		174	108	
SGY	1257	573	479	397	333	333	240	283	231		214	146	58
YAK	1409	828	658							276		276	

RATE PER FOOT FOR VEHICLES OVER 21 FEET (Driver not included)

	BEL	YPR	KTN	WRG	PSG	KKE	SIT	PEL	ANG	GUS	HNH	JNU	HNS
KTN	43.2	7.8											
WRG	48.4	12.5	6.1										
PSG	51.9	15.6	9.7	4.1									
KKE	55.2	18.7	12.9	8.3	5.2								
SIT	56.8	20.2	14.4	9.7	6.3	5.7							
PEL	68.2	34.2	26.2	21.1	17.4	13.6	10.3						
ANG	60.5	26.3	18.6	13.8	10.3	7.1	5.0	9.7					
GUS		29.9	24.6					4.5					
HNH	62.1	28.0	19.9	15.0	11.8	9.8	5.7	5.5	4.7	3.9			
JNU	62.1	25.2	19.9	15.0	11.8	11.8	6.3	8.3	5.6	4.7	4.5		
HNS	67.2	29.6	24.9	19.7	16.7	16.7	11.1	13.5	10.6		9.7	5.7	
SGY	69.1	31.5	27.0	22.2	18.6	18.6	13.4	15.8	12.7		11.8	7.7	3.3
YAK	77.7	47.5	37.8							15.6		15.6	

Port Abbrev: Bellingham (BEL), Prince Rupert (YPR), Ketchikan (KTN), Wrangell (WRG), Petersburg (PSG), Kake (KKE), Sitka (SIT), Angoon (ANG), Gustavus (GUS), Hoonah (HNH), Tenakee (TKE), Juneau (JNU), Haines (HNS), Skagway (SGY), Pelican (PEL), Yakutat (YAK).

Vessel key (facing page): Columbia (COL); Malaspina (MAL); Matanuska (MAT); Taku (TAK)
See pages 734-741 for additional ferry service between Petersburg, Sitka, Pelican, Angoon, Gustavus, Tenakee, Hoonah, Juneau, Haines, Skagway. See also Kennicott service, page 722.
The State of Alaska reserves the right to alter, revise or cancel schedules and rates without prior notice, and assumes no responsibility for delays and/or expenses due to such modifications.

Southeast Alaska
Cabin Rates Summer 2014, May 1-Sept. 30

Four Berth Cabin-Sitting Room-Outside-Facilities

MV's: COL, MAL

	BEL	KTN	WRG	PSG	SIT	JNU	HNS
KTN	394						
WRG	431	88					
PSG	456	103	72				
SIT	506	134	103	90			
JNU	533	158	134	118	84		
HNS	580	208	178	161	128	93	
SGY	580	208	178	161	128	93	75

Three Berth Cabin-Outside-Complete Facilities

MV: MAT

	YPR	KTN	WRG	PSG	KKE	SIT	JNU	HNS
KTN	70							
WRG	92	69						
PSG	104	80	56					
KKE	124	91	74	63				
SIT	133	97	80	70				
JNU	154	111	90	84	77	63		
HNS	188	151	125	111	106		72	
SGY	188	151	125	111	106		72	59

Four Berth Cabin-Outside-Complete Facilities

MV's: COL, KEN, MAL, MAT, TAK

	BEL	YPR	KTN	WRG	PSG	KKE	SIT	JNU	HNS
KTN	359	88							
WRG	395	120	83						
PSG	416	135	94	65					
KKE		155	109	83	74				
SIT	458	170	125	93	84	76			
JNU	484	196	149	120	99	92	74		
HNS	535	238	194	163	151	129	118	86	
SGY	535	238	194	163	151	129	118	86	69
YAK	623		273					139	

Two Berth Cabin-Outside-Complete Facilities

MV's: COL, MAL, MAT, TAK

	BEL	YPR	KTN	WRG	PSG	KKE	SIT	JNU	HNS
KTN	257	66							
WRG	281	88	58						
PSG	296	97	71	53					
KKE		110	84	63	55				
SIT	327	125	89	72	63	57			
JNU	352	144	104	88	76	70	58		
HNS	393	178	135	111	100	98	86	65	
SGY	393	178	135	111	100	98	86	65	53

Four Berth Cabin-Inside-Complete Facilities

MV's: KEN, MAL

	BEL	KTN	WRG	PSG	SIT	JNU	HNS
KTN	304						
WRG	336	74					
PSG	360	87	61				
SIT	396	109	86	74			
JNU	421	129	99	90	65		
HNS	462	170	146	132	99	75	
SGY	462	170	146	132	99	75	61
YAK	539	236				118	

Two Berth Cabin-Inside-Complete Facilities

MV's: COL, MAL, MAT, TAK

	BEL	YPR	KTN	WRG	PSG	KKE	SIT	JNU	HNS
KTN	227	59							
WRG	254	83	55						
PSG	260	90	65	47					
KKE		98	74	57	49				
SIT	288	108	83	65	56	52			
JNU	308	124	92	79	69	63	53		
HNS	337	156	124	100	93	92	79	59	
SGY	337	156	124	100	93	92	79	59	50

Two Berth Cabin-Outside-No Facilities

MV: KEN

	BEL	KTN	JNU
KTN	208		
JNU	281	87	
YAK	365	159	84

Two Berth Roomette-Outside-No Facilities

MV: KEN

	BEL	KTN	JNU
KTN	66		
JNU	88	31	
YAK	118	53	30

Two Berth Cabin-Inside-No Facilities

MV: KEN

	BEL	KTN	JNU
KTN	186		
JNU	253	79	
YAK	328	144	75

Two Berth Roomette-Inside-No Facilities

MV: KEN

	BEL	KTN	JNU
KTN	56		
JNU	74	27	
YAK	99	45	25

Port Abbrev: Bellingham (BEL), Haines (HNS), Juneau (JNU), Kake (KKE), Ketchikan (KTN), Petersburg (PSG), Prince Rupert (YPR), Sitka (SIT), Skagway (SGY), Wrangell (WRG), Yakutat (YAK)
Vessels: Columbia (COL), Kennicott (KEN), Malaspina (MAL), Matanuska (MAT), Taku (TAK)

The State of Alaska reserves the right to alter, revise or cancel schedules and rates without prior notice, and assumes no responsibility for delays and/or expenses due to such modifications.

Cross Gulf

Passenger, Vehicle and Cabin Fares-Summer 2014 May 1–Sept. 30

ADULTS 12 YEARS OR OLDER (Meals and berth not included).
Children under 6 travel free. Children 6 through 11 years
approximately1/2 adult fare. Senior rates may be available on some sailings.

	BEL	YPR	KTN	JNU, GUS	YAK
KOD	638	463	411	312	254
HOM	706	531	479	380	322
SEL	710	535	483	384	326
WTR	547	372	320	221	163
CHB	636	461	409	310	252

VEHICLES UP TO 15 FEET (Driver not included)

	BEL	YPR	KTN	JNU, GUS	YAK
KOD	1438	1034	924	699	568
HOM	1591	1187	1077	852	721
SEL	1606	1202	1092	867	736
WTR	1247	843	733	508	377
CHB	1406	1002	892	667	536

VEHICLES UP TO 19 FEET (Driver not included)

	BEL	YPR	KTN	JNU, GUS	YAK
KOD	1706	1230	1095	829	674
HOM	1889	1413	1275	1012	857
SEL	1904	1428	1293	1027	872
WTR	1481	1005	870	604	449
CHB	1671	1195	1060	794	639

VEHICLES UP TO 21 FEET (Driver not included)

	BEL	YPR	KTN	JNU, GUS	YAK
KOD	2172	1554	1384	1039	851
HOM	2399	1781	1611	1266	1078
SEL	2422	1804	1634	1289	1101
WTR	1882	1264	1094	749	561
CHB	2123	1505	1335	990	802

VEHICLES UP TO 10 FEET (Driver not included)

	BEL	YPR	KTN	JNU, GUS	YAK
KOD	852	615	550	421	340
HOM	939	702	637	508	427
SEL	947	710	645	516	435
WTR	735	498	433	304	223
CHB	836	559	534	405	324

Rate per foot for VEHICLES OVER 21 FEET (Driver not included)

	BEL	YPR	KTN	JNU, GUS	YAK
KOD	121.0	88.3	78.6	58.4	31.8
HOM	124.0	102.0	91.9	71.7	60.5
SEL	136.0	104.0	94.5	74.3	63.1
WTR	105.0	72.4	62.7	42.5	31.3
CHB	118.0	85.3	75.6	55.4	44.2

Bicycles (No Trailers)

	BEL	YPR	KTN	JNU, GUS	YAK
KOD	109	83	73	56	45
HOM	115	89	79	62	51
SEL	116	90	80	63	52
WTR	89	63	53	36	25
CHB	104	78	68	51	40

Kayaks/Inflatables

	BEL	YPR	KTN	JNU	YAK
KOD	162	124	110	82	67
HOM	170	132	118	90	75
SEL	173	135	121	93	78
WTR	132	94	80	52	37
CHB	156	118	104	76	61

Four Berth Cabin-Outside-Complete Facilities
MV: KEN

	BEL	KTN	JNU	YAK
YAK	623	273	139	
KOD	998	647	514	420
WHT	838	487	354	260
CHB	972	621	488	394

Two Berth Cabin-Inside-No Facilities
MV: KEN

	BEL	KTN	JNU	YAK
YAK	328	144	75	
KOD	531	345	278	228
WHT	442	256	189	139
CHB	517	331	264	214

Four Berth Cabin-Inside-Complete Facilities
MV: KEN

	BEL	KTN	JNU	YAK
YAK	539	236	118	
KOD	851	546	430	353
WHT	717	412	296	219
CHB	827	522	406	329

Two Berth Roomette-Outside-No Facilities
MV: KEN

	BEL	KTN	JNU	YAK
YAK	118	53	30	
KOD	190	123	102	86
WHT	156	89	68	52
CHB	185	118	97	81

Two Berth Cabin-Outside-No Facilities
MV: KEN

	BEL	KTN	JNU	YAK
YAK	365	159	84	
KOD	592	383	311	255
WHT	493	284	212	156
CHB	577	368	296	240

Two Berth Roomette-Inside-No Facilities
MV: KEN

	BEL	KTN	JNU	YAK
YAK	99	45	25	
KOD	160	105	86	74
WHT	130	75	56	44
CHB	155	100	81	69

Port Abbrev: Bellingham (BEL), Chenega Bay (CHB), Gustavus (GUS), Homer (HOM), Juneau (JNU), Kake (KKE), Ketchikan (KTN), Kodiak (KOD), Prince Rupert (YPR), Seldovia (SEL), Whittier (WTR), Yakutat (YAK)
Vessel: Kennicott (KEN)

The State of Alaska reserves the right to alter, revise or cancel schedules and rates without prior notice, and assumes no responsibility for delays and/or expenses due to such modifications.

May 2014

Southeast Alaska Dayboats:

MV's: *Fairweather* (northbound)/*LeConte* (eastbound)

For updated schedules and fares, go to www.ferryalaska.com

	PETERSBURG	SITKA	ANGOON	TENAKEE	HOONAH	JUNEAU	GUSTAVUS	HAINES	SKAGWAY	PELICAN
LEC						Th1 7:00A				Th1 2:00P
LEC				F2 2:30P	F2 6:15P	F2 9:30P				
LEC						S3 7:00A	S3 11:15A			
LEC			M5 7:00A	M5 10:00A		M5 3:00P				
LEC					T6 9:30A	T6 12:45P				
LEC					W7 11:15A	W7 2:30P				
LEC						Th8 7:00A	Th8 11:15A			
LEC				F9 2:30P	F9 6:15P	F9 9:30P				
LEC						S10 7:00A	S10 11:15A			
LEC			M12 7:00A	M12 10:30A		M12 3:30P				
LEC					T13 9:30A	T13 4:30P	T13 12:15P			
LEC						W14 7:00A	W14 12:45P			W14 4:00P
FWX		Th15 1:15P				Th15 5:45P				
FWX	F16 12:00P					F16 4:00P				
LEC				F16 2:30P	F16 6:15P	F16 9:30P				
LEC						S17 7:00A	S17 11:15A			
FWX		S17 1:00P	S17 4:30P			S17 7:15P				
FWX		Su18 12:00P				Su18 4:30P				
LEC			M19 7:00A	M19 10:00A		M19 3:00P				
LEC					T20 9:30A	T20 12:45P				
LEC					W21 11:15A	W21 2:30P				
LEC						Th22 7:00A	Th22 11:15A			
FWX		Th22 11:30A	Th22 3:00P			Th22 5:45P				
FWX		F23 12:00P				F23 4:30P				
LEC				F23 2:30P	F23 6:15P	F23 9:30P				
LEC						S24 7:00A	S24 11:15A			
FWX		S24 1:15P				S24 5:45P				
FWX		Su25 12:00P				Su25 4:30P				
LEC			M26 7:00A	M26 10:30A		M26 3:30P				
LEC					T27 9:30A	T27 4:30P	T27 12:15P			
LEC						W28 7:00A	W28 12:45P			W28 4:00P
FWX		Th29 1:15P				Th29 5:45P				
FWX		F30 12:00P				F30 4:30P				
LEC				F30 2:30P	F30 6:15P	F30 9:30P				
LEC						S31 7:00A	S31 11:15A			
FWX		S31 11:30A	S31 3:00P			S31 5:45P				

Vessel key: Fairweather (FWX); LeConte (LEC). *Arrivals noted in red.*

The State of Alaska reserves the right to alter, revise or cancel schedules and rates without prior notice, and assumes no responsibility for delays and/or expenses due to such modifications.

Southeast Alaska Dayboats:
MV's: *Fairweather* (northbound)/*LeConte* (eastbound)

ALASKA MARINE HIGHWAY SCHEDULES & TARIFFS

	PETERSBURG	SITKA	ANGOON	TENAKEE	HOONAH	JUNEAU	GUSTAVUS	HAINES	SKAGWAY	PELICAN
FWX		Su1 12:00P				Su1 4:30P				
LEC			M2 7:00A	M2 10:00A		M2 3:00P				
LEC					T3 9:30A	T3 12:45P				
LEC					W4 11:15A	W4 2:30P				
LEC						Th5 7:00A	Th5 11:15A			
FWX		Th5 11:30A	Th5 3:00P			Th5 5:45P				
FWX		F6 12:00P				F6 4:30P				
LEC				F6 2:30P	F6 6:15P	F6 9:30P				
LEC						S7 7:00A	S7 11:15A			
FWX		S7 1:15P				S7 5:45P				
FWX		Su8 12:00P				Su8 4:30P				
LEC			M9 7:00A	M9 10:30A		M9 3:30P				
LEC					T10 9:30A	T10 12:45P				
FWX		T10 12:00P	T10 3:30P			T10 6:30P				
LEC						W11 7:00A	W11 12:45P			W11 4:00P
FWX		Th12 1:15P				Th12 5:45P				
FWX		F13 12:00P				F13 4:30P				
LEC				F13 2:30P	F13 6:15P	F13 9:30P				
LEC						S14 7:00A	S14 11:15A			
FWX		S14 1:00P				S14 5:30P				
FWX		Su15 1:45P				Su15 6:15P				
LEC			M16 7:00A	M16 10:00A		M16 3:00P				
LEC					T17 9:30A	T17 12:45P				
LEC					W18 11:15A	W18 2:30P				
LEC						Th19 7:00A	Th19 11:15A			
FWX		Th19 11:30A	Th19 3:00P			Th19 5:45P				
FWX		F20 12:00P				F20 4:30P				
LEC				F20 2:30P	F20 6:15P	F20 9:30P				
LEC						S21 7:00A	S21 11:15A			
FWX		S21 1:15P				S21 5:45P				
FWX						Su22 6:00A		Su22 8:15A		
LEC			M23 7:00A	M23 10:30A		M23 3:30P				
LEC					T24 9:30A	T24 4:30P	T24 12:15P			
LEC						W25 7:00A	W25 12:45P			W25 4:00P
FWX		Th26 1:15P				Th26 5:45P				
FWX		F27 12:00P				F27 4:30P				
LEC				F27 2:30P	F27 6:15P	F27 9:30P				
LEC						S28 7:00A	S28 11:15A			
FWX		S28 11:30A	S28 3:00P			S28 5:45P				
LEC						Su29 7:00A	Su29 11:15A			
FWX		Su29 12:00P				Su29 4:30P				
LEC					M30 11:00A	M30 2:15P				
FWX		M30 12:00P				M30 4:30P				

Vessel key: Fairweather (FWX); LeConte (LEC). *Arrivals noted in red.*

The State of Alaska reserves the right to alter, revise or cancel schedules and rates without prior notice, and assumes no responsibility for delays and/or expenses due to such modifications.

July 2014
Southeast Alaska Dayboats:
MV's: *Fairweather* (northbound)/*LeConte* (eastbound)

For updated schedules and fares, go to www.ferryalaska.com

	PETERSBURG	SITKA	ANGOON	TENAKEE	HOONAH	JUNEAU	GUSTAVUS	HAINES	SKAGWAY	PELICAN
LEC					T1 9:30A	T1 12:45P				
FWX	T1 11:00A					T1 3:00P				
LEC					W2 11:15A	W2 2:30P				
FWX		W2 12:00P				W2 4:30P				
LEC						Th3 7:00A	Th3 11:15A			
FWX		Th3 1:15P				Th3 5:45P				
FWX		F4 12:00P				F4 4:30P				
LEC				F4 2:30P	F4 6:15P	F4 9:30P				
LEC						S5 7:00A	S5 11:15A			
FWX		S5 11:30A	S5 3:00P			S5 5:45P				
FWX		Su6 12:00P				Su6 4:30P				
LEC			M7 7:00A	M7 10:30A		M7 3:30P				
FWX		M7 12:00P				M7 4:30P				
LEC					T8 9:30A	T8 4:30P	T8 12:15P			
FWX	T8 11:00A					T8 3:00P				
LEC						W9 7:00A	W9 12:45P			W9 4:00P
FWX		W9 12:00P				W9 4:30P				
FWX		Th10 11:30A	Th10 3:00P			Th10 5:45P				
FWX		F11 12:00P				F11 4:30P				
LEC				F11 2:30P	F11 6:15P	F11 9:30P				
LEC						S12 7:00A	S12 11:15A			
FWX		S12 1:15P				S12 5:45P				
FWX		Su13 12:45P				Su13 5:15P				
LEC			M14 7:00A	M14 10:00A		M14 3:00P				
FWX		M14 1:45P				M14 6:15P				
LEC					T15 9:30A	T15 12:45P				
FWX	T15 11:00A					T15 3:00P				
LEC					W16 11:15A	W16 2:30P				
FWX		W16 12:00P				W16 4:30P				
LEC						Th17 7:00A	Th17 11:15A			
FWX		Th17 12:45P				Th17 5:15P				
FWX		F18 12:00P				F18 4:30P				
LEC				F18 2:30P	F18 6:15P	F18 9:30P				
LEC						S19 7:00A	S19 11:15A			
FWX		S19 11:30A	S19 3:00P			S19 5:45P				
FWX		Su20 12:00P				Su20 4:30P				
LEC			M21 7:00A	M21 10:30A		M21 3:30P				
FWX		M21 12:00P				M21 4:30P				
LEC					T22 9:30A	T22 4:30P	T22 12:15P			
FWX	T22 11:00A					T22 3:00P				
LEC						W23 7:00A	W23 12:45P			W23 4:00P
FWX		W23 12:00P				W23 4:30P				
FWX		Th24 11:30A	Th24 3:00P			Th24 5:45P				
FWX		F25 12:00P				F25 4:30P				
LEC				F25 2:30P	F25 6:15P	F25 9:30P				
LEC						S26 7:00A	S26 11:15A			
FWX		S26 1:15P				S26 5:45P				
FWX		Su27 12:00P				Su27 4:30P				
LEC			M28 7:00A	M28 10:00A		M28 3:00P				
FWX		M28 12:00P				M28 4:30P				
LEC					T29 9:30A	T29 12:45P				
FWX	T29 11:00A					T29 3:00P				
LEC					W30 11:15A	W30 2:30P				
FWX		W30 12:00P				W30 4:30P				
LEC						Th31 7:00A	Th31 11:15A			
FWX		Th31 1:15P				Th31 5:45P				

Vessel key: Fairweather (FWX); LeConte (LEC). *Arrivals noted in red.*
The State of Alaska reserves the right to alter, revise or cancel schedules and rates without prior notice, and assumes no responsibility for delays and/or expenses due to such modifications.

*For updated schedules and fares,
go to www.ferryalaska.com*

August 2014

Southeast Alaska Dayboats: MV's: *Fairweather* (northbound)/*LeConte* (eastbound)

	PETERSBURG	SITKA	ANGOON	TENAKEE	HOONAH	JUNEAU	GUSTAVUS	HAINES	SKAGWAY	PELICAN
FWX		F1 12:00P				F1 4:30P				
LEC				F1 2:30P	F1 6:15P	F1 9:30P				
LEC						S2 7:00A	S2 11:15A			
FWX		S2 11:30A	S2 3:00P			S2 5:45P				
FWX		Su3 12:00P				Su3 4:30P				
FWX						M4 6:30A		M4 8:45A		
LEC			M4 7:00A	M4 10:30A		M4 3:30P				
FWX						M4 1:00P		M4 3:15P		
LEC					T5 9:30A	T5 4:30P	T5 12:15P			
FWX	T5 11:00A					T5 3:00P				
LEC						W6 7:00A	W6 12:45P			W6 4:00P
FWX		W6 12:00P				W6 4:30P				
FWX		Th7 11:30A	Th7 3:00P			Th7 5:45P				
FWX		F8 12:00P				F8 4:30P				
LEC				F8 2:30P	F8 6:15P	F8 9:30P				
LEC						S9 7:00A	S9 11:15A			
FWX		S9 1:15P				S9 5:45P				
FWX		Su10 12:00P				Su10 4:30P				
LEC			M11 7:00A	M11 10:00A		M11 3:00P				
FWX		M11 12:30P				M11 5:00P				
LEC					T12 9:30A	T12 12:45P				
FWX	T12 11:00A					T12 3:00P				
FWX		W13 11:00A				W13 3:30P				
LEC					W13 11:15A	W13 2:30P				
LEC						Th14 7:00A	Th14 11:15A			
FWX		Th14 2:00P				Th14 6:30P				
FWX		F15 12:00P				F15 4:30P				
LEC				F15 2:30P	F15 6:15P	F15 9:30P				
LEC						S16 7:00A	S16 11:15A			
FWX		S16 11:30A	S16 3:00P			S16 5:45P				
FWX		Su17 12:00P				Su17 4:30P				
LEC			M18 7:00A	M18 10:30A		M18 3:30P				
FWX		M18 12:00P				M18 4:30P				
LEC					T19 9:30A	T19 4:30P	T19 12:15P			
FWX	T19 11:00A					T19 3:00P				
LEC						W20 7:00A	W20 12:45P			W20 4:00P
FWX		W20 12:00P				W20 4:30P				
FWX		Th21 11:30A	Th21 3:00P			Th21 5:45P				
FWX		F22 12:00P				F22 4:30P				
LEC				F22 2:30P	F22 6:15P	F22 9:30P				
LEC						S23 7:00A	S23 11:15A			
FWX		S23 1:15P				S23 5:45P				
FWX		Su24 12:00P				Su24 4:30P				
LEC			M25 7:00A	M25 10:00A		M25 3:00P				
FWX		M25 12:00P				M25 4:30P				
LEC					T26 9:30A	T26 12:45P				
FWX	T26 11:00A					T26 3:00P				
LEC					W27 11:15A	W27 2:30P				
FWX		W27 12:00P				W27 4:30P				
LEC						Th28 7:00A	Th28 11:15A			
FWX		Th28 1:15P				Th28 5:45P				
FWX		F29 12:00P				F29 4:30P				
LEC				F29 2:30P	F29 6:15P	F29 9:30P				
LEC						S30 7:00A	S30 11:15A			
FWX		S30 11:30A	S30 3:00P			S30 5:45P				
FWX		Su31 12:00P				Su31 4:30P				

September 2013 (to 15th)

Southeast Alaska Dayboats: MV's: *Fairweather* (northbound)/*LeConte* (eastbound)

	PETERSBURG	SITKA	ANGOON	TENAKEE	HOONAH	JUNEAU	GUSTAVUS	HAINES	SKAGWAY	PELICAN
LEC			M1 7:00A	M1 10:30A		M1 3:30P				
FWX		M1 12:00P				M1 4:30P				
LEC					T2 9:30A	T2 4:30P	T2 12:15P			
FWX	T2 11:00A					T2 3:00P				
LEC						W3 7:00A	W3 12:45P			W3 4:00P
FWX		W3 12:00P				W3 4:30P				
FWX		Th4 1:15P				Th4 5:45P				
FWX						F5 1:00P			F5 3:30P	
LEC				F5 2:30P	F5 6:15P	F5 9:30P				
LEC						S6 7:00A	S6 11:15A			
FWX		S6 11:30A	S6 2:30P			S6 5:45P				
FWX		S6 3:00P								
FWX						Su7 6:30A			Su7 9:00A	
LEC			M8 7:00A	M8 10:00A		M8 3:00P				
FWX		M8 12:00P				M8 4:30P				
LEC					T9 9:30A	T9 12:45P				
FWX	T9 11:00A					T9 3:00P				
LEC					W10 11:15A	W10 2:30P				
FWX		W10 1:00P				W10 5:30P				
LEC						Th11 7:00A	Th11 11:15A			
FWX		Th11 1:15P				Th11 5:45P				
FWX		F12 11:15A				F12 3:45P				
LEC				F12 2:30P	F12 6:15P	F12 9:30P				
LEC						S13 7:00A	S13 11:15A			
FWX		S13 1:15P				S13 5:45P				
FWX		Su14 12:00P				Su14 4:30P				
FWX		M15 12:00P				M15 4:30P				

May 2014

Southeast Alaska Dayboats:

MV's: *Fairweather* (southbound)/*LeConte* (westbound)

For updated schedules and fares, go to www.ferryalaska.com

	PELICAN	SKAGWAY	HAINES	GUSTAVUS	JUNEAU	HOONAH	TENAKEE	ANGOON	SITKA	PETERSBURG
LEC	Th1 4:00P				Th1 11:00P					
LEC					F2 7:00A	F2 10:45A	F2 2:00P			
LEC				S3 12:45P	S3 5:00P					
LEC					Su4 7:00A	Su4 11:15A	Su4 3:00P	Su4 5:15P		
LEC					M5 4:00P	M5 7:15P				
LEC					W7 7:00A	W7 10:15A				
LEC				Th8 12:45P	Th8 5:00P					
LEC					F9 7:00A	F9 10:45A	F9 2:00P			
LEC				S10 12:45P	S10 5:00P					
LEC					Su11 7:00A	Su11 11:15A	Su11 3:00P	Su11 5:15P		
LEC					M12 4:30P	M12 7:45P				
FWX					Th15 6:30A				Th15 9:45A	Th15 12:45P
LEC	Th15 7:00A			Th15 11:15A	Th15 3:30P					
LEC					F16 7:00A	F16 10:45A	F16 2:00P			
FWX					F16 7:30A					F16 11:30A
FWX					S17 7:30A				S17 12:30P	
LEC				S17 12:45P	S17 5:00P					
FWX					Su18 6:30A				Su18 11:00A	
LEC					Su18 7:00A	Su18 11:15A	Su18 3:00P	Su18 5:15P		
LEC					M19 4:00P	M19 7:15P				
LEC					W21 7:00A	W21 10:15A				
FWX					Th22 6:30A				Th22 11:00A	
LEC				Th22 12:45P	Th22 5:00P					
FWX					F23 6:30A				F23 11:00A	
LEC					F23 7:00A	F23 10:45A	F23 2:00P			
FWX					S24 6:30A			S24 9:45A	S24 12:45P	
LEC				S24 12:45P	S24 5:00P					
FWX					Su25 6:30A				Su25 11:00A	
LEC					Su25 7:00A	Su25 11:15A	Su25 3:00P	Su25 5:15P		
LEC					M26 4:30P	M26 7:45P				
FWX					Th29 6:30A			Th29 9:45A	Th29 12:45P	
LEC	Th29 7:00A			Th29 11:15A	Th29 3:30P					
FWX					F30 6:30A				F30 11:00A	
LEC					F30 7:00A	F30 10:45A	F30 2:00P			
FWX					S31 6:30A				S31 11:00A	
LEC				S31 12:45P	S31 5:00P					

Vessel key: Fairweather (FWX); LeConte (LEC). *Arrivals noted in red.*
The State of Alaska reserves the right to alter, revise or cancel schedules and rates without prior notice, and assumes no responsibility for delays and/or expenses due to such modifications.

*For updated schedules and fares,
go to www.ferryalaska.com*

June 2014

Southeast Alaska Dayboats:
MV's: *Fairweather* (southbound)/*LeConte* (westbound)

	PELICAN	SKAGWAY	HAINES	GUSTAVUS	JUNEAU	HOONAH	TENAKEE	ANGOON	SITKA	PETERSBURG
FWX					Su1 6:30A				Su1 11:00A	
LEC					Su1 7:00A	Su1 11:15A	Su1 3:00P	Su1 5:15P		
LEC					M2 4:00P	M2 7:15P				
LEC					W4 7:00A	W4 10:15A				
FWX					Th5 6:30A				Th5 11:00A	
LEC				Th5 12:45P	Th5 5:00P					
FWX					F6 6:30A				F6 11:00A	
LEC					F6 7:00A	F6 10:45A	F6 2:00P			
FWX					S7 6:30A			S7 9:45A	S7 12:45P	
LEC				S7 12:45P	S7 5:00P					
FWX					Su8 6:30A				Su8 11:00A	
LEC					Su8 7:00A	Su8 11:15A	Su8 3:00P	Su8 5:15P		
LEC					M9 4:30P	M9 7:45P				
FWX					T10 6:30A				T10 11:00A	
FWX					Th12 6:30A			Th12 9:45A	Th12 12:45P	
LEC	Th12 7:00A			Th12 11:15A	Th12 3:30P					
FWX					F13 6:30A				F13 11:00A	
LEC					F13 7:00A	F13 10:45A	F13 2:00P			
FWX					S14 7:00A				S14 12:00P	
LEC				S14 12:45P	S14 5:00P					
FWX					Su15 6:30A			Su15 9:45A	Su15 12:45P	
LEC					Su15 7:00A	Su15 11:15A	Su15 3:00P	Su15 5:15P		
LEC					M16 4:00P	M16 7:15P				
LEC					W18 7:00A	W18 10:15A				
FWX					Th19 6:30A				Th19 11:00A	
LEC				Th19 12:45P	Th19 5:00P					
FWX					F20 6:30A				F20 11:00A	
LEC					F20 7:00A	F20 10:45A	F20 2:00P			
FWX					S21 6:30A			S21 9:45A	S21 12:45P	
LEC				S21 12:45P	S21 5:00P					
LEC					Su22 7:00A	Su22 11:15A	Su22 3:00P	Su22 5:15P		
FWX			Su22 9:15A		Su22 11:30A					
LEC					M23 4:30P	M23 7:45P				
FWX					Th26 6:30A			Th26 9:45A	Th26 12:45P	
LEC	Th26 7:00A			Th26 11:15A	Th26 3:30P					
FWX					F27 6:30A				F27 11:00A	
LEC					F27 7:00A	F27 10:45A	F27 2:00P			
FWX					S28 6:30A				S28 11:00A	
LEC				S28 12:45P	S28 5:00P					
FWX					Su29 6:30A				Su29 11:00A	
LEC				Su29 12:15P	Su29 4:30P					
LEC					Su29 6:00P	Su29 9:15P				
FWX					M30 6:30A				M30 11:00A	
LEC					M30 4:00P	M30 7:15P				

Vessel key: Fairweather (FWX); LeConte (LEC). *Arrivals noted in red.*
The State of Alaska reserves the right to alter, revise or cancel schedules and rates without prior notice, and assumes no responsibility for delays and/or expenses due to such modifications.

July 2014

For updated schedules and fares, go to www.ferryalaska.com

Southeast Alaska Dayboats:

MV's: *Fairweather* (southbound)/*LeConte* (westbound)

	PELICAN	SKAGWAY	HAINES	GUSTAVUS	JUNEAU	HOONAH	TENAKEE	ANGOON	SITKA	PETERSBURG
FWX					T1 6:30A					T1 10:30A
FWX					W2 6:30A				W2 11:00A	
LEC					W2 7:00A	W2 10:15A				
FWX					Th3 6:30A			Th3 9:45A	Th3 12:45P	
LEC				Th3 12:45P	Th3 5:00P					
FWX					F4 6:30A				F4 11:00A	
LEC					F4 7:00A	F4 10:45A	F4 2:00P			
FWX					S5 6:30A				S5 11:00A	
LEC				S5 12:45P	S5 5:00P					
FWX					Su6 6:30A				Su6 11:00A	
LEC					Su6 7:00A	Su6 11:15A	Su6 3:00P	Su6 5:15P		
FWX					M7 6:30A				M7 11:00A	
LEC					M7 4:30P	M7 7:45P				
FWX					T8 6:30A					T8 10:30A
FWX					W9 6:30A				W9 11:00A	
FWX					Th10 6:30A				Th10 11:00A	
LEC	Th10 7:00A			Th10 11:15A	Th10 3:30P					
FWX					F11 6:30A				F11 11:00A	
LEC					F11 7:00A	F11 10:45A	F11 2:00P			
FWX					S12 6:30A			S12 9:45A	S12 12:45P	
LEC				S12 12:45P	S12 5:00P					
FWX					Su13 6:45A				Su13 11:45A	
LEC					Su13 7:00A	Su13 11:15A	Su13 3:00P	Su13 5:15P		
FWX					M14 7:45A				M14 12:45P	
LEC					M14 4:00P	M14 7:15P				
FWX					T15 6:30A					T15 10:30A
FWX					W16 6:00A				W16 11:00A	
LEC					W16 7:00A	W16 10:15A				
FWX					Th17 6:00A			Th17 9:15A	Th17 12:15P	
LEC				Th17 12:45P	Th17 5:00P					
FWX					F18 6:30A				F18 11:00A	
LEC					F18 7:00A	F18 10:45A	F18 2:00P			
FWX					S19 6:30A				S19 11:00A	
LEC				S19 12:45P	S19 5:00P					
FWX					Su20 6:30A				Su20 11:00A	
LEC					Su20 7:00A	Su20 11:15A	Su20 3:00P	Su20 5:15P		
FWX					M21 6:30A				M21 11:00A	
LEC					M21 4:30P	M21 7:45P				
FWX					T22 6:30A					T22 10:30A
FWX					W23 6:30A				W23 11:00A	
FWX					Th24 6:30A				Th24 11:00A	
LEC	Th24 7:00A			Th24 11:15A	Th24 3:30P					
FWX					F25 6:30A				F25 11:00A	
LEC					F25 7:00A	F25 10:45A	F25 2:00P			
FWX					S26 6:30A			S26 9:45A	S26 12:45P	
LEC				S26 12:45P	S26 5:00P					
FWX					Su27 6:30A				Su27 11:00A	
LEC					Su27 7:00A	Su27 11:15A	Su27 3:00P	Su27 5:15P		
FWX					M28 6:30A				M28 11:00A	
LEC					M28 4:00P	M28 7:15P				
FWX					T29 6:30A					T29 10:30A
FWX					W30 6:30A				W30 11:00A	
LEC					W30 7:00A	W30 10:15A				
FWX					Th31 6:30A			Th31 9:45A	Th31 12:45P	
LEC				Th31 12:45P	Th31 5:00P					

Vessel key: Fairweather (FWX); LeConte (LEC). *Arrivals noted in red.*
The State of Alaska reserves the right to alter, revise or cancel schedules and rates without prior notice, and assumes no responsibility for delays and/or expenses due to such modifications.

For updated schedules and fares, go to www.ferryalaska.com

August 2014

Southeast Alaska Dayboats: MV's: *Fairweather* (southbound)/*LeConte* (westbound)

	PELICAN	SKAGWAY	HAINES	GUSTAVUS	JUNEAU	HOONAH	TENAKEE	ANGOON	SITKA	PETERSBURG
FWX					F1 6:30A				F1 11:00A	
LEC					F1 7:00A	F1 10:45A	F1 2:00P			
FWX					S2 6:30A				S2 11:00A	
LEC				S2 12:45P	S2 5:00P					
FWX					Su3 6:30A				Su3 11:00A	
LEC					Su3 7:00A	Su3 11:15A	Su3 3:00P	Su3 5:15P		
FWX			M4 9:45A		M4 12:00P					
FWX			M4 4:15P		M4 6:30P					
LEC					M4 4:30P	M4 7:45P				
FWX					T5 6:30A					T5 10:30A
FWX					W6 6:30A				W6 11:00A	
FWX					Th7 6:30A				Th7 11:00A	
LEC	Th7 7:00A			Th7 11:15A	Th7 3:30P					
FWX					F8 6:30A				F8 11:00A	
LEC					F8 7:00A	F8 10:45A	F8 2:00P			
FWX					S9 6:30A			S9 9:45A	S9 12:45P	
LEC				S9 12:45P	S9 5:00P					
FWX					Su10 6:30A				Su10 11:00A	
LEC					Su10 7:00A	Su10 11:15A	Su10 3:00P	Su10 5:15P		
FWX					M11 6:30A				M11 11:30A	
LEC					M11 4:00P	M11 7:15P				
FWX					T12 6:30A					T12 10:30A
FWX					W13 5:30A				W13 10:00A	
LEC					W13 7:00A	W13 10:15A				
FWX					Th14 7:15A			Th14 10:30A	Th14 1:30P	
LEC				Th14 12:45P	Th14 5:00P					
FWX					F15 6:30A				F15 11:00A	
LEC					F15 7:00A	F15 10:45A	F15 2:00P			
FWX					S16 6:30A				S16 11:00A	
LEC				S16 12:45P	S16 5:00P					
FWX					Su17 6:30A				Su17 11:00A	
LEC					Su17 7:00A	Su17 11:15A	Su17 3:00P	Su17 5:15P		
FWX					M18 6:30A				M18 11:00A	
LEC					M18 4:30P	M18 7:45P				
FWX					T19 6:30A					T19 10:30A
FWX					W20 6:30A				W20 11:00A	
FWX					Th21 6:30A				Th21 11:00A	
LEC	Th21 7:00A			Th21 11:15A	Th21 3:30P					
FWX					F22 6:30A				F22 11:00A	
LEC					F22 7:00A	F22 10:45A	F22 2:00P			
FWX					S23 6:30A			S23 9:45A	S23 12:45P	
LEC				S23 12:45P	S23 5:00P					
FWX					Su24 6:30A				Su24 11:00A	
LEC					Su24 7:00A	Su24 11:15A	Su24 3:00P	Su24 5:15P		
FWX					M25 6:30A				M25 11:00A	
LEC					M25 4:00P	M25 7:15P				
FWX					T26 6:30A					T26 10:30A
FWX					W27 6:30A				W27 11:00A	
LEC					W27 7:00A	W27 10:15A				
FWX					Th28 6:30A			Th28 9:45A	Th28 12:45P	
LEC				Th28 12:45P	Th28 5:00P					
FWX					F29 6:30A				F29 11:00A	
LEC					F29 7:00A	F29 10:45A	F29 2:00P			
FWX					S30 6:30A				S30 11:00A	
LEC				S30 12:45P	S30 5:00P					
FWX					Su31 6:30A				Su31 11:00A	
LEC					Su31 7:00A	Su31 11:15A	Su31 3:00P	Su31 5:15P		

September 2014 (to 15th)

Southeast Alaska Dayboats: MV's: *Fairweather* (southbound)/*LeConte* (westbound)

	PELICAN	SKAGWAY	HAINES	GUSTAVUS	JUNEAU	HOONAH	TENAKEE	ANGOON	SITKA	PETERSBURG
FWX					M1 6:30A				M1 11:00A	
LEC					M1 4:30P	M1 7:45P				
FWX					T2 6:30A					T2 10:30A
FWX					W3 6:30A				W3 11:00A	
FWX					Th4 6:30A			Th4 9:45A	Th4 12:45P	
LEC	Th4 7:00A			Th4 11:15A	Th4 3:30P					
LEC					F5 7:00A	F5 10:45A	F5 2:00P			
FWX		F5 4:30P			F5 7:00P					
FWX					S6 6:30A				S6 11:00A	
LEC				S6 12:45P	S6 5:00P					
LEC					Su7 7:00A	Su7 11:15A	Su7 3:00P	Su7 5:15P		
FWX		Su7 10:00A			Su7 12:30P					
FWX					M8 6:30A				M8 11:00A	
LEC					M8 4:00P	M8 7:15P				
FWX					T9 6:30A					T9 10:30A
LEC					W10 7:00A	W10 10:15A				
FWX					W10 7:30A				W10 12:00P	
FWX					Th11 6:30A			Th11 9:45A	Th11 12:45P	
LEC				Th11 12:45P	Th11 5:00P					
FWX					F12 5:45A				F12 10:15A	
LEC					F12 7:00A	F12 10:45A	F12 2:00P			
FWX					S13 6:30A			S13 9:45A	S13 12:45P	
LEC				S13 12:45P	S13 5:00P					
FWX					Su14 6:30A				Su14 11:00A	
FWX					M15 6:30A				M15 11:00A	

MV Fairweather dining area. (©Sharon Nault)

Prince William Sound
Summer 2014 MV *Chenega*

For updated schedules and fares, go to www.ferryalaska.com

DATE: DAY	Eastbound		
	Whittier	Valdez	Cordova
May 1-12 **Th, Sat, Mon**	11:30A	3:15P	6:00P
May 2-11 **Su, Wed, Fri**	3:00P		6:15P
May 15-Sept. 11 **Th**	3:00P		6:15P
May 12-Sept. 29 **Mon**	11:30A	3:15P	6:00P
May 13-Sept. 10 **Su, Tue, Wed, Fri, Sat**	12:15P		3:30P
Sept. 8-30 **Mon, Wed*, Fri**	11:30A	3:15P	6:00P
Sept. 14-30 **Su, Tue, Th**	2:45P		6:00P

*Wed: Begins Sept. 17

DATE: DAY	Westbound		
	Cordova	Valdez	Whittier
May 1-11 **Su, Wed, Fri:**	7:15A	11:15A	2:00P
May 1-13 **Sat, Mon, Tue, Th:**	7:15A		10:30A
May 15-Sept.13 **Su, Mon, Tue, Wed, Fri, Sat:**	7:15A		10:30A
May 15-Sept. 11 **Th:**	7:15A	11:15A	2:00P
Sept. 14-30 **Su, Tue, Th:**	7:15A	11:00A	1:45P

Prince William Sound
Summer 2014 MV *Aurora*

DATE: DAY	Eastbound		
	Whittier	Valdez	Tatitlek
May 15-Sept. 11 **Su, Mon, Wed*, Th, Fri, Sat**	1:45P	7:30P	
May 15-Sept. 11 **Tue.**	2:15P	8:00P	
May 21; June 4, 18; July 2, 16, 30; Aug. 13, 27; Sept. 10 **Wed**		7:00A	9:45A

*NO sailings from Whittier Wed.'s: May 21; June 4, 18; July 2, 16, 30; Aug. 13, 27; Sept. 10.

DATE: DAY	Westbound		
	Tatitlek	Valdez	Whittier
May 15-Sept. 11 **Su, Mon, Tue, Wed*, Th, Fri, Sat**		7:00A	12:45P
May 21; June 4, 18; July 2, 16, 30; Aug. 13, 27; Sept. 10 **Wed.**	10:15A	1:00P	

*NO sailings from Valdez Wed.'s: May 21; June 4, 18; July 2, 16, 30; Aug. 13, 27; Sept. 10.

The State of Alaska reserves the right to alter, revise or cancel schedules and rates without prior notice, and assumes no responsibility for delays and/or expenses due to such modifications.

Southwest and Aleutian Chain
Westbound Summer 2014: MV's *Kennicott* and *Tustumena*

ALASKA MARINE HIGHWAY SCHEDULES & TARIFFS

Month		Seldovia	Homer	Port Lions*	Kodiak	Sand Point	King Cove	Cold Bay	False Pass	Akutan	Dutch Harbor
MAY	TUS	T29 5:45P	T29 10:30P		W30 4:45P	Th1 11:45P	F2 7:45A	F2 12:45P	F2 6:45P	S3 5:45A	S3 9:15A
MAY	KEN		S3 2:00A		S3 11:00A						
MAY	KEN	Su4 6:30A	Su4 10:45A †		Su4 10:45P †						
MAY	TUS	T6 8:15P	W7 12:30A	W7 11:30A	W7 2:00P						
MAY	TUS	Th8 4:30P	Th8 8:45P	F9 7:45A	F9 10:45A						
MAY	TUS		S10 10:30A		S10 8:15P						
MAY	TUS	Su11 4:30P	Su11 8:45P	M12 7:45A	M12 10:15A						
MAY	TUS	T13 5:45P	T13 10:30P		W14 4:45P	Th15 11:45P	F16 7:45A	F16 12:45P	F16 6:45P	S17 5:45A	S17 9:15A
MAY	KEN		S17 2:00A		S17 11:00A						
MAY	KEN	Su18 6:30A	Su18 10:45A †		Su18 10:45P †						
MAY	TUS		T20 9:15P		W21 6:45A						
MAY	TUS		Th22 2:45A		Th22 12:15P						
MAY	TUS		F23 5:45A	F23 4:30P	F23 7:00P						
MAY	TUS	S24 3:00P	S24 7:30P		Su25 5:00A						
MAY	TUS		Su25 10:30P	M26 9:15A	M26 11:45A						
MAY	TUS	T27 10:30P	W28 3:15A		W28 4:45P	Th29 11:45P	F30 7:45A	F30 12:45P	F30 6:45P	S31 5:45A	S31 9:15A
MAY	KEN		S31 2:00A		S31 11:00A						
MAY	TUS	T28 10:30P	W29 3:15A		W29 8:15P	Th30 11:45P	F31 7:45A	F31 12:45P	F31 6:45P	S1 5:45A	S1 9:15A
JUNE	KEN	Su1 6:30A	Su1 10:45A †		Su1 10:45P †						
JUNE	TUS	T3 8:15P	W4 12:30A	W4 11:30A	W4 2:00P						
JUNE	TUS	Th5 4:30P	Th5 8:45P	F6 7:45A	F6 10:45A						
JUNE	TUS		S7 10:30A		S7 8:15P						
JUNE	TUS	Su8 4:30P	Su8 8:45P	M9 7:45A	M9 10:15A						
JUNE	TUS	T10 5:45P	T10 10:30P		W11 4:45P	Th12 11:45P	F13 7:45A	F13 12:45P	F13 6:45P	S14 5:45A	S14 9:15A
JUNE	KEN		S14 2:00A		S14 11:00A						
JUNE	KEN	Su15 6:30A	Su15 10:45A †		Su15 10:45P †						
JUNE	TUS	T17 8:15P	W18 12:30A	W18 11:30A	W18 2:00P						
JUNE	TUS	Th19 4:30P	Th19 8:45P	F20 7:45A	F20 10:45A						
JUNE	TUS		S21 10:30A		S21 8:15P						
JUNE	TUS	Su22 4:30P	Su22 8:45P	M23 7:45A	M23 10:15A						
JUNE	TUS	T24 5:45P	T24 10:30P		W25 4:45P	Th26 11:45P	F27 7:45A	F27 12:45P	F27 6:45P	S28 5:45A	S28 9:15A
JUNE	KEN		S28 2:00A		S28 11:00A						
JUNE	KEN	Su29 6:30A	Su29 10:45A †		Su29 10:45P †						
JULY	TUS	T1 8:15P	W2 12:30A	W2 11:30A	W2 2:00P						
JULY	TUS	Th3 4:30P	Th3 8:45P	F4 7:45A	F4 10:45A						
JULY	TUS		S5 10:30A		S5 8:15P						
JULY	TUS	Su6 4:30P	Su6 8:45P	M7 7:45A	M7 10:15A						
JULY	TUS	T8 5:45P	T8 10:30P		W9 4:45P	Th10 11:45P	F11 7:45A	F11 12:45P	F11 6:45P	S12 5:45A	S12 9:15A
JULY	KEN		S12 2:00A		S12 11:00A						
JULY	KEN	Su13 6:30A	Su13 10:45A †		Su13 10:45P †						
JULY	TUS	T15 8:15P	W16 12:30A	W16 11:30A	W16 2:00P						
JULY	TUS	Th17 4:30P	Th17 8:45P	F18 7:45A	F18 10:45A						
JULY	TUS		S19 10:30A		S19 8:15P						
JULY	TUS	Su20 4:30P	Su20 8:45P	M21 7:45A	M21 10:15A						
JULY	TUS	T22 5:45P	T22 10:30P		W23 4:45P	Th24 11:45P	F25 7:45A	F25 12:45P	F25 6:45P	S26 5:45A	S26 9:15A
JULY	KEN		S26 2:00A		S26 11:00A						
JULY	KEN	Su27 6:30A	Su27 10:45A †		Su27 10:45P †						
JULY	TUS	T29 8:15P	W30 12:30A	W30 11:30A	W30 2:00P						
JULY	TUS	Th31 4:30P	Th31 8:45P	F1 7:45A	F1 10:45A						
AUGUST	TUS		S2 10:30A		S2 8:15P						
AUGUST	TUS	Su3 4:30P	Su3 8:45P	M4 7:45A	M4 10:15A						
AUGUST	TUS	T5 5:45P	T5 10:30P		W6 4:45P	Th7 11:45P	F8 7:45A	F8 12:45P	F8 6:45P	S9 5:45A	S9 9:15A
AUGUST	KEN		S9 1:00A		S9 10:00A						
AUGUST	KEN	Su10 5:30A	Su10 10:45A †		Su10 10:45P †						
AUGUST	TUS	T12 8:15P	W13 12:30A	W13 11:30A	W13 2:00P						
AUGUST	TUS	Th14 4:30P	Th14 8:45P	F15 7:45A	F15 10:45A						
AUGUST	TUS		S16 10:30A		S16 8:15P						
AUGUST	TUS	Su17 4:30P	Su17 8:45P	M18 7:45A	M18 10:15A						
AUGUST	TUS	T19 5:45P	T19 10:30P		W20 4:45P	Th21 11:45P	F22 7:45A	F22 12:45P	F22 6:45P	S23 5:45A	S23 9:15A
AUGUST	KEN		S23 1:00A		S23 10:00A						
AUGUST	KEN	Su24 5:30A	Su24 10:45A †		Su24 10:45P †						
AUGUST	TUS	T26 8:15P	W27 12:30A	W27 11:30A	W27 2:00P						
AUGUST	TUS	Th28 4:30P	Th28 8:45P	F29 7:45A	F29 10:45A						
AUGUST	TUS		S30 10:30A		S30 8:15P						
AUGUST	TUS	Su31 4:30P	Su31 8:45P	M1 7:45A	M1 10:15A						
AUGUST	TUS	T2 5:45P	T2 10:30P		W3 4:45P	Th4 11:45P	F5 7:45A	F5 12:45P	F5 6:45P	S6 5:45A	S6 9:15A
AUGUST	KEN		S6 12:00A		S6 9:00A						
SEPTEMBER	KEN	Su7 4:30A	Su7 9:45A †		Su7 10:45P †						
SEPTEMBER	TUS	T9 8:15P	W10 12:30A	W10 11:30A	W10 2:00P						
SEPTEMBER	TUS	Th11 4:30P	Th11 8:45P	F12 7:45A	F12 10:45A						
SEPTEMBER	TUS		S13 10:30A		S13 8:15P						
SEPTEMBER	TUS	Su14 4:30P	Su14 8:45P	M15 7:45A	M15 10:15A						
SEPTEMBER	TUS	T16 5:45P	T16 10:30P		W17 4:45P	Th18 11:45P	F19 7:45A	F19 12:45P	F19 6:45P	S20 5:45A	S20 9:15A
SEPTEMBER	KEN		S20 9:30A		S20 9:30A						
SEPTEMBER	KEN	Su21 5:00A	Su21 10:45A †		Su21 10:45P †						
SEPTEMBER	TUS	T23 8:15P	W24 12:30A	W24 11:30A	W24 2:00P						
SEPTEMBER	TUS	Th25 4:30P	Th25 8:45P	F26 7:45A	F26 10:45A						
SEPTEMBER	TUS		S27 10:30A		S27 8:15P						
SEPTEMBER	TUS	Su28 4:30P	Su28 8:45P	M29 7:45A	M29 10:15A						
SEPTEMBER	TUS	T30 5:45P	T30 10:30P		W1 8:15P						

*Old Harbor MV *Tustumena* departures on June 26 Th1:15A; August 21 Th1:15A. **Ouzinkie** MV *Tustumena* departures at 9:15A on May 9; June 6 & 20; July 4 & 18; August 1, 15 & 29; Sept 12 & 26. † Cross Gulf southbound sailing, see page 722. Arrivals noted in red.

Southwest and Aleutian Chain

Eastbound Summer 2014: MV's *Kennicott* and *Tustumena*

ALASKA MARINE HIGHWAY SCHEDULES & TARIFFS

Month	Ship	Dutch Harbor	Akutan	Cold Bay	King Cove	Sand Point	Kodiak	Port Lions*	Homer	Seldovia
MAY	KEN						F2 12:00P		F2 9:00P	
	KEN						S3 3:00P		Su4 4:00A	Su4 5:15A
	TUS	S3 5:15P	S3 9:45P	Su4 10:45A	Su4 1:45P	Su4 9:00P	T6 4:15A		T6 5:00P	T6 6:30P
	TUS						W7 7:30P	W7 10:45P	Th8 11:45A	Th8 1:15P
	TUS						F9 5:00P	F9 8:45P	S10 7:00A	
	TUS						S10 11:15P		Su11 11:45A	Su11 1:15P
	TUS						F16 12:00P		F16 9:00P	
	TUS						M12 5:30P	M12 8:45P	T13 11:45A	T13 1:15P
	KEN						S17 3:00P		Su18 4:00A	Su18 5:15A
	TUS	S17 5:15P	S17 9:45P	Su18 10:45A	Su18 1:45P	Su18 9:00P	T20 4:15A		T20 1:45P	
	TUS						W21 2:15P		W21 11:45P	
	TUS						Th22 5:15P		F23 2:45A	
	TUS						F23 10:00P		S24 10:15A	S24 11:45A
	TUS						Su25 8:00A		Su25 5:30P	
	KEN						F30 12:00P		F30 9:00P	
	TUS						M26 11:30P		T27 4:30P	T27 6:00P
JUNE	KEN						S31 3:00P		Su1 4:00A	Su1 5:15A
	TUS	S31 5:15P	S31 9:45P	Su1 10:45A	Su1 1:45P	Su1 9:00P	T3 4:15A		T3 5:00P	T3 6:30P
	TUS						W4 7:30P	W4 10:45P	Th5 11:45A	Th5 1:15P
	TUS						F6 5:00P	F6 8:45P	S7 7:00A	
	TUS						S7 11:15P		Su8 11:45A	Su8 1:15P
	TUS						F13 12:00P		F13 9:00P	
	TUS						M9 5:30P	M9 8:45P	T10 11:45A	T10 1:15P
	KEN						S14 3:00P		Su15 4:00A	Su15 5:15A
	TUS	S14 5:15P	S14 9:45P	Su15 10:45A	Su15 1:45P	Su15 9:00P	T17 4:15A		T17 5:00P	T17 6:30P
	TUS						W18 7:30P	W18 10:45P	Th19 11:45A	Th19 1:15P
	TUS						F20 5:00P	F20 8:45P	S21 7:00A	
	TUS						S21 11:15P		Su22 11:45A	Su22 1:15P
	KEN						F27 12:00P		F27 9:00P	
	TUS						M23 5:30P	M23 8:45P	T24 11:45A	T24 1:15P
	KEN						S28 3:00P		Su29 4:00A	Su29 5:15A
	TUS	S28 5:15P	S28 9:45P	Su29 10:45A	Su29 1:45P	Su29 9:00P	T1 4:15A		T1 5:00P	T1 6:30P
JULY	TUS						W2 7:30P	W2 10:45P	Th3 11:45A	Th3 1:15P
	TUS						F4 5:00P	F4 8:45P	S5 7:00A	
	TUS						S5 11:15P		Su6 11:45A	Su6 1:15P
	KEN						F11 12:00P		F11 9:00P	
	TUS						M7 5:30P	M7 8:45P	T8 11:45A	T8 1:15P
	KEN						S12 3:00P		Su13 4:00A	Su13 5:15A
	TUS	S12 5:15P	S12 9:45P	Su13 10:45A	Su13 1:45P	Su13 9:00P	T15 4:15A		T15 5:00P	T15 6:30P
	TUS						W16 7:30P	W16 10:45P	Th17 11:45A	Th17 1:15P
	TUS						F18 5:00P	F18 8:45P	S19 7:00A	
	TUS						S19 11:15P		Su20 11:45A	Su20 1:15P
	KEN						F25 12:00P		F25 9:00P	
	TUS						M21 5:30P	M21 8:45P	T22 11:45A	T22 1:15P
	KEN						S26 3:00P		Su27 4:00A	Su27 5:15A
	TUS	S26 5:15P	S26 9:45P	Su27 10:45A	Su27 1:45P	Su27 9:00P	T29 4:15A		T29 5:00P	T29 6:30P
	TUS						W30 7:30P	W30 10:45P	Th31 11:45A	Th31 1:15P
	TUS						F1 5:00P	F1 8:45P	S2 7:00A	
AUGUST	TUS						S2 11:15P		Su3 11:45A	Su3 1:15P
	KEN						F8 12:00P		F8 9:00P	
	TUS						M4 5:30P	M4 8:45P	T5 11:45A	T5 1:15P
	KEN						S9 2:00P		Su10 3:00A	Su10 4:15A
	TUS	S9 5:15P	S9 9:45P	Su10 10:45A	Su10 1:45P	Su10 9:00P	T12 4:15A		T12 5:00P	T12 6:30P
	TUS						W13 7:30P	W13 10:45P	Th14 11:45A	Th14 1:15P
	TUS						F15 5:00P	F15 8:45P	S16 7:00A	
	TUS						S16 11:15P		Su17 11:45A	Su17 1:15P
	KEN						F22 11:00A		F22 8:00P	
	TUS						M18 5:30P	M18 8:45P	T19 11:45A	T19 1:15P
	KEN						S23 2:00P		Su24 3:00A	Su24 4:15A
	TUS	S23 5:15P	S23 9:45P	Su24 10:45A	Su24 1:45P	Su24 9:00P	T26 4:15A		T26 5:00P	T26 6:30P
	TUS						W27 7:30P	W27 10:45P	Th28 11:45A	Th28 1:15P
	TUS						F29 5:00P	F29 8:45P	S30 7:00A	
	TUS						S30 11:15P		Su31 11:45A	Su31 1:15P
	KEN						F5 11:00A		F5 8:00P	
	TUS						M1 5:30P	M1 8:45P	T2 11:45A	T2 1:15P
	KEN						S6 1:00P		Su7 2:00A	Su7 3:15A
SEPTEMBER	TUS	S6 5:15P	S6 9:45P	Su7 10:45A	Su7 1:45P	Su7 9:00P	T9 4:15A		T9 5:00P	T9 6:30P
	TUS						W10 7:30P	W10 10:45P	Th11 11:45A	Th11 1:15P
	TUS						F12 5:00P	F12 8:45P	S13 7:00A	
	TUS						S13 11:15P		Su14 11:45A	Su14 1:15P
	KEN						F19 11:00A		F19 8:00P	
	TUS						M15 5:30P	M15 8:45P	T16 11:45A	T16 1:15P
	KEN						S20 1:30P		Su21 2:30A	Su21 3:45A
	TUS	S20 5:15P	S20 9:45P	Su21 10:45A	Su21 1:45P	Su21 9:00P	T23 4:15A		T23 5:00P	T23 6:30P
	TUS						W24 7:30P	W24 10:45P	Th25 11:45A	Th25 1:15P
	TUS						F26 5:00P	F26 8:45P	S27 7:00A	
	TUS						S27 11:15P		Su28 11:45A	Su28 1:15P
	TUS						M29 5:30P	M29 8:45P	T30 11:45A	T30 1:15P

*Old Harbor MV *Tustumena* departures on June 16 M 7:30P; August 11 M 7:30P. Ouzinkie MV *Tustumena* departures at 7:00P on May 9; June 6 & 20; July 4 & 18; August 1, 15 & 29; Sept. 12 & 26. Arrivals noted in red.

For updated schedules and fares, go to www.ferryalaska.com

Southcentral/Southwest/Aleutians
Passenger & Vehicle Fares Summer 2014

ADULTS 12 YEARS OR OLDER (Meals and berth not included)
Children under 6 travel free. Children 6 thru 11 years approximately 1/2 adult fare. Senior rates may be available on some sailings.

	UNA	AKU	FPS	CBY	KCV	SDP	CHG	OLD	K/O	PTL	HOM	SDV	WHT	CHB	V/T
AKU	31														
FSP	72	54													
CBY	89	76	33												
KCV	107	97	54	33											
SDP	147	134	89	66	50										
CHG	192	182	134	111	97	66									
OLD	259	249	201	178	164	133	67								
K/O	293	281	237	215	200	163	111	44							
PTL	293	281	237	215	200	163	111	44	33						
HOM	351	343	295	272	256	221	173	106	74	74					
SDV	357	347	301	279	260	227	178	80	80	80	33				
WHT								91	91	91	159	163			
CHB								91	91		159	163	89		
V/T								147	147	147	202	206	89	89	
CDV								147	147	147	202	206	89	89	50

VEHICLES UP TO 10 FEET (Driver not included)

	UNA	AKU	FPS	CBY	KCV	SDP	CHG	OLD	K/O	PTL	HOM	SDV	WHT	CHB	V/T
AKU	36														
FSP	91														
CBY	122		37												
KCV	142		68	37											
SDP	189		114	84	63										
CHG	256		183	151	129	84									
OLD	347		274	242	220	175	91								
K/O	387	348	316	284	264	219	151	60		40					
PTL	387		316	284	264	219	151	60	40						
HOM	461	415	392	362	341	294	228	137	94	94					
SDV	469		399	367	350	301	236	145	102	102	32				
WHT								275	117	117	204	212			
CHB									117		204	212	101		
V/T								231	189	189	268	275	75	101	
CDV								231	189	189	268	275	75	101	58

VEHICLES UP TO 15 FEET (Driver not included)

	UNA	AKU	FPS	CBY	KCV	SDP	CHG	OLD	K/O	PTL	HOM	SDV	WHT	CHB	V/T
AKU	60														
FSP	150														
CBY	201		57												
KCV	238		105	53											
SDP	317		186	134	99										
CHG	432		301	248	215	134									
OLD	581		450	397	364	283	149								
K/O	662	596	528	478	445	365	248	99		58					
PTL	662		528	478	445	365	248	99	58						
HOM	796	716	667	617	579	492	383	234	152	152					
SDV	812		680	628	593	509	398	249	166	166	46				
WHT								475	191	191	344	359			
CHB									191		344	359	159		
V/T								395	317	317	451	463	105	159	
CDV								395	317	317	451	463	105	159	94

VEHICLES UP TO 19 FEET (Driver not included)

	UNA	AKU	FPS	CBY	KCV	SDP	CHG	OLD	K/O	PTL	HOM	SDV	WHT	CHB	V/T
AKU	70														
FSP	174														
CBY	238		68												
KCV	280		125	63											
SDP	376		222	157	115										
CHG	510		360	295	251	157									
OLD	687		537	472	428	334	177								
K/O	787	708	635	572	524	433	295	118		68					
PTL	787		635	572	524	433	295	118	68		179				
HOM	949	854	793	731	688	593	451	274	179	195					
SDV	966		810	745	705	608	465	288	195	225	54				
WHT								564	225		408	423			
CHB									225		408	423	190		
V/T								474	376	376	536	553	123	190	
CDV								474	376	376	536	553	123	190	110

VEHICLES UP TO 21 FEET (Driver not included)

	UNA	AKU	FPS	CBY	KCV	SDP	CHG	OLD	K/O	PTL	HOM	SDV	WHT	CHB	V/T
AKU															
FSP	224														
CBY	304		88												
KCV	360		158	79											
SDP	479		282	201	147										
CHG	658		455	379	325	201									
OLD	885		682	606	552	428	227								
K/O	1018	916	817	736	680	555	379	152		88					
PTL	1223		1024	941	888	764	587	152	229		229				
HOM	1246	1101	1042	962	907	784	605	360	248	248		66			
SDV								378	290	290	517		540		
WHT								729	290		517	540		241	
CHB									290	479	696	714	157		241
V/T								612	479	479	696	714	157	241	
CDV								612	479	479	696	714	157	241	138

RATE PER FOOT FOR VEHICLES OVER 21 FEET (Driver not included)

	UNA	AKU	FPS	CBY	KCV	SDP	CHG	OLD	K/O	PTL	HOM	SDV	WHT	CHB	V/T
AKU	5.0														
FSP	12.4		4.6												
CBY	16.9		8.6	4.0											
KCV	19.7		15.5	11.0	7.9										
SDP	27.2		25.8	21.4	18.1	11.0									
CHG	37.3		46.1	41.5	38.3	31.4	21.4								
OLD	50.1		38.6	34.2	30.9	23.8	12.8								
K/O	57.5	5.0	46.1	41.5	38.3	31.4	21.4	9.0		4.6					
PTL	57.5		57.8	53.3	50.1	43.0	32.9	8.6	12.6		12.6				
HOM	69.1	5.0	59.0	54.4	51.1	44.2	33.6	20.1	13.8	13.8		3.4			
SDV	70.4							20.8	15.9	15.9	29.2		31.8		
WHT								41.2	15.9		29.2	31.8		12.9	
CHB									27.0	27.0	38.9	40.4	8.3		12.9
V/T								34.6	27.0	27.0	38.9	40.4	8.3	12.9	
CDV								34.6	27.0	27.0	38.9	40.4	8.3	12.9	7.5

Additional fees for bicycles (no trailers) and kayaks/inflatables. Check www.ferryalaska.com for more information.

Port Abbreviations: Akutan (AKU), False Pass (FPS), Dutch Harbor/Unalaska (UNA), Cold Bay (CBY), King Cove (KCV), Sand Point (SDP), Chignik (CHG), Kodiak (KOD), Kodiak & Ouzinkie (K/O), Old Harbor (OLD), Port Lions (PTL), Homer (HOM), Seldovia (SDV), Whittier (WHT), Chenega Bay (CHB), Valdez (VDZ), Tatitlek (TAT), Valdez & Tatitlek (V/T), Cordova (CDV)

The State of Alaska reserves the right to alter, revise or cancel schedules and rates without prior notice, and assumes no responsibility for delays and/or expenses due to such modifications.

Southcentral/Southwest/Aleutians
Cabin Rates Summer 2014, May 1-Sept. 30

*For updated schedules
and fares, go to
www.ferryalaska.com*

Four Berth Cabin-Outside-Complete Facilities
MV's: *KENNICOTT, TUSTUMENA*

	UNA	AKU	FPS	CBY	KCV	SDP	KOD	OUZ	PTL	HOM	WHT
AKU	37										
FPS	120	87									
CBY	160	127	47								
KCV	180	188	104	66							
SDP	223	239	159	118	98						
KOD	490	426	344	302	282	241					
OUZ							66				
PTL	409	426	344	302			66	66			
HOM	563	492	411	369	351	302	129	66	129		
SDV	581	503	422	381	360	313	143	129	143	66	
WHT							160	143		249	
CHB							160			249	134

Two Berth Cabin-Outside-WCA Facilities
MV's: *TUSTUMENA*

	UNA	AKU	FPS	CBY	KCV	SDP	KOD	OUZ	PTL	HOM
AKU	30									
FPS	84	61								
CBY	109	89	33							
KCV	127	134	80	52						
SDP	161	170	111	87	72					
KOD	336	304	250	220	206	173				
OUZ							52			
PTL	381	304	250	220			52	52		
HOM	389	344	288	259	245	211	90	90	90	
SDV	396	353	297	268	254	219	97	97	97	52

Two Berth Cabin-Outside-No Facilities
MV's: *KENNICOTT, TUSTUMENA*

	UNA	AKU	FPS	CBY	KCV	SDP	KOD	OUZ	PTL	HOM	WHT
AKU	24										
FPS	72	53									
CBY	93	79	31								
KCV	109	118	70	46							
SDP	149	144	92	71	63						
KOD	311	280	229	206	189	161					
OUZ							46				
PTL	259	280	229	206			46	46			
HOM	361	320	271	247	230	199	80	80	80		
SDV	370	326	280	256	238	203	86	86	86	46	
WHT							99			158	
CHB							99			158	84

Four Berth Cabin-Outside-No Facilities
MV: *TUSTUMENA*

	UNA	AKU	FPS	CBY	KCV	SDP	KOD	OUZ	PTL	HOM
AKU	32									
FPS	97	72								
CBY	134	104	42							
KCV	154	159	89	57						
SDP	186	202	134	97	87					
KOD	410	356	288	254	237	202				
OUZ							57			
PTL	342	356	288	254			57	57		
HOM	475	411	344	309	294	254	106	106	106	
SDV	488	421	354	317	301	260	120	120	120	57

Four Berth Cabin-Inside-Complete Facilities
MV: *KENNICOTT*

	KOD	HOM	WHT
HOM	108		
SDV	128	59	
WHT	134	207	
CHB	134	207	110

Two Berth Roomette-Outside-No Facilities
MV: *KENNICOTT*

	KOD	HOM	WHT
HOM	29		
SDV	31	20	
WHT	34	50	
CHB	34	50	29

Two Berth Cabin-Inside-No Facilities
MV: *KENNICOTT*

	KOD	HOM	WHT
HOM	72		
SDV	76	42	
WHT	89	136	
CHB	89	136	75

Two Berth Roomette-Inside-No Facilities
MV: *KENNICOTT*

	KOD	HOM	WHT
HOM	24		
SDV	25	19	
WHT	30	41	
CHB	30	41	25

Ports: Akutan (AKU), False Pass (FPS), Unalaska/Dutch Harbor (UNA), Cold Bay (CBY), King Cove (KCV), Sand Point (SDP), Kodiak (KOD), Port Lions (PTL), Homer (HOM), Seldovia (SDV), Whittier (WHT), Ouzinkie (OUZ)

The State of Alaska reserves the right to alter, revise or cancel schedules and rates without prior notice, and assumes no responsibility for delays and/or expenses due to such modifications.

Basic Itinerary #1:

Inbound: Alaska Highway via West Access Route

Outbound: Inside Passage

The classic itinerary for Alaska-bound travelers on the West Access route is to drive the Alaska Highway one-way, and take the Alaska Marine Highway the other way via the Inside Passage from Haines, AK, to Bellingham, WA. The ferry portion of the itinerary requires advance reservations. Travelers should work backwards from their ferry departure date when estimating travel time for the driving portion of the trip.

Depart Seattle on the West Access Route, but cross the international border at Blaine (instead of Sumas), and follow Highway 99 through Vancouver to Horseshoe Bay and the start of the Sea to Sky Highway. This stunning highway, a former logging road, is a slight twist in the traditional West Access approach to the Alaska Highway. And it is, indeed, a twisting road, but Highway 99 also offers an exciting route into British Columbia's Cariboo country. Stop at the historic Hat Creek Ranch before joining Highway 97 north from Cache Creek to Prince George.

Leave Prince George via the Hart Highway to Dawson Creek. Stop in Chetwynd for a root-beer float and a look at some amazing chainsaw sculptures. Take a Tumbler Ridge side trip to see Kinuseo Falls or drive the Hudson's Hope Loop and tour the huge W.A.C. Bennett Dam.

Heading north up the Alaska Highway, allow enough time to stop and enjoy wildlife viewing, scenic lakes and historic lodges along the way. Stop for a soak at Liard River Hotsprings. At Watson Lake, first stop in Yukon, photograph the famous Signpost Forest. From Watson Lake it is just 164 miles to Teslin, home of the George Johnston Museum and the Tlingit Heritage Centre.

Next stop is Whitehorse, capital of Yukon and home to many of Yukon's best known attractions, including the SS *Klondike*, Yukon Beringia Interpretive Centre and Miles Canyon. Side trips include scenic Atlin on Atlin Road and Emerald Lake and Carcross on the South Klondike Highway. The White Pass & Yukon Route Railway offers train trips from Carcross to Skagway.

Driving north from Whitehorse, you'll visit Haines Junction, the Kluane Lake area and Beaver Creek. Just north of Beaver Creek you'll cross into Alaska at Port Alcan. Your first stop in Alaska will probably be Tok, which has all services and 2 visitor information centers. Delta Junction also has all services and is the official end of the Alaska Highway. Stop at Rika's Roadhouse just outside Delta Junction before driving to Fairbanks via the Richardson Highway.

Explore the many attractions of Fairbanks. Allow time for side trips to gold mines, hot springs, the trans-Alaska pipeline,

the Arctic Circle and points North.

Plan on at least 2 days (or more) to drive the Parks Highway from Fairbanks south to Anchorage. There's quite a bit to see and do on this highway, from horseback riding to touring sled dog kennels. Denali National Park is a must stop. Side trips along the Parks Highway include Petersville Road and Talkeetna. Anchorage side trips include Hatcher Pass Road, Prince William Sound and the Kenai Peninsula.

From Anchorage, take the Glenn Highway Scenic Byway, past Matanuska Glacier, to the Tok Cutoff. At Tok, go east on the Alaska Highway to Haines Junction, YT, then take Haines Highway south to the port of Haines, where you will catch the Alaska state ferry south to Bellingham, WA. If time allows, include stopovers at Southeast ports along the Inside Passage/Alaska Marine Highway portion of your trip.

Inbound mileage: 2,701 miles
Detail: Seattle to Dawson Creek 853 miles
 Dawson Creek to Fairbanks 1,486 miles
 Fairbanks to Anchorage 362 miles

Outbound mileage: 771 miles. Ferry travel is 68 hours (about 3 days).
 Detail: Anchorage to Tok 328 miles
 Tok to Haines 443 miles

Major Attractions

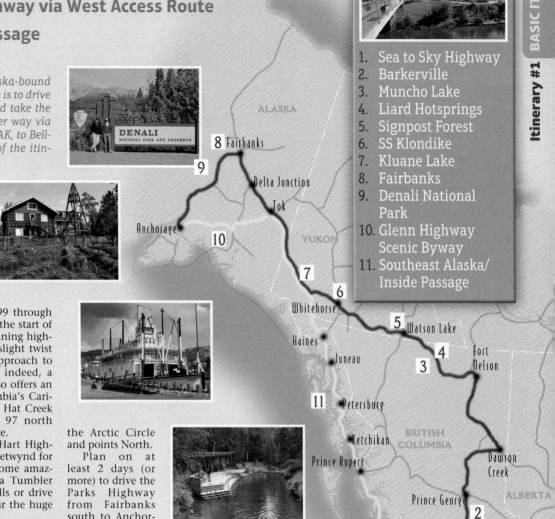

1. Sea to Sky Highway
2. Barkerville
3. Muncho Lake
4. Liard Hotsprings
5. Signpost Forest
6. SS Klondike
7. Kluane Lake
8. Fairbanks
9. Denali National Park
10. Glenn Highway Scenic Byway
11. Southeast Alaska/ Inside Passage

FOLLOWING THIS ITINERARY IN The MILEPOST.

NOTE: For reverse itinerary, read sections from bottom to top and reverse page numbers.
Page numbers for major attractions and side trip options are found on the Contents page and/or in the Index.

Basic Itinerary #2:

Inbound: Central Access/Hart Hwy. to Alaska Hwy. and Klondike Loop

Outbound: Inside Passage to Yellowhead Hwy. to Icefields Parkway

An itinerary using the Central Access route and part of the West Access route inbound to reach the Alaska Highway. Driving north to Whitehorse and entering Alaska via the Klondike Loop. On the return, take the Alaska Marine Highway from Haines to Prince Rupert, BC, and drive east on the Yellowhead Highway to Jasper and follow the Icefields Parkway south. The ferry portion of this itinerary requires advance planning. Check current summer schedules and time your itinerary accordingly.

Head up the Central Access Route from Ellensburg, WA, through British Columbia's Okanagan region. Follow Yellowhead Highway 5 north to Clearwater, making time to stop and see the spectacular waterfalls at Wells Gray Provincial Park. At Tete Jaune Cache, where Yellowhead 5 junctions with Yellowhead 16, drive west to Prince George and follow the Hart Highway northeast to Dawson Creek, BC, Mile Zero of the Alaska Highway.

Head north on the Alaska Highway, allowing enough time to stop and enjoy wildlife viewing, rivers, historic lodges, beautiful Muncho Lake and Liard River Hotsprings. At Watson Lake, first stop in Yukon, don't miss the famous Signpost Forest. Continue on to Whitehorse, capital of Yukon and home to many of Yukon's best known attractions, including the SS *Klondike*, Yukon Beringia Interpretive Centre and Miles Canyon.

Just northwest of Whitehorse, you'll turn off the Alaska Highway onto the Klondike Highway, which leads to the historic gold rush town of Dawson City. After exploring Dawson, line up early for the ferry ride across the Yukon River to the Top of the World Highway. The ride only takes a few minutes,

but on busy summer days, Alaska-bound traffic can stack up. You'll also want to allow plenty of time to drive the Top of the World Highway; winding road and gravel breaks make this scenic drive a slow one.

After crossing into Alaska, you'll junction with the Taylor Highway, which leads north to Eagle on the Yukon River and south through Chicken to the Alaska Highway. At Chicken, don't miss the Pedro gold dredge, Tisha's schoolhouse or Beautiful Downtown Chicken. The Taylor Highway from Chicken south to the Alaska Highway junction is paved. It is only 12 miles from the junction to Tok.

Tok is an important service stop on the Alaska Highway and it is also decision-making time: Do you first head southwest on the Tok Cutoff/Glenn Highway to Anchorage, or continue on the Alaska Highway to Delta Junction and on to Fairbanks? Since any driving tour of Alaska should include Anchorage, Fairbanks and Denali National Park, it may be a question of timing, with events like Fairbanks' Midnight Sun Baseball Game (June 21st), or the Russian River red salmon run on the Kenai Peninsula playing a role in your decision.

Outbound from Tok, take the Alaska south to Haines Junction and the Haines Highway to Haines (or take the South Klondike Highway to Skagway). Arrange for ferry passage through Southeast Alaska to Prince Rupert, BC. From Prince Rupert, it is a 682-mile drive via Yellowhead Highway 16 to Jasper and the Icefields Parkway south to Banff. Drive east to Calgary via Trans-Canada Highway 1 to rejoin the East Access

Route and continue to Great Falls, MT. (Or you may choose to follow Trans-Canada Highway 1 west or BC routes 93/95 south.)

Inbound mileage: 2,985 miles
Detail: Ellensburg to Dawson Creek 1,012 miles
Dawson Creek to Whitehorse 895 miles
Whitehorse to Tok 510 miles
Tok to Fairbanks 206 miles
Fairbanks to Anchorage 362 miles

Outbound mileage: 2,018 miles. Ferry travel is 42 hours.
Detail: Anchorage to Haines 771 miles
(or Anchorage to Skagway 948 miles)
Prince Rupert to Jasper 682 miles
Jasper to Calgary 245 miles
Calgary to Great Falls 320 miles

Major Attractions

1. The Okanagan
2. Wells Gray Park
3. Mile 0 Alaska Highway
4. Liard Hotsprings
5. Signpost Forest
6. SS Klondike
7. Dawson City
8. Fairbanks
9. Denali National Park
10. Anchorage
11. Inside Passage

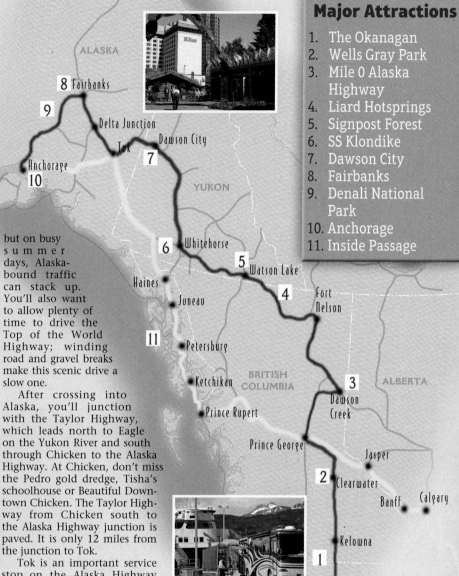

NOTE: For reverse itinerary, read sections from bottom to top and reverse page numbers.
Page numbers for major attractions and side trip options are found on the Contents page and/or in the Index.

Basic Itinerary #3:

Inbound: Inside Passage/Klondike Loop

Outbound: Alaska & Cassiar highways to West Access

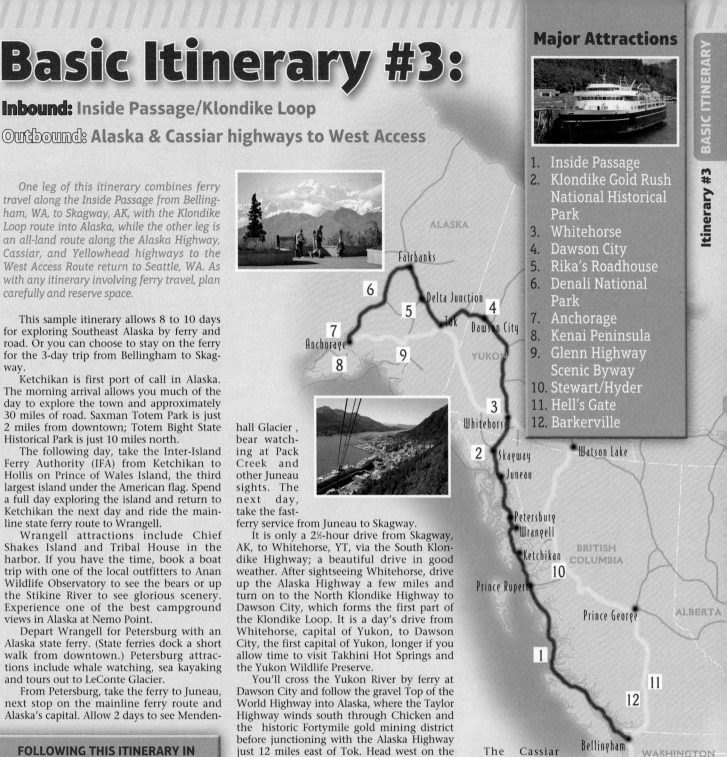

Major Attractions

1. Inside Passage
2. Klondike Gold Rush National Historical Park
3. Whitehorse
4. Dawson City
5. Rika's Roadhouse
6. Denali National Park
7. Anchorage
8. Kenai Peninsula
9. Glenn Highway Scenic Byway
10. Stewart/Hyder
11. Hell's Gate
12. Barkerville

One leg of this itinerary combines ferry travel along the Inside Passage from Bellingham, WA, to Skagway, AK, with the Klondike Loop route into Alaska, while the other leg is an all-land route along the Alaska Highway, Cassiar, and Yellowhead highways to the West Access Route return to Seattle, WA. As with any itinerary involving ferry travel, plan carefully and reserve space.

This sample itinerary allows 8 to 10 days for exploring Southeast Alaska by ferry and road. Or you can choose to stay on the ferry for the 3-day trip from Bellingham to Skagway.

Ketchikan is first port of call in Alaska. The morning arrival allows you much of the day to explore the town and approximately 30 miles of road. Saxman Totem Park is just 2 miles from downtown; Totem Bight State Historical Park is just 10 miles north.

The following day, take the Inter-Island Ferry Authority (IFA) from Ketchikan to Hollis on Prince of Wales Island, the third largest island under the American flag. Spend a full day exploring the island and return to Ketchikan the next day and ride the mainline state ferry route to Wrangell.

Wrangell attractions include Chief Shakes Island and Tribal House in the harbor. If you have the time, book a boat trip with one of the local outfitters to Anan Wildlife Observatory to see the bears or up the Stikine River to see glorious scenery. Experience one of the best campground views in Alaska at Nemo Point.

Depart Wrangell for Petersburg with an Alaska state ferry. (State ferries dock a short walk from downtown.) Petersburg attractions include whale watching, sea kayaking and tours out to LeConte Glacier.

From Petersburg, take the ferry to Juneau, next stop on the mainline ferry route and Alaska's capital. Allow 2 days to see Mendenhall Glacier, bear watching at Pack Creek and other Juneau sights. The next day, take the fast-ferry service from Juneau to Skagway.

It is only a 2½-hour drive from Skagway, AK, to Whitehorse, YT, via the South Klondike Highway; a beautiful drive in good weather. After sightseeing Whitehorse, drive up the Alaska Highway a few miles and turn on to the North Klondike Highway to Dawson City, which forms the first part of the Klondike Loop. It is a day's drive from Whitehorse, capital of Yukon, to Dawson City, the first capital of Yukon, longer if you allow time to visit Takhini Hot Springs and the Yukon Wildlife Preserve.

You'll cross the Yukon River by ferry at Dawson City and follow the gravel Top of the World Highway into Alaska, where the Taylor Highway winds south through Chicken and the historic Fortymile gold mining district before junctioning with the Alaska Highway just 12 miles east of Tok. Head west on the Alaska and Richardson highways to Fairbanks. After taking in Fairbanks area attractions like Pioneer Park, Chena Hot Springs and the University of Alaska's Museum of the North, drive down the Parks Highway to Denali National Park and Anchorage.

Explore the Kenai Peninsula before heading out the Glenn Highway/Tok Cutoff from Anchorage to Tok. At Tok, take the Alaska Highway east to its junction with the Cassiar Highway, just 13 miles west of Watson Lake. Make the short drive into Watson Lake to see the Signpost Forest before heading south on Highway 37 into British Columbia.

Cassiar Highway 37 is popular with motorists who have driven the Alaska Highway and are looking for an alternate route for the drive back. The Cassiar accesses Stewart, BC, and Hyder, AK, an interesting side trip with glaciers (Bear and Salmon) and bear viewing (at Fish Creek).

The Cassiar junctions with Yellowhead Highway 16, which takes you east to Prince George, where you'll take the West Access Route south. Don't miss Barkerville or Hell's Gate before continuing south to the international border at Sumas and back down I-5 to Seattle, WA.

Inbound mileage: 1,195 miles plus 3 to 10 days ferry travel time.
Detail: Skagway to Dawson City 442 miles
Dawson City to Fairbanks 391 miles
Fairbanks to Anchorage 362 miles

Outbound mileage: 2,320 miles
Detail: Anchorage to Tok 328 miles
Tok to Watson Lake 669
Watson Lake to Prince George 761
Prince George to Seattle 562

FOLLOWING THIS ITINERARY IN The MILEPOST.

NOTE: For reverse itinerary, read sections from bottom to top and reverse page numbers.
Page numbers for major attractions and side trip options are found on the Contents page and/or in the Index.

Basic Itinerary #4:

Inbound: Deh Cho Route, Alaska Highway, Klondike Loop
Outbound: Cassiar & Yellowhead highways to East Access

This all-land itinerary features a lot of wilderness driving and offers an off-the-beaten-path choice on the inbound portion via the Deh Cho Route through Northwest Territories to junction with the Alaska Highway. Also in the mix: The less traveled Bighorn Route coupled with the wildly popular Icefields Parkway.

Head up the East Access Route from Great Falls, MT, crossing into Alberta at Sweetgrass, MT/Coutts, AB, and drive north through to Calgary, one of the province's 2 largest population centers. Head east on Trans-Canada Highway 1 to the spectacular Icefields Parkway. From Jasper, at the north end of the Icefields Parkway, drive east 45 miles and catch the Bighorn Highway north to Grande Prairie. (Calgary to Grande Cache is about a day's drive).

Continue north through Grande Prairie, one of the portals to Alberta's Peace River region and keep driving north. Stop at Dunvegan historic park en route to Grimshaw, which is Mile Zero of the Mackenzie Highway. The Mackenzie Highway is part of the Deh Cho Route itinerary through Northwest Territories.

A well-maintained, two-lane highway, the Mackenzie Highway travels straight through northern Alberta, and into Northwest Territories about 400 miles north of Grande Prairie. From the Alberta/NWT border, the Deh Cho Route continues as NWT Highway 1, the aptly named Waterfalls Route, featuring the spectacular Alexandra and Louise waterfalls.

A number of NWT highways connect with the Deh Cho Route, each with its own attractions. Don't miss the Frontier Trail (Highway 3) to Yellowknife: herds of bison, and a highway across the pre-Cambrian shield to a modern city on the territory's largest lake, make this a unique experience.

The Deh Cho Route follows Highway 1 to junction with the Liard Trail south to the Alaska Highway. Make the 76-mile round-trip side trip to Fort Simpson before continuing on to Fort Liard and the Alaska Highway. The Deh Cho Route ends for northbound travelers 17 miles northwest of Fort Nelson.

From the Liard Trail junction, you'll drive north 312 miles to Watson Lake, first stop in the Yukon. At Watson Lake, you continue west on the Alaska Highway to just beyond Whitehorse, where it junctions with the Klondike Highway to Dawson City (for more detail see Itinerary #2).

After exploring Dawson City, the first capital of Yukon and a Klondike Gold Rush heritage site, take the 5-minute ferry ride across the Yukon River. (See the KLONDIKE LOOP section for details on when the customs station is open here.) On the other side you'll follow the Top of the World Highway into Alaska, then the Taylor Highway south through Chicken and the historic Fortymile gold mining district to the Alaska Highway just southeast of Tok. From Tok, head up the Alaska/Richardson Highway to Fairbanks, then down the Parks Highway to Anchorage.

The outbound portion of this trip takes the Glenn Highway/Tok Cutoff from Anchorage to Tok, then the Alaska Highway from Tok east and south to the Cassiar Highway/Highway 37. The Cassiar offers the remote Telegraph Creek Road. Easy access to Stewart, BC, and Hyder, AK, via Highway 37A, an interesting side trip with glaciers (Bear, Salmon) and bear viewing (Fish Creek).

The southern terminus of the Cassiar Highway junctions with Yellowhead Highway 16, which takes you east to Edmonton and the East Access Route to Calgary (with possible side trip to Canadian Badlands) and Great Falls, MT.

Major Attractions

1. Icefields Parkway
2. Alexandra Falls
3. Yellowknife
4. Dawson City
5. Fairbanks
6. Anchorage
7. Salmon Glacier

Inbound mileage: 3,875 miles.
*Detail: Great Falls to Calgary 320 miles
Calgary to Grande Cache 374 miles
Grande Cache to Yellowknife 843 miles
Yellowknife to Fort Simpson 390 miles
Fort Simpson to Watson Lake 595 miles
Watson Lake to Whitehorse 275 miles
Whitehorse to Dawson City 323 miles
Dawson City to Fairbanks 390 miles
Fairbanks to Anchorage 364 miles*

Outbound mileage: 2,669 miles
*Detail: Anchorage to Tok 328 miles
Tok to Whitehorse 396 miles
Whitehorse to Dease Lake 395 miles
Dease Lake to Prince George 602 miles
Prince George to Edmonton 454 miles
Edmonton to Great Falls 494 miles*

FOLLOWING THIS ITINERARY IN The MILEPOST.

NOTE: For reverse itinerary, read sections from bottom to top and reverse page numbers.
Page numbers for major attractions and side trip options are found on the Contents page.